DICTIONARY OF AMERICAN SLANG

DICTIONARY OF AMERICAN SLANG

THIRD EDITION

Edited by
Robert L. Chapman, Ph.D.

HarperCollins*Publishers*

This work is based on the *Dictionary of American Slang* by Harold Wentworth and Stuart Berg Flexner.

DICTIONARY OF AMERICAN SLANG (*Third edition*). Copyright © 1995 by HarperCollins Publishers, Inc. All rights reserved. Printed in the United States of America. No part of this book may be used or reproduced in any manner whatsoever without written permission except in the case of brief quotations embodied in critical articles and reviews. For information address HarperCollins Publishers, Inc., 10 East 53rd Street, New York, N.Y. 10022.

Designed by C. Linda Dingler

Library of Congress Cataloging-in-Publication Data
Chapman, Robert L., 1920–
   Dictionary of American slang / [re-written and] edited by Robert L. Chapman.
      p.   cm.
      Rev. ed. of: Dictionary of American slang / compiled and edited by Harold Wentworth and Stuart Berg Flexner. 2nd supplemented ed. 1975.
   ISBN 0–06–270107–X
   1. English language—United States—Slang—Dictionaries. 2. Americanisms—Dictionaries. I. Wentworth, Harold. 1904– Dictionary of American slang. II. Title.
   PE2846.C46 1997   97-2771
   427'973'03—dc21   CIP

00 01 ❖/RRD 10 9 8 7 6 5

Contents

. . . banish plump Jack, and banish all the world.

Henry IV, Part 1

Considering Language then as some mighty potentate, into the majestic audience-hall of the monarch ever enters a personage like one of Shakespere's clowns, and takes position there, and plays a part even in the stateliest ceremonies. Such is Slang, or indirection, an attempt of common humanity to escape from bald literalism, and express itself illimitably.

Walt Whitman, "Slang in America"

Preface to the Second Edition

The editor of a new dictionary of slang owes explanations to people at large and to those who use the book. To the public he should explain *why* such a book is made and deserves to be made. To the users he must explain *how* the book was made and how to use it. Finally, to all these and to himself, he must attempt to explain *what* slang is, anyway. (For a brief working answer to this last question, the reader may look up *slang* in this dictionary; for a more considered account, see below.)

Why This Book Was Made

The question will be: Why does a serious scholar devote himself to this uncouth sort of language, and why does he connive, worse yet, in foisting it on us and our innocent youth? Even though to a lexicographer that question is not very relevant, it is far from trivial. Dictionaries are popularly thought to have strong influence. They are thought to give validity and authority to their entries, and therefore to have social and moral impact. A dictionary like this, which specializes in terms not to be lightly used in polite society, is therefore thought of as teaching and advocating these terms, and hence akin to pornography.

The question may be answered in two veins, the theoretical and the historical. Theoretically, in linguistics any corpus or body of vocabulary is worth recording, and all are equally worthy. Linguistics, lexicography, is like a science in that its values have to do with accuracy, completeness, and demonstrability rather than with moral or social good. As a lexicographer I collect and record slang because it is there, and I take as much professional delight in a faithful transcript of all this nasty talk as I do in capturing and recording for our descendants the differing elegancies of standard language.

So, as a lexicographer I answer that I will collect every slang term I can get my hands on, will treat these as carefully and responsibly as I am able, and will leave their use up to others, who will have been warned against the undeliberate wielding of these powerful and provocative words. Yes, children will sneak off into corners with this book, and find the dirty words, and have dirty thoughts. If I believed that our whole culture could be made the least bit more decent, more respectful, more harmonious, happier, and mentally healthier by not making a slang dictionary, I might refrain. But I do not believe that and have not refrained.

This line of justification is nicely summed up in a story I heard Elie Wiesel tell: A magisterial historian was challenged with the question "Why does a scholar like you occupy himself with a silly and contemptible subject like X?" To which the savant replied, "X is, as you say, silly and contemptible; but the history of X is scholarship!"

History of Slang Lexicography

In historical justification, this book joins itself to an Anglo-American tradition going back just over two hundred years, and of which the high spots may be mentioned.

Credit as founder of general slang lexicography, as distinct from those who dealt in specialized lexicons, goes to the distinguished British antiquarian Francis Grose, who published *A Classical Dictionary of the Vulgar Tongue* in 1785. After two further editions, the book became the basis of an 1811 updating and expansion called *Lexicon Balatronicum: A Dictionary of Buckish Slang, University Wit, and Pickpocket Eloquence,* of about 260 pages, with nearly five thousand defined entries. A half-dozen or so earlier compilations exist from as early as the 1560s, but they deal only in the special vocabularies of thieves and tramps. Grose's book and its successor include the slang of the so-called *balatrones*—"jesters, buffoons, contemptible persons; literally, babblers," who are urban dandies or men-about-town— and of the learned humorists of and from the universities, as well as of thieves.

Grose's work held the field until 1859, when it was superseded by John C. Hotten's *A Dictionary of Modern Slang, Cant, and Vulgar Words,* which had new editions in 1860, 1864, and 1874. The attribution to Hotten is not certain, since the book was anonymous, but it is generally accepted. Henry Bradley of the *Oxford English Dictionary* judged it "a work of considerable merit" and praised its scholarly authority.

In 1887 Albert M.V. Barrere, Professor of French at the Royal Military Academy in Woolwich, published at his own expense *Argot and Slang: A New French and English Dictionary.* Two years later the Ballantyne Press brought out for subscribers only *A Dictionary of Slang, Jargon & Cant,* in two volumes totaling 956 pages. Barrere had as collaborator Charles Godfrey Leland, an American. Leland had been a Philadelphia lawyer, a journalist and editor, a three-day barricades veteran of the 1848 Revolution in Paris, on the whole a rather Hemingwayish character, and was the first American to figure prominently in general slang lexicography. He had made a particular study of British gypsies and their language, and was the first to describe Shelta, a jargon of certain Irish and Welsh gypsies. The dictionary embraces "English, American, and Anglo-Indian slang, Pidgin English, tinkers' jargon and other irregular phraseology."

One year later the first volume of John Stephen Farmer and William Ernest Henley's *Slang and Its Analogues* was published, without Henley's name on the title page. Henley let his name be used on Volume 2 in 1891 and on the subsequent five volumes through 1904. He was a poet and editor, now undervalued as a poet though popularly known for the stirring Invictus, set to music as a virile baritone solo and ending "I am the master of my fate; I am the captain of my soul." Contemporary brief biographies of Henley refrain from mentioning the slang dictionary, and indeed his part in it is not well understood. Farmer, probably the originator and major author, was a prodigious scholar and editor, especially of Tudor drama and other texts of that epoch. His production comes to more than twenty volumes in that field alone. He also collected and edited six volumes of songs, especially of the "merry" sort. He wrote three books on spiritualism, a late Victorian craze. More to the point here, in 1888 he published *Americanisms Old and New,* "by J.S.F.," surely written as a preliminary by-product of his work on the seven-volume slang dictionary. An American authority on our national English, Richard H. Thornton, discovered that nine-tenths of the examples in Farmer's 564-page book came from material published in 1888. This indicates very great efficiency and/or a white-hot pace of work. When the Farmer and Henley work was completed in 1904, it amounted to 2,736 pages.

A less useful contribution to general slang lexicography was James Maitland's 308-page *The American Slang Dictionary of 1891.* This book is not a jewel in the tradition, perhaps for the reasons that caused an anonymous reviewer in the *Nation* to observe that most of the entries were not American and not slang, and that the philological grounding of the editor was meager indeed. The review concluded, in cruelly measured words that make any slang lexicographer cringe in a nightmare, ". . . it must be said of the present work that it not only has no reason to show for its existence, but furnishes a good many reasons to suggest the desirability of its non-existence."

After Farmer and Henley, good general slang lexicography was not resumed until 1937, when Eric Partridge brought out the first edition of his masterwork, *A Dictionary of Slang and Unconventional English*, which was updated and enlarged in seven editions and numerous reprintings by Partridge himself through 1980 and has recently been posthumously revised and published in an eighth. Eric Partridge— New Zealander, Australian, Englishman, soldier, scholar, university teacher, essayist, novelist—is the lofty star at whose work and book all other slang lexicographers must hopelessly aim. He is also, for the twentieth century, the one who made slang lexicography more or less respectable and enabled us to cease lurking behind pseudonyms or anonyms or initials, or being privately and furtively printed.

The first full-scale dictionary of American slang had to wait until 1960, when Harold Wentworth and Stuart Berg Flexner's *Dictionary of American Slang* was published by Thomas Y. Crowell (a company now incorporated into HarperCollins). Professor Wentworth had previously written an *American Dialect Dictionary,* portions of which were adapted for the slang dictionary. Mr. Flexner added thousands of slang definitions from other sources and wrote the invaluable preface, our best treatment of the sociolinguistics of slang. The preface to that edition is reprinted in this book. He also did the immense analytical work reflected in the appendix, which treats the processes of word-formation in slang with unequaled authority and exhaustiveness. Flexner was responsible for final defining and editing of all the entries in the seven-hundred-page volume, which at once became the standard work in its field. Wentworth and Flexner, as it is usually called, was enlarged and updated in 1967 and 1975 and is the basis of the present book.

These are the theoretical and historical justifications of this book, to which a practical note must be added. First, obviously the book has a primary utility for people who find slang terms in their reading, or who overhear them, and need help with their meaning. Finally, it means to serve people who just plain enjoy slang and are curious about it and where it came from.

How This Book Was Made

This dictionary came into being in a five-stage process that may be quickly explained but was only slowly carried out.

1. Policies were determined and a "style manual" made that embodied these decisions on the format of the entries, their typefaces, their punctuation, the ordering of information, etc. The basic policies of the book are that it means to be a general dictionary of current American slang, rather than a collection of special vocabularies, a scholarly historical treatment, or a book with regional or other bias.

2. The Wentworth and Flexner *Dictionary of American Slang* was "recycled" and its wealth of material retained, altered, or discarded according to the new policies.

3. A corps of collectors was recruited for the accumulation of new material. At its most numerous this group consisted of fifty or more collectors, these dwindling as the years passed to an indefatigable hard core who are still submitting material as this preface is written. The collectors are listed, gratefully, at the end of the preface.

4. The definitions were written, rewritten, and then edited and reedited by gimlet-eyed faultfinders whose crucial work is also acknowledged, gratefully, below.

5. Computers were used throughout in many ways. Citations were stored and sorted in computers. Entries were coded and typed directly onto disks, making editing and checking more easy, fast, and reliable. The text was hand-encoded to prepare it for use with desktop publishing software.

Working by these stages and with this copious help, and having the advantage of standing on the strong shoulders of predecessors, making a dictionary is not the momentous and Olympian task it is popularly thought to be. It is simply an affair of knowing it can be done and knowing the practical steps to take. And working and worrying.

The style and apparatus of this dictionary are explained in the section called "Guide to the Dictionary."

What Is Slang?

In linguistics, where definitions at best are often imprecise and leaky, that of slang is especially notorious. The problem is one of complexity, such that a definition satisfying to one person or authority would seem inadequate to another because the prime focus is different. Like the proverbial blind men describing an elephant, all correctly, none sufficiently, we tend to stress one aspect or another of slang. My own stress will be on the individual psychology of slang speakers.

Sociolinguistic Aspects of Slang

The external and quantitative aspects of slang, its sociolinguistics, have been very satisfactorily treated, nowhere more so than in Stuart Berg Flexner's masterful preface to the *Dictionary of American Slang*. Readers may also consult Eric Partridge's 1954 book *Slang To-Day and Yesterday,* in particular parts III and IV.

Updating Flexner's discussion of the social milieu from which American slang emerges would involve no real correction of his findings, but only an account of the historical shifts that twenty-five years have brought.

Recorded slang emerged, as the sketch of dictionaries has shown, from the special languages of subcultures, or perhaps we should call the more despised of them "undercultures." The group studied longest and most persistently has been the criminal underworld itself, including the prison population, whose "cant" or "argot" still provides a respectable number of unrespectable terms. Other undercultures contributing heavily are those of hoboes, of gypsies, of soldiers and sailors, of the police, of narcotics users, of gamblers, of cowboys, of all sorts of students, of show-business workers, of jazz musicians and devotees, of athletes and their fans, of railroad and other transportation workers, and of immigrant or ethnic populations cutting across these other subcultures.

In the 1990s, we must note that some of these traditional spawning grounds for slang have lost their productivity, and that other subcultures have emerged to replace them. For example, general adoption of terms from hoboes, from railroad workers, from gypsies, and from cowboys has very nearly ceased, although the contributions of all these persist in the substrata of current slang. Criminals and police (cops and robbers) still make their often identical contributions, and gamblers continue to give us zesty coinages. Teenagers and students can still be counted on for innovation and effrontery. Show-business workers, although they have largely shed the raffish image of their roving and carnival past, are still a fertile source of slang. But several centers of gravity have shifted greatly during the past fifty or so years, as reflected in the entries of this book.

For example, the adoption of military, naval, and merchant marine slang has slowed to a relative trickle, not surprisingly. World Wars I and II probably gave us more general slang than any other events in history, but they are now history, and the Korean and Vietnam wars have had in comparison a meager effect. Railroad slang has been replaced, though on a lesser scale, by the usage of airline workers and truck drivers. The jazz world, formerly so richly involved with drug use, prostitution, booze, and gutter life, is no longer so contributory, nor has rock and roll quite made up the loss, but taken as a whole, popular music—rock, blues, funk, rap, reggae, etc.—are making inroads.

Terms from "the drug scene" have multiplied astronomically, and a specialized book this size could easily be made from them alone. The "counterculture" helped disseminate many drug terms that might otherwise have remained part of a special vocabulary. Sports also make a much larger contribution, with football and even basketball not challenging but beginning to match baseball as prime producers. Among the immigrant-ethnic bestowals, the influx from Yiddish continues strong in spite of the sociological shifting of the Jewish population. The old Dutch and German sources have dried up. The Italian carries on in modest proportion. The Hispanic has been surprisingly uninfluential, although a heavier contribution is surely predictable. All these are far outstripped by increased borrowing from black America, and this from the urban ghetto rather than the old Southern heartland. Close analysis would probably show that, what with the prominence of black people in the armed forces, in music, in the entertainment world, and in street and ghetto life, the black influence on American slang has been more pervasive in recent times than that of any other ethnic group in history. This can be conjectured, of course, without any implication that black Americans constitute a homogeneous culture.

Some sources of the slang in this book will be entirely or relatively new. Examples of this are the computer milieu and the hospital-medical-nursing complex. In the first case an exciting technological inundation is at the base, and in the other, as in so many other trends of our era, the reason is television.

In the matter of sex, our period has witnessed a great increase in the number of terms taken over from homosexuals, especially male homosexuals. And it would be wrong to restrict the range of their contribution to sex terms alone, since the gay population merges with so many others that are educated, witty, observant, acerbic, and modish.

The "growth sector" hardest to characterize just now is in linear descent from the people old Captain Francis Grose, and Ben Jonson and others before him, called "university wits." Today, trying to mark off this most fecund assemblage, I need a clumsy compound like "the Washington-Los Angeles-Houston-Wall Street-Madison Avenue nexus." Our culture occupies these centers, and they occupy the culture through pervasive and unifying communications media. They give us the slang of the brass, of the execs, of middle management, of dwellers in bureaucracies, of yuppies, and of the talk shows and the "people" sort of columns and magazines. Bright, expressive, sophisticated people, moving and prospering with our lively popular culture, and not entirely buying it. They are the trend-setters and source of the slang that seems to come from everywhere and not to be susceptible of labeling. We will need more historical perspective before we can be usefully analytic about them, but they, whoever they are, clearly make up the wave of the present.

This new emphasis in the fortunes of American slang, by the way, points to one of its important distinctions, that between what I call "primary" and "secondary" slang. Primary slang is the pristine speech of subculture members, so very natural to its speakers that it seems they might be mute without it. Of course they would not be, since we know that slang is by definition always an alternative idiom, to be chosen rather than required. Much of teenage talk, and the speech of urban street gangs, would be examples of primary slang. Secondary slang is chosen not so much to fix one in a group as to express one's attitudes and resourcefulness by pretending, momentarily, in a little shtick of personal guerrilla theater, to be a member of a street gang, or a criminal, or a gambler, or a drug user, or a professional football player, and so forth—and hence to express one's contempt, superiority, and cleverness by borrowing someone else's verbal dress. Secondary slang is a matter of stylistic choice rather than true identification. The increasing currency of the "Washington-Los Angeles-Houston, etc." sort of slang may mean that in the future secondary or acquired slang will be our major variety. That is, the old disreputable groups will blend gradually into the mass, and slang will become more a matter of individual wit and self-advertisement, with its sources no more apparent than those of, say, a dirty joke. In fact it may be conjectured that even now the strong influence of black slang and gay slang has less to do with those subcultures per se than with the fact that both put a very high premium on verbal skill. Blacks, for example, are particularly given to rhyme and other prosodic features that seem to be increasingly prominent in slang.

Individual Psychology of Slang

Obviously an individual in one of the groups or subcultures mentioned above, or any of many others, resorts to slang as a means of attesting membership in the group and of dividing him- or herself off from the mainstream culture. He or she merges both verbally and psychologically into the subculture that preens itself on being different from, in conflict with, and superior to the mainstream culture, and in particular to its assured rectitude and its pomp. Slang is thus an act of bracketing a smaller social group that can be comfortably joined and understood and be a shelter for the self. It is simultaneously an act of featuring and obtruding the self within the subculture—by cleverness, by control, by up-to-dateness, by insolence, by virtuosities of audacious and usually satirical wit, by aggression (phallic, if you wish). All this happens at fairly shallow levels in the psyche and can be readily understood. It explains most of what we know and feel about slang.

But what explains "it"? If, as the authorities agree, slang is a universal human trait and as old as the race itself, and if it came into being in the same human society where language itself was born, can we not seek deeper and more generalized explanations? Authorities also agree, as it happens, that the roots of slang must be sought in the deepest parts of the mind, in the unconscious itself. Although that territory is perilous ground for a working lexicographer, a few conjectures and a few relationships can be proposed for consideration.

It seems to me that the deeper psychodynamics of slang have to do with two things: (1) defense of the ego against the superego, and (2) our simultaneous eagerness and reluctance to be human.

Surely wounded egos are the most common human nonanatomic possession. Slang might be seen as a remedy for them, as a self-administered therapy old as the first family that spoke. The family, like society, entails a hierarchy of power and of right, against which the healthy growing self of the child needs measures to compensate for its weakness and sinfulness. Slang as a remedy denies the weakness and brags about the sinfulness.

In this view, it would not be too much to claim that therapeutic slang is necessary for the development of the self; that society would be impossible without slang. It is curious that a linguistic phenomenon that seems so fleeting and so frivolous, as slang undeniably does, should at the same time be so deep and so vital to human growth and order. This is only one of the paradoxes of slang.

This aspect of slang is "deeper" than the matters mentioned above, like group identification and so on, only because it existed before groups, and it persists as groups themselves chop and change in the flux of history. In this aspect slang is similar to, and perhaps the same as, profanity. Like profanity, slang is a surrogate for destructive physical action. Freud once remarked that the founder of civilization was the first man who hurled a curse rather than a rock or spear at his enemy. Slang also has this usefulness, and I suspect that profanity is a subcategory of slang, the more elemental phenomenon.

Hence, slang is language that has little to do with the main aim of language, the connection of sounds with ideas in order to communicate ideas, but is rather an attitude, a feeling, and an act. To pose another paradox: Slang is the most nonlinguistic sort of language.

"Our simultaneous eagerness and reluctance to be human"—what can that have to do with slang? My notion here is that when you try to consider it deeply slang seems to join itself with several other phenomena: with Freud's "dream-work," with comedy, with elements of myth.

It seems to me that slang (I mean the slang impulse of the psyche) shares with all these the salvational and therapeutic function of both divorcing us from and maintaining our connection with genetic animality. Dream-work relieves us of the need to be reasonable and discharges the tension of the great burden with which our angelic rationality charges us. Although we are uncomfortable with paradox in ordinary language, we easily tolerate it in slang, where it seems as much at home as it is in the study of logic.

Slang links itself with comedy in the respect that it exploits and even celebrates human weakness, animality, without working to extirpate it. It makes room for our vileness, but only so much room. The great comic figures of our culture usually come in pairs, each member having its legitimacy, and each limiting the other: Sancho Panza and Don Quixote; Falstaff and Prince Hal; Huck Finn and who?—Tom Sawyer, Aunt Polly, even Jim. To these we may add the Wife of Bath, whose counterfigure was a part of herself, making her more like most of us than Sancho or Falstaff or Huck are. We may add, without too much strain, the comic figure Dante Alighieri over against Beatrice and the lightweight devil Mephistopheles over against Faust. What we seem to have in the comic heroes and in our own slang impulse is a reaching for or clinging to the primal earth, a *nostalgie de la boue*, which helps make tolerable the hard aspiration to be civilized and decent.

As to myth, Sancho, Alice of Bath, and Falstaff are modern myths themselves. For ancient myth we might think of Antaeus, whose strength was valid only while he had his feet on the earth, and of Silenus and the satyrs, and even of the Devil himself, who must, when he is not quoting scripture, speak a great deal of slang. We may also attend to the intriguing "trickster" figure who is so prevalent in world mythology. C.G. Jung reminds me of the slang impulse when he asserts, for example, ". . . [the trickster's] fondness for sly jokes and malicious pranks, his powers as a shape-shifter, his dual nature, half animal, half divine, his exposure to all kinds of tortures, and— last but not least—his approximation to the figure of a saviour." In the same essay, "On the Psychology of the Trickster-Figure," Jung relates the trickster to the medieval Feast of Fools and other manifestations of the comic and slang spirit, especially those that deflate pomp, that prick presumption, that trip up our high horses. Jung believed that the civilizing process began within the framework of the trickster myth, which is a race memory of the human achievement of self-consciousness.

As the literary scholar Wylie Sypher said, ". . . man is not man without being somehow uneasy about the 'nastiness' of his body, [and] obscenity. . . is a threshold over which man enters into the human condition." For *obscenity* we might read slang, and observe that we are not so far beyond the threshold that we cannot always reach it with our foot, which is of clay.

Slang is also the idiom of the life force. That is, it has roots somewhere near those of sexuality, and it regularly defies death. What I have in mind is partly the "dirty" and taboo constituent of slang, but even more its tendency to kid about being hanged, electrocuted, murdered, or otherwise annihilated. Gallows humor is, from this point of view, more central to slang than may have been thought.

One changing pattern that has obvious connections with both socio- and psycholinguistics is the relation of slang to gender. In these times, and partly because of the feminist movement, women are more and more using the taboo and vulgar slang formerly accounted a male preserve. Sociologically this shows the determination of some women to enter the power structure by taking on this badge, among others, that denotes "maleness," and simultaneously to shed the restrictions of the "ladylike" persona. Psychologically the implications are not that clear, but it may be that some women are determined to replicate at the core of their psyches the aggressive and ordering nature we have usually identified as a part of profound maleness, or else to show that these masculine traits do not lie as deep as we thought.

Apologies

Our aim has been to make a dictionary of current general American slang, but even a cursory look will show that we have retained from the *Dictionary of American Slang* many entries that are only dubiously current and not very general. We have done so for two reasons: (1) We felt that these would be helpful to readers baffled by slang found in earlier writings or writings that use earlier slang, and (2) some of these obsolete terms are aids in understanding the derivation of current terms.

In the absence of a litmus test for slang and nonslang we must ask some indulgence. Slang shares misty boundaries with a relaxed register usually called informal or colloquial, and we have inevitably strayed across the boundary. Eric Partridge spared himself the embarrassment of this apology by calling his book the dictionary of "slang and unconventional English." This book should probably have the same title.

Slang also shares a boundary with a stylistic register we might call figurative idiom, in which inventive and poetic terms, especially metaphors, are used for novelty and spice, and incidentally for self-advertisement and cheekiness, in relief of a standard language that is accurate and clear but not personal and kinetic. Here again we beg the indulgence of those who disagree with our choices, as we would hope to be indulgent of theirs.

We are interested in getting the book right, and would be grateful for corrections and suggestions. These can be addressed to the publisher.

Robert L. Chapman
May 1986

Preface to the Third Edition

Much of the original preface will also serve here, and is reprinted. The only meaningful addition is a new list of collectors (new although two of them also contributed to the first edition).

Since only six zealots collected for the second edition, their offerings were individually more numerous than those of the first, and my debt of gratitude is heavier.

George Avgeris of Denver, Colorado, proffered many sheaves of examples, and was particularly useful in giving quotations from televisions programs.

Jean Billman, one of the earlier collectors, combed and winnowed the newspapers of Macon, Georgia, and a number of magazines for teenagers.

Miven Booth of Los Angeles, California, kept me more or less abreast of California usage.

Bernard Kane of Ridley Park, Pennsylvania, also an earlier collector, did his best to swamp me with quotations from here, there, and everywhere, all meticulously edited.

Robert Perkins of Fort Atkinson, Wisconsin, sent so much that I regard him as a chief collaborator, without whom the book would be quite slim.

Lee Russell of Mesa, Arizona, sent not only masses of useful terms but also instructive essays to ensure my accurate comprehension.

These are friends and colleagues whom I will miss now that the book is finished. I hope I have served them as well as they have me.

I would also like to thank Josie Cook of the Drew University Library for all her assistance.

I cannot possibly express my full debt to Barbara Ann Kipfer of Essex, Connecticut, who has been the Developmental Editor of this book. She has been my conscience and my benign instructress throughout its preparation, and will be the guardian of its future.

And again, of course, I thank my dear wife Sarah for her patience and fortitude.

Robert L. Chapman
February 1997

Guide to the Dictionary

The editors have tried to make the apparatus of this book clear and self-explanatory, but a few guidelines may help the reader. These are given more or less in the order of the elements in the definition block itself.

The Main Entry

The main entry sometimes contains portions that do not appear in boldface and are not taken into account in alphabetization. These include the articles *a, an*, and *the*, when they appear at the beginning of an entry, and the variable pronoun in a phrase, indicated by *someone, someone's, something, one's*, etc. Variant forms following or and variants found within parentheses appear in boldface but do not affect alphabetization.

Impact Symbols

Main entries considered to have strong social or emotional impact are indicated by delta symbols bracketing the entry itself or the separate definition numbers if the impact symbol does not apply to all senses of the term. The symbols are assigned on a two-level principle, corresponding to what have usually been called taboo and vulgar levels. Taboo terms are *never* to be used, and vulgar terms are to be used only when one is aware of and desires their strong effect. In this book terms of contempt and derision for racial or other groups have been included among the taboo terms.

Terms of strongest impact are marked with the symbols ◀▶ and those of lesser impact with the symbols ◁▷. The assignment of these is a matter of editorial judgment, and not everyone will agree with us. In some places it was difficult to assign impact symbols to terms that are acceptable within a group but are considered offensive when used by those outside the group. We have taken account of recent changes in the currency and acceptability of terms previously unspeakable, and some may feel we have gone too far with the trend.

Pronunciations

Words are respelled for pronunciation only when "normal" pronunciation cannot be readily ascertained or when pronunciation is crucial to the meaning of the term. The system of respelling is designedly very simple, depending on what we regard as a majority pronunciation of the respelled syllable and showing stressed syllables in capital letters.

Part-of-Speech Labels

Parts of speech and a few other grammatical particulars are indicated by rather self-explanatory abbreviations or labels:

n	noun	modifier	
v	verb	infix	
pron	pronoun	phr	phrase
adj	adjective	sentence	
adv	adverb	pres part	present participle
affirmation		past part	past participle
negation		prefix	
conj	conjunction	suffix	
prep	preposition	combining form	
interj	interjection	combining word	

Variant Forms

Variation is shown in three ways:

1. In the main entry itself, up to three variants are shown, separated by *or*.

2. Where there are more than three variants, or they apply to various parts of the main entry, they are shown in parentheses with the label *Variations*.

3. Where variant forms apply to particular numbered definitions, this is shown by printing the form or forms at the beginning of the numbered sense, introduced by *also*.

Dating Labels

Even though this is not meant to be a full-fledged historical dictionary, the time of origin and/or special currency of the terms is shown by a dating phrase. These usually designate the early, middle, or late part of a century, or in more recent times they indicate decades of origin when known. All labels are based upon evidence found in published scholarship or lexicography, and most are of course subject to correction where better evidence is found.

When an entry does not carry a dating label, the inference is either that the date was undiscoverable or that the term is relatively recent and would have to be labeled *1980s* or *1990s*.

Provenience Labels

When the social group or milieu from which a term emerged is known, it is indicated by a labeling that is often intermixed with the dating labels; for example, *fr late 1800s cowboys*, or *esp 1960s teenagers*. Two abbreviations are used in provenience labels: *fr* for *from* and *esp* for *especially*. Some attempt at precision has been made in these labels, but they are regrettably sometimes rather vague and general. Nevertheless, no label has been applied without evidence.

Definitions

Definitions were written in what most users will accept as a normal form. A few explanations need to be made, however:

1. The usual distinction between transitive and intransitive verbs has not been used, in the belief that the definitions and the examples will make that distinction clear when useful.

2. After the label *sentence*, another sentence has been provided that translates the main entry sentence.

3. Interjections, prefixes and suffixes, and combining forms and words have been explained "objectively," with no attempt made to provide a strictly substitutable version of the form.

4. When a word is defined in one part of speech but is often used in others, it may be "defined by example" in this book. The most common case is the one where a noun is often used as an attributive modifier, which in this book is shown by the label *modifier* followed by a colon and by an example of the use. Definitions by example apply strictly only to part-of-speech shifts from the definition immediately preceding them.

5. Definitions are not always given in chronological order, even when that is known. The order is rather a logical-semantic one that attempts to show how senses have grown from previous senses. Sometimes the order can hardly be anything but arbitrary.

6. Occasionally when a printed example itself fully defines the term, it will stand as the definition without further ado.

Slang Synonyms

Often slang synonyms will be provided at the ends of definitions, after an equal sign. This is meant to be an aid in definition rather than a serious comprehensive collection of synonyms.

Slang synonyms are also used as quick definitions when a full definition is given elsewhere, at a synonymous entry, usually at a more current or frequently used or interesting term. Slang synonyms are not used as cross-references to variant terms, although sometimes this distinction may not be a sharp one.

Editorial Notes

When certain information seems useful but does not fit into the normal format of the definition block, it is included as an editorial note. These are introduced by a large black dot.

Examples

In this book usage examples are given either when they have been collected from the media or when an invented example seems to help in definition or in showing context and structure. Examples thus have a double function: to illustrate usage and to validate usage and the inclusion of the term.

Examples are attributed to authors, especially when these are well known; when newspapers or magazines are cited, authors are generally not named, even though the articles may have had bylines. Attributions are to be taken essentially as evidence that the material quoted did in fact appear in the place or under the name cited. They are not, of course, to be taken as characterizing the typical style of the source.

Derivations

Derivations are given in square brackets at the end of the definition block proper, before the cross-references.

Slang etymology is less certain and precise than standard etymology, for two chief reasons: (1) Because of the moral and social dubiousness of slang, relatively little of it was printed over the centuries, yielding less evidence than one needs; and (2) it is an etymology of meaning rather than form, and semantic connections are seldom as public, positive, and knowable as are formal relations. Hence slang etymology must be to an uncomfortable degree a matter of assessing probabilities.

Derivations are not given here when they are deemed to be obvious. When they are accepted and demonstrable, they are stated as fact. When probability, or even possibility, proposes them, they are stated tentatively. The ruling criterion has been common sense and occasionally another sense that in German is called Sprachgefühl, a sort of personal linguistic intuition.

In cases where a derivation seems patently necessary, but none can be discovered or surmised, the notation *origin unknown* is used. This must not be taken absolutely, but only to mean that the derivation is not now known to the editor.

A part of the fun of making a slang dictionary is the exercise of ingenuity and insight for derivations, especially those that have not apparently been proposed before. The editor does not apologize for his attempts, although he asks to be enlightened if ignorant and corrected if perverse.

Cross-References

An extraordinary attempt has been made to help the user find the term in question by cross-referencing nearly every important term in every phrase (prepositions, particles, articles, and the like are, of course, not cross-referenced). Since this book defines a very great number of phrasal entries, much space has been given to this purpose, and we hope these merely utilitarian features will not get in the way.

A

A *narcotics* **1** *n* Amphetamine **2** *n* LSD; =ACID
  See FROM A TO Z, Q AND A

AA (pronounced as separate letters) *armed forces fr WWI* **1** *n* An antiaircraft weapon, or antiaircraft fire; =ACK-ACK, FLAK **2** *modifier*: *an AA barrage*

abbot *n narcotics* Nembutal™, a barbiturate; =DOWNER [fr the name of the pharmaceutical company that produces it]

Abe's cabe *n phr jive talk fr 1930s & rock and roll fr 1950s* A five-dollar bill [fr the portrait of Lincoln on the bill, and perhaps fr a shortening and repronouncing of "cabbage"]

◀**Abie**▶ **1** *n* Any Jewish male **2** *n* A tailor

A-bomb **1** *n* An atomic bomb **2** *n hot rodders* A car especially modified for quick acceleration and speed; =HOT ROD **3** *n narcotics* A combination of drugs, typically marijuana or hashish plus opium

abortion *n* Something of very poor quality; a messy failure; *That show is a real abortion*

about that **See** SORRY ABOUT THAT

about town **See** MAN-ABOUT-TOWN

above one's **head** **See** IN OVER one's HEAD

academy **See** LAUGHING ACADEMY

Acapulco gold *n phr narcotics* Marijuana of high quality grown near Acapulco, Mexico, and having leaves with a golden hue

accidentally on purpose *adv phr* As if by accident, but really by intention: *She missed the meeting accidentally on purpose*

accommodation collar *n phr police* An arrest made to fulfill a quota, usu in response to pressure for strong police action against crime

account **See** NO-ACCOUNT

accounting **See** CREATIVE ACCOUNTING

AC-DC (Variations: **AC/DC** or **ac-dc** or **ac/dc**) **1** *adj* Practicing both heterosexual and homosexual sex; bisexual **2** *adv*: *I think she does it AC-DC* [fr the abbreviations for the two types of electrical current, alternating and direct; an appliance that can operate with either type is marked *AC-DC*]

ace **1** *n* A person of extraordinary skill, usu in a specified activity: *poker ace/ the ace of headwaiters* **2** *modifier*: *an ace mechanic/the ace professor* **3** *adv*: *He did it ace every time*—Richard Merkin **4** *n fr WWI* A combat pilot who has shot down five or more enemy aircraft **5** *n* An unusually pleasant, generous, and decent person, esp a male; =PRINCE **6** *n black & street gang* A very close friend; =BUDDY, PAL **7** *n black* A man who favors flamboy-ant, up-to-the-minute dress; =DUDE **8** *n narcotics* A marijuana cigarette; =JOINT **9** *n* A dollar bill **10** *n golf* A hole scored in one stroke **11** *n racquet games* An unreturnable serve that scores a quick point **12** *v sports* To score by an ace: *He aced the fifth hole/ She aced him six times in one set* **13** *v* (also **ace out**) *college students* To make a perfect or nearly perfect score: *My sister aced the chemistry exam/ Ace the test and you go on to the next subject*—Flying **14** *n restaurant* A table for one; also, a single customer **15** *n lunch counter* A grilled cheese sandwich [fr the name of the unitary playing card]
  See CASE ACE, CHINESE ACE, COME WITHIN AN ACE, COOL AS A CHRISTIAN WITH ACES WIRED

◁**ace boon coon**▷ or **ace boon** or **ace buddy** *n phr black* A very good friend; best friend

ace-deuce *n* Three, esp a three of playing cards

ace-high *adj* Of the best; first rate: *His reputation is ace-high*

ace in **1** *v phr* To use strategy in getting oneself into a good or profitable position **2** *v phr* To understand; =DIG

ace in the hole *n phr* Something held privately in reserve until needed, esp for a winning stroke; a hidden reserve or advantage [fr poker term *in the hole* for a card dealt face down in a stud game]

ace of spades ◀**1**▶ *n phr* A black person, esp a very dark one ◁**2**▷ *n phr* The female genitals [fr the color and shape of the playing-card symbol]

ace out **See** ACE

aces *adj* Of the very best quality; superior; finest: *I said it in this very sincere voice. "You're aces. . . ."* —JD Salinger

aces wired **See** COOL AS A CHRISTIAN WITH ACES WIRED

ace up one's **sleeve** *n phr* A hidden advantage, esp a tricky one [fr a common technique of magicians and cardsharps]

acey-deucey **1** *adj* Of mixed quality; having both good and bad, high and low; ambiguous: *an acey-deucey proposition* **2** *adj* So vague, generalized, or inclusive as to offend no one; satisfactory; mediocre; =SO-SO [fr card games in which the **ace** is the highest and the **deuce** the lowest card in value]

acid *narcotics* **1** *n* The hallucinogen LSD, which is chemically an acid; =A **2** *modifier*: *an acid party*
  See AUGUSTUS OWSLEY, BATTERY ACID

acid freak or **acidhead** *n phr* or *n narcotics* A person who uses LSD, esp one who uses the drug heavily or habitually: *He has suggested that some of our recent Presidents were acidheads*—Saul Bellow

acid pad *n phr* narcotics A place, esp someone's home or apartment, where LSD is taken

acid rock 1 *n phr* A form of very loud rock music featuring electronic sound effects and often accompanied by stroboscopic and other extraordinary lighting to suggest the hallucinatory impact of LSD **2** *modifier*: *acid-rock guitar*

acid test narcotics **1** *n phr* A party at which LSD is added to food and drink **2** *v phr* To provide special effects at a party, usu of a psychedelic sort: *He acid tested his place with colored strobe lights* [a punning adaptation of the standard phrase, "a final and decisive test"]

ack-ack armed forces fr WWI **1** *n* Antiaircraft gun or guns; antiaircraft fire; =AA, FLAK **2** *modifier*: *ack-ack positions*

across the board 1 *adj phr* horse-racing Designating a bet in which the same amount of money is wagered on the horse to win, place, or show **2** *adv phr*: *Marcus bet $2 across the board on Duck Giggle in the fifth* **3** *adj phr* Designating an equal alteration to each member of a related set, esp an equal raising or lowering of related wages or salaries: *They got an across-the-board increase of 80 cents an hour* **4** *adv phr*: *The fees were lowered across the board* [fr the **totalizator board** that shows the odds at horse-racing tracks]

act 1 *n* A display of pretended feeling; an affected pretense: *His elaborate grief was just an act* **2** *n* A dramatic mimicking; =SHTICK, TAKEOFF: *You oughta see my Brando act*
   See a CLASS ACT, CLEAN UP one's ACT, DO THE DUTCH, GO INTO one's DANCE, SISTER ACT

acting jack *n phr* Army An acting sergeant; soldier wearing the insignia of and having the authority of a sergeant but without the official rank

action 1 *n* Gambling activity; a crap game or other game of chance: *Most people now go to Atlantic City for the action* **2** *n* Activity or entertainment: *looking for the local action* **3** *n* The, or a, sex act: *He was ogling the girls, looking for a little action*
   See a PIECE OF THE ACTION, WHERE THE ACTION IS

◁**act like** one's **shit doesn't stink**▷ *v phr* To behave with self-assured haughtiness; show a sense of superiority

actor *n* sports An athlete who is good at pretending he has been hurt or fouled; esp, a baseball player who very convincingly mimes the pain of being hit by a pitch
   See BAD ACTOR

Ada from Decatur *See* EIGHTER FROM DECATUR

Adam *See* NOT KNOW someone FROM ADAM

add one's **two cents in** *See* PUT one's TWO CENTS IN

ad lib 1 *v phr* To speak, play, dance, or otherwise perform a passage not in one's prescribed plan, often with an original and spontaneous effect: *The Senator ad libbed for ten minutes waiting for the President to show* **2** *n phr* A passage or comment, etc, given spontaneously: *He forgot his lines and did a stupid ad lib* **3** *modifier*: *an ad-lib gag/ a quick ad-lib put-down* **4** *adv*: *They danced ad lib until the conductor found his place again* [fr Latin *ad libitum* "as one wishes"]

◁**adobe dollar**▷ *n phr* A Mexican peso

advantage *See* HOME-COURT ADVANTAGE

African black *n phr* narcotics A grade of marijuana grown in Africa

◀**African dominoes**▶ **1** *n phr* Dice **2** *n phr* The game of craps; =AFRICAN GOLF [fr the racist presumption that the game of craps is a specialty and a special weakness of blacks]

◀**African golf**▶ *n phr* The game of craps

Afro 1 *n* A hair style worn by many blacks and some whites, usu with an exaggerated bouffant style of tightly curled hair **2** *n* A black person **3** *modifier*: *an Afro social club*

◁**Afro-Saxon**▷ *n* black A black person who has assumed the behavior and values of the dominant white society; =OREO, TOM

against the wall *See* UP AGAINST THE WALL

age out *v phr* narcotics To reach an age, usu in the 30s or 40s, when drugs no longer have the desired effect, whereupon the user gradually stops taking them voluntarily

a-go-go esp 1960s & 70s **1** *n* A discotheque or other venue for rock-and-roll dancing **2** *modifier*: *a-go-go music* **3** *adj* Rapid and dizzying tempo: *our crazy a-go-go pace of life* **4** *adj* In the newest style; faddish; =TRENDY: *his a-go-go opinions about sexual freedom* [fr French *à gogo* "galore," used in the name of a Parisian club, *Whisky à Gogo*]
   See GO-GO

agreement *See* SWEETHEART CONTRACT

ah *See* OOH AND AH

ahead *See* COME OUT AHEAD, STRAIGHT-AHEAD

A-head narcotics **1** *n* A frequent user of amphetamines **2** *n* =ACIDHEAD

ahead of the game *adv phr* In a winning or advantageous position: *Hard as I try, I can't seem to get ahead of the game*

-aholic *suffix used to form nouns and adjectives* Addicted to and overengaging in what is indicated: *fuckaholic/ sleepaholic/ workaholic*

something or someone ain't *negation* Something or someone emphatically is not •Said as a wry and intensive negator in a comparative statement: *My joint? Buckingham palace it ain't/ Well, she sings OK, but Joan Sutherland she ain't* [perhaps fr a Yiddish syntactic pattern]

ain't hay *See* THAT AIN'T HAY

air *v* To broadcast by radio or television: *to air a new miniseries*
   See a BEAR IN THE AIR, DANCE ON AIR, FULL OF HOT AIR, GET THE AIR, GIVE someone THE AIR, GO UP IN THE AIR, GRAB A HANDFUL OF AIR, HOT AIR, SUCK AIR, UP IN THE AIR

air one's **belly** *v phr* To vomit

air one's **dirty linen** *See* WASH one's DIRTY LINEN

airhead or **airbrain** *n* A stupid or silly person; =BUBBLEHEAD, DITZ: *The steel-belted airheads were in Lonnie's suite*—Dan Jenkins

airheaded or **airbrained** *adj* Stupid; silly; vapid; =BUBBLEHEADED, DITZY: *the delightfully airbrained Mickie*—Village Voice

airmail *n* Garbage thrown out of a window

air out 1 *v phr black* To stroll; saunter **2** *v phr* To leave; =SCRAM, SPLIT

airplane *n narcotics* A tweezerlike clip for holding a marijuana cigarette stub; =ROACH CLIP

airs *See* PUT ON AIRS

aisles *See* LAY THEM IN THE AISLES

◁**AK** or **ak**▷ (pronounced as separate letters) **1** *n* =ALTER KOCKER **2** *n* =ASS-KISSER

aka (pronounced as separate letters) *prep phr* Also known as; alias: *He's an asshole, aka a big deal*

Al or **Alfred** *n shoeshop* The shoe width A

Albert *n outdated pawnshop & underworld* A watch chain, esp a gold one [probably fr the common portraits of Albert, the Prince Consort of Queen Victoria of Great Britain, where he is shown wearing a conspicuous gold watch chain]
See FAT ALBERT

Alibi Ike *n phr* A person who habitually offers excuses and plausible explanations for dubious actions

alike *See* LOOK-ALIKE

alkied or **alkeyed** (AL keed) *adj* Drunk

alky or **alki** (AL kee) **1** *n* Alcohol **2** *n esp 1920s* Inferior or bootleg whiskey **3** *n* A chronic alcoholic, esp one who is a homeless drifter or street denizen; =BUM

all bases *See* TOUCH ALL BASES

all by one's **lonesome** *adv phr* Alone; solo: *She did it all by her lonesome*

all ears *adj phr* Very eager to hear; keenly attentive: *Something juicy's coming, and they're all ears*

alley *See* BACK ALLEY

Alley *See* TIN PAN ALLEY

alley apple 1 *about 1910* (also **road apple**) A piece of horse manure **2** *n phr* A rock put into a stocking and used as an impromptu blackjack; =GROUND BISCUIT

alley cat 1 *n phr* A homeless cat; stray cat **2** *n phr* A sexually promiscuous person, esp a woman

all-fired *fr early 1800s* **1** *adv* To an extreme or extravagant degree: *Don't be so all-fired stupid* **2** *adj*: *He's got an all-fired lot of nerve* [a euphemism for *hell-fired*]

all fired up *See* FIRED UP

all fours *See* DOWN ON ALL FOURS

all get out or **all get up** *n phr fr late 1800s* The extreme or absolute case of what is indicated: *overwhelmingly white, and affluent as all get-out*—Ebony

all hanging out *See* HAVE IT ALL HANGING OUT

all hang out *See* LET IT ALL HANG OUT

all hell broke loose *sentence* Things became very turbulent, dangerous, noisy, etc: *All Hell Breaking Loose*—Time

all hollow *See* BEAT ALL HOLLOW

alligator 1 *n black* An assertively masculine, flashily dressed, and up-to-the-minute male; =DUDE, SPORT **2** *n esp 1930s jive talk* An active devotee of swing and jive music, dancing, and speech ●The salutation "See you later, alligator" was commonly heard **3** *n black jazz musicians* A white jazz musician or jazz enthusiast

◁**alligator bait**▷ *n phr black* A black person, esp one from Florida or Louisiana

alligators *See* UP TO one's ASS IN something

all in *adj phr fr early 1900s* Tired; exhausted; =BEAT, POOPED

all in one piece or **in one piece** *adv phr* Intact; unharmed: *She came out of it in one piece*

all (or **all stuff**) **like that there** *n phr* Other such things; etcetera: *They sold boots and shoes and all like that there*

all-nighter *See* PULL AN ALL-NIGHTER

all of a doodah *adj phr fr early 1900s British* Upset; nervous; confused

all-originals scene *n phr black* A party or other occasion where only blacks are present: *I dig you holding this all-originals scene at the track*—Malcolm X

all-out 1 *adj* Holding nothing back; sparing nothing: *an all-out effort* **2** *adv*: *He ran all-out for ten minutes*

all over *See* HAVE IT ALL OVER someone or something

all over someone **1** *adj phr* Very affectionate; eagerly amorous: *The wife went to get some popcorn and the husband was all over me*—Playgirl **2** *adj phr* Aggressively smothering or battering; assaulting: *They broke through the line and were all over the quarterback*

all over the lot (or **the ballpark**) *adv phr* Very unfocused and inconsistent; confused: *His answers are all over the lot/ But otherwise. . .you were all over the ballpark*—Philadelphia

all-pro *adj* Of first quality; blue-ribbon; stellar: *an all-pro team of Washington super-lobbyists*—Washingtonian [fr the annual designation of certain professional football players to the putative team of the best]

all quiet on the Western front *adj phr fr WWI* Calm; peaceful; uneventful [fr the title of a WWI novel by Erich Maria Remarque reflecting the stagnation and stability of trench warfare]

all reet (or **reat** or **root**) *interj esp 1930s jive talk* An exclamation of approval: *"All reat". . .is the rug-cutters' way of saying "all right"*—New Yorker

all (or **aw**) **right** (aw RĪT) **1** *interj* An exclamation of strong approval, esp of something well done or successful; =WAY TO GO **2** *affirmation* Yes; I agree: *All right, I'll go when you want*

all-right *adj* Good; commendable; of the proper sort ●Most often used of persons: *all-right guys trying to make a living*—James M Cain

all right already *interj* A comment protesting that one has heard or had enough or a bit too much [fr Yiddish idiom patterns, and translating Yiddish *genuk shoyn*]

all righty *affirmation* (Variations: **rightie** or **righ-tee** or **rightey** may replace **righty**) A humorous or deliberately cute and childish way of saying "all right"

all she wrote *See* THAT'S ALL SHE WROTE

all shook up or **all shook** *See* SHOOK UP

all six *See* HIT ON ALL SIX

all one's **switches** *See* NOT HAVE ALL one's SWITCHES ON

all that jazz *n phr* Other such things; etcetera: *baseball, apple pie, Chevrolet, and all that jazz*

◁**all that kind of crap**▷ *n phr* (Variations: **shit** or **stuff** or **bull** may replace **crap**) Other such stupid and boring things; the depressing remainder: *what my lousy childhood was like, and how my parents were occupied before they had me, and all that kind of crap*—JD Salinger

all that meat and no potatoes *interj* An exclamation of pleasure and appreciation, by a man, on seeing a well-built woman •Has the sense of a wolf-whistle; regarded by many women as offensive

all the answers *See* KNOW ALL THE ANSWERS

all the marbles *See* GO FOR BROKE

all the moves *See* HAVE ALL THE MOVES

all there *adj phr* Intelligent; =TOGETHER: *At least Prudence is all there*
See NOT ALL THERE

all the way *adv phr* Without reservation; to the end: *I'll back her all the way*
See GO ALL THE WAY

all the way live *adj phr* *high school students* Exciting; vibrant and animated: *That party was all the way live* [fr the sense of immediacy and tension of *live* in its television use]

all thumbs *adj phr* Very awkward; inept: *I'm all thumbs when it comes to drawing*

all together *See* GET IT TOGETHER, HAVE IT ALL TOGETHER

all to hell *See* EXCUSE ME ALL TO HELL, PARDON ME ALL TO HELL

all washed up *See* WASHED UP

all wet *adj phr* *fr 1920s* Incorrect; wrong: *Your idea is all wet, I'm afraid*

the **almost** *n phr* *1950s beat & cool talk* Nearly the best or greatest person or thing: *He's not top line, but he's sure the almost*

alone *See* GO IT ALONE

along for the ride *See* GO ALONG FOR THE RIDE

Alps *See* JEWISH ALPS

already 1 *adv* Without further ado; such being the case: *Let's go already* **2** *adv* Right now; at once: *Shut up already* **3** *adv* Very specifically; precisely: *Drop dead already* •The full semantic range of *already* is broad and the distinctions are subtle. It is used chiefly for a humorous exasperated effect and to suggest Yiddish speech patterns

also-ran *n* A person, competitive product, etc, that does not succeed; a person of mediocre talents; =LOSER [fr the term for a race-horse who runs fourth or worse]

◁**alter kocker (or cocker)**▷ (AL tə KAH kər) *n phr* An old man, esp a disgusting and querulous one; =AK: *You young bloods have got it all over us alter cockers*—Bernard Malamud [fr Yiddish, literally "old shitter"]

the **altogether** *See* IN THE ALTOGETHER

alum (ə LUM) *n* An alumnus or alumna

alvin or **Alvin** *n* *carnival, circus, & underworld* A person who can be fooled or defrauded easily; =MARK, PATSY, SUCKER

alyo *underworld & sports* **1** *n* Any routine task **2** *n* A person not easily disconcerted; =COOL HAND **3** *n* A condition of calm or safety **4** *n* An arrangement between criminals and the police giving the former immunity from arrest or harassment; =the **fix** [possibly fr Italian **aglio** "garlic," in the idiom **mangiare aglio**, literally "to eat garlic," meaning to be outwardly calm and placid although perhaps inwardly angry; perhaps related to the folk belief that garlic averts evil]

am *See* PRO-AM

-ama *See* -RAMA

amateur night 1 *n phr* Any occasion on which professionals do a bad or mediocre job: *After the third inning it was strictly amateur night* **2** *n phr* A casual sex act done with a person who is not a prostitute [fr the special occasions or evenings when *amateurs* perform at theaters or on television or radio programs]

ambidextrous *adj* Bisexual; =AC-DC

ambish (am BISH) *n* *esp theater* Ambition; aggressiveness

ambulance chaser 1 *n phr* *fr late 1800s* Any unethical lawyer, or one who is too aggressive in getting clients; =SHYSTER **2** *n phr* *fr early 1900s* A lawyer or lawyer's helper who urges accident victims to sue for damages, negligence, etc

ammo (AM oh) **1** *n* *fr around 1930* Ammunition: *The platoon is out of ammo* **2** *modifier*: *The fat ammo barge rocked up and down*—This Week **3** *n* Information and other material that may be used in a debate, campaign, exposé, etc: *Your shabby personal life gives lots of ammo to the opposition*

amp 1 *n* An ampere, the electrical unit of measurement **2** *n* An audio amplifier, esp one used for electronic musical instruments **3** *n* *narcotics* An ampoule of a narcotic

amscray *v* To leave at once; =BEAT IT, SCRAM [pig Latin for *scram*]

◁**Amy-John**▷ *n* *homosexuals* A lesbian, esp one who plays the dominant role; =BUTCH, DIESEL-DYKE [origin uncertain; perhaps fr French *ami Jean* "friend John," or fr a corruption of *Amazon* "female warrior"]

anchor *See* SWALLOW THE ANCHOR

anchor man 1 *n phr* *college students fr 1920s* The student having the lowest academic standing in the class **2** *n phr* (also **anchor**, **anchor person**) A television news broadcaster who has the principal and coordinating role in the program

and *n* *lunch counter* The second of two items that normally go together •"Coffee and" means "coffee and doughnuts," "ham and" means "ham and eggs," etc

and change *n phr* An additional smaller amount: *It*

happened an hour and change before midnight/ That'll run the taxpayers $6 billion and change [fr dollars plus *change,* "coins"]

and counting *adj phr fr 1960s aerospace* Plus more, gradually: *$840 million and counting*—New York Times [first used in the countdown to a rocket launching]

and how *interj fr early 1900s* An exclamation of emphatic agreement or confirmation: *Are we happy? And how!*

angel 1 *n fr about 1920* A person who contributes to a politician's campaign fund **2** *n fr theater fr 1920s* A financial contributor to any enterprise, esp a stage production; =BUTTER-AND-EGG MAN **3** *v: My doctor angeled one of Hansberry's plays* **4** *n underworld* A thief's or confidence man's victim; =MARK, PATSY **5** *n homosexuals fr 1930s* A homosexual male **6** *n* A vague and illusory image on a radar screen, often due to bird flights, rare atmospheric conditions, or electronic defects **7** *n Vietnam War Navy* A helicopter that hovers near an aircraft carrier to rescue air crew who crash into the water

angel dust *narcotics* **1** *n phr* The powdered form of PCP, a tranquilizer used in veterinary medicine, which as a narcotic is either sniffed or smoked in a tightly rolled cigarette **2** *n phr* A synthetic heroin

Angelino or **Angeleno** (an jə LEE noh) *n* A resident or native of Los Angeles

◁**angel teat (or tit)**▷ **1** *n phr* A mellow whiskey with a rich aroma: *Distillery workers smacked their lips over angel teat*—Labor's Special Language **2** *n phr* Any pleasant or easy task

angle *n* Something one does for profit or advantage, esp a devious action disguised as altruism: *That guy never does anything unless there's an angle*

◁**Anglo**▷ *n Hispanics* A white person; =PADDY

animal *n fr Army & students fr 1940s* A brutal or aggressive person, esp one given to excessive sexuality or violence

ankle *v* To walk: *I ankled over to the bar* [perhaps in part from *angle,* cited fr 1890s in sense of "to walk"]
See BEATEN DOWN TO THE ANKLES

Ann *See* MARY ANN

Annie *See* BASEBALL ANNIE

Annie Oakley or **Annie** *n phr* or *n fr early 1900s sports & show business* A free ticket or pass to a game or entertainment [fr the name of a 19th-century trick-shot artist who could riddle a playing card tossed into the air so that it looked like an often-punched ticket]

another country (or **county** or **precinct) heard from** *sentence* Still another voice makes itself heard •Usu an irritated and contemptuous response to a new or unwanted contribution of opinion

another pretty face *See* NOT JUST ANOTHER PRETTY FACE

answers *See* KNOW ALL THE ANSWERS

ante *See* PENNY ANTE, UP THE ANTE

ante up *v phr fr middle 1800s* To contribute money one is responsible for or is expected to give: *On April 15 we all ante up to Uncle Sam* [fr the poker term for an initial contribution to the pot as a game begins]

anti (AN ti) *n* A person opposed to a particular plan, position, action, etc: *The vote showed three pros and six antis*

antifreeze *n narcotics* Heroin

antinuke 1 *adj* Antinuclear; opposed to nuclear energy and nuclear armaments **2** *n: The antinukes assaulted Wall Street, holding hands, singing, and sitting in*—New York Daily News

ants or **ants in** one's **pants 1** *n* or *n phr* An unrelaxed, disturbed condition; anxiety; acute restlessness: *After two days at sea she began to get ants* **2** *n* or *n phr* Sexual excitement; =the **hots**

antsy 1 *adj* In an anxious, disturbed state; nervous; jittery: *But when things are quiet, I get antsy*—Jackie Friedrich **2** *adj* Sexually aroused; lustful; =HOT

A-number–1 or **A-number-one** *adj* Of the highest or best quality; first class; excellent

anyhoo (EN ee hoo) *adv* Anyhow •Mispronunciation used for presumed humorous effect

any old *adj phr* Having only ordinary or mediocre quality; of no special distinction: *Any old car will do me*

A-OK or **A-Okay** or **A O-K** *fr astronautics fr 1960s* **1** *adj* Proceeding or functioning properly; giving no cause for worry; =COPACETIC, GO: *Your X rays are A-OK* **2** *adv: The plan's going A-OK*

A–1 or **A-one** *adj* =A-NUMBER–1

ape ◀**1**▶ *n* A black person **2** *n beat talk & rock and roll* The best or greatest; the ultimate: *Her paintings are truly ape* **3** *adj* (also **ape-shit**) Stupid and destructive; irrational; berserk: *You acted like you were ape, pounding the wall* **4** *adj* (also **ape-shit**) Very enthusiastic; highly excited; =BANANAS: *He's ape about my new symphony* **5** *n* An especially strong and pugnacious hoodlum; a strong-arm man or muscle man; =GOON, GORILLA
See BRUSH APE, DRAPE APE, GO APE, HOUSE APE, RUG APE

the **ape** *adv phr beat talk & rock and roll* Very well; best: *Maybe we could dig each other the ape*—S Boal

aped *adj early 1900s* Drunk

ape hangers *n phr motorcyclists* High swooping motorcycle handlebars

◁**ape-shit**▷ *See* APE, GO APE

apparatchik *n* An aide, staff member, etc, esp of a bureaucratic sort; flunky; =RUNNING DOG: *the politicians and their technocratic apparatchiki on both sides*—Philadelphia [fr Russian, "member of the Communist party, or *apparat*"]

apple 1 *n* A man; fellow; =ARTICLE, GUY •Always preceded by an adjective: *He's a real slick apple* **2** *n* A ball, esp a baseball **3** *n esp 1930s jazz musicians* A street or district where excitement may be found **4** *n esp 1930s jazz musicians* Any large town or city ◁**5**▷ *n Native American* A Native American who has taken on the values and behavior of the white community; =UNCLE TOMAHAWK

See ALLEY APPLE, the BIG APPLE, HORSE APPLE, SAD APPLE, SMART APPLE, SURE AS GOD MADE LITTLE GREEN APPLES, SWALLOW THE APPLE, WISE GUY

the Apple *See* the **big apple**

applehead *n* A stupid person; idiot: *You, sir. . .are an applehead*—Arthur Daley

applejack cap *n phr black* A round, usu knitted and bright-colored cap with a wide peak and a pom-pom; =BOP CAP

◁**apple-knocker**▷ **1** *n* Any fruit picker, esp a migratory orchard worker **2** *n* A rural person; unsophisticated rustic; =HICK [fr the practice of *knocking apples* out of trees]

apple-pie-and-motherhood *modifier* Having obvious and unexceptionable virtue: *They'll always vote yes on an apple-pie-and-motherhood issue*

apple-pie order *n phr* A condition of neatness, correctness, and propriety: *MacFarlane finds in this "apple-pie order of oppositeness". . .a singular problem*—Toronto Life

apple-polish *v* To flatter and pamper in order to gain personal advantage; curry favor; =BROWN-NOSE, SUCK UP TO someone: *He started apple-polishing the Skipper as soon as he got on board*

apple-polisher *n* A person who apple-polishes [fr the traditional figure of the pupil who brings the teacher a shiny red apple]

apples *See* HOW DO YOU LIKE THEM APPLES

applesauce *n fr early 1900s* Nonsense; pretentious talk; =BULLSHIT, BUNK: *"Ideologies". . .freely translated into American means "applesauce"*—Max Eastman [fr the fact that relatively cheap, hence worthless, **applesauce** would be copiously served instead of choicer food in boarding houses]

appropriate *v esp WWI Army* =LIBERATE

AR (pronounced as separate letters) *n police* Armed robbery

-arama *See* -RAMA

arcadenik (ar KAYD nik) *n* A habitué of video-game arcades: *video-game mags. . .which. . .are a surprise hit with arcadeniks*—Washington Post

Archie Bunker 1 *n phr* A bigoted lower-middle-class American; =HARD HAT, REDNECK **2** *modifier*: *He has the support of the traditional Republican establishment, and is adding the Archie Bunker vote*—James Reston [fr the name of the leading character of a television comedy series *All in the Family*, who exhibited the traits indicated]

argle-bargle *n middle 1800s fr Scottish* Silly debate, esp specious objections; trivial arguing: *turn questions of sense into mere argle-bargle*—Newsweek [fr a Scottish phrase, "to bandy words"]

-arino *See* -ERINO

Arkansas lizard *n phr hoboes* A louse

Arky or **Arkie 1** *n* A migratory worker, esp one from Arkansas **2** *n* Any poor Southern farmer, esp a white sharecropper **3** *modifier*: *the Arky drawl of the CB radio user* **4** *n* =OKIE

arm 1 *v cabdrivers* =HIGHFLAG **2** *n* A police officer [police sense fr *arm of the law*]
See AS LONG AS YOUR ARM, CROOKED ARM, GLASS ARM, HOOK ARM, ONE-ARM BANDIT, ONE-ARM JOINT, RIDE THE ARM, SHORT-ARM INSPECTION, STIFF, TWIST someone's ARM

the arm *See* PUT THE ARM ON someone, RIDE THE ARM, a SHOT IN THE ARM

an arm and a leg *n phr* An exorbitantly high price: *The trip cost an arm and a leg*

armchair general (or **strategist**) *n phr* A person who speaks authoritatively but not convincingly on matters where that person lacks practical experience; =BLOWHARD, KNOW-IT-ALL

arm it *v phr cabdrivers* To convey a customer and collect the fare without using the meter; =HIGHFLAG, RIDE THE ARM [fr the vertical *arm* of the taxi meter, turned horizontal to start the meter]

armored cow (or **heifer**) *n phr esp armed forces fr WWII* Canned milk

armpit *n* A very undesirable place; geographical nadir; =ASSHOLE, THE PITS *My home town is the armpit of the universe*
See PULL TEETH THROUGH THE ARMPIT

Armstrong [1] or **armstrong** *n* A high note or run played on the trumpet [fr Louis **Armstrong**, who was among the first to exploit the high register of the trumpet in jazz]

Armstrong [2] or **armstrong** *n railroad* A locomotive fired by hand [fr the **strong arms** required for such work]

Armstrong heater *n phr* The encircling arms of one's girl- or boyfriend

Armstrong mower *n phr* A scythe

Armstrong starter *n phr* A crank for starting an engine

arm-waver *n* An excitable or emphatic person

army chicken *n phr WWII Army* Beans and frankfurters

the (or the **old**) **army game** *n phr* Any swindle or confidence game; a dishonest gambling game; =FLIMFLAM: *It's nothing but. . .the army game*—James M Cain

army strawberries *n phr WWII Army* Prunes

-aroo *See* -EROO

-arooney or **-erooney** *suffix used to form nouns* A suffix added to the term indicated to imply familiarity or humor: *This little cararooney's got only 10,000 miles on her*

around the axle *See* WRAPPED AROUND THE AXLE

around the bend 1 *adv phr* With most or the hardest part done; =OVER THE HILL: *Two more days and we'll be around the bend on this project* **2** *adj phr chiefly British* Insane; =BONKERS: *The Free Islamic Revolutionary Movement and all its around-the-bend comrades*—New Yorker
See ROUND-THE-BEND

someone has been around or **around the block** *sentence first variant 1920s, second variant by 1990s* The subject is not naive, but is experienced and clever: *We've all been around*—Ernest Hemingway/ *Having been around the block, Sylvia not only writes stories but dispenses advice. . .*—New York Times/ *Oliver's been* *around the block and won't be seduced by money*—Time

around the bush *See* BEAT AROUND THE BUSH

around (or round) the horn **1** *adv phr* *underworld fr 1930s* Legally detained on a minor charge but suspected and not yet charged for a more serious crime **2** *adj phr* *baseball* Of throws from third base to second base to first base: *a brilliant round-the-horn double play* [fr the length and circuitousness of a voyage around Cape Horn at the southern tip of South America]

around the world *See* GO AROUND THE WORLD

arrow *See* STRAIGHT ARROW

art *n* *police* A photograph or photographs of criminals, esp wanted criminals; =MUG SHOT: *Information began to appear under art of Karpis on post office bulletin boards*—A Hynd

    See STATE OF THE ART, TIT ART

article *n* A person, esp one considered to be clever, cute, or resourceful; =NUMBER •Always preceded by an adjective, or by the locution "Quite an": *He is some slick article/ Your little sister's quite an article*

artillery **1** *n* *underworld fr early 1900s* A weapon or weapons, esp a handgun carried by a criminal **2** *n* *narcotics* A drug user's hypodermic syringe

    See HEAVY ARTILLERY

artist *See* BULLSHIT ARTIST, BUNCO ARTIST, BURN ARTIST, CLIP-ARTIST, DIT-DA ARTIST, GYP, HEAT ARTIST, MAKE-OUT ARTIST, PUT-ON, RIPOFF, SACK ARTIST, SHORT-CHANGE ARTIST

artsy-craftsy or **artsy** or **arty** *adj* *fr 1940s* Pretentiously and self-consciously artistic; straining for esthetic effect: *an artsy-craftsy little boutique on Nantucket*

artsy-fartsy or **artsy-smartsy** *adj* Pompously or blatantly esthetical •The superlative degree of *artsy-craftsy*: *The. . .pianist veers toward the artsy-fartsy*—Village Voice

asap or **ASAP** (pronounced either as separate letters or as an acronym AY sap) *adv* *armed forces* Right away; immediately: *Our job is simple—to liberate US POWs from Asia, ASAP*—Washington Post [fr *as soon as possible*]

ash can *n phr* *Navy fr WWI* An antisubmarine depth charge

    See KNOCK someone FOR A LOOP

ash cat *n phr* *railroad* An engine stoker

ashes *See* GET one's ASHES HAULED

◁**Asiatic**▷ *adj* *Navy & Marine Corps fr before WWII* Crazy; wild; violent: *He could wind up some tapped-out old Asiatic rumdum*—Earl Thompson [fr presumed unstable character of those who had served too long in *Asiatic* posts]

ask for it *v phr* *fr early 1900s* To behave in a way that invites and deserves trouble; provoke: *I'm sorry you had that wreck, but with no brakes you were asking for it*

asleep at the switch *adj phr* *fr railroad* Not attending to one's duty and risking safety; unvigilant; inattentive

as long as your arm *adj phr* Very extensive; remarkably long: *The guy's a jailbird, a record as long as your arm*—WT Tyler

as per usual *adv phr* As usual

◁**ass**▷ **1** *n* The buttocks; posterior; =BUTT: *a kick in the ass* **2** *n* The anus; =ASSHOLE: *You can take it and shove it up your ass* **3** *n* A person regarded solely as a sex partner or target; =TAIL: *She looks like good ass* **4** *n* Sexual activity; sexual gratification: *He was out looking for ass* **5** *n* The whole self; the person •Used for emphasis and euphony: *Get your ass out of here pronto/ I'm out in Kansas for the first time. . .eighteen or nineteen, my ass drafted*—WT Tyler

    See one's ASS IS DRAGGING, someone's ASS IS ON THE LINE, BAG ASS, BARREL ASS, BET YOUR BOOTS, BURN someone's ASS, BUST one's ASS, CANDY ASS, CANDY-ASSED, CHEW someone's ASS, COLD AS HELL, COVER one's ASS, DEADASS, DRAG ASS, DRAG one's TAIL, DUMB-ASS, FALL ON one's ASS, FLAT-ASS, FLAT ON one's ASS, GET one's ASS IN GEAR, GET one's HEAD OUT OF one's ASS, GET OFF one's ASS, GET THE LEAD OUT, GET THE RED ASS, GIVE someone A PAIN, GO POUND SALT, GRIPE one's ASS, one HAS HAD IT, HAUL ASS, HAVE A BUG UP one's ASS, HAVE someone's ASS, HAVE one's ASS IN A SLING, HAVE one's HEAD PULLED, HAVE LEAD IN one's PANTS, one's HEAD IS UP one's ASS, HORSE'S ASS, IN A PIG'S ASS, JUMP THROUGH one's ASS, KICK ASS, a KICK IN THE ASS, KISS MY ASS, MAN WITH A PAPER ASS, MY ASS, NO SKIN OFF MY ASS, NOT HAVE A HAIR ON one's ASS, NOT KNOW one's ASS FROM one's ELBOW, ON one's ASS, OUT ON one's ASS, a PAIN IN THE ASS, PIECE OF ASS, PISSY, PULL something OUT OF one's ASS, PUT one's ASS ON THE LINE, RAGGEDY-ASS, a RAT'S ASS, RATTY, SHAG ASS, SHIT-ASS, SIT ON one's ASS, SIT THERE WITH one's FINGER UP one's ASS, SMART-ASS, SOFT-ASS, SORRY-ASS, STACK ASSES, STAND AROUND WITH one's FINGER UP one's ASS, STICK IT, SUCK ASS, TEAR OFF A PIECE, THROW someone OUT ON someone's ASS, TIRED-ASS, UP THE ASS, UP TO one's ASS IN something, WHAT'S-HIS-NAME, WILD-ASS, WORK one's ASS OFF

◁**-ass** or **-assed**▷ **1** *suffix used to form adjectives* Having buttocks of the specified sort: *big-ass/ fat-assed* **2** *suffix used to form adjectives and nouns* Having a specified character or nature to a high degree: *badass/ wildassed/ silly-ass*

◁**ass backwards**▷ **1** *adv phr* In a reversed position or confused manner: *You installed it ass backwards/ She had it all ass backwards* **2** *adj phr*: *The whole plan is ass backwards*

◁**assbite**▷ *n* A strong rebuke; reprimand: *I took the assbite without looking at him*—Joseph Wambaugh

◁**assed**▷ *See* HALF-ASSED, PUCKER-ASSED, RED-ASSED

◀**assfuck**▶ **1** *v* To do anal intercourse; =BUGGER, BUNGHOLE **2** *n* An act of anal intercourse

◁**asshole** or **butthole**▷ **1** *n* The anus; rectum **2** *n* *middle 1930s* A despised person; =BASTARD, SHIT-HEAD: *Oh, Christ, what ass-holes be Americans*—Norman Mailer/ *Better not, you butthole*—Cameron Crowe **3** *n* =ASSHOLE BUDDY **4** *n* The most despised

and loathsome part; =ARMPIT: *This town's the ass-hole of the North*
See BLOW IT OUT, BREAK OUT INTO ASSHOLES, FLAMER, TANGLE ASSHOLES

◁**asshole** (or **buttfuck**) **buddy**▷ *n phr* A very close friend; best friend; =PAL ●Usu with only a humorous connotation of homosexuality: *The big cheese who teaches you butt-fuck buddies how to blow a few of the Baptists away*—Richard Merkin

◁**asshole deep**▷ See UP TO one's ASS IN something

◁**ass in a sling**▷ See HAVE one's ASS IN A SLING

◁one's **ass is dragging**▷ *sentence* The subject is very tired; one is exhausted, and hence sluggish

◁one's **ass is getting light**▷ *sentence Army* The subject has been repeatedly and thoroughly rebuked; one has been severely chastened [fr the concept that when one is thoroughly rebuked one's anus is chewed or reamed out]

◁one's **ass is grass**▷ *sentence fr 1940s* The sub-ject is in trouble; one will be ruined, undone, etc: *Give me a title, in short, or your ass is grass*—Boston Magazine

◁someone's **ass is on the line**▷ *sentence* Someone is at risk; someone has taken a perilous responsibility: *A friend's ass is on the line and I promised I'd talk to you*—Lawrence Sanders /*I bet-ter be right this time, because my ass is on the line* [fr the notion of a *line* separating hostile per-sons, such that encroaching on it is a challenge and a risk]

◁**asskicker**▷ *fr Army* **1** *n* An energetic person, esp an officer who harasses subordinates **2** *n* Something that functions very well: *That little motor's a real ass-kicker* **3** *n* An exhausting experience

◁**asskicking**▷ *adj Army* Functioning or performing well: *That's an asskicking little heater*

◁**ass-kisser**▷ *n* (Variations: **licker** or **sucker** may replace **kisser**) A person who flatters and serves obse-quiously to gain favor with a superior; sycophant; =AK, BROWN-NOSE, YES-MAN

◁**ass-kissing**▷ *n* Flattery; currying favor with superi-ors; *It's a short step from lip service to ass-kissing*—Saul Bellow

◁**ass man**▷ **1** *n phr* A man with an extraordinary and consuming interest in doing the sex act; lecher; satyr; =COCKSMAN **2** *n phr* A man whose favorite part of female anatomy is the buttocks

◁one's **ass** (or **buns** or **tail**) **off**▷ *adv phr* Very hard; one's best; to one's utmost: *I worked my ass off for that ungrateful jerk/ listen to Oscar Peterson play his buns off*—Down Beat

◁**ass over tincups** (or **teacups** or **teakettle**)▷ *adv phr* In or into helplessness; head over heels: *She's so beautiful she'll knock you ass over tincups* [a variant of the early–20th-century British *arse over tip,* "head over heels"]

◁**ass peddler**▷ *n phr* A prostitute, of either sex

◁**ass-wipe** or **ass-wiper**▷ **1** *n* Toilet paper or something similarly used **2** *n* Idiot, fool; =ASSHOLE

◁**assy**▷ *adj homosexuals* Malicious; nasty; mean; =BITCHY

-ateria *suffix used to form nouns* (Variations: **-teria** or **-eria** or **-eteria**) Place or establishment where the indicated thing is done or sold: *bookateria/ caviarteria*

Atkins See TOMMY ATKINS

at liberty *adv phr* Unemployed

-atorium or **-torium** or **-orium** *suffix used to form nouns* Place where an indicated thing is done: *drinkatorium/ lubritorium/ printorium*

attaboy or **attagirl** *interj* An exclamation of approval or encouragement; =WAY TO GO [fr *that's the boy*]

at the double See ON THE DOUBLE

at the switch See ASLEEP AT THE SWITCH

attitude *n fr black & prison* A resentful and hostile manner; pugnacity
See HAVE AN ATTITUDE

attrit 1 *v* To dispose of or dispense with gradually; subject to attrition: *Workers never retire, resign, or die. . .they are attritted*—New York Times **2** *v* To kill: *Well, if we can attrit the population base of the Vietcong, it'll accelerate the process of degrading the VC*—Frances FitzGerald **3** *n Air Force* An expected rate of loss or attrition: *Attrit. . .is now sometimes seen in Air Force publications to refer to an expected rate of loss or attrition*—American Speech

auction See JAM AUCTION

audible 1 *n football* A play or formation announced at the line of scrimmage and different from the one called in the huddle **2** *n* Any sudden or impromptu change of instructions, esp when issued orally: *The boss said if anything went wrong he'd give us an audible*

Augustus Owsley *n phr narcotics* A high-grade form of LSD [fr the name of the man who first pro-duced this high-grade variety]

aunt or **Aunt 1** *n* The madame of a brothel **2** *n homosexuals* An elderly male homosexual

auntie [1] *n fr early 1800s* Any elderly black woman

auntie [2] *n Air Force* An antimissile missile [fr humor-ous mispronunciation of **anti**]

Aunt Tom *n phr* A woman who does not support or sympathize with the women's liberation movement [fr the analogy with *Uncle Tom*]

ausgespielt (OUS kee speelt) *adj* Thoroughly exhausted; enervated; =FRAZZLED, PLAYED OUT [fr German, "played out"]

Aussie 1 *n* An Australian **2** *adj*: *the Aussie movie industry*

Aussie steak *n phr* Mutton

avoirdupois (AV ər də poyz) *n* Body weight; fat or fatness: *too much avoirdupois, so I'm dieting*

aw *interj* An exclamation of entreaty, disappoint-ment, disbelief, regret, and various other uncomfort-able feelings ●Used either alone or before certain fixed expressions like "come on," "hell," "man," "shit," or "shoot"

awash 1 *adj* Full of a liquid; full to surfeit: *Dr Johnson was awash in tea, drinking thirty cups each day* **2** *adj* Overwhelmed with; drowning in:

The dean was awash in niggling student complaints
See DECKS AWASH

away 1 *adv* baseball Out: *Two away in the top of the eighth* **2** *adv* underworld In prison

awesome *teenagers* *adj* Excellent; wonderful; outstanding; =COOL, NEAT

awful 1 *adj* Extremely unpleasant or objectionable **2** *adv* Very; intensely: *I feel awful bad about that*
See GOD-AWFUL

awfully *adv* Very; very much: *It's awfully dark here*

AWOL or **awol** (pronounced either as separate letters or as an acronym AY wawl) *armed forces fr WWI* **1** *adj* Absent without leave **2** *n* A person who is absent without leave

aw right **See** ALL RIGHT

aw shucks 1 *interj* An exclamation of embarrassment, self-abnegation, regret, and various other mildly uncomfortable feelings •Usu used in imitation of rural or extremely naive, boyish males **2** *v phr*: *good-ole-boy aw shucksing*—Time •euph for aw shit

awshucksness *n phr* Modesty; self-abnegating embarrassment: *Young Crosby displayed all the easygoing awshucksness of his late father*—Time

ax or **axe 1** *v* To dismiss someone from a job, a team, a school, a relationship, etc; =CAN, FIRE: *who suggested to Reagan that Deaver be axed*—Washingtonian **2** *v* To eliminate; cut: *They axed a lot of useless stuff from the budget* **3** *n jazz musicians fr 1950s* Any musical instrument, esp the saxophone: *The piano player noodled on his ax* **4** *n rock and roll* A guitar [sense 3 originally fr the resemblance in shape between a saxophone and an ax, and possibly fr the rhyme with *sax*; also related to the transferred idea of *chops*, originally related to a musician's embouchure, then thought of as blows with an ax]
See MEAT-AX

the ax **See** GIVE someone THE AX

axle **See** WRAPPED AROUND THE AXLE

axle grease *n phr* Butter

Aztec two-step *n phr* Diarrhea; =MONTEZUMA'S REVENGE, TURISTA

azul (ah zōōl) **1** *n* A police officer; =COP **2** *n* The police; =FUZZ [fr Spanish "blue"]

B

b *See* SON OF A BITCH

B narcotics **1** *n about 1950* Benzedrine™; =BENNY **2** *n by 1970s* =BEE **3** *n 1990s students* The game of Frisbee

babe *n by 1915* A girl or woman, esp a sexually desirable one; =CHICK, DOLL •Used almost entirely by men, and considered offensive by many women; having a strong resurgence of use in the 1990s

baby 1 *n early 1900s* A wife, girlfriend, or other cherished woman; also, less frequently, a husband, boyfriend, or cherished man: *My baby don't love me no more* **2** *n early 1900s* Any cherished or putatively cherished person •A shortening of earlier *warm baby* **3** *n by 1930s* A mean and dangerous man; =TOUGH GUY •*Babe* "a tough; a rowdy; blackguard" is attested in the 1860s, and attributed to Baltimore: *I did not want them babies to think they had me under contract*—John O'Hara **4** *n about 1910* A term of address for man or woman; =BUD, MAC, PAL •In stereotype, much used by show-business people: *And this is maximum security, baby*—Joseph Wambaugh **5** *n by 1900* Anything regarded with special affection, admiration, pride, or awe: *Those babies'll turn on a dime/ What we had heard was the firing of those big babies a mile and a half from shore*—Time **6** *n by 1930s* A thing referred to, esp something one does not know the name of; =GADGET, SUCKER: *What's this baby over here supposed to do?*
See BOTTLE BABY, HOT BABY

Baby Bell *n phr late 1980s* One of several regional telephone companies formed upon the fragmentation of the American Telephone and Telegraph Company: *The consent decree that broke up AT&T and created the Baby Bells*—New York Times [so called because they are progeny of *Ma Bell*]

baby blues *n phr by 1970s* Blue eyes: . . . *lookin' up into the baby blues of some sweet-faced Army nurse*—Gary Trudeau [perhaps influenced by *baby blue eyes*, a plant name attested in the 1880s]

baby boom *fr 1960s, despite an isolated occurrence in 1941* **1** *n phr* A significant rise in births, esp after 1945 **2** *modifier*: . . . *the millions of baby-boom couples who work for wages*—Los Angeles Times

baby boomer *n phr 1970s* A person born during the baby boom following World War II

baby bust *n phr early 1970s* A significant decline in the birth rate, esp the one beginning in the 1970s

[fr the common phrase *boom or bust*, said of the economy]

baby buster *n phr* (also **buster**) *1980s* A person born during a baby bust

babycakes or **honeycakes** *n 1960s* A sweetheart or other cherished person •A term of endearment: *Hey, babycakes, let's see those pecs*—Milwaukee Journal/ *"Ain't that right, baby?" "Sure is, honeycakes"*—New Yorker

baby doll *n phr early 1900s* A pretty woman, esp one cherished by a man as his own

baby-sit 1 *v 1940s* To attend and care for a child, or by extension, for anyone or anything: *Which is why she has one of us baby-sitting twenty-four hours a day*—Robert B Parker **2** *v 1960s narcotics* To be a guide and companion to someone undergoing a psychedelic drug experience [back formation from *baby-sitter*, "nursemaid, nanny," attested before 1940]

baby-sitter *n Navy fr Vietnam War* A destroyer that guards an aircraft carrier

baby split *n phr bowling* A split where two pins are left standing side by side

bach or **batch 1** *n by 1850s* A bachelor **2** *v* (also **bach it**) *1860s* Of a man, to live without a woman's help

bachelor girl 1 *n phr 1890s* An unmarried young woman, usu with a career or a profession; =CAREER GIRL **2** *modifier*: *a bachelor-girl apartment*

back 1 *v middle 1500s* To give one's support to some effort or person: *I'll back your application* **2** *v late 1600s* To bet on: *He backed Green Goo in the eighth* **3** *v by 1880s* To contribute money for; =BANKROLL: *My cousin backed the rock show in the park* **4** *n* (also **backup** or **backup for a beef**) *1980s teenagers* Someone who will support and assist; a trusty ally **5** *adv bartenders and waitresses by 1980s* As a chaser: *She wants whiskey with water back*
See BIRDYBACK, FISHYBACK, GET one's or someone's BACK UP, GET OFF someone's BACK, GET THE MONKEY OFF, GIVE someone THE SHIRT OFF one's BACK, KNOCK BACK, LAID-BACK, MELLOW-BACK, MOSSBACK, ON someone's BACK, PIGGYBACK, PIN someone's EARS BACK, RAZORBACK, YOU SCRATCH MY BACK, I SCRATCH YOURS

back alley 1 *n phr early 1860s* An alley or street in a mean and disreputable neighborhood; slum street or area **2** *modifier*: *a back-alley saloon/ back-alley language*

backasswards *adv* =ASS BACKWARDS

11

backbencher *n British by 1874* An occupant of a rear seat in a legislature; an obscure legislator •Still chiefly British: *No one I know of in modern times has gone from being a backbencher to being this much in the center of things in that short a time*—Newt Gingrich

back-breaker *n early 1900s* A very difficult job or task; =BALLBUSTER, BITCH, PISSER

back-burner 1 *v by 1980s* To put a project, idea, suggestion, etc, in reserve: *Shall we just back-burner that one?* **2 modifier**: *a back-burner crisis*—Elizabeth Drew

backchannel *n 1990s* A secret conduit for information: *Clinton's backchannel during the trouble was the Russian Embassy*—TV show *FirstNews*

backchat *n late 1800s British military* Impertinent and provocative replies, esp to a superior, elder, etc; =BACK TALK, SASS

back door 1 *n phr by 1643, and probably before* A devious, shady, and perhaps illegal means: *. . . an unhappy software vendor charges that he improperly used a "back door" to make good on a campaign promise. . .* —Newark Star-Ledger ◁**2**▷ *n phr late 1600s* The anus; =ASSHOLE

back-door *adj early 1900s* Dishonest; dubious •Earlier senses were "secret, clandestine" and "illegitimate, bastard": *. . . a sleazy little back-door business*

backdoor man *n phr 1960s black* A married woman's lover; =JODY

backdoor trots *n phr late 1700s British, now chiefly Canadian* Diarrhea

back down *v phr by 1850s* To retreat from one's position; surrender; retract: *He wouldn't back down even when they beat him up*

backgate (or backdoor) parole *n phr fr 1920s prison* The death of a prisoner from natural causes

backhouse *n by middle 1800s* An outdoor toilet house without plumbing; outhouse; =FIRELESS COOKER, PRIVY

back in the saddle *adj phr by 1940s* Operational again; restored to function: *. . . the economy is back in the saddle*—Milwaukee Journal/ *I have aspirations to get back in the saddle. . .* —Milwaukee Journal Sentinel [fr a popular cowboy song *Back in the Saddle Again*]

back number *n phr by 1880s* Someone or something out of date; =HAS-BEEN: *Mr Stale is a back number*—H McHugh

back off *primary sense, "retreat" by 1930s* **1 v phr** To stop annoying or harassing someone •Often a command or threat **2 v phr** To soften or moderate; relent: *The president backed off a little from his hardnosed line* **3 v phr** To slow down; go easier: *Hey, back off a little, I don't get you*

back someone **off** *v phr* To order someone to leave; eject someone: *The bouncer backed him off real quick*

back out *v phr fr early 1800s* To cancel or renege on an arrangement; =CRAWFISH, FINK OUT: *We can't back out just because we're scared*

back-pedal *v about 1900* To retreat, esp from a stated position; =BACK OFF, BACK OUT: *This news caused the candidate to back-pedal hastily*

backroom *adj by 1940s* Having to do with political expediency; from the inner circles of party affairs: *a backroom decision/ backroom motives* [fr *See what the boys in the back room will have*, suggesting a secret conclave in the rear of a saloon]

backscratch or **backscratching** *n late 1800s* A helping or accommodating of one by another: *It's got to be a mutual backscratch*—American Libraries *See* YOU SCRATCH MY BACK, I SCRATCH YOURS

back seat *See* TAKE A BACK SEAT

backseat driver *n phr 1920s* A person who gives unwanted and officious advice; =KIBITZER

back-slapper *n by 1924* A demonstratively friendly person: *Bob and Bill, they're back-slappers*—Milwaukee Journal Sentinel

back-slapping *adj by 1777* Demonstratively friendly: *. . . the back-slapping jocosity that passes for humor here*—Sinclair Lewis

back talk *n phr middle 1800s* Impudent response; impertinent comment; =SASS

one's **back teeth are floating** *sentence 1890s* One needs very urgently to urinate

back to square one *adv phr 1960s British* Returned to the starting point, usu having wasted a great deal of effort; no farther ahead: *Which means. . . we're basically back to square one*—Stan Cutler [origin uncertain; perhaps fr a pre-television system of designating parts of a soccer or rugby field by numbered squares to facilitate radio commentaries; perhaps fr one of various board games]

back to the old drawing board *sentence* The matter must be reconsidered; it's time to start again: *So back to the drawing board. Find another way to go*—Stan Cutler [fr the caption of an early 1940s Peter Arno *New Yorker* cartoon showing a crashed airplane]

back to the salt mines *adv phr 1920s* Returned to hard work and unremitting discomfort, after a period of relative ease and pleasure: *I had a week off, then back to the salt mines* [fr the tradition of Russian penal servitude in Siberian salt mines]

back-track *See* BOOT

backup 1 *n 1950s* A replacement, substitute, or something or someone in reserve •This sense was popularized by 1960s astronautics: *We can't afford to lose her because we've got no backup* **2 modifier**: *a backup system/ backup wide receiver*

back up 1 *v phr 1860s British* To support or confirm, esp to verify the statement of: *You explain it, and I'll back up your version* **2 v phr** To refer to some earlier place; reverse oneself a little: *They couldn't understand, so he backed up and told 'em once more* [first sense fr cricket "go behind a fielder in case he misses the ball"]

back someone **up 1** *v phr 1860s British* To confirm what someone says; support what someone does: *If you want to go in to complain, I'll back you up* **2 v phr 1950s** To be someone's substitute; be in reserve: *We've got three other drivers to back him up* **3** *v phr* baseball by 1940s To play behind a fielder to retrieve balls that might be missed

the **back yard** *n phr* circus by 1950s The performers as distinguished from the management

bacon *See* BRING HOME THE BACON

bad *adj* esp teenagers fr 1920s black Good; excellent; admirable: *real bad licks/ bad nigger* •The use is attested from slavery times, when this sense was marked by a lengthened vowel and a falling tone in pronunciation

    See SO BAD one CAN TASTE IT

bad actor *about 1900* **1** *n phr* A vicious animal **2** *n phr* A malicious or deceitful person **3** *n phr* A habitual criminal

◁**badass**▷ *1950s* **1** *n* A belligerent and worthless person; =BAD ACTOR, BAD EGG, BUM: *It's the badasses who don't want him back*—Philadelphia Journal/ *He still burned with a desire to show us Mad Dogs what a badass we'd passed up*—Easyriders **2** *adj*: *. . . sounds as bad-ass as John Denver singing "Macho Man"*—Aquarian **3** *adj* 1980s college Excellent; wonderful; =RAD, SLAMMIN'

bad boy *n phr* 1980s An impressive and perhaps dangerous device; =SUCKER: *You have written plenty of checks for your Harley. . . maybe even a few while right in the saddle of your bad boy*—Milwaukee Journal

bad cop *See* GOOD COP BAD COP

bad day at Black Rock *adj phr* An unhappy time: *It will be a bad day at Black Rock when the players. . . gather for the last time. . .* —Wisconsin State Journal [fr the 1955 cowboy-suspense movie *Bad Day at Black Rock*]

baddie or **bad guy** *1930s motion pictures* **1** *n* Someone or something that is bad, esp a movie, television, or sports villain **2** *n* A criminal or other habitually reprehensible person; =BAD MAN

bad egg *n phr* by 1855 A villain, criminal, or other deplorable person; =BAD ACTOR, BADDIE

badge *n* 1920s underworld A police officer

    See SCARE BADGE

badge bandit *n phr* hot rodders A police officer

badger game **1** *n phr* about 1880 A method of extortion in which a woman entices the victim into a sexually compromising situation, whereupon a male accomplice appears and demands payment for keeping the situation quiet **2** *n phr* A means of blackmail, extortion, or intimidation, esp one based on a sexually compromising situation [fr earlier *badger*, a thief who crawled through the detachable wall-panels of a panel house to rob the man bedded with his accomplice]

bad hair day *n phr* early 1990s The sort of day when nothing goes right; the sort of day that is not one's day: *They had a bad hair day, a bad CD-ROM day, who knows?*—Los Angeles Times [fr the notion that one's well-being depends on the neatness and order of one's hair]

bad man (or **guy**) *n phr* fr middle 1800s western A villain; a desperado: *. . . supposed to pick up a*

vehicle containing a suitcase full of cash this morning from a "bad guy". . . —New Yorker

bad-mouth *1930s* **1** *v phr* To disparage; denigrate: *He bad-mouthed everybody*—James Thurber **2** *n phr*: *If you can't say anything good, at least don't be a bad mouth*

bad news **1** *n phr* 1920s The bill for goods or services, esp a restaurant check; =BEEF **2** *n phr* 1930s Any unfortunate or regrettable situation or event: *That meeting was strictly bad news* **3** *n phr* 1960s An ominous person; a menace: *Their big new linebacker is bad news* **4** *n phr* 1970s An unpleasant or depressing person, esp a persistently annoying one: *Isn't she bad news since her old man left her?* [all senses extended from the literal]

◀**bad nigger**▶ *fr 1960s black* **1** *n phr* A black person, usu a male, who wins the respect of his own people by resisting the dominant white society: *A bad nigger was a nigger who "didn't take no shit from nobody"*—Claude Brown **2** *n phr* A belligerent black male, esp one who mistreats women •These illustrate the contradictory senses of *bad*, and both the taboo and acceptable senses of *nigger*, which depend upon who is using the word

bad paper **1** *n phr* by 1940s Worthless or counterfeit money, checks, etc: *They passed some bad paper* **2** *1970s fr Vietnam War veterans* A less-than-honorable discharge from military service

bad patch *n phr* 1920s British A period of difficulty, suffering, etc: *You went through a real bad patch. . . a shaky time*—TV show Geraldo

bad rap **1** *n phr* underworld An erroneous conviction or sentence; wrongful punishment; =BUM RAP **2** *n phr* Any unjustified condemnation: *Mobil has taken a bad rap from Congress*—Newsweek

bad scene *n phr* fr 1950s jazz musicians Something unpleasant, esp a displeasing and depressing experience or situation •The term was popularized by the 1960s counterculture [fr the jazz sense of *scene*, "center of activity for musicians," attested fr about 1925]

◁**bad shit**▷ **1** *n phr* by 1950s Something menacing and nasty: *A lot of bad shit goes down at the track, man*—Harry Crews **2** *n phr* by 1950s Bad luck: *Breaking my leg was just bad shit* **3** *n phr* 1960s narcotics A toxic or contaminated narcotic: *But it's bad shit, or too strong*—Stan Cutler

bad time *n phr* armed forces fr WWII Time spent in the guardhouse and therefore not a part of one's required period of service

bad (or **bum** or **down**) **trip** **1** *n phr* fr 1960s narcotics A frightening or depressing drug experience, esp a nightmarish time with LSD **2** *n phr* fr 1960s counterculture Any unpleasant occasion or experience; =BUMMER, DOWNER: *The party was a real bad trip*

bafflegab *n* late 1951 The pompous and opaque prose style affected by bureaucrats and certain scholars [coined by Milton Smith of the US Department of Commerce, fr standard *baffle* and slang *gab*, first attested in January 1952]

bag ◁1▷ *n by 1920s* The scrotum ◁2▷ *n by 1950s* A condom; =RUBBER, SCUMBAG **3** *n middle 1800s baseball* The cushionlike marker that serves as a base **4** *n 1960s narcotics* A portion of narcotics, often wrapped in a paper or glassine envelope: *They found three nickel bags of marijuana on him* ◁5▷ *n middle 1600s* A woman's breast •*Bag* has long meant an animal's udder **6** *v by 1814* To get or capture: *to bag a gold medal/ They bagged the mugger in the next block* **7** *v early 1800s* To arrest; =BUST, COLLAR: *You don't have to bag nuns*—Philadelphia Journal **8** *n 1920s* An unattractive girl or woman; ugly woman **9** *n fr 1950s jazz musicians* That which one prefers or is doing currently; =KICK, THING •Said to be fr *bag of tricks* **10** *n 1950s jazz musicians* An environment; milieu; =SCENE: *That fox comes out of a very intellectual bag*—W M Kelley **11** *v middle 1800s* To discharge; =CAN, FIRE, SACK: *Just, say the author was willing to bag an old friend*—Philadelphia Journal **12** *v 1960s* To suppress; get rid of; discard: *Let's bag the whole notion, okay?* **13** *v* (also **bag it**) *students by 1892* To avoid; not attend; =SKIP: *We can bag gym class*—William Goldman/ *Like bag this movie, for sure*—Newsweek **14** *v* (also **bag it**) *1980s students* To abandon; cease; give up: *I had to bag it. . . I had to give up all that stuff*—New York Magazine **15** *v 1960s* To include; categorize; group with: *We're always bagged in England with bands like Iron Maiden*—Rolling Stone **16** *v by 1990s* To break into for a clandestine investigation; do a black-bag job on: *. . . to pick up conversations by traveling execs, then "bagged" their hotel rooms to rummage through attaché cases*—New York Daily News **17** *v by 1990s* =BAG ON someone **18** *v narcotics by 1960s* To inhale fumes of an intoxicating substance: *. . . the dangers of inhaling, sniffing, and "bagging" such chemicals. . .*—Macon Telegraph

See BROWN-BAG, DIME BAG, DITTY BAG, DOGGY BAG, DOUCHE BAG, FAG BAG, FLEABAG, GRAB-BAG, GROUCH-BAG, HAIR BAG, HALF IN THE BAG, HAVE A BAG ON, IN THE BAG, JIFFY BAG, LET THE CAT OUT OF THE BAG, NICKEL BAG, OLD BAG, RUM BAG, SANDBAG, SLEAZEBAG, SLIMEBAG, STASH BAG, TIE A BAG ON, TOTE BAG, WINDBAG

bag and baggage *adv phr fr British military by 1600* Entirely; leaving nothing; with all one's possessions: *We threw her out bag and baggage/ It all went up in smoke, bag and baggage*

◁**bag ass**▷ *v phr Navy by 1960s* To leave quickly; get out; hurry; =HAUL ASS

bagel *n by middle 1980s* A tennis set won 6–0 •The term, said to have been coined by Eddie Gibbs, has spread to other sports, where it often means "zero, zip" [fr the shape of a *bagel*, a leavened, doughnut-shaped roll, fr Yiddish *beygl*, of uncertain origin but attested fr the early 1600s]

baggage *See* BLIND BAGGAGE, EXCESS BAGGAGE

baggage smasher *n phr fr middle 1800s* A baggage-handler at a railroad station, airport, etc

bagged 1 *adj by 1950s* Drunk **2** *adj by 1940s* Prearranged; **3** *adj* Exhausted; =BEAT, POOPED: *I'm too bagged to breathe*—comic strip "For Better or for Worse" [second sense fr the phrase *in the bag*]
See HALF-BAGGED

bagger *See* BROWN BAGGER, DOUBLE-BAGGER, FOUR-BAGGER, ONE-BAGGER, THREE-BAGGER, TWO-BAGGER

baggies 1 *n early 1960s surfers* A pair of loose-cut boxer-type men's bathing trunks: *. . . girls in bikinis and boys in "baggies"*—New York Times **2** *n by 1970s* A pair of full trousers with cuffs, resembling those of the 1930s: *Then comes a pair of "baggies," very baggy trousers*—New Yorker

bag job *n phr by 1970s* A theft or burglary, esp of files, documents, etc •Became current during the early–1970s Watergate affair: *Someone had done a bag job on his precious files*—C McCrystal/ *The spectators. . . sure know a bag job when they see one*—Sports Illustrated

bag lady or **shopping-bag lady** or **bag woman** *n phr early 1970s* A woman who goes about the streets collecting discarded objects and taking them home in shopping bags: *. . . a bag lady whose tiny room was crammed with garbage*—New York Post **2** *n phr* A homeless woman, often elderly, who lives in public places and carries her possessions in shopping bags: *. . . bag ladies, the Big Apple's discarded, homeless women*—New York Post

bagman 1 *n fr 1920s underworld* A person who collects money for bribers, extortionists, mobsters, etc: *And he was meeting the bagman and it went haywire*—Robert B Parker **2** *n fr 1960s narcotics* A person who peddles drugs; =PUSHER

bag or **load of wind** *n phr 1890s* =WINDBAG

bag of worms *See* CAN OF WORMS

bag on someone *v phr* (also **bag**) *1980s college students* To criticize someone; insult; =DUMP ON, PUT DOWN: *He's not like smart. I'm not trying to bag on him. . .*—Los Angeles Times/ *Far be it from us to bag, but we must say Cher's. . . book. . . leaves something to be desired*—Sassy

bags 1 *n middle 1800s British* Trousers ◁2▷ *n middle 1600s* A woman's breasts; =TITS **3** *n about 1920* A great quantity: *He's got bags of money*
See MONEYBAGS

bag some rays *v phr by 1980s* To sunbathe

bag your face *sentence early 1980s high school students* Conceal your face; you are repulsive •A generalized insult, perhaps related to *bag your head*, "shut up," attested fr the middle 1800s

bag Zs *See* COP ZS

bail *v 1970s college students* To leave; =CUT OUT, SPLIT: *Nicole Eggert. . . has bailed from the scene entirely*—Buzz/ *Most of my friends had bailed to stay with other relatives. . .*—Sassy
See JUMP BAIL

bail on someone *1980s college students* **1** *v phr* To break a date with someone; =STAND someone UP **2** *v phr* To tease someone; speak spitefully about someone; criticize someone

bail out *v phr by 1940s* To abandon an effort, project, relationship, etc, in order to minimize losses: *"Toddy" has bailed out of his geek house. . .* — Douglas Coupland [fr the 1920s aviation use, "to parachute from an aircraft"]

bail someone **out** *v phr by 1970s* To get someone out of a difficult plight; relieve someone of debt, embarrassment, etc: *I'll bail you out this time, but next time bring enough money* [fr paying someone's *bail* for release fr confinement]

bait money *n phr 1990s* Money given to a thief containing a device that will dye the money and the thief

bake and shake 1 *n phr 1980s* A search, esp a body search for narcotics **2** *v phr by 1990s* To cremate a body and scatter the ashes: *It's going to be tough to bake and shake that guy; he must weight 400 pounds*—Los Angeles Times [two of several slang variations on the name of a popular brand of pre-baking food coatings]

baked *adj middle 1980s* Intoxicated with narcotics; =HIGH, STONED
See HALF-BAKED

Baker flying *See* HAVE THE RAG ON

bald-headed row *1880s* **1** *n phr* The front row in a burlesque or other theater **2** *n phr* Any group of men, esp old men, who ogle women

Baldwin *n 1990s teenagers* An attractive male; =HUNK: *Baldwin. . . An attractive guy*—Macon Telegraph [said to refer to the actors William or Alec *Baldwin*]

baldy or **baldie 1** *n fr middle 1800s* A bald man **2** *n by 1970* A worn automobile tire

ball ◁1▷ *n fr 1300s* A testicle; =NUT ◁2▷ *v 1940s jazz musicians* To do the sex act; copulate with; =SCREW **3** *n 1890s underworld* A dollar, esp a silver dollar •Attested in the late 1980s as high-school student use in Delaware **4** *v early 1940s black* To have an especially good time; enjoy oneself in a relaxed and uninhibited way: *A good-time town, where everybody comes to ball*—New York Daily News **5** *n 1860s* The game of baseball
See BALL UP, BEANBALL, BUTTERFLY BALL, CANNON-BALL, CARRY THE LOAD, EMERY BALL, FIREBALL, FLY COP, FORKBALL, FOUL BALL, GET ON THE BALL, GO FOR THE LONG BALL, GOOFBALL, GOPHER BALL, GREASEBALL, GREEDBALL, HAVE A BALL, JUNK-BALL, KEEP one's EYE ON THE BALL, MEATBALL, NOT GET one's BALLS IN AN UPROAR, NUTBALL, ODDBALL, ON THE BALL, PLAY BALL, PLAY CATCH-UP, RED BALL, SLEAZEBAG, SLIMEBAG, SLUDGEBALL, SOFTBALL, SOURBALL, THAT'S THE WAY THE BALL BOUNCES

-ball 1 *combining word* A person who is obnoxious or strange because of what is indicated: *oddball/ goofball/ dirtball/ dizzball/ sleazeball* **2** *combining word 1970s* Baseball of a specified sort: *Billyball/ greedball* [first sense probably fr 1930s *screwball*, "eccentric person," fr late 1920s name of a baseball pitch, suggesting *screwy*, "crazy, eccentric"; second sense fr the kind of baseball played by the teams of the manager *Billy* Martin]

a **ball** *n phr 1930s black college students* An espe-cially good time; a loud, funny party: *The concert was a ball/ Man, we had us a ball*

◁**ball-and-chain**▷ *n early 1920s* One's wife; =OLD WOMAN

◁**ball-buster**▷ (Variations: **breaker** or **wracker** may replace **buster**) **1** *n by 1950* Something that is very difficult to accomplish; a Herculean task; =KILLER **2** *n by 1970* Someone who assigns and monitors extremely difficult tasks: *a real ball-buster of a skipper* **3** *n 1970s* An intimidating man; ruffian; =ENFORCER, GORILLA: *. . . it had been a mistake allowing these two ball-breakers in*—Michael Grant **4** *n 1970s* A woman who saps or negates a man's masculinity; castrating female

◁**ball-busting**▷ *1970s* **1** *n* The sapping or destruc-tion of masculinity; =NUT-CRUNCHING **2** *adj*: *. . . his lily-black reputation with that ball-busting wife of his*—Charles Beardsley

balled up *adj phr 1880s* In a thoroughly confused and futile condition; erroneous and useless because of perverse incompetence; =FUCKED UP, SCREWED UP: *Things were totally balled up when the alarm went* [probably fr the helplessness of a horse on a slippery street when its shoes have accumulated *balls* of ice; somehow the term has come to be associated with the testicles, as the related term *bollixed up* shows]

ball game 1 *n phr 1960s* A given set of conditions; complex of circumstances; situation: *What we do and what they do isn't the same ball game* **2** *n phr late 1960s* A competition; rivalry: *It's NBC ahead in the network ratings ball game, NBC says*—R Doan/ *Goodbye, ball game, he said*—R Grossbach **3** *n phr late 1960s* The decisive ele-ment or event, esp in a competition or encounter; =the NAME OF THE GAME: *The third ward vote is the ball game in this town*
See THAT'S THE BALL GAME, a WHOLE NEW BALL GAME, a WHOLE 'NOTHER THING

balling *n black fr 1930s* Fun, esp of an uninhibited sort

the **ball is in** someone's **court** *sentence early 1960s* The next action, decision, response, etc, belongs to the person or persons indicated: *That's my offer. The ball is in your court* [fr tennis]

ball of fire *n phr about 1900* A dazzling per-former; spectacularly successful striver; overachiever; =GO-GETTER, HOT SHOT [perhaps fr earlier *ball of fire*, "a very fast train"]

ball of wax *See* the WHOLE BALL OF WAX

balloon 1 *n fr 1920s hoboes* A hobo's bedroll; =BINDLE **2** *n by 1960s* A condom **3** *v fr 1920s the-ater* To lose one's lines completely during a perfor-mance; =BLOW UP, GO UP **4** *n 1970s* A dollar bill; one dollar: *It'll cost you six balloons* **5** *n Army by 1970s* A platoon **6** *n 1840s* The floating blob with a line to a speaker's mouth, used to show speech in comic strips
See LEAD BALLOON, WHEN THE BALLOON GOES UP

balloonhead *n 1930s* A stupid person; =AIRHEAD

balloonheaded *adj 1930s* Stupid; oafish: *Listen, you balloon-headed fool*—Jerome Weidman

balloon room *n phr* 1960s *narcotics* A room where marijuana is smoked; =BEAT PAD [probably because one gets high in such a place]

ballot box *See* STUFF THE BALLOT BOX

ballpark or **park** *n* by 1963 Claimed or designated special territory; =TURF: *Aren't you a little out of your ballpark here?/ . . . I've played mostly your game. But now we're in my park*—Robert B Parker *See* ALL OVER THE LOT, IN THE BALLPARK

ballpark figure (or **estimate**) *n phr* 1960s A rough numerical approximation: *I'd say forty, but that's a ballpark figure*

balls ◁1▷ *n* early 1300s The testicles ◁2▷ *n* by 1920s Courage; nerve; =GUTS: *They have balls but not soul*—Richard Goldstein/ *I admire a woman with the balls to bare her breasts*—Playboy **3** *interj* by 1940s An exclamation of incredulity, disappointment, or disgust **4** *n* chiefly British 1880s Nonsense; =POPPYCOCK: *That story is just such patent balls that I've written a letter*—Interview/ *He was talking high-minded balls. Twaddle!*—Saul Bellow •Frequently an interj of disbelief, contempt, etc *See* BLUE BALLS, BUST one's ASS, the CAT'S MEOW, DOES HOWDY DOODY HAVE WOODEN BALLS, GRIPE one's ASS, HAVE BRASS (or CAST-IRON) BALLS, HAVE someone BY THE BALLS, HAVE THE WORLD BY THE BALLS, NOT GET one's BALLS IN AN UPROAR, PUT BALLS ON, TIGHT AS KELSEY'S NUTS

◁**ballsiness** or **balliness**▷ *n* 1950s Courage; =BALLS, GUTS: *. . . a dangerous ethic of ballsiness in international affairs*—Newsweek

balls-out *adj* 1940s Very great; extreme; total: *That was more like a crazy, balls-out terrain, a whack course*—Sassy [probably fr *balls to the wall*]

balls to the wall *fr* 1960s *Air Force* **1** *adv phr* At or to the extreme; at full speed; =ALL-OUT, FLAT OUT: *. . . driving balls to the wall* **2** *adj phr*: *They are not the cigar-chomping "balls to the wall" warmongers of popular perceptions*—Newsweek [fr the thrusting of an aircraft throttle, topped by a ball, to the bulkhead of the cockpit to attain full speed]

balls-up *n* fr late 1930s *British* A confused and inept blunder; =FUCK-UP: *. . . a world-class balls-up*—Lawrence Sanders

◁**ballsy**▷ *adj* late 1950s Courageous; spunky; =GUTSY: *Valerie Green's a very ballsy lady*—Anne Bernays

ball the jack 1 *v phr* To move or work very rapidly **2** *v phr* To gamble or risk everything on one stroke or try [fr railroad term meaning "to go full speed"; related to the railroad sense of highball and of jack]

ball up 1880s **1** *v phr* To confuse; mix up; lead astray: *This guy has balled me up totally* •Attested fr 1856 in the sense "to fail an examination" **2** *v phr* To wreck or ruin by incompetence; botch; =BOLLIX UP, FUCK UP, SCREW UP: *I managed to ball up the whole project* **3** *n* about 1900 Confusion; blundering: *The ball-up abroad has been supervised by Harry's advisers*—Robert C Ruark

ball-wracker *See* BALL-BUSTER

bally *n* and *v* =BALLYHOO

ballyhoo by 1908 **1** *n* Advertising or publicity, esp of a raucous and colorful sort; =FLACK, HYPE: *to peddle a product with sheer ballyhoo* **2** *modifier*: *. . . a ballyhoo expert* **3** *v* about 1900: *They ballyhooed him right into office* [origin unknown; immediately fr carnival and circus use fr about 1900, "a short sample of a sideshow, presented with a barker's spiel"]

ballyhooed *adj* 1920s Much publicized: *. . . two ballyhooed mergers between telephone companies and cable-TV outfits. . .* —New Yorker

bally show *n phr* carnival & circus fr about 1910 A sideshow

bally stand *n phr* carnival & circus fr about 1910 The platform in front of a sideshow where the barker presents the ballyhoo

baloney or **balony** or **boloney** late 1920s **1** *n* Nonsense; pretentious talk; bold and deceitful absurdities; =APPLESAUCE, BULLSHIT, HOOEY: *No matter how you slice it, it's still baloney*—Carl Sandburg **2** *v*: *And don't try to baloney me, either* **3** *n* A stupid person: *You dumb baloney*—Jerome Weidman [perhaps fr Irish *balonie*, "nonsense"; however, about 1920 the word meant "an unskilled boxer; palooka," as reflected in the third sense above]

Baltimore chop *n phr* baseball fr late 1890s A batted ball that hits the plate or close in front of the plate and bounces high in the air

bam¹ by 1918 **1** *v* To strike or hit: *Heads may be biffed or bammed*—M Doolittle **2** *interj* (also **bamm, bammo**) An exclamation imitating a hard blow: *I got tested. . . and bammo! The bad news*—Elle **3** *n* The sound of a hard blow: *. . . it struck the desk with a resounding bamm*—Macon Telegraph *See* WHAM-BAM THANK YOU MA'AM

bam² *n* fr 1970s *narcotics* A mixture of a depressant with a stimulant drug, esp of a barbiturate with an amphetamine [fr barbiturate + amphetamine]

◁**bam** or **BAM**▷³ *n* fr WWII A woman Marine [fr broad-assed Marine]

bam-and-scram *n* 1990s A hit-and-run accident

bambino early 1920s **1** *n* A baby or young child **2** *n* A ruffian; an intimidating man; =GORILLA, TORPEDO •In the middle 1800s *babe*, "rowdy, blackguard," is attested in Baltimore slang; the identification of infant and goon is durable [fr Italian, "baby," literally "silly little one"]

bamboo *adj* Navy Crazy; erratic •Sense related to *Asiatic*

bamboo curtain *n phr* The barrier of secrecy and exclusion that once cut the People's Republic of China and other Asian Communist countries off from the rest of the world [modeled on *iron curtain*]

bamboozle *v* underworld fr about 1700s To hoax; trick; swindle; =FLIMFLAM: *My worthy opponent thrives by bamboozling the public* [origin unknown and much disputed; some claim a Romany source]

banana 1 *n* fr show business by 1950s A comedian, esp in a burlesque show •These performers were

ranked as "top banana," "second banana," etc **2** **n** **fr** black by 1940s A sexually attractive light-skinned black woman •Considered offensive by the women to whom this term is applied ◁**3**▷ **n** by 1916 The penis ◁**4**▷ **n** by 1980s An Oriental sympathetic with and part of the white majority society •Because white on the inside though yellow on the outside **5** **n** medical by 1980s A patient with jaundice ◁**6**▷ **n** by 1920 A fool; an idiot •Attested as college slang in 1989, probably based on bananas rather than on the earlier use◁**7**▷ **n** 1970s A crazy person; =LOONY
See HAVE one's BANANA PEELED, TOP BANANA

banana ball **n phr** 1960s A hit or thrown ball that curves off to the right; . . . can go to a golf course and. . . hit a banana ball supreme—Milwaukee Journal [fr the shape of a banana]

bananahead **n** by 1950s A stupid person

banana oil **n** about 1910 Nonsense, esp when used to flatter and mislead; =BUNK [perhaps fr the oily smoothness and fruity odor of banana oil, amyl acetate]

◁**banana republic**▷ **n phr** 1930s A small country, esp Central American, dominated by foreign companies [fr the fact that such places were typically under the control of the United Fruit Company, and grew bananas]

bananas **1** **adj** 1970s Crazy; =NUTS: I could see that my calm was driving him bananas—Stan Cutler **2** **adj** 1960s Very enthusiastic; highly excited; =APE **3** **adj** underworld fr 1930s Homosexual
See GO BANANAS

band **See** BIG BAND

Band-Aid 1960s **1** **n** A temporary or stop-gap remedy: All they did to rectify the problem was to put a Band-Aid on it—Wall Street Journal **2** **modifier**: a Band-Aid expedient [fr Band-Aid, trademark for a brand of small adhesive bandages]

bandbox **n** fr 1930s prison A small or rural jail, esp one that seems easy to escape from [fr the lightly built box formerly used by ladies to carry bits of finery]

B and D **n phr** 1960s Bondage and discipline; sadomasochistic sexual practice; =S AND M

bandit **1** **n** armed forces fr WWII An enemy aircraft **2** **n** prison by 1970s An aggressive homosexual who often resorts to violence
See BADGE BANDIT, LIKE A BANDIT, MAKE OUT LIKE A BANDIT, ONE-ARM BANDIT, SPACE BANDIT

bandwagon **n** railroad A car from which railroad workers are paid

the **bandwagon** by 1890s **1** **n phr** The strong current popularity and impetus of a person, idea, party, etc: the Reagan bandwagon/ the antinuke bandwagon **2** **modifier**: the bandwagon phenomenon
See GET ON THE BANDWAGON

bang **1** **n** about 1930 A very pleasurable sensation; surge of joy; thrill; =KICK, RUSH: This'll give you a big bang **2** **n** narcotics fr about 1910 An injection of a narcotic, esp an intravenous shot of heroin **3** **v** about 1920: They banged some horse and got high ◁**4**▷ **v** by 1916 To do the sex act with or to; cop-

ulate with: He banged her twice and left happy ◁**5**▷ **n** The sex act: The wedding night, you idiot. The first bang. How was it?—Lawrence Sanders **6** **adv** 1820s Precisely; exactly: . . . bang on the hour **7** **n** printers by early 1930s, computer by early 1980s An exclamation point; =SHRIEK: Let's stick a bang on it to dress it up—Los Angeles Times **8** **n** 1990s A drink of liquor; =SHOT: Give me a bang of Jaeger Meister—Los Angeles Times **9** **v** late 1980s Los Angeles gangs To be in a youth gang; be a gangbanger [last sense from the rhyme, but influenced by gang bang, "serial sex act done by a group of males to one woman," attested fr 1950s]
See BIG BANG, GANG BANG, GET A BANG OUT OF someone or something, GO OVER WITH A BANG, WHIZBANG

bang away **v phr** 1840s **1** To fire a gun or guns: The hunters banged away at the fleeing wolf **2** To attack as if by shooting: The defense kept banging away at the lack of an eye-witness

banger **1** **n** 1950s hot rodders A cylinder in an automobile engine: . . . a souped-up four-banger **2** **n** early 1960s A car, esp an old and decrepit vehicle; =HEAP, JALOPY: . . . this wonderful banger—Sports Illustrated **3** **n** 1980s Los Angeles gangs =GANGBANGER: They're all crowded, that's all. Lots of bangers, traffic accidents—Buzz
See BIBLE-BANGER, BIT BANGER, EAR-BANGER, FOUR-BANGER, WALL BANGER

bangers and mash **n phr** 1990s A minor car accident; =BUMPER-THUMPER, FENDER-BENDER [an adaptation of the British food phrase bangers and mash, "sausages and mashed potatoes," probably triggered by banger, "a car"]

bang for the buck **n phr** late 1960s Value for what one pays: You get the best bang for the buck right here—Chicago Magazine/ Yet the bang we are getting for our buck is worth whimpering about—Philadelphia [fr a frivolous way of referring to the national defense budget and the destructive power it produces]

bang out **v phr** by 1940s To make or compose something, esp to write something, in a hurry; cobble up

bangtail **n** about 1920 A racehorse [fr the manner of cropping and tying the tail of a racehorse as if it were chopped square in a bang; bang-tailed is attested fr 1861]

bang the hostess **v phr** airline by 1980s To ring for the cabin attendant

bang to rights **See** DEAD TO RIGHTS

bang-up **adj** 1830s fr about 1810 British Excellent; superior: I have some bang-up gin—Gene Fowler/ You've done a bang-up job on that report, Smythe

banjax **v** by 1939 To defeat utterly; =CLOBBER •Popularized in Great Britain by the Irish broadcaster Terry Wogan in the 1970s: She upped and banjaxed the old man—New Yorker [origin unknown]

banjo **n** (also **Irish banjo**) fr hoboes & railroad fr early 1900s A shovel

banjo hit **n phr** 1930s baseball A hit between the infield and outfield; =BLOOPER, TEXAS LEAGUER

banjo hitter *n phr 1930s baseball* A player who gets banjo hits and usu has a low batting average: *Banjo Hitter Plunks Brewers*—Milwaukee Journal

bank *n late 1980s teenagers* Money

bankable *adj 1960s* Having a reputation or influence that insures the success of a project: *. . . after a decade when bankable stars have all but monopolized movies*—New York Magazine/ *She had established herself as the most bankable female actress in Hollywood*—Philadelphia

bank on *v phr 1880s* Depend or rely on: *You can bank on his word*

bankroll *v 1920s* To finance; put up the money for, esp for a theatrical production; =ANGEL: *Whoever bankrolled this turkey will go broke*

banner *See* CARRY THE BANNER

bar *See* HERSHEY BAR, NUTBALL, SIDEBAR, SISSY BAR

barbecue *n outdated fr 1920s jazz musicians* A sexually attractive young woman

barber **1** *n 1920s baseball* A talkative baseball player **2** *v by 1940s* To converse; chat: *I shouldn't ought to barber with you*—Raymond Chandler **3** *n late 1940s baseball* A pitcher who forces the batter back from the plate by throwing at his head [first baseball sense reflects the fact that *barbers* were noted for talking to their customers; pitching sense fr Sal "*the Barber*" Maglie, late 1940s and 1950s New York Giants pitcher, who was known for this sort of pitch; the nickname probably reflects the fact that a *barber* gives a close shave]

barber chair *n phr fr 1960s astronautics* The adjustable seat used by an astronaut in a space craft

barber-shop *about 1910* **1** *modifier* Designating close-harmony singing, esp by a male quartet **2** *modifier*: *I've never sung barber-shop* [fr the presumed and archetypal male-quartet singing that occurred in *barber shops*]

Barbie Doll *early 1970s* **1** *n phr* A mindless man or woman; a person lacking any but typical, bland, and neatly attractive traits: *a Barbie Doll. . . programmed to sing, dance, and fall in love*—Time **2** *modifier*: *Our Barbie Doll president with his Barbie Doll wife*—Hunter S Thompson [fr the trademark of a very popular blue-eyed blonde teenage doll for young children]

barbs *n fr late 1950s narcotics* Barbiturates

barby or **barbie** *n 1980s Australian* A barbecue: *Put a shrimp on the barby for me*—Gary Trudeau/ *. . . which is sure to have Aussies everywhere ducking under their barbies*—Sassy

◁**bare-ass** or **bare-assed**▷ *adj 1930s* Naked; =BUCK NAKED

bareback *by 1950s* **1** *adv* Without using a condom **2** *adj*: *a bareback lay*

bareback rider *n phr by 1950s* A man who does the sex act without using a condom

bare-bones *adj by 1970s* Unadorned; spare; minimally accoutered: *. . . as it attempts to upgrade its image from a bare-bones discounter. . .*—Milwaukee Journal [fr the phrase *bare bones*, "mere skeleton," which is attested fr the 1600s]

barefaced or **bareface** *late 1600s adj* Bold; shameless; unscrupulous ●Nearly always seen in *barefaced lie* or *barefaced liar*, attested from 1850

barf **1** *v chiefly students fr 1950s* To vomit **2** *interj 1970s* An exclamation of strong disgust: *You want to know what I think of it? Barf!* **3** *v computer by early 1980s* To respond strangely or with an error warning after unacceptable input: *This machine barfs when I ask for a simple sort* [probably echoic]

barf bag **1** *n phr by 1960s* A paper bag provided on airplanes, ambulances, etc, to catch and hold vomit ◁**2**▷ *n phr 1980s teenagers* A disgusting person; something disgusting; =DOUCHE BAG, SCUMBAG **3** *adj*: *. . . Dicky Barrett's barf-bag vocal stylings*—Entertainment Weekly

Barf City *adj phr chiefly 1980s students* Disgusting; loathsome; =YUCKY

bar-fly *n about 1910* A heavy drinker; =LUSH, SOUSE

barf me out *interj 1980s high school students* An exclamation of disgust; =YUCK

◁**barfola**▷ *n 1980s college students* An unattractive woman; =DOG, DOUBLE-BAGGER

bargain *See* NO BARGAIN

bargaining (or **gambling) chip** *n phr 1960s* Something to be offered, conceded, threatened, etc, in negotiations: *He is using his information like a bargaining chip*—New York Times/ *The boy isn't just a gambling chip, Walter*—Hugh Pentecost [fr the *chip* used in gambling]

barge in or **into** *by about 1910* **1** *v phr* To enter a place without hesitation or ceremony, esp when not invited: *You can't just barge into the Yale Club* **2** *v phr* To interrupt; esp to intrude with unwanted counsel; =BUTT IN, KIBITZ [fr the slow, heavy impact of a *barge,* and the sense "bump heavily into," attested fr the 1880s]

bar-girl *n* =B-GIRL

bargle *See* ARGLE-BARGLE

barhop *v* (also **bar crawl** or **pub crawl**) *first form 1940s; third form by 1915* To go drinking from bar to bar

barker **1** *n fr late 1600s British* A person who attracts customers, esp to a circus or carnival sideshow, with a spiel and a sample **2** *n early 1800s* A pistol

barking dogs *n phr by 1930s* Tired or sore feet

bark up the wrong tree *v phr by 1830s* To be mistaken; be seeking in the wrong direction: *You're barking up the wrong tree if you think the cause is entirely economic*

barmy or **balmy** *adj first form chiefly British fr about 1600, second fr middle 1800s* Mildly crazy; =CRACKED: *One of your balmier notions* [fr *barm*, "froth on fermenting beer," hence "flighty, ditsy"; fell in with *balmy*, said to be fr St. *Bartelemy*, the patron of mad folk, perhaps because the words are homophones on British English]

barn *See* someone CAN'T HIT THE SIDE OF A BARN, GO AROUND ROBIN HOOD'S BARN

barn-burner *n by 1940s* Anything sensational or exciting; a great success: . . . *whether they have a barn burner of a natural gas well or a dry hole—*Newsweek/ *George's Bank has proved to be, in the words of one oil-company executive, "no barn-burner"*—Boston Globe

barney 1 *n middle 1800s* A prize fight or race whose outcome has been prearranged; a fixed fight or race: *looked like a barney, as if there were some collusion—*A J Liebling **2** *n 1980s college students* A despised person; =NERD [second sense fr the name of a character in the TV show *The Flintstones*]

barnstorm 1 *v 1880s* To travel as an entertainer, making short or one-night appearances in small towns **2** *v fr 1920s aviators* To travel about in an airplane or with an air show, doing aerobatics, giving rides, etc, esp in rural places [back formation fr earlier *barnstormer*]

barnstormer *n by 1860s* A person who barnstorms, esp a traveling actor

barnyard golf *n phr 1920s* The game of horseshoe pitching

barracks bag *See* BLOW IT OUT

barracks lawyer *See* LATRINE LAWYER

barrel or **barrel along** *v or v phr late 1920s* To speed, esp to drive a car very fast; career
See CRACKER-BARREL, IN THE BARREL, LIKE SHOOTING FISH IN A BARREL, OVER A BARREL, SCRAPE THE BOTTOM OF THE BARREL

◁**barrel ass**▷ *v phr 1950s hot rodders* To barrel: *We're barrel-assing toward Van Nuys—*Esquire

barrelhouse 1 *n by 1880s* A cheap saloon, esp one in combination with a brothel: *Barrelhouse kings, with feet unstable—*Vachel Lindsay **2** *n 1920s jazz musicians* A jazz style marked by strong beat and ensemble improvisation; also, music in this style **3** *modifier*: *barrelhouse jazz/ barrelhouse beat*

barrelhouse bum *n phr 1920s hoboes* =SKID ROW BUM

bar the door *See* KATIE BAR THE DOOR

base *See* GET TO FIRST BASE, OFF BASE, OFF one's BASE, TOUCH BASE WITH someone

baseball *See* OLDER THAN GOD

baseball Annie *n phr 1960s* A young female baseball fan, esp one who courts the players: *He was a big hit even with the Baseball Annies memorialized in Bull Durham—*People/ *. . . the groupies known as Baseball Annies who hang around the players' hotels—*New York Times

basehead *n 1980s* A narcotics addict, esp one who uses freebase cocaine

bases *See* TOUCH ALL BASES

bash 1 *v 1860s* To hit; =CLOBBER, SOCK **2** *n 1940s* A party, esp a good, exciting one: *Her little soiree turned into a real bash* **3** *n 1940s British* An attempt; =CRACK, WHACK: *Let's have a bash at moving this thing*

-basher *combining word 1880s British* A person who harasses or beats the person or item indicated: *Japan-basher/fag-basher/honkybasher*

-bashing *combining word esp since late 1950s* Hating and attacking what or who is indicated: *Clinton-bashing/faggot-bashing/geezer-bashing/gringo-bashing/ Paki-bashing*

basket 1 *n late 1800s* The pit of the stomach; =BREADBASKET: . . . *a blow flush in the basket—*Joseph Auslander **2** *n 1940s homosexuals* The male genitals, esp when prominently displayed in tight pants: *Steep enthusiastic eyes, Flicker after tits and baskets—*W H Auden

basket case *fr 1960s* **1** *n phr* A helpless, hopeless, distraught person: *If I worried after a decision. . . I'd be a basket case—*Time **2** *n phr* Anything ruined and hopeless: *Those are only the best-known corporate basket cases—*Toronto Life/ *the reconstitution of the East Wing as an autonomous. . . nation and international basket case—*Time [fr a 1919 term describing a person, usu a wounded soldier, without either arms or legs, who needed to be carried in a *basket*; use revived in 1939 by Dalton Trumbo's novel *Johnny Got His Gun*]

◁**bassackward** or **bassackwards**▷ *1930s* **1** *adj* Backwards; reverse; =ASS BACKWARDS: *sort of bassackward hydraulic gimcrackery—*Car and Driver **2** *adv*: *He got it all bassackwards*

basser *n early 1990s teenagers*: *"Bassers". . . drive around . . . playing recordings of what sound like above-ground nuclear tests. . .* —Dave Barry

basshead *n by 1990s* A dancer in a "rave" who stays near the speakers: *Some ravers are dubbed "bassheads" because they dance next to the 10-foot stereo speakers. . .* —Wisconsin State Journal

◁**bastard**▷ **1** *n late 1600s* A man one dislikes or disapproves of, esp a mean, dishonest, self-serving man; =PRICK, SON OF A BITCH **2** *n 1930s* Anything unpleasant or arduous; =BITCH: *Ain't it a bastard the way it keeps raining*

basted *adj 1920s* Drunk

bastille (ba STEEL) *n 1880s* A jail or prison [fr the former French royal prison]

bat ◁**1**▷ *n fr early 1600s* A prostitute; a loose woman •Probably so-called because she works at night◁**2**▷ *n* =OLD BAT ◁**3**▷ *n by 1880s* A woman, esp an ugly one **4** *n 1840s* A spree; carousal; =BINGE
See GO TO BAT AGAINST, GO TO BAT FOR, HAVE BATS IN one's BELFRY, LIKE A BAT OUT OF HELL, RIGHT OFF THE BAT, TAKE OFF LIKE A BIGASS BIRD

not bat an eye *See* NOT BAT AN EYE

bat around *v phr late 1800s* To do nothing in particular; go about in idle pursuit of pleasure; =FART AROUND, GOOF AROUND: *I want the kids home instead o' battin' around the street—*Elmer Rice [perhaps fr the erratic movements of a *bat*]

bat something around *v phr by 1940s* To discuss the pros and cons of an idea, project, etc =KICK something AROUND: *We batted around the notion of a sick-out*

bat boy *n phr early 1990s* A person who beats homeless people [fr the *bat boy* who looks after bats for a baseball team]

bat one's **brains out** *v phr by 1940s* To puzzle or study intensely; cogitate painfully: *I've been batting my brains out all day, but still can't figure it out*

bat carrier *n phr outdated underworld fr 1920s* A police informer; =STOOL PIGEON

batch *See* BACH, LAY A BATCH

batch out *v phr 1950s hot rodders* To start and accelerate a car from a standstill

bat one's **gums** *v phr* (Variations: **beat** or **hump** or **flap** may replace **bat**; **chops** or **jaw** or **jowls** or **lip** may replace **gums**) *entry form fr WWII armed forces; beat form fr 1940s black* To talk, esp idly or frivolously: *He didn't mean it—he was just batting his gums/ Well, you weren't just flapping your lip that time*—Peter De Vries

bath *See* TAKE A BATH

bathroom humor *n phr* Very gross and puerile wit: *But bathroom humor, especially vile bathroom humor illustrated in full and graphic detail, has never appealed to me. . .* —Mesa Tribune

bathtub gin *n phr outdated, esp 1920s* Gin made at home by mixing alcohol with flavoring, often literally in a bathtub

bat out *v phr by 1940s* To write something more quickly than one ought; =WHOMP UP: *He kept batting out scenes*—Budd Schulberg/ *Bat me out a memo, please*

bats or **batty** *adj first form about 1920, second about 1900* Crazy; =BATTY, NUTS: *He was grinning like he was bats/ . . . funnier than you'd expect, fairly batty*—Village Voice

See HAVE BATS IN one's BELFRY

batten down the hatches *v phr late 1800s* To get ready for trouble; take precautions; =BUCKLE YOUR SEAT BELTS: *So we batten down the hatches and wait it out*—Hugh Pentecost [fr the action of a ship's crew, securing wooden *battens* over the hatches in anticipation of a gale]

battery acid *n phr WWII armed forces* Coffee

bat the breeze *v phr WWII armed forces* To chat; converse, esp easily and idly; =RAP, SHOOT THE BREEZE: *a couple of cops batting the breeze*

battle-ax *n 1890s* An ill-tempered woman, esp a mean old woman; virago

Battle of the Bulge *n phr by 1960s* The constant struggle to keep slim, to eliminate the bulge around one's waist [fr the name of the Ardennes campaign of late 1944 in World War II]

battle royal *n phr by 1670s* A general quarrel or fight; =BRANNIGAN, DONNYBROOK: *What began as a mild disagreement escalated into a battle royal*

battlewagon **1** *n fr 1920s Navy* A battleship **2** *n outdated 1920s underworld* A police patrol wagon

batty *See* BATS

bat one's **wings** *v phr 1990s* To be futile; waste one's effort: *I've got to get people away from denial. Until I can do that I'm kind of batting my wings*—Milwaukee Journal

bawl someone **out** *v phr fr early 1900s* To reprimand severely; rebuke; =CHEW someone OUT

bay window *n phr by 1870s* A protuberant stomach; paunch; =POTBELLY: *He's lean and mean, no bay window and no patience*

bazillion *n by 1980s* A very large number; a zillion: *. . . lavished bazillions of dollars. . .* —Milwaukee Journal

◁**bazongas** or **bazoongies** or **bazookas**▷ (bə ZAHN gəz, bə ZOON geez) *n 1970s* A woman's breasts; =BAZOOM, JUGS: *. . . what difference would it make that her bazookas were twice the size of mine?*—Sue Grafton [all based on *bazooms*]

bazoo (bə ZOO) *n fr early 1900s* The mouth, esp regarded as a speech organ •The meaning shifted from "horn, trumpet," in phrases like "blow one's own bazoo" and "the silvery tinkle of his bazoo," attested in the middle 1800s: *if you would close that big bazoo*—Walt Kelly [apparently fr Dutch *bazuin*, "trumpet"]

See SHOOT OFF one's MOUTH

bazooka¹ (bə ZOO kə) **1** *n fr WWII Army* A small anti-tank rocket launcher **2** *n 1990s* A very successful enterprise; =BLOCKBUSTER: *. . . its big bazooka, Home Improvement*—Los Angeles Times [first sense fr its resemblance to a tubular musical instrument played by the 1940s comedian Bob Burns, who invented and named it in 1905]

bazooka² *n late 1980s narcotics* A marijuana cigarette impregnated with bazuco, a coca paste [fr Sp *bazuco*, "bazooka"]

◁**bazoom** or **bazooms**▷ (bə ZOOM) *n 1950s* A woman's breast or breasts: *Whatever Julie Andrews wants to do with her bazooms is OK with me*—Susan Rausch [fr comic mispronunciation of bosom, and association with the excitement of zoom]

bazuco or **basuco** *n late 1980s narcotics* A cheap cocaine paste: *Also on the horizon are "croak". . . and "basuco," a cocaine derivative. . .* —Milwaukee Journal [fr Sp *bazuco*, "bazooka," suggesting the effect of the drug]

B-bag *See* BLOW IT OUT

b-boy *late 1980s* **1** *n* A devotee of rap music •Originally applied to middle 1980s *break dancers*: *. . . b-boys with business cards*—New York Times **2** *n* A stylish dresser [perhaps abbreviation of *break boy*, perhaps of *beat boy* or *bad boy*]

be *v early 1990s* To say; =GO: *He's Oates, Oates, I'm going to get you*—New York Times/ *I was "Bart, Bart, get these guys going*—New York Times

beach blanket bingo *n phr 1960s* Sexual activity on the beach; the love game pursued semi-nude amidst sun and sand [fr the title of a 1965 movie]

beach bum *n phr early 1960s* A man who frequents beaches, esp one who is a surfer, who conspicuously shows his muscles, etc

beach bunny *n phr 1960s* A girl who, whether or not a surfer, spends time with surfers; =GREMLIN

beached whale *n phr medical by 1980s* A very obese person, esp one who cannot get out of bed or a chair without assistance

bead *See* DROP BEADS, GET A BEAD ON something or someone

the beads *n phr 1960s* Fate; destiny: *. . . fate, or*

whatever else you called it: "the beads"—John Rechy

beady eye *See* GIVE someone THE FISH-EYE

be a friend of Dorothy's *v phr* *1990s Canadian students* (also **know Dorothy**) To be homosexual [fr *Dorothy*, the main character in *The Wizard of Oz*, played in the movie by Judy Garland; the actress is a great favorite of many homosexuals]

beak 1 *n outdated fr 1830s* A mayor, magistrate, or trial judge •Outdated in US use, though still current in British slang •Attested in 1573 as *beck* **2** *n* The nose: *The beak-buster in the opening round was the first punch Moore had thrown*—Associated Press

See EAGLE-BEAK

the beam *See* OFF THE BEAM, ON THE BEAM

beam me aboard or **up** *v phr* (also **beam me up, Scotty**) *1980s students* **1** Tell me what is happening **2** Get me away from here [fr the TV series *Star Trek*, in which a character called *Scotty* teleported other characters by means of a "transporter beam"]

bean 1 *n 1850s underworld* A five-dollar gold piece **2** *n about 1900* A dollar: *. . . without a coat on his back or a bean in his pocket*—J Lilienthal **3** *n about 1900 gambling* A poker chip **4** *n about 1900* The head, esp the human head and brain: *Whistling at a crook is not near as effective as to crack him on the bean with a hickory stick*—Will Rogers **5** *v about 1910* To strike someone on the head, esp to hit a baseball batter on the head with a pitch: *Not the first time I've been beaned*—Stan Cutler ◀**6**▶ *n about 1920* A person of Spanish-American background, esp a Chicano

See FULL OF BEANS, JELLYBEAN, LOOSE IN THE BEAN, MEAN BEAN, SPILL THE BEANS, USE one's HEAD

beanball *n about 1900* A baseball pitch that hits or nearly hits the batter's head and is sometimes used to intimidate the batter: *Mr Bender places much reliance on the bean ball*—C Dryden

bean counter *n phr 1970s* A statistician or arithmetical clerk in government or business; an accountant; =GNOME, NUMBER CRUNCHER: *Even in Britain, the bean counters couldn't tolerate a negative cash flow forever*—Car and Driver/ *. . . the bean counters always spoil our fun*—Brian Di Salvatore [In the middle 1800s a popular comedian called Mose the Bowery Boy ordered pork and beans: "Say, a large piece of pork, and don't stop to count de beans," which became a much-quoted line]

bean-counting *modifier* Having to do with bureaucratic statistics and calculations: *We have our bean-counting ways; they, Russians, Cubans, etc, have their bean-counting ways*—National Public Radio/ *This bean-counting approach is an easy way to score debating points*—New York Times

bean-eater 1 *n about 1800* A resident of Boston ◀**2**▶ *n about 1920* A person of Spanish-American background, esp a Chicano; =BEAN

◀**beaner**▶ *n* A person of Spanish-American background, esp a Chicano; =BEAN, BEANEATER: *I was called a wetback, a beaner, a spic*—Los Angeles Times

beanery *n by 1890s* A restaurant or diner, esp a cheap one: *a beanery in Hell's Kitchen*—John McCarten

beanie *n about 1920* A skull cap, esp one worn by schoolboys and college freshmen; =DINK

beanpole *n 1830s* A tall, thin person; =HATRACK: *She was tall, but no beanpole*—Raymond Chandler

beans 1 *n by 1830s* Nothing; a minimal amount; =DIDDLY: *I wouldn't give you beans for that idea/ She would get all of her famous friends to appear and pay them beans*—Time [A *bean* in this sense is attested fr the 1200s. Semantically the same as *bubkes*] **2** *interj early 1900s* An exclamation of disbelief or contempt

See FULL OF BEANS, a HILL OF BEANS, KNOW one's ONIONS, NOT KNOW BEANS

bean-shooter *n by 1940s* A small-caliber pistol; =POPGUN

Bean Town *n phr about 1900* Boston, Massachusetts

bean wagon *n phr about 1900* A small restaurant or diner, esp a cheap one [perhaps fr the mid–19th-century inception of prepared food selling from *wagons*, noted, for example, in Providence, Rhode Island]

bear 1 *n 1960s narcotics* A capsule containing a narcotic **2** *n students by 1960s* A difficult school or college course **3** *n by 1950s* Anything arduous or very disagreeable; =BITCH: *It's been a bear of a morning*—Radio traffic report •*Bear* is attested fr 1915 in a similar sense, "doozie, humdinger" **4** *n* =BEARCAT: *Stokovich. . . was a bear for records. . .*—Carsten Stroud **5** *n by middle 1700s* A large, gruff man [third sense perhaps influenced by jazz 1930s musicians' use, "an unhappy state or condition; impoverishment," in which it was rhyming slang for "nowhere"]

See DOES A BEAR SHIT IN THE WOODS

Bear *See* SMOKEY BEAR

bearcat *by 1916* **1** *n* A durable and determined person; tough fighter or worker: *. . . a bearcat for jobs like this* **2** *n* Something remarkable, wonderful, superior, etc; =BEAUT, HUMDINGER

beard 1 *n 1950s beat & cool talk* An up-to-the-minute, alert person; =HIPSTER **2** *n by 1980s fr gambling* A person used as an agent, to conceal the principal's identity: *Use him as a beard, is what Donny thought he'd do*—Dan Jenkins/ *He's the beard. That's what they call the other man who pretends to be the lover*—Lawrence Sanders **3** *v*: *She says Rollins was supposed to beard for him. . .*—Stan Cutler **4** *n by early 1700s* A bearded man, esp someone of apparent dignity and authority: *I can't believe the sainted beards would bang me with a manufactured case*—Paul Sann **5** *n by late 1600s* The pubic hair; =BEAVER, BUSH

See GRAYBEARD

◁**bearded clam**▷ *n phr by 1960s* The vulva

bear hug 1 *n phr by 1930s* A crushing embrace **2**

n phr 1970s business A takeover bid so enticing that directors are forced to accept it

a **bear in the air** *n phr* middle 1970s A police officer in a helicopter [fr Smokey Bear]

bearish *adj* Showing a negative and unhopeful attitude; disheartening •Often used with "on" or "about": *He's quite bearish on our chances/ She's not entirely discouraging but rather bearish* [fr the stock market term *bear market*, "market in which price, sales, etc, tend to decrease"]

bear trap *n phr* 1970s citizens band A police radar trap for speeders [related to Smokey Bear, "policeman"]

beast ◁1▷ *n* esp WWII armed forces A cheap prostitute ◁2▷ *n* (also **beastie, beasty**) 1940s teenagers An especially unattractive woman **3** *n* jazz musicians by 1960s Any woman whatever, but esp a young attractive one **4** *n* by 1860s Anything regarded as difficult and misbegotten: *But that is part of the beast that was created*—Milwaukee Journal

beat 1 *n* fr middle 1800s A loafer; drifter; =DEADBEAT, MOOCHER **2** *v* 1830s To baffle; nonplus: *It beats me how she can do so much* **3** *v* fr 1920s underworld To avoid a fine or conviction: *He beat the burglary rap* **4** *n* news media about 1900 News printed or broadcast first, before one's competitors; =SCOOP: *The News scored an important beat* **5** *n* early 1700s The area or subject matter that one is assigned to handle: *cop on his beat/ a reporter on the courthouse beat* **6** *modifier*: *. . . anything I knew that I hadn't told the beat man at the news conference*—Robert B Parker **7** *adj* by 1830s Very tired; =ALL IN, POOPED: *You. . . have been on the go right around the clock. You look beat*—Hugh Pentecost **8** *n* by 1930s The basic meter of a piece of music, esp the insistent percussive rhythm of some jazz styles and rock and roll **9** *adj* 1950s beat talk Alienated from the general society, and expressing this by a wandering life, the avoidance of work, the advocacy of sexual freedom, the use of narcotics, a distinctive style of dress and grooming, and the adoption of certain aspects of Far Eastern religions: *the beat generation/ beat poets* **10** *n* =BEATNIK **11** *v* by 1850 To rob or defraud: *I sure got beat when I bought that old clunker* **12** *adj* 1980s teenagers Boring; stupid; =LAME **13** *n* theater by 1950s A short pause; heartbeat: *I waited a beat, then started for the garage*—Stan Cutler/ *. . . it may take a couple of beats to absorb the shock of this new length. . .*—Harper's Bazaar

See DOWNBEAT, UPBEAT

beat a dead horse *v phr* middle 1800s To continue arguing, discussing, or broaching a matter that is settled or proved unavailing [*Dead horse* as something not revivable is attested fr the middle 1600s]

beat all *v phr* 1830 To surprise one; be a wonder: *Doesn't it beat all how Fred is always first in line?*

beat all hollow *v phr* fr middle 1800s To defeat easily; surpass completely: *His story beats mine all hollow* [*Beat hollow*, "beat entirely, clobber" is attested fr 1769]

beat around (or about) the bush *v phr* middle 1500s To avoid speaking directly and precisely; evade; tergiversate

beat one's **brains out** *v phr* late 1500s To labor strenuously with the mind, often with a sense of having failed: *I beat my brains out getting ready for it, but flunked anyway*

beat someone or something **by a country mile** *v phr* by 1940s To win or prevail by a comfortable margin: *Her cherry pie beats mine by a country mile/ He beat the throw by a country mile*

beat-down 1 *n* 1990s A quick body search for weapons, drugs, etc: *What you gonna do. . . give me a beat-down right here?*—New York Times **2** *n* 1990s street gang A beating given to a member who decided to leave the gang: *So I didn't have to go through the beat-down or be jumped out*—Milwaukee Journal Sentinel

beaten down to the ankles *adj phr* by 1950s Totally exhausted; =BEAT, POOPED

beaten-up *See* BEAT-UP

beater *n* by 1980s A car, esp an old and used one: *. . . when he's stolen the beater off the streets*—Ann Rule

See EGGBEATER, GUM-BEATER, WORLD-BEATER

beat one's **gums** *See* BAT one's GUMS

beat someone **in** *v phr* 1990s street gang To initiate someone into a gang by assaulting them: *"When you're getting 'beat in' or 'quoted,'" one female "G" explains. . .*—LA Weekly

beating *See* GUM-BEATING, TAKE A BEATING

beat something **into** someone's **head** *v phr* by 1880 To teach something persistently and rigorously: *How often must I beat it into your head that dragons are dangerous?*

beat it *v phr* early 1900s To go away; depart; =SCRAM •Often a command: *When the cop told us to beat it we didn't waste any time*

◁**beat** one's **meat**▷ *v phr* (Variations: **flog** or **pound** may replace **beat**; **dummy** or **log** may replace **meat**) 1960s To masturbate

beatnik *n* fr 1950s A person who is beat in the sense of alienation from society, etc [*See* beat and -nik; coined by San Francisco newspaper columnist Herb Caen in 1958]

◁**beat off**▷ *v* 1960s To masturbate

beat-out *adj* fr 1870s Tired; exhausted; =BEAT, POOPED

beat someone **out** *v phr* by 1840s To surpass or best someone, esp by a narrow margin: *She just beat me out for the job, probably because she had more schooling*

beat someone **out of** something *v phr* early 1880s To take something away by cheating or fraud: *He was so simple they beat him out of his money before he knew it*

beat pad *n phr* 1960s narcotics A place where marijuana may be bought and smoked, esp inferior marijuana; =BALLOON ROOM

beats me *sentence* 1880s I don't know; I don't understand: *Why was he hired? Beats me/ . . . why* *don't they take the whole investigation. . . ? Beats the shit out of me*—Michael Grant

be at square one *See* GO BACK TO SQUARE ONE

beat the bushes *v phr by 1940s* To search diligently; seek ardently: *You beat the bushes and beat the bushes for years*—National Public Radio [fr the practice of driving game out by *beating the bushes*]

beat the drum *v phr early 1600s* To broadcast emphatically and constantly; insistently feature: *He's beating the drum for that pet idea*

◁**beat the hog**▷ *v phr by 1970s* To masturbate

beat the rap *v phr fr 1920s underworld* To go unpunished; be acquitted: *Every time they arrest him he beats the rap*

◁**beat the shit out of** someone or something▷ *v phr* (Variations: **bejabbers** or **bejesus** or **daylights** or **hell** or **kishkes** or **living daylights** or **living shit** or **stuffing** or **tar** or **whey** may replace **shit**; **kick** or **knock** or another term denoting assault or punishment may replace **beat**) *entry form by 1950; others generally earlier* To defeat or thrash thoroughly; trounce; =CLOBBER: *. . . tried to blackmail him, he's beat the shit out of you*—Elmore Leonard/ *He went up against palooka and they beat the stuffing out of him*—National Public Radio/ *"I'll sue the shit out of her," vowed Professor Gold*—Joseph Heller

beat the socks off someone *v phr by 1970s* To defeat decisively; trounce; =CLOBBER: *In a surprising upset, Hart beat the socks off Mondale*

beat someone's **time** *v phr about 1930* To win out over a rival, esp to take someone's girlfriend or boyfriend away

beat someone **to the draw (**or **to the punch)** *v phr* To act sooner or quicker than someone else; forestall: *If we. . . beat 'em to the punch, they're not going to look too good*—Stan Cutler

beat to the ground *adj phr* (Variations: **a frazzle** or **the socks** may replace **the ground**) *entry form by 1940s; second form early 1900s* Totally exhausted; =POOPED: *Frankie Machine, looking beat to the ground, brushed past*—Nelson Algren

beat-up *adj 1930s* Battered and damaged, esp by age and use: *He drove a beat-up Volvo/ an old beat-up dog*

beat someone **up** *v phr about 1900* To thrash someone soundly

beat up on *v phr about 1900* To attack and damage; criticize harshly; trounce; =CLOBBER: *. . . a message to people who beat up on the public programs*—New York Times

beat one's **way** *v phr 1870s* To travel without paying; travel in the cheapest possible way

beaut (BY$\overline{oo}$T) *n by 1860s* A person or thing that is remarkable or extraordinary; =HUMDINGER, LOLLAPALOOZA: *While the president doesn't go off on these tangents often, when he does, they are beauts*—Drew Pearson/ *That black eye was a beaut*

beautiful 1 *interj middle 1800s* An exclamation of approval and gratification **2** *n 1920s* A good-looking woman •Used in direct address: *Where've you been all my life, beautiful?*

the **beautiful people** *n phr 1960s* People who are fashionable, wealthy, admired for style and opulence, etc; =the JET SET

beauty *adj Canadian by 1970s* Excellent; superior; =GREAT: *I thought the guy was beauty*

beauty contest *n phr 1960s* A canvass or occasion that reveals preference, without the force of an election: *the mini-convention billed as a beauty contest for those seeking the presidential nomination*—Village Voice/ *Today's primary is considered a beauty contest because no delegates to the convention will actually be chosen*—National Public Radio

beaver 1 *n early 1900s British* A bearded man **2** *n early 1900s British* A full beard ◁**3**▷ *n 1920s British* The female genitals, esp with a display of pubic hair•First attested when the cry *Beaver!*, usu uttered at the sight of a bearded man, is uttered at the sight of a woman's pubic hair, seen through a keyhole ◁**4**▷ *n 1960s Pornography: The editor. . . lovingly runs his beaver one column over from his furious tirade*—New York Times ◁**5**▷ *n* (also **beaver movie** or **beaver flick**) *1960s* A pornographic film; =SKIN FLICK ◁**6**▷ *n 1970s citizens band* A woman **7** *n middle 1800s* A person who works hard and diligently

See SPLIT BEAVER

◁**beaver loop**▷ *n phr 1960s* A pornographic film strip in a coin-operated viewing machine

◁**beaver-shooter**▷ *n 1960s* A man obsessed with peering at female genitals: *A beaver shooter is, at bottom, a Peeping Tom*—Jim Bouton

◁**beaver shot**▷ *n phr 1960s* A photograph showing the female genitals prominently, esp one focusing on the vulva

be big on someone or something *v phr 1960s* To be enthusiastic about or laudatory of someone or something: *The boss is very big on this guy, as of now*

bebop *See* BOP

not **be caught dead** *See* NOT BE CAUGHT DEAD

bed *See* GO TO BED, GO TO BED WITH someone, HOTBED, MUSICAL BEDS, one SHOULD HAVE STOOD IN BED

bedbug *See* CRAZY AS A LOON

beddy *n late 1980s California* A pretty young girl, esp one considered sexually complaisant: *. . . a group of pretty teen-age girls skips down the sidewalk. "Hey, look at those little beddies"*—Los Angeles Times

bedpan commando *n phr WWII armed forces* A medical orderly

bedposts *See* the **devil's bedposts**

bedrock *1870s* **1** *n* The basic facts; the crucial elements; =THE BOTTOM LINE, THE NITTY-GRITTY **2** *modifier*: *a bedrock discussion/ bedrock decision* [fr *bedrock* "the solid rock underlying strata and detritus"]

bedroom or **come-hither eyes** *n phr* by *1940s* Seductive eyes: *I left them holding hands and gazing at each other with bedroom eyes*—Lawrence Sanders/ *Courage and come-hither eyes / Have a genius for taking pains*—W H Auden

bee[1] *n middle 1800s* =BEE IN one's BONNET

bee[2] *n 1960s narcotics* Enough narcotic to fill a penny match box, a unit used in selling drugs; =B [fr *box*]

See PUT THE BITE ON someone

beef 1 *n by 1890s* A complaint; grievance: *Her mother called up to register a beef*—Billy Rose **2** *v by 1880s*: *The hospital beefed when the city announced plans*—Philadelphia Bulletin **3** *n underworld about 1910* A criminal charge or indictment: *"What was your beef, Jim?. . . " "Robbery"*—Joseph Wambaugh **4** *n by 1930s* A quarrel; argument: *I've got no beef with you, buddy* **5** *v by 1930s* To quarrel: *We started beefing with each other*—TV show Geraldo **6** *n 1930s* A customer's bill or check; =BAD NEWS, DAMAGE **7** *n middle 1800s* Muscle; strength; huskiness **8** *n middle 1800s* Bulkiness; fleshiness; mass: *The old chorus girls had lots of beef, not like now* ◁**9**▷ *n by 1890* The penis

See CUT A BEEF, SQUARE THE BEEF

beefcake *n 1940s* A photograph or photographs of a muscular male body with little or no clothing: *The actor has no objections to male cheesecake, or beefcake as it is called in Hollywood*—Bob Thomas [based on *cheesecake*]

beefcakery *n 1940s* Photography showing the nude or nearly nude male body

beefeater *n by early 1600s* An Englishman; =LIMEY [fr the preeminence of beef, esp roast beef, in the traditional English diet]

beefer 1 *n 1930s* A complainer; malcontent **2** *n by 1890s* A police informer; =STOOL PIGEON

◁**beef injection**▷ *n phr* (also **hot beef injection**) *by 1980s* The sex act; penile penetration; =BOP, SCREW: *Maybe she care to try my famous African beef injection*—Robert B Parker/ *He asked if my boyfriend had ever slipped me the hot beef injection*—UCLA Slang [fr *beef*, "penis," and *injection*, attested in this sense by the 1740s]

beef squad *n phr by 1950s* A group of fighters or hoodlums, esp as used in labor disputes; =GOON SQUAD

beef trust *n phr 1920s* Any group of stout or fat people, esp a chorus line of hefty women [fr the late 1800s muckraker term for those who controlled the meat business]

beef up *v phr WWII armed forces and industry* To strengthen; reinforce •*Beef up!* is attested as an exhortation to use more strength by 1890: *The Patriots beefed up their defense by adding an all-star lineman*

beefy *adj middle 1700s British* Heavy-set; strong; bulky: *I tried to avoid the three beefy characters just ahead/ Reborn for a new calling, the beefy bikes came to be known as "clunkers"*—Los Angeles Times

bee in one's **bonnet** *n phr middle 1800s* A particular idea or notion, esp a fantastic or eccentric one; obsession: *He's got a bee in his bonnet about wheat germ curing all the world's ills* [Attested as *bee in one's head* fr early 1500s]

beely bopper *See* DEELY BOPPER

been there, done that *sentence 1990s college students* That is nothing new; tell me something else; =SO WHAT ELSE IS NEW [*Been there*, "experienced," is attested fr 1870]

beep 1 *v 1920s* To sound the horn of a car **2** *n 1920s*: *The car gave a few hearty beeps* **3** *n 1950s aerospace* A usu high-pitched short burst of sound emitted by an electronic device on a satellite, rocket, telephone answering machine, etc: *Please leave your message when you hear the beep* **4** *v by 1970s* To notify someone by a beep that attention or action is needed: *So I called the doctor and they beeped him and he called me* [echoic]

beeper *by 1970s* **1** *n* A tiny radio receiver that gives a coded signal to a person being notified of a telephone call, a voice message, or other summons: *Beepers proliferate, tolling for many besides the doctor*—Wall Street Journal **2** *n* Any very small electronic device used to control garage doors, car doors, etc: *The gate. . . was open, but I could see. . . that one could close and open it with a beeper*—Robert B Parker

beer *See* CRY IN one's BEER, DRINK one's BEER, SLING BEER, SMALL POTATOES

beer and skittles *See* NOT ALL BEER AND SKITTLES

beer belly *by 1940s* **1** *n* A protuberant paunch **2** *n* A man with a prominent paunch

beer bust (or **blast**) *n phr by 1910* A party where beer is the featured drink; =BREWOUT: *It was supposed to be a party, a beer bust*—James Jones

beer goggles or **beernoculars** *n phr late 1980s college students* Impaired vision and judgment due to drunkenness: *I must have had beer goggles on last night to think he was handsome*—New York Times

beer jerker *n phr outdated fr about 1870* A person whose work is drawing draught beer and serving it: *. . . waiter girls, popularly known as "beer-jerkers"*—H Asbury

beer joint *n phr by 1940s* A tavern or bar serving primarily beer

beer run *n phr by 1990s* A venturing out to buy beer: *. . . a proud holder of three drunk-driving convictions, really had to go on a beer run*—Sassy

beerslinger *n fr late 1800s* A bartender

Beer City or **Beertown** *n by 1940s* Milwaukee, Wisconsin: *. . . tiny minimum-security prisons right in the midst of Beertown*—Milwaukee Journal

beer up *v phr 1920s* To drink a lot of beer, esp enough to get drunk: *. . . the mechanics, beering up with the guys and driving off to Detroit*—John Clellon Holmes

bees *See* the BIRDS AND THE BEES

beeswax *n by 1940s* Business; concern: *If they did, that's their own beeswax*—Milwaukee Journal

beetle 1 *n outdated fr 1920s* A girl; young woman: *We could find plenty of nice beetles to rub ourselves against*—James T Farrell **2** *n fr horse-racing by 1930s* A racehorse; =ROACH: . . . *some beetle whose neck will feel the caress of a floral horseshoe*—S McLemore **3** *n middle 1940s* Trademark of an early model of Volkswagen car, with a squat body curving down at front and rear

beeveedees *n* =BVDS

beezer *n fr prizefight by 1915* The nose

beggar's velvet *n phr by 1860s* =GHOST TURDS, HOUSE MOSS, SLUT'S WOOL

be good *interj by 1908* A parting salutation •Later expanded with "if you can't be good, be careful, and if you can't be careful, don't name it after me"

behind *n about 1830* The buttocks; rump; =ASS: . . . *her broad, plain Slavic face, absence of waistline, and enormously broad behind*—Vogue

behind the curve *adj phr 1990s* Lagging; not abreast of current things
See AHEAD OF THE CURVE

behind the ears *See* NOT DRY BEHIND THE EARS

behind the eight ball *adv phr early 1930s* In a losing or endangered position: *He was sick and broke, right behind the eight ball* [fr the position of a pool player behind the black eight ball, which he must not hit]

behind the stick *See* WORK BEHIND THE STICK

beige *adj 1980s high school students* Boring; insipid; =HO-HUM

be-in *n esp 1960s counterculture* A large, peaceable gathering of young people, esp of hippies, where they don't do anything in particular: *a San Francisco "Be-in" attracted more than 100,000 persons*—New York Times/ . . . *with buttons and beards and Be-Ins*—WH Auden [modeled on *sit-in*]

be in someone's **face** *v phr by 1980s fr black* To confront and bother someone •The expression may come from the aggressive confrontations of basketball players: *He was totally in her face*—UCLA Slang/ *I was up in Hedda's face*—New York Times

be in the swim *v phr by 1869* To be fashionable, up-to-date, etc: *Don't use stale slang if you're in the swim*

be in the weeds *v phr by 1980s* To be in difficulty; be struggling: . . . *the corporation that issues your hubby's paycheck is. . . in the weeds*—comic strip "Mary Worth" [probably fr the plight of a golfer who has sent the ball into the rough]

be in the zone *v phr sports by middle 1980s* To play, esp tennis, effortlessly and without concentrated thought

the **bejesus** *See* BEAT THE SHIT OUT OF someone or something

belch 1 *n about 1900* A complaint; =BEEF **2** *v*: *All she did was belch about how bad he treats her* **3** *v underworld about 1900* To inform; =SQUEAL: *I feel good that I didn't belch on my friend*

belfry *See* HAVE BATS IN one's BELFRY

believe *See* YOU BETTER BELIEVE something

believer *See* MAKE A BELIEVER OUT OF someone

bell *See* DUMBBELL, HELL'S BELLS, MA BELL, RING A BELL, RING someone's BELL, RING THE BELL, SAVED BY THE BELL, WITH BELLS ON

bellcow *n 1980s baseball* A pitcher who can both start and win a game: . . . *the one with the time and the talent to be that "bellcow" remains Al Leiter. . .* —New York Times

bellhop *See* SEAGOING BELLHOP

bellied *See* YELLOW-BELLIED

bells *See* HELL'S BELLS, WITH BELLS ON

bells and whistles *1970s* **1** *n phr* Unessential elements, esp when impressive and decorative; frills: *the latest "bells and whistles," as high-tech frills are called*—Time/ . . . *you strip away the technological bells and whistles. . .* —New York Times **2** *n phr* Accessories and accoutrements, esp of the flashier sort; refinements; adornments; finishing touches: *Maserati. . . with all the bells and whistles*—Wall Street Journal **3** *modifier*: *If you are a bells and whistles guy, you will probably find these cars to be of more value*—New York Times

bells go off *sentence by 1950s* Alarming recognitions and associations emerge: *What started to slow me down, though, was the little bells going off at the sight of a young black guy. . .* —Stan Cutler

belly *n 1920s* =BELLY LAUGH
See AIR one's BELLY, BEER BELLY, JELLY-BELLY, LOW-BELLY STRIPPERS, POSSUM BELLY, POTBELLY, POTBELLY STOVE, SOURBALL, SOW-BELLY, YELLOW-BELLY

bellyache *by 1880s* **1** *v* To complain, esp to do so habitually; =BITCH: *You may exit the theater bellyaching about the show's unsubtleties. . .* —Newark Star-Ledger **2** *n* A complaint; =BEEF, BELCH

belly-buster *See* BELLY-WHOPPER

belly button *n phr 1870s* The navel

belly-crunch *v by 1990s* To be in intimate embrace: . . . *candle light, chilled wine, soft music. . . you and me belly-crunching in front of the fire*—Wisconsin State Journal

belly flop *n phr by 1930s* A dive in which one strikes the water stomach first; =BELLY-WHOPPER

belly-flopper *See* BELLY-WHOPPER

bellyful *n 1830s* The limit of what one can stand; an overplus; surfeit: *I've had a bellyful of your bellyaching*

belly gun *n phr 1920s* A short-barreled pistol inaccurate at any long range, but quite effective at very close range, like a shot in the belly: . . . *about .32 caliber, a belly gun, with practically no barrel*—Raymond Chandler

belly laugh *n phr about 1920* An especially loud, vigorous, and appreciative laugh; =BELLY, BOFFOLA [coined by the writer Jack Conway of *Variety*]

belly out *v phr by 1980s* =BELLYACHE: *Dixon had bellied out his trouble to somebody*—Scott Turow

belly-robber or **belly-burglar** *n armed forces fr WWI* A cook or a mess sergeant [Cowboys had a very similar term, *belly-cheater*]

belly-rub *1920s* **1** *n* A dance, esp at a public dance hall where one pays for each dance **2** *n* A dancing party

belly-rubbing *modifier* Intended or used for dancing: *That's some fine belly-rubbing music*—Atlanta Journal-Constitution

belly-smacker *See* BELLY-WHOPPER

belly stove *See* POTBELLY STOVE

belly telly *n phr by 1980s* A small television set, such as might be perched on one's stomach for viewing as one lies flat

belly up *1870s cowboys* **1** *v phr* To die; be down and out; collapse; =GO BELLY UP: *. . . were the schools to belly up tomorrow*—Philadelphia **2** *adj phr*: *The whole project's belly up*
See GO BELLY UP

belly up to *v phr fr early 1900s cowboys* To push or come up close to, esp to a bar for a drink: *Sammy Davis Jr. bellied up to the bar*—People Weekly/ *Meat Loaf bellies up to Billy Joel at a softball showdown*—Rolling Stone

belly-wash *n about 1900* Any drink one holds in contempt; =SWILL

belly-whopper (Variations: **-buster** or **-flopper** or **-smacker** may replace **-whopper**) **1** *n entry term by 1940s* A sled ride begun by running with the sled held at one's side, then leaping onto it stomach down **2** *n* =BELLY FLOP

below the belt *about 1890 fr prizefighting* **1** *adv phr* Not according to decent and usual practice; unconscionably irregular: *to hit below the belt/ aim below the belt* **2** *adj phr* Nasty; malicious; =DIRTY: *That remark was below the belt/ his below-the-belt tricks* [fr boxing where blows to the lower part of the body are forbidden]

belt **1** *v 1830s* To hit; strike; =SOCK: *Ed belts him in the kisser/ He belted the ball a mile* **2** *n about 1900* A blow; stroke; =WHACK: *She gave it a good belt* **3** *n by 1930s* A thrill; transport of pleasure; =KICK: *You'll get a belt out of this one* **4** *n 1950s narcotics* A marijuana cigarette; =JOINT **5** *v middle 1800s* (also **belt down**) To drink, esp vigorously and often: *. . . I seen him come in this joint lots of times and belt them down until he's cross-eyed. . .* — Mike Royko **6** *n by 1920s* A drink; swig; swallow: *He handed me the bottle and I took a belt at it*—H Allen Smith
See BORSCHT BELT

belt around *v phr by 1890s* To travel or move fast: *As for Godfrey's belting around in Air Force planes. . .* —John Crosby

belt out *v phr early 1950s* To sing in a loud and vigorous style

belt up *v phr chiefly British fr 1930s air force* To hold one's peace; be quiet; =SHUT UP: *Maybe he can get Pauline Kael to belt up once in a while*—New Republic

Beltway *modifier by 1980s* Connected with the federal government or the huge complex it occupies [fr the *Beltway*, the peripheral highway that is supposed to help one avoid the city's traffic]

Beltway bandit *n phr by 1980* One of the horde of businesses, consultants, lobbyists, etc who cluster about the federal government

BEM (pronounced as separate letters) *n by 1930s* Any of many bizarre extraterrestrial creatures found in early pulp science fiction: *From Amazing Stories, a Deco-costumed hero throttles a green alien, turning it into a classic BEM (Bug-Eyed Monster)*—Milwaukee Journal

be my guest *sentence 1950s* Do as you please •Often an ironic acquiescence to something ill-advised: *You want to tell the cop he's wrong? Be my guest*

bench warmer *n phr 1880s theater* A person not among the most active and important members of an enterprise; esp, a substitute athlete who seldom plays

bend **1** *v jazz musicians by 1940s* To slur a note: *. . . they alter pitch. . . they call it "bending"*—Stephen Longstreet **2** *n 1870s* =BENDER
See AROUND THE BEND

bend someone's ear *v phr by 1940s* To talk to someone insistently and at length: *He was bending my ear about his new car*

bender **1** *n 1840s* A spree, esp a drinking spree; =BAT, BINGE: *That three-day bender left Jim hurting all over/ a carrot-juice bender* **2** *n underworld by 1940s* A stolen car [first sense fr *hell-bender*, "alligator," of obscure origin, which came to mean "anything spectacular and superior" and was applied to a great spree in the middle 19th century]
See EAR-BENDER, ELBOW-BENDER, FENDER-BENDER, MIND-BLOWER, PRETZEL-BENDER

bending *See* ELBOW-BENDING, MIND-BLOWING

bend (or lean) over backwards *v phr first form 1940s, second form 1920s* To make every effort; strive mightily; =GO OUT OF ONE'S WAY •Several British sources identify the *lean* form as peculiarly US: *I bent over backwards trying to be fair*

the bends *n phr about 1900* Caisson disease, a painful result of rapid decompression after a deep dive

bend the (or one's) elbow (Variations: **crook** or **tip** may replace **bend**) *by 1825* **1** *v phr* To drink frequently and heavily, esp whiskey: *They cautioned him that maybe he was bending the elbow a little too often* **2** *v phr* To have a drink: *We'll tip the elbow over at my place*

bend the rules *v phr by early 1970s* To alter the rules slightly; to interpret loosely: *Let's bend the rules a bit and have another dessert*

bend the throttle *v phr Air Force fr WWII & 1940s teenagers* To drive or fly very fast

bennies or **benies** *n fr 1970s* Employer benefits such as health care, insurance, etc; =FRINGES, PERKS: *I like the pay, but the bennies stink*

benny or **bennie** *1950s narcotics* **1** *n* Any amphetamine pill, esp Benzedrine™ **2** *modifier*: *The kid was a benny addict*

Benny[1] *n shoeshop* The shoe size B

Benny[2] or **Benjamin** *n first form about 1900; second form fr early 1800s British underworld* A man's overcoat [said to be fr the name of a tailor]

bent **1** *adj 1830s* Intoxicated, either from alcohol or narcotics **2** *adj by 1940s* Having very little money: *I'm not quite broke, but quite bent* **3** *adj by*

1940s Eccentric; odd; =CRACKED, WACKY **4 adj** by *1930* Homosexual **5 adj** by *1930* Sexually aberrant; =KINKY: *Charley got bent bad over women. . . he was kinky when it came to ladies*—Harry Crews **6 adj** *early 1900s* Dishonest; shady; =CROOKED: *. . . look a little bent. . . look like you were up for a little whoremongering and black-marketing and smuggling*—Richard Merkin **7 adj** *underworld fr early 1900s* Stolen, said esp of a car **8 adj** *Air Force by 1970s* Angry; upset; =BENT OUT OF SHAPE

bent-eight *See* FORKED-EIGHT

bentnose *n* A criminal; a Mafioso: *. . . this bentnose in their town, a crud with a long drug sheet*—Lawrence Sanders/ *. . . once Cifelli and his band of bentnoses were in, Lefcourt had less control than ever*—Stan Cutler

bent out of shape 1 *adj phr* *1980s students* Intoxicated; drunk; =BENT, STONED **2 adj** *fr 1960s Air Force and college students* Extremely upset; very angry: *He is so far bent out of shape by the press reaction*—Washington Post/ *Why are you bent out of shape?*—Armistead Maupin

Benzo *n* *1980s teenagers* A Mercedes-Benz car

be or **get real** *interj* *esp 1980s college students* An exhortation to be sane and sensible: *John, are you going fishing this weekend? Be real, Smitty, I have to study for a test*—UCLA Slang

Bernie *n* *1980s police* A crime victim who is armed and might resist [fr *Bernhard* Goetz, who shot several young men he said threatened him on a New York City subway]

the **berries** *n phr* *about 1915* The best; =the MOST [fr early 1900s college slang *berry*, "something easy and pleasant, a good thing"]

berry *n* *fr early 1900s* A dollar [perhaps fr the notion of a small unit of something good, and alliterating with *buck*; see the *berries*]
See OYSTER-BERRY

berth *n* *late 1700s nautical* A job, appointment, situation, etc: *Dissatisfied with his prewar truck-driving berth*—Newsweek

Bertha *See* BIG BERTHA

beside oneself *adj phr* *late 1400s* Undergoing a surge or transport of emotion, esp of anger; half-crazy: *She was beside herself when she found out he was cheating/ He was beside himself with despair*

best *See* someone's LEVEL BEST

best bib and tucker *n phr* *middle 1700s* One's best clothes; =GLAD RAGS

best girl *n phr* *1880s* One's sweetheart; =MAIN SQUEEZE

best shot *See* GIVE something one's BEST SHOT

the **best** (or **greatest**) **thing since sliced bread** *n phr* *1960s* A person or thing that is superlative; a paragon; =WINNER: *I thought she was the best thing since sliced bread*—Washington Post

bet *See* IF BET

bet one's **bottom dollar** *v phr* *1860s Western* To be absolutely sure of something; be totally con-

vinced; =BET THE FARM: *I'll bet my bottom dollar she'll be back*

bet one's **life** *v phr* *1840s* =BET one's BOTTOM DOLLAR

Bete *See* PHI BETE

be there *v phr* *1880s* To have the experience; learn first-hand: *You have to be there to know what I mean/ I can tell you, because I've been there myself*

betsy or **Betsy** or **Betsey** *n* (Variation: often preceded by **old**) *1830s* A firearm of any sort: *I got a lot of votes in ol' Betsey here*—Walt Kelly
See IRON BETSY

better *See* GO something or someone ONE BETTER, NO BETTER THAN one OUGHT TO BE, YOU BETTER BELIEVE something

better half *n phr* *late 1500s* One's wife; occasionally, one's husband [either because the beloved is more than *half* of one, or is the superior part, the soul]

bet the farm (or **the ranch** *v phr* (Variations: **ranch** or **franchise** or **house** or **left nut** or **rent** or **shop** may replace **farm**) *chiefly 1980s* Bet everything one has; =GO FOR BROKE, BET one's BOTTOM DOLLAR: *I wouldn't have bet the farm. . . but I'd sure bet the back forty*—Washingtonian/ *I wouldn't bet the ranch that he'll be reappointed*—National Public Radio/ *You can bet the rent the Jacksons will go where the big money is*—Washington Post/ *. . . Horowitz. . . says he'll bet his house that Ginsburg won't vote to overturn Roe v Wade*—National Review/ *. . . nothing less than betting the franchise on this project*—Milwaukee Journal

betty *1980s students* **1** *n* A pretty girl, esp one regarded as sexually biddable; =BEDDY: *Betty. . . A beautiful woman*—Macon Telegraph **2** *n* An eccentric person; =FREAK [perhaps fr *Betty*, a character in the TV show *The Flintstones*]

between a (or **the**) **rock and a** (or **the**) **hard place** *adv phr* *by 1940s fr cowboys* In a dilemma; baffled: *So a writer is caught between the rock and the hard place*—New York Times/ *informants, caught between the rock of prison and the hard place of the snitch*—Washington Post

bet your boots *v phr* (Variations: **ass** or **sweet ass** or **bibby** or **bippy** or **bottom dollar** or **buns** or **left nut** or **life** or **shirt** or **whiskers** may replace **boots**) *entry form fr early 1800s, variants fr then until middle 1900s* To be absolutely assured; count on it: *You can bet your boots I'll be there/ You bet your sweet ass it was easier at the museum*—Leslie Hollander/ *I'll bet my left nut that's what was happening*—Lawrence Sanders

bevels *n* *gambling by 1960* A pair of dishonest dice with some edges beveled to affect the roll [fr *beveled suction shapes*]

bfd or **BFD** (pronounced as separate letters) *n* Something or someone of importance •Usually said sarcastically or dismissively [fr *big fucking deal*]

B-girl *n* *1930s* A promiscuous girl or woman, esp one who works in a bar as a sort of hostess to stimulate the sale of drinks; =BAR-GIRL

bi (BĪ) *1960s* **1** *adj* Bisexual; =AC-DC **2** *n*: *I think maybe Vi is a bi*

bib *See* BEST BIB AND TUCKER

bibby *See* BIPPY

bible or **Bible** *See* CALIFORNIA PRAYER BOOK, SWALLOW THE BIBLE, SWEAR ON A STACK OF BIBLES, TIJUANA BIBLE

Bible-banger *n* (Variations: **-pounder** or **-puncher** or **-thumper** or **-walloper** may replace **-banger**) *entry form fr Australian by 1940s; other forms fr 1880s on* A strict religionist, esp a Protestant fundamentalist preacher: . . . *to ensure it doesn't offend some Bible-banger in Mississippi*—Playboy/ . . . *Americans send millions of dollars to fast-talking TV bible thumpers*—Milwaukee Journal

◁**bicho**▷ (BEE choh) *n* The penis: . . . *this little girl, she's leading you around by your bicho*—Elmore Leonard [fr Spanish, literally "bug, beast," and more]

bicoastal *by 1980s* **1** *adj* Active on both the Atlantic and Pacific coasts: . . . *a pair of bicoastal type A males*—Time **2** *adj* Bisexual; =AC-DC, BI

bicycle *See* GET ON one's BICYCLE

biddle *See* BINDLE

biddy 1 *n late 1700s* A woman, esp an old shrewish woman •Nearly always with "old": *Charley had met an old biddy named Zoe Winthrop*—W Fuller **2** *n 1780s* =CHICK [diminutive of the name *Bridget*]

biff 1 *n about 1890* A blow with the fist; =SOCK •*Biff* as the sound of a blow is attested in 1847 **2** *v about 1890*: *He wouldn't quit, so she biffed him* **3** *n 1980s college students* A stupid young woman **4** *v 1980s college students* To fail; =FLUNK ◁**5**▷ *n* =BIFFER

◁**biffer**▷ *n black by about 1930* A homely woman who compensates by being promiscuous

biffy *n by 1940s* A toilet; bathroom •Chiefly Canadian use: . . . *announces in all earnestness the new biffies being installed at a . . . dormitory*—Milwaukee Journal

big 1 *adj late 1500s* Important; powerful: *the big names in this business/ the big guy* **2** *adj about 1910* Popular; successful: *If I do say so, we were very big*—Bing Crosby/ *The book's big in Chicago* **3** *adv by 1886* Successfully; outstandingly well: *The wing-dancing and funny acts catch on big*—The Lantern *See* BIG WITH someone, **go over big, make it big, take it hard, talk big**

Big *adj* Good; decent; admirable •Used as an epithet for an admired person: *Hey, what's up, Big Eddy? See* MISTER BIG

Big A 1 *n phr* The Atlanta federal penitentiary **2** *n phr* The Aqueduct racetrack in New York City

big ape or **baboon** *n phr by 1940s* A large, dangerous man •Nearly always used affectionately of a man by a woman

the **Big Apple** or **the Apple 1** *n phr by 1909* New York City •Popularized in the 1970s as a "boosterish" nickname: *New York is the Big Apple*—Stephen Longstreet/ *young musicians storming into the Apple*—Village Voice **2** *n phr* A jitterbug dance of the middle 1930s [apparently fr jazz musicians' term **apple** for a city, esp a city in the North; the dance may be so-called from a Harlem club of the same name]

bigass *by 1940s fr black and WWII armed forces* **1** *adj* Pretentiously large: *Abraham opened the door of his bigass Cadillac*—Hugh Selby Jr. **2** *adj* Pretentious; self-important: . . . *his goddam big-ass face*—New Yorker [in these and other senses *-ass* and *-assed* are used virtually as intensifiers; they may be suffixed to nearly any adjective]

bigass bird *See* TAKE OFF LIKE A BIGASS BIRD

big band *1920s* **1** *n phr* A large band of dance or swing musicians, esp like the Benny Goodman or Tommy Dorsey bands of the 1930s **2** *modifier*: *the big-band sound/ big-band era*

big bang *by 1950* **1** *n phr* The primordial explosion by which the universe was hypothetically created [The term was coined, or at least popularized, by the British astronomer Fred Hoyle in a 1950 book] **2** *modifier*: *the big-bang theory/ big-bang cosmology*

Big Bertha *n phr fr WWI* Any very large cannon [said to be fr *Frau Bertha Krupp*, a member of the German armaments-making family]

big boy 1 *n phr about 1910* You there; man; =MAC •A term of address variously used with the intention to challenge, flatter, attract, etc: *Want a little fun, big boy?* **2** *n phr 1920s* An important man; =BIGGIE, BIG SHOT: *He tried to shake down one of the big boys*—Raymond Chandler **3** *n phr* An adult male; grown-up man •Most often used in rebuke: *Cut that out—you're a big boy now*

Big Blue *n phr 1980s* IBM, International Business Machines Corporation [because the cover of one of its computers was *blue*]

Big Brother or **big brother 1** *n phr 1949* The faceless and ruthless power of the totalitarian or bureaucratic state personified **2** *n phr airline by 1970s* The tracking radar used by ground controllers [*Big brother*, "protector," is attested fr at least the 1860s. First sense fr its use by George Orwell in his novel *Nineteen Eighty-Four*; second sense quite benign]

big brown eyes *n phr* A woman's breasts; =HEADLIGHTS

big bucks *n phr about 1970* A large amount of money; great sums of money; =MEGABUCKS: *That car would cost you big bucks today*

big bug *n phr 1820s* An important person; =BIG SHOT: . . . *even among the big bugs of his own Cabinet*—Robert Lynd

big butter-and-egg man *See* BUTTER-AND-EGG MAN

big buzz *n phr by 1970s* Loudest current rumor: . . . *the big buzz around Broadway is the announcement*—Aquarian

Big C 1 *n phr late 1960s* Cancer **2** *late 1950s narcotics* Cocaine

the **big cage** *n phr underworld by 1940s* A state or federal prison or reformatory; =THE BIG HOUSE

big cheese 1 *n phr* early 1900s =BIG BUG, BIG SHOT **2** *modifier*: . . . *but without the big-cheese attitude*—Buzz **3** *n phr* 1920s A stupid or rude man; lout [for first sense, see the *cheese*]

big D *n phr* by 1970s LSD

Big D 1 *n phr* 1960s Detroit, Michigan **2** *n phr* 1930s Dallas, Texas

Big Daddy or **big daddy 1** *n phr* 1940s You there; man; =BIG BOY, MAC •Term of address used to any man, usu with a view to flattering him **2** *n phr* jazz musicians fr 1920s =DADDY **3** *n phr* jazz musicians fr by 1940s =DADDY-O

the **Big Dance** *n phr* early 1990s The NCAA basketball tournament: . . . *the prize will be an automatic bid to the Big Dance*—Milwaukee Journal

big deal 1940s students and WWII armed forces **1** *n phr* Anything very important; consequential event or circumstance •Often used ironically to deflate someone or something, esp in the retort "Big deal" after someone has made an earnest reference: *Getting good grades is a big deal around here/ So you just bought an Audi. Big deal* **2** *n phr* An important person; =BIG SHOT: *Thinks he's a big deal 'cause he's got that fucking paper backing him up*—Robert B Parker **3** *modifier*: *a big-deal salary/ . . . any big-deal Boston wiseass dick. . .* —Robert B Parker [probably fr the Yiddish sarcastic dismissal *a groyser kunst*, "some big art," as translated and used, for example, by the comedian Arnold Stang]

See MAKE A BIG PRODUCTION, NO BIG DEAL

Big Dick *n phr* crapshooting by 1940s The point or roll of ten

the **Big Ditch** *n phr* Variously the Erie Canal (fr 1823), Atlantic Ocean (by 1909), or Panama Canal (by 1915)

big do *n phr* 1980s An important or popular person: *He was the big do in Green Bay*—Milwaukee Journal [perhaps a shortening of *big doolie*]

big dog *n phr* by 1840s An important and dominating person: *This is going to be the year of the Big Dog!*—Milwaukee Journal

bigdome *n* 1980s An important person, esp a manager or business executive; =BIG SHOT: . . . *if the NBA bigdomes are concerned about their image and popular appeal*—New York Daily News

big doolie *n phr* 1980s An important person, esp a winning athlete; =BIG SHOT: *I got a gold today, so I'm a big doolie*—New York Times [perhaps related to the earlier term *dooly*, "dynamite"]

the **Big Drink** *n phr* Variously the Mississippi River (fr 1840s) or the Atlantic Ocean (fr 1880s)

big drive *n phr* 1950s narcotics A heavy or comparatively pure injection of a narcotic: . . . *man, their eyes when that big drive hits*—Nelson Algren

the **Big Easy** *n phr* 1970s New Orleans

big enchilada *n phr* 1970s The chief; the head person; =BOSS: *The Big Enchilada is tied up with the Chief Honcho at the moment, but the Little Enchilada can see you now*—New Yorker cartoon

big eyes *n* jazz musicians fr about 1950 Desire; lust

big fat *adj phr* by 1970s Embarrassingly obvious; blatant and humiliating: *I couldn't keep my big fat mouth shut/His big fat trademark heart greets you in this show*—Village Voice

big fish (or frog or tuna) *n phr* 1830s An important person; =BIG SHOT: . . . *landed herself a big fish—an old guy with money and power*—Los Angeles Times/ . . . *the sports authoritarian and local big tuna said*—Milwaukee Journal

big fish (or frog) in a little (or small) pond by 1970s *n phr* An important person in a relatively unimportant place •*Big toad in the puddle* is attested fr 1877

big foot 1 *n phr* 1980s newspaper office A senior editor, important editorialist or columnist, etc: . . . *but many an editor or pundit, a "big foot" in the parlance of the bus*—Time **2** *modifier*: *George Will used his Big Foot status to get himself invited to sessions that a mere sportswriter wouldn't have been allowed near*—New Republic **3** *n phr* 1990s =BIG SHOT: . . . *much unlike the national policy big foot she is*—Washington Post **4** *v*: *DeeDee Myers was relegated to the sidelines, a victim of David Gergen's Bigfooting in the White House*—Vanity Fair [fr *Bigfoot*, one of the designations of Sasquatch, a large hairy humanoid creature thought by some to inhabit the forests of the Pacific Northwest, and probably applied to senior newspaper persons because of metaphorical size and menace]

big George *n phr* by 1950s A quarter of a dollar [fr the portrait of George Washington on the coin]

bigger (or other) fish to fry *n phr* Other and more pressing matters to attend to; more important things in prospect: *Anyway. . . we've got bigger fish to fry*—W T Tyler/*Tell him to relax, we've got bigger fish to fry*—Ed McBain

biggie 1 *n* by 1930 A prominent or stellar person; =BIG SHOT: *Sullivan continues putting the bee on other Government biggies*—Variety **2** *n* by 1940s Something important and successful; =BIG DEAL: . . . *a tubular biggie, not only in LA and NY, but in Chicago, Detroit, and Atlanta*—Time **3** *n* by 1940s Anything large and important: . . . *if a real biggie, like Brazil, went to the wall*—Playboy/ *The next earthquake might be the biggie*

See NO BIGGIE

biggity or **biggidy** chiefly black by 1880 **1** *adj* Haughty; conceited; =UPPITY **2** *adv*: *Don't talk so biggity*

biggums *adj* 1990s teenagers Overweight; obese •This reflects that *fat* is now generally avoided as a matter of sensitivity, and that it has taken on a new meaning, "cool, attractive," in youthful speech

big gun by 1830 *n phr* =BIG SHOT

big guns *See* HEAVY ARTILLERY

big guy *n phr* by 1980 Man; fellow •Used in direct address, usu with a flattering or genial purpose: *So, big guy, how's it going?*—Stan Cutler/ *How's it look up there, big guy?*—New Yorker

big H *n phr* 1950s narcotics Heroin

a **big hand** *n phr* by 1880s Enthusiastic applause: *Let's give the little lady a big hand, folks*

Big Harry *n phr* 1950s narcotics Heroin

big hat, no cattle *n phr* western by 1980s A pretender; a pompous poseur: *Most of 'em are only good at. . . hanging around the Fort Worth Club. Big hat, no cattle*—Dan Jenkins

bighead *n* by 1840s A self-important, conceited person

a **big head** 1 *n phr* by 1850s Conceit: *The promotion gave him a big head* 2 *n phr* by 1890 The discomfort consequent upon drinking too much liquor; =HANGOVER: *The rum gave me a big head next morning*

bigheaded *adj* by 1940s Conceited

big heat *n phr* by 1980s An ostentatiously important person: *I am into so many big things, such a big heat, that I must deal as I wheel*—Mike Royko [perhaps a synonym for *hot shot*]

big hole *n phr* truckers by 1940s The low gear of a truck

the **big house** or the **Big House** *n phr* underworld by 1915 A state or federal penitentiary; =the BIG CAGE •The term meant "workhouse" in middle 1800s London, which may or may not be relevant: *to go to the big house for the rest of his life*—Morris Bishop

the **big idea** *See* WHAT'S THE BIG IDEA

big John *n phr* 1960s narcotics A police officer or the police

the **big joint** *n phr* underworld by 1920s =the BIG HOUSE

big kahuna or **kahoona** *n phr* by 1950s An authoritative person; the chief; =BIG ENCHILADA, HONCHO: *Take the word "interim" out of Al Fisher's job description. . . and insert "big kahuna"*—Milwaukee Journal [fr Hawaiian *kahuna*, "shaman, medicine man, priest"; the term was apparently disseminated by surfers]

big-league *adj* by 1940s Serious; important; professional: *No more fooling around, now it's big-league stuff*

big-leaguer *n* by 1910 =BIG-TIMER

the **big leagues** 1 *n phr* 1890s In baseball, the major leagues 2 *n phr* by 1940s The higher, more serious and arduous reaches of a profession, business, government, sport, etc; =the BIG TIME, HARDBALL

the **big lie** by 1940s 1 *n phr* A major political untruth, usu of a demagogic sort, uttered frequently by leaders as a means of duping and controlling the constituency 2 *modifier*: *the big-lie technique/ a big-lie approach* [fr a notion of Adolf Hitler in *Mein Kampf* (1924), that a *big lie* is often easier to foist on the masses than a little one]

big man *n phr* fr students by 1920s A male school or campus leader: *. . . the prep school "big man"*—F Scott Fitzgerald

big man on campus 1 *n phr* college students by 1930s A male college student leader; =BMOC 2 *n phr* by 1990s Any preeminent man: *. . . Griffey is the Mariners' big man on campus. . .*—Milwaukee Journal Sentinel

big moment *n phr* 1930s students One's sweetheart or lover

big money *See* HEAVY MONEY

big-mouth 1880s 1 *n* A person who talks constantly and loudly 2 *n* A person who freely announces personal opinions and judgments; =KNOW-IT-ALL, SMART-ASS 3 *n* A person who can't keep a secret *See* HAVE A BIG MOUTH

big name by 1920s 1 *n phr* A celebrated person, personality, or entity, esp a star entertainer: *Hollywood figures only the big names are bankable* 2 *n phr* A prominent reputation; fame: *The group has a big name in the Boston area* 3 *modifier*: *a big-name star/ They get a big-name fee*

big nickel *n phr* 1950s gambling A $5,000 bet

big noise *n phr* early 1900s British An important person; most influential person: *Who's the big noise around here?*

the **big O** *n phr* 1960s An orgasm

big one *n phr* fr 1930s gambling A thousand dollars, esp as a bet: *The highjackers are handed 50 cents a gallon, which is 15 big ones and OK for a couple hours' work*—Time/ *The next time you want me to do the Today show, it's going to cost you ten big ones*—Art Buchwald

the **big picture** *n phr* by 1970s The large strategic situation as distinct from little details; inclusive of the surrounding circumstances

big pipe *n phr* cool musicians fr 1950s A baritone saxophone

the **Big Pond** *n phr* by 1830s The Atlantic Ocean

big potatoes *n phr* by 1940s Someone or something important or impressive: *Commencement is still big potatoes around here* [a deliberate antonym of *small potatoes*]

the **Big Pretzel** *n phr* by 1970s Philadelphia

Big Pretzelite *n phr* by 1970s A Philadelphian: *several reasons for Big Pretzelites to swing into the Franklin Plaza*—Philadelphia

big production *See* MAKE A BIG PRODUCTION

the **big rag** *n phr* circus by 1930s =the BIG TOP

the **bigs** *n phr* by 1960s The major leagues, in baseball or other areas; =the BIG TIME: *When Backman was in the bigs, he wasn't your regular Mr. Sunshine*—Village Voice

the **big school** *n phr* hoboes & underworld fr 1920s =the BIG HOUSE

Big Science *n phr* early 1960s Scientific work that is extremely costly, productive of huge machines, etc

the **big score** *n phr* by 1940s Huge financial success; spectacular profits: *Jobs' entrepreneurial flair and his instinct for the big score*—Time

big shot or **bigshot** fr 1920s 1 *n phr* or *n* A very important person; influential person; leader; =BIG CHEESE, BIGGIE •Thought to have been taken over from the idiom of Prohibition-age gangsters: *. . . eight big shots of various farmers', manufacturers', or veterans' organizations*—H L Mencken/ *"Hey, bigshot," his father would bellow on the tele-*

phone—Joseph Heller **2 *modifier*** •Often used sarcastically: *a big-shot chest surgeon/ big-shot notions*

big stiff *n phr* by *1890s* A large, rough man, esp one who is somewhat stupid as well •Sometimes used as a term of affection by a woman of a man

big talk *middle 1800s* **1** *n phr* Boastful and extravagant talk; esp promises or claims beyond one's capacity: *His promises were just big talk* **2** *v*: *Don't big-talk a big-talker, man*

big-tent *adj 1990s* Welcoming all sorts; hospitable: *NOW itself is a big-tent organization, abidingly tolerant of all attitudes*—David Shiflett

big (or **high**) **ticket** *early 1970s salespersons* **1** *adj phr* Expensive; high-priced: *. . . very low for the promotion of a big-ticket item*—Fortune/ *More and more complete-text services are becoming available, especially in high-ticket fields like law*—Philadelphia **2** *n phr* The sale of an expensive item: *He wrote up a couple of big tickets yesterday*

big time **1** *adv* Army by *1970s* Very much; totally: *. . . where does it say. . . that a congressman has the right to be on the take big time?*—Mike Royko/ *. . . it sticks big-time to any smooth surface*—Toronto Globe and Mail **2** *adj* by *1910* Important; notable: *. . . so my single was big-time*—Julio Franco [ultimately fr the outdated theater sense]

the **big time** **1** *n phr* by *1920* The upper reaches of a profession, business, government, sport, etc; =the BIG LEAGUES **2** *modifier*: *a big-time outfit/ big-time crime* [fr theater use of about 1910 designating certain important vaudeville circuits or houses]

big-time operator *n phr* by *1940s* A person conspicuously active in affairs where trade-offs, special favors, private understandings, etc, are crucial; machinator; =BTO, MACHER, WHEELER-DEALER

big-timer *n* by *1930* =BIG-LEAGUER

big or **big-time spender** *n phr* *1920s* nightclubs A person who is generous and extravagant, esp for lavish entertainment; =HIGH ROLLER

the **big top** *n phr circus* by *1890s* The main tent of a circus; also, the circus and circus life in general: *hypnotized by life under the big top*—Hamilton Basso

big wheel by *1940s* **1** *n phr* An important person; =BIG SHOT: *Up to that juncture I was boss man of the family and big wheel*—S J Perelman **2** *modifier*: *a big-wheel attitude/ Look at the big-wheel label on those jeans* [probably connected with Chicago underworld use *wheels*, "gang chief, big shot," attested in 1932]

big with someone *adj phr* Popular with; preferred by; relished by: *That's big with her*—Armistead Maupin [In this sense *big* goes back to about 1910]

bike **1** *n 1880s* A bicycle **2** *n 1940s* A motorcycle; =IRON, SCOOT •Short for earlier *motorbike* **3** *1950s police* A motorcycle police officer
See DIRT BIKE

biker *n* A motorcycle rider, racer, enthusiast, etc •Short for earlier *motorbiker*: *Bikers in black leather roared through the town*

biker chic *n phr 1990s* The dressing style of motorcyclists: black leather garments and boots, menacing helmets, etc: *. . . the ghosts of all the cattle that had died in the name of biker chic*—New York Times

bikinis *n* by *1980s* Very brief underpants [named for the very brief 1940s bathing costume, which was named in turn after *Bikini* atoll, where nuclear bombs were tested in 1946]

bilge **1** *n early 1900s* Nonsense; worthless and vain matter; =TRIPE, BLAH **2** *v* (also **bilge out**) *college students* about 1900 To fail or expel a student [short for *bilgewater*]

bilk joint *n phr* A business place, esp a shop, that overcharges and cheats its customers; =GYP JOINT: *. . . the Times Square tenderloin, the porno shops, the bilk joints, the freaks*—Pulpsmith [fr 17th century *bilk*, "cheat, fraud" plus *joint*]

bill **1** *n about 1910* A single dollar: *Can I borrow a couple of bills until tomorrow?* **2** *n 1920s* A hundred dollars: *I laid out four bills for that shearling* **3** *n 1990s football* A hundred yards of gain in football: *Coach Jackson told me I needed two bills to win*—Milwaukee Journal
See HALF BILL, PHONY AS A THREE-DOLLAR BILL

Bill Daley *n phr 1940s horse-racing* A long lead in a race: *She might go out on the Bill Daley and hang on*—J Lilienthal [after a jockey instructor who advised taking a long lead and holding it]

billies *n high school students* by *1980s* Bills; currency; money

billy or **billy-club** *n 1840s* A club or truncheon, now esp one carried by the police •Associated with the police fr the 1850s, but a reference of the 1880s still describes only what would now be called a blackjack, definitely a criminal's weapon [Said to be a burglar's pet or secret name for his crowbar, along with *Jemmy* or *Jimmy*; he also used it as a weapon]

billycan or **billy** *n hoboes* fr *1880s Australian usage* A container for heating water or for cooking

billy doo *n phr about 1900* A love letter: *To help me polish off this billy doo*—Wallace Irwin [fr French *billet doux* "love letter"]

bim *n esp 1920s* A girl or woman, esp one's girlfriend: *John took his bim to a dance*—Roy W Cowden [fr *bimbo*]

◁**bimbette**▷ *n early 1980s* A frivolous or stupid young woman; a man's plaything: *. . . itching to play something more demanding than bimbettes and stand-by wives*—Times/ *. . . could have any bimbette. . . in the state of California*—Douglas Coupland [fr *bimbo* plus French feminine suffix *-ette*]

bimbo **1** *n about 1920* A man, esp a mean and menacing one; =BABY, BOZO: *The bimbos once helped pluck a bank*—Dashiell Hammett/ *one of them bimbos which hurls a mean hammer*—H Witwer **2** *n about 1920* An insignificant person; =NEBBISH: *Nobody listened to the poor bimbo* ◁**3**▷ *n middle 1920s* A woman, esp a young woman of hedonistic aspect: *What kind of a bimbo did he think I am?*—Hal Boyle/ *. . . a bimbo with* *legs that go all the way up*—George V Higgins ◁**4**▷ *n fr 1920s* A prostitute; =HOOKER: *Some escort services are just fronts for prostitution. . . men call up and the service just sends out some bimbo in blue jeans from Brooklyn*—New York Magazine [fr Italian, "baby, bambino"; see *babe*]

Bimmer *n 1980s* A BMW car: *Bum out a Bimmer driver. Unleash a Chevette*—Car and Driver

bimmy *n 1980s* =BIMBO: *What do you suggest instead? A bimmy?*—Christopher Zenowich

the bin *n phr 1930s* =LOONY BIN
See WEENIE BIN

bind *n middle 1800s* A very tight and awkward situation; cleft stick; =BOX, JAM: *This is a nasty sort of bind*
See IN A BIND

binder **See** HIGH-BINDER

binders *n 1940s British* The brakes of a car

bindle or **biddle** **1** *n hoboes fr before 1900* A blanket-roll holding one's possessions; =BALLOON **2** *n hoboes fr before 1900* Any package or bundle **3** *n narcotics about 1920* A packet of narcotics, esp when folded as an envelope [probably an alteration of *bundle*]

bindlestiff *fr early 1900s* **1** *n* A migrant harvest worker, esp a hobo with his bindle: *I was a bindlestiff. That's the class that will do some work once in a while*—J R Kennedy **2** *n* Any hobo or derelict [fr *bindle*, "blanket-roll, bundle" and *stiff*, "worker, migratory worker"]

bing **1** *interj early 1900s* An exclamation in reaction to something sudden; =BINGO **2** *n by 1920s* A packet of narcotics; =BINDLE **3** *n prison by 1950s* A prison cell used for solitary confinement; =the HOLE

binge *n* **1** *middle 1800s* A spree, esp a drunken spree; =BAT, BENDER: *with the studios on an economy binge*—Variety/ *. . . one last banana binge*—Philadelphia Bulletin **2** *v early 1900s* To carouse; consume inordinately [perhaps fr Lincolnshire dialect *binge*, "to soak"]

binged (BINGD) *adj armed forces fr WWI* Vaccinated

binger[1] (BIN jər) *n early 1900s* A person who goes on a spree or sprees: *. . . situational sketches about stage mothers. . . and food bingers*—Village Voice

binger[2] (BING ər) *n 1980s baseball* A home run

bingle *n* (also **bingo**) *baseball by 1902* A base hit, esp a single

bingo[1] *interj* An exclamation in reaction to something sudden and unexpected, or expressing sudden success: *Have your contracts and debts declared void and, bingo, you're back in business*—Newsweek [echoic]

bingo[2] *n Canadian* Cheap wine [fr late 1600s *bingo*, "brandy," and US middle 1800s *bingo*, "liquor"]

bingo[3] *n 1930s* A more or less benign gambling game
See BEACH BLANKET BINGO

bingo-boy *n 1880s* A drunkard ●Some revived use

in 1940s by New York City street gangs [fr contemporary *bingo*, "liquor"]

binny *n about 1910 underworld* A large or concealed pocket in a shoplifter's coat where stolen things may be hidden [an alteration of *Benny*, "overcoat"]

bio or **biog** *n first form by 1950s, second by 1940s* A biography, esp a brief one in a yearbook, theater program, etc: *By now Jenny had read my bio in the program*—Erich Segal

bioflick or **biopic** *n by 1980s* A movie or television show based on some person's life story: *. . . star in a bioflick on. . . Charlie Parker*—People Weekly/ *. . . a big-budget Hollywood biopic*—Wired

bippy or **bibby** *n 1960s* The buttocks; =ASS
See BET YOUR BOOTS

bird **1** *n middle 1800s* A person of either sex, usu a man and often elderly: *I'm a literary bird myself*—F Scott Fitzgerald/ *She was a tall old bird with a chin like a rabbit*—Raymond Chandler **2** *n middle 1800s* Somebody or something excellent; =BEAUT, LULU **3** *n college students by 1900* A young woman; =CHICK ●Much commoner in British usage; regarded by some women as offensive **4** *n middle 1800s* An odd or unusual person; an eccentric; =FLAKE, WEIRDO: *He was a funny bird in many ways*—Armistead Maupin ◁**5**▷ *n late 1800s* A male homosexual; =GAY ◁**6**▷ *modifier late 1800s*: *a gaggle of the guys in a Third Avenue bird bar*—Judith Crist **7** *n armed forces fr WWI* The eagle as an insignia of a colonel's rank **8** *modifier*: *a bird colonel* **9** *n by 1918* Any aircraft, esp a helicopter **10** *n 1950s astronautics* A rocket or guided missile **11** *n 1970s aerospace* A communications satellite: *A VTR operator in Vancouver is editing a local piece for The National. "Gotta make the bird," the guy says confidently*—Toronto Life/ *. . . an agreement to put Satellite News Channel up on its bird*—Village Voice [homosexual senses may be based on or be revived by Yiddish *faygele*, "homosexual," literally "bird"]
See EARLY BIRD, FOR THE BIRDS, HAVE A BIRD, JAILBIRD, LOVEBIRDS, RAILBIRD, TAKE OFF LIKE A BIGASS BIRD, WHIRLYBIRD, YARDBIRD

the bird **1** *n phr 1860s British* A rude flatulatory noise made with the tongue and lips to express disapproval, derision, or contempt; =BRONX CHEER, RASPBERRY: *Give him the boid, the raspberry*—Eugene O'Neill **2** *n phr 1960s* =the FINGER [first sense fr the mid-1800s expression *give the big bird*, "hiss someone like a goose"]

birdbrain *n by early 1940s* A person of meager intelligence; idiot: *. . . whatever bird-brain is rendering one of the ditties of the day*—Robert Ruark

birdbrained *adj by early 1940s* Stupid: *Nancy Fox, an abducted bride, is unquestionably birdbrained*—Village Voice

bird colonel *n phr* =CHICKEN COLONEL

bird course *n phr Canadian students* An easy college course; =GUT COURSE

bird dog **1** *n phr about 1930* A person, like a

detective, talent scout, etc, whose job is to find something or someone **2** *v* about 1930 To act as a bird dog: . . . *Leo Browne, who was doing some "bird-dogging" for the Yankees. . .* —Joe Garagiola **3** *n phr* 1930s *students* A chaperon at a dance, or a third person on a date, appointed to be vigilant **4** *n phr* 1930s *service academy* A tactical office, enforcing order and discipline **5** *n phr* A fighter or interceptor aircraft **6** *n phr* *WWII Army Air Forces* An aircraft that spotted and marked targets **7** *n phr* airline *by 1970s* The automatic direction-finding instrument of an aircraft **8** *n phr* 1970s *citizen band* A radar detector: . . . *if my dog barks—a radar detector, or "bird dog". . .* —Brian Di Salvatore **9** *v* 1990s *teenagers* To seduce or go out with another girl's boyfriend: *Sorry to bird-dog you, Cecelia, but the guy. . . asked me to the Afghan Whigs show. . .* —Sassy

birdfarm *n* *Vietnam War Navy* An aircraft carrier: *The days are gone when a carrier was called a flattop. The craft is now a "birdfarm"*—New York Times

birdie or **birdy** *adj* 1950s *teenagers* Eccentric; weird; =FLAKY

birdies or **bird legs** *n* *by 1950s* Thin, bony legs   *See* HEAR THE BIRDIES SING

birds   *See* FOR THE BIRDS, LOVEBIRDS

the **birds and the bees** *n phr* The basic facts about sex and reproduction, esp as explained to children

birdseye *n* 1960s *narcotics* A small packet or portion of a narcotic

◁**birdseye maple**▷ *n phr* *black fr* 1920s A light-skinned black girl, esp if sexually attractive

◁**birdshit**▷ *n* =CHICKEN SHIT

◁**birdturd**▷ *n* 1950s A despicable person; =PRICK, SHIT: *Suppose those birdturds come back here today*—Bernard Malamud

birdwood **1** *n* 1960s *narcotics* Marijuana **2** *n* *by* 1940s A cigarette

birdyback *n* 1970s The transport of loaded containers or semitrailers by airplane

birthday suit *n phr* *by* 1730s What one is wearing when completely nude; the state of nakedness: *Naked as a jaybird, with nothing on over his birthday suit*

biscuit **1** *n* 1930s *black* The buttocks; =ASS, BUNS **2** *n* 1980s *students* A small person; =PEANUT   *See* DOG BISCUIT, GROUND BISCUIT

biscuit-eater *n* 1960s *black* A moderate, integrationist black person =OREO [perhaps fr *biscuit,* "buttocks," with the implication of ass-kissing the whites]

biscuit hooks *n phr* *by* 1940s The hands

biscuit-shooter *n* 1890s *cowboy* A cook, esp on a ranch

bissel (BISS əl) *n* A bit; a little: *I'd hold onto your God's little acre a bissel longer*—Village Voice [fr Yiddish]

bistro (BEE stroh) *n* *by* 1940s A restaurant or cafe [fr French]

bit **1** *n* *underworld* about 1860 A prison sentence:

Ferrati, whose "bit" was three to seven years—P L Quinlan **2** *n* (also **bit part**) *early 1900s theater* A small part in a play or other show **3** *n fr theater* A display of pretended feeling, or an outright imitation; =ACT, SHTICK: *So he does his hurt-puppy-dog bit/ You should see my Jimmy Cagney bit* **4** *n fr* 1950s *beat & cool talk* A person's particular set of attitudes, reactions, behavior patterns, etc; style; life style; =THING: *Zen never was my real bit* **5** *adj* 1970s *teenagers* Disappointed and resentful ●Perhaps the same semantics as middle 1800s *bit,* "cheated"   *See* FOUR-BIT, SIX-BIT, TWO-BIT

bit banger 1980s *computer* **1** *n phr* A programmer who works out details of a computer program, rather than a subordinate or assistant programmer **2** *n phr* Assembly-language programmers as distinct from applications programmers

bitch ◁**1**▷ *n* about 1400 A woman one dislikes or disapproves of, esp a malicious, devious, or heartless woman ●The equivalent of the masculine *bastard* as a general term of opprobrium: . . . *a cold-hearted bitch*—Budd Schulberg ◁**2**▷ *n* 1990s *black teenagers* A girl: *Some boys commonly use the word "bitch" as a synonym for "girl". . .* —New York Times ◁**3**▷ *n* 1930s *homosexuals* A waspish or insolent male homosexual **4** *n* about 1900 The queen of any suit in playing cards **5** *v* (also **bitch and moan**) *by* 1930 To complain; gripe; =BEEF, BELLYACHE: *College students always bitch about the food* **6** *n* about 1910: *What's your bitch today?* **7** *n by* 1814 Anything arduous or very disagreeable: *That wind's a bitch*—Lawrence Sanders **8** *v* 1920s To cheat; =CHISEL: *You never tried to bitch me out of anything*—Budd Schulberg **9** *v* also **bitch up** *by* 1820s To ruin; mess up   *See* BULL BITCH, DRUNK AS A FIDDLER'S BITCH, IT'S A BITCH, SON OF A BITCH

bitch box *n phr* *armed forces fr WWII* A public-address system; =SQUAWK BOX

bitchen or **bitchin'** or **bitching** **1** *adj* 1950s *teenagers* Good; excellent; superior: *A bitchen new single from Southern California has been riding the airwaves to the max this summer*—Newsweek/ *Because of your bitchin' body, I'm going to put you on hold for a couple of days*—Easyriders **2** *adv* Very; extremely: *That was a bitching good party*

◁**bitch in heat**▷ *n phr* A sexually predatory woman; promiscuous woman

bitch kitty ◁**1**▷ *n phr* about 1930 An especially disliked or disagreeable woman **2** *n phr* about 1930 An especially unpleasant or difficult task: *Taking the rusty muffler off the car was a bitch kitty* **3** *n phr* *by* 1940s Anything especially pleasant or admirable; =HUMDINGER: *a real bitch kitty of a performance*   *See* IT'S A BITCH

a **bitch of a** or **one bitch of a** *adj phr* *by* 1960s Very remarkable, awful, admirable, distressing, etc; =A HELL OF A, SOME KIND OF: *Getting the thing together was a bitch of a job/ She's wearing one sweet bitch of a dress!*

bitch session *by 1960s* **1** *n phr* A meeting where complaints and grievances are voiced, esp by labor union representatives; =GRIPE SESSION **2** *n phr* =BULL SESSION

bitchy ◁**1**▷ *adj 1930s* Having the traits of a bitch; mean; nasty; vindictive **2** *adj 1930s* Good-looking; chic; =CLASSY **3** *adj 1920s* Sexually provocative: . . . *two bitchy strip queens*—Time

bite 1 *v* To accept a deception as truth: *She said she was rich, and he bit* **2** *v 1920s* Australian To borrow money from; =PUT THE BITE ON: *He bit me for six bills and left town/ You think I come here to bite you for money*—Elmore Leonard **3** *v* early 1900s To anger; annoy; vex: *She wouldn't tell me what was biting her* **4** *v* (also **bite on**) *1980s* To appropriate; steal; take over: . . . *to bite a popular expression from Cornel West*—Village Voice **5** *n by 1950s* One's share of, or the amount of, a sum owed or demanded: *We owe ten thousand, so what's my bite?* **6** *v 1970s* teenagers =SUCK **7** *n 1980s* A short excerpt or film-clip shown on television news

the **bite** *n by 1950s* Expense; charge; cost; =DAMAGE: *It's a good place, but the bite is fierce*
See PUT THE BITE ON someone

bite someone's **ass** *v phr 1950s* To anger; annoy: *How the hell should I know what's biting his ass?*—Michael Grant

bite someone's **head off** *v phr by 1850s* To react angrily; =JUMP DOWN someone's THROAT ●**Bite someone's nose off** is attested fr 1599, and **eat someone's head off** in 1703: *Don't mention the survey or she'll bite your head off*

bite me *interj* (also **bite it, bite moose, bite this**) *variously fr 1940s* =FUCK YOU, GO TO HELL [these are all invitations to perform fellatio on the speaker, hence to be humiliated]

◁**bite my ass**▷ *interj by 1970s* =KISS MY ASS

bite off more than one **can chew** *sentence by 1870s* To undertake more than one can do; overreach oneself

bite the big one 1 *v phr 1970s* To be a total failure ◀**2**▶ (also **bite the big wazoo**) *1970s & 1980s* teenagers To perform fellatio; =SUCK

bite the bullet *v phr 1700s* military To accept the cost of a course of action; do something painful but necessary: *Will he bite the bullet and become the. . . leader that Philadelphia's black community wants and needs?*—Philadelphia/ . . . *the only thing John can do is bite the bullet*—Scott Turow [fr the early surgical practice of having the patient bite hard on a bullet to divert the mind from pain and prevent screaming]

bite the dust 1 *v phr* middle 1700s To die or be killed **2** *v phr by 1940s* To fail; be destroyed: *The ledgers showed too much red ink, and the company bit the dust*

bite one's **tongue** *v phr fr 1500s* To restrain one's speech, often with difficulty: *Hillary bit her tongue when asked that*—C-Span television

bite your tongue *sentence* Retract or be ashamed of what you just said

bit-grinding *n* computer *by 1980s* The processing of data into a computer

◁**bit (or piece) of fluff**▷ *n phr by 1840s* A girl or young woman; =CHIT

bit part *See* BIT

bitty *See* LITTLE BITTY

biz *n by 1860s* Business
See SHOW BIZ, THAT'S SHOW BUSINESS

bizarro *adj by 1970s* Bizarre: . . . *along comes a bizarro piece of work like Trudy*—Carsten Stroud/ *But subsequent experts on Bizarro World cinema rejected that view. . .* —Entertainment Weekly [fr a character *Bizarro* in the "Superman" comic strips]

bizzer *n by 1980s* An entertainer; veteran of show business: *It's kind of neat for a bizzer who's pushing 40. . . to come on as a dirty teen dream*—Village Voice

blab 1 *v* (also **blab off**) middle 1500s To talk on and on, without necessarily making sense **2** *n* about 1400: *That's stupid, pure blab* **3** *v* (also **blab off**) middle 1500s To say more than one ought; esp to incriminate oneself or others; =SING, SQUEAL: . . . *the gym lady blabbed to Todd*—Douglas Coupland/ . . . *anyone who might have something to blab to them would not be under the influence of the target's lawyer*—Scott Turow

blabbermouth *n* middle 1930s A person who talks too much, esp one who reveals personal or secret matters indiscreetly; =BIG-MOUTH ●*Blabmouth* is found in the middle 1920s: . . . *the blabbermouths are likely to have the whole wretched truth beat out of them. . .* —Seamus Deane

black *adj 1960s* Secret: *The plans for the Stealth bomber were kept in the military's black budget*—Nation
See IN THE BLACK

black and tan *adj phr* outdated *fr 1920s* Occupied or patronized by both blacks and whites; interracial; =SALT AND PEPPER: *My place was black and tan, for colored and white alike*—A Lomax [perhaps fr the same phrase used to describe an 1860s faction of southern Republicans who proposed proportional representation for black and white voters]

black and white 1 *n phr 1970s* narcotics A capsule of an amphetamine and a sedative, or of two amphetamines **2** *n phr 1960s* A police car: *Hanger was patrolling Interstate 35 in his black-and-white*—Los Angeles Times

black-bag job *n phr 1970s* A burglary or robbery done by government agents: *In the FBI. . . he'd never had anything to do with the famous black bag jobs*—New York Review of Books/ *The involvement of foreign nations or companies in corporate black-bag jobs also has soared up*—New York Daily News

blackball or **blacklist** *v* To punish someone by denial of work, boycotting of products, etc ●Both terms come fr the 1700s, and meant "to ostracize'; the modern specialized sense appears to have developed in the labor troubles of the 1890s: *Some mem-*

bers of the Twilight Zone *movie crew say they are being blackballed*—Washington Post

blackbirder *n by 1880s* A trader in black slaves: *The stinking ships of the blackbirders crossed the bars*—Stephen Longstreet [Originally used of traders in Polynesian captives, esp Hawaiians sold into slavery]

black book *See* LITTLE BLACK BOOK

black box *n phr by 1970s* Secrecy; classified material; intelligence interests: . . . *suspected the project might involve secret military operations. "I knew there was black box involved with it"*—Milwaukee Journal/ *A highly confidential annex, placed. . . in a black box, contains selected "raw material"*—M Hastings and S Jenkins [fr the use by British intelligence agencies of a *black box* for highly secret material for the Prime Minister and the Defense and Foreign Secretaries]

black diamonds *See* DIAMONDS

the **black dog** *n phr by 1820s* Melancholia; =the BLUES: *The black dog's got you chewed to the bone*—Harry Crews

black eye 1 *n phr by early 1600s* An eye surrounded with darkened areas of contusion; =MOUSE, SHINER **2** *n phr by 1880s* A bad reputation; an adverse and damaging public image: *That story gave me a black eye*

black gang *n phr by 1890s* The fireroom and boiler room crew of a ship

black hat *1970s* **1** *n phr* A villain; =HEAVY: *The only way I can do that is to make you the black hat*—Philadelphia Journal/ *This time, perhaps, there are black hats on both sides*—New York Times **2** *v*: *They do not try to penetrate security systems or conduct clandestine tests. . . "There is no black-hatting"*—Associated Press **3** *modifier*: *the black-hat rustler in the horse opera* **4** *n phr* The badge or symbol of a villain: *Companies have this black hat on when they go to court*—New York Times [fr the Hollywood tradition that villains in Western movies always wore *black hats*]

black hole *n phr 1990s* A place where things mysteriously disappear •An extension of the 1960s astrophysics term for a region of such extreme gravitational attraction that not even light can escape; in some minds also perhaps evoking the *Black Hole of Calcutta,* a prison cell in which some 179 Europeans were kept in 1756, and where most died: *Bureaucracy is the great black hole of both modern capitalism and modern socialism*—John Kenneth Galbraith/*Banks have found a new black hole for their customers' money: leveraged buyouts*—New Republic

blackjacking *n late 1980s* The business practice of buying an interest in a company and then announcing a takeover, for the purpose of increasing the value of the stock and taking a quick profit: *Blackjacking has made the family a fortune but has also brought controversy*—Milwaukee Journal [fr *blackjack,* the stunning weapon, perhaps influenced by *blackjack,* the card game]

blacklist *See* BLACKBALL

Black Maria (mə RĪ ə) *n phr by late 1830s* A patrol wagon used to carry police prisoners [origin unknown]

black money (or cash) *by 1970s* **1** *n phr* Money obtained illegally, esp by politicians and organized crime operations, that must be "laundered" before it can be used: *Money that derives from an illegal transaction. . . is considered "dirty" or "black" cash*—Philadelphia **2** *n phr* Income not reported for tax purposes; =SKIM

black-on-black *adj 1990s* Committed by black people against other blacks: . . . *damage now being done by crack, AIDS, and black-on-black violence*—New York Times

black operator *n phr by 1980s* A secret agent: *At the Central Intelligence Agency, he was a "black operator" who never quite made it*—New York Times

blackout *modifier 1990s* A period during which discount or favorable prices on airlines are arbitrarily canceled: . . . *flight from LA to NYC for free (depending on availability, blackout dates and routings)*—Time

black out 1 *v phr 1930s fr aviation* To faint; lose consciousness: . . . *he slugged me with something and I blacked out*—Hugh Pentecost **2** *v phr 1930s* To lose one's memory of something: *He totally blacked out that evening* **3** *v phr by 1980s* To exclude an area from television coverage, esp of a sports event: *The whole region was blacked out for the final game*

blackshoe *n Navy by 1940s* A nonflying member of an aircraft carrier's complement

blackstrap *n early 1900s armed forces and lumberjack* Coffee

black stuff 1 *n phr narcotics by 1940s* Opium **◄2►** *n phr* (also **black velvet**) *by 1960s* A black woman or women as sex partner(s), esp for a white man; =POON TANG •*Black velvet* is found in Australian and New Zealand slang in the 1890s

black tar *n phr by middle 1980s* Distilled and concentrated heroin; =SHRIEK

bladder *n by middle 1930s* A newspaper [fr German *Blatt,* "leaf, page, newspaper"]

blade 1 *n esp underworld by 1940s* A knife considered as a weapon; =SWITCHBLADE •This sense dates back to the early 1300s **2** *n hospital by 1970s* A surgeon **3** *v by 1980* To skate on in-line skates: *Concerned that Mrs Onassis' son was blading on the day before her funeral*—New York Times [sense 3 a shortening of *Rollerblade*™]
See SWITCHBLADE

blah (also **blah-blah** or **blah-blah-blah**) **1** *n by 1918* Idle and meaningless talk; falsehoods and vanities; =BALONEY, BUNK: *a lot of romantic blah*—Wolcott Gibbs **2** *interj early 1920s* An expression of disagreement, contempt, etc; =BULLSHIT **3** *adj* (also **bla**) *by 1919* Unstimulating; bland; featureless; dull: . . . *make one ponder the value of crawling out of bed on such a blah day*—Lawrence Sanders

4 *adj* Tired; mildly depressed; enervated: *fever, chills, sore throat. . . and an allover "blah" feeling*—M Fishbein [echoic; but third sense said to be fr French *blasé*, "indifferent, bored"]

blahly *adv* by 1970s In a tedious, colorless way; insipidly: *. . . someone whose footsteps are blahly familiar*—New York Magazine

the **blahs** *n phr* late 1960s A condition of dullness, fatigue, malaise, etc: *The radicals are suffering from a case of the blahs*—Life

blamed *adj* fr middle 1800s =DARN

blame game *n phr* 1990s The reciprocal process of assigning blame; ritual exchange of accusations: *Charles was the clear loser in the royal blame game*—Time

blank 1 *n* 1970s narcotics A weakened or diluted narcotic, or a non-narcotic substance sold as a narcotic; =FLEA POWDER **2** *v* sports by 1970s To hold an opponent scoreless; =SCHNEIDER, SHUT OUT, SKUNK: *The hapless Tigers were blanked twice last week* **3** *v* underworld by 1980s To kill; =RUB OUT, WHACK: *. . . the woman Loftus was with the night he was blanked*—Lawrence Sanders [first sense probably fr *blank cartridge*, "a cartridge without a bullet"]
See DRAW A BLANK, SHOOT BLANKS

blanket 1 *n* by 1950s A pancake; hotcake **2** *n* by 1950s A cigarette paper **3** *n* by 1940s An overcoat •A shortening of *blanket overcoat*, which is attested in the early 1820s
See BEACH BLANKET BINGO, CALIFORNIA BLANKET, SECURITY BLANKET, WET BLANKET

blanket drill *n phr* Army fr 1920s Sleep; =SACK TIME

blanket stiff *n phr* fr late 1800s hoboes A hobo or migratory worker, esp one who carries his belongings in a blanket roll; =BINDLESTIFF

blankety-blank *adj* or *n* or *v* by 1880s A generalized euphemism substituted for a taboo or vulgar term; =BLEEP: *You blankety-blank idiot!/ Stick it up your blankety-blank*

blap 1960s **1** *n* Stroke; bit: *little blaps of revelation and no affect*—Philadelphia **2** *v* To strike; =SOCK: *continually blapped about the head and shoulders with pig bladders wielded by clowns*—Philadelphia Bulletin [echoic]

blast 1 *n* by 1950s A blow; =SOCK: *a blast in the kisser* **2** *v* by 1950s To hit: *She blasted him in the gut* **3** *v* by 1920s To shoot: *They blasted him with a sawed-off shotgun* **4** *n* by 1950s In baseball, a long or strong hit, esp a home run **5** *v* by 1950s: *So the Babe blasts it right out of there* **6** *v* by 1940s To attack, esp with strong verbal condemnation: *He blasted the Secretary for saying that* **7** *n* by 1940s: *He figures the opposition's blast won't hurt him* **8** *v* by 1960s To defeat utterly; trounce; =CLOBBER **9** *v* (also **blast off**) 1930s To leave; =BOOK, PEEL OUT, SPLIT: *He got in the Porsche and blasted out of there* **10** *v* 1930s narcotics To take narcotics, esp to smoke marijuana; use: *. . . to start blasting opium from a water pipe*—H Braddy **11** *n* 1950s narcotics A single dose or portion of a nar-

cotic or other stimulant; =BELT, FIX: *Maybe it's a little early in the day for that first blast*—D Harris **12** *n* 1960s A thrill; a transport of pleasure; =CHARGE, KICK: *Meeting her was a blast* **13** *n* 1950s A noisy and jolly party or other especially exciting occasion; =BALL **14** *n* by 1970s Anything good or admirable; =GASSER **15** *interj* by 1630s An exclamation of dismay, irritation, frustration, etc; an imprecation •Chiefly British
See FULL BLAST

blasted 1 *adj* and *adv* by late 1680s =DARN **2** *adj* by 1940s Intoxicated by drugs or alcohol; =STONED

blaster underworld by 1940s **1** *n* A gunman; =HIT MAN **2** *n* A firearm
See GHETTO BOX

blast from the past *n phr* 1960s =GOLDEN OLDIE

blastissimo *adj* and *adv* musicians by 1970s Very, very loud; fortississimo: *You ought not to sing the berceuse blastissimo* [modeled on *fortissimo*]

blast off 1950s aerospace *v phr* To ignite rockets and rise from the launchpad: *The shuttle blasted off cleanly*

blast (or **blasting) party** *n phr* 1950s narcotics A social gathering of narcotics users, esp of marijuana smokers; =POT PARTY

blat 1 *v* by 1870s =BLAB **2** *n* by middle 1930s A newspaper; =BLADDER

blather *n* by 1780s Noisy nonsense; =BULLSHIT

blaxploitation early 1970s **1** *n* The commercial exploitation of putative black experience, esp in films with blacks in sensational heroic roles of police officers, criminals, gamblers, etc **2** *modifier*: *Most of the blaxploitation films. . . have been shoddy ripoffs*—Village Voice [blend of *black* and *exploitation*]

blaze 1 *v* by 1980s To speed; rush; =BARREL: *She blazed around in it like Chuck Yeager, but it scared me half to death*—Robert B Parker **2** *v* 1980s teenagers To leave; =BOOK, SPLIT
See LET'S BOOGIE

blaze away *v phr* by 1770s To shoot at, either literally or figuratively: *The cops blazed away at the crouchiung villains/ The candidates blazed away on television and radio*

blazer *n* by 1840 A remarkable person; =HOT SHOT, PISSER: *His competition was suspect, but he is a blazer*—Milwaukee Journal

blazes *See* BLUE BLAZES

as **blazes** or **as hell** or ◁**as shit**▷ *adv phr* first form by 1830s To a very great degree; =TO THE MAX: *the life now. . . hard as blazes*—Village Voice/ *cold as hell/ tough as shit*

blazing *adj* 1990s black teenagers Seductive in dress and action; =HOT

bleached blonde *See* CHEMICAL BLONDE

bleachers *n* by 1889 The most distant and cheapest seats in a baseball park, overlooking the outfield •Virtually standard English now, partly because there is no other word for them

blech (BLEKH or BLECH) *interj* 1960s An exclamation of disgust, revulsion, etc: *The House Democratic Caucus launched its response to Reaganomics:*

"BLECH!"—National Review [perhaps fr the use of the term to lampoon *Breck™* shampoo in a joke advertisement in *Mad* magazine]

bleed *v by 1680s* To take someone's money by overcharging or extortion: *His creditors bled him to death*

bleeder 1 *n baseball by 1930s* A lucky or weak base hit; =BLOOPER, TEXAS LEAGUER **2** *n by 1800* A hemophiliac

bleeding heart *by 1950s* **1** *n phr* A person regarded as unduly softhearted, esp towards idlers who do not merit sympathy •Very commonly used by the politically conservative to condemn the politically liberal **2** *modifier*: *a bleeding-heart wimpy liberal* [fr religious pictures showing the *bleeding heart* of Jesus]

bleed someone **white** *v phr* To take all of someone's money; exact everything: *. . . it looks like they were bled white and dumped*—Carsten Stroud

bleep or **bleeping** or **blipping** *adj* or *n* or *v 1970s* A generalized euphemism substituted for a taboo or vulgar term; =BLANKETY-BLANK: *. . . your bleeping black ass*—Jane Leavey/ *. . . they're a bunch of arrogant bleeps who think their stuff doesn't stink*—Milwaukee Journal/ *The 270. . . ain't no blipping good*—Sports Afield [fr the practice of erasing objectionable material on a tape or in a sound track with a high-pitched sound called echoically a *bleep*]

bletcherous *adj 1980s computer* Disgusting; nasty; ugly: *The whole design is bletcherous* [fr *bletch* or *blecch,* a comic-book expression of disgust similar to *yuck*]

blimp *n by 1940s* An obese person [fr the WWI term for a nonrigid dirigible, based on *limp*]

blimp boat *n phr 1980s college students* =BLIMP

blind 1 *adj by 1630s* Very drunk; =BLIND DRUNK, ZONKED **2** *adv esp students fr early 1900s* Completely; =COLD •Most common in the expression *steal someone blind*: *Goddam car was eating me blind*—George V Higgins **3** *adj homosexuals by 1920s* Uncircumcised
See STEAL someone BLIND

blind baggage or **blind** *n phr* or *n 1890s hoboes* A railroad baggage car or mail car with no door or a locked door at one end; also, the relatively safe space thus provided, where hoboes may hide or ride: *to catch the blind baggage on the west-bound overland*—Jack London

blind date (or **drag)** *esp students fr 1920s* **1** *n phr* An arranged appointment for a show, dance, etc, where one's partner is a previously unknown person, usu the friend of a friend **2** *n phr* One's partner on such an occasion

blind drunk or **blinded** *adj phr* or *adj by 1840* Very drunk

blindgate *v 1990s* To drive far enough behind a car to stop if it stops, but not far enough to miss something in the road if it swerves [based on *tailgate*]

blind pig (or **tiger)** *n phr by middle 1880s* An unlicensed or illegal saloon; =SPEAKEASY

the **blinds** *See* RIDE THE BLINDS

blind-side (also **blind-pop)** *1960s football* **1** *v* To tackle or block someone from an unseen quarter: *have to worry about gettin' blind-popped from a corner blitz*—Dan Jenkins **2** *v* To be burdened or attacked unexpectedly: *Businessmen began to be blind-sided by enormous legal bills*—Newsweek/ *The state. . . will be coming back sometime in the future to blind-side us*—Milwaukee Journal

blind tiger *n phr by 1850s* =BLIND PIG, SPEAKEASY [In order to evade liquor laws, the originator posted a sign by a hole in the wall "*Blind Tiger,* ten cents a sight," and passed out a glass of whiskey when given a dime]

Blind Tom *n phr baseball by 1940s* An umpire [perhaps fr earlier *Blind Tom,* "blind-man's buff"]

blinger (BLING ər) *n by 1900* Something remarkable, wonderful, superior, etc; =HUMDINGER: *. . . real blingers going through to the phase of secondary infection*—Paul de Kruif [fr *bling,* "ring," perhaps referring to ringing the bell in some carnival contest]

blink *v by middle 1980s* To blink one's eyes in a face-to-face confrontation, a sign of weakness; =BACK DOWN: *NBC Entertainment President. . . thinks ABC has blinked*—Los Angeles Times
See ON THE BLINK

blinkers *n by 1816* The eyes

blip 1 *adj 1930s jive talk* Excellent; very good **2** *adj 1950s cool talk* =HIP **3** *n 1940s* A luminous signal on a radar screen: *Birds can cause blips on radar screens*—P Wagner **4** *n 1980s* A rapid increase and decrease; quick peaking: *The bond bulls argue that commodities' rally is a blip. . .*—Los Angeles Times/ *. . . despite temporary blips up and down*—Time **5** *v 1980s* To encroach upon, as one aircraft's image on a radar screen might enter the territory of another aircraft: *Cartridge-makers blip into Atari's airspace, attracted by the enormous profit potential*—New York Magazine **6** *v 1960s* To censor a taped word or passage by erasing it electronically from the tape and substituting a "bleep": *Occasionally Mr Carson's lines are "blipped"*—New York Times [most senses fr earlier *blip,* "a sharp blow or twitch"]

blip (or **ping) jockey** *n phr armed forces by 1970s* A person who monitors electronic detection devices

blip someone **off** *v phr outdated 1920s underworld* To kill, esp by shooting: *If he blipped Beno off, he knows me*—Dashiell Hammett

blipping *See* BLEEP

blissed out *adj phr early 1970s* In a state of exaltation or blissful ecstasy: *. . . blissed-out young pilgrims*—DS Greene/ *. . . and lives a blissed-out life with Sue*—Washington Post

bliss ninny *n phr 1970s* A person ecstatic to the point of seeming idiocy

blissed or **bliss out** *v phr 1970s* To become ecstatic; go into a mystic daze, esp under the influence of a guru: *Misty. . . was blissed and became Dusty's instant lifelong fan*—Douglas Coupland/

Don't get high, don't space out, don't get blissed out—National Review

blissout *n 1970s* A state of exaltation or ecstasy; mystic daze

blister 1 *n early 1800s* An annoying person without whom one could do nicely: *He's not quite a jerk, just a blister* **2** *n middle 1800s* A prostitute **3** *n 1940s* A bubble-shaped transparent covering on an aircraft cockpit, roof opening, etc

blisterfoot *n WWI Army* An infantry soldier; =PADDLEFOOT

blitz[1] *v students around 1900* To absent oneself from a class or examination; =CUT, SHINE

blitz[2] *v WWII armed forces* To polish one's brass buttons, etc; prepare for inspection [fr *Blitz Cloth*, trademark for a brand of metal-polishing cloth]

blitz[3] **1** *v 1970s* To defeat without being scored upon; =BLANK, SHUT OUT: *They blitzed the Mariners 12–zip* **2** *v 1960s football* To rush the quarterback in force, hoping to prevent him from completing a pass **3** *n 1940s* Any heavy onslaught or attack: *His best strategy was a blitz of TV spots just before the election* **4** *v 1940s*: *We blitzed her with questions* **5** *n 1990s* An electronic-mail (email) message **6** *n by 1990s* A chess game that must be played within ten minutes [fr German *Blitzkrieg,* "lightning war," an overwhelmingly heavy and rapid attack, using tanks and other armor, bombers, etc]

blitzed (also **blitzed out**) **1** *adj college students by 1960s* Drunk: *. . . where are they going to find room in overcrowded jails for a blitzed driver?*—Sassy/ *We were pretty blitzed out by the time Lee walked in*—Richard Merkin **2** *adj 1970s* Completely exhausted; =WIPED OUT [probably fr *blitz*[3], perhaps influenced by *bliss out*]

blivit *n WWII armed forces* Anything superfluous or annoying ●Examples like the one following, though differing in the number of pounds, were ordinarily given as an explanation of the word, and the explanation was the fun: *Gerber's confession was what Keisman called a "blivit," four pounds of shit in a two-pound bag*—Lawrence Sanders

blizzard-head *n 1940s television studio* A very blonde person for whom studio lighting must be subdued

bloated *adj outdated fr 1920s* Drunk

blob 1 *n students about 1900* A mistake **2** *v*: *He blobbed the second question* **3** *n early 1700s* A mass of viscous matter; an amorphous portion; =GOB

block 1 *n by 1630s* The head **2** *adj 1980s students* Stupid

See GAPER'S BLOCK, KNOCK someone's BLOCK OFF, NEW KID ON THE BLOCK

blockbust *v 1960s* To persuade white property owners to sell their houses quickly by arousing a fear that blacks are moving into the neighborhood

blockbuster[1] *n 1950s* A great success; a lavish and popular film, show, etc: *A gangster movie can be a box-office blockbuster*—Saturday Review [fr the large high-explosive aerial bombs of World War II called *blockbusters*]

blockbuster[2] *n 1960s* A real estate dealer who blockbusts

blockhead *n by middle 1500s* A stupid person; =KLUTZ ●Considered standard by some, slang by others: *No man but a blockhead ever wrote except for money*—Samuel Johnson [that is, a head no more intelligent than the *block* on which hats are made; a *woodenhead*]

blocks *See* PUT THE BLOCKS TO someone

bloke[1] *n middle 1800s* A man; fellow; =GUY ●Chiefly British use: *Look at the bloke ridin'*—Theodore Dreiser [perhaps fr Celtic *ploc,* "large stubborn person"]

bloke[2] *n narcotics by 1970s* Cocaine [probably echoic *blow*]

blonde and sweet *n phr WWII Navy* Coffee with sugar and cream

blood 1 *n college students fr early 1900s* A fashionable and popular man: *crew cut like the college blood*—John O'Hara **2** *n black* A fellow black; =BLOOD BROTHER: *and these cats. . . well, we was all bloods*—D Evans

See MAKE one's BLOOD BOIL, SMELL BLOOD, TIRED BLOOD, TOO RICH FOR someone's BLOOD

blood brother *n phr black fr about 1960* A fellow black; =BLOOD

blood chit *n phr Korean War armed forces* A cloth badge that identifies a military aviator as American and promises a reward for aiding him: *Seven crew members survived. One of them produced a "blood chit". . .* —Milwaukee Journal

blood on the floor *n phr 1990s* The emotional residue of an intense struggle: *Women in the upper ranks of big companies are making it, but there's blood on the floor*—New York Times/*I don't know if there's blood on the floor after Clinton's NAFTA victory, but Democrats will reunite*—George Stephanopoulos

bloody (or **blue**) **murder 1** *n phr by 1970* A shattering defeat; total destruction: *After the second quarter it was bloody murder* **2** *adv phr by 1850s* As if announcing general slaughter and universal destruction: *. . . screaming blue murder on the arms of their seats*—Village Voice

blooey *See* GO BLOOEY

bloom *n television studio* A glare from some white object in a television image

bloomer *n Australian by 1880s* A blunder; =BONER, GOOF: *. . . a "bloomer" by Truman and Marshall about a grave that was not there*—United Press/ *This dictionary, I'm afraid, is scarcely free of bloomers* [said to be Australian fr the phrase "a *blooming* error"; however, it is not listed in dictionaries of Australian slang, while *blue,* "an error, a bloomer," is; the relation is unclear]

bloomer boy *n phr WWII armed forces* A paratrooper [fr the baggy style of their pants, reminiscent of the roomy trousers devised for women and worn by Amelia *Bloomer* (1818–1894), the American feminist leader]

bloomers *n* WWII Navy Gun covers [see *bloomer boy*]

blooming *adj* and *adv* by 1880s =DARN ●Chiefly British use [fr the notion of full-blown or -*bloomed*]

bloop 1 *n* about 1930 An unwanted sound in a phonograph record, resulting from a poor splice between two pieces of magnetic tape **2** *v* 1940s baseball To hit a ball relatively weakly and slowly: *He blooped a lob over her head* **3** *v* by 1950s To launch and land a long, curving blow: *Turner blooped a bolo to the heart*—New York Daily News

blooper 1 *n* A blow with the fist, esp a long, looping punch: *So I could hang a blooper on your kisser*—John O'Hara **2** *n* baseball A high, looping pitch, throw, or hit: *I poked an easy blooper over third* **3** *n* A blunder; =BONER, BOO-BOO: *He may have felt he pulled a blooper*—J Marlow

blotter 1 *n* police by 1880s The daily record of arrests at a police station **2** *n* (also **blotter acid**) 1970s narcotics A sheet of absorbent paper to which liquid LSD has been applied and then allowed to dry

blotto *adj* early 1900s Drunk: *. . . the drivers who are blotto*—Philadelphia

bloviate *v* middle 1800s To talk loudly and bombastically; =BLOW OFF one's MOUTH, TALK BIG ●This appears to be a revival of old frontier tall-talk coinage: *Just more bloviating by the Senator about cutting the budget*—Milwaukee Journal/ *Limbaugh chortles, crows, bloviates and denounces*—Norristown Times Herald [fr *blow* made into a fancy word by adding the suffix]

blow 1 *v* jazz musicians fr early 1900s To play a musical instrument, esp in jazz style and not necessarily a wind instrument: *There will be three kids blowing guitar, banjo, and washboard*—Ed McBain/ *This music is the culmination of all my writing and blowing*—Duke Ellington **2** *n* esp 1950s beat & cool talk To do or perform something, esp to do it well: *He blows great conversation*—E Horne ◁**3**▷ *v* by 1930s To do fellatio or cunnilingus; =SUCK OFF ◁**4**▷ *v* by 1970s To be disgusting, nasty, worthless, etc; =BITE, SUCK: *This blows and you do too*—National Lampoon **5** *v* by 1870s To treat someone to something; buy something expensive or unusual for someone: *I blew myself to a new pair of shoes* **6** *v* (also **blow** something **in**) by 1890s To spend money, esp foolishly and all at once: *The state blew my money buying votes for Roosevelt*—Westbrook Pegler/ *And blow it in on smokes*—Joseph Auslander **7** *v* about 1920 To take a narcotic, esp but not necessarily by inhalation: *Jimi blew every kind of dope invented*—New York Times/ *I don't know how you can blow dust and eat*—Harry Crews **8** *n* 1960s narcotics Cocaine: *OK, he gets busted for blow eight times. . .* —Milwaukee Journal/ *Hell, half the people doing blow are reacting to the cut. . .* —Robert B Parker **9** *v* 1960s narcotics To smoke marijuana; =BLOW SMOKE: *He enjoys sex; he does not blow grass*—Commonweal **10** *v* by 1902 To leave; depart; =SPLIT: *I'm blowing, I got a job in Detroit*—Dorothy

Parker **11** *v* about 1920 To lose or ruin something by mistake, inattention, incompetence, etc; =BLOW IT: *I blew the best chance I ever had* **12** *v* theater by 1920s To forget or botch one's part in a show **13** *v* =BLOW OFF **14** *v* by 1840s To inform against someone; =SING **15** *v* by late 1500s To expose or publicize something secret, esp something scandalous: *Treat me right or I'll blow it about the love nest* **16** *v* early 1900s To lose one's temper; =BLOW one's TOP **17** *v* also **blow off** by 1400 To brag; =TOOT one's OWN HORN **18** *v* 1980s college students To sing, esp to sing well

See BLOW someone AWAY, BLOW one's COOL, BLOW someone's or something's COVER, BLOW someone's HAIR, BLOW someone's MIND, BLOW OFF one's MOUTH, BLOW ONE, BLOW OUT OF THE WATER, BLOW SMOKE, BLOW THE GAFF, BLOW THE LID OFF, BLOW THE WHISTLE, BLOW one's TOP, BLOW UP, BLOW UP A STORM, BLOW something WIDE OPEN, LET OFF STEAM, LOW BLOW, ONE-TWO, TOOT one's OWN HORN

Blow *See* JOE BLOW

blow a fix *v phr* 1960s narcotics To lose the effect of a narcotic injection by missing the vein

blow a gasket *v phr* (Variations: **gasket** may be replaced by **fuse** or **gut**) by 1940s To lose one's temper, esp to the point of insanity; =BLOW one's TOP: *The higher-ups blew a gasket when they heard*—Bing Crosby/ *. . . wants more than she will give. He blows a gasket*—Scott Turow/ *If Barbara sees a subpoena notice. . . she'll blow a gut*—Scott Turow

blow away *v phr* by 1950s To depart; =BLOW, TAKE OFF

blow someone **away 1** *v phr* early 1900s To kill; assassinate; get rid of; =OFF: *. . . and boom, Jack Blumenfeld gets blown away*—Philadelphia **2** *v phr* To defeat utterly; trounce; =CLOBBER: *And they blew away some of the best long-distance runners in the world*—New York Times **3** *v phr* To overcome, often with admiration; =FRACTURE: *I read the book and it blew me away*—Philadelphia Bulletin/ *The cow connection just blew us away*—Milwaukee Journal

blow by or **past** *v phr* baseball by 1950s To pitch a ball so hard and fast that the batter cannot hit it: *He blew it right by the slugger*

blow by blow 1 *adv phr* 1930s In a complete and detailed way: *I'll tell you what happened blow by blow* **2** *adj*: *a blow-by-blow account*

blow chunks *v phr* (Variations: **chow** or **cookies** or **grits** or **lunch** may replace **chunks**) 1980s college students To vomit; =BARF, TOSS one's COOKIES

blow one's **cool** *v phr* 1960s counterculture To lose one's composure; become flustered, excited, or angry: *I always blow my cool when they honk at me*

blow one's **cork** *See* BLOW one's TOP

blow someone's or something's **cover** espionage & police by 1970s **1** *v phr* To ruin or nullify one's disguise or assumed role; reveal one's true identity: *The undercover cop had to blow his cover by pulling his gun when he thought they might have spotted him/She called out my name, which* *blew my cover* **2** *v phr* To reveal something, esp inadvertently or mischievously: *I'm not blowing the movie's cover story by giving you this information*—Philadelphia

blower *n by 1920* A supercharger for a car or airplane engine; =HUFFER
See MIND-BLOWER

blow someone's **hair** *v phr by 1970s* To frighten someone; be scary: *When I think. . . things. . . could have happened, it blows my hair*—Playboy

blowhard *by 1820s* **1** *n* A braggart; self-aggrandizer: *. . . his reach often does exceed his grasp, in a town of blowhards*—Buzz **2** *n* An insistent and aggressive talker

blow hot and cold *v phr by 1570s* To be indecisive; dither

blow in 1 *v phr by 1890s* To arrive and enter, esp from a distance: *Look who just blew in from Sri Lanka* **2** *v phr by 1880s* To spend recklessly; squander: *He blew his whole month's pay in on that one pair of shoes*

blow-in card *n phr by 1990s* A reply card inserted among the pages of a magazine: *. . . blow-in cards make flipping through the magazine like opening a garbage can*—Time [fr the fact that they are *blown in* by an air-insertion machine]

blow something **in** *See* BLOW
blowing *See* MIND-BLOWING

blow it *v phr about 1920* To fail; make a botch; ruin one's chances: *We are winning. If we don't blow it*—Village Voice/*I think I blew it. I talked too much and said too little*—Erma Bombeck

blow it off *v phr college students by 1970s* To fail to deal with or attend to something; neglect something deliberately: *He felt sort of blah, so he decided to blow it off and skip his morning classes*

blow it out *interj* (Variations: **your asshole** or **your B-bag** or **your barracks bag** or **your ear** or **your tailpipe** may be added) *fr WWII armed forces* A generalized exclamation of contempt, anger, incredulity, etc ●Most often uttered in challenge or rebuke

◁**blow job**▷ *n phr* An act of fellatio or of cunnilingus: *. . . whether a blow job from a married woman is the same as committing adultery*—Elmore Leonard [origin unknown; perhaps fr the use of the mouth; perhaps for the reason that Walt Whitman called semen *white-blow*]

blow one's **lines** *v phr theater by 1970s* To perform badly, esp by misspeaking: *Before the week was out he had blown his lines as President, and perhaps blown the Democratic Party out of office*—Time

blow someone's **mind** *v phr fr narcotics & 1960s counterculture* To evoke deep feelings of awe, admiration, strangeness, etc; stir one profoundly: *The simplicity of the thing blew my mind*

blown *adj 1950s hot rodders* Having a supercharger: *. . . a blown engine*

blown-out *adj 1960s narcotics* In a state of narcotic intoxication, trance, or exhilaration; =HIGH, STONED

blowoff 1 *n early 1900s* A climax; a final provocation: *She said I was late, and that was the blowoff* **2** *n early 1900s* A quarrel: *She and Hobart have had a big blow-off*—J Kelly **3** *n 1970s teenagers* Something very easy; =PIECE OF CAKE

blow off 1 *v phr by 1960s* To avoid or shirk; not attend or attend to; ignore: *. . . I'm not going to tell you to blow off any standing-room-only. . . events*—Sassy/ *. . . it was just something he was going through, so we blew it off*—Rocky Mountain News

blow someone **off** *v phr by 1990s* To rebuff; slight; treat dismissively: *Before you blow them off with a snotty comment, examine yourself*—Vanity Fair/ *Mike blows off Sharon Stone*—Gary Trudeau

blow off one's **mouth** or **blow** one's **mouth off** *v phr* (Variations: **trap** or **yap** may replace **mouth**) *by late 1800s* =SHOOT OFF one's MOUTH

blow off steam *See* LET OFF STEAM

blowout 1 *n by 1820s* A noisy, festive occasion; =SHINDIG, WINGDING **2** *n early 1900s* An explosive rupture of a car tire **3** *n by 1980s* A massive defeat; =LAUGHER

blow someone **out** *v phr by 1860s* To kill or destroy; =BLOW someone AWAY: *The Redskins got blown out*—CBS Sports

blow someone **out of the water 1** *v phr by 1960s* To defeat utterly; =SHOOT someone DOWN IN FLAMES: *Are you afraid of being blown out of the water?*—Playboy/Bradlee *"blew him (Tavoularas) out of the water"*—Washingtonian **2** *v phr by 1990s* To astonish utterly; =KNOCK one's SOCKS OFF: *. . . these kids just blow you out of the water with the work they've done*—Milwaukee Journal Sentinel

blow one's **own horn** *See* TOOT one's **own horn**

blow smoke 1 *v phr by 1940s* To boast; brag; exaggerate: *. . . four cops sitting around drinking, blowing smoke, and kidding*—Lawrence Sanders **2** *v phr* (also **blow smoke up** someone's **ass** or **blow heat**) *by 1940s* To mislead; confuse; deceive: *Anybody who tells you different's just blowing smoke up your ass*—George V Higgins **3** *v phr by 1940s* To flatter; =SWEET-TALK: *Do you mean it, or are you just blowing smoke?*—comic strip "Sally Forth" **4** *v phr by 1930s* To smoke marijuana or hashish: *Everybody blew smoke there. You could buy hash*—New Yorker [fr both the presumed effects of smoking opium and the confusing and concealing effect of making a smokescreen]

blow someone's **socks off** *See* KNOCK someone's SOCKS OFF

blow the gaff *v phr outdated underworld fr early 1800s* To inform on someone; =SING: *didn't mind if I blew the gaff on this "common practice"*—Village Voice [to reveal the concealed cheating mechanism of a carnival game]

blow the lid off *v phr by 1920s* To expose a scandal, esp political or governmental corruption

blow the whistle 1 *v phr underworld by 1940s* To inform; =SING: *She hadn't been Dutch Schultz's wife for four years not to know the penalty for blowing the whistle*—NY Confidential/ *How come* *you're blowing the whistle?*—Robert B Parker **2** *v phr* by 1950s To expose or begin to resist wrongdoing: *The detective who blew the whistle was also transferred*—Village Voice [fr the *whistle* once used by police officers to signal "Stop!"; influenced by the signal of a sports official that an infraction, foul, etc, has been committed]

blow one's **top** (Variations: **cork** or **lid** or **topper** or **stack** or **wig** may replace **top**) *entry form by 1920s* **1** *v* To go insane; become violently mad **2** *v* To become wildly excited or enthusiastic: *Here's an idea'll make you blow your cork* **3** *v* To become violently excited by narcotics; =FLIP, FREAK OUT **4** *v* To become violently and suddenly angry; have a tantrum: *. . . a "quiet, mild-mannered man" who "blew his lid". . .*—Milwaukee Journal Sentinel [perhaps fr the violence of an oil well that *blows* as a gusher]

blowtorch *n 1950s Air Force* A jet aircraft or jet engine

blowup 1 *n early 1800s* A fit of anger **2** *n early 1800s* A quarrel; violent rift between persons **3** *n by 1930s* A photographic or other enlargement: *He already has a blowup of your proverb. . . on a wall of his breakfast room*—Joseph Heller

blow up 1 *v phr by 1930s* To enlarge a photograph **2** *v phr* =BLOW one's TOP **3** *v phr* =BLOW one's COOL **4** *v phr early 1900s theater* To forget or garble one's lines on stage; =BALLOON: *Barrymore "blew up" in his lines*—Gene Fowler

blow something **up** *v phr by 1970s* To assign too much importance to; exaggerate; =MAKE A FEDERAL CASE OUT OF something, PUMP UP: *He'll blow it up into a world-class scandal*

blow up a storm 1 *v phr 1930s jazz musicians* To play, esp jazz trumpet, cornet, clarinet, etc, with great skill and verve: *I first heard Buddy Bolden play. . . . He was blowing up a storm*—Louis Armstrong **2** *v phr* =PISS UP A STORM

blow something **wide open** *v phr by 1970s* To expose a scandal, esp political or governmental corruption; =BLOW THE LID OFF: *That'll be the perfect time to blow this thing wide open*—Washington Post

blow (or **cut**) **Zs** *v phr armed forces by 1970s* To sleep; =SACK OUT [*Z*, "snore," is attested from the 1920s]

BLT (pronounced as separate letters) *n 1950s* A bacon, lettuce, and tomato sandwich: *. . . the Lodge. . . where MTV V.J.'s get B.L.T.'s A.S.A.P.*—Vanity Fair

blubber 1 *v by 1300s* To weep; snivel **2** *n by 1700s* Fat; =AVOIRDUPOIS

◁**blubber butt**▷ *n phr by 1950s* A very fat person, esp one with big buttocks; =BUFFALO BUTT, FAT-ASS: *. . . we can't have blubber butts like her on the payroll*—Mike Royko

blubberhead *n by 1870s* A stupid person

blue 1 *adj fr early 1800s* Drunk: *When you were blue you got the howling horrors*—Dorothy Parker **2** *adj by 1840* Lewd; rude; suggestive; =DIRTY

•The term covers the range from obscene to slightly risqué: *. . . blue humor has long been a staple of black audiences*—New York Times **3** *adj early 1500s* Melancholy; depressed; woeful: *I feel a little blue and blah this morning* ◀**4**▶ *n 1920s* A very dark-skinned black person **5** *n by 1860s* A police officer: *By the time the first blues got there, there's like maybe ten people milling about*—Lawrence Sanders **6** *n computer by 1980* An IBM™ computer

See BAYOU BLUE, HEAVENLY BLUE

Blue *n by 1930s* The University of Michigan football team •Most often heard in the exhortation "Go Blue!"

blue-and-white *n 1970s* A police car, esp in New York City; =BLACK-AND-WHITE: *. . . those blue-and-whites rolling slowly up and down in front of her house*—Carsten Stroud

blue around the gills *See* GREEN AROUND THE GILLS

◁**blue-ball**▷ *n by 1970s* A sexually frustrated male: *. . . and a fellow blue-ball did things to each other that they wanted the girls to do to them*—Penthouse

◁**blue balls**▷ **1** *n phr early 1900s* A turgid and painful condition of the testicles due to sexual excitement and frustration: *Sex will relieve testicular congestion, or blue balls*—Playboy **2** *n phr by 1930s* Any of various venereal diseases, esp gonorrhea or lymphogranuloma inguinale

blue blanket *n phr by 1970s* A personal possession that gives a sense of safety; security blanket: *I like my stick closer to me. . . it's my blue blanket*—Joseph Wambaugh

blue blazes *early 1800s* **1** *n phr* Hell: *What in blue blazes are you up to?* **2** *adv phr* Like hell: *. . . lying blue blazes*—Ken Kesey [fr the sulfurous blue blazes of Hell, an extreme environment]

blue bomb or **bomber** *n phr by 1980s* A tablet of Halcion™, a sleeping pill: *"Time for a blue bomb," he announces before naps*—Time

bluebook *n college students by 1890s* A college examination: *I'm cramming for a bluebook in Econ* [fr the color of the examination booklet]

blue box *n phr 1970s college students* An electronic device enabling one to make long-distance telephone calls without paying: *. . . the alleged use of an electronic "blue box" to avoid telephone tolls*—Arizona Wildcat

blue cheer *n phr 1960s narcotics* LSD [fr *Blue Cheer*™ laundry soap]

blue-chip *adj by 1920s* Of the best sort; first rate: *a blue-chip stock/ a blue-chip school* [fr the color of the highest denomination of gambling chip]

blue chipper *n phr by 1970s* A person or thing of the highest quality, ability, etc, esp an athlete: *But the crop does not contain many blue chippers*—Inside Sports/ *. . . he did not necessarily appear to major colleges as a blue-chipper*—Milwaukee Journal

bluecoat *n by 1870s* A police officer: *He told the damn bluecoat. . . he'd punch him all over the corner*—James T Farrell

blue-collar *modifier by 1940s* Working-class: *a blue-collar neighborhood/ blue-collar concerns* [fr the color of the traditional work-shirt]

blue-collar ballet *n phr by 1990s* Professional wrestling

blued *See* SCREWED, BLUED, AND TATTOOED

blue darter *n phr* baseball *by 1940s* A low, hard-hit line drive: *A hard line drive is a blue darter, frozen rope, or an ungodly shot*—Jim Bouton

blue-devil *See* BLUE HEAVEN

Blue Dog *n phr by 1990s*: *GOP leaders are courting a group of 21 House Democrats, the self-proclaimed Blue Dogs. . .* —Associated Press

blue-eyed boy *See* FAIRHAIRED BOY

◁**blue-eyed devil**▷ *n phr 1960s* black A white person; a Caucasian

blue-eyed soul *n phr 1970s* musicians Black music with its style and mannerisms, as performed by white musicians: *Boz came on like an inspired amateur of blue-eyed soul*—Village Voice/ *. . . a composer devoted to extending the chromatic vocabulary of blue-eyed soul. . .* —New York Times

blue flags *n phr 1970s* narcotics LSD

blue flick *See* BLUE MOVIE

blue flu *n phr 1960s* A mythical disease epidemic during a police job action when numbers of officers telephone to say that they are ill; =SICK-OUT

blue funk British *by 1860s* **1** *n phr* A profoundly timorous or nervous state **2** *n phr* A profoundly depressed state •Both senses more common in British use but equally outdated

bluegrass 1 *n* Music based on the songs and dances of the Southern Appalachians and played usu at a fast tempo by a string group **2** *modifier*: *the bluegrass sound/ bluegrass mandolin* by Bob Applebaum [fr the nickname of Kentucky, the *bluegrass* state]

blue-hair *n by 1980s* An old woman; =WRINKLY: *One old blue-hair even struggled up the steps with her walker*—Jane Leavy [fr the *blue hair* tint of those who use a blue haircolor rinse on gray or white hair]

blue heaven or **blue-devil** *n phr* or *n 1950s* narcotics A capsule of Amytal™, a type of barbiturate [perhaps fr a 1920s popular song *My Blue Heaven*]

blue hell *n phr by 1970s* An extremely nasty and trying situation; =UNSHIRTED HELL •*Blue* here is almost an intensifier, although it carries the infernal suggestions of *blue blazes*: *It was more than tough, it was blue hell*

blue ice *n phr* airlines *by 1990s* Waste water discharged from aircraft in flight, which freezes on the way to the ground [fr the *blue* toilet disinfectant used]

blue in the face *See* TILL one IS BLUE IN THE FACE

blue-light special *n phr by 1980s* A bargain; a good buy; =STEAL: *. . . Paramount may look like a blue-light special in five years. . .* —Milwaukee Journal [fr the marking by a *blue light* of a particular bargain or discount in Kmart stores]

blue meanie or **meany** *1960s* **1** *n phr* A very nasty person; =BASTARD: *It's not that all landlords are blue meanies*—Washington Post **2** *n phr* Depression; melancholy; =BLUE FUNK, THE BLUES [fr cartoon characters in the 1968 film *The Yellow Submarine* of the English rock group The Beatles]

blue movie (or **flick**) *n phr 1960s* A pornographic movie; erotic film; =SKIN FLICK

blue murder *See* BLOODY MURDER

bluenose *n 1920s* A prude; prig; self-appointed moral arbiter: *The moral bluenoses were sniffing around*—Stephen Longstreet

Bluenose *n by 1830s* A native of Nova Scotia, esp a Maritimes fisherman [fr the color of a very cold nose]

blue note *n phr 1890s* musicians A flatted note of the sort common in blues music

blue ruin *n phr* outdated early 1800s British Inferior gin

the blues 1 *n phr by 1830s* A state of melancholy; depression **2** *n phr by 1912* A usu slow style of singing, guitar-playing, and jazz originally reflecting in its melancholy and resignation the special plight of black people and the general vicissitudes of life and love; esp songs having in each stanza a repeated opening statement and single closing statement **3** *n phr* middle *1800s* The police [first sense ultimately fr late 1700s term *the blue devils,* "a fit of melancholy"]

blue sky 1 *v phr by 1980s* To hold a brainstorming session with no limit on the strangeness of the ideas proposed **2** *n phr 1980s* Speculation; guesswork: *That may sound great, but it's just blue sky* **3** *n phr 1980s* narcotics Heroin: *. . . ex-psychiatric case. . . from Bellevue with a minor in blue sky and toot*—Carsten Stroud

blue-sky *adj* about *1900* finance Having no sound factual or value basis; recklessly imaginative: *. . . a budget figure, as it turned out, and a blue-sky one at that*—Time [perhaps fr the purveyor's fanciful description being as appealing and unclouded as the wide *blue sky*]

a blue streak *by 1890s* **1** *adv phr* (also **like a blue streak**) In a very rapid or excessive manner; extravagantly: *she talked a blue streak/ he split out like a blue streak* **2** *n phr* An extreme amount, speed, etc: *He yelled a blue streak/We ran a blue streak* [fr the *blue streak* of a lightning bolt]

blue ticket *n phr 1930s* Army A discharge without honor, a dismissal not as condemnatory as a dishonorable discharge

◁**blue veiner**▷ *n phr by 1970s* A very stiff penile erection: *Even the Dragon Lady couldn't have given you a blue veiner*—Joseph Wambaugh

blue velvet *n phr 1960s* narcotics A mixture of paregoric with Pyrabenzamine™, an antihistamine, used as an injection

bluff 1 *v by 1670s* To use confident pretense as a means of winning or succeeding •The 1674 definition is "to blindfold or hoodwink"; the game of poker was originally known as *bluff* **2** *n by 1870s*: *His courage was all bluff* •A noun sense fr 1849 is "an excuse"[perhaps related to, though not derived fr a

late 1700s *bluff,* "a blindfold or blinker for a horse"]
See CALL someone's BLUFF

blunt *n 1980s narcotics* A cigar hollowed out and filled with marijuana [fr the *Phillies Blunt™* cigars eponymously used]

blurb *n about 1910* A statement in praise of something or somebody; esp an encomious passage from a book or theater review, used as advertising [said to have been coined by Gelett Burgess (1866–1951), US humorist and illustrator; also attributed to Brander Matthews (1852–1929), US scholar and critic]

◁**BMO**▷ (pronounced as separate letters) *n 1990s Desert Storm Army* An Arab woman [fr *black moving object,* describing the shrouded appearance of such women]

BMOC (pronounced as separate letters) *n phr 1930s* A college-student leader or idol [fr *big man on campus*]

B movie *n phr 1930s* A usu low-budget movie intended for the broad middle ground of taste and meant to be primarily entertaining and narrative rather than serious, artistic, etc [fr their being the second movie in a double feature]

BMX (pronounced as separate letters) *n 1980s bicyclists* Cross-country bicycle racing [fr *bicycle motocross,* fr *moto-cross,* "cross-country motorcycle racing over a laid-out course," fr French *moto,* "motorcycle," and English *cross,* "cross-country"]

bo¹ or **'bo** *n late 1800s hoboes* A hobo: *From some bo on the drag I managed to learn what time a certain freight pulled out*—Jack London

bo² **1** *n early 1900s prison* A boy or young man, esp a prisoner's catamite; =PUNK **2** *n by 1825* A man; fellow •Now outdated, but once used in direct address, like "mac" or "dad"[origin uncertain; perhaps fr *boy,* perhaps fr *beau*]

BO¹ (pronounced as separate letters) *n 1930s* Body odor, esp from underarm perspiration •Popularized by extensive use in ads for Lifebuoy™ soap

BO² *1930s show business* **1** *n* Box office, the gauge of how well a show is doing by its receipts **2** *adj* Theatrical appeal: *The show is really big BO*

board **1** *n show business by 1950s* A ticket to a show or game; =PASTEBOARD **2** *n basketball by 1990s* A rebound, the catching of a ball that bounces off the backboard or the basket: *We did a heck of a job on Shaq. He had 10 boards*—Milwaukee Journal **3** *v*: *If we rebound, we've got a chance. . . If we don't board we can hang it up*—Milwaukee Journal **See** ACROSS THE BOARD, IDIOT CARD, JINKY-BOARD, PASTEBOARD, PUNCHBOARD, SANDWICH BOARD, TOTE³

boards *n gambling by 1920s* Playing cards; =PASTEBOARDS

boat **1** *n about 1915* A car: *The little boat (automobile, in the argot of '22)*—S J Perelman **2** *n about 1920* A big car: *. . . whyn't you park that boat there, hop inside with me*—Carsten Stroud **See** GRAVY TRAIN, LIFEBOAT, MAN IN THE BOAT, MISS THE BOAT, ON THE GRAVY TRAIN, RIDE THE GRAVY TRAIN, ROCK THE BOAT

boat people *n phr middle 1970s* Political refugees who escape by small boat

boat race *n phr horse-racing about 1915* A race with a prearranged winner

bob **See** BOOB JOB, DITTYBOP, FLY COP, NOSE JOB

Bob **1** *n 1990s Desert Storm Army* A Bedouin or Iraqi **2** *modifier*: *Bob car/ Bob clothes*

bob and weave *v phr 1920s prize fighting* To behave evasively; =ROLL WITH THE PUNCHES: *For months Ross bobbed and weaved with Time's negotiators*—New York Review of Books

bobber **See** DEELY BOPPER

Bobbittry *n 1990s* Militant feminism so extreme as to seem to approve sexual mutilation of the male •This may be an ephemeral nonce coinage, although the Bobbitt case was hugely publicized and popular [fr John Wayne *Bobbitt,* whose wife was convicted of cutting off his penis]

bobble *about 1900* **1** *v* To blunder, esp in baseball, to mishandle or drop the ball **2** *n*: *The President's denial was a bad bobble*

bobby socks *n phr esp 1940s students* White cotton socks worn below the knee, and esp worn folded over shoes [origin unknown; perhaps related to *bobbed,* "short, cut short," influenced by the diminutive name *Bobby*]

bobby-soxer *n esp 1940s* An adolescent girl [fr the 1930s and 40s fashion of wearing *bobby socks* folded down over saddle shoes]

bobo *n baseball by 1950s* Someone perceived to be rewarded by favoritism: *. . . I expect him to be a teacher, not a bobo whose only job is to pick up baseballs*—Whitey Herzog

bobtail **1** *n Army by 1870s* A dishonorable discharge •So called because the phrase "service honorable and faithful" was deleted from the discharge form **2** *n 1940s truckers* A truck tractor without a semitrailer **3** *v*: *Returning with just the tractor (bobtailing) represented a loss*—Smithsonian [sense 2 considers the semitrailer as the *tail* of the rig]

◁**Boche**▷ (BAHSH) *WWI armed forces* **1** *n* A German, esp a soldier **2** *modifier*: *the Boche infantry* [fr French, a shortening of *Alboche,* a contemptuous modification of *Allemand,* "German"]

bod **1** *n 1930s British* A person •Chiefly British use **2** *n 1960s* The body; physique: *Pamela Anderson (Brigitte Bardot hair, pouty lips, sex-doll bod)*—Buzz/ *. . . there are women who don't know any other way to relate except with their bods. . .* —Stan Cutler **See** WARM BODY

bodacious (boh DAY shəs) *adj chiefly Southern fr 1840s* Extreme; audacious; blatant: *as complicated as "Gaucho's" bodacious cowboy Custerdome business*—Village Voice [fr early 19th-century *bodyaciously,* "bodily, totally"]

bodacious tatas *n phr 1980s college students* Prominent attractive breasts [*tatas* is a pronunciation of "taters, potatoes," and a euphemism for "tits"; the phrase was used in the 1982 movie *An Officer and a Gentleman*]

bodega (boh DAY gə) *Mexican Spanish by 1850s* **1** *n* A liquor store **2** *n* A grocery store, esp in Puerto Rican areas of New York City [fr Spanish, "shop"]

bodice-ripper or **bodice-buster** *n* *1980s* A romantic-erotic novel, esp one with a historical plot; =HEAVY BREATHER: . . . *the offensive term bodice-ripper*—Publishers Weekly/ . . . *literary set that swoons over such bodice-busters as "Rapture's Slave," "Love's Sweet Agony"*—Philadelphia Journal

body *See* KNOW WHERE THE BODIES ARE BURIED, WARM BODY

body and soul *n phr* *1930s* One's boyfriend or girlfriend [probably fr the title of a 1930s song, "Body and Soul"]

body bag *n phr* *1990s* A kind of heroin [because if you use it you will be carried out in a *body bag*, 1960s term for the zippered plastic shroud used by persons transporting corpses]

body packer or **internal** *n phr* *1990s* narcotics: *These "internals" or "body packers". . . swallow heroin encased in condoms or other packaging, disgorging their contraband to drug dealers, if they are not killed by leaking packages first*—New York Times

body-shake *See* SKIN-SEARCH

body-up *v* *1990s* To be aggressive; muscular: . . . *I like to play a physical game, you know, body-up, go to the hole*—Milwaukee Journal

boff **1** *n* *by 1920s* A blow with the fist or open hand **2** *v*: *LaGuardia bade his cops to muss them up and boff them around on sight*—Westbrook Pedler **3** *v* *by 1930s* To do the sex act: . . . *professors boffing coeds in their offices*—New York Magazine/ *I was trying for the world boffing championship*—John D MacDonald **4** *n* *by 1950s* A sex act; coupling: . . . *a quick bathroom boff*—Playgirl **5** *v* To vomit; *by 1950s* =BARF **6** *n* *1940s* show business A laugh, esp one following a comedian's joke; =BOFFOLA **7** *n* *1940s* show business A joke or witty remark **8** *n* *1940s* show business A show that pleases the audience; =SOCKEROO [first and sex sense echoic; show business senses probably a shortening of *boffo*]

See THROW A FUCK INTO someone

boffer *n* *by 1930s* A man who does the sex act; =COCKSMAN: *The All-American boffer*—John D MacDonald

boffin *n* *WWII British aviators* An expert, esp in a scientific or technical field: *Computer boffins. . . play a game called hunt the wumpus*—Time [origin unknown; conceivably fr a humorous comparison between the laboratories and shops of experts and the enormous trash heaps of Mr and Mrs Boffin in Dickens's *Our Mutual Friend*]

boffo **1** *n* *by 1920s* A dollar or dollar bill: *That's worth a million boffos*—Joel Sayre **2** *n* *1920s* underworld A year, esp a one-year prison sentence; =BOPPO **3** *n* *1940s* show business A laugh, esp a loud laugh in response to a comedian; =BOFF, BOFFO-LA **4** *n* *1940s* show business A joke or a witty remark; =BOFF **5** *adj*: *Hey, that's a very boffo line/ The zany Brewsters. . . still get laughs, boffo laughs*—Philadelphia Evening Standard **6** *n* *1940s*

show business A successful entertainment; =BOFF, HIT: . . . *her string of box-office boffos*—Bob Thomas **7** *adj*: *"Crimson Tide" rolls in as the first boffo box office/ Red-blooded boffo entertainment for both sexes*—S J Perelman **8** *adj* Highly favorable; laudatory [fr a 19th-century carnival term based on the idea of a good *box office*]

boffola or **buffola** *1950s* show business **1** *n* A loud appreciative laugh; =BELLY LAUGH, BOFF: *This ability brought out the old boffola from coast to coast*—B Herndon **2** *n* A joke or remark that provokes such laughter: *All I need is a funny hat and a buffola*—Fred Allen

bogart or **Bogart** or **bogard** *1960s black* **1** *v* To behave truculently; get something by intimidation: *The little old lady bogarted her way into the grocery line*—Delcastle High School dictionary/ . . . *some hotshot from Brooklyn trying to Bogart a game from the regulars*—Village Voice **2** *v* (also **bogart a joint**) To take more than one's share, esp of a marijuana cigarette; =HOG [fr the tough roles played in films by Humphrey *Bogart*]

bog down *v phr* *by 1920s* To become helpless and immobile, as if mired in a bog: . . . *on the one hand a threat had been neutralized, but. . . we were bogging down again*—Stan Cutler

bogey or **bogie** or **bogy** **1** *n* *underworld by 1930s* A police officer **2** *n* *WWII Army Air Forces fr British RAF* An enemy aircraft, esp an attacking fighter plane **3** *n* *fr late 1800s British* A golf score of one stroke over par on a given hole [all senses fr *bogy* or *bogey,* "evil spirit, hobgoblin," the *boogy* or *boogy-man* invoked to frighten children; the golf sense originated in 1890 when Dr Thomas Browne, a naval surgeon, compared his opponent, the "ground score," to the "Bogey Man" of a popular song, at any rate, so it is said]

bogsatt *n* *1980s Pentagon and government* An informal and congenial method of making decisions [acronym fr "a bunch of guys sitting around a table talking"]

◀**bog-trotter** or **bog-hopper**▶ *n* *by 1680s* An Irishman or -woman or person of Irish extraction; =MICK

bogue¹ **1** *adj* *1960s narcotics* In need of narcotics; suffering from deprivation: *I'm bogue. . . . I'm trying to kick*—Clarence Cooper **2** *adj* *by 1950s* False; fake; =BOGUS, PHONY [origin unknown]

bogue² *adj* *esp 1950s teenagers* Disgusting; unattractive; =GROSS [fr *bogus*]

bogue³ *1980s high school students* **1** *n* A cigarette **2** *v* To smoke a cigarette [fr Humphrey *Bogart,* who smoked so often in his films]

bogue out *v phr* *1980s computer* To become bogus, that is, false, misleading, useless, etc

bogus **1** *adj* *by 1830s* False; fake; counterfeit; =PHONY **2** *adj* *1980s teenagers* Ignorant; not up-to-date; unattractive; =LAME, SQUARE: *"Bogus" is a different shading of "lame"*—Time **3** *adj* *1980s computers* Not to be trusted; useless, false, wrong, silly, incredible, etc [origin unknown; certainly connected with *bogus*, attested as name of a counterfeiting machine in 1827, whence a connection has been made with *bogy*]

boho 1 *n 1960s* An ineffectual person; =LOSER: *Leave it to bohos like the Clash to give the class war its first cavalry charge*—Village Voice/ *Jamie Lee as a goofball boho intellectual*—Washington Post **2** *n 1980s college students* A person who is outdated, behind the times [apparently fr *hobohemian,* found by 1919 and revived in the 1960s to mean "member of an out-of-date avant-garde"]

◀**bohunk**▶ *fr loggers* **1** *n about 1900* An immigrant from central or eastern Europe, usu a Czech, Slovak, Hungarian, or Pole; =HUNKY **2** *n by 1920* A stupid, clumsy person; lout

boiled *adj by 1890s* Drunk

  See HARD-BOILED, HARD-BOILED EGG

boiled shirt (or rag) *1850s western* **1** *n phr* A dress shirt, esp with a starched front; =FRIED SHIRT **2** *n phr* Stiff, chilly, and pompous behavior; stuffiness: *. . . not arrayed in the "boiled shirt" of formality*—Robert Lynd

boiler *See* POTBOILER

boilermaker 1 *n* (also **boilermaker and his helper**) *by 1930s* A drink of whiskey with or in a glass of beer **2** *n* =BOILERMAKER'S DELIGHT

boilermaker's delight *n phr about 1910* Any very strong or rough drink; inferior whiskey; =ROTGUT [because it would clean the scales from the inside of a *boiler*]

boiler room 1 *n phr by 1930s* A site of illegal operations, often the telephone sale of stocks, real estate, etc, by charlatans **2** *modifier: The county is home to hundreds of "boiler room" telephone operations*—New York Times/ *. . . what law enforcement officials call a "boiler room" operation*—Time **3** *n phr by 1980s* A shady and provocative gathering-place; a hotbed: *. . . the tendency of their young people to congregate in places that. . . are boiler rooms for drugs and violence*—Milwaukee Journal

boil someone **in oil** *v phr* To punish or rebuke severely

boing 1 *interj* (also **boing-boing**) *WWII armed forces* An exclamation of appreciative delight and intentness at the sight of an attractive woman •An uttered equivalent of a *wolf whistle*: *. . . dropped what they were doing and their eyes went "Boing, boing"*—Pete Martin **2** *v* (also **boink**) *1980s* To do the sex act with or to; =BOFF, BONK: *. . . previously it was more important whether I was boinging Paula Abdul*—Time/*. . . chicks he claims he's boinked*—Carsten Stroud [fr the sound a plucked spring makes, suggesting tenseness and quivering response, with a hint perhaps of penile erection; sense 2 related to *bang* and *bonk*]

boinker *n 1980s* An encounter or engagement that ends in a sex act

boite (BWAHT) *n early 1920s* A nightclub: *With boites such as Smalls, the Olive, Swingers, and Jones Hollywood under their collective belts. . .* —Buzz [fr French *boîte de nuit,* "nightclub"]

bojie *See* BOOJIE

boke or **boko** *n underworld by 1850s* The nose

bollixed (or bolaxed or bolexed) up *adj phr 1930s* In a thoroughly confused and futile condition; =BALLED UP, FUCKED UP: *You're getting your cues all bollixed up*—Jerome Weidman [fr *bollocks* or *ballocks,* "testicles," ultimately fr old English *bealluc,* "testicle"]

  See BALLED UP

boll weevil *n phr fr early 1900s but esp 1980s* A conservative Southern Democrat who votes with Republicans in Congress [fr the insidious reputation of the *boll weevil,* an insect that eats cotton bolls]

bolo 1 *n armed forces fr 1920s* A very inaccurate rifleman **2** *n prizefight by 1950s* A long, looping punch: *Turner blooped a bolo to the heart of Jim Jennings*—New York Daily Mirror [sense 2 perhaps fr *bolo,* the long, heavy knife of the Philippines, as suggesting a looping stroke]

bolo badge *n phr 1990s Desert Storm Army* A Purple Heart, esp one awarded posthumously after an injudicious maneuver [fr the notion that one was killed because he was a poor shot]

boloney *See* BALONEY

bolt *v 1970s students* To leave; =BOOK, SPLIT •Very close to standard, but entered as slang in glossaries

bolts *See* BUCKET OF BOLTS, NUTS AND BOLTS

bolus *n underworld fr middle 1800s* A physician [fr Latin *bolus,* "pill"]

bomb 1 *n 1950s show business* A conspicuous and total failure; =BLAST, FLOP **2** *v 1960s show business*: *The show bombed everywhere on the road/ I took the test, and bombed* **3** *v 1960s students* To do very well at or on: *I really bombed the math test, aced it* **4** *n 1950s hot rodders* A car, esp a hot rod **5** *v 1960s* To go very fast; plunge: *found. . . the discarded relics ideal for bombing down the dirt slopes of Mt Tam*—Los Angeles Times **6** *n* (also **bomber**) *1950s narcotics* An especially big marijuana cigarette **7** *n 1950s narcotics* Heroin **8** *v 1980s* To paint graffiti on; =TAG: *His favorite stylin'-and-bombin' wall, tagged with the rebellious urban scrawl of graffiti artists. . .* —Los Angeles Times **9** *n 1990s teenagers* Something very good: *. . . teenagers come home from a movie and say it was a "bomb," yet insist on seeing it again and again*—KRT News Service [in the sense of failure, perhaps fr the outdated expression *make a baum of it,* "fail"]

  See DROP BOMBS, DUMB BOMB, STINK BOMB

the bomb 1 *n phr 1960s football* A very long forward pass intended to score a quick touchdown **2** *n phr 1990s teenagers* Something wonderful, outstanding, etc

bombed *adj 1950s* Drunk

bombed out *adj phr 1960s narcotics* Very much intoxicated by narcotics; very dozy or exhilarated; =SPACED-OUT, STONED

bomber *n 1980s* A crude cocktail: *The kids had*

been chugging "bombers"—a mixture of liquors, wine and beer. . . —Milwaukee Journal

bombiosity or **bombosity** *n by 1930s* The buttocks; =ASS, DUFF [fr *bombous,* "rounded, belly-shaped," fr the shape of a *bomb*]

bombita (bahm BEE tə) *n 1960s narcotics* Any amphetamine pill or capsule used by addicts [fr Spanish, "little bomb"]

bomb out *v phr by 1970s* To fail; =BOMB: *Stephanie Moody. . . "bombed out" last year: failed to complete her opening lifts*—New York Magazine

bombshell 1 *n by 1920s* A startling, striking event; something that makes one gape: *Her entrance astride the crocodile was a bombshell* **2** *n by 1940s* A sexually stimulating woman ●Often in the expression "blonde bombshell"

bond *See* JUNK BOND

bondage *n 1960s* Sexual practice in which a participant is tied up or otherwise restrained, usu for whipping or other "discipline"

bone¹ 1 *n 1970s teenagers* Money; cash **2** *n by 1860s* A dollar, esp a silver dollar ◁**3**▷ *n middle 1800s n* The erect penis ◁**4**▷ *v* (also **bone away**) *1980s students* To do the sex act; =SCREW: *Shit! he thought. He coulda been boning by now*—GQ
See HAVE A BONE ON, JAWBONE, PRAYER BONES, TAIL BONE

bone² ** *college students by 1880s* **1 *n* A diligent student **2** *v* (also **bone up**) To study, esp to study intensely for an examination [fr the student's use of *bohns,* "translations, ponies," named after *Bohn's Classical Library*]

bonehead *early 1900s* **1** *n* A stupid person: *. . . four sons, all bone-heads*—F Scott Fitzgerald **2** *modifier*: *. . . I should have been in bonehead English*—Los Angeles Times [fr the notion of the head being all *bone,* no brain]
See PULL A BONER

boneheaded *adj early 1900s* Stupid

bonehead play *n phr chiefly sports by about 1910* An error, esp one caused by bad judgment: *Merkel's throw was the most renowned bonehead play in history*

◁**bone-on**▷ *n by 1940s* An erect penis: *Sometimes he could still get a pretty respectable bone-on*—Stephen King

bone-orchard *n by 1870s* A cemetery

bone out *v phr early 1990s teenagers* To lose one's nerve; quit; =CHICKEN OUT

bone-polisher *n 1920s hoboes* A vicious dog

boner 1 *n fr baseball about 1910* A blunder; error; =BLOOPER, HOWLER **2** *n college students about 1900* A diligent student; =BONE ◁**3**▷ *n 1950s* An erect penis; =BONE-ON, HARD-ON: *. . . the time you coveted your neighbor's wife. You had a big boner*—Stanley Elkin/ *He walks around with a boner all the time*—Cameron Crowe
See PULL A BONER

bones 1 *n by 1880s* Dice ●Chaucer referred to dice as "bitched *bones*" about 1390 **2** *n by late 1500s* Two sticks or bones held between the fingers and used to make a clacking rhythm ●Best known fr their use in post-Civil War minstrel shows, where they were wielded by a character named Mr. *Bones* **3** *n by early 1900s* Dollars; money
See MAKE NO BONES ABOUT, PRAYER BONES, SAWBONES

Bones *n merchant marine by 1940s* A ship's doctor

bone-shaker *n 1860s* Any badly sprung, springless, or violently jerking vehicle, esp a very early form of bicycle

bone-top *n early 1900s* A stupid person; =BONEHEAD

bone up *See* BONE²

boneyard *n by 1860s* A cemetery: *. . . lie on a blanket out on the boneyard*—Tennessee Williams

bong 1 *n 1960s narcotics* A water pipe for smoking narcotics ●Said to have been introduced by returning Vietnam veterans: *. . . the array of glass and plastic water pipes or bongs*—New York Times **2** *v 1960s teenagers* To smoke marijuana using a water pipe **3** *v 1980s teenagers* To drink beer from a keg through a hose

bonged-out *adj 1970s* Intoxicated by a narcotic, esp one smoked through a bong: *You feel like a bonged-out Cubist painting*—Penthouse

bongo or **bongoed** *adj by 1940s* Drunk

bonk 1 *n 1930s* A blow; =BASH, SOCK **2** *v 1930s* To hit; strike; =BANG, BIFF **3** *v 1970s British* Do the sex act with or to; =BOFF, SCREW: *And I asked him if he was still sneaking around bonkin' that secretary. . .*—Mike Royko/ *What's this I hear about you bragging to friends that you bonked Kate Moss?*—Vanity Fair **4** *n 1980s British* A single sex act; =BANG, FUCK, PIECE

bonkers *adj fr 1950s British* Crazy; insane; =NUTS: *Folks are going slightly bonkers these days over anything that glitters*—Newsweek/ *. . . suffering stress-related ailments like eczema or colitis, or just plain going bonkers*—New York Times [probably fr *bonk,* "to hit on the head," plus the British slang suffix *-ers*]

bonnet *See* BEE IN one's **bonnet**

bonzer *WWII armed forces fr Australian* **1** *adj* Good; excellent **2** *n* Anything superior or useful

bonzo *by 1970s* **1** *adj* Crazy; =NUTS: *. . . almost drove me bonzo*—Philadelphia Bulletin **2** *n*: *This guy is a real bonzo*—Lawrence Sanders [origin unknown; perhaps influenced by *bonkers* and *gonzo;* perhaps related to a British puppy named *Bonzo,* originated in 1922]

boo¹ 1 *adj esp early 1950s* Excellent; remarkable ●Probably fr second sense: *Something that used to be known as the cat's whiskers is now called. . . "deadly boo"*—Hal Boyle **2** *n 1930s jazz musicians* Marijuana or another narcotic: *I got over there and she lays this dynamite boo on me, I mean super shit*—Richard Price [second sense said to be fr black English *jabooby,* "marijuana, so called because it induces a state of fear or anxiety," of unknown origin; but possibly fr *Budda,* "marijuana"]
See TICKETY-BOO

boo² 1 *interj* *by 1890s* An exclamation of disapproval, the equivalent of a hiss 2 *v*: *Next time at bat he was roundly booed* 3 *interj* *by 1940s* A supposedly frightening exclamation, such as a ghost might give: *She jumped out of the closet and hollered "Boo!"*

boob¹ 1 *n* *by 1908* A stupid person; =DIM-WIT: *There are still boobs, alack, who'd like the old-time gin-mill back*—Sinclair Lewis 2 *n* *1920s* A person who is too innocent and trusting; =SUCKER: *The poor boob fell for his line and gave him the money*

◁**boob²**▷ *n* *by 1940s* A woman's breast; =BUB, KNOCKER [probably fr *boobie²*]

boob³ *1930s* 1 *n* A blunder; error; =BOO-BOO 2 *v*: *If I boob, I expect you. . . to protect me*—Wendy Leigh

boobie¹ or **bubbie** *See* BUBBY

◁**boobie²** or **bubbie**▷ (Bōō bee) *n* *by late 1600s* A woman's breast [perhaps ultimately fr Latin *puppa,* literally "little girl," which in child language became "breast"; whence Old French *pope, popel,* "breast," German dialect *Bubbi,* and so on]

boo-bird *by 1970s* 1 *n* A sports spectator who boos; a noisy heckler: *A trade might satisfy the boo-birds*—New York Daily News 2 *modifier*: *More often than not, I've joined the boo-bird chorus*—Sandy Grady

boob job (or **bob**) *n phr* *1980s* A surgical breast enlargement: *. . . saying that Julie had had a boob job*—Playboy

boo-boo¹ 1 *n* *1950s* An error or misstep, esp one with embarrassing consequences; faux pas: *The original boo-boo that started all this public confusion*—H R King [perhaps fr *boob³*; perhaps fr Yiddish *bulba,* "potato," fr Polish, which came to mean "malapropism, faux pas"]

boo-boo² *n* *by 1900* A minor flesh wound or blemish [perhaps fr *boo-hoo,* a child's crying over a minor hurt]

boob trap *n phr* *by 1950s* A nightclub; =BOITE

the **boob tube** *n phr* *middle 1960s* Television or a television set; =the TUBE

booby hatch 1 *n phr* *by 1890s* An insane asylum; mental hospital: *King Bolden cut hair in the booby-hatch*—Stephen Longstreet 2 *n phr* (also **booby hutch**) *outdated fr 1950s underworld* A police station [first sense perhaps connected with *Colney Hatch,* a village near London where an insane asylum was opened in 1851; the name became generic for a mental hospital]

booby trap *esp WWII Army fr middle 1800s British* 1 *n phr* A hidden explosive charge designed to be set off by some ordinary act, such as starting a vehicle or driving down a street, used originally in wartime to harass invaders •The British schoolboy's booby trap was a pitcher of water poised atop a door so that whoever opened the door would be doused 2 *v*: *They booby-trapped his car and six people died* 3 *n phr* The seemingly harmless appearance that conceals vexations arranged for an unsuspecting opponent: *Don't debate him, it's a booby trap*

boodle 1 *n* *by 1830s* An entire lot; a large number or amount; =CABOODLE 2 *n* *underworld by 1850s* Counterfeit money 3 *n* *1880s* Bribe money or other money obtained by graft and corruption: *. . . a few trees are planted. What happens to most of the boodle?*—New York Times 4 *n* *by 1890* Money in general 5 *n* *prison & students about 1900* Sweets; treats; delicacies 6 *v* *1940s students* To hug, kiss, etc; =NECK [fr Dutch *boedel,* "estate, lot"]

boodler *n* *by 1870s* A corrupt and venal politician: *Weiss claims that the Fink boodlers were continued on the state payroll*—Village Voice

boog *v* *1930s* To dance: *. . . to go booging*—Life [fr *boogie-woogie*]

boogaloo or **bugaloo** (BŌŌG a lōō, BŌŌG-) *by 1960s* 1 *n* A shuffling, shoulder-swinging dance: *. . . feet doing a fast boogaloo in the grass*—Stephen King 2 *v*: *They boogalooed down the street* 3 *modifier*: *That's really voodoo music, man, boogaloo music*—Rolling Stone 4 *v* To carry on jocularly; play; tease; =FOOL AROUND 5 *modifier*: *. . . go out and have a bugaloo good time*—Village Voice [apparently a rhyming form based on *boog,* like *boogerboo*]

booger or **boogie** *n* *by 1890s* A piece of nasal mucus [an extension of *bugger,* "nasal mucus"] *See* BUGGER

boogerboo (Bōō gər bōō, Bōō-) *black by 1940s* 1 *v* To pretend; fake 2 *n* An insincere person; =PHONY

boogered or **boogered up** *adj* *1920s* Damaged; inoperable: *I can't use this bolt; the threads are all boogered/ That car is all boogered up*

boogie or **boogey** (Bōō gee, Bōō-) 1 *n* (also **boogie-woogie**) *fr early 1900s black* Syphilis, esp advanced syphilis ◀**2**▶ *n* *1920s* A black person ◁**3**▷ *modifier*: *a boogie hairstyle/ boogie music* 4 *n* *by 1940s* =BOOGIE-WOOGIE 5 *v* *1940s* To move, shake, and wriggle the body in time to rock-and-roll music; do a sort of boogaloo: *Amanda boogies and bangs a tambourine while her 39 sisters sit on steps and force shattered smiles*—G Mitchell 6 *v* *1970s* To move; go; leave; =LIGHT OUT: *Let's boogie, Mama*—*Right behind you, Big Daddy*—TV commercial/ *F16D, a jet that can really boogie*—Milwaukee Journal/ *He was here on June 16. . . then boogied before we got on the record*—Milwaukee Journal 7 *v* *by 1930s* To carry on jocularly; play; tease; =FOOL AROUND: *back from a long weekend and ready to boogie*—Philadelphia Journal 8 *v* *1960s* To do the sex act: *. . . a lot of heavy boogieing going on at Iowa State*—Playboy ◁**9**▷ *n* *1960s* The vulva; =CUNT ◁**10**▷ *v* *by 1970s* To do anal intercourse; =BUGGER: *Would Ronnie be averse to being boogied by Kiss during his acceptance speech*—National Lampoon 11 *n* *WWII Army Air Forces* An enemy aircraft, esp a fighter plane; =BOGEY 12 *n* A piece of solid mucus from the nose; =BOOGER *See* FADED BOOGIE, LET'S BOOGIE

boogie board *1970s* 1 *n phr* A skateboard 2 *n phr* A kind of surfboard

boogie box *See* GHETTO BOX

boogie-woogie (Bŏŏ gee Wŏŏ gee, Bōō-, Wōō-) **1** *n fr early 1900s black* Syphilis, esp advanced syphilis **2** *n 1920s jazz musicians* A fast jazz piano style with a heavy rolling bass played eight beats to the measure, often used as a song accompaniment **3** *modifier*: *Jimmy Yancey. . . created the boogie woogie blues*—Stephen Longstreet **4** *v 1930s black* To enjoy oneself thoroughly [origin uncertain]

boojie (Bōō zhee, Bŏŏ-) (Variations: **bojie** or **boochie** or **booj** or **boojy** or **bourgie** or **buzhie**) *1970s black* **1** *n* A middle-class black person; also, such persons collectively: *the black bourgeoisie. . . better known to most of us as the bourgie*—Washington Post **2** *n* Any middle-class person **3** *modifier*: *a bourgie couple mourning their 20-year-old daughter's comatose state*—Village Voice/ *exaggerating the slumminess of the tenements and playing down the boojy trappings of our apartment*—Richard Price

book 1 *n gambling by 1860s* =BOOKIE **2** *n gambling by 1860s* A bookie's function and place of business: *Joey keeps a book* **3** *v* =MAKE BOOK **4** *n police by 1840s* The daily logbook of a police station **5** *v police by 1840s* To charge someone with a crime or misdemeanor at a police station: *They took the bum in and booked him for vagrancy* **6** *v by 1820s* To engage or reserve in advance: *They booked eight readings in three days for the visiting poet/ Book me a table for six* **7** *v* =HIT THE BOOKS **8** *v 1980s students* To run or depart, esp rapidly: *. . . and the couple booked off into the sunset for their honeymoon*—Easyriders

See BY THE BOOK, CALIFORNIA PRAYER BOOK, CRACK A BOOK, HIT THE BOOKS, IN someone's BAD BOOKS, LITTLE BLACK BOOK, ON BOOK, ONE FOR THE BOOK, POUND THE BOOKS, READ someone LIKE A BOOK, STROKE BOOK, TAKE A PAGE FROM someone's BOOK, THROW THE BOOK AT someone, WRITE THE BOOK

the **book 1** *n phr 1920s underworld* A life sentence to prison **2** *n phr 1950s* Instructions or conventional wisdom about someone's performance; =FORM: *The "book" on this player. . . was to leave him alone, treat him politely, and pick him up if you happened to block him*—Lou Cannon [first sense fr *throw the book at someone*; second sense fr the accumulated knowledge about horses and jockeys that gamblers study]

See THROW THE BOOK AT someone

bookend *1980s* **1** *v* To precede and follow; bracket: *all this. . . is somehow bookended by the secret, shadow manuscripts of his mother and his wife*—New Yorker/. . . *eight big star duets, bookeneded by solo performances*—Macon Telegraph **2** *n*: *. . . two black bodyguards, macho bookends*—Vanity Fair **3** (also **bookend ad**) A television commercial having two parts, separated by other unrelated commercials: *Bookends are intriguing to people because they set up a scenario. . .* —Milwaukee Journal

bookie *n 1880s gambling* A person who accepts and handles bets on horse-races; bookmaker

book it 1 *v phr 1970s students* To depart quickly; =BOOK **2** *v phr* To be confident of something; count on something; =MAKE BOOK ON something: *I'll be back. Book it*—Albuquerque Tribune

book-smarts *n 1990s* Learning; erudition: *They not only have the "book-smarts" that it takes, but the acting and drama ability*—Milwaukee Journal

boola-boola *n by 1960s* Noisy partisan support for one's college teams: *. . . too much panty-raiding, fraternities, and boola-boola and all of that*—Malcolm X [fr a Yale University song]

boom 1 *v 1860s* To flourish; show vigor ●Opinion as to whether this is still slang would be divided. Brander Matthews was not sure in 1893: *Business is booming!* **2** *v by 1890s* To promote aggressively: *There he goes booming that brand of soap* **3** *v* (also **boom along**) *1600s nautical* To sail fast, under full canvas **4** *n 1950s narcotics* Marijuana **5** *adj 1990s Canadian students* Wonderful; fashionable; outstanding; =GREAT

See FALL DOWN AND GO BOOM, LOWER THE BOOM

◁**boom-boom**▷ *n 1960s armed forces* Sexual activity; copulation; =ASS: *. . . dragging girls into the woods "for a little boom-boom"*—Time

boom box *n phr* (also **boom**) *1980s* A loud stereo cassette player: *Violators risk. . . confiscation of their boom boxes*—New York Times

See GHETTO BOX

boomer 1 *n 1890s hoboes* A migratory worker **2** *n 1890s hoboes* A railroad or construction worker, logger, etc, who continually shifts from one place of work to another **3** *n esp 1930s* A womanizer; ladies' man **4** *n 1880s* An enthusiastic advocate of land development: *What consumes the attention of most Idahoans is the battle between the boomers (developers) and the greenies (environmentalists)*—Milwaukee Journal **5** *n 1980s* A member of the post-WWII baby boom; =BABY BOOMER: *Two quirky tales of adolescence, rooted in boomer history and sanitized for the boomer market*—Village Voice

boomerang *v 1980s* To return to the parental nest: *. . . there's a 40 percent chance you'll "boomerang" back to live with your parents at least once*—Atlantic Monthly

boomerang baby (or **kid**) *n phr 1980s* A child who returns to the parental home even after college and other mature training; a reoccupant of the empty nest

booming or **boomin'** *1980s teenagers* **1** *adj* Excellent; wonderful; =BOOM, FLY, RAD **2** *adj* Playing loud bass tones on a stereo

boomlet *n by 1880* A minor upsurge; a small access of vigor: *. . . sustains the boomlet in comedy-dramas about Irish village life. . .* —Newark Star-Ledger

boom sticks *n phr 1950s cool musicians & rock and roll* Drumsticks

◁**boon coon**▷ *See* ACE BOON COON

boondagger *n by 1970s* A tough woman or aggressive lesbian; =BULLDYKE: *. . . the boondaggers, you know, like bulls that come offa the street*—L Berry

boondock *modifier* WWII Navy and Marine Corps Suitable for rough outdoor use: *Marines use boondock clothes and boondock shoes for hikes and maneuvers*—H L Miller

boondocker *n* WWII Navy and Marine Corps A person who lives or works in a remote region, esp by preference

boondockers *n* 1930s Marine Corps Shoes suitable for rough outdoor use, esp heavy duty military shoes or boots

the **boondocks** or the **boonies** *n* Marine Corps about 1900 Remote places; rural regions: *The people out there in the boonies may not know you're past it*—Washingtonian [fr Tagalog *bundok,* "mountain"]

boondoggle middle 1930s **1** *v* To spend public funds outlandishly or on futile activity **2** *n*: *The public's got the idea that this is a boondoggle, a Rube Goldberg*—Time [origin uncertain; verb said to be fr the iron-smelting industry, meaning "make unprofitable attempts to retrieve good iron from slag"; noun found by 1940s meaning "an ornamental thong made by Boy Scouts," and suggesting mere makework]

boonie rat *n phr* Vietnam War armed services A combat soldier, esp an infantry private; =DOGFACE, GRUNT

booshwa or **booshwah** *See* BUSHWAH

boost 1 *v* by 1908 To steal, esp by shoplifting: *Someone had boosted my tape recorder out of the room*—Harry Crews/ *. . . slept on park benches and boosted from the A&P*—Herbert Gold **2** *v* about 1900 To praise highly: *to boost one's home town* **3** *n*: *I'll give you a good boost* **4** *v* 1980s students To do the sex act with or to; =BONK, SCREW

booster 1 *n* by 1908 A shoplifter; pilferer: *Got a booster for you. The chunky girl in blue at the lace counter*—Dashiell Hammett/ *He knew they couldn't be boosters or creepers. . .*—Joseph Wambaugh **2** *n* carnival fr about 1905 A huckster's or auctioneer's assistant who pretends to buy in order to stimulate others; =SHILL **3** *n* by 1890 A person who praises extravagantly; =FAN

boot 1 *v* 1870s To kick, esp to give a hard kick: *Let's boot a football around* **2** *n* by 1940s: *Give him a boot in the ass* **3** *v* by 1880s To discharge; eject; =FIRE, SACK **4** *v* (also **boot away**) by 1950s To lose or waste by incompetence, inattention, etc; botch; bungle; =BLOW: *I booted three good chances* **5** *v* early 1900s baseball To commit an error, esp in handling a ground ball **6** *n*: *Dark atoned for his boot by making a good play on Kiner's slow roller*—J McCulley **7** *n* by 1930 A thrill; surge of pleasure; =BANG, KICK: *I get a boot from boats* **8** *v* (also **back-track**) 1960s narcotics To inject a narcotic gradually by pulling back and reinjecting blood again and again to increase the drug's effect: *The technique, known as "booting," is believed to prolong the drug's initial effect*—J Mills **9** *n* Navy & Marine Corps about 1900 A recruit ◄**10**► *n*

1950s black A black person **11** *v* computer by 1980 =BOOT UP **12** *n* (also **Denver boot**) late 1960s A metal locking device put on the wheels of a scofflaw's car to prevent driving

See HARDBOOT, RUBBER BOOTS, TO BOOT

the **boot** *n phr* by 1880s Dismissal, discharge

boot camp 1 *n phr* WWI Navy & Marine Corps A basic training center **2** *n phr* 1980s A penal camp, resembling a military boot camp in rigor, used as a substitute for imprisonment: *. . . penal system is moving toward separate drug-treatment facilities, boot camps for young offenders*—Time **3** *n phr* 1990s Any very strict training facility: *. . . militant pro-life boot camp*—Time

booted *adj* 1900s narcotics Intoxicated by narcotics; =HIGH, STONED

bootleg 1 *v* by 1906 To make or sell illegal whiskey and other illegally repackaged products such as music recordings, movies, etc **2** *n* by 1880s Whiskey illegally made or sold **3** *modifier*: *. . . a bottle of bootleg hooch* **4** *v* football by 1950s To carry the ball deceptively by holding it against the leg, esp after pretending to hand it off to another player [fr the idea of concealment in the upper part of one's boots]

bootlegger or **booter** or **bootie** *n* by 1880s A person who bootlegs: *. . . 5,000 booters on Manhattan Island alone*—HL Mencken/ *That new bootie. . . carries a powerful line of hooch*—Saturday Evening Post

bootlick *v* by 1840s To serve and flatter a superior; curry favor; =APPLE-POLISH, BROWN-NOSE: *Boss kisser-uppers will always be with us, boot-licking their way through the workplace. . .*—Saundra Smokes

boot party *n phr* 1990s street gang Savagely kicking an offender as a form of punishment

boots *n* by 1840s A bootblack, esp in a hotel

See BET YOUR BOOTS, JESUS BOOTS, RUBBER BOOTS

boot strapper *n phr* by 1960s A person who succeeds by his own efforts; self-made person: *. . . black "boot strappers," teachers, city workers, professionals who have to struggle to make it*—George Vecsey [fr the expression *lift oneself by one's own bookstraps*]

boot up or **boot** *v phr* or *v* 1970s computers To start up or input a computer's operating system: *The typical first step in working with a computer, then, is to load the DOS programs; this is called "booting up"*—Computers at Home/ *. . . showed me how to log in and boot the operating system*—New York Times [fr earlier *bootstrap,* because after a simple action like pressing one key, the computer loads the operating system itself, as if it were *raising itself by its own bootstraps*]

◁**booty** or **boody**▷ black by 1920s **1** *n* The female body as a sex object **2** *n* The vulva **3** *n* The sex act; sex; =ASS: *The heroines are giving up some booty*—San Francisco **4** *modifier*: *It's about snappin' all the booty rap*—Macon Telegraph/ *You can listen to it, but you can shake your booty to it too*—Macon Telegraph

boo-word *n phr* 1990s A word or phrase that

frightens: . . . *his scholarly interests—traditional, historical, and, to use a radical boo-word, Eurocentric*—New York Times

booze 1 *n by 1880s* Any alcoholic drink, esp whiskey and other spirits **2** *v by 1760s* To drink alcoholic beverages, esp to drink whiskey heavily [fr Middle English and dialect *bowse* (pronounced like *booze*), "drink, carouse," reinforced by the name of a 19th-century Philadelphia distiller, E G Booze]

See HIT THE BOTTLE

boozed or **boozed up** *adj* or *adj phr first form by 1850, second by 1880s* Drunk •Included as *bowz'd* in Benjamin Franklin's 1722 list of 228 words meaning "drunk"

boozehound or **booze-fighter** *n first form by 1940s; second by early 1900s* A person who habitually drinks a great deal of whiskey; =LUSH: *Among American governors, the booze-fighters are plainly the best*—H L Mencken

boozer *n by 1819* A heavy drinker; =ALKY, LUSH

boozery *n by 1915* A saloon, esp an illegal or after-hours saloon; =SPEAKEASY

booze up *v phr by 1940s* To drink a great deal of liquor

booze-up *n 1890s British* A drinking spree; =BINGE: . . . *the morning booze-up. . . which was still fouling his blood*—Robert Stone

boozy *adj about 1720* Drunk •Found in the 225 terms meaning "drunk" that Benjamin Franklin published in 1722

bop 1 *v by 1930s* To strike, esp with the fist: *Nina reached out and bopped her on the head*—Hal Boyle/ *I kept my temper in check, since bopping police chiefs wasn't good PR. . .* —Stan Cutler **2** *n by 1930s*: *a bop on the beezer* **3** *v 1980s* To defeat: *The home team got bopped again* **4** *n 1950s street gang* A fight among gangs; =RUMBLE **5** *v*: *You gotta go on bopping and hanging around street corners all your life?*—Life **6** *n 1970s* The sex act; =SCREW **7** *v*: *You told Esteva the cop was bopping his wife*—Robert B Parker **8** *n 1940s jazz musicians* (also **bebop**) A style of modern jazz characterized by complex harmonics, sudden changes in register, the use of fast and nearly unintelligible lyrics, etc: *Bop is "cool" jazz*—American Speech **9** *modifier*: *a bop musician* **10** *v 1950s students* To walk or go, esp in a slow and relaxed mood: *They bopped over to the bar* [echoic]

See DIDDLYBOP, DITTYBOP, HARD BOP, TEENYBOPPER, THROW A FUCK INTO someone

bop cap *n phr 1960s* =APPLEJACK CAP

bop (or bopper) glasses *n phr 1940s jazz musicians* Horn-rimmed spectacles: *The horn-rims of the intellectual came to be known as bop glasses*—Herbert Gold

bop off *v phr 1950s students* To depart; =BOOK, SPLIT

bopper 1 *n 1960s* A street-gang fighter **2** *n 1940s* A bop musician **3** *n 1970s* A baseball power hitter; =SLUGGER: *Now I've got a big bopper at the*

plate. . . —Milwaukee Journal **4** *n 1960s* =TEENY-BOPPER

See DEELY BOPPER

bopping *1970s Philadelphia cabdrivers* **1** *n* Tampering with taxicab meters to register illegally high charges: *The United Cab Association here has expelled about 40 cab drivers in the last two years for "bopping"*—Philadelphia Inquirer **2** *modifier*: . . . *"bopping" cabbies expelled*—Philadelphia Inquirer

boppo *n 1930s underworld* A one-year prison sentence, or one year of a longer sentence

boppy *adj 1980s* Bouncy; zesty; =JAZZY: . . . *an MTV-like newscast—everything is boppy, the pace is snappy and the graphics flashy*—New York Times

borax *1920s furniture business* **1** *n* Cheap or inferior material; shoddy merchandise **2** *n* Exaggeration; misrepresentation; =HORSESHIT •This may derive fr sense 1 as the talk of borax salesmen, or it may be the ultimate source of all other senses: *borak* or *borax*, an aboriginal language, has been used in Australia since at least the 1840s to mean "nonsense"; hence it might have developed (pejorated) to mean "horseshit," and found its way to the US **3** *n by 1940s* Any gaudy item; tasteless bric-a-brac **4** *modifier*: *strictly a piece of borax junk* [origin unknown; it has been suggested that sellers of cleansers based on the mineral *borax* gave away cheap furniture to customers]

border *See* SOUTH OF THE BORDER

bored out of one's **skull** *adj phr 1960s* =BORED TO DEATH: *Stratford High School, where he was bored out of his skull for four years*—New Yorker

bored to death *adj phr by 1880* Extremely bored

bored stiff *adj phr 1920s* =BORED TO DEATH

bork or **Bork** *late 1980s* **1** *v* To mount an intense campaign against a political appointee; =BUSHWHACK: *"We're going to Bork him,"* proclaimed a feminist advocate—New Republic **2** *n*: . . . *close ranks to coordinate a huge preemptive bork*—New Republic [fr the experience of Judge Robert Bork, whose 1987 nomination to the Supreme Court was rejected by strong concerted opposition]

born loser *See* LOSER

born to *adj phr 1980s* Seemingly destined and compelled to perform something indicated: . . . *my born-to-shop bride is disappointed that all the shops are closed on Sunday*—Motor Cyclist/ *This guy was born to run*/ *Weeb was born to coach*

borscht belt 1 *n phr 1930s* The region in and near the Catskill Mountains north of New York City where many predominantly Jewish resort hotels are found **2** *n phr 1990s* Any neighborhood peopled by Russians or Russian emigrants: *Just South of the Fairfax borscht belt and across the street from the Farmer's Market. . .* —Los Angeles Reader [fr Russian *borshch*, "beet soup" (in its Yiddish spelling), a focus of the cuisine]

borscht circuit *n phr 1930s* The resort hotels of the Catskills borscht belt, regarded as a circuit for entertainers, lecturers, etc

bosh *n 1830s* Nonsense; poppycock; =BULLSHIT

[apparently fr Turkish, "empty," popularized by an 1834 British novel]

bosom buddy *1920s* **1** *n phr* A very close friend; best friend; =MAIN MAN **2** *modifier*: *IBM has entered a series of bosom-buddy pacts with Novell, Lotus and Borland*—New York Times

boss 1 *n late 1500s* The chief; the person in charge **2** *v by 1850s*: *That little guy bosses the whole operation* **3** *n 1860s* The head of a political machine **4** *adj by 1880s* Excellent; wonderful; =THE MOST ●This old use seems to have been revived independently by 1950s jazz musicians and teenagers: *Aw, this is boss*—Rolling Stone/ *Japan has leaped into the implements-for-bosser-living gap*—San Francisco [fr Dutch *baas*, "master"]
See CRUMB BOSS, STRAW BOSS

boss someone **around** *v phr by 1850s* To direct or control someone in an offensively authoritarian way: *I don't mine being told, but I hate being bossed around*

boss trick *See* CHAMPAGNE TRICK

bossy[1] *adj by 1880s* Domineering; autocratic: *She's very bossy, a take-charge gal*

bossy[2] **1** *n* A cow **2** *n 1930s* lunch counter Beef [fr Latin *bos*, "cow"]

bothered *See* HOT AND BOTHERED

both hands *n phr 1930s underworld* A ten-year prison sentence

both sides of the desk *n phr 1990s* The faculty and students of a school or university: *. . . and both sides of the desk challenged the established canon. . .* —Los Angeles Times

both sides of the street *See* WORK BOTH SIDES OF THE STREET

both ways *See* HAVE IT BOTH WAYS, SWING BOTH WAYS, WORK BOTH WAYS

bottle 1 *n by late 1600s* A bottle or bottle's amount of liquor; =JUG: *He had a bottle on him* **2** *n early 1900s line repairers* A glass insulator for electric or communications line **3** *n 1920s radio operators* A vacuum tube
See FIGHT A BOTTLE, HIT THE BOTTLE, POP BOTTLE

the **bottle 1** *n phr 1600s* Liquor; =BOOZE: *In life he battled wives, producers, bankruptcy, and the bottle*—People **2** *n phr by 1960s* Male prostitution [sense 2 perhaps fr cockney rhyming slang *bottle and glass*, "ass"]
See HIT THE BOTTLE

bottle baby *n phr 1920s police* A derelict alcoholic; =SKID ROW BUM [fr the term for an infant fed with a bottle]

bottle club *n phr 1930s* A social club where members may drink after legal hours

bottom *n by 1790s* The buttocks; =ASS

Bottom *See* FOGGY BOTTOM

bottom dollar *See* BET one's BOTTOM DOLLAR, BET YOUR BOOTS

the **bottom dropped out** *sentence by 1935* The market collapsed; disaster struck: *". . . some funds intended for a new project were used to com-*plete the old. And then the bottom dropped out of the market"*—Sue Grafton

bottom-end *n 1950s hot rodders* The crankshaft, main bearing, and connecting rod bearings of an automobile engine

bottom feeder *1990s* **1** *n phr* A despicable, predatory person who exploits and fancies the squalid; =SCUMSUCKER, SLEAZEBAG: *Jesse Helms, David Duke, and other political bottom feeders*—New Republic **2** *n phr* (also **bottom fisher** or **bottom troller**) A person or company that deliberately exploits those in difficulty and profits by their poverty or misfortune: *. . . which has made the bottom trollers. . . start to take notice*—Milwaukee Journal Sentinel [fr the presumed disgusting habits of fish and other marine forms that *feed* on the *bottom*, hence eat slime, excrement, etc; the fact that *bottom* means "ass" may not be entirely irrelevant]

bottom-feeding *modifier 1990s* Showing the instincts and practice of a bottom feeder: *. . . bottom-feeding biographies have existed as long as people have been able to write*—Time

bottomless *by 1960s* **1** *adj* Wearing nothing; nude: *. . . a bottomless waitress* **2** *adj* A bar, club, restaurant, etc, featuring unclad females [by comparison with *topless*, which means nude above the waist]

the **bottom line** *by 1960s* **1** *n phr* The bookkeeping figure showing profit or loss **2** *n phr* The result of any computation or estimate, esp one showing total costs: *I'll go half if the bottom line's OK* **3** *n phr* Any final decision or judgment: *Let me tell you the bottom line* **4** *n phr* A fundamental or crucial point of fact; the essence; =the NITTY GRITTY: *The bottom line is I am paid to win games, not for goodwill*—Inside Sports **5** *modifier*: *a bottom-line matter* [perhaps fr Yiddish *untershte shure*, "bottom line," as used in the financial-commercial community]

bottom of the barrel *See* SCRAPE THE BOTTOM OF THE BARREL

bottom out *v phr by 1970s* To get as low or bad as possible; reach nadir: *If [Watergate] ever bottoms out, we might be all right*—Time

◁**bottoms up**▷ *adv phr by 1950s* =DOG FASHION

bottom woman *n phr by 1960s* The best patronized and most dependable woman in a pimp's covey of prostitutes

bounce 1 *v by 1870s* To expel; throw out: *When he started swearing, they bounced him* **2** *v by 1880s* To discharge or dismiss; =FIRE **3** *n by 1940s* Energy; vitality; =PISS AND VINEGAR, PIZZAZZ ●Perhaps fr a 1930s term for a lively jazz tempo: *more bounce to the ounce* **4** *v 1920s* To be rejected for lack of funds in the bank: *His checks never bounce* **5** *v early 1600s* To intimidate; bully; =ROUST ●Esp police use: *. . . and I'll want to bounce this Nadine kid, see what she has to say*—Carsten Stroud **6** *n underworld by 1950s* A prison sentence: *You're going down as an accessory to assault and battery. . . it's a serious bounce*—James Lee Burke **7** *n* (also **bump**) *by 1980* A sudden and sometime brief increase in rating, popularity, value, etc: *. . . the*

Republicans got a three-point bounce out of their convention—Nation

the **bounce** *by 1870s* **1** *n phr* Forcible ejection, esp by a person hired to remove unwanted customers; =the BUM'S RUSH **2** *n phr* A dismissal, polite or otherwise; =KISS-OFF: *After a brief dialogue with my boss I got the bounce*

bounce something **around** *v phr by 1970s* To think about and discuss an idea, project, etc: *Let's bounce it around a little before we decide*

bounce back *v phr by 1950s* To recover; return to action: *She had a bad case of flu, but bounced back in two days*

bounce for *v phr by 1930s* To pay for; treat; =PICK UP THE TAB: *. . . somewhere that doesn't bounce for bluecoats*—Joseph Wambaugh

bounce something **off** someone *v phr by 1970s* To try out an idea or scheme by seeing how someone reacts; seek a quick evaluation: *He likes working with people, bouncing off people and having them bounce off him*—Rolling Stone

bounce off the walls *v phr* Army and medical *by 1970s* Be in a nervous and confused condition

◁**bounce-on**▷ *n 1990s* A sex act; a copulation; =FUCK, SCREW: *I want a bounce-on*—TV program *Married with Children*

bouncer 1 *n 1880s* A person employed to eject unwanted customers from a saloon, restaurant, dance hall, etc **2** *n 1920s* A check that is returned for lack of funds; =RUBBER CHECK **3** *n 1920s* underworld A forged check
    See CHECK BOUNCER

◁**bouncy-bouncy**▷ *n by 1950s* The sex act
    See PLAY BOUNCY-BOUNCY

bouquets **See** THROW BOUQUETS AT someone or something

bourgie **See** BOOJIE

bow-and-arrow squad *n phr by 1970s* A police assignment involving unarmed duty: *They pull an officer's weapon and send him off to a desk-bound bow-and-arrow squad*—Newsweek

bowels **See** GET one's BALLS IN AN UPROAR

Bowery bum *n phr by 1940s* =SKID ROW BUM

bowl **See** CHILI-BOWL, GOLDFISH BOWL, RUST BOWL

bowlegs *n* Army *by early 1900s* A cavalry soldier

bow out *v phr by 1940s* To depart, voluntarily and often gracefully: *We wanted her to take the role, but she bowed out*

bow tie *n phr* baseball *by 1990s* =BRUSHBACK: *"Dykstra needs a bow tie." Nolan pitched the next day, and, sure enough, Lenny got his present*—New Yorker

bowwow 1 *n by 1890s* A dog ◁**2**▷ *n by 1970s* An unattractive or obnoxious young woman; =DOG **3** *n about 1900* A frankfurter

bowwows 1 *n 1920s* The feet **2** *adj by 1930s* Beautiful; attractive: *. . . an athletically built blonde who was just bow-wows*—James T Farrell

bowzed *adj* =BOOZED ●Included as *bowz'd* in Benjamin Franklin's 1722 list of 225 words meaning "drunk"

box 1 *n 1600s* A coffin **2** *v 1970s* medical To die: *Oh, she boxed last night*—New York Times **3** *adj* (also **boxed**) *1970s* medical Dead **4** *v by 1970s* To kill: *Samalson planned to go back Monday morning, but. . . he got boxed*—Ed McBain **5** *n* early *1900s* underworld A safe; vault; bank vault ◁**6**▷ *n 1600s* The vulva; vagina: *Her box ain't no rose blossom*—Joseph Wambaugh ◁**7**▷ *n 1960s* homosexuals The male genitals, esp as displayed by tight pants; =BASKET **8** *n* jive & cool talk fr *1930s* jazz musicians Any stringed instrument, esp a guitar **9** *n by 1950s* An accordion; =GROAN BOX **10** *n 1920s* A phonograph **11** *n 1970s* =GHETTO BOX: *Hey, man, don't mess with my box*—Wall Street Journal/ *. . . were allowed to keep their boxes because their age exempted them from normal court procedures*—New York Times **12** *n* A very tight and awkward situation; cleft stick; =BIND: *Those guidelines put me in a hell of a box*
    See BITCH BOX, BLUE BOX, COLD-MEAT BOX, FIRST CRACK OUT OF THE BOX, GIT-BOX, GO HOME FEET FIRST, GOOLA BOX, GROAN BOX, IDIOT BOX, IN A BIND, NUT HOUSE, OUT OF THE BOX, PETE, SHINE BOX, SOAPBOX, SQUAWK BOX, STUFF THE BALLOT BOX, THINK-BOX

the **box** *1950s* *n phr* Television or a television set

boxcar 1 *n* WWII Army Air Forces A large cargo aircraft or bomber **2** *modifier* gambling *by 1950s* In high numbers: *boxcar odds* [second sense from the high numbers seen on the sides of railroad boxcars]

boxcar numbers (or **figures**) *n phr by 1940s* Very high numbers: *. . . bringing in the kind of boxcar numbers that advertisers like*—Village Voice

boxcars 1 *n* crapshooting *by early 1900s* A throw of two sixes **2** *n by 1940s* Very large shoes
    See GRAB AN ARMFUL OF BOXCARS

boxed *adj by 1940s* Drunk

boxed out *adj phr* narcotics *by 1940s* Totally free and uninhibited, esp because of narcotic intoxication: *"Brush 'em easy, he boxed out," he says of a Pensacola dude, a dealer in contraband*—Village Voice

boxer *n 1920s* hoboes A box car

box someone **in** *v phr by 1940s* To put someone in a tight and awkward situation; incapacitate someone

◁**box lunch**▷ *n phr by 1950s* Cunnilingus

box man 1 *n phr* (also **box-worker**) underworld *about 1900* A criminal specializing in opening safes; =PETE-MAN **2** *n phr* gambling *by 1950s* A professional blackjack or twenty-one dealer **3** *n phr* gambling *by 1950s* A cashier or croupier at a gambling table: *. . . the box men, who are the cashiers of the tables*—J Cannon

box office *n phr* show business *by 1930s* A popular and financial success, esp in the entertainment field: *. . . just because you're no longer box office*—Roddy McDowall

boy ◁**1**▷ *n by 1850* A black man: *Don't call me "boy". . . I'm as old as you are if not older*—Langston Hughes ◁**2**▷ *n* Any male, regardless of age, working as a porter, elevator operator, etc

•With the implication that it is not the job for a man. *Boy* has been used as a term of contempt since about 1300 **3** *n homosexuals by 1970s* A male who takes the subservient role in a homosexual relationship; =PEG BOY **4** *n narcotics fr 1920s* Heroin: *But now he had the boy; he could lie around*—C Cooper **5** *interj* (also **boy howdy, boy o boy, boys**) *by 1890s* An exclamation of amazement, shock, happiness, intensification, etc; =JEEZ, MAN, WOW: *Boy, that was a close one!/ Boy o boy, isn't this great?*

See BIG BOY, BLOOMER BOY, BUG BOY, CLINKER BOY, FAIRHAIRED BOY, FLY-BOY, GOOD OLD BOY, JEWBOY, OLD BOY NETWORK, ONE OF THE BOYS, PADDY, PEG BOY, PERCY, POOR BOY, PRETTY-BOY, THAT'S MY BOY, TOMBOY, WALKBOY

boychik or **boychick** *n by 1960s* A boy; youngster; =KID: *Maybe you're crazy about one boychick*—Sassy [fr Yiddish]

boyfriend *n early 1900s* A girl's or woman's sweetheart, lover, male friend, etc

boyo *n by 1970* A fellow; man; friend •Often used in address[fr Anglo-Irish]

the **boys** *by 1880s* **1** *n phr* Any group of men, esp a group of drinking companions, poker players, etc: *an evening out with the boys* **2** *n phr* A group of criminals or other disreputable types

See ONE OF THE BOYS

the **boys in the backroom** *n phr by 1880s* Any group of men, esp politicians and their aides, who are privy to and control the inner workings of an enterprise or place: *. . . the salad boys in the back room, oiling up the cabbage*—W T Tyler

the **boys uptown 1** *n phr by 1880s* The political bosses of a city, and their staffs; =CITY HALL **2** *n phr by 1880s* Any group of influential and unnamed criminals: *The tricksters. . . were "the boys uptown," not yet identified*—New York Daily News

boy-toy 1 *n 1980s* A young woman used like the plaything of a man: *. . . when she plays boy-toy to all your crush objects. . .* —Seventeen **2** *n 1980s* A young man used like the plaything of a woman: *Paul Newman's 69 now and thinks being the boy toy of yet another generation of women is "undignified"*—New York Times/ *. . . a has-been silent screen legend and her young screenwriter boytoy*—Newark Star-Ledger **3** *modifier*: *. . . the times Madonna has whupped her boy-toy dancers on stage*—Los Angeles Times

bozette *n by 1970s* A girl; a woman, esp a somewhat vulgar one; a female bozo; =BIMBO: *A drunk babe is a happy babe, whether it's Babe Ruth or some bozette you've snagged at the five-and-dime*—National Lampoon

bozo *n about 1910* A fellow; a man, esp a muscular type with a meager brain: *This bozo right here next to me [Rep. Thomas P. O'Neill incognito] could probably be a better Congressman than those guys in Congress*—TV show Cheers [origin unknown; perhaps fr Spanish *bozal*, used in the slave trade and after to designate someone who speaks Spanish badly, hence a stupid person]

bozo filter *n phr 1990s computer* A desirable but non-existent device that would automatically exclude fools and louts from computer networks: *Do you know where I could get a good bozo filter?*—New Yorker

bra (BRAH) *n 1930s* A brassiere

◁**bra-burner**▷ (BRAH bər nər) *n 1970s* A very militant feminist: *The media decided henceforth to label feminists as "braburners"*—Esquire [fr the putative symbolic burning of brassieres as a protest against the restriction of women's freedom]

brace 1 *v about 1890* To stop or approach a person and beg for money: *This panhandler came up to me and braced me*—John O'Hara **2** *v by 1950s* To confront someone with an accusation: *. . . this would be a good chance to brace Bellsey's wife without her husband being present*—Lawrence Sanders **3** *n armed forces and service academies by 1930s* A very stiff and exaggerated standing at military attention **4** *v*: *The sergeant ordered her to brace*

See SPLICE THE MAIN BRACE

bracelet *n 1990s* A radio transmitter in a band fitting on the ankle, and emitting signals so that the whereabouts of the wearer may be monitored: *. . . drug dealer was released on the condition that he wear an ankle bracelet*—New York Times

bracelets *n underworld by 1840s* A pair of handcuffs •Old-fashioned fetters were so called in the 1600s

bracer *n by 1820s* A drink of liquor

bracket creep *n phr 1970s* The raising of wage-earners into higher income-tax brackets, esp because of wage-raises triggered by inflation: *Tax payments will mount next year from "bracket creep," the tendency of inflation to push people into higher tax brackets*—Wall Street Journal

bragging rights *n phr sports by 1980s* The privilege of boasting about one's accomplishments; the warrant of superiority: *. . . the burning question of the bragging rights to the world's hottest chilies*—ABC World News/ *A town of 2,000 or more had a number of teams vying for local bragging rights. . .* —Robert F Perkins

brag-rags *n by 1950s* =FRUIT SALAD

braid *See* GOLD BRAID

brain 1 *n by 1914* An intelligent person; intellectual; good scholar: *The publicity of being a brain did not further her movie career as a glamour girl*—Bob Thomas **2** *v* To injure with a hard blow to the head •Attested fr 1382 in the full sense, "kill by knocking out the brain": *The left hook really brained him*

See BIRDBRAIN, BUBBLE BRAIN, HAVE something ON THE BRAIN, LAMEBRAIN, NOT HAVE BRAIN ONE, PICK someone's BRAIN, RATTLEBRAIN, SCATTERBRAIN

brain bucket 1 *n phr 1950s armed services* A steel helmet **2** *n phr* =HARD HAT

braindead *adj 1980s students* Stupid; =DUMB [The more technical term designating biological death as cessation of brain activity dates fr the 1970s]

brain dish *n phr 1990s* A helmet worn for motorcycling, bicycling, in-line skating, etc: *Do I really have to wear this brain dish?*—comic strip "Sally Forth"

brain drain *n phr 1960s British* The loss of useful educated persons, esp professionals, because they can find better conditions elsewhere: *Stalled Economy Speeds Puerto Rico's Brain Drain*—New York Times

brain dump *n phr 1990s computer* To talk, explain, expatiate: *Go hang around a mouse potato and see if you can get him to geek out and do a brain dump*—Macon Telegraph [based on *screen dump*, a computer command to print everything appearing on the monitor screen]

brained *See* AIRHEADED, BIRDBRAINED, CRACK-BRAINED, DICK-BRAINED, LAMEBRAINED, NUMB-BRAINED

brainery *n by 1890s* A college or university

brain-fade **1** *n by 1980s* Stuporous boredom; tedium: *She and her colleagues fight brain-fade by sizing up customers*—Time **2** *v by 1990s* To become confused; lose coherence: *". . . I just brain-faded. . . I got a little confused*—Milwaukee Journal

brainiac *1980s* **1** *n* An intelligent person; =BRAIN: *Hugo is such a brainiac he got 100% on the algebra test*—Leah Beatty, Canadian college student **2** *n* An intellectual; =DOUBLE-DOME, EGGHEAD **3** *modifier*: *. . . since you've been quoting every brainiac dumb-dumb to make your points. . .* —Village Voice [fr a smart and nasty character in the Superman comics]

brain one *n phr by 1970s* The most elementary intelligence; a minimum of sagacity: *Our leader doesn't exhibit brain one*
  See NOT HAVE BRAIN ONE

brain-picker *n by 1880s* A person who exploits the creative notions of others: *. . . nothing but scorn for brain-pickers and imitators*—A Lomax

brains **1** *n by middle 1700s* Intelligence; mind; =SAVVY, SMARTS **2** *n 1920* The person who does the thinking and planning; guiding mind: *Father Paul Lucano, the real brains of the organization*—Milwaukee Journal
  See BEAT one's BRAINS OUT, FUCK someone's BRAINS OUT, HAVE SHIT FOR BRAINS, SHIT-FOR-BRAINS

one's **brains out** *adv phr* To one's utmost; extremely much; spectacularly; =one's HEAD OFF: *So I played his brains out in spring training*—Milwaukee Journal/*Xing his brains out*—Homo

brainstorm **1** *n 1920s* A sudden idea, esp one that is apt and useful; a happy insight ●*Brainstorm* was a medical term for "mental explosion" by the 1890s **2** *v by 1920s* To examine and work on a problem by having a group sit around and utter whatever relevant thoughts they have, spontaneously: *We'll brainstorm the drop in enrollment*

brain surgeon *See* YOU DON'T HAVE TO BE A BRAIN SURGEON

brain surgery *n phr 1990s* Anything very difficult and technical: *This game isn't brain surgery, but it teaches them to vent without hurting someone*—New York Times/ *If a guy doesn't know he's being*

tailed. . . tailing is not brain surgery—Robert B Parker

brain tablet *n phr 1930s cowboys* A cigarette

brain-teaser *n* (also **brain-twister** and **brain-scratcher**) *1920s* A puzzle; a hard or tricky question: *. . . here is today's social brain-scratcher*—Los Angeles Times

brain-tap *n 1990s* An instance of brain-picking [probably based on the operation called *spinal tap*, in which spinal fluid is drawn off for medical analysis]

brainwash *early 1950s* **1** *v* To cause profound attitudinal changes, usu in a prisoner, by psychological conditioning, supplemented by drugs and physical abuse **2** *v* To change or influence someone's opinions or attitude by methods less stringent than those used on prisoners: *They were brainwashed into joining that crazy cult* **3** *n*: *Your line is persuasive, virtually a brainwash* [fr Chinese *hsi nao*, "wash brain," which came into US use during and after the Korean War, apparently because of its use by North Koreans and their Chinese allies as custodians of US prisoners of war]

brain wave *n phr by 1890s* A sudden useful idea; =BRAINSTORM: *Lou had a brain wave. He offered the boy a C note to let him drive*—Raymond Chandler

brainy *adj by 1840s* Intelligent; sagacious

brakes *See* STAND ON one's BRAKES

brakie or **brakey** *n 1880s hoboes* The brake operator of a train

brand X **1** *n phr 1970s Army* The infantry insignia, crossed rifles **2** *n phr 1970s narcotics* Marijuana [fr the phrase used in television advertising for unnamed and inferior products]

brannigan or **branigan** *by 1903* **1** *n* A spree: *a prolonged crossword puzzle brannigan*—Benjamin de Casseres **2** *n by 1940* A brawl or fracas; =DONNYBROOK: *Republicans and Democrats alike are guilty of this brannigan*—P Edson [fr the Irish surname, for unclear reasons]

brass **1** *n 1700s* Impudence; effrontery; =CHUTZPA ●Fr the late 1500s *brass* had the same meaning, in the phrase *face of brass*, that is, "brazen-faced" **2** *n late 1500s* Money ●Common in British usage, obsolete on the US **3** *n by 1899* High officials or managers in general; =the BRASS: *There's lots of vice presidents here but they're not really brass*

the **brass** *n phr armed forces fr WWII* The upper ranks of the military or other uniformed services: *Many a GI hated the brass and the enemy*—J B Douds [probably a shortening of *brass hat*]
  See the TOP BRASS

◁**brass balls**▷ *n phr 1960s* Courage; audacity; =GUTS: *But I had the brass balls to hold out for a piece of the action*—Rolling Stone

brass collar *n phr 1930s railroad* A railroad officer or high manager

brassed off *adj phr fr WWII Royal Air Force* Ready to quit; sated; bored; =FED UP

brass hat **1** *n phr British by 1890s* A high-ranking officer in the military or other uniformed services

2 *1930s n phr* Any high-ranking official; manager; chief; =BOSS

brass-pounder *n 1920s* A telegrapher; amateur radio operator [because sending keys are made of *brass*]

brass tacks *See* DOWN TO BRASS TACKS

brat[1] *n by 1505* A child, esp an obnoxious or troublesome one [origin unknown]

brat[2] *n by 1980s* Bratwurst, a kind of sausage: . . ./. *a neighborhood more attuned to baseball, brats, and beer*—Milwaukee Journal

-brat *combining word by 1940s* Designating a child raised in a stated environment: *Army brat/ opera brat/ Navy brat/ faculty brat/ Air Force brat*: *Masako led a normal life—normal, that is, for a diplomatic brat with an ambitious father*—New Yorker

brat pack *n phr 1980s* A group of young metropolitan males deemed worthy of media attention: *Richard Price was a one-man Bronx-boy Brat Pack*—Vanity Fair [modeled on *rat pack*]

brat-sit *v 1990s*: *baby-sit*

braver than Dick Tracy *adj phr by 1970s* Audacious; too brave for one's own good; =BALLSY, GUTSY [fr the stoic detective hero of a comic strip, whose courage was acknowledged when Al Capp satirized him as Fearless Fosdick]

brawl *n 1920s* A noisy, riotous party [fr *brawl,* "a noisy fight," of obscure origin; perhaps related to Dutch *brallen,* "brag," and Low German *brallen,* "shout, roar"; perhaps fr French *branle,* "an energetic circle dance"]

bread *n by 1940s, but esp cool talk & 1960s counterculture* Money; =DOUGH [probably fr *dough*; perhaps related to earlier *gingerbread,* "money"]
  See the BEST THING SINCE SLICED BREAD, SMALL POTATOES

bread and butter *by middle 1735* **1** *n phr* The simple necessities of life; basic needs **2** *modifier*: *. . . a routine, bread-and-butter type of case*

breadbasket *n by 1750s* The stomach; abdomen; =KISHKES, LABONZA

bready *See* WHITE BREADY

break 1 *n by 1830s* An escape or attempt to escape **2** *n by 1860s* A brief period of rest or relaxation: *Take a five-minute break* **3** *v*: *Let's break while I think about it all* **4** *v by 1400* To interrupt or abandon some regular practice: *to break training/ break an old routine* **5** *n by 1911* A stroke of luck, good or bad •Probably fr the *break* in billiards, when balls arrange themselves in either a good or bad way: *I got a break and made it on time/ Football's a game of breaks to some extent* **6** *n* A stroke of mercy or favor: *Give me one break and I'll never flunk again* **7** *v by 1914* To happen; occur; fall out: *If things break right I'll be OK* **8** *v by late 1400s* To tame a wild horse; subdue someone's spirit **9** *v by 1612* To bankrupt a company or person **10** *v late 1600s* To demote; reduce in rank; =BUST: *They broke him back to buck private* **11** *v by 1890s* To separate, esp from a clinch: *The boxers broke and came at each other again* **12** *n 1930s* jazz musicians An improvised passage; solo; =LICK **13** *v 1980s black teenagers* (also **breakdance** or **boogie**) To do a kind of dancing that evolved in the inner-city ghettos, and characterized esp by intricate writhings and shows of balance and strength close to the floor •*Break down* was used by 1819 to describe very energetic black dancing: *You can go running. You can swim. Or you can break*—New York Times **14** *v* (also **service break**) *tennis by 1950s* To win a game from an opponent who is serving
  See COFFEE BREAK, EVEN BREAK, TAKE A BREAK

break a hamstring *v phr 1930s loggers* To do one's best; =BUST one's ASS, BUST HUMP

break a leg *sentence fr theater* Best wishes; good luck; I hope you do very well [perhaps fr German *Hals und Bein brechen,* "break your neck and leg," a similar good-luck formula; the same grim warding-off spell is expressed in Italian *in bocca al lupo,* "good luck!"]

break one's **arm patting** oneself **on the back** *v phr by 1990s* To be very self-gratulatory; bask in smugness: *I think we've improved the Met a great deal. I don't mean I'm breaking my arm patting myself on the back*—New Yorker

◁**break** one's **ass**▷ (or ◁**balls**▷ or **buns** or **butt** or **cork** or **hump** or **nut** or ◁**sweet ass**▷) *See* BUST one's ASS

break (or **pop) a sweat** *v phr prizefight by 1970s* To perspire from exercise or exertion; exert oneself: *Students were not the only ones breaking a sweat Sunday*—Wisconsin State Journal/ *They want to feel great and look great and not pop a sweat*—Robert B Parker

breakaway 1 *modifier theater by 1950s* Made to break or collapse easily: *bashed with a breakaway chair* **2** *adj by 1930s* Unconventional; rebellious: *a breakaway rock group/ breakaway mind-set*

break bad *v phr 1970s black* To become hostile and menacing: *I don't want to make eye contact with this sucker because he may break bad on me*—New York Times

break someone's **brains** *v phr by 1990s* Injure someone severely: *. . . any more of that shit and I'm gonna break your brains*—Stan Cutler

break (or **bust) chops** *v phr 1970s* To injure; punish; literally, to break someone's face or mouth: *But busting Luana's chops by busting her boyfriend's wasn't going to exactly get me in her good graces*—Stan Cutler

break (or **bust) someone's chops** *1970s* **1** *v phr* To verbally assault someone; harass: *I love it here. I can work hung over and nobody busts my chops*—National Lampoon/ *Well, she turned absolutely livid, and ever since she's been busting my chops*—Lawrence Sanders **2** *v phr* =BUST one's ASS

breakdance *See* BREAK

break something **down** *v phr 1960s black* To explain something; present something in detail: *Break it down for me, Baby*—Eldridge Cleaver

breaker *n 1980s black teenagers* A person who dances with intricate writhings and shows of balance

and strength close to the floor, esp and originally to rhythmic, staccato songs spoken rather than sung, in a style indigenous to the urban ghetto: . . . *the night he and other breakers showed up. . . ready to boogie*—New York Times
See BACK-BREAKER, JAWBREAKER

breakfast *See* FROM HELL TO BREAKFAST, MEXICAN BREAKFAST, SHOOT one's COOKIES

break-in *n by 1850s* A burglary; forcible entry

break someone or something **in** *v phr by 1840s* To put through an initial period of easy use or training before requiring full function

break it up *v phr by 1930s* To stop fighting, quarreling, chatting, etc •Usu a stern command

break luck *v phr* prostitutes *by 1950s* To get the first client of the day

break out 1 *v phr* To escape from prison or some other confining situation **2** *v phr by 1530s* To show symptoms of disease or discomfort: *He broke out in a purple rash* **3** *v phr by 1890s* To bring out; produce for use •Originally fr nautical use where it referred to the freeing of cargo prior to unloading: *When I came he broke out the Scotch* **4** *v phr 1990s* To be the case; be apparent: *We need donations; that's how it breaks out here*—Colorado Public Radio

◁**break out into assholes**▷ *v phr by 1970s* To become very frightened [an allusion to the loose bowels associated with fear]

break out the jams *See* KICK OUT THE JAMS

the **breaks** *by 1911* **1** *n phr* Good luck; special favors: *If I get the breaks I'll prevail* **2** *n phr* Bad luck: *Them's the breaks*

break the back *v phr* **1** *by 1970s* To make ineffective; cripple: *The UN's mission is to break the back of the warlords in Somalia*—ABC radio news **2** *v phr by 1890* To do the hardest part, or most, of a job

break the ice *v phr late 1500s* To dissipate the sense of strain among people who do not know each other: *I broke the ice by saying she looked like Charlemagne's mother*

break the points *v phr* sports & gambling *by 1970s* To score enough points to cover the point-spread

breakthrough *n 1930s* An abrupt solution or surge of progress: *Understanding the reaction was a breakthrough* [fr earlier military term for a successful attack]

break up 1 *v phr middle 1700s* To separate or to cause separation or dissolution of a close relationship: *to break up a marriage/ After ten years they broke up* **2** *v phr by 1920s* To laugh or cause to laugh uncontrollably; =FRACTURE, SLAY •The synonymous phrase *break all up* is attested in the 1890s: *His doctor shtick broke them up*

break-up *n middle 1700s* A separation or dissolution

break wind *v phr middle 1600s* To flatulate; =FART

◁**breastworks**▷ *n by 1860s* The female breasts; =BAZOOM

breath *See* CHANGE BREATH

breathe easy *v phr by 1950s* To be relieved of concern; relax

breather *n by 1970s* A person who makes harassing telephone calls and merely breathes, rather than talking, into the mouthpiece
See HEAVY BREATHER, MOUTH-BREATHER

breathing *adj by 1970s* Alive, at least: *They'll take any warm body that's breathing*
See MOUTH-BREATHING

breeder *n* homosexuals *by 1980s* A heterosexual person; =STRAIGHT: *the scornful term "breeders," used by some urban gays about heterosexual couples with children*—New Republic

breed of cat *n phr by 1970s* Sort; kind; species: *But Trent is another breed of cat entirely*—Lawrence Sanders

breeze 1 *n 1920s* baseball An easy task; anything easy; =CINCH, CAKEWALK **2** *v by 1907* To go or move rapidly and easily: *to breeze through work/ I breezed out* **3** *v* prison *by 1940s* To escape from prison **4** *n*: *They had a breeze today at Ossining*

the **breeze** *See* BAT THE BREEZE, BURN THE BREEZE

breeze off *v phr by 1920s* To leave; depart; =BOOK

breezy *adj by 1870* Very easy-going and jovial; cheery: *a breezy "Good morning"*

brekkie *n by 1980s* Breakfast: *It was brekkie with Ed Meese*—Washington Post [perhaps modeled on Oxford *brekker*, attested by 1890]

a **brew (or brewhaha or brewskie)** *n phr* first form *by 1940s*, second *by 1970s*, third *by 1980s* A glass, bottle, or can of beer; a beer •*Brewhaha* has its own variants: *brewha, haha,* and *ha*: *She treated me to a brew* [second form fr French *brouhaha*, "fuss, ado"]

brew-out *n* college students *by 1970s* A beer party; =BEER BUST

briar *n 1830s* underworld A file or hacksaw

brick 1 *n 1830s* British students A decent, generous, reliable person **2** *n 1970s* narcotics A kilogram (2.2 pounds) of tightly compacted marijuana **3** *n 1980s* students A very inaccurate basketball shot [first sense said to be a clever student version of Aristotle's phrase *tetragonos aner*, "foursided-man, four square man," used in the *Nichomachean Ethics* to describe a person of public merit whose praise might appear on a square monument of tribute]
See DROP A BRICK, HIT someone LIKE A TON OF BRICKS, HIT THE BRICKS, PRESS THE BRICKS, SHIT A BRICK, THREE BRICKS SHY OF A LOAD

brick agent *n phr by 1970s* An FBI agent of the lowest rank: *. . . brick agent, the Federal infantry who. . . knock on doors, track down mysterious émigrés*—Philadelphia [because they walk the streets and sidewalks, the *bricks*]

brickhouse *n 1980s* students A very busty woman [because she is *built like a brick shithouse*]

bricklayer *n 1990s* sports An inaccurate basketball shooter: *His drawback is that he's a bricklayer from the free throw line*—Milwaukee Journal

the **bricks** *n phr by 1940s* The streets and sidewalks of a city: *I had to get out on the bricks and hustle* **See** HIT THE BRICKS, PRESS THE BRICKS

bricks and mortar *n phr by 1850s* Buildings and construction, esp as an item of expenditure and administrative emphasis for an institution

◁**brick shithouse**▷ **See** BUILT LIKE A BRICK SHITHOUSE

bricktop *n by 1850s* A redheaded person

brickyard **See** HOGAN'S BRICKYARD

the **Brickyard** *n phr by 1970s* The motor speedway at Indianapolis, Indiana, site of the annual 500-mile race [fr the *brick* construction of the track]

bridesmaid syndrome *n phr 1990s* Misfortune of being very close, but never the winner: *Suffering from bridesmaid syndrome, which had left her the loser in 6 of the 8 finals she reached last year*—New York Times

brief *v 1860 lawyers* To instruct someone: *They briefed him very carefully before they let him comment*

brig **1** *n* The detention cell of a ship **2** *n 1850s nautical* A naval prison **3** *n by 1890s* Any military jail or prison

bright *n 1930s black* Day; the daytime

bright-eyed and bushy-tailed *adj phr 1950s Air Force adj phr* Eager and energetic; in splendid fettle

See STREET-SMART

bright-line *v 1980s* Single out; focus on; emphasize: *My final comment, and I want to bright-line it* [fr the use of a usu yellow felt pen to mark important passages]

brights *n by 1970s* The bright or upper-beam headlights of a car: *. . . into the brights of an oncoming car*—Village Voice

brig rat *n phr 1940s armed forces* A military prisoner

brill *adj by 1981* Brilliant: *John Turturro is brill as gawky Jew who takes a dive. . .* —Sassy

◀**Brillo** or **Brillo-pad**▶ *n by 1980s* A black person: *a black woman admitted that white teenagers called her "Brillo-pad" while she was standing at a bus stop*—New Republic [fr *Brillo*™, a brand of scouring pad with tight wiry fibers resembling tight curly hair]

bringdown *esp 1950s beat & cool talk fr 1940s jazz musicians* **1** *n* A cutting rebuke or comment; a deflation: *Polite applause is a bit of a bringdown* **2** *n* A disappointing or depressing performance **3** *modifier*: *a bringdown scene* **4** *n* A morose person: *A "bringdown" is a depressing character*—Stephen Longstreet **5** *modifier*: *that bringdown face*

bring someone **down** *v phr 1960s students fr beat & cool talk* To depress; dispirit; sadden: *I'm afraid your jolly word brings me down*

bring down the house *v phr 1840s theater* To score a resounding theatrical success: *Old Man Dillinger strode onto the stage and brought down the house*—A Hynd/ *first heard on a Broadway stage in 1930, when she brought down the house singing "I Got Rhythm"*—New York Times

bring home the bacon (**groceries** may replace **bacon**) *by 1908* **1** *v phr* To achieve a tangible goal or task: *Their new tailback brought home the bacon* **2** *v phr* To earn enough to support oneself and one's family

bring it **1** *v phr 1980s baseball* To throw a baseball fast **2** *v phr 1900s* To play very well; do the job: *He's a heck of a football player. . . He can bring it*—Milwaukee Journal

bring money *sentence by 1970s* What we are talking about is quite expensive: *They have plans for two more hotels. Bring money. Breakfast for two, without champagne, can run to $50 or $60*—Time

bring scunnion (or **smoke**) *1970s Army* **1** *v phr* To inspire fear or anxiety in others **2** *v phr* To concentrate fire, esp artillery fire [origin unknown]

bring something **to a screeching halt** *v phr 1970s* To end or cease something immediately: *If I were you, I'd bring that association to a screeching halt*—Lawrence Sanders

bring (or **get** or **keep**) **someone up to speed** *v phr* To give necessary information; =FILL someone IN, PUT someone IN THE PICTURE: *Well, look, I appreciate your keeping me up to speed*—Washingtonian/ *Johnson's teammates have gone out of their way to help him get up to speed*—Milwaukee Journal [fr the need to increase gradually the speed of a machine or phonograph turntable, video recorder, etc, to the proper rate]

the **briny** *n phr by 1850s* The ocean; the sea

Brit *1960s fr about 1900 British* **1** *adj* British: *the Brit rock scene* **2** *n*: *two Brits and a Yank*

bro' or **bro** **1** *n by middle 1600s* Brother **2** *n black by 1960s* A black person: *. . . the slick-speaking bro who scores points off the ofay*—Time **3** *n by 1970s* A man; =GUY: *. . . the pack of twenty-seven bros jamming along the freeway*—Easyriders/ *Hawk murmured, "Right on, bro," and drank some champagne*—Robert B Parker

◁**broad**▷ *about 1910* **1** *n* A woman •Used almost entirely by men, and considered offensive by many women: *Sorry lady, no broads allowed in here: So here was this suburban broad*—Saul Bellow **2** *n* A promiscuous woman; prostitute [probably from the notion "broad in the beam"]

See SQUARE BROAD

broad-assed or **broad-beamed** *by 1916* Wide in the buttocks

broad-gauge *adj by 1970s* Very versatile and competent: *We're looking for a few broad-gauge people for an exciting project*

the **broad strokes** *n phr by 1980s* General details; basic facts: *I don't want any details. I understand your hesitation. Just the broad strokes*—Sue Grafton

brodie or **Brodie** **1** *n late 1800s* A fall; tumble **2** *n 1920s theater* A total failure; fiasco; =FLOP, TURKEY **3** *n 1920 students* A mistake **4** *n 1950s* motorcyclists A squealing, rubber-burning skidding of a motorcycle or car [fr Steve *Brodie,* who claimed to have leaped off the Brooklyn Bridge in 1886, but failed to have the act witnessed]

broke *adj* by 1660s Entirely out of money; destitute
See ALL HELL BROKE LOOSE, DEAD BROKE, FLAT BROKE, GO BROKE, GO FOR BROKE

broken arrow *n phr* by 1980s An accident involving nuclear weapons: *The idea that this is a "broken arrow" never released is incorrect*—Milwaukee Journal

broken-bat bleeder *n phr* baseball by 1990s A weak blow on which the hitter breaks his bat, and which trickles out for a hit: *It's appropriate that we should lose that game on a frickin' broken-bat bleeder up the middle*—Milwaukee Journal

the **broken-nose crowd** *n phr* by 1990s The organized-crime syndicates; =MOB •Compare *bent-nose: There is. . . a big-time problem here that wouldn't be one if the broken-nose crowd still ran the gambling houses*—Los Angeles Times

broken record *n phr* Something or someone repetitive, tedious, and importunate: *He kept asking for a raise, like a broken record*

broken-striper *n* Navy by 1914 A naval warrant officer

broke to the curb *adj phr* 1990s teenagers Ugly; ill-favored; =BUCKLED, CRUSHED, PISS-UGLY

brolly *n* 1870s British schools An umbrella •Thoroughly British, with some US use

bromide outdated fr early 1900s **1** *n* An old, stale joke or scrap of wisdom: *. . . a rolling illustration of the bromide that beggars can't be choosers*—New York Times **2** *n* A boring, tedious person: *Clutterbuck, with his wilted wit, was a total bromide* [fr the use of *bromide* as a sedative]

bronc or **bronk 1** *n* =BRONCO **2** *n* hoboes A catamite; =PUNK

bronco 1 *n* 1840s southwest traders A horse not tamed for riding; unruly mount **2** *n* homosexuals by 1970s A young male not accustomed to nor complaisant in homosexual relations [fr Spanish *bronco,* "coarse, rough"]

bronco buster 1 *n phr* (Variations: **peeler** or **snapper** or **twister** may replace **buster**) cowboys by 1880s A cowboy who tames broncos to riding; also, a rodeo performer who rides unruly horses in competition **2** *n phr* homosexuals by 1970s =CHICKENHAWK

Bronx cheer 1920s **1** *n phr* A loud, rude, flatulating noise made with the tongue and lips; =the BIRD, RASPBERRY: *The Duchess was startled but serene when the crowd greeted her with a fortissimo Bronx cheer* **2** *n phr* Any outright and precise expression of derision: *That book will get Bronx cheers from every critic*

brookie *n* by 1950s A brook trout

Brooklyn side *n phr* bowling by 1940s The left side of the bowling alley as one faces the pins [fr the location of *Brooklyn* as one looks south along the East River]

broom *v* outdated fr early 1800s To run or walk away, esp to escape by running
See HAVE A BROOM UP one's ASS

brother 1 *n* by about 1910 A man; fellow; =GUY •Used in addressing strangers: *I don't know you, brother, but you said a mouthful* **2** *n* black about 1920 A black person; =BLOOD •Common and significant fr 1960s: *All you brothers here, and you white people too, got to take care of business* **3** *n* by middle 1300s A fellow professional; colleague: *I'd like to ask Brother Donaldson something, if I may*—George Will **4** *interj* by 1920s An exclamation of surprise, amusement, vehemence, etc; =BOY, JEEZ, MAN: *". . . the lady was prepared to take it if it did." "Brother!"*—Hugh Pentecost
See SOUL BROTHER

Brother *See* BIG BROTHER

brouhaha (BREW hah hah)*n* 1950s A noisy clamor; fuss; =FLAP [fr French; possibly ultimately fr Hebrew *baruch haba* "blessed are those who come (in the name of the Lord)," Psalm 118, although the line of derivation is complex and tenuous]

brow *See* HIGHBROW, LOWBROW, MIDDLEBROW

browbeat *v* by 1830s To intimidate; =STRONG-ARM

browbeater by 1830s One who intimidates: *. . . alternately a party-throwing cheerleader and a sadistic browbeater*—New York Times

brown 1 *adj* by 1990s Opposed to environmental preservation and restoration •The opposite of *green*: *. . . the chairman of the Council of Economic Advisers is judged brown, rather than green, on the issue of timetables for climate control*—New Yorker ◁2▷ *v* also **brown-hole** by 1930s To do anal intercourse; =BUGGER, BUNGHOLE

brown-bag or **brown-bag it** *v* by 1960s To take one's lunch to the office, or one's liquor to a club or restaurant, in a paper bag: *. . . for brown-bagging booze at places that allow this practice*—Esquire/ *. . . to reduce the dangers of brown-bagging it for lunch*—Wall Street Journal

brown bagger 1 *n* by 1960s A person who brown-bags **2** *n* by 1970s A very ugly person; =DOUBLE-BAGGER [second sense fr the notion that such a person should wear a bag over the head to hide the face]

browned off 1 *adj phr* British armed forces since WWI Restless from waiting or wasting time; bored; =BRASSED OFF **2** *adj phr* 1930s Angry; =PISSED OFF: *He got browned off at the way they treated the kids*

brown eyes *See* BIG BROWN EYES

brownie[1] *n* WWII armed forces =BROWN-NOSER [fr the color of feces]

brownie[2] *n* by 1980s A traffic-control and parking-violation officer [fr the color of the uniform]

Brownie points *n phr* 1960s A fancied unit of credit and approval: *I'll get Brownie points for helping him: . . . a place where you get big shiny brownie points, cash, sex, and adulation*—Village Voice [fr merit points awarded to *Brownies* toward promotion to Junior Girl Scouts]

brown-nose *1930s military academy students*
1 *v* To flatter and pamper in order to gain approval
and advantage; curry favor; =APPLE-POLISH: *He's just
like any other person who's in a position to screw
you. You gotta brown nose*—John R Powers **2** *n*
also **brown-noser** : *He got there by being a pious
and effective brown-nose* [fr the color of feces presumably acquired when one has one's nose at the flat-
teree's anus]

bruh or **brud** *n by 1940s* Brother: *The man had
me and I know what it's like, bruh*—Rolling Stone

bruiser *n fr middle 1700s* A big, strong man, esp a
pugilist

brunch *n 1890s British students* A meal taken
between breakfast and lunch •Probably standard
now, since no other single term exists

brush 1 *n by 1820s* A mustache **2** *n by 1840s* A
fight; squabble; disagreement: *. . . have had drug or
alcohol problems, and have experienced a "brush
with the law"*—Milwaukee Journal

the **brush 1** *n phr by 1770s* The backwoods; jungle; =the BOONDOCKS **2** *n phr by 1930s* A snub;
quick dismissal; =BRUSH-OFF
See GIVE someone THE BRUSH

brush ape *n phr by 1930s* A rustic or backwoods
person; =HILLBILLY

brushback *1950s baseball* **1** *modifier* Pitched
very close to the batter, as if to hit him: *. . . knocked
me over like a good brushback pitch*—New Yorker
2 *n* =BEANBALL, DUSTER: *Throw another brushback
and you're out of the game*

brush someone **back** *v phr 1950s baseball* To
pitch close to a batter in order to force him or her
away from home plate and upset the batting poise

brusher *See* SAGEBRUSHER

brush-fire war *n phr 1950s* A small-scale war that
erupts suddenly, and might spread

brush-off *n by 1930s* =the BRUSH

brush someone **off** *v phr 1930s* To snub or dismiss someone pointedly; =GIVE someone THE BRUSH

brush up 1 *v phr by 1600* To clean; make neat and
clean **2** *v phr* (also **brush up on**) *by 1830s* To
improve, review, or perfect one's mastery: *Brush up
your Shakespeare. Start quoting him now*—Cole
Porter

bruss *n Army by 1950s* An extremely stiff and exaggerated military position of attention; =BRACE [fr
brace]

brutal *adj 1960s students* Excellent; great

BS or **bs** (pronounced as separate letters) *n about
1900* =BULLSHIT

BSer *n about 1900* =BULLSHIT ARTIST: *He's not a big
BSer*—Milwaukee Journal

B-side *n 1960s* The second or other side of a phonograph record, of an issue, etc; =FLIP SIDE

BTO or **bto** (pronounced as separate letters) *n by
1940s* =BIG-TIME OPERATOR

BTW (pronounced as separate letters) *adv computer
network by 1990s* By the way

bub[1] *n by 1960* =BOOB, TIT

bub[2] *n by 1830s* A man; fellow; brother; =GUY •Used

in direct address, with a slightly insulting intent:
Okay, bub, get the hell outta my way [fr *bubba* fr
brother]

bubba 1 *n Southern by 1860s* Brother •Not
uncommon as a nickname: *Here comes big Bubba
Jones* **2** *n* also often **Bubba** *1980s* A person of
simple Southern rural culture; =CRACKER, GOOD OLD
BOY •Occurrence increased enormously during the
early years of the Clinton Administration: *People
watching "Jeopardy!" aren't just bubbas out
there*—Milwaukee Journal/ *He doesn't have your
typical "Bubba" approach to state government*—
San Antonio Express-News [Imitation of baby-talk]

Bubbafest *n* A celebration of Southern rural culture:
*Greer, SC, is holding a Bubbafest. . . complete with
country music, sports, wading pools full of grits, a
Moon Pie toss, and the crowning of the royal
Bubba and Bubbette*—Milwaukee Journal

Bubbette *n 1990s* A woman Bubba

bubble brain *n phr by 1960s* A stupid and vapid
person; =AIRHEAD: *Did I want to establish that, bubble brain though I seemed to him, there were
sound reasons?*—Saul Bellow

bubble-brained *adj by 1960s* Stupid; vapid:
Suzanne Somers' bubble-brained Chrissy—
Wisconsin State Journal

bubble-butt *n 1990s* The bulbous stern found on
many 1990s cars: *. . . Chryslers and Tauruses and
Toyotas. . . they all have "bubble-butts"*—Douglas
Coupland

bubble-dancer *n lunch counter & WWII Army* A
dishwasher; =PEARL-DIVER [fr the ironic relation
between the bubbly soapsuds of the dishwasher and
the balloons used artistically by a cabaret *bubble-
dancer*]

bubble economy *n phr 1990s* An economy that
overexpands and must burst: *. . . the bubble economy of the '80s*—New York Times

bubblegum machine *n phr 1960s* The flashing
colored lights on the roof of a police car; =GUMBALL,
PARTY HAT: *Many of us come to the same realization
as the bubblegum machine lights up behind us
while we cruise at 85 mph. . .* —Milwaukee Journal

bubblegummer *n 1960s* A young teenager;
=TEENYBOPPER

bubble-gum music or **bubble gum** *1960s* **1**
n phr Rock-and-roll music that appeals to young
teenagers: *young adult audience dissatisfied with
"bubblegum music"*—New York Times/ *. . . so fundamental that one might refer to it as "heavy bubble gum"*—Aquarian **2** *modifier*: *The rap itself is
sheer bubble-gum monotony*—Variety/ *The new
album is less bubblegum, something kids and
adults can relate to*—Los Angeles Times

the **bubble-gum set** *n phr 1960s* Young
teenagers; =TEENYBOPPERS

bubblehead *n 1950s* A stupid person, esp one who
is frivolous and flighty; =AIRHEAD, BUBBLE BRAIN:
*Linda was, a polite word for dumb cunt, a bubble-
head*—Richard Merkin

the **bubbles** *adj phr by 1990s* All fun; all beer and

skittles: *Think life is the bubbles when you're Batman?*—Milwaukee Journal

bubble the pot *v phr by 1990s* To try something out; learn by experiment: *You have to bubble the pot, stand back and see what floats to the top*—Washington Post

bubbly *n by 1920* Champagne; sparkling wine

bubby (also **boobie, bubbe, bubbie, bubeleh**) (BU bee) *by 1940s* Darling; =BABY, SWEETIE, TOOTS •A term of affection with general application: *Bubby. . . it's Hollywood. A little mistake. . .* —Stan Cutler [fr Yiddish *bubele,* an endearing epithet, fr Hebrew *buba,* "doll," which is much like Latin *pupa,* "doll"]

bubkes or **bobkes** or **bupkes** (BOoB kəs, BOoP) *by 1940s* **1** *n* Something trivial; nothing; =BEANS: *We've gone from bubkes to big deals in a year*—People Weekly/ *They've waved bye-bye to the likes of Julius Irving. . . and gotten bubkes in return*—Village Voice/ *. . . paying bupkes for rent*—Lawrence Sanders **2** *adv* Absurdly little: *That it sold bubkes. . . may say just as much for his laziness and his hubris*—Village Voice [fr Yiddish, "goat dung," fr Russian, "beans"]

◁**bubs**▷ (BOoBZ) *n about 1900s* A woman's breasts; =BOOB

buck 1 *n by 1850s* A dollar **2** *n gambling by 1960s* A hundred dollars, esp as a bet **3** *n* =BUCK PRIVATE **4** *n 1920s hoboes* A Roman Catholic priest **5** *n by 1800* A young male Indian; Native American brave **6** *n by 1830s* A young black man **7** *n by middle 1700s* Any young man, esp a strong and spirited one; =BUCKO **8** *v by 1850s* To resist; defy; go up against •Often in the negative: *You can't buck the system: Life is a combination hard to buck, a proposition difficult to beat*—Wallace Irwin **9** *v by 1880s* To work for personal advancement; aspire eagerly; covet: *I'm bucking for that dealership* **10** *v fr WWII armed forces* To pass along a letter, memorandum, problem, etc, usu without taking action; =PASS THE BUCK: *Let's buck this one to the Committee on Hot Potatoes* [all senses ultimately fr *buck,* "male animal, usually horned"; the semantics are complex: for example, the first sense is said to be fr the fact that a *buck* deer's skin was more valuable than a female's skin; the other senses have most to do with male behavior of a butting and strutting sort] **See** BANG FOR THE BUCK, BIG BUCKS, THE BUCK STOPS HERE, FAST BUCK, PASS THE BUCK, SAWBUCK

bucked *adj by 1907* Pleased; proud; braced: *After that win they were really bucked with themselves*

bucket 1 *n by 1930s* A car, esp a big, old car **2** *n merchant marine & Navy by 1840s* A ship, esp an old and slow ship; =RUST BUCKET **3** *n Navy by WWII* A destroyer; =CAN, TIN CAN **4** *n by 1930s* The buttocks; rump: *Knocked him on his bucket* **5** *v by 1860s* To speed; =BARREL: *The kids were bucketing along. . .* —WNYC radio **6** *n 1920s basketball* The basketball net **7** *n 1920s basketball* A basketball goal: *He'll make ten buckets a game* **8** *n baseball by 1913* The rearmost part of the batter's box •The

source expression was "have his foot in the water-bucket": *. . . had his foot way back in the bucket/ Emily steps into the bucket when going for a pitch*—New York Times **9** *n Los Angeles police by 1990s* Jail: *These days, the Gray Bar Motel is a synonym for "the bucket," which means jail*—Los Angeles Times **See** BRAIN-BUCKET, someone CAN'T CARRY A TUNE IN A BUCKET, DROP one's BUCKETS, FOR CRYING OUT LOUD, GO TO HELL IN A HANDBASKET, GUTBUCKET, KICK THE BUCKET, LARD-BUCKET, RUST BUCKET, SLEAZE-BUCKET, SLIMEBAG

the bucket *n phr late 1800s* Jail; =the COOLER: *These days, the Grey Bar Motel is a synonym for "the bucket," which means jail*—Los Angeles Times

buckethead *n by 1950s* A stupid person; =BLOCKHEAD •Probably originally fr the blunt thickish head of a donkey or mule

bucket of blood *n phr by 1915* A nasty saloon, filthy restaurant, etc: *It was about what he figured: a real bucket of blood. White tiled walls slick with grease*—Lawrence Sanders

bucket of bolts *n phr by 1940s* An old car, airplane, etc; =JALOPY

bucket shop *by 1880* **1** *n phr* A place where very dubious stocks, commodities, real estate, etc, are sold, often by telephone solicitation **2** *modifier*: *A sleazy bucket-shop operation* [origin uncertain; *bucket,* "cheat, swindle," is attested in 1812, and may be the source; another account has illicit traders sending down by elevator for "another *bucketful*" of dupes]

buck general *n phr Army by 1940s* A brigadier general [modeled on *buck private* and *buck sergeant,* all three denoting a soldier of the lowest rank within the category]

buckle *v 1990s teenagers* To hit; =CLOBBER

buckled *adj 1990s teenagers* Ugly; =CRUSHED, PISS-UGLY

buckle down *by 1860s v phr* To set seriously to work; put slothful ease behind one

buckle your seat belts *v phr by 1970s* To get ready for trouble; take precautions; =BATTEN DOWN THE HATCHES [fr the pilot's order to passengers as an airplane approaches danger]

buck naked *n phr by 1920s* Entirely nude; =BARE-ASS: *My God, Sal, them women is buck naked in them magazines*

◀**buck nigger**▶ *n phr by 1830s* A black man, esp a strong young one

bucko *fr 1800s merchant marine* **1** *n* Fellow; friend; comrade; buddy; guy **2** *n* A mean and dangerous man: *The mate aboard the Pride of Hoboken was a notorious bucko* **3** *modifier*: *The bucko skipper was a nasty sadist*

buck private *n phr Army by 1870s* An Army private; soldier of the lowest rank [origin unknown]

buckra *n outdated black British about 1790* A white man, esp a poor and mean one; =CRACKER, PADDY [probably fr *mbakara,* "master," fr several West African languages]

bucks *See* BIG BUCKS, LIKE A MILLION BUCKS

buck sergeant *n phr* Army *fr* WWI An Army sergeant, wearing three stripes [origin unknown]

buck slip *n phr esp* WWII Army A note, memorandum, printed form, etc, that passes an item of business along to someone else [*fr* pass the buck]

the **buck stops here** *by* 1940s *sentence* This is the place where responsibility must be accepted; a decision must be made here ●Attributed usually to President Harry S Truman [The *buck* is the same as in *pass the buck*]

buck up *v phr* British schools *by* 1850s To cheer up; brace: . . . *immigrant life lets people down as soon as it bucks them up*—New York Times

buckyball *n* 1990 A buckminsterfullerene, a molecule shaped like a geodesic dome [*fr* R. Buckminster "Bucky" Fuller, who designed the geodesic dome]

bud[1] **1** *n by* 1850s Friend; fellow; =GUY ●Used only in direct address, often with hostile intent: *Okay, bud, that'll do* **2** *n by* 1930s A very close friend; =BUDDY, PAL: *Just be glad I'm your bud*—Cameron Crowe/ *She hid out with various buds and in runaway shelters. . .* —Sassy [*fr* buddy, a childish pronunciation of *brother*]

bud[2] *n* 1980s teenagers Marijuana: *There was no pain yet, just numbness, kind of like smoking bud*—Buzz [*fr* Budda, Buddha sticks, earlier terms for marijuana]

◀**buddahead** or **buddhahead**▶ *n* black & police *by* 1940s An Asian person

buddy *by* 1850 **1** *n* =BUD[1] **2** *n* A man's closest male friend; =PAL ●During WWI this term took on a particularly strong sentimental value **3** *n* A male's partner in work or sport **4** *v* =BUDDY UP [*fr* earlier *butty*, "partner, chum," said to be *fr* Romany; probably influenced by a childish pronunciation of *brother*] *See* ACE BOON COON, ASSHOLE BUDDY, GOOD BUDDY

buddy-buddy 1 *n* 1940s A close friend; =BUDDY **2** *n* 1960s A person who is too friendly; an importunate acquaintance **3** *v*: *Look at that guy buddy-buddying Joe* **4** *adj*: . . . *some are buddy-buddy with the players*—Whitey Herzog/ *He is not buddy-buddy. . . although he. . . insisted that the photographer take their pictures together*—Irwin Shaw

buddyroo *n* 1940s =BUDDY, PAL: *You should've seen the way they said hello. . . . Old buddyroos*—J D Salinger

buddy seat *n phr by* 1950s A passenger portion on a motorcycle seat *See* IN THE DRIVER'S SEAT

buddy store *n phr* Vietnam War Air Force & Navy A military refueling facility for aircraft

buddy up *by* 1930 *v phr* To share living quarters and conditions with; form a close association or two-person team: *These guys are alike; OK if they buddy up?/ Swimmers, buddy up*

buddy up to someone *v phr by* 1950s To become close and comradely with; ingratiate oneself with: *He's hanging out with Watson now and buddying up to him*—Edmund Wilson/ *Lawrence*

smarmily buddies up to these women—Washington Post

buff[1] *n* A devotee or enthusiast; hobbyist; =FAN, NUT: *I like to think I'm a people buff* [originally *fire buff*, because New York City volunteer firefighters about 1820 wore *buff*-colored, light brownish-yellow, coats; transferred to persons who like to watch fires, then to enthusiasts in general]

buff[2] *adj by* 1604 Naked [probably *fr* the pale yellowish color of the leather called buff, likened to skin] *See* IN THE BUFF

buff[3] **1** *adj* (also **buffed**, **buffed out**) 1980s teenagers Well-built; muscular; =HUNKY: . . . *looking mighty buff, by the way. . .* —Seventeen **2** *v* also **buff out** 1980s teenagers To do body-building; put on muscle; become brawnier: *Fudgie wondered if Tweezer had buffed out in San Quentin*—Buzz **3** (also **buff up**) 1990s Hollywood To be ingratiating and attentive, so as to keep on good terms: *Gotta go. Gotta buff*—New Yorker [probably *fr* buff, "polish, make attractive," a process originally done with a leather *buff stick*; the first sense may be derived *fr* buffalo, as an image of strength]

buff[4] or **buff up** *v* or *v phr* medical *by* 1970s To make a patient's chart look good, esp in preparing him or her for discharge [*fr* buff, "to polish"]

Buff *n* 1960s Air Force An HH53 long-range rescue helicopter, called a "big ugly fat fellow"

buffalo 1 *v* about 1870 To confuse someone purposely, esp in order to cheat or dupe **2** *v* about 1890 To intimidate; cow; =BULLDOZE ◀**3**▶ *n by* 1950s A heavy or fat woman; =COW ◀**4**▶ *n by* 1870s A black person ●This sense reflects that black troopers were called *buffalo soldiers* by the Indians

buffalo butt *n phr* students *by* 1970s A person with large buttocks; =FAT-ASS: *I mean "buffalo butt" could be a term of, uh, endearment*—Seventeen

buffalo chips *modifier by* 1840 Like the feces of a buffalo; =COWFLOP: . . . *give you that stretch valise buffalo chips thing*—Milwaukee Journal Sentinel

buffaloed *adj* about 1870 Baffled; puzzled: *I didn't think Pierre would be buffaloed by it*—Hugh Pentecost

◀**buff the helmet**▶ *v phr* 1990s black To fondle one's penis; masturbate

◀**bufu**▶ (BOO foo) *n* 1980s students A male homosexual; sodomite; =BUGGER [*fr* butt-fucker]

bug[1] **1** *n* British *by* 1642 Any insect whatever ●Now US only **2** *n by* 1919 Any bacterium, microbe, virus, etc: *Syph is caused by a bug* **3** *n by* 1960s Any upper-respiratory or flulike complaint, esp one that is somewhat prevalent: *There's a bug going around* **4** *n by* 1870s Any fault or defect in a machine, plans, system, etc: *You've got to get the bugs out of the program before trying to run it on the computer* **5** *n* early 1800s circus & carnival Any small, cheap item sold by a vendor or huckster **6** *n* poker *by* 1940s A joker or a wild card **7** *n* 1960s teenagers A girl: *Boys prowl for "bugs"*—Time **8** *n* 1920s radio operators A semiautomatic or automatic radiotelegraph key used for fast sending **9** *n* print *shop by 1950s* Any small symbol or label, such as a copyright or trademark symbol **10** *n horse-racing by 1940s* An asterisk printed beside the weight a horse is to carry, showing that a five-pound decrease has been granted because the jockey is an apprentice **11** *n horse-racing by 1940s* An apprentice jockey who has ridden his or her maiden race during the current year or has not yet won his or her fortieth race **12** *n horse-racing by 1940s* A horse that has never won a race; =MAIDEN **13** *n 1950s hot rodders* A hot rod **14** *n by 1919* A small foreign car, esp the Volkswagen beetle **15** *n 1960s astronautics* A small two-person lunar excursion vehicle **16** *n by 1841* An enthusiast; devotee; hobbyist; =FAN, NUT: *Momma's a football bug* **17** *n about 1900* A compelling idea or interest: *His bug is surf-casting* **18** *n by 1880s* An insane person; =NUT: *Only a bug is strong enough for that*—Eugene O'Neill **19** *n prison fr 1930s* An irrational, touchy mood; bad mood **20** *n prison by 1950s* A psychiatrist **21** *v prison by 1950s* To do a psychiatric evaluation; pronounce one insane **22** *v 1940s jazz musicians* To irritate or anger someone; pester or harry someone: *I suspected something was bugging her*—Louis Armstrong **23** *n underworld about 1925* A confidential message or signal; confidential information **24** *n 1920s underworld* A burglar alarm **25** *v*: *They've got that safe bugged eight ways* **26** *v about 1920* To prepare a room or other place for electronic surveillance by installing hidden microphones; equip for electronic eavesdropping: *to bug a room/ bug the Secretary's telephone* **27** *n by 1940s*: *The team planted bugs in about six flowerpots* [the sense "irritate, pester" may be a shortening of black English *humbug,* attested in such uses as "Him wife de humbug him too much"; *humbug* itself, attested in English fr the mid–18th century, is apparently found in and may derive fr Pacific Pidgin English and West African Pidgin English]

See BIG BUG, FIREBUG, HAVE A BUG UP one's ASS, JITTERBUG, LITTERBUG, PUT A BUG IN someone's EAR, SHUTTERBUG

bug² *dialect by 1870s* (also **bug out**) To protrude; bulge: *Her eyes bugged out when she saw the bill* [fr humorous or dialectal pronunciation of *bulge*]

-bug *combining word by 1920s* A devotee or energetic practitioner of what is indicated: *firebug/ money-bug/ hockey bug*

bugaboo *n by 1820s* Something that frightens or defeats one; bugbear; hobgoblin; bogy [probably fr *Bugibu,* a demon cited in the Old French poem *Aliscans,* of 1141]

bugaloo *See* BOOGALOO

bug boy (or **rider**) *n phr horse-racing by 1940s* An apprentice jockey [fr the fact that an asterisk, or *bug,* appears beside their names in racing programs, showing that the horses are carrying reduced weight]

bug doctor *n phr prison by 1950s* A psychologist or psychiatrist; =SHRINK

bugeyed 1 *adj* Having protruding eyeballs; exophthalmic; =POPEYED **2** *adj* Startled; astonished:

. . . gets very bugeyed about details of a failed real estate development—Mike Royko [fr humorous or dialectal pronunciation of *bulge*]

◀**bug-fucker**▶ *n by 1970s* A man with a tiny penis

bugged *adj by 1919* Fitted with a concealed microphone or otherwise equipped for electronic surveillance: *. . . do-it-yourself sex manuals, bugged phones*—WH Auden

bugged up *adj phr black by 1940s* Confused; flustered; upset

bugger¹ (BUH gər) *n by 1950s* A person who bugs, esp one who installs electronic surveillance devices

bugger² (BUH gər, Bŏŏ-, Bōō-) **1** *n by 1719* A despicable man; =ASSHOLE, JERK **2** *n by 1850s* Fellow; man; child; thing ●Used affectionately: *What have you been up to, you old bugger?/ Ain't he a cute little bugger?* **3** *n by 1940s* An object, esp something admired, wondered at or scorned; =FUCKER, SUCKER: *. . . the little buggers would outlast anything humans threw at them and dance on our graves*—New Yorker ◁**4**▷ *n by 1550s* A male with a taste for anal intercourse; sodomite ◁**5**▷ *v by 1590s* To do anal intercourse or sodomy; sodomize; =BUNGHOLE: *The proprietor. . . wins the right to bugger him*—Newsweek/ *. . . who immediately announced that the Reverend Mr. Alger had been "buggering" him*—Village Voice **6** *v* (also **booger up, bugger up**) *cowboys about 1880s* To spoil; ruin; confuse; abuse; impair; =BOLLIX UP: *Between them they buggered up the mimeo machine: The practice of how you bugger these numbers of US-Soviet armaments*—Village Voice **7** *n 1930s* An arduous, painful or difficult thing; =BITCH

bugger³ or **booger** or **boogie** (BUH gər, Bŏŏ-, Bōō-) *n* A piece of solid mucus from the nose

buggered *adj by 1850s* Damned; confounded; =FUCKED: *. . . I'm buggered if I can see anything busted on that truck*—Carsten Stroud

buggerlugs *n Canadian by 1990s* An ineffectual or contemptible person; =JERK, WIMP

bugger off *v phr British by 1920s* To leave; depart; =FUCK OFF ●Often a contemptuous command; rare in US, although adopted by the Air Force in the Korean War: *. . . pay no attention to my piteous Don'ts, but bugger off quickly*—W H Auden

bugging or **buggin'** *n 1990s teenagers* Irrational behavior; overreacting: *buggin'. . . Irritated, perturbed. . . Flipping out*—Macon Telegraph

bugging out *n phr 1990s black teenagers* Male sexual response to attractive females; protrusion of the trousers

buggy¹ 1 *n 1890s railroad* A caboose **2** *n about 1925* A car, esp an old and rickety one; =HEAP, JALOPY: *I wouldn't exactly call my Maserati a buggy See* BUZZ-BUGGY, HELL BUGGY, HORSE-AND-BUGGY, IRISH BUGGY, STRUGGLE-BUGGY

buggy² *adj about 1900* Crazy; =BUGHOUSE, NUTS

buggy whip 1 *n phr by 1940s* A long radio antenna on a car **2** *modifier: a buggy-whip antenna* **3** *adj by 1970s* Old-fashioned; outmoded; antique; =OLD-TIMEY: *. . . still manages to epitomize buggy-*

whip thinking in an increasingly sophisticated high-tech communications world—Village Voice

bughouse 1 *n about 1900* An insane asylum: *Who cares whether you're free or locked in a bughouse?*—Calder Willingham **2** *adj by 1895* Crazy; =NUTS: *He's a bughouse pimp*—William Kennedy/ *The local constabulary haul the bughouse blighter off to prison*—Washington Post
See GO BUGHOUSE

bug-hunter *n 1880s* An entomologist; naturalist; lepidopterist; =BUGOLOGIST

bugjuice 1 *n by 1860s* Liquor, esp inferior whiskey; =ROTGUT **2** *n by 1950s* A synthetic and highly colored soft drink [fr resemblance to the *juice* secreted by grasshoppers]

bugle *n by 1865* The nose; =BEAK, SCHNOZZ

bug money *n phr by 1990s* Money bet on a policy operation: *A person that. . . takes illegal bug (numbers) money. . .* —Macon Telegraph

bug off *v phr by 1950s* To leave; depart ●Often an irritated command: *I'm done with you, so bug off* [perhaps fr *bugger off*; perhaps fr early–19th-century US **bulge** "to rush, dash"]

bugologist *n by 1870s* An entomologist

bugology *n by 1840s* Entomology

bugout *fr Korean War Army* **1** *n* A person who usually withdraws and evades; a slacker **2** *n* A military retreat **3** *modifier*: *a bugout plan*

bug out[1] *v phr by 1880s* To bulge; protrude: *His eyes bugged out like a frog's* [fr bulge]

bug out[2] **1** *v phr fr Korean War Army* To retreat; turn one's back and run **2** *v phr 1950s teenagers & hot rodders* To leave rapidly, esp to drive away in a hurry **3** *v phr 1980s students* To behave crazily; =FREAK OUT

bugs or **bugsy** *adj about 1900* Crazy; =NUTS: *The idea is so bugs it might work/ Don't act bugsy*
See STIR-CRAZY

bug someone **up** *v phr prison by 1950* To agitate someone; upset someone

build 1 *n by 1850s* One's physique, esp one's figure or shape; =BOD: *a husky build/ sexy build* **2** *n theater by 1950s* A show whose earnings continue to increase: *The revue was a build once word-of-mouth took hold* **3** *v underworld by 1920s* To prepare someone for swindling, extortion, etc; =SET someone UP **4** *n*: *It's been a long build, but we can make our move now* [first sense perhaps influenced by earlier *build*, "the look and shape of tailored clothing"]

build a collar *v phr police by 1950s* To gather evidence for an arrest

build a fire under someone *v phr by 1950s* To encourage and incite someone forcibly: *Let's get those people moving if we have to build a fire under them*

builder-upper *n 1930s* Anything or anyone that strengthens someone or increases someone's confidence

buildup 1 *n 1920s* Publicity and other provisions for introducing a new product, entertainer, etc: *the buildup for a concert* **2** *n by 1940s* The careful preparation of a potential customer or victim

built *adj* Physically well-developed, esp in a sexually attractive way; =HUNKY, STACKED: *She wasn't especially smart, but she was built*

◁**built like a brick shithouse** (or **chickenhouse**)▷ *by 1940s adj phr* Very solidly and well constructed; =BUILT, HUNKY ●Said usually of a woman with a sturdy and attractive body, esp with large breasts

bulb *n by 1960s* =DIM BULB

bulge 1 *n by 1840s* An advantage; a lead: *running up a 20–0 bulge*—New York Daily News/ *. . . the Californians fashioned a two-run bulge of their own*—Milwaukee Journal **2** *n by 1940s* A usu fatty surplus on the waist, buttocks, etc; =SPARE TIRE
See BATTLE OF THE BULGE

bull 1 *n by 1850s* A peace officer of any kind, esp a uniformed police officer ●London police constables were called *bull-dogs* by 1710 **2** *n circus by 1920s* An elephant, of either sex **3** *n poker by 1940s* An ace ●Short for *bullet* **4** *n by 1930s* Bull Durham™, a very popular brand of tobacco for rolling cigarettes **5** *n railroad by 1880s* A locomotive **6** *n loggers & cowboys by 1940s* The chief; head man; =BOSS, BULL OF THE WOODS **7** *n early 1700s stock market* A dealer who favors higher prices and quicker selling **8** *modifier*: *a bull market* **9** *n 1960s* =BOONDAGGER, BULLDAGGER **10** *n about 1900* =BULLSHIT **11** *v*: *We were sitting around bulling/ He was bulling about his enormous talent*
See ALL THAT KIND OF CRAP, BULL OF THE WOODS, BULL SESSION, BULLWORK, COCK-AND-BULL STORY, FULL OF SHIT, HARNESS BULL, SHOOT THE BULL, SLING IT, THROW THE BULL, YARD BULL

◁**bull bitch**▷ *n phr by 1960s* A woman with masculine traits; virago; =BULLDYKE

bull cook *n phr early 1900s cowboys and loggers* A male cook

bulldagger *n black by 1920s* A lesbian, esp a tough and aggressive one; =BOONDAGGER, BULLDYKE: *That's a bull-dagger, baby*—Claude Brown/ *. . . passing time with another girl and a bull-dagger*—Joseph Wambaugh

bulldog 1 *n newspaper office by 1920s* The earliest daily edition of a newspaper **2** *modifier*: *the bulldog edition* **3** *v gambling by 1950s* To advertise horse-race winners falsely; =DYNAMITE **4** *v fr early 1800s & esp cowboys* To attack like a bulldog, esp to wrestle a steer to the ground by the horns **5** *n 1880s police & underworld* A snub-nosed revolver

bulldoze *v 1870s* To intimidate; overcome by force ●Early use of the term is connected with Southern politics of the Reconstruction period, and describes the intimidation of black men who wished to vote: *to bulldoze employees* [fr *bulldose*, "to beat, flog with a strip of leather," perhaps fr the notion of the *dose* of force needed to cow a *bull*]

bulldozer 1 *n 1870s* A person who bulldozes **2** *n about 1880s* A revolver

bulldyke *n 1920s black* A lesbian, esp an aggressive one; =BOONDAGGER, BULLDAGGER, DYKE

bullet 1 *n* card games by 1807 An ace **2** *n* underworld about 1900 Money; dollars **3** *n* WWII aircraft workers A rivet **4** *n* by 1940s Anything thrown or hit so as to travel very fast, esp a baseball: *He's throwing bullets out there* **5** *n* 1970s recording industry A record rising very fast on the popularity charts **6** *v*: . . . *currently bulleting up the charts*—Rolling Stone **7** *n* police by 1990s A one-year prison sentence; =BOFFO
See BITE THE BULLET

bullet bait *n phr* WWII armed forces Soldiers, esp young novice soldiers; =CANNON FODDER

bullets *early 1900s prison & Navy* **1** *n* Beans **2** *n* Peas, esp chickpeas and cowpeas
See SHIT BULLETS, SWEAT BULLETS

bullfest *n* 1920s students =BULL SESSION

bull fiddle *n phr* 1870s The double bass; bass fiddle

bullfrog *n* truckers by 1960s A male hitchhiker

bullgine *n* by 1840s A locomotive

bullhead *n* about 1850 A stupid, obstinate person

bullheaded *adj* by 1818 Obstinate

bullhockey *n* by 1960s =BULLSHIT ●Perhaps earlier, since *hockey, hawky,* "shit," is attested as a dialect verb in 1902

bullhorn *n* WWII Navy An electronic megaphone; loud hailer

bullish 1 *adj* stock market by 1880s Favoring and exhibiting high prices and relatively quick turnover: *a bullish market/ bullish advice* **2** *adj* Showing a positive and hopeful attitude; encouraging ●Often used with "on" or "about": *She tends to be bullish about our prospects/ He's quite bullish on the new restaurant*

bull of the woods 1 *n phr* 1920s loggers & truckers The foreman or chief; =BOSS **2** *n phr* by 1940s Any chief or supervisor: *Oakes is bull of the woods in the proofroom* [perhaps because the *Bull of the Woods* was the first locomotive used in logging, in 1852]

bullpen 1 *n* by 1880s A cell or secure area where prisoners are kept temporarily; =TANK: *We're in the bullpen waiting to go to court* **2** *n* about 1900 A military stockade; military prison **3** *n* baseball by 1915 A usu enclosed area where pitchers practice and warm up: *The bullpen's getting active now* **4** *n* baseball The relief pitching staff of a baseball team: *They've got starters but no bullpen* **5** *n* loggers about 1930 A bunkhouse **6** *n* 1940s students A living room, lounge, etc, where a girl's escorts and suitors are appraised by friends and family [baseball sense perhaps fr a boys' game called *bullpen*, attested fr 1857, in which opponents lined up in a rectangle and threw balls at each other; similarly, the pitchers in the bullpen are vulnerable to being hit by thrown and hit balls]

bullrag 1 *n* by 1970s Bovine excrement; =BULLSHIT, COWFLOP: . . . *didn't mean bullrag in a pasture to him*—Stephen King **2** *v* also **bullyrag** first form 1880s; second form 1820s To intimidate; domineer over; tease [second sense origin unknown; earlier

forms included *balrag, ballarag, ballyrag,* of obscure origin]

bull session *n phr* college students about 1920 A discussion, esp one among good companions passing time idly but investigating important topics [perhaps influenced by *bull,* "discuss, visit another student to pass the time," attested as college slang by 1850]

bull's-eye *interj* An exclamation of admiration over a perfect answer, guess, solution, etc; =BINGO
See HIT THE NAIL ON THE HEAD

bullshine *n* by 1970s Nonsense; pretentious talk; =BULLSHIT: . . . *the perpetual motion, nonstop, all-American bullshine machine*—Washington Post [a euphemism for *bullshit*]

◁**bullshit**▷ **1** *n* by 1915 Nonsense; pretentious talk; bold and deceitful absurdities; =BALONEY: *I'm afraid your theory is chiefly bullshit* **2** *v* by 1942 *He tried to bullshit his way out of it* **3** *interj* An exclamation of disbelief, derision, and contempt in retort to some proposition

◁**bullshit artist**▷ *n phr* by 1940s A person who habitually and effectively exaggerates, cajoles, seduces verbally, etc: . . . *seen as a talented maverick. "She's not a bullshit artist"*—New Yorker

◁**bullshitter**▷ *n* by 1930s Someone who bullshits

bullshooter *n* A person given to exaggeration, boasting, or pompous inanity [fr *shoot the bull,* and a euphemism for *bullshitter*]

bullsmoke *n* by 1990s =BULLSHIT ●Attributed to the football coach Vince Lombardi, who died in 1970: *It's all blocking and tackling. Everything else is bullsmoke*—Milwaukee Journal

bullwork *n* by 1970s Tedious work requiring little thought or skill; =DONKEYWORK, GRUNT WORK, SCUT: . . . *sees computers taking over only the bullwork of secretaries*—Westworld

bully 1 *adj* by 1840s Excellent; good **2** *interj* by 1780s: *Bully for you!* **3** *n* railroad about 1900 A track worker; =GANDY DANCER [first two senses fr *bully,* "a beloved person, darling," of obscure origin, attested fr 1538. *Bully,* "worthy, admirable," used of persons, is attested in 1681]

bully pulpit *modifier* late 1980s Using high office or fame as a splendid standpoint for one's teaching or preaching: *At the least, they hoped that his "bully pulpit" approach would help rally public support*—New York Times service/ *Theodore Roosevelt, rejoicing in the president's bully pulpit, drowned out every other voice in the United States*—New Republic/ *Madonna has used her bully pulpit to preach scantily clad homilies on bigotry, abortion, civic duty, power, death, and safe sex*—Time [Said to have been originated by Theodore Roosevelt, and lately popularized by Ross Perot]

bully up *v phr* by 1970s To press one's way forward; =BELLY UP: *Sharkey. . . was bullying up to the bar*—George Warren [probably fr *belly up*]

bum[1] **1** *n* by 1860s A person who seldom works, seldom stays in one place, and survives by begging and petty theft; drifter; vagrant; hobo **2** *v* by 1860s To live as a tramp, drifter, etc: *It wasn't easy bumming*

that winter/ He bummed for a couple of years, then got a job **3** *v* by 1850s To beg or borrow; cadge: A schooner can be grafted. . . if you're fierce at bumming—Wallace Irwin **4** *v* (also **bum** one's **way, bum a ride**) by 1920s To hitchhike: They bummed all the way to Alaska **5** *adj* 1850s Inferior; defective; =LOUSY: That's a real bum notion you have there **6** *n* by 1930 A promiscuous woman, esp a cheap prostitute: . . . picking up bums in public dance halls—James T Farrell **7** *n* about 1920 Any male who is disliked by the speaker, esp for lack of energy, direction, or talent •Often used of inept or despised athletes: The bum strikes out three times in a row **8** *n* 1950s A person who lives or tries to live by his or her sports talent and charm, usu without being genuinely professional: Developed by volleyball bums who hated the regimentation of the indoor game. . . —Buzz **9** *n* about 1930 An inferior animal, breed, racehorse, etc **10** *n* by 1950s Anything inferior or ineffectual: Money is a bum, a no-good bum—Hal Boyle **11** *adj* by 1859: I told a bum story first—James M Cain/ . . . he just didn't want me to think he had a car with a bum clutch—Joseph Wambaugh **12** *v* by 1960s To deceive; victimize: . . . anyone who's seen this halfbaked ode to mixed marital relations realizes that the star has been bummed into a bit role—Us **13** *v* computer To improve something, esp by exploiting its full potential or rearranging its parts: I bummed the whole program to show up all possible mistakes **14** *v* (also **bum out**) by 1960s To become depressed, discouraged, or irritated: You don't want to pull off the information superhighway because you're already. . . dialed into an on-line service. Don't bum—Macon Telegraph [probably fr German Bummler, "loafer"]
See BEACH BUM, CRUMB-BUN, SKID ROW BUM, STEW-BUM, STUMBLEBUM

bum² *n* late 1300s The buttocks or anus; =ASS •More common in British usage: . . . after getting a shot of something in her bum—Philadelphia [fr Middle English "anus"]

bum around *v phr* by 1940s To go about idly; loaf: I just bummed around last summer

bumble-bee See KNEE-HIGH TO A GRASSHOPPER

bumblepuppy 1930s cardplayers **1** *n* A bridge game played haphazardly **2** *n* An indifferent or erratic player [fr a late–1800s British term for inexpert whist]

bumf *n* 1880 British schoolboys Paper; paperwork; toilet paper •Chiefly British: Most of the bumf he handles himself—Lawrence Sanders [fr bum fodder]

◁**bum fodder**▷ *n phr* by 1650s Toilet paper or other material of the same use •Later, for obvious reasons, this became a term for a newspaper or magazine

◀**bumfuck**▶ *v* by 1860s =ASSFUCK

◀**Bumfuck, Egypt**▶ (also **East Bumfuck**) 1970s Army **1** *n phr* A very distant and remote place; dead-end **2** *n phr* The destination of or a point along a long and circuitous march

bummed or **bummed out** *adj* or *adj phr* 1960s In a bad mood; dejected; depressed: I'm heavily bummed. . . if I've realigned anybody's karma—Playboy/ . . . belonging to the most bummed-out generation—Chicago [fr narcotics and teenager senses of bummer]

bummer 1 *n* by 1855 A bum: . . . an old bummer named Rumson—A J Lerner **2** *n* 1960s narcotics An unpleasant or depressing experience with a narcotic, esp with LSD; =BAD TRIP **3** *modifier*: Zonk is rushed to the Woodstock bummer tent—Gary Trudeau **4** *n* 1960s counterculture Any bad experience or occasion; bad situation or place: May 17—Trip was a bummer. Instead of being off by ourselves, we met another couple—Erma Bombeck **5** *interj* An exclamation of dismay: Ms. Riner is too docile, too scared, too unsexy for the role, and—bummer!—there seems to be a real possibility that she's innocent—Nation [first sense probably fr German Bummler, "loafer"]

bum someone **out** *v phr* 1960s To depress; discourage; irritate: At a fraternity. . . the things you observe totally bum you out—Esquire/ It bums the fuck out of me sometimes—Rolling Stone

bum-out *n* 1940s prison & Army An assignment to easy work

bump 1 *v* about 1915 To discharge; dismiss; =FIRE: They bumped him for insubordination **2** *v* railroad about 1860 To take away one person's status in order to accommodate someone of greater importance or seniority: A person is bumped by someone with a larger number of retention points—Jane Eads **3** *v* by 1940s To cancel a reserved seat on an airline, bus, etc, because the vehicle has been oversold: To be bumped. . . means to be put off a flight because too many seats have been sold—Wall Street Journal **4** *v* by 1950s To displace a sports opponent by defeat: The Indians bumped the Tigers out of third place **5** *v* by 1910 To kill; =BUMP OFF **6** *v* by 1930s To make pregnant; =KNOCK someone UP: She had to blame someone for bumping her—Len Yinberg **7** *v* 1980s students To do the sex act with or to **8** *v* by 1930s To promote: He got bumped to assistant manager **9** *n* by 1930s: I see old Pipkin has got the bump to full professor—Morris Bishop **10** *v* 1930s poker To raise a bet **11** *v* show business by 1940s In dancing, esp in striptease, to thrust the pelvis forward and up •Nearly always in combination with grind **12** *n*: She unreeled about fifty bumps in dazzling staccato **13** *n* by 1980s A drink; =SLUG: They go out. . . and have a bump of whiskey—Garrison Keillor **14** *n* 1980s teenagers A party
See HUMP AND BUMP, LIKE A BUMP ON A LOG

the **bump** *n phr* about 1920 Murder; assassination; =BUMPOFF

bump along *v phr* by 1960s To progress haltingly: The interest rate has been bumping along—New York Times

bump and grind 1 by 1940s *v phr* To thrust out and rotate the pelvis in dancing, esp the striptease; an imitation of the sex act: *She bumped and ground faster as the bass drum upped its tempo* **2** *v phr* hockey by 1980s To play roughly; stress the physical game rather than strategy: *We have to bump and grind. That's how the puck went in for us*—Milwaukee Journal **3** *n phr* by early 1990s The wearing tedium of life and work; =RAT RACE: *. . . the ordinary bump and grind we call civilization*—Milwaukee Journal/ *Let us get you through the bump and grind tomorrow*—Denver radio ad

bump belly *v phr* by 1990s To oppose; confront; =GO UP AGAINST: *And while bumping belly with Bob Dole may prove tough. . .* —Milwaukee Journal

bumpdrafting *n* car racing by 1990s In a race, pushing the car ahead, in order to increase speed: *Bumpdrafting, as the name implies, involves actually pushing the car in front*—Milwaukee Journal

bumper[1] *n* show business by 1950s A striptease dancer or other erotic dancer

bumper[2] *n* 1990s A black upwardly mobile person

bumper music *n phr* radio by 1990s Music played before a radio show esp a talk show [probably by analogy with the *bumper* of a car]

bumper-thumper *n* 1990s A minor car accident; =BANGERS AND MASH, FENDER-BENDER

bump fuzz *v phr* by 1990s To do the sex act; =BOFF, SCREW: *Little did he know, all I wanted was to bump fuzz*—Details

bump one's **gums** *See* BAT one's GUMS

bumping *adj* 1980s students Excellent; wonderful; =COOL, RAD: *. . . with kickin' taste and bumpin' packaging. (That means it tastes good and looks good)*—Macon Telegraph

bump into someone *v phr* by 1880s To meet someone unexpectedly: *Guess who I bumped into downtown*

bumpman 1 *n* 1920s underworld A professional killer; =HIT MAN **2** *n* by 1930s A pickpocket

bumpoff *n* 1920s underworld A killing; murder; assassination; =HIT

bump someone **off** *v phr* underworld by 1908 To kill, esp to murder; =WHACK

bump on a log *See* LIKE A BUMP ON A LOG

bumps *See* DUCK BUMPS, GOOSE BUMPS

bumpy *See* GOOSE-BUMPY

bump zone *n phr* football by 1990s A five-yard space downfield from the line of scrimmage, within which a wide receiver can be bumped once, and beyond which he may not be bumped at all: *. . . the '94 rules strictly enforcing the bump zone*—Milwaukee Journal

bum rap 1 *n phr* underworld by 1920s An erroneous conviction or sentence **2** *v*: *he had been bum-rapped*—Stephen King **3** *n phr* by 1980s Any unjustified condemnation: *Reagan said, "Nancy's taken a bit of a bum rap on that buying White House china"*—Newsweek **4** *v*: *the Philadelphia Navy Yard has been bum-rapped*—Philadelphia

bum-rush *v* To eject someone, esp from a restaurant or other public place: *Your posse bumrushed Tatum*—Village Voice

the **bum's rush** early 1920s **1** *n phr* The ejection of a person by force, esp from a public place: *Dey gimme de bum's rush*—Eugene O'Neill/ *You want us to give 'em the bum's rush?*—Hugh Pentecost **2** *n phr* Any discourteous or summary dismissal: *Those not in sympathy with the strike got the bum's rush*—Westbrook Pegler / *. . . with Stanfill telling the press that she had given her husband "the bum's rush"*—Washington Post

bum steer *n phr* by 1924 Erroneous guidance or advice

bum trip *See* BAD TRIP

bun 1 *n* about 1900 A state of drunkenness; alcoholic exhilaration: *A bun is a light jag*—R Connell **2** *n* by 1530s The buttocks; =BUM ●Originally "the tail of a hare, scut" first seen applied to persons in Scottish poetry **3** *n* by 1970s A single buttock; =CHEEK: *. . . a boil on my left bun*

See CHEESE BUN, CRUMB-BUN, HAVE A BUN IN THE OVEN, HAVE A BUN ON

bun-buster *n* by 1970s A very hard task or job; =BALL-BUSTER: *This job is a bun-buster*—People Weekly

bunch 1 *n* by early 1600s A group of people **2** *n* by 1902 A particular group or set, family, etc: *I like my bunch, but yours is elitist* **3** *n* by 1950s =MOB **4** *n* Money, esp a large sum; =BUNDLE: *He must have paid a bunch for that mink*

a **bunch** *adv phr* by 1980s Very much; a lot; =HEAPS: *. . . your CIC'll be a bunch happier this way*—Stan Cutler

buncher *n* 1990s A dognapper who steals dogs in quantity for sale to research laboratories or pet shops: *Organizations that help dog owners. . . are often thwarted by teams of thieves called "bunchers"*—Milwaukee Journal

bunch of fives *n phr* by 1825 A fist

bunco or **bunko 1** *v* by 1875 To swindle; defraud; =FLIMFLAM: *He was buncoed out of his seat in the House*—Greenough and Kittredge **2** *n* (also **bunco game**) by 1872 A swindle; =CON GAME, SCAM **3** by 1872 *modifier*: *a bunco scheme/ the police bunco squad* [said to be fr *Banco*, the name given in the 1850s by a crooked US gambler to the older game "Eight-Dice Cloth"; *Banco* was probably based on Spanish *banca*, a card game similar to monte]

bunco (or **bunko**) **artist** *n phr* by 1901 A professional swindler; =CON MAN: *Sleep, like a bunco artist, rubbed it in*—Wallace Irwin/ *The other fellow is, in most instances, a bunko artist*—Time

buncombe *See* BUNK

bunco-steerer *n phr* by 1875 An accomplice in a confidence game, esp one who makes the first contact with the victim; =SHILL: *became entangled with a bunco-steerer*—Theodore Dreiser

bundle 1 *n* by 1905 A large amount of money ●Originally the loot from a robbery: *Can the Pentagon Save a Bundle?*—New York Times/ *He's dropped a bundle that way*—W T Tyler **2** *n* about

1930 An attractive woman •This term has improved: In the early 1800s it designated a camp-follower, then a fat woman: *I saw Charley yesterday with this cute bundle* **3** *n 1960s* narcotics Twenty-five $5 packets of a narcotic, esp marijuana or cocaine **4** *v 1980s* To gather up small political contributions into a large and influential amount: *His preferred strategy is a controversial practice known as bundling, which. . . means rounding up contributions from friends and other. . .* —Common Cause/ *. . . the PAC bundles all the checks for presentation to the individual campaigns*—Nation
See DROP A BUNDLE

bungee (BUN jee)**1** *n late 1800s* British schoolboys Rubber; a rubber eraser **2** *modifier*: *bungee cord/ bungee jump* [origin unknown]

◁**bung fodder**▷ *n phr* Toilet paper; =BUM FODDER

◁**bunghole**▷ **1** *n by 1600s* The anus **2** *v by 1940s* To do anal intercourse; =BUGGER

bung up *v* or *v phr by 1830s* To dent; damage; bruise; =BANG: *He bunged up the left fender pretty good/ My knee is all bunged up* [Used in the 1500s to mean "close the eyes or mouth with a blow, as the *bung* of a barrel is closed"]

bunk 1 *n about 1900* Nonsense; pretentious talk; =BALONEY, BULLSHIT **2** *v by 1870s* To cheat; defraud; =BUNCO: *. . . couldn't possibly have done a better job of bunking the American people*— Chicago Tribune [fr the explanation by a 1800s politician that his extraordinary statements were meant only for his constituents in *Buncombe* County, North Carolina]

Bunker *See* ARCHIE BUNKER

bunker mentality *n phr 1980s* A sense of impending doom, stimulating the innermost defenses [Probably recalling the last days and delusions of Hitler in his Berlin *bunker*]

bunk fatigue (or habit) *n phr* WWII armed forces A period of sleep or rest in bed; =BLANKET DRILL, SACK TIME

bunk flying *n phr* WWII Army Air Forces Talk, esp dramatic and exaggerated talk, about one's flying

bunkie *n* students fr WWII armed forces A roommate or bunkmate; a close friend: *OK, bunkies, let's raise our right hands and make a solemn pledge*— Milwaukee Journal

bunk lizard *n phr* WWII armed forces fr Navy A habitual shirker; =GOLDBRICK, GOOF-OFF

bunko *See* BUNCO

bunkum or **buncombe** *n by 1840s* =BUNK

bunned *adj by 1908* Drunk

bunny 1 *n early 1900s* students Welsh rabbit **2** *n 1920s* A habitually puzzled or victimized person: *She is always criticizing some poor bunny*—Sinclair Lewis **3** *n by early 1600s* Any young woman, esp a pert and attractive one **4** *n 1960s* A young woman who associates with the men in some exciting, daring, or otherwise glamorous activity, sometimes as a participant; =GROUPIE: *. . . to eliminate any chance that newsroom chauvinists could tag her as an electronic bunny*—Time ◁**5**▷ *n* homosexuals by

1950s A prostitute who serves his or her own sex **6** *n* basketball by 1970s A layup shot
See BEACH BUNNY, CUDDLE-BUNNY, DUMB BUNNY, DUST KITTY, GUNBUNNY, JUNGLE-BUNNY, PLAY SNUGGLE-BUNNIES, QUICK LIKE A BUNNY, SEX KITTEN, SKI BUNNY

bunny (or rabbit) food *n phr by 1936* Lettuce, salad, green vegetables, etc [*Bunny grub* is attested in British schoolboy use by 1890]

◀**bunny fuck**▶ *by 1960s* **1** *n phr* A very quick sex act; =QUICKIE **2** *v*: *They pulled beside the road and bunny-fucked* **3** *v* To stall; waste time; =FUCK THE DOG: *Quit bunny-fucking and let's move*

bunny hill *n phr by 1980s* The beginners' slope at a ski resort: *The people on the bunny hill are having just as much fun as those on the moguls*— Milwaukee Journal

bunny suit *n phr 1960s* A protective flight suit, sanitary coveralls, or other raiment of astronauts, nuclear workers, etc

buns *n by 1960s* The buttocks, esp male buttocks: *I'll grab Ron's or Alan's buns sometimes and they're firm and hard*—Playboy [*Bun*, "buttocks," is found in the 1500s, based on an early sense, "the tail of a hare"; this later use is probably not related, being rather based on the full, round shape of an eating bun; note that *biscuit* and *crumpet* exemplify this baked-goods analogy in other milieux]

one's **buns off** *adv phr 1970s* Very energetically; with maximum effort; =TO THE MAX: *You'll be playing your buns off with your left hand*—Toronto Life
See one's ASS OFF, BUST one's ASS, WORK one's ASS OFF

bun-struggle *n by 1890* A formal tea

buppie *n 1980s* A black yuppie: *. . . two proto-buppies slide instantly into Coney Island life*—Nation

'burb *1970s* **1** *n* A suburb: *. . . the 'burbs my pet name for LA-Boston-Frisco*—Village Voice/ *If he chooses to bolt to the 'burbs that's his business*— Milwaukee Journal **2** *mofifier*: *. . . starring Teri Garr and Robert Urich as burbs newcomers. . .* — Entertainment Weekly

burbed out *adj phr 1970s* teenagers Middle-class; bourgeois; pretentious: *. . . non-stop wisecracks about burbed-out or boojy students*—Richard Price

burg *n 1840s* theater A city; town; village •Usu expresses contempt: *. . . stuck two days in this ghastly burg*

-burger *combining word 1930s* A sandwich made with cooked portions of what is indicated: *beefburger/ cheeseburger/ snakeburger* [The definition does not apply to *hamburger*, the source of the term. The suffix was probably first used by the comic-strip artist E C Segar, who coined *goonburger* in the middle 1930s]

burger-flip *1990s* **1** *v* To work at a fast-food restaurant **2** *v* To work for low and insufficient wages: *. . . the average Proctor worker has a family, which a burger-flipping job won't feed*

burger-flipper *n 1990s* A person who burger-flips: *. . . pay himself wages that could be topped by a burger-flipper at McDonald's*—New York Times

burglar *n* 1920s A person who cheats or victimizes others: *Don't shop there, he's a burglar*
See GUT-BURGLAR

burgle *v* by 1870 To break into a place to rob; burglarize

buried 1930s underworld & prison **1** *adj* Serving a life sentence or other long prison sentence **2** *adj* Languishing in solitary confinement; incommunicado

burleycue (also **burley-cue, burlecue, burlicue**) by 1920s **1** *n* A burlesque show; the burlesque stage or circuit: *. . . earned him the reputation of being the funniest second banana in burley-cue*—Lawrence Sanders **2** *modifier*: *burleycue top banana/ burlicue stripper*

burly[1] *n* Burlesque: *even when Buttons was in burly*—Gilbert Milstein

burly[2] *adj* 1990s snowboarders & skateboarders Very difficult; tricky; dangerous: *Check out his burly disaster slide*—Los Angeles Times

burn 1 *v* by 1950s To cook or heat food: *Let's burn a couple of hot dogs* **2** *v* by 1925 To put or be put to death in the electric chair; =FRY **3** *v* by 1930s To kill; assassinate **4** *v* by 1930s To become angry; =BURN UP: *He began making cracks. . . I burned but went on singing*—John O'Hara **5** *n* 1930s: *He didn't blow up, just did a slow burn* **6** *v* by 1935 To anger; infuriate; =PISS-OFF: *You must have done something to burn him*—Elizabeth Morgan **7** *v* by late 1600s To cheat; swindle; victimize; rob; =RIP OFF: *If you go along with that guy you'll get burned* **8** *n*: *It was a burn, but it didn't start out to be*—Rolling Stone Interviews **9** *v* 1950s street gang To assault or fight a rival gang or gang member **10** *v* by 1950s To harass a person relentlessly; hound: *I'll burn you right off the force*—Ira Wolfert **11** *v* 1970s teenagers & students To insult; =PUT DOWN
•This seems to be a spontaneous verb form that coincides with the much older noun: *I burned this chick. . . . "Whereja get those jeans, like Sears or something?"*—The Valley Girls' Guide to Life/ *The Administration only turned to her after it felt burned by two "Eastern elitists"*—New York Times **12** *n* by middle 1890s: *I didn't mean it as a burn* **13** *interj* 1980s students An exclamation of delight at a successful insult **14** *v* by 1500s To infect or become infected with a venereal disease **15** *v* To pass; spend; waste; =KILL: *I'll start a conversation just to burn time*—Washington Post/ *. . . if it burns tomorrow afternoon*—George V Higgins **16** *v* by 1880s To move very rapidly; speed; =BARREL: *He wasn't just running, he was burning* **17** *v* 1950s jazz musicians To perform, esp to improvise, superbly; excel: *The cat was getting down and burning* **18** *v* by 1970s To borrow; beg **19** *v* by 1940s To throw something, esp a baseball, very fast: *He burned the fastball right down the middle* **20** *v* To outdo; outshine in competition: *. . . in the direction of the Spanish kids, who are already looking humiliated. Tony has burned the guy*—Village Voice/ *. . . the way Dex burned Eddie on that last number*—Los Angeles Times **21** *v* Army by 1980s To make a xerographic copy: *Will you burn me ten copies of this?* **22** *v* police by 1950s To expose as an informer: *Do you really want. . . to spend valuable man-hours trying to find out who burned him?*—Lawrence Sanders
See BURNOUT

a **burn** *n phr* by 1970s A cigarette; =a SMOKE: *They stepped outside for a burn*
See DO A SLOW BURN

burn artist *n phr* 1960s narcotics A professional swindler or confidence man; a person who makes fraudulent sales, esp of spurious narcotics

burn someone's **ass (** or **butt)** *v phr* first form by 1950s To anger someone; irritate someone extremely: *It burns a girl's ass. . . when she's not supposed to go around with anybody else*—Noel Gerson/ *Still, it burns my ass to be so close and miss it*—Lawrence Sanders/ *That arrogance burns my butt for sure*

burn someone **down** by 1930s **1** *v phr* To shoot someone **2** *v phr* To deflate; humiliate: *He's so cocky someone has to burn him down*

burned or **burnt** *adj* by 1930s Very angry: *Everyone is sitting there really pissed, really burned*—W T Tyler/ *My dad would be burned if he knew we bought it at a Chevron*—New York Times

burned out 1 *adj phr* by 1940s Tired; exhausted; =POOPED **2** *adj phr* by 1883 At the end of one's vigor and productivity; =PLAYED OUT: *The coach said he quit because he was burned out/ an old burned-out teacher* **3** *adj phr* 1960s narcotics Depressed and exhausted after the effects of a narcotic have worn off

burned-out (or **burnt-out) case** *n phr* by 1960s A person who is exhausted and ineffectual; =BURNOUT: *. . . once a superior foreign correspondent but by then a burnt-out case*—New York Review of Books [fr the title of a 1961 Graham Greene novel about a leper whose case was arrested and cured only after loss of fingers and toes]

burner 1 *n* 1920s The electric chair **2** *n* by 1950s A superlative performer; =the TOPS: *He showed he was a burner at the combine*—Milwaukee Journal **3** *n* 1920s A pistol, esp a .22 caliber revolver
See COOK WITH GAS, FAST BURNER, GREASE-BURNER, HAY BURNER, OAT-BURNER, ON THE BACK BURNER

burnie 1960s narcotics **1** *n* A partially smoked marijuana cigarette **2** *n* A marijuana cigarette shared among smokers

burning out *n phr* 1960s narcotics An older addict's voluntary withdrawal from narcotics after years of use

burn one *v phr* about 1930 To draw a glass of beer

burn one in (or **over)** *v phr* by 1940s In baseball, to throw a fastball

burnout 1 *n* 1970s Total and incapacitating exhaustion; inability to go on •The term apparently originated among psychotherapists, describing their own overstressed condition: *Many report lawyer burnout after two or three years in practice/ high rate of teacher burnout* **2** *n* 1970s Boredom; apathy; satiation; •The currency of this and the previous sense are due to the various narcotics-users' meanings of *burn out: I feared polka burnout, but it never happened. . . I became a polkaholic*—Village Voice **3** *n* (also **burn**) *1970s teenagers* A user or abuser of drugs, liquor, etc: *There are two groups in my school, the jocks and burn-outs. The burn-outs smoke and take pills and drink*—New York Times/ *except for the long hairs (or"burns," short for "burnouts") who hang out on the steps and smoke*—Washington Post **4** *n 1950s hot rodders* A very high-speed hot rod race **5** *n* An informal match where players try to throw a baseball so hard that it cannot be caught without undue pain **6** *n 1950s astronautics* The point where a rocket or missile has exhausted its fuel

burn rubber *v phr by 1970s* To leave; depart, esp very precipitately: *When I got back to the flat, you had burned rubber out the back*—Village Voice [fr the scorching of tires in the fast acceleration of a car]

burn the breeze *v phr about 1930* To run or drive at very high speed

burn the road *v phr about 1930* To drive a car very fast

burn up 1 *v phr about 1940* To perform very well; do superbly well: *His club is burning up the league this season* **2** *v phr by 1940s* To go very fast on •*Burn* in the same sense dates from the 1870s: *to burn up the base paths/ burn up the road* **3** *v phr by 1940s* To become angry

burn someone **up 1** *v phr* (also **burn** someone **off**) *by 1930s* To anger someone: *His egocentricity burns me up* **2** *v phr 1920s* To put someone to death in the electric chair **3** *v 1930s circus* To cheat; swindle; victimize

burp *by early 1930s* **1** *n* A belch, esp a gentle one **2** *v*: *She burped thrice and smiled* **3** *v* To cause a baby to belch, esp by holding it over the shoulder and patting its back

burp gun *WWII Army* **1** *n phr* A German Schmeisser machine pistol, with a very high rate of fire **2** *n phr* Any submachine gun; =TOMMY GUN

◀**burrhead**▶ *n about 1900* A black person

burr under the saddle (or **up one's rear end)** *by 1990s* A constant annoyance; obsessive nuisance: *General Noriega has been a burr under the saddle of this Administration*—ABC News/ *Sasha Schneider has always been a burr under the saddle of musical complacency*—New York Times/ *For some reason, though, he had a burr up his rear end*—Milwaukee Journal

bury 1 *v underworld about 1900* To sentence someone to a very long prison term or to solitary confinement **2** *v sports by 1940s* To defeat decisively; =CLOBBER

bury the hatchet *v phr by 1750s* To make peace; cease hostilities: *He and Chambrun hadn't buried the hatchet after all*—Hugh Pentecost [fr an American Indian custom of burying such a weapon as a sort of peace treaty]

bus 1 *n by 1919* A car: *Whose old bus is in the drive?* **2** *n by 1916* An aircraft **3** *n police by 1980s* An ambulance: *Roger one-oh-four, do we need a bus?*—Carsten Stroud **4** *v by 1913* To clear dirty dishes and tableware from the tables in a restaurant or cafeteria [the restaurant sense probably fr the four-wheeled cart often used to carry dishes]
See JITNEY, MISS THE BUS, RUBBERNECK WAGON

busboy *n by 1913* A person who clears dirty dishes and tableware from restaurant tables: *Talking very tough to a bus boy*—Damon Runyon

buscar *early 1900s armed forces* **1** *n* Borrowed money **2** *n WWII armed forces* Unexpected or forbidden pleasure; =BOODLE [fr Spanish *buscar*, "to seek, hunt"]

bush 1 *n by 1640s* A beard; whiskers ◁**2**▷ *n by 1745* The pubic hair, esp of a female; =BEAVER ◁**3**▷ *modifier*: *Bush shot. You could see the pubic hair, but not the sex parts*—John Irving **4** *adj fr 1650s* Rural; provincial; =BUSH LEAGUE •The sense has gradually developed from "the wilderness" to "the country as distinct from the city"; coincidentally it has taken on the same value judgment: *The city is superior, the country is inferior: a bush town* **5** *adj fr 1650s* Mediocre; second-rate; amateur: *seemed pretty bush for. . . pros*—John D MacDonald **6** *v by 1870* To fatigue; exhaust; sap; =POOP: *The climb bushed him/ Our dialogues always bush me*
See BEAT AROUND THE BUSH, BEAT THE BUSHES, TAKE THE RAG OFF THE BUSH

the bush or **bushes** *n phr fr 1670;* The back country: *When I was. . . working 12-hour tricks as a newspaper cub in the bushes*—Westbrook Pegler
See BUSH

bushboy *n by 1980s* A young, new, and naive prisoner: *That damn bushboy beats his gums too much*—Anthropological Linguistics

bushed *adj loggers by 1870* Tired out; exhausted; =BEAT, FRAZZLED, POOPED [perhaps fr middle–19th-century meaning "lost in the woods"]

busher or **bush leaguer 1** *n* or *n phr by 1910* A baseball player in a minor league •A 1907 example of *bush leaguer* applies to basketball rather than baseball players **2** *n* or *n phr by 1920s* Any mediocre or second-rate performer; amateur: *He's a busher at the piano*

bush league 1 *n phr by 1908* A baseball minor league of professional or semiprofessional players **2** *n phr by 1908* Any subordinate, apprentice, or amateur enterprise: *The road companies are sometimes bush leagues for aspirants to Broadway* **3** *adj phr* Mediocre; second- or third-rate; =BUSH, SMALL-TIME: *a bush-league hoodlum/ Your ideas are invariably bush league*

the bush leagues *n phr by 1908* The mediocre and inferior reaches of business, entertainment, sports, etc; =the SMALL TIME: *For years he made a perilous living as a singer in the bush leagues*

bush parole *n phr* prison about 1920 An escape from prison

bush patrol[1] *n phr* Hugging and kissing; =NECKING [fr the notion that a couple might hide in the *bushes*]

◁**bush patrol**[2]▷ *n phr* by 1950s The sex act; copulation [fr *bush,* "pubic hair"]

bush pilot *n phr* 1930s An airplane pilot who flies in very remote territory, like the back country of Alaska

bushwah (BŏŏSH wah, BŏŏSH-) *n* (Variations: **booshwah** or **bushwa** or **booshwa**) by 1906 Nonsense; pretentious talk; bold and deceitful absurdities; =BALONEY, BULLSHIT: *But the President's own managers concede this is so much bushwah*—Washingtonian [seemingly a euphemism for *bullshit* fr a cowboy corruption of French *bois-de-vache,* "dried cow dung"; in some users possibly influenced by French *bourgeois* taken pejoratively]

bushwhack by 1860s **1** *v* To assault, esp from ambush: *Two guys jumped out and bushwhacked him* **2** *v* To attack violently: *After that speech the President felt bushwhacked* [fr the action of cutting the bush in order to get through the forest or along an overgrown stream]

bushy-tailed *See* BRIGHT-EYED AND BUSHY-TAILED

busier than a one-armed paperhanger (or **a tall horse in flytime)** *v phr* first form by 1920s Extremely busy: *Since taking over last June, Schofield has been busier than the proverbial one-armed paperhanger*—New York Times

business *n* by 1645 Excrement, esp that of a house pet
See IN BUSINESS, KNOW one's ONIONS, MONKEY BUSINESS, TAKE CARE OF BUSINESS, THAT'S SHOW BUSINESS

the **business** *n phr* narcotics by 1930s The equipment used for giving oneself a narcotic injection
See GET THE BUSINESS, GIVE someone THE BUSINESS

business as usual *n phr* by 1885 Persistence in the ordinary course of events, despite difficulties, morality, and other hindrances: *. . . the team that is supposed to drag America from the path of business as usual*—Nations/ *The riot is over, and it's back to business as usual*—New York Times/ *If you bribe a public employee it's corruption; if he works in a private company it's business as usual*—Nation

the **business end** *n phr* by 1878 The dangerous or operative part of something, esp the muzzle of a gun

businessman's bounce *n phr* 1930s *jazz musicians* Dance music or a popular song played in a soft, smooth style

busk *v* by 1840s To perform music in subway stations or other public places, taking the contributions of listeners •Very common in Great Britain, but spreading to the US

buss *v* 1980s *teenagers* To talk about; gossip over: *Quit bussin' about my shoes* [perhaps a survival of British dialect *buss,* "mutter, murmur busily, buzz," attested from the 1500s]

bussy *n* by 1970s A bus driver: *Where the blazes was that bussy?*—Sports Illustrated

bust 1 *v* by 1806 To break: *I busted my nose* **2** *v* Army by late 1800s To reduce in rank; demote: *He got busted from buck sergeant to buck private* **3** *v* cowboys by 1890s To tame a wild horse for riding: *Two rides will usually bust a bronco so that the average cow-puncher can use him*—Harper's Magazine **4** *v* underworld by 1890s To break open a safe, vault, etc; also, burglarize a place **5** *n* 1950s *street gang* To disperse or chase a rival street gang **6** *n* by 1930s A police raid: *One whiff of marijuana and we get a bust*—Meyer Berger **7** *n* by 1918 An arrest; =COLLAR: *Beating a Bust: Two Views*—Rolling Stone **8** *v*: *I've been busted, bring bail* **9** *v* 1950s *teenagers* To catch someone in an illegal or immoral act **10** *v* by 1808 To hit someone: *She busted me in the kishkes* **11** *n*: *That one bust decked me* **12** *n* by 1840s A failure; fiasco: *My try for her sweet favors was a total bust* **13** *n* by 1920s A person who fails; =NONSTARTER, LOSER: *At baseball I was a risible bust* **14** *v* *college students* about 1900 To fail an examination or course; =FLUNK •The standard form *burst* is found in the 1850s: *I miserably busted the econ final* **15** *n* by 1840 A spree; drinking bout: *. . . took his paycheck and went on a bust* **16** *adj* by 1840s Out of funds; destitute; =BROKE
See BEER BUST, GO BROKE

bust a cap 1 *v phr* by 1840s To shoot off a firearm: *Otherwise I'd have busted a cap in his goddamn head*—Joseph Wambaugh **2** *v phr* 1950s *narcotics* To take a narcotic, esp heroin: *Why don't you bust a cap with me? It's choice*—C Cooper [first sense fr the breaking of the percussion *cap* of a pistol; second sense probably fr the same, in the sense "have a shot, take a shot"]

bust a gut (or **hamstring)** *v phr* first form by 1912; =BUST one's ASS

bust along *v phr* by 1940s To travel fast; speed: *Ab Jenkins. . . busting along at 120 or so*—Sports Illustrated

bust ass *v phr* by 1980s To thrash; punish by beating; =CLOBBER, KICK ASS: *A little belly, sure. . . But I can still bust ass*—Harry Crews

◁**bust** one's **ass**▷ *v phr* (Variations: **break** may replace **bust**; ◁**balls**▷ or **buns** or **butt** or **chops** or **conk** or **hump** or **nuts** or **stones** or ◁**sweet ass**▷ or **tail** may replace **ass**) first form by 1940s To work or perform to one's utmost; exert oneself mightily: *Yeah but, what if he busts his ass, goes to a lot of trouble. . .*—Elmore Leonard/ *If They Break Their Asses They Might Get into College Program*—John R Powers/ *I'm finished busting my hump on that kind of work*—Rolling Stone/ *I busted my butt to get those business people to sponsor me*—Los Angeles Times/ *We're really busting our buns*—Milwaukee Journal/ *Here I was, busting my tail to develop young players*—Whitey Herzog

◁**bust balls**▷ *v phr* by 1950s To discipline harshly; punish: *They gonna be bustin' balls, man*—David Rabe

bust one's **buttons** *v phr* To be ostentatiously proud and happy: *Dolores Rogan of Bay View is busting her buttons these days*—Milwaukee Journal

bust caps *1970s Army* **1** *v phr* To fire the main gun of a tank **2** *v phr* To have a fire-fight
See BUST A CAP

bust chops **See** BREAK CHOPS

bust someone's **chops** **See** BREAK someone's CHOPS

bust clothes *v phr 1980s teenagers* To dress up

busted *adj by 1860s* Penniless; =BROKE

busted flush *n phr by 1909* A failure; a sad disappointment: *Beaverbrook dismissed Churchill as a busted flush*—New Republic [fr the name of a poker hand with four cards of one suit, but lacking the fifth to make a *flush*]

buster[1] **1** *n by 1840s* A splendid person, esp a robust one; =BEAUT, CORKER: *He was a buster. . . nigh as big as his Mammy*—Robert Penn Warren **2** *n* (also **Buster**) *by 1860s* Man; fellow; =GUY, BROTHER ●Used in direct address with a somewhat hostile tone: *Down the hall to the back room, buster*—Hugh Pentecost **3** *combining word by 1930s* Someone or something that destroys, thwarts, or otherwise defeats what or who is indicated ●Revived by an early 1980s film comedy called *Ghostbusters: blockbuster/ chartbuster/ gangbuster/ gridlock buster/ fuzz buster/ troll buster/ virus buster*
See BALL-BUSTER, BELLY-WHOPPER, BRONCO BUSTER, BUN-BUSTER, CLOUD-BUSTER, CONK-BUSTER, KIDNEY-BUSTER, SKULL-BUSTER

buster[2] *n 1990s street gang* A weak or treacherous gang member; =MARK: *Bogard accused Compton of being. . . a "buster," meaning he was weak and unwilling to defend the gang's interests*—Los Angeles Times/ *No fucking way. I ain't no buster!*—Buzz [probably fr *gangbuster*]

busthead *outdated fr 1850s* **1** *n* Cheap or inferior whiskey; =PANTHER PISS **2** *n* A drunkard, one who is a hobo or drifter; =SKID ROW BUM

bust hump *v phr by 1970s* To work extremely hard; =BUST one's ASS: *Nobody's ever accused you of being unwilling to bust hump*—Hannibal Boris

bustier (BOO stee ay) *n 1990s* A brassiere that enhances the size of the breasts: *. . . a sex-bomb blonde in a push-up bustier*—Morris County Daily Record/ *So it's jarring when she hands you a short rubber skirt and bustier. . .* —Elle [fr French, "strapless brassiere"]

busting out *adj phr 1980s black teenagers* Doing well; looking good

bustlebutt *n by 1980s* A very busy energetic person; =EAGER BEAVER

bust out **1** *v phr about 1920* To be dismissed from a school for academic failure **2** *v phr by 1960s* To lose all one's money gambling, esp at craps; =TAP OUT **3** *v phr by 1930* =BREAK OUT

bust someone **out** *v phr by 1960s* To win all of someone's money in a crap game, esp by cheating

bust-out *n police by 1950s* The climax of a swindle, when the victim hands over the money

bust-out joint *n phr gambling by 1950s* A dishonest gambling house

bust-outs *n gambling by 1950s* Loaded or otherwise tampered-with dishonest dice

bust up *v phr by 1920s* To end a marriage, friendship, or other association

busty *adj by 1940s* Having large breasts; bosomy; =CHESTY: *But she looked like the others, busty, too slender, bony hips*—Joseph Wambaugh

busy bee *n phr 1970s narcotics* The powdered form of phencyclidine, a tranquilizer used in veterinary medicine, which as a narcotic is either sniffed or smoked in a tightly rolled cigarette; =ANGEL DUST: *. . . angel dust, also known as busy bee*—New York Times [fr the fact that a low dosage produces a *buzz*]

but *adv by 1930s* Really; definitely: *He noticed it and began making cracks but loud*—John O'Hara [perhaps fr a Yiddish speech pattern]

butch **1** *n by 1902* A rough, strong man; =TOUGH ●Often used as a nickname **2** *n homosexuals by 1940s* An aggressive lesbian; =BULLDYKE, DYKE: *Even if she has turned butch on me and twisted the family name on you*—Harry Crews **3** *adj*: *. . . short round blonde of butch self-sufficiency*—Saul Bellow [fr *butcher*]

butcher **1** *n middle 1800s* A surgeon, esp an incompetent one **2** *n by 1529* A brutal and sanguinary ruler: *They called Bokassa a worse butcher than Amin* **3** *v by 1640s* To do crudely and clumsily what should be done with finesse: *I butcher their language/ I try to paint but butcher the canvas* **4** *n*: *As a carpenter I'm a butcher*
See WOOD BUTCHER

butcher boy hit *n phr baseball by 1940s* A ball hit sharply downwards so as to bounce high; =BALTIMORE CHOP

bute (BYOOT)*n 1960s* Butazolidin™, a drug sometimes used to stimulate race horses

but good *adv phr by 1930s* Very well; extremely; really: *They hate us but good: Your brother fucked you but good*—Saul Bellow [perhaps fr a Yiddish speech pattern]

butt **1** *by 1450 n* The buttocks; rump; =ASS ●This sense is attested as Western US in 1860. Oddly enough, *butt* looks like a diminutive of *buttock*, but to judge by the suffix, the opposite must be the case: *So drunk he couldn't find his butt with both hands*—H Allen Smith **2** *n by 1930s* The remainder of a smoked cigarette or cigar **3** *n about 1900* A cigarette: *a pack of butts* **4** *n armed forces & prison about 1915* The final year of a prison sentence or a term of military enlistment **5** *adj 1990s students* Bad; undesirable **6** *adv 1980s students* Very; extremely; =STONE: *That furniture is butt ugly*—Drew Slang
See DUCK-BUTT, DUSTY BUTT, GET OFF one's ASS, GOOD BUTT, GOOFY-BUTT, GRIPE one's ASS, SCUTTLEBUTT

butt can *n phr esp WWII armed forces* A large tin can hung in a barracks or elsewhere to receive cigarette butts

butt-end Charlie *n phr WWII air forces* The rear gunner in a bomber; =TAIL-END CHARLIE

butter 1 *v* (also **butter up**) *by 1700* To flatter shamelessly and fulsomely **2** *n by 1823* Flattery; cajolery; =SOFT SOAP

See LIKE SHIT THROUGH A TIN HORN

butter-and-egg man *1920s* **1** *n phr* A wealthy business executive or farmer from the provinces: *The visiting Butter and Egg Men had their Whoopee in New York*—C Bragdon **2** *n phr* A person who finances a theatrical production; =ANGEL

butterball *n by 1940s* Any plump person: *Short and plump. A real butterball*—Lawrence Sanders/ *. . . but butterball? That's on a par with pleasingly plump*—Stan Cutler [The simile "as fat as a *butterball*" occurs from the middle 1800s]

butter bar *n phr 1970s Army* A second lieutenant [fr the gold color of the insignia *bars*, and the fact that butter is sold in quarter-pound *bars*]

butterfingered *adj by 1615* A clumsy person who drops things as if his fingers were slick with butter

butterfingers *n 1850s cricket* A clumsy, unhandy person, esp one who regularly drops things [Adopted by baseball players in the 1880s]

butterflies *n by 1908* Dull spasms in one's stomach, caused by anxiety and nervousness; flutters: *I sure got butterflies thinking about it*

butterfly *See* PUSSY BUTTERFLY

butterfly ball (or **pitch**) *n phr baseball by 1940s* A slow and erratic pitch; =KNUCKLEBALL: *All this exertion took the butter off his butterfly ball*—New York Daily News

butterfly case *n phr by 1970s* An insane person; =NUT: *At first Rupert Pupkin. . . doesn't seem like a butterfly case*—Philadelphia [fr the conceit that insane persons go about chasing *butterflies*]

butterfly kiss *n phr by 1871* A caress made by winking an eye so that the lashes brush one's partner: *She worked her eyelashes and made butterfly kisses on my cheeks*—Raymond Chandler

◁**butterhead**▷ *n black by 1960s* A black person regarded by others as a discredit to the black community

Butternut *n by 1863* A Confederate soldier [fr the fact that many such soldiers, esp fr rural areas, were dressed in homespun colored with dye made fr *butternuts*]

butter no parsnips *v phr by 1639* To have no practical effect; be unavailing: *Subtlety, Madonna well knew, butters no parsnips in the pop marketplace*—New Republic [The source expression is "Fair words butter no parsnips"]

◀**buttfuck**▶ *v* and *n* =ASSFUCK, BUMFUCK: *. . . to sue us for. . . his two-thirds contingency fee and all the troopers he can butt-fuck*—Carsten Stroud

◀**buttfuck buddy**▶ *See* ASSHOLE BUDDY

◁**butthead**▷ *n 1980s students* A stupid person; oaf; =BONEHEAD, DUMDUM, SPAZZ: *Howdy is a depressingly stupid butthead. . .*—Carsten Stroud [probably fr *butthead*, "ass-headed," influenced by the 1960s student term *butterhead*, "stupid person"]

butt heads *v phr* To vie strongly; contend: *. . . NBC's new* John Laroquette Show *butted heads with ABC's Roseanne*—USExpress

◁**butthole**▷ *n by 1950s* The anus; =ASSHOLE: *Did those buttholes score again?*—Dan Jenkins

butt in *v phr by 1900* To intrude oneself; proffer unwanted counsel; =BARGE IN: *The Wagner Act forbade any employer to butt in on such matters*—Westbrook Pegler/ *"Greenspan, don't butt in,"* said Gold—Joseph Heller

buttinsky *n* (Variations: **butterinsky** or **buttinski** or **butt-in**) *by 1902* A person who rudely intrudes himself, esp one who does so habitually [fr *butt in* plus the Slavic or Yiddish suffix -**sky**, added for humorous effect]

butt-kicker *n 1980s students* A very effective person •Compare asskicker: *He's a real butt-kicker in soccer*—UCLA Slang

buttload *n 1980s students* A large quantity; a lot of; =SHITLOAD

buttlegger *n by 1960s* A cigarette smuggler: *. . . expected to concentrate on apprehending buttleggers who plied a trade between the low-tax, tobacco-growing South and the high-tax, tobacco-consuming North*—New Yorker

button 1 *n by 1920* The chin; point of the chin: *I got clipped square on the button* **2** *n by 1870s* The clitoris; =CLIT **3** *n narcotics by 1960s* A small quantity of a narcotic: *There exists some traffic, however, in "buttons," or small amounts*—H Braddy **4** *n narcotics by 1960s* The rounded top of the peyote plant **5** *n by 1920s* A police officer's badge; =POTSY, TIN **6** *n* (also **buttons**) *about 1900* A police officer •Blue and buttons was used of the police **7** *n phr 1960s underworld* (also **button man** or **button player** or **button soldier**) A low-ranking member of the Mafia; =SOLDIER

See BELLY BUTTON, CHICKEN SWITCH, HIT THE PANIC BUTTON, ON THE BUTTON

button chopper *n phr WWII Army* A laundry; also, a laundry owner or worker

buttondown or **buttoned-down** *adj 1960s* Conventional; of unmistakable respectability; conservative; =SQUARE: *The button-down, dispassionate, country club racism of the nouveau riche*—Paul Good/ *One of the most squeaky-clean and buttoned-down of US corporations is a partner*—Wall Street Journal [fr the wearing of *buttondown* collars by business executives and other conservatives]

button down *by 1950s* **1** *v phr* To classify; =PEG, PIGEONHOLE: *I buttoned him down from the start as a probable bore* **2** *v phr* To make precise; discard all but one alternative: *First we decide to buy, then we button down the price* **3** *v phr* To prepare for action; get ready: *He was all buttoned down and ready to go* [third sense fr a military term for closing all ports and hatches for action]

buttoned-up *adj by 1970s* Neat; trim; prim: *Betty Crocker's very serious, buttoned-up, orderly*—Wall Street Journal

buttonhole *v by 1880* To get someone's attention

as if by taking hold by a buttonhole: . . . *listening to and buttonholing other researchers*—New York Times [*Button* in the same sense is attested from the early 1860s]

buttonhook *n football by 1970s* A maneuver in which a pass receiver runs downfield and then suddenly spins and runs back toward the line of scrimmage [fr the resemblance of the path to a *hook* used for pulling *buttons* through the buttonholes of a pair of shoes]

button one's **lip** *v phr by 1847* To stop talking; not tell what one knows: *I wish Jim Quello would button his lip*—Mesa Tribune

buttons *See* HAVE ALL one's BUTTONS

button up 1 *v phr by 1850s* To keep quiet; =BUTTON one's LIP, CLAM UP: *If you don't button up they'll shut you up* **2** *v phr by 1940s* To finish something, esp tidily and handsomely: *We buttoned it up in a couple days* **3** *v phr by 1940s* To lock up, close up, or make secure: *I told John Sanderson to button up the generator*—J C Clark

butt out 1 *v phr by 1930s* To stop intruding; reverse one's butting in •Usu an exasperated command, based on opposition to *butt in:* . . . *and four other guys told me I should butt out*—Robert B Parker **2** *v phr by 1940s* To depart, esp abruptly; =BUG OUT: *I butted right out of there when it went off*

butt pack *n phr* =FANNY PACK

◁**buttplug**▷ *n 1980s* A despised person; =ASSHOLE, JERK

butts or **butts on** *interj by 1930s* The declaration that one has or wants first rights to something; =DIBS: *The kids hollered "Butts on the drumstick!"* [fr the claiming of a cigarette *butt* seen in the street]

butt ugly *adj phr 1980s students* Very ugly; repulsive: *That furniture is butt ugly*—Drew Slang/ . . . *the "I feel butt-ugly" days*—Sassy

buy 1 *v* To believe; accept as true: *These guys bought the myth and now it's costing them dearly*—Toronto Life/ *I buy it. What you told me is between us*—Robert B Parker **2** *v by 1920s* To agree to; acquiesce in: *If that's the plan, I'll buy it* **3** *v by 1940s* To do; effectuate: *She pointed her gun at me. I said, "What are you trying to buy with that?"*—J Evans **4** *v by 1650s* To hire; engage: *He bought him a lawyer and filed suit* **5** *v* (also **buy off**) *by 1650s* To induce by money; bribe: *He tried to buy a couple of jury members*

buy-and-bust operation *n phr 1980s* A police operation in which an undercover officer buys narcotics and then arrests the seller: *The case began with a routine buy-and-bust operation*—Milwaukee Journal

buy a pig in a poke *v phr by 1562* To accept or agree to something without careful examination; risk the unknown: *It is unfair for anyone running for president "to ask people to buy a pig in the poke"*—Associated Press [fr dialect *poke,* "bag, sack"]
See CAN'T BUY

buy-in *n by 1990s* Acceptance; acquiescence: . . . *not everyone adheres to the strategy. They hedge. There's a lack of buy-in*—Time

buy into *v phr* To accept; acquiesce in •Thought of and perhaps coined as the opposite of *sell out,* which has a more contemptuous suggestion of betrayal: *lots of guilt and I bought into that*—San Francisco/ *I bought into the whole materialistic trip*—San Francisco/ . . . *the degree with which you bought into the pop culture of the Fifties*—Nation

buy it *See* COP IT

buy jawbone *v phr by 1860s* To buy on credit [perhaps fr the notion that one has to *jawbone* the merchant into taking a credit risk]

buy off on *v phr 1970s Army* To agree to; =BUY: *Will you buy off on letting us go back to the garrison?*

buy the farm (or **the ranch**) *v phr armed forces by 1950s* To be killed; die: *the cat that bought the farm when Harvey hit him on his bike*—Cyra McFadden/ *Luna crash confirmed. They bought the ranch*—Playboy [fr earlier Air Force term *buy a farm,* "to crash"; probably from the expressed desire of wartime pilots to stop flying, buy a farm, and live peacefully]

buy time *v phr by 1960s* To be dilatory or evasive in order to gain time; temporize; =STALL

buzhie *See* BOOJIE

buzz 1 *v about 1910* To call someone on the telephone; =RING: *Why not buzz Eddy for the brawl?*—H T Webster **2** *n about 1910: I think I'll give the Guided Child a buzz*—K Brush **3** *v by 1832* To talk; converse: *The crowd was buzzing about some pretty raunchy divorces* **4** *n by 1605* Subject of talk; gossip; rumor: *What's the buzz, cuz?* **5** *n about 1935* A feeling or surge of pleasure, esp a pleasant sense of intoxication; =HIGH: *After two Scotches he got a nice buzz* **6** *n teenagers fr 1950s* A police squad car **7** *v about 1900* To flatter; court **8** *v by 1950s* To inform someone in confidence, esp by whispering: *You'll buzz me later*—Mickey Spillane **9** *v by 1950s* To announce one's arrival or summon someone by or as if by sounding a buzzer: *Buzz when you want me* **10** *v 1920s hoboes* To beg **11** *v underworld by 1812* To pilfer; rob; =HOLD UP **12** *v 1930s police & underworld* To question or investigate someone **13** *v WWII air forces* To fly an aircraft alarmingly close to something, esp to the ground •A sense "to flutter or hover about, over, etc," is attested from 1650 **14** *v WWII armed forces* To roister drunkenly at: *They were all buzzing the bar* **15** *v 1990s street gang* Kill; =WASTE: *They buzz the kid and her baby?*—Robert B Parker

buzz along *See* BUZZ OFF

buzzard 1 *n 1600s* A dislikable person, esp an old man: *a stingy and predatory old buzzard* **2** *n 1930s armed forces* The eagle worn as insignia by a colonel or a naval captain
See JUNGLE BUZZARD

buzzard colonel *n phr 1930s armed forces* =CHICKEN COLONEL

buzz bomb *n phr middle 1940s* A German WWII V–1 winged robot bomb powered by a ramjet engine

buzz book *n phr by 1970s* A best-selling book; a book everyone is talking about: *The nation's latest buzz book is not a fast summer read*—Time

buzz-buggy or **buzz-wagon** *n first form by 1906, second by 1914* A car

buzz-buzz *n by 1908* Unintelligible or tedious noise, esp continuous vociferation: *All the buzz-buzz from without may be said to go in one ear and out the other*—Atlantic Monthly

buzz-crusher or **buzz-kill** *n 1980s students* Someone or something that ruins or dampens one's pleasure; =KILLJOY, PARTY-POOPER

buzz cut or **buzzed hair** *1990s* **1** *n phr* A cutting off of all or most of the hair; a total or near-total dehairing: *A woman cadet could conceivably get a buzz cut*—New Yorker/ *Nowicki. . . received a buzz cut from his swimmers*—Milwaukee Journal **2** *modifier*: *Some have buzz-cut spiked haircuts*—New Yorker/ *Fitness guru Susan Powter, she of the platinum buzz-cut hair*—Milwaukee Journal

buzzed *adj by 1950s* Intoxicated, esp mildly so; =TIDDLY: *Getting a little buzzed on a second Bloody Mary*—Peter de Vries

buzzer *n by 1914* A police or other law-enforcement badge: *I brought out the 1928 deputy sheriff's star I carried to show people who wanted to see a buzzer*—J Evans
See MOLL-BUZZER

buzzin' *adj 1980s teenagers* Drunk
See WHAT'S BUZZIN', COUSIN

buzz in *v phr by 1930s* To arrive: *Old JK buzzed in from Syracuse*

buzz someone in *v phr by 1970s* To unlock an outer door for someone by actuating an electric unlatching device

buzz off (or **along**) *v phr by 1914* To depart; •First form often a command

buzzword or **buzzphrase** *n by 1946* A modish technical or arcane term used to make one appear sophisticated: *The rhetoric has sputtered with buzzwords like "anticolonialist" and "progressive"*—Time/ *I avoid buzzphrases like "this point in time"/ Buzzword of the Month Dept*—PC Magazine [coined in the middle 1940s by students at the Harvard Business School, and meaning "a word used to describe the key to any course or situation" in their specialized and amusingly stilted vocabulary; hence, *buzz* may be a shortening and repronouncing of *business*]

buzzy *adj by 1700s* Drunk

BVDs (bee vee deez) *n 1920s* Underwear, esp long underwear; =BEEVEEDEES: *I opened the door and caught her in her BVDs* [fr the 1870s trademark of a brand of long underwear, the initials of the manufacturers Bradley, Voorhees, and Day]

by *by 1920s* **1** *prep* With; as far as concerns: *Five skins is jake by me*—American Mercury **2** *prep* At; to; at the place of: *I'll buy you a drink by Antek*—Nelson Algren [fr direct transcription of Yiddish prepositional use into English]
See GET AWAY WITH something, GET BY

not by a long shot (or **a jugful**) See NOT BY A LONG SHOT

by a nose *adv phr by 1908* By a narrow margin; barely: *win by a nose*

by-a-whisker *adj by 1970s* Very nearly tied; very close: *. . . the House of Representatives' by-a-whisker vote. . .* —New York Times

by cracky *interj fr early 1800s* By Christ •A euphemistic form: *By cracky, he hit the jackpot!*

bye See TAKE A BYE

by ear *adv phr* He sort of made his judgments by ear [fr the playing of music without the use of graphic notation, a term used since at least the 1840s]
See PLAY IT BY EAR

by George *interj by 1731* A mild exclamation of surprise, approval, determination, emphasis, etc: *By George, I'll do it/ I think she's got it, by George* [A euphemism for *by God*]

-by God- *infix* Used for emphasis: *I was born in West-by God-Virginia*

by guess and by God *adv phr by 1940s* By approximation and instinct; not by precise or infallible means: *She didn't know exactly how to make a quiche, so had to do it by guess and by God*

BYOB (pronounced as separate letters) *by 1950s* **1** *v phr* Bring your own bottle, or your own booze **2** *modifier*: *a BYOB party*

◁**by the balls**▷ See HAVE someone BY THE BALLS

by the bell See SAVED BY THE BELL

by the book *adv phr by 1840s* According to correct procedures; as one should under regulations, law, contract, etc: *He said there would be no more corner cutting, we'd do everything strictly by the book*

by the numbers *adv phr WWI armed forces* In a prescribed way; mechanically: *He even makes love by the numbers* [fr the military training device of analyzing a complex action by breaking it into a numbered series of simpler actions, performed as the numbers are called out]

by the seat of one's **pants** *adv phr 1930s aviators* By instincts and feelings, without the benefit of formal training or procedures; =BY GUESS AND BY GOD, BY EAR: *. . . pushing his luck, living on the edge, playing brilliantly by the seat of his pants*—New Yorker
See FLY BY THE SEAT OF one's PANTS

by the short hairs See HAVE someone BY THE SHORT HAIRS

by the truckful *adj phr* (Variations: **boxcar** or **carload** may replace **truckful**) *by 1960s* In great quantity; numerous

C

C *n* Cocaine

See BIG C, C-NOTE, GENTLEMAN'S C, H AND C

caballo *n 1950s narcotics* Heroin [fr Spanish, "horse," translating *horse*, "heroin"]

cabbage *n about 1900* Money; =LETTUCE: *. . . the salad boys in the back room, oiling up the cabbage. And it's big cabbage, too*—W T Tyler

See FOLDING MONEY, HAPPY-CABBAGE

cabinet **See** KITCHEN CABINET

cabin fever *n phr by 1918* Restlessness, impatience, and other signs of having been restrained too long

caboodle *n by 1840* A totality; discrete unit; =BOODLE: *Keep the whole caboodle* [perhaps fr *boodle*]

See KIT AND CABOODLE

caboose *n by 1860s* A jail [prob fr *calaboose*, "jail"]

ca-ca or **caca** or **kaka** (KAH kah) **1** *n by 1870s* Excrement; =SHIT: *Overweight is kaka*—Village Voice **2** *n 1950s narcotics* Heroin; =HORSE, SHIT [origin uncertain; perhaps fr late–1800s *cack*, "to defecate"; perhaps fr dialect *cacky*, "excrement," attested by 1899; perhaps fr Latin *cacavi*, "to defecate," used as a euphemism in the presence of children; perhaps fr Modern Greek; ultimately fr the Indo-European root *kakka* or *kaka*, designating defecation]

cackle *v by 1530* To laugh; giggle: *Later on, Susan and Karla were cackling together*—Douglas Coupland

cackle-broad or **cack-broad** *n by 1940s* A wealthy woman or society woman: *I knocks de pad with them cack-broads up on Sugar Hill*—Zora Neale Hurston

cackle factory *n phr by 1940s* An insane asylum; =LAUGHING ACADEMY

cackler *n 1920s hoboes* An office worker; white-collar worker

Cad or **Caddy** or **Caddie** *n 1920s* A Cadillac car: *And we'll rent a black Caddy. . .* —Ed McBain

cadet *n 1980s students* A despised person; =GEEK: *Ignore him, he's such a cadet*—UCLA Slang

See SPACE CADET

cadge (CAJ, CAYJ) *v early 1800s* To borrow; beg; =BUM, MOOCH

Cadillac **1** *n 1950s narcotics* An ounce of heroin **2** *n* The best of its kind; standard of excellence; paragon: *Republicans call New York the Cadillac of welfare states*—New York Times/ *Revos are the Cadillac of sunglasses*—Milwaukee Journal **3** *modifier*: *It's Cadillac all the way. . . It's a Cadillac operation*—Milwaukee Journal

cafe-au-lait (KA fay oh lay) *modifier by 1939* A brownish cream color, like that of coffee mixed with milk: *The glamorous cafe-au-lait singer-dancer had been stabbed. . .* —Stan Cutler [fr French, "coffee with milk"]

cafeteria *modifier by 1980s* Allowing a range of choice: *. . . cafeteria insurance plans*—New Republic

cafeteria Catholic *n phr 1980s* A Roman Catholic who observes church prescriptions and prohibitions at his or her own discretion: *You know, cafeteria Catholics who want to pick and choose . . . what they want to believe of. . . Catholic teaching*—Mike Wallace

cage **1** *n by 1630s* A prison **2** *v*: *The punk concealed a genuine terror of being caged*—Nelson Algren **3** *n motorcyclists by 1970s* A car or van: *The cage behind me bleated its horn*—Easyriders **4** *v* =CADGE **5** *n sports by 1920s* A basketball basket or net **6** *n sports by 1920s* Basketball **7** *modifier*: *a big cage star/ the cage standing*

See MONKEY CAGE, RATTLE someone's CAGE, RATTLE CAGES

cager *n sports by 1930s* A basketball player: *The eight-foot cager sped down the court like a maddened giraffe*

cage rattler *n phr 1970s* A person not content with the humdrum or conventional: *The governor wants "cage rattlers". . . thinkers, dreamers, and gadflies*—Newsweek

cagey or **cagy** *adj by 1890s* Shrewd; wary; pawky: *a quiet, cagy observer* [perhaps fr the expression *play a caged game*, "be careful, keep your intentions concealed," attested in 1890s]

cahoots **See** IN CAHOOTS

Cain **See** RAISE CAIN

caj or **cas** or **cazh** (CAZH, CAYZH) *adj 1980s teenagers* Casual; acceptable

Cajun *n by 1860s* Descendants of the Acadians, French occupants of the Canadian Maritime Provinces, who in the US live mostly in Louisiana •This term was regarded as offensive by most Louisianans, but with the recent popularity of Cajun culture it has largely lost its impact [dialect pronunciation of *Acadian*]

cake ◁**1**▷ *n black by 1940s* The female genitals **2** *n black by 1940s* A sexually attractive woman;

=FOX **3** *n esp 1920s* (also **cake-eater**) A ladies' man; =DUDE: . . . *his brown hat, fixed square-shaped the way the cakes were wearing them*—James T Farrell **4** *n about 1910* =PIECE OF CAKE *See* BABYCAKES, COFFEE AND CAKES, FRUITCAKE, ICE THE CAKE, NUTBALL, PIECE OF CAKE, TAKE THE CAKE

cake-cutter *n circus by 1930s* A cashier or other person who gives short change

cake job *n phr by 1990s* An easy job; sinecure: *Meter maids have a cake job*—Denver radio talk show

cakewalk *n by 1890s* Something very easy; =BREEZE, CINCH, PIECE OF CAKE: *Casey on his way to a cakewalk with the Senate Intelligence Committee*—Time/ *Our players thought this season was going to be a cakewalk*—Sports Illustrated [fr the name of a 19th-century dance contest, influenced by *piece of cake*]

calaboose (KAL uh boos) *n late 1700s* A jail or prison; cell [fr Spanish *calabozo*]

calf *See* SHAKE A WICKED CALF

calf love *n phr by 1890s* =PUPPY LOVE

calico *See* PIECE OF CALICO

California blanket *n phr hoboes by 1920s* Newspapers used as bedding: . . . *spent his nights on park benches under California blankets*—World's Work

California kiss-off *See* KISS-OFF

California prayer book (or **bible**) *n phr by 1850s* A deck of playing cards

California stop *n phr* (also **Michigan stop**) *by 1960s* An instance of rolling slowly past a stop sign, rather than stopping

Californicate *by 1990s* **1** *v* To overdevelop the land: . . . *bumper sticker: Don't Californicate Montana*—Utne Reader **2** *v* To seduce and infect with the moral and social standards of southern California: *McKellen was, in the tradition of expatriate Englishmen, Californicated into a greater sense of individual freedom*—Vanity Fair

Californication *n by 1990s* A Californicating: *Gogarty said that his task was to prevent the Californication of Ireland*—The Atlantic

calk off *See* CAULK OFF

call *n by 1980s* A decision: *It was my call*—Les Aspin [fr the playing decisions of managers, quarterbacks, etc, and the officiating decisions of umpires, referees, etc] *See* CATTLE CALL

call someone's **bluff** *v phr by 1870s* To force someone to justify or validate a pretense; require the truth: *When she called his bluff, he had to admit he was lying*

call-down *n by 1890s* A reprimand; rebuke

call someone **down** *v phr by 1890s* To reprimand; rebuke

call girl *n phr about 1900* A prostitute, esp one who may be engaged by telephone

call house (or **joint**) *n phr about 1910* A brothel, esp one where a prostitute may be engaged by telephone: *that call joint*—Jerome Weidman

call in one's **chits** (or **markers**) *v phr by 1980s* To collect what is owed to one, esp tit-for-tat political or other favors: *I have no chits to call in from politicians*—New York Times/ *You're calling in your chits, Ivar*—Lawrence Sanders/ *For the Titian show, Michel Laclotte, soon to retire as director of the Louvre, has called in all his markers at once. . .* —Time [fr *chit*, "notation of something owed, IOU," attested fr the 1770s; the source is Hindi *chitti*; a *marker* is also a notation of debt, esp in gambling]

call it a day (or **quits**) *v phr* first form by 1840s, second by 1940s To stop or terminate something; declare one has had enough: . . . *the Iraqi leadership has hunkered down; time to call it a day*—New Republic/ *Any sensible assassin would have called it quits*—Billy Rose [*Call quits* is attested from the 1890s]

call it like one **sees it** *v phr by 1980s* To be honest and unbiased; be deaf to influence

call off the dogs *v phr by 1930s* To relent; ease one's demands •A metaphor from hunting, where a trapped quarry is beset by *dogs*: . . . *Holmgren basically called off the dogs in the third quarter. . .* —Milwaukee Journal

call of nature or **nature's call** *n phr by 1761* The need to use the toilet, esp when urgent: *Where'd he go so quickly? To answer the call of nature, naturally*

call someone **on the carpet** *v phr by 1890s* To reprimand or summon for a reprimand; =CHEW someone OUT [probably fr early–19th-century British *walk the carpet*, having the same sense and based upon a servant's being called into the parlor to be reprimanded]

call someone **pisher** *sentence by 1940s* It's no big deal, so let's drop it •Often response to a rebuke one regards as trivial or undeserved: *So I'm five minutes late. Call me pisher/ And what can I do if he refuses? Call him pisher?*—Julius G Rothenberg [fr Yiddish; a *pisher* is a little kid, a bed-wetter]

call one's **shots** *v phr by 1930s* To explain or predict what one will do: *She'll never try to trick you; she always calls her shots* [fr a target-shooter's announcement of where the next *shot* will hit]

call the shots *v phr by 1960s* To be in charge: *Who's calling the shots around here?*

cally *n hoboes by 1920s* A jail or police station [fr *calaboose*]

calm as a Christian with aces wired *See* COOL AS A CHRISTIAN WITH ACES WIRED

◀**Cambo**▶ *n Vietnam War armed forces* A Cambodian

camelback or **camel** *n railroad* A locomotive having the cab in the center rather than at the rear

◀**camel-jammer**▶ *n 1970s* An Arab or Iranian [fr *jam*, "copulate with"]

the camera loves someone *sentence* The person named is very photogenic or telegenic: *The camera loved her dark good looks*—Time

cammies or **camies** *n by 1970s* A camouflage suit

or uniform: . . . *they said they would kill just to peel off their ripe desert cammies*—Newsweek/ *There were kids whose cammies (camouflage suits) were still on fire*. . . —Milwaukee Journal

cammo *n by 1980s* Camouflage: *The Cammo Dudes are here*—New York Times

camp 1 *n homosexuals by 1940s* A male homosexual **2** *adj*: *a camp bar/ the camp scene* **3** *n homosexuals by 1920s* Effeminate behavior, such as mincing gait, fluttering gestures, or pronounced lisp **4** *v* (also **camp it up**): *Malcolm was camping perilously in the blue-collar bar* **5** *n by 1960s* Something, esp in art, decoration, theater, etc, so naively stylized, artificial, affected, old-fashioned, and inadequate to good modern taste as to be highly amusing and inviting to parody: . . . *television's inexhaustible supply of crash courses in camp*—Washington Post **6** *adj a camp advertisement/ camp clothing* **7** *v* (also **camp it up**) *by 1960s* To behave in a humorously affected, exaggerated way, esp imitating the acting and oratorical styles of the 1800s: *She started camping, vamping me like Theda Bara* [origin uncertain; perhaps, as noted in 1909 referring to a sense "actions and gestures of exaggerated emphasis," it is fr French *se camper*, "put oneself in a bold, provocative posture," attested fr the middle 1600s; the more modern senses were revived, introduced, and popularized in Susan Sontag's essay "Notes on Camp," published in 1964] *See* BOOT CAMP, BUNYAN CAMP, HIGH CAMP, LOW CAMP, MITT-CAMP

campaign *See* WHISPERING CAMPAIGN

campus *v 1920s college students* To confine a student to the college premises as a disciplinary measure; =GROUND

campy 1 *adj homosexuals by 1940s* Effeminate; overtly homosexual **2** *adj by 1960s* Displaying naive, affected, and old-fashioned style: *a campy evocation of WWI patriotism*

can 1 *n about 1900* A toilet; =JOHN •Said to be a shortening of *piss-can* **2** *n about 1910* The buttocks; rump; =ASS: *And that's when I asked her about her fat can*—Mike Royko **3** *v by 1905* To discharge an employee; =FIRE: *He is not the first commentator to be canned by an editor*—Heywood Broun **4** *v by 1906* To stop; cease, esp some objectionable behavior •Usu a stern command: *Let's can the noise* **5** *n about 1910* A jail or prison; cell **6** *v*: *They caught him and canned him for two weeks* **7** *n Navy by 1930s* A destroyer; =TIN CAN **8** *n 1950s hot rodders* A hot rod **9** *n narcotics by 1930s* An ounce of marijuana or other narcotic **10** *v basketball by 1980s* To score by throwing a basket: . . . *Sander*. . . *canned another 20-footer*. . . **11** *n by 1990s* A canvasback duck: *I know there are a lot of hunters here this weekend to try for cans*—Milwaukee Journal *See* ASH CAN, BUTT CAN, GET A CAN ON, IN THE CAN, KICKING CAN, OIL CAN, SHITCAN, TIE A CAN ON someone, TIN CAN

canal water *See* SUCK CANAL WATER

canary 1 *n by 1880s* A girl or woman; =CHICK **2** *n*

by 1919 A woman singer, esp of popular music **3** *v*: *She used to canary with Stan Kenton* **4** *n 1920s underworld* An informer; =STOOL PIGEON •Because a *canary* sings *See* MOUNTAIN CANARY

can be *See* EASY AS PIE

cancelbot *n computer by 1990s* A computer program that intercepts and destroys a network message automatically when triggered by elements of the message: *Even*. . . *users who applaud such a use of what they call a "cancelbot" acknowledge that the situation raises broad and troubling issues*. . . —Milwaukee Journal [fr *cancel* plus ro*bot*]

cancer stick *n phr 1950s* A cigarette: . . . *you find some cancer sticks hidden*—Sassy [The origin of the term coincides with the first national awareness of the relationship between cigarette smoking and lung *cancer*]

can do 1 *sentence about 1900s* I can do it; I'm the one you want •The noun phrase *can do*, "good and willing worker," is attested from the 1830s: *We asked them to design a whole new bridge in a week, and they said "Can do"* **2** *modifier*: *The CIA was a can-do outfit*—The New Republic/ *So far it's been mostly a can-do spring for the 24-year-old righthander*—Milwaukee Journal *See* NO CAN DO

candy 1 *n about 1900* Cocaine or hashish **2** *n narcotics by 1960s* A sugar cube soaked with LSD; LSD **3** *n narcotics by 1960s* Any barbiturate drug **4** *n by 1940s* Something easily done; =BREEZE, CINCH, PIECE OF CAKE *See* NEEDLE CANDY, NOSE CANDY

candy ass *n phr by 1960s* A timid person; weakling; =WIMP

candy-assed or **candyass** *adj by 1950s* Timid; feeble; cowardly; =WIMPY: . . . *not that candy-assed dreck played by legions of Spandexed clones*—Worcester Magazine/ *Some candyass Barry Manilow type might be at ease in this setting*—New York Times

candy man *n phr 1960s narcotics* A narcotics supplier; =CONNECTION, PUSHER

candy store *by 1990s* **1** *n phr* A place where wide-eyed dreams are or may be fulfilled: *The US market is the candy store for one and all*—New Yorker **2** *n phr* Personal territory or property; =TURF: *It's Aidid's candy store*—Denver radio talk-show caller

candy stripe *n phr 1970s Army* A secondary road on a map [fr its pink color]

candy striper *n phr by 1960s* A young woman who is a volunteer nurse's aide in a hospital [fr the *stripes* on her uniform, resembling those on peppermint *candy*]

can house *n phr early 1900s* A brothel: *him playing the races and going to can houses*—James T Farrell [fr *can*, "buttocks, ass"]

I **can live with that** *sentence by 1980s* That's acceptable; I'll buy that: *You want 10 percent? I can live with that*

canned 1 *adj* (also **canned up**) *about 1910* Drunk: *They was already pretty canned*—James M Cain/ *They got canned up a little more*—James M Cain **2** *adj about 1900* Recorded; played from a phonograph record or magnetic tape: *canned music* **3** *adj 1890s* Not fresh for the occasion; kept for easy and general use: *The candidate uttered one or two canned one-liners, to small effect* **4** *adj* movie studios *by 1950s* Filmed; completed •That is, put into one of the large flat circular tin *cans* used for holding movie film: *That scene is already canned*

canned cow *n phr* cowboys *by 1920s* Canned milk; condensed milk

canned goods *n phr by 1918* A virgin, either male or female

canned hunt *n phr 1990s* A hunt arranged at a hunting ranch: *Farms and ranches offering what critics call "canned hunts" are springing up across the country*—Milwaukee Journal

cannery *n by 1920s* A jail

cannibal *n by 1970s* =SIXTY-NINE

cannon[1] *n* underworld *about 1900* A pistol; firearm; =PIECE: *He holstered his own cannon*—Raymond Chandler
See LOOSE CANNON

cannon[2] **1** *n* underworld *by 1910* A professional thief, esp a pickpocket: *. . . grand larceny, when a cannon lifts a wallet from a pocket*—New York Times **2** *v* underworld *by 1920s* : *You're too small to cannon the street-cars*—Nelson Algren [based on *gun*, "thief," fr Yiddish *gonif*]

cannonball 1 *n* hoboes *about 1915* A fast express or freight train **2** *n* prison *by 1920* A message sent from one prisoner to another, or from a prisoner to friends outside

cannonball day *n phr 1990s* lifeguards A day of bad weather such that you could shoot a cannonball down the beach without hitting anyone

cannon fodder *by 1930s* **1** *n phr* Common soldiers, esp young and relatively untrained infantry soldiers; =BULLET BAIT **2** *n phr* Any relatively low-ranking employee, associate, etc: *But I'm still cannon fodder when the crunch comes*—Douglas Coupland

canoe *v by 1930s; now outdated* To kiss and caress, etc; =MAKE OUT, NECK •Probably not connected with the later sense of *canoe* used just below: *Her old man had been hearing about me and Daisy canoeing*—Louis Armstrong [probably fr *canoodle*]

◁**canoe inspection**▷ *n phr by 1960s* Examination of the vulva and vagina for evidence of venereal disease •The female equivalent of the *short-arm inspection*

can (or tall can) of corn *n phr* baseball *by 1930s* A high, easy fly ball

can (or bag) of worms *n phr by 1950s* A complex and troublesome matter; a Pandora's box: *. . . leave it alone, don't kick the crawly old can of worms*—Stan Cutler/ *. . . the current bag of worms*—Armistead Maupin
See OPEN UP A CAN OF WORMS

canoodle or **kanoodle** *by 1850s* **1** *v* To hug, caress, etc; make love **2** *v* To coax, esp by lavishing affection [origin uncertain; said to be Oxford University slang, "paddle a canoe," which might lead to amorous behavior and blandishment, as little as this seems likely in an unstable watercraft]

can-opener *n* underworld *about 1910* Any tool used to open a safe

one can really (or one sure knows how to) pick 'em *sentence by 1960s* One is very selective, accurate, and successful in choices •Nearly always used ironically: *Is this turkey your idea of a good show? You can really pick 'em*

cans ◁1▷ *n by 1950s* A woman's breasts; =TITS: *. . . that chanteuse with the huge cans* **2** *n 1920s* Earphones worn over the ears [second sense perhaps fr the toy telephones made by punching a hole in the bottom of a tin *can* and connecting it to another such can by a string. When drawn taut, the string would carry the vibrations of a voice from one can and reproduce it in the other]
See KNOCK someone FOR A LOOP

can't buy *v phr by 1960s* To have no possibility of; be totally denied: *From then on, I couldn't buy a good review*—Saturday Review/ *You couldn't find a job. You couldn't buy a job*—Newsweek

someone can't carry a tune in a bucket *sentence later 1800s* Someone is tone-deaf; someone sings very badly: *Ashley can't carry a tune in a bucket*—New York Times

you can't fight city hall **See** YOU CAN'T FIGHT CITY HALL

can't fight (or punch) one's way out of a paper bag *v phr* prizefight *by 1940s* To be a very weak or ineffective puncher; put up a poor showing

he can't find his ass with both hands *sentence* (Variations: **butt** may replace **ass**; **hold** may replace **find**; **in his back pocket** may be added) *by 1940s* He is very stupid indeed; he is hopelessly drunk: *So drunk he couldn't find his butt with both hands*—H Allen Smith/ *. . . I'm a no-good scumbag from IAD who couldn't find his ass with both hands in his back pocket*—Michael Grant

you can't get there from here **See** YOU CAN'T GET THERE FROM HERE

someone can't hit the side of a barn (or a barn door) *sentence by 1930s* Someone is unable to throw accurately enough to hit anything at all

you can't make an omelet without breaking eggs **See** YOU CAN'T MAKE AN OMELET WITHOUT BREAKING EGGS

canto *n* sports *about 1910* A round, inning, period, or other division of a contest: *Lefty got decked in the third canto* [fr Italian, "song," with reference to the 100 poetic divisions of Dante's *Divina commedia*]

someone can't win for losing *sentence by 1970s* Someone seems entirely unable to make any sort of success; someone is persistently and distressingly bested: *We busted our humps, but we just couldn't win for losing*

Canuck 1 *n by 1840s* A Canadian, esp a French-Canadian **2** *modifier*: *Canuck booze/ my Canuck pal* •Regarded as offensive by some, but apparently becoming more acceptable

the **canvas** *n phr by 1910* A boxing ring

can you read lips *See* READ MY LIPS

cap[1] *by 1840s* **1** *n* Captain **2** *n* Mister; sir •Used in direct address to a man one wishes to flatter

cap[2] **1** *n 1920s narcotics* A capsule of narcotics: *I didn't have the money to buy a cap with*—D Hulburd **2** *v 1950s narcotics* To buy narcotics; =COP: *I capped me some more pot*—H Braddy **3** *v 1950s narcotics* To open or use a capsule of narcotics; =BUST A CAP
See BUST CAPS

cap[3] **1** *v by 1940s* To best or outdo, esp with a funnier joke, stranger story, etc; =TOP: *She told a lie that capped mine* **2** *v 1960s* To shoot; kill by shooting •Compare *bust a cap*: *I should just cap you right now*—Rocky Mountain News/ . . . *I think I'm going to cap myself today*—Milwaukee Journal Sentinel **3** *v 1980s teenagers* =CAP ON someone [all in one way or another fr *cap*, "head covering"]
See APPLEJACK CAP, BUST A CAP, GIMME CAP, GO-TO-HELL CAP

◁**cap**[4]▷ *n by 1960s* Fellatio; =HEAD: *Give Jerry some cap*—Donald Goines

Cape Cod (or **Cape Ann) turkey** *n phr by 1865* Codfish

capeesh or **coppish** or **capiche** (kə PEESH) *by 1940s* **1** *question* Do you understand?: *All right, class, that's all there is to it. Capeesh?/ I owe it all to you. Strip Dealers School, capiche?*—Mesa Tribune/ . . . *fixed me with a pair of very cold eyes. "Capish?" he said*—Stan Cutler **2** *affirmation* I understand: *Ten tonight? Capeesh* [fr Italian *capisci*, "Do you understand?"]

caper 1 *n by 1870s* A drunken spree; a carouse; =BINGE **2** *n by 1840s* A prank; stunt **3** *n underworld by 1920s* A crime, esp a robbery

caper-juice *n by 1880s* Whiskey

capo (KA poh, KAH-) *n* The head of a local unit of the Mafia; Mafia captain: . . . *identified as. . . Mafia capo by whatever's current crime commission*—Stan Cutler [fr Italian, "head, chief"]

capo di tutti capi (KAH poh dee toot ee KAH pee) *n phr by 1970s* The chief of all chiefs; =HEAD OF ALL THE HEADS, HONCHO, MISTER BIG, TOP DOG: . . . *the dissidents convened an extraordinary meeting of every capo di tutti baseball capi*—Time/ *Salvatore (Toto) Riina, the capo di tutti capi of the Sicilian mob*—New York Times

cap on someone *by 1980s* **1** *v phr* To outdo someone; =CAP, TOP **2** *v phr* To insult someone; =DIS, PUT someone DOWN

capper 1 *n by 1750s* A huckster's or professional gambler's helper, who attracts clients; =SHILL **2** *n by 1940s* The climax or end of something **3** *n by 1940s* A story, joke, etc, that outdoes another one

car *n 1980s prison* A group of prisoners from the same city or other place; locational clique: *All these kids were in the Sacramento car*
See FUNNY CAR, POP CAR, PROWL CAR, WAY CAR

carbo *n 1970s* A carbohydrate food: *She knew she shouldn't be munching out on carbos like this*—Cyra McFadden

carborundum *See* ILLEGITIMATI NON CARBORUNDUM

car bra *n phr 1980s* A protective covering for the front of a car, often made of black plastic

car clout *n phr 1990s* A thief who breaks into parked cars, esp at national parks: *We don't get a lot of sophistication in car clouts. They smash the window, grab the stuff, and high-tail it out of there*—Milwaukee Journal

card 1 *n by 1830s* A remarkable person, esp an eccentric or amusing one **2** *n 1920s narcotics* A portion of a narcotic; =DECK **3** *n sports by 1930s* A schedule; program of events: *six fights on the card* **4** *v by 1970s* To require someone to show identification, esp at a bar or liquor store: *So far my only success was not getting carded at the Wheaton Liquor Store*—Robert B Parker
See FACE CARD, GET one's CARD PUNCHED, IN THE CARDS, MEAT CARD, PAINT CARDS, PIE CARD, STACK THE DECK, WILD CARD

card-carrying *adj by 1960s* Authentic; genuine and long-standing: *These women tend not to be card-carrying feminists*—New York Daily News/ . . . *a service for all us card-carrying optimists*—James Michener [fr the *carrying* of a membership card in an organization; first used of Communists during the 1950s period of political inquisition]

card sharp (or **shark) *n phr by 1880s* A very clever cardplayer, esp an unscrupulous poker or bridge player •Shortening of earlier *card sharper*

cardy or **cardi** or **cardie** *n by 1960s* A cardigan sweater: *Blue cardy, $100, by Lacoste*—Sassy

care *See* TAKE CARE OF BUSINESS

care and feeding *n phr by 1960s* Solicitous care and nurturing, like that given an infant: *Sununu devoted himself to the care and feeding of a five-member Executive Council*—Vanity Fair

career girl *n phr by 1940s* A woman, esp a young woman, who pursues a business or professional career, and often remains unmarried

care package *n phr by 1980s* Gifts, money, etc, given to a relative or friend: *They try to help their son with occasional care packages* [fr CARE package, a parcel of food, clothing, etc, sent to needy persons overseas through the Cooperative for American Relief Everywhere, in the aftermath of World War II]

carhop *1930s* **1** *n* A waitress or waiter who serves food to patrons in parked cars at a drive-in restaurant; =CURBIE **2** *v*: *She carhopped at Beef Babylon* [formed on the model of *bellhop*]

carjacking *n 1990s* The armed and violent stealing of a car from its driver; =GANKING: *At 15 he was arrested for carjacking and assault*—New York Times [fr *car* plus hi*jacking*]

carny or **carney** or **carnie** *by 1930s* **1** *n* A carnival **2** *n* A carnival worker or member of such a worker's family: *outdoor show people, the "carnies," who travel from town to town with carnivals*—AJ Liebling **3** *modifier*: *carny talk/ a carney family* **4** *n* The occupational idiom or jargon of carnival people: *I thought you talked carney by now*—F Brown

carpet *See* CALL someone ON THE CARPET, RED CARPET, ROLL OUT THE RED CARPET

carpetbag *v 1930s students* To try to make a good impression

carpet-bomb *v 1980s* To mount a highly destructive and intense opposition; =CLOBBER: *. . . the Bush campaign carpet-bombed Dukakis from Labor Day onward*—New Republic [fr a 1950s term for total area bombing, laying as it were a *carpet* of *bombs*]

◁**carpet-muncher**▷ *n by 1980s* A lesbian

carpet-rat *See* RUG APE

carps *n theater by 1920s* A stage carpenter ●Used as a nickname, as *Chips* is for a ship's carpenter

carrier *See* BAT CARRIER, JEEP CARRIER

carrot-top *n by 1880s* A redhead

carry 1 *v 1920s narcotics* To have narcotics on one's person **2** *v underworld by 1950s* To be armed [fr the 1920s phrase *carry iron*, "to be armed"]

carry a load *v phr by 1890s* To be drunk

carry a lot of weight *v phr by 1690s* To be important; have authority: *My opinions don't carry a lot of weight*

carry a tune in a bucket *See* someone CAN'T CARRY A TUNE IN A BUCKET

carrying 1 *adj by 1950s* Armed, esp with a pistol: *He carrying, Mr Esteva*—Robert B Parker **2** *adj 1920s narcotics* Having narcotics on one's person *See* CARD-CARRYING

carry the ball *v phr football by 1940s* To assume the active leading role: *While the boss is away, you must carry the ball*

carry the banner *v phr hoboes by 1890s* To walk the street all night for lack of a bed: *I have "carried the banner" in infernal metropolises*—Jack London

carry the something chromosome *v phr by 1990s* To have the characteristics indicated: *My husband, who knows I carry the restaurant chromosome, suggested that I get up on the steel catwalk that ran along one long wall to make a toast*—Los Angeles Times [fr the X and Y *chromosomes* that determine sexual and hence other characteristics]

carry the difference *v phr early 1900s* To be armed: *If you're going to fool around with that guy, don't you think you ought to carry the difference?*—movie Johnny Eager

carry the load (or the ball) *v phr by 1950s* To do or be responsible for the major part of a job: *His wife carried the load in that family*

carry (or haul) the mail 1 *v phr by 1950s* =CARRY THE LOAD **2** *v phr by 1920s* To go very fast; =BARREL

carry the stick *v phr hoboes by 1940s* To be a hobo; =BUM AROUND [fr the *stick* on which the hobo carried his or her bindle]

carry the torch *v phr by 1927* To love in a suffering way, esp because the desired one does not reciprocate: *She was carrying the torch for W C Fields*—E Johnson [origin unknown; said to have been coined by a Broadway nightclub singer named Tommy Lyman, when he said, "My famous torch song, 'Come to me, my melancholy baby'"; Venus, of course, carried a torch regularly]

carry someone's **water** *v phr by 1980s* To do the menial jobs; be an underling, esp in politics: *I have carried the water for the Democratic Party for years*—Denver radio talk-show caller/ *The White House doesn't have to call. . . . They have other people carrying their water for them*—New York Times

car-surf *v by 1990s* To ride on the outside of a car, esp on the trunk: *The boy. . . was thrown from the trunk early Saturday morning while "car-surfing". . .* —Milwaukee Journal

car-surfing *n by 1990s* Riding on the outside of a car: *. . . he and a 12-year-old girl tried a round of "car-surfing". . .* —Milwaukee Journal

cart *v by 1880s* To transport; move; take: *I carted him over to the drug store: Jesse James could have waltzed in there and carted off all the patio furniture*—Lawrence Sanders *See* COLD-MEAT CART

cartload *n by 1570s* A large amount; lots; =HEAPS, SHITLOAD: *. . . government documents tend (especially when there are cartloads of them) to induce a certain myopia*—Nation

car toad *n phr 1920s railroad* A terminal worker who inspects or services railroad cars

cartwheel *n about 1850* A dollar, esp a silver dollar

carve *v outdated 1930s jive talk* To give one a thrill; =SEND: *He carves me. Does he carve you?*—Max Shulman

not **carved in stone** *See* NOT CARVED IN STONE

cas (CAZH) *adj* (also **caj, cazh**) *1980s teenagers* Casual; informal; =LAID-BACK: *It's gonna be a very mellow night; laid back and cazh*—Slang Bag 93

◁**casabas**▷ *n by 1970s* A woman's breasts [fr *casaba*, a kind of melon, fr *Kassaba*, a Turkish town that exported them]

Casanova or **casanova** *n by 1880s* A ladies' man and seducer; =LOVER-BOY: *Do ravish me, you wicked casanova you* [fr the name of Giacomo Girolamo *Casanova*, 1725–98, a writer and legendary debaucher]

case 1 *n by 1833* An odd, eccentric person; =CARD, CHARACTER **2** *v* (also **case out**) *underworld by 1914* To inspect, scrutinize, esp with a view to robbery or burglary ●*Keep the cases* in the sense "keep close watch" is attested fr 1856, with reference to faro: *I've cased this one and it's ripe*—Joseph Wambaugh **3** *n*: *Lefty gave the bank a case See* BUTTERFLY CASE, COUCH CASE, DROP CASE, FIVE-CASE NOTE, GET DOWN TO CASES, GET OFF someone's CASE, GET ON someone's CASE, HAVE A CASE OF THE DUMB-ASS, HAVE A CASE ON someone, HEADCASE, MAKE A FEDERAL CASE out of something, NUTBALL, OFF someone's CASE, ON someone's CASE, SHOWCASE, WORST-CASE SCENARIO

case ace *n phr* cardplayers by 1950s The fourth ace after three have been dealt, esp in stud poker [fr the dealing box or *case* used in the game of faro, where the last card of each denomination left in the box is the *case card*]

case dough *n phr* by 1940s A small amount of money set aside for emergencies; =MAD MONEY

case note *n phr* by 1880s A dollar; dollar bill

case out *v phr* outdated fr 1940s To accompany someone, esp in order to share winnings, luck, etc: *Can't I case out wit' you, Frankie?*—Nelson Algren

cash *See* COLD CASH

cash cow *n phr* 1970s A source of money, esp a generous one: *But all this leaves The New Republic Inc without a cash cow*—New Republic/ *For a fairly blatant cash cow,* Pisces Iscariot *delivers some fine milk*—Entertainment Weekly

cash-for-trash *modifier* 1990s Sordid, and told only for payment: *The White House is not going to comment on any cash-for-trash stories*—Milwaukee Journal Sentinel

cash in one's **chips** **1** *v phr* (also **cash it in**) by 1870s To die; =KICK THE BUCKET **2** *v phr* by 1890s To withdraw from some arrangement, esp a business deal [fr the redeeming of gambling chips for money, signifying the end of the game]

cash in on something *v phr* by 1920s To get profit or advantage from something, esp from something unexpected

casino *modifier* by 1990s Marked by risk-taking and the gambling spirit: *. . . contradiction between the real economy and the casino economy of Wall Street*—Atlantic Monthly

cast *n* 1990s Interpretation; opinion; =SPIN, TAKE •In the sense of a personal turn or inclination of mind, *cast* is attested by 1711: *He has his own cast on this*—National Public Radio news

cast a kitten *See* HAVE KITTENS

not **cast in concrete** *See* NOT CARVED IN STONE

casting couch *n phr* by 1920s The fancied sofa in a theatrical or film decision-maker's office upon which he appraises the talent of young women seeking roles: *. . . only slightly detoured by a refusal to join Darryl F Zanuck on the casting couch*—New York Times

cast-iron balls *See* HAVE BRASS BALLS

cat[1] **1** *n* outdated hoboes fr 1890s A hobo or a migrant worker **2** *n* by 1535 A prostitute ◁**3**▷ *n* by 1730s The vulva; =PUSSY **4** *v* (also **cat around**) by 1725 To spend time with women for amatory purposes; chase and stalk women; =TOMCAT **5** *n* by 1760s A woman who, often subtly, attacks and denigrates other women; a spiteful and malicious woman: *Dorothy Parker was a super cat* **6** *n* 1950s black & teenagers A man who dresses flashily, and ostentatiously pursues worldly pleasure; =DUDE, HEPCAT, SPORT: *. . . I was a sharp cat*—Louis Armstrong/ *The cool chick down on Calumet has got herself a brand new cat*—Gwendolyn Brooks

7 *v* black by 1960s To move stealthily: *. . . began to cat toward the door*—Donald Goines **8** *v* by 1920s To loaf and idle; spend one's time on street corners admiring young women **9** *n* 1920s jazz musicians A jazz musician: *It was all right to the early cats*—Stephen Longstreet **10** *n* 1960s =HIPSTER **11** *n* by 1940s Any man; fellow; =GUY: *Who's that cat sitting next to the Pope?* **12** *n* by 1880s A sailboat with one fore-and-aft sail; a catboat: *He sails a little cat* **13** *n* 1990s Metcathenone, an addictive synthetic narcotic similar to but more powerful than cocaine: *For a few hundred dollars, dealers can produce thousands of dollars' worth of cat*—National Public Radio [black sense, "dude," may be influenced by a Wolof term]

See ALLEY CAT, ASH CAT, FAT CAT, FRAIDY CAT, HELLCAT, HEPCAT, HIP CAT, HOLY CATS, KICK AT THE CAT, LET THE CAT OUT OF THE BAG

cat[2] or **Cat** *n* by 1940s A bulldozer or Caterpillar tractor [fr *Caterpillar,* trademark for a kind of continuous-track tractor]

cat[3] *n* by 1960s A catamaran boat

Cat *n* black by 1940s A Cadillac: *Tia Juana pulled up in his long green Cat*—C B Himes

catbird seat *n phr* by 1930s An enviable position; a controlling position: *The owners are in the catbird seat*—Sports Illustrated

See SIT IN THE CATBIRD SEAT

catch **1** *v* by 1906 To see, hear, or attend a particular entertainment: *I caught Mickey Rooney on TV* **2** *v* by 1880s =CATCH ON **3** *n* by 1740s A highly desirable acquisition or engagement: *Getting Von Karajan for our benefit would be a catch* **4** *n* by 1855 A hidden cost, qualification, defect, etc; something to make one think twice: *It looks like all gravy, but there's a catch to it* **5** *v* police by 1950s To do desk duty, answering the telephone and receiving complaints: *Thompson was catching in the squad room at Manhattan South*—Richard Lockridge **6** *v* homosexual by 1970s To be penetrated in an anal sex act

See SHOESTRING CATCH

catch someone somewhere, doing something, etc *sentence* by 1830 You will never discover this person in the situation or activity named •A vigorous denial with nearly interjectional force: *Catch Eddie allowing himself to be dated like that!*—Saul Bellow/ *Catch me in a tux!*

catch a Herb *v phr* 1990 To look for an easy robbery victim

catch a rail *See* TAKE GAS

catch-as-catch-can *modifier* by 1880s Precarious; requiring keen readiness: *We lived a catch-as-catch-can life those first few years*

catch dog *n phr* by 1980s A scapegoat: *We are the catch dogs for everyone who comes along looking for something to kick at*—New York Times [evolved fr Southern dialect *catch dog,* "dog used to round up animals, herd dog," perhaps because the herded animals would kick at the dogs]

catch fire *v phr* by 1980s To become markedly successful; =CATCH ON: *It was a good idea, but it never really caught fire*

catch someone **flat-footed (**or **on** their **heels** *v phr* by 1940s To surprise someone; catch someone unprepared: *When the market crashed they were caught flat-footed/ Milwaukee was caught on its heels as. . . Doran added his second goal. . .* Milwaukee Journal [fr baseball, referring esp to a base-runner who is caught off-base and thrown out]

catch flies 1 *v phr* theater by 1940s To distract the audience's attention from another performer by making unnecessary gestures and motions **2** *v phr* by 1940s To gape and yawn, esp from boredom

catch hell (Variations: **holy hell** or **merry hell** may replace **hell**) by 1920s **1** *v phr* To be severely rebuked or punished **2** *v phr* To be severely damaged or injured: *The dock caught holy hell in that last approach*

catch it *v phr* by 1835 To be very severely rebuked or punished: *Uh-oh! This time we'll catch it!*
See GET IT IN THE NECK

catch on 1 *v phr* by 1880s To see and understand, esp with insightful suddenness; grasp; =DIG, GET: *As long as they don't catch on, we can cheat them forever* **2** *v phr* by 1880s To be accepted and approved; succeed with the public: *The wing-dancing and funny acts catch on big*—The Lantern

catch–22 or **Catch–22** 1960s **1** *n* A condition or requirement very hard to fulfill, esp one which flatly contradicts others: *It was a classic catch–22. . . The problem was that it was a top-secret project they weren't supposed to know about*—Associated Press **2** *modifier*: *. . . puts me in a Catch–22 fix*—William Appel [fr the title of a 1961 satirical novel by Joseph Heller]

catch-up *See* PLAY CATCH-UP

catch someone **with** someone's **hand in the till (**or **the cookie jar)** *See* WITH one's HAND IN THE TILL

catch someone **with their pants down** *v phr* by 1920s To find someone in the wrong with no possibility of evasion; catch someone in flagrante delicto: *Every time someone catches us with our pants down, catches us in an outright lie, up pops Ron to admit it*—Earl Thompson/ *The insensitive, bumbling male senators caught with their political pants down suggested a watershed in American politics*—Nation

catch some rays *v phr* 1980s To sunbathe: *. . . the prince seized the opportunity to leave his chilly isle behind and catch some rays*—Milwaukee Journal

catch the wave *v phr* by 1990s To seize an opportunity; take advantage of present trends: *. . . television is the central fact of political life: deal with it or die*—catch the wave—New York Times [fr surfing, with a possible echo of Hamlet: "There is a tide in the affairs of men/ Which, taken at the flood, leads on to fortune"]

catchy *adj* by 1830s Seizing attention or admiration; attractive: *You need a really catchy logo*

catch Zs *See* COP ZS

cat fight *n phr* by 1970s A particularly noisy and vicious struggle or squabble: *. . . to judge from the cat fight that erupted among members of the advisory council*—Washington Post

catfit *n* by 1890s A violent fit of rage or other strong feeling; =CONNIPTION FIT, DUCK-FIT: *If he doesn't get that job he'll have a catfit*

cathauling *n* Prolonged and rough questioning: *Brafferton's cathauling by the Harford Committee*—Richard Starnes [fr the mid–19th-century literal term *cathaul,* "drag a clawing cat down the bare back of a prone victim"]

Catholic *See* IS THE POPE POLISH

cathouse 1 *n* hoboes about 1915 A cheap lodging house; =FLOPHOUSE **2** *n* by 1890s A brothel: *New Orleans was proud and ashamed of its cathouses*—Stephen Longstreet [second sense fr earlier *cat,* "prostitute, vulva"]

cat-nap *n* by 1850s A short doze while sitting up: *The Senator was enjoying a cat-nap at the time* [Attested in form *cat's nap* by 1823]

cats and dogs *n phr* outdated 1870s stock market Low-priced stocks, such as those returning no dividends at all
See RAIN CATS AND DOGS

the cat's meow *n phr* (Variations: **ass** or **balls** or **eyebrows** or **nuts** or **pajamas** or **whiskers** may replace **meow**; the phrase may be shortened to **the cat's**) about 1920 Something or someone that is superlative •Not quite outdated: *The cat's pajamas!*—anything that is very good—Philadelphia Evening Bulletin/ *. . . that you are on top of things and that you are, therefore, the cat's ass*—Robert B Parker [the entry form and *pajamas* form are said to have been coined by the cartoonist and sports writer Tad Dorgan, who died in 1929]

catsuit *n* by 1990s A tight-fitting garment covering the entire body: *Michelle is wearing a skintight black catsuit and short high-heeled boots*—Vanity Fair [Perhaps suggested by the seeming-epidermal garb of a character named *Catwoman,* played by Julie Newmar in the 1970s televison show *Batman,* and by characters in the show *Cats*]

cattle call show business by 1950s **1** *n phr* An audition announcement, esp for a number of extras; also the crowd resulting from such an announcement: *Mr Allen is having what is known in show business as a cattle call*—Wall Street Journal/ *I can't speak for the other agencies,. . . but we've just about done away with the cattle call*—Toronto Life **2** *modifier*: *Nonprofessionals may vie for spaces. . . in "cattle-call" auditions*—Washington Post

cattle show *n phr* by 1970s A convention or other occasion where political candidates display their notions, charisma, etc: *. . . raise money for themselves by holding "cattle shows"*—Washingtonian

catty *adj* by late 1800s Inclined to discredit others;

malicious; spitefully gossipy: *Karla and Susan were being catty about Dusty*—Douglas Coupland [But *cat*, "spiteful woman," is attested from the 1760s]

catty-cat *See* CAT[1]

be **caught dead** *See* NOT BE CAUGHT DEAD

caught in a rundown *adj phr fr baseball by 1970s* In an embarrassing and untenable plight: *The imperilled Cuomo seemed to be constantly in motion. Sometimes he moved so desperately that he seemed to be caught in a rundown—a reminder that he had briefly been a center fielder with a Pittsburgh Pirates farm team*—New Yorker

caught looking *adj phr baseball by 1970s* Called out on strikes from not swinging

cauliflower ear *n phr fr early 1900s* A boxer's or wrestler's ear deformed by injuries and accumulated scar tissue

caulk (or calk or cork) off *Navy by 1890s* **1** *v phr* To sleep; go to sleep •*Caulk* in the same sense is noted as British Navy use by 1818 **2** *v* To rest from work; =TAKE A BREAK

cavalry *n by 1980s* Last-minute rescue forces; a deus ex machina: *Powell likened the Somalia operation to "the cavalry coming to the rescue"*—Harper's/ *. . . not the time for a President who avoided the draft to call up the cavalry*—New York Times/ *Democrats hear hoofbeats—the cavalry's arrival, in the nick of time*—New York Time [fr the numerous cases in cowboy movies when the US Cavalry would arrive to rescue various beleaguered persons]

cavalier *n prizefight fr 1920s* A skillful boxer as distinct from a slugger or caveman

cave **1** *v* (also **cave in**) entry form by 1850s, variant by 1830 To surrender; give way; =CHICKEN OUT: *The Russians will cave when they find we are in earnest*—Hawley Smart/ *OK, so I caved in on the white suger, the TV, the war toys*—New York Times **2** *n by 1930s* A room; =PAD

caveman **1** *n early 1900s* A strong, crude man, esp one who is sexually rough and masterful; =MACHO **2** *n 1920s prizefight* A strong hitter or slugger

cayuse (KĪ yōōs) *n cowboys by 1860s* A horse, esp a small and hardy beast descended from the wild horse of the Pacific Northwest: *From Oregon came the horse's name, "cayuse." That state was the home of the Cayuse tribe of Indians, an equestrian people*—P A Rollins

CCM (pronounced as separate letters) *n 1990s black* Money; cash [fr *cold cash money*]

Cecil or **Cee** *n narcotics by 1930s* Cocaine

ceiling *n by 1930s* An upper limit: *The Gov put a two-billion-dollar ceiling on office expenses* [probably fr *ceiling*, "the highest an airplane can go," which is attested from 1917]
See HIT THE CEILING

cel *n by 1990s* A celluloid sheet made for an animated cartoon, now prized by collectors: *. . . cartoon lovers have been buying drawings and celluloids, or "cels". . .*—Milwaukee Journal

celeb (sə LEB) *n by 1913* A celebrity: *. . . each a certified celeb from the realms of cafe, style, or the-atrical society*—New York Daily News/ *. . . surrounded by giggling celebs*—New York Magazine

celestial discharge *n phr 1990s medical* Death: *Mr Jones got his celestial discharge. . . today*—Los Angeles Times

the **cellar** *n phr early 1900s* The lowest standing in a sports league, esp in a baseball league: *. . . struggling not to finish in the cellar*

cellar-dwellers *n by 1970s* The team in last place in a sports league

cellphone *n 1990s* A cellular telephone: *. . . a pall of melancholy introspection descends on the cell-phones of the media facilities*—New Yorker

cementhead **1** *n 1980s* A stupid person; dolt; =BOOB, DOOFUS, SPAZ **2** *n 1990s hockey* A player known more for his combative than athletic skills; =GOON: *That cementhead gave him a lumber facial, but the ref didn't call it*—Los Angeles Times

cement mixer **1** *n phr by 1940s* A dance or other act that includes a swiveling of the pelvis; =GRIND **2** *n phr 1930s truckers* A noisy car or truck: *Some jerk pulls alongside and guns his cement mixer*—comic strip "There Oughta Be a Law"

cement overcoat (or kimono) *n phr by 1940s* A casing of cement containing a corpse for disposal in deep water

cent *See* a RED CENT

center *See* DEAD CENTER, FRONT AND CENTER

centerfold *n by 1960s* A sexually desirable person: *. . . a woman with a centerfold's chest going for her*—Dan Jenkins [fr the photographs of such persons decorating the *centerfolds* of erotic magazines]

center stage *n phr by 1990s fr theater* The place of maximum visibility; forefront: *. . . when women's issues were brought to center stage, the Democrats caved*—Time

central *n by 1990s* The most important site of what is indicated: *. . . Israel Claims U.S. Is Terror Central*—Nation/ *. . . quickly turned the Odessa into Mob Central*—Vanity Fair/ *This is a small town, but if its cocaine central then it's a pretty tough town. . .*—Robert B Parker

Central Casting *n phr by 1980s* The putative office whence ideal and stereotypical persons, products, recipes, etc, come: *. . . white, male, married Protestant, middle to upper class, with children and dogs. He comes straight out of Central Casting*—New York Review/ *This is salsa from Central Casting*—John Willoughby [fr the Hollywood office that provides actors for film producers]

cents *See* PUT one's TWO CENTS IN, TEN CENTS

centurion *n by 1990s* A dependable defender; loyal soldier: *Adm William Crowe, the Democrats' favorite centurion*—Nation [the Roman officer who commanded 100 legionaries]

century *n by 1850s* A hundred dollars: *For two centuries a week I had me a bodyguard*—Jerome Robbins

Cessna repellent *n phr airline by 1970s* The landing lights of an airliner when switched on in a busy area to warn other aircraft of its presence [fr

Cessna, trademark for a line of relatively small airplanes, and *repellent* fr the model *insect repellent*]

CGI (pronounced as separate letters) *n 1990s* Computer-generated imagery: . . . *blend computer-generated imagery (CGI, new buzzword) and full-size mock-up dinos. . .*—Macon Telegraph

◀**cha-cha**▶ *n 1970s* A Latino person

chain *See* BALL-AND-CHAIN, DAISY CHAIN, PULL someone's CHAIN

chain-drink *v by 1970s* To have drink after drink without pause: . . . *a man who chain-drinks Pepsis*—C See [modeled on *chain-smoker*]

chain gang *n phr by 1980s* The football officials who carry and set the chain that marks off the ten yards needed for a first down

chain lightning *n phr by 1843* Inferior whiskey

chain locker *n phr nautical by 1960s* A wretched dockside bar [fr the filthy and dangerous compartment where anchor *chain* is stowed aboard ship]

chain-smoke *v fr early 1900s* To smoke cigarette after cigarette, lighting the next one from the current one

chain-snatcher *n* A petty thief; =PUNK: . . . *the buppie asks Yolanda what she's doing with this chain-snatcher*—New York Times

chair *See* BARBER CHAIR

the chair *by 1895* **1** *n* The electric chair; =the HOT SEAT **2** *n* Death by legal electrocution: *They convicted him, and he got the chair*

chair-warmer *n by 1909* An untalented and dispensable person; =WARM BODY

chalk *n horse-racing by 1950s* A horse favored to win [References to winning by *a long chalk,* an allusion to scoring points by a chalk mark, date from the 1830s]

chalk-eater or **chalk-player** *n horse-racing by 1950s* A person who bets only on the horse favored to win

chalk-talk *n by 1880s* A lecture, lesson, etc, accompanied by sketches: *The coach gave us a chalk-talk about the blitz*

chalk something **up** *v phr by late 1500s* To record credit or debit, as if by a chalk mark: *She won easily, and we must chalk it up to her careful preparation*

Chamber of Commerce *n phr by 1900* A toilet [fr *chamber pot*]

champ *n by 1868* A champion, esp a boxing titleholder

champagne (or **boss) trick** *n phr prostitutes by 1970s* A rich or high-paying client: *I take only champagne tricks, $100 an hour*—Gail Sheehy

chance *See* CHINAMAN'S CHANCE, OUTSIDE CHANCE, a SNOWBALL'S CHANCE IN HELL

chandelier sign *n phr medical by 1980s* The diagnostic sign for pelvic inflammatory disease: the patient surges up from the table, toward the chandelier, when her cervix is moved

change *n by 1880s* Money: . . . *a sizable chunk of change*—Bob Thomas
See LOOSE CHANGE, PIECE OF CHANGE, SMALL POTATOES

and **change** *n phr by 1980s* A small additional amount: . . . *the book value of the Thunderbird was $3,900 and change*—New York Times/ *At an hour and change before midnight there was still a line of people waiting to get into the Opera Cafe*—New York Times/ . . . *an average sentence is 27 words and change*—Spy

change breath *v phr by 1940s* To have a drink of liquor

change hats *v phr by 1990s* To change one's affiliations, role, etc: . . . *changed hats and supported Maggie Thatcher*—Russell Baker

change the channel *v phr 1950s teenagers* To shift the topic of conversation

change-up **1** *n 1950s baseball* A slow pitch delivered after a motion that might precede a fast pitch; a change of pace **2** *v 1950s baseball* : *Holy cow! He changed him up for a strike!* **3** *n by 1970s* Any change, esp a pronounced one: *McDowell exhibits a first-rate change-up*—Richard Schickel/ *Four costume changes served as a change-up in the manic pace*—Rolling Stone

channel **1** *n 1950s narcotics* A vein, usu in the crook of the elbow or the instep, favored for the injection of narcotics; =MAIN LINE **2** *v 1950s hot rodders* To lower the body of a car by opening channels around parts of the frame: *Johnny Slash, the punk in wraparound shades, lusts for a chopped and channeled '49 Merc*—Village Voice **3** *v 1980s* To be a medium of communication for a unbodied spirit: *Just some guy she channels for. Don't worry, the viewers love him*—Gary Trudeau

channel surf *v phr 1990s* To shift rapidly from one television channel to another: . . . *people who channel surf, using a remote control*—Hippocrates [*Channel-hop,* in the same sense, is attested from 1971, but did not thrive]

channel surfer *n phr 1990s* A person who channel surfs; =GRAZER, TRAWLER

chap or **chappie** *n by early 1700s* A man; fellow; =GUY, JOE ●Predominantly British use: *Which of you chaps is ready?/* . . . *which may amuse the chappies around Labuses*—John O'Hara [fr a shortening of *chapman,* "peddler; peddler's·customer," hence analogous with *customer* in the same sense]

chap someone's **ass** *v phr by 1950s* To irritate or annoy someone; =BE IN someone's FACE, GRIPE

chaplain *See* SEE THE CHAPLAIN

chapped *adj 1960s* Angry; =PISSED OFF

chaps *See* CHOPS

chapter *by 1940s* **1** *n* A division of a sports contest, esp an inning of baseball; =CANTO **2** *n* An episode, period, or passage: *Please don't remind me of that revoltingly squalid chapter in my life*

chapter and verse *by early 1700s* **1** *n phr* An exact detailed account: *I can give you chapter and verse about that night* **2** *adv phr*: *He knew it chapter and verse* **3** *n phr* The guiding documents or principles; rules: *I know the chapter and verse of the university's policy*

character **1** *n by 1770s* A person who behaves

oddly and often amusingly; an eccentric: *My uncle's quite a character* **2** *n by 1920s* A person; =JOKER: *You know a character name of Robert Ready?*

charge 1 *n 1920s narcotics* An injection of a narcotic **2** *n* (also **large charge**) *1930s jazz musicians* An acute thrill of pleasure; =BLAST, KICK, RUSH: *What kind of ol' creep'd get a charge out of this stuff?*—S J Perelman **3** *n narcotics by 1950s* Marijuana **4** *v underworld by 1930s* To rob
 See GET A BANG OUT OF someone or something, LARGE CHARGE

charged up 1 *adj phr narcotics by 1920s* Intoxicated by a narcotic; =HIGH **2** *adj phr* In a state of excited preparedness and heightened keenness; =PUMPED UP: *They lost, the coach declared, because they were not charged up*

charger *n 1950s hot rodders* A driver, esp of a hot rod

chariot *n by 1930s* A car

charity *See* COLD AS HELL

charity girl *n phr by 1940s* A sexually promiscuous young woman

charity stripe (or **line**) *n phr basketball by 1930s* The free-throw line: *. . . the Hawks knew the game would be decided at the charity stripe*—Jefferson County Union

charity toss *n phr basketball by 1940s* A free throw

Charley *n* =CHARLEY HORSE
 See GOOD-TIME CHARLEY

Charley coke or **Charlie** *narcotics by 1940s* **1** *n phr* or *n* Cocaine **2** *n phr* or *n* A cocaine addict

charley (or **Charley**) **horse** *n phr by 1887* A stiff and painful inflammation of a muscle, esp of the large thigh muscle

Charley Noble *n phr by 1840s* The galley chimney, funnel, or exhaust pipe of a ship or boat

◁**Charlie**▷ *n Vietnam War armed forces* The Vietcong or a Vietcong soldier [fr Victor *Charlie*, military voice alphabet designation for VC]
 See MISTER CHARLIE

Charlies *n Army by 1970s* Army C-rations, packages of tinned and dried food [fr *Charlie*, the letter C in the military phonetic alphabet formerly used for voice communication]

chart 1 *n horse-racing by 1940s* Figures and other material showing past performance, esp of a race horse; =FORM, TRACK RECORD **2** *n 1950s cool musicians* A musical arrangement or score

the **charts** *n phr 1960s* The listings that show the popularity of a song, a record, etc: *Stevie's latest single is way, way up on the charts*
 See OFF THE CHARTS

chase *v by 1906* To take a usually milder drink after a drink of liquor: *Let's chase this with a little Perrier*
 See GO CHASE yourself, PAPER CHASE

chase one's **own tail** *v phr 1960s* To go on frantic and futile pursuits: *. . . it's been fun watching the press chase its own tail on the persistent rumors of his extramarital escapades*—Nation

chaser 1 *n by 1897* A drink, often water, taken immediately after a drink of liquor **2** *n by 1894* A man in amatory pursuit of women; =SKIRT-CHASER: *Mark always was a lady-killer, a chaser*—A R Hilliard **3** *n truckers by 1920s* An employee assigned to hurry others in their work **4** *n show business by 1930s* An exit march; music played as the audience is leaving; recessional **5** *n prison by 1960s* A guard
 See AMBULANCE CHASER, FLY-CHASER, MONKEY-CHASER, SKIRT-CHASER, WOMAN-CHASER

chase the dragon *v phr 1970s narcotics* To inhale heroin fumes: *I was chasing the dragon, strung out on junk*—Philadelphia Journal

chassis *n by 1920s* The human physique, esp the body of a well-built woman; =BUILD
 See CLASSY CHASSIS

chat *n 1980 computer* The capability of exchanging personal messages on a computer network: *As you play, you can exchange typed messages—that's a feature called "chat" in computer lingo—with other players*—Milwaukee Journal

chat group *n phr computer by 1990s* A designated topic on a computer network, under which interested users may subscribe themselves; new group; interest group: *Or, as gunnies on the Internet chat group rec.guns put it. . .* —New York Times

chat line 1 *n phr 1980s* A telephone service on which one may converse, often in a lurid fashion, with other subscribers or with an employee of the service **2** *n phr* (also **chat room**) *computer by 1990s* A computer-network news or interest group mostly devoted to personal messages: *. . . and drops in on "chat lines" where his far-flung customers argue, banter, console, consult, wheel, deal, and sometimes fall in love. . .* —Baltimore Sun/ *Chat rooms can be a great forum. . . But more often than not, it's a stop for compusex, that information-age version of phone sex*—Macon Telegraph

chattering classes *n phr by 1990s* Sets of persons who are habitually and professionally garrulous: *. . . writers, scholars, politicians and other members of the chattering classes*—New York Times

chat up *v phr 1960s* To charm and seduce with talk
 •More common in British use, in which *chat* in the same sense is attested from 1898: *You hear Elvis laughing, chatting up the crowd*—Rolling Stone/ *. . . while Dartmouth seniors, a little tight, chatted up Smithies*—Time

chauvinist pig *See* MALE CHAUVINIST PIG

chaw-head *n by 1990s* A person who chews tobacco or something else habitually: *I used to watch baseball. . . then I witnessed one too many newsclips of brawling, drunken chaw-heads*—Sassy

cheap 1 *adj by 1827* Stingy; overly frugal; =CHINTZY: *Cheap old bastard won't give you the time of day* **2** *adj by 1950s* Reputedly easy of sexual conquest; =ROUNDHEELED: *a cheap tramp with a heart of gold*
 See DIRT CHEAP, ON THE CHEAP

cheap date (or **drunk**) *n phr by 1940s* A person who needs very few drinks to become intoxicated: *All* *it took was one small sherry; she's such a cheap date*

cheapie or **cheapo** *first form by 1898, second by 1950s* **1** *n* Any cheaply made or cheaply sold item: *No ticket in town is a cheapie these days/ The problem with retreads, ethnic shoes, and Woolworth cheapos is. . .* —Village Voice/ *. . . Wood made this fairly ordinary cheapie a mere year after. . .* Glenn or Glenda—Entertainment Weekly **2** *modifier*: *. . . cheapie ripoffs of* The Godfather—T Meehan/ *Our Tenth Annual Cheapo Guide*—Toronto Life **See** EL CHEAPO

cheap is cheap *sentence* You get what you pay for: *Russian movie annoyingly narrated. . . In culture as in commerce, cheap is cheap*—Nation

cheapjack or **Cheap John** *modifier* Inferior and cheap; obscure and third-rate; shoddy [*Cheap Jack* and *Cheap John*, "itinerant huckster, merchant of shoddy," are attested from about 1850]

◁**cheapshit**▷ *adj by 1970s* Inexpensive and inferior: *. . . ten million pair of cheapshit jeans without any labels on them*—National Lampoon

cheap shot *sports by 1960s* **1** *n phr* (also **shot**) A malicious insult or action; something crude, underhanded, and damaging: *Well, the race for governor isn't a festival of cheap shots*—New York Magazine/ *Keenan shouted, "Didn't you just take what is known as a cheap shot?"*—New York Times **2** *v phr*: *. . . see his players take illegal runs at his son. He'd say "Hey, don't cheap shot my son"*—Philadelphia Journal/ *If a person's going to cheap-shot me, it just shows how low he is*—Playboy **3** *modifier*: *. . . some dirtymouth comedian who made cheap-shot race jokes*—Village Voice

cheap-shot artist or **cheap-shotter** *n first form by 1960s, second by 1970s* A person who takes cheap shots: *Immigrant bashing is a handy charge for cheap-shotters and fear-mongers*—Los Angeles Times

cheapskate *n by 1896* A nasty stingy person; =TIGHTWAD: *. . . and cheapskate Goodman's not going for a renewal*—Stan Cutler

cheat *v by 1930s* To be sexually unfaithful; =GET A LITTLE ON THE SIDE

cheaters 1 *n about 1920* Spectacles •Attributed to the cartoonist and sports writer Tad Dorgan, who died in 1929 **2** *n by 1940s* Marked playing cards

cheat sheet 1 *n phr students by 1950s* A paper used to replace or reinforce one's memory; =CRIB: *. . . his notes and data on enemy hitters, which he consults in preparing game notes—a cheat sheet*—New Yorker/ *During cooking demonstrations, a paper cheat sheet sits nearby on the counter*—Milwaukee Journal **2** *n phr* =SWINDLE SHEET

check 1 *interj by 1922* An expression of understanding, approval, etc: *I'll say check to that!/ It's time to leave? Check!* **2** *v* (also **check that**) *sports broadcasting by 1950s* To cancel; introduce a correction: *He made eight yards; check that, six yards* **3** *v by late 1700s* To look at; pay attention to; =CHECK OUT •The date refers to use in phrases like

"*I have checked this account*": *Check the guy at the end of the counter* **4** *n narcotics by 1950s* A small quantity of a drug
See GIVE someone A BLANK CHECK, PICK UP THE TAB, RAIN CHECK, RUBBER CHECK, TAKE A RAIN CHECK

check bouncer *n phr by 1920s* A person who writes checks on bank accounts with insufficient funds or none whatever

check (or checkerboard) crew *n phr by 1930s* A work crew having black and white members [fr the black and white squares of a *checkerboard*]

checkerboard *n by 1940s* A neighborhood, town, or other place with both black and white people; an integrated place

checkers *See* PLAY CHECKERS

check in 1 *v phr by 1912* To die; =CHECK OUT **2** *v phr by 1918* To indicate one's arrival at a hotel, motel, etc

check into the net *v phr 1970s Army* To announce one's arrival or departure; keep others informed

check it *v phr 1990s teenagers* To leave; =BUG OFF, SPLIT •Usu an irritated command

check out 1 *v phr by 1960s* To look closely at, esp for evaluation; scrutinize; =GIVE someone or something THE ONCE-OVER: *. . . for this style of music, if you prefer twang to snarl, check it out live at the Rodeo Bar*—The Atlantic **2** *v phr by 1940s* To prove valid; be accurate: *Your story checks out* **3** *v phr by 1940s* To examine and approve one's competence: *I'm checked out on that machine* **4** *v phr by 1960s* To add up purchases and collect money at a supermarket or similar store: *I'll check you out over here* **5** *modifier*: *a check-out counter/ check-out person* **6** *n*: *express check-out/ slow sloppy check-out* **7** *v phr by 1960s* To pay for one's purchases at a supermarket or similar store: *It took me an hour to check out of that place* **8** *v phr by 1920s* To pay one's bill and leave a hotel or motel: *When did Almendorfer check out of this fleabag?* **9** *modifier*: *When's check-out time tomorrow?* **10** *v phr by 1920s* To leave; depart; =BOOGIE, BOOK, SPLIT: *Let's check out of this joint and find a livelier one* **11** *v phr by 1920s* To die: *She checked out before they reached the hospital*

check the plumbing *v phr by 1940s* To go to the toilet; =SEE A MAN ABOUT A DOG

check one's wallet *v phr by 1960s* To make sure that one has not been robbed or deluded: *. . . too eloquent for his own good. Sometimes you want to check your wallet when he's done talking*—New York Times

cheeba or **chiba** or **chiba chiba** *n 1970s narcotics* Marijuana

cheechako *n by 1890s* A newcomer; =GREENHORN [fr Chinook jargon *chee chahco*, "newcomer"]

cheek 1 *n by 1840* Impudence; audacity; =BRASS, CHUTZPA: *She had the infernal cheek to stick out her tongue at me* **2** *n by 1600* A buttock; =BUN: *I* *took the injection in the left cheek* [first sense apparently related to *jaw*, suggesting insolent speech]

cheek it *v phr* *students by 1895* To deceive by pretending more knowledge than one has; =BLUFF, FAKE IT, WING IT

cheeky *adj by 1850s* Impudent; impertinent; rude

cheer *See* BRONX CHEER

cheerio or **cheery-bye** *interj about 1910* Goodbye •Used as a conscious amusing Briticism: *Cheerio, pip-pip, and all that!*

cheers *interj* *British by 1919* A salute or toast on taking a drink: *Cheers and bottoms up, one and all!*

cheese 1 *n by 1950s* Nonsense; lies; exaggerations; =BALONEY: . . . *what a line of cheese*. . . —Richard Bissell **2** *n 1980s baseball* A fastball **3** *v* =CHEESE IT **4** *v* (also **cut the cheese**) *by 1970s* To flatulate; =FART **5** *v by 1970s* To vomit; =BARF **6** *n*: *There was cheese all over the floor in the subway station* **7** *n 1980s students* Something out of date; often something so appallingly out of date that it has a certain chic appeal; =CAMP, CORN: *That brown dress you're wearing is total cheese*—UCLA Slang/ *Lime-green shag carpeting is Cheese. Wide-bodied neckties are Cheese*—New York Times **8** *v by 1990s* To make someone look outlandish; make cheesy: *A lot of actresses want to preserve the integrity of their characters, but I said "Cheese me up! Go ahead"*—Milwaukee Journal

See BIG CHEESE, EAT CHEESE, HARD CHEESE, MAKE THE CHEESE MORE BINDING

the cheese *n phr by 1818* A superior person or thing: *She's the real cheese*—A Lewis [perhaps fr Anglo-Indian slang *chiz* fr Hindi fr Persian, "the thing"]

cheeseball *modifier by 1980s* Stupid; inferior; =CHEESY: *One theater near city hall played the kind of cheeseball samurai movies that never quite made it to the more respectable Japanese theaters*—Los Angeles Times

cheese bun (or **eater**) *n phr* (also **cheese eater, cheesy rider**) *by 1940s* An informer or other despicable person; =RAT

cheesecake 1 *n 1930s* Photographs and photography of women in clothing and poses that emphasize their sexuality: *a magazine full of cheesecake* **2** *modifier*: . . . *unless one perceives in cheesecake photographs illicit and limitless pleasures*—Toronto Life **3** *n by 1940s* A woman's legs, breasts, hips, etc: *standing on the corner scoping out the cheesecake* [apparently fr the appreciative comments of one or another New York City newspaper photographer at the ocean-liner docks who posed women so that their legs were featured, and pronounced the pictures to be "better than *cheesecake*"]

cheesed off *adj phr WWII Air Forces fr British armed forces* Bored; disgusted: . . . *if superbored, you're "cheesed off"*—American Mercury

cheesehead 1 *n by 1920* A stupid person: *You let this cheesehead. . . insult me?*—Raymond Chandler **2** *n by 1980s* A native or resident of Wisconsin: . . . *how much one of these jets costs the average*

Wisconsin taxpayer. Why should he upset us cheeseheads needlessly. . . —Milwaukee Journal

cheese it *underworld by 1811* **1** *interj* An exclamation of alarm and warning uttered when properly constituted authorities are approaching: *Cheese it, Muggsy, the cops!* **2** *v phr* To leave; depart; =SCRAM

◁**cheese whiz**▷ (also **cheez whiz**) *1980s students* **1** *n phr* An unattractive girl; =DOG, TWO-BAGGER **2** *modifier* Out of date; =CHEESY: *Her shoes were total cheez whiz*—UCLA Slang [fr the trademark name of a kind of soft cheese spread]

cheesy 1 *adj by 1950s* Lacking in taste; vulgarly unesthetic: . . . *an altogether hideous room, expensive but cheesy*—J D Salinger/ . . . *the acting. . . was so cheesy. It was like porn acting*—Douglas Coupland **2** *adj by 1896* Of inferior workmanship; shoddy: *This is accomplished through some really cheesy special effects*—Milwaukee Journal **3** *adj by 1896* Shabby; ugly: *"I thought that was kind of cheesy," Harding said*. . . —Milwaukee Journal **4** *adj by 1970s* Not real or genuine; false; =FAKE, PHONY **5** *adj 1980s students* (also **cheese dog**) Out of date; often so appallingly so that it has a certain chic appeal; =CAMPY, CORNY: *The runway stuff? Cheese dog.*—Sassy/ *I included the big hair to cause a little friction. . . they both almost unanimously referred to it as "cheesy"*—Sassy/ . . . *and the Cheesy Award goes to*. . . *Tony Bennett*—Seventeen

chef *n narcotics by 1911* A person who prepares opium for smoking

chemical blonde *n phr* (also **bleached blonde, peroxide blonde**) *by 1990s* A blonde whose hair is given its colors by a bleach or another compound;: *That's why both the chemical blonde and the ponytailed pugilist made my stomach perform a nauseous little flip*—Milwaukee Journal

chemical machine *n phr by 1990s* A bodybuilder who used steroids and other drugs: *In bodybuilding slang, Gordon Kimbrough is known as "a chemical machine"*—Milwaukee Journal

chemistry *n* Feelings between persons; attractions and repulsions, but mainly attractions: *Miss McElderry feels the unusual chemistry between her and Mr Pfeiffer has been beneficial*—New York Times/ *He also struck up what one aide calls "instant chemistry" with US Secretary of State George Shultz*—New York Times

chemotherapy look *n phr by 1990s* A hair style resembling the look of a chemotherapy patient: *Packard likes such incorrect things as fur coats, especially on women with long hair (as distinct from the chemotherapy look)*—New York Times [Chemotherapy patients typically lose much of their hair]

cher (SHEHR) *adj teenagers by 1960s* Personable; attractive: *He's a real cher cat* [fr French "dear"]

cherries *n by 1980s* The flashing lights atop a police car or other emergency vehicle; =GUMBALL, PARTY HAT

cherry ◁1▷ *n by 1935* A virgin, of either sex ◁2▷ *n by 1928* Virginity: *Does he still have his cherry?* ◁3▷ *adj* Virgin; sexually uninitiated: *She confessed she was cherry* ◁4▷ *n* The hymen **5** *adj* In an unproved or maiden state of any sort: *He hasn't published anything yet; still cherry* **6** *modifier 1950s hot rodders* In mint condition; pristine: *Mint is what I'm saying. Cherry*—George V Higgins/ . . . *including cherry restorations of Belairs and Fairlanes from the Fifties*—New Yorker **7** *n Army* An inexperienced soldier sent to the front lines as a replacement: *A Cherry who survived long enough earned the right to harass the next rookie*—New York Times Magazine [sexual senses fr the fancied resemblance between the hymen and a *cherry*]

See COP A CHERRY, HAVE one's CHERRY, POP someone's CHERRY

cherry-pick *v by 1990s* To select the best and most profitable elements; =PICK AND CHOOSE: *When a bank fails, a healthy competitor often buys it and cherry-picks the safest and most profitable loans*—Milwaukee Journal/ . . . *small insurance companies survive by cherry-picking their clients*—New Republic

cherry-picker ◁1▷ *n by 1950s* A man who especially prizes the sex act with young girls **2** *n railroad by 1940s* A switch operator **3** *n by 1940s* An articulated crane with a bucket-like platform: *a guy in a cherry-picker fixing the phone lines*

cherry-picking *n by 1990s* The selection of only what is most helpful to one's case: *The Justice Department report on the Waco raid was cherry-picking*—Art Bell

cherry pie *by 1950s* **1** *n phr* Something easily done or gotten; =PIECE OF CAKE **2** *n phr circus* Money easily obtained

cherry-top *n 1960s teenagers* A police car; =PROWL CAR

chest *See* PLAY CLOSE TO THE CHEST

chestnut *n by 1816* A trite old story, joke, song, etc [probably fr a play, *The Broken Sword*, in which one character tells a story 27 times, naming a *chestnut* tree, then abruptly changes it to a cork tree, whereupon another character recalls the repetition of *chestnut*, and the first says "well, a chestnut be it then"]

chesty **1** *adj by 1950s* Having large breasts; bosomy; . . . *watching two chesty girls in tube tops*. . . —Ed McBain **2** *adj by 1899* Prone to boast about one's virility, boldness, etc: *When you have money in the bank it will be time enough to get chesty*—The Slang-Dic

chev *See* SHIV

chevy *See* CHIVVY

Chevy or **Chev** (SHEH vee, SHEHV) *n by 1930* A Chevrolet car

chew **1** *v by 1930s* To chew tobacco **2** *n by 1920s*: *He had big chew in his cheek* **3** *v by 1890* To eat **4** *v* (also **chew over**) *by 1890s* To talk; converse; discuss; =JAW: *We got together to chew about the election/ Drop up and chew it over*—Raymond Chandler

chewallop or **chewalloper** (chee WAH ləp) *n by 1836* A fall or dive that makes a loud splat

◁**chew** someone's **ass (**or **ass out)**▷ *v phr WWII armed forces* =CHEW someone OUT

chew someone's **ear off** *v phr by 1919* To talk overlong and tediously to someone: *I just wanted the time, not to get my ear chewed off*

chewed *adj 1940s black* Tired; defeated; =BEAT: *I know you feel chewed*—Zora Neale Hurston

chewed up **1** *adj phr by 1930s* Badly damaged or worn: *The transmission's all chewed up* **2** *adj phr 1940s black* =CHEWED

chew gum at the same time *See* NOT HAVE BRAINS ENOUGH TO WALK AND CHEW GUM AT THE SAME TIME

chewing *See* RAG-CHEWING

chewings *n hoboes by 1930s* Food

chew light-bulbs *v phr by 1990s* To do something extremely painful and nasty: *Would you rather chew light bulbs than go shopping for jeans?*—Los Angeles Times

chew nails *v phr by 1970s* To be very angry; be livid: *We'd better get out before he starts chewing nails*

chew someone **out** (or **up**) *v phr WWII armed forces* To reprimand severely; rebuke harshly; =EAT someone OUT, REAM: *He got chewed out for it more than once by the platoon sergeant*. . . —Elmore Leonard

chew the fat (or **the rag**) *v phr early 1900s* To converse, esp in a relaxed and reminiscent way ●In earlier senses the terms meant "to complain; wrangle": *You want a press conference, or do you want to chew the fat?*—Hugh Pentecost

chew someone **up and spit them out** *v phr about 1920* To demolish someone; treat someone very harshly

chew up the scenery *v phr 1930s show business* To overact; =HAM: *Beery. . . and Lionel Barrymore chew up all the scenery that isn't nailed down*—Village Voice/ . . . *Neeson doesn't chew up the scenery when he works*—New York Times [originally fr a 1930 theater review by Dorothy Parker: ". . . more glutton than artist. . . he commences to *chew up the scenery*"; in an 1881 glossary a loud actor is said to "eat scenes," which may or may not be related]

chewy *1920s* **1** *adj* Substantial and desirable; rich: *Hepburn. . . may have a less chewy part than has Fonda*—Richard Schickel/ *"chewy wordplay" on Elvis Costello's new LP*—Nation **2** *adj* Needing thought and discussion; challenging; tricky: *The hegemony of CNN. . . raises lots of chewy questions*—New York Times

chib *See* SHIV

chiba *See* CHEEBA

chiba shop *See* SMOKE SHOP

Chicago *n 1930s lunch counter* A pineapple sundae or soda [fr gangsters' use of *pineapple*, "hand grenade"; Chicago was the most famous gangster milieu during the 1920s and '30s]

Chicago overcoat *n phr* *1920s* A coffin: *A Chicago overcoat is what blasting would get you*—Raymond Chandler

Chicago piano *n phr* *1930s* A submachine gun [Used in WWII in British Navy for a rapid-fire automatic antiaircraft gun]

Chicago pineapple *n phr* *1930s* A small grenade or bomb

chichi (SHEE SHEE, CHEE CHEE) *by* *1940* **1** *n* Something frilly, fancy, precious, and overdecorated: *Another bit of chichi that has come to our notice lately is Eleanor Roosevelt's letterhead*—New Yorker/ *So much chichi. The pretty glass people*—New York Magazine **2** *adj*: *. . . Fifth and 57th is no longer so chi-chi*—New York Times [fr French fr *chic*]

◁**chi-chi**▷ (CHEE chee) *late 1940s & Korean War armed forces* **1** *n* A woman's breasts; =TITS **2** *n* Anything sexually attractive [fr a corruption of Japanese *chisai chichi,* "little breasts"]

chick *n* *black by 1927* A woman, esp a young woman [fr *chicken*; popularized in the beat and hippie movements]
See HIP CHICK, SLICK CHICK

chickabiddy *n* *British by 1785* =CHICK

chicken **1** *n* *by 1711* =CHICK **2** *n* *homosexuals by 1940s* An adolescent boy regarded as a sexual object for an adult homosexual; catamite; =PUNK **3** *modifier*: *. . . had I written extensively about the mechanics of chicken sex*—Village Voice **4** *n by 1707* A coward; an overly timid person; =SISSY: *Don't be a chicken; dive right in* **5** *adj*: *He seems like a chicken guy* **6** *n 1950s hot rodders* A trial of valor in which two persons drive cars at each other down the middle of a road, the first to swerve aside being designated "chicken" **7** *n Army fr 1920s* The eagle worn as insignia of rank by an Army colonel **8** *n by 1940s* **9** *adj* =CHICKENSHIT **10** *n underworld by 1950s* The victim of a robbery or swindle; =MARK, SUCKER [homosexual senses perhaps fr late 19th-century sailor term for a boy who takes a sailor's fancy and whom he calls his *chicken*]
See RUBBER-CHICKEN

chicken colonel *n phr WWI Army* A full colonel; =BIRD COLONEL

chicken coop *n phr truckers by 1970s* A weighing station for trucks
See RAIN CATS AND DOGS

chicken feed (or **money**) *n phr by 1830s* A small amount of money; =PEANUTS, SMALL POTATOES: *Two million? That's chicken feed in this milieu*

chickenhawk **1** *n homosexuals by 1960s* An adult homosexual who relishes young boys as sex partners: *. . . a "chickenhawk," a man who likes sex with "chickens," that is, boys in their middle teens*—New York Times **2** *n police by 1980s* A child molester; =SHORT EYE

chickenhead **1** *n by 1950s* A stupid person **2** *n police by 1990s* A petty criminal; =PUNK **3** *n* or *n*

phr A crack-addicted woman who prostitutes herself for narcotics: *. . . someone who would trade her body for crack, in street lingo, a chicken head. . .* —Macon Telegraph

chickenheart *n* A coward

chickenhearted *by 1680s* **1** *adj* Cowardly; =SISSIFIED: *Here's a potbellied, chickenhearted slob*—J & W Hawkins **2** *adj* Squeamish; overly fastidious

chicken-livered *adj* *by 1870s* Cowardly; =CHICKENHEARTED

chicken out *v phr 1960s* To cancel or withdraw from an action because of fear; =HAVE COLD FEET: *You'll think of something to chicken out*—Erma Bombeck/ *But I chickened out. . . I felt sorry for him*—Elmore Leonard

chickens come home to roost *sentence* (Variations: other things may replace **chickens**) *by 1810* Consequences, although delayed, will happen: *The chickens are coming home to roost on Reagan economics*—Newsweek/ *However the Gulf affair is resolved, it represents large chickens of the 1980s coming home to roost*—New Republic/ *Higher interest rates are coming home to roost*—National Public Radio

◁**chickenshit**▷ **1** *modifier by 1930s* Contemptible; trivial; petty **2** *n WWI armed forces, but esp WWII* The rules, restrictions, rigors, and meanness of a minor and pretentious tyrant, or of a bureaucracy: *The new regulations are so many parcels of chicken shit* **3** *n WWI armed forces, but esp WWII* An excessive display of authority; a hectoring insistence **4** *modifier WWI armed forces, but esp WWII*: *a chicken-shit requirement/ chicken-shit new task force* **5** *n by 1940s* A coward **6** *modifier by 1940s* Cowardly; =CHICKEN

chicken (or **egads**) **switch** (or **button**) *1950s astronautics* **1** *n phr* A control used to destroy a malfunctioning rocket in flight; a destruct switch **2** *n phr* A control used to eject an astronaut or pilot from a damaged vehicle [*chicken* fr the sense "coward"; *egads* an acronym for *electronic ground automatic destruct sequencer* and coincides with an archaic interjection of dismay]

chicken tracks **See** HEN TRACKS

chick movie (or **flick**) *n phr 1990s* A motion picture that appeals to women but not to men: *"Chick movie" is simply a shorthand term. . . to describe the genre of films that do not feature car chases, explosions, sports, or battle scenes*—Milwaukee Journal/ *. . . starring alongside Meryl Streep in the ultimate "chick flick"*—Wisconsin State Journal

chickie **1** *n about 1920* A young girl; =CHICK: *But I do not really envy the guys my age who. . . are making out with the young chickies*—San Francisco **2** *interj 1940s New York City teenagers* An exclamation of alarm and warning, uttered when properly constituted authorities are approaching; =CHEESE IT, JIGGERS
See LAY CHICKIE

chicklet or **chiclet** *n about 1920* A young girl; =CHICK: *Teenies and chicklets came into fashion—*Gail Sheehy [a normal diminutive form, reinforced by *Chiclet,* trademark of a brand of chewing gum sold as small sugared bits]

Chic Sale *n phr outdated 1920s* An outhouse; privy [fr the name of a humorist who wrote of such amenities]

chief **1** *n by 1930s* A man; fellow; =GUY, MAC •Usu in direct address to a stranger, with a sense of ironic deference **2** *n 1960s narcotics* LSD

See TOO MANY CHIEFS AND NOT ENOUGH INDIANS

chief cook and bottle washer *n phr by 1830s* The person in charge; =HONCHO

chief itch and rub *n phr outdated 1920s* The most important person about; =BIG ENCHILADA, BOSS

chief of staff *n phr 1970s Army* An army officer's wife

child *See* FLOWER CHILD

children *See* FLOWER CHILDREN

chili[1] *interj 1950s teenagers* An exclamation of agreement, pleasure, congratulation, etc; =GOOD DEAL [probably related to *chilly* and *cool*]

◄**chili**[2]► *adj by 1960s* Mexican [fr the *chili* bean]

chili-bowl **1** *n by 1940s* A haircut that looks as if someone had put a bowl over one's head and cut off what hair showed below **2** *n by 1960s* A dirty, slovenly person; =DIRTBALL

chill **1** *v boxing by 1930s* To render someone unconscious; =KNOCK someone OUT: *She chilled him with a kick on the chin* **2** *v by 1930s* To kill; murder: *Remember the night Stein got chilled out front?—*Raymond Chandler **3** *v 1920s* To quench enthusiasm and amiability abruptly; snub: *He chilled me with a glance* **4** *v 1970s students* =CHILL OUT: *As my daughter often tells me, I need to learn how to "chill"—*Working Mother **5** *n 1960s students* A glass or can of beer **6** *adj* (also **chilled**) *1980s teenagers* Excellent; wonderful; =COOL, FRESH, RAD: *A "chill" outfit for a girl is tight Sergio Valente or Tale Lord jeans—*New York Times/ *. . . the top accolades (in 1986) include cool, chill or chilly, although froody and hondo also get high marks—*UPI **7** *v 1980s students* To stay or become calm; relax; =COOL IT, KICK BACK •Often a command or exhortation

chiller or **chiller-diller** *n 1950s* A film, play, etc, intended to evoke delicious shudders of fear; horror show or story

chillin' *1980s teenagers* **1** *adj* Excellent; the best; =COOL, RAD: *But, Ma, this is "the style"! This is chillin'—*comic strip "Curtis" **2** *adj* Relaxing; being quiet and carefree: *She told the magazine she was chillin', just having fun. . . —*Milwaukee Journal

chill out *v phr 1980s teenagers* To relax; calm oneself; =COOL OUT, KICK BACK: *. . . offers her a lit joint. "Chill out," he says—*New York Magazine/ *. . . she has become synonymous with bingeing celebrities who need to chill out—*Milwaukee Journal

chill pill *n phr by 1990s* A tranquilizer: *They seem to have taken a chill pill musically, but the lyrics are as biting as ever—*Sassy

chilly or **chili** *adj 1980s teenagers* Wonderful; excellent; =COOL, NEAT: *. . . you're chilly. You're okay, Sarge—*Carsten Stroud

chilly mo *n phr 1980s black* An aloof and unengaged person; =COLD FISH [fr *mo,* "motherfucker"]

chime in *by 1840s* **1** *v phr* To interrupt and intrude one's counsel; =BUTT IN, KIBITZ **2** *v phr* To offer comment: *Chime in whenever you want*

chin **1** *v by 1870s* To talk; converse: *happily chinning in the corner* **2** *n by 1890s* A talk; a chat **3** *v by 1880s* To talk to: *The cop was chinning. . . a nurse—*James M Cain

See TAKE IT ON THE CHIN, WAG one's CHIN

china **1** *n by 1940s* The teeth **2** *n jazz musicians by 1930s* Money **3** *n lunch counter by 1960s* A cup of tea

China Cat *n phr 1990s* A strong kind of heroin: *Police say a potent batch of heroin called China Cat may be to blame for at least 13 deaths in Manhattan in just six days—*Milwaukee Journal

china chin *See* GLASS JAW

china-clipper *n WWII armed forces* A dishwasher; =PEARL-DIVER [fr the *China Clipper,* a Pan American Airways seaplane that flew a regular service to the Far East beginning in the 1930s, because the dishwasher was apparently thought to be *clipping,* "hitting, bashing," the dishes]

China (or **china**) **doll** *n phr by 1940s* A woman of very delicate beauty; a pretty and fragile woman

◄**Chinaman**► **1** *n merchant marine by 1950s* A sailor who works in a ship's laundry **2** *n police by 1970s* A police officer's patron and influential political friend; =RABBI: *police officer. . . needed a Chinaman, or sponsor—*Chicago Magazine

◄**a Chinaman's chance**► *n phr about 1910* No chance at all •Nearly always in the negative: *He hasn't got a Chinaman's chance of landing that job* [said to be fr the unfortunate situation of Chinese prospectors in the 1940s California gold rush, who were forced to work exhausted or unpromising claims, although no contemporary examples of use remain]

China White *n phr 1970s narcotics* A very high grade of heroin: *"It's China White," he said. . . . Jesus, I thought, I'm out here with junkies—*Hunter S Thompson

chinch or **chintz** *n by 1625* A bedbug

chinch pad *n phr black by 1950s* A cheap hotel or lodging house; =FLOPHOUSE

chinchy *adj by 1300* Parsimonious; stingy; mean; =CHINTZY [Middle English fr Old French *chiche* in same sense]

'chine (SHEEN) *n 1960s teenagers* A machine, esp a car

◄**Chinee**► **1** *n by 1870s* A Chinese person **2** *n* (also **chinee** [or **Chinese**] **ducket**) *by 1930s* A complimentary ticket; =ANNIE OAKLEY: *. . . a chinee being a ducket with holes punched in it like old-fashioned Chink money—*Damon Runyon

◄**Chinese ace**► *n phr WWI aviators* A pilot who

lands an airplane with one wing low [fr the possible *Chinese* name Wun Wing Low or the purportedly humorous invention Wun Hung Low referring to the low wing]

◀**Chinese fire drill**▶ *n phr* Something incredibly confused and confusing: *. . . an eight-page letter with a Chinese fire drill of your life*—Chicago Tribune/ *. . . did their Chinese fire drill of calling the fix-it man*—Richard Merkin [perhaps fr the WWII Marine Corps expression "fucked up like *Chinese fire call*"]

◀**Chinese homer**▶ *n phr* baseball by 1920s A home run hit to the closest fence; a very short home run [attributed to the cartoonist and sports writer Tad Dorgan, who died in 1929]

◀**Chinese landing**▶ *n phr* WWII *aviators* A landing made with one wing low

   See CHINESE ACE

◀**Chinese opera**▶ *n phr* 1970s Army An extremely elaborate event, parade, briefing, etc

Chinese pagodas *See* KNOCK someone FOR A LOOP

◀**Chinese three-point landing**▶ *n phr* WWII *aviators* An airplane crash, esp one due to pilot error

chinfest *n* by 1940s A session of talk and gossip; =BULL SESSION, GABFEST

◀**Chink** or **chink**▶ *about 1900* **1** *n* A Chinese person **2** *adj*: *Chink food/ a chink chick*

chin music 1 *n phr* by 1830s Talk, esp inconsequential chatter; =CHITCHAT: *. . . chin music calculated to allay her trepidation*—S J Perelman **2** *n phr* baseball by 1880s Various kinds of raucous shouting at a baseball game, from the crowd, from the players to each other, from the players or manager to the umpires, etc **3** *n phr* baseball by 1980s A pitched ball that passes close to the batter's face; =BEANBALL: *You ever face major league pitching, Berkowitz? You ever face chin music?*—Jane Leavy

◀**Chino** or **chino**▶ (CHĬ noh) *n* by 1890s A Chinese person; =CHINEE, CHINK

chintzy¹ *adj* by 1950s Parsimonious; stingy; =CHEAP, CHINCHY •The spelling imitates follows that of *chintzy²*; a dialect spelling *chinsy* is attested from 1940: *Ask them to validate both tickets, she'd think I was chintzy*—Stan Cutler [probably fr *chinchy*]

chintzy² by 1850s **1** *adj* Cheap and ill-made, but showy: *the window filled with chintzy plastic couches* **2** *adj* Lacking chic and style; unfashionable: *White shoes with a dark dress is considered very definitely. . . "chintzy"*—Syracuse Post-Standard [fr Hindi fr **chintz**, a printed cotton fabric regarded as cheap, gaudy, and unstylish]

chin-wag *n* by 1870s A conversation, esp a long and intimate chat: *You haven't had a good chin-wag with your sister-in-law since she got the joystick for her Apple*—Washington Post

chip 1 *n* by 1848 A flat piece of dung **2** *v* golf by 1920s To hit a short, usu high shot onto the green **3** *v* 1960s *narcotics* To use a drug or drugs clandestinely while abstaining from using the drug for

which one is being treated or is undergoing psychotherapy: *The men and women of the group. . . also look at the man who is chipping. There is some palpable dismay*—Washington Post *See* BARGAINING CHIP, BLUE-CHIP, HAVE A CHIP ON one's SHOULDER

chiphead *n* 1980s *computer* A computer enthusiast: *I'm not a chiphead, but if you don't keep up with the new developments. . . you're not going to have the competitive edge*—Time [fr silicon *chip* plus *head*, "addict"]

chip in 1 *v phr* by 1861 To contribute, esp a share of some expense: *We each chipped in twenty bucks and got him a new suit* **2** *v phr* by 1970 To interject a comment; contribute to a colloquy: *She chipped in some honeyed reminiscences* [fr the adding of poker *chips* to the pot]

a **chip off the old block** *n phr* by 1920s A child that resembles one or both parents, esp a boy that resembles his father [The form *chip of the old block* is attested fr the 1620s]

chipper¹ *n* 1960s *narcotics* An occasional, non-addicted user of narcotics; =JOY-POPPER: *Amy, who is only a "chipper,". . . wanted to meet somebody*—Rolling Stone [fr *chip*, "small quantity, bit"]

chipper² *adj* by 1830s Energetic and jaunty; lively; =PERKY [fr British dialect *kipper*]

chippy or **chippie 1** *n* by 1880s A woman presumed to be of easy virtue; woman who frequents bars, public dance halls, etc: *. . . the same as in Storyville except that the chippies were cheaper*—Louis Armstrong **2** *v* by 1930 To be sexually unfaithful to one's wife; =CHEAT, GET A LITTLE ON THE SIDE **3** *n* early 1900s A simple buttoned dress: *A chippie is a dress that women wore, knee length and very easy to disrobe*—A Lomax **4** *v* 1920s *narcotics* To take narcotics, esp cocaine, only occasionally; =CHIP [origin unknown; senses relating to women possibly from the chirping sound of a sparrow, squirrel, or other small creature, suggesting the gay frivolity of such women]

chippy house or **joint** *n phr* by 1920s A brothel

chips *n* by 1850s Money *See* CASH IN one's CHIPS, IN THE CHIPS

Chips *n* nautical by 1785 A ship's carpenter •Used as a nickname, as Sparks is for a radio officer and Bones for a ship's doctor

the **chips are down** (or **on the table**) *sentence* by 1940s The time of final decision and hard confrontation has come; resolution is at hand •Usu with *when*: *When the chips are down he goes to pieces/ For a change, when the chips were on the table, came up with some good stuff*—Milwaukee Journal [fr the final bets of a poker hand]

chip shot 1 *n phr* golf by 1909 A shot, usu a high shot made onto the green **2** *n phr* football by 1970s An easy field goal or field goal opportunity **3** *modifier*: *I liked my chances of kicking a chip-shot field goal*—Milwaukee Journal [perhaps fr hitting under the ball as if to chop a *chip* from it]

chirp 1 *v* about 1930 To sing: *She chirps with the orchestra*—Bob Thomas **2** *v* underworld by 1830s To inform; =SING, SQUEAL

chirpy *adj* by 1830s Bright and energetic; vivacious: *a nice, wholesome, chirpy, reasonably intelligent woman*—Philadelphia Magazine

chisel 1 *v* by 1808 To cheat or defraud, esp in a petty way; deal unfairly; =SCAM: *Every time I buy a car part, he chisels a buck or two* **2** *v* by 1920s To get without necessarily intending to repay or return; =BUM, MOOCH: *Can I chisel a cigarette from you, pal?*

chisel in *v phr* 1920s underworld To intrude oneself; =MUSCLE IN

chit[1] *n* by 1640s An impudent and spirited young woman: *a saucy chit* [origin uncertain]

chit[2] *n* by 1920s A bill for food or drink, which one signs or initials instead of paying immediately [In the sense "note," chit is attested from the 1780s; shortening of Anglo-Indian *chitty*, "letter, note," fr Hindi]

chitchat *n* by 1710 Talk, esp relaxed and idle conversation; =CHIN MUSIC: *The members were enjoying a bit of chitchat when the gavel sounded*

◁**chitlin circuit**▷ *n phr* by 1970s Theaters and clubs featuring black entertainers [fr *chitlins*, a form of *chitterlings*, the entrails of a hog, which when fried are a great delicacy among poor people, esp in the South]

chiv or **chive** *See* SHIV

chivvy or **chivey** or **chevy** (CHIH vee, CHEH vee) *v* by 1821 To harry and annoy; badger; =BUG, HASSLE [perhaps fr *Chevy Chase*, site of a skirmish between the English and the Scots, which came to mean "a running pursuit" in Yorkshire dialect; *chivy* came to mean "pursue"]

◁**chocha**▷ (CHOH chah) *n* by 1960s The vulva [fr Spanish, literally "woodcock"]

chockablock *adj* 1840s nautical Crammed; crowded full: *The plays and stories. . . are chockablock with figures*—Washington Post [fr a nautical rhyming phrase used to mean that the two *blocks* of a block and tackle are touching after the device has been tightened to its limit]

chock-full *adj* perhaps by 1400, certainly by 1751 Absolutely full; crammed; =CHOCKABLOCK [origin uncertain; perhaps "full to the point of choking"]

chocolate *n* by 1950s Opium; =BIG O

◀**chocolate drop**▶ *n phr* by 1912 A black person

chocolate tide *n* 1990s narcotics A kind of marijuana

chog *n* Midwestern by 1990s An Easterner

chogie (CHOH gee) *v* 1960s Army To go fast [fr Korean]

chogue *n* Korean War armed forces A Korean: *Regardless of whether the man's a spic, a wop, mick, wog, dago, coon, slope, chogue, towelhead*—Esquire [fr Korean *chogi*]

choi oy *interj* Vietnam War armed forces An exclamation of disgust, dismay, etc [fr Vietnamese]

choirboy *n* by 1970s *. . . brilliant, coldly efficient crime boss makes John Gotti look like a choirboy*—Vanity Fair

choke *v* by 1980s To become ineffective because of tension or anxiety; =CHOKE UP: *. . . I studied all night for my test and I totally choked*—UCLA Slang

choke a horse *v phr* by 1900 To be very large: *That bankroll would choke a horse* *See* ENOUGH TO CHOKE A HORSE

choke-dog *n* by 1820s Strong raw whiskey, usu homemade

choked out *adj phr* 1990s narcotics Intoxicated by narcotics; =HIGH, STONED

choke point *n phr* 1960s A place where activity, passage, etc, cannot continue; *The choke point is in the few blocks between our homes. . . and the telephone company's switch*—New York Times/ *Processing plants, with antiquated equipment and unable to deal with large shipments, are another choke point*—New York Times

choker 1 *n* by 1840s Anything worn about the neck, such as a collar or necktie **2** *n* by 1920s A short necklace **3** *n* by 1980s A person who becomes ineffective because of tension or anxiety: *Still, Jansen can't forget the sting of being called a "choker"*—Milwaukee Journal *See* HERRING CHOKER

◁**choke the gopher**▷ *v phr* by 1970s To masturbate

choke up 1 *v phr* sports by 1940s To become tense and ineffective under pressure; =CHOKE, SWALLOW THE APPLE, TAKE THE PIPE: *He choked up, lost his concentration, and got clobbered in the third* **2** *v phr* baseball by 1940s To hold the bat high on the handle, in effect shortening the bat **3** *v phr* by 1960s To cause one to be speechless with pleasure: *Your new book doesn't exactly choke me up* **4** *v phr* by 1960s To become speechless with grief

cholo 1 *adj* by 1970s Very virile; =MACHO **2** *n* prison by 1980s A fellow gang member: *A cholo (street-wise young Latino male). . .* —MM [fr Spanish, literally "mestizo, half-breed," used contemptuously of a lower-class Mexican]

chomp *v* by 1840s To chew [By 1640s in form *champ*]

chomp (or champ) at the bit *v phr* by 1640s To be eager for action; be impatient: *He'd been chomping at the bit real hard the last three weeks*—Los Angeles Times

◁**chooch**▷ *n* 1920s The vulva; =CHOCHA: *Ah, yuh mudduh's chooch*—Sidney Kingsley

choo-choo *See* PULL A TRAIN

chop *n* by 1823 Grade or quality: *The food here is first chop* [fr Hindi, "seal"]

chop block *n phr* football by 1990s A dangerous and illegal block made at the knees: *I can tolerate the holding, the chop blocks I can't tolerate*—Milwaukee Journal

chop-chop *adv* by 1830s Quickly; at once ●Used as a command or exhortation as well as a modifier: *They cut out chop-chop* [fr Pidgin English, "fast," fr Chinese]

chopped 1 *adj 1950s hot rodders* Of a car, having the chassis lowered or the fenders removed or both **2** *adj 1950s motorcyclists* Of a motorcycle, having the front brake and fender removed, the wheel fork extended forward, and the handlebars raised

chopped liver *n phr by 1930s* An insignificant person or thing; nothing •Often in the negative: *We have spent $25 million to adapt. And that isn't chopped liver*—New York Times/ *. . . it ain't chopped liver*—movie *Slightly Honorable/ I'm not chopped liver. I feel too good to retire*—Milwaukee Journal/*What the hell is the faculty lounge. . . Chopped liver?*—Drew Acorn
See THAT AIN'T HAY

chopped top *n phr 1950s hot rodders* A car with the windshield, windows, upper body, etc, removed

chopper 1 *n 1920s* A submachine gun, esp a Thompson; =TOMMY GUN **2** *n 1920s* A gangster who uses a submachine gun: *Johnny Head had met the "chopper"*—John Gunther **3** *n 1950s* A helicopter: *the traffic reporter from the chopper* **4** *n 1950s hot rodders & motorcyclists* A chopped car or motorcycle
See BUTTON CHOPPER, PORK-CHOPPER

choppers or **chompers** *n by 1930s* Teeth, esp false teeth

chops 1 *n* (also **chaps**) *by about 1500* The jaws; the mouth; the cheeks beside the mouth; jowls: *old turkey with pendulous chops/ Open your chops and sing* **2** *n jazz musicians by 1960s* Musical technique or ability: *With electronically amplified music you lose your chops, your right hand, you lose your dexterity*—Philadelphia Journal **3** *n* Talent or skill in general: *We'll see what kind of chops they got*—Jimmy Breslin/ *First of all, you got the chops for it, bod-wise*—Gary Trudeau [senses related to skill fr notion of a jazz musician's lips, *chops,* the essential for technique in "blowing" the instrument]
See AX, BREAK CHOPS, BREAK someone's CHOPS, BUST one's ASS, KLOP IN THE CHOPS, LICK one's CHOPS

chop shop 1 *n phr* A place where stolen cars are dismantled to be sold as parts •A slang dictionary of 1883 defines *chopped up* as "Stolen goods divided into small lots and hidden in different places": *. . . in Detroit, where Axel and his fellow cops are about to raid a chop shop*—Macon Telegraph/ *I started off takin' 'em to a chop shop for $100*—Philadelphia Magazine **2** *modifier*: *. . . mixed up with chop shop operators in the Midwest*—Saul Bellow

chop one's **teeth** *v phr* =BAT one's GUMS

chord *See* PINK CHORD

chorine *n 1920s* A chorus girl; =PONY

chow 1 *n by 1856* Food; meals; fare: *How's the chow at Maxim's these days?* **2** *v about 1900*: *OK gang, let's chow* [origin uncertain; fr Pidgin English *chow-chow,* "a mixture (of foods)," but also a dog of China that is eaten by the poor]

chowderhead *n by 1830s* A stupid person

chow down *v phr WWII Navy* To eat; have a meal: *They should bundle up, chow down, and stay home*—Fran Lebowitz

chow hall *n phr Army by 1940s* A room where meals are served, esp a military mess hall

chow hound *n phr Army by 1920s* A person keenly and actively interested in eating; glutton

chow line *n phr armed forces by 1920s* A line of persons waiting to get food

Christer *n college students about 1920* A straitlaced person, esp a religious one: *Nondrinkers are called all sorts of names, one in popular use is "Christer"*—Cornell Daily Sun

Christian with aces wired *See* COOL AS A CHRISTIAN WITH ACES WIRED

Christmas goose *See* as FULL OF SHIT AS A CHRISTMAS GOOSE

Christmas tree 1 *n phr oilfield by 1920s* The assembly of valves, pipes, and gauges used to control the output of an oil well **2** *n phr 1950s car-racing* A display of colored lights that flash in sequence, used to start drag races **3** *n phr Navy by 1940s* The control panel of a submarine
See LIT UP

chrome-dome *by 1960s* **1** *n* =EGGHEAD: *. . . just to catch up on what the liberal chrome-domes are thinking*—Mike Royko/ *The Carter Center has its share of chrome-domes, eggheads, incompetents and hangers-on*—New York Times **2** *modifier*: *. . . Reggie Rivers doesn't have a fancy name for his chrome-dome hairdo. . .* —Milwaukee Journal

chrome pony *n phr by 1990s* A motorcycle; =BAD BOY, IRON, SLED

chronic *n early 1990s* Marijuana; =POT: *Smoking a spliff of high-octane chronic. . .* —People

chub¹ *n by 1960s* A Texan [origin unknown]

chub² *n by 1870s* A baby or child: *In all your life you never saw such a chub—22 pounds, with cheeks like a chipmunk in September*—New York Times [fr resemblance in shape to a fish called a *chub*]

chubbette *n by 1970s* A chubby woman, esp a small one: *The poor thing was petrified that Graig would find out what a chubbette she'd become*—Armistead Maupin/ *. . . a chubbette with "railroad tracks" across her teeth*—New York Magazine

chubbo *n 1980s students* An obese person

chuck 1 *n British by 1850* Food; a meal; =CHOW, EATS: *She invited us in for some chuck* **2** *v by 1590s* To throw, esp to throw or pitch a ball: *chuck a mean slider* **3** *v by 1850* To discard; throw away: *Is it possible she has chucked her aloofness*—Sinclair Lewis **4** *v by 1940s* To vomit; =UPCHUCK: *He looked like he was going to chuck his breakfast*

chuck-a-lug *See* CHUG-A-LUG

chucker-out *n by 1880s* =BOUNCER •More common in British use

chuck habit or **chuck horrors** or **chucks** *by 1920s* **1** *n phr* or *n* The intense hunger felt by a drug addict whose narcotics intake is cut off: *He'd gotten the chuck horrors: for two full days he'd eaten candy bars, sweet rolls and strawberry malteds*—Nelson Algren **2** *n phr* or *n* The voracious eating that comes from extreme hunger: *the "chuck horrors," that awful animal craving for food that*

comes after missing half a dozen meals—J Black
3 *n phr* or *n* Insanity resulting from imprisonment or fear of imprisonment

chucklehead *n by 1730s* A stupid person

chuckleheaded *adj by 1764* Stupid; =DIMWITTED, DUMB: . . . *so strangely assembles, so Britishly chuckle-headed*—Robert Louis Stevenson

chuck you, Farley *interj* (Variation: **and your whole famn damily** may be added) *by 1970s* May you and yours be reviled, abused, humiliated, rejected, etc; =FUCK YOU, UP YOURS •This amusing variant of the damning formula goes beyond the brevity of an interjection but retains the force [based on earlier *fuck you, Charley* and the euphemism *whole famn damily*]

chug *v about 1900* To move along, esp slowly and laboriously: *The USS Saratoga came chugging up the Delaware*—Philadelphia [echoic of an engine, esp a steam engine, operating]

chug-a-lug or **chug** or **chuck-a-lug** *v by 1940s* To drink the whole of what is in a glass or bottle without pausing: *I tried to chug-a-lug a quart bottle of Schaefer. . .*—Lawrence Sanders/ *He chugged a liter of vodka and dropped dead* [echoic of the sound of repeated swallowing; perhaps related to Scots dialect *chug*, "a short tug or pull"]

chug out *v phr by 1990s* =GRIND OUT: . . . *cheerfully sifted through hard copy of the bug-checked code he'd been chugging out*—Douglas Coupland

chukker *n sports* A division of a sports contest; =CANTO, STANZA [fr a division of a polo game, fr Hindi *cakkar*, "circular running course"]

chum¹ 1 *n students by 1680s* A very close friend; =BUDDY, PAL **2** *v* (also **chum around**) *by 1880s*: *He chums with Georgie Ogle* **3** *n by 1940s* Man; fellow; =GUY •Used in direct address esp to strangers, usu with mildly hostile overtones: *Keep guessing, chum*—Hugh Pentecost [origin uncertain, but earlier uses strongly suggest *chamber*-mate or *chamber*-fellow as the etymon]

chum² by 1850s 1 *v* To throw ground-up bait into the water to attract fish: *to chum for blues* **2** *n*: *Augie, start dumping the chum over* [origin unknown]

chum-buddy *n by 1950s* A particularly close friend: *Yesterday's villains are tomorrow's chum-buddies*—Robert Ruark

chummy 1 *n by 1840s* =CHUM **2** *adj by 1880s* Very friendly; =BUDDY-BUDDY, PALSY-WALSY

chump 1 *n by 1877* A stupid person, esp a dupe; =SUCKER: *I look like a chump these days*—William Kennedy **2** *modifier*: . . . *the honest, hardworking immigrant was a chump game*—New York Magazine **3** *v by 1920s*: *You were chumped, Donna Rice and Marla Trump*—Macon Telegraph [origin unknown; perhaps an alteration of *chunk* referring to blockheadedness]

chump change 1 *n phr black by 1950s* A small or relatively small and meager amount of money; a pittance: . . . *a hundred dollars a day to the town is chump change*—Bryan Di Salvatore/ *Latinos*

rejecting $4.50 an hour as chump change—The Atlantic **2** *n phr carnival* Carnival tokens customers can redeem for cash

◄**chungo bunny**► *n phr by 1970s* A black person: . . . *looked like he hadda be the biggest chungo bunny inna world*—George V Higgins [fr *jungle bunny*]

chunk *v by 1830s* To throw; =CHUCK

chunk up *v phr by 1990s* To gain weight; become chunky

chuppie *n by 1990s* A Chinese yuppie: *Some Chinatown residents call the Planning Council Chuppies*—New Yorker

church key *n phr by 1950s* A bottle or can opener

churn *v by 1940s* To artificially increase the level of activity in a law firm, insurance company, or other enterprise in order to increase commissions, feign busyness, etc: . . . *policyholders have launched class-action suits alleging churning. . .*—US News & World Report

churn out *v phr by 1912* To produce written matter very rapidly and mechanically; =CRANK OUT: *The sci/fi fantasy cartoons being churned out in Japan these days. . .*—TV Guide

chute *n by 1920* A parachute
See POOP CHUTE

chutzpa (HŏŏTS pə, KHŏŏTS-) *n* (Variations: **chuzpa** or **hutzpa** or **hutzpah**) *by 1892* Extreme and offensive brashness; arrogant presumption; hubris: *Chutzpa is that quality enshrined in a man who, having killed his mother and father, throws himself on the mercy of the court because he is an orphan*—Leo Rosten/ *The hutzpah of using Studio 54. . . was much commented on*—Pulpsmith

ciao (CHOW) *interj by 1920s* A salutation either on meeting or parting [fr Italian, fr *schiavo*, "I am your slave"]

cig *n by 1880s* A cigarette

cigarette or **cigarette boat** *n phr by 1970s* An open-cockpit inboard power boat used for offshore racing, and to some extent for transporting contraband: . . . *the look on Bush's face as he pushes up the throttle on his cigarette boat: demonic*—Vanity Fair/ . . . *a speedboat, one of those cigarettes like the black one out there. . .*—Ed McBain [fr their elongated shape]

cigaroot *n* A cigarette [influenced by *cheroot*]

cinch 1 *n cowboys by 1880s* A certainty; something sure to happen; =SURE THING: *It's a cinch they'll win* **2** *v by 1883* To make something certain; =CLINCH, NAIL something DOWN: *We cinched it with a last-second field goal* **3** *n about 1890* Something easily done; =BREEZE, PIECE OF CAKE: *Going up is a bother, coming down's a cinch* [fr Spanish *cincha*, "saddle girth," which, when tight, fosters certainty]
See HAVE something CINCHED, LEAD-PIPE CINCH

cinched *See* HAVE something CINCHED

cinchers *n 1930s truckers & bus drivers* The brakes of a truck, car, or bus; =BINDERS

cinder dick (or **bull**) *n phr 1920s hoboes* A railroad police officer or detective

circ *n by 1990s* A circumcision

◁**circle jerk**▷ *by 1940s* **1** *n phr esp teenagers* A sex party of mutual masturbation **2** *n phr* Any futile occasion, meeting, session, etc

circle the wagons *v phr by 1980s* To take up a defensive posture or position: *"It's time to circle the wagons and suck it up," veteran guard Mark Bortz said. . .* —Milwaukee Journal/*You might say Polaroid Corp circled the wagons to repel a $3.2 billion assault. . .* —Associated Press [fr the action taken in a cowboy movie when a *wagon* train is threatened by hostile Indians]

circle the drain *v phr medical and police by 1980s* To be dying; *And how do some cops describe the condition of a traffic victim who is near death? Circling the drain*—Los Angeles Times

circuit *See* BORSCHT CIRCUIT, CHITLIN CIRCUIT, CLOUT FOR THE CIRCUIT, STRAW-HAT CIRCUIT

circuit breaker *n phr by 1990s* A computer or other mechanism for halting the operation of a stock market in cases of instability: *. . . barely 17 minutes after the opening, one circuit breaker was triggered, suspending program trading*—Philadelphia Inquirer [fr the mechanism used to open an electrical *circuit* in case of an overload]

circuit clout (or **blow** or **wallop**) *n phr baseball by 1908* A home run

circuit slugger *n phr baseball by 1940s* A talented homerun hitter: *Gil Hodges. . . became the greatest circuit slugger ever to wear Dodger flannels*—New York Daily News

circular file *n phr by 1940s* A wastebasket

circus 1 *n by 1885* Any bright and uproarious occasion: *You should have been there—it was a circus* **2** *n by 1870s* A sex show, often featuring bestial couplings

circus catch *n phr 1880s baseball* A spectacularly good and difficult catch [fr the seemingly superhuman feats of *circus* performers]

circus play *n phr 1880s baseball* A spectacularly good play

citizen *n 1960s black & counterculture* A person of a more conservative, established, and prosaic caste than oneself; =SQUARE

Citizen *See* JOHN Q CITIZEN

cits *n by 1829* =CIVVIES

city *1930s jazz musicians* **1** *combining word* The place or milieu of what is indicated: *hamburger city* **2** *combining word* A prevalence or instance of the thing indicated: *trouble city/ dumb city/ fat city* [coined on the model of the *-sville* suffix]

See FAT CITY, FUN CITY, SOUL CITY, TAP CITY, WRINKLE CITY, YUCKO CITY

city cow *n phr WWII armed forces* Canned milk; =ARMORED COW

city hall *n phr by 1890s* The political powers and their haunts; those who control purse strings and patronage: *see how city hall reacts*

See YOU CAN'T FIGHT CITY HALL

city slicker *n phr by 1920s* A shrewd and modish urban person, esp as distinct from the honest and gullible provincial: *A small-town beauty shop, where city slickers can really let their hair down*—New York Times

civvies *n by 1880s* Civilian dress; mufti

clam 1 *n by 1860s* A silent, secretive person, esp one who can be trusted with a confidence **2** *v by 1916* =CLAM UP ●The term must be earlier than the date given, although no examples can be provided. In fact one wonders whether Middle English *clum*, "be quiet! shut up," of obscure origin, may not be related to *clam* **3** *n by 1930s* A dollar: *That'll be eight clams for the oil* **4** *n 1940s jazz musicians* A wrong or sour note; =CLINKER **5** *n by 1916* The vulva; =BEARDED CLAM ●The term is probably older than indicated. An English dialect dictionary of 1857 hints as much with two senses of *clam*: "a slut"; "to snatch, to shut"

See BEARDED CLAM, HAPPY AS A CLAM

clambake 1 *n by 1940s* Any gathering, meeting, convention, party, etc, esp a happy and noisy one **2** *n 1930s jazz musicians* =JAM SESSION

◁**clam bumper**▷ *n phr by 1990s* A lesbian

clamp down *v phr by 1940s* To increase the severity of measures against persons who break rules and laws; punish rather than tolerate: *The whole country's clamping down now on drunk drivers*

the clamps *See* PUT THE CLAMPS ON

clam shells (or **trap**) *n phr by 1830* The mouth and jaws

clam up *v phr by 1916* To stay or become silent; stand mute; =BUTTON UP: *When I ask for details he just clams up*—H L Wilson

clank or **clank up** *v* or *v phr WWII Air Force* To panic; be paralyzed by fear

clanked *adj 1960s students* Exhausted; =BEAT, POOPED

clanker *n outdated hoboes & circus* A dollar

the clanks *n phr by 1943* Delirium tremens; =the SHAKES: *He told me he had the clanks from Purple Passions*—Hal Boyle

the clap *n by 1587* Gonorrhea: *If a guy said 'I ride bareback,' I'd tell him he needs a raincoat. Instead of gonorrhea, I'd talk about the clap*—US News & World Report [fr early French *clapoir*, "bubo, swelling"]

See NO-CLAP MEDAL

clapped-out *adj 1940s Royal Air Force* Worn-out; ready for the junk heap; =BEAT-UP: *The civilian jumped into his clapped-out Mercury*—Car and Driver

clapped-up *adj by 1960s* Infected with gonorrhea: *In reality she's a gotch-eyed. . . clapped-up. . . hooker*—Dan Jenkins

claptrap *n by 1819* Nonsense; mendacious cant; =BULLSHIT [fr early 1700s theatrical use, literally "a *trap* to get a *clap*," a device, verbal or otherwise for milking applause]

claret *n prizefight by 1604* Blood [fr the red color of *claret* wine]

class 1 *n by 1870s* High quality; admirable style;

cachet: *quiet dignity under fire, real class* **2** *modifier*: *a real class joint*
See HIGH-CLASS, WORLD-CLASS

a **class act** *n phr* by 1970s A person or thing of admirable style, quality, competence, etc: *48 HRS clicks anyway. It's a class act*—Playboy/ *Monaco was, as Arthur Lewis said, a class act*—Philadelphia

classic *n* narcotic by 1980s Powdered cocaine; =BLOW, COKE: *Grain, glass, classic, Jock, motor, harp, what you need is what we got*—Robert B Parker

classy by 1891 **1** *adj* Of high quality; first-rate; superior: *That's a very classy speech you just made* **2** *adj* Having or showing prestige; aristocratic; =POSH: *a classy school/ classy manners*

classy chassis *n phr* by 1950s A good figure; trim body: *sassy lassie with a classy chassis*

Claus **See** SANTA CLAUS

claw underworld by 1917 **1** *n* A police officer **2** *v* To arrest
See HAVE one's CLAWS OUT

◀**clay eater**▶ *n phr* by 1841 A native of southern US low country

Claymore *n* by 1990s A danger; an unpredicted peril: . . . *skipping from television to a feature-film career has its built-in Claymore.* . . —Knight-Ridder Newspapers [fr the US *claymore* antipersonnel mine, named in turn for a Scottish broadsword]

clay pigeon **1** *n phr* by 1920s A person who is easily duped; =EASY MARK **2** *n phr* Navy by 1940s An aircraft catapulted from a ship **3** *n phr* by 1950s Something easily done; =CINCH

clean **1** *adj* by 1926 Not carrying anything forbidden, esp a firearm: *Cops gave him a body-shake and he came out clean* **2** *adj* by 1300 Innocent; unincriminated **3** *adj* by 1950s Not producing radioactive contamination: *a clean bomb* **4** *adj* late 1900s Lacking money; =BROKE, CLEANED OUT **5** *adj* by 1867 Not lewd or obscene; morally unexceptionable: *a couple of clean jokes/ a clean old man* **6** *adj* by 1400 Trim; neat; elegant: *Mies' clean lines and crisp angles* **7** *adv*: *I was crazy about Lester. He played so clean and beautiful*—Charlie Parker **8** *adj* 1950s narcotics Free of drug addiction **9** *adj* black by 1960s Well-dressed; clad in the latest style: *Danny, he was really clean. He had new clothes*—Claude Brown
See COME CLEAN, KEEP one's NOSE CLEAN, WIPE THE SLATE CLEAN, SQUEAKY-CLEAN

Clean **See** MISTER CLEAN

clean and green *adj phr* 1970s citizens band Clear of police and other obstructions

clean as a whistle (or **a hound's tooth**) *adj phr* first form by 1828, second by 1940s Perfectly clean

clean someone's **clock** by 1960s **1** *v phr* To attack and punish someone: *Carlson suddenly really wanted to clean Ron Connelly's clock*—Earl Thompson **2** *v phr* To defeat; trounce: *The DA. . . had his clock cleaned for him*—George V Higgins/ *"She just cleaned my clock,"* Mrs King

said—New York Times [perhaps fr the notion of *clock* as "face"; perhaps fr the earlier underworld and railroad term *clean the clock*, "stop, esp suddenly"]

clean dozens *n phr* black by 1930s An elaborate word game in which personal insults are bandied, but without reference to the opponent's mother •As contrasted with the *dirty dozens*

cleaned out *adj phr* by 1812 Lacking money, esp having lost it gambling or speculating; =BROKE, TAPPED OUT: *Georgie was cleaned out after the third race*

the **cleaners** **See** GO TO THE CLEANERS, TAKE someone TO THE CLEANERS

cleaning **See** HOUSE-CLEANING

clean someone **out** *v phr* by 1812 To win all of someone's money at gambling, esp in a crap game **2** *v phr* by 1860s To require or use up all of someone's money: *Buying the condo just about cleaned them out*

cleanup **1** *n* by 1920s An intensive effort or campaign against crime, filth, etc, of the sort periodically undertaken by the authorities: *The Mayor vowed another definitive cleanup of the Times Square area* **2** *modifier*: *another cleanup campaign* **3** *modifier* baseball about 1910 Batting fourth in the lineup: *He did better as the cleanup hitter* [baseball sense fr the sanguine notion that the first three hitters will reach base and the bases will be emptied, *cleaned up*, by the fourth hitter]

clean up *v phr* by 1830s To make a large profit; get an impressive return for one's money; =MAKE A KILLING: *The West today knows many a ghost town where men of too much enterprise cleaned up and cleared out*—Sierra Club Bulletin

clean up one's **act** (or ◀**shit**▶) *v phr* 1960s To correct one's behavior; act properly and decently; *I told the kid to clean up his act or leave*

clean up on someone *v phr* by 1860s To defeat someone decisively; trounce; thrash; =CLEAN someone's CLOCK: *We really cleaned up on them in the second half*

the **cleanup spot** (or **slot**) *n phr* baseball about 1910 The fourth position in the batting order: *The manager didn't have a very reliable hitter for the cleanup spot* [fr the fact that the batter in this position may, or ought to, get a hit and *clean* the runners off the bases by driving them in to score]

clean (or **wipe**) **up the floor with** someone *v phr* by 1890s To defeat someone decisively; =CLEAN UP ON someone: *If he said that to me I'd clean up the floor with the bastard*

clear someone *v* by 1940s To show or declare someone free of suspicion: *He looked guilty, but the investigation cleared him*
See READ someone LOUD AND CLEAR

clear as mud *adj phr* by 1880s Entirely unclear; lacking lucidity: *I think I get it, though your explanation is as clear as mud*

clear out *v phr* by 1839 To depart; =HIT THE ROAD: . . . *obliged every coloured man to "clear out" of the streets.* . . —Bentley's Miscellany

clear sailing *n phr by 1850s* Easy and unimpeded progress; easy going: *After a rough couple of months it was clear sailing*

clear up *v phr 1960s narcotics* To stop using narcotics; get help in withdrawing from drug addiction

clem *circus & carnival by 1920s* **1** *n* A fight between show people and the local citizenry: *It'd start a clem, with me in the middle*—F Brown **2** *v* To disperse rioting customers at a circus or carnival

Clem *circus by 1920s* **1** *n* A small-town resident; rural person, esp one who is easily duped **2** *n* An inhabitant of the place where the circus is playing **3** *interj* A cry used by circus people to rally forces in a fight with townspeople

clemo *prison by 1950s* **1** *n* Executive clemency **2** *n* A prison escape

clerks and jerks *n phr 1970s Army* Soldiers in other than front-line units; rear-echelon troops

Cleveland *n by 1990s* A thousand dollars; a thousand-dollar bill: *The British publicist offered me an exclusive with King Freddy for a Cleveland—$1,000—but I passed*—New York Times [fr the Presidential portrait on the bank note]

click **1** *v theater by about 1910* To succeed; please an audience or constituency: *If I can click with wholesalers I should be ready to open up in about 3 weeks*—George Orwell **2** *v by 1930s* To evoke or precede a flash of insight: *Something clicked. . . I thought, This is what I want to do for the rest of my life*—New York Times **3** *n* An insight, esp a sudden one; flash of comprehension: *She gifts us with this click: Most men want their wives to have a jobette*—Gloria Steinem/ *And finally to a click when it began adding up. . .* —Stan Cutler **4** *v by 1920s* To fit together precisely; go well together: *Those two really click, like a well-oiled machine* **5** *n by 1920s* A clique **6** *n* (also **klick**, **klik**) *1960s armed forces* A kilometer: *. . . a hundred and sixty clicks north of Saigon*—George Warren

clicker *n by 1980s* The remote-control device of a television set

cliffhanger *n by 1937* A very suspenseful story, film, game, situation, etc: *The election was a cliffhanger, right through the recount* [fr the fact that the actress Pearl White actually ended some episodes of her early serial movies *hanging* from the Palisades above the Hudson River]

climb someone *v phr WWI Army* To reprimand severely; =CHEW OUT, REAM •*Climb over someone's frame* has the same sense in college slang of the 1890s: *The old man really climbed me for that stupid trick*

climb on the bandwagon *See* GET ON THE BANDWAGON

climb (or go up) the wall *v phr by 1970s* To become frantic, esp from frustration or anxiety; =GO OUT OF one's SKULL: *By the time the cops came I was about to climb the wall*

clinch **1** *n prizefight by 1870s* A close contact of two boxers, where they hold each other's arms to stifle blows **2** *v*: *Two palookas clinched through six rounds* **3** *n by 1899* An embrace; passionate hug **4** *v by 1716* To determine conclusively; finish definitively and positively; =NAIL something DOWN: *They claim new evidence that'll clinch their case* [fr the bending over, clinching, of the point of a nail to ensure it does not pull out; ultimately fr *clench*]

clincher *n by 1830s* The deciding or conclusive element; =BOTTOM LINE: *One smudged fingerprint was the clincher*

◁**clink**▷ *n black* A black person; =BROTHER

the **clink** *n phr by 1770s* A jail or prison; =the SLAMMER [fr the old prison on *Clink* Street in the Southwark district of London]

clinker **1** *n by 1900* A biscuit **2** *n by 1920s* =the CLINK **3** *n 1930s musicians* A squeak or unintended reed sound made on the clarinet, saxophone, or oboe **4** *n 1930s musicians* An obvious wrong or sour note: *One of the louder sopranos hit an excruciating clinker* **5** *n by 1934* An error; =BONER **6** *n by 1940s* Anything inferior in workmanship, esp a play, movie, or other show; =LEMON, TURKEY **7** *n by 1940s* An incompetent person; a failure; =DUD, LOSER: *There have been some ultraconservative judges, but there has been an absence of real clinkers*—Time **8** *n by 1960s* Something damaging, esp when unseen or unforeseen; a hidden flaw: *There was a clinker in the works apart from his writing, a sort of catch*—Earl Thompson [fr *clinker*, "unburnable cinder"]

clinker boy *n phr railroad by 1940s* A fire stoker

clip **1** *v* To hit; strike sharply and neatly: *He clipped and decked the local goon* **2** *n by 1850s*: *You hit him a good clip*—P Starnes **3** *v by 1930s* To steal; =SWIPE: *Where'd you clip the new car?* **4** *v by 1920s* To cheat someone, esp by overcharging: *That joint'll clip you every time* **5** *v by 1940s* To arrest **6** *v underworld by 1920s* To kill, esp by shooting: *You think he clipped three people, including a seventeen-year-old kid*—Robert B Parker ◀**7**▶ *n by 1940s* =CLIPPED DICK **8** *v* (also **clip it**) *by 1830s* To move rapidly; run; =BARREL, CARRY THE MAIL **9** *n by 1860s* Pace; rate: *She took off at a real good clip* **10** *n by 1801* Each one; each occasion; =POP: *two treatments at $100 a clip/ Every clip cost him half a day's pay* **11** *n by 1920s* A clipping from a newspaper, magazine, etc: *Thanks for sending the clips about the kid's wedding* **12** *n by 1960s* A portion of a movie or television tape: *. . . television clips from the period of the accident*—New York Times **13** *v by 1970s* To cut a car into sections, usu in an illegal operation **14** *n by 1970s* A cut-apart or dismantled section of a car: *Salvage yards will pay $5,000 for the front end, back clip, engine, radio, doors, and bumpers*—Time [senses denoting fraud and theft are probably fr the practice of *clipping* bits of metal off coins and passing them at face value] *See* ROACH CLIP

clip-artist *n underworld by 1940s* A professional swindler or thief: *A gentle clip-artist, Abadaba robbed bookmakers as well as bettors*—T Betts

clip joint *n phr by 1920s* **1** A gambling establishment where the customer is regularly cheated **2** Any business establishment that regularly overcharges, or where one is likely to be cheated: *One man's gourmet noshery is another man's clip joint*

◀**clipped dick**▶ *n phr by 1940s* A Jewish male

clipper *n police by 1970s* A pickpocket: *. . . accused her of being a clipper, or pickpocket—*New York Times

clipping 1 *n football by 1930s* Illegal blocking from behind **2** *n by 1970s* The repairing of a car by joining together two undamaged halves after either the front or rear end has been damaged: *Front and rear clips are attached to the remains of vehicles that have been seriously damaged. . . but clipping. . . is dangerous—*Washingtonian

◁**clit**▷ *n by 1960s* The clitoris; =BUTTON

◁**clit-licker**▷ *n by 1970s* A person who does cunnilingus; =MUFF-DIVER

clobber *by 1940s* **1** *v* To hit or attack very hard; •Appears to have been popularized by WWII RAF use; Eric Partridge gives a date of about 1910, but no example of use=BASH **2** *v* To defeat decisively; trounce; =MURDER, WIPE OUT: *Rommel got clobbered at El Alamein* [origin unknown; perhaps fr Scots *clabber*, "spatter, cover with mud"]

clobbered *adj esp 1950s* Drunk: *. . . those who are, to use a word presently popular with the younger drinking set, clobbered—*James Thurber

clock 1 *v 1920s Australian* To hit; =SOCK: *. . . who clocked me when I wasn't looking—*R Starnes/ *She clocked him with the portable telephone—*GQ **2** *v by 1880s* To time, esp with a stopwatch: *They clocked her at 6:05:03.65* **3** *v by 1892* To achieve a specified time: *I clocked a two-minute lap yesterday* **4** *v 1980s teenagers* To get; amass: *Malcolm Forbes is clockin' megadollars—*Delcastle Dictionary of Slang **5** *n 1980s teenagers* To waste one's time; detain one: *Why're you clockin' me? I got people to see—*New York Magazine **6** *n 1980s teenagers* To watch; keep one's eye on: *He is always clockin' girls—*Delcastle Dictionary of Slang [first sense probably related to *clock*, "face"]
See CLEAN someone's CLOCK

clocker *n by 1990s*: *A clocker is a nickel-and-dime crack dealer who hustles round the clock—*New York Times

clock in (or **out**) *v phr by 1920s* To come or go at a certain recorded time, esp to or from a job where a time clock is used; =PUNCH IN (or OUT)

the **clock** (or **meter**) **is ticking** (or **running**) *sentence* or *v phr by 1990s* A decreasing amount of time is available; the end draws near: *Baker and Aziz were preparing to hold last-minute talks, and the clock was ticking toward war—*Time/ *But the clock is ticking down for the 49-year-old ex-lineman—*Los Angeles Times/ *One of the banks has suffered twenty million dollars in unrecoverable loans and the meter is still running—*New Yorker [fr sports, astronautics, bomb disposal, and other contexts where a *clock* measures the time remaining]

clock-watcher *n phr by 1890* A person who

vouchsafes more attention to the time of quitting than to work: *. . . a hard worker, no clockwatcher—*Ira Wolfert

clod *n by 1605* A stupid person [fr *clodpate* or *clodpole*, "clodhead"]

clodhopper 1 *n by 1690* A farmer; rustic; =SHIT-KICKER •Originally a plowman **2** *n by 1940s* An old vehicle, suitable for only short passages; =CLUNKER, JALOPY

clodhoppers *n by 1830s* Strong, heavy shoes, esp workshoes; =BOONDOCKERS, SHIT-KICKERS

clone *n 1970s* An imitation, esp a person who imitates or emulates another; a mindless copy: *Not a clone in sight. No one has the same color hair—*Village Voice [fr clone, "the asexually produced offspring of an organism," ultimately fr Greek *klun*, "twig, branch"]

clonesome *adj 1970s* Tending to copy; unoriginal; robot-like: *. . . a tall, dark, clonesome actor—*Village Voice

clong *n 1980s politics* The impact of a powerfully inept speech, line, phrase, etc: *Clong is speechwriter talk for "the rush of shit to the heart when a line drops dead in the hall"—*Toronto Globe and Mail/ *"Clong" is the rush of shit to your heart when you see the state's evidence—*Scott Turow/ *His call is a grand clong—*Washington Post [probably echoic of something falling with a loud, dull clang, like *clonk* and *clunk*]

cloning *n 1990s* A cellular telephone fraud in which a personal code is stolen and sold to someone else

clonish *adj 1970s* Inclined to copy; unoriginal and duplicative: *The crowd was decidedly clonish—*Armistead Maupin

clonk *v by 1930s* =CLUNK

close 1 *adj early 1600s* Parsimonious; stingy **2** *adj 1960s students* Very good; extraordinary: *Oh, man, this is crazy close!—*Milwaukee Journal
See THAT'S CLOSE

close but no cigar *adv phr by 1970s* Very nearly correct; not quite the thing: *. . . one package that was acceptable, too many amounted to her idea of close-but-no-cigar—*Washington Post/ *If you answered George Lucas' Star Wars you're close, but no cigar—*Washingtonian [fr carnival feats where one gets a *cigar* as a prize]

close-fisted *adj by 1608* Unwilling to give; niggardly; stingy; =CLOSE

closer (KLOH zer) *n baseball by 1980s* A relief pitcher who usu comes in for the ninth inning: *You can't expect your closer to go out and save 60 games—*Milwaukee Journal

close shave (or **call**) *n phr by 1834* A very narrow avoidance or evasion of some danger; =SQUEAKER

closet *modifier by early 1600s* Secret; unsuspected •Although this sense is much earlier, it has recently been revived by the homosexual use: *Puddin' calls me his closet red neck—*Dan Jenkins/ *. . . fellow who was known around the White House as a "closet liberal"—*New York Times

the **closet** *n phr* *by 1960s* The condition of concealment in which a homosexual or other nonconforming person lives: *If you're out of the closet, you're out of the armed service*—Ms
See COME OUT OF THE CLOSET

close to the chest (or **vest**) *adj phr* *by 1950s*: *Janet Reno is very close to the vest about her personal feelings*—MacNeill/Lehrer News Hour
See PLAY CLOSE TO THE CHEST

closet queen (or **queer**) *n phr* *1960s* A secret male homosexual

close-up **1** *n by 1913* A photograph or movie or television sequence shot close to the subject **2** *modifier* Made or done from very near: *a close-up view/ close-up study* **3** *n 1930s* A biography: *It is becoming commonplace for a literary critic to describe a biography as a "close-up"*—Ernest Weekley

clothes **See** SSUNDAY CLOTHES

clotheshorse *n by 1850* A fashionably dressed person; a person who wears clothes becomingly and perhaps does nothing else

clothesline **1** *n 1930s baseball* A very flat, fast line drive; =FROZEN ROPE, ROPE **2** *v 1960s football* To block or tackle by holding out one's arm in the path of a running player: *He clotheslined him*—Esquire

cloud **See** ON CLOUD NINE

cloud-buster *n baseball by 1950s* A very, very high fly ball

cloud nine (or **seven**) *n phr 1950s* A state of total euphoria: *Capriati's coach. . . knew he had to "get her off Cloud 9"*—New York Times [fr the notion of *clouds* as heavenly locations]
See ON CLOUD NINE

clout **1** *n by 1400* A heavy blow: *She gave him a clout on the snoot* **2** *v by 1890s* To hit; strike; =BASH: *My old man would have clouted the hell out of me*—Calder Willingham **3** *v baseball by 1910* To hit the ball, esp to hit it hard **4** *v by 1940s* To steal, esp to shoplift or steal a car **5** *n by 1950s* Force; power; impact; =PUNCH: *This wimpish paragraph lacks clout* **6** *n 1950s* Influence or power, esp of a political sort: *He has lots of friends in high places, but no clout*

clout (or **hit**) **for the circuit** *v phr baseball by 1940s* To hit a home run in baseball

clover **See** IN CLOVER, LIKE PIGS IN CLOVER

clover-kicker *n by 1940s* =SHITKICKER

clown **1** *n by 1920s* A person for whom the speaker feels mild contempt, esp one whose behavior merits its derision: *. . . get this clown off my back and let me help you. . .*—Hugh Pentecost **2** *v* (also **clown around**) *by 1940s* To behave frivolously; persist in inappropriate levity

club **See** BOTTLE CLUB, DEUCE OF CLUBS, KEY CLUB, MILE-HIGH CLUB, RAP CLUB, SCRUB CLUB, WELCOME TO THE CLUB

Club Fed *n phr 1980s* A minimum-security Federal prison: *Set on 42 campus-like acres, Club Fed had neither walls nor armed guards*—New York Times [after *Club Med*, trademark name of a chain of holiday resorts]

clubhouse *modifier by 1960s* Having to do with routine and sometimes shady urban partisan politics: *Dinkins, 62, is a classic clubhouse politician*—Time

clubhouse lawyer *n phr baseball by 1940s* A baseball player who is a prominent self-appointed authority on the game and its regulations, and who generously instructs his associates

cluck or **cluckhead** or **kluck** **1** *n by 1920s* A stupid person; idiot: *The champion cluck of all time*—Joel Sayre/ *. . . if I defend myself you two clucks are going to need a lot more backup*—Robert B Parker ◀**2**▶ *n black by 1950s* A very dark black person
See DUMB CLUCK

cluck and grunt *n phr lunch counter by 1950s* Ham and eggs

cluckish *adj by 1920s* Stupid

clue *v* or *v phr* (also **clue in**) *by 1940s* To inform someone of pertinent facts; =PUT someone IN THE PICTURE: *I'll clue ya*—Newsweek/ *Neil Sheehan and I were terribly clued-in. We had a lock on that story*—David Halberstam
See GET A CLUE, HAVE A CLUE, NOT HAVE A CLUE

clued out *adj phr 1990s* Unaware; ignorant: *I like Elvissa, but she can be so clued out*—Douglas Coupland

clueless *adj 1980s students fr 1930s Royal Air Force* Ignorant; hopelessly unaware: *. . . we'll have to endure loads of clueless reporters raving on*—New York Times/ *You're probably just a clueless newbie*—Macon Telegraph [Perhaps a revival, perhaps a new coinage]
See TOTALLY CLUELESS

cluelessly *adv 1990s* In a clueless way: *. . . the Bumbling Around Cluelessly Phase. . .*—Dave Barry

clunk **1** *v* (also **clonk**) *by 1940s* To hit; strike; =CLOCK: *She clunked him in the teeth* **2** *n*: *He hit me a good clunk* **3** *n by 1940s* A stupid person; dupe; =CLUCK: *. . . scheming maids who have been working on the poor clunks all spring*—Robert Ruark **4** *n by 1940s* An old and worn-out machine, esp a car; =CLUNKER: *Look at that fuckin' broad in the clunk next to us*—Rolling Stone/ *. . . hauled a junk car on the ice and took bets. . . This contest was called "Dunk the Clunk"*—Village Voice **5** *v by 1970s* To move awkwardly and slowly: *The plot just clunks forward, for two hours and 10 minutes*—Entertainment [probably all based on *clunk*, "make a dull sound," found by 1796]

clunk down **See** PLANK DOWN

clunker **1** *n by 1940s* Anything inferior; =LEMON, TURKEY: *His last clunker was Lolly Madonna*—New York Magazine **2** *n by 1950s* An old, worn-out machine, esp a car; =CLUNK, JALOPY: *. . . let in someone in an old clunker with a broken muffler and a fuming exhaust*—New York Times **3** *n by 1940s* A clumsy person, esp an unskillful athlete; =DUFFER, HACKER: *Tell one of those clunkers what a great stroke he has*—G Edson
See MOUNTAIN BIKE

clunkhead *n* by 1950s A stupid person: *Some clunkhead sent me three live quail*—Arthur Godfrey

clunkily *adv* by 1970s Ungracefully; stolidly: *Her clunkily earnest lyrics are very big on concepts like the Necessity of Being Your Own Person*—Ms

clunky or **clunkish** *adj* by 1970s Blockish and ungraceful; stolidly unsophisticated: *. . . a pair of clunky Sonora biker boots*—Buzz/ *a clunkish magazine called Pick-Up Times*—Village Voice/ *The ads are so clunky and quaint that they transport one back to a seemingly more innocent consumer past*—Washington Post

clutch 1 *n* by 1950s An embrace; =CLINCH **2** *n* by 1908 A group; bunch: *a clutch of drunken sailors* **3** *n restaurant* by 1950s A customer who does not tip, or tips too little; =STIFF **4** *v* (also **clutch up**) by 1950s To panic; be seized with anxiety: *If that's what's got you clutched up, don't worry about it*—Elmore Leonard

the clutch 1 *n phr* by 1920s A moment when heroic performance under pressure is needed: *You could always depend on Gladys when the clutch came* **2** *modifier*: *a clutch hitter/ clutch play*

clutched *adj* by 1950s Nervous; tense; =UPTIGHT

clutcher *See* DOUBLE-CLUTCHER

clutching *See* DOUBLE-CLUTCHING

clutchy by 1960s **1** *adj* Likely to become nervous or anxious **2** *adj* Difficult; dangerous; =HAIRY

clutz *See* KLUTZ

clyde *n* 1940s *students* A person who does not appreciate the current music, culture, etc; =SQUARE

C-note *n* by 1920s A hundred-dollar bill; =FRANKLIN: *. . . staring at that C-note*—Elmore Leonard

coach *See* SLOW COACH

coal *See* DEAL IN COAL, HAUL someone OVER THE COALS, POUR ON THE COAL

coalhole *n* by 1835 A prison, guardhouse, cell, etc

coast 1 *v* by 1880s To go along without effort: *I coasted through the two exams* **2** *v* by 1940s To be exhilarated by a narcotic, by music, etc; be euphoric: *That first fix. . . had sent him coasting one whole week*—Nelson Algren **3** *n*: *The flip side gave us a coast*

the coast (or Coast) *n phr* by 1870s The Pacific coast, esp California, or the Atlantic coast
See LEFT COAST

the coast is clear *sentence* by 1630s Danger is past; resistance no longer impends: *I'll be back here as soon as the bomb squad says the coast is clear*—Hugh Pentecost

coat *See* PINE OVERCOAT

coattail 1 *v musicians* by 1950s To keep the same musical tempo: *You're still keeping the same time. We called it coattailing*—Downbeat **2** *modifier* Based on another person's achievement or quality; derivative: *. . . but the Sephardim are not likely to remain contented with coattail power for long*—Newsweek

cob *See* OFF THE COB, ROUGH AS A COB

cobble together *v phr* by 1830s To make or construct, esp by assemblage: *. . . van Zylen still rejects computers for production, preferring to cobble together layouts by hand*—Vogue

cock ◁1▷ *n* by 1618 The penis; =PRICK: *The youth's cock was by now rock hard. . .*—Xaviera Hollander **2** *n* by 1830s A friend; =PAL •Chiefly British: *How goes it, old cock?* [origin uncertain; perhaps based on *cock,* "spigot"]
See DROP YOUR COCKS AND GRAB YOUR SOCKS, HORSE COCK, POPPYCOCK

cockalorum *See* HIGH COCKALORUM

cockamamie or **cockamamey** or **cockamamy** (kahk ə MAY mee) *adj New York City* children by 1920s Crazy; confused: *The picture ends with a cockamamie implication that love will conquer all*—Time/ *. . . this cockamamie little tort. . .*—New York Times [fr New York City dialect, perhaps fr British; somehow connected with *decalcomania*; perhaps because decalcomanias as given in candy boxes and chewing-gum packets were used by children for antic self-decoration]

cock-and-bull story *n phr* by 1620 An improbable account, often an alibi; a mendacious farrago: *He gives me this cock-and-bull story about six flat tires* [origin uncertain; the French term "cock and donkey" is analogous]

cock a snook *v phr* by 1791 To show derision and contempt by thumbing one's nose: *. . . the "world's Greatest Rock and Roll Band" took the occasion to cock a snook at their chief competitors*—Newsweek [origin unknown; the spread hand resembles a rooster's head, and the dialect verb *snook* means "to seek by smelling," but the semantics are not otherwise useful]

cocked *adj* by 1730s Drunk
See HALF COCKED

cocked hat *See* KNOCK something INTO A COCKED HAT

cocker *See* ALTER KOCKER, OLD COCKER

cockeye *n baseball* by 1940s A lefthanded pitcher; =SOUTHPAW

cockeyed 1 *adj* by 1820 Crosseyed; walleyed; strabismic **2** *adj* by 1930s Crazy; weird; all wrong; =SCREWY: *Anybody who thinks I'm kidding is cockeyed*—Heywood Broun/ *In this cockeyed caravan called the 90s. . .*—Mademoiselle **3** *adj* by 1722 Drunk: *He is in a doghouse at home on account of coming home cockeyed on his wedding anniversary*—Joseph F Dinneen **4** *adj* by 1920s Unconscious: *Izzy knocks him cockeyed* **5** *adv* by 1910s Askew; crooked; =SLONCHWAYS: *He put his hat on cockeyed and got a polite chuckle* **6** *adj* by 1920s Genuine; absolute; =FUCKING: *You're a cockeyed wonder, you know that?*—Stan Cutler
See I'LL TELL THE WORLD

◁**one's cock is on the block**▷ *sentence* by 1970s One is in grave and imminent peril: *. . . he'll cop a plea if you tell him his cock is on the block for the murder. . .*—Lawrence Sanders

cockpit queen *n phr* by 1990s A flight attendant who dallies with the pilots: *I couldn't get that cockpit queen to help me with the cart*—Los Angeles Times

◁**cocksman** or **cock hound**▷ *n* *first form by 1916, second by 1940s* An ardent womanizer and copulator; =STUD: *In those days Harry was a big cocksman. . .* —Stan Cutler/ *Valdez was a cock hound, no question. . .* —Robert B Parker

cocksmanship *n* *by 1990s* The practice of being a cocksman: *In "Mambo Mouth," cocksmanship is portrayed as the only surviving romance in lives bereft of other dreams*—New Yorker

◀**cocksucker**▶ **1** *n* *by 1890s* A person who does fellatio, esp a male homosexual **2** *n* *by 1920s* A man held by the speaker in extreme contempt; =BASTARD, PRICK: *Oh, Sid, you fucking cocksucker. . . . You nailed me again*—Joseph Heller

◀**cocksucking**▶ *by 1910* **1** *adj* Despicable; contemptible: *So I told the cocksucking little pimp to get lost* **2** *adj* Wretched; =DAMNED ●A very general intensive use, often for euphony: *Don't give me no cocksucking grief/ Here, take your cocksucking money* **3** *adv*: *Don't talk so cocksucking silly*

cocktail *1960s narcotics* **1** *n* A cigarette of marijuana and tobacco, with marijuana put into the end of an ordinary cigarette **2** *n* A cigarette of more than a single narcotic

  See MOLOTOV COCKTAIL

◁**cock-tease**▷ *v* *by 1950s* To permit sexual familiarities but deny the sex act: *. . . chivying a string of suitors and behaving like overage sorority sisters. They cock-teased*—New Yorker

◁**cock-teaser** or **prick-teaser** or **prick-tease**▷ *n* *entry form by 1891, variants by 1960s* A woman or a male homosexual who arouses a man sexually by granting certain favors, then denies him the sex act

coco *n* *by 1835* The head

coconut **1** *n* *by 1834* The head **2** *n* *by 1920s* One dollar: *. . . the whole hundred thousand coconuts*—Joel Sayre **3** *n* *by 1970s* A Hispanic person who truckles to or imitates the values of the non-Hispanic majority; =TIO TACO: *Maldonado ridicules him for selling out, for being a coconut, brown on the outside, white on the inside*—New York Times

cocoon *1980s* **1** *v* To stay at home, and, often, to be inactive: *The couch potatoes are going to be cocooning in their families' personal oases*—New York Times **2** *n* One's cozy home: *Each morning he leaves his domestic cocoon in Rancho Palos Verdes. . .* —People

codger *n* *by 1756* An old man, esp an eccentric one ●Usu with *old*: *Look at those happy codgers on the shuffleboard court* [probably fr *cadger*, "moocher, wheedling beggar"]

coffee *See* COWBOY COFFEE, CUP OF COFFEE

coffee-and-cake joint *n phr* (Variations: **layout** or **place** or **spot** may replace **joint**) *by 1950s* A business or place of business that is not very remunerative

coffee and cakes or **coffee-and-cake money** *n phr* *by 1920s* Small wages; a pittance; =PEANUTS: *playing for coffee and cakes in an obscure Washington nightspot*—A Lomax

coffee break *n phr* *1940s* A respite of ten or twenty minutes during the workday

coffee cooler *n phr* *by 1876* A person devoted to easy work; shirker; =GOLDBRICK

coffee grinder *n phr* *by 1950s* A strip teaser or other performer who features slow pelvic gyration; =CEMENT MIXER

coffee pot *n phr* *by 1920s* A lunch counter or diner: *. . . a cheap quick lunch emporium. . . frequently called a "greasy spoon"*—Time/ *The Marx brothers ate in coffee pots and greasy spoons*—Joel Sayre

coffin **1** *n* *by 1830s* A ship regarded as unsafe; later, any unsafe vehicle **2** *n* *WWII Army* A tank or armored car

coffin corner *n phr football by 1940s* Any corner of the football field [because any player running the ball upfield from a corner is dangerously trapped]

coffin nail (or **tack) ** *n phr* *by 1880s* A cigarette; =BUTT

coffin varnish *n phr* *by 1908* Inferior whiskey, esp bootleg or homemade whiskey

coin *n* *by 1870s* Money; =BREAD, LOOT

co-inky-dinky or **coinkidink** *n* *by 1940s* A coincidence: *My, oh, my, what a coinky-dinky*—New Yorker/ *What a coinkidink that we have two classes together*—UCLA Slang

coin money *v phr* *by 1840s* =MAKE MONEY HAND OVER FIST

co-jock *n* *1980s students* A computer science major [fr computer *jockey*]

cojones (coh HOH neez) *n* *by 1932* Courage; audacity; =BALLS: *. . . requiring cojones the size of the award-winning cabbages at the state fair*—Car and Driver/ *You've got stainless steel cojones, Dave*—James Lee Burke [fr Spanish "testicles"]

coke **1** *n* *by 1908* Cocaine **2** *modifier*: *coke peddlers/ coke sniffer* **3** *n* =COKE

Coke *n* *by 1909* Coca-Cola, trademark name of a soft drink

Coke-bottle (or **Coke-bottle-bottom) glasses** *n phr* *by 1970s* Very thick eyeglass lenses: *He had thinning hair, Coke-bottle glasses, a big nose*—New York Review/ *Every maladjusted sociopath with Coke-bottle-bottom glasses has no trouble finding this stuff*—Milwaukee Journal [fr their resemblance to the thickness of the bottom of a soft-drink bottle]

coked or **coked-up** or **coked-out** *adj* *1920s narcotics* Intoxicated with cocaine; =HIGH: *. . . the new generation of "coked". . . gunmen*—E Lavine/ *. . . the pair of strippers, a coked-out Pakistani princess and a coked-up Fire Island queen*—Village Voice/ *Marvella, you coked-out cunt. . .* —Harry Crews

cokehead *n* *1920s narcotics* A cocaine addict

coke slut *n phr* *late 1980s* A woman who exchanges sexual favors for narcotics: *A coke slut, she said, would do anything for drugs*—Milwaukee Journal

cokie or **cokey 1** *n* *1920s narcotics* A narcotics addict, esp a cocaine addict: *the horde of Hollywood cokies* **2** *modifier*: *a cokey friend/ cokie chat* **3** *adj* *black about 1930* Relaxed and sleepy-looking; inattentive

cola 1 *n* *by 1910s* A soft drink flavored with cola nut seeds **2** *n* *narcotics by 1970s* Cocaine: . . . *paying upwards of $75 for a gram of cola*—Head [second sense a word-play on *Coca-Cola*, a trademark]

colaholic *n* *by 1970s* A person who drinks a great deal of cola: *Many colaholics revealed that they would find it difficult to give up the habit*—P Horn

cold 1 *adj* *by 1896* Unconscious; =OUT: *The snowball knocked him cold* **2** *adj* Undergoing a spell of bad luck: *I got out of that game because I was cold and Pop was hot* **3** *adj* *by 1890s* Without rehearsal, practice, or warmup: *When the star got sick, this woman had to take over the part cold* **4** *adv* *by 1890s* Perfectly; in every detail; =BLIND: *She knew the subject cold* **5** *adv* *by 1908* With no possibility of evasion; definitively; =DEAD TO RIGHTS: *After that slip they had him cold* **6** *adj* *1980s* Insulting; cruel: *That's really cold, Duffy*—Harry Crews **See** BLOW HOT AND COLD, HOT AND COLD

cold as (or **colder than**) **hell** *adj phr* (Variations: **charity** or **Kelsey's ass** or **a welldigger's ass** or **a witch's tit** may replace **hell**) *charity* form *by 1835, witch's tit by 1932, welldigger's ass by 1940's, Kelsey was often identified as the welldigger* Very cold: *In Chicago, that December 1955, it was cold as a well-digger's ass in the Klondike*—Earl Thompson/ *It's cold as a witch's tit outside*—Van Wyck Mason

cold-blooded *adj* *1960s black teenagers* Absolutely first-rate; the very best; =ZERO COOL

cold-call 1 *v* *by 1970s* To make a sales call without an appointment: *It's difficult to cold-call a corporation and ask them to give you five figures up front*—Photo District News **2** *n*: *Canvassing is the equivalent of cold calls in the sales field*—Sue Grafton

cold cash *n phr* *by 1884* Unmistakably valid money, as distinct from checks, promises, etc; *The place wants payment in cold cash, nothing less* [fr the notion that definite and inalterable things, like gold and silver coins, are *cold* and hard]

coldcock *by 1918* **1** *v* To knock someone unconscious; =KNOCK someone OUT: *He told me to step aside and I wouldn't, so he cold cocked me*—Village Voice/ . . . *he was going to die like some effengee, cold-cocked and kicked senseless by a couple of redneck ranchers*—Carsten Stroud **2** *n* The act of knocking someone unconscious quickly before the victim can resist [origin uncertain; perhaps fr the hammering of *caulking* into a boat's or ship's seams; perhaps related to Canadian loggers' *put the caulks to* someone, "stamp in someone's face with spiked boots"]

a cold day in hell *n phr* *by 1940s* An impossible time; never: *It'll be a cold day in hell when you catch me smoking dope*

cold deck 1 *n phr* *by 1856* A dishonest deck of playing cards, usu stacked or marked **2** *v phr* *by 1884* To take advantage of someone; dishonestly assure one's own winning; =RIG, STACK THE DECK

cold-decker *n* *by 1920* A swindler; cheat

cold-dis *v* *1980s teenagers* To snub; behave dismissively toward: *Why did you cold-dis me at the party and leave without me?*—Washington Post

◁**cold enough to freeze the balls** (or **nuts**) **off a brass monkey**▷ *adj phr* *by 1928* Very cold indeed [A politer version citing the *tail of a brass monkey* is attested in 1928]

cold feet *See* HAVE COLD FEET

cold fish *by 1920s* **1** *n phr* A person who lacks emotional warmth, compassion, sociability, etc; =ICEBERG **2** *modifier*: *Jackson offered a cold-fish handshake to Antrim after the game*—Milwaukee Journal

cold haul *v phr* (also **cold haul it**) *black by 1940s* To leave; depart; =HAUL ASS: *He cold hauled it!*—Zora Neale Hurston

cold in hand *adj phr* *black by 1950s* Lacking money; =BROKE

cold meat *n phr* *by 1819* A cadaver; corpse; =DEAD MEAT

cold-meat box *n phr* *1880s* A coffin

cold-meat cart *n phr* *by 1820* A hearse

cold-meat party *n phr* *by 1908* A wake or funeral: *You were at that cold-meat party; I spotted you coming out of the cemetery*—J Evans

a cold one *n phr* *by 1990s* A bottle or glass of beer; =BREW, BREWSKIE: . . . *when someone from far away stops in for a cold one. . .* —Milwaukee Journal Sentinel

cold-out *v* *1980s teenagers* To insult, esp to insult a woman

cold pack 1 *n phr* *prizefight by 1920s* A knockout or knockout punch **2** *n phr* *1920s* A certainty; =SURE THING, CINCH

cold pricklies *n phr* *by 1970s* Unpleasant and unwelcome comments; adverse criticism: *The cast needed strokes, but they got cold pricklies* [the opposite of *warm fuzzies*]

cold shoulder 1 *n phr* *by 1816* A deliberate snub; display of chilly contempt **2** *v* *by 1845*: *I cold-shouldered him and he looked puzzled*

cold shower *by 1990s* **1** *n phr* A remedy for illusions; an imposer of reality; a dampener of spirits: . . . *turning a cold shower on the grimy, corrosive residue of 73 years of communism*—Time **2** *modifier*: . . . *hard-line, cold-war, cold-shower Republican Protestants*—New York Times [Attested in 1866 in the form *a douche of cold water*; it should also be recalled that *cold baths* and *showers* have been a traditional prescription for calming the rampant male]

cold snap *n phr* *by 1776* A short spell of cold weather

cold sober *adj phr* *by 1930s* Completely sober **See** STONE COLD SOBER

cold storage *See* IN COLD STORAGE

cold turkey 1 *n phr by 1928* The plain truth; =the STRAIGHT SKINNY **2** *modifier by 1920s* Basic; unadorned; =HARD-CORE: *Stalin didn't like certain cold-turkey facts Kennan reported*—New York Daily News **3** *v by 1920s*: *I'll cold-turkey right now: the butler did it* **4** *adv phr by 1940s* Without warning, rehearsal, overture, etc; =COLD: *. . . simply walk in cold turkey and talk things over*—D H Beetle **5** *n phr by 1921* Total and abrupt deprivation of narcotics, as distinct from gradual withdrawal **6** *adv phr*: *He kicked his habit cold turkey* **7** *adj by 1921* Requiring abrupt and complete deprivation: *They tried the cold-turkey cure* **8** *v phr auctioneers by 1940s* To stop auction bidding and sell at a previously set price
See TALK TURKEY

collar 1 *v by 1830s* To seize or take, later esp to arrest: *He collared the muggers in the next block* **2** *n by 1865* An arrest •The earliest form is *put the collar on*: *The bull makes a collar on me*—American Mercury/ *The best collar in recent years. . .* —Time **4** *v teenagers by 1940s* To comprehend; grasp; =DIG: *I don't collar your meaning, Sam*
See ACCOMMODATION COLLAR, BRASS COLLAR, DOG COLLAR, HOT UNDER THE COLLAR, WHITE-COLLAR

collar a nod *v phr black by 1940s* To sleep: *You can't collar nods all day*—Zora Neale Hurston

collar the jive *v phr 1930s jive talk* To understand and approve; =DIG

college *n underworld by 1850s* A jail, prison, or reformatory: *Say, I'm no punker. Wasn't I in college?*—American Mercury
See COW COLLEGE, NUTHOUSE

College **See** JOE COLLEGE

college try **See** the OLD COLLEGE TRY

collision mat *n phr Navy fr WWII* A waffle or pancake

collitch *n by 1940s* College •A humorous mispronunciation

colly *v black by 1930s* =COLLAR THE JIVE

the **collywobbles** *n phr by 1823* A stomachache

colonel **See** CHICKEN COLONEL, LIGHT COLONEL

color *n media by 1938* Interesting background, esp details about players, etc, as used in sports coverage •A scholar in the middle 1920s wrote of *color stuff* as the enlivening human interest and spicy, inventive language used by sports writers to avoid mere facts: *. . . doing color, spoke of a shot put up by one of the players by calling it "a Perot hook": in, out, and in*—personal letter/ *I told him I need some color for a magazine piece I'm doing. . .* —Elmore Leonard
See OFF COLOR

Colorado koolaid *n by 1970s* Coors™ beer: *Colorado koolaid is always advertised on television*—Delcastle Dictionary of Slang [fr *Kool-Aid*™, a soft-drink powder; the beer is brewed in *Colorado*]

color me something *sentence by 1980s* I am what is indicated: *Color me gone*—College Slang 101/ *Color me ready*—TV show Murphy Brown [fr a child's book in which *colors* are added to outline drawings]

colors *n motorcyclists by 1960s* Dress and insignia that identify members of motorcycle clubs and other gangs: *. . . many bars had signs on their doors listing their dress codes or other rules. . . The phrase "no colors" was almost always part of such a list*—Lee Russell/ *I've never seen anything that resembled colors or signs or whatever*—Wisconsin State Journal
See WITH FLYING COLORS

color-struck *adj black by 1970s* Harboring prejudice against darker-skinned black persons

Columbia **See** HAIL COLUMBIA

combination-platter *modifier 1980s* Containing a little of everything; =GRAB-BAG: *. . . legislature submitting gigantic combination-platter spending bills*—Time

combo 1 *n musicians by 1920s* A musical group or band: *a combo like Led Zeppelin* **2** *n by 1920s* The combination of a safe, lock, vault, etc **3** *n by 1920s* Any combination: *gin and tomato juice combo/ boy-girl combo* **4** *n 1980s students* A bisexual: *. . . we had deep concerns that Andy was becoming a combo*—UCLA Slang

◁**come**▷ **1** *v by 1650* To have an orgasm; ejaculate semen **2** *n* (also **cum**) *by 1920s* Semen, or any fluid secreted at orgasm
See HOW COME

come a cropper *by 1870s* **1** *v phr* To take a sudden violent fall **2** *v phr* To fail; suffer a setback •Some US use, chiefly as a conscious Briticism [origin uncertain; perhaps fr a British dialect word *crop*, "neck"]

come across 1 *v phr by 1908* To give something, esp to do so somewhat reluctantly: *When will you come across with the rent?* **2** *v phr by 1930s* To accede to the sex act; bestow oneself sexually: *She came across without more fuss* **3** *v phr by 1930s* To seem to be; give the impression •Often with as or like: *Walter doesn't come across as a crusader, or muckraker*—Esquire/ *This guy always comes across very hostile*

come again *v phr by 1884* To repeat something; =RUN something BY AGAIN •Nearly always a request, or an expression of disbelief at what one has heard: *Come again? Did I hear what I hope I didn't?*

come apart at the seams *v phr* To lose coherence; disintegrate: *It was rather a long kiss. Silas felt himself coming apart at the seams*—S McNeil/ *I would choose not to give the Republicans any advice, rather just stand back and watch them coming apart at the seams*—New York Times

come at someone **like six headlights (or like a Mack Truck)** *v phr by 1980s* To confront someone honestly and forcibly: *I'd rather sit in a room with a guy that comes at you like six headlights, like a Mack Truck. . .* —Los Angeles Times

comeback 1 *n by 1889* A quick and witty retort; a withering riposte: *Dorothy Parker was famous for devastating comebacks* **2** *n by 1908* A regaining of success, fame, health, etc: *He's trying another comeback at 38* **3** *n salespersons by 1950s* A customer who returns merchandise; also, the returning itself **4** *n* 1970s citizens band A response to a call: *Thanks for your comeback, Dead Duck*

come back *v phr* by 1910 To regain success, renown, health, etc; make a comeback: *It's hard to come back after a fiasco like that*

come back and bite one *v phr* (Variations: **in the ass** or **in the fanny** may be added) by 1990s To reappear as punishment or retribution; boomerang; backfire: *It has come back to bite him*—overheard in Denver/ . . . *they don't want any of their used boxes to come back and bite them in the fanny*—Milwaukee Journal

come back for more *v phr* by 1950s To return repeatedly, either bravely or foolishly, to a bad situation; not know when one is beaten: . . . *pathetically, no matter how treacherously venomous they were, Lady Ottoline came back for more*—New Yorker

come clean *v phr* by 1919 To tell the truth, esp the whole truth; make a plenary confession

comedian *See* STAND-UP COMIC

comedown 1 *n* by 1840 A reduction of one's status; loss of prestige: *Riding the bus was a comedown for her* **2** *n* 1950s narcotics The ending of a drug experience: *I cooled it with Quaalude. . . the comedown wasn't too bad*—Saturday Review **3** *n* by 1950s =LETDOWN

come down 1 *v phr* 1950s narcotics To experience the ending of a drug intoxication: . . . *as if he had just come down off methedrine*—J Bradshaw **2** *v phr* narcotics by 1960s To become firmly established: . . . *when a chick's habit came down on her*—Claude Brown **3** *v phr* black by 1960s To happen: *Sir Morgan's cove, where the Great Event was coming down*—Worcester/ *Something weird had to be coming down*—Cyra McFadden

come down on someone **(or something)** *v phr* by 1881 To criticize severely; savage: *If I did that, the press would come down on me very hard*

come down on someone **like a ton of bricks** *v phr* by 1920s To punish or suppress severely; =CLAMP DOWN: *When he heard about it he came down on them like a ton of bricks* [The earlier version *like a thousand of bricks* is found by 1836]

come down the pike *v phr* by 1950s To appear; come on the scene: . . . *every dumbass little news story that comes down the pike*—Armistead Maupin

come hell or high water *adv phr* fr cowboys by 1916 No matter what happens; in any event: *I'll find out come hell or high water*

come high *v phr* by 1880s To be expensive: . . . *he says everything is lovely and their booze comes high*—The Lantern

come-hither eyes *See* BEDROOM EYES

come-in circus **1** *n* The line of people waiting to buy tickets **2** *n* The time between the opening of the main tent and the beginning of the entry procession

come in for *v phr* by 1665 To receive; be given something: *He came in for a lot of grief after that decision*

come in from the cold 1 *v phr* by 1960s To

retire from espionage service: . . . *coming in from the cold and staying free might be out of reach for Markus Wolf*—Time **2** *v phr* by 1980s To return to comfort, acclaim, etc, after a period of relative obscurity: *An Osmond comes in from the cold*—Milwaukee Journal [popularized by the John le Carré 1963 novel *The Spy Who Came In from the Cold*]

come-lately *See* JOHNNY-COME-LATELY

come off 1 *v phr* by 1590s To succeed: *To everybody's astonishment, the scheme came off* ◁**2**▷ *v phr* by 1650 To have an orgasm; ejaculate semen; =COME **3** *v phr* by 1855 To happen; =GO DOWN **4** *v phr* by 1990s To seem to be; give the impression; =COME ACROSS ●Often with *as*: *Geronimo comes off as ersatz tragedy*—Bill Gallo/ *She comes off softer than you would think*

come off something *v phr* by 1880s To stop doing or saying something immediately ●Usu a stern command, most often *Come off it!*: *Come off that crap. Keep your jaw shut*—Calder Willingham/ *Give me a break and come off it*

come off one's **perch** *v phr* by 1890s To stop behaving in a superior or haughty manner; =GET OFF one's HIGH HORSE

come on 1 *v phr* about 1950 To show as; present oneself as; act; =COME ACROSS: *Your friend comes on real dumb* **2** *interj* by 1603 An exclamation of disbelief, disapproval, request, etc: *Come on, Arnold, don't give me that shit*

come-on by 1902 **1** *n* Anything designed to attract or seduce; an enticement: *I gave her a big grin, but she knew it was a come-on* **2** *modifier*: *football bowls baited with $100,000 or so of come-on money*—Arthur Daley

come on like gangbusters *v phr* by 1942 To begin or proceed in a vigorous fashion: . . . *I come on like the Gang Busters and go off like The March of Time*—Zora Neale Hurston [fr the radio program *Gangbusters* of 1937–1942, which was introduced by a noisy miscellany of sirens, shots, screeches, music, etc]

come on strong 1 *v phr* horse-racing by 1940s To gain steadily and rapidly in a race **2** *v phr* by 1970s To be vehement and positive: *He always comes on a little too strong about taxes*

come on to someone *v phr* by 1980s To make a sexual advance; =PROPOSITION, PUT A MOVE ON: *The way I came on to you the other night; I thought you'd be miffed*—Lawrence Sanders

come out 1 *v phr* by 1840s To declare oneself; take a position ●The action of the above date is that of declaring a religious conversion: *Did she come out for the Equal Rights Amendment?* **2** *v phr* by 1896 To end; eventuate: *How'd that whole deal come out?* **3** *v phr* homosexuals by 1970s To acknowledge one's homosexuality; =COME OUT OF THE CLOSET: *Their eldest son had "come out"*—Shana Alexander

come out ahead (or on top) *v phr* by 1930s To win: *Who came out ahead in the poll?*

come out of a bag *v phr* *black by 1990s* To act contrary to expectation

come out of the chute *v phr* *by 1980s* To begin; inaugurate something: *If we had come out of the chute conservatively, we would have been projecting a sense of doubt*—Milwaukee Journal [fr the rodeo, where bucking horses, rampaging bulls, etc, *come out of a chute* at the edge of the arena]

come out of the closet 1 *v phr* *homosexuals by 1960s* To acknowledge one's homosexuality; =COME OUT: *He came out of the closet last year and his parents damn near died* **2** *v phr* To reveal or acknowledge some personal conviction, political position, etc: *In 1978 Timmy came out of the closet and showed a genuine interest in the club*—Sports Illustrated/ *James Robinson, a fiery, red-faced orator with a Bible clenched in his upraised hand, thundered that it was "time for God's people to come out of the closet and the churches and change America"*—Washington Post

come out of the woodwork *See* CRAWL OUT OF THE WOODWORK

come out swinging (or smoking) *v phr* *by 1990s* To be eager and aggressive; =COME ON STRONG: *Labor chief comes out swinging*—Milwaukee Journal Sentinel/ *... the fighter came out smoking, trying to dazzle the audience with a flurry of quips*—Milwaukee Journal

come over someone *v phr* *by 1609* To convince or influence, esp by force or fraud: *Then I realized he was just trying to come over me, not inform me*

◁**come-queen**▷ *v* *by 1970s* A person who prefers and practices fellatio: *... a nutty come-queen named Linda Lovelace*—Deep Throat Papers

comer *n* *by 1880s* A person doing very well and promising to do better in a certain field: *She's a comer, a potential champ*

come running *v phr* *by 1596* Join one in a hurry; appear immediately: *Once you've asked her these questions, let her make up her own mind, and be there if she comes running*—Seventeen

come through 1 *v phr* *by 1899* To succeed as expected and desired: *Jim Thorpe always came through to win*—Bill Stern **2** *v phr* *by 1899* To cope successfully with perils and troubles; weather adversity: *All seems bleak, but we'll come through unscathed* **3** *v phr* *by 1907* =COME ACROSS

come (or bring) to a screeching halt *v phr* *by 1970s* To be finished abruptly and immediately: *... when the 1994 season came to a screeching halt*—Milwaukee Journal Sentinel/ *I've got to bring this to a screeching halt*—Wayman Tisdale

come unglued (or unstuck or unwrapped) *v phr* *about 1910* To go out of control; deteriorate to chaos; disintegrate; =COME APART AT THE SEAMS: *Mr Foster... succeeded in keeping the proceedings from coming unglued*—New York Times/ *Dole's constant anxiety that it could all come unstuck has set the dynamics of his campaign...*—New Yorker/ *Everybody knew she was bound to come unwrapped*—John Farris

comeuppance or come-uppings *n* *by 1958* A deserved chastening, esp some event that checks a wrongdoer; just desserts

come up roses *v phr* *by 1960s* To turn out well; succeed: *Will Dodgers' crop come up roses?*—Milwaukee Journal

come up short *v phr* *by 1980s* To be deficient; not add up to what it ought: *Shelton slugged 15 aces, but the rest of his game came up short*—Newark Star-Ledger

come up smelling like a rose (or with the five-dollar gold piece) *v phr* *by 1950s* To have extraordinarily good luck; emerge from peril with profit [fr the traditional image of the happy person who "falls in the shitpile and *comes up smelling like a rose*"]

come up to the wire *v phr* *by 1970s* To approach the finish; come near the end: *The crucial project is coming up to the wire and we're a bit nervous* [fr the *wire* that marks the finish line of a race]

come within an ace *v phr* *by 1704* To come very near to doing something, winning something, etc: *She came within an ace of getting the world title* [probably a version of the 13th-century term *within ambs ace*, "very close to," *ambs ace* being the lowest point in dice, two ones or snake-eyes, fr Old French fr Latin *ambas as*, "both ace"]

come with the territory (or turf) *See* GO WITH THE TERRITORY (or TURF)

comfy *adj* *by 1829* Comfortable and comforting; pleasant and easy: *Just reeling off their names is ever so comfy*—W H Auden

comic 1 *n* *by 1619* A comedian, esp one who does a solo act in clubs, etc **2** *n* *about 1910* A comic book or comic strip

See HEAD COMIC, STAND-UP COMIC

the **comics** *See* the FUNNIES

coming from *See* WHERE someone IS COMING FROM

coming out of one's **ass (or ears)** *adj phr* *by 1960s* In surfeit; in overplenteous supply; *I got plenty of problems, problems coming out of my ass/ We had weekly updates: We had statistics coming out of our ears*—New Republic

See STEAM WAS COMING OUT OF someone's EARS

comma-counter *n* *by 1940s* A person who overstresses minor details; a pedantic and picayune perfectionist

commando *n* *students fr WWII Army* A person who behaves roughly and overeagerly, esp in lovemaking [fr the *Commandos*, elite British shock troops of WWII]

See BEDPAN COMMANDO, PICCADILLY COMMANDO

Commerce *See* CHAMBER OF COMMERCE

commercial 1 *n* *by 1930s* Any endorsement or recommendation: *I like the idea, so spare me the commercial* **2** *n* *1920s jazz musicians* Obviously designed for wide audience approval: *How can it be commercial? It's Jelly Roll*

Commie or Commy *by 1930s* **1** *n* A communist **2** *adj*: *Commy plot/ Commie rhetoric*

commish *n* by 1908 A commissioner, esp a police commissioner: *. . . create a high school that would focus on criminal justice studies, a kind of High School for the Commishes of tomorrow*—New York Times

See OUT OF COMMISH

commo[1] *n* prison by 1950s Treats, cigarettes, etc, from the prison commissary

commo[2] *n* Army by 1970s Communications: *Commo okay?* **2** *modifier* fr Army : *. . . went over the commo signals for the fiftieth time*—Richard Merkin/ *Murphy's selling commo systems out of a place out in Rockville*—W T Tyler

commy *n* by early 1900s A cheap glass playing marble: *Commies was our word for those cheap ten-for-a-cent marbles*—James Thurber

comp 1 *n* by 1885 A complimentary ticket; =ANNIE OAKLEY **2** *n* by 1930s A nonpaying guest at a hotel, restaurant, casino, club, etc **3** *n* by 1960s Something given free to a privileged guest or customer: *The first was the comps he got in the casino for dropping his $2,000*—Philadelphia Journal **4** *v*: *The hotel will comp you for just about anything you want*—Elmore Leonard/ *Now, because I'm a high roller, everything is comped. I don't pay for anything*—Philadelphia **5** *n* by 1970s Compensation, esp workman's compensation or unemployment compensation: *I've got three more weeks of comp coming*

the **Company** *n phr* by 1960s The US Central Intelligence Agency

company man *n phr* labor union by 1920 One who is, esp from the point of view of union members, devoted to the interests of the employer

comped *modifier* by 1960s Given free; free of charge; complimentary: *Including the bill for the comped room at the Oaks and Pines. . .* —W E B Griffin

compleat *See* REET

compo *n* by 1940s A cheap dress shoe that is pasted or nailed together rather than sewn [fr *composition*]

compusex *n* by 1990s Sexual talk, innuendo, proposals, titillations, etc, on a computer network: *But more often than not, it's a stop for compusex, that information-age version of phone sex*—Macon Telegraph [fr *computer* plus *sex*]

computer nerd (or Moonie) *n phr* by 1980s A computer enthusiast and expert, esp one who seems out of touch with the rest of the world; =HACKER, PROPELLER HEAD: *Remember the computer nerd who shut down the US Army? . . . the costly supermicros still lack appropriate software and will be used only by "computer Moonies and propeller heads"*—Washington Post

con[1] *n* by 1893 A convict or former convict; prison inmate: *You're a "con," you've no rights*—New Republic

con[2] **1** *v* by 1896 To swindle; work a confidence game: *We conned the old fart out of three big ones* **2** *n* =SCAM: *It's a clever con and you're a greedy rat* **3** *n* by early 1900s A dishonest sort of persuasion; =PUT-ON: *. . . a slick young man with a line of deferential con*—Pete Hamill **4** *v*: *He conned her into thinking he'd marry her*

con artist *See* CON MAN

concern *See* a GOING CONCERN

conchy or **conchie** *n* WWI British A conscientious objector to military service

condo *n* by 1960s A condominium apartment, house, etc

cone *See* GIVE CONE

conehead 1970s **1** *n* An intellectual; *These coneheads are retards*—Village Voice **2** *n* A stupid person

Coney Island whitefish *n phr* by 1930s A discarded condom, esp a floating one; =MANHATTAN EEL

confab (KAHN fab) **1** *n* by 1701 A talk; discussion **2** *v* by 1740: *Let's confab a bit about that idea* [fr *confabulation*]

confetti *See* IRISH CONFETTI

confisticate *v* by 1780 To confiscate

con game (or job) *n phr* by 1880s A confidence game; swindle; =SCAM

conk[1] **1** *n* by 1860s The head •*Conk* designated the nose earlier, by 1812 **2** *v* by 1925 To hit on the nose or head: *I got conked by the bat* **3** *v* by 1950s To defeat utterly; =CLOBBER [probably fr *conch*]

See BUST one's ASS

conk[2] or **gonk** black by 1940s **1** *v* To apply a mixture sometimes containing lye to the head in order to straighten kinky hair **2** *n*: *I couldn't get over marveling at how their hair was straight and shiny like white men's hair; Ella told me this was called "conk"*—Malcolm X [probably fr *Congolene*, trademark of a preparation used to straighten hair, influenced by *conk*[1]]

conk[3] *v* WWI Royal Flying Corps To die; cease to operate; =CONK OUT: *. . . a year after that, a spinster aunt conked*—Lawrence Sanders

conk-buster black by 1940s **1** *n* Cheap and inferior liquor **2** *n* Any difficult problem **3** *n* An intellectual

conked *adj* black by 1940s Of hair, straightened by application of lye or other chemicals: *. . . pegged pants, conked heads, tight skirts*—Village Voice

conk off 1 *v phr* by 1940s To go to sleep; sleep: *You been conking off for eight hours*—Mickey Spillane **2** *v phr* by 1950s To stop work; rest when one should work; =GOOF OFF

conkout *n* An act or instance of conking out: *I did a swift conkout when I got to bed*

conk out 1 *v phr* WWI Royal Flying Corps To stop running or operating: *. . . if this plane conked out*—Village Voice **2** *v phr* by 1920s To lose energy and spirits suddenly; become abruptly exhausted **3** *v phr* by 1940s To go to sleep; =CONK OFF **4** *v phr* by 1920s To die: *So she's conked out, eh?*—Agatha Christie/ *John Le Mesurier wishes it to be known that he conked out on Nov 15. He sadly misses family and friends*—Time [probably echoic]

con man (or artist) 1 *n phr* by 1889 A confidence man **2** *n phr* by early 1900s One adept at persuasion, esp at dishonest or self-serving persuasion

connect 1 *v* by 1930s To hit someone very hard: *He connected with a rude one to the jaw* **2** *v* 1960s narcotics To buy narcotics or other contraband **3** *v* by 1940s To get along with; establish rapport with; =CLICK: *She's never been able to connect with her tenant*

connection *n* narcotics by 1925s A seller of narcotics; a person who can get drugs; =PUSHER
See KILO CONNECTION

connect the dots by 1980s **1** *v phr* To draw a conclusion from disparate facts: *. . . he calls this connecting the dots because it links bits of information to form a big picture*—New York Times **2** *modifier* From one fixed point to another: *. . . rarely venture out of their own connect-the-dots puzzle: from home to work, on to local haunts, and home again*—New Yorker **3** *v phr* To do something very simple: *He couldn't even figure out how to connect the dots* [fr a child's puzzle, where a picture emerges when one *connects* a number of dispersed *dots* on the paper]

conniption fit or **conniption** *n phr* first form by 1833, second by 1848 A violent tantrum; hysterics; =CATFIT, DUCK FIT: *Please don't throw a conniption fit over the news* [origin unknown; the later term *catnip fit* is a stab at folk etymology]

cons *See* MOD CONS

constant *See* FINAGLE FACTOR

constitutional *n* by 1829 A healthful walk or other exercise

constructed *adj* by 1950s Having an attractive body; generously built; =STACKED

contact high *n phr* 1950s narcotics A seeming intoxication induced by being with persons who are intoxicated with narcotics: *that sympathetic vibration known as the "contact high"*—Tom Wolfe

contract 1 *n* by 1930s An arrangement to have someone murdered by a professional killer: *The word is there's a contract out for Taffy Taylor* **2** *n* police by 1950s Any illegal or unethical arrangement: *. . . contract, any favor one policeman says he'll do for another*—G Y Wells
See SWEETHEART CONTRACT, YELLOW DOG CONTRACT

contraption *n* by 1820s A contrivance or device; piece of machinery: *What's this ugly contraption in the corner?*

conversation piece *n phr* by 1784 Something unusual or bizarre, esp in the decoration of a room, which can at least be justified as a topic of discussion

conversation pit *n phr* by 1960s A sunken area in the floor of a living room where people may gather to chat

convict *n* circus by 1940s A zebra

cooch 1 *n* by 1920s Any sexually suggestive or imitative dance, esp a strip-tease dance; =HOOTCHIE-COOTCHIE **2** *modifier*: *an old-time circus cooch show* ◁3▷ **3** *n* by 1950s The female crotch; vulva

coo-coo *See* CUCKOO

cook 1 *v* by 1930s To be put to death in the electric chair; =FRY **2** *v* 1940s jive talk To happen; occur: *Is anything cooking on the new tax rule?* **3** *v* jazz

musicians about 1930 To do very well; excel: *. . . if the performers begin cooking together and most of the director's intuitions and skills pay off*—Washington Post **4** *v* by 1636 To falsify; tamper with: *The British government cooked press stories shamelessly in order to deceive the Argentine enemy*—Newsweek/ *She cooked the statistics*—New York Times **5** *v* 1960s narcotics To dissolve heroin in water over a flame before injecting it
See BULL COOK

cookbook 1 *n* students by 1950s A chemistry laboratory manual **2** *n* by 1970s Any guide, manual, protocol, etc: *We use a cookbook of procedures*—National Public Radio news **3** *modifier* by 1970s Routine; mechanical; unimaginative: *All he did was adopt the cookbook solution*

cooked 1 *adj* by 1850 Ruined; hopelessly beaten; =FINISHED: *After the fourth fumble they were cooked* **2** *adj* by 1860 Altered; falsified; =DOCTORED: *. . . his miracle rise turned out to be based more on cooked books than shampooed rugs*—Los Angeles Times

cooked-up *adj* by 1940s Specially contrived; expedient and dishonest: *It's insane why we give ourselves cooked up reasons for not moving the issue*—Westworld

cooker *See* FIRELESS COOKER, PRESSURE COOKER

cook someone's **goose** *v phr* by 1845 To ruin or destroy someone; =FINISH ●Very often in the passive form, "our goose is cooked": *I know I've basically cooked my own goose here*—Parade [origin uncertain; one legend has it that a Swedish King Erik was mocked, as he approached a town, by a goose hanging over the wall, the goose being a symbol of folly and stupidity. The king thereupon burnt the town and cooked the goose!]

cookie or **cookey 1** *n* (also **cookee**) by 1840s A cook or cook's helper **2** *n* narcotics by 1950s A person who prepares opium for smoking; opium addict **3** *n* by 1920 An attractive young woman **4** *n* by 1930 A person; =GAL, GUY ●Most often modified by *smart* or *tough*: *"What do you really want?" Smart cookie*—Stan Cutler ◁5▷ *n* (also **cookies**) black by 1950s The female genitals; vulva **6** *n* baseball by 1970s A base hit: *knowing I was going to get at least one cookie every game*—Sports Illustrated
See GRIPE one's ASS, THAT'S THE WAY THE BALL BOUNCES, TOUGH COOKIE

cookie-cutter or **cooky-cutter 1** *n* circus by 1920s A police officer's badge; =POTSY, TIN **2** *n* by 1950s A weak and unenterprising person; =COOKIE-PUSHER, WIMP **3** *n* by 1950s An inadequate weapon, esp a knife **4** *modifier* (also **cookie-cut**) Identical and unoriginal; standardized; stereotyped: *Each store is a cookie-cutter copy, laid out according to plans devised at the corporate headquarters*—New York Times/ *I'd never want to read that kind of cookie-cut magazine*—Philadelphia

cookie jar *See* WITH one's HAND IN THE TILL

cookie monster *n phr* by 1970s Someone who is voracious and destructive: *The policy got eaten up* by a Cookie Monster named Richard Darman, director of OMB—New York Times [fr a televison hand-puppet character so named who noisily devours huge amounts of cookies]

cookie-pusher or **cooky-pusher** by early 1940s **1** *n* A weak and unenterprising person; =WIMP **2** *n* A person who pampers and flatters superiors; =APPLE-POLISHER, BROWN-NOSE **3** *n* A government career person, esp in the Department of State

cookies *See* COOKIE, SHOOT one's COOKIES

cookout *n* by 1947 An outdoor meal at which food is cooked, usu grilled on charcoal

cooks *See* WHAT'S COOKING

cook the books *v phr* by 1940s To tamper with and falsify records, esp financial accounts: *The managers had cooked the books to the tune of $34 million*—Newsweek/ *He's been cooking the books for so many of those companies*—W T Tyler

cook up *v phr* by 1750 To devise; fabricate; =HOKE UP: *We'll cook up a story to explain your swollen lip*

cook up a pill *v phr* 1960s narcotics To prepare opium for smoking

cook with gas (or **on the front burner**) *v phr college students fr 1930s jive talk* To perform very commendably; =GROOVE

cool 1 *v* by 1950s To postpone; await developments in: *Let's cool this whole business for a week or so* **2** *v* about 1920 To kill: *... who knew what he wanted to make it look like when he cooled her*—Scott Turow **3** *adj* by early 700s In control of one's feelings; stoic: *Learn to be cool under fire* **4** *n* by 1960s: *He lost his cool and bolted like a rabbit* **5** *adj* by 1940s Aloof and uninvolved; disengaged, as an expression of alienation; =BEAT, HIP: *He's cool, don't give a shit for nothing* **6** *n*: *My guru drifted me to a total spiritual cool* **7** *n* 1940s cool musicians Jazz marked by soft tones, improvisation based on advanced chord extensions, and revision of certain classical jazz idioms **8** *adj*: *cool jazz/ a real cool passage* **9** *adj* by 1940s Excellent; good: *a cool shirt/ cool sermon* **10** *adj* by 1950s Pleasant; desirable; =COPACETIC: *You enjoying it? Is everything cool?*—Douglass Wallop
    See BLOW one's COOL, LOSE one's COOL, PLAY IT COOL, ZERO COOL

cool as a cucumber *adj phr* by 1730s Very calm, and often haughty or callous

cool (or **calm**) **as a Christian with aces wired** *adj phr* by 1970s Serenely assured; tranquilly confident: *"We will take care of that," he says, cool as a Christian with aces wired*—Edward Abbey

cool beans *modifier* 1980s *students* Excellent; wonderful; =COOL, FRESH, RAD: *Cool Beans "superlative, a highly desirable situation"*—North Jersey Herald and News

cooled-out *adj* by 1970s Relaxed; passionless: *... a cooled-out sign linked to the mass media*—Time

the **cooler** by 1880s **1** *n* A jail; =the SLAMMER **2** *n prison* A cell or cellblock for solitary confinement
    See COFFEE COOLER

cool guy *n phr* 1990s *teenagers* A conventional, tedious, or pretentious person who thinks he is up-to-date, aware, interesting, etc

cool hand early 1600s **1** *n phr* A person not easily disconcerted •Sir Thomas Overbury, who died in 1613, wrote that a *cool hand* is "one who accounts bashfulness the wickedest thing in the world, and therefore studies impudence" **2** *modifier*: *... these four cool-hand lunatics*—Newsweek

cool one's **heels** *v phr* by 1608 To wait, esp to be kept waiting: *I cooled my heels for two hours before the great one would see me*

cool it 1950s *beat & cool talk* **1** *v phr* To relax; stop being excited or angry **2** *v phr* To slow one's pace; stop being strenuous **3** *v phr* To stop what one is doing, esp what is annoying the speaker •In all three senses often an exhortation or irritated command

cool million *n phr* by 1890s A whole big million dollars [*Cool* as applied to a large sum of money is attested by 1728; with currency inflation the use has progressed from hundred to thousand to million to (very likely) billion, on the way to *cool trillion*]

cool off 1 *v phr* by 1860s To become calmer and less explosive; moderate: *When he cooled off I spoke sweet reason* **2** *v phr* To kill; =COOL: *Somebody cools off Mr Justin Veezee*—Damon Runyon

cool out 1 *v phr horse-racing* about 1910 To walk a horse after a race to calm and moderate it gradually **2** *v phr beat & black* by 1970s To do the sex act **3** *v phr* by 1980s To relax; become calm; =COOL IT: *He was cooling out now, not sprinting, just sitting straight up on the seat, riding without hands at a lazy relaxed rhythm*—Harry Crews

cool-out *n* by 1940s A device or strategy intended to relax someone, esp to calm justified apprehensions: *... cooperating in an Uncle Tom cool-out this late in the game*—Eldridge Cleaver/ *... begins what he calls the "cool out." This prepares the man to accept defeat philosophically*—Wall Street Journal

cool someone **out 1** *v phr* by 1940s To mollify and appease someone; calm someone's apprehensions or anger: *White Americans found a new level in which to cool the blacks out*—Eldridge Cleaver/ *He is the one who has to cool people out and pay off State officials*—New York Magazine **2** *v phr* early 1900s To relax; calm someone **3** *v phr* by 1830s To kill someone; =COOL, OFF •The date is based on an 1833 text by Davy Crockett; the use has been extremely rare in the interim and is rare now

coolster *n* 1990s *teenagers* A stylish and admirable person; =DUDE, STUD: *... if you see said coolsters in the cafeteria, ask if it's OK to sit with them*—Sassy

coolville or **Coolville** *modifier* (also **coolsville** or **Coolsville**) by 1950s Excellent; splendid: *Your little scheme's coolville*

◄**coon►** **1** *n* by 1862 A black person **2** *n* (also **coon's ass**) *carnival* by 1990 A carnival worker who is too aggressive and mistreats the customers
    See ACE BOON COON

◀**coon-ass**▶ *n by 1950s* A person of Acadian heritage; =CAJUN [origin uncertain; perhaps fr French *connasse*, "silly bitch"; perhaps based on *coon*, "black person"]

◀**coon box** ▶ *See* GHETTO BOX

a **coon's age** *n phr by 1843* A very long time: *I haven't seen her in a coon's age*

◀**coon-shouter**▶ *n by 1906* A singer of songs in a presumed loud black style

◀**coon-shouting**▶ *adj early 1900s* A loud singing style thought to be typical of Southern blacks: *Dorsey thought of Mahalia Jackson as one of those coon-shoutin' singers*—New York Review of Books

◀**coon song**▶ *n phr by 1887* A song thought to be typical of Southern blacks, and of the sort sung in minstrel shows

coop¹ **1** *n by 1785* A jail or prison **2** *n police by 1960s* A place, esp a patrol car, where police officers sleep while on duty: *. . . all the. . . cops will be in the coop*—Lawrence Sanders **3** *v*: *There were the cats, the milkmen, and the cops cooping in a police car at the corner*—Earl Thompson [police senses based on earlier *coop*, "any shelter used by the police to avoid the elements"; fr *chicken coop*]
See CHICKEN COOP, FLY THE COOP, HENCOOP, IN THE COOP, RAIN CATS AND DOGS

coop² *n by 1930* A coupe car: *It's a Plymouth convertible coop*—John O'Hara

co-op or **coop** (KOH ahp) **1** *n by 1870s* A cooperative apartment house, store, etc **2** *modifier*: *co-op prices/ coop apartment complex* **3** *v by 1950s* To convert an apartment or building from a rental to a cooperative unit: *The old Sussex Arms got co-oped last year*

coop-happy *adj prison by 1950s* =STIR-CRAZY

coot *n by 1760s* A stupid or silly person, usu an aged one: *a harmless old coot*
See CRAZY AS A LOON

cootchie *See* HOOTCHIE-COOTCHIE

cootie or **cooty** *n WWI Army fr British* A body louse [origin uncertain; perhaps fr Malay *kutu*, "dog tick"; one study suggests London cockney slang as the source]

◁**cooz**▷ (Variations: **cooze** or **cou** or **couz** or **couzie** or **couzy** or **cuzzy**) *by 1920s* **1** *n* A woman: *. . . killed two quarts of tequila last night in Olvera Street, this Mexican cooz and I*—S J Perelman/ *He runs. He screams like a cooze*—Robert Stone **2** *n* The female genitals; vulva **3** *n* A person, esp a woman, viewed solely as a sex object: *. . . a piece of beautiful, dumb eighteen-year-old cooze*—Jackie Collins

cop **1** *n by 1850s* A police officer **2** *v by 1850s* To arrest **3** *v about 1900* To steal: *He copped six PCs from the shop* **4** *v by 1914* To win; be awarded: *to cop second place* **5** *v by 1940s* To comprehend; grasp: *I don't quite cop your sense, pal* **6** *v 1960s narcotics* To buy or get narcotics: *The pusher has appeared,. . . they will make their round-about way to him to "cop"*—J Mills [origin uncertain; perhaps

ultimately fr Latin *capere* "seize," by way of French; police officer sense a shortening of *copper*; second sense "seize, catch" attested by 1704]
See GOOD COP BAD COP

copacetic (KOH pə SET ik) *adj* (Variations: **copesetic** or **kopasetic** or **kopesetic** or **kopasetee** or **kopesetee**) *by 1919 fr black* As it should be; quite satisfactory; =COOL, OK [origin unknown; perhaps fr Louisiana Creole French *coupe-sétique* in the same sense, semantically related to *cope*, attested fr about 1880; perhaps fr Hebrew *kol ba seder*, "all in order," which may have been acquired by black customers of a Jewish merchant]

◁**cop a (or someone's) cherry**▷ *v phr by 1930s* To deprive someone of virginity; deflower someone

cop a feel *v phr by 1930s* To feel or caress someone's body, esp the sex organs, usu in a sly or seemingly inadvertent way: *I thought he wanted to help me into the car, but I think he just wanted to cop a feel*

cop an attitude *See* HAVE AN ATTITUDE

cop a plea *v phr 1920s police & underworld* To plead guilty to a lesser charge than one might otherwise be tried for; escape a worse punishment by accepting a lesser one

cop a tude *See* HAVE AN ATTITUDE

copeck *n about 1900* Money, esp a silver dollar [fr the name of a Russian coin]

cop-heat *n by 1970s* Police activity: *When there's cop-heat here, the prostitutes go there*—Los Angeles Times [*Heat* in this sense is attested from 1931]

copilot *n 1960s truckers* An amphetamine taken in order to stay awake

cop (or buy) it *v phr WWI British forces* To die, esp to be killed in battle or otherwise; =BUY THE FARM: *He had a feeling he wouldn't cop it that day/ The guy who buys it. . . does it off camera*—Washington Post

cop-killer *n by 1980s* A bullet capable of penetrating bullet-proof vests: *. . . the apple-green bullets they call cop-killers*—Chicago Tribune

cop out **1** *v phr underworld by 1940s* To be arrested **2** *v phr by 1940s* To confess; plead guilty; =COP A PLEA: *I copped out*—John Lardner **3** *v phr 1960s counterculture* To avoid trouble and responsibility; evade an issue or problem; disengage oneself: *When his friends really needed help he copped out*

cop-out *n 1960s counterculture* An evasion; an excuse for inaction: *. . . arguing about standards is a "cop-out"*—P Sourain

copper¹ **1** *n by 1846* A police officer **2** *n underworld by 1897* An informer; =STOOL PIGEON **3** *n underworld by 1908* Time taken off a prison sentence for good behavior or because one has informed on colleagues

copper² *v gambling by 1864* To bet against a card, roll of the dice, person, etc [fr the use of a special metal chip, often a *copper* cent, by a gambler to indicate a bet with the bank in faro]

copper-bottomed *adj* by 1890 Genuine; authentic: *a copper-bottomed scoundrel* [fr the covering of a ship's *bottom* with *copper* plates to frustrate the shipworm]

copper-hearted *adj* underworld by 1920s Likely to be an informer; untrustworthy

copper-on copper-off *n phr* gambling by 1940s A system where one alternatively bets for and against, or bets and doesn't bet, etc

cop shop *n phr* fr 1940s Australian A police station

cop to something *v phr* by 1990s To confess to; plead guilty to: *He cops to bimbo massages, but insists he didn't go "coital"*—Gary Trudeau/ *This gave students an opportunity to cop to secretly held feelings. . .*—Los Angeles Times [a shortening of *cop out*]

copy 1 *v* 1980s To send a copy of a message to someone other than the immediate addressee: *Copy Tina and tell her the mag is fast turning to compost*—New Yorker **2** *n* by 1880s A subject for an article in a newspaper, magazine, etc: *She knew that Miss Gould was good "copy"*—Literary Digest

copycat 1 *n* by 1890s An imitator; mimic •The 1890s source indicates that the word was at least forty or fifty years older **2** *modifier*: *a copycat inventor/ copycat crime* **3** *v* by 1930s: *. . . Sally traps her there, and copycats the first murder, gore and all. . .*—Stan Cutler **4** *n* by 1960s A copycat crime or criminal: *Could be a copycat. . . Guy wants to do his wife in, covers it up by making it look like Red Rose. . .*—Robert B Parker/ *I knew enough. . . to bet the farm that this was no coincidence or copycat*—Stan Cutler

copycat crime *n phr* A crime committed in imitation of another crime, esp one which is sensational and highly publicized: *Copy-Cat Crimes of the Heart*—Time

copy the mail *v phr* 1970s citizens band To listen to radio traffic; monitor

cop Zs (or **some Zs**) *v phr* (Variations: **bag** or **catch** or **cut** or **get** or **pile up** or **stack** may replace **cop**) black by 1950s To take a nap; sleep; =SNOOZE: *. . . got to peck a little, and cop me some Z's*—Malcolm X/ *. . . sits around all day cutting Zs*—Motorcross Action Magazine

core *See* HARD-CORE, SOFT-CORE

core dump 1980s computers **1** *v phr* To empty out the central memory of a computer **2** *v phr* To explain oneself fully; say one's piece, esp in the mode of complaint: *One of the semiconductor makers here went to see her manager the other day. Later she told a friend that she had "core dumped" on the boss*—New York Times

Corine *n* narcotics by 1970s Cocaine

cork *See* BLOW one's TOP, POP one's CORK

corked *adj* by 1896 Drunk

corker *n* by 1882 A person or thing that is remarkable, wonderful, superior, etc; =HUMDINGER, PISS-CUTTER: *What a corker, this guy*—Stan Cutler [fr earlier sense "something that definitively settles a matter," perhaps fr *caulk*]

corking by 1891 **1** *adv* Extremely; very: *to have a corking good time* **2** *adj* Excellent; wonderful: *a corking party*

corking mat *n phr* WWII Navy A sleeping pad or a mattress

cork off *See* CAULK OFF

cork out *v phr* early 1990s To behave very strangely; =FREAK OUT: *"Hey, he/she's corking out." (acting really weird)*—Wisconsin State Journal

corksacking *adj* Disgusting; depraved; =COCKSUCKING •Euphemistic form of *cocksucking*; others, probably attested only in dirty jokes, are *cokesacking* and *socktucking*: *. . . you effing corksacking limey effer*—Anthony Burgess

corn 1 *n* by 1820 Corn whiskey; moonshine **2** *n* jazz musicians about 1930 Music, poetry, sentiment, etc, that is maudlin and naively affirmative of old-fashioned values; banal and emotionally overwrought material; =SCHMALTZ [second sense probably from the notion of *cornfed* as indicating rural simplicity and naivete]

cornball by 1940s **1** *n* A person who admires or produces markedly sentimental material and utters relatively simpleminded moral convictions: *Eisenhower on no account can be called a cornball*—Robert Ruark **2** *adj*: *Where did you get those cornball notions?*

corn bill *See* CORN WILLIE

corndog *n* 1980s students An eccentric and socially inept person; =DWEEB, GEEK

corned *adj* by 1785 Drunk
See HALF-CORNED

corner *See* COFFIN CORNER, HOT CORNER

corn-fed 1 *adj* by 1787 Plump and sturdy; rural or as if rural: *a corn-fed beauty* **2** *adj* by 1920s Naive and sentimental; =CORNY

◄**cornhole** ► *v* by 1930s To do anal intercourse; =BUGGER, BUNGHOLE: *. . . so the Germans would get castrated when they cornholed him*—Trevanian/ *Bartley had corn-holed the Irish maid in full view of wife and child*—Gore Vidal

corn juice (or **mule**) *n phr* by 1840s Corn whiskey; moonshine

corn willie (or **bill**) *n phr* WWI Army Corned beef: *You must try the corn willie, Rusty*—Scott Turow [origin unknown]

corny *adj* jazz musicians about 1930 Overly sentimental; banal; devoted to or expressing old-fashioned moral convictions; =CORNBALL [the writer Mari Sandoz (1896–1966) suggested as possible origin the corn-seed catalogs sent to Midwestern farmers before and after 1900, which were larded with tired old jokes; the jokes were called *corn jokes* and *corny*]

corporal *See* HOLLYWOOD CORPORAL

corporal's guard *n phr* by 1815 A very small group: *a corporal's guard of adherents*

corpse *v* theater by 1860s To embarrass a fellow performer by forgetting one's lines and failing to deliver a cue

corral (kə RAL) *v* by 1850s To find; gather: *to corral votes* [fr Spanish]

corset *n* 1920s *police & underworld* A bulletproof vest; =FLAK JACKET

cosh 1860s *British* **1** *n* A bludgeon; blackjack **2** *n*: . . . *as these samurai cosh, ignite, bludgeon and blow away a host of contemptible nincompoops*—Washington Post

cost the earth *v phr* by 1924 To be very expensive: *The large bed at stage center is made up with sheets and blankets that cost the earth*—New York Times

cotics *n* *narcotics* Narcotics

cottage cheese thighs *n phr* by 1990s Fat thighs; =THUNDER THIGHS: . . . *in Los Angeles, cottage cheese thighs are nothing to snicker about*—Los Angeles Times

cottage industry by 1920s **1** *n phr* Productive work done at home using computers or computer terminals **2** *n phr* A local, esp a rural, concern or enthusiasm: . . . *great supporter of the contras, an occupation that appears to have been an Arkansas cottage industry*—New Republic [based on the name given to the system of having piecework done at home, rather than in factories, at the beginning of the Industrial Revolution]

cotton *See* SHIT IN HIGH COTTON

cotton mouth *n phr* by 1970 Dryness of the mouth caused by a hangover, use of marijuana or drugs, fear, etc

cotton-picking or **cotton-pickin'** *adj* by 1950s Despicable; wretched; =DAMNED: *They're out of their cotton-picking minds*—Washington Post/ *I don't think it's anybody's cotton-pickin' business what you're doing. . .* —New York Post [fr the inferior status of the field hand or poor farmer in southern US society]

cotton to *v phr* by 1605 Approve of; like; appreciate; fancy: *"That's a thing I didn't cotton to anyhow," said Miss Fuschia Leach, who had found her talent did not lie that way*—Ouida [perhaps fr Welsh *cytuno,* "agree, consent"]

◁**cou**▷ *See* COOZ

couch *See* CASTING COUCH

couch case *n phr* by 1960s An emotionally disturbed person [fr the psychoanalyst's stereotypical use of the *couch* for a reclining patient]

couch commander *n phr* 1990s *teenagers* A television remote control

couch doctor *n phr* by 1950s A psychoanalyst; =SHRINK

couch potato or **sofa spud** *n phr* entry form by 1970s, variant by 1990s A habitual lounger, esp a person who spends much time watching television: *They're not couch potatoes. They're mobile, they go out*—Washington Post/ . . . *the period that Anglophile couch potatoes find most fascinating*—Book World

cough syrup *n phr* *underworld* about 1925 Bribe or blackmail money paid to silence someone

cough up 1 *v phr* by 1894 To pay or give something, esp with some reluctance: *Coughing it up: Dunleavy was not happy that the Bucks committed 26 turnovers*—Milwaukee Journal **2** *v phr* by about 1393 To tell or relate, esp under interrogation ●Modern use, which may not truly represent a continuity with the medieval occurrence, begins in the 1890s

coulda-been *modifier* by 1990s Suggesting, often lamenting, what might have been: . . . *other coulda-been sad-sack tales*—LA Village View

could be *sentence* by 1930s It is possible ●Often a reply to a speculative question: *Is he still alive? Could be/ Could be they don't like us out there See* EASY AS PIE

could not (or could) care less *v phr* One simply does not care; one is sublimely indifferent ●In a curious development, the original British negative form has been changed to affirmative by many US speakers, without change of meaning; such contradiction is more common in slang than in standard speech: *I couldn't care less if you like me or not/ I could care less if you like me or not*

count *See* DOWN FOR THE COUNT, NO-COUNT

be counted *See* STAND UP AND BE COUNTED

counter *See* COMMA-COUNTER

not count for spit *See* NOT COUNT FOR SPIT

country *adj* Quite competent; reliable: *He's a pretty good country ball player; gets his pitches over the plate* ●The phrase is meant as moderate yet distinct praise of a person who might not be as spectacular as a big city or downtown performer

See ANOTHER COUNTRY HEARD FROM, GO OUT IN THE COUNTRY

country club *modifier* by 1890s Characteristic of the wealthy: *Tax cheating is a country-club crime, like insider trading*—New Republic [The date is based on the earliest potential use, that is, on the first occurrence of such primarily golfing clubs of generally exclusive membership]

country cousin *n phr* by 1770 A distant though related person or thing: *This was country cousin to a myth that floated around St. Louis earlier, about a major utility that ordered six thousand body bags with its name imprinted on them*—New Yorker [The date refers to the sense "an unsophisticated rustic relative"]

country-fried *adj* by 1990s Rural; unsophisticated; countrified; =SHIT-KICKING: *Atwater, a Southerner, a country-fried Sammy Glick who learns the error of his ways*—New York Times

a country mile by 1940s **1** *n phr* A very long distance: *She made it home first by a country mile* **2** *modifier*: *Dennis Conner's country-mile victory in the first America's Cup race. . .* —Associated Press *See* BEAT someone or something BY A COUNTRY MILE

county mounty *n phr* *citizens band* A police officer. esp one patrolling the highway; a sheriff, deputy sheriff, state police officer, etc [second element fr *Mounty* or *Mountie,* "member of the Royal Canadian Mounted Police"]

coupe *See* DEUCE

a **couple** something **short of** *modifier* by 1980s Stupid; mentally deficient •A very flexible and productive formula for gently expressing an adverse judgment: *The manager is a couple cans short of a six-pack/ He's a couple bricks short of a load/ She's a couple sandwiches short of a picnic/ They were all a couple dogies short of a corral*

courage *See* DUTCH COURAGE

course *See* BIRD COURSE, CRIB COURSE, GUT COURSE, PAR FOR THE COURSE, PIPE COURSE, SNAP COURSE

court *See* the BALL IS IN someone's COURT, FULL COURT PRESS, HOME-COURT ADVANTAGE, KANGAROO COURT

court-in *n* street gang by 1990s A rigorous initiation ceremony into a girls' gang: *At her court-in, a girl is christened with the nickname by which she will be known*—Milwaukee Journal

court-out *n* street gang by 1990s Severe physical punishment for a gang member deemed disloyal: *. . . she can face a "court-out," in which there is no time limit to the beating*—Milwaukee Journal

cousin **1** *n* by 1430 Friend; person •An amiable form of address: *How you doin', cousin?* **2** *n* underworld by 1552 A dupe; =MARK, PIGEON *See* KISSING COUSIN, WHAT'S BUZZIN', COUSIN

◁**couz** or **couzie** or **couzy**▷ *See* COOZ

cove *n* British by 1560s A man; fellow; =GUY •Very rare in US usage [origin uncertain; perhaps fr Romany *kova*, "thing"; perhaps fr Scots *cofe*, "peddler, chapman"]

cover **1** *v* newspaper by 1893 To report on regularly; monitor the news at: *Who's covering the White House now?* **2** *v* (also **cover up**) by 1940s To protect someone with one's testimony: *I'll cover for you if you're caught* **3** *v* by 1960s To substitute for someone; replace someone temporarily and protectively: *Bini was the designated cover for Placido Domingo in La Gioconda*—Time **4** *v* by 1970 To attend to, esp temporarily: *Will you cover the switchboard while I'm at the dentist?* **5** *v* by 1818 To travel: *I covered two miles in one minute* **6** *v* by 1793 To include; account for: *That about covers what happened* **7** *v* by 1687 To aim at with a firearm: *Freeze, I got you covered* **8** *n* by 1970s A popular song recorded by artists other than those who made it famous: *. . . third album, like the first two, contains many covers of recent chart-busters*—Rolling Stone **9** *v*: *They did best covering Springsteen and Stones hits* **10** *n* espionage by 1940s An identity, usu an elaborate falsification, assumed by a secret agent for concealment: *To improve his cover he "resigned" from the agency*—C McCrystal

cover all bases *v phr* baseball by 1940s To guard against or supervise all contingencies: *The baking is done on the premises, and Ms Scherber covers all the bases*—New Yorker

◁**cover** one's **ass**▷ (or **tail**) (also **CYA**) **1** *v phr* To provide or arrange for exculpation; devise excuses and alibis: *Some call it "risk management," others "covering your ass"*—Toronto Life/ *The FBI may have to let you be destroyed to cover its own ass*—Nat Hentoff/ *CYA, you know, that old French expression that means making sure that when historians write about it all it won't be seen as happening on your shift*—Washington Post **2** *modifier*: *. . . writing long cover-your-ass memos*—Village Voice

covered wagon *n phr* WWII Navy An aircraft carrier

cover girl by 1915 **1** *n phr* A model or celebrity whose likeness appears on the cover of a magazine; a beautiful and glamorous young woman **2** *modifier*: *. . . it doesn't seem fair that their cover-girl looks. . . should obscure the vast athletic skills displayed between the lines*—Buzz

cover story **1** *n phr* espionage by 1940s The biography and plausible account devised for a secret agent for concealment; =COVER **2** *n phr* by 1940s An alibi; a false narrative explanation: *We agree on the cover story, that you haven't seen me for three weeks*

cover the waterfront *v phr* by 1930s To be a complete account of something; be the whole story: *Lake covers premarital agreements, no-fault divorce. . . even a. . . will. That covers the waterfront*—Playboy [fr the title of a 1932 book by Max Miller, a journalist, exposing crime and corruption on the *waterfront*]

cover-up *n* by 1935 Anything designed to conceal or obfuscate the truth by replacement: *Sending the Navy south instead of north was an obvious cover-up*

cow **1** *n* by 1900 Milk ◁**2**▷ *n* by 1696 A woman: *The silly cow believed everything she heard* ◁**3**▷ *n* 1930s underworld A young woman *See* ARMORED COW, BLACK COW, CANNED COW, CASH COW, CITY COW, HOLY CATS, SEA COW

cowabunga **1** *interj* 1950s surfers A surfer's exclamation of delight and commitment at the beginning of a ride, often used as a generalized cry of delight: *It was the real Andy Griffith, too: cowabunga*—Village Voice **2** *n* by 1980s Energetic popular plaudits: *. . . make their most open bid yet for commercial cowabunga*—Village Voice [apparently coined by Eddie Kean, writer of the television *Howdy Doody Show* as a distress call for one of the characters]

cowboy **1** *n* by 1920s A reckless driver or pilot: *City Subway Mishaps Attributed To Speeding "Cowboy" Motormen*—New York Times/ *. . . a pilot with a history of recklessness and a reputation as a "cowboy"*—Milwaukee Journal **2** *n* gambling by 1940s The king of a suit of playing cards **3** *n* underworld by 1920s A violent gun-brandishing criminal: *Apparently the same cowboy. . . a young punk with a Fu Manchu mustache, waving a nickel-plated pistol*—Lawrence Sanders **4** *v* underworld by 1920s To murder recklessly and openly: *. . . even if we had to cowboy them (which) means that we were to kill them any place we found them even if it was in the middle of Broadway*—C A Wyer *See* DRUGSTORE COWBOY

cowboy (or Navajo) Cadillac *n phr by 1970s*
A pickup truck; =WAUSAU WAGON

cowboy coffee *n phr by 1940s* Black coffee:
*. . . air, self-esteem, cigarette butts, cowboy
coffee*—Joseph Mitchell

cowboy job *n phr underworld by 1920s* A robbery
done recklessly, clumsily, and violently

cow chip *n phr by about 1840* =COWPAT, MEADOW
MUFFIN: *Blue chips into cow chips. . . Investor loses
money*—Milwaukee Journal Sentinel

cow college (or tech) *n phr college students by
about 1900* A college rurally located and of humble
distinction, esp an agricultural college: *Every instructor in every cow college is trying to get to be an
assistant professor*—Philadelphia

cowflop or **cowflap** or **cowplop** *by about
1900* **1** *n* Cattle dung: *He is dumb as cowflop and
hopeless at foot shufflin' and finger snappin', but
he tries hard*—John Skow **2** *n* Nonsense; pretentious talk; =BULLSHIT: *I don't believe that cowflap*—
Paul Theroux/ *Urban Cowplop*—Rolling Stone

cow out *v phr 1990s students* To lose control

cowpat or **cow pie** *n* or *n phr by 1940s* A disk
of cattle dung; =MEADOW MUFFIN: *. . . the meadow
muffin, better known as the cow pie. . .* —Daily
Jefferson County Union

cowpats *interj by 1990s* An exclamation of scorn,
disbelief, vexation, etc; =BULLSHIT: *Cowpats!. . . He's
just trying to make my life miserable. . .* —
Lawrence Sanders

◁**cow pilot**▷ *n phr airline by 1940s* An airline stew-
ardess; woman cabin attendant

cowpuncher or **cowpoke** *n first form by
1870s, second by 1880s* A cowboy [fr the use of
metal-tipped prods to drive cattle into railroad cars]

cow-simple *adj 1930s underworld* In love with a
woman or with women in general

coyote *n by 1920s* A person who smuggles illegal
immigrants across the Mexican-US border: *. . . the
"coyotes," the smugglers who bribe or otherwise
contrive to get their charges past border authorities. . .* —US News & World Report

coyote ugly *adj phr 1980s students* Extremely
ugly or nasty; =PISS-UGLY: *I had a coyote ugly date*—
UCLA Slang

cozy up *v phr by 1930s* To become very friendly;
court: *I find myself, too, on about the fifth
trip. . . to the hardware store, cozying up to the
proprietor*—New Yorker

crab **1** *v by 1812* To complain, esp to do so regularly; nag; =BITCH: *Crab, crab, crab, that was all she
ever did*—Dorothy Parker/ *So us crabbing about
our zero-life factors isn't up for debate, really*—
Douglas Coupland **2** *n*: *He's an awful crab, never
gives her a moment's peace* **3** *n by 1920s* A resident of Annapolis, Maryland **4** *v by 1890s* To spoil;
ruin: *He's trying to crab the deal*

crabs *n by 1840* An infestation of crab lice in the
pubic area: *Her friends slobbered, ripped off girls'
dresses at parties, had crabs*—Philip Wylie

crack **1** *v by 1830s* To open a safe or vault by force
2 *n by 1836* A try; attempt; =SHOT: *It looks impossible, but I'll take a crack at it* **3** *v by 1950s* To go
uninvited to a party; =CRASH **4** *v by 1950s* To gain
admittance to some desired category or milieu: *He
finally cracked the best-seller list* **5** *v by 1930s* To
solve; reveal the secret of: *They never cracked the
case*—Raymond Chandler **6** *v* (also **crack up**) *by
1880s* To suffer an emotional or mental collapse; go
into hysteria, depression, etc: *After six months of
that it's a wonder she didn't crack* **7** *v about 1850*
To break down and give information, or to confess,
after intense interrogation: *Buggsy cracked and
spilled everything* **8** *v by 1315* To speak; talk;
make remarks: *Listen, Ben, quit cracking dumb*—
James M Cain **9** *n by 1725* A brief, funny, pungent,
and often malicious remark; =WISECRACK: *One more
crack like that and I'm going to sock you*—K Brush
◀**10**▶ *n unknown date, but very old* The vulva;
=CUNT ◁**11**▷ *n unknown date, but very old* The
deep crease between the buttocks **12** *n* (also **crack
cocaine**) *narcotics by 1985* Cocaine freebase, a very
pure crystalline cocaine intended for smoking rather
than inhalation; =COKE: *Crack's low price and quick
payoff make it especially alluring to teenagers*—
Time [all senses are ultimately echoic; narcotics sense
fr the sound of breaking crystals or the cracking
sound the crystals make when smoked]
See FALL BETWEEN THE CRACKS, GIVE something A
SHOT, HAVE A CRACK AT something, WISECRACK

crack a book (or the books) *v phr 1920s students* To study •Nearly always in the negative: *He
tried to pass the course without cracking a book/
The exam's coming up and I better crack some
books*

crack a deal **See** CUT A DEAL

◁**crack a fart**▷ *v phr 1980s students* To flatulate;
express gas anally; =LAY A FART: *What's that smell?
Did someone crack a fart?*—UCLA Slang

crack a smile *v phr by 1840* To smile; start to
smile: *I even wiggled my ears, but she wouldn't
crack a smile*

crackbrained *adj by 1634* Crazy; eccentric; wild;
=CRACKPOT

crackdown *n 1930s* A particular instance or severity of punishment, law enforcement, etc: *The Mayor
again vowed a crackdown on the porn shops*

crack down *v phr 1930s* To enforce the law or
rules more vigorously; =CLAMP DOWN: *Cops will
crack down on drunk drivers*

cracked *adj by 1692* Crazy; eccentric: *You're
cracked if you think I'll stay now*
See GET one's NUTS

cracked up *part phr by 1836* Said; praised •Most
often in the negative: *This beer ain't all it's cracked
up to be* [fr 1300s sense of *crack,* "boast, brag"]

cracker *n by 1766* A Southern rustic or poor white;
more particularly, a Georgian; =REDNECK [The dated
sense refers to "a lawless set of rascals on the fron-
tiers of Virginia, Maryland, the Carolinas, and
Georgia," who were great *crackers,* "boasters"; these

would be nearly the original frontier "tall talkers" of the Davy Crockett ilk]

See JAWBREAKER, SAFECRACKER

cracker-barrel *by 1877* **1** *adj* Unsophisticated; basic: *a cracker-barrel philosophy* **2** *adj* Intimate; gossipy: *a cracker-barrel discussion of family* [fr the archetypical image of rural discussants sitting on or around the *cracker barrel* in the general store]

cracker box 1 *n phr* Army *by 1930s* An Army ambulance **2** *n phr by 1930s* Any small and not overly substantial building or vehicle: *Wausaukee will have a new gym next year. . . but Saturday its 35-year-old crackerbox has to suffice*—Milwaukee Journal

cracker factory *n phr by 1970s* A mental hospital; =LOONY BIN, NUTHOUSE [because insane people are *cracked*, or in British slang *crackers*]

crackerjack *or* **crackajack** *late 1880s* **1** *n* A person or thing that is remarkable, wonderful, superior, etc: *Signorelli is a crackerjack* **2** *modifier*: *Orne. . . estimates that a crackerjack examiner working under optimum conditions would find 10 to 15 percent of his cases to be inconclusive*—Washingtonian/ *I'm a crackerjack story teller*—Pulpsmith [origin uncertain; perhaps a fanciful extension of *cracker* in the mid–19th-century British sense "something approaching perfection," which is also reflected in terms like *crack shot, crack troops*, etc, and based on an echoic expression of speed; hence also *cracking*; the term is reinforced in the US by late–19th-century trademark *Cracker Jack* for a popcorn and peanut confection]

Cracker Jack prize *n phr by late 1800s* Something of very little value: *The Whitney show is full of works that bring to mind gigantic gift boxes containing plastic Cracker Jack prizes*—New York Times [fr the fact that each box of Cracker Jacks™ contains a little gift among the glazed popcorn]

crackers *adj by 1928* Crazy; =CRACKED •Chiefly British use: *Also he was plain crackers*—Saul Bellow [formed with the British suffix *-ers*, like *bonkers, preggers*, etc]

crackhead *n 1980s narcotics* A user of cocaine freebase

crackheaded *adj by 1796* Crazy; =CRACKED, CRACKERS, NUTS

crackhouse *or* **crackshack** *n by 1985* A place where crack cocaine is sold or smoked

cracking *by 1830* **1** *adj* Excellent; first-rate: *a cracking meal* **2** *adv* Very: *a cracking good meal* **3** *n 1990s teenagers* : *Ragging, bagging, snapping, and cracking, these are all word games teens use as a way of competing with one another*—NEA Today

See GET CRACKING

crack one's **jaw** *v phr black by 1930s* To brag

crack off *v phr by 1970s* To make nasty or boastful remarks

crack on someone *v phr black by 1990s* To insult someone; =DIS, DUMP ON, TRASH

crackpot *by 1883* **1** *n* A crazy idiot; an addled fool; eccentric: *He's a crackpot about flying saucers* **2** *adj*: *my colleague's crackpot notions*

cracks *See* FALL BETWEEN THE CRACKS

crack the whip *v phr by 1940s* To command peremptorily and fiercely; intimidate: *He has made great industrial corporations jump. . . when he cracks the whip*—Time [fr the use of a whip to control animals, esp in the circus]

crackup 1 *n by 1926* A collision, crash, etc: *a bad car crackup/ airline crackup* **2** *n by 1930s* A mental or emotional breakdown: *Have you read Fitzgerald's* The Crackup? **3** *n by 1960s* A very funny person or thing: *His Cagney sketch is a crack-up*

crack up 1 *v phr by 1920s* To collide; crash: *The trucks cracked up head-on* **2** *v phr* (also **crack**) *by 1930s* To suffer an emotional or mental breakdown; go into hysteria, depression, etc: *Jimmy felt that he was cracking up*—Calder Willingham **3** *v phr by 1940s* To have a fit of uncontrollable laughter: *It may crack you up, but that's all*—Milwaukee Journal

crack wise *v phr by 1920s* To make quick, pungent, witty, and often malicious remarks: *All you do is crack wise*—Raymond Chandler

cradle *See* ROB THE CRADLE

cradle-robber *or* **cradle-snatcher** *by 1926* **1** *n* A person who prefers relatively younger sex or courtship partners **2** *n* A recruiter or sports scout who solicits very young persons

See ROB THE CRADLE

cram *British students by 1803* **1** *v* To study intensively for an upcoming examination **2** *modifier*: *a cram session/ cram book* **3** *n by 1900s* A very diligent student; =GRIND

cram it *See* STICK IT

cramp someone's **style** *v phr by 1917* To be a hindrance or distraction: *Your blank stare cramps my style* [Charles Lamb had written "cramps the flow of the style" as early as 1819]

crank 1 *n by 1881* An eccentric person, esp one who is irrationally fixated; =NUT, FREAK: *That crank wants a yogurt shampoo/ All kinds of cranks took credit for the murder* **2** *modifier*: *crank letters/ crank phone calls* **3** *n 1960s narcotics* Methamphetamine, a stimulant; =SPEED: *Ain't no calories in crank*—Harry Crews **4** *modifier*: *It's connected to a crank factory, and the case goes to New Jersey, so the FBI is all over it*—Carsten Stroud [first two senses perhaps fr the *crank* of a barrel organ, by which one can play the same tune over and over again; applied by Donn Piatt to the publisher Horace Greeley]

crank back *v phr by 1970s* To return to an earlier stage: *Let's crank back to where we started*

cranked *by 1980s* **1** *adj* Excited and eager; keen for action; =CHARGED UP, CRANKED UP, PUMPED UP: *I was cranked. I was geared*—Milwaukee Journal **2** *adj* Angry; =PISSED OFF: *He opened up. . . the casket. . . and man, was he cranked about that!*—Carsten Stroud

cranked up 1 *adj phr by 1950s* =CRANKED **2** *adj*

phr by middle 1980s Intoxicated by narcotics such as cocaine, esp by methamphetamine: *Was he cranked up when he did it?*—Carsten Stroud

cranking *adj* 1980s students Excellent; wonderful; first-rate; =COOL, RAD, TITS: *That party last night was so cranking*—UCLA Slang

crank on someone *v phr* by 1980s To vent one's anger on; =HASSLE: *She must have needed someone to crank on, and I was elected*—Sue Grafton

crank something **out** *v phr* by 1950s To produce or make something, esp with mechanical precision and regularity: *. . . with the kind of junk the studios are cranking out*—J Bell

crank someone or something **up 1** *v phr* by 1960s To get someone or something started; initiate action: *The people around Reagan. . . talk about "We'll crank him up on this"*—Washington Post/ *Let's crank up the dog project tomorrow* **2** *v phr* by 1950s To make excited, eager, keenly ready for action, etc: *You better crank the quarterback up if you want this team to score*

cranky *adj* by 1821 Very irritable; touchy: *The baby was cranky all day*

◁**crap**▷ **1** *v* by 1846 To defecate; =SHIT: *Where's the bathroom? I have to crap* **2** *n* by 1898 Feces; excrement; =SHIT: *The bad news is, I look like crap*—US Express **3** *interj* by 1930s An exclamation of disbelief, disgust, disappointment, rejection, etc; =FUCK, SHIT: *Oh, crap, I broke it again* **4** *n* by 1898 Nonsense; pretentious talk; bold and deceitful absurdities; =BULLSHIT: *I'm not interested in stories about the past or any crap of that kind*—Arthur Miller **5** *v* by 1930 To lie, exaggerate; try to deceive: *You're crapping me*—Lawrence Sanders **6** *n* by about 1910 Offensive and contemptuous treatment; overt disrespect: *. . . but I don't take crap from anybody*—Us **7** *n* by 1920s Anything of shoddy quality; pretentious and meretricious trash: *Her new show is pious crap* [by extension fr Middle English *crap*, "chaff, siftings of grain, residue"]

See ALL THAT KIND OF CRAP, FULL OF SHIT, SHOOT THE BULL

◁**crap around**▷ *v phr* by 1930s To waste time foolishly; lack seriousness; =FUCK AROUND, MESS AROUND: *Quit crapping around and get to work*

crape-hanger *n* by 1920 A habitually morose person; pessimist; =KILLJOY, PARTY-POOPER, WET BLANKET [fr the earlier funeral practice of hanging swaths of *crape* as a sign of mourning]

crap game *See* FLOATING CRAP GAME

◁**crap list**▷ *See* SHIT LIST

◁**crapoid**▷ *adj* by 1970s Disgusting; nasty; wretched; =CRAPPY: *Clover said they were crapoid for thinking that*—Paul Theroux [fr *crap* plus the suffix *-oid*, which became increasingly popular from the 1960s]

◁**crapola**▷ **1** *n* by 1950s Lies and exaggeration; =BULLSHIT: *. . . odious even by the usual standards of feminist crapola*—Village Voice/ *. . . grinding out the old heartfelt crapola*—Peter De Vries **2** *modifier*: *the latest trends in crapola entertainment* [fr *crap* plus suffix *-ola*]

crap out 1 *v phr* by 1930s To lose; fail **2** *v phr* by 1950s =COP OUT **3** *v phr* by 1940s To succumb to exhaustion; =CRASH, SACK OUT: *. . . then come back up here and crap out in that polo-field-size bed*—W E B Griffin [fr the failure of a crapshooter to make the winning point, and to roll 2, 3, or 7 instead]

◁**crapper**▷ **1** *n* by 1920s A toilet: *We'd just like to know if the governor of the state is aware of that damned thing in the crapper*—Earl Thompson **2** *n* by 1940s A person who regularly lies and exaggerates; a boaster and self-advertiser: *I call your great guru a mean little crapper* **3** *n* by 1970s Something disgusting, nasty, or shoddy: *Oh, Mondays are a crapper*—Westworld [fr *crap*]

◁**crappy**▷ by 1846 **1** *adj* Of inferior quality; shoddy: *the crappiest shoes I ever had* **2** *adj* Very unpleasant; nasty: *Don't you feel crappy?*—Buzz

crapshoot *n* by 1970s A risky gamble; something very chancy: *But who knows? It's such a crap shoot that nobody can really call it*—Milwaukee Journal/ *. . . such reforms would subject students to a crapshoot. . .* —Wisconsin State Journal

crash 1 *v* by 1920s To break into a building; enter by force: *Hoover's men crashed Doc's apartment*—A Hynd **2** *v* by 1920s To rob a place, esp by breaking in; =CRACK **3** *v* by 1922 To gain admittance to some desired category or milieu: *In LA she tried to crash TV* **4** *v* (also **crash the gate**) by 1922 To go to a party or other event uninvited or without tickets **5** *v* 1960s counterculture To sleep or live at a place for a day or so, usu without invitation: *I heard about this place and hoped I could crash here for a day or two*—P Curtis **6** *v* 1960s counterculture To go to sleep **7** *v* 1960s students To lose consciousness from narcotics or alcohol **8** *n* 1960s narcotics The empty feeling, depression, etc, felt when a euphoric intoxication ends; =LETDOWN: *The "crash" from coke. . . is grim*—Time **9** *v* 1970s computer To fail suddenly: *The spacecraft's No 1 computer . . . "crashed" or shut down*—Time/ *. . . computers that can alert a mainframe owner to an impending computer "crash"*—New York Times

crash and burn by 1970s **1** *v phr* (also **crash in flames**) To fail entirely; =BLOW IT: *. . . you'd think his presidency had already crashed in flames*—New Republic **2** *v* To collapse from exhaustion; =POOP OUT: *I was just about to crash and burn*—Armistead Maupin

crash-and-dash *See* SMASH-AND-GRAB

crash cart *n phr* medical by 1970s A hospital cart with drugs, defibrillator, etc, summoned in cases of cardiac arrest: *Get the crash cart. We've got a code blue in 516A*—Los Angeles Times [probably based on *crash wagon*, an airport ambulance or emergency vehicle, so called from the 1930s]

crashed *adj* by 1970s Drunk

crashout *n* underworld & prison by 1940s A prison escape; jailbreak [perhaps based on earlier *crushout* in the same sense]

crash out *v phr* underworld & prison by 1940s To escape from prison

crash pad *n phr* 1960s counterculture A place to sleep or live for a day or so, esp for young people traveling about more or less aimlessly and with little money: . . . *discouraging intinerant filmmakers, homeless poets, and hangers-on of all kinds from using the room as a crash pad*—New Yorker

crash program (or **project) *n phr* by 1940s** An intense and extraordinary effort to a specific end: *Getting the refugees housed needed a crash program* [fr the urgency of a submarine's *crash-dive* ordered in extreme danger; *crash-dive* dates from about 1918]

crash with someone *v phr* by 1990s To do the sex act with someone; sleep with someone; =BOFF, BONK, BOP: *You crashed with my sister*—TV show *Night Court*

crate 1 *n* about 1920 A car, bus, airplane, etc, esp an old rickety one ●Seems to have been used for airplanes before cars; this may be because early airplanes were literally wooden and cloth *crates*: *A "crate" is a "junker" with one surge left*—New York Times **2** *n* hoboes by 1920s A jail **3** *v* by 1990s To arrest and jail: *We crate Major and they'll go. . . But they won't leave him there*—Robert B Parker

crate of sand *n phr* 1930s truckers A truckload of sugar

crater *v* by 1980s To abandon; give up; =FOLD: *He doesn't crater. . . When he has a tough inning, he comes back. . .*—Milwaukee Journal

crawfish *v* by 1842 To renege; retreat; =BACK OUT: *He started to crawfish when he realized who the competition was*

crawl ◁**1**▷ *v* by 1940s To do the sex act with; mount ●Actually used by the 1890s to mean "mount and manage a horse": *I finally crawled Mary Jane Cummings last night*—Calder Willingham **2** *v* WWI Army To reprimand severely; =CHEW OUT: *"To crawl" meant what Second World War troops meant by "chew out"*—A J Liebling **3** *n* 1920s A dance; =HOP **4** *n* 1960s Text that scrolls up the television screen, esp explaining what happened to the characters of a "based on fact" docudrama: *And a crawl going up the screen saying she's pleaded no contest. . .*—Milwaukee Journal/ *The use of crawl to finish a quasi-historical story. . .*—Washington Post

See PUB CRAWL

crawl someone's **hump** *v phr* early 1900s cowboys To assault someone; =CLOBBER

crawl (or **come) out of the woodwork** *v phr* by 1960s To appear, materialize, interfere, etc, as or like something very loathsome: *A lot of them are weirdos who just crawled out of the woodwork*—WT Tyler/ *Any time there's a juicy scandal a lot of creeps come out of the woodwork* [fr the notion that worms, spiders, maggoty creatures, rats, etc, dwell in hidden places]

crawl with *adj phr* by 1576 To be well provided with: *The place was suddenly crawling with cops*

Crayola (or **crayon-box) colors** *n phr* by 1990s Intense, saturated primary colors: . . . *arrayed himself in billowy zoot suits of Crayola colors, with a long gold chain*—New Yorker [fr *Crayola*™, the name of a kind of childrens' crayons]

crazy 1 *adj* 1940s jazz musicians Excellent; splendid; =COOL: *If you like a guy or gal, they're cool. If they are real fat, real crazy, naturally they're real cool*—Newsweek **2** *n* by 1867 An insane or eccentric person; =LOONY: *We're going to prevent the right-wing crazies from bombing and destroying*—Playgirl

See LIKE CRAZY, STIR-CRAZY

-crazy *combining word* Inordinately devoted to or manic over what is indicated: *boy-crazy/ kill-crazy/ speed-crazy*

crazy about (or **over** or **for) *adj phr* by 1904** Very enthusiastic about; infatuated with; =NUTS ABOUT: *I'm crazy about Ronnie*

crazy as a loon (or **a coot** or **a bedbug) *adj phr*** first form by 1845, third by 1832 Insane; =NUTTY: *If you think that, you're crazy as a loon* [fr the *loon's* or *coot's* cry, like an insane laugh, and the *bedbug's* frantic rushing about when exposed]

crazy-house *n* by 1887 A mental hospital; insane asylum

crazy like a fox *adj phr* by 1908 Very bright and canny

crazy quilt *n phr* by 1880s Something confused and patternless; a hodgepodge ●Originally a bed quilt made of odd bits and pieces of cloth: *The Crazy Quilt of American Politics*—New York Times/ *More bizarre turns in the last decade, relations among Iran, Iraq, and the US form a crazy quilt*—New Yorker

creak *v* by 1930s To show signs of wear; be near collapse: . . . *indications that their marriages are creaking*—Philadelphia Journal

cream 1 *v* by 1920s To cheat or deprive someone of something, esp by silky glibness: *I got creamed out of the hotel spot in Ohio*—John O'Hara/ . . . *a smoothie who wolfed on a friend and creamed his lady*—World's Work **2** *v* by 1929 To do very well against; overcome; =CLOBBER: *You didn't stop by just to tell me how you creamed the Irish*—Lawrence Sanders ◁**3**▷ *v* by 1940s To be sexually aroused, esp so as to secrete sexual fluids, either semen or lubricants ●*Cream* has meant "semen" since at least the middle 1800s: *He thinks we're gettin' all agitated. . . over here creamin' in our drawers*—John Sayles/ *It made me cream in my panties, isn't that fun?*—Interview **4** *n* black by 1980s A white person; =PADDY: . . . *he was a "cream" in a car full of home boys and bloods from the black projects. . .*—Carsten Stroud

See ICE CREAM, ICE CREAM HABIT

CREAM *n* 1990s black teenagers Money [fr *cash rules everything around me*]

creamie *n* A white or clear playing marble

◁**cream** one's **jeans (**or **silkies)**▷ *v phr* by 1940s To become sexually excited; exude sexual fluids: . . . *any idea how them ladies cream their silkies watching a muscular and handsome guy*—Tom Aldibrandi *See* CREAM

cream puff 1 *n phr by 1930s* A weakling; =SISSY, WIMP: *Opponents might get the idea. . . Lemonick is a cream puff*—D Cresan **2** *n phr salespersons by 1940s* Something for sale, esp a used car in splendid condition and a tremendous bargain: *. . . before you believe, much less see, any of the "creampuffs" in the. . . classifieds*—Philadelphia

cream-puff hitter *n phr baseball by 1950s* A weak hitter

cream up *v phr by 1940s* To execute perfectly: *You guys know what you're supposed to do and when, so let's cream this up*—New Yorker

creative accounting *n phr by 1970s* Fraudulent or dubious bookkeeping; falsification of financial records in imaginative ways: *. . . secret takeover deals, creative accounting just this side of Internal Revenue Service rules*—New York Times/ *. . . through some very creative accounting the. . . corporations were both depriving. . . governments of all sorts of taxes*—W E B Griffin

creek *See* UP SHIT CREEK

creep or **creepo** *n first form 1930s students, second by 1950s* A disgusting and obnoxious person; =CRUD, JERK, NERD •An isolated 1886 use seems to refer specifically to a cringing sycophant rather than a generally repulsive person: *The man is nothing but a creep*—Quentin Reynolds/ *. . . poets loyal to Blake and Whitman, the "holy creeps"*—Saul Bellow/ *How to spend our money on making some creepo more creative in the growing world of weirdness*—Mike Royko [origin uncertain; perhaps fr one who makes one's flesh *creep*; perhaps generalized fr one who cringes and curries favor]

-creep *combining word by 1980s* A gradual increase in the thing named: *My cost-of-living allowance put me into bracket-creep on my income tax*/ *In Somalia we saw mission-creep*—New Yorker

creeper 1 *n 1930s truckers* The lowest gear on a truck **2** *n radio studio by 1940s* A performer who moves closer and closer to the microphone **3** *n underworld by 1930s* A sneak thief: *He knew they couldn't be boosters or creepers, not flashing their bread the way these two were doing*—Joseph Wambaugh

creepers *n underworld about 1900* =SNEAKERS

Creepers *n* or *interj by 1940s* Christ •A euphemistic form: *Creepers, but that was a nasty moment* *See* JEEPERS CREEPERS

creepette *n by 1990s* A female creep: *Surrounded by creeps and creepettes*

creeping crud *n phr WWII armed forces* Any disease, esp an unnamed and prevalent flulike disorder or an unexplained and nasty rash [a reduplicating expansion of *crud*]

creep-joint *n underworld by 1920s* A gambling meet that moves about to avoid arrest; =FLOATING CRAP GAME

the creeps 1 *n phr by 1864* Sensations of fear and loathing, such that one's flesh seems to formicate; revulsion; =WILLIES: *The willies or the creeps. Call it what you like*—Scott Turow **2** *n phr by 1940s* Delirium tremens: *He was not in with the creeps but with a broken leg*—John McNulty

creep someone **out** *v phr by 1990s* To frighten and disgust someone: *flirt alert: My teacher's creeping me out*—Seventeen

creepy 1 *adj by 1831* Frightening; scary; =HAIRY: *a creepy show about necrophiles* **2** *adj by 1880s* Loathsome; disgusting: *a creepy little chap with an enormous bow tie*

creepy-crawly 1 *adj by 1880s* Loathsome; repellent; =CREEPY: *The trio plunges into the creepy-crawly high life of Acapulco*—Richard Grenier **2** *n by 1920s* A nasty creature, esp the caterpillar, snake, or centipede sort: *. . . the lair, maybe, Of creepy-crawlies or a ghost*—W H Auden

cremains *n by 1990s* The remains of a cremated body

cretin maggot *n phr 1990s teenagers* A despicable disgusting person; =DICKWAD, SCUMBAG

cretinoid *1970s college students* **1** *n* A cretin; idiot; =SPASTIC **2** *modifier: El Presidente, and others too cretinoid to mention*—Drew Acorn [In the standard sense "resembling a cretin" attested from 1874]

cretinous *adj computer by 1980s* Wrong; inoperative; wretchedly designed; =BLETCHEROUS

crew *See* CHECK CREW

crib 1 *n students by 1827* A translation or a set of answers used to cheat on an examination **2** *v by 1778: He cribbed on the econ exam and got caught* **3** *n underworld by 1857* A place where thieves and hoodlums congregate; cheap saloon: *a sleazy crib on Second Ave* **4** *v by 1748* To steal **5** *n by 1930s* A nightclub; =DIVE: *I am singing for coffee and cakes at a crib on Cottage Grove Avenue*—John O'Hara **6** *n 1960s teenagers* Home

crib course *n phr college students by 1970s* An easy college course; =GUT COURSE: *Even at Stanford or Johns Hopkins the student in desperate need of a crib course can be sure to find one*—Washington Post [fr student senses of *crib*]

crib crime (or job) *n phr by 1970s* The robbing or mugging of an old person

cricket *See* NOT CRICKET

cried out *adj phr 1980s students* Exhausted; =BEAT, POOPED: *I was cried out after practice*—Delcastle Dictionary of Slang

Crikey *n* or *interj by 1838* Christ •Chiefly British euphemism; an obsolete US form *crickey* is attested in 1839: *Crikey but it was a rum go*

crill *n by 1990s: The traffic gets worse in the spring and peaks by summer. The youths come to sell "crills," or hits of crack wrapped in plastic, for $15 to $20*—New York Times

crime *See* COPYCAT CRIME

a crime *n phr* college students by 1895 A misfortune; a shame: *It would be a crime if they elected that guy*

Criminy or **Crimus** (KRI mə nee, KRĪməs) *n* or *interj* by 1700 Christ •A euphemistic form: *Criminy, I've been hoodwinked/ Crimus but it's cold*

crimp by 1896 **1** *n* A restriction; obstacle: *He kept putting crimps into my plan* **2** *v*: *I'll crimp him good with this nasty new rule*

crip 1 *n* hoboes & underworld by 1918 A cripple; =GIMP: *"Phony crips" as the fraudulent cripples call each other*—New Yorker **2** *n* (also **crip course**) 1920s college students An easy course; =CRIB COURSE, GUT COURSE, SNAP

Cripes or **Cripus** *n* or *interj* by 1910 Christ •A euphemistic form: *Cripes, what a rotten deal*

crip-faker *n* hoboes by 1940s A professional beggar who feigns being badly crippled

crippin' *n* 1980s street gangs Forming and joining the sort of teenage drug-criminal street gangs typified by the Los Angeles Crips and Bloods; =GANGBANGING: *Moe has been credited with bringing "crippin'" to Little Rock in 1987. . .* —Los Angeles Times [fr the gang name *Crips*]

crippleware *n* computer by 1990s A computer shareware program that is deliberately left incomplete so that the user must petition the maker

Crisco *n* by 1930s An obese person; =FATTY [fr *Crisco*, trademark for a kind of shortening sold in cans, hence, "fat in the can"]

Crisco disco *n phr* by 1970s A nightclub or discotheque frequented by male homosexuals [fr the presumed use of *Crisco* as a lubricant for anal intercourse]

crispy *adj* 1980s students Suffering the morning-after effects of alcohol; =HUNG OVER

crispy critter *n phr* 1960s Army A person, car, etc, that has been very severely burned: *Some of the soldiers wandering the graveyard joked a bit. "Crispy critters," said one, looking at the incinerated*—New Republic [fr *Crispy Critters*, trademark of a breakfast cereal resembling little toasted animals]

critter *n* by 1815 An animal or person; =CUSS, CUSTOMER: *That dog is a nasty critter/ Jane's a friendly old critter* [fr creature]

croak 1 *v* by 1812 To die: *I had the horse trained, then he up and croaked on me* **2** *v* by 1848 To kill; murder: *He croaked a screw at Dannemora*—Joel Sayre **3** *n* 1980s narcotics A mixture of crack cocaine and cocaine: *A new wave of narcotics with names such as "croak" and "parachute" is hitting the nation's streets*—Associated Press

croaker *n* by 1859 A physician: *Don't say "croaker," say "doctor"*—Nelson Algren

crock 1 *n* by 1876 A disliked person, esp an old person: *. . .a lot of old crocks with baggy eyes*—R Starnes **2** *n* medical by 1950s A hypochondriac and whining patient **3** *n* WWII Navy A bargelike cargo ship made of cement **4** *v* by 1918 To hit; =CLOBBER, CLOCK: *I crocked the orderly with a bed-*spring—Raymond Chandler **5** *v* by 1918 To ruin; wreck; kill; =QUEER: *Calling the pitch. . . lies, as you might imagine, crocked the job*—Philadelphia **6** *n* =CROCK OF SHIT: *Spook the sponsors. What a crock*—New Yorker/ *Bonny Loo giggles, "That's a crock"*—Carolyn Chute **7** *n* 1980s computer Something, esp a program, that functions, but in an ugly or awkward manner

crocked *adj* by 1927 Drunk

crockery 1 *n* early 1900s The teeth **2** *n* baseball by 1950s A pitcher's arm that becomes lame and ineffective; =GLASS ARM

◁**crock of shit**▷ *n phr* by 1940s Nonsense; lies and exaggerations; mendacious cant; =BULLSHIT: *. . .characterized reports of TJ Club activity in Weinstein's campaign as a "crock of shit"*—Village Voice/ *Asked about Burns's contention. . . he replied, "That's a crock of shit"*—Toronto Life

cronk *adj* about 1850 Drunk [fr German *krank*, "ill"]

crook 1 *n* by 1870s A habitual or professional criminal; a consistently dishonest person: *The chief said, "I'm not a crook"* **2** *v* by 1940s To steal: *He crooked my socks*—E Kasser

crooked (KRŏŏ kəd) *adj* by 1870s Dishonest; fraudulent; criminal [Attested from 1225 in the larger sense "immoral, perverse, not orthodox"]

crooked arm *n phr* baseball by 1940s A lefthanded pitcher; =SOUTHPAW

crooker *See* PINKY-CROOKER

crook the elbow *See* BEND THE ELBOW

croon by 1460 **1** *v* To sing in a relaxed and mellow style: *Rudy Vallee crooned his way to immortality* **2** *v* To sing [fr Scots dialect; related to Dutch *kreunen*, "groan, whimper"]

cropper *See* COME A CROPPER

cross someone **1** *v* by 1589 To act contrary to someone's wishes; attempt to thwart someone; contradict: *You must not cross me on this* **2** *v* by 1823 =DOUBLE CROSS [both senses fr the distinction between "straight, square," and *cross*; *cross* meant "illegal practices" by 1812]
See DOUBLE CROSS

cross-dresser *n* by 1960s A transvestite: *I'm constantly getting calls from cross-dressers who think I could use their talents*—Village Voice

crossed idiotsticks *n phr* 1970s Army The crossed rifles of the infantry branch insignia

cross-eyed *See* LOOK AT someone CROSS-EYED

cross my heart or **cross my heart and hope to die** *sentence* by 1908 I am telling the truth; I swear this is the truth: *I love you, baby. Cross my heart*

crossover 1 *n* 1970s musicians A shift from one musical style to another or a deliberate mixture of disparate styles **2** *modifier*: *. . .a series of absurd moments straight outta crossover hell*—The Source **3** *modifier* by 1990s Bridging some gap of medium, "lifestyle," etc: *. . . Rose Troche and Guinevere Turner created a lesbian comedy that. . . is likely to be a crossover hit*—Vogue

cross someone's **palm** *See* GREASE someone's PALM

crossroader *n* *police by 1950s* A person who cheats at casino games, esp at slot machines: . . . *one of the world's greatest crossroaders, or slot-machine cheats*—Wall Street Journal

cross the aisle *v phr by 1980s* To change one's affiliations, loyalties, politics, etc: *GM asked me to cross the aisle*—Ralph Nader [fr the *aisle* that separates Republicans and Democrats in both houses of Congress]

cross-up *by 1940s* **1** *n* An error, esp one caused by misunderstanding: *nobody's fault, just a cross-up* **2** *n* =DOUBLE CROSS

cross someone **up** *v phr by 1940s* To confuse or deceive someone: *He had to cross the blockers up*

crotchcutter *n by 1990s* A woman's bathing suit with leg openings that reach above the hips and even the waist: *"Crotchcutters," the Village Voice called the suits*—Knife and Fork Menuzine

crotch job *n phr by 1990s* A book, television show, etc, of vulgar sensationalism: *The latter is a Fox crotch job. . . "Roseanne: An Unauthorized Biography"*—Los Angeles Times

crotch worker *n phr police by 1970s* A shoplifter who conceals loot under her dress

crow 1 *n WWI Navy* The eagle on naval insignia **2** *n WWI Navy* A naval petty officer or captain who wears the eagle insignia **3** *n WWII armed forces* Chicken **4** *v by 1522* To boast in exultation; flatter oneself: *That poem's nothing to crow about* *See* JANE CROW, JIM CROW

crowbait *n by 1857* An old, mean, or ugly horse

crowd 1 *n by 1840* A group, faction, clique, etc: *The Hip Sing and On Leong crowds. . . —*E H Lavine **2** *n by 1863* An audience: *To watch Dick Enberg work the crowd. . . —*ABC Radio *See* GO ALONG WITH THE CROWD

crowd someone *v by 1839* To press or importune someone; encroach on someone's territory or safety: *Don't crowd me now, just let me handle it*

crowd someone **out** *v phr by 1652* To push or force someone by pressure as of a crowd: *I think he's trying to crowd me out of the board membership*

crowd-pleaser *n by 1943* A performer, sport, show, etc, that is very popular with the multitude: . . . *the triumph of the superior woman over the crowd-pleaser*—New York Times/ *Soccer is not an instant crowd pleaser*—New Yorker

crowd-surf *v by 1990s* To be passed along overhead by the people at a "moshing" session: *The mosh pit. . . started going full speed, complete with crowd-surfing*—Milwaukee Journal Sentinel

crow-hop *n baseball by 1980s* A little forward jump made by an outfielder to increase the distance of a long throw: *Mike Knight. . . shouted to him to use a crow-hop*—Milwaukee Journal

Crow Jim *n phr* Strong antiwhite prejudice among blacks: . . . *the form of reverse prejudice known as Crow Jim*—Esquire [the obverse of *Jim Crow*]

crown *v by 1746* To hit someone, esp on the head; =BEAN, CONK: *If she finds out she'll crown me*

crow tracks *n phr Army by 1940s* Chevrons showing non-commissioned officers' rank; =STRIPES

crud or **crut 1** *n Army by 1920s* Any venereal disease **2** *n* (also the **crud**) *1930s college students* Any disease, esp one featuring a rash or obvious skin eruption; any unnamed disease: *I probably picked up the crud that's going around* **3** *n by 1930s* A dirty and slovenly person; =DIRTBALL: *I used to be a smelly crud* **4** *n by 1930s* Anything loathsome or markedly inferior: *His new show's a piece of crud* **5** *modifier*: *It's in your ballpark, since you love the crud detail*—Erma Bombeck [fr Middle English, "coagulated milk or other substance, curd," of unknown origin] *See* CREEPING CRUD

cruddy *by 1940s* **1** *adj* Nasty; loathsome; repellent: . . . *a bar band playing cover tunes in a cruddy dive*—Milwaukee Journal **2** *adj* Somewhat ill and indisposed; under par; =BLAH: *I'm not exactly sick, I just feel cruddy*

cruft *computer by 1980s* **1** *n* A repellent substance; =CRAP, CRUD: *The dust that gathers under your bed is cruft*—The Hacker's Dictionary **2** *n* The consequences of inferior construction: *He tried for elegance in that design, but ended up with cruft*

crufty *computer by 1980s* **1** *adj* Unpleasant; repellently viscid; =YUCKY **2** *adj* Poorly built; perhaps overly complex: *This is standard old crufty DEC software*—The Hacker's Dictionary

cruise 1 *v by 1903* To drive slowly and watchfully in the streets, walk about vigilantly in bars and parties, etc, looking for a sex partner ●Streetwalkers were called *cruisers* by about 1900: *He started cruising the singles bars* **2** *v by 1940s* To make a sexual approach: *I dated girls but at the same time was still cruising guys*—Deviant Reality/ *But what happens if, after cruising chicks. . . you find yourself with a more cerebral companion?*—Milwaukee Journal **3** *v by 1960s* To be smoothly going about one's business: *He was still "cruising nice and mellow" from an acid trip two nights before*—New York Magazine *See* LET'S BOOGIE, SHAKEDOWN CRUISE

on **cruise control** *adj* or *adv phr by 1980s* Behaving or seeming to behave smoothly without conscious effort; *In the 8th inning Clemens is on cruise control. Pitching with a 4–0 lead makes him all the more effective*—New York Times [fr *Cruise Control*, a trademark device for setting the speed of a car so that it does not vary and one does not need to touch the controls]

cruise patrol *n phr 1980s* A strolling about, usu looking for girls [possibly influenced by *cruise control*]

cruiser *n* A person who cruises: *"Looking for Mr Goodbar," which was told from a female cruiser's point of view*—New York Magazine

cruising for a bruising *v phr teenagers by 1951* Looking for trouble; courting violence, esp while riding about in a car [perhaps fr or influenced by black English *cruising,* "strolling, parading," attested by 1942]

cruit or **croot** (KRⓞⓞT) *n WWI Army* A recruit; =ROOKIE, YARDBIRD

crumb or **crum 1** *n by 1863* A louse or bedbug **2** *n hoboes about 1910* A blanket roll or pack; =BINDLE **3** *n by 1918* A dirty, slovenly person; =CRUD, DIRTBALL **4** *n by 1918* A loathsome, contemptible person; =CREEP [fr the resemblance of a louse to a *crumb*]

crumb boss *by 1920s* **1** *n phr* A bunkhouse janitor **2** *n phr railroad* A person in charge of a work-crew's car

crumb-bun or **crum-bun** *n* A contemptible person; =BUM, CRUMB: *Unlike the other critic crumb-buns, he has a soul*—Saul Bellow [based on earlier *crumb-bum,* "lice-ridden bum"]

crumbcrusher *n* (also **crumbcruncher** or **crumb-grinder** or **crumbsnatcher**) *1930s black* A baby; small child: *... when your own li'l crumbcrushers suffered through fatherless periods*—Douglas Turner/*Here comes one crumbsnatcher, then two*—Joseph A Walker

crumb-roll *n hoboes by about 1915* A bedroll or blanket roll; bed

crumbs *n by 1856, but current fr 1950s* A very little, esp of money; a pittance; =CHUMP CHANGE, COFFEE AND CAKES, PEANUTS: *Hell no. I won't work for crumbs—I want bread*

crumb (or **crum**) **the deal** *v phr by 1918* To spoil a plan; =LOUSE UP

crumb (or **crum**) **up** *WWI Army* **1** *v phr* To spoil; confuse; =LOUSE UP, MESS UP: *He tried too hard and crumbed up the whole thing* **2** *v phr* To clean clothing thoroughly, esp to delouse

crummy or **crumby** *adj by 1850s* Infested with body lice; lousy **2** *adj by 1850s* Loathsome; disgusting; =LOUSY: *I'd be dead of the dirty monotony around this crummy neighborhood*—Nelson Algren **3** *adj by 1850s* Of inferior quality; shoddy; =CHEAP: *This crumby razor doesn't work/ Where'd you get that crummy camera?*

crunch 1 *n by 1930s* A crisis; a desperate climax; =SQUEEZE: *Then came the political conventions that summer, and more crunches*—Clay Felker/ *A "crunch" is characterized by a skyrocketing of interest rates and a choking off of the availability of credit*—L Silk/ *The "crunch" between press and Government is inevitable in American affairs*—J Raymond **2** *modifier*: *PARKS: It's Crunch Time in the Havens*—Los Angeles Times **3** *v 1980s computer* To process, usu in a wearisome way **4** *n 1990s* A kind of exercise for the stomach, in which one pulls the head off the floor while lying on one's back: *Actress Julianne Phillips keeps her stomach flat by doing 6,000 "crunches" a week*—Milwaukee Journal **5** *v 1980s students* To study intensely; =PULL AN ALL-NIGHTER

cruncher *See* NUMBER CRUNCHER

crunchie 1 *n 1970s Army* An infantry soldier ◁**2**▷ *n 1980s students* A lesbian ●The quotation

crunching *See* NUMBER-CRUNCHING, NUT-CRUNCHING

crunch numbers *v phr fr 1980s computer* To do arithmetic or mathematics; calculate: *But if the general reader is up to crunching some numbers, Sportsbiz could be a pleasing ticket to understanding the money in sports*—Milwaukee Journal

crunchy (also **crunchy granola, granola**) **1** *adj 1980s students* Having a healthy diet and way of living; natural; earthy: *She's a crunchy granola girl*—UCLA Slang/ *... drew directly on their college days at Connecticut's slightly crunchy (as in granola) Wesleyan University*—Los Angeles Times **2** *n 1990s students* A person who is disagreeably intent on environmental matters, personal bodily simplicity, walking in the forest, etc ●The term altered to pejorative as the student ethos altered and "political correctness" became repellent: *crunchy granola: a person who is emotionally or temperamentally still living in the 1960s...* —Los Angeles Times/ *Hippie parents, you know. Rill crunchy*—Douglas Coupland [fr the 1876 trademark of a "cooked, granulated wheat"; *crunchy,* candylike modern versions of the cereal were much prized by some elements of the 1960s counterculture]

crush 1 *n by 1895* A passing infatuation: *That's a crush, Manny is love*—New York Times **2** *n by 1806* A thick crowd; heavily crowded place **3** *v by about 1610* To humiliate someone; reduce someone to helpless dismay: *Her snub crushed me*
See HAVE A CRUSH ON someone, ORANGE CRUSH

crushed *adj 1990s teenagers* Ugly; =BUCKLED, PISS-UGLY

crush out *v phr 1920s underworld* To escape from prison: *... who had crushed out of Leavenworth*—Dashiell Hammett

crush-out *n 1920s underworld* An escape from prison

crust *n by 1890s* Bold audacity; gall; =CHUTZPA: *You've got a hell of a crust assuming I'll go down there*—Raymond Chandler
See the UPPER CRUST

crusty *adj by 1834* Gruff; surly; ill-tempered; =FEISTY: *Crusty George Meany.... The downturned lips, the jowls, the half-closed lids, all were dour*—Time

crut *See* CRUD

crutch 1 *n 1960 narcotics* A container for a hypodermic needle **2** *n 1960s narcotics* =ROACH CLIP

crybaby 1 *n by 1852* A person given to weeping or lamenting at the least adversity, esp from self-pity **2** *modifier*: *The Georgetown basketball team... has continued its crybaby act*—Milwaukee Journal

cry in one's **beer** *v phr by 1940s* To indulge in a session of lamentation or weeping; feel keenly sorry for oneself: *You can't make something like this make you cry in your beer*—Milwaukee Journal Sentinel

crying *See* FOR CRYING OUT LOUD

crying jag *n phr by 1904* A fit of uncontrollable weeping, often accompanying drunkenness: *Florence got regular crying jags, and the men sought to cheer and comfort her*—Dorothy Parker

crying room *n phr by 1940s* A fancied place where one can go to bewail a defeat, disappointment, etc

a **crying shame** *n phr by 1881* A great misfortune; a very distressing thing; =DIRTY SHAME: *That's a crying shame. I'll have to go see him*—Lawrence Sanders

crying towel *n phr by 1920s* A fancied towel offered in ironic sympathy to one who laments undeserved ill fortune, unbearable reverses, etc: *Get out the crying towel, old Frank got another parking ticket*

crystal or **crystal meth** *n 1960s narcotics* Narcotics in powdered form, esp amphetamines; =SPEED

crystalhead 1 *n 1960s narcotics* A person addicted to amphetamines; =SPEEDFREAK 2 *n 1980s* A follower of New Age beliefs; a New Ager [second sense because such persons prize crystals for various putative powers]

C-section *n 1980s* A Caesarean section: *I took three weeks off for a C-section*—Milwaukee Journal/ *Although doctors have long advised against repeated C-sections, the high rate has continued*—Time

C-sex *n 1990s* Computer sex; sexual talk, provocation, etc, on a computer network

C-Span-head *n by 1990s* A devotee of the cable-television channel *C-Span,* a channel showing political events, conferences, and discussions

◁**ct** or **CT**▷ *n* =COCK-TEASER

CTD *adj medical by 1980s* Nearly dead [fr *circling the drain,* that is, about to go down]

cub[1] 1 *n newspaper office by 1890s* A novice reporter 2 *n by 1840* Any novice or apprentice 3 *modifier*: *a cub reporter/ cub professor* [fr *cub,* "the young of certain animals"]

cub[2] or **cubby** *n first form by 1546, second by 1860s* A room or dwelling; =PAD: *Let's go to my cub*—Delcastle Dictionary of Slang [origin uncertain; related to Low German of the same meaning; the 1500s form refers to an animal's stall or shed; these senses are preserved more often in black English than in standard English]

cube 1 *n* (also **cubesville**) *by 1950s* A very conformistic and conventional person; =SQUARE 2 *n 1950s narcotics* A portion of LSD, hashish, or morphine: *He wanted a couple cubes, two cubes I had*—Prison

cubed out *adj phr 1980s military* Filled to capacity

cubehead *n 1950s narcotics* A frequent user of LSD [fr sugar *cube,* into which LSD can be soaked before taking]

the **cubes** *n phr* Dice; a pair of dice: *He chose to stake his hopes. . . on one throw of the cubes*—G Talbot [The use is very, very old: the word *cube* derives from the Greek word meaning "a die for gambling"]

cuckoo or **coo-coo** 1 *n by 1581* A crazy or eccentric person 2 *adj by 1918* Crazy; very eccentric; =NUTTY: *Where do you get these cuckoo ideas?* [perhaps because of the bird's monotonous, silly-sounding call]

cuddle-bunny *n 1940s teenagers* An attractive young woman, esp one who is generous with sexual favors

cuddle chemical *n phr by 1990s*: *Oxytocin, the 'cuddle chemical,' seems to control a woman's pleasure during orgasm, childbirth, cuddling and nursing her baby*—New York Times

cuddle (or **cozy**) **up to** someone *v phr by middle 1700s* To become friendly or cozy with someone: *Now we have the Senator cuddling up to his former opposition*

cueball *n WWII armed forces & students* A man or boy with a bald, shaven, or close-clipped head

cuff *by 1920s* 1 *v* To borrow money from someone, usu in an urgent way 2 *v* To charge something, esp on an expense account: *No man. . . feels he is getting ahead until he can cuff a few tabs on the firm*—Hal Boyle 3 *v by 1693* To put handcuffs on someone: *Cuff him and book him, Flanagan* [first two senses fr the notion of keeping track of debts by notations on the *cuff* of one's shirt]

See OFF THE CUFF, ON THE CUFF, STUFF CUFF

◁**cuff one's meat**▷ *v phr by 1970s* To masturbate: *He'd still be cuffing his meat in Spain*—Tom Aldibrandi

cuffo or **cufferoo** *adj by 1930s* Free of charge; nonpaying; on credit: *. . . not a spending party, strictly cufferoo*—John O'Hara/ *. . . before you caught your cuffo flight*—Paul Sann

cuffs *n by 1663* Handcuffs

Cuisinart *by 1980s* 1 *n* Anything that obliterates distinctions and creates homogeneity: *Europeans chafe at depositing their identities into the EC Cuisinart to be homogenized into bland Euromush*—New York Times 2 *modifier*: *. . . written in Cuisinart prose, language-by-committee: wooden and self-parodic*—Nation [fr the trademark of a well-known food slicer and blender]

culture vulture *n phr about 1940* An enthusiastic devotee of the arts and of intellectual pursuits, esp a pretentious one: *Culture vultures to the contrary, there is more integrity to the guy*—San Francisco

◁**cum**▷ *See* COME

cume (KYUM) *n college students by 1960s n* The cumulative academic average of a student: *. . . saying he didn't care about flunking, she would say "And what about your cume?"*—Christopher Zenowich

◀**cunt**▶ 1 *n by 1325* The vulva 2 *n by 1670s* Sexual favors and indulgence; =ASS, FUCKING: *But some of their daughters were giving away more cunt than Dixie was selling*—Claude Brown 3 *n by 1920s* A woman: *Why didn't he spin off this stupid cunt*—Saul Bellow 4 *n by 1920s* A fellow male one dislikes, esp a homosexual: *. . . and this one is from Max, the cunt*—Arthur Maling

◀**cuntface** or **cunthead**▶ *n first form by 1940s, second by 1960s* A despicable person; =BASTARD:

. . . cunthead. . . you wretched fart—John Irving

◄**cunt-hair**► *n by 1920s* A very small amount or distance; minute amount; =SMIDGEN, TAD: *. . . knows when it's off center, even when it's only a cunt hair off*—William Kennedy

◄**cunt-lapper**► *n by 1920s* A person who does cunnilingus; =MUFF-DIVER

◄**cunt-lapping**► *n by 1916* Cunnilingus: *. . . nor induced Maurice White to advocate cunt-lapping*—Village Voice

◄**cunt meat**► *n phr by 1970s* Women; women's quality: *He was drowning in cunt meat. Tina's and his mother's, waves of it*—Patrick Mann

◄**cuntmobile**► *n* =RAPE WAGON

◄**cunt-struck**► *n by 1891* Dominated by a woman; henpecked; =PUSSY-WHIPPED

cupcake 1 *n by 1970s* An eccentric person; =NUTBALL: *. . . regarding puppeteers as kind of weird cupcakes who play with dolls*—Washington Post/ *. . . the publishing cupcake. . . who nailed you on the couch and then fired you*—R Grossbach **2** *n by 1930s* An attractive young woman; =CHICK: *Flossie was a saucy blonde cupcake then*—William Kennedy/ *In her. . . don't-think-I'm-just-another-cupcake suit, Geraldine A. Ferraro. . . gave a pep talk*—Philadelphia **3** *modifier by 1990s* Weak; soft; =WIMPISH: *On cupcake opponents: It doesn't matter who you play. When you cross those black lines you should come out and play hard*—Milwaukee Journal

cup of coffee *n phr early 1900s baseball* A very short visit or tenure with a team or in a major league: *After his years with the Tigers, the outfielder had a cup of coffee with the Yankees in 1950 and the Giants in 1952*—New York Daily News/ *I just wanted a cup of coffee, I just wanted my foot in the door*—New York Times

one's **cup** (or **dish**) **of tea** *n phr British fr 1920s* One's special taste, predilection, etc; =THING: *Harlem is. . . his forte and his dish of tea*—Carl Van Vechten

cups *See* IN one's CUPS

curbie *n by 1930s* =CARHOP: *Us curbies don't get no salary for banging these trays*—New Yorker

curbstone *v car dealers by 1990s* To pretend to sell a car for a private person while actually selling it for a dealer

curdle *v by 1940s* To offend; disgust: *"It curdles me" = "I loathe it"*—Life

curl someone's **hair** (or **toes**) *v phr by 1940s* To shock or appall •A somewhat earlier sense is "to injure; batter": *The prices here will curl your hair* [fr a supposed reaction to intense fear]

curlies *See* HAVE someone BY THE SHORT HAIRS

currency *See* SOFT MONEY

the **curse** *n phr by 1920s, and probably earlier* A woman's menstrual period; menstruation: *Is it any wonder that menstruation is commonly called "the curse"*—Saturday Review

curtain *See* BAMBOO CURTAIN, LACE-CURTAIN IRISH

curtain climber *n phr by 1960s* A baby or small child, esp one who is just learning to walk; =CRUMBCRUSHER, RUG APE

curtains *n late 1800s* Death; disaster; the bitter end: *It looked like curtains for Ezra then and there*—J Lilienthal [fr the final *curtain* of a show; or perhaps fr the crape *curtains* formerly hung by undertakers at the dead person's door]

curvaceous *adj by 1935* Having a generously formed female body; =BUILT LIKE A BRICK SHITHOUSE, STACKED

curve ball *n phr by 1940s* Something tricky and unexpected; a sly maneuver: *Barring another last-minute curve ball from. . . Frank Lorenzo, Peter V Ueberroth is expected to win the battle for Eastern Airlines*—Associated Press

cush (KŏoSH) *n late 1900s* Money; cash: *They've put up their good cush to send me on tour*—H McHugh [probably fr *cash*]

cushion 1 *n by 1940s* One of the bases in baseball; =BAG **2** *n by 1950s* Anything, esp money, kept as a safeguard against hard times: *He kept one bank account just as a cushion*
See the KEYSTONE, WHOOPEE CUSHION

the **cushions** *n phr hoboes about 1910* A passenger coach or train; first-class train travel

cushy (KŏoSH ee) *British by 1915* **1** *adj* Easy; easeful; supplying comfort and pleasure: *I landed a cushy post, a soft sinecure at the foundation* **2** *adj* Fancy; luxurious; =HIGHFALUTIN, POSH: *I may not know a lot of cushy words*—Budd Schulberg [perhaps fr Hindi *khush,* "pleasure" or Romany *kushto,* "good," or perhaps fr a shortening of *cushiony*]

cuspy *adj 1980s computer* Neat and clean; elegant; efficiently designed [fr *commonly used system program,* a program designed for wide use and typically with a useful simplicity]

cuss *n by 1775* A man; fellow; =GUY •Most use since the 1860s [a shortening of *customer*; or perhaps "one who *curses*"]

customer *n by 1580s* A person; =COOKIE •The word has a tinge of disapproval: *a tough customer/ She's a shrewd customer* [perhaps an expansion of *cuss*]

cut 1 *v British university by 1794* To absent oneself from without permission or legitimate excuse: *She cut choir practice twice/ to cut class* **2** *n*: *Anybody with more than four cuts flunks* **3** *n early 1900s* A share or portion, esp of criminal or gambling profits **4** *v*: *They cut the million eight ways* **5** *v by 1920s* To dilute something, esp whiskey or narcotics: *They cut the pure stuff before they sell it on the street* **6** *adj*: *cut whiskey/ heavily cut cocaine* **7** *v by 1865* To shorten a movie, book, manuscript, etc **8** *n*: *How much of a cut did you make?* **9** *adj*: *a brutally cut film/ a cut version* **10** *v by 1913* To edit a film or other script **11** *n*: *Welles had surrendered the right of final cut in his contract*—New York Review of Books **12** *v movies by 1913* To recur to a scene shown before •The dated form is *cut back*: *Cut back to Jazz at Lincoln Center*—Nation **13** *v by 1582* To injure someone with an insult or sarcasm: *That crack really cut me* **14** *n*: *What a nasty cut she gave me* **15** *v by 1634* To ignore someone pointedly, esp an acquaintance: *Next time I saw him I cut him* **16** *n*: *That wasn't a snub, it was a cut* **17** *v by 1880s* To remove someone from a team, cast, group, etc •The date reflects cowboy use for removing some cattle from a herd: *I'll be happy if Coach doesn't cut me* **18** *n*: *I made the cut!* **19** *v* (also **cut it, cut it out**) *by 1859* To stop doing something; desist •Usu an irritated command: *Cut the crap, Martinez*—W E B Griffin **20** *v by 1612* To leave; depart: *Let's cut. . . We ain't no more than just time, providing we step lively*—W Henry **21** *v by 1855 v* To speed; =BARREL: *. . . and "cut" about the streets like Tom Thumb's coach*—G M Musgrave **22** *n by 1940s* A turn; time; =CRACK, SHOT: *Have a cut at it yourself* **23** *v baseball by 1940s* To swing at the ball **24** *n*: *What a thunderous cut that was!* **25** *v by 1880s* To outdo someone; best; surpass: *Lydia Lunch, who I feel cuts Yoko on every possible level*—Village Voice **26** *v black by 1940s fr jazz musicians* To do something well; =GROOVE **27** *v by 1937* To make a phonograph record, CD, or tape recording; record: *He cut a couple of demos yesterday* **28** *n 1930s* A phonograph record or side, or a separate band on a record: *Osmond will perform cuts from "Donny Osmond"*—Milwaukee Journal **29** *n by 1990s* An opinion or interpretation; viewpoint; =SLANT, TAKE: *I got a different cut from an American general*—TV program *Roundtable*

the cut *See* MAKE THE CUT

cut a (kut AY) *See* CUT ASS

cut a beef *v phr underworld about 1900* To complain; =BEEF, BITCH

cut someone **a break** *v phr by 1970s* To give someone special favor: *He petitioned. . . Judge Michael Wallace to cut me a break*—Philadelphia Journal

cut (or **crack**) **a deal** *v phr by 1970s* To make or conclude an arrangement; transact an agreement: *Doesn't it make more sense to cut a deal with the Soviets?*—Philadelphia Journal/ *The city has done its entrepreneurial turn by cutting a deal with the Republicans in which it must approve all souvenirs*—New Republic

◁**cut a fart**▷ *See* LAY A FART

cut a figure *v phr by 1759* To be important; be imposing; make an impression: *I cut quite a figure in this town, but nowhere else*

cut and dried (or **dry**) *adj phr by 1710* Regular, predictable, and uninteresting; pro forma

cut-and-paste *modifier* Crude; improvised; haphazard; =SLAPDASH: *. . . a slapdash, cut-and-paste feel*—Jack Garner

cut and run *v phr by 1704* To leave; depart, esp hastily: *If you hear a whistle, cut and run at once* [fr the *cutting* of the anchor cable in the swift departure of a ship]

◁**cut** someone **a new asshole**▷ *v phr by 1970s* To rebuke someone harshly; reprimand severely; =REAM

◁**cut ass** (or **a**)▷ *v phr 1950s* To leave; depart; =HAUL ASS, SHAG ASS

cut a take 1 *v phr 1930s recording industry* To record a performance, song, number, etc **2** *v phr 1950s cool talk* To explain something carefully

cutback *n by 1940s* A reduction or decrease: *no cutback in prices*

cut back *v phr by 1940s* To reduce; decrease: *They'll cut back the interest rate*

cut bait *v phr by 1970s* To cease some activity; stop; discontinue: *Westway Trial: Lawyers Cut Bait*—Village Voice
See FISH OR CUT BAIT

cut didoes (DĪ dohz) *v phr by 1807* To frivol and frolic; =HORSE AROUND [origin uncertain; the notion of reference to the notorious behavior of the crew of HMS *Dido* has no confirmation]

cut someone or something **down to size** *v phr by 1930s* To counter and neutralize; deflate: *A few words from the judge cut him down to size*

cute 1 *adj by 1730s* Shrewd; sly; tricky **2** *adj by 1950s* Disrespectfully frivolous; =SMART-ASS: *Don't be cute with me, you slimy pimp*

cute as a bug's ear (or **as a button**) *adj phr* first form *by 1920s*, second *by 1940s* Very attractive; pretty; =DISHY

cuter or **kyuet** or **quetor** (KYoo tər) *n by middle 1920s* A quarter; 25-cent piece

the cutes *by 1940s* **1** *n phr* Arch and simpering behavior; kittenish ways: *Lina began flapping her dress to give herself air. Then she got the cutes and asked if that was allowed*—James M Cain/ *Some of the musical background, like the narration, also suffers from the cutes*—New York Times **2** *n phr* The tendency or habit of constant joking; tasteless frivolity: *. . . born with an incurable case of the cutes*—Time

cutesey or **cutesie** *by 1970s* **1** *adj* Designedly attractive in a pert way; overtly charming •One dictionary shows a 1914 date, but this seems isolated: *. . . and the children cutesy freaks*—Judith Crist/ *. . . Dutch doors. . . partly ivy-covered, and mostly cutesy*—Stan Cutler **2** *n*: *The author oversimplifies everything and gets carried away with his own cutesies*—Playboy

cutesy-poo or **cutesy-pie** *adj* Designedly arch and simpering to a nauseating degree: *. . . saying anything narsty about so cutesy-poo an endeavor*—Judith Crist/ *McWilliams writes in a cloying cutesy-pie style*—New Republic

cutie or **cutey** or **cuty 1** *n by 1917* A person or thing that is charming, attractive, clever, etc: *I'm no beauty, but am counted a cutie* **2** *n by 1920s* A person who is shrewd, deceptive, and wily: *Watching a cutey spar with an ordinary dull fighter*—A J Liebling

cutie-pie *n by 1940s* A very attractive person, esp a doll-like woman: *. . . my new cutie pies*—Dan Jenkins

cut in 1 *v phr* by 1819 To intrude into a conversation or discussion; =BARGE IN **2** *v phr* by 1896 To take someone's partner away while dancing

cut-in *n* by 1931 The right to share something: *We've each got a cut-in on the profits*—Jerome Weidman

cut someone **in** *v phr* by 1930s To award someone a share, esp of winnings, loot, etc: *They cut me in for 25 percent of the take*

cut it *v phr* jazz musicians by 1960 To achieve or finish something; succeed; =HACK IT: *They've been warned that a string group won't cut it with jazz fans*—Peter Occhiogrosso/ *But I think that you probably could cut it*—National Review

cut it up *v phr* by 1950s To analyze and discuss something; take a close look: *Come on, guys, cut it up*—Rick Morgan

cut something **loose** *v phr* black by 1970s To give something up; free oneself from something: *I want to save some bread so I can cut the hustling thing loose altogether*—New York Magazine

cut one's **losses** *v phr* To make the best compromise in a losing siuation; salvage or extricate at least something: *You'd better sell right now and cut your losses*

cut no ice (or **smoke**) *v phr* by 1895 To have no influence or effect; make no difference: *His Nobel Prize don't cut no ice with me/ . . . but that doesn't cut any smoke with the Gov*—New York Daily News

the **cut of** one's **jib** *n phr* fr nautical by 1790s One's general character and appearance

cut someone **off** *v phr* by 1970s To drive abruptly in front of someone in traffic: *He says she cut him off at the toll booth, so he shot her*

cut oneself **off at the knees** *v phr* by 1970s To disable oneself; =SHOOT oneself IN THE FOOT: *I don't want to cut myself off at the knees by giving figures*—Washingtonian

cut someone **off at the knees** *v phr* by 1970s To deflate or reduce someone, esp surprisingly; =TAKE someone DOWN A PEG: *. . . the nebbish with a disarming wit that could cut you off at the knees*—Philadelphia

cut-offs *n* by 1970s Pants, usu blue jeans, cut off above the knees and left to unravel

cut (or **turn**) **off** someone's **water** *v phr* by 1950s To subdue someone; deal decisively and damagingly with someone: *I just smiled sweetly and turned off his water*

'cutor or **cutor** (KYOO tər) *n* by 1920s A prosecuting attorney: *. . . beg the kid off with the US 'cutor*—Raymond Chandler

cut out 1 *v phr* by 1797 To leave; depart, esp hastily: *So you think you're cutting out? You're not leaving until I leave with you*—Tennessee Williams **2** *v phr* about 1900 To stop doing something; desist: *If you cut out the booze maybe it'll work*

cut-out *n* espionage by 1960s A person, business, etc, used to conceal the identity or purpose of a secret operation; =COVER: *The firm operated as a cut-out, or front, for the FBI's purchase*—Time/

. . . he can serve as your cut-out—Lawrence Sanders

cut out dolls (or **paper dolls**) *v phr* by 1940s To be insane; behave dementedly: *She has her cutting out paper dolls*—Raymond Chandler

cut one's **own throat** *v phr* by 1583 To ruin oneself; hoist oneself with one's own petard; =SHOOT oneself IN THE FOOT: *If you try to get him that way you'll cut your own throat*

cut someone's **papers** (or **orders**) *v phr* police & Army by 1970s To prepare and distribute official papers such as warrants, writs, assignment orders, etc: *They're still cutting her papers*—movie *The Gauntlet* [probably fr the *cutting*, perforation by typing, of a duplicating-machine stencil]

cut someone **some slack** *v phr* 1980s To stop pressuring or importuning someone; let someone be; *Clinton should lie low for a while, and the rest of us should cut him some slack*—National Public Radio news/ *I probably cut him more slack than I have with other guys*—Milwaukee Journal

cutter *See* CAKE-CUTTER, COOKIE-CUTTER, DAISY-CUTTER, FOG-CUTTER, PISS-CUTTER, RUG-CUTTER

cut the cheese *See* CHEESE

cut (or **cut up**) **the melon** (or **the pie**) *v phr* by 1930s To divide and share out receipts, profits, loot, etc

cut the mustard *v phr* by 1907 To succeed; be qualified; =CUT IT ●Very often in the negative: *. . . groups who have special vested interests. And that's not gonna cut the mustard*—Philadelphia [probably fr *cut*, "achieve," and *the mustard* in the earlier slang sense of "the genuine thing, best thing," perhaps based on the fact that *mustard* is hot, keen, and sharp, all of which mean "excellent"]

cut the (or **a**) **rug** *v phr* 1930s swing talk To dance, esp in jitterbug style

cutthroat *adj* by 1567 Very harsh and barbarous: *a cutthroat game/ cutthroat competition*

cutthroat defense *n phr* by 1990s A courtroom defense in which two counsels work against each other: *The two defense counsels were working in opposition to each other—a cutthroat defense, as it is known*—New Yorker

cut throats *v phr* 1990s To lower corporate costs by reducing the number of employees; downsize: *. . . new philosophy: cutting throats is the best way of cutting costs*—New York Times

cut to the chase *v phr* (also **go straight to dessert**) by 1990s To go to the essential matter; focus on what is most important: *It grows late, and we must cut to the chase, but further attention to the Blue Jays here is not out of place*—New Yorker/ *Want to write irresistible love letters? As you write, cut to the chase, broach the erotic. Share astonishingly intimate secrets*—Harper's/ *Let's go straight to dessert, Marco*—Carsten Stroud

cut two ways *See* WORK BOTH WAYS

cut up 1 *v phr* by 1837 To behave frivolously; be rowdyish; =HORSE AROUND **2** *v phr* underworld by 1930s To divide profits, loot, etc **3** *v phr* by 1759

To speak ill of; analyze maliciously; insult: *Or they can collectively "cut up" the girls they see around*—Sexual Behavior

cut-up 1 *n by 1880s* A prankster; practical joker; antic rogue: *Uncle is a cut-up, owner of all kinds of gimmicks* **2** *n by 1880s* An energetic and entertaining person: *. . . a great cut-up. He could dance a bit, sing better than average, and had a sense of comedy*—H R Hoyt **3** *adj by 1844* Upset; hurt; distressed: *She was pretty cut up about not getting a paper*—Richard Peck

cut up the touches (or **jackpots** or **pipes**) *v phr underworld by 1920s* To divide loot, spoils, etc, esp at a special meeting

cuty *See* CUTIE

cut Zs *See* COP ZS

◁**cuzzy**▷ *See* COOZ

CYA *See* COVER one's ASS

cyber- *combining word late 1980s* Having to do with computers and computer operations: *cybergroup, cybermuffin, cyberphobe, cybersex* [fr Greek *kyber*, "rudder"; used by the mathematician Norbert Wiener in 1948 about his work on automatic control]

cybercrat *n 1990s* A person in government who is becoming a powerful player on information-policy matters: *A new term, "cybercrat". . . is now a vicious epithet*—New Republic [fr *cyber-* plus bureau*crat*]

cyberfeelies *n 1990s* The computer-network equivalent of fondling and groping: *. . . a guy out to see how many cyberfeelies he can grab*—Washington Post

cybermuffin *n 1990s* A young man who frequents computer networks: *. . . wuss-o-rama New-Age computer stud hombre cybermuffin*—Dave Barry

cyberphobe *n by 1990* A person who does not like computers

cyberporn or **compu-smut** *n 1990s* Pornography on computer networks: *Last week it approved a ban on cyberporn. . .* —Macon Telegraph

cyberpunk 1 *n middle 1980s* A kind of science fiction, mode of discourse, set of attitudes, etc, that combine scientific interests, esp computers, with the punk ethos: *. . . pieced togather from cybernetics. . . and punk. Within this odd pairing lurks the essence of cyberpunk*—Time/ *Cyberpunk caters to the wish-fulfillment requirements of male teenagers*—New York Times **2** *n late 1980s* A person who admires computers, esp one who uses them recreationally

cyberpunkish *adj* Resembling or exemplifying cyberpunk: *The magazine's cyberpunkish design also exhibited plenty of attitude*—Vogue

cyber sleaze *n phr early 1990s* Pornography disseminated on computer networks

cyberslut *n early 1990s* A wanton woman dressed in futuristic garb: *Betsey Johnson's vinyl-clad cyberslut*—Elle

cyberspace *n by middle 1980s* The putative or apparent "space," be it mental, electronic, or "virtual," in which computer phenomena, operations, and experiences take place; in particular, the universe of computer networks [seemingly coined by the science-fiction writer William Gibson, and used in his 1986 book *Count Zero*]

cybertag *n early 1990s* A nickname used on the computer network: *You'll need a cybertag. Mine is "Dancer"*—Gary Trudeau

cyberthief *n by 1990s* A computer hacker who breaks the laws against entry into private databases, telephone networks, etc: *A Most-Wanted Cyberthief Is Caught in His Own Web*—New York Times

cyber-tweaker *n by 1990s* A devoted computer user; =COMPUTER NERD: *. . . techno-nerds and cyber-tweakers sporting pocket protectors. . .* —Sassy

the cycle *See* HIT FOR THE CYCLE

czar *n fr 1890s* A person appointed or elected to have great authority over a certain sport or other area; the commissioner of a sport or government department: *baseball czar/ czar of boxing/ drug czar* [fr the title of the Russian emperors; used as the nickname of T B Reed (died 1902), authoritarian Speaker of the House of Representatives]

czarina *n by 1990s* A female czar: *. . . the AIDS czar or czarina will probably work out of the White House*—Nation

D

D *n* A dollar
    See BIG D, TAKE A D, THREE D
DA (pronounced as separate letters) **1** *n* *by 1920s* District Attorney **2** *n* *by 1951* A ducktail haircut
daaa *See* TAH-DAH
dab *See* SMACK
dab hand *n* *phr* *British by 1828* An expert; a skilled person; an adept: *He is reportedly a dab hand at setting lofty prices*—New York Magazine [fr late 1600s *dab*, "an expert," of unknown origin]
dad **1** *n* *by 1950s* An old man •Used as a disrespectful term of address towards older men. The similar term *pop* is not similarly disrespectful: *Okay, dad, outta the way and you won't get hurt* **2** *n* *by 1670s* God •Used euphemistically as an element in various old-fashioned mild oaths like *dad-blamed*
    See HO-DAD
dad-blamed or **dad-blasted** *adj* (also **dag-blamed** or **dag-blasted**) *by 1840s* Wretched; accursed; =DARN: *Git outta my dad-blamed way*
dad (or dag) burn *interj* *by 1829* An exclamation of surprise, irritation, frustration, etc •A euphemism for *goddamn*: *Well, dad burn it, come on*
daddy **1** *n* *black by 1920s* A male lover, esp one who keeps a younger mistress; =SUGAR DADDY **2** *n* *by 1901* The most respected man in a field; cynosure; dean: *Gary Cooper, the daddy of all cowboys*
    See DISNEYLAND DADDY, HO-DAD, ZOO DADDY
Daddy-o or **daddy-o** *1940s bop talk* **1** *n* Man; old guy; =GUY •Used in addressing men, sometimes older men, respectfully and amiably **2** *n* An older male patron, esp of a young woman; =SUGAR DADDY: *. . . like a young beauty swept out of a small Nebraska town by some Hollywood Daddy-O. . .* —Douglas Coupland
daddy track *n* *phr* *by 1990s* An arrangement of work, working hours, etc, made by men who wish to spend more than the ordinary time with their children: *. . . the Daddy Track, about devoted dads voluntarily choosing to temper their career ambitions. . .* —Milwaukee Journal
daffy *adj* *by 1884* Crazy; =NUTS: *He tries to convince her that she is not daffy*—SJ Perelman [fr British dialect *daff*, "fool, simpleton"; *daffish* is attested fr the 15th century]
    See STIR-CRAZY
daffydill *n* *by 1930s* An insane person; =NUT: *Take your pick whether Cecil is a genius or a daffydill*—Damon Runyon

dag-blamed or **dag-blasted** *See* DAD-BLAMED
dag burn *See* DAD BURN
dagged *adj* Drunk
dagger *See* BULLDYKE
daggone *See* DOGGONE
dagnab *See* DOGGONE
◀**dago** or **Dago**▶ *by 1823* **1** *n* An Italian or person of Italian descent •First used chiefly of Hispanics; noted as "chiefly Italians" by 1900: *Hey, Fiorello, you're a dago*—Fiorello H LaGuardia **2** *adj* Italian **3** *n* The Italian language **4** *n* A person of Hispanic birth or descent [fr *Diego*, "James," used in the 17th century to mean "Spaniard"]
◀**dago (or Dago) bomb**▶ *n* *phr* *1930s* A white spherical firecracker
◀**dago (or Dago) red**▶ *n* *phr* *by 1906* Cheap red table wine, esp of Italian origin or type
dagwood *n* *by 1940s* A large thick sandwich of many ingredients [from *Dagwood* Bumstead, a comic-strip character who made tall and complex sandwiches]
dah *See* TAH-DAH
daisies *See* PUSH UP DAISIES
the daisies *n* *phr* *1940s baseball* The outfield
daisy **1** *n* *by 1757* A person or thing that is remarkable, wonderful, superior, etc; =DILLY, DOOZIE, HONEY: *My new car's a daisy* ◀**2**▶ *n* *about 1940* A male homosexual; =PANSY
daisy chain **1** *n* *phr* *by 1941* Sexual acts shared or partly shared by more than two people at the same time in the same place; group sex **2** *v* *phr* *by 1990s* To connect; link; chain: *Up to 8 EXP–16's may be daisy-chained together for a total of 128 differential inputs*—MetraByte Corp
daisy-cutter **1** *n* (also **daisy-clipper**) *baseball by 1866* A grounder or very low line drive **2** *n* *tennis by 1897* A very low tennis shot **3** *n* *by 1791* A horse that trots with its hooves near the ground **4** *n* *WWII Army* An antipersonnel bomb or mine that ejects shrapnel close to the ground
dally *See* DILLY-DALLY
the damage *n* *phr* *by 1755* The price; cost; esp, a bill at a restaurant or bar
damaged *adj* *by 1851* Drunk
◁**damaged (or used) goods**▷ *n* *phr* *by about 1910* A woman who is not a virgin: *Once they find out I have kids, they think of me as used goods. . .* —TV show Montel Williams
◁**dame**▷ *n* *by 1900* A woman; =BROAD, DOLL

damn *by 1770s* **1** *interj* (also **damn it**) An exclamation of disappointment, irritation, frustration, etc: *Damn, it's gone!* **2** *adj* (also **damned**) Cursed; accursed; wretched: *What do I do with this damned thing?* **3** *adv*: *You seem damn stupid all of a sudden* **4** *v* To execrate; condemn; curse: *Damn this dictionary!*—Henry Cecil Wyld
  See HOT DAMN

a **damn** *n phr by 1760* Nothing; very little; =A FUCK, A RAT'S ASS, A SHIT: *Oh, we don't give a damn for the whole state of Michigan; we're from O-hi-o*—college song
  See NOT GIVE A DAMN

damned *See* I'LL BE DAMNED

damned if you do and damned if you don't *adj phr by 1970s* Condemned, whatever decision one makes: *Investigating is delicate: Companies feel they're damned if they do, damned if they don't*—New York Times

damn right *adj* and *adv phr* (also **damn skippy, damn straight, damn tootin'**) *entry form by 1940s, probably much earlier* Certain; certainly: *Damn right I was mad, who wouldn't be?/ You're damn skippy. . . let's go for the best record in the league*—Milwaukee Journal/ *Damn straight we used cowboy logic, if that's what you want to call it*—Time
  See YOU'RE DAMN TOOTIN'

damper 1 *n by 1748* A person or thing that depresses, takes the edge off joy, chills one's enthusiasm, etc: *The news was a damper on our hopes* **2** *n by 1848* A cash register or till; cash drawer **3** *n* A bank or money depository; treasury: . . . *dropping bonds into the damper which are then sold to the public*—Westbrook Pegler

damper pad *n phr underworld by 1920s* A bankbook

damp rag *n phr by 1940s* A disappointment; a blighted hope: *That. . . was a little bit of a damp rag*—Washington Post

Dan *See* DAPPER DAN

dance *n street gang by 1940s* A fight between rival gangs; =RUMBLE: . . . *the kids have plenty of time for pushing a dance*—Collier's
  See GET THE LAST DANCE, GO INTO one's DANCE, RAIN DANCE, SONG AND DANCE, TAP DANCE

dance around *v phr by 1970s* To improvise, tergiversate, etc, in order to avoid a question or issue; =TAP DANCE: *Larson dances around the real issue of gun control*—Atlantic/ . . . *there's always an owner willing to cave in or dance around*—National Public Radio news

dance card *n phr by 1980s* A putative list of priorities, engagements, etc: *Kissinger's dance card that week included a party for Margaret Thatcher*—New Yorker/ *Suddenly, the Iraqi leader had maneuvered himself to the top of Mr. Clinton's dance card*—New York Times

dancehall *n prison by 1920s* A death-house or execution chamber; =DEATH ROW: *I'm layin' in the dance-hall when he sends me a lifeboat*—American Mercury [fr *dance*, "to die by hanging," attested by 1837]

dance off *v phr by 1930s* To die, esp by legal execution: *If you don't dance off up in Quentin*—Raymond Chandler

dance on air (or **on nothing**) *v phr first form by 1870s, second by about 1800* To die by hanging

dancer *n prizefight by 1940s* A boxer who spends most of his time and energy nimbly evading the opponent
  See BUBBLE-DANCER, DOLLY DANCER, GANDY DANCER, GO-GO GIRL

dancing *See* TOUCH DANCING

D and B *n phr by 1980s* A credit investigation or report: *Our salesman comes in with a $500,000 order. . . I run a D&B and find out the customer's in over his head*—Time [Initials of *Dun and Bradsreet*, a credit-rating firm]

dander *See* GET one's DANDER UP

dandy *by 1880s, very popular by 1900* **1** *n* A person or thing that is remarkable, wonderful, superior, etc ●Attested from 1784 in the form *the dandy*: *You should get one, it's a dandy* **2** *adj*: *a dandy idea* **3** *adv*: *He does it dandy/ We get on just dandy*
  See HOTSIE-TOTSIE, JIM-DANDY

dang *by 1840* **1** *interj* (also **dang it**) An exclamation of disappointment, irritation, frustration, etc: *Dang, we missed the Welk show* **2** *adj* (also **danged**) Wretched; nasty; accursed **3** *adv* Absolutely; extremely: *You looked dang silly/ "Purchase what the customer intends to buy?" "Dang right"*—Scott Turow [a euphemism for *damn*, which is regarded by some as taboo]

a **dang** *See* NOT GIVE A DAMN

danged *adj by 1870s* Wretched; accursed; =DAMN: *It can tell you almost anything, but the danged thing doesn't speak in English*—Bill Husted
  See I'LL BE DAMNED

dangle *n by 1980s* An unanswered question; a loose end: *And I guess the biggest dangle is how could a trained psychologist. . . possibly be an insane killer herself*—William Bayer

dangler *n circus by 1930s* A trapeze artist; =FLYER

dap 1 *adj black by about 1950* Stylish; well-dressed; dapper **2** *adj black by about 1950* Aware; up-to-date; =HEP: *You want somebody to know a man is sharp, is au reet, you say he's dap*—A Jazz Lexicon **3** *n 1930s students* A white person; =PADDY

dapper (or **fancy**) **Dan** *n phr by 1940s* An ostentatiously well-groomed man, usu one not inured to hard work: . . . *the fancy Dans, dressed fit to kill*—A Lomax

darb *n by 1915* A person or thing that is remarkable, wonderful, superior, etc; =LULU, PEACH [perhaps fr Ruby *Darby*, the name of an Oklahoma showgirl much admired by oil-drillers, who would praise a new gusher as a "Ruby Darby" or "a Darb"; perhaps fr *dab*, "an expert," since earlier *darb* meant "skilled, competent"]

darbies or **derbies** *n by 1673* Handcuffs [fr a form

of British usurer's bond called *Father Derby's* (or *Darby's*) bands, attested from 1592]

dark *adj* theater by 1916 Closed; not in operation: *Monday is a "dark" day at Heinz Hall*—New Yorker **See** IN THE DARK

dark horse by 1842 fr horse-racing **1** *n phr* A person or team, esp in sports or politics, that seems very unlikely to win but might nevertheless do so **2** *modifier*: *a dark-horse candidate/ dark-horse odds*

◄**dark meat**▶ by 1920s **1** *n phr* A black person, esp a woman, regarded solely as a sex partner **2** *n phr* A black person's body and genitals [fr the distinction between the *white meat* and *dark meat* of a roasted fowl, attested from the 1850s]

dark-thirty **See** OH-DARK-THIRTY

◄**darky**▶ *n* by 1775 A black person

darn or **dern** or **durn** by 1780s **1** *interj* (also **darn it** or **dern it** or **durn it**) An exclamation of disappointment, irritation, frustration, etc: *Darn, I've dropped my glockenspiel!* **2** *adj* (also **darned** or **darnfool** or **derned** or **durned**) Wretched; nasty; silly: *. . . sentimental songs, darnfool ditties, revival hymns*—Virgil Thompson **3** *adv*: *She was darn excited* [euphemism for *damn*, which is regarded by some as taboo; probably based on earlier *darnation*, "damnation," attested by 1798]

-darn- *infix* by 1918 Used for emphasis: *absodarnlutely*

a **darn** or a **dern** or a **durn** **See** NOT GIVE A DAMN

darned **See** I'LL BE DAMNED

darning needles **See** RAIN CATS AND DOGS

darn tootin' **See** YOU'RE DAMN TOOTIN'

darter **See** BLUE DARTER, JOE-DARTER

dash *n* by 1867 The dashboard of a car or other vehicle: *I keep a gun under the dash* **See** SLAPDASH

dash it or **dash it all** *v phr* by 1800 =DAMN, DARN ●Chiefly British use: *Dash it, old fellow, we're dished!*

dat or **DAT** (pronounced as separate letters) *n* 1970s Army A tank-crew member [fr *dumbass tanker*]

data highway or **dataway** *n phr* about 1993 The immense global telephone network that transmits voice, fax, computer, cable television, and other electronic communications; =INFOBAHN: *. . . what the new regime calls America's "data highway"*—Time/ *. . . the fusion of cable and telephone companies would result in the emergence of a robust dataway. . .* —New Yorker

data rape *n phr* early 1990s The electronic theft of private information: *. . . those powerful converter boxes will know your habits: Who would protect citizens from what has been called data rape?*—New Yorker [a pun on *date rape*]

date 1 *n* by 1885 An engagement or rendezvous, esp with a member of the other sex **2** *n* by 1925 A man or woman with whom one has an engagement or rendezvous: *He's her date for tonight* **3** *v* by 1902: *How many girls have you dated this week?* **See** BLIND DATE, CHEAP DATE, HEAVY DATE

date bait *n phr* 1940s teenagers A popular and attractive young woman

date mate *n phr* 1940s teenagers One's partner on a social rendezvous, esp a regular partner: *. . . finds himself a date mate who'll wait to be dated*—S J Daly

date someone **up** *v phr* To schedule a social engagement or rendezvous with someone

day **See** EAGLE DAY, HAVE A FIELD DAY, MAKE MY DAY, MOTHER'S DAY, NINETY-DAY WONDER, NOT GIVE someone THE TIME OF DAY, PUNK DAY

day-glo *adj* by 1950s Blatantly gaudy; cheaply flashy: *. . . smoldering pageant turns totally day-glo*—Village Voice/ *. . . plenty of sequins and day-glo fur*—Rolling Stone/ *. . . day-glo glamor*—Us [fr the trademark of a brand of paint that makes things glow under a black light and produces lurid, psychedelic color effects]

a **day late and a dollar (**or **dime) short** *adj phr* by 1990s Inadequate; overdue and lacking; too little too late: *Yankee traders will be a day late and a dollar short: Visa cards are already welcome in Saigon*—New Republic/ *Clinton's attempt to explain Whitewater is several days late and a dollar short*—Howard Fineman/ *"Dante Jones is a day late and a dime short," Butkus said when the linebacker failed to cover Sterling Sharpe*—Milwaukee Journal

daylight 1 *n* by 1820 A clear and open space between two things, horses, players, boats, etc: *Daylight began to open between the two leaders/ He went into the line, but couldn't find any daylight* **2** *v* by 1970s To work at a second job during the day: *. . . who is daylighting in an ad agency as a producer of commercials*—Playboy [second sense based on *moonlight*] **See** PUT DAYLIGHT BETWEEN

the **daylights** or the **living daylights** **See** BEAT THE SHIT OUT OF someone or something

◄the **day the eagle shits**▶ (or **screams**) *n phr* armed forces & theater by 1940s Payday [fr the eagle as symbol of the US government]

dazzle **See** RAZZLE-DAZZLE

dazzle someone **with footwork** *v phr* by 1980s To impress someone with facile virtuosity: *Hailey's 10th novel is a literary example of an old boxing adage: If you don't have the power, dazzle them with footwork*—New York Times

DDT (pronounced as separate letters) *interj* 1940s teenagers An exclamation of severe and abrupt rejection; =GET LOST, DROP DEAD: *In Chicago last year's "DDT" (drop dead twice) is still fashionable*—Time

dead 1 *adj* by 1813 Very tired; =BEAT, POOPED **2** *adj* by 1902 Not operating; not startable: *Damn battery's dead* **3** *adj* by 1400 Ruined; destroyed; =FINISHED, KAPUT: *As far as another chance goes, I'm dead/ The ERA's dead again* **4** *adj* by 1000 Dull; tedious and uninteresting: *another dead sermon* **5** *adj* by 1530 Lacking brilliance and overtones; flat; dull: *The trumpets sounded dead* **6** *adj* by 1589 Absolute; assured: *It's a dead certainty* *he'll run again* **7** *adv* by 1589 Extremely; very much: *I'm dead broke/dead set against it* **8** *n post office* by 1950s A letter or package that can neither be delivered nor returned •*Dead letter* in this sense is attested from 1703 [the sense "absolute, assured, certain" probably developed fr expressions like Middle English *ded oppressed,* "completely overcome," 16th-century *dead drunk,* and others suggesting the inertness of death; when inertness suggested fixedness, unchangingness, certainty, etc, the term took on these present senses]

   See DROP DEAD, KNOCK someone DEAD, NOT BE CAUGHT DEAD, STONE DEAD, STOP someone or something DEAD IN someone's or something's TRACKS

dead air *n phr* broadcasting by 1950s A sudden and undesirable silence

dead as a dodo (or **doornail**) *adj phr* first form by 1904, second by 1350 Absolutely lifeless; entirely hopeless •Doornail form fr 1300s: *The Philadelphia Bulletin is dead, dead as a doornail*—Philadelphia

◁**deadass**▷ by 1950s **1** *n* A stupid, boring person; an absolute dullard: *Get some action going among these deadasses in the loony bin*—Tom Wolfe **2** *adj*: *There are so many deadass people out there, boring each other to death*—San Francisco **3** *adv* Completely; totally: *You're deadass wrong when you say I got nothing to go on*—William Brashler

   See GET OFF one's ASS

deadbeat by 1863 **1** *n* A person who habitually begs or gets money from others, does not pay his or her debts, etc; =MOOCHER, SCHNORRER: *. . . a chance to demand immediate payment if the clerk looks like a deadbeat*—Time **2** *v* To sponge, loaf, etc: *Living off interest is not exactly deadbeating* [fr *dead,* "complete, completely" and *beat,* "sponger"]

dead beat *adj phr* by 1821 Completely exhausted: *My poor ass is draggin' and I'm dead beat*

deadbeat dad (or **daddy**) *n phr* by 1990s A man who is delinquent in paying child support awards: *The champion deadbeat dad of all owes over $500,000*

dead broke by 1842 *adj phr* Totally without money; destitute

dead cat *n phr* circus by 1930s A lion, tiger, etc, that does not perform but is only exhibited

dead-cat bounce *n phr* stock market by 1990s A tiny rise or recovery after a decline: *Economists are arguing fiercely over whether it is a solid long-term recovery or just a dead-cat bounce*—The Atlantic [fr a Wall Street saying that even a *dead cat* will bounce a little if you drop it from a high building]

dead center *n phr* by 1920s A point at which nothing is happening: *Let's try to get this negotiation off dead center*

a **dead cert** or **dead cinch** *n phr* first form fr horse-racing by 1889, second fr cowboys by 1893 A certainty; a foregone conclusion; =SURE THING: *Given Mamet's Shavian morality, it was a dead cert that one of his heroes would wind up in Hell. . .* —New Yorker/ *Just why a dead cinch should be the*

securest of any, I confess I do not know—Brander Matthews

dead drunk *adj phr* by 1602 Very drunk

dead duck (or **pigeon**) *n phr* by 1844 A person or thing that is ruined; =a GONER, GONE GOOSE: *Just one more little push and she was a dead duck*—Changes/ *Unless somebody would start this mob to the sugar bowl, I was a dead pigeon*—Max Shulman

deadfanny *modifier* Dull; stupid •A sort of euphemism for *deadass*: *. . . the hilariously deadpan, deadfanny fall guy*—Newsweek

dead-fish *modifier* by 1980s Limp; lifeless; unresponsive: *This yacht gives no sensory return. It's like getting a dead-fish handshake*

dead from the neck up *adj phr* by 1920s Stupid; dull; =KLUTZY

dead giveaway *n phr* by 1882 An unmistakable and definitive clue: *His blushing was a dead giveaway*

deadhead **1** *n* by 1841 A nonpaying spectator at a game, show, etc; =FREELOADER **2** *n* railroad by 1869 A nonpaying passenger **3** *n* by 1911 A train, bus, tractor truck, etc, carrying no passengers or freight, usu returning from a paying trip **4** *modifier*: *a deadhead cab/deadhead freight train* **5** *v*: *I'll deadhead your hack back to the garage* **6** *n* by 1950s A stupid person; an incompetent; =KLUTZ **7** *n* by 1940s An extremely boring person

Deadhead *n* by 1970s A devotee of the rock-and-roll group The Grateful Dead: *Tipper Gore, Deadhead and wife of Vice President Al Gore. . .* —Milwaukee Journal

dead heat *n phr* horse-racing by 1796 A tied race, contest, etc: *The election ended in a dead heat* [fr *dead,* "absolute, total, thorough," related to the finality of death, and *heat,* "a single course of a race," related either to a single firing or heating of a mass of metal, or to the heating of the body in running, or to both]

dead horse *See* BEAT A DEAD HORSE

dead hour *n phr* college students about 1920 A college period during which one has no class: *By dead hour I didn't mean Professor Chapman's class, only that I had no class at all at 9*

dead in the water *adj phr* Unable to move; stalled; defunct: *Right now, the economy is dead in the water, with 10.8 percent unemployment*—New York Times/ *Once I saw you, you were dead in the water*—TV movie The Lost Honor of Kathryn Beck [fr the image of a disabled ship, unable to proceed]

dead letter *n phr* by 1663 A matter no longer of concern or currency; a bygone issue

deadlights *n* by 1877 The eyes [fr the heavy glass set in a ship's hull to admit light]

deadly **1** *adv* by 1300 Extremely: *She is deadly serious about it* **2** *adj* by 1300 Boring; extremely tedious; dull as death itself: *I came prepared for a long and deadly meeting* **3** *adj* 1940s swing talk Excellent; admirable; =COOL

dead man's hand *n phr* poker fr late 1800s A

hand containing a pair of aces and a pair of eights [fr the tradition that Wild Bill Hickock held such a hand when Jack McCall shot him in 1876]

dead man switch *n phr* *railroad* A throttle control on a train or other vehicle that automatically goes to the "stop" position if not gripped and held

dead meat *n phr* *by 1860s* A corpse: *We don't believe in geography, teacher. Say one more word and you're dead meat*—Milwaukee Journal/ *But tell that to Toddy and you're dead meat*—Douglas Coupland

deadneck *n* *by 1930s* A stupid person; dullard: *They were awake and lively; they weren't deadnecks*—James T Farrell [probably fr the expression *dead from the neck up*]

dead nut *adj phr* *by 1980s* Exactly right; precisely as desired; [*Dead nuts* in a similar sense is attested at about the same time. Both *dead on* and *dead nuts on* are attested as meaning "having complete mastery over; sure hand at" in 1871]

dead-on *adj* *marksmen* *by 1889* Exactly right; =DEAD NUT: *One reason for the dead-on quality is the way the experiences of the Buchmans parallel. . . the lives of its creators*—Milwaukee Journal

dead on arrival *adj phr* *by 1980s* Invalid and rejected: *The President's budget was dead on arrival even before it got to Congress*

dead one *n phr* *by 1904* A dull, ineffective person; =DULL TOOL

deadpan *by 1930s* **1** *n* An expressionless face; =POKER FACE **2** *n* A person with an expressionless face: *Buster Keaton and Fred Allen were classic deadpans* **3** *v*: *With kids packing his audiences, he deadpanned "I promise to lower the voting age to 6"*—Newsweek **4** *adj*: *. . . my wife's New York ironies or her deadpan humor*—New York Times/ *This is known as the deadpan system of prevarication*—AJ Liebling

dead pigeon *See* DEAD DUCK

dead president *n phr* *by 1950s* Any US banknote [fr the fact that banknotes show portraits of US presidents]

dead ringer *n phr* *by 1891* An exact duplicate, esp a person who is the double of another: *He was such a dead ringer for my ex-boss*—Jerome Weidman [fr *dead*, "precise, exact," and *ring in*, "substitute, esp fraudulently," an early–19th-century slang term for gambling]

dead sexy *adj phr* *1990s* *students* Very attractive; =SEXY

dead soldier (or marine) 1 *n phr* *by 1913* An empty or emptied bottle, esp a liquor bottle •*Dead man* in the same sense is attested from 1738 **2** *n phr* *about 1920* Food or plates of food only partially eaten: *. . . on the way to the kitchen with the dead soldiers, or leftovers*—Louis Armstrong

deadsville *adj* *by 1970s* Dull; boring: *. . . the young people who always felt that cruises were deadsville*—Newsweek

dead (or bang) to rights *adv phr* *by 1859* With no possibility of escape or evasion; in flagrante delic-

to; redhanded: *. . . was caught "dead to rights" and now languishes in the city Bastille*—San Francisco City Argus

dead to the world 1 *adj phr* *by 1899* Fast asleep **2** *by 1926* *adj phr* Drunk, esp stuporous from drink

dead wagon *n phr* *by 1894* A hearse; vehicle for carrying dead bodies: *. . . calling the dead wagon for a nice ride downtown to the morgue*—H Johnson

dead white European male or **DWEM** *n phr* *about 1990* A type of person viewed as unjustly dominant in literature and culture, and hence archetypally despised by feminists, multiculturalists, etc: *The scientific method, largely produced by those hated demons, dead white European males*—Time/ *. . . challenged the established canon, which too often focused. . . on DWEM's (Dead White European Males)*—Los Angeles Timer

deadwood *by 1887* **1** *n* Unproductive persons; lazy and useless staff **2** *n* Anything useless, esp something useless that must be kept [fr the fact that *dead* or *rotten* wood does not produce much heat when burned]

deal 1 *v* *by early 1500s* To make arrangements, tradeoffs, sales, etc; =WHEEL AND DEAL: *Sophie did all the dealing there*—Nelson Algren **2** *v* *narcotics* *by 1920s* To sell narcotics; be a peddler **3** *v* *baseball* *by 1970s* To pitch a baseball •In the game of hurling, *deal*, "throw the ball", is attested by 1602: *The big lefthander deals a smoker* **4** *n* *by 1860s* A usu secret arrangement between politicians, rulers, business executives, etc: *He made a deal with the Republicans. . . to suppress the charges*—R G Spivack **5** *n* *students* *by 1940* Situation; thing in hand or at issue; affair: *Hey, what's the deal here? My car's gone/ The deal is that I'm tired of this sorry farce*

See BIG DEAL, CRUMB THE DEAL, GOOD DEAL, MAKE A BIG PRODUCTION OUT OF something, **no big deal, not make deals, play with a full deck, raw deal, sweetheart deal**

deal someone **a poor deck** *v phr* *by 1970s* To treat someone cruelly and unjustly: *Take a thirty-year-old nurse. . . who's bitter and thinks she's been dealt a poor deck*—A T Fleming

dealer 1 *n* *gambling* *by 1950s* A person who makes a living from gambling, whether or not an actual dealer-out of cards •*Dealer*, "player who distributes the cards," is attested from 1600: *A bookmaker, who is known as a dealer in refined usage*—T Betts **2** *n* *by 1950s* A person involved actively and aggressively in a range of negotiations, trades, purchases, etc; =WHEELER-DEALER **3** *n* *narcotics* *by 1920s* A person who sells narcotics; peddler; =CONNECTION, PUSHER: *The "dealer" (not "pusher") is the man who sells all this*—New York Times

See JUICE DEALER

deal someone **in** *v phr* *by 1940s* To make someone a participant; let someone share: *He heard we were going and said deal him in*

◁**deal in coal**▷ black by 1930s **1** **v phr** To mix and consort with black persons when one is not black oneself **2** **v phr** To associate with very dark-skinned black persons

dealing *See* DOUBLE-DEALING

deal with a full deck *See* PLAY WITH A FULL DECK

deaner *See* DEEMER

deano *n* underworld A month [perhaps fr *deaner, deemer,* etc, because a month is about as much of a year as a dime is of a dollar]

dearie *n* by 1888 Dear person; cherished one •A somewhat vulgar term of address used chiefly by women: *If you wore it you can't return it, dearie*

Dear John 1 *n phr* fr WWII armed forces A letter or other means of informing a fiancé, spouse, boyfriend, etc, that one is breaking off the relationship **2** *modifier*: *Dear-John letter*

death *See* LOOK LIKE DEATH WARMED OVER, SUDDEN DEATH

death metal *n phr* by 1980s A style of rock and roll music

death on something or someone *adj phr* by 1839 Very effective against something or someone; fatal to something or someone •Another nearly contemporary sense was "fond of; addicted to": *The Senator is death on any suggestions of compromise*

death row *n phr* by 1940s The part of a prison housing convicts condemned to death; =DANCEHALL

death warmed over *See* LOOK LIKE DEATH WARMED OVER

deb 1 *n* by 1920 A debutante **2** *n* 1940s street gang A member of a girl's street gang: *The Assassins. . . were organized with sub-gangs of. . . "debs"*—New York Times

◁**de-ball**▷ *See* DE-NUT

debunk *n* by 1923 To clear away lies, exaggerations, vanities, etc: *The author neither glorifies nor debunks*—Saturday Review [coined by W W Woodward in a book published in 1923]

decaf *n* by 1980s Decaffeinated coffee; =UNLEADED COFFEE

decaffeinated *adj* by 1990s Inauthentic; enfeebled •Decaffeinization of coffee dates from the 1920s: *Dress like Hemingway, but confine yourself to drinking Lite: This decaffeinated style is horrible*—Vanity Fair

Decatur *See* EIGHTER FROM DECATUR

deceivers *See* FALSIES

deck 1 *n* by 1853 The roof of a railroad car **2** *n* narcotics by 1922 A package of narcotics; portion of a drug, esp three grains of heroin; =BAG: . . . *a deck of nose candy for sale*—J Evans **3** *n* by 1940s A package of cigarettes **4** *v* by 1940s To knock someone down, esp with the fist; =FLOOR: *Remember that guy I decked in the restaurant?*—Lawrence Sanders **5** *n* skateboarders by 1990s A skateboard
See COLD DECK, DEAL someone A POOR DECK, HIT THE DECK, ON DECK, PLAY WITH A FULL DECK, WET DECK

decker *See* JOKER

decks awash by 1940s *adj phr* Drunk

decode *v* by 1950s Explain: *Hans, will you please decode that?*

decoder ring *n phr* by 1990s A ring that can decode secret messages •Radio programs of the 1930s and 40s offered secret *decoder rings* to their juvenile listeners, upon the submission of a box-top and a little money: *It would take effortful misconstruction, if not a secret decoder ring, to read 'apartheid is dead' into those sentences*—Nation

decompress *v* about 1970 To be relieved of stress; regain equilibrium; relax; =LAY BACK: *He'll be whisked away to some undisclosed place where he can decompress*—Rocky Mountain News [fr the gradual lowering of atmospheric pressure as one returns from a deep underwater dive]

decruit *v* by 1990s To discharge from a job; terminate employment; =CAN, FIRE: . . . *and when you're decruited, you're fired*—Los Angeles Times

deduck (DEE duck) *n* by 1950s A deduction, esp from one's taxable income: *more deducks or we're dead ducks*

deejay *See* DISC JOCKEY

deek *n* by 1920s A detective; =DICK

deely bopper or **deely bobber** or **beely bopper** *n phr* about 1975 A small hat equipped with bobbing wire antennas like those of an insect or some extraterrestrial creature: . . . *a decor of remaindered Deely Bobbers and airsick bags*—Newsweek

deemer or **dimmer** or **deener** about 1910 **1** *n* A dime **2** *n* A niggardly tip **3** *n* A person who gives an insufficient tip; =CHEAPSKATE **4** *n* Ten [fr *dime,* perhaps influenced by *deaner,* earlier British tramps' term for "shilling"]

deep *adj* by 1980s Copious, esp well-supplied with good athletes: *They may not be very deep on the bench, but they're. . . smart*—Westword/ *Fudgie's set was deep, and fifty people showed up. . .* —Buzz
See KNEE DEEP

deep doo-doo (or **foo-foo**) *n phr* by 1980s Serious trouble; =DEEP SHIT: *Deep Doo-Doo or Shallow?*—New Republic/ . . . *you're in a bigger paradigm, and if you break that you're in deep foo-foo*—Wisconsin State Journal

deep end *See* GO OFF THE DEEP END, JUMP OFF THE DEEP END

deep freeze *See* IN COLD STORAGE

deepie or **depthie** *n* 1950s A three-dimensional movie: *The deepies released so far have been gimmick pictures*—Associated Press

deep pocket by 1951 **1** *n phr* Wealth; available riches and financial security: *He felt more comfortable with the deepest pocket available*—Wall Street Journal/ . . . *a deep pocket, that of an insurance company*—New York Times **2** *modifier*: *No matter what fathers (deep-pocket lads) and schoolteachers (wardens) may think of current slang, to teenagers it is real George all the way*—Newsweek

deep pockets *n phr* Sources of much money; rich

persons: *. . . why should she waste time with a turd-kicker like him when there are so many other applicants with deep pockets*—Lawrence Sanders/ *. . . greater news-gathering assets than CNN and deeper pockets to offset losses*—Time

deepsea turkey *n phr* WWII armed forces Salmon

◁**deep shit**▷ (or **trouble**) *n phr* by 1972 Very serious trouble: *If they do that there'll be deep shit: He was in deep shit with Big Lou*—Rolling Stone

deep six 1 *n phr* underworld by 1920s A grave **2** *v phr* nautical by 1940s To discard; jettison; throw overboard: *One White House disposal crew even unblushingly planned to deep six a file in the Potomac*—Jack Anderson/ *If any publication is deep-sixed, it will almost certainly be "The Car Book"*—Mother Jones [probably fr the combined notions of a grave as *six feet deep* and a fathom as six feet in *depth*]
See GIVE something THE DEEP SIX

deep-think by 1963 **1** *n* Profound intellectuality •Used ironically: *a good example of university deep-think* **2** *modifier*: *do some deep-think social criticism* [probably based on *goodthink, crimethink,* and other terms coined by George Orwell in *Nineteen Eighty-Four*]

deep throat *n phr* 1974 An important source of secret information: *The real "deep throat" of the rumors was someone believed to be peripherally connected with Sony or Columbia*—Esquire [fr the name of a popular 1973 pornographic film, where the reference was to fellatio, applied to the prime source of secret information in the Watergate affair, where the reference was to copiousness of speech]

deep water *See* IN DEEP WATER

def or **deaf** *adj* black by 1983 Excellent; wonderful; =COOL, RAD: *She is really def*—UCLA Slang/ *He's got a def girlfriend*—Delcastle Dictionary of Slang [origin uncertain; perhaps fr Black English (Jamaican) pronunciation of *death*, where the semantics would resemble those of *killer, murder,* etc; certainly interpreted by many as a shortening of *definite*]

defense *See* NICKEL DEFENSE

defi or **defy** (DEE fi) *n fr* late 1880s Defiance; notice of act of defiance •Use has not been continuous since the first attestation in 1580: *. . . on a signboard, a defi to the On Leongs*—E Lavine [apparently fr French *défi*]

defuse *v* 1950s To ease or eliminate the danger of something menacing •Extension of the 1940s use "to remove the fuse from an unexploded bomb": *We might not stop it, but we might defuse it*

degree *See* THIRD DEGREE

déja vu all over again (DAY ZHAH VOO) *n phr* by 1970s The repetition of an old story; a recurrence: *Listening to Bob Dole carp about the Democrats is déja vu all over again*—New York Times [fr the French name for paramnesia or proamnesia, said to have been used by the baseball player and manager Yogi Berra in this reduplicated form; Mr Berra is a favorite putative source of such solecisms]

deke or **deke out** *v* Canadian hockey by 1950s To trick, esp by decoying; =FAKE someone OUT: *My friend, you deked me. You're not supposed to do that*—George V Higgins/ *. . . deked out all the troopers*—Carsten Stroud [fr *decoy*]

delay *See* GAPER'S BLOCK

delayering *n* early 1990s To eliminate one layer of management in the effort to reduce costs: *Delayering, the smart-bomb version of cutback*—Wisconsin State Journal

Delhi belly *n phr* by 1944 Diarrhea

deli or **delly** or **dellie** (DELL ee) by early 1950s **1** *n* A delicatessen: *a nice smelly deli* **2** *n* Delicatessen food: *Feel like deli for lunch?* **3** *modifier*: *deli food/ treat from the deli counter*

delight *See* BOILERMAKER'S DELIGHT

delish (dee LISH) *adj* Delicious

deliver or **deliver the goods** *v* or *v phr* by 1909 To perform successfully, esp after promising; =COME THROUGH: *It's a very tough assignment, but he thinks he can deliver/ He talks big, but can he deliver the goods?*

Dem or **Demo** first form by 1840, second by 1793 **1** *n* A Democrat **2** *adj*: *the Dem boss/ Demo congressmen*

dementoid 1980s teenagers **1** *n* A crazy person; =CUCKOO, NUT **2** *adj*: *. . . that was a totally dementoid movie*—Dictionary of Contemporary Slang

demi-rep *n* by 1750 A woman of somewhat shady reputation

demo (DEH moh) **1** *n* by 1950s A record or tape made to demonstrate the abilities of musicians, the quality of a song, etc: *Mark's got a good demo to pitch the new song with* **2** *n* by 1980s A computer disk or tape cassette made to demonstrate the abilities of a particular program: *I tried out their software demo before I bought their package* **3** *modifier*: *Let's try the demo disk* **4** *n* by 1936 A demonstration of protest or other conviction, esp by a large crowd with banners, etc: *a no-nukes demo*

demolition derby *n phr* by 1950s A scene or event of utter destruction and confusion: *Spectacular demolition derbies taking place in Russia, China, Cuba and Eastern Europe*—Nation [fr a chaotic entertainment where drivers crash their old cars into each other until only one, the winner, is still running]

Denmark *See* GO TO DENMARK

den mother *n phr* homosexuals by 1970s The head and sometimes provider or supporter of a group of male homosexuals, often an older man: *They had a sort of den mother. A middle-aged writer type who had given up the straight life*—Patrick Mann [sardonic adoption of the term fr *den mother*, the adult leader of a group of Cub Scouts]

◁**de-nut** or **de-ball**▷ *v* by 1940s To castrate

Denver boot *See* BOOT

depthie *See* DEEPIE

derail *v* by 1950s To throw off the proper course; wreck: *He managed to derail the proposal just before Christmas*—Time [The source term, "To leave or cause a car or engine to leave the railroad tracks" was adopted fr French by 1850]

derbies *See* DARBIES

Derbyville *n by 1950s* Louisville, Kentucky

dern *See* DARN

a **dern** *See* a DARN

derned *See* DARN

derrick 1 *n underworld by 1908* A shoplifter 2 *v baseball by 1943* To remove a player from a game: *Shotton derricked him in favor of Cookie Lavagetto*—Arthur Daley [fr the notion of lifting on a *derrick*; the contrivance commemorates a Tyburn hangman of that name, who practiced about 1600]

derriere or **derrière** (deh ree EHR) *n by 1774* The buttocks; rump: *. . . what Mr Irvine would no doubt delicately call our derrieres*—A E Gower/ *So gangway everybody, mother's off her derriere again*—American Home [fr French]

desert rat *n phr by 1907* A person who lives in or frequents the desert

designated something *n phr 1973* A person formally appointed to a certain function •The date indicates the first use in American League baseball of the *designated hitter*: *'Let us be your Designated Driver' campaign, to keep drunk drivers off the road*—Town Talk/ *Dornan, the Bush campaign's designated viper*—New Republic/ *Dinkins was being treated this spring as a designated loser*—New Yorker/ *. . . his minority whip and designated spitball thrower, Rep David Bonior of Michigan*—John J Farmer

designer 1 *n underworld by 1940s* A counterfeiter 2 *modifier 1960s* Of high quality; bearing a famous label: *Ah, designer ennui*—Village Voice

designer drug *n phr early 1980s* A synthesized narcotic, often of much higher potency than those produced from plants: *These new "designer drugs" or "super narcotics" are triply dangerous*—Good Housekeeping/ *Out here. . . urine testing has spawned the "designer" drug game. . .*—Village Voice

desk jockey *n phr by 1950s* An office worker: *Let some desk jockey in the home office envy you*—Hal Boyle

desperado *n gambling by 1950s* A person who gambles or borrows more than he can pay, and is certain to default, or who gambles with money he cannot afford to lose •Such money is called *desperate* or *scared*[fr earlier *desperado*, "outlaw, fugitive," literally "desperate man," fr Spanish]

detox (DEE tahx) *v narcotics* To free someone of a narcotics addiction; detoxify: *I jumped in and out of opium habits but eventually de-toxed for good*—Saturday Review/ *We can detox a heroin addict. . . in three weeks*—G Hoenig

deuce 1 *n by 1680* A two of playing cards 2 *n about 1920* Two dollars •Formerly, and still in Canada, a two-dollar bill 3 *n prison by 1950s* A two-year prison sentence: *. . . did a deuce together at Joliet*—Kansas City Confidential 4 *n 1940s street gang* A quitter; coward; petty thief 5 *n* (also

deuce coupe) *1940s hot rodders* A powerful or handsome specially prepared two-door car, esp a 1932 Ford [hot rod sense probably fr the *two* or *deuce* of 1932]

See ACEY-DEUCEY, FORTY-DEUCE

the **deuce** 1 *n phr by 1776* =the HELL 2 *n phr 1970s teenagers* Forty-second Street in New York City, mecca for many teenage runaways; =FORTY-DEUCE: *. . . in the peep shows and urinals and bars of the Deuce*—Village Voice

deuce and a half *n phr WWII Army* A two-and-a-half ton truck

deuce of clubs *n phr reformatory by 1950s* Both fists

deucer *n by 1950s* Two dollars; a two-dollar bill

deuce spot *by 1940s* 1 *n phr theater* The second act in a vaudeville show 2 *n phr* Second place in a contest

deuces wild *n phr baseball by 1980s* A team's situation with two men out, two strikes on the batter, and two men on base [fr the dealer's call in poker that all *deuces* may be valued as any other card]

Devil *See* RED

the **devil** *See* the HELL

devil-may-care *adj by 1790s* Reckless; cavalier: *a devil-may-care insouciance*

the **devil's bedposts** *n phr 1930s cardplayers* The four of clubs

devil's dozen *n phr by 1831* Thirteen; baker's dozen

devoon (də VŏoN) *adj 1940s teenagers* Divine; great: *"Devoon," said Jeanie languidly*—Billy Rose

dew *n 1960s narcotics* Marijuana

See MOUNTAIN DEW

dexie or **dexy** *n 1950s students* A tablet of Dexedrine, trademark of a brand of amphetamine: *You can take dexies, but you can get hooked on them*—Stephen Longstreet

dexter *n 1980s teenagers* A despised person who is a zealous student, computer user, etc; =CHIPHEAD, PROPELLER HEAD: *A dexter, that's your basic nerd, dork, or pud. . .*—North Jersey Herald & News

D-girl *n Hollywood by early 1990s* A young woman who aids in developing film scripts: *The job of a D-Girl is to talk on the phone a lot, take writers and directors out to breakfast, lunch and dinner, and attend all the screenings and parties*—Buzz

DI (pronounced as separate letters) *n Marine Corps by 1913* A drill instructor; non-commissioned officer in charge of recruits

dialed in *adj 1990s* Concentrating; focused: *It's hard to believe how fully she's dialed in*

dial something **out** *v phr by 1980s* To put firmly out of one's mind; ignore designedly: *All I had to do was concentrate on driving. I had a real excuse to dial it all out*—Sports Illustrated

diamond lane *n phr by 1990s* A highway lane designated for "high-occupancy" cars, esp for carpool cars: *The code in most states is that a carpooling vehicle can use the usually much faster diamond* *lane*—New Yorker [because the lane is designated by *diamond*-shaped signs on the pavement]

diamonds 1 *n* (also **black diamonds**) *by 1849* Coal: *. . . throwing diamonds in the firebox*—Casey Jones **2** *n* The testicles; =FAMILY JEWELS [the second sense reflects the idea "precious stones"]

diarrhea of the mouth *See* VERBAL DIARRHEA

dib 1 *n by 1829* A share, esp a share of money: *I ought to collect the kid's dib, too*—Dashiell Hammett **2** *n by 1930s* A dollar: *. . . fifty sweet dibs*—Samuel Hopkins Adams [probably fr *divvy*]

dibs 1 *n by 1807* Money: *How did you make your dibs?*—Raymond Chandler **2** *n* (also **dibs on**) A claim; a preemptive declaration: *It's mine, I said dibs first/ Dibs on the front seat* [perhaps fr *dibstones*, a children's game played with small bones or other counters]

dice *v 1950s* car-racing To jockey for position in a race: *I had no really sharp feeling about dicing with Parnelli*—Sports Afield [fr the notion of taking risks] *See* LOAD THE DICE, NO DICE, SLICE AND DICE FILM

dice house *n phr 1920s* cowboys A bunkhouse

dicer *n by 1890* A stiff hat, or a military helmet

dicey *adj 1940s* British Risky; perilous: *African investment is dicey*—Newsweek/ *Updike indulged in many dicey curlicues*—Commonweal/ *the dicey art of writing a farce*—New York Times

dick[1] or **deek** *by 1908* **1** *n* A detective **2** *n* Any police officer; =BULL [fr a shortening and altering of *detective*] *See* HARNESS BULL

◁**dick**[2]▷ **1** *n* British armed forces *by 1880s* The penis: *Now why don't you pull the weight down with your dick*—Robert B Parker **2** *v by 1940s* To do the sex act with; =SCREW: *If he went and dicked your twelve-year-old sister. . . he wouldn't tell you all about it*—Richard Merkin/ *He was dicking everything that wiggled*—Robert B Parker **3** *v* (also **dick around**) *by 1940s* To potter or meddle; play; =MESS, SCREW AROUND: *That's federal merchandise you're dicking with, right, marshal?*—W T Tyler/ *. . . still in the kitchen, dicking around with the sushi*—Armistead Maupin **4** *n by 1960s* A despised person; =PRICK: *You dick!*—Cameron Crowe **5** *n by 1950s* Nothing; =SQUAT, ZILCH, ZIPPO: *So far we got dick*—Carsten Stroud/ *Look, I didn't have any money, the Feds wouldn't do dick, nobody was helping out*—Vanity Fair [perhaps fr the nickname *Dick,* an instance of the widespread use of affectionate names for the genitals; perhaps fr earlier British *derrick,* "penis"; perhaps fr a dialect survival of Middle English *dighten,* "do the sex act with," in a locution like "he dight her," which would be pronounced "he dicked her"] *See* CLIPPED DICK, DOES A WOODEN HORSE HAVE A HICKORY DICK, DONKEY DICK, LIMP-DICK, STEP ON IT

Dick *See* BIG DICK, EVERY TOM, DICK, AND HARRY

◁**dick-brained**▷ *adj 1980s* Stupid; crazy; =NUTTY: *. . . coke-snorting super freaks, dick-brained Bob Marley tribute, and jive ooh-la-la*—Village Voice

◁**dickhead**▷ *n 1960s* A despised person; =BASTARD, PRICK: *Why would I possibly want to check out a dickhead like you?*—Richard Merkin/ *Drum the dickhead right out of the Republican party*—Stan Cutler

◁**dicklicker** or **dickey-licker**▷ *n by 1940s* A person who does fellatio, most often a male homosexual; =COCKSUCKER

◁**dickoid**▷ *n by 1990s* A despised person; =DICK, PRICK: *Dickoids like Martin who snap like wolverines on speed when they can't have a. . . window seat*—Douglas Coupland

◁**dick** someone **over (or around)**▷ *v phr 1980s* students To victimize and maltreat someone, sexually or otherwise; =FUCK OVER

dicty or **dickty** or **dictee** black *by 1926* **1** *adj* Stylish; wealthy; =CLASSY: *"Dicty" is high-class*—Stephen Longstreet **2** *adj* Haughty; snobbish; imperious: *These dickty jigs around here tries to smile*—Zora Neale Hurston **3** *n* A snob; aristocrat: *I don't want to be a dicty*—Mezz Mezzrow [origin unknown]

◁**dickwad** or **dickweed**▷ *n 1980s* A despised person; =JERK, PRICK, ASSHOLE: *All right, you dickweeds, we gotta talk*—Carsten Stroud

diddle 1 *v* (also **diddle around**) *by 1825* To waste time; idle; loaf **2** *v by 1806* To cheat; swindle; victimize; =SCAM **3** *v by 1980s* To alter illicitly or illegally; =COOK, DOCTOR: *But I thought Tommy must have diddled the phone records*—Scott Turow ◁**4**▷ *v by 1879* To do the sex act with or to; =SCREW: *Diddle your sister? Circle jerk?*—Douglas Coupland ◁**5**▷ *v* (also **diddle oneself**) *by 1950* To masturbate ◁**6**▷ *v by 1960* To insert a finger into a woman's vulva; =FINGERFUCK **6** *v 1980s* computer To correct or adjust a program in various small ways; =TWEAK: *I diddled the text editor to ring the bell before it deletes all your files*—Hacker's Dictionary [cheating sense said to be fr Jeremy Diddler, a character in the 1803 novel *Raising the Wind,* by James Kenney]

diddler *n* prison *by 1980s* A child molester; =SHORT EYES

diddle with *by 1940s* **1** *v phr* To handle casually, idly, or nervously; play with: *Stop diddling with the silverware* **2** *v phr* (also **diddle around with**) To interfere with; have to do with; =FOOL AROUND WITH: *Don't diddle with that button, it controls the power for the whole building*

diddly or **diddley** (Variations: **doo** or **eye** or **damn** or **poo** or **poop** or **shit** or **squat** or **squirt** or **whoop** may be added) *by 1960s* **1** *adj* Trivial; insignificant: *Tennis was a diddly sport back then*—Sports Illustrated/ *If you had a choice between. . . IBM or a diddly-squirt upstart*—Newsweek **2** *n* Nothing at all; very little; =ZILCH: *Rock critics don't mean diddley*—Rolling Stone/ *I don't know a diddly damn about theater*—Washingtonian/ *And Hannibal, he didn't do diddly-squat*—Pulpsmith/ *They take this very seriously. . . it isn't just "diddley-eye" to them*—Rocky Mountain News *See* NOT GIVE A DAMN, NOT KNOW BEANS

diddlybop *1960s students* **1** *v* To waste time; idle **2** *v* To do something pleasant and exciting **3** *n*: *They had a nice diddlybop at Gino's after work*

diddy bag *See* DITTY BAG

diddybop *See* DITTYBOP

diddybopper *See* DITTYBOPPER

didie *n by 1902* A baby's diaper

DIDO (DĪ doh) *1980s computer* **1** *sentence* A product can be no better than its constituents; esp, the validity of a computer's output cannot surpass the validity of the input; =GIGO **2** *modifier*: *The DIDO principle still applies to its contents*—Village Voice [fr the abbreviation of *dreck in, dreck out,* "shit in, shit out"]

didoes *See* CUT DIDOES

die 1 *v by 1596* To laugh uncontrollably: *When he puts a lampshade on his head you could die*—Max Shulman **2** *n by 1591* To desire very strongly: *She was dying to become Miss Pancake* **3** *v baseball by 1908* To be left on base at the end of an inning
See CROSS MY HEART, ROOT HOG OR DIE

died and gone to heaven *v phr by 1890* In paradisiacal euphoria; =HAPPY AS A CLAM: *Looking around bug-eyed like she'd died and gone to heaven*—Elmore Leonard

die for something *v phr by 1709* To have a very strong desire for something: *I'm dying for a drink/ Kids die for Sugar Glops*

die on someone *v phr by 1907* To die or cease to function, to the disadvantage of the speaker: *Damn motor died on me halfway up*

die on one's **feet** *v phr by 1940s* To become absolutely exhausted; carry on although one can hardly move

◁**diesel dyke**▷ *n phr* An aggressive, masculine lesbian; =BULLDYKE: *The women regarded themselves either as butches (alternatively diesel dykes and truck drivers) or femmes*—New Republic/ *. . . a man fighting with a diesel-dyke over a girl they both wanted*—Maledicta

die standing up *v phr show business by 1920s* To fail in a show or performance; =BOMB

die with one's **boots on** *v phr by 1873* To die while still active and vital

diff or **dif** *n fr middle 1800s* Difference: *What's the diff?*—Owen Johnson

difference *See* the SAME DIFFERENCE

the **difference** *n phr by 1903* A clear advantage; something that gives an advantage, esp a gun
See CARRY THE DIFFERENCE

different animal (or **breed of cat**) *n phr by 1970s* A different thing or person; =SOMETHING ELSE AGAIN: *This is a different animal*—CBS television news/ *In the pros you're dealing with a different breed of cat than when you're in the college scene*—Milwaukee Journal

different strokes for different folks *n phr black by 1970s* A comment on the inevitable and tolerable variety of people and their ways: *Different strokes for different folks, I remarked*—Arthur Maling/ *Different strokes for different folks, he chirped mentally*—Earl Thompson

diffugalty (dih FYŏŏ gəl tee) *n fr 1920s* Difficulty; trouble; problems [a humorous mispronunciation]

dig 1 *v by 1940s* To interrogate or inquire vigorously: *She won't tell you, no matter how hard you dig* **2** *n by 1840* A derogatory, irritating, or contemptuous comment: *It wasn't quite an insult, more a dig* **3** *n by 1896* An archaeological excavation **4** *v 1930s black* To understand; comprehend: *Nobody ain't pimping on me. You dig me?*—Zora Neale Hurston **5** *v 1930s black* To like; admire; prefer: *Do you dig gazpacho and macho?* **6** *v* =DIG UP **7** *v 1930s black* To hear or see in performance; =CATCH: *dug a heavy sermon at Smoky Mary's last week* [the cool senses, originally black, are probably related to the early–19th-century sense, "study hard, strive to understand"]
See TAKE A DIG AT someone

dig at *v phr by middle 1800s* To derogate; harass verbally; =PUT DOWN: *Why are you always digging at me about my mustache?*

dig dirt *v phr by 1920s* gossip

digerati *n early 1990s* Persons who use and enjoy computers; computer-literate people; =CHIPHEAD: *Unix computers connect to the Well, a convivial gathering spot for San Francisco's digerati*—New York Times/ *Wired offers in-depth reporting, fiction and profiles of the digerati*—Milwaukee Journal [fr digital plus literati]

digger 1 *n WWI Australian and New Zealand* An Australian or New Zealander **2** *n by 1920* =GOLDDIGGER: *She was just a plain digger*—W R Burnett **3** *n by 1930s* A pickpocket **4** *n by 1970s* A person who buys tickets to be sold at prices higher than is legally permitted; =SCALPER: *They use diggers, dozens of guys who stand in lines and buy the maximum*—New York Times

diggety or **diggity** *See* HOT DIGGETY

digging *See* EASY DIGGING

dig in *v phr by 1912* To begin to eat: *It's on the table, so dig in*

dig oneself **into a hole** *v phr by 1970s* To weaken or undermine one's own position, esp by a dogged defense; =SHOOT oneself IN THE FOOT: *Every time the fool opens his mouth he digs himself deeper into a hole*

◁**digital sex**▷ *n phr by 1990s* Masturbation by hand

digit head *n phr early 1990s* A very expert computer user; =CHIPHEAD, HACKER: *Mitchell's favorite jargon terms include digit head (the computer nerd's computer nerd)*—Macon Telegraph

dig out *v phr by 1855* To leave; depart; =CUT OUT, SPLIT: *Supposing we dig out*—Owen Johnson

digs¹ or **diggings** *n by 1890s* Lodgings; quarters: *Your digs, or mine?*

digs² *interj 1990s students* A exclamation of approval and affirmation; =GREAT

dig someone or something **the most** *v phr by 1950s* To like or prefer; have the closest affinity: *Adam and I dig each other the most*—Hazel Scott

dig up *v phr by 1888* To find or discover, esp after effort: *She dug up a shirt and we went out/ What sort of evidence have they dug up?*

dike *See* DYKE

dikey *See* DYKEY

dildo or **dildoe** **1** *n* by 1593 An artificial substitute for an erect penis **2** *n* (also **dill** by 1950s) by 1638 A stupid and despicable person; =JERK, PRICK: *Yeah, I know that dildo. What's your problem with him?*—Carsten Stroud [fr Italian *diletto*, in the particular sense "a women's delight"]

diller *See* CHILLER-DILLER, KILLER, THRILLER-DILLER

dillion by 1950s **1** *n* A very large sum; =JILLION, ZILLION **2** *modifier*: *I'd walk a dillion miles*

dilly or **dill** *n* by 1935 A person or thing that is remarkable, wonderful, superior, etc; =BEAUT, LULU: *The last one is a dilly if you don't have an appointment*—R S Prather

dilly-dally *v* by 1741 To idle; dither in an aimless or pointless fashion: *Folks who dilly-dally with dessert. . .*—United Press

dim *adj* by 1892 Stupid; uncomprehending: *Anybody. . . who pays to watch these teams has to be considered just a bit dim*—Mike Royko

dimbo *n* 1980s students A stupid person; =DIM BULB: *That dimbo probably couldn't find her way home from her own backyard*—UCLA Slang [perhaps a blend of *dim* and *bimbo*]

dim bulb *n phr* 1920s A stupid person; =DIMWIT: *. . . a peculiar combination of dim bulb and bump-on-a-log*—Washington Post/ *Heroes meant to be swankily sexy tend to come off as tight-lipped dim bulbs*—Village Voice

dime 1 *n* underworld by 1960s A ten-year prison sentence **2** *n* gambling by 1960s A thousand dollars, esp as a bet **3** *v* underworld & prison by 1960s (also **drop a dime**) To inform on someone; =SING, SQUEAL: *Frankie would have been okay if somebody hadn't dimed on him* [final sense from the *dime* dropped into the pay telephone for the call to the police]
See FIVE-AND-TEN, GET OFF THE DIME, NICKEL AND DIME, ON someone's DIME, STOP ON A DIME, a THIN DIME, TURN ON A DIME

a **dime a dozen** *adj* by 1920s Very common; very cheap; in surplus: *Copycats are a dime a dozen*—Sports Illustrated

dime bag or **dime** *n phr* or *n* 1960s narcotics Ten dollars' worth of a narcotic

dime dropper *n phr* underworld & prison by 1960s An informer; =FINK: *Somebody that talks, turns state's evidence on you, a dime dropper*—Village Voice

dime-note *n* by 1940s A ten-dollar bill; =TEN-SPOT

dime store *n phr* by 1920s =FIVE-AND-TEN

dime up *v phr* hoboes by 1920s To offer a dime for a meal, then try to get the dime back as well as the meal

dimmer *n* (also **dimbo**, **dimmo**) about 1910 A dime; =DEEMER: *Neither of us can make a thin dimmer*—Dashiell Hammett

dim view *See* TAKE A DIM VIEW OF someone or something

dimwit *n* about 1917 A stupid person; =BOOB: *She's the worst dim-wit on campus*—Bryn Mawr slang

dinch by 1920 **1** *v* To crush out a cigar or cigarette **2** *n* A cigarette or cigar butt

din-din *n* about 1900 Dinner: *. . . kisses, candlelight, din-din, liqueurs*—Philadelphia

dine (or **lunch**) **out on** *v phr* by 1923 To receive hospitality on the basis of one's particular knowledge or experience: *She dined out all year on that little adventure in the mountains/ Hitchens visited wartime Sarajevo once, two years ago. Ever since, he has been lunching out on the emotional and political insight he supposedly garnered*—New Republic

dinero (dee NAIR oh) *n* by 1856 Money: *That's gonna set you back mucho dinero* [fr Spanish]

ding 1 *v* hoboes by 1950s To go on the road as a hobo; =BUM: *When you go bumming, you go ding-ing*—New Yorker **2** *modifier*: *. . . in the ding camp at San Jose*—New Yorker **3** *v* hoboes by 1950s To beg; =BUM, PANHANDLE **4** *n* by 1825 A blow; a buffet: *We get a ding a day from the Chinese*—Time **5** *v* college students about 1930 To vote against a candidate for membership; blackball •An 1812 sense was "to drop someone's acquaintance totally" **6** *n*: *She got six yeahs and five dings* **7** *n* college students about 1930 A letter rejecting one's application for a job or interview: *. . . most disappointed in the dings that come on postcards*—Wall Street Journal **8** *v* Army by 1970 To administer a reprimand or an adverse appraisal: *If we dinged people, very seldom did they get jobs*—Washingtonian **9** *n* by 1960s A dent: *Not a nick. Not a ding. Nary a scratch*—Milwaukee Journal
See RING-A-DING-DING, RING-DANG-DO, RING-DING

ding-a-ling[1] **1** *n* by 1930s An eccentric person; =NUT, SCREWBALL: *The impression left by all this is that Wolman and Kuharich must be a couple of ding-a-lings*—True/ *. . . great for teeny-boppers and cute little ding-a-lings*—Jackie Collins **2** *adj* by 1930s: *. . . to maintain the dingaling Holly Goheavily manner of life*—Life/ *It's the ding-a-ling capital of the universe*—Dan Jenkins [fr the notion that such a person hears bells ringing in the head]

ding-a-ling[2] *n* by 1980s The penis; =COCK, DOODLE [probably fr *dingus*]

dingbat 1 *n* by 1905 An unspecified or unspecifiable object; something one does not know the name of or does not wish to name; =DINGUS, GADGET: *I don't think any wire and glass dingbat is going to "oontz" out cheek-to-cheek dancing*—Billy Rose **2** *n* by 1915 A stupid person, esp a vague and inane simpleton; =DIMWIT: *All in the Family was reexported to the BBC complete with "Polack pinko meatheads,". . . "dingbats," and "spades"*—D Taylor **3** *n* print shop by 1930s Any of various typographic symbols used as decorations, separators, emphasizers, trademark and union-done indicators, etc [first sense fr German or Dutch *dinges*, "thing"; second sense fr Australian *have the dingbats, be dingbats*, "be crazy"]

ding-ding *n* *by 1970s* A stupid person; idiot; =DINGBAT: . . . *or have that ding-ding of a driver inform the cops*—Glendon Swarthout

ding-dong 1 *adj by 1870* Vigorous and spirited; =KNOCK-DOWN-DRAG-OUT •Used adverbially, "with a will" by 1672: *A ding-dong battle is in prospect*—Fortune 2 *n by 1920s* An eccentric person; =DING-A-LING, NUT ◁**3**▷ *n by 1940s* The penis; =DONG: . . . *couldn't find his own ding-dong if you told him to look between his legs*—Calvin Trillin/ *Forget his ding-dong. Think of it as a technically superior game*—Village Voice

ding-donger *n* *hoboes by 1940s* An energetic and aggressive hobo

◀**dinge**▶ (DINJ) **1** *n* A black person **2** *modifier by 1848*: *You say this here is a dinge joint?*—Raymond Chandler [fr *dingy*, "dark," used as a term for black persons fr early 1900s]

dinger 1 *n by 1809* =HUMDINGER: *That was a dinger, chaplain*—New York Herald Tribune **2** *n* baseball *by 1970s* A home run: . . . *five hacks, five dingers*—Jane Leavy/ *The Brewers go into the afternoon with one dinger in more than two weeks*—Milwaukee Journal Sentinel **3** *modifier*: *He was in an 11-game dinger drought*—Sports Illustrated [fr an early (by 1500) sense of *ding*, "to surpass, excel"]

ding how (or **hao**) *adj phr* WWII armed forces Very good; splendid: *It was a ding how operation all the way* [fr Chinese]

dingleberry *n by early 1920s* A despised person; =JERK, NERD •Revived by 1980s students: *Tell that dingleberry I'm not here*—College Slang 101 [originally one of several similar derogatory terms ending -*berry*, for example *huckleberry*, attested by 1835; in later use probably influenced by *dingleberry*, "a fragment of feces clinging near the anus"]

dingo *n hoboes by 1920s* A hobo; tramp: *One dingo got a dollar*—Meyer Berger [related to the hobo sense of *ding* and probably ultimately to the 17th-century British slang *ding-boy*, "rogue, sharper"]

ding-swizzled *See* I'LL BE DAMNED

dingus 1 *n by 1876* Any unspecified or unspecifiable object; something one does not know the name of or does not wish to name; =GADGET, GIZMO: *What's that dingus in the corner?* ◁**2**▷ *n by 1940s* The penis [fr Dutch *dinges*, of the same meaning, essentially "thing"]

ding ward *n phr by 1970s* The psychiatric ward of a hospital [probably because *ding-a-lings* are treated there]

dink¹ 1 *n college students by 1920* A tiny cap worn by freshmen; =BEANIE •*Dinky cap* is attested from 1893 ◁**2**▷ *n by 1880s* The penis •A child's term 3 *n by 1960s* A despised person; =DORK, JERK, PRICK: *Nor, he insists, does he believe that any witless dink could learn to play like Ringo Starr within a week*—Rolling Stone 4 *n by 1950s* Very little; nothing; =DICK, ZILCH: *He knows dink about weapons* 5 *v* tennis *by 1939* To make small exasperating movements, tennis shots, etc •First exam-

ple may reflect 1920s *dinky*, "a trolley car having a short route": . . . *after finding that the campaign was dinking along like a Toonerville trolley*—Time/ *They're not letting the. . . combination dink them into submission anymore*—Wisconsin State Journal/ *He dinked the kid to death with left-handed backspin junk. . .* —Elmore Leonard [fr *dinky*]

◀**dink²**▶ *n Vietnam War armed forces* A Vietnamese; =GOOK, SLOPE [related to Australian *Dink*, "a Chinese," perhaps fr *dinge* or fr *Chink*]

dink³ *n about 1900* A yacht's tender; dinghy [probably fr *dinghy*, but see *dinkey*]

dink⁴ *n by 1986* One of a childless couple, both of whom are employed: . . . *a friend referred to two young professionals as "a couple of dinks"*—New York Magazine [acronym fr *double income no kids*]

dink⁵ *See* RINKY-DINK

dinkey 1 *n railroad by 1874* A small locomotive for switching, etc 2 *n by 1849* A small boat; =DINK

dinkum *adj* =FAIR DINKUM

dinky *by 1788* 1 *adj* Small; undersized •The earliest sense meant "small, neat, trim," and is related to later college use *dink*, "a dude": *a dinky foreign car/ dinky little town* 2 *adj* Inadequate; substandard: *What a dinky joint!*

dinner *See* SHOOT one's COOKIES

◀**dino¹**▶ (DEE noh) *n by 1918* An Italian or other southern European, or a person of such extraction; =DAGO: *Someday he'll shake down the wrong dino*—Nelson Algren [probably fr *Dino*, a common Italian given name; the term became confused with *dyno*, "railroad section hand who works with dynamite," probably because southern European immigrants became construction laborers in great numbers; similarly, *wop* and *spick* are outdated terms for railroad section hands]

dino² *by early 1990s* 1 *n* A dinosaur: . . . *a dino who wants to be a detective. . .* —Milwaukee Journal 2 *modifier*: *In film, the dino craze looks to remain healthy for awhile*—Milwaukee Journal

dino³ *See* DYNO

dip¹ 1 *n underworld by 1850* A pickpocket: *Since he seemed to remind me of a dip I'd helped bust years before*—Stan Cutler 2 *v*: *Frankie dipped two men on the 37 bus* [fr dipping one's hand into a pocket]

dip² 1 *n by 1920s* A stupid person; simpleton; =DIPSHIT: *That goddamned dip's worse than the Cowboys*—W T Tyler 2 *n by 1920s* An eccentric person; =NUT: *My grandmother was a woefully crazy lady. . . a bit of a dip*—Carol Burnett 3 *n 1960s* teenagers A slovenly, untidy person; =DIRTBAG 4 *adj by 1917* =DIPPY

dip³ *n by 1940s* Diphtheria

dip⁴ *n by 1940s* =DIPSO

dip⁵ *v by 1848* To chew tobacco or take snuff

dip⁶ *See* DOUBLE-DIP, I'LL BE DAMNED, SKINNY-DIP

diphead *n students by 1973* A stupid person; =DIP, DIPSHIT: *That means "the Democrats are dipheads,"* *Phil*—comic strip "Wild Life"

dipped or ◁**dipped in shit**▷ *See* I'LL BE DAMNED

dipper *n* =DIPPERMOUTH
See FANNY-DIPPER, HIPPER-DIPPER

dippermouth *n by 1920s* A person with a large mouth: *Dipper, that was my nickname, short for Dippermouth*—Louis Armstrong

dippiness *n about 1900* Craziness; silliness: *the sweet season of general dippiness*

dippo *n by 1970s* A stupid person; =DIP, DIPSHIT

dippy *adj about 1900* Crazy; foolish; whimsically silly; =KOOKIE: *. . . so strange and dippy as to have come from the brain of Tolkien*—Toronto Life/ *Depardieu at his dippiest*—Village Voice [origin unknown; perhaps fr *dip*, "head," in the expression *off one's dip*, "crazy"; perhaps fr *dipsomaniac*; perhaps fr Romany *divio*, "mad, madman"]

dipsey *n 1920s hoboes* A short jail sentence

◁**dipshit**▷ or **dipstick** *by 1960s* **1** *n* A stupid, obnoxious person; =JERK: *You dipshit dog*—Stephen King/ *The other guy is the dipshit*—Village Voice/ *We're broke, dipstick*—Toronto Sun **2** *modifier*: *The dipshit broads took their lives in their own hands*—Easyriders/ *Listen, you toadying dipshit scumbag*—New Yorker [*dipshit* is an emphatic form of *dip²*; *dipstick* may be a euphemism, or may reflect putative *dipstick*, "penis"]

dipso *n by 1880* A drunkard; dipsomaniac; =LUSH: *Madeline Kahn is his dipso wife, Gilda Radner his ditsy daughter*—Time/ *But dipsos don't count years; you take it day by day*—Lawrence Sanders

dipsy 1 *adj* Drunken; bibulous; alcoholic; =DIPSO: *Beryl Reid's appearance as a dipsy researcher*—Time **2** *adj* Foolish; silly; =DITSY: *Kelly, her dipsy counterpart at NBC*—Pulpsmith **3** *n by early 1950s* =DIPSY-DOODLE

dipsy-do 1 *n baseball by 1940s* A curve ball that dips sharply; a downcurve: *[Babe Ruth] had good stuff, a good fast ball, a fine curve, a dipsy-do that made you think a little*—Casey Stengel

dipsy-doodle *by 1940s* **1** *n* Fraud; deception; chicanery: *I opened the front door, leaving the key in the lock. I wasn't going to work any dipsy-doodle in this place*—Raymond Chandler/ *This dipsy-doodle allowed the Democratic candidate to preach a different sermon in every church*—Rolling Stone **2** *n* A deceiver; swindler; =CON MAN: *He's a marriage counselor, this dipsy-doodle*—New York Magazine **3** *v*: *That smooth chap might just have dipsy-doodled us* **4** *n sports* =DIPSY-DO **5** *n prizefight* A fight with predetermined outcome; a fixed fight **6** *n* A dance featuring dipping motions **7** *v hockey* To weave among players on the ice: *Kurri dipsy-doodled down center ice to the net*—Los Angeles Times [most senses seem to have evolved fr the baseball *dipsy-do*, the semantic common thread being deception]

dipwad *n 1970s students* A despised person; =JERK

◁**dip** one's **wick**▷ *v phr late 1800s* To insert one's penis; do the sex act; =SCREW: *You dipped your wick just like the rest of them*—movie Sudden Impact

[Tony Thorne says: Wick is either a shortening of the rhyming slang *Hampton Wick*, "prick," or a straightforward metaphor from candle-wick]

dirt 1 *n by late 1500s* Obscenity; pornography: *All you see in the movies these days is dirt* **2** *n by 1920s* Gossip; intimate or scandalous intelligence; =SCOOP: *What's the dirt about your neighbors?* **3** *n by 1300* A despicable person; scum; filth: *He's dirt, no better*
See DIG DIRT, DISH THE DIRT, DO someone DIRT, EAT DIRT, HIT THE DIRT, PAY DIRT, TAKE SHIT

dirtbag or DIRTBALL **1** *n WWII armed forces* A garbage collector **2** *n phr by 1970s* A despicable person; filthy lout; =CRUD, SCUMBAG: *Those people in the store must have thought I was some kind of dirt bag*—New York Times/ *Why don't you throw this dirtbag in jail, deputy?*—Playboy/ *He ended up being chased down the hall by a dirtball with a knife*—Your Week in Ocean City **3** *n medical by 1990s* A dirty, smelly patient brought into the emergency room off the street

dirt bike *n 1960s motorcyclists* =SCRAMBLER

dirt cheap *by 1830s* **1** *adj phr* Very cheap: *dirt-cheap prices* **2** *adv phr*: *buy it dirt cheap*

dirt chute *n phr by 1940s* The anus; =ASS-HOLE, WINKIE

dirt me *sentence rock-climbers by 1990s* Lower me to the ground

dirt track *n phr by 1960s* The anus; =ASS-HOLE, GAZOOL, WAZOO: *. . . is your dirt track hanging hemorrhoids?*—Harry Crews [a pun on the early 1900s phrase for a race track with a dirt surface; hobo slang *dirt road* was semantically similar]

dirty 1 *adj by 1670* Corrupt; dishonest; shady •Often used of corrupt police officers: *If I was dirty. . . I would take what that Cadillac cost*—W E B Griffin/ *Maybe he's not dirty on Nijinsky, but he's dirty on something*—Stuart Woods **2** *adv*: *They fight dirty/ play dirty* **3** *adj by 1599* Lewd; obscene; =BLUE, RAUNCHY: *This dictionary dotes on dirty words/ Eschew dirty thoughts* **4** *adv*: *He talks dirty* **5** *adj 1920s jazz musicians* Sexually insinuating in sound and intonation; =CATHOUSE, BARRELHOUSE: *dirty blues* **6** *adj by 1920s* Personally malicious or snide; nasty: *a dirty crack* **7** *adj 1960s narcotics* Addicted to narcotics **8** *adj 1960s narcotics* Having narcotics in one's possession: *Cops did a bodyshake and he was real dirty* **9** *adj by 1919* Well supplied with money; =FILTHY RICH: *Paddy was dirty with fifteen thousand or so*—Dashiell Hammett **10** *adj 1950s* Leaving much radioactive contamination or waste: *dirty bombs*
See DO THE DIRTY ON someone, DOWN AND DIRTY, QUICK-AND-DIRTY

the **dirty dozens** *See* PLAY THE DOZENS

dirty heavy *n phr 1920s movie studio* A villain, esp in the movies; =HEAVY

dirtyleg *n by 1960s* A promiscuous woman or prostitute; =FLOOZY: *. . . flirting with a dirtyleg while in the company of a lady*—Dan Jenkins

dirty linen (or **wash**) *n phr by 1860s* Personal or

family matters; intimate details: *I won't hang out our dirty linen in front of this bunch*
See WASH one's DIRTY LINEN

dirty little secret 1 *n phr* Something shameful that must be concealed; an embarrassing fact: *Power. . . has been a dirty little secret among modern economists*—New York Times **2** *n phr* Anything held secret personally or communally because it is patently shameful; a skeleton in the closet: *Everybody will know the dirty little secret of American journalism*—Time/ *Class Act: America's Last Dirty Little Secret*—New York Times [phrase propagated by D H Lawrence, esp in his long essay "Pornography and Obscenity"]

dirty mind *n phr* by 1930s A head full of sexual, malicious, and other reprehensible thoughts, fantasies, and implications

dirty-minded *adj* by 1930s Inclined toward sexual, odious, or dubious notions

◁**dirty-neck**▷ *by 1940s* **1** *n* A laborer or farmer **2** *n* An immigrant

dirty old man 1 *n phr* by 1930s A lecherous man, esp an elderly one; =OLD GOAT **2** *n phr* homosexuals by 1960s A male homosexual whose partner is much younger than himself: *Christopher is 20 years younger than Leo. . . He asks Leo to be his dirty old man*—New York Times

dirty pool *n phr* by 1956 Unethical and dubious practice; =DIRTY TRICKS: . . . *triggered ugly accusations of dirty pool*—TV Guide

a **dirty (or low-down dirty) shame** *n phr* A person or thing that is much to be lamented; a pity; a disgrace: *He did? Ain't that a dirty shame?/ Man, you're a low-down dirty shame, you're nasty*

dirty tricks 1 *n phr* Dishonest or underhanded practices, esp in politics; malicious tactics: . . . *make into federal crimes many "dirty tricks" in presidential and congressional elections*—Time/ *Mr Clarke called the indictment "one of the greatest political dirty tricks of all times"*—New York Times **2** *modifier*: *the Senate Watergate Committee's chief "dirty tricks" investigator*—Newsweek

dirty work *n phr* Dishonest, unethical, underhanded, or criminal acts; =SKULLDUGGERY

dis *v* (also **diss; on** may be added) *1980s black teenagers* To show disrespect; insult by slighting; =CAP ON someone: *The boys on the bus were dissing that girl*—Washington Post/ *Yet "dissin',"	showing real or apparent disrespect, is cited as the motive in an amazing number of murders*—Miss Manners/ *I'm tired of John dissin' on her all the time*—College Slang 101

disathon *n* 1980s teenagers A prolonged exchange of insults between two teenagers in the presence of their peers ●This sport of reciprocal vilification is also called *playing the dozens* when it includes insults to families as well as individuals; a medieval *flyting* and a *slanging match* were the same sort of diversion, suggesting that such logomachy is a widespread culture trait

disc or **disk** *n* by 1888 A phonograph record; =PLATTER

disc jockey *n phr* (Variations: **deejay** or **Dee-Jay** or **DJ** or **dj**) *by 1941* A radio performer who plays and comments on phonograph records; also, the person who plays records at a discotheque: . . . *the thunder-voiced DJ*—Saturday Review

disco 1 *n* by 1964 A discotheque, a kind of nightclub where patrons dance to recorded music, sometimes with synchronized psychedelic and strobe lighting: *There's not much jazzing around at the disco*—Vogue **2** *modifier*: *show up. . . for a disco party and fashion show*—Look **3** *v*: *We discoed the night away* **4** *n* (also **disco music**) *1970s* A musical style based on black soul music and marked by a strong rhythmic bass guitar
See CRISCO DISCO

discombobulate or **discomboberate** *by 1830s* **1** *v* To disturb; upset; =BUG **2** *v* To perplex; puzzle: *The fancy words discombobulated me*

discombobulated *adj* by 1830s Disturbed; upset; weird: *In this discombobulated society, it is far easier to get a piano shipped out to sea and lowered into the water beside the drowning man*—Washington Post

discombobulation *n* by 1830s The condition of being discombobulated: . . . *the Skinner course responsible for their emotional discombobulation*—Time

disconnect *n* 1990s A disagreement: *Disconnect. . . It means a breakdown in communication*—Wall Street Journal

disease **See** FOOT-IN-MOUTH DISEASE

disgusto *adj* by 1970s Disgusting: . . . *disgusto special effects aside*—Village Voice

dish 1 *v* by 1798 To cheat; thwart: *I'm afraid that blackguard has dished us again* **2** *n* by 1920s A particularly attractive woman ●Regarded by some women as offensive: *This was going to be my favorite dish*—John O'Hara/ *I love this book and I think its 80-year-old author is a dish*—Washington Post **3** *n* about 1900 A person or thing that one especially likes; what exactly meets one's taste; =CUP OF TEA: *Now, there is a book that is just my dish*—George S Kaufman **4** *n* baseball by 1907 The home plate of the baseball diamond **5** *v* by 1920s To gossip; have an intimate chat; =DISH THE DIRT: *She sat and dished with the girls*—H Selby/ . . . *now I feel free to dish about First Hair*—Liz Smith **6** *v* by 1940s To disparage; denigrate; =DIS: *The President-elect played on the beach while his snobby neighbors dished*—Time/ *We have no reason to do an anti-CBS film. There's no dishin' going on here*—Washington Post **7** *v* (also **dish out**) by 1641 To give; purvey: *He took everything we gave and dished it right back*—D Cresap **8** *v* basketball by 1970s To pass the ball: . . . *a goateed Magic in butt-tight shorts twists, whirls and dishes through his career as maestro of five NBA championships*—People
See one's CUP OF TEA

dish it out *v phr* by 1930 To administer punishment, injury, or abuse: *Jenny, you can dish it out, but you can't take it*—Erich Segal

one's **dish of tea** *See* one's CUP OF TEA

dish out (or **up**) by 1652 **1** *v phr* To distribute; issue: *The brand of drool they dished out*—Joseph Auslander/ *What line are they dishing up today?* **2** *v phr* To inflict; give: *They dished her out a horrid trouncing*

dishrag *See* LIMP DISHRAG

dish the dirt by 1920s **1** *v phr* To enjoy a cozy chat about personalities: *So, dish the dirt. What was Hillary like in high school?*—Milwaukee Journal Sentinel **2** *modifier*: *The first lady told her dish-the-dirt guests she called them together "to announce my candidacy"*—Milwaukee Journal

dishwater *n* by 1719 Weak and scarcely drinkable soup, coffee, etc
See DULL AS DISHWATER

dishy *adj* by 1940s Very attractive •Chiefly British use; regarded by some women as offensive; the dated sense is "excellent, first rate; sharp, snaky, trim and slim, smooth": . . . *exactly what it is to be a dishy girl bored stiff*—Penelope Gilliatt/ . . . *we certainly don't live in one of the dishier neighborhoods. . .*—Douglas Coupland/ *With a new job at a ritzy club and the attentions of two dishy men. . .*—Waldenbooks catalog

disk *See* DISC

Disneyland daddy *n phr* by middle 1980s A divorced or separated father who sees his children rarely; =ZOO DADDY

dispatcher *n* gambling by 1798 A dishonest pair of dice

disposable (or **throwaway**) **worker** *n phr* by early 1990s A temporary or flexibly assigned employee: *Some labor economists. . . call them disposable or throwaway workers*—Milwaukee Journal

dissolve 1 *n* by 1912 The gradual blending of one scene into the next in motion pictures or television; also, a device that causes this effect **2** *v*: *Dissolve to a closeup of the house* [The use of the term in Victorian magic lantern shows is attested in 1845]

ditch 1 *v* by 1900 To dispose of; get rid of; =CHUCK: *We'll ditch this Greek and blow*—James M Cain **2** *v* by 1940s To land an aircraft on the water in an emergency **3** *v* 1920s To play truant; fail to go to school or to a class

Ditch *See* the BIG DITCH

ditsy or **ditzy** *adj* middle 1970s Vapid and frivolous; silly; =AIRHEADED: *Charles Ruggles's ditsy bimbo*—Village Voice/ *Is there something in the air that makes Washington wives ditsy?*—Philadelphia Journal [perhaps a blending of *dizzy* and *dotty*]

dittohead *n* early 1990s A person who totally agrees with a proffered system of belief, esp with the uncomplex notions of the talk-show host Rush Limbaugh: *They. . . are happy to be known as dittoheads, from the . . . shorthand that callers use to signify 100% agreement. . .*—Milwaukee Journal/ *Dittoheads: people who are in perfect agreement on an issue, an idea, or a belief system*—Wired

ditty (or **diddy**) **bag** *n phr* nautical by 1850s A small bag for one's personal belongings, usu exclusive of clothing [origin uncertain; perhaps short for *commodity*, fr the earlier British naval term *commodity box*, which became *ditty box*]

dittybop or **dittybob** or **diddybop** ◁1▷ *n* black by 1950s A stupid person, esp a crude and unsophisticated black person **2** *modifier*: . . . *the diddybop image of JJ*—Amsterdam News **3** *v* by 1980s To move, sway, etc, to music; =BOP: *A young man with earphones on his head. . . was ditty bopping in front of Saks*—New York Magazine

dittybopper or **diddybopper** black by 1980s **1** *n* A person who dittybops ◁2▷ *n* A pretentious or pompous black person, esp one who aspires to enter the mainstream white culture **3** *n* =DITTYBOP

ditz *n* middle 1970s A silly and inane person; a frivolous ninny: . . . *a brainy ditz involved with a vulnerable hunk*—Village Voice/ . . . *little more than a likable, spoiled ditz who allows herself to ruled by. . . chemicals*—New York Review of Books

ditzo *n* 1980s students A person who is out of touch with reality; =LUNCHBOX

diva *n* early 1990s A male transvestite; esp, a homosexual cross-dresser; =DRAG QUEEN: *Salt-N-Pepa's divas are checking out designer creations* [fr Italian, "goddess, lady love," used by the 1880s to designate a distinguished woman singer]

dive 1 *n* by 1871 A vulgar and disreputable haunt, such as a cheap bar, nightclub, lodging house, or dancehall; =CRIB: . . . *the girl who danced in a dive in New Orleans*—K Brush **2** *n* esp 1920s =SPEAKEASY **3** *n* prizefight by 1940s A knockdown or knockout, esp a false prearranged knockout: *A dive is a phantom knockout*—Arthur Daley **4** *v*: *They fixed it so that he'd dive in the fourth* [origin of first sense uncertain; perhaps fr the notion that one could *dive* into a disreputable cellar haunt (called a *diving bell* in an 1883 glossary) and lose oneself among lowlifes and criminals; perhaps a shortening of *divan*, "a smoking and gaming room," a usage popular in London in the middle and late 19th century; the places were so called because furnished with *divans*, "lounges," the name ultimately fr Turkish]
See NOSE DIVE, TAKE A DIVE

diver *See* MUFF-DIVER, PEARL-DIVER

divot (DIV ət) *n* by 1950s A toupee; =RUG [fr the Scottish word, "a piece of turf or sod, esp one cut out by a golf club," of unknown origin]

divvy by 1872 **1** *v* (also **divvy out** or **divvy up**) To divide; apportion: *The governor and the Paris crook divvy the swag*—Alva Johnson/ *We would pass our hats and divvy up*—Louis Armstrong **2** *n* A share of profits or spoils **3** *n* A dividend

dixie *n* Army by 1970s A mess tin or small pot

Dixie by 1980s **1** *n* The southern United States **2** *modifier*: *a Dixie drawl* [origin obscure; perhaps because the region is south of the Mason-*Dixon* line]
See NOT JUST WHISTLING DIXIE, WHISTLING DIXIE

Dixieland 1 *n* by *1850s* The southern United States; =DIXIE **2** *n* about *1920* The style of jazz played by the street bands in New Orleans, marked by a simple two-beat rhythm, ragged syncopation, improvised ensemble passages, etc **3** *adj*: *Dixieland trumpet*

Dixie mafia *n phr* by *1970s* A confederation or category of criminals operating in the southern United States, esp in urban centers and esp in the narcotics traffic: . . . *a new criminal class, which some Southern law officials, for lack of a better term, term the Dixie mafia*—New York Times

dizzball *n* by *1990s* An inane person; a ninny; =DITZ: . . . *Victoria Jackson, the ex-dizzball from* Saturday Night Live. . . —Newark Star-Ledger

dizzy *adj* by *1501* Silly; foolish; inane; =DITSY •Found as a noun meaning "foolish man" by 1825; now mostly used of women, and esp, since the 1870s, of blondes: . . . *some dizzy broad*—Jerome Weidman

dizzy-wizzy *n* early *1900s* narcotics Any narcotic in pill form

DJ or **dj** *See* DISC JOCKEY

DK *v 1980s* To claim that one does not know someone or something: . . . *plunges the younger Sheen into trouble on a D-K (in which the buyer reneges by insisting that he "doesn't know".* . . — Milwaukee Journal

DMT *n 1960s* narcotics Dimethyltryptamine, a hallucinogen like LSD but with shorter effects

DMZ *n 1980s* An area now peaceful but recently and perhaps soon again the scene of violence: *They had long since passed Ninety-sixth Street, the infamous DMZ.* . . —William Bayer/ *Traversing Brooklyn's DMZ to go to a steak house.* . . —Esquire [fr the region between North and South Korea designated the *Demilitarized Zone* when the Korean War ended]

do 1 *v* by *1641* To cheat; swindle: *He is hated by all the beggars above him, and they do him every chance they get*—J Flynt **2** *v* by *1853* To eat or drink; partake of •The dated sense has to do mainly with drinks; the revived sense is usually in the phrase *do lunch: That was where.* . . *I'd be "doing lunch" with Mark Bradley*—Stan Cutler/ *The expressions "doing lunch" and "fun".* . . *lead the 11th annual list of "banished words".* . . —Washington Post **3** *v 1960s* narcotics To use or take narcotics: *Hell, half the people doing blow are reacting to the cut.* . . —Robert B Parker/ *I'd wonder why and do another line. But I never looked at it as if I were some big drug addict*—Playboy **4** *v* by *1860s* To serve a prison sentence: *He did six years up at San Quentin* **5** *n* by *1824* A party or other gathering; affair; =SHINDIG: . . . *a few of the other main do's*—Budd Schulberg/ *The Tweed do was held early last December*—Village Voice **6** *n* (also **doo**) black by *1960s* A haircut or styling: *Your hair, your doo*—Jane Leavy/ *Yuppie bikers favor short fashion-boy dos or neat ponytails*—Los Angeles Times **7** *n* by *1920s* Excrement; feces: *I stepped in doggy-do* •A childs' term, perhaps first

used in *dog-do* or *doggy-do* **8** *n* Something one should do or must do •Always in the phrase *dos and don'ts: Being friendly is a do, but being possessive is a don't* **9** *v* by *1888* To visit; make the rounds of: *Shall we do Provence this summer?* **10** *v* by *1350* To kill; do to death; =SCRAG, OFF, RUB OUT: *The guy she's having cocktails with is the one who done her?*—Scott Turow/ *I'm the guy doing these colored girls*—Robert B Parker **11** *v* by *1913* To do the sex with or to; =BOFF, FUCK: *Heidi Does Hollywood*—Time & Vanity Fair

See DO someone DIRT, DO-GOODER, DO IT ALL, DO one's NUMBER, DOODAD, DO someone OUT OF, DO-RAG, DO one's STUFF, DO one's THING, DO TIME, DO UP, DO something UP BROWN, WHOOP-DE-DO

DOA (pronounced as separate letters) **1** *adj* Dead on arrival **2** *n*: *Don't risk being a DOA by driving drunk*

do a brodie *v phr* motorcyclists by *1950s* To fall while doing a skidding turn

do a bunk *v phr* by *1860s* To run away; escape; =LIGHT OUT, MAKE TRACKS: . . . *nothing could look so much like guilt as to do a bunk at this juncture*—Lee Thayer [By 1891 the phrase also meant "to defecate, crap"; the semantic relation is not immediately apparent]

do a deal *v phr* by *1913* To complete a negotiation or mutual arrangement; =DEAL •Chiefly British; the US phrase is *make a deal: He had not thought about what kind of deal he wanted to do*—Harry Crews

do a job on someone by *1960s* **1** *v phr* To injure; treat roughly: *Those motherf..in' scorpions really do a job on you*—New York Times **2** *v phr* =DO A NUMBER ON **3** *v phr* To destroy: *The pup did a job on the rug*

Doakes *See* JOE BLOW

do (or **run**) **a number on** *1970s* **1** *v phr* To take advantage of, esp by deception; mistreat; =SCREW: *You people ran a number on us. Whenever we brought it up, you walked away*—New York Times/ . . . *get even with Leonard for doing that.* . . *number on her*—Cyra McFadden **2** *v phr* To affect adversely, esp as to morale and self-esteem: *He really did a number on her when he told her the boss didn't like her report* **3** *v phr* To beat; trounce; =CLOBBER: . . . *he tells me to work this guy over, do a number on him*—Milwaukee Journal/ *Duke Does Number on Michigan*—Milwaukee Journal

do a slow burn *v phr* by *1930s* To become very angry gradually: *And I do a real slow burn*—Leo Rosten [Identified with the film actor Edgar Kennedy]

do bad things *v phr 1990s* To commit crimes of violence •An arch, childish way of euphemizing and emphasizing such atrocities: *You may have noticed there are some nuts out there who do bad things to people who deliver abortions*—Newark Star-Ledger

do one's **business** *v phr* by *1645* To defecate or urinate; ease oneself: *It's about time I let Roscoe out to do his business*—comic strip "Pickles"

doc[1] **1** *n by 1850s* A physician; doctor **2** *n by 1940s* Man; fellow; =GUY •Used in address to strangers: *What's up, doc?*—Bugs Bunny

doc[2] *n by 1990s* A movie or televison documentary: *. . . as many as 65 feature-length docs qualified for consideration*—Wisconsin State Journal

doc in the box *n phr medical by 1980s* A walk-in clinic

dock *v by 1822* To reduce one's pay for some infraction: *I'm docking you six bucks for being sassy* [fr *dock*, "to cut off part of the tail," fr a Middle English word meaning "docked tail"]

dock rat *n phr by 1860s* A vagrant; drifter; =BUM

dock-walloper *n by 1838* A dockworker: *. . . strolled among the dock-wallopers swinging a cane*—O O McIntyre/ *As a dock-walloper he was the king of Greenpernt's waterfront*—Time

doctor 1 *n horse-racing by 1940s* A person who drugs racehorses to improve their performance **2** *v by 1774* To alter or tamper with something dishonestly; =COOK: *We doctored the receipts/ He doctored the booze* **3** *v by 1828* To repair; mend: *Somebody's got to doctor this furnace*
See BUG DOCTOR, COUCH DOCTOR, PLAY DOCTOR, SPIN DOCTOR, ZIT DOCTOR

Dr Feelgood *black by 1940s* **1** *n phr* A physician who prescribes amphetamines, vitamins, hormones, etc, to induce euphoria: *No Dr Feelgood was in the White House administering amphetamines*—William Safire **2** *n phr* Any person who soothes and pleases by hedonic ministrations: *. . . the Dr Feelgood of American politics*—New York Times [fr the title of a 1960s song popularized by Aretha Franklin]

docu or **docudrama** (DAKH yoo) *n by 1950s* A documentary film, TV program, play, etc: *Each of the. . . programs is half docu, half drama*—People/ *. . . one vidfilm, plus a docu on Theodore Roosevelt*—Variety

docu-schlock *See* INFOTAINMENT

do-dad *See* DOODAD

do one's **damndest** *v phr by 1918* To do one's best; exert oneself: *He swore he'd do his damndest to find her*

doddle *n British by 1960s* Something easily done; =CINCH, PICNIC, PIECE OF CAKE: *It was a doddle for Joe. He arrived back fresh as a daisy before their fax came through*—Milwaukee Journal [*Doddle it*, "to win a horse-race very easily," is attested in US slang by the 1940s]

dodge *n by 1842* A person's way of making a living, esp if illegal or dubious •Often ironically and deprecatingly used of one's own perfectly ordinary line of work: *We used to run gin, but when prohibition ended we had to give up that dodge: One of the better practitioners of the dictionary dodge*

dodger *See* ROGER

do someone **dirt** *v phr by 1893* To cause someone trouble or embarrassment, esp by malice and slander; serve someone ill: *Don't repeat that unless you want to do him dirt*

dodo 1 *n by 1880s* A stupid, inept person; =TURKEY **2** *n by 1880s* A boring person; =FOGY: *I'm a respectable old dodo*—Philip Wylie **3** *n 1940s Army Air Corps* A student pilot who has not yet made a solo flight [fr the extinct *dodo* bird, rather sluggish and flightless; oddly enough, the word is fr the Portuguese name *doudo*, "simpleton, fool," given to the bird]
See DEAD AS A DODO

do doors (or **a door) ** *v phr by early 1990s* To raid drug sites illegally: *. . . "doing doors." illegally raiding drug dens for plunder*—New York Times

doer *n by early 1990s* A person who commits a crime; =PERP: *Police talked about having captured most of the "doers" in the bombing*—Time

◁**does a bear shit in the woods**▷ *sentence by 1970s* That was a stupid question; isn't the answer very obvious?

◁**does a wooden horse have a hickory dick**▷ *sentence by 1970s* That was a stupid question; isn't the answer very obvious?; =DOES A BEAR SHIT IN THE WOODS

◁**does Howdy Doody have wooden balls**▷ *sentence by 1970s* That was a stupid question; isn't the answer very obvious?; =DOES A BEAR SHIT IN THE WOODS

do for someone *v phr by 1740* To harm or ruin someone; destroy someone

do-funny *See* DOODAD

dog 1 *n by 1930s* An unappealing or inferior person or thing; =DUD, LOSER: *The new show's a total dog* ◁**2**▷ *n by 1930s* An unattractive woman: *And she was a dog*—Joseph Wambaugh **3** *n jazz musicians by 1960s* An attractive woman; =FOX **4** *n by 1596* A man; fellow; =GUY: *dirty dog/ handsome dog* **5** *n black by 1950s* An untrustworthy man; seducer **6** *n black by 1950s* A sexually aggressive man: *. . . before the dogs on the ward showed their hand*—Donald Goines **7** *n by early 1900s* A foot: *His left dog pained* **8** *n by 1900* =HOT DOG **9** *v* (also **dog around, dog on**) *fr 1970s Army* To pester; taunt; =BUG, HASSLE: *You were fully doggin' him about his hair*—Miven Booth/ *My roommate was dogging on me for using up her shampoo*—College Slang 101/ *In the verbal dueling of the speeded-up poetry, he doesn't bite rhymes and he doesn't get dogged or dissed*—Los Angeles Times **10** *n 1990s black teenagers* A teenager: *. . . girls refer to boys as "dogs," and both refer to sex as a function*—New York Times **11** *v 1980s students* To perform well; defeat an adversary: *I dogged him at racquetball, though*—College Slang 101
See BARKING DOGS, BIRD DOG, CATS AND DOGS, DOG IT, DOG-ROBBER, DOG SHOW, DOG'S-NOSE, DOG TAGS, DOG UP, DOG-WAGON, FUCK THE DOG, the HAIR OF THE DOG, HOT DIGGETY, HOT DOG, HOUND DOG, IT SHOULDN'T HAPPEN TO A DOG, LINE DOG, PUP TENT, PUT ON THE RITZ, RAIN CATS AND DOGS, RED DOG, ROAD DOG, SEE A MAN ABOUT A DOG, SHORT DOG, TOP DOG, YELLOW DOG CONTRACT

the **dog** *n phr* black by 1940s Syphilis: *He was so far gone with the dog. . .* —Eubie Blake

the **Dog** *See* the HOUND

dog and pony act (or **show**) *n phr* by 1970s An elaborately prepared or staged presentation, event, etc, intended to sway or convince: *Bring them in here and do a dog and pony act*—Ed McBain [by the 1920s, *dog and pony show* was a derisive name for a small circus]

See GO INTO one's DANCE

◁**dog-ass**▷ *adj* Wretched; inferior; pitiable;: *. . . that dog-assed motel*—George V Higgins

dog biscuit 1 *n phr* 1920s Army & students Hardtack, a hard biscuit or bread made of flour and water ◁**2**▷ *n phr* 1940s students An unattractive woman

dog collar *n phr* by 1883 A collar fastening at the back, like a Roman collar; also, a very high collar like the one on a Marine Corps uniform

dog-ear *v* by 1886 To fold back the corner of a page to mark one's place in a book: *. . . those of us who still dog-ear and reread her books say "Who cares?"*—New Yorker [Found as *dog's-ear* by 1659]

dog-eared by 1894 **1** *adj* Worn, creased, and rumpled; shabby; unkempt **2** *adj* Old; outworn; hackneyed: *. . . even a clean reading of a dog-eared tune is deepened*—Village Voice [fr the look of a book whose pages have been repeatedly folded at the corners; found in this sense by 1824]

dogface 1 *n* Army by 1930s A soldier, esp an infantry private: *Few wanted to be dogfaces*—Time **2** *modifier*: *a dogface, paddlefoot private*

◁**dog fashion** (or **style**)▷ *adv phr* by late 1800s With one partner in a sex act entering the other from the rear; =BOTTOMS UP

dogfight 1 *n* WWI air forces An aerial combat among fighter planes **2** *n* by 1880 Any confused and riotous brawl; =DONNYBROOK

dog food *n phr* WWII Navy Corned-beef hash

◀**dogfuck**▶ *v* by 1960s To do a sex act with one partner entering the other from the rear: *. . . including how to 69 and dogfuck*—Playboy

dogger *See* HOT DOGGER

doggie *n* by 1930s =DOGFACE

See LINE DOG

doggo *adj* British by 1893 In hiding; quiet and unobtrusive; low-profile: *Hamilton, lying doggo since killing the Chicago detective*—A Hynd/ *Even doggo prospects like anthropologists and landscape architects, we learn, are still in demand*—Washington Post

See LIE DOGGO

doggone or **daggone** or **dagnab 1** *interj* (also **doggone it** or **daggone it** or **dagnab it**) by 1851 An exclamation of disappointment, irritation, frustration, etc; =DANG, DARN: *Doggone it, leave me be!* **2** *adj* (also **doggoned** or **daggoned** or **dagnabbed**) by 1860 Wretched; nasty; silly: *This doggone thing's busted* **3** *adv* by 1871: *They left here doggone fast* [probably a euphemism for *God damn*]

doggy *adj* by 1889 Stylish; well dressed and groomed: *. . . selling off the doggy companies Geneen had bought*—Newsweek

doggy bag *n phr* by 1964 A paper or plastic bag or box given a restaurant customer to take home leftovers

doghouse 1 *n* Any small structure resembling in some way a dog's individual kennel: *The boat has a doghouse over the main cabin* **2** *n* 1920s jazz musicians The bass viol: *When the bull-fiddler plucks the strings he is slapping the doghouse*—H T Webster

See IN THE DOGHOUSE

dogie *n* cowboys by 1888 A motherless calf in a herd; =BUM

dog it 1 *v phr* =PUT ON THE RITZ **2** *v phr* by 1905 To avoid or evade work; refuse to exert oneself; =COAST: *He had his troubles all year long, dogging it on us and complaining all the time*—Whitey Herzog/ *The impression comes through clearly that I was dogging it*—Scott Turow **3** *v phr* To leave hastily; flee **4** *v phr* To live as a parasite; =SPONGE: *He was dogging it, mooching his room and board* **5** *v phr* 1980s students To behave wantonly or promiscuously

dogmeat *n* by 1890s Something or somebody inferior or worthless; =CRAP, SHIT: *Your car is a piece of dogmeat*—Milwaukee Journal/ *Columbus was dogmeat after he discovered America*—National Examiner [The dated form is *dog's meat*]

dognaper or **dognapper** *n* by 1940s A stealer of dogs, esp for profitable selling

do-good *adj* Overtly benign and altruistic: *This "do-good" laundry list draws sneers*—Saturday Review

do-gooder *n* by 1927 A person whose selfless work may be more pretentiously than actually altruistic; an ostentatiously rightminded citizen: *. . . a professional do-gooder*—Billy Rose

dog out (or **up**) *v phr* by 1930s To dress fancily; =DOLL UP: *He would have been feeling much better if he were dogged out in a new outfit*—James T Farrell

dog someone **out** *v phr* by early 1990s To chide someone; criticize adversely: *Johnson is not afraid to be critical, and. . . had heard things like "Hey, you dog me out"*—Milwaukee Journal

dogpile *v* by 1940s To heap oneself on top of a person who is on the ground; =PILE ON

dog-robber *n* Army by 1860s An officer's orderly [fr the notion that these soldiers, who ate at the second table in the officers' mess, were *robbing the dogs* of the table scraps]

dogs *n* by 1919 The feet [said to be short for *dog's meat*, "feet" in rhyming slang; also attributed to the writer and cartoonist Tad Dorgan]

See BARKING DOGS, CATS AND DOGS, GO TO THE DOGS, RAIN CATS AND DOGS

the **dogs** *n phr* by 1930s The greatest thing; a marvel: *Wouldn't it be the dogs to be paged like that?*—James T Farrell

dogsbody *n by 1922* A menial; lowly pawn •Chiefly British usage: *Oh, I'm the general dogs-body around here*—Stuart Woods [apparently fr early 1800s naval slang for peas boiled in a cloth sack, although the semantic relation is not obvious]

dog's breakfast (or **dinner) n phr** *first form by 1934, second by 1960s* A wretched mixture; an unpalatable combination; =MESS: . . . *that dog's breakfast of fact and fancy. . . docudrama*—Meg Greenfield/ *The plot is a dog's breakfast of half-baked ideas*—San Francisco

◁**dogshit**▷ *n by 1960s* Despicable matter; pretentious trash; =CRAP, DOGMEAT, SHIT: . . . *none of this fancy-pants bullshit, poodle-top haircuts and flashy clothes. None of that dogshit*—Rolling Stone

dog show *n phr* *WWII Army* Foot inspection

a **dog's life** *n phr by 1607* A wretched existence; a miserable life

dog's-nose *n by 1891* A drink of beer or ale mixed with gin or rum

dog style *See* DOG FASHION

dog tags *n phr* *WWI armed forces* Identification tags, esp metal tags worn around the neck by members of the armed forces: *Vets, if you still have your dog tags*—New York Sunday News [each soldier had two: one to be taken from his body if he died, the other to be left with it]

dog tent *See* PUP TENT

dog-tired *adj by about 1809* Very tired; exhausted; =BEAT, POOPED, WASTED [as tired as a *dog* after a hunt; Bayard Taylor called it "a German phrase" in an 1876 letter]

dog up *See* DOG OUT

dog-wagon 1 *n college students by 1900* A modest or cheap diner, such as might occupy an old railroad car or street car, that serves hot dogs **2** *n truckers by 1940s* An antiquated truck

dogwash *n computer by early 1990s* : *Dogwash: A project of minimal priority undertaken as an escape from more serious work*—Kansas City Star

do-hickey or **do-hinky** *See* DOODAD, DOOHICKEY

do one's **homework** *v phr by 1930s* To be ready and informed, esp for a meeting, interview, report, etc: *Shana Alexander has done her homework well*—National Public Radio

do someone **in** *by 1905* **1** *v phr* To kill someone: *She did in the old woman, too*—Agatha Christie **2** *v phr* To ruin someone; destroy: . . . *why you let your brother do you in the way he did*—Saul Bellow

doing *See* NOTHING DOING, TAKE SOME DOING

do it *v phr by 1913* To do the sex act; =FUCK •An arch euphemism very popular for a time in a series of bumper-stickers: *Divers do it deeper/ Professors do it fifty minutes at a time/. . . let alone comprehend that sexual intercourse is more than two bodies "doing it"*—Milwaukee Journal

do it all 1 *v phr underworld by 1940s* To serve a life term in prison **2** *v phr by 1960s* To be versatile; be variously skilled: *Take that shortstop. He'll do it all for you*

do it the hard way *v phr by 1920s* To do something in the most difficult and painful manner: *"He did it the hard way," said Johnny Croll*—New York Times [fr *the hard way* in craps, making the points of 4, 6, 8, or 10 with throws of a pair of 2s, 3s, 4s, or 5s]

do it up or **do it up brown** *v phr by 1880* To do something decisively and well: *Some of us really did it up in grand style*—Saturday Review

do-jigger *See* DOODAD

doke or **dokey** or **dokie** *See* OKEY-DOKE

dokle *See* OKEY-DOKE

dolf *n 1980s teenagers* A despised person; =DORK, JERK, NERD

doll 1 *n* (also **dolly**) *by 1860* A conventionally pretty and shapely young woman, esp a curly, blue-eyed blonde, whose function is to elevate the status of a male and to inspire general lust; =BABE, BABY DOLL, BIMBO: *If a blonde girl doesn't talk we call her a doll*—F Scott Fitzgerald/ . . . *the subservient dolly without a thought in her head. . .* —Buzz **2** *n by 1778* Any woman, esp an attractive one; =BABE, CHICK •Considered offensive by many women **3** *n by 1950s* A notably decent, pleasant, generous person; =LIVING DOLL: *Isn't he a doll?* **4** *n by 1940s* An attractive boy or young man **5** *n* (also **dolly**) *1960s narcotics* An amphetamine or barbiturate drug in pill or capsule form

See BABY DOLL, CHINA DOLL, LIVING DOLL

Doll *See* BARBIE DOLL

dollar *See* BET one's BOTTOM DOLLAR, HOT AS A THREE-DOLLAR PISTOL, PHONY AS A THREE-DOLLAR BILL, TOP DOLLAR

dollar-spinner *n by 1970s* Commercial success; seller: *All spectator sports combined to become the No 1 dollar-spinner. . . in entertainment*—People

dollars to doughnuts *adv phr by 1904* Very probably; almost certainly: *Dollars to doughnuts, there are more people this morning day-dreaming about old lovers than are reading this newspaper*—New York Times [*dollars to buttons* is found in 1884, and *dollars to a doughnut* in 1890; the most common phrase is *It is dollars to doughnuts that*]

dollar to rub against another *See* NOT HAVE ONE DOLLAR TO RUB AGAINST ANOTHER

dollface *n by 1940s* A person with regularly pretty features of a feminine sort

dollop *by 1812* **1** *n* A lump or glob **2** *n* A portion, esp a small portion of food [origin unknown]

dolls *See* CUT OUT DOLLS

doll up (or **out**) *v phr by 1906* To dress fancily and in one's best clothes; =GUSSY UP: *This year the girls are dolling up in calico patchworks*—New York Magazine

dolly *See* DOLL

dolly dancer *n phr* *WWII Army* A soldier who gets easy duty, esp by pleasing officers

do lunch *See* DO

DOM (pronounced as separate letters) *n by 1959* A dirty old man

-dom *suffix* **used to form nouns** The range, establishment, scope, or realm of what is indicated: *fandom/ moviedom/ klutzdom*

dome *n by 1880s* The head: *But when the messenger's got a gat pointed at your dome, what are you gonna do?*—Macon Telegraph
See IVORY-DOME, MARBLE-DOME

do me feminist *n phr early 1990s* A feminist who is overtly interested in appearance, style, sex, etc: *New generation of women thinkers who are embracing sex (and men!). Call them "do me" feminists*—Nation/ . . . *the "Do Me" feminists who have it all: good looks, good connections, no hang ups about sex (or capitalism). . .* —Extra [*do me* is a blunt invitation to the sex act]

dominoes *n by 1920s* Dice
See GALLOPING DOMINOES

donagher **See** DONNICKER

donar or **donah** (DAH nər, -nə) *n 1950s street gang* A girl, esp one's steady girl or fiancee, or a street-gang girl [prob fr Italian *donna*, "woman, lady"; used in London slang fr middle 1800s, and Australian fr late 1800s; the route to US slang is unclear]

done deal *n phr by 1980s* Something unlikely to be altered; a fait accompli: *If Ben shook your hand, it was a done deal*—Dan Jenkins/ *President Bush's enormous popularity may appear to make his re-election a done deal*—New York Times

done for *adj phr by 1842* Ruined; doomed; =FINISHED, KAPUT, SOL: *Once this gets out, we're done for*

done in *by 1917* **1** *adj phr* (also **done up**) Very tired; =POOPED: *I was done up*—SJ Perelman **2** *adj phr* Killed **3** *adj phr* Ruined; wrecked: *My plans are done in but good*

◁**dong**▷ *n by 1891* The penis [origin unknown; possibly fr *ding-dong* fr *dingus*, a euphemism for the unnamable thing; perhaps echoic to suggest striking; compare *wang*]
See FLONG one's DONG, PULL one's PUD

donk *n by 1920s* Whiskey, esp raw or corn whiskey [because it has a kick like a *donkey*]

◁**donkey dick**▷ **1** *n phr WWII armed forces* Salami and other cold-cut sausages; =HORSE COCK **2** *n phr 1960s narcotics* A very durable penile erection, due to an effect of heroin use: . . . *a reward known in smack circles as "donkey dick"*—High Times

donkey roast *n phr by 1960s* A large, fancy, or noisy party: . . . *at $100 a ticket. . . promises to be a real fine donkey roast*—New York Post

donkey's breakfast *n phr merchant marine by 1940s* A straw mattress

donkey's years (or **ears**) *n phr by 1917* A very long time ●Chiefly British use: *I got interested in his apprenticeship donkey's years ago*—Robert Ruark [a punning allusion to the long *ears* of a *donkey*]

donkeywork *n by 1920* Tedious work needing little skill or wit; =SCUT: *He uses computers to do what the "whiz kids" call their "donkey work"*—US News and World Report

donna **See** PRIMA DONNA

donnicker or **doniker** or **donagher** *n underworld, carnival & circus by 1930s* A toilet [fr diminutive of 18th-century British *danna*, "feces," applied to a privy]

donnybrook *n by 1852* A riotous scene, esp a general and energetic brawl; =BRANNIGAN: *A donnybrook began when police arrested the operators*—R McCarthy [fr the reputation of a fair held annually at the Dublin suburb of *Donnybrook*]

do someone **nothing** *v phr by 1950s* To leave one unaffected, unmoved, unpleased, etc: *This book does me nothing* [probably a play on the Yiddish phrase *tu mir eppes*, "do me something"]

don't *n* Something one should not or must not do; =NO-NO: *The do's and don'ts of sailing a leaky barge*

don't-blink *adj by early 1990s* Very small; =ONE-HORSE: . . . *maybe east or west through the don't-blink communities of LeRoy or Elmore*—Milwaukee Journal [because if you *blink* you will miss them entirely]

someone or something **don't get no respect** *sentence by 1970s* The subject is not treated with proper regard: *Although Luisa Miller has edged into the semi-standard repertory, it still doesn't get much respect*—New York Times/ *We Republicans are not getting any respect from the White House*—New Republic/ *Among superpower currencies, the Soviet ruble gets no respect*—Time [fr the tag line of the comedian Rodney Dangerfield]

◁**don't get your balls in an uproar**▷ *sentence by 1930s* Don't get so excited; be calm; =COOL IT: *Don't get your balls in an uproar. This isn't the first crime commission and it won't be the last*—Michael Grant

◁**don't get your testicles in a twist**▷ *sentence by 1990s* =COOL IT: *I'm coming, Mr McAllister! Don't get your testicles in a twist!*—Carsten Stroud [perhaps influenced by British *Don't get your knickers in a twist*, which is attested from 1971]

don't get your wig pushed back *sentence 1990s teenagers* Don't get so excited; be calm; don't overreact; =DON'T GET YOUR BALLS IN AN UPROAR, KEEP one's HAIR ON

don't give it a second thought *sentence by 1960s* Don't worry unduly about what you said or did; =FORGET IT: *You didn't mean to, I know. Don't give it a second thought*

don't give up (or **quit**) **your day job** *sentence by 1990s* What you are planning or doing may not pan out; you may be making a mistake: *If you consider yourself to the left of, say, Michael Kinsley, then don't give up your day job*—Lingua Franca

don't go there *sentence 1990s teenagers* Don't bring that up; don't broach that topic: *Don't go there: increasingly popular catch phrase among teenagers*—New York Times

don't have a baby (or **cow**) *sentence 1980s*

teenagers Calm down; relax; =COOL IT: *Don't have a cow; I'm only five minutes late*—Delcastle Dictionary of Slang

don't hold your breath *sentence* by *1960s* Don't count on a certain event or outcome; be patient and skeptical: *Will Clinton's vague and toothless form of workfare dissolve the welfare-based underclass? Don't hold your breath*—New Republic

don't knock it *sentence* Don't be critical of it; appreciate its value: *Don't knock it. Nobody who lived in the past would want to live in the past*—A Brien/ *Don't knock it. . . Good bucks there*—Lawrence Sanders

don't pop the champagne corks yet *sentence* (also **don't uncork the champagne yet**) by *1990s* Don't celebrate a victory prematurely; don't count your chickens before they're hatched: *It didn't happen, but don't pop the champagne corks yet*—John J Farmer/ *. . . the S&L industry posted earnings of $1.97 billion, the first gain in five years. But don't uncork the champagne yet*—Time [fr the custom of pouring champagne over the victors in a sports contest]

◁**don't shit a shitter**▷ *sentence* by *1970s* Don't try to hoodwink an expert hoodwinker: *"Don't shit a shitter," said Dubie*—Stan Cutler/ *. . . you can play it any way you like. But don't try to shit a shitter, okay?*—Elmore Leonard

don't take any wooden nickels *sentence* by *1915* Take care of yourself; goodbye, and watch yourself •Used as an amiable parting salutation

◁**don't try to shit a shitter** (or **bullshit a bull-shitter**)▷ *sentence* Never try to deceive a deceiver: *We get there you can play it any way you like. But don't try and shit a shitter, okay?*—Elmore Leonard

do one's **number** *v phr* by *1920s* To behave in an expected way; play a role; =GO INTO one's ACT: *He was doing his number about how you have to alienate no one* [fr *number*, "theatrical act or routine, shtick," which is attested by 1885]

doo *See* HOOPERDOOPER, DO-RAG

doobie or **dubee** or **duby** *n 1960s narcotics* A marijuana cigarette; =JOINT: *I smoke a doobie at lunch*—Armistead Maupin/ *. . . and rolled myself an ample doobie*—Richard Merkin **2** *n computer* by *1980s* A database [first sense, origin unknown; second sense probably fr *database*, influenced by first sense]

doodad by *1905* **1** *n* (Variations: **do-dad** or **do-funny** or **doofunny** or **do-hickey** or **doohickey** or **do-hinky** or **doohinky** or **do-jigger** or **doojigger** or **doowhangam** or **do-whistle** or **doowhistle** or **do-willie** or **doowillie**) Any unspecified or unspecifiable thing; something one does not know the name of or does not wish to name; =GADGET, THINGAMAJIG: *We may have turned into what looks like a nation of doohickeys*—Time/ *Imagination and art aren't worth those little doowhangams you put under a sofa leg*—National Review **2** *n* Something useless or

merely ornamental: *There was not one photograph, not a doodad, not a toy, not a cup, of my own*—Stan Cutler

doodah *See* ALL OF A DOODAH

doodle 1 *v* by *1823* To cheat; swindle; =DIDDLE **2** *v 1935* To make drawings and patterns while sitting at a meeting, talking on the telephone, etc: *From your doodle, the shrink sees what's in your noodle* **3** *n* Wretched material; =SHIT: *How can he write such doodle?*—Washington Post ◁**4**▷ *n* by *1780s* The penis •A child's term [second sense apparently coined by Robert Riskin, screenwriter for the movie *Mr Deeds Goes to Town*; third sense perhaps fr *doo*, childish word for "shit"]

See DIPSY-DOODLE, WHANGDOODLE, WHOOP-DE-DO

doodle-brained *adj* by *1970s* Stupid; silly: *. . . singing a doodle-brained folk song about "travelin'"*—Village Voice [fr *doodle*, "fool, simpleton," attested by 1628, whence *Yankee Doodle*]

doodlebug 1 *n railroad* by *1940s* A self-propelled railroad car; a one-car train **2** *n WWII armed forces* A small reconnaissance car **3** *n WWII armed forces* A military tank, esp a light tank **4** *n WWII British armed forces* A German jet-propelled robot bomb, the V1 **5** *n* by *1924* A divining rod or other device used for locating underground water, gas, etc [all senses connected with *doodlebug*, "the larva of the tiger-beetle or various other insects"]

◁**doodle-shit**▷ *n* (Variations: **doodily-shit** or **doodley-shit** or **doodly-squat** or **doodly**) *entry form* by *1960s*; -squat *forms* by *1930s* Nothing; very little; =SQUAT, ZILCH: *I don't care doodily-shit about Jews and Nazis*—Ira Levin/ *A whole lot of doodley-shit*—Richard Fariña

doodling *n* by *1970s* Idle playing: *When Sinatra entered the wings. . . the doodling ceased*—Village Voice

doodly-squat or **diddly-squat 1** *adj carnival* by *1930s* Penniless; =BROKE **2** *n* =DOODLE-SHIT

doo-doo *n* by *1940s* Excrement; =DO, SHIT •A child's term; see do: *I think doo-doo is coming out of your ears*—R Grossbach

doo-doo head *n phr* by *1970s* A stupid person; an idiot; =SHIT-FOR-BRAINS, SHITHEAD: *Let's face it, we're doo-doo heads for playing*—Washington Post

doofunny *See* DOODAD

doofus by *1960s* (also **doof** or **doofis** or **dufus**) **1** *n* A fool; idiot; =AIRHEAD, BIRDBRAIN, BOOB: *. . . he'll do his best to make you feel like a doofus/ But this is the doofus you have to deal with. . . so hush up*—Elle/ *I have to be in front of this self-important doofis with his portable phone*—comic strip "Shoe"/ *I felt like such a dufus*—comic strip "Sally Forth"/ *. . . when some big, loud, popcorn-chuggin' doof and his date sit in front of me*—comic strip "Curtis" **2** *modifier*: *. . . many another dufus play among friends*—Richard Merkin [probably related to *doo-doo* and *goofus*]

doohickey *n* (Variations: **do-hickey** or **do-hinky** or **doohinky**) by *1914* Any unspecified or unspecifiable

thing; something one does not know the name of or does not wish to name; =GADGET, THINGAMAJIG
See DOODAD

doohinky *See* DOODAD, DOOHICKEY

doojee or **doojie** or **dujie** (Dōō jee) *1960s narcotics* **1** *n* Heroin **2** *n* A baby born addicted to heroin [perhaps fr *do,* "feces," since heroin is also called "shit"]

doojigger *See* DOODAD

dooky *n* (also **dookie, dukie**) *1980s teenagers* Excrement; =SHIT: *I would have stomped the dooky out of him*—New Yorker [fr *doo*]

doolie *n 1950s Air Force Academy* A first-year cadet [origin uncertain; perhaps fr Greek *doulos,* "slave," which is the source of the early 1800s British schoolboy term *doul,* "fag, senior boy's personal menial among the junior boys"; perhaps fr the West Point term *ducrot,* "inferior or despised cadet"]
See BIG DOOLIE

do something **on top of** one's **head** *v phr* To accomplish something easily: *You can do that shit on top of your head*—Donald Goines

doop *See* WHOOP-DE-DO

dooper *See* HOOPERDOOPER, SUPER-DUPER, WHOOPER-DOOPER

door *See* someone CAN'T HIT THE SIDE OF A BARN, KATIE BAR THE DOOR, REVOLVING-DOOR, SHOW someone THE DOOR, SIDE-DOOR PULLMAN

doorkey child *See* LATCHKEY CHILD

doormat **1** *n* A person who is regularly and predictably exploited by others; constant victim: *. . . the soulful Earth Mother doormat of the kind played by Shirley MacLaine in the fifties*—New York Magazine/ *. . . the wife a rape victim, slave, doormat*—Mike Royko **2** *modifier*: *Cornell University's doormat status on the gridiron*—People
See TREAT someone LIKE A DOORMAT

doorstep *v 1990s* To confront someone for a media interview on the very doorstep: *Mrs. Ashdown, doorstepped by a TV team, gave an impassive nod before disappearing into her house*—New Yorker/ *The first time I went to meet Kunayev, I tried to doorstep him; this was not a wise maneuver*—New York Review of Books

do someone **out of** *v phr* by 1825 To deprive by cheating, fraud, stealing, etc: *They did the poor jerk out of his pay*

doowhangam or **doowhistle** or **doowillie**
See DOODAD

doo-wop or **do-whop** **1** *n 1950s black musicians* A style of street jazz-singing, esp by black ensembles **2** *modifier*: *. . . from the do-whop music and lovingly customized cars*—Time/ *. . . lead singer of her Sixties doo-wop outfit, Patti Labelle and the Bluebelles*—Rolling Stone [echoic fr a common rhythm phrase of the songs]

doozie or **doozy** or **doosie** *n by 1916* A person or thing that is remarkable, wonderful, superior, etc; =BEAUT, HUMDINGER: *. . . a little 30-page doozey called "Making Chicken Soup"*—Village Voice/

Want a swell Naval Air Station? I got two doozies up for grabs—Esquire [origin uncertain; perhaps fr a humorous repronunciation of *daisy;* certainly reinforced by *dusy, duesie,* and other shortenings of *Duesenberg,* the name of a very expensive and desirable car of the 1920s and 30s]

dope **1** *n by 1895* Any narcotic drug, legal or illegal •First applied to opium, by 1889: *They searched him for dope/ The doctors kept him full of dope* **2** *modifier*: *a dope fiend/ dope stash* **3** *v by 1889*: *The nurse doped him so that he could sleep* **4** *v by 1909* To use narcotics: *I like to dope*—Stan Cutler **5** *v by 1875* To give drugs, vitamins, etc, to horses or athletes to improve their competitive prowess: *He couldn't run that fast if he wasn't doped* **6** *n by 1915* Coca-Cola™: *Jim Bob sat down and ordered a large dope* **7** *n by 1872* Any liquid, esp a viscous one, used for a special purpose *. . . massaged his lamps with fragrant drug store dope*—Wallace Irwin **8** *n by 1909* =DOPER **9** *n British dialect by 1851* A stupid person; idiot; =TURKEY: *Only a dope would refuse that chance* **10** *n by 1901* Information; data; =the LOWDOWN: *Get me all the dope you can on her colleagues/ What's the latest dope about Ruth?* **11** *n by 1901* A prediction, esp about a race or a game, based on analysis of past performance; =FORM: *The dope says Dream Diddle in a romp* **12** *v by 1920s*: *I dope it like this, Ali all the way* **13** *modifier 1980s teenagers* Wonderful; excellent; =COOL, RAD, SUPER: *It's a dope day, dude!*—Gary Trudeau/ *Redman was one of the people Andre said was dope*—Vanity Fair/ *. . . have, in the parlance of the street, become "dope" and "phat," i.e. cool, greatest*—New York Times [fr Dutch *doop,* "sauce for dipping," with elaborate semantic shifts]
See HIT THE DOPE

dopenik *n 1960s narcotics* A narcotics addict

dope off **1** *v phr WWI Navy & Marine Corps* To sleep; fall asleep: *I fill my stomach before I go in there and I'll start to dope off and yawn or something*—Earl Thompson **2** *v phr WWII armed forces* To neglect one's duty and concerns; =GOOF OFF

dope out *v phr by 1906* To explain or clarify; figure out: *I doped that all out myself*—Bryn Mawr Slang

doper *narcotics by 1889* **1** *n* A narcotics addict or user: *. . . alerting dopers of every stripe that where the penalties had been stiff, they would now be feudal*—T Ferris/ *. . . I think to myself, some dopers're having a disagreement. . .*—Elmore Leonard **2** *modifier*: *. . . with all these doper cops loose*—Rolling Stone/ *. . . seemed merely a statement of doper hipness*—Rolling Stone

dope sheet *n phr by 1903* Printed information or instructions, esp about the past performance of race horses; =FORM

dopester *n by 1907* A person who makes predictions based on available information, esp about races and games

dope stick *n phr about 1915* A cigarette

dopey or **dopy** *by 1896* **1** *adj* Stuporous, esp

from narcotic intoxication: *I was dopy after they gave me the shot* **2 adj** Stupid; idiotic: *. . . most movies are written for women in their 20s and 30s, and these are sort of dopey parts*—New York Times [fr *dope*; the word has also meant "a thief's or beggar's woman" since at least the 1850s, and this may in some minds have influenced the modern senses]

Dora *See* DUMB DORA

do-rag 1 *n* black by 1960s A cloth or scarf worn over a processed hairdo or "conk": *. . . wears a "do-rag" on his new hairdo as he pours out hatred of whites*—Life/ *Plaid work shirt, do-rag, pointy-toed shoes. . .*—Carsten Stroud **2 modifier**: *that famous do-rag militant, Sammy Davis*—Village Voice

do-re-mi *n* by 1920s Money: *Get the rubber band off the do-re-mi*—John Kieran [fr the first three sol-fa notes, with a pun on *dough*, "money"]

◁**dork**▷ **1** *n* by 1964 The penis: *. . . the glorious acrobatics she can perform while dangling from the end of my dork*—Philip Roth **2** *v* by 1970s To do the sex act with or to; ruin or confound as if by violating sexually; =FUCK, SCREW: *I said to myself, "I dorked him," but the ball just kept floating like it was floating on air. . .*—Milwaukee Journal **3** *n* students by early 1970s A despicable person; =JERK, PRICK: *. . . a frightened, virtuous dork*—New Yorker

dorky *adj* students by early 1970s Stupid; =DOPEY, DUMB: *. . . a dorky kid with Dumbo ears*—Armistead Maupin/ *Casually include them in chitchat about how dorky the principal's speech was. . .*—Sassy

dorm by 1900 **1** *n* A dormitory, esp at a college **2 modifier**: *a dorm picnic/ dorm rule*

dory *See* HUNKY-DORY

dosage index *n phr* fr horse-racing by 1990s A performance record; winning potential: *. . . there is that troubling dosage index: Dole ran and lost twice before*—Milwaukee Journal Sentinel/ *Keep your eye on Afternoon Deelites. . . good dosage index ("pedigree" to the uninitiated)*—Milwaukee Journal Sentinel

dose *v* by about 1914 To infect with a venereal disease, esp gonorrhea: *What's going to happen is that you'll get dosed*—Richard Fariña

a **dose** *n phr* by 1914 A case of venereal disease, esp of gonorrhea: *Don't Give a Dose to the One You Love Most*—New York Daily News
See LIKE SHIT THROUGH A TIN HORN

do-se-do or **do-si-do** (DOH see DOH) **1** *n* prize-fight by 1930s A dull fight, with more dancing than punching: *The guys who are supposed to do the fighting go in there and put on the old do-se-do. . .*—Damon Runyon **2** *n* by 1960s A regular alternation; predictable shift: *Fashion always does a do-si-do between artifice and the natural*—New York Times [fr the square-dance figure, fr French *dos-à-dos*, "back to back," in which dancers pass each other back-to-back and return to their places]

dose of salts *See* LIKE SHIT THROUGH A TIN HORN

doss 1 *n* hoboes by 1890s Sleep: *find good barns for a doss at night* **2** *n* (also **doss house**) by 1888 A cheap lodging house; =FLOPHOUSE **3** *n* by 1789 A bed; =KIP [ultimately fr Latin *dorsum*, "back"]

do something **standing on one's head** *v phr* by 1896 To do something easily [the dated form is *do it on one's head*]

do one's **stuff** *v phr* 1920s To perform one's role, esp something one does very well: *Get in there and do your stuff*

the **dot** *See* ON THE DOT

do tell *interj* by 1840 An exclamation of surprise, incredulity, etc: *You shot the dog? Do tell!*

◁**dot head**▷ *n phr* by 1980s A Hindu Indian: *He refers to Asian Indians as "dot heads"*—Bergen Record [fr the *dot* caste mark worn on the forehead by some Hindu Indians]

◁**do the bone dance** (or **the nasty**)▷ *v phr* 1980s students To do the sex act; =BOFF, BONE, SCREW: *My parents walked in while I was doing the bone dance and grounded me for forty years*—UCLA Slang

do the dirty on someone *v phr* by 1914 =DO someone DIRT

do the Dutch (or **the Dutch act**) *v phr* by 1904 To commit suicide: *Why did the old man do the Dutch?*—Lawrence Sanders/ *She only came aboard to do the Dutch act*—John O'Hara [narrowed meaning of an earlier phrase meaning "to depart, abscond, go south"]

do the nasty *v phr* 1980s students To do the sex act; =BOFF, BONE, SCREW

do the wild thing *v phr* 1980s students To do the sex act; =BOFF, BONE, SCREW: *Elliot Gould. . . first did the wild thing with. . . Barbra Streisand. . . in the early 1960s*—Denver Post/ *It was a bad thing to do the wild thing without a blessing from the Almighty*—P K McCary

do one's (or one's **own**) **thing** *v phr* fr black by 1960s To follow one's special inclinations, esp despite disapproval; fulfill one's peculiar destiny: *Doing your own thing may be all right in prescribed doses*—A J H Brown

do time *v phr* about 1860 To serve a prison sentence

do tricks *See* GO DOWN AND DO TRICKS

dotted Q sign *n phr* medical by 1980s A sign that the patient is comatose or dead [the Q is the open mouth with the tongue hanging out; the *dot* is a fly on the tongue]

dot the Is and cross the Ts *v phr* by 1885 To work meticulously, esp to make something clear and accurate: *Extraneous to my investigation, but I like to dot the i's and cross the t's*—Lawrence Sanders

dotty *adj* by 1885 Crazy; insane; feebleminded: *a dotty old fellow* [origin uncertain; perhaps related to *dotty*, "of unsteady, uneven, or feeble gait," and this is the dated sense above; perhaps related to *dote* and *doat*, attested in the 1200s as "silly, crazy"; *dote* is also an early spelling of *dot*, so the matter seems quite complex]

double *n* by 1543 A person or thing that strongly or

exactly resembles another; duplicate; =DEAD RINGER, LOOK-ALIKE: *She's Grace Kelly's double*

See ON THE DOUBLE

a **double** *n phr* A double portion or pair of anything: *. . . scored a double, riding the winners of the fourth and seventh races*—New York World-Telegram

double (or **double in brass**) **as** *v phr* circus by about 1920 To perform or work as, in addition to one's primary job: *He doubled in brass as a waiter when the cooking was done* [fr the skill of a circus performer who does an act and also plays in the band]

double-bagger *n* 1970s teenagers A very ugly person; =TWO-BAGGER [fr the fact that one needs two *bags* to obscure the ugliness, one to go over the subject's head and one over one's own head]

double-barreled name *n phr* by 1889 A name made up of two names, usu hyphenated: *An elderly Englishwoman with a title and a double-barreled surname*—New York Times

double-clutcher *n* black by 1950s A despicable person; =BASTARD, PRICK [a rhyming euphemism for *motherfucker*]

double-clutching *adj* black by 1950s =MOTHERFUCKING

double cross by 1834 **1** *n phr* A betrayal or cheating of one's own colleagues; an act of treachery, often in an illicit transaction: *The two suspected dealers were planning a double-cross*—New York Magazine **2** *v*: *I would never double-cross a pal* [fr the reneging on an agreement to lose, a *cross*, by actually winning]

See GIVE someone THE DOUBLE CROSS

double dare or **double dog dare** *v phr* by 1940s To challenge provocatively: *The movie double-dared its audience to find sympathy in its dour or manic characters*—Time/ *. . . I double dog dare ya to find out which three!*—Toronto Globe and Mail [fr a boys' response to "I dare you!," "I double dare you!"; double dog dare is still higher defiance]

double-dealing by 1529 **1** *n* Deceitful or treacherous behavior **2** *modifier*: *a double-dealing little crum*

double-dip *v* 1970s To collect more than one income at a time, esp by simultaneously drawing a government pension and holding a job [fr an ice-cream cone with two *dips*, scoops, of ice cream]

double-dipper *n* 1970s A person who double-dips: *Federal pensioners are "double-dippers" who also collect Social Security checks*—Time

double-dome by 1930s **1** *n* An intellectual; scholar; =EGGHEAD: *Princeton, NJ, where the double domes congregate*—New York Post **2** *modifier*: *None of your double-dome pomp, please* **3** *v*: *legitimate double-doming I suppose, but totally without fact*—Philadelphia

double Dutch *n phr* by 1864 Language that cannot be understood, esp overly technical jargon: *Plain English will do; cut the double Dutch* [Dutch, "German," being unintelligible, *double Dutch* is twice as opaque]

double-gaited by 1930s **1** *adj* Bisexual; =AC-DC: *Duilio is not double gaited as far as I know*—John O'Hara/ *Was Danny simply double-gaited?*—Charles Beardsley **2** *adj* Strange; eccentric; =WEIRD: *These double-gaited gonzos are perpetrating a plague of best-selling takeoffs*—Newsweek [fr the various *gaits* of a horse]

doubleheader *n* sports by 1890s Two contests, esp baseball games, played at one meeting [fr earlier railroad use for a train drawn by two engines]

double nickel **1** *n phr* 1970s citizens band The 55-mile-per-hour speed limit **2** *n phr* by 1980s Interstate highway 55, running south from Chicago

double-o *v* by 1917 To examine carefully; scrutinize: *I stop a second to double-o the frame*—Lionel Stander [fr the abbreviation of *once-over*]

the **double-o** *n phr* by 1917 A close examination; =the ONCE-OVER: *You mean give him the double-O*—John O'Hara

double-R *n* by 1990s A Rolls-Royce car: *I crossed back to the Union 76, paid my ransom for Full Service, and got back in the double-R*—Stan Cutler

double sawbuck (or **saw**) *n phr* by 1850 Twenty dollars; a $20 bill: *. . . so many sheets of dollars, ten-spots and double saws*—Westbrook Pegler

double scrud **See** SCRUD

double (or **fast**) **shuffle** by 1891 **1** *n phr* =DOUBLE CROSS **2** *n phr* Deception; duplicity; =RUNAROUND: *I don't want you to think I'm giving you a fast shuffle*—Lawrence Anderson **3** *v*: *He was fast shuffling me, but I caught him* [fr the deceptive *shuffle* of a card sharp]

double-take by 1940s **1** *n* A sudden second look or a laugh or gesture over something one has at first ignored or accepted; a belated reaction: *She suddenly caught the reference and did a double-take* **2** *v*: *I double-took a little bit when she ordered a cigar*—Robert Ruark

double talk by 1938 **1** *n phr* A sort of gibberish or patter that seems plausible but is nonsense, done for amusement: *Danny Kaye excelled at double talk* **2** *n phr* Deceptive and insincere speech: *Don't be put off by his double talk*

double-team *v* by 1860 To attack or defend against someone, esp a formidable athlete, with twice the usual forces: *He was gaining every play till they double-teamed him* [originally fr *doubling* the *team* of horses used for a purpose]

double-time *v* =DOUBLE CROSS, TWO-TIME

double-trouble by 1940s **1** *n* Serious difficulty; =DEEP TROUBLE •This was the name of a black shuffle dance as early as 1807, showing the potential of the rhyme **2** *modifier*: *a double-trouble day* **3** *n* A source or cause of great difficulty or menace; =BAD NEWS: *Watch that clown, he's double trouble*

double turkey *n phr* bowling by 1940s Six strikes bowled one after another

double whammy *n phr* by 1940s A two-part or two-pronged difficulty; a dual disadvantage: *. . . the*

double-whammy of steep home prices and steeper interest rates—Washingtonian
See the WHAMMY

double X *n phr* by 1920s =DOUBLE CROSS

◁**douche bag**▷ *n phr students* by 1950s A despicable and loathsome person; =SCUMBAG: *. . . dirty, filthy douchebag*—Herbert Kastle/ *Either this guy is a bigger douche bag than I even remember or something is way out of line*—Scott Turow [recorded in the 1940s meaning "a military misfit"]

dough 1 *n* by 1851 Money; =BREAD: *And to get the dough we'll put our watch and chain in hock*—H S Canby **2** *n* =DOUGHBOY
See CASE DOUGH, HEAVY MONEY

doughboy *n* by 1867 An infantry soldier; =GRUNT, PADDLEFOOT [origin unknown; perhaps fr a resemblance between the buttons of the infantry uniform and *doughboys*, "suet dumplings boiled in seawater," a term fr the British merchant marine]

doughfoot *n* WWI =DOUGHBOY

dough-head *n* by 1838 A stupid person; idiot; =KLUTZ

doughnut 1 *n truckers* by 1930s A truck tire **2** *n* by 1980s The driving of a car in tight circles, esp by hoodlums who have stolen the car: *Perform doughnuts, in which they lock the brakes, step on the gas, and send the car spinning in circles*—Time/ *. . . spotted about 7:20 doing doughnuts in the parking lot of Taco Bell. . .*—Macon Telegraph
See TAKE A FLYING FUCK

doughnut factory (Variations: **foundry** or **house** or **joint** may replace **factory**) by 1940s, foundry form by 1920s **1** *n phr* A cheap eating place; luncheonette **2** *n phr hoboes* A place where free food is distributed

dough-pop *v* by 1970s To defeat; hit; =CLOBBER, WHACK: *. . . dough-popped Arkansas 37 to 21*—Dan Jenkins

do up 1 *v phr* by 1846 To pummel and trounce; =CLOBBER **2** *v phr* 1960s narcotics To take narcotics: *We'll do up some hash*

do something **up brown** *v phr* by 1840 To do something very thoroughly: *He didn't just finish it, he did it up brown* [fr the brown color of something well baked]

douse or **dowse** *v* by 1807 To extinguish a light, lamp, candle, etc [specialized fr an earlier sense, "hit"]

dove (DUHV) **1** *n* by 1596 Dear one; honey; love: *There at once, my dove* **2** *n* by 1962 A person who advocates peace and nonviolence; an irenic soul
See TURTLEDOVES

dovetail *v* 1970s Army To say something linked and sequential: *Let me dovetail on what you just said*

dovey *n* by 1796 =LOVEY-DOVEY

dovish *adj* by 1960s Tending to advocate peace over war; irenic: *. . . more and more room for dovish interpretations*—Stewart Alsop

dow **See** ROW-DOW, ROWDY-DOW

dowd *n* by 1330 A woman who dresses unfashionably and dully: *. . . a sweet pug up against the system, and in love with a dowd*—Washington Post

dowdy **See** ROWDY-DOW

do what comes naturally *v phr* by 1940s To do the simple obvious thing; respond unthinkingly: *As might have been expected, the Joint Chiefs of Staff did what came naturally*—New York Review [Popularized by a song "Doing What Comes Naturally," which celebrates wholesome instinctive behavior]

do-whistle or **do-willie** **See** DOODAD

do whop **See** DOO-WOP

down 1 *v* by 1860 To eat or drink: *I downed an enormous pizza* **2** *v* by 1960s To criticize; complain of; =PUT someone or something DOWN: *My friends downed me for listening to country music*—H E Roberts **3** *adj* by 1645 Depressed; melancholy; =BLUE: *He's real down about losing that chance* **4** *adj* by 1950s Depressing; pessimistic; dampening; =DOWNBEAT: *I don't see the point of making such a "down" picture*—Xaviera Hollander **5** *adj* by 1970s Not functioning; =ON THE BLINK: *The power plant has been down for two months/ The computer's down again today* **6** *adj* by 1970s Coolly cognizant; at ease in one's own skin; =COOL: *To show how "down" you are to youthful consumers. . .*—Washington Post/ *Of course if you are "with it,". . . you "be down"*—New York Times **7** *adj jazz musicians* about 1950 Excellent; good; profoundly satisfying **8** *n* 1960s narcotics =DOWNER **9** *adj* (also **down-ass**) 1930s jazz musicians Having special affinity; linked; in league ●The term was strongly revived in the 1990s by black teenagers and street gangs: *It wasn't her turf, but she wasn't down special with one gang. . .*—Robert B Parker/ *You're down with the heavy metal crowd now*—New Yorker/ *. . . I am probably one of the few down-ass females on his team. . .*—The Source/ *You're down hard for the 'hood*—televison show Hill Street Blues [cool and teenager senses perhaps fr jazz musicians' terms like *low down* and *down and dirty* used to praise gutbucket and other jazz when especially well played]
See DOWN ON someone, GET DOWN, GO DOWN ON someone, HAVE something DOWN PAT, LOOK DOWN ON someone, the LOWDOWN, LOW-DOWN, MELTDOWN, PUT-DOWN, PUT someone DOWN FOR something, UP-AND-DOWN

down (or **up**) someone's **alley** *adv phr* entry form by 1941, variant by 1931 Of the sort one prefers or is best at; =TAILOR-MADE: *That job's right down his alley*

down and dirty *adj phr* by 1950s Nasty; low; vicious and deceptive ●Also uttered in seven-card stud poker as the last cards are dealt face down: *Mississippi: A Down and Dirty Campaign*—Newsweek/ *This is down-and-dirty time. Just witness Rizzo's angry characterization of Goode*—Philadelphia

down and out *adj phr* by 1889 Penniless and hopeless; destitute: *When you're down and out, remember what did it*—Arthur Miller [fr the condition of a fighter who is knocked down unconscious]

down-and-outer *n* by 1909 A complete failure; derelict; =BUM

down a peg *See* TAKE someone DOWN A PEG

downbeat *adj* by 1950s Depressing; pessimistic: . . . *a triumph of upbeat pictures over the downbeat*—Bob Thomas [fr the *downbeat* of an orchestra leader's hand or baton, taken as the direction of dejection]

down-dressed *adj* by 1970s Avoiding the obvious appearance of luxury or formality; understated; casual

down-dresser *n* by 1990s A person who dresses caually: *Jack Sterk, faculty president of Vallejo College and notorious down-dresser.* . . —Los Angeles Times

downer 1 *n* 1950s narcotics A depressant drug, esp a barbiturate; sedative; =DOWN **2** *n* 1960s narcotics A depressing experience; =BAD TRIP, BUMMER, DRAG: *The opening scene's a downer*

down for the count *adj phr* by 1922 Utterly defeated; ruined; =DOWN AND OUT [fr the *count* of ten made over a *downed* boxer]

downhill 1 *n* prison about 1930 The final half of a prison sentence or a military enlistment **2** *adj* by 1719 Simple and easy: *nearly done and all downhill from here* **3** *adv* by 1795 To a worse condition; to the bad: *all trends ineluctably downhill* **4** *adj*: *a downhill prospect*
See GO DOWNHILL

down home by 1848 **1** *adv phr* In the southern US; in Dixie **2** *n phr*: *old buddy from down home* **3** *modifier*: *He was getting away from all that old down-home stuff*—Claude Brown **4** *adv phr* In a Southern regional or ethnic manner: . . . *funkier than blues and playing about as down home as you can get*—Rolling Stone **5** *adj phr* Simple; homey: *a down-home meal of roast chicken, potatoes, and peas*

down in flames *See* GO DOWN IN FLAMES

down in the dumps *adj phr* by 1785 Depressed; melancholy; =BLUE, DOWN [in text of 1529, *in a dump* means "melancholy, dejected"; modern use probably influenced by US *dump*, "rubbish heap," etymologically unrelated, which is attested from 1865]

down in the kitchen *adv phr* 1930s truckers Driving in lowest gear, the "creeper" gear

down one's **nose** *See* LOOK DOWN one's NOSE

down on someone or something *adj phr* by 1843 Angry with or critical of: *Everybody's down on Mary since she reported Sue to the boss*

down on all fours *adv phr* by 1710 In an equal situation; not superior: . . . *Du Pont found itself down on all fours with the rest of the industry*—M Ways

downplay *v* by 1968 To de-emphasize; minimize; =SOFT-PEDAL: *They're downplaying the role of bias in all this*

downputter *n* by 1950s A person who regularly criticizes and disparages; =KNOCKER

downside *n* by 1980s The depressing or deflating aspect of something; the bad news: . . . *the more ability and ambition you need to survive the "down-side" of this evolutionary process*—Milwaukee Journal/ *It sounds a little too perfect. What's the downside?*—New Yorker/ . . . *developments of the past decades have surely had their down side*—New Republic

downsize *v* early 1980s To reduce the size of a company by eliminating employees, in order to increase profits

down the drain *adv phr* by 1930 To a futile end; to waste: *All his best efforts seemed to go down the drain*
See POUR MONEY DOWN THE DRAIN

down the Goodyears (or the rollers) *v phr* airline by 1970s To lower the landing gear ●Esp the command to do so

down the hatch *interj* by 1931 A toast, followed by the swallowing of a whole drink

down the pike *See* COME DOWN THE PIKE

down the river *See* SELL someone DOWN THE RIVER

down the road *adv phr* by 1960s Later; in the future: *It might save us a little now, but it'll cost us down the road*

down the tube (or tubes or chute) *See* GO DOWN THE TUBE

down someone's **throat** *See* JUMP DOWN someone's THROAT

down ticket or **down ballot** *adj phr* by 1990s Having a lower place on the ballot, hence contending for less important or local offices: *A great deal of creative savagery is to be found in the down ticket races in campaigns from North Carolina to Washington*—New York Times/ *As a down ballot candidate, try to attend senatorial and gubernatorial events in your state*—Harper's

downtime 1 *n* by 1950s Time during which a machine, factory, etc, is not operating **2** *n* Time away from work; leisure time: *He spends most of his downtime with Toby, his wife*—People/ *He has more downtime than he did four years ago*—Time

down to brass tacks *adv phr* by 1897 Dealing with the essentials; concerned with the practical realities: . . . *highbrow sermons that don't come down to brass tacks*—Sinclair Lewis [apparently fr the *brass tacks* that were used to measure cloth on the counter of a dry goods store, hence represented precision]

down to the ankles *See* BEATEN DOWN TO THE ANKLES

down to the ground *adv phr* by 1878 Totally; utterly: *That'll suit me down to the ground*

down to the wire *adv phr* horse-racing by 1901 Near the finish; at or to the last possible moment: *The project is getting down to the wire and things are getting frantic* [fr the imaginary line marking the end of a horserace; horses were said to pass "under the *wire*"]
See GO TO THE WIRE

downtown *n* narcotics by 1980s Heroin; =HORSE, SHIT

down trip *See* BAD TRIP

Down Under *by 1890s* **1** *adv phr* In Australia and/or New Zealand; in the Antipodes **2** *n phr*: *They're from Down Under*

downwinder *n by 1980s* People who live where nuclear fallout reaches them on the wind: *Bush signed a bill to compensate downwinders and some workers who participated in above-ground atomic tests*—New York Times/ *The studies have not yet confirmed what the downwinders say they know*—Cable News Network

down with it *adj phr 1930s jazz musicians* Coolly cognizant; absolutely in touch; =WITH IT

down yonder *adv phr by 1840s* =DOWN HOME

do you want an engraved invitation *question by 1970s* Must you be especially asked and pleaded with?; you are being too standoffish and scrupulous

dozen *See* CLEAN DOZENS, DEVIL'S DOZEN, a DIME A DOZEN, PLAY THE DOZENS

dozer **1** *n by 1950s* A powerful blow, esp with the fist; =BELT, BIFF **2** *n by 1950s* =DOOZIE **3** *n by 1940s* A bulldozer [except for sense 3, the sources do not clarify pronunciation; senses 1 and 2 may be pronounced *DOOzer*, which would make them different in origin from sense 3]

DPT (pronounced as separate letters) *n 1970s narcotics* Dipropylphyptamine, a hallucinogen like LSD but having an effect lasting only an hour or two

Dracula clause *n phr by 1980s* A statutory clause that prevents an impeached official from running for the office again: *They have voted to impeach, but they don't get to go home yet. Now they have to vote on whether to invoke the Dracula clause*—Arizona television [fr the horrid but very popular vampire Count *Dracula,* who kept coming back to life after being killed]

draft *v 1970s car racing* To drive close behind a vehicle so as to be drawn by reduced air pressure: *The point person takes on the wind, allowing those behind him to draft and save as much as 20% of their energy*—New York Times
See FEEL A DRAFT

draft bait *n phr by 1940s* A person subject to immediate conscription

drag **1** *n by 1896* Influence; weight; =CLOUT, PULL: *We had a big drag with the waiter*—Ernest Hemingway **2** *n by 1851* A street: *. . . from some bo on the drag I managed to learn*—Jack London **3** *n by 1914* An inhalation of smoke; puff; =TOKE: *The ponies took last drags at their cigarettes and slumped into place*—F Scott Fitzgerald **4** *v by 1919*: *dragging on cigars and feeling grown up* **5** *n by 1940s* A cigarette; =BUTT: *. . . a drag smoking on your lip*—Stephen Longstreet **6** *n* (also **drag party**) *homosexuals by 1920s* A party or gathering, usu of homosexuals, where everyone wears clothing of the other sex; a clustering of transvestites **7** *n homosexuals by 1870* Clothing worn by someone of the sex for which the clothing was not intended; transvestite costume, esp women's clothing worn by

a man: *We shall come in drag, which means wearing women's costumes*—Reynolds Newspaper/ *Mother walked in, a little Prussian officer in drag*—Tennessee Williams **8** *modifier*: *a drag queen/ drag party* **9** *v 1950s hot rodders* To race down a straightaway **10** *n* =DRAG RACE **11** *n police* A roll of money, purse, etc, used to lure the victim in a confidence game **12** *n 1940s jazz musicians* A situation, occupation, event, etc, that is tedious and trying; =DOWNER: *Life can be such a drag one minute and a solid sender the next*—Louis Armstrong/ *Keeping things at the cleaners was sometimes a last-minute drag. . .* —Stan Cutler **13** *n by 1940s* A dull, boring person: *Don't ask John to the party; he's such a drag* **14** *modifier*: *Take the quiz and unearth your drag quotient*—Sassy **15** *v computer by 1980s* To move an image, a file designation, etc, or expand a designated menu on the computer screen by using the mouse: *I copied the whole file onto a floppy disk. . . dragged the original file into the electronic trash can*—New Yorker
See MAIN DRAG

◁**drag ass**▷ *by 1940s* **1** *v phr* To depart, esp in a hurry; =HAUL ASS **2** *v phr* To be morose, sluggish, and whiny: *Quit drag-assing and get to work* **3** *n*: *. . . we had twenty-five good guys on the club, no more drag-asses, no more prima donnas*—Whitey Herzog

drag one's **feet** *v phr fr loggers* To shirk; make less than a good effort, perhaps in the spirit of sabotage: *She spent a lot of time dragging her feet*—New York Times/ *I'm not dragging my feet. I'm just scared*—Elmore Leonard [fr the action of an unenergetic member of a two-person sawing team, who would *drag his feet* or "ride the saw" rather than contribute the proper effort]

drag one's **freight** *See* PULL one's FREIGHT

dragged out *adj phr by 1831* Exhausted; =BEAT: *I feel awful dragged out today*

dragger *See* KNUCKLE-DRAGGER

dragging *See* one's **ass is dragging**

draggy *adj by 1922* Slow; monotonous; sluggish: *a draggy movie*

drag in *v phr by 1940s* To arrive: *Where'd you drag in from?*

drag someone **kicking and screaming into the twentieth century** *v phr* To force someone to recognize or adapt to change; educate a rigid reactionary: *. . . the group that drags the ABA kicking and screaming into the 20th century*—New York Times

Dragon Lady *n phr by 1940s* A powerful, intimidating woman [fr a character in the popular comic strip "Terry and the Pirates," which originated in the 1930s]

drag out **1** *v phr by 1842* To extend something tediously; make something last too long: *He dragged out the story excruciatingly* **2** *v phr by 1940s* To extract; elicit: *She couldn't drag the truth out of him*

drag-out *See* KNOCK-DOWN-DRAG-OUT

drag queen *homosexuals by 1941* **1** *n phr* A male homosexual who enjoys dressing like a woman: *. . . a rabidly right-wing congressman, a demented Southern drag queen, a pushy leather dyke. . .* —Penguin Books catalog **2** *n phr* A male homosexual who affects pronounced feminine behavior; =QUEEN

drag race *n phr* *1950s hot rodders* A speed competition between or among cars, esp vehicles with very powerful engines and very elongated, skeletal bodies

dragster *n* *1950s hot rodders* A car used in drag races, esp one purposely built for such competition

drag strip *n phr* *1950s hot rodders* The straight track or portion of highway on which a drag race is held

dragsville *adj* *by 1960s* Very dull; tedious; =DRAGGY, DULLSVILLE: *My much touted party proved dragsville*

drag-tail *v* *by 1940s* To move or work sluggishly; =DRAG ASS: *Jimmy is drag-tailing it up Main Street*—Billy Rose

drag one's **tail** (or ◁**ass**▷) *v phr* *by 1930s* To work sluggishly; loaf; =DRAG ASS, DRAG-TAIL: *Two hours off with pay, why the hell are they draggin' their tails?*—Pietro di Donato

drain *See* BRAIN DRAIN, DOWN THE TUBE, POUR MONEY DOWN THE DRAIN

drama *See* DOCU, DROOPY DRAMA

drape *1940s jive talk* **1** *n* A suit; ensemble of suit, shirt, necktie, and hat **2** *n* A young man wearing black, narrow-cuffed slacks, a garish shirt, a loose jacket without lapels, and no necktie: *Drapes resent any comparison with zoot-suiters*—Time
See SET OF THREADS

drape ape *n phr* *college students* A baby or small child

drapes *n* *black by about 1935* Clothes; dress

drape shape *1940s jive talk* **1** *n phr* A severely draped garment, as worn by zoot-suiters **2** *modifier*: *. . . designing the first drape-shape coat*—New Yorker

draw **1** *n* *by 1876* A puff on a pipe, cigarette, etc; =DRAG, TOKE **2** *n* (also **drawing card**) *by 1881* Something that attracts: *A skin flick is always a good draw*
See BEAT someone TO THE DRAW, GET A BEAD ON someone or something, the LUCK OF THE DRAW, QUICK ON THE DRAW, SLOW ON THE DRAW

draw a blank **1** *v phr* *by 1940s* To fail completely in recall: *I'm trying to remember, but keep drawing a blank* **2** *v phr* *by 1825* To get nothing; have a negative result; fail: *I drew a blank when I solicited him*

draw a picture (or **diagram**) *v phr* *by 1960s* To explain something in very simple terms; make things transparently clear: *I just don't like him. Do I have to draw you a picture?*

drawer *See* TOP-DRAWER

drawers *See* MAGGIE'S DRAWERS

dreadlock or **dredlock** *by 1960* **1** *n* (also **dread**) A mat or clump of long ungroomed hair as worn by Rastafarians, reggae musicians, etc: *. . . grown his hair in long dredlocks, Rasta style*—Village Voice/ *Her dark-brown dreads. . . are very thick and practically matted to her head*—Sassy **2** *modifier*: *. . . a British skinhead playing the dreadlock music of Jamaica*—Playboy [fr the *dread* presumably aroused by the wearers]

dream *See* PIPE DREAM, WET DREAM

dream and cream *v phr* *by 1970s* To have sexual fantasies: *. . . the kind of man you dream and cream about*—Tom Aldibrandi

dream bait (or **puss**) *n phr* *1940s students* An attractive, desirable person

dreamboat *1940s* **1** *n* Any very desirable vehicle: *A dreamboat for hot-rodders is a chromed roadster*—Life **2** *n* A very attractive person: *. . . will star opposite James Mason, who she says is a "dreamboat"*—Associated Press

dream up *v phr* *by 1940s* To invent; confect in the mind: *Julian has to start dreaming up a story*—Budd Schulberg/ *. . . conceptions of living dreamed up by such groups as the Mormons*—J B Roulier

dreamy *adj* *by 1920s* Very desirable; beautiful: *What a dreamy house you've got!*

dreck or **drek** *by 1920s* **1** *n* Wretched trash; =GARBAGE, JUNK, SHIT: *. . . the ugliness, dreck and horror of New York City*—People/ *They may bring with them a pile of overfinished drek*—Toronto Life/ *the sad glitter of desert drek*—WH Auden **2** *modifier*: *. . . no point in my keeping every drek album*—Rolling Stone/ *an opponent of the ticky-tacky world of dreck-tech architecture*—Toronto Life [fr Yiddish, "feces"]

dredge up *v phr* *by 1950s* To find or discover by effort and persistence: *Let's dredge up more dirt on the candidate*

dress *See* GRANNY DRESS

dress down **1** *v phr* *by 1715* To reprimand; rebuke; =CHEW OUT **2** *v phr* *by 1960* To dress less formally or arrestingly than one might: *Casual Fridays raise new fashion issues. How much should you dress down?*—Milwaukee Journal

dress-down Friday or **jeans day** *n phr* *1990s* The last day of the work week, when one can dress informally: *He cites the business community's adoption of dress-down Friday as an example. . .* —Los Angeles Times/ *It's Friday, jeans day, pal*—Douglas Coupland

dressed to the teeth (or **to kill** or **to the nines**) *first form by 1970s, second by 1940s, third by 1859* **1** *adj phr* Extremely well and fancily dressed or decorated: *She's dressed to the teeth in magenta silks*—Village Voice **2** *modifier*: *. . . our dressed-to-the-teeth test car*—Car and Driver **3** *v phr*: *. . . when she wrote articles about textured stockings and dressed to the nines*—Gloria Steinem [*to the teeth* implies "completely, from the bottom up"; *to the nines* is probably based on *nine* as a nearly perfect number just under ten, or

on *nine* as a mystical or sacred number in numerology, the product of three times three]
See the WHOLE NINE YARDS

dress-off *n black by 1960s* A competition among flashily-garbed persons

dress something **up** *v phr by 1691* To alter something, usu with an aim to misleading: *It's an ugly story, no matter how you try to dress it up*

dribs and drabs *n phr by 1850s* In skimpy bits; piecemeal: *Details about Whitewater are coming out in dribs and drabs*—Thomas Friedman [*drib* is probably a shortening of *dribble; drab* earlier meant "a small debt"]

dried *See* CUT AND DRIED

drift 1 *n 1950s car racing* A controlled sidewards skid: *. . . puts his Maserati or Ferrari into a corner with a four-wheel drift*—Life **2** *n by 1526* Meaning; intent: *Get my drift, chum?* **3** *v underworld & prison by 1960s* (also **drift out, drift away**) To leave; depart: *Beat it. . . Drift*—Raymond Chandler
See GET THE DRIFT

drifter *n by 1908* A derelict; =BUM

drift off track *v phr by 1970s* To deviate from proper conduct: *I sometimes drift off track a bit, but I really try to do what is right*—Westworld

drifty *adj by 1970s* Stupidly inattentive; silly; =SPACED-OUT: *It makes Dede and me both look a little drifty*—Armistead Maupin

drill 1 *v by 1674* To speed with force, esp through obstacles: *. . . skimmed by his head and drilled through the closed window*—New York Daily News **2** *v by 1808* To shoot; kill by shooting: *Go drill the mutt. He's strictly stool*—American Mercury **3** *v baseball by 1940s* To hit a hard, straight grounder or line drive: *Lockman drilled a single past Hodges*—Associated Press **4** *n by 1940* The way of doing something; the plan of action •Still chiefly British use: *Pain in the ass, but that's the drill*—Stan Cutler
See BLANKET DRILL, MONKEY DRILL, SACK DUTY

drink *See* CHAIN-DRINK, I'LL DRINK TO THAT, TAKE A DRINK

Drink *See* the BIG DRINK

the **drink** *n phr by 1832* A body of water; the water: *She tripped and fell into the drink*

drink one's **beer** *v phr by 1940s* To stop talking; =SHUT UP •Usu an exasperated command: *Finally I had to tell him to drink his beer*—Hal Boyle

drink like a fish *v phr by 1747* To drink too much; overindulge in alcohol; =BOOZE, HIT THE BOTTLE

drink one's **lunch** *v phr by 1960s* To drink too much, esp during the working day: *I had to counsel Ames on the extent to which he was drinking his lunch*—Vanity Fair

drink of water *See* a LONG DRINK OF WATER

drip 1 *n 1930s teenagers* A tedious, unimaginative, conventional person; =SQUARE, WIMP •The term was apparently used a decade earlier in British schoolboy slang: *. . . the biggest drip at Miss Basehoar's, a school ostensibly abounding with fair-sized drips*—J D Salinger/ *such drips. . . they're just sort of*

dull—Calder Willingham **2** *n hoboes about 1930* Useless and idle talk; gossip

drippy *teenagers by 1940s* **1** *adj* Tedious; unimaginative; conventional; =WIMPY **2** *adj* Sentimental; lachrymose; =CORNY

dripwad *n teenagers by 1990s* An ineffectual, despised person; =JERK, LOSER, WIMP: *Jason, have I ever told you what a total loser you are?. . . Geek?. . . Nerdboy?. . . Dripwad?*—comic strip "Fox Trot"

drive 1 *n by 1908* Dynamism; insistent power: *a song with drive* **2** *v jazz musicians by 1930s* To play music, esp jazz, with strong forward impetus and rhythms **3** *n narcotics by 1927* A thrill or transport of pleasure and energy; =KICK, RUSH
See BIG DRIVE

drive-by *modifier 1990s* Performed casually and callously while or as if while merely driving past: *Chicago woman convicted of the drive-by shooting of a teenage boy*—Time/ *Broder and Woodward correctly chide the political press for practicing quick, drive-by journalism rather than trying to elevate the level of discussion*—New York Times/ *. . . a drive-by debate*—Lani Guinier

drive-in *by 1930* **1** *n* A place where one eats, watches movies, worships, etc, while sitting in one's parked car **2** *modifier: drive-in bank/ drive-in church/ drive-in movie*

driven *adj by 1887* Pressed along by some despotic or urgent force; hag-ridden: *She works as if driven*

-driven *combining word* Controlled or caused by what is indicated: *ego-driven, profit-driven, tax-driven, publicity-driven*

drive someone **over the hill** *v phr by 1970s* To drive to distraction; drive mad: *That kid is going to drive me over the hill. I'm at my wits' end*—Psychology Today

driver *n Vietnam War Air Force & Navy* An airplane pilot
See BACKSEAT DRIVER, HACK-DRIVER, PENCIL-PUSHER, SUNDAY DRIVER

driver's seat *See* IN THE DRIVER'S SEAT

drive the big bus *v phr students by 1970s* Vomit into the toilet, esp from drunkenness; =BARF [fr the resemblance of a toilet seat to a steering wheel]

drive-thru childbirth (or **delivery**) *n phr middle 1990s* The practice of allowing only one day of hospitalization for a childbirth: *. . . new laws designed to stop so-called drive-thru childbirth*—Milwaukee Journal Sentinel/ *Drive-through delivery: Shortened hospital stay after childbirth*—Macon Telegraph [fr restaurants, banks, etc, which provide quick service to customers in cars]

drive someone **up the wall** *v phr* To cause someone to become irrational or hysterical; madden: *It drives most women right up the wall*—Milwaukee Journal/ *Leave him alone and let him work. Quit driving him up the wall*—J J Roget

driving at *See* WHAT one IS DRIVING AT

◁**driving while black** or **DWB**▷ *v phr by 1990s* A putative motor vehicle offense committed by blacks:

Most middle-class citizens don't know about the de facto driving violation known as DWB, driving while black—Progressive Review

drizzle or **drizzle-puss** *n by 1930s* =DRIP

droid *1970s teenagers* **1** *n* An inferior, mechanical sort of person; robot; a semihuman drone; =CLONE: *. . . for all its ecumenical menagerie of creatures and droids*—People **2** *modifier*: *. . . tends to get people in the droid positions. . . and pay little*—San Francisco [fr *android*, "humanlike," esp as used by science-fiction writers]

drone **1** *n 1930s students* A boring person; =DRIP, WIMP **2** *n by 1940s* A small unmanned aircraft used as a target for gunnery practice

drool **1** *v by 1900s* To talk foolishly or stupidly; utter inanities **2** *n*: *It gives me sharp and shooting pains, to listen to such drool*—Morris Bishop **3** *n by 1930s* =DRIP

drool for (or **over**) *v phr by 1940s* To show keen appreciation; show desire: *He's still drooling for Marilyn Monroe*

drooly **1** *adj 1940s teenagers* Very attractive; =YUMMY: *Rain can turn the sharpest dressed drooly dreamboat into a drizzly drip from the knees down*—New York Daily News **2** *n 1940s teenagers* A popular and attractive boy: *Who's the chief drooly at Cooley?* **3** *adj by 1940s* Stupid; driveling: *. . . ought to shut their fat, drooly mouths and stick their opinions in their wax-infested ears*—Mike Royko

droop or **droopy-drawers** *n 1930s teenagers* A somewhat dull and stupid person: *He's such a droop, he can't even discuss the weather intelligently*

droopy drama *n phr 1940s* A radio or television daytime serial

drop **1** *v underworld by about 1900* To be arrested; be caught with loot; =FALL **2** *v by 1812* To knock someone down; =DECK **3** *v by 1726* To kill someone, esp by shooting; =BUMP, OFF, WHACK **4** *v by 1676* To lose, esp money: *He dropped a bundle in the market yesterday* **5** *v by 1400* To collapse, esp with fatigue: *I'll drop if I don't sit down* **6** *v by 1605* To stop seeing or associating with someone: *She dropped her boyfriend* **7** *v 1960s narcotics* To take any narcotic, esp in pill or capsule form: *We want a society where you can smoke grass and drop acid*—New York Times **8** *n* (also **drop joint**) *underworld by 1930s* A seemingly honest place used as a cover for illegal matters, esp as a depot for stolen goods; =FENCE **9** *n by 1950s* =MAIL DROP **10** *n by 1775* A drink or drinks: *I could see by his careful walking he'd taken a drop* **11** *n black by 1950s* A homeless slum boy: *. . . accepting anywhere from 25 cents to $1 a week for taking in drops, rustles, fetches*—W Davenport **12** *n cabdrivers by 1950s* A paying passenger **13** *n cabdrivers by 1950s* The base fee on a taxi meter registered when the cabdriver activates the meter

See CHOCOLATE DROP, GET THE DROP ON someone, **knockout drops**

drop a brick *v phr British students by 1905* To blunder; commit a gaffe: *He rather dropped a brick when he mispronounced Lady Fuchs' name*

drop a bundle *v phr by about 1900* To lose a large amount of money, esp by gambling: *He's dropped a bundle that way*—W T Tyler

drop a (or **the**) **dime** **1** *v phr 1960s* To inform; give information, esp to the police; =DIME, RAT •New York City teenagers have equated *dime* with an amount of information, and also speak of dropping a quarter, more information, and dropping a dollar, the maximum of information: *Chaney questioned the man who had dropped the dime on Madison*—Washingtonian/ *. . . and then he dropped the dime (made the phone call) and turned Vinnie in*—Village Voice **2** *v phr Army by 1970s* To point out the faults and failures of another; criticize [fr the *dime* put into a pay telephone in that era]

drop beads (or **hairpins**) *homosexuals by 1960s* **1** *v phr* To use homosexual code words to elicit whether someone is homosexual **2** *v phr* To reveal oneself as homosexual inadvertently, esp during conversation

drop one's **beads** *v phr 1990s street gangs* To leave a gang

drop bombs *v phr 1940s jazz musicians* To place accents in music, esp during improvised passages, using the foot pedal of a bass drum: *Joe Jones? He was the first drummer to drop bombs*—A Basie Dozen (radio program)

drop one's **buckets** *v phr by 1970s* To make an embarrassing mistake; =DROP A BRICK, GOOF: *You really dropped your buckets when you replied*—Washington Post

drop-by *n 1990s* A quick visit by a celebrity, political figure, etc: *Also, his people are trying to limit this thing to a drop-by. . .* —Gary Trudeau

drop case (or **shot**) *n phr by 1970s* A stupid person; idiot; =TURKEY: *Nobody. . . was a big enough drop case to bet*—Dan Jenkins/ *Mr Williams called Mr Mallard a drop shot, which had been established as a derogatory term*—New York Times [perhaps fr the notion that a stupid person had been *dropped* on his head when a baby, with some added connection with the ignominious *drop shot* in tennis]

drop one's **cookies** **See** SHOOT one's COOKIES

drop dead **1** *interj by 1930s* Go to hell; =GET LOST •Nearly always an exclamation of curt refusal or sharp disapproval: *At that rude suggestion she told him to drop dead* **2** *adj phr 1970s* Unusually striking; sensational: *A drop-dead mansion in Beverly Hills, complete with his-and-hers whirlpools*—People/ *. . . the soulful voice and the drop-dead campiness*—Time **3** *adj phr 1980s* Absolutely final: *Schedule the announcement for December 23rd, one day before the drop-dead date, and close to the holidays*—New Yorker [so called because it is an impudent affront to some canons of taste]

drop-dead list *n phr by 1970s* A usu fancied list of persons one does not wish to associate with or favor; =SHIT LIST

drop (or **throwaway**) **gun** *n phr police by*

1980s A pistol dropped by police in order to justify a dubious shooting by claiming that the victim was carrying it;: *Was Wolfie stupid enough to think that a drop gun was going to help anybody out of the shit-storm?*—Carsten Stroud

drop-in 1 *n by 1950s* A place of temporary and sometimes dubious resort: *. . . drop-ins for youths wishing marijuana revels*—NY Confidential **2** *n 1960s students* A person who attends classes and other college events without being registered: *NBC did some research on college drop-ins*—D Kallman **3** *n by 1990s* A new car engine as a replacement: *If you have a current model-year car, you can get a "drop-in." That's a brand new engine. . .* —Tom and Ray Magliozzi [sense 2 is the opposite of a *dropout*]

drop someone **in** someone's **tracks** *v phr by 1820s* To knock down or kill someone suddenly and sharply: *One kick dropped him in his tracks*

drop it *v phr by 1844* To discontinue or cut off a certain topic •Often an irritated command: *I'm not interested, so let's drop it*

drop joint *See* DROP

drop someone or something **like a hot potato** *v phr by 1846* To discontinue or get rid of very quickly: *When she frowned I dropped the topic like a hot potato*

drop like flies *v phr by 1940s* To fall down in great numbers: *All over the hot theater people were dropping like flies* [*like flies* meant "in great numbers" by 1595]

dropout *n by 1920s* A person who withdraws; voluntary self-excluder, esp from school or college

drop out *v phr 1960s* To remove oneself from the conventional competitive world of politics, business, education, etc: *. . . rush back from every excursion into Big Power and drop out with town meetings and backyard picnics*—Hugh Sidey

dropper 1 *n underworld by 1920s* A paid assassin; criminal who injures or kills his victims; =HIT MAN: *We got to send East for a couple of droppers*—American Mercury **2** *n underworld by 1920s* A thief who treats his victims violently; =COWBOY, MUGGER **3** *n by 1785* A confidence man who drops something of value, appears to find it, and offers the dupe a share, for a price

drops *See* KNOCKOUT DROPS

drop one's **teeth** *v phr by 1980s* To be very astonished; be gapingly shocked: *I do drop my teeth at the notion that Shakespeare is busted and needs to be fixed*—Washington Post

drop the ball *v phr by 1980s* To fail, esp to fail in one's entrusted job or duty; =FLUB THE DUB: *I think the State Department dropped the ball on Iraq*

drop (or put) the lug on someone *v phr by 1920s* To beg money; =PUT THE BITE ON someone: *How's about dropping the lug on you for thirty-five thousand?*—C Carson

drop the other shoe *v phr* (occasionally **let the other shoe drop**) *by 1980s* To conclude or round

out something in suspense: *The city. . . dropped the other shoe*—Village Voice/ *. . . get with Martinez and drop the other shoe*—W E B Griffin

◁**drop your cocks and grab your socks**▷ *sentence WWII armed forces* Get out of bed immediately •A jovial instruction issued by a noncommissioned officer or barracks orderly to troops quite early in the morning

drownder *See* GOOSE-DROWNDER

drowned rat *See* LOOK LIKE A DROWNED RAT

drown one's **sorrows** (or **troubles**) *v phr by 1674* To alleviate or obscure the chagrins of one's life, esp by getting drunk

drug[1] *v by 1970s* To annoy and nag at; =BUG: *His constant bitching really drugs me*
See DESIGNER DRUG, HARD DRUG, LOVE DRUG, ORPHAN DRUG, SOFT DRUG

drug[2] *adj jazz musicians by about 1940* Displeased; angry; =PISSED OFF: *If other players are drug about it or feel that I'm trying to horn in. . . then it's not much fun*—Downbeat [past participle of *drag*, in a dialect variation]

drug-chugging *adj by 1990s* Drug-using; narcotic-addicted: *None of that hippy-dippy, war-protesting, free-loving, drug-chugging stuff for him*—Los Angeles Times [fr *drug* plus *chug*, "drink, gulp"]

druggie or **druggy** *n 1960s narcotics* A narcotics user or addict; =DOPER

drughead *n 1960s narcotics* A heavy user of narcotics or other drugs; =HOPHEAD: *. . . every front-page report of violence by some freaked-out drug-head*—P Horn

drugola *n 1960s narcotics* Money paid by narcotics dealers for protection, esp to the police [based on *-ola* terms like *payola, plugola,* and *gayola*]

drugstore cowboy 1 *n phr middle 1920s* A young man who frequents public places trying to impress and entice women; a Romeo of the street corners: *. . . bell-bottom trousers so much in vogue with the drugstore cowboys*—A Hynd **2** *n phr Hollywood* An extra in a Western film [attributed to the cartoonist and humorist Tad Dorgan, who died in 1929]

drum *See* BEAT THE DRUM

drum-beater *n by 1940s* A person, esp a press agent, who insistently lauds someone or something: *I'm something of a drum-beater for my Alma Mater* [*beat the drum,* "to make loud advertisement or protest," is attested by 1611]

drummer *n by 1827* A traveling salesperson [fr the practice of going about with a *drum* to gain attention for recruiting and other purposes; for example, the sale of fish was announced by *drumming* in the London streets]

drum up *v phr by 1849* To stimulate; promote: *Go drum up a little enthusiasm for this turkey*

drunk 1 *n by 1779* A drinking bout; spree; =BENDER, BINGE **2** *n by 1849* A case or occasion of intoxication: *Took him an hour to get a good drunk* **3** *adj by 1340* Intoxicated by alcohol; =PLASTERED, SCHNOCKERED, SHIT-FACED **4** *n by 1852* A drunken person, esp a habitual alcoholic; =LUSH [in all senses *drunk* verges on being standard English]

See CHEAP DATE, PUNCH-DRUNK

drunk as a boiled owl *adj phr* by 1888 Very drunk

drunk as a fiddler's bitch *adj phr* middle 1800s Very drunk: *It's all over, and nobody knows it but me, drunk as a fiddler's bitch, lasted too long*—Washington Post

drunk as a skunk *adj phr* by 1940s Very drunk; =SCHNOCKERED: *They bring beer and cigarettes, are drunk as skunks*—Village Voice

drunk tank *n phr* by 1940s A police detention cell for intoxicated persons: *A police reporter had to pick him out of the collection in the drunk tank*—A R Bosworth

druthers *n* by 1895 Wishes; desires; preferred alternatives: *We know your druthers, The Marketplace*—Philadelphia [fr a dialect pronunciation of *rather* or *had rather*; used by Bret Harte in the form *drathers* in 1875]

See HAVE one's DRUTHERS

dry 1 *n* by 1888 A person who favors the prohibition of alcoholic drink **2** *adj* by 1887 Not permitting the sale of alcoholic drink: *North Carolina has dry counties* **3** *adj* by 1406 Thirsty

dry as a bone *adj phr* by 1649 Very dry: *Drink, please, I'm dry as a bone*

not **dry behind the ears** *See* NOT DRY BEHIND THE EARS

◀**dry fuck (or hump)**▶ by 1930s **1** *n phr* To approximate the sex act, without penetration or divestiture, and typically without orgasm: *. . . what he would call. . . the dry humps*—Stephen King **2** *v*: *Did attack-crazy kamikazes crash into dry-humping kids on the Hell's Kitchen shore?*—Village Voice

dry-gulch 1 *v* Western by 1930 To murder, esp by pushing over a cliff **2** *v* by 1940s To knock senseless; =BUSHWHACK, CLOBBER: *Then one of them got into the car and dry-gulched me*—Raymond Chandler [origin uncertain; perhaps fr the practice of killing the animals of another rancher by stampeding them over a cliff into a *gulch;* perhaps fr attacking sheepherders out of a *gulch* and killing their animals]

dry out by 1967 **1** *v phr* To refrain from alcohol, esp in a medical facility as a part of treatment for alcohol abuse: *He dried out a couple of weeks up in the Valley* **2** *v phr* To be treated for narcotics abuse; be detoxified

dry run 1 *n phr* 1940s A tryout, practice version, or rehearsal of something planned: *One more dry run, then tomorrow we do it* **2** *v*: *. . . so the medical staff could "dry run" their equipment*—Associated Press

dry up *v phr* by 1852 To stop talking; =SHUT UP ●Usu an irritated command: *Finally I just told him to dry up*—Hal Boyle

DT *n* by 1920s A detective; =DICK, TEC: *"You DT?" "No." "So what you care who piped Devona?"*—Robert B Parker

DTs *n* by 1858 Delirium tremens; =the CLANKS: *When*

Bix got the DT's Whiteman treated Bix to a drunk cure—Stephen Longstreet

duals *n* truckers by 1970s A pair of wheels and tires mounted as a unit on a truck or semitrailer axle

dub¹ 1970s **1** *n* A form of reggae music marked by weird, unexpected, and discontinuous sounds: *The hypnotic weirdness of such music has helped make dub the most popular form of reggae*—Newsweek **2** *modifier*: *A flood of dub versions followed*—Newsweek [probably fr the electronic technique of *dubbing,* "doubling," sound tracks]

dub² by 1920s **1** *v* To replace or augment an original sound track with another, esp to substitute a movie sound track in a language other than the original **2** *v* To add a singer, instrumental part, etc, to the tape for a recording: *They dubbed the final vocals last week* [fr *double*]

dub³ *n* by 1887 An awkward performer; novice; =DUFFER: *. . . planned by destiny for dubs and has-beens and that solemn brood*—Wallace Irwin

See FLUBDUB, FLUB THE DUB

dubage (DOO bij) *n* 1980s teenagers Illegal narcotics: *He hid the dubage in my locker*—Delcastle Dictionary of Slang

dubich (DOO bich) *n* 1980s teenagers Marijuana; =POT, WEED: *The drug dealer sold a bag of dubich to a tourist*—Delcastle Dictionary of Slang

dubee or **duby** *See* DOOBIE

dubok (Doo bahk) *n* underworld by 1970s fr espionage A seemingly innocent place where clandestine activity may be shielded; =DROP [fr Russian, "oak tree"]

ducat or **ducket** or **duket** (DUH kət) **1** *n* by 1874 A ticket or pass to a show, game, race, etc **2** *n* by 1775 Money; dollars: *. . . keep him in ducats for the rest of his life*—Ellery Queen [fr the name of an originally Venetian gold coin; adoption probably influenced by its prominence in *The Merchant of Venice*]

See CHINEE

duchess *n* 1950s street gang A female member of a street gang

duck 1 *n* by 1846 A man; fellow; =GUY: *That duck isn't a critic*—H McHugh **2** *n* (also **ducks**) by 1590 Dear one; precious; pet; =DUCKY: *. . . and his wife, a darling duck of a homebody*—Village Voice **3** *n* by 1868 =DUCK-EGG **4** *n* by about 1917 A hospital bedpan **5** *n* WWII armed forces An amphibious vehicle, esp a WWII troop carrier designated DUKW 1942, whence the nickname **6** *v* by 1530 To move, weave, squat, etc, so as to avoid a blow **7** *v* (also **duck out**) by 1896 To evade or escape: *He ducked over the wall/ They always felt she was trying to duck work*

See DEAD DUCK, FUCK A DUCK, HAVE one's DUCKS IN A ROW, KNEE-HIGH TO A GRASSHOPPER, LAME DUCK, RUPTURED DUCK, SITTING DUCK

duck bumps *n phr* by 1940s =GOOSE BUMPS

duck-butt *n* by 1930s A person of short stature

duck-egg *n* by 1868 A score or grade of zero; =GOOSE EGG, ZIP

duck-fit *n* *by 1881* A noisy fit of anger: *Clarice. . . would throw a duck-fit, if she knew*—Elmer Rice

ducks *n* *by 1930s* Dear one; precious •Chiefly British use: *Try this one, ducks*
See HAVE one's DUCKS IN A ROW

◁**duck's ass**▷ *by 1951* **1** *n phr* =DA, DUCKTAIL **2** *modifier*: *He had a 1950 duck's-ass haircut with enough grease to lubricate the QE2*—Lawrence Sanders

duck-shoot *n* *1970s* Something very easy; =CINCH, PIECE OF CAKE, PICNIC [fr the notion of shooting a *sitting duck*]

duck soup *n phr* *by 1908* Anything easily done; =CINCH, PIECE OF CAKE: *It would be duck soup for him to have led Willis into a trap*—Hugh Pentecost/ *Only duck soup for a guy like you*—Stan Cutler

duck squeezer *n phr* *1970s college students* A conservationist and environmentalist; =ECOFREAK

ducktail *n* *1950s teenagers* A haircut tapered in back so that it resembles a duck's tail; =DA, DUCK'S ASS

duck-walk *v* *by 1930s* To move forward while squatting on one's haunches: *Maybe that reporter. . . should duck-walk up Olympia ski hill. . .* —Milwaukee Journal

ducky or **duckie 1** *adj* *by 1897* Excellent; splendid •Often used ironically: *Everything was just ducky until Lally went into that dame's house. . .* —James O'Hanlon/ *Oh, me? I'm just ducky*—Scott Turow **2** *adj* *by 1897* Cute; too cute; =CORNY: *Pastel phials tied with ducky satin bows*—Raymond Chandler **3** *n* *by 1819* Dear one; precious; =DEARIE, DUCKS: *Are you quite ready, duckie?*

ducrot (DOO kraht) *n* *West Point by 1900* Anything or anyone, esp a first-year cadet, whose name is not known and not worth knowing; =DUMBJOHN [fr French *du crotte,* "a portion of excrement"]

dud 1 *n* *by 1908* A failure: *The show's a dud/ He was a bit of a dud* **2** *n* *WWI armed forces* A shell or bomb that fails to explode **3** *modifier*: *a dud bomb*

duddy **See** FUDDY-DUDDY

dude 1 *n* *by 1883* A dapper man, esp one who is ostentatiously dressed; dandy •In earliest use, to quote an 1891 source, a *dude* was "not a dandy; there is nothing gallant or dashing about him. . . He is soberness itself;. . . heis as respectable as an undertaker. Yet. . . your real dude is irresistibly comic" **2** *n* *by 1883* A guest at a Western or Western-style ranch **3** *n* *by 1918* A man; fellow; =CAT, GUY •In the 1960s and 70s *dude* became preeminently a black term: *I'm sittin' in the bus stop. . . just me an' these other three dudes*—D Evans [origin unknown; perhaps an invented word]

dude up *v phr* *by 1899* To don fancy clothes, or one's best clothes; =DOLL UP

Dudley **See** YOUR UNCLE DUDLEY

Dudley Do-Right *n phr* *by 1980s* A person of exceptional virtue; social and moral paragon; =MISTER CLEAN: *Bush's carefully managed image as a square-shouldered Dudley Do-Right*—Time/ *. . . a '90s breed of Dudley Do-Right is back in the saddle*—Milwaukee Journal Sentinel [fr a character in a television cartoon series, *Dudley Do-Right of the Mounties*]

duds *n* *by about 1300* Clothing; =THREADS: *To see them washed and put in and out of their duds was perhaps the greatest pleasure of her life*—Anthony Trollope [origin unknown; perhaps fr one or another English or Celtic words meaning "cloth, rag"]

dues **See** PAY one's DUES

duff *n* *by 1830s* The buttocks; rump; =ASS: *A bunch of lazy guys sitting around on our duffs*—Time [origin uncertain; perhaps black slang for *fud*, "buttocks," attested by 1785; perhaps fr *duff*, "a (sailors') pudding boiled in a bag," which bag may have suggested a human fundament in shape; in this sense *duff* is a Northern pronunciation of *dough*]

duffer *by 1840s* **1** *n* An elderly man; =GEEZER, JASPER •Used rather affectionately: *He's a sweet old duffer, isn't he?* **2** *n* A mediocre or downright poor performer, esp at golf; =HACKER [perhaps fr Scots *duffar,* "dolt"]

duh or **duhh** *interj* *by 1940s* A sound imitating that of a weak-minded person collecting his thoughts •The gesture of flapping one's lower lip with one's fingers while uttering a droning sound is used to the same effect: *Bill Cosby doesn't really serve Jell-O chocolate pudding at dinner parties? Duh*—Time/ *. . . white male artists continue to dominate (duhhh) the blue-chip market*—Village Voice

dujie **See** DOOJEE

du jour (DOO ZHOOR or JOO) *adj phr* *1990s* Of today; of the day; current: *Thought du jour*—Toronto Globe and Mail/ *. . . Kennedy. . . would quiz aides about the crisis du jour. . .* —New York Times/ *. . . where would the management gurus du jour find grist for their latest bestsellers?*—Wall Street Journal [fr French, "of the day," used to identify the day's specialties in restaurants]

duke 1 *n* *by 1874* A hand, esp when regarded as a weapon **2** *n* *prizefight by 1930s* The winning decision in a boxing match, signaled by the referee's holding up the victor's hand: *Even if I lose the duke I get forty percent*—Jim Tully **3** *v* *by 1940s* To hand something to someone: *Duke the kid a five or ten*—George V Higgins **4** *v* *by 1940s* To fight with the fists **5** *v* *circus by 1940s* To try to collect money from a parent for something given to a child **6** *v* *circus by 1940s* To short-change someone by palming a coin owed him **7** *v* *by 1965* To shake hands; =PRESS THE FLESH **8** *v* *street gang by 1990s* To do the sex act with or to; =BOFF, SCREW: *. . . she might even have duked one of the Hobart Street Fros sometime*—Robert B Parker [perhaps fr Romany *dook,* "the hand as read in palmistry, one's fate"]
See DUKES

duke breath *n phr* *1990s teenagers* Fetid breath; halitosis [fr the notion of *duke* as someone or something very strong; in prison slang, for example, a *duke* is a strong habitual criminal, and on the farm the bull was the *duke*]

duke it out *v phr* by 1960s: *More than 90 percent of the fugitives. . . don't want to duke it out. . .* —Macon Telegraph

duke someone **out** *by 1970s* **1** *v phr* To beat someone unconscious; =KNOCK someone OUT: *What should I do, duke him or her out?*—National Review **2** *v phr* To damage or injure someone: *Dirk Hamilton dukes himself out, adopts a. . . style in which he's inferior*—Village Voice

dukes *n by 1859* The fists or hands: *I imagine you can handle your dukes, Jim*—Joseph Wambaugh [said to be Cockney rhyming slang fr *Duke of Yorks,* "forks, hands"]

dukes-up *adj by 1970s* Combative; =FEISTY: *Her salty language and dukes-up style endeared her*—Time

duket *See* DUCAT

dull as dishwater *adj phr by 1940s* Very tedious and unexciting; boring: *The sermon today was dull as dishwater, Your Eminence* [the original form, and current British form, is *dull as ditchwater* attested by the 1840s]

dull out *v phr by 1980s* To live a quiet life; eschew excitement: *Fewer distractions, fewer parties, fewer people. "I need to dull out for a year"*—Christopher Zenowich

dullsville *adj by 1960* Very dull; tedious; =DRAGSVILLE: *a dullsville wimp*
See -SVILLE

dull tool *n phr by 1700* An ineffective person; =DEAD ONE, LOSER

dumb 1 *adj by 1823* Stupid; mentally sluggish; =DIM: *You think I'm pretty dumb, don't you?*—F Scott Fitzgerald **2** *adj* or *adv by 1787* =DAMN, DARN [fr Pennsylvania German *dumm*]

◁**dumb-ass**▷ *by 1950s* **1** *adj* Stupid; inane; tedious: *Our private life has to take a backseat to every dumbass little news story*—Armistead Maupin **2** *n*: *to understand how a dumb-ass like Newton can have a following*—Playboy
See HAVE A CASE OF THE DUMB-ASS

dumbbell *n by about 1918* A stupid person; idiot: *She's an awful dumb-bell*—Bryn Mawr slang [fr *dumbbell,* a kind of weightlifter's bar-bell, attested from the 1880s]

◁**dumb blonde**▷ *n phr by 1950s* A pretty but rather stupid blonde young woman; =BIMBO, DUMB BUNNY, DUMB DORA: *Robelot's not just another dumb blonde out there; she's very aggressive*—Delaware Valley

dumb bomb (or **missile**) *n phr by 1970s* A bomb or missile lacking a sophisticated and accurate guidance system [fr contrast with *smart bomb*]

dumb bunny *n phr about 1917* A naive and unwary person; silly little fool: *My dear, you are the preshest old dumb-bunny*—Bryn Mawr slang

dumb cluck *n phr by 1929* A stupid person; clumsy bungler; =CLUCK, KLUTZ: *. . . all those dumb clucks snickering at you*—Sinclair Lewis

dumb Dora *n phr by 1890s* A stupid or vapid young woman; =BIMBO, DUMB BUNNY: *You're just an average Dumb Dora from north-suburban Chicagoland*—Saul Bellow [said to have been coined by Anita Pines, the first woman stage manager of a burlesque theater]

dumb down *v phr by 1940s* To make simpler and easier, esp to alter a textbook to make it more elementary •Apparently first used of movies: *There has been a real "dumbing down" of the texts*—Village Voice/ *. . . what some educators have called the "dumbing down" of textbooks*—New York Times/ *There are jobs that will be dumbed down*—Associated Press [attributed to Los Angeles Times reporter William Trombley]

dumbhead *n by 1887* A stupid person: *This dumbhead has just gone nuts*—Ellery Queen [perhaps fr German *Dummkopf*]

dumbjohn 1 *n by 1950s* A person easily duped; =EASY MARK, PATSY **2** *n by 1900* =DUCROT **3** *n* Army *by 1940s* A recruit; =CRUIT

dumbo (DUM boh) **1** *n by 1950s* A stupid person: *. . . an ace dumbo friend named Cleo*—Time **2** *n by 1970s* A blunder; stupid mistake; =BLOOPER: *if you think you've seen dumbos pulled on the highways*—Saturday Evening Post

dumb ox *n phr by 1847* A stupid, sluggish person, esp a hulking one [oddly enough, this was the nickname given by his schoolfellow to Thomas Aquinas, not for stupidity but for stolid silence]

◁**dumbshit**▷ *n by 1960s* Stupid; =CRETINOID, DOOFUS: *Yeah, right. Dumbshit, two-term Reagan*—New Republic

dumb something **up** *v phr by 1960s* To make something simpler and easier; leach out all but the most puerile substance; =DUMB DOWN: *They handed him the script and told him to dumb it up still more*

dum-dum or **dumdum** or **dumb-dumb** *by 1940s* **1** *n* A stupid or foolish person **2** *adj*: *The only man safe enough to see is this dumdum cop*—Saul Bellow

dummy 1 *n by 1796* A stupid person; idiot; =CLUCK ◁**2**▷ *n by 1874* A deaf-mute or a mute **3** *n* hoboes *by 1890s* Bread **4** *n* railroad *by 1890s* A train carrying railroad employees **5** *n 1960s* narcotics A weakened or diluted narcotic; also, a non-narcotic substance sold as a narcotic; =BLANK **6** *n* newspaper office & publishing *by 1858* A pasted-up page, a blank book, or other preliminary representation of material to be published **7** *v*: *The designer dummied the new book* **8** *n by about 1845* A model or representation; =MOCK-UP **9** *modifier*: *a dummy machine gun/ dummy windows*
See BEAT one's MEAT,

dummy dust *n phr by 1980s* Cocaine

dummy up *v phr by 1926* To keep silent; =CLAM UP: *You can't dummy up on a murder case*—Raymond Chandler/ *When questioned, they invariably dummy up*—S J Perelman

dump 1 *n by 1899* Any place so shabby or ugly as to

be comparable to a depository for trash and garbage; a repulsive venue: *What a dump my hometown is now!* **2** *n by 1930s* Any building or place: *Nice little dump you got here/ fanciest dump in town* **3** *n underworld by 1904* A prison **4** *v by 1868* To sell goods, stock, etc, in order to manipulate or depress a market **5** *n gambling by 1940s* A race, game, etc, that is intentionally lost, usu for gambling advantage; =FIX: *When he took a dive in the first I knew we had a dump on our hands* **6** *v*: *Players accepting bribes to "dump" games*—Associated Press **7** *v baseball about 1920* To bunt a baseball: *Dehoney dumped one toward third* **8** *v 1930s underworld* To kill **9** *v by 1848* To rid oneself of someone or something; =DEEP SIX: *He dumped the whole cabinet* **10** *n by 1940s* A defecation: *To start the morning with a satisfactory dump is a good omen*—W H Auden **11** *v medical by 1980s* To admit someone to a hospital without proper cause ●Often done as a way of avoiding responsibility for a patient **12** *n politics by 1990s* A fund-raising event that allows many contributions to be given at once; =SCOOP: *The chief has a breakfast dump at the Century Plaza, then a stump speech at 2 p.m.*—Los Angeles Times **13** *v police by 1990s* To assign vulnerable novices and officers with disciplinary infractions to drug-ridden precincts **14** *v by 1990s* To speak openly and volubly: *I shake my head and proceed to start dumping about my mom. . .*—Sassy [origin uncertain; perhaps related to a Scandinavian term meaning "to fall suddenly," the connection being the tipping out of a load from a cart]
See CORE DUMP, TAKE A DUMP

◁**dump a load**▷ *v phr by 1940s* To defecate; =CRAP

dumper 1 *n gambling by 1950s* An erratic and extravagant gambler: *Professional gamblers describe the Colonel as a dumper*—Albert Goldman **2** *n by 1970s* A container for trash; Dumpster™: *It was determined. . . that disco would be in the dumper*—Playboy
See IN THE DUMPER

dumping *n by 1950s* Harsh criticism; severe derogation: *A coupon is provided on page 47 for your dumping*—Diner's Choice

dumping ground *n phr by 1885* A place to which unwanted persons and things are relegated: *Because of such appointments the Department came to be seen as "a dumping ground". . .*—New York Times

dump job *n phr by 1990s* A derogatory attack; =HATCHET JOB: *They did a dump job on her*—Denver talk-show caller

dump on (or **all over)** *v phr by 1940s* To criticize harshly, often unfairly; complain and carp at; =PUT DOWN: *If he does something right, I'm not going to dump on him*—Time/ *Don't dump on the teachers we have*—New York Times/ *. . . an acknowledgement of the fact that he had dumped on us all year*—Judith Martin [perhaps fr *dump*, "defecation"]

Dumpster diving or **urban mining** *n phr late 1980s* Searching through trash for something of value: *Low-end thefts range from so-called*

Dumpster diving, searching the garbage for discarded carbons, to old-fashioned card theft—Milwaukee Journal/ *On Dumpster Diving: Eighner offered a sophisticated essay on the theme of surviving on refuse*—New Yorker [fr the trademark of a type of refuse receiver]

dune buggy *n phr 1960s* A small and squat open car, usu with a Volkswagen engine, equipped with very fat tires for traveling on sand

duner *n by 1970s* A dune-buggy driver or rider: *Duners go out on runs, trips by a half-dozen dune buggies*—Calvin Trillin

dunk 1 *v by 1919* To dip something into a liquid, esp to dip food into a drink: *Scientific temperature readings cannot be taken just by dunking a thermometer on a string*—G Hill **2** *v by 1940s* To go into the water: *Be right back, just want to dunk* **3** *n*: *Leroy had a quick dunk in the creek* **4** *n basketball by 1937* A basketball field goal scored by putting the ball into the hoop from just beside or above it: *Almost all of the baskets were dunks*—Sports Illustrated/ *. . . basketball courts. . . where the dunks have been so fierce lately*—Philadelphia **5** *v*: *He jumped up and dunked another one* [fr Pennsylvania German *dunken,* "dip"]
See SLAM DUNK

dunkie butt *n phr 1990s rappers* A large fundament . . . *what is a dunkie butt?. . . It's a big butt that's shapely*—Macon Telegraph

dunk on someone *v phr by 1990s* To attack someone: *He talked about my mother, talked about my shoes, my shorts, so I dunked on him*—Cox News Service [probably fr the notion of a violent basketball *dunk* or *slam dunk*]

dunnigan *n by 1970s* A repulsive thief who plies his trade in public toilets: *Sam is not like the sleazy dunnigans, who work toilets*—Los Angeles Times [fr earlier *dunnakin,* "toilet"]

dupe *n by 1902* A duplicate copy of a film or text

duper *See* SUPER-DUPER

durn or **durned** *See* DARN

a **durn** *See* NOT GIVE A DAMN

dust 1 *v by 1850* To leave quickly; flee; fly: *Dillinger. . . used a Ford. . . when dusting from a job*—A Hynd **2** *v by 1612* To hit; swat: *. . . dusted one of the lieutenants with an old shoe for trying to talk them back to work*—Time **3** *v* (also, earlier, **dust off**) *by 1970s* To kill: *Watch me dust this bitch*—movie Revenge on the Highway/ *Don't suppose you just want to dust Esteva and go home*—Robert B Parker **4** *n 1960s narcotics* Narcotics in powder form **5** *v 1930s* To spray insecticide from a low-flying aircraft
See ANGEL DUST, EAT someone's DUST, HAPPY-DUST, HEAVEN DUST

the **dust** *See* BITE THE DUST

duster *n 1920s baseball* A pitch purposely thrown at or close to the batter, to intimidate him or force him back from the plate; =BRUSHBACK
See EAR-DUSTER, KNUCKLE-DUSTERS

dust someone's **jacket** *v phr* by 1698 To beat and pummel someone

dust kitty (or **bunny) ** *n phr* by 1980s One of the tufts of dust that accumulate under beds, tables, etc; =GHOST TURDS

dust someone **off** *v phr* 1920s baseball To pitch a ball at or close to the batter; =BRUSHBACK

dust something **off** *v phr* (also **dust the cobwebs off**) by 1940s To use or re-use something old; reclaim something: *Why don't we dust off a few of the good ideas our parents had?/ Hey, let's dust the cobwebs off the Declaration of Independence and take it seriously*

dustup *n* by 1897 A quarrel or fight; altercation; =SCRAP: *a big dustup in the office of a vice-president*—New Yorker

dusty *See* RUSTY-DUSTY

Dusty by 1940s **1** *n* A common nickname for a person named Rhodes, Rhoades, Rodes, etc **2** *n* A nickname for a short person, a "dusty butt"

dusty butt *n phr* by 1940s A person of short stature; =SHORTY

Dutch 1 *adj* by 1460 German •This use died out in the UK long ago, but persists in parts of the US: *Ann Arbor's a Dutch town* **2** *n* by 1920s A nickname for anyone with a German surname: *Big Dutch Klangenfuss* **3** *adv* (also **dutch**) by 1887 With each person paying his or her own share: *This meal is Dutch, okay?*
See DOUBLE DUTCH, GO DUTCH, IN DUTCH, TO BEAT THE BAND

the **Dutch act** *See* DO THE DUTCH

Dutch courage *n phr* by 1820s False or fleeting bravery resulting from liquor: *A man in liquor. . . is full of Dutch courage*—F K Secrist [like many other pejorative uses of *Dutch,* this comes from the 17th century, when the English and the Hollanders were chronically at war. In some uses, though, *Dutch* means "German" rather than "Netherlandish," and the cases are not easily sorted]

Dutch rub *n phr* about 1910 The trick or torment of holding someone's head and rubbing very hard and painfully at a small area of scalp with the fist; =NOOGIE

Dutch treat by 1887 **1** *n phr* A meal, show, etc, where each person pays his or her own way **2** *adv*: *We'll eat Dutch treat tonight*
See GO DUTCH

Dutch twins *n phr* by 1980s Two people having the same birthday

Dutch uncle *n phr* by 1838 A severely censorious person, usu a man: *A "Dutch uncle" whose every word is reproof*—F K Secrist

the **Dutch way** *n phr* by 1908 Suicide

duty *See* PAD DUTY, RACK DUTY, SACK DUTY

◁**DWB**▷ *v phr* by 1990s: *Nor does William Julius Wilson wonder why he was stopped near a small New England town by a policeman. There's a moving violation that many African-Americans know as DWB: Driving While Black*—New Yorker
See DRIVING WHILE BLACK

dweeb or **dweebo** 1980s teenagers **1** *n* A despised person; =CREEP, NERD **2** *modifier*: *. . . biggest dweeb award of all*—Kathy Hogan Trocheck

dweeby *adj* 1980s teenagers Revolting; silly; =NERDLY: *. . . wear a visor (or something less dweeby). . .* —Sassy

dying quail *n phr* baseball by 1980s A batted ball that sinks suddenly

◁**dyke** or **dike**▷ by 1930s **1** *n* A lesbian, esp one who takes an aggressive role; =BULLDYKE **2** *modifier*: *That woman lives with her dyke daughter and her dyke daughter-in-law*—Armistead Maupin [origin uncertain and much debated; perhaps fr a shortening of *morphodyke,* dialectal and substandard pronunciation of "hermaphrodite," perhaps influenced by *dick,* "penis"; a source of 1896 lists *dyke,* "the vulva"]

◁**dykey** or **dikey**▷ *adj* by 1960s Resembling or having the nature of an aggressive lesbian: *. . . doing calisthenics with the dikey-looking brunette*—Earl Thompson

dynamite 1 *n* 1920s narcotics Heroin or cocaine of high quality: *. . . a connection who deals in good-quality stuff, "dynamite"*—J Mills **2** *n* 1950s narcotics Marijuana, esp a marijuana cigarette **3** *adj* (also **dyno-mite**) Excellent; superior; =SUPER: *"Dynamite. . . I knew we'd get along*—Robert B Parker/ *DYN-O-MITE! The Blammo 12-gauge has a precision-cast hollow-core slug with stabilization tail fins for accuracy at long range*—Harper's **4** *n* by 1930s Something very disturbing or dangerous; a sensation: *Don't talk about it, it's dynamite*

dynamite charge *n phr* (also **Allen charge, deadlock charge**) lawyers by 1990s A very strong charge given by a judge to a jury, seeking to insure a verdict: *. . . might have been better off had the jury been instructed with a dynamite charge*—Court TV [fr a punning use of *charge*]

dynamiter *n* truckers by 1940s A driver who abuses a truck by rough handling or speeding

dyno or **dino** (DI noh) *n* railroad by 1940s A railroad section hand or any other construction or excavation worker, esp one who uses dynamite [fr *dynamite*]
See DINO[1]

E

each *See* PER EACH

eager beaver 1 *n phr by 1940s* An energetic and willing worker; ambitious striver **2** *modifier*: her *eager-beaver sincerity/ eager-beaver gung-ho spirit*

eagle *See* the DAY THE EAGLE SHITS, LEGAL EAGLE

◄**eagle-beak**► *n by 1920* A Jew: *Catch me workin' for one of them eagle-beaks*—James T Farrell

eagle day *n phr WWII armed forces* Payday [fr the *eagle* depicted on US currency, and the fact that the eagle is said to fly or shit or scream on payday]

eagle-eye 1 *n* A person noted for keen vision or one who keeps a close watch: *It took a real eagle-eye to catch that* **2** *n railroad* A locomotive engineer **3** *n* A detective, esp one assigned to watch for shoplifters or pickpockets

eagle-eyed *by 1601* **1** *adj* Having very keen vision **2** *adj* Keeping a close watch

eagle freak *n phr by 1970s* A conservationist and environmentalist; =ECOFREAK, DUCK SQUEEZER

the **eagle screams** *sentence by 1950s* It is payday: *The old eagle screams today*—comic strip "Arlo and Janis"

ear *v by 1583* To listen; hear: *Rosen Tapes To Be Eared By The Judge*—New York Daily News
See ALL EARS, BEND someone's EAR, BLOW IT OUT, CAULIFLOWER EAR, CHEW someone's EAR OFF, ELEPHANT EARS, HAVE something COMING OUT OF one's EARS, IN A PIG'S ASS, NOT DRY BEHIND THE EARS, PIN someone's EARS BACK, PLAY IT BY EAR, POUND one's EAR, PRETTY EAR, PULL IN one's EARS, PUT A BUG IN someone's EAR, PUT IT IN YOUR EAR, RABBIT EARS, STAND AROUND WITH one's FINGER UP one's ASS, STEAM WAS COMING OUT OF someone's EARS, STICK IT, TALK someone's EAR OFF, WARM someone's EAR

ear-banger *n armed forces by 1930s* A person who tries to advance himself by flattery; =BROWN-NOSE

ear-bender *n by 1930s* An overly loquacious person; =GABBER, WINDBAG: *James Joyce was something of an ear-bender, no?*

ear candy *n phr 1980s* =ELEVATOR MUSIC

ear-duster *n baseball by 1930s* =DUSTER

eared *See* DOG-EARED

an **earful** *n phr by 1917* A large or impressive quantity of talk, esp of a rambling or gossipy sort

ear-grabber *n by 1990s* Something that catches one's attention; =HOOK: *It's one of those short items that are perfect ear-grabbers for radio and TV...* —Mike Royko

early bird *by 1883* **1** *n phr* A person who habitually gets up early in the morning; one who greets the dawn ●Based on the proverb "The early bird catches the worm," attested fr the 1670s **2** *modifier*: an *early-bird session/ early-bird radio program* **3** *n phr* A person who arrives early at a gathering, the office, etc **4** *n phr* The first train, bus, airplane, etc, of the day

earn one's **wings** *v phr by 1940s* To prove oneself competent and reliable in one's work [fr the *wing*-shaped badge awarded to graduating air cadets]

ears *n by 1940s* Small boxed announcements at the upper right and left hand of a newspaper page: . . .space in the small boxes known as "ears" on the tops of. . .front pages—Milwaukee Journal

earth muffin or **granola** *n phr 1980s students* A person who is not stylish; for example, a woman who does not wear cosmetics ●Shows a mocking attitude towards "natural-looking" people and environmentalists

ease on (or **out** or **on out**) *v phr by 1920s* To depart; =MOSEY ALONG: *easing on down the road to the Land of Oz*—Philadelphia

ease someone **out** *v phr by 1940s* To dismiss or remove someone from a post or place gradually and gently

ease up 1 *v phr by 1915* To become less stringent or punishing: *Let's ease up on them; they've got no fight left* **2** *v phr by 1945* To become less tense, exertive, etc; =GO EASY, LIGHTEN UP, TAKE IT EASY: *Come on, ease up now, it's all over*

Eastern Western *n phr by 1970s* A Japanese or Chinese movie featuring the sort of violence and machismo typical of cowboy movies

East German coaches *n phr by 1990s* Anabolic steroids and other drugs prohibited in amateur sports: *"East German coaches" is a euphemism. . .for illegal performance-enhancing drugs*—Milwaukee Journal

East Jesus *n phr* An archetypical small rural town; =PODUNK

East Jesus State *n phr students by 1940s* Any small college regarded as inferior and backward; the mythical, archetypical small provincial college; =SIWASH

easy *See* BREATHE EASY, FREE-AND-EASY, GO EASY, OVER EASY, SPEAKEASY, TAKE IT EASY

easy as pie *adj phr* and *adv phr* (Variations: **can be** or **could be** or **falling off a log** or **hell** or **rolling off a log** may replace **pie**) *entry form by*

163

1921, log forms by 1840 Very easy or easily: *He did it easy as pie/ The thing's easy as can be*

easy digging *n phr by 1950s* Anything easily done; =PIECE OF CAKE [perhaps fr earlier sense, "sugar"]

easy eight *n phr by 1990s* An easy job; sinecure: *Smith doesn't relish the work; he tells himself the job's an easy eight, but wastes his nights drinking away the haunting images of the day*—Nation

easy lay *n phr by 1934* A person easy to convince and control; =PUSHOVER: *Don't expect Stone to direct: Oliver's been around the block and won't be seduced by money. He's not an easy lay*—Time

easy make 1 *n phr* (also **easy lay**) A woman easily persuaded to engage in the sex act **2** *n phr* =EASY MARK

easy mark *n phr by 1896* A person easily victimized or cheated; =PATSY, SUCKER: *He was. . .an "easy mark"*—Jack London

easy meat 1 *n phr by 1920s* Something done or acquired very easily **2** *modifier*: *. . .their easy-meat score in the aerial spraying issue*—Los Angeles Times **3** *n phr by 1986* A person easily duped; =MARK, PATSY, SUCKER [fr the earlier sense that something or someone is vulnerable, easily hunted and caught, etc, esp in the sexual sense where *meat* means "sexual victim, conquest, object, etc"]

easy street *See* ON EASY STREET

eat 1 *v by 1893* To preoccupy or upset; engross; fret: *She asked what was eating me when I frowned so* **2** *v by 1382* To be forced to swallow or recant something: *He mouths off a lot, and lately has had to eat many of his grand pronouncements*—John J Farmer **3** *v sports by 1970s* To be unable to pass the ball along: *They blitzed and the quarterback had to eat the ball* **4** *v by 1919* To accept and enjoy; =EAT UP: *You really eat this shit, don't you?*—C D B Bryan ◁**5**▷ *v* (also **eat up**) *by 1916* To do fellatio or cunnilingus; =GO DOWN ON someone: *So Little Red Riding Hood said to the wolf "Eat me"*

eat cheese *v phr 1970s Army* To inform on someone; tattle; =RAT [fr the *cheese-eating* of the rodent]

eat crow *v phr by 1872* To admit that one was wrong; recant and atone [said to have originated during an armistice of the War of 1812, when an American soldier shot a crow while hunting across the Niagara River from his post; he was forced by guile to take a bite of it; he in return forced the English landowner to consume a portion]

eat dirt *v phr by 1857* To accept rebuke or harassment meekly; swallow one's pride; =EAT SHIT: *I ate dirt and apologized to that bastard*—Calder Willingham

eat someone's **dust** *v phr by 1940s* To be behind someone in a race or chase: *After two laps they ate Coghlan's dust*

eater *See* CHALK-EATER, CHEESE BUN, CLAY EATER, FIRE-EATER, FROG, GRASS EATER, MEATEATER, MOTHERFUCKER, PETER-EATER, SAWDUST EATER, SNAKE EATER

eatery *n about 1900* A restaurant

eatery/drinkery *n by 1980s* A bar that serves food: *He opened an eatery/drinkery called the Chelsea Street Pub. . .*—New York Times

eat one's **hat** *See* EAT one's WORDS

eat high on (or **off**) **the hog** *v phr by 1940s* To live very well; thrive; prosper; =SHIT IN HIGH COTTON: *You will. . .eat high on the hog, as a member of the ruling mob*—Westbrook Pegler/ *The institute will eat high off the hog*—Harvey Breit

eating *See* FROG, MOTHERFUCKING

◁**eatin' stuff**▷ *n phr* (also **eating pussy, table grade**) *by 1940s* A woman of great sexual appeal •Although the reference is ambiguous, these terms need not connote cunnilingus

eat someone's **lunch** *v phr* (**catch** or **have** may replace **eat**) *about 1960* To defeat decisively and humiliatingly; =CLOBBER, FINISH: *They are destroying the America that ate the world's lunch because we were the masters of change*—Lowell Weicker/ *The hitters have been having his lunch*—New Yorker

eat out *v phr by 1933* To have a meal away from home, esp at a restaurant

eat someone **out 1** *v phr by 1940s* To reprimand someone severely; rebuke harshly; =CHEW someone OUT: *Out came Joe McCarthy from the Boston dugout all set to eat me out*—Gilbert Millstein ◁**2**▷ *v phr by 1960s* To do cunnilingus or analingus

eats *n* Food; provender: *A soft bed and good eats were paradise enow*

◁**eat shit**▷ **1** *v phr* =EAT DIRT **2** *v phr* To be accursed, humiliated, etc •Usu a loud oral insult; in WWII, Japanese troops attempted to arouse US troops to a reckless frenzy by shouting "Babe Ruth eats shit!": *You eat shit, you son of a bitch!* *See* TAKE SHIT

eat the Bible *See* SWALLOW THE BIBLE

eat the carpet *v phr by 1990s* To be obsequious; truckle: *"Eat the carpet" is what endangered nominees do at confirmation hearings to make amends: They crawl*—Milwaukee Journal

eat up 1 *v phr by 1535* To use entirely; deprive of completely; =GOBBLE UP: *The rent ate up half my pay* **2** *v phr by 1909* To accept and enjoy; have delectation for; =EAT: *When a man receives wolf whistles, he eats it up*—Denver talk radio caller

eat one's **words** (or **hat**) *v phr* Words form by 1891, hat by 1836 To be forced either to retract or to suffer for what one has said: *They showed him proof and he had to eat his words/ I'll eat my hat if I'm wrong*

eat your heart out *sentence by 1581* Look at me and be envious; suffer vexation over my situation •A rather nasty taunt: *Eat your heart out, Aaron Lebedeff!*—Joel Grey [current use influenced by Yiddish *es dir oys s'harts*, "eat out your heart"]

ech (EK) *See* YUCK

eco- *combining word 1960* Having to do with ecology: *eco-activist/ ecofreak/ eco-terrorist/ eco-warrior*

ecofreak or **econut** *n by 1972* An environmentalist and conservationist; =DUCK SQUEEZER, EAGLE FREAK: *Eco-freaks will love the clean-burning engine*—National Review

econobox *n by 1990s* A cheap car without frills: *The sleek and brightly painted Paseo's body wraps a core that is strictly econobox*—New York Times

ecstasy or **X** *n 1980s narcotics* A variety of amphetamine narcotic: *Ecstasy. . .by emergency order of the Drug Enforcement Administration, illegal*—Washington Post

Ed *See* OP-ED PAGE

edge 1 *n by 1896* An advantage: *. . .soaking up that famous New York "edge". . .* **2** *n by 1908* An irritated or sarcastic tone; sharp timbre: *She answered with a slight edge to her voice*
See HAVE AN EDGE ON someone

the **edge** *n phr by 1980s* Perilous territory; a risky situation: *Living closer to the edge somehow makes you more than just a pampered Hollywood pretty boy*—New York Times

Edge City or **technoburb** *n phr by 1990s* A sprawling suburb lacking a downtown core but well-provided with malls and other consumer amenities, and serving as a place of high-tech employment: *This is the most obvious truth of family life in Edge City: The old idea of neighborhood is dead*—Esquire/ *They're called edge cities, or technoburbs, suburbs a dozen or twenty miles outside old downtown cores that have burgeoned into . . .centers for high-tech employment*—Esquire [the term was originated and propagated by Joel Garreau in his 1992 book *Edge City: Life on the New Frontier*]

edged 1 *adj by 1894* Drunk: *When he was nicely edged he was a pretty good sort of guy*—Raymond Chandler **2** *adj 1980s teenagers* Very angry; =PISSED OFF

edge someone **out** *v phr by 1940s* To defeat by a close margin; barely surpass: *We edged them out by just three votes*

edgy 1 *adj* (also **on edge**) *by 1837* Tense and irritable; nervous; =UPTIGHT: *I saw he was getting a bit edgy, so I agreed to include him* **2** *adj 1990s* Daring advanced; on the cutting edge: *Spurred by the sudden obsession with youth culture, these editors are producing a series of visually edgy, culturally progressive new glossies. . .*—Vogue

edifice complex *n phr by 1940s* The keen desire of public and educational administrators to build buildings: *NY Gov. Nelson Rockefeller's edifice complex left a legacy of overly large and torpid buildings around the state*—New York Times [a pun on Freud's 1890s *Oedipus complex*]

Edsel *n 1950s* Something useless; a fiasco: *We have to win out. We're not selling Edsels, you know*—Time [fr the *Edsel* car, so named in 1956, which fell short of commercial success]

educated guess *n phr by 1954* A guess made with some basis of fact and knowledge: *Economists offer some educated guesses on why the adjustment in unemployment is so skewed*—New York Times

-ee *suffix used to form nouns* The object of what is indicated: *baby-sittee/ kickee/ muggee*

eel *See* MANHATTAN EEL

◁**eff**▷ *v* or *n by 1920s* =FUCK ●This curt euphemism is also the base for equivalents of *fucked, fucking,* and *fucker*: *. . .eff off back to effing Russia*—Anthony Burgess/ *. . .otherwise effed around until. . .Bill Veeck was forced to. . .*—Playboy/ *. . .this is the stupidest effing stunt you've ever pulled*—Douglas Coupland

egads switch (or button) *See* CHICKEN SWITCH

egg 1 *n by 1853* A person: *Evelyn's a good egg* **2** *n by 1589* Anything roughly egg-shaped, such as the head, a baseball, an aerial bomb, etc: *bopped him on the egg/ reared back and chucked the old egg* [first sense altered fr the mid–19th-century term *bad egg*, "bad or rotten person"]
See BAD EGG, DUCK-EGG, FRIED EGG, GOOSE EGG, HARD-BOILED EGG, HAVE EGG ON one's FACE, LAY AN EGG, NEST EGG, SUCK EGGS, WALK ON EGGS, YOU CAN'T MAKE AN OMELET WITHOUT BREAKING EGGS

eggbeater 1 *n WWII Army Air Force* An aircraft propeller **2** *n by 1937* A helicopter ●Now almost entirely superseded by *chopper*: *The "egg-beater" took off for Inchon with its burden*—Associated Press **3** *n by 1940s* An outboard motor; =KICKER: *. . .wouldn't be caught dead with an eggbeater on their boat*—R W Carrick

egger *See* HAM-AND-EGGER

egghead 1 *n by 1950s* A bald man **2** *n by 1907* An intellectual; thinker; =DOUBLE-DOME ●Revived in the 1950s to designate the followers of Adlai Stevenson: *An egghead is "one who calls Marilyn Monroe Mrs Arthur Miller"*—P Sann [second sense presumably fr the putative high, domed, *egg*-shaped heads of such persons; the term was used in a letter of Carl Sandburg about 1918]

egg in someone's **beer** *n phr by 1940s* The height of luxury or pleasure; everything one could desire ●Often part of an impatient question addressed to someone who asks for more than is merited or available: *So it's got no air-conditioning. You want egg in your beer?/ I don't call two weeks' vacation exactly egg in my beer*

egg-sucker *n by 1950s* A person who seeks advancement through flattery; =BROWN-NOSE

ego trip *1960s* **1** *n phr* Something done primarily to build one's self-esteem or display one's splendid qualities: *The pie-thrower. . .said the guru was on an ego trip*—Time/ *This isn't any ego trip, taking a job in this administration*—W T Tyler **2** *v*: *I was showing off, ego-tripping* [based on *trip*, "psychedelic narcotic experience"]

eight *See* FORKED-EIGHT, FORTY-EIGHT, NINETY-EIGHT

eightball ◀**1**▶ *n by 1919* A black person **2** *n by 1940s* A chronically unfortunate and ineffective person; =LOSER, SAD SACK **3** *n 1950s jive talk* =SQUARE [because the pool ball numbered eight is black, and unlucky if it blocks one's cue ball]
See BEHIND THE EIGHT BALL

eighteen wheeler *n phr* 1970s *citizens band* A semitrailer truck; cab and trailer: *The driver of the eighteen-wheeler to my left was wearing the uniform of the West Virginia Highway Patrol*—Penthouse

eighter (or Ada) from Decatur *n phr* *crap-shooting & poker by* 1940s The card, roll, or craps point of eight

eight-hundred-pound gorilla *See* SIX-HUNDRED-POUND GORILLA

◀**eight-rock**▶ *n* *black by* 1950s A very dark-skinned black person

eighty-four *n* *WWII Navy* A naval prison

eighty-one or **eighty-two** *n* 1930s *lunch counter* A glass of water

eighty-seven *n* 1930s *lunch counter* A signal meaning "a good-looking woman has come in; take note"

eighty-six 1 *n* 1930s *lunch counter* A cook's term for "none" or "nix" when asked for something not available **2** *v*: *We had to eighty-six the French dip*—John Sayles **3** *n* *bartenders by* 1930s A person who is not to be served more liquor: *. . .known as an "eighty-six," which. . .means: "Don't serve him"*—Gene Fowler **4** *v* (also **eight-six**) *by* 1959 To eject or interdict someone: *I'll have you eighty-sixed out of this bar*—John Rechy/ *I been eighty-sixed out of better situations*—George V Higgins **5** *v by* 1980s To reject; refuse; eschew: *Kids, eighty-six those video games*—Rocky Mountain News **6** *v by* 1970s To kill; destroy; annihilate: *There'd been serious pragmatic reasons for not eighty-sixing the man then and there*—Richard Merkin [probably fr the rhyme with "nix"]

eighty-two *See* EIGHTY-ONE

el bonzo *adj phr by* 1990s Crazy; hectic; frenetic; =BONZO: *At dinner time, this restaurant goes el bonzo*—Warren Byrne

elbow 1 *n* A police officer or detective **2** *v* To associate with someone as a friend; =RUB ELBOWS
See BEND THE ELBOW, NOT KNOW one's ASS FROM one's ELBOW, RUB ELBOWS

elbow-bender *n* A convivial person; drinker

elbow-bending *n* Drinking liquor: *the gentlemanly art of refined elbow-bending*—Esquire

elbow grease *n phr by* 1710 Muscular exertion; physical effort

elbow someone **out** *v phr* To eliminate or replace someone by aggressive pressure: *She looked pretty secure, but he elbowed her out of the vice presidency*

elbow room *n phr fr* 1700s Barely enough space for the occupant; a minimum of space: *This office is so crowded I couldn't find elbow room for anyone else*/ *Don't crowd so, give me elbow room* [propagated in the US because it was a nickname for General John Burgoyne, who boasted in the 1770s that he would find *elbow room* in this country]

el cheapo 1960s **1** *n phr* A cheap product; a piece of shoddy merchandise: *They bought the El Cheapos and found they didn't work*—New York Times **2** *modifier*: *Beware of plaid shirts, el cheapo haircuts and candidates who talk r-e-a-l slow. . .*—Philadelphia Daily News [probably first applied like *El Ropo*, to cheap cigars, since many cigars have Spanish names; see *el -o*, mock-Spanish combining form]

electric horseman *n phr early* 1990s A kind of dancing based on a cowboy motif: *. . .it's the individual dances that are most popular: the tush push, slapping leather, and the electric horseman*—Milwaukee Journal

elephant *See* SEE PINK ELEPHANTS, WHITE ELEPHANT

elephant ears *n phr* 1950s *astronautics* Large, thick metal discs on the outer shell of a rocket or missile

elephant linebacker (or position) *n phr* *football by* 1990s A linebacker or defensive end who specializes in rushing the quarterback on pass plays: *Now comes "elephant position"*—Milwaukee Journal/*Paup started the first nine games at elephant, or rush, outside linebacker*—Milwaukee Journal

elephant tranquilizer *n phr* 1960s *narcotics* =ANGEL DUST

elevate *v* 1920s To rob: *go out and "elevate" a bank*—J Black [probably a play on *heist*]

elevated *adj by late* 1600s Drunk

one's **elevator doesn't go to the top floor** *sentence by* 1980s One is not very bright: *Those people, doesn't sound like their elevators go to the top floor*—Lawrence Sanders/ *But they should come down now. If they don't, their elevator doesn't go to the top*—Milwaukee Journal

elevator music *n phr by* 1970s Bland, pretty music, of the sort played over speakers in elevators; =EAR CANDY, MUZAK

elevator surfing *n phr* 1980s The bold prank of riding on the roof of an elevator car

el foldo *n phr* 1940s *college students* Academic failure, either general or in a course
See PULL AN EL FOLDO

Elk *n* 1950s *beat talk* A conventional person; =SQUARE: *kill themselves later with laughter over the amount of money the Elks spent*—S Boal [fr a scornful judgment of the Benevolent and Protective Order of *Elks*]

el -o *combining form by* 1940s An amusing variation of whatever is infixed: *. . .travel el cheapo*—Time/ *. . .flatchested el birdos in long dresses*—Stephen King/ *You still seeing El Sleazo these days?*—Cyra McFadden/ *. . .universal emptiness. . . el zilcho*—Stephen King/ *Our President. . .did his famous el foldo*—Sports Illustrated/ *If it is calm, it is el snoro*—Time [fr a common pattern in Spanish]

El Ropo *n phr by* 1940s A name for any inferior cigar, or for any cigar at all that one does not like [imitation of a typical cigar name, of a cigar made of rope]

else *See* OR ELSE

Elsewhere *See* MOUNT SAINT ELSEWHERE

embalmed *adj* Drunk

embalming fluid *n phr by 1890s* Strong coffee, whiskey, or other potent drink

emcee *See* MC

emery ball *n phr baseball by 1914* A pitch thrown with the ball partially roughened

emote *by 1917* **1** *v* To play a theatrical role, esp one calling for a strong display of emotion; =HAM: . . .*all been panting to see her emote in the gangster film*—Louella Parsons **2** *v* To indulge in a display of feeling, esp a pretense: *Now she's emoting about the electric bill*

emoticon *n computer by 1990s* Symbols made from punctuation marks, used to denote emotion: :-) – *smile;* ;-) – *smile with a wink;* 8-) – *smile from a person who wears glasses;* :-(– *frown*—Los Angeles Times

empty-nester *n early 1980s* A person whose children have grown up and moved away from home: . . .*when my older boys were grown and I'm an empty-nester*—Milwaukee Journal/ *We are getting a lot of empty-nesters moving into a Leisure World development*—Washingtonian/ . . .*elderly "empty nesters" who sell their suburban homes and come to the city*—New York Times

empty suit *n phr 1980s* A person of some seeming distinction who is actually a product of publicity: *Steven Brill calls him an "empty suit" whose main talent is getting his name in the papers.* . .—Us Magazine

enchilada *See* BIG ENCHILADA, the WHOLE ENCHILADA

end 1 *n by 1903* A share; =CUT: *Eddie would be entitled to half an end*—E DeBaun/ *I muscle in for an end of the beer racket*—American Mercury **2** *n by 1909* Particular concern or portion; sector: *Selling's his end of it*

See GO OFF THE DEEP END, HIND END, JUMP OFF THE DEEP END, the LIVING END, REAR END, SEE THE LIGHT AT THE END OF THE TUNNEL, SHORT END OF THE STICK

the **end** *n phr 1950s beat & cool talk* The best; the greatest; =the LIVING END: *Mr Secretary General, you're the end!*

end run *by 1950s fr football* **1** *n phr* An attempt to avoid or evade higher authority by acting outside authorized channels: *McLarty gave Shalala a dressing down about doing end runs around the White House*—New Yorker **2** *v*: *Special interests have found new ways to end-run our system*—New York Times/ . . .*the label chiefs would no longer be allowed to end-run Morgado*—Vanity Fair

ends 1 *n 1950s beat & cool talk* Shoes: *When a hipster buys clothes, he begins with "ends"*—E Horne **2** *n motorcyclists by 1980s* A complete turning over of the motorcycle

endville or **endsville** *adj 1950s cool talk* Superb; unsurpassed: *Endville means the best*—E Horne [see -**sville**]

the **Energizer bunny** *n phr 1990s* Someone or something that never runs out of energy: *Nixon, like the Energizer bunny, just goes on and on and on*—New York Times [fr television ads for Energizer™ bat-

teries, which show a mechanical rabbit carrying on endlessly]

enforcer *n by 1930s* A person, esp a gangster, hockey player, or other athlete assigned to intimidate and punish opponents; =POLICEMAN

English[1] *n 1950s lunch counter* An English muffin

English[2] *n by 1860s* A spin imparted to a billiard ball, tennis ball, etc, to make it curve [fr French *anglé,* "angled," similar to *Anglais,* "English"]

English spliff *n phr 1960s narcotics* A cigarette combining tobacco with some narcotic: . . .*rolls an English spliff, tobacco mixed with hashish*—Rolling Stone

an **engraved invitation** *See* DO YOU WANT AN ENGRAVED INVITATION

enjoy *interj by 1980s* An exhortation to be happy, to enjoy oneself: *Go. Read. Enjoy. It couldn't hurt*—Time/ *The trooper grinned. "Enjoy," he said, and walked on toward the cruiser*—Robert B Parker [fr a Yiddish speech pattern, recorded but not approved by Leo Rosten]

enough is enough *interj by 1546* An exhortation to be done, to desist: *More than a few descendants of immigrants are saying enough is enough*—New York Times

enough to choke a horse *by 1940s* **1** *adv phr* To a very great degree; in a very large quantity: *His ego is big enough to choke a horse* **2** *n phr* A very large quantity; a plethora: *Does he have money? Enough to choke a horse*

enough to gag a maggot *adv phr by 1970s* Very disgusting; repulsive: *His excuse was enough to gag a maggot/ "Oh, gross," Lou Ann said. "Gag a maggot"*—Barbara Kingsolver

enviro *n 1990s* An environmentalist: *Even Beltway enviros not promised jobs expected something.* . .—Nation **2** *modifier*: *Attending an enviro benefit because he cared about the rain forest*—New Republic

equalizer *n about 1900* A pistol or other firearm; =the DIFFERENCE

erase *v by 1940s* To kill; =RUB OUT

eraser *n prizefight by 1940s* A knockout or a knockout punch

-erino *suffix used to form nouns* (also **-arino** or **-orino**) *by 1900* A humorous version or a remarkable specimen of what is indicated: *peacherino/ bitcherino* [probably fr the Italian diminutive suffix *-ino* combined with the agentive suffix *-er*]

-eroo *suffix used to form nouns* (also **-aroo** or **-roo** or **-oo**) *by 1930s* Emphatic, humorous, or affectionate form of what is indicated: *babyroo/ floperoo/ jivaroo/ screameroo/ sockeroo*

-ers *suffix used to form adjectives and nouns by 1860s* In the condition humorously indicated •These are all British imports, coming ultimately from public school slang: *bonkers/ champers/ preggers/ starkers*

-ery 1 *suffix used to form nouns by 1920s* Place or establishment where the indicated thing is used, done, sold, etc: *boozery/ eatery/ minkery* **2** *suffix*

used to form nouns The collectivity or an instance of what is indicated: *claptrappery/ jerkery*

-ess *suffix used to form nouns* by 1400s A woman member of the indicated group or calling •A standard suffix now used most often in slang partly because the standard use is regarded as, and sometimes meant to be, offensive: *loaferess/ muggess/ veepess*

etaoin shrdlu (ə TAY oh ən SHƏRD loŏ) *n phr* by 1931 Confusion; mistakes: *98 percent accurate and 2 percent etaoin shrdlu*—New York Post [fr the phrase typeset by sweeping one's finger down the two left-hand columns of Linotype keys, in a gesture made by compositors when they have erred and must begin again]

-eteria *See* -ATERIA

Ethel *1920s* **1** *n* A coward, esp a cautious prizefighter **2** *n* An effeminate man; =PERCY, SISSY

euchre *v* by 1855 To outwit, esp by cheating; =SCAM

Euro *adj* or **combining word** by 1950s European: *The majority of the Euro children hit the black box first*—Psychology/*Eurobrat/ Eurobucks/ Eurofunk/ Eurojargon/ . . .dancing Europop strings*—Village Voice

even *adj* by 1637 On the same footing: *When you hit me we'll be even*
See GET EVEN

even break *n phr* by 1911 A fair and equal chance; honest treatment; =a FAIR SHAKE: *The Bible, I think it is, says never to give a sucker an even break*

evened out *adj phr* by 1970s Restored to balance and health; rational: *"I was really emotionally fucked up." "Are you evened out now?"*—Diana Clapton

evening *See* LARGE EVENING

even-stephen or **even-steven** by 1866 **1** *adj* Fair; even; equable: *Give me the hundred and fifty and we'll call it even-steven*—Dashiell Hammett **2** *adv*: *And we'll do likewise for San Francisco and Odessa, or any places we want, always even-stephen*—D Fairbairn

even the score *v phr* by 1940s =GET EVEN

ever *adv* Really; truly; certainly •Used postpositively for emphasis: *Boy, has it ever!*—Mike Royko/ *Clinton's generation has already had its chance to make its tastes the country's tastes. Has it ever—*Time/ *Did we win? Did we ever!*

evergreen 1 *n* (also **think piece, thumbsucker**) *print & broadcast journalism* by 1980s A story that is not news, but penetrating analysis, etc: *Such articles, the desperate resort of editorial writers everywhere, are. . .known as evergreens and think pieces*—James J Kilpatrick **2** *modifier*: *. . . .desperately searching the shelf of "evergreen" pieces, hoping to find some picture story that we could tie in with what was happening*—Sam Donaldson **3** *n* A perennial favorite, esp a song; by 1940s =GOLDEN OLDIE [journalism senses so called because such material is perdurably useful]

evergreen contract *n phr* *sports* by 1980s A contract always written with a time extension: *It was an "evergreen" contract on which he'd always have two years to go. . .automatically*—Milwaukee Journal

ever-loving by 1930s **1** *adj* Devoted; faithful: *And this is my ever-loving bride* **2** *intensifier*: *Say that again and I'll bust your ever-loving ass*

everybody and his uncle *n phr* by 1940s Absolutely everyone: *Everybody and his uncle came to the party/ Parvin received advice from everybody and his brother. . .*—Time/ *"Will enough people see that?" "Everybody and his dog will see that,"* Smith says—New Yorker [in earlier versions going back to the 1860s, *his cousin* or *their mothers-in-law* could replace *uncle*]

every man jack *n phr* by 1840 Everyone; every male; =EVERY TOM, DICK, AND HARRY: *I'll have you in irons, every man jack*

every Tom, Dick, and Harry *n phr* by 1734 Every and any man, esp a very ordinary one: *. . .letting every Tom, Dick, and Harry in on the election*—Max Shulman

every which way *adv phr* by 1824 In all ways; in all directions: *Mrs Bush now has it every which way: she's the American queen mother and the master politician*—New Republic

everything's coming up roses *sentence* by 1980s Everything is going marvelously well

everything but the kitchen sink *WWII armed forces* **1** *n phr* Everything imaginable •First used in such phrases as "They hit us with everything but the kitchen sink" **2** *adj phr*: *Sunday dinner—salads with an everything-but-the-kitchen-sink touch*—New York Times

evil 1 *adj* by 1950s Excellent; splendid; =MEAN, WICKED: *Geoffrey beats an evil set of skins* **2** *adj* *homosexuals* by 1970s Biting and sarcastic; catty; =BITCHY

ex¹ or **x** *n* by 1929 A former wife or husband, girlfriend or boyfriend, etc: *He introduced his ex rather casually, considering they were together 27 years*

ex² *n* *carnival & circus* by 1940s An exclusive concession

exam by 1848 **1** *n* An examination **2** *modifier*: *exam results/ exam book*

excess baggage *n phr* *theater* by 1909 A person or thing regarded as unnecessary and likely to impede: *He thought his wife and kids were excess baggage*

ex-con *n* by 1906 A former convict

excuse *n* by 1940s A version or example of: *He's a rotten excuse for a lawyer*

excuse (or **pardon**) **me all to hell** *sentence* I apologize; I am sorry •Most often said ironically, when one thinks an accusation has been undeserved or too strong

excuse-me hit *n phr* *baseball* by 1980s A hit made with a checked swing or other unlikely contact

exec 1 *n Navy* by 1920s An executive officer **2** *n* by 1896 A business executive: *They'd never heard of female execs*—New York Magazine/*I find parking* space for senior execs—New Yorker **3 modifier**: exec perks/ exec burnout

executive modifier by 1970s Stylish; luxurious; costly; =POSH: executive housing/ executive bus/ executive class

exo n by 1990s An exhibition game or match: I mean she's playing a freaking exo—New York Times

expedition   See GO FISHING

extra 1 n by 1793 A special edition of a newspaper or a special broadcast of news made immediately on learning of an important event; news-break **2 n** theater by 1880 A person appearing in a crowd scene or otherwise in a minor capacity in a play or movie: I was an extra in the Budapest showcase of "Godot"

extracurricular adj Irregular; irresponsible: not an affair, but an extracurricular fling [fr the college sense "outside the academic curriculum"]

the **extra mile   See** GO THE EXTRA MILE

-ey   See -IE

eye n by 1930 A private detective; =PRIVATE EYE: . . . an eye named Johnny O'John—Anthony Boucher **See** BIG BROWN EYES, BLACK EYE, EAGLE-EYE, FOUR-EYES, GIVE someone THE EYE, GIVE someone THE FISH-EYE, GIVE someone THE GLAD EYE, a GLEAM IN THE EYE, GOO-GOO EYES, HAVE EYES FOR, IN A PIG'S ASS, KEEP AN EYE ON, MAKE GOO-GOO EYES, MUD IN YOUR EYE, NOT BAT AN EYE, PRIVATE EYE, PULL THE WOOL OVER someone's EYES, PUT THE EYE ON someone, REDEYE, the RED-EYE, ROUND-EYE, SHORT EYES, SHUT-EYE, SNAKE EYES, STONED TO THE EYES, a THUMB IN one's EYE

the **Eye** or the **eye n** by 1914 The Pinkerton National Detective Agency, or one of its detectives [fr the eye used as the trademark symbol of the agency]

eyeball v 1940s black To look at; look over; =SCOPE ON •An isolated instance is attested in 1901: He would eyeball the idol-breaker. . .—Zora Neale Hurston/ You locate trophies before they eyeball you—Sports Afield **See** GIVE someone THE FISH-EYE, UP TO one's EYE-BALLS

eyeball to eyeball by 1950s **1 adv phr** Face to face; in confrontation: We're eyeball to eyeball and I think the other fellow just blinked—Dean Rusk **2 adj phr**: our eyeball-to-eyeball chat

eyed   See COCKEYED, GOTCH-EYED, HOARY-EYED, ONE-EYED MONSTER, PIE-EYED, WALL-EYED

◁**eye-fuck**▷ **v** by 1916 To stare intently, esp at a sex object: That's what he believed the trio was doing, eye-fucking Callaway and Nguyen. . .—Vanity Fair

eyeful 1 n by 1914 A good look; close scrutiny; =GANDER: Get an eyeful of that place over there **2 n** by 1922 A very good-looking woman; =DISH

eyegrabber n by 1980s Something or someone that strongly attracts attention; =GRABBER, HOOK: Daily News front pages have been eye-grabbers on the newsstands for 70 years—New Republic

eye-grabbing adj by 1980s Strongly attractive; magnetic: Geena's so statuesque, she's so eye-grabbing on the screen—Vanity Fair

eye in the sky 1 n phr gambling by 1960s In casinos, a security guard or video camera watching games from concealment above **2 n phr** by 1970s A police officer, reporter, etc, who watches traffic from above, usu in a helicopter **3 n phr** 1980s baseball A coach, coordinator, etc, who watches a game from the press box and calls plays and suggestions to the coaches on the ground: Teams have the "eye in the sky" to get an edge on defense. . .—Joe Garagiola

eye-opener 1 n by 1818 A drink of liquor taken upon awaking: He fumbled for the jug and slurped an eye-opener **2 n** 1960 narcotics An addict's first injection of the day **3 n** by 1863 Anything that informs or enlightens one: Listening to that story was a real eye-opener

eyepopper n by 1940s Something that makes one's eyes bulge in astonishment; =EYE GRABBER: The president added a further eyepopper—Washington Post

◁**eyes like pissholes in the snow**▷ **n phr** by 1940s Very bleary eyes; tired and dim eyes, esp those of a severe hangover •**Pissholes in the sand** is found by 1932: Your eyes look like two piss holes in the snow—Rex Burns

eyes only adj phr by 1960s Very personal and confidential [fr the government security phrase "for your eyes only"]

eyewash 1 n by 1884 =HOGWASH •Eye, "nonsense, humbug," is attested by 1859, and all my eye a century earlier; although the connection is not clear, these probably led to eyewash **2 n** by 1919 Flattery; cajolery: eyewash to soften him up for the touch

◁**Eytie** or **Eyetie**▷ (Ī tee; Brit Ī tī) British armed forces by 1925 **1 n** An Italian **2 adj**: an Eytie village/ Eyetie chick

F

fab *adj* or *interj* *1950s teenagers* Excellent; wonderful; fabulous: . . . *a man who would think it a fab idea to rent a silver limo*—Village Voice

face 1 *n* *show business by 1960s* A celebrity, esp a show-business notable **2** *n* *1950s cool talk* A person: . . . *bad face. . . a surly, mean, no-good cat*—E Horne **3** *n* *black by 1940s* A white person; =FAY: *Don't see why we need some high-priced face down here telling us how to live*—Robert B Parker **4** *v* *students by 1980s* To insult; embarrass; humiliate; =BURN ●This sense probably originated in basketball, where aggressive players put their hands in front of other players' faces: . . . *face, which means to embarrass. . .* —Philadelphia Inquirer
See BAG YOUR FACE, DOLLFACE, FEED one's FACE, FLANGE-FACE, GET OUT OF someone's FACE, GET OUT OF someone's FACE, GO UPSIDE one's FACE, HAVE A RED FACE, HAVE EGG ON one's FACE, LAUGH ON THE OTHER SIDE OF one's FACE, LET'S FACE IT, NOT JUST ANOTHER PRETTY FACE, PALE-FACE, PIEFACE, POKER FACE, RED FACE, SHE CAN SIT ON MY FACE ANY TIME, SHIT-FACED, SHOOT OFF one's MOUTH, a SLAP IN THE FACE, STRAIGHT FACE, SUCK FACE, TILL one IS BLUE IN THE FACE, WHAT'S-HIS-NAME, WHITE-FACE

face card *n phr* *by 1970s* An important person; star; =BIG SHOT: *Oh, don't be so modest. . . you're a face card yourself now*—Philadelphia Journal

faced *adj* *by 1960s* =SHIT-FACED
See POKER-FACED, RED-FACED, SHIT-FACED

face someone **down** *v phr* *by 1530* To disconcert in a direct confrontation: *I am being faced down by a ten- or twelve-year-old boy*—Hugh Pentecost

face fungus *n phr* *by 1972* A beard; whiskers: *Which do you fancy, the blue-eyed chap in the tux or the loser with the face fungus?*—New Yorker

face-off *n* *by 1896* Confrontation, esp one before action: . . . *continuing face-off and stalemate*—Philadelphia [the date reflects use in hockey and lacrosse, where play begins with players scrabbling for the puck or ball]

a **face that would stop a clock** *n phr* *by 1891* A very ugly face: *Unfavored of nature indeed must be that member of the gentler sex whose face would "stop a clock". . .* —Charles L Hildreth

face the music *v phr* *by 1850* To endure whatever punishment or rigors one has incurred; take what one has coming [origin uncertain; perhaps fr the necessity of forcing a cavalry horse to face steadily the regimental band; perhaps fr the plight of a performer on stage]

face time *n phr* *early 1990s* Time spent face-to-face or in close proximity, esp with persons useful to one's career: *Getting 'face time,' as insinuating your way into a photograph with the President is known*—New York Times/ *He recently spent some "face time" chatting with his new pig*—Los Angeles Times

face up *v phr* *by 1920* To confront boldly; acknowledge: *It's time you faced up to how wrong you've been*

fack *black by 1940s* **1** *v* To tell the truth; utter facts: *Negroes know. . . that facking means speaking facts*—Time **2** *sentence* That's a fact: . . . *she'll die a Turnipseed. Fack*—Harry Crews [fr the normal pronunciation of *fact* in Black English]

facockta *adj* *by 1990s* Accursed; wretched; =CRAPPY, SHITTY: *Robbed. Upstairs in your facockta parking lot*—Esquire [fr Yiddish, literally "shitty"]

factoid *n* *early 1970s* A presumed fact of dubious validity; a popular assumption or belief: *Of the eight factoids pertaining to the present Administration. . .* —New York Times/ . . . *a paragraph, part human interest, part factoid*—Anna Quindlen [fr *fact* plus *-oid*]
See -OID

factor *See* FINAGLE FACTOR

factory 1 *n* *narcotics by 1940s* The apparatus used for injecting narcotics; =WORKS **2** *combining word* *by 1920s* Place where what is indicated is done, pursued, used, etc ● A jocular appropriation of the term: *brain factory/ freak factory/ nut factory*
See CRACKER FACTORY, GARGLE-FACTORY, JOINT FACTORY, NUT HOUSE

facts *See* HARD FACTS

faddle *See* FIDDLE-FADDLE

fade 1 *v* *by 1848* To leave; depart: *He faded to Chicago*—A Hynd **2** *v* *crapshooting by 1890* To take one's bet; cover one's offered bet: *When I saw I was faded, I rolled the dice* **3** *v* *by 1450* To lose or cause to lose power and effectiveness: *And I would try to fade the heat off me*—Milwaukee Journal **4** *n* *black by 1970s* A white person **5** *n* *black by 1970s* A black person who prefers white friends, sex partners, attitudes, etc; =OREO **6** *n* *1980s black teenagers* A hair style with a thick upright flat top that tapers toward the ears: *Will has a fresh fade*—Delcastle Dictionary of Slang

fadeaway *n* *baseball by 1908* A pitch that moves away from the batter so that he would have to reach

171

out for it [identified esp with the pitcher Christy Mathewson]

fade away (or **out**) *v phr* by 1820 To depart, esp gradually

◁**faded boogie**▷ *n phr* black by 1940s A black police informer [fr the suggestion that the subject is no better than a white person]

fade-out *n* motion picture by 1923 The end of a scene, film, etc, where the picture gradually disappears

fag 1 *n* by 1888 A cigarette; =BUTT, COFFIN NAIL: *He passed them swell fags around*—Langston Hughes ◁**2**▷ *n* by 1923 A male homosexual; =FAGGOT, QUEER: *. . . and fags are certain to arouse the loathing of all decent fiction addicts*—Gore Vidal/ *. . . sicker by a long shot than any fag, drag, thang, or simple gay man or woman*—Ebony ◁**3**▷ *modifier*: *. . . frenetic hot-rhythm dancing, the cheap fag jokes*—Playboy/ *. . . like a fag party*—Raymond Chandler **4** *v* (also **fag out**) by 1930 To fatigue; exhaust ●The sense "to study hard, go without sleep," is attested in Cambridge University slang by 1803: *This sort of work fags me quickly* [origin unknown; the "homosexual" sense may be connected with the British term *fag*, "the boy servant, and inferentially the catamite, of a public-school upperclassman"; perhaps influenced by Yiddish *faygele*, "homosexual," literally "bird, little bird"]

◁**fag bag**▷ *n phr* homosexuals by 1960s A woman married to a homosexual

fag end *n phr* by 1622 The useless, dreary, or extreme end of something: *The fag ends of my days are irretrievably grungy* [origin uncertain; one early sense of *fag* was "end, dragging end," and in the earliest dated example *fag end* means "ass end"; later use influenced by *fag*, "cigarette, cigarette butt," found by 1888]

fagged out *adj phr* by 1833 Exhausted; =BEAT, POOPED

◁**faggot**▷ *n* by 1914 A male homosexual: *Hot faggot queens bump up against chilly Jewish matrons*—Albert Goldman/ *. . . an amazing job of controlling the faggots*—Tennessee Williams [origin unknown; perhaps fr *fag*; perhaps fr *faggot*, "woman," found by 1591]

◁**faggotry** or **faggery**▷ *n* by 1970s Male homosexuality: *Faggotry was at the very least a terrible embarrassment*—R A Arthur/ *. . . I have a feeling he was arrested sometime in his life. For faggery if nothing else*—Michael Grant

◁**faggoty** or **faggy**▷ *adj* first form by 1928, second by 1950s Homosexual, esp in an overt way ●Used only of males: *. . . who lives with his faggoty American friend*—Playboy

◁**fag hag** or **faggot's moll**▷ *n phr* by 1969 A heterosexual woman who seeks or prefers the company of homosexual men: *Zeffirelli seems to have created a sort of limp-wrist commune, with Clare as the fag hag*—Judith Crist/ *Michael once referred to her. . . as "the fag hag of the bourgeoisie"*—Armistead Maupin

◁**fagocite**▷ *n* New York City boys by 1930s An effeminate boy or man; =SISSY [modeled, surprisingly, on *phagocyte,* "a cell that ingests and destroys foreign particles," altered by *fag*]

fag tag *n phr* (also **fairy loop, fruit loop**) by 1970s A cloth loop sewn into the middle pleat of the upper back of a shirt [*fruit loop* variant fr a breakfast cereal called *Froot Loops*™]

fair dinkum *adj phr* Australian by 1894 Honest; fair and just ●Still chiefly Australian use

fair-haired (or **blue-eyed** or **white-haired**) **boy** first form by 1918, second by 1924, third by 1923 **1** *n phr* A favored or favorite man or boy: *. . . the latest "fairhaired boy" of the musical world*—D Bittan/ *the white-haired boy of the happy family*—Budd Schulberg **2** *n phr* A man destined for and being groomed for principal leadership or other reward; =COMER: *A job had to be found for Patten, the blue-eyed boy of British politics*—New Yorker

a **fair shake** *n phr* by 1830 Equal treatment; the same chance as others; =EVEN BREAK: *He complains he didn't get a fair shake* [fr an honest *shake* of the dice]

◁**fairy**▷ *n* 1895 A male homosexual, esp an effeminate one; =FAG, QUEER: *Too bad you weren't a fairy*—Philip Wylie

fairy godfather *n phr* by 1930s A potential sponsor, advertiser, or financial backer, esp in show business

◁**fairy godmother**▷ *n phr* homosexuals by 1970s A male homosexual's homosexual initiator and tutor

◁**fairy lady**▷ *n phr* about 1950 A lesbian who takes a passive role in sex: *Then there was the fairy lady who said "Argyle it to me!"*—Gay Talk

fake 1 *n* by 1827 A sham or deception; something spurious **2** *v* by 1812 To make something spurious; imitate deceptively: *He was good at faking Old Masters* **3** *adj* *It was a fake Uccello battle scene* **4** *v* theater by 1909 To improvise lines in a play **5** *v* =FAKE IT [origin uncertain; perhaps fr earlier *feak, feague,* or *fig,* "to spruce up, esp by deceptive artificial means"; perhaps ultimately fr German *fegen,* "clean, furbish," or Latin *facere,* "to do"]

fake-bake 1980s students **1** *n* A tanning salon **2** *n* A tan acquired in a salon: *Look at Tiffany's fake-bake!*—UCLA Slang

fake it 1 *v phr* To make a pretense of knowledge, skill, etc; bluff; =CHEEK IT **2** *v phr* (also **fake**) jazz musicians fr about 1915 To improvise more or less compatible chords or notes as one plays or sings something one really has not learned

fake off *v phr* by 1950s To loaf; idle; =GOOF OFF

fake someone **out** *v phr* sports by 1940s To bluff or deceive someone; mislead: *Bailey. . . had faked out Keuper into using a preempt*—John D MacDonald

faker See POODLE-FAKER

fall 1 *v* underworld by 1879 To be arrested; be imprisoned; =DROP: *When you have bad luck and* *you fall, New York is the best place*—New York Times/ . . . *the best thief in the city till he fell*—W R Burnett **2** *n* by 1893: *This your first fall, ain't it?*—The American Scholar/ *Another fall meant a life sentence*—D Purroy **3** *v* by 1906 To become enamored; become a lover: *Once Abelard saw her he fell*

See PRATFALL, the ROOF FALLS IN, TAKE A FALL, TAKE THE RAP

fall all over oneself *v phr* by 1895 To be confusedly effusive: *He fell all over himself trying to apologize/ . . . Administration analysts "fell over themselves" whenever he or his staff sought information. . .* —Los Angeles Times

fall apart *v phr* about 1945 To lose one's usual poise and confidence; lose control; =LOSE one's COOL: *Even the seasoned troupers fall apart*—A Hirschfeld

fall (or slip) between (or through) the cracks *v phr* by 1970s To be ignored, overlooked, mismanaged, or forgotten, esp because of ambiguity in definition or understanding: *The entire problem. . . simply fell between the cracks*—New Yorker/ *. . . a conviction that otherwise might have fallen through the cracks*—Washingtonian

fall down and go boom by 1930s **1** *v phr* To take a tumble; fall heavily **2** *v phr* To fail, esp utterly and obviously

fall down on the job *v phr* by 1898 To fail at one's responsibilities; shirk an obligation

fall for by 1903 **1** *v phr* To become enamored with; become a lover of: *He's constantly falling for long-legged brunettes* **2** *v phr* To be deceived or duped by; acquiesce to: *Americans would continue to "fall for" this*—Robert Lynd

fall guy by 1906 **1** *n phr* An easy victim; =EASY MARK, SUCKER **2** *n phr* A person who willingly or not takes the blame and punishment for another's misdoings; =PATSY: *He said he would not be the president's fall guy*

falling-down drunk *adj phr* by 1980s Too drunk to stand up; very drunk: *O'Hara was fired from most of the jobs he held; he was a falling-down, no-holds-barred, contentious drunk*—New Yorker/ *. . . some rather large, falling-down drunk individuals. . .* —Drew Acorn

falling off a log See EASY AS PIE

fall money *n phr* underworld by 1893 Money set aside to deal with the expenses of being arrested: *Mike set aside a percentage of his takings for "fall money"*—T J Courtney

fall off the map *v phr* by 1980s To disappear from view and attention; drop out of sight: *This show marks a return of sorts for a figure who fell off the map*—New York Times [off the map in this sense is found by 1904]

fall off the roof *v phr* by 1930s To menstruate, esp to begin a menstrual period [probably a fanciful way to explain bleeding]

fall off the wagon *v phr* by about 1905 To begin drinking liquor again after a period of abstinence;

also, to breach abstinence or moderation in anything: *. . . but like most of us, she falls off the wagon from time to time, and heads for a stadium hot dog*—Toronto Life

◁**fall on** one's **ass**▷ **1** *v phr* (also **fall flat on** one's **ass**) by 1940s To fail, esp ignominiously and spectacularly: *They want to see you fall on your ass*—Interview/ *Pratt and Murphy fell on their ass*—George V Higgins **2** *v phr* airline by 1970s To deteriorate beneath operational limits •Said of the weather conditions at an airport

fall on one's **face** *v phr* (also **fall flat on** one's **face**) by 1970s To make an embarrassing mistake, failed attempt, catastrophic decline, etc; =FALL ON one's ASS: *Trying to be stately, I fell flat on my face/If the dollar was stumbling, the Japanese stock market was falling on its face*—Time

fall on one's **sword** *v phr* by 1990s To commit suicide, esp after a defeat and for the good of the general cause: *Cells that become irreparably damaged are expected to fall on their swords for the greater good of the organism*—Time [fr the ancient Roman mode of self-immolation, reflected in Horatio's noble sentiment "I am more an antique Roman than a Dane"]

fallout 1950s **1** *n* An accompanying or resultant effect of something; an aftermath: *Talking to oneself is a fallout of watching too many primaries on TV*—Goodman Ace **2** *n* Incidental products, esp when copious and of little value: *reports, memoranda, and other printed fallout from the executive suite*—Saturday Review [fr the radioactive dust and other debris of a nuclear explosion]

fall out 1 *v phr* 1950s narcotics To go to sleep or into a stuporous condition from narcotic intoxication: *Only those who are uptight fall out*—Saturday Review/ *If you resist falling out and pass the barrier, the curve is up to a mellow stupor*—New York **2** *v phr* by 1950s To become helpless with laughter or emotion; =CRACK UP: *I tried double tempo and everybody fell out laughing*—Charlie Parker/ *. . . sizing up audiences and delivering the goods that would make them fall out, whether in church or not*—Nation

fall through *v phr* by 1879 To fail; miscarry; =FIZZLE: *Our plans for the building fell through*

fall up *v phr* (Variations: **by** or **down** or **out** may replace **up**) 1930s black To come for a visit; arrive: *The bash is in the basement, Dad. Fall up anytime*—E Horne

faloosie See FLOOZY

falsie or **falsy** by 1940s **1** *n* Anything false or artificial; a prosthesis: *Its tail, a falsy, fell off*—Newsweek **2** *n* A brassiere padded to give the appearance of large breasts; also, padding worn in other places to increase the generosity of a woman's body

falsies or **gay deceivers** *n* by 1940s A pair of breast pads worn to give the appearance of large breasts

family See PLAY THE DOZENS

family jewels *n phr by 1920s* The testicles; =NUTS: *A kick in the family jewels will often dampen a man's ardor*

famous last words *n phr by 1940s* Something said that proves singularly wrong or inappropriate •An ironic reference to the final deathbed utterances of famous people: *"I certainly hope this won't be made public,"* North said. Famous last words—Time

fan[1] *n baseball by 1889* A devotee or enthusiast, esp of a sport; aficionado; =BUFF, BUG: *a tennis fan/ cathedral fan* [origin uncertain; perhaps fr *fanatic*, or perhaps fr *the fancy*, "sports followers or fanciers"]

fan[2] **1** *n WWII Army Air Forces* An aircraft propeller or engine **2** *v baseball by 1886* To strike out; =WHIFF **3** *v police by 1920s* To search someone; =FRISK: *The gendarmes fan them to see if they have any rods on them*—Damon Runyon **4** *n underworld by 1847* A quick brush or pat used by pickpockets to find the place of the victim's wallet **5** *v*: *You will be fanned by hands feeling for an impression of your wallet*—New York Magazine **6** *v by 1940s* To chat; gossip; =BAT THE BREEZE: *. . . all the other chauffeurs I'd stand around fanning with*—H Larkin **7** *v by 1970s* To manipulate the coin-return lever of a pay telephone in the hope of dislodging coins: *Mary was embarrassed at being observed at her fanning activities*—New York Post

See BAT THE BREEZE, FAN someone's TAIL, IRISH BANJO, the SHIT HITS THE FAN

fancy Dan 1 *n phr prizefight by 1940s* A skillful boxer with a weak punch **2** *n phr baseball by 1927* A player who makes every play seem spectacular; =HOT DOG, SHOWBOAT **3** *n phr by 1980s* A skillful, polished ball player: *. . . called Bush's abilities "absolutely superb, a real fancy Dan"*—Milwaukee Journal

See DAPPER DAN

fancy-Dan *adj by 1930s* Pretentious; =HIGHFALUTIN: *It's fancy-Dan nomenclature*—National Review

fancy (or fast) footwork *n phr sports by about 1900* Very adroit evasion; clever dodging and maneuver: *It will take fancy footwork to explain this one/ The American Medical Association tried a little fast footwork before Congress last week*—New York Times

fancy man *n phr by 1811* A lover, esp the adulterous sex partner of a married woman

fancy pants *by 1940s* **1** *n phr* A dressed-up or overdressed person **2** *n phr* An effete man; =SISSY **3** *modifier*: *one of your fancy-pants diplomats*

fancy-schmancy *adj by 1970s* Very elegant or ornate, esp pretentiously so; =HIGHFALUTIN: *. . . mostly fancy-schmancy Roman numbers like IIs and IIIs*—Philadelphia [fr the humorous and derisive Yiddish rhyming of a first word with a second one beginning *shm-*, as in "Oedipus-shmoedipus, just so he loves his mother"]

fandangle[1] *n by 1835* An ornamental object; gewgaw

fandangle[2] *n middle 1800s* A confused profusion; generous lively miscellany: *. . . cranes, firebirds, foxes, flamingos, a fauna fandangle hard to believe*—New York Magazine [fr eastern US dialect *fandango*, "a boisterous assembly," fr the Spanish dance]

fandom *n by 1903* Devotees and aficionados collectively: *All fandom welcomes the new summer football*

faniggle *See* FINAGLE

fanner 1 *n underworld by 1847* A person who locates wallets for a pickpocket to steal **2** *n by 1970s* A person who manipulates coin-return levers on pay telephones, hoping to dislodge coins: *little old lady of about 80 who was dubbed Mary the Fanner*—New York Post

Fannie Mae *n phr by 1948* A publicly traded security backed by the Federal National Mortgage Association (FNMA), established in 1938

fanny *n about 1920* The buttocks; rump; =ASS: *I can hardly sit down, my fanny is so sore*—Associated Press [fr earlier British *fanny*, "vulva," perhaps fr John Cleland's 18th-century heroine *Fanny* Hill]

fannybumper *by 1970s* **1** *n* A crowded occasion; =MOB SCENE: *The reception was a fannybumper* **2** *modifier*: *organized a fannybumper vernissage*—Interview

fanny-dipper *n 1960s surfers* A conventional swimmer, as distinct from a surfer

fanny pack *n phr* (also **butt pack**) *middle 1980s* A small crescent-shaped cloth bag worn about the waist on a belt [a 1971 use is found in *Outdoor Life*, before use of the fanny pack became general]

fan someone's **tail** *v phr by 1884* To spank someone; =TAN: *Don't let him out of your sight or I'll fan your tail*—Ellery Queen

fan the breeze *v phr by 1950s* =BAT THE BREEZE

the fantods *n phr by 1880s* Fidgety nervousness; uneasy restlessness; =the WILLIES: *You just got the fantods, that's all*—W Henry [fr British dialect, "indisposition, restlessness," perhaps fr *fanteague*, "commotion, excitement," or fr *fantasy*]

fanzine (FAN zeen) *by 1940s* **1** *n* A fan magazine: *wants to start his own fanzine*—Village Voice **2** *modifier*: *The fanzine set is not scared off by raunchy lyrics*—Rolling Stone

FAQ (pronounced as separate letters) *n 1990s computer* A set of frequently asked questions, often with their answers: *. . . the best thing to do first is to read the FAQ, the list of frequently asked questions*—New Yorker

fare-thee-well or **fare-you-well** *See* TO A FARE-YOU-WELL

Farley *See* CHUCK YOU, FARLEY

farm[1] *v 1970s Army* To be killed in action; die in the armed services; =BUY THE FARM: *Just about the whole company farmed that day* [fr buy the farm]

See BET THE FARM, FAT FARM, FUNNY FARM, NUT HOUSE

farm[2] *n baseball by 1898* A minor league club used as a training ground by a major league club: *Columbus is a Yankee farm*

◁**farmer**▷ *n by 1902* A stupid person; ignorant rustic; clown

Farmer *See* JOHN FARMER

farmisht (far MISHT) *adj by 1970s* Confused; mixed up; ambivalent and/or ambiguous: *I'm afraid she's a little farmisht* [fr Yiddish]

far out *1950s* **1** *adj* Very unconventional; unorthodox and strange; =WEIRD: *Drake liked "Suzie Q." Which to us was really far out*—Rolling Stone/ *. . . a curious combination of far-out medicine, pampering, and very shrewd doctoring*—Fortune **2** *adj* Excellent; splendid; =COOL: *The next thing I heard from her was "Far out!"*—American Scholar

◁**fart**▷ **1** *v by 1250* To expel gas through the anus; relieve flatulence by the most immediate expedient; =TOOT **2** *n by 1930s* A man; fellow; person; =GUY: *What's that stupid fart up to?* **3** *n by 1460* The least thing; nothing; =DIDDLY, ZILCH: *It isn't worth a fart See* LAY A FART, OLD FART

◁**fart around**▷ *by 1930s* **1** *v phr* =HORSE AROUND **2** *v phr* =GOOF AROUND [perhaps fr Yiddish *arum-fartzen*, "fart around"]

◁**fart sack**▷ *n phr Army by WWII* A sleeping bag

fascinoma *n medical by 1970s* An interesting, difficult, or unusual disease or condition [fr *fascinating* plus *-oma*, the suffix used to form the names of tumors]

fashion plate *n phr by 1920s* A well-dressed person, esp a stylish one: *The present-day. . . racketeer is a veritable fashion plate*—E Lavine

fast *adj by 1859* Morally lax; libertine: *. . . on Long Island with the fast younger married set*—F Scott Fitzgerald

fast (or quick) buck *by 1940s* **1** *n phr* Money gotten quickly, esp without too fine a concern for ethics or the future: *. . . tryin' to hustle me for a fast buck*—Arthur Kober **2** *modifier*: *Fast-buck speculators were getting rich on inflated FHA appraisals*—Reader's Digest/ *Fast-buck artists, dreamers, and even some well-heeled companies. . .* —Milwaukee Journal

fast burner *n phr 1970s Army* A person whose success is rapid; =BALL OF FIRE

fasten one's **seat belt** *sentence by 1940s* Prepare for difficulties; get ready for a rough time: *Fasten Your Seat Belts for the Fare War*—Time [fr the pre-flight instructions of airliners]

fast-feed *v 1990s* To dispense fast food: *. . . a culinary wasteland that seemed to exist totally to fast-feed the captive audiences. . .* —Buzz

fast food *by 1951* **1** *n phr* Food like hamburgers, fried chicken, etc, cooked and served very rapidly and uniformly, usu by large catering corporations **2** *modifier*: *a fast-food chain*

fast footwork *See* FANCY FOOTWORK

fast-forward *adj by 1980s* Very much up-to-date; socially and intellectually dynamic; proactive; =AHEAD OF THE CURVE: *. . . hip, fast-forward people. . .* — New Republic [fr the control on a tape player that advances the tape very rapidly]

fast lane (or track) *1960s* **1** *n phr* A pace and quality of life emphasizing quick success against strong competition, along with the trappings of wealth and style: *. . . amazing woman, lives on a fast lane*—Village Voice/ *Jean Piaget. . . started academic life on a fast track*—Time/ *. . . certainly influenced the 1960s expression "life in the fast lane"*—City in Slang **2** *modifier*: *. . . its glittery fast-lane image*—Time/ *New York's fast-track, high-yield high culture*—New Republic [fr the left-hand or *fast lane* of a superhighway, which slower drivers enter at their risk, and a horse-racing *track* in good, dry condition]

fast one *n phr by 1924* A trick or deception; clever subterfuge; =DIPSY DOODLE: *That was sure a fast one, you wearing the false mustache* [probably fr *fast shuffle*] *See* PULL A FAST ONE

fast on one's **feet** *v phr fr prizefight by 1970s* Ready and resourceful; skillful in debate and repartee: *. . . he is a man who knows how to ask questions and answer them. He showed himself to be fast on his feet*—Milwaukee Journal

fast shuffle *See* DOUBLE SHUFFLE

fast talk *n phr by 1950s* Talk meant to deceive or confuse: glib and plausible nonsense: *Ignore the fast talk and don't sign a thing*

fast talker *n phr by 1950s* A person who engages in fast talk: *Loose Manhattan from its moorings and let it float out to sea. Good-bye dirt, noise, crack dealers, street peddlers, fast talkers*—New York Times

a **fast track** *n phr by 1990s* A very rapid and urgent information requirement: *This is on a fast track. . . and we hope to have more information by next week*—Milwaukee Journal Sentinel

fat 1 *n by 1570* The best and most rewarding part; =CREAM: *He just took the fat; screw the long term* **2** *adj*: *fat profits/ fat prospects* **3** *adj by 1700* Wealthy; in funds, esp temporarily so; =FLUSH: *Hit him up now, he's pretty fat* **4** *n by 1970s* A fat person; =FATTY: *I met the other 18 women or fellow fats*—A D Botorff **5** *adj* (also **phat**) *teenagers by 1951* Attractive; up to date; =COOL, DOPE, RAD ●*Fat* is recorded by 1932 a meaning "hot," in US dialect, and this may underlie the teenage use: *If they are real fat, real crazy, naturally they're real cool*—Newsweek/ *Timberland boots have, in the parlance of the street, become "dope" and "phat," i.e. cool, greatest*—New York Times **6** *adj* (also **phat**) *1980s students* Sexy; having a shapely body ●Some think this, when spelled *phat*, is an acronym for *pretty hips and thighs: The three boys thought that Carolyn looked fat as she walked down the street*—Delcastle Dictionary of Slang **7** *adj baseball by 1940s* Slow and easy to hit: *Williams then leaped on a fat pitch to knock the baseball 400 feet*—New York Times

See BIG FAT, CHEW THE FAT

fat Albert 1 *n phr 1970s* A kind of guided bomb **2** *n phr airlines by 1980s* A Boeing 747 jet aircraft, or other jumbo jet [fr a character used in stories by the comedian Bill Cosby]

◁**fat-ass**▷ *by 1916* **1** *n* A fat person **2** *adj*: *Get your fat-ass self out of here* **3** *n* A person with large buttocks; =BUFFALO BUTT

fatback *adj by 1930s* Redolent of Southern rural tastes; =FUNKY: *The song became progressively funkier with Guerin laying down a dirty fatback beat*—San Francisco

fat cat *by 1928* **1** *n phr* Any privileged and well-treated person, esp a wealthy benefactor; tycoon: *. . . a millionaire fat-cat who, when the revolution comes, will probably be allowed to keep at least one of his chauffeurs*—New York Magazine/ *. . . the late arrival even of such famous "fat cats"*—New York Times/ *. . . had jousted with Nelson Rockefeller at a formal dinner for fat cats*—Joseph Heller **2** *modifier*: *. . . the fat-cat cases, where big money is involved*—New York Times/ *. . . whether fat-cat contributors or New Hampshire coffee-klatschers*—Meg Greenfield **3** *v . . . "fat-catting". . . a term applied. . . to higher leaders who try to pad themselves with special privileges and comforts*—Hal Boyle

fat chance *n phr by 1906* No chance at all: *. . . entry without prior permission fell into the category of fat chance*—Stan Cutler

fat city 1 *n phr early 1960s* An ideal situation; splendid state of affairs ●In earlier use *fat city* meant "vulva": *You're in fat city while other poor slobs sweat on assembly lines*—Sports Illustrated/ *Johnny came marching home from college. . . and announced he was in "fat city"*—New York Times **2** *n phr by 1970s* Poor physical condition, esp because of being overweight: *Its principal characters wind up in "fat city" (argot for "out of condition")*—American Scholar

fat, dumb, and happy *adj phr by 1970s* Blissfully and rather bovinely contented

fat farm *n phr by 1960s* A resort or treatment center where people go to lose weight: *It'll be adventures of me, and takes place at a fat farm*—Blair Sabol/ *I went to a California fat farm a couple years ago*—New York Times

fathead *n by 1842* A stupid person; =BLUBBERHEAD

fatheaded *adj by 1748* Stupid: *. . . some fatheaded motorist*—J Evans

◀**fatherfucker**▶ *n homosexuals by 1970s* =MOTHERFUCKER

fatigue *See* BUNK FATIGUE

fat lady sings *See* the OPERA AIN'T OVER TILL THE FAT LADY SINGS

fat mouth *n phr by 1942* One who talks incessantly; =MOTOR-MOUTH: *With very little prodding Jimmy began the conversation because he was feeling like a fat mouth*—Joseph Wambaugh [probably fr the locution *I had to open my big fat mouth*]

fat-mouth *by 1970s* **1** *v* To blab and chatter; =CHEW THE FAT **2** *v* To cajole verbally; =BULLSHIT, SWEET-TALK: *I ain't asking you to fatmouth me, just as I am not interested in getting into any argument*—Bernard Malamud

fat part *n phr theater by 1901* A prominent role sure to delight the audience

Fats *n* (Variations: **Fat** or **Fatty** or **Fatso** or **Fat stuff**) *by 1940s* A nickname for a fat person

fatso *adj by 1940s* Fat, in any sense: *. . . a fatso deal in six figures*—New York Daily News

fatter *See* HAM-FATTER

fat-tire bike *See* MOUNTAIN BIKE

fatty 1 *n by 1797* A fat person: *. . . designed to keep all us fatties from committing hara-kiri*—Esquire **2** *n narcotics by 1980s* A thick marijuana cigarette

faunet or **faunlet** (FAW nət, FAWN lət) *n homosexuals by 1970s* An adolescent or preadolescent boy as a homosexual sex object [on analogy with *nymphet*, probably influenced by *fawn*]

faust (FOUST) *adj 1950s cool talk* Ugly; disgusting: *"Faust". . . means ugly*—Stephen Longstreet

faux *adj by 1980s* False; =FAKE, PHONY: *. . . a British conglomerate told Ms Tabb to shelve her plans to sell the faux burger*—New York Times/ *. . . the facade drops, revealing them as the faux funsters they really are*—Buzz/ *She had a faux art clock that ran on a battery. . .*—Robert B Parker [fr French]

fave or **fave rave** *first form by 1938, second by 1967* **1** *n* or *n phr* A favorite song or musical number, film, person, etc: *. . . group scats Mozart, Vivaldi, Bach, and other fave raves*—Saturday Review/ *. . . includes many of the quintet's faves*—Variety **2** *modifier*: *My absolute fave-rave model was printed boldly*—Village Voice

fax attack *n phr by 1980s* Unsolicited advertising received over facsimile machines: *A Connecticut state legislator is going on the offensive against "fax attacks". . .*—Milwaukee Journal

◀**fay**[1]▶ *n 1920s black* A white person; =HONKY, PECKERWOOD [fr *ofay*]

fay[2] *adj homosexuals by 1950s* Homosexual; =GAY [fr earlier *fay*, "fairy"]

featherbed *by 1920s* **1** *v* To work languidly and sluggishly; seek easy tasks **2** *v* To create or retain unnecessary jobs; do essentially fictitious jobs: *. . . featherbedding clauses in labor agreements*—Labor's Special Language

featherheaded *adj by 1647* Empty-headed; silly: *The Color Purple speaks to the heart, and no featherheaded translation is needed*—Los Angeles Times

feather merchant *WWII armed forces* **1** *n phr* A civilian, esp one who evades military service **2** *n phr* A reserve officer, or a person commissioned directly into the Navy **3** *n phr* A sailor who has a desk job [perhaps fr a group of small rather parasitic persons called *feather merchants* in the comic strip "Barney Google"]

feather (or line) one's nest *v phr by 1590* To be primarily concerned with one's own gain; take care of oneself

feathers *See* HORSEFEATHERS

Fed *n by 1912* Any federal government worker or agent, esp in law enforcement or taxation: *. . . right* *up to the day the Feds dragged him into court*—Esquire

the **Fed** *n phr by 1960s* The Federal Reserve System, Board, or Bank: *Now the Fed has apparently decided to let the market carry interest rates upward*—New York Times/ *The Fed was reluctant to raise its discount rate*—Wall Street Journal

Federal case *See* MAKE A FEDERAL CASE OUT OF something

fed up *adj phr by 1900* Disgusted; tired; surfeited; =BRASSED OFF: *A number of people suddenly became fed up with a slang phrase like "fed up"*—J Greig [the related form *fed up to the eyelids* is found by 1882]

feeb *n by 1914* A feeble-minded person; idiot: *Then why are you treating me like a feeb?*—Life

Feeb or **Feebie** *n by 1970s* An agent of the Federal Bureau of Investigation; =G-MAN: *the agents of the Federal Bureau of Investigation, whom they call "Feebs"*—F C Shapiro/ *make sure the Feebies didn't get any credit for it*—Patrick Mann

feed 1 *n by 1830* A meal: *Stop by for a feed, anytime* **2** *v by 1895* To board; take one's meals; eat **3** *n about 1900* Money **4** *n early 1990s* Contributions of opinion, advice, etc; input: *They put their feed into the project*—National Public Radio news
See CHICKEN FEED, OFF one's FEED

feedback *n by 1950s* Response, esp information and opinion: *We'll wait for feedback before we try anything else* [fr the portion of output *fed back* to the input in an automatic control circuit or system]

the **feedbag** *n phr by 1920s* A meal; food: *I'm ready for the feedbag*—W R Burnett [fr the *bag* of *feed*, or nosebag, hung on the head of a horse]
See PUT ON THE FEEDBAG

feedbox (or **feedbag**) **information** *n phr* horse-racing *by 1940s* Supposedly dependable advance information on a horse race: *Neither of us had ever heard of Clam giving out feed-box information to anybody*—J Lilienthal [because such information was virtually from the horse's mouth]

feed one's **face** *v phr by 1930s* To eat

feeding frenzy *n phr by 1980s* A scene of frantic competition, unexampled greed, etc: *First the feeding frenzy begins. We did the story for two days, then the media angle on the story, and then the legal angle*—New York Times [fr the phrase used to describe the behavior of sharks who smell blood, find meat, etc]

feed the fish *v phr by 1880s* To vomit over the side of a vessel, from seasickness

feed the kitty *v phr* poker *by 1940s* To contribute to a fund, esp to put what one owes into the pot of a card game

◁**feel** or **feel up**▷ *v* or *v phr by 1930* To touch, caress, or handle the buttocks, breasts, legs, crotch, etc; =COP A FEEL

◁a **feel**▷ *n phr by 1932* A caress or touch, esp of the buttocks, breasts, or crotch: *The eager amorist entreated a quick feel*
See COP A FEEL

feel a draft *v phr* black *by 1940s* To feel unwelcome, snubbed, etc; esp, to sense racial prejudice against oneself

Feelgood or **feelgood** *by 1940s* **1** *n* =DR FEELGOOD **2** *n* A condition of contentment or euphoria: *a purveyor of religious feelgood* **3** *modifier*: *. . . a general "relax, feelgood" vibe*—Village Voice/ *The President is running a feel-good campaign*—Charles MacDowell

feel good *v phr by 1930s* To be slightly and pleasantly drunk: *Old Charley was feeling good that night*—Mickey Spillane

feelie *See* TOUCHIE-FEELIE

feelies *n by 1931* A sort of motion picture that has tactile as well as visual and auditory effects: *When the holograms acquire tactile capability, they fulfill Huxley's vision of 'feelies'*—New Yorker [modeled on *movie* and *talkie*; most prominently employed by Aldous Huxley in his 1932 novel *Brave New World*]

feel no pain *v phr by 1940s* To be drunk: *. . . three men who were feeling no pain*—Christopher Morley/ *The anticipated audience. . . should be feeling no pain*—GQ

feel one's **oats** *v phr by 1831* To be active and high-spirited; act brashly and confidently: *The manufacturer was just feeling his oats, having accomplished his happy intention*—Village Voice [fr the vigor of a just-fed horse]

feel out *v phr by 1920s* To inquire or investigate tentatively: *Let's feel out the possibilities first*

feened out *adj phr* students *by 1980s* Surfeited or overdosed with caffeine

feep *1980s* computer **1** *n* The electronic bell- or whistle-like sound made by computer terminals **2** *v*: *The machine feeped inexplicably but insistently*

feet *See* DRAG one's FEET, GET one's FEET WET, GO HOME FEET FIRST, HAVE COLD FEET, HOLD someone's FEET TO THE FIRE, VOTE WITH one's FEET

fegelah or **feygelah** (FAY gə lə) *n by 1960s* A male homosexual; =FAG: *The guy must be a real whacko. A fegelah, you figure?*—Lawrence Sanders [fr Yiddish, "little bird"]

feh or **fehh** *interj by 1950s* An exclamation of disgust: *Thus, soccer. Feh*—Village Voice/ *Well, fehh, Petro thinks that Dr Scholl's spray seems to work*—Village Voice [fr Yiddish]

feisty *adj by 1896* Truculent; irascible: *They said the president was a feisty little chap/ He was having trouble with a feisty old lady who didn't want to move* [fr *feist*, found by 1770, "small, worthless cur, esp a lapdog"]

fellow *See* REGULAR FELLOW

fellow traveler *n phr by 1930s* A person who sympathizes with a cause or doctrine, without openly identifying himself with it: *These people are not hipsters, they are fellow travelers*—Eugene Burdick [said to have been coined by Leon Trotsky in Russian as *sputnik*, and translated into English as "fellow traveler"]

fem or **femme 1** *n* students *by 1900* A woman: *He has aired the fem that got him the job*—John

O'Hara **2** *modifier*: . . . *looks more like a post deb than a femme comic*—H Gardner/ . . . *whereas women with big heads of fat hair always look femme*—San Francisco **3** *n homosexuals by 1970s* A lesbian who takes a passive, feminine role in sex **4** *modifier*: . . . *butch-femme role players are sad relics of the uptight past*—Village Voice **5** *n homosexuals by 1970s* An effeminate homosexual male: . . . *active or passive, manly ("stud") or womanly ("fem")*—Saturday Review [fr French, "woman"]

fenagle *See* FINAGLE

fence 1 *n by 1700* A person or place that deals in stolen goods: . . . *but even big fences like Alphonso can get stuck*—New York Magazine/ *The loot had disappeared and been handled by a fence*—Associated Press **2** *v by 1610*: *The clown that stole the Mona Lisa found it hard to fence* [all senses are shortenings of *defence*; in the case of criminal act, the notion is probably that of a secure place and trusty person, well defended]
See GO FOR THE FENCES, ON THE FENCE

fence-straddler or **fence-hanger** *n by 1940s*

fender-bender *n by 1960s* A minor car accident; trivial collision: *I've only had one fender-bender since I got it*—Don Pendleton

fer instance *See* FOR INSTANCE

fer sure (or **shure** or **shurr**) *See* FOR SURE

fess (or **'fess**) **up** *v phr by 1840* To confess; admit the truth: *Then why doesn't the judge come clean and fess up?*—Village Voice/ *He finally fessed up to something that I've known a long time*. . . —Douglas Coupland

-fest *combining form by 1880s* A celebration or extensive exercise and indulgence of what is indicated: *slugfest/ gabfest/ fuckfest/ jazzfest/ schmoozefest/ splatterfest* [fr German, "festival"]
See BULL SESSION

fetching *adj by 1902* Attractive: *a fetching appearance*

fetch-me-down *See* HAND-ME-DOWN

fever *gambling by 1940s* **1** *n* The five of a playing-card suit **2** *n* Five or the point of five; =PHOEBE
See CABIN FEVER

a **few** *See* HANG A FEW ON, WIN A FEW LOSE A FEW

a **few quarts low** *adj phr by 1980s* Stupid; mentally deficient; =NOT WRAPPED TIGHT, OUT TO LUNCH

a **few tacos short of a combination plate** *adj phr by 1990s* Stupid; mentally deficient; =NOT WRAPPED TIGHT, OUT TO LUNCH: . . . *clearly a few tacos short of a combination plate in the intelligence area*—Milwaukee Journal Sentinel

feygelah *See* FEGELAH

fi *See* HI-FI, LOW-FI

the **fickle finger of fate** *n phr by 1940s* The dire and unpredictable aspect of destiny: *It wasn't anything she specially deserved, just the fickle finger of fate at work* [regarding *finger* as both a pointer and a violator of the body]
See FUCKED BY THE FICKLE FINGER OF FATE

fiddle 1 *v* (also **fiddle around** or ◁**fiddle fart around** or **fiddle-fart**▷) *entry form by 1663* To waste time; =GOOF AROUND, FART AROUND: . . . *and the school board*. . . *fiddled*—New York Times **2** *v by 1604* To cheat; defraud **3** *n by 1874*: *His new boat is a tax fiddle*
See BULL FIDDLE, GIT-BOX, PLAY SECOND FIDDLE, SECOND FIDDLE, STEAM FIDDLE

fiddled *adj phr by 1604* Illegally altered; =COOKED: . . . *how a Park Avenue corporation based on fiddled data might have no more financial stature than an Orchard Street pushcart*—Lawrence Sanders

fiddle factor *n phr by 1980s* A cheating maneuver; tricky move: *The Navigation Foundation's study "has more fiddle factors than the New York Philharmonic"*. . . —Associated Press

fiddle-faddle 1 *n by 1577* Nonsense; foolishness; =BULLSHIT: . . . *such homemade fiddle-faddle*—Alexander Woollcott **2** *interj by 1671* An exclamation of irritation, disapproval, dismissal, etc

◀**fiddlefucking**▶ *adj by 1960s* Particular and accursed; =DAMN ●Used for vehement and vulgar emphasis: *Not one swingin' dick will be leavin' this fiddlefuckin' area*—Philip Roth

fiddler's bitch *See* DRUNK AS A FIDDLER'S BITCH

fiddlesticks *n by 1857* Nonsense; foolishness; =BULLSHIT: *When I explained, she only said, "Fiddlesticks!"* [the singular form is found by 1600]

field *v by 1902* To handle; receive and answer; cope with: *The secretary fielded the questions rather lamely*
See OUT IN LEFT FIELD, PLAY THE FIELD

field day *See* HAVE A FIELD DAY

fiend 1 *combining word by 1865* A devotee or user of what is indicated: *camera fiend/ dope-fiend/ sex fiend* **2** *v underworld by 1980* To use a choke hold on a robbery victim: *They'd take out a bodega, or fiend a few housewives*. . . —Carsten Stroud

fierce *adj by 1903* Nasty; unpleasant; awful: *Gee, it was fierce of me*—Sinclair Lewis
See SOMETHING FIERCE

fifth wheel *n phr by 1902* A superfluous person or thing: *I feel as though I'm a fifth wheel*—Wall Street Journal [the date reflects the full form *fifth wheel of the coach*]

fifty-seven varieties *n phr by 1896* A very great number; a large assortment: *She's sampled just about all 57 varieties of excess and illumination available in Western civilization*—Time [fr the trademark designation of products made by the H J Heinz Company]

fifty-six *n police by 1950s* The time off that substitutes for the weekends of those who work Saturdays and Sundays [because the time adds up to *fifty-six* hours]

fifty-two *n lunch counter* An order for two cups of hot chocolate

fig *n gambling by 1990s* The amount of money won or lost by a gambler [fr *figure*]
See MOLDY FIG

fight *n by 1891* A party; =STRUGGLE: . . . *the cocktail fights attended by the old man*—R Starnes
See CAT FIGHT, DOGFIGHT, YOU CAN'T FIGHT CITY HALL

fight a bottle *v phr* by 1940s To drink liquor, esp to excess: . . . *after fighting a bottle all evening*—R Starnes

fighter *See* BOOZEHOUND, HOP FIEND, NIGHT PEOPLE

fightin' tools *n phr* WWII armed forces Eating utensils; silverware

fightin' words *n phr* by 1917 Provocative speech; words inviting combat •Often said in a broad cowboy style: *I can go along with a little ribbing, but them is fightin' words, son*

fight shy *v phr* by 1821 To avoid: *We had better fight shy of the chaos in the Balkans*

can't fight one's **way out of a paper bag** *See* CAN'T FIGHT one's WAY OUT OF A PAPER BAG

figure 1 *v* by 1950s To make sense; be plausible and reasonable: *It figures he'd be next in line* **2** *v* by 1930s To be expected; be very likely: *The pup figured to be in the room when Einstein discussed the bomb with the president*—Billy Rose *See* BALLPARK FIGURE

file 1 *n* underworld by 1754 A pickpocket **2** *n* by 1940s A wastebasket •Often humorously called *file 17, the circular file,* etc [first sense perhaps fr the tool; perhaps related to French *filou,* "pickpocket"] *See* CIRCULAR FILE

file 17 (or 13) *n phr* WWII armed forces A wastebasket; =CIRCULAR FILE

filk music *n phr* 1950s A set of songs and parodies sung by assembled science-fiction fans: *Their performances. . . can be divided into "bardic" filk. . . and "chaos" filk. . .*—Los Angeles Times [apparently fr the misspelling of *folk* on a 1950s poster]

fill in *v phr* by 1940s To substitute; replace temporarily: *I'll fill in for you*

fill-in 1 *n* by about 1945 A summary account; information meant to supply what one does not know: *A friend gives me a fill-in on how Costello is running the country*—Saturday Evening Post **2** *n* by 1920s A substitute, esp a substitute worker: *Get a fill-in, I gotta split*

fill someone **in** *v phr* by about 1945 To complete someone's knowledge; brief someone; =PUT someone IN THE PICTURE: *Fill me in so I know what's up here*

filling station *n phr* by 1940s A very small town; =JERKWATER TOWN

fill the bill *v phr* by 1861 To suffice; meet the requirement: *I'd like the job, if you think I fill the bills*

fill the squares *v phr* 1970s armed forces To finish a set of compulsory routine tasks

filly *n* by 1616 A girl; young woman [fr French *fille,* "girl"]

film *See* SLICE AND DICE FILM, SNUFF FILM, SPLAT MOVIE

filthbag *n* by 1970s A despicable person; =DIRTBAG, SCUMBAG: *Tony called Strumpet a filthbag*—San Francisco

filthy 1 *adj* by 1930s Wealthy; rich; =LOADED: *He's filthy with dough*—Eugene O'Neill **2** *adj* by 1535 Obscene; salacious; =BLUE, DIRTY: *filthy movies/ filthy minds* **3** *adj* 1990s teenagers Excellent; desirable; =COOL, RAD

the filthy *n phr* by 1930s Money; =FILTHY LUCRE: *just trying to make a bit of the filthy*—P G Wodehouse

filthy lucre *n phr* by 1526 Money [fr the Pauline epistle to Titus]

filthy rich *adj phr* Very rich; =LOADED

fin¹ by 1840 **1** *n* The hand: *Reach out your fin and grab it* **2** *n* The arm and hand

fin² *n* 1920s underworld A five-dollar bill; five dollars: *I gave my pal a fin*—John O'Hara/ *It was the fin seen round the world. Where Reagan got the five bucks is a mystery*—Time [fr Yiddish *finif,* "five"]

finagle (fə NAY gəl) (also **faniggle** or **fenagle** or **finigal** or **finagel** or **phenagle**) by 1920s **1** *v* To manage or arrange, esp by dubious means; contrive: *Well, she's always trying to finagle me out of it*—Ed McBain/ *He finagled the driver into doing it for him*—Hannibal and Boris **2** *v* To acquire, esp by trickery: *She finagled a couple of choice seats* [origin unknown; perhaps related to British dialect *finegue,* "to evade," or *fainague,* "to renege"]

finagle factor or **Fink's constant** *n phr* by 1950s The putative mathematical constant by which a wrong answer is multiplied to get a right answer

find *n* by 1872 A remarkable discovery, esp of something unexpected *See* IF YOU CAN'T FIND 'EM, GRIND 'EM

fine *adj* 1990s teenagers Attractive; =DISHY, HUNKY: *. . . if a guy or girl is cute, they're a "hottie" or "fine"*—KRT News Service [a revival of 1940s bop and cool use, from black, "pleasing, wonderful, exciting, cool"]

a fine how-de-do (or how-do-you-do) *n phr* by 1835 A situation; set of circumstances: *. . . which is a fine how-de-do in a country that prides itself on progress*—David Dempsey [the dated instance is pretty *how do you do*]

fine kettle of fish *n phr* by 1800 A nasty predicament; lamentable situation

the fine print *See* the SMALL PRINT

the finest *n phr* by 1890s The police force •Often in city name plus *finest* phrases like *San Francisco's finest, Madison's finest*

fine-tune *v* 1960s To make delicate and careful adjustments; =TWEAK: *. . . knowledge and techniques to fine-tune the economy*—New York Times

finger 1 *v* 1920s underworld To locate and point out someone: *You're the guy that fingered Manny Tinnen*—Raymond Chandler/ *. . . artificially heightening the tale's drama (by fingering the sponsor)*—Washington Post **2** *v* 1920s underworld To tell thieves about the location, value, etc, of potential loot: *I fingered the robberies*—movie *Scene of the Crime* **3** *n* underworld by 1930s A police informer; =STOOL PIGEON **4** *n* 1920s underworld A person who tells thieves about potential loot ◁**5**▷ *v* by 1970s To insert a finger into the vulva; =FINGERFUCK: *With one hand Larry was fingering me*—Xaviera Hollander **6** *n* by 1856 About a half-inch of liquor in a glass: *Maybe I'd better have another finger of the hooch*—Raymond Chandler

See BUTTERFINGERS, FIVE FINGERS, FUCKED BY THE FICKLE FINGER OF FATE, GIVE FIVE FINGERS TO, GIVE someone THE FINGER, NOT LAY A GLOVE ON someone, PLAY STINKY-PINKY, PUT one's FINGER ON something, PUT THE FINGER ON someone, STAND AROUND WITH one's FINGER UP one's ASS

the **finger 1** *n phr* *1920s underworld* The act of identifying or pointing out potential loot, a hired killer's victim, a wanted criminal, etc **2** *n phr* by *1950s* A lewd insulting gesture made by holding up the middle finger with the others folded down, and meaning "fuck you" or "up yours"; =the BIRD, ONE-FINGER SALUTE

See GIVE someone THE FINGER, PUT THE FINGER ON someone

fingered *See* LIGHT-FINGERED, STICKY-FINGERED

◄**fingerfuck►** *v* by *1970s* To insert a finger into the vulva; =FRIG, PLAY STINKY-PINKY: *She wants you to fingerfuck her shikse cunt till she faints*—Philip Roth

finger man *n phr* *underworld* by *1920s* A person who points out potential loot, potential victims, wanted criminals, etc

finger of fate *See* FUCKED BY THE FICKLE FINGER OF FATE

finger-pointing *n* by *1990s* The assessing of blame, guilt, etc: *Criticism of the President's foreign policy has produced a spate of finger-pointing within the Administration*—New York Times

finger-popper *n* *1950s cool talk* A listener who is sent into finger-snapping transports by music; an enthusiastic devotee

fingerprint *v* *truckers* by *1970s* To load or unload a truck oneself, without using paid dockside labor •Said of independent truckers: *An independent driver. . . may "fingerprint" the boxes on or off the trailer himself*—Smithsonian

fingers *See* BUTTERFINGERS, FIVE FINGERS, GIVE FIVE FINGERS TO

finger up one's **ass** *See* STAND AROUND WITH one's FINGER UP one's ASS

finif or **finiff** or **finnif** *n* by about *1850 fr British* A five-dollar bill; five dollars; =FIN [fr Yiddish *finif*, "five"]

finigal *See* FINAGLE

finish *v* by *1755* To put a disastrous end to something or to someone's prospects; =COOK someone's GOOSE: *If she doesn't like you, you're finished around here*

finished *adj* Ruined; no longer able to function or compete; =DEAD, KAPUT: *After two tries he was finished/ She couldn't act any longer and was finished at thirty*

finisher *n* *prizefight* by *1827* A blow that knocks one unconscious; quietus

finish last *See* NICE GUYS FINISH LAST

fink 1 *n* fr *1890s* A strikebreaker; =SCAB **2** *n* by *1902* A labor spy; worker who is primarily loyal to the employer: *. . . unpopular with the other waiters, who thought him a fink*—New Yorker **3** *n* by *1925* A police officer, detective, guard, or other law enforcement agent: *This Sherlock Holmes. . . this fink's on the old yocky-dock*—J Cannon **4** *n*

1920s underworld An informer; =STOOL PIGEON: *Now he's looking for the fink who turned him in*—Raymond Chandler/ *The glossary runs to such pejorative nouns as fink, stoolie, rat, canary, squealer*—Time **5** *v* *1920s*: *Dutch knew I worked for his friend. . . and I wouldn't fink*—George Raft **6** *n* by *1894* Any contemptible person; vile wretch; =RAT FINK, SHITHEEL: *All men are brothers, and if you don't give, you're a kind of fink*—Bennett Berger [origin unknown; perhaps fr *Pink*, "a Pinkerton agent engaged in strikebreaking," or fr German *Fink*, "finch," a university students' term for a student who did not join in dueling and drinking societies; first sense said to have been used during the Homestead Strike of 1892; sixth sense was unaccountably revived by sub-teens in the early 1960s]

See RAT FINK

fink out 1 *v phr* *1960s counterculture* To withdraw from or refuse support to a project, movement, etc, esp in a seemingly cowardly and self-serving way; =BACK OUT: *. . . or if he will "fink out," as Kauffman believed he had done so far*—Society **2** *v phr* by *1960s* To become untrustworthy and a potential informer **3** *v phr* by *1970s* To fail utterly

Fink's constant *See* FINAGLE FACTOR

Finn *See* MICKEY FINN

finnagel *See* FINAGLE

finiff or **finnif** *See* FINIF

fire 1 *v* by *1887* To discharge someone from a job; dismiss, usu with prejudice; =CAN, SACK **2** *v* by about *1910* To throw something with great force: *The big left-hander fired a fastball down the middle* **3** *v* by *1850s* To ask or utter with bluntness and vehemence: *The panel fired questions at me and I soon wilted*

See BALL OF FIRE, HOLD someone's FEET TO THE FIRE, ON THE FIRE, PULL something OUT OF THE FIRE, SURE-FIRE

fire away by *1775* **1** *v phr* To begin; go ahead •Usu an invitation: *"Maybe this is something you can help me with". . . "Fire away"*—Sue Grafton **2** *v phr* To attack verbally: *As soon as I walked into the room he began to fire away at me*

fireball *n* =BALL OF FIRE

Fireball flasher *n phr* *police* by *1970s* The emergency display of lights atop a police car; =GUMBALL, PARTY HAT: *He moved down the line of squad cars looking back past Fireball flashers revolving slowly. . .* —Elmore Leonard

fire blanks *See* SHOOT BLANKS

fire-breathing *adj* by *1591* Fierce; menacing; dragon-like: *ABC now planned to swap Ellen with Wednesday's fire-breathing Grace Under Fire*—USExpress

firebug *n* by *1872* An arsonist; pyromaniac [fr *fire* plus *bug*, "maniac"]

firecracker *n* *WWII armed forces* A bomb; torpedo

fired up 1 *adj phr* about *1850* Drunk **2** *adj phr* by *1824* Angry **3** *adj phr* (also **all fired up**) by *1970s* Full of enthusiasm, energy, and resolve: *If he gets fired up he's unbeatable*

fire-eater 1 *n* by 1804 A quarrelsome and energetic person **2** *n* by 1920s A fire fighter; =SMOKE-EATER

fire in the belly *n phr* by 1951 Zealous ambition; energy; high spirits: *You want someone with fire in the belly*—Milwaukee Journal/ *It's hard to get fire in the belly over health insurance when it's stuffed with pate*—Time [probably fr the French phrase *avoir quelque chose dans le ventre*, "to have something in the gut"]

fireless cooker *n phr* by 1920s An outdoor toilet; privy; =BACKHOUSE [fr a device for cooking with stored-up heat, found by 1908]

fireman *n baseball* by 1940s A relief pitcher, esp an effective one: *. . . a four-run blast against fireman Joe in the eighth inning*—Associated Press
See VISITING FIREMAN

fire on *v phr black* by 1960s To strike; hit: *. . . looking at this one dude Huey had fired on*—Bobby Seale

fire on all cylinders *v phr* by early 1990s To operate or proceed at maximum speed and efficiency: *Europe's economy will fire on all cylinders*—television panel *Wall Street Week*/ *. . . a world firing on all cylinders, where the US, Japan, and Europe are all growing simultaneously*—Milwaukee Journal

fire stick *n phr* 1950s *street gang* A firearm; gun; =PIECE

firestorm *n* An intense and often destructive spate of action or reaction: *. . . report. . . has already generated a firestorm of criticism*—New York Times/ *A lawyer from Time-Warner expected a firestorm of protest from the shareholders after the vote*—New Yorker [fr the catastrophic and unquenchable *fires* caused by aerial bombing of cities in World War II]

fire someone up *v phr* by 1970s To fill someone with energy and enthusiasm; excite someone: *She fired them up with promises of huge winnings*

firewall 1 *n computer* by early 1990s A computer that protects internal networks from outside intrusion: *Firewalls, in recent years, have become the bulwark against computer break-ins*—Knight-Ridder Newspapers **2** *n* by 1990s A strong safeguard between one operation or area and another: *Impenetrable firewalls between federally insured banking activities and their nonbanking commercial activities would prevent stock manipulation*—Nation [fr a *firewall* built to contain a fire in a building, a meaning found by 1851, and a barricade between an engine and a passenger compartment, found by 1947]

firewater *n* by 1826 Liquor; =BOOZE [the term is attributed to North American Indians]

fireworks 1 *n* by 1883 Excitement; furor; noisy fuss; =HOOPLA: *. . . speeches that. . . would produce the "fireworks" supporters have demanded*—J Devlin **2** *n* by 1880s Anger; quarrels; rancorous rhetoric **3** *n* by 1860s Shooting; gunfire or cannon fire: *The riot ended when the National Guard showed up and the fireworks began*

first base *n phr* 1980s *school children* In early sexual play, holding hands: *"In sixth grade," she said, "first base is holding hands, and second base is kissing on the mouth"*—New York Times
See GET TO FIRST BASE

first crack out of the box *adv phr* by 1940s Immediately; before anything else: *Get him back home and, first crack out of the box, he's run away again*

firstest (or fustest) with the mostest *adv phr* First with the most; soonest and best equipped [fr explanation said to have been given by Confederate General Nathan B Forrest of how he won a skirmish; he actually said "Get there first with the most men"]

first john *n phr Army* by 1940s A first lieutenant

first luff *n phr Navy* by about 1850 A naval lieutenant, senior grade

first man (or shirt or soldier) *n phr Army* by 1940s A first sergeant; =TOP-KICK

first off *adv phr* by 1880s First in order; to begin with: *I said that first off I wanted an apology*

first-of-May *circus & carnival* by 1920s **1** *n* A novice; neophyte, esp one who stays on the job only a short time: *A beginner at barking is known as a "first of May"*—M Bracker/ *a short-timer, a "First-of-May"*—Society **2** *adj*: *These first-of-May guys are a little off time*—R L Taylor [related to the early *May* beginning of the season]

first-rate 1 *adj* by 1697 Excellent; of best quality **2** *adv*: *That'll do first-rate* [fr the rating of warships in the 1600s]

first sacker *n phr baseball* by 1911 A first baseman

fish 1 *n prison* by 1870s A new inmate: *As a "fish". . . at Charlestown, I was physically miserable*—Malcolm X **2** *n* 1950s *street gang* A nonmember of a street gang; a person regarded as inimical and distasteful by a street gang **3** *n* by 1753 A weak or stupid person, esp one easily victimized; =PATSY, SUCKER: *Why should he be the fish for the big guys?*—Ira Wolfert/ *The superteams get stronger. They can pad their schedules with the occasional fish*—Sports Illustrated **4** *n* by 1885 A person, esp a criminal, thought of as being caught like a fish: *The cops catch a lot of very interesting fish*—Life **5** *n homosexuals* by 1970s A heterosexual woman **6** *n* by 1930s A prostitute; =HOOKER
•*Fish* meant "vulva" by the 1890s, retained the meaning, at least in black English, until at least the 1930s **7** *n* by 1920 A dollar: *The job paid only fifty fish*—Lionel Stander **8** *n* by 1928 =TIN FISH
•*Fish torpedo* is found by 1876 **9** *v* by 1563 To seek information, esp by a legal or quasi-legal process having a very general aim; =GO FISHING **10** *v* by 1803 To ask for something, usu a compliment, esp in an indirect and apparently modest way
See BIG FISH, BIGGER FISH TO FRY, COLD FISH, FINE KETTLE OF FISH, GO FISHING, KETTLE OF FISH, LIKE SHOOTING FISH IN A BARREL, POOR FISH, QUEER FISH, TIN FISH, YELLOWFISH

fishery *n* hoboes by 1920s A religious mission in a working-class neighborhood [ultimately fr the concept of St Peter as a *fisher* of men]

the **fish-eye** *See* GIVE someone THE FISH-EYE

fish-eyed *adj* by 1836 Cold, staring, and inhuman •The dated form is *fishy-eyed*: . . . *have to persuade a fish-eyed insurance claims adjustor*—New York

fishhooks *n* by 1846 The fingers

fishing *See* GO FISHING

fishing expedition *n phr* by 1961 An attempt, on the part of the police, a prosecutor, etc, to discover evidence where it may or may not be; a sort of inquisition: *She had nothing special in mind to ask Joan Tesell; it was just a fishing expedition*—Lawrence Sanders
See GO FISHING

fish music *n phr* by 1950s An early form of rock and roll, not as fast and loud as the developed version

fish or cut bait *sentence* by 1876 Do one thing or another, but stop dithering; take action; =SHIT OR GET OFF THE POT •Usu a firm or irritated demand: *The union leader warned that the city had until Feb 1 to "fish or cut bait"*—New York Times

fishskin 1 *n* by 1930s A dollar bill 2 *n* by 1930s A condom

fish story (or tale) *n phr* by 1819 A series of lies or exaggerations; a false or improbable explanation: *His whole alibi is a fish story* [fr the tendency of an angler to exaggerate the size of the catch]

fishtail 1 *n* 1950s A women's dress or skirt style featuring a flare at the bottom 2 *n* 1950s hot rodders Flaring rear fenders on a car 3 *v* by 1927 To swing a car, motorcycle, etc, from side to side at the rear: *. . . causing his rear wheels to spin or the rear end to fishtail, that is swing back and forth*—Life

fish to fry *See* BIGGER FISH TO FRY

fishwife *n* homosexuals by 1970s The wife of a homosexual man

fishy *adj* by 1840 Very probably false or dishonest; very dubious: *The whole proposition is decidedly fishy* [probably fr the unpleasant odor of spoiled *fish*]

fishyback *n* by 1954 The transport of loaded containers or semitrailers by ship or barge [modeled on *piggyback*]

fist 1 *n* 1930s telegraphers & radio operators The hand used for operating a telegraphic key 2 *n* by 1842 A signature
See MAKE MONEY HAND OVER FIST

fisted *See* HAM-HANDED

◄**fist-fucking** 1 *v* by 1890s Male masturbation 2 *n* (also **fisting**) by 1970s Anal intercourse, usu homosexual, in which the hand is inserted into the partner's anus

fistful 1 *n* by 1611 A handful, usu a large amount: *I've got a fistful of overdue bills* 2 *n* by 1950s A large amount of money: *The digital stereo set me back a fistful* 3 *n* underworld by 1940s A five-year prison sentence

fistiana *n* by 1840 The sport or business of prizefighting; the boxing game: *. . . that hotbed of fistiana known as Las Cruces*—New York Daily News

fit *n* 1950s narcotics The devices used for injecting narcotics; drug paraphernalia; =WORKS [probably a shortening of *outfit*]
See CATFIT, DUCK-FIT, HAVE A SHIT FIT, THROW A FIT

fit as a fiddle *adj phr* by 1616 In very good condition; in fine fettle

fit to be tied *adj phr* by 1894 Very angry; =STEAMED

five *n* 1950s jive talk The hand; the five fingers
See GIVE someone FIVE, HANG FIVE, NINE-TO-FIVE, NINETY-FIVE, SLIP (or GIVE) ME FIVE, TAKE FIVE

five-and-ten or **five-and-dime** by 1908 1 *n* A variety store selling relatively cheap items; =DIME STORE 2 *adj* Cheap; paltry; second-rate: *Dr Ruth is strictly a five-and-dime affair*—New York Magazine

five-by-five 1 *adj* by 1940s Fat 2 *adj* (also **five square**, **five five**) radio operators by 1940s [second sense fr the military radio operator's double scale, of one to *five*, for reporting both strength and clarity of a signal]

five-case note *n phr* by 1920s A five-dollar bill

five-dollar gold piece *See* COME UP SMELLING LIKE A ROSE

five-finger discount *n phr* 1960s teenagers Shoplifting

five fingers underworld by 1940s 1 *n phr* A five-year prison sentence 2 *n phr* A thief
See GIVE FIVE FINGERS TO

five it *v phr* by 1970s To refuse to answer on grounds of the Fifth Amendment: *How many questions would they be able to get in before DeMeo began to "five it"*—New York Magazine

Five-O *n* 1980s teenagers A police officer; the police: *Why you think you and the flap can shut the Deuce down? Five-oh can't do it*—Robert B Parker [fr the television police-adventure series *Hawaii Five-O*]

five-ouncers *n* prizefight by 1940s The fists [fr the minimum weight of boxing gloves]

five-pound bag *See* BLIVIT

fiver 1 *n* by 1843 A five-dollar bill; five dollars: *For a fiver, cash, you could ride*—Nelson Algren 2 *n* prison by 1940s A five-year prison sentence; =FIVE FINGERS
See NINE-TO-FIVER

fives *See* BUNCH OF FIVES

five-sided puzzle palace *n phr* Army by 1970s The Pentagon

five-spot 1 *n* by 1890s A five-dollar bill 2 *n* underworld by 1900 A five-year prison sentence

fix 1 *v* by 1790 To prearrange the outcome of a prizefight, race, game, etc 2 *n* by 1890s A fight, game, etc, of which the winner has been fraudulently predetermined: *The World Series that year was a blatant fix* 3 *v* by 1872 To arrange exoneration from a charge, esp by bribery; have a charge quashed: *He had a pal could fix tickets for five bucks* 4 *n* (also **fix-up**) narcotics by 1930s A dose of a narcotic, esp an injection of heroin; =BLAST: *. . . a fix to calm her jittery nerves*—San Francisco Examiner 5 *n* by 1970s Anything needed to appease a habitual need or craving •One of the common transfers of narcotics terms, like *junkie*: *He had to have his daily fix of flattery* **6** *v* by 1940s To castrate an animal, esp a cat **7** *v* by 1800 To punish; injure; =FIX someone's WAGON: *Make him wash the dishes, that'll fix him* **8** *n* by 1809 A difficult situation; a nasty position or dilemma: *I'm afraid her lying has gotten her into quite a fix* **9** *n* by 1902 A clear idea; an accurate notion •The dated use refers to the determination of a point or line in navigation: *I can't get a fix on this guy's intentions*

See QUICK FIX

the **fix 1** *n phr* by 1940s Arrangements, esp illicit payments, assuring the prearranged outcome of a prizefight, game, race, etc;: *It's in the bag. The fix is on*—W R and F K Simpson/ *If he doesn't get the Nobel, the fix is in*—Milwaukee Journal **2** *n phr* by 1920s Arrangements assuring exoneration from a police charge: *The super hisself couldn't put the fix in any faster*—Nelson Algren

fixer *n* by 1889 A person who arranges shady and illegal affairs: *He's a fixer you have to see if you want to open a gambling hall*—Raymond Chandler

fix someone's **hash** *See* SETTLE someone's HASH

fixings *n* by 1842 Things, esp food, normally accompanying some central or focal object: *turkey and all the fixings*

Fixit *See* MISTER FIXIT

fix someone **up** *v phr* by 1861 To provide or arrange what is needed: *We can fix you up with a nice new car/ If you want a date I can fix you up with Gert*

fix someone's **wagon** *v phr* by 1940s To punish; injure; ruin; =CLEAN someone's CLOCK

FIZBO *n* 1980s A person who attempts to sell property without a real-estate broker, or the arrangement for doing so: *Another is their dislike for brokers who offer their services at a discount to FIZBOS, which stands for For Sale By Owner*—Chicago Tribune

fizz *n* by 1940s A failure; =FIZZLE: *"It was a big fizz,"* the ambassador said—Time

fizzle college students by 1840s **1** *v* To fail; lose effect; =FLOP, PETER OUT: *. . . and I bail out of all my commitments and things fizzle*—Douglas Coupland **2** *n*: *Our monster bash was a fizzle* [fr the lackluster sibilance of a damp firecracker]

flabbergast *v* by 1772 To amaze; perplex; =THROW

flack or **flak 1** *n* by 1940s Publicity; public relations material; =BALLYHOO, HYPE: *Mr Mogul's latest epic was preceded by wheeling galaxies of affecting flack* **2** *modifier*: *The flack description is also worth quoting*—Variety **3** *n* (also **flacker**) A publicity person or press agent: *. . . something that would cause your basic, self-respecting flack to want to slit his throat*—Calvin Trillin/ *. . . "He's shown steady improvement," said a medical flak*—New York Daily News **4** *v*: *. . . his publishers, who flack it. . . into a best seller*—Atlantic Monthly/ *He's not flakking for ulterior motives*—Toronto Life [origin unknown; said to be fr the name of Gene *Flack*, a

moving picture publicity agent, and first used in the show-business paper *Variety*; probably influenced by *flak*]

flack or **flack out** 1950s cool & beat talk **1** *v* or *v phr* To fall asleep; lose consciousness **2** *v phr* To be tired or depressed **3** *v phr* To die

flackery *n* by 1960s Publicity; =FLACK, HYPE: *A White House insider's name, with enough flackery, can be sold like mouthwash*—Hugh Sidey

flag 1 *v* (also **flag down**) by 1850s To hail a vehicle, person, etc; signal a stop: *He was barreling along till she flagged him down* **2** *v* underworld by 1940s To arrest; =BUST: *They flagged my reefer man yesterday*—New York Magazine **3** *n* baseball by 1883 The pennant awarded annually to a league championship team **4** *n* underworld by 1930s An assumed name; alias **5** *v* by 1980s To designate as someone who will not be served more liquor; =EIGHTY-SIX: *. . . Babris asked Pilone whether the men were "the local troublemakers" and then demanded that they be "flagged," the bartender testified*—Newark Star-Ledger

See JEWISH FLAG

flagged *adj* by 1980s Forbidden further drinks, because already drunk

flag it *v phr* 1950s college students To fail an examination or a course; =FLUNK

flagpole *See* RUN something UP THE FLAGPOLE

flagship by 1955 **1** *n* The most imposing constituent; premier specimen: *This car's the flagship of the line* **2** *modifier*: *. . . and not one damn word in the nation's flagship papers*—Village Voice

flag-up *adj* cabdrivers by 1960s With the taxi meter not started: *a flag-up ride*

flag-waver by 1890s **1** *n* A conspicuously patriotic person; superpatriot **2** *n* A book, play, etc, that is strongly patriotic

flak 1 *n* WWII armed forces An antiaircraft gun or guns; antiaircraft fire; **2** *n* (also **flack**) by 1960s Severe criticism; angry blame: *This order provoked little political flack*—Harper's/ *. . . Joe took considerable flak from white co-workers. . .*—New York Magazine **3** *n* by 1960s Trouble; fuss; dissension; =STATIC: *Let's not have a lot of flak about this* [fr German *Fliegerabwehrkanonen*, "antiaircraft gun"]

flake 1 *n* baseball by 1950s An eccentric person, esp a colorful individualist; =BIRD: *. . . what is known in the trade as a flake, a kook, or a clubhouse lawyer*—Christopher Lehmann-Haupt/ *Users and flakes clung to her*—New York Magazine **2** *n* baseball by 1960s The quality of flamboyant individualism: *The Yankees have acquired. . . an amount of "flake"*—Leonard Koppett **3** *adj* baseball by 1960s : *Don't act so flake* **4** *n* 1960s teenagers A stupid, erratic person; =RETARD **5** *n* narcotics by 1920s Cocaine **6** *v* police by 1970s To arrest someone on false or invented charges; =FRAME **7** *v* police by 1970s To plant evidence on a suspect: *I have a throwaway gun. We're going to flake him*—Michael Grant **8** *n* police by 1970s An arrest made in order to meet a quota; =ACCOMMODATION COLLAR **9 v** *1980s students* To cancel an appointment without notice; =STAND someone UP: . . . *it is already seven o'clock; I guess he flaked*—UCLA Slang [all except police senses ultimately fr an attested phrase *snow flakes,* "cocaine"]

flaked-out *adj 1950s beat & cool talk* Asleep; unconscious

flake off *v phr 1960s teenagers* To leave; depart •Often an irritated command: *Want to brush off such friends? Suggest that they. . . flake off*—J Gray [probably a euphemism for *fuck off*]

flake out *1970s* **1 v phr** =FLACK OUT **2 v phr** =FLAKE OFF **3 v phr** To fail [origin uncertain; *flax out* in the third sense is found in New England dialect by 1891, and is probably related]

flake-out *n 1970s* A total failure; =FLOP

flak jacket *n phr by 1950s* A bulletproof vest or other protective garment for the chest: . . . *the flak jacket Oiler QB Dan Pastorini wore last year*—New York Daily News/ *Nebraska officials said that Berringer, who was wearing a flak jacket, was not in pain but was held out in the second half*—Milwaukee Journal [fr the protective *jacket* worn by air-crew members in WWII]

flaky or **flakey** **1** *adj baseball by 1960s* Colorfully eccentric; buoyantly individualistic **2** *adj 1960s* Insane; =SCREWY, WACKY: . . . *a flaky old professor, a snake expert*—New York Magazine **3** *adj 1960s* Disoriented; barely conscious; dizzy: . . . *played the last 23 minutes of the game in a condition that was described as "flaky" and "fuzzy"*—New York Times *See* FLAKE

flam *See* FLIMFLAM

flamdoodle *See* FLAPDOODLE

flame **1** *n by 1647* A sweetheart; beloved **2** *v* (also **flame it up**) *homosexuals by 1970s* To flaunt or exaggerate effeminate traits; =CAMP **3** *v esp 1980s computer* To rant angrily and often obscenely on a computer bulletin board or other network: . . . *you may even get the chance to "flame" someone else*—New York Times **4** *n* (also **flame-mail**) *1980s computer* An angry and often obscene message on a computer network: . . . *countless scornful messages, called "flames" on the network*—New York Times/ *Bill. . . sent Michael this totally wicked flame-mail from hell. . .* —Douglas Coupland *See* SHOOT someone DOWN

flame-out or **flame out** **1** *v phr by 1940s* Of a jet engine, to fail by losing the flame of its fuel **2** *v phr by 1990s* To lose energy; falter; collapse: *The Stevens Point native flamed out in the 1500 meters. . .* —Milwaukee Journal Sentinel **3** *n by 1940s* The failure of a jet engine where the flame is extinguished **4** *n by 1990s* A person of fleeting fame; =HAS-BEEN, FLASH IN THE PAN: . . . *he is the Russian Hotspur, a fiery flameout who will soon become a historical footnote*—New York Times/ *Michael Jackson was a flame-out, too*—Milwaukee Journal **5** *modifier*: *Gramm, flame-out Jack Kemp. . .* —Los Angeles Reader

◁**flamer** or **flaming asshole** or **flaming fruit-bar**▷ *n or n phr homosexuals by 1970s* A male homosexual; =QUEEN: *It doesn't have anything to do with me being a flamer*—Richard Merkin

flames *See* GO DOWN IN FLAMES

flamethrower *n baseball by 1970s* A pitcher with a very fast fastball

flame war *n phr computer by 1990s* An extended outbreak of vituperation on a computer network: . . . *the whole net will basically collapse through flame-wars*—New York Times/ *They flame back, and then a flame war begins*—New Yorker

flaming ◁**1**▷ *adj homosexuals by 1970s* Blatantly homosexual, esp in an effeminate way; =SWISH: . . . *in hiding the fact that Babe Ruth and Lou Gehrig were flaming homosexuals*—National Lampoon **2** *adv by 1895* Very •Used as an intensifier, usu preceded by "so": *I can't believe he'd be so flaming stupid* **3** *n* (also **flamage**) *1980s computer* The use of rude, strong, obscene, etc, language on a computer bulletin board, in computer mail, etc •This sort of verbal license is said to be common and apparently to be an effect of the medium itself

◁**flaming pisspot**▷ *n phr Army by 1970s* The insignia of the Ordnance Corps, a flaming grenade bomb

flammer *See* FLIMFLAMMER

◁**flange-face**▷ *n WWII Navy* An ugly sailor

◀**flange-head**▶ *n WWII Army Air Forces* A Chinese person

flap **1** *n British by 1916* Disturbance; tumult; fuss: *Law was one direction open to me with the least amount of flap*—Good Housekeeping **2** *v by 1920s* To become flustered; lose one's composure: *I've seen him under hostile pressure before. He doesn't flap and he doesn't become a doormat*—D E Kneeland **3** *n 1950s street gang* A fight between street gangs; =RUMBLE **4** *n black street gang by 1990s* A white person: . . . *I wouldn't give a fuck what you or the flap or anybody thought 'bout it*—Robert B Parker

flapdoodle or **flamdoodle** *n by 1833* Nonsense; foolishness; =BALONEY: *He then goes on to utter other flapdoodle for the nourishment of the mind*—New York Times

flap one's **gums** *See* BAT one's GUMS

flapjack *n by 1600* A pancake

flapjaw *by 1950s* **1** *n* Talk; discourse; chat: *We caught Mannone and Moore for a moment's flapjaw before we left*—New Yorker **2** *n* A loquacious person; =MOTOR-MOUTH

flapjawed *adj by 1950s* Talkative; notably loquacious: . . . *to describe the flap-jawed Turner as outspoken*—People

flap one's **lip** *See* FLIP one's LIP

flapper **1** *n by 1770s* The hand; =FLIPPER **2** *n by 1893* A young woman of the type fashionable in the 1920s, with pronounced worldly interests, relatively few inhibitions, a distinctive style of grooming, etc •The date refers to two senses, "a young whore," and "a young girl"; the 1920s revival seems to blend these **3** *modifier*: *the flapper era/ flat flapper chest* [origin uncertain; perhaps from the idea of an unfledged bird *flapping* its wings]

flash 1 *n* by 1718 Thieves' argot **2** *n* about 1900 A look; quick glance: *We slid into the cross street to take a flash at the alley*—James M Cain **3** *n* by 1603 A person who excels at something, esp in a showy and perhaps superficial way; =WHIZ: *He's a flash at math* **4** *n* circus by 1920s A display of gaudy merchandise or prizes: . . . *expensive flash that the mark couldn't win*—E Brown **5** *v* circus by 1920s To set up a display of presumed prizes •*Flash it*, "to show the bargains offered," is found by 1849: *Flash the joint*—American Mercury **6** *v* by 1811 To vomit •The dated example is *flash the hash* **7** *v* 1960s narcotics To have a hallucinatory experience from a narcotic: *He flashed he was as big as a mountain* **8** *v* 1960s narcotics To feel the sudden pleasurable effect of a narcotics injection: *As soon as the needle went in, she flashed* **9** *n* 1960s narcotics =RUSH: *Harry shot up a couple of the goof balls and tried to think a bigger and better flash than he got*—Hubert Selby Jr **10** *adj* teenagers by 1970s Excellent; wonderful; =DYNAMITE **11** *n* by 1970s Distinctive personal style and charm; charisma: *Flash is in the clothes, the cars, the walk, the talk*—R Woodley **12** *v* by 1920s To have a sudden idea, insight, or impulse **13** *n*: . . . *if he should get a sudden flash to commit Cat. . . and wants to call her*—S Werbin/ . . . *the joy when I get the flash, figure out who did it. . .* —William Bayer **14** *n* by 1970s Something one is currently doing; =BAG, THING: *His current "flash," as he calls it, tends toward gaucho suits*—New York Post **15** *v* by 1846 To expose one's genitals, breasts, etc •The earlier British forms were *flash it* and *flash one's meat*: *Judy thought she was gonna flash me. She started unbuttoning her blouse*—Dolly Parton **16** *n*: *He gave her a flash and she squawked* **17** *v* To display suddenly and briefly: *We flash our tin and ask him if he's lost a ball-peen hammer. . .* —Lawrence Sanders **18** *n* by 1970s Urination; =PISS: . . . *and said he'd pay double in case of a "flash," which is a delicate way of describing one of nature's indelicate imperatives*—Washington Post **19** *v* rock climbing by 1990s To climb a route on the first try **20** *n* by 1990s Showiness; superficiality; =GLITTER, GLITZ: *For all the flash. . . Carlito's Way is pretty tame*—Bill Gallo **21** *adj* by early 1600s =FLASHY

flashback 1 *n* by 1916 A scene or passage in a novel, movie, etc, that depicts events earlier than those in the main time frame **2** *n* 1960s narcotics A hallucination or sensation originally induced by LSD or other drugs but recurring after the drug experience has ended

flasher *n* by 1960s A person who exposes the genitals in public; exhibitionist [male exhibitionists were known as *meat-flashers* by the early 1890s]

flashforward *n* by 1949 A scene or passage in a novel, movie, etc, that depicts events later than those of the main time frame

flash in the pan *n phr* by 1809 A person or thing that does not fulfill an apparent potential: *If he's not a flash in the pan he'll be the best poet we ever had* [fr the igniting charge in an old gun that goes off *in the pan* or holder without igniting the main charge]

flash on *v phr* 1960s To recall; realize vividly: *I flashed on all that stuff in basic about it being better dead than captured*—Rolling Stone/ *She just flashed on it for once in her life, she ought to put her own needs right up front*—Cyra McFadden

flash point *n phr* by 1990s The place or time when something "takes fire," becomes exciting and exemplary: . . . *we want the White House to function as a flash point for whatever's great in this couintry. . .* —Macon Telegraph [in the technical sense, "lowest point of ignition of a fluid, compound, etc," the term is found by the 1870s]

flash roll or **flash money** or **front money** *n phr* by 1970s A bundle of cash shown as proof that the holder is in funds: . . . *thinking it would make for a fatter looking flash roll*—Joseph Wambaugh/ . . . *showed suspects six million in cash as front or flash money to prove that they indeed had funds*—Portland Journal

flashy *adj* by 1690 Gaudy; meretriciously showy: *flashy rings/ a flashy new car*

flat 1 *adj* by 1833 =FLAT BROKE **2** *adj* carnival by 1940s Having to do with any gambling game, esp one in which money rather than prizes may be won [carnival sense fr earlier meaning of *flats*, "playing cards" or fr earlier meaning "dishonest dice"]
See GRANNY FLAT, IN NOTHING FLAT

flat as a pancake *adj phr* by 1761 Very flat: *The car was squashed flat as a pancake* [the form *flat down as pancakes* is found by 1611]

◁**flat-ass**▷ *adv* by 1960s Totally; absolutely: *Some farmers are absolutely flat-ass broke*—Time/ *It's not just that. I'll flat-ass leave her*—Leonard Gardner

flatbacker *n* by 1960s A prostitute: *His prostitutes are well known for being unhooked flatbackers*—I Ianni

flat broke *adj phr* by 1842 Entirely without funds; penniless

flatfoot *n* by 1899 A police officer or detective: *The flat-feet scratched their heads*—NY Confidential

flatfooted 1 *adj* baseball by 1912 Unprepared; surprised •Usu in the phrase *catch someone flatfooted*: *He just stood there flatfooted and watched it roll in* **2** *adj* by 1828 Straightforwardly; without ceremony: *If they were going to turn it down, they would have just flatfooted done it*—Milwaukee Journal

flathead 1 *n* by 1862 A stupid person; =FATHEAD **2** *n* by 1950s A police officer; =FLATFOOT **3** *n* restaurant by 1950s A nontipping patron at a restaurant or club **4** *n* 1950s hot rodders An L-head or side-valve car engine

flatheaded *adj* by 1880 Stupid: *The speaker was a flatheaded idiot*—P Curtiss

flat-joint or **flatstore** *carnival by 1940s* **1** *n* A game one plays for money rather than a prize **2** *n* Any gambling concession, esp a dishonest one

flatline *by 1980s* **1** *v* To die: *State government is in a coma. We're going to flat-line at any moment*—Harper's **2** *modifier* Dead: *The defendant's face was flatline*—Denver television news [fr the *flat line* showing no waves, hence no heartbeat, on a heart monitoring machine]

flatlined *adj by 1990s* Drunk; =PLASTERED, SHIT-FACED: *I've had so many reebs I'm flatlined*—Los Angeles Times

flatliner 1 *n by 1980s* A dead person **2** *n restaurant by 1990s* A nontipping customer; =FLATHEAD

◁**flat on** one's **ass**▷ **1** *adj phr by 1960s* Penniless and exhausted; =DOWN AND OUT: *He blew his pay pack and he's flat on his ass* **2** *adj phr 1970s Army* Incompetent; feckless: *That platoon's a loser, flat on its ass*
See FALL ON one's ASS

flat out *adv phr by 1932* At full speed; =ALL-OUT, WIDE OPEN: *The economy is running flat out and revenues are pouring in*—Wall Street Journal/ *Flat out, working on it myself, it will take a week*—John McPhee [perhaps fr the elongated shape of a horse going at top speed]

flat-out 1 *adj* Open and direct; unambiguous; plain: *Bunuel resorts to flat-out assertions in the last scene*—American Scholar/ *This time a flat-out demand*—Stuart Woods **2** *adj* Total; unrestricted •The noun *flat-out*, "a failure," is found by 1870; the following example is an unconscious redundancy: *. . . a husband who was a flat-out failure*—Time/ *Despite its creepshow pretensions, much of it is flat-out dull*—Los Angeles Times

flats 1 *n horse-racing by 1840s* Horse-racing in which the jockey is mounted and the horse runs, rather than trotting **2** *n gamblers by 1591* A pair of dishonest dice

flat-tailed *adv by 1990s* Totally; completely: *They controlled the game. They just flat-tailed beat us*—Milwaukee Journal

flattener *n prizefight by 1920s* A blow that knocks one down and unconscious; knockout punch

flat tire (or **hoop**) *n phr early 1920s* A tedious person; an insipid companion

flattop *n WWII armed forces* An aircraft carrier

flatty or **flattie 1** *n by 1899* A police officer; =FLATFOOT **2** *n carnival by 1950s* A gambling concession; =FLAT-JOINT **3** *n carnival by 1950s* A concession agent who operates a flat-joint: *Performers suggest that "flatties" are no more than common thieves*—Society

◁**flavor** or **flava**▷ *black by 1960s* **1** *n* A sexually attractive woman **2** *adj*: *That's a very flava lady*

flavor of the month *n phr by early 1990s* Something ephemeral; a short-lived phenomenon: *That 23 percent could dwindle, Mr. Perot could be the political flavor of the month*—New York Times/ *She's not seeing him any more; turned out to be another flavour of the month*—Slang Bag 93 [fr the Baskin and Robbins ice cream chain's marketing of a new *flavor* each *month*]

FLB (pronounced as separate letters) *n medical by 1970s* Strange or arrhythmic heartbeats [fr *funny-looking beats*]

fleabag or **fleahouse** or **fleatrap 1** *n by 1839* A bed; mattress; bunk or hammock **2** *n horse-racing by 1950s* An inferior racehorse **3** *n by late 1820s* A cheap and wretched hotel or rooming house; =FLOP, FLOPHOUSE: *. . . my last French hotel of the war: a fleabag two rooms wide*—Albert Guerard/ *He has transformed the motel from the old wayside fleabag into the most popular home away from home*—Time **4** *modifier*: *. . . will no longer take her dates to fleabag hotels*—New York Times **5** *n by 1950s* Any cheap, dirty, or ramshackle public place: *. . . unveiled at an owl show in a Forty-second Street flea bag*—S J Perelman

flea-flicker *n 1920s football* A play combining a lateral pass and a forward pass: *You won't get the flea-flickers and special-teams gambles from Holmgren. . .*—Milwaukee Journal

flea powder *n phr 1960s narcotics* A weakened or diluted narcotic, or a nonnarcotic substance sold as a narcotic; =BLANK

fleece *v by 1577* To cheat or swindle: *. . . get back the money he'd fleeced me out of*—J Scarne/ *For these traders the function of the outside public speculator is to be fleeced*—Washington Post

flesh *See* IN THE FLESH, PRESS THE FLESH

flesh flick *See* SKIN FLICK

flesh-peddler 1 *n by 1940s* A pimp or prostitute •The earlier version, *flesh-monger*, is found by 1603 **2** *n 1930s* An actor's or athlete's agent: *The old Hollywood flesh peddlers never stop talking money*—Raymond Chandler **3** *n by 1960s* A person working at an employment agency; =HEADHUNTER

flesh-pressing *modifier by 1920s* Handshaking, meeting and flattering voters, etc, in politics: *The flesh-pressing process remains invariable, as you will glean from the weekly schedule of City Alderman Joe Pantalone*—Toronto Life

flex one's **muscles** *v phr by 1960s* To give a sample of one's power, esp in a threatening way: *I'm not sure they mean harm, probably just flexing their muscles*

flextime or **flexitime** *n by 1970s* Flexible working time that varies as to hours and days worked: *. . . flextime for working mothers and fathers in business*—Time [fr the trademark of a device used to record the hours an employee works]

flic (FLICK, FLEEK) *n* A police officer: *. . . if the flic had the slightest suspicion*—R Fish [fr French slang]

flick *1920s* **1** *n* A movie: *. . . a cheapie hard-core porno flick*—Saturday Review/ *He will play a role in the flick*—Associated Press **2** *n* A movie theater [fr the *flickering* of early movie images]
See SKIN FLICK

flicker *n by 1910* =FLICK

the **flicks** or **flickers** or **flix** *n phr by 1920s* The movies; the cinema: *When I went to the flicks, I was forced to sit far back*—Goodman Ace/ *. . . the getting-away-from-it-all surcease we seek at the flicks*—Judith Crist

flier *See* FLYER

flies *See* CATCH FLIES, NO FLIES ON

flight *n 1960s narcotics* A hallucinogenic drug experience; =TRIP
 See WHITE FLIGHT

flimflam *by 1538* **1** *v* To cheat or swindle; defraud; =BAMBOOZLE, CON: *We've been flimflammed*—James M Cain/ *He talked like some hick. . . begging to be flimflammed*—Joseph Wambaugh **2** *n*: *Don't fall for that flimflam* **3** *modifier*: *a flimflam game/ flimflam man*

flimflammer *n by 1880s* A confidence man; cheater; swindler: *. . . an expert flimflammer who worked up crime's ladder*—New York Daily News

flimsy *n by 1857* A copy of a bill, art work, etc, on thin paper

fling **1** *n by 1827* A period of pleasure and indulgence, often as relaxation after or before stern responsibilities: *He had a last fling before going to the monastery* **2** *n by 1592* A try; =CRACK, GO, SHOT: *Will you have a fling at climbing that wall?* **3** *n 1940s students* A dance; party; =SHINDIG

fling woo *See* PITCH WOO

flip[1] *adj by 1847* Flippant; impudent; =CHEEKY: *Mr Lawrence. . . is flip and easy*—Clive Barnes/ *Someone else thought he was too flip at press conferences*—New York Times

flip[2] **1** *v by early 1900s* To change or switch diametrically; =FLIP-FLOP: *So I flipped over to the opposite opinion* **2** *v by 1950* To respond enthusiastically; feel great excitement and pleasure: *"They flipped over it," Riveroll recalls*—Forbes/ *I flip over this record*—T Brown **3** *v by 1950* To cause one to respond with enthusiasm; give one great pleasure: *My imitation of Mr Kissinger flipped the assemblage* **4** *n about 1950* Something that causes hilarity or pleasure: *The big flip of the year is Peter Arno's book of cartoons*—Gilbert Milstein **5** *v by 1940s* To become angry: *When he told me what he had done, I flipped* **6** *v 1950s cool talk* To go insane; behave irrationally; =FLIP OUT: *I was flipping at first. . . but then the marvelous vibes got to me*—Whitney Balliett **7** *v police by 1980s* To become an informer; =FINK OUT, SING: *Someone had tipped the police off to where they should look: a suspect who had been persuaded to flip, become a government informant, on the night of his arrest*—New Yorker/ *It was the easiest flip Stone ever made. The man rolled over like a puppy. . .*—Joseph Wambaugh **8** *v by 1980s* To vomit: *Many jockeys have to "flip" (regurgitate) their meals to make weight*—Milwaukee Journal **9** *v by 1990s* To exchange one for another; trade in: *You buy one. . . get it out of your system, flip it for a gray Lexus or Infiniti. . .*—Douglas Coupland

flip-flop *by about 1900* **1** *n* A complete reversal of direction; about-face •The primary meaning is "som-

ersault": *Commodities have been doing flip-flops on the price ladder*—K Scheibel **2** *v*: *So Kennedy's flip-flopped again*—Time **3** *modifier*: *. . . flip-flop views and reluctance to confront the issues*—New Yorker

flip-flops *n 1960s* Bathing sandals, esp the kind where a strap fits between one's toes: *. . . in a flowered housedress and Dr Scholl flip-flops*—New York Times

flip one's lid (or wig or raspberry) *1940s jazz musicians* **1** *v phr* To become violently angry; =BLOW one's TOP: *When she told him he flipped his lid* **2** *v phr* To go insane; behave irrationally: *When he started mumbling I was sure he'd flipped his wig/ flipped his lid and blew a whole list of nuclear warhead targets*—W T Tyler **3** *v phr* To show great enthusiasm and approval: *When she finished reading, the crowd flipped its raspberry*

flip (or flap) one's lip *v phr 1940s students* To talk, esp idly or foolishly

flip-lipped *adj 1940s students* Flippantly loquacious; =FLIP, SMART-ASS: *Pine was a flip-lipped bastard who should have had his ears pinned back long ago*—J Evans

flip on *v phr by 1990s* To turn on; activate: *. . . was vacationing in Norway recently when he flipped on the telly*—Milwaukee Journal

flip on someone *v phr 1990s street gang* To rob; hold up

flip out *1950s bop & cool talk* **1** *v phr* To evoke an enthusiastic response: *I flipped out these guys with my crazy stories*—Xaviera Hollander **2** *v phr* To display enthusiasm; crow: *My junkie brother continues to flip out about what a cool dude I am*—Saturday Review **3** *v phr* To go insane; =FLIP, FREAK OUT: *. . . and I flipped out and went crazy*—Rolling Stone

flip-out *1950s bop & cool talk* **1** *n* A spell of anger, disturbance, craziness, etc: *Harriet has a minor flip-out and flees*—New Yorker **2** *n* An exciting or wondrous experience: *Her performance was a real flip-out*

flip one's pancake *v phr by 1990s* To delight one; inspire on; =TURN ON: *MTV's Real World does not flip my pancake either*—Macon Telegraph

flipper **1** *n by 1832* A hand; =FLAPPER: *I manfully gripped his flipper* **2** *n stock market by 1990s* Traders who buy initial public offerings as the market opens and sell them when vigorous trading begins: *It's been a boom year for initial public offerings, just the right environment for "flippers". . .*—Bloomberg Business News

flip phone *n phr by 1990s* A cellular telephone with a mouthpiece that folds up to decrease total size

flipping *adj British by 1911* Accursed; wretched; =DAMN, FREAKING: *Give me the flipping thing and I'll get it fixed* [a euphemism for *fucking*]

flip side **1** *n phr* The reverse surface of a phonograph record; =B-SIDE: *a golden oldie on the flip side* **2** *n phr* The other side of a question, issue, etc: *. . . it is true that. . . the flip side is that*—People/

As usual, there is a flip side. Any of the films revered by men are detested by women—Milwaukee Journal

flip the bird *v phr* (also **flash the bird, flick off, flip off**) *1980s students* To make a contemptuous sign with the hand, middle finger extended; =GIVE someone THE FINGER: *The six ladies flipped the bird to all their earthling viewers, lifting their minis*—National Lampoon/ *He's like the jerk who whips around traffic. . . flashing the bird as he passes*—C W Gusewelle/ *How did it feel to you when Mr Harrington stared you down and flipped you off in that manner?*—Court TV

flip the script *v phr 1990s* To reverse a role or situation; turn a circumstance around: *But is that still true if we flip the script?*

flip-top *See* POP-TOP

◁**flit**▷ *n by 1940s* A male homosexual; effeminate man

◁**flitty**▷ *adj by 1940s* Homosexual; effeminate; =GAY: *This isn't some weird kind of flitty pass, is it?*—Toronto Life/ *Do you know the ballet? All those flitty people up on their toes*—John Irving

fliv **1** *n by 1920s* =FLIVVER **2** *v show business by 1914* To fail; =FLOP

flivver **1** *v show business by 1910* To fail; =FLOP: *If the production flivvers, I'll need that thirty cents*—L J Vance **2** *n by 1914* A failure **3** *n by about 1914* A Model-T Ford car **4** *n by 1920s* Any car, airplane, or other vehicle, esp a small or cheap one [origin unknown]

the flix *See* the FLICKS

FLK (pronounced as separate letters) *n medical by 1960s* An abnormal, sick, or ugly child [fr *funny-looking kid*]

float **1** *v about 1930* To loaf on the job; =GOOF OFF **2** *n salespersons by 1950s* A customer who leaves while one is looking for merchandise **3** *v by 1970s* To disseminate; send out: *Reporters have been told to float their resumes*—Washingtonian

floater **1** *n by 1958* A person who habitually moves about; vagabond; =DRIFTER **2** *n British universities by 1913* A blunder: *. . . made an error, slip. . . or floater*—Sterling North **3** *n baseball about 1906* A slow pitch that appears to float in the air **4** *n by 1852* A corpse taken from the water

floating **1** *adj by 1940s* Drunk **2** *adj narcotics & black by 1950s* Intoxicated with narcotics; =HIGH

floating crap game *n phr by 1940s* A professional crap game that moves about to thwart police interference: *The floating crap game run by an underworld gambling syndicate*—W R and F K Simpson

a flock *n phr by 1920s* A large number; =HEAPS: *. . . buys him a flock of drinks afterwards, and hopes for the best*—John Crosby

flog *v British by 1919 fr armed forces* To offer for sale; peddle, esp in the sense of public hawking: *I went to the. . . convention to flog a new book*—Art Buchwald/ *Motel and bus companies flog special charter rates*—Newsweek [fr British slang *flog the clock*, "move the clockhands forward in order to

deceive," applied later to the illicit selling of military stores]

◁**flog** one's **meat**▷ *See* BEAT one's MEAT

◁**flong** one's **dong**▷ *v phr by 1970s* To masturbate: *If it weren't for flonging my dong, I don't know what I'd do*—Playgirl

flood pants *See* HIGH WATERS

flooey *See* GO BLOOEY

flookum or **flookem** *See* FLUKUM

floor **1** *v by 1812* To knock down; =DECK **2** *v by 1830* To shock, surprise, or hurt to the point of helplessness: *I was floored when some of our players accepted their offer*—Buzz **3** *v* (also **floorboard** or **floor it**) *by 1950s* To drive at full speed; push the throttle pedal to the floorboard; =PUT THE PEDAL TO THE METAL: *She floored the Porsche on the freeway and got caught/ You better floor it and get out of here*

See CLEAN UP ON someone, IN ON THE GROUND FLOOR, MOP THE FLOOR WITH someone, PUT someone ON THE FLOOR

floozy (Variations: **faloosie** or **floogy** or **floosie** or **floozie** or **flugie**) *by 1911* **1** *n* A self-indulgent, predatory woman, esp one of easy morals; cheap and tawdry woman: *He'd learn more about their psychology by taking a floozie to Atlantic City*—W B Johnson/ *. . . the central figure of an adult whodunit, an obviously no-good floosie*—S Helfrich **2** *n* A prostitute: *You been with some floozy, George*—Robert B Parker [origin uncertain; said to be an alteration of *flossy*]

flop **1** *v hoboes by 1907* To lie down for rest or sleep; sleep; =CRASH: *"Kip," "doss," "flop," "pound your ear," all mean. . . to sleep*—Jack London **2** *n* A place to sleep, esp a cheap and sordid hotel or shelter; =FLOPHOUSE: *I went into the flops and the shelters and was shocked*—New York Magazine *. . . in a three-dollar-a-week flop*—J Roebert **3** *v by 1893* To fail completely; =BOMB: *The show flopped, ran one night only* **4** *n*: *My great idea was a total flop* **5** *v police by 1980s* To transfer a police officer from one station to another, one assignment to another, etc: *That's funny. Abbott's giving me advice and he's about to be flopped*—Michael Grant

See BELLY FLOP

flophouse *n by 1923* A cheap and sordid rooming house or hotel, esp one with dormitories for men; =CHINCH PAD, FLEABAG: *I'm spending my nights at the flophouse*

flopper *See* BELLY-FLOPPER

flopperoo *n by 1931* A particularly spectacular failure; =FLOP: *three subdivisions: flop, flopperoo, and kerplunk*—W Holbrook

floppola *n by 1940s* A failure, esp a severe one; =FLOPPEROO: *And Fortune's worst floppola seems apocalyptic. Who will care for the poor?*—Washington Post

flop sweat *n phr by 1960s* An actor's anxiety; fear of failure: *Flop sweat is what an actor gets when he's nervous on stage*—Henny Youngman/ *Lights, camera, and flopsweat*—Independent Press

flossy or **flossie** *adj by 1890s* Fancy; frilly; =HIGHFALUTIN: *It may be highly important to know a flossy name for the boss*—F Tripp

the **flow** *See* GO WITH THE FLOW

◁**flower**[1]▷ *by 1950s* **1** *n* An effeminate man or boy; =SISSY ●Horticultural metaphors are favored here: *lily, pansy* **2** *n* A male homosexual

flower[2] *See* HEARTS AND FLOWERS, WALLFLOWER

flower child *n phr 1960s* A member of the hippie movement or counterculture, who typically advocated love, peace, and nonviolence: *. . . a caricature of a London flower child who is about as interesting as a boiled potato*—New Yorker

flower children (or **people**) *n phr 1960s* Members of the 1960s hippie movement collectively: *Woodstock is long over, and the bloom has gone off these flower children*—Penelope Gilliatt/ *. . . the flower people of the late 1960s, mostly middle-class kids trying to create a gaudy secular religion*—Time

flower power *n phr* The influence and merits of the pacifistic, altruistic values of the 1960s hippie movement

the **flu** *n by 1839* Influenza

flub *1920s* **1** *n* A stupid blunderer; =LUMMOX, KLUTZ: *Pick up your feet and don't be such a flub* **2** *v* To blunder; err; commit a gaffe; =GOOF: *I flubbed as soon as I opened my big mouth* **3** *v* To ruin by blundering; spoil with mistakes: *She flubbed the introduction, but did okay afterwards* **4** *n*: *The flub, as generally defined, is a mistake*—Pulpsmith **5** *v* To avoid work or duty; shirk; =GOOF OFF

flubdub *1920s* **1** *n* Incompetence; ineptitude: *They would remove much of the amateur flub-dub*—New York Daily News **2** *n* An awkward person; blunderer; =GOOF-UP, KLUTZ **3** *v*: *I made flubdubbed and increasingly abashed efforts to make myself feel good again*—St Clair McKelway [first sense found by 1888 in the sense "foolishness, bunk, hot air"]

flub the dub *esp WWII armed forces* **1** *v phr* To avoid one's work or duty; shirk; =GOLDBRICK: *He learned to flub the dub, but still stay pals with his associates* **2** *v phr* To think, work, move, etc, sluggishly and haplessly **3** *v phr* To fail by blundering; ruin one's best chances: *I think I flubbed the dub again, bidding so late*

flub-up *by 1950s* **1** *n* A blunder: *The attempt was one big flub-up* **2** *n* A blunderer; =GOOF-UP, KLUTZ: *. . . a kooky police cadet flub-up*—People

FLUF (FLUHF) *n airline by 1970s* the Boeing 737 airliner [fr *fat little ugly fucker*]

fluff ◁**1**▷ *n by 1903* A girl or young woman ●Found in the sense "female pubic hair, bush, beaver" by the 1890s: *A wan little fluff steals a dress so as to look sweet in the eyes of her boyfriend*—R L Woods/ *Thanks for the great interview with Cindy Crawford. It brings the word fluff to a new low*—Buzz **2** *n by 1891* An oral error, esp one made by an actor, announcer, etc; lapsus linguae: *A hell of a fluff, talking about Montezuma's revenge to the president of Mexico*

3 *v*: *Show me an actor that never fluffed a line* **4** *n by 1920s* A blunder; misplay

See BIT OF FLUFF, GIVE someone THE FLUFF

◁**fluffhead**▷ *n by 1970s* A frivolous or stupid young woman; =DITZ: *To judge masculinity you need a woman, and not some little fluffhead either*—Village Voice

fluff off *v phr WWII armed forces* To avoid work or duty; shirk; =GOOF OFF [probably a euphemism for *fuck off*]

fluff-off *n WWII armed forces* A sluggard; shirker; =GOLDBRICK, GOOF-OFF

fluff someone **off** *v phr by 1940s* To snub or cut someone; reject someone haughtily: *He thought he was pretty good, so he fluffed us all off*

flugie *See* FLOOZY

fluke *n by 1857* A good or bad stroke of luck; an extraordinary and unpredictable event: *My winning was just a fluke/ We got onto that flight by a fluke* [origin unknown, but perhaps fr *fluke* "flatfish" by way of an early 1800s British slang sense of *flat*, "easy dupe, victim," altered in billiards jargon to *fluke*, to characterize the seeming chicanery of a good stroke of luck]

flukum or **flookum** or **flookem** (FLOO kəm) *early 1920s pitchmen* **1** *n* Cheap and gaudy merchandise **2** *n* Powder to which sugar and water are added to make a soft drink

fluky or **flukey** *adj by 1867* Uncertain, unpredictable, and often unexpected: *It would have been a very fluky shot, even if he happened to have the camera in his hand*—Raymond Chandler

flummadiddle *n by 1854* Nonsense; foolishness; =BOSH

flummox **1** *v by 1837* To spoil; upset; confound: *Fu-Manchu tries to abduct a missionary who has flummoxed his plans in China*—S J Perelman **2** *n by 1851* A failure; disaster; =FUCK-UP: *The solemn commemoration was a total flummox* [fr British dialect, "maul, bewilder"]

flummoxed *adj by 1837* Confused and turbulent; baffling or baffled: *"One never knows, do one," I said, and left him flummoxed*—Lawrence Sanders

flunk *college by 1823* **1** *v* To fail; make a botch of: *I tried selling, but flunked at that* **2** *v* To fail an examination, a course, etc; =BUST: *He flunked the final but passed the course* **3** *v* To give a student a failing grade **4** *n*: *I've got three passes and two flunks* [origin unknown; perhaps a blend of *fail* with *funk*, perhaps echoic of a dull collapse]

flunk out *by 1838* **1** *v phr* To fail; make a botch **2** *v phr* To be dismissed from school for failing work: *The great man had flunked out of Wittenberg*

flush **1** *adj by 1603* Having plenty of money; affluent, esp temporarily; rich: *It took money, and the jazzman wasn't ever too flush*—Stephen Longstreet **2** *v college students by 1940s* To stay away from class; =CUT **3** *v college students by 1960s* =FLUNK **4** *v by 1960s* To reject or ignore someone socially

See FOUR-FLUSH

flusher *n by 1970s* A toilet: *. . . right in the old flusher*—Dan Jenkins
See FOUR-FLUSHER

flush it 1 *v phr college students by 1960s* To fail a course, examination, etc; =FLUNK **2** *interj by 1970s* An exclamation of contempt and disbelief: *I started to explain, but the cop told me to flush it*

◁**flute** or **fluter**▷ *n by 1940s* A male homosexual [fr metaphor of *flute* as "penis," and a homosexual as one who *plays the skin flute*]
See PLAY THE SKIN FLUTE, SKIN FLUTE

fly 1 *adj by 1811* Clever; knowing; alert; shrewd **2** *adj black by about 1900* Stylish; very attractive; =SHARP, SUPERFLY: *. . . driving a Cadillac that's fly*—R Woodley/ *They tell each other they're fly when they look sharp*—Philadelphia Inquirer **3** *v 1960s narcotics* To act in a strange or bizarre way: *The broad must be flying on something*—Philadelphia Journal **4** *v 1960s narcotics* To feel the effects of narcotic intoxication: *About a minute after the fix he was flying* **5** *v by 1970s* To succeed; persuade; =GO OVER •Often in the negative: *They're experts on what will fly and what won't*—Art Buchwald/ *He glanced at Keenan to see if that statement was going to fly*—Playboy **6** *v* To run or travel very fast [the first sense, "clever, alert, etc," is of unknown origin, though it is conjectured that it may refer to the difficulty of catching a *fly* in midair, that it may be cognate with *fledge* and hence mean "accomplished, proven, seasoned," and that it is a corruption of *fla,* a shortening of *flash;* the fifth sense, "succeed, persuade, etc," is fr a cluster of jokes and phrases having to do with the Wright Brothers' and others' efforts to get something off the ground and make it *fly;* the two adjective senses involve either a survival or a revival of an early-19th-century British underworld term of unknown origin]
See BAR-FLY, CATCH FLIES, FRUIT FLY, LET FLY, NO FLIES ON, ON THE FLY, SHOO-FLY, SUPERFLY

fly a kite *v phr underworld by 1940s* To smuggle a letter into or out of prison
See GO FLY A KITE

fly-bait *n by 1940s* A member of Phi Beta Kappa [fr a pun on the name]

fly blind *v phr fr 1920s aviation use* To proceed or make decisions without enough information: *Like most benefits executives, she is largely flying blind when it comes to comparing the performances of health plans*—New York Times

fly-boy *n WWII armed forces* An aircraft pilot, esp an intrepid one in the US Air Force: *The generals are no full-throttle "fly-boys"*—Time

flyby *n by 1950s* A ceremonial or demonstrational passage overhead by an airplane or a group of airplanes: *They saluted the President with a flyby of the newest jets*

fly by the seat of one's **pants 1** *v phr 1930s aviators* To pilot an airplane by feel and instinct rather than by instruments: *The old-time barnstormers had to fly by the seat of their pants* **2** *v phr by 1970s* To proceed or work by instinct and improvisa-

tion, without formal guides or instructive experience: *The teachers are not trained to recognize it. . . . They're flying by the seat of their pants*—Washington Post/ *Every case is different, and every investigator ends up flying by the seat of his (or her) pants*—Sue Grafton
See SEAT-OF-THE-PANTS

fly-chaser *n baseball by 1930s* An outfielder

flychick *n 1940s black* =HIP CHICK

fly cop *n phr* (Variations: **ball** or **bob** or **bull** or **dick** or **mug** may replace **cop**) *by 1859* A detective; plainclothes police officer: *. . . an offer to make him a "fly-cop" or detective*—E Lavine [probably fr *fly,* "clever, shrewd," because of the presumed intelligence of detectives]

flyer or **flier** *n circus by 1890s* A trapeze performer
See TAKE A FLYER

fly high *v phr by 1906* To live in an affluent fashion; live as a successful person

flying *adj by 1940s* Useless; worthless •Used to emphasize terms meaning "something of little value," all probably variations and euphemisms of a *flying fuck*
See HAVE THE RAG ON

flying colors **See** WITH FLYING COLORS

◁**flying frig**▷ **See** TAKE A FLYING FUCK

◂a **flying fuck**▶ *n phr about 1800* Something of very little value; =a DAMN, DIDDLY, a FUCK: *Your take on this isn't worth a flying fuck* [the dated instance, describing a sex act done on horseback, occurs in a broadside ballad called *New Feats of Horsemanship;* the semantics are no more nor less clear than those of simple *fuck*]
See NOT GIVE A DAMN, TAKE A FLYING FUCK

flying-jinny *n by 1906* A merry-go-round; carousel: *The wooden horses of the flying-jinny revolved in the circle to the mechanical music*—Carson McCullers [because the machine was powered by a *jenny* or *jinny,* a mule]

flying time *n phr WWII armed forces* Sleep

fly mug **See** FLY COP

fly off the handle *v phr by 1825* To lose one's temper; =LOSE ONE's COOL

a **fly on the wall** *n phr by 1949* An unseen observer; inconspicuous witness: *A lot of people in NATO would have given a lot to be a fly on the wall at the Warsaw Pact discussions*—ABC World News

fly out *v phr baseball by 1893* To hit a fly ball that is caught for an out

fly right *v phr by 1940s* To be honest, dependable, etc: *He's my son. . . . I want him to fly right*—J and W Hawkins

fly the coop *v phr about 1910* To leave, esp to escape from confinement: *He had flown the coop. . . via a fire-escape*—A Hynd/ *Our Dubie done flew the coop*—Stan Cutler

fly trap *n phr by 1795* The mouth

fly under the radar *v phr by 1990s* =KEEP A LOW PROFILE: *We do our best to fly under the radar of the media and professions so they don't know* *what hit them until it's too late, Reed told them—*Time

FOAF (FOHF) *n by* 1990s: *These colorful experiences always seem to happen to a FOAF (friend of a friend), hardly ever a person with a name, address, and telephone number*—Milwaukee Journal

fodder *See* BUNG FODDER, CANNON FODDER

foe one one *n phr* 1990s *black* Information; facts; =the 411, the SCOOP, the SKINNY [fr *411*, the telephone number called for customers' telephone listings]

fofarraw *See* FOOFOORAW

fog 1 *v* (also **fog it**) *Western by* 1914 To run; speed; hurry **2** *v baseball by* 1930s To throw with great force: *Ole Diz was in his prime then, fogging a fast-ball*—Hal Boyle **3** *v Western by* 1920s To attack; shoot ●Also recorded as 1920s racketeer talk: *I takes me heat an' fogs 'em*—American Mercury [origin unknown; probably a substitution for *smoke* in all senses]
See IN A FOG

fog away *v phr Western by* 1914 To commence shooting; shoot: *I fogged away with my gun*—C G Givens

fog-cutter *n by* 1833 A drink of liquor taken in the morning [supposed to protect one against the danger of the morning *fog*]

fogged out *adj phr narcotics by* 1970s Befuddled and deluded by narcotics: *A lot of people were fogged out and superegotistic in that drugged-out way*—Milwaukee Journal

the **foggiest** *See* NOT HAVE THE FOGGIEST

Foggy Bottom *n phr by* 1950 The US Department of State: *. . . little affinity for the "career boys" of Foggy Bottom*—H S Villard [fr the name of a marshy region in Washington, DC, where the State Department and other federal buildings are located; also an allusion to the murkiness of some policies and pronouncements]

fog it in *v phr baseball by* 1930s To pitch a fastball

fogy or **fogey 1** *n by* 1785 An old person; any very conservative, outdated person; =DODO: *College students today are young fogies* **2** *n armed forces by* 1881 A military longevity allowance, awarded for units of service: *He got his pension and eight fogies* [origin uncertain; perhaps fr French *fougeux,* "fierce, fiery," referring to the doughty spirit of an invalid soldier, whence *fogy,* "fierce, fiery," found by the 1860s; veteran soldiers were called *foggies* in the late 1700s, perhaps because they were regarded as moss-covered with age, *fog* being Scots dialect for "moss"]

Fogeyville *n by* 1990s Old age; senility: *I mean we are talking Fogeyville here!*—comic strip "For Better or for Worse"

foil *n* 1960s *narcotics* A small packet of narcotics; =BAG

fold 1 *v by* 1930s To fail or close, esp in business or show business ●The usual term earlier was *fold up*: *If the club folds. . .*—A J Liebling **2** *v by* 1250 To collapse; surrender; give way; =CAVE: *After the*

President jawboned him unmercifully, the Senator folded **3** *v poker by* 1940s To drop out of a poker game, indicated by putting all one's cards face down on the table

folding *n by* 1930s Money; =FOLDING MONEY: *The socialites lose a handsome wallet stuffed with a liberal supply of folding*—John O'Hara
See GREEN FOLDING

folding money *n phr* (Variations: **cabbage** or **green** or **lettuce** may replace **money**) *by* 1920s Paper money; banknotes, esp in large quantities: *They leave their folding money at home*—John O'Hara/ *. . . lacks the folding green to pick up a nightclub tab*—Hal Boyle

fold out *v phr by* 1980s To abdicate responsibilities; slough off; =COP OUT: *. . . he was not a guy who would just fold out*—Ann Landers column [fr the act of *folding,* dropping out of a poker game]

folkie *n* 1960s A folk singer or folk-music devotee: *The precious youth audience was lost to the folkies and the rockers*—New York Magazine

folkiehood *n by* 1990s The milieu, attitudes, etc, of folk-music performers and devotees: *. . . as sure as she rejects that of ether-dwelling, confessional folkiehood*—Vogue

folknik *n* 1960s A folk-music devotee or enthusiast
See -NIK

folks 1 *n* 1880s *underworld* A band of hoodlums **2** *n* 1990s *street gangs* A gang; one's own gang: *"What does 'folks' mean now?" Grober asks. In unison: "Gangs"*—Milwaukee Journal **3** *n by* 1940s Parents ●Usu used affectionately: *I want to introduce her to my folks* **4** *n by* 1619 Ordinary people; common people; =JUST FOLKS

follow-home robbery *n phr by* 1990s The usually violent robbery of a person whom the criminal has followed home: *As the fear of violent and once-unheard-of crimes such as car-jackings and follow-home robberies permeate the consciousness of suburban America. . .*—Los Angeles Times

follow one's **nose** *v phr by* 1620 To go in the most obvious direction; go straight along

follow something **straight out the window** *v phr by* 1980s To go to the extreme; follow obsessively: *When she gets hold of an idea, she'll follow it straight out the window*

follow through (or **up**) *by* 1940s **1** *v phr* To carry on with the next useful action; finish an action completely; pursue: *Follow up these hints, and you'll find the answer* **2** *n*: *What's the logical follow-through to what he said?*

follow something **up** *by* 1940s **1** *v phr* To carry one's investigation further; pursue a lead **2** *v phr* (also **follow**) To do something appropriate subsequent to something else, or better than something already done: *How will she follow up her best-seller?/ I can't follow that line*

fonk *See* FUNK

fonky *See* FUNKY

food *See* BUNNY FOOD, DOG FOOD, FAST FOOD, JUNK FOOD, SOUL FOOD, SQUIRREL-FOOD

foodaholic *n* by 1980s A compulsive eater; glutton *See* -aholic

food fight *n phr* by 1970s A messy and childish fight among people who smear and spatter each other with food: *It makes for the kind of nice, political food fight that television politics specializes in serving up*—John J Farmer

food for the squirrels *n phr* by 1940s =SQUIRREL-FOOD

foodie 1980s **1** *n* A person who pays unusual attention to food, cuisine, etc; devotee of healthy gourmet cooking and eating: *To be a proper foodie, it little matters where you live as long as you own a "serious" vegetable knife*—New Yorker **2** *adj*: *... San Francisco, foodie capital of the USA*—New York Times [perhaps modeled on *groupie*]

fooey *See* PHOOEY

foofooraw or **fofarraw** or **foo-foo-rah** or **foofaraw** (Foo fə raw) *Western* by 1848 **1** *n* A loud disturbance; uproar: *Ivar, what's all the foofaraw about the Ellerbee case?*—Lawrence Sanders **2** *n* Gaudy clothing and accessories, esp the latter **3** *n* Ostentation; proud show: *The refreshing thing about it is the lack of drumbeating and foo-foo-rah*—Saturday Evening Post [origin uncertain; perhaps fr Spanish *fanfarrón*, "braggart"; perhaps fr French *frou-frous*, "frills"]

fool *n* by 1920s An adept or enthusiast in what is indicated: *Lindy was a flying fool* [perhaps because the person is devoted to the extent of *fool*ishness] *See* TOMFOOL

fool around **1** *v phr* by 1875 To pass one's time idly; putter about; loaf **2** *v phr* by 1875 To joke and tease; =KID AROUND: *Mark, stop fooling around and get to work* **3** *v phr* by 1970s To adventure sexually, esp adulterously; =PLAY AROUND, SLEEP AROUND: *He had never fooled around or seen a prostitute until he came to us*—Xaviera Hollander/ *As I told Lipranzer a long time ago, Carolyn did not fool around*—Scott Turow

fool around with *v phr* by 1875 To play or tamper with; coquette with: *I told you not to fool around with that gun; now you've shot Aunt Bessie/Better not fool around with him, he's a karate black belt*

foolish powder *n phr* 1930s *underworld* Heroin

◁**foop**▷ *v* 1970s *college students* To do homosexual sex acts [probably a backward version of British *poof*, "male homosexual, effeminate male," fr early 1900s Australian; perhaps fr the exclamation *poof* or *pooh*, regarded as effeminate]

◁**fooper**▷ *n* 1970s *college students* A homosexual

foot *See* BIG FOOT, BLISTERFOOT, DOUGHFOOT, FLATFOOT, GIVE someone THE FOOT, HAVE ONE FOOT IN THE GRAVE, HEAVY-FOOT, HOTFOOT, PADDLEFOOT, PUT one's FOOT IN IT, PUT one's FOOT IN one's MOUTH, RABBITFOOT, SHOOT oneself IN THE FOOT, SLEWFOOT, TANGLEFOOT, TENDERFOOT, WEB-FOOT

football *See* GUINEA FOOTBALL, ITALIAN FOOTBALL

football around *v phr* by 1980s To tout or hawk loudly and often: *The decreased sales of housecoats is caused by being footballed around too much*—National Public Radio news [perhaps fr the notion of *kicking something around* rather than dealing with it sensibly and seriously]

footed *See* LEAD-FOOTED, LIGHT-FOOTED

foot-in-mouth disease *n phr* by 1960s The uttering of embarrassing, stupid, or indiscreet speech: *... Pat Robertson, who regularly displays symptoms of foot-in-mouth disease*—Milwaukee Journal [blend of the veterinary term *hoof-and-mouth disease* and the idiom *put one's foot in one's mouth*; *put one's foot in it*, "blunder foolishly," is found by 1858]

foot it by 1831 **1** *v phr* To walk: *A bus is OK during non-rush-hours if you've been footing it too long*—New York Times **2** *v phr* To escape by running; =BEAT IT: *He stopped all of a sudden and said, "Foot it, Sonny! Foot it!"*—Claude Brown

footprint **1** *n* 1990s A history of activity; record; =TRACK RECORD: *Reporters were wondering about the Justice's footprint* **2** *n* 1990s The horizontal space needed for a machine, appliance, etc: *The new computers have a very small footprint*

footshot *n Army* by 1970s An act, choice, utterance, etc, that damages one's reputation or standing: *Saying "stuff it" out loud was a real footshot* [fr *shoot oneself in the foot*]

foot soldier *n* 1990s A lower-ranking member of a corporation, regime, etc: *Goth's role as an SS officer and faithful foot soldier of the Third Reich is preserved*—New Yorker/ *... filtered through the hazy surmises of the Cleveland footsoldiers*—New York Times

foot the bill *v phr* by 1819 To pay the charges; =PICK UP THE TAB

footwork *See* FANCY FOOTWORK

fooy *See* PHOOEY

foozle **1** *v* by 1890s To blunder; spoil by bungling; botch: *I rather foozled my first attempt at acting* **2** *n* by 1890s An error; =BONER **3** *n* by 1855 A conservative, out-of-date person, esp an old man; =DODO, FOGY [sense 3 is perhaps a humorous pronunciation of *fossil*]

for a loop *See* THROW someone FOR A LOOP

for all it (or one) is worth *adv phr* by 1899 To the utmost; with all one's might: *She's playing the wronged woman game for all she's worth/ Push that idea for all it's worth*

for cat's (or Pete's) sake *interj* first form by 1921, second by 1903 An exclamation of emphasis, surprise, impatience, disbelief, dismay, etc; =FOR CRYING OUT LOUD: *For cat's sake, get moving!* [euphemisms for *for God's sake, for Christ's sake*]

for crying out loud (or in a bucket) *interj* 1920s An exclamation of emphasis, surprise, disbelief, impatience, etc; =FOR THE LOVE OF PETE: *For crying out loud, what half-assed thing has he done now?* [a euphemism for *for Christ's sake*]

forecastle (or sea) lawyer *n phr nautical* by 1829 A sailor or other person who habitually complains and criticizes, pretends to have an intricate knowledge of rules and regulations, demands rights, etc; =LATRINE LAWYER

for free *adv phr* by 1940s Without charge; gratis; =FREE GRATIS: *They gave him a sandwich absolutely for free*—Arthur Daley [based on Yiddish *far gornisht,* "for nothing"]

forget about it *interj* (also **fuhgedaboudit, fuhgeddabaudit**) by 1940s An exclamation of dismissal and scorn •The variants represent New York City pronunciations: *Omerta. The code of silence for a sacred brotherhood. Well, fuhgeddaboudit. Every time you turn around lately, a member of the Mafia is testifying at a trial*—Time/ *The latest on Joey Buttafuoco's comedic debut: Fuggeddabautit*—Milwaukee Journal [said to be also a euphemism for *fuck it*]

forget it by 1900 **1** *interj* An injunction to put something out of one's hopes, concern, etc, esp because it is impossible: *If you thought you were next in line around here, forget it/ Forget it, she never did intend to go/ I can get up there most of the time, but in winter, forget it* **2** *interj* An exclamation of pardon; a token of forgiveness; =DON'T GIVE IT A SECOND THOUGHT: *Hell no, I didn't mind. Forget it*

forget you teenagers by 1970s **1** *interj* An invitation or command to leave; =BUG OFF **2** *interj* An exclamation of rejection or refusal; =NO WAY

for one's **health** *adv phr* by 1900 Lightly or frivolously; for one's delightful good •Always used ironically and in the negative: *I didn't make this damn stupid trip for my health, you know*

for (or **fer**) **instance** *n phr* by 1940s An example; an instance: *I'd understand the point better if you gave me a couple of concrete for instances* [fr a Yiddish pattern]

◁**fork**▷ *v* by 1940s To cheat; maltreat; take advantage of; =FUCK, SHAFT: *I hoped he'd take care of us, but we got forked* [a euphemism for *fuck*]

forkball 1920s baseball **1** *n* A pitch thrown from a forklike finger grip that drops sharply as it comes to the plate **2** *n* (also **forked ball**) A spitball; =SPITTER

forked-eight or **bent-eight** *n* 1950s hot rodders A V–8 engine or a car having such an engine

for keeps *adv phr* by 1884 Forever; permanently: *They put him away for keeps/ She wanted to be married for keeps*
See PLAY FOR KEEPS

forkhander *n* baseball by 1950s A left-handed pitcher; =SOUTHPAW

◁**forking**▷ by 1940s **1** *adj* Wretched; disgusting: *I won't eat this forking stuff* **2** *adv* Very; extremely: *He sounded forking mad* [a euphemism for *fucking*]

fork over (or **up** or **out**) *v phr* first form by 1835 To pay; give; contribute: *Fork up the cash*—E Conradi/ *I imagine he used a picture. . . to make you fork over the dough*—R S Prather

forks *n* by 1848 Fingers: *Get your forks off that*
See RAIN CATS AND DOGS

◁**fork you**▷ by 1940s *interj* =FUCK YOU

for laughs (or **kicks**) *adv phr* by 1940s For sim-

ple pleasure, usu a wicked pleasure: *Girl mobsters beating up other girls simply for laughs*—Newsweek

form *n* horse-racing by 1940s The record of past performances by a horse, team, competitor, etc; =the BOOK, TRACK RECORD: *What's the form on General Electric this quarter?/ The form on the little gelding is super* [fr *form,* "the fitness or condition of a racehorse," which is found by 1760]

form sheet *n phr* horse-racing by 1940s A printed record of past performance; =CHART, DOPE SHEET

for openers (or **starters**) *adv phr* by 1960s As a beginning; as a first move or suggestion: *For openers, there's the approach via the Staten Island ferry*—New York Times/ *So, try this for openers*—Pulpsmith/ *expensive. . . for starters*—Armistead Maupin [fr the *openers,* "cards of a certain value," required in draw poker for beginning the betting]

for real by 1940s **1** *adj phr* Believably existent; as good or bad as seems; authentic: *But if you ask if they are for real, the answer is right there. . . I often wondered if the bastard was for real*—Milwaukee Journal **2** *adv phr* Really; truly: *I'm gonna for real do it, right now* [based on Yiddish *far emmes,* "for true?"]

for serious by 1950s **1** *adv phr* Seriously; with a sober intent: *The Yanks took the field for serious*—Robert Ruark **2** *adj phr*: *He was for serious but she wasn't* [perhaps based on *for real*]

◁**for shit**▷ *adv phr* by 1940s At all; in the least degree; =TO SAVE one's NECK: *They can't drive for shit*—Elmore Leonard

for (or **fer**) **sure** (or **shure** or **shurr**) by 1553 **1** *adv phr* Definitely; certainly •This old phrase was briefly resurrected in the California Valley Girls talk of the 1980s: *He is for sure a nerd* **2** *affirmation* Yes: *When he asked if I'd do it I said fer sure I would*

for the birds *adj phr* WWII armed forces Inferior; undesirable; of small worth; =LOUSY: *I won't buy it. . . It's for the birds*—John Crosby/ *A single bed is for single men, it's for the birds*—Sidney Skolsky [a euphemistic shortening of *shit for the birds;* because some birds eat animal feces, it is the equivalent of *bullshit* or *horseshit*]

for (or **just for**) **the hell of it** *adv phr* by 1934 For no definite or useful reason; for fun; casually: *He does it, apparently, just for the adrenaline hell of it*—New Yorker

for the long ball **See** GO FOR THE LONG BALL

for (or **over**) **the long haul** *adv phr* by 1930s For a long while; for a period of difficulty and strain: *. . . the slump in sales of women's apparel is here for the long haul*—Milwaukee Journal [the *long haul,* "a transcontinental run," is found in bus-drivers' talk by 1938]

for the love of Pete (or **Mike**) *interj* by 1910 An exclamation of emphasis, surprise, impatience, disbelief, dismay, etc; =FOR CRYING OUT LOUD: *I already did it, for the love of Pete!*

forthwith *n* police by 1950s An order to report immediately

◀**fortune cookie**▶ *n phr early 1990s* A person of Asian origin or descent; =BUDDAHEAD: *In the Korean market dispute, blacks taunted the Koreans with cries of "Fortune cookies!"*—New Yorker

forty-deuce *n 1970s* Forty-second Street in New York City: *Forty-deuce is what its seamy inhabitants call 42d Street*—Newark Star Ledger

forty-eight *n WWII Navy* A weekend pass

forty-four *n by 1950s* A prostitute [fr the rhyme with *whore*]

forty-'leven *by 1860* **1** *n* An indefinite large number **2** *modifier*: *about forty-'leven times*

fortysomething *late 1980s* **1** *n* A person between forty and fifty years old; =BABY BOOMER: *The fortysomething reminisced about seeing them on the same bill with Sonny and Cher*—Newsweek **2** *modifier*: *the fortysomething generation/ fortysomething self-indulgence* [based on *Thirtysomething*, the title of a television series]

forty (or **six) ways to Sunday** *adv phr by 1840* In every possible manner, direction, etc; comprehensively: *She had him beat forty ways to Sunday* [origin unknown]

forty winks *n phr by 1828* A short sleep; nap: *He caught forty winks and perked right up*

forward in the saddle *See* LEAN FORWARD IN THE SADDLE

forwards *n 1960s narcotics* Pills of amphetamine or its derivatives [probably an allusion to *speed* in the same sense, with perhaps a by-reference to the *fast forward* control of a tape player]

FOS (pronounced as separate letters) *medical by 1980s* A patient whose symptoms are psychosomatic [abbreviation of *full of shit*]

fossil *n by 1850s* An old or very conservative person; =ALTER KOCKER, FOGY: *If I got to kiss old fossils to hold this job I'm underpaid*—Hal Boyle

fotog *See* PHOTOG

foul ball **1** *n phr prizefight by 1920s* An inferior fighter; =PALOOKA **2** *n phr by 1920s* A useless and inadequate person; =DULL TOOL, LOSER: *It is Scotty's boast that he hasn't sent a sponsor a foul ball yet*—J McCallum **3** *n phr by 1930s* A person having deviant convictions and attitudes; outsider; =ODDBALL [fr baseball]

fouled up *by 1940s* **1** *adj phr* Spoiled by bungling; confused; hopelessly tangled; =FUCKED UP: *. . . never seen anything more fouled up than what happened yesterday at the White House*—J Marlow **2** *adj phr* Damaged; impaired: *The kids were fouled up. . . came from bad homes, went to bad schools*—New York Times [a euphemism for *fucked up*]

foulmouth *n by 1640* A person inclined to utter obscenities, profanity, etc

foulmouthed *adj by 1596* Obscene and profane in speech; filthy: *a foulmouthed retort*

foul out *v phr basketball by 1980s* To be removed from a game after committing too many fouls

foul up *v phr by 1940s* To ruin and confuse a project, assignments, etc; display one's ineptitude and futility; =FUCK UP, SNAFU: *I fouled up my very first chance to be a reporter* [a euphemism for *fuck up*; possibly of naval origin, since *foul* is used of ropes, lines, anchors, sea bottoms, etc, in ways not characteristic of non-nautical speech]

foul-up *by 1940s* **1** *n* A confused, tangled, hopeless situation; botch: *It's supposed to be a concert series, but it's a total foul-up* **2** *n* A person who consistently blunders; bungler; =FUCK-UP: *Why put that notorious foul-up in charge?* [a euphemism for *fuck-up*]

foundry *See* HASH FOUNDRY, NUT HOUSE

four *See* TEN FOUR

four-and-one *black by 1950s* **1** *n* Friday, the fifth day of the week **2** *n* Payday

four-bagger *n baseball by 1883* A home run: *It was Bobby's 31st four-bagger and his fourth at Ebbets Field*—J Reichler

four-banger *n 1950s hot rodders* A four-cylinder motor or car

four-bit *adj by 1840s* Costing 50 cents; half-dollar: *. . . to smoke four-bit cigars*—James T Farrell

four bits *n phr by 1840s* Half a dollar; 50 cents [originally a *bit* was a Mexican or Spanish *real*, worth $12\frac{1}{2}$ cents, or a part of a more valuable coin, such that eight would make a dollar; ultimately fr 18th-century British slang *bit*, "a small piece of money"]

four-by-four *n Army & truckers by 1940s* A four-wheel-drive vehicle having four forward gears

four-corner town *n phr by 1980s* A very small town; a crossroads: *We were flabbergasted by these four-corner towns with four bars*—Milwaukee Journal

four-eyes *n by 1874* A person who wears eyeglasses

four-flush *by 1896* **1** *v* To live by sponging off others, or by pretense and fraud **2** *v* To cheat; swindle; victimize **3** *modifier*: *Four-flushing hustlers who really knew how to gamble*—Louis Armstrong [fr poker player's attempt to bluff when he has *four* cards of one suit showing and one of another suit not showing]

four-flusher *n by 1904* A bluffer or fraud; cheat; swindler

the four hundred *n phr about 1890* The set of socially prominent people, esp in a given place; the social elite [fr the list, attributed to Ward McAllister, of *four hundred* socially desirable people]

four-letter man *by 1920s* **1** *n phr* A stupid man •From the four letters of *dumb* **2** *n phr* A detestable man; a contemptible wretch; =PRICK, SHIT •From the four letters of *shit* [fr the notion of *four-letter word*, "dirty words," influenced in the US by athletic *letters*, "school initials," awarded to athletes and worn on a sweater]

four nines *n phr by 1970s* Something pure or very nearly pure: *That is four nines, or 99.99 pure gold*—Time

four-O *adj WWII Navy* Perfect; splendid; =A-OK [fr the point system used in Navy efficiency ratings, where 4.0 is the top rating; it is also the numerical equivalent of the grade A in most colleges]

the 411 *n phr* *1990s black* The facts; the information; =FOE ONE ONE, the SCOOP, the SKINNY: *The 4–1–1 on Urban Cool*—New York Times [fr *411*, the telephone number called for information on customers' telephone listings]

four on the floor *n phr* *1970s* A gearshift lever emerging from the floor of a car, and controlling four speeds; hence, standard as distinct from automatic shift: *This little baby's got four on the floor and leather bucket seats*

four-pointer *college students by 1960s* **1** *n* A grade of A for an examination or course **2** *n* A superior student [fr the grade-point system where an A rates at four points]

fours *See* DOWN ON ALL FOURS

four sheets to the wind *See* THREE SHEETS TO THE WIND

four-striper *n WWI Navy* A naval captain, wearing four stripes as insignia

four-time loser *See* THREE-TIME LOSER

four-wheeler *n truckers by 1960s* An automobile; =CAGE

four wide ones *n phr baseball by 1970s* A base on balls; a walk, esp an intentional pass

fox 1 *v by 1631* To deceive; mislead; outwit; =OUTFOX: *He tried to fox me with that phony accent, and did* **2** *n teenagers & black by 1940s* A beautiful, sexually attractive woman, or in teenage use, man [fr *foxy*]

foxhole *n WWII armed forces* A hole in which one conceals oneself, esp one dug for that purpose by a soldier

fox paw *n phr by 1785* A faux pas

foxy *adj college students by 1895* Attractive; stylish; sexually desirable; =DANG[1]: *She was 22 years old, a real foxy little chick with auburn hair*—J Eszterhas/ *. . . but she must be one foxy lady*—Lawrence Sanders

fracture *by 1940s* **1** *v* To elicit loud laughter from; =LAY THEM IN THE AISLES: *We're a riot, hey. We play all kinds of funny stuff. We fracture the people*—Max Shulman **2** *v* To evoke a strong reaction: *That flips me out and fractures me, man*

fractured *adj by 1940s* Drunk

frag *Vietnam War armed forces* **1** *v* To kill or wound someone, esp a detested officer of one's own unit, typically by throwing a fragmentation grenade at him **2** *v* To kill; =ICE, WASTE: *If I hadn't've done it, he would've fragged me*—George V Higgins

fragged *adj car-racing by 1970s* Ruined; blown-out: *. . . countless fragged Ferrari engines, including two that disintegrated under a CD tester's heavy foot*—Car and Driver

fraidy (or 'fraidy) cat *n phr by about 1910* A timorous person, esp a boy; coward

frail *n by 1905* A woman, esp a young woman: *. . . in persuading frails to divulge what they know*—E Lavine

frail eel *n phr black by 1940s* An attractive woman;

=FOX: *I can get any frail eel I wants*—Zora Neale Hurston

frame 1 *n by 1600* The human body; physique; build, esp that of a woman **2** *n homosexuals by 1950s* A heterosexual man attractive to homosexuals; hunk **3** *n by 1910* A unit of a game or other contest; =STANZA: *Mel Queen lined a single to right field to open that frame*—R McGowen **4** *n by 1914* The incrimination of an innocent person with false evidence; =FRAME-UP: *. . . just the victim of a frame*—J Evans **5** *v*: *I was framed*—Joseph Auslander

frame-up 1 *n by 1913* The incrimination of an innocent person with false evidence: *I'll prove to you it's a frame-up*—W Weeks **2** *n pitchmen by 1940s* A display of goods for sale

frame up *v phr by 1899* To concoct; fabricate: *What lie are you going to frame up for your father*—James Forbes [perhaps fr the carpenter's term for erecting the *frame* of a new building]

frame someone up *v phr about 1900* To incriminate an innocent person with false evidence: *They couldn't get him legally, so they framed him up with a phony burglary charge*

the franchise *n phr sports by 1980s* A superstar athlete who constitutes the drawing and earning power of a team: *He's not just the front runner, he's the franchise/ There goes the franchise*—New York Times

frank *n 1920s* A frankfurter; =WEENIE

Franken- *combining word 1990s* Designating what is indicated as being genetically engineered or otherwise strangely produced: *Frankenchips*—Time/ *Frankenfood*—MacNeill/Lehrer News Hour/ *Frankentomato*—New York Times [shortening of *Frankenstein*, name of the scientist in Mary Shelley's novel]

Franklin *n by 1990s* A hundred-dollar bill; =C-NOTE: *He peels off another five Franklins*—New Yorker [fr its portrait of Benjamin *Franklin*]

frantic *jazz musicians about 1940* **1** *adj* Excellent; wonderful; =COOL **2** *adj* Conventional; bourgeois; =UNCOOL: *The man who cares is now derided for being "frantic"*—Herbert Gold

◁**frapping**▷ *adj 1960s* Wretched; accursed; =DAMN, FUCKING: *I need a frapping medic like a hole in the head*—People [a euphemism for *fucking*]

frat 1 *n college students by 1895* A college fraternity **2** *n* (also **frat rat**) *college students by 1895* A fraternity member **3** *n 1960s teenagers* A male student who conforms to middle-class norms of conduct and dress: *A "frat". . . is a youth who dresses neatly and conforms to the accepted patterns*—New York Times

fraternize *v WWII armed forces* To associate closely with inhabitants of an enemy country, esp to consort sexually with the women

frau (FROU) *n by 1902* One's wife: *. . . and escort your incomparable frau to a tea dance*—K Brush/ *. . . his reward from the frau*—Hal Boyle [fr German] a **fraud** *n phr* by 1850 A deceptive person; one posing as what he is not; =PHONY

to a **frazzle** *adv phr* by 1865 Completely; totally; to a ruined condition: *After the marathon I was beat to a frazzle* [fr dialect *frazzle,* "frayed end of a rope"]

frazzled 1 *adj* (also **on the frazz**) by 1872 Exhausted; tired in nerve and flesh; =PLAYED OUT: *He was frazzled after three weeks without a break* **2** *adj* by 1940s Drunk

freak ◁**1**▷ *n* by 1891 A strange or eccentric person **2** *n college students* by 1895 An expert; specialist; very good student **3** *n* by 1908 A devotee or enthusiast; =BUFF, FAN ◀**4**▶ *n jazz musicians* by 1940s A male homosexual: *"Freak" is a homosexual*—Stephen Longstreet **5** *n* by 1960s =HIPPIE **6** *v* 1960s To behave strangely and disorientedly as if intoxicated by a psychedelic drug; =FREAK OUT: *His publisher for the last two books "sort of freaked" when they got a look at this one*—New York Magazine **7** *v* (also **freak off**) *prostitutes* by 1960s To do violent and deviant sex acts **8** *n* 1990s *teenagers* An attractive person

-freak *combining word* A devotee or enthusiast; addict; =BUG, BUFF, NUT: *plant freak/ radio freak/ porn-freak*

See ACID FREAK, ECOFREAK, HARD-ROAD FREAK, JESUS FREAKS, METH HEAD, PEEK FREAK, SPEEDFREAK

◁**freak-ass**▷ *adj* by 1990s Strange; freakish: *Some freak-ass accident*—Carsten Stroud

freaker *n* 1990s =PHONE PHREAK

freaking by 1920s **1** *adj* Wretched; accursed; =DAMN, FUCKING: *. . . who's got so much freaking talent it just turns your stomach*—Car and Driver/ *. . . all the freaking way to the bank*—Playboy **2** *adv*: *The ball just freaking found its way through*—Milwaukee Journal **3** *n* 1960s Violent and deviant sex acts: *And there were numerous reports of lewd behavior; "freaking," after all, is a slang term for adventuresome sex*—Los Angeles Times [a euphemism for *fucking*]

freak out (or **up**) 1960s *narcotics* **1** *v phr* To have intense and disturbing hallucinations and other reactions from psychedelic drugs **2** *v phr* To go out of touch with reality, with or without narcotics; become irrational, esp frantically so; be intoxicated; =FLIP OUT: *. . . plus the chance to freak out, speak in tongues or talk nonsense*—Herbert Gold/ *I saw those golden arches and I freaked out, because I'd just seen the buttes and all that great stuff*—New Yorker **3** *v phr* To become very excited and exhilarated, as if intoxicated with narcotics **4** *v phr* To abandon conventional values and attitudes; =DROP OUT

freak-out 1960s *narcotics* **1** *n* An instance of freaking out: *. . . a period which one feminist writer has called one of "mass freak-outs all over the place"*—Esquire/ *. . . the same freakouts, the same strange clothes*—New Yorker **2** *n* A person who is freaked out **3** *n* A frightening or nightmarish drug experience; =BAD TRIP, BUMMER **4** *n* A congregation of hippies

freak someone **out** *v phr* 1960s *narcotics* To cause someone to show the irrationality, lethargy, excitement, withdrawal, etc, of a psychedelic experience: *The heavy metal sound freaked him out*

freak trick *n phr prostitutes* by 1970s A man who demands very exotic or brutal sexual activity: *. . . the victim of a "freak trick," a customer who gets his kicks from brutally beating girls*—Xaviera Hollander

freaky *adj* 1960s *narcotics* Having the qualities of a freak or a freak-out; =FAR OUT: *I think it would be freaky to have an affair with my barber*—Playboy/ *There is nothing bohemian, or beat, or hippie, or freaky about them. They are straights, uptight*—Saturday Review

freckles *n* WWII *Navy & Marines* Tobacco for rolling cigarettes

fred *n* 1980s *students* A despised person; =GEEK, JERK: *When Mark missed an easy shot. . . his friends called him a fred* [fr the name of a character in the television show and movie *The Flintstones*]

Freddie Mac *n phr* by 1980s The Federal Home Loan Mortgage Corporation, which buys mortgages from lenders

Freddy *n* by 1990s An employee of the National Forest Service: *"Not much to hunt around here with that type of ammo except Freddies." "Freddies?" "Employees of the. . . Forest Service, that's what the eco-terrorists call us"*—TV show X-Files

free *See* FOR FREE, HOME FREE

free-and-easy *n* fr late 1700s A saloon or other bibulous social center

freebase or **free base it** *v* or *v phr* 1970s *narcotics* To use cocaine by heating it and inhaling the smoke, its most powerful essence: *The addiction problem seems to be compounded by the fact that so many cokeheads are freebasing it*

freebie or **freebee** or **freeby** *n black* about 1900 Anything given or enjoyed free of charge: *That meal was a freebie and it didn't cost me anything*—Louis Armstrong/ *Holiday Inn bartenders are enjoined from giving freebies to customers, no matter how much they spend*—Time

free fall *n phr* by 1919 An extremely rapid and unhindered descent ●First used of a rocket returning to earth; then mainly of a parachutist who had not yet opened the parachute: *the bank is trying to slow the free fall of the Mexican peso/ the Russian economy is in free fall*

free gratis (GRA təs) **1** *adv phr* by 1883 Without charge; =FOR FREE ●In earliest form *free, gratis, and for nothing*: *The Congressmen traveled free gratis* **2** *adj phr*: *a free-gratis perk/ free-gratis tickets* [fr combination of *free* with Latin *gratis,* "free"]

freek *n* by 1940s Frequency: *Check the freek meter/ . . . the coroner's dispatch freek*—Michael Connelly

freeload by 1940s **1** *v* To be fed, entertained, supported, etc, without charge; live parasitically; =SPONGE: *They will successfully free load the rest of their lives*—Hal Boyle/ *. . . who gives freeloading* *off a famous father a bad name*—Milwaukee Journal **2** *n*: *During the depression women free loads were rare*—J Cannon

freeloader *by 1930s* **1** *n* A person who freeloads; =MOOCHER: *Congressmen are great freeloaders*—L Mortimer **2** *n* A gathering or party with free refreshments: *Somebody was tossing a free-loader over on Park Avenue*—J Bainbridge

freeloading *by 1940s* **1** *v* Eating, drinking, etc, without paying: *Free loading has diminished*—J Cannon **2** *modifier*: *my freeloading cousins/ your freeloading pals*

free lunch *n phr by 1854* Something had without paying for it; an uncompensated pleasure; a perquisite or gratuity •The date shows first occurrence of the saloon-food sense mentioned in the etymology: *... pushing the free lunch*—Wall Street Journal [fr the former custom of giving customers free food called *free lunch* in saloons]
See THERE'S NO FREE LUNCH

free-o *n by 1980s* Something received without charge; =FREEBIE: *So he picks up a few free-o's here and there*—California

free (or **freeworld**) **people** *n phr* prison *by 1970s* People who are not prison inmates, esp guards, wardens, etc

free-range *adj by 1960s* Unconfined; free to roam: *The Mall of America is not just one more amalgam of frozen-yogurt stands and packs of free-range adolescents in Guess jeans*—New York Times [fr the distinction between *free-range* chickens and battery chickens, which are raised in confinement]

free ride **1** *n phr* baseball *by 1980s* A base on balls; a walk **2** *n phr* poker *by 1940s* A card received without betting, because no one wished to start the betting on the previous round **3** *n phr by 1899* Something received without paying
See GET A FREE RIDE

free-rider *n* labor union *by 1950s* A nonunion worker who benefits from the pay and advantages gained by a union

freeside *adv* prison *by 1950s* Outside the walls of a prison: *He yearns to live freeside again*

free skate *n phr by 1990s* Something simple and easy; =PICNIC, PIECE OF CAKE: *This lawsuit isn't a free skate*—Denver radio talk show [fr the skating-rink custom of occasionally allowing an unpaid period of skating]

free ticket **1** *n phr by 1940s* General freedom of action, esp of forbidden action; license; carte blanche: *He thinks the uniform gives him a free ticket to be a shitheel* **2** *n phr* (also **free ride, free transit, free transportation**) baseball *by 1917* A base on balls; walk

free-vee *n by 1970s* Nonpay television: *Well, pay-TV proved free-vee wrong*—Toronto Star

free-wheeling **1** Independence of action and initiative; blithe and unconstrained indulgence: *No free-wheeling here, you do things strictly our way* **2** *modifier*: *Jonathan himself tries opium, hash, freewheeling sex, gliders*—Playboy **3** *n* Liberal

spending; easy munificence: *the free-wheeling of the new rich* **4** *modifier*: *... the free-wheeling out-of-towner*—Hal Boyle [fr the feature of certain 1930s cars permitting them to coast *freely* without being slowed by the engine]

freeworld **1** *n* prison *by 1950s* Life outside prison; unincarcerated living **2** *modifier*: *... what they called free-world punks, guys who'd been queer even before they got sent up*—Ezra Hannon

freeze **1** *n by 1930s* A stopping of change, esp in various monetary matters: *a freeze on profits/ nuclear freeze* **2** *v*: *The government denies it wants to freeze interest rates* **3** *v by 1848* To stay or become motionless: *The cop hollered to him to freeze right there/ Your best bet is to freeze and wait. You can't get away*—Nelson Algren **4** *v by 1861* To treat someone with deliberate hauteur; snub; cut; =PUT THE FREEZE ON someone: *Next time she froze me mercilessly* **5** *v by 1607* To inspire terror: *His scream froze me* **6** *v* (also **freeze up**) *by 1970s* To become immobile and ineffective from fear; =CLANK, PANIC: *The lifeguard should have dived in for the boy, but she froze*
See IN COLD STORAGE

freeze one's **ass** *v phr by 1940s* To become cold; freeze: *Get into your winter coat, before you freeze your ass*—Elmore Leonard

freeze frame *n phr 1990s* A stopped or suspended condition: *Secret police files provide the historian of intelligence with a freeze frame from the secret world*—New York Times/ *The L.A. riots put the mayoral campaign into freeze frame*—New York Times [fr the stopping of a movie, video cassette, etc, on one image]

freeze-out *n by 1883* The absence of cooperation, information, etc; a blank: *... this total freeze-out on details for big Ray*—Erich Segal

freeze someone **out** *v phr by 1891* To exclude someone; discriminate against someone: *When I wanted to get into the game they froze me out*

freight **See** PAY THE FREIGHT, PULL one's FREIGHT

◁**French**▷ *by about 1917* **1** *n* Cunnilingus or fellatio; =the FRENCH WAY **2** *v*: *Then the perverse chap actually Frenched her!*
See PARDON MY FRENCH

French-inhale *by 1940s* **1** *n* The trick of exhaling smoke by mouth and immediately reinhaling it by nose **2** *modifier*: *He continued to smoke in this "French inhale" style*—J D Salinger

French kiss *by 1920s* **1** *n phr* A kiss in which the tongue of one person explores the oral cavity of another, and vice versa; =SOUL KISS **2** *v*: *They French-kissed and perhaps more*

French leave *n phr by 1771* Departure without notice or permission, esp going AWOL from a military post

French letter (or **safe**) *n phr by 1856* A condom; =RUBBER: *He was too shy to go in and buy a French letter*

French postcard *n phr by 1920s* A pornographic photograph, such as was fancied to be sold by furtive characters pulling at one's sleeve in the streets of Paris [found by 1849 in the form *French print*]

◁**French tickler**▷ *n phr by 1916* A condom with added variegated surfaces, spirals, fins, etc, to increase vaginal stimulation

French (or Spanish) walk *by 1940s* **1** *n phr* A painful and humiliating means of hurrying one by holding his seat and neck forcing him to walk; =the BUM'S RUSH **2** *v* (also **walk Spanish**) : *Mike Spanish-walked him swiftly across the little space*—W R Burnett/ *Smith. . . was an expert at walking 'em Spanish*—New Yorker •*walk Spanish* is attested from the early 1800s [said to be fr the custom of pirates, in the *Spanish Main*, of forcing prisoners to *walk* while holding them by the neck so that their toes barely touched the deck]

◁the **French way**▷ *n phr* Cunnilingus or fellatio [fr the conviction expressed in the classic couplet: The French they are a funny race/ They fight with their feet and fuck with their face]

fresh 1 *adj by 1848* Impudent; disrespectful; saucy; =CHEEKY: *Don't be fresh to your Momma or I'll belt you one* **2** *adj by 1870s* Flirtatious; sexually bold; =FAST: *I'm not that kind of girl, so don't be fresh* **3** *adj 1980s* black and teenage Aloof and uninvolved; =COOL •In 1990s use increasingly modified: *funky fresh, stupid fresh*, etc: *"We hang out with him because he's fresh," said Jesse. . .* —New York Daily News/ *Word up, fool. We be fresh tonight*—Carsten Stroud [first two senses perhaps related to German *frech*, "impudent"; third sense said to have originated with a 1970s rock group called the Fantastic Romantic Five MCs, who said "We're *fresh* out of the pack, you gotta stand back, we got one Puerto Rican and the rest are black"]

fresh as a daisy *adj phr by 1815* Brisk; vigorous; unfatigued: *He arrived back fresh as a daisy before their fax came through*—Milwaukee Journal

fresh dip *n phr 1990s teenagers* Casual clothing

freshie *n college students by 1847* A first-year college student [fr *freshman*]

fresh meat 1 *n phr* prison *by 1930s* New inmates ◁**2**▷ *n phr* homosexuals *by 1970s* A new homosexual partner

fresh one 1 *n phr* prison *by 1930s* A new prisoner **2** *n phr* homosexuals *by 1970s* =FRESH MEAT

fresh out *adv phr by 1830s* Without; recently not available; =OUT: *We're fresh out of bananas, Missus*

fribble *n by 1832* A trifle; a piece of inanity: *For every zappow fribble, there were equal servings of socially redeeming food for thought*—Newsweek

Friday *See* GAL FRIDAY, TGIF

fried 1 *adj by 1926* Drunk **2** *adj* underworld *about 1930* Electrocuted **3** *adj 1980s teenagers* Exhausted; =BURNED OUT; FRAZZLED: *Apparently, Maurice White's voice is fried*—Milwaukee Journal/ *Yeah, I know that fix destroyed the file system, but I was fried when I put it in*—Hacker's Dictionary

fried egg 1 *n phr* West Point *by 1908* A showy brass military hat decoration **2** *n phr* WWII armed forces The Japanese flag: *. . . sunk about everything the Japs owned with a fried egg on its masthead*—Robert Ruark

fried shirt *n phr by 1905* =BOILED SHIRT

friendly 1 *n* WWII armed forces In wartime, a plane, ship, soldier, civilian, etc, of one's own side: *Friendlies. . . sometimes used to designate townspeople who cooperate with the Americans*—New York Times **2** *n* sports *by 1980s* An exhibition game: *Even if some current 18-year-old blossoms in the so-called friendlies, exhibition games. . .* —Milwaukee Journal

-friendly *combining word 1980* computer Easy, convenient, or amenable for what is specified: *The new PCs are quite user-friendly/ Works of art like these are more viewer-friendly than post-modernist art of 10 years ago*—New York Times/ *The Saudi desert is not exactly visitor-friendly*—New Republic [based on *user-friendly*]

◁**frig**▷ **1** *v by 1785* To masturbate **2** *v by 1598* To do the sex act; =FUCK **3** *v 1920s* To cheat or trick someone; take advantage of someone; =DIDDLE, FUCK, SHAFT [ultimately fr Latin *fricare*, "rub"] *See* TAKE A FLYING FUCK

◁**frigging**▷ *by 1930* **1** *adj* Wretched; accursed; =DAMN, FUCKING: *. . . if we could find the frigging truck*—Arthur Hailey/ *You're a walkin', friggin' combat zone*—Time **2** *adv*: *They friggin' loved it*—Washington Post

fright mail *n phr 1990s* Mail designed to resemble official government documents, in order to fool the receiver into opening it: *You threw out today's fright mail, scanned a magalog, then picked up some trash cash. . .* —New York Times

◁**frill**▷ *n 1920s* A woman, esp a young woman; =FRAIL

fringe *n about 1960* A benefit, like insurance coverage, added to one's pay; fringe benefit

frisbee (FRIZ bee) *1930s college students* **1** *n* A game played in many variations by skimming a platelike disc among players: *Frisbee. . . was well on its way this week to becoming America's latest sports craze*—Newsweek **2** *n* The usu plastic disc used in the game [said to have originated at Middlebury College where students tossed pie plates from the Frisbie Pie Co, of Bridgeport CT; the present spelling is a trademark of the Wham-O Co; students at Yale and Princeton have also claimed credit]

Frisco *n by 1854* San Francisco, California: *Ever been to Frisco?*—James M Cain •This nickname is said to be disapproved by the residents of the place

frisk *by 1781* **1** *v* (also **frisk down**) To search, esp for firearms or contraband, by patting or rubbing the person in places where these might be concealed: *. . . raise your hands high, frisk him*—R Wallace/ *. . . without getting taken-off, frisked-down or punched-out*—New York Times **2** *n*: *They did a quick frisk and let him go* **3** *v* To inspect a building, apartment, etc, for evidence or loot: *Let's go up and frisk the apartment*—Raymond Chandler

frit *n by 1960s* A male homosexual; =FLIT

fritter away *v phr by* 1728 To squander and dissipate, esp little by little: *These politicians are frittering away whatever credit they still possess with the public* [fr earlier sense of *fritter*, "to break into small pieces"]

fritz *v by* 1903 To make something inoperative; put out of working order: *Lightning hit some wires and fritzed the generator*—F Brown
See ON THE BLINK

◁**Fritz**▷ *n by* 1883 A German, esp a German soldier; =KRAUT

fritz out *v phr by* 1960 To become inoperative; break down; =GO DOWN

frivol *v by* 1866 To behave frivolously; jape and frolic: *I wish I could frivol away my summer*

'fro or **fro** *n by* 1960s A frizzy style of coiffure; =AFRO: *... the curly 'fro which has found particular favor among the men*—Ebony

frobnitz *n* 1980s computer An unspecified or unspecifiable object; something one does not know the name of or does not wish to name; =GADGET, GIZMO

frog ◁**1**▷ *n* (also **Frog** or **froggy** or **Froggy** or **frog-eater**) *by* 1778 A Frenchman or -woman: *My dad was in France during the last war. He knows those Frogs*—Calder Willingham ◁**2**▷ *modifier by* 1778: *frog wine/ a Frog chick* ◁**3**▷ *n by* 1778 The French language: *He asked me in Frog* **4** *n* 1950s teenagers A dull and conventional person: *Anybody who still wears saddle shoes is... a "frog"*—New York Times [senses referring to the French fr their eating of *frog-legs*]
See BIG FISH, BIG FISH IN A LITTLE POND, KNEE-HIGH TO A GRASSHOPPER

frogman *n* WWII Navy A scuba diver, esp a professional or military diver

frogskin *by* 1902 **1** *n* A one-dollar bill; one dollar: *I'll give you five hundred frogskins for the good will and fixtures*—SJ Perelman **2** *n* Any piece of paper money; =FOLDING MONEY: *He not only got his quail, but a handful of frogskins as well*—Associated Press [fr the green color]

frog-sticker **1** *n by* 1836 A long-bladed knife, esp a pocket knife: *Out comes your liver on the end o' this frogsticker*—Chicago Tribune **2** *n* WWII Army A bayonet

frog up *v phr* 1930s black To become confused; be deceived [probably fr humorous mispronunciation of *fog up*]

from Adam **See** NOT KNOW someone FROM ADAM

from Hell *adj phr* early 1980s Accursed; wretched; infernal: *... they struck on the title "Zarda, Cow from Hell"*—Associated Press/ *... a certified, notarized, top-of-the-line day from hell*—Jean Billman [popularized by a comedian named Richard Lewis]

from hell to breakfast *adv phr by* 1920s Thoroughly and vehemently; violently: *Police... clubbed the Gophers from hell to breakfast*—H Asbury

from hunger 1930s musicians **1** *adj phr* Inferior; unpleasant; contemptible: *I started giving the three witches at the next table the eye again. That is, the blonde one. The other two were strictly from hunger*—J D Salinger **2** *adv phr*: *... playing from hunger... in a style to please the uneducated masses*—Peabody Bulletin [fr Yiddish *fun hoonger*]

from jump street *adv phr by* 1970s =FROM THE GIT-GO: *He was lying from jump street*

from nothing **See** KNOW FROM NOTHING

from scratch **1** *adv phr by* 1876 From the earliest stages; from the very beginning: *We had to do it all again, from scratch* **2** *adj phr*: *... his first from-scratch musical venture*—Philadelphia **3** *adv phr by* 1950s Using the separate basic ingredients or parts: *I never tired of watching my grandmother make the bread "from scratch" to feed the whole family*—San Francisco [fr the mark or *scratch* indicating the starting line of a race]

from the git-go (or **get-go**) *adv phr* fr black From the very beginning: *It was his bust from the git-go*—R Woodley/ *Right from the get-go he came out smoking... It all went down in milliseconds*—New York Times [perhaps based on *from the word go*, found by 1883]

from the hip **See** SHOOT FROM THE HIP

from (or **out of** or **straight from**) **the horse's mouth** *adv phr by* 1930 From the most authentic source: *I got the tip straight from the horse's mouth*—W R Burnett [perhaps fr the fact that a *horse's* age can be determined most precisely and directly by examining its teeth]

from the shoulder **See** STRAIGHT FROM THE SHOULDER

from the top *adv phr* musicians *by* 1950s From the beginning: *Let's hear it again from the top* [perhaps fr the musical instruction *da capo*, "from the beginning," literally, "from the head"]

from the word go *adv phr by* 1883 From the very beginning; ab ovo: *He was lying from the word go*

from way back *adj phr by* 1887 Genuinely; entirely; from a long time ago: *My Dad is a Yankee fan from way back*

from where I sit *adv phr by* 1980s From my point of view; according to my notion: *Contrary to what Bernstein says, it is not clear that the idiot culture is taking over. From where I sit, we call the things he is fretting about "change"*—New Republic

front **1** *n by* 1896 The appearance and impression one presents publicly; facade: *This and his stickpin, his two diamond rings, and his shirts and the gabardine suit composed his "front"*—Ira Wolfert/ *... a real coon type, but that's just front*—Lawrence Anderson **2** *n* (also **front man**) *by* 1920s A respectable and impressive person who represents or publicly supports persons lacking social approval: *Inability to hire a professional bondsman and "good front" results in a quick trial*—E Lavine/ *Ian Anderson, the band's flute-playing front man...*—Milwaukee Journal Sentinel **3** *v*: *If you ask them to front for you, they know you're going*

to do something—Playboy **4** *v* (also **front man**) by 1990s To be the leading figure of: *Terry Frank, who fronted the blues outfit Bone Deluxe since 1980. . .*—Milwaukee Journal Sentinel **5** *n* by 1920s An ordinary and unexceptionable business used as a cover for gambling, extortion, etc, esp as a way of decontaminating ill-gotten money: *The candy store was a front for his bookie business* **6** *v* 1960s narcotics To give something, esp narcotics, on promise of payment: *I'll front you some of this shit if you pay me by Thursday* **7** *v* by 1990s To behave in a hostile manner; confront **8** *v* 1990s teenagers To lie; renege on an agreement; =COP OUT
See OUT-FRONT, UP FRONT

frontal *adj* by 1980s Candid; direct; open: *He's a very direct and forceful guy, a very frontal person*—Washington Post [fr *up front*]
See FULL FRONTAL

front and center *adv phr* fr armed forces by 1940s To the position of maximum prominence: *Because of political instability and a lack of moral leadership, race has once again moved front and center in the American mind*—New York Times [fr the position in *front* of a military formation where a singled-out soldier presents himself or herself]

front money *n phr* by 1920s An initial and impressive amount of money; cash as an earnest: *He had agreed. . . to help the manufacturer get the $1.2 million loan in return for 7 percent of the total, plus "green" or "front money"*—New York Times/ *. . . in the drive for $4.5 million in "front money" by Labor Day*—New York Times
See FLASH ROLL

front name *n phr* by 1877 The first name; given name: *What is your front name?*—Groucho Marx

front office 1 *n phr* by 1930s The chief administrative offices of a company **2** *n phr* by 1930s Managers; executives: *What's the front office think?* **3** *adj phr*: *front-office memos* **4** *n phr* underworld by 1900 A police station

front runner *n phr* by 1914 from racing The leader in a contest, election, etc: *That left as front runners Runcie and England's second-ranking churchman*—Time

front-running 1 *adj* by 1940s from racing Leading; first in a competition: *. . . universally considered to be the GOP's front-running candidate*—Time **2** *n* commodities market by 1980s A type of fraud in which a trader withholds a large customer order so that he can personally profit from its effect on the market: *. . . found David E Sitzmann guilty on eight counts of "frontrunning" in the live cattle and live hog futures markets*—Wisconsin State Journal

frood *n* 1980s college students An admirable person [fr the book *A Hitchhiker's Guide to the Galaxy*]

froody *adj* 1980s college students Admirable; =COOL: *He's really froody*—The Levi's 501 Report

frosh *n* students by 1915 A first-year student, or such students collectively

frost 1 *n* by 1885 A total failure; something not well received: *My idea was a dismal frost* **2** *n* by 1635 Social hauteur; chill; =COLD SHOULDER: *He smiled at her and got frost* **3** *v* by 1896: *For nifty Mame has frosted me complete*—Wallace Irwin **4** *v* by 1940s To anger; irritate: *That tone of voice really frosts me*

frostback *n* by 1980s An illegal immigrant from Canada [modeled on *wetback*]

frosted over by 1970s *adj phr* Irritated; annoyed

frosty 1 *adj* by 1970s Unperturbed; =COOL: *Stay frosty. Relax*—Joseph Wambaugh **2** *adj* by 1833 In a reserved manner; haughty; cool: *her frosty glance*

frou-frou *n* by 1870 Frilly dress and adornment; frivolous bedizenment: *Is that what you want in a girl, chi-chi, frou-frou, fancy clothes, permanent waves?*—Max Shulman [fr French, imitative of the rustling of silk]

frowsy *n* about 1900 A slovenly, unkempt woman: *. . . a few frowsies in skirts*—New Yorker

frozen rope *n phr* baseball by 1960s A hard line drive: *A hard line drive is a blue darter, frozen rope, or an ungodly shot*—Jim Bouton

the frug *n phr* 1960s A discotheque dance derived from the twist: *The dignified dances include. . . the Frug (the movement is in the hips, the derivation of the name is shady)*—New York Times [origin unknown; perhaps a blend of *frig* and *fuck*]

fruit 1 *n* by about 1910 An eccentric person; =FRUITCAKE, ODDBALL: *I'll bet we get a lot of fruits*—O Johnson ◁**2**▷ *n* by 1935 A male homosexual; =FAIRY [first sense short for *fruitcake*, as in "nutty as a fruitcake"]
See HEN-FRUIT

fruitbar *See* FLAMER

fruitbasket *n* by 1990s An insane person; =FRUITCAKE, NUT, WACK: *Touched the wound, rubbed the blood on his cheeks and his forehead. Total fruitcake*—Carsten Stroud

◁**fruit boots**▷ *n phr* by 1970s Shoes favored by homosexual males: *Throughout the '50s, fruit boots were white tennies or white suede shoes*—Bruce Rodgers

fruitcake 1 *n* by 1950s An insane person; =NUT: *The shrink himself is a certified fruitcake* **2** *n* by 1950s An eccentric person; =FRUIT, ODDBALL **3** *modifier*: *. . . those fruitcake sandal makers in the tractor-gear factory*—Calvin Trillin ◁**4**▷ *n* by 1960s A male homosexual; =FRUIT **5** *modifier*: *his fruitcake mannerisms*
See NUTTY AS A FRUITCAKE

◁**fruit fly**▷ *n phr* homosexuals by 1970s =FAG HAG

◁**fruit-picker**▷ *n* homosexuals by 1970s A basically heterosexual man who occasionally seeks out homosexual partners

fruit salad 1 *n phr* WWII armed forces Ribbons and other badges worn on the breast of a military jacket: *You can recognize the boys from Korea by the new decoration added to the war "fruit salad"*—Syracuse Post-Standard **2** *n phr* 1960s narcotics A mixture of tranquilizers, painkillers, and other drugs from the family medicine cabinet used secretly by adolescents ◁3▷ *n phr* (Variations: **potato patch** or **rose garden** or **vegetable garden**) *medical by 1980s* A group of stroke victims or otherwise totally disabled patients

fruit-salad party *n phr 1960s narcotics* A party at which adolescents experiment with drugs garnered from the family medicine cabinet

fruit wagon *n phr dockworkers by 1950s* An ambulance: *If you squawk you leave the docks, most likely in the fruit wagon*—M H Vorse

fruity 1 *adj 1930s teenagers* Eccentric; odd; =NUTTY, WEIRD ◁2▷ *adj by 1930s* Homosexual; =GAY

frump *n by 1817* A dowdy woman: *. . . that floppy-looking frump he left you for*—James M Cain

frumpy *adj by 1845* Dowdy; run-down; unattractive: *The message is that soft frumpy fellows are not only lovable but sexually attractive*—Village Voice

fry 1 *v by 1929* To be executed in the electric chair, or to execute someone in the electric chair: *I built up a case against Sandmark. You probably could have fried him with it, too*—J Evans/ *Apparently everybody in Texas thinks everybody should be fried*—Washington Post **2** *v about 1920* To punish severely; =KICK ASS, ROUGH UP: *I'll call the CFTC, the FBI, George Bush. . . and I'll beg them to fry your ass*—Scott Turow **3** *v by 1960s* To upset; anger; =PISS OFF **4** *v computer by 1980s* To fail; =GO DOWN **5** *v black by 1950s* To remove the kinks from hair with a hot comb or curling iron **6** *v 1980s teenagers* To take LSD; =DROP
See BIGGER FISH TO FRY, SMALL FRY

FTA (pronounced as separate letters) *sentence Army fr 1950s* Fuck the Army; also, fuck them all

FTL (pronounced as separate letters) *sentence* Fuck the law: *The graffiti on the walls everywhere said "FTL"; I was told that it stood for "Fuck the Law"*—New Yorker

F2F or **f2f** *modifier computer by 1990s* Face-to-face; in actual personal contact rather than computer network contact: *Cyberspace reader has been involved in serious romances, which culminated in F2F experiences*—Time

fu (Foo) *n narcotics by 1940s* Marijuana [perhaps a shortening of Portuguese *fumo d'Angola,* "Angola smoke," referring to marijuana and the smoking habit brought by slaves from Angola to Brazil]

fubar (Foo bar) *adj WWII armed forces* Totally botched and confused; =SNAFU [fr *fucked up beyond all recognition*]

fubb *adj WWII armed forces* =FUBAR, SNAFU [fr *fucked up beyond belief*]

fubis (Foo bis) *sentence Army fr 1950s* An irritated or defiant comment [fr *fuck you, buddy, I'm shipping*]

◀**fuck▶ 1** *v by 1200s* To do the sex act with or to someone **2** *n by 1680* An instance of the sex act: *a quick fuck* **3** *n by 1874* A sex partner: *She said he's not a bad fuck* **4** *n by 1920s* A despicable person; =BASTARD, PRICK: *Why don't you fucks find a cure for*

that already?—Joseph Heller/ *"Oh yes, of course," said the fuck. . .*—Stan Cutler **5** *v by 1860s* To cheat; swindle; maltreat; take advantage of; =FUCK OVER, SCREW: *I was with them twenty years, but they fucked me anyhow* **6** *v by 1920s* To curse and vilify; revile extremely; =DAMN •Strongest of the cursing terms that include wishing the person or thing to eternal damnation; "damn," "to hell with," and mentally subjecting the person or thing to an act of sodomy: "fuck, screw," and British "bugger" and "sod"; has the elaborate variant *fuck them all but six and save them for pallbearers/Fuck the money, I'm gone go on this ride*—Claude Brown/ *Ah, fuck that noise*—Philip Roth **7** *interj by 1940s* An exclamation of disgust, disappointment, dismay, etc: *. . . and yelled against the moan of the wind as loud as he could, "Fuck!"*—Elmore Leonard **8** *v by 1920s* To botch and confuse; ruin; =FUCK UP: *My God, if the doctor sent out a bill. . . it might fuck the whole thing*—Lawrence Sanders [origin unknown; perhaps fr or related to German *ficken,* "strike, copulate with"]
See DRY FUCK, FINGERFUCK, a FLYING FUCK, GOAT FUCK, GO FUCK oneself, HONEY-FUCK, MIND-FUCK, NOT GIVE A DAMN, NOT GIVE A FUCK FOR NOTHING, RAT FUCK, TAKE A FLYING FUCK, THROW A FUCK INTO someone

◀**a fuck▶** *See* NOT GIVE A DAMN, NOT GIVE A FUCK FOR NOTHING

◀**the fuck▶** *See* the HELL

◀**fuck a duck▶** *interj by 1940s* An exclamation of surprise and incredulity: *He did? Well, fuck a duck!*

◀**fuck-all▶** *n by 1960* Nothing; =ZILCH •Chiefly British: *A good extra. . . can pull in good money to not do fuck-all*—Playboy

◀**fuck around▶** *by 1929* **1** *v phr* To idle and loaf about; =MESS AROUND: *Although I do fuck around in home studios and things like that, I think that it's of no importance*—Rolling Stone **2** *v phr* To tease; fool around annoyingly; =HORSE AROUND
See FUCK WITH

◀**fuck book▶** *n phr by 1940s* A pornographic book or magazine

◀**fuck** someone's **brains out▶** *v phr by 1970s* To do the sex act busily and for a long time: *We can spend the whole night together, fuck our brains out*—Earl Thompson/ *. . . two people who'd just fucked each other's brains out*—Richard Grossbach

◀**fucked▶** *adj by 1940s* Confounded; victimized; =BUGGERED, DAMNED: *I'll be fucked if he's not right!*

◀**fucked by the fickle finger of fate▶** *adj phr by 1940s* Victimized by bad luck; very unfortunate

◀**fucked out▶** *adj phr by 1940* Exhausted; =PLAYED OUT, POOPED

◀**fucked up▶** *by 1940s* **1** *adj phr* Confused; botched; ruined; =BALLED UP: *Now isn't that as fucked up as a Chinese fire drill?*—Lawrence Sanders **2** *adj phr* Mentally and emotionally disturbed; neurotic: *I was so fucked up I couldn't talk sense* **3** *adj phr* Intoxicated, esp by narcotics: *I was so drunk and fucked up and shaken with tenderness*—Rolling Stone

◀**fucker▶** *by 1893* **1** *n* A detestable person;

=BASTARD, PRICK: *And the fuckers are really, really twisting us up*—Rolling Stone/ *The fucker stole my money*—Sue Grafton **2** *n* Any person or thing •Often used affectionately: *Look at that little fucker go!/ Jiggs doesn't like to have anything to do with boats. . . "I don't want no parts of them fuckers"*—Elmore Leonard

See FATHERFUCKER, MIND-FUCKER, MOTHERFUCKER, PIG-FUCKER

◄**fuck film►** *n phr by 1960s* A pornographic movie; =SKIN FLICK: *Calling it an erotic film festival made it possible for people. . . to dig a good fuck film*—Changes

◄**fuckhead►** *n by 1960s* A despicable person; =JERK: *. . . some back-country fuckhead with a stetho-scope*—Stephen King

◄**fucking►** *by 1893* **1** *adj* Wretched; rotten; accursed; =DAMN: *. . . hectic fuckin' business*—Changes **2** *adj* Genuine; absolute; =COCKEYED: *Ain't that a fucking shame?* **3** *adv* Extremely; very: *It's fucking difficult to get a raise these days* **4** *intensifier*: *Why don't we go downtown and fucking get it done?*—Elmore Leonard

See MOTHERFUCKING, a ROYAL FUCKING

◄**-fucking-►** *infix* Used for emphasis •Often printed as a separate word without hyphens: *non compos fuckin' mentis*—George V Higgins/ *in-fucking-cred-ible*—Dan Jenkins/ *"Un-fucking-believable,"* they say in the booth—Toronto Life

◄**fucking a (or ay)►** *by 1940s fr British* **1** *affirmation* Absolutely; definitely: *Fucking a, no one's gonna shoot Keith*—Playboy **2** *adv phr*: *Fucking ay right I did*—Patrick Mann **3** *interj* An exclamation of pleasure, triumph, joy, etc; =GREAT: *We won? Fucking a!* [fr an affirmatory phrase *your fucking arse*]

◄**fucking well►** *intensifier by 1920s* Absolutely: *. . . not afraid of fucking well anything*—George Warren

◄**fucking well told►** *adv phr by 1940s* Absolutely right; =FUCKING A: *"You're fucking well told,"* he replied—Stan Cutler

◄**fuck like a mink►** *v phr by 1930s* To copulate readily and vigorously •Said only of women

◄**fuck-me or do-me►** *adj by 1980s* Blatantly seductive: *. . . a brand-new pair of rhinestone fuck-me shoes*—Jane Leavy

◄**fuck off►** **1** *v phr by 1940s* =FUCK AROUND **2** *v phr by 1940s* =FUCK UP **3** *v phr by 1929* To leave; depart •Often an irritated command: *Tell 'em to fuck off, I don't want anything to do with them*—Xaviera Hollander

◄**fuck-off►** *n WWII armed forces* A habitual shirker; sluggard; =GOOF-OFF: *I mean, everybody's a fuck-off*—Rolling Stone

◄**fuck over►** *v phr by 1960s* To victimize and mal-treat, sexually or otherwise; =FUCK: *. . . so accus-tomed to being used and fucked over that they probably would do nothing*—Howard S Becker/ *. . . let people know who might be fucking them over*—Village Voice

◄**fuck-stick►** *n by 1950s* A despised person; =ASSHOLE, JERK: *. . . real pompous little fuck-stick*—Westword

◄**fuck the dog►** *v phr by 1930s* To waste time; idle about; temporize: *We better quit fucking the dog and get cracking*

◄**fuck up►** *by 1940s* **1** *v phr* To fail by blundering; ruin one's prospects: *They are the prime reasons that people fuck up in bands*—Rolling Stone **2** *v phr* To confuse; botch; =BALL UP: *I had it right, but he fucked it up*

◄**fuck-up►** *by 1940s* **1** *n* A bungler, esp a chronic one: *The sergeant was a confirmed fuck-up* **2** *n* A confused situation; botch; =MESS: *The operation was a royal fuck-up* **3** *n* A blunder; =GOOF: *These things are my ideas. . . they've all got the same fuck-ups*—Rolling Stone

◄**fuck someone up►** *v phr by 1960s* To injure or maltreat someone; =FUCK OVER: *If anybody was to mess with your sister, you had to really fuck him up*—Claude Brown/ *They didn't do it, so they fucked me up*—Rolling Stone

◄**fuck up (or screw up) a two-car funeral►** *v phr by 1990s* To mismanage completely; botch: *D'Amato says Federal banking regulators could screw up a two-car funeral*—New York Times

◄**fuck up, move up►** *sentence Army by 1970s* If you blunder badly, you'll be promoted

◄**fuck (or fuck around) with►** *by 1940s* **1** *v phr* To play or toy with; meddle with: *Floyd was a lit-tle crazy and just liked to fuck with people by talk-ing a lot of nonsense*—Claude Brown/ *. . . every harebrain east of the Mississippi River will be fuck-ing around with this thing. . .*—Robert B Parker **2** *v phr* To defy or challenge; provoke; =MESS AROUND WITH: *"They don't fuck with me,"* the old man said—Robert B Parker/ *. . . to see if Buck Rogers was real and had come down here to fuck with Texas*—Dan Jenkins

◄**fuck-witted►** *adj by 1990s* Stupid; moronic; =DUMB: *. . . it's a pretty fuck-witted thing to do. . .*—Douglas Coupland

◄**fuck you►** *interj by 1940s* An exclamation of very strong defiance and contempt: *Fuck you, friend, if that's your attitude*

Fudd *See* WILLIE FUDD

fuddy-duddy or fuddy-dud *by about 1900* **1** *n* An old-fashioned, esp a meticulous, person; an out-dated conservative: *To this little squab, I evidently rated as a fuddy-duddy*—Billy Rose **2** *adj*: *There were a few fuddy-duddy requests for documenta-tion*—Village Voice

fudge **1** *v by 1660s* To cheat or misrepresent slight-ly; deviate somewhat: *. . . so I could fudge three or four inches on my height*—James M Cain/ *. . . if you're fudging on your income tax return*—Associated Press **2** *interj by 1766* A mild exclama-tion of surprise, disappointment, etc; =DARN **3** *v by 1950s* To rub someone to orgasm; =FRIG [first sense said to be fr the name of a Royal Navy Captain *Fudge*, "by some called Lying Fudge"; sailors, hear-ing a lie told, exclaimed "You *fudge* it!"]

fudge factor *n phr by 1962* An arbitrary percentage added to a proposed contract or estimate, to allow for adverse contingencies: *How many will die? Current projections are pure darts at a board, an enormous extrapolation coupled with a fudge factor*—New York Times

fudge one's **pants (or undies)** *v phr by 1970s* To become frightened; =SHIT one's PANTS

fuggle *See* HONEY-FUCK

fugly *adj 1980s* Very ugly; =BUTT UGLY: *That ski suit Mary has on is not just ugly, it's fugly*—Slang Bag 93 [fr *fucking ugly*]

fuie *See* PHOOEY

full *adj by 1872* Drunk

full blast *by 1839* **1** *adv phr* To the limit of capacity; with no restraint; =ALL-OUT **2** *adj*: *a full-blast campaign for mayor*

full bore *by 1936* **1** *adv phr* At maximum speed and power; =ALL-OUT, FULL BLAST: *We're going full bore Sheriff Wells says*—People **2** *adv phr* Absolutely; totally: *. . . and I already full-bore suspected old Ronny*—Stan Cutler [fr the condition of an unchoked carburetor in an engine, where the *full bore* of the gas line is being used; influenced by the unchoked condition of a shotgun]

full-bore *adj by 1936* Large; fully developed: *And this track here. . . big, a full-bore male*—Carsten Stroud

full Cleveland *adj phr by 1991* Of a man, dressed in white shoes and a white suit

full court press *n phr* Very great or maximum pressure: *. . . an inclination not to resume a full court press for the peace plan*—Wall Street Journal [fr an aggressive *pressing* defense in basketball, using both halves of the *court*]

full deck *See* PLAY WITH A FULL DECK

full fig *n phr by 1838* Full official or ceremonial attire; full dress •Chiefly British: *Arrivals from a Swissair flight: two lushly draped, satiny ladies, a squire in noisy tweeds, a bishop in full fig*—New Yorker [origin uncertain; perhaps fr *full figure*, used of fashion illustrations showing the full front of the wearer]

full frontal *adj phr by 1970s* Total; complete; unrestricted: *. . . a variety of forms including iambic pentameter, full frontal rhyme and ballads*—New York Times [fr the phrase *"full frontal nudity"* used to describe the ultimate grade of nakedness, as seen in art, moving pictures, television, etc]

full hank *n phr 1980s teenagers* A tedious, contemptible person; =DORK, DWEEB, JERK

full-moon day *n phr librarians by 1990s* A day when many disturbed patrons visit

full-mooner *n by 1980s* An insane or very eccentric person; =LOONY, NUT: *. . . in San Francisco, where there are full-mooners on every street corner*—Washingtonian/ *This issue goes beyond the full-mooners*—Robert Nowak [fr the belief that some people go crazy at the time of the *full moon*]

full of beans 1 *adj phr by 1854* Vibrant with energy; peppy: *The old guy was still full of beans*

2 *adj phr* (also **full of hops**) *by 1940s* Wrong; mistaken, esp chronically so; =FULL OF SHIT: *. . . maybe Ted Williams was full of beans*—Mike Royko [first sense fr the belief that a *bean*-fed horse is particularly frisky and strong; second sense fr a connection with *beans,* hops, prunes, etc., as promoting excretion]

full of hot air *adj phr by 1940s* Wrong; mistaken; pompously in error: *If she says that, she's full of hot air*

◁**full of piss and vinegar**▷ *adj phr by 1940s* Brimming with energy; very peppy and assertive; =FULL OF BEANS: *. . . full of the piss and vinegar her mother lacks*—Village Voice/ *. . . full of piss and vinegar and occasionally now, a little weed*—Inside Sports

full of prunes 1 *adj phr by 1887* Vibrant with energy; peppy: *The old guy was still full of prunes* **2** *adj phr by 1894* Wrong; mistaken, esp chronically so; =FULL OF SHIT
See FULL OF BEANS

◁**full of shit**▷ *adj phr* (Variations: **crap** or **bull** or **it** may replace **shit**) *by 1940s* Wrong; mistaken; not to be credited: *Oh, he's so full of shit, that self-seeking schmuck*—Joseph Heller/ *Anyone who says it doesn't matter is full of it*—Erich Segal/ *They're all fulla shit anyway, all them goddam politicians*—W T Tyler

◁as **full of shit as a Christmas goose**▷ *adj phr by 1940s* =FULL OF SHIT •An intensive use

full ride *by 1950s* **1** *n phr* A full college scholarship: *. . . seven of them got full rides to Division 1 schools*—Milwaukee Journal Sentinel **2** *modifier*: *. . . accused of receiving a full ride scholarship from Michigan*—B Fay

full steam ahead *adj phr by 1960s* Eager and energetic; =GUNG HO: *BJ's rehab has gone well. . . He's full steam ahead*—Milwaukee Journal Sentinel

full-tilt-boogie *adv by 1980s* At full speed; headlong; =FULL BORE: *I would rather that my state run full-tilt-boogie into gambling proprietorship. . .*—Daily Jefferson County Union

full up *adj phr by 1892* Completely full: *The plane was full up by then*

fully *adv by 1990s* Really; certainly: *That was fully the best movie I've ever seen*—Drew Slang/ *He was fully flailing on the guitar. You were fully doggin' him about his hair*—Miven Booth

full yard *See* GO THE FULL YARD

fumble-fingered *adj by 1980s* Clumsy; =BUTTERFINGERED: *. . . directions for the fumble-fingered*—Time

fumblerooski *n football by 1980s* A play in which the quarterback leaves the ball between the center's legs and fakes a hand-off, whereupon a guard takes the ball and runs with it: *. . . and make the guard-around or "fumblerooski" play illegal*—Milwaukee Journal/ *I got you on the fumble-rooski, didn't I?*—Milwaukee Journal

fumfer or **fumper** *v by 1980s* To temporize and

mumble; dither; =WAFFLE: *Orrin Hatch with his quotes from* The Exorcist, *Howard Metzenbaum fumfering on about leaks*—Nation/ *When questioned, they fumpered around*—Sue Cameron [fr Yiddish]

fumtu (FUHM tŏŏ) *adj phr WWII armed forces* Totally confused; botched; =SNAFU [fr *fucked up more than usual*]

fun *adj by 1950s* With which, with whom, in which, etc., one can have fun: *Mickey and his chums introduce each other as "a real fun guy"*—Saturday Review

See LIKE HELL, POKE FUN

fun and games *n phr by 1920* Pleasure; delightful diversion; amatory dalliance ●More commonly British than US, and most often ironic: *We had some fun and games a few months ago*—Rex Burns/ *What happens to Romanov after that is fun and games for you, Hardy*—Hugh Pentecost [based on the talk and attitude used toward children by hearty people, and analogous with *show and tell*]

Fun City or **fun city** *n phr late 1960s* Any city, esp New York City, fancied to be a venue for pleasure, often ironically [first used as a public-relations motto for the administration of New York City Mayor John Lindsay, and felt to be in ironic contrast with increasing urban shabbiness, poverty, crime, etc]

fund *See* SLUSH FUND

fun fur *n phr by 1962* Cheap synthetic fur for casual use

fungo *baseball by 1867* **1** *n* A ball hit to give practice to fielders, usu by tossing it up and swinging **2** *v*: *They used to fungo that ball over your head*—Philadelphia Journal **3** *n* A long, light bat used to hit practice balls to fielders [origin unknown; perhaps fr dialect *fonge*, "catch," fr Old English *fon*, "seize, catch," or fr the German cognate *fangen*, in the same sense; the *-o* ending might indicate a shouted warning, the whole meaning "Now catch!"; Paul Dickson, the baseball lexicographer, describes five theories of origin]

fungo stick *n phr baseball fr 1860s* A bat used to hit balls for fielding practice

fungus-faced *adj 1980s teenagers* Repulsive; =GROSS: *The kids call Baker a fungus-faced toadsucker*—Washington Post

funk[1] **1** *v by 1737* To fail through panic; be frightened to immobility ●Chiefly British: *She would have won, but suddenly funked* **2** *n 1743* Depression; moroseness; =the BLUES: *This levelheaded man of logic, however, is also a creature of moods and funks*—Playboy/ *You guys are in a funk*—New Yorker [perhaps fr Flemish *fonck*, "perturbation"]

See BLUE FUNK, IN A FUNK

funk[2] or **fonk** *musicians by 1950s* **1** *n* A style of urban black music that relies heavily on bass guitar and exhibits elements like African rhythms, the blues, early rock and roll, jazz, etc: *There is no denying. . . the influence of Instant Funk*—Aquarian/ *. . . the Minister of Super Heavy Funk, the legendary James Brown*—Afrika Bambaataa/ *He is*

New Orleans "fonk"—record jacket **2** *v* To play or move to an urban black music that features a dominant bass guitar: *I think it's all right to funk all night*—Aquarian [fr *funky*]

funkadelic *adj by 1980s* Musically hard-edged and urban while also reminiscent of the effects of hallucinogenic drugs; =FUNKY: *. . . breaks into his best funkadelic solo as the mood changes*—Village Voice [fr a blend of *funky* and *psychedelic*]

funk hole *n phr by 1900* A hiding place when one is frightened

funkified *adj by 1970s* Tending toward a hard-edged, urban, black 1970s style in music: *Ornette Coleman, whose current funkified direction*—Downbeat

funkiness *n by 1980s* The excited, hard-edged, soulful, or rhythmically compelling mood associated with funk: *Cannonball's alto sax has lost its old zesty funkiness*—Time

funky (also **fonky** or **funky-butt** or **funkyass**) **1** *adj by 1784* Repulsive; malodorous; stinking: *What a stinking, dirty, funky bitch she was*—Claude Brown/ *The Baths, though, are funky enough without booze*—Saturday Review **2** *adj black musicians by 1954* In the style of the blues; earthy; simple yet compelling, with a strong beat and powerful bass guitar: *He has combined a basically funky sound with experimentation*—Ebony/ *. . . the funky-butt tune high wide an' lonesome*—George Warren **3** *adj late 1960s* Excellent; effective; =COOL: *He wanted to get down and get funky*—Sports Illustrated/ *There's a funkyass biker after my own heart*—George Warren **4** *adj 1960s* Old-fashioned; quaintly out-of-date; having a nostalgic appeal: *. . . for those of you who are not familiar with its funky splendor*—Village Voice/ *. . . my love for funky Forties clothes*—Playboy **5** *adj 1960s* Pleasantly eccentric or unconventional; =OFFBEAT **6** *adj* Deviant; =KINKY: *That guy's a little too funky for my taste* **7** *adj 1960s* Highly emotional; lacking affective restraint: *He hints that it may have its funky moments*—New Republic

funky fresh *adj phr late 1980s* Superb; the very greatest: *Funky fresh describes something that is super, exceptional, superior to fresh*—Geneva Smitherman

the **funnies** (or **comics**) *n phr by 1928* Comic strips; section or page of a newspaper with comic strips

funny *by 1806* **1** *adj* Eccentric; odd; =WEIRD ●Once derided as a US Southernism **2** *adj* Insane; =NUTS **3** *adv* In a strange way: *He looked at her real funny*

a **funny** *n by 1950s* A joke; wisecrack; witty remark

See DOODAD

funny business *See* MONKEY BUSINESS

funny car *1980s n phr* A dramatically modified car, usu having a powerful engine, oversized wheels, a raised rear suspension, etc, esp a drag racer so modified: *. . . the "funny" car, built for speed*—"Dick Tracy comic" strip

funny farm (or **house**) *n phr by 1963* A mental hospital, rest home for alcoholics, etc; =LAUGHING ACADEMY: *Who put me in your private funny house?*—Raymond Chandler/ *They must all have died in flop-houses or on state funny-farms*—Saul Bellow

funny ha-ha or funny peculiar *question by 1938* Do you mean something funny that's amusing, or something funny that's strange?: *Gore Vidal: You can see it in the career of Woody Allen, who was wildly funny. Kopkind: Funny ha-ha or funny peculiar?*—Nation

funny money *n phr by 1938* Worthless, counterfeit, or play money

funsies *n early 1960s* Fun; =FUN AND GAMES: *The driver said they must not leave the parking area. "Oh, funsies!" said Boots*—New Yorker

funster *n by 1784* A person who has or makes fun: *. . . the facade drops, revealing them as the faux funsters they really are*—Buzz

◁**fur**▷ *n by 1893* The vulva; pubic hair

◁**furburger**▷ *1960s college students* **1** *n* The vulva **2** *n* A very attractive woman; =EATIN' STUFF

◁**fur pie**▷ *by 1940s* **1** *n phr* The vulva **2** *n phr* Cunnilingus

fuse *See* BLOW A GASKET, HAVE A SHORT FUSE

fuss *See* KICK UP A FUSS

fusspot *n by 1921* A very meticulous and finicky person; fussbudget

fustest with the mostest *See* FIRSTEST WITH THE MOSTEST

◁**futy**▷ (Foo dee) *by 1940s* **1** *n* The vulva **2** *v* To do the sex act; =FUCK **3** *v* =FUTZ AROUND **4** *v* To fuss; grumble; =BITCH

◁**futz**▷ (FUTS) *by 1930s* **1** *n* The vulva **2** *v* =FUCK **3** *v* (also ◁**futz with**▷) To meddle or alter wrongfully; damage; =FUCK UP: *What is clear is that this movie has been futzed with*—Newsweek **4** *n* A repulsive man, esp an old one; =ALTER KOCKER: *Inside of every American. . . is a scrawny, twanging old futz like me*—Kurt Vonnegut Jr [origin uncertain; perhaps fr Yiddish *arumfartzen*; mainly perceived as a euphemism for *fuck*]

futz around *by 1932* **1** *v phr* To loaf and idle; =FUCK OFF: *Stop futzing around and get to work* **2** *v phr* To experiment; try tricks; play; =MESS AROUND: *The foundation folk may get to futzing around with their computers*—Book World/ *You never really had time to sort of futz around in the sets*—Playbill **3** *v phr* To defy or challenge; provoke; =FUCK WITH: *I am nobody to futz around with*—Philip Roth

futzed up *adj phr by 1940s* Confused; botched; ruined; =FUCKED UP: *I've got her all futzed up. She does everything I tell her*—Calder Willingham

fuzz *n about 1930* A police officer; the police: *Cops must be annihilated. Kill the Fascist fuzz*—Newsweek [origin unknown; the form *fuzey* is found at about the same time]

fuzzbuster *n by middle 1970s* A device that detects police radar signals: *Rauch discovered that I had a Fuzzbuster, designed to warn me of radar traps*—Penthouse [fr a trademark name]

fuzzled *adj by 1621* Drunk

◁**fuzznuts**▷ *n by 1940s* A contemptible person; =JERK

◁**fuzz nutted**▷ *adj phr by 1970s* Inexperienced; callow; green: *. . . a fuzz nutted rookie*—Joseph Wambaugh [fr *fuzznuts*]

fuzzy **1** *n* (also **fuzzie**) *by 1940s* A police officer; =FUZZ **2** *n gambling by 1950s* A certainty, esp a horse sure to win; =SURE THING

the F-word *n by 1980s* A euphemized version of the taboo word "fuck"

F/X or FX *n movies by 1980s* Visual and other special effects •Best known after the 1986 movie *F/X: The FX were tops, the tone tender*—Milwaukee Journal Sentinel [fr *effects* pronounced a FX]

G

G *n* 1990s *street gangs* A member of a gang; =GANGBANGER, GANGSTA: *In a world of so much hate, another white "G" explains. . .* —L A Weekly

gab 1 *v by 1786* Talk, esp of a long, prattling sort [fr Scots or Northern English dialect; perhaps related to the Old French *gab*, "mockery, boasting"]

gabber *n by 1793* A talkative person; =GASBAG, MOTOR-MOUTH

gabby *adj by 1719* Talkative; noisily garrulous; gossipy: *They have spoken of any gabby party*— Westbrook Pegler

gabfest *n by 1897* A session of conversation; a loquacious occasion; =CHINFEST

gab (or talk) line *n phr 1980s* A telephone service allowing one to talk with someone in a designated subject area, for a considerable charge per minute •A sort of forerunner of the "interest groups" or "chat groups" of the computer Internet

gabs *See* GOB¹

gack *interj by 1990s* An exclamation of disgust; =YUCK [perhaps imitating vomiting]

gacky *adj by 1990s* Disgusting; =BLETCHEROUS, CRUDDY, SHITTY: *The milk is gacky; throw it out!*— Miven Booth

gadget *nautical fr middle 1800s* **1** *n* Any unspecified or unspecifiable usu small object; something one does not know the name of or does not wish to name; =THINGAMAJIG **2** *n* An unnecessary but presumably impressive item added as decoration or inducement: *The car's full of silly gadgets* [origin unknown; perhaps fr French *gâchette*, "a small mechanical part of a rifle, lock, etc"; perhaps fr a dialect pronunciation of *gorget*]

gadgetry *n by 1920* Ingenious or impressive devices, esp electronic or mechanical: *an age in love with gadgetry*

gaff 1 *n carnival & hawkers by 1893* A concealed device or operation that makes it impossible for the customer to win; =GIMMICK: *People started looking for a gaff*—New Yorker **2** *v carnival & hawkers by 1893* To cheat; swindle; trick, esp by short-changing **3** *v carnival & hawkers by 1893* To use a concealed device, esp for an illusion: *The volcano was "gaffed" with steampipes*—A J Liebling **4** *v Navy by 1950s* To reprimand; rebuke severely [fr *gaff*, "a hook"]
See BLOW THE GAFF, STAND THE GAFF

gaffer 1 *n by 1659* One's father; =OLD MAN: *Studs felt that Mr O'Brien was different from his own gaffer*—James T Farrell **2** *n by 1575* An old man: *Look at that gaffer trying to stand on his head* **3** *n by 1841* A foreman or boss, such as the manager of a circus, head glassblower, chief electrician on a movie set, etc [fr British dialect, "grandfather, godfather"; the dated meaning of first sense is actually "master, governor," often synonyms of "father"]
See OLD COCKER

gag 1 *n by 1823* A joke; wisecrack; trick: *I'll tell you gags, I'll sing you songs*—Mel Brooks **2** *n by 1777* To deceive; hoax; =SCAM, TAKE IN: *. . . his skills at what is called "social engineering" by some and "gagging" by others*—Los Angeles Times [perhaps fr obsolete *geck*, "dupe," related to German *geck*, "fool"; in the late 19th century a *gag* was "a line interpolated into a play"]

gaga *adj by 1905* Crazy; silly; irrational: *When prohibition comes up, the wets go gaga*—A Briggs/ *. . . not to mention a ga-ga French gamine in Mickey Mouse ears*—Village Voice [fr French, "fool"]

gag a maggot *See* ENOUGH TO GAG A MAGGOT

gage or gauge (GAYJ) **1** *n by 1940s* Cheap whiskey **2** *n by 1676* Tobacco •Also "a pipeful of tobacco," since *gage* meant "pipe" **3** *n narcotics by 1950s* Marijuana •Perhaps related to sense 2 and the old meaning, "pipe": *I could not see how they were more justified in drinking than I was in blowing the gage*—Eldridge Cleaver **4** *adj (also gaged) narcotics by 1950s* Intoxicated with marijuana
See GET one's GAGE UP, STICK OF GAGE

gage (or gauge) butt *n phr narcotics by 1930s* A marijuana cigarette; =JOINT

gaged (GAYJD) *adj by 1940s* Drunk
See GAGE

gagers (GAY jərz) *n by 1859* The eyes

gaggy *adj by 1990s* Funny; cleverly amusing; =JOKEY: *. . . MediHEAT's A Little Comfort (gaggy name, oh well). . .* —Sassy

gag me with a spoon *sentence 1980s teenagers* I am disgusted; I am about to retch

gaited *See* DOUBLE-GAITED

gak *v 1990s* To speak, esp to babble on; =YAK: *The pet lady then gakked on about the merits of ferrets. . .* —Milwaukee Journal Sentinel

gal *n by 1795* A woman •The female equivalent of *guy*: *She's a good gal, don't you think?/ a tough old gal*

gal (or girl) Friday *n phr by 1940* A woman assistant or secretary, esp in an office; female factotum; =GOFER [fr Daniel Defoe's novel *Robinson Crusoe,* where the servant and companion was named *Friday*]

gall *n by 1882* Arrogant self-assurance; effrontery; =CHUTZPA: *How do you like the gall of those Aussies*—S Smith

gallery *See* PEANUT GALLERY, ROGUE'S GALLERY, SHOOTING GALLERY

galley-west *See* KNOCK someone or something GALLEY-WEST

galloping dominoes *n phr by 1920* Dice

galoot (gə LōōT) *n by 1864* A person, esp an awkward or boorish man •Very often in the phrase *big galoot*: *. . . large enough for the galoots to fit through and take over*—New York Times/ *"I really love that galoot," said Harry*—Stan Cutler [fr early 1800s British, "soldier," of unknown origin; perhaps fr the Sierra Leone Creole language Krio *galut* fr Spanish *galeoto,* "galley slave"]

galumph *v by 1872* To move or cavort ungracefully; crash heavily about: *Linda Evans galumphing around the edges. . . like a wounded rhino*—Village Voice/ *. . . who had seen him practically every day of his life galumphing around the house naked. . .* —Harry Crews [coined by Lewis Carroll in *Through the Looking Glass*]

galumphing *adj by 1891* Ungraceful; heavy and cumbersome: *. . . his dead eyes, croaky voice, and large galumphing body*—Village Voice

gam[1] **1** *v black by 1950s* To boast; show off **2** *v black by 1950s* To flirt **3** *v by 1893* To gossip; visit **4** *n by 1893* A social visit; party [origin unknown; perhaps fr nautical use, "a meeting of whaling ships at sea, with attendant talk and exchange of news" found by 1850; perhaps fr 18th-century *gammon,* "talk, chatter"; probably ultimately fr Middle English *gamon,* "to play, frolic"]

gam[2] *n by 1781* A leg, esp a woman's leg •Most often in the plural: *. . . regarding her superb gams with affection*—V Faulkner/ *Gavilan has spindly gams, a thin neck, and a wasp waist*—New York Daily News [perhaps fr Northern French *gambe,* "leg"]

gambler *See* TIN HORN

game *n by 1860s* One's occupation; business; =RACKET: *He's in the computer game these days* *See* AHEAD OF THE GAME, BADGER GAME, BALL GAME, CON GAME, FLOATING CRAP GAME, the NAME OF THE GAME, ON one's GAME, the ONLY GAME, PLAY GAMES, SKIN GAME, a WHOLE NEW BALL GAME, a WHOLE 'NOTHER

game face *n phr by 1980s* The determined face one adopts in a contest; a mask of hardihood: *Just keep your game face. . . We've come this far*—Harry Crews/ *The advancing Knicks needed to wear their game faces in a hurry, and they did*—New York Times

game plan *n phr football by 1940s* A strategy for winning; plan for conducting some project or affair: *That type of a game plan gave us the option to point out how badly we need a responsible press*—Tom Wicker

gamer *n baseball & football by 1980s* A brave and enterprising player, esp one who works with pain or against the odds: *. . . what is known in the business as a gamer, a guy who pitches with pain. . . who wants the ball*—New York Daily News/ *When Jean Fuggett played for the Dallas Cowboys. . . his teammates called him a gamer*—Arthur Pincus [probably fr *game,* "brave, determined"; in the 1620s the word meant "an athlete," and the current sense is conceivably though improbably a survival]

game, set, and match *adv phr by 1990s* Thoroughly; completely •Chiefly British: *Major announced that Britain had won game, set and match, achieving everything it wanted*—New York Times/ *Game, Anne thought, and I think probably set and match*—Penelope Lively [fr tennis]

gamy *adj by 1843* Daring; racy; slightly risqué: *. . . will be shown in its gamy uncut version*—New Yorker [based on the taste and odor of game that has slightly decayed]

gander 1 *n by 1887* A look; close scrutiny; glance: *I'll have a gander at the prices* **2** *v by 1914*: *Want to gander at TV for a while?* [fr the stretched, goose-like neck of someone gazing intently] *See* TAKE A GANDER

gandy dancer 1 *n phr hoboes, railroad & lumberjacks fr about 1915* A railroad track worker **2** *n phr loggers by 1940s* Any manual laborer, esp a pick-and-shovel digger **3** *n phr carnival by 1930s* A seller of novelties [origin unknown; a 1935 source says that the third sense was "mentioned by George Borrow in his descriptions of early nineteenth-century street fairs"]

ganef or **ganof** *See* GONIFF

gang *See* BLACK GANG, JERRY GANG

gangbang *v street gang by 1960s* To belong to a street gang: *What would you be doing if you wasn't gangbanging?*—Buzz/ *To Mr Shakur, gangbanging (engaging in gang activities) was a career. . .* —New York Times [an adaptation of *gang bang,* changing the meaning of *bang* from the sexual to the generally violent]

◁**gang bang**▷ (Variations: **shag** or **shay** may replace **bang**) *by 1953; the variant* gang shag *by 1927* **1** *n phr* An occasion when several males do the sex act serially with one woman; =TRAIN **2** *v phr*: *. . . tear the place apart, leave the owner for dead, gangbang the waitress*—Joan Didion **3** *n phr* A group-sex orgy: *We all ended up in a big profitable gangbang*—Xaviera Hollander

gangbanger *n street gang by 1960s* A member of a street gang; =BANGER: *He lives where the city's most violent gangs. . . live, where gangbangers cover walls, houses, even trees with arcane graffiti*—Los Angeles Times

gangbusters *by 1970s* **1** *n* Superlative; very successful: *. . . and "Breakfast Time" does that well. I think it's going to be gangbusters*—Newsweek **2** *adv*: *The big investigation still going gangbusters?*—Scott Turow/ *Dad is still alive and going great gangbusters. . .* —Elle [fr

the name of a radio series that lasted from 1936 to 1957]
See LIKE GANGBUSTERS

◀**gang fuck**▶ *n phr by 1916* =GANG BANG

gangland *by 1908* **1** *n* The world of organized crime; the gangster milieu **2** *modifier*: *a gangland-style slaying/gangland gorillas*

gangsta (GANG stuh) *modifier by 1980s* Showing the rapacious, violent, and misogynistic values of street gangs: *The group was one of the first to record "gangsta" lyrics, which focus on crime and violence*—Milwaukee Journal [fr *gangster*]

gangsta (or **gangster**) **rap** *n phr 1990s* A kind of "rap," speaking words to a strong rhythmic beat, marked by rapacity, violence, and misogyny: *. . . flirtation with gangsta rap, a style known for its profanity, violence and derogatory treatment of women*—Milwaukee Journal/ *. . . clean up violent "gangsta rap" lyrics that they said demean and threaten women*—Macon Telegraph/ *The stars of gangster rap have become dangerous emblems for an immensely popular, primarily black musical genre*—New York Times

gangster **1** *n by 1908* A member of a criminal gang; an organized-crime figure; =MOBSTER, WISEGUY **2** *modifier*: *gangster movie/ the gangster menace* **3** *n 1950s narcotics* A marijuana cigarette: *Just go on and smoke that gangster and be real cool*—C Cooper

gangster glide or **pimp roll** *n phr by early 1990s* A style of walking used by street gang members: *Sometimes it's called "the pimp roll," sometimes it's called the "gangster glide." It's a very exaggerated walk that some street gang members affect*—Court TV

gang up on someone or something *v phr by 1925* To combine against a single opponent: *The nonaligned nations ganged up on Sri Lanka*

ganja (GAHN jə) *n narcotics by 1800* A strong type of marijuana obtained from a cultivated strain of Indian hemp: *He remembers an uncle getting "so mean on ganja, he kills his girlfriend. . . "*—People [fr Hindi; adopted from West Indian use]

ganking *n 1990 teenagers* The armed and violent stealing of a car from its driver; =CARJACKING: *Teens engaged in "ganking" spree*—Milwaukee Journal

ganze macher (GAHN sə MAH kər) *by 1970s* **1** *n phr* A person busy with many affairs, esp officiously and conspiratorially; =BIG-TIME OPERATOR **2** *n phr* An important person; =BIG SHOT, VIP [fr Yiddish, "total busybody"]

gaper *n 1930s jive talk* A mirror

gaper's block or **gaper delay** *n phr by 1960s* Traffic congestion caused by drivers slowing down to inspect an accident or other matter of interest

garage *n 1980s* A kind of house music

garbage (GAR bəj, gar BAHZH) **1** *n hoboes & loggers by 1940s* Food or meals **2** *n by 1592* Anything inferior and worthless, esp a literary text or other artistic work; =CRAP, JUNK: *You call that piece of garbage a sonnet?* **3** *modifier*: *She uses a lot of*

tricky garbage shots to win games and sets/ I call it a garbage movie

garbage down *v phr WWII Navy* To eat; have a meal; =CHOW DOWN

garbage fee *n phr real estate by 1990s* An unwarranted fee charged by some escrow companies: *We found out too late that our escrow officer is the queen of garbage fees*—Los Angeles Times

garbage furniture **See** STREET FURNITURE

garbage habit *n phr narcotics by 1970s* The taking of narcotics in medleys and mixes: *. . . an increase in the garbage habit, where people mix a variety of drugs to achieve a high*—New York Times

garbage head *n phr narcotics by 1970s* A person who mixes various narcotics

garbage time *n phr basketball by 1980s* The last few minutes of a game whose outcome has already been decided, and when players try individually for scores to increase their averages: *Baker also played the final 2:26 of garbage time*—Milwaukee Journal

garbonzas *n by 1980s* A woman's breasts; =BAZONGAS, HOOTERS, TITS [perhaps fr Spanish *garbanzo*, "chickpea"]

garbology *n by 1946* The study of the refuse of a modern society [coined by W Rathje]

garden **1** *n baseball by 1869* =OUTER GARDEN **2** *n railroad by 1940s* A freight yard

garden carpet *n phr real estate by 1990s* A carpet so dirty it could grow vegetables

gardener **1** *n baseball by 1902* An outfielder **2** *n narcotics by 1970s* A person who plants narcotics on an airplane for smuggling

garden-variety *adj by 1928* Of the usual kind; ordinary; =RUN-OF-THE-MILL

gargle **1** *n by 1864* A drink, esp of liquor **2** *v truckers by 1930s* To drain and flush the radiator of a truck

gargle-factory *n by 1940s* A saloon; bar

garlic-burner *n motorcyclists by 1980s* A motorcycle made in Italy

garmento *n by 1980s* A person in the business of designing and manufacturing garments •A deprecating term for old-fashioned practitioners, and a self-deprecating term, like *the rag trade*, for the whole industry

gas **1** *n by 1847* Empty and idle talk; mendacious and exaggerated claims; =BULLSHIT: *Most of what I say is pure gas, my friend* **2** *n by 1852* Talk of any sort, esp conversation: *Let's get together for a good gas* **3** *v*: *I haven't gassed this long for a year*—Sinclair Lewis **4** *n by 1905* Gasoline **5** *n hoboes by 1940s* Denatured alcohol or some other substitute for liquor **6** *v 1940s cool talk* To impress one's hearers very favorably; overcome with admiration: *Bird gassed them*—Metronome Yearbook/ *She gassed me, she was that good*—P Martin **7** *v by 1970s* To impress an audience very unfavorably; fail with: *Our show appears to have gassed both the critics and the public* **8** *n baseball by 1980s* A fastball: *He got him out on the high gas*—Los Angeles Times **9** *n by 1957* =GASSER: *"What a gas!" she* *cried on the way from the courthouse*—Scott Turow **10** *n athletes by 1980s* Anabolic steroids, used to increase body bulk: . . . *Terry Bollea, said about 60 percent of the wrestlers he knew during the 1980s used steroids, commonly known as "juice" or "gas"*—Milwaukee Journal

See COOK WITH GAS, RUN OUT OF GAS, STEP ON IT

a **gas** *n phr 1940s cool talk* Something very impressive, pleasurable, effective, etc: *Therefore it's a gas for me to be the scribe of this weekly space*—Amsterdam News/ *She told me she'd been functionally fulfilled dispensing data, and it'd been a gas interfacing me*—Stan Cutler

gasbag *by 1888* **1** *n* An energetic and persevering talker; =WINDBAG **2** *v* To talk energetically and perseveringly: . . . *although we have of course plenty of gasbagging about morality*—Newsweek

gas-guzzler *n by 1970s* A car, esp a large American model, that uses a great deal of gasoline [*gas eater* and *gas hound* are found by the 1940s]

◀**gash¹**▶ **1** *n by middle 1700s* The vulva: *Plus ball the gash off a real foxy chick?*—Easyriders **2** *n by 1914* Women regarded as sex partners: . . . *that St Paul gash*—Richard Bissell/ . . . *all that fine gash, just wasted*—Esquire **3** *n by 1918* The sex act; =ASS: *Don't you ever think of anything but gash?*—James T Farrell **4** *v 1980s students* To do the sex act: *We gashed*—UCLA Slang

gash² *n WWII Army fr early 1900s British Navy* Extra or unexpected portions, bits of luck, etc; dividends; bonuses [origin unknown; perhaps fr French *gaché,* "spoiled," since it occurs in *gash bucket,* "garbage bin"]

gas hound 1 *n phr hoboes by 1940s* A person who drinks denatured alcohol or other substitutes for liquor **2** *n phr by 1940s* A big car; =GAS-GUZZLER

gas house *n phr WWII armed forces* A saloon; bar; beer tavern

gasket *See* BLOW A GASKET

gaslight *v by 1950s* To deceive someone systematically: *He set me up and has been gaslighting me*—TV show *Hunter* [fr the 1944 movie *Gaslight,* in which a man attempts to drive his wife mad by causing her to mistrust her senses]

gas man *n phr by 1950s* A publicist; press agent; =FLACK

gas-passer *n medical by 1960s* An anesthesiologist

gasper *n by 1914* A cigarette: . . . *handed Lt Edward Psota a nice, fresh marijuana gasper*—A Smith

gassed *by 1940s* **1** *adj* Drunk: *I begged them not to get gassed or start any fights*—Bing Crosby **2** *adj* Overcome with admiration: *After her speech the crowd was gassed*

gasser 1 *n by 1912* =GASBAG **2** *n 1930s cool talk* Anything or anyone exceptionally amusing, effective, memorable, etc; =a GAS: . . . *or examine this gasser*—Leo Rosten **3** *n 1940s cool talk* Anything or anyone exceptionally dull, mediocre, inept, etc; =CORNBALL, BOMB: *We planned a blast, and got a gasser* **4** *n 1960s rock and roll* =GAS-GUZZLER: *She*

beats the gassers and the rail jobs—Ronny and the Daytonas

gassy *adj by 1863* Garrulous; loudly self-important and pretentious

gas something **up** *v phr by 1950s* To make more interesting, exciting, etc; =GIN UP, JAZZ something UP: *Warner Brothers has been around to gas things up a little*—John McCarten

gat *n underworld by 1904* A pistol: . . . *poking his gat your way*—Saturday Evening Post [probably fr *Gatling gun*]

gate 1 *n by 1886* The money collected from selling tickets to a sporting or other entertainment event: . . . *the winner to take seventy-five and the loser twenty-five percent of the gate*—The Lantern **2** *n jazz musicians by 1940s* A performing engagement; =GIG **3** *n jazz musicians fr early 1920s* A musician, a musical devotee, or any man; =CAT **4** *v by 1940s* =GIVE someone THE GATE [musicians' senses fr the simile *swing like a gate,* "play or respond to swing music well and readily," with some influence of *'gator* and *alligator;* or perhaps fr *gatemouth,* a nickname for Louis Armstrong; first musical sense said to have been coined by Louis Armstrong]

See CRASH, GET one's TAIL IN A GATE, GIVE someone THE GATE, SWING LIKE A RUSTY GATE

-gate *combining word 1970s* An exposed affair of corruption, venality, etc, of the sort indicated: *Allengate/ Billygate/ Koreagate/ Lancegate/ Irangate* [fr the *Watergate* scandal of the early 1970s]

gate-crasher *n by 1927* A person who attends a party, entertainment, etc, without invitation or ticket; uninvited guest: *"There are bound to be gate-crashers,"* Mike said—Hugh Pentecost

gatemouth *n black by 1930s* A person who knows and tells everyone else's business; a chronic and active gossip

gatoring *n by 1970s* A sort of ballroom divertissement in which the participants writhe about among one another on the floor: *Gatoring is over*—Parade

gat up *v phr underworld by 1930s* To arm oneself with a pistol

gat-up *n 1920s underworld* An armed robbery; holdup

gauge¹ *n underworld & police by 1970s* A shotgun: . . . *a shotgun is called "the gauge,"* explained Officer Phil Lee—Los Angeles Times/ *This man took a gauge (Armond pantomimes holding a gun, then bends over to dodge from it) and two people end up dead*—Esquire [fr the use of *gauge* to designate the caliber of a shotgun]

gauge² or **gage** *n narcotics by 1930s* Marijuana; =GRASS, POT, WEED [origin unknown; perhaps from *gaged,* "drunk"]

gauge butt *See* GAGE BUTT

gawk *v by 1785* To stare; gape stupidly: . . . *locals gathered to gawk at strange lights. . .* —New York Times/ *They went in and out of the garage to gawk at the body. . .* —Scott Turow [fr dialect *gawk, gouk,* "fool, idiot," literally "cuckoo"]

gawky *adj* by 1759 Awkward; ill-coordinated

gay 1 *adj* homosexuals by 1920s Homosexual; homoerotic: *gay men and women/ gay attitudes* **2** *adj* homosexuals by 1920 Intended for or used by homosexuals: *gay bar/ gay movies* **3** *n* homosexuals by 1920s A male homosexual or a lesbian •Widely used by heterosexuals in preference to pejorative terms: . . . *a hideaway for live-together couples and middle-aged gays*—Albert Goldman ◁**4**▷ *adj* 1980s students Ugly; =CORNY, WEIRD: *The clarinet player looked totally gay in his USC band uniform*—UCLA Slang [perhaps by extension fr earlier British *gay*, "leading a whore's life"]

gay-bashing by 1980s **1** *n* The harassment of homosexuals **2** *modifier*: . . . *after his arrest in a gay-bashing case*—Village Voice

gay boy 1 *n phr* by 1990s A young male homosexual; =GAY: . . . *those of you who have friendships with sweet gay boys will certainly relate*—Sassy **2** *modifier*: *Raoul, 24, is a cute gayboy filmmaker*—Sassy

gay-cat 1 *n* hoboes by 1893 A hobo, esp a novice: *Were not these other tramps mere dubs and "gay-cats"?*—Jack London **2** *n* (also **gey-cat**) by 1902 A homosexual boy; catamite **3** *n* underworld by 1916 A novice criminal who acts as lookout, decoy, etc

gay deceivers *See* FALSIES

gay (or Gay) lib by 1960s **1** *n* The movement that advocates the rights and protection of homosexual persons: . . . *the presence of Gay Lib and advocates for legalization of abortion*—Commentary/ *Your reporter needs to open his closet a little wider to find out how great gay lib is*—Rolling Stone **2** *modifier*: *gay-lib banners/ a gay lib alliance* [modeled on *women's lib*]

gayola by 1950s **1** *n* Bribery, blackmail, and extortion paid by homosexuals and homosexual businesses, esp to police: . . . *for blackmail and for shakedowns by real or phony cops, a practice known as "gayola"*—Time/ *Homosexual bars. . . pay "gayola" to crime syndicates and to law enforcement agencies*—Saturday Review **2** *adj* Homosexual; =GAY: *There have to be some fulfilling alternatives to the gayola fun fair*—Village Voice [first sense modeled on *payola*]

gazabo (gə ZAY boh) *n* by 1896 A man; fellow; =GUY: *The gazabos they put on the jury'll know all about me*—WE Weeks [fr Mexican Spanish *gazapo*, "smart fellow"]

gazer *n* 1930s narcotics A federal narcotics agent; =NARC

See SHADOW GAZER

gazillion *n* by 1990s A very large number; =JILLION, ZILLION: *This is a movie adaptation of John Grisham's gazillion-copy bestseller*—Time/ . . . *some supermodel making gazillions of dollars each year. . .*—Sassy

◁**gazongas** or **guzungas**▷ *n* A woman's breasts; =GARBONZAS, HOOTERS, TITS: *I don't get these women to sweat their gazongas off*—Village Voice

gazoo or **gazool** *See* KAZOO

gazooney or **gazoonie 1** *n* about 1915 A catamite; =PUNK **2** *n* hoboes by about 1920 A young and callow tramp **3** *n* merchant marine by 1940s An ignorant man **4** *n* baseball by 1940s A recruit; =ROOKIE [said to be a variant of *gunsel*]

See GUNSEL[1]

GB or **gb** (pronounced as separate letters) *n* 1940s narcotics =GOOFBALL

gd or **g-d** (pronounced as separate letters) *adj* by 1920s God-damned: *The biggest gd engine in the West*—Stephen Longstreet

GDI *n* 1980s students A person who is not a member of a fraternity or sorority •Stands for "god-damned independent": . . . *I'm a GDI!*—UCLA Slang

gear *adj* early 1950s British Excellent; wonderful; superb: *The opposite of "gear" is "grotty"*—Village Voice [fr the WWI British Army phrase *that's the gear*, "that's right"]

See IN HIGH GEAR, SHIFT INTO HIGH GEAR

gearbox *n* by 1970s A stupid person; idiot; =DIMWIT: . . . *only gearboxes greet strangers*—Toronto Life

geared 1 *adj* Excited; ecstatic; =HIGH: . . . *a sexy rock star, and he got the audience so geared*—Rolling Stone/ *So I was cranked. I was geared*—Milwaukee Journal **2** *adj* prison by 1930s Homosexual

gearhead *n* by 1970s A devotee of cars, car-racing, etc: . . . *translating that into monosyllables for you gearheads*—Car and Driver/ *Robin Yount. . . has always been a gearhead*—Milwaukee Journal

gear-jammer (or -bonger or -grinder or -fighter) *n* 1930s truckers A truck or bus driver

gear up *v phr* by 1890 To prepare; equip oneself: . . . *seem ready to gear up realistically for the very tough political fight ahead*—New York Daily News/ *Geriatric Gearing Up*—New York Daily News [fr *gear up*, "to put the harness on a horse," found by 1886]

gedunk (gee DUNK) *n* WWII Navy Ice cream, pudding, and the like

gee[1] or **g** (JEE) *n* by 1907 A fellow; man; =GUY: *He was the mayor, and he was one smart gee*—James T Farrell [abbreviation of *guy*]

See HIP GEE, WRONG GEE

gee[2] or **g** (JEE) *n* hoboes by 1940s A gallon of liquor [abbreviation of *gallon*]

gee[3] or **g** (JEE) **1** *n* by 1928 A thousand dollars; =GRAND **2** *n* by 1940s Money [abbreviation of *grand*]

gee[4] (JEE) *interj* by 1895 An exclamation of surprise, pleasure, sheepishness, etc; =GEE WHIZ [a euphemism for *Jesus*]

See HOLY CATS

gee[5] *adj* 1970s teenagers Disgusting; rebarbative; =GROSS [abbreviation of *gross*]

◀**geechee** or **geechie**[1]▶ (GEE chee) black by 1905 **1** *n* A black person, esp a Southern rural black: . . . *obsessed with hatred for the "geechees," those he feels are holding back the race*—Washington Post **2** *n* The dialect, culture, etc, of Southern rural or sea-coast blacks **3** *n* A low-country South Carolinian, esp one from the Charleston area [origin uncertain or mixed; perhaps fr the *Ogeechee* River in northern Georgia or another place name and ultimately fr a Native American language; perhaps fr *geejee,* "the Gullah dialect or a speaker of that dialect," and ultimately fr the name of a language and tribe in the Kissy region of Liberia]

◀**geechie²**▶ (GEE chee) *n WWII armed forces* A woman of the South Pacific region, esp of the islands occupied by US forces in World War II [fr *geisha girl,* perhaps influenced by *geechee*]

geed (or g'd) up¹ (JEED) *hoboes by 1940s* **1** *adj phr* Crippled **2** *adj phr* Battered and bent [perhaps from *gimp,* "limp"]

geed (or g'd) up² (JEED) *adj phr narcotics by 1940s* Intoxicated with narcotics, esp stimulants [perhaps fr *geared up*]

gee-gee (JEE jee) *n by 1869* A horse, esp a mediocre race horse ●British child's word for *horse: I like to follow the gee-gees*—J Evans/ *You can go to bet the gee-gees at Hialeah or Gulfstream*—Washingtonian [perhaps fr the command *gee* given to a horse]

geek 1 *n 1920s carnival & circus* A sideshow freak, esp one who does revolting things like biting the heads off of live chickens **2** *n 1920s carnival & circus* A snake charmer **3** *n 1920s carnival & circus* A pervert or degenerate, esp one who will do disgusting things to slake deviant appetites; =CREEP, WEIRDO **4** *n* (also **geekoid**) *by 1990s* A devotee; fan; =FREAK, NERD: *. . . and assorted science-fiction geeks around the world who actually call themselves cyberpunk*—Time [origin unknown; perhaps related to British dialect *geck, geke,* "fool"; according to David Maurer, "said to have originated with a man named Wagner of Charleston, WV, whose hideous snake-eating act made him famous"] *See* GINK

geek out *1990s computer* **1** *v phr* To speak about computers in specialized technical language, esp among noninitiates: *Go hang around a mouse potato and see if you can get him to geek out and do a brain dump*—Macon Telegraph **2** *v phr* To do programming with obsessive intensity: *Not infrequently, Michael locks himself inside and geeks out on code*—Douglas Coupland

geekspeak *n 1990s computer* The jargon and slang of computer users: *The lingo: Geekspeak on the information highway*—Mesa Tribune

geeky or **geekazoid** *adj by 1980s* Eccentric and repulsive; =WEIRD, CREEPY, NERDLY: *Kia. . . sets her up with geeky granola-type Ely. . .* —Vogue/ *. . . the geeky game played a company picnics*—Buzz/ *Maybe you have a geekazoid freshman brother who is the designated wedgie-victim of the entire 11th grade*—Sassy

gee string *See* G-STRING

geetus or **geetis** or **geedus** (GEE təs) *n* (also **geedus, geetis, geets**) *1930s underworld & hawkers* Money: *Pitchman must give the store a 40 percent cut on the "geedus"*—M Zolotow/ *I'm spendin' my hard-earned geets*—The Jazz Word

gee whiz¹ 1 *interj* (also **Gee whiz, gee whillikins, gee willikers**) main entry form by 1885; others somewhat earlier An exclamation of approval, surprise, mild disapproval, emphasis, etc; =GOSH: *But gee willikers, he does arithmetic like lightning*—Washington Post **2** *adj by 1980s* Enthusiastic; very much impressed; youthfully optimistic: *With a very gee-whiz kid, you're not talking about a very long period*—Philadelphia Journal/ *Finch's willed naiveté frequently leads to gee-whiz insights*—Village Voice **3** *adj by 1990s* Very impressive, esp in a gaudy way: *. . . a windowless conference room that felt gee-whiz, a little Big Brother by way of Virginia. One wall was filled with a couple of dozen television sets. . .* —New York Times [a euphemism for *Jesus*]

gee whiz² *n phr underworld by 1950s* An armed pickpocket [fr *gee,* "gun," and *whiz,* "pickpocket"]

geez or **geeze** (GEEZ) *v narcotics by 1940s* To have or give a dose of narcotics, esp an injection: *They drop acid, go up on DMT and "geeze" (mainline meth)*—Newsweek/ *I need to geez now, Bumper. Real bad*—Joseph Wambaugh/ *I geezed that scum*—Newark Star Ledger

geezed or **geezed up** *by 1940s* **1** *adj* or *adj phr* Drunk **2** *adj* or *adj phr* Intoxicated with narcotics; =GEED UP, HIGH

geezer¹ *by 1885* **1** *n* A man, esp an old man; =DUFFER, GAFFER, GUY: *It gave him all kinds of confidence just to hear the big geezer spout*—J Lilienthal/ *He is a tall geezer with chin whiskers*—H Allen Smith **2** *modifier*: *Van Dyke's comeback is part of a multinetwork trend toward what could be called geezer mysteries*—Milwaukee Journal/ *"Geezer rock" goes on tour*—Milwaukee Journal [fr earlier and possibly Cockney *giser,* "mummer, one who puts on a guise or mask," hence, a quaint figure; the origin resembles that of *guy*]

geezer² **1** *n prison by 1920s* A drink of liquor; =SNORT **2** *n narcotics by 1940s* A dose or injection of a narcotic

geezer-bashing *adj by 1990s* Denigrating and blaming old people: *. . . major media have provided ample amplification for Lead or Leave's geezer-bashing message*—Extra!

geezo *n prison by 1920s* An inmate, esp an experienced one [probably fr *geezer¹*]

gel or **jell** **1** *v by 1950s* To come to a firm and useful form; =WORK: *In this highly partisan county, it just didn't gel*—Chicago Tribune/ *If this doesn't gel, the local people. . . will be stuck*—Philadelphia Journal/ *Frost's saga fails to jell either as compelling drama or convincing social portraiture. . .* —Newark Star-Ledger **2** *v* (also **jell out**) *1980s students* To relax; =CHILL OUT, KICK BACK: *After having five hours of class today I think I'll just go home and gel*—UCLA Slang [second sense perhaps fr the notion of productively sitting still as a *gelatin* pudding does]

gelt (GELT) *n* by 1529 Money: *To let you guys get away with the gelt?*—W E Weeks [fr German and Yiddish, literally "gold"]

gendarme *n* by 1906 A police officer; =COP, FUZZ: *Can you drive the Viper without being stopped by every other gendarme?*—New York Times [fr French]

gender bender by 1980 **1** *n phr* A person who tends to reverse or alter traditional notions of sex roles, dress, etc **2** *modifier*: . . . *a two-day search for Boy George, the 25-year-old "gender-bender" pop star. . .* —Washington Post

gender-bending 1980s **1** *n* The reversal or alteration of sex roles, dress, etc; androgyny: *A decade or so ago, cinematic gender-bending reached unprecedented levels*—Milwaukee Journal **2** *modifier*: *Madonna is known for her gender-bending antics*—Denver Public Radio

general *See* ARMCHAIR GENERAL, BUCK GENERAL

generic *adj* 1980s students Inferior; =CHEESY, GROTTY: *Larry King doesn't appear to be generic: he has a distinctive voice, and he doesn't look like anybody else*—New York Times

gent (JENT) *n* by 1564 A man; fellow; =GUY: *A hefty, tough-talking gent of not quite 50*—P Edson

gentleman's C *n phr* by 1940s A satisfactory rating, but not a high one: *The Sierra Club gives Ruckelshaus only a "gentleman's C"*—Time [fr the passing but mediocre grade traditionally given in college to well-bred but not serious students]

the **gents** *n phr* by 1938 The men's toilet •Chiefly British

Gen-X or **twentysomethings** *n* early 1990s Generation-X, the set of white middle-class people born after the baby-boom generation: *He has a bunch of the Gen-X jargon in there. . .* —Macon Telegraph [fr the title of a 1991 book by Douglas Coupland]

george *v* black by 1950s To invite to sexual activity; =PROPOSITION: *One of the girls georged him, just for kicks*—C Cooper

George 1 *interj* by 1731 =BY GEORGE **2** *adj* (also **george**) teenagers by 1951 Excellent; great; superb: *She's real George all the way*—Newsweek **3** *n* British aviators by 1931 The automatic pilot of an aircraft **4** *n* 1950s rock and roll A theater usher [aviation sense because *George* became the term for any airman in the British forces, like "Jack" for a sailor and "Tommy" for a soldier] *See* BIG GEORGE, LET GEORGE DO IT, the REAL GEORGE, SHORTY GEORGE

George Washington *n phr* by 1990s A dollar; a dollar bill [fr the portrait on the bill]

gerbil tube *n phr* 1980s An enclosed overpass for pedestrians [fr devices used in *gerbil* cages]

◁**German goiter**▷ *n phr* by 1940s A protuberant paunch; =BEER BELLY

gerpin' *adj* 1990s teenagers Behaving violently and irrationally; crazy: *If you're crazy, east side teens may say you're "trippin,'" "postal," or "gerpin'"*—KRT News Service

get 1 *v* by 1892 To seize mentally; grasp; understand: *Do you get me?*—Zora Neale Hurston **2** *v* by 1950s To take note of; pay attention to: *Get him, acting like such a big shot* **3** *v* by 1853 To kill or capture; take vengeance; retaliate destructively against: *He can't say that. I'll get him* **4** *n* by 1320 Offspring; progeny •Used contemptuously, as if of an animal **5** *n* show business by 1950s =GATE, TAKE **6** *n* underworld by 1940s The route taken by criminals in fleeing the scene of their efforts: *The get, or getaway route*—E DeBaun

get one's **1** *v phr* by 1910 To get the punishment one deserves: *Don't worry, he'll get his before this is all over* **2** *v phr* by 1940s To become rich; get one's large share of worldly goods: *She went into this business determined to get hers by the time she was thirty* [probably fr the notion of *getting one's deserts*]

get a bag on *See* TIE A BAG ON

get a bang (or **charge) out of** someone or something *v phr* about 1930 To enjoy especially; get a thrill out of: *The younger set is not "getting a bang" out of things anymore*—New York Times

get (or **draw) a bead on** someone or something *v phr* by 1841 To take very careful aim at something or someone; concentrate successfully; =ZERO IN: *She has, however, got a bead on her five original characters*—Washington Post [fr the bead-like appearance of the front sight of a rifle; the date is for the *draw* form]

get a broom up one's **ass** *See* HAVE A BROOM UP one's ASS

get (or **have) a can on** *v phr* 1920s To get drunk: *A gal used to throw herself out the window every time she got a can on*—Dorothy Parker

get a clue *v phr* teenagers by 1980s To understand; grasp; become aware; =DIG, WISE UP •Often in the imperative: *Get a Clue Dept: Rockwell and AT&T have revolutionized telecommunications. . .* —PC Magazine

get something **across (** or **over)** *v phr* by 1894 To explain successfully; =PUT something ACROSS: *He decided to devote all his energy to getting his own platform across*—Howard Fast [fr a stage term for success, *to get it across the footlights*]

get a crush on someone *See* HAVE A CRUSH ON someone

get one's **act (** or ◁**shit**▷**) together** *See* GET IT TOGETHER

get (or **have) a free ride 1** *v phr* by 1927 To enjoy something without paying; get something gratis **2** *v phr* poker by 1940s To get the next card without betting, because no one in the game wishes to start the betting **3** *v phr* baseball by 1980s To get a base on balls

get a handle on someone *v phr* by 1972 To begin to understand someone; have a clue as to someone's character, behavior, etc: *That's right. I can't get a handle on him*—Lawrence Sanders

get a handle on something or someone *v phr* by 1972 To find a way of coping; discover how to proceed: *Sometimes I think I haven't got a handle on things anymore*—Armistead Maupin/ *They've just got to get a handle on this thing*—Whitey Herzog

get (or take) a hinge at *v phr* by 1930s To look at; glance at: *I only write you letters instead of getting a hinge at yr. . . kisser*—John O'Hara/ *. . . a fast hinge at the sodden courtyard*—R Starnes [perhaps fr the action of turning the head, as if on a *hinge*]

get a hump on *v phr* by 1890s To speed up; hurry; get busy; =GET A MOVE ON: *Get a hump on with that assignment, OK?*

get a hustle on *See* GET A MOVE ON

get a kick out of someone or something *v phr* by 1903 To enjoy immensely; take great pleasure in: *I sure get a kick. . . out of the way you guys kid each other along*—Joseph Heller/ *I get a kick out of you*—Cole Porter (from a song lyric)

get a life *teenagers and students by middle 1980s* **1** *v phr* To do something significant; stop wasting time on trivia: *When someone calls the NBA office and says "What are you going to do about Calvin Murphy putting voodoo on that man?" that person needs to get a life*—Milwaukee Journal/ *"Get a life," Captain Kirk once told some Trekkies*—Nation **2** *interj* An exclamation of disgust and impatience •The exhortation is very much like "Get out of my face" or "Get lost" or "Stop bugging me!": *Upon reading Donald Trump's response to the article, I have but three words for him: Get A Life!*—Vanity Fair

get (or have) a little on the side *v phr* by 1940s To be sexually unfaithful; =CHEAT

get a load of *v phr* by 1929 To examine; attend to; =GET: *Let him get a load of the new suit of clothes*—James M Cain

get along (or on) **1** *v phr* by 1888 To live without any great joy nor grief; pass through life more or less adequately; cope; =GET BY **2** *v phr* by 1856 To be compatible; associate easily: *He didn't get along with the boss*

get a move on *v phr* (Variations: **hump** or **hustle** or **wiggle** may replace **move**) *entry form by 1891;* hump by 1892; wiggle by 1896 To hurry; speed up;: *Tell him to damn well get a wiggle on*—Laurence Stallings & Maxwell Anderson

get an attitude *v phr black by 1960s* To become hostile and resentful: *At first I got an attitude about it. . . I thought it had to do with race*—Baltimore Sun

get an offer one **can't refuse** *See* MAKE AN OFFER one CAN'T REFUSE

get another kick at the cat *v phr* by 1980s To have another chance: *. . . an attorney could lose one trial strategy, then present a new one to "get another kick at the cat"*—Milwaukee Journal

get a rise out of someone *v phr* by 1886 To get a response from someone, esp a warm or angry one: *His limp joke got a rise and some projectiles out of the crowd* [fr the *rising*, the appearance, of a fish or other quarry]

get around *v phr* by 1928 To be socially active and desirable •With often a hint of sexual promiscuity: *. . . she was a beautiful woman and one of modern temperament. Carolyn, we know, got around*—Scott Turow

get around someone *v phr* by 1891 To persuade or fool someone, often with an illicit motive: *Somehow she managed to get around the jury*

◁**get (or have) one's ashes hauled**▷ *v phr* by 1910 To do the sex act: *. . . that spider climbin' up that wall, goin' up there to get her ashes hauled*—Jelly Roll Morton [*ashes* is probably a euphemism for *ass*]

◁**get one's ass in a sling**▷ *See* HAVE one's ASS IN A SLING

◁**get one's ass in gear**▷ *v phr* by 1940s To get into action; stop loafing and wasting time; =PUT A VERB IN IT: *I'd best get my ass in gear and pull this case out of sewer city. . .*—Stan Cutler

get at someone *v phr* by 1865 To influence someone illicitly: *They found there was no way to get at the judge*

get (or have) a toehold *v phr* by 1940s To get or have a precarious grip on something; get or have an uncertain command: *You've got a good toehold on the job; now let's see you take over* [fr the sort of unsure footing one has when only the *toes* are planted and the precarious seizure one has made when only the *toe* of the quarry is in one's grip]

getaway by 1890s **1** *n* The act of fleeing, esp from the scene of a crime: *How about a quiet getaway from this mad scene?* **2** *modifier*: *our getaway car/ getaway route/ getaway vacation package* *See* MAKE one's GETAWAY

getaway day *n phr horse-racing by 1940s* The last day of a race meeting

get away with something by 1878 **1** *v phr* (also **get by with** something) To go uncaught and unpunished after doing something illegal or indiscreet: *I didn't get away with hassling the committee* **2** *v phr* To steal or run off with something: *He came for a friendly visit and got away with my stereo*

get away with murder *v phr* by 1920 To go unpunished or unharmed after some risk or impudence: *. . . bitter complaints that Reagan was getting away with murder in the press*—Washingtonian

get one's or someone's **back up** *v phr* by 1887 To become angry or make someone angry, esp in a way to cause one to resist: *When they said he was lying, that got his back up*

◁not **get** one's **balls in an uproar**▷ *See* NOT GET one's BALLS IN AN UPROAR

get one's **banana peeled** *See* HAVE one's BANANA PEELED

get (or groove) behind **1** *v phr 1960s narcotics* To have a pleasurable narcotic intoxication **2** *v phr* by 1970s To enjoy something: *I can't get behind this, I keep trying to tell you*—Cyra McFadden

get behind something or someone *v phr* by 1903 To support or advocate a person, cause, etc;

=PUSH: *If we all get behind the amendment, it'll pass*

get one's **bell rung** *v phr* sports by 1960s To be injured; esp to get a head injury: *Conlon got his bell rung Tuesday night. . . when he was accidentally kicked in the head*—Milwaukee Journal Sentinel

get bent *interj* 1980s students An exclamation of scorn and dismissal; =DROP DEAD, GET A LIFE, GO FUCK YOURSELF, GO TO HELL

get one's **bones** *v phr* prison by 1980s To earn the tattoo of an underworld gang

get busy (or **down) ** *v phr* 1980s students To do the sex act; =SCREW: *Let's get busy*—UCLA Slang [fr *get down to business*]

get by 1 *v phr* by 1918 To do just acceptably well; neither succeed nor fail, but survive; =MAKE OUT: *We were barely getting by on two salaries* 2 *v phr* by 1904 To barely escape failure; scrape by 3 *v phr* by 1914 To pass inspection; stand up to scrutiny: *His work didn't get by the manager*

get someone **by the short hairs (** or **curlies** or **knickers)** *See* HAVE someone BY THE SHORT HAIRS

get by with something *See* GET AWAY WITH something

get (or **have) ** one's **card punched** *v phr* by 1960s To have one's credentials, merit, etc, verified: *I'm not here to get my civil-rights card punched*—Walter Mondale [fr the periodic punching of one's union card to show that one has paid one's dues]

get one's **clock cleaned** *v phr* by 1960s To be assaulted and injured; be pummeled: *. . . you could get your clock cleaned by a Boy Scout if you started chasing him incautiously*—Robert B Parker

get cold feet *See* HAVE COLD FEET

get one's **cookies (** or **jollies** or **kicks)** *v phr* by 1950s To enjoy one's keenest pleasure; indulge oneself; =GET OFF ●Usually with a hint of perversion: *The owner. . . gets his jollies by walking around. . . in a Sioux war bonnet*—D Welch/ *This how you get your cookies?*—George V Higgins

get cracking (or **cutting) ** Royal Air Force about 1925 1 *v phr* To commence: *. . . made a mental note to get cracking on Kenneth Bodin*—Lawrence Sanders 2 *v phr* To go or work faster: *. . . and if we don't get cracking, get serious, and get leadership*—Washingtonian

get crosswise with someone *v phr* by 1990s To be in conflict with someone: *He had got himself crosswise with the boss*—National Public Radio

get one's **dander (** or **Irish) up** dander by 1831; Irish by 1834 1 *v phr* To cause anger; infuriate; =PISS-OFF: *That law gets my dander up* 2 *v phr* To become angry; =BLOW one's TOP: *They got their dander up and decided to fight the case in court*—Washington Post [origin of *dander* form unknown; the form *rise my dandee up* is found in a nautical context in 1839, and is probably related]

get digits *See* PULL NUMBERS

get down 1 *v phr* gambling by 1901 To stake one's money or chips; bet: *All right, get down on this card*—A Lomax 2 *v phr* black musicians by 1960s To make an effort; get serious; attend to the task: *. . . so I get down now and then to try to block a couple of shots*—Village Voice/ *She's gonna get down. She just plans for it*—Cameron Crowe 3 *v phr* 1970s black To let oneself be natural and unrestrained: *. . . to really get down and relate*—Cyra McFadden/ *It's really egalitarian that you can come here and just get down with regular people*—CoEvolution Quarterly 4 *modifier*: *. . . a get down player for those who enjoy that thumping sound*—Downbeat 5 *v phr* 1970s teenagers To enjoy oneself; have fun: *Shoot yo' cuffs, boy, jack-knife yo' legs. Get down*—Buzz 6 *v* 1950s narcotics To use a narcotic, esp heroin 7 *v phr* (also **get busy**) by 1960s To do the sex act; =BOFF, SCREW: *. . . a chapter on sex straightforwardly called "All About Getting Down"*—Time 8 *v phr* 1990s teenagers To join oneself to; get in the good graces of ●Used by jazz musicians in the 1930s, and revived by teenagers in the 1990s: *Groups of amateur performers can "get down with God" by recording a rap song based on the Ten Commandments. . .*—Milwaukee Journal [perhaps fr *get down to it* and *get down to business,* "begin to work seriously"; perhaps from an unattested *get down and dirty*] *See* DOWN

get someone **down** *v phr* by 1930 To depress or annoy; =MIFF: *That constant whine gets me down*

get down and boogie *v phr* by 1980s To enjoy oneself; =HAVE A BALL, PARTY: *That said, we're ready to get down and boogie*—Gary Trudeau

get down on someone *v phr* by 1875 To show strong disapproval or lack of trust; rebuke; upbraid: *Mama used to get down on me about hanging out with Reno*—Claude Brown *See* GO DOWN ON someone

get down to brass tacks *See* DOWN TO BRASS TACKS

get down to cases *v phr* by 1930s To talk seriously; =TALK TURKEY

get (or **have) ** one's **ducks in a row** *See* HAVE one's DUCKS IN A ROW

get even *v phr* by 1858 To take revenge; =EVEN THE SCORE: *His motto was "Don't get mad, get even"*

get one's **feet wet** *v phr* by 1960s To initiate oneself or be initiated into something; have a first and testing experience of something: *Try one or two, just to get your feet wet* [fr the image of a person who goes into the water very carefully rather than plunging in]

◄**get fucked**► *interj* by 1970s A rude utterance of rejection, scorn, dismissal, etc: *And Robbie said, "Get fucked, Tony," and hung up*—Elmore Leonard [possibly modeled on British *get stuffed,* found by 1952]

get one's **gage up** 1 *v phr* =GET one's DANDER UP 2 *v phr* To become drunk [probably from the condition shown by a rising pressure *gauge* on a steam boiler, influenced by *gaged,* "drunk"]

get someone's **goat (** or **nanny) ** *v phr* by 1910

To annoy: *His bitching gets my goat sometimes* [perhaps fr depriving a racehorse of its goat mascot; perhaps fr French *prendre sa chèvre*, "take one's source of milk or nourishment"]

◁**get** one's **head out of** one's **ass**▷ (or **tuckus**) *v phr* To start paying attention; become aware and active; =GET ON THE BALL: *Make the system work. Get your head out of your Hollywood ass—* Pulpsmith/ *Now get your head outta your tuckus!—* Milwaukee Journal

get hep *v phr by 1906* To become aware; become up to date; =GET WISE, WISE UP

get one's **hooks into** (or **on**) *v phr by 1926* To get possession of, esp in a predatory way; get hold of: *If they get their hooks into you, you're a goner* ●Often used of a woman who has pursued and caught a man: *Once I got my hooks into those books I kept them* [fr *hooks*, "hands, fingers"]

get horizontal *v phr by 1980s* To do the sex act; =BOFF, SCREW: *I'll remember this when it's time to get horizontal—*New York Times

◁**get in** (or **it in**)▷ *v phr by 1888* To succeed in penetrating someone sexually; =GET INTO someone's DRAWERS (or PANTS)

get in (or **into**) **a jam** *v phr* (also **get jammed up**) *by 1914* To encounter trouble; =GET INTO HOT WATER: *Call me if you get into a jam/ . . . stay away from those guys. You're only going to get jammed up—*Michael Grant

get something **in edgewise** (or **edgeways**) *v phr by 1824* To succeed in saying or interjecting something: *You can't even get a "Yeah, I'm still alive" in edgewise—*Seventeen

get in someone's **face** *v phr by 1970s* To confront someone; be present and provocative: *Don't you get in my face no more. . . I'll kill you—*Donald Goines/ *. . . the perpetrators bumped off someone who was apparently getting in their faces—* Milwaukee Journal

get in someone's **hair** *v phr by 1851* To annoy someone; nag at someone: *But with him always being away, we don't have time to get into each other's hair—*New Yorker [the dated instance is *have in one's hair*]

get in on the ground floor *v phr business & finance by 1904* To be an original participant, esp in something profitable: *Sign up today if you want to get in on the ground floor* [*ground floor* meaning "the very basis or beginning" is found by 1864]

get into the act *v phr by 1940s* To join in; participate; esp to intrude where one is not wanted [popularized by Jimmy Durante's lament, "Everybody wants to get into the act"]

◁**get into** someone's **drawers** (or **pants**)▷ *adv phr by 1960s* Into the venue of venereal delight; enjoying sex with someone; =GET IN: *You wouldn't believe how easy it is to get into her drawers*

get into hot water *v phr by 1848* To encounter trouble; incite hostility to oneself: *. . . which reportedly got van Zuylen into hot water with the designer—*Vogue

get in wrong *adv phr by 1910* In trouble; in disfavor: *I don't get in wrong with no fuzz/ He must have done something horrible to get that much in wrong*

get one's **Irish up**   *See* GET one's DANDER UP

get it 1 *v phr by 1851* =GET IT IN THE NECK ◁**2**▷ *v phr by 1889* To do the sex act; =BOFF, SCREW **3** *v phr by 1892* To understand; =DIG: *I read it to him twice before he got it*

get (or **catch**) **it in the neck** *v phr by 1887* To be severely punished or injured: *The poor wimp got it in the neck again* [probably an allusion to hanging]

◁**get it off**▷ *by 1960s* **1** *v phr* To have an orgasm; ejaculate semen; =COME OFF **2** *v phr* To do the sex act **3** *v phr* To masturbate

get it on *by 1960s* ◁**1**▷ *v phr* To become sexually excited; get an erection: *Or, in the words of the young, they can get it on—*Mike Royko ◁**2**▷ *v phr* To do the sex act; =GET IT OFF: *If Eric Valdez had gotten it on with Mrs Esteva, he was a major leaguer—* Robert B Parker **3** *v phr* (also **get it off**) To enjoy something greatly; have a good time; =JAM: *. . . three, five, fifteen guys in a studio just get it off—*Ringo Starr/ *And they overlay their daring with pure joy. They're getting it on—*Sports Illustrated

get it together (or **all together**) *v phr* (Variations: one's **act** or one's **head** or one's **shit** or one's **stuff** may replace **it**) *1960s counterculture fr black* To arrange one's life or affairs properly; integrate and focus oneself: *Get your shit together, said Junior Jones—*John Irving/ *. . . why the executive departments of government don't get their act together—*Lewis Powell/ *Congress has to get its shit together—*W T Tyler

◁**get it up**▷ *v phr by 1950s* To achieve and retain an erection; =GET IT ON: *I couldn't get it up in the State of Israel—*Philip Roth/ *He was so bashful he could not get it up—*Xaviera Hollander

get one's **jollies** (or **kicks**)   *See* GET one's COOKIES

get one's **knickers in a twist** *v phr* (Variations: one's **panties in a bunch** or one's **pants in a wad** or one's **shorts in a knot** may replace **knickers in a twist**) *entry form by 1971* To become very agitated and angry: *It's the right-wingery of the Ayatollah's death sentence that gets people's knickers in a twist—*New York Times/ *This kind of crap really gets my pants in a wad—*Sassy *See* NOT GET one's BALLS IN AN UPROAR

get lost *by 1940s* **1** *v phr* To leave; depart; =SCRAM ●Usually an exasperated command: *. . . if the cops or I ask her a direct question. . . she'll tell us to get lost—*Lawrence Sanders **2** *interj* An exclamation of severe and abrupt rejection; =DROP DEAD

get one's **lumps** *v phr by 1935* To be severely beaten, punished, rebuked, etc: *Their greatest fun is to see a cop getting his lumps—*H Lee

get naked *v phr by 1980s* To have a good time; really enjoy oneself; =JAM, PARTY

get next to someone *v phr by 1896* To become familiar with someone, esp in view of sexual favors:

I'm telling you, you were liable to get next to that broad—A Lomax

get nowhere fast *v phr* by 1920s To make no progress whatever; be stuck: *He was getting nowhere fast and was more depressed*—Charles Beardsley

◁**get one's nuts**▷ *v phr* (Variations: **cracked** or **off** may be added) *by 1940s or earlier* To have an orgasm; ejaculate semen: *He'd get his nuts just looking at her/ When I'd gotten my nuts off about six times, we got hungry*—Claude Brown

get off 1 *v phr* narcotics by 1950s To get relief and pleasure from a dose of narcotics: *How we s'posed to get off with no water to mix the stuff with?*—Philadelphia Bulletin ◁**2**▷ *v phr* by 1860s To do the sex act; have an orgasm; =GET IT OFF: *It is led by trendy bisexual types, who love to get off amidst the chic accouterments of a big smack-and-coke party*—Albert Goldman **3** *v phr* musicians by 1930s To play an improvised solo **4** *v phr* by 1835 To avoid the consequences of; =GET AWAY WITH something: *He thinks he might get off with probation* **See** TELL someone WHERE TO GET OFF

get someone off ◁**1**▷ *v phr* by 1860s To bring someone to sexual climax: *She was really eager and it didn't take long to get her off* **2** *v phr* by 1960s To please greatly; move and excite: *Ron sings so fast because it gets us off*—Village Voice/ *I've got to write stuff. . . that will get people off*—Aquarian

◁**get off one's ass**▷ *v phr* (Variations: **butt** or **dead ass** or **duff** may replace **ass**) *by 1940s* To stop being lazy and inert; =GET CRACKING: *He wasn't able to get his class off their dead ass*

get off someone's **back** (or **neck**) *v phr* by 1880 To leave alone; stop nagging or annoying: *All they need is for Government to get off their backs*—Time/ *. . . get this clown off my back. . .* —Hugh Nightingale [the date is very imprecise; the notion of being a burden, *on one's back,* is found by 1677]

get off someone's **case** *v phr* black by 1960s To leave alone; =GET OFF someone's BACK: *I hope you will. . . tell your mother to get off your case*—Ann Landers/ *Get off my case, O.K., Dad?*—New Yorker

get off one's **high horse** *v phr* by 1928 To stop being haughty and superior; deal informally; =COME OFF one's PERCH [the notion of *high horse,* "pretentious arrogance," is found by 1716]

get off on *v phr* by 1950s To enjoy greatly; like very much: *. . . you get the impression she got off on it, like she wanted to roll a little in the dirt*—William Bayer/ *She really got off on Eddings*—Cyra McFadden [fr earlier *get off,* and less frankly sexual] **See** TELL someone WHERE TO GET OFF

get off the block *v phr* by 1980s To start, esp to start quickly: *My game plan was to get off the block first and stay out there*—Toronto Life [fr the *starting blocks* used by runners for initial impetus]

get off the dime *v phr* by 1925 To start; stop wasting time; =GET OFF THE BLOCK: *How do we get off the dime we're on?*—New York Times/ *. . . with*

word from the Mayor to get off the dime—Philadelphia Journal [alteration of the expression *stop on a dime,* used to praise the brakes of a car]

get off the ground *v phr* by 1940s To succeed, esp to do so initially: *. . . projects misfired or didn't get off the ground at all*—Saturday Review [fr the take-off of a plane]

get something **off the ground** *v phr* by 1940s To make a successful start: *As Wilbur said to Orville, "You'll never get it off the ground"*

get someone **off the hook** *v phr* by 1864 To aid someone in evading or preventing punishment, responsibility, etc: *He falls for Ilona. . . and winds up trying to get her off the hook*—J Kelly

get on (or **along**) *v phr* by 1885 To grow old; age **See** GET ALONG

get on someone *v phr* by 1940s To deride; harass; =HASSLE, RAG: *. . . it helps them stay cool when their boss gets on them*—New York Times

get on one's **bicycle** *v phr* 1920s prizefight To keep retreating from one's opponent in the boxing ring; fight defensively

get on someone's **case** *v phr* black by 1960s To meddle in someone's affairs; pay unwanted, annoying attention to someone; criticize; =BUG, HASSLE: *There are times when I get on his case pretty hard*—Sports Illustrated [fr early 1900s black expression *sit on someone's case,* "make a quasi-judicial study and judgment"]

get on one's **high horse** *v phr* by 1856 To become dignified and formal; assume a haughty and arrogant mien: *As soon as I said a little slang to her she got on her high horse* [*ride the high horse* is found by 1716]

get on one's **horse** *v phr* by 1940s To hurry; start at once: *You better get on your horse if you're going to make that plane*

get on someone's **nerves** *v phr* by 1903 To be an irritant; annoy: *This word processor's humming gets on my nerves*

get on the ball *v phr* by 1940s To pay closer attention to doing something right; improve one's performance ●Often an exasperated command [fr *keep your eye on the ball,* fr baseball or other ball sports]

get on the bandwagon *v phr* (Variations: **climb** or **hop** or **leap** or **jump** may replace **get**) *by 1899* To join a person, party, cause, etc, esp one that is currently popular [fr the large circus *wagon* that carried the *band*]

get on the stick (or **wood**) *v phr* by 1940s To get busy; get to work; =GET OFF one's ASS: *She said he'd better get on the stick or she'd dump him*

get on to someone or something *v phr* by 1880 To learn the truth about; come to understand; =GET WISE: *Be careful they don't get on to your little tricks*

get out (or **out of here**) *interj* by 1940s An exclamation of disbelief; =GO ON: *He really said that? Get out!/ . . . didn't we feel just wunderbar. Get out of here*—Stan Cutler **See** ALL GET OUT

get out from under *v phr* by 1875 To extricate oneself from troubles, esp financial troubles: *They'll never get out from under that debt*

get out of someone's **face** *v phr* black by 1942 To leave alone; stop annoying; =GET OFF someone's CASE: *Get out of my face, Jelly!*—Zora Neal Hurston

get out of the gate *v phr* fr horse-racing by 1980s To start; get under way; =GET OFF THE BLOCK: *I think it was important. . . to get out of the gate quickly*—Milwaukee Journal [fr the starting *gate* of a horse track]

get outside of *v phr* by 1888 To eat or drink heartily: *. . . as he got outside of a bowl of chili*—AJ Liebling

get over something *v phr* by 1687 To recover or rebound from something; be restored to the previous norm; surmount: *. . . the 1954 equivalent of "you lost, now get over it"*—Newark Star-Ledger/ *My suggestion is: GET OVER IT! and conduct a decent interview*—Buzz

get something **over** *See* GET something ACROSS

get (or have) someone **over a barrel** *v phr* by 1930s To have someone in a helpless position: *Okay. . . you got me over a barrel*—Robert B Parker/ *It may look like you got me over a barrel now*—Stan Cutler

get something **over with** *v phr* by 1765 To finish or end something without procrastination; come to the stopping point: *It was a very tough job, but we had to get it over with* [the date refers to the phrase *over with*]

get physical *v phr* by 1970s To use the body and body contact, esp roughly or amorously: *The type who might want to get physical early in a relationship, like during the first five minutes*—New York Times

get psyched *v phr* 1950s teenagers To get excited; become enthusiastic

get (or be) real *interj* by 1970s An exhortation to be sensible, to eschew illusion: *"I'll trade them for your Reuben Kincaid sleep goggles." "Get real, pal"*—Douglas Coupland/ *Be real, Smitty, I have to study for a test*—UCLA Slang/ *What other city has both a large number of Quaker activists and a dreadlocked black cult whose house the city has bombed? Get real*—Nation

get religion *v phr* by 1884 To be chastened; learn proper behavior, at last; become a convert: *It appears that Mr. Reagan has got religion on the subject of environmentalism*—National Public Radio [in the strict sense of religious conversion, found by 1772]

◁**get** one's **rocks (or** one's **rocks off)**▷ **1** *v phr* by 1930s To have an orgasm; =GET one's NUTS: *Go out, have a few drinks, and if you're lucky, maybe even get your rocks off*—Advocate/ *. . . people who'd never be caught dead at a 42d Street skinflick to get their rocks off and feel intellectual about it*—E McCormack **2** *v phr* by 1948 To enjoy very much; =GET one's COOKIES: *. . . while everyone else was getting. . . their rocks off at the Muse concerts*—Village Voice/ *I think she gets her rocks off turning squid inside out*—John Irving

◁**get** one's **shit together**▷ *v phr* by 1960s To organize and manage one's affairs and life properly; =HAVE one's DUCKS IN A ROW
 See GET one's ACT TOGETHER

not get one's **shorts in a knot** *See* NOT GET one's SHORTS IN A KNOT

get small *v phr* police by 1980s To disappear; disperse and vanish; =MAKE oneself SCARCE: *Those suspects got small in a hurry*—Los Angeles Times

get smart *v phr* by 1940s To become wisely aware of one's situation, the possibilities, etc; =WISE UP: *Tell him if he doesn't get smart he'll get clobbered*

◁**get stuffed**▷ *interj* British by 1953 =FUCK YOU
 •Chiefly British

get stupid *v phr* 1980s teenagers To have fun; enjoy oneself: *We got stupid at that picnic*—Delcastle Slang

get one's **tail in a gate** ◁**(or tit in a wringer)**▷ *v phr* by 1940s To get into a perilous plight; be in a painful situation: *With the whole bunch against it you got your tail in a gate/ Katie Graham's gonna get her tit caught in a big fat wringer if that's published*—John Mitchell [variant form refers to the old-fashioned washing machine with a hand- or machine-operated *wringer* having counter-rotating cylinders]

get taken off at the knees *v phr* by 1970s To be severely injured; be destroyed: *That guy is just waiting to get taken off at the knees*—Peter Gent

getter *See* GO-GETTER

not get one's **testicles in a twist** *See* NOT GET one's TESTICLES IN A TWIST

get the air *v phr* (Variations: **ax** or **can** or **boot** or **chop** or **heave-ho** or **old heave-ho** may replace **air**) by 1900; ax form by 1883, boot by 1888 To be dismissed, esp to be jilted: *When she found out, he got the air/ Lefebvre got the can in Seattle after building the Mariners to their first over-.500 finish*—New Yorker

get the bird *v phr* vaudeville by 1922 To be greeted with catcalls, hisses, boos, etc [fr the fancied attack by *big birds*, "hissing geese," when a show is radically disliked, a notion found by 1825; the form *get the big bird* is found by 1886]

get the business *v phr* by 1940s To be treated roughly; be punished or rebuked: *When they found out his record he got the business*

get the call *v phr* by 1940s To be appointed or designated: *Boyce got the call. So it's his*—William Bayer

get the (or one's**) drift** *v phr* by 1927 To see the tendency of discourse, esp what one is hinting at: *And it won't show up. Get my drift?* [*drift* in this sense is found by 1549]

get the drop on someone *v phr* by 1869 To get someone in an inferior or threatened position; seize the advantage: *I got the drop on him with that question about oil*

get the goods on someone *v phr* by 1913 To find or collect decisive evidence against: *"Why did you ask me to hire a private detective?". . . "To get the goods on him"*—Ed McBain

get the hang of something *v phr* by 1847 To master the particular skill needed: *If I could get the hang of it, I could live as well for $2500 as in Boston for $5000*—John Lathrop Motley

get the hook *v phr* show business by 1940s To be dismissed, silenced, or rejected, esp suddenly: *Just when he thought he was doing so well, he got the hook* [fr the notion that a wretched performer, esp at an amateur night, was pulled forcibly off the stage with a *hook*]

get the hungries *v phr* by 1980s To become hungry: *I get the hungries for some breakfast*—TV ad

get the jump on someone or something *v phr* by 1912 To get the lead, or an advantage, esp by alert early moves: *Never let the other guy get the jump on you*—Village Voice

get the last dance *v phr* by 1970s To be the winner in the end; triumph finally: *But Dorsey got the last dance, telling jurors Mary had "died a noble death"*—Washington Post [fr the awarding by the belle of the *last dance* at the ball to the favored suitor]

get the lead out *v phr* (Variations: **of** one's **ass** or **of** one's **pants** or **of** one's **feet** may be added) by 1920s To stop loafing; =GET one's ASS IN GEAR, HUSTLE ●Often an irritated command: *Get the lead out and start writing*

get the monkey off (or **off** one's **back**) *v phr* narcotics by 1860 To break a narcotics habit: *. . . so hooked on morphine that there would be no getting the monkey off without another's help*—Nelson Algren

get the munchies *See* HAVE THE MUNCHIES

get the nod *v phr* by 1940s To be approved; be chosen: *There were a dozen other bids. . . but McCulloch got the nod*—Saturday Review

get the picture by 1922 **1** *v phr* To understand; =CAPEESH, DIG ●Often a question: *After I told him about six times he got the picture/ Well, you won't ever be promoted here. Get the picture?* **2** *v phr* To mentally grasp something injurious or repellent to oneself; =GET WISE: *After she caught him with that whore she got the picture*

get the pink slip *v phr* by 1915 To be dismissed or discharged: *When they discovered the shortage of funds he got the pink slip*

◁**get** (or **have**) **the red ass** (or **the ass**)▷ *v phr* Southern by 1940s To become irritated and angry; be irritable: *If any of us gets the red ass about something, then we ought to talk it over*—Dan Jenkins/ *An angry man has the red ass or the RA*—Jim Bouton/ *Has he got the ass?*—American Speech

get there from here *See* YOU CAN'T GET THERE FROM HERE

get the sack *v phr* British by 1825 To be dismissed, with prejudice: *If they protested, they got the sack*

get the shaft *v phr* by 1950s To be ill-treated; be abused, esp by cruel deception: *He thought he'd get promoted, but he got the shaft instead* [a euphemism for sodomization]

◁**get the shitty end of the stick**▷ *v phr* (Variations: **crappy, cruddy, dirty, little, mucky, rough, shit, shitten, short, thick** or **wrong** may replace **shitty**) entry form by 1846, others later To be badly and unfairly treated; have the worst of an arrangement or of luck: *Pastorini got the shit end of the stick, as usual*—Rolling Stone

get the show on the road *v phr* by 1940s To get started; get under way: *Good. Then I can get the show on the road*—Lawrence Sanders

get one's **ticket punched** *v phr* by 1970s To be sent on one's way; be rejected or even killed: *Well, I thought my ticket had been punched*—Whitey Herzog/ *. . . a bus-station sit-com looking not to get your ticket punched*—US Express

get one's **time** *v phr* (Variations: **time** may be replaced by the number of years: **20, 30,** etc) police by 1980s To reach retirement age: *You said you'd retire when you got your time*—Michael Grant

◁**get** one's **tit in the wringer**▷ *See* GET one's TAIL IN A GATE

get to someone **1** *v phr* by 1927 To bribe someone: *I think maybe we can get to the Governor's butler* **2** *v phr* by 1950s To distress or anger someone; =BUG, HASSLE: *It's impossible to "get to" Oliver Barrett III*—Erich Segal/ *I think it is starting to get to me*—Eliot Fremont-Smith **3** *v phr* by 1960s To affect; make an impression: *The puppy really got to me; I couldn't send him to the shelter*

get to first base 1 *v phr* by 1930s To begin well; take a successful first step ●Usually in the negative: *I couldn't get to first base with the committee* **2** *v phr* 1970 teenagers To initiate sexual activity successfully, esp by hugging, caressing, kissing, etc ●In the same baseball analogy, get to third base means touching and toying with the genitals, and get to home plate means to do the sex act, that is, "score"

get-together *n* by 1911 A meeting or session, often social; party

get under someone's **skin** *v phr* by 1896 To trouble or irritate; annoy; =BUG: *That cackle of his soon got under my skin*

get-up 1 *n* underworld by 1925 The end of a prison term **2** *n* by 1861 Dress; costume and grooming: *Why the fancy get-up today?*

get someone **up** *v phr* by 1940s To inspire and energize someone, esp for a game, examination, or other ordeal; =PSYCH oneself UP: *Steinbrenner thinks he can get the players up for games*—Inside Sports [*up* in a similar sense, "excited, vivacious," is found by 1815]

get-up-and-go *n* by 1940s Energy and initiative; pep; =PISS AND VINEGAR, PIZZAZZ: *My get-up-and-go has got up and went* [in the form *get up and get* found by 1884]

get up someone's **nose** *v phr* by *1940s* To irritate someone; provoke hostility: *Put us together and we'd get up each other's noses in a minute*—George Warren

get someone **where** one **lives** *v phr* by *1860* To affect someone profoundly; clutch at the vitals: *. . . the psychological reaction resulting. . . was that it got this nut and this guy where they lived*—Living Age

get someone **where the hair is short (or by the short hairs)** *v phr* first form by *1872*, second by *1888* To have complete control over a person; have a painful advantage: *We've got them where the hair is short, and they can't squirm out*

get wise *v phr* by *1890s* To become impudent or defiant; be saucy: *Get wise with me, punk, and you're dead* [the sense found in *wiseass, wiseguy,* and *wiseacre*]

get wise to *v phr* by *1896* To become aware of; discover: *Had you gotten wise to me, or was it an accident?*—Hugh Pentecost

get with it *v phr* by *1940s* To pay active attention to what is happening or what needs doing; =GET ON THE BALL: *We'll all have to get with it if we want this to turn out right*

get Zs *See* COP ZS

gevalt (gə VAHLT) *interj* by *1960s* An exclamation of woe, distress, shock, etc: *He breaks open a mezuzah, nothing inside, gevalt! but a piece of paper that says "Made in Japan"*—R Alter [fr Yiddish, "powers," hence an invocation of a higher force]

gey-cat *See* GAY-CAT

◁**ghetto box**▷ *n phr* (Variations: **beat box** or **boogie box** or **box** or **coon box** or **ghetto blaster** or **jambox**) *1980s* A large portable stereo radio and cassette player often carried and played loudly in public places: *Hey, man, don't mess with my box*—Wall Street Journal/ *. . . that guy in the streets with his ghetto blaster*—Village Voice

ghost 1 *n* *1920s* A writer paid for a book or article published under someone else's name; professional anonymous author **2** *v* by *1922*: *I "ghosted" my wife's cookbook*—P Darrow **3** *n* by *1833* The mythical paymaster of a theatrical company, who distributes pay as he walks [theater sense said to be fr a line in *Hamlet:* "The *ghost* walks," implying that pay is at hand; analogous with "the eagle shits" referring to the source of pay]

◁**ghost turds**▷ *n phr* Army by *1970s* =HOUSE MOSS

GI (pronounced as separate letters) **1** *adj* WWI armed forces Of, in, or from the US armed forces, esp the Army; government issue: *GI shoes/ His officious ways are very GI* **2** *n* armed forces A member of the US armed forces, esp an enlisted Army soldier serving since or during World War II: *The GIs fought furiously to hold Taejon*—Associated Press **3** *v* WWII Army To scrub and make trim: *They Gled the barracks every Friday night*

See GI PARTY, the GIS

GIB (pronounced as separate letters) *adj* by *1980s* Sexually proficient [fr *good in bed*]

gidget *n* middle *1950s* A lithe and pert young woman [fr *girl midget*]

gift *See* GOD'S GIFT

gift of gab (or the gab) *n phr* by *1650* The ability to talk interestingly, colorfully, and/or persuasively

gig¹ 1 *n* jazz musicians by about *1915* A party for jazz musicians and devotees; =JAM SESSION: *Kid Ory had some of the finest gigs, especially for the rich white folks*—Louis Armstrong **2** *n* jazz musicians by about *1905* A playing date or engagement, esp a one-night job: *. . . on a gig, or one night stand*—Louis Armstrong/ *We found some musicians and I was able to finish the gig*—Whitney Balliett **3** *v*: *. . . their glam-rock band, Nancy Boy, which has already gigged on both coasts. . .*—Vogue/ *. . . I forget whether we're gigging in Basin Street or Buenos Aires*—Dizzy Gillespie **4** *n* *1950s* Any job or occupation: *. . . it's better to take some kind of main gig for their sake*—New York Magazine **5** *n* A criminal act; swindle; =JOB, SCAM: *It ain't no gig, lady, and I don't really care what you think*—Sports Illustrated/ *On my first solo gig I was bagged. . . beaten shitless, and dumped in jail*—Bernard Malamud **6** *n* armed forces by *1940s* A demerit; report of deficiency or breach of rules [origin unknown; musicians' senses are extensions of earlier meanings, "spree, dance, party," found by 1777]

See LIVING-ROOM GIG

◁**gig²**▷ *n* by *1689* =GIGGY [origin unknown; perhaps fr Irish or Anglo-Irish, as attested by the name *sheila-na-gig* given to carved figures of women with grotesquely enlarged vulvae found in English churches; fr Irish *sile na gcioch*, "Julia of the breasts"]

See UP YOURS

gig³ *n* about *1950* An old car [fr *gig,* "one-horse carriage"]

gigabucks *n* by *1990s* Very much money •Much inflated from *megabucks*: *. . . Silicon Valley, where the winners down-loaded giga-bucks. . .*—Los Angeles Times

giggle water *n phr* by *1929* Any alcoholic drink, esp champagne

◁**giggy** or **gigi**▷ by *1950s* **1** *n* The vulva **2** *n* The anus

See UP YOURS

GIGO or **gigo** (GĪ goh) *sentence* computer by *1966* The output is no better than the input [fr *garbage in, garbage out*]

See MEGOGIGO

GI Joe *n phr* WWII armed forces A US soldier, esp an enlisted soldier of and since World War II; =DOGFACE

gilguy (GILL gī) *n* nautical by *1886* =THINGAMAJIG [origin uncertain; used in the mid–19th century to designate a *guy* rope or wire supporting a boom, and often applied to an inefficient *guy*]

gilhickey *n* by *1940s* =THINGAMAJIG

gilhooley 1 *n* by *1940s* =THINGAMAJIG: *I forgot to*

press the hickeymadoodle on the gilhooley—Billy Rose **2** *n* car-racing by 1950s A skid in which a car ends up facing in the reverse direction

gillion *See* JILLION

gills *See* GREEN AROUND THE GILLS, LIT TO THE GILLS, SOUSED, STEWED

Gilroy's kite *See* HIGH AS A KITE

gimcrack or **jimcrack** *n* by 1632 A gaudy trifle; gewgaw; curiosity

gimme or **gimmie 1** *n* by 1927 An acquisitive tendency; greed: *With her it's always gimme, gimme, gimme* **2** *modifier*: *The extent to which the "gimme" spirit has banished rationality*—New York Times **3** *n* golf by 1920s A short putt that is conceded as sunk without actually being tried **4** *n* 1970s A gift; something freely given **5** *n* sports by 1980s A sure win; an easy victory: *Not all that long ago, this was a gimme for the National League*—Milwaukee Journal **6** *n* 1990s police A pistol: *A "gimme" is a pistol, because they're often seen in the hands of somebody saying "gimme your money"*—Los Angeles Times [fr *give me*]
See GIVE ME A BREAK

gimme game *n phr* sports by 1980s An easily won game; a sure victory; =LAUGHER: *We don't have any gimme games in our schedule*—Bob Knight/ *We thought this was going to be a gimme game*—Milwaukee Journal

gimmick 1 *n* by 1926 A secret device or hidden trick that causes something to work and assures that the customer will not win; =GAFF: *A new gimmick, infra-red contact lenses, which. . . enabled a card player to read markings on the backs of cards*—Billy Rose **2** *n* by 1930s Any device; =GADGET **3** *n* 1960s narcotics Apparatus used for preparing and injecting narcotics; =WORKS: *A small red cloth bag with his spike needle and "gimmicks" fell out*—New York Magazine **4** *n* by 1950s A feature in a product, plan, presentation, etc, believed to increase appeal, although it is not necessarily useful or important; =GRABBER, HOOK: *This promo isn't bad, but we sorely need a gimmick* **5** *v*: *Get a fairly good item, then gimmick the hell out of it* **6** *n* by 1950s One's selfish and concealed motive; =ANGLE, PERCENTAGE: *This looks fine, Mr Mayor. What's your gimmick, anyhow?* [origin unknown; perhaps fr *gimcrack*]

gimmickery or **gimmickry** *n* by 1950s The use of gimmicks: *To juxtapose this. . . is sheer gimmickry*—Time

gimmie cap (or hat) *n phr* (also **feed cap**) 1970s A peaked cap like a baseball cap, bearing the trademark or name of a manufacturer and distributed as an advertising device: *She made him stop wearing his John Deere gimmie hat in public places*—New Yorker/ *. . . a "macho" gimmie cap emblazoned with "Cat" (for Caterpillar Tractors)*—New York Times [probably fr the request *"gimme one of those!"* heard when these were available free from dealers]

the **gimmies** *n phr* by 1940s An acquisitive zeal; greed: *They got da gimmies. . . always take, never*

give—James M Cain/ *What they all have in common. . . is a galloping case of the gimmies*—Lawrence Sanders

gimp 1 *n* by 1920s A limp **2** *v*: *The old guy was gimping across the street* ◁**3**▷ *n* by 1920s A lame person; =CRIP: *He'd just kick a gimp in the good leg and leave him lay*—J K Winkler **4** *n* by 1901 Vitality; ambition: *All he needs is a wife with some sense and some gimp*—Donald Henderson Clarke

gimper *n* Air Force by 1940s A competent and efficient airman [see early 1900s British Army phrase *gimp up*, "dress oneself up smartly," fr British dialect *gimp*, "neat"]

gimpy *adj* by 1920s Having a limp or being lame

gin black & street gang by 1950s **1** *n* A street fight; =RUMBLE **2** *v* To fight; scuffle [origin unknown]
See BATHTUB GIN

◁**ginch**▷ *esp motorcyclists* **1** *n* A woman, esp solely as a sexual object; =CHICK: *the fifth ginch I'd had on those eerie sand barrier islands*—Easy Riders/ *. . . cop can't afford that kind of ginch*—George V Higgins **2** *n* The vulva, and sexual activity; =ASS, CUNT: *all the free groupie ginch south of Bakersfield*—George Warren/Hagen. . . *prowls the Stampede for ginch ahoof*—Tom Wolfe [origin uncertain; perhaps related to 1950s Australian and British sense, of surfer origin, "elegance, smartness, skill"]

ginchy *adj* early 1960s Excellent; admirable; elegant; =SEXY: *Annie and I were the cat's pajamas and ginchy beyond belief*—Richard Merkin

ginder *See* CRUMBCRUSHER

◀**ginee**▶ *See* GUINEA

ginger *n* by 1843 Energy; pep; =PIZZAZZ: *. . . the effervescent quality that used to be called "ginger"*—L F McHugh [fr the practice of putting ginger under a horse's tail to increase its mettle and showiness, noted by 1785]

gingerbread 1 *n* by 1700 Money **2** *n* by 1757 Fussy decoration, esp on a house; frillwork **3** *modifier*: *the gingerbread stacks of the old river steamers*

ginger-peachy *adj* teenagers by 1940s Excellent; splendid; =NEAT

ginhead *n* by 1930s A drunkard; =LUSH: *. . . a busted romance that makes her become a ginhead*—Damon Runyon

gink (GINK) by 1908 **1** *n* A man; fellow; =GUY: *Does a gink in Minsk suffer less from an appendectomy?*—Hal Boyle **2** *n* A tedious, mediocre person; =JERK [origin unknown; perhaps somehow fr Turkish, "catamite, punk," found in early 1800s sources both British and US]

gin mill *n phr* by 1860 A saloon; barroom; tavern: *There still are some boobs, alas, who'd like the old-time gin-mill back*—Sinclair Lewis/ *In some gin mill where they know the bartender*—New York Times [certainly influenced by *gin mill*, "cotton mill where a cotton *gin* is used"]

ginned or **ginned up** *adj* or *adj phr* by 1900 Drunk: *Hold me up, kid; I'm ginned*—P Marks

◀**ginnee** or **ginney**▶ *See* GUINEA

Ginnie Mae *n phr by 1970* A government agency that buys Federal Housing Administration loans from lenders, and sells shares to investors [formed from the initials *GNMA,* Government National Mortgage Association]

gin up *v phr by 1887* To enliven; make more exciting; =JAZZ UP: *To gin up support for his embattled plan, the President went to Capitol Hill on Wednesday*—Time/ *Numbers of voters ginned up by the revelations may throw the bums out*—ABC Radio [probably fr earlier *ginger up*]

◀**ginzo** or **guinzo**▶ *by 1931* **1** *n* An Italian or person of Italian descent: *Gonna have at least eight hot ginzos looking for me*—George V Higgins **2** *adj*: *What ginzo broad didn't?*—Patrick Mann **3** *n* Any apparently foreign person; =HUNKY: . . . *a Roumanian or some kinda guinzo*—Joel Sayre [fr *Guinea*]

gip *See* GYP

GI party *n phr WWII Army* A bout of scrubbing and cleaning, esp of the barracks

girene *See* GYRENE

girl 1 *n homosexuals by 1970s* A male homosexual **2** *n narcotics by 1950s* Cocaine: *They call cocaine girl because it gives 'em a sexual job when they take a shot*—C Cooper
 See BACHELOR GIRL, BAR-GIRL, BEST GIRL, B-GIRL, CALL GIRL, CHARITY GIRL, GAL FRIDAY, GLAMOR GIRL, GO-GO GIRL, IDIOT GIRL, OOMPH GIRL, PLAYGIRL, SWEATER GIRL, TOMBOY, V-GIRL, WORKING GIRL

girl Friday *See* GAL FRIDAY

◁**girlie**▷ **1** *n by 1860* A girl: . . . *this girlie and her mother*—Sinclair Lewis **2** *adj by 1950s* Featuring nude or otherwise sexually provocative women: *To some extent, "girlie" magazines are information-getting*—US News & World Report

the **girl next door** *n phr by 1961* A sweet and ordinary young woman, in romance regarded as preferable to a talented, sophisticated, seductive woman

the **GIs** (or ◁**GI shits**▷) *n phr WWII Army* Diarrhea: *An all-night bout with the GIs left him weak and weary*—Time [so called because soldiers often got diarrhea after eating with unclean mess-gear]

gism *See* JISM

gismo *See* GIZMO

git *interj by 1864* A command to leave; =BLOW, SCRAM

git-box or **git-fiddle** *n 1920s jazz musicians* A guitar

git-go *See* FROM THE GIT-GO

give *interj by 1956* A command to speak, to explain, etc: *She said, "Give!," so I told all*
 See WHAT GIVES

give (or **write**) someone **a blank check** *v phr by 1884* To give someone leave to do whatever he or she wishes; give carte blanche: *The man gave me a blank check to order whatever I needed*

give someone **a buzz** *v phr by 1925* To call someone on the telephone: *Just give me a buzz*—Scott Turow

not **give a damn** *See* NOT GIVE A DAMN

◀not **give a fuck**▶ *See* NOT GIVE A DAMN

◀not **give a fuck for nothing**▶ *See* NOT GIVE A FUCK FOR NOTHING

give someone **a grease job** *v phr by 1940s* To flatter

give someone **a hand 1** *v phr by 1860* To help: *Gimme a hand with this huge crate* **2** *v phr by 1890* To applaud someone by clapping the hands: *Give the little lady a big hand, folks!*

give someone **a hard time** *by 1940s* **1** *v phr* To scold or rebuke; quarrel with; =GIVE SOMEONE GRIEF: *He was giving her a hard time about drinking too much* **2** *v phr* To make difficulties for someone, esp needless ones; =GIVE SOMEONE GRIEF, HASSLE: *Jesus, everybody was giving him a hard time*—Elmore Leonard

give a holler *v phr by 1940s* To inform, alert, or summon someone: *You need me, Mama, just give a holler*—Stan Cutler

give someone **a hotfoot** *by 1930s* **1** *v phr* To do the practical joke of clandestinely sticking a match into the crevice between the heel or sole and upper of the victim's shoe, then lighting the match and watching the pained and startled reaction: *Kids give them hotfoots with kitchen matches*—Joseph Mitchell **2** *v phr* To arouse someone from lethargy; stimulate someone sharply to activity: *The project's stalled and we'd better give Joe a hotfoot*

give someone **a jump** *v phr by 1980s* To do the sex act to or with; =BOFF, SCREW: . . . *went in a bedroom there with the broad, gave her a jump*—Elmore Leonard

give someone or something **a miss** (or **the go-by**) *v phr first form by 1919, second by 1659* To avoid; not opt for •*The go-by variant is attested from the mid–1600s: Give these girls a miss*—Pan American Travel Guide/ . . . *become fed up with a slang phrase. . . and resolve to give it the go-by in the future*—J Greig [*miss* form is fr billiards]

give someone **a pain** *v phr* (Variations: **in the neck** or **in the ass** may be added) *entry form by 1891, neck by 1921, ass by 1940s* To be distasteful, repellent, tedious, etc: *That guy gives me a royal pain in the neck/ one of those bragging polymath types who gave everybody a pain in the ass*—Saul Bellow

give someone **a piece of** one's **mind** *v phr by 1865* To rebuke someone severely

give someone **a ring** *v phr by 1940s* To call on the telephone

give something **a shot** *v phr* (Variations: **crack** or **go** or **rip** or **ripple** may replace **shot**) *entry form by 1840* To have a try at; make an attempt: *He gave the exam a good shot, but flunked it/ Let's give it a rip. We've nothing to lose*

give someone **a slap on the wrist** *v phr by 1914* To give a light and insufficient punishment;

=RAP someone's KNUCKLES: *They caught a couple more Mafiosi and I'm sure they'll give them a real good slap on the wrist*

give someone **a tumble** *v phr* by 1921 To show a sign of recognition or approval; acknowledge: *The newspaper guys had the Bone Crusher pegged as a plant and wouldn't give him a tumble*—H Witver/ *Both knew me, but neither gave me a tumble*—Dashiell Hammett [probably fr the earlier *take a tumble to oneself,* "examine oneself closely, esp with respect to one's faults," after which *tumble* was taken to mean "scrutiny, acknowledgment"]

giveaway 1 *n* by 1882 Anything that reveals something concealed; clue; =DEAD GIVEAWAY: *She talked harsh, but the smile was a giveaway* **2** *n* by 1872 A gift, prize, etc, esp one given to attract business; =FREEBIE **3** *modifier*: *a giveaway show/ giveaway offer*

give someone **away** *v phr* by 1862 To expose oneself; show one's opinion, guilt, etc: *I tried to be serious, but a grin gave me away*

give away the store (or shop) *v phr* (also **give away the keys to the store**) by 1980s To concede too much; be overly generous: *His opponents complained that Dinkins would give away the store to his friends in labor*—New York Times/ *. . . to reinforce the president. . . without giving away the shop*—Washington Post/ *. . . the Republican Congressional leaders had given them "the keys to the store"*—New York Times

giveback *n* 1990s Something previously granted, esp in a labor contract, that must now be forfeited: *The new contract has no raises and several givebacks, especially in health-care benefits*

give something one's **best shot** *v phr* by 1840 To try one's hardest; do the best one can; =BUST one's ASS: *For three months, they had given it their best shot*—Toronto Star/*Anyway, I gave it my best shot*—Village Voice/*The whole thing is not easy. . . . But you must give it your best shot*—New York Times/*This house was built for himself by Bruant. Naturally enough, he gave it his best shot*—New York Times

◁**give cone**▷ *v phr* teenagers by 1970s =GIVE HEAD

give one's **eyeteeth** *v phr* (Variations: **left ball** or **left nut** may replace **eyeteeth**) entry form by 1905, variants by 1940s To pay a very high price; sacrifice much; give anything: *She said she'd give her eyeteeth for the role/ I'd give my left nut to get into NET*—Michael Grant/ *I'd give my left ball for a case like that*—William Bayer

give someone **five** *v phr* (Variation: **slap** can replace **give**) black by 1960s To shake hands with someone or slap someone's hand in greeting, congratulation, etc; =GIVE ME SOME SKIN: *Reno put out his hand for me to give him five*—Claude Brown *See* HIGH FIVE, LOW FIVE

give five fingers to *v phr* by 1940s To thumb one's nose at: *Then you could give five fingers to every cop*—A Hynd

give good something *v phr* 1990s To be very effective at something; work well at or as something: *Zoe Baird gives good daughter*—New Yorker/ *Mozart gives good sound track*—Time [based on *give (good) head*]

give someone **grief (or heat)** *v phr* by 1920s To make difficulties for someone; harass; =HASSLE: *Don't let the prof give you any grief about this/ . . . though she gave me heat about it not being "man's work"*—Erich Segal

◁**give head**▷ *v phr* by 1950s To do fellatio; =BLOW, SUCK: *Not that Linda has anything against balling customers. . . but she just loves to give head*—Xaviera Hollander/ *She must give extra good head or something*—Joseph Wambaugh

give someone **hell (or merry hell or holy hell)** *v phr* by 1851 To rebuke or punish severely; =CHEW OUT: *The skipper gave him merry hell for crud and drunkenness*

give (or read) someone **his (or her) rights** *v phr* by 1960s To inform an arrested person formally of his or her legal rights, esp by reading him or her a "Miranda card" detailing them: *The judge threw it out because they hadn't given the crook his rights* [fr the requirement based on the Supreme Court decision in the Miranda case of 1966]

give someone **his (or her) walking papers** *v phr* (Variation: **running shoes** or **walking ticket** may replace **walking papers**) entry form by 1825 To dismiss or discharge; reject: *If he doesn't stop seeing other women she'll give him his walking papers/ When he objected to the new policy they gave him his running shoes*

give it a rest (or a break) *v phr* first form by 1882 To stop; ease up on •Often a firm command: *OK, give it a rest, huh, Joe?/ You won't get anything tonight. Give it a break, okay?*—Carsten Stroud

don't give it a second thought *See* DON'T GIVE IT A SECOND THOUGHT

give it the gun *v phr* by 1917 To speed up an engine abruptly; accelerate to highest speed; =FLOOR, PUT THE PEDAL TO THE METAL

give it to someone **1** *v phr* by 1864 To rebuke harshly; punish: *He really gave it to me yesterday after I totaled his car* ◁**2**▷ *v phr* by 1940s To do the sex act with or to someone: *. . . one minute he'd be giving it to her in his cousin's Buick*—J D Salinger

give someone **leg** *v phr* by 1970s To deceive someone; fool someone; =PULL someone's LEG: *Last time I saw you, you're giving me a little leg about there's nothing going on*—George V Higgins

give someone **lip** *v phr* by 1821 To speak to someone in an impertinent and offensive way: *People get on here all day long and all they do is give me lip*—Washington Post/ *Don't be giving me lip*—James T Farrell

give me (or gimme) a break *sentence* (Variations: **cut** may replace **give me**) 1980s That's enough of such foolishness; please stop it; =ALL RIGHT ALREADY, GIVE IT A REST, PUT A SOCK IN IT: *Gimme a* break here, Mr C—comic strip "Shoe"/ *Western journalists declare in a triumphant voice that capitalism has won. Gimme a break. I can see that socialism lost—Nation/ . . . a religious sect whose secrets are known only to a few. Give me a break!—Michael Grant/ Jamie, cut me a break. I've thought about it since—Scott Turow*

give me five *See* SLIP ME FIVE

give me (or **gimme) some skin** *sentence* black by 1940s Let's shake hands: *Hi there, Sweet Back. . . Gimme some skin—Zora Neale Hurston*

give odds *v phr* by 1591 To bet or speculate confidently, from a point of advantage: *It may not seem so, but I'd give odds those people are faking it*

give out *v phr* by 1523 To collapse; cease to function; fail: *His old ticker gave out/ The bus gave out halfway up the hill*
  See PUT OUT

gives *See* WHAT GIVES

give some skin *v phr* black by 1930s To shake or slap hands in salutation: *Everybody gave some skin all around—Richard Fariña/ "Hi there, Sweet Back!. . . Gimme some skin!—Zora Neal Hurston*

give someone **the air** *v phr* by 1904 To jilt or reject: *His last girl gave him the air*

give someone **the ax** *v phr* (Variations: **the boot** or **the chop** may replace **the ax**) ax form by 1883; boot by 1888; chop by 1940s To dismiss or discharge; =CAN, CUT, FIRE: *The school gave six profs the ax yesterday/ The Oval Office should give him what he really deserves: the boot—Newsweek/ A vast trade and business complex. . . was given the chop—Westworld*

◁**give** someone **the bird**▷ **1** *v phr* vaudeville by 1922 To greet someone with boos, hisses, catcalls, etc **2** *v phr* (also **give** someone **the bone) 1980s students** To show contempt and defiance by holding up the extended middle finger toward someone; =FLIP THE BIRD: *Do you have to give everyone who cuts you off the bone?—UCLA Slang*

give someone **the brush** *v phr* by 1930s To snub; treat icily and curtly; =KISS OFF: *I got the brush in about two seconds in that fancy dump*

give someone **the business** *v phr* by 1920s To give someone rough treatment; punish; rebuke: *I really gave him the business when I caught him cheating on my exam* [to do one's business for one, "to kill," is found by 1773]

give someone **the cold shoulder** *v phr* by 1840 To snub someone socially; be chilly toward someone

give someone **the creeps** *v phr* by 1849 The feeling that loathsome things are creeping on one's skin; nervous apprehension: *His smile gives me the creeps*

give something **the deep six** *v phr* nautical by 1940s To dispose definitively of; jettison; throw overboard: *They gave those files the deep six* [probably fr the *six* feet of a fathom, the unit for measuring *depth*]

give someone **the double cross** *v phr* by 1834 To betray or cheat one's own colleagues; act treacherously: *. . . if you feel tempted to give the old gentleman the double cross—H McHugh*

give someone **the eye** by 1940s **1** *v phr* To look at in an insinuating and seductive way: *I could see he was giving you the eye* **2** *v phr* To signal with a look: *Get up when I give you the eye*

◁**give** someone **the finger (**or **middle finger)**▷ by 1940s **1** *v phr* To treat unfairly, dishonestly, etc; =SCREW, SHAFT: *Let me show you how to give that guy the finger—Budd Schulberg* **2** *v phr* To show contempt and defiance by holding up the extended middle finger toward someone; =FLIP THE BIRD: *. . . leers into the rear-view mirror and gives you the finger—Milwaukee Journal/ It's a sort of collective giving of the finger to liberalism in all its forms—Toronto Life/ . . . gave me the middle finger and stormed off the set—Milwaukee Journal* [fr the figurative insertion of a finger punitively into the anus]

give someone **the fish-eye (**or **beady eye** or **hairy eyeball)** *v phr* fish-eye by 1940s, others by 1960s To look or stare at someone in a cold, contemptuous, or menacing way: *A well-fed man in tails opened the door, gave them the fish eye—G Homes/ . . . who gave me such hairy eyeballs that I want to slink back—Village Voice*

give someone **the fluff** *v phr* by 1940s To snub; dismiss; =BRUSH-OFF: *I gave him the fluff—Hal Boyle*

give someone **the foot** *v phr* by 1940s To dismiss or eject someone

give someone **the gate** *v phr* by 1918 To discharge, jilt, or eject someone: *After the last goof, they gave him the gate*

give someone **the glad eye** *v phr* by 1903 To look or glance at invitingly; gaze enticingly at: *A tipsy actress gives her man, Donald, the glad eye—New York Times*

give someone **the glad hand** *v phr* by 1895 To greet and welcome effusively: *I gave 'em all the glad hand, but they voted for the other bum anyway*

give someone or something **the go-by** *See* GIVE someone or something A MISS

give someone **the heave-ho** *v phr* by 1940s To dismiss or reject someone; =GIVE someone THE AIR: *It took Lisa two years to give her boyfriend the heave-ho—Seventeen*

give someone **the hook** *v phr* show business by 1940s To dismiss, silence, or otherwise reject someone, esp suddenly: *The teacher gave him the hook—Mike Royko*
  See GET THE HOOK

◁**give (**or **slip) someone the hot beef injection**▷ *v phr* 1980s students To do the sex act with or to someone

give someone **the needle** *v phr* by 1940s To nag at someone; criticize regularly and smartingly; =HASSLE, NEEDLE: *The only needle she knows is the one she gives grandpa for stopping off at the bar on his way home—Hal Boyle*

give the nod *v phr* by 1940s To give approval; confer permission: *Detroit has tightened the* *reins. . . on the boys in the sheet metal design department. . . while giving the nod to the engineers*—Ebony

give someone or something **the once-over** *v phr* by 1915 To examine quickly; glance at, esp with a view to evaluation or identification; =CHECK OUT: *That guy in the corner is giving us the once-over/ I gave her papers the once-over and figured she qualified*

give someone **the pink slip** *v phr* by 1915 To discharge or dismiss; =CAN, FIRE

give someone **the runaround** *v phr* by 1924 To be deceptive and persistently evasive with someone: *Don't give me the runaround*—Sherman Billingsley

give someone **the sack** *v phr* by 1825 To dismiss someone; terminate employment •Chiefly British [origin uncertain; the phrase *donner son sac*, "to give him his sack," has been current in French since the 1600s; *sack* may be "traveling bag, bindle"]

give someone **the shaft** *v phr* by 1940s To swindle, maltreat, or otherwise deal punishingly with someone; =FUCK, SHAFT: *He wasn't expecting much praise, but he sure didn't think they'd give him the shaft like that*

give someone **the shake** (or **the shuck**) *v phr* by 1940s To rid oneself of someone; get away from someone: *He gave the cops the shake a block or so away/ I've been expecting Tish to give you the shuck*—Harry Crews

give someone **the shakes** (or **shivers**) *v phr* by 1940s To instill fear and trembling; intimidate: *. . . he's being paid $5.4 million by the New York Yankees to give opposing batters the shakes*—React [*the shakes*, "a fit of trembling fear," is found by 1837]

give someone **the shirt off** one's **back** *v phr* by 1771 To be extremely generous •Usu in a conditional statement: *Open-handed? Why he'd give you the shirt off his back if you needed it*

give someone **the slip** *v phr* by 1567 To evade or escape someone: *They had him cornered, but he gave them the slip*

not **give** someone **the time of day** *See* NOT GIVE someone THE TIME OF DAY

give someone **the works** *v phr* by 1920 To mistreat or beat severely; =CLOBBER, WORK someone OVER: *They took him into the adjoining room and gave him the works*
See the WORKS

give someone **what for** *v phr* British by 1873 To beat or punish severely; drub either physically or verbally; =CLOBBER, LET someone HAVE IT: *. . . two or three of us would pitch on him and give him "what-for"*—Jack London

give with something *v phr* 1940s jive talk To give; impart: *He wouldn't give with the information*—I, Mobster/ *gives with the big blue eyes as if to say: "He didn't mean to"*—E DeBaun [perhaps modeled on *make with* fr Yiddish *machen mit*]

gizmo or **gismo** or **giz** WWII Navy & Marine Corps **1** *n* An unspecified or unspecifiable object; something one does not know the name of or does not wish to name; =DINGUS, GADGET: *"Why weren't you using the gismo?" "I was. It didn't work"*—New York Times/ *"What's this gizmo?" I asked. "The hand brake"*—Billy Rose/ *Guy tried to shove a Pepsi bottle in his wife's giz*—Joseph Wambaugh **2** *n* gambling =GIMMICK **3** *n* A man; fellow; =GUY: *What's this gizmo have in mind?* [origin unknown; it has been suggested that it is fr Moroccan Arabic *ki smuh*, learned during the invasion of North Africa in 1942]

GKW (pronounced as separate letters) *n* Something unknown or unidentifiable: *The water contains GKW, God knows what*—Milwaukee Journal/ *. . . known to paleontologists as GKWs or God knows whats*—Smithsonian

glad-hand by 1903 **1** *modifier* Effusive and warm; cordial: *He gave me that glad-hand business* **2** *v*: *After. . . glad-handing the local dignitaries, he heads for the fence*—Associated Press
See GIVE someone THE GLAD HAND

glad-hander *n* by 1929 A person who evinces a warmth and heartiness that is probably insincere; one who is designedly cordial: *He is what is known as a glad-hander, meaning that he merely shakes hands and talks*—TV Guide

glad rags by 1902 **1** *n phr* One's best and fanciest clothing; party clothes: *He was piking around in his glad-rags, with the buy-bug in his ear*—The Slang-Dic **2** *n phr* Formal evening wear

glahm *See* GLOM

glam 1 *v* by 1937 To be glamorous; glamorize oneself **2** *modifier* by 1940s Glamorous; exhibiting beauty, sexiness, etc: *"Glam" is a term I'm having a little trouble with. Is this short for "glamorous"?*—Denver Post/ *. . . the super-sexy glam vixens of the '80s*—Los Angeles Times/ *The glam plan is neat and polished*—Sassy **3** *modifier* middle 1970s Playing a kind of rock music called "glam-rock": *They've been asked to open a show for new glam fave Suede*—Rolling Stone

glamazon *modifier* by 1980s Exhibiting the attractions of a robust woman; Junoesque: *We're getting back to the glamazon look of the '80s: bigger, taller, busty models*—Los Angeles Times

glam it up *v phr* by 1990s To dress and behave glamorously; =GLAM: *I haven't done the black-tie bit in ages. Why don't we glam it up just for the fun of it?*—Lawrence Sanders/ *Ellen Barkin and Naomi Campbell glammed it up at New York City's fall fashion shows. . .*—People

glamour (or **glam**) **girl** *n phr* first form by 1935, second by 1940s A woman whose looks and life are glamorous, esp a movie star or other professional beauty: *She was a beautiful thing when she started her career as a glamour girl*—New York Daily News/ *. . . the three delivered flawlessly rhythmic patter with the charm of tom-boy glam-girls*—Los Angeles Times

glamour-puss or **glamor-puss** by 1941 **1** *n* A

person whose looks and life are regarded as glamorous **2 *modifier***: *They are augmented by Daryl Hannah as Rourke's glamorpuss girlfriend*—Washington Post

glass narcotics *by 1980s* **1 *n*** Methedrine capsules **2 *n*** Rock cocaine

glass arm 1 *n phr* baseball *by 1891* A pitcher's arm that is prone to injury and inflammation; =CROCKERY **2 *n phr*** dock workers *by 1940s* An inferior worker; weakling

glass ceiling *n phr* *by 1990* A solid but invisible barrier against women's advancement in business and other institutions: *Women could all stop wearing lipstick and blusher tomorrow, and I doubt it would help them break through the glass ceiling*—New York Times/ *. . . the sound of glass ceilings breaking as women empowered by the Clinton Administration rise to new positions of influence. . .* —Time

glasses *See* BOP GLASSES, GRANNY GLASSES

glass jaw or **china chin *n phr*** prizefight *by 1920* A boxer's chin that cannot tolerate a hard punch

glass-jawed *adj* prizefight *by 1920* Having a very tender or vulnerable chin: *. . . the glass-jawed bimbo which can't take it and dives into a clinch when shook up*—H Witwer

glaum *See* GLOM

glaze someone **over *v phr*** *by 1980s* To make someone ecstatic; intoxicate: *Said one enthusiastic participant: "Doesn't this just glaze you over?"*—Washington Post

a **gleam (**or **glimmer** or **twinkle) in the eye *n phr*** *by 1940s* A potential child; a passionate impulse with portent: *At that time he wasn't even born, wasn't even a gleam in his father's eye/ Your weight was genetically programmed when you were only a glimmer in your parents' eye*—Sassy/ *No, I was not even a twinkle in my mother's eye*—Burckfeldt

glim 1 *n* *by 1700* A light, lamp, etc: *"Douse the glim, Mugsy," said a voice from my youth* **2 *n*** (also **glimmer**) truckers *by 1950s* A headlight **3 *n*** (also **glimmer**) *by 1789* An eye **4 *v*:** *I glimmed her from across the room*

glims *n* *1920s* underworld & hoboes Eyeglasses: *Dark glasses, of course, are rimmed dimmed glims*—Philadelphia Bulletin

glitch 1 *n* aerospace *by 1962* An operating defect; malfunction; a disabling minor problem: *. . . despite such "glitches" (a spaceman's word for irritating disturbances)*—Time/ *Most had assured themselves that the trouble signal was only a "glitch"*—Newsweek **2 *n*** computer *by 1980s* A sudden interruption of electrical supply, program function, etc: *. . . the term "bug" to refer to a computer glitch*—Newsweek [fr German *glitschen* (or Yiddish *glitshen*), "slip"]

glitter *n* *by 1960s* A gaudy style of dress and grooming affected by some musicians, comprising dyed hair, jewels on face and body, and refulgent jumpsuits and cowboy suits

the **glitterati *n*** *by 1940* Famous and glamorous people; outstanding celebrities: *. . . among the glitterati*—People/ *. . . to film the glitterati at a Derby bash*—Newsweek [based on *literati*; in the 1920s the presumed suffix *-ati* was used to form *hustlerati* and *flitterati*]

Glitter City *n phr* *by 1980s* Las Vegas, Nevada: *. . . the triumph of the sturdy Midwest over Glitter City*—Milwaukee Journal

Glitter Gulch 1 *n phr* *by 1940s* Reno, Nevada **2 *n phr*** *by 1950s* =GLITTER CITY

glitter rock *n phr* *by 1972* Music played by rock groups that affect a spectacular style of dress

glitz *by middle 1970s* **1 *n*** High gaudy finish; flashy surface: *. . . some optional Hollywood glitz*—Car and Driver/ *. . . applied Vegas and hot tub glitz to the old Jack La Lanne*—Village Voice **2 *v*** (also **glitz up**) : *. . . the Pirates of Penzance newly glitzed*—California
See GLITZY

glitzy *adj* *by 1966* Blatantly scintillant; flashy; gaudy: *and a glitzy sister. . . who has backed into degeneracy*—New York Times [fr German or Yiddish *glitzern*, "glitter, glisten"]

globaloney *n* *1943* Policies and ideals based on international concern rather than nationalism [a blend coined by Clare Booth Luce fr *global* plus *baloney*]

◁**globes**▷ *n* *by 1889* A woman's breasts: *I'd even seen Elena's soft globes*—H K Fink

globocop *n* *1990s* A global police officer, esp a government or group of governments that seeks to order and pacify the world: *No globocop, however powerful, can force implacable enemies to cry uncle*—Time [probably based on *robocop*]

glom or **glaum** or **glahm** underworld & hoboes *by 1907* **1 *n*** A hand, regarded as a grabbing tool **2 *v*** To grasp; seize: *. . . a contingency plan of creating wider seats for their popcorn-glomming customers*—Los Angeles Times **3 *v*** =GLOM ON TO **4 *v*** To steal: *"Where'd you glahm 'em?" I asked*—Jack London/ *. . . under the pretext of glomming a diamond from the strongbox*—S J Perelman **5 *v*** To be arrested **6 *v*** To look at; seize with the eyes; =GANDER, GLIM: *. . . or walk around the corner to glom old smack heads, woozy winos and degenerates*—New York Times/ *. . . two new collections for the fashionable to glom*—Village Voice **7 *n*:** *Have a glom at that leg, won't you?* [fr British dialect *glaum, glam,* "hand," ultimately fr Old English *clamm,* "bond, grasp," related to *clamp*]

glommer or **glaumer** or **glahmer** *See* MITT-GLOMMER

glom (or **glaum** or **glahm) on to *v phr*** underworld & hoboes *by 1907* To acquire; grab; seize; =LATCH ON TO: *. . . how many times the authorities might have glommed onto this man but didn't*—Washington Post

gloomy gus *n phr* *by 1940s* A morose, melancholic person; pessimist; =CRAPE-HANGER [as the name of a comic-strip character, *Gloomy Gus* is found by 1904]

glop 1 *n by 1943* Any viscous fluid or mixture; =GOO, GOOK, GUNK: . . . *dimes that rolled into the glop*—William Kennedy **2** *n* Sentimentality; maudlin trash; =SCHMALTZ: *That is very dull. I hate glop*—Hal Boyle **3** *v by 1980s* To smear; daub: *By glopping strings and chorales onto Tin Pan Alley lyrics, Nashville responded to rock's commercial success*—Nation

glorified *adj by 1821* Transformed into something illustrious; glamorized: *The Chrysler van is much more than a glorified golf cart*—Time

glory days (or **years**) *n phr by 1980s* A time of great success and acclaim; halcyon days: *Gorelick knows the lore of the glory days*—New York Times/ *Natori's Glory Days*—Harper's Bazaar/ *George Romney, the man who led the Rambler glory years at American Motors. . .* —Milwaukee Journal

glory hog *n phr by 1960s* A person who blatantly seeks adulation; =GLORY HOUND: *Our self-abnegating chief turned out to be a glory hog*

glory hole *homosexuals by 1940s* **1** *n phr* A hole between stalls in a toilet, through which the penis may be put for oral sex **2** *modifier*: *A private glory-hole club makes a lot more sense*—Playboy

glory hound *n phr by 1940s* =GLORY HOG

glossy 1 *n by 1940s* A magazine printed on shiny coated paper; a high-quality magazine; =SLICK: *. . . female editors of the powerful "glossies"*—K Fraser/ *. . . start their own glossies in three very different cities*—Vogue **2** *n by 1920s* A photograph printed on shiny paper

glove *v baseball by 1887* To catch and hold the ball
   See NOT LAY A GLOVE ON someone

glow *n by 1940s* Mild intoxication: *After a couple of bourbons she had a nice glow*

gluepot *n by 1950s* A racehorse: *. . . pay the cost the old gluepot rates when he toes the line*—Robert Ruark [fr the conventional belief or suspicion that horses go to the *glue* factory as raw material when no longer of use]

glug 1 *n by 1768* An imitation of the sound of liquid pouring from a bottle held upside down and vertical **2** *n by 1940s* The quantity of liquor poured as the bottle makes one dull gurgle

glurp *v by 1990s* =SLURP: *She glurped a milkshake*—Douglas Coupland

g-ma *n by 1990s* Grandmother: *. . . and cook the g-ma some special grub*—Sassy

G-man *n by late 1920s* A Federal Bureau of Investigations agent; =FEEB

gnarly *1980s teenagers* **1** *adj* Excellent; wonderful; =COOL, HAIRY, GREAT: *That girl is gnarly. She goes to every party there is*—UCLA Slang **2** *adj* Disgusting: *So, when the halls. . . became a little too gnarly for Principal Charles Lutgen. . .* —Gazette Telegraph/ *"Gnarly" means disgusting*—New York Times [said to have originated among 1970s surfers, describing a dangerous wave; this sense persisted among skateboarders until at least 1988]

gnome *n by middle 1960s* An anonymous expert, esp a statistician or an industrious observer of trends; =BEAN COUNTER: *The Gnomes of Baseball*—Time/ *. . . the inhibitions of sports announcers whose minds have been studied by small-town station managers and network gnomes*—New York Times [the term is being extended from the first use, *gnomes of Zurich,* coined in 1964 and designating the faceless little men who take account of and in part determine the curiosities of the international money market]

go 1 *n by 1890* A fight: *. . . a ripsnorting go*—W R Burnett **2** *n by 1835* A try; =CRACK, WHACK: *She gave it a good go, and made it* **3** *v by 1390* To die **4** *v by 1891* To rule; be authoritative: *Whatever he says goes around here* **5** *v by 1926* To relieve oneself; go to the bathroom: *The dog had to go. We set him in the sink*—Nelson Algren **6** *v by 1940s* To happen; transpire; =GO DOWN: *What goes here?*—W R Burnett **7** *v 1960s teenagers* To say; utter: *You wake up one morning and you go, "Wait a minute"*—Playgirl **8** *v by 1816* To yield; produce: *She'll go maybe 300, 400 pounds* **9** *adj 1950s astronauts* Functioning properly; going as planned; =A-OK: *As the astronauts say. . . all signs are go in the National League*—Sporting News **10** *adj by 1960s* Appropriate; fitting •The phrase *all the go,* "the fashion," is found by 1893: *. . . beatniks, whose heavy black turtle-neck sweaters had never looked particularly go with white tennis socks*—Time
   See FROM THE GIT-GO, FROM THE WORD GO, GIVE something A SHOT, HAVE A CRACK AT something, have something GOING FOR someone or something, LET FLY, LET oneself GO, NO GO, NO-GO, ON THE GO, TELL someone WHERE TO GET OFF, THERE YOU GO, WAY TO GO, WHAT GOES AROUND COMES AROUND

the go-ahead 1 *n by 1940s* Permission or a signal to proceed; consent: *She pleaded her case before state officials and got the go-ahead*—Associated Press/ *His wife Joan had given him the go-ahead to make the race*—Time **2** *modifier baseball by 1960s* Putting a competitor in the lead: *The Tigers got the go-ahead run in the eighth and held the lead to win 9 to 8*

goal **See** KNOCK someone or something FOR A LOOP

go all the way 1 *v phr by 1940s* To do the utmost; make a special effort; =GO THE EXTRA MILE: *If you decide to do it, I'll go all the way for you* **2** *v phr* =GO THE LIMIT

go along for the ride *v phr by 1940s* To do something or join in something in a passive way: *I don't expect much, but I'll go along for the ride*

go along with *by 1940s* **1** *v phr* To agree with some suggestion or statement **2** *v phr* To accept or comply with some proposal; acquiesce

go along with the crowd *v phr by 1940s* To lack or eschew individual judgment; do what everyone else does: *What the hell, I figured I'd go along with the crowd and vote yes*

go ape (or ◁**ape-shit**▷) *by 1950s* **1** *v phr* To behave stupidly, irrationally, and violently; go wild: *When they told him, he went ape and wrecked his* room **2** *v phr* To be very enthusiastic; admire enormously: *People are going quietly ape over the girl*—H G Brown/ *Everyone we met, experienced native and green tourist alike, went ape for it*—Popular Science

go around Robin Hood's barn *v phr by 1854* To act or speak in a roundabout way; make complexity out of something simple; =MAKE A FEDERAL CASE OUT OF something [fr the fact that *Robin Hood's barn* would be a large and pathless forest]

go around the bend *v phr by 1920s* To become insane; go crazy; =FREAK OUT: *Jessica Lange, who goes around the bend with more style, insight, and intensity*—Washingtonian

◁**go around the world**▷ *v phr by 1970s* To kiss or lick the whole body of one's partner, esp as a prelude to fellatio or cunnilingus

go around with someone *v phr by 1950s* To be someone's frequent escort or date; be linked romantically or sexually

goat 1 *n 1950s hot rodders & teenagers* A car, esp an old one or one with an especially powerful engine **2** *n by 1894* A person who takes the blame for failure or wrongdoing; scapegoat; =PATSY: *After the latest flop they elected me goat* **3** *n Army by 1970s* The most junior officer in an Army unit **4** *n railroad by 1916* A switch engine or yard engine **5** *n horse-racing by 1940s* A racehorse, esp an aged or inferior beast *See* GET someone's GOAT, OLD GOAT

◀**goat fuck (**or **screw** or **rope)**▶ *n phr Army by 1970s* A very confused situation, operation, etc; =CHINESE FIRE DRILL

go at it hammer and tongs *v phr by 1833* To do something, esp to quarrel or fight, with great energy [fr the tools of a blacksmith]

goat-roper *n by 1960s* A rustic; hick; =SHITKICKER

goat-smelling *adj Army by 1970s* Malodorous; stinking: *Get your goat-smelling ass out of here*

gob¹ 1 *n by 1382* A mass of viscous matter; =BLOB: *She chucked a big gob of plaster at me* **2** *n* (also **gabs**) *by 1839* A quantity, esp a large quantity: *I think he's got gobs of money*

gob² *n by 1550* The mouth •Chiefly British use [fr Irish]

gob³ *n by 1915* A US Navy sailor; =SWABBY [perhaps fr earlier British *gabby*, "coast guard; quarterdeckman," of unknown origin]

go back on *v phr by 1859* To renege; fail to keep one's word

go back to (or **be at) square one** *v phr by 1960* To be forced to return to one's starting point, usu after a waste of effort; make a new beginning [probably fr the first or starting *square* of a board game; an elaborate suggestion that it refers to a British grid system for locating places on the soccer field, for radio broadcasting of games, cannot be verified]

go back to the well *v phr by 1980s* To return to a reliable source: *We just kept going back to the well and he just kept making it*—Milwaukee Journal

go ballistic *v phr middle 1980s* To become very

angry and irrational; =BLOW UP, HIT THE CEILING: *Either way, some constituents will go ballistic*—Milwaukee Journal/ *Henry George would go ballistic over the idea of reopening the capital gains tax break for real estate*—New Republic [fr the extreme height attained by a *ballistic* missile, and the idea that upward motion is associated with anger]

go balls out *v phr 1980s students* To make a supreme effort; =GO FOR BROKE: *I went balls out on my term paper*—UCLA Slang *See* BALLS-OUT, BALLS TO THE WALL

go bananas *by late 1960s* **1** *v phr* To become wildly irrational; =FREAK OUT, GO APE: *. . . speculation that maybe old Strom had gone bananas at last*—John Corry **2** *v phr* To be extremely enthusiastic; admire enormously: *She went bananas over the dress and bought one in every color* [fr the spectacle of an ape greedily gobbling *bananas*]

go bare *v phr insurance by 1990s* To be uninsured

go batshit *v phr Army by 1940s* To become wildly irrational; =GO BANANAS: *Sal took a look at the page and went batshit*—Jane Leavy/ *The President said that Perot went batshit and has never forgiven him*—Vanity Fair

gobble 1 *v baseball by 1873* To make a catch ◁**2**▷ *v by 1920s* To do fellatio or cunnilingus

gobbledegook or **gobbledygook** *n* Pretentious and scarcely intelligible language, esp of the sort attributed to bureaucrats, sociologists, etc [coined in 1944 by Representative Maury Maverick of Texas]

◁**gobbler**▷ *n by 1920s* A person who does fellatio or cunnilingus

gobble up *v by 1601* =EAT UP

go belly up *v phr by 1870s* To die; collapse; cease to operate; =BELLY UP: *. . . two major credit-card firms had gone belly up*—Wall Street Journal

go blooey *v phr* (Variations: **flooey** or **kablooey** or **kerflooey** or **kerflooie** or **kerfooey** may replace **blooey**) *by 1920* To end abruptly in failure or disaster; break down; collapse; =GO DOWN THE TUBE: *Will I make it. . . without the air conditioner in the car going kablooey*—Washington Post/ *Then, of course, the whole thing all goes flooey*—Village Voice [echoic imitation of an explosion]

go boom *See* FALL DOWN AND GO BOOM

go broke (or **bust)** *v phr by 1895* To become penniless; become insolvent; =GO BELLY UP, TAKE A BATH: *His newest escapade into the fashionable world of trade and manufacturing had again gone bust*—Joseph Heller

gobs *See* GOB

gob-stick *n by 1936* A clarinet [a *stick* to put in the *gob*, "mouth"]

go bughouse *v phr by 1896* To become insane; go crazy: *Four years earlier, Travis. . . had gone bughouse*—Washington Post

go bust *See* GO BROKE

the **go-by** *See* GIVE someone or something **a miss**

go chase yourself *sentence by 1893* Don't be so stupid; let me alone; =GET LOST •Almost always a command

go coast-to-coast *v phr* basketball by 1990s To take the ball alone from one end of the court to the other, and usu score: *He went coast-to-coast for the lay-in*—Robert Perkins

go critical *v phr* 1955 To become unstable and dangerous: *He felt that the Salvadoran situation was about to go critical* [fr nuclear physics, "to approach chain reaction"]

God *See* BY GUESS AND BY GOD, OLDER THAN GOD

god-awful by 1878 **1** *adv* Extremely: *Ain't it god-awful cold in here?* **2** *adj* Wretched; miserable; inferior: *. . . cases that would never have come up but for this god-awful legislation*—Toronto Life

God-damn or **God-damned** *adj* by 1851 Accursed; wretched; nasty; =FUCKING ●Often used for euphony and rhythm of emphasis: *Take your God-damn foot off my God-damn toes* [much older than the date given; as an oath, found by 1640]

goddess *See* SEX GODDESS

godfather *n* by 1970s The chief; highest authority; =BOSS: *He was Life's first publisher, the godfather of the radio and film March of Time series*—Time [fr the Mafia term, "head of a Mafia family," voguish after a book and a movie]
See FAIRY GODFATHER

godmother *See* FAIRY GODMOTHER

go down[1] *v phr* 1980s computer To become inoperative; stop functioning
See WHAT'S GOING DOWN

go down[2] *v phr* black by 1940s To happen; =GO: *He wanted this scam to go down as rigged*—Lawrence Sanders/ *You can't define it in terms of what kind of rap is going down*—Bobby Seal

go down[3] *v phr* by 1906 To be convicted and punished; =FALL: *I want somebody to go down for killing the kid and her baby*—Robert B Parker/ *You going down on this thing?*—Scott Turow

◁**go down and do tricks**▷ *v phr* =GO DOWN ON someone

go downhill *v phr* by 1922 To deteriorate; worsen; =GO TO POT: *It looks like his health is going downhill fast*

go down in flames *v phr* by 1940s To be utterly ruined; be wrecked: *The . . . Ballet. . . has gone down in flames after two years*—Milwaukee Journal/ *He became Washington bureau chief of ABC News and promptly went down in flames*—Washingtonian [fr the fate of WWI combat pilots, who wore no parachutes]

◁**go down on** someone▷ *v phr* by 1916 To do fellatio or cunnilingus; =SUCK: *Only she won't go down on me. Isn't that odd?*—Philip Roth/ *When I try to go down on my girlfriend, she routinely blocks my head with her thighs. . .* —GQ

go down swinging *v phr* by 1930s To refuse surrender; show fight; nail one's colors to the mast: *The President promised he would go down swinging on that issue* [fr baseball, "to strike out, but swing at the third strike"]

go down the line *v phr* by 1940s To do whatever is necessary; =GO ALL THE WAY: *Will unions go down the line for Clinton on the health bills?*—Charlie Rose TV show

go down the rabbit hole *v phr* 1990s students To use narcotics [fr *Alice in Wonderland*, where Alice follows the White Rabbit *down the rabbit hole* to a land of fantasy]

go down the tube (or **tubes** or **chute**) entry form by 1963; chute by 1940s; drain by 1925; gurgler by 1990s; toilet by 1980s; tubes by 1970s To go to wrack and ruin; be lost or destroyed: *Bache was in danger of going down the chute with the price of silver*—Nicholas von Hoffman/ *. . . speaks of a whole generation going down the tube*—New York Times/ *. . . and all of that is going right down the drain*—Whitey Herzog/ *Should the Government sanction the act of simply sending taxpayers' dollars straight down the gurgler?*—New York Times/ *. . . our foreign policy would not be down the toilet*—Milwaukee Journal

God's gift *n phr* by 1938 A very special blessing; premier offering ●Nearly always ironical: *Wall Street tells MBA's they are God's gift to investment banking*—Time/ *. . . he is becoming God's gift to columnists*—New Republic

God's medicine *n phr* narcotics by 1940s Narcotics of any sort: *The joy-poppers had the willpower, they felt, to use God's medicine once or twice a month and forget it the rest of the time*—Nelson Algren

God Squad **1** *n phr* students by 1969 A campus religious organization **2** *n phr* by 1990s A federal government committee that may set aside parts of the Endangered Species Act: *It was the first exemption ever granted by the committee, known as the "God Squad" because its rulings can doom a species*—Milwaukee Journal

go Dutch (or **Dutch treat**) *v phr* by 1914 To pay one's own way at a dinner, show, etc: *Nobody had much money, so we all went Dutch*

go easy by 1885 **1** *v phr* To restrain oneself; control one's anger: *Go easy, fellow, he was just jiving* **2** *v phr* To be lenient with; spare: *Why do the judges go so easy with these perverts?*

goes around *See* WHAT GOES AROUND COMES AROUND

go eyeball to eyeball *v phr* by 1960 To confront and contend with one another; =GO HEAD TO HEAD: *. . . he went eyeball to eyeball with a Soviet delegation. . .* —US News & World Report

gofer or **go-for** or **gopher** *n* by 1967 An employee who is expected to serve and cater to others; a low-ranking subordinate: *. . . running the robo machine and acting as a receptionist, secretary, and general go-for*—Nicholas von Hoffman/ *. . . attractive go-fers for executive editor Frank Waldrop*—Washingtonian [*gofor*, an underworld term for "dupe, sucker," is found by the 1920, and is probably related semantically]

gofer (or **gopher**) **ball** *n phr* baseball by 1932 A pitch likely to be hit for a home run [said to have been coined by the pitcher Vernon Louis "Lefty" Gomez; when hit, the pitch will *go for* a home run]

go figure *v phr* To try to understand, esp something contradictory or astonishing: *Evidence that drug abuse and street crime derive principally from absence of strong fathers. Go figure*—Nation/ *Who knows. Go figure people*—Scott Turow [fr Yiddish *gey vays*, "go know"]

go fishing (or **on a fishing expedition**) *v phr* by 1960 To undertake a search for facts, esp by a legal or quasi-legal process like a grand-jury investigation

go flatline *v phr* by 1980s To die: *In the ambulance he went flatline*
See FLATLINE

go flippo *v phr* by 1980s =FLIP OUT: *. . . and the TV people and politicians went flippo*—Mike Royko

go fly a kite *sentence* by 1940s Cease annoying me; =GO TO HELL, GET LOST: *I asked for more, and he told me to go fly a kite*

go for 1 *v phr* by 1835 To be in favor of; admire; be attracted to: *I really go for her*—John O'Hara **2** *v phr* by 1838 To attack: *Three of the villains went for me*
See HAVE something GOING FOR someone or something

go for all the marbles *v phr* by 1970s =GO FOR BROKE: *He goes for all the marbles*—CBS News

go for broke *v phr* Hawaiian English by 1940s To make a maximum effort; stake everything on a big try •This was the battle-cry of the 442d Regimental Combat Team, made up of Japanese-Americans, in World War II [fr a gambler's last desperate or hopeful wager]

go for it *v phr* by 1871 To make a try for something, esp a valiant and risky one •Often an encouraging imperative: *Will we play it safe, or go for it?/ Go for it! You've almost got it knocked!*

go for the fences *v phr* baseball by 1970s To try to make long base hits, esp home runs; =SLUG

go for the gold *v phr* by 1980s To strive for the highest reward; =GO FOR BROKE: *. . . everything else looks real. They were going for the gold*—Ed McBain/ *Any time Hollywood goes for the gold there are bound to be contestants that finish dead last*—Los Angeles Times [fr the *gold medal* awarded to the first-place finisher in Olympic competitions]

go for the jugular *v phr* by 1980s To compete in dead earnest; give or take no quarter: *They were a tough team that always went for the jugular* [fr the *jugular vein* in the neck, severance of which is usually fatal; the image is of a wolf or other attacking animal]

go for the long ball *v phr* fr football by 1970s To take a large risk for a large gain; =GO FOR BROKE: *. . . entering the fall campaign might decide to go for the long ball*—Washingtonian [fr a *long pass*, the "bomb," thrown in a football game]

◄**go fuck** (or **impale**) oneself► by 1960s **1 sentence** May you be accursed, confounded, humiliated, rejected, etc; =GO TO HELL: *Oh, go fuck yourself, Stern*—Scott Turow/ *Ah, go impale yourselves, the*

bunch of you—John Le Carré **2** *v phr*: *If people were only interested in it 'cause she balled Paul McCartney "then they could go fuck themselves"*—Village Voice

go full bore *v phr* by middle 1930s To go at the utmost speed: *We're going full bore, Sheriff Wells says*—People
See FULL BORE

go full term *v phr* by 1990s To reach completion or fruition: *Although today's test did not go full term, we were impressed with the professional manner with which the launch team responded*—Time [fr the obstetrical designation *full term*, "full development of the fetus at birth"]

go-getter *n* by 1921 A vigorous and effective person; =WINNER: *. . . sometimes enviously referred to as a go-getter, a hot shot, a ball of fire*—Fact Detective Mysteries

gogglebox *n* 1980s students An eager, rather idealistic, person; =GOO-GOO: *Those do-goody goggleboxes in student government didn't help me at all*—College Slang 101 [probably fr the notion that such people wear *goggles*, "glasses"; used in the 1984 movie *Repo Man*]

goggles *n* by 1836 Eyeglasses: *I can't read that without my goggles*

go-go 1 *adj* esp 1960s Having to do with discotheques, their music, style of dancing, etc **2** *adj* Stylish; modish; =TRENDY: *She may be getting on in years, but she certainly is a go-go dresser* **3** *adj* Showing vitality and drive, esp in business and commerce; urgent and energetic: *Religion is a really go-go growth industry these days*—LR Hills/ *Japan's go-go entrepreneurs can turn their operations into the new Goliaths*—Newsweek **4** *n* by middle 1980s A bar or club with go-go girls: *It surely won't keep minors out of go-gos*—Milwaukee Journal **5** *n* by 1990s The penis: *Mrs Bobbitt cut off her husband's go-go*—Paul Harvey
See A-GO-GO

go-go girl (or **dancer**) *n phr* by 1967 A scantily clad or partly naked young woman employed to do solo gyrational dancing in a discotheque or club on a small stage or platform, in a cage, etc

go gold *v phr* by 1990s To sell enough copies to become a gold record: *A rerelease of his album. . . recently went gold*—Milwaukee Journal

go great guns *v phr* by 1913 To do extremely well; succeed remarkably: *He's going great guns as a wine-taster* [fr the early 1800s nautical expression *blow great guns*]

go gunning for someone **See** GUN FOR someone

go halfies (or **halvies** or **halvsies**) *v phr* by 1940s To award an equal share; divide in two equal parts: *I may go halvsies*—Atlantic Monthly/ *If he stonewalled them or went halvsies with the truth. . . . . .*—Scott Turow [*go halves* is found by 1848]

go haywire by 1929 **1** *v phr* To become inoperative; break down unexpectedly; =GO BLOOEY: *This radio's gone haywire*—J C Hixson **2** *v phr* To go crazy; become confused and disoriented: *Remember that I tried to talk you out of it, and don't go hay-*

wire—S McNeil [fr the ramshackle condition of something that must be hastily repaired with *haywire*]

go head to head *v phr* by 1960s To confront and contend with one another; =GO EYEBALL TO EYEBALL: *Lawyers Susan Sarandon and Tommy Lee Jones go head to head over the fate of an eleven-year-old boy...* —Seventeen

go (or **run**) **hog-wild** *v phr* by 1904 To be wildly excited and unrestrained: *I'm going to take a roundhouse wallop at the first thing I see and run hog-wild on the bases*—Everybody's Magazine/ *A person easily excited... goes "hog-wild and crazy"*—American Speech

go Hollywood *v phr* by 1929 To affect arrogance, gaudy dress, and other presumed traits of motion-picture success: *It is at this point that the Hollywood ingenue goes Hollywood*—Writer's Digest

go home feet first (or **in a box**) *v phr* by 1940s To die: *Make one wrong move and you go home feet first*

goifa *See* GREEFA

going *See* HAVE something GOING FOR someone or something

a **going concern** *n phr* by 1881 A project, business, operation, etc, that is successfully launched and functioning smoothly: *Just an idea last year, now it's a going concern*

going down *See* WHAT'S GOING DOWN

going out of style *See* LIKE IT'S GOING OUT OF STYLE

a **going-over 1** *n phr* by 1940s A beating; trouncing: *The goons gave him a brutal going over* **2** *n phr* by 1919 An examination; scrutiny: *Give these records a going-over, please* [related to the first sense, "a scolding, a dressing-down" found by 1872]

go into one's **act** *v phr* by 1940s =DO one's NUMBER

go into one's **dance** *v phr* (Variations: **dog and pony show** or **song and dance** may replace **dance**) by 1980s To begin a prepared line of pleading, explanation, selling, seduction, etc: *He went into his dance, but she wasn't convinced*

go into orbit *v phr* by 1960s To reach very extreme and apparently uncontrolled heights: *those whose stocks can absorb, say, $50 million or more without going into orbit*—Fortune

go into the dumper *v phr* by 1990s To fail utterly; be discarded: *... Gone to Carnival had gone straight into the dumper*—Stan Cutler [*dumper* is probably a shortening of *Dumpster*, trademark for a refuse bin]

go into the tank *v phr* prizefight by 1940s To lose a fight, game, etc, deliberately; =THROW: *Some night you went inna tank?*—George V Higgins [fr the resemblance between a fighter hitting the canvas and a person *taking a dive into a tank*]

go it alone *v phr* by 1842 To do something arduous or tricky by oneself: *She tried going it alone but found it scary* [fr the game of euchre, where one may play against combined opponents]

goiter *See* GERMAN GOITER, MILWAUKEE GOITER

go jump in the lake *sentence* by 1912 May you be accursed, confounded, humiliated, etc; =DROP DEAD, GO FUCK oneself: *Go jump in the lake (or perhaps something a little stronger), Wauwatosa Ald Joseph Ptaszek essentially told several people...* —Milwaukee Journal/ *'So far,' Rothschild said, 'Nader hasn't told us to jump in the lake.'*—New York Times

go kerplunk *v phr* by 1940s To fail; =FLOP, GO BLOOEY: *If they go kerplunk, someone will have to scrape up the pieces*—Arthur Daley

gold *n* 1960s narcotics A high grade of marijuana *See* ACAPULCO GOLD

◀**Goldberg**▶ *n* black by 1960s A Jew, esp one who employs blacks or has a shop in a black neighborhood: *... sweeping the floors for Goldberg*—Claude Brown

See RUBE GOLDBERG

gold braid *n phr* by 1940s Naval officers, esp high-ranking ones: *It is evident that the gold braid doesn't think enough of the order*—G W Hibbitt

goldbrick 1 *n* (also **goldbricker**) WWI armed forces A shirker; a person who avoids work or duty; =GOOF-OFF **2** *v*: *She made him promise to quit goldbricking* **3** *v* by 1902 To swindle; cheat; =CON [fr the convention of the confidence trickster who sells spurious *gold bricks*]

gold-digger *n* by 1920 A woman who uses her charms and favors to get money, presents, etc, from wealthy men: *Lorelei Lee... the crazy-like-a-fox gold-digger*—Billy Rose

gold dust twins *n phr* by 1940s Any two persons thought of as a pair or who share a common interest: *Eddie Einhorn and Jerry Reinsdorf, the gold-dust twins of the Chicago White Sox and Bulls*—New York Times/ *They called me and my buddy the gold dust twins* [fr the picture of a grinning pair on the label of a household cleanser]

golden boy *n phr* by 1937 A favored and especially gifted boy or man; =FAIRHAIRED BOY: *Casey regarded Inman as a brittle golden boy, worried about his image*—Esquire [popularized by the title of Clifford Odets's 1937 play about a boxer]

golden handcuffs *n phr* by 1976 Arrangements, options, perquisites, etc, that induce one to stay in one's job: *These ties that bind have become known in industry as golden handcuffs*—Time

golden oldie or **oldie but goodie** *n phr* by middle 1960s An old record, song, person, etc, still regarded as good, esp one that has revived or sustained popularity: *... a golden oldie like "Honeysuckle Rose"*—F P Tullius/ *All the golden oldies are replayed and the untied threads neatly resolved*—Newsweek/ *Oldies but Goodies Could Put Success in Senior Tours: There's a golden patch of oldies who can still play great tennis*—New York Times/ *... oldies but goodies such as "Down by the Riverside"*—Pulpsmith [probably influenced by association with the *gold* phonograph record struck for a recording that has sold a million copies and more]

golden parachute (or **handshake**) *n phr first form by 1980s, second by 1960* Very high sums, benefits, etc, offered for taking early retirement: *"Golden parachutes" or severance package. . . are all becoming more common*—New York Times/ *. . . parting golden handshake with GM included a valuable Cadillac franchise*—Time

golden retriever *n phr by 1990s* A successful motion-picture executive: *A golden retriever is a studio executive with the ability to outrun everyone else and bring in the hottest scripts, actors, or directors*—New Yorker [fr the name of a kind of dog]

◁**golden shower**▷ *n phr homosexuals & prostitutes by 1940s* Urination on someone who sexually enjoys such a wetting: *. . . what girls do through the bladder, which is otherwise known as the "golden shower"*—Xaviera Hollander/ *Golden showers. . . Not me*—Philadelphia

goldfinger *n 1960s narcotics* A type of synthetic heroin

goldfish *n WWI Army* Canned salmon

goldfish bowl *n phr by 1935* A place or situation where one is exposed; a venue without privacy: *Celebrities must live in a goldfish bowl*

goldilocks **1** *n by 1598* Any pretty blond woman •Often used ironically: *Well, thought Jimmy, it won't be because of you, goldilocks*—Calder Willingham **2** *n by 1990s* A burglar who breaks into a house, eats, and otherwise makes himself at home, but takes nothing of value [second sense fr the folk tale *Goldilocks and the Three Bears*]

a **gold mine** *n phr by 1882* A fortunate or unexpected source of great wealth: *I didn't think much of the book, but the royalties have been a gold mine* [a somewhat ambiguous use in 1664 probably refers to an actual *gold mine*]

gold piece *See* COME UP SMELLING LIKE A ROSE

gold time *n phr by 1990s* Double overtime pay: *When TV crews work past midnight on Friday and Saturday, they are normally paid gold time. . .* —New York Times

go levers *n phr airline by 1970s* The throttles of an aircraft

golf *See* BARNYARD GOLF

golf widow *n phr by 1908* A woman often left alone while her mate plays golf

go like sixty *v phr by 1860* To go very fast; =BARREL: *They all went like sixty to the nearest exit*

golly *interj by 1775* A mild exclamation of surprise, dismay, pleasure, etc; =GOSH: *Golly, Mom, did you really win it?* [a euphemism for *God*]

go-long *n black by 1940s* A police patrol wagon; =PADDY WAGON: *Joe Brown had you all in the go-long last night*—Zora Neale Hurston

goma (GOH mah) *n 1960s narcotics* Crude opium

go mahoola *v phr by 1970s* =GO DOWN THE TUBE [origin unknown; the verb *mahula*, "to fail, go bankrupt," is found by the 1940s]

gomer **1** *n medical by 1960s* A patient needing extensive care; a vegetative comatose patient: *We got a real gomer in from ICU yesterday*—Los Angeles Times/ *He says the guy's a total gomer now*—Carsten Stroud **2** *n 1950s* A first-year Air Force Academy cadet, esp a clumsy trainee [origin uncertain; medical sense said to be an acronym of "get out of my emergency room"]

goms *n 1920s underworld* A police officer

gon or **gond** *See* GUN[2]

go native *v phr by 1901* To take on the behavior and standards of the place one has moved to or is visiting, esp when this means a loss of rigor, respectability, etc: *On Bleecker Street he went native and donned a black sweatshirt and sneakers*

gone **1** *adj jazz musicians by 1940s* Intoxicated, esp with narcotics **2** *adj 1940s cool talk* In a trancelike condition; meditative: *. . . gurgling forth a flow of words, a "gone" expression on his face*—Calder Willingham **3** *adj 1940s cool talk* Excellent; wonderful; =COOL: *a real gone chick*

gone coon *n phr by 1839* =GONE GOOSE

gone goose *n phr by 1830* =DEAD DUCK

gone on (or **over**) *adj phr by 1885* In love with; enamored of: *I was so gone over her*—Louis Armstrong

a **goner** *n by 1850* Someone or something that is doomed; someone dead or about to die; =DEAD DUCK: *pray. . . or you're a goner*—San Diego Herald/ *. . . for Rome will be a goner*—WH Auden

gong **1** *n* (also **gonger**) *narcotics by 1914* An opium pipe **2** *n British WWII use* A military decoration; medal or ribbon [both senses probably fr *gong*, "saucer-shaped metal bell," of Malayan origin; the sense "opium pipe" may be related to the general association of *gongs* with Chinese matters, and the military sense to the notion that a decoration is something like the ceremonial sounding of a *gong*] *See* KICK THE GONG AROUND

gonged **1** *adj narcotics by early 1900s* Intoxicated with narcotics; =HIGH, STONED: *She's sitting in the front row gonged to the gills with acid*—Albert Goldman **2** *adj 1980s* Dismissed: *Just ask Pat Sheridan, who was gonged by WISN last fall*—Milwaukee Journal [second sense fr television *Gong Show*, where performers were dismissed by the sound of a *gong*]

goniff (GAH nəf) **1** *n* (Variations: **gonef** or **gonif** or **gonof** or **gonoph** or **ganef** or **ganof** or **guniff**) *by 1845* A thief; a person who is in effect a thief, like an unethical salesperson: *And who is this arch-goniff?*—Dashiell Hammett/ *. . . a gonof like Glick*—Budd Schulberg/ *. . . all the other gonophs, consultants who peddle bullshit, builders who build badly*—Village Voice **2** *v*: *Are you trying to goniff me, pal?* [fr Yiddish, "thief," fr Hebrew *gannabh*, "thief"]

gonk *See* CONK

go no-go *adj phr 1960s astronauts* Pertaining to the last critical moment at which a project, plans, etc, can still be canceled; relating to the point of no return: *It's go no-go. Either we do it or we kill it*

go nowhere fast *v phr by 1940s* To proceed very slowly; be stalled: *The proposal is officially still pending but going nowhere fast*—New York Times

gonsil or **gonzel** *See* GUNSEL

go nuclear *v phr by 1990s* =GO BALLISTIC: *. . . Susan and poor, meek little Emmett Couch. . . went nuclear*—Douglas Coupland

gonzo (GAHN zoh) *by 1971* **1** *adj* Insane; wild; bizarre; confused; =CUCKOO, BANANAS, NUTSO: *. . . established Hunter Thompson as the father of gonzo journalism, a flamboyant if controversial style*—New York Daily News/ *. . . the gonzo idea of a cross-country street race*—Car and Driver **2** *n*: *The Gonzo and the Geeks*—Vivian Gornick/ *These double-gaited gonzos are perpetrating a plague of best-selling takeoffs*—Newsweek [fr Italian, "credulous, simple, too good"]

goo **1** *n by 1903* Any sticky and viscous substance; =GLOP, GUNK: *. . . fell in the goo rounding third*—New York Daily News/ *. . . a layer of goo on the skin*—R Adler **2** *n by 1922* Sentimentality; maudlin rubbish; =GLOP, SCHMALTZ **3** *n* Fulsome flattery; overly affectionate greetings: *They ladle out the old goo*—Bing Crosby [perhaps sound symbolism, influenced by *glue;* perhaps fr *burgoo,* "oatmeal porridge"]

goob or **goob-a-tron** *n 1980s students & teenagers* A tedious, contemptible person; =DORK, NERD: *Nerds can be "goobs" or "tools". . .* —New York Times/ *A Goob-a-tron's Guide to Rad Speak*—New York Times [fr *goober*]

goober *1970s teenagers* **1** *n* A minor skin lesion; =ZIT: *. . . whiteheads, blackheads, goopheads, goobers, pips*—New York Times **2** *n* A stupid and bizarre person; =GEEK, WEIRDO [fr *goober,* "peanut," fr Kongo *nguba,* "kidney, peanut"; first sense probably because the first syllable describes the *goo* that exudes from or is squeezed from the lesion]

◁**goober-grabber**▷ *n phr by 1867* A native or resident of Georgia [fr the general association of Georgia with its important product, the peanut]

goob someone out *v phr 1980s students* =GROSS someone OUT: *Joe got sick in the car; he really goobed me out*—College Slang 101

good *See* BE GOOD, DO-GOOD, DO-GOODER, FEEL GOOD, HAVE IT GOOD, MAKE GOOD, NO-GOOD

good buddy **1** *n phr 1970s citizens band* The person one is cordially addressing **2** *n phr homosexuals by 1970s* One's homosexual lover **3** *n phr citizens band by 1980s* A male homosexual: *It turns out that the most famous term in the CB vocabulary. . . has become slang for "homosexual"*—Brian Di Salvatore

good butt *n phr 1950s narcotics* A marijuana cigarette; =JOINT

good-bye *See* KISS something **good-bye**

good cop bad cop or **nice cop tough cop** *modifier* Marked by alternations between friendliness and hostility, easiness and rigor, etc: *Successful management requires a variation of the "good cop, bad cop" routine*—New York Times/ *In short, a "nice cop" Rousseau and a "tough cop" Rousseau*—New York Review of Books/ *I think that she's the good cop and he's the bad one, and*

I think it's quite deliberate—New York Magazine [fr the interrogation technique by which one police officer pretends to sympathize with the suspect and to protect him from a pitiless and menacing fellow officer]

good deal *WWII armed forces* **1** *n phr* A pleasant and favorable situation, life, job, etc: *He had a good deal there at the bank, but blew it* **2** *interj* An exclamation of agreement, pleasure, congratulation, etc: *You made it? Good deal!*

good egg *n phr by 1903* A decent and kindly person; a reliable and admirable citizen: *Henry Fonda frequently was cast as the good egg* [modeled on *bad egg,* found by 1855]

gooder *See* DO-GOODER

good-for-nothing **1** *n by 1751* A worthless person; scoundrel; =BUM **2** *adj by 1711*: *You good-for-nothing bastard, you*

good golly Miss Molly *interj 1950s* An exclamation of emphasis, surprise, indignation, etc; goodness gracious: *Good golly, Miss Molly! Lascivious lyrics were not, after all, introduced to the lower orders from above*—New York Times [fr the title of a 1950s song by Little Richard (Richard Penniman)]

good hair *n phr black by 1942* Straight nonkinky hair; =RIGHTEOUS MOSS: *Good hair: Caucasian type hair*—Zora Neale Hurston

good hair day *n phr 1990s* A day when things go right; good day: *She said she was having a good hair day as she arranged the seating for the photos during the interview*—Madison Eagle
See BAD HAIR DAY

good head *n phr teenagers about 1950* A pleasant and agreeable person

goodie or **goody** **1** *n* =GOODY-GOODY **2** *n by 1940s* A special treat; something nice to eat: *. . . a huge basket of goodies*—New Yorker **3** *n by 1940s* Something nice; a pleasant feature; something very desirable: *. . . headlight with a middle beam, the goodie you've been waiting for*—Popular Science/ *The local population took to the goodies of Western culture with avidity*—J Williams **4** *modifier*: *Then I got out my goodie bag*—Xaviera Hollander **5** *n* (also **good guy**) *1930s motion pictures* Someone on the side of virtue and decency, in contrast with a villain: *It's much easier to make a girl a baddie than a goodie*—Time
See GOLDEN OLDIE

good Joe *n phr by 1940s* A pleasant, decent, reliable man; =GOOD EGG

good-looker *n by 1893* Someone or something that is handsome and attractive, esp a woman; =LOOKER: *Is she a good looker?*—S Smith

good night *interj by 1880s* An exclamation of surprise, irritation, emphasis, etc: *Good night! Must you chew that gum so loud?* [a euphemism for *good God*]

good old (or ole) boy *by 1970s* **1** *n phr* A white Southerner who exemplifies the masculine ideals of the region; =BUBBA: *The helpful truck driver was a good old boy from around Nashville* **2** *modifier*:

Kevin Baker and Fred Ward have good-ol'-boy chemistry. . . —Macon Telegraph

goods *n* narcotics Narcotics of any sort
See CANNED GOODS, GREEN GOODS, PIECE OF CALICO, STRAIGHT GOODS

the goods 1 *n phr by 1904* Something or someone of excellent quality; just what is wanted: *She's the real goods*—A Lewis **2** *n phr by 1908* The evidence needed to arrest and convict a criminal: *We've got the goods on him*—Erle Stanley Gardner **3** *n phr by 1900s* Stolen property; contraband: *They caught him with the goods in his pocket*
See DELIVER THE GOODS, GET THE GOODS ON someone

good shit *by 1950s* **1** *interj* =GOOD DEAL **2** *n phr* Anything favorable or pleasant; something one approves of: *This place is real good shit, ain't it?*

good sport *n phr by 1917* A person who plays fair, accepts both victory and defeat, and stays amiable: *I just want to be a good sport and get along with people*—Hal Boyle

good time *n phr* prison *fr about 1870* Time deducted from a prison term for good behavior: *. . . a period of solitary confinement and a loss of "good time"*—American Scholar

good-time Charlie *n phr by 1927* A man devoted to partying and pleasure; bon vivant

good to go *interj* Persian Gulf War Army A rallying cry; battle cry; =GUNG HO: *. . . has a ring that is still missing in the similar "good to go" that came out of the Gulf*—Retired Officer Magazine

good word **See** WHAT'S THE GOOD WORD
Goodyears **See** DOWN THE GOODYEARS

goody-goody 1 *n by 1873* A prim and ostentatiously virtuous person: *I'm not a mammy boy nor a goody-goody*—O Johnson **2** *modifier by 1871*: *. . . what might have been a goody-goody role*—Time

goody two-shoes 1 *n phr by 1766* An obviously innocent and virtuous young woman; =GOODY-GOODY •Most often used mockingly or contemptuously **2** *modifier*: *in spite of its Goody Two-Shoes ecological image*—Toronto Life [fr the name of the heroine of a 1760s child's story, probably by Oliver Goldsmith, about a little girl who exulted publicly at the acquisition of a second shoe]

gooey *adj by 1906* Consisting of, covered with, or resembling goo: *These passages seem affected and a bit gooey*—New Yorker/ *. . . the story of Teresa Stratas, without gooey heaviness*—Toronto Life

goof 1 *n by 1916* A stupid person; =BOOB, KLUTZ, SAP: *. . . two goofs can't agree on how many orgasms they should have. . .*—Mike Royko/ *. . . high school girls now talk of the "goofs we go with"*—Time **2** *n by 1940s* An insane person; mental case: *He couldn't have acted more like a goof*—James M Cain **3** *n 1930s* prison One's cellmate **4** *n 1950s* jive talk A blunder; bad mistake; =BOO-BOO: *. . . they covered their goof quite well*—Esquire **5** *v by 1941*: *You goofed again; it's a one-way street* **6** *v by 1932* To pass one's time idly and pleasantly; =GOOF OFF: *In Sarajevo, members of a*

student volunteer brigade goofed and joked as they worked*—Time **7** *v by 1940s* =GOOF AROUND **8** *v by 1940s* To fool; =KID: *Don't goof your grandpa*—James T Farrell [fr British dialect *goof, goff,* "fool"]

goof around *by 1940s* **1** *v phr* To pass one's time idly and pleasantly; potter about; =FART AROUND **2** *v phr* To joke and play when one should be serious; =FUCK AROUND, HORSE AROUND: *The monarch ordered the field marshal to quit goofing around and win the goddamn war*

goofball 1 *n by 1959* A stupid and clumsy person; =GOOF: *. . . roles that earned him the affectionate labeling as a "goof ball"*—Washington Post **2** *n by 1959* An eccentric person; =ODDBALL, WEIRDO **3** *n 1940s* narcotics A pill or capsule of Nembutal™ **4** *n* narcotics *by 1940s* A barbiturate, tranquilizer, etc, used as a narcotic: *. . . took over three hundred goof balls*—A Stump **5** *n 1930s* narcotics A portion or dose of a narcotic; =BALL, GB: *A goof ball is a narcotics preparation which is burned on a spoon and inhaled*—New York Daily News **6** *n 1930s* narcotics Marijuana

goof-butt **See** GOOFY-BUTT

goofed *adj* narcotics *by 1950s* Intoxicated with a narcotic, esp marijuana; =HIGH, STONED

goofer or **goopher 1** *n by 1925* A fool; =GOOF: *Don't be a critical goopher or you can't go*—F Scott Fitzgerald **2** *n WWII Army Air Forces* An intrepid fighter pilot

◁**go off**▷ *v phr by 1928* To have an orgasm; =COME OFF

go off half-cocked *v phr by 1833* To make a premature response, esp an angry one: *Let's not go off half cocked*—Joseph Wambaugh/ *But before I went off half-cocked, I had to check the alibis. . .*—Stan Cutler [fr the accidental firing of a gun at *half cock*]

go off on someone *v phr 1980s* students To lose one's temper; attack someone: *. . . now think about this before you go off on me. . .*—Judy Markey

go off the deep end *v phr by 1921* To go into a violent rage; =BLOW one's TOP [perhaps fr the notion of jumping into a pool at the *deep end,* hence being in *deep* water, in trouble]
See JUMP OFF THE DEEP END

go off the rails *v phr by 1848* To behave abnormally; lose stability: *Most of what she said was okay, but she went off the rails with that last remark*

goofiness *n by 1920s* The acts, ways, ideas, etc, of those who are goofy: *. . . an unparalleled tolerance for goofiness*—A J Liebling

goofnut *modifier by 1990s* =GOOFY, NUTTY: *Those goofnut Shorewood boys. . . are back with another spitfire satirical comedy. . .*—Milwaukee Journal

goof off *v phr WWII armed forces* To pass one's time idly and pleasantly; potter about; shirk duty; =GOOF AROUND: *My goofing off in the final period had knocked down a possible A average*—Life/ *Are you trying to tell me my son is goofing off?*—Erma Bombeck

goof-off *WWII armed forces* **1** *n* A person who regularly or chronically avoids work; =BUNK LIZARD, FUCK-OFF: *. . . getting kicked out of seminary as a goof-*

off—Inside Sports **2** *n* A period of relaxation; respite: *A little goof-off will do you good*

goof on someone *v phr* teenagers by 1970s To play a joke on someone; fool someone

goof-proof *v* by 1970s To insure against mistakes; forestall errors: *. . . her own formulas for goof-proofing a party*—Philadelphia

goof up by 1960 **1** *v phr* To spoil; disable; =QUEER: *He goofed up the whole deal by talking too soon* **2** *v phr* To blunder; =GOOF: *. . . that can look at a child when he goofs up and reflect, "I understand and I love you"*—Erma Bombeck

goof-up by 1960s *n* A blunder, esp a serious one; =FUCK-UP, SNAFU

goofus 1 *n* by 1940s =THINGAMAJIG **2** *n* circus by about 1915 A small calliope **3** *n* by middle 1920s A saxophone-shaped, breath-operated reed instrument with a keyboard covering two octaves, intended as an easy aid to the musically uneducated ●The name may have been given by the jazz saxophonist Adrian Rollini, who led a group called *The Goofus Five*, featuring the instrument; it was originally known as the Couesnophone after the French manufacturer Couesnon et Compagnie **4** *n* by 1918 A stupid person; =DIMWIT, DOPE, SPAZ: *The networks always remind me of slow-witted goofuses squatting out there in the L A glare. . .* —Washington Post **5** *n* circus & carnival by about 1920 A rural person; naive spectator; =EASY MARK **6** *n* show business by 1950s Tasteless and meretricious material or entertainment designed for the unsophisticated

goofy *adj* by 1921 Silly; foolish; crazy; =DOTTY ●Nearly always has an affectionate and amused connotation: *. . . a goofy grin*—H C Witwer/ *. . . a goofy awkward kid*—Chances/ *And he looked, well, goofy*—J D Salinger

goofy about by 1921 *adj phr* =CRAZY ABOUT

goofy-butt or **goof-butt** *n* narcotics by 1950s A marijuana cigarette; =JOINT

googly *adj* by 1901 Protruding; exophthalmic: *. . . her great big googly eyes* [origin uncertain; perhaps fr *goggle*, which meant "stare at admiringly or amorously"; perhaps fr mid–1800s *google*, "the Adam's apple," where the eyes are thought of as similarly protruding; perhaps influenced by *goo* in the sense of "sentimental, amorous"; popularized by the hero of a comic strip]

goo-goo¹ *n* by 1895 A good-government advocate; a reformer: *Well, many of my friends are do-gooders, or goo-goos as they are known in Chicago politics*—Mike Royko/ *. . . while neighboring Wisconsin has so many goo-goos (a Chicago word for do-gooders and reformers)?*—Milwaukee Journal

goo-goo² or **gu-gu** ◀**1**▶ *n* 1920s Navy =GOOK² **2** *adj* by 1863 Infantile; cooing: *. . . talking goo-goo talk to her, like you would to a baby*—Saturday Evening Post

goo-goo eyes *n phr* by 1897 Eyes expressing enticement, desire, seduction, etc [probably fr *googly*, with which it is synonymous in early uses]

See MAKE GOO-GOO EYES

goo-goo face *n phr* by 1990s An enticing, seductive expression; =COME-ON: *. . . hunched over with a hand stuck in my jeans while making goo-goo faces, my new husband would lead me to the bed. . .* —Donna Britt [modeled on *goo-goo eyes*]

googs *n* by 1940s Eyeglasses [probably fr *goggles*]

gook¹ or **guck** (GŏŏK) *n* by 1940s Dirt; grime; sediment; =GOO, GLOP, GUNK: *Glim gets the gook off*—New York Daily News/ *Joan has white guck all over her face*—Philadelphia

◀**gook²**▶ (GŏŏK, GŏŏK) Army by early 1900s **1** *n* An Asian or Polynesian; =SLOPE ●Originally a Filipino insurrectionary, then a Nicaraguan, then any Pacific Islander during WWII, embraced Koreans after 1950, Vietnamese and any Asian fr 1960s; sometimes used of any colored person: *. . . take it on the chin better than an American or a Zulu or a gook*—Hal Boyle/ *. . . the way he felt about Vietnam. The gooks. . .* —New York Times/ *It was there that I first heard of dinks, slopes, and gooks*—New Yorker **2** *modifier*: *Give it to the gook hospitals*—New York Times [fr *gugu*, a term of Filipino origin, perhaps fr Vicol *gugurang*, "familiar spirit, personal demon," adopted by US armed forces during the Filipino Insurrection of 1899 as a contemptuous term for Filipinos, and spread among US troops to other places of occupation, invasion, etc; probably revived after 1950 by the Korean term *kuk*, which is a suffix of nationality, as in *Chungkuk*, "China," etc]

gooky (GŏŏK ee) *adj* by 1940s Sticky; viscid; greasy: *Greaseless. Nongooky*—Cosmetics advertisement

goola *n* jazz musicians by about 1917 A piano [origin unknown]

goola box *n phr* black by about 1917 A juke box

goombah (GŏŏM bah) (also **goombar** or **gumba** or **gumbah**) **1** *n* A friend; companion; trusted associate; patron; =PAL: *They called him Joey Gallo's rabbi or his goombah*—Saturday Evening Post/ *. . . trying to make these old goombars understand*—Patrick Mann/ *We want all our gumbahs to come over and get rich*—George V Higgins **2** *n* An organized-crime figure; Mafioso: *I'm gonna kill any greasy Guinea goombah that tries to stop me*—George Warren/ *This big dumb gumba can send you home with your nuts in a paper bag*—Scott Turow [fr dialect pronunciation of Italian *compare*, "companion, godfather"]

goomer *n* medical by 1970s A hypochondriac [fr *get out of my emergency room*]

See GOMER

go on *interj* by 1940s A mild exclamation of disbelief, esp when one is praised: *Oh, go on, I'm not that good*

goon by middle 1930s **1** *n* A strong, rough, intimidating man, esp a paid ruffian: *Fondled, pinched, handled by a big red-haired goon who was our jailer*—Hugh Pentecost **2** *modifier*: *goon squad/ his goon tactics* **3** *n* Any unattractive or unliked person; =JERK, PILL: *He had the face of a pure goon*—H Allen Smith [origin uncertain; perhaps entirely fr the name of Alice the Goon, a large hairy creature who appeared in E C Segar's comic strip "Thimble Theatre" in 1936, but who had a very gentle disposition; perhaps connected with Frederick Lewis Allen's term for "a person with a heavy touch," that is, a literary or stylistic touch, found by 1921; perhaps fr *gooney*]

goon boy *n phr* 1950s students A despised person; =GEEK, JERK, NERD

go something or someone **one better** *v phr* gamblers by 1845 To surpass or outbid; raise the standard: *That wasn't a bad offer, but I'll go you one better* [fr the raising of bets in poker]

gooned or **gooned out** *v phr* by 1960s Intoxicated; =HIGH, STONED: *Getting gooned on Nyquil*—Los Angeles Times

gooney *n* by 1895 A stupid person; simpleton; fool [fr earlier *goney, gonus,* "simpleton," found by 1580, and of obscure origin]

gooney bird *n phr* WWII aviators The DC-3 airplane: *Pilots everywhere refer to it with great affection as the "Gooney Bird" after the albatross*—New York Post [fr the slow but sure flight of the *gooney bird,* "black-footed albatross," the bird so called by seamen because of its foolish look and awkward behavior when on the ground]

goonk *See* GUNK

goonlet *n* by 1940s A young hoodlum or ruffian: *Cops handle young goonlets gently*—W Davenport

goon-out *n* by 1980s A lapse; momentary loss of control: *He had one little goon-out. In three innings, that's pretty good*—Milwaukee Journal

goon squad *n phr* by middle 1930s A group of ruffians •Used of the opposition by both sides in labor disputes: *A few weeks later, another "goon squad," as they have been rightly labeled*—New York Times/ *What some doctors deride as investigative "goon squads"*—Time

go on the hook for something *v phr* by 1950s To go into debt: *So you'll go on the hook for one of those eighty-dollar sports-car coats*—S McNeil

go on track *v phr* prostitutes by 1970s To patrol an area seeking prostitution customers; =HOOK: *Then I'd go on track till 4 AM, sleep two more hours, and start over*—Milwaukee Journal

goop[1] or **goup** by 1940s **1** *n* A nasty viscid substance; =GLOP, GOO: *. . . suck up the goop and then spill it over*—John D MacDonald **2** *n* Stupidly sentimental material; sugary rubbish: *. . . who can't transcend the Positive Mental Attitude goop she is forced to utter*—Village Voice [probably fr *goo*]

goop[2] *n* by 1900 A stupid and boorish person; =CLOD, KLUTZ [fr the name of an unmannerly creature invented by the humorist Gelett Burgess in the late 1800s]

goophead *n* teenagers by 1980 A minor skin lesion; =ZIT: *. . . whiteheads, blackheads, goopheads, goobers, pips*—New York Times

goopher *See* GOOFER

goopy by 1940s **1** *adj* Viscid; nastily sticky: *You certainly tend to get goopy fancy food these days*—Arizona Republic **2** *adj* Stupidly sentimental;

maudlin; =GOOEY: *There's no way to talk about that without sounding goopy*—Tom Wolfe/ *. . . please, not another goopy eulogy to the past*—Village Voice

goose ◁1▷ *v* by 1881 To prod someone roughly and rudely in the anal region, usu as a coarse and amiable joke: *As she was bending over her lab table, a playful lab assistant goosed her*—Max Shulman ◁2▷ *n*: *He threatened a goose, and I cringed* **3** *v* by 1930s To exhort strongly and irritably; goad harshly: *. . . and goosed the media into hyping them*—Washington Post/ *. . . every once in a while goose it with defense spending*—Village Voice **4** *n*: *The whole bunch needed a good goose* **5** *v* by 1940s To run an engine at full speed or with spurts of high speed; =GUN: *Vroom-vroom-vroom, he goosed the engine to full-throated life*—Earl Thompson [fr the presumed prodding action of an angry *goose*; influenced by an earlier sense, "to do the sex act to; screw," where the instrument is a tailor's *goose,* a smoothing iron with a curved handle, found by 1690] *See* COOK someone's GOOSE, as FULL OF SHIT AS A CHRISTMAS GOOSE, GONE GOOSE

goose bumps (or **pimple**) *n phr* first form by 1930s, second by 1914 A roughness of the skin or the production of small pimples on the skin as the result of fear, cold, or excitement; gooseflesh

goose-bumpy *adj* by 1930s Frightened; panicky: *. . . goes goose-bumpy at the thought of hooking a 50-pound sailfish*—Time

goose-drownder *n* South and Southwest by 1929 A very heavy rainstorm; cloudburst

goose egg *n phr* baseball by 1866 Zero; nothing; a score of zero; =ZILCH: *My contribution appears to have been a great big goose egg*

goose something **up** *v phr* by 1970s To make something more exciting, intense, impressive, etc; =JAZZ something UP: *If we tried to goose it up too much. . . it wouldn't help anybody*—Newsweek

goo spot *n phr* police by 1980s A thoroughly decomposed body: *. . . goo spots, bodies that have been left so long that they don't even look like bodies. . .*—Steven Naifeh & Gregory White Smith

goosy or **goosey** *adj* by 1906 Touchy; jumpy; sensitive: *I feel a little goosy about the whole thing*—Time/ *Hennessey was goosey anyway, and he jumped*—James T Farrell *See* LOOSE AS A GOOSE

go out 1 *v phr* by 1888 To die **2** *v phr* (also **go out like a light**) by 1930s To lose consciousness; =PASS OUT: *Last thing I heard before I went out was the siren/ Something swished and I went out like a light*—Raymond Chandler

go out of one's **skull** by 1960s **1** *v phr* To become very tense; get nervous: *You can go out of your skull while they're doing that*—R Musel **2** *v phr* To become very excited; be overcome with emotion; =GO APE: *They went out of their skulls when she grabbed the mike to sing* **3** *v phr* To be overcome with tedium; fret with boredom: *The silence made him go right out of his skull*

go out of one's **way** *v phr* by 1876 To make a special effort; try very hard; =BEND OVER BACKWARDS: *I went out of my way to be nice to the guy*

go out on a limb *v phr* by 1897 To put oneself in a vulnerable position; take a risk: *OK, I'll go out on a limb and vouch for you*

go over *v phr* by 1910 To succeed; be accepted: *This demonstration will never go over with the hard hats* [go in this sense is found by 1742]

go over big *v phr* by 1920s To succeed very well; be received with great approval: *Her proposal went over big with the biggies* [the form go big is found by 1903]

go overboard by 1931 **1** *v phr* To be smitten with love or helpless admiration: *He went overboard for her right away* **2** *v phr* To commit oneself excessively or perilously; overdo: *Take a couple, but don't go overboard* **3** *v phr* =JUMP OFF THE DEEP END

go over like a lead balloon *v phr* by 1940s To fail miserably; =FLOP: *The whole thing went over like a lead balloon*—Buzz

go over the hill *v phr* armed forces by 1920s To go absent without leave from a military unit

go over with a bang *v phr* by 1928 To succeed splendidly; be enthusiastically approved: *My idea for a new bulletin board went over with a bang*

goozle *n* by early 1800s The throat

See WET one's **goozle**

go pfft (or phffft or poof) *v phr* by 1930s To end; dissolve; break up; =FIZZLE: *Their romance went pfft after that/ This year, two ballyhooed mergers. . . have gone phffft. . .* —New Yorker/ *. . . new opportunities are emerging even as old ones go poof. . .* —Los Angeles Times [used by gossip columnists; fr the British echoic phrase go phut, "come to grief, fizzle out," found by 1888]

gopher[1] 1 *n* by 1893 A young thief or hoodlum: *. . . tough West Side gophers who wouldn't hesitate to use a gun*—E Lavine **2** *n* underworld by 1901 A safecracker **3** *n* underworld by 1870s A safe or vault **4** *n* =GOFER

gopher[2] *v* baseball by 1970s gofer ball: *. . . only about the fifth or sixth that Orosco had gophered home the eventual gamer*—Village Voice

gopher[3] *n* computer by 1990s A system of menus allowing easy access to many resources on the Internet: *Gopher: An Internet tool that allows users to locate information and retrieve it. . .* —Mesa Tribune [fr the mascot of the University of Minnesota, where the first computer gopher originated]

gopher ball *See* GOFER BALL

◁**go piss up a rope**▷ *sentence* by 1940s Go away and do something characteristically stupid; =GET LOST, GO FLY A KITE: *He asked for another contribution and I told him to go piss up a rope*

go pittypat *v phr* (also **pit-a-pat** or **pitterpat**) by 1601 To beat strongly and excitedly; pump with joy and anticipation: *My veteran heart went pittypat*—San Francisco

go places *v phr* by 1930s To do very well in one's work; have a successful career; make good

go postal *v phr* computer by 1990s To succumb to tension and fatigue; =LOSE IT, STRESS OUT [a grim reference to "the unfortunate number of postal employees in recent years who have snapped or gone on shooting rampages"—Macon Telegraph]

go pound salt (or sand) *v phr* (Variation: **up** one's **ass** may be added) by 1950s To do something degrading and humiliating; =GO FUCK oneself: *. . . told Glazer and the feds to go pound sand, in legal terms, of course*—Philadelphia [the date should probably be earlier]

go public *v phr* To reveal oneself; acknowledge openly; =COME OUT OF THE CLOSET: *. . . how she adjusted to going public as a single-breasted woman*—Ms/ *Rumor is that the FBI is about to go public with another suspect* [fr the financial idiom go public, "offer stock for sale in the stock market after it had previously been held in a family or otherwise privately"]

gorilla 1 *n* (also **gorill**) by 1904 A ruffian; =GOON: *Strong-arm men, gorillas, and tough gangsters*—E Lavine/ *Those gorills do not care anything about law*—John O'Hara **2** *n* by 1920s A hired killer; =HIT MAN **3** *v* by 1960s To steal or rob with threat and violence: *. . . if you let somebody gorilla you out of some money*—Claude Brown **4** *v* by 1960s To beat someone up; savage someone; =CLOBBER: *If that doesn't work, we'll gorilla a little bit*—New York Times/ *You ain't gonna gorilla anybody*—Milwaukee Journal **5** *n* by 1980s Anything very powerful and unstoppable; anything very forceful and intimidating: *It is very simple to create the appearance of a "gorilla," a product with a lot of momentum*—Wall Street Journal

See SIX-HUNDRED-POUND GORILLA

gorilla juice *n phr* by 1980s Anabolic steroids and other substances used by body-builders, weight-lifters, etc, to increase bulk and musculature

gork 1 *n* medical by 1980s A stuporous or imbecilic patient; patient who has lost brain function: *The gork in that room has the "O" sign, did you notice?*—Elizabeth Morgan/ *By any definition, a gork. Lived a few minutes. . .* —Carsten Stroud **2** *v* medical by 1980s To sedate a patient heavily ◁**3**▷ *n* 1980s students A despised person; =GEEK, DORK, JERK: *Hubert is such a gork. His glasses are always falling off his nose, and he wears plaids with stripes*—UCLA Slang [said to be fr God only really knows, referring to a patient with a mysterious ailment]

gorked or **gorked out** *adj* or *adj phr* medical by 1980s Stuporous; semi-conscious; heavily sedated; =SPACED-OUT

gork out *v phr* medical by 1980s To become stuporous or comatose

gorm *v* students by about 1850 To eat voraciously [fr gormandize]

gormless *adj* British by 1746 Stupid; slow-witted; =DUMB [fr British dialect gaumless, "half-silly," lacking gaum, "understanding"; the dated sense is in the form gaumless; the entry spelling is found by 1883]

go-round *n* by 1960s A turn; a repetition: *That was nice. . . let's have another go-round*

go round and round *v phr* by 1970s To quarrel; squabble; fight: *They went round and round on the same issues for hours* [go-round, "a fight," is found by 1891]

gorp[1] *v* by 1940s To eat greedily; =GOBBLE, GORM [probably fr British *gawp up*, "to devour"]

gorp[2] *n* by 1980s A food mixture of dried fruit, nuts, and seeds, consumed esp by hikers, alpinists, etc [said to be fr *good old raisins and peanuts* and probably related to *gorp*[1]]

gorp gobbler *n phr* by 1980s A hiker; backpacker: *A Nature-Loving Backpacker is a Gorp Gobbler*—Nevada

go screw *sentence* or *v phr* =GO FUCK oneself: *Until that time, all those more experienced guys could go screw*—Lawrence Sanders

gosh *interj* by 1757 A mild exclamation of pleasure, disbelief, surprise, etc: *Gosh but I'm tickled, Reverend* [a euphemism for *God*]

go shank's mare *See* RIDE SHANK'S MARE

gosh-awful by 1900 **1** *adv* Extremely: *Wasn't it gosh-awful dark in there?* **2** *adj* Wretched; miserable; =DARNED: *Isn't that picture gosh-awful?*

◁**go shit in your hat**▷ *See* SHIT IN YOUR HAT

go sit on a tack *sentence* by 1900 Cease annoying me; =GO FLY A KITE, GO TO HELL

go slumming *See* SLUM

go snooks (or **snucks**) *v phr* by 1970 To share equally; go half-and-half: *We are going to go snooks on an electric golf cart*—Milwaukee Tribune [fr British *go snacks*, found by 1693, where *snacks* is related to earlier US *snook*, "a bite to eat"; hence the idiom has to do originally with sharing something to eat; the entry date should probably be earlier]

go soak yourself (or **your head**) *sentence* by 1884 Cease annoying me; =GO TO HELL: *When I asked for a date she told me to go soak my head*

go some *v phr* by 1911 To go very fast: *By the first turn we were going some*

go sour *v phr* by 1935 To become unsatisfying; fail; disappoint: *After a couple of years of fame it all went sour*

go south (also **head south, take a turn south**) **1** *v phr* by 1940s To disappear; fail by or as if by vanishing: *He played unbelievably. . . then all of a sudden he just went south*—Sports Illustrated/ *North Goes South*—New Yorker/ *Royals' offense heads south when Cone takes turn on mound*—Milwaukee Journal **2** *v phr* by 1925 To abscond with money, loot, etc: *She went south with a couple of silk pieces*—Dashiell Hammett/ *I hope he doesn't go South with the winnings*—American Speech **3** *v phr* underworld by 1950 To cheat, esp to cheat at cards: *go south 1: Palm cards or chips 2: Quit a game while winning, pretending to have suffered losses*—American Speech **4** *v phr* by 1980s To lessen; diminish: *. . . concern about injury went south*—Sports Illustrated/ *. . . his salary request needs to take a turn south*—Milwaukee Journal/

. . . the price immediately heads south in a highly competitive market—New York Times [probably fr the notion of disappearing *south of the border*, to Texas or to the Mexican border, to escape legal pursuit and responsibility; probably reinforced by the widespread Native American belief that the soul after death journeys to the south, attested in American Colonial writing fr the middle 1700s; GTT, "Gone to Texas, absconded," is found by 1839]

gospel *See* BIBLE

gospel-pusher *n* A preacher; minister

go steady *v phr* by 1905 To have a constant and only boyfriend or girlfriend: *Going steady means taking out one girl until a better one comes along*—Woman's Day

go straight *v phr* underworld by 1919 To renounce a life of crime; reform

go straight to dessert *See* CUT TO THE CHASE

gotcha 1 *n* A wound or injury, usu minor like a slight razor slice incurred while shaving: *Remember the gotchas you got from that worn old wrench?* **2** *n* A capture; a catch; an arrest: *"This is a gotcha," Johnson allegedly told Jaffee*—Time **3** *n* 1980s Gleeful and persistent faultfinding and personal recrimination, esp a particular fault loudly found: *The Admissions office at Georgetown revealed that blacks on average had lower test scores. "Gotcha!" was the attitude among critics*—New Republic/ *. . . a gigantic game of "gotcha," leading the Senate into what he described as "uncharted waters". . .*—Milwaukee Journal **4** *modifier*: *. . . a gotcha campaign*—American Speech [fr *got you*]

gotch-eyed *adj* by 1970s Having protuberant eyes; exophthalmic: *. . . she is a gotch-eyed. . . clapped up. . . hooker*—Dan Jenkins/ *. . . a real firebrand with that gotch-eyed look in his right eye. . .*—Carsten Stroud [fr British dialect *gotch*, "big-bellied jug"; the date should probably be earlier]

gotchie *n* Canadian children by 1980s The prank of pulling the underwear upward from behind by the waistband; =WEDGIE

go the distance *v phr* by 1940s fr horse-racing To finish an arduous effort; persist to the end: *Don't start this if you can't go the distance*

go the extra mile *v phr* by 1980s To make an extra effort; do more than usual: *It is time to communicate that. It is time to go that extra mile*—Garrison Keillor/ *. . . but for women, you have to go the extra mile to prove your credibility*—Nancy Landon Kassebaum

go the full yard *v phr* by 1980s To do the utmost; pursue something to the limit; =GO THE WHOLE HOG *See* the WHOLE NINE YARDS

go the hang-out road *v phr* 1960s To make a complete disclosure; abandon all concealment; =LET IT ALL HANG OUT

go the limit (or **all the way**) *v phr* by 1925 To do the sex act, as distinct from heavy petting, foreplay, etc: *. . . all-American girl must not. . . "go the limit"*—Frederic Morton [entry form fr poker, "to bet the maximum allowed"]

go the whole hog or **go whole hog** *v phr by 1828* To do the utmost; not slacken; pursue to the limit; =GO THE FULL YARD: *He decided to go the whole hog and buy a real big boat* [fr the notion of buying an entire animal and not a butchered part of it; *go the whole animal* is found as a variant by 1890]

go the whole nine yards *v phr by 1960s* To do the utmost; =GO THE LIMIT, GO THE WHOLE HOG: *I went the whole nine yards*—TV show *St. Elsewhere*
See the **whole nine yards**

go through changes *black about 1952* **1** *v phr* To work very hard; strive; =HUSTLE **2** *v phr* To pass through various emotional difficulties; be unstable and unsure: *Since last July 31, he has "gone through every change, from suicidal to who gives a shit"*—Toronto Life

go through the cellar *v phr by 1980s* To plummet; fall disastrously; =GO SOUTH: *The ratings went through the cellar*—Bob Denver

go (or **be**) **through the mill** *v phr by 1859* To have practical experience of something; be thoroughly seasoned: *I think you can rely on her; she's been through the mill*

go through the motions *v phr by 1816* To imitate some action rather than perform it; simulate a feeling, stance, etc: *Are you really remorseful, or just going through the motions?*

go through the roof *v phr by 1950s* To become very upset and angry; =GO BALLISTIC, HIT THE CEILING: *All I said was "Cool it," and she hit the roof*

go to bat *v phr underworld by 1940s* To be tried for a crime

go to bat against *v phr by 1940s* Oppose; contend against: *None of her victims would go to bat against her*—Dashiell Hammett

go to bat for *v phr* To support or defend; help: *. . . to judge by how he'd gone to bat for him*—Stan Cutler

go to bed *v phr newspaper office by 1930s* To be in final form ready for the press: *I can predict before the paper goes to bed*—Westbrook Pegler

go to bed with someone *v phr by 1940s* To do the sex act with someone; =SLEEP WITH someone

go to blazes *sentence by 1853* =GO TO HELL

go to Denmark *v phr by 1960s* To have a sex-change operation; become a transsexual [fr the fact that such operations were originally done primarily in Denmark]

go-to guy **1** *n phr basketball by 1990s* A player to whom the ball is thrown for a fairly sure score: *He was our go-to guy down low. And you knew if he got fouled he'd make his free throws. . .* —Milwaukee Journal/ *He's once again the go-to guy on the best team in the conference*—Los Angeles Times **2** *n phr* (also **go-to office**) *1990s* The best person or place to go for information, action, etc: *Professor Wilson is the main go-to guy on race and poverty for the institutions that shape agendas*—Nation/ *His became the go-to office for getting things done*—New York Times

go toe to toe *v phr by 1940s* To fight, esp to fight hard; =SLUG IT OUT: *They are going toe-to-toe with Cosmo, Glamour*—Philadelphia/ *Men in the courtroom can go toe to toe and then go off patting each other on the back*—Philadelphia

◁**go to hell**▷ **1** *v phr by 1930s* To deteriorate; be ruined: *The whole town's gone to hell, with that new mayor/ Old Joe's gone to hell a bit lately* **2** *sentence by 1836* May you be accursed, confounded, humiliated, etc; =DROP DEAD, GO FUCK oneself: *He wanted me to lie, but I told him to go to hell*

go-to-hell cap *n phr WWI armed forces* A military garrison cap; overseas cap

go to hell in a handbasket (or **a bucket**) *v phr 1980s* To deteriorate badly and rapidly; =GO DOWNHILL: *White people can go to hell in a handbasket. . . they can go to Burger King and not have their way*—Washington Post

go to pot *v phr by 1831* To deteriorate; worsen; =GO DOWNHILL, GO TO HELL: *A group of men who had literally and figuratively let themselves go to pot get back into good physical condition*—Psychology Today/ *A middle-aged man going to pot gets more than muscle tone from heavy exercise*—Psychology Today [fr the condition of an animal no longer useful for breeding, egg-laying, etc, that will now be cooked in the *pot*]

go (or **be taken**) **to the cleaners** *v phr by 1907* To lose all one's money, esp gambling at craps; =TAKE A BATH

go to the dogs *v phr by 1864* =GO TO HELL, GO TO POT [fr the notion that something unfit for human food would be given to the lowly *dogs*]

go to the glass *v phr basketball by 1990s* To shoot for a basket [fr the *glass* backboard of the basket]

go to the mat *v phr by 1908* To fight; contend mightily: *They soon stopped sparring and went to the mat* [fr the *mat* used as a wrestling site]

go to the wall **1** *v phr by 1589* To be ruined and destitute; collapse: *. . . if a real biggie, like Brazil, say, went to the wall*—Playboy **2** *v phr by 1858* To do sacrifice oneself; give way to another's interest; =GO ALL THE WAY: *We've gone to the wall for you*—TV program *Cagney and Lacey* [first sense fr the plight of someone being executed by being shot, against a *wall*]

go to (or **down to**) **the wire** *v phr by 1901* To be in very close competition until the very end: *The 1928 pennant race between the As and the Yanks went to the wire*—Philadelphia

go to town *by 1933* **1** *v phr* To do very well; succeed; perform impressively **2** *v phr* To throw off restraint; let go

got up on (or **out of**) **the wrong side of the bed** *v phr by 1930s* To be peevish, perverse, etc; be in a nasty mood: *He just about bit my head off, must have got up on the wrong side of the bed*

gouge *v by 1875* To cheat; =FLIMFLAM, SCAM: *Looks respectable, but this place regularly gouges the customer*

goulashes or **goolashes** (Gōō lash əz) *n by 1930s* Galoshes, as amusingly mispronounced

go under *v phr by 1880* To fail; sink; esp to lose consciousness

goup *See* GOOP

go up 1 *v phr 1960s narcotics* To become intoxicated from narcotics **2** *v phr theater about 1920* =GO UP IN one's LINES

go up against *v phr by 1940s* To confront; face; challenge: *So that's the kind of piffle actors have to go up against*—H McHugh

go up in one's **lines** *v phr theater about 1920* To forget or badly misspeak one's lines during a performance; =GO UP IN THE AIR

go up in smoke *v phr by 1933* To be ruined; be destroyed: *He just saw his beautiful scam go up in smoke*

go up in the air 1 *v phr theater about 1920* To miss a cue, forget one's lines, etc; =FLUFF **2** *v phr by 1906* To lose one's composure; become angry; =LOSE one's COOL: *You will rouse his anger, and he may "go up in the air"*—D S Martin

go (or **hit**) **upside** one's **face** (or **head**) *black by 1960s* **1** *v phr* To beat and pummel, esp around the head **2** *v phr* To defeat utterly; trounce; =CLOBBER

go up the spout *v phr by 1884* To be lost; be fruitlessly gone; =DOWN THE TUBE: *Fifty dollars tuition, all our plans. . . just gone up the spout*—Tennessee Williams [fr an earlier meaning, "pawned, in hock," because the pawnbroker had a tube or spout through which to convey pawned articles upstairs]

go up the wall *See* CLIMB THE WALL

gourd *n by 1844* The head; skull

See LOSE one's **gourd, out of** one's **head**

gow (GOU) **1** *n underworld about 1915* Opium **2** *n underworld about 1915* Any narcotic **3** *n by middle 1950s* Pictures of unclad or scarcely clad women; =LEG ART: *. . . this type of artwork, which in the newspaper field is called cheesecake and in the paperbooks field is "gow"*—Publishers Weekly [fr Canton Chinese, *yao-kao*, "sap, opium"]

gowed up *adj phr narcotics by 1940s* Intoxicated with a narcotic; =HIGH, HOPPED UP: *. . . some gowed-up runt*—Raymond Chandler

go whistle *v phr by 1453* To do anything one wants, but not to expect satisfaction, payment, etc; =GET LOST: *When I asked him again for my pay, he said I could go whistle*

go whole hog *See* GO THE WHOLE HOG

go with the flow *v phr 1960s counterculture* To consign oneself to the order and pace of things; be passive: *They pondered a while and decided to go with the flow and they all went back to sleep*—Tom Wolfe/ *Really, I'm just trying to go with the flow*—Milwaukee Journal [probably a reference to Taoism]

go (or **come**) **with the territory** (or **turf**) *v phr by 1960s* To be an integral part of some occupation or status, esp a part that is not especially delightful: *At EPA It Goes With the Territory*—New York Times/ *Tierney's answer was that such speculation "goes with the territory"*—New York Magazine/ *Such embarrassments come with the turf, however. . .*—New York Times [fr the conditions implicit in a sales representative's covering of a certain *territory*, popularized by use in the Requiem section of Arthur Miller's 1949 play, *Death of a Salesman*]

gow job *n phr 1950s hot rodders* =HOT ROD [in a somewhat earlier teenage sense, a *gow job* was "a flashy girl"]

gowster *n narcotics by 1930s* A marijuana user; =POTHEAD

grab 1 *n police by 1753* An arrest; =BUST, PINCH: *We will get credit for the grab, and we will also profit*—Lawrence Sanders/ *The only thing worse than no grab is a bad grab*—Cosmopolitan **2** *v by 1966* To seize the admiration or attention of; impress: *How does that grab you?*—New Yorker/ *. . . to reflect on a whole lot of things that had been grabbing me*—New York Times

grab a handful of air *v phr truckers by 1930s* To apply the brakes of a truck or bus quickly [fr the fact that such vehicles have *hand*-operated *air* brakes]

grab a handful of rods *v phr hoboes by 1920s* To ride on the rods of a freight car; =RIDE THE RODS: *I grabbed myself a handful of rods*—Jack Dempsey

grab an armful of boxcars *v phr hoboes by 1920s* To jump on a moving freight train

◁**grab-ass** or **grabarse**▷ *n by 1940s* Sexual touching and clutching: *. . . less anxious, less suspicious about my merry games of grabarse*—John Cheever *See* PLAY GRAB-ASS

grab-bag *n by 1855* A miscellaneous mixture; random collection: *the grab-bag of memories in my muddled head* [dated sense refers to a carnival game in which one may reach inside a bag of small prizes, after paying a fee]

grabber *n by 1966* Anything that seizes and rivets the attention; something that commands immediate admiration; =HOOK: *Dance within the regular format is a solid grabber*—Variety/ *He's found a real grabber*—Westworld

See GOOBER-GRABBER, MOTHERFUCKER

grabby 1 *adj by 1910* Greedy; acquisitive; selfish: *Share that, don't be grabby* **2** *adj by 1960s* Seizing; arresting; riveting: *. . . spent hours working on a goddamn grabby lead*—Armistead Maupin

grabs *See* UP FOR GRABS

grab shot *n phr by 1980s* A photograph taken in great haste, without time for proper focusing, exposure-setting, etc; a photograph of opportunity

grab your socks *See* DROP YOUR COCKS AND GRAB YOUR SOCKS

grad *students by 1871* **1** *n* A graduate: *college grad* **2** *modifier*: *a grad student/ grad reunion*

grade *See* EATIN' STUFF

the grade *See* MAKE THE GRADE

graffiting *n by 1980s* The spraying of graffiti: *When people stopped graffiting on the subways, they turned more to walls*—New York Times

graft 1 *n British by 1853* One's occupation; =GAME, RACKET **2** *n by 1865* The acquisition of money by dishonest means, esp by bribery for political favors: *the usual charges of graft at City Hall* [origin unknown; an 1883 source connects the two senses: *Graft.* To work. *Grafting.* Helping another to steal]

G-rag *n by 1990s:* . . . *NFL executive Gene Washington called for a ban on players wearing bandannas, known as do-rags (hair-do rags) or G-rags (gang rags) because they. . . promote the fashion and violent images that leap from America's street gangs*—New York Post

grain *n narcotics by 1980s* Marijuana; =GRASS, POT: *You been smoking too much grain. You head is juiced*—Robert B Parker

gramps *n by 1940s* Grandfather; any old man: *Need any help, gramps?* [*gramp* is found by 1898]

grand *n underworld & sports by 1920* A thousand dollars; =GEE: *A banker would scarcely call one thousand dollars "one grand"*—J C Hixson [said to have originated with Peaches Van Camp, a criminal who flashed such *grand* notes for ostentation]

the **grand bounce** *n phr* =the BOUNCE

Grand Central Station *n phr* Any place that is overcrowded and busy; =MOB SCENE: *My office was like Grand Central Station this morning*

granddaddy of all something *n phr by 1956* The most venerable, most impressive, largest, etc, of what is named; doyen; dean; =MOTHER OF ALL something: *The Newport is the granddaddy of all jazz festivals*

grandfather *v by 1900* To give someone a special status or privilege because of service prior to the time a new or definitive arrangement is made: *Some farmers just got grandfathered in, that's true*—Milwaukee Journals [fr the *grandfather clause* often written into new arrangements in order to be fair to older incumbents or practitioners; the date indicates the earliest instance of *grandfather clause*]

grandma 1 *n truckers by 1940s* The lowest and slowest gear of a truck; =CREEPER **2** *n by 1940s* Any old woman: *Can I carry your groceries, grandma?* [the second sense date must be much earlier]

grand slam 1 *n phr by 1814* The winning of all the goals, games, prizes, etc, available; total comprehensive victory: *Nobody won the tennis grand slam last year* **2** *n phr baseball by 1940* =GRAND SLAMMER **3** *modifier*: *grand-slam home run* [fr a bridge term for the winning of all the tricks in one hand]

grand slammer *n phr baseball by 1940* A home run hit when all the bases are occupied, and scoring four runs

grandstand *students by 1895* **1** *v* To play or perform in a brilliant and spectacular way, esp in order to get the approval of an audience; =HOT DOG, SHOW OFF: *Coach told him to stop grandstanding and take care of business* **2** *modifier*: *a grandstand catch*

grandstander *n students by 1895* A person who habitually grandstands; =HOT DOG, SHOW-OFF

grandstand play *baseball by 1888* **1** *n phr* A play made with special brilliance and brio, esp in order to impress the spectators **2** *n phr* Any action, speech, tactic, etc, designed to appeal to spectators; a tour de force: *The President's pronouncement's just a grandstand play*

granny dress *n phr 1960s* A floor-length dress, usu with long sleeves and a high neckline

granny (or grampa) dumping *n phr by 1991* The abandonment of helpless and destitute old people by families that cannot care for them: *Some overwhelmed families turn to granny dumping, abandoning their relatives at hospital emergency rooms*—Philadelphia/ *John Kingery, 82, victim of Alzheimer's, found abandoned in his wheelchair at a dog track, drew national attention to the phenomenon of grandpa dumping*—Time

granny flat *n phr by 1965* A small cottage or apartment where elderly people may live near but not actually with their children's family; =MOTHER-IN-LAW APARTMENT

granny glasses *n phr 1960s* Eyeglasses with small, circular steel or gold frames

granny tax *n phr by early 1990s* A state tax on nursing-home beds: *Groups who represent the elderly consider Thompson's proposal a "granny tax"*—Milwaukee Journal

◁**granola**▷ *late 1980s students* **1** *n* A person who is objectionably or prissily devoted to the 1960s values of environmental awareness, multiethnic tolerance, healthy "natural" diet, usu vegetarian, precious antiquated tastes, etc; =EARTH MUFFIN: *Stephanie turned into a granola when she started college. She won't even eat at McDonald's*—UCLA Slang/ *Elizabeth was far too granola for Jason, what with her herb garden and Celtic record collection*—Slang Bag 93 **2** *modifier*: . . . *geeky granola-type Ely*—Vogue/ *Fort Collins isn't really into. . . hard. . . music. . . There's a granola scene here*—Dave Nesheim [fr a multigrain W K Kellogg breakfast cereal devised around 1886]

grape *n by 1636* Wine or champagne

grapefruit league *n phr baseball by 1937* The association of major league teams as they play each other in preseason training [fr the fact that most spring training camps are held in citrus-growing regions]

grapevine *adj by 1863* Coming from an unofficial source of rumor or news: *a grapevine item/ grapevine gossip*

the **grapevine** *n phr Civil War* The source and route of rumors and unofficial news: *I heard it through the grapevine*—Norma Whitfield & Barrett Strong

grass 1 *n black by 1950s* The straight hair typical of Caucasians **2** *n* (also **grass weed**) *narcotics by 1930s* Marijuana; =POT: . . . *smoking a little grass and passing on venereal disease*—New York Times/ *Scoring grass here is easier than buying a loaf of bread*—New Yorker

See one's **ass is grass**

grass-cutter or **grass-clipper** *n baseball by 1868* A very hard ground ball

grasseater *n police by 1970s* A corrupt police officer who accepts graft money but does not demand it: *. . . repeated the distinction between the "grass eater" and the "meat eater"*—New York Times/ *The grasseaters are turning themselves in*—New York Post

grasshopper *n 1960s narcotics* A person who smokes marijuana; =POTHEAD: *My wife was a little grasshopper herself. But she didn't go on to become an addict*—R V Winslow

grass widow *n phr by 1839* A woman who is alone because of divorce, separation, rejection, etc [because her husband is still above the *grass* rather than under it]

gratis *See* FREE GRATIS

graum *v by 1950s* To worry; fret: *All a bookmaker graums about is they don't drop an atom bomb*—J Cannon [perhaps fr Middle English *gramen,* "be afflicted or tormented," fr Old English]

grave *See* HAVE ONE FOOT IN THE GRAVE

gravel *See* HIT THE DIRT

graveyard shift *n phr by 1907* A working shift that begins at midnight or 2 AM

graveyard watch *n phr railroad & Navy by 1927* A period of guard or watch duty from midnight to 4 AM or 8 AM

gravy *n by 1910* Money or other valuables beyond what one actually earns or needs; a bonus or excess: *Once we make back our expenses, everything else is gravy*

the **gravy train (** or **boat)** *n phr fr railroad by 1927* A chance, job, business, etc, that gives a very ample return for little or no work; an obvious sinecure; =the LIFE OF RILEY: *His job's a permanent gravy train/ Thus, railroad workers referred to a short haul that paid well as a. . . "gravy train"*—Hartford Courant

See ON THE GRAVY TRAIN, RIDE THE GRAVY TRAIN

◀**gray**▶ *black by about 1930* **1** *n* A white person; Caucasian; =OFAY **2** *adj*: *What about that gray girl in San Jose who had your nose wide open?*—Eldridge Cleaver

Gray Bar Motel *n phr Los Angeles police by 1990s* Jail; prison: *These days, the Gray Bar Motel is a synonym for "the bucket," which means jail*—Los Angeles Times [said to have been the name of the Lincoln Heights police station; a place displaying *gray* prison *bars;* earlier terms like *Graybar Hotel* and *Graystone College* are found by the 1930s]

graybeard *n airline by 1970s* A very senior pilot

gray market *n phr 1960s* The sale of reputable products, esp cameras and electronic equipment, by persons who have not bought them from the manufacturers' authorized distributors, and hence offer lower prices because the products do not qualify for the makers' guarantees: *There is a growing "gray" market for Levi's. . .* —Rocky Mountain News

gray matter *n phr by 1899* Intelligence; =BRAINS, SMARTS

gray mule *See* WHITE MULE

graze *v by 1980s* To eat small amounts often: *"I don't eat meals," she said. "I graze all day long"*—New York Times/ *. . . Cindy Crawford grazing at the salad bar*—Vanity Fair

grazer *by 1980s* **1** *n* A person who grazes rather than eats meals **2** *n* A person who shifts rapidly from one television to another; =CHANNEL SURFER: *Comedy will come in quick bursts, aimed at TV grazers who flip around the dial with their remotes*—Time

greafa or **greapha** *See* GREEFA

grease **1** *n esp 1800s* Money **2** *n by 1823* Bribe or protection money; money given for corrupt purposes: *They get so much grease it takes them half a block just to change direction*—Carsten Stroud **3** *n WWII Army* Butter **4** *n Persian Gulf War Army* Food **5** *v WWII armed forces* To shoot, esp to kill by shooting: *He has a gun and might try to grease you*—Rolling Stone **6** *n*: *You handled the grease real good, but not good enough, you didn't kill them*—Robert Daley [the verb *to grease,* "to bribe," is found by 1557; last two senses fr *greasegun,* a WWII submachine gun]

See AXLE GREASE, ELBOW GREASE, GREASE someone's PALM

greaseball ◀**1**▶ *n by about 1915* A dark-skinned, dark-haired person of Mediterranean or Latin American origin; =DAGO, GREASER: *. . . taking knives away from greaseballs in zoot suits*—Raymond Chandler/ *This time the greaseball smacked her. They were taking turns smacking her*—Ed McBain **2** *n hoboes by 1920s* A dirty tramp **3** *n WWII Navy* A cook or kitchen worker **4** *n circus by 1940s* A hamburger stand or concession **5** *n theater fr 1920s* An actor who uses too much makeup or greasepaint

grease-burner *n by 1940s* A cook, esp one who fries food at a lunch counter

greased lightning *n phr by 1848* Something or someone extraordinarily fast; =a BLUE STREAK: *He got out of there like greased lightning*

greasegun *n phr WWII armed forces* A submachine gun, esp one with a cylindrical body resembling a lubricating grease gun: *The Army's present standard model, the M–3 "greasegun"*—Associated Press/ *You had an automatic weapon. Like a grease gun*—Elmore Leonard [because its cylindrical body resembled the *greasegun* used to lubricate cars]

grease it *v phr WWII aviators* To land an aircraft smoothly: *He greased it!*—TV report of a Voyager space shuttle landing

grease job *n phr WWII aviators* A very smooth landing

See GIVE someone **a grease job**

grease joint **1** *n phr circus & carnival by 1920s* The cookhouse and eating tent **2** *n phr by 1914* A hamburger stand

grease monkey *by 1920s* **1** *n phr* A worker who lubricates machines, esp automobiles: *Good grease monkeys all, they could think better with a grease rack to lean against*—J Ellison **2** *n phr merchant marine* A stoker, oiler, or wiper on a ship **3** *n phr* Any mechanic, esp an automotive mechanic

grease (or **cross** or **oil**) someone's **palm** *v phr* by 1581 To pay someone for a corrupt purpose; bribe; buy favors: *If you grease the commissioner's palm, you can get anything fixed*—Jim Tully/ *Officials whose palms have been crossed*—A Hynd

grease-pusher *n* theater by 1940s A theatrical makeup person

greaser ◀1▶ *n* by 1849 =GREASEBALL •Used esp in referring to a Mexican or an Italian **2** *n* 1950s teenagers A hoodlum, petty thief, etc; =PUNK: *Stradazzi. Looks like a greaser, too*—Carsten Stroud **3** *n* aviators by 1980 A very smooth landing [second sense fr the *grease* used for their typical combed-back hairstyle]

grease the wheels *v phr* by 1809 To make things go smoothly; facilitate

grease trough (or **pit**) *n phr* by 1940s A lunch counter or lunch room: *Imagine yourself in the grease trough again*—Saturday Evening Post/ *. . . a shadowy grease pit midway between. . .*—Time

greasy 1 *adj* by 1529 Repellent in an unctuous and cunning way; =OILY **2** *adj* horse-racing by 1950s Muddy and slippery: *. . . to negotiate a "greasy" mile before an approving audience*—Morning Telegraph

◀**greasy grind**▶ *n phr* about 1930 A very diligent student

greasy spoon *n phr* by 1925 A small, cheap restaurant, lunchroom, or diner: *The Marx brothers ate in coffee pots and greasy spoons*—Joel Sayre/ *. . . your above-average greasy spoon in Boston's Back Bay*—Time

great 1 *adj* by 1848 Excellent; wonderful: *Hey, that's really great* **2** *n* by 1400 A famous person, esp an athlete or entertainer: *Weiss, a former football "great"*—Philadelphia Inquirer

the **greatest** *n phr* 1950s bop & cool talk A person or thing of superlative quality; =the MOST

the **greatest thing since sliced bread** *See* the BEST THING SINCE SLICED BREAD

great guns *See* GO GREAT GUNS

Great something or somebody **in the Sky** *n phr* by 1970s Heaven; God; the ultimate authority: *Senator Levin will be in the Great Committee Room in the Sky before Congress revisits the lobbyist mess*—Nation/ *We'll leave this play to that Great Critic in the Sky*

Great Mentioner *n phr* by 1990s A mythical personage who suggests names when an important appointment is to be made: *There are two or three names the Great Mentioner has come up with*—C-Span television

great shakes *See* NO GREAT SHAKES

greedball *n* by 1980s Professional baseball as administered and played by very high-paid and wealthy persons

greedhead *n* by 1970 An avaricious person; =GREEDYGUT: *The man's corrupt! A total greedhead!*—Gary Trudeau

greedygut or **greedyguts** *n* by 1546 A glutton; =CHOW HOUND, PIG: *One has no problem with*

Clifford Irving, a mere greedyguts—William Hampton

greefa *n* (Variations: **goifa** or **greafa** or **greapha** or **greefo** or **greeta** or **grefa** or **griefo** or **griffa** or **grifo**) narcotics by 1930s Marijuana or a marijuana cigarette [fr Mexican Spanish *griffa*, "weed"]

Greek 1 *n* college students by 1900 A Greek-letter fraternity member **2** *n* gambling by 1528 A professional gambler, esp a card-sharp

◀the **Greek way** (or **style**)▶ *n phr* Anal intercourse, esp heterosexual: *Another request is for Greek style. That is, anal sex*—Xaviera Hollander

green 1 *n* 1920s underworld & sports Money, esp ready cash; =FOLDING MONEY: *. . . plus "green" or "front money" to pay off others*—New York Times **2** *adj* by 1970s Advocating environmental protection; pro-ecological •The opposite of *brown*

See FOLDING MONEY, LONG GREEN, MEAN GREEN, SHIT GREEN

green apples *See* SURE AS GOD MADE LITTLE GREEN APPLES

green (or **blue**) **around the gills** *adj phr* by 1930s Sick-looking; pale and miserable; nauseated: *He was looking green around the gills, so I told him to lie down* [the date should probably be earlier; *gills*, "face," is found by 1626]

◀**green-ass**▶ *adj* by 1940s New and inexperienced; callow; green: *I spent thirty-four months havin' green-ass corporals chew me up*—Nelson Algren

greenback *n* 1870 A dollar bill [said to have been coined by Salmon P Chase, who died in 1873]

green folding *n phr* by 1950s =FOLDING MONEY

green goods *n phr* by 1887 Counterfeit paper money

greenhorn *n* by 1753 An inexperienced person; newcomer; neophyte; =ROOKIE

greenhouse *n* WWII aviators The transparent cockpit cover of an airplane

green ice *n phr* underworld by 1950s Emeralds

greenie 1 *n* by 1830s =GREENHORN **2** *n* 1960s narcotics A heart-shaped green stimulant pill of dextroamphetamine: *Do you take something, like greenies?*—Sports Illustrated/ *Greenies are pep pills. . . and a lot of baseball players couldn't function without them*—Jim Bouton **3** *n* Los Angeles police by 1990s A traffic ticket

the **green light** *n phr* by 1937 Permission, esp a superior's approval to proceed; =the GO-AHEAD: *When she got the green light, she invited the couple to see her in Washington. . .*—New York Times/ *. . . have also been given the green light to advertise special plates*—Los Angeles Times

green-light *v* by 1968 To approve; sanction: *Who in the world thought that Levinson's screenplay should be greenlighted?*—New Republic

greenmail *n* by 1983 The buying, at a premium price, of the stock holdings of someone who is threatening to take over a company, in order to induce the person to cease the attempt: *The most cited recent case of greenmail. . . occurred this spring and summer as Walt Disney Productions fought to escape a* *takeover*—New York Times/ *But Wall Street analysts agreed that CBS was unlikely to consider such action, since it amounts to "greenmail"*—New York Daily News [modeled on *blackmail*]

green money *n phr by 1940s* Paper money; ready cash; *by 1940s* =FOLDING MONEY: . . . *shooting for green money*—A Hynd

green one *n phr by 1980s* A dollar bill; dollar; =BUCK, CLAM: *Alphamassage, only 15,000 green ones at Hammacher Schlemmer, plus 125 for shipping and handling*—New Yorker

the **green stuff** *n phr by 1880s* Money; ready cash; paper money; =FOLDING MONEY, LONG GREEN: *He really poured the green stuff to the bookies*—S Frank

a **green thumb** *by 1940s* **1** *n phr* A special talent for gardening **2** *n phr* The ability to make projects succeed, like flourishing plants: . . . *possessor of a green thumb when it comes to making musicals blossom*—H Ormsbee

greeta or **grefa** *See* GREEFA

gremlin 1 *n WWII Army Air Forces fr British* An imaginary imp who caused malfunction in machines, problems in projects, confusion in arrangements, etc •The Royal Naval Air Service apparently used the term in WWI **2** *n* (also **grem, gremmie**) *1960s surfers* A person, esp a girl, who frequents surfing beaches without surfing; =BEACH BUNNY: . . . *gremlins, usually girls, those hangers-on who may never get wet*—Time [origin unknown; probably modeled on *goblin*, with the first syllable perhaps fr Irish *gruaimin*, "irascible little creature"]

greyhound therapy *n phr by middle 1980s* The practice by some municipalities or other governmental groups of ridding themselves of the homeless and other potentially burdensome persons by giving them a bus ticket to another place: *Greyhound therapy. . . giving the homeless a one-way bus ticket to Los Angeles*—New York Times [fr the trademark name of the *Greyhound* bus company]

grid or **gridiron 1** *n* A football field **2** *modifier*: *the grid squad/ gridiron victories*

G-ride *n Los Angeles police by 1990s* Car theft; grand theft auto

gridlock *n by 1980* A blockage; paralysis: *Until the emotional and psychological gridlock over the Federal deficit is broken*—Newsweek [fr the traffic term designating a total blockage of traffic caused by cars stopping in intersections behind other stopped cars, and blocking traffic on the intersecting street]

grief *n by 1929* Complaints; faultfinding; reprimand: *I don't want no grief from the fourteenth floor*—Michael Grant

See GIVE someone **grief**

griefo or **grifo** or **griffa** *See* GREEFA

grievous bodily harm or **GHB** *n phr by 1990s* An illegal steroid substance, gamma hydroxybutyric acid; =SCOOP: . . . *GHB crossed over onto the club circuit, where users refer to it as Grievous Bodily Harm*—Milwaukee Journal

grift *carnival & circus by 1914* **1** *n* Money gotten dishonestly and by one's wits, esp by swindling **2** *n* Any dishonest way of getting money by cunning, esp the deceptions of confidence tricksters, hawkers, etc **3** *v*: *He grifted a couple years then got a regular job*

grifter *carnival & circus by 1915* **1** *n circus* A gambler **2** *n* A confidence trickster, hawker, minor criminal, etc **3** *n* A hobo; vagabond; =DRIFTER

grin and bear it *v phr by 1864* To exercise forbearance and fortitude; =TOUGH IT OUT

grinch *n by 1980s* A person who spoils a happy occasion, esp Christmas; spoilsport; =SCROOGE: *The grinch at City Hall*—US News & World Report/ . . . *Mecham of Arizona is drawing fire as a new kind of grinch*—New York Times [fr a character in Dr Seuss' 1957 book *How the Grinch Stole Christmas*]

grind 1 *v by 1940s* To rotate one's pelvis in the sex act or in imitation of the sex act •Nearly always in combination with *bump: the strippers bumping and grinding away* **2** *n by 1940s*: . . . *to wow the audience with her bumps and grinds*—Trans-Action **3** *v students by 1864* To study diligently: *Five days to grind and two days to be social. . . the way it was at Yale*—Sexual Behavior **4** *n students by 1864*: *No one except a few notorious grinds studied that night*—P Marks **5** *v circus by about 1925* To attract and address a crowd at a show or concession; =SPIEL **6** *n*: *They heard the hawker go into his grind* **7** *n circus by about 1925* A hawker or barker **8** *n by about 1890* Any obnoxious or annoying person; =JERK, PAIN IN THE NECK, PILL: *The prof's a tedious old grind* **9** *n by 1852* Any very difficult and trying task, esp one that lasts a long time and is slowly and painfully done: *Writing dictionaries is indeed a grind*

See BUMP AND GRIND, GREASY GRIND, IF YOU CAN'T FIND 'EM, GRIND 'EM

grindcore *n by 1990s* A variety of hard-rock music: . . . *this veteran quintet may be the purest and most primal grindcore band. . .* —Los Angeles Times

grinder 1 *n circus & carnival by about 1925* A barker or hawker **2** *n by 1950s* A stripteaser; =STRIPPER **3** *n by 1940s* A car, esp an old and ramshackle one: . . . *bought a brand new Chev to take the place of her old grinder*—J Lilienthal **4** *n by 1950s* =HERO SANDWICH **5** *n Marine Corps by 1940s* A parade ground; drill field

See COFFEE GRINDER

grind-house or **grind movie** *n or n phr 1930s theater* A theater that runs continuously without intermissions, holidays, etc: *Four years ago, it would have been restricted to a few downtown grind-houses*—Time/ *He dragged me to the Times Square grind-house to which it had been relegated*—San Francisco [probably fr *grind show*, perhaps influenced by the burlesque and sexual connotations of *grind*]

grinding *See* BIT-GRINDING

grind something **out** *v phr by 1940s* To produce

or make something, esp with uninspired precision or long and painful effort: *They sat down and ground the script out in two days/ They just grind them out. . . ten a day*

grind show *n phr* 1930s *carnival* A show that runs continuously [probably because the show *grinds* along like a machine]

grip 1 *n theater & movie studio by 1888* A stagehand or stage carpenter: *. . . crowded with assistant directors, character actors, movie stars, grips and electricians*—H Niemeyer **2** *n by 1879* A traveling bag; valise: *Gonna pack my grip and make my getaway* [second sense a shortening of *gripsack*]

gripe 1 *v by 1932* To complain, esp habitually and trivially; groan; =BITCH, KVETCH, PISS: *He got good and sore and griped*—Morris Bishop **2** *n by 1934*: *I want to clear my desk of various matters, mostly gripes*—Bernard DeVoto **3** *v by 1559* To annoy or disgust; afflict; distress: *What's griping him is that he can't do anything for the kids*—James T Farrell **4** *n by 1930s* =GRIPER [ultimately fr *griping of the gut,* "colic, bellyache, stomach cramp"]

◁**gripe** one's **ass**▷ *v phr* (Variations: **balls** or **butt** or **cookies** or **left nut** or **middle kidney** or **soul,** or some other organ or possession at the whim of the speaker, may replace **ass**) *by 1940s* To disgust or annoy someone extremely: *His sycophancy gripes my ass*

griper *n by 1938* A chronic complainer; malcontent; =KVETCH

gripe session *n phr by 1940s* A conversation or discussion consisting primarily of complaints

grip'n'grin *modifier by 1980s* Showing someone, esp a politician, shaking hands and smiling: *. . . "grip'n'grin" photographs and mind-numbing meeting minutes. . .* —Milwaukee Journal

gripper *See* GROUND-GRIPPER

grit 1 *n by 1825* Courage; fortitude and stamina **2** *n railroad by 1950s* The roadpath beside a railroad track **3** *v black by 1930s* To eat **4** *n* (also **grits**) *black by 1930s* Food ◁**5**▷ *n by 1960s* A Southerner: *He's a hotshot down here among the grits. A good Yankee guard would eat him alive*—Pat Conroy **6** *n* (also **Grit**) *black by 1960s* A white person: *It's a God's wonder some Grit didn't kill us*—Harry Crews [food senses at least partially fr *hominy grits,* although *grit* was British military slang for "food" in the 1930s; Southern dialect sense probably ironically fr Civil War use of the expression *true Yankee grit* by Northern soldiers and writers]
See HIT THE DIRT

gritty *See* the **nitty gritty**

groady or **groaty** or **groddy** *See* GROTTY

groan box *n phr by about 1930* An accordion

groaner *See* GRUNT-AND-GROANER

groceries *n by 1940s* A meal or meals: *I got hooked for the groceries*—Sherman Billingsley
See BRING HOME THE BACON

grogged 1 *adj* Drunk **2** *adj* Sleepy; =GROGGY [fr British naval *grog,* "rum and water," so called because it was introduced in the mid–18th century as a sailor's

ration by "Old *Grog,*" Admiral Sir Edward Vernon, who habitually wore a *grogram* coat]

groggy *adj by 1832* Sleepy; dazed; semi-conscious: *Conlon was so groggy that he wanted to know why Nelson was not coaching the Warriors*—Milwaukee Journal Sentinel

grog-mill *by 1940s* **1** *n* A saloon; tavern **2** *modifier*: *. . . no grog-mill cuties*—J Evans

◀**groid**▶ *n students by 1970* A black person: *The groids sure love to fish*—John McPhee [fr *Negroid*]

grok (GRAHK) **1** *v counterculture & students by 1961* To communicate sympathetically: *. . . all rapping and grokking over the sound it made*—Tom Wolfe/ *All the Romans grokked like Greeks*—Pulpsmith **2** *v* (also **grok on**) *counterculture & students by 1961* To get into exquisite sympathy with: *She met him at an acid-rock ball and she grokked him*—Playboy/ *. . . the Handbook of Highway Engineering. . . They totally grokked on it*—Douglas Coupland **3** *v computer by 1980s* To understand: *You've come to grok that Cronenberg's narrative is merely the pretense for his imagery*—Village Voice [coined by Robert A Heinlein as a Martian word in the 1961 science-fiction novel *Stranger in a Strange Land*]

grollo *n* =GROWLER

grommet *n by 1986* An early teenage or subteen person in a surfing milieu •Apparently a borrowing from Australia, where it is also spelled *grummit*: *. . . an ersatz club scene for junior high-schoolers, grommets, kiddies. . .* —Los Angeles Times [origin unknown; *grummit* and *grommet* are found by the 1890s in the sense "vulva," where the reference is probably to various rings used in ship's rigging, but the semantic connection here is uncertain]

gronk out *v phr computer by 1980s* To cease functioning; =GO DOWN: *The terminal gronked out about ten minutes ago*

grooby *adj teenage by 1943* Excellent; =GROOVY: *You, too, can get on the grooby side*—Time

groove 1 *n by 1958* Any habitually preferred activity; what excites and gratifies one; =BAG, KICK **2** *v 1960s* To enjoy intensely; take gratification, esp rather passively and subjectively; =GO WITH THE FLOW: *To groove means to yield yourself to the flow of activity around you*—New York Times/ *I just like to get out there and groove a little*—New York Times **3** *v 1960s* To like and approve; =DIG: *They see the spade cats going with ofay chicks and they don't groove it*—R DeWolf **4** *v by 1935* To perform very well; be effective: *. . . really grooving on that funny trumpet* [fr the sense that a musician is in a definite and exciting track, has hit a perfect stride, when playing well, esp a solo; perhaps influenced by the *grooves* of a phonograph record]
See IN THE GROOVE

a **groove** *n phr 1960s* Something excellent, desirable, exciting, etc: *Working at ABC is "a groove"*—New York Magazine/ *Your hat is a groove*—Harper's Bazaar

groove on something or someone *v phr 1960s*

To enjoy intensely; =GROOVE: *I can really groove on the Beatles*—New York Times/ *She walks for blocks grooving on Reality*—Gail Sheehy

groovy 1 *adj* 1930s jive talk Playing and enjoying music well and with concentration; =HEP, IN THE GROOVE **2** *adj* teenagers by 1944 Excellent; wonderful; =FAR OUT: *"Hey, groovy," said Sally*—Max Shulman **3** *adj* 1980s teenagers Obsolete; out-of-date: *. . . a way of describing, with heavy sarcasm, maroon polyester suits: "Groovy!"*—New York Times

grope *v* by 1250 To touch, feel, caress, fondle, etc, with seeming or actual sexual intent *See* GROUP-GROPE

grope-in *n* by 1960s =GROUP-GROPE

gross *adj* teenagers by 1958 Disgusting; rebarbative; =GROTTY: *. . . at this moment (how gross!) blowing kisses into the phone*—Erich Segal

grossed out *adj phr* teenagers by 1960s Disgusted; revulsed

gross-out teenagers fr 1960s **1** *n* Something particularly disgusting; repellent trash: *He attempts. . . the ultimate gross-out: "self-expression" of the kind found in Greenwich Village*—Newsweek **2** *modifier*: *The Animal House gross-out movies are all about groups*—New York Magazine/ *. . . gross-out scenes of the Dalmatian mounting the smaller dog*—Toronto Life

gross someone **out** *v phr* teenagers by 1968 To disgust or offend, esp with crude and obscene language and behavior: *They're grossing me out, too, you know*—Cyra McFadden/ *Being a mother really grosses me out*—Erma Bombeck

grotacious *adj* by 1990s =GROSS, GROTTY: *No; grotacious, or what*—Douglas Coupland

grotty (GROH dee, -tee) middle 1960s teenagers **1** *adj* (Variations: **groady** or **groaty** or **groddy** or **grody; to the max** may be added) Disgusting; nasty; repellent; bizarre; =GRUNGY, SCUZZY: *The magazines had covers with those grotty weirdos on them*—Philadelphia **2** *n*: *. . . the introspective hedonism and political individualism of the second group. . . called groddies*—Trans-Action [fr *grotesque*; popularized by the Beatles in the 1960s; perhaps fr Merseyside dialect]

grouch-bag circus by 1908 **1** *n* A small bag in which money for an emergency is carried: *Circus roust-abouts took their money out of grouch-bags, pouches. . . like tobacco pouches*—Nelson Algren **2** *n* The money in a grouch-bag; =MAD MONEY

ground *See* BEAT TO THE GROUND, DOWN TO THE GROUND, NOT KNOW one's ASS FROM one's ELBOW, NOT KNOW someone or something FROM A HOLE IN THE GROUND, RUN something INTO THE GROUND, STAMPING GROUND

ground someone *v phr* by 1940s To deny privileges to someone, esp to keep someone confined at home as a punishment: *If my father got a pair of bell-bottoms, I think I'd ground him*—McCall's [fr the practice of not permitting a pilot to fly, as a punishment, the word found by 1931]

ground biscuit *n phr* by 1920s =ALLEY APPLE

grounder 1 *n* hoboes by about 1930 A cigarette butt **2** *n* baseball by 1861 A batted baseball that rolls along the ground **3** *n* police by 1980s A homicide case that be easily and quickly solved: *. . . decided to hand Kennedy the 23rd Street jumper, which he thought was a grounder. . .*—Carsten Stroud

ground floor *See* IN ON THE GROUND FLOOR

ground-gripper WWII Navy **1** *n* A landlubber **2** *n* A sailor who neither flies in an airplane nor sails in a ship

ground rations *n phr* black by 1950s The sex act [probably fr the sexual sense of *grind* plus the frequent association of the sex act with eating]

group *See* IN-GROUP, RAP GROUP

group-grope by 1960s **1** *n* Mutual touching and caressing by a group of people, either plainly orgiastic or with some sort of psychotherapeutic intent; =GROPE-IN **2** *n* Intimate intertwining of entities: *Harvard will reestablish an independent department of sociology, ending 24 years of interdisciplinary group-grope*—John Leonard

groupie 1960s rock and roll **1** *n* A young woman who seeks to share the glamour of famous persons, esp rock musicians, by offering help and sexual favors; =BUNNY: *No fool, no groupie, no teeny-bopper, she takes rock music, rightly, seriously*—Vogue **2** *n* An ardent devotee and votary; =FAN: *. . . like many of Hollywood's young trendies, a political groupie*—Newsweek/ *. . . the American literary groupies*—Saturday Review **3** *modifier*: *. . . the "groupie" syndrome, personified by adulatory novices of science flocking around the luminaries*—Dan Greenberg

grouse *v* British armed forces by 1887 To complain; =BITCH: *No grousing, no foot-dragging, both signs of a solid pro*—Harper's

growl *v* by 1707 To complain; mutter angrily

growler 1 *n* (also **grollo**) by 1888, now obsolete A container used to carry beer home from a bar: *A can brought in filled with beer at a barroom is called a growler*—B Matthews **2** *n* WWII Navy A public-address loudspeaker or system; =BITCH BOX, SQUAWK BOX **3** *n* by 1912 A small iceberg **4** *n* police by 1980s A police squad car; =PROWL CAR: *They got back into the growler and took off*—Jay J Armes

growler-rushing by 1880s, now obsolete **1** *n* A drinking spree **2** *modifier*: *Heslin was the contemptible, growler-rushing type of petty thief*—E Lavine

grrrl *modifier* 1990s Aggressively feminist, as expressed in music, fashion, ideas, etc: *. . . leader of the hard-core feminist riot grrrl movement. . .*—Los Angeles Times/ *. . . media overkill about the Riot Grrrl fashion trend. . .*—Sassy [a blend of the angry animal-like utterance *grr!* with *girl*]

grrrldom *n* 1990s The realm and principles of an aggressive feminism: *. . . the humorless man-hating axis of riot-grrrldom. . .*—Vogue

grub 1 *n* by 1659 Food: *. . . goods one can exchange at the kitchen door for grub*—Jack

London/ . . . nonchalantly gobble up mounds of this grub—CoEvolution Quarterly **2 v** black : Come over and grub with us—O Johnson

grubbin' *n* 1990s teenagers Good food

grub-pile *n* cowboys by 1863 A meal

grub-slinger *n* cowboys by 1912 A cook

grubstake *n* by 1863 The money needed for a new venture, new start, etc: *Nobody knows how much he gave away in grubstakes*—T Betts

grudge fight (or **match) n phr** by 1930s A sports contest in which personal animosity figures: *. . . their every match is a grudge match. . .* —New York Times

gruesome twosome n phr 1940s teenagers A couple going steady

grunge or **grunch** (GRUHNJ, GRUHNCH) **1** *n* A dull, tedious person; =NERD, PILL **2 adj** 1960s teenagers Boring **3 adj** 1960s teenagers =GRUNGY **4** *n* 1960s teenagers Slovenliness; sloppiness **5** *n* 1960s teenagers Something nasty: *Those globs of guitar grunge get me off every time*—Village Voice **6** *n* early 1990s A style of dress featuring mismatched and rumpled garments, mostly suggesting lumberjacks, and appearing to have been bought at thrift shops and donned at random, and favored by grunge rock musicians: *"Stuff We Hate". . . grunge as high fashion*—Sassy/ *Garth's wardrobe is mostly grunge*—Slang Bag 93 **7** *n* early 1990s A kind of rock music originally associated with Seattle, WA: *Nirvana and Pearl Jam are two of the best grunge bands*—Slang Bag 93

grungy (GRUHN jee) **adj** 1960s teenagers Shabby; squalid; dirty; =GROTTY, SCUZZY: *I put down in my grungy little notebook that Max Frisch was a wise man*—C Vetter/ *. . . the peerless, fearless, slightly grungy Grodin to investigate*—Richard Grenier [origin unknown; perhaps sound symbolism resembling *gross, mangy, mung, stingy*, etc]

grunt 1 *n* line repairers by about 1900 A line repairer's helper who works on the ground and does not climb poles **2** *n* railroad by 1940s A locomotive engineer; =HOGGER **3** *n* Vietnam War armed forces An infantry soldier; =PADDLEFOOT: *I was drafted. . . and served twelve months as a grunt in Vietnam*—Newsweek/ *Now there's a willingness to tell the story of the poor grunt who got his tail shot off*—New York Times **4** *n* by late 1960s Any low-ranking person, neophyte, etc: *The attitude among the reporter grunts was pretty much "them against us"*—Washingtonian **5** *n* by 1940s A bill for food or drink: *I just hope Toots didn't bring along any of the grunts I must have left in that oasis*—Paul Sann **6** *n* by 1980s A diligent student; =GRIND: *A grunt is a student who gives a shit about nothing except his sheepskin*—Stephen King *See* CLUCK AND GRUNT

grunt-and-groaner *n* by 1940s A wrestler

grunter *n* by 1940s A wrestler

grunt-horn or **grunt-iron** *n* musicians by 1940s A tuba

grunt work (or **labor) n phr** by 1977 Hard and/or tedious toil; =BULLWORK: *The machine will do the grunt work, filing, typing lists, comparing, sorting*—San Francisco/ *Congress returned to Washington. . . and settled down for a month of grunt work. . .* —New York Times/ *Whereas Agassi's every second of court time is grunt labor*—New York Times

G-string or **gee string n phr** or **n** by 1878 A breech-cloth, or brief covering for the genitals, worn esp by striptease dancers: *Thus the G-string became an integral part of a stripper's apparatus*—Toronto Life [origin unknown; the dated use refers to Plains Indian use of a loin cloth; the stripper sense is found in the 1930s]

guard *See* CORPORAL'S GUARD, HOME GUARD

guardhouse lawyer n phr Army by 1888 =LATRINE LAWYER

Gucci Gulch n phr early 1990s A fashionable shopping street or mall in Washington, Los Angeles, etc: *. . . I'm gonna have to kill some time at Gucci Gulch*—Gary Trudeau/ *Yes, Wisconsin's red and white army shopped the gold and jewels of Gucci Gulch. . .* —Milwaukee Tribune [fr the posh and pricey Florentine retail house of *Gucci*]

guess what or **who** or **why v** by 1930s To feign a conjecture when the truth is blatantly obvious; =SURPRISE SURPRISE: *The only one bold enough to call the proposal a smoke screen disguising congressional complicity was Colorado Republican Armstrong. Guess what? He's retiring this year*—New Republic/ *Kissinger's scheme outlined a framework between the two superpowers to be arranged by a secret envoy (guess who?)*—New Republic/ *The stoppages were unpopular; the Western press—guess why?—is no longer keen on Polish strikes*—Nation *See* BY GUESS AND BY GOD

guesstimate by 1934 **1** *n* An approximation based on calculation and guesswork **2 v**: *Let's guesstimate a yield of four percent*

guest shot n phr by 1980s A guest appearance on a television show: *. . . I get a big guest shot for big bucks on his next special. . .* —Stan Cutler

guff 1 *n* by 1888 Nonsense; pretentious talk; bold and deceitful absurdities; =BULLSHIT: *. . . his ability to listen to all the guff, through all the tedium*—Time **2 v** To lie; exaggerate; =BULLSHIT: *Quit your guffing and tell it right* **3** *n* Complaints, abuse: *Don't take any guff from him*—New Yorker [perhaps fr Scots *gaff*, "loud, rude, merry talk"; *gaff* in the first sense, now obsolete, is found by 1825]

guide *See* TOUR GUIDE

Guido or **guido** *n* 1980s teenagers A gaudy macho type: *Guido:. . . a greasy, pimpy, open-shirted, hairy-chested, gold-chain-danglin' sleazoid*—Sassy/ *It's not my fault I look like a Guido*—Montel Williams TV show [the name of a character in the 1983 movie *Risky Business*]

the **guilties n phr** by 1980s Feelings or pangs of guilt: *Sometimes. . . we get the guilties on this account*—Newsweek

◄**Guinea**► (GIHN *ee*) (also **ghinney** or **ginee** or **gin-nee** or **ginney** or **guin** or **guinea** or **guinie**; any of the variants may begin with a capital letter) **1** *n by 1896* An Italian or person of Italian descent **2** *adj*: . . . *a tough Ginney bootlegger*—Damon Runyon **3** *n* WWII armed forces A native of a Pacific island, including Japan [perhaps fr contemptuous association with the outdated term *Guinea Negro,* "black slave from the Guinea coast"]

◄**guinea football**► *n phr* WWI Army A small bomb, esp a homemade one; =ITALIAN FOOTBALL

◄**guinzo**► *See* GINZO

gulch *See* DRY-GULCH

gull 1 *n merchant marine by 1950s* Chicken or other fowl **2** *n* WWII Navy A prostitute

gully-low *adj jazz musicians by about 1910* Sensuous; insinuating; =DIRTY, SEXY

gum 1 *v by 1940s* To talk; chatter: *The he-gossips at the Press Club have been gumming about another romance*—R Starnes **2** *v by 1901* =GUM UP *See* BAT one's GUMS, BUBBLE-GUM MUSIC, the BUBBLE-GUM SET

gumbah *See* GOOMBAH

gumball *by 1970s* **1** *n* The lights carried atop a police car; =PARTY HAT: *Don't believe in gumballs. I kinda like to sneak around, you know*—Car and Driver **2** *v*: . . . *a dozen police cars blocking the streets, their red-and-blue lights gumballing in all directions*—Playboy

gum-beater *n black by 1930s* A persistent talker, esp a pompous braggart; =BLOWHARD

gum-beating *black by 1930s* **1** *n* A conversation; chat; =RAP **2** *n* Vain and exaggerated talk; =BALONEY, BULLSHIT

gumbies 1 *n 1970s students* Black tennis shoes **2** *n by 1990s* Rubber wet suits as worn by divers, sailboarders, etc

gumby ◄**1**► *n 1970s Canadian teenagers* A dull, tedious person, esp one out of touch with current fashions; =NERD, PILL: *You can become a gumby. . . by wearing the wrong plaid stretch pants*—The Globe and Mail **2** *n 1980s teenagers* A slanted box haircut: *Murph has a gumby. . .* —Delcastle Dictionary of Slang [first sense fr a repulsive character, Mr *Gumby,* in the television series "Monty Python's Flying Circus"; second sense fr a person-shaped toy rubber (gum) figure named *Gumby,* seen in TV shows and also portrayed by the comedian Eddie Murphy on the television series *Saturday Night Live*]

gummixed (or gummoxed) up *adj phr by 1950s* Confused; chaotic; ruined; =BOLLIXED UP, FUCKED UP [perhaps from a blend of *gummed up* with *bollixed up*]

gummy 1 *adj by 1922* Inferior; tedious; unpleasant: *He found himself in a very gummy situation, with both of them berating him* **2** *adj about 1940* Sentimental; maudlin; =CORNY: *a gummy, gooey tearjerker of a film* [like *icky* and *sticky,* fr the unpleasant feel of glue or slime]

gump 1 *n by 1825* A fool; dolt; =KNUCKLEHEAD **2** *n hoboes by 1899* A chicken, esp a stolen one **3** *n prison by 1950s* A male homosexual [fr British dialect, "fool"]

gumption *n by 1831* Initiative; enterprise; courage; =SPUNK

gums *See* BAT one's **gums**

gumshoe *by 1906* **1** *n* (Variations: **gum boot** or **gumfoot** or **gumheel** or **gumshoe man**) A police officer, esp a detective or plainclothes officer: *It made him a good gumshoe*—New York Times **2** *v* (also **gumheel**) To work as a police officer or detective: *Still gumheeling?*—R Starnes **3** *v* To walk a police beat: *Police now ride prowl cars instead of gumshoeing around the block*—E B White **4** *v* To walk quietly and stealthily [fr *gumshoe,* "rubber-soled shoe"]

gum up or **gum up the works** *v phr by 1890* To ruin; spoil; throw into confusion; =BOLLIX UP, FUCK UP [fr dialect *gaum,* "handle improperly, damage," found by 1656, influenced by the stickiness and clogging capacity of *gum*]

gun¹ 1 *n by 1859* An armed criminal: *They hired a gun to blast the competition* **2** *v by 1898* To shoot someone: *Canales had no motive to gun Lou*—Raymond Chandler **3** *n by 1830* An important person; =BIG GUN: *He's quite a gun around there now* **4** *n early 1900s* The throttle of a car, airplane, etc: *Get your stupid foot off the gun* **5** *v by 1940s* To speed up an engine or vehicle, esp abruptly; =GOOSE: *He gunned the Rolls into the parking spot* **6** *n 1930s narcotics* A hypodermic needle **7** *n 1960s surfers* A long, heavy surfboard **8** *n baseball by 1929* Throwing arm, esp a strong and accurate one *See* BIG GUN, BURP GUN, GIVE IT THE GUN, GREASEGUN, JUMP THE GUN, SCATTERGUN, SIX-SHOOTER, SMOKING GUN, SON OF A BITCH, TOMMY GUN, ZIP GUN

gun² ** *n* (also **gon) *by 1858* A professional thief, esp a pickpocket [fr Yiddish *gonif*]

gunboats *by 1886* **1** *n* A pair of shoes or galoshes, esp of large size: *He brought some of the 14EE gunboats with him from the States*—Associated Press **2** *n* A pair of large feet

gunbunny *n 1970s Army* An artillery man

gunch *by 1970s* **1** *n* An attempt to influence the roll of a pinball **2** *v*: . . . *the body English, the nudging, gunching, and infinite alternations of the ways to flip the flipper*—Time

gun someone **down** *v phr by 1898* To shoot so as to fell or kill: *They gunned him down in a barber chair*

gun (or go gunning) for someone **1** *v phr by 1888* To seek out or pursue with harmful intent; aim to punish: *He gunned for her after she slapped him with a lawsuit* **2** *v phr by 1940s* To pursue actively: *She's gunning for a new image*—USExpress

gung ho *adj phr* WWII Marine Corps Very zealous; totally committed; enthusiastic: *They were gung ho about the opportunity, their talk charged with an eagerness*—New Yorker/ . . . *reminiscent of the gung-ho shot making that brought him so many* *grass-stained knees at Wimbledon*—New York Times [fr the name of a Chinese industrial cooperative organization, *kung ho,* "work together," adopted as *Gung ho!* to be the battle cry of a Marine Corps raiders group in World War II]

guniff	*See* GONIFF

gunk or **goonk** *by 1932* **1** *n* Any sticky, viscous liquid, esp hair tonic, cosmetics, lubricants, or cleaning fluids; =GLOP, GOOK[1] **2** *n* Dirt; slime; oily grime; muck: *The anchor was clotted in noisome gunk* [fr a trademark, *Gunk,* for a degreasing compound, and part of a cluster of nearly synonymous terms beginning with *g*]

gunkhole *yachting by 1908* **1** *v* To cruise rivers, creeks, tidal estuaries, etc, in a small yacht, anchoring in remote spots **2** *n*: *We found a nice gunkhole near the Kennebec*

gun moll *n phr by 1908* A female criminal or a criminal's consort [fr *gonif* rather than fr the firearm; *Moll* is a diminutive of *Mary,* and has been identified with notorious women since the early 1600s]

gunner **1** *n basketball by 1960s* A flashy performer; =GRANDSTANDER, HOT DOG: . . . *the reputation of a gunner and a hot dog, playground terms for players who showboat*—New York Times **2** *n students by 1990s* A student who aggressively courts attention in class •In earlier use, *gunner* meant a sexually aggressive student: *"Gunners" are people who raise their hands in class repeatedly just to impress*—St Louis Post-Dispatch

gunny **1** *n Marine Corps by 1940s* A gunnery sergeant: *Whenever you try to explain something. . . the gunny accuses you of trying to skate*—New York Times **2** *n* An armed criminal: *Tell us the rest about the two gunnies*—Raymond Chandler **3** *n by 1950s* A proponent of gun possession: *How did gunnies cling so ferociously to beliefs. . . that were completely at odds with majority opinion?*—New York Times/ *Or, as gunnies on the Internet chat group rec.guns put it. . .*—New York Times

gunpoke *n by 1930s* An armed criminal: . . . *sends a gunpoke around to take the money*—Raymond Chandler

guns	*See* HEAVY ARTILLERY

gunsel[1] (also **gonsil** or **gonzel** or **guncel** or **guntzel** or **gunzl**) **1** *n underworld by 1914* A sexually vulnerable boy or young man; catamite; =PUNK **2** *n by 1931* A male homosexual [fr Yiddish *gantzel,* "gosling"]

gunsel[2] *n* (Variation: see **gunsel**[1]) *by 1950s* An armed criminal; hoodlum: *The reformed gunzl took a quick gander*—Paul Sann/ *The gunsels killed each other off*—Don Pendleton [fr a blend of *gonif, gunsel*[1], *gunman,* etc]

gun-shy *adj by 1884* Apprehensive; reluctant; fearful: . . . *he's still gun-shy about putting things on paper*—Scott Turow

gunslinger **1** *n by 1920s* An armed criminal: *The gun-slinger will spend. . . his life behind bars*—Associated Press/ *He thought of himself as a lone gunslinger, like John Wayne*—Newark Star-Ledger **2** *n prison by 1990s* An inmate who habitually exposes himself to female guards: . . . *the sexually aggressive inmates, known as "gunslingers" in prison lingo*—Macon Telegraph

guppy *n airlines by 1980s* A Boeing 737 airliner: *Southwest Airlines has a fleet of guppies*—Los Angeles Times

guru **1** *n 1960s* A leader, expert, or authority in some field, esp a charismatic or spiritual figure who attracts a devoted following: . . . *turning for guidance to such gurus as Paul Goodman and Herbert Marcuse*—John Fischer/ *That genial guru of the right, Barry Goldwater*—Tom Wicker **2** *n 1960s* A psychiatrist; =SHRINK **3** *n 1960s narcotics & counterculture* A person who aids and supports someone having a psychedelic drug experience **4** *n computer by 1990s* A computer expert: . . . *when you were with gurus (read: seasoned computer veterans)*—Kansas City Star [fr Sanskrit, "venerable"]

Gus	*See* GLOOMY GUS

gussy up *by late 1940s* **1** *v phr* To dress in one's best clothes; adorn oneself; =DOLL UP **2** *v phr* To clean or make neat: *The freak had the little apartment all gussied up. . .* —Joseph Wambaugh **3** *v phr* To decorate or elaborate on a plain design **4** *v phr* To refurbish, renovate; polish: *They're gussying up the same old tiredness*—Village Voice **5** *v phr* To decorate; make fancy: *It resembled a gussied-up Studebaker*—Philadelphia [origin unknown; perhaps fr *gusset,* a triangular insert that might be used to prettify a dress; perhaps fr someone or some place named *Augusta*]

gut **1** *n by 1000* The stomach; abdomen; paunch; =BAY WINDOW, POTBELLY **2** *adj by 1964* Basic; essential; most immediate: . . . *the gut issues in the forthcoming election*—Newsweek **3** *adj by 1968* Deep and not essentially rational; visceral; intuitive: . . . *this deep, gut feeling that they want to be part of things*—W H Honan/ *He has to convince me on a gut level that I can do things my mind resists*—Playboy/ *Whether the messenger is a top Government official or an ordinary Russian with a gut instinct. . .* —Time **4** *n students by 1916* =GUT COURSE: . . . *considered a gut by at least 50 percent of the students*—Atlantic Monthly **5** *adj students by 1916*: . . . *a "gut" humanities course where the professor is said to put on a good show*—David Riesman **6** *v by 1950s hot rodders* To remove all unessentials; =STRIPPED DOWN

See BUST A GUT, PINCH-GUT, POTBELLY, PUS-GUT, ROTGUT, SPILL one's GUTS, SPLIT A GUT, TUB OF GUTS

gutbucket *jazz musicians by about 1910* **1** *n* A strongly rhythmic, emotionally evocative, uninhibited style of jazz: . . . *puts toe-tapping tunes atop the complicated counterpoint. . . I've started calling this music avant-gutbucket for its brains, historical sweep, and down-home emotion*—New York Times **2** *n* A fat, pompous person [first sense fr a New Orleans name for a low resort, where a *gutbucket,* that is, a beer bucket or a chamber pot, would be used to collect contributions for the musicians; second sense fr the notion of *a bucket of guts*]

gut-burglar *n loggers by 1920s* A cook

gut course *n phr* (also **gut**) *college students by 1916* An easy course in college [perhaps fr earlier sense *gut*, "a feast," hence, a course that one can "eat up"]

gut-hammer *n loggers by 1940s* A gong or iron triangle used as a dinner bell

gut it out *v phr by 1970s* To be strong and resistant; be sturdily stoic; persist; =TOUGH IT OUT: *Cook claimed that he was innocent of any wrongdoing and until last week insisted that he would "gut it out"*—Time

gutless *adj by 1915* Cowardly; feeble; =CHICKEN

gut reaction *n phr by 1968* An immediate and instinctive response; an intuition; =HUNCH: *if the public-opinion polls and gut reaction count for anything*—Philadelphia

guts 1 *n by 1580* The insides of a person, machine, etc; viscera; =INNARDS: *He removed the cover and exposed the guts* **2** *n by 1950s* The most essential material or part; essence: *The guts of the matter is that they are not here* **3** *n by 1893* Courage; nerve; =BALLS: *. . . the guy who had guts enough to croak "Tough Tony"*—E Lavine

See HATE someone's GUTS, SPILL one's GUTS, TUB OF GUTS

gutsy *by 1930s* **1** *adj* Brave: *a gutsy lady* **2** *adj* Energetic and tough; =ZINGY: *a gutsy car*

gutter *n by 1950s* A dive in which one lands flat on the water; =BELLY-WHOPPER

See HAVE one's MIND IN THE GUTTER

the **gutter** *n phr by 1846* A wretched and lowly venue; =THE PITS: *Without jobs they'll never get out of the gutter*

gutter language *n phr by 1890* Profanity and obscenity; scabrous speech: *This dictionary has a selection of gutter language* [*gutter*, "appropriate to the gutter or sewer," is found by 1849]

guttersnipe or **gutterpup** *n by 1869* A vulgar person; a vile wretch [in the sense "a curbside stock broker" found by 1856]

gut-thumper *n by 1980s* An exciting and suspenseful occasion; =CLIFFHANGER: *It wasn't a cakewalk. . . but it wasn't exactly a gut-thumper either*—Milwaukee Journal

gutty 1 *adj by 1939* Forceful and assertive: *. . . a good gutty rock number*—John Clellon Holmes **2** *adj by 1950s* =GUTSY **3** *adj 1950s hot rodders* Capable of high speed; having a powerful engine

gut-wrenching *adj by 1990s* Emotionally shattering; extremely disturbing: *. . . graphic, gut-wrenching description of gang violence*—New York Times/ *Thursday's gut-wrenching roll-call victories represented a down payment on Clinton's campaign promises to get the country moving again*—New York Times

gut-wrenchingly *adv by 1990s* In a gut-wrenching way; shattering: *Many of Breyten's poems included*

gut-wrenchingly vivid evocations of his actual situation—New Yorker

guy 1 *v by 1869* To mock; ridicule **2** *n by 1876* A person of either sex, esp a man; fellow ●Used of and to women in address, and then almost invariably in the plural, but seldom in reference or in the singular **3** *n by 1940s* A woman's fiancé, husband, lover, etc: *Just remember he's my guy* **4** *n by 1980* A thing referred to, esp something one does not know the name of; =BABY, GADGET, SUCKER: *I'll have this guy, this guy, and this guy*—New Yorker [ultimately fr the name and reputation of *Guy* Fawkes, and esp of his ugly effigies burnt in England on November 5 to commemorate the foiling of the Gunpowder Plot, his plot to blow up the houses of Parliament]

See FALL GUY, JIGGER-MAN, ONE OF THE BOYS, REGULAR FELLOW, RIGHT GUY, SMART GUY, TOUGH GUY, WISE GUY

guyed out *adj circus about 1930* Drunk [fr *guy out*, "tighten"]

guyness *n by 1990s* Maleness; masculinity: *. . . Busfield's rustic, feely guyness*—Sassy

guzzle 1 *v fr 1500s* To drink, esp rapidly: *He guzzled a Coke* **2** *v* To drink liquor, esp to excess: *He guzzled a lot when he got worried* **3** *n* =GOOZLE [fr French *gosier*, "throat," or perhaps like that French word, echoically based on the sound of swallowing]

guzzlery or **guzzery** *n by 1890s* A saloon or bar; =GIN MILL

guzzle shop *n phr by 1890s* A saloon or bar: *No lower guzzle shop was ever operated*—H Asbury

gweebo *n 1980s college students* A tedious and contemptible person; =DORK, NERD

gym rat *n phr by 1970s* An athlete; a person who frequents gymnasiums: *. . . a thin, fortunate group of very highly paid gym rats. . .*—Milwaukee Journal

gyp or **gip** or **jip 1** *n* (also **gyp artist** or **gypster**) *by 1889* A swindler; cheater; =CROOK: *. . . denunciations of punks, tinhorns, and gyps*—Westbrook Pegler **2** *modifier*: *a gyp joint/ gyp terms* **3** *v* To cheat; swindle; =CON: *We got gypped out of it all in two days*—F Scott Fitzgerald **4** *n by 1914*: *. . . the victim of any such gyp*—James M Cain **5** *n cabdrivers by 1930* A cabdriver who does not start the meter, hence can pocket the fare [fr *gypsy*]

gyp joint *n phr about 1935* Any business place that overcharges, cheats, etc; =CLIP JOINT: *Cops tried to shut down the midtown gyp joint*

gyppo or **jippo** *1920s* **1** *n* Part-time work **2** *n* An itinerant worker or pieceworker **3** *modifier*: *They discussed gyppo logging*—Time **4** *v* To cheat; swindle; =GYP: *The contract worker is. . . being unmercifully gyppoed by the boss*—American Mercury

gyppy tummy *n phr by 1943* Diarrhea, esp as it afflicts travelers ●Chiefly British, reflecting former Empire territory: *In the Middle East, it's gyppy tummy and Basra belly*—New York Times [fr British *gyppy*, "Egyptian"]

gypsy 1 *n by 1940s* =GYPSY CAB **2** *n truckers by 1942* A truck driven by its owner rather than a union driver **3** *n truckers by 1942* An owner-driver; an independent trucker **4** *v gambling by 1950s* To make a risky bet or call: *You will find players consistently gypsying, flat-calling with kings up or less*—Gambling Times

gypsy cab *n phr* by *1970s* A taxicab operating without a taxi license or medallion, or with only a livery license that does not entitle them to pick up passengers on the street: *. . . the advent of the latest taxi competitor: the gypsy cab*—Society

gypsy moth *n phr* *1980s* A Republican from the Northern states who votes against an incumbent conservative President and with the more liberal Democrats, esp on budgetary matters [based on *boll weevil,* as a sort of Northern equivalent]

gyrene or **girene** (jī REEN) *n* by *1894* A US Marine; =LEATHERNECK

gyve *See* JIVE

H

H *n narcotics by 1940s* Heroin
 See BIG H

hab *n Canadian by 1980s* A French-speaking resident of Quebec [fr French *habitant,* "a French settler or a descendant of one"]

haba-haba (HAH bə HAH bə) *interj WWII armed forces* An exhortation or request for speed or immediate action
 See HUBBA-HUBBA

habit *n narcotics by 1897* Drug addiction: *I had a great big habit*—Nelson Algren
 See BUNK FATIGUE, CHUCK HABIT, GARBAGE HABIT, ICE CREAM HABIT, OFF THE HABIT

ha-cha-cha **See** HOTCHA

hack¹ 1 *n by 1704* A taxicab ●The dated reference is to a coach for hire **2** *v by 1931*: *I worked in an office for years. . . Then I took to "hacking"*—Hal Boyle **3** *n bus drivers by 1950s* A bus **4** *n railroad by about 1915* A caboose [ultimately fr *hackney,* "horse", fr *Hackney,* a village incorporated into London, fr Old English "Haca's island" or "hook island"; presumably the horses were associated with the place]
 See YARD BULL

hack² 1 *n by 1885* A persistent, often nervous, cough: *. . . oughta see someone about that hack* **2** *v*: *If you quit smoking maybe you won't hack like that* **3** *n by 1836* A try; attempt; =WHACK: *Let George take a hack at it* **4** *v by 1940s* To cope with, esp successfully; manage; =HANDLE ●Most often in the negative: *"I can't hack this," Sandy remarked*—New Yorker/ *I couldn't hack the lines, so I used Mother Nature's privy*—Andy Gordon **5** *v* (also **hack at**) *by 1940s* To attempt; do persistently but mediocrely: *Do I play tennis? Well, I hack at it* **6** *n by 1700* A mediocre performer or worker; tiresome drudge: *. . . they are not the hacks that Eric's scholarship would make them*—Changes **7** *v by 1813*: *They hacked for some of our most respected. . . leaders*—Washington Post **8** *n* (also **hack writer**) *by 1810* A professional, usu freelance, writer who works to order ●This sense belongs to hack¹, reflecting the notion that such a writer was for hire like a horse, but is placed here because its own derivatives blend with those of hack², esp "try, stroke, etc" **9** *n computer by 1980s* A computer program, esp a good one: *A well-crafted program, a good hack, is elegant*—Rolling Stone **10** *v computer by 1980s* To work with a computer or computer program, esp to do so cleverly, persistently, and enthusiastically ●The term has many specialized senses in computer slang, which alter too rapidly for practical account **11** *v by 1892* To annoy; anger; =BURN: *That attitude really hacks me* **12** *n prison by 1940s* A guard: *The guards, the hacks, as they called them*—Claude Brown/ *The hacks didn't worry about the old convicts too much*—Donald Goines **13** *n black & prison by 1940s* A white person; =HONKY, OFAY [nearly all senses ultimately fr *hack,* "cut, chop"; black and prison senses fr identification of prison guards with white persons in the pattern identical with that of *the man;* prison guards perhaps so called because they sometimes beat prisoners]

hack around *v phr by 1960s* To do nothing in particular; idle; loaf: *He says he's been hacking around in some bar*—George V Higgins/ *So I quit Butter, hacked around for a while*—Rolling Stone

hack-driver *n WWII Navy* A chief petty officer

hacked *adj* (also **hacked off**) *black by 1892* Annoyed; angered; chagrined: *How come you're so hacked off about Combs?*—W T Tyler

hacker¹ *n by 1950s* A persistent but generally unskillful performer or athlete; =DUFFER

hacker² 1 *n computer by 1976* A skillful but not necessarily elegant computer programmer ●The term has many senses in computer slang, which change too rapidly for practical account; the core notion is simply "someone who enjoys messing with computers, cleverly or not": *When a hacker programs, he creates worlds*—Rolling Stone/ *As a hacker, McLachlan is a member of an intense, reclusive subculture of the computer age*—Time **2** *n computer by 1980* A person who with evil, inquisitive, or self-aggrandizing intent intrudes into computer networks and files: *He said computer intruders, commonly referred to as hackers, who take over a router can do whatever they want. . .* —Knight-Ridder Newspapers [said to be fr *hack²,* computer jargon for a clever and subtle correction of a flow in a computer program]

hackery *n by 1970s* Routine mediocrity; esp the dull performance and tone of an average political professional: *. . . the grey, self-serving hackery of previous City Councils*—Toronto Life

hackie *n* (also **hacker** or **hacky**) *by 1937* A taxicab driver: *He enriched another hacker by an even $5,000*—Associated Press/ *He actually found a hackie named Louis Schweitzer*—World

253

hack it *v phr* by 1940s To cope successfully; =CUT IT, HANDLE ●Often in the negative: *John Fist can't hack it anymore*—Webster Schott

hack on someone *v phr* 1990s students To ridicule someone; =PUT someone DOWN

be **had** (or **taken** or **took**) **1** *v phr* by 1594 To become a partner in the sex act **2** *v phr* by 1805 To be duped or cheated; be victimized: *You practically need a finance degree to know that you are being had*—Newsweek

had it *See* one HAS HAD IT

ha-ha by 1940s **1** *n* A joke; something funny; stroke of wit: *That's a ha-ha all right*—Ira Wolfert **2** *adj*: *. . . even made a ha-ha pass at him*—Psychology Today/ *. . . ha-ha candles made to look like penises*—Saturday Review [ha-ha represented the sound of laughter by 1000]

See the MERRY HA-HA

the **Haight** *n phr* 1960s =HASHBURY

hail Columbia by 1854 **1** *interj* A mild exclamation of emphasis, annoyance, etc: *Hail Columbia, can't I ever go?* **2** *n phr* Punitive measures; a rebuke; =HELL: *They'll give me hail Columbia when they know* [a euphemism for *hell*]

Hail Mary *modifier* football by 1980s Done in pious hope and desperation: *Staubach hurls a Hail, Mary pass into the end zone*—National Public Radio/ *"We did what could be described as the Hail Mary play," Gen. Schwarzkopf says*—New York Times/ *You know a Hail Mary moment when you see one: It happened at the Redskins-Cardinals game*—New York Times [fr the liturgical prayer *Hail, Mary, full of grace, etc*]

haimish or **heimish** (HAY mish) *adj* by 1960s Friendly and informal; unpretentious; cozy: *No one in his right mind would ever call Generals de Gaulle or MacArthur haimish*—Leo Rosten [fr Yiddish, with root of *haim,* "home"]

hair *n* computer by 1980s Complexity: *a system with a lot of hair*

See CURL someone's HAIR, FAIRHAIRED BOY, GET IN one's HAIR, GOOD HAIR, HAVE A BUG UP one's ASS, HAVE someone BY THE SHORT HAIRS, IN someone's HAIR, LET one's HAIR DOWN, LONGHAIR

hair bag police by 1950s **1** *n phr* A veteran police officer: *Hair bag—A veteran policeman, especially knowledgeable about the inner workings of the Police Department*—G Y Wells **2** *modifier*: *Hairbag is police slang for men who don't care anymore, who are waiting out retirement*—Robert Daley **3** *n phr* police by 1980s An unreliable novice police officer: *Hair bag: a cop. . . the sloppy new gun who acts like he's an old timer. . .*—Street News

hairball **1** *n* 1980s students A noisy, destructive drunk: *Jon was being a hairball last night. He got heated and thrashed the whole upstairs*—UCLA Slang **2** *n* by middle 1980s A repulsive person; =SLEAZEBAG: *. . . makes a nice change from the hairballs featured in most crime novels*—Book World

haired *See* LONGHAIR

the **hair of the dog** (or **of the dog that bit one**) by 1546 **1** *n phr* A drink of liquor taken as a remedy for a hangover; in general, the use of a harmful agent against itself **2** *modifier*: *Does the presence of IgG block the IgE response? Or does the hair-of-the-dog procedure eventually desensitize key cells in the immune system to the offending allergen?*—Time [fr the belief that the bite of a dog could be healed by applying its *hair* to the wound]

◁**hair pie**▷ by 1930s **1** *n phr* Cunnilingus; =BOX LUNCH **2** *n phr* The female genitalia; the vulva; =PUSSY [a pun on *hare pie*]

hairpin *See* DROP BEADS

hair-pounder *n* loggers by about 1925 The driver of a team of horses; teamster

hair wrap *n phr* early 1990s A hair braid interwoven with colored thread: *. . . doing hair wraps, those vaguely Rastafarian braids woven with Technicolor threads*—New York Times

hairy **1** *adj* by 1940s Old; hoary: *a hairy tale* **2** *adj* by 1848 Difficult; rough; =TOUGH: *We had a hairy time getting it all organized* **3** *adj* 1940s teenagers Frighteningly dangerous; hair-raising; scary: *. . . campus guards would comb the dorm. . . "It was hairy"*—New Yorker/ *. . . the hairy strip of 42d Street*—New York Times [last sense probably fr the *hairy* monsters of horror films, but the sense of "difficult" was used at 19th-century Oxford, and that of "dangerous" in the British armed forces of the 1930s]

hairy eyeball *See* GIVE someone THE FISH-EYE

half *See* BETTER HALF, DEUCE AND A HALF, a LAUGH, ONE-AND-A-HALF-STRIPER, the OTHER HALF

◁**half-and-half**▷ *n* prostitutes by 1960s Fellatio plus copulation

half a shake *n phr* by 1930s A moment; a trice: *I'll be there in half a shake* [fr the expression *two shakes of a lamb's tail,* "a very short time"]

◁**half-assed** or **half-ass**▷ *adj* by 1932 Ineffectual; incompetent; half-hearted; =HALF-BAKED: *You first ran into censorship problems with the words "half-assed games"*—Rolling Stone/ *. . . so far it's been a half-ass investigation*—Lawrence Sanders [perhaps fr a humorous mispronunciation of *haphazard*]

half a yard *n phr* by 1940s Fifty dollars: *. . . a "yard" and "half a yard" meaning one hundred dollars and fifty dollars respectively*—Society

half-bagged *adj* by 1950s Drunk: *They keep half-bagged all day and bore their new friends silly with stories*—Lawrence Sanders

half-baked *adj* by 1621 Foolish; ill-conceived; not completely thought out; =HALF-ASSED

half bill or **half a bill** *n phr* 1920s Fifty dollars: *Half an hour after I'd lent Reno the half bill, he was back uptown*—Claude Brown

half Cleveland *adj phr* by 1991 Of a man, wearing white shoes or a white suit

half cocked by 1940s **1** *adv* Prematurely; unpre-

pared: . . . *not going into this half cocked*—Max Shulman **2** *adj*: *a half-cocked start*
See GO OFF HALF COCKED

half-corned *adj by 1950s* Drunk

half crocked *adj phr by 1920s* Drunk; half-drunk: . . . *laying around on a settee, sort of half crocked*—S J Perelman/ *I came out at twelve, one o'clock, half-crocked, really snockered*—W T Tyler

halfies or **halvies** or **halvsies** *n by 1960s* One half of what is indicated, esp as an equal share: *She found it, but I claimed halvsies because I did most of the work*
See GO HALFIES

half in the bag *adj phr by 1920s* Drunk; half-drunk: *He was half in the bag. He always is at Christmas*—Playboy/ . . . *Billy Small was half in the bag even that early*. . . —Joseph Wambaugh

half load *n phr 1960s narcotics* Fifteen packets of a narcotic, esp of cocaine or heroin

half-pint *by middle 1920s* **1** *n* A short person: . . . *the little half-pint that she was*—John O'Hara **2** *modifier*: . . . *half-pint showman*—United Press **3** *n* A boy

half seas over *adj phr by 1736* Drunk [fr the notion that one is like a ship low in the water and burdened so that relatively low waves, *half seas*, sweep over its deck]

half-shot *adj by 1837* Drunk; half-drunk: . . . *when they were half shot with beer*—James M Cain

half-stewed *adj* (Variations: **screwed** or **slewed** or **snapped** or **sprung** may replace **stewed**) *by 1737* Drunk; half-drunk

hall **See** CHOW HALL, JOHN HALL

ham[1] *by 1928* **1** *n* An amateur radio operator **2** *modifier*: *a ham radio operator/ ham network* [fr *amateur*]

ham[2] **1** *n by 1882* An actor who overacts, dramatizes himself, emotes too broadly, etc: . . . *had been roasted by the critics as a ham*—Russell Baker/ *Variety never referred to actors as "hams"*—Abel Green **2** *modifier*: *ham actor/ ham performance* **3** *v* (also **ham it up**) *by 1933*: *The famous star was hamming all the way* **4** *n by 1940s* A person who uses overtheatrical and overly expressive airs and actions: *Miss Moment was no doubt the biggest ham of a teacher*—A Lomax **5** *v* (also **ham it up**) *by 1940s*: *The prof strode into the lecture hall hamming and mugging* [fr *ham-fatter*]

ham and or **ham an** *n phr lunch counter by 1940s* Ham and eggs

ham-and-egger **1** *n by 1920s* An average, predictable person or thing: *The new People Wieners album is a ham and egger*—Sassy **2** *n 1920s prizefight* An average or mediocre prizefighter

hambone *by 1893* **1** *n* A person who fancies himself an actor; histrionic self-advertiser; =HAM: *Every hambone from the deep sticks was constrained to make a speech for the benefit of the cameras*—Robert Ruark **2** *modifier*: *The night's most ebullient winner. . . was Fyvush Finkel, who plays Fences hambone attorney*—Milwaukee Journal

hamburger *by 1940s* **1** *n* A scarred and unvictorious prizefighter **2** *n* A hobo or mendicant **3** *n* An inferior racing dog
See MAKE HAMBURGER OUT OF someone or something

ham-fatter *n by 1882* =HAM, HAMBONE [fr a minstrel song of 1887, "The Hamfat Man," having to do with a second-rate actor, and the use of *ham fat* as greasepaint to remove makeup]
See HAM JOINT

hamfist *n by 1920s* A large fist, big as a ham: *His huge hamfist had landed me a vicious blow*—Xaviera Hollander

ham-handed or **ham-fisted** *adj first form by 1918, second by 1928* Crude and clumsy; lacking in finesse: . . . *his hamfisted approach to a delicate matter*

ham-handedness *n by 1928* Crudeness; clumsiness; lack of polish: *In selecting the rottenest apples. . . one seeks the pretension and the exploitation rather than mere ham-handedness*—Judith Crist

ham joint *n phr 1920s* A cheap restaurant or pool hall, used as a loitering and gathering spot by criminals: . . . *rendezvous is a "ham joint"*—H McLellan

hammer **1** *n black by 1960s* A sexually desirable woman; =FOX ●Regarded by some women as offensive **2** *n truckers by 1960* The accelerator of a truck **3** *n by 1960s* The penis: *How's your hammer hangin', Tiger?*—George Warren **4** *v by 1900* To denigrate severely; =DUMP ON: . . . *you can be playing outside the pearly gates and you're still going to get hammered*—Whitey Herzog **5** *v stock market by 1846* To beat down the price of a stock: *Beverly's stock was being hammered by the company's persistent losses*—New Republic
See GUT-HAMMER

hammer and tongs *adv phr by 1708* Very violently; with full force: *We went at each other hammer and tongs* [reflecting use of both the blacksmith's main tools]

hammer away at someone or something *v phr by 1887* To persist in a line of questioning or declaration; attempt to persuade or break down by force: *The prosecutor kept hammering away at the alibi/ He hammered away at my credibility*

hammer down *adv phr truckers by 1960* Going full speed; with throttle to the floor; =WIDE OPEN: . . . *a herd of L A rednecks, all of 'em pie-eyed and hammer down*—Esquire

hammered *adj by 1950s* Drunk: . . . *I don't get hammered anymore*—Baltimore Sun

hammerhead *n by 1930s* A stupid person: *The best way out is for one of the three to be a hammerhead*—Jerome Weidman

hammer lane *n phr truckers by 1980s* The fast lane of a superhighway: . . . *the passing lane can be "centerfield," "the hammer lane," or "the showoff lane"*—Brian Di Salvatore [fr the trucker sense *hammer*, "accelerator"]

hammer-man *n black by 1950s* An authoritative person; strong man [perhaps an echo of *John Henry*]

ham up *v phr* by 1929 To make histrionic; overexpress; =HAM: *The baseball umpire was hamming up his signals for the benefit of the television audience*—New Yorker

hand *v* by 1919 To give, esp something not desired; bestow forcefully, fraudulently, etc: *The Red Sox handed the Yankees a 12 to 3 shellacking*/ *What kind of con job was he trying to hand you?*
See BOTH HANDS, COLD IN HAND, COOL HAND, DEAD MAN'S HAND, GIVE someone THE GLAD HAND, GLAD-HAND, HAVE one's HANDS FULL, NOT LAY A GLOVE ON someone, SOFT HANDS, TIP one's MITT, WITH one's HAND IN THE TILL, WITH ONE HAND TIED BEHIND one's BACK

a **hand** 1 *n* by 1838 A round of applause: *Well she got a big hand*—John O'Hara 2 *n* by 1960 Help; aid
See GIVE someone A HAND

hand someone **a lemon** *v phr* by 1860s To take advantage of; cheat; =GYP: *. . . if they hand me a lemon*—Erle Stanley Gardner

handbasket *See* GO TO HELL IN A HANDBASKET

handbook *horse-racing & gambling* by 1894 1 *n* A place, other than a legal betting office, where bets are made away from the racetrack; =HORSE ROOM: *I was in the handbook near Loomis and Madison*—Fact Detective Mysteries 2 *n* =BOOKIE [probably fr the fact that betting records were kept in small, concealable notebooks for secrecy and portability]

H and C *n phr* 1960s *narcotics* A mixture of heroin and cocaine; =HOT AND COLD, SPEEDBALL

handcuffs *See* GOLDEN HANDCUFFS

handed *See* HAM-HANDED, LEFT-HANDED, RIGHT-HANDED

hander *See* FORKHANDER, GLAD-HANDER

handful 1 *n underworld* by 1930 A five-year prison sentence or term 2 *n* by 1887 A great deal to manage; burdensome task: *That kid of yours is a handful*
See GRAB A HANDFUL OF AIR

hand someone **his head** *v phr* by 1970s To destroy; figuratively to decapitate someone and hand him his own head; =CLOBBER: *Do what they want, or they'll hand you your head*—Village Voice/ *. . . when the press is handing Francis Coppola his head*—Village Voice

hand-holding *n* by early 1908 Support; reassurance; encouragement: *Congress wants some hand-holding from Clinton on Somalia*—National Public Radio

handies *See* PLAY HANDIES

hand it to someone *v phr* by 1906 To compliment; praise someone for a success •Often said with overtones of reluctance: *I got to hand it to you*—James M Cain

◁**hand job**▷ *n phr* by 1940s An act of masturbation, usu done for one person by another: *. . . rolled over on top of me and started giving me a real good hand job*—Lon Albert/ *. . . if you were unlucky, all you got was a hand job*—Philadelphia

◁**handkerchief-head**▷ *black* by 1940s 1 *n* A black person who is obsequious towards white people; =UNCLE TOM: *A "handkerchief-head" is an old-fashioned Negro who doesn't know his rights*—Stephen Longstreet 2 *modifier*: *She fought often with TV directors who were inclined to present her in the Hollywood handkerchief-head tradition*—New York Review of Books

handle 1 *n* by 1870 A person's name, nickname, or alias: *He is known by that handle ever since to all his pals*—Associated Press/ *Many people use handles for themselves instead of their real names*—New Yorker 2 *n* 1920s The gross receipts or the profit of a sporting event, a gambling game, an illegal operation, etc: *A total handle . . . between 4 and 10 billion a year in the handbooks, the numbers, and the slots*—Westbrook Pegler 3 *n* 1920s *gambling* The amount of money bet on a specific race or game, or in a particular day or week, etc: *The handle at Belmont dropped today on account of the blizzard* 4 *n* by 1972 A way of approaching or grasping something; an initial and relevant insight: *Women. I don't seem to have a handle on them*—Carsten Stroud/ *So we may have less handle on him than we did before*—Robert B Parker 5 *v* by 1970s To cope with; manage; =HACK: *He can handle Tom's temper tantrums very well*/ *My wife left me and I don't know how to handle it*
See FLY OFF THE HANDLE, GET A HANDLE ON something, LONG-HANDLE UNDERWEAR, PANHANDLE

handler *n prizefighting* by 1950 A person who seconds, supports, advises, etc, a principal: *Bush and his political handlers believe, as Reagan did, that the way to the people's heart is paved with unshucked corn*—New Republic [the term was used of those who handled game-cocks, dogs, etc, by 1825]
See PANHANDLER

handles *See* LOVE HANDLE

hand-me-down or **fetch-me-down** by 1874 1 *n* Something, esp clothing, used by one person and then passed to another, esp to a younger sibling: *I wore mostly my brother's hand-me-downs* 2 *modifier*: *a pair of hand-me-down pants*/ *fetch-me-down ski boots*

handout 1 *n hoboes* by 1882 Food, money, or other donations received or given •Nearly always with the implication that the giver is overgenerous or self-interested, and the recipient undeserving: *Damn hippies lived on food stamps and other bleeding heart handouts* 2 *n* A leaflet or flyer passed out on the streets 3 *n* by 1941 An official press release or communiqué: *The newspaperman's slightly derogatory slang term for the news release is "handout"*—Daniel J Boorstin

hand over fist *adv phr* by 1833 Very energetically, persistently, and rapidly: *It was a treat to see them go at it hand over fist*
See MAKE MONEY HAND OVER FIST

hands *See* BOTH HANDS, HAVE one's HANDS FULL, SIT ON one's HANDS

one's **hands are tied** *sentence* by 1940s One is unable to act: *I'd like to help, but my hands are tied*

hands down *adv phr* fr horse-racing by 1867 Very easily; without effort •Most often in the phrase *win hands down: She entered the race unheralded, and won it hands down/ We just loafed along, but beat them hands down* [fr the gesture of a jockey who drops his hands and lets the reins go loose in an easy victory]

handshaker *n* by 1900 A person who characteristically gets on by being amiable, making friends, pleasing superiors, etc; =GLAD-HANDER

hands-off *adj* by 1902 Noninterfering; passive: *. . . the president's hands-off policy*

handsome *See* HIGH, WIDE, AND HANDSOME

hands on by 1960s **1** *adv phr* Manually, by direct control rather than automatic control: *The ship was then flown hands on* **2** *modifier*: *. . . hands-on landing of the aircraft* **3** *adj* Practical and active rather than theoretical: *. . . what we labeled a hands-on mayor*—San Francisco/ *No Hands-On Achiever Need Apply*—Newsweek

hand trouble *n phr* by 1940s A pronounced tendency to touch and caress; generalized tactile amorousness: *Bonnie had encountered men with hand trouble*—A Hynd

hand up *v phr* by 1893 To testify against; betray; =RAT ON: *He said he'd do life before he'd hand up his associates*—Michael Grant/ *This, like the problem of cops refusing to hand up other cops*—Newark Star-Ledger [the dated instance is from British schoolboy slang]

hand-wringing *n* by 1603 An ostentatious show of grief, remorse, etc: *Hand-wringing. . . on the part of the press*—Howard M Paul

handyman's special *n phr* by 1970s Something, esp a house, in dire need of major repair; a wreck: *"Hudson River Castle for Sale: Handyman's Special with View"*—New York Times

hang 1 *v* teenagers by 1951 To spend time; frequent; =GOOF OFF, HANG OUT: *Who runs the coffeepot where they hang?*—movie Scene of the Crime/ *If a person is goofing off, he's hanging*—Newsweek **2** *v* 1980s students To endure a situation; survive; handle pressure: *No one ever chants I am somebody. . . If you weren't, you couldn't hang*—New York Times/ *This is so stressful. I can't hang*—UCLA Slang
See HAVE IT ALL HANGING OUT, LET IT ALL HANG OUT

hang a few on *v phr* by 1950s To have several drinks of liquor: *He had only hung a few on and was, for him, slightly sober*—Stephen Longstreet

hang a left (or **a right**) *v phr* 1960s teenagers To turn left or right, to round a corner: *Bellsey hung a left on 53rd Street. . .* —Lawrence Sanders [perhaps fr surfers' phrases *hang five, hang ten*]

hang around by 1847 **1** *v phr* To idle about; loiter; =HACK AROUND **2** *v phr* To stay where one is; remain: *I decided to hang around and see what went down*

◁**hang-down**▷ *n* by 1970s The penis; =PRICK: *. . . like the horse's hang-down that I am, get myself shit-faced*—George V Higgins

hanged *See* I'LL BE DAMNED

hanger *See* CLIFFHANGER, CRAPE-HANGER, FENCE-STRADDLER, PAPERHANGER

hangers *See* APE HANGERS

hang five *v phr* 1960s surfers To ride forward on the surfboard so that the toes of one foot are over the edge

hang in (or **in there**) *v phr* by 1969 To endure in some difficult action or position; persist tenaciously; =HANG TOUGH: *He didn't pack it up, of course, he hung in there and saw the story through*—Playboy/ *Rosemary Woods is hanging in*—Nora Ephron

hanging *See* HOW THEY HANGING

hang it *v phr* medical by 1970s To administer intravenous medicine: *As soon as the nurse is free, he'll be in to hang it*

hang it easy *v phr* 1950s hot rodders =TAKE IT EASY

hang it up *v phr* by 1874 To retire; cease working, competing, etc: *. . . since Joe Namath and Sonny Jurgenson hung it up*—Dan Jenkins/ *After a serious injury they wanted me to hang it up*—Washington Post

hang (or **stay**) **loose** *v phr* 1950s hot rodders To be relaxed and nonchalant; be uninvolved; =COOL IT •Often heard as a genial exhortation: *I needed to hang loose, breathe free, get lost, take a trip*—Xaviera Hollander/ *You're healthier and happier when you hang loose*—Harper's/ *Stay loose, man*—Richard Fariña

the **hang of** something *See* GET THE HANG OF something

hang on 1 *v phr* To endure; persist; =HANG IN **2** *v phr* To make an accusation; inculpate: *They can't hang a Murder One on me*—TV show Matlock

hang (or **tie** or **pin**) **one on 1** *v phr* by about 1900 To get very drunk; go on a drinking spree **2** *v phr* by 1908 To hit someone hard; =CLOBBER: *Will you hang one on my jaw?*—James M Cain

hangout¹ 1 *n* by 1893 A place for loitering, loafing, and passing time, esp with congenial companions: *a grad student hangout on Mirandola Lane/ a gay hangout* **2** *n* 1920s One's home; =DIGS

**hangout² ** *n* by 1960s Complete disclosure; total openness: *a "modified limited hang-out," meaning a response that would satisfy Watergate investigators while disclosing as little as possible*—Newsweek
See GO THE HANG-OUT ROAD

hang out *v phr* by 1844 To pass time; loaf pleasantly about; loiter; =HANG: *. . . just us five hangin' out*—Rolling Stone/ *. . . The best hours of my youth were spent loitering in front of Simon's Candy Store. . . doing nothing, just hanging out*—Saturday Review
See HAVE IT ALL HANGING OUT, LET IT ALL HANG OUT

hang out the laundry *v phr* WWII Air Forces To drop paratroops from an aircraft

hang out the wash *v phr* baseball by 1930s To hit a hard line drive [because the ball's path resembles a taut clothesline]

hang someone **out to dry** *by 1980s* **1** *v phr* To punish someone severely, esp as a scapegoat: *. . . the company silently took the fall; Storms was hung out to dry*—New York Times/ *J R Rider says he was "hung out to dry" by Nevada-Las Vegas officials. . .* —Milwaukee Journal **2** *v phr* To defeat utterly; =CLOBBER: *. . . hang Sox out to dry. . .* —Daily Jefferson County Union **3** *v phr baseball by 1980s* To catch a base-runner in a run-down; pick off a base runner: *I was hacking because I didn't want to leave Listach out to dry*—Milwaukee Journal

hangover *n by 1912* The headache, morbid sensitivity, nausea, etc, felt upon awakening some hours after drinking too much liquor

hang ten *v phr 1960s surfers* To ride forward on a surfboard so that the toes of both feet are over the edge

hang time *n phr football by 1980s* The time that a punted ball stays in the air: *He's got lots of great stats, hang time*—Milwaukee Journal

hang tough *v phr by 1960s* To endure in a difficult plight; show plucky and stoic persistence; =HANG ON, TOUGH IT OUT: *You've got a friend at Chase Manhattan, if you've still got a traveler's check to cash. Otherwise, hang tough*—J Horn/ *Mr Shannon glorifies Kennedy for his ability to "hang tough"*—Book World

hang up *v phr 1960s* To become fixated: *Why did you get hung up on Proust, anyhow?*

hang-up *by 1959* **1** *n* A mental block; a psychological disturbance, fixation, or problem: *. . . ribald anecdotes concerning his hang-up on strong women*—Changes **2** *n* Anything encumbering, frustrating, distressing, etc; an impediment: *You couldn't carry around an amplifier and electric guitar and expect to survive, it was just too much of a hang-up*—Bob Dylan/ *. . . The only hang-up we can see right now is that business of paying the doctors*—Lawrence Sanders

hang someone or something **up** *v phr fr middle 1800s* To stall or immobilize; frustrate; paralyze: *The four would not be able to hang the entire jury up*—Ebony/ *. . . or some other means of transcending the realities that hang one up*—Trans-Action

hang something **up** *v phr by 1854* To abandon one's efforts; =CALL IT QUITS: *Police have hung it up*—Robert B Parker

hang up (or out) one's **shingle** *v phr by 1871* To commence professional practice; open up a law office, doctor's office, etc: *He's passed his bar exam now, so he can hang up his shingle*

hang with *v phr by 1950s* To seek and prefer the company of; consort with: *Sondra didn't hang with nobody but doctors*—Ms

hankie or **hanky** *n by 1895* A handkerchief

hankty *See* HINCTY

hanky-pank *carnival by 1950s* **1** *n* Any game that is cheap to play, esp one where the customer gets a prize each time he or she plays: *Typical hanky-panks are the fish-pond, the ring-toss and dart-throwing games*—Society **2** *n* A barker's exhortations; =SPIEL **3** *adj* Cheap and gaudy; trashy; =SCHLOCKY: *hanky-pank costume jewelry*

hanky-panky *n by 1841* Anything dishonest, deceptive, or unethical; esp, in recent use, sexual infidelity; =MONKEY BUSINESS: *She seems just to be along for some hanky-panky with her pal, General Von Griem*—Ms/ *. . . can be an assurance against clandestine wrongdoing and political hanky-panky*—Nation

happening *1980s students* **1** *adj* Up-to-date and desirable; chic; =COOL, HIP, WITH IT: *That dress is definitely happening; you look great*—UCLA Slang/ *This music is happening*—Slang Bag 93 **2** *adj* Lively; vibrant: *It's a way happening town*

happenings *n narcotics by 1950s* Narcotics; =JUNK

happy *adj by 1893* Drunk, esp slightly so; =TIDDLY

-happy *combining word by 1930s* Somewhat insane over or excessively wrought upon by what is indicated: *bomb-happy/ car-happy/ power-happy/ trigger-happy* [probably modeled on *slap-happy*]

happy as a clam *adj phr by 1636* Very happy; euphoric: *. . . she's happy as a clam with contractor Roe Messner*—Milwaukee Journal/ *. . . on a posing dais in front of a full-length mirror, happy as a clam*—Douglas Coupland [fr earlier locution *happy as a clam at high tide,* that is, when it cannot be dug]

happy as a pig in slop *adj phr by 1970s* Very happy; euphoric: *. . . happy as a pig in slop just to be playing in the National Football League. . .* —Milwaukee Journal [a euphemism for *happy as a pig in shit,* found by 1896]

happy-cabbage *n by 1940s* Money; =CABBAGE

happy camper *n phr by 1980s* A contented person; someone well pleased: *. . . Quayle called the people of American Samoa "happy campers". . .* —Milwaukee Journal [said to have originated among California movie and show-business people; the reference is probably to child clients of summer camps]

happy-dust *1920s narcotics* **1** *n* Cocaine **2** *n* Morphine

happy face *n phr 1960s* A stylized circular smiling face, drawn or pasted up as a talisman: *I don't want to put one of those Chuck Tanner happy faces on this season*—Whitey Herzog

happy hour *by 1980s* **1** *n phr* The hour or so of relaxation with drinks after work; cocktail hour **2** *n phr* A specified period of time, usu in early evening, in some restaurants and bars when drinks are sold at lower prices or when free food is provided

happy-juice *n by 1950s* Liquor: *The increased taxes on happy-juice has cut the revenues from liquor sales*—Robert Ruark

happy pill *n phr by 1956* A tranquilizer pill

happy talk *television studio by 1980s* **1** *n phr* Informal chat and chaffing among news broadcasters during the program, as an element of entertainment: *Later, happy talk evolved, to break the tension created by the action, that is the violence, shown on TV news*—Washingtonian **2** *modifier*: *. . . as for the happy-talk format that sandwiches cheerful repartee between the fire and robbery reports*—

Philadelphia [fr the title of a song in the 1949 Rodgers and Hammerstein musical *South Pacific*]

the **haps** *n phr* 1990s Events; happenings; attractions: *Free Haps*—Noise/ *E-mail our trend hotline with the haps in your town. . .* —Seventeen

hard 1 *adj* by 1960s Demonstrable; verifiable; not dependent on subjective judgment, emotion, etc: *A comprehensive set of hard figures emerged for the first time*—Time **2** *adj* by 1818 =TOUGH **3** *adj* 1930s jive talk Excellent; good; =COOL ◁**4**▷ *n* by 1893 =HARD-ON
   See TAKE IT HARD

hard as nails *adj phr* by early 1850s Extremely durable and grim; =TOUGH

◁**hard-ass** or **hard-assed**▷ *by 1940s* **1** *n* A severe and often pugnacious person;: *I've gotten the reputation as being a hard-ass*—Aquarian **2** *adj*: *. . . some are hard-ass disciplinarians. . .* —Whitey Herzog/ *. . . even your most hardassed rightwingers had some showboat in them*—Elmore Leonard

hard at it *adj phr* by 1749 Doing the sex act: *Was you and she not hard at it before I came into the room?*—Henry Fielding

hardball by 1973 **1** *n* Serious and consequential activity, work, etc; perilous and responsible doings: *It's hardball now, it's not games anymore*—Philadelphia Journal/ *It's going to be hard ball. . . We're talking about physicians losing income*—New York Times **2** *modifier*: *. . . fields hardball questions in a practice TV interview*—Time/ *. . . despite his hardball attitude toward sponsors of offensive TV shows*—Time **3** *v* =PLAY HARDBALL

hard-boiled *adj* by 1886 Severe and uncompromising; strict and pugnacious; =TOUGH: *The rather hard-boiled painting that hangs in Father's office*—F Scott Fitzgerald [fr *hard-boiled egg*]

hard-boiled egg *n phr* by 1880s A severe and pugnacious person; =TOUGH GUY: *Our basic idea of a hero is really a "hard-boiled egg"*—P Curtiss [because "it can't be beat"]

hardboot by 1940s **1** *n* A Kentuckian, esp a Kentucky horse rider **2** *n* A devotee of horses and of horse-racing: *Granted hardboots can be sentimental about a horse on the lead*—Time

hard bop *n phr* jazz musicians by 1950s A type of music resembling the blues that is related to, but more earthy and modal in approach than, straight bop: *. . . swing, bop, cool jazz, hard bop, funky jazz*—B W Bell

hard (or **heavy) breathing** *n phr* by 1970s Passionate love-making

hard case *n phr* by 1836 A rough and dangerous person; =TOUGH GUY: *Most of the hardcases knew their rights better than the cops*—Carsten Stroud

hard cheese 1 *n phr* by 1876 An unfortunate outcome or situation •Still chiefly British; often an interjection: *This is hard cheese indeed*—Village Voice **2** *n phr* baseball by 1980s A fastball; =SMOKE

hard coin *n phr* by 1970s Large amounts of money; =MEGABUCKS: *There's some hard coin being made by the music magnates*—Motive

hard copy *n phr* by 1964 A printed copy of a computer document; printout: *Millie, can you give me a hard copy of that?*—Michael Grant

hard-core 1 *adj* by 1951 Essential and uncompromising; unmitigated: *a hard-core Republican/ hard-core pornography* **2** *n* by 1970s Pornography that openly depicts complete sex acts: *He sort of likes dirty stuff, but not real hard core*

hard drug *n phr* 1960s narcotics A narcotic, like heroin or morphine, that is powerfully addictive and injurious: *The American problem is heroin, as "hard" a drug as there is*—New York Times [probably modeled on *hard liquor*]

hard facts *n phr* by 1887 Information that is dependable and verifiable

hard hat 1 *n phr* by 1935 A derby hat: *The boys with the hard hats always ask a lot of questions about murders*—J Evans **2** *n phr* (also **brain bucket**) by 1953 The steel or plastic helmet worn by various sorts of workers, esp construction workers: *From here on we wear hard hats/ . . . they lay aloft at 1930 with their "brain buckets" (hard hats) and bags of tools*—Smithsonian **3** *modifier*: *Caution, this is a hard-hat zone* **4** *n phr* by 1960s A worker who wears a hard hat: *The hard hats sat around and whistled at the passing girls* **5** *n* early 1970s A very conservative right-winger; a reactionary: *He knows he can count on the hard hats to support him* **6** *n phr* Vietnam War armed forces A regular Viet Cong soldier, who wears a military helmet, as distinct from a guerrilla or reservist: *. . . some 50,000 are "hard-hats" (full-time fighters)*—Time [the political sense fr the vocal and sometimes violent opposition of many construction workers to the US peace movement during the Vietnam War, reinforced by terms like *hard line* and *hard core*]

hardhead *n* by 1519 An obstinate or stupid person

hard-headed 1 *adj* by 1583 Obstinate; stubborn; =PIG-HEADED **2** *adj* by 1779 Realistic; practical; unevasive; =HARD-NOSED

hard line by early 1960s **1** *n phr* A policy or attitude based on severity and lack of compromise: *Take a hard line with them or they'll murder you* **2** *adj*: *. . . the President's hard-line views on abortion*

hard liquor *n phr* by 1879 Whiskey, rum, gin, brandy, as distinct from wine and beer; spirits; strong waters

a **hard look 1** *n phr* 1960s An intense and unblinking scrutiny; strict examination: *Take a hard look at what's going on upstairs/ We'll have a hard look at the income and expenses* **2** *n phr* by 1888 A menacing or hostile stare: *She gave me a real hard look when I blurted her name*

hard-luck story *n phr* by 1900 A tale calculated to gain sympathy and help: *He gives me the same old hard-luck story every time*

hard news *n phr* by 1938 Information that is definite and verifiable, free of conjecture

hard-nosed 1 *adj* middle 1920s Stubborn; obstinate **2** *adj* by 1940s Severe and practical; harshly realistic; =HARD-HEADED, TOUGH: *They'll take a hard-nosed look, then report*

◁**hard-on**▷ **1** *n* by 1893 An erection of the penis: *It was another one of those subway things. Like having a hard-on at random*—Saul Bellow **2** *n* by 1980s A severe and intolerant person, esp a martinet leader or superior: *Stone is turning into a world-class hard-on*—Michael Grant

See HAVE A HARD-ON FOR someone or something

hard-road freak *n phr* 1960s A drifting young person who has rejected conventional society and has typically been arrested for vagrancy, drug use, etc; =HIPPIE

hard rock *n phr* 1960s rock and roll A form of rock and roll music with a simple, driving beat, usu played on heavily amplified guitars

hard-rock *adj* by 1923 Severe; dour and pugnacious; =TOUGH: *... the old hard-rock guy who would line up all the cocaine users and shoot them*—Time [probably fr the difficulty of *hard-rock* mining as distinct fr other kinds; influenced by *rock-hard*]

a **hard (**or **tough) row to hoe** *n phr* by 1835 A difficult task; a period of trouble and travail; =HARD TIMES: *If he focused on Rwanda, where would he get the interest and support? It's going to be a hard row to hoe*—New Republic

hard science *n phr* by 1960s A science such as chemistry or physics where the data and conclusions are supportable by objective criteria

hard sell *n phr* 1950s An act or policy of selling aggressively, forcibly, loudly, etc: *Joe is a master at hard sell*

hard-shell *adj* Strict; conservative; =HARD-CORE: *... her hard-shell manner, her hipped-up weariness*—Scott Turow

hard stuff **1** *n* by 1891 Whiskey and other strong liquors; spirits; =HARD LIQUOR: *The troubles the hard stuff inflicts on men with no defense against it*—John McCarten **2** *n phr* 1960s narcotics =HARD DRUG **3** *n phr* underworld about 1910 Money, esp loot or other illicit gain

hard swallow *n phr* 1990s Something hard to accept: *Clinton's change of policy is a hard swallow for Ghali*—National Public Radio

hard time *n phr* underworld by 1930s Time actually spent in prison by a sentenced criminal: *Hard men are serving hard time 10 miles down the road*—A M Rosenthal

See GIVE someone A HARD TIME

hard times *n phr* by 1705 A period of economic depression, poverty, etc

hardtop **1** *n* by 1940s A car resembling a convertible, but having a metal roof **2** *n* by 1950s A paved area or road: *Park over there on the hardtop*

hard up **1** *adj phr* by 1821 Poor; penniless: *It was no disgrace to be hard up in those times* **2** *adj phr* by 1940s Sexually frustrated; needing sexual gratification; =HORNY: *He declared he was so hard up he'd fuck mud* [apparently fr a nautical expression meaning the helm is *hard up,* that is, held all the

way to windward while beating and so pinched as tight as possible]

hard up for something *adj phr* by 1840 Lacking; deficient in: *We're hard up for booze around here*

hardware **1** *n* by 1865 Weapons and other war matériel: *... military "hardware," tanks, planes, guns, rockets, weapons*—W F Arbogast **2** *n* WWII armed forces Military insignia or medals worn on a uniform **3** *n* 1930s Badges and other identification jewelry

the **hard way** **1** *n phr* crapshooting by 1950s The repetition of an even number that came up on the first roll, made by rolling two even dice that add up to it **2** *n phr* by 1931 The most difficult and strenuous way of doing anything: *Wideman is building a picture of the world the hard way—person by person, life by life*—New Republic

hard-wired *adj* early 1970s Determined by innate brain functions; not a matter of choice: *These individuals seem hard-wired only to show up at work, do their task and leave with a paycheck*—Milwaukee Journal Sentinel/ *We're hard-wired to be social creatures*—Milwaukee Journal [fr the definiteness of an actual wired connection in a computer, as distinct from something depending on a program]

the **hardwood** *n* basketball by 1940s A basketball court

harness *n* by 1841 The dress and equipment of special categories of persons, such as telephone line repairers, police officers, train conductors, motorcyclists, etc: *Wise detectives, who dread going back into "harness" or uniform*—E Lavine

See IN HARNESS

harness bull (or **cop** or **dick) 1** *n phr* by 1903 A uniformed police officer **2** *modifier*: *... the harness-bull secretary*—W R Burnett

harp ◄**1**► *n* by 1904 An Irish person or one of Irish descent **2** *n* by 1887 A harmonica **3** *n* narcotics by 1990s Phencyclidine or PCP, a narcotic

harrumph *v* by 1940s To speak disparagingly or indignantly: *Louise Trubek... harrumphed that title insurance is regarded... as a "consumer rip-off"*—Wisconsin State Journal/ *She harrumphed and slammed her door closed*—Douglas Coupland

Harry **See** BIG HARRY, EVERY TOM, DICK, AND HARRY

harsh *v* 1990s teenagers To nag and complain; =NUDGE

Hart, Schaffner and Marx *n phr* poker by 1960s Three jacks [fr the name of a men's clothing manufacturer]

has-been **1** *n* by 1786 A person who was once famous, successful, courted, etc, but is no longer so: *Some has-beens make spectacular comebacks* **2** *n* =BACK NUMBER

hash **1** *v* by 1920 To discuss, esp at length; =HASH OVER: *... they had hashed and rehashed for many a frugal conversational meal*—F Scott Fitzgerald **2** *v* by 1663 =HASH UP **3** *n* 1950s narcotics Hashish **4** *adj* 1960s cool talk Excellent; wonderful; =COOL

See MAKE HAMBURGER OUT OF someone or something, SETTLE someone's HASH, SLING HASH

one has had it *WWII armed forces* **1** *sentence* (Variations: **up to here** or **up to** one's **ass** or **up to** one's **eyebrows** or some other anatomical feature may be added) One is exhausted, disgusted, unwilling to put up with any more: *All at once I've had it up to here with psychiatry*—New Yorker **2** *sentence* One has been given a last chance and has failed: *That's the ball game, buddy, you've had it* [fr shortening of World War II British Royal Air Force slang: He's *had his time*, "He's been killed"]

Hashbury *n 1960s counterculture* The Haight-Ashbury section of San Francisco, a haunt of hippies during the 1960s; =the HAIGHT

hasher *by 1916* **1** *n* A waiter or waitress: . . . *going to give them jobs as hashers*—G Weisberg **2** *n* A cook or kitchen worker

hashery *n by 1870* A restaurant or lunch counter, esp a small or cheap place: *We'll inhale a few hamburgers at some fashionable hashery*—"Our Boarding House" comic strip

hash foundry **1** *n phr by 1940s* =HASHERY **2** *n phr* hoboes *by 1950s* A charitable establishment where free meals may be had

hash head *n phr 1950s narcotics* A frequent user of hashish or marijuana

hash-house *n by 1875* A restaurant or lunch counter, esp a cheap one; =HASHERY: . . . *the sort of language that one would expect to hear from a hobo in a Bowery hash-house*—Bookman

hash mark (or stripe) **1** *n phr armed forces by 1909* A service stripe, worn on the sleeve of a military uniform to mark each four-year period of service: . . . *the voice of a subaltern of God, hashmarks running down his arm for a thousand miles*—Pat Conroy **2** *n phr football by 1960s* An inbounds line marker used to help fix the point where the ball is put in play, and spaced one yard from the next mark [military sense apparently fr the number of years one has had free food from the Army]

hash over (or out) *by 1931* **1** *v phr* To discuss, esp repeatedly and lengthily: *We kept hashing over the same tired old topics/ She thought we should hash it out right now* **2** *v phr* To rehash, review: *Asked him in to hash over a point or two*—New Yorker [fr the notion of chopping something fine]

hash session *n phr by 1940s* =GABFEST

hash-slinger *by 1868* **1** *n* A waiter or waitress, usu in a cheap restaurant or lunch counter: *Hash-slingers are plentiful, but well-trained waitresses are scarce*—Associated Press **2** *n* A cook or kitchen worker

hash up *v phr by 1940s* To ruin; spoil; =FUCK UP, MESS UP

hassle or **hassel** *by 1920s, but mainly since 1940s* **1** *n* A disagreement; quarrel; fight: *A hassle between two actors touched off. . . the riot*—Billy Rose/ *The hassle over putting fluoride in drinking water*—N Boynton **2** *v*: *They were hassling about who would pay the bill* **3** *v* (also **hass**) To harass; treat rudely and roughly: *I went to an assistant DA and told him I wanted to discuss being hassled by the police/ What you going to do. . . you find the hobo that hassed him?*—Robert B Parker **4** *n* A difficult or tedious task or concern: *Getting those tickets was a real hassle* **5** *v 1950s narcotics* To get narcotics with difficulty: *He finally hassled one bag* [origin unknown; probably fr *hatchel*, "to harass," found by 1800, a *hatchel* being an instrument for beating flax, and related to *heckle*; perhaps fr *hazel*, with a variant *hassle*, the switch used for beatings; *hazel oil* meant "a beating" by 1678]

hassle-free *adj by 1980s* Without difficulties and worries: *The bliss of hassle-free existence depends first and foremost on other people who can dispense with all the pesky minutiae of daily life. In other words, you need staff*—New Republic

hat *n 1990s teenagers* A condom

See BRASS HAT, GIMMIE HAT, HARD HAT, HERE'S YOUR HAT WHAT'S YOUR HURRY, HIGH-HAT, IRON HAT, KNOCK something INTO A COCKED HAT, OLD HAT, PARTY HAT, PASS THE HAT, PLUG HAT, SHIT IN YOUR HAT, STRAW HAT, TALK THROUGH one's HAT, THROW one's HAT IN THE RING, TIN HAT, UNDER one's HAT, WEAR TWO HATS, WHITE HAT, WOOL HAT

hatch *n by 1931* The mouth and throat: *DeCasseres would hurl the first legal drink down his hatch*—H A Smith

See BOOBY HATCH, DOWN THE HATCH, NUT HOUSE

hatchet job *by 1940s* **1** *n phr* A malicious attack; a diatribe or indictment meant to destroy: *By hatchet job is meant here. . . a calculated attempt to demolish the author*—Wilfred Sheed **2** *n phr* A discharge or dismissal; =AX

hatchet man **1** *n phr* (also **hatchet**) *by 1880* A professional killer; =HIT MAN ●The date refers to California Chinese assassins **2** *n phr by 1944* A person whose task and predilection is to destroy an opponent, often by illegitimate means

hate someone's **guts** *v phr by 1918* To have an extreme hatred for someone; absolutely execrate someone: *I dislike him, but I don't hate his damn guts*

hate-jock *n 1990s* A radio talk show host who encourages bigotry: . . . *a protest. . . against the racism of white hate-jock Bob Grant. . .*—Extra!

hat in hand *adv phr* Obsequiously; tamely; pleadingly: *The President stands there, hat in hand, begging the Congress for their votes*—National Public Radio

hatrack *n by 1930s* A thin or frail person; =BEANPOLE

hat trick **1** *n phr British sports by 1877* The scoring of three goals in a single game by the same player in hockey or soccer **2** *n phr baseball by 1980s* The feat of hitting a single, double, triple, and home run in one game [fr cricket, "the bowling down of three wickets with successive balls," probably compared with the magician's trick of pulling a rabbit out of a hat; also said to be a feat which entitled the player to the proceeds of a collection, i.e., a passing of the *hat*, or to a new *hat*]

hatty *See* HIGH-HAT

haul *n by 1776* Profits or return, esp illicit ones; loot: *The show yielded a huge haul* [fr the contents of a fish net that is *hauled*]
See COLD HAUL, FOR THE LONG HAUL, GET one's ASHES HAULED, LONG HAUL, OVER THE LONG HAUL

haul one's **ashes** *v phr by 1950s* To leave; depart; =HAUL ASS

haul someone's **ashes** *by 1950s* **1** *v phr* To harm or injure someone, esp by beating ◁**2**▷ *v phr* To do the sex act with someone
See GET one's ASHES HAULED

◁**haul ass**▷ **1** *v phr* (also **haul a**) *WWI Navy* To leave; depart; =BUG OUT, CLEAR OUT, DRAG ASS: *. . . if you're smart you'll haul ass out of here before you get in big trouble*—Robert B Parker/ *Time to haul a, man!*—Gary Trudeau **2** *v phr* To act quickly, esp in response to a command: *. . . being ready to haul ass when the ball was hit. . .*—Whitey Herzog **3** *v phr 1950s hot rodders* To drive or travel very fast: *They were really hauling ass when they hit that curve*

hauler *n 1950s hot rodders* A very fast car; =HOT ROD

haul someone **in** *v phr by 1940s* To arrest someone; =RUN someone IN: *The police decided to haul them all in*—Life

haul it *v phr black by 1940s* To run away; flee; escape [fr haul ass]

haul off *v phr by 1870* To launch an attack, diatribe, etc: *The parson hauled off and told that bunch of jerks they were a bunch of jerks* [probably fr the action of drawing away to make more room for launching the fist, and *haul* suggests a nautical origin]

haul off on someone *v phr by 1930s* To hit or beat someone; launch a blow at someone: *. . . counting fifty before they hauled off on a Red*—James T Farrell

haul (or **rake)** someone **over the coals** *by 1719* **1** *v phr* To rebuke someone harshly; castigate; =CHEW OUT **2** *v phr* To put someone through an ordeal [fr the old ordeal by fire]

haul the mail *See* CARRY THE MAIL

hausfrau (HOUS frou) *n by 1918* A woman whose primary interests are keeping house, raising children, etc ●Often used in mild contempt, and to suggest a lack of chic [fr German, "housewife"]

have ◁**1**▷ *v by 1594* To do the sex act with; possess sexually: *I had Mary Jane in her own bathtub ten times*—Calder Willingham **2** *v by 1805* To cheat; deceive; =DIDDLE: *I'm afraid it's a scam, they have had us* **3** *v by 1596* To gain an advantage over: *I have you there, old man!*
See be HAD

have a bag (or **half a bag) on** *v phr by 1940s* To be drunk: *He had half a bag on and looked it*—Mickey Spillane

have a ball *v phr by 1940s* To enjoy oneself particularly well and uninhibitedly: *After the dean left we had us a ball*

have a bellyful *v phr by 1886* To get more than one wants; be unpleasantly surfeited: *I've had a bellyful of your bitching*

have a big foot *v phr by 1990s* To be important; have much influence: *We have a big foot in Asia*—TV show *Washington Week in Review*

have a big mouth *v phr by 1960s* To be inclined to say embarrassingly too much, esp about others' personal affairs: *Marcel Proust sure had a big mouth/ When he heard that, my pal told me I had a big mouth* [popularized by the comedian Jackie Gleason, who often said it of himself]

have a bird *v phr by 1960s* To exhibit shock or anger; =HAVE KITTENS: *Charlie will have a bird when he learns she died*—William Goldman

◁**have a bone on**▷ *v phr by 1920s* To have an erect penis [fr a hubristic anatomical misstatement]

have a bone to pick with someone *v phr by 1565* To have a matter to complain about or go into with someone

◁**have a broom up** one's **ass**▷ *v phr* (Variations: **get** may replace **have**; **stick** may replace **broom**; **in** one's **tail** may replace **up** one's **ass**; **butt** may replace **ass**) *by 1930s* To work diligently and eagerly; be an overachiever [fr the willing or harried worker in a joke, whose hands are full, but who would sweep the floor if one placed a *broom* in the worker's nether cavity]

◁**have a bug (**or **hair) up** one's **ass (**or **up** one's **nose)**▷ *v phr by 1940s* To be very irascible and touchy: *These people with little bugs up their ass, they come here to cause trouble. . .*—Elmore Leonard/ *Obviously the chief had a bug up his ass, and this was not the time to start an argument*—Michael Grant/ *Cheatham had a hair up his ass, was the consensus*—Earl Thompson/ *He had some bug up his butt and insisted I come down last night*—Sue Grafton

have a bun in the oven *v phr by 1940s* To be pregnant: *The outspoken Miss Bow, who. . . had a bun in the oven, replied*—Ms

have a bun on *v phr by about 1900* To be drunk

have a can on *See* GET A CAN ON

◁**have a case of the dumb-ass**▷ *v phr Army by 1970s* To do something stupid; err idiotically

have a case on someone *v phr by 1852* To be infatuated with or in love [*case* was specialized to mean "a case of being in love" by the mid–19th century]

have a chip on one's **shoulder** *v phr by 1855* To be very touchy and belligerent; be easily provoked

have a clue *v phr WWII British armed forces* To know; be aware or apprised of ●Often in the negative: *Do you have a clue about what's going on here?*
See NOT HAVE A CLUE

have a cow *See* HAVE KITTENS

have (or **take) a crack at** something *v phr* (Variations: **go** or **rip** or **ripple** or **shot** or **whack** may replace **crack**) *by 1836* To make an attempt at something; have a try: *He said he wasn't sure he could, but he'd have a crack at it*

have a crush on someone *v phr* by 1913 To be infatuated or enchanted with someone, esp to be secretly in love with someone older and more worldly than oneself

have a field day *v phr* by 1827 To indulge oneself freely and successfully; have it entirely one's way; go all out: *When the news gets out, the press will have a field day/ I'm afraid the bunnies have had a field day with the hyacinths* [fr middle 1700s *field day,* "a military review"]

have a finger in the pie *v phr* by 1659 To participate in an intrusive way; meddle: *I'm afraid the Commissioner has a finger in this pie*

have a free ride *See* GET A FREE RIDE

have a full (or **much on** one's) **plate** *v phr* by 1924 To be very busy; be preoccupied and overburdened: *I know you have a full plate and can't give any one case the coverage it needs*—Lawrence Sanders/ *I have so much on my plate and so little time. . .* —Working Mother

have a go *v phr* by 1835 To make an attempt; have a try; =HAVE A CRACK AT something: *Thought I'd have another go at friend Gary*—Hugh Pentecost

◁**have a hair up** one's **ass**▷ *See* HAVE A BUG UP one's ASS

◁**have a hard-on for** someone or something▷ *v phr* by 1970s To have antipathy for; hate: *He knows I'm a federal cop, so he's got to figure I got a hard on for Panthers*—George V Higgins/ *. . . couple heavy-duty Cubans worked for the CIA when the CIA had a hard-on for Castro*—Elmore Leonard

have a heart *interj* by 1916 A pleading exclamation: *Have a heart, baby, I only did it once!*

have a hole in one's **head** (or **wig**) *v phr* by 1940s To be very stupid; be insane; =HAVE ROCKS IN one's HEAD

have a lech for someone or something *v phr* by 1796 To be especially desirous of; lust after [*lech* is a shortening of *lechery* or *lecherous*]

have a leg up on someone or something *v phr* by 1940s To have a good start on some project, process, in some competition, etc; be well on the way to a goal: *She just started, and they already have a leg up on it*

have a little on the side *See* GET A LITTLE ON THE SIDE

have all one's **buttons** (or **marbles**) *v phr* by 1860 To be normal or mentally sound; be sane; be shrewd and aware •Most often in the negative: *When I'm sure I no longer have all my buttons I'll quit this line of work/ The old guy doesn't seem to have all his marbles, the way he mumbles to himself* [buttons probably refers to the neatness and completeness of a normal mind compared with the uncertainty and slovenliness of clothes lacking buttons] *See* LOSE one's MARBLES

have all one's **ducks in a row** *See* HAVE one's DUCKS IN A ROW

not **have all** one's **switches on** *See* NOT HAVE ALL one's SWITCHES ON

have all the answers *See* KNOW ALL THE ANSWERS

have all the moves *v phr* by 1970s To be very skillful; be expert, esp and originally in a sport or game

have a load on *v phr* by 1598 To be drunk; =FEEL NO PAIN

have a lock on something *v phr* by 1970s To be assured of some result; be certain of success: *. . . Catholics constantly yearn for moral conviction, and Mr Powell's got a lock on that*—New Yorker [fr *lock,* "a wrestling hold"]

have a mind like a sieve *v phr* by 1893 To be very forgetful

have a monkey on one's **back** *v phr* 1930s narcotics To be addicted to narcotics [perhaps related to the same phrase, meaning "to be angry," found by 1860]

have (or **cop**) **an attitude** (or **tude**) *black* by 1980s **1** *v phr* To dislike and complain about one's plight; =BITCH, KVETCH: *If you'd put up as many bonds for nothing. . . as I have, you'd have a fucking attitude too*—Donald Goines/ *"Go ahead, cop an attitude," she says and pulls away from him*—Village Voice/ *If you're going to cop a tude because I was a few minutes late, then I'll just go home*—College Slang 101 **2** *v phr* To be arrogant or haughty

have an (or **the**) **edge on** someone *v phr* by 1896 To have an advantage; enjoy a superior or winning position: *The slim and handsome will always have the edge on the rest of us*

have a (or **one's**) **nerve** *v phr* by 1890 To be impudently aggressive: *You sure have your nerve, telling him off that way*

have another think (or **thing**) **coming** *v phr* by 1901 To be wary of a fixed opinion; be skeptical of one's certainty: *For lo! I have another think a-coming*—Wallace Irwin

not **have any** *See* NOT HAVE ANY

have a party *v phr* by middle 1930s To do the sex act; =SCREW

◁not **have a pot** (or **without a pot**) **to piss in**▷ *See* NOT HAVE A POT TO PISS IN

have a prayer *v phr* by 1941 To have a chance; be able •Very often used in the negative: *The Eagles don't have a prayer, and neither will Murray*—Philadelphia

have a problem with something *v phr* by 1970s To find hard to accept; be unable to agree immediately: *I said we'll split it. You got a problem with that?*

have a red face *v phr* by 1937 To be embarrassed; have a guilty and sheepish mien; =HAVE EGG ON one's FACE: *The Chief had a red face when. . . he was found in possession of stolen property*—A Hynd

◁**have a rod on**▷ *v phr* by about 1900 To have an erect penis; =HAVE A BONE ON

have a screw loose *v phr* by 1810 To be crazy; be eccentric: *. . . that his brains, in her opinion,* *were twisted, or that he had a screw loose—Joseph Heller/ Sometimes I think she must have a screw loose*

have one's **ashes hauled** *See* GET one's ASHES HAULED

◁**have a shit fit**▷ *v phr by* 1970s To become very upset or furious; =SHIT A BRICK, SHIT GREEN: *Some people are going to have a shit fit when they read it—Anne Bernays*

have a short fuse *v phr by* 1960s To have a quick temper; be irascible; =SHOOT FROM THE HIP

◁**have someone's ass**▷ *v phr by* 1940s To punish someone; retaliate severely: *If you utter one word, I'll have your ass*

have one's **ass handed to** one *v phr* 1990s To be decisively defeated: *If he runs again he'll have his ass handed to him*

have one's **ass** (or **tail**) **in a crack** *v phr by* 1980s To be in a bad situation; be in trouble

◁**have** one's **ass in a sling**▷ *v phr* (Variations: **get** or **put** may replace **have**; the locution may be one's **ass is, was,** etc, **in a sling**) 1930s To be in serious trouble: *Allen has taken an introspective, but not innocent, bystander, and put his ass in a sling—Playboy* [the similar *have one's eye in a sling* is found by 1909]

◁**have** one's **ass to the wind**▷ *v phr by* 1980s To be vulnerable, as if naked: *They're telling Harold he's wearing a beautiful suit, and he's got his ass to the wind—Philadelphia*

have a thing about *v phr by* 1936 To be especially concerned with, in love, hate, or fascination; be strongly emotional about: *She really has a thing about pyramids*

have a tiger by the tail *v phr by* 1972 To be in a nasty situation, esp innocently or unexpectedly, that will get much worse before it gets better

have oneself **a time** *v phr by* 1882 To enjoy oneself hugely: *Everybody had himself a time—Billy Rose*

have a toehold *See* GET A TOEHOLD

have a turkey on one's **back** *v phr by* 1980s To be drunk

◁**have** (or **get**) one's **banana peeled**▷ *v phr by* 1889 To do the sex act; copulate

have bats in one's **belfry** *v phr about* 1901 To be crazy; be eccentric

not **have brain one** *See* NOT HAVE BRAIN ONE

◁**have brass** (or **cast-iron**) **balls**▷ *v phr by* 1970s To have audacity; be foolhardy: *Which one of you worthless nits had the brass balls enough to cough when I was talking—Pat Conroy*

◁**have someone by the balls**▷ *v phr by* 1940s To have someone in a very perilous and painful position; have a firm grip on someone; =HAVE someone BY THE SHORT HAIRS: *I didn't want to do it, but they had me by the balls*

◁**have** (or **get**) someone **by the short hairs** (or **curlies** or **knickers**)▷ *v phr by* 1891 To have someone in a painful and helpless situation; have absolute control over; =HAVE someone BY THE BALLS:

When life gets you by the short hairs, it doesn't let go—Playboy/ Someone nasty and ruthless has him by the short hairs—Village Voice/ You're in no position to make deals. We got you by the curlies—Joseph Wambaugh/ We've got him by the knickers and he's hurting—Wall Street Journal [fr the *short hairs* growing on the scrotum]

have someone or something **by the tail** **1** *v phr by* 1940s =HAVE someone BY THE BALLS **2** *v phr by* 1796 To have control of: *I know all young people are sure they can have it by the tail—Stephen Longstreet*

have one's **card punched** *See* GET one's CARD PUNCHED

◁**have** one's **cherry**▷ **1** *v phr by* 1889 To be a virgin **2** *v phr by* 1970s To be unproved or untried in the sense indicated: *He's never been bankrupt; still got his cherry*

have something **cinched** *v phr* (Variations: **iced** or **knocked** or **made** or **taped** or **wired** may replace **cinched**) *entry form by* 1900, *most others by* 1950s To be entirely sure of a favorable outcome; be sure of success, well-being, etc: *Then you see the helicopter. . . and you know you've got it knocked—movie The Bridges at Toko-ri/ . . . a veteran bank shot artist who has the back boards at West 4th Street wired, does anything he pleases—Village Voice/ I thought I had it iced—Washington Post* [*have* something *cinched* is fr cowboy usage, referring to a tightly and securely *cinched* saddle; the variants *have* something *made, taped,* and *wired* fr poker terms, also fr cowboy use]

have one's **claws out** *v phr by* 1940s To be intent on committing injury; be in a damaging or fighting mood: *Maggie Siggins certainly had her claws out when she wrote about Bill*

have (or **get**) **cold feet** *v phr by* 1893 To be timorous or afraid; have second thoughts: *Ella was coming too, but she had cold feet*

have someone **coming and going** *v phr by* 1903 To have someone in an inescapable situation: *What could I do? They had me coming and going*

have something **coming out of** one's **ears** *v phr by* 1940s To have something in great abundance: *He's got talent coming out of his ears*

have deep pockets and short arms *v phr by* 1980s To be rich and parsimonious

have dibs on *v phr by* 1930s To have a claim or option on: *No, sorry. . . This guy has dibs on me—Stan Cutler*

◀**have** one's **dick in** one's **zipper**▶ *v phr by* 1980s To be in a difficult and embarrassing plight: *And Buster's got his dick in his zipper now—George V Higgins*

have something **down pat** (or **cold**) *v phr first form by* 1896, *second form by about* 1915 To know something or be able to do something perfectly; be perfect master of something: *I had my story down pat, so I almost believed it myself*

have one's **druthers** *v phr by* 1895 To have one's preference; have it one's way: *. . . if George*

Bush had his druthers—National Review/ *But personally, if I had my druthers, I would like nothing better than to run off to the country with some guy*—Washington Post
See DRUTHERS

have (or get) one's ducks in a row *v phr* (Variations: **have** [or **get**] **one's ducks all in a row** or **have** [or **get**] **all one's ducks in a row**) *Army by 1970s* To be fully prepared; to be organized; =DO one's HOMEWORK: *You have five years to get all your ducks in a row*—Time/ *Want to get all your ducks in a row? Get ChemPlus...*—New York Times [perhaps fr a mother duck's marshaling of her ducklings in a neat flotilla behind her; perhaps fr some game]

have one's ears on *v phr 1970s citizens band* To have one's receiver turned on

have egg on one's face *v phr by 1950s* To be caught in an embarrassing or guilty plight; be rueful and embarrassed: *Steve Brill, the editor... should have egg on his face this week*—Village Voice/ *He left President Reagan with egg on his face*—Washington Post

have eyes for *v phr by 1810* To desire; wish for; =HAVE A LECH FOR someone or something: *But the chick who has eyes for some cat would be uncool if she told him so directly*—S Boal/ *...then suddenly she finds out he's got eyes for another woman...*—Lawrence Sanders

have (or eat) someone for lunch *v phr by 1980s* To defeat and destroy someone; =CLOBBER, EAT someone's LUNCH: *Then Ronald Reagan... had Walter Mondale for lunch*—New York Times

have something going (or working) for someone or something *v phr by 1960s* To enjoy a certain advantage; have particular assets: *You've got more going for you with NTS home training*—Popular Science/ *The best thing this mall has going for it is it's just a test*—New Yorker

have something going with someone *v phr by early 1970s* To be amorously tied to someone

have one's hands full *v phr by 1546* To be occupied up to one's limit, esp in an emergency: *When the water main burst, the utility workers had their hands full*

have one's head handed to one *v phr by 1980s* To be severely punished: *The emir said nothing at all, and sped off to his palace. This is just the sort of thing that has gotten other rulers their heads handed to them*—New Republic

have one's head pulled *v phr* (Variation: **out of one's ass** may be added) *Army by 1970* To be intelligent and sensible; be aware

have one's head screwed on right *v phr by 1821* To be sane and sensible: *No matter what he sounds like, he really has his head screwed on right*

◁**have one's head up one's ass**▷ *v phr by 1970s* To behave stupidly and blindly; be chronically wrong: *Why you gommy, stupid shit... Your head is up your ass*—William Kennedy/ *...he's one of the few bosses in this job who doesn't have his head up his ass*—Michael Grant

have hot pants *v phr by 1935* To be very lustful; crave carnally: *He has hot pants for her and she for someone else, alas*

have someone in the palm of one's hand *v phr by 1940s* To have control of someone; have someone at one's command: *We had her in the palm of our hands*—Stuart Woods

have it *v phr by 1940s* To be talented; be competent and effectual: *He tries hard, but he just doesn't have it* [probably a shortening of *have it on the ball*]
See LET someone HAVE IT

have it all *v phr by 1970s* To enjoy everything life might offer: *These days women are telling her they can't have it all. You've spent so long getting where you are—how does a baby fit in?*—New York Times

have it all hanging out *v phr 1960s* To be concealing nothing; be entirely candid and undefensive; =LET IT ALL HANG OUT: *As the current saying goes, NCR has it all hanging out*—Forbes

have it all over someone or something *v phr by 1922* To be superior; surpass or outstrip: *In advanced technology, the North has it all over the South*

have (or get) it all together *v phr 1960s* To have one's life, feelings, energies, etc, satisfactorily arranged; be free of emotional and behavioral dysfunctions: *Dr Jung says we'll all be OK when we have it all together*

have it bad *v phr by 1872* To be very much in love; be powerfully infatuated: *They would say that mouse has got it for Joey but bad*—John O'Hara/ *He warbled the old song, "I got it bad and that ain't good"*

have it both ways *v phr by 1914* To hold or esp to profit from two contrary positions; =WORK BOTH SIDES OF THE STREET ●Usu in the negative: *Make up your mind which one you'll support, because you can't have it both ways*

have it going on *v phr 1990s* To be attractive; be chic and up-to-date: *So you think you've got it going on, huh?*—Milwaukee Journal

have it good *v phr by 1940s* To enjoy prosperity, health, regular meals, and pleasures, etc: *I had it real good up there, till they canned me/ We never had it so good!*

have it in for someone *v phr by 1849* To be angry with; feel vindictive towards; bear a grudge: *Hatfield had it in for McCoy*

have it made **See** HAVE something CINCHED

◁**have it off**▷ *v phr 1930s British* To do the sex act; copulate ●Still chiefly British: *...who has had it off with both of them*—Us [fr earlier use, "to achieve a crime or shady transaction, pull something off," probably transferred to sexual activity on analogy with *cheating* and *hanky panky*, and by psychological suggestions related to *pull off* and *come off*]

have kittens or **cast a kitten** *v phr* (Variations: **a cat** or **a cow** or **pups** may replace kittens) *by*

1900 To manifest strong and sudden feeling; have a fit of laughter, fear, anger, etc: *He got so mad I thought he was going to have kittens/In addition to shy clients and those who don't want their parents to have a cow. . .* —Milwaukee Journal

have lead in one's **pants (**or ◁**in** one's **ass**▷**)** *v phr by 1950s* To be very sluggish and lazy; move or work slowly; be unresponsive: *Frank's got lead in his ass, go jazz him up*

◁**have lead in** one's **pencil**▷ *by 1916* **1** *v phr* To be sexually potent; have an erect penis **2** *v phr* To be keenly needful of sexual gratification

have lockjaw *v phr by 1980* To be silent or reticent: *PUSH is not an organization that has lockjaw when it comes to issues*—Jesse Jackson

have loose lips *v phr by 1940s* To be unable to keep a secret or keep quiet

have someone's **lunch** *See* EAT someone's LUNCH

have something **made** *See* HAVE something CINCHED

have one's **mind in the gutter** *v phr by 1940s* To be preoccupied with or devoted to crudeness and smut

have money to burn *v phr by 1896* To be wealthy; have more money than one needs: *Last year he was a bum, but he hit the lottery and has money to burn*

have no bones about *See* MAKE NO BONES ABOUT

have someone's **nose open** *v phr black by 1960s* To excite someone's sexual appetite: *What about that gray girl in San Jose who had your nose wide open?*—Eldridge Cleaver [perhaps fr the involuntary flaring of the nostrils as a symptom of strong desire, anger, etc]

have-not *by 1919* **1** *n* A poor person, region, etc **2** *modifier*: *the have-not nations of the Third World*

have someone's **number** *v phr by 1853* To know the exact truth about someone, though it be disguised; know someone completely: *She knew what I meant, and she knew I had her number*—James M Cain/ *. . . they'd all had Dixon's number for years*—Scott Turow

have one foot in the grave *v phr by 1621* To be nearly dead; be doomed

have one in the hopper *v phr by 1970s* To be pregnant; have a pregnant wife: *I've only been married a short time. . . but we've got one in the hopper*—Joseph Wambaugh

have something **on the ball** *v phr by 1912* To be talented; =HAVE IT [fr the skill of a baseball pitcher, who puts speed, motion, etc *on the ball*]

have something **on the brain** *v phr by 1862* To be obsessed with: *She's got folk-dancing on the brain*

have papers (or **papers on)** *v phr black by 1970s* To be married, or married to: *I will not be number two; I got papers on you*—Washington Post

have one's **plate full** *See* HAVE one's HANDS FULL

have pups *See* HAVE KITTENS

have rocks in one's **(**or **the) head** *v phr by 1940s* To be wrong, stupid, crazy, etc: *Kid, you got rocks in your head*—Max Shulman
See ROCKS IN one's HEAD

◁**have shit for brains**▷ *v phr by 1940s* To be very stupid

have the edge on someone *See* HAVE AN EDGE ON someone

not **have the foggiest notion** *See* NOT HAVE THE FOGGIEST NOTION

have the goods *v phr by 1980* To be talented; be effective; =HAVE IT, HAVE WHAT IT TAKES: *. . . she had the goods to hold on to a tried. . . and true audience*—New York Times

have the goods on someone *v phr by 1913* To have incriminating evidence: *They can't convict him because they don't have the goods on him*

have the hots for someone *v phr by 1940s* To desire someone sexually: *. . . the stocky instructress was glaring at them. "Think she's got the hots for you"*—Earl Thompson/ *. . . I know Grodin has the hots for you*—Village Voice

have the inside track *v phr by 1857* To have a strong advantage, esp one based on some fortuitous circumstance: *All the candidates look OK, but Hester has the inside track because she's single* [fr the advantage that a racer has by being nearest the *inside* of the *track* and having therefore the shortest distance to run]

have the jump (or **jump on)** *v phr by 1912* To enjoy a lead or advantage; be ahead of: *Who has the jump in this election?*

have them in the aisles *See* LAY THEM IN THE AISLES

have (or **get) the munchies** *v phr 1960s narcotics & counterculture* To be hungry, esp for sweets and starches after using marijuana: *I just smoked the smoke and got the munchies and I got real fat*—New York Times

◁**have the rag on (**or **Baker flying)**▷ *v phr by 1940s* To menstruate; =FALL OFF THE ROOF [*Baker flying* is fr the red-colored B flag, called *Baker* flag in the military phonetic alphabet]

◁**have the red ass**▷ *See* GET THE RED ASS

have the shorts *v phr by 1930s* To be short of money: *I told him I had the shorts*—Lionel Stander/ *This partnership. . . still has a severe case of the shorts*—Village Voice

◁**have the world by the balls**▷ *v phr* (Variations: **by the tail** or **on a string** may replace **by the balls)** *by 1970s* To be in a very profitable and dominant situation; =HAVE something CINCHED, SHIT IN HIGH COTTON: *Dunning had the world by the balls*—Don Pendleton/ *With a good agent, you've got the world by the balls*—John Irving

have one's **ticket punched** *v phr by 1970s* To be a legitimate member of something; be fully warranted in experience, qualification, etc; =PAY one's DUES: *These women have had their "tickets punched" in the corporate world*—Washington Post

◁**have** one's **tits in a wringer**▷ *v phr by 1940s* To be in trouble; be distressed: *. . . even as she* *watched her tits being pulled into the wringer*—Elmore Leonard [referring to the old fashioned *wringer* for wet laundry]

have something **to burn** *v phr* by 1896 To have something in great abundance; =HAVE something COMING OUT OF one's EARS: *This guy has chutzpah to burn*

have what it takes *v phr* by 1934 To have the right abilities, personality, etc, for success: *Do you have what it takes? Let me enhance your gifts!*

Hawaiian *n* 1990s narcotics A kind of marijuana

hawk¹ *v* by 1583 To clear one's throat; cough up and spit: *. . . let out of their cells to wash . . . hawk. . . stretch*—Nelson Algren

hawk² **1** *n* by 1960s A person who advocates a strong and bellicose policy or action: *Some were doves on Vietnam and hawks on Iran* **2** *n* homosexuals by 1970s A person who attracts and procures young men and boys for homosexuals, esp older men: *The police believe he was acting the role of a "hawk," finding "chickens" (young boys) for older men*—New York Times

hawk³ *n* by 1980s A imitation Indian hair cut affected by punk rockers; the Mohawk: *. . . egg or soap it into the hawk*—New York Times

the **hawk** or **hawkins** *n phr* black by about 1900 The cold winter wind: *Well, looks like the hawk is getting ready to hit the scene and send temperatures down*—Ruby Dee [origin unknown; perhaps fr the strong biting quality of such a wind]

hawking *n* 1990s teenagers To drive slowly and watchfully in the streets, walk about vigilantly in bars and parties, etc, looking for a sex partner; =CRUISE: *If. . . you're out searching for a date, you're "cruising," "hawking," or "macking"*—KRT News Service [perhaps related to *hawk²*, "a pimp for homosexuals"]

Hawkins *See* MISTER HAWKINS

hawkish *adj* by 1965 Having the attitude of one who advocates strong action on national policy: *These people. . . are as hawkish as Lyndon Johnson*—Stewart Alsop

hawkishness *n* by 1967 The quality of being an advocate of a bellicose policy; belligerence: *A few of the Republicans objected to Nixon's hawkishness*—Saturday Evening Post

hay by 1940s **1** *n* narcotics Marijuana; =HERB *See* HIT THE HAY, INDIAN HAY, ROLL IN THE HAY, THAT AIN'T HAY

the **hay** *n* by 1912 Bed: *He is in his hotel room in the hay*—Damon Runyon *See* HIT THE HAY, ROLL IN THE HAY

haybag *n* by 1851 A woman

hay burner **1** *n phr* (also **oat-burner**) by 1904 A horse, esp a race horse: *. . . preferred the company of hay-burners to that of humans*—Billy Rose **2** *n phr* by 1940s A person who smokes marijuana: *About half the guys in the troupe were hay burners*—New Yorker

haymaker by 1912 **1** *n* A very strong blow with the fist: *Smashes the. . . kid with a wild haymaker*—H Witwer **2** *n* Any powerful stroke or felling blow:

Having her arrested. . . would be a haymaker to your father—J Evans **3** *n* Any supreme or definitive effort, performance, etc; =WINNER: *Her blues number was a haymaker* [probably fr the wide swinging stroke of a scythe in cutting hay]

hayseed by 1888 **1** *n* (also **hayseeder**) A farmer; country person: *There's still a lot of hayseed in Senator Chance*—R Starnes **2** *adj*: *a hayseed routine/ hayseed simplicity* **3** *adj* Rural; provincial: *The bad actors perform worse plays in hayseed theaters*—Robert Ruark

haywire loggers by 1905 **1** *adj* Functioning erratically; out of order; =ON THE BLINK: *This meter's haywire* **2** *adj* Makeshift; precariously operative: *What sort of haywire gadget are you using for a pump?* **3** *adj* Crazy; confused; =COCKEYED: *He never looked inside an almanac, and was sure that anyone who did was haywire*—Stewart Holbrook *See* GO HAYWIRE

haze *See* IN A FOG

hazmat *n* by 1990s Hazardous material: *The ambulance crew checked the site for hazmats*

head **1** *n* by 1893 A headache, esp as a component of a hangover; =a BIG HEAD: *You won't believe the head I had next morning* **2** *n* by 1893 The foam on a glass of beer **3** *n* by 1551 A person: *. . . at twenty-five cents a head, no reserved seats*—J Lilienthal/ *One head that used to claim to sell stockings called*—A J Liebling ◀**4**▶ *n* Fellatio or cunnilingus; =BLOW JOB, HAIR PIE: *Some quiff is going to give you head*—Lawrence Sanders **5** *n* narcotics by 1911 A narcotics user, esp an addict: *My trip is to reach as many heads in this country as I can, and turn them around*—New York Times **6** *n* narcotics by 1960s The feeling of euphoria produced by a narcotic; =HIGH, RUSH: *I take two Tuinals and get a nice head*—New York Magazine/ *. . . much of the head, or psychic lift, that users experience*—Wall Street Journal

See ACID FREAK, ACIDHEAD, AIRHEAD, APPLEHEAD, BALLOONHEAD, BANANAHEAD, BIGHEAD, a BIG HEAD, BITE someone's HEAD OFF, BLIZZARD-HEAD, BLOCKHEAD, BLUBBERHEAD, BONEHEAD, BUBBLEHEAD, BUCKETHEAD, BULLHEAD, BURRHEAD, BUSTHEAD, CHEESEHEAD, CHICKENHEAD, CHIPHEAD, CHOWDERHEAD, CHUCKLEHEAD, CLUNKHEAD, COKEHEAD, DEADHEAD, DOO-DOO HEAD, DUMBHEAD, FATHEAD, FLATHEAD, GARBAGE HEAD, GET one's HEAD OUT OF one's ASS, GINHEAD, GIVE HEAD, GOOD HEAD, GO SOAK YOURSELF, HANDKERCHIEF-HEAD, HARDHEAD, HASH HEAD, HAVE A HOLE IN one's HEAD, HAVE one's HEAD PULLED, HAVE ROCKS IN one's HEAD, one's HEAD IS UP one's ASS, HEAD SHOP, HEADSHRINKER, HIT THE NAIL ON THE HEAD, HOPHEAD, HOTHEAD, IN OVER one's HEAD, JARHEAD, JUICEHEAD, KNOTHEAD, KNUCKLEHEAD, LUNKHEAD, MEATHEAD, METAL HEAD, METH HEAD, MUSCLEHEAD, MUSH-HEAD, MUTTONHEAD, NEED someone or something LIKE A HOLE IN THE HEAD, NOODLEHEAD, NUMBHEAD, OFF THE TOP OF one's HEAD, OPEN one's YAP, OUT OF one's HEAD, OVER one's HEAD, PIGHEAD, PILLHEAD, PINHEAD, POINTHEAD, POINTY-HEAD, POTATO-HEAD, POTHEAD, PUDDINGHEAD, PUMPKIN-

HEAD, PUTTY-HEAD, RAGHEAD, ROCKHEAD, ROCKS IN one's HEAD, ROTORHEAD, SAPHEAD, SHITHEAD, SOFT IN THE HEAD, SOREHEAD, STAND ON one's HEAD, TALKING HEAD, TREADHEAD, USE one's HEAD, WEEDHEAD, WHERE someone's HEAD IS AT, WOODENHEAD, YELL one's HEAD OFF

-head *combining word* narcotics by 1911 Addicted to or using the narcotic specified: *acidhead/ pothead*

the **head** *n phr* nautical by 1748 The toilet; =CAN [fr the location of the crew's toilet in the bow or *head* of a ship]

headache *n* by 1934 Any trouble, annoyance, vexation, etc: . . . *another headache for pro coaches*—Associated Press

headbanger *n* by early 1970s A devotee of heavy metal rock music, a style dating from the middle 1960s: *Hip headbangers, it seems, want nothing more than to see Bon Jovi fall off the face of the earth*—Milwaukee Journal/ *The show's naked emotionality feels as false and forced as an arena full of headbangers holding their lighters aloft during a power ballad*—Time [fr the frenetic reactions of such persons to the music, including actual *banging of the head*]

headbone *n* by 1000 The skull

headcase *n* by 1970s An insane or very eccentric person; =NUT: . . . *dedication to a cause that marked them as fanatics of a sort. . . the wealthy headcases and professional haters*—Don Pendleton

head (or **underground**) **comic** *n phr* 1960s counterculture An underground comic book designed to be read while smoking marijuana, and featuring bizarre drawings, black humor, sex, etc

-headed *combining word* by 1386 Having a head, esp a mind, of the specified defective sort
See AIRHEADED, BALLOONHEADED, BIGHEADED, BONE-HEADED, BULLHEADED, FATHEADED, FLATHEADED, MEAT-HEADED, MUSH-HEADED, MUTTONHEADED, NUMBHEADED, PIGHEADED, PINHEADED, POINTY-HEADED, WOOLLY-HEADED

header 1 *n* by 1849 A head-first dive, fall, or plunge **2** *n* soccer by 1906 A pass, shot at the goal, etc, made by batting the ball with one's head
See DOUBLEHEADER

head for *v phr* by 1835 To start out for or toward; =HIT FOR: *I headed for the door/ He's headed for a disappointment* [fr the pointing of a ship's bow or *head* toward a destination]

head game *n phr* by 1990s A process of manipulation, something like brainwashing; =MIND-FUCK: *I was playing head games*—Ed Rollins/ *Coach Riley is a head-gamer who uses players as pieces in a board game*—New York Times

headhunt *v* To act as a headhunter

headhunter *n* by middle 1960s A person or agency that seeks out and recruits employees, esp business executives and highly paid professionals, as candidates for usu high-paying or prestigious jobs: *Headhunters head for Washington as a capital place to find executives*—Wall Street Journal

head in a bed *n phr* medical by 1990s A patient with no chance of recovery: *In neurosurgery slang, Dimas would spend his life as a head in a bed, with a body that was more or less irrelevant*—New York Times

◁one's **head is up** one's **ass**▷ *sentence* by 1970s One is behaving stupidly and blindly: . . . *were even saying that, skill-wise, the FBI's head was up its ass*—Village Voice

◁**head job**▷ *n phr* by 1960s Fellatio or cunnilingus; oral sex: . . . *receiving a listless headjob from an aging black prostitute*—Joseph Wambaugh

head kit *n phr* narcotics by 1960s The set of implements used for taking narcotics; drug apparatus; =WORKS: *Head kits are constantly being found*—L J Berry

headlight 1 *n* black by 1950s A light-skinned black person **2** *n* by 1940s A large diamond, esp in a ring or clasp: *A lurid "headlight" in his tie*—Abel Green

headlights 1 *n* 1920s prizefight The eyes ◁**2**▷ *n* by 1940s A woman's breasts

headline-grabbing *adj* by 1980s Newsworthy; prominently publicized: *The science community is demoralized; the atmosphere has been fouled by a multitude of headline-grabbing incidents*—Time

headliner *n* show business by 1896 The main or chief performer; main attraction: *She was the headliner last week at the Seven Seas*

head of all the heads *n phr* by 1970s The highest ranking chief; the big chief; =CAPO DI TUTTI CAPI: *Head of all the heads, you understand my meaning?*—Stan Cutler
See CAPO

one's **head off** *adv phr* by 1920 To one's utmost; extremely much; spectacularly; =one's ASS OFF, one's BRAINS OUT: . . . *one time when Joey was vomiting his head off*—San Francisco

head someone or something **off at the pass** *v phr* by 1930s To forestall or prevent by anticipation: *A single mother has to establish control fast. . . Before the coercive cycle builds. . . you have to head it off at the pass*—New York Times [fr the stock situation in Western movies, where typically the leader of a force pursuing thieves or rustlers through rough ground declares "We'll head them off at the pass"]

head of steam *n phr* by 1835 Full speed and impetus: *Stephanopoulos acknowledges a steady series of peaks and valleys: "You get up a head of steam and then—oops! What's coming around the corner?"*—Vanity Fair [the date refers to the actual boiler pressure of a machine]

headrush *n* narcotics by 1960s The feeling of euphoria produced by a narcotic; =HEAD, RUSH: *There are so many people packed into one place it almost gives you a headrush*—Macon Telegraph

head shop *n phr* 1960s counterculture A shop selling various accessories of the drug culture and hippie culture, such as water pipes, holders for marijuana cigarettes, psychedelic posters, incense, etc

headshrinker or **headpeeper** *n* medical by

1950 Any psychotherapist, psychiatrist, psychoanalyst, etc; =SHRINK: . . . *with a good deal more understanding than any clergyman or headshrinker*—Sports Afield/ . . . *you lousy smug headpeeper*—Stephen King

head south *See* GO SOUTH

heads up *interj by 1940s* A warning of some impending danger or need to be alert: *Heads up, for heaven's sake*—New York Times

heads-up 1 *adj by 1940s* Clever; alert; shrewd: *They're playing real heads-up football* **2** *n by 1990s* A warning; a meeting where warning is given: *. . . blamed Young for not giving. . . regents a "heads up" about the controversy*—Los Angeles Times/ *Altman called a brief heads-up designed to tell the White House what procedures the RFC would follow*—Time **3** *modifier*: *Daschle was on Mitchell's heads-up list for good reason*—New Republic

heads will roll *sentence by 1930* People will be dismissed, punished, ruined, etc: *If eventually the authorities catch up with you, no heads will roll*—Punch/ *I promise you: if this package is not delivered on time, heads will roll* [the source is a quotation from Adolf Hitler]

head trip 1 *n phr* A mental exploration; an adventure of thought, esp of a new sort; a delectable fantasy: *Private head trips seemed to be adjuncts or companions of social movements*—Andrew Kopkind **2** *modifier*: *The Head-Trip Dodge, verbalizing without involvement, the educated filibuster*—New York Magazine **3** *v phr*: . . . *man seeks companion for headtripping, studying together, Scrabble, etc*—Psychology Today **4** *n phr* =HEAD GAME, MIND-FUCK: *Considering the estrangements and head trips your family has put you through, it's a wonder you can still smile*—Vanity Fair

head up 1 *v phr by 1930s* To be the chief of; supervise; direct: *Stan Baker will head up our new Verbal Economy Division* **2** *v phr black by 1990s* To confront or attack someone: *Fudgie wouldn't want to head up with him*—Buzz/ *You niggers burn those ribs, I'm a head you up*—Buzz

heap *by 1924* **1** *n* A car, esp an old ramshackle one; =JALOPY: *I keep hoping somebody will steal this heap*—Lawrence Sanders **2** *n* Any old vehicle [a motorcyclists' shortening of *scrap heap*]
See JUNK HEAP

a **heap** *adj phr by about 1930* Very much: *Thanks a heap, old buddy*

heaps *by 1547* **1** *n* Very many; =a FLOCK, OODLES: *I've got heaps of scratch* **2** *adv* Very much: *She loved him heaps, but kept mum*

heart *n 1960s narcotics* A tablet of an amphetamine, esp Dexedrine™
See BLEEDING HEART, CROSS MY HEART, HAVE A HEART, PURPLE HEART

hearted *See* CHICKENHEARTED, COPPER-HEARTED

hear the birdies sing *v phr by 1940s* To be knocked unconscious; be unconscious

hear the wheels going around *v phr by 1970s* To be aware of another's thought process; notice cerebration: *Kennedy could hear the wheels going around*—Carsten Stroud

hearts and flowers 1 *n phr by 1920s* Sentimentality; maudlin appeals, etc: *I believed all the hearts and flowers you gave me about being in love with your husband*—J Evans **2** *n phr prizefight by 1940s* A knockout [fr the name of a mournful and sentimental song of about 1908]

heart-throb *n by 1920s* One's deeply beloved: *Who's your heart-throb this week?*

heat 1 *n underworld by 1928* Pursuit, prosecution, and other sorts of involvement with the law: *. . . types of cash mark which do not involve federal heat*—E DeBaun **2** *n* (also **heater**) *baseball by 1980s* A good fastball **3** *n by late 1920s* Any sort of trouble and recrimination, esp the angry complaining of irritated persons; =FLAK, STATIC: *We better expect heat when this report gets out* **4** *n* (also **heater**) *by late 1920s* A firearm, usu a pistol: *I was packing about as much heat as you find in an icicle. . . without a gun*—J Evans **5** *n sports by 1940s* A round in boxing, inning in baseball, etc ●*Heat,* "a horse race," is found by 1663
See BITCH IN HEAT, DEAD HEAT, GIVE someone HEAT, PACK HEAT

the **heat** *n phr by 1937* The police; a police officer: *Try operating an American city without the heat, the fuzz, the man*—Eldridge Cleaver/ . . . *until the heat pulls up in one of those super paddy wagons*—Esquire
See IF YOU CAN'T STAND THE HEAT STAY OUT OF THE KITCHEN, PUT THE HEAT ON someone, TAKE HEAT

heat artist *n phr hoboes* A drinker of jellied alcohol [jellied alcohol is called *canned heat*]

the **heat is on** *sentence by 1934* Extreme pressure and pursuit are afoot, esp by the police against criminals: *The heat is on dope. That's a big bust if they get hold of you*—New York Magazine

heave 1 *v by 1868* To vomit; =BARF **2** *n police by 1950s* A shelter: *Heave. Any shelter used by a policeman to avoid the elements*—G Y Wells

the **(or the old) heave-ho** *n phr* Forcible ejection; summary and emphatic dismissal; =the BOUNCE: *If you make any noise. . . you get the heave-ho*—W J Slocum/ *And he gave me the old heave-ho*—Whitey Herzog [*heave and ho,* the sailors' cry when hauling, is attested from the 1500s]
See GET THE AIR, GIVE someone THE AIR

heaven *See* BLUE HEAVEN, HOG HEAVEN, NIGGER HEAVEN, STINK TO HIGH HEAVEN, TO HELL

heaven dust *n phr narcotics by 1940s* Cocaine

heavenly blue *n phr 1960s narcotics* Morning glory seeds, used as a narcotic

heavy 1 *n by 1920s* A thug; hoodlum; =GOON **2** *n theater by 1880* The villain in a play, movie, situation, action, etc; =BADDIE, DIRTY HEAVY: *It mattered not at all that his employers were the heavies of the piece*—Don Pendleton **3** *adj by 1971* Serious; intense ●*The ancient sense was revived during the*

1920s: *heavy petting/ heavy correcting* **4 adj** *1960s counterculture* Excellent; wonderful; =COOL: *These guys were not simply cool. . . they were heavy, totally hip, and totally trustworthy*—San Francisco **5 adj** *by 1842* Important; consequential; prominent: *The heaviest art form on the planet is certainly films*—D Crosby/ *You said we were meeting this heavy actress*—Paul Theroux/ *He must have been blowing some heavy politics*—Bobby Seale **6 n** *by 1940s* An important person; =BIG SHOT, HEAVYWEIGHT: *. . . will continue to stitch up the local heavies*—Village Voice **7 n** *1970s surfers* A big wave: *. . . good set of heavies*—Life

See ON THE HEAVY, WALK HEAVY

heavy artillery or **big guns** *n phr first form by 1809* The most impressive and persuasive arguments, evidence, persons, etc, available: *The Republicans are rolling out their heaviest artillery for this debate/ Against these big critics' big guns I offer Serban & Co some shelter*—Village Voice

heavy breather *n phr by 1970s* =BODICE-RIPPER

heavy breathing *n phr by 1990s* Pompous opinionating; punditry: *Give us the tabloids, and even transcripts in the serious newspapers, but spare us the prime-time writhing and op-ed heavy breathing*—New Republic

See HARD BREATHING

heavy click time *n phr 1990s television* The moment when television viewers most likely change the channel: *They ponder "pod positioning". . . and "heavy click time" (the moments when most viewers reach for their remote controls)*—Los Angeles Times

heavy date *by 1923* **1 n phr** A very important rendezvous, esp with someone of the other sex for sex: *A heavy date with a light lady*—K Brush **2 n phr** One's partner on a heavy date **3 n phr** Any important, urgent engagement: *. . . a heavy poker date for this afternoon*—W C Burnett

heavy-duty *adj by 1940s* Very active; highly productive: *The sting identified 46 "heavy-duty taggers"*—Milwaukee Journal [fr the term for a particularly strong and durable machine, found by 1914]

heavy-foot *n police by 1940s* A habitually fast driver; speeder

heavy (or **long-ball**) **hitter** *n phr by 1980s* A person of achievement; an expert; =MAJOR LEAGUER: *. . . there was no one-upmanship dealing with a heavy hitter like Cifelli*—Stan Cutler/ *Hitler was a heavy-hitter if there ever was one*—Carsten Stroud/ *I knew immediately that Annette Bening was a long-ball hitter, emotionally, intellectually and artistically*—New York Times [fr a baseball term, "player who hits the ball hard," found by 1883; *long-ball* variant found in baseball by 1950s]

heavy (or **heavily**) **into** *adj phr by 1970s* Much engaged in; prominent in: *. . . his family very heavy into potato chips*—A Arthur/ *Us niggers be very heavy into stockings over our faces doing houses and Seven Elevens*—Harry Crews

heavy leather *by 1970s* **1 n phr** Leather clothing and various metal accoutrements as or in imitation of motorcycle gangs, esp by extravagantly masculine homosexuals: *He's gone beyond butch, won't wear anything but heavy leather these days* **2 modifier**: *A psychopathic killer cruises heavy-leather homosexual bars*—New York Times

heavy lifter *n phr by 1990s* The one who does the heavy lifting "heavy lifting": *The NRA is the heavy lifter. . . —*Art Bell

heavy lifting *n phr by 1990s* The hardest work: *Baker reckons that he has done most of the heavy lifting, whereas it is his friend who got first prize*—New Yorker/ *It's going to be some really heavy lifting*—New York Times

heavy metal *1960s rock and roll* **1 n phr** A style of simple music characterized by extreme loudness, distortion, pounding drums, and played through great banks of amplifiers and speakers: *With all the sudden interest in heavy metal. . . Deep Purple has decided to give it a go once again*—Aquarian/ *. . . a degree of internal intricacy that belies popular conceptions of heavy metal*—Rolling Stone **2 modifier**: *As the prototypical heavy metal band, Led Zeppelin has created its fair share*—Rolling Stone

heavy money *n phr* (Variations: **big** or **important** or **real** may replace **heavy**; **dough** or **jack** or **sugar** may replace **money**) *by 1924* A large amount of money; impressive sums; =MEGABUCKS: *Why did she walk out on a movie career which was paying her heavy money?*—P Martin/ *I've been busy cleaning up some heavy dough*—Jerome Weidman/ *So nobody's about to pay big money for the site fee of a Tyson versus Ribalta*—New York Times

heavy petting (or **necking**) *n phr by 1940s* Very passionate kissing, fondling, etc, stopping short of the sex act proper

heavy sugar *n phr by 1926* A possession or condition indicating wealth: *Six Mercedeses is heavy sugar*

See HEAVY MONEY

heavy up *v phr by 1990s* To become obtrusively friendly: *After he won. . . people at the gym started to heavy up with him, so Mike began working out in a garage*—Charles Gaines & George Butler

heavyweight *n by about 1890* An important person; =BIGGIE: *He's some sort of heavyweight in the rag trade*

◄**Hebe** or **Heeb**► *n by 1932* A Jew

heck *interj by 1887* =HELL

the **heck** **See** the HELL

hedge 1 *v* (also **hedge off**) *by 1672* To transfer part of one's bets to another bookmaker as a means of reducing possible losses if too many of one's clients were to win: *Big banks use derivatives to hedge their bets on which way the markets are going. . .* —Gannett News Service **2 n** Something that offsets expected losses: *People were buying gold as a hedge against inflation*

H-E-double toothpicks *n phr by 1940s* Hell: *I caught H-E-double toothpicks for saying I liked the* perfume-scented inserts in magazines—Ann Landers

the **heebie-jeebies** (Variations: **the heebies** or **the jeebies** or **the leaping heebies**) by 1923 **1** **n phr** A very uneasy and jumpy feeling; nagging frets; =the WILLIES: ... Mr Perot worked off his heebie-jeebies by trashing Mr Bush's chance for re-election—New York Times/ His several disquisitions on the jeebies—H Allen Smith/ I always get the heebies there—Harold Robbins **2** **n phr** Delirium tremens [said to have been coined by a cartoonist named Billy De Beck]

heel 1 **n** underworld by 1914 A sneak-thief; petty criminal; =PUNK **2** **n** carnival by about 1930 A petty hawker; =SHILL **3** **n** by 1925 A contemptible man; blackguard; =BASTARD, PRICK, SHITHEEL: His friend turned out to be a heel, and ran off with his wife and money **4** **v** underworld by 1950s To escape from prison **5** **n**: They made a clean heel from Leavenworth **6** **v** by 1873 To get a gun for oneself or another person [last sense fr heel, "arm a fighting cock with a gaff or spur," found by 1755]

See COOL one's HEELS, ROUNDHEEL, RUBBER HEEL, SHITHEEL, TARHEEL

heeled 1 **adj** by 1866 Armed; carrying a weapon: I can talk better when I know this guy isn't heeled—J Evans **2** **adj** by 1880 Wealthy; in funds; =FLUSH: Having two bills in the kick I counted myself heeled **3** **adj** 1960s narcotics Possessing narcotics; =DIRTY, HOLDING

See WELL-HEELED

heeler **n** newspaper office by 1960s An apprentice; novice reporter; =CUB [perhaps fr the obedience of a trained dog who stays at the heel of the master]

See WARD HEELER

heeltap **n** by 1780 A few drops of liquor left in a glass: ... drink three martinis... absolutely no heeltaps—American Mercury [origin uncertain; a heeltap glass was one without a flat base, so that it could not be set down until entirely empty (such was presumably also a tumbler), and probably so called because the narrow bottom resembled the narrow tap of a shoe heel]

heesh **n** 1960s narcotics Hashish

heft **n** by 1848 Importance; weight in political or other terms: ... the person really has to have some heft—Los Angeles Times

hefty by 1871 **1** **n** A stout or obese person: While other hefties count their calories, he counts the dollars—Hal Boyle **2** **adj**: a hefty matron over at the corner table **3** **adj** Large; considerable: ... not only romance, but a hefty dose of fantasy these days—New York Magazine

◄**heifer**► **n** by 1853 A young woman, esp an attractive one; =FILLY

See ARMORED COW

heifer dust **n phr** by 1927 =BULLSHIT: "That's pure heifer dust," quoth the Governor

height **adj** hip-hop by middle 1980s Excellent; unsurpassed; =GREAT: The gloves I got for Christmas are height—New York Magazine [probably a shortening of the height of fashion]

heimish *See* HAIMISH

heinie **n** by 1930s The buttocks; =ASS, BUTT, KEISTER: I think it was her heinie... That high, insolent ass... —Elmore Leonard [probably fr hind end]

heinous **adj** 1980s students Bad; =CRAPPY, GROSS, LAME

a **Heinz 57 variety** **n phr** by 1896 A mutt; a dog of no discernible lineage; a mongrel: Chloe's her dog... "a Heinz 57 variety," says Ivey—New York Daily News

See FIFTY-SEVEN VARIETIES

heist (HĪST) **1** **v** underworld by 1931 To steal; stick up; rob **2** **v** underworld by about 1920 To highjack **3** **n** underworld by 1930 A robbery or hold-up: Led Zeppelin... was the victim of the heist—New York Post [fr an early and dialectal pronunciation of hoist; in an 1883 source hoist is defined as "to rob houses by climbing in a window," because one thief climbs or hoists himself up over another]

See SHORT HEIST

heist man **n phr** underworld by 1930s A professional thief or hold-up man

helium hands **n phr** by 1990s A student who frequently volunteers in class: There's a nickname for people like that, "helium hands," their hands are always in the air—Milwaukee Journal

hell 1 **interj** by 1678 An exclamation of disgust, regret, emphasis, etc: Oh hell, they're back/ Hell, darling, I didn't mean it **2** **n** by 1851 Strong rebuke or punishment; =MERRY HELL: Your old man'll give you hell/ I caught hell from the tax people **3** **n** by 1374 A bad experience: Dinner with my in-laws is usually pure hell **4** **v** by 1897 =HELL AROUND **5** **v** by 1929 To speed; =BARREL: An ambulance, helling out the state road—R Starnes **6** **interj** by 1893 An exclamation of strong denial, disbelief, defiance, etc; =IN A PIG'S ASS, MY EYE: "Retreat hell!" said the general

See ALL HELL BROKE LOOSE, BEAT THE SHIT OUT OF someone or something, as BLAZES, BLUE HELL, CATCH HELL, COME HELL OR HIGH WATER, EASY AS PIE, EXCUSE ME ALL TO HELL, FOR THE HELL OF IT, FROM HELL TO BREAKFAST, GIVE someone HELL, GO-TO-HELL CAP, GO TO HELL IN A HANDBASKET, LIKE A BAT OUT OF HELL, LIKE HELL, MERRY HELL, PLAY HELL WITH something, RAISE HELL, a SNOWBALL'S CHANCE IN HELL, TAKE OFF LIKE A BIGASS BIRD, TO HELL

the **hell** by 1911 **1** **adv phr** (also ◄**the fuck**►) Completely and immediately •A hostile intensifier: The hell're we doing sitting here?—Elmore Leonard/ Anybody who hasn't learned this yet had better grow the fuck up—The Source/ Kid, shut the fuck up—Carsten Stroud **2** **adv phr** (Variations: **deuce** or **devil** or ◄**fuck**► or **heck** may replace **hell**; **in God's name** or **in hell** may replace **the hell**) In fact; really •Mainly used for rhythmic fullness in a hostile question: What the hell do you mean by that?/ What the deuce are you about, you blackguard?/ Tell me what the devil you have in *mind/ How the fuck would he meet the taxes and pay so many salaries?*—Joseph Heller [probably derived from expressions of incredulity like "in the world," which altered to "in hell"]

hellacious *adj 1930s college students* Excellent; wonderful; =GREAT: *It was a hellacious picnic*

hell around *v phr by 1897* To lead a life of low pleasures; frequent bars, chase sex partners, etc: *I'd like to hell around a couple years, then settle down*

hell-bender *n by 1889* A wild spree

hell-bent *adj by 1835* Strongly determined; recklessly eager: *They are hell-bent to cut taxes again before election*—New Republic

hell-bent-for-leather *See* HELL-FOR-LEATHER

hell-buggy *n WWII Army* A military tank

hellcat *n by 1605* A volatile and dangerous woman

heller *n students by 1895* An energetic and aggressive person, esp one who is mischievous and menacing: *He was quite a heller when young*

hell-for-leather or **hell-bent-for-leather** *adv by 1889* Rapidly and energetically; =ALL-OUT, FLAT OUT: *Frank and Pat had gone hell-for-leather over this territory*—Carsten Stroud [origin unknown; perhaps related to British dialect phrases *go hell for ladder, hell falladerly, hell faleero,* and remaining mysterious even if so, although the *leather* would then be a very probable case of folk etymology with a vague sense of the *leather* involved in riding tack]

hellhole *n by 1866* Any unpleasant or morally degenerate place; =DUMP: *I was so glad to get out of this hellhole*—Calder Willingham/ *Emerson is a hellhole*—New York Times

a **hell of a** or **helluva** or **one hell of a** *adj phr first form by 1776* Very remarkable, awful, admirable, distressing, etc; =a BITCH OF A, SOME KIND OF: *They could have done a helluva lot better than cold cereal*—Armistead Maupin

a **hell of a note** *n phr by 1940s* Something amazing, disgusting, surprising, etc: *She drank it, ain't that a hell of a note?/ What a hell of a note this is, a lousy flat tire*

a **hell of a (or no) way to run a railroad** *n phr by 1940s* An incompetent, overcomplex, or disastrous way of doing something; a flawed and botched methodology: *When she saw how our department was organized she told us it was a hell of a way to run a railroad, and she suggested some improvements*

the **hell of it** *n phr by 1940s* The worst part of something; what makes something very nasty: *The hell of it is that I tried all week to renew my license before they caught me*

hell on wheels *n phr by 1843* A very impressive, nasty, violent, etc, event, person, etc: *This house is going to be hell on wheels in six months*—Lawrence Sanders/ *And considering what hell on wheels she'd been during our divorce. . .* —Stan Cutler [origin uncertain; said to be fr mid–1800 characterization of the gambling places and houses of prostitution loaded on flat-cars for railroad workers in

the West, but the first instances predate this; perhaps fr earlier *on wheels,* "smooth, rapid, impressive"]

hell or high water *See* COME HELL OR HIGH WATER

hell-raiser *by 1914* **1** *n* A person likely to cause trouble and disturbance, esp by an active and defiant spirit: *This town needs a few hell-raisers to liven it up* **2** *n* A person who leads a life of low pleasures; profligate; libertine; =HELLER: *He was barred from the Muskie train after lending his press pass to a drunken hell-raiser*—Saturday Review

hell's bells *interj by 1912* An exclamation of impatience, anger, emphasis, etc: *Hell's bells, Maude, I did that two whole years ago*

hell to pay *n phr by 1901* A very large fuss with dangerous implications; violent repercussions: *Hell to pay, in other words, for anyone who was unyielding*—Scott Turow

hell to split *adv phr by 1867* Very rapidly; =HELL-FOR-LEATHER, LICKETY-SPLIT: *She looked back, and I piled after her hell to split*—James M Cain

helper *See* BOILERMAKER

he-man *by 1859* **1** *n* A very masculine man; =HUNK, MACHO **2** *modifier*: *. . . a regular he-man cop*—E Lavine

hem and haw *v phr by 1580* To hesitate; tergiversate; temporize: *Stop hemming and hawing and do something*

hemp *n narcotics by 1940s* Marijuana; Indian hemp *See* INDIAN HAY

hen *by 1626* **1** *n* A woman, esp a fussy or gossipy woman •This and other senses regarded as offensive to some women: *That old hen made him sick*—P Marks **2** *n* A young woman; =CHICK **3** *modifier* By, of, and for women: *hen party/ hen talk*

hencoop or **hen ranch** *n* or *n phr college students by 1900* A woman's dormitory

hen-fruit *n by 1854* Eggs

hen party *n phr by 1887* A party for women only: *Men have stag parties; girls have hen parties*—J G Rothenberg

henpecked *adj by 1690* Dominated by women, esp by one's wife; =PUSSY-WHIPPED

hen-pen *n 1940s students* A girl's school, esp a private boarding school

hen tracks *n phr* (Variations: **chicken** may replace **hen**; **scratches** or **scratchings** may replace **tracks**) *by 1907* Illegible handwriting; scrawl

hep *adj underworld by 1908* Aware; up-to-date; =HIP, WITH IT •Taken up by jazz musicians to the extent of being identified with them: *By running with the older boys I soon began to get hep*—Louis Armstrong/ *. . . but I'm hep, man; for example, I had my vasectomy already*—Herbert Gold [origin unknown; a 1914 source says it is based on the name of "a fabulous detective who operated in Cincinnati"] *See* UNHEP

hepcat *n 1920s jive talk* A man who appreciates the right sort of music, leads a life of fashionable pleasure, etc; =CAT, DUDE: *. . . a big-timer, a young sport, a hep cat, in other words, a man-about-town*—Langston Hughes [fr *hep cat;* a possible supplementary origin fr Wolof *hipicat,* "man who is aware," has been suggested]

hepster *n 1930s jive talk* A hep person; =HEPCAT

hep to *adj phr underworld by 1908* Aware of; cognizant of: *How little we've been personally hep to what's actually going on*—New Yorker
See HEP

hep to the jive *adj jazz musicians by about 1915* Aware; informed; initiated; =WITH IT: *I commenced getting hep to the jive*—Louis Armstrong

herb *n 1990s students* A tedious, contemptible person; =DORK, GEEK, NERD: *. . . think you're a couple of reality-impaired herbs*—Time

herb or **herbs** *n 1960s narcotics* Marijuana; =POT: *So you get fines to pay and you've lost your herbs*—Wall Street Journal

herd *See* RIDE HERD ON someone

herder *n prison by about 1930* A prison guard

here *See* UP TO HERE

here's mud in your eye *See* MUD IN YOUR EYE

here's your hat what's your hurry *sentence by 1940s* Why are you leaving so soon? but leave at once •Ironic and jocular combination of a polite question and rude request

Herkimer Jerkimer *n phr by 1940s* Any rustic, fool, or eccentric [based on a *jerk* from Herkimer, that is, from a distant provincial place]

herky-jerky *adj by middle 1950s* Jerky; spasmodic; not smooth: *. . . bellow and quiver with those herky-jerky spasms*—Village Voice/ *. . . herky-jerky instability of Shepard's plays*—New Yorker/ *. . . producing a herky-jerky style of governing*—Bob Woodward

hero sandwich or **hero** or **Hero** *n phr* or *n by 1955* A sandwich made with a loaf of bread cut lengthwise and filled with a variety of cheeses, sausages, vegetables, etc; =GRINDER, HOAGIE, POOR BOY, SUBMARINE, TORPEDO [perhaps because one needs to be a bit of a *hero* to eat the whole *sandwich*]

herpie *n by 1970s* A person infected with genital herpes

◁**Herring Choker** or **herring chocker**▷ **1** *n by 1940s* A Scandinavian **2** *n by 1899* A New Brunswick native or ship **3** *n phr by 1899* A Nova Scotian person or ship; =BLUENOSE: *No price for lobster, cause of the Herring-Chokers*—Philip Wheelwright

the **herring pond** *n phr by 1686* The Atlantic Ocean

Hershey bar *n phr WWII armed forces* A yellow stripe, worn on a military uniform to indicate units of time spent on overseas service [fr a *bar* of Hershey™ chocolate, some of which have yellow wrappers; probably influenced by the name of General Lewis B *Hershey,* director of the selective service system from 1941 to 1970]

hess *See* a MELL OF A HESS

hetero *adj by 1933* Heterosexual

hex *n by 1909* A jinx or curse; =the INDIAN SIGN, WHAMMY: *I lose every time, must be a hex on me* [ultimately fr German *Hexe,* "witch"]

hey *interj by early 1980s* An exclamation used to underscore mildly what is said: *Pennzoil has been arguing that, hey, they are reasonable people*—American Speech/ *I tried explaining. . . that, hey, basically a goose is just a big duck. . . .*—Dave Barry/ *Hey, I'm only human*—Stan Cutler [the use is attenuated from the ancient call for attention found by 1225]

hey Rube *n phr carnival by 1935* The traditional warning and rallying cry of circus and carnival people, used esp when they are attacked by righteously indignant citizens [fr *hay-rube,* "hayseed, rube, rustic," found by 1908]

hi or **hiya** *interj first form by 1862, second by 1940* A salutation upon meeting: *The staccato cry of "Hi!," which we. . . judged to be the almost universal greeting*—New Yorker [probably based on *hi,* "hey," exclamation used to call attention, found by 1475]

hiccup *n by 1980s* A brief interruption; spasmodic stoppage: *The violence in Moscow is another hiccup in Russia's drive for democracy*—TV show Sunday Morning

hick *by 1565* **1** *n* A rural person; a simple, countrified man or woman; =APPLE-KNOCKER, RUBE: *The automobile. . . largely nullified the outward distinctions between hick and city slicker*—D L Cohn **2** *modifier*: *. . . wasn't bad looking in a hick way*—H Witwer/ *. . . that hick chief of police*—Erle Stanley Gardner [fr a nickname of Richard, thought of as a country name, as Reuben is the base of "rube"]

hickey or **hickie** **1** *n by 1909* Any unspecified or unspecifiable object; something one does not know the name of or does not wish to name; =DOODAD, DOOHICKEY, GADGET: *We have little hickeys beside our seats*--Atlantic Monthly **2** *n by about 1915* A blackhead, pimple, or other minor skin lesion; =ZIT **3** *n by 1956* A mark on the skin made by biting or sucking during a sex act: *. . . line of hickeys, or love bites*—John Irving/ *. . . Violet came home from the mall with a leather bustier and a hickey. . .*—Seventeen

◁**hickory dick**▷ *See* DOES A WOODEN HORSE HAVE A HICKORY DICK

hick town *n phr by 1920* A small or rural town: *. . . any hick town in Kansas*—American Mercury

hickville or **hicksville** or **Hicksville** *by 1940s* **1** *adj* =DULLSVILLE •Capitalized form fr an actual New York city **2** *adj* =CORNY

hicky *adj by 1940s* Rural; mean and meager: *This man is from some hicky farm in Shit Creek, Georgia*—Eldridge Cleaver

hide *n baseball by 1940s* =HORSEHIDE
See TAKE IT OUT OF someone's HIDE, TAN

hideaway **1** *n by 1930* A private retreat; personal refuge; =HIDEOUT **2** *n by 1929* A small, remote place, esp a small nightclub, restaurant, etc: *The vaudeville performer on the two-a-day has played to punks in the hideaways*—World's Work

hide or hair *n phr* (also **hide nor hair**) *by 1830*

No sign or part of the person mentioned: *No one has seen hide or hair of him since*—Time

hideout 1 *n prison by about 1915* An inmate who hides with the intention of escaping at night **2** *n by 1885* A place of relative obscurity and safety; =HIDEAWAY: *The gang had a hideout in a ruined warehouse near Hoboken*

hide out *v phr by 1884* To hide, esp from the police or other pursuers

hides 1 *n 1920s jazz musicians* Drums, esp a complete drum set as used by a jazz musician **2** *n by 1980s* Automobile or truck tires; =SKINS

◁**hide the weenie**▷ *See* PLAY HIDE THE WEENIE

hidey hole *by 1817* **1** *n phr* A place to hide; =HIDEAWAY **2** *modifier*: . . . *conceal themselves in one of the hidey hole apartments of their proliferating step-parents*—Village Voice

hi-fi or **hi fi** or **high-fi** *late 1940s* **1** *n* or *n phr* A record player that reproduces sound without much distortion or alteration from the original **2** *modifier*: *a hi-fi amplifier/ hi fi recording* [fr *high fidelity*]

higgledy-piggledy *adj by 1598* Confused; chaotic; =MESSY: *I was walking in dark corridors that were all higgledy-piggledy*—San Francisco [origin uncertain; perhaps fr the disorderly herding configuration of *pigs*]

high 1 *adj by 1627* Drunk, esp slightly so: . . . *high, slightly alcoholic, above the earth!*—Arthur Miller **2** *adj narcotics by 1932* Intoxicated by narcotics, esp in an easy and lighthearted condition induced by drugs; =GEEZED: *An actor has less license to get high during working hours than does a musician*—Saturday Review/ . . . *the smoker uses them in big puffs getting high*—Stephen Longstreet **3** *n narcotics by 1960s* : *He took a few tokes and got a pretty good high* **4** *n by 1960s* A nonintoxicated feeling of exhilaration or euphoria; =LIFT: *Weddings are a high*—Saturday Review **5** *adj by 1960s*: *The congregation was all high on gospel enthusiasm* ***See*** MILE-HIGH CLUB, SHIT IN HIGH COTTON

high as a kite *adj phr by 1939* Intoxicated or exhilarated to an important degree

highball 1 *n railroad by 1897* A signal denoting a clear track or clearance to start or accelerate **2** *n railroad* A train running on schedule, or an express train **3** *v railroad by about 1925* To speed; rush: *A train was thirty yards away, highballing down the track*—Calder Willingham/ *One New York distributor highballed 30 trucks through the Holland Tunnel*—Associated Press **4** *n by 1898* An iced, mixed alcoholic drink taken in a high glass: *He quaffed a couple of rye highballs and left* **5** *n WWI Army* A military salute [fr the former use of a railroad track side signal using a two-foot globe, raised or lowered, to instruct the engineer; the military sense fr the use of a railroad conductor's raised hand or fist as a signal to the engineer to start, the term transferred from the mechanical signal; the drinking sense is probably fr a *ball*, "drink of whiskey" in a *high* glass]

high-binder *n by 1835* A corrupt politician or functionary: . . . *covered the winter meeting of the grand inner circle of high-binders at Miami Beach*—Westbrook Pegler [of obscure origin, at first (by 1906) referring to ruffians and gang members]

highbrow 1 *n about 1902* An intellectual; person of notable education and culture; =DOUBLE-DOME, EGGHEAD: *One does not need to be a "highbrow" to read this book*—A G Kennedy **2** *adj* (also **high-browed**) *by 1891*: . . . *all them high-brow sermons*—Sinclair Lewis **3** *adj* Impractical; idealistic; unrealistic: . . . *another silly highbrow scheme* [said to have been coined by the humorist Will Irwin, as a back-formation fr *high-browed*]

high camp *n phr by 1954* Art work, theater performance, items of decoration, etc, that are so outrageously old-fashioned, so blatantly injurious to good contemporary taste, as to assume a sort of special value by their very egregiousness: *His way of lisping Shirley Temple lyrics is high camp* ***See*** CAMP

high-class *adj by 1864* Of first quality; esp of refined and elevated culture; =CLASSY: *a high-class show/a very high-class guy*

high cockalorum *n phr by 1881* A pompous, self-important person [ultimately fr a mid–1800s British schoolboys' game in which boys leap-frogged on top of one another, and the highest was called *high cockalorum,* suggesting a triumphant, crowing rooster]

high cotton *See* SHIT IN HIGH COTTON

higher-up *n by 1916* One of the persons in charge; a member of the upper echelon; =BIG SHOT •Most often in the plural: *A conference with the Higher-ups and Tammany Hall*—E Lavine/ *She always fought with the movie higher-ups*—Associated Press

highfalutin or **highfalutin'** or **hi-foluting** *adj by 1848* Overblown and pretentious; bombastic; stilted: . . . *take one with ideas less "highfalutin"'*—Scribner's/ . . . *stilted, overstrained, and as the Americans would say, hi-foluting*—Anthony Trollope [origin unknown; originally a gerund, seemingly based on a verb *high falute,* suggesting a humorous alteration of *flute;* perhaps fr a blend of *highflown* with some other element; perhaps fr Dutch *verlooten,* "stilted"]

high five 1 *n phr* A way of greeting or congratulating by slapping raised palms together •Chiefly used by and adopted from athletes, who themselves adopted the style from black colleagues: . . . *handshaking, even a few high-fives from the younger alums*—Rutland Herald **2** *v phr* =GIVE someone FIVE: . . . *Roberts is not the kind to engage in trash-talking or high-fiving*—Milwaukee Journal

highflag *v cabdrivers by 1970s* To convey a customer and collect the fare without using the meter; =ARM IT, RIDE THE ARM

high flyer *n phr by 1690* A very adventuresome and impressive person

high gear *See* IN HIGH GEAR, SHIFT INTO HIGH GEAR

high-hat 1 *n* (also **high-hatter**) *by about 1925* A person who behaves arrogantly and snobbishly; a putatively important person: *a lot of lowbrows pretending to be intellectual high-hats*—P Marks **2** *v by about 1925:* *How come you're high-hatting me, old buddy?* **3** *adj* (also **high-hatty**) *by about 1925: his high-hat posturings/ high-hatty pretentions* **4** *n* jazz musicians *by about 1932* A set of two cymbals, the upper of which is crashed on the lower by operating a foot-pedal; =SOCK

high-hatter *n by 1930* =HIGH-HAT

high heaven *See* STINK TO HIGH HEAVEN, TO HELL

high horse *See* GET OFF one's HIGH HORSE, GET ON one's HIGH HORSE

highjack *See* HIJACK

high-jinks *See* HI-JINKS

high muckety-muck *n phr* (Variations: **muck-a-muck** or **muckie-muck** or **mucky-muck** or **monkey-monk** may replace **muckety-muck**) Western *by 1856* A very important person, esp a pompous one; =BIG SHOT, HIGHER-UP: *I'm gonna meet a couple of the high muckety-mucks at the university tomorrow* [fr Chinook jargon *hiu muck-amuck,* "plenty to eat," transferred to the important individual who has plenty to eat; the *monkey-monk* variant is a case of folk etymology]

high-octane *adj by 1980s* Forceful; energetic; =HIGH-POWERED, PUNCHY: *A pompous classical overture gives way to a jittery, high-octane beat and frayed guitar riffs*—Time [fr the *octane* rating of motor fuels, from about 1930]

a **high old time** *n phr by 1834* A very pleasant occasion; =a BALL: *They had them a high old time on that trip*

high on someone or something **1** *adj phr by 1942* Very favorable towards; enthusiastic about: *I'm not as high on Wallace Stevens as I once was* **2** *adj phr by 1932* Intoxicated by; exhilarated with: *He says he's high on Jesus/ She gets high on wine and pot*

high on the hog *See* EAT HIGH ON THE HOG

high pitch *n phr* pitchmen *by 1930s* A hawker's street display set up on a box, wagon, or car: *40,000 men standing on the sidewalks...with high pitch*—J T Flynn

highpockets *n by 1912* A tall person, esp a man or boy

high-powered *adj by 1930s* Forceful; energetic; =HIGH-OCTANE, PUNCHY: *George is a real high-powered salesman* [used of cars by 1903]

high puller *n phr* gambling *by 1980s* Frequent and inveterate players at slot machines: *...the "high pullers" at the dollar machines*—Elmore Leonard [modeled on *high roller*]

high-rent *adj phr by 1970s* Chic and expensive; =CLASSY, HIGH-CLASS: *...with some kind of high-rent bitch from a women's magazine*—Dan Jenkins

high rider *n phr by 1980s* A car or truck that has been fitted with very large tires: *A high rider is a normal sized car, camper, or pickup that is mounted on oversized, "monster" tires*—Lee K Russell

high roller 1 *n phr* gambling *by 1902* A person who gambles for high stakes: *...for the high rollers in the mysterious world of wheat and corn futures*—Time **2** *n phr by 1881* =BIG-TIME SPENDER [gambling sense probably influenced by the idea of *rolling* the dice in craps]

the **high sign** *n phr by 1903* A signal to an associate, esp one given inconspicuously by gesture: *...waiting by prearrangement in the dark blue Lincoln Town Car, and George gave him the high sign*—San Francisco

hightail or **hightail it** cowboys *by 1925* **1** *v* or *v phr* To leave quickly; =LIGHT OUT: *She took one look and hightailed for home* **2** *v* or *v phr* To speed; rush; =HIGHBALL: *We better hightail it if we want to make the first show*

high tech or **hitech** *by 1972* **1** *n phr* or *n* Advanced technology: *From OPEC to High Tech*—Washington Post **2** *adj: ...takes us through three high tech happenings, a computer room, a radiology unit, an intensive care unit*—Village Voice/ *...a chic, high-tech version of The Creature from the Black Lagoon*—New York Magazine/ *a downsized, hitech, ultraswoopy model next year*—Car and Driver **3** *n phr* or *n* An object or design, usu of synthetic or fabricated material, designed to look like an example of high technology: *This chair is high tech*

high ticket *See* BIG TICKET

high-toned or **high-tony** *adj by 1888* Very refined and genteel; aloof and superior; =TONY: *Look at the high-tony bum*—Toots Shor [the term had meant "excellent, superior" by 1855]

high-up *n by 1868* An important person; =BIG SHOT, HIGHER-UP ●Most often plural: *Rico got in touch with some of the high-ups*

high water *See* COME HELL OR HIGH WATER

high waters *n phr* (also **high water pants** or **high waders** or **flood pants**) Trousers that are shorter than current fashion dictates, esp that end above the ankles: *Look at his high waters!*—Delcastle Slang Dictionary [fr the notion that the trousers have been chosen or rolled up for walking through *high water*]

highway robbery *n phr by 1886* An unconscionable price asked by a merchant: *Highway robbery is no name for it*—The Lantern/ *100 bucks? That's highway robbery!*

high, wide, and handsome *by 1907* **1** *adv phr* Easily, triumphally, and masterfully; =WITH FLYING COLORS **2** *adj phr: a high-wide-and-handsome win*

high-wire act *n phr by 1970s* A perilous policy, procedure, etc: *Nixon remained skeptical of Kissinger's high-wire act in Vietnam*—New Republic [fr *high wire,* an 1880s term for the funambulist's high tight rope]

◁**high yellow (or yaller)**▷ *n phr* black *by 1923* A light-skinned black person, esp an attractive young woman: *I mean high-yellow girls*—Langston Hughes/ *...took some little high-yaller girl in the closet one day*—Claude Brown

hijack or **highjack 1** *v by 1923* To rob, esp to

rob a vehicle of its load: *Hijack the truck*—E Lavine **2** *v by 1960s* To commandeer a public vehicle, esp an airliner, for some extortionary or political purpose: *Two more planes were hijacked to Cuba last week* **3** *v by 1980s* To appropriate unjustifiably; annex; steal: *The 40th anniversary of D-day was hijacked by Reagan's PR men*—Nation/ *When Petersen, the director, is stuck, he just hijacks an idea or two from Hitchcock to get him to the next point in the picture*—New Yorker/ *How was the Bharatiya Janata Party able to hijack Hinduism?*—New Republic [origin uncertain; said to be fr the command *High, Jack,* telling a robbery victim to raise his hands; an early–1900s hobo sense, "traveling hold-up man," is attested, which suggests that the source may be railroad and hobo slang; said to have originated in the California wheat fields and among the Wobblies; the name of the 1875 skit *High Jack the Heeler* is interesting but probably coincidental]
See ball the jack

hi-jinks or **high-jinks** *n by 1861* Boisterous fun; uninhibited jollification; pranks and capers: *...the dashing hi-jinks of the Katzenjammer Kids*—Ebony/ *...the out-of-towner...cuts the hi-jinks here*—Hal Boyle [fr the name of a dice game played for drinks, found from 1690]

hike 1 *v by 1867* To raise; increase; boost: *They won't hike our wages this year* **2** *n*: *The government got a big tax hike* **3** *v* =HIKE A CHECK [fr mid–1800s term *hike up,* "go or raise up," related to *hoick* of the same meaning, both probably fr the basic dialectal sense "go, go about"]

hike a check *v phr underworld by 1940s* To illegally raise the amount shown on a check; =KITE: *Did you hike those checks?*—Associated Press

hiker 1 *n line repairers by 1940s* A telephone or electric line repairer **2** *n hoboes by about 1925* A town marshal

hill *n baseball by 1908* The pitcher's mound
See DRIVE someone OVER THE HILL, GO OVER THE HILL, OVER THE HILL

Hill *See* SAM HILL

the Hill *by 1970s* **1** *n phr* Capitol Hill in Washington, DC: *They're all over the Hill, and can frighten members*—Fortune **2** *n phr* The US Congress: *Republicans or Democrats on the Hill*—Playboy

hillbilly 1 *n by 1900* A southern Appalachian hill dweller •Regarded as offensive by some **2** *adj*: *hillbilly music/ hillbilly crafts* **3** *n* A country bumpkin **4** *adj* Countrified; unsophisticated; =HICK: *This ain't no hillbilly joint. We got some class here*—J Cannon

a hill of beans *See* NOT GIVE A DAMN

hi-lo *n by 1970s* A forklift vehicle

himself *See* HIS NIBS

hincty (Variations: **hinkty** or **hinktyass** or **hankty**) *black by 1924* **1** *adj* Snobbish; aloof; =STUCK-UP: *hinkty motherfucker*—George Warren/ *...like you do a hankty heifer in the bed and make her like it*—Village Voice **2** *adj* Pompous; overbearing

3 *adj* =HINKY **4** *n* A white person; =OFAY [origin unknown]

hind end *n phr by 1915* The buttocks; =ASS, HEINIE

hinders or **hind legs** *n* or *n phr by 1940s* The legs •Often in phrases connoting resistance or defiance: *He stood up on his short little hinders and got himself a lawyer*—F Brown/ *The Packer defense rose on its hind legs again*—Milwaukee Journal

hind hook *n phr railroad by 1940s* A train's brake operator

hindsight *See* TWENTY-TWENTY HINDSIGHT

◁**hind tit**▷ *See* SUCK HIND TIT

hinge *n by 1930s* A look or glance; =GANDER
See GET A HINGE AT

hinky *adj by 1970s* Suspicious; curious: *Something hinky is going down*—TV show *The Renegades*/ *...driver of the pimpmobile looks hinky*—Joseph Wambaugh [origin unknown]
See DOODAD

hip 1 *adj black by 1904* =HEP **2** *adj by 1951* Being and/or emulating a hipster, hippy, beatnik, etc; =COOL, FAR OUT: *"I'm hip"...means...Cool*—Herbert Gold/ *...to be hip is to be "disaffiliated"*—Eugene Burdick **3** *v by 1932* To make aware; inform: *...educating the masses of America, hipping black people to the need to work together*—Bobby Seale [fr *hep*]
See SHOOT FROM THE HIP

hip cat or **hipcat** *beat & cool talk by 1944* **1** *n phr* or *n* =HEPCAT **2** *n phr* or *n* =HIPSTER

hip chick *n phr beat & cool talk by 1944* An alert and up-to-date young woman, esp in matters of popular culture, music, etc; =FLYCHICK

hipe *See* HYPE

hip gee[1] *n phr by 1940s* A man who can be trusted; a well-informed man [fr *hip* plus *gee,* "guy"]

hip gee[2] *n phr by 1950s* Money well used or bet; =the SMART MONEY [*gee* meaning "grand," hence a large amount of money]

hip-hop or **Hip Hop** *1980s* **1** *n* or *n phr* =RAP SONG **2** *n* or *n phr* =BREAK DANCING **3** *adj* or *adj phr* Of or pertaining to contemporary black urban youth culture **4** *n* or *n phr* The activities that are emblematic of contemporary black urban youth culture: *What is "hip-hop"? That phrase includes such activities as break dancing, rap music, and graffiti art*—New York Daily News/ *Most of them...are young Hispanics, more connected to Hip Hop than High culture*—New York Daily News [echoic, said to have originated with a New York disk jockey called Hollywood]

hip-huggers *n by middle 1960s* Pants having a low waistline, usu below the navel

hipped *See* UNHEP

hipped on *adj phr by 1920* Enthusiastic about; obsessed with: *I ain't hipped on her, sort of hypnotized by her, anymore*—Sinclair Lewis/ *I'm hipped on Freud and all that*—F Scott Fitzgerald [ultimately fr *hip* or *the hip,* "hypochondria," hence obsession]

hipper-dipper *by 1930s* **1** *adj* Excellent; superb; =SUPER-DUPER: *...a hipper-dipper display*—John

Kieran **2** *n prizefighting* A prizefight where the result is prearranged: *...the last fight being a "hipper-dipper"*—Philadelphia Record [the boxing sense perhaps related to *dipper,* "small swimming pool," in which one goes up to the *hips;* modeled on *take a dive* and *tank*]

hippie or **hippy** *1960s counterculture* **1** *n* One of a group of usu young persons who reject the values of conventional society and withdraw into drifting, communes, etc, espouse peace and universal love, typically wear long hair and beards, and use marijuana or psychedelic drugs; =BEAT, BEATNIK **2** *modifier*: *Saigon has acquired an elaborate hippie culture*—New Yorker [fr *hip*]

hippie-dippy *adj by 1990s* Hippie; of the 1960s hippie culture: *None of that hippie-dippy, war-protesting, free-loving, drug-chugging stuff for him*—Los Angeles Times [fr *hippie* + *dippy,* "weird, crazy"]

hippiedom or **hipdom** *1960s counterculture* **1** *n* Hippies collectively **2** *n* The hippie movement, world, culture, etc

hippings *n hoboes by 1940s* Anything used as bedding under the hips

hippity-clippity *adj by 1980s* Rapidly; at once: *I ran hippity-clippity down the siding*—Richard Whittingham

hip-pocket bookie *n phr gambling by 1960s* A betting agent who has only a few large bettors as clients

hippy *adj by 1919* Having wide and prominent hips **See** HIPPIE

hip shooter *n phr by 1904* A person inclined to act and respond impulsively and aggressively; =HOTHEAD [fr the habit of shooting as one draws from the holster, rather than taking aim]

hipster *by 1941* **1** *n* =HEPCAT, HEPSTER, HIP CAT **2** *n* =BEATNIK, HIPPIE

hip to *adj phr by 1920s* Aware of; knowledgeable and informed of: *Why don't you get hip to yourself?*—P Dunning & G Abbott/ *They were hip to me too and just waiting for the right moment*—Macleans

hired gun **1** *n phr by 1958* A professional killer; =HIT MAN **2** *modifier*: *...elaborated on his "hired gun" reference in an interview*—Washingtonian **3** *n phr by 1970s* An employee or agent, esp in some aggressive capacity: *We're not just "hired guns" out to raise a few bucks for the place*—Washingtonian/ *Keith is not going anywhere as a hired gun for one year*—Wisconsin State Journal

his nibs or **himself** *n phr by 1812* A very important person; supervisor or chief, esp one who insists on deferential treatment; =the MAN: *Take it in to his nibs yourself/ Has himself seen this?* [origin unknown]

hissing match *n phr 1990s* A disagreeable confrontation; spat: *...refused to get into a hissing match with former union director Marvin Miller*—Milwaukee Journal [probably a euphemism for *pissing contest*]

hissy fit *n phr 1990s* A noisy fit of anger; =CATFIT, CONNIPTION FIT, DUCK-FIT: *...the vile, know-nothing hissy fit loose in our land*—New York Times/ *...and write that memo before the boss has a hissy fit that registers on the Richter scale*—Milwaukee Journal Sentinel [*hissy* in the same sense is found by the 1940s as a Southwestern usage]

hist or **histed** *adj* =HISTORY: *Hist! Goodbye!*—UCLA Slang

history *adj 1980s students* Finished; done with; =HIST: *It's been history, I'd say, four months*—Scott Turow

hit **1** *n by 1815* Anything very successful and popular, esp a show, book, etc: *He wrote two Broadway hits* **2** *v*: *I think this show will hit* **3** *modifier*: *a hit musical/ a hit song* **4** *n by 1666* A stroke of good fortune at gambling, on the stock market, etc; =LUCKY BREAK: *...a big hit on the commodities exchange* **5** *v*: *She hit real big at the track last week* **6** *n underworld by 1970* A premeditated murder or organized-crime execution, esp one contracted for with a professional killer: *"He can order a hit," a police officer says*—New York Times/ *There is no set price for a hit*—Playboy **7** *v by 1955* =RUB OUT, WHACK: *The mob figure got hit last night in his car* **8** *n by 1668* A stroke of severe criticism; attack; assault: *...the club hired the...firm to counter the hits it was taking in the media*—New York Times/ *Zavala took a double hit because her husband...also refused to cross the picket line*—Los Angeles Times **9** *n narcotics by 1951* A dose, inhalation, etc, of narcotics; =FIX ●*Hit the pipe,* "smoke opium," is found by 1886: *The current price of cocaine was about $10 a "hit"*—H M Schmeck/ *He held a long hit in his mouth, then expelled it slowly*—Cameron Crowe **10** *n by 1950s* A drink; swallow; =SNORT: *...a tall glass of thick, slightly green fluid, and said, "Take a big hit off this, Felix"*—Harry Crews **11** *n 1960s narcotics* A pleasurable sensation; =RUSH: *People jockeyed for position around the foyer to get a little hit of darshan*—Ramparts **12** *n 1960s narcotics* A cigarette into which heroin has been introduced: *GIs sit smoking the mixed tobacco-and-heroin cigarettes called "hits"*—Iver Peterson **13** *n narcotics by 1970s* A dilution or "cutting" of a narcotic: *You give it a full hit, you already double your price*—Ed McBain **14** *v by 1888* To reach; visit; attain: *His new book...hit the best-seller list*—Philadelphia Bulletin/ *...The market hit a new high today* **15** *n by 1980s* Each separate occasion; each time; =POP, SHOT: *You should be on a tour, where you can get 2,000 people a hit* **16** *v students by 1950s* To pass an examination, esp with a good grade; =ACE: *I really hit the eco final* **17** *v by 1891* To cause a strong reaction; have a strong impact: *The injection hit the heart like a runaway locomotive*—Nelson Algren **18** *n medical by 1980s* An unwanted, unwarranted, hospital admission: *The ambulance people asked which hospital would take the hit* **19** *n computer by 1990s* A match between a

search item and an item in a data base: *That year, Popcorn racked up 58 Nexis hits*—New Republic **20 n** *by* 1990s An interpretation; idea; =TAKE: *...my hit on this is he heard about Brian*—Sue Grafton
See BANJO HIT, CLOUT FOR THE CIRCUIT, MAKE A HIT, PINCH HIT, SMASH

hit someone **1 v phr** (also **hit** someone **up**) *by* 1882 To solicit money, a favor, etc: *I'll hit Joe for ten bucks/ She hit him up for a big raise* **2 v phr** *by* 1891 To have a strong impact on; distress; overwhelm: *Kennedy's death hit me pretty hard* **3 v phr** *by* 1960s To present; reveal: *I wanna hit you with a very profitable idea* **4 v phr** cardplaying *by* 1940s To deal another card **5 v phr** *by* 1940s To serve another drink: *He signaled the bartender. "Hit us again"*—J E Grove **6 v phr** 1940s narcotics To administer a narcotic, esp by injection

hit a brick wall *v phr by* 1960s To encounter an insuperable obstacle: *Negotiations seem to have hit a brick wall this week* [*brick wall* in this sense is found by 1886]

hit by a Mack truck *adj phr by* 1940s Astonished; stunned; bowled over: *What's up? You look like you been hit by a Mack truck* [*Mack* is a trademark make of *truck*]

hitch 1 n *by* 1748 A problem or difficulty; delaying defect; =CATCH, GLITCH: *Everything went off without a hitch* **2 n** armed forces *by* 1835 A period of enlistment: *42 percent have "reupped" for another hitch*—New York Times **3 n** *by* 1923 A ride, esp one gotten by hitchhiking; =LIFT **4 v** *by* 1940s =HITCHHIKE **5 v** *by* 1844 To marry; be married

hitch a ride (or **a lift**) *v phr by* 1940s To get a free ride, esp by hitchhiking

hitched *adj by* 1857 Married

hitchhike *v by* 1923 To get free rides by standing beside a road and signaling drivers; =HITCH, THUMB

hitchy *adj by* 1872 Nervous; twitchy; jumpy

hitfest *n by* 1950s A baseball game with many hits and runs; =SLUGFEST: *...pathetic parodies of the old hitfests*—Robert Ruark

hit for (or **out for**) *v phr by* 1905 To start for or toward; =HEAD FOR: *One time we hit for KC*—James M Cain

hit for the circuit *See* CLOUT FOR THE CIRCUIT

hit for the cycle *v phr* baseball *by* 1960s To hit personally a single, a double, a triple, and a home run all in one game

hit it *v phr* 1930s jazz musicians To begin playing music; attack

hit it a lick *v phr by* 1940s To hit something very hard

hit it big *v phr by* 1940s To succeed splendidly: *Pitchers who hit it big as soon as they escaped from the Trappers' pocket-sized park*—Scott Turow

hit it off *by* 1780 **1 v phr** To like one another: *The pair hit it off right from the start*—Billy Rose **2 v phr** To work well together **3 v phr** To succeed with others: *He hit it off with the whole class*

hit someone **like a ton of bricks** *v phr by* 1920s To have a great sudden impact on, esp by sur-

prise: *Then the answer hit me like a ton of bricks* [based on the mid–1800s term *fall upon someone like a thousand bricks*]

hit list *n phr by* 1976 A putative or actual list of persons who are to be removed from office, punished, murdered, etc: *EPA officials maintained a "hit list" of employees*—New York Times

hit man *n phr by* 1970 An assassin, esp a professional killer; =HIRED GUN, MECHANIC: *Like every professional hit man I've ever known, I've always used a gun*—Playboy/ *...a State Police detective, posing as a hired killer "flown in as a hit man"*—New York Times

hit on someone **1 v phr** *by* 1970s To ask for a favor; solicit; pester; =HIT someone: *Everyone's been hitting on her lately to help save something or other*—Lawrence Sanders **2 v phr** 1980s students To make advances to; =PROPOSITION: *What if musclebound jocks hit on her all day long?*—Cameron Crowe/ *I fired my last studio manager for hitting on one of the girls*—Susan Peters/ *It's amazing that a man of my own age would be hitting on me*—San Francisco

hit on all six (or **on six**) *v phr by* 1916 To do very well; operate smoothly and effectively: *He's sure hittin' on all six*—Literary Digest [fr the smooth operation of a six-cylinder engine]

hit pay dirt *v phr by* 1850s To find what one is looking for or needs; garner profit; =STRIKE OIL: *I didn't hit pay dirt until near the bottom of the second box*—J Evans

hit (or **slap**) **skins** *v phr* black teenagers *by* 1990s To do the sex act; =SCREW: *She'd be like, "Did you ever hit skins?"*—New York Times

hit squad *n phr by* 1976 A group of assassins, severe critics, "hatchet men," etc: *André Breton commanded and organized literary hit squads, practicing intimidation in the name of Surrealist dogma*—New Republic

hitter *n by* 1970 =HIT MAN
See CREAM-PUFF HITTER, NO-HITTER, SWITCH-HITTER

hit the books *v phr* students *by* 1920s To study, esp in an intensive way

hit the bottle (or **the booze** or **the sauce**) *v phr* 1889 To drink liquor, esp rapidly and to excess; =BOOZE: *If he keeps hitting the bottle they'll have to dry him out*

hit the bricks *by* 1931 **1 v phr** To go out and start walking on a street or sidewalk **2 v phr** prison To be released from prison: *He'll hit the bricks tomorrow, having been paroled* **3 v phr** To go out on strike: *...teachers...won't be as quick to hit the bricks*—New York Times **4 v phr** hoboes To live in the streets because one is homeless

hit the bullseye *v phr by* 1940s =HIT THE NAIL ON THE HEAD

hit (or **kiss**) **the canvas** *v phr* entry form by 1922, variant by 1919 To be knocked down in a fight

hit the ceiling (or **roof**) *v phr by* 1914 To become violently angry; =BLOW UP: *...and, according* *to one source, hit the ceiling with rage*—New York Times

hit the deck 1 *v phr* by 1940s To be knocked down **2** *v phr* by 1940s To get down on the ground quickly; duck down flat: *When I heard that airplane shoot, I hit the deck* **3** *v phr* WWI armed forces To get out of bed; rouse oneself

hit the dirt (or **gravel) 1** *v phr* baseball To slide into a base **2** *v phr* hoboes (also **hit the grit**) To jump off a train, esp a moving one **3** *v phr* To get down and take cover, esp from gunfire

hit the Dixie highway *v phr* baseball by 1960s To be dismissed from a team: *Five major league managers have already been told to hit the Dixie Highway this season*—Milwaukee Journal [the *Dixie Highway* is US Route 1, going South; when the term was first used, the only teams in the South were minor league]

hit the dope *v phr* by 1920s To use narcotics [*hit the pipe*, "smoke opium," is found by 1886]

hit the fan *v phr* To cause or experience extensive trouble and chaos: *A month later it all hit the fan*—Esquire/ *Meanwhile the mailings had hit the fan*—New York Magazine **See** the SHIT HITS THE FAN

hit the ground running *v phr* Marine Corps by 1950s To make a quick and eager start; not waste time: *Boot camp legislation hits the ground running*—Newark Star-Ledger/*The new Administration should hit the ground running*—Time

hit the hay (or **the sack) ** *v phr* first form by 1912, second by 1943 To go to bed; =CRASH, FLOP, SACK OUT

hit the hump *v phr* by 1940s To escape from prison, desert from military service, etc; =GO OVER THE HILL

hit the jackpot *v phr* by 1944 To win or succeed spectacularly; get the most available: *I hit the jackpot with this new job*

hit the nail on the head *v phr* by 1574 To be exactly right; say precisely the most accurate thing: *His few quiet remarks hit the nail on the head*

hit (or **push) the panic button** *v phr* Air Force by early 1950s To give way to alarm and terror; declare a general emergency: *He hit the panic button when he saw the month's figures/ a move characterized by many as pushing the panic button*—Inside Sports

hit the pipe *v phr* by 1886 To smoke a narcotic, esp opium

hit the road by 1873 **1** *v phr* To leave; get on one's way: *We better hit the road, it's a long way home* **2** *interj* An irritated request that one leave: *Hit the road, Jack, and don't you come back no more*—Percy Mayfield

hit the rods **See** RIDE THE RODS

hit the sauce **See** HIT THE BOTTLE

hit the silk *v phr* WWII paratroops & Army Air Forces To make a parachute jump

hit the skids by 1918 **1** *v phr* To fail; =GO BELLY UP: *But if HBJ hit the skids, could the building*

ensure the integrity of retirees' pensions?—Newsweek **2** *v phr* To show a precipitous decline; fall disastrously: *Home sales are down and sales of large cars have hit the skids*—Time/ *Eventually they had hit the skids*—A J Liebling [*skids* are various planks or rollers used to move heavy objects]

hit the spot *v phr* by 1940s To be very satisfying, esp to some appetitive need: *That cup of coffee really hit the spot*

hit the ties *v phr* by 1907 To travel by walking along railroad tracks: *It was up to me to hit the ties to Wadsworth*—Jack London

hit the wall *v phr* sports by middle 1980s To come to one's limit of energy and capability, esp in a marathon or other arduous race: *...I hit a wall of shock and pain*—New York Times/ *Sampras Slams Into the Wall...*—Los Angeles Times/ *...if he wears down and "hits the wall" as Avent did last season*—Milwaukee Journal

hit up *v phr* narcotics by 1940s To inject a narcotic; =SHOOT UP [an earlier related sense, "to drink to excess," found by 1900]

hit someone **up** *v phr* by 1917 To request something, esp a loan; importune: *...I'm sure your only salvation is to hit up your rents*—Sassy

hit upside one's **face (**or **head) ** **See** GO UPSIDE one's FACE

hit someone **where** one **lives** *v phr* by 1860 To deliver a very painful blow, insult, insinuation, etc; have a strong impact: *The Third Movement hits me right where I live*

hive *v* West Point by about 1935 To understand

hivey *adj* West Point by about 1935 Sharp-witted; perceptive

hiya **See** HI

hizzoner *n* The mayor: *Hizzoner, looking game but a tad uncertain...*—Milwaukee Journal

◄**HMFIC**► (pronounced as separate letters) *n* Persian Gulf War Army Commanding officer; officer in charge: *HMFIC can be rendered politely as "head military person in charge"...*—Retired Officer's Magazine [fr *head motherfucker in charge*]

◁**HN**▷ (pronounced as separate letters) *n* black by 1970s A black person who adopts or reflects white society's values; =OREO, UNCLE TOM [fr *house nigger*, a reference to the slavery-era distinction between slaves who worked in the plantation house and those who worked in the fields]

◄**HNIC**► (pronounced as separate letters) *n* by 1990s A black person sponsored as a leader by white people: *There's a part of West that wants to be the next HNIC; it's not just white folks making him a hero*—Time [fr *head nigger in charge*; perhaps influenced by *HN*]

ho[1] or **hoe** *n* by 1960s A prostitute or other disreputable woman: *...like many of her sisters of the streets (she calls them "hos")*—New York Times/ *The bar was a hangout for players and hos*—Time [fr Southern or black pronunciation of *whore*]

ho[2] **See** the HEAVE-HO, RIGHT-O

hoagie *n by 1967* =HERO SANDWICH

hoary-eyed or **orie-eyed** or **orry-eyed** *adj by 1940s* Drunk: *He would be orry-eyed before night-fall*—H Allen Smith [origin uncertain; perhaps fr *hoary*, "frosty, hence icy, glazed," with later dropping of the *h* to avoid *whore*]

hobnob with someone *v phr by 1866* To be on friendly terms with someone [fr earlier *hob and nob*, "to drink familiarly together," suggesting two men calling each other by nicknames]

hobo *n by 1889* A person who wanders from place to place, typically by riding on freight trains, and who may occasionally work but more often cadges sustenance •The hobo is sometimes distinguished from bums and tramps by the fact that he works [origin unknown; perhaps fr the call "Ho, boy," used on late-1800s Western railroads by mail carriers, then altered and transferred to vagrants; perhaps putative *hoe-boy*, a migrant farm worker in the West, who became a *hobo* after the harvest season]

hock[1] **1** *v by 1878* To pawn: *I hocked my diamond ring*—John O'Hara **2** *n* The state of pawn: *I've got to get my typewriter out of hock* [apparently fr Dutch *hok*, "prison"; the earliest US use was *in hock*, "in prison"; perhaps also fr the underworld phrase *in hock*, "caught," fr the notion that one is taken "by the heels," or *hocks*]
See IN HOCK

hock[2] or **hok** *v by 1940s* To pester; nag; chatter incessantly: *...whom my mother kept hocking my father to promote to director*—Budd Schulberg/ *Stop already hocking us to be good*—Philip Roth/ *...with her hokking and her kvetching*—National Lampoon [fr Yiddish *hok* in the idiom *hok a chynik*, "knock a teapot," meaning "chatter constantly, talk foolishness," perhaps because such talking resembled the loud whacking of a pot]

hockable *adj by 1878* Pawnable: *The "ice" was always hockable*—Abel Green

◁**hockey** or **hocky**▷ *by 1923* **1** *n* Feces; excrement; =SHIT: *Great big blooping hunks of dog hockey*—William Styron/ *But it's a lot of horse hockey, on both sides*—John J Farmer **2** *n* Empty and pretentious nonsense; =BULLSHIT: *...any of that hocky about being a white man*—Calder Willingham **3** *n* Semen; =CUM [origin unknown; perhaps fr a variant pronunciation of the *hokum*, *hokey*, *hocus-pocus* cluster, suggested by some spellings, and hence originally "falsehood, pretentious exaggeration, etc," whence "bullshit," whence "shit"; the first term is probably earlier; related *hawky*, "filthy; defiling," and "go to the toilet" are found by 1902]

hockshop *n by 1871* A pawnshop

hocktooey *interj by 1990s* An imitation of hawking and spitting, taken as a sign of machismo: *...masculine in a cigar-smoking, crotch-grabbing, hocktooey! way*—New York Newsday

hocus-pocus *n by 1694* Sleight-of-hand; trickery; =MONKEY BUSINESS [originally a term for a juggler, and probably derived fr a juggler's spoken formula imitat-ing the Church Latin phrase *hoc est corpus*, "this is the body"]

◀**hod**▶ *n cabdrivers fr 1920s* A black passenger; =SCUTTLE [probably because a *hod* is a container for coal]

ho-dad (also **hodad** or **ho dad** or **ho-daddy**) *1960s surfers* **1** *n* A person who claims knowledge and authority he or she does not possess; =BLOWHARD, WISE GUY: *..."ho-daddy" (intruding wise guy)*—Life **2** *n* A nonparticipant who seeks the company of athletes and performers; hanger-on: *The true surfer is scornful of the "ho-daddies"*—Time **3** *n* An obnoxious and contemptible person; =JERK, PHONY, WIMP [origin unknown; perhaps fr a surfer's cry *Ho, dad!*]

hoe *See* A HARD ROW TO HOE

hoedown 1 *n* (also **hoe-dig**) *by 1807* A country square dance; **2** *n by 1950s* A lively and noisy argument **3** *n by 1950s* A riotous fight; brawl: *Mr Clinton has put more energy into such old-politics hoedowns...*—New York Times **4** *n 1950s street gangs* A fight between gangs; =RUMBLE: *Anything can start a hoedown*—H Lee

hog 1 *n railroad & hoboes by about 1915* A locomotive, originally a heavy freight engine **2** *n railroad & hoboes by about 1915* =HOGGER **3** *n 1960s motorcyclists* A Harley-Davidson™ motorcycle: *Harley, perhaps best known for its big-engine "hogs"*—Time/ *...a hundred Hell's Angels on their Hogs*—Esquire **4** *n black by 1950s* A large car, esp a Cadillac™: *"I got a Hog...a Cadillac"*—Clarence Cooper **5** *v by 1884* To take or eat everything available, for oneself; claim and seize all: *...appeared simultaneously with ET and suffered as the little fungiform geek hogged the box office*—Washington Post/ *...Mara had deliberately hogged the spotlight*—Michael Grant **6** *n* (also **the hog**) *1960s narcotics* PCP or a similar addictive drug: *...climbed on stage and threw thousands of caps of "the hog"...into the crowd*—Esquire **7** *n 1980s students* A sexually appealing male; =ADONIS, HUNK [railroad and hobo sense fr the fact that large locomotives consumed a great deal of coal]
See EAT HIGH ON THE HOG, ON THE HOG, ROOT HOG OR DIE, WHOLE HOG

Hogan's brickyard *n phr early 1900s baseball* A rough baseball diamond; =SANDLOT

hogger *n* (also **hog** or **hog-head** or **hogshead** or **hog-jockey**) *railroad & hoboes by about 1915* A railroad engineer; =GRUNT

hog (or pig) heaven (or paradise) *n phr by 1940s* A place of total bliss, esp for the gluttonous; =FAT CITY: *For the sports junkie, this is Mecca. For the gambler, it is hog heaven*—Philadelphia Journal/ *It doesn't put Wisconsin in pig heaven...*—Milwaukee Journal/ *Jesse Helms must be in pig paradise*—Time

hog (or hog's) leg *n phr cowboys by 1940s* A pistol, esp a large one: *...his hog's leg looking like a fire plug against his ribs*—Raymond Chandler/ *He got his hog leg out and came over*—R V Winslow/ *...a .45-caliber hogleg out of his coat* pocket—Stephen King [probably fr the curved shape of the weapon]

hogs *n* 1940s bop talk Dollars, esp only a few dollars

◁**hog's-breath**▷ *n* by 1990s A despicable person; disgusting wretch; =CRUD, GEEK, SCUMSUCKER: *The unshaven hog's-breath of a transient thief...stands out like a green-glowing extraterrestrial...*—Milwaukee Journal

hogster *n* by 1980s An owner, admirer, etc, of Harley-Davidson™ motorcycles, which are called "hogs": *The unlikely collection of hogsters arrived in Milwaukee last month...*—Milwaukee Journal

hogwash or **hogslop** *n* first form by 1882, second by 1990s Empty and pretentious talk; nonsense; =BALONEY, BULLSHIT: *It's hogwash. There's no such thing...*—Los Angeles Times/ *...Bradley is too soft, too fragile. Hogslop*—Milwaukee Journal [fr the house waste fed to hogs; the date of *hogslop* is probably earlier; *hogslosh* in the same sense is found by the 1940s]

hog-wild *See* GO HOG-WILD

ho-hum 1 *interj* by 1924 An expression of boredom **2** *adj* by 1960s Unexciting; mediocre; dull: *...ho-hum sex and the dregs of countless six-packs*—R J Battaglia/ *After a ho-hum second quarter, stocks have perked up*—Time **3** *v* by 1960s To be bored with; be indifferent to: *On the other hand, we shouldn't ho-hum the situation*—Paul Engeler **4** *n* by 1960s Boring matter; dull tripe

hoist 1 *v* underworld fr 1708 To rob; steal; =HEIST: *The stall...distracts the sales force while the hoister hoists*—R L Woods **2** *n*: *Crooks...speak of a job of hold-up as a "hoist"*—J Wilstach **3** *v* by 1940s To drink some beer or liquor: *Let's stop at Harry's and hoist a few*

hoisted *adj* underworld fr 1708 Stolen: *...among the hoisted articles recently*—C Adams

hoister *n* by 1847 A shoplifter

hoity-toity 1 *adj* by 1668 Snobbishly exclusive; haughty; uppish; =SNOOTY: *...in the hoity-toitiest of Fifth Avenue shops*—S Dawson/ *Will he go all hoity-toity on us?*—Washington Post **2** *interj* (also **highty-tighty**) by 1695: *Highty tighty! What a debil of a rage...*—Bentley's Miscellany [fr earlier *highty-tighty*, "peremptory, quarrelsome," perhaps related to the notion of being *high* in the sense of "superior"]

hoke 1 *n* by 1921 =HOKUM **2** *v* (also **hoke up**) by 1935 To make fun of; treat insincerely; overplay: *...but don't hoke it too hard, Beatrice*—Saturday Review/ *It's all right to hoke the incident, but not the theme*—Associated Press/ *Halaby hoked up a special ceremony*—R G Sherrill

hoked-up *adj* by 1940s False; dishonestly confected; =PHONY: *...hoked-up or fictionalized biographies*—Jay Jacobs/ *...a zest for hoked-up violence*—Playboy

hokey *adj* by 1927 False and meretricious; very dubious; =PHONY: *...hokey confections that public taste ought to repudiate*—Albert Maltz/ *The radio is jammed with hokey copies of US and European rock and roll songs*—New Republic

hokey-dokey *See* OKEY-DOKE

hokey-pokey or **hoky-poky 1** *n* by 1884 Cheap ice cream and sweets made primarily to attract children **2** *modifier*: *...candy bars on the hokey-pokey counter*—Westbrook Pegler **3** *n* by 1840s False and meretricious material; deception; =HOKUM: *...too much of..."Hollywood hokey-pokey"*—Philadelphia Bulletin **4** *adj*: *It might sound weird or hokey pokey, but it works*—Milwaukee Journal [fr an earlier sense of *hokey-pokey*, "cheat, swindle," ultimately fr *hocus-pocus*; the ice cream is said to have been named in Italian, *O, che poco*, a child's cry at the paucity of the portion]

the **hokey-pokey** *n phr* by 1960s A simple, informal sort of circle dance: *...people across the globe will join hands, form huge human circles...The hokey-pokey*—Philadelphia

hokum by 1917 **1** *n* Pretentious nonsense; inane trash; =BUNK: *...more hokum from the Department of State* **2** *n* theater A trick, gag, routine, etc, sure to please a gullible public: *There is some hokum in "King Penguin"*—New York Times **3** *n* =HOKEY-POKEY [origin unknown; perhaps a blend of *hocus-pocus* and *bunkum*]

hokus *n* narcotics by about 1930 Any narcotic

hold 1930s narcotics **1** *v* To have narcotics for sale **2** *v* To have narcotics in one's possession *See* ON HOLD

◁**hold** someone **by the nuts**▷ *v phr* by 1940s =HAVE someone BY THE BALLS: *Would you rather have the cops holding you by the nuts?*—Elmore Leonard

hold someone's **coat** *v phr* by 1940s To stand back and let others fight: *A lot of people are willing to hold our coats and let those 200,000 soldiers in the Persian Gulf go to war*—TV show Washington Week in Review

holder *See* ROACH CLIP

hold everything *sentence* by 1924 Stop what you are doing; let's stop right now: *Hold everything, here's new evidence!*

hold someone's **feet to the fire** *v phr* by 1980s To subject someone to strong and painful persuasion; use maximum pressure: *...helping hold the President's feet to the fire*—New York Times

hold one's **horses** *v phr* by 1844 To be patient; stop importuning; =HOLD one's WATER • Often an irritated command: *Wait a second, Bradley, hold your horses*—Stan Cutler

holding 1 *adj* by 1940s Wealthy: *Respect...for people who are "holding"*—A J Liebling **2** *adj* 1930s narcotics Possessing narcotics

holding pattern *See* IN A HOLDING PATTERN

hold onto your hat *v phr* by 1970s To get ready for trouble; take precautions; =BUCKLE YOUR SEAT BELTS: *Hold onto your hats for the craziest ride through the truth that's ever been done on television*—New York Times

holdout 1 *n* by 1911 A person, esp a professional athlete, who refuses to sign a contract until the salary is raised **2** *n* by 1940s A person who refuses to agree to something: *...coerce reluctant hold-outs into "kicking in"*—E Lavine **3** *n* gambling by 1894 A playing card sneakily kept from the deck by the dealer

hold out 1 *v phr* by 1907 To refuse to do something until one gets certain conditions: *The union held out for a 10 percent raise* **2** *v phr* by 1593 To endure; persist: *This tire won't hold out another mile*

holds *See* NO HOLDS BARRED

hold the phone *v phr* by 1930s To wait a minute; delay; =HOLD EVERYTHING ●Often a request for respite and thinking space: *...body jerked back in a kind of W C Fields double take. "Hold the phone,"* I said—Newsweek

holdup 1 *n* by 1851 A robbery, esp the armed robbery of a person, bank, store, etc; =STICKUP: *Give us no nonsense. This is a holdup*—Philadelphia Bulletin **2** *modifier*: *...the full-fledged hold-up business*—E Lavine **3** *n* The demanding of exorbitant prices, wages, etc: *That was no sale, it was a holdup* **4** *n* by 1843 A delay; stoppage; cause of delay: *...a brief holdup in our magnificent progress/ What's the holdup?*

hold up 1 *v phr* by 1851 To rob, esp at gunpoint: *They were holding an old man up at the corner* **2** *v phr* To extort or demand higher prices, wages, etc: *That shop held me up!* **3** *v phr* by 1843 To delay; cause a delay or stoppage: *The strike held up our flight for six days* **4** *v phr* by 1602 To point to; single out: *Is this the one you held up as such a great example?*

hold one's **water** *v phr* To be patient; stop importuning; =HOLD one's HORSES ●Often an irritated command: *I know that, fuckface. Just hold your water*—Paul Sann/ *Hold your water, Mr McAllister!*—Carsten Stroud

hole 1 *n* by 1616 Any nasty or unpleasant place; =DUMP, JOINT: *The restaurant turned out to be a loathsome little hole* ◁**2**▷ *n* by 1340 The vulva or anus

See ACE IN THE HOLE, BIG HOLE, BROWN, BUNGHOLE, CORNHOLE, IN A HOLE, IN THE HOLE, the NINETEENTH HOLE, NOT KNOW one's ASS FROM one's ELBOW, NOT KNOW someone or something FROM A HOLE IN THE GROUND, RATHOLE

the **hole 1** *n* prison by 1535 Solitary confinement or a cell used for it; =BING: *I was slapped with the organizing label and put in the "hole"*—Huey P Newton/ *I was thrown in the hole for it*—Eldridge Cleaver **2** *n phr* underworld by 1950s A subway

See ACE IN THE HOLE, IN THE HOLE

hole card *n phr* poker by 1908 A card dealt face down in stud poker

the **hole in the doughnut** *n phr* by 1990s What is lacking; an obstacle of omission: *The hole in the doughnut...in helping the homeless is substance-abuse treatment*—National Public Radio

hole in the ground *See* NOT KNOW one's ASS FROM one's ELBOW, NOT KNOW someone or something FROM A HOLE IN THE GROUND

a **hole in the (**or one's**) head** *See* HAVE A HOLE IN one's HEAD, NEED someone or something LIKE A HOLE IN THE HEAD

hole in the wall *n phr* by 1822 A small and usu unpretentious dwelling, shop, etc: *Nothing fancy, just a hole in the wall on Park Lane*

hole out *v phr* golf by 1867 To finish a hole by putting the ball in the cup

hole up (or **in) by** 1875 **1** *v phr* To hide; take refuge; =HIDE OUT: *Long Island, where...he might hole up for a day or two*—NY Confidential **2** *v phr* To stay for a time; lodge; =CRASH: *...thinking about holing up for the night*—Sinclair Lewis

-holic *See* -AHOLIC

holiday Navy by 1935 **1** *n* A small area missed while painting **2** *n* A forgotten or neglected task

holler 1 *v* by 1699 To shout **2** *v* by 1940s To inform; =SING, SQUEAL: *You think he wouldn't holler if they turned the heat on him?*—W R Burnett **3** *v* by 1904 To complain; =BITCH: *What's he hollering about now?* **4** *n* (also **holler-song**) by 1930s A Southern black folk song with spoken or shouted words, a precursor of the blues song: *You find hollers in many of Leadbelly's recordings and songs*—Stephen Longstreet

hollow *See* BEAT ALL HOLLOW

Hollywood corporal *n phr* WWII Army An acting corporal

holy cats *interj* (Variations: **cow** or **gee** or **mackerel** or **Moses** or **schmutz** or **shit** or **smoke** or **sox** may replace **cats**) entry form by 1900, cow by 1940s, gee by 1895, mackerel by 1903, Moses by 1900, schmutz by 1990s, shit by 1940s, smoke by 1889, sox by 1909 An exclamation of surprise, wonder, dismay, admiration, etc: *All he could manage to say upon seeing the nude blonde was "holy cow!"*—B Price/ *...holy shit, the police*—Richard Fariña/ *And I think holy shit, this could be a Hitler*—Village Voice/ *Holy schmuts, that would be the pride and glory*—Milwaukee Journal Sentinel [euphemisms for *holy Christ*]

holy hell *n phr* by 1940s Vehement rebuke; severe punishment; =HELL, MERRY HELL: *I caught holy hell when the thing broke*

See CATCH HELL, GIVE someone HELL

Holy Joe 1 *n phr* by 1874 A clergyman; chaplain: *...needs twelve Holy Joes to get him past them Pearly Gates*—J Evans **2** *n phr* by 1889 A sanctimonious, pietistic person: *In the east they're all holy Joes and teach in Sunday schools*—Stephen Longstreet **3** *modifier*: *...these Holy Joe voices*—J D Salinger

holy terror *n phr* by 1887 A troublesome, energetic, and aggressive person: *He's a holy terror around the house*

hombre (HAHM bray, AHM bray) by 1846 **1** *n* A Hispanic person **2** *n* A man; fellow; =GUY: *a real cool hombre* [fr Spanish, "man"]

See WISE GUY

home *See* BRING HOME THE BACON, HOME BOY, MONEY

FROM HOME, NOBODY HOME, NOTHING TO WRITE HOME ABOUT

home boy or **homeboy** 1 *n phr* or *n* black by 1940s A person from one's hometown 2 *n phr* black by 1940s A simpleton; naive bumpkin: *Youse just a home boy, Jelly. Don't try to follow me—* Zora Neale Hurston 3 *n phr* or *n* (also **home**) black by 1970s A close friend, or someone accepted like a friend •Used also by Chicanos in Los Angeles, some of whom apparently dispute the black origin: *Home boy, them brothers is taking care of business!*—Eldridge Cleaver/ *...he stormed outside with two homeboys: one called "Gino," and Kevin Baca, 17, whom he'd met a month before*—MM 4 *n phr* or *n* by 1980s A black male; =BRO, BLOOD, HOME SLICE: *...black faces...fucking home boys with skin the color of bunker oil and the threat coming off them in waves*—Carsten Stroud 5 *n phr* or *n* college students by 1970s An easygoing, unpretentious person

homebuddy *n* black by 1980s =HOME BOY: *Don't want what you can't have, or what your homebuddy has...*—Milwaukee Journal

home-court advantage *n phr* sports by 1970s The psychological and other favorable elements that come from being in familiar surroundings, with a sympathetic audience, etc: *Yojimbo is less than sympathetic here (it's clear who has the home-court advantage)*—Village Voice

home free *adj phr* Successfully arrived or concluded; at or assured of one's goal; out of trouble: *I hear things been a little tight. Well, you home free now*—Harry Crews/ *I think you're home free. If you'll forgive me for saying this...*—New York Times

home guard *n* circus & hoboes by early 1900s A resident of a place; native; =LOCAL

home in on someone or something *v phr* by 1950s To approach purposefully; go straight toward: *I saw these two guys homing in on her at the bar* [fr the movement of an airplane, ship, missile, etc, that follows a radio beam or other signal to approach a destination or target; *home* is found by 1920; perhaps reinforced by the behavior of a *homing* pigeon]

home plate *n phr* Air Force by 1950s The landing field, aircraft carrier, etc, where an aircraft is based [fr the baseball sense, regarded as a goal and safe haven] **See** GET TO FIRST BASE

homer 1 *n* baseball by 1891 A home run; =CIRCUIT BLOW 2 *v*: *Kaline homered in the sixth* 3 *n* sports by 1980s An official who favors the home team: *A lot of refs get reputations as "homers", which means...they give all the tough calls to the home team*—Whitey Herzog

Homes or **Holmes** *n* black & students by middle 1980s Close friend; =HOME BOY •Most often as a term of address: *Put a charge on his head, Homes*— Robert B Parker/ *What's happenin', Holmes?*— Los Angeles Times [second form fr *Sherlock Holmes* by homophony]

homeskillet *n* students by 1990s A good friend; =HOME BOY: *...a "homeskillet," a good friend*

homeslice or **home slice** 1 *n* or *n phr* 1980s teenagers A good friend; one's best friend; =BUDDY, HOME BOY: *That's my homeslice out on the court* 2 *n* or *n phr* black by 1990s A black person; =BROTHER, BLOOD: *And "home slice" is a black person*—Baltimore Sun

homework **See** DO one's HOMEWORK

homie 1 *n* (also **homey**) black by 1970s A close friend or a fellow townsperson; =BUDDY, HOME BOY: *...is expecting more than her homies to support her*—Amsterdam News/ *Then get yourself a job, homie*—Sassy 2 *modifier*: *...and "homie love," the camaraderie among members of his gang*—Los Angeles Times 3 *n* by 1940s A male homosexual; =FAGGOT, QUEER

◁**homo**▷ 1 *n* by 1929 A homosexual man or woman: *I knew nothing about "homos" at that time*—H K Fink 2 *modifier*: *homo slang/ a homo bar*

◁**homorock**▷ *modifier* by 1990s Featuring rock music played by homosexuals: *...Pansy Division, the San Francisco homorock band that celebrates queer horniness...*—LA Weekly

hon (HUHN) *n* by 1906 Sweetheart; honey •Used in direct address: *What's that, hon?*

the Hon (HAHN) *n phr* by 1873 The Honorable: *I want you to meet the Hon P Jensen, our mayor*

honcho (HAHN choh) 1 *n* by 1947 The person in charge; chief; =BIG ENCHILADA, BOSS: *...better known as the honcho of Scientific Anglers, Inc*—Sports Afield 2 *v*: *...honcho a staff*—Lawrence Sanders [fr Japanese *hancho*, "squad leader"; *han*, "small group," and *cho*, "leader"]

hondo *adj* 1980s students Excellent; desirable; =CHILL, COOL: *...froody and hondo also get high marks at some schools*—Webster K Nolan/ *If a guy is better than cool..."he's really hondo"*—Levi's 501 Report [fr Spanish, "deep"]

honest-to-God *adj* by 1916 Genuine; real; =NO SHIT: *What is certain is the damage of an honest-to-God fight to the finish involving the debt ceiling*— John J Farmer

honey 1 *n* by 1880 One's sweetheart, beloved, spouse, etc 2 *n* by 1880 Any pleasant, decent person; =PUSSY CAT, SWEETIE 3 *n* by 1888 A person or thing that is remarkable, wonderful, superior, etc; =DILLY, HUMDINGER: *Ain't this a honey of a show?*

honey barge *n phr* Navy by 1950s A garbage scow

honey bucket *n phr* Canadian by 1931 A chamber pot or other container for excrement

honeycakes **See** BABYCAKES

◀**honey-fuck**▶ by 1950s 1 *v* To do the sex act in a romantic, idyllic way 2 *v* (also **honey-fuggle**) To do the sex act with a very young girl: *...mysterious pains and penalties attached to "honeyfuggling"*—Philip Wylie [fr the early–19th-century *honeyfuggle*, of obscure origin, which meant "cheat, swindle"; the present sense must come fr assimilation with *fuck*]

honey man *n phr* by 1940s A kept man; pimp

honeymoon burger *n phr* lunch counter by

1980s A sandwich made with only bread and lettuce [fr *lettuce alone*, heard as *let us alone*]

◁**honeypot**▷ *n by 1719* The vulva or vagina

honey wagon 1 *n phr by about 1915* A manure wagon or manure spreader **2** *n phr WWII Army* A garbage truck

honk 1 *v by 1895* To sound the horn of a car **2** *v by 1960s* To make a sexual, esp a homosexual, advance by handling or pressing a man's genitals: *He's making a move to honk you, just grab his hand*—Joseph Wambaugh **3** *v by 1990s* To vomit; =BARF, HURL

honked or **honked off** *adj by 1980s* Angry; =PISSED OFF: *I'm going to have people really honked at me no matter what I do*—comic strip "Sally Forth"/ *...a honked-off Torcivia wrote to Wineke*—Milwaukee Journal
See HONK OFF

honker *n by 1940s* The nose; =SCHNOZZ: *...and she has a honker as big as yours*—Mike Royko

honking *adj 1980s students* Large; =HUMONGOUS: *We have a honking textbook in my management class...*—UCLA Slang

honk off *v phr by 1980s* To anger; =PISS OFF: *...he honked off some natives, who thought the Veep was being more than a tad condescending*—Milwaukee Journal/ *While that's honking off some bird lovers...*—Milwaukee Journal [origin unknown; perhaps fr the annoyance shown by *honking* the horn of a car]

◀**honky** or **honkie**▶ **1** *n black by 1967* A white person; =GRAY, OFAY **2** *modifier*: *No talkin' or we'll bust your honky heads*—Time [fr *hunky¹*, as often normally pronounced in black English]

honky-tonk *by 1894* **1** *n* A cheap, usu disreputable saloon and gambling place; =JOINT: *...rode to my honky-tonk on a bus*—Philip Wylie **2** *v*: *...his honky-tonking ended, naturally, at Filly's, the urban cowboy saloon*—Philadelphia Journal **3** *modifier*: *...wisely emphasizes Brown's down-and-dirty honkytonkin' side...*—Dan DeLuca **4** *n* A cheap, small-town theater: *...playin' the sticks...the honky-tonks*—Gypsy Rose Lee **5** *n* A brothel **6** *modifier*: *the honky-tonk district* [origin unknown]

hon-yock or **hon-yocker 1** *n by about 1875* A rustic person; farmer; =HICK: *speaking as a purebred hon-yock out of the Middle West*—H Allen Smith **2** *adj*: *...a kind of dumb hon-yock accent* [origin unknown]

hoo-boy *interj by about 1950* An exclamation of surprise, consternation, amazement, etc: *Hoo-boy! The cheapest way to have your family tree traced...*—comic strip "The Small Society" [perhaps a blend of *hoo ha* with *oh boy*; popularized by Walt Kelly's comic strip "Pogo"]

hooch¹ *n by 1897* Liquor; strong drink; =BOOZE: *...and the bottles of hooch, and the free food on the job*—New York Times/ *...or guzzles hooch that he hides inside a big toy duck*—Time [fr the liquor made by the *Hoochinoo* Indians of Alaska]

hooch² or **hootch** *Korean & Vietnam War armed forces* **1** *n* A Korean house, room, shack, etc: *...giggle timidly and plead: "Come on to my hooch"*—Time **2** *n* A Vietnamese village hut **3** *n* An American barracks, esp a Quonset-style barracks in Vietnam [fr Japanese *uchi*, "house"]

hooch³ *See* the HOOTCHIE-COOTCHIE

hood¹ (HŌŌD, HŎŎD) **1** *n by 1930* A hoodlum: *...those St Louis hoods*—American Mercury/ *the procession of hoods...on the witness stand*—Bruce Bliven **2** *modifier*: *...has been in the hood hierarchy for decades*—New York Post

hood² or **'hood** *n by middle 1980s* Neighborhood •Esp associated with black Los Angeles neighborhoods: *...who know the defendant from the 'hood. It's part of the job*—Scott Turow

hoodge *v by 1980s* To take someone's nipple between thumb and forefinger and squeeze it painfully; =RAT

hoodlum *n by 1868* A petty criminal; a street tough [origin unknown, although many suggestions have been made; the term appears to have originated in San Francisco]

hoodoo *n by 1882* A person or thing that brings bad luck; jinx: *A mascot...and a hoodoo, meaning one who brings ill fortune, are terms invented in the theater...*—Brander Matthews [said to be an alteration of *voodoo*]

hoody *adj by 1970s* Hoodlumish; like a hood: *...imitating a hoody Tony Curtis*—Time

hooey *n by 1889* Nonsense; foolishness; =BALONEY: *...lip-smacking imps of mawk and hooey write with us what they will*—W H Auden/ *...a dangerous mix of electioneering hooey and religious claptrap*—Time [origin unknown]

hoof 1 *n by 1598* A foot: *Take your goddam hoof the hell off my fender*—J Evans **2** *v by 1888* To walk; =HOOF IT: *I better hoof over to the garage* **3** *v by 1921* To dance: *She's hoofing in that show about cats*
See SHAKE A WICKED CALF

hoofer *n by 1921* A dancer, esp a professional dancer in nightclubs, musical plays, etc: *The hoofers and the chorines of a cabaret*—John Mason Brown

hoof-in-mouth disease *n phr by 1960s* A tendency to speech before thought; the habit of opening one's "big fat mouth": *Among the most notable practitioners of hoof-in-mouth disease in the past year...*—Milwaukee Journal [fr *put one's foot in it* with a pun on the *hoof-and-mouth disease* of farm animals, so designated by 1887]

hoof it 1 *v phr by 1728* To walk: *...get off the bus...and hoof it home*—Philadelphia **2** *v phr by middle 1920s* To dance: *...then hoofed it a bit herself with old friend Gene Kelly*—Newsweek

hoo-ha¹ *interj by 1930s* An exclamation of astonishment, admiration, envy, scorn, deflation, etc: *Does she gossip? Hoo-ha*—Leo Rosten [fr Yiddish]

hoo-ha² *by 1931* **1** *n* Disturbance; brouhaha; uproar: *What was I supposed to do in the middle of* such a hoo-ha?—Leo Rosten/ ...in case you're wondering what all the hoo-ha is about—A Sainer **2** **n** A noisy celebration; a raucous fete: *But Northampton, Mass, held a week-long hoo-ha for its favorite son*—Newsweek [perhaps influenced by *hoo-ha¹*; first attested in early 1900s British armed forces as "an argument; an artillery demonstration," and probably echoic-symbolic of a loud fuss, like *hoopla, to-do, brouhaha, foofaraw,* and *hooley*]

hoohaw **n** by 1970s An important person; =POOH-BAH: *...and the rest of the town's hoohaws*—William Brashler

hook 1 **n** *nautical* by 1940s An anchor **2** **n** *baseball* by 1910 A curveball **3** **n** *narcotics* by 1950s A hypodermic needle or bent pin used for injecting a narcotic **4** **n** *narcotics* by 1950s A narcotic, esp heroin **5** **v** by 1615 To steal, esp to shoplift: *Hooking merchandise from department stores requires no training*—Forum **6** **v** by 1940s To get; find: *Where can we hook a good meal around here?* **7** **v** by 1920s To arrest; stop and ticket: *My cab driver got hooked for speeding*—W R Burnett **8** **v** by 1764 To entice successfully; procure more or less against one's will: *They hooked me for the main speech* **9** **v** by 1940s To cheat; deceive •Most often in the passive voice: *He got hooked into paying the whole bill* **10** **n** by about 1915 A prostitute; =HOOKER: *Janie Ruth looked at the hook*—Dan Jenkins **11** **v** by 1959 To work as a prostitute; whore: *They stress the fact that they strip and don't hook*—Trans-Action/ *Carl supplemented their income by...hooking from the notorious bus bench*—San Francisco **12** **n** by about 1930 Something that strongly attracts, esp something catchy in the lyrics or music of a song: *...the musicians push a good hook, a high, ragged guitar line*—Rolling Stone/ *You just won't tell me much at a time about life. It's your hook*—Larry McMurtry/ *...There are no hooks, either, like the mechanical bull or dancing*—Milwaukee Journal **13** **v** by 1880s To drink, esp quickly at a gulp: *You pour a half-glass of Dewar's, hook it down and fan out the flames with a bottle of beer*—Albert Goldman **14** **n** *police* by 1980s A patron; a helpful connection: *Why have I been in a radio car for over twenty years? Because I don't have a hook...*—Michael Grant **15** **n** *students* by 1960s A grade of C

See BUTTONHOOK, HIND HOOK, MUD-HOOK, ON one's OWN HOOK, SHITHOOK, SKYHOOK

the **hook** **n** **phr** *football* by 1970s A violent football tackle in which the head of the ball-carrier is caught and held in the crook of the tackler's arm

See GET someone OFF THE HOOK, GET THE HOOK, GIVE someone THE HOOK, GO ON THE HOOK FOR something, LET someone OFF THE HOOK, OFF THE HOOK, ON THE HOOK, RING OFF THE HOOK

hook arm *baseball* by about 1930 **1** **n** **phr** A pitcher's throwing arm **2** **n** **phr** A left-handed pitcher; =SOUTHPAW

hooked 1 **adj** *narcotics* by 1925 Addicted to a narcotic: *Once a week wasn't being hooked*—Nelson Algren/ *I was the pusher who got you hooked*—W H Auden **2** **adj** by 1960s Captivated as if drug-addicted: *...a shock to discover my wife was hooked on needlepoint*—Good Housekeeping/ *...Once you buy his preposterous premise and get to know his pleasantly insane characters, you're hooked*—Playboy **3** **adj** by 1889 Married; =HITCHED

hooker 1 **n** by 1845 A prostitute: *...drunken sportswriters, hard-eyed hookers, wandering geeks and hustlers*—Hunter S Thompson/ *...the thirtyish ex-hooker was answering questions*—New York Post **2** **modifier**: *hooker district* **3** **n** by 1850s A person who recruits, enlists, snares, etc: *Hooker, a person who induces union members to act as spies*—Labor's Special Language **4** **n** by 1887 A drink of liquor; =SNORT: *It took a stiff hooker of whiskey...to thaw her*—Dashiell Hammett [first sense apparently fr the notion that such women are "*hookers* of men"]

hook someone **for** **v** **phr** by 1940s To cheat someone out of; take away, esp by shady means: *At Atlantic City they hooked him for everything he had*

hooking up **adj** **phr** *motorcyclists* by 1980s Daydreaming; pleasantly euphoric; =IN A ZONE

hook (or rook) someone **into** something **v** **phr** by 1940s To obligate or involve someone by force or trickery: *They hooked me into paying for everybody's lunch*/ *She got rooked into a very boring cocktail party*

hook it **v** **phr** by 1851 To depart hastily; run away: *Better hook it, Joan, the heat's arrived*

hook a **ride** **v** **phr** by 1940s To get or beg a ride: *Since Swede had no car, he either hooked rides from the waiters who did, or walked*—New Yorker [probably fr hobo *hook a rattler*, "get a ride on a freight train," where *hook* means "seize with the hands"]

hooks **n** by 1846 The hands

See BISCUIT HOOKS, FISHHOOKS, GET one's HOOKS INTO, LUNCH-HOOKS, MEATHOOKS, POTHOOKS

hookshop **n** by 1889 A brothel, esp a cheap one: *...one of the cheap hookshops*—American Mercury

◁**hookup**▷ **n** by 1990s A sex act; =SCREW, PIECE OF ASS

◁**hook up**▷ **v** **phr** by 1990s To do the sex act; =DO THE WILD THING, SCREW: *We didn't do nothing wrong, 'cause it's not illegal to hook up*—Milwaukee Journal

hook someone **up** **v** **phr** *police* by 1990s To arrest someone; =COLLAR, PINCH [probably fr the act of handcuffing someone]

hooky 1 **adj** by 1930s Captivating; very attractive; catchy: *It's also more insinuatingly hooky than Led Zep ever was*—Village Voice/ *After the first few merely hooky tracks...*—Macon Telegraph **2** **v** by 1950s =PLAY HOOKY

hooligan 1 **n** by 1898 A hoodlum; ruffian; street tough; =GOON: *Beat me up with your hooligans*—Ira Wolfert **2** **n** =GUN **3** **n** *circus* by 1940s The Wild West tent of a circus or show [origin unknown; perhaps fr a rowdy Irish family named *Hooligan* of Southwark, London, England; perhaps fr Irish *Uillegán*, a nickname for William, with confusion by Americans over vocative "Oh, Willie," spread term to all Irishmen; circus sense perhaps related to Western *hoolian* or *hooley-ann* or *hoolihan*, "throw a steer by leaping on its horns, bulldog"; all senses perhaps related to Irish *hooley*, "noisy party, carousal"]

Hooligan Navy *n phr* nautical by 1922 The US Coast Guard

hoop 1 *n* fr underworld by 1859 A finger ring: *...the old hoop on that finger*—Joseph Auslander **2** *n* basketball by 1930s The basketball net or basket; =BUCKET **3** *n* basketball by 1940s A basketball goal; =BUCKET: *He made six hoops last night* **4** *modifier* basketball by 1940s Having to do with basketball: *a hoop team/hoop scores* **5** *v* by 1980s To vomit; =BARF, OOPS: *One of the guys from Emergency Services hooped into his boots over it*— Carsten Stroud

See FLAT TIRE

hoop-a-doop or **hoop-de-doop** or **hoopty-do** *See* WHOOP-DE-DO

hooperdooper or **hooperdoo 1** *n* by 1940s A person or thing that is remarkable, wonderful, superior, etc; =HONEY, HUMDINGER: *Next Saturday's Barn Dance is going to be another hooper-doo*— "National Barn Dance" radio program **2** *modifier*: *...we got a hooperdoo quarter hour left*— "Uncle Walter's Doghouse" radio program **3** *n* by 1920s A very important person; =BIG SHOT: *He may be a Hooperdooper to Ann, but he's not to me*—K Brush

hoopla or **whoopla** by 1877 **1** *n* A joyous and boisterous clamor; =HOO-HA: *Is this hoopla for my birthday?* **2** *n* A noisy fuss; a commotion: *His arrival started a big hoopla* **3** *n* Advertising or promotion; =BALLYHOO, FLACK: *I say this is a lot of unnecessary hoopla*—Sports Afield [perhaps fr *hoop-la!*, the stagecoach driver's exhortation to his horses]

hoop-man or **hoopster** *n* basketball by 1940s A basketball player

hoops *See* JUMP THROUGH HOOPS

hoopty-doo *See* WHOOP-DE-DO

hoopy *n* used car sales by 1990s A hopelessly defective car; =LEMON [fr 1920s *hoopie*, "an old car, jalopy"]

hoosegow (HŌŌS gou) *n* by 1911 A jail [fr Mexican Spanish *juzgao*, "tribunal, court"]

hoosier 1 *n* by 1846 A rustic; =HICK **2** *n* 1930s prison A prison guard [origin uncertain; perhaps related to southern Appalachian *hoozer*, "anything unusually large, humdinger"]

Hoosier *n* by 1826 A native or resident of Indiana

hoot *n* A person; =COOT: *Milo O'Shea makes a canny old hoot of the judge*—People Weekly

a **hoot** *n* students by about 1915 Something or somebody very funny and pleasant: *Life is a hoot*— Village Voice/ *Wouldn't it be a hoot to wake up one morning and find yourself in Gracie Mansion?*—Denison Hatch

See NOT GIVE A DAMN

a **hoot and a holler** *n phr* by 1940s A short distance: *The gas station's just a hoot and a holler that way*

hootch *See* HOOCH

◁**hootchee** or **hotchee**▷ *n* Korean War armed forces The penis

the **hootchie-cootchie (** or **hootchy-kootchy** or **hooch)** by 1890 **1** *n* An erotic dance in which the woman rotates her hips, etc **2** *n* A woman who dances the hootchie-cootchie [origin unknown; "The Hootchy-Kootchy" was the name of a song associated with the dancer Little Egypt at the Chicago World's Fair of 1893, but the term is found several years earlier in the context of the minstrel show]

hootenanny (HŌŌT ən annee) **1** *n* by about 1925 Any unspecified or unspecifiable object; something one does not know the name of or does not wish to name; =GADGET, GIZMO: *He took a little hootenanny off the shelf and blew into it* **2** *n* by 1940s A folk music entertainment, esp one where the audience participates [one of many fanciful coinages for something unspecified; probably related to *hooter*, "anything trifling," found fr the mid–1800s, and to *hewgag*, "an indeterminate, unknown mythical creature," similarly found; the syllable *hoo-*, which is prominent in such coinages, probably represents the interrogative pronoun *who*; the folk music sense is based on this, in spite of a fanciful explanation by the singer Woody Guthrie, involving a loud singer called *Hootin' Annie*]

hooter *n* 1960s students A marijuana cigarette

◁**hooters**▷ *n* by 1980s A woman's breasts: *Hooters (a synonym, I learn, for knockers)...is a nice little play*—New York Magazine

hoot it up *v phr* by 1980s To laugh; cackle: *Goodman and Francie were hooting it up...*—Stan Cutler [*hoot*, "to laugh," is found by 1925]

hooty *adj* by 1980s Excellent; delightful; amusing: *Wasn't that a hooty rendition?*

hoover by 1980s **1** *v* To eat or drink up, esp greedily: *...instead of the moussaka and lamb that everyone else was hoovering*—Car and Driver ◁**2**▷ *v* To do fellatio or cunnilingus with or to; =EAT: *Will you hoover me immediately, before I pay any attention to you*—National Lampoon **3** *v* To elicit information from: *...a chance to hoover your brains*—George V Higgins [fr the *Hoover™* vacuum cleaner]

Hoover blanket *n phr* 1930s A newspaper used as a blanket: *...when newspapers were called "Hoover blankets" and were valued as much for their warmth as for their information*—Charles Panati

See HOOVERVILLE

Hooverville *n* 1930s A slum of makeshift shacks where unemployed workers live [fr President Herbert Hoover, who was president during the early years of the Great Depression]

hop[1] **1** *n* by 1731 A dance or dancing party: *We went to a hop*—James T Farrell **2** *n* by 1940s A hotel desk porter; =BELLHOP: *The hop was tall and*

thin—Raymond Chandler **3** *n* by 1909 A trip; stage of a journey; airplane flight: *a long hop to Singapore* **4** *v*: *They hopped over to Brussels* **5** *v* by 1909 To board: *to hop a plane*
See CARHOP, SEAGOING BELLHOP, SOCK HOP, TABLE-HOP

hop² **1** *n* narcotics by 1887 Opium: *So long as any smoker can obtain his hop*—The Lantern **2** *n* narcotics by 1898 Any narcotic; =DOPE: *A little hop or dope was slipped to an anxious prisoner*—E Lavine **3** *modifier*: *a hop fiend/ hop dream* [fr a shortening of Cantonese Chinese *nga pin,* pronounced HAH peen, "opium," literally "crow peelings," a Chinese folk etymology for English *opium;* in a subsequent US folk etymology this was changed to *hop* by assimilation with the plant used to make beer, with its suggestions of intoxication]

hope to die **See** CROSS MY HEART

hop fiend (or fighter) *n phr* narcotics by 1898 A drug addict; =HOPHEAD

hophead *n* narcotics by 1911 A drug addict; =HEAD: *...deprive a "hophead" of narcotics*—E Lavine/ *...the bench with its bittersweet words: winos, hopheads, the omnipresent graffiti*—New York Magazine

hop it *v phr* British by 1914 To leave; depart hastily; =BEAT IT

hopjoint *n* by 1887 An opium den

hop on the bandwagon **See** GET ON THE BANDWAGON

hopped up **1** *adj phr* narcotics by 1924 Intoxicated by narcotics; =GEEZED, GOWED UP: *The newer generation of "coked" or "hopped up" gunmen*—E Lavine **2** *adj phr* by 1923 Excited; highly stimulated: *What are you so hopped up about?* **3** *adj phr* by 1940s Made very exciting; deliberately intensified; =JAZZED UP: *...those hopped-up novels in which passion is named but not felt*—W G Rogers **4** *adj phr* by 1942 =SOUPED UP

hopper *n* baseball by 1940s A ground ball that hops along

the hopper *n phr* by 1950s The imagined place where proposed ideas, actions, etc, are placed; the place where proposed bills are filed for legislative consideration; =PIPELINE: *Can't look at it now, put it in the hopper* [fr the *hopper* device that feeds mills, etc, so called fr its shaking]

hopping mad *adj phr* by 1840 Very angry; livid; =STEAMED

hops *n* by 1930 Beer
See FULL OF BEANS

hopscotch *v* by 1970s To leap about; make long and diverse transits: *The show...hopscotches from Toronto and Boston to Lake Tahoe and Las Vegas*—R K Doan [fr the childrens' game]

hopup (HAHP up) *modifier* 1950s hot rodders Used to increase the power and speed of a car engine: *...a pretty good selection of hopup and speed equipment*—Village Voice

hop up **1** *v phr* narcotics by 1940s To administer narcotics: *He hopped himself up on heroin* **2** *v phr* horse-racing by 1940s To drug a horse for

speed; =DOPE: *...to hop up or slow down their horses*—A Hynd **3** *v phr* by 1940s To increase the speed and power of a car; =SOUP UP: *How to Hop Up Chevrolet and GMC Engines*—Floyd Clymer Motorbook

the horizontal bop *n phr* (Variations: **mambo** or **rhumba** may replace **bop**) by 1980s The sex act; copulation: *...while he did the horizontal bop with this girl...*—Carsten Stroud/ *Clark, you can do the horizontal rhumba with the entire Metnet cheerleading squad if you want...*—Time [*horizontal refreshment* in the same sense is found by 1893]

hork *v* by 1980s To vomit; =BARF, HURL: *It's enough to make you hork*—Carsten Stroud [echoic]

horn **1** *n* jazz musicians by 1940s Any wind instrument **2** *n* jazz musicians by about 1900 The trumpet ◁**3**▷ *n* by 1785 A penile erection; =HARD-ON: *I could have beat up five guys with the horn I had on*—George V Higgins **4** *n* by 1940s The telephone: *I get straight on the horn to Eckert...*—Sue Grafton
See GRUNT-HORN, LIKE SHIT THROUGH A TIN HORN, TIN HORN, TOOT one's OWN HORN

the horn *n phr* by 1940s The telephone: *Regional representatives got on the horn with the Louisville headquarters*—Philadelphia

horner *n* 1960s narcotics A person who has a tender, runny nose from inhaling cocaine

horn in *v phr* by 1912 To intrude; thrust oneself in; =BUTT IN: *Some wallie tried to horn in on our gang*—Philadelphia Bulletin

◁**horniness**▷ *n* by 1960s Sexual craving; lust and lustfulness; =HOT ROCKS: *...the lure of High Art to mask the visceral odors of simple human horniness*—New York Magazine

hornswoggle *v* by 1829 To cheat; swindle; dupe; =CON

◁**horny**▷ *adj* by 1889 Sexually excited and desirous; keenly amorous; lustful; =HOT ●Of recent years applied to women as well as men, despite being derived fr *horn,* "erect penis": *...his horny teen-age daughter*—Time/ *At first it eased my head and made me less horny*—Mike Aron/ *...a few scenes between a horny housewife and a guy in a Lone Ranger mask*—Playboy

the horrors *n phr* by 1860 Delirium tremens; =the SHAKES
See CHUCK HABIT

horse **1** *n* narcotics by 1940s Heroin; =SHIT: *They shoot horse in the john at the local high school*—Judith Crist/ *After about 1952, nobody called it horse any more*—Claude Brown **2** *n* narcotics by 1940s A hard-drug addict **3** *n* prison by 1960s A prison guard paid by inmates to smuggle letters and other contraband in and out ●See *mule,* "a person paid to carry smuggled drugs" **4** *n* truckers by 1940s A truck or a tractor **5** *n* police by 1960s An honest, hard-working police officer: *We know who the horses are around here, every cop in the department knows*—Providence Journal-Bulletin **6** *v* by 1927 To play and idle; =FOOL AROUND, HORSE

AROUND: *He wasn't just horsing now*—W Henry/ *...the Badgers lapse into their old ways, horsing up shots...*—Milwaukee Journal Sentinel ◁**7**▷ *v* To do the sex act with or to; =SCREW: *...there ain't goin' to be any immoral horsin' goin' on*—Stephen Longstreet **8** *v* by 1901 To fool; ridicule; trick [the sense "heroin" may have derived fr *shit*, "heroin," by way of *horseshit*, although the derivation might well have gone in the other direction; or perhaps the sense is based on the sobriquet of a Damon Runyon character *Harry the Horse* by way of the partial rhyme of *Harry* with *heroin*; seventh sense used of stallions and mares by 1420]

See DARK HORSE, DEAD HORSE, DOES A WOODEN HORSE HAVE A HICKORY DICK, ENOUGH TO CHOKE A HORSE, FROM THE HORSE'S MOUTH, GET ON one's HIGH HORSE, GET ON one's HORSE, IRON HORSE, ONE-HORSE, ONE-HORSE TOWN, SALT HORSE, WARHORSE

horse-and-buggy *adj* by 1927 Old-fashioned: *a horse-and-buggy leisureliness*

horse apple by 1940s **1** *n phr* A ball of horse feces **2** *n phr* Pretentious trash; =HORSESHIT: *...all that particular pile of horseapples boiled down to...*—Stephen King

horse around *v phr* by 1927 To joke and caper pleasurably; indulge in horseplay; =FOOL AROUND: *He was horsing around and he got caught*—Sue Grafton

◁**horse cock**▷ *n phr* WWII Navy Salami and other cold-cut sausages; =DONKEY DICK

horsefeathers by 1928 **1** *interj* An exclamation of disbelief, rejection, contempt, etc: *Mail comes urging that something be done to "rescue children from guns, daggers, and soldier worship." Horsefeathers!*—F Tripp **2** *n* Nonsense; =BALONEY, BUNK, HORSESHIT: *Don't give me that horsefeathers about your saintly momma*

horsehide *n* baseball by 1895 A baseball

the **horselaugh** *n phr* by 1738 A loud, nasty, and dismissive laugh at someone; =the MERRY HA-HA: *When I asked for more time I just got the horselaugh*

horse opera (or **opry**) **1** *n phr* by 1927 A cowboy movie; Western; =OATER **2** *n phr* circus by 1857 A circus show featuring horses

horse piano *n phr* circus by 1940s A steam calliope

horseplay *n* by 1589 Rough and boisterous playing; coarse physical merriment

horseplayer *n* by 1940s A person who bets on horse races

horse-race *n* by 1970s A serious contest; a hard-fought competition: *Suddenly what looked like a shoo-in turned into a real horse-race*

horse room (or **parlor**) *n phr* horse-racing by 1940s A bookmaker's establishment; =HANDBOOK

horses *n* gambling by 1940s A pair of dishonest dice, esp of mismatched dice that can produce only specific combinations: *Karnov explained the use of "horses"*—Associated Press

See HOLD one's HORSES

◁**horse's ass** (or **derriere**)▷ *n phr* A contemptible person; a persistent and obnoxious fool; =JERK: *I just regard the critic privately as being the biggest horse's ass in the western world*—Interview/ *If, however, he wanted to present himself in Texas as a real horse's ass, none of us would dispute him*—Joseph Heller/ *We just hope history will prove we were visionaries and not horses' derrieres*—Time

◁**horseshit**▷ by 1940s **1** *n* Nonsense; pretentious talk; bold and deceitful absurdities; =BALONEY, BULLSHIT: *You give me all that horseshit about the conditions here*—Calder Willingham **2** *n* Something of very poor quality; =DRECK, GARBAGE: *I'm not a cheerleader; if we're horseshit, I'll say so*—Whitey Herzog **3** *modifier* (also **horsebleep**) : *Superstar! What a horseshit idiot!*—Saul Bellow/ *...and the overall horsebleep pitching*—Wisconsin State Journal **4** *v*: *He was horseshitting about what a great sailor he is* **5** *interj* An exclamation of disbelief, disapproval, and contempt: *Horseshit! I'll never believe that* **6** *n* Trivialities; nonessentials; =CHICKENSHIT: *Don't bother me with that niminy-piminy horseshit*

◁**horseshit and gunsmoke**▷ *n phr* Army by 1970s Excitement and confusion; chaos [fr an evocation of a cavalry skirmish or a cowboys-and-Indians battle]

horse's mouth *See* FROM THE HORSE'S MOUTH

horse-trading *n* by 1940s Negotiating reciprocal concessions and benefits, esp of a political sort: *...vintage Washington politics as usual was not good enough anymore, that horse-trading, your bill for mine, was part of the old-time religion*—Milwaukee Journal

hos and trix (HOHZ *n* TRIX) *n phr* 1990s rap lyrics Women; females [idiosyncratic pronunciation and spelling of *whores and tricks*, where *trick* means "a prostitute's sexual transaction"]

hose ◁**1**▷ *v* by 1940s To do the sex act with or to; =BONK, JAZZ, SCREW: *...do you still want to hose her some more tonight?*—Harry Crews **2** *v* by 1940s To cheat; deceive; dupe; =SCREW, SHAFT: *He's not going out of his way to hose Nico*—Scott Turow/ *I got news for you. You got hosed*—Sue Grafton **3** *v* students by 1960s To turn down; reject; snub: *They're afraid of getting hosed*—New York Times **4** *n* 1980s students A sexually promiscuous woman [origin uncertain; perhaps fr a rare but found *hose*, "penis," whereupon the term would be analogous to *diddle, fuck, screw, shaft,* etc]

◀**hose job**▶ *n phr* by 1980s =BLOW JOB: *Looks like the hooker was doing a hose job on one of the truckers...*—Carsten Stroud

◁**hoser**▷ **1** *n* 1980s students A contemptible and obnoxious person, esp a man; =DORK, JERK: *Reagan is a hoser*—Drew University graffito **2** *n* (also **hosehead**) Canadian by 1980s A Canadian, esp a simple and durable northern type ●Originated by comedians Dave Thomas and Rick Moranis for the television skits called "The Great White North," where it was used by the mentally challenged Mackenzie brothers: *...unavailable to us hosers, but can be bought down south*—Westworld/ *...unlike their hoser cousins*—Toronto Star **3** *n* 1980s students A very sexually active male; =COCKSMAN: *Bill has slept with three girls this week. What a hoser!*—UCLA Slang

hosing *n* prison by 1931 Abuse, esp a beating with a hose

See TAKE A HOSING

hoss *n* by 1940s A strong and dependable person; superior person; strong man; =PISSER: *We didn't have a hoss in the bullpen until Mark Littell...started coming through for us*—Whitey Herzog

hostess *See* BANG THE HOSTESS

the **hostess with the mostest** *n phr* 1950s The most successful, lavish, and well-connected party-giving woman [fr a popular song fr the 1950s show *Call Me Madam*, "The Hostess with the Mostest on the Ball"]

hot 1 *adj* by 1868 Capable of high speed; moving very fast: *Hot crate, a fast plane*—A Ostrow **2** *adj* by 1960s Selling very rapidly and readily, hence very much in demand: *...paralleled the rise of the "hot" ticket*—New York Times/ *Xaviera Hollander...is the hottest thing in the business promoting her own work*—New York Magazine **3** *adj* by 1895 Performing extremely well; certain to win: *When you're hot you're hot/ The big fork-baller is real hot today, folks* **4** *adj* by 1225 Angry; furious; =PISSED OFF: *Don't get so hot about it, it was just a goof* **5** *adj* by 1911 Lively; vital; vibrant: *This is a hot town*—Ernest Hemingway/ *A "hot" magazine is one that's sizzling and bubbling with activity*—New York Herald Tribune **6** *adj* by about 1500 Sexually excited; afire with passion; lustful; =HORNY: *Hot faggot queens bump up against chilly Jewish matrons*—Albert Goldman/ *...the hottest little devil I ever met*—P Marks **7** *adj* by 1892 Pornographic; salacious; =DIRTY: *a real hot movie* **8** *adj* by 1971 Eager; =ANTSY: *Why so hot to get started?* **9** *adj* jazz musicians by about 1920 Exciting, rapid, strongly rhythmical, eliciting a visceral response: *The old jazz was mostly hot, then it was cool, and now even cool cats blow hot licks now and then* **10** *adj* underworld by 1925 Stolen, esp recently stolen; contraband: *Stolen bonds are "hot paper"*—H McLellan **11** *adj* underworld by 1931 Wanted by the police: *Where would a hot can of corn like Dillinger hide out*—A Hynd **12** *adj* by 1618 Dangerous; menacing; potentially disastrous: *Things were getting too hot*—Erle Stanley Gardner/ *It's so hot out there, man, I'm thinking about getting into another game*—New York Magazine **13** *adj* medical by 1990s Extremely infectious; having lethal potential: *The garbage bags held seven dead monkeys, and they were hot as hell. Presumably lethal*—New Yorker **14** *adj* by 1908 New, esp both brand-new and interesting: *a hot tip/ the hot news from upstairs* **15** *adj* by 1925 Having electrical potential; live; switched on: *Is this mike hot?/ Can I touch this wire, or is it hot?*

16 *adj* by 1942 Radioactive **17** *adj* 1980s teenagers Excellent and very good-looking: *...hot means...cool and extremely good-looking...*—New York Times [stolen goods sense may derive fr *hot*, "too well known," found by 1883]

See BLOW HOT AND COLD, NOT SO HOT, RED HOT, SQUAT HOT

a **hot** *n phr* jive talk by 1940s A meal: *He might have staked him to a hot*—Zora Neale Hurston

hot air by 1900 **1** *n phr* Nonsense; pretentious talk; bold and deceitful absurdities; =BALONEY, BULLSHIT: *The Jefferson family tree will never be blown down by any hot air from me*—H McHugh **2** *n phr* Pomposity and vanity; bombast: *The old fraud talks a lot of hot air*

See FULL OF HOT AIR

hot and bothered *adj phr* by 1921 Angry; fiercely indignant; =PISSED OFF, STEAMED UP: *Now don't get all hot and bothered just because he didn't call*

hot and cold *n phr* 1960s narcotics A mixture of heroin and cocaine; =H AND C, SPEEDBALL

See BLOW HOT AND COLD

◁**hot-and-cold running secretaries**▷ *n phr* by 1960s Secretaries stereotypically regarded as easy available sex objects: *...one of those glass cages on the fortieth floor of the IBM building, with hot-and-cold running secretaries and a bunch of megabuck partners...*—Scott Turow

hot as a three-dollar (or **two-dollar**) **pistol** *adj phr* by 1940s Very hot; red-hot: *The rumor is hot as a three-dollar pistol*

hot as blazes (or **hell**) *adj phr* first form by 1849, second by 1912 Very hot indeed

hot baby *n phr* students by about 1900 A wild and sexy young woman

hot bed or **hotbed 1** *n phr* or *n* by 1945 A bed used both day and night, by shifts of sleepers **2** *n* or *n phr* by 1768 A place that produces or is prominently rich in specified things: *College these days is a hotbed of sobriety*

hot button 1980s **1** *n phr* An inflammatory topic or area; a tender public nerve: *...the Horton spot hit a "hot button"*—Milwaukee Journal/ *...more low-income housing, a political hot button in town*—Madison Eagle **2** *modifier*: *...his subtle tilts to the center on hot-button issues such as abortion and gun control*—Milwaukee Journal [perhaps fr the earlier *hot button*, "the clitoris"; perhaps fr the button or key of a news teletype that sounded a bell to announce "hot" news]

hotcha by 1933 **1** *interj* (also **hotcha-cha** or **ha-cha-cha**) An expression of pleasure, approval, relish, etc **2** *adj* Sexually attractive and energetic: *He run Sternwood's hotcha daughter, the young one, off to Yuma*—Raymond Chandler [a derivation fr Yiddish *hotsa*, "hop!" has been suggested, based on the joyous repetition of the word as one bounces an infant on one's knees; perhaps fr *hot*; according to Gelett Burgess, *hot-cha-cha* was coined by the comedian Jimmy Durante, with whom one identifies the utterance]

hot corner 1 *n phr* by 1854 Any very dangerous and crucial place: *The North African front…is a "hot corner"*—Word Study **2** *n phr* baseball by 1889 Third base, esp as a fielding position [baseball sense reflects the time when most sluggers were right-handed hitters]

hot damn *interj* by 1936 An exclamation of pleasure, gratification, etc; =HOT DOG, HOT SHIT

hot diggety (or diggity) *interj* (Variations: **dog** or **doggety** or **damn** may be added; **ziggety** or **ziggity** may replace **diggety**) by 1924 =HOT DOG

hot dog 1 *interj* by 1906 An exclamation of delight, gratification, relish, etc; =HOT DAMN, HOT SHIT: *Did you have a good time? "Hot dog!"*—Philadelphia Bulletin **2** *n phr* by 1900 A frankfurter or a frankfurter sandwich **3** *modifier*: *a hot-dog stand/ embattled hot-dog vendor* **4** *n phr* by 1900 =HOT SHOT **5** *v phr* by early 1960s To perform in a brilliant, spectacular way, esp in order to seize the admiration of an audience; =GRANDSTAND, PLAY TO THE GRANDSTAND, SHOW OFF: *…a little careless against Bob Cousy's Royals, hot-dogging their passes and loosening their defenses*—New York Times **6** *n* by 1966: *Walter is one of the good guys, not a hot dog*—John Chancellor **7** *modifier*: *I don't appreciate that hot-dog garbage in my ball park*—Newsweek **8** *v phr* 1960s surfers To surf spectacularly: *Surfers may…"hot dog," do acrobatics*—National Geographic **9** *v phr* skiers by early 1970s To do hot-dog skiing

hot dogger *n phr* by early 1960s =GRANDSTANDER, HOT SHOT

hot-dog skiing *n phr* skiers by early 1970s Freestyle skiing that features somersaults, midair turns, ballet-like figures, and other feats rather than speed: *A whole new style of baroque skiing has developed. Known as "free-style," "exhibition," or "hot-dog" skiing*—Time

hotfoot 1 *v* (also **hotfoot it**) by 1838 To go fast; hurry: *The boys would hotfoot back…when they heard the mess call*—Louis Armstrong/ *Tell him to hotfoot it to the sheriff's office*—G Homes **2** *adv* by 1835 At once; immediately: *I'll walk hotfoot to the doctor's office* **3** *v* =GIVE someone A HOTFOOT

hot for by 1667 **1** *adj phr* Very desirous of; lusting for; wishing to possess: *She seemed hot for you*—Calder Willingham/ *…a young outfielder everyone in the Mets' organization was hot for*—Whitey Herzog **2** *adj phr* Very eager over; enthusiastic about: *He's real hot for the new promotion policy*

hothead by 1660 **1** *n* An irascible person; one quick to anger; **2** *n* A fanatical, emotional person; fiery militant

hot iron *n phr* 1950s hot rodders =HOT ROD

hot knife through butter *See* LIKE SHIT THROUGH A TIN HORN

hot line or **hotline** *n phr* or *n middle* 1950s An emergency telephone line or number: *Clearly, hot lines are no cure for the complex, overall problem of drug abuse*—Parent/ *…a community "hot line"* to head off gang wars—New York Times [popularized by the telephone line between the White House and the Kremlin]

hot-load *v* narcotics by 1980s To poison or otherwise treat a drug dose to render it fatal; give someone a "hot shot": *You hot-loaded the cocaine, knowing it would kill her*—Michael Grant

hot number (or item) by 1930s **1** *n phr* A very sexy man or woman; =HOT PANTS **2** *n phr* salespersons Something that is selling rapidly and well

hot one 1 *n phr* by 1913 A very funny story, piece of news, etc **2** *n phr* by 1919 A despised person; =ASSHOLE, JERK: *You are a hot one, you are*—Elmer Rice

hot pants 1 *n phr* by 1927 Strong sexual desire; lust; carnal craving: *His hot pants will get him in trouble* **2** *n phr* by 1966 A very passionate, lustful, and potentially promiscuous person: *Catherine the Great was apparently an imperial hot pants* **3** *n phr* 1960s Very brief women's shorts
See HAVE HOT PANTS

hot patootie *n phr* by 1928 A sexually attractive and sexy woman: *He calls the object of his affection a "hot patootie"*—Nation [fr hot potato, with a play on potato as used, like tomato, to mean "a person"]

hot (or hot-rock) pilot *n phr* WWII Air Forces A very skillful and daring aviator: *Gabreskie was a very hot pilot; …a vanishing breed of hot-rock pilot in an age of increasingly automated flight*—Time

hot poo by 1950s **1** *n phr* or *interj* =HOT SHIT **2** *n phr* (also **hot poop**) Recent and authoritative information; the latest word

hot potato *n phr* by 1846 Something embarrassing and troublesome; a tricky and sticky matter: *Everyone can see how the boss looks when he handles a hot potato*—Associated Press
See DROP someone or something LIKE A HOT POTATO

hot property *n phr* by 1958 Someone or something very valuable and marketable, esp an athlete, desirable executive, entertainer, etc: *Timmons and Co, knowing a hot property when it signs one up*—Washington Post

hot rock *n phr* =HOT SHOT

◁**hot rocks (or nuts)**▷ *n phr* Male sexual craving; powerful lust; =HORNINESS

hot rod 1 *n phr* hot rodders by 1945 A car specially modified and fitted with a powerful or rebuilt engine so as to be much faster than one of the same stock design; =A-BOMB, CAN, ROD: *Special Racing Cars and Hot Rods, a technical book…explains the principles of supercharging, carburetion, suspension, shock absorbers. A complete speed manual*—advertisement for Floyd Clymer books **2** *modifier*: *hot-rod manual/ hot-rod club* **3** *n phr* (also **hot rodder**) hot rodders by 1949 A driver or devotee of hot rods: *Right away he thinks he's a hot rod*—J A Maxwell

the hots by 1947 **1** *n phr* Strong liking; predilection: *I'd never got the deep undying hots for that rah rah collitch boy*—Hal Boyle/ *If a girl calls and asks me out, she's got the hots for me*—Milwaukee

Journal Sentinel **2 *n phr*** Lust; =HOT PANTS: *A bare-chested photograph of this guy can give 2,300 women the hots*—Philadelphia Journal

See HAVE THE HOTS FOR someone

the **hot seat 1 *n phr*** *by 1925* The electric chair; =the HOT SQUAT: *He draws the hot-seat for taking that rat*—American Mercury **2 *n phr*** *by 1942* A place where one is under uncomfortable scrutiny and pressure, esp the witness stand: *Deane was succeeded in the hot seat by a very small pot from the State Department*—R Starnes/ *...always on the cutting edge, always in the hot seat*—Washington Post

See ON THE HOT SEAT

hot sheet *modifier* *by 1980s* Catering to quick assignations; permitting short-term occupancy: *The "Strip Tease" murder includes a brief, touching appearance of the forlorn manager of a hotsheet place called the Flightpath Motel*—New York Times/ *Investigating shady insurance claims lands Jack in the usual hot-sheet motels in North Dallas*—New York Times [modeled on *hot bed*]

◁**hot shit**▷ *by 1940s* **1 *n phr*** or ***interj*** =HOT DOG **2 *n phr*** Someone or something very remarkable and attractive, irresistible, etc; =HOT STUFF: *He thinks he's real hot shit* **3 *modifier***: *Thought he was a hot shit basketball player*—Buzz/ *...to get the hotshit, thick-book education he could well afford*—Dan Jenkins **4 *n phr*** An aggressive, self-assured person; =BIG SHOT: *...something sensitive and probing like all the rest of these hot shits*—Rolling Stone

hot short *n phr* *1920s underworld* A stolen car [fr earlier *short*, "car," possibly reflecting the earlier sense "street car," found by 1897, based on a street car being *short* compared with a railroad car]

hot shot 1 *n phr* *by 1933* An especially gifted and effective person; a notably successful person; =BALL OF FIRE, WINNER ●Often used ironically: *What has been written about executives has usually dealt with the hot shots*—C W Morton/ *You're not pushing around some crummy client to show him what a hot-shot you are*—J Evans **2 *modifier***: *In just a year I'm claiming to be a hot-shot Columbia man myself*—Dwight David Eisenhower/ *...a young, hot-shot second lieutenant*—American Legion Magazine **3 *n phr*** *railroad by about 1930* A fast train or express train **4 *modifier***: *a hot-shot freight* **5 *n phr*** *by 1940s* A news bulletin; a news flash: *When that hot-shot came in about Monahan's death*—movie *Scene of the Crime* **6 *n phr*** *narcotics by 1950s* A narcotics injection that is fatal because of an impurity or poison: *You got a hot shot! You're dead*—C Cooper

hot-shot Charlie *n phr* *WWII Air Forces* A flashy braggart; egotist

hotsie-totsie or **hotsie-dandy *adj*** (also **hotsy-totsy**) *by 1926* Satisfactory; fine; =COPACETIC: *All's hotsie-totsie here, thank you so much*

hot sketch *by 1921* **1 *n phr*** A remarkable, colorful person; =CARD **2 *n phr*** An attractive young woman; =HOT NUMBER

hot spit *n phr* or ***interj*** *by 1960s* =HOT SHIT

hot spot 1 *n phr* *by 1932* =TIGHT SPOT **2 *n phr*** *by 1941* A dangerous place, esp a combat zone: *Sarajevo is a hot spot again* **3 *n phr*** *by 1931* A popular night club, esp one with sexy entertainment: *...became 52d Street's hot spot*—Louis Sobol

the **hot squat *n phr*** *by 1890s* The electric chair: *You couldn't ever rise from the hot squat*—A Hynd

hot stove league *n phr* *by 1912* The off-season entity of devotees, arguments, etc, that keeps baseball serious and topical from October to April [as applied to horse-racing, the term is found by the 1870s]

hot stuff 1 *n phr* *by 1889* A person of exceptional merit, talents, attractions, etc; =HOT SHOT ●Almost always used ironically: *I guess they think they are hot stuff*—John O'Hara/ *...Don't you think I'm hot stuff*—R S Prather **2 *n phr*** *by 1904* Material, entertainment, etc, that is very exciting, esp salacious: *Those magazines are real hot stuff* **3 *n phr*** *underworld by 1924* Stolen goods; contraband **4 *n phr*** *by 1931* News or information that is very important, fresh, sensational, forbidden, etc: *I peeked in your briefcase, and that's hot stuff!* **5 *n phr*** *by 1940s* Food, drinks, etc, that are very hot: *Hot stuff coming through*

hotter than a pistol (or **three-dollar pistol**) ***adj phr*** *by 1940s* Very hot, in various senses: *Big hog lots? "It's hotter than a pistol in Iowa..."*—Milwaukee Journal Sentinel

hot ticket *by 1960s* **1 *n phr*** A very popular show; =HIT: *Mr. Martins's staging of Sleeping Beauty was such a critical success at its premiere that it became an instant hot ticket*—New York Times **2 *modifier***: *Willenson is a hot ticket item in the media these days*—Milwaukee Journal

hottie *n* *1990s teenagers* An attractive person; =BEDDY, DISH: *...if a guy or girl is cute, they're a "hottie" or "fine"*—KRT News Service

hot to trot *adj phr* *1950s black* Afire with craving, esp for sexual activity; lustful: *...to ask her bluntly if she was hot to trot*—Cyra McFadden/ *Somebody...was hot to trot for a Japanese sedan*—Car and Driver/ *...who claims her hot-to-trot boss gave her a chase around the office*—New York Post

hot under the collar *adj phr* *by 1895* Very angry: *The Puerto Ricans who get hot under the collar and curse aloud if anyone should question their being Puerto Rican*—Village Voice

hot up 1 *v phr* *by 1936* To become more exciting and dangerous; heat up: *Then things really hot up and January falls in love with an aging macho novelist*—Saturday Review **2 *v phr*** *by 1903* To make something hot or hotter: *I'll just hot up some soup for lunch*

hot walker *n phr* *horse-racing by 1960s* A person who walks a horse after a race or strong exercise in order to cool it off gradually: *She has worked at the King Ranch and at Churchill Downs as a "hotwalker" grazing thoroughbreds*—Washingtonian

hot war *n phr* *by 1947* A war with combat and

killing; =SHOOTING WAR •An isolated use in 1768 means "a vigorous war," lacking the modern contrast with *cold war*

hot water *n phr by 1875* Difficulty; trouble; embarrassment: *...got herself into hot water by marrying a Siamese prince*—Time
See IN HOT WATER

hot-wire 1 *v by 1961* To start a car, truck, etc, by electrically bypassing the ignition lock: *He could hot-wire any car in about 20 seconds* **2** *v by 1970s* To activate illegally; tamper with: *...let the affected corporations hot-wire the regulatory process*—New York Times [fr the notion of attaching an electrically *hot* wire to the starter-motor relay]

hound *v by 1605* To harass, pester, or annoy someone; =BURN: *I hounded him. Oh fuck, what a loser I was*—Douglas Coupland
See BOOZEHOUND, CHOW HOUND, GAS HOUND

-hound *combining word* A person devoted to or addicted to what is indicated: *autograph hound/ boozehound/ newshound/ nicotine hound/ thrill-hound*

the **Hound** or the **Dog** *n phr by 1960s* A Greyhound™ bus

hound dog *n phr by 1940s* A contemptible man, esp a woman-chaser [a Southernism popularized by an Elvis Presley song lyric: "Ain't nothin' but a hound dog"]

hounds *adj 1950s teenagers* Very satisfying; wonderful; great; =NEAT

hound the beef *v phr by 1980s* To cruise for sex: *Me and Stick were out hounding the beef*—Jane Leavy

hour **See** DEAD HOUR

house 1 *n by 1865* A brothel; =CATHOUSE, WHOREHOUSE •Earlier occurrences, from 1726 on, have modifiers: *of ill repute, of ill fame, of assignation, of accommodation, etc*: *A House is not a Home*—Polly Adler **2** *n by 1921* The audience at a theater **3** *n middle 1980s* A kind of dance music derived from soul, rock, and jazz, with a strong percussive beat, originally a black Chicago style •Comes in many varieties: deep house, garage, tribal, progressive, etc: *...to introduce Southern California to "house," the technologically sophisticated dance music that has taken the country by storm...*—Buzz/ *For years, dance-club regulars have been expecting the boom-chucka-boom beat of house music to conquer pop*—New York Times [third sense fr the *Warehouse*, a Chicago club]
See BARRELHOUSE, the BIG HOUSE, BRING DOWN THE HOUSE, BUGHOUSE, CALL HOUSE, CAN HOUSE, CATHOUSE, CHIPPY HOUSE, CRAZY-HOUSE, CRACK HOUSE, DICE HOUSE, DOSS, FLEABAG, FLOPHOUSE, FUNNY FARM, GAS HOUSE, GRIND-HOUSE, HASH-HOUSE, JAG HOUSE, JOY HOUSE, JUKE HOUSE, NOTCH-HOUSE, NUT HOUSE, ON THE HOUSE, POWERHOUSE, ROUGHHOUSE, ROUNDHOUSE, SCRATCH HOUSE, SKIN HOUSE, SPORTING HOUSE, STROKE HOUSE, WHEELHOUSE, WHOREHOUSE

house ape *n phr by 1980s* A small child; an infant; =CURTAIN CLIMBER, RUG APE

housebroken *adj by 1932* To be generally observant of the amenities; tame [fr the condition of a pet who will soil the house with excreta]

house-cleaning *n by 1928* A reorganization of a business or government department, esp with dismissal of incompetent or dishonest employees; =SHAKE-UP: *Honest cops, instead of welcoming a house-cleaning...resent it*—E Lavine

house larry *n phr salespersons by 1940s* A man who frequents a store without buying: *The "house larry"...drops in two or three times a week not to buy*—G Milstein

house moss *n phr by 1940s* The tufts and whorls of dust that accumulate under beds, tables, etc; =BEGGAR'S VELVET, GHOST TURDS, SLUT'S WOOL

House of Pain *n phr sports by 1980s* The Houston Astrodome, opened in 1964

house-sit *v by 1970s* To live in and care for a house free of charge or for a fee while the owner is away [modeled on *baby-sit*]

how **See** AND HOW, DING HOW, KNOW-HOW

how about (or **what do you know about**) **that** *interj* first form by 1939, second by 1920s An exclamation of surprise, pleasure, admiration, etc: *We've only got a year to go. How about that!; ...I should worry. What d'yuh know about that?*—Living Age [first form popularized by the baseball announcer Mel Allen]

how something **can you get** *sentence by 1951* It is impossible to be or behave to a more extreme degree; this is the utmost: *"How tacky can you get?" Maddie said disgustedly*—Lawrence Sanders/ *He did? How stupid can you get?*

how come *sentence by 1848* What is that?; what is the reason?: *"Change of plans. We move today" "How come?"*—Elmore Leonard

how do you like (or **how about**) **them apples** *interj by 1940s* An exclamation of pleasure and triumph, usu inviting admiration for something one has done or acquired: *How do you like them apples, huh, Ma?!*—Robert B Parker/ *How about them apples, Goodman?*—Stan Cutler

howdy *interj by 1843* An exclamation upon greeting: *Howdy, pardner, what's up?* [fr *how do you do*]

Howdy Doody **See** DOES HOWDY DOODY HAVE WOODEN BALLS

how it shakes out *adv phr by 1990s* The consequences; the fate of an idea, experiment, endeavor, etc: *This may or may not fly; we'll just wait and see how it shakes out*

a **howl 1** *n by 1934* Something amusing; a funny event; =a HOOT **2** *n by 1886* =BEEF, STINK: *I do not want any...friends to make a howl through the press*—The Lantern

howler *n by 1844* A very funny mistake, esp in something written or spoken rather solemnly: *His misuse of "Rappaport" for "rapport" was the season's howler*

howling *adj by 1887* Conspicuously successful: *The Peoples' theatre...is doing a howling biz*—The Lantern

how's about *prep phr* *by 1925* What do you feel or think about: *How's about a drink?*—Budd Schulberg

how's tricks *sentence* *by 1904* How are you?; how are things going for you?

how they hanging or **how's it hanging** *sentence* *1940s* How are you? •A genial greeting, usu from one man to another; an inquiry as to the condition of the genitals: *Madeline Kurnitz said, "How they hanging, kiddo"*—Lawrence Sanders

HUA (pronounced as separate letters) *adv phr* *by 1980s* Stupidly; blindly; inattentively: *You're driving pretty HUA today* [fr *head up ass*]

hubba-hubba *WWII armed forces* **1** *interj* An exclamation of delight, relish, etc, esp at the sight of a woman **2** *adv* Quickly; immediately; =HABA-HABA, ON THE DOUBLE [origin unknown; perhaps a version of a Chinese greeting *how-pu-how*, apparently adopted by US airmen from Chinese pilot trainees; perhaps originally a bit of gibberish used to imitate the clamor of conversation, esp when soldiers get the command "Parade rest," after which one can talk, as distinct from the command "At ease," after which one must remain silent and contribute to no *hubbub*]

hubby *n* *by 1798* Husband

huck *v* *by 1990s* To throw; =CHUCK: *...we'd each huck a dart standing on one foot, gulping a beer...*—Douglas Coupland

huckleberry **1** *n* *by 1883* A man; fellow; =GUY: *Well, I'm your huckleberry, Mr Haney*—Jim Tully **2** *n students* *by 1895* A sweet, agreeable person, hence sometimes a dupe •A very mild and affectionate insult

huckster *n* *by 1945* An advertising person or publicity agent: *...so the television hucksters can peddle their shaving cream*—New York Times [popularized by the 1946 novel about advertising, *The Hucksters*, by Frederick Wakeman]

huddle *by 1929* **1** *n* A conference; closed and intense discussion: *He went into a huddle with his aides* **2** *v*: *We'll have to huddle on that one* [fr the *huddle*, esp of the offensive team, before most plays in football]

Huey *n* *Vietnam War armed forces* A US military helicopter, model HU–1B: *The Huey...a combination of shuttle bus, supply truck, ambulance, and weapon of war*—New York Times

huff *v narcotics* *by 1980s* To inhale glue, gasoline, or aerosol fumes for intoxicating effect: *The deaths of three Wisconsin teenagers after they inhaled aerosol fumes to get high, the practice known as "huffing"...*—Milwaukee Journal

See IN A HUFF

huff-duff *n* *WWII Army Air Forces* A high-frequency radio direction finder [fr the initials making up the name]

huffer **1** *n* *1950s hot rodders* An automobile supercharger; =BLOWER **2** *n narcotics* *by 1980s* A person who inhales various chemical fumes for intoxicating effect: *Huffers: Youngsters who inhale gasoline,* hair spray, butane or any of a variety of household poducts to get high—Toronto Globe and Mail

huffy *adj* *by 1848* Angry; petulant; irritable; =IN A HUFF: *I didn't mean to get huffy*—Sinclair Lewis

huggy-huggy *adj* (also **kissy-huggy** or **kissy-kissy**) *by 1980s* Very affectionate; =BUDDY-BUDDY, PALSY-WALSY: *We are all very huggy-huggy with each other*—People Weekly/ *This is not gonna be a kissy-huggy book*—Edward I Koch/ *...the kissy-kissy socials had all but disappeared*—Vanity Fair

the **hully-gully** *n phr* *1960s* A discotheque dance derived from the twist: *The dignified dances include...the Hully-Gully (like Wyatt Earp drawing his guns, Dean Martin downing drinks, and Esther Williams knocking water out of her ear)*—New York Times [origin unknown; perhaps related by some of its gestures to a southern children's game, *hull-gull*, in which the players guessed at the number of chinquapin nuts held in a closed hand]

hum (or **hmmm**) **babe** *interj* *baseball* *by 1980s* An utterance of various meanings, often of encouragement: *Piece of cake, can of corn, hum babe*—Milwaukee Journal [perhaps fr exhortations to the pitcher to throw a devastating *hummer*]

humdinger *n* *by 1905* A person or thing that is remarkable, wonderful, superior, etc; =BEAUT, LOLLA-PALOOZA: *Arnold Moss gave us a humdinger of a talk*

humdinging *adj* *by 1930s* First-rate; superior: *...a real, humdinging comer*—Ira Wolfert

hummer **1** *n* *by 1907* A person or thing that is remarkable, wonderful, etc; =HUMDINGER: *This is Mason's first book, and it's a hummer*—Village Voice **2** *n baseball* *by 1940s* A fastball

hummy **1** *adj* *black* *by 1970s* Content; happy; ignorant of danger **2** *adv*: *She lives real hummy*

humongous (hoo MAWN gǝs) *adj students* *by 1960s* Very large; gigantic: *...a humongous chain*—Industrial Research [perhaps a sort of echoic-symbolic blend of *huge* with *monstrous*]

hump **1** *v* (also **hump it**, **hump along**) To move or go, esp with difficulty; slog: *...lack the nerve to hump it through to the end*—Partisan Review/ *...put on that pack and hump for miles through the boonies*—Life ◁2▷ *v* *by 1785* To do the sex act with or to; =FUCK: *...from the brave pilots who hump the nubile hostesses to the dialect-spouting steerage passenger*—Judith Crist **3** *v* *by 1835* To exert oneself mightily; work hard •To work as if carrying something on one's back, or *hump*: *...and humped the big tractor trailer right off 128 and down ramp...*—Robert B Parker/ *The groundskeepers have been humping to prepare the stadium for the big game*—Rick Barber **4** *n police* *by 1990* A contemptible constable; an incompetent •Apparently sometimes used jovially to mean simply "cop": *I don't believe that hump! I'm trying to develop a case, and he acts like I'm a hysterical old maid looking for rapists under the bed*—Michael Grant

See BUST one's ASS, BUST HUMP, CRAWL someone's

HUMP, DRY FUCK, GET A HUMP ON, GET A MOVE ON, HIT THE HUMP, OVER THE HILL

hump oneself *v phr* by 1883 To hurry: *You better hump yourself over to the police station and explain*

hump and bump *v phr* by 1970s To work hard and progress or propel haltingly: *He says it costs him $10,000 a month to hump and bump his business along*—Village Voice

hump day *n phr* by 1960s Wednesday

◁**humpery**▷ *n* by 1970s The sex act; coupling; =FUCKING: *...refused to change the X rating on* Fritz the Cat *on the ground that it depicted "anthropomorphic humpery"*—Judith Crist

humpin' *adj* black by 1990s Attractive; good-looking; =DISHY

◁**humpy**▷ *adj* by 1970s Sexually arousing; lubricious; sexy: *...flashy, precise, and humpy as...in a Czardas*—Village Voice

humvee or **hummer** *n* by 1990s A small military vehicle: *...she and others were traveling in a humvee when one of the Jeeplike vehicles...rolled over a mine*—Milwaukee Journal/ *Some 20,000 Humvees were used in the Persian Gulf War*—Time [fr high mobility multipurpose wheeled vehicle]

hunch by 1904 **1** *n* An intuitive premonition; a shrewd idea or notion: *I gotta hunch she won't come back* **2** *modifier*: *This was too good a hunch play to let drop*—E Selby **3** *v*: *As I hunch it, the answer is triple*—Billy Rose [said to be fr a gamblers' belief that touching a *hunchback's* hump would bring good luck]

hung 1 *adj* by 1958 =HUNG OVER **2** *adj* rock 'n' roll about 1955 In love ◁**3**▷ *adj* by 1641 Having impressive male genitals; =HUNG LIKE A BULL, WELL-HUNG

hunger *See* FROM HUNGER

◁**hung like a bull** (or **a horse**)▷ *adj phr* by 1960s Possessing large genitals; =HUNG, WELL-HUNG

hung over *adj phr* by 1940s Suffering the ill effects of a hangover: *...looking as hung over as you can get*—R Starnes

the **hungries** *See* GET THE HUNGRIES

hungry *adj* Very ambitious; extremely eager to succeed: *He won't make it because he's not hungry enough*

hung up 1 *adj phr* jazz musicians by 1940s Limited by conventional beliefs and attitudes; =SQUARE, UNCOOL: *Either you're way out, pops, or you're hung up*—E Klein **2** *adj phr* fr beat & cool talk Agitated or immobilized by emotional disturbance; stalled: *She suddenly got all hung up around Christmas* **3** *adj phr* by 1712 Delayed; detained: *He got hung up with a phone call as he was leaving*

hung up on *adj phr* beat & cool talk by 1957 Obsessed with; stalled or frustrated by; suffering a hangup over: *I'm hung up on fried rice*—Harper's Bazaar

hunk 1 *n* by 1940s A man or woman considered primarily as a sex partner; =PIECE, PIECE OF ASS: *He*

came back to the hot little hunk he used to run around with—J Evans **2** *n* by 1945 A very attractive man, esp a muscular and sexually appealing one; =STUDMUFFIN: *Wherever she goes she always manages to pick up a hunk*—Aquarian

hunker down 1 *v phr* (also **hunker**) by 1720 To squat on one's haunches: *He heads for the inevitable mariachi square, hunkers down in the dark, wet and shivering*—Tom Wolfe/ *Fiona had just hunkered down, abandoned all caution...*—Scott Turow/ *Jon...was hunkered in the dark, silently chain-smoking*—New Yorker **2** *v phr* by 1970s To get into the mood and posture for hard work: *Now that summer's gone we must hunker down and get that report finished* **3** *v phr* by 1970s To take a sturdy defensive attitude; become hard to move: *As the public responds...the defense lawyers hunker down*—Philadelphia/ *..."We'll just have to hunker down," said Jody Powell*—Newsweek [fr Southern US fr northern British dialect *hunker*, "haunch"]

hunk of change *See* PIECE OF CHANGE

hunk of cheese *n phr* by 1940s A stupid, obnoxious person

hunkorama or **hunkster** *n* first form by middle 1980s, second by 1990s A very attractive man, esp a muscular and sexually appealing one; =HUNK, STUDMUFFIN: *...all 6 feet 2 inches of blond hunkorama...*—Washington Post/ *Holy Hunksters! It's* Batman *forever!*—Liz Smith

◀**hunky¹**▶ (also **hunkie** or **Hunky** or **Hunkie** or **Hunk** or **hunks**) **1** *n* by 1910 A foreigner, esp a Hungarian, Slavic, or Baltic laborer; =BOHUNK, GINZO **2** *modifier*: *hunky talk/ dumb hunkie brain* **3** *n* black by 1960s =HONKY: *99 white workers got killed in a coal-mine disaster, man! Do you know what I mean? So I can't call everybody no Hunkie*—Ishmael Reed [fr *bohunk*]

hunky² *adj* by 1978 Attractive, esp sexually desirable; =MACHO: *...hunky, bearded actor-troubadour*—Time/ *...the hunky blond who cranks the ferry*—Advocate [the related sense, "thick-set, solidly built," is found by 1911]

hunky-dory *adj* by 1866 Satisfactory; fine; =COPACETIC: *That may be hunky-dory...with the jumping and jiving youngsters*—Bosley Crowther [origin uncertain; *hunky* was a generalized term of approval by 1861; as to *dory*, according to one proposal of 1876 it was brought back by sailors from Yokohama, Japan, where *Honcho dori* is a street where they found their diversions; the term was popularized by a Christy Minstrels song of about 1870]

hunter *See* HEADHUNTER, IVORY-HUNTER, POTHUNTER

hunt up *v phr* by 1791 To search for diligently; search out: *Let's see if we can hunt up a place to get this fixed*

hurl 1 *v* baseball by 1908 To pitch: *...after hurling five frames in three games*—F Eck **2** *v* by 1992 To vomit: *Somebody hurled, which was so gross it made somebody else hurl...*—Milwaukee Journal

hurler *n* baseball by 1908 A pitcher

a **hurrah's nest** *n phr by 1829* Confusion; chaos; =SNAFU

hurry *See* HERE'S YOUR HAT WHAT'S YOUR HURRY

hurt *adj 1980s teenagers* Ugly; ill-favored; =PISS-UGLY: *I never saw anyone as hurt as her boyfriend*—Delcastle Dictionary of Slang

hurtin' for certain *adj phr college students by 1980s* =HURTING

hurting *adj armed forces & students fr black by 1940s* In great need; in distress: *Guys, the last thing we want…is to seem to be hurting for money*—Douglas Coupland

husband **1** *n prostitutes by 1960s* A pimp: *She has a pimp she calls her "husband"*—New York Times **2** *n homosexuals by 1960s* The dominant, masculine member of a homosexual couple, male or female

hush-hush *by 1916* **1** *adj* Very secret; classified: *…a hush-hush border meeting*—Associated Press **2** *n*: *Why all the hush-hush about Walden?*—Raymond Chandler

hush money *n phr by 1709* Money paid to insure silence: *…you can't give "hush money" to someone who's already talked*—Milwaukee Journal Sentinel

hustle **1** *v by 1844* To hurry: *We better hustle, the thing leaves in five minutes* **2** *n*: *Put a little hustle in it now* **3** *v by 1888* To behave, play, perform, etc, very energetically and aggressively: *The reason they're losing is they don't hustle* **4** *v by 1891* To beg: *You'll hustle for an overcoat*—J Flynt **5** *v by 1930* To work as a prostitute; =HOOK: *…whores that hustle all night long*—Louis Armstrong **6** *v by 1887* To cheat; swindle; victimize; =CON: *It took a hell of a caddy to hustle a pro and a greenskeeper*—Saturday Evening Post/ *Larabee, he decided, was trying to hustle him*—WT Tyler **7** *n by 1963*: *I guess one man's "hustle" is another man's "promotion"*—Village Voice **8** *v by about 1915* To steal: *We must hustle us a car* **9** *n*: *You know I can't pay out five bills for a wash if I wasn't planning a hustle*—Lawrence Sanders [criminal senses may be related to early 19th-century *hustle*, "do the sex act, fuck"]

See GET A HUSTLE ON, GET A MOVE ON, ON THE HUSTLE

hustler **1** *n by 1825* A thief or a dealer in stolen goods: *…and sells to hustlers like Tommy at about one-third its retail value*—New York Magazine **2** *n by 1914* A confidence trickster or swindler, esp one who pretends ignorance of a game where he or she is in fact an expert and sure to win; =CON MAN, SHARK **3** *n by 1924* A prostitute; =HOOKER: *I ain't nothing but a hustler*—Langston Hughes **4** *n by 1882* An energetic, aggressive performer or worker: *An active and successful businessman achieves the honorable distinction of a "hustler" or a "rustler"*—Charles L Hildreth

hutzpa or **hutzpah** *See* CHUTZPA

◀**Hymie**▶ *n by early 1980s* A Jewish male •Apparently chiefly black use: *A little curly-haired Hymie pleading his case*—Elmore Leonard [fr the Jewish given name *Hyman*]

hype¹ **1** *n narcotics by 1913* A hypodermic needle; =HYPE-STICK **2** *n narcotics by 1925* An injection of narcotics **3** *n narcotics by 1924* An addict who injects narcotics: *…and heroin substitutes don't work with a stone hype*—Joseph Wambaugh **4** *n* A seller of narcotics; =CONNECTION: *…any hype that wants to get you hooked*—D Hulburd [fr *hypodermic* referring to a needle or an injection]

hype² **1** *v by 1937* To blatantly promote:…*exercises no stock options, hypes no quick secondary stock offering*—New York Magazine/ *…unless Margaret's hyping the gate for a rematch*—Sports Illustrated **2** *n* Advertising or promotion, esp of a blatant sort:…*without any advance PR hype*—H Smith **3** *v by 1914* To trick; deceive; originally, to short-change **4** *v by 1938* =HYPE UP [origin unknown; perhaps related to *hyper*, "hustle," of obscure origin, found from the mid-1800s; recent advertising and public relations senses probably influenced by *hype¹* as suggesting supernormal energy, excitement, etc, and by *hyper²* and *hyperbole*; sense 4 supported by a 1914 glossary: "*Hyper*, current among money-changer. A flim-flammer"]

See MEDIA HYPE

a **hype** **1** *n phr by middle 1960s* A high-pressure advocacy or urging; a publicity or public relations invention: *The nostalgia for the Fifties is not entirely a media hype*—New York Times/ *This is gonna sound like a hype*—Rolling Stone **2** *n phr by middle 1960s* A person or thing promoted by hype **3** *n phr by 1962* A swindle; =CON, SCAM

hyped-up **1** *adj by 1940s* False; fake; =HOKED-UP, PHONY: *…no hyped-up glamour*—Billy Rose/ *…the woman's archly hyped-up language*—Village Voice **2** *adj by 1938* Excited; overstimulated; =HYPER: *I leave early…hyped-up, impressed, nauseated*—Commentary/ *…The game gets him "hyped up," and "releases energy" in the same way that football does*—Games

hyper¹ or **hype artist** *n* or *n phr by 1960* A publicist; promoter; advertiser; =FLACK [fr *hype²*]

hyper² **1** *adj by 1942* Overexcited; manic; overwrought; =HYPED-UP: *She tells how the grownups gave her Nembutal when she was eight years old, because "I was hyper"*—New York Magazine/ *It's this flaky hyper hour*—New York Magazine/ *She's a hyper-person, accustomed to constant activity*—Good Housekeeping **2** *adj by 1970s* Exceeding most; very superior;: *…with harem cushions, a hyper-hi-fi set, ha-ha candles*—Saturday Review [fr Greek *hyper*, "super," and in the first sense probably fr medical terms like *hyperactive, hyperkinetic, hyperthyroid*, etc; in some sources this term is associated with *hipped* and *hippish*, fr *hypochondriac*, "melancholic," first found in the early 18th century]

See THROW A FIT

hype-stick *n narcotics by 1940s* A hypodermic needle

hype up *by 1940s* **1** *v phr* To fake; manufacture; invent; =HOKE: *They had to hype up a convincing* *story* **2** *v phr* To promote or advertise by blatant, obnoxious means **3** *v phr* To give something a false impact, appeal, energy, etc: *...other chemicals to hype up the produce and fool the buyer*—Saturday Review

hypo *by 1904* **1** *n* A hypodermic needle **2** *n* A hypodermic injection **3** *n narcotics by 1940s* A drug addict who injects narcotics; =HYPE **4** *v by 1960s* To stimulate or strengthen; =BEEF UP: *...a wilted record player hypoed by a pooped-out public address system*—John R Powers [fr *hypodermic,* referring to a needle or an injection]

I

IC (pronounced as separate letters) *n* *lunch counter by 1950s* An irate customer: *There were usually about two ICs a night*—Cameron Crowe

I Can Catch *n phr truckers by 1930s* The Interstate Commerce Commission

ice 1 *n by 1906* Diamonds; a diamond: *a two-carat hunk of ice* **2** *n by 1906* Gems and jewelry in general: *Gonna wear your ice?* **3** *n by 1927* Extra payment given for a desirable theater ticket: *. . . a slight fee, say $100 worth of tickets for $120. The $20 is the "ice"*—M Zolotow **4** *n by 1948* Protection money; bribery; =PAYOFF: *. . . syndicate that paid out $1,000,000 in ice to the police*—New York Times **5** *v by 1930s* To make something certain; =CINCH, SEW something UP: *They iced the game in the ninth with two more runs* **6** *v* (also **ice** someone **out**) *by 1836* To ignore someone; snub; cut; =COLD SHOULDER: *. . . how women were "iced" by peers during corridor conversations*—Newsweek/ *I've had doors closed and I've been iced out*—Associated Press **7** *v sports by 1960s* To defeat utterly; trounce; =CLOBBER: *Nebraska iced Kentucky 55 to 16* **8** *v underworld by 1960s* To kill; =OFF •Probably a shortening of *put on ice*: *Ice a pig. Off a pig. That means kill a cop*—Robert Daley **9** *adj 1960s cool talk* Excellent; fine; =COOL **10** *n 1980s narcotics* Methamphetamine crystals

See BREAK THE ICE, CUT NO ICE, GREEN ICE, ON ICE

iceberg *n by 1840* An unemotional, chilly person; =COLD FISH

icebox 1 *n prison by 1920s* A solitary confinement cell; =the HOLE: *When a prisoner is sent to the "icebox"*—E Lavine **2** *n prison by 1920s* A prison **3** *n by 1940s* The imagined place where persons and things are held in reserve; =ON THE BACK BURNER: *I got a left-hander in the icebox* **4** *n by 1940s* A very cold place: *This building's an icebox*

ice cream *n phr narcotics by about 1910* The crystalline form of a narcotic: *. . . the ice cream eaters, who chewed the crystal*—H Asbury

ice cream (or **snow**) **cone** *n phr baseball by 1980s* A ball that is caught but can be seen protruding from the glove or mitt; a barely caught ball

ice cream habit *n phr 1960s narcotics* The occasional, nonaddicted, use of narcotics

iced *See* HAVE something CINCHED

iced jeans *n phr* (also **acid jeans** or **frosted jeans**) Jeans streaked with white

ice maiden (or **queen**) *n phr by 1970s* A very cool and composed woman; a chilly woman; =ICEBERG: *Margaret Thatcher, the Ice Maiden, branded the conservative Gorsuch "the Ice Queen"*—Newsweek/ *Ms Stone plays Sally, a powerful woman, another ice queen whose roiling emotions remain contained*—New York Times [perhaps modeled on the title of Hans Christian Andersen's tale *The Snow Queen*]

iceman 1 *n by 1940s* A jewel thief **2** *n by 1940s* A very calm person, performer, etc: *An iceman. . . is a gambler who never loses his head*—J Lilienthal **3** *n underworld by 1970s* A professional killer; =HIRED GUN, HIT MAN: *Maybe I hadn't seen the iceman with Bobb*—Richard Merkin/ *Go play iceman*—TV show *T J Hooker*

ice princess 1 *n phr by 1970s* A chilly, reserved woman; =ICEBERG, ICE MAIDEN: *. . . the travails of growing up with a politician for a father and an ice princess for a mother*—Milwaukee Journal **2** *modifier*: *Blond, beautiful, smart, impeccably dressed, ice-princess cool and very direct. . .* —New York Times

ice (or **put the icing on**) **the cake** *v phr by 1940s* To put a victory beyond question; insure a favorable result: *He iced the cake with a knockdown in the seventh*

ick *interj by 1948* An exclamation of disgust; =GROSS, YECCH, YUCK

icky (Variations: **ickie** or **icky-poo** or **icky-sticky** or **icky-wickey**) **1** *adj jive talk by 1939* Overly sentimental; maudlin; =SCHMALTZY: *That music pleased my icky, lachrymose sensibility*/ *The prose gets a mite too icky-poo for comfort*—New York Magazine **2** *n by 1935* A conventional, tedious person; =SQUARE: *She turned out to be an icky* **3** *adj by 1960s* Unpleasant; revolting; nasty; =GROSS, GRUNGY: *Those cool comedies and quizzes became dumb, boring, icky, weird*—Good Housekeeping/ *. . . refuse to get involved in anything outside their own little ickey-wickey bailiwicks*—Village Voice/ *The acting is icky*—San Francisco [fr baby-talk "sticky, nasty"; although perhaps fr Yiddish *elken* or *iklen*, "to nauseate, revolt"]

icy *adj 1980s teenagers* Excellent; good; =COOL: *. . . the old Valley Girl terms "rad" and "icy" still describe the very cool*—New York Times

ID (pronounced as separate letters) *by 1950s* **1** *n* An identity card **2** *n* Identification; evidence for one's identity: *You can't cash it here without ID* **3** *v* To identify: *Police ID driver killed in chase*—Newark Star-Ledger

idea *See* WHAT'S THE BIG IDEA

idiot box *n phr by 1959* A television set; television; =the BOOB TUBE

idiot card (or board) *n phr television studio by 1952* A large sheet of heavy paper held up out of range of the television camera, to prompt actors or speakers; cue card: *"Idiot boards" are held out of camera range*—Saturday Evening Post/ *The scripts are gone, but now there are idiot cards*—Saturday Review

idiot girl *n phr television studio by 1950s* A young woman who holds up idiot cards for television performers

idiot light *n phr by 1968* A usu red light on a car's dashboard that glows to announce some sort of fact, such as the discharge of a battery, overheating, etc: *... replaced by too-late-to-react idiot lights*—Car and Driver

-ie (also **-ey** or **-y** or **-sie** or **-sey** or **-sy**) **1** *suffix used to form nouns* Diminutive, affectionate, or familiar versions of what is indicated: *auntie/ cubby/ thingy/ tootsie/ folksy* **2** *suffix used to form adjectives* Having the quality indicated: *comfy/ creepy/ swanky* **3** *suffix used to form nouns* Coming from the place or background indicated: *Arky/ Okie/ Yalie* **4** *suffix used to form nouns* A person of the sort indicated: *weirdie/ hippy/ sharpy*

if bet *n phr gambling by 1940s* A bet on two or more horses, stipulating that part of the winnings be wagered on one or more later races

iffy *by 1937* **1** *adj* Uncertain; doubtful; improbable: *His chances. . . were a bit iffy*—Time/ *Would the DA take the case, knowing the chances of a conviction would be iffy?*—Lawrence Sanders **2** *adj* =DICEY

-ific or **-iffic** *suffix used to form adjectives* Extremely marked by what is indicated: *horrific/ beautific* [fr *terrific*]

if I had a nickel (or dime) for every time something happens *adv clause by 1970s* A somewhat rueful complaint about the frequency of the named event: *If I had a nickel for every time I'm called homophobic, I could buy New York*—Rick Roberts

if it ain't broke, don't fix it *sentence by 1970s* If it is functioning, don't meddle; leave well enough alone: *The economy ain't broke, so don't fix it*—Nation

if looks could kill *adv clause by 1922* The extreme fanciful gauge of a disapproving look: *If looks could kill, she would have been guilty of my murder*

if you can't find 'em, grind 'em *sentence by 1970s* If something cannot be done smoothly or readily, do it roughly; let push come to shove if necessary [fr the action of a truck driver who, if the gears do not shift smoothly, forces them and lets them *grind*]

if you can't stand the heat stay out of the

kitchen *sentence by 1940s* Do not undertake a hard job if you lack the stamina and thick skin to endure sharp criticism [a favorite saying of President Harry S Truman, referring to the Presidency]

ig or **igg** *v 1940s jive talk* To ignore; refuse to notice

iggle *v 1950s teenagers* To persuade: *See if you can iggle him into it*

I only (or just) work here *sentence by 1950s* I can't answer your question; I don't know what is going on, even though I probably should

Ike *See* ALIBI IKE

◀**Ikey**▶ *n by 1835* A Jew [fr a nickname for *Isaac*]

I kid you not *sentence by 1950s* I am perfectly serious; I am not misleading nor joking with you: *There were daily departures of a yacht called, I kid you not, the Alter Ego*—Nation/ *It's rough out there, I kid you not*—Elmore Leonard [popularized by the television comedian Jack Paar]

ill 1 *adj underworld by 1960s* Arrested or detained on suspicion; jailed **2** *adj 1980s black teenagers* Very good; excellent; =COOL: *Ill: very good or bad. . .* —Los Angeles Times **3** *adj 1980s black teenagers* Very bad: *Ill: very good or bad. . .* —Los Angeles Times

I'll be damned *sentence* (Variations: **danged** or **darned** or **ding swizzled** or **dipped** or ◀**dipped in shit**▶ or ◀**fucked**▶ or **jiggered** or **jigswiggered** or **hanged** or **hornswoggled** or **a monkey's uncle** or **switched** may replace **damned**; **damned** may also be omitted) *entry form by 1920s,* ding swizzled *by 1940s,* dipped *by 1940s,* jiggered *by 1837* May I be maltreated, confounded, accursed, etc; an exclamation of surprise or determination: *I'll be damned, we made it!/ I will be dipped in shit*—Larry Niven and Jerry Pournelle/ *I'll be a monkey's uncle if you put that over on me!/ Well I'll be, he made it!* [dipped forms fr 1600s British *be dipped* or *dipped in wing*, "get into trouble; be defeated"]

I'll drink to that *sentence by 1960s* I agree; you are quite right; I approve

I'll eat my hat *sentence by 1837* I am absolutely convinced that a given statement is true, a named event will occur, etc: *I'll eat my hat if he doesn't come back tomorrow*

illegitimati (or illegitimis) non carborundum *sentence by about 1939* Don't let the bastards grind you down ●Offered as a proposed motto or a pearl of wisdom [fr mock-Latin *illegitimatus*, "bastard," and *Carborundum*, trademark of a brand of abrasives]

illin or **illen** *1980s teenagers fr rap groups* **1** *adj* Really terrible or really good; =ILL: *Illin: Vague term meaning something really terrible or really cool*—Los Angeles Times **2** *adj* Stupid; insane

I'll tell the world (or the cockeyed world) *sentence 1900s esp WWI armed forces* You are absolutely right; it is entirely correct: *I'll tell the cockeyed world he's a crook*

I love it *sentence by 1990s* Believe it or not: *... they want to search us on the way out. I love it*—New York Times

I'm Audi 5000 *sentence* 1990s teenagers =I'M OUTA HERE [a pun on the car name *Audi 5000*™]

I may be stupid, but I'm not dumb *sentence* by 1990s: From a distance, Brett looked as if he would run right over McClelland, but the umpire stands 6 foot 6, weighs 250 pounds, has protective equipment on and is holding a bat in his hand. As Brett said, "I'm stupid, but I'm not dumb"—New York Times

IMHO *adv phr* computer network by 1990s In my humble opinion: *The roast quail with polenta was dynamite, IMHO*—Los Angeles Times

immatesticle *adj* by 1940s Of no concern; not relevant; immaterial: *Whether I get called or not is immatesticle* [a play on *immaterial*]

immie by 1940s **1** *n* A kind of playing marble: *The correct answer is marble aggies and immies*—Jack Paar **2** *n* An eye: *. . . a guy who could be junked up to where his immies turn into little beads*—Rocky Graziano

I'm outta or **outa here** *sentence* by 1984 I am leaving now: *. . . if it gets into blamin' me or stuff like that, I'm outta here*—Carsten Stroud/ *"So what are you going to do?" "I'm outa here. . . "*—Robert B Parker

import *n* students by 1940s An out-of-town date brought to a dance, party, etc

important *adj* by 1980s Impressive; imposing; =HEAVY, SERIOUS: *. . . wear short dresses made of metal and leather and have important hair*—New Yorker

important money *See* HEAVY MONEY

I'm sideways *sentence* 1990s teenagers =I'M OUTA HERE

in 1 *n* underworld by 1920s An advantage, esp through an acquaintance; entree: *Get me an in with the skipper of that precinct*—American Mercury **2** *n* by 1768 A person who holds office or other power or position: *Will the Democrats ever be the ins again?* **3** *adj* by 1960 In fashion at the moment; now preferred: *Violence is in, sentiment is out* **4** *adj* by 1960 Accepted; acceptable; belonging to a select group; =IN LIKE FLYNN: *one of the in people Bullock made it to the "in" crowd a few years later. . . —React*

See GET IN, HAVE IT IN FOR someone

-in *combining word* 1960s A communal occasion where one does what is indicated: *be-in/ lie-in/ love-in/ pray-in*

in a bad way *adj phr* by 1809 In great difficulty; badly damaged or injured: *I'm afraid our poor friend is in a very bad way after the wreck*

in a big way *adv phr* by 1903 Very much; extremely: *The soldiers went for pin-ups in a big way*—United Press International

in a bind (or **box**) *adj phr* loggers by 1940s In a very tight and awkward situation; stalled by a dilemma; =IN A BOX: *I'm in a bind, damned if I do and damned if I don't* [fr the situation of a logger whose saw is caught and held tight by the weight of a tree or branch]

in a box *adv phr* by 1913 In an awkward situation; =IN A BIND: *No, and don't put me in a box*—Rick Barber talk show [the related and perhaps original sense "short of money" is found by 1891]

See GO HOME FEET FIRST

in a bucket *See* FOR CRYING OUT LOUD

in a fix *adv phr* by 1837 In difficulty; in a tight spot: *. . . under a cloud, up a tree, quisby, done up, sold up, in a fix*—Household Words

in a fog (or **haze**) *adj phr* by 1888 In a dazed, disoriented, confused state; inattentive: *He was so tired he was walking around in a haze*

in a funk British by 1743 **1** *adv phr* In a depressed, nervous, or frightened state: *Jackson left San Francisco in a funk, he. . . looked tired and sounded like a morose, defeated candidate*—Washington Post **2** *adj phr* Depressed; melancholy: *Steve's been in a funk since he lost his dog*

in a holding pattern *adv phr* by 1950s In abeyance; not in an active status; =ON THE BACK BURNER [fr the aviation term, found by 1948, for airplanes that are flying a prescribed circling route while awaiting clearance to land]

in a hole *adj phr* by 1762 In grave and probably insurmountable difficulties; =UP SHIT CREEK: *The death of my brother leaves me in a deep legal-financial hole*—Saul Bellow

in a huff *adj phr* by 1694 Angry; petulant; grumpy [fr a *huff* or gust of anger]

in a jam *adj phr* by 1914 In trouble, esp serious trouble: *If you're in a jam, he'll fight for you*—P Jones

in a lather (or **lava**) *adj phr* by 1828 Angry; upset; =IN A SWEAT: *. . . this business of your being in a lather about it*—J Evans/ *The editors say they are not in a lava over the coincidence*—Time [fr the resemblance between an agitated sweat, esp the frothy sweat of horses, and frothy washing *lather* thought of as the result of vigorous agitation; found by 1660 in the form *lavour*]

◁**in-and-out** or **in-out**▷ *n* first form by 1620 The sex act; copulation; =FUCKING: *The pages of romances offered less in-and-out than a downtown parking garage*—San Francisco/ *Her refreshing answers about the old in-and-out bluntly demystified any last glitches*—Village Voice/ *. . . the endlessly hypnotic spectacle of the old in-out*—Changes [fr the 1600s idiom *play at in-and-out*, "do the sex act, copulate"]

in-and-outer *n* by 1905 An erratic performer: *30 knockouts among his 52 victories, but he has been an in-and-outer*—Associated Press

in an uproar *See* NOT GET one's BALLS IN AN UPROAR

in a pickle *adj phr* by 1585 In a disagreeable situation; in a sad predicament: *Today I find myself in a pickle, bind, and jam*

◁**in a pig's ass**▷ *adv phr* (Variations: **asshole** or **ear** or **eye** may replace **ass**) Not at all; never; LIKE HELL ●Used for vehement denial: *In a pig's ass, I did*—Village Voice/ *Yeah, we'll get it back. In a pig's eye*—Jerome Weidman/ *In a pig's asshole!*—Robert Stone

in a pinch *by 1903* **1** *adv phr* If necessary; if need be: *In a pinch we could make that do* **2** *adv phr* =IN A JAM

in a poke *See* BUY A PIG IN A POKE

in a row *See* HAVE one's DUCKS IN A ROW

in a state 1 *adj phr by 1837* Agitated; upset; tense: *She got home and found her husband in a state* **2** *adj phr by 1879* Untidy; disheveled; chaotic: *I'm afraid my room's in a state*

in a stew *by 1809* **1** *adj phr* Chaotic and muddled; in disarray: *The whole place is in a stew about the new appointment* **2** *adj phr* Angry and irritable; upset; =IN A SWEAT: *Well don't get in such a stew about it*

in a sweat *adj phr by 1753* Upset; irritated; tense; scared: *Don't get in a sweat, I'll return it at once*

in a tail spin *adj phr by 1928* Dangerously out of control: *I knew he'd be upset, but he's gone into a tail spin over this* [fr the downward spinning of an airplane, for which the term is found by 1917]

in a tizzy *adj phr by 1935* Very much upset; distractingly disturbed; in a state: *I have been in a tizzy since reading his accusations*—Saul Bellow [origin unknown]

in at the kill *adv phr by 1814* Participating in the finish of something, esp when it is very satisfying and vindictive: *Tell me when the thing'll be signed, I want to be in at the kill* [fr a fox-hunting term]

in a walk *See* WIN IN A WALK

in a whoosh *adv phr by 1970s* Very rapidly; in an easy rush: *He went through in a whoosh and obviously with attention to all the arcane mumbo jumbo he had to memorize*—William Kennedy [echoic]

in a zone *adj phr by 1970s* Daydreaming, esp from narcotics; =SPACED-OUT [said to be fr *ozone*, implying very high up in the sky or towards outer space]

in bad *adj phr by 1911* In difficulty; embroiled: *When did you get in bad with the cops?*

in someone's **bad books** *adv phr chiefly British by 1861* Regarded as hostile by someone; hated and menaced by someone: *... nervous about getting in the bad books of the mob guys*—Toronto Life

in bed *See* one SHOULD HAVE STOOD IN BED

in bed with someone *adj phr by 1970s* In close association with; on good terms with: *Lefcourt, who was in bed with the mob, as you know*—Stan Cutler

in one's **book** *adv phr by 1964* In my opinion; as I believe: *"Is he a competent investigator?" "In my book?"*—Scott Turow

in business *adj phr by 1950s* In operation; under way: *One more day or so of prep and we're in business/ The space shuttle is finally in business*

in cahoots *adj phr by 1829* In partnership; acting in a common purpose: *Louise Peccoralo... and her husband... claim they were not in cahoots with William Perone of Arizona*—Newark Star-Ledger [origin uncertain; perhaps fr French *cahute*, "cabin"]

in clover *adv phr by 1710* In a position of ease and affluence; =HAPPY AS A CLAM

include one **out** *v phr by 1937* To exclude one: *Counties began asking the DNR to include them out...*—Milwaukee Journal [said to have been uttered by the movie mogul Samuel Goldwyn, upon resigning from the Hays organization that monitored Hollywood films for moral content]

in cold storage (or **the deep freeze**) *adv phr by 1940s* Held in abeyance; reserved to be dealt with later; =ON HOLD, ON THE BACK BURNER: *The plan's in cold storage for now/ Well, let's just keep that one in the deep freeze for a few months*

in concrete or **cement** *adj phr by 1960s* Firmly set; fixed and determined: *The most recent thing I heard is 45 days to two months, but nothing's in concrete*—Robert F Perkins/ *The President seems to be in cement*—Congressman Thomas P O'Neill

in one's **cups** *adj phr by 1561* Drunk

indeedy *adv by 1856* Indeed; certainly: *No, indeedy*—Sinclair Lewis

in deep ◁**doo-doo** (or **shit**)▷ *n phr by 1970s* Very serious trouble: *He was in deep shit with Big Lou*—Rolling Stone/ *Boy, is your ass in deep shit*—W E B Griffin

in deep water *adv phr by 1861* In a difficult situation, esp where one is not fitted to cope

Indian hay (or **hemp**) *n phr by 1876* Marijuana: *... a couple of Indian hay cigarettes*—American Journal of Psychiatry

Indians *See* TOO MANY CHIEFS AND NOT ENOUGH INDIANS

the **Indian sign** *n phr baseball by 1908* A baleful spell or curse; =HEX, JINX, WHAMMY: *You'd think the Indian sign was on the whole operation*

indie 1 *n movie studio by 1928* An independent, esp an independent movie producer **2** *modifier*: *... one indie pic company*—Variety **3** *adj by 1990s* Playing indie rock: *Really they're just five soft-spoken indie prepsters who happen to rule nice-kid noise pop*—Seventeen

indie rock 1 *n phr early 1990s* A kind of rock music of no particular style but of the small-company, college radio, etc, milieu **2** *modifier*: *... its purposeful indie-rock slag at commerciality...*—Los Angeles Village View/ *Stars of the indie-rock scene dig into...*—formidable pop catalogue—Buzz [fr *indie*, "independent," for the relatively small companies and labels involved]

indigo *n narcotics by 1990s* A kind of marijuana

industrial 1 *adj 1980s students* Very masculine; manly; =MACHO, STUDLY: *If you can get a date with Bambi, you'll be so industrial, dude!*—UCLA Slang **2** *n 1990s* A variety of rock music: *... industrial music is "the sounds our culture makes as it comes unglued"*—Time **3** *modifier*: *... and the harsh industrial pop of Nine Inch Nails...*—Macon Telegraph **4** *adj by 1980s* =INDUSTRIAL-STRENGTH: *... an industrial dose of Thorazine*—George V Higgins

industrial-strength *adj by 1980s* Powerful, sturdy, weighty, etc, as if fit for use in industry; heavy duty: *... drinking a cup of industrial-strength coffee out of a pig-shaped mug*—Carsten Stroud/

... industrial-strength smog—Stan Cutler/ ... ripe for heavy, industrial-strength investigation—New York Times [the descriptive and advertising term is found by about 1920]

in Dutch *adj phr* by 1912 In disfavor; in trouble: *You have to promise, Pop, not to get me in Dutch with Mrs Skoglund*—Saul Bellow [origin uncertain; perhaps fr bookmaking: *Dutch book*, "a bad risk with a bookmaker," is found by 1915]

the **Indy** or **Indy 500** *n phr* by 1960s The annual Indianapolis 500 car race

in one's **ear** *See* STAND AROUND WITH one's FINGER UP one's ASS, STICK IT

in one's **eye** *See* a THUMB IN one's EYE

in flames *See* GO DOWN IN FLAMES

info *n* by 1906 Information; =POOP: *I can slip you the info*—Saturday Evening Post

infobahn *n* 1990s The Information Superhighway, a projected system of linked computer networks; =I-WAY: *... Walt is already ahead of everyone on the Infobahn...* —Buzz [fr *info* plus *bahn*, fr German *Autobahn*, "multi-lane automobile highway"]

infomercial *n* by 1983 A television program that tells or teaches something and is also advertising a product: *... has been doing infomercials, a Taco Bell ad...* —Milwaukee Journal/ *Infomercials got their initial boost in 1984, when the FCC freed local stations from limits on the amount of commercial time they could air*—Time [fr *information* plus *commercial*]

in for it *adj phr* by 1698 Committed willy-nilly; about to suffer trouble, attack, etc: *When they saw the black clouds they knew they were in for it/ If they nab us with the pope's ring, we'll really be in for it*

information *See* FEEDBOX INFORMATION

infotainment *n* by 1983 Televisions programs that teach while entertaining: *... "infotainment," an information-entertainment program...* —Associated Press [fr *information* + *entertainment*]

in front *See* UP FRONT

in God's name *See* the HELL

in-group *n phr* by 1907 An exclusive group or clique, esp of influential persons

in-groupy *adj* by 1980s Catering to or like an ingroup: *When a show sets out to achieve cult status, can it avoid becoming self-consciously clubby and clever, in-groupy?*—New Yorker

in someone's **hair** *adj phr* by 1851 Constantly annoying; nagging at: *You'll have one of these... professors in your hair*—Mark Twain

inhale *v* by 1924 To eat or drink, esp rapidly: *I inhaled my lunch because I didn't have much time to eat*—UCLA Slang
See FRENCH-INHALE

in harness *adj phr* by 1875 Working; actively employed rather than resting, retired, on holiday, etc: *He didn't know how to relax after all those years in harness*

in heat *See* BITCH IN HEAT

in heck *See* the HECK

in hell *See* the HELL

in high (or tall) cotton *adj phr* Southern by 1920s Happy; pleased; fortunate; =FAT, DUMB, AND HAPPY: *We're in high cotton tonight to have with us Mr...* —Denver radio talk show/ *... would greet them from this office, this desk, this chair, high and dry in tall cotton*—Washington Post [fr the double fact that the crop is well-developed and is easier to pick because the picker need not stoop over]

in high gear *adj phr* by 1940s In the most active, rapid, impressive phase; at full tempo: *The advertising campaign is in high gear*
See SHIFT INTO HIGH GEAR

in hock by 1883 **1** *adj phr* Accepted for pawn; in a pawnshop **2** *adj phr* In debt; mortgaged: *We're deeply in hock to the bank*
See HOCK¹

in hot water by 1765 **1** *adv phr* In trouble, esp with the law, one's superiors, etc: *I'm in hot water with the cops again* **2** *adv phr* In difficulties, esp in serious trouble; =IN THE SOUP: *I got you in some hot water with the boss*—Scott Turow

in jigtime *adv phr* by 1916 Immediately; very quickly: *They worked together and got it done in jigtime* [fr *jig*, "rapid dance," found by 1560]

ink 1 *n* hoboes by 1940s Coffee **2** *n* black by 1930s Cheap wine: *... a cheap local "ink"*—Meyer Berger ◄**3**► *n* by 1940s A black person **4** *v* by 1940 To write; sign, esp a contract: *He also inked the plays*—New York Daily News/ *... has inked to helm two more pictures*—Variety **5** *n* by 1980s Press notices; print publicity: *New York Days got lots more ink than Paul will get for his memoir*—Nation/ *NBC thought it might as well hang onto the one show that was getting good ink*—New York Times
See PINK INK, RED INK

ink-slinger by 1877 **1** *n* A writer; author; newspaper reporter or writer **2** *n* lumberjacks, cowboys & hoboes fr early 1900s A clerk; office worker

ink-stained wretch *n phr* by 1980s A newspaper writer: *He doesn't care for radical gay writers, Allen Ginsburg and the ink-stained wretches of the Village Voice*—New Republic/ *That's when Ben might have guessed he had an ink-stained wretch on his hands*—Dan Jenkins

inkstick *n* hawkers by 1940s A fountain pen: *At 15, Nellie was "making a pitch" with inksticks*—S S Jacobs

in like Flynn *adj phr* by 1940s, perhaps fr US Army Air Corps Accepted; acceptable; belonging to a select group; =IN: *"Are you in or out right now?" "I'm in like Flynn. Didn't you notice the picture on my desk?"*—Art Buchwald [origin uncertain; perhaps merely a rhyming phrase; perhaps associated with the sexual and other exploits of the actor Errol *Flynn*]

in line by 1920s **1** *adj phr* Within appropriate bounds; acceptable; =IN THE BALLPARK: *Yes, those prices are about in line* **2** *adj phr* Behaving properly; out of trouble: *Can't you keep your kids in line?*

in line for *adv phr* by 1940s In position to get; about to get: *Hey, you're in line for a big bonus*

in living color *adj phr* by 1990s Displayed with complete accuracy and life-like tones: *The rules and rituals of life inside IBM are all here, and in living color: the army of lawyers, tangle of procedures and endless slide presentations*—New York Times

in luck *adj phr* by 1857 Lucky [the opposite of earlier *out of luck*]

in mothballs *adj phr* late 1940s In reserve; =ON ICE

innards 1 *n* by 1825 The viscera; =GUTS, INSIDES, KISHKES: *. . . got a feeling in my innards it won't work* **2** *n* by 1921: *The inner parts or workings*; =INSIDES: *Let's look at the innards of this gizmo and see what's going on*

innie 1 *n* by 1980s A concave navel **2** *modifier*: *. . . a tidy innie belly button*—Stan Cutler/ *I suspect that the Cardinal arts editor has an outie belly button, and I have an innie belly button*—Wisconsin State Journal [probably a children's term]

inning 1 *n* by 1884 A chance for action or participation **2** *n* by about 1920 A round of a prizefight [fr baseball; the British term, fr cricket, is always *innings*, and is found by 1836]

in nothing (or no time) flat *adv phr* by 1940s Very quickly: *When I heard the signal, I got over there in nothing flat*

-ino *See* -ERINO

in one piece *See* ALL IN ONE PIECE

in on the ground floor *adv phr* by 1872 Engaged early and profitably in a project, investment, etc: *You better act now if you want to be in on the ground floor*

in orbit *adj phr* 1960s teenagers Having a free and exhilarating experience; =HIGH, WAY OUT: *One slurp of gin and he's in orbit*

in over (or above) one's head *adv phr* by 1622 In a situation one cannot cope with; helplessly committed and likely to lose: *He tried to stop, but he was in over his head*

in one's pants *See* ANTS

in pictures *adv phr* by 1920s Acting or otherwise engaged in the movies: *You ought to be in pictures, as the old song says/ After years in pictures he went back to the theater and bombed*

in someone's pocket or hip pocket *adv phr* by 1940s Under someone's absolute control: *Don't worry, I have him in my pocket/ He's in the hip pocket of the networks*—Washington Post

inside *adv* prison by 1888 In prison
See ON THE INSIDE

inside job *n phr* by 1908 A robbery, stroke of espionage, etc, done by someone or with the aid of someone within the target organization: *The cops think the hotel murder is an inside job*

insider *n* by 1850 A person who has special knowledge, authority, etc, because he is within or part of some privileged group: *The insiders are saying that the President will veto it*

insides *n* =INNARDS

inside skinny *n phr* by 1972 The confidential and little-known truth: *This guy gave us the inside skinny on Prozac*

inside the Beltway *adv phr* by 1980s In US government and other Washington circles: *You don't know this yet, but it's an old story inside the Beltway*

the inside track *See* HAVE THE INSIDE TRACK

in one's sleep *adv phr* by 1953 Very easily: *There's a lot of prose so negligent that Mr. Leithauser could have written it in his sleep*—New York Times

in spades *adv phr* by 1929 To the utmost; in the highest degree: *What Aleksandr Solzhenitsyn did for the Gulag he has now done in spades for the Soviet Union as a whole*—National Review/ *I detest them right back, in spades*—Saul Bellow

inspection *See* SHORT-ARM INSPECTION

instant replay *n phr* by early 1970s Immediate repetition and additional judgment: *If anyone mistakes the new regimen for freedom, the full trappings of martial law remain available for instant replay*—New York Times [fr the re-viewing of a sports play on television, sometimes in order to confirm or change an official's call]

in stir *adv phr* by 1851 In prison; =INSIDE

in sync (or synch) *adv phr* by 1940s In order; in harmony; synchronized; without jar or clash: *. . . to bring the author back into sync with his existentialist colleagues*—National Review/ *. . . perfectly in sync with Thicke's outrageous style*—Newsweek [fr *in synchronism*, used in radio, television, etc, to express exact matching and timing between audio and video]

inta *See* INTO

intense *adj* 1970s teenagers Excellent; =COOL

intercom *n* by 1940s An intercommunication system: *Marc yelled into the intercom*—Billy Rose

internal *See* BODY PACKER

in the air *See* a BEAR IN THE AIR

in the altogether *adj phr* by 1894 Naked

in the bag 1 *adj phr* by 1926 Certain; sure; =ON ICE: *It's in the bag. The fix is in*—W R and F K Simpson **2** *adj phr* by 1970s Ruined; destroyed; =FINISHED, KAPUT, OUT OF THE BOX: *If an actor is hurt or killed doing a stunt the whole film is in the bag*—TV show Entertainment Tonight [fr game shot and stuffed *into the game bag*; second sense fr the use of the heavy plastic body bag for the handling of military and other casualties]
See HALF IN THE BAG

in the ballpark *adj phr* by 1968 Within general appropriate limits; not exorbitant, outrageous, etc: *. . . react to an analyst's estimate by telling him whether it is too high, too low, or "in the ballpark"*—Fortune

in the barrel *adj phr* black by 1940s Without money; =BROKE: *A red hot pimp like you ain't got no business being in the barrel*—Zora Neale Hurston [fr the archetypal image of a destitute man who wears a *barrel* for clothing]

in the belly of the beast *adv phr* *1990s* In an extremely difficult plight; beleaguered: *Esa-Pekka Salonen is in the belly of the beast. The brilliant young Finnish conductor has begun his third season as music director of the Los Angeles Philharmonic...* —New York Times [perhaps an allusion to the plight of Jonah, swallowed by a great fish]

in the black *adj phr* *by 1928* Profitable; solvent; not in debt: *We toyed with bankruptcy for a while, but now we're in the black* [fr the color of ink traditionally used by bookkeepers to record assets, profits, etc]

in the bubble *adj* *sports* *by middle 1980s* In winning form; playing very well; =IN THE ZONE, ON A ROLL [said to have been the reply of basketball player Julius Irving when he was asked what a winning streak felt like]

in the bucks *adj phr* *by 1920s* Having money, esp a lot of it; in funds; =FLUSH, LOADED: *... right after Christmas and we're not in the bucks*

in the buff *adj phr* *by 1960s* Naked; =BARE-ASS, BUCK NAKED, IN THE ALTOGETHER: *There we stood, in the buff and abysmally embarrassed* [*in buff*, "in the bare skin," is found by 1602]

in the can *adj phr* *movie studio* *by 1940s* Successfully finished; ready for release, consumption, etc [fr the large, flat, circular tin *can* into which finished movie film is put]

in the cards *adj phr* *by 1936* Very probable; likely to or about to happen: *Another tax cut is in the cards*

in the catbird seat *See* SIT IN THE CATBIRD SEAT

in the chips *adj phr* *by 1938* Having money; affluent; =FLUSH, LOADED [*chips*, "money," is found by 1859]

in the chops *See* KLOP IN THE CHOPS

in the clear *adj phr* *by 1901* Apparently not involved; not suspected of wrongdoing; =CLEAN: *After thorough investigation they declared him in the clear*

in the clutch *adv phr* *by 1920s* At the moment when heroic performance under pressure is needed: *He's a good one to have around in the clutch* [probably a baseball term originally]

in the coop *adj phr* *police* *by 1960s* Sleeping on the job; off duty for unauthorized rest: *The cruise car for that street was supposed to be in the coop*— Lawrence Sanders

in the cross-hairs *adv phr* *by 1884* Fixed as a target; aimed at: *Detroit's Big Three found themselves again in the media cross hairs*—New York Times [the date shows the earliest use of the term for a telescope or telescopic sight indicator]

in the cut *adj phr* *1990s* *street talk* Relaxed; calm; =COOL, LAID-BACK [perhaps fr the confidence of one who *makes the cut*; perhaps a version of *in the groove*]

in the dark *by 1838* **1** *adj phr* Uninformed; ignorant; uncognizant: *We'll keep 'em in the dark about this until the time is right* **2** *adj phr* Mystified; puzzled: *You maybe told me, but I'm still sort of in the dark*

in the (or a) doghouse *adj phr* *by 1932* In a position or status of obloquy; out of favor, esp temporarily: *The press secretary is in the doghouse for cussing out a reporter/ He was in a doghouse at home on account of coming home cockeyed on his wedding anniversary...* —Joseph F Dinneen

in the driver's (or buddy) seat *adj phr* In the position of authority; in control: *With that kind of vote, we're in the driver's seat/ You don't make it very easy, do you? Always in the driver's seat*—W T Tyler

in the dumper *by 1970s* **1** *adj phr* Bankrupt; ruined; insolvent; =IN THE TUB **2** *adj phr* Lost; irretrievably forfeited or taken away: *Fifteen years plus, and his pension, in the dumper*—Scott Turow

in the face *See* A SLAP IN THE FACE, TILL one IS BLUE IN THE FACE

in the flesh *by 1865* **1** *adv phr* In person; in propria persona: *The great movie star appeared there in the flesh* **2** *adj phr*: *an in-the-flesh presentation* [an allusion to the corporeal resurrection of Jesus]

in the foot *See* SHOOT oneself IN THE FOOT

in the groove *1930s* *jive talk* **1** *adj phr* Making good sense; saying what needs saying: *Right! You're in the groove now* **2** *adj phr* In good form; working smoothly and well: *The professor of Classics was, as she would have put it, "in canaliculo," in the groove* **3** *adj phr* *jive musicians* Playing well and excitingly; =HEP

in the gutter *See* HAVE one's MIND IN THE GUTTER

in the hay *adv phr* *by 1940s* In bed, either sleeping or cavorting: *Joe's in the hay, zonked out/... a toss in the hay with her boss*—Neal Travis [probably fr *hit the hay*, found by 1912]
See ROLL IN THE HAY

in the hole **1** *adv phr* *poker* *by 1915* Dealt face down, in stud poker: *What's he got in the hole?* **2** *adv phr* *by 1890* In debt: *He is in the hole to the tune of $9,000*
See ACE IN THE HOLE

in the hopper *See* IN THE PIPELINE

in the hot seat *See* ON THE HOT SEAT

in the know *adj phr* *by 1902* Well informed, esp having current, advance, or confidential information: *Those in the know tell me to sell*

in the life *adj phr* *by early 1970s* Occupied or engaged in some specialized and usu socially despised way of living, such as the homosexual subculture or prostitution: *By the time strippers are "in the life" they have developed an exploitative attitude to men and people in general*—Trans-Action

in the long run *adv phr* *by 1768* After a long period of time, trial, endurance, etc: *It looks grim now, but in the long run you'll see it'll get better* [the form *at the long run* is found by 1627]

in the loop *by 1980s* **1** *adv phr* In a select company, esp in the communicating circle of the powerful: *... no force in the administration, observes simply, "He's not in the loop"*—Chicago Tribune/

Sometimes they are not even "in the loop" to get important information—New York Times **2 adv phr** Being circulated and processed; =IN THE PIPELINE: *It's in the loop now, and who knows when I'll get it back*—George Avgeris [probably an alteration of the military idiom *in the net,* of the same meaning, fr the use of radio *nets* or communications nexuses that include or exclude certain headquarters]

in the money 1 *adj phr* by 1902 Having money, esp in large amounts; =IN THE BUCKS, FLUSH: *I'm in the money at last*—H Allen Smith **2 adv phr** gambling & horse-racing by 1928 Providing winnings to bettors: *None of his horses finished in the money today at the track*

in the mud *See* STICK IN THE MUD

in the paint *adv phr* basketball by 1990s The area of a basketball court extending from the basket to the three-point line, hence the site of most action: *... "In the Paint" refers to being in the center of the action of a basketball game*—Milwaukee Journal/ *... who can crash the boards, feed and run the break, wheel and deal in the paint, and shoot from the three-point range...* —Milwaukee Journal [fr the fact that it is often painted a different color from the rest of the floor]

in the picture 1 *adv phr* by 1900 In a position to understand what is happening; in an informed position •Chiefly British: *OK, now that you're one of us, I want you in the picture* **2 adj phr** by 1923 Probable; distinctly conceivable: *It just isn't in the picture that they'll get married/ I'd like to travel, but it doesn't seem like it's in the picture for a year or so See* PUT someone IN THE PICTURE

in the pink *adj phr* by 1914 In good health; ruddy and in fine fettle

in the pipeline 1 *adj phr* (also **in the hopper** or **in the works**) by 1955 Being prepared, processed, or worked on; =ON THE FIRE: *... almost 10 times that amount in infrastructure projects were in the pipeline*—Milwaukee Journal/ *We got a little gizmo in the works that'll give them a duck-fit* **2 adv phr** surfers by 1963 Riding inside the curled-over front of a wave

in the pocket 1 *adj phr* 1960s narcotics Enjoying the best part of a psychedelic intoxication: *It was a golden time, and I was right in the pocket*—Rolling Stone **2 adj phr** jazz musicians by 1990s Playing precisely on the beat: *Jimmy Knepper, the trombonist, lays way back rhythmically. He rarely plays on the beat, or in the pocket, as musicians say. He places his notes in the cracks*—New Yorker

in the raw by 1930s **1** *adj phr* Naked; =IN THE BUFF: *... Leonotra always liked sleeping "in the raw," as she called it*—Carson McCullers **2 adj phr** Without amenity or polish; relatively crude and primitive: *Up there they lived life in the raw/ His work is sculpture in the raw*

in there by 1940s **1** *adv phr* =IN THERE PITCHING **2** *adv phr* baseball Pitched across home plate for a strike *See* HANG IN

in the red *adj phr* by 1926 In debt; losing money; insolvent: *The huge corporation has been in the red for eight years* [fr the color of ink traditionally used by bookkeepers to record debts, losses, etc]

in there pitching *adv phr* (also **in there** or **right there** or **right in there**) by 1940s Making a great effort; coping energetically and successfully; =ON TOP OF: *I'm on the go night and day, and I'm in there pitching*—Calder Willingham/ *When they needed a strong guide, he was in there*

in the ring *See* THROW one's HAT IN THE RING

in the road *See* WIDE PLACE IN THE ROAD

in the sack *adv phr* by 1960s Doing the sex act; making love: *Like Kirkland's book, Tharp's even includes a discussion of what Baryshnikov is like in the sack*—New Yorker

in the saddle 1 *adv phr* by 1738 In a controlling position; in charge: *I see old Wilcox is in the saddle again* **2 adv phr** by 1940s On duty; working; =IN HARNESS: *... on duty since six that morning. Close to eighteen hours in the saddle*—Carsten Stroud **3 adv phr** by 1940s Doing the sex act; in flagrante: *Maybe Caroline... caught old Bailey in the saddle up there*—Robert B Parker

in the same boat *adv phr* by 1550 Equally sharing a situation, plight, etc: *City, country, slum, farm, we're all in the same boat*

in the soup (or ◁the shit▷) *adv phr* first form by 1888, second by middle 1800s In trouble; in peril; =IN DEEP DOO-DOO: *He'd better clear this one fast or he's in the soup...* —Lawrence Sanders/ *Maybe that's why I'm in this soup to begin with*—Scott Turow/ *Jeeves cocks an eyebrow, and Bertie knows he's in the soup*—Village Voice

in the spotlight *adj phr* by 1904 Singled out for close attention; prominent: *He was a public figure, but hated being in the spotlight*

in the straight lane *adv phr* by 1970s Of a normal and respectable sort, esp not criminal nor homosexual nor drug-addicted: *... referred her to Booth Street for another chance at life in the straight lane*—Milwaukee Journal

in the tank *adv phr* 1990s Woefully ineffectual; inept; =LAME: *The Rockies are in the tank; they have lost twelve games in a row*—Denver radio news [a 1930s sports sense was "losing games or fights intentionally"] *See* GO INTO THE TANK, TANK

in the toilet *adj phr* by 1980s In very dire straits; standing a clear last: *Thirty-one years ago, when the Mets were really in the toilet, sportswriters rallied New Yorkers by touting the Mets' incompetence as symbolic of underdog struggle*—New York Times

in the tooth *See* LONG IN THE TOOTH

in the trenches *adv phr* by 1970s In the workplace; in contact with the people or problems in a situation; unprotected by distance or illusion: *I needed to be back in the trenches where I could really relate to a community*—Philadelphia Journal/ *More retrospective accounts are elegant and noble. Watson told it like it was in the trenches*—Edward Yoxen

in the tub *adj phr by 1940s* Bankrupt; ruined; =IN THE DUMPER

in the water *See* DEAD IN THE WATER

in the wind *See* TWIST SLOWLY IN THE WIND

in the woods *See* DOES A BEAR SHIT IN THE WOODS

in the works *See* IN THE PIPELINE

in the wrong *by 1400* **1** *adj phr* Mistaken; wrong; erring: *He's usually in the wrong when he discusses music* **2** *adv phr* In an unfavorable light or position: *This guy is always putting me in the wrong*

in the zone *adj phr* (also **zoned**) *tennis by 1980s* Playing easily and spontaneously: *Just that one time, I was in the zone/ She is zoned in the second set*—NBC television

into or **inta** (IN tōō, IN tə) *prep by 1960s* Currently interested or involved in; now practicing or absorbed in: . . . *a former Ivy Leaguer named Crimpcut who is into Buddha*—Russell Baker/ *Cool it, woman, I'm inta my thang*—D Evans/ . . . *if you're into Chinese cuisine*—Esquire

into oneself *adj phr by 1990s* Absorbed; introspective: *If a bear appears when you are into yourself*. . . —TV show *Trailside*

into someone for *adj phr by 1970s* In debt to; owing, esp money: *The guy's into me for five grand!*

into the ground *See* RUN something INTO THE GROUND

into the twentieth century *See* DRAG someone KICKING AND SCREAMING INTO THE TWENTIETH CENTURY

in transition *adj phr by early 1990s* Unemployed; =AT LIBERTY: *in transition: A many-headed euphemism*. . . *read: unemployed*—Wall Street Journal

intro *by 1923* **1** *n* An introduction or prelude of any sort: *"Listen to that intro," she says. "How awful"*—Whitney Balliett/ . . . *the kind of intro which is important*—Rolling Stone **2** *v*: *Who'll intro the archbishop?*

invent the wheel *v phr* To labor unnecessarily through the obvious and elementary stages of something: *Hey, cut to the chase! You don't have to invent the wheel*

invitation *See* DO YOU WANT AN ENGRAVED INVITATION

invite (IN vīt) *n by 1615* An invitation: *You can't go in there without an invite*

in-your-face *adj 1980s* Confrontational; hostile; impudent; =SASSY: *We're just playing in-your-face football, and we feel we can stand up to anybody*—Milwaukee Journal/ . . . *verbal mud-wallowing that proudly wears its in-your-face machismo smut*—Los Angeles Times/ . . . *takes its title from "Seasons in the Sun," which is as in-your-face as it gets*—Macon Telegraph

in your ear *See* PUT IT IN YOUR EAR

IOU (pronounced as separate letters) *n by 1618* A promise to pay; written acknowledgment of a debt: . . . *had won $800,000, in cash, not IOUs*—John Scarne

◁**Irish**▷ *n black street gangs by 1990s* A white person; =GRAY, OFAY: *You call all white people Irish?*—Robert B Parker

See GET one's DANDER UP, LACE-CURTAIN IRISH, SHANTY IRISH

Irish banjo *See* BANJO

◁**Irish buggy** (or **local**)▷ *n phr by about 1915* A wheelbarrow

◁**Irish confetti**▷ *n phr by 1935* Bricks, stones, Belgian paving blocks thrown in an altercation

Irisher *n by 1807* An Irish person or one of Irish descent: . . . *the most exemplary Irisher in Hollywood*—J Bacon

◁**Irish pennant**▷ *n phr nautical by 1883* The end of a rope, sheet, etc, carelessly left loose or trailing off a boat or ship: *Always loose ends. You know what they call them in the Navy? Irish pennants*—Lawrence Sanders [the form *Irish pendant* is found by 1840]

◁**Irish turkey**▷ *n phr hoboes by 1930s* Corned beef and cabbage

◁**Irish twins**▷ *n phr by 1980s* Two children born in short order: *Having two children as close as 10 to 18 months is comparable to having unequal twins, and they are even called Irish twins*—Milwaukee Journal

iron **1** *n motorcyclists by 1920s* A motorcycle; motorcycles collectively; =BIKE, SCOOT: . . . *competing on old British and American iron*—Cycle World **2** *n by 1935* A car: *On this big piece of German iron there's a bumper sticker*. . . —Elmore Leonard **3** *n by 1775* A firearm, esp a pistol; =SHOOTING IRON **4** *n by 1972* The weights used in weight-lifting *See* HAVE BRASS BALLS, HOT IRON, PUMP IRON, SHOOTING IRON, WAFFLE-IRON

iron betsy *n phr Army by 1940s* An Army rifle

iron-fisted *adj by 1828* Having a fist or grip strong as iron: . . . *the company appears to have iron-fisted control of the market*—Minneapolis-St Paul Star-Tribune

iron hat *n phr by 1940s* A derby hat; =HARD HAT

iron horse **1** *n phr fr middle 1800s* A railroad engine: *It seems he does have an affinity for the iron horse*—Milwaukee Journal **2** *n phr WWII Army* A military tank

iron man **1** *n phr by 1908* A dollar: . . . *two hundred iron men snatched*. . . *out of his mitt*—Charles MacArthur **2** *n phr by 1914* A very durable and tough man; tireless worker and player, esp in sports **3** *n phr musicians by 1960s* A West Indian musician who plays an instrument made out of an oil drum

iron out **1** *v phr* To kill, esp with a gun, an "iron": *You weren't at home when he was ironed out*—J Evans **2** *v phr by 1920s* To arrange satisfactorily; straighten out; =WORK OUT: *Ironing out the kinks this way made them aware of just how weak their endgame was*—Games

iron pony *n phr by 1940s* A motorcycle

iron-pumper *n by 1972* A weight lifter

iron up *v phr truckers by 1940s* To put on tire chains

is *See* BE

ish kabibble (ISH kə BIB əl) *interj by 1921* An exclamation of indifference, nonchalance, etc: *"Ishkabibble," or "I should worry"*—C T Ryan/ *It was a pretty abrupt transition from la belle époque into the Space Age, but ish kabibble*—S J Perelman [origin unknown; perhaps an alteration of Yiddish *nit* or *nisht gefidlt;* apparently introduced and perhaps coined by the comedienne Fanny Brice]

iso *n prison* Solitary confinement or isolation cells

isotope *n 1990s* A nearly identical person; near double: *Like his isotope Paglia, Rush Limbaugh can be counted on to bury the occasional nugget of truth beneath his avalanche of infuriating extrapolation and phony statistics*—New Republic/ *. . . actually IS you. Or an isotope of you. Or a photocopy of you*—Douglas Coupland [fr the term denoting nearly identical atoms in a chemical element]

Isro (IZ roh) *See* JEWFRO

Is the Pope Polish (or **Italian** or **Catholic) sentence** *by 1970s* That was a stupid question; isn't the answer very obvious?; =DOES A BEAR SHIT IN THE WOODS [first variant used since the accession of John Paul II]

it 1 *n by 1904* Sex appeal, esp female: *a girl with lots of it* **2** *modifier*: *Clara Bow, the original it girl* **3** *n by 1611* The sex act; copulation; =SCREWING •Used in numberless unmistakable but quasi-euphemistic contexts like *do it, go at it, want it, have it off, make it,* etc

it ain't over till it's over *sentence by 1970s* Don't give up hope; the decision is not yet made: *It ain't over 'til it's over. So reason America's steel-makers, who began a broad campaign last week to reverse recent tariff rulings*—New York Times [fr a heartening observation by the New York Yankees catcher and manager Yogi Berra]

◀**Italian football**▶ *n phr 1920s* A bomb; grenade, as used by criminals; =GUINEA FOOTBALL: *He gets out of line, so they kick an Italian football round his dump*—American Mercury

itch *See* SCRATCH

itch and rub *See* CHIEF ITCH AND RUB

itchy *adj by 1940s* Eager; restless; =ANTSY

it couldn't happen to a nicer guy *sentence by 1940s* What punishment or damage was received was richly deserved •The sentiment is quite ironic: *Joe got canned? It couldn't happen to a nicer guy!*

item *See* HOT NUMBER

an item *n phr by 1970* An unmarried but sexually linked couple; =A NUMBER: *Book Says Ava and Adlai Were An Item*—New York Magazine/ *. . . Carolyn and Larren used to be an item a long time ago*—Scott Turow [probably a shortening of "an *item* in the gossip columns"]

it girl *n phr 1920s* A young woman with sex appeal

-itis *suffix used to form nouns by 1903* An excessive and probably unhealthy involvement with or prevalence of what is indicated: *committeeitis/ symbolitis*

it is dollars to doughnuts *See* DOLLARS TO DOUGHNUTS

it rules *sentence 1980s teenagers* It is wonderful, impressive, awesome

it's a bitch (or **bitch kitty) sentence** *by 1814* The thing referred to is very impressive, very difficult, very complicated, very sad, or in some other way extraordinary: *She shook his knee playfully. "It's a bitch, isn't it?"*—Armistead Maupin/ *The last couple of laps are a real bitch kitty*

it's one's **ass** *sentence 1940s Army* One is doomed, or in great difficulty; =one's ASS IS GRASS •Usu a conditional statement: *. . . but I lend you my iron and it's my ass*—Lawrence Sanders/ *You write anything about me in an article again and it'll be your ass*—Joseph Heller/ *We have to find this outlaw an hour after daybreak or it's our asses!*—Don Pendleton

it's at *See* KNOW WHERE IT'S AT

it's been real or **it's been** *sentence by 1950s* It has been nice to meet you; it has been a nice time or party, etc •Often used ironically

it shouldn't happen to a dog *sentence by 1940s* What has happened, often to the speaker, ought not to happen even to the lowliest of creatures; it is atrocious: *The trouble I had getting this ticket, it shouldn't happen to a dog* [fr Yiddish speech patterns]

it's (or **the opera's) never over till the fat lady sings** *sentence fr 1970s baseball* Things are never finished until they are finished; further possibilities of action exist here: *Like they say around here, "The opera's never over till the fat lady sings." What hotel are you staying at, little lady?*—W T Tyler [originated by Dan Cook, a San Antonio broadcaster, and based on Yogi Berra's "It ain't over till it's over"]

itsy-bitsy or **itty-bitty** *adj by late 1930s* Tiny; esp, small and cute; =LITTLE BITTY, TEENSY-WEENSY: *. . . I can't find even an itty-bitty scrap of paper to show who these Wunderkinds are*—Scott Turow [fr baby talk]

it's you *sentence by 1960s* The thing is precisely appropriate or integral to you: *Oh my sweet, that mauve cummerbund, it's you!*

it's your nickel *sentence early 1940s students* Its is your prerogative to act, speak, etc, since you are paying for it: *"Go ahead, it's your nickel," he said quaintly. . .*—Stan Cutler [fr the (former) 5-cent charge for a telephone call]

it takes two to tango *sentence by 1952* This cannot happen or have happened without more than one person; cooperation or connivance is indicated: *It takes two to tango, said the mediator*—Philadelphia Journal/ *Now, it takes two to tango, but I still think it was more her fault*—San Francisco [the name of a 1950s song]

it up *suffix used to intensify verbs* Doing energetically, vehemently, loudly, etc, what is indicated: *camping it up/ hamming it up/ laughing it up*

ivories 1 *n by 1782* The teeth: *. . . as fine a display of ivories as we've seen in our time*—New Yorker **2** *n by 1830* Dice; a pair of dice

the **ivories** *n by 1918* Piano keys; the piano
  See TICKLE THE IVORIES

ivory-dome 1 *n about 1915* A stupid person;
=BONEHEAD **2** *n about 1940* An intellectual;
=DOUBLE-DOME, EGGHEAD

ivory-hunter *n baseball by 1915* A recruiter or
scout, esp a baseball scout

ivory-thumper *n by 1940s* A piano player:
. . . some cheap little ivory thumper—James M
Cain

I-way *n early 1990s* The Information Superhighway,
a projected system of linked computer networks;
=INFOBAHN: *. . . our current overhyping of the
InfoBahn, the I-way*—Douglas Coupland

ixnay *negation by 1930* No; no more; none: *Ixnay
on the kabitz*—American Mercury [pig Latin for *nix*]

izzatso *interj by 1900* An exclamation of defiance
or disbelief: *I'm a crud? Izzatso!*

J

J *n* (also **jay** or **jay smoke** or **J smoke**) *1960s narcotics* A marijuana cigarette; =JOINT [fr the *J* of *Mary Jane*, "marijuana," or the *j* of *joint*]

jab a vein *v phr narcotics by 1950s* To inject narcotics, esp heroin; =SHOOT UP: *...smoke marijuana or opium...or jab a vein*—Stephen Longstreet

jabber 1 *n narcotics by about 1915* A hypodermic needle **2** *v by 1499* To talk incessantly; chatter on *See* JIBBER-JABBER

jabberjack *n by 1970s* Foolish talk; nonsense; =BULLSHIT: *When I hear all the false jabberjack, all the phony cries and squawks*—Newsweek

jab-off *n 1920s narcotics* An injection of a narcotic

◁**jaboney** or **jiboney** or **jibone**▷ **1** *n* A newly arrived immigrant; a naive person; =GREENHORN: *Vinny, you're a real jibone, you know that?*—Richard Price **2** *n* A hoodlum; thug; =GORILLA: *He had a couple of his jiboneys with him*—Lionel Stander **3** *n 1990s television* A frequent television guest expert: *"Nightline" is desperate for a jaboney tonight. They tried for Kissinger...*—Los Angeles Times [origin uncertain; perhaps fr Italian dialect *giappone*, literally "a Japanese," but extended to any strange- or foreign-looking person]

jack 1 *n by 1859* Money: *...the fans which paid their jack*—H Witwer/ *I figured it would be an easy way to make some jack*—Village Voice **2** *v Vietnam War Air Force* To take twisting evasive action in an airplane; =JANK, JINK **3** *n 1980s students* Nothing; =JACK SHIT, ZIP: *What did you do today? Jack*—UCLA Slang **4** *v esp 1990s teenagers* To steal; rob: *Two men who "jacked," or stole, a 1991 Plymouth Colt...*—Macon Telegraph [money sense probably fr the expression *hard Jackson*, or *hard Jackson money* referring to President Andrew Jackson, and found by 1838; second sense perhaps related to mid–1800s British criminal slang *jack*, "run away, escape," or perhaps by folk etymology fr *jank*, an echoic companion of *jink*; compare *jink-jank* with *yin-yang* and *zig-zag*; stealing sense probably fr *hijack*, and related to *carjacking*] *See* BALL THE JACK, HEAVY MONEY, HIJACK, PIECE OF CHANGE

Jack *n by 1889* Man; friend; fellow; =MAC •Used in addressing any man, whatever his name: *Man, he's murder, Jack*—Max Shulman/ *That supposed to be funny, jack?*—Robert B Parker

jack around *students by 1960s* **1** *v phr* To idle about; =FART AROUND, SCREW AROUND: *He and LD had been jacking around in practice and LD fell on his leg*—Peter Gent **2** *v phr* To meddle with; =FOOL AROUND: *...and jack around with somebody else's wife*—Dan Jenkins/ *...until the lawyers started jacking around with the structure*—Toronto Life [origin uncertain; perhaps fr *jack off*]

jack someone **around** *students by 1960s* **1** *v phr* To tease; =KID: *These guys are only trying to jack you around*—Dan Jenkins **2** *v phr* To victimize; =HASSLE, JERK someone AROUND: *Don't you think I know when people are jacking me around?*—Armistead Maupin

◁**jackass**▷ *n by 1823* A stupid person; idiot; dolt; fool; =LUNKHEAD, SHIT-FOR-BRAINS

jackass rig (or **harness**) *n phr police by 1980s* A shoulder holster: *The butt of a large revolver was hanging out of a molded-leather Jackass rig on Maksins' left side*—Carsten Stroud [probably fr the resemblance of the harness to that of a horse or jackass]

jacked in *adj phr early 1990s* Up-to-date and aware; =ON TOP OF: *...I'm impressed by the level of techiness: people here are fully jacked in*—Douglas Coupland [fr *jack*, "male plug used in telephone and electronic patching," hence, "totally connected"]

jacked up *by 1970s* **1** *adj phr* Stimulated; exhilarated; =HIGH: *...all the parents jacked up on coffee*—Cameron Crowe/ *I was jacked up, coming in, then I faced reality...*—Milwaukee Journal **2** *adj phr* Elevated, esp by artifice; =JUMPED-UP: *That he is a jacked-up cowboy and minor film star is a libel*—National Review [first sense probably fr *jagged up*, "drunk," found by 1737]

jacket *police by 1940s* A criminal record; =RAP SHEET [fr the cardboard folder or *jacket* used to hold the papers] *See* DUST someone's JACKET, MONKEY JACKET, YELLOW JACKET

jack (or **jake**) **it** *v phr baseball by 1970s* To play half-heartedly, claiming an injury; malinger: *...Piniella's charge that Henderson was "jacking it"*—Milwaukee Journal [fr earlier *jake*, "a player who loafs or stalls," apparently based on the name of Jake Stahl, who played and managed various teams between 1903 and 1913, because his surname rhymes with "stall"]

jackleg *n by 1853* An incompetent and unscrupulous person; =PHONY: *You don't think I hang out with jacklegs like that*—Harry Crews

309

jack Mormon *by 1890* **1** *n phr* A non-Mormon who associates with or imitates Mormons **2** *n phr* A non-observant or backsliding Mormon: *Sure I have coffee in the house. I'm only a jack Mormon*—Lee Russell

◁**jack off**▷ *v by 1916* To masturbate; =JERK OFF •Said chiefly of males [ultimately fr *jack*, "penis"]

◁**jack-off** or **jagoff**▷ *n by 1930s* A stupid, incompetent person; =JERK: *What's that jack-off up to now?/ ...those two slick-haired jagoffs*—William Brashler

jack out *v phr by 1940s* To pull out; seize and expose: *...could jack his gun out kind of fast*—Raymond Chandler

jack party *n phr sports by 1970s* A neglectful or indifferent participant: *Coach Phillips was a jack party, didn't even have headphones on*—Denver radio commentator
See JACK IT

jackpot *n gambling by 1940s* The largest win available in a slot machine [fr the *progressive jack pot* in poker, which stipulates that if no player has a pair of jacks or better to open, then on the next hand, after anteing again, someone must have queens or better, and so on; thus the *pot* could become quite large; the outdated poker use, "a very large win," is found by 1881]
See CUT UP THE TOUCHES, HIT THE JACKPOT

jack-rabbit *v by 1990s* To advance by leaps, like a jack-rabbit: *...a stock market jack-rabbiting past the Dow Jones 5,000*—Milwaukee Journal Sentinel

jackroll *v by about 1915* To rob, esp a drunken man; =ROLL: *Father had recently been "jackrolled" while drunk*—W J Slocum

◁**jack shit**▷ *n phr Southern students by 1970s* Nothing at all; =DIDDLY, ZILCH: *They had it, but jack shit was what they had*—Robert Stone/ *I didn't know jackshit about it*—Richard Merkin/ *"Ex-model" means jackshit*—Jessica Lange

jack up **1** *v phr 1960s narcotics* To inject a narcotic; =SHOOT UP **2** *v phr by 1970s* To stimulate; exhilarate: *Aren't you getting jacked up?...Ain't it great?*—Washington Post **3** *v phr by 1904* To raise; increase: *Did they jack up the price again?*

jack someone **up** **1** *v phr by 1896* To rebuke, esp to revive a sense of duty: *The sergeant had to jack the whole platoon up* **2** *v phr by 1960s* To rob, esp at gunpoint **3** *v phr by 1960s* To thrash; trounce; =CLOBBER **4** *v phr black by 1960s* Of the police, to stop and search someone, demand identification, question harshly, etc; =ROUST, TAKE ON

jag *by 1887* **1** *n* A drinking spree; =BENDER **2** *n* A spell or spree of a specified sort: *One had a "crying jag"*—P Marks/ *...the annual Christmas gift-buying jag*—Hal Boyle [fr *jag*, "a load," found by 1597, whence "as much liquor as a man can drink," found by 1678]
See CRYING JAG

Jag *n by 1950s* A Jaguar car

jagged (JAGD) *adj by 1737* Drunk

jag house *n phr homosexuals by 1960s* A house of male prostitution [probably fr *jack*, "penis"]

jagoff *See* JACK-OFF

jail *v by 1980s* To live tolerably in jail; survive imprisonment: *Roy taught me how to jail*—Elmore Leonard

jail bait *by 1934* ◁**1**▷ *n phr* A girl below the legal age of sexual consent, copulation with whom would constitute statutory rape; =SAN QUENTIN QUAIL **2** *n phr* Any person or thing likely to tempt one to crime and imprisonment

jailbird *n by 1618* A convict or ex-convict

jailhouse lawyer *n phr by 1940s* A prisoner who, authoritative or not, is disposed to lengthy discussion of his legal rights and those of other inmates; =GUARDHOUSE LAWYER: *...an avid reader of good literature and a "jailhouse lawyer"*—E Ranzal

jake *underworld by 1914* **1** *adj* Excellent; very satisfactory; =HUNKY-DORY: *She said the whole college seemed jake to her*—P Marks **2** *adv*: *You never can tell on a day like this, things could be goin' jake one minute, then presto, before you know it you're history*—Village Voice [origin unknown]

jalopy or **jaloppy** or **jalop** *by 1924* **1** *n* An old and battered car or airplane; =HEAP: *A jalopy is a model one step above a "junker"*—New York Times **2** *n* Any car; any vehicle; =BUGGY: *Let them search every jalop on the road*—radio show "Gangbusters" [origin unknown; perhaps fr *Jalapa*, a Mexican city to which many US used cars were sent]

jam[1] **1** *n by 1914* A predicament; =BIND, TIGHT SPOT **2** *n* (also **traffic jam**) *by 1917* A tight crush of cars, people, etc; =JAM-UP **3** *n underworld by 1925* Small objects like rings and watches that are easy to steal **4** *v 1930s jazz musicians* To play jazz with great spontaneity, esp to improvise freely with other musicians and usu without an audience **5** *modifier*: *Jam bands do have styles*—C Smith **6** *n 1930s jazz musicians* A party or gathering where jazz musicians play for or with one another; =JAM SESSION: *Bix and the boys would blow it free and the jam was on*—Stephen Longstreet **7** *v students fr 1930s black* To have a good time; party joyously; =GET IT ON: *As for us, we danced, we jammed, and we wondered*—Buzz **8** *n students fr 1930s black* A party: *Are you going to the jam tonight?*—Delcastle Dictionary of Slang **9** *v New York teenagers by 1970s* To make up a rap song, esp in a competitive situation **10** *v by 1960s* To make trouble for; coerce or harass, esp with physical force: *...than when they're jammin' me for a penny every time I walk down the street*—Newsweek/ *He knows what to say that will jam you and not jam you*—New York Magazine ◁**11**▷ *n by 1896* The vulva; a woman's genitals ◁**12**▷ *v students by 1970s* To do the sex act; copulate; =SCREW: *Did what? Jammed*—Paul Theroux **13** *n 1960s narcotics* Cocaine; =NOSE CANDY **14** *v hawkers by 1950s* To auction; act as an auctioneer **15** *v by 1914* To send an interfering signal on a broadcast channel one wishes to make unintelligible: *An attempt was made to jam*—The Voice of America **16** *v by 1990s* To run away; =SKEDADDLE: *Let's jam!*—TV show *Land of the*

Lost/ ...I shifted into high gear and jammed it...up to Santa Teresa...—Sue Grafton **17** v baseball by 1960s To pitch the ball close to the batter, so that he is forced to hit it close to the gripped end of the bat **18** v basketball by 1990s =SLAM DUNK [all senses have some relation to the basic notion of squeezing or crushing so as to make *jam*]
See IN A JAM, JIM-JAM, LOGJAM, TOE JAM

jam² n homosexuals by 1970s A heterosexual man [said to be fr *just a man*]

jam auction (or pitch) n phr hawkers by 1940s A hawker's business carried on in a store, esp one where cheap knickknacks, souvenirs, jewelry, etc, are sold

jamble **See** JIMBLE-JAMBLE

jambox **See** GHETTO BOX

jammed adj by 1922 Drunk: He got jammed—Philadelphia Bulletin

jammed up adj phr by 1940s =IN A JAM: You are jammed up—R Starnes

jammer n 1930s jazz talk A musician who takes part in jam sessions: ...the likely jammers being the four ex-Beatles, Leon Russell, Mick Jagger, and a few other "friends"—Rolling Stone
See CAMEL-JAMMER, GEAR-JAMMER

jammies n by 1980s Pajamas: ...who conclude the revue clad in jammies—Milwaukee Journal/ ...into the bedroom, into his jammies, into the bed...—Stan Cutler

jammy¹ n (also **jammies**) by 1980s A gun: Also a jammy, a smoker, a heater, a piece—Street News/ ...jammies was street terminology for gun—New York Times [origin unknown]

jammy² adj by 1853 Excellent ●Chiefly British [fr jam, the sweet conserve]

jamoke¹ or **Jamoke** (jə MOHK) n by 1914 Coffee [perhaps a blend of java and mocha]

jamoke² or **jamoche** n A despised man; =JERK: I don't rate your chances none too good if that jamoke's going to defend you—George V Higgins/ ...you really think this jamoche is gonna give you somethin'?—Scott Turow [origin unknown]

jam-packed adj by 1925 Very tightly packed; very crowded: ...those jam-packed suburban classes—New York Magazine

the jams **See** JIM-JAMS, KICK OUT THE JAMS

jam session n phr 1930s jazz musicians A gathering of musicians, esp jazz musicians, playing freely and for one another, but sometimes in a public performance; =JAM: Here's Dodo on the piano and Tiny on the bass. Looks like we'll have a fine jam session—Slim Gaillard

jam up v phr by 1940s To encumber; disable by overburdening: ...to file complaints. It was a sure way to jam up a cop...—Michael Grant

jam-up n by 1940s A tight crush of people, cars, etc, preventing normal movement; =JAM: ...to forestall the possibility of another jam-up—James M Cain

jane by 1906 **1** n A young woman; =CHICK, DOLL: ...some jane that was kind of simple—A Lomax/

Ladies from Long Island, janes from New Jersey—New York Times **2** n A man's sweetheart, fiancée, etc: ...make earrings for our janes out of them studs—Langston Hughes
See MARY JANE

Jane Crow n phr by 1960s Discrimination against women: ...segregation by sex, describing it as "Jane Crow"—Life [fr Jim Crow]

Jane Q Citizen (or Public) n phr by 1940s Any woman, esp the average or typical woman: The president seems very popular with Jane Q Citizen

janfu n WWII armed forces Confusion; chaos; =SNAFU [fr joint Army Navy fuck-up]

◁**jang**▷ n The penis
See YING-YANG

jangle **See** JINGLE-JANGLE

jank v Vietnam War Air Force To maneuver an airplane about evasively; =JACK, JINK: I was janking...when I got hit—Time [perhaps fr jink and jank on the model of zig and zag]
See JINK

◀**Jap**▶ (JAP) n by 1902 A Japanese or person of Japanese descent; =NIP

◀**JAP** or **Jap**▶ (JAP) **See** JEWISH AMERICAN PRINCESS

jarhead 1 n by 1918 A mule **2** n WWII armed forces A US Marine; =GYRENE

jasper by 1914 **1** n A fellow; man; =GUY: ...two jaspers with a grudge—H Birney **2** n A rustic; =HICK

java or **Java** n by 1907 Coffee [fr Java, an Indonesian island whence some coffee was exported]

jaw 1 v by 1760 To talk; chat; converse: Can't stand here jawing with you all day—S J Perelman **2** n by 1842: ...ain't had a good jaw together—W R Burnett **3** v by 1810 To exhort; lecture; strive to persuade orally; =JAWBONE: ...had kept sober for several months by jawing drunks, unsuccessfully—J Alexander
See BAT one's GUMS, CRACK one's JAW, FLAPJAW, GLASS JAW, RATCHET-MOUTHW

jawbone 1 v by 1862 To borrow; obtain on credit: He jawboned enough...to set up an office—Robert Ruark **2** n by 1862 Credit or trust, esp financial: Try as he might he got no jawbone from the bankers **3** v by 1966 To discuss; talk over, esp extensively and profoundly: ...a distinguished group of presidential biographers to jawbone about the situation—Washington Post **4** v by 1969 To exhort and earnestly urge in order to persuade ●Used predominantly to describe high-level pressure applied on economic issues, and popularized under President Lyndon Johnson: ...the Presidential promise not to "jawbone" business into not raising prices—Commonweal/ ...chiefly direct controls on all pay and prices or "jawboning" against individual wage and price rises—Wall Street Journal **5** n: The President launched a sustained and hot jawbone on the budget cuts **6** v WWII Army To fire a weapon in practice, esp for formal qualification to use it

jawboning n by 1960s Strong exhortation; potent oral pressure: The technique was called "jawboning." *Lyndon Johnson and Mr Nixon used it*—Newsweek

jawbreaker or **jawcracker 1** *n by 1835* A long word or a word difficult to pronounce: *Diphenyl-pentoactomaggetoneplangianoliosis is something of a jawbreaker* **2** *n by 1875* A piece of hard candy, esp a spherical piece with bubble gum in the center

jaw dropper *n phr 1990s* Something astonishing; an awesome event: *Wasn't that a jaw dropper! Imagine Ted being elected Dalai Lama!*—Slang Bag 93/ *That first show was a jaw-dropper...*—Milwaukee Journal [fr the instinctive gaping response to such an event]

jawed *See* GLASS-JAWED

jaw-hanging *adj by 1990s* Causing the jaw to gape in awe; riveting: *...you have to have cutting-edge, jaw-hanging graphics*—Los Angeles Times

jay[1] *n by 1523* A rustic; simpleton; =HICK, RUBE **2** *n underworld by 1884* An easy victim; =MARK, PATSY, SUCKER [fr the raucous bird]

jay[2] *n 1960s narcotics* Marijuana or a marijuana cigarette; =J: *Let's do up a jay and truck on down to the libo*—Esquire

Jayhawker *n by 1858* A native or resident of Kansas [fr a term for "freebooter, guerrilla," applied during the Civil War to pro-slavery raiders]

jay smoke *See* J

jaywalk *v by about 1916* To walk into or across a street at a forbidden place or without the right of way [fr the naive behavior of a *jay*, "rustic"]

jazz ◁1▷ *v fr late 1800s black* To do the sex act with or to; =FUCK: *I jazzed her, too*—James T Farrell/ *...what he's going to do to a guy he finds out's been jazzing his wife...*—Elmore Leonard **2** *v black by about 1875* To increase the tempo, animation, or excitement of something; =JAZZ something UP: *Come on, jazz yourself, we're late* **3** *n*: *This place needs more jazz and pizzazz* **4** *n early 1900s jazz musicians* A kind of popular, often improvised, and emotive instrumental music originating among Southern black people in the late 19th century, and still evolving as an American and a world style **5** *v* To arrange or play in a jazz style: *They jazzed the National Anthem* **6** *modifier*: *a jazz trumpet/ jazz riffs* **7** *n by 1918* Empty talk; nonsense; lies; =BALONEY, BULLSHIT, JIVE: *You mean her most eloquent pledges were jazz?* **8** *v*: *Stop your jazzing and merely adduce the data* **9** *n by 1960s* Ornamentation; embellishment, esp when merely superficial: *a clean design, without a lot of jazz* [origin unknown; *jass* was an earlier spelling]

See ALL THAT JAZZ

jazz-bo 1 *n by 1923* A flashily groomed man or woman; =CAT, DUDE: *...her stage image as a witchy little jazz-bo with a boxer's shuffle and a baseball player's kick*—Time ◁2▷ *n by 1919* A black man, esp a black soldier

jazzed *adj 1960s teenagers* Eager and energetic; =PSYCHED UP: *...I'm really jazzed. I want to train for '96*—Milwaukee Journal

jazzed up *adj phr by 1930s* Made faster, more exciting, interesting, active, etc; =HOPPED UP, HYPED-UP: *They were riding motorcycles, the big jazzed-up ones*—New York Times

jazz something **up** *by 1930s* **1** *v phr* To make faster, more exciting or stimulating, etc: *He tried to jazz the meeting up* **2** *v phr* To play in the musical style indicated

jazzy *by about 1915* **1** *adj* Resembling or partaking of the musical style indicated: *He could turn a Beethoven sonata into a jazzy little number* **2** *adj* Exciting; stimulating; =SEXY: *He wore bow ties and...jazzy suits*—Truman Capote

jeans 1 *n by 1843* Trousers; pants: *I had the price in my jeans*—Jack London **2** *n by 1950s* Blue denim work pants or trousers that are modifications of these [fr *jean fustian*, a cloth originating in *Gene (Genoa)*, Italy]

See STRETCH SOME JEANS

jeasly or **jeasely** *adj by 1920s* Of little worth; trivial; =MEASLY: *...here is his jeasely ol' pie and biscuit irons*—Stewart Holbrook [probably echoic-symbolic]

◁**Jebby**▷ *n by 1950s* A Jesuit

jeebies *See* the HEEBIE-JEEBIES

jeep *WWII Army* **1** *n* A useful and durable small open US military vehicle of World War 2, later adapted to civilian use and still evolving **2** *v*: *...jeeping...through Maquis-held territory*—Time **3** *n* =JEEP CARRIER [fr the name and cry of a small versatile creature first appearing in the comic strip "Thimble Theatre" by E C Segar on March 16, 1936, and the military designation *GP*, "general purpose" in the designation of the little vehicle]

jeep carrier *n phr WWII Navy* A US Navy escort aircraft carrier

Jeepers Creepers or **Jeepers** *interj by 1929* An exclamation of surprise, dismay, emphasis, etc: *Jeepers Creepers, another busted leg!* [a euphemism for *Jesus Christ*]

jeep-jockey *n WWII Army* A jeep driver

Jeez *interj* (also **jeez** or **Jeeze** or **jeeze** or **Jees** or **jees** or **jeezy-peezy** or **Jeezy-peezy**) *entry form by 1923, jeeze by 1920, jees by 1931, jeezy-peezy by 1942* An exclamation of surprise, dismay, emphasis, etc; =JEEPERS CREEPERS [fr *Jesus*]

jeff or **Jeff 1** *n 1930s black* A white person **2** *v black by 1940s* To take on the values of the dominant white society; =TOM: *...same people Profilin' and Jeffin' for their survival*—Amsterdam News **3** *n black by 1940s* A tedious person; =SQUARE [fr *Jefferson* Davis, president of the Confederacy during the Civil War]

See SILVER JEFF

jelloid *n by 1990s* A weak and indecisive person; jellyfish: *If Clinton shows more policy spine this year, he'll be a stronger candidate against a jelloid George Bush this fall*—New Republic [fr *jelly* plus *-oid*]

jelly *by 1940s* **1** *n* An easy, pleasant task; sinecure; =CINCH **2** *n* Anything gotten free or without effort; =GRAVY **3** *n* =JELLY-ROLL

jellybean 1 *n by about 1919* A gaudily dressed

man; faddish dresser **2** *n by about 1915* A stupid person; fool; =SAP: *The jelly beans I went to school with*—Richard Bissell **3** *n baseball by 1950s* A novice; =ROOKIE

jelly-belly *n by 1896* A fat person

jelly-roll ◁**1**▷ *n black fr about 1870s* The vulva; vagina ◁**2**▷ *n black fr about 1870s* The sex act; copulation; =FUCKING **3** *n black fr about 1870s* A man obsessed with women; woman-chaser; =COCKSMAN, LOVER-BOY **4** *n black fr about 1870s* A lover or mistress; =SWEET MAMA **5** *n by 1980s* Large round hay bales; big round bales [sexual senses perhaps related to *jelly*, "semen," found by 1622]

jerk 1 *n by 1892* A short branch railroad line: *...a small "jerk" with only two locals a day*—Jack London **2** *n cabdrivers fr 1920s* A short ride **3** *n carnival by 1935* A tedious and ineffectual person, esp a man; fool; ninny; ass; =BOOB, TURKEY: *Jeez, what a jerk!*—American Scholar **4** *n by 1935* A contemptible and obnoxious person, esp a man; =ASSHOLE, BASTARD: *Dr Johnson admired Goldsmith's literary talent, although he considered him a jerk*—Dwight MacDonald/ *...a jerk not only bores you, but pats you on the shoulder as he does so*—Heywood Broun **5** *modifier*: *...a couple of jerk wops*—I, Mobster **6** *n by 1923* =SODA JERK ◁**7**▷ *v by 1940s* =JERK OFF [the derogatory term comes fr *jerk off*, "masturbate"; the form *soda jerker* is found by 1883]
See CIRCLE JERK, KNEE-JERK, PULL someone's CHAIN, SODA JERK

jerk around *v phr by 1980s* To idle about; play casually; =FOOL AROUND: *...if kids are jerking around and enter a system as a lark with no intent to deprive*—Newsweek

jerk someone **around** (or **off**) *v phr by 1980s* To victimize or harass: *Salespeople feel that men who want hand holding are often jerking them around*—Philadelphia/*...bumming cigarettes...and generally jerking him around throughout the broadcast*—Rolling Stone/ *I think Coyle was jerking you off*—George V Higgins

jerk (or **yank**) someone's **chain** *v phr by 1980s* To victimize or dupe; harass; =JERK someone AROUND: *You came out to jerk my chain tonight*—George V Higgins/ *... the perception white voters got that Jackson was jerking their chains*—David Broder/ *Are you guys yanking my chain?*—TV show *Hill Street Blues* [fr the notion of a chained man, monkey, etc, being harassed]

Jerkimer *See* HERKIMER JERKIMER

Jerk McGee *n phr by 1950s* A stupid person; =JERK: *Some Jerk McGee like you just got off the boat*—J Cannon

◁**jerk off**▷ **1** *v phr by 1916* To masturbate; =JACK OFF: *I went ahead as usual and jerked off into my sock*—Philip Roth/ *KB was always trying to jerk off*—Claude Brown **2** *v phr by 1950s* To idle about; =FUCK OFF, GOOF OFF

◁**jerk-off**▷ **1** *modifier* Useful for masturbation: *...an electric suction jerk-off device*—Village Voice

2 *adj* Stupid; =JERKY: *It's too much of a jerk-off idea*—Rolling Stone/ *...preparing an answer to the jerkoff question*—Easyriders **3** *n by 1960s* A person who jerks off, either literally or figuratively: *I'd be tickled to death to lose the jerk-offs*—Rolling Stone

jerk over *v phr by 1980s students* To victimize; treat disrespectfully; =DIS: *My professor jerked me over when he refused to accept my paper two days late*—UCLA Slang **2** *v phr by 1980s* To treat ineffectually; =FUCK UP, MESS UP: *Well, you know, just generally jerking it over*—Carsten Stroud

jerk soda *v phr by 1883* To work at a soda fountain: *They had spent their tender years jerking sodas*—American Mercury

◁**jerk the gherkin**▷ *v phr by 1940s* To masturbate; =PULL one's PUD: *Your gherkin is for firkin', not for jerkin'*—Folk saying

jerk (or **jerkwater**) **town** *n phr by 1899* A small town; an insignificant village: *...to fool around a jerk town*—J Flynt

jerkwater *adj by 1897* Insignificant; trivial: *These seem like jerkwater sentiments*

jerk water (or **soup**) *v phr railroad by 1890s* To take on boiler water, esp by scooping from a trough between the rails [whence *jerk* or *jerkwater town*, because the train doesn't stop]

jerky *adj by 1940s* Having the traits of a jerk: *...any jerky Joe*—Billy Rose
See HERKY-JERKY

jerry 1 *n railroad by about 1915* A track laborer; =GANDY DANCER **2** *n hoboes by about 1915* Any laborer **3** *n underworld by 1940s* A small pistol that can be easily concealed

Jerry *n WWI Army fr British* A German soldier; =KRAUT, KRAUTHEAD [fr the German helmet, which was likened to a *jerry*, "chamber pot," found by 1827]

jerry gang *n phr railroad by about 1915* A track-laying crew

jerry-rigged *adj by 1980s* Patched or cobbled; =HOKED-UP: *...these would be much better than something jerry-rigged on my Olivetti*—Sara Paretsky [a blend of *jerry-built*, "badly or flimsily built," found by 1869, with *jury-rigged*, "rigged temporarily or in an emergency," found by 1788; the origin of both of these is unknown]

Jersey lightning *n phr by 1852* Applejack brandy [fr the fact that applejack brandy was (and still is) distilled in New Jersey]

Jerusalem Slim *n phr hoboes by 1920s* Jesus Christ

the **Jesus** *n by 1940s* =BEJESUS
See EAST JESUS, EAST JESUS STATE

Jesus boots *n phr 1960s counterculture* Men's sandals

Jesus Christ *interj by 1592* An exclamation of surprise, dismay, emphasis, etc; =JEEPERS CREEPERS

Jesus freaks (or **people**) *n phr 1960s counterculture* Members of an evangelical Christian religious movement among young people, esp ex-hippies and drug addicts: *...in this light the herds of Jesus*

freaks—M Rossman/ *Jesus freaks, gypsies, lunatic right-wingers, leering conventioneers*—Psychology Today

Jesus H Christ *interj by 1840s* An exclamation of surprise, dismay, emphasis, etc; =JEEPERS CREEPERS [the intrusive *H* may reflect *IHC*, fr Greek *IHSOUS,* "Jesus Christ," found by 950 and still embroidered on vestments of the Church of England; or it may be an infix for oral emphasis]

jet *v 1990s teenagers* To leave; =AIR OUT, SPLIT

the **jet set** *n phr by 1951* The group of wealthy, chic people who move about from one costly venue to another: *...a charter member of the international jet set*—Time

the **jetties** *n phr by 1970s* Jet fatigue; jet lag: *She was disoriented a couple days by a bad case of the jetties*

◀**Jewboy**▶ *n by 1796* A Jewish boy or man

◀**Jew (or jew) down**▶ *v phr by 1848* To bargain and haggle in an attempt to get a lower price: *...but then the guy started jewin' me down*—Philadelphia [*jew* in the same sense is found by 1824]

the **jewel in** one's **crown** *n phr by 1873* One's most precious and distinguished possession: *Once the jewel in Luce's crown,* Time *was seen by its new managers as just another rhinestone*—New York Review of Books

jewels *See* FAMILY JEWELS

◁**Jewfro** or **Isro**▷ *n police by 1960s* A hairstyle similar to the Afro;: *...wild curly hair that stood out from their heads like pyramids of Brillo, what police slang called a Jewfro*—Beth Gutcheon

Jewish Alps *n phr by 1920s* The Catskill Mountains in southern New York State; =BORSCHT BELT: *I could never go back to the Jewish Alps with any woman whose name was Birdye*—Paul Sann [the term was originally applied to Washington Heights, a steep rocky neighborhood in northern Manhattan, where many Jews settled]

◀**Jewish American Prince**▶ *n phr by 1970s* A pampered and usu wealthy young man who feels he deserves special treatment

◀**Jewish American Princess** or **JAP** or **Jap**▶ *n phr by 1970s* A pampered and usu wealthy young woman who feels she deserves special treatment: *...plenty of Jewish American Princesses in their wigs and false eyelashes*—Xaviera Hollander/ *...the unofficial, secret JAP within me*—Village Voice

◀**Jewish flag**▶ *n phr 1920s hoboes* A dollar bill

◀**Jewish lightning**▶ *n phr by 1960s* What causes buildings, usu old ones, to burn so that insurance can be collected; arson

◁**Jewish penicillin**▷ *n phr by 1950s* Chicken soup, regarded as a panacea

Jheri curl (or Kurl) *black by 1990s* **1** *v phr*: *It's a wonder we don't have a national holiday for Madame CJ Walker, who invented the process of straightening kinky hair. Call it JheriKurled or call it relaxed. It's still fried hair*—New Yorker **2** *n* Staightened kinky hair: *He was a tall motherfucker with a Jheri curl, looked like a baboon*—Buzz

◀**jibagoo**▶ *See* JIGABOO

jibber-jabber **1** *v* To talk nonsense; =JABBER: *Time for Congress to quit jibber-jabbering*—Philadelphia Bulletin/ *We just jibber-jabbered these things all day*—Wall Street Journal

jiboney *See* JABONEY

a **jiffy** **1** *n phr* (Variations: **jif** or **jiff** or **jiffin** or **jiffing**) *by 1793* A short space of time; an instant: *...drop off to sleep for a jiffy*—S J Perelman/ *I'll have coffee ready in a jiff*—Lawrence Sanders **2** *modifier*: *Let's make a jiffy dessert* [said to be fr thieves' slang *jeffey* or *jiffey,* "lightning"]

jiffy bag **1** *n phr WWII armed forces* A small canvas or leather bag for carrying toilet articles, etc, while traveling **2** *n phr* (also **Jiffy,** a trademark) *by 1970* A heavy-walled paper bag used for mailing items, esp books

jig **1** *n* A dancing party or public dance ◀**2**▶ *n by 1923* =JIGABOO

◀**jigaboo**▶ (also **jibagoo** or **jigabo** or **jig** or **zig** or **zigaboo** or **zigabo**) *by 1909* **1** *n* A black person **2** *modifier*: *a jig band*

jigger **1** *n hoboes by 1890s* An artificially made sore, usu on the arm or leg, useful in begging: *...whether it will pay to use his "jigger"*—J Flynt **2** *n by 1857* A liquor glass of one-and-a-half ounce capacity; =SHOT GLASS **3** *v hoboes by 1890s* To interfere with; =QUEER: *...jigger our riding on the railroad*—J Flynt **4** *v by 1970s* To tamper with or falsify; =DOCTOR: *There is pressure from Casey...to jigger estimates*—New York Times/ *...how the gold trading was jiggered*—Lawrence Sanders **5** *n by 1874* =THINGAMAJIG [*giger,* "lock," is found by 1612, apparently coined by Thomas Dekker, and is probably the source of the fifth sense]

See DOODAD, I'LL BE DAMNED

jiggered *See* I'LL BE DAMNED

jigger-man or **jiggers guy** *n* or *n phr underworld by 1940s* A lookout: *...acted only as "the two-block jiggers guy"*—LF McHugh

jiggers or **jigs** *interj* An exclamation of alarm and warning: *Jiggers, the heat's here* [probably connected with British dialect *jigger,* "constable, police officer," found by 1857]

jiggery-pokery *n by 1893* Deception; trickery; =SKULLDUGGERY: *...or what some term jiggery-pokery*—Time/ *...could have prevented most of the jiggery-pokery*—New Yorker [probably fr Scottish *joukery-paukery* fr *jouk,* "trick"]

jiggins *See* JUGGINS

jiggle or **jiggly** *by 1970s* **1** *n* The bouncing and shaking of a woman's parts, esp of the breasts ●Hence the whole tone and style of blatant female sexual exploitation: *...help put the jiggle back in the series "Charlie's Angels"*—People **2** *modifier*: *...the ads for comedies in the jiggle genre*—TV Guide/ *...a brand of show so dependent on buxom starts and wet T-shirts that it was called...jiggle television*—Macon Telegraph **3** *v*: *She swims, jumps rope, and practices jiggling in front of the* mirror—Philadelphia **4** *n* A TV program featuring the bouncing and shaking of a woman's parts: *...when advertisers see wall-to-wall jigglies in prime time*—New York Times

the jig is up *sentence* by 1800 The criminal enterprise is discovered

◁**jig-jig** or **zig-zig**▷ *n* first form by 1932, second by 1918 The sex act; copulation; =FUCKING [the earlier form is US military slang from WWI, and represents a French-like pronunciation of British *jig-a-jig*, "do the sex act," found by 1893]

jig-swiggered *See* I'LL BE DAMNED

jihad *n* by 1980s A violent attack; destructive assault: *...we'll call these guys Tinker, Evers, and Chance, to protect them from jihad by the Elvis cult...*—Milwaukee Journal [fr Arabic, "holy war"]

jillion *n* (also **gadzillion** or **gillion** or **kajillion** or **skillion** or **zillion quadzillion**) by 1940s A great many; an indefinitely large number; =SCADS: *...a jillion jackpots*—Time/ *The beautiful people who would be at her cocktail party ("A zillion horny studs!")*—Lawrence Sanders/ *All those years we paid no official notice to those gadzillions of Chinese*—Newark Star-Ledger/ *This instant, in fact, quadzillions of these particles may be streaking harmlessly through our bodies*—Time

jimble-jamble *adj* by 1970 Mixed; motley: *...a jimble-jamble sort of crowd*—Village Voice [modeled on *skimble-skamble*, found by 1826]

Jim Crow ◁**1**▶ *n phr* by 1828 A black man; African-American **2** *n phr* by 1940s Segregation and discrimination against black people, and the laws and practices that accompany them: *My first experience with Jim Crow*—Louis Armstrong/ *Jim Crow killed Bessie Smith*—Tennessee Williams **3** *modifier*: *Jim Crow laws* **4** *v*: *I would like to...say that the people who Jim Crow me have a white heart*—Langston Hughes [fr a character in a minstrel-show song by T D Rice]
See CROW JIM

jim-dandy **1** *n* by 1844 A person or thing that is remarkable, wonderful, superior, etc; =BEAUT, HUMDINGER **2** *adj*: *Anacin is a jim-dandy remedy*—Philip Hamburger [perhaps fr an early 1840s song *Dandy Jim of Caroline*]

jim-jam *v* by 1940s =JAZZ, JAZZ something UP

jim-jams *n phr* by 1880 =the HEEBIE-JEEBIES: *...two-seaters are high therapy from life's imbalances, emotional dross and other colitis-causing jimjams*

jimjick *n* by 1940s Something one does not know the name of or does not wish to name; =GIZMO, THINGAMAJIG: *...this jimjick here, the trigger*—S J Perelman [perhaps a blend of *jim hickey* with *jigger*, both meaning "thingamajig"]

jimmies *n* by 1960s Bits of candy put onto ice cream as a topping

the jimmies *n phr* by 1900 Nervous frets; =the HEEBIE-JEEBIES, JIM-JAMS: *Frankly it gives me the jimmies*—Wolcott Gibbs

jimmy or **jimmy hat** *n* 1990s teenagers A condom: *That's right, condom fashions...with small pockets for what kids call jimmys*—Milwaukee Journal

jimmy up or **jim** *v phr* by 1940s To spoil something; damage; =BUGGER: *This scale's all jimmied up*

jingle *n* A telephone call; a ring; =TINKLE: *We never hear from you, not even a jingle*—movie Any Number Can Play

jingle-jangle **1** *n* (also **jing**) by 1950s Money; coins: *I've got some jingle-jangle in my jeans*—radio show Corliss Archer/ *A lot of bars have fundraisers and donate a big chunk of their jing to AIDS groups*—George T Avgeris **2** *adj* by 1970s In poor condition; ramshackle: *...driving down to Big Sur in their funky bus or some jingle-jangle car*—Rolling Stone

jink *v* by 1785 To take evasive action; dodge; zig-zag: *...went jinking down the field, shot and missed*—Paul Theroux/ *She jinked sideways to avoid an oncoming truck*—Penelope Lively [fr northern English dialect *jink*, "make a quick evasive turn," adopted into the idiom of Rugby football; popularized by Vietnam War Air Force use]

jinks *See* HIGH-JINKS

jinny *n* about 1920 A speakeasy
See FLYING-JINNY

jinx **1** *n* by 1911 A cause of bad luck: *Somebody around here is a jinx* **2** *n* by 1911 A curse; assured ill fortune: *Looks like the place has a jinx on it* **3** *v* by 1917: *Somebody jinxed him* [apparently fr *jynx* or *iynx*, "wryneck woodpecker," fr the use of the bird in divination]

jip *See* GYP

jippo *n* British military by 1920s Fat or grease; drippings: *He dipped his bread in the jippo and sighed with pleasure* [fr the mid–1800s nautical sense "gravy," of obscure origin]
See GYPPO

jism ◁**1**▶ *n* by 1899 =CUM **2** *n* (also **gism**) by 1842 Liveliness; excitement; spunk; =ZING [origin unknown]

◁**jit**▶ *n* by 1931 A black person

jitney or **jit** **1** *n* by 1903 A nickel; **2** *n* (also **jitney bus**) by 1914 A small bus used as public transportation •Formerly, jitneys were cars operating for low fare in more or less unregulated competition with taxis, buses, and street cars **3** *modifier*: *...cracked down today on illegal jitney service*—Philadelphia Bulletin **4** *n* by 1917 Any car, esp a small or cheap one **5** *adj* by 1916 Cheap: *...a jitney dance hall*—G Millburn [origin unknown; perhaps fr Yiddish]

jitter **1** *v* by 1931 To tremble; quiver: *A line of...half-washed clothes jittered on a rusty wire*—Raymond Chandler **2** *v* by 1932 To be nervous; be agitated; fret: *I jittered around the house...unable to concentrate on anything*—H Allen Smith [echoic-symbolic]

jitterbug 1930s jive talk **1** *n* A devotee of swing music, esp one who dances to swing: *Jitterbugs are the extreme swing addicts*—Life **2** *v* To dance to swing music: *Do you feel like jitterbugging a little bit?*—J D Salinger

the **jitterbug** *n phr* *1930s jive talk* A fast, freely improvisational, and vigorous dance done to swing music, with passages where the couple separates to do more or less spectacular solo figures

the **jitters** *n phr* *by 1925* A state of nervous agitation; acute restless apprehension: *I had the jitters*—Philip Wylie

jittery *adj* *by 1931* Nervous: *He felt all jittery and uptight*

jive¹ **1** *v* *black by 1938* To banter; jest; tease; =KID: *She told him to quit jiving* **2** *v* *by 1928* To deceive, but not seriously; mislead, esp playfully **3** *n* *by 1929* Empty and pretentious talk; foolishness; =BALONEY, BULLSHIT: *Sugar Mouth Sammy with the same ol' tired jive*—D Evans/ *...male chauvinist, damsel in distress, and all that jive*—Village Voice **4** *n* *by about 1920* Trifles; trash: *I bought a lot of cheap jive at the five and ten cent store*—Louis Armstrong **5** *n* *by 1938* Swing music of the 1930s and '40s, esp as played by the big bands and played fast and excitingly: *Man, what solid jive!*—Max Shulman **6** *modifier*: *jive records/ jive dancers* **7** *v* *by 1938* To play or dance to fast, exciting swing music **8** *n* (also **gyve**) *by 1938* Marijuana or a marijuana cigarette: *So Diane smoked jive, pot, and tea*—Orville Prescott [origin unknown; perhaps fr Wolof *jev*, "talk disparagingly"]
See JUKING AND JIVING, SHUCK

jive² *v* *by about 1940* To jibe; chime •The form **gibe** is found by 1813: *The two answers do not jive* [origin uncertain; perhaps related to *chime*; the form *gibe* is found by 1813]

jive and juke *v phr* *college students by 1970s* To have a very good time
See JUKING AND JIVING

◁**jive-ass**▷ *black by about 1940* **1** *n* Pretentious and deceitful talk; =BULLSHIT, JIVE: *That's like jive-ass*—Rolling Stone **2** *adj* Deceitful; undependable: *Damn his lazy, jiveass soul*—Armistead Maupin/ *You better find out some place else, you jiveass punk*—Society [in the phrase *jive-ass motherfucker* said to have originated with the musician Charlie "Bird" Parker]

jive stick *n phr* *1960s narcotics* A marijuana cigarette

jive talk *n phr* *1930s jive talk* A rapid, pattering way of talking, accompanied with finger-snapping and bodily jerks, and using the swing and jive vocabulary, affected by teenagers during the swing and jive era of the 1930s and '40s

◀**jizz** or **jizzum**▶ *n* *by 1960s* Semen; =CUM, JISM: *...puts a little body in his jizz, pumps a baby a year into the wife*—John Sayles

◁**J/O**▷ *modifier* *by 1980s* Masturbation: *Since the confusing days of AIDS, one of the main attractions of group J/O scenes was precisely the ecstatic sexual energy that only a group can generate*—Utne Reader [abbreviation of *jack off*]

joanie *adj* *1970s teenagers* Out-of-date; passé

job 1 *n* (also **jobbie**) *by 1927* A specimen or example, either of a thing or a person: *I lost two $110*

imported jobs before a locksmith told me what I was doing wrong*—Saturday Review/ *She's a tough little job*—Dashiell Hammett/ *...one of those big 18-wheel jobbies* **2** *n* (also **jobbie**) *by 1940s* A car: *She was driving a little red job* **3** *n* *underworld by 1667* A crime; a criminal project; =CAPER: *a big payroll job* **4** *v* *by 1731* To deceive; cheat; =DOUBLE CROSS, FRAME: *Crying...that he had been jobbed*—H Asbury/ *...got absolutely jobbed out of the Heisman*—Sports Illustrated
See BAG JOB, BLOW JOB, BOOB JOB, COFFEE-AND-CAKE JOB, CON GAME, COWBOY JOB, DO A JOB ON, GIVE someone A GREASE JOB, GOW JOB, GREASE JOB, HAND JOB, HATCHET JOB, INSIDE JOB, LAY DOWN ON THE JOB, LUBE, MENTAL JOB, NOSE JOB, PUT-UP JOB, SEX JOB, SHACK JOB, SNOW JOB, STRAIGHT JOB, TORCH JOB, TURNKEY JOB

◁**jobbie**▷ *v* To befoul: *...any ladies out there who will jobbie their pants for the camera*—Village Voice

job pop *v phr* *1960s narcotics* To inject narcotics intravenously, usu into the arm

jock 1 *n* *by 1670* A jockey **2** *n* *by 1970s* =DISC JOCKEY **3** *n* *by 1790* The penis; the crotch: *I'll be beating the bushes with snow to my jock*—George V Higgins **4** *n* *by 1952* An athletic supporter; =JOCKSTRAP: *I asked him if he wanted some sweat clothes, or a jock*—Esquire **5** *n* (also **jocko**) *by 1963* An athlete •Now used of both men and women, despite the phallic derivation: *The players themselves are a curious blend of woman and jock*—New York Times/ *...the lucrative job proper to an all-Ivy jock*—Clara Park [the basic etymon is *jock*, "penis," fr *jack*, probably the diminutive of *John*, which fr the 14th century has been applied to males, male-like things, and male organs; the sense "athlete" is fr *jockstrap*]
See VIDEO JOCK

jocker *hoboes by 1893* **1** *n* A homosexual hobo who lives off the begging of his boy companion **2** *n* An aggressive male homosexual; =WOLF: *When he was a kid in some juvenile place some black guy musta been his jocker*—Joseph Wambaugh

jockey *n* *by 1912* The driver or pilot of any vehicle: *airplane jockey/ tank jockey*
See BLIP JOCKEY, DESK JOCKEY, DISC JOCKEY, HOGGER, JEEP-JOCKEY, PSYCH-JOCKEY, SOUP JOCKEY

jockocracy *n* *by 1980s* The athletes and former athletes who play a large role in television broadcasting: *...bored with the games, utterly bored with the jockocracy*—Washington Post

jockstrap 1 *n* *by 1897* An athletic supporter **2** *n* *by 1960s* An athlete; =JOCK **3** *v* *by 1960s* To make one's living in the less glamorous and lucrative reaches of professional sports: *He spent a couple of years jockstrapping in the minor leagues*

jody *WWII Army fr black* **1** *n* A civilian who is thought to be prospering back home with a soldier's sweetheart, wife, job, etc: *Jody was the guy going in the back door while you were walking down the front walk*—Soldiers **2** *n* =JODY CALL [fr the full name *Jody Grinder,* that is, fornicator, probably fr an earlier black and prison character of similar import *Oolong the Chinese Grind-boy* or *Chinese Joe the Grinder*]

jody call *n phr WWII Army* An antiphonal song or chant done while marching or running [fr the character *Jody* used in the chant]

Joe or **joe 1** *n by 1940s* Coffee **2** *n by 1846* Man; fellow; =GUY: . . . *never seemed to share much of the problems of the ordinary joe*—Robert Ruark **3** *n WWII Army* =GI JOE **4** *adj* underworld by 1940s Informed; aware; =HEP **5** *v* underworld by 1940s : *Let me Joe you to that racket*—D W Maurer **See** GI JOE, GOOD JOE, HOLY JOE, LITTLE JOE, OLD JOE, SLOPPY JOE

Joe Average *n phr by 1990s* The ordinary or typical citizen: *For Joe Average. . . the game simply doesn't exist*—Milwaukee Journal

Joe Beige *n phr by 1980s* A bland, colorless person: ". . . *I don't find you very interesting.*" "*Joe Beige*"—Charles M Schulz

Joe Blow *n phr* (Variations: **Doakes** or **Storch** or **Zilch** may replace **Blow**) entry form 1920s jazz musicians, Doakes by 1943, Storch by 1960s, Zilch by 1925 Any man; the average man; =JOHN DOE: . . . *the average black "Mr Joe Blow"*—Ebony [fr the *blowing* of the musician, later probably thought of as referring to big talk]

Joe College *n phr by 1932* A young man whose dress and manner betoken the nonacademic aspects of college life: . . . *a real Joe College type*—Leonard Feather

joe-darter *n by 1851* =HUMDINGER

Joe Lunch Bucket *by 1990s* **1** *n phr* The ordinary or typical working man: *Three years ago the Packers got Jim Thorpe in the draft, and now they get Joe Lunch Bucket*—Milwaukee Journal Sentinel **2** *modifier*: *Royko's Joe Lunchbucket persona may lie at the heart of his appeal*—Washington Post

Joe Sad *n phr black by 1934* An unpopular person

Joe Schmo (or **Schmoe) *n phr by 1960s* An undistinguished and unfortunate person [fr *schmo*, a Yiddish or quasi-Yiddish word meaning "unfortunate person, *schlemiel*"]

◁**Joe Shit the Ragman**▷ *n phr* (Variations: **Snuffy** or **Tentpeg** may replace **Shit the Ragman**) *Army by 1970s* An ordinary soldier; =BUCK PRIVATE, GI

Joe Six-pack *n phr* An ordinary American male; =JOE, JOE AVERAGE, JOE BLOW: *Do you think that Joe Six-pack in Illinois cares?*—National Public Radio/ . . . *a sleazy bar where go-go girls perform for goggle-eyed Joe Six-packs*—New York Times [fr the six-bottle or -can packets of beer these men typically consume]

joey or **Joey** *n by 1896* A clown [fr the nickname of *Joseph* Grimaldi, famous early–1800s British clown and pantomimist]

Joe Yale *modifier by 1940s* Betokening by dress and manner the nonacademic aspects of life in the Ivy League: . . . *this very Joe Yale-looking guy*—JD Salinger

jog *v teenagers by 1970s* To annoy; bother

john[1] *n fr 1930s* A toilet; =CAN: *I made a brief visit to the john*—J Evans [probably an amusing euphemism for *jack* or *jakes,* 16th-century terms for toilet; some say fr Sir *John* Harington (1561–1612), who originated a form of water closet, but evidence for the attribution is lacking; *cuzjohn,* "cousin john," in the same sense is found in 1735]

john[2] *n WWII Army* An Army lieutenant **See** FIRST JOHN, SECOND JOHN

john[3] or **John 1** *n black by 1920s* Any man; an average man; =JOE: *We don't want no poor johns on here*—A Lomax **2** *n by 1946* A man regarded as an easy victim, a potential easy sale, etc: *He's pretty smart at figurin' out what a John'll pay*—Langston Hughes **3** *n Army by 1940s* An Army recruit **4** *n by 1950s* A man who keeps a girl; =DADDY, SUGAR DADDY **5** *n* (also **john, johnson**) prostitutes by 1911 A prostitute's customer: . . . *even for girls turning their first tricks, pulling their first real John*—Claude Brown/ . . . *shot an 18-year-old hooker. . . then plugged a john who was present*—New York Times **6** *n homosexuals by 1950s* An older homosexual male who keeps a younger one **7** *n* =JOHN LAW **See** BIG JOHN, DEAR JOHN, PLAY WHO SHOT JOHN, SQUARE JOHN

John B *n phr by about 1920* A hat [fr *John B* Stetson, the hat maker]

John Doe or **Richard Roe** *n phr by 1768* Any man; the average man; =JOE [originally the fictitious plaintiff and defendant in a lawsuit]

John Dogface *n phr WWII Army* A recruit

John Farmer *n phr by 1940s* A farmer

John Hall *n phr by 1940s* Alcohol

John Hancock (or **Henry) *n phr by 1903* One's signature [fr the fact that *John Hancock* of Massachusetts was the first to sign the Declaration of Independence in 1776; *John Henry,* possibly by confusion with *Patrick Henry,* because of the prominence of *John Henry* as a folklore hero, and by near-rhyming resemblance]

John Hollowlegs *n phr hoboes by 1940s* A hungry man

John Law *n phr by 1907* A police officer; the police: . . . *had been gathered in by John Law*—Jack London

John L's *n phr by 1940s* =LONG JOHNS

Johnny or **johnny** *n by 1673* Any man; =JOE, JOHN ●Chiefly British: *The big johnny came over to talk*

Johnny-come-lately *by 1839* **1** *n* A person or thing only recently arrived, esp as compared with the more seasoned: *Postwar planning. . . was no Johnny-come-lately*—Max Shulman **2** *modifier*: *a Johnny-come-lately quasi-solution* **3** *n* An upstart

Johnny-one-note *modifier by 1930s* Like someone who has only one idea, one method, one explanation, etc: *One of the great bogus management concepts is consensus; Johnny-one-note thinking is just what corporations don't need*—New York

Times [fr the title of a pre-WWII popular song about a musician with only one note]

Johnny-on-the-spot *n by 1896* A person who is ready and effective when needed: *Ed was Johnny-on-the-spot and we got it cleaned up quick*

John Q Citizen (or **Public**) *n phr by 1940s* Any man, esp the average or typical man; =JOE AVERAGE: *John Q Citizen seems to yearn for the big cars*

John Roscoe *See* ROSCOE

johns *See* LONG JOHNS

◁**johnson** or **Johnson** or **jones**▷ *n by 1863* The penis: *. . . beat out time with their titties and their johnsons*—Village Voice/ *I've only got one Johnson, and he winks*—Village Voice/ *Enough is enough, turn my jones loose*—Donald Goines [origin unknown; such a use is recorded fr Canada in the mid–1800s, perhaps as a euphemism for the British euphemism *John Thomas,* "penis"]

Johnson or **Johnson man** *n hoboes by about 1905* A hobo; drifter; =BUM, YEGG [fr *Johnson bar,* a steel crowbar used by railroad laborers to pull up spikes, and by criminal hoboes to pry open safes]

Johnson rod *n phr by 1950s* A mythical and fragile part of a machine •Used jocularly, esp to confuse novices: *Could it be that the Johnson rod is bent?*

John Wayne 1 *adj phr Army by 1970s* Very tough and durable; militarily exemplary **2** *v phr Army by 1970s* To handle a weapon, esp a machine gun, in an ostentatiously unconventional way **3** *n phr by 1990s* An aggressive police officer

John Wayne it *v phr by 1980s* To be very tough, taciturn, and virile: *I'm supposed to go around John Wayneing it all the time*—San Francisco

John Wayne's brother *n phr Army by 1970s* A good soldier; ideal fighting man

John Wayne's sister (or **mother**) *n phr Army by 1970s* A weak, lazy, self-indulgent person

joined at the hip *adj phr by 1990s* Very closely associated; inseparable; symbiotic: *Weldon writes as if she were Virginia Woolf and Roseanne Arnold joined at the hip*—New York Times/ *Frequently in the past, Main Street and Wall Street have had their differences, but today as never before they are joined at the hip*—New Republic [fr the condition of some Siamese twins]

join out *v phr circus by 1914* To join; join up

joint 1 *n by 1821* Any disgusting or disreputable place; =DIVE, DUMP: *That evening the joint buzzed with sedition*—American Scholar/ *. . . a vile Kansas "joint"*—Literary Digest **2** *n by 1905* Any place or venue, including a home: *It's a swell joint, all right*—H McHugh **3** *n 1950s narcotics* A marijuana cigarette; =REEFER: *inhale a joint or two of cannabis*–Time/ *I've had to hold joints in my hand. . . but I never smoked even one*—New York Times **4** *n narcotics by 1940s* The apparatus for injecting narcotics; =HEAD KIT, WORKS ◁**5**▷ *n by 1960s* The penis **6** *n carnival by 1940s* A concession [place senses fr early–1800s Anglo-Irish *joint,* "low resort," perhaps from its being a nearby, joined room rather than a main room]

See BEER JOINT, the BIG JOINT, BUST-OUT JOINT, CALL HOUSE, CLIP JOINT, CREEP-JOINT, EAT HIGH ON THE HOG, FLAT-JOINT, GREASE JOINT, GYP JOINT, HAM JOINT, HOPJOINT, JUICE-JOINT, JUKE JOINT, MITT-CAMP, MUG JOINT, ONE-ARM JOINT, PULL one's PUD, PUT someone's NOSE OUT OF JOINT, RIB JOINT, RIGHT JOINT, RUG JOINT, SCHLOCK SHOP, SQUARE

the joint *n phr by 1927* Jail; prison: *. . . in the joint*—Joseph Wambaugh

joint factory *n phr 1960s narcotics* =SMOKE SHOP

joke *See* SICK JOKE

a joke *n phr by 1791* Someone or something not to be taken seriously; a laughing-stock: *So nobody's about to pay big money for the site fee of a Tyson versus Ribalta. I mean, Ribalta's a joke*—New York Times

joker 1 *n* (also **joker in the deck**) *by 1904* A hidden cost, qualification, defect, nasty result, etc; =CATCH: *It all looks very sweet, but there's a joker* **2** *n by 1811* A man; fellow; =GUY, CHARACTER, CLOWN •Often derogatory: *Ask that joker who the hell he thinks he is* [first sense fr the *joker* card included in a new deck, which may be used as a trump or a wild card]

jokey or **joky** *adj by middle 1800s* Fun-loving; jocular; giving to joking;: *George is too jokey for a responsible slot*

jollies *n by 1957* Pleasure and gratification; thrills, esp when somewhat disreputable; =BANG, KICKS: *People that drive Buicks are getting some kind of jollies*—A Sherman

See GET one's COOKIES

jolly *v by 1876* To cajole with humor and bonhomie: *I was pretty upset, but she jollied me along/ We jollied her into coming along with us*

jolt 1 *n narcotics by 1916* The initial impact of a narcotic injection; =RUSH **2** *n narcotics by 1916* A narcotic injection **3** *v*: *We didn't want to jolt*—D Hulburd **4** *n narcotics by 1950s* A marijuana cigarette; =JOINT **5** *n by 1904* A drink of liquor; =SNORT: *. . . a wee jolt of Bourbon*—F Scott Fitzgerald **6** *n underworld by 1912* A prison sentence: *to get a jolt in the stir*—E Booth

jone or **joan** *v black by 1930s* To play a game of verbal abuse, esp against the opponent's mother and family; =JIVE, PLAY THE DOZENS: *All kinds of kids jone, says 11-year-old Hamani*—Milwaukee Journal/ *. . . readers howling in outrage that we had dared to suggest. . . that the verb "joan" (meaning to insult) was possibly derived from Joan Rivers*—Washington Post [origin unknown]

Jones or **jones** *1960s narcotics* **1** *n* Heroin; =HORSE, SHIT **2** *n* A drug habit: *. . . works at two jobs to keep up with the "Jones"*—J Lelyveld **3** *n* Any intense interest or absorption: *The twentysomething elite definitely has a jones for Jones*—Buzz **4** *v*: *She's jonesing for those diamond earrings*—UCLA Slang [origin unknown; perhaps an innocent code word used by addicts and dealers]

See JOHNSON, SCAG JONES

Joneses *See* KEEP UP WITH THE JONESES

joning or **joaning** *n* black by 1930s Playing a game of verbal abuse, esp against the opponent's mother and family: *My sons, 11 and 8, call it "jon-ing,"* which rhymes with toning—Milwaukee Journal/ *Whether it's jonin', or joanin', it apparently didn't start with Joan Rivers*—Washington Post

jook *See* JUKE

Jose *See* NO WAY

josh 1 *v* by 1845 To joke; banter; =KID: *. . . continued Brian, unwilling to be joshed out of it*—Stan Cutler 2 *n* by 1978: *It was just a tasteless little josh* [origin unknown; the earliest example is capitalized, suggesting a proper name; Eric Partridge gives "a country man; a rustic," as one sense, so perhaps the primary meaning is "to behave like a bumpkin" or "to fool one by seeming to be a rural simpleton"]

joskin *n* by 1811 A rustic; =HICK •Still chiefly British [fr British dialect *joss*, "bump," with wordplay on *bumpkin*]

jostle *v* by 1929 To pick pockets: *a junkie vocation known as "jostling"*—J Markham/ *. . . always looking for cats who were down there jostling*—Claude Brown

journo *n* by 1990s A journalist; =INK-STAINED WRETCH: *Another part of his pedigree had been unknown even to Mr Blair himself until the journos started trampling over his life*—New Yorker

jowls *See* BAT one's GUMS

joy house *n phr* by 1940 A brothel: *I ain't been in a joy house in 20 years*—Raymond Chandler

joy-juice *n* by 1950s Liquor

joy pop *v phr* 1930s narcotics To take narcotic injections occasionally, esp intramuscularly

joy-popper 1930s narcotics 1 *n* A newcomer among narcotics users, esp among marijuana smokers 2 *n* A person who takes, or claims to take, only an occasional dose of narcotics: *For the "joy-poppers" had no intention of becoming addicts in the true sense*—Nelson Algren

joy-powder *n* narcotics by 1950s Morphine

joy ride *n phr* by 1908 A ride or trip taken solely for pleasure, esp a fast and merry junket that is in some way forbidden: *They stole the police car and had themselves a joy ride*

joy-rider *n* narcotics by 1940s An occasional and nonaddicted user of narcotics

joy smoke *n phr* narcotics by 1940s Marijuana

joy-stick 1 *n* by 1910 The control lever of an airplane 2 *n* 1950s hot rodders The steering wheel of a car, esp a hot rod 3 *n* by 1967 The control lever for a computer or video game 4 *n* narcotics by 1940s An opium pipe ◁5▷ *n* (also **joy-knob**) by about 1920 The penis [the origin of the control-lever senses is uncertain; perhaps fr the tremulous shaking of the stick, perhaps fr the joyful sensation experienced while flying]

j-school *n* by 1990s A school or college of journalism: *I did not say that j-school was a worthless educational experience, only that the degree was not highly regarded by potential employers*—Nation/ *. . . Truman is trying to entertain J-school questions about the future of American magazines. . .* —Los Angeles Times

J smoke *See* J

juane *n* narcotics by 1930s Marijuana or a marijuana cigarette: *. . . a half-smoked juane on the side*—Philip Wylie

juco (JOO koh) by 1939 1 *n* A junior college; community college 2 *n* A junior college student or graduate: *. . . those fugitives from a real education, those, those. . . "jucos"*—Milwaukee Journal

Judas Priest *interj* by 1914 An exclamation of surprise, dismay, emphasis, etc [a euphemism for *Jesus Christ*]

judy 1 *n* by 1823 A sexually promiscuous girl or woman 2 *n* by 1885 A girl or woman

Judy *sentence* WWII Air Forces I have you in sight or on the radar screen [origin unknown]

jug 1 *v* by 1834 To put in jail; imprison: *I get jugged for parking in the wrong places?*—Lawrence Sanders 2 *n* by 1886 A bottle of liquor: *Fetch me my jug, son* 3 *n* by 1980s A relatively cheap wine, usu bought in large bottles; =JUG WINE: *Far more people drink jugs these days*—San Francisco 4 *n* underworld by 1925 A vault or safe; 5 *n* underworld by 1845 A bank 6 *n* 1960s hot rodders A carburetor 7 *n* rock climbers by 1990s A good holding place: *. . . "jug"—a nice big hold (relative to the rest of the route)*—Macon Telegraph [rock-climbing sense fr *jug-handle* in the same sense, found by 1955]

the jug *n phr* by 1834 Jail; prison: *Refusal will result in a quick trip to the jug*—Rolling Stone

jugful *See* NOT BY A LONG SHOT

juggins or **jiggins** 1 *n* British schoolboys by 1882 A stupid person; dolt; =JUGHEAD 2 *n* underworld by 1940s A dupe; =EASY MARK, PATSY, SUCKER

juggle *v* by 1813 To alter, esp with a view to deception and advantage: *Owners Might Juggle Lineup Before Facing Players*—New York Times/ *They discovered that the CEO had been juggling the books*

juggler *n* 1960s narcotics =PUSHER

jughandle *n* by 1961 A tightly curved portion of road shaped like the handle of a jug, used for making turns from and into a busy highway

jughead *n* by 1926 A stupid person; fool; =KLUTZ

Jughead *n* computers by 1990s An Internet search tool for files in the public domain

See ARCHIE

◁**jugs**▷ *n* Australian by about 1920 A woman's breasts; =HOOTERS [abbreviation of *jugs of milk*]

jugular by 1960s 1 *adj* Bent on destruction; ruthless; savage; =CUTTHROAT: *. . . inert and inept troop of Democrats unable to beat back an aroused and jugular band of Republicans*—New York Times 2 *adj* Vital; crucial; life-and-death: *. . . a jugular issue for the industry*—New Yorker/ *Barbara has a very strong respect for power and position. She will not ask the ultimate jugular question*—New York Times [based on the phrase *go for the jugular*]

jug wine *n phr* by 1980s A relatively cheap domestic wine, usu bought in large bottles

juice[1] or **juicer** *n theater & movie studio* by 1928 A stage or studio electrician: *He treated the grips and juicers the way he had always treated them*—A Morgan

juice[2] **1** *n* by 1828 Liquor; =BOOZE, the SAUCE: *. . . liquor much stronger than the present-day juice*—Louis Armstrong/ *. . . those people just don't hold the juice*—Elmore Leonard **2** *n underworld* by 1940s Money, esp illegally obtained and used by gamblers, loan sharks, etc: *The juice, the C, the commission*—T Betts **3** *modifier*: *a juice dealer/ juice man* **4** *n underworld* by 1940s The interest paid on a usurious loan: *. . . interest, known in the trade as vigorish, vig, or juice*—Wall Street Journal **5** *n* by 1896 Electricity; current and voltage: *Turn on the juice so we can see something* **6** *n* by 1909 Gasoline; motor fuel: *If you have a light supply of juice you climb at about 200 mph*—New York Times **7** *n hot rodders & car-racing* by 1960s A fuel additive for cars, esp hot rods; =POP **8** *n* by 1925 Nitroglycerin; =SOUP **9** *n* by 1935 Influence; =CLOUT, PULL: *"What's juice?" "I guess you'd call it pull. Or clout"*—John Gregory Dunne **10** *n* 1960s narcotics Methadone, often administered in fruit juice **11** *n* by 1980s Anabolic steroids: *. . . about 60 per cent of the wrestlers he knew during the 1980s used steroids, commonly known as "juice". . .*—Milwaukee Journal **12** *n black 1980s hip-hop & street talk* Authority; power: *. . . the stuff of cool and ultimate victory. The Redskins have the juice, the Broncos don't*—Los Angeles Times/ *As one of the oldest gangsters in the neighborhood, Bogard had the credibility, or "juice," to call the shots*—Los Angeles Times **13** *v baseball* by 1960s To hit the ball hard and far; =SLUG: *. . . the club starts struggling a bit, so he starts trying to juice the ball*—Milwaukee Journal **See** BUGJUICE, CAPER-JUICE, CORNJUICE, HAPPY-JUICE, JOY-JUICE, JUNGLE-JUICE, JUNIPER-JUICE, LIMEY, MOO-JUICE, TORPEDO JUICE

juiced or **juiced up[1]** **1** *adj* or *adj phr* by about 1937 Intoxicated, either by liquor or narcotics; =HIGH, STONED: *Crabs was already pretty juiced up*—Easyriders/ *You been smoking too much grain. You head is juiced up*—Robert B Parker **2** *adj* or *adj phr* by 1960s Excited, perhaps overly so; enlivened; inspired; =PUMPED UP: *When they get into (regular season) games, they get all juiced up. You try to protect them*—Milwaukee Journal Sentinel **3** *adj phr baseball* by 1980s Manufactured or tampered with so as to travel longer and farther: *One thing about the ball that never changes is the occasional claim that it's "juiced up"*—Joe Garagiola/ *When. . . a little singles hitter like the Mets' Howard Johnson connects for a tape-measure homer, all you hear is "The ball is juiced, it's hot"*—Joe Garagiola

juice dealer *n phr underworld* by 1960s A racketeer who loans money at very high interest; usurer; =LOAN SHARK, SHYLOCK

juiced up[2] **1** *adj phr* by 1990s Using anabolic steroids **2** *adj phr hot rodders* by 1940s =SOUPED UP

juicehead *n* by 1955 A heavy drinker; =LUSH: *He had a raving juice-head for a wife*—Rolling Stone/ *All wayfarers, outlaws, broken-down poets and juiceheads looking for a free drink were welcomed*—Changes

juice-joint **1** *n circus* by 1940s A soft-drink concession or stand **2** *n* 1920s =SPEAKEASY

juice loan *n phr underworld* by 1960s A loan made by a racketeer; a usurious loan

juice man *n phr underworld* by 1950s A hoodlum who collects money owed to a racketeer: *. . . a "juice man" (loan collector) for syndicate hoodlum bosses*—Chicago Tribune

juice up **1** *v phr* To energize; invigorate; =PUMP oneself UP: *A thing like that can really juice you up*–Time/ *He seems, if anything, to be juicing up the pace these days*—Philadelphia Journal **2** *v phr* To fuel: *They juiced the car up and set out* **3** *v phr hot rodders* by 1940s =SOUP UP **4** *v phr* by 1980s To use anabolic steroids

juicy *adj* by 1883 Interesting in a sexy or scandalous way; sensational; =RACY: *He spared us none of the juicy details*

juke[1] or **jook** *fr early 1900s* **1** *n* =JUKE HOUSE **2** *n* =JUKE JOINT **3** *n* =JUKEBOX **4** *v* To tour roadside bars, drinking and dancing: *I want you to go juking with me*—Tennessee Williams **5** *v college students* by 1970s To have a good time; disport oneself, esp at a party **6** *v college students* by 1970s To dance **7** *v college students* by 1980s To do the sex act; =BOFF, SCREW: *"Did you juke?" "No, we just met"*—UCLA Slang **8** *v* by 1980s To kill; =OFF, SCRAG: *A man. . . said the lady who got juked was Alice Carmody*—Ed McBain **9** *v Canadian teenagers* by 1970s To absent oneself from school; =PLAY HOOKY **10** *n black street talk* by 1990s Liquor; =BOOZE: *. . . that is some juke, man. That is some bad beverage*—Robert B Parker [fr Gullah fr Wolof and/or Bambara, "unsavory"] **See** JIVE AND JUKE, JUKING AND JIVING

juke[2] *v sports* To swerve and reverse evasively; trick a defender or tackler; =JINK: *. . . rather than to juke a defensive back, then duck inside*—Sports Illustrated/ *Zaffuto juked past. . . Peters on the right side*—Sports Illustrated [fr Scots *jouk*, of uncertain origin]

jukebox *n* by 1930s A coin-operated record player in a restaurant, bar, etc

juke house *n phr* by 1940s A brothel [the date should probably be earlier]

juke joint *n phr* by 1935 A usu cheap bar, roadside tavern, etc, with a jukebox

juking and jiving *college students* by 1970s **1** *n phr* Frivolity and evasiveness; triviality and inanity **2** *modifier*: *Hart despises "the jukin' and jivin' phoniness of politics"*—Time **See** JIVE AND JUKE

jumbo *adj* by 1897 Very large; gigantic; =HUMONGOUS: *I had a jumbo portion* [fr the London

Zoo's great elephant, sold in 1882 to PT Barnum; *Jumbo* is a version of the word for "elephant" in various West African languages, for example, Kongo *nzamba*]

jump 1 *v by 1789* To attack; assault: *We jumped him as he left the place* **2** *v by 1859* To rob, esp at gunpoint; =HOLD UP **3** *v 1930s jive talk* To be furiously active; be vibrant with noise and energy: *Before long the joint was jumpin'*—H Allen Smith **4** *n 1930s jive talk* =SWING **5** *modifier*: *a jump tune/ jump music* **6** *n 1930s jive talk* A dance where the music is swing or jive; =HOP **7** *n 1950s street gangs* A street fight between teenage gangs; =RUMBLE ◁**8**▷ *v by 1638* To do the sex act with or to; =SCREW: *She admitted she always wanted him to jump her* **9** *n newspapers by 1920s* The continuation of a news story on a later page: *Wednesday's Times had to concede, in the jump, that Kennedy didn't make any Cabinet appointments until December 1st. . .* —New Yorker **10** *n baseball by 1960s* A base runner's lead off base in a possible steal
See GET THE JUMP ON someone or something, HAVE THE JUMP

jump all over (or **up and down on**) someone *v phr by 1950s* To rebuke and berate someone very severely; savage someone: *He jumped all over her for not telling him/ The critics loved to jump up and down on Brubeck: He only once won a Down Beat critics' poll*—New Yorker

jump at *v phr by 1769* To agree eagerly: *They all jumped at the idea of a picnic*

jump bail *v phr underworld 1872* To default on one's bail

jump band *n phr 1930s jive talk* A band playing fast and heavily accented swing music: *A "jump band" is a big and powerful jazz band*—Stephen Longstreet

◁ **jump** (or **jump on**) someone's **bones**▷ *by 1960s* **1** *v phr* To make strong sexual advances; sexually assault: *All these spades is gonna jump on your bones and pull your pants off*—Playboy/ *Have I tried to. . . jump your bones?*—movie *The Gauntlet* **2** *v phr* To do the sex act with someone: *. . . how you wish to deal with the question of me jumping your bones*—Robert B Parker

jump down someone's **throat** *v phr by 1916* To make a violent and wrathful response: *When I hinted he might be mistaken he jumped down my throat*

jumped-up *adj by 1835* Elevated above one's proper status; =JACKED UP ●Chiefly British: *The elite regard me as a jumped-up interloper*

jumper *See* PUDDLE-JUMPER, STUMP-JUMPER, TREE JUMPER

jump someone **in** *v phr 1990s street gangs* To initiate a gang member by beating: *. . . gang members asked if she wanted to be "jumped in" to their gang*—Mesa Trubune

jump it *v phr 1930s jive talk* To play in a swing music style: *. . . then the band would "jump it" and*

O'Connell would join in a swinging rendition— Milwaukee Journal

jump (or **go**) **off the deep end** *v phr by 1940s* To act precipitately; take drastic action: *He jumped off the deep end and got married again*
See GO OFF THE DEEP END

jump on someone *v phr by 1868* =JUMP ALL OVER someone: *. . . when severe reproof is administered, the culprit is said to be jumped on*—Brander Matthews

jump on someone's **meat** *v phr by 1970s* To rebuke severely; savage; =CHEW someone OUT: *Chickenshit lieutenant. . . used to jump on our meat every night at roll-call*—Joseph Wambaugh

jump on the bandwagon *See* GET ON THE BANDWAGON

jump someone **out** *v phr 1990s street gangs* To eject someone from a gang, usu with beating: *So I didn't have to go through the beat-down or be jumped out (practices in which the gang members are physically beaten if they decide to leave)*— Milwaukee Journal Sentinel

jump out of one's **skin** *v phr by 1798* To react vehemently from joy or fear: *If that promotion comes through, he'll jump out of his skin/ When it thundered she jumped out of her skin*

jump page *n phr newspapers by 1920s* A page on which stories are continued: *. . . the mixup of several paragraphs appearing on the inside "jump page"*—Milwaukee Journal

the **jumps** *n phr by 1899* =the JITTERS

jump salty *v phr black by 1938* To lose one's temper: *. . . if you're trying to jump salty*—Zora Neale Hurston

jump ship *v phr by 1940s* To desert or abandon one's job; change jobs: *Why did CBS' Deborah Norville jump ship to replace Bill O'Reilly. . .* — Milwaukee Journal

jump smooth *v phr 1950s street gang* To give up crime and violence; adhere to the law: *. . . tells why he decided to "jump smooth"*—Life

jump-start 1 *v by 1980s* To start a car by attaching cables to the battery from a car that runs; start anything that resists going: *. . . they finally jump-start that poor dumb animal*—Bryan Di Salvatore/ *Mubarak Tries to Jump Start Stalled Mideast Peace Talks*—New York Times **2** *n*: *Linden teacher gives kids jump-start on information highway*— Newark Star-Ledger

jump street *n phr by 1980s* The very beginning; =GIT-GO, SQUARE ONE: *One usually starts at the beginning of the endeavor, or from Jump Street*— Irving Lewis Allen [*at the first jump* in the same sense is found by 1577]

jump suit *n phr by 1948* A one-piece coverall modeled on those worn by paratroopers and parachute jumpers

jump the gun *v phr by 1940s* To act prematurely: *We planned it well, but jumped the gun and ruined it* [*beat the pistol* is found by 1905]

◁**jump through** one's **ass**▷ *v phr Army by*

1970s To make a very quick response to a sudden difficult demand: *Old Man says we'll have to jump through our ass to get that done by tomorrow*

jump through hoops *by 1917* **1** *v phr* To serve, obey, or accommodate someone without question, esp in a harried, frantic way: *You had to jump through hoops to please that guy* **2** *v phr* To exert oneself mightily; strain: *I had to jump through hoops to get you that job* [fr the image of a trained animal *jumping through hoops* in a show, circus, etc]

jump-up *n Army by 1970s* A job that must be done at once, with little time to think and prepare

jumpy *adj by 1879* Nervous; apprehensive; =JITTERY: *One of our pals. . . is jumpy and he needs a bodyguard tonight*—George Raft

jungle **1** *n hoboes by 1914* A camp or regular stopping place near the railroad on the outskirts of a town: *. . . always leaves the jungle like he found it*—James M Cain **2** *n by 1906* Any place of notable violence, lawlessness, etc: *The neighborhood's becoming a jungle*

◀**jungle-bunny**▶ *n by 1950s* A black person: *It's no longer open season on jungle bunnies. That day is gone*—Milwaukee Journal

jungle buzzard *n phr hoboes by 1940s* A hobo who lives permanently in a camp or regular stopping place and begs from transient hoboes

jungle-juice *n WWII Army fr earlier nautical* Liquor made by prisoners, soldiers, etc, from any available alcohol and flavorings [originally *African rum*]

jungle stiff *n phr hoboes by 1940s* A hobo living or staying in a camp or regular stopping place

junk **1** *n by 1842* Worthless and shoddy things; useless and inept productions; trash; =DRECK, SHIT: *Why do you always buy such junk?* **2** *modifier*: *junk jewelry/ junk mail* **3** *n tennis by 1970s* Tricky serves and lobs; soft, hard-to-reach shots: *He is a master of control and of dealing "junk"*—New York Times/ *. . . looping junk, the players' term for soft, short shots*—Esquire **4** *n baseball by 1950s* =JUNK-BALL **5** *n 1920s narcotics* Narcotics; =DOPE: *Canales has a noseful of junk a lot of the time*—Raymond Chandler/ *Sherlock Holmes. . . All he does is play a fiddle and take junk*—J Cannon **6** *modifier*: *. . . one of the most dangerous junk neighborhoods in the city*—Esquire **7** *n* Unspecified heaps and objects; stuff; crap: *Men carry more junk in their pockets than women do in their pocketbooks*—Associated Press [fr a British nautical term for old or weak rope or cable, found by 1485]

junk-ball **1** *n baseball by 1950s* A deceptive and unorthodox pitch; =JUNK **2** *modifier*: *Eddy Lopat, another "junk ball" pitcher*—R Roden

junk bond *n phr by middle 1970s* A bond having high yield but relatively little security, used as a payment for one company by another in a corporate merger: *Fed adopts "Junk Bond" curbs*—New York Times

junked up *adj phr narcotics by 1940s* =HOPPED UP

junker **1** *n narcotics by 1920s* =JUNKIE **2** *n narcotics by 1920s* A narcotics dealer; =CONNECTION, JUGGLER **3** *n by 1950s* A car or other machine that is worn out and ready to be discarded, or that has been discarded; something that ought to be discarded; =PIECE OF SHIT: *You can't litter the countryside with the kind of crap that the junkers are*—Fortune/ *driving a junker around and around one of the chicken coops*—Newsweek

junket **1** *n by 1886* A tour undertaken by a government official, at public expense, and often for no public benefit: *An agricultural junket through nine European countries*—Newsweek **2** *v*: *. . . junketed like contemporary tourists*—Herald Tribune [fr *junket*, "feast; merrymaking," found by 1530 and of obscure origin; the verb is found by 1821, meaning "take a pleasure trip," without the US political sense]

junk food *n phr early 1970s* Foods like potato chips, popcorn, sugar-coated cereals, and the like, esp popular with children and having little nutritional value

junk heap **1** *n phr by 1940s* A worn and ramshackle old car; =HEAP, JALOPY **2** *n phr by 1906* Any unsightly or chaotic place: *His room was always a mephitic junk heap*

junkie or **junky** **1** *n narcotics by 1923* A narcotics addict: *I didn't want to be a junkie*—Saturday Review/ *The man I was to find was both a junkie and pusher*—A Halsey **2** *modifier*: *Junkie logic is the ability to justify whatever needs to be done to support an addiction*—Los Angeles Times **3** *n* A devotee or addict of any sort: *Zuckerman describes himself as a "newspaper and magazine junkie"*–Time/ *Growth junkies, snipes one former insider, go-go boys*—Wall Street Journal

junk mail *n phr by 1950s* Mail, usu third class, consisting of advertising circulars, appeals for money, etc, and sometimes addressed to "resident"

junk shop *n phr by 1940s* A shop where old discarded things and miscellaneous bits of potential trash are sold; second-hand store

junk sports *n phr by 1980s* Professional wrestling, "gladiator" contests, big-wheel trucking, and other quasi-sports events seen on television: *He hosts. . . occasional "junk sports" specials on network TV. . .* —Milwaukee Journal

junkyard dog *n phr by 1980s* A particularly vicious dog or person: *If the unions took over our plants, we would turn as mean as a junk-yard dog*—New Yorker/ *He's a junkyard dog. . . He's tough. He's nasty*—Milwaukee Journal

junque *n* Old and discarded odds and ends; rummage; =JUNK: *a wonderful collection of white elephants, trash, treasures and, as the antique dealers spell it, "junque"*—Washington Post/ *. . . ever since the self-described "junque" jeweler arrived in New York*—Town and Country [the pseudo-French spelling lends a certain chic and dignity to the material]

the **jury is still out** *sentence by 1980s* No decision has yet been made; the question is open: *The jury is still out on whether he's fitting in—*

Milwaukee Journal/ *The jury is still out on whether the traditional union is necessary for the new workplace*—Nation/ *The jury may remain out on Mr. Clinton's contradictory character for a long time*—New York Times

not **just another pretty face** *See* NOT JUST ANOTHER PRETTY FACE

just around the corner *adv phr* by 1914 Nearby; imminent: *Prosperity is just around the corner, the President said*

just fallen off the turnip truck *adj phr* by 1980s Unfledged; inexperienced; ignorant: *Detective Benjamin Calazo was not a cop who had just fallen off the turnip truck*—Lawrence Sanders [the agricultural source suggests an earlier date]

just folks *n phr* by 1908 Ordinary people; common people; hoi polloi: *. . . the Mayor moved about in a warm-up jacket, playing just folks*—New Yorker

just for the hell of it *See* FOR THE HELL OF IT

just one of those things *n phr* by 1930s Something that can hardly be predicted, justified, explained, or avoided, but is an intrinsic and sometimes a distressful part of living ●The gestural equivalent is a shrug: *Their divorce was just one of those things*

just what the doctor ordered *n phr* by 1914 Exactly what is needed: *Account Supervisors: We're just what the doctor ordered for your career*—New York Times

just whistling Dixie *See* NOT JUST WHISTLING DIXIE, WHISTLING DIXIE

juve or **juvie** or **juvey** *adj* by 1940s Juvenile; youthful: *the next monster juve act would be. . .* —Village Voice **2** *n* by 1940s A young person; child; juvenile, esp a juvenile offender: *I'm a juve*—TV show *Hill Street Blues* **3** *n* by 1935 An actor who plays youthful roles; a juvenile lead: *No juve in this show?* **4** *modifier*: *Andrews became the archetypal juve lead on British television* **5** *n* by 1940s A juvenile court or a reformatory: *I was desperate. You ever been in juvie?*—Sue Grafton **6** *modifier*: *juvey hall/ juvey books*

K

K 1 *n* by 1970s A thousand dollars: *Four bastards no smarter'n you and me got ninety-seven K out of some little bank*—George V Higgins **2** *n* 1960s narcotics A kilogram, esp such a quantity of narcotics; =KEY: . . . *even occasional Ks (kilograms) of cocaine*—New York Times **3** *n* baseball by 1861 A strikeout [fr the Greek prefix *kilo-*, "one thousand"; baseball sense said to have been originated in a scorecard notation system either by Henry Chadwick or MJ Kelly]

kabibble *See* ISH KABIBBLE

kablooey *See* GO BLOOEY

kafooster *n* by 1940s Useless talk; babble; =BULLSHIT: *There has been a great deal of kafooster about emasculating the price-control act*—Robert Taft

kaka *See* CA-CA

kale or **kale-seed** *n* by 1902 Money; =the GREEN STUFF: . . . *trite slangisms, among 'em kale, dough, mazuma, etc*—Abel Green

kamikaze *modifier* by 1960s Violent and reckless; self-destructive: . . . *his kamikaze style would lead to fine, suspension, or tragic injury*—Milwaukee Journal

kangaroo *v* prison To convict someone with false evidence; =FRAME

kangaroo court or **club 1** *n phr* by 1853 A mock court: *The toughest prisoner announced that he was president of the Kangaroo Club and would hold court*—E Lavine **2** *n phr* by 1940s A small-town police court where traffic fines to transients are high, and usu divided among the police [origin unknown]

kaput or **kapoot** (kah PŏoT) *adj* by 1914 Inoperative; ineffective; =FINISHED: *I would be "kaput" without a folding machete*—S J Perelman/ *Only sixteen of us. After that, kapoot*—Sue Grafton [fr echoic-symbolic German slang]

karma *n* =VIBES [fr Sanskrit, "work"]

Katie bar the door *sentence* by 1930s Get ready for trouble; a desperate situation is at hand: *If you fall too far behind, it'll be Katie-bar-the-door real quick*—New York Times/ *If they were on to him, well, that's all she wrote. Katie bar the door*—William Kennedy

katrinka *n* by 1990s An old car: . . . *makes it clear that some of the old katrinkas are worth their weight in gold*—Ann Landers

kayo or **kay** *n* prizefight by 1923 A knockout; =KO

kazoo or **gazoo** or **gazool** by 1970s **1** *n* The buttocks; anus; =ASS: . . . *an impossible, unreliable, self-destructive pain in the kazoo*—Washington Post/ *We have subcommittee staff running out the kazoo*—New York Times/ . . . *you know he's off balance and you'd like to stick it in his gazoo*—Alan K Simpson **2** *n* Toilet; =CAN: *I tore it up and flushed it down the kazoo*—Lawrence Sanders [origin unknown; perhaps fr Louisiana French *zoozoo*, "buttocks, ass"; perhaps *kazoo,* known in its standard sense fr the 1880s, suggested the anus in being tubular and emitting sounds]

kee *See* KEY

keed *n* by 1920 =KID

keel over *v phr* by 1876 To fall down; collapse: *He was so tired he was about to keel over* [fr nautical careening of a ship so that the *keel* is raised]

keen *adj* teenagers & students by 1900 Excellent; wonderful; =NEAT: *I think she's a keen kid*—Max Shulman/ *"Keen?" Blanche said. "I haven't heard that word in 20 years"*—Lawrence Sanders *See* PEACHY

keep someone *v phr* by 1560 To support and maintain someone for sexual purposes: *She has "an old man". . . who "keeps" her*—New York Times/ *Maybe some day some guy'll even keep me*—Xaviera Hollander

keep (or maintain) a low profile *v phr* by 1975 To stay inconspicuous; try not to attract much attention: *Better keep a low profile until this blows over* [originally a military term, based on the idea of offering a small target; *low profile* is found by the 1960s]

keep an eye on someone or something *v phr* by 1818 To watch; guard over: . . . *so I paid her a visit so as I could keep an eye on the house*—The Lantern

keep one's **cool** *v phr* 1950s beat & cool talk To retain one's composure; stay calm; =COOL IT: *We'd all better keep our cool and not provoke him*

keep one's **eye on the ball** *v phr* by 1907 To pay strict attention to what one is doing; be alert and undistracted

keep one's **eye peeled (or skinned)** *v phr* entry form by 1853, second by 1833 To be vigilant; look carefully: *I keep my eye peeled for bargains*

keep one's **hair on** *v phr* by 1885 To stay unruffled; be calm; =COOL IT: *I'm coming. Just keep your hair on, won't you?*

keep someone **honest** *by 1960s* **1** *v phr* To pose a requirement or test so that someone does not go unchallenged: *We'll ask her a few questions just to keep her honest* **2** *v phr* baseball To pitch close to a batter; throw at a batter: *Keep him honest, which means, make the batter afraid of you*—Jim Bouton

keep it down to a dull (or **loud**) **roar** *v phr by 1940s* To be quiet, or quieter: *... how about keeping the noise level down to a dull roar?*—Michael Grant/ *Earl thrives on controversy, and we're trying so hard to go the other way or, at least, keep it to a loud roar*—New Yorker

keep it on the D L *v phr 1990s teenagers* To keep something secret [fr *keep it down low*]

keep one's **nose clean** *v phr by 1887* To avoid doing wrong or seeming to do wrong; stay above reproach: *... if you only keep your nose clean, you'll have it*—The Lantern [fr a traditional injunction of a mother to a child to wipe its *nose*, wash behind its ears, etc]

keep someone **on a short leash** *v phr by 1970s* To keep someone under close control: *We must keep that crazy kid on a short leash*

keep someone **on ice** *v phr by 1894* To keep someone under one's authority: *... complete control to keep Dubie on ice indefinitely*—Stan Cutler

keep on keeping on *v phr by 1970s* To persist; hold one's course; =KEEP ON TRUCKING: *... he would keep on keeping on and worry later about his destination*—New York Times

keep someone **on the reservation** *v phr by 1990s* To insure and require orthodoxy, esp in politics: *White House chief of staff McLarty kept Penny, McCurdy and Stenholm completely on the reservation*—Time [fr the notion of confinement to an Indian *reservation*]

keep on trucking *v phr by 1972* To carry on; continue what one is doing, esp working, plugging away, etc; =KEEP ON KEEPING ON

keep one's **pecker** (or **rocket**) **in** one's **pocket** *v phr by 1990s* To refrain from the sex act; practice continence: *... another professor remarked crudely, "You had better teach your husband to keep his pecker in his pocket, so you can get your research done*—Wisconsin Magazine

keeps *See* FOR KEEPS, PLAY FOR KEEPS

keep several balls in the air *v phr by 1980s* To be involved on multiple jobs, projects, etc [fr the image of a juggler]

keep one's **shirt** (or **pants**) **on** *by 1854* **1** *v phr* To stay unruffled; be calm; =COOL IT: *He was beginning to holler, so I told him to keep his shirt on* **2** *v phr* To be patient; wait a bit; =HOLD one's HORSES: *Keep your pants on and the guy will be back*

keep tabs on *v phr by 1888* To keep informed about; keep watch on or over: *Who's gonna keep tabs on the receipts?* [fr *tab*, "bill, account"]

keep one's **trap shut** *v phr by 1899* To stay or become silent; =SHUT UP: *... otherwise you do yourself a favor and keep your trap shut, you understand?*—Robert B Parker

keep something under one's **hat** *v phr by 1885* To keep something quiet, or a secret; keep to oneself: *Payne, keep this under your hat, will you?*—W E B Griffin

keep up with the Joneses *v phr by 1913* To strive, esp beyond one's means, to keep up socially and financially with others in the same neighborhood or in the same social circle: *Never keep up with the Joneses; drag them down to your level... it's cheaper*—Quentin Crisp [fr the title of a 1913 comic strip by Arthur R Momand]

kee-rect (KEE rekt) *adj by 1950s* Correct

kef (KEEF, KAYF) *n* (also **keef** or **kief** or **kif**) narcotics *by 1878* Marijuana, hashish, or opium [fr Arabic, "pleasure"]

kegger *n teenagers & students by 1960s* A beer party; =BEER BUST

keister (KEE stər) (also **keester** or **keyster** or **kiester** or **kister**) **1** *n by 1931* The buttocks; rump; =ASS: *I've had it up to my keister with these leaks*—Ronald Reagan/ *What a sensation; we'll knock them on their keister*—Stan Cutler **2** *n* pickpockets *by 1930s* A rear trousers pocket **3** *n* hawkers *by 1930s* A suitcase that opens into a display of goods: *... the typical "keister" of the street hawker*—Collier and Westrate **4** *n* underworld *by 1914* A safe; strongbox; =CRIB [fr British dialect *kist* or German *Kiste*, "chest, box," transferred to the buttocks perhaps by the pickpocket sense or by the notion that something may be concealed in the rectum]

◁**Kelsey's ass**▷ *See* COLD AS HELL

◁**Kelsey's nuts**▷ *See* TIGHT AS KELSEY'S NUTS

◁**kelt** or **keltch**▷ *black by late 1920s* **1** *n* A white person **2** *n* A light-skinned black person who might or does pass as white [origin unknown; some connection with *Irish* in the same sense is possible]

Ken or **Ken-doll** *n* A conformist, conventional man; a man lacking any but bland typical characteristics: *Mr Quayle has been called a sort of Ken*/: *Bergin, the male villain, is reprising his role as the Ken-doll monster of Sleeping With the Enemy*—Nation [fr the male counterpart of the Barbie doll]

kennel *n by 1837* A house or room ●In British underworld slang usu *ken* [fr *kennel*, "doghouse," found by 1440]

Kentucky windage *n phr by 1940s* A slight adjustment made on instinct rather than strict measurement: *Let's apply some Kentucky windage and raise that figure just a tad* [fr the skillful adjustments of aim made by good sharpshooters]

keptie *n by 1940s* A woman kept as a mistress: *... the place to hole up your "keptie"*—NY Confidential

ker- (KURR or KUH) *prefix by 1840s* A particle that intensifies echoic terms for blows, splashings, hard efforts, etc: *kerbang/ kerblam/ kerplunk/ kerslosh/ kerwallop*

kerflooie or **kerflooey** *See* GO BLOOEY

kerflummoxed *adj* =FLUMMOXED

kerfuffle *n by 1813* Disorder; confusion: *Don Imus. . . has thrown the capital into a kerfuffle*—Maureen Dowd [fr Scots dialect; often spelled *curfuffle*]

kerplunk *See* GO KERPLUNK

kettle of fish *See* FINE KETTLE OF FISH

kevork or **kervork** *v early 1990s* To terminate; kill; nullify: *This is going nowhere. I'm going to kervork it*—Kansas City Star/ *This kind of kevorks the idea of blood sucking. But mosquitoes come prepared*—Milwaukee Journal [fr Dr Jack *Kevorkian*, a Michigan physician who assists suicides; the *ker-* variant is based on simple misspelling or perhaps a subliminal influence of the *ker-* prefix]

key[1] **1** *n 1950s college students* A typical Ivy League student; =WHITE SHOE **2** *adj by 1980s* Essential; crucial: *U.S. commitment and pressure are key to what happens next*—Time/ *The attendance of cute guys at this party is key*—UCLA Slang **3** *adj 1980s students* Excellent; splendid; =FRESH, KILLER, AWESOME **4** *n basketball by 1990s* The area on the court legal for free throws: *Best way to choose a nominee? "Personally," said Bradley, "I favor a jump shot from the top of the key"*—Time/ *. . . knocked home a 19-footer from the top of the key*—Milwaukee Journal Sentinel **5** *v by 1980s* To vandalize a car by scratching it with a key: *Well, did you key her car?*—Lee K Russell
See CHURCH KEY

key[2] or **kee** or **ki** *n narcotics* A kilogram (about 2.2 pounds) of a narcotic: *. . . enough opium to produce a key (kilo) of heroin*—Time/ *Anybody who can handle a key of pure coke is dealing big*—New York Magazine [fr *kilo*]

key club 1 *n phr* A loose association of married couples in which keys to dwellings are exchanged more or less at random, for sexual purposes **2** *n phr* A private social organization to which one can purchase a membership

key on something *v phr by 1990s* To regard something as important; discover that something is "key": *. . . one of the things I kept keying on was this notion of a distinctly hand-oriented society*—New Yorker

keyster *See* KEISTER

the keystone or **keystone sack** or **keystone cushion** *n phr baseball by 1917* Second base

ki *See* KEY

kibbles and bits *n phr 1990s teenagers* Crumbs of cocaine [fr *kibbles*, "products of a kind of grinding," found by 1891; the verb is found by 1790; today chiefly a form of dog-food pellets]

kibitz or **kabitz** *by 1920s* **1** *v* To give intrusive and unrequested advice while watching a game, performance, etc: *He was kibitzing us all the way*—Leo Rosten **2** *n*: *Ixnay on the kabitz. Get me?*—American Mercury **3** *v* To banter, comment: *We were kibitzing around*—Leo Rosten [fr Yiddish fr German *Kiebitz*, "peewit, lapwing," a noisy little bird]

kibitzer *n by 1920s* A person who gives intrusive advice: *I don't mind admitting that a good kibitzer has 20–20 hindsight*—New York Post

kibosh (KĪ bahsh) *v by 1884* To eliminate; terminate; =KEVORK, KILL: *. . . that was kiboshed promptly by the White House spokesman*—Philadelphia Journal

the kibosh *n phr by 1834* The termination; sad end; sudden doom: *This latest goof is probably the kibosh* [origin unknown, and very extensively speculated upon; perhaps, e.g., fr Irish *cie bais,* "cap of death," referring to the black cap a judge would don when pronouncing a death sentence; perhaps fr Yiddish]
See PUT THE KIBOSH ON someone or something

kick 1 *v by 1388* To complain; protest; =BITCH: *She can just kick all she wants to*—Sinclair Lewis **2** *n by 1839*: *If you got any kicks, you can always quit* **3** *n by 1849* A pocket, esp a pants pocket: *I have a hundred thousand boo-boos in the kick*—H McHugh **4** *n by 1941* A surge or fit of pleasure; a feeling of joy and delight; =BELT, CHARGE: *He was having a real kick*—R S Prather/ *I get a kick out of you*—Cole Porter **5** *n by 1941* Anything that gives one a feeling of pleasure, joy, etc: *That's a kick. . . . Ridin' a guy down Wilshire in daylight*—Raymond Chandler **6** *n by 1940s* A strong personal predilection; =THING: *Arthur. . . is on the Paris kick*—John Crosby/ *. . . several opportunities to let her wail on a comic kick*—Bob Salmaggi **7** *n by 1844* Power; impact; potency: *One of those. . . stories with a kick*—P Marks **8** *n by 1904* A shoe: *Hey, nice kicks* **9** *v narcotics by 1936* To end one's drug habit; become "clean" **10** *n sports by 1980s* A spurt of speed at the end of a footrace: *Full into his kick as he passed them. . .* —Harry Crews [pocket sense fr late 17th-century *kicks,* "breeches"]
See GET A KICK OUT OF someone or something, ON A ROLL, SIDEKICK, TOP-KICK

kick a lung out of someone *v phr by 1880s* To defeat or thrash thoroughly; trounce; =BEAT THE SHIT OUT OF someone, CLOBBER

kick around *by 1940s* **1** *v phr* To idle about; drift around rootlessly; =BAT AROUND: *He put in a couple years just kicking around California* **2** *v phr* To acquire experience; become seasoned: *. . . sound like a band that's kicked around for a long time*—Changes [the sense "walk around" is found by 1839]

kick someone **around** *v phr students by 1912* To abuse; repeatedly maltreat: *Mr Nixon said the press wouldn't have him to kick around anymore*

kick something **around** *v phr by 1940s* To discuss or think about something; consider from all angles: *It's something we've been kicking around for about 10 years*—Milwaukee Journal

kick ass *Army by 1970s* **1** *v phr* To assert power; be rough; punish: *He once again kicked ass with the Wagner 6 to 1 triumph*—Village Voice/ *Geometry and algebra were kicking my ass*—Claude Brown/ *We kicked a little ass last night*—George Bush **2** *v phr* To have power; have unpolished vigor: *. . . just country that kicks ass and entertains*—Aquarian

kick-ass *Army by 1970s* **1** *adj* (also **kick-butt** or

kick-yer-ass) Rough; powerful; =ROUGH-ASS, TOUGH: *. . . that kick-ass attitude*—Sports Illustrated/ *. . . gave up its last drop of kick-ass Gewurztraminer*—Car and Driver/ *. . . the only team without a kick-butt run blocker on their line*—Milwaukee Journal **2** *n* Power; energy; virility: *He's the guy who coaxed the kick-ass back into the torque*—Car and Driver/ *. . . with the gall to label such Muzak kick-ass*—Worcester

◁**kick ass and take names**▷ *v phr Army by 1970s* To behave very roughly and angrily; =KICK ASS: *screaming, berating, threatening, kicking ass and taking names*—Sports Illustrated/ *Paschal ain't gonna do nothing but kick ass and take names*—Dan Jenkins [fr the image of a rough and punitive police officer, drill sergeant, prison guard, etc]

kick at the cat *n phr by 1970s* A turn; a chance: *When the pages are pasted up, the Engraving Department gets its second kick at the cat*—Milwaukee Journal/ *. . . give everyone an opportunity to take a kick at whatever cat is up for study*—Milwaukee Journal

kickback *n by 1934* Money given to someone illegally or unethically: *Buying another poor devil's job for $50 or a kick-back from his pay*—Westbrook Pegler/ *All the cops were on the pad, getting kickbacks from the hookers*

kick back 1 *v phr underworld by 1926* To return or restore, esp to give back stolen property: *Stolen goods returned to the rightful owner are "kicked back"*—H McLellan **2** *v phr by 1934* To give part of wages, fees, etc, illicitly to another in return for one's job or other advantage: *The cabbies had to kick back a lot to the dispatchers* **3** *v phr 1980s students fr black* To relax; =CHILL OUT: *Use the pool, kick back. . . . Who knows?*—Armistead Maupin/ *That's when I started kicking back with my brothers and homeboys*—MM

kick booty *v phr by 1980s* =KICK ASS

kick down *v phr truckers by 1960s* To shift into a lower gear in a truck or car

kicker 1 *n by 1876* A complainer; =KVETCH **2** *n by 1928* A small motor, esp an outboard, used for a boat; =EGGBEATER **3** *n by 1940s* Anything that gives great pleasure; =KICK: *The kicker. . . was the station wagon*—R Starnes **4** *n by 1970s* A hidden cost, qualification, defect, etc; =CATCH: *The kicker is that if you are subject to this requirement. . . your homeowner's policy will not cover the injuries*—Washingtonian/ *The kicker to this one is simple*—Gilbert Milstein [fourth sense probably fr poker, "a high card kept, along with a pair, in draw poker," found by 1892]

kickers *n 1950s college students* Shoes, esp tennis shoes

kickin' *adj 1980s black teenagers* Excellent; =BAD, COOL: *. . . a creamy Italian dressing with kickin' taste and bumpin' packaging*—Macon Telegraph/ *The game was kickin'*—Delcastle Dictionary of Slang

kick in 1 *v phr by 1908* To pay up money; make one's proper contribution; =FORK OVER: *to ask you guys to kick in your share of the expenses*—Jerome Weidman **2** *v phr by 1980s* To begin action; take effect; begin to function: *. . . the endorphins were beginning to kick in*—Stan Cutler/ *Now the morphine was kicking in. . .*—Carsten Stroud/ *The motel kitchen was kicking into action*—Robert B Parker [second sense perhaps fr earlier phrase *kick it in gear*, "shift the gears of a car"]

◁**kicking ass**▷ *n phr 1980s college students* A good time; =a BALL: *We went downtown and had a kicking ass*

kicking can *n phr by 1980s* An object of attack, esp a habitual object; whipping boy: *The young alderman's chief kicking can has been four oil companies*—Toronto Life [fr the child's game *kick the can*]

◁a **kick in the ass** (or **the pants**)▷ *by 1940s* **1** *n phr* A surprising and dampening rebuff, misfortune, etc; a slap in the face **2** *n phr* A strong stimulus or impetus; =a SHOT IN THE ARM: *If this campaign doesn't get a kick in the ass we're dead*/ *The sizzle of the 24-valve V8 Mercedes M3 assures the driver of the right kind of kick in the pants*—New York Times

kick it 1 *v phr narcotics by 1936* To rid oneself of narcotic addiction: *I don't think anybody knew anyone who had kicked it*—Claude Brown **2** *v phr jazz talk & jive talk* To play swing or jazz very vigorously **3** *v phr 1980s black teenagers* To idle about with nothing much to do: *Dude canceled his party, so we'll probably end up kickin' it*—Washington Post/ *I didn't really have any friends at school, I just used to kick it by myself*—Rocky Mountain News

kick line *n phr by 1990s* A theatrical chorus line: *Who does not know Madonna's latest stage show, complete with tubular-breasted males and a kickline of Dick Tracies?*—New Republic

kickoff 1 *n by 1875* The beginning; inauguration: *He planned the kickoff of his campaign for Texas* **2** *modifier*: *kickoff dinner/ kickoff speech*

kick off 1 *v phr by 1921* To die: *. . . after his wife kicked off*—New Yorker **2** *v phr by 1950* To leave; depart **3** *v phr* To begin something; inaugurate: *the chain of thought kicked off by it*—Eldridge Cleaver/ *. . . a relative newcomer who kicked off her film career with Menace II Society*—USExpress

kick-out *n WWII armed forces* A dishonorable discharge

kick someone **out** *v phr by 1711* To eject, expel, or dismiss someone; =BOUNCE: *She kicked Peter out of the apartment*—New York Magazine

kick (or **break**) **out the jams** (or **jambs**) *v phr 1960s musicians* To behave in an unrestrained way; be uninhibited; =LET oneself GO: *Kick out the jams, motherfookers*—Village Voice/ *On Side Two they kick out the jams, or at least shake the Jello*—Rolling Stone [said to be fr *jams*, "chocks under the wheels of a dragster, used to hold it in place"]

kick over See KNOCK OVER

kick pad *n phr 1960s narcotics* A place where one

is detoxified from narcotics: *I was clean three more days, left the kick pad*—Joseph Wambaugh

kick party *n phr* 1960s narcotics A party where LSD is used

kicks 1 *n* by 1950s Pleasure and gratification; =BANG, JOLLIES: *Sock cymbal's enough to give me my kicks*—Douglass Wallop **2** *n* by 1891 Shoes **See** GET one's COOKIES

kick-start *n* by 1990s To inaugurate; launch, esp vigorously: *Clinton's speech was a kick-start for his health plan*—National Public Radio [fr the starting of a motorcyle by a *kick* downward on the start pedal]

kick stick *n phr* 1960s narcotics A marijuana cigarette

kick the bucket *v phr* by 1785 To die: *Old man Mose done kicked the bucket* [origin uncertain; perhaps fr the *bucket* a suicide might kick from beneath him in hanging himself]

kick-the-cat *modifier* by 1990s Angry and frustrated: *... puts the IRS in a surly, kick-the-cat mood*—Newark Star-Ledger [fr the image of one who *kicks the cat* when the real target of anger is unknown or unreachable]

kick the gong around *v phr* narcotics by 1930s To smoke opium or marijuana: *He helped the world kick the gong around, Jack did*—William Kennedy [fr *gong*, "opium pipe"]

◁**kick the shit out of** someone or something▷ **See** BEAT THE SHIT OUT OF someone or something

kick the tires *v phr* by 1970s To make a quick and superficial inspection; do cursory checking: *... simplistic agrarian vision bought by the war-weary nation without kicking the tires*—Michael M Thomas/ *... has asked* PC Magazine *to kick the tires and slam the doors* [fr such an examination made while appraising a car]

kick someone **to the curb** *v phr* by 1990s To be no longer employed or wanted; made surplus: *... be rendered, as the British say, redundant. Or as my contemporaries would observe... kicked to the curb*—Los Angeles Times

kick-up 1 *n* by 1778 A dance or dancing party **2** *n* by 1793 A commotion; disturbance; =RUCKUS

kick up a fuss (or **a row**) *v phr* entry form by 1848, variant by 1759 To make a disturbance; complain loudly and bitterly; =RAISE CAIN: *I don't want his lawyer to kick up a fuss about this*—E Lavine/ *I'm afraid the opposition will kick up a row over this*

kick someone **upstairs** *v phr* by 1821 To remove someone from office by promotion to a nominally superior position: *It is conceivable but not likely that Mr Gromyko has been kicked upstairs where... he'll no longer influence Soviet foreign policy*—New York Times

kicky by 1950s **1** *adj* Very chic and modish: *... a lot of kicky clothes, many of them imports*—New York Times/ *... so easy and smooth in their short, kicky skirts, pantyhose*—Village Voice **2** *adj* Exciting; ravishing; =FAR OUT: *It's very kicky to be able to drive right over sand dunes*—Playboy/ *... a kicky way to spend a couple of years*

kid 1 *n* by 1599 A child: *She's a cute little kid* **2** *n* by 1884 A young or relatively young man or woman: *the kids in college* **3** *modifier*: *his kid sister/ my kid cousin* **4** *v* by 1891 To joke; jest; banter; =JOSH: *a funny guy, always kidding* **5** *v* by 1811 To attempt to deceive; try to fool: *Are you kidding me?* **6** *n*: *That's no kid, neither*—Dunning and Abbott [fr *kid*, "an infant goat"; bantering and fooling senses perhaps fr an alteration of dialect *cod*, "hoax, fool"] **See** I KID YOU NOT, NEW KID ON THE BLOCK, WHIZ KID

the **Kid** *n phr* WWII Army Air Forces A copilot; =METER-READER

kid around *v phr* by 1940s To jest and banter; avoid seriousness; =FOOL AROUND

kiddie or **kiddy** *n* by 1889 A child [the form *kiddey* is found by 1823]

kidding See NO KIDDING

kiddo or **Kiddo** *n* by 1905 A person, esp one younger than oneself •Used nearly always in direct address: *Look, kiddo, I don't think you quite understand*—Hugh Pentecost/ *There's a lot of loot there, kiddo*—Lawrence Sanders

kidney See GRIPE one's ASS

kidney-buster truckers by 1940s **1** *n* A rough road **2** *n* A hard-riding truck

kidpic *n* by 1990s A movie made primarily for children: *... all the purer-than-thou preteens and tots from kidpics like* Angels in the Outfield. . . —Los Angeles Times

kid show *n phr* circus by 1930 A sideshow

kid stuff by 1923 **1** *n phr* Something too easy to challenge an adult; =CINCH, PIECE OF CAKE: *That swim to Catalina's kid stuff* **2** *n phr* Activity not appropriate for an adult; childish concerns: *Give up the kid stuff and find a real job*

kid top *n phr* circus by 1930 The sideshow tent

kidvid 1 *n* by 1955 Children's television: *... a year when kidvid is being publicly scolded*—TV Guide/ *The three networks are offering the public more kidvid*—New York Times **2** *modifier*: *The trade journals call the children's program segment on television the "kidvid ghetto"*—American Scholar

kief or **kif See** KEF

kiester See KEISTER

kife *v* circus by 1940s To swindle; cheat

◀**kike▶ 1** *n* by 1904 A Jew •Sometimes used by Jews of other Jews they regard with contempt; several early occurrences are found in a theatrical context **2** *adj*: *kike neighborhood* **3** *n* by 1916 A low or shady merchant or shop •The 1916 advertisement quoted here was placed by a Jewish merchant: *Go into any little kike, little hole-in-the-wall. . .* —Joplin Globe [origin unknown and much speculated upon; the most plausible explanation, published by J H A Lacher, a former traveling salesman, is that the established German-American Jewish salesmen ridiculed their Eastern European colleagues in the 1890s with the name *kiki*, because so many of their surnames ended in "ki" or "ky," whence *kike*]

kill 1 *v* by 1833 To drink or eat up: *The lady killed a dozen oysters*—The Lantern **2** *v* by 1573 To spoil or ruin: *One bad grade killed his chances for med school* **3** *v by 1940s* To demoralize totally; make hopeless: *The third defeat killed him* **4** *v by 1899* To be extremely successful with: *The Evergreen Review kills him*—Eldridge Cleaver **5** *v by 1856* To make an audience helpless with laughter; =FRACTURE: *My McEnroe act kills 'em* **6** *v students by 1900* To do very easily; =ACE: *I killed the geology final* **7** *v by 1865* To eliminate a newspaper story or part of it **8** *v by 1934* To extinguish a light **9** *v by 1886* To stop or turn off a motor **10** *n by 1930s* A murder: *. . . for the Shannon kill*—Raymond Chandler **11** *n WWII armed forces* An enemy airplane, ship, tank, etc, destroyed

See IN AT THE KILL, KILLER

to **kill** *See* DRESSED TO KILL, DRESSED TO THE TEETH

killer 1 *n by 1937* A very attractive person: *Ain't she a killer?* **2** *n* (also **killer-diller**) *by 1930s* A person or thing that is remarkable, wonderful, superior, etc; =BEAUT, DOOZIE: *The song's a killer!/ The famed quartet. . . steams out "killer-dillers"*—New Yorker **3** *adj* (also **killer-diller**) *by 1970s*: *. . . not only was it a killer version*—Village Voice/ *The killer idea of the century is about to be laid on you*—William Goldman **4** *n narcotics by 1940s* A marijuana cigarette; =JOINT

See LADY-KILLER

killing *adj 1980s teenagers* Excellent; =FRESH, GREAT, KILLER: *. . . and good things are known as "rad, tough, booming, legit, fly, kill, killing, chilling, fresh or nasty"*—Daily News [the sense "fascinating, bewitching, irresistible" is found by 1619, but the current use is an independent phenomenon rather than a survival]

See MAKE A KILLING

killjoy *n* A morose pessimist; =CRAPE-HANGER, GLOOMY GUS

killout *n black by 1950s* A remarkable person or thing; =KICK

kill the clock *v phr sports by 1960s* To use delaying tactics and plays at the very end of a period or game: *. . . and ran double tight-end formations sets to kill the clock*—Milwaukee Journal

kill (or **shoot**) **the messenger 1** *v phr by 1980s* To punish the bearer of bad news: *Dreyfus is right. Let's not make the mistake of killing the messenger*—Time **2** *modifier*: *In a shoot-the-messenger diversionary tactic, the spotlight swung away from Clarence Thomas and smack onto Totenberg*—Vanity Fair

kilo connection *n phr 1960s narcotics* A wholesale narcotics dealer, who dilutes the pure drug by about 50 percent

kilter *See* OUT OF KILTER

kimono *See* PINE OVERCOAT

kin *See* KISSING COUSIN, SHIRTTAIL KIN

the **kind** *adj phr 1980s teenagers* Excellent; superior; =SOME KIND OF: *He's got the kind car*

kind (or **sort**) **of** *See* SOME KIND OF

king 1 *n* (also **king pin**) *entry form by 1382, variant by 1867* The leader; chief: *king of the motorcy-*

cle jumpers **2** *n underworld by 1940s* A prison warden **3** *n railroad by 1940s* A yardmaster or freight conductor

king-hell *modifier by 1990s* Very severe; outstanding; =WORLD-CLASS: *. . . the poor fool is pushing a stroller around the zoo in 90-degree heat with a king-hell hangover*—Milwaukee Journal

King Kong 1 *n phr by 1955* Something huge and threatening; =SIX-HUNDRED-POUND GORILLA: *"It wouldn't matter if you put King Kong in the Treasury," complained Sir Teddy Taylor. "The Germans control our economy"*—Time **2** *n phr black by 1960s* Cheap and strong liquor: *No six-year-old child got no business drinking that King Kong*—Claude Brown [fr the 1933 movie *King Kong*, about a gargantuan gorilla]

king-size or **king-sized** *adj by 1940s* Very large; extra large: *Your nagging gives me a king-size headache/ The new king-sized rockets stopped three Red tanks*—Associated Press

kink 1 *n* (also **kinko**) *by 1960s* A person with deviant or bizarre tastes, esp sexual: *I'm not some kind of kink*—John D MacDonald **2** *modifier*: *. . . a kinko diner who tries to attract Chong's attention*—Washington Post **3** *n* A deviant practice or predilection, esp sexual: *. . . a Nazi with a kink for prepubescent girls*—A Bailey/ *. . . the female staffer whose kink is making love down in the morgue*—New York Magazine **4** *n by 1990s* A style featuring deviation and oddness: *. . . blend of leaden TV-style melodrama and deadpan modernist kink*—Newark Star-Ledger **5** *n by 1868* A defect or flaw, esp a minor one; =BUG: *We'll work the kinks out of the plan before we announce it*

kinky 1 *adj by 1927* Dishonest; illegal; =CROOKED: *. . . "kinky" gambling paraphernalia*—W R Simpson **2** *adj underworld by 1927* Stolen: *a kinky car* **3** *adj by 1860* Eccentric; crotchety **4** *adj by 1950s* Bizarre; weird: *. . . no offense so kinky that the Maximum Enchilada and his consigliores wouldn't commit it*—G Wolff **5** *adj by 1950s* Deviant and abnormal, esp sexually: *. . . a very kinky guy, likes being beat up* **6** *adj* Showing or pertaining to sexual deviation: *kinky photos/ kinky porn* [the stronger, fifth sense is said to have originated among British homosexuals in the 1920s]

kip *by 1859* **1** *n* A bed: *. . . in the kip*—John O'Hara **2** *n* Sleep; a sleep or nap **3** *v*: *. . . find a place to "kip"*—Jack London **4** *n* A night guard [origin uncertain; perhaps fr Danish *kippe*, "hut, mean alehouse," whence the early–1800s sense "brothel"]

kishkes or **kishkas** *n by 1959* The entrails; innards; =GUTS: *His kishkas were gripped by the iron hand of outrage and frustration*—Philip Roth [fr Yiddish]

kiss *n by 1950s* =KISS-OFF

See BUTTERFLY KISS, FRENCH KISS, SOUL KISS

KISS (KIS) *sentence by 1980s* Keep it simple, stupid, or keep it simple and stupid

kiss and make up *v phr by 1940s* To become reconciled; forget past animosity: *Mandela and his* rival Chief Buthelezi, whose followers have been slaughtering one another by the thousands, have kissed and made up—New Republic

kiss and tell 1 *modifier* by 1695 Gossiping about one's friends, esp about sexual exploits: . . . *Reagan condemned these "kiss and tell" books by former government servants. . .* —Milwaukee Journal/ *. . . those juicy kiss-and-tell escapades that seem so much a part of the professional athlete's life*— Milwaukee Journal **2** *n phr* by 1980s: *Don't look for a kiss-and-tell from Ulichny*—Milwaukee Journal [the dated instance for the first sense is in the original verb form]

kiss-and-tell book *n phr* by 1980 A book of intimate gossip and revelation: *It will not be a kiss-and-tell book. . . I will preserve the confidentiality of my conversations with the president*—Milwaukee Journal

◁**kiss ass**▷ *v phr* by 1930s To flatter one's superiors; =BROWN-NOSE: *He likes to be perfect and kiss ass*— Pat Conroy

◁**kiss-ass**▷ or **kiss-butt** by 1960s **1** *n* A toady; sycophant; =BROWN-NOSE, ASS-KISSER: *and not have people think, "Oh, what a kiss-butt"*—Washington Post **2** *modifier* (also **kissy-ass**) : . . . *another kiss-ass review of an extremely bad album*—Rolling Stone/ *. . . his tone much different, being efficient and a little kissy-ass*—Elmore Leonard **3** *n* Sycophantic flattery: *using the old kiss-ass with the colonel*

◁**kiss someone's ass**▷ *v phr* by 1749 To flatter someone; curry favor with superiors: *I didn't kiss anybody's ass and I didn't expect anybody to kiss mine*—People Weekly

kisser *n* by 1860 The mouth; the face: *It would be a pleasure to drop one on your kisser, I admit*—Leo Rosten/ *. . . show the good side of my kisser*— John O'Hara/ *Reagan had that quizzical "do I talk now?" look on his kisser*—Washington Post
See ASS-KISSER, MOTHERFUCKER

kiss something goodbye *v phr* by 1930s To take leave of something, often unwillingly; bid farewell: *I figure, this is it, say your prayers and kiss your butt goodbye*—Carsten Stroud

kissing *See* MOTHERFUCKING

kissing cousin (or **kin**) by 1940s **1** *n* A relative close enough to be kissed in salutation, hence anyone with whom a person is fairly intimate: *The two species will often prove to be kissing cousins, for they'll crossbreed*—Sports Afield/ *You guys talk like kissing cousins*—movie *The Tanks Are Coming* **2** *n* A close copy: *He had a kissing cousin of Montgomery's mustache*—JA Kugelmass

kissing trap *n phr* by 1854 The mouth; =TRAP

◁**kiss my ass**▷ *sentence* by 1705 An invitation to perform an obsequious and humiliating act; =GO FUCK oneself, FUCK YOU ●Always an insulting challenge and rejection: *"What should I say?" asked Belle. "Tell him to kiss my ass"*—Joseph Heller/ *I want him to kiss my ass in Macy's window and tell me it smells like roses*—New Republic

kiss off 1 *v phr* by 1930s To dodge; evade: *. . . had kissed off all raps*—J Evans **2** *v phr* by 1940s To kill: *. . . who kissed off Martin*—J Evans

kiss-off 1 *n* (also **California kiss-off** or **New York kiss-off**) A dismissal, esp a rude one; =the BOUNCE, BRUSH-OFF, KISS: *He got up out of his chair, the standard kiss-off*—Stan Cutler **2** *v* black by 1940s To die

kiss someone or **something off** by 1930s **1** *v phr* To dismiss rudely; =BRUSH someone OFF: *The receptionist kissed me off quite cheekily* **2** *v phr* To let go of, to attempt to forget; =KISS something GOODBYE: *You can kiss that money off*

kiss someone out *v phr* 1920s underworld To deny someone their share: *When a member of a mob is deprived of his share he is "kissed out"*—H McLellan

kiss the canvas (or **the resin**) *v phr* by 1919 To be knocked unconscious, esp in a boxing match

kiss the dust *v phr* by 1940s =BITE THE DUST

kissy-face (also **kissy-huggy** or **kissy-kissy** or **kissy-poo**) by 1980s **1** *n* Displays of affection; cuddling; blandishments: *From now on it's all PR work and kissy-kissy here and kissy-kissy there*— Milwaukee Journal **2** *n* A kiss: *The symbol of welcome. . . is a handshake, not a kissy-poo*— Washington Post **3** *modifier*: *But she was such a kissy-face up person. . .* —Stan Cutler/ *. . . Pauley and Norville's kissy-poo exchange on* Today— Milwaukee Journal/ *For two weeks after that kissy-face weekend, our love connection continued*— Details/ *. . . is not gonna be a kissy-huggy book*— Edward I Koch/ *Many of the rich and famous, the kissy-kissy socials had all but disappeared*—Vanity Fair **4** *v*: *I've trained poodles so that they won't kissy-face everybody*—Time
See PLAY KISSIE

kister *See* KEISTER

kit *See* HEAD KIT

kit and caboodle (or **boodle**) *n phr* by 1861 The totality; everything: *. . . the whole kit and caboodle, go hang*—George Jean Nathan/ *. . . the whole kit and boodle of 'em*—Ellery Queen [fr 1700s British *kit*, "outfit of equipment," plus early 1800s *boodle*, "lot, collection," perhaps fr Dutch *boedel*, "property, effects"]

kitchen 1 *n* railroad by 1940s The cab of a locomotive **2** *n* hoboes by 1940s The stomach **3** *n* baseball by 1970 The space over home plate where a batter finds it easiest to hit a fair ball; a batter's preferred point of delivery; =WHEELHOUSE: *He'd throw it in my kitchen, so I moved up a step toward the plate*—Associated Press [baseball sense perhaps ultimately fr *kitchen*, "stomach," found by 1594
See DOWN IN THE KITCHEN, IF YOU CAN'T STAND THE HEAT STAY OUT OF THE KITCHEN

kitchen cabinet *n phr* by 1832 An unofficial set of advisers to a president or chief, made up of close friends and cronies, originally of President Andrew Jackson

kite 1 *n* underworld by 1851 A letter or note, esp

one smuggled into prison **2** *n* *by 1917* An airplane ●Chiefly British **3** *v by 1934* To write a check when one does not have the funds to cover it, hoping to find them before the check is cashed: *The bill was due before payday, so I had to kite the check* [*fly a kite* in the third sense is found by 1808]
See FLY A KITE, GO FLY A KITE, HIGH AS A KITE

kitsch or **Kitsch** (KITCH) *n by 1925* Literature or art having little esthetic merit but appealing powerfully to popular taste: *It stands unchallenged as a masterpiece of kitsch*—Playboy/ *The closest I can come to America is through its Kitsch*—Harper's [fr German, "trash, rubbish"]

kitschy *adj by 1960s* Being or resembling kitsch: *Visconti's kitschy film*—Harvey Gross/ *Its kitschy Lupe Velez ambiance*—Armistead Maupin

kitten **See** HAVE KITTENS, SEX KITTEN

kitty *n gambling by 1891* The pot or pool of money in a gambling game, made up of contributions from the players; a contributed fund: *Each put $25,000 in the kitty*—Philadelphia
See BITCH KITTY, DUST KITTY, FEED THE KITTY, IT'S A BITCH

Kitty *n by 1940s* A Cadillac car: *If I had my way I'd take a Kitty*—CB Himes

kiwi **1** *n by 1918* A New Zealander **2** *n Air Force fr WWI British* An Air Force member, esp an officer, who shuns airplanes [fr the name of a flightless bird of New Zealand, fr Maori]

Kleenex *n by 1990s* Something to be used once and discarded: *Presidents and champions who used women like Kleenex were merely exercising an aspect of their power*—New York Times/ *The freeways might open up in an earthquake, causing roadways to fall. He called them disposable Kleenexes good for one blow*—New Yorker/ *Delors himself says that the French go through politicians like Kleenex*—New Yorker [the name of a brand of disposable tissues, a trademark since 1925]

klepto *n by 1940s* A kleptomaniac: *"Bloody klepto,"* says Siddhartha*—New Yorker [fr a Greek combining word *klepto-*, "thief"]

klick or **klik** **See** CLICK

klop in the chops *n phr by 1960s* A blow to the face; a severe attack: *. . . starting with a klop in the chops from San Francisco*—Ann Landers [fr Yiddish *klop*, "a blow," plus the *chop* phrase for rhyme]

kluck **See** CLUCK, DUMB CLUCK

kludge or **kloodge** or **kluge** (KLŌŌJ, KLUJ) *computer by 1962* **1** *n* A term of endearment for a favorite computer, esp a somewhat defective one **2** *n* A computer program that has been revised and tinkered with so much that it will never work **3** *n* A ludicrous assortment of incompatible and unworkable components: *You see this mechanical kluge (contraption), stop, think, and decide to do something*—Newsweek [apparently fr German *klug*, "clever," with an ironic reverse twist]

klutz or **clutz** (KLUTS) *by 1968* **1** *n* A stupid person; idiot; =BLOCKHEAD: *Now, klutz that I am, I thought of Neal*—Esquire/ *A small crowd of first-*

class clutzes—John D MacDonald **2** *n* A clumsy person; a lubberly lout: *I am the world's biggest klutz. . . I trip over my own feet, drop things*—New York Post [fr Yiddish, "blockhead," literally "block"]

klutz around *v phr by 1960s* To behave stupidly; tamper with clumsily

klutzy *by 1968* **1** *adj* Stupid; idiotic: *. . . any clever kid playing a klutzy kid*—New York Times **2** *adj* Clumsy; unhandy

kneecap *by 1975* **1** *v* To shoot someone in the kneecap or legs ●Typically done by terrorists or gangsters as a disabling measure short of assassination: *There was another drive-by and one of the deacons got kneecapped*—Robert B Parker **2** *v* To disable as if by kneecapping: *The law-and-order issue, which Republicans have used for a generation to kneecap Democrats at will, has been coopted*—New Yorker

knee deep *adj phr by 1940s* Overwhelmed; oversupplied; very much involved; =UP TO one's ASS IN something: *I never even tried to make money, and now I'm knee deep in the stuff*—Saul Bellow

knee-high to a grasshopper *adj phr* (Variations: **bumble-bee** or **duck** or **frog** or **mosquito** or **spit** or **splinter** or **toad** may replace **grasshopper**) *by 1851* Very short or small, esp because young: *He's been smoking since he was knee-high to a grasshopper* [*knee high to a toad* is found by 1814]

knee-jerk **1** *n by 1958* A reflexlike action or response: *Being nasty to women is a knee-jerk with him* **2** *modifier*: *. . . one more gesture to the knee-jerk hawks in the Congress*—W Jackson/ *Yet McDonald is no mere knee-jerk critic of the evangelicals*—Washington Post **3** *n by 1958* A person who reacts with a reflexlike response: *. . . a seventy-year old knee-jerk best remembered for castigating the Reverend Bill Moyers for dancing the frug in the White House*—L L King **4** *v by 1980s*: *We need less kneejerking on both sides in these arguments about the environment*—National Public Radio [fr the patellar reflex, described as *knee jerk* by 1876]

knees **See** CUT oneself OFF AT THE KNEES, CUT someone OFF AT THE KNEES

kneesies *n by 1951* Clandestine amorous friction of the knees: *We got back to the table and played kneesies while we talked*—Mickey Spillane [modeled on *footsie*]

knee-slapper *n by 1966* Something very funny, esp a joke; =BOFFOLA: *That's a knee-slapper*—Matt Crowley/ *If she ever told a knee-slapper, I wasn't there*—Washingtonian

knickers **See** HAVE someone BY THE SHORT HAIRS

knife and gun club *n medical by 1990s* A hospital emergency room [modeled on *fish and gun club*]

one's **knitting** **See** STICK TO one's KNITTING

knob **1** *n by 1725* The head: *Can you get that through your ugly knob?* **2** *n by 1990s* A despised person; =DORK, JERK, PRICK: *Don't they know what a knob he is?*—Milwaukee Journal [*knob*, "penis," was British use in the 1800s, according to Tony Thorne]

knobber *n by 1970s* A male homosexual transvestite prostitute: *It is where the knobbers, or transvestites, hang out*—New York Times [perhaps fr their wearing of false *knobs*, "female nipples or breasts"; perhaps because they give *knob jobs*]

knobby *See* NOBBY

◁**knob job**▷ *n phr by 1960s* An act of fellatio; =BLOW JOB

◁**knobs**▷ *n by 1970s* A woman's breasts or nipples; =KNOCKERS

See WITH BELLS ON

knock 1 *v by 1896* To deprecate; criticize severely; dispraise; =PUT someone or something DOWN: . . . *by knocking Hymie Salzman*—Potash and Perlmutter **2** *n*: *It wasn't a disinterested comment—it was a knock/ The knock on Fernandez is he can't field* **3** *v black by 1950s* To borrow or lend; ask or beg **4** *v black by 1944* To give: *C'mon, baby, knock me a kiss*

See BEAT THE SHIT OUT OF someone or something, DON'T KNOCK IT, HAVE something CINCHED

the **knock** *n phr by 1970s* The bill for food, drinks, etc; check; =the DAMAGE, TAB: *By the way, I'm picking up the knock*—Lawrence Sanders

knockabout 1 *adj by 1880* Casual; informal: *These are my knockabout clothes* **2** *adj by 1892* Noisy; raucous; crude: *Beverly Hillbillies has knockabout humor*—National Public Radio/ . . . *in the contest of a knockabout comedy it's deeply offensive*—Los Angeles Times

knock around *v phr by 1834* To idle about; loaf; =KICK AROUND

knock back *v phr by about 1915* To drink in one gulp: *The Colonel got his drink, and after he had knocked it back with one swift motion, he began to feel better*—A J Liebling . . . *there to mull their downside risks and knock back free champagne*—Toronto Life

knock someone's **block off** *v phr by 1908* To hit very hard; give a severe trouncing; =CLOBBER: *One more word and I'll knock your block off* [block, "head," is found by 1635]

knock someone **cold** (or **cuckoo**) *v phr by 1896* To knock unconscious or semiconscious

knock someone (or **knock 'em**) **dead** *v phr by 1917* To delight or impress someone extremely; =KILL, KNOCK someone's SOCKS OFF, WOW: . . . *a fantastic scenery number for my life's movie. Something that'll knock 'em dead*—Washington Post

knockdown 1 *n by 1865* An introduction: *You want a knockdown to something*—Jerome Weidman **2** *n by 1940s* An invitation **3** *n by 1860s* Money stolen from one's employer: . . . *considered the "knock-down" a perfectly legitimate source of profit*—E A Powell **4** *modifier by 1795* Designed to be sold unassembled, and be easy to assemble and disassemble: *a knockdown kitchen set*

knock down 1 *v phr by 1850s* To pocket money taken from one's employer: . . . *clerk who was knocking down on the till*—J Evans **2** *v phr by 1929* To earn: *Hommuch he knock down a week?*—Arthur Kober

knock something **down** *v phr by 1760* To sell something at auction: *I'll knock it down to you for three bucks* [probably fr the gavel-blow given by an auctioneer to signal and conclude a sale]

knock-down-drag-out *by 1827* **1** *adj phr* Very violent; unrestrained; =ALL-OUT: *They were having a knock-down-drag-out argument when I got there* **2** *n*: *Seems the neighbors were having a knock-down-drag-out*—Washington Post

knocked *adj* police *by 1920s* Arrested

See HAVE something CINCHED

knocked out 1 *adj phr by 1940s* Drunk **2** *adj phr* narcotics *by 1940s* Intoxicated with a narcotic; =HIGH, STONED **3** *adj phr by 1940s* Overcome with delight; extremely pleased: *and were really knocked out with it*—Rolling Stone/ *Everybody was knocked out to be asked*—Rolling Stone **4** *adj phr by 1950s* Very tired; exhausted; =POOPED

◁**knocked up**▷ *adj phr by 1813* Pregnant

knocker[1] *n by 1898* A consistently negative critic; detractor: . . . *that pack of knockers that have been howling*—The Billboard

See APPLE-KNOCKER

knocker[2] or **k'nocker** (KNAH kər) *n by 1960s* A very important person; =BIG SHOT, MACHER: *Knocker means a big shot, either real or imagined, and you pronounce that first "k"*—C McHarr [fr Yiddish, literally "one who cracks or snaps a whip"]

◁**knockers**▷ *n by 1941* A woman's breasts; =HOOTERS: *Dumb broads with big knockers, that's what guys go for*—A Leslie

knock someone's **eyes out** *v phr by 1930s* To astonish and delight someone: *But wa-ait a minute! I'm going to knock your eyes out!*—New Yorker

knock someone or something **for a loop** (Variations: **throw** may replace **knock**; **goal** or **row** or **row of ashcans** or **row of milk cans** or **row of Chinese pagodas** or **row of tall red totem poles** may replace **loop**) *by 1920* **1** *v phr* To hit someone or something very hard; =CLOBBER: *We knocked the villain for a row of ash cans*—H Witwer/ *You certainly knocked him for a row of tall red totem poles*—K Brush **2** *v phr* To unsettle severely; disrupt calm and confidence; =DISCOMBOBULATE: *It must have thrown him for a loop, but he asked*—Earl Thompson **3** *v phr* To delight extremely; thrill and amaze; =KILL, KNOCK someone's SOCKS OFF: *if this climactic sequence doesn't knock you for a loop*—Playboy/ *Wouldn't that knock the boys for a row or two*—James T Farrell/ . . . *guaranteed to knock the keenest mind for a loop*—Raymond Chandler **4** *v phr* To cope with very well; =ACE, CREAM: *Would he hit Math 1 in the eye? He'd knock it for a loop*—P Marks

knock someone or something **galley-west** (or **skywest**) *v phr by 1875* To hit someone or something very hard, esp to knock unconscious; trounce; =CLOBBER: *Jimmy likewise knocked him galley-west*—Foy and Harlow/ . . . *something that* *will knock somebody around here skywest*—L Ford **See** GALLEY-WEST

knock heads together *v phr* by 1940s To exercise persuasive or punitive force; =KICK ASS: *Oakley has spent much of his time in Somalia opening dialogue between different elements trying to get them to talk—New York Times*

knock something **into a cocked hat** *v phr* by 1833 To demolish, esp to disprove, invalidate, or show the falsity of a statement, plea, etc: *This knocks our whole case into a cocked hat* [literally "flatten," since a naval officer's cocked hat could be flattened]

knock someone or something **into the middle of next week** *v phr* by 1836 To hit extremely hard; =CLOBBER

knock it off or **knock it** *v phr* by 1902 To stop doing or saying something; desist •Often a stern command: *I told you creeps to knock it off, now I'm gonna waste you*

knock someone's **lights out** by 1940s **1** *v phr* To beat severely; =BEAT THE SHIT OUT OF someone, CLOBBER **2** *v phr* To impress enormously; =KNOCK someone's SOCKS OFF: *I have a story that would knock your lights out—Sam Shepard* [probably based on the expression *liver and lights*, "liver and lungs" used of animals by at least 1704; influenced by *lights*, "eyes"]

knockoff 1 *n* by 1966 A copy or close imitation: *Clint Eastwood's* Pale Rider *is a contemporary knockoff—People Weekly* **2** *modifier*: *. . . extra pieceworkers to turn out knockoff blouses—New York Times/ . . . at dovegray tables in knockoff Marcel Breuer chairs—Jane Leavy*

knock off 1 *v phr* by 1649 To stop, esp to stop working; desist **2** *v phr* by 1820 To produce, esp with seeming ease and rapidity: *He knocked off a couple of portraits at $40,000 each* **3** *v phr* by 1811 To delete; shorten by: *Let's knock off this last paragraph/ If you do that I'll knock off half the purchase price* **4** *v phr* by 1950s To consume, esp to drink; =KNOCK BACK, KNOCK DOWN: *. . . after knocking off a glass of. . . wine—John McCarten/ . . . while I knock off two or three or four drinks—*Esquire **5** *v phr* by 1919 To kill; murder; assassinate; =RUB OUT: *Before long the spiders knock off Michael—Judith Crist/ . . . sent to a lonely spot and knocked off—E Lavine* **6** *v phr* by 1704 To die; pass away **7** *v phr* by 1926 To arrest, esp after a raid: *Local cops. . . had free authority to knock them off—Westbrook Pegler* **8** *v phr* by 1919 To rob; =HOLD UP, KNOCK OVER: *The pair knocked off several shops, a bank, and jewelry stores—*Associated Press ◁**9**▷ *v phr* by 1940s To do the sex act with, esp as a prostitute; satisfy a sex client: *. . . if you're a street hooker and knock off twenty or thirty guys a day—Xaviera Hollander/ She couldn't see anybody just knocking her off one time—Claude Brown* **10** *v phr* by 1950s To defeat; overcome: *The Tigers knocked off the Yankees today*

11 *v phr* by 1940s To attain; operate at: *The old tub was knocking off 12 knots and groaning like a cow in labor*

◁**knock off a piece**▷ *v phr* by 1940s To do the sex act; copulate; =SCREW

knock someone or something **off** one's **pins** *v phr* by 1880 To stun; bowl over; invalidate: *Nature knocked our theories off their pins—TV show* Nova

knockout 1 *n* by 1906 An especially attractive person or thing; =DISH: *Saaay, you know, you're a knockout—Jerome Weidman* **2** *modifier*: *That was a knockout plot—K Brush/ . . . a knockout wife and two daughters—Ira Levin*

knock oneself **out** by 1936s **1** *v phr* To work very hard; do one's utmost: *They like "knocking themselves out" for* Variety—Abel Green **2** *v phr* To have a splendid and exhausting time: *They knocked themselves out drinking and dancing* [perhaps fr Yiddish *aroysshlogn zikh*]

knock someone **out 1** *v phr* (also **knock** someone **stiff**) by 1896 To make someone unconscious, esp with a blow **2** *v phr* by 1942 To delight or impress someone extremely; =KILL, KNOCK someone's SOCKS OFF: *I read a lot of war books and mysteries and all, but they don't knock me out too much—J D Salinger/ He knocked me out. He just killed me!—Rolling Stone*

knock something **out** *v phr* by 1856 To make or produce, esp rather quickly and crudely: *I haven't got time to knock the script out myself—Budd Schulberg*

knockout drops *n phr* by 1876 Chloral hydrate or another stupefacient drug, esp when put into a drink of liquor; =MICKEY FINN

knockover *n* underworld by 1940s A robbery; =HEIST

knock over 1 *v phr* (also **kick over**) entry form by 1928, variant by 1930 To rob; =HOLD UP, KNOCK OFF: *. . . made regular sweeps by jet, knocking over airport motels—Time/ We kick over the spot—American Mercury/ . . . to prevent people from coming in to case the joint so they can knock it over later—Washington Post* **2** *v phr* by 1931 To raid: *. . . knocked over a reputed. . . bookmaking parlor—J Martin*

knocks *n* Extreme pleasure; gratification; =COOKIES, JOLLIES, KICKS: *They get their knocks that way—Pete Martin*

knock (or blow) someone's **socks off** *v phr* by 1845 To delight extremely; thrill and amaze; =KILL, SEND: *It's undressing that really knocks your socks off—Playboy/ We got a sound that's gonna knock your socks off—Rolling Stone/ . . . a "surprise special" that we think will blow your socks off—Playboy* [these senses fr mid-1800s sense "defeat utterly," fr the notion of hitting someone so hard that he is lifted right out of his shoes and socks]

knock them in the aisles **See** LAY THEM IN THE AISLES

knock the props from under (or out from under) *v phr* by 1910 To make a position, argument, opinion, etc, invalid; call into serious question: *What he found out knocks the props from under her story*

◁**knock the shit out of** someone or something▷ *See* BEAT THE SHIT OUT OF someone or something

knock the spots off someone *v phr* by 1950 To defeat someone decisively; =CLOBBER

knock (or **throw**) **together** *v phr* by 1874 To make or produce something quickly: *. . . what you said about knocking something together that we could eat*—James M Cain/ *In the few minutes available they threw together a cover story*

knock someone **up** ◁1▷ *v phr* by 1813 To make pregnant **2** *v phr* by 1663 To awaken someone; arouse by knocking •Used with arch jocularity by Americans who know that it is a British term, meaning to awaken someone with a knock at the door, with a vulgar US meaning

knothead *n* by 1940 A stupid person: *Look at Petey, a knothead*—Max Shulman/ *The movie states the knothead's case in its early passages*—Time

know *See* IN THE KNOW

know (or **have**) **all the answers** by 1940s **1** *v phr* To claim or affect special intimate knowledge: *That little creep over there always thinks he knows all the answers* **2** *v phr* To have a jaded, cynical, spiritless sort of wisdom: *She don't bother anymore, knows all the answers* **3** *v phr* To know a case or subject thoroughly •Most often in the negative: *Even your doctor doesn't have all the answers*

◁not **know** one's **ass from** one's **elbow** (or **from a hole in the ground**)▷ *See* NOT KNOW one's ASS FROM one's ELBOW

know a thing or two *v phr* by 1792 To have practical sagacity; be worldy wise; =KNOW WHAT'S WHAT

not **know beans** *See* NOT KNOW BEANS

know Dorothy *See* BE A FRIEND OF DOROTHY'S

know from *v phr* by 1940s To know about; be acquainted with: *I don't know from trees much*—George V Higgins [fr Yiddish *vos vayz ikh fun*]

not **know** someone **from Adam** *See* NOT KNOW someone FROM ADAM

not **know** someone or something **from a hole in the ground** *See* NOT KNOW someone or something FROM A HOLE IN THE GROUND

know (or **not know**) **from nothing** *v phr* by 1936 To be ignorant; be deeply uninformed or ill-informed: *Gallo knows from nothing*—Jim Hays [fr Yiddish *nit zu wissen fin gornisht*]

know-how *n* by 1838 Skill, esp technical skill; practical competence: *Takes know-how to run that thing*

know-it-all *n* by 1895 A person who pretends to virtual omniscience; =BIG-MOUTH, SMART-ASS: *Just what we need around here, another know-it-all*

know one's **onions** *v phr* (Variations: **beans** or **business** or **stuff** may replace **onions**) by 1922 To be very competent and authoritative in one's work: *I'm glad the tax accountant knows his onions*

◁not **know shit from Shinola**▷ *See* NOT KNOW SHIT FROM SHINOLA

know the ropes *v phr* fr nautical by 1874 To be seasoned and informed; know the intricacies of a job, situation, etc; =KNOW one's WAY AROUND [fr the myriad *ropes* of a sailing vessel]

know the score *v phr* by 1940s To have essential and current information; understand what is important: *You look like a smart lad who knows the score*—J Evans

know one's **way around** *v phr* by 1940s To be informed and experienced; be seasoned and reliable: *He's been at the job for two years but still doesn't know his way around*

know what one **can do with** something *v phr* (Variations: **where** one **can put** [or **shove** or **stick** or **stuff**] may replace **what** one **can do with**) by 1950s To know that one's offer, request, possession, etc, is held in extreme contempt •A euphemized way of saying that one can take something and stick it up his or her ass: *I saw the contract, and he knows what he can do with it/ I told him where he can shove that great idea of his*

know what's what *v phr* by 1553 To have practical sagacity; =KNOW WHICH WAY IS UP

know when to hold them and when to fold them *v phr* by 1980s To be aware of probabilities and consequences; =KNOW THE SCORE: *Jackson knows instinctively how to bluff and bargain, when to hold 'em and when to fold 'em*—Time [fr a Kenny Rogers song, and fr poker]

know where it's at *v phr* 1960s counterculture To be up-to-date and cognizant: *the NOW generation, who, like, know what's happening and where it's at*—Trans-Action

know where the bodies are buried *v phr* by 1960s To have intimate and secret knowledge, esp of something criminal, scandalous, etc: *The president reckoned he had to keep that lawyer quiet, because he knew where the bodies were buried*

know which way (or **end**) **is up** *v phr* by 1891 To have practical sagacity; =KNOW WHAT'S WHAT: *Beneath the tunes and the glories, Mozart knew which way was up, and had a first-class comic imagination*—New Yorker/ *. . . they was all badly scared and muddled, and didn't know which end was uppermost*—Robert Louis Stevenson

knuckle *See* WHITE KNUCKLE

knuckleball or **knuckler 1** *n* baseball by 1906 A pitch thrown from the knuckles that moves slowly and erratically; =BUTTERFLY BALL: *Leonard's tantalizing knucklers*—L Effrat **2** *modifier*: *a knuckleball artist*

knuckled *See* WHITE-KNUCKLED

knuckle down *v phr* by 1866 To work hard and seriously; stop loafing; =BUCKLE DOWN [fr the act of putting one's *knuckles down* to the taw or marble preparing for a careful shot in the game of marbles, a use dating fr the mid–18th century]

knuckle-dragger *n* college students by 1970s A

rough, somewhat stupid and crude man; =GORILLA, STRONG-ARM MAN: . . . *the tendency of some covert agents, "the knuckledraggers" of the Special Operations Group, to revel in deception*—Washingtonian [from the image of a gorilla whose knuckles drag on the ground when it walks]

knuckle-dusters *n* by 1858 Brass knuckles

knucklehead *n* by 1940s A stupid person; =BONEHEAD: *Movies are made by unappreciative knuckleheads*—Pete Martin [fr earlier *knuckle*, "bone"]

knuckler *See* KNUCKLEBALL, WHITE KNUCKLER

knuckles *See* RAP someone's KNUCKLES

knuckle sandwich *n phr* by 1973 A hard blow to the mouth or face: *I feed him a knuckle sandwich*—Lawrence Sanders/ *You keep that up and you're going to get a knuckle sandwich*—Newsweek

knuckle under *v phr* by 1860 To yield; =THROW IN THE SPONGE: *It's a shame she had to knuckle under to those bigots*

knuckle up *v phr* 1990s teenagers To fight with the fists; =MIX IT UP

knucks *n* by 1897 Brass knuckles; =KNUCKLE-DUSTERS: *The "knucks" were hidden in the heel*—Associated Press

KO (pronounced as separate letters) **1** *n* prizefight by 1922 A knockout; =KAYO **2** *v*: *He KOed six in a row* **3** *modifier*: *a KO punch*
See TKO

kocker *See* ALTER KOCKER

Kojak light *n phr* by 1980s A flashing light magnetically attached to the roof of an unmarked police car [fr its use in the TV show *Kojak*]

Kong or **kong** *n* black by 1960s =KING KONG

kook (Ko͞oK) **1** *n* 1950s teenagers An eccentric person; =NUT, SCREWBALL: *The bomb cannot be exploded by a single "kook"*—Nation/ *The early Streisand played kook*—Look **2** *modifier*: . . . *did a kook piece with dancers*—Village Voice **3** *n* surfers by 1961 A novice surfer [fr *cuckoo*]

kookie or **kooky** *adj* fr 1950s teenagers Crazy; eccentric; =DIPPY, GOOFY: . . . *make you seem a little kookie*—David Halberstam/ . . . *the kooky stunt so pleased him*—Time

kootchy *See* the HOOTCHIE-COOTCHIE

kopasetic *See* COPACETIC

kosh *n* =COSH

kosher *adj* by 1896 Proper; as it should be; legitimate: *Everything looks kosher*—Lawrence Sanders [fr Yiddish fr Hebrew *kasher*, "fit, proper"]

◄**kraut** or **Kraut** or **krauthead**► **1** *n* WWI armed forces A German, esp a German soldier: *Oh, that kraut-head*—Tennessee Williams **2** *adj*: *kraut wine* [fr *sauerkraut*, regarded as a favorite and characteristic German food]

kvell (KVEL) *v* by 1967 To display pride and satisfaction; beam: *The elderly couple. . . kvell also. . . upon making contact with a Jewish airstrip*—Philip Roth/*Hollywood agents, kissing and kvelling*—New York Magazine [fr Yiddish, literally "gush, flow forth"]

kvetch (kə VECH) by 1960s **1** *v* To whine; complain; be consistently pessimistic: *I know you know. . . I'm just kvetching*—Robert B Parker/ *Dealing with a controversial idea of public importance, Mobil kvetched*—Village Voice **2** *n*: *I am another kvetch when it comes to wind chimes*—Ann Landers/ . . . *right in tune with the city medical spirit, which is basically one of kvetch*—New York Magazine [fr Yiddish, literally "squeeze, press"]

kyuter (KYo͞o tər) *See* CUTER

L

lab 1 *n* by 1895 A laboratory **2** *modifier*: *a lab report* **3** *n* (also **Lab**) by 1960s A Labrador retriever

lab jockey *n phr* A laboratory scientist: *. . . lab jockeys showed stannous fluoride was better than other fluoride compounds. . .* —Milwaukee Journal Sentinel

labonza *n* by 1950s The belly; =GUT, KISHKES: *She let him have it right in the labonza* [probably fr Italian *pancia,* "paunch," with attached article and dialectal pronunciation]

labor *See* GRUNT WORK

labster *n* 1990s narcotics A designer and maker of illicit narcotics: *Among "labsters," as clandestine drug producers are known. . .* —Milwaukee Journal

◁**lace-curtain Irish**▷ *n phr* by 1934 Prosperous and respectable persons of Irish extraction: *. . . become lace-curtain Irish. . . across the tracks*—AE Hutson [fr the fact that *lace curtains* in the windows would be a sign of prosperity and of social superiority relative to the laboring class]

lace into *v* by 1920s To attack and beat; thrash; =CLOBBER: *I rushed at the fellow and fairly laced into him*—Robert Graves/ *Reviewers laced into the play*—Time [*lace* in the same sense is found by 1599]

la-de-da (also **lah-de-dah** or **la-di-da** or **lah-di-dah**) **1** *n* by 1883 A dandyish or sissified man; super-refined and delicate person: *Some lah-de-dah with a cane*—Hecht and MacArthur **2** *adj*: *. . . lunch place of the la-de-dah literary set*—NY Confidential **3** *adj* by 1940s Very refined and respectable: *Nobody weren't going to make her live in a lah-di-dah place like that*—RGG Price **4** *adj* by 1970s Carefree and nonchalant: *Her emotions at the dissolution of her 25-year marriage are anything but la-de-da*—Us **5** *v* by 1970s To treat in a nonchalant, off-hand manner: *The outfielder la-di-da'd the catch* **6** *interj* by 1970s A phrase used to mean the equivalent of "It doesn't matter": *You're canceling our date? Oh well, lah-di-dah* [an imitation of casual and aristocratic speech]

ladies' (or **lady's**) **man** by 1842 **1** *n phr* A man who pursues and otherwise devotes himself to women to an unusual degree; =LOVER-BOY **2** *n phr* A man who is attractive to many women: *He's so conceited. . . thinks he's a real ladies' man*

ladies who lunch *n* by 1970 Women who are well-off, style-conscious, and somewhat conservative in dress: *The title character, played by Mia Farrow,* is a pampered Upper East Side lady who lunches— New Yorker/ *Chic fleet—for tony ladies who lunch*—Buzz [fr a song by Stephen Sondheim]

lady *n* by 1400, US use since 1890s Any woman; any grown-up female ●Used increasingly since the 1970s, perhaps as a sort of response to feminism: *That's a very smart lady*
  See BAG LADY, FAIRY LADY, OLD LADY, the OPERA AIN'T OVER TILL THE FAT LADY SINGS

the lady *n phr* 1960s narcotics Cocaine

Lady H *n phr* 1960s narcotics Heroin: *. . . urging teens to stay away from Lady H*—Los Angeles Times

lady-killer *n* by 1811 =LADIES' MAN

laff (or **laugh**) **riot** theater by 1940s **1** *n phr* A very funny show, event, etc: *. . . the "Tristan und Isolde" of laff riots*—New Yorker **2** *n phr* Something very amusing; an occasion for hilarity ●Often used ironically: *Otherwise I might have turned into a "laff riot,". . . a zany*—Saul Bellow/ *This LA doomsday film is an unintentional laugh riot*—Los Angeles Times [fr a cliché based on an advertising misspelling of *laugh* for humorous effect; the spelling is found by 1681; *riot,* "great success," is found by 1909]

lag 1 *n* underworld by 1930s A convict: *Lags who escape from the county pokey. . .* —Damon Runyon **2** *v* underworld by 1940s To arrest or imprison a criminal

lagniappe (LAN yap) *n* by 1849 A dividend; something extra: *I hit her with a few real hard ones for lagniappe (or good measure)*—Louis Armstrong/ *From the company's point of view, of course, safety is a lagniappe*—New York Times [fr New Orleans Creole, origin unknown and much speculated; originally a little present or gratuity given to a customer by a New Orleans merchant]

laid-back *adj* 1960s Relaxed; easy-going: *. . . a sort of laid-back, not insane Janis Joplin*—V Aletti/ *. . . relatively upbeat moods, laid-back-in-the-South-Seas*—New Times [perhaps fr the reclining posture of highway motorcyclists]

laid out *adj* by 1929 Drunk

la-la (or **la la** or **lala**) **land** (also **Lotus Land**) by 1980s **1** *n phr* Los Angeles and Southern California in their reputed glamour and trendiness: *Suddenly the real Los Angeles intrudes itself. La-la land with its beaches and movie stars, Rolls Royces and Evian, Italian suits and car phones,* *coke-sniffing boy-girl bimbos, was gone*—Time/ *I just wanted to show you we ain't asleep down here in Lotusland*—Carsten Stroud **2** **n phr** An unreal and hallucinatory place; dreamland; Never-Never Land; Lotus Land/ *After the operation I was in la-la land*—TV show Today/ *This is directed at President Clinton, Mike McCurry, and anyone else in that la la land they call Washington. . .* —StarLedger/ *Stanford is a multicultural lala land; it's not the real world*—New York Times

lallygag *See* LOLLYGAG

lam *underworld by 1886* **1** **v** To depart; go, esp hastily in escaping: *lammed for Cleveland*—H Witwer **2** **v** To escape from prison [ultimately fr British sense "beat," found by 1596, hence the same semantically as *beat it*]
See ON THE LAM, TAKE IT ON THE LAM

lamb **n** *by 1923* A dear, sweet person: *Mary is such a lamb*

lambaste or **lambast** (lam BAYST, lam BAST) *by 1637* **1** **v** To hit very hard; thrash; =CLOBBER: *They lambasted the suspect mercilessly* **2** **v** To disparage strongly; castigate: *A woman psychologist today lambasted the idea that "mom is to blame"*—AL Blakeslee [ultimately fr British *lam* and *baste*, both "beat"]

lambie or **lambie-pie** **n** *by 1940s* One's sweetheart; beloved: *. . . a dithering meditation on a lackluster Don Juan. Are Reynolds and Edwards such unmanly lambie-pies?*—Washington Post

lame 1 **adj** *by 1942* Socially awkward; clumsy; =KLUTZY: *Cindy normally tells such great jokes, but that last one was really lame*—UCLA Slang **2** **adj** *1950s students* (also **lamed** or **lame-o**) Stupid; inept: *. . . I automatically inherit this lame "slacker" attitude. . .* —Los Angeles Times/ *. . . don't try and sell us this lame-o "throwback to a bygone era" argument*—Milwaukee Journal **3** **n** *1950s teenagers fr jazz musicians* An old-fashioned, conventional person; =SQUARE: *. . . and not worry about anybody naming me a lame*—Claude Brown/ *. . . not have been as quick to judge him as a lame*—Rolling Stone **4** **adj** *1950s teenagers fr jazz musicians* : *. . . a lame assault on boomers. . .* —Macon Telegraph/ *Their performances were sloppy, sometimes even lame*—Saturday Review

lamebrain **n** *by 1929* A stupid person; =DOPE, KNUCKLEHEAD: *Not all the lamebrains on Capitol Hill frequent the House or Senate*—Washington Post

lamebrained **adj** *by 1929* Stupid; =KLUTZY

lame duck 1 **n phr** *by 1863* A public official who has lost an election or one who is not permitted by law to seek reelection for an additional term but is serving out a term **2** **modifier**: *lame-duck president* **3** **n phr** *stock market by 1751* A speculator who has taken options on stocks he or she cannot pay for [political sense attributed to Vice-President Andrew Johnson, referring to a Colonel Forney]

lamp 1 **n** *by 1590* An eye: *. . . a beefsteak. . . for this lamp of mine*—P Marks **2** **v** *by 1916* To see;

look at: *Lamp the lad in blue*—F K Secrist **3** **n** *by 1920s* A look; glance; =GANDER

lamster **n** *underworld by 1904* An escaped convict [fr *lam*]

landing *See* CHINESE LANDING

landsman (LAHNTS mən) **n** *by 1940s* A fellow countryman, townsman, etc; compatriot; =HOMEBOY, PAESAN: *You from Kalamazoo? Landsman!* [fr Yiddish]

lane *See* FAST LANE, HAMMER LANE, IN THE STRAIGHT LANE

lap 1 **n** *about 1920* A round of a prizefight **2** **n** *by 1940s* A swallow of liquor; =SLURP

lap-dance **v** *by 1990s*: *To lap-dance, you undress, sit your client down, order him to stay still and fully clothed, then hover over him, making a motion that you have perfected by watching Mister Softee ice-cream dispensers*—New Yorker

lap dancer **n phr** *by 1990s* A woman who does "lap dancing": *Of course, not every coming film exalts women: audiences will also see them as lap dancers, strippers, and phone-sex workers*—New York Times

lapdog **n** *by 1980s* A subservient person; eager sycophant: *The leading Singapore newspaper, the Straits Times, enthusiastically fills the role of government lapdog*—New Yorker/ *. . . employee committees that labor leaders charge will be lapdogs of management*—Milwaukee Journal Sentinel

lapel-grabber **n** *by 1980s* A person who seizes and holds one's attention by grasping one's lapels, either actually or in effect: *The style is the man; Hoving of the Met has always been a lapel-grabber*—New York Review of Books/ *Margaret Mead is the most famous of these lapel-grabbers*—New Republic

lapper *See* CUNT-LAPPER

lapping *See* CUNT-LAPPING

lap something up **v phr** *by 1922* To accept or believe eagerly: *Tell 'em you'll lower their taxes and they'll lap it up*

lard *See* TUB OF GUTS

◁**lard-ass** or **lard-bucket**▷ **n** *by 1946* A fat person; =CHUBBO, TUB OF GUTS

large **n** *by 1980s* A thousand dollars; =BIG ONE, GRAND: *. . . with new Beverly Hills basic wheels going for fifty large. . .* —Stan Cutler

large car **n phr** *truckers by 1980s* A truck, esp a tractor-trailer truck: *. . . you got a bear at the three-four-one stick draggin' his hooks looking for large cars*—Brian Di Salvatore

large charge *1940s students fr jive talk* **1** **n phr** Great pleasure; =CHARGE, KICK: *I can hardly do justice to the large charge I get out of you* **2** **n phr** =BIG SHOT

large evening **n phr** *by 1896* A festive, pleasant, exciting, etc, evening: *The good doctor had himself a large evening*—L F McHugh

large one **n phr** *underworld by 1970s* A year in prison: *The Tiger got fifteen large ones*—George V Higgins

lark 1 **n** *by 1811* A merry time ●Chiefly British **2** **v**

by 1813: *This is no time to go larking* [origin uncertain; perhaps fr an allusion to the bird, since *skylark* in the same sense is found somewhat earlier]

larky *adj* by 1841 Playful; frolicsome; bantering •Chiefly British: *. . . began making larky plunges into show business*—Time

larrup (LEH ruhp) *v* by 1839 To beat; thrash; =CLOBBER, LAMBASTE, LATHER

larry *See* HOUSE LARRY

lash-up *n* WWII Army fr British Living quarters; barracks; =DIGS [fr British, "something improvised," found by 1898]

last *See* NICE GUYS FINISH LAST

the last dance *See* GET THE LAST DANCE

last-ditch *modifier* by 1940s Ultimate; final and heroic: *They pumped themselves up for a last-ditch effort* [fr earlier *last-ditcher*, ultimately fr *die in the last ditch*, "die at the last defense line," found by 1715 and attributed to William of Orange]

last hurrah *n phr* by 1956 The end for someone or something: *Last hurrah for some write-offs*—Milwaukee Journal/ *I want this book to be my last hurrah* [fr the title of Edwin O'Connor's 1956 novel about a politician's final campaign and bow]

the last of the big-time spenders *n phr* by 1970s The last lavish spender and host •Always ironical, meaning its opposite [*big spender* is found in the New York night-life milieu in the 1920s]

lat *modifier* by 1980s For exercising the latissimus dorsi muscles: *. . . did a handstand on the seat of the lat pull down machine*—Robert B Parker

latchkey (or **doorkey**) **child** or **kid** *n phr* by 1944 A child whose parents are working and who must spend part of the day unsupervised at home: *A latchkey child, Nikki would always go home, stay inside, and do her homework*—Milwaukee Journal/ *Personally, I always wanted to be a latchkey kid, or at least have a key*—Lee K Russell

latch on to or **latch on** 1930s black **1** *v phr* To get; obtain; =GLOM ON TO: *Latch on to the first seat that's empty* **2** *v phr* To comprehend; grasp; =DIG: *He finally latched onto the truth* **3** *v phr* To attach oneself to; be dependent on: *He latched on to me as soon as I arrived*

lately *See* JOHNNY-COME-LATELY

later *interj* 1980s teenagers fr black A parting salutation: *I dug right away what the kick was, so I said, "Later," and he split*—Eldridge Cleaver/ *Later, baby. Catch you later*—Joseph Wambaugh

lather *v* by 1797 To hit; strike: *He lathered the ball out of the park* [fr the notion that frothy washing *lather* is produced by vigorous agitation or beating] *See* IN A LATHER

latrine (or **barracks**) **lawyer** *n phr* Army by 1940s A soldier who is argumentative, esp on fine points, and tends to be a meddler, complainer, and self-server

latrine rumor *n phr* WWI Army An idle rumor that probably has no basis in fact

lats *n* by 1980s The latissimus dorsi muscles: *. . .*

checking the cut of their lats in shiny windows—San Francisco

laugh *See* BELLY LAUGH, the HORSELAUGH

a laugh or **a laugh and a half** *n phr* Something funny; a cause of amusement, esp of contemptuous derision: *You're gonna cook? That's a laugh*

laugh all the way to the bank *v phr* by 1970s To be amused and gratified by a victory where a defeat was predicted: *The film, with horrible reviews, grossed more than $30 million. Disney laughed all the way to the bank*—New York Times

laugher *n* sports by 1960s A laughing matter, esp a game in which one team scores an annihilating victory: *The two games he mentioned were laughers, Oklahoma 41–7 over North Carolina. . .* —Sports Illustrated/ *I like to see it about 16–0. I like laughers*—Inside Sports

laughing academy *n phr* by 1960s A mental hospital; =FUNNY FARM, NUT HOUSE

laughing soup *n phr* by 1934 Liquor; =BOOZE

laugh something **off** *v phr* by 1715 To dismiss something with a laugh: *It's hard to laugh that insult off, isn't it?*

laugh on (or **out of**) **the other side of** one's **face** *v phr* by 1779 To lament and moan; suffer a change of mood from joy to distress; undergo a defeat: *When they get through with him he'll be laughing out of the other side of his face*

laugh up (or **in**) one's **sleeve** *v phr* by 1560 To laugh covertly: *After you had that accident she was laughing up her sleeve*

launching pad *n phr* 1960s narcotics =SHOOTING GALLERY

launder *v* by 1961 To transfer or convert funds so that illegal or dubious receipts are made to appear legitimate: *. . . the account money that had been "laundered" by being siphoned from this country into Mexico and returned under an alias*—W Barthelmes

laundry 1 *n* by 1960s A bank or other place used for legitimizing illegal or dubious money **2** *n* WWII Air Forces A board of faculty members that passes on flying cadets [second sense from the fact that some cadets were *washed out*, "failed," by such a board] *See* HANG OUT THE LAUNDRY

laundry (or **shopping**) **list** *n phr* by 1958 A long bill of items to be obtained, discussed, done, or not done: *This "do-good" laundry list draws sneers*—Maurice Moskowitz/ *The cadets didn't need a laundry list of prohibitions*—New York Times/ *A shopping list is not a strategy*—New York Review of Books

lava *See* IN A LATHER

lavender *adj* by 1970s Homosexual: *Alberta Maged had marched with a coalition of groups including the Lavender Left and the Commie Queers*—Randy Shilts/ *Clinton dropped the gays like a flaming potato, suggesting they might serve in special lavender units*—Time [both blue and lavender are colors associated with homosexuality]

law *See* SUNSET LAW, SUNSHINE LAW

Law *See* JOHN LAW

the law *n phr* underworld by 1920s Any police officer, prison guard, etc; =the HEAT

lawnmower *n* baseball by 1891 A hard-hit grounder

lawyer *See* CLUBHOUSE LAWYER, FORECASTLE LAWYER, JAILHOUSE LAWYER, LATRINE LAWYER, SEA LAWYER

lay ◁**1**▷ *n* by 1932 A person regarded merely as a sex partner or object: *The two girls looked like swell lays*—James T Farrell/ *She's a great lay*—Saturday Review ◁**2**▷ *n* by 1936 A sex act; =PIECE OF ASS: *Anyone who is looking for an easy lay*—New York Magazine ◁**3**▷ *v* by 1934: *. . . five cadets who swore they'd all laid the girl one night*—Calder Willingham **4** *v* by 1300 To bet: *I laid her six to one he wouldn't show up* *See* EASY MAKE

lay a batch *v phr* teenagers by 1940s To leave black rubber marks on the road by accelerating a car rapidly

◁**lay a fart**▷ *v phr* (Variations: **cut** or **let** or **rip** may replace **lay**) by 1940s To flatulate; =FART: *This guy. . . laid this terrific fart*—J D Salinger

not **lay a glove** (or **finger** or **hand**) on someone *See* NOT LAY A GLOVE ON someone

lay an egg *v phr* by 1929 To fail; =BOMB, FLOP: *The plan's going to lay an egg unless we give it a shot in the arm* [fr earlier British *lay a duck's egg*, "make a score of zero"]

lay a trip (or **scene**) **on** someone *v phr* 1960s counterculture fr black To attribute something to someone; burden someone with something; accuse someone of something: *But if you try and lay a trip on somebody through psychoanalysis, it's nonsense*—Changes/ *Don't lay this scene on me. I did the best I could*—Paul Sann/ *Vote for. . . Walker. . . But don't lay any undue trips on him*—Amsterdam News

lay back *v phr* by 1970s fr black To relax; take one's ease: *. . . not a Southern-rock band. They don't lay back*—Rolling Stone

lay chickie *v phr* street gang by 1940s To act as a lookout for criminals: *. . . not having anyone to lay chickie for me*—Claude Brown [origin unknown]

lay down on the job *v phr* by 1918 To loaf; dawdle and shirk

lay down the law *v phr* by 1762 To cite the rules, or one's rules, sternly: *He overheard a father laying down the law to three sheepish kids*

lay for someone *v phr* by 1494 To watch for one's chance to take revenge; vigilantly stalk: *I'd lay for him in town some night*—Calder Willingham

lay into someone *v phr* by 1838 To attack someone, physically or verbally: *That's why I laid into Eckert and made him drive me down that night*—Sue Grafton

lay it on *v phr* by 1560 To exaggerate; overstate; •Often used of flattery and cajolement: *I overheard you laying it on to the boss. Shame!*

lay it on someone *v phr* by 1960 To tell; inform; =CLUE: *If you know it, please lay it on me*

lay (or **put**) **it on the line** (or **on the table**) *v phr* by 1940s To speak candidly and straightwardly; =TELL IT LIKE IT IS: *They are more likely to give it to you if you lay it on the table*—CoEvolution Quarterly

lay it on thick *v phr* by 1740 To exaggerate; overstate; hyperbolize; =LAY IT ON: *"I tell them it's something their father and I always talked about" "That's laying it on a bit thick, isn't it?"*—Sue Grafton

lay it on with a trowel *v phr* by 1600 =LAY IT ON THICK: *The film has too many slow spots, and its message is laid on with a trowel*—Time

lay low *v phr* by 1839 To stay out of sight; remain inconspicuous; =KEEP A LOW PROFILE, LIE DOGGO: *We're layin' low a couple days*—Nelson Algren

layoff 1 *n* by 1919 A dismissal or furlough from a job **2** *n* gambling by 1950s The part of a bookmaker's bets placed with another agent to forestall catastrophic loss **3** *n* theater by 1950s An unemployed actor: *A couple of layoffs. . . were walking out of the hotel*—Lionel Stander

lay off 1 *v phr* by 1908 To stop troubling or harrying someone; leave someone in peace •Often an irritated command or entreaty: *So lay off or I'll split your head, baby*—Changes **2** *v phr* by 1868 To dismiss or furlough an employee: *Half the staff at IBM has been laid off* **3** *v phr* gambling by 1950s To place a portion of bets or debts with other agents, so as to reduce one's possible losses: *. . . that's a lot of cash to come up with. We could lay some of it off, you know. . . it'd be easier for us*—Ed McBain

lay someone **off** *v phr* by 1868 To terminate someone's job

lay something **on** someone 1960s counterculture fr 1930s black **1** *v phr* To present; give: *And the sisters laid the revolutionary ideology right on them*—Bobby Seale/ *. . . will suck his dick to oblivion if he lays some coke on them*—Ed McBain **2** *v phr* To tell or inform: *I have something heavy to lay on you, I'm afraid* **3** *v phr* =LAY A TRIP ON someone: *. . . the media says I'm not a journalist. I never said I was. They're laying something on me I never laid on myself*—Larry King

lay one on someone *v phr* by 1940s To hit hard; punch; =HANG ONE ON: *She laid one on him, when he least expected it*

lay (or **put**) something **on the line** *v phr* by 1950s To put deliberately at risk; put in peril as a wager or hostage: *If you try this, remember you are laying your ass on the line*

layout 1 *n* by 1869 A place; house; living arrangements: *Nice little layout you got here* **2** *n* by 1886 Place, equipment, apparatus, etc, for a particular purpose: *. . . who may never have seen such a layout. . .*—The Lantern *See* COFFEE-AND-CAKE JOINT

lay paper *v phr* underworld by 1940s To pass counterfeit money, worthless checks, etc

lay pipe (or tube) ◁1▷ *v phr* black by 1967 To do the sex act; copulate; =SCREW: *If you're up all night, laying pipe, you won't be worth a shit to me on the court*—Tom Aldibrandi/ *About eighty a them's gonna lay more tube than the motherfuckin' Alaska Pipeline*—Playboy **2** *v phr* by 1970s To specify; spell out: *You can't just infer that; you gotta lay pipe*—TV show *Don't Touch That Dial*

lay rubber *v phr* teenagers by 1940s To accelerate rapidly and speed in a car, so as to leave black tire marks on the road

lay the skin on someone *v phr* black by 1940s To shake or otherwise deploy hands in greeting; =GIVE someone FIVE: *Lay the skin on me, pal*—Zora Neale Hurston

lay them in the aisles *v phr* (Variations: **have** or **knock** or **put** may replace **lay**) by 1934 To entertain, amuse, or impress an audience extravagantly; =WOW

lazybones *n* by 1593 An indolent person; slug-a-bed

lead *n* by 1809 Bullets; gunfire
See GET THE LEAD OUT, HAVE LEAD IN one's PANTS, HAVE LEAD IN one's PENCIL

lead balloon *n phr* by 1940s A dismal failure; =FLOP: *His run for office was a lead balloon*
See GO OVER LIKE A LEAD BALLOON

lead someone **down the garden path** *v phr* by 1870 To deceive someone; hoodwink someone: *Will anyone know who led whom down the garden path?*—New Yorker

leaded coffee *n phr* by 1980s Coffee with caffeine, as distinct from decaffeinated coffee: *Coffee? You want leaded or unleaded?*

lead-foot (LED foot) *v* truckers by 1940s To drive fast: *Starting Friday, speeders will pay an extra $20 when caught lead-footing*—Milwaukee Journal

lead-footed (LED foot əd) **1** *adj* by 1596 Sluggish and awkward; clumsy: *The bungling, lead-footed fellow*—R Wallace **2** *adj* truckers by 1940s Tending to drive very fast [the first dated form is *leaden-footed*]

lead-pipe (or lead-tight) cinch by 1898 **1** *n phr* A certainty; inescapable fact: *. . . not early enough to move no tables, that's a lead-pipe cinch*—Nelson Algren/ *. . . calls Coleco Vision a "lead-pipe cinch" for making a strong showing at Christmas*—Toronto Life **2** *n phr* Something very easy; =CINCH, PIECE OF CAKE: *. . . a lousy lead-tight cinch that any freshman in law school could have won*—Harry Crews [fr the fact that a *lead pipe* can be easily bent, in case one has bet on such a feat]

lead-poisoning *n* by 1940 Gunshot wounds

lead with one's **chin** *v phr* by 1940s To make oneself vulnerable: *If you tell him that right away you'll be leading with your chin*

the **leaf** *n phr* 1960s narcotics Cocaine

league *See* BIG-LEAGUE, BUSH LEAGUE, GRAPEFRUIT LEAGUE, HOT STOVE LEAGUE, OUT OF one's LEAGUE

leaguer *See* TEXAS LEAGUER

leagues *See* the BIG LEAGUES, the BUSH LEAGUES

leak 1 *v* by 1859 To give information to the press or other recipient secretly: *Then the FCC report was "leaked" to the press*—RG Spivack **2** *n* by 1873 The divulgence or divulger of secret information: *A famous leak was called Deep Throat* ◁3▷ *n* by 1930s An act of urination ◁4▷ *v* by 1930s To urinate; =PISS: *He said he had to leak; his back teeth were floating*
See TAKE A LEAK

lean and mean *adj phr* by 1970s Desperately and somewhat menacingly ambitious; =HUNGRY: *"Lean and mean" is the byword in publishing these days*—New York Magazine/ *A fat and lazy firm must become lean and mean, or see its capital redeployed*—Nation

lean forward in the saddle *v phr* Army by 1970s To be eager and anxious; =be RARING TO GO

lean on someone *v phr* by 1950s To put pressure on someone, esp with violence or the threat of it: *. . . and he thinks he can lean on me!*—Hannibal & Boris/ *. . . Several restaurants and clubs. . . were being leaned on*—Jackie Collins

lean over backwards *See* BEND OVER BACKWARDS

the **leaping heebies** *See* the HEEBIE-JEEBIES

leap on the bandwagon *See* GET ON THE BANDWAGON

leap tall buildings at (or **in**) **a single bound** *v phr* by 1940s To do something impossible: *She is under the impression that you can leap tall buildings at a single bound*—Robert B Parker [one of the feats of the comic-strip character Superman]

learn the ropes *v phr* by 1977 To learn the elements of a task or profession; serve one's apprenticeship: *Stokovich and a mope from Justice who was at the time learning the ropes. . .*—Carsten Stroud

leary *See* LEERY

the **least** *n phr* 1950s beat & cool talk The worst; the dullest, most conventional, etc

leather 1 *n* by 1980s The clothing and trappings of overt sado-masochism **2** *n* homosexuals by 1970s A kind of male homosexual behavior, costume, etc, based on exaggerated masculinity as symbolized esp by black-leather-clad motorcycle gangs **3** *modifier*: *. . . jokes about the heroine's harmless male roommate, leather men, etc*—New Republic/ *. . . becomes part of the leather-bar homosexual underworld*—New York Times/ *. . . the sex clubs and leather bars of the gay ghetto*—New York Magazine
See HEAVY LEATHER, HELL-FOR-LEATHER, THROW LEATHER

leather-lunged *adj* by 1846 Loud; bellowing; raucous: *. . . tested by two leather-lunged fans seated behind the Bucks' bench*—Milwaukee Journal

leather medal *n phr* by 1831 An award of very little value; an ironic token decoration: *John, in order to get a leather medal, ran the prices up too fast. And now they're paying the price*—Vanity Fair

leatherneck *n* Navy by 1914 A US Marine; =GYRENE [fr the *leather* collars of their early uniforms;

the term is found by 1890 as British sailor's name for a soldier]

leave *See* FRENCH LEAVE

leave a strip *v phr* *1950s hot rodders* To brake or decelerate a car very rapidly, so as to leave black rubber marks on the pavement

leave a calling card *v phr* *by 1940s* To defecate in a public or inappropriate place: . . . *after a passing horse had left its calling card on the street*—Milwaukee Journal

leave someone **flat (or cold)** *v phr* *by 1902* To leave a person suddenly and definitively: *When he lied once too often she left him flat*

leave someone **holding the bag 1** *v phr* *by 1906* To cause someone to take all the losses; dupe someone to his disadvantage: *Don't you let them leave you holding the bag*—Erle Stanley Gardner **2** *v phr* To maneuver so that one takes individual blame for a failure or a crime [fr 1600s *give the bag to hold*, "victimize in a game of snipe-hunt"; the form *hold the sack* in the first sense is found by 1904]

leave someone **in the lurch** *v phr* *by 1596* To abandon someone in a difficult plight: *They all cleared out and left me in the lurch*

leaves *n* *1950s teenagers* Denim dungarees; =LEVIS [fr *Levis*™]

lech or **letch 1** *n* *by 1796* Strong desire, esp sexual; lust; =the HOTS: . . . *his lech for cam shafts and turbines*—James M Cain/ *He had a lech for his fifteen-year-old daughter*—Lawrence Sanders **2** *v* *by 1911*: . . . *when Henry goes letching after Anne*—Vincent Canby/ *keep Junior from leching*—Time **3** *n* *by 1943* A lecher: . . . *under the illusion that the lech is as enamored as she is*—Inquiry/ *who also appears as a good-natured lech*—Newsweek [fr *lecher, lechery*, ultimately fr the notion of licking]
See HAVE A LECH FOR someone or something

leech 1 *n* *by 1784* A human parasite **2** *v* *by 1960s*: . . . *insisted that MCI was not leeching off the successful campaign of its competition*—Philadelphia Journal

leery or **leary** *adj* *by 1718* Untrusting; suspicious; wary: *He was leery of toting so much money*—Dashiell Hammett/ *Cheyfitz and Farrell exchanged leery glances*—Hannibal and Boris [probably fr British dialect *lere*, "learning, knowledge"]

left *See* HANG A LEFT

Left Coast *n phr* The Pacific Coast: *That's not what they're saying out on the Left Coast*—Playboy

left-field *adj* *by 1950s* Unorthodox; unexpected; =WACKY: *Abril stuffs her first starring role in an American movie with the kind of willful, left-field behavior that she learned from working with Almodovar*—New Yorker
See OUT IN LEFT FIELD

left-handed 1 *adj* *merchant marine by 1940s* Undesirable; unlucky **2** *adj* *by 1612* Irregular; illicit; dubious: . . . *left-handed honeymoons with someone else's husband*—J Evans

left-handed compliment *n phr* *by 1881* Praise that is subtle dispraise; reluctant and dubious praise: *Telling her she has the constitution of a horse is maybe a left-handed compliment*

left nut *See* GRIPE one's ASS

lefty or **leftie 1** *n* *by 1886* A left-handed person, esp a left-handed pitcher or other athlete **2** *modifier*: *a lefty hurler/ leftie tennis ace* **3** *n* *by 1930s* A person of liberal or socialist political beliefs; radical; liberal: . . . *such urban lefties as Bella Abzug*—National Review

leg 1 *v* (also **leg it**) *by 1601* To go; travel: *I was legging down the line* **2** *n* *Vietnam War Army* An infantry soldier; =GRUNT **3** *n* *1960s college students fr black* A woman, esp a sexually promiscuous one
See an ARM AND A LEG, BOOTLEG, DIRTYLEG, GIVE someone LEG, HAVE A LEG UP ON someone or something, HOG LEG, MIDDLE LEG, PEG LEG, PULL someone's LEG, SHAKE A LEG, SHAKE A WICKED CALF, TANGLE-FOOT

legal eagle (or beagle) *n phr* A lawyer, esp a clever and aggressive one: *In 1979 Davis' legal eagles got him acquitted again*—Newsweek/ *Software turns you into a regular legal beagle*—Milwaukee Journal

leg art *n phr* *by 1930s* Pictures of women in clothing and poses that emphasize their sexuality; =CHEESECAKE: *The magazine was once sought for its leg art*

leg-biter *n* *1980s college students* A small child or infant; =CRUMB-CRUSHER

lege (LEDGE) *n* *by 1990s* A preeminent and awe-inspiring person: *A few hours after she had beaten the "lege," the legend of her chosen field. . .* —New York Times [probably influenced by the phrase *a legend in one's own time*, applied to personages like Ernest Hemingway]

leggy *adj* *by 1848* Having prominent legs, esp long and shapely ones •Nearly always used of women, although the dated instance refers to a horse: *She looked tall and leggy. . .* —Ed McBain

legit (lə JIHT) **1** *adj* *by 1931* Legitimate; =KOSHER: *She's a legit farmer*—H Allen Smith/ . . . *by legit, or honest, people*—E DeBaun **2** *n* *by 1897* The legitimate theater, or one such theater **3** *adj* *by 1923* Having to do with or being of the legitimate theater: . . . *specialists in legit reviewing*—Abel Green
See ON THE LEGIT

leg man 1 *n phr* *newspaper office by 1923* A newspaper reporter who goes out to gather facts, and may or may not write the story **2** *n phr* *by 1950s* Any person who works actively and outside, rather than in, an office **3** *n phr* *by 1940s* A man whose favorite part of the female body is the legs

legperson *n* *by 1990s* A newspaper leg man or woman •The nonsexist version: *Either Breslin or his legperson combed old city directories to track Runyon from his boyhood in Colorado through his rise to journalistic stardom in New York*—Nation

leg-pull *n* *by 1915* The act of deceiving or fooling someone; =PUT-ON: . . . *the wisecrack and the gag, the leg pull and the hotfoot*—James Thurber

Legree *See* SIMON LEGREE

legs *n show business by 1970s* The ability of a show, song, public figure, etc, to be an enduring success; staying power: . . . *whether a movie will have legs, the power to entice audiences week after week*—New York Times/ . . . *runaway success, bigger than disco, with stronger legs*—Newsweek/ . . . *there is no other theory with legs*—New York Times

See BIRD LEGS, HINDERS

leg show *n phr by 1882* A performance featuring the bare legs, etc, of dancers or models

legs that go all the way up *n phr* (Variations: many, some of which are shown below) *by 1980s* Long and shapely legs: . . . *a bimbo with legs that go all the way up*—George V Higgins/ . . . *legs that go all the way to heaven*—Carsten Stroud/ *Only the floor kept her legs from going on forever*—New York Times/ *Huston and Bening both have scintillating street wit and legs that go on for days*—Time/ *Tits out to here, legs that won't quit.* . . —Ed McBain

a leg up 1 *n by 1837* Aid; a boost: *He'll do OK, but he needs a financial leg up to get started* **2** *n phr by 1901* An advantage: *You can go in with a leg up on other people*—Washington Post

See HAVE A LEG UP ON something

legwork *n phr newspaper office by 1891* Peripatetic work done outside the office: *I figured Wendell must be somewhere close, and I did a little legwork*—Sue Grafton

lemon¹ 1 *n by 1909* Anything unsatisfactory or defective, esp a car; =CLINKER: *His tale brought back memories of my first lemon*—Mother Jones/ *That show's a lemon* **2** *n black by 1940s* A light-skinned and attractive black woman; =HIGH YELLOW **3** *n by 1925* A sour, disagreeable person **4** *n 1960s narcotics* (also **lemonade**) Weakened or diluted narcotics, or a nonnarcotic substance sold as a narcotic; =BLANK

See HAND someone A LEMON

lemon² *n 1960s narcotics* A Quaalude™ [*Lemmon* is the name of a pharmaceutical company that once manufactured the drug]

lens louse *n phr by 1925* A person who obtrusively puts himself into a photograph, television shot, etc, esp by clowning behind the speaker

◁**les** or **lez** or **lezzie**▷ (LEZ) **1** *n by 1929* A lesbian: *Mary is a les and John is a fairy*—Joe E Lewis/ *I'd have figured you for a lez*—Lawrence Sanders **2** *modifier*: *It was a fantastic turn-on, watching a lezzie scene*—Herbert Kastle

◁**lesbo**▷ (LEZ boh) *n by 1940* A lesbian: . . . *where the Lesbos even come and watch the dress rehearsals*—John O'Hara/ . . . *a carefree single lesbo looking for love*—Vogue

let a fart *See* LAY A FART

letch *See* LECH

letdown 1 *n by 1889* A disappointment; =COMEDOWN: *Actually meeting him was something of a letdown* **2** *n by 1945* The gradual descent of an airplane toward a landing

let fly (or go) 1 *v phr by 1654* To launch vigorously into something; begin with projective energy: *She took a deep breath and let fly* **2** *v phr by 1624* To hurl; shoot; fire: *The gunman let go with both automatics*—E Lavine

let George do it *sentence by 1910* Let someone else besides me take care of it [perhaps fr a learned journalist's recall of the French *laissez faire à Georges,* "let George do it," referring to Cardinal Georges d'Amboise, a church and government official under Louis XII in the late 15th and early 16th centuries]

let oneself **go** *v phr by 1926* To behave in an unrestrained way; be uninhibited: *Come on, Herbert, let yourself go, have another cookie*

let one's **hair down** *v phr* To be very open and candid, esp about personal matters: *A lot of men that I have been with do not let their hair down*—Sexual Behavior/ *A small-town beauty shop, where city slickers can really let their hair down*—New York Times

let someone **have it 1** *v phr by 1840* To hit someone, esp powerfully; =CLOBBER: *Then let him have it, right on the chin*—James M Cain **2** *v phr by 1891* To attack verbally, esp punitively; =GIVE IT TO someone: *He allows me to count on his affection. Then he lets me have it*—Saul Bellow

let her (or 'er) rip *v phr by 1879* To let something go at full speed; take off all restraints: *He decided to buckle his seat belt and let her rip*

let it all hang out *1960s counterculture fr black* **1** *v phr* To be entirely candid; be free and unrestrained; =LET one's HAIR DOWN: *You'll feel better if you let it all hang out* **2** *modifier*: *I enjoy our let-it-all-hang-out relationship*—Mademoiselle

let it go at that *v phr by 1898* =LET IT SIT: *You'll eat half of it? OK, let it go at that*

let it sit *v phr by 1990s* To decline to object or interfere; acquiesce: *"He wasn't perfect, but he tried." I let that one sit there, unwilling to challenge her version of events*—Sue Grafton/ *"Let it sit, then," he said with the slightest of shrugs*—Sue Grafton

let someone **off** *v phr by 1828* To decline to pursue or prosecute someone: *The prosecutor let him off because he was a pal of the mayor*

let (or blow) off steam *v phr by 1837* To talk loudly and angrily, as a method of relieving the pressure of one's feelings; express one's anger or frustration: *He's not serious, just letting off steam/ I've blown off steam*—Woman's Home Companion/ *They're bored, just blowing off steam*—W T Tyler

let someone **off the hook** *v phr by 1960s* To relieve someone of responsibility or menace: *They had already given me a lot. I wanted to let them off the hook*—Philadelphia

let on *v phr by 1825* To reveal; hint: *Guys fool around, they sort of joke about it, they sort of let on, you know?*—Robert B Parker

letout 1 *n by 1940s* Dismissal from a job: . . . *other Metro executive letouts*—Variety **2** *n by 1935* =OUT

let out (or slip) *v phr by 1870* To reveal: *They let out that they were already married*

let something **ride** *v phr by 1921* To let something go on as it is; decline to change or intervene: *Let the same order ride for now*

let's boogie *sentence 1950s teenagers* (Variations: **cruise** or **blaze** may replace **boogie**) Let us leave [originally "let's dance to boogie-woogie music"]

let's face it *sentence by 1911* Let us freely admit it; let us accept the unhappy truth: *Let's face it, kids, we're all to blame some*

let's get the (or this) show on the road *sentence by 1957* We should get started; we should become active

letter *See* DEAD HORSE, FRENCH LETTER, POISON-PEN LETTER

letterbox *v television by 1990s* To show a wide-screen movie on the television screen, by reducing its size and putting black bars above and below: *Today we'll see a wide-format, letterboxed edition, which is rarely telecast*—Teri Garr/ . . . "letterboxing," *which retains theatrical images on a rectangular shape*—Milwaukee Journal

letter man *See* FOUR-LETTER MAN

let the cat out of the bag *v phr by 1760* To reveal a secret, usu without intending to: *Her guilty smile pretty much let the cat out of the bag*

let the good times roll *v phr jazz musicians fr about 1900* To enjoy oneself; be joyous, gregarious, and bibulous [the phrase is still associated with New Orleans]

lettuce *n by 1929* Money, esp paper money; =CABBAGE: *That's a lot of lettuce*—New York Review of Book/ *the man who nipped all this lettuce from the* Playboy *patch*—Newsweek
See FOLDING MONEY

level **1** *v by 1920* To tell the truth; be honest and candid: *Don't laugh. I'm leveling*—Joel Sayre/ *It's on this level that they tell you that they are "leveling" with you*—Saul Bellow **2** *adj* True: *There's never a place for guys like me.. . . That's level*—H Lee
See ON THE LEVEL

someone's **level best** *n phr by 1851* The utmost one can do; one's honest greatest effort: *I'll do my level best to keep you*

level playing field *n phr by 1981* Equality of opportunity; fair terms on all sides: *It's no level playing field if you always get to pick first*

'leven *See* FORTY-'LEVEN, SEVENTY-'LEVEN

levers *See* GO LEVERS

levies or **Levis** (LEE vīz) *n by 1940s* Blue denim dungaree pants; blue jeans [fr *Levi* Strauss™, a mid–1800s Western company that made and makes such garments]

lez *See* LES

◁**lezzie**▷ *See* LES

liaise (lee AYZ) *v by 1916* To cooperate; get into regular contact: . . . *told her to liaise with the FBI*—Lawrence Sanders [shortening of *liaison*]

lib *n by 1960s* Liberation, esp as the aim of various movements: *animal lib*
See GAY LIB, MEN'S LIB

libber *n by 1960s* A member of one of the liberation movements, esp of the women's lib movement: *Thus. . . did Golda Meir vent her view of women's libers*—Newsweek/ *"The libber and the lobber." All those lines are mine*—Nora Ephron

libe *students by 1915* **1** *n* A library, esp a college library **2** *v* To study in a library

liberate *v WWII Army* To steal or appropriate, originally something in conquered enemy territory

liberty *See* AT LIBERTY

a **license to print money** *n phr* A very lucrative business: *The railways are not, like some predecessors, a license to print money*—Nation/ *In the past, owning a movie studio was like having a license to print money*—Vanity Fair

lick **1** *n by 1678* A blow; stroke: *I got in a couple good licks before he decked me* **2** *v by 1563* To beat; pummel; =LAMBASTE, LARRUP **3** *v by 1800* To defeat; =CLOBBER: *Next time we'll lick 'em for good* **4** *n by 1739* Censure; adverse criticism; =HIT, KNOCK: *The show is no winner, but doesn't deserve the licks it's taken* **5** *n by 1863* A try; attempt; =CRACK, SHOT, WHACK: *I probably won't make it, but I'll give it a good lick* **6** *n baseball by 1883* A time at bat: *So the Yankees come up for their last licks* **7** *n 1920s jazz musicians* A short figure or solo, esp when improvised; =BREAK, RIFF: . . . *a few solid licks on the sliphorn*—C Smith/ . . . *that I know are exactly the licks that I play*—Rolling Stone
See HIT IT A LICK

a **lick and a promise** *n phr by 1860* A hasty job; a cursory performance [fr the notion that one does one *lick* or stroke of what is appropriate, and *promises* to do the rest]

lick one's **chops** *v phr by 1655* To display hunger and anticipation, for food or for something else desired: *We all sat licking our chops as the turkey was carved: I licked my chops when I thought of that huge bonus*

licker *See* ASS-KISSER, CLIT-LICKER, DICKLICKER

lickety-split or **lickity-split** *adv by 1859* Very fast: *Felt he just had to get a lawyer lickity-split*—Scott Turow [fr *lick*, "speed, a spurt of speed," found by 1809; earlier forms *lickety-cut, lickety-click, lickety liner*, and *lickety switch* are found in the 1830s and 1840s]

licorice stick *n phr 1930s jive talk* The clarinet

lid **1** *n by 1896* A hat **2** *n 1960s narcotics* One ounce of marijuana: . . . *a shutdown on grass, lids were going for thirty dollars*—Saturday Review/ . . . *lifted out the back seat and found a lid of marijuana*—Rolling Stone
See BLOW THE LID OFF, FLIP one's LID, PUT A LID ON something or someone, SKID LID

lie *See* THE BIG LIE, a PACK OF LIES

lie doggo *v phr by 1893* To stay in hiding; secrete oneself; =LAY LOW ●Chiefly British: *You better lie doggo a while till it blows over* [probably fr the silent and unobtrusive behavior of a hunting or herding *dog* when stalking]

lie like a rug (or wet rug) *v phr* by 1940s To be very mendacious: *They say the truth is not in us, first of all. They say we lie like wet rugs*—Milwaukee Journal

lie through one's **teeth (or dentures)** *v phr* by 1940s To be radically untruthful; =LIE LIKE A RUG: *Carl, what you already did is called lying through your dentures*—Sue Grafton

lieut (LōōT) *n* by 1843 Lieutenant; =LOOEY, LOOT

lieutenant *See* THIRD LIEUTENANT

life *See* BET YOUR BOOTS, LOW-LIFE, NOT ON YOUR LIFE

a **life** *n phr* baseball by 1868 Another chance to get a hit, score, etc, esp after a fielding error: *The Tigers got a life when the second baseman bobbled an easy one*

the **life** or **the Life** by 1970s **1** *n phr* Prostitution, esp as a business: *. . . a hooker from L A who knows this is her ticket out of the life*—Ed McBain/ *. . . this latter often purchased "hot" from others in the life*—Xaviera Hollander **2** *n phr* The homosexual life, esp that of an effeminate transvestite male prostitute: *She had lived the life so long now*—Patrick Mann
See IN THE LIFE

lifeboat *n* underworld by 1940s A pardon from a prison or other sentence; a retrial

the **life of Riley** *n phr* by 1919 An easy, luxurious, and pleasant life; =the GRAVY TRAIN: *I took the money, went to Mexico, and lived the life of Riley* [origin uncertain; perhaps fr an 1880s song about a man named *O'Reilly*, who became rich and sybaritic]

lifer 1 *n* by 1830 A convict serving a life sentence **2** *n* WWII Army A career Army officer: *. . . "lifers" (the contemptuous GI term for career officers)*—New York Times

lift 1 *n* by 1861 A surge or feeling of exhilaration; a transport of exuberance; =HIGH, KICK, RUSH: *I get a lift from watching that kid* **2** *v* by 1526 To steal: *He got caught lifting a chicken from the convenience store* **3** *v* by 1892 To plagiarize: *whole pages lifted from my book* **4** *n* by 1712 A ride: *I need a lift to the bus terminal downtown*
See HITCH A RIDE

lifted *adj* 1990s narcotics Intoxicated by narcotics; =HIGH, STONED

lifties or **lifts** *n* by 1940s Men's shoes built up so as to increase the wearer's height: *Male movie stars are said to wear "lifties"*—Associated Press

light *See* the GREEN LIGHT, IDIOT LIGHT, OUT LIKE A LIGHT, REDLIGHT, SEE THE LIGHT AT THE END OF THE TUNNEL

light colonel *n phr* WWII Army A lieutenant colonel

lighten up *v phr* by late 1960s To become less serious; be easy; relax •Often a more or less gentle admonition: *Schofield lightens up and improves at bat*—New York Times/ *Aw, come on, everybody, lighten up a little. It wasn't that bad. The decade, I mean*—New York Times/ *You have to lighten up,*

Chief. *The men are giving it everything they have*—Michael Grant

light-fingered 1 *adj* by 1547 Inclined to steal; thievish; =STICKY-FINGERED **2** *adj* by 1804 Having a light and nimble touch: *The light-fingered thoughtfulness, the ironic lyricism of the most civilized playwright of the era*—Time

light-footed *adj* by about 1955 Homosexual; effeminate

light into *v phr* by 1878 To attack; excoriate; =LAY INTO: *He lit into the Administration's tax bill with some sparkling epithets*—Wall Street Journal

lightly *See* a ONCE-OVER

lightning *n* by 1781 Cheap, raw whiskey; =WHITE LIGHTNING
See CHAIN LIGHTNING, GREASED LIGHTNING, JERSEY LIGHTNING, RIDE THE LIGHTNING, WHITE LIGHTNING

light on one's **feet** *adj phr* by 1960s Homosexual; effeminate: *Some models are light on their feet*—TV show *Geraldo*

light out *v phr* by 1870 To leave, esp hastily; =TAKE OFF, HIGHTAIL: *Jack, estranged from his father by his brother's death in a helicopter crash, lights out for the territories*—New York Times •This allusion to Huck Finn is not quite accurate. Mark Twain wrote "the territory" [fr earlier nautical *light out*, "move out, or move something out," of obscure origin; perhaps "move or move something lightly, quickly, handily"]

lights *n* 1980s teenagers A police car: *There were five lights at Dunkin' Donuts*—Delcastle Dictionary of Slang

lights out 1 *n phr* Bedtime: *Lights out is at 10:30* **2** *n phr* The end; death; =CURTAINS: *. . . otherwise lights out for me*—Dashiell Hammett
See PUNCH someone's LIGHTS OUT, SHOOT THE LIGHTS OUT

lightweight 1 *adj* by 1809 Inconsequential; unserious **2** *n* by 1882: *He seems like a lightweight to me, don't pay him any attention*

like 1 *adv* 1950s counterculture & bop talk As if; really; you know; sort of •A generalized modifier used to lend a somewhat tentative and detached tone to the speaker, to give the speaker time to rally words and ideas: *Like I was like groovin' like, you know what I mean?* **2** *v* by 1950s To pick; bet on: *I liked Felton. I took his folder and read it again*—Robert B Parker
See MAKE LIKE

like a bandit *adv phr* by 1960s Very successfully; thrivingly: *. . . coming out of the battle with Bendix like a bandit*—New York Times
See MAKE OUT LIKE A BANDIT

like a bat out of hell *adv phr* by 1921 Very rapidly; =LICKETY-SPLIT: *They split like a bat out of hell*
See TAKE OFF LIKE A BIGASS BIRD

like a blue streak *See* a BLUE STREAK

like a bump on a log *adv phr* by 1863 Idly; uselessly; inertly: *He just sits there like a bump on a log*

like a bunny *See* QUICK LIKE A BUNNY

like a hole in the head *See* NEED someone or something LIKE A HOLE IN THE HEAD

like a house afire *adv phr* by 1863 Forcefully and without delay: *The crowd burst through the gate, like a house afire*—American Idioms Dictionary

like a million bucks *adv phr* by 1930s Very good; superb: *In that blouse she looks like a million bucks*

like a streak *adv phr* by 1839 =LIKE GREASED LIGHTNING

like a ton of bricks *See* COME DOWN ON someone LIKE A TON OF BRICKS

◄**like fuck**► *adv phr* by 1990s =LIKE MAD: *. . . coding like fuck every day. . .* —Douglas Coupland

like gangbusters *adv phr* by 1942 Very energetically and successfully: *Everyone knows I'm getting into your pants like gangbusters*—Earl Thompson/ *The rest of the year the economy will be going like gangbusters*—Newsweek
See COME ON LIKE GANGBUSTERS

like greased lightning *adv phr* by 1833 Very rapidly; =LIKE A STREAK: *The little car went by like greased lightning*

like hell (or **blazes) 1** *adv phr* entry form by 1855, variant by 1845 In an extravagant way; very forcefully: *. . . walleyes feed like crazy and "bite like hell"*—Sports Afield/ *Started screaming like hell*—Joyce Carol Oates **2** *adv phr* (Variations: **fun** or **shit** may replace **hell**) entry form by 1925, fun by 1909 Never; it is impermissible; =IN A PIG'S ASS: *Like hell you will!/ . . . when the prostitute says "Like fun you are"*—D Costello

like it is *See* TELL IT LIKE IT IS

like it or lump it *adv phr* by 1833 Whether or not one wishes: *We have to go now, like it or lump it*

like it's going out of style or **like there's no tomorrow** *adv phr* by 1970s Extravagantly; wildly; recklessly; with abandon: *spending money like it was going out of style/ boozing like there was no tomorrow*

like mad (or **crazy) *adv phr* entry form by 1653, variant by 1924 Extravagantly; wildly; violently: *. . . tearing around like crazy*—P Marks/ *Then everybody laughs like mad*—A J Liebling

like nobody's business *adv phr* by 1938 Very much; extraordinarily: *He loves her like nobody's business/ That hurts like nobody's business*

like pigs in clover *adj phr* early 1800s Very happy; euphoric: *Paramount's general counsel laughs, "This part of the job I enjoy. We're like pigs in clover"*—Vanity Fair [probably a euphemized version of *happy as a pig in shit*; *pigs in clover* is a child's game first marketed in 1889]

like pulling teeth *adj phr* by 1970s Very slow and arduous: *Interviewing movie stars can be like pulling teeth, but Nicole Kidman was a delightful surprise: relaxed, natural, and a lot of fun*—Vanity Fair [*like pulling gum-teeth* in the same sense is found by 1872]

◄**like shit through a tin horn**► *adv phr* (Variations: **a dose of salts** or **a hot knife through butter** may replace **shit through a tin horn**) *dose of salts by 1837, others by 1940s* Very rapidly and easily; effortlessly: *He went through the defense like shit through a tin horn/ The pension bill went through like a dose of salts*

like shooting fish in a barrel *adj phr* by 1940s Very easy; much too easy: *Home shopping is like shooting fish in a barrel*—New York Times

like sixty *adv phr* by 1839 Very rapidly; =LIKE A BAT OUT OF HELL: *They went after him like sixty* [*sixty* is probably used as an indefinite large number, as *forty* was in similar 1800s contexts, to express extreme briskness]

like something the cat dragged in *adj phr* Revolting; rebarbative; =GROSS, YUCKY: *Jesus, get cleaned up. You look like something the cat dragged in/ . . . sometimes the glue smells like something the cat dragged in*—Lawrence Sanders

◄**like tits on a boar (** or **boar hog)**► *adj phr* by 1940s Absolutely useless: *A relief pitcher without confidence is like tits on a boar hog*—Whitey Herzog

◄**like ten pounds of shit in a five-pound bag**► *See* BLIVIT

like that *See* ALL LIKE THAT THERE

lily ◄**1**► *n* by 1940s A homosexual; =PANSY, QUEER **2** *n* Something superior, etc; =LULU: *I told my best joke. . . it's never missed, it's a lily*—Lionel Stander

lily-white *adj phr* by 1903 Desiring or having only Caucasian residents, workers, etc: *. . . the thugs would never think to look for him in a lily-white suburb*—USExpress

lily whites *n phr* by 1950s Bed sheets

limb *See* GO OUT ON A LIMB, OUT ON A LIMB

◄**limey** or **lime-juicer**► **1** *n* by 1888 An English person: *The "Doctor" was a lime-juicer*—Scribner's **2** *n* by 1919 A British ship [fr the ration of *lime-juice* given to British sailors as an antiscorbutic; the dated use for the first sense is strictly "an English immigrant to the Antipodes"; the generalized term probably reflects the US use, "English sailor or soldier," found by 1918]

the limit *n phr* college students by 1900 A person, thing, etc, that exceeds or outrages what is acceptable: *I've seen some stupid things, but this is the limit/ Ain't he awful, ain't he just the limit?* *See* GO THE LIMIT

limo (LIHM oh) **1** *n* by 1946 A limousine: *. . . disapproves of this vast fleet (789 limos) of luxury transportation*—Saturday Review **2** *v*: *Check your reso before you limo to Manhattan*—American Speech *See* STRETCH LIMO

limousine liberal *n phr* by 1969 A wealthy person of liberal political convictions: *The limousine liberals of the record industry complain that it's censorship. . .* —Mesa Tribune/ *After her Academy Award speech, Susan Sarandon was dismissed by some as a limousine liberal*—New York Times

◁**limp-dick**▷ **1** *n* by 1970s An ineffectual man; an impotent man; =WIMP **2** *adj*: *I called myself every limp-dick name I could think of*—Richard Price

limp dishrag *n phr* by 1970s An ineffectual person; =NEBBISH, WIMP: *Sandy is discarded. . . as if she were, well, a limp dishrag*—Village Voice

limp noodle 1 *n phr* by 1970s Something or someone feeble, tasteless, and without distinction: . . . *Warren Christopher has shown himself to be a limp noodle of a persuader*—William Safire **2** *adj*: *. . . outdated postures, overused jokes, and limp-noodle romantic ballads*—Village Voice

limp wrist 1 *n phr* by 1950s A male homosexual: *I reminded her that Boke Kellum was a limp wrist*—Dan Jenkins/ *Barbara Hutton could only marry herself seven or eight limp wrists*—Paul Sann **2** *modifier*: *a limp-wrist hangout*

limp-wristed *adj* by 1950s Effeminate; slack and sinuous; homosexual: *His art always has this subtle, limp-wristed style to it*—Village Voice/ *. . . the most limp-wristed "stud" in the Philadelphia metropolitan area*—Philadelphia

line 1 *n* by 1903 One's way of talking, esp when being persuasive or self-aggrandizing; =SPIEL: *. . . of what in a later generation would have been termed her "line"*—F Scott Fitzgerald/ *You've got some line*—Ira Wolfert **2** *n* by 1655 One's occupation, business, etc; =RACKET: *What's my line? Herring in brine* **3** *n* 1930s jazz musicians A musical solo or figure, esp personal and innovative: *Coasters talk of "lines," not licks, breaks, or riffs*—Artie Shaw **4** *v* baseball by 1892 To hit the ball in a line drive **5** *n* gambling by 1970s A bookmaker's odds on a sports event: *Baseball, basketball, and hockey lines are available on the day or night of the games*—Harper's **6** *n* narcotics by 1980 A dose of cocaine, usu formed into a thin line to be nasally ingested **7** *v*: *They lined twice last night, no wonder they're tired* *See* someone's ASS IS ON THE LINE, the BOTTOM LINE, CHOW LINE, HARD LINE, HOT LINE, IN LINE, IN LINE FOR, LAY IT ON THE LINE, MAIN LINE, ON LINE, ON THE LINE, OUT OF LINE, PULL A LINE, PUNCH LINE, PUT one's ASS ON THE LINE, REDLINE, SHOOT someone A LINE, STAG LINE, TOE THE MARK

the **line** by 1940s **1** *n phr* The chorus girls of a show **2** *n phr* An assembly line *See* TOE THE MARK

line dog (or doggie) *n phr* Army by 1970s A soldier, esp a sergeant, in a combat unit [combat units are trained to operate in the front *line*]

linen *See* DIRTY LINEN, WASH one's DIRTY LINEN

line one's **nest** *See* FEATHER one's NEST

line out 1 *v phr* by 1970s To sing, esp in a loud strong voice; =BELT OUT **2** *v phr* baseball by 1890s To hit a line drive that is caught [musical sense perhaps fr church practice of having a hymn read one line at a time, then having the congregation sing the line]

liner *See* HEADLINER, ONE-LINER

lines *See* GO UP IN one's LINES

line-up 1 *n* police by 1907 A number of persons displayed in line across a platform to find whether witnesses can pick a suspect from among them; =SHOW-UP **2** *n* baseball by 1889 The roster of a team, esp for a particular game: *Just before the game started, the managers showed their line-ups to the umpires*

line up with *v phr* by 1940s To support; take sides with: *Who will you line up with on this thorny issue?*

lingo (LING goh) *n* by 1660 Language; jargon; idiom

◁**linthead**▷ *n* Southern by 1933 A despised person; =TRASH [literally "a worker in a cotton mill"]

lip 1 *n* by 1821 Insolent, impertinent, or presumptuous talk; =SASS, SAUCE: *I don't want none of your lip*—W Moore **2** *n* underworld by 1929 A lawyer; =MOUTHPIECE **3** *v* jazz musicians by 1950s To play a musical instrument, esp in jazz; =BLOW: *He couldn't lip anything proper anymore*—Stephen Longstreet *See* BAT one's GUMS, BUTTON one's LIP, FLIP one's LIP, ZIP one's LIP

lip lock *n phr* by 1990s A kiss: *. . . the Rubbles in a passionate lip lock. . .* —Wisconsin State Journal

lip-locking *n* by 1990s Kissing: *. . . then you might enter into some serious lip-locking*—Milwaukee Journal

lip mover *n phr* by 1980s A dull and stupid person; =BLOCKHEAD: *. . . between those countless millions of lip-movers and the minuscule audience for better novels*—New York Times [fr the habit of uneducated or dull people of *moving their lips* while reading to themselves]

lippie *n* by 1990s Lipstick: *. . . you should find a lippie that's as dark as or even a bit darker than your skin*—Sassy

lippy 1 *adj* by 1875 Insolent; brash and arrogant: *He's smart, but much too lippy* **2** *adj* by 1893 Talkative

lip-splitter *n* jazz musicians by 1950s A musician who plays a wind instrument

lip-sync or **lip-synch** (LIP sink) *v* by late 1950s To move the lips silently in synchronism with recorded singing or speaking, to give the illusion of actual performance: *Having taped his lines before the show, he lip-synched his pronouncements*—Time/ *. . . staying home with her sister lip synching to Leon Russell records*—Village Voice

liquidate *v* by 1924 To kill •A Soviet euphemism [based on Russian *likvidirovat*, "liquidate, wind up"]

liquid crack *n phr* by 1990s: *. . . 40-ounce bottles of malt liquor sometimes have a nickname among the young people who drink them dry in one sitting: "liquid crack"*—Milwaukee Journal

liquor *See* HARD LIQUOR, POT LIQUOR

liquored up *adj* by 1921 Drunk

list *See* HIT LIST, SHIT LIST, SUCKER LIST, WISH LIST

listen *v* by 1930s To sound right; seem right; make sense; =FIGURE: *It don't listen*—Raymond Chandler/ *That listens, doesn't it?*—Lawrence Sanders

listen-in *n by 1940s* An instance of eavesdropping or wire-tapping: . . . *an occasional listen-in on the. . . line*—Philadelphia Bulletin

listen up *v phr 1960s armed forces fr black* To listen closely; pay strict attention •Often a brusque command: *He can make you listen up with that violin of his*—Village Voice

listserv *n 1990s computers* : *Now there's a listserv, or electronic mailing list, for those few Internet denizens who are classical music aficionados*—Washington Post

lit¹ *n by 1850* Literature: *comp lit/ black lit*

lit² *adj by 1917* Drunk

lit-crit 1 *n by 1963* Literary criticism **2** *modifier*: *Gallop, a celebrity in lit-crit circles, could be described as a sort of post-structural Mae West. . .*—Milwaukee Journal

lite *adj by 1980s* Not serious; not scholarly; watered down; popularized: . . . *there's myth lite apres Joseph Campbell, Pinkola Estes, etc*—New York Times [fr the misspelling of *light* used to identify less fattening, less intoxicating, etc, products, esp beer]

litter *See* POCKET LITTER

litterbug *n about 1947* A person who throws trash in the streets, parks, etc [coined for a New York Police Department campaign against littering; modeled on *jitterbug*]

little bitty *adj phr by 1940* Very small; =ITSY-BITSY: *I got four little bitty kids*—American Scholar

little black book *n phr by 1940s* The private notebook in which one is supposed to keep telephone numbers and details of potential and actual sex partners; secret record

someone's **little game** *n phr by 1884* Someone's devious scheme; someone's wretched stratagem: *The crowd dropped to his little game*—The Lantern

little green apples *See* SURE AS GOD MADE LITTLE GREEN APPLES

little green men *n phr by 1961* Aliens from outer space, said to have been seen descending from flying saucers: . . . *Search for Extraterrestrial Intelligence, which has long been derided as a quest for "little green men"*—Milwaukee Journal

Little Joe *n phr crapshooting by 1890* The point four, or four on the dice [a shortening of *Little Joe from Kokomo;* the relation to four is not patent]

a **little low on wattage** *adj phr by 1990s* Stupid; uncomprehending; =DIM . . . *who is obviously a little low on wattage above the neck*—Los Angeles Times

little Michael (or Mickey) *n phr by 1960s* =MICKEY FINN

little Phoebe (or fever) *See* PHOEBE

little school *n phr underworld & hoboes by 1940s* A reformatory; reform school

little secret *See* DIRTY LITTLE SECRET

little shaver *n phr by 1843* A young boy

little tin god *n phr by 1886* A petty and self-important figure

the **little woman** *n phr by 1881* One's wife •Once regarded as affectionate, this term is now patronizing and demeaning: . . . *tooling along with the kiddies and the little woman in his costly can*—Westbrook Pegler

lit to the gills *adj phr by 1917* Drunk

lit up or **lit up like a Christmas tree 1** *adj phr by 1902* Drunk: *I found Uncle Peter and he was also lit up*—H McHugh **2** *adj phr 1960s narcotics* Intoxicated with narcotics; =HIGH

live (LĪV) **1** *adj by 1934* Not recorded or taped: *live music/ a live telecast* **2** *adj by 1900* Of current importance; still to be decided: *Is metrication really a live issue today?*
See ALL THE WAY LIVE

live high on the hog *See* EAT HIGH ON THE HOG

live-in 1 *adj by 1955* Sharing one's domicile: *Coe's former live-in girlfriend*—Newsweek/ *J Edgar's "longtime live-in lover"*—Village Voice **2** *n by 1955* A housekeeper or caregiver who lives in one's home: *After they had their second child, they hired a live-in*

live it up *v phr by 1951* To live joyfully and extravagantly: *After retirement we decided to live it up for a while*

live one 1 *n phr by 1920s* A lively person; up-to-date person; =LIVE WIRE **2** *n phr carnival by 1920s* A likely target for a confidence scheme or fast sell: *Hey, Eddie, looks like we got us a live one here*

live on the edge *v phr by 1990s* To life dangerously; court disaster: . . . *dumped about a quarter-cup of salt on top. "I like to live on the edge," she explained*—Los Angeles Times/ . . . *pushing his luck, living on the edge, playing brilliantly by the seat of his pants*—New Yorker

live park *v phr by 1980s* To park a car with the motor running

liver *See* CHOPPED LIVER, THAT AIN'T HAY

liver rounds *n phr medical by 1980s* An after-hours gathering of doctors at a cocktail lounge, bar, or party

lives *See* HIT someone WHERE HE LIVES

live wire *n phr by 1909* An energetic, vibrant person: *Jimmy's a live wire, all right*—P Marks

the **living daylights** *See* BEAT THE SHIT OUT OF someone or something

living doll *n phr by 1960s* A notably decent, pleasant person: *Isn't the emcee a living doll?*

the **living end** *n phr 1950s beat & cool talk* A person, thing, etc, that is about as much as one can stand; =the END, the LIMIT •Usu highly complimentary

living-room gig *n phr 1950s jazz musicians* A television appearance: . . . *living room gig, a guest shot on television*—E Horne

◁**the living shit**▷ *See* BEAT THE SHIT OUT OF someone or something, SCARE THE SHIT OUT OF someone

lizard *See* BUNK LIZARD, LOUNGE LIZARD

lizzie or **Lizzie** *n by 1913* A car, esp a cheap or ramshackle one: . . . *the luxurious lizzie I've always dreamed about*—Billy Rose
See TIN LIZZIE

load 1 *n* Enough liquor to make one drunk: *He's tak-*

ing on a load again **2** *n esp teenagers* A dose of narcotic smoked in a water pipe ◁3▷ *n* The semen of a single orgasm **4** *n 1980s teenagers* A car **5** *n by 1990s* An obese person; =CHUBBO: *It's sort of OK to be a load, because it's what's inside that counts. . .* —Milwaukee Journal/ *I'm not going to camp with a bunch of fat loads*—Macon Telegraph **6** *n* (also **load of shit**) *by 1990s* Nonsense; lies and exaggerations; mendacious cant; =BULLSHIT, CROCK OF SHIT: . . . *the whole thing about O J threatening to blow his head off was a load*—Esquire
See CARRY A LOAD, CARRY THE LOAD, FREELOAD, GET A LOAD OF, HALF LOAD, HAVE A LOAD ON, a SHITLOAD, SHOOT one's LOAD, TAKE A LOAD OFF YOUR FEET, THREE BRICKS SHY OF A LOAD

loaded 1 *adj by 1886* Drunk: . . . *men should act different. . . when they get loaded*—The Lantern/ *Jerry got so loaded at the party last night that we were afraid to let him drive home*—UCLA Slang **2** *adj by 1930s* Containing whiskey or other liquor: *We sipped our loaded coffee*—Raymond Chandler **3** *adj narcotics by 1940s* Intoxicated with narcotics, esp heroin; =HIGH, STONED: *And then you get loaded and like it*—D Hulburd **4** *adj by 1709* Well supplied; abounding in; =LOUSY WITH: *She's loaded with talent/ He died loaded with honors* **5** *adj by 1910* Wealthy; =FILTHY RICH: *They're all loaded in that neighborhood* **6** *adj students by 1895* Full of information; prepared **7** *adj by 1942* Carrying significance beyond the obvious or surface meaning: *That was a loaded remark* **8** *adj by 1940s* Prearranged; biased: *The interview was loaded in my favor*

loaded dice *n phr by 1781* Dice of which the weight distribution has been altered so that the roll is predictable

loaded for bear *adj phr* Ready and anxious for a fight; heavily prepared for conflict, debate, etc: *I went to the board meeting loaded for bear* [fr the notion that a hunter must use particularly powerful ammunition, or *load*, to kill a *bear*; the phrase meant "very drunk" by 1896]

loader *See* FREELOADER

loadie or **loady 1** *n 1970s teenagers* A person who uses narcotics, drinks beer and liquor, etc: *for every high school loadie you will find a National Merit Scholar*—Time **2** *n 1970s college students* A drunkard; an alcoholic; =LUSH

loading *See* FREELOADING

a **load off** someone's **mind** *n phr by 1852* A great mental and emotional relief; an end to fretting: *When I heard she was OK it was a great load off my mind*

a **load of VW radiators (or post holes or wind)** *n phr truckers by 1940s* An empty truck; no cargo whatever [fr the fact that VW engines were air-cooled and had no *radiators*]

loads of something *n phr by 1880* A great number; many; much: *The old lady has loads of charm and loads of money*

load the dice *v phr by 1714* To prearrange or bias some result: . . . *a man who helped load the dice*

against the dissidents within the government— David Halberstam [the date applies to the literal sense; the metaphorical is hard to date]

load up 1 *v phr baseball by 1980s* To tamper with the ball by covertly applying spit, hair oil, Vaseline, etc **2** *v phr 1980s students* To drink heavily; get drunk: *John always loads up before he goes to fraternity parties*—UCLA Slang

loan *See* JUICE LOAN

loan shark *n phr by 1905* An underworld usurer; =JUICE DEALER, SHYLOCK

lobo *n by 1940s* A hoodlum; thug: *A lobo's a gun, thug, hoodlum, downstate*—movie Scene of the Crime [fr Spanish, "wolf"]

lobster shift (or trick) *n phr newspaper office fr 1920s* A working shift beginning about midnight [perhaps fr *lobster*, "fool, dupe," found by 1896]

local *See* IRISH BUGGY

local yokel 1 *n phr 1970s citizens band* A town or city police officer **2** *n phr by 1940s* A resident of a small town or rural area

lock *v by 1990s* To be seemingly paralyzed and helpless; =CHOKE: *He locked on Letterman*—National Public Radio

a **lock** *n phr by 1940s* A certainty; =SURE THING, SHOO-IN: *This guy looks like a lock now*—New York Post/ *no longer a lock to win the NFC East*—New York Daily News [fr *lock*, "wrestling hold"]
See HAVE A LOCK ON something, **mortal lock**

-lock *combining word by 1980* A stoppage or restriction of or by the indicated thing: *gridlock/ job lock/ marriage lock/ timelock* [modeled on *gridlock*; perhaps based on wrestling holds called *locks*]

lock down *v phr prison by 1980s* To confine all prisoners to their cells: . . . *the prison was locked down and sharpshooters. . . were aiming their guns at the barred windows*—New Yorker

locker *See* CHAIN LOCKER

lock horns *v phr by 1839* To contend with; fight: *They had locked horns with a better man*—Albert Goldman/ *She has also locked horns with the network*—New York Daily News

lockjaw *n by 1980s*: *McKellen's Richard, his defects minimized and with a ruling-class lockjaw accent, is elegantly carved in ice*—Vanity Fair
See HAVE LOCKJAW, LOCUST VALLEY LOCKJAW

lockup *n by 1839* A cell, esp a detention cell or holding cell; =the COOLER, TANK

lock someone **up and throw away the key** *v phr by 1940s* To imprison someone for a very long time: *A lot of people feel good when you lock these criminals up and throw away the key*—NBC Evening News

loco[1] **1** *adj by 1887* Crazy; =NUTS: *He took one look and just went loco* **2** *n*: *She's acting like a loco* [fr Spanish, "insane"]

loco[2] *n railroad by 1940s* A locomotive

locomotive 1 *n students by 1950s* A cheer that resembles a steam locomotive starting: *We all had to stand up. . . and give him a locomotive*—J D Salinger **2** *n* A strong motive force; prime mover: . . . *free* *trade, which has been a locomotive of prosperity since World War II*—Time

Locust Valley (or Larchmont) lockjaw *n phr by 1980s* A somewhat stifled way of speaking, associated with US and British aristocracy [the places named are affluent suburbs of New York City]

log *See* BEAT ONE'S MEAT, EASY AS PIE

logjam *n by 1890* An immovable static situation; =GRIDLOCK: *He broke the logjam of negotiations with the cable companies*—Toronto Life

logo *n by 1937* A distinctive graphic image adopted as the symbol of a company, school, organization, etc: *He claims to have designed the HarperCollins logo*

log roll *n phr medical by 1970s* A way of carefully turning a patient out of a cart onto a bed: *She said she needed my help with a log roll in Room 643*

logrolling *n by 1823* The Congressional practice of canny reciprocal assistance in getting votes: *Thus, when members of Congress find themselves not able. . . to secure the passage of a measure of purely local interest, they are apt to resort to logrolling. . .* —Encyclopaedia Britannica [said to be based on a proverbial phrase, "You *roll* my *log* and I'll *roll yours*"]

loid 1 *v by 1958* To open a locked door by moving the catch with a strip or card of celluloid: *The cards. . . could be used to loid any door with a spring latch*—Ezra Hannon 2 *v by 1960s* To burglarize an apartment, building, etc [fr *celluloid*]

lol *v phr computer by 1990s* Computer network abbreviation for "laughed out loud"

lollapalooza (lah lə pə LŌō zə) *n by 1904* A person or thing that is remarkable, wonderful, superior, etc; =BEAUT, HUMDINGER: *He's got a lollapalooza of a cold*

loll (or laze) around *v phr by 1940s* To dispose or comport oneself idly; =GOOF OFF, LOLLYGAG, LOUNGE AROUND: *We were lolling around at the pool when the thing fell* [*loll*, "lean idly," is found by 1377]

lollipop *n baseball by 1960s* A pitch that is easy to hit: *. . . will they chuckle when out-of-shape lefties lob up lollipops?*—Milwaukee Journal

lollygag or **lallygag** (LAH lee gag) 1 *v by 1862* To idle about; =GOOF OFF: *. . . the summer free for play, swimming, berry picking, and general lally-gagging*—Frank Sullivan/ *. . . when my nephew and his companion lollygagged back to my house*—Washington Post 2 *v by 1868* To kiss and caress; dally; =MAKE OUT, NECK

loner *by 1940s* 1 *n* (also **lone wolf**) A person who prefers to be alone, do things alone, etc; a solitary or recluse: *He became more of a "loner," almost a man apart from the rest of the team*—Arthur Daley/ *. . . that breed of loners who wandered through the Rockies in the first half of the nineteenth century*—Esquire 2 *n* One person or thing by itself: *"Make it two and I'll be true." "Here's a loner to get you started"*—Lawrence Sanders

lonesome *See* ALL BY ONE'S LONESOME

as long as your arm *See* AS LONG AS YOUR ARM

the long arm *n phr by 1940s* A police officer; =the LAW [fr the phrase *the long arm of the law*]

long ball *See* GO FOR THE LONG BALL

long block *v phr car mechanics by 1990s*: A *"long block" is a complete engine minus the oil pump and oil pan*—Milwaukee Journal

a long (or tall) drink of water *n phr by 1940s* A very tall, thin person: *Bill Bradley is sure a long drink of water/ We have an expression in the Midwest: "a tall drink of water"*—Johnny Carson

long dry spell *n phr by 1970s* A period of disappointment; sterile period: *It's been a long, dry spell for Atari game players*—Milwaukee Journal

long green *n phr by 1891* Paper money; bills; =FOLDING MONEY: *. . . that dear old affectionately regarded long green*—Amsterdam News [perhaps influenced by earlier sense "home-grown, home-cured tobacco"]

longhair 1 *n by 1920* An intellectual; =EGGHEAD 2 *adj* (also **long-haired**): *longhair tastes in poetry* 3 *n 1920s jazz musicians* Classical music •Originally the term was used for musicians who play from written music, and for the music they play: *. . . sometimes called Western music, sometimes European music, and sometimes just longhair*—Stephen Longstreet 4 *adj* (also **longhaired**): *sonatas and other longhair stuff* 5 *n 1960s* A young man with long hair, esp a hippie: *. . . another longhair, a member of our commune*—J Jerome [earlier senses fr the stereotype of an intellectual or esthete as being strange and wearing *long hair*]

long-handle (or long-handled) underwear *n phr by 1940s* Long winter underwear: *. . . coats and long-handle underwear to fill Norway's needs*—Time

long haul *n phr by 1940s* A long and arduous period: *It looks like it'll be a long haul*
See FOR THE LONG HAUL, OVER THE LONG HAUL

Longhorn *n by 1903* A Texan; a cattleman [fr the breed of cattle particular to Texas and the Southwest, the name found by 1834]

longies *n by 1950s* Long underwear; =LONG JOHNS: *. . . that day's version of today's longies*—C Lawry

long in the tooth *adj phr by 1852* Aged; advanced in age: *The actor is a bit long in the tooth to be playing Tom Sawyer* [fr the practice of judging the age of horses by the *length of teeth*]

longjohn *n prison by 1990s* A man who is copulating with a prisoner's wife; =JODY: *That longjohn out there is gonna die when I hit the street*—Anthropological Linguistics

long johns or **long ones** *n phr by 1940s* Long winter underwear: *A generation or so ago, men, women, boys and girls put on long ones in October and wore long ones until spring*—Wall Street Journal/ *Pop, will you dig that dish out of your long johns*—Saul Bellow

long pig *n phr by 1883* A person regarded as meat for cannibals: *. . . he offered mammoth marrow, and, perhaps, Long Pig*—W H Auden [translation of Fijian *puaka balava*]

the **long run** *See* IN THE LONG RUN

long shot 1 *n phr* by 1869 A person, horse, project, etc, that seems not likely to win or succeed; =DARK HORSE: . . . *but it's a pretty long shot I'm afraid*—Hugh Pentecost **2** *modifier*: *a long-shot victory* **3** *n phr* by 1940s A scene photographed from a distance; a long-range photograph
See NOT BY A LONG SHOT

someone's **long suit** *n phr* by 1895 Someone's best gift or quality; forte; strong point: *His gift of gab is his long suit. He can call a bird off a tree*—Slang-Dic [fr cardplaying "suit in which you hold originally more than three cards," found by 1876]

long time no see *sentence* by 1900 I haven't seen you for a long time

long underwear 1930s jazz musicians **1** *n phr* Jazz music played in a sweet or commercial way: . . . *"long underwear" for concert stuff*—Stephen Longstreet **2** *n phr* An incompetent jazz musician **3** *n phr* Classical music; =LONGHAIR **4** *adj*: *She found out he was a long-underwear platterbug*—C Mason [fr the quaint antiquity of wearing such underwear]

loo¹ *n* by 1940 A toilet •Chiefly British: . . . *everything you'd find in a powder room except the loo*—Toronto Life [origin uncertain; perhaps fr *Waterloo* in proportionate analogy with *water closet*; perhaps fr the Edinburgh cry "Gardyloo" uttered when one threw the contents of the slopjar into the street; Mrs. Virginia Burton of Lynchburg, VA, suggests it may be a pronunciation of French *lieu*, "place," in the phrase *lieu d'aisance*, "toilet, lavatory"]

loo² *n* (also **Loo**) by 1990s A lieutenant, esp of police: *All lieutenants were called Loo*—Michael Grant

looey or **looie** or **louie** *n* WWI Army A lieutenant; =LOOT: *They demoted me to second looey*—Stephen Lewis

loogan 1 *n* by 1929 A stupid person; =BOOB **2** *n* A thug; =GOON, HOOD: *What's a loogan? A guy with a gun*—Raymond Chandler [origin uncertain; perhaps fr Irish *luigean*, "a weak person"]

loogan left *n phr* Chicago by 1980s A left turn made in front of traffic just as the light turns green

look *See* a HARD LOOK

look-alike 1 *n* by 1947 A person who closely resembles another; =DEAD RINGER, DOUBLE: *Barratt had an interview with his noted look-alike*—B Thomas **2** *n* computer by 1980s A compatible machine: *an IBM PC look-alike*

look at someone **cross-eyed** *v phr* by 1940s To commit even a tiny fault; offend in the least way: . . . *who would yell copper if you looked at them cross-eyed*—Raymond Chandler

look daggers *v phr* by 1833 To look at with anger; glare at: *I wondered why they were looking daggers at me*

look down one's **nose** *v phr* by 1921 To behave with hauteur; act condescendingly: *He looked down his nose at me as if I were some loathsome thing in his path*

look down on someone or something *v phr* by

1711 To hold in contempt; scorn: *He looks down on us as newcomers*

looker 1 *n* by 1902 A good-looking person of either sex, but esp a woman: *That waitress is a looker, a real dish* **2** *n* salespersons by 1940s (also **lookie-loo**) A person who inspects merchandise but does not buy: *A "looker" is to the used car lot what a browser is to a bookstore*—New York Times/ . . . *yard/garage/tag sales are. . . plagued by "lookie-loos"*—Lee K Russell
See GOOD-LOOKER

looking *adv* baseball by 1970s Watching the pitch without swinging the bat: *The Russian infielder struck out three times, looking*—New York Times

be **looking at** (or **talking**) *v phr* by late 1970s To have as a subject; direct the mind to; specify; contemplate: *We're looking at about 3 billion here/ John Glenn, not known for his humor, slammed Reagan's top aides. Instead of serving four more years, he said, some are looking at ten to 20*—Time/ *What we're talking here. . . is seventy-five a key*—Ed McBain/ *Rita Rose. You're talking Rita Rose, right?*—Stan Cutler

looking good *interj* by 1970s An exclamation of encouragement, praise, reassurance, etc; =WAY TO GO: *They hollered "Looking good!" as the leader passed*

look like a drowned rat *v phr* by 1508 To have a singularly disheveled, subdued, and unsightly appearance: *When they got off the boat after a weekend they looked like drowned rats*

look like death warmed over *v phr* by 1939 To look miserable; look ill and exhausted; have a wretched mien: *I don't know what the news was, but Frank looks like death warmed over*

◁**look like ten pounds of shit in a five-pound bag**▷ *See* BLIVIT

look see *v phr* by 1930s To look; have a look: *I'm dropping down to look see*—Raymond Chandler [the same redundancy was used by Ben Jonson in *Volpone* (1605): *Look, see these petulant things*]

a **look-see** *n phr* by 1883 A look; an inspection: *Let's have a look-see at our friend*—Ellery Queen/ *I stopped in at Jerry's for a lager and a look-see*—Billy Rose

loon *See* CRAZY AS A LOON

loony or **looney** or **luny 1** *adj* by 1853 Crazy; =NUTTY: . . . *you looney punk*—Ira Wolfert/ *"I think, sir, he's a little luny," replied Ginger Nut, with a grin*—Herman Melville **2** *n* (also **loon** or **loonball**) by 1884: . . . *the inspired looney who hated killing*—Billy Rose/ . . . *would have shown up in a Mel Brooks epic had that loonball thought of it first*—Toronto Life [probably fr both *lunatic* and *crazy as a loon* (found by 1845)]

loony bin *n phr* by 1919 A mental hospital; =NUTHOUSE: . . . *that fugitive from a loony-bin*—Arthur Kober/ *So how come I felt like a loony in a loony-bin?*—Esquire

loony-tune or **loony-tunes** (Variations: **looney** may replace **loony**; **toon** may replace **tune**) **1** *n* by

1980s A crazy person; =NUT: *Jesus, what a loony tune*—Richard Merkin/ *Loony-tunes Dennis Hopper wires a city bus to blow up. . .* —Seventeen **2 modifier**: . . . *the loony-toon acting debut of writer Stephen King*—Flare/ *It's been kind of a looney-tunes week*—William Goldman [fr *Looney Tunes™*, a series of short cartoon-film comedies, a paraphrasing of Silly Symphonies, also short cartoon-film comedies]

loop *n sports by 1940s* An athletic league or conference: *the Big Ten loop*

See IN THE LOOP, KNOCK someone or something FOR A LOOP, OUT OF THE LOOP, THROW someone FOR A LOOP

looped or **looping** *adj by 1934* Drunk: *The end result is a looped group*—Hal Boyle/ *Was she drunk? Looping*—Irwin Shaw

looper *n baseball by 1937* A flyball hit between the infield and outfield

loopy or **loopy-loo** *adj by 1925* Crazy; silly; =NUTTY: . . . *that loopy guy whose handkerchief you cry into*—Raymond Chandler/ . . . *visually complemented the singer's loopy Balkan bop*—Rolling Stone/ . . . *even loopier bids for the few works in Wood's small mature oeuvre*—Time

loose 1 *adj 1950s cool talk* Relaxed; easy; =COOL: *No wonder you guys were really loose*—Rolling Stone/ *You are loose in the rush, misty and safe*—New York Magazine **2 adj** *by 1595* Sexually promiscuous

See ALL HELL BROKE LOOSE, HANG LOOSE, a SCREW LOOSE

loose as a goose 1 *adj phr 1950s cool talk* (also **loosey-goosey**) Very relaxed; perfectly easy; =COOL: *loose-as-a-goose. . . completely relaxed on the field*—Dickson Baseball Dictionary/ . . . *a big party place; people slept with each other, it was loosey-goosey*—New York Magazine **2 adj phr** *1950s hot rodders* Of a car engine, needing new bearings and other repairs [probably both fr the rhyme and the perception that a *goose* has *loose* bowels; first sense may be related to an earlier "weak, flimsy," with the notion of "loosely articulated," hence relaxed to the point of languor]

loose cannon *n phr by 1977* A person who is quite likely to cause damage; a wildly irresponsible person: *Haig is a loose cannon on a pitching deck*—Time/ *His detractors call him a loose cannon. . . who makes recommendations in public before consulting*—Washington Post

loose change *n phr by 1827* Money at hand and to spare; available money: *I wanted to help, but didn't have any loose change*

loose in the bean (or **upper story**) *adj phr by 1940s* Crazy; =NUTTY

loosen (or **loose**) **up** *v phr by 1911* To speak more freely; become loquacious; loosen one's tongue: *Fatigue and a drink or two loosened him up and he told us the whole story*/ *Debating Perot is a mistake. They will loose him up*—TV show Washington Week in Review

loot[1] *n jazz musicians about 1930* Money, esp a large amount of money: *Rich planters would come and spend some awful large amounts of loot*—Louis Armstrong/ *There's a lot of loot there, kiddo*—Lawrence Sanders

loot[2] *n by 1898* A lieutenant; =LIEUT

lop *n 1980s teenagers* A tedious, contemptible person; =DORK, JERK, NERD: *Lop: a dork*—Los Angeles Times [origin unknown]

lord **See** TIGHT

lose one's **ass** *v phr by 1960s* To be badly defeated; lose everything: . . . *we would have lost our ass if we had gone in the way Colin wanted*—Newsweek

lose one's **cookies** **See** SHOOT one's COOKIES

lose one's **cool** *v phr 1950s cool talk* To become angry or flustered; lose composure; =LOSE IT: *Easy, dude, don't lose your cool*

lose one's **gourd** *v phr by 1960s* To become insane; go crazy; =GO APE, FREAK OUT: *Have you lost your gourd?*—Pat Conroy [fr *gourd*, "head"]

lose it *v phr by 1990s* To become very distraught; lose control of oneself; suffer a kind of breakdown; =CRACK UP: . . . *told me to keep an eye on Dennis, that he looked like he was losing it*—Milwaukee Journal/ . . . *of being totally stressed out, of "losing it"*—Kansas City Star/ *Thieu was really tough, but that day he lost it. . . His spirit was broken*—Time [probably fr the notion of *losing one's grip* on reality]

lose one's **marbles** *v phr by 1920s* To become foolish, irrational, forgetful, etc, as if senile [fr an earlier phrase *let his marbles go with the monkey*, fr a story about a boy whose marbles were carried off by a monkey; *lose one's taw* (a choice playing marble), "go crazy," is found by 1902]

loser 1 *n students by early 1950s* (also **born loser**) A person or thing that fails, esp habitually; =BUST, DUD, LEMON, NONSTARTER **2** *v*: *I don't want them to think I'm losered out*—New York Times

lose sleep over something *v phr by 1942* To worry overmuch about something; be very anxious about something •Often in the negative: *Murray doesn't seem to have lost a lot of sleep over working without a strong black literary tradition to rely on*—New Republic/ *Do you lose sleep over your investments?*—American Idioms Dictionary

lose one's **wig** *v phr 1950s cool talk* =BLOW one's TOP

losing **See** someone CAN'T WIN FOR LOSING

losses **See** CUT one's LOSSES

lost **See** GET LOST

lot **See** ALL OVER THE LOT

lot louse *n phr circus by 1940s* A person who wanders and watches but does not spend money: *The men who never spend a dime to visit the sideshow are "lot lice" to her*—Joseph Mitchell

lot of weight **See** CARRY A LOT OF WEIGHT

a lot of white showing *n phr fr baseball by 1990s*: *"Yesterday Ron's response to something Alice said was 'A lot of white showing'." "That's a* baseball term. It means that you almost dropped the ball"—comic strip "Sally Forth"

See ICE CREAM CONE

lots of luck or **good luck** *interj* A rueful and ironic way of wishing someone success when it is obviously impossible: *Vance played a key part in negotiating the Camp David agreements on the Middle East, but lots of luck in getting him to say so*—Time/ *Looking for a lady loan shark? Good luck; mob jobs remain male turf*—Time [the first form is sometimes uttered in a jokey Asian way: "Rots of ruck"]

Lotus Land *See* LA-LA LAND

loud *adj* by 1849 Vulgar and gaudy in taste; garish: *Isn't his dress rather loud?*—Slang-Dic

See FOR CRYING OUT LOUD, READ someone LOUD AND CLEAR

loudmouth 1 *n* by 1934 A loud and constant talker, esp a braggart and self-appointed authority; =WINDBAG: *Maybe poking Loud Mouth in the kisseroo would solve everything*—D Decker **2** *v*: *Don't you loudmouth me!*

loud-talk *v* prison by about 1920 To provoke trouble by talking loudly about real or supposed violations of rules

louie *See* LOOEY

lounge around *v phr* by 1940s =LOLL AROUND: *What are you lounging around here for? Get to work!*

lounge lizard *n phr* by 1918 =LADIES' MAN [fr the notion that such a man *lounges,* frequents cocktail *lounges,* and is as colorful, indolent, and reptilian as a *lizard* in the sun]

louse *n* by 1633 An obnoxious and despicable person, esp one who is devious and undependable; =BASTARD, CRUMB: *We kicked the dirty louse out when he said that*

See LENS LOUSE, LOT LOUSE

louse up by 1938 **1** *v phr* To ruin or spill; botch; =BOLLIX UP: *Boy, you certainly loused that up*—John O'Hara **2** *v phr* To fail; =SCREW UP: *He'll get promoted next month if he doesn't louse up*

lousy 1 *adj* by 1690 Bad; nasty; =CRUMMY: *Crab was all she ever did. What a lousy sport*—Dorothy Parker/ . . . *yuh lousy boob*—Eugene O'Neill **2** *adv*: *I did pretty lousy on that test*—F Brown

lousy with *adj phr* by 1843 Well provided with; swarming with: *Everybody will come home lousy with cash*—Dashiell Hammett/ *That hotel was lousy with perverts*—JD Salinger

love *See* CALF LOVE, FOR THE LOVE OF PETE, PUPPY LOVE

a **love** *n phr* by 1841 Any notably decent, pleasant, generous person; =LIVING DOLL: *Be a love and bring me another drink*

love affair *n phr* by 1970s An attraction or affinity that is strong but not sexual: *The fishing industry. . . is well aware of the love affair anglers have with records*—Milwaukee Journal

lovebirds *n* by 1911 Lovers: . . . *the two lovebirds* —Raymond Chandler

love bug 1 *n phr* by 1937 An imagined insect whose bite causes one to fall in love **2** *n phr* by 1975 A notably decent, pleasant, generous person; =DOLL, LIVING DOLL, LOVE: . . . *but once you know her, she's a love bug*—Milwaukee Journal

love drug *n phr* 1960s students A drug thought to be an aphrodisiac, such as methaqualone

love handle 1 *n phr* by 1960s A bulge of fat at the side of the abdomen: . . . *when I have strapped the metal thing to my love handles*—George V Higgins **2** *modifier*: . . . *who come in rarely, and mostly for love-handle removal*—Village Voice

love-in *n* 1960s counterculture A gathering, esp of hippies, devoted to mutual love and understanding: *Tulsa. . . recently had its first love-in*—Jack Newfield

lovely *n* by 1940s An attractive woman: . . . *where flabby lovelies in polka-dot bikinis lobbed beach-balls around*—New York Magazine

love me, love my dog *sentence* by 1546 If you accept me, you must accept what belongs to me or comes with me: *Our stations are not for sale separate from the network. Our attitude is Love me, love my dog*—New Yorker

◁**love-muscle**▷ *n* by 1930s The penis

love nest *n phr* by 1930s A place where two can make love, esp adulterous love

lover *See* MOTHERFUCKER

lover-boy by 1940s **1** *n* A handsome man; matinee idol **2** *n* A womanizer; woman-chaser; =LADIES' MAN, CASANOVA, STUD

◁**lovesteak**▷ *n* 1980s students The penis; =COCK, DONG, DORK: *Playgirl always has men with big lovesteaks as their centerfolds*—UCLA Slang

love (or like) the sound of one's **own voice** *v phr* by 1960s To have a high opinion of one's self; enjoy self-esteem: *Clifford was a man who clearly loved the sound of his own voice*—Nation

lovey-dovey by 1904 **1** *adj* Affectionate; amorous: *My, aren't they lovey-dovey?* **2** *n* Affection; friendship: . . . *a reign of peace, prosperity, and lovey-dovey*—H L Mencken **3** *n* A wife, mistress, sweetheart, etc: . . . *their foreign lovey-doveys*—D Fairbairn

loving *See* EVER-LOVING, MOTHERFUCKING

low 1 *adj* by 1744 Sad; melancholy: *I was so. . . low and depressed*—Bill New Yorke **2** *n* 1960s narcotics A bad reaction to a narcotic; =BUMMER

See GULLY-LOW, KEEP A LOW PROFILE, LAY LOW

low-ball *v* To report as lower; reduce: *Had Feldstein deliberately low-balled the original numbers?*—Newsweek/ *But he apparently lowballed the amount of money he gave Medlar*—Milwaukee Journal

low-belly strippers *n phr* gambling about 1960 Marked playing cards; a marked deck

low blow *n phr* by 1940s An unfair and malicious stroke; =CHEAP SHOT: *"They'd be rendered mute if they couldn't use sports analogies." "Low blow, Alice"* [fr the illegal blow below the belt in boxing]

low-bridge *v* baseball by 1937 To pitch so near the

batter that he has to lean sharply back to avoid the ball: *Joe Carter was then low-bridged by another pitch before striking out*—Milwaukee Journal

lowbrow 1 *n about 1902* A person lacking education and refinement; an ignorant lout **2** *adj*: *What are you always pulling that lowbrow stuff for?*—P Marks [said to have been coined by the humorist Will Irwin]

low camp *n phr by 1960s* Entertainment or art characterized by very broad and vulgar features: *Low camp. . . would mean doing it with winks and leers at the audience, in jeering collusion*—John Simon

low-down 1 *adj by 1888* Vulgar; despicable; vile: *a dirty low-down trick* **2** *adj* jazz musicians by about 1900 Intense and insinuating, in the blues style: *. . . a babe with a low-down voice*—Mickey Spillane *See* a DIRTY SHAME

the lowdown *n phr by 1915* The truth; the authentic facts: *. . . eager to get the low-down on new aircraft*—Philadelphia Bulletin

low-down dirty shame *See* a DIRTY SHAME

lower the boom *by 1940s* **1** *v phr* To deliver a knockout punch: *. . . when he got his Irish up, Clancy lowered the boom*—popular song **2** *v phr* To punish; exact obedience and docility: *. . . if we lower the boom on every nonconformist in society*—Arthur Schlesinger/ *My patience evaporated and I lowered the boom on them*—S J Perelman

low-fi or **low fi 1** *n* or *n phr by 1950s* Record- or tape-playing or other equipment that reproduces sound rather badly **2** *modifier*: *a room full of low-fi components* [based on *hi-fi*]

low five 1 *n phr by 1980s* A greeting or gesture of approval made by slapping hands at about waist level: *San Diego hand-slapping, high fives, low fives*—Newsweek **2** *v phr* =GIVE someone FIVE

low-key 1 *v by 1960* To treat with little emphasis; =PLAY DOWN: *They were low-keying it because of the controversy*—Thomas H Kean **2** *adj by 1965* Quiet; modest; unassertive: *She is low-key but is happy to talk about things that Wayans doesn't do for himself. . .* —USExpress [in second sense, a technical term in photography, "with tones lying in the gray scale," found by 1907]

low-life 1 *adj by 1794*: *. . . fancies himself in love with the raucous, lowlife Doreen*—New Yorker **2** *n by 1909* A person of reprehensible habits; =BUM

low-octane *adj by 1990s* Feeble; ineffectual; low-powered: *The songs earned the obligatory pan from Rolling Stone: "low-octane operatic drivel"*—Time

low pitch *n phr* hawkers by 1940s A street display set on the sidewalk or pavement

low profile 1 *n phr by 1960s* Inconspicuousness; recessiveness; modesty: *He thought he'd do better with a low profile the first year or so* **2** *adj*: *a low-profile discreetness See* KEEP A LOW PROFILE

low-rent or **low-end** *adj* Cheap; second-rate; inferior: *. . . and from that low-rent lunch at the Century Plaza*—Dan Jenkins/ *Plug themselves into*

some low-rent section of the brain. Some dud bit of the brain—Martin Amis/ *I'm having trouble deciding whether he's classically Rabelaisian or just low-end*—New Yorker

low rent *n phr 1960s students* A sexually promiscuous woman; =PUSHOVER

low ride *adj phr* southern California by 1950s Socially inferior; vulgar; =TRASHY: *For teenagers any mixing with the Indians or low ride Mexicans down in the valley is slumming*—Time

low rider southern California by 1950s **1** *n phr* A person who drives a car with a radically lowered suspension **2** *n phr* A car with a lowered suspension **3** *n phr* A motorcyclist, esp one who rides a customized motorcycle with the handlebars very high **4** *n phr* A rough young man from a black ghetto: *A group of low riders from Watts assembled on the basketball court*—Eldridge Cleaver/ *There are what the blacks call low riders, these people who run around pushing their weight around*—Lewis S Nelson [extended fr the ghetto style, among blacks and Chicanos, of the cool young man who wished, according to Calvin Trillin, "to *lower* his car to within a few inches of the ground, make it as beautiful as he knows how. . . and drive it very slowly"]

lox *n by 1940s* Liquid oxygen, as a fuel [*LOX*, "liquid oxygen explosive," is found by 1923]

LSD *n 1960s narcotics* Lysergic acid diethylamide, a hallucinogenic drug; =ACID: *There is no rite of passage, such as smoking pot or tripping with LSD*—Trans-Action [found as a chemical abbreviation by 1947 in a Swiss journal]

L7 1 *n black by 1950s* An unpopular misfit; =SQUARE **2** *adj*: *an uncool L7 wimp* [fr the square visual pattern made by the joining of the capital *L* and the number 7]

LT[1] (pronounced as separate letters) *n college students by 1970s* Living together: *. . . the subject of living together ("LT" in college lingo)*—Washington Post

LT[2] (pronounced as separate letters) *n by 1990s* Lieutenant; =LOO, LOOEY: *I still say there's something rocky in his bedroll, LT*—Carsten Stroud

lube 1 *n* (also **lube job**) *by 1950s* A lubrication; grease job; a greasing: *. . . accused the Packers. . . of giving their jerseys a lube job to prevent offensive linemen from holding*—Milwaukee Journal **2** *modifier*: *lube rack* **3** *n students* (also **lubricant**) Butter [last sense from the likening of *butter* and *grease*]

lubricated *adj by 1927* Drunk; =OILED

luck *interj by 1980s* A wish that one have good lick: *"Luck," I said. "You too," Conway said. . .*—Robert B Parker *See* BREAK LUCK, IN LUCK, OUT OF LUCK, POT LUCK, SHIT OUT OF LUCK

luck into *v phr by 1950s* To get something by luck: *Alain lucked into a goldmine with an idea for a magazine*—New York Times

the luck of the draw *n phr by 1967* The way fortune would have it; =THAT'S THE WAY THE BALL BOUNCES

luck out 1 *v phr* WWII Army To be very unlucky; be doomed **2** *v phr* by 1954 To be lucky; get something by good luck: *. . . that he will. . . luck out after his search and create operation*—Commonweal [one of the slang expressions that can mean opposite things]

luck up *v phr* by 1954 To become lucky: *Before I lucked up*—Louis Armstrong

lucky break *n phr* by 1938 A stroke of good luck; =HIT: *Finding the guy was sure a lucky break*

lucky stiff (or **dog)** *n phr* first form by 1914, variant by 1844 A fortunate person: *You've done it again, you lucky stiff*

lucre *See* FILTHY LUCRE

lude or **'lude** *n* 1960s narcotics Quaalude™, a depressant drug; any methaqualone capsule or pill: *Only this year "ludes" (Quaaludes or "downs") were the hot sellers*—Judy Klemesrud/ *Dropping the Last 'Lude*—Time

luded out *adj phr* 1960s narcotics Intoxicated with depressants, esp Quaalude™: *The folks who use it are usually too luded out or preoccupied*—Playboy

luff *See* FIRST LUFF

lug 1 *n* by 1924 A stupid man; dull fellow; =BOZO: *Those lugs in the band would begin to kid me about it*—John O'Hara/ *. . . a simple-minded lug like Moose Malloy*—Raymond Chandler **2** *n* by 1934 A demand for money, esp bribe or protection money: *. . . a captain of detectives who was collecting the lug from the gambling houses*—Westbrook Pegler **3** *v* To solicit money; borrow [origins and derivations uncertain; the first sense is probably fr *lug*, "something heavy and clumsy," attested in the 16th century and retained in several English dialects where it is used derogatorily of persons]
See DROP THE LUG ON someone

LUG (LUHG) *n* by 1990s: *At colleges as diverse as Smith and Ohio State, for example, episodic lesbians are numerous and open enough to have spawned an acronym: LUG, short for Lesbian Until Graduation*—Glamour

lugger *n* horse-racing by 1951 A racehorse that bears into or away from the inner rail: *. . . a rapid lugger*—A J Liebling

lug in *v phr* horse-racing by 1951 To bear into the inner rail of a racetrack

lug out *v phr* horse-racing by 1951 To bear away from the inner rail of a racetrack

lulu¹ *n* by 1886 A person or thing that is remarkable, wonderful, superior, etc; =DARB, HUMDINGER, PISSER: *He said the aquarium was a lulu*—A J Liebling/ *Burrows was permitted his own bower, and it was a lulu*—S J Perelman [origin unknown; earlier *looly*, "beautiful girl," is attested; perhaps fr the cowboy term *loo loo*, "a winning hand," explained as a hand invented by local people in order to win a game from a stranger "for the good of the *loo*," where *loo* means "party, set, community"; this sense of *loo* is related to the popular 18th-century card game of the same name, fr *lanterloo* fr French *lanterlu*, a nonsense phrase in the refrain of a song]

lulu² *n* New York State by 1966 A legislator's perquisite of goods, services, or a stipend "in lieu" of basic legitimate compensation: *decision to abandon the "lulus" of legislators*—New York Times/ *He may also get a "lulu" (a stipend in lieu of expenses)*—Village Voice [fr *lieu*, influenced by *lulu¹*]

LULU *n phr* by 1989 An undesirable use of land [acronym of *locally undesirable land use*]

lumber 1 *n* baseball by 1940s A bat **2** *v* by 1845 To take advantage of someone; make someone a scapegoat ●Chiefly British: *He was totally lumbered. It was a terrible travesty*—Washingtonian [second sense fr *lumber*, "to fill up or obstruct with lumber," found by 1642]

lumber facial *n phr* 1990s hockey A blow to the face with a hockey stick: *That cementhead gave him a lumber facial, but the ref didn't call it*—Los Angeles Times

lumberman *n* hoboes by 1940s A beggar with a crutch: *The "lumbermen" can beg $30 a day with ease*—W J Slocum

lummox or **lummux** *n* by 1841 A stupid, clumsy person; =KLUTZ [fr British dialect fr *lummock*, "lump"]

lump 1 *n* hoboes by 1912 A packet of food: *"Lumps". . . are possible at any time during the day*—HF Kane **2** *n* by 1597 A dull, stupid person; =CLOD, KLUTZ: *What an unspeakable lump I was*—Max Shulman

lumper *n* truckers by 1940s A person who loads and unloads trucks: *"Lumpers" unload the trailer for him*—Smithsonian [found by 1796 as "those who load and unload ships"]

lump it *v phr* by 1791 To accept or swallow something one does not like: *It was a lousy deal, but I just had to lump it* [fr earlier sense of *lump*, "dislike, reject," probably related to the sense "strike, thrash"]
See LUMPS, LIKE IT OR LUMP IT

lumps *n* by 1935 Severe treatment; punishment; a beating: *Somebody was out to give him his lumps*—J Roeburt [ultimately fr late–1700s *lump*, "beat, thrash"]
See GET one's LUMPS, TAKE one's LUMPS

lumpy *adj* cool talk Badly played

lunatic fringe *n phr* by 1913 The radical and irresponsible sector of a group or party: *The party has been turned over to its lunatic fringe* [apparently coined by Theodore Roosevelt in *History as Literature*]

lunch 1960s students (also **lunching** or **lunchy**) **1** *adj* Stupid; ineffectual; useless: *A lunch guy might as well be out to lunch for all the good he's doing*—R Scott **2** *adj* Old-fashioned; passé; out of style: *That bow tie is stone lunchy*
See EAT someone's LUNCH, OUT TO LUNCH, SHOOT one's COOKIES

lunchbox or **lunchsack** *n* 1960s students A confused or ignorant person; someone out of touch with reality; =DITZO

lunch-bucket or **lunch-pail** by 1990s **1** *modifier* Working-class; blue-collar; proletarian and ordinary: *Phillips. . . is a regular commentator on NPR, that bastion of lunch-bucket values*—New Republic/ *. . . the fight. . . made Tomashek a lunch pail hero*—Milwaukee Journal/ *. . . hard worker, good player, overlooked contributor. A lunch-pail guy*—Milwaukee Journal **2 modifier** Favoring the political interests of the working class: *Traditional lunch-pail liberals and progressive Democrats are beginning to question the vitality of their own programs*—New York Times

lunch-hooks *n* by 1896 The hands; fingers; =MEATHOOKS: *. . . get a set of predatory lunch-hooks into him*—Gilbert Milstein

lunch (or fatten) up on *v phr* by 1980 To profit from; take great advantage of: *They proceeded to lunch up on a carnival of bad pitching and sloppy fielding*

lunger (LUNG ər) *n* by 1893 A person with tuberculosis: *. . . at once a lunger and lifer*—J Black
See ONE-LUNGER

◁**lung-hammock**▷ *n* by 1940s A brassiere

◁**lungs**▷ *n* A woman's breasts; =BOOBS, KNOCKERS: *. . . pushed a whole blouse full of lungs against my arm*—Dan Jenkins/ *She has a great pair of lungs*—Lawrence Sanders

lunk 1 *n* by 1867 A stupid person; =LUNKHEAD: *Lunks, Hunks and Arkifacts*—Time/ *. . . a character whom Tristan describes as "a big lunk"*—Village Voice **2 modifier**: *. . . four books about a lunk hero Carlo Reinhart*—Time

lunker 1 *n* by 1920 A very big fish, often the apocryphal one that got away: *In the ocean there's nothing but lunkers*—New York Times **2** *n* by 1970s An old car; =CLUNKER, HEAP: *. . . in old cars known as clunkers, lunkers, winter rats*—New York Times

lunkhead *n* by 1852 A stupid person; =BOOB, DOPE, LUNK: *. . . a bulky, duckfooted lunkhead*—John Cheever/ *Tenors have been traditionally stereotyped as vain lunkheads*—Newsweek

lunky *adj* by 1940s Stupid: *. . . conflict between paternal authority and lunky adolescent waywardness*—Time

lurk 1 *v* 1960s black To ride about looking for sex partners; =CRUISE: *Me and the boys are going lurken' tonight to pick up some foxy broads*—Current Slang **2** *v* computer by 1990s: *Lurk: To log onto a bulletin board and read the discussion without participating or making your presence known*—Los Angeles Times

lurker 1 *n* computer by 1990s A person who "lurks": *. . . according to David Brooks, a pro-gun control lurker*—New York Times/ *You just sneak around and listen without revealing your presence, thus becoming what internauts pejoratively call a lurker*—New Republic **2** *n* computer by 1970s A person who enters a computer system illegally; an uninvited computer eavesdropper: *Ian had found a lurker in the system*—Toronto Life

luscious *adj* by 1748 Very attractive; =DISHY, SEXY, ZOFTIG

lush 1 *n* by 1890 A drunkard; an alcoholic; =DIPSO: *She is still plastered, the little lush*—John O'Hara/ *The father was by no means a lush, but the son carried temperance to an extreme*—Joseph Mitchell **2** *v*: *. . . lushing, stowing wine into our faces*—Henry Seidel Canby [origin unknown; probably related to *lush*, "liquor, booze," which is found by 1790 and may be fr Romany or Sehlta (tinkers' jargon)]

lushed or **lushed up** *adj* or *adj phr* by 1926 Drunk

lusher *n* by 1895 A drunkard: *City editors are roughnecks and urbane gentlemen, lushers and Puritans*—Stanley Walker

lush roller (or worker) *n phr* underworld by 1930s A thief who specializes in robbing helpless drunks: *A lush roller rolls lushes*—A J Liebling *. . . when a. . . lush worker picks the pocket of a sleeping drunk*—New York Times

luxo *adj* by 1970s Luxurious; =POSH: *Sapporo/ Challenger luxo-coupe*—Westworld

luxobarge or **luxomobile** *n* by 1990s A large, showy car; =BOAT: *The era of the luxobarge has been scuttled*—Automotive Industries/ *Cadillac remains Nation's leading luxomobile*—New York Times

M

M 1 *n* narcotics by 1912 Morphine: *You've got to get M to get that tingle-tingle*—Nelson Algren **2** *n* 1960 narcotics Marijuana

ma'am *See* WHAM-BAM THANK YOU MA'AM

ma-and-pa *See* MOM-AND-POP

Ma Bell *n phr* by 1970s A wry nickname for the Bell Telephone system •Now of primarily historical use, since the communications monolith has been fragmented: *Ma Bell, for instance, is fair game to many*—American Scholar/ *The quality of some phone lines is often below what Ma Bell promised*—Fortune

mac¹ *n* by 1940s A mackintosh raincoat: *His simple dream of naked girls in wet macs* *See* MACK

mac² *n* by 1928 Man; fellow; =BUSTER, JACK •Used in direct address, often with a mildly hostile intent: *Take it easy, mac* [fr the many surnames beginning *Mac* or *Mc*]

mac³ *v* (also **mac out**) students by 1980s To eat; gorge: *Let's go mac*—UCLA Slang/ *He really macked out last night*—UCLA Slang [fr the McDonald's™ chain of fast-food restaurants]

macaroni 1 *n* loggers by 1940s Sawdust **2** *n* by 1980s A gangster; mafioso: *. . . the macaronis are shooting each other*—Elmore Leonard [*macaroni*, "an Italian," is found by 1845]

MacGuffin or **McGuffin** *n* by 1930s A plot or movie device that raises a seemingly crucial question in the minds of the audience, but may well be a cunning deception: *Traditionally in British scandals the MacGuffin was,. . . what if an errant minister should be blackmailed by a foreign power?*—Vanity Fair/ *. . . the writers wanted a MacGuffin which would set up a series of absurd rules for us*—New York Times/ *You still haven't told me what the McGuffin is. Why were the government and Mr D so interested. . .* —Lawrence Sanders [first used by the director Alfred Hitchcock, and perhaps suggested by *McGuffin*, "a gift that is not to be opened until Christmas," hence something tantalizing, found by 1925]

macher (MAH kər, -khər) *n* by 1909 An active, usu self-important person; =BIG SHOT, OPERATOR: *the Muse to numerous folk-rock machers*—New Yorker/ *Stan had made Mel a big macher*—Scott Turow [fr Yiddish, literally "maker, doer"]

machinery 1 *n* narcotics by 1940s A drug user's paraphernalia; =ARTILLERY **2** *n* by 1980s The male genitals: *. . . you could see the bulge of his machinery there at the crotch*—Ed McBain

machisma (mah CHIZ mə) *n* by 1970s The female counterpart of machismo: *Machisma, Women, and Daring*—Grace Lichtenstein

machismo (mah CHIZ moh) *n* by 1960s Aggressive masculinity; blatant virility: *. . . machismo, a he-man complex*—Time/ *with Chicago machismo, also universal adolescent horniness*—Harper's [fr Spanish]

macho (MAH choh) by 1970s **1** *n* An aggressively masculine man; =HE-MAN **2** *n* Aggressive maleness; =MACHISMO: *It was not just a question of executive macho*—New York Magazine **3** *adj*: *. . . a typical macho Mailerism*—Pauline Kael/ *. . . list of macho jobs as long as a master sergeant's sleeve of hash marks*—Nation [fr Spanish]

macho it out *v phr* by 1970s To behave with masculine courage and stamina; =TOUGH IT OUT: *I machoed it out all the way into the men's room before I threw up*—Time

Machree *See* MOTHER MACHREE

mack *n* by 1887 A pimp; =MACKMAN: *. . . copped you a mack*—Donald Goines [fr 15th-century *mackerel*, "pimp," fr Old French *macquerel*, perhaps related to Dutch *makelaar*, "trade, traffic," hence ultimately to *make, macher* etc] *See* MAC

mackerel *See* HOLY CATS

macking 1990s teenagers **1** *n* Heavy petting and other sex play: *Mackin' Making Out*—People Weekly **2** *n* To drive slowly and watchfully in the streets, walk about vigilantly in bars and parties, etc, looking for a sex partner; =CRUISE [perhaps related to *mack*, "pimp"]

mackman 1 *n* black by 1950s A pimp; =MACK: *. . . went back to. . . that young mackman?*— C Cooper *. . . a mere player masquerading as a mack-man*—Village Voice **2** *modifier*: *. . . for all his jackass mackman shit*—Village Voice

Mack truck *n phr* by 1980s Something very powerful; =SIX-HUNDRED-POUND GORILLA: *Marilyn Horne, the greatest coloratura mezzo of our time, is a Mack truck of a voice with awesome flexibility*—New York Times [fr the trademark of a line of heavy trucks]

mac on something *v phr* 1980s students To eat; =CHOW, SCOFF: *We'll mac on hamburgers and fries tonight*—UCLA Slang *See* MAC³

mad 1 *adj* *by 1400s* Angry **2** *adj* *1950s bop & cool talk* Excellent; exciting; =CRAZY
> *See* LIKE MAD

-mad *combining word* Devoted to, manic over, obsessed with what is indicated: *money-mad/ computer-mad/ horse-mad*

mad about someone or something *adj phr by 1744* =CRAZY ABOUT: *Aren't you just mad about her new book?*

madam or **madame** *n by 1871* The female manager or owner of a brothel

mad as a wet hen *adj phr by 1823* Very angry; infuriated; =PISSED OFF: *When he got the letter he was mad as a wet hen*

mad-dog *v 1990s street talk* To stare at someone steadily and provocatively; stare someone down: *Torres thought the man had challenged or "mad-dogged" him*—MM/ *He kept his stare on Hawk. It was what the gang kids called mad-dogging*—Robert B Parker

made *n black by 1950s* Straightened hair; a head of straightened hair
> *See* HAVE something CINCHED, TAILOR-MADE

be **made** *v phr by 1950s* =be HAD

made for someone *adj phr* Exactly fitted to one's desires, looks, etc: *Mr and Mrs Smith were not exactly made for each other*—American Idioms Dictionary

made man (or **guy**) *n phr by 1960s* A man who has been initiated into the Mafia: *He was a mob hanger-on, but not a made man/ . . . a made guy, one of them*—Elmore Leonard

made of money *adj phr by 1849* Very rich; =LOADED: *Well off? Why the guy's made of money*

Madison Avenue or **Mad Ave 1** *n phr by 1950s* The values, behavior, business, milieu, etc, of advertising and public relations **2** *modifier*: *Madison Avenue hype*

mad money *by 1922* **1** *n phr* Money carried by a woman with which to pay her way home if her escort becomes offensive **2** *n phr* Money saved by a woman against the time when she wants to make an impulsive or therapeutic purchase

Mae West *n phr 1930s British aviators* A bulky life preserver [fr the generous bosom of the actress]

mafia *n by 1960s* A group prominent in and suspected of controlling some organization, institution, etc: *Chernenko was a member of the Brezhnev mafia in the Politburo*—National Public Radio [fr Italian *mafia* or *maffia*, designating the Sicilian secret society supposed to be deeply involved in organized crime both in Italy and the US; the Italian word derives fr Old French *mafler*, "to gluttonize, devour," perhaps cognate with German *maffelen*, "chew"]
> *See* DIXIE MAFIA

mag 1 *n by 1801* A magazine **2** *n by 1920* A magneto **3** *n by 1960s* A car wheel made of a magnesium alloy **4** *v by 1990s* To search someone with a magnetometer device: *. . . no unscheduled stops and limited contact with people who haven't been magged*—Milwaukee Journal

magazine *See* SKIN MAGAZINE

Maggie or **maggie** *n underworld by 1940s* A semi-automatic pistol [perhaps fr the fact that bullets are put into a *magazine,* which fits into the pistol]

Maggie's drawers *n phr Army by WWII* A blatant red flag waved on a military firing range when the target is missed completely

maggot *n black by 1980s* A white person; =GRAY, OFAY: *Maggot: street slang for anyone white*—Carsten Stroud
> *See* ENOUGH TO GAG A MAGGOT

magic *See* TRAGIC MAGIC

magic bullet *n phr by 1960s* A miraculous remedy for some social, economic, etc, ill: *We know no one chancellor has a magic bullet to turn the school system around*—New York Times [fr the name given in 1910 to salvarsan, formerly a trademark, discovered and proposed by the bacteriologist Paul Ehrlich as a cure for syphilis]

magnum-force *adj* Very powerful: *. . . one of Thomas Hearns's magnum-force punches* [fr the powerful *Magnum* revolver (a trademark since 1935)]

magoo (mə Gōō) *show business by 1940s* **1** *n* Custard pie, esp as used in comic stage and movie scenes **2** *n* An important person; =BIG SHOT: *Darryl Zanuck, chief magoo of the studio*—T M Pryor

mahoff *n Philadelphia by 1940s* An important person; personage; =BIG SHOT, MACHER: *Ogden-Allied sent a mahoff down from the corporate office in New York yesterday to look into the case*—Philadelphia Inquirer/ *He used to be a big marketing mahoff at Dorney Park*—Philadelphia Inquirer [origin unknown]

maiden *n horse-racing by 1880* A racehorse, regardless of sex, that has never won a race; =BUG

mail *See* AIRMAIL, CARRY THE MAIL, GREENMAIL, JUNK MAIL

mail drop *n phr by 1959* A place or address where one can receive mail clandestinely

main *adj black by 1960s* Favorite; most admired; beloved: *This is my main nigger, my number one nigger*—Claude Brown
> *See* MAINLINE

main brace *See* SPLICE THE MAIN BRACE

main drag (or **stem**) *n phr entry form by 1851, variant by 1900* The major street of a town or city
> •**Main stem** was used of a railroad line by 1832: *We begged together on the "main drag"*—Jack London/ *We sifted along the main stem*—Raymond Chandler

mainline or **main 1** *v narcotics by 1930s* To inject narcotics into a blood vessel; =SHOOT UP: *. . . after mainlining heroin the night before*—New York Post **2** *v* To take or administer stimulants or depressants of various sorts: *. . . because the economy was mainlining bigger and bigger fixes of inflation*—Philadelphia/ *LA and the San Joaquin valley mainlined northern California water and couldn't wait for the next fix*—New York Times

main line 1 *n phr* (also **Main Line**) *by 1930s* The wealthy and fashionable elements of a place; high society and its area of residence, esp that of Philadelphia: . . . *so young and handsome and so popular with the Main Line*—Stephen Longstreet **2** *n phr* narcotics by 1920s A vein in the arm, the median vein, into which narcotics may be injected [first sense fr the railroad between Philadelphia and the wealthy suburbs to the west]

main man 1 *n phr* black by 1960s One's best friend: *Lou Reed, he my main man*—Aquarian **2** *n phr* by 1990s The most important player, person, etc: . . . *the team's main man*—New Yorker

main queen 1 *n phr* by 1950s One's steady girl-friend **2** *n phr* homosexuals A male homosexual who takes the passive role, esp one much sought after by other homosexuals

main squeeze 1 *n phr* by 1896 The most important person; =BIG ENCHILADA, BOSS: *Vance seems to be the main squeeze*—Dashiell Hammett **2** *n phr* by 1980 One's sweetheart, lover, etc: . . . *which center on his main squeeze, a girl in his Shakespeare class*—Publishers Weekly

mainstream *adj* 1980s students Conventional; materialistic: *It's a mainstream movie; don't waste your time*—College Slang 101

maintain a low profile *See* KEEP A LOW PROFILE

maisie *See* S AND M

major *adj* by 1990s Impressive; weighty; =IMPORTANT, SERIOUS: *The TV pictures of the smoking problem showed over-accessorized secretaries with major hair smoking in dark doorways of an office building*—Nation

major league *adv* by 1990s Very much; totally; =BIG TIME: *We've been major-league screwed. I just found out the trains are stopped*—New Yorker

major leaguer *n phr* A person of achievement; an expert; =HEAVY HITTER: *If Eric Valdez had gotten it on with Mrs Esteva, he was a major leaguer*—Robert B Parker

majorly *adv* by 1990s Very; extremely: *Both are majorly distraught over the wife/mommy's death*—Sassy/ *I remember once when I was majorly depressed. . .* —Douglas Coupland

make 1 *v* underworld by 1700 To rob; steal; =HEIST **2** *v* underworld & police by 1906 To recognize or identify; make an identification: *The dealer-suspect "made" (i e, correctly identified) one of the staked-out 53 cars*—New York Times/ *He made me the minute he saw me*—John O'Hara **3** *n*: *The woman gave us a make on the guy who slugged her* **4** *v* by 1912 To understand; grasp; =DIG: *I don't make you, kid. . . What did the boy do?*—H Witwer **5** *v* by 1460 To bring fame, success, wealth, etc: *That one show made her* ◁**6**▷ *v* by 1918 To do the sex act with; =LAY, SCREW: *Not only is the King in love with me, but the Queen tried to make me too*—Newsweek/ . . . *in the sense of "making" handsome men*—Faubion Bowers ◁**7**▷ *n* by 1918 A person regarded merely as a sex partner; =LAY: *an easy make* **8** *v* by 1624 To arrive at; =HIT: *We'll never make Padanaram before dark* **9** *v* by 1950s To defecate; =DUMP, SHIT **10** *v* by 1960s To initiate

one into the Mafia: . . . *the purpose of a particular meeting. . . had been to make us. . . "to incorporate individuals as new members of the family"*—American Speech **11** *v* (also **make up**) To shuffle playing cards: *Peter made the cards and handed them to Stern to deal*—Scott Turow

See EASY MAKE, ON THE MAKE, ON THE TAKE, PUT THE MAKE ON someone, **run a make**

make a believer out of someone *v phr* by 1960s To convince someone, esp by forceful or harsh means: *I never worried about it much, but that one wreck made a believer out of me*

make a big production (or **big deal**) **out of** something *v phr* by 1960s To overdo; overreact; overplan, etc; =MAKE A FEDERAL CASE OUT OF something: *All she wanted was a simple wedding, but he had to make a big production out of it*

make a bundle *v phr* by 1905 To acquire a lot of money; =CLEAN UP: *John really made a bundle on the deal*—American Idioms Dictionary

make a Federal case out of something *v phr* by 1950s To overemphasize the importance of something; exaggerate or overreact; =BLOW UP: *I merely bought a new car. . . so don't try to make a Federal case out of it*—S McNeil [popularized after being spoken by a judge in the 1959 movie *Anatomy of a Murder*]

make a hash of something *v phr* by 1735 To make a jumble of; mangle; botch: *The newspapers made a total hash of what I had said*

make a hit *v phr* by 1829 To be successful; be received with approval, gratitude, etc: *She made a hit with my family*

make a killing *v phr* by 1888 To get a large, quick profit; win hugely: *Where did he get all that money? Made a killing on the stock market, he says*

make a mess *v phr* by 1903 To defecate; =CRAP, SHIT: *I'm afraid the kid has made a mess in his pants*

make a mess of something *v phr* by 1862 To make a jumble of; mangle; botch; =MAKE A HASH OF something: *He gave it his best shot, but made a mess of it*

make a monkey out of someone *v phr* by 1900 To make someone seem stupid or inept; make a fool of someone: *Are you trying to make a monkey out of me?*—American Idioms Dictionary

make a move on someone *See* PUT A MOVE ON someone

make (or **get**) **an offer** one **can't refuse** *v phr* by 1960s To coerce or menace, esp with an ostensibly plausible offer: *"He's a businessman," the Don said blandly. "I'll make him an offer he can't refuse"*—Mario Puzo/ *The North Atlantic allies last week got an offer they couldn't brusquely refuse*—New York Times [popularized by Mario Puzo's 1969 novel *The Godfather* and the subsequent movie]

make an omelet *See* YOU CAN'T MAKE AN OMELET WITHOUT BREAKING EGGS

make a pass at someone *v phr* by 1928 To

make a sexual advance; =PROPOSITION, PUT A MOVE ON someone: *He got high one time and made a pass at her*—Raymond Chandler [fr early 1800s in the sense of "strike at, attack"]

make a pitch *v phr* by 1960s To make a persuasive case; advocate strongly •**Do a pitch** in the same sense is found by 1876: *The theatrical agent came in and made a pitch for her client*—American Idioms Dictionary

make a pit stop *v phr* by 1970s To urinate [fr the *pit stop* for refueling, etc, in a car race, found by 1932]

make a play for *v phr* by 1905 To attempt to get or seduce, esp by applied attractiveness: *He's making a play for that cute millionaire*

make a scene (or **a stink**) *v phr* entry form by 1804, variant by 1812 To exhibit anger, indignation, fiery temper, hysterics, etc, in a public outburst: *I asked her to be quiet and not make a scene/ Why don't these pay cable services make a public stink about the Time Inc-Manhattan Cable monopoly?*—Village Voice/ *"I never made a big stink about it," says Righetti*—Village Voice

make a score 1 *v phr* 1960s narcotics To buy narcotics; =SCORE: *... this Jewish cat looking to make a score*—New York Times 2 *v phr* gambling by 1950 To win a bet: *But I make scores and they keep me going for a while*—New York Post/ *... ran wild in the cabaret as soon as they made a big score*—Jimmy Cannon

make a splash *v phr* by 1820 To produce a strong and usu favorable impression; be very conspicuous: *That's the book that made such a big splash a couple of years ago*

make (or **have**) **a stab at** something *v phr* by 1895 To make an attempt; have a try: *I've never done this before, but I'll make a stab at it*

make one's (or **the**) **blood boil** *v phr* by 1859 To make one very angry; infuriate one: *... a devastating combination of logic, analysis, and case studies, makes the blood boil*—Fortune

make one's **bones** *v phr* by 1990s: *"In order to be a real mobster, you have to kill somebody," Matt said evenly. "They call it 'making your bone'"*—W E B Griffin

make book on something *v phr* by 1940s To bet on; offer odds on: *This time she really means it, and you can make book on that*

◁**make** one's **butt pucker**▷ *v phr* by 1990s To frighten one; =SCARE someone SHITLESS: *Some criminals have faces that'll make your butt pucker*—Denver radio talk show

make one's **day** *v phr* by 1909 To insure the pleasure and distinction of one's whole day: *Getting the notice of her selection really made her day: "Momma, if I tell you, you won't like it."... "So go ahead, make my day"*—comic strip "Momma" *See* NOT MAKE DEALS

not **make deals** *See* NOT MAKE DEALS

make for 1 *v phr* by 1633 =HEAD FOR 2 *v phr* by 1526 To encourage; promote: *This will make for renewed confidence*

make one's **getaway** *v phr* by 1893 To escape; flee; fly, esp from the scene of a crime: *The thugs made their getaway in a souped-up Sherman tank*

make good *v phr* by 1899 To succeed; do what one set out to do in career or life

make goo-goo eyes *v phr* by 1900 To look at someone longingly, lovingly, seductively, etc: *... make goo-goo eyes near a tropical lagoon*—People Weekly

make hamburger (or **hash** or **mincemeat**) **out of** someone or something *v phr* entry form by 1980s, mincemeat variant by 1708 To defeat definitively; trounce; =CLOBBER: *They made hamburger out of the wilting opposition* [make meat of, "to kill," is found by 1841]

make it 1 *v phr* by 1925 To succeed; =GO OVER: *The charts showed we had made it, and big* 2 *v phr* by 1940s To survive; live: *He's so sick, I don't think he'll make it* 3 *v phr* by 1885 To get to a particular goal or place: *He didn't quite make it to the john*

make it big *v phr* by 1960s To succeed extraordinarily well •*Big* in this adverbial sense is found by 1886

make it (or **things**) **hot for** someone *v phr* by 1830 To make things unpleasant for someone: *Maybe if we make it hot for them they'll leave*—American Idioms Dictionary/ *... citizens of obvious substance, who might make things hot for them*—New Yorker

make it snappy *v phr* by 1915 To hurry; go faster; act quickly; =GET THE LEAD OUT, SNAP TO IT

make it with someone 1950s cool talk ◁1▷ *v* To do the sex act with or to someone; =SCORE: *Man, don't think I didn't make it with her*—S Boal 2 *v phr* To succeed with someone: *Talking that way he'll never make it with the committee*

make kissy-face *v phr* by 1980s To purse the lips and imitate a kiss; give an "air kiss": *Rush guffaws, he blusters, he bats his eyes, he makes kissy-face*—Time

make like *v phr* by 1940s To pretend to be; imitate: *A cop picked it up and made like a bookie*—NY Confidential/ *Brewster's gonna make like a canary*—Hannibal & Boris [fr Yiddish *makh vi*]

make mincemeat out of someone or something *See* MAKE HAMBURGER OUT OF someone or something

make money hand over fist *v phr* by 1888 To earn a large income; prosper hugely; =COIN MONEY •*Hand over fist* used about winning money by 1833

make one's **move** *v phr* by 1970s To take a first and crucial action, esp one that will start a chain of reactions: *The cops are just waiting for the guy to make his move* [probably fr sports, where opponents watch the person with the ball to see where he moves]

make my day *sentence* by 1971 Go ahead and do what you appear to threaten, so that I can trounce you and have a successful day: *"Make my day" is much used in the New York subway system, where* *life is raw and tempers are short*—Mary McGrory [popularized by the movie star Clint Eastwood, who used the line in one of his *Dirty Harry* police thrillers]

make nice *v phr by 1970s* To pet; cosset, caress: *Public officials. . . make nice to politicians they cannot stand. . . because they need their goodwill*—New York Times [perhaps fr Yiddish syntax]

make (or **have**) **no bones about 1** *v phr by 1548* To be entirely candid about; to be open about: *They make no bones about what they're going to do*—Washington Post **2** *v phr* To show or feel no doubt or hesitation about: *This spirited Labrador. . . had no bones about venturing out*—Milwaukee Journal [origin unknown; the form *find no bones,* found by 1459, may indicate that the reference is to bones in soup or stew, which would hinder the eating, hence hold the matter up]

make noises *by 1951* **1** *v phr* To express oneself; speak, esp initially and somewhat vaguely: *The Russians began to make noises about leaving* **2** *v phr* To talk insincerely or uselessly: *Do they mean it, or are they making noises?*

make no never mind *v phr black by 1940s* To make no difference; be insignificant: *Makes no never mind what he thinks, I'm going*

make out 1 *v phr by 1646* To understand; =DIG: *I couldn't quite make out what he was getting at* **2** *v phr by 1776* To succeed, esp by a slim margin; manage; =GET BY: *Did you make out OK with that new machine?* **3** *v phr* teenagers & students *by 1940s* To pet heavily; kiss and caress; =NECK: *. . . holding hands, slow dancing, making out to a point*—Playboy/ *. . . nostalgic for duck-tail haircuts, and making out in the back seat*—New York Magazine **4** *v phr by 1939* To succeed in sexual conquest

make-out artist 1 *n phr by 1940s* A man known for sexual success; =COCKSMAN, STUD: *The correct description for such a fellow is "make-out artist"*—New York Times **2** *n phr by 1950s* A man who tries to charm and impress his superiors

make out like a bandit *v phr by 1960s* To emerge very successfully; win everything: *You'd make out like a bandit*—George V Higgins/ *Some of the people who came on early were making out like bandits*—Sue Grafton/ *"How did you make out?" "Like a thief"*—Lawrence Sanders [based on Yiddish *bonditt,* "bandit; clever, resourceful fellow"]

make one's **pile** *v phr by 1975* To earn or win a fortune: *George made his pile investing in Microsoft*

make (or **score**) **points with** someone *v phr by 1960s* To be more highly prized with someone: *That's no way to make points with the voters these days*

maker *See* WAVE-MAKER, WIDOW-MAKER

make oneself **scarce** *v phr by 1749* To depart, esp hastily and under threat; =BUG OUT, SKEDADDLE: *Yonder comes the law; we better make ourselves scarce*

make something out of *v phr by 1940s* To interpret as a cause for combat; regard as a challenge or insult: *So you heard what I said, huh? You want to make something out of it?*—John McNulty

make something **stick** *v phr by 1932* To cause an accusation, assertion, etc, to be believed; validate or prove something: *They accused him of rape, but they'll never make it stick*

make the cheese more binding *v phr by 1960s* To make things more difficult or complicated; clutter or snarl the matter: *And just to make the cheese more binding, they're also sold through mail order*—Lawrence Sanders [a humorous pun based on the fact that cheese is thought to be *binding,* "constipating," and certain elements of a situation are also *binding,* "constraining"]

make the cut *v phr by 1980s fr sports* To survive an elimination, when a team or group is being chosen: *. . . Holly Hunter, Rosie Perez and Anjelika Huston, none of whom even made the cut*—Milwaukee Journal

make the fur fly *v phr by 1834* To promote a lively conflict; stir things up: *When the Senator hears about this, he'll make the fur fly*

make the grade *by 1912* **1** *v phr* To succeed: *He made the grade as a lawyer* **2** *v phr* To meet certain standards: *His work just didn't make the grade* [perhaps fr a train's ability to climb up the *grade* or slope of the track]

make the rounds *v phr by 1970s* To be passed from person to person; circulate: *A theory about the cause is making the rounds now* [*go the rounds* in the same sense is found by 1669]

make the scene *1950s beat & cool talk* **1** *v phr* To arrive; appear: *I hope I can make the scene Saturday night*—American Idioms Dictionary **2** *v phr* To succeed; achieve something: *With this album they'll sure make the scene* **3** *v phr* To do; experience: *I think I'll make the political scene next*

make time *v phr by 1887* To go fast; travel at a good speed: *They really made time after they let the passengers off*

make time with someone *v phr by 1934* To succeed sexually with someone, esp to make or approach a rapid conquest: *He was making time with Ezra's girl*

make tracks *v phr by 1839* To depart; =CLEAR OUT, MAKE oneself SCARCE: *If you know what's good for you, make tracks right now*

makeup *n by 1821* The composition; constituents: *What's the makeup of that club?*

make up for lost time *v phr by 1774* To work, play, travel, etc, very fast to compensate for a slow start

make waves *v phr by 1962* To cause trouble; upset things: *What he said has made waves*—Milwaukee Journal/ *John Quinn had always been a team player who didn't make waves*—San Francisco/ *The case continues to make waves in the state*—New York Times [fr the joke in which a person just arrived in hell, and hearing beautiful serene singing, finds that it is being done by inmates standing in chin-high excrement and cautiously chanting "Don't make waves"]

make whoopee 1 *v phr by 1928* To have a very good time; =PARTY: *. . . 70 degrees and humidity 50 percent, which is when fleas make serious whoopee*—Los Angeles Times ◁**2**▷ *v phr* To copulate; =SCREW: *"What do you mean, done, Ethan?" "You know, made whoopee, for Christ's sake"*—Douglas Coupland

make with *v phr by 1939* To use; exercise: *The poor man's Bing Crosby is still making with the throat here in Chi*—John O'Hara [fr Yiddish *machen mit,* "swing or wave something about, brandish something"]

-making *combining word by 1970s* Causing what is indicated: *nervous-making/ puke-making/ shy-making/ sick-making*

the **makings** *n phr by 1613* The ingredients; what is necessary for: *He's young, but he's got the makings of a real pro*

makkes (MAW kuss or **MAH** kuss) *n by 1940s* Nothing; =BUBKES, DIDDLY, ZIP [fr Yiddish fr Hebrew *makot,* "plagues, blows, troubles"]

malarkey *by 1929* **1** *n* Lies and exaggerations; empty bombastic talk; =BALONEY, BULLSHIT: *Hollywood is in the business of manufacturing malarkey as well as movies*—Bob Thomas/ *That's a lot of malarkey*—Newsweek **2** *interj* =BULLSHIT [origin unknown]

male chauvinist pig or **porker 1** *n phr entry form by 1972, variant by 1990s* A man who believes in and proclaims the superiority of men over women; =MCP: *Is it all right to call a priest a male chauvinist pig?*—New York Times/ *And the men who ran the AVP were even worse oinking porkers. . .*—Buzz **2** *modifier*: *. . . male-chauvinist-pig-type man to the contrary notwithstanding*—New York Magazine/ *. . . the arrogant male chauve resident. . .*—Village Voice

male member *See* MEMBER

mallie or **mall rat** (MAW lee) *n* or *n phr first form by early 1980s, second by 1986* A person, esp a teenager, who frequents shopping malls for sociability, excitement, etc: *"Mallies" always hang around the pay telephone*—comic strip "Peanuts"/ *A mall rat is someone who is here every day*—Smithsonian

malling *n by late 1980s* The shopping and social activity of visiting a mall: *. . . everyone in South Florida decided to go malling*—Lawrence Sanders

mama 1 *n black by 1925* A sexually attractive or sexually available woman: *"Say, baby, you sportin' tonight?" "Yeah, Mama, if I could find somebody to sport with"*—Claude Brown **2** *n 1960s motorcyclists* A woman who belongs to a motorcycle gang: *If a girl wants to be a mama and "pull a train,". . . she'll be welcome at any Angel party*—Saturday Evening Post **3** *n homosexuals by 1970s* The passive partner of a homosexual couple

See RED-HOT MAMA, SWEET MAMA

mama-and-papa *See* MOM-AND-POP

mama's boy or **mammy boy** *n phr by 1896* A soft or effeminate boy or man; a male overly attached to his mother: *. . . the stale old mama's-boy-liberated-by-looney-lovely*—Judith Crist

◁**mammyrammer**▷ *See* MOTHERFUCKER

man 1 *interj by 1896* An exclamation of surprise, delight, emphasis, etc; =JEEZ, WOW: *Man! I almost missed it!* **2** *n by 1921* A dollar; =IRON MAN: *You oughta grab about 300 men*—H Witwer [in the first sense, the very similar *man alive* is found by 1839]

See ASS MAN, BACKDOOR MAN, BOX MAN, BUTTER-AND-EGG MAN, CANDY MAN, COMPANY MAN, CON MAN, DIRTY OLD MAN, FANCY MAN, FINGER MAN, FIRST MAN, FOUR-LETTER MAN, G-MAN, HAMMER-MAN, HATCHET MAN, HEIST MAN, HE-MAN, HIT MAN, HONEY MAN, HOOP-MAN, IRON MAN, JIGGER-MAN, JUICE MAN, LADIES' MAN, LEG MAN, MONDAY MAN, OUNCE MAN, PANMAN, PETE-MAN, PETER-MAN, POINT, POOR MAN'S something, ROD-MAN, SANDWICH MAN, SEE A MAN ABOUT A DOG, SHACK MAN, STRAIGHT MAN, SWEET MAN, TIT MAN, TOMMY MAN, TRIGGER MAN, VENT MAN, WHEEL MAN

the **man** or **the Man 1** *n phr by 1918* Any man in authority; =BOSS, HIS NIBS: *See the guy in front? That's the man* **2** *n phr 1960s narcotics & underworld* A police officer, detective, prison guard, etc; =the HEAT: *Careful, here's the man* **3** *n phr 1960s narcotics* A supplier of narcotics; =DEALER **4** *n phr black by 1963* A white man; the white establishment: *. . . a super nigger who spends his life trying to prove he's as good as the Man*—Saturday Review/ *That's what "the man" wants you to do. . . to riot, so he can shoot you down*—New Yorker

a **man about a dog** *See* SEE A MAN ABOUT A DOG

man-about-town *n by 1734* A sophisticated urban man and cynosure; boulevardier

manage *v by 1655* To cope satisfactorily; survive; =GET BY: *It's a lot to pay, but we'll manage*

mangy with *adj phr by 1940s* =LOUSY WITH

manhandle *v by 1865* To treat roughly; beat; =BANJAX, CLOBBER: *They manhandled him pretty thoroughly before they let him go*

Manhattan eel *n phr by 1980s* A condom; =CONEY ISLAND WHITEFISH [fr the fact that so very many of these are seen floating amongst the offal in New York Harbor]

Manhattan side *n phr bowling by 1940s* The right side of the bowling alley as one faces the pins [fr the location of Manhattan as one looks south along the East River]

manicure *v by 1922* To care for meticulously •The standard sense "care of the hands and fingernails," is found by 1889: *Dutch farmers' constant manicuring of the land has driven out numerous native plant and animal species*—New York Times/ *. . . the manicured playing fields of international finance*—John Connolly

mano a mano *n phr by 1970s* A hand-to-hand fight or duel: *Hemingway's subject. . . was the mano a mano between Spain's two leading matadors*—New York Times/ *. . . a literary mano a mano with some good books as weapons*—New York Times [fr Spanish, "hand-to-hand"]

man on (or in) the street 1 *n phr by 1830* The average person; the ordinary person; =JOE AVERAGE, JOHN Q CITIZEN 2 *modifier*: . . . *and some man-on-the-street TV commercials for post-convention use*—New York Magazine

man-sized or **man-size** *adj by 1934* Large; =HEFTY: *Crump bet man-sized money*—J Lilienthal

◁**man with a paper ass**▷ *n phr black by 1970s* A person whose ideas are not important; a trivial man; =LIGHTWEIGHT

many *See* ONE TOO MANY

map 1 *n by 1908* The face: *A funny look. . . spread over Kenney's crimson map*—H Witwer 2 *n gambling by 1950s* A bank check

maple *See* BIRDSEYE MAPLE

map out *v phr by 1853* To plan: *Let's map out what we're gonna do tomorrow*

maps *n 1950s cool musicians* Sheet music; written arrangements

◁**maracas**▷ *n by 1939* A woman's breasts; =BOOBS: *. . . gams and a pair of maracas that will haunt me in my dreams*—John O'Hara

marble-dome *n by 1940s* A stupid person; =BLOCKHEAD

marble orchard *n phr by 1929* A cemetery: *You'll get your names in this marble orchard soon enough*—James M Cain

marbles *See* GO FOR ALL THE MARBLES, GO FOR BROKE, HAVE ALL one's BUTTONS, LOSE one's MARBLES, MISSISSIPPI MARBLES

mare *See* RIDE SHANK'S MARE

marge 1 *n homosexuals by 1970s* The passive, "feminine" partner in a lesbian couple; =MAMA 2 *n by 1940s* Margarine

Mari *See* MARY

Maria *See* BLACK MARIA

◁**maricón**▷ (MAH rih kahn, MA-, -KOHN) *n by 1932* A male homosexual: *"This it is, maricón," snarled the Puerto Rican*—High Times [fr Spanish]

Marines *See* TELL IT TO THE MARINES

mark 1 *n by 1883* The target or victim of a swindle, esp one who is easily duped; =PATSY, SUCKER: *. . . not that he's more of a mark than other horse nuts*—J Lilienthal/ *. . . his "marks," as the gullible are called by a pitchman*—New York Times 2 *n carnival by 1940s* An outsider or member of the local community; =HOME GUARD: *Marks. . . aren't allowed in*—F Brown 3 *v teenagers by 1970s* To inform; =SQUEAL: *He swore he wouldn't mark if they caught him*
See EASY MARK, HASH MARK, TOE THE MARK, UP TO SCRATCH

marker 1 *n by 1887* =IOU: *He is willing to take Charley's marker for a million*—Damon Runyon 2 *n sports by 1940s* A point or score: *eight markers in the first period*

market *See* GRAY MARKET, MEAT MARKET, SLAVE MARKET

marks the spot *See* X MARKS THE SPOT

marmalade *n by 1950s* =MALARKEY

marquee *by late 1980s* 1 *adj* Famous and influen-tial; star; stellar: *Sawyer is likely to escalate demands from other marquee names*—New Yorker/ *When you play a marquee player like Shaquille O'Neal, if you block his shot, you want to let him know*—New York Times 2 *modifier* Publicity; =HYPE: *That Pasolini was offered these public forums suggests that there was a certain marquee value attached to his name*—New Republic [fr the important names featured on a theater *marquee*]

marriage *See* SHOTGUN WEDDING

marry *v by 1526* To join; bring together: *He tries to marry the Canadian producers with the foreign buyers*—Toronto Life

◁**marshmallow**▷ *n black by 1960s* A white person: *. . . an Oreo fronting for a "marshmallow"*—R Levine/ *Not bad for a kid whose mother was probably knocked up by a marshmallow*—James Lee Burke

marshmallow shoes or **marshmallows** *n phr* or *n by 1960s* Shoes with very thick white platform soles

martooni *n by 1950s* A martini cocktail [fr a spoonerized protestation like "I only had tee martoonis"]

Marx *See* HART, SCHAFFNER AND MARX

Mary 1 *n homosexuals by 1970s* A male homosexual who takes the passive, "feminine" role: *He passed two willowy-looking queers, Mary's who'd decided to settle for each other*—George V Higgins 2 *n (also **Mari**) 1960s narcotics* Marijuana

Mary Ann or **Mary Jane** *n phr 1920s narcotics* Marijuana or a marijuana cigarette

Mary Warner *n phr 1920s narcotics* Marijuana

mash 1 *n by 1920s* Love or a love affair: *. . . just another mash*—Louis Armstrong 2 *n by 1879* A lover, of either sex: *her latest big mash* 3 *v by 1882* To make a sexual advance to; =PROPOSITION: *I wouldn't try to mash anybody like you* 4 *v 1980s students* To neck, pet, etc; =MAKE OUT: *My blind date and I felt just a little uncomfortable when you guys started mashing in the backseat last night*—UCLA Slang [apparently fr Romany, "allure, entice," and so used in mid–1800s vaudeville by a Gypsy troupe]
See MISH-MASH

masher *n by 1875* A man who habitually makes sexual approaches to women; =LADY-KILLER, WOLF

mash note *n phr by 1880s* A very flattering letter, esp one proposing or offering sex: *He gets mash notes by the ton*—W R Burnett/ *. . . showered him with embroidered pillows, mash notes, and cigars*—Reader's Digest

massage 1 *v by 1924* To beat; drub; =ROUGH someone UP: *. . . caught and massaged with rubber hoses*—H F Pringle 2 *v by 1966* To handle, process, or manipulate data, esp computer data: *The results all depend on how you massage it*

massage someone's **ego** *v phr by 1980s* To soothe and flatter someone; =STROKE: *He felt all strong and confident after she massaged his ego at lunch*

massage parlor *n phr by 1970s* A place that provides sexual services under the guise of legitimate body massage; =RAP CLUB

master *See* RINGMASTER

masters *See* SLAVES AND MASTERS

mat *n Navy by 1950s* The floor; deck

See COLLISION MAT, CORKING MAT, GO TO THE MAT, ON THE MAT

match *See* the WHOLE SHOOTING MATCH

mate *See* DATE MATE

math *n students* Mathematics

matter *See* GRAY MATTER

Mau-Mau (MOU MOU) *v* (also **mau-mau** or **mao-mao**) *by 1970* To coerce with rough treatment; terrorize: *The pressure ladies half-successfully mao-maoed Communications Minister Francis Fox. . . to censure the offending shows*—Toronto Life/ *I've been a mayor for nine years and I've been Mau-Maued by the best*—Milwaukee Journal [fr the *Mau Maus,* a terrorist group in Kenya in the 1950s]

mavin or **mayvin** or **maven** (MAY vən) *n by 1960s* An expert; an authority; a connoisseur: *. . . growing clientele of pizza mavins*—L Goldberg/ *A real advertising mavin must have thought that up*—Leo Rosten [fr Yiddish fr Hebrew, "understanding"]

max 1 *adv by 1970s* At the most; at the highest limit: *I do three cars a week, max*—George V Higgins **2** *v college students by 1950s* To win; do the very best [fr *maximum*; in the second sense *max,* "the highest possible grade," is found by 1851]

See TO THE MAX

maxed *adj 1960s narcotics* Intoxicated with a narcotic; =STONED [perhaps related to *max,* "gin, brandy, liquor," found from 1811]

maxed out *adj phr by 1990s* Having reached a specified upper limit: *People have less money and are maxed out on their credit cards*—Nation

maxi *1960s* **1** *n* A below mid-calf or ankle-length skirt or coat **2** *n* The ankle-length depth of hemline: *Is the new length a midi or a maxi?*—Life **3** *adj*: *. . . long black pants under a maxi coat*—G Emerson [fr *maximum*]

max out 1 *v phr Army by 1970s* =MAX To make the best score, or one's best score **2** *v phr* To do or contribute the maximum possible amount: *. . . go to the people with the potential of, as they say in the business, "maxing out"*—Newsweek **3** *v phr 1970s college students* To go to sleep **4** *v phr by 1990s* To reach the highest possible point; peak: *It doesn't look to be a trend that's maxed-out*—Milwaukee Journal **5** *v phr by 1990s* To be used to the maximum: *There's been a great outpouring of affection. The phones have been maxed out*—Los Angeles Times/ *. . . teen angst is something that happens when your credit cards max out*—Rene Rodriguez

May *See* FIRST-OF-MAY

mayo *n by about 1930* Mayonnaise

maytag *prison by 1980s* **1** *v* To rape a weaker prisoner: *. . . good looks had been a problem at Rikers, getting him "maytagged" at least eight times*—Carsten Stroud **2** *n*: *Maytag Prison slang for a weak male unable to protect himself from homosexual rape. . .* —Carsten Stroud

mazel (MAH zəl) *n by 1968* Luck: *When a man has mazel, even his ox calves*—Leo Rosten [fr Yiddish fr Hebrew]

mazuma (məe ZOO mə) *n* (also **mezuma** or **mazume** or **mazoomy** or **mazoo** or **mazoola** or **mazula**) *by 1901* Money: *You have to leave your mazuma behind*—George Jean Nathan [fr Yiddish fr Hebrew; perhaps fr a Chaldean word meaning "the ready necessary"]

Mc- *prefix by 1980s* Indicating various qualities associated with the McDonald's™ restaurant chain and its food, such as rapidity, brevity, disposable packaging, small size, strict standardization, etc ●The prefix reflects a scornful comparison with the things: *McFirm/ McJob/ McLibrary/ McLunchroom/ McMyth/ McNews/ McPublisher/ McSchool/ McSurgery center/ McTheater/ McWine/ McWorld*

MC or **emcee** (pronounced as separate letters) **1** *n by 1929* A master of ceremonies **2** *v*: *MC'd by Bob Hope*—New York Magazine/ *George Jessel emceed the event*—Variety

McCoy *adj by 1930* Genuine; legitimate; =KOSHER: *. . . like every other McCoy biz*—Variety

the McCoy *See* the REAL MCCOY

McCrea *See* MOTHER MACHREE

McDucks *n 1980s college students* McDonald's™, a fast-food restaurant [reference to Disney's *Donald Duck*]

McGee *See* JERK MCGEE

MCP or **mcp 1** *n by 1971* =MALE CHAUVINIST PIG **2** *modifier*: *. . . a sort of anarcho-Marxist MCP*—Village Voice/ *Somehow his senior mcp act doesn't really threaten women*—Herbert Gold

MD *n lunch counter by 1970s* Dr Pepper™, a soft drink

MDA *n 1960s narcotics* Methyl diamphetamine, a stimulant that is somewhat like LSD

meadow muffin *n phr by 1980s*: *. . . the meadow muffin, better known as the cow pie. . .* —Daily Jefferson County Union

meal *See* SQUARE

meal ticket 1 *n phr sports by 1905* A superstar athlete who constitutes the drawing and earning power of a team, manager, etc; =the FRANCHISE: *. . . with his meal ticket, the Brown Bomber himself*—Arthur Daley **2** *n phr by 1902* Any person, skill, part of the body, instrument, etc, that provides one's sustenance: *His looks are his meal ticket*

mean *adj black by about 1900* Excellent; wonderful; =CLASSY, WICKED: *This. . . girl has already proved she can play a mean game of tennis*—Inside Sports/ *And Wheelright had a great, mean ear for dialect*—Peter Schjeldahl

See LEAN AND MEAN, SHAKE A WICKED CALF

mean bean *n phr* by 1980s An expert; =MAVIN: *John, who's a mean bean at squash and horseback riding*—People

mean gene *n phr* by 1990s A postulated genetic basis for a violent personality

mean green *n phr* black by 1970s Money: *Mean green won out over neighborhood purity in the end*—Village Voice

meany or **meanie** *n* by 1927 A cruel, unkind person; villain; =HEAVY
See BLUE MEANIE

measly *adj* by 1864 Contemptibly inadequate; petty: *Should I work for a measly five bucks an hour?*

meat ◁1▷ *n* by 1597 A person considered merely as a sex partner or object; =ASS ◁2▷ *n* by 1611 The vulva; =CUNT ◁3▷ *n* by 1595 The penis; =PRICK **4** *n* students by 1970s A stupid person; =MEATHEAD: *. . . to see a bunch of meats play*—Sports Illustrated **5** *n* car-racing by 1970s The depth of tread on a car tire **6** *n* by 1886 Solid value or meaning; substance: *The ones that contained real meat were milked capably by the cast*—Variety **See** ALL THAT MEAT AND NO POTATOES, BEAT one's MEAT, COLD MEAT, DARK MEAT, EASY MEAT, JUMP ON someone's MEAT, MAKE HAMBURGER OUT OF someone or something, PIG-MEAT, WHITE MEAT

one's **meat** by 1899 **1** *n phr* An easy and favorite opponent; a chosen opponent: *He wins every time, guess I'm his meat* **2** *n phr* One's preferred work, play, effort, etc: *Tennis is his meat* [probably based on the older sense of *meat*, "food, sustenance, game"]

the **meat** *n phr* by 1901 The essential part; core: *Now we see the meat of the problem*

meat and potatoes 1 *n phr* by 1940s The simple fundamentals; =the NITTY GRITTY **2** *modifier*: *It's the meat-and-potatoes appeal, the old pull at the heart-strings*—S J Perelman
See ALL THAT MEAT AND NO POTATOES

meat-ax *v* by 1940s To assault brutally; chop down: *. . . the jobless refugees from Doubleday's meat-axing of Dial and Delacorte*—Village Voice [the date should probably be earlier; the noun phrase *meat ax* indicating something savage and extreme is found by 1834]

meatball 1 *n* by 1940 A stupid, tedious person; an obnoxious or disgusting person; =CREEP, JERK: *"How come?" "Because he's a meatball"*—W T Tyler **2** *n* WWII Navy A signal flag with a black dot on a yellow field **3** *n* WWII Navy The Japanese flag

meat card *n phr* by 1950s =MEAL TICKET [as a card entitling one to meat, the term is found by 1870]

meateater *n* police by 1970s A corrupt police officer who aggressively seeks illicit spoils: *Meat eaters. . . spend a good deal of their working hours aggressively seeking out situations they can exploit*—New York Times
See GRASSEATER

meat grinder *n phr* by 1951 A place or situation of extreme destruction: *An Iraqi battalion had blundered badly, sending thinly armored personnel car-* *riers across the border into a meat grinder, where Saudi and American missiles had all but demolished the invaders*—New York Times

meathead *n* by 1945 A stupid person; =MEATBALL: *The copper. . . was a big meathead*—J B Martin *Take your hand off that door, you meathead*—Tom Wolfe

meatheaded *adj* by 1949 Stupid: *. . . some meat-headed tart*—W R Burnett

meathooks *n* by 1919 The hands or fists; =BISCUIT HOOKS

meat market 1 *n phr* by 1896 A place where one looks for sex partners; the milieu of the singles; =MEAT RACK: *. . . men, who are now in the meat market, just like women have always been*—New York Times/ *They go out to the meat markets, then come back and say how awful it was*—Washingtonian **2** *n phr* by 1980s Any place where people are displayed, appraised, etc, and generally treated like cattle: *. . . the free gear, the summer job, the horrific meat market of the Nike summer camp for prime national hoop prospects*—New Yorker

meat rack *n phr* homosexuals by 1972 A gathering place, often public like a park bench or a shopping mall, where one seeks out sex partners; =MEAT MARKET: *. . . trailers parked near the river in Greenwich Village, the strip some people call "the meat rack"*—Washington Post/ *Crescent Beach was the local meat rack. . . where the beautiful young women from the university drifted across the sand. . .*—Harry Crews

meat run *n phr* railroad by 1950s Any fast train

meat show *n phr* by 1940s A cabaret floor show featuring nude or nearly nude women: *. . . a divertissement known in the trade as a meat-show*—Westbrook Pegler

meat wagon 1 *n phr* by 1925 An ambulance: *He woke up in the meatwagon*—Forum/ *I got a lift in the meat wagon to the hospital where I got the treatment of a fuckin' king*—Carolyn Chute **2** *n phr* by 1950s A hearse: *They have the meat wagon following him around*—Raymond Chandler **3** *n phr* prizefighting by 1980s A group or stable of second-rate fighters: *Montoya was known for running a meat wagon, a wholesale source of journeymen opponents*—New York Times

mechanic 1 *n* gambling by 1909 An expert card player, esp one adept at cheating; =CARD SHARP: *No "mechanics" (sharps) were tolerated*—T Betts **2** *n* by 1973 A professional killer; =HIRED GUN, HIT MAN: *. . . some prison mechanic will take him out on the lunch line*—Carsten Stroud

MECCA *n* medical by 1980s Any university hospital [fr *Mecca*, the supreme goal of Muslims]

med 1 *n* by 1851 A medical student **2** *modifier* by 1933 Medical: *med school/ a med alert*

medal *v* sports by 1980s To win a medal: *Flo-Jo medaled in the 100-meter*—Bryant Gumbel
See NO-CLAP MEDAL

media blitz *n phr* by 1990s An intensive publicity campaign: *A new coalition of fiscally conservative*

groups is planning a $10 million media blitz. . . —
Newark Star-Ledger

media circus *n phr by 1990s* An occasion of very extravagant media coverage, esp television: *. . . it'll be a media circus*—Lawrence Sanders

media hype *n phr by 1970s* Concentrated favorable publicity for a person, corporation, candidate, etc: *Instead of dealing in the media hype, Coplon should have. . . pursued the reasons*—Village Voice

medic 1 *n by 1823* A medical student **2** *n armed forces by 1925* A military medical orderly, attendant, stretcher-bearer, etc **3** *n* (also **medico**) *by 1661* A physician

medicine *See* GOD'S MEDICINE, TAKE one's MEDICINE

meds *n medical* Medications: *. . . an angry, alienated 25-year old who swallows anti-psychotic "meds" to curb his demons. . .* —Milwaukee Journal

the **meemies** *See* the SCREAMING MEEMIES

meet 1 *n railroad by 1940s* A point where trains are scheduled to meet **2** *n by 1879* A meeting, esp for some illegal purpose: *She went out to make a "meet" to buy more bogus bills*—Fact Detective Mysteries/ *I'll call you next Friday, same time, and set up a meet*—Lawrence Sanders **3** *n 1950s bop musicians & cool musicians* =JAM SESSION

meets the road *See* WHERE THE RUBBER MEETS THE ROAD

mega *1980s students & teenagers* **1** *adj* Much: *I got mega homework tonight* **2** *adv* Very: *This dude is mega gross*

mega- *prefix by 1981* A very large specimen, quantity, etc, of what is indicated: *megabitch/ megablitz/ mega-cost/ megafame/ megagreed/ megahopes/ megamodel/ megatravel*

megabucks *n* (also **megageeters**) *by 1946* Much money, literally, "millions of dollars" •**Megabuck,** "a million dollars," was coined by nuclear scientists in 1946, but the plural form was not popularized until the 1960s and 70s: *. . . the simple faith that moves mountains and grosses megabucks*—Village Voice/ *He was doing okay, but she's got megabucks of her own*—Lawrence Sanders/ *. . . after two years on the road. . . you'll be knocking down megageeters*—Christopher Zenowich

the **megillah** or the **whole megillah** (mə GILL ə) *n phr by 1909* Something very long and tedious told or explained exhaustively: *I've been listening to all this here Megillah*—Potash and Perlmutter/ *Let's not have the megillah*—C McHarry/ *. . . a whole megilla (song and dance)*—New York Times [fr Yiddish fr Hebrew, "scroll, volume," esp the Book of Esther read aloud in its entirety at Purim celebrations]

MEGO (MEE goh) *sentence chiefly news media by 1980s* This is a smashingly boring affair [fr *mine eyes glaze over*]

MEGOGIGO (MEE goh GĬ goh) *sentence 1980s teenagers* This is totally tedious [fr *mine eyes glaze over, garbage in garbage out*]

-meister *combining word* Very active in, adept at, or in charge of what is indicated •These words have proliferated hugely since the 1960s, apparently on the model of **schlockmeister**: *admeister/ attackmeister/ blurbmeister/ budgetmeister/ burgermeister/ coupmeister/ dealmeister/ frissonmeister/ hypemeister/ kinkmeister/ megadealmeister/ mudmeister/ mushmeister/ opinionmeister/ ordealmeister/ packmeister/ perkmeister/ processmeister/ quotemeisters/ rapmeister/ schlockmeister/ shuttlemeister/ sleazemeister/ spinmeister/ spookmeister/ symbolmeister/ talkmeister/ trashmeister/ yakmeister* [fr German, or fr Yiddish *mayster*, "master"; what was probably a Yiddish word was given, as is the custom, a German spelling]
See SCHLOCKMEISTER

a **mell of a hess** *n phr* A dire situation; =SNAFU: *You better come over, Doc, there's a mell of a hess here/ Some mell of a hess you got us into* [spoonerism for *hell of a mess*]

mellow 1 *adj by 1690* Slightly drunk; =TIDDLY **2** *adj jazz musicians by about 1935* Sincere and skillful •Said of a musical performance **3** *adj 1950s cool use* Relaxed; at ease; =LAID-BACK **4** *adj 1950s cool use* Very friendly; intimate **5** *n 1950s cool use* A close friend; =BUDDY **6** *v 1980s students* =MELLOW OUT

mellow-back *adj 1930s black* Smartly dressed

mellow out *v phr* (also **mellow**) *1970s students* To become relaxed and easy: *. . . wondering why the family in "The Grapes of Wrath" didn't move to LA and mellow out*—Washington Post/ *Even the testiest groups and crews can be mellowed out after spending time at Alpine*—Milwaukee Journal

melon *n by 1906* The sum of profits, loot, etc, to be divided: *The stockholders have a meager melon to share this year*

melonhead *n by 1980s* A stupid person; =KNUCKLEHEAD, MEATBALL: *She called Greenwood a "melonhead"*—Milwaukee Journal

meltdown *n by 1970s* A disaster: *They are. . . facing a credibility meltdown*—Toronto Life/ *The Glenn campaign has achieved almost total meltdown*—NBC News [fr the nuclear power-plant disaster in which the core of radioactive material *melts down* into the earth below, the term found by 1963]

melt down *v phr by 1990s* To be disastrously affected: *When you put on that kind of outfit, boys are going to melt down*—Julie Newmar

melted out *adj phr gambling by 1950s* Penniless, esp from gambling; =BROKE, TAPPED OUT

Melvin or **melvin 1** *n 1950s teenagers* A disgusting and contemptible person; =CREEP, NERD **2** *n 1980s students* The prank of pulling the underwear upward from behind by the waistband; =WEDGIE, MURPHY

member 1 *n black by about 1958* A fellow black person; =BROTHER, SISTER ◁**2**▷ *n by 1356* The penis [second sense, a euphemism for the even more euphemistic *membrum virile*]

mend one's **fences** *v phr by 1880s* To establish or restore good relations: *I had better get home and mend my fences*—American Idioms Dictionary

mensch or **mensh** *by 1909* **1** *n* An admirable and substantial person; a decent and mature person: *. . . wear good clothes and look like a mensch*—Potash and Perlmutter/ *A generous little mensch. . . gets French manicure gift certificates for his girlfriend*—Sassy **2** *n* A virile man •Can also be used of women: *. . . mensch, a stand-up he-man*—C McHarry/ *Trigere, almost alone, is mensch enough to candidly dismiss the misogynous midi*—Stephanie Harrington [fr Yiddish, literally "person, man"]

men's lib *n phr by 1970* Men's liberation, the counterpart, and possibly reaction, to women's liberation: *Only men's lib and women's lib can alert society*—Rosemary Park

mental **1** *n British by 1913* A deranged person; =NUT **2** *adj British by 1927* Crazy; deranged; =NUTTY: *. . . and the son, William, went absolutely mental*—New York Magazine

mental job *n phr by 1950s* A neurotic or psychotic person; =NUT

meow *See* the CAT'S MEOW

merchant *combining word by 1914* A person who esp indulges or purveys in what is indicated: *heat merchant/ speed merchant*

merge *v* To marry

the **merry ha-ha** *n phr by 1906* A ridiculing and dismissive laugh at someone; =the HORSELAUGH

merry hell *n phr by 1911* A severe rebuke or punishment: *He gave us merry hell for that caper* *See* CATCH HELL, GIVE someone HELL

merv *n 1980s students* A student who studies hard; =GREASY GRIND, PENCIL NECK, POINDEXTER

mesc *n 1960s narcotics* Mescaline, a hallucinogenic drug

meshegoss or **meshugas** *See* MISHEGOSS

meshuga (mə SHŏŏ gə, -SHIH-) *adj* (also **meshigga** or **meshugah** or **meshiggah** or **mishugah** or **mishoogeh**) *by 1892* Crazy; =NUTTY: *Mishoogeh or mishugah. . . spelled either way means crazy*—C McHarry [fr Yiddish fr Hebrew; the variant pronunciations reflect major dialects of Yiddish]

meshugana or **meshiggana** or **meshiganer** (mə SHŏŏ gə nə, -SHIH-) *n* A crazy person; =NUT [fr Yiddish fr Hebrew]

mess **1** *n by 1834* A desperately confused situation; trouble; chaos; =FOUL-UP, FUCK-UP: *"You seem to have got into a mess," said the officer*—Robert Louis Stevenson **2** *n by 1936* An incompetent, disorganized, and confused person: *Honey, I'm a mess* **3** *n by 1851* Dirt, garbage, trash, etc; a dirtying: *Clean up your damn mess*

message *v computer by 1990s* To send a message on the Internet •The sense "to send a message" is found by 1583: *". . . I need to do it," Baker messaged a man with whom he had been discussing rape, torture, and murder. . .*—Macon Telegraph

mess around *v phr by 1932* To idle about; loaf; work indolently; =GOOF OFF: *Stop messing around and get to work*

mess someone **around** (or **over**) *v phr black by 1960s* To victimize and exploit; maltreat; =FUCK OVER: *. . . being messed over by Goldberg all the time*—Claude Brown/ *Here's a young black dude in a Cadillac, we'll just mess him around*—New York Magazine

mess around with or **mess with** **1** *v phr by 1913* To become involved with: *I don't mess with married or attached women*—New York Post **2** *v phr by 1950s* To defy or challenge; provoke; =FUCK WITH: *Nobody dared to mess around with Slippers*—Louis Armstrong/ *They go around messing with us, because we're trying to do something*—Ishmael Reed **3** *v phr by 1940s* To play or tinker with: *I caught him messing around with the heating control*

mess up **1** *v phr by 1909* To disarrange; muddle: *Who messed up these figures?* **2** *v phr by 1919* To injure; damage: *The drugs and booze messed up her mind* **3** *v phr by about 1915* To get into trouble; make a botch; =FUCK UP: *If you don't mess up you get an automatic promotion*

mess someone **up** *by 1940s* **1** *v phr* To thrash; beat up; =WORK someone OVER: *They sent a couple of goons to mess him up when he wouldn't pay* **2** *v phr* To damage or injure someone: *The wreck messed him up so he can't walk*

messy *by 1940s* **1** *adj* Confused; chaotic; =FUCKED UP **2** *adj* Nasty; =DIRTY: *There'll be a lot of messy publicity about this*

metal *by 1973* **1** *n* =HEAVY METAL **2** *v* To play loudly amplified rock and roll music: *Nobody can metal like Blue Oyster Cult*—B Malamut *See* HEAVY METAL, PUT THE PEDAL TO THE METAL

metal head *n by 1970s* A devotee of heavy-metal rock music: *. . . the standard uniform of the metalhead: Led Zeppelin T-shirt, jeans, shoulder-length hair*—Toronto Star

metallurgist *n by 1970s* A heavy-metal musician

meter-reader *n WWII aviators* The copilot of an airplane; =the KID

meth *n 1960s narcotics* Methedrine™; methamphetamine: *Eight hours after snorting cocaine for two days and doing crystal meth. . .* —Ann Landers column

meth head (or **freak**) *n phr 1960s narcotics* A habitual user of Methedrine™

me-too or **me-tooistic** *adj by 1940s* Imitative; =COPYCAT: *. . . big companies brought out many me-too drugs and had to slim down. . .* —Los Angeles Times

◄**Mex**► *by 1854* **1** *n* A Mexican **2** *adj* Mexican: *Ensenada is all Mex*—James M Cain

◄**Mexican breakfast**► *n phr by 1950s* A cigarette and a glass of water

◄**Mexican infantry**► *n phr Army by 1970s* Military intelligence

◄**Mexican promotion** (or **raise**)► *n phr by 1950s* Advancement in rank or status with no raise of salary

Mexican standoff *n phr by 1891* A stalemate; deadlock; =STANDOFF •The dated use refers to a tie baseball game

mezonny (mee ZUHN ee) *n* Money, esp money spent for narcotics [fr *money* disguised by insertion of *-ez-* in the carnival people called "Carnese"]

mezuma *See* MAZUMA

mezz *jazz musicians by 1938* **1** *n* A marijuana cigarette; =REEFER **2** *adj* Excellent; =MELLOW [fr the name of the jazz clarinetist *Mezz Mezzrow*]
See the MIGHTY MEZZ

MF or **mf** *n black by 1960s* A despicable person; =MOTHERFUCKER: *He used to look right at them MFs*—Pete Hamill/ . . . *kill some of the Uncle Tomming mfs*—Eldridge Cleaver

mice *n television studio by 1950s* Children [fr the popular children's program *The Mickey Mouse Club*]

Michigan bankroll (or **roll**) *n phr by 1932* A bankroll having a note of large denomination on the outside and small notes or paper making up the rest [the date is probably earlier; in the 1850s, Michigan bankers outwitted auditors by taking barrels of nails, with a thin top layer of silver coins, from bank to bank ahead of them]

mick[1] *1980s students* **1** *n* An easy course; =GUT COURSE, PIPE COURSE: *I heard that Astro 3 is a mick*—UCLA Slang **2** *modifier: Russian 27A is a mick course*—UCLA Slang [fr *Mickey Mouse*]

◄**mick**[2] or **Mick**► *by 1856* **1** *n* An Irishman or person of Irish descent **2** *adj: a mick politician* **3** *n* A Roman Catholic **4** *adj:* . . . *my one mick friend, although he isn't Irish*—P Marks [fr the nickname of the common Irish name *Michael*]

mickey or **Mickey** **1** *n by 1940s* A potato: *We stole our first mickies together from Gordon's fruit stand*—Claude Brown/ . . . *roast mickies in the gutter fires*—Joseph Mitchell **2** *n by 1915* =MICKEY FINN: *Mickeys act so drastically that one may kill a drunk with a weak heart*—A J Liebling **3** *n by 1914* A half-bottle of liquor **4** *n* (also **Mickey Mouse**) *black by 1970s* A white person; =IRISH, OFAY: . . . *and the Mickey, which is you, be dead a long time ago, except he says no*—Robert B Parker [potato sense probably by association with the common phrase *Irish potato*]
See SLIP someone A MICKEY

Mickey Ds *n phr 1970s teenagers* A McDonald's™ fast-food restaurant

Mickey Finn or **mickey finn** **1** *n phr by 1890s* A strong hypnotic or barbiturate dose, esp of chloral hydrate, put secretly into a drink; =KNOCKOUT DROPS: *The drug, sometimes known as "knockout drops" or Mickey Finn is a sedative*—New York Times/ *Sometime during the nineties, technology finally brought refinement to the art, in the form of the Mickey Finn*—New York Magazine **2** *n phr by 1935* A purgative similarly administered [origin unknown and richly conjectured, chiefly being fathered on various bartenders or saloon proprietors with names like *Mickey Finn*]

Mickey Mouse or **mickey mouse 1** *adj phr* (also **micky-mouse**) *musicians by about 1935* Sentimental and insincere: *A "micky-mouse band" is a real corny outfit*—Stephen Longstreet/ . . . *to the*

dead beat of mind-smothered Mickey Mouse music—Eldridge Cleaver **2** *adj phr by 1951* Showy; meretricious, merely cosmetic;: *And I don't think Mickey Mouse changes are going to work*—Walter Mondale **3** *n by 1960s: It's hard to get past the mickey mouse and see what the hell they're driving at* **4** *adj phr by 1960s* Shoddy; inferior: *The carpentry work was just Mickey Mouse* **5** *adj phr 1950s students* Simple; elementary; easy: *A "Mickey Mouse course" means a "snap course"*—M Crane **6** *adj phr students by 1951* Petty; inconsequential: *A Mickey Mouse survey of popular culture/ A lot of the Mickey Mouse stuff has been eliminated from the program*—New York Times/ . . . *got picked up on a Mickey Mouse thing in August by the State Patrol*—Ann Rule **7** *n phr by 1960s: That book's pure mickey mouse* **8** *n phr armed forces by 1960s* A blunder due to confusion and stupidity; =SCREW-UP: *The only big Mickey Mouse. . . was a brief shortage of. . . jungle boots*—Time **9** *n phr* (also **Mickey**) *black by 1970s* A stupid person, esp a white person or a police officer **10** *v phr by 1980s* To treat someone shabbily; ill-use someone; =SCREW, SHAFT: *"I think we got Mickey Moused," Williams said. "My best pitcher is washed right down the drain, and I don't like it"*—Milwaukee Journal [apparently this pejorative trend began after the wide distribution of cheap *Mickey Mouse* wrist watches, showing the cartoon character on the face, with his arms as the watch's hands, which were regarded as shoddy, gimmicky, etc, at that time; the diminutive rodent continues to be extremely popular with children]

Mickey Mouse around *v phr by 1970s* To waste time; =FOOL AROUND: *We can't Mickey Mouse around while faced with technological challenges*—R G Hummerstone

Mickey Mouse ears *n phr students* Lights, siren, etc, on the top of a police car; =GUMBALL, PARTY HAT [members of the TV *Mickey Mouse Club* wore large black rodent *ears* on their heads]

microskirt *n by 1990s* A very short skirt, shorter than a miniskirt: *Lena, 20, has dyed blond hair, a black microskirt and black high-heeled boots*—New York Times

middle-aged crazies *n phr by 1990s* A kind of foolishness that afflicts middle-aged persons: . . . *the middle-aged crazies take possession of America's first neurotic and No. 1 storyteller*—Los Angeles Times [perhaps a slang variant of *mid-life crisis*]

middlebrow 1 *n by 1925* A person of average intelligence and taste **2** *adj: a middlebrow magazine/ middlebrow audience*

middle kidney *See* GRIPE one's ASS

◄**middle** (or **third**) **leg**► *n phr by 1922* The penis

someone's **middle name** *n phr by 1920* Someone's most characteristic feature, gift, ,concern, etc; someone's forte or "trademark": *The CIA's middle name is intelligence, which Webster defines as the faculty of understanding*—Time/ . . . *baseball is my middle name*—Nation

the middle of nowhere *n phr by 1960* A very remote area; an isolated place; =the BOONDOCKS: *They moved out of Manhattan way into Jersey, the middle of nowhere*

middy *n nautical by 1818* A midshipman

midnight requisition *n phr WWII armed forces* A wrongful acquisition, esp of military property in a nonregulation manner: *One of our sergeants was quite skillful at the midnight requisition*

miff *v by 1811* To anger; offend: *The way I came on to you the other night; I thought you'd be miffed*— Lawrence Sanders

miffed *adj by 1824* Angered; offended ●Sir Walter Scott calls this a "women's phrase": *. . . miffed over failure of pleas to raise his bail*—New York Daily News/ *. . . Dad, although miffed, took pity on Ethan and decided not to get huffy*—Douglas Coupland

miffy *adj by 1810* Angry; =MIFFED, PISSED OFF: *. . . after a good bit of miffy correspondence*—A Logan [the earlier form *mifty* is found by 1700]

miggle 1 *n by 1940s* A playing marble **2** *n 1960s narcotics* A marijuana cigarette; =JOINT

the mighty mezz *n phr jazz musicians by 1930s* Marijuana

mike 1 *n by 1927* A microphone **2** *v* To amplify with a microphone: *The club was so small they decided not to mike the show* **3** *n railroad by 1950s* A Mikado engine, a type of locomotive having eight drive wheels, produced in the 1890s for the Japanese state railroad and also used in the US **4** *n by 1970* A microgram; a millionth of a gram: *I feel like I've been up on 300 mikes of acid*—Saturday Review

mike fright *n phr by 1937* A disabling fear felt when one tries to speak into a microphone; stage fright

mile *See* GO THE EXTRA MILE, STICK OUT

mileage *n by 1945* Profit; productive potential: *Do they think there's any mileage in my idea?*

mile-high club *n phr airline by 1970s* The putative association of persons who have done the sex act more than a mile high in the sky: *They had stayed behind to renew their membership in the mile-high club by sinking into one of the leather banquettes and making passionate love*—Newlook

military marriage (or wedding) *n phr by 1940s* =SHOTGUN WEDDING

militia *See* RAGGEDY-ASS MILITIA

milk 1 *v show business by 1921* To exploit something to the utmost: *The ones that contained real meat were milked capably by the cast*—Variety **2** *v by 1532* To get something, esp money, unfairly or fraudulently: *The agents had regularly been milking the tenants for exorbitant rents* ◁**3**▷ *v by 1970s* To masturbate

milk cans *See* KNOCK someone or something FOR A LOOP

milk run 1 *n phr airline by 1970s* A scheduled airline passage with many stops,: *. . . followed by a milk run to Charleston, Jacksonville, Daytona Beach, and Tampa*—Saturday Review **2** *n phr WWII Air Forces* An easy bombing mission: *It looked like a milk run*—C Macon [fr the stopping of a train at every rural station to pick up *milk* for delivery to the cities]

◁**milk the lizard**▷ *v phr by 1990s* To masturbate; =JACK OFF, SPANK THE MONKEY

milk wagon *n phr by 1950s* A police van; =PADDY WAGON

mill[1] *n by 1955* A million dollars: *That'll cost the government a cool six mill*

mill[2] 1 *n prizefighting by 1842* A prizefight: *. . . the night of the KO Kelly mill*—Joseph Auslander **2** *n WWI armed forces* A military prison or guardhouse **3** *n by 1918* A car or motorcycle engine: *Has it got the magnum mill?*—George V Higgins/ *They both chuckled and fired up their mills*—Easyriders **4** *n 1950s teenagers* A car: *. . . a squirrel is a reckless driver of a mill (automobile)*—Newsweek **5** *n railroad by about 1925* A locomotive **6** *n newspaper office by 1919* A typewriter
See GIN MILL, GO THROUGH THE MILL, GROG-MILL, RUMOR MILL, RUN-OF-THE-MILL, THROUGH THE MILL

million bucks *See* LIKE A MILLION BUCKS

milquetoast or **milktoast** *n by 1924* A mild, ineffectual person; a timid person; =WIMP [fr or popularized by the comic-strip character Caspar Milquetoast in "The Timid Soul" by HT Webster]

Milwaukee goiter (or tumor) *n phr by 1940s* A protuberant belly; =BEER BELLY, GERMAN GOITER, POTBELLY [fr the fame of the *Milwaukee* breweries]

Milwaukee iron *n phr by 1980s* A Harley-Davidson™ motorcyle, manufactured in Milwaukee: *Had it not been for the unsung efforts of a trio of Harley partisans. . . bikers on Milwaukee iron might be riding Yamahas instead*—Milwaukee Journal

mince *n 1960s students* An unfashionable or tedious person; bore; =DRIP: *Anybody who still wears saddle shoes is. . . a "mince"*—New York Times

mincemeat *See* MAKE HAMBURGER OUT OF someone or something

mind *See* BLOW someone's MIND, DIRTY MIND, HAVE A MIND LIKE A SIEVE, a LOAD OFF someone's MIND, MAKE NO NEVER MIND, ONE-TRACK MIND, a PIECE OF one's MIND

mind-blower or **mind-bender** *1960s counterculture & narcotics* **1** *n* A hallucinogenic drug **2** *n* Something exciting, beautiful, shocking, etc: *That little book's a mind-bender*

mind-blowing or **mind-bending** *1960s counterculture & narcotics* **1** *adj* Hallucinogenic; psychedelic **2** *adj 1960s counterculture & narcotics* Overwhelming; exciting; staggering: *The speech was mind-blowing*

mind-boggling *adj by 1964* So astonishing or complex as to overwhelm the mind: *The school problem is absolutely mind-boggling* [*boggle*, "to be disablingly frightened, take alarm," is found by 1598; a *bogle* or *boggle* was a spook that horses were reputed to see]

minded *See* DIRTY-MINDED

◀**mind-fuck**▶ **1** *v* by 1970s To manipulate someone to think and act as one wishes; =BRAINWASH: *He was totally mind-fucked. . . but he seemed to know his stuff*—John Sayles **2** *n*: *. . . such supposedly Caucasian specialties as stance and persona and pop mind-fuck*—Village Voice

◀**mind-fucker**▶ **1** *n* by 1970s A person who manipulates others, esp for his or her own profit: *Most gurus are magnificent and filthy-rich mind-fuckers* **2** *n* by 1970s A distressful situation; =BAD SCENE

mind game *n phr* by 1990s A toying with psychological influence for one's advantage: *. . . she was moving with a fast bunch of kids who did drugs and played mind games and had group sex and I don't know what else*—William Bayer/ *It isn't a subtle mind game to make the. . . airport seem bigger than it is*—Rocky Mountain News **2** *v* =PSYCH: *. . . they try to mind-game you*—PowerTeam Show

mind one's **ps and qs** *v phr* by 1779 To take care of one's affairs carefully and exclusively: *What the hell are you staring at, madam, you mind your p's and q's*—H Donohue [fr the fact that the two similar letters are particularly hard to distinguish in type, where their ordinary shapes are reversed]

mind the store *v phr* by 1970s To attend to routine business; carry on: *Who'll mind the store while Mr Clinton is overseas?* [fr the joke about the dying man who, finding by patient inquiry that all his children are at his deathbed, inquires testily who is *minding the store*]

mine *See* RUN-OF-THE-MILL

mingy (MIN jee) *adj* by 1911 Parsimonious; mean; tight-fisted [said to have been coined by the author Noel Busch; perhaps a blend of *mean* and *stingy*]

mini by 1965 **1** *n* A very short dress, skirt, or coat ending well above the knee **2** *adj*: *She looked out of place in her mini dress* **3** *n* The fashion or style of wearing such short garments

mini- *prefix used to form nouns* by late 1930s Small; miniature; short: *minibus/ minicab/ minivan/ minicam/ mininuke/ minisemester/ miniskirt* [fr *miniature*]

mink by 1940s **1** *n* A sexually promiscuous person; lecher; nymphomaniac: *The. . . doctor was a regular mink*—W R Burnett **2** *n* A pert and attractive young woman; =DISH, FOX ◀**3**▶ *n* A woman's genitalia, pubic hair, etc; =BEAVER

See FUCK LIKE A MINK, TIGHT

Minnie *n* by 1940s Minneapolis

minor league *adj phr* by 1926 Not of the highest quality or type; second-rate: *This author exhibits a minor-league talent/ . . . with my 50-word vocabulary I'd be a busher in that company, having had no minor league experience*—Variety [the original baseball use is found by 1884]

a **mint** *n phr* by 1874 Very much money; =MEGABUCKS: *The old guy must be worth a mint* [the full phrase *mint of money* is found by 1655]

minuteman *n* street gang by 1990s : *Youth gangs use minors as gun runners, calling them "minute-*

men" because if they're caught they're out (of jail) in a minute—Wisconsin State Journal

Mirandize *See* GIVE someone HIS RIGHTS

mishegoss (MISH ə gahs) *n* (also **mishigas** or **meshegoss** or **meshugas**) by 1890s Craziness; absurdities: *. . . a mishegoss of mixed-up crap*—Philip Roth/ *. . . and free-lance mishigas*—Village Voice/ *Mailer's old meshugas about cancer*—Changes [fr Yiddish fr Hebrew]

mish-mash (MISH mahsh) *n* (also **mish-mosh**) by 1450 A confused mixture; an indiscriminate miscellany: *. . . regarded as a hopeless mishmash*—Brooks Atkinson/ *. . . as untidy as untangling the Starrett mishmash*—Lawrence Sanders [apparently originally fr German *Mischmasch,* but probably in its modern use chiefly fr Yiddish]

mishugah or **mishoogeh** *See* MESHUGA

a **miss** *See* GIVE someone or something A MISS

Miss Emma *n phr* narcotics by 1940s Morphine: *She got sent to the principal for suspicion of having some Miss Emma*—Delcastle Dictionary of Slang

missile *See* DUMB BOMB

missionary position *n phr* by 1960s The sexual posture in which the male lies over the female between her spread legs: *Most of them have never gone beyond three furtive minutes in the missionary position*—Village Voice/ *. . . enjoying sex in that reliable missionary position*—Ruth Westheimer [fr the fancied distinction between this coital configuration of Christian *missionaries* and those of the peoples among whom they labored]

Mississippi marbles *n phr* by 1940s Dice

miss out on something *v phr* by 1929 To fail to see, enjoy, etc, something; =MISS THE BOAT: *I'm sorry I missed out on the ice cream*—American Idioms Dictionary

Miss Right *See* MISTER RIGHT

miss the bus or **boat** *v phr* by 1940s To lose an opportunity; fail; =BLOW IT: *Tom really missed the boat when it came to making friends*—American Idioms Dictionary/ *. . . in Bartlett's book the Byzantine Empire and Kievan Russia seem to have missed the bus*—New York Review of Books

the **missus** (or the **missis**) *n phr* by 1833 One's wife; =the LITTLE WOMAN: *He wanted the missus to get some sleep*—E Lavine

mister *n* by 1760 Man; fellow; =GUY ●Always used in direct address, usu to a stranger: *Hey, mister, where's the turn-off for Bogota?*

Mister Big *n phr* by 1940 The chief or most important person; =BIG ENCHILADA, HONCHO: *I predict in three or four years he'll be Mister Big*

Mister Blewit *n phr* Canadian by 1987 A man who has failed in some effort

Mister Charlie *n phr* black by 1960 A white man; =the MAN

Mister Clean 1 *n phr* by early 1970s A man, esp a politician, unsullied by suspicion of corruption or bad character; =DUDLEY DO-RIGHT: *. . . a female version of a managerial Mr Clean*—Toronto Life **2** *modifier*: *Ramos operated in the cutthroat*

Marcos administration and emerged with his Mr Clean reputation largely intact—Time [fr the trademark name of a household detergent]

Mister Fixit *n phr* A person who can and does repair, adjudicate, resolve, etc, difficulties: *. . . has earned a reputation as an ingenious Mr Fixit*—Newsweek/ *Peter Ueberroth, the Mr Fixit of the 1984 Olympics, was called upon to save Los Angeles even as the fires were raging*—New Yorker

◁**Mister Happy**▷ *n phr* students by 1980 The penis; =COCK, DORK: *Is Mr. Happy taking longer to snap back to attention? Sexually speaking, a man is never what he used to be*—Esquire

Mister Hawkins *n phr* black by about 1900 The cold winter wind; =the HAWK

Mister Man *n phr* street gang by 1990s The leader of a gang: *He was trying to be Mister Man*—TV show Geraldo

Mister (or Miss or Ms) Right *n phr* by 1937 The person one would and should happily marry; one's dream mate: *The Kathleen Norris heroine who didn't wait for Mr Right*—New Yorker

Mister Tom *n phr* black by 1960s A black man who wishes to be or has been assimilated into the white middle-class culture; =UNCLE TOM

Mister Whiskers *See* UNCLE WHISKERS

mitt 1 *n* by 1896 The hand: *snatched right out of his mitt*—Charles MacArthur **2** *n* prizefighting by 1812 A boxing glove: *. . . have the big mitts on*—W R Burnett **3** *v* prizefighting by 1920s To clasp hands above one's head as a sign of victory and acknowledgment of applause: *. . . sitting in his corner and mitting the crowd*—W R Burnett **4** *v* by 1924 to shake hands: *Mitt me, pal, I done it* **5** *n* circus & carnival by 1914 =MITT-READER [fr *mitten*] *See* TIP one's MITT

mitt-camp or **mitt-joint** *n* circus & carnival by 1914 A fortuneteller's tent

mitt-glommer or **mitt-glaummer** or **mitt-glahmer** *n* by 1940s A handshaker; =GLAD-HANDER

mitt-reader *n* circus & carnival by 1914 A palmist; fortune-teller *. . . every confounded swami-woman and mitt-reader in the nation*—Joseph Mitchell

mitts *n* underworld by 1950s A pair of handcuffs

Mitty *See* WALTER MITTY

mix 1 *n* (often **the mix**) by 1959 A mixture; combination of components; medley: *. . . most important element in an auto maker's marketing mix*—New York Magazine/ *I enjoy what callers bring into the mix*—Denver talk show host Tom Jensen **2** *v* by 1921 To fight; =MIX IT: *Them last two babies mixed. . . many times a month*—H Witwer

mixed up 1 *adj phr* by 1862 Confused; chaotic; =MESSY: *His mind's all mixed up* **2** *adj phr* by 1912 Involved; implicated: *I think he was mixed up somehow in the failure of those banks*

mixer 1 *n* by 1896 A person who easily becomes acquainted and sociable with others; a gregarious person **2** *n* by 1920s A party or other gathering intend-

ed as an occasion for people to meet and become acquainted with one another *See* CEMENT MIXER

mix it or **mix it up** *v phr* by 1900 To fight; =HASSLE: *Candidates for the Milwaukee School Board took off their gloves and mixed it up a little with each other. . .* —Milwaukee Journal/ *. . . didn't seem to want to mix it*—W R Burnett/ *Richards, the traditional marketing man, mixing it up with the culture gang*—Toronto Life

mixologist *n* by 1856 A bartender

mix-up 1 *n* by 1898 Confusion; chaos; =MESS: *There's an awful mix-up over at the plant today* **2** *n* by 1841 A fight, esp a free-for-all

MJ *n* 1960s narcotics Marijuana [fr Mary Jane, an earlier name for marijuana]

mo *n* by 1896 A moment: *Give me half a mo*

mob 1 *n* by 1688 Any group, gathering, class, etc; =BUNCH: *. . . as a member of the ruling mob*—Westbrook Pegler **2** *n* by 1839 An underworld grouping; organized-crime family ●The dated instance refers to "a number of thieves working together"; the organized crime sense is found by 1927: *a narcotics mob/ the Genovese mob* **3** *modifier*: *mob infiltration/ a mob boss*

the mob (or **Mob**) *n* by 1927 Organized crime; the Mafia; the syndicate: *I heard it's controlled by the mob*

mobbed up *adj phr* by 1970 Controlled by or implicated with organized crime: *. . . real hard evidence. . . that Schiavone or Donovan are mobbed up*—Newsweek

mobile *adj* 1990s teenagers Attractive; =DISHY *See* NERDMOBILE, PIMPMOBILE

mob scene *n phr* fr motion pictures by 1922 A very crowded place or occasion; =FANNYBUMPER: *And the secretaries soon report that the reception room is a mob scene. . .* —Scott Turow

mobster *n* by 1917 A member of a criminal grouping; a Mafioso; =GANGSTER: *. . . nickname he got from the mobsters*—John O'Hara

moby *adj* 1980s computer Very large, complicated, and impressive: *Some MIT undergrads pulled off a moby hack at the Harvard-Yale game*—The Hacker's Dictionary [probably fr the white whale in Herman Melville's *Moby Dick*]

◀**mockie** or **mocky**▶ **1** *n* by 1931 A Jew: *. . . crashed their fists into a mockie*—James T Farrell **2** *adj*: *I have a mockie accent?*—Saul Bellow [origin unknown; perhaps fr *macher*; perhaps fr underworld slang "fake, phoney"; probably fr *mock*]

mock-up 1 *n* by 1920 A model; a simulation, often full-sized: *They made a mock-up of the wing to study the lift* **2** *modifier*: *. . . blend computer-generated imagery. . . and full-size mock-up dinos seamlessly*—Macon Telegraph

mod *adj* 1960s Modern; up-to-date, esp in the styles of the 1960s: *. . . shows off her attributes in a mod wardrobe*—Bosley Crowther

mod cons *n phr* by 1934 The amenities and furnishings of a house or apartment: *The place has a* good view and all mod cons [fr *modern conveniences*]

Model-T *adj by 1940s* Old-fashioned; =OLD-TIMEY: . . . *a real Model-T speakeasy out of an early Warner Brothers movie*—Stephen Longstreet [fr the *Model T* Ford car of the early 1900s]

modoc (MOH dahk) **1** *n carnival by 1930s* A dummy set up to be knocked down with a thrown baseball **2** *n carnival by 1930s* A stupid person; =BOOB, KLUTZ **3** *n aviators by 1930s* (also **modock**) A person who becomes or pretends to be an aircraft pilot for the glamour and status of the occupation [origin unknown]

Moe, Larry, and Curly *n phr airline stewardesses by 1990s* The pilot, copilot, and navigator of an airliner

mohasky *narcotics by 1940s* **1** *n* Marijuana **2** *adj* Intoxicated with marijuana; =STONED [fr *mohoska*]

Mohawk *n by 1970s* A haircut in which the side hair is shaved off, leaving a brush-like line of hair down the middle of the scalp: . . . *like this guy that comes into Mattie's all the time with a Mohawk*—Barbara Kingsolver/ . . . *all make a good Mohawk*—New York Times [fr its fancied resemblance to the hair style of *Mohawk* Indian males; the style was much affected by the punk-rockers]

mohoska *n WWII merchant marine* Energy; strength; =MOXIE, PIZZAZZ [origin unknown]

mojo[1] *n black by 1920s* A charm or amulet worn against evil; hence, power, luck, effectiveness, etc: *When you got the mojo, brother, when you're on the inside, the world is fantastic*—Robert Stone/ . . . *gets his mojo going for conventions and elections*—Washington Post/ *The office bears a sort of superstitious, bad-mojo stamp*—Penthouse [origin unknown; probably fr an African language]

mojo[2] *n narcotics by 1935* Any narcotic, esp morphine [perhaps fr Spanish *mojar*, "celebrate by drinking"]

moke ◀**1**▶ *n by 1856* A black person ◀**2**▶ *n 1930s Navy* A Filipino **3** *n by 1871* A dolt; fool; ass **4** *n by about 1900* An easygoing person, esp one who solicits favors and gifts; =MOOCHER [origin unknown; perhaps fr Romany *moxio* or *moak*, "donkey," with intermediate sense of "ass, fool"; perhaps related to British dialect *moke*, "murk, darkness"; perhaps fr *mocha*, "coffee-colored"] **See** JAMOKE

moldy fig *1940s bop & cool talk* **1** *n phr* A prude; pedant **2** *n phr* A person who prefers traditional jazz to the more modern styles: *Barry Ulanov and Rudi Blesh hit upon the idea of having a battle of styles, Moldy Figs vs Moderns*—Mark Gardner **3** *adj*: *my moldy-fig tastes*

moll **1** *n fr 1700s British* A woman **2** *n by 1604* A prostitute **3** *n by 1823* A criminal's woman companion, accomplice, girlfriend, etc; =GUN MOLL [fr *Molly*, nickname for Mary]

moll-buzzer **1** *n underworld by 1859* A thief who preys on women, esp a purse-snatcher **2** *n hoboes fr 1920s* A hobo or tramp who begs from women

Molly Do-Gooder *n phr by 1980s*: . . . *I am no Molly Do-Gooder. I'm not swayed by propagandized emotionalism, do not weep crocodile tears over media sob stories, and am highly disturbed that each year creates a more violent and vicious society.* . . .—Milwaukee Journal

Molotov cocktail *n phr WWII* A grenade made by pouring gasoline into a bottle, adding a cloth wick and igniting [fr Vyacheslav *Molotov*, Soviet premier, used and satirically named by Finnish fighters against the Soviet invasion of 1940]

momaflage *v 1990s students*: *And don't forget to "momaflage the kind" when you go home* (hide whatever kind of drug you use in your suitcase, so your mother can't find it)—Macon Telegraph

mom-and-pop *adj by 1951* Run by a couple or a family; small-scale: . . . *still seem wedded to the "mom and pop store," small-business approach*—Albert P Blaustein/ *All kinds of neighborhoods have them, mom-and-pop stores, laundromats*—San Francisco/ *The constitution says nothing about a mom and pop presidency*—Ms

moment *See* BIG MOMENT

momism (MAHM izm) *n by 1942* Maternal domination; matriarchalism; mother worship •Disseminated by Philip Wylie's book *Generation of Vipers*

momma *n black by 1970s* Any specified object, esp a large, admirable, or effective one; =MOTHER, MOTHERFUCKER: *It's time to put this momma in the oven*—TV program *Cher*

mommick up (MAHM ək) *v phr by 1906* To confuse and botch; =BOLLIX UP, FUCK UP: *She's wanting to do it all by herself, then she mommicks things up*—Gail Godwin [fr British dialect, "cut awkwardly, maul," fr the disheveled and sloppy appearance of a *mommick*, "scarecrow," fr *mammet* or *maumet*, "doll, puppet, grotesquely dressed figure," fr earlier "idol, figure of a pagan deity," fr *Mohamet*, the name of the Muslim prophet]

mommy track *n phr by 1987*: *Should corporations set up a two-track system for women managers, a fast track for childless women and a slower "mommy track" for women with children?*—Milwaukee Journal

mom-word *n by early 1990s* =MOTHERFUCKER: *"Hit the ground, you (obscenity)." (All right, if you must know, he was using the mom-word)*—Mike Royko

momzer or **momser** (MUHM zər, MAHM-) *by 1562* **1** *n* A person who expects many loans and favors; =MOOCHER **2** *n* A contemptible person; =BASTARD, SHITHEEL: *A very cool customer, this momzer*—Ira Levin [fr Yiddish fr Hebrew, "bastard"; used in the 4th-century Latin Vulgate Bible; despite this ancient lineage, modern use is ordinary demotic Yiddish]

mon or **mun** (MUHN) *n by 1894* Money

Monday man *n phr hoboes by 1940s* A person who steals clothes from clotheslines [fr the fact that *Monday* was customarily the day for doing the laundry]

Monday morning quarterback *n phr* by 1932 A person who is good at predicting things that have already happened and at pointing out the errors of quarterbacks and other leaders; =ARMCHAIR GENERAL [fr the fact that *Monday* is the first weekday or business day after the weekend, when school and college football games are played]

mondo or **mundo** or **mongo** by 1979 **1** *adj* Very large; =HUMONGOUS, IMPORTANT: *She had a lot of things on her desk top, including a mondo-size slo-mo printer*—radio ad WABC/ *I've got a mongo bruise on my leg from field hockey*—UCLA Slang/ *. . . you'd think it took some kind of miracle, or some mondo engineering breakthrough. . .*—Patricia McLaughlin **2** *adv* Very; =FULLY, WAY: *Your dad is mondo cool!*—UCLA Slang [fr Italian *mondo*, "world"; the *mongo* variant is probably just imitative]

money *See* BAIT MONEY, BLACK MONEY, BUG MONEY, CHICKEN FEED, COIN MONEY, FALL MONEY, FOLDING MONEY, FRONT MONEY, FUNNY MONEY, GREEN MONEY, HEAVY MONEY, IN THE MONEY, a LICENSE TO PRINT MONEY, MAD MONEY, MAKE MONEY HAND OVER FIST, ON THE MONEY, PUT one's MONEY WHERE one's MOUTH IS, RIGHT MONEY, the SMART MONEY, SOFT MONEY, THROW MONEY AT something, TIGHT MONEY, WHITE MONEY

moneybags **1** *n* by 1818 A rich person: *. . . some aged moneybags*—J Evans **2** *n* WWII Navy A military paymaster

money from home *n phr* by 1913 Something very welcome and useful, esp when gratis and unexpected: *. . . but for the TV news boys. . . this was money from home*—Washington Post

money pit *n phr* by 1990s A project, possession, etc, that costs more and more money: *See that boat? I call it my Money Pit*

moneypuker *n* by early 1990s An automatic teller machine; ATM: *Frank went to get some cash from the moneypuker at Becker's*—Slang Bag 93

money talks **1** *sentence* by 1891 Wealth is power: *In New York, boy, money really talks, I'm not kidding*—J D Salinger **2** *sentence* (also **money talks, bullshit walks**) =PUT UP OR SHUT UP, PUT one's MONEY WHERE one's MOUTH IS: *Money talks and you know what walks. . .*—National Geographic/ *Money talks, bullshit walks*—Robert Stone [the second sense variant is found by 1987]

money tree *See* SHAKE THE MONEY TREE

money-washing *n* by 1972 The "laundering" of illicit money to make it seem legitimately earned: *Soon the Caymans became a great capital of money-washing*

mongo *n* by 1979 Something valuable found in an abandoned building, a trash bin, etc [origin unknown] *See* MONDO

monicker *n* (also **moniker** or **monniker** or **monacer** or **monica** or **monaker**) British street talk by 1849 A person's name, nickname, alias, etc; =HANDLE: *His "monica" was Skysail Jack*—Jack London/ *Ricord picked up a new moniker among US narcotics agents*—Time [origin unknown and very broadly speculated upon; perhaps fr transfer-

ence fr earlier sense, "guinea, sovereign," when used by hoboes as an identifying mark; perhaps related to the fact that early–1800s British tramps referred to themselves as "in the monkery," that monks and nuns take a new name when they take their vows, and *monaco* means "monk" in Italian; perhaps, as many believe, an alteration of *monogram*]

monk **1** *n* by 1843 A monkey ◀**2**▶ *n* by 1925 A Chinese or Chinese-American: *. . . known to their Occidental neighbors, the Irish especially, as monks*—R L McCardell

monkey **1** *n* by 1914 A man; person; =GUY ●Mildly contemptuous: *. . . a smart monkey*—Raymond Chandler **2** *n* by 1605 A child or young person ●An affectionate use ◁**3**▷ *n* by 1912 A Chinese or Chinese-American **4** *n* hoboes by 1940s A person who is not a hobo, carnival worker, etc; ordinary person **5** *n* carnival by 1940s A victim; =MARK **6** *n* 1940s narcotics Narcotics addiction; a drug habit: *. . . went from monkey to nothin' in twenty-eight days*—Nelson Algren **7** *n* 1960s narcotics A kilogram of a narcotic: *. . . and you call and you want 100 monkeys*—Washington Post **8** *v* by 1881 To tinker or tamper; intrude one's action: *Look, it's running fine, don't monkey with it* **9** *v* =MONKEY AROUND
See GET THE MONKEY OFF, GREASE MONKEY, HAVE A MONKEY ON one's BACK, POWDER MONKEY

monkey around **1** *v phr* by 1891 To idle about; loaf; =GOOF AROUND: *I'm just monkeying around, nothing special* **2** *v phr* by 1894 To tinker or tamper; attempt to use or repair: *Please stop monkeying around with that machine*

monkey (or funny) business by 1883 **1** *n phr* Frivolous pranks; japes and jests, etc: *He was full of monkey business, the clown* **2** *n phr* Dubious and dishonest stratagems; trickiness: *Show these kids that you're going to stand for no monkey business*—Time

monkey cage *n phr* prison by 1940s A prison cell

monkey-chaser ◀**1**▶ *n* black by about 1920 A West Indian **2** *n* by 1952: *Monkey chasers are gin and ice, with a little sugar and a trace of water*—New Yorker

monkey drill *n phr* armed forces by late 1800s Calisthenics; physical training exercises [fr the fact that the exercisers follow the movements of the instructor, as *"monkey see, monkey do"*]

monkey jacket **1** *n phr* by 1830 Any tight, short jacket, esp one that is part of a uniform **2** *n phr* medical by 1970s A medical patient's gown [fr the fact that *monkey* was a nautical term for anything small, in this case a short, informal jacket as distinct from a formal frock coat; *monkey jackets* are also the traditional garb of an organ-grinder's *monkey*]

monkey-monk *See* HIGH MUCKETY-MUCK

monkeyshines *n* by 1832 Tricks; japes and capers; pranks

monkey suit **1** *n phr* by 1886 A fancy uniform or formal suit; tight uniform: *Neither of my two hats* *went well with the monkey suit*—J Evans **2** *n* baseball *by 1929* A baseball uniform

monkey's uncle *See* I'LL BE DAMNED

Monkey Ward *n phr by 1930s* The Montgomery Ward retail company

monkey-wrench *modifier by 1975* Promoting preservation of the environment by sabotage [fr Edward Abbey's novel *The Monkey-Wrench Gang;* ultimately fr *throw a monkey-wrench into the machinery*]

monkey-wrencher *n by 1980s: They call themselves monkey-wrenchers, the guys who drive spikes into trees, sabotage logging equipment, and otherwise make life miserable for lumberjacks and lumber mills*—TV show *X-Files*

monniker *See* MONICKER

mono (MAH noh) **1** *n students by 1960s* Mononucleosis **2** *n by 1950s* A monophonic recording

monokini *n by 1964* A one-piece bathing suit that leaves the breasts bare [fr *bikini,* interpreting *bi-* as "two" referring to the number of pieces]

monster 1 *n 1960s narcotics* A narcotic that acts on the central nervous system **2** *modifier: users of scag and monster drugs*—American Scholar **3** *n by 1970s* A bestseller, esp a recording **4** *modifier by 1837* Enormous; overwhelming; =HUMONGOUS: *his monster ego/ a monster rally* **5** *modifier 1990s teenagers* Very good; =COOL, KILLER, RAD
See ONE-EYED MONSTER

Montezuma's revenge *n phr by 1962* Diarrhea, esp traveler's diarrhea =AZTEC TWO-STEP, TURISTA: *It was regarded as unfortunate that the President joked about Montezuma's revenge when he introduced the president of Mexico*

a **month of Sundays** *n phr by 1841* A very long time: *He hadn't seen the family in a month of Sundays*

moo[1] **1** *n by 1916* Beefsteak: *. . . slab of moo*—Max Eastman **2** *n by 1940s* Milk

moo[2] *n by 1945* =MOOLA

moocah *n narcotics by 1940s* Marijuana [origin unknown; perhaps an alteration of *mooter, moota*]

mooch 1 *v by 1857* To beg; borrow; =CADGE, SPONGE: *The geisha girls are forever mooching chocolates. . .* —Philadelphia Bulletin **2** *n by 1914* =MOOCHER **3** *v by 1862* To steal **4** *v by 1851* To stroll; loaf along **5** *n carnival by 1929* A gullible customer; dupe; =MARK **6** *n carnival by 1940s* A person who listens to the pitch, but does not buy **7** *n salespersons by 1940s* A customer who painstakingly examines the merchandise before buying [fr earlier *mowche,* "to pretend poverty; play truant," found by 1460, fr Old French *muchier,* "to hide, skulk"]

moocher *n by 1857* A beggar; borrower; =DEADBEAT: *He heard a moocher deliver the following spiel*—Billy Rose/ *Minnie the moocher, she was a low-down hootchy-cootcher*—Cab Calloway

moo-juice *n lunch counter & Army by 1941* Milk or cream

moola or **moolah** *n by about 1920* Money: *So put a little moola in your portfolio and get yourself a cash cow*—Time/ *He who rips off jazz makes mucho moolah*—Albert Goldman [origin unknown]

moon 1 *n by 1928* Cheap whiskey, esp whiskey made by unlicensed distillers; =MOONSHINE: *. . . a couple of pints of moon*—J B Martin/ *. . . using it to transport moon*—George V Higgins **2** *v by 1848* To behave in a pleasantly listless and dreamy way: *I was sitting there mooning over her latest letter* **3** *v 1960s teenagers & students* To exhibit one's bare buttocks as a defiant or amusing gesture, usu out a window [third sense fr *moon,* "buttocks," found by 1756]

mooner 1 *n police by 1950s* A criminal or eccentric active during the period of the full moon **2** *n 1960s teenagers & students* A person who "moons"
See FULL-MOONER

moonlight *v by 1957* To work at a job in addition to one's regular job: *. . . a million guys moonlighting, holding a little back*—World

moonshine 1 *n by 1877* Whiskey made by unlicensed distillers; corn whiskey; =MOUNTAIN DEW: *. . . the moonshine distilled in the mountains*—Ernie Pyle **2** *n by about 1920* Any cheap, inferior whiskey; =ROTGUT **3** *n by about 1920* Any liquor or whiskey **4** *n by 1843* Exaggerated talk; vain chatter; =BALONEY, BULLSHIT: *His story's plain moonshine*

moony *adj by 1848* Behaving in a pleasantly listless and dreamy way: *. . . in a back booth at Caballero's where Carolyn and I talked and became drunk and moony*—Scott Turow

◁**Moony** or **Moonie**▷ *n* A member or disciple of the Unification Church [fr the name of the leader, Sun Myung *Moon*]

moose[1] *n by 1940s* A large, powerful man; =HOSS: *The man fills a doorway. Oh, he's a big man. They should call him Bob Moose*—New York Times [fr Narraganset *moos,* fr *moosu,* "he trims or cuts smooth," referring to the animal's feeding on the lower banches of trees]

moose[2] *n Korean War armed forces* A prostitute [fr Japanese *musume,* "girl"]

moosh (MOOSH) *v by 1990* To mash; squash: *I see it's all mooshed out of shape*—New York Times [the date should certainly be much earlier, since this is a variant spelling of *mush,* which is found by 1781]
See MUSH[2]

mooter *n* (also **moota** or **mootie** or **mutah** or **mu**) *1930s narcotics* A marijuana cigarette; =JOINT [fr Mexican Spanish *mota,* "marijuana," of uncertain origin; since the word also means "bundle of herbs" and "sheaf of hay," it seems semantically akin to *grass, hay, bale of hay,* and *herb,* all of which are disguising names for marijuana or marijuana cigarettes]

mop *n black by 1944* The last item or act; the final result: *And the mop was he got caught* [probably from the notion of *mopping* or cleaning up, influenced by earlier jazz use "the last beat at the end of a jazz number"]

mope 1 *n by 1540* A stupid person; fool; =BOOB: *They. . . weren't a bunch of mopes*—James T

Farrell/ . . . *make it easy for regular mopes to use the Internet*—Mike Royko **2** *n* police by 1980s A criminal; suspect; =PERP

mopery *n* A trivial or fabricated offense against the law: *If he'd lived long enough they'd have had him up for mopery*—Raymond Chandler/ *Gotti sanctioned guilty pleas for what he called malicious mopery, minor offenses that had nothing to do with the existence of La Cosa Nostra*—New Yorker

mopped *adj* 1990s teenagers Thoroughly beaten; =CLOBBERED

mop (or **mop up**) **the floor with** someone *v phr* by 1940s To defeat thoroughly; trounce; =CLOBBER

mop top 1 *n phr* by 1990s A person with a thick head of hair: *Those with only a receding hairline are in no greater danger than the mop tops* **2** *modifier*: . . . *curly-haired mop-top headshop owner*—New York Times [*mop-head* in the same sense is found by the late 1700s, so the date is probably earlier than shown]

more fun than a barrel of monkeys *adj phr* by 1895 A very good time; a pleasant occasion

more than you can shake a stick at *n phr* by 1818 Much; a lot: *He's got more money than you can shake a stick at*

morph 1 *n* narcotics by 1912 Morphine **2** *n* by 1940s =MORPHADITE **3** *v* early 1990s To change one image into another by a computer technique: *One of the most popular techniques in TV ads has been to "morph" a Democratic rival into Clinton, employing special effects to have the candidate's face change into the President's*—Los Angeles Times/ *One thing morphs into another before your very eyes*—New York Times [fr Greek *morphe*, "form"]

morphadite *n* (also **mophrodite** or **morphrodite**) by 1896 A hermaphrodite: *You morphadite*—Richard Bissell [fr a probably naive rather than humorous mispronunciation of *hermaphrodite*]

mortal lock *n phr* gambling by 1950s A certainty; =CINCH, SURE THING: *Brown is what bettors would call a mortal lock to win*—Time/ . . . *a mortal lock to get on the front page*—Jane Leavy [fr a wrestling hold]

mortar *See* BRICKS AND MORTAR

Moses *See* HOLY CATS

mosey or **mosey along** (MOH zee) *v* or *v phr* by 1829 To move along, esp to walk slowly; saunter; =EASE ON: *A mild river that moseyed at will*—W H Auden/ *The Wheaton cruiser moseyed on by me and turned back toward town*—Robert B Parker [perhaps fr Spanish *vamos;* perhaps fr British dialect *mose about,* "walk in a stupid manner"]

See VAMOOSE

mosh (MAHSH) *v* by late 1980s fr British To dance to heavy metal music in a tight-packed arena called a "mosh pit," with a certain amount of physical violence: *They don't dance. They mosh. They slam. They skank and thrash, too*—Wisconsin State Journal/ *Gearshift would give the crowd some-*

thing to mosh to. . . —Macon Telegraph [fr British dialect, "mash, smash," found by 1848]

moshing *n* by late 1980s: . . . *Pearl Jam pulled out of a concert. . . in a dispute with security forces over how to handle "moshing," the rowdy, high-contact dancing common at their shows*—Macon Telegraph

mosh pit *n phr* by late 1980s The place where "moshing" is done: *It's unspeakably hot, often painful, certainly claustrophobic, all in all, just another night in the mosh pit*—New York Times/ *Mosh pits are a lot like armpits; they both are sweaty, hairy, and they stink*—Angela Vogel

mosquito *See* KNEE-HIGH TO A GRASSHOPPER

moss *n* 1940s black Hair; among black people, straightened or processed hair: *Moss is hair*—Jim Bouton

See HOUSE MOSS, RIGHTEOUS MOSS

mossback *n* by 1878 A very conservative person; =FOGY: *The real mossbacks will vote for the governor* [said to have been a description of a group of poor white Carolina swamp-dwellers who had lived among the cypresses until the *moss* grew on their backs]

the **most** *n phr* 1950s beat & cool talk The best; =the GREATEST: *New Jetliner The Most, Reds Say*—New York Daily News

the **mostest** *n phr* by 1885 =the MOST [fr Southern dialect and black normal superlative of *much*]

See FIRSTEST WITH THE MOSTEST, the HOSTESS WITH THE MOSTEST

most rickety-tick *adv phr* Army by 1970s Immediately; without delay: *Please respond most rickety-tick* [probably a simple rhyme with *quick*]

mothball *v* by 1949 To take something out of active use and preserve it for the future, as clothing is stored with mothballs: *"It's really sad to see Buran on the ground." It was used in 1988 and then mothballed. . .* —Milwaukee Journal

See IN MOTHBALLS

mother 1 *n* homosexuals by 1970s The leader, usu the elder and mentor, of younger homosexuals **2** *n* fr black A despicable person; =MOTHERFUCKER: *I looked into the wallet of one of the mothers*—New York Magazine **3** *modifier*: *Every mother other one of 'em cried foul*—H Norris **4** *n* black by 1950s A fine, interesting, or remarkable event, object, or person; =MOMMA: *Grab these mothers. They'll really do the job*—Joseph N Sorrentino/ *When a good-looking girl passes a "big man" on the street, instead of a whistle she gets an approving Motha Higby, especially if she's a cool mother*—Newsweek [both black senses fr the very useful and general *motherfucker*]

See JOHN WAYNE'S SISTER

◀**motherfucker**▶ (Variations: **eater** or **grabber** or **jumper** or **kisser** or **lover** or **nudger** or **rammer** or some other two-syllable agent word may replace **fucker**; **mammy** or **mama** or **momma** may replace **mother**; other alliterating or rhyming terms like **motorscooter** may replace the whole form) *black by*

1950s **1** *n* A detestable person; =BASTARD, SHITHEEL: *"You motherfucker!" she screamed, "You bastard!"*—Rolling Stone/ *. . . blew this motherfucker's brain out*—Bobby Seale **2** *modifier*: *. . . a mammyrammer blowhard fart that has no respect*—Bernard Malamud **3** *n* An admirable or prodigious person: *We will joyfully say, "Man, he's a motherfucker"*—Bobby Seale/ *You old benevolent motherjumper, I love you*—Richard Fariña **4** *n* A fine, interesting, or remarkable event, object, or person; =MOMMA, MOTHER, SUCKER: *We had a motherjumper of a winter. Snow up the yin-yang*—George V Higgins

◀**motherfucking**▶ *adj* (Variations: see *motherfucker* for base forms from which *-ing* forms may be made) *black by 1950s* Detestable; disgusting; nasty; accursed; =GOD-DAMN ●Often used for rhythmic and euphonious emphasis: *. . . went down there with his motherfucking gun, knocked down the motherfucking door*—Bobby Seale/ *what he describes as "three hard mothergrabbin' years"*—Time

motherhood *See* APPLE-PIE-AND-MOTHERHOOD

mothering *adj black by 1968* Disgusting; accursed; =MOTHERFUCKING: *. . . till you put them motherin' dogs on me*—R Lorning

mother-in-law apartment *n phr* A cottage or apartment where, typically, a widowed mother-in-law or other parent may live near but not actually with their children's family; =GRANNY FLAT

Mother Machree (or McCrea) *n phr by 1940s* An alibi, esp a sad story inviting sympathy and leniency; =SOB STORY [fr the name of a sentimental Irish song]

mother-nudger *See* MOTHERFUCKER

mother of all something *n phr 1991 Gulf War* The largest, most impressive, utterly unsurpassable example of something; =GRANDDADDY OF ALL something: *The plan to fix the Hubble telescope in orbit is the mother of all repair missions*—Time/ *I have the mother of all pains in the back*—Army [Muslim tradition fr Ayesha, second wife of Mohammed, and the *Mother of Believers*; used by Iraqi President Saddam Hussein to describe the battle in which he would annihilate invading forces]

mother's day or **Mother's Day** *n phr by 1960s* The day when welfare checks come: *We had picked this day because it was Mother's Day*—Robin Moore/ *Mother's Day in Watts comes on the first and sixteenth of every month*—Current Slang

motor **1** *v by 1970s* To perform well, and without apparent effort; =CRUISE: *Agassi is motoring through the match*—New York Times **2** *v 1980s* teenagers To leave; =BOOGIE, BOOK, SPLIT: *I have to motor if I want to be ready for the funeral*—movie Heathers **3** *n 1990s* narcotics An amphetamine, esp Methedrine™ =SPEED: *"What's motor? Speed?" ""Un huh"*—Robert B Parker

motor-mouth **1** *n by 1971* A very talkative person; a compulsive jabberer; =FLAPJAW, WINDBAG: *What else can you do with this motor-mouth but grin and bear it?*—Village Voice/ *He keeps on talking. A motor-mouth, this guy*—W T Tyler **2** *adj*: *I didn't know he was motor-mouth*—George V Higgins/ *The gangsta rapper is wrecking the mike with motormouth rhymes*—Nation

mountain bike *n phr by 1980s*: *I still ride a bicycle, but it's one of a new and sturdy breed that goes by many names: mountain bike, fat-tire bike, clunker, and all-terrain bike (ATB)*—Frank Staub

mountain (or Rocky Mountain) canary *n phr by 1905* A donkey; burro

mountain dew *n phr by 1839* Raw and inferior whiskey, esp homemade bootleg whiskey; =MOONSHINE

mountain (or prairie) oysters *n phr by 1890* Sheep or hog testicles used as food

Mount Saint Elsewhere or **Saint Elsewhere** *n phr medical by 1970s* A place, not so prestigious, to which a patient, esp a hopelessly ill one, might be transferred

mounty *See* COUNTY MOUNTY

mouse **1** *n by 1842* A bruise near the eye, caused by a blow; =BLACK EYE, SHINER: *One of the Kid's eyes has a little mouse under it*—H Witwer **2** *n by 1655* A young woman: *. . . a little mouse I got to know up in Michigan*—John O'Hara/ *I'm pouring Dom Pérignon and black eggs into this little mouse*—Woody Allen **3** *n by 1520* A term of endearment for a woman: *Just stepping out for a minute, mouse* **4** *n computer by 1965*: *The program employs a "mouse," a pointing device about the size of a pack of cigarettes*—Time/ *. . . a mouse, a handheld device that when slid across a table top, moves the cursor on Mac's screen*—Philadelphia Inquirer

mouse potato *n phr by early 1990s*: *Mouse potato, the digital age's version of the couch potato: a person who is habitually on-line or otherwise occupied at the computer*—Parade

mousetrap **1** *n by 1950s* A small, inferior theater or nightclub: *He walked out on the stage of a mousetrap called the Blue Angel*—John Crosby **2** *v sports by 1950s* To trick someone into a trap, esp by various feints

mouth **1** *n by 1926* Impudence; backtalk; =SASS: *I've had about enough of your mouth* **2** *v*: *They jounced and mouthed each other*—Ray Bradbury *See* BAD-MOUTH, BIG-MOUTH, BLOW OFF one's MOUTH, COTTON MOUTH, FOOT-IN-MOUTH DISEASE, FOULMOUTH, FOULMOUTHED, FROM THE HORSE'S MOUTH, LOUD-MOUTH, MOTOR-MOUTH, MUSHMOUTH, POOR-MOUTH, RATCHET-MOUTH, RUN OFF AT THE MOUTH, SHAD-MOUTH, SHOOT OFF one's MOUTH, SMARTMOUTH, TALK POOR MOUTH, WATCH one's MOUTH, ZIP one's LIP

mouth-breather *n by 1970s* A stupid person; moron; idiot: *Some mouth-breather in the office told me it would be OK* [fr the noisy breathing of an adenoidal idiot]

mouth-breathing *adj by 1970s* Stupid; moronic: *If the dumb mouth-breathing bastards in the street only understood*—Patrick Mann/ *. . . a quirky Canadian sport run by morons, played by barbar-*

ians, and watched by mouth-breathing, two-fisted slobbers—Milwaukee Journal

a **mouthful** *n phr* by 1884 Something hard to pronounce or speak; =JAWBREAKER: *Diphosphopyridine nucleotide is a mouthful*
See someone SAID A MOUTHFUL

a **mouth full of South** *n phr* by 1970s A Southern accent: *. . . a man with a mouth full of South*—Washington Post

mouth off by 1970s 1 *v phr* To talk; make comments; chat 2 *v phr* =SHOOT OFF one's MOUTH

mouth on someone *v phr* by 1960s To inform on; =SQUEAL: *He got busted, and he mouthed on everybody he knew*—Claude Brown

mouthpiece 1 *n* by 1857 A lawyer; =LIP: *inability to hire a professional bondsman and "good front," "mouth-piece" or lawyer*—E Lavine 2 *n* by 1805 A spokesperson: *Each tong has an official "mouth-piece"*—E Lavine

move by 1950s 1 *v* To steal; pilfer 2 *v* To sell merchandise; dispose of a stock: *We better move these monster Teddy Bears quick* 3 *v* To be desirable to customers; sell quickly: *Those pet rocks are not moving any more*
See MAKE one's MOVE, PUT A MOVE ON someone

move someone **back** *v phr* by 1930s To cost someone; =SET someone BACK: *. . . a chinchilla flogger that moves Israel back thirty G's*—Damon Runyon

move into high gear **See** SHIFT INTO HIGH GEAR

moves **See** HAVE ALL THE MOVES

move up *v phr* by 1970s To buy a more expensive or more cherished thing: *The smoker is exhorted to "move up" to a particular brand of cigarettes, the motorist to a new car*—Russell Baker

movie **See** BLUE MOVIE, B MOVIE, GRIND-HOUSE, SNUFF FILM, SPLAT MOVIE

moviedom *n* by 1916 The motion picture industry; Hollywood

mower **See** LAWNMOWER

moxie by 1908 1 *n* Courage; =GUTS: *You're young and tough and got the moxie and can hit*—Dashiell Hammett 2 *n* Energy; assertive force; =PIZZAZZ: *We knew you had the old moxie, the old get out and get*—Max Shulman 3 *n* Skill; competence; shrewdness: *. . . showed plenty of moxie as he scattered seven hits the rest of the way*—Associated Press [the semantic history is not entirely clear; best known fr the advertising slogan "What this country needs is plenty of *Moxie*," used for a brand of soft drink registered in 1924; but other Moxie drinks preexisted this: a patent "nerve medicine" of the same name was marketed in 1876; the name may be based on a New England Indian term found in several Maine place names and perhaps in the name of a plant, *moxie-berry*]

Ms Right **See** MISTER RIGHT

mu **See** MOOTER

muck *n* =HIGH MUCKETY-MUCK •Always used with *big, high,* etc: *. . . the way some of these big mucks do*—Ellery Queen

muck-a-muck **See** HIGH MUCKETY-MUCK

muck around *v phr* To tinker or tamper; interfere in; =FUCK AROUND: *I found myself mucking around my life as well as Jean's*—Philadelphia Journal/ *. . . he believed that. . . other Brewer coaches were mucking around too much in his area of expertise*—Milwaukee Journal [a euphemism for *fuck around*]

mucker *n* by 1891 A crude and unreliable man; lout: *. . . cheap muckers with fine bodies*—P Marks [fr German, "sanctimonious bigot"]

mucket *n* by 1920s =THINGAMAJIG

muckety-muck **See** HIGH MUCKETY-MUCK

muck-mouthed *adj* by 1990s Given to uttering obscenities; foul-mouthed: *Def Comedy Jams begins its fourth season. . . with Joe Torry replacing muck-mouthed Martin Lawrence. . .*—Los Angeles Times

muck up *v phr* To damage; ruin; =FUCK UP: *And let's not muck up our public spaces before we find the answers*—Philadelphia Journal/ *Mucking up the enterprise are fatuous passages about smugglers, espionage, and computers*—New York Times [a euphemism for *fuck up,* probably influenced by mid–1800s *mucks,* "disarrange, discompose, make a muddle" fr British dialect *muxen,* "make filthy"]

mucky-muck **See** HIGH MUCKETY-MUCK

mucky-muckdom *n* by 1970s High circle of power: *. . . the stratosphere of Washington mucky-muckdom*—Washington Post

mud 1 *n* by 1786 Defamatory assertions and accusations: *Watch out, they'll throw a lot of mud at you* 2 *n* narcotics by 1922 Opium before it is readied for smoking 3 *n* hoboes by 1925 Coffee
See someone's NAME IS MUD, STICK IN THE MUD

mud bogging *n phr* by 1980s An entertainment event in which trucks with huge tires drive through mud

mudder *n* horse-racing by 1905 A racehorse that runs very well on a muddy track

mud-hook *n* by 1827 An anchor

mud (or **here's mud**) **in your eye** *interj* by 1927 A toast; a health: *He raised his glass and said, "Mud in your eye"*

mud-slinging *n* by 1884 The use of defamation, insinuation, etc, esp in politics; =SMEAR

mud wrestle (or **wrestling**) *n phr* by 1980s Low and slanderous political devices; =DIRTY TRICKS: *The mud wrestle was mostly over how to craft a law that would fatten the ranks of new Democratic voters at the expense of Republicans*—New York Times/ *What we have now is mud wrestling and dirty tricks and Willie Horton*—Time [fr a form of entertainment in which lightly clad women *wrestle* in *mud*]

muff 1 *v* by 1837 To fail; botch, esp by clumsiness •The dated example refers to playing cricket: *This is a ripe one. Don't muff it, Billy*—Joseph Wambaugh 2 *n*: *. . . dropped the ball, "the $75,000 muff," as it was called*—Arthur Daley 3 *n* by 1940s A wig; a toupee; =RUG: *. . . wasn't wearing his muff—*

Raymond Chandler ◁**4**▷ *n by 1699* The vulva and pubic hair; =BEAVER [first sense fr the clumsiness of someone wearing a *muff* on the hands]

◁**muff-dive**▷ *v by 1935* To do cunnilingus •Sometimes used as a plain insult: *You muff-diving, mother-fucking son of a bitch*—Philip Roth

◁**muff-diver**▷ *n by 1935* A person who does cunnilingus; =CLIT-LICKER

muffin *n Canadian by 1856* A young girl, esp one's girlfriend
See STUDMUFFIN

◁**muffins**▷ *n by 1950s* A woman's breasts

mug or **mugg** 1 *n by 1708* The face: . . . *showing so unperturbed a face. . . so impudent a "mug"*—Henry James 2 *v by 1899* To photograph a person's face, esp for police records: *When crooks are photographed they are "mugged"*—H McLellan 3 *n by 1887* A photograph of the face; =MUG SHOT: . . . *a police mug, front and profile*—Raymond Chandler 4 *v by 1855* To make exaggerated faces, grimaces, etc, for humorous effect: *while Danny mugs through his program*—Time 5 *n by 1895* A man; fellow, esp a tough, rude sort or a pugilist or hoodlum: *Those mugs on the corner seem menacing* 6 *v by 1818* To assault and injure someone in the course of a robbery: *The victims were mugged in the hallways of their homes*—New York Times [probably fr drinking *mugs* made to resemble grotesque human faces; the sense of violent assault comes fr mid–1800s British specialization of the term "rob by violent strangulation," probably fr *mughunter,* "a thief who seeks out victims who are mugs" (easy marks); the sense 6 of *mug* occurs in *mug's game*]
See FLY COP

mugger 1 *n by 1892* An actor or comedian who makes exaggerated faces, grimaces, etc, for humorous effect: *where this trivial mugger is performing*—Gene Fowler 2 *n by 1865* A thief who uses extreme physical violence: . . . *apparently the victim of muggers*—New York Times/ *A knife or an armlock around the throat has been the favorite technique of muggers*—New York Post

muggle *n 1920s narcotics* A marijuana cigarette: . . . *desk clerk's a muggle-smoker*—Raymond Chandler

muggles *1920s narcotics* 1 *n* Marijuana, esp dried and unshredded leaves: *Some kid was shoving muggles*—Ed McBain 2 *n* A marijuana cigarette [origin unknown]

mug joint *n phr circus & carnival by 1940s* A tent or booth where one's photograph is taken and printed

mug's game *n phr by 1910* A futile effort; a sure failure •Chiefly British: *All this case-making and courtroom argument and laying out of certain facts is a mug's game, a no-win proposition*—Newsweek/ *Reliving past glory is. . . a mug's game*—Dick Cavett [fr British sense of *mug,* "dupe, fool, sucker," found by 1851]

mug shot *n phr by 1940s* A photograph of a person's face, esp the front and side views made for police records; =ART: . . . *passed around a mug shot of Willie*—J Randolph/ *She had identified a "mug shot" from the books as the man who attacked her*—New Yorker

mug up 1 *v phr Canadian by 1897* To have a snack 2 *v phr WWII Navy* To have a cup of coffee

◁**muh-fuh** or **mo-fo**▷ *n black by 1970s* A despicable person; =MOTHERFUCKER: *Them muh-fuhs are superbad*—D James

mule 1 *n by 1848* A stubborn person: *He's a hard-headed mule* 2 *n by 1926* Crude raw whiskey; =MOONSHINE, WHITE MULE 3 *n narcotics by 1935* A person who carries, delivers, or smuggles narcotics or other contraband: *The danger to the mule is that a packet may rupture*—Time/ *"Mules". . . carry coke in picture frames and sealed in the sides of suitcases*—New York Times/ *American currency was spirited out of the country then, often by "mules"*—Philadelphia 4 *v:* *Sometimes they mule it in small amounts*—Robert B Parker/ . . . *otherwise law-abiding countrymen into performing muling favors*—Newsweek 5 *n narcotics by 1970s* A condom stuffed with narcotics, carried in the vagina or rectum
See CORN JUICE, WHITE MULE

mule-skinner *n by 1870* A mule-driver; muleteer

mulligan 1 *n hoboes by 1904* A stew, esp one made of any available meat and vegetables 2 *n golf by 1940s* : *A mulligan is the taking of an extra shot contrary to the rules*—Milwaukee Journal [perhaps fr the proper name *Mulligan*]

the **mulligrubs** *n by 1619* =the BLUES [origin unknown]

mullion *n baseball by 1970s* An unattractive person: *Either you're a mullion, a dog. . .* —Jane Leavy [origin unknown]

multi-culti *modifier by 1990s* Multicultural; expressing or advocating multiculturalism: *Kalman wasn't hired by Benetton because they hoped his multi-culti graphics would put the company out of business*—New York Times

mum *n by 1926* A chrysanthemum

munchies *n by 1950s* Snacks; food: . . . *take the joy out of America's favorite munchies, from burgers to pasta to popcorn*—Los Angeles Times

the **munchies** *n phr by 1971* Desire for food after smoking marijuana
See HAVE THE MUNCHIES

Munchkin *n by 1970s* A low-ranking employee, staff-member, etc; a menial: *Justice Department spokesman Thomas De Cair sniffed that Honegger was "a low-level Munchkin"*—Newsweek/ *Most of the munchkins, junior campaign aides, won't make it to the transition staff*—New Republic [fr the name of the dwarfish helpers in L Frank Baum's 1900 book *The Wonderful Wizard of Oz*]

munch out (or up) *v phr* To eat, esp to consume hungrily; =PIG OUT: *You'll get together with your friends, right, and you'll be munching up or some-*

thing—San Francisco/ *She knew she shouldn't be munching out on carbos like this*—Cyra McFadden

mung 1 *n* *1960s students* Anything nasty; filth; =GLOP: *Jones noticed the mung on Lydon's never-brushed teeth*—Rolling Stone/ *Fold the table down, and generations of crud and mung appear*—Scottsdale Daily Progress **2** *v* (also **mung up**) *1960s students* To spoil; botch **3** *v* *1980s computer* To make changes, often undesirable ones, in a file **4** *v* *1980s computer* To destroy: *The system munged my whole day's work* [origin unknown]

mung up *v phr* *teenagers by 1970s* To make filthy: *I munged up my shoes walking across the field*

◁**munjacake**▷ *n* *1990s Canadian* A Canadian of English descent; a WASP Canadian •Used by Italo-Canadians: *What does he know about style? He's such a munjacake*—Slang Bag 93 [fr Canadian Italian *mangiakekka*, "cake-eater"]

murder 1 *n* *jive talk by about 1935* =the MOST, the GREATEST •Sometimes pronounced with equal stress on each syllable, as noted by 1943 **2** *n* A very difficult or severe person or thing: *Baseball is murder on families. . .* —Whitey Herzog **3** *v* *by 1950s* To defeat decisively; trounce; =CLOBBER: *They murdered them all season*—G Talbot **4** *v* *by 1970s* To make someone helpless with laughter; =FRACTURE, KILL: *This one'll murder you*
See BLOODY MURDER, GET AWAY WITH MURDER

murder board *n phr* *by 1980s* A committee or board convened esp to examine a candidate for presidential appointment before the name goes to the Senate for confirmation: *. . . grilled by lawyers at the Justice Department in a ritual known as "a murder board"*—New York Times/ *With Senator Mitchell, even the murder board and the whole business may be unnecessary*—C-Span. . .

murderer's row *n phr* *baseball by 1858* A set of formidable athletes or other persons: *Gathered at the 92nd Street Y, a murderer's row of poets came together for an evening in hell: to read from their joint translation of Dante's* Inferno—New York Times [fr the part of New York City's Tombs prison where *murderers* were housed; most recently used of the New York Yankees lineup of 1927: Lou Gehrig, Babe Ruth, Earl Combs, Tony Lazzeri, and Bob Meusel]

murder one *n phr* *by 1971* The criminal offense of murder in the first degree: *. . . when he did get to trial, and they were going to go for murder one*—Easyriders

murphy 1 *n* *by 1811* A potato **2** *n* *underworld by 1960s* A confidence game in which the victim is left with a sealed envelope supposed to contain something valuable, but in fact filled with blank paper **3** *v*: *Mayor Smitherman was "murpheyed" by the Negro confidence man*—New York Times **4** *n* *1980s students* =WEDGIE

Murphy's Law *n phr* *by 1958* The supposed principle that if anything can go wrong, it will •Called "an old military maxim" in the earliest known printed example

muscle 1 *n* *by 1929* A strong-arm man; =GORILLA: *. . . some gowed-up muscle*—J Evans **2** *n* *by 1931* Power; influence; =CLOUT: *DiBona will have a lot of muscle when it comes to Penn's Landing*—Philadelphia
See FLEX one's MUSCLES, LOVE-MUSCLE, ON THE MUSCLE

muscle car *n phr* *by 1980s* A powerful car, esp one admired by teenagers: *Chrysler's hot-selling Viper muscle car is $50,000*—Time/ *. . . the Sacramento Valley is "car country," where blue-collar kids drive "muscle cars" (old Pontiacs, newish Corvettes if they're making money) and are slurred. . . as "the Camaro crowd"*—Joan Miller/ *. . . undercover cops had a sporty muscle car. . . It was mean. It was fast. It was cool*—Milwaukee Journal Sentinel

musclehead *by 1950s* **1** *n* A stupid person; =KLUTZ **2** *n* A strong-arm man; =MUSCLE: *I saw three or four muscleheads gleefully beat up on a kid*—Village Voice

muscle in *v phr* *underworld by 1929* To force one's way in, esp into someone's criminal operation: *. . . attempt to muscle in on some graft out of his own domain*—E Lavine/ *. . . afraid you're muscling in on his scam*—W T Tyler

muscle out *v phr* *by 1950s* To force out: *If she persists. . . she'll be muscled out of the movement*—F Sparks

museum piece *n phr* *by 1950s* Something old-fashioned: *His hat's a museum piece*

mush¹ 1 *n* *by 1841* Empty and exaggerated talk; =BALONEY: *Don't hand me that mush, pal* **2** *n* *by 1908* Sentimentality; saccharinity; =CORN, SCHMALTZ: *They were all weeping over the Dickensian mush* [perhaps an alteration of *mash,* "something soft and pulpy"]

mush² or **moosh** (often Mo͞oSH) *n* *by 1859* The face, esp the mouth and jaws: *He pulled his mush away from the plate and sighed*—Jerome Weidman [origin unknown; perhaps fr Romany, "man"]

mush-head *n* *by 1888* A stupid person

mush-headed or **mushy-headed** *adj* *by 1890* Stupid: *. . . some really mushy-headed, or at least questionable, rationalizations*—Washington Post

mushmouth *n* *by 1950s* A person who talks indistinctly and slurringly: *Say it again so I can hear it, mushmouth*

mushroom *n* *by late 1980s*: *The growing contempt for accidental victims is even indicated by the name killers give them: "mushrooms" who "pop up" in the line of fire*—Milwaukee Journal

mushy or **mushy-gushy** *adj* *by 1839* Sentimental: *The kid got mushy with the broad*—Dashiell Hammett/ *If you expected Al Unser Sr to get all mushy-gushy and misty-eyed. . . you don't know Al Unser Sr*—Milwaukee Journal

music **See** BUBBLE-GUM MUSIC, CHIN MUSIC, ELEVATOR MUSIC, FACE THE MUSIC, FISH MUSIC, RAP SONG, SOUL

musical *modifier* *by 1924* Changing rapidly from one to another possessor: *At night in Port-au-Prince a massive game of musical houses is going on*—

New Republic/ *The revolving cast of* Love Letters *has become something of a game of musical celebrities*—New York Times/ *Neither partner will relinquish the co-op; this is black comedy, a wickedly funny tale of musical apartments and malfunctioning appliances*—New York Times [the date refers to the first occurrence of *musical chairs*, the game in which players circle a set of chairs and sit in any one available when the music stops]

musical beds *n phr* Sexual promiscuity; =SLEEP AROUND: *The soaps were conspicuous for their preoccupation with musical beds*—TV program *Entertainment Tonight*
See MUSICAL.

muso (MYoo zoh) *n Australian by 1967* A musician: *. . . a superb band. . . no musos to be fooled with*—Village Voice

muss or **muss up** *v* or *v phr by 1899* To disarrange; dishevel: *He mussed his hair all up* [fr *mess*]

mussy *adj by 1899* Disarranged; rumpled: *. . . rumpled now, and mussy*—James M Cain

a **must 1** *n phr by 1892* Something that must be seen, experienced, done, etc: *Having two cars is a must these days* **2** *adv* Necessarily; imperatively: *Solaris is definitely a must-have game*—Milwaukee Journal/ *I don't think the element of fantasy ruins the movie, which in my book is a must-see*—Nation

mustang *n armed forces by 1847* A commissioned officer who has been promoted from the enlisted ranks: *A mustang who had worked his way up from the ranks in 13 years*—Time [fr *mustang*, "wild, sturdy horse of the Western US," fr Mexican Spanish *mestengo*, "stray animal"]

mutah *See* MOOTER

mutant *n 1980s student* A weird and disgusting person; =SHPOS: *Marvin is a mutant; he's constantly licking his nose in public*—UCLA Slang

mutt 1 *n by 1906* A dog, esp a hybrid; mongrel **2** *n by 1901* A stupid person; =KLUTZ, MUTTONHEAD: *A mutt? Yeah, he's that all right. Not too much brains*—Lawrence Sanders **3** *n police by 1980s* A criminal; suspect; =MOPE, PERP

muttonhead or **mutton-top** *n by 1803* A stupid person

muttonheaded *adj by 1833* Stupid

muzak or **Muzak** *n by 1954* Sweet and bland background music; uninteresting taped music; =ELEVATOR MUSIC: *. . . the theatre of media-buzz where ideas normally melt down into verbal muzak*—Toronto Life/ *. . . a nice guy with all the charisma of Muzak in a minor key*—Time [fr the trademark of a company that provides prerecorded music to be heard in offices, elevators, etc]

muzzler *n by 1930s* A police officer [probably fr *muzzle*, "get, take," attested from the mid–19th century]

◁**my ass**▷ *interj by 1796* An exclamation of strong denial, disbelief, defiance, etc; =IN A PIG'S ASS: *"Looks like you had a pretty good hunch, Mr Light". . . Pretty good hunch, my ass*—Stan Cutler [a dysphemism for *my eye*]

my bad *interj 1990s teenagers*: *My bad: My fault or my mistake. A term of apology*—Daily Record

my boy *See* THAT'S MY BOY

my eye or **my foot** *interj first form by 1842* =IN A PIG'S ASS, MY ASS: *She's the greatest my eye/ You'll do that my foot* [in the early and obsolete meaning "nonsense," perhaps fr a Joe Miller joke in which a Latin nonsense phrase *O mihi, beate Martine* ("O, to me, blessed Martin") is pronounced as *all my eye and Betty Martin*]

my man *n phr black jazz musicians by about 1930* One's particular friend; =BUDDY, HOMIE, PAL: *"Serve it up, my man," said Tump. Tump never even saw it*—Harry Crews

mystery *n by 1885* Hash

mystery meat *n phr students by 1970s* Meat not readily identifiable, esp as served in a student dining hall, fraternity house, etc: *Parents must follow the rules: They are forbidden to smoke or leave the building, must show up at homeroom and eat mystery meat at lunch like the rest of their classmates*—New York Times [meat loaf was called *mystery loaf* by the 1940s]

N

nab 1 *v* by 1686 To catch; seize; arrest; =COLLAR: *The officers nabbed him around the corner* **2** *n* (also **nabs**) 1950s street gang A police officer or detective [fr dialect *nap* as in *kidnap*, perhaps related to Swedish *nappa*, "catch," or Danish *nappe*, "pull"; probably related to *nip*; the second sense is recorded in British criminal slang by 1813]

nabe 1 *n* by 1937 A neighborhood; =HOOD: *The nabe is a honey, architecturally*—Village Voice **2** *n* by 1935 A neighborhood movie theater: *The current films. . . eventually make their way to the nabes*—A D Copleman

◁**nads** or **'nads**▷ *n* by 1980s The male gonads; testicles; =BALLS, FAMILY JEWELS: *Apparently I was no longer rousing his 'nads*—Details/ *When we found him his nads were gone*—Robert B Parker [*nard*, "testicle," is found in 1960s student slang and is probably also a shortening of *gonad*]

nag *n* by 1400 A horse, esp an old and worn-out racehorse: *. . . to make dough on the nags*—New York Daily News [origin unknown]

nail 1 *v* by 1766 To catch; seize; =NAB: *. . . the feared and famous Batman and Robin who'd nailed him*—New York Magazine **2** *n* 1960s narcotics A hypodermic needle ◁**3**▷ *v* To do the sex act to someone; =FUCK: *. . . the publishing cupcake in the Florsheims who nailed you on the couch and then fired you*—Richard Grossbach **4** *v* =NAIL something DOWN: *We've got it nailed*—Newark Star-Ledger

See HARD AS NAILS

nail-biter *n* by 1990s Something very worrying and suspenseful: *If Lucas looked this nervous as the Spurs were blowing out the Clippers, how would he react during a nail-biter?*—Milwaukee Journal/ *The gain in compliance cases brought by the SEC has been a nail-biter for brokerage executives*—New York Times

nail-down *n* by 1980s: *. . . defines a "nail-down" as "an advertised price to lure you into the store that is attached to exactly one item." And the saleperson will move heaven and earth to keep you from buying that item. It's as if the goods are nailed down to the floor*—Milwaukee Journal

nail in the coffin *n phr* by 1824 Something that hastens defeat or death: *The Houston convention was one very big nail in Bush's re-election coffin*—New York Times/ *Whittle's proposal is the first nail in the coffin of public education*—Nation

nail something down *v phr* by 1880 To make something securely final; =CINCH: *They nailed down the arrangement and had a drink*

nail someone or something to the cross (or **the wall**) *v phr* by 1990s To punish severely and publicly; make an example of; crucify: *We are going to nail them to the cross*—Time/ *We would not nail an airline to the wall if it made its best effort*—New York Times/ *I wonder why nobody tried to nail his hide to the wall for the Irish jokes he told over the years*—Milwaukee Journal

naked *See* BUCK NAKED

naked as a jaybird *adj phr* by 1930s Entirely unclothed; =BARE-ASS

Nam or **'Nam** *n* Vietnam War armed forces Vietnam: *. . . not like the gooks back in 'Nam who always got their goddam hands out*—M Sayle/ *I was in Nam and Nam made me like that*—New York Magazine

name 1 *n* by 1611 A very important person, esp in entertainment; =HEADLINER: *I saw three or four names there: He's a name in the carpet business* **2** *modifier* by 1938 Being well-known or prestigious: *a name band/ name brand*

See BIG NAME, FRONT NAME, WHAT'S-HIS-NAME, YOU NAME IT

name-calling *n* by 1853 The assigning of malicious designations in politics, debate, etc; character assassination; vilification: *They soon sank to simple name-calling*

name-drop *v* by 1955 To mention the names of important persons as if they were friends and associates [back formation fr *name-dropper*]

name-dropper *n* by 1947 A person who ostentatiously mentions the names of important people as if they were friends and associates: *Well, she may know Barbra Streisand, or she may just be a name-dropper*

name-dropping *n* by 1949 The practice of a "name-dropper"

someone's name is mud *sentence* by 1823 One is in trouble; one is doomed: *If they catch him, his name is mud* [fr earlier British dialect *mud*, "fool"]

name names *v phr* by 1950s To make accusations, esp against one's former associates: *A genuinely guilty collaborator in Czechoslovakia can now, it seems, easily save his or her own hide by "naming names" and implicating independent-minded dissidents*—Nation

the **name of the game** *by 1966* **1** *n phr* What matters most; the essence: *In business, the name of the game is the bottom line*—Philadelphia/ *Good gun dogs are the name of the game*—Sports Afield **2** *n phr* The inevitable; the way things are: *Telling lies in politics? Hell, that's just the name of the game*

names *See* KICK ASS AND TAKE NAMES

◁**nance** or **nancy** or **Miss Nancy**▷ **1** *n by 1904* A male homosexual who takes the passive role **2** *n by 1883* An effeminate man; =LILY: *Where you need desperately a man of iron, you often get a nance*—Philip Wylie **3** *modifier*: . . . *with his talk of nancy poets, his anti-intellectualism*—Esquire [said to be fr the nickname of Miss Anna Oldfield, an actress who died in 1730 and was noted for her extreme vanity, fashionable dress, etc]

nanny *See* GET someone's GOAT

nanny tax *n phr by 1980s* The legal requirement, enacted in 1951, that full-time domestic child-minders be treated like other employees under the Social Security law: *The Social Security "nanny tax," made famous last year in confirmation hearings. . . will be eased under legislation Congress passed Thursday*—Wisconsin State Journal [fr British *nanny*, "childrens' nurse," a nickname for *Ann*, and found by 1795]

-naper or **-napper** *See* DOGNAPER

-napping *combining word by 1939* The stealing of the indicated animal: *The judge was told of the monkeys' disappearance; the monkey-napping had its serious side*—New Yorker [based on *kidnapping*; the dated example is *dognapping*]

nappy *adj 1980s students* Dirty; messy: . . . *Kelly's panties are nappy. No doubt, she's been wearing them for a week*—UCLA Slang

naps *n black by 1950s* The hair, esp kinky hair: *His naps aren't together*—Ebony

narc or **narco** **1** *n 1960s narcotics* A narcotics agent or police officer; =GAZER: *another drug-scare hoax promulgated by the "narcs"*—New York Times/ . . . *the ritual of dodging the "narcos"*—John Ciardi **2** *modifier*: . . . *down to the narco police on the beat*—Esquire

narcodollars *n by 1980s* Money made by selling narcotics: *Narcodollars circulate through Panama's financial system; how do they expect them not to circulate through ours?*—New Yorker

nark **1** *n by 1860* A police informer; =STOOL PIGEON **2** *v* (also **narc**) : *He will nark on him if the first guy doesn't keep playing games*—Lawrence Sanders/ . . . *felt the Fraynes and their youngsters had narced on them*—New York Times **3** *n by 1950s* =KIBITZER, BUTTINSKY **4** *n gambling by 1960s* A decoy; =SHILL: . . . *information about known gamblers, little bookmakers, and their narks*—Fortune [fr Romany *nak*, "nose"]

narrowcast *v by 1970s* To plan a TV program for a special audience rather than the masses: *This "narrowcasting" approach may win NBC an unusual distinction*—Time

nash *See* NOSH

nasty **1** *n by 1971* Something unpleasant, repulsive, etc: . . . *pathos, poverty, and other real-life nasties*—Village Voice **2** *n by 1930s* A vicious person; villain: . . . *takes her family on a river trip, where they are taken prisoner by nasties*—Milwaukee Journal/ . . . *a few of the nasties. . . are scenery-chomping, world-class scum*—Los Angeles Times **3** *adj by 1834* Good; stylish; admirable [third sense revived in 1930s jive use, retained in 1980s teenager and student use]

natch *by 1945* **1** *adv* Naturally; certainly: . . . *will be in riding clothes (habits of the rich, natch)*—John Chapman/ *The two men, natch, are soul buddies*—Judith Crist **2** *affirmation* Of course; right: *Do I like it? Natch, what else?*

native *See* GO NATIVE

the **natives are restless** *sentence by 1930s* One can expect some opposition; discontent appears to be afoot: *Meanwhile, the natives are restless: Polls indicate rising feeling that the President is paying too much attention to foreign matters*—New Yorker [fr a trite line in many old jungle movies as native drums throb]

natty *adj by 1806* Neat; spruce; stylish: *The fitted shirt gave him a natty appearance/ A natty convertible*—Morris Bishop

natural **1** *n by 1897 fr crapshooting* A first throw of the dice that yields seven or eleven **2** *n by 1925 fr prizefighting* Something or someone that is obviously and perfectly fitting; just the thing: *A novel which looks like a natural for Lassie*—New York Times **3** *n prison by 1940s* A jail sentence of seven years **4** *n black fr 1960s* =AFRO

natural-born *adj black fr 1930s* Total; absolute; innate: *The man's a natural-born spaz/ a natural-born artist*

nature's call *See* CALL OF NATURE

the **nature of the beast** *n phr by 1678* The innate characterisitcs of someone or something: *The shared experience is the value of network television; it's the nature of the beast*—Time [the earliest occurrence is in a collection of English proverbs]

Navajo Cadillac *See* COWBOY CADILLAC

navigate *v by 1843* To walk, esp when drunk

navy *See* HOOLIGAN NAVY

neat **1** *adj teenagers by 1920s* Excellent; wonderful **2** *adj by 1579* Without water or another mixer; undiluted; =STRAIGHT, STRAIGHT-UP ●Used to describe spirits: *I'll take my Scotch neat, please*

neatnik *n by 1959* A neat or tidy person, as distinct from a "beatnik"
See -NIK

neato *adj teenagers by 1968* =NEAT: . . . *with nothing to his name but a variety of neat-o consumer electronics. . .* —Douglas Coupland

nebbie *See* NIMBY

nebbish or **neb** *n by 1941* A person without charm, interesting qualities, talent, etc; =WIMP: *"Nebbish". . . is simply the one in the crowd that you always forget to introduce*—Budd Schulberg/

Don't be a nebbish—W T Tyler/ . . . *poor little nebs like Julian*—Budd Schulberg [fr Yiddish fr Czech *neboky*]

nebbishy *adj* Having the character of a nebbish: . . . *plays a nebbishy student who. . . acquires telekinetic powers*—People Weekly/ *Paul Reiser stars as a nebbishy playwright*—Los Angeles Times

the **necessary** *See* the NEEDFUL

neck *v by 1825* To kiss, embrace, and caress; dally amorously; =MAKE OUT, SMOOCH: *At least you'd want to neck me*—Philip Wylie/ . . . *You "spooned," then you "petted," after that you "necked"*—E Eldridge

See DEAD FROM THE NECK UP, DIRTY-NECK, GET OFF someone's BACK, GIVE someone A PAIN, LEATHERNECK, NO-NECK, a PAIN IN THE ASS, REDNECK, ROUGHNECK, RUBBERNECK, STICK one's NECK OUT

necked *See* RED-NECKED

necking *n by 1825* The pleasures and procedures of those who engage in kissing, embracing, and caressing: . . . *pupils. . . resort to necking*—H L Mencken/ . . . *It was the closest we ever got to necking*—J D Salinger

See HEAVY PETTING

neck of the woods *n phr by 1839* An area, neighborhood, etc: *Hey, you live right in my own neck of the woods*

necktie *n by 1871* The noose used in a hanging: *They'll put a necktie on you*—W R Burnett

necktie party (or **social** or **sociable**) *n phr by 1871* A hanging or lynching

the **needful** (or **necessary**) *n phr by 1774* Money

needle 1 *v by 1940* To nag at someone; criticize regularly and smartingly; =HASSLE: *He keeps needling the guy about his looks* **2** *n*: *a really nasty needle* **3** *v 1920s* To age or strengthen an alcoholic beverage artificially, esp by using an electric current passed through a needlelike rod **4** *n by 1943* A hypodermic injection; =SHOT

the **needle 1** *n phr by 1940* Injurious and provocative remarks; nagging criticism: *He's always ready with the needle* **2** *n phr* narcotics *by 1940s* Narcotics injections; the narcotics habit: *The needle finally killed him*

See GIVE someone THE NEEDLE, OFF THE NEEDLE, ON THE NEEDLE

needle beer *n phr by 1928* Beer reinforced with alcohol or ether

needle candy *n phr* narcotics *by 1950s* A narcotic taken by injection, esp cocaine: *Holmes has need of greater stimulants than needle candy*—W F Miksch

needle park *n phr by 1966* A public place where addicts regularly gather to deal in drugs and to take injections; =SHOOTING GALLERY: *Drug addicts have turned the Platzspitz in Zurich, once elegant, into a needle park*—New York Times

needles *See* RAIN CATS AND DOGS

need someone or something **like a hole in the head** *v phr by 1951* To have emphatically no

need whatsoever for someone or something [fr Yiddish *loch in kop*, "hole in head"]

neg *v 1980s* teenagers To reject; turn down: *I was negged from Princeton but accepted at Yale*—Washington Post

negative *n by 1647* A negative element in judgment; a minus: . . . *"drove up Dukakis' negatives" in voter surveys*—Milwaukee Journal

negatory *negation* Air Force *by early 1950s* No; =NIX, NOPE: *Mrs. Shrub sternly took Shrub's arm. "Were you really going to ruin his daughter's wedding?" The Shrub said, "Negatory"*—New Republic [an adjective sense, fr French *négatoire,* is found by 1580; the modern sense was popularized by the citizens band phenomenon of the 1970s]

Nellie or **Nelly** *by 1960s* **1** *adj* Homosexual; effeminate; =GAY, SWISH: *Well, his backstroke is a little Nellie*—Armistead Maupin/ *What in the past. . . would have been described as a Nelly queen*—New York Times **2** *adj* Overfastidious; finicky; school-marmish: *"As follow" is Nellie usage and probably incorrect*—Red Smith

See NERVOUS NELLIE

nemmie or **nemish** *See* NIMBY

neo-con *adj by 1970s* Neo-conservative: . . . *the neo-con idol, George Orwell*—Village Voice

nerd or **nurd 1** *n* (also **nerdboy**) teenagers *by 1951* A tedious, contemptible person; =DORK, DWEEB, JERK: *In Detroit, someone who once would be called a drip or a square is now, regrettably a nerd, or in a less severe case, a scurve*—Newsweek/ *What about a total dweeb? Yup. Geek? Yup. Nerdboy? Yup.*—comic strip "Fox Trot" **2** *n 1980s* students An overstudious person, esp a computer devotee, usu pictured with horn-rimmed spectacles and often buck teeth •In some uses nearly synonymous with "hacker" **3** *modifier*: *Norton represents a new type of American rich person: the nerd tycoon*—New Yorker/ . . . *"a mix between journalism and nerd heaven," with its sophisticated desktop equipment and absence of paper*—Los Angeles Times [probably fr the 1950 childrens' book *If I Ran the Zoo*, by "Dr. Seuss," where a *nerd* is one of the desired animals]

nerdacious or **nerdly** *adj by 1990s* Nerdlike; =NERDY: . . . *and nerdacious mutterings full of buried Hobbit references*—Douglas Coupland

nerdling *n by 1980s* An inexperienced and naive computer "hacker"

nerdmobile *n* teenagers *by 1970s* A large ostentatious car

nerdpack *n 1980s* teenagers A plastic shield worn to keep ink off shirt pockets

nerdy *adj 1970s* teenagers Characteristic of a nerd: *Above all, stay away from anything nerdy*—Philadelphia Magazine/ *When the trendy become mainstream, the hip go nerdy*—Newark Star-Ledger

nerf *v 1950s* hot rodders To bump a car out of one's way [origin unknown]

nerts or **nertz** *See* NUTS

nerty *See* NUTTY

nerve 1 *n by 1809* Courage; =GUTS **2** *n by 1887* Audacity; =CHUTZPA
See GET ON someone's NERVES, HAVE A NERVE

nervous *1950s beat & cool talk* **1** *adj* =COOL, FAR OUT **2** *adj* =JAZZY

nervous Nellie *n phr by late 1930s* A timid or cautious person; a worrier: . . . *a nervous Nellie a bit like Jeanne Dixon*—Village Voice [perhaps fr *Nervous Nellie*, the nickname of Frank B Kellogg, secretary of state 1925–29, who negotiated the Kellogg-Briand differences]

nervous pudding *n phr lunch counter by 1936* Molded gelatin

nervy 1 *adj by 1891* Nervous; =JUMPY **2** *adj by 1896* Impudent; bold

nest *See* FEATHER one's NEST, LOVE NEST

nest egg *n phr by 1700* Saved money, esp for use in retirement or an enterprise, emergency, etc

nester *See* EMPTY-NESTER

the **net (or Net)** *n 1990s computers* The Internet: *Like many newcomers to the "net," which is what people call the global web that connects more than thirty thousand on-line networks. . .*

net down *v phr by 1980s* To be equivalent to; amount to: *Hostile takeovers net down to a power grab. . .*—US News & World Report

netiquette *n by 1990s* The etiquette of the Internet; polite on-line behavior: . . . *the "netiquette" that prevailed in its early days is breaking down*—New Yorker/ *This clash isn't even about the future of "netiquette". . .*—Los Angeles Times

net-sex *n by 1990s* Sexual expression and interchange on the Internet: *I think I'll head back to the house for a little Net-sex and a nap*—New Yorker

netter *n by 1932* A tennis player: *The Jefferson High School netter took second in the Southern Lakes Conference tournament last year. . .*—Jim Schlender

network *v by 1980s* To solicit opinion and aid from associates with common interests: *I'm networking this question, but nobody has a certain answer*—CoEvolution Quarterly
See OLD BOY NETWORK

networking *n by 1980s* The forming of an association of mutual interest: *Building friends and contacts is what everybody is referring to as networking these days*—New York Daily News/ *And More Jewish Networking*—Nat Hentoff

never follow a dog act *sentence show business by 1960s* Be very careful about whom you are to be immediately compared with •Often a rueful comment after one has been outshone

never mind *See* MAKE NO NEVER MIND

never-was *n by 1950s* A person who never succeeded or captured notice; =LOSER [based on *has-been*]

new *See* WHAT ELSE IS NEW

new ball game *See* a WHOLE NEW BALL GAME

newbie *n 1990s computer* A person new to computers and computer networks; computer neophyte: *You'd copy it because you didn't want to seem like*

a newbie (read: clueless computer rookie)—Macon Telegraph/ *Newbies sometimes get flamed just because they are new. . .* —New Yorker

new boy *n phr by 1970s* A novice; beginner: *Not a bad start for a new boy*—Time [fr the British term for a beginning school student, found by 1847]

Newfie *n by 1940s* A Newfoundlander

new fish *n phr prison by 1940s*: *For first-time prisoners ("new fish," in prison parlance), once bail is revoked the darkness descends quickly*—New York Times

new kid on the block *n phr* Any newcomer or recent arrival: *The newest kid on that ostentatious block is O'Neal, who, after signing with Orlando, was snatched up by Reebok. . .* —Philadelphia

the **new look** *n phr 1947* A new fashion; new practice, fad, etc: *Here's the new look in computer software, folks* [fr a fashion sensation notable chiefly for the long skirts of Christian Dior dresses]

a **new one on** someone *n phr by 1887* Something not heard or experienced before: *Isn't this a new one on you, Messrs. Police?*—The Lantern

news *See* BAD NEWS, NOSE FOR NEWS

newshawk or **newshound** *n first form by 1929, second by 1936* A newspaper reporter

newshen *n by 1980s* A woman newspaper reporter: *Our heroine is a no-nonsense reporter who likes to call herself a newshen*—Milwaukee Journal

newsie or **newsey** *n by 1875* A newspaper seller: *Beno, a hophead newsie*—Dashiell Hammett

new wrinkle *n phr by 1899* A novel idea or technique; expedient; trick: *Hey, that little gismo is a new wrinkle*

newy or **newey** or **newie** *n by 1940s* Something new; a novelty: *You'll like this one, it's a newy and a goody*

New Yawky *adj phr by 1990s* Like New York; New Yorkish •The spelling imitates a New York pronunciation: . . . *the New Yawky-voiced beauty will play a transsexual*—Sassy

New York kiss-off *See* KISS-OFF

New York minute *n phr by 1990s* A very short time; =a JIFFY: *In the computer world, nouns like modem and fax become verbs in a nanosecond, almost as short as a New York minute*—New York Times/ *I would sign a woman in a New York minute*—Milwaukee Journal

next *See* GET NEXT TO someone

next off *adv phr by 1920s* Next; at that point: *Next off, Hutch give a yell*—James M Cain

next to nothing *n phr by 1656* Almost nothing; a very little bit: *It's been very useful and cost me next to nothing*

next week *See* KNOCK someone or something INTO THE MIDDLE OF NEXT WEEK

NG or **ng** (pronounced as separate letters) *adj by 1839* No good: *She is NG*—A Lomax/ *This gadget's ng, so give me another one*

nibbled to death by ducks *adj phr by 1950s* Subject to constant petty annoyances: *Writing in* *such an editor-dominated environment was like being nibbled to death by ducks—New York Review of Books/ . . . is being nickeled-and-dimed. . . nibbled to death by ducks—Washington Post*

nibs *See* HIS NIBS, TOUGH SHIT

nice *See* MAKE NICE

as **nice as pie** *adj phr* *by 1922* As pleasant and harmless as could be: *It didn't make any difference to her. You know? She was as nice as pie—Scott Turow*

nice cop tough cop *See* GOOD COP BAD COP

nice guys finish last *sentence by late 1940s* It is foolish to be fair and decent; look out only for yourself [attributed to the baseball manager Leo Durocher]

nice Nelly 1 *n phr by 1930s* An overfastidious person; =BLUENOSE **2** *adj*: *I've got to use "heck" because practically all my editors are. . . being more rabidly nice Nelly than usual—G Dixon* [fr a stock character in Franklin Pierce Adams' column "The Conning Tower"]

nice work if you can get it *sentence by 1930s* That would be a very pleasant thing to do; wouldn't that be fun? •An admiring comment made when one sees something easy, pleasant, attractive, etc, used esp with sexual overtones: *They're paid salaries totaling millions, they get the best tables in restaurants, the valets never keep them waiting for their Mercedes, they glide from one studio job to another. Nice work if you can get it—New York Times* [this was the title of a George and Ira Gershwin song of 1937]

nicey-nice (also **nicey-nicey** or **nicety-nice**) **1** *adj* Affectedly amiable and wholesome: *This little kid here with all her nicey-nice talk—W R Burnett/ You flip the book over and you see all nicey, nicey things—Bobby Seale/ Renegades who questioned this nicety-nice world were locked in deep freeze—Los Angeles Times* **2** *adj* Effeminate; overly fastidious

nic-fit *v by 1990s* To crave nicotine; suffer from withdrawal: *It's so incredibly bad to nic-fit, it's not even funny—Parade*

nick 1 *v by 1869* To rob or steal •Much more common in British than US use: *The bank is gonna be nicked—Dashiell Hammett* **2** *v by 1921* To charge; overcharge; exact: *I think you can nick her for one fifty if you get tough—James M Cain* **3** *n 1990s narcotics* =NICKEL BAG

nickel 1 *n underworld by 1960s* A five-year prison sentence **2** *n 1960s narcotics* =NICKEL BAG
See BIG NICKEL, DON'T TAKE ANY WOODEN NICKELS, DOUBLE NICKEL, PLUGGED NICKEL

nickel and dime 1 *v phr by 1970s* To drain in small increments; nibble away at: *The mack started nickel-and-diming him into the poorhouse—George Warren/ He said the grizzly habitat was being nickeled-and-dimed out of existence—New York Times* **2** *v phr by 1970s* To quibble; niggle; bring up all sorts of trivia: *. . . is being nickeled-and-dimed. . . nibbled to death by ducks—Washington Post* **3** *modifier by 1970* Inconsequential; trivial;

=TWO-BIT: *. . . you realize you've smashed a grape with a hammer. . . Whacking some nickel-and-dime guy—Mike Royko*

nickel back *n phr* *football by 1980s* The fifth backfield player in the "nickel defense": *When peace was restored, the officiating crew ejected end Tom Briggs and nickel back Leroy Axem—New York Times*

nickel bag *n phr 1960s narcotics* A five-dollar packet of narcotics

nickel defense *n phr* *football by 1980s* A defensive formation in which a fifth defensive back is added, to cover an almost certain pass receiver

nickel-nurser *n by 1924* A miser; =PENNY-PINCHER

nickels and dimes *n phr by 1893* Very small amounts of money; =PEANUTS: *We can get the improved roads for nickels and dimes*

nickel (or dime) up *v phr hoboes by 1940s* To offer a merchant five or ten cents for food or other goods worth more

nifty 1 *adj by 1868* Smart; stylish; =NEAT, SLICK: *. . . a great many niftier and hotter words—H L Mencken/ a nifty way to upstage the president—Wall Street Journal* **2** *n*: *. . . his six blonde nifties—Jerome Weidman/ Another nifty is the circularization of telephone subscribers—R Littell* **3** *adv*: *You did that real nifty* [origin unknown; called by Bret Harte, in the 1868 example, "Short for *magnificat*"]

◀**nig**▶ *n by 1932* A black person

◀**nigga**▶ (NIGG uh) *n by 1925* A black person •Not a taboo word as used by one black person to or about another, esp by rap singers: *For several years, it has become common for young blacks to greet each other as "nigga"—Robin Kelley*

◀**nigger**▶ **1** *n by 1786* A black person •Not a taboo word as used by one black person to or about another **2** *modifier*: *a nice nigger lady*
See BAD NIGGER

◀**nigger heaven**▶ *n phr by 1878* The topmost gallery or balcony of a theater

◀**nigger rich**▶ *adj phr by 1940s* Having much money, esp suddenly; =FLUSH: *I'm either nigger rich or stone poor—George V Higgins*

◀**niggra** or **nigra**▶ *n by 1944* =NIGGER

night *See* AMATEUR NIGHT, GOOD NIGHT, SATURDAY NIGHT SPECIAL

nightcap 1 *n by 1818* A drink taken just before going to bed or the last drink of the evening, esp an alcoholic drink: *Let's stop at Joe's for a nightcap* **2** *n baseball by 1917* The second game of a doubleheader

nightery *See* NITERY

nightie *n by 1894* A nightgown: *Aphrodite in her nightie, Oh my God what a sightie—Howard Moss*

night-night or **nightie-night** *interj by 1896* An amiable parting salutation at night

night owl or **nighthawk** *n* first form *by 1846*, second *by 1868* =NIGHT PERSON

night people (or **fighters**) *n phr by 1950s* People who work at night or prefer to be up late at night: *I happen to be "night people" and I'm always up late*—Xaviera Hollander/ *Night people, the professor and his wife used to retire about 2:30 to 3 AM*—F Marja

night person *n phr by 1950s* One of the night people: *She's a night person, never gets up before the afternoon*

night spot *n phr by 1936* A nightclub; cabaret; =BOITE, NITERY

-nik *suffix used to form nouns by 1940s* A person involved in, described by, or doing what is indicated: *beatnik/ computernik/ peacenik/ no-goodnik* [fr Yiddish fr Russian and other Slavic languages]

nimby *n* (also **nimbie** or **nebbie** or **nemmie** or **nemish**) *narcotics by 1950* Nembutal™ or any barbiturate

NIMBY (also **Nimby** or **nimby**) **1** *n by 1980* not in my back yard: *Institutions that no organized community wants in its backyard, prisons, sanitation works and other NIMBYs, have followed*—Nation **2** *modifier* Exclusivist; fiercely protective: *The local perspective is a recipe for disaster: ignorance, Nimby selfishness, isolationism, tribal and racial strife*—New York Times [fr "not in my backyard"]

nimrod *n 1980s teenagers* : *Of course, there's always the middle ground, reserved for friends who commit a blunder. For these, we have "nimrod," "klutz," and "geek"*—North Jersey Herald & News [fr the name of *Nimrod*, the "mighty hunter before the Lord" in *Genesis*]

NINA *sentence by early 1900s*: *There were businesses in Boston that needed employees but put up signs in the windows saying NINA, which, as we all know, meant No Irish Need Apply*—Tip O'Neill

nine 1 *n by 1990s* A nine-millimeter semiautomatic pistol: *. . . there was a fight. . . I saw a man running with a nine*—Milwaukee Journal/ *People seeking guns for personal combat want reliable stopping power, revolvers or semiautomatic pistols known as "nines"*—New York Times **2** *v*: *Motherfucker tried to stiff me on a buy and I nined him right there*—Robert B Parker

nine-days' wonder *n phr by 1594* A marvel of rather short duration; =FLASH IN THE PAN [the notion of a wonder lasting nine nights appears in Chaucer's *Troilus and Criseyde* of 1374]

nine-hundred-pound gorilla *See* SIX-HUNDRED-POUND GORILLA

the **nines** *See* DRESSED TO THE TEETH

the **nineteenth hole** *n phr golf by 1901* A drink or a spell of drinking after finishing a golf game

nine-to-five 1 *adj by 1950s* Occupying the time period of a regular, salaried, probably dull office job: *a nine-to-five drag of a job* **2** *v by 1962* To be regularly employed, esp in an office job: *. . . even when he was nine-to-fiving*—R Woodley

nine-to-fiver *by 1959* **1** *n* A person who is steadily employed: *As early as the 1920s they were called white-collar slaves . . . and by the 1950s nine-to-fivers*—The City in Slang **2** *n* A regular job, esp a salaried office job

ninety-day wonder *WWI armed forces* **1** *n phr* An Army or Navy officer commissioned after a three-month course at an officer candidate school **2** *n phr* Any very youthful officer **3** *n phr* A reserve officer put on active status after three months of training **4** *n phr* Any person doing a job with minimal training ●Usu used sarcastically: *They sent us another ninety-day wonder to run the department* [based on *nine-days' wonder*]

ninety-eight *n lunch counter by about 1935* The manager of a lunch counter

ninety-five *n lunch counter by about 1935* A customer who leaves without paying

ninety-nine 1 *n lunch counter by about 1935* The chief fry cook or chief soda jerk **2** *n salespersons by 1940s* Out-of-style or damaged goods that a salesperson is paid extra for selling

nine yards *See* the WHOLE NINE YARDS

◁**ninnies**▷ *n by 1990s* A woman's breasts; =JUGS, HOOTERS: *Ordell saw what looked like a swimsuit bra covering her ninnies*—Elmore Leonard

nip *n by 1796* A small quantity, a taste, of a drink: *Well, give me just a nip, then* [apparently fr *nipperkin*, "small measure of drink," found by 1694]

◀**Nip**▶ **1** *n WWII* A Japanese or person of Japanese ancestry **2** *adj*: *a Nip waitress* [fr *Nippon*, "Japan," which derives fr a Chinese word for "rising-sun place"]

nip and tuck *by 1857* **1** *adj phr* Equally likely to win or lose; even; neck and neck: *Near the finish they're nip and tuck* **2** *adj phr* Of equal probability; equally likely: *It's nip and tuck whether I'll get there in time or not* [earlier versions included *rip and tuck, nip and chuck*, and *nip and tack*, making the original semantics somewhat difficult to assess; the term might be from sailing or from sewing and tailoring]

nipper *n by 1859* A small boy; lad ●In British dialect, the youngest child of a family: *. . . warning that America's nippers are turning into microchip golem*—Washington Post [perhaps because he *nips*, "moves quickly"]

nippers *n by 1821* Handcuffs: *A newly appointed policeman. . . has to buy. . . a pair of nippers*—Outlook

◁**nips**▷ *n by 1970s* The nipples: *Barb's nips are not big and dark*—Dan Jenkins

nit *n* Nothing; =ZILCH: *If you're wondering about their homosexual records, it's nit*—Lawrence Sanders [fr Yiddish or perhaps German dialect]

nitery or **nightery** *n by 1934* A nightclub; =BOITE

nitpick *v* To quibble over trivia; niggle: *. . . so all that remains is for them to sit and lie there and nitpick over trivialities or talk about what's on TV. . .*—Douglas Coupland

nitpicking 1 *n* The act and pleasure of one who quibbles over trivia **2** *adj*: *a highly nit-picking attitude* [from the very slow and attentive work of a person or a simian picking tiny *nits*, "insect eggs," out of hair or fur]

nitro (NĪ troh) **1** *n by 1935* Nitroglycerin; =SOUP **2** *n 1960s hot rodders* Nitromethane, a fuel additive for cars

the **nitty gritty** or the **nitty 1** *n phr* black by 1960s The most basic elements, esp when unwelcome or unpleasant; harsh realities: . . . *from what they call the nitty gritty and the grass roots*—Bobby Seale/ . . . *the awesome and awful nitty gritty of today's urban condition*—Ada Louise Huxtable/ . . . *and shifting from ideology to the nitty*—National Review **2** *adj phr*: . . . *a lot of nitty-gritty campaigning as well*—Newsweek **3** *n phr* Practical details [fr the repellent association of *nits,* "the eggs of hair lice, young hair lice," and *grit,* "abrasive granules"]

nitwit *n* by 1922 A stupid person; fool; =BOOB [perhaps fr *nit,* fr German dialect, "no," found by 1909, plus *wit*]

nix 1 *n* by 1789 Nothing: . . . *wasn't taking her out here in the park for nix*—James T Farrell **2** *negation* by 1909 No: *I asked her for one and she said nix* **3** *n* by 1951 A refusal; veto: . . . *if the Petrillo nix stands*—Variety **4** *v* by 1903 To veto; reject: . . . *had been considering marriage but have apparently nixed the idea*—Washington Post/ . . . *and he was afraid that might nix his CBS deal*—Stan Cutler [fr German *nichts,* "nothing"]

nixie *n* post office by 1885 A piece of mail that cannot be delivered because of damage, illegibility, etc

nix on *v phr* by 1902 To forbid ●Used only as an imperative: *Nix on the hurry talk*—H McHugh/ *Nix on swiping anything*—E B White

nix sign *n phr* by 1990s: *A local cafe sells a T-shirt showing a howling coyote in a circle with a slash through it—the international nix sign*—New Yorker

no-account or **no-count 1** *adj* by 1845 Worthless; untrustworthy; incorrigible: *I'm a lazy no-account bum* **2** *n*: *A no-count that never did a right thing in his life*

nob *n* by 1755 A rich and important person; =SWELL [origin unknown]

no bargain *n phr* by 1940s A person or thing that is not especially desirable or good; =NO PRIZE PACKAGE: *Well, he's OK, but no bargain* [fr Yiddish *nit ka metsie*]

nobbler *n* by 1854 A person who drugs a racehorse or racing dog or otherwise tries to fix the outcome of a race ●Chiefly British: . . . *the nobblers who drugged dogs*—P Jones [origin unknown; perhaps fr *hobble,* "make lame," by the same interesting variation that gives *Hob* and *Nob* as nicknames for *Robert*]

nobby or **knobby** *adj* by 1788 Stylish; fashionable; smart: *Polo shirts, nobby ties*—James T Farrell/ *In 1903 Larkin picked up a nobby one-cylinder Winton*–New Yorker [fr *nob*]

no better than one **ought to be** *adj phr* by 1815 Sexually promiscuous; loose

no big deal *n phr* Nothing important; no problem: *I kept telling him that it wasn't any big deal*–New Yorker

no biggie *n phr* teenagers by 1970s =NO BIG DEAL

a **nobody** *n* by 1581 A person lacking fame, status, importance, etc; an uninteresting person; =NEBBISH

nobody home 1 *sentence* by 1919 This person is crazy, stupid, or feeble-minded; =OUT TO LUNCH **2** *modifier*: *Forrest Gump wears an expression of nobody's-home innocuousness throughout the picture*—New Yorker

◁**nobody likes a smart-ass (**or **wise-ass)**▷ *sentence* by 1980s What you just said is very offensive; you are too smart and acid for your own good: *Nobody likes a minority smart-ass*—Robert B Parker/ *"And you will notice that I am not sweating." "No one loves a smartass"*

no bones *See* MAKE NO BONES ABOUT

no-brain *adj* by 1980s Stupid; vapid: *The show was a loser right up to its no-brain ending*

no-brainer 1 *n* by middle 1980s Something very simple, requiring no intelligence: *The question of which CAD program to buy is a no-brainer; Autodesk's AutoCAD dominates the market*—PC World/ *Passing it seemed like a no-brainer, but it failed*—Macon Telegraph **2** *modifier*: *Alden Essex is currently the undisputed king of no-brainer novels*—comic strip "Mary Worth"/ *Lansing, with the help of no-brainer sequels such as* Wayne's World 2 *and* Addams Family Values, *has the studio back on track*—Vanity Fair

no can do *sentence* by 1923 I am unable or unwilling to do that: *On that schedule? No can do* [a phrase in pidgin English probably adopted and disseminated by seamen; popularized in the 1940s by a song having the phrase as a title]

no chicken or **no spring chicken** *modifier* first form by 1720, second by 1910 No longer young ●Usu said of a woman: *She looks great, but she's no spring chicken*

no-clap medal *n phr* WWII Army The Good Conduct Medal [fr the sardonic notion that not having *clap,* "gonorrhea," is sufficient evidence of good conduct]

no-count *See* NO-ACCOUNT

nod *v* 1960s narcotics To be intoxicated with narcotics to a very drowsy or stuporous state: . . . *with slews of rich kids nodding in the Scarsdale woods*—New York [the underlying sense, "let the head fall forward when drowsy," is found by 1562]

a **nod** *n phr* 1960s narcotics A stuporous state following an injection of narcotics: *He goes on a "nod," his head drooping, eyelids heavy*—J Mills/ *Here was Pimp in a nod*—Claude Brown *See* COLLAR A NOD

the **nod** *n phr* sports by about 1920 The affirmative decision; the signal of choosing or preference; =THUMBS UP: *Bold Ruler gets the nod over Gallant Man in today's renewal of the Carter Handicap*—The Morning Telegraph *See* GET THE NOD

noddle *See* NOODLE

no dice 1 *negation* by 1931 No; absolutely not; =NO SALE, NO SOAP, NO WAY: *A Nuevo Laredo judge said no dice*—G Spagnoli/ *Nice, but no dice*—W T Tyler **2** *adj* Worthless; =CRUMMY: . . . *a little no-dice paper called the Rome American*—Westbrook

Pegler [fr the call of a crapshooter that the roll just made is not valid]

no flies on someone or something *n phr* by *1888* Nothing impeding one's energy, awareness, soundness, up-to-dateness, etc: *There's no flies on Jersey. It's got more and better bookmakers. . .* — Joseph F Dinneen [fr the image of an active cow, horse, etc, on which *flies* cannot settle; the similar term *no flies about* is found in Australia by 1848]

no-frills *adj* by *1960* Restricted to the essentials; without frivolous ornamentation or flourishes: *Imagine a no-frills warehouse crossed with an abattoir*—Toronto Life

noggin *n* by *1866* The head: *. . . . . . the psychiatrist after diagnosing his noggin*—H Allen Smith [fr *noggin*, "mug," itself used for "face"] *See* MUG

no glove no love *modifier* by *1990s* Forbidding sex without a condom: *Female rappers have become front-line teachers of the "no glove, no love" school*—New York Times

no go *n phr* by *1825* An unlikely success; a sure failure; an impossibility: *We tried to save him, but it was no go*

no-go *adj* by *1960s* Not ready to proceed; inauspicious; blocked: *This looks like a no-go situation* [probably stimulated recently by astronauts' use] *See* GO NO-GO

no-good or **no-gooder** *1 n* first form by *1924*, second by *1950s* An unreliable or deplorable person; =BUM, NO-ACCOUNT, NO-GOODNIK: *A high-living no-good in a derby hat*—Hal Boyle *2 adj*: *His father was a no-good drunk*—Life [*no-good-boy* is found by 1908]

no-goodnik *n* by *1924* =NO-GOOD *See* -NIK

no great shakes *adj phr* by *1819* Mediocre; not outstanding; rather ineffective; =NOTHING TO WRITE HOME ABOUT: *I'm no great shakes at serve-and-volley* [origin unknown]

no-hitter *n* baseball by *1948* A game in which at least one side gets no base hits

no holds barred *1 adv phr* by *1940s* Free and uninhibited; with no limits or reservations: *They went at it no holds barred 2 adj phr*: *The commission was to produce a "no-holds-barred" study*—Washington Post [fr the rules of a wrestling match]

no-hoper *n* by *1957* A person who has no hope of success: *Stand-ins are the film industry's no-hopers, the ones who never made it*—Roger Tredre [found in Australian racing slang by 1943 as "a horse with no hope of winning"]

nohow *adv* by *1775* In no way; under no circumstances: *We tried, but couldn't manage to score nohow*

noise *1 n* by *1940s* Empty talk; meaningless verbiage; bluster: *That press release is plain noise 2 n* *1920s narcotics* Heroin *See* BIG NOISE, MAKE NOISES

no kidding or **no joke** *adv phr* first form by *1914*, second by *1880* Really; factually ●Often a question asked when one hears something astonishing or doubtful [the earlier form *no kid* is found by 1873]

no-knock *adj* by *1970s* Providing for or including the police right of entry without a search warrant: *The cops demanded a no-knock statute so that they could catch criminals in the lair*

no more Mister Nice Guy *n phr* by *1970s* No longer a decent, fair, trustworthy, amiable, etc, person: *If I get the nomination, it'll be no more Mr. Nice Guy*–Toronto Life/ *No More Mr. Nice Guy. . . Shevardnadze declares war on Georgia's rebels*—Time

nonbook *n* by *1960* A printed effort lacking literary value and normal publishing validity, usu one blatantly ghost-written and/or put out for reasons of sensation, meretricious chic, or brazen and high-pitched publicity

noncom (NAHN kahm) *n* by *1747* A noncommissioned officer

no-neck *1 n* by *1970s* A stupid, bigoted person; a brute =REDNECK: *. . . the moral and intellectual sleaziness of the media and its no-necks in residence*—Village Voice *2 modifier*: *Andrew Giuliani, the executive moppet, strolled uninvited to the lectern, as uninhibited as one of Tennessee Williams's no-neck monsters*—New York Times [fr the thick, *neckless* aspect of very muscular men, gorillas, etc]

nonevent by *1962 1 n* An apparent event staged or produced for or by the media *2 n* Something invalid; something that in effect did not happen: *"As a practical matter" the new rules are "a nonevent"*—Newsweek

no never mind *See* MAKE NO NEVER MIND

a **no-no** *n phr* by *1940s* Something forbidden; something very inadvisable: *The company says mustaches are a no-no*—Charlotte Observer/ *. . . allowing members to enjoy such former no-nos as corn on the cob*—Newsweek

non-sked *n* by *1946* An airline that has no fixed schedule of flights

nonstarter *n* by *1909* A failure; =ALSO-RAN, LOSER: *The proposed travel book. . . now seemed. . . to be a nonstarter*—Humphrey Carpenter/ *Compromises. . . should be considered "nonstarters"*–New Yorker

non-techie *n* by *1980s* A person who is unversed and uninterested in technical matters, esp in computers and electronics: *This network is aimed at non-techies, so I begged Amanda to try it*—Milwaukee Journal

noodge *See* NUDGE

noodle[1] *1 n* by *1914* The head; the mind: *Most of the fellows running television today are sick in the noodle*—Philip Hamburger *2 v* musicians by *1937* To play idly at an instrument; improvise lazily: *I noodled a bit on it and instantly realized I could express me*—Down Beat/ *Members of an avian orchestra are already softly noodling*—W H Auden *3 v* (also **noodle around**) by *1970s* To think, esp in a free and discursive way; indulge in mental play:

. . . as many drafts and as much noodling as I wanted to—Avery Corman/ . . . still noodling around with our. . . calculators and the latest census data—Fortune **4 v** by 1970s To play; toy: . . . noodling nervously with a glass of water—Aquarian [origin unknown; the "play around" senses perhaps influenced by doodle; noddle in the first sense is found by 1579]

noodle² **n** by 1753 A stupid person; fool; simpleton •Still predominantly British when not entirely outdated: Something that noodle at Interior might reflect on—Washington Post [origin unknown; perhaps fr noodle the food, fr German nudel, because of its limp and wormlike connotations]

noodlehead **n** by 1950s A stupid person; =NOODLE

noodlework **n** by 1940s Mental work or effort; thinking; studying: This job's going to need plenty of noodlework

noogie (Nŏŏ gee, Nŏŏ-) **n** 1960s teenagers A painful rubbing of the scalp with the knuckles; =DUTCH RUB: Tomashek. . . was probably the first challenger in heavyweight history whose most effective tactic was a noogie—Milwaukee Journal
See TOUGH SHIT

◁**nookie** or **nookey** or **nooky**▷ (Nŏŏk ee) by 1928 **1 n** Sexual activity; the sex act; =ASS, COOZ: . . . a young kid tryin' to get his first nookey!—Budd Schulberg/ . . . if you can't give her a little nooky—People Weekly **2 n** A woman regarded as a sex partner; =ASS, CUNT [origin unknown; perhaps fr Dutch neuken, "to fuck"]

◁**no one loves a smart-ass**▷ **See** NOBODY LIKES A SMART-ASS

nooner **n** by 1980s A sex act done at midday: . . . putting a tax on anyone who checks into a motel for what is crudely called a "nooner"—Mike Royko/ . . . so she invited this boy. . . here for a nooner—Harry Crews

nope **negation** by 1888 No [fr no plus an intrusive stop resulting from the closure of the lips, rather than the glottis as is normal]

no picnic **n phr** by 1888 A difficult or trying experience; a hard time or task: While the ground crew didn't exactly have to carry me onto the plane kicking and screaming, it was no picnic—Playboy/ It's no picnic, teaching people to play—Washington Post

noplaceville 1950s students **1 adj** Dull and tedious; =DEADSVILLE **2 n** A small, unimportant town; =JERK TOWN

no potatoes **See** ALL THAT MEAT AND NO POTATOES

no prize package or **no prize** **n phr** by 1940s A person or thing of little worth, interest, charm; =NO BARGAIN: He's well qualified on paper, but no prize package

no problem or **no prob** **interj** by 1963 An assurance that everything is under control, that no difficulties are at hand in spite of appearances; =NO SWEAT: You'd like a red one? No problem—American Idioms Dictionary

north **adv** by 1864 In the direction of increase; upward:

A few months ago the cost of a 4-megabit memory chip was $11 on the spot market. Last week, it was $20 and heading north—New York Times

north of **adj phr** by 1990s More than; above: Credit Lyonnais will probably pay Ovitz north of $30 million—Time/ . . . a good guess would be somewhere north of $5 million—Milwaukee Journal

northpaw **n** baseball by 1922 A righthanded person, esp a baseball pitcher [based on southpaw]

no sale **negation** by 1934 No; absolutely not; =NO DICE, NO SOAP, NO WAY: Sorry, Still No Sale; Assad still denied that terrorism had been discussed with the White House—Time [fr the sign which arose into the glass indexing window of a cash register when the No Sale key was punched]

nose **n** underworld by 1830 A police informer; =STOOL PIGEON

See BLUENOSE, BY A NOSE, DOG'S-NOSE, HARD-NOSED, HAVE A BUG UP one's ASS, HAVE someone's NOSE OPEN, KEEP one's NOSE CLEAN, LOOK DOWN one's NOSE, NO SKIN OFF MY ASS, ON THE NOSE, PAY THROUGH THE NOSE, POKE one's NOSE INTO something, POPE'S NOSE, PUT someone's NOSE OUT OF JOINT

nose around **v phr** by 1879 To show strong inquisitiveness; investigate, esp closely and slyly; pry: Why are you nosing around in my life in the first place?—Robert B Parker

the **nosebag** **See** PUT ON THE FEEDBAG

nosebleed **1 n** sports by middle 1980s Putative nasal bleeding caused by high altitudes: $50. This is the dreaded 400 section of Madison Square Garden. Short of flying on the Concorde, a seat here offers one of the most glamorous nosebleeds available anywhere—New York Times **2 modifier**: Sitting next to Bob Uecker up there in Nosebleed Heaven—Milwaukee Journal/ I passed the evening of January 1 in the nosebleed section of the Louisiana Superdome watching Alabama claim the championship—New Republic/ . . . were forced to watch the show standing behind nosebleed seats in the balcony—Milwaukee Journal

nose candy **n phr** narcotics by 1930s A narcotic, esp cocaine, taken by sniffing: . . . a deck of nose candy for sale—J Evans

nosed **See** HARD-NOSED

nose dive **1 n phr** by 1920 A sudden and large decrease: The price of gold took a nose dive **2 v**: Our morale nose-dived yesterday [fr the precipitate descent of an airplane, found by 1912]

no see **See** LONG TIME NO SEE

no-see-um **n** by 1847 Any tiny biting insect; midge; gnat [fr a presumed Indian term]

nose for news **n phr** by 1893 Special ability and eagerness for learning news: A good reporter has, first of all, a keen nose for news

nose job (or **bob**) **n phr** by 1963 Plastic surgery to beautify a nose; rhinoplasty

nose someone **out** **v phr** by 1940s To defeat by a small margin; barely win over; win by a nose: He nosed out the leading candidate in Iowa

nose out of joint *See* PUT someone's NOSE OUT OF JOINT

nose tackle or **nose guard** *n phr* football by 1970s A lineman whose position is just opposite the center: *"I don't want to celebrate yet,"* said nose tackle Jeff Wright—Time/ *Charlie Krueger, a former nose tackle, retired from the San Francisco 49ers in 1973*—Nation

nosh or **nash** (NAHSH) *by 1957* **1** *v* To have a snack; nibble: *. . . noshing on more fruits and veggies. . .* —Sassy **2** *n*: *He always liked a little nosh between meals* [fr Yiddish]

noshery *n by 1963* A restaurant or delicatessen, esp for snacking

◁**no shit**▷ **1** *interj by 1940s* Is that right; you wouldn't "shit" me, would you; =NO KIDDING: *"No-o,"* said Gold with extravagant amazement, "shit"—Joseph Heller/ *Uh. . . now, you mean? No shit*—Armistead Maupin **2** *modifier* Genuine; real; =HONEST-TO-GOD: *. . . the man from Santo Domingo, a no-shit revolutionary full of zeal*—Elmore Leonard

no-show **1** *n by 1941* Someone or something that fails to keep an appointment, use a reserved seat, etc: *Snowstorm a no-show*—Morris County Daily Record/ *The airline figures about 20 percent no-shows* **2** *adj* Designating a nonexistent worker or job, usu on the public payroll: *. . . a no-show job Sonny got him*—George V Higgins

no siree or **no siree bob** *negation* first form by 1848, second by 1890 No; absolutely no: *Nope, never, no way. No siree bob*—Milwaukee Journal

◁**no skin off my ass**▷ *adj phr* (Variations: **butt** or **ear** or **nose** may replace **ass**) entry form by 1920, nose form by 1909 Of no concern, esp damaging concern, to me; immaterial: *. . . and if you fall on your face, no skin off my nose*—W T Tyler

no slouch *adj phr by 1796* Very able or competent; skilled ●Often followed by *at* something: *She's no slouch at finding good restaurants/ When it comes to golf he is definitely no slouch* [fr British dialect *slouch*, "awkward, lazy person," found by 1515]

no soap *negation by 1924* No; absolutely not; =NO DICE, NO SALE, NO WAY: *"No soap,"* said the assistant warden—New York Times/ *. . . tried to talk her out of it, but no soap*—Lawrence Sanders [origin unknown; perhaps fr the question *how are you off for soap?*, found by 1834, but of no obvious relevance]

no spring chicken *See* NO CHICKEN

no strings attached *adj phr by 1940s* Free of conditions, limitations, etc: *He's giving us the house with no strings attached* [fr *string*, "a restriction," found by 1888; the similar form *"no strings to something"* is found by 1909]

no sweat *n phr by 1950s* No problem or difficulty; an easy thing: *No sweat, though!*—New York Times/ *It was no sweat for me*—Claude Brown

nosy or **nosey** *adj by 1882* Inquisitive, esp overly so; prying: *. . . everyone on the staff must be super nosy*—Hugh Pentecost/ *We shall not be nosey*—W H Auden

not *negation by 1990s* What has just been stated is emphatically not true: *Millions of animals in experimental labs die annually. Shock value? NOT!*—Utne Reader/ *Hooray for Pat Buchanan, not!*—New Yorker/ *Dan Quayle has already filmed a commercial declaring Murphy Brown his favorite show. . . not*—Vanity Fair

not a dime's worth of difference *n phr by 1990s* Hardly any difference: *There's not a dime's worth of difference between the candidates on health care*

not all beer and skittles *adj phr* (also **not all skittles and beer**) *by 1857* Not entirely pleasant or easy; not a picnic, cinch, piece of cake, etc [fr *skittles*, a bowling game played in taverns and pubs; Dickens used the form *all porter and skittles* in 1837]

not all there *by 1864* **1** *adj phr* Stupid; feebleminded: *The poor creature who's not quite all there. . .* —Agatha Christie **2** *adj phr* Crazy; eccentric; =NUTS, OUT TO LUNCH

not a one-way street *n phr by 1950s* A situation, arrangement, etc, where reciprocal fairness is desired or required; =IT TAKES TWO TO TANGO: *Remember, this negotiation is not a one-way street*

not bat an eye *v phr by 1904* To not show surprise, reluctance, etc: *"I'm leaving,"* she said. He didn't bat an eye

not be caught dead *v phr by 1940s* To be defiantly set against; be extremely reluctantly found or seen: *I wouldn't be caught dead in that dress*

not (or **barely**) **break a sweat** *v phr* prizefighting by 1970s To do something very easily; be entirely nonchalant; =NOT TURN A HAIR: *The touring Soviet squad barely broke a sweat in the 6–2 victory over the Badgers. . .* —Milwaukee Journal

not buttoned up too tightly *adj phr by 1980s* Feeble-minded; eccentric; =NOT ALL THERE, NOT WRAPPED TIGHT: *. . . a nice old gentleman, but not buttoned-up too tightly, as you've noticed*—Lawrence Sanders

not by a long shot *adv phr by 1861* Not at all; emphatically not: *It's not my best work, not by a long shot*

not carved (or **etched**) **in stone** *adj phr* (also **not cast in concrete**) *by 1970s* Not having ultimate and permanent authority; able to be altered: *It's a good policy, but it's neither carved in stone nor set in concrete* [fr the *carved stone* tablets of the Decalogue]

notch **1** *v by 1623* To score; achieve: *. . . a pacy serve that's notched a few aces in its time*—Toronto Life ◁**2**▷ *v by 1970s* To do the sex act ●Use attributed to volleyball players: *Guys don't fuck, they notch*—Playboy [first sense fr use of the term in cricket, and influenced by the cowboy tradition of filing a *notch* in the handle of one's pistol for each man killed]

See NOTCHERY, TOP-NOTCH

notch baby *n phr by middle 1980s* A person born between 1917 and 1921, and who is said to receive less of Social Security benefits thereby

notchery or **notch-house** *n by 1931* A brothel [fr earlier *notch*²]

not count for spit *v phr by 1980s* To be very insignificant; be trivial: *Aptitude for speaking. . . amusingly doesn't count for spit*—Fran Lebowitz [*spit* is a euphemism for *shit*; *count*, "to be of importance," is found by 1857]

not cricket *adv phr British by 1900* Improper; dubious; unethical; unfair: *Something not quite cricket happened*—Washington Post [fr inadmissible actions in the game of *cricket*]

not dry behind the ears *adj phr* (also **wet behind the ears** and **still wet behind the ears**) *entry form by 1939,* wet forms *by 1931* Not mature; inexperienced; callow: *He's not dry behind the ears yet, but he's learning* [perhaps an allusion to the wet condition of newborns]

note *See* BLUE NOTE, CASE NOTE, C-NOTE, DIME-NOTE, FIVE-CASE NOTE, a HELL OF A NOTE, MASH NOTE, SWAP NOTES

no-tell motel *n phr by 1980s* A discreet motel for sexual rendezvous: *He goes to a no-tell motel at least twice a week*—Denver radio talk show/ *The last six Presidents combined do not conjure up enough erotic energy to fill a single room at the No-Tell Motel*—Time

not enough Indians *See* TOO MANY CHIEFS AND NOT ENOUGH INDIANS

◁**not get** one's **balls** (or **bowels**) **in an uproar**▷ *v phr by 1930s* To avoid becoming excited or upset; stay calm; =COOL IT ●Often an attempt to soothe someone: *Come on! Don't get your feminist balls in an uproar*—Lawrence Sanders

not get one's **knickers in a twist** *v phr British by 1971* To avoid becoming tense and upset

not get one's **shorts in a knot** *v phr by 1990s*: *Don't get your shorts in a knot, it's only a suggestion*

◁ **not get** one's **testicles in a twist**▷ *v phr by 1990s* To avoid becoming tense and upset; =NOT GET one's KNICKERS IN A TWIST: *I'm coming, Mr. McAllister! Don't get your testicles in a twist!*—Carsten Stroud

not give a damn *v phr* (Variations: **dang** or **darn** or **dern** or **durn** or **diddly-damn** or **diddly-shit** or ◀**flying fuck**▶ or ◀**fuck**▶ or **hill of beans** or **hoot** or **piss** or ◁**rat's ass**▷ or **rat's behind** or **rat's rump** or **rip** or ◁**shit**▷ or **spit** or **squat** or **two hoots in hell** may replace **damn**) *entry form by 1895,* fuck *by 1929,* hill of beans *by 1863,* hoot *by 1878,* rip *by 1940s* To be indifferent to or contemptuous of; not care one whit: *I don't give a damn what they do to me/ Nobody gave a flying fuck who their influences were—Aquarian/ When do celebrities give a hoot about people who interview them?*—Philadelphia/ *We all busted up because George didn't give a rat's ass*—William Kennedy/ *The average American child does not give a rip*

about O J Simpson—Milwaukee Journal Sentinel/ *Me, I don't give a shit, high road, low road, I go either way*—W T Tyler/ *Anyway, who gives a fuck, actually?*—Ed McBain

◀**not give a fuck for nothing**▶ *v phr by 1940s* To be absolutely indifferent and unafraid: *Ole Bobby Joe don't give a fuck for nothing*

not give someone **the time of day** *v phr by 1593* Not do the slightest favor for; not greet or speak to; have contempt for: *Like him? I wouldn't give that bastard the time of day* [the dated instance, from Shakespeare, is not in the negative]

not have a clue *v phr WWII British armed forces* To be uninformed or ignorant about something; be "clueless": *"You know who I was?" "Haven't got a clue"*—W T Tyler

not have a leg to stand on *v phr by 1594* To lack support for one's position. arguments, etc: *My lawyer told me I didn't have a leg to stand on, so I shouldn't sue the company*—American Idioms Dictionary

not have all one's **buttons** *v phr by 1860* To be feeble-minded; be "not all there": *I'm afraid the old fellow doesn't have all his buttons*

not have all one's **switches on** *v phr by 1970s* To be retarded or demented; be mentally subnormal ●Used as a jocular insult rather than a clinical judgment: *Reasonable people come to the movies to watch the movie. . . the movietalker. . . doesn't have all his switches on*—Washington Post

◁**not have a pot** (or **without a pot**) **to piss in**▷ *v phr by 1930s* To be very poor and deprived; be penniless: *. . . entering their middle years without a pot to piss in*—Ed McBain

not have a prayer *See* HAVE A PRAYER

not have brain one *v phr by 1960s* To be very stupid

not have brains enough to walk and chew gum at the same time *v phr by 1960s* To be lacking the most elementary intelligence

not have nickel one *v phr by 1942 black* To be without money: *You ain't got nickel one*—Zora Neale Hurston

not have one dollar to rub against another *v phr by 1930s* To lack money: *When we came from West Virginia we didn't have one dollar to rub against another*

not have the foggiest notion (or **the foggiest**) *v phr British by 1917* To be entirely ignorant and uncertain: *. . . I didn't have the foggiest notion what "the right thing" was*—Hugh Pentecost

not having any *v phr by 1903* To refuse to accept; reject; ignore: *Home buyers weren't having any and more than a few developers went belly-up*—Apartment Life

'nother *See* a WHOLE 'NOTHER

nothing *adj by 1950s* Inane; lacking charm, talent, interest, etc; worthless: *That was a real nothing experience*
See DANCE ON AIR, DO someone NOTHING, KNOW FROM NOTHING

a **nothing** *n phr by 1950s* Someone or something that lacks all talent, charm, qualities, etc; =NEBBISH: *This show's a total nothing*

nothing doing 1 *negation by 1910* No; absolutely not; =NIX, NO WAY: *Buy that piece of crap? Nothing doing* **2** *n phr by 1827* A lack of activity; stasis: *Nothing doing on the job front*

nothing flat *See* IN NOTHING FLAT

nothing to write home about *n phr by 1914* A very ordinary or mediocre person or thing; nothing special; =NO GREAT SHAKES: *His pitch was nothing to write home about*

not just another pretty face *n phr by 1970s* Not someone or something of no particular distinction; not a specious person or thing: *He had a time convincing them he was a genuine expert, not just another pretty face* [fr the plight of a young woman, esp in popular fiction or film, who has intelligence, talent, etc, but fears she is being treated by males as only an ordinary sex object]

not just whistling Dixie *v phr* To be saying something important or useful: *When they warned us about this they weren't just whistling Dixie* *See* WHISTLE DIXIE

◁**not know** one's **ass from** one's **elbow**▷ *v phr* (Variations: **a hole in the ground** or **third base** may replace one's **elbow**) *by 1930* To be very ignorant; be hopelessly ill-informed; be stupid; =KNOW FROM NOTHING: *Well, he obviously didn't know his ass from a hole in the ground*—Village Voice/ *He doesn't know his ass from third base*—George V Higgins

not know beans *v phr* (Variations: **diddly** or **diddley** or **diddly-damn** or **diddly-poo** or **diddly-poop** or **diddly-shit** or **diddly-squat** or **diddly-squirt** or **diddly-whoop** or **shit** or **squat** or **zilch** or **zip** may replace **beans**) *by 1833* To be very ignorant; not know even the fundamentals ●In each case the positive and negative idiom have the same meaning: *You don't know beans, do you?*—Russell Baker/ *. . . may have been England's greatest mathematical puzzle inventor, but he knew beans about spiders and flies*—Games [entry form fr an old joke question, found by 1830, "How many blue beans make five white?"]

not know enough to come in out of the rain *v phr by 1884* To be quite stupid, esp in practical matters: *Ross thought that people with talent didn't in general know enough to come in out of the rain*—New Yorker [the positive form is found by 1599]

not know someone **from Adam** *v phr* (also **Adam's off ox** or **from Adam's house cat**) *entry form by 1843*, ox *by 1890*, cat *by 1908* To be entirely unacquainted with or uncognizant of: *We're bigger than 90 percent of the companies on the Big Board, but nobody knows us from Adam*—Fortune/ *I didn't know from Adam's house cat who Nolan Ryan was*—Milwaukee Journal

not know from nothing *See* KNOW FROM NOTHING

not know something **if it bit** someone *v phr by 1990s* To be quite ignorant and unperceptive: *Kuttner wouldn't know a strategic trade policy if it bit him on the leg*—Atlantic Monthly

◁**not know shit from Shinola**▷ *v phr by 1930* =NOT KNOW one's ASS FROM one's ELBOW ●Often euphemized: *. . . a tightfisted banker who doesn't know what from Shinola*—New York Times/ *In high school I didn't know shoot from Shinola*—TV show Geraldo [fr *Shinola*™, a brand of shoe polish; used partly for a suggestion of brown color, mainly for alliteration]

not lay a glove (or **finger** or **hand**) **on** someone *v phr* prizefighting *by 1940s* To leave unscathed; fail to hurt: *To this point, they haven't laid a glove on him*—Philadelphia Inquirer

not make deals *v phr by 1960s* To refuse to operate by or tolerate clandestine or unethical arrangements: *I don't make deals, especially not with crooks*

no tomorrow *See* LIKE IT'S GOING OUT OF STYLE

not on your life *negation by 1896* No; absolutely not; =NOTHING DOING, NO WAY: *Drink that? Not on your life*

not play for someone *v phr by 1990s* To be unappealing or unconvincing for one: *I like the idea, but it may not play for you*

not play with a full deck *See* PLAY WITH A FULL DECK

not put it past someone *v phr by 1870* To believe someone capable of an indicated act, opinion, etc: *I wouldn't put it past you to believe such hogwash*

not say boo *v phr by 1940s* To keep silent; not respond: *He didn't say boo when I called him a thief* [perhaps fr earlier *not say boo to a goose*, "to be afraid or too timid to speak"]

not so hot *adj phr* teenagers *by 1926* Not very good; mediocre; poor: *I didn't flunk, but my record isn't so hot*—P Marks [the form *not so warm* is found by 1900]

not to be sneezed at *adj phr by 1813* Not to be underrated; of considerable value: *It's not a big salary, but still not to be sneezed at*

not too shabby *adj phr by 1980s* Quite good; highly acceptable: *The Angels train in Palm Springs, California, which isn't too shabby*—Whitey Herzog

not touch someone or something **with a ten-foot pole** *v phr by 1909* To be loath to have anything to do with; be suspicious or apprehensive; reject: *If I were you I wouldn't touch that proposition with a ten-foot pole* [semantically akin to the proverb advising us to use a long spoon when we eat with the devil; an earlier and once more-common version spoke of a *forty-foot pole*]

not to worry *sentence by 1958* There is nothing to worry about ●Still chiefly British: *Not to worry, I bought plenty of food for everybody*

not turn a hair *v phr by 1897* To remain unruffled; stay cool; =NOT BREAK A SWEAT: *Surprisingly, he* *did not turn a hair when I told him about the threat* [fr the same phrase applied to a horse's unruffled hair, found by 1798]

not worth a bucket (or **pitcher) of warm spit** *adj phr* (Variations: **spit in the wind** or **dry spit on a hot day** may replace **a bucket of warm spit**) *by 1970s* Of very little value; worthless: *The new telephones are not worth a bucket of warm spit/ . . . a cable TV contract for the Bronx, Brooklyn, Queens, and Staten Island that's worth about as much as a bucket of warm spit*—Village Voice/ *Some is good. Really worthwhile. But a lot of it ain't worth spit in the wind*—Milwaukee Journal/ *In the great scheme of things, woodchucks are not worth dry spit on a hot day*—Milwaukee Journal

not worth a damn (or **a shit)** *first variant by 1817; second by 1920s* **1** *adv phr* Not well at all: *This guy doesn't sing worth a damn/ She doesn't like me worth a shit* **2** *adj phr*: *Those promises aren't worth a damn*

not worth a hill of beans *adj phr by 1863* Worthless; useless

not worth a plugged nickel *adj phr by 1940s* Valueless: *His word isn't worth a plugged nickel* [a *plugged* coin was counterfeit or had an insertion of inferior metal]

no two ways about it *adv phr by 1818* Clearly; definitely: *No two ways about it, this guy is nuts*

not wrapped tight *adj phr by 1968* Crazy; eccentric; =NOT ALL THERE, NOT BUTTONED UP TOO TIGHTLY: *Your father was not wrapped real tight. His loaf was missing several slices*—Harry Crews/ *Some MEs, who weren't wrapped too tightly to begin with. . .* —Michael Grant [fr the image of something *wrapped* neatly without loose ends, spillage, etc]

nougat *n* A stupid or crazy person; =BOOB, NUT, SAP: *I told her not to be a nougat*—K Brush [because nuts are the principal ingredient of *nougat*, the candy]

nouveau punk *n phr by 1993* Newer aspects of the "punk" style

Nova *n by 1970s* Nova Scotia smoked salmon; lox

now *adj by 1967* Up-to-date; very much au courant; thoroughly modern: *tripping out on now words*—Newsweek/ *the Right On, Now Generation*—Gail Sheehy

no way or **no way, Jose** or **no way in hell** **1** *negation by early 1960s* No; absolutely not; =NO DICE: *No good. No go. No way, Jose*—Village Voice/ *You absolutely no way in hell can use my name*—Brian Di Salvatore **2** *adv phr* Never; under no circumstances: *No way will I resign. You'll have to fire me*

See THERE'S NO WAY

no way to run a railroad **See** A HELL OF A WAY TO RUN A RAILROAD

nowhere or **nowheresville** *adj by 1940* Inferior; tedious; drab: *If you're not with it, you're nowhere*—L Lipton/ *. . . rows of folding chairs, nowheresville decor*—New York Magazine

See the MIDDLE OF NOWHERE

no-win *adj* Impossible to win; hopeless: *This tax business is a no-win situation/ Furious Volley in a No-Win Match*—Time

nozzle *n prizefighting by 1871* The nose; =SCHNOZZ

nubblies *n by 1935* Bumps; lumps; scattered protrusions: *Instead of a green plastic pad with little plastic nubblies. . .* —Douglas Coupland

nudge (NŏŏJ, NŏŏD jə) (also **noodge** or **nudjh** or **nudgy** or **nudzh**) **1** *n by 1960s* A chronic nagger, kibitzer, or complainer: *He's not a writer, he's a nudge*—New York Times/ *. . . not as an assassin, but as a nudge and a nerd*—Time **2** *v*: *Usually he comes up to nudgy me while I'm writing*—Bernard Malamud/ *. . . and oh nudjh, could he nudjh!*—Philip Roth [fr Yiddish fr Slavic "fret, dully ache"; perhaps influenced by English *nudge*]

nudge elbows **See** RUB ELBOWS

nudging **See** MOTHERFUCKING

nudie *by 1935* **1** *n* A movie, play, etc, in which players appear naked **2** *n* A nude or nearly nude female performer: *. . . some of the worried little nudies*—Westbrook Pegler **3** *n* A magazine, book, etc, featuring pictures of nudes; =SKIN MAGAZINE **4** *modifier*: *I bought a couple of nudie magazines*

nudnik (NŏŏD nihk) *n* An annoying person; pest; nuisance; =NUDGE: *the story of a gang of nudniks trying to defeat the establishment*—Newsweek/ *. . . remains an unreconstructed nudnik throughout*—Wilfred Sheed [fr Yiddish *nudne*, "boring"]

See -NIK

nuff said *sentence by 1841* Enough has been said; that closes the topic: *I will not go, never. Nuff said*

nuke **1** *n by 1959* A nuclear device or facility; nuclear weapon; nuclear power plant **2** *v by 1969* To destroy with a nuclear weapon or weapons: *The global village has been nuked*—Time **3** *v by 1986* To destroy; eliminate; =KILL: *Jesus Christ, I can nuke this guy*—Mike Royko/ *Nuke this whole paragraph*—Julie Downs/ *. . . she didn't seem like someone who's contributed to the community. Nuke*—Sassy **4** *v by 1987* To cook or heat in a microwave oven

See ANTINUKE

nuke oneself *v phr 1980s students* To go to a tanning salon

nuke and puke *n phr by 1989*: *Anything except a nuke and puke. . . A microwavable frozen dinner*—comic strip "Sally Forth"

numb *adj by 1950s* Stupid; unresponsive

numb-brained *adj by 1930* Stupid; dull-witted: *. . . recruits from the numb-brained hanger-on*—E Lavine

number **1** *n by 1919* A person, esp one considered to be clever and resourceful or attractive; =ARTICLE, HOT NUMBER ●Always preceded by an adjective or by the locution "quite a": *. . . some dizzy broad that must have been a snappy number*—Jerome Weidman/ *. . . bored-looking number*—J Evans **2** *n by 1894* A piece of merchandise, esp of clothing; =ARTICLE: *I found a number I liked pretty well*—James M Cain **3** *n show business by 1885* A theatrical act or routine, esp a song; =SHTICK: *He does that number with the tablecloth* **4** *n* by 1970s A tactic or trick; =ACT: *When he's pulling one of his numbers, he knows what he's doing*—H Hertzberg **5** *n* homosexuals A casual homosexual partner; =TRICK **6** *n* 1960s narcotics A marijuana cigarette: *. . . smoked a couple of numbers in the room*—Richard Merkin [merchandise sense fr the model *number* that most retail items have]

See A-1, BACK NUMBER, BOXCAR NUMBERS, BY THE NUMBERS, DO A NUMBER ON, DO one's NUMBER, HAVE someone's NUMBER, HOT NUMBER

a **number** *n phr* by 1980s Something noted, esp a sexual relationship; =an ITEM: *Hey, we're a number. . . . We have a non-casual relationship now*—Leslie Hollander

number cruncher 1 *n phr* by 1966 A computer or mechanical calculator **2** *n phr* (also **numbers cruncher**) by 1971 One who regularly processes or works with figures, statistics, records, etc, esp with a computer: *As a veteran numbers cruncher, I find that good research often raises more questions than it answers*—Playboy/ *. . . promote clerks rather than bring in fancy number-crunchers from outside*—Village Voice **3** *adj* Requiring mathematics, statistics, etc: *number-cruncher course*

number-crunching *n* computer by 1980s Doing serious and difficult mathematics by computer: *. . . played chartered accountant for a few sessions of number crunching*—Toronto Life

someone's **number is up** sentence by 1899 One is dead or about to die: *I'm glad we never know when our number is up until it's up*

Number One or **number one 1** *n phr* by 1704 One's own self, esp as competitive with others; =NUMERO UNO: *Always look out for Number One, he says* **2** *n phr* by 1902 Urination **3** *v*: *The little kid had to number one real bad*

number-one boy by 1950s **1** *n phr* The chief; =BOSS, HONCHO **2** *n phr* The chief lieutenant or assistant of a leader or ruler: *He's the president's number-one boy*

numbers *n* sports A player's averages, statistics, etc; =STATS: *. . . I've always thought numbers were a hill of beans. The only numbers that matter are wins and losses*—Milwaukee Journal

See BY THE NUMBERS

the **numbers** *n phr* by 1897 An illegal gambling game in which players bet that a certain number will appear somewhere; the policy racket: *Poor people lose a lot playing the numbers*

number two 1 *n phr* by 1902 Defecation **2** *v phr*: *He ran off into the woods, having to number two*

numbhead or **numbie** *n* first form by 1876 A stupid person

numbheaded *adj* by 1847 Stupid; =NUMB-BRAINED

◁**numb-nuts**▷ by 1960s **1** *n* A despicable person; =JERK, LIMP-DICK: *You gotta get a better job, numbnuts*—George V Higgins **2** *modifier*: *. . . not the numbnuts chatter cornballs like Bob Hope or Yellowman peddle*—Village Voice

Numero Uno or **numero uno** by 1883 **1** *n phr* One's own self, esp as the object of one's best efforts; =NUMBER ONE **2** *n phr* The chief; leader; =BOSS, HONCHO: *. . . a clear understanding between the brothers about who is Numero Uno*—Toronto Life **3** *n phr* The most distinguished person in a field or endeavor: *. . . now an also-ran. . . but for many years Numero Uno*—Toronto Life [fr Italian or Spanish]

See TAKE CARE OF NUMERO UNO

nurd **See** NERD

nurse 1 *v* by 1942 To consume one's drink slowly: *He ordered a highball and nursed it all evening* **2** *v* by 1980s To handle or drive slowly and carefully: *I nursed it away from the curb and went out Main Street. . .* —Robert B Parker

nut 1 *n* by 1846 The head **2** *n* by 1903 A crazy or eccentric person; maniac; =FLAKE, SCREWBALL: *It is forbidden to call any character a nut; you have to call him a screwball*–New Yorker **3** *n* by 1934 A very devoted enthusiast; =BUG, FREAK: *He's a nut about double crostics* **4** *n* by 1912 The investment needed for a business; capital and fixed expenses: *. . . producing a daily income that barely met the nut*—A J Liebling/ *Our nut is high, but our variable expenses are practically nothing*—New York Magazine **5** *n* 1960s underworld Any illegal payoff to a police officer: *. . . what they called "the nut," payoffs to the police*—M Arnold **6** *n* 1960s underworld A share in the graft collected by police officers ◁**7**▷ *n* by 1899 A testicle; =BALL: *He said it griped his left nut* [insanity sense probably fr late 1800s *off* one's *nut*, that is, head; senses 4, 5, and 6 fr the custom of taking the retaining *nut* from the wheel of a circus wagon, to be returned when all bills were paid]

See GRIPE one's ASS, a TOUGH NUT TO CRACK

-nut *combining word* by 1930s A devotee or energetic practitioner of what is indicated; =BUFF, FREAK: *. . . when one football nut writes a book*—Arthur Daley/ *. . . But he's not just a word nut*—Playboy

nutball (Variations: **bar** or **cake** or **case** may replace **ball**) **1** *n* entry form, bar, and cake by 1970s, case by about 1950 A crazy or eccentric person; =NUT: *A lot of nutballs accost you at that corner/ The Protestants in Ireland also have their share of nutcakes*—Boston Globe/ *I'm not a nut case*—Xenia Field **2** *adj*: *. . . murdered by nutball moneybags Harry K Thaw*—Newsweek/ *Use the nutbar examples we've provided here*—National Lampoon/ *. . . not such a nutcake question*—William Goldman

nutburger *modifier* by 1980s Crazy; very eccentric: *Here are the nutburger remedies, my fellow sufferers*—Esquire/ *It was a complete nutburger case*—Rocky Mountain News ["a sort of hamburger made with nuts" found by 1934]

nut-crunching *n* by 1970s The sapping or destruction of masculinity; figurative castration; =BALL-BUSTING: *Adrienne Barbeau, playing a government investigator whose best defense is nut-crunching*—Village Voice

nuthouse *n* (Variations: **box** or **college** or **factory** or **foundry** or **hatch** may replace **house**) *entry form by 1920s, box by 1960s, college by 1934, factory by 1915, foundry by 1932, hatch by 1940s* A mental hospital; insane asylum: *He has been recalled by the nut college. . .* —comic strip "Major Hoople"/ *. . . goes away to the nut house*—Jim Tully/ *. . . exceptional privacy and independence even in a nut hatch*—Earl Thompson/ *. . . a general air of having been redecorated by a parolee from a nut hatch*—Raymond Chandler

nuts or **nerts** or **nertz** 1 *adj first form by 1914, second by 1932* Crazy; very eccentric; =BUGHOUSE, MESHUGA: *Are you nuts to turn your back on a deal that could mean life or death?*—Philip Roth/ *Heir Rejected 400G, Is He Nuts?*—New York Daily News 2 *interj by 1931* An exclamation of disbelief, defiance, contempt, dismay, etc: *General McAuliffe replied "Nuts!" to the Germans at Bastogne* ◁3▷ *n by 1899* The testicles; =BALLS, FAMILY JEWELS: *They want to get their nuts out of the sand*—Eldridge Cleaver

See BUST one's ASS, the CAT'S MEOW, GET one's NUTS, HOT ROCKS, NUMB-NUTS, TIGHT AS KELSEY'S NUTS

the **nuts** or the **nerts** or the **nertz** *n phr first form by 1932, second by 1934* The very best; =the GREATEST: *. . . eulogizing anything. . . as "the nuts"*—English Journal [probably a shortening of *the cat's nuts*]

See the CAT'S MEOW

nuts about (or **over** or **on**) *adj phr* (Variation: **nutty** may replace **nuts**) *by 1918* Very enthusiastic about; devoted to; =CRAZY ABOUT: *I think I'm nuts about you*—S McNeil/ *I'd be simply nutty about the quadrangles at Oxford*—Sinclair Lewis [fr British slang *nutty,* "piquant, fascinating," fr earlier sense "rich, tasty, desirable, like the kernel of a delicious nut," altered in slang to *nuts* and originally in the phrase *nuts upon,* found by 1785; the US form *nuts about* may be based on all this or on the notion *crazy about,* and probably on both]

nuts and bolts 1 *n phr by 1960* The fundamentals; the practical basics: *. . . the nuts and bolts of wildland preservation*—CoEvolution Quarterly/ *. . . men who are dealing with the nuts and bolts of negotiations*—Fortune 2 *modifier*: *Berger's nuts-and-bolts discussion of film-TV music*—Village Voice

nutshell *v by 1883* To condense; sum up: *If I'm forced to nutshell it, the show is about community, it's about the workplace and the town*—New York Times [fr the idiom *put something in a nutshell*]

nutso or **nutsy** *adj first form by 1975, second by 1923* Crazy; =NUTTY: *I have to keep up with 29 (mostly nutso) ballot initiative. . .*—New York Times/ *. . . drove each other nutsy with crashing self-confidence*—Village Voice

nutsville *adj by 1980s* crazy: *This city is nutsville*—Lawrence Sanders

nutter *n by 1958* A crazy person; =NUT, NUTBALL: *. . . the Zodiac killer or some nutter on the loose*—Rolling Stone/ *Mick Jagger says there will always be the nutters*—Philadelphia Journal [a British coinage and still chiefly British; perhaps influenced by *Nutter,* trademark name of a butter made from nuts, found by 1906]

nuttiness *n by 1916* Craziness; insanity; =GOOFINESS: *Booth's capacity for nuttiness became. . . a legend*—Billy Rose

nutty *adj by 1898* Crazy; very eccentric; =NUTS: *I was just about nutty, I was so lonely*—Sinclair Lewis
See SLUG-NUTTY

nutty as a fruitcake *adj phr by 1935* Crazy as can be; extremely eccentric: *"That's me," Calazo said. "Nutty as a fruitcake"*—Lawrence Sanders

nut up *v phr college students by 1970s* To go crazy; =GO APE-SHIT: *He'll just about nut up when you tell him that*

nympho *n by 1935* A nymphomaniac: *. . . no boozing broad, no nympho, no psycho, no bitch*—Pauline Kael

O

-o by 1960s **1 suffix used to form adjectives** Having the indicated characteristics: berserko/ luxo/ neato/ sicko/ wrongo **2 suffix used to form nouns**: foldo/ freako/ klutzo/ muso ●This fanciful formation is increasingly current [fr a humorous imitation of Spanish or Italian words, more probably Spanish because of the similar el -o pattern of coinage]
See the BIG O, DOUBLE-O, FIVE-O, FOUR-O

oak See OK

Oakley See ANNIE OAKLEY

oar See PUT one's **oar in, row with one oar**

oat-burner See HAY BURNER

oater or **oateater** or **oat opera** n or n phr movie studio by 1951 A cowboy movie; Western; =HORSE OPERA: . . . horse operas, also known as sagebrushers or oaters—Bob Thomas/ . . . the deputy marshall in the oateater—Paul Sann

OBE (pronounced as separate letters) **adj** Army by 1970s Overcome by events

Obie¹ n by 1956 An award given to a meritorious off-Broadway production [fr off Broadway]

Obie² n 1960s narcotics A narcotic combining four amphetamines: The brother makes tea, and they talk about Obies—Gail Sheehy [fr Obetrol™, probably a portmanteau form of obesity control]

obit (OH bit) **1** n by 1874 An obituary, esp in a newspaper: . . . getting left out of the pious obits in The Times—Albert Goldman **2 modifier**: This is not the obit page—Harvey Breit

OD¹ (pronounced as separate letters) n Army by 1921 Olive drab; olive drab cloth

OD² (pronounced as separate letters) 1960s narcotics & medical **1** n An overdose of narcotics: I guess he'd taken a light OD—Claude Brown **2** v: met Jesus one day when I was ODing on speed in my room—Village Voice **3** v To overindulge in or on anything: Viewers may have OD'd on athletics and turned to reruns—Time

oddball by 1940s **1** n An eccentric person; a strange one; =WEIRDO: This little guy, opinionated, emotional, sensitive, was definitely an oddball—Saul Bellow/ This weird guy. . . this oddball with his long neck and his funny talk—Joseph Wambaugh **2 adj**: . . . sensible drug users and the odd-ball drug users—Saturday Review **3** n A nonconformist; outsider; odd man out: We were generally considered to be a family of hopeless odd-

balls—San Francisco **4 adj**: He had some pretty oddball ideas

odd couple n phr by 1965 Two people who seem unlikely as partners, mates, etc: The odd couple, Gen. Humberto Ortega and President Violeta Barrios de Chamorro of Nicaragua, have arrived at a working relationship—New York Times [fr the title of a 1965 Neil Simon play]

odd man out n phr by 1889 Someone who is not included in a game, arrangement, business deal, etc: United Artists seemed the odd man out in Transamerica's financial services game—Business Week

odds and ends n phr by middle 1700s A miscellany of leftovers, outsizes, scraps, unmatched bits, etc

odds-on adj gambling by 1898 Favorable; sure to win: This one's so successful the odds-on betting was it'd never burn down—Stan Cutler

ODs (OH DEEZ) n Army by 1920s The former olive drab uniform of the US Army, or the trousers of that uniform

of (əV) v by 1844 Have, in verb constructions ●Used for humorous or dialect effect: I must of gone crazy or something—Joyce Carol Oates

◁**ofaginzy**▷ n black by 1950s A white person; =OFAY: The white visitor is. . . known as an "ofaginzy"—Stephen Longstreet [fr ofay; the second element may be fr ginzo, "an Italian," fr guinea, or unattested ginzy, "Jew," fr Ginsberg]

◁**ofay**▷ **1** n black by about 1917 A white person; =FAY, GRAY: Let the ofays have Wall Street to themselves—B Brown/ . . . a white boy, an ofay—Louis Armstrong **2 modifier**: . . . ofay business men and planters—Louis Armstrong [probably fr pig Latin for foe]

off 1 adj by 1846 Not performing well;: Perot had an off-night—Denver radio talk show **2 adj** by 1896 Spoiled; not fresh: the milk's a bit off **3 adj** by 1866 Eccentric; abnormal; =WEIRD: That girl is off—Delcastle Dictionary of Slang **4 adj** by 1882 Canceled; not going to happen: Let's call the whole thing off/ The deal's off **5 adj** by 1861 Not working; not engaged: The cook is off today **6** v by 1930 To kill or destroy; =WASTE: . . . ordered him to mess up a couple of guys, but instead he offed them—John Godey/ We'll off any pig who attacks us—Bobby Seale ◁**7**▷ v black by 1950s To do the sex act with or to; =SCREW: When I off a nigger bitch, I close my eyes and concentrate real hard—Eldridge Cleaver **8 prep** narcotics by 1930s Not

397

using; no longer addicted to: *She's off H now/ I've been off the sauce for four years*

off and running *adj phr* horse-racing by 1960s Started and making good headway: *. . . by hitting one of his rare home runs, and I thought we were off and running*—Whitey Herzog [*they're off!* to signal the start of a race is found by 1833]

off one's **ass** *adv phr* 1980s students Extremely; =TO THE MAX: *My roommate was wasted off his ass by the time the party was over, and I had to carry him to bed*—UCLA Slang

off at the knees *See* CUT oneself **off at the knees**

off base 1 *adj phr* fr baseball by 1936 By surprise; unawares: *The lawyer tried to catch him off base with some unexpected questions* **2** *adj phr* Not appropriate; uncalled for: *Some of his questions were way off base* **3** *adj phr* by 1950s Presumptuous; impudent; =OUT OF LINE: *When I asked for her number she said I was off base* **4** *adj phr* by 1947 Incorrect; inaccurate: *These stats are a mile off base*

off one's **base** *adj phr* by 1891 Seriously out of touch with reality: *Professor McClintock is quite off his base in knocking the use of slang*—Washington Post

off one's **bean** *adj phr* by 1940s Crazy; demented; =OFF one's **chump**: *. . . and a turkey-necked freak who was at least half off his bean*—Joseph Wambaugh

offbeat *adj* by about 1935 Unusual; unconventional; strange: *. . . the off-beat death. . . in an off-Broadway hotel*—New York Daily News/ *. . . its off-beat ad seeking 10 Renaissance-type men*—Wall Street Journal [fr the interruption of a regular rhythm in music]

off someone's **case** *See* GET OFF someone's CASE

off color *adj phr* by 1875 Somewhat salacious; risqué; =BLUE: *a couple of off-color jokes/ Some of his observations were a bit off color*

offer *See* MAKE AN OFFER one CAN'T REFUSE, PUTTER-OFFER

off one's **feed** *adj phr* by 1862 Not feeling or looking well; indisposed [used of animals by 1816]

off one's **head (**or **chump** or **conk** or **nut)** *adj phr* entry form by 1889, chump by 1877, conk by 1870, nut by 1873 Crazy; demented; =NUTS

office *n* aviators by 1917 The cockpit of an airplane *See* BOX OFFICE, FRONT OFFICE

off one's **noodle (**or **onion** or **rocker)** *adj phr* entry form by 1945, onion by 1890, rocker by 1897 Crazy; deluded; =MESHUGA, NUTS: *I've been as near off my noodle as a. . . sane man can get*—K Brush/ *I suppose he was off his rocker*—New York Daily News

off one's **plate** *adv phr* by 1980s No longer a matter of one's responsibility and concern: *Congress would like to get the abortion issue off its plate*—National Public Radio

off-putting *adj* by 1828 Distressing; unsettling; discomfiting: *. . . nor do I find pubic hair ugly or off-*putting—A Brien/ *. . . an off-putting chip on the shoulder*—Esquire

off-road 1 *v* by 1990s To drive in deserts, mountains, forests, beaches, etc, away from roads: *People with a little too much enthusiasm for nocturnal off-roading were a problem for the Santa Monica Mountains Conservancy*—Vanity Fair **2** *modifier*: *This baby is an off-road, all-terrain vehicle*

off the bat *See* RIGHT OFF THE BAT

off the beam *adv phr* by 1940s Distant from truth or accuracy; in error: *That idea is way off the beam* [fr the radio *beam* that guides aircraft to an airport or runway]

off the charts *adj phr* by 1980s Too great to be measured; off the scale: *His popularity, high before, is now way off the charts* [fr the published *charts* that show the best-selling musical records and albums]

off the cob *adj phr* 1940s teenagers Conventional and unexciting; =CORNY: *The music was strictly off the cob*—F Brown

off the cuff 1 *adv phr* by 1938 Extemporaneously; without rehearsal: *I don't speak well off the cuff* **2** *adj*: *a good off-the-cuff talker* [fr the notion of speaking from notes made on one's shirt cuff]

off the deep end *See* GO OFF THE DEEP END, JUMP OFF THE DEEP END

off the ground *adj phr* by 1970s Started; in operation; =OFF AND RUNNING: *We have to decide how to get the project off the ground* [fr the putative conversation of airline pilots at takeoff: "Let's see if we can get this thing *off the ground*"]

off the habit *adj phr* 1960s narcotics Cured of drug addiction; =CLEAN

off the hog *See* EAT HIGH ON THE HOG

off the hook *adj phr* by 1954 Free of responsibility, blame, punishment, etc; =CLEAR: *Shagan gets Harry off the hook*—Pauline Kael/ *In brief, parents are off the hook*—Faubion Bowers
See LET someone OFF THE HOOK, RING OFF THE HOOK

off the needle *adj phr* 1960s narcotics No longer injecting or using narcotics; =CLEAN

off the pace *adv phr* by 1951 Behind the leader or leaders: *The red car is about two laps off the pace*

off-the-rack *adj* by 1963 Mass-produced or ready-made; not tailored or specially designed: *Buying an off-the-rack reno is expensive and not very adventurous*—Toronto Life

off the record *adv phr* by 1933 Confidential; not for publication or attribution: *The mayor would only speak off the record, and very cryptically at that*

off-the-shelf *modifier* by 1936 Readily available from retail sources; not customized: *. . . a drastically scaled-down program that involves purchasing off-the-shelf computer software*—Los Angeles Times

off the top *adv phr* by 1970s Before any deductions are made; =UP FRONT: *He demanded his percentage right off the top*

off the top of one's **head** *adv phr* by 1939 Without thought or calculation; impromptu: *I can't* give you the figure off the top of my head, but it's around, say, 500

off the wagon (or **water wagon**) *adj phr* by about 1904 Drinking liquor, after a period of abstinence: . . . *like the bartenders, they fall off the wagon*—A J Liebling
See FALL OFF THE WAGON

off the wall 1 *adj phr* by 1968 Unusual; outrageous; =ODDBALL, OFFBEAT: . . . *his off-the-wall sense of humor*—J Landau/ . . . *the totally off-the-wall absurdity of existence*—Bruce Malamut **2** *adj phr* Crazy; very eccentric; =OFF one's NOODLE: *Mrs Morea was "very, very distraught, really incoherent, off the wall"*—New York Times/ *They're describing him as "off the wall"*—Arizona Republic [probably fr the medical term *bounce off the walls,* referring to the behavior of a psychotic patient]
See BOUNCE OFF THE WALLS, PING OFF THE WALLS

offtish **See** OOFTISH

off one's **trolley** *adj phr* by 1896 Crazy; demented; =NUTS: *You're off your trolley*—Max Shulman [fr the helpless condition of a streetcar of which the *trolley,* a spring-loaded shaft with a wheel at the top to engage the electric wires, has come *off* the wires]

OG (pronounced as separate letters) *n phr* 1980s street talk A leading gang member; prime "gang-banger": *Eager to achieve the supreme title OG (Original Gangster), he put in long hours on the streets, trying at least to get off a few shots at an enemy gang member*—New York Times/ *He's as mean as they come. An Original Gangster, or OG, he bears the most exalted of titles bestowed for the most heinous of crimes*—Milwaukee Journal

oh-dark-thirty or **zero-dark-thirty** *n* Army by 1970s An early morning hour

oh-so- *adv* Very; extremely; =WAY: *Patriotism provides an oh-so-convenient way to confuse the higher ideals it announces with the narrow interests it claims to transcend*—Nation/ *The administration's bank regulators are moving oh-so-slowly in seizing insolvent banks*—New Republic

oh yeah *interj* by 1930 An exclamation of defiance or disbelief; =IZZATSO: *I told her I'd make her a star, and she said, "Oh yeah?"*

-oid 1 *suffix used to form nouns* Something resembling or imitating what is indicated: *flakoid/ fusionoid/ Grouchoid/ klutzoid* **2** *suffix used to form adjectives* Resembling or imitating what is indicated: *blitzoid/ cheesoid/ technoid/ zomboid* •This suffix is increasingly current, probably because of the popularity of fantasy and science fiction, esp among teenagers [fr the scientific suffix *-oid,* fr Greek *-oeides,* ultimately fr *eidos* "image, form"; dictionaries list over 1800 *-oid* compounds, most of which date from the 1700s and 1800s]

oil 1 *n* by 1917 Flattering and unctuous talk; =BALONEY, BUNK: *Stop the oil, will you?*—Jerome Weidman/ . . . *marinated in good old Hollywood oil*—John McCarten **2** *n* by 1903 Money, esp money paid for bribery and acquired by graft **3** *v*: *We'll have to oil the mayor to get that permit*

See BANANA OIL, BOIL someone IN OIL, PALM OIL, STRIKE OIL

oiled *adj* by 1737 Drunk: . . . *choose your companions, and get properly oiled as well*—New York Times
See WELL-OILED

◄**oiler**► *n* by 1907 A Mexican; =GREASER

oil someone's **palm** **See** GREASE someone's PALM

oily *adj* by 1879 Cunning and ingratiating; sly and unctuous: . . . *his perfect-pitch portrayal of Artie, the oily producer of The Larry Sanders Show.* . . —Buzz

oink ◄**1**► *n* (also **oinker**) by 1960s A police officer; =PIG **2** *v* To sound and behave like a pig: . . . *and sends masculine outrage oinking into overdrive*—Newsweek [verb sense related to *male chauvinist pig*]

oinker scale *n phr* by 1990s: *On an oinker scale of 1 to 10, 10 being that mythical guy who willingly cleans the house and does the laundry.* . . *I'd give my husband a solid 7*—Los Angeles Times [related to *male chauvinist pig*]

oinking porker *n phr* by 1990s A "male chauvinist pig": *And the men who ran the AVP were even worse oinking porkers determined to annihilate the WPVA, marginalize the women's game, and monopolize pro beach volleyball*—Buzz

OJ¹ or **oj** (pronounced as separate letters) *n* lunch counter by 1940s Orange juice: *trying to persuade the public to refer to orange juice as "OJ"*—Russell Baker

OJ² *v* by 1990s To displace or cancel a media program or appearance in order to broadcast the O J Simpson murder trial: *I'm meant to do a radio interview at 11:30. Live. But it says here they'll tape it if I get OJed*—Martin Amis

OK (also **ok** or **okay** or **oka** or **okeh** or **okey** or **oak** or **oke**) by 1839 **1** *affirmation* Yes; I agree; I accept that; I will do that **2** *adj* Agreeable; =COPACETIC: *He made an OK decision* **3** *adj* Acceptable but not excellent; satisfactory: *The play's okay, but I still prefer the book* **4** *adj* Good; excellent: *He had worked with Sergeant Boone before and knew he was an okay guy*—Lawrence Sanders **5** *affirmation* or *question* Is that all right?; is that understood?; =CAPEESH: *I'm going now, okay?* **6** *adv* Right; that's understood, let's get on: *So I told you about that, okay, so the next thing was he jumped the fence* [origin uncertain and the subject of essay after essay; Allen Walker Read is the great authority and has shown that the locution began as a bumpkin-imitating game among New York and Boston writers in the early 1800s, who used *OK* for "oll korrect"]

okey-doke *affirmation* or *question* (also **hokey-dokey** or **okie-doke** or **okey-dokey** or **okie-dokie** or **okle-dokle**) students by 1932 Yes, satisfactory, alright, etc; =OK: *Suppose I pick you up at seven? Okie doke*—Peter De Vries

Okie¹ by about 1935 **1** *n* A migratory worker, esp one in the 1930s who had to leave home because of dust storms; =ARKY **2** *n* A native or resident of Oklahoma; =SOONER

Okie² *n WWII armed forces* A native or resident of Okinawa

-ola or **-olo** *suffix used to form nouns by 1940s* An emphatic instance or humorous version of what is indicated: *buckola/ crapola/ schnozzola* [probably modeled on *pianola* and *Victrola*, both found by 1905; *-ola* compounds proliferated after the Charles Van Doren *payola* scandal of 1959; *-ola* compounds, numbering about 40, offer no real semantic core]

old *adj by 1598* Good; dear; well-liked: *What's old Donald up to now?*
See ANY OLD

the **old army game** *See* the **army game**

◁**old bag** or **old bat**▷ *n phr first form by 1920s, second by 1940s* An old woman, esp a repulsive, gossipy old shrew [both *bag* and *bat* earlier meant "prostitute"]

◁**old biddy**▷ *n phr by 1940s* An old woman, esp an unpleasant one: *Talk to the old biddy for me. . . She likes you*—Lawrence Sanders [ultimately fr *biddy*, "chicken, hen," found by 1601]

old bird *n phr by 1853* An old man; =GAFFER, GEEZER

old boy *n phr British schools by 1868* A graduate; alumnus: *. . . thousands of Princeton old boys flexed their wrists and learned to Frisbee*—Newsweek
See GOOD OLD BOY

old boy network or **old boys' system** *n phr British by 1959* A reciprocally supportive, exclusive, and influential group of men, esp those who were friends at some prestigious school or college; =IN-GROUP: *. . . an "old-girl" network to rival the much-ballyhooed "old-boy" network*—Washingtonian/ *It's an old boys' system. Once you have a few commissions under your belt, one architect recommends you to another*—Philadelphia

old cocker *n phr by 1980s* =ALTER KOCKER: *. . . I said good morning to the two Old Cockers who ambled along every day kidding themselves they were exercising*—Stan Cutler/ *. . . a lot of old cockers out there who wanted to hear a ball game*—New York

the **old college try** *n phr by 1927* One's utmost effort; =GIVE something one's BEST SHOT: *It's not going to be the end of the world. You give it the old college try*—Washingtonian [fr the early and innocent legends of college football]

◁**old crock**▷ *n phr by 1880* An old person, esp a man, who is broken down and physically debilitated: *That old crock still plays tennis?* [*crock* is found in several Germanic languages as "a broken-down horse"; noted in 1969 as medical slang for a neurotic complainer]

older than God (or **baseball** or **dirt**) *adj phr* Very, very old: *Robert Penn Warren is older than God*—Mary Lee Settle/ *Dick James, who remem-*bers the Philadelphia Athletics, older than dirt—WFLN-FM Philadelphia

◁**old fart**▷ *n phr by 1968* An old man; a superannuated man; =ALTER KOCKER, POOP: *I feel like an old fart. My back's stiff, my knees hurt, my teeth hurt*—Sierra

◁**old fogy** (or **fuddy-duddy**)▷ *n phr first form by 1790, second by 1899* An old man, esp one who clings to old-fashioned ways [of *fuddy-duddy*, origin unknown]
See FOGY

◁**old geezer**▷ *n phr by 1897* An old man, esp an unpleasant one: *Get that old geezer out of here*
See GEEZER

◁**old goat**▷ *n by 1598* =DIRTY OLD MAN

old hand *n phr by 1785* An experienced person; a seasoned veteran: *She's an old hand at these diplomatic remedies*

old hat *adj phr British by 1911* Out of style; old-fashioned: *Tubular stuff is now old hat*—R M Coates

old head *n phr chiefly black by 1940s* : *A generation ago urban black neighborhoods contained the figure of the "old head," defined as a man of stable means who believed in hard work, family life, and the church*—New Republic

the **old heave-ho** *See* the HEAVE-HO

oldie or **oldy** *n by early 1930s* An old thing or person, esp an old song, movie, or story: *Our pet oldie concerns the India rubber skin man*—Walter Winchell/ *. . . as good as a W C Fields oldie*—New York Post [the late pianist Eubie Blake dated this phrase from about 1900]
See GOLDEN OLDIE

oldie but goodie *See* GOLDEN OLDIE

old Joe *n phr by 1960s* Any venereal disease; syphilis; gonorrhea: *Twice I got old Joe, you know, a dose*—T Rubin

old lady 1 *n phr by 1836* One's wife; a wife: *Losin' his old lady is what crazied him*—Nelson Algren **2** *n phr by 1950s* A girlfriend, mistress, woman living companion, etc: *He introduced this chick as his old lady* **3** *n phr by 1836* One's mother; a mother: *The little kid went to ask his old lady if he could come along*

old man 1 *n phr by 1895* One's husband; a husband: *She can't bear to see her old man lose his money*—J Cannon **2** *n phr by 1950s* A boyfriend or lover: *Her old man was a bass guitar player in a rock group* **3** *n phr by 1768* One's father; a father: *My old man wasn't mean*—Calder Willingham **4** *n phr by about 1935* A man who supports a mistress; =JOHN, SUGAR DADDY: *"Old Man," the name we used to have for a common-law husband*—Louis Armstrong/ *She has an "old man" who "keeps" her*—New York Times **5** *n phr prostitutes* A pimp **6** *n phr by 1870* Old friend
See DIRTY OLD MAN, SO'S YOUR OLD MAN

the **old man** *n phr by 1830* The chief, esp the captain of a ship or aircraft or the commander of a military unit; =HONCHO

old money *n phr by 1963* Inherited wealth, as distinct from that of the nouveaux riches: *Bush attended two fund-raisers in Highland Park, the center of what passes in Dallas for old money, rooted in real estate, cotton, and oil in the early years*—New Yorker

the old one-two *See* ONE-TWO

old pro *See* PRO

old-shoe *adj by 1825* Comfortable and familiar: *. . . a relationahip that has evolved from open hostility to the old-shoe clubbiness of rivals drawn by shared personalities*—Milwaukee Journal

old Siwash *See* SIWASH

Old Smoky (or **Sparky**) *n phr* prison *by 1920s* The electric chair: *A half dozen men are alive today who otherwise would have ridden "Old Sparky"*—Publishers Weekly/ *Lethal injection or Old Sparky?*—New Yorker

Old Sol *n phr by 1940s* The sun

old stick *n phr by 1886* A rather stiff old person •Chiefly British

old thing *n phr by 1852* Old friend: *. . . in conversation address you as "Old Thing"*—Robert Lynd

old timer *n phr by 1860* A seasoned veteran, esp a man •Often used in direct address, generally affectionately: *Although younger agents find them exciting. . . old-timers resist them*—Chicago Tribune

old-time religion *n phr by 1930s* The tried-and-true way of doing things; hallowed wisdom: *. . . that horse-trading, your bill for mine, was part of the old-time religion*—Milwaukee Journal/ *If Cuomo does run, he will have money, eloquence, labor unions and the power of old-time Democratic religion behind him* [fr a hymn tune "Give me that old-time religion"]

old-timey *adj by 1850* Old-fashioned, esp in a pleasant and nostalgic way: *. . . dripping with old-timey decorations*—N Winters

old woman *n phr* =OLD LADY

olive *See* SWALLOW THE APPLE

-olo *See* -OLA

omelet *See* YOU CAN'T MAKE AN OMELET WITHOUT BREAKING EGGS

on 1 *adj by 1885* Aware; informed; alerted: *I saw he was on, and quit talking*—James M Cain **2** *adj by 1908* Not canceled; scheduled to happen: *The deal's still on: It's on for tomorrow night* **3** *adj by 1812* Accepted and confirmed as a partner, competitive bettor, etc: *He said he bet he could do it, and I told him he was on: You want to go up there with us? You're on* **4** *adj by 1793* Performing; presenting a talk, appeal, etc, as if one were on stage: *She's never relaxed, she's always on/ Better review your points, since you're on next* **5** *prep by 1871* Paid for by; with the compliments of: *This was to be on him*—James M Cain **6** *prep* narcotics *by 1936* Taking; using; adicted to: *He had her on penicillin/ He was on acid and barbiturates at the time*

on a cloud *adj phr by 1950s* Very happy; euphoric; in a blissful transport: *Oh, world, I'm on a cloud today!*

on a dime *See* STOP ON A DIME, TURN ON A DIME

on a roll 1 *adj phr by 1976* Having great success; enjoying a winning impetus: *The tax cut's a smash. You're on a roll, Mr President*—Philadelphia Daily News/ *But Brad was on a roll now*—Cameron Crowe **2** *adj phr* (also **on a kick**) *by 1970s* Doing something enthusiastically and constantly: *She was on a philosophy roll*—Rolling Stone [fr a crapshooting term meaning "very, very lucky; unbeatable with the dice"]

on a shingle *See* SHIT ON A SHINGLE

◁**on** one's **ass**▷ (or **ear**) *adv phr* entry form *by 1950s*, variant *by 1940s* In or into a sad and helpless condition; supine; =DOWN FOR THE COUNT: *He lost three jobs, and now he's on his ass/ His hat store went kerflooie, and he's on his ear now*—James T Farrell

    See FALL ON one's ASS, FLAT ON one's ASS, SIT ON one's ASS

◁**on** someone's **ass**▷ *adj phr by 1980s* Annoying or harassing one: *The paparazzi have been on my ass all day*—Stuart Woods

on a tear (TAIR) *adj phr by 1880s* Very angry, esp punitively so; =PISSED OFF: *Ronald Reagan is on a tear over leaks*—National Review [the dated example is *in a tear*]

on someone's **back** *adv phr by 1776* Persistently annoying or harassing someone; =ON someone's CASE: *The cops were on my back after that*

on board *adv phr by 1980s* Serving as a member of a team, government, or other group: *The President said he was glad to have the new Secretary on board*

on book *adj phr* theater *by 1970s* Reading one's lines from the script, before having memorized them: *Most of the actors are still "on book," clutching scripts in hand*—Toronto Life

on someone's **case** *adv phr* black *by 1970s* Paying close and esp meddling or punitive attention to someone: *Maybe the world isn't on my case. Maybe the problem is me*—Garrison Keillor/ *These people got on my case heavy the first day the ol' man was dead*—Joseph Wambaugh [fr the black expression *sit on someone's case,* "discuss and judge someone's problems, behavior, etc," based on a judicial analogy]

once in a blue moon *adv phr by 1864* Very rarely: *Herb? I only see him once in a blue moon*

a **once-over** or **once-over lightly** *n phr by 1940s* A hasty cursory performance or preparation; =a LICK AND A PROMISE: *. . . a razor for a hasty once-over*—Meyer Berger

the **once-over** *n phr by 1915* A look or glance of inspection; scrutiny; =the DOUBLE-O: *The first thing we went to buy after giving all the pavilions the once-over was tomatoes*—Art Buchwald

    See GIVE someone or something **the once-over**

on cloud nine (or **cloud seven**) *adj phr by 1950s* At the very pinnacle of bliss; euphoric; =ON A CLOUD: *She came back home and he's on cloud nine*

on someone's **coattails** *adv phr by 1909* Profiting from someone else's success, esp in a decisive election: . . . *when all these rube politicians come riding in on Reagan's coattails*—W T Tyler [Abraham Lincoln used *under that coattail* in the same sense in 1848, referring to the winning influence of Andrew Jackson]

on deck 1 *adv phr* baseball by 1867 Waiting to be the next batter, usu in a special circle marked for the purpose **2** *adj phr*: *the on-deck hitter* **3** *adj phr* by 1889 Present and ready; on hand and prepared: *If you need anybody else, I'm on deck*

on someone's **dime (or nickel)** *adv phr* At someone's expense other than the speaker's: *On the dime of Universal*—GQ/ *Hicks and Sims went home, on their own nickel, to their own miseries*—Esquire [fr the *dime* or *nickel* formerly needed to activate a pay telephone]

one *See* BIG ONE, DEAD ONE, FAST ONE, FOUR-AND-ONE, FRESH ONE, HANG ONE ON, HOT ONE, NUMBER-ONE BOY, SQUARE ONE

One *See* MURDER ONE, NUMBER ONE, TRACK ONE

one-and-a-half striper *n phr* Navy by about 1925 A lieutenant, junior grade

one and only *n phr* by 1906 One's beloved, fiancee, sweetheart, etc: *My one and only, what am I going to do if you turn me down when I'm so crazy over you*—Ira Gershwin

on one's **ear** *See* ON one's ASS

one-arm (or one-armed) bandit *n phr* by 1938 A slot machine

one-arm joint or **one-arm** *n phr* or *n* by 1915 A cheap restaurant, esp a small one with chairs having an enlarged right arm that serves as a table: *She went with me to this one-arm where I eat*—John O'Hara

on easy street *adv phr* by 1901 In a condition of solvency, ease, and tranquility

one-bagger *n* baseball by 1880s A one-base hit; single

one better *See* GO something or someone ONE BETTER

on edge *See* EDGY

one dollar to rub against another *See* NOT HAVE ONE DOLLAR TO RUB AGAINST ANOTHER

187 (pronounced as separate numbers) *n phr* Los Angeles police by 1990s : *In the lines you quote, "1-8-7" is Los Angeles police slang for homicide. . . so it means that the narrator is boasting about shooting an undercover cop to death*—Los Angeles Times

◁**one-eyed demon (or snake)**▷ *n phr* by 1990s The penis: *Safe sex education blew it. The emphasis should be on the psychology that goes into wrestling with that one-eyed demon*—Nation [fr regarding the meatus as an eye]

one-eyed monster *n phr* by 1958 A television set; television; =the boob tube

one-finger salute *n phr* by 1980s A lewd insulting gesture made by holding up the middle finger with the others folded down, and meaning "fuck you" or "up yours"; =the FINGER: *Then he put his arm out*

the window and raised his hand in the one-finger salute—Mike Royko

one foot in the grave *See* HAVE ONE FOOT IN THE GRAVE

one for the book (or books) *n phr* by 1922 Something remarkable; an amazing thing, case, etc: *That storm was really one for the book*

one for the road *n phr* by 1943 A last drink of the evening, party, carouse, etc

one hell of a *See* A HELL OF A

one-horse *adj* by 1853 Insignificant; inferior: *It's a one-horse operation he's got there*

one-horse town *n phr* by 1855 A small town; =JERKWATER TOWN

one-liner *n* by 1964 A quick joke or quip; a funny observation; =WISECRACK: *. . . a new neighbor who exchanges one-liners with Lianna in the laundry room*—Toronto Life

one-lunger by 1908 **1** *n* A one-cylinder engine **2** *n* A car, boat, etc, with a one-cylinder engine

one-man show (or band) *n phr* entry form by 1921, variant by 1938 An enterprise, business, etc, controlled by one person: *The company had previously been run as a "one-man show"*—Fortune

one-night stand 1 *n phr* by 1880 A performing engagement for one evening only: *Not a bad gig, but just a one-night stand* **2** *n phr* by 1963 A casual sex act; a brief sexual encounter: *He never enjoyed one-night stands* **3** *n phr* A person who has a casual sexual encounter: *. . . emerges as less the femme fatale than a one-night stand gone wrong*—Time

one oar *See* ROW WITH ONE OAR

one-off *n* by 1934 Something unique; something not repeated: *. . . encouraged band member Jim Warchol. . . to think of 5th and National as more than a one-off*—Milwaukee Journal

one of the boys (or the guys) *n phr* by 1893 An ordinary, amiable man; a man without side or lofty dignity: *His Eminence was trying hard to be one of the boys*

one of those things *See* JUST ONE OF THOSE THINGS

something 101 *n phr* by 1980s The introductory course in something: *You should be teaching police-amatic Bullshit 101 at John Jay*—Michael Grant/ *College Slang 101*—Connie Eble/ *Is Pistol-Packing 101 the 80s equivalent of Drivers' Ed?*—New York Times

one on one 1 *adv phr* by 1967 In immediate confrontation; person to person; =EYEBALL TO EYEBALL, MANO A MANO: *I go on the basketball court and have a 15-year-old guy beat me one on one*—San Francisco/ *John Rhodes was very effective, one-on-one*—Wall Street Journal **2** *n phr*: *. . . have a one-on-one with him*—Lawrence Sanders

one piece *See* ALL IN ONE PIECE

oner *n* by 1840 A remarkable person or thing: *I've heard some bullshitters, but this guy's a oner*

one red cent *See* A RED CENT

one-shot 1 *n* by 1942 A story or article that appears once, with no sequel **2** *n* by 1937 Any transaction, event, etc, that occurs only once: *He was doing poetry readings, one-shots* =ONE-OFF **3 modifier**: *He put her in a one-shot whodunit*—Newsweek/ *Maybe it was a one-shot shakedown*—J Ellison **4 n** by about 1950 A woman who accedes to the sex act once, then refuses repetitions

one size fits all *adj phr* by 1990s Of broad or universal application: *Social Security is a one-size-fits-all program, run entirely out of Washington*—New Republic/ *A one-size-fits-all approach in public education is unfair to youngsters with disabilities*—New Republic [fr the labels on caps, gloves, and other products that accommodate all wearer sizes]

one smart apple *See* SMART APPLE

one-stoplight town *n phr* by 1980s =ONE-HORSE TOWN: *. . . no one seemed interested in how many "steppenwolfs" were playing one-stoplight towns. . .* —Milwaukee Journal

one-stop shopping *n phr* by 1980s Getting whatever one needs at a single place: *The days of diplomatic one-stop shopping are over; Washington will now have to take into account not only the Kremlin, but the Ukraine, Byelorussia or Kazakhstan* —New York Times/ *The BCCI ran a one-stop shopping center for criminals, corrupt leaders and official intelligence agencies around the world*—Time [*One-stop* was used of service stations by 1934]

one-striper 1 n *Navy* by about 1920 An ensign **2 n** *WWII Army* A private first class

in **one swell foop** *adv phr* anytime after 1605 All at once: *How many times have you wanted to copy all your files to another directory and then delete the old files in one swell foop?*—Ventura Tips and Tricks [Shakespeare's reference in *Macbeth* to the fatal *swoop* of a raptor]

one thin dime *See* a thin dime

one too many *n phr* by 1937 Enough liquor to make one drunk, and possibly more: *Its driver had obviously had one too many*—D McFerran

one-track mind *n phr* by 1927 A mind limited to or obsessed with a single idea, theme, etc

one-trick pony *n phr* by 1990s A person having a single accomplishment: *. . . as he proved during exquisite ballads and mid-tempo tunes, he's no one-trick pony*—Milwaukee Journal/ *For years, Twentieth Century Fund has been known to investors as a one-trick pony*—New York Times

one-two 1 n (also **the old one-two** or **one-two punch** or **one-two blow**) by 1811 A combination of two blows with the fists, a short left jab plus a hard right cross, usu to the chin: *zipping "one-twos" to the jaw*—Jim Tully **2 modifier**: *good potent one-two punches*—New Yorker

one-up 1 *adv phr* by 1919 In a superior position; at an advantage: *I always try to be one-up* **2 v** To get the advantage over: *I wasn't trying to one-up Arthur Schwartz*—M Williams **3 adv phr** Ahead by one: *The Pinks were one-up on the Puces, 109 to 108*

one-upmanship *n* by 1952 The technique and practice of having the advantage over one's opponent, esp keeping a psychological advantage by low cunning and subtle brilliance: *. . . a wide-open but good-humored game of political one-upmanship*—Tom Wicker [coined by the late British humorist Stephen Potter as a book title]

one-way street *See* NOT A ONE-WAY STREET

on one's **game** *adj phr* by 1920 Performing very well; =HOT: *When I was out in the water and on my game, nothing existed but the wave*—Washington Post

on one's **head** *See* STAND ON one's HEAD

on one's **high horse** *adj phr* by 1805 Behaving arrogantly and pompously [the form *ride the great horse* is found by 1716]

on hold *adv phr* In postponement or abeyance; suspended; =IN COLD STORAGE: *Our plans are on hold for a while* [fr the button on a telephone marked *hold,* used to switch temporarily from the conversation]

on ice 1 *adj phr* by 1890 Certain of being won, or of turning out well; =IN THE BAG: *The deal's on ice* **2 adv phr** by 1931 In prison, esp in solitary confinement **3 adj phr** (also **on tap**) by 1894 In reserve; ready to play a role; =IN COLD STORAGE: *If this one fails, I've got another on ice/ Who arranged Dubie to be on tap. . .* —Stan Cutler
See PISS ON ICE

onion *n* by 1890 The head
See KNOW one's ONIONS, OFF one's NOODLE

on line 1 *adj phr* *computers* by 1980s Computerized; accessible by computer: *We have the whole card catalog and about 200 books online* **2 adj phr** by 1980s Available; ready for use; installed: *The Navy's announced plans for a new destroyer class are on line* [perhaps fr the connecting *lines* on a flow chart used to indicate a computer and its attached apparatus]

only *See* EYES ONLY, ONE AND ONLY

the **only game** *n phr* (also the **only ball game**) The only choice available: *For export industries "development bank" projects are the only game in town*—New York Times/ *They are the only ball game for maintenance*—Star Tribune [a shortening of the expression *I know it's crooked, but it's the only game in town*]

on one's **own hook** *adv phr* by 1812 By one's own efforts; on one's own account: *You'll have to do it on your own hook* [origin unknown and much speculated upon; perhaps fr *fishhook*]

on paper *adv phr* by 1795 Only by abstract report or reputation; theoretically: *It works on paper, but I've never actually tried it*

on sked *adv phr* by 1940s On schedule: *Aside from minor setbacks. . . "Street Trash" has been proceeding smoothly and on sked*—New York Times

on spec *adv phr* by 1832 As a venture or gamble; hoping to profit: *They said they would take the case on spec*

on tap *See* ON ICE

on the back burner *adv phr* by 1960 Not being actively considered; in reserve; =ON HOLD: *I have some good projects on the back burner right now*

on the ball *adj phr* by 1912 Skillful, alert, and effective; =WITH IT: *FBI agents were very much on the ball in the Bremer snatch*—A Hynd [fr the advisability of keeping one's eyes *on the ball* when playing a ball game]

See GET ON THE BALL, KEEP one's EYE ON THE BALL, something ON THE BALL

on the beach *See* PEBBLE ON THE BEACH

on the beam *adv phr* by 1941 On the proper track or course; performing correctly: *It took a while, but he's on the beam now* [fr the radio *beam* used to guide aircraft]

on the blink *adj phr* (Variations: **bum** or **fritz** or **Fritz** may replace **blink**) *entry form* by 1904, fritz by 1903, bum by 1896 Not functioning properly; in poor condition: *His pacemaker just went on the fritz*—W T Tyler [origin unknown; perhaps fr the notion that defective eyes or lights *blink*]

on the brain *See* HAVE something ON THE BRAIN

on the bubble *adv phr* by 1980s In a precarious position: *. . . that could place guard Conner Henry on the bubble*—Milwaukee Journal [because the *bubble* might burst]

on the button by 1937 **1** *adv phr* Precisely; exactly; =ON THE DOT, ON THE NOSE: *The meter says 35 on the button* **2** *adj phr* Perfectly placed; absolutely correct; =ON THE MONEY, ON THE NOSE, SPOT-ON: *Your estimate was right on the button*

on the carpet (or mat) *adv phr* by 1899 In the situation of being reprimanded: *Next time they caught him asleep he was on the carpet* [probably fr *walk the carpet* or *carpet* "reprimand, rebuke," found by 1823]

on the cheap 1 *adv phr* by 1859 cheaply: *. . . selling. . . just about anything on the cheap*—Milwaukee Journal **2** *adj phr*: *Prices still delight the on-the-cheap set*—Toronto Life

on the cuff by middle 1920s **1** *adv phr* On credit: *The mutt puts me on the cuff for the drinks*—American Mercury **2** *adv phr* Free of charge: *He promised me lodging on the cuff* **3** *adj phr*: *On-the-cuff drinks are delicious* [fr the practice of noting debts on the *cuff* of the shirt, esp on a detachable *cuff*]

on the dot *adv phr* by 1909 At the exact moment; punctually: *I got there on the dot*

on (or at) the double by 1892 **1** *adv phr* At twice the rate of ordinary marching **2** *adv phr* Quickly; rapidly: *When I holler, come on the double*

on the draw *See* SLOW ON THE DRAW

on the edge *See* LIVE ON THE EDGE

on the fence *adv phr* by 1828 Not taking a stand or making up one's mind; straddling

on the fire 1 *adj phr* Pending; in preparation; =IN THE PIPELINE: *We've got a great new model on the fire for next year* **2** *adj phr* lunch counter Being cooked; in preparation

on the fly (or the gallop) 1 *adv phr* entry form by 1851, variant by 1693 Hastily in passing; without preparation or forethought: *We had to make up our minds on the fly/ . . . he objected to disposing of the case "on the gallop"*—Milwaukee Journal **2** *adj phr*: *an on-the-fly decision*

on the fritz *See* ON THE BLINK

on the front burner *adj phr* by 1970 Getting immediate attention

on the go by 1843 **1** *adj phr* Active; energetic; indefatigable: *I'm on the go day and night*—Calder Willingham **2** *adj phr* Always moving about; restlessly in motion: *I'm on the go all the time and don't see my family*

on the gravy train (or boat) *adv phr* by 1927 Enjoying an effortless and prosperous life; =FLUSH: *After a couple of years on the gravy train the bottom fell out of things*

on the ground floor *See* IN ON THE GROUND FLOOR

on the head *See* HIT THE NAIL ON THE HEAD

on the heavy *adv phr* underworld by 1940s Engaged in and living on crime

on the hog *See* EAT HIGH ON THE HOG

on the hook by 1940s **1** *adv phr* In trouble; liable to blame: *You're on the hook for this mess, junior* **2** *adv phr* Trapped; ensnared: *She had the old fool on the hook right soon*

on (or in) the hot seat *adv phr* by 1960s In an uncomfortable situation; =IN A JAM: *You're on the hot seat every day in that job*—Los Angeles Times

on the house *adj phr* by 1889 Free of charge; =FREE GRATIS: *Breakfasts, luncheons, and dinner. . . . All "on the house"*—advertisement for Northwest Airlines

on the hustle *adj phr* by 1970s Living by constant petty frauds and crimes; watchful for dupes: *. . . sleeping till ten in the morning, on the hustle in the streets or the poolrooms*—Stewart Alsop

on the inside *adv phr* by 1932 Having access to the most confidential information; near the focus of power and influence

on the lam or on the run *adj phr* first form by 1931, second by 1887 In hiding from the police; wanted as a fugitive: *So I went on the lam*—D Purroy [the form *on a lam* is found by 1904]

See TAKE IT ON THE LAM

on the legit *adj phr* or *adv phr* by 1931 Lawful; legal; =ON THE LEVEL: *. . . strictly on the legit*—Nelson Algren

on the level 1 *adj phr* by 1875 Honest; candid; =ON THE LEGIT: *. . . to swear that I'm on the level*—H McHugh **2** *adv phr*: *. . . and would fight on the level*—A J Liebling

on the line *adv phr* by 1968 In a risky or vulnerable position; at risk, esp deliberately; up for grabs: *The whole season's on the line this inning* [origin unknown; perhaps fr a gambling game where the bet is placed *on a line*; perhaps fr the commercial slang expression *lay (the price or payment) on the line*, "pay, pay up"; perhaps fr the sense of *line* as separating combatants or duelists]

See LAY IT ON THE LINE, LAY something ON THE LINE, PUT one's ASS ON THE LINE

on the make 1 *adv phr* by 1869 Aspiring and ambitious, esp in a ruthless and exploitive way; careeristic; =HUNGRY: *The rookies are very much on the make* **2** *adv phr* by 1929 Offering and seeking sexual pleasure and conquest; openly amorous: *. . . whether they are on the make, and they all are*—Sexual Behavior

See ON THE TAKE

on the map *adj phr* 1990s teenagers Excellent; =COOL: *That movie was on the map*—Macon Telegraph

on the mat *See* ON THE CARPET

on the money *adj phr* by 1971 Absolutely perfect; precisely as desired; accurate: *. . . good hit, right on the money*—New York Times

on the muscle *adj phr* by 1930 Truculent; inclined to violence

on the needle *adj phr* narcotics by 1940s Using narcotics, esp as an addict

on the nose by 1937 **1** *adv phr* Precisely; exactly; =ON THE DOT: *It's six on the nose* **2** *adj phr* Perfectly placed; exactly as desired; =ON THE MONEY: *Your guess was right on the nose*

on the outs *adj phr* by 1887 Estranged; alienated: *The young couple are on the outs now. . .* —The Lantern

on the pad *adv phr* police by 1970 Taking bribes and graft; =ON THE TAKE [fr the *pad*, a notebook listing the names of corrupt police officers]

on the pan *adj phr* by 1923 Being severely criticized and deplored

on the pipe *adj phr* 1980s narcotics : *The common slang term we're hearing now when we talk to arrested people is that they're "on the pipe". . . That means they're smoking crack* [the same phrase, found by 1926, meant "smoking opium"]

on the prowl 1 *adj phr* by 1836 Actively seeking; abroad and searching, esp for prey **2** *adv phr* by 1940 Seeking sexual pleasure and conquest; =ON THE MAKE

on the QT 1 *adv phr* by 1884 Secretly; quietly: *We did it on the QT* **2** *adj phr*: *Remember, what I said is on the QT* [fr the first and last letters of *quiet*]

◁**on the rag**▷ **1** *adj phr* by 1940s Menstruating: *Maybe I'm on the rag*—Richard Merkin **2** *adj phr* 1960s students Irritable; in a bad mood [fr *rag* used as a sanitary napkin]

on the rims *adv phr* by 1970s As close as possible to insolvency [fr the image of a car with ruined tires running on its *rims*]

on the road *adv phr* show business by 1870 Traveling from place to place with a show, musical program, etc

on the rocks 1 *adv phr* by 1889 In a ruined condition; hopelessly wrecked; =KAPUT: *My little enterprise is on the rocks* **2** *adv phr* by 1946 Poured over ice: *Scotch on the rocks'll be fine*

on the ropes *adj phr* by 1924 Defeated; bested; =CLOBBERED: *His career as a promoter is on the ropes*—Milwaukee Journal Sentinel [fr the plight of a boxer who must lean on the *ropes* of the ring or fall down]

on the same wavelength (or **page)** *adj phr* by 1962 In agreement; in harmony: *Her door's open, but we are not on the same wavelength*—San Francisco/ *. . . we do now have a long-range plan. Everybody's on the same page*—Milwaukee Journal

on the sauce *adj phr* by 1970s Drinking liquor, esp heavily: *. . . on the sauce in a charming schoolboy way*—Stephen Longstreet [*sauce*, "liquor," is found by 1940]

on the shake *adv phr* by 1940s Practicing extortion, blackmail, etc: *You knew they was on the shake*—A J Liebling [fr *shakedown*]

on the shelf *adv phr* by 1815 Not in active use or consideration; deferred; =ON THE BACK BURNER: *We'll have to put some of those plans on the shelf for a while*

on the side *adv phr* by 1893 Extra; additionally: *He moonlights as a hackie on the side*

on the skids *adj phr* by 1921 On a failing or declining course; deteriorating: *After that scandal his whole career was on the skids* [ultimately fr the *skids*, "long pieces of timber," on which barrels, logs, and other heavy objects were rolled or slid, sometimes on a downgrade]

on the spot 1 *adj phr* by 1928 Expected to cope, explain, react, etc, at once; under sharp pressure: *She can't make it, so I guess you're on the spot* **2** *adj phr* by 1884 Available and ready; keen and at hand: *When I need him he's never on the spot* **3** *adv phr* by 1687 Immediately; at once and at the place in question: *I was able to fix it on the spot* [the third dated form is *upon the spot*]

See JOHNNY-ON-THE-SPOT

on the square *adv phr* by 1689 In an honest manner; fairly and justly: *I always treated you on the square*

on the take (or the **make)** *adv phr* by 1930 Amenable to bribery and graft; =ON THE PAD: *spent 30 years fighting everything from pigeons to cops on the make*—Time

on the town *adv phr* by 1712 Enjoying the pleasures of a city, esp the night life; roistering and reveling urbanly [the dated example is *upon the town*]

on the up and up *See* UP AND UP

on the uptake *See* SLOW ON THE DRAW

on the wagon (or the **water wagon)** *adj phr* by 1904 Abstaining from liquor; teetotal, at least temporarily: *Monty didn't drink, and Clifton James went on the wagon*—This Week [first attested as *on the water cart* in 1902]

on the warpath *adj phr* by 1880 Truculent; looking for a fight ●The original Native American sense is found by 1841

on tick *adv phr* 1668 On credit: *. . . getting his liquor "on tick"*—Russell Janney [fr *on ticket*, which is found by 1600]

on to someone *adj phr* by 1877 Aware of, esp of something shady or forbidden; =WISE TO: *Watch it now, I think the guard is on to you*

on top *See* COME OUT AHEAD

on top of *by 1970s* **1** *adv phr* Actively coping with the problem; able to guide and control the matter; =JACKED IN: *It's a nasty outlook, but I think we can get on top of it* **2** *adv phr* Fully informed about something: *Get on top of this latest development right away*

on track *See* GO ON TRACK

on one's **uppers** *adj phr* by 1891 Penniless; destitute; =DOWN AND OUT [fr the notion that one has worn out the soles of one's shoes and is walking *on the uppers* only]

on velvet *adv phr* by 1769 In easy circumstances, such as those applying when one gambles only winnings: *. . . in order to be able to work on "velvet"*—E Lavine

on someone's **watch** *adv phr* by 1980s During someone's tenure of responsibility; while someone is in charge, esp of protection: *Jerusalem and the West Bank were lost to Jordan and the Arab world on his watch*—New Yorker [fr the nautical setting of *watches,* the designating of officers and crew members who run the ship for a specified period]

on wheels *adj phr* by 1940s To the utmost extent; of the purest sort; =IN SPADES: *We agreed she was a bitch on wheels/ He thinks he's shit on wheels* [modeled on *hell on wheels,* found by 1843] *See* SHIT ON WHEELS

oo *v* =DOUBLE-O •In written use only

-oo *See* -EROO

ooch or **oonch** *See* SCRUNCH

oodles *n* by 1869 A large amount; lots; =a SHITHOUSE FULL, a SHITLOAD: *They have oodles of charisma* [perhaps fr *boodle, caboodle*]

oof *n* by 1860s Money [shortening of *ooftisch*]

oofay *See* OFAY

ooftish or **offtish** *n* by 1860s Money, esp money available for gambling or investment [fr Yiddish *oyf tishe,* "on the table," meaning "show your money"]

oofus *n* 1950s black & jive talk A stupid person; oaf; =GOOF: *. . . oofus, a dope*—E Horne [perhaps fr *goof, goofus*]

oogley *adj* 1930s jive talk Attractive; worth ogling with admiration: *It's oogley. Also Bong*—D Willens

ooh ah factor *n phr* by 1980s: *Canham has dismissed notions that the university needs a big-name athletic director, an attribute referred to as the "ooh, ah" factor*—Milwaukee Journal

ooh and ah *v phr* by 1953 To express wonder, amazement, etc: *. . . the spectators, the oohers and aahers*—Chester County Calendar

ook *n* 1940s students A detestable, insipid person; =NERD, WIMP: *Does even an "ook" give out with a wolf whistle?*—Time

ooky *adj* by 1964 Repellent; slimy; =YUCKY: *The Addams family are definitely mysterious and undoubtedly ooky*—Vanity Fair

oomph by 1937 **1** *n* Sexual attractiveness; compelling carnality; =IT **2** *n* Energy; =CLOUT, PIZZAZZ: *. . . substance, drive, authority, emotional power, and oomph*—Frank Sullivan [an echoic coinage suggesting the gasp of someone hit hard by a blow, a transport of desire, etc]

oomph girl *n phr* by 1939 A young woman who is notably sexually attractive; sex goddess or queen; =DISH: *. . . the oomph-girl of the Romance Language Department*—Morris Bishop [a sobriquet given by press agents to the film actress Ann Sheridan]

oops 1 *interj* 1933 An exclamation of surprise, dismay, apology, etc, esp when one has done something awkward: *Mr Belve, oops, I mean Webb, is ecstatic*—B Thomas **2** *n* by 1980s A blunder; serious mistake; =GOOF, WHOOPS: *Might have saved her life. Basic oops*—Stan Cutler **3** *v* (also **oops up**) by 1980s To vomit; =BARF [echoic, fr the involuntary lip-rounding and expulsion of breath that accompanies a regrettable mistake, and from an approximation of the sound of vomiting]

ooze *v* black by 1940s To move or walk slowly; glide or slide; saunter: *I'd ooze across the street and into the bar*—R Starnes

op 1 *n* railroad by 1931 A telegrapher **2** *n* by 1926 A private detective: *. . . one of your ops*—Dashiell Hammett [fr *operator* or *operative*]

OP or **op** (pronounced as separate letters) *adj* by 1901 Other people's: *OP. Other people's money*—T Betts [perhaps a translation of Yiddish *yenems*]

Op-Ed (or **op-ed**) **page** *n phr* by 1970 A newspaper page, usu appearing across from the editorial page, made up of columns and short essays [fr *opposite editorial*]

opener *See* CAN-OPENER, EYE-OPENER

openers *See* FOR OPENERS

open season *n phr* by 1914 The time when persons may be harmed, insulted, etc, with impunity: *If we leave, it will be open season on Americans globally*—President Clinton [fr the time when game may be legally hunted, the term found by 1896]

open up 1 *v phr* by 1921 To speak and inform candidly; =SPILL one's GUTS: *You must open up and tell us all about what happened* **2** *v phr* To cause or induce someone to speak: *. . . the DA, who opens Leo up with the threat of a perjury charge*—William Bayer

open up a (or **that**) **can of worms** *v phr* by 1962 To broach a very complicated and troublesome matter; set something messy in motion: *Merit pay? Let's not open up that can of worms* *See* CAN OF WORMS

open one's **yap** *v phr* by 1937 To open one's mouth, esp to speak; speak up; say something: *. . . every time you open your yap to say something*—Jerome Weidman

the opera ain't over till the fat lady sings *sentence* about 1977 Things are never finished until they are finished; =IT AIN'T OVER TILL IT'S OVER [coined by Dan Cook, a San Antonio sportscaster, and modeled on the Yogi Berra dictum entered here as a synonym]

opera *See* HORSE OPERA, OATER, SOAP OPERA, SPACE OPERA

operate with a full deck *See* PLAY WITH A FULL DECK

operator 1 *n* *by 1875* A person who busily deals and manipulates, often self-importantly; =DEALER, MACHER, WHEELER-DEALER **2** *n* *by 1950s* =LADIES' MAN

opry *See* HORSE OPERA

oral diarrhea *See* VERBAL DIARRHEA

-orama *See* -RAMA

orange crush *n phr* *by 1980s* A special squad of police or prison guards, clad in orange jumpsuits, used to deal with prison riots and other such disturbances [fr a punning reference to the soft drink *Orange Crush*™]

Orange Sunshine *n phr* *1970s narcotics* A kind of LSD: *"Orange Sunshine" began to appear in acid-starved New York City and in New England communes*—MJ Warth

orbit *See* GO INTO ORBIT, IN ORBIT

orc or **orch** *See* ORK

orchard *See* BONE-ORCHARD, MARBLE ORCHARD

order *See* APPLE-PIE ORDER

orders *See* CUT someone's PAPERS

◁**O'Reilly's balls**▷ *See* TIGHT AS KELSEY'S NUTS

or else *prep phr* *by 1833* Otherwise; or this unhappy thing will follow •Used at the end of a command or warning to encourage compliance: *Get that damn thing out of here or else*

◁**Oreo**▷ *n black fr 1960s* A black person whose values, behavior, etc, are those of the white society; =AFRO-SAXON: *I've been called a "zebra" and an "Oreo"*—React [fr the trademark of a brand of sandwich cookies that have a white cream between round chocolate biscuits]

org *n* *by 1936* An organization: *The Joe Breen (Hays org) influence on pix*—Abel Green

organized *adj* *by 1914* Drunk [perhaps fr *hoary-eyed*]

orie-eyed or **orry-eyed** *See* HOARY-EYED

-orino *See* -ERINO

-orium *See* -ATORIUM

ork or **orc** or **orch** *n* *by 1936* An orchestra

ornery *adj* *by 1816* Mean and irascible; ill-tempered: *He was confident and ornery on the mound*—Inside Sports [fr a dialect pronunciation of *ordinary*]

orphan *n* *by 1940s* A model of a car, boat, computer, etc, which is no longer being manufactured, and for which spare parts are hard to find

orphan drug *n phr* *by 1980s* A pharmaceutical drug that may not be commercially feasible, though it may be very useful or necessary to a relatively small number of people: *Program to Spur "Orphan" Drugs Proves a Success*—Wall Street Journal

or what *question* *by 1990s* Or is it not?; what else can it be?: *Was that exciting, or what?*—Milwaukee Journal/ *Is this the old trickle-down theory or what?*—Daily Record

oscar *n underworld by about 1930* A pistol; firearm [perhaps fr *roscoe* by resemblance]

Oscar 1 *n* *by 1931* Any of a set of annual awards, and the statuette signifying it, from the Academy of Motion Picture Arts and Sciences **2** *n* Any award [said to have been coined by a woman named Margaret Herrick, who said that the figure reminded her of her Uncle *Oscar* Pierce, a farmer]

O sign *n phr medical by 1980s* A sign of death: the patient's mouth is wide open

ossifer *n* *by 1831* An officer, esp a police or Army officer [an ignorant or drunken spoonerism]

ossified *adj* *by 1901* Drunk; =STONED

other fish to fry *See* BIGGER FISH TO FRY

the other half *n phr* *by 1532* One large sector of population, usu the rich as distinct from the poor or the poor as distinct from the rich •Nearly always in the expression "see how *the other half* lives": *Young people from West Berlin now spend their weekends "over there," trying to find out how the other half lives*—Joseph Wechsberg [the dated example is from Rabelais]

other side of one's **face** *See* LAUGH ON THE OTHER SIDE OF one's FACE

ouch *n* *by 1873* An injury; a hurt: *A very serious injury is a "big" ouch*—David Dempsey [fr the pained interjection *ouch* fr German, probably Pennsylvania German, *autsch,* found by 1838]

one **ought to have** one's **head examined** *sentence* *by 1940s* One has done something very stupid or strange: *He paid full price? He ought to have his head examined*

ounce *See* VIG OUNCE

ounce man *1960s narcotics* **1** *n phr* A narcotics dealer who cuts or adulterates heroin **2** *n phr* A narcotics seller who buys from a wholesale drug seller; =CONNECTION, DEALER

out 1 *adj beat & cool talk by about 1942* Attractive; au courant; =HIP, WAY OUT: *Man, that Modigliani is really out* **2** *adj* *by 1966* Not modern, popular, or in accord with current taste: *Those neckties are out this year* **3** *adj homosexuals by 1970s* Openly avowing homosexuality; =OUT OF THE CLOSET **4** *v by late 1980s*: *Some gay activists have undertaken a campaign of outing, exposing well-known people who are believed to be gay*—Time **5** *adj* (also **out cold**) *by 1936* Unconscious or intoxicated: *The folks who use it are usually too luded out or preoccupied*—Playboy **6** *n* *by 1919* A way of escape; a plausible alibi or evasive course; =LETOUT: *You have an out, though. You can talk*—Hugh Pentecost **7** *adj* *by 1923* Rejected; not to be considered •Said to be fr the editing or cutting room in a movie studio: *Ask him again? No, that's out* **8** *adv* *by 1990s* To the point of surfeit or exhaustion: *. . . I'm coffeed out for the time being*—Sue Grafton/ *I don't want them to think I'm losered out*—New York Times

See ALL GET OUT, FAR OUT, GET OUT, WAY OUT

out-and-out *adj* *by 1813* Thorough; complete: *an out-and-out idiot* [as an adverb, found by 1325]

outasight *See* OUT OF SIGHT

outercourse *n by 1990s* Non-invasive sex: *Thousands of American women have told Ann Landers, in their sex lives they would like more talking, more hugging, more outercourse*—Atlantic Monthly

outer garden *n phr baseball by 1907* The outfield

outfox *v by 1962* To outwit; outsmart; =FOX

out from under *See* GET OUT FROM UNDER

out-front *adj by 1960s* Honest; candid; unevasive; =UP FRONT: *. . . intelligent, very open, out-front people*—Tom Wolfe

outie *1 n by 1980s* A convex navel *2 modifier*: *I suspect that the Cardinal arts editor has an outie belly button, and I have an innie belly button*—Wisconsin State Journal [probably a childrens' term]

outing *1 n sports by 1980s* A particular game or performance: *Eldred rebounds from his lone poor outing*—Milwaukee Journal *2 n* (also **outage**) *by late 1980s* The exposure of someone as homosexual

out in left field *1 adj phr by 1959* Very unorthodox and wrong; weirdly unconventional; crazy *2 adj phr medical by 1960* Disoriented; confused

out like a light *adj phr by 1934* Unconscious; fast asleep

out loud *See* FOR CRYING OUT LOUD

out of commish *adj phr by 1939* Not in order or repair; out of commission

out of one's **ears** *See* HAVE something COMING OUT OF one's EARS

out of gas *adj phr by 1975* Exhausted; =BEAT, POOPED: *So I started the second game, damn near out of gas*—Whitey Herzog

out of one's **head** (or **skull** or **gourd**) *entry form by 1825, variants by 1950s* *1 adj phr* Insane; crazy; =NUTS: *You're out of your head if you think I'll do that 2 adj phr* Dazed; delirious; =OFF one's NOODLE: *He took one sniff and went right out of his gourd*

out of hell *See* TAKE OFF LIKE A BIGASS BIRD

out of it *1 adj phr by 1940s* Unable to win or succeed: *The Hawks are out of it this season 2 adj phr by 1960* Not a part of the trend or scene; uninitiated: *Everyone was out of it in the Fifties*—New York Times *3 adj phr by 1963* Unattending, because of drugs, disease, etc: *. . . prefer him dreamy to guilty. We could accept him as being out of it*—John Irving

out of joint *See* PUT someone's NOSE OUT OF JOINT

out of kilter *adj phr by 1628* Not in order or repair; =OUT OF WHACK [fr British dialect *kilter* or *kelter*, "condition, state, frame," of obscure origin]

out of one's **league** (or **ballpark**) *by 1966* *1 adj phr* Not comparable or equal in talent, importance, remuneration, etc: *I'd love to have Reba McEntire, but she's completely out of our ballpark*—Milwaukee Journal *2 adj phr* Not in one's proper province: *The matter's fortunately out of my league*

out of left field *adv phr by 1953* Unexpectedly; suddenly and surprisingly: *When they needed a new idea, this guy appeared out of left field*

out of line *by 1940* *1 adj phr* Not in accordance with what is appropriate or expected: *You was considered out of line if your coat and pants matched*—A Lomax *2 adj phr* Behaving improperly, esp presumptuously: *Maybe I'm out of line. I just feel. . .*—William Bayer

out of luck *adj phr* Having no chance of success; already too late for what one wants: *Those looking for New Jersey organic turkeys. . . are out of luck*—New York Times
See SHIT OUT OF LUCK

out of pocket (or **the pocket**) *adj phr by 1974* Absent or otherwise unavailable: *I'm out of the pocket for a bit, but I'll get back at ya*

out of shape *adj phr by 1970s* Very upset; angry; hysterical
See BENT OUT OF SHAPE

out of sight *1 adj phr* (also **outasight**) *by 1891* Excellent; superior; =WAY OUT *2 adj phr by 1940s* Very high-priced; exorbitantly priced: *That hat's out of sight*

out of style *See* LIKE IT'S GOING OUT OF STYLE

out of sync *adj phr by 1961* Not coinciding or compatible; arrhythmic, esp in relation to something else, a context, etc: *. . . his presence just self-consciously regular enough to be out of sync*—Toronto Life [fr the lack of *synchronism* sometimes noted between a movie or TV image and its soundtrack]

out of the bag *adj phr police by 1990s* In plainclothes; not in uniform

out of the box *1 adj phr by 1970s* Out of contention; ruined; =FINISHED, KAPUT *2 adv phr by 1990s* In an original and creative manner: *Thinking out of the box. Creating new processes, not just tinkering with old formulas*—Wall Street Journal [first sense fr the condition of a baseball pitcher who has been *knocked out of the box* and hence has probably lost the game; second fr the notion that conventional thinkers are *in a box*]

out of the closet *by 1970s* *1 adj phr* Openly avowing homosexuality *2 adj phr* No longer secret: *The last American taboo, that of talking about indebtedness, may be out of the closet at last*—New York Times
See COME OUT OF THE CLOSET

out of the fire *See* PULL something OUT OF THE FIRE

out of the gate *adv phr by 1990s* Immediately: *The booing began in the first inning, when Cal Eldred spotted the Detroit Tigers three runs right out of the gate*—Milwaukee Journal [fr the start of a horse race]

out of the loop *adj phr by late 1980s* Not one of the inner and influential group; not in the network: *George Bush was out of the loop. . . an ineffective second in command*—Newsweek [probably fr the military notion of radio *nets*, conceptually like *loops*, connecting various commanders]

out of the water *See* BLOW someone OUT OF THE WATER

out of the woods *adj phr* by 1792 Out of danger; safe: *This does not get us out of the woods in terms of the growth curve of prison costs*—Rocky Mountain News [the dated example reads *out of the wood*]

out of the woodwork *See* CRAWL OUT OF THE WOODWORK

out of this world *adj phr* by 1938 Excellent; wonderful; superior; =the GREATEST, WAY OUT: *She had a figure that was out of this world*—H Witwer

out of one's **tree** *adj phr* by 1966 Insane; crazy; =APE: *I think she's got to be out of her tree*—Washington Post

out of turn *adj phr* underworld by 1930 Behaving improperly: *You're strictly out of turn. Get in line*—American Mercury
  See TALK OUT OF TURN

out of one's **way** *See* GO OUT OF one's WAY

out of whack by 1885 **1** *adj phr* Not operating; out of order; =ON THE BLINK, OUT OF KILTER: *My car's out of whack, so I'll take yours* **2** *adj phr* Not in adjustment, harmonious synchronism, etc; not in proper order: *Our priorities are out of whack*—Washingtonian **3** *adj phr* Strange; inexplicable; not right: *It seems out of whack to me, then, that Jakobek was the only aldermanic candidate who had a great deal of support from the young*—Toronto Life [probably fr *whack*, "share, a just proportion," so called perhaps fr the blow that divides something or like the auctioneer's hammer-rap signals a fair share or deal]

out of one's **wig** *adj phr* by 1960s Crazy; =OUT OF one's HEAD: *If he thinks he's going to get more, he's out of his wig*—Milwaukee Journal

out on a limb *adv phr* by 1841 In a very vulnerable position; exposed; in peril: *The announcement put the Mayor out on a limb*
  See GO OUT ON A LIMB

◁**out on** one's **ass**▷ *adj phr* (also OUT ON ONE'S EAR) by 1940s Discharged; rejected; superseded; =FINISHED: *She's the First Lady now, and I'm out on my ass*—Interview

outside *See* GET OUTSIDE OF

outside chance *n phr* by 1909 A remote possibility; a slim likelihood: *He may have an outside chance to pass*

outtake *n* by 1977 An excerpt; an extracted passage: *Is this an outtake from the $1.98 Beauty Show?*—Playboy [originally, by 1960, a rejected part of a film]

out the wazoo *adv phr* by 1990s =UP THE ASS: *. . . you can be full of warts, have a scarred-up body. . . have disadvantages out the wazoo. . .*—Macon Telegraph

out the window *adj phr* by 1939 Wrecked and futile; =GO DOWN THE TUBE, KAPUT: *All our plans are out the window now, so forget it*

out to lunch *adj phr* students by 1955 Insane; crazy; eccentric: *On critical issues of fact and analysis he is out to lunch*—Washington Post

out to pasture *See* PUT someone or something OUT TO PASTURE

out year *n phr* by 1970s One of the six or so years affected by a budget or an action in question: *. . . will rise even more sharply in the near future, or what the Pentagon calls the "out years"*—New York Times

over *See* the ONCE-OVER, QUICK-OVER

over a barrel *adv phr* by 1939 In a helpless situation: *I knew enough about him that I had him over a barrel* [perhaps fr the tying *over a barrel* of a person about to be flogged]

over-amp *v* by 1990s To intensify unduly; overblow; =PUMP UP: *. . . the uncomfortable sense that things are being artificially over-amped. . .*—Los Angeles Times

over-amped *adj* by 1990s Unduly stimulated; too expectant; =PSYCHED UP, PUMPED UP: *Couples who fall in love and marry instantaneously often find themselves "over-amped"*—Los Angeles Times

overboard *See* GO OVERBOARD

overcoat *n* WWII Air Forces A parachute
  See CHICAGO OVERCOAT, PINE OVERCOAT

over easy *adj phr* by 1940s Of eggs, fried on both sides, lightly on one

over someone's **eyes** *See* PULL THE WOOL OVER someone's EYES

over one's **head 1** *adj phr* by 1622 Too difficult for one mentally; incomprehensible: *The concept's way over my head* **2** *adv phr* by 1970s Better than one's usual standard; in an inspired way: *The team played over its head, and by God they won*
  See IN OVER one's HEAD

overkill *n* by 1958 An excess, esp of needed action: *Going twice would be overkill, don't you think?* [fr the use of the term in connection with the *killing* potential of nuclear arms and arsenals]

over the coals *See* HAUL someone OVER THE COALS

over the hill 1 *adj phr* by 1940s Middle-aged or past middle age: *. . . a film for, and about, the over-the-hill gang*—Time **2** *adj phr* by 1940s No longer effective; worn out; =AUSGESPIELT **3** *adj phr* by 1970s Most of the way to success or completion: *I think that you can say that we're over the hill*—Ebony **4** *adj phr* Army by 1940s Absent without leave; =AWOL [first three senses fr the notion that one is no longer going upwards towards the summit, but is descending the far side of the imagined *hill*]
  See DRIVE someone OVER THE HILL

over the hump *adj phr* by 1925 Most of the way to success or completion; =OVER THE HILL [a 1914 source defines *hump* as "the half-way point in a prison sentence"]

over the long haul *See* FOR THE LONG HAUL

over the top *adj phr* by 1968 Beyond reason; outlandish: *Makes no sense at all. Simply hilarious and over the top*—Liz Smith/ *It would be over the top! It would be redundant! It would be ridiculous*—Buzz

owl show *n phr* by 1940s A performance, movie, etc, presented late at night: *. . . an owl show in a fleabag*—S J Perelman

the **owner** *n phr* Navy by 1950s The captain of a naval vessel

one's **own hook** *See* ON one's OWN HOOK

one's **own horn** *See* TOOT one's OWN HORN

Owsley *See* AUGUSTUS OWSLEY

ox *See* DUMB OX

oy *interj* by 1892 An exclamation of multiple significance: *Oy. . . may be employed to express anything from ecstasy to horror*—Leo Rosten [fr Hebrew]

oy gevalt *interj* (also **oy vay** or **oy vey iz mir**) An intensification of "oy" as an exclamation of alarm, distress, etc: *Oy Gevalt! New Yawkese An Endangered Dialect?*—New York Times/ *Oy Vay! Bigamy on the Lower East Side*—New York Times/ *The Six-Day War altered my mindset for good: from Oy vey iz mir to Never again!*—Nation

oyster *See* MOUNTAIN OYSTERS, the WORLD IS one's OYSTER

ozone or **zone** *n* 1960s college students A psychedelic condition, usu due to drugs: *He wasn't making much sense because he was way up there in a zone* [fr the notion of being as high as the *ozone* layer of the atmosphere]

P

P or **p** or **pee** *n* by 1966 Any of the various units of currency whose designations begin with "p," such as the Mexican peso or the Vietnamese piastre
See PEE

pace *See* OFF THE PACE

pack *v* by 1890 To carry, esp a weapon
See COLD PACK, NERDPACK, RAT PACK

package 1 *n* by 1956 A large sum of money; =BUNDLE: *That must have cost a package* 2 *n* by 1952 The collective terms of a contract or agreement: *The lefthander signed for a package including 10 million in two years, three McDonald's franchises, and the state of South Dakota* 3 *n* by 1931 A particular combination or set: *That rental car is part of the vacation package* 4 *n* by 1947 The manner and quality of presentation, the trappings and ornamentation, etc, of something: *It isn't what you've got, it's the package that impresses people* 5 *v* by 1947: *He never peddled his idea because he didn't know how to package it*
See NO PRIZE PACKAGE

package deal *n phr* by 1955 An agreement, arrangement, purchase, etc, that comprises various separate items: *In their package deal you get hotel and breakfast but no tours*

packed or **packing** *modifier* first form 1980s teenagers, second by 1990s Armed, esp with a pistol; =CARRYING: *The policeman was packed before he raided the building*—Delcastle Dictionary of Slang

packer *n* 1980s students A male homosexual: *There were a few packers at the party last night. . .*—UCLA Slang [fr homosexual slang *pack fudge*, "do anal intercourse," found by the 1940s]

packet sniffer *n phr* 1990s computers : *Packet sniffers—programs, favorite among illegal hackers, that watch packets of data going by and record user names and passwords for later illicit use*—Mesa Tribune

pack heat *v phr* underworld by 1940s To carry a gun: *They knew all along that Elvis was packin' heat*—Albert Goldman/ *If you pack heat, you got to know what you're doing*—W R Burnett

packie *n* by 1980s A package liquor store

pack in (or **up**) *v phr* by 1940s To cease; give up; retire from: *I intended to pack up playing all together*—Rolling Stone/ *. . . told the FBI men he is "packing in"*—Robert M Yoder

pack it in *v phr* by 1940s To stop; desist; give up what one is doing: *I decided to pack it in and move to New York*—David Standish/ *Who can fault them for not quite yet wanting to pack it in and quietly go home*—Saturday Review

a **pack of lies** *n phr* by 1763 A set or series of lies; =COCK-AND-BULL STORY: *That whole eyewitness account is a damn pack of lies*

pack rat *n phr* by about 1850 A person who cannot discard anything acquired; a compulsive keeper and storer

packtripper *n* by 1960s A person who travels with a rucksack or backpack; backpacker

pact by 1930s 1 *n* An employment contract: *. . . a settlement of his Metro pact*—Variety 2 *v*: *MG Pacts Gable*—Abel Green

pad 1 *n* by 1718 A bed or place to sleep temporarily; =CRASH PAD ●Revived and popularized in 1960s: *The girl shares her pad with other hippies*—TransAction 2 *n* narcotics by 1930s A room, apartment, etc, where narcotics addicts and users gather to take drugs: *There were plenty of pads*—New York Post 3 *n* by 1973 One's home; residence: *He and I used to live in the same pad for two years*—Douglas Wallop 4 *n* prostitutes by about 1915 A prostitute's working room; =CRIB 5 *n* by 1948 An automobile license plate: *The job was wearing California pads*—J Evans 6 *v* by 1913 To increase the amount or length of: *He was padding his expense account*
See BEAT PAD, CHINCH PAD, CRASH PAD, DAMPER PAD, KICK PAD, LAUNCHING PAD, ON THE PAD

the **pad** police by 1960s 1 *n phr* Graft and bribe money taken and shared by police officers 2 *n phr* The list of those police officers who share graft and bribe money
See ON THE PAD

padding *n* by 1861 Text added, often gratuitously and for mere bulk, to an essay, book, speech, etc

paddle *See* UP SHIT CREEK

paddlefoot *n* WWII Army An infantry soldier; rifleman; =DOGFACE: *Murray was a paddlefoot in Europe*—Bill Mauldin

paddle one's **own canoe** *v phr* by 1828 To deal with one's own problems, advancement, etc: *My Dad kicked me out and told me to paddle my own canoe*

pad down by 1950s 1 *v phr* (also **pad out**) To sleep; go to bed; =SACK OUT 2 *v phr* To search; =FRISK

pad duty *n phr* WWII Navy Sleeping; reclining; =SACK DUTY

◄**paddy** or **Paddy**► **1** *n by 1780* An Irish person or person of Irish extraction **2** *n* (also **patty**) *black by 1946* A white person: *Even a drunken black shoeshine man could handle the likes of this paddy*—Joseph Wambaugh **3** *modifier*: *I know I can't be tight with this paddy boy*—Claude Brown [fr the nickname of the given name *Patrick*]

paddy wagon *n phr by 1930* A police patrol wagon or van; =BLACK MARIA: *The cooperative family was being escorted into the paddy wagon*—Philadelphia Bulletin [fr *patrol wagon*, perhaps influenced by the fact that many policemen were of Irish extraction, hence *paddies*]

padre (PAH dray) *n by 1898* Any military chaplain [fr Spanish or Portuguese, "father, priest"]

paesan (pī ZAHN) *n by 1930s* A fellow native of one's country or town; compatriot; =HOMIE, LANDSMAN [fr Italian dialect]

page *See* OP-ED PAGE, TAKE A PAGE FROM someone's BOOK

page turner *n phr by 1976* A book that is so absorbing that one reads it without stopping, although not necessarily for serious literary or intellectual quality: *. . . a book that unquestionably deserves the description page turner*—New York Daily News

pail *n black by 1950s* The stomach

pain *See* FEEL NO PAIN

a **pain** *by 1908* **1** *n phr* Annoyance; irritation; =HEADACHE: *Marvin is a real pain* **2** *n phr* =a PAIN IN THE ASS: *It's very much like the Internet equivalent of having your windows soaped. But it's still a pain to clean up after*—Newark Star-Ledger

See GIVE someone A PAIN

◁a **pain in the ass**▷ (or **neck**) *n phr* entry form *by 1934, variant by 1924* An annoying, obnoxious person or thing: *This proved a major pain in the ass as too many casual favorites fell to the wrong side*—Village Voice

See GIVE someone A PAIN

paint *n* (also **paint cards**) *by 1931* Playing cards, esp picture cards

See RED PAINT, WAR PAINT

the **paint** *n basketball by 1990s* The foul zone; lane: *. . . get the hell out of the paint*—New Yorker

paint-by-numbers *modifier by 1970* Simple; obvious: *Clark's second Regan Reilly mystery has a paint-by-numbers plot with characters who collide in wildly improbable ways*—New York Times [fr the kits with which one paints a picture by coloring numbered patches]

paint oneself **into a corner** *v phr by 1980s* To put oneself into a frustrating or helpless situation: *Paul has painted himself into a corner with that unlikely explanation*

paint the town or **paint the town red** *v phr by 1884* To go on a wild spree; carouse: *Well, sport, let's go out and paint the town a new color*—Hal Boyle

◁**pair**▷ *n by 1922* A woman's breasts ●Regarded as offensive by many women

paisano (pī ZAHN oh) *n by 1844* =PAESAN [fr Spanish, "countryman"]

pajamas *See* the CAT'S MEOW

pal 1 *n by 1681* A friend, esp a very close male friend; boon companion; =BUDDY: *. . . has many devoted friends, but he is nobody's "pal"*—New York Times **2** *v by 1899* =PAL AROUND [fr Romany *phral, phal,* "brother, friend," ultimately fr Sanskrit *bhratr,* "brother"]

palace *n by 1834* A grand venue for something ●Always ironically used of a fairly seedy though perhaps ornate place

See FIVE-SIDED PUZZLE PALACE

pal around *v phr by 1915* To be "pals"; consort as "pals": *. . . the people he palled around with*—Ira Wolfert

pale *n black by 1940s* A white person; =GRAY

paled or **paled out** *adj* or *adj phr Canadian teenagers by 1970s* Completely exhausted, esp by drugs or liquor; =WASTED

paleface 1 *n black homosexuals by 1970s* A white homosexual **2** *n circus by 1940s* A circus clown

palimony 1 *n by 1979* Money awarded, property shared, etc, when an unmarried couple separate **2** *modifier*: *a much-heralded palimony suit* [fr *pal* plus *alimony*; coined for or at least popularized by a lawsuit against the film star Lee Marvin]

pally or **pallie 1** *adj by 1895* Very friendly; affectionate and familiar; =PALSY-WALSY **2** *n by 1940* =PAL

palm *v by 1673* To conceal a playing card against the palm in order to use it in a gambling hand: *It was five cards that he palmed, three aces and a pair of queens*—Calder Willingham

See GREASE someone's PALM

palm something **off** *v phr by 1822* To bestow something inferior as if it were of good quality; foist; fob off: *He palmed the leaky old place off like it was the Ritz*

palm oil *n phr by 1627* Money used for bribery and graft [because it is used to *grease one's palm*]

palmtop *n computers by 1990s* A very small computer: *Silicon Valley's future may hinge on winning the palmtop computer race*—New York Times [modeled on *desktop, laptop*]

palooka or **paluka** or **palooker** (pə LOO Kə) **1** *n by 1925* A mediocre or inferior boxer: *. . . a paluka who leads with his right*—Dashiell Hammett **2** *n by about 1940* A professional wrestler **3** *n by 1940s* Any large and stupid man [origin unknown; said to have been coined by the sports writer and humorist Jack Conway]

palsy-walsy (PAL zee WAL zee) **1** *adj by 1940s* Very friendly; =CHUMMY: *. . . breezy, palsy-walsy with Baskerville, who's not a breezy type*—Nation **2** *n*: *Hey, palsy-walsy, what's going down?*

pan¹ 1 *n by 1923* The face; =MUG: *. . . too great for them to keep their pans shut*—Jerome Weidman

2 *v by 1909* To criticize severely and adversely; derogate harshly; =ROAST: *The Daily Worker panned his first novel*—Leonard Lyons **3** *n*: . . . *an out-and-out pan*—Billy Rose [sense 2 and 3 fr the fact that roasting is done in a *pan*]
See DEADPAN, FLASH IN THE PAN, ON THE PAN

pan² or **pam** *movie studio by 1922* **1** *v* To move the camera across a visual field to give a panoramic effect or follow something moving **2** *modifier*: *a pan shot* [fr *panorama*]

panhandle *v by 1903* To beg, esp by accosting people on the street: *The boys deal drugs or panhandle, even become male prostitutes*—Time [fr *panhandler*]

panhandler *n by 1897* A person who begs, esp by accosting people on the street; beggar: *This panhandler came up to me and braced me*—John O'Hara [fr the stiff arm held out by the beggar]

panic 1 *v by 1910* To become frightened and confused, esp suddenly; =FLIP: *He panicked and dropped the ball* **2** *v by 1920* To get a strong favorable reaction, esp to get loud laughter from an audience; =FRACTURE: *Mr Todd knows how to panic the rubes*—Brooks Atkinson **3** *n by 1924* A very funny person; an effective comedian; =a STITCH

panic button *See* HIT THE PANIC BUTTON

panic rack *n phr Air Force by 1951* A pilot's ejection seat: *The jockey is in the panic rack and ready to go*—Associated Press

panky or **pank** *See* HANKY-PANKY

panman *n by 1960s* A drummer in a West Indian steel band, whose players strike xylophonelike instruments made from the ends of steel containers such as oil drums

pan out *v phr by 1868* To be productive; succeed; =PAY OFF: *Ryan thought about what he'd be living with if the FBI profile panned out*—Philadelphia [fr the practice of *panning* gold in river sediments]

◁**pansified**▷ (PAN zi fid) *adj by 1941* Effeminate; =SISSIFIED

◁**pansy**▷ *by 1929* **1** *n* A male homosexual; =QUEEN: *. . . if someone had bluntly said that her friends. . . were pansies*—Philip Wylie **2** *n* A weak or effeminate male; =LILY, SISSY **3** *adj*: *Stage and screen voices in recent years have become so pansy*—H W Seaman

◁**panther piss (or sweat)**▷ or **panther** *n phr* or *n by 1929* Raw and inferior whiskey; =ROTGUT

pantry *n prizefight by 1950* The stomach; =BREADBASKET: *. . . another real fine left to the pantry*—R Starnes

pants *See* ANTS, CATCH someone WITH THEIR PANTS DOWN, CREAM one's JEANS, FANCY PANTS, FLY BY THE SEAT OF one's PANTS, FUDGE one's PANTS, GET THE LEAD OUT, HAVE LEAD IN one's PANTS, HIGH WATERS, HOT PANTS, RAGGEDY-ASS, SEAT-OF-THE-PANTS, SHIT one's PANTS, SMARTY-PANTS

the **pants off** someone *adv phr* (also **someone's pants off**) *by 1933* To the utmost; to an extreme degree: *I'm going to sue the pants off you this time, meathead*—Washington Post [the intensifier became

popular in the 1930s, mostly with menacing verbs like *beat, bore,* and *scare,* but also with *charm* and *flatter;* the semantics are not apparent, except perhaps that one feels helpless with one's pants off]

panty raid *n phr 1950s students* A male invasion of a women's dormitory, the purpose being to take underwear as trophies

pantywaist *n by 1936* A weak or effeminate male; =PANSY: *The hurt. . . pantywaist ran off a number of copies of his letter*—Bernard DeVoto [fr a child's garment with short *pants* buttoned to the *waist* of a shirt]

pap *n by 1844* Father; =PAPPY

papa *n esp black by about 1922* A male lover; =DADDY
See SWEET MAN

paparazzi 1 *n by 1968* A freelance photographer who hounds celebrities: *. . . out of the public spotlight and away from the paparazzi*—Parade **2** *modifier*: *. . . one of the most paparazzi-plagued women of this American century. . .* —Mesa Tribune [plural of Italian *paparazzo*]

paper 1 *n by 1850* A forged or worthless check **2** *v by 1925* To use or pass counterfeit money or worthless checks; =LAY PAPER: *. . . papered Queens and Long Island with. . . bum checks*—New York Daily News **3** *n theater by 1785* A pass or free ticket; =ANNIE OAKLEY **4** *v theater by 1879* To give out free tickets in order to get a large audience: *The show was not doing well, so they papered the theater* **5** *v police by 1960s* To write traffic and parking tickets: *The captain complained that the patrolmen were not papering enough* **6** *n 1960s narcotics* A packet of narcotics; =BAG
See BAD PAPER, LAY PAPER, ON PAPER, PEDDLE one's PAPERS, WALKING PAPERS

◁**paper ass**▷ *See* MAN WITH A PAPER ASS

paper bag *See* CAN'T FIGHT one's WAY OUT OF A PAPER BAG

◁**paper bag case**▷ *n phr 1980s students* An ugly woman

paper (or brown paper) bag test *n phr black by 1980s* A criterion for admission to certain clubs, parties, etc: *If you are darker than a standard paper bag, you are simply rejected*—Atlantic/ Black Washingtonians remember the days when upper-crust black folks used to do the brown paper bag test to determine who could come to a particular party*—New Yorker

paper chase *n phr British by 1932* An intense searching and collation of files, books, documents, etc, esp for the needs of bureaucratic pomp: *Manuel's history of ideas carries the reader not on a paper chase but on a fascinating voyage*—New Republic [fr the game of hare and hounds in which the quarry would leave a trail of scraps of *paper,* the term found by 1856; popularized in the US as the title of a film and a TV series, where the *paper* was a Harvard Law School degree]

paper dolls *See* CUT OUT DOLLS

paperhanger or **paper-pusher** *n underworld by 1914* A person who passes counterfeit money or worthless checks: *The FBI's suspect was a master paperhanger, the last of a breed*—Philadelphia

paper over *v phr* by 1955 To conceal or gloss over; fail to deal with: *If the tiff were nothing but a clash of personalities. . . it might be quickly papered over*—Newsweek [based on *paper over the cracks*, found by 1910 and based on a phrase of Bismarck's]

paper profits *n phr* by 1940s Monetary gains recognizable by accounting but not realized in palpable money or goods

papers *See* CUT someone's PAPERS, PEDDLE one's PAPERS, PUT one's PAPERS IN, WALKING PAPERS

paper tiger *n phr* by 1952 A menacing person or thing that in fact lacks force; a blusterer: . . . *doing battle with a paper tiger when he aims his wrath at the white liberal*—New York Times [fr the Chinese expression *tsuh lao fu*, "paper tiger" given currency by Mao Zedong]

paper trail *n phr* by middle 1980s Records, documents, etc, that lead to a conclusion: *Officials. . . had expected to find a damning paper trail of incriminating evidence*—New York Times

pappy *n* Father; =PAP: *Harry Light? His pappy*—Stan Cutler

parachute *n* 1980s narcotics : A mixture of crack cocaine and heroin known as "parachute". . . —Associated Press
See GOLDEN PARACHUTE

parade *See* RAIN ON someone's PARADE

paralyzed *adj* by 1888 Very drunk

parboiled *adj* by about 1935 Drunk

pard *n* by 1872 Friend; partner; =PAL

pardon me all to hell *See* EXCUSE ME ALL TO HELL

pardon me for living *interj* by 1960s An ironic riposte from someone who feels wrongly accused and badgered

pardon (or excuse) my French *interj* entry form by 1895, variant by 1940 An exclamation of apology for the use of profane or taboo language: *That Goddamned. . . pardon my French*—Tennessee Williams/ *You will excuse my French. I am only quoting Mr Clemens*—Donald Henderson Clarke

par for the course *n phr* by 1947 What is to be expected: *He had to take a little crap from the clerk, but that's par for the course*

park 1 *v* by 1922 To put or place; locate: *Park yourself anywhere, I'll be right back* 2 *v* by 1990s To manipulate records illegally so as to conceal true ownership of stocks: . . . *if you're caught "parking" stock, your defense is . . . everybody does it but I didn't know it was going on*—Gary Trudeau
See BALLPARK, BALLPARK FIGURE

park one *v phr* baseball by 1940s To hit a home run: *A cheer would go up across the street, and someone who had a transistor radio would holler, "Mantle just parked one"*—New York Times

parlay *v* by 1942 To build or increase something from a small initial outlay or possession: *She parlayed her dimples into movie superstardom* [fr horse racing, "place a series of increasing bets," found by 1895, fr *paralee* or *parlee*, an early–1800s

faro term fr Italian *parole*, "words, promises"]

parley-voo *v* WWI Army To speak, esp a foreign language: *She wondered if he parley-vooed Chinese* [fr French *parlez-vous*, "do you speak?"]

parlor *See* HORSE ROOM, MASSAGE PARLOR, RAP CLUB, RUB PARLOR, SAWDUST PARLOR

parlor pink *n phr* by about 1935 A mildly radical socialist; political liberal

parole *See* BACKGATE PAROLE, BUSH PAROLE

the parson's nose *See* the POPE'S NOSE

part *See* BIT

party 1 *n* by 1460 A person 2 *n* by about 1935 A bout of sex play or sexual activity 3 *v* by 1922 To go to or give parties; be energetically social; =LIVE IT UP, MAKE WHOOPEE: *You don't party with the right people, kiss your ass good-bye*—Elmore Leonard
See BLAST PARTY, COLD-MEAT PARTY, GI PARTY, HAVE A PARTY, HEN PARTY, KICK PARTY, NECKTIE PARTY, POP PARTY, POT PARTY, STAG, TAILGATE PARTY

party animal (or reptile) *n phr* by 1980s An enthusiastic party-goer: *Apparently Salman has turned into a major party animal*—Dave Barry

party hat 1 *n phr* by 1960s The array of lights on the roof of a police car or emergency vehicle; =GUMBALL 2 *n phr* 1980s students A condom: *In the heat of the moment he realized he didn't have a party hat*—UCLA Slang

party hearty *n phr* by 1990s =PARTY ANIMAL: *He attracted a Hollywood set of Hawaiian-shirt party hearties who sunned themselves like alligators down in Key West*—Vanity Fair

the party is over *sentence* by 1937 The fun is finished; reality impinges

the party line *n phr* by 1942 The accepted view; conventional wisdom: *The party line on Matisse. . .* —New Yorker [popularized in the 1930s as "the official dogma of the Communist Party"]

party pooper or **party poop** *n phr* by 1951 A morose, pessimistic person; =KILLJOY, WET BLANKET: *No one can call Mr Bulganin and Mr Kruschchev party poopers*—Edmund Wilson/ *What a party poop you are today, Sally*—Anne Bernays

party record (or album) *n phr* by 1980s A salacious recording originally meant to be played at parties: *Long before Richard Pryor, Foxx was making X-rated party records*—New York Times

pash by 1921 1 *n* Passion: . . . *insisted that he get some "pash" into it*—P Marks 2 *n* One's current absorbing love object: *She's my pash this week* 3 *adj* Passionate: *That isn't as pash as some of the poems*—F Scott Fitzgerald

pass 1 *v* by 1940s To be thought to be something one is not, esp to be thought white when one is actually black: . . . *the oldest daughter, so fair she could pass* 2 *v* by 1565 To suffice or be adequate, only just barely: *It's not great pasta, but it'll pass* 3 *n phr* by 1928 A sexual advance; =PROPOSITION 4 *v* by 1869 To decline to do something, take something, etc: *I'll pass on the French fries, but take the onions* [in the first sense, *pass oneself off* as found by 1809]
See MAKE A PASS AT someone

passion pit 1 *n phr* teenagers by 1951 A drive-in movie theater: . . . *taking his buxom daughter off to the local passion pit*—Stephen King **2** *n phr* by 1970s A room used for seduction: . . . *some minorleague Don Juan's passion pit*—Stephen King

passout *n* by 1950s A person who has passed out, esp from drinking: . . . *finding yourself with an 18-year-old passout on your hands*—Esquire's Handbook for Hosts

pass out 1 *v phr* (also **pass out cold**) by 1918 To lose consciousness; faint; go to sleep, esp from drinking too much liquor **2** *v phr* by 1899 To die: *He left us a lot of jack when he passed out*—P Marks

pass the buck *v phr* by 1865 To refer a problem or responsibility to someone else, esp to a higher authority; decline to take action: *We chickened out and passed the buck to the dean* [fr poker games where one would *pass the buck,* usu a pocketknife with a *buck* horn handle, on to the next person, thereby passing the deal on]

pass the hat *v phr* by 1762 To ask for contributions of money; collect money from a group: *We passed the hat until we had her plane fare*

pass something **up** *v phr* by 1896 To choose not to take, attend, etc; =GIVE someone or something A MISS: *I guess I'll pass up the concert tonight*

paste 1 *v* by 1846 To hit; strike very hard: *She grabbed the broom and pasted me* **2** *v* sports by 1940s To defeat decisively; trounce; =CLOBBER: *The Jets got pasted* [origin unknown; perhaps an alteration of earlier *baste,* "strike, trounce," of obscure origin and preserved in *lambaste*]

pasteboard 1 *n* by 1934 A ticket of admission; =ANNIE OAKLEY, BOARD: *He studied the coveted pasteboard*—P Jones **2** *n* by 1837 A business card or calling card **3** *n* by 1859 A playing card: *Okay, shuffle the pasteboards and let's commence* [by 1856 in the first sense, "railroad ticket"]

pasties *n* by 1961 Adhesive patches worn over the nipples by nude dancers

pasting *n* by 1851 A beating; drubbing

pasture *n* baseball by 1891 The outfield of a baseball field
    See OUTER GARDEN, PUT someone or something OUT TO PASTURE

patch out *v phr* 1960s students To make a quick start in a car, so as to spin the wheels and leave patches of rubber on the pavement

pat-down search *n phr* by 1974 A search made by patting the outer clothing: *During a pat-down search, a female Milwaukee police officer felt something soft in one of Guy's pockets*—Milwaukee Journal

◁**pato**▷ (PAH toh) *n* by 1960s A male homosexual [fr Puerto Rican Spanish, "duck"]

patoot or **patootie** or **ptoot** (pə TooT) *n* by 1960s The buttocks; fundament; =ASS: *You hear with your patoot, curlylocks*—Earl Thompson/ *Talk about a horse's ptoot. . .*—Daily Jefferson County Union [origin unknown; perhaps fr dialect *tout,* "buttocks," fr Middle English, pronounced *toot,*

and altered to conform with *sweet patootie* by folk etymology]

patootie or **sweet patootie** by 1921 **1** *n* or *n phr* One's girlfriend or boyfriend; sweetheart: *. . . tell their patooties how pretty they are*—NY Confidential **2** *n* or *n phr* A young woman: *. . . a batch of pretty-panned patooties*—G Dixon [perhaps fr a play on *sweet potato* suggested by *sweetheart* and *potato* as used, like *tomato,* to mean a person]

patsy by 1903 **1** *n* A victim; dupe; =SUCKER: *. . . a patsy, a quick push, a big softie*—W R Burnett/ *But to retain lawyers is clear proof that you're a patsy*—Saul Bellow **2** *n* A person who takes the blame for a crime, who is put up against a superior opponent in order to lose, etc; =FALL GUY [apparently fr the name of *Patsy Bolivar,* a character in a minstrel skit of the 1880s, who was blamed for whatever went wrong]

pattern *See* IN A HOLDING PATTERN

patty *See* PADDY

patzer or **potzer** (PAHT zər) *n* by 1926 A mediocre but often enthusiastic chess player [probably fr Yiddish]
    See POTCHKIE

the **pavement** *See* POUND THE PAVEMENT

paw 1 *n* by 1605 A hand: *You let me get my paws on the money*—Raymond Chandler **2** *v* by 1701 To touch and handle, esp in a crude sexual way
    See NORTHPAW, SOUTHPAW

pax *n* by 1970s A passenger: *There were twenty pax listed for the trip*—John Ball [apparently derived fr *passenger* as *prexy* is fr *president*]

pay *See* HELL TO PAY

payback *n* by 1970 Revenge; retaliation: *Payback is the idiom of East Africa, but the rule is that innocents always get hurt*—New Republic

pay dirt *n phr* by 1873 Profit and success: *I'll try a fast-food franchise, where there's sure to be pay-dirt* [in the sense "richly yielding ore," found by 1856]
    See HIT PAY DIRT

pay one's **dues** *v phr* by 1943 To serve and suffer such that one deserves what good comes to one; =GO THROUGH THE MILL: *We elderly have paid our dues*—New York Times [an isolated example is found in 1878]

payoff 1 *n* underworld by 1930 Payment, esp of bribery, graft, etc: *The villains were waiting for their payoff* **2** *n* by 1926 The final outcome or bit of information, esp when it is surprising or amusing: *OK, here's the payoff, she's the Albanian consul!*

pay off 1 *v phr* underworld by 1930 To give someone bribe money, blackmail money, or the like: *We'll have to pay them off handsomely to keep quiet* **2** *v phr* by 1951 To bring in profit; succeed; pay: *Getting another degree will pay off someday*

payola *n* by 1938 Graft; extortion money; bribery, esp that paid by recording companies to disc jockeys for playing their records on the radio [coined probably fr *payoff* and the ending of *Pianola,* trademark of an automatic piano-playing device, or *Victrola,* trademark of a gramophone]

pay the freight *v phr* by 1970s To pay for; compensate for; bear the expense of; =PICK UP THE TAB: *We may have to "pay the freight for well-meant efforts at improvement"*—New Yorker

pay through the nose *v phr* by 1672 To pay exorbitantly; give too much in recompense

pay up *v phr* by 1434 To pay in full; settle one's account: *Pay up and be done with it*

pay-wing *n baseball* by 1950s A pitcher's throwing arm

pazzazza (pə ZAZ ə) *n* by 1921 A piazza: *. . . young woman is sitting on the pazzazza*—H Witwer

PC 1 *n airline* by 1970s A pilot check flight or ride, where a pilot's continued qualification to fly is periodically tested **2** *n computer* by 1978 A personal computer: *Turn on your PC and type in. . . CHKD-SK*—Mesa Tribune **3** *n* by 1990s Political correctness; conformity with a set of progressive social ideals **4** *adj phr*: *He found my strictures politically correct*

PCP *n* 1960s *narcotics* Phencyclidine, an animal tranquilizer smoked as a narcotic; =ANGEL DUST

p'd *See* PISSED OFF

PDQ *adv* by 1875 Pretty damn quick

pea *See* SWEET PEA

peacenik *n* by 1965 A member of a peace movement; pacifist; antiwar demonstrator

See -NIK

peach 1 *n* by 1754 An attractive young woman: *She really was a "peach"*—S A Clark **2** *n* by 1904 Any remarkable, admirable, amiable, or attractive person: *You're a peach*—Dorothy Parker **3** *n* by 1870 Anything superior or admirable: *The hotel was a peach*

peacherino *n* by 1900 =PEACH: *Ain't this show a peacherino?*

peach-fuzz *modifier* by 1990s Young; inexperienced: *. . . I asked one of Clinton's peach-fuzz counselors how they could still be learning to govern after running the country for two years*—Maureen Dowd

peachy or **peachy-keen** *adj* first form by 1900, second by about 1955 Excellent; wonderful; =GREAT, NEAT: *. . . this president's political health, which Wirthlin thinks is peachy*—George Will

peanut 1 *n* by 1934 A small or trivial person; something insignificant **2** *adj*: *a peanut operation*

peanut gallery 1 *n phr* by 1888 The topmost rows of a theater **2** *n phr* A group or individual whose opinion is considered inconsequential

peanuts *n* by 1934 A small amount of money; a trivial sum; =NICKELS AND DIMES: *They got you working for peanuts*—Budd Schulberg

See THAT AIN'T HAY

pearl-diver *n* by 1913 A person who washes dishes, esp in a restaurant

pea-shooter 1 *n* by 1950s A firearm, esp one so-called by a person who scorns its small caliber **2** *n WWII Army Air Force* A fighter pilot or plane [fr a

child's toy, a long tube through which he *shoots peas,* found by 1803]

pea soup (or **souper)** *n phr* by 1849 A thick fog, esp one plaguing London

peat *See* PETE

pebble on the beach *n phr* by 1896 A person, esp as reduced in significance by being of a numerous sort: *Remember, you're not the only pebble on the beach*

pec *n* by 1966 A pectoral muscle: *All the male weight lifters love her a bushel and a pec*—Playboy

peck ◁1▷ *n black* by 1940s =PECKERWOOD **2** *v black* by 1960s To eat **3** *n teenagers* by 1960s Food **4** *n* by 1893 A perfunctory kiss: *She gave him a friendly peck and got back to work*

See a PECK OF TROUBLE

◁**pecker**▷ *n* by 1902 The penis

pecker checker *n phr medical* by 1980s A urologist

◁**peckerhead**▷ *n* by 1955 A despicable person; =ASSHOLE, JERK: *Do you hear me, peckerhead?*—Andrew Coburn

◁**pecker tracks**▷ *n phr* Traces on a man's pants showing that he has had an orgasm or near orgasm: *. . . then what would he be looking for, pecker tracks?*—Elmore Leonard

◁**peckerwood**▷ *esp black* by 1929 **1** *n* A poor Southern white, esp a farmer; =CRACKER, REDNECK **2** *n* Any white Southern man: *Any white man from the South is a "peckerwood"*—Stephen Longstreet [fr rural black use of the red-headed *woodpecker,* with dialect inversion of the word elements, as a symbol for white persons in contrast with the blackbird as a symbol for themselves; the red head may be the semantic base, suggesting *redneck*]

peckings (or **pecks)** *n black* by 1950s Food

peckish *adj* by 1785 Hungry •Chiefly British

a **peck of trouble** *n phr* by 1535 Much difficulty: *Looks like that young fellow got himself into a peck of trouble. . .* —Sue Grafton

pedal *See* PUT THE PEDAL TO THE METAL, SOFT-PEDAL

peddle one's **papers** *v phr* by 1936 To go about one's business •Often an irritated command that one leave the speaker alone: *I told him to go peddle his papers*—Hal Boyle

peddler *n narcotics* by 1929 A narcotics seller; =DEALER

See ASS PEDDLER, FLESH-PEDDLER, PILL-PUSHER

ped scramble or **Barnes dance** *n phr* by 1960s A system of urban traffic control in which in a cycle all traffic lights turn red to stop cars, while pedestrians can cross in all directions [variant named for Henry Barnes (died 1968), Traffic Commissioner of New York City; *ped,* "pedestrian, speed walker," is found by 1863, and among traffic engineers by 1962]

pee by 1880 **1** *v* To urinate; =PISS, WHIZ **2** *n* Urine

See P

peed off *See* PISSED OFF

peejays *n* by 1964 Pajamas; =PJS

peekaboo *adj* by 1895 Made of a sheer fabric or decorated with holes; =SEE-THROUGH

peek freak *n phr by 1960s* A voyeur; Peeping Tom

peel 1 *v by 1785* To undress; strip **2** *v 1950s* hot rodders =PEEL OUT **3** *v 1980s* street talk: *Many of the young people describe stealing a vehicle as "peeling it"*—Milwaukee Journal

peeler *n by 1940s* A striptease dancer; =STRIPPER: *. . . grinders, peelers, and bumpers*—Louis Sobol
See BRONCO BUSTER

peel out *v phr* (also **peel rubber** or **peel wheels**) *1950s* hot rodders To leave quickly; =SPLIT [fr the notion of *peeling* off the tread of a tire]

◁**peenie**▷ **See** POUND one's PEENIE

peep *n by 1903* A word; the slightest sound: *If I hear a peep out of you, you've had it*

peeper *n by 1940* A private detective; =PI, PRIVATE DICK: *. . . and don't bother to call your house peeper*—Raymond Chandler
See HEADSHRINKER

peepers 1 *n by 1700s* The eyes: *If anything was wrong with my peepers the army wouldn't of took me*—Nelson Algren **2** *n by 1970s* A pair of sunglasses; =SHADES: *I'd come through the employee door with one of my peepers on*—D James

peep show 1 *n phr by 1914* A supposedly private view, as if through a hole in the wall, of some forbidden sexual activity **2** *n phr by 1940s* =LEG SHOW [found by 1851 as "an exhibition of pictures viewed through a lens in a small hole"]

peet **See** PETE

peeties *n gamblers by about 1890* Loaded dice [fr *repeaters*]

peeve 1 *v by 1908* To annoy; irritate: *That crap really peeves me* **2** *n by 1911*: *You probably have a long list of peeves* [by back formation fr *peeved,* which in turn derives by back formation fr *peevish,* fr Middle English *peivish,* "perverse, wayward, capricious," perhaps fr Latin *perversus*]
See PET PEEVE

peeved or **peeved off** *adj* or *adj phr by 1908* Annoyed; irritated; irked: *He got peeved*—Billy Rose

peewee *n by 1877* A short or small person, animal, etc: *That peewee doesn't scare me*

peezy **See** JEEZ

peg 1 *v by 1920* To identify; classify; pick out; =BUTTON DOWN: *I could peg a joint like that from two miles away*—John O'Hara **2** *v by about 1935* To taper or bind a pair of trousers at the lower end: *Pants must be pegged to fit snugly around the ankle*—Max Shulman **3** *n baseball by 1862* A throw, esp a hard one: *His peg missed and the runner scored* **4** *v*: *He pegged it sharply to first* **5** *v 1980s* students To derogate; speak unfavorably of; =BAG ON someone, PUT-DOWN, TRASH: *It's good he wasn't at the party, because he was really pegged*—College Slang 101
See SQUARE PEG, TAKE someone DOWN A PEG

◁**peg boy**▷ *n by 1950s* A boy used as a catamite by a man, esp a sailor [fr the notion that sailors' young catamites were forced to sit on *pegs* to dilate their anuses; the date must be considerably earlier]

peg leg 1 *n phr by 1872* A person who wears a wooden leg **2** **modifier**: *Watch me pass that peg-leg gimp*—Nelson Algren

peg out *v phr by 1855* To die: *Harrison. . . actually pegged out in 1841*—H L Mencken [fr the ending of play in cribbage by *pegging*]

pegs *n by 1847* Legs; =PINS: *He was wobbly on his pegs*

Pelican *n by 1890* A native or resident of Louisiana [the flag of Louisiana shows a *pelican* feeding her young]

pellet *n baseball by 1907* The ball used in a ball game: *Berra. . . searched the premises for the pellet*—Associated Press

pelter 1 *n by 1856* An inferior horse; =HAY BURNER **2** *n by 1901* A fast horse

pen *n by 1845* A prison of any sort, esp a penitentiary
See BULLPEN, HEN-PEN, PIGPEN, POISON-PEN LETTER, PUSH A PEN

pencil *v by 1990s* To work out details; study: *Let me pencil this idea for a while*
See HAVE LEAD IN one's PENCIL

pencil someone or something **in** *v phr by 1940s* To make a tentative arrangement: *Why don't I pencil in an appointment for next Thursday?*

pencil neck 1 *n phr by 1973* A weak person; =WIMP: *Catch you later, you pencil-neck motherfucker*—Joseph Wambaugh **2** *n phr* (also **pencil geek** or **pencil-necked geek**) *1980s* students A studious person; =GRIND, MERV: *The pencil neck answered every question correctly*—Delcastle Dictionary of Slang

pencil-pusher (or **-driver** or **-shover**) *n by 1881* An office worker, esp a clerk, bookkeeper, or the like; =DESK JOCKEY: *The number of pencil pushers and typists has increased*—S Dawson

penguin 1 *n Royal Air Force by 1918* A nonflying member of an air force; =KIWI **2** *n movie studio by 1950s* An actor who wears a tuxedo as part of a crowd scene

penguin suit *n phr by 1967* A tuxedo; =TUX . . . *yes, it is possible to do serious rock'n' roll in a penguin suit*—Milwaukee Journal

penicillin **See** JEWISH PENICILLIN

penman 1 *n underworld by 1965* A forger **2** *n 1950s* teenagers A student who signs his or her parents' names to made-up excuses

pennant **See** IRISH PENNANT

the **Pennsy** *n by 1940s* The Pennsylvania Railroad

penny ante 1 *n phr by 1935* A trivial transaction; a cheap offer, arrangement, etc **2** *adj*: *I despised his penny-ante ideas* [fr the minimal *ante* required in a cheap poker game]

penny loafers *n phr by 1970* A kind of mocassin-like shoe with a slot that can hold a coin, and generally worn by well-off people: *We are not poor, we wear penny loafers, ride mountain bikes and have large discretionary incomes*—Nation

penny-pincher *n by 1934* A stingy person; miser; =TIGHTWAD

penny pool *n phr by 1940s* A paltry game or affair; =PENNY ANTE: *I told him to shove his deal, it*

was penny pool
See PLAY PENNY POOL

penny stock *n phr by 1932*: *That minimum would exclude penny stocks, which are cheap, risky stocks that usually have prices below $1 a share*—Milwaukee Journal

pennyweighter *n outdated underworld* A jewel thief or shoplifter

pen-pusher *n by 1913* =PENCIL-PUSHER

pen yen *n phr narcotics by about 1920* Opium [probably a shortening of Cantonese Chinese *nga pun-yin,* "opium"]
See HOP[2]

◁**peola**▷ *n black by 1942* A very light-skinned black person, esp a young woman

people *n by 1926* A person: *She's great people*—Lawrence Sanders
See the BEAUTIFUL PEOPLE, BOAT PEOPLE, FLOWER CHILDREN, FREE PEOPLE, JESUS PEOPLE, NIGHT PEOPLE, ROAD PEOPLE, STREET PEOPLE

the **people** *n phr 1960s narcotics* Narcotics dealers on a large or wholesale scale; =KILO CONNECTION

people person *n phr by 1990s* A sociable and compassionate person: *And the fact that he could tolerate a query about personality flaws. . . proved he's not all that bad a "people person"*—Los Angeles Times

Peoria **See** PLAY IN PEORIA

pep 1 *n by 1912* Energy; vitality; =PISS AND VINEGAR, PIZZAZZ **2** *modifier*: *pep talk/ pep pill* [fr *pepper*]

pepped out *adj phr by 1920* Exhausted; sapped: *I'm tired and pepped out*—F Scott Fitzgerald

pepper 1 *n by 1895* Energy; vitality; =PEP: *The old moral support is what gives we players the old pepper*—Westbrook Pegler **2** *v baseball by 1920s* To throw a baseball very hard; =BURN **3** *n baseball by 1920s* A fast and hard session of pitch-and-catch; =BURNOUT ◀**4**▶ *n* (also **pepper belly**) *by 1920s* A Mexican or person of Mexican extraction
See SALT AND PEPPER

pepper-upper *n by 1937* A thing, food, drink, person, etc, that imparts pep; stimulant: *"Say, fellows,"* said a uniformed pepper-upper to a bunch of GI assault troops*—M Mayer

pep pill *n phr 1930s narcotics* Any amphetamine pill; =UPPER

peppy *adj by 1918* Energetic; vital; =ZINGY

pep rally *n phr* A meeting where the participants are stimulated to some activity, harder effort, etc: *Ceausescu's. . . pep rally becomes a revolution*—New Republic

pep talk *n phr* A hortatory speech, usu given by a team coach or other leader: *I always had to give myself a pep talk before I went out to sing*—Peggy Lee

pep up *v phr by 1925* To stimulate; energize; brighten; =JAZZ something UP: *. . . pep up your winter wardrobe*—Philadelphia Bulletin

perc **See** PERK

percentage *n by 1862* Profit or advantage: *I don't*

see any percentage in doing it that way

perch 1 *v by 1930s* To kiss and caress; =NECK: *Now you may "smooch" or "perch"*—E Eldridge **2** *v 1990s teenagers* To do the sex act; =HIT SKINS [fr the activity of lovebirds]
See COME OFF one's PERCH

percolate 1 *v by about 1925* To run smoothly and well: *The little engine was percolating nicely* **2** *v black by 1942* To saunter; stroll; =OOZE: *. . . percolate on down the Avenue*—Zora Neale Hurston [all senses fr the coffee-making device; sense of "run well," for example, fr the steady cheery bubbling of the coffeemaker]

percolator *n black by 1946* A party where one sells drinks and food to friends in order to pay one's rent; =RENT PARTY: *You could always get together and charge a few coins and have a percolator*—Stephen Longstreet

Percy or **Percy boy** or **Percy-pants** *n* or *n phr by 1916* An effeminate male; =LILY, PANSY: *He never prated about his Oedipus complex like the Percy boys*—S J Perelman

per each *adv phr by 1906* For each; apiece; =a THROW: *Those are $8 per each, to you* [fr a humorous insertion of Latin *per* in imitation of pretentious business use]

perform *v by 1916* To do a sex act; function sexually: *She didn't love him, but liked the way he performed*

perk[1] or **perc 1** *n by 1950s* Percolated coffee **2** *v by about 1925* To run smoothly and well; =PERCOLATE: *The project's perking now*

perk[2] or **perc** *n by 1824* Extra money, privileges, fringe benefits, etc, pertaining to a job or assignment: *His men were delighted to be in Afghanistan, he said, mostly because of the perks*—Time [fr *perquisite*]

perk (or **perc**) **along 1** *v phr by about 1925* To run smoothly and easily: *The outboard's perking along sweetly* **2** *v phr 1930s jive talk* To move at a relaxed pace; =PERCOLATE: *I'm not hurrying, just perking along* [fr the persistent and even sound of a coffee *percolator*]

perker-upper *n by 1950s* =PEPPER-UPPER

perk (or **perc**) **over** *v phr by 1920s* To run slowly; idle; =TICK OVER
See PERK ALONG

perk up 1 *v phr by 1965* To stimulate; invigorate: *Gotta perk up this class* **2** *v phr by 1706* To recuperate; recover; gain energy: *He's perked up after a two-week illness* [origin uncertain; perhaps related to *perch*, and semantically to the notion of being placed high]

perky *adj by 1855* Energetic and jaunty; lively; =CHIPPER

Perot jumper *n phr by 1990s*: *. . . Eddie Doucette. . . has coined a term for a jumper that almost goes in, comes out, then goes in. Doucette. . . calls it a "Perot jumper"* [fr the on-again off-again presidential candidate H Ross Perot]

peroxide blonde **See** CHEMICAL BLONDE

perp *n* A criminal engaged in a specific crime: *The perp stood up, stepped back, took out a handgun and fired at least two shots*—New York Daily News [shortened form of *perpetrator*]

perp parade (or walk) *n phr* by 1940s; see walk example A public display of a criminal defendant by the police: . . . *an extended jaunt around the block, which is known as a perp parade*—New York Times/ . . . *term used for at least 5 decades. The perp walk is a ritual, a vital part of New York's criminal-justice system.* . . —New York Times

persnickety or **pernickety** *adj* first form by 1905, second by 1814 Overfastidious; finical; fussy [fr Scots dialect]

persuader *n* by 1884 A handgun; =HEAT

per usual *See* AS PER USUAL

pesky *adj* by 1775 Vexatious; annoying; pesty [origin unknown]

pet 1 *v* by 1924 To kiss and caress: . . . *torrid hugging, smooching, and petting*—Calder Willingham **2** *n* by 1755 Darling; sweetheart; =DOLL: *It's you, pet! How frightfully tickety-boo!*
See HEAVY PETTING

pete *n* (also **pete-box** or **peet** or **peat**) *underworld* by 1911 A safe; =CRIB [fr *peter¹*]

Pete *See* FOR THE LOVE OF PETE, PISTOL PETE, SNEAKY PETE

pete-man *n underworld* by 1931 A criminal who specializes in opening safes; =BOX MAN

peter¹ *n underworld* by 1859 A safe; strongbox; vault [origin unknown]

peter² *n narcotics* by 1897 =KNOCKOUT DROPS

◁**peter³**▷ *n* by 1902 The penis [fr the association with *pee*, "urine"]

◁**peter-eater**▷ *n* by 1970s A person who does fellatio, esp homosexually; =COCKSUCKER

peterman *n underworld* by 1900 A safe-cracker; =PETE-MAN: . . . *the petermen of half a century ago*—E DeBaun

peter out *v phr* by 1858 To become exhausted; dwindle away in strength, amount, etc: *They ran well the first mile or so, then petered out* [origin unknown; a 1908 article says it may be fr *peterboat*, a sharp double-ended vessel, hence, "grow small or thin"]

pet peeve *n phr* by 1919 One's particular and most cherished dislike or annoyance: . . . *long been one of my pet peeves*—Word Study

petrified *adj* by 1903 Drunk; =OSSIFIED, STONED

petting *n* by 1924 The activity of those who pet: *Petting is necking with territorial concessions*—Frederick Morton
See HEAVY PETTING

petting party *n phr* by 1920 A spell or session of fondling and caressing: . . . *great American phenomenon, the "petting party"*—F Scott Fitzgerald

pfft *See* GO PFFT

pfui *See* PHOOEY

P-funk *n* 1980s *narcotics* : *They said users already were able to buy a synthetic form of heroin known as "P-funk"*—Associated Press

PG (pronounced as separate letters) **1** *n* 1960s *narcotics* Paregoric, an opium product **2** *adj* by 1980s Pregnant; =PREGGERS

phat *See* FAT

phenagle *See* FINAGLE

phenom (FEE nahm) *n baseball* by 1890 A phenomenally skilled or impressive person; a performing wonder, esp in sports: *Veeck was a phenom, too*—Sports Illustrated

Phi Bete (FĪ BAYT) **1** *n phr* by 1924 The academic honor society Phi Beta Kappa **2** *n phr* A member of Phi Beta Kappa

a **Philadelphia lawyer** *n phr* by 1834 One who makes things unnecessarily complicated and obfuscates matters [fr a traditional reputation for the shrewdness of such attorneys, and the phrase *it would puzzle a Philadelphia lawyer*, found by 1788]

Philly or **Phillie** *n* by 1891 Philadelphia

phiz or **phizog** (FIZ, FIZ ahwg) *n* by 1688 The face; =MUG [fr *physiognomy*]

◁**phlegmwad** or **flemwad**▷ *n* by 1990s A despised person; =JERK, PRICK, ASSHOLE
See -WAD

Phoebe or **little Phoebe (or fever)** *n* or *n phr crapshooting* by 1940s Five or the point of five

phone *See* CELLPHONE, FLIP PHONE, HOLD THE PHONE

phone it in *modifier sports* by 1980s Lackadaisical and half-hearted in playing

phone phreak *n phr* by 1972 A computer hacker who illegally enters the telephone system for fun and profit: *Mitnick also became a skilled "phone phreak" who was able to manipulate the telephone system to pull pranks on friends and enemies.* . . —Los Angeles Times

phone tag *n phr* by 1990s A repetitive cycle of telephoning, leaving messages, missing replies, etc •referring to the pervasive round-robin of messages left and phonecalls missed: *"Having computers in our volunteers' homes has eliminated phone tag," says Power.* . . —Modern Maturity

phoniness *n* by 1940s Falseness: . . . *fed up on the phoniness of Hollywood films*—Bob Thomas

phono 1 *n* by 1940s A phonograph **2** *modifier*: *a phono album/ phono cartridge*

phonus bolonus (or balonus) 1 *n phr* by 1929 Something false and meretricious: *Phonus bolonus, he said*—Irwin Shaw **2** *adj*: *What a phonus-balonus smile he's got on*

phony or **phoney 1** *adj* by 1900 Not real or genuine; false; fake: *You phony little fake*—Arthur Miller **2** *n* by 1902 A fake thing: *That window's a phony, it don't open* **3** *v* by 1942: *I ain't phoneying them woids*—Jimmy Durante **4** *n* by 1902 A person who affects some identity, role, nature, etc; poseur: . . . *some phony calling himself a writer*—James M Cain [fr late 1700s British underworld slang *fawney* fr Irish *fáinne*, "ring," referring to a swindle in which the *fawney-dropper* drops a cheap ring before the victim, then is persuaded to sell it as if it were valuable; as the sequence of spellings, *phoney* and later *phony*, indicates, the US spelling is probably based on an attested folk etymology revealing the notion that one's feelings or even identity could be readily falsified on the *telephone*]

phony as a three-dollar bill *adj phr* by 1940s Very false indeed; not remotely genuine

phooey *interj* (also **phoo** or **pfui** or **fooey** or **fooy** or **fuie**) by 1929 An exclamation of disbelief, rejection, contempt, etc [fr Yiddish fr German; popularized by the newspaper columnist Walter Winchell]

photog or **fotog** (FOH tahg) *n* by 1913 A photographer: *The Swedish fotogs were actually saving film*—R Montgomery

photo op *n phr* by 1980s A brief period during which the press is allowed to photograph a dignitary or celebrity; a photographic opportunity

phreaking (FREE king) *n* by 1972 The imitation of telephone touch-tone signals by whistling or by using mechanical devices, so that free calls may be readily made: . . . *and "phreaking," the art of using the telephone for fun but no profit for the company, came into being*—Toronto Life

physical *adj* by 1970 Using the body, esp roughly or intimately: *Vanderbilt is a lot better than last year and more physical*—Birmingham News
See GET PHYSICAL

PI *n* (pronounced as separate letters) **1** by 1931 A pimp **2** by 1960 A private detective; =OP

piano *n* black by 1940s Spareribs, esp a single section of broiled spareribs: . . . *cornbread with a piano on a platter*—Zora Neale Hurston
See HORSE PIANO

piano legs *n phr* by 1960s Thick calves and ankles: *Claudia Schiffer, the Bardot look-alike with a slight case of piano legs, stumps down the runway appallingly clumsy*—New Yorker

pic *n* by 1884 A picture, and later esp a movie; =FLICK: *Raft's next pic*—Abel Green

Piccadilly commando *n phr* WWII Army A London prostitute

◁**piccolo player**▷ *n phr* by 1950s A person who likes and does fellatio [fr a double reference to the *picklelike* shape of a penis, and the fact that fellatio is referred to as "playing the skin *flute*"]

pick *See* NIT-PICK

pick and choose *v phr* by 1577 To select very carefully

pick someone's **brain** by 1885 **1** *v phr* To question someone closely for one's own profit; exploit someone's creativity by imitation; be an intellectual parasite **2** *v phr* To inquire of someone; ask someone for information, advice, etc

pick 'em *See* one CAN REALLY PICK 'EM

pick 'em up and lay 'em down *v phr* by 1940s To run fast: *When he went by he was really picking 'em up and laying 'em down*

picker *See* BRAIN-PICKER, CHERRY-PICKER, FRUIT-PICKER, PRUNE-PICKER

picker-upper *n* by 1936 A person or thing that picks up: *A hitchhiker caught a ride. . . The picker-upper was soon arrested*—Associated Press

picking *See* COTTON-PICKING

pickings *See* SLIM PICKINGS

pickle 1 *n* (also **picklement**) by 1609 A parlous situation; predicament; dilemma: *I was in a sad pickle when I lost my job* **2** *v phr* baseball by 1908 To hit the ball very hard **3** *n* WWII Navy A torpedo **4** *n* by 1940s A bullet: *He fired six pickles at the knob*—Westbrook Pegler **5** *v* by 1950s To ruin; wreck: *This will promptly pickle her college chances*—F Sparks [first sense fr 1500s British slang *in a pickle,* and may refer to the situation of a mouse fallen into a pickling vat; *picklement* is a handy echo of *predicament*]

pickled *adj* by 1842 Drunk; =SOUSED

picklepuss *n* by 1940s A frowning and pessimistic person; =SOURPUSS

pick-me-up by 1867 **1** *n* A drink or snack that invigorates; =PEPPER-UPPER, PERKER-UPPER **2** *n* A drink of liquor taken to restore tone and morale

pick off *v phr* by 1810 To shoot, esp with careful aim

pick someone or something **to pieces** *v phr* by 1859 To be exquisitely critical: *We were sitting around picking the speech to pieces*

pickup 1 *n* by 1926 A person accosted and made a companion, esp in a bar, on the street, etc, for sexual purposes: *His next girlfriend was a pickup he made at Rod's* **2** *n* by 1908 An arrest **3** *n* (also **pickup truck**) by 1932 A small truck having a cab, and cargo space with low sidewalls **4** *n* by 1909 The ability of a car to accelerate rapidly, esp from a halt **5** *n* by 1938 The act of getting or acquiring something: *He made the pickup at the post office* **6** *adj* by 1859 Impromptu; unceremonious: *We'll have a pickup lunch in the kitchen* **7** *adj* by 1936 For one occasion; temporary; ad hoc: *a pickup band/ pickup corps of waiters*

pick up 1 *v phr* by 1608 To get; acquire: *He picked up a few thou hustling* **2** *v phr* by 1874 To make things clean and neat; tidy up: *You'd better pick up in your room. . . it's a godawful mess* **3** *v phr* by 1970s To answer the telephone

pick someone **up 1** *v phr* by 1871 To arrest someone: *The cops picked up six muggers and hauled their asses in* **2** *v phr* by 1698 To make someone's acquaintance boldly, esp in a bar, on the street, etc, for sexual purposes: *She lets the soldiers pick her up*—Associated Press

pick something **up** *v phr* by 1857 To notice; discover; learn: *Did you pick that wink up?/ He picked up pitching in no time*

pick up on something **1** *v phr* by about 1935 To notice; become aware of: *I pick up on people's pain, Alexander*—New Yorker **2** *v phr* by 1970s To refer to and add to; bring back to notice, esp in order to query: *I want to pick up on what you just said about Philadelphia*

pick up the tab (or **check**) *v phr* by 1945 To pay; assume the expense; =PAY THE FREIGHT: . . . *also somebody to pick up the tab. She admitted that this was important*—Saul Bellow

picky *adj* by 1917 Very niggling; =CHICKENSHIT, PER-

SNICKETY: *For growing a beard. A lot of little picky things like that*—Elmore Leonard

picnic 1 *n by 1880s* Something very easy; =CINCH, PIECE OF CAKE: *That job's a picnic* **2** *n by 1909* An enjoyable time; =a BALL, BLAST: *The last week we had a picnic*
See NO PICNIC

picture **See** DRAW A PICTURE

the **picture** *n phr by 1922* The situation; present shape of things
See the BIG PICTURE, GET THE PICTURE, PUT someone IN THE PICTURE

pictures **See** IN PICTURES

piddle 1 *v by 1796* To urinate; =PEE: *So you piddled on the floor. But you don't have to have your face wiped in it*—Time **2** *n by 1901* Urine **3** *v by 1545* To waste; idle: *You just piddle the day away*—Washington Post [a euphemism for *piss*]

piddling or **piddly** or ◁**pissy-ass**▷ *adj first form by 1559, second by 1940s* Meager; trivial; paltry: *It was an effort, though a piddling one/ The case was "a piddly little misdemeanor"*—Milwaukee Journal/ *Make your pissy-ass point again*

pie *n by 1889* An easy task or job; =GRAVY: *That's pie for him*—Baltimore Sun
See APPLE-PIE ORDER, CUTESY-POO, CUTIE-PIE, EASY AS PIE, FUR PIE, HAIR PIE, SWEETIE-PIE

piece 1 *n by 1929* A share; portion; financial interest; =a PIECE OF THE ACTION, SLICE: *. . . a piece of the racket*—American Mercury **2** *n by 1581* A gun; pistol: *They step up to the driver's side and shove a piece in his ear*—Time ◁**3**▷ *n by 1785* =PIECE OF ASS **4** *n 1960s narcotics* An ounce of heroin or other narcotic: *He buys heroin in "pieces"*—J Mills **5** *n by 1970s* A graffito on a subway car: *A train rumbles in. . . and we all pause to view its pieces*—M Blaine [second sense, US underworld use since about 1930]
See ALL IN ONE PIECE, COME UP SMELLING LIKE A ROSE, CONVERSATION PIECE, KNOCK OFF A PIECE, MOUTHPIECE, MUSEUM PIECE, TEAR OFF A PIECE, THINK-PIECE

◁**piece of ass** (or **tail**)▷ *first form by 1930s, variant by 1917* **1** *n phr* The sex act; a completed sex act **2** *n phr* A person regarded as a sex object, organ, or partner [the date should probably be earlier, in view of the 1785 occurrence of *piece* in the first sense]
See TEAR OFF A PIECE

piece of cake *n phr by 1936* Anything very easy; anything easily or pleasantly done; =BREEZE, DUCK SOUP •Originally and chiefly British: *It's a piece of cake because you don't have the fear that they are going to pitch out on you*—Inside Sports

piece of calico (or **goods**) *n phr first form by 1880, variant by 1751* A woman [piece meant "woman" as long ago as the 1400s]

piece of change *n phr* (Variations: **hunk** may replace **piece**; **jack** may replace **change**) *by 1914* Money, esp a large amount: *. . . which would come to quite a piece of change*—Village Voice

piece of fluff **See** BIT OF FLUFF

piece of meat *n phr by 1940s* A person regarded as merely a physical body; unaccommodated man: *I'm just a piece of meat. . . but I know I'm a good piece of meat*—Sports Illustrated

a **piece of** one's **mind** **See** GIVE someone A PIECE OF one's MIND

◁**piece of shit** (or **junk** or **crap**)▷ *by 1950s* **1** *n phr* Something or someone inferior or worthless: *. . . as a film he didn't want to make, about nothing, and was a piece of shit*—New Yorker **2** *n phr* A lie; hypocrisy; =a PACK OF LIES: *Everything she said is a big piece of shit*

◁**piece of tail**▷ **See** PIECE OF ASS

a **piece of the action** (or **pie**) *n phr first form by 1966, variant by 1970s* A share of something, esp in profits, a business, or speculation, etc: *. . . a piece of the "Gunsmoke" action*—L Raddatz/ *Health expenditures. . . consume an ever growing piece of the pie*—New Republic [fr *action*, "gamble, gambling"]

piece of trade *n phr by 1940s* A prostitute; a promiscuous woman: *. . . with some good-natured piece of trade*—Nelson Algren

piece of work *n phr by 1928* A person remarkable either for good or ill; a prodigious person: *. . . and pow along comes a bizarro piece of work like Trudy the dietitian*—Carsten Stroud [fr Hamlet's paean "What a *piece of work* is a man"; the date belongs to the first occurrence of *nasty piece of work*, but it should probably be earlier; the phrase is listed among those children like in a 1900 compilation, and seems to refer to persons]

pie-eyed 1 *adj by 1904* Drunk: *. . . the pie-eyed brothers*—P Marks **2** *adj by 1940* Astonished; wide-eyed: *Randall was pie-eyed. His mouth moved, but nothing came out of it*—Raymond Chandler

pieface *n by 1920s* A stupid or foolish person

pie-faced *adj by 1923* Stupid; foolish: *. . . a pie-faced boy from Minnesota*—Pulpsmith

pie in the sky *by 1911* **1** *n phr* The reward one will get for compliant behavior, later; hence, wishful thinking or utopian fantasies **2** *modifier*: *It was a bit of a pie-in-the-sky idea*—Newark Star-Ledger [fr a Wobbly expression of contempt for those who maintained that suffering and penury on earth would be compensated by bliss and luxury in heaven; the *locus classicus* is a 1911 parody of the hymn "In the Sweet By and By," by the Wobbly martyr Joe Hill]

pie wagon *n phr by 1898* =PADDY WAGON

piffed or **piffled** *adj first form by 1900, second by 1934* Drunk

piffle 1 *n by 1890* Nonsense; =BALONEY, BUNK: *. . . the kind of piffle actors have to go up against*—H McHugh **2** *interj by 1914* A mild exclamation of disbelief, contradiction, rejection, etc

pifflicated *adj by 1905* Drunk

◁**pig**▷ **1** *n underworld by 1811* A police officer **2** *n by 1890s* A glutton **3** *v* =PIG OUT: *When you eat too much, you can say "I pigged"*—Milwaukee Journal **4** *n by 1927* A promiscuous woman, esp one who is blowsy and unattractive: . . . *spoke of a pig he had recently picked up*—James T Farrell **5** *n* horse-racing *by 1940s* A racehorse, esp an inferior one; =BEETLE: . . . *why the hell that pig didn't win*—Fortune

See BLIND PIG, PIGS IN CLOVER, LONG PIG, MALE CHAUVINIST PIG, RENT-A-PIG

pigboat *n WWI Navy* A submarine: . . . *the archaic "pigboat" of the First World War*—J L Riordan

pigeon 1 *n underworld by 1849* An informer; =STOOL PIGEON: *I don't like pigeons*—Raymond Chandler **2** *n by 1593* The victim of a swindle; dupe; =MARK, SUCKER: *I'm your pigeon now and you guys are gonna rip me off*—W T Tyler **3** *n by 1586* A young woman; =CHICK **4** *n by 1980s* A former alcoholic in the care of a helpful sponsor or guardian [for first sense see **stool pigeon**; the second sense probably derives fr the expression *pluck a pigeon* and may be based on a notion that *pigeons* are easy to catch; the sense "young woman" is probably fr or related to *quail* and again suggests an easy victim]

See CLAY PIGEON, DEAD DUCK, STOOL PIGEON

pigeon drop *n phr underworld by 1937* A swindle in which the confidence man tells the victim that he has found a large amount of money, which he will share if the victim proffers money as a show of good faith

pigeonhole 1 *v by 1870* To classify; identify; =BUTTON DOWN, PEG: *I pigeonhole this clown as a total bigmouth* **2** *v by 1855* To put away or aside [fr the separate compartments of a desk or sorting system, likened to the orifices in a *pigeoncote*]

◀**pig-fucker**▶ *n by 1940s* A despicable person; =BASTARD, FUCKER, SHITHEEL

piggyback 1 *n by 1953* The transport of loaded containers or semitrailers on railroad flatcars **2** *v by 1968* To originate or prosper with the help of something else: *Aerobic dancing piggybacked on the jogging craze* [fr the term for carrying someone, esp a child, on one's back derived by folk etymology fr *pick-a-back,* of unknown origin]

piggy bank *n phr by 1941* A source of funds: *Portland GE has $25 million in the company's piggy bank*—New York Times [the date refers to the first notice of pig-shaped banks for children]

pighead *n by 1889* A stubborn person

pigheaded *adj by 1620* Stubborn; stupidly obstinate

pig in a poke **See** BUY A PIG IN A POKE

◁**pig-meat**▷ *black by 1950s* **1** *n* A woman, esp a sexually promiscuous one **2** *n prizefighting* A defeated or moribund person; =LOSER

◁**pigmobile**▷ *n by 1960s* A police car; squad car; =BLACK AND WHITE: . . . *that took one pigmobile off patrol*—Niven and Pournelle

pig out *teenagers by 1979* **1** *v phr* To overeat; =PIG: . . . *we ordered a pizza and totally pigged out*—UCLA Slang **2** *v phr* To overindulge in anything: *It was time to pig out on rock and roll*—Village Voice

pig-out *n teenagers by 1979* A gluttonous occasion Thanksgiving was a total pig-out

pigpen *n* (also **pigsty**) *by 1872* Any filthy, littered place: *His room's a pigpen*

◁**pig's ass** (or **ear** or **eye**)▷ **See** IN A PIG'S ASS

◁**pig shit**▷ **See** STRONGER THAN PIG SHIT

pigskin 1 *n by 1894* A football **2** *modifier*: *the pigskin parade/ a pigskin superstar*

pig-sticker *n by 1890* A bayonet, lance, etc

pig sweat *by 1950* **1** *n phr* Beer **2** *n phr* Inferior whiskey; =PANTHER PISS

pike **See** COME DOWN THE PIKE

piker 1 *n by 1872* A mean and stingy person; miser; =TIGHTWAD **2** *n by 1889* A shirker; loafer [originally a vagrant, esp a gambler, who wandered along the *pike;* hence a poor sport, a cheapskate]

pile *v by 1948* To dash; run; thrust oneself: *I piled after her hell to split*—James M Cain

See GRUB-PILE, WOODPILE

a or **one's pile** *n phr by 1741* A large amount of money; a fortune; =BUNDLE

◁**pile of shit**▷ *by 1940s* **1** *n phr* =CROCK OF SHIT **2** *n phr* Something inferior or worthless; a shabby performance or product; =PIECE OF SHIT: *The whole project's a pile of shit*

pile on 1 *v phr football by 1980s* To throw oneself on a downed opponent unnecessarily: *It constitutes what is known in football as piling on, and they penalize you for it*—New York Times **2** *modifier*: *Contributing to the pile-on tactics, both big corporate media (including the* Washington Post) *and putative defenders of free expression strafed Moldea I from the start*—Nation [*pile onto,* "assail," is found by 1894]

pileup *n by 1929* A wreck, esp one involving a number of cars: *6-car, end-to-end pile-up on the New Jersey Turnpike*—Associated Press

pile up *v phr by 1899* To wreck; =RACK UP, TOTAL: . . . *after he piled up his car*—J Evans

pile up Zs **See** COP ZS

pill 1 *n by 1871* A boring, disagreeable person; =a PAIN IN THE ASS: *Oh, don't be a pill, Valerie*—S J Perelman **2** *n by 1906* A baseball or golf ball **3** *n narcotics by 1887* An opium pellet for smoking **4** *n narcotics by 1950s* A Nembutal™ capsule; =NIMBY **5** *n by 1626* A bomb, cannonball, bullet, etc: *He was drinking coffee when the big pill came down*—New York Daily News

See COOK UP A PILL, PEP PILL

the pill or **the Pill** *n phr* Any oral contraceptive for women: . . . *now that the joint and the pill are with us*—Society

pillhead or **pill popper** *n 1960s narcotics* A person who habitually takes tranquilizers, amphetamines, barbiturates, etc, in pill or capsule form: *Papoose and me were a bunch of pillheads*—Rolling Stone

pillow 1 *n prizefight by about 1900* A boxing glove **2** *n baseball by 1940s* A base; =BAG, SACK

pillow talk *n phr by 1939* Intimate talk, esp that between a couple in bed

pill pad *narcotics* **1** *n phr by about 1925* A place where addicts gather to smoke opium; opium den **2** *n phr 1950s narcotics* A place where narcotics users gather to take drugs of any sort; =PAD

pill-popping *1960s narcotics* **1** *adj* Addicted to or using narcotics in pill or capsule form: *The prostitute is now a suicidal, pill-popping* Newsweek *reporter*—Saturday Review **2** *n phr* The use of narcotics in pill form

pill-pusher or **pill-roller** or **pill-peddler** *first form by 1945, second by 1926, third by 1927* **1** *n* A physician: *. . . gynecological phenomena you pill-peddlers are always talking about*—Ellery Queen **2** *n* A pharmacist or student of pharmacy

pilot *by 1940s* **1** *n* The manager of a sports team **2** *n* A jockey
See COW PILOT, HOT PILOT, SKY-PILOT

pimp **1** *n 1990s teenagers* : *Pimp. . . A cool guy who's popular with girls*—People Weekly **2** *n loggers by about 1915* A boy who does menial jobs at a logging camp

pimping *n medical by 1980s* Rapid questioning of a trainee by a superior [fr initials of *put in my place*]

pimpish *adj 1980s teenagers* Stylishly dressed

pimple *n by 1818* The head

pimpmobile *by 1973* **1** *n* A fancy car used by a prostitute's procurer and manager: *There's a red Cadillac pimpmobile parked outside*—New York Magazine **2** *n* Any very fancy and overlavish car **3** *modifier*: *The pimpmobile mantle will be donned by the 1983 Cougar*—Car and Driver

pin **1** *n by 1530* A leg **2** *v by 1960s* To classify and understand someone; =PEG, PIGEONHOLE: *He was pinned as a bad doctor*—Dean Edel **3** *v by 1960s* To look over; survey; =DIG: *. . . just pinning the queer scene*—John Rechy **4** *v students by about 1935* To declare a serious commitment to someone by giving or taking a fraternity pin
See HAIRPIN, KING, PIN someone DOWN, PIN something DOWN, PIN someone's EARS BACK, PIN ON, PINS, PIN-SHOT

pinball *v by 1980s* To move about erratically: *Robin Williams' comedy routines pinball from one manic impression to another*—Time [fr the game of *pinball*, found by 1911, in which a spring-propelled ball bounces about among obstacles]

pinch **1** *v by 1656* To steal; =SWIPE: *Who pinched the script?*—L Ford **2** *v by 1837* To arrest; =BUST: *The stores will invite ill will if they pinch indiscriminately*—Fortune **3** *n by 1900*: *. . . make a respectable number of pinches to stay off the transfer list*—Rolling Stone
See IN A PINCH

pincher *See* PENNY-PINCHER

pinch-gut *n by 1659* A miser; =TIGHTWAD

pinch hit *n phr baseball by 1907* A hit made by a player who bats in place of another

pinch-hit **1** *v baseball by 1927* To bat for a player who has been removed from the lineup, usu at a critical point in the game **2** *v by 1927* To substitute for someone else: *Silvey has been pinch-hitting as an assistant director*—Variety

pinchpenny **1** *n by 1412* A miser; =PINCH-GUT, TIGHTWAD **2** *adj*: *your pinchpenny budgets*

pin someone **down** **1** *v phr by 1951* To get a definite answer, commitment, piece of information, etc, from someone: *He wouldn't say just when, I couldn't pin him down* **2** *v phr by 1940s* To make someone immobile, esp to keep soldiers in place with constant or accurate fire **3** *v phr by 1960s* To identify or classify someone definitely; =PEG, PIN: *I can't pin her down, but I've seen her before*

pin something **down** *v phr by 1951* To recognize, identify, or single out something definitely; make explicit: *I can't quite pin my feeling down*

pineapple *n WWI Army* A fragmentation grenade or small bomb; =CHICAGO PINEAPPLE, ITALIAN FOOTBALL: *Nobody tried to throw a pineapple in my lap*—Raymond Chandler [fr the resemblance of a fragmentation grenade, with its deeply segmented ovoid surface, to a *pineapple*]

pin someone's **ears back** *v phr by 1941* To punish someone, either by words or blows; chasten: *. . . a flip-lipped bastard who should have had his ears pinned back long ago*—J Evans

pine (or **wooden**) **overcoat** *n phr entry form by 1896, variant by 1903* A coffin, esp a cheap one: *. . . what they call in the army a pine overcoat*—R H Thornton

◁**pinga**▷ (PEEN gah) *n by 1960s* The penis; =BICHO [fr Cuban Spanish]

ping jockey *See* BLIP JOCKEY

ping off the walls *v phr Army by 1970s* To be very nervous; be tense and excited: *Better stop pinging off the walls and start making some plans*

ping-pong *v medical by 1972* To refer a patient, esp a Medicaid recipient, to other doctors, in order to maximize fees: *"Medicaid mills" or clinics. . . reap enormous profits by such practices as "Ping Ponging"*—Time [fr *Ping-Pong*, trademark for a manufacturer's table tennis set and game]

Ping-Ponging *modifier*: *The modeling world's shifting tastes is nothing new. FIT's Steele offers a thumbnail sketch of the Ping-Ponging changes in America's dream girl*—Los Angeles Times

ping-wing *n narcotics by 1950s* A narcotics injection, esp in the arm

pinhead *n by 1896* A stupid person

pinheaded *adj by 1901* Stupid

pink **1** *n black by 1926* A white person; =GRAY **2** *n by 1927* A politically liberal or mildly socialist radical; =PARLOR PINK **3** *adj by 1837*: *pink perspective on Palestine* **4** *n 1950s hot rodders* A legal certificate of car ownership **5** *adj homosexuals by 1972* Homosexual
See IN THE PINK, TICKLED PINK

pink chord *n phr 1930s musicians* A mistake in reading or improvising music

pink collar *by 1977* **1** *adj phr* Traditionally held by women of the middle class: *Mature women tended to gravitate toward pink collar jobs as secre-*

taries, teachers, nurses, and saleswomen—New York Times **2 adj phr** Working in a job traditionally held by women of the middle class: . . . *the TV character to whom real-life blue- and pink-collar working women most relate*—Time [modeled on *blue collar* and *white collar*]

pink elephants *See* SEE PINK ELEPHANTS

Pinkerton or **Pink** or **Pinkie** *n by 1850* An operative or agent of the Pinkerton detective agency: . . . *how you suppose Pinkies get trainin'*—Nelson Algren

pink ink *n phr by 1970s* Romance novels; =BODICE-RIPPER

pinko 1 *n by 1936* A person of liberal or mildly radical socialist political opinions; =PINK: . . . *pinko James J Matles and pinko Julius Emspak*—Time **2 adj** *by 1957*: *How come those Niggers and those creepy pinko hippies call us names like "pigs"?*—Ebony

pink puffer *n phr medical by 1970s* A thin emphysema patient

pink slip 1 *n phr by 1915* A discharge notice; =WALKING PAPERS: *All 1,300 employees got pink slips today*—Associated Press **2 v** *by 1915*: *They had pink-slipped Hartz one brutal afternoon*—Washingtonian **3** *n phr 1950s* hot rodders A legal certificate of car ownership; =PINK: *I got the pink slip, daddy*—Beach Boys song
See GET THE PINK SLIP, GIVE someone THE PINK SLIP

pink tea *n phr by 1887* A very exclusive party or event

pink-toes *n black by 1942* A light-skinned black woman

pinky[1] or **pinkie 1** *n by 1860* The little finger: *Pardon my lifted pinky*—Hy Gardner **2 modifier**: *pinky ring* [fr an earlier adjective sense, "small, tiny"]
See PLAY STINKY-PINKY

pinky[2] or **pinkie** *n black by 1942* =PINK-TOES

Pinky *n* (also **Pink**) *by 1930s* Nickname for a redheaded person

pinky-crooker *n by 1970s* A person of affectedly refined tastes and manners: *You'll find only the pinky-crookers at the concerts*—Time

pinky-ringed *adj by 1980s* Wearing a ring on the little finger, taken as an indication of raffishness or criminality: *A bespectacled, pinky-ringed chain-smoker, he used lingo straight out of Damon Runyon. . .* —Los Angeles Times

pinned 1 *adj narcotics by 1970s* Having eye pupils contracted to a pinpoint: . . . *he could see that her eyes were pinned from the dope. . .* —Harry Crews **2 adj** *students by about 1935* Seriously involved, by the act of taking or giving a fraternity pin

pin on *v phr* To make an accusation; inculpate; =HANG ON: *Police indicated they had little to pin on them*—Associated Press

pin one on *See* HANG ONE ON

pins *n by 1530* The legs: . . . *knocked clean off his pins*—O Johnson

pin-shot *n narcotics by 1940s* A narcotics injection made with a safety pin and an eyedropper

pint *See* HALF-PINT

pin-up *by 1941* **1** *n* A picture, usu a provocative photograph, esp of a pretty young woman **2 modifier**: . . . *pin-up collections and books*—Playboy **3** *n* A young woman shown in a pin-up: *Dorothy Lamour was the Army's favorite pin-up*

pin-up girl *See* SWEATER GIRL

pip *n by 1676* A minor skin lesion, esp of teenagers: . . . *whiteheads, blackheads, goopheads, goobers, pips, acne trenches*—New York Times

a pip (or **a pipperoo** or **a pippin**) **1** *n phr* first form *by 1912*, second *by 1942*, third *by 1897* A person or thing that is remarkable, wonderful, superior, etc; =BEAUT, HUMDINGER: *His wildest dreams have to be pips*—Washington Post **2 modifier**: *a pipperoo flick* [fr *pippin*, a prized kind of apple; the shift was probably fr *peach* as one kind of excellent fruit to *pippin* as another]

the pip *n phr by 1896* A severe case of being annoyed or depressed: *People gave him the pip*—P Marks [fr a disease of birds, extended to mean various human ailments]

pipe[1] *n students by 1902* Something easily done; =CINCH, PIECE OF CAKE: *Getting in is a pipe* [apparently fr *pipe dream*, suggesting something as easily or magically done as in a wishful dream]

pipe[2] **1** *n underworld by 1940s* A signal; letter or note **2 v**: *Bill Johnson pipes from Frisco that times are hard*—D W Maurer **3** *n by 1960s* A telephone **4 v** *by 1784* To speak up; say something; =PIPE UP: *But I am not suppose to know that and do not pipe*—John O'Hara **5 v** *by 1846* To look at; see; notice: *Did you pipe her hands?*—Eugene O'Neill **6** *n* (also **pipeline**) *surfers by 1963* The tubular inner section of a breaking wave **7 v** *underworld by 1970s* To hit someone on the head, esp with a metal pipe: *Someone was gonna pipe me*—Prison **8 v** *black street talk by 1990s* To shoot or kill with a gun; =NINE: *So what do you care who piped Devona?*—Robert B Parker [all senses probably derived fr *pipe* as a conduit or a musical instrument; the sense "look at" is related to criminal slang "follow, keep under surveillance," of obscure origin and difficult to relate to any sense of *pipe*; *pipe-gun*, "crude gun made of a pipe," is found by 1973]
See BIG PIPE, DOWN THE TUBE, HIT THE PIPE, LAY PIPE, LEAD-PIPE CINCH ·

pipe course *n phr college students by 1927* An easy course; =GUT COURSE: *You are all freshmen and you may not be familiar with the term "pipe course"*—Max Shulman

pipe down *v phr by 1900* To stop talking; speak more quietly: *The others got sore at him and told him to pipe down*—John O'Hara [fr naval jargon, probably related to the use of the boatswain's *pipe* for giving commands, or to its shrill noise]

pipe dream *n phr by 1896* An improbable and visionary hope, ideal, scheme, etc, such as an opium smoker might have: *He has some ambitious plans, mostly pipe dreams*

pipe-jockey *n* 1950s Air Force A jet fighter pilot

pipeline 1 *n* by 1921 A channel of communication, esp a direct and special one: *You'd think he has a pipeline to Jesus* **2** *n* by 1955 A channel or course for routine production, processing, etc: *We'll have fewer men in what we call the "pipeline" who are moving*—US News & World Report **3 modifier**: *a pipeline review*
See IN THE PIPELINE, PIPE

pipe someone **off** *v phr* nautical by 1940s To blacklist someone [fr the nautical practice of blowing the boatswain's *pipe* to welcome someone aboard or usher someone off a ship]

pipes or **set of pipes** *n* or *n phr* The voice, esp the singing voice: *. . . to bring that great set of pipes into your very own living room*—Changes
See CUT UP THE TOUCHES

pipe up *v phr* by 1889 To speak up; raise one's voice; =SING OUT: *He piped up with a couple of smart-ass cracks* [perhaps fr a play on the nautical *pipe down;* perhaps fr the playing of the *pipe* or *pipes*]

pippy-poo *adj* by 1970s Small; teeny: *That's just a pippy-poo minuscule example of what I mean*—Washington Post

pisher by 1942 **1** *n* A young, insignificant person; =SQUIRT: *Roth's rise in a few short years from Hollywood pisher to Hollywood mogul was a classic movie scenario*—Vanity Fair **2** *adj* Insignificant; trivial; =PIDDLING: *I'm only sad that critics take it seriously. It's just a little pisher half-hour*—Maury Povich [fr Yiddish, "bed-wetter"]
See CALL someone PISHER

◁**piss**[1]▷ **1** *n* by 1386 Urine **2** *v* by 1290: *He had to piss* **3** *v* (also **piss and moan**) by 1940s To complain; grumble; =BITCH, KVETCH: *Angie's mother pissed and moaned about it for months*—Easyriders **4** *adj* by 1970s Of wretched quality; =PISS POOR: *Europe is a piss place for music*—Rolling Stone
See EYES LIKE PISSHOLES IN THE SNOW, FULL OF PISS AND VINEGAR, NOT HAVE A POT TO PISS IN, PANTHER PISS, TICKLE THE SHIT OUT OF someone

◁**piss**[2]▷ *combining word* by 1940s A term placed before an adjective to intensify its meaning: *piss-awkward/ piss-elegant/ piss-poor/ piss-ugly*

◁**piss and vinegar**▷ *n phr* by 1942 Energy; vitality; =PEP, PIZZAZZ: *I was seventeen years old. . . and 150 pounds of piss and vinegar. . .* —Whitey Herzog [*full of vinegar,* "interesting, entertaining," is found in college slang by 1926]
See FULL OF PISS AND VINEGAR

◁**piss and wind**▷ *n phr* by 1922 Pretentious but feeble show; gaudy display: *They strut with the piss and wind traditional among victors in political intrigues*—Village Voice [perhaps fr the situation of a person who can urinate and flatulate, but not achieve a substantial defecation]

◁**pissant**▷ (PIHS ant) by 1903 **1** *n* A despicable person; an insignificant wretch: *That sorry damn pissant*—Pat Conroy **2** *adj* Insignificant; paltry: *. . . this little pissant country*—New York Times

[extension of *pissant,* "ant," which is found by 1661]

◁**piss** something **away**▷ *v phr* by 1930s To waste and dissipate something foolishly; squander: *There was a part of him that wanted to piss it away and be a loser*—Washingtonian

◁**piss call**▷ *n phr* armed forces by 1940s Reveille, the military signal to get out of bed in the morning

◁**piss-cutter**▷ *n* by 1940s A person or thing that is remarkable, wonderful, superior, etc; =BEAUT, HUMDINGER, PIP, PISTOL: *Isn't our new colleague a piss-cutter?*

◁**pissed off**▷ *adj phr* (Variations: **pissed** or **p'd** or **peed off** or **po'd**) Angry; profoundly annoyed; indignant: *His face got all red-colored whenever he was pissed off*—Rolling Stone/ *He gets a little pissed like I'm making fun of him*—Rex Burns

◁**piss-elegant**▷ *adj* (Variations: ◁**piss-ass** or **pissy** or **pissy-ass**▷) by 1972 Ostentatiously elegant; affecting great refinement; =HOITY-TOITY: *. . . a piss-elegant new wave Chinese restaurant and bar*—Rolling Stone/ *He was a jerk for needing to hang around with pissy queens*—Armistead Maupin

◁**pisser**▷ by 1940s **1** *n* A very difficult job or task; =BALL-BUSTER, BITCH: *That climb was a pisser* **2** *n* A person or thing that is remarkable, wonderful, superior, etc; =PISS-CUTTER, PISTOL: *You're a pisser, you are*—Lawrence Sanders **3** *n* A very funny person or thing: *What a pisser when he opened the wrong door by mistake* **4** *n* A toilet: *. . . windowless with a pisser and no benches*—Rolling Stone [third sense fr the notion that one laughs hard enough to *piss* in one's pants]

◁**pisshead**▷ *n* by 1970s A despicable person; a stupid bore; =ASSHOLE: *. . . who made such a pisshead of herself*—Stephen King

◁**pissholes in the snow**▷ **See** EYES LIKE PISSHOLES IN THE SNOW

◁**piss ice water**▷ *v phr* by 1980s To be very cool; exhibit sangfroid: *. . . Patrick Stone had a reputation for pissing ice water at times like these*—Michael Grant

◁**pissing contest** (or **match**)▷ *n phr* by 1970s An argument; disagreement; confrontational debate: *. . . warned him against getting into a pissing contest with Bittman*—Washingtonian/ *I'm not going to sit here and get in a pissin' match about petty problems like work shoes*—Philadelphia Journal [perhaps fr actual vying among boys as to who can project the urinary stream farthest]

◁**piss into the wind**▷ *v phr* by 1980s To waste one's time and effort: *Why do you think the smart people get out of the job? Because. . . they realize they're pissing into the wind*—Michael Grant [*he who pisseth against the wind, wetteth his shirt* is found as an Italian proverb by 1642]

◁**piss-off**▷ *n* WWII armed forces Anger; indignation: *There's a basic, well-justified piss-off all over the country*—Newsweek

◁**piss** someone **off**▷ *v phr* WWII armed forces To make angry; arouse indignation

◁**piss on** someone or something▷ *v phr* by 1720

To dismiss or treat contemptuously; defile or violate; =DAMN, FUCK, SOD ●Often used as an angry and defiant dismissal: *I said thanks for the flower. He said piss on the flowers*—Stan Cutler

◁**piss on** one's **foot** (or **in** one's **pocket) and call it rain**▷ *v phr by 1980s* To lie and mislead cajolingly: *You're not just pissing on my foot and calling it rain, are you?*—Harry Crews/ *You know the people up there. They'd piss in my pocket and tell me it's raining*—Michael Grant

◁**piss on ice**▷ *v phr by about 1950* To live well; =EAT HIGH ON THE HOG, SHIT IN HIGH COTTON [fr the practice of putting cakes of *ice* in the urinals of expensive restaurants and clubs]

◁**piss poor**▷ **1** *adj phr* (also **pea-poor**) *by 1946* Of wretched quality; inferior; bad: *. . . outgrow its status as one of the many piss-poor modern dance groups playing college campuses*—Village Voice/ *I thought the tight ends were pea-poor*—Milwaukee Journal **2** *adj phr by 1957* Penniless; in pauperdom: *They're all born piss-poor*—Lawrence Sanders

◁**piss-ugly**▷ *adj by 1970s* Very ugly; nasty and menacing: *Beer-bellied brutes. . . peered at the world through piss-ugly eyes*—Village Voice

◁**piss up a rope**▷ *See* GO PISS UP A ROPE

◁**pissy** or **pissy-ass**▷ *adj by 1973* Stupid; silly; offensive: *Oh, don't be so pissy. . . You know I will when I'm sure*—Robert B Parker
See PIDDLING, PISS-ELEGANT

pistol 1 *n by 1984* A person or thing that is remarkable, wonderful, superior, etc; =BEAUT, PIP, PISS-CUTTER: *That Ruby Jean, she's a pistol*—New York Times **2** *n by 1990s* A woman's breast; =BAZOOKA, JUG, TIT: *Whoa! Look at the pistols on that new French teacher*—Gary Trudeau **3** *n lunch counter by 1950s* Hot pastrami [first sense probably a euphemism for *pisser*; lunch counter sense because the eater feels as if shot in the stomach soon after eating hot pastrami]
See HOT AS A THREE-DOLLAR PISTOL

pistol Pete *n phr by 1940s* A zealous and effective lover; =COCKSMAN [fr the usual jocular analogue between *pistol* and "penis," "shooting" and having an orgasm, etc, reinforced by alliteration and the fact that *Peter* means "penis"]

pit *v by 1970s* To take a racing car into the pit: *He pitted for fresh rubber and thus lost a lap*—Sports Illustrated
See CONVERSATION PIT, GREASE TROUGH, PASSION PIT

pit bull *n phr by 1980s* An extremely vicious and aggressive person ●*Rottweiler* is more common in British use: *Perot hired legal pit bull Roy Cohn to sandbag the Vietnam Memorial because he hated the design*—New York Times

pitch 1 *n by 1849* A hawker's or street vendor's place of business; =HIGH PITCH, LOW PITCH **2** *n by 1876* The sales talk or spiel of a hawker: *He recited a part of his pitch*—New Yorker/ *other gifts to prospective brides, along with a pitch to honeymoon at Holiday Inns*—Time **3** *v: Louie. . . pitches kitchen gadgets*—M Zolotow/ *He pitches house-*

hold items like the Magic Towel—New Yorker **4** *n by 1930s* A sexual approach, esp a tentative one; =PASS: *I never made a pitch with Herta*—John O'Hara **5** *v: I wouldn't try to pitch to that Ice Maiden* **6** *v homosexuals by 1970s* To penetrate the anus in sex
See BUTTERFLY BALL, HIGH PITCH, IN THERE PITCHING, LOW PITCH, MAKE A PITCH, PURPOSE PITCH, THROW

pitchforks *See* RAIN CATS AND DOGS

pitch in *v phr by 1843* To set to work vigorously; help: *Let's all pitch in and get it done*

pitch into someone or something *v phr by 1829* To attack; assail forcibly

pitching *See* IN THERE PITCHING

pitchman *by 1926* **1** *n* A person who sells novelties, household items, clever toys and tricks, etc, on the streets or at a fair or carnival **2** *n* Any advocate, promoter, persuader, spokesman, etc: *chief pitchman for Big Oil*

pitchout 1 *n baseball by 1910* A pitch thrown wide of the plate so that the catcher can more easily throw to one of the bases to forestall an attempted steal **2** *n football by 1947* A lateral pass from one back to another

pitch out *v phr baseball by 1910* To make a pitchout

pitch (or **fling**) **woo** *v phr 1930s teenagers* To kiss and caress; =NECK: *And she pitches some more woo with Dr Jan*—S J Perelman

the **pits** *n phr by 1953* The most loathsome place or situation imaginable: *This school is the pits* [fr armpits]

pit stop *n phr* A stop so that people may go to the toilet: *Pit stop. Head run*—Pat Conroy [fr the *pit stops* made by racing cars for service, repair, rest, etc; possible pun on *piss stop*]

pivot *n Army by 1970s* A soldier with the rank of private [fr the abbreviation *pvt*]

pix[1] *by 1932* **1** *n* Movies; the movies; =the FLICKS: *You ought to be in pix* **2** *n* Photographs, esp the artwork of a newspaper, magazine, book, etc; graphics **3** *modifier: pix credit*

pix[2] *n by 1972* A male homosexual [fr *pixie*, suggested by *fairy*]

pixilated 1 *adj by 1848* Crazy; eccentric; confused **2** *adj by 1955* Drunk [fr enchantment by *pixies*; revived and popularized by the 1936 movie *Mr. Deeds Goes to Town*]

pizzazz *n by 1937* Energy; power; =PEP, PISS AND VINEGAR: *What's missing is overall pizzazz and pace*—Judith Crist [origin unknown; perhaps echoically suggested by *piss, ass,* and *piss and vinegar*]

PJs or **pjs 1** *n by 1964* Pajamas; =JAMMIES, PEEJAYS: *New arrivals like me still flapped about in pj's and robes*—New York Magazine/ *. . . as though I were running around in my PJs*—Sports Afield **2** *n 1990s black teenagers* Housing projects: *We always lived in the PJs*

place *See* COFFEE-AND-CAKE JOINT

places *See* GO PLACES

plain Jane *adj phr* by 1912 Unadorned; stark; =NO-FRILLS: *"Plain Jane" is how one gun collector describes the look*—New York Times [the earliest examples read *plain Jane and no nonsense*]

plain vanilla *adj phr* by 1970s Unadorned; simple; basic: *. . . more lushly appointed variants of plain vanilla family cars are due to arrive*—New York Times [fr *vanilla* ice cream, considered less fancy than other flavors]

plain (or **plain white**) **wrapper** *n phr* 1970s citizens band An unmarked police car

plane *n* 1980s teenagers A big car; =BOAT: *My dad bought a plane from a used car dealer*—Delcastle Dictionary of Slang

◁**plank**[1]▷ *v* by 1970s To do the sex act with or to; =SCREW: *. . . had witless good fun with his children while his wife was out getting planked*—John Irving [origin unknown]

plank[2] *See* WALK THE PLANK

plank down (Variations: **plunk down** or **plump down** or **clunk down** or **plank out** or **plank**) by 1839 **1** *v phr* To put down with a thud or crash; place decisively: *. . . an overstuffed chair some admirer had planked down next to the booth*—A J Liebling **2** *v phr* To pay money; put down or put up money; offer or bet money: *. . . planked down a cool $8,000,000*—R H Fetridge/ *. . . plunked down. . . $65,000*—Bob Thomas [fr the hard striking of the *plank* of a table]

plant 1 *v* by 1610 To bury; hide **2** *v* by 1865 To place evidence secretly so that someone will be incriminated: *Someone is planting evidence*—Erle Stanley Gardner **3** *n* by about 1925 =SHILL **4** *n* by 1785 A cache, esp of stolen goods **5** *n* by 1912 Evidence placed so as to incriminate **6** *n* by 1812 A spy, esp a police spy: *The new guy turned out to be a plant* **7** *v* by 1920 To place a blow: *He planted a left on my poor snoot*

planting *n* by 1940s A funeral: *I get in on a lot of these plantings*—J Evans

plaster 1 *n* by 1940s A banknote, esp a one-dollar bill: *If you need a couple of plasters until Ed gets out, tell me*—Lawrence Sanders **2** *v* by 1585 To cover or apply generously: *They plastered the city with leaflets* **3** *n* by 1940s A person who surreptitiously follows another; shadow; =TAIL: *He probably knew he had a plaster by this time*—J Evans **4** *n* by 1950s A subpoena or summons; arrest warrant [money sense fr *shinplaster*, an early 19th-century term for "currency of little value or very small denomination"]

plastered *adj* by 1912 Drunk

plastic 1 *adj* 1960s counterculture False and superficial; meretricious; =HOKED-UP, SLICK, PHONY: *. . . in California. . . a plastic society*—B W Dipple **2** *n* by 1979 A credit card; monetary credit afforded by the use of credit cards [second sense fr *plastic money*, which is found by 1974]

plate *See* HAVE one's HANDS FULL, HOME PLATE, OFF one's PLATE

plater *n* horse-racing by 1920s A race horse, esp an inferior one; =BEETLE, PIG
See SELLING PLATER

platforms or **pyramids** *n* by 1970s Shoes with extremely thick soles and heels [in the sense "very thick soles," found by 1945]

platter *n* by 1931 A phonograph record; =DISC

the **platter** *n* baseball by 1940s Home plate

play 1 *v* by 1937 To acquiesce; cooperate; =PLAY BALL: *They'd come back and get her, if I didn't play with them*—Raymond Chandler **2** *v* show business by 1980s To go very well; succeed: *The O'Connor appointment's playing. . . you're on a roll, Mr President*—Philadelphia Daily News **3** *n* by 1929 Publicity; media coverage: *The dangers of the Free Trade Agreement are getting more play*—Denver radio talk show
See BONEHEAD PLAY, GRANDSTAND PLAY, MAKE A PLAY FOR

play along *v phr* by 1929 =PLAY BALL

play around 1 *v phr* by 1960 To do something, esp one's job, casually or frivolously; =HORSE AROUND: *Quit playing around and start playing hardball* **2** *v phr* by 1929 To be sexually promiscuous; =SLEEP AROUND: *She plays around*—Raymond Chandler

play around with someone **1** *v phr* by 1929 To flirt or dally with; have a sexual involvement with **2** *v phr* by 1960 To treat lightly or insultingly; challenge or provoke: *I wouldn't play around with that gorilla if I were you*

play at something *v phr* by 1840 To pretend to do something: *Play tennis? Well, I play at it*

play ball 1 *v phr* by 1867 To begin; get started: *Let's play ball now; it's time* **2** *v phr* by 1903 To cooperate; collaborate; acquiesce: *I might have played ball just a little, but I scorned to*—Agnes DeMille **3** *v phr* by 1944 To deal honestly and fairly: *He was playing ball with Artrim*—Erle Stanley Gardner [fr baseball; the first date refers to the first record of a baseball umpire's call *Play ball!*]

◁**play bouncy-bouncy**▷ *v phr* by 1960s To do the sex act, esp in the superior position; copulate: *He keeps cool. . . while she plays bouncy-bouncy on him*—Herbert Gold

playboy *n* by 1829 A man devoted to amusement; bon vivant; =GOOD-TIME CHARLIE, MAN-ABOUT-TOWN

play catch-up (or **catch-up ball**) by 1971 **1** *v phr* To play a game determinedly and desperately when one is losing: *. . . when college wishbone teams go to the air to play catch-up*—Sports Illustrated **2** *v phr* To work to recover from a disadvantage, defeat, etc: *For the last two years it's been a matter of playing catch-up ball with the budget*—Washington Post

play checkers (or **chess**) *v phr* homosexuals by 1972 To move about from seat to seat in a movie theater, soliciting possible sex partners

play close to the chest (or **the vest**) *v phr* by 1950s To be secretive and uncommunicative; keep one's counsel: *So you had to play your cards very close to your chest*—Ed McBain/ *. . . nominees* *have played their cards close to the vest*—Milwaukee Journal [fr the practice of a careful card player]

play dirty *v phr* by 1940s To use unethical, illegal, or injurious means; be deceptive and tricky; chicane: *When he started in politics he didn't mean to play dirty* [the related form *play dirt* is found by 1908]

play doctor *n* theater by 1940s A writer who specializes in altering and improving other writers' plays

play down *v phr* by 1934 To treat with little emphasis; =LOW-KEY: *They decided to play down the chief's faux pas*

played out by 1862 **1** *adj phr* Exhausted; worn out; =AUSGESPIELT, FRAZZLED: *I was played out, and quit at once* **2** *adj phr* No longer useful, viable, fashionable, etc: *I think the alienation theme is about played out*

player 1 *n* by 1483 A bettor: *A lot of players are avoiding OTB* **2** *n* by 1974: *. . . some of his fellow "players" (as pimps refer to themselves)*—F Ianni **3** *n* by middle 1980s An active participant: *Man, I'm a player. I gotta be watched*—Carsten Stroud **See** CHALK-EATER, HORSEPLAYER, PICCOLO PLAYER

play footsie (Variations: **footsy-footsy** or **footsy-wootsy** or **footy-footy**, or all these spelled with **ie** replacing the final **y**) by 1935 **1** *n* Amorous and clandestine touching and rubbing of feet between a couple; pedal dalliance: *I played footsie with her during Carmen*—Gene Fowler **2** *n* Any especially close relationship between persons or parties: *Truman is plenty burned up over the way Chiang Kai-shek. . . played footy-footy with the Republicans*—Drew Pearson

play someone **for a sucker** *v phr* by 1881 To take advantage of someone's gullibility, greed, etc: *Some blokes can never see when they are being played for suckers*—The Lantern

play for keeps (or **rough**) *v phr* by 1861 To be intent and serious to the point of callousness; =PLAY HARDBALL: *We're out here man for man and playin' for keeps*—Claude Brown [fr the game of marbles and other childrens' games where the tokens may be either returned or *kept* by the winner]

play games *v phr* by 1970s To maneuver and manipulate cunningly; toy and gamble: *Don't play games with me, Linda*—National Lampoon

playgirl *n* by 1934 A woman devoted to amusement

◁**play grab-ass**▷ *v phr* by 1940s To indulge in sexual clutching and touching; to feel and fondle; =GROPE •Sometimes used metaphorically: *. . . were currently inside a doughnut shop, playing grabass with the counter girl*—Easyriders/ *His reluctance to play what he called grab-ass with Congress*—Newsweek

play handies *v phr* by 1960s To indulge in the mutual fondling of hands: *Beneath the counter they were playing handies*—Christopher Morley

play hardball *v phr* by 1973 To be intent and serious to the point of callousness; =PLAY FOR KEEPS: *You want to play hardball, here we go*—George Warren [fr the presumed distinction in difficulty, severity, and manliness between baseball, that is, *hardball*, and softball]

play hell (or **merry hell**) **with** something *v*

phr by 1803 To damage or destroy: *The rain had played hell with business*—Armistead Maupin/ *Gloria. . . played merry hell with the filing system*—Penelope Lively [fr *play hell and Tommy,* attested in the mid–19th century and said to be fr earlier *play Hal and Tommy,* in reference to the behavior of Henry VIII and his minister Thomas Cromwell]

◁**play hide the weenie** (or **salami**)▷ *v phr* by 1980s To do the sex act; copulate; =SCREW: *. . . so Craig suggested that we play hide the salami*—UCLA Slang

play hooky (or **hookey**) *v phr* by 1848 To stay away from work and duty, or esp from school without an excuse; be truant [probably fr *hook it*]

play in Peoria *v phr* by 1970s To succeed in areas distinct from such focuses of power as Washington and New York or the Northeast in general: *When you're under a deadline, it's hard to judge what will play in Peoria*—Art Buchwald [fr the theater sense of *play,* to succeed on the stage; perhaps echoing Harold Ross' criterion that he wanted *The New Yorker* to appeal to "a little old lady in *Peoria*"]

play in the family *See* PLAY THE DOZENS

play into someone's **hands** *v phr* by 1705 To give an advantage to one's opponent: *Signing that is just playing into their hands*

play inside oneself *v phr* by 1990s To play nicely within one's capacity: *Jon. . . did a nice job. He played right inside himself*—Milwaukee Journal

play it by ear *v phr* by 1961 To handle a situation instinctively and extemporaneously, rather than by informed planning; improvise: *We didn't have much to go on, so we just had to play it by ear* [fr the playing of music imitatively, without training and notation; the phrase is found by 1674]

play it cool *v phr* by 1955 To behave in a calm, controlled, uncommitted way; be watchful and impassive: *We asked for a price and the agent "played it cool"*—Publishers Weekly

play it (or **play**) **safe** *v phr* by 1919 To choose a cautious line of behavior; avoid much risk: *Now we're ahead, let's play it safe*

play kissie (Variations: **kissy-face** or **kissy-facey** or **kissie-kissie** or **kissy-poo** or **lickey-face** or **smacky lips** may replace **kissie**) by 1970s **1** *v phr* To kiss and caress; =MAKE OUT, NECK: *Salesmen got them to buy an awful lot of perfume when they weren't busy playing lickey-face*—New York Post/ *Newlyweds play kissy-poo in a resort hotel*—People Weekly **2** *v phr* To be friendly and flattering; =PLAY UP TO someone: *We have to play kissie with him*—New Yorker

playmate *n* by 1970s One's companion in the pursuit of pleasure, esp of sexual delight

play (or **play Man**) **on** someone *v phr* by 1970s To treat roughly; intimidate physically: *If Tony stole your woman. . . you'll get your chance to play on him*—Donald Goines/ *Dreamer can't play Man on Shake. . . Shake'll dust his ass*—Dan Jenkins

play out *v phr* by 1854 To develop; transpire; =BREAK OUT, SHAKE OUT: *How do you see this playing out in your own State?*—National Public Radio [fr the finishing of a stage *play*]

play pattycake *v phr* by 1976 To cooperate cozily; =PLAY FOOTSIE: *They point to the hypocrisy of local law enforcement that plays pattycake with the Mafia up on the Strip*—Nation [fr a game one plays with infants]

play penny pool *v phr* by 1940s To deal in paltry matters; be concerned with childish trivia: *This isn't penny pool these guys are playing*—George Warren

play rough *See* PLAY FOR KEEPS

plays *See* the WAY IT PLAYS

play second fiddle *v phr* by 1809 To be in an inferior position; lack power or will to lead: *They won't play second fiddle to their spouses anymore*

play snuggle-bunnies *v phr* by 1970s To kiss and caress; cuddle amorously; =PLAY KISSIE: *Mr De Varennes is playing snuggle-bunnies with Mrs Martin*—Washington Post

◁**play stinky-pinky** (or **stink-finger**)▷ *v phr* by 1903 =FINGERFUCK

play the something **card** *v phr* by 1886 To use an exploitive or inflammatory maneuver: *Milosevic saw that the best way to hold on to power was to play the nationalist card*–New Yorker

play the deuce (or **devil**) **with** something *v phr* by 1834 To wreck or damage something: *That will play the deuce with his election chances*

play the dozens (or **the dirty dozens**) black by about 1925 **1** *v phr* To play an elaborate word-game of reciprocal insult, esp against the opponent's mother: *Don't play in de family, Sweet Back. I don't play de dozens*—Zora Neale Hurston **2** *v phr* To take advantage of; deceive; =DO A NUMBER ON: *He burst into tears, crying, "You all played the dozens on me"*—Joseph Wambaugh [origin unknown; the form *slipping in the dozens* is found by 1928, and *putting them in the dozens* by 1935]

play the field *v phr* by 1936 To have a number of sex or love partners, rather than settling on one [fr gamblers who bet on other horses than the favorites]

play the ponies *v phr* by 1908 To bet on horse races

◁**play the skin flute**▷ *v phr* by 1940s To do fellatio

play to the grandstand *v phr* baseball by 1888 To try ostentatiously to please the audience; =HOT DOG

play up *v phr* by 1909 To emphasize; feature; make the most of: *Hey, don't play up your bad points* [fr the featuring of a story in a newspaper]

play up to someone *v phr* by 1826 To flatter; be compliant: *If you play up to him he'll think you're brilliant* [fr the behavior of an actor who gives featuring support to another]

play who shot John *v phr* Army by 1970s To bandy excuses, recriminations, accusations, etc

◁**play with** oneself▷ *v phr* by 1896 To masturbate; =JACK OFF: *I was going with girls. . . and I didn't feel the urge to play with myself*—H K Fink

play (or **deal** or **operate**) **with a full deck** by 1970s **1** *v phr* To be sane and reasonable; have normal intelligence ●Usu in the negative: *Neither of the poor things was playing with a full deck*—Saul Bellow/ *. . . but she is dealing with a full deck, as it were*/—Philadelphia Journal/ *He wasn't playing with a full deck of cards*—John Irving **2** *v phr* To be honest and straightforward; avoid deception: *He has bluffed you into thinking he was playing with a full deck*—Playboy

play with someone's **head** *v phr* by 1990 To toy with psychological influence for one's advantage; play a "mind game": *He's playing with my head, and I don't like it*—Milwaukee Journal

plea *See* COP A PLEA

pleat *See* REET PLEAT

plebe *n* service academy by 1833 A first-year student at Annapolis or West Point [fr *plebeian,* "lower-class person," fr Latin]

pledge 1 *n* students by 1901 A student who has agreed to join a certain college fraternity or sorority **2** *v*: *Without a second thought MacCrimmon pledged Xi Phi*

plenty *adv* by 1842 Very; very much; extraordinarily: *I was plenty cautious*—Erle Stanley Gardner

plink *v* by 1966 To shoot: *I could walk up to him, plink his eyes out. . .* —Lawrence Sanders

plonk 1 *n* British fr Australian by 1930 Inferior wine; cheap wine: *It's a humble plonk, but you'll like it* **2** *n* by 1960s A boring and obnoxious person; =PILL [wine sense fr French *vin blanc,* "white wine"; second sense perhaps fr the dull sound *plonk*]

plonked *adj* by 1943 Drunk

plotz (PLAHts) *v* by 1967 To burst with emotion, frustration, anger, etc: *She's so stoked she could plotz* *See* PLOTZED

plotzed *adj* by 1962 Drunk: *. . . even smashed as you were, friend, plotzed out of your wits*—John D MacDonald [probably fr Yiddish *plotzen,* German *platzen,* "burst, split," reflecting the same notion of violent destruction as *smashed, bombed,* etc]

◁**plow** or **plough**▷ *v* by 1606 and probably before To do the sex act with or to a woman; =SCREW

plow (or **plough**) **into 1** *v phr* by 1972 To collide with very hard; ram: *. . . so long as they don't fry in the sun or plow into an atmosphere*—CoEvolution Quarterly **2** *v phr* by 1940s To attack heartily; assault

ploy *n* by 1722 A device or stratagem; a move, esp one designed to disconcert an opponent while keeping one's position; a shrewd maneuver [apparently fr Scots dialect; popularized by the late British humorist Stephen Potter]

PLU (pronounced as separate letters) *adj* by 1970 Admirable and fitting; discriminating: *The wife admires their living room ("Very PLU, people like us")*—Judith Crist [fr *people like us*]

pluck[1] *v* by 1400 To rob or cheat; fleece: *These bimbos once helped pluck a bank*—Dashiell Hammett [fr the image of *plucking* a chicken]

◁**pluck²**▷ *v* *by 1950s* To do the sex act with or to; =SCREW [a euphemism for *fuck*]

plug¹ **1** *n* *by 1860* An inferior old horse; =NAG **2** *n* *by about 1915* An average or inferior prizefighter [perhaps fr Dutch *plug*, "a sorry nag," related to Swiss-German *pflag* and to Danish *plag*, "foal"]

plug² **1** *n* *by about 1900* A silver dollar **2** *adj* (also **plugged**) *by 1888* Worthless; =PHONY: . . . *and furthermore the author does not give a plug damn*—Pauline Kael **3** *v* *by 1870* To shoot, esp shoot to death: *The mugger got plugged by an indignant onlooker* **4** *v* *by 1901* To do the sex act to; =BOFF, POKE, SCREW [all senses fr the notion of *plug* as holefiller; the second sense may be influenced by the notion of inferiority in *plug¹*]

See PULL THE PLUG, SPARK PLUG

plug³ **1** *v* (also **plug along** or **plug away**) *by 1888* To work or study steadily and fairly hard; keep busy but not excitingly so: *She's plugging away, though. . .*—New York Magazine **2** *v* *by 1906* To give a flattering appraisal, esp with a view to selling something; advocate and support; cry up: *Cosmetic manufacturers plugged products to give women ersatz tan*—R Adler/ *If you'll plug my book, I'll plug yours* **3** *n* *by 1902*: *I certainly would appreciate him giving me a plug in the owners*—John O'Hara [fr Oxford University slang, apparently in imitation of heavy plodding steps, or perhaps the steps of an old and tired horse; sense of selling or advocating fr the fact that such commendation was originally constant and repetitive]

plug for *v phr* *by 1900* To support actively; cheer for; =ROOT FOR: *She was plugging for the coalition candidate*

plugged in (or **into**) *by late 1960s* **1** *adj phr* In direct touch with; sensitive to and aware of: *She's plugged in, in ways I don't quite understand*—Vogue **2** *adj phr* =TURNED ON [fr the metaphor of a person as an electrical or electronic device]

plugged nickel *See* NOT WORTH A PLUGGED NICKEL

plugger **1** *n* *by 1900* A diligent but not brilliant worker or student; dependable drudge **2** *n* *underworld* *by 1940s* A hired killer; =HIT MAN **3** *n* *football* *by 1990s*: . . . *the Packers reluctantly shifted George Koonce from the inside linebacker (plugger) position. . .*—Milwaukee Journal Sentinel

plug hat *n phr* *by 1863* A top hat

plug in (or **into**) *by late 1960s* **1** *v phr* To become a part of; participate in; gain access to: *Parents were beginning to be plugged directly into the decision-making process*—Toronto Life **2** *v phr* To discover and exploit to one's advantage; tap: *Nixon. . . has plugged into a great national yearning*—Hugh Sidey [fr the notion of the electrical *plug* and socket]

plugola **1** *n* *by 1959* Illicit payment, often not in money, given to media people for mentioning commercial products in noncommercial contexts **2** *n* Such a mention; =PLUG [based on *payola*]

plug-ugly **1** *n* *by 1856* A rowdy; tough; =GORILLA, HOOD **2** *n* *by 1940s* A prizefighter; =PUG [origin unknown; perhaps fr rowdy fire companies in Baltimore, hence fr *fireplug*; perhaps fr New York toughs of the 1830s who wore top hats over their ears as helmets; perhaps related to *plug-muss*, "a fight," found by the early 1950s]

plum **1** *n* *by 1825* Something highly prized, esp an easy job with high pay and prestige, often given for political favors: *The winners get to pick all the plums* **2** *modifier*: . . . *who recently got the plum job of heading the county's Department of Human Resources*—Milwaukee Journal [probably influenced by Little Jack Horner's feat of reaching in his thumb and pulling out a *plum* (in fact a raisin); compare early–1800s British *plummy*, "good, desirable"]

plumb *adv* *by 1748* Completely; entirely; =STONE: *What he said was plumb silly* [fr notions of exact extent and precision associated with the *plumb bob* or sailor's *plumb line* (for measuring depth of water), ultimately fr Latin *plumbum*, "lead"]

plumber **1** *v* *by 1930s* To botch; ruin: *I tho't I plumbered it*—John O'Hara **2** *n* *medical* *by 1950s* A urologist **3** *n* *by 1972* A member of a White House group under President Richard M Nixon, which exerted itself to stop various leaks of confidential information: *One of the jobs carried out by the plumbers was burglarizing the office of Dr Daniel Ellsberg's former psychiatrist*—New York Times

plumbing **1** *n* *jazz musicians* *by about 1930* A trumpet **2** *n* *by 1950s* The digestive, excretory, and reproductive systems and organs

plummy *adj* *by 1881* Rich and sonorous; orotund and fruity; unctuous; =SMARMY: . . . *the rich, plummy voice of Edward Arnold*—K Harris

plump or **plunk** *adv* *by 1734* Precisely; exactly; squarely; =SMACK [fr *plumb*]

plump down *See* PLANK DOWN

plump for someone or something *v phr* *by 1834* To choose; support; advocate

plumpie or **plumpy** *n* *by 1970s* An overweight person; a chubby person: *A studio of plumpies!*—Esquire [the adjective is found by 1606]

plunge *v* *by 1876* To bet or speculate recklessly

plunk **1** *n* *by 1891* A dollar: . . . *my five thousand plunks*—H McHugh **2** *v* *by 1888* To shoot [echoic]

plunk down *See* PLANK DOWN

plush or **plushy** **1** *adj* *by 1927* Luxurious; stylish; costly: . . . *a swank, plush, exclusive cabaret club*—Westbrook Pegler/ . . . *singer Ella Logan at the plushy Casablanca*—Budd Schulberg **2** *n*: *All the plush in the world won't tidy up his vulgar soul* [fr the soft and costly fabric, fr French *pluche*]

plushery *n* *by 1951* A plush hotel, nightclub, restaurant, etc

plute *n* *by 1908* A rich person; plutocrat: *The tutoring sections were only for "plutes"*—P Marks

po *See* PISSED OFF

pocket *See* DEEP POCKET, HIGHPOCKETS, IN someone's POCKET, IN THE POCKET, OUT OF POCKET

pocket litter *n phr* *by 1973* The usual miscellany

in a person's pocket: . . . *just a driver's license and some pocket litter*—H Hunt

◁**pocket pool** (or **polo**)▷ *n phr* entry form by 1930s, variant by 1980s The fondling of one's own genitals with a pocketed hand

po'd *See* PISSED OFF

pod *n* narcotics by 1952 Marijuana; =POT: *Diane smoked jive, pod, and tea*—Orville Prescott [origin unknown; perhaps fr the *pod*, or seed container, the flowering and fruiting head of the female cannabis plant; perhaps an alteration of *pot*]

pod people (or **person**) *n phr* by 1956 Stupid, unfeeling, machinelike people; =ZOMBIE: *Have body snatchers invaded America's airwaves? Is this pure pop for pod people?*—Newsweek/ *And find you're a bug. A pod person?*—Christopher Zenowich [fr the extraterrestrial creatures depicted in the 1956 movie *Invasion of the Body Snatchers,* who spawn in *pods* and take over the bodies of human beings; based on a novel by Jack Finney]

PODS *n* by 1990s: . . . *a car for PODS, Poor Old Dumb Slobs. . . traditional domestic-car buyers who couldn't afford Cadillacs*—New York Times

podspeak *n* by 1960s Automatic, meaningless, ritual talk, the idiom of pod people; tedious bromides: *Clerks utter such podspeak as the inescapable "Have a nice day"*—Washington Post

Podunk (POH dunk) *n* by 1843 The legendary small country town; =EAST JESUS, JERK TOWN [originally an Algonquian place name, meaning "a neck or corner of land," used for several places in New England; also the name of a small tribe]

poetry slam *n phr* by 1990s: *A poetry slam is a contest for poets. Anyone who spends his or her leisure hours pouring his or her soul onto paper can enter a slam*—Macon Telegraph

po-faced *adj* British by 1934 Without expression; showing a neutral mask; =DEADPAN, POKER-FACED, STRAIGHT-FACED: *The famous portraits of the Father of our Country as an unsmiling, po-faced stuffed shirt do him an injustice*–Time [fr *poker-faced*]

pog *n* by 1990s A small cardboard disk used by children in games: *Hey, gimme back my pog!*—comic strip "Ernie"

pogey or **pogie** or **pogy** (POH gee) **1** *n* hoboes by 1891 A poorhouse, workhouse, or old folks' home **2** *n* by 1940s A jail; =POKEY **3** *n* by 1918 =POGEY BAIT **4** *n* =POGUE [origin unknown; perhaps fr the common name of the trash fish menhaden, as suggesting something cheap, common, and to be caught with bait; perhaps fr the Southern pronunciation of *porgy,* another fish of a similar quality; both fish names are of obscure origin]

pogey bait *n phr* (Variations: **pogie** or **pogy** or **poggie** or **poggy** may replace **pogey**) by 1918 Candy and cake, etc; sweets; nonmilitary food and delicacies carried on field exercises [so called because they could be used in the seduction of boys and young men, *pogues,* into homosexual acts]

◁**pogue**▷ (POHG) **1** *n* by 1940s A youthful homosexual male, or either willing or unwilling partner of a homosexual male; =PUNK: *The kid was a pogue*—Robert Stone **2** *n* Vietnam War armed forces Any despicable boy or young man; =PUNK: *I was just a pogue, humpin' connex containers at a depot in Long Binh*—Gary Trudeau [shortened form of *pogey*]

poindexter *n* 1980s students An overly studious person; =MERV, NERD, PENCIL NECK

point 1 *n* prizefighting by about 1925 The jaw **2** *n* 1960s narcotics A hypodermic needle; =SPIKE **3** *n* (also **point man**) armed forces & underworld by 1940s A forward reconnaissance man; lookout man; scout who warns his associates of danger, and may get the first shock of attack: *He is the point man for organized labor*—Philadelphia Journal *See* BROWNIE POINTS

pointed head 1 *n phr* by 1940s A stupid, duncelike mind; a brainless cranium: *I hope you got that idea into your pointed head, creep* **2** *n phr* by 1972 An intellectual; =BIGDOME, EGGHEAD: . . . *the guys who think we're all a bunch of pointed heads and all we want is poetry*—Washington Post

pointer *n* by 1883 An item of advice or instruction: *She gave me a few pointers about how to say it* *See* FOUR-POINTER

pointhead or **pointy-head** by 1972 **1** *n* A stupid person; =TURKEY **2** *n* An intellectual; =EGGHEAD: *The "pointy heads" are impractical as politicians*—Newsweek

point-shaving *n* sports & gambling by 1971 The illegal practice, esp on the part of athletes, of controlling the score of a game, match, series, etc, so that professional gamblers will have to pay less to the bettors or will win for themselves

point-spread *n* sports & gambling by 1973 The difference between the handicapping points added or subtracted for various teams in football and basketball betting

point the finger *v phr* by 1829 To accuse or vilify: *Don't be too quick to point the finger in his case* [the dated instance refers to *the finger of scorn*]

pointy-headed by 1968 **1** *adj* Intellectual; cultured: . . . *uninterested in. . . any of the pointy-headed criticism generated in the last two decades* **2** *adj* Stupid; idiotic [said to have been coined by Governor George Wallace of Alabama]

poison 1 *n* by 1918 A situation, person, event, etc, that portends harm and evil; =MURDER: *Don't try that route, it's poison* **2** *n* by 1805 Liquor, esp cheap whiskey *See* SNAKE POISON

poisoning *See* LEAD-POISONING

poison-pen letter *n phr* by 1929 A malicious anonymous letter; an obscene crank letter

poison pill *n phr* business & finance by middle 1980s Any financial stratagem that causes a company to be unattractive to takeover bidders: *Time Warner's poison pill effectively bars an investor from owning more than 15 percent of the company's outstanding shares*—New Yorker

poke[1] **1** *v* by 1940s To herd cattle **2** *n* by 1928 A cowboy: *Each poke pays his own transportation to* *the Rodeo*—Ithaca Journal **3** *n* by *1940s* =SLOWPOKE **4** *v* baseball by *1880s* To hit the ball, esp to hit fairly lightly with precise aim: *He just poked it into the hole* ◁5▷ *n* by *1700* The sex act; =PIECE OF ASS ◁6▷ *v* by *1868* To do the sex act with or to; =SCREW

See BUY A PIG IN A POKE, COWPUNCHER, GUNPOKE

poke² **1** *n* by *1859* A wallet, pocket, or purse: *. . . with only about $85 in my poke*—John O'Hara **2** *n* by *1926* Money; one's bankroll [fr Southern dialect, "pocket, bag," fr Middle English, ultimately fr Old Norman French]

poke around *v phr* by *1809* To examine or search, esp in a dilatory way: *. . . he might know we've been poking around the computer files*—Stan Cutler [the dated instance reads *poke about*]

poke fun *v phr* by *1840* To tease; jape; mock

poke one's **nose into** something *v phr* by *1860s* To pry and meddle; examine: *. . . and to poke your nose into all the most interesting places*—Philadelphia

poker face by *1885* **1** *n phr* An expressionless face; neutral mask; =DEADPAN **2** *n phr* A person whose face is usually expressionless

poker-faced *adj* by *1923* Without expression; showing a neutral mask; =DEADPAN, STRAIGHT-FACED: *She's great at poker-faced zingers*

pokery **See** JIGGERY-POKERY

pokey¹ or **poky** *n* by *1919* A jail; =CLINK, SLAMMER: *My thoughts centered around the prospect of the "Pokey"*—James Simon Kunen [origin unknown]

pokey² or **poky** **1** *adj* by *1856* Slow; dawdling; sluggish: *What a pokey waiter* **2** *adj* by *1849* Insignificant; paltry: *a pokey little town*

See HOKEY-POKEY

pol (PAHL) *n* by *1942* A politician: *. . . only another pol on the take*—Newsweek

◀**polack**▶ (POH lahk) (also **Polack** or **pollack** or **Pollack** or **pollock** or **Pollock**) *n* by *1879* A Pole or a person of Polish extraction ●It is curious that this word is somewhat pejorative in English even though it is the Polish word for "Pole"

pole **See** BEANPOLE, NOT TOUCH someone or something WITH A TEN-FOOT POLE

polgeek *adj* by *1990s* Featuring political pundits: *. . . television's polgeek show "Crossfire"*—Milwaukee Journal

police or **police up** *v* or *v phr* Army by *1851* To clean up a camp, barracks, parade ground, etc; make neat and orderly

policeman *n* by *1980s* =ENFORCER: *. . . you had to bring in somebody who was as tough, or brutal, as they were. The kind of terminology for this role in hockey was "policeman". . .* —Milwaukee Journal

Polish **See** IS THE POPE POLISH

polisher **See** APPLE-POLISHER, BONE-POLISHER

polish off **1** *v phr* by *1873* To eat; consume, esp quickly and heartily: *I had polished off a platter of beans*—Boston Post **2** *v phr* by *1837* To finish; accomplish: *He polished off the week's quota in four days* **3** *v phr* by *1829* To put out of action;

defeat; kill: *. . . polish him off by crowning him with a Coca-Cola bottle*—Life [fr the notion of finishing a piece of work by giving it a final *polish*]

politician *n* by *1592* A person who succeeds through charm, diplomacy, mutual favors, etc ●The term is mildly derogatory in suggesting a lack of true substance: *If you called him an asshole to his face you're no politician*

politico (pə LI ti koh) *n* by *1630* A politician, esp a spectacular or unscrupulous one: *the heavy-duty Bay State politicoes* [fr Spanish or Italian]

◁**pollack** or **pollock** or **Pollock**▷ **See** POLACK

polluted *adj* by *1912* Drunk

Pollyanna *n* by *1913* An irrepressibly cheery person; undaunted optimist: *. . . or were we all a crowd of Pollyannas?*—Hugh Pentecost [fr the title and heroine of a novel by Eleanor Hodgman Porter, 1868–1920]

po-mo *adj* by *1990s* Post-modern; up-to-date; trendy: *. . . in a politically correct, bias-free, po-mo (post-modern) way*—Los Angeles Times

◁**pom-pom**▷ *n* WWII Army The sex act; =SCREWING [perhaps fr the echoic name *pom-pom* of various rapid-fire automatic guns, found by 1889]

ponce **1** *n* chiefly British fr *1872* A pimp, or any man supported by a woman **2** *v*: *He quit work and took to poncing* [origin unknown; perhaps fr French *pensionnaire*, "boarder, lodger, person living without working"]

the **pond** *n* by *1641* The ocean

See the BIG POND, the HERRING POND

◁**pong¹** or **Pong**▷ *n* Australian by *1906* A Chinese or a person of Chinese extraction

pong² *n* by *1919* A smell; a stink: *. . . when I catch that pong in the air*—Robert Stone [origin unknown; perhaps fr Romany *pan*, "stink"]

pony **1** *n* students by *1827* A literal translation of a foreign-language school text, used as a cheating aid; **2** *n* by *1970s* Any cheating aid as used by a student **3** *n* by *1849* A small, bell-shaped liquor glass, used esp for brandy and liqueurs **4** *n* by *1907* A racehorse: *Do you follow the ponies?* **5** *n* by *1905* A chorus girl or burlesque dancer: *The ponies. . . slumped into place*—F Scott Fitzgerald [in all senses fr the thing being small like a *pony*; the student senses, which have or have had *horse* and *trot* as synonyms, may also suggest something that carries one, gives one a free ride]

pony act **See** DOG AND PONY ACT

pony up *v phr* by *1824* To pay; =FORK OVER: *He had ponied up a silver quarter*—Jack London [fr earlier British *post the pony*, "pay," fr 16th century *legem pone*, "money," fr the title of the Psalm for Quarter Day, March 25, the first payday of the year]

poo or **pooh** **1** *interj* by *1602* A mild exclamation of disbelief, dismay, disappointment, etc: *Oh poo, I dropped it* **2** *n* by *1950s* Excrement; =DO, POO-POO ●Along with *poop*, this is a euphemism used by and to children: *Zoo Poo garden fertilizer is made from the waste of all manner of exotic creatures*—Toronto Life

See CUTESY-POO, HOT POO, ICKY

-poo *combining word* by *1970s* Little; silly little •A nonsense word used after diminutive forms to give an arch baby-talk effect: . . . *settled down for a well-bred nappy-poo*—Village Voice

pooch[1] *n* by *1924* A dog: . . . *a card for. . . your pooch*—Associated Press [origin obscure]
See SCREW THE POOCH

pooch[2] *v* football by *1980s* To kick a high and relatively short punt: *Bracken has not been much of a coffin-corner kicker, choosing instead to pooch the ball in hopes that it gets downed. . . near the goal line*—Milwaukee Journal [origin obscure]

pooched out *adj phr* by *1970s* Protruding: . . . *round shoulders, pooched out stomach*—Glamour [perhaps related to British dialect *pooch*, "to thrust out the lips sullenly"]

poochy by *1920s* **1** *n* =POOCH **2** *adj* Doggy; dog-like: *a poochy smell*

poodle-faker 1 *n* by *1902* =LADIES' MAN **2** *n* WWI Army fr British A self-important newly commissioned officer [first sense fr the notion that such a man would emulate a *poodle* or other lapdog to ingratiate himself with women]

◁**poof**▷ *n* (also **poofter** or **poove** or **pouffe**) British by *1850*, first variant Australian by *1903* A male homosexual; =FAGGOT, QUEER [origin unknown; perhaps fr *puff*, attested in mid–1800s British hobo slang as "homosexual"]

pooh-bah *n* by *1888* An important person; a self-important person; =BIG SHOT, HONCHO, VIP: . . . *where presidents and pooh-bahs commune*—Westword [fr the character in Gilbert and Sullivan's *The Mikado* who holds many high offices, the name probably coined fr two exclamations of contempt and derision]

poohed or **poohed out** *adj* or *adj phr* by *1940s* =POOPED

pooh-pooh or **poo-poo** *v* by *1827* To dismiss lightly and contemptuously; airily deprecate; deride: *I don't poo-poo his talent, just his character*

pool *See* DIRTY POOL, PENNY POOL, PLAY PENNY POOL, POCKET POOL

poolroom *n* horse-racing & gambling by *1875* An illegal bookmaker's establishment: . . . *a poolroom. . . from auction-pool betting*—T Betts

◀**poon tang** or **poon**▶ *n phr* or *n* by about *1910* A black woman regarded as a sex object or partner: *Eye that poon tang there*—Calder Willingham/ *just about to get a little poon*—Village Voice/ *watching all that young poon*—Joseph Wambaugh [probably fr French *putain*, "prostitute," by way of New Orleans Creole]

poop[1] *n* *1930s* Army & students Information; data; =SCOOP: *The girl's given us the complete poop*—G Cotler
See POOP SHEET

poop[2] **1** *n* by *1744* Excrement; =POO •Along with *poo*, this is a euphemism for use to and by children **2** *v* by *1903*: *The dog pooped on the rug* **3** *n* by *1915* A contemptible, trifling person; =PILL •Often used ironically and affectionately, esp of an old person: . . . *a sweet old poop who was seventy-six*—Kurt Vonnegut Jr **4** *v* by *1932* To tire; fatigue; =BUSH: *Being with him poops me exceedingly* [probably fr a merging of 14th-century *poupen*, "to toot," with 15th-century *poop*, "the rear part of a ship," fr Latin *puppis* of the same meaning; the fatigue sense may be related to the condition of a ship that is *pooped*, "has taken a wave over the stern"]

◁**poop chute**▷ *n phr* by *1970s* The anus: *I fingered her pussy and poop chute*—Penthouse

pooped or **pooped out** *adj* or *adj phr* by *1930* Exhausted; deeply fatigued; =BEAT, BUSHED: . . . *starting to get pooped out*—James T Farrell [fr a British nautical term describing a ship that has been swept by a wave at the stern; perhaps related to *pooped*, "overcome, bested," found by 1551]

pooper *n* by *1970s* The posterior; =ASS, BUTT: *What a fuckin' pooper on that little snatch*—Joseph Wambaugh

pooper (or poop) scooper *n phr* by *1972* A shovel and container set designed for cleaning one's dog's feces off the sidewalk, and, by extension, anything so used: . . . *to buy a pooper scooper or something like it*—Village Voice

poopicate *v* by *1990s* To defecate; =SHIT: . . . *you're sure to be wondering how bats poopicate when they sleep upside down*—Milwaukee Journal

poo-poo *n* by *1970s* Excrement; =POO, POOP •A euphemism used to and by children: *He reverts to that childishness of poo-poo caca*—Time [fr *poop*]

poop (or poo) out *v phr* by *1926* To fail; lose energy and impetus; =FIZZLE: *They would have won, but they suddenly just pooped out*

poop sheet *n phr* Army & students by about *1935* Any set of data, instructions, official notices, etc: *Here's the poop sheet from the comptroller* [origin unknown; perhaps fr *poop*, "excrement"; improbably but possibly an unaccounted shortening of *liripoop*, "lore, tricks of the trade," as found in the 1500s phrases *to know one's liripoop, to teach someone his liripoop*, perhaps related to *lerrie*, "something learned or spoken by rote"]

poopsie or **poopsie-woopsie** *n* by *1940s* Sweetheart; =BABE, HONEY •Often a term of endearment: *I hear you, poopsie*

poop someone up *v phr* Army by *1970s* To inform; brief; =FILL someone IN, PUT someone IN THE PICTURE

◁**poor-ass**▷ *adj* by *1960s* Wretched; nasty; =LOUSY: . . . *a poor-ass place to live*—Earl Thompson

poor boy *n phr* by *1921* A very large sandwich; =DAGWOOD, HERO SANDWICH [coined and invented by Clovis and Benjamin Martin, who opened a New Orleans restaurant in 1921]

poor-boy it *v phr* by *1970s* To be forced to impoverished extremities; be severely deprived: *We're poor-boying it in Criminal Court*—New York Times

poor deck *See* DEAL someone A POOR DECK

poor fish (or simp) *n phr* entry form by *1919*, variant by about *1900* An ordinary person, esp regarded as a victim of existential perversity: *The* *poor fish is damned if he does and damned if he doesn't/ They've tricked you again, you poor simp*

poor man's something or someone *n phr by 1854* A thing or person less glamorous, desirable, famous, etc, than the top grade: . . . *the Poor Man's Palm Beach*—Ring Lardner

poor-mouth 1 *v by 1965* To deny one's wealth and advantages; emphasize one's deficiencies; =TALK POOR MOUTH: *Richard Nixon often poor-mouthed his chances*—J Rekkanen **2** *v by 1967* To deprecate severely; =BAD-MOUTH: *I'm not going around poor-mouthing the war*—A Shuster [*make a poor mouth*, "to whine, make the worst of things," is found as Scots dialect by 1822]

◁**poot**▷ *black by 1970s* **1** *n* Excrement; =CRAP, SHIT: *Did she think I usually walked around festooned in pigeon poot?*—Village Voice **2** *interj*: *I checked my watch. Poot. It was only twelve forty-five*—Sue Grafton **3** *n* A contemptible person; =PILL, POOP: . . . *some old poots patrolling with a dog or two*—John Farris **4** *v* To flatulate; =FART **5** *n*: *The dog laid a loud poot* [probably a variant of *poop*]

poot around *v phr black by 1970s* To waste time; behave frivolously; =CRAP AROUND: *There's been a lot of pootin' around but very little maximum effort*—Pat Conroy

◁**pootbutt**▷ *n black by 1970s* A callow and ignorant person; a stupid and unfledged youth, esp one lacking the cunning of the ghetto: . . . *show Chester that he wasn't a poot-butt*—Donald Goines

poove *See* POOF

pop[1] or **pops 1** *n by 1838* Father; =POPPA **2** *n by 1889* An older or elderly man •Used in informal, yet respectful, direct address: *Hey, pop, slow down a bit*

pop[2] **1** *n by 1882* Flavored carbonated water; soda; soda pop **2** *n by 1923* Ice cream or flavored ice on a stick; Popsicle™ **3** *n car-racing & hot rodders by 1960s* Nitromethane or any other fuel additive for cars: . . . *fuel additives. . . called pop*—Fort Worth Star-Telegram **4** *v 1950s narcotics* To take narcotics by injection; =SHOOT UP **5** *v 1960s narcotics* To take pills, esp barbiturates, amphetamines, etc, and esp habitually **6** *n 1960s narcotics* A quantity of narcotics; =BAG: *Each of them had a couple of pops on 'em*—New York Magazine ◁**7**▷ *v by 1950s* To do the sex act with or to; =JAZZ, SCREW: *Well, did you pop her?*—Claude Brown ◁**8**▷ *n by 1950s* The sex act; sexual activity; =ASS **9** *v by 1386* To hit; smack: *She popped him on the snoot* **10** *v 1762* To shoot; kill; =DRILL: *You might avoid going to the joint, or getting popped, today's term for murder, if caught*—Milwaukee Journal Sentinel **11** *v by late 1960s* To catch; arrest: *But what I need is probable cause to pop a guy. . .* —Carsten Stroud **12** *n baseball by 1895* =POP-UP [all senses related to *pop* as an echoic term for a sharp noise or a sharp blow; in the first sense, "ginger beer" found by 1836]

pop[3] *adj by 1910* Popular; having a very broad audience: *Tom Wolfe, the pop journalist*—New York Times [found by 1862 in the senses "a popular concert," "popular music"]

a **pop** *n phr by 1939* A time; each occasion; =CRACK: *Steinem gets $3000 a pop for talking*—New York Times [fr *pop*, "blow, stroke, crack," and according to Eric Partridge used by the Australians in the 1920s] *See* DOUGH-POP

pop a sweat *See* BREAK A SWEAT

pop a wheelie *v phr 1960s motorcyclists & bicyclists* To raise the front wheel of a motorcycle or bicycle off the ground in order to ride on the rear wheel only

pop bottle *n phr photography by 1940s* An inferior lens in a camera or photo-enlarger

pop car *n phr railroad by about 1934* A small, motor-driven open car used by track workers [fr the *pop-pop* sound of the one-cylinder engine]

◁**pop** someone's **cherry**▷ *v phr by 1930s* To terminate someone's virginity: *I would definitely pop his cherry*—Xaviera Hollander

◁**pop** one's **cookies (or rocks)**▷ *v phr by 1970s* To have an orgasm; climax; =COME •The variant is chiefly British: *Madam Gray, who couldn't ever pop her cookies enough*—Paul Sann

pop one's **cork** *v phr by 1930s* To become furious; explode angrily; =BLOW one's TOP: *I didn't expect her to pop her cork either*—Dennis Day

popcorn *by 1973* **1** *n* Something trivial and insubstantial: *Gimbel called the charges "popcorn". . .* —Milwaukee Journal **2** *n* Something easily done; =BREEZE, PIECE OF CAKE: *As for Streep, she does what she is asked to do. But the role is popcorn*–New Republic

Pope *See* IS THE POPE POLISH

Popemobile *n by 1979* A car specially designed and built to display and protect the Pope: . . . *I had chased his Popemobile as he toured western Sicily on a weekend pastoral jaunt*—Vanity Fair

the **pope's** (or the **parson's**) **nose** *n phr by 1785* The triangular tailpiece of a cooked fowl

popeyed 1 *adj by 1830* Having protuberant eyes; exophthalmic; =BUGEYED **2** *adj by 1906* Astonished; amazed: *I just stood there popeyed*

pop for *v phr by 1940s* To pay for, esp as a treat to others; =PICK UP THE TAB: . . . *go to a veterinarian or pet groomer and pop for the flea dips*—Los Angeles Times

popgun *n by 1849* A pistol

popoff 1 *n by 1880s* A death or killing **2** *n by 1940s* A bragging, blatant, brash, and/or stupid declaration: *It was a typical senatorial popoff*—Ithaca Journal **3** *n by 1940s* =BIG-MOUTH, LOUDMOUTH

pop off 1 *v phr by 1764* To die: *If he had popped off sooner, less trouble for all* **2** *v phr by 1933* To talk loudly and perhaps prematurely; =SHOOT OFF one's MOUTH: *I'm not popping off about the pennant until we get it*—Casey Stengel **3** *v phr by 1919* To leave; depart

pop someone **off** *v phr by 1824* To kill someone, esp by shooting: *The police never found who popped the informer off*

popout *n surfers by 1960s* A mass-produced surfboard

poppa 1 *n by 1765* One's father **2** *n by 1765* Any older man [fr *papa*, which is found by 1681]

pop party *n phr 1960s narcotics* A gathering or party for the purpose of taking narcotics

popper 1 *n by 1889* A pistol **2** *n 1960s narcotics* A pill or capsule of amyl or butyl nitrite: *I'm just giving you a harmless popper*—Xaviera Hollander
See EYEPOPPER, FINGER-POPPER, JOY-POPPER, PILL-POPPER

poppy *adj by 1990s* Resembling "pop" music rather than rock'n'roll: *. . . a more youthful, poppy, idealistic sound*—New York Times

poppycock *n by 1865* Nonsense; foolishness [apparently fr Dutch *pappekak*, "soft dung"]

poppy love *n phr black teenagers by 1980s* An elderly Jewish man: *Ain't no hymie poppy love be on The Deuce Monday night, fool!*—Carsten Stroud

pop quiz or **shotgun quiz** or **pop test** *n phr college students by 1940s* A surprise test; an unexpected examination [*pop*, "to announce or produce unexpectedly," is found by 1529]

pops *See* POP

the **pops** *n phr by 1957* Popular records, songs, etc: *the best of the pops*

popskull *n by 1867* Raw inferior whiskey; =MOONSHINE

pop the question *v phr by 1826* To propose marriage

pop-top *by 1970* **1** *n* A small sailboat, camper, etc, whose top rises to provide headroom and sleeping room **2** *n* (also **flip-top**) A beverage can with a preperforated opening and a ringlike lever on the top for access to the liquid

pop up 1 *v phr by 1706* To appear suddenly: *. . . for the universe to pop up tackily out of nowhere. . .*—New York Times **2** *v phr baseball by 1867* To hit a high fly ball in the infield, either fair or foul

pop-up *n baseball by 1908* A high fly ball in the infield

pop wine *n phr by 1971*: *. . . "pop" wines, low-alcohol, fruit-flavored wines specially designed for the soda- and fruit-punch palate*—New York Magazine

porcelain god *See* PRAY TO THE PORCELAIN GOD

porcupine *n WWII Navy* A frayed wire rope

pork 1 *n by 1862* Federal appropriations obtained for particular localities or interests ◁**2**▷ *v by early 1980s* To do the sex act; copulate; =SCREW: *I decided to lay some groundwork for porking her brains out*—National Lampoon [origin uncertain; perhaps fr *poke*]

pork and *n phr lunch counter by 1940s* Pork and beans

pork-chopper *n labor union by 1940s* A person, like a venal officer or friend or relative of an officer, on a union's payroll with a sinecure

pork out *v phr 1980s students* To eat overheartily; overeat; =PIG OUT: *We were porking out on three sweet rolls*—Clark County Press

pork up *v phr by 1990s* To put on weight; fatten oneself: *Jeff Daniels porked up for* Dumb & Dumber *role*—US Express

porky *adj by 1852* Obese; porcine: *. . . a porky, middle-aged waitress with a mustache and bad feet*—Lawrence Sanders

porn or **porno** *first form by 1970, second by 1952* **1** *n* Pornography; a pornographic film, book, etc: *. . . the merry world of pimps and porno*—Judith Crist/ *. . . or witness the amount of porn around*—Saturday Review/ *. . . I found out about the porno Rita'd made. . .*—Stan Cutler **2** *adj*: *The very best porn film ever made*—New York Times/ *. . . little prospect of pay-TV turning our homes into porno palaces*—David Lachenbruch

porny *adj by 1961* Pornographic

portsider 1 *n by 1934* A lefthanded person; =SOUTHPAW: *We despair that portsiders will ever get their rights*—Philadelphia Record **2** *n baseball by 1926* A lefthanded baseball pitcher

poser *n 1980s teenagers* A person who pretends to have various desirable traits and tastes; poseur: *My son also told me that there are also people called "posers" who DRESS like "bassers" but are, in fact, secretly "preppies"*—Dave Barry [the revival of a term found by 1888]

posh *adj by 1903* Luxurious; fancy; chic; =CUSHY: *The apartment. . . is now rather posh*—A Logan [origin uncertain; perhaps fr the mid–1800s term *posh*, "money," fr Romany *pash*, "a half," referring to a half-penny; perhaps fr mid–1800s *posh*, "a dandy," of unknown origin; perhaps fr early 1900s Cambridge University slang *push* or *poosh*, "stylish"; perhaps a mispronunciation of *polish*; improbably an acronym for *port out starboard home*, said to be the formula for choosing the side of the ship with the most comfortable cabins on the steamer route from England to India or return; perhaps none of the above]

posse *n 1980s black teenagers*: *I thought posses were Jamaican. . . Language changes very fast here, now it just means a small gang*—Robert B Parker [probably fr the sheriff's *posse* seen so often in cowboy movies]
See PUSSY POSSE

possum belly *n phr hoboes by 1940s* An extra storage compartment under a railroad car [fr the marsupial pouch of an *opossum*]

postal *teenagers by middle 1990s* **1** *n*: *postal–1) A state of irrational, psychotic anger and disorientation*—Macon Telegraph **2** *adj*: *postal–2) Whacko, flipped*—Macon Telegraph
See GO POSTAL

postcard *See* FRENCH POSTCARD

posted *adj by 1850* Informed; =IN THE PICTURE: *If you hear anything, you might keep me posted*

poster boy (or **girl** or **child**) *n phr by 1980s* Someone given prominence in a certain cause: *The Bible-thumpers portray Col. North as the poster boy for the religious right*—Nation/ *Mary Matalin, for all her new visibility as a GOP poster girl, is actually a moderate*—Vanity Fair/ *Marky Mark* *became the poster child of the baby teens, smiling with sweet innocence in his Calvin Klein underwear from billboards around the country*—New York Times [fr the appealing children appearing on posters in the 1930s and following, soliciting money for various disease-fighting organizations]

post holes *See* A LOAD OF VW RADIATORS

pot[1] **1** *n gambling by 1847* The total amount bet on a hand of poker or some other gambling matter; =KITTY: *The goulashes' takeout was 5 percent of the pot*—T Betts **2** *n by about 1930* A rather obnoxious person, esp an unattractive woman; =PILL: *. . . one of the pots that sat at the table*—Jerome Weidman **3** *n by 1928* =BEER BELLY, POTBELLY **4** *n by 1941* A carburetor **5** *n 1950s hot rodders* A car engine **6** *n railroad by about 1930* A locomotive **7** *v by 1860* To shoot: *He potted a woodchuck* [all senses fr cooking *pot*, as something containing a *pot*-luck mess of food, something sooty and unattractive, something fat-looking, something to be filled by hitting the hunt's prey, etc]

See COFFEE POT, GO TO POT, NOT HAVE A POT TO PISS IN, RUMPOT, SEXPOT, a SHITLOAD, STEEL POT, TINPOT

pot[2] *1930s narcotics* **1** *n* Marijuana; =GRASS, TEA: *Most of the parties I had been invited to recently, pot had been passed around freely*—New York Times **2** *modifier*: *a pot party* [perhaps fr Mexican Spanish *potiguaya*, "marijuana leaves"]

pot[3] *n by 1940s* A potentiometer

the pot *n phr by 1705* The toilet; =CRAPPER: *. . . closed the stall door, and sat down on the pot*—Richard Fariña [fr *chamber-pot*, which is found by 1570]

See SHIT OR GET OFF THE POT

potato **1** *n by 1931* A dollar: *You can get this wonderful coat for 497 potatoes*—Time **2** *n baseball by 1940s* A baseball

See ALL THAT MEAT AND NO POTATOES, COUCH POTATO, HOT POTATO, MEAT AND POTATOES, SMALL POTATOES, SWEET POTATO

potato-head *n by 1832* A stupid person

potato patch *See* FRUIT SALAD

potato-trap or **tater-trap** *n by 1843* The mouth

potbelly or **potgut** *first form by 1714, second by 1909* **1** *n* A protuberant belly; paunch; =BEER BELLY, POT **2** *n* A person with a potbelly, esp a man

potbelly (or **belly) stove** *n phr middle 1800s* An old-fashioned stove, esp a rotund one: *. . . rickety armchairs around the big belly stove*—Joseph Mitchell

potboiler *n by 1864* A book, play, etc, written just to get money, esp something done rather badly by a writer who can do very well [fr the notion that one does such work only to keep the food *pot boiling* in the domicile]

potch *by 1892* **1** *n* A slap, esp to a child **2** *v* To slap or spank a child **3** *v* To slap; bump: *. . . potching against the waves in a plastic foam Sunflower*—Philadelphia Journal [fr Yiddish fr German *patsch*, "smack, splash"]

potchkie or **potchky** or **potsky** (PAHCH kee) *v*

(Variation: **around** may be added) *by 1950* To putter; tinker; =MESS: *The dentist potchkied around in Stanley's mouth*—Esquire/ *. . . how you could potsky around with such superstitions*—Billy Rose [fr Yiddish fr German *patschen*, "splash, slap"]

pot-gutted *adj by 1773* Having a paunch; big-bellied

pothead *n 1960s narcotics* A user of marijuana, esp a heavy user: *a few potheads who don't move up from marijuana*—New York Times

pothooks *n by 1795* One's handwriting; scribble; =HEN TRACKS

pothunter *n by 1958* A person who scavenges in abandoned buildings, towns, fields etc: *Cemeteries are also considered fair game for pothunters*—Wall Street Journal [probably an informal term for "archeologist," since *pots* and *pot* fragments are so crucial to their work]

pot liquor *n by 1744* The residue left in a pot after cooking: *. . . rubbed him. . . with pot liquor to give him strength*—Carson McCullers

pot luck *by 1600* **1** *n phr* A meal composed of odds and ends of leftovers, or of whatever turns up **2** *adv phr*: *Come on and dine pot luck* **3** *modifier*: *pot-luck supper*

pot out *v phr 1950s hot rodders* To stop running; fail; =CONK OUT

pot party *n phr 1960s narcotics* A gathering or party for the purpose of smoking marijuana in company; =BLAST PARTY

potshot *See* TAKE A POTSHOT AT someone

potsy **1** *n New York City by 1931* The game of hop-scotch **2** *n police by 1932* A police badge: *Ernie goes in the lobby and flashes his potsy*—Lawrence Sanders [game name perhaps a variant of the nickname *Patsy*; police sense fr resemblance of the badge to a *potsy*, the piece of squashed tin used in the game]

potted or **potted up** **1** *adj* or *adj phr by 1922* Drunk **2** *adj* or *adj phr 1960s narcotics* Intoxicated by marijuana or another narcotic: *. . . all potted up on something*—E Trujillo

◁**a pot to piss in**▷ *See* NOT HAVE A POT TO PISS IN

potty **1** *n by 1940s* A young child's toilet seat and chamber pot **2** *n*: *. . . failure to perform potty at the proper hour*—Time **3** *n by 1940s* Any toilet **4** *modifier*: *. . . time out for a potty break*—Playboy **5** *adj by 1920* Slightly crazy; eccentric; =DOTTY, GOOFY

potty-mouth *n by 1960s* A person who uses foul and scatological language: *Margaret Cho describes herself as a kind of potty-mouth in her standup act*—New York Times

potty talk *n phr by 1990s* Foul and scatological language: *. . . the use of profanity, epithets and potty talk on TV jumped 45 percent from 1990 to '94*—Wisconsin State Journal

pot-walloper **1** *n by 1860* A pot and pan washer **2** *n loggers by 1902* A cook

potzer *See* PATZER

pouffe *See* POOF

pound ◁1▷ *v* by 1970s To do the sex act to or with; =SCREW **2** *v* by 1980s To drink, esp beer: *Let's knock off and go pound some Budweiser*—Bryan Di Salvatore

pound brass *v phr* telegraphers & radio operators by 1940s To transmit telegraph or radio-telegraph signals with a key

◁**poundcake**▷ *n* by 1970s An attractive young woman [fr the vulgar sense of *pound*]

pound one's **ear** *v phr* by 1894 To sleep, esp heavily

pounder *n* by 1938 A police officer, esp one who walks, "pounds," a beat
See BRASS-POUNDER, HAIR-POUNDER

◁**pound** one's **meat**▷ *See* BEAT one's MEAT

◁**pound** one's **peenie**▷ *v phr* by 1970s To masturbate; =BEAT one's MEAT: *Who is he mooning over as he pounds his peenie?*—John Farris

pound salt (or **sand**) *v phr* by 1950s =GO FUCK oneself: *The Brooklyn strike force seemed unwilling to share any information. They told Giacalone to pound sand*—Vanity Fair
See GO POUND SALT

pound the books *v phr* students by about 1935 To study hard; =HIT THE BOOKS

pound the pavement (Variations: **pavements** or **the sidewalks** or **the streets** may replace **the pavement**) by 1940s **1** *v phr* To walk a police beat **2** *v phr* To trudge about the streets, esp looking for work: *... the liberal arts graduates... pounding the Park Avenue pavements*—New York Magazine

poured into one's **garment** *adj phr* by 1940s Wearing very tight and revealing clothing: *She's in those TV commercials, poured into her jeans*

pour it on by 1940s **1** *v phr* To make an intense effort; maximize striving: *Henry Gonzalez was pouring it on thick*—New Republic **2** *v phr* To exert all one's charm and persuasiveness; =COME ON STRONG: *He was really pouring it on to that judge* **3** *v phr* To speed; =POUR ON THE COAL: *The driver was pouring it on to close the gap*—J Evans

pour money down the drain (or **the rathole**) *v phr* by 1970s To waste money utterly; spend hugely for nothing: *The Legislature is not going to pour more money down that rathole*—Philadelphia Journal

pour on the coal *v phr* by 1937 To travel very fast; speed up; =STEP ON IT: *The pilot apparently decided to go around again and poured on the coal*—Associated Press

pout-out *n* 1950s hot rodders Engine failure in a hot rod

pow 1 *interj* by 1881 An imitation of a blow, collision, explosion, etc, used for sudden emphasis or to show sudden understanding: *Suddenly bells went off and I knew that was it! Pow!*—New York Post **2** *n* by 1960s Power; influence; =CLOUT: *... only be apprehended by government action, that is, by political "pow"*—Gus Tyler [second sense reinforced by *power*]

powder 1 *v* underworld by 1920 To leave; depart hastily, esp in escaping: *We better powder* **2** *n*: *Bonnie murdered a constable during the powder*—A Hynd **3** *v* baseball by 1940s To hit very hard; =PULVERIZE: *... after he had powdered the second pitch*—Associated Press **4** *n* baseball by 1932 The speed of a pitch, esp very high speed; =STUFF [sense of running away probably fr similar *dust* fr the notion of raising dust as one runs; perhaps, in view of *take a powder* and *run-out powder,* the basic notion is reinforced by that of taking a medicinal *powder,* esp a laxative, so that one has to leave in a hurry, or perhaps a magical *powder* that would cause one to disappear]
See FLEA POWDER, FOOLISH POWDER, JOY-POWDER, RUN-OUT POWDER, TAKE A POWDER

powder city *adj phr* baseball by 1970s Pitching very fast: *The big lefthander's really powder city today!*

powderman *n* by 1980s An explosives expert: *That's powderman... in the trade*—Elmore Leonard

powder monkey *n phr* loggers & miners by 1926 A person who works with explosives in mining, construction, etc [found by 1682 designating a boy who handles gunpowder aboard a warship]

powderpuff 1 *n* prizefighting by 1940s A cautious, agile fighter as distinct from a slugger **2** *v*: *He just powderpuffed his opponent until he tired* **3** *adj* by 1930s For or involving women; women's: *... the pampered, powderpuff existence of the Ultra-feminine*—Eldridge Cleaver **4** *adj* by 1930s Trifling; insignificant: *Reagan offers reporters only powder-puff photo opportunities*—New York Magazine

power *v* baseball by 1940s To hit the ball very hard: *He powered that one to the wall*
See FLOWER POWER

powerhouse by 1915 **1** *n* A formidable team, organization, etc: *Georgia Tech, another powerhouse*—Associated Press/ *Texas Instruments, a powerhouse in electronics* **2** *n* An energetic and effective person **3** *n* A vigorous, muscular person, esp an athlete **4** *n* Anything that constitutes winning force: *If you control six votes that's a powerhouse*

power lunch *n* (Variations: **breakfast** or **feeding** may replace **lunch**) by middle 1980s A meal calculated to increase or negotiate influence; a feed where important matters are on the table: *Mr. Trump was seen at both a power breakfast and a power lunch yesterday/ If you still believe that the Four Seasons and 44 are the only places that matter for Manhattan media power feeding...*—Vanity Fair

power pop *n phr* by 1990s A kind of music: *The Riverdales' self-titled debut is about as straight ahead and unalienated as punk-derived power pop gets*—Macon Telegraph

power trip *n phr* by middle 1960s A show of personal power, esp of a blatant sort: *... the classic Latin American dictator's power trip*—Toronto Life [based on the narcotics sense of *trip*]

pow-wow *n* by 1625 A meeting; discussion: *The directors are having a crucial pow-wow* [ultimately fr an Algonquian word for "medicine man," meaning "he dreams," extended to mean counsel and a council]

PR or **pr** (pronounced as separate letters) **1** *n* by 1940s Public relations **2** *modifier*: *the PR department*

practice *See* SKULL PRACTICE

prairie oysters *See* MOUNTAIN OYSTERS

prat or **pratt** *n* by 1567 The buttocks; =ASS: *He does not fall on his prat*—Time [origin unknown]

pratfall *fr theater* **1** *n* by 1939 A fall on one's rump, esp by a clown or comedian: *. . . a perfect pratfall*—Edmund Wilson **2** *n* by 1950 A humiliating defeat; an embarrassing humiliation: *. . . the principles and pratfalls of the rhyming racket*—Billy Rose

prayer *See* HAVE A PRAYER

prayer bones *n phr* by 1889 The knees

prayer book *See* CALIFORNIA PRAYER BOOK

pray to the porcelain god *v phr* 1970s *college students* To vomit in the toilet

preem *theater* by 1937 **1** *n* A first showing or performance; premiere: *. . . set for an Oct 4 preem*—Variety **2** *v*: *. . . show which preems via ABC*—New York Daily News [fr *premiere*]

preemie or **preemy** or **premie** *n* by 1927 A premature baby: *. . . like a human preemie, it was placed in an Isolette*—Time

preggers *adj* by 1942 Pregnant: *Meredith gets preggers by Jos*—Playboy

preggy **1** *adj* by 1938 Pregnant **2** *n*: *Six preggies were waiting to see the doctor*

pregnant duck *See* RUPTURED DUCK

prego by 1980s **1** *n* A pregnant teenager **2** *adj* Pregnant: *. . . as if one-half the female population is. . . prego*—Ebony

prelim (PREE lim) **1** *n* *prizefighting* by early 1930s A professional boxing match coming before the main match in a given program **2** *n* by 1891 A preliminary qualifying examination

premed (PREE med) *college students* by 1940s **1** *n* A premedical student **2** *n* A premedical course of study or major **3** *modifier*: *a required premed course*

pre-nup *n* by 1990s A pre-marital agreement, primarily about money and property, made by persons about to marry: *A Federal court decision may mean hundreds of thousands of pre-nups are irrelevant*—New York Times [shortening of *pre-nuptial*]

prep **1** *adj* by 1895 Preparatory; preparing a student for college or university **2** *n* by 1895 A preparatory school: *She went to Georgetown Prep* **3** *v* *students* by 1915 To go to preparatory school: *Where'd you prep?*—F Scott Fitzgerald **4** *n* by 1980s =PREPPIE: *If you don't listen to Green Day or Nirvana, then you're a "prep"*—React **5** *n* *medical* by 1927 Preparation; preliminary steps: *The nurses did the prep for the operation* **6** *v* by 1934 To prepare; get ready: *. . . a pitcher who has prepped earnestly for many years*—Arthur Daley [prep, "stu-

dent at a preparatory school," is found by 1890, and *prepster* by the 1940s]

preppie or **preppy** **1** *n* (also **prepster**) by 1970s A student or graduate of a preparatory school: *Wouldja please watch your profanity, Preppie?*—Erich Segal/ *. . . five soft-spoken indie prepsters who happen to rule nice-kid noise pop. . .*—Seventeen **2** *adj* Typical of the manners, attitudes, folkways, etc, of preppies: *The handshake is firm and preppy*—J Cameron [preppy, "silly, immature," is found by 1900]

prep school **1** *n phr* by 1895 A preparatory school, usu rather expensive and aristocratic **2** *adj*: *prep school grad*

prequel *n* by 1973 A book, episode, etc, that precedes an existing work in time ●Not very precisely differentiated from *flashback*: *. . . what Hollywood calls a "prequel," an adventure that takes place at the start of his career*—Time [based on *sequel*]

pres (PREZ) *n* (also **prez** or **prex** or **prexy** or **prexie**) by 1940s, *prex* by 1828, *prexy* by 1871 A president

press *See* FULL COURT PRESS

press roll *n phr* *musicians* by 1934 A snare-drum roll in which the loosely-held sticks are pressed onto the drumhead and allowed to vibrate

press the bricks **1** *v phr* *loggers* by 1940s To loaf in town **2** *v phr* by 1920s To walk a police beat; =POUND THE PAVEMENT: *Go press the bricks*—WR Burnett

press the flesh (or **the skin**) **1** *v phr* by 1926 To shake hands ●Used chiefly of politicians and others who ingratiate themselves with the public **2** *adj*: *Williams conducted a press-the-flesh campaign*—Newsweek

pressure cooker **1** *n phr* by 1958 A place or situation of great personal stress: *. . . the pressure cooker on the Hudson*—Gore Vidal **2** *modifier*: *. . . flung into the pressure-cooker existence of live TV*—Pauline Kael

pretty *adv* by 1565 Quite; more than a little: *The weather's pretty rotten* *See* be SITTING PRETTY

pretty boy **1** *n* by 1885 A man who is good-looking in an epicene way; an effeminate dandy **2** *modifier*: *. . . their "pretty boy" young preacher*—Malcolm X **3** *n* *circus* by about 1931 A bouncer or professional strong man

pretty ear *n phr* *prizefighting* by 1930 An ear deformed from blows; =CAULIFLOWER EAR: *. . . busted bones and pretty ear*—W R Burnett

pretty face *See* NOT JUST ANOTHER PRETTY FACE

pretty kettle of fish *n phr* by 1742 A new and probably unfortunate circumstance: *Here's a pretty kettle of fish; his teeth went down the drain*

a **pretty penny** *n phr* by 1768 A lot of money: *That car cost him a pretty penny*

pretzel *n* *musicians* by 1936 A French horn *See* the BIG PRETZEL

pretzel-bender *n* *musicians* by 1936 A French horn player

previous *n* by 1935 An earlier conviction: *Kid looks clean; no previous*

prexy or **Prexy** or **prexie** or **Prexie** *See* PRES

prez or **Prez** *See* PRES

pricey or **pricy** *adj* by 1932 Expensive; dear •Chiefly British: *Godiva chocolates and other pricey goodies*—Philadelphia Journal

◁**prick**▷ **1** *n* by 1592 The penis; =COCK **2** *n* by 1929 A detestable person, esp a man; obnoxious wretch; =ASSHOLE, BASTARD: *He's an antagonistic prick*—Rolling Stone [Farmer and Henley's *Slang and its Analogues* includes six and a half pages of synonyms in the 1896 volume]

pricklies *See* COLD PRICKLIES

◁**prick-teaser**▷ *See* COCK-TEASER

pricky or **prickish** *adj* by 1960s Obnoxious; detestable: *What a pricky kid*—Philip Roth/ *. . . a prickish man*—Changes

prima donna *n phr* by 1936 A person of great and touchy self-esteem; a person who requires to be the sole focus of adulatory attention and who indulges in temperamental displays [fr Italian, literally "first lady," a title for superstar opera singers and the like]

primo *n* 1990s narcotics Crack cocaine smoked with marijuana

prince *n* by 1911 A very decent and admirable person; =ACE •Often used ironically: *He told me he thinks you're a goddam prince*—J D Salinger

Prince *See* JEWISH AMERICAN PRINCE

Princess *See* JEWISH AMERICAN PRINCESS

print 1 *n* by 1924 A fingerprint: *My prints ain't on that gun*—Erle Stanley Gardner **2** *v* by 1938: *They printed me*—Erle Stanley Gardner
See FINGERPRINT, the SMALL PRINT

print money *See* a LICENSE TO PRINT MONEY

prior *n* by 1978 An earlier conviction; =PREVIOUS: *"Any priors on him?" "Dinged once, in Rapid City"*—Carsten Stroud

prissy 1 *adj* by 1895 Overfastidious; primly censorious: *He has a prissy distaste for heavy shoes* **2** *n*: *. . . these do-gooding prissies*—Newsweek [origin uncertain; perhaps a blend of *prim* or *precise* with *sissy*]

private *See* BUCK PRIVATE

private dick or **private eye** *n phr* entry form by 1908, variant by 1938 A private detective; a private investigator; =PI

privates *n* by 1846 The genitals; private parts

privy *n* by 1662 An outdoor toilet without plumbing; =BACKHOUSE, CHIC SALE

no **prize package** *See* NO PRIZE PACKAGE

pro[1] **1** *n* by 1866 A professional in any field, as distinct from an amateur, and mainly distinguished by superior and dependable performance: *. . . hear his song played and sung by pros*—C Lowry **2** *modifier*: *pro ranks* **3** *n* by 1937 A prostitute: *He treats all women like pros and all men like enemies*—Budd Schulberg [the last sense perhaps fr *professional* reinforced by *prostitute*, or vice versa]

pro[2] *n* WWII armed forces A prophylactic for preventing venereal disease; condom; =RUBBER

pro[3] **1** *n* by 1950s Probation, as a judicial sentence **2** *n* A person on probation

pro-am *adj* by 1949 Admitting or including both professional and amateur performers, esp athletes; open: *a pro-am golf tournament*

process *n* black by 1960s =CONK

production *See* MAKE A BIG PRODUCTION OUT OF something

production line *n phr* hockey by 1940s A high-scoring offensive line [based on the industrial *production line*, the term found by 1935]

prof *n* college students by 1838 Professor

professor 1 *n* by 1940s An orchestra leader **2** *n* by 1930s The piano player in a saloon, brothel, etc: *. . . the job of regular professor*—A Lomax

profile black by 1960s **1** *v* To strut and attitudinize; =SHOW OFF: *Now, right now, you're profiling. . . And I'm being bored* **2** *v* To display prominently and proudly; =SHOW OFF: *He was profiling his new Mercedes*—Delcastle Dictionary of Slang [fr the notion of displaying one's handsome *profile*]
See KEEP A LOW PROFILE, LOW PROFILE

prog *n* by 1655 Food [origin unknown; perhaps fr obsolete *prog*, "poke and forage about," of obscure origin]

program *v* fr computers by 1966 To train; predispose by rigorous teaching, condition: *He's programmed to be polite to old ladies and all*
See CRASH PROGRAM

project *See* CRASH PROGRAM

projo or **pro Joe** *n* or *n phr* Army by 1970s An artillery projectile

pro-kit or **pro-pack** *n* WWII armed forces A kit for preventing venereal disease, including condoms and a medicament to be injected into the meatus [fr *prophylactic kit*]

prole (PROHL) *n* by 1887 A member of the lower or working class: *Chez Tom Wolfe proles, for example, wear new down coats*—Atlantic Monthly [fr *proletarian*, "member of the working class," ultimately fr Latin; popularized by George Orwell's 1949 novel *Nineteen Eighty-Four*]

prom 1 *n* students by 1894 A dance, esp a formal ball in celebration of graduation from high school: *. . . neither the fraternity dance nor the Prom*—P Marks **2** *modifier*: *prom queen* [fr *promenade*]

promise *See* a LICK AND A PROMISE

promo (PROH moh) by 1963 **1** *n* Advertising and promotion: *Who's handling the promo for this show?* **2** *n* A film, tape, printed piece, etc, for promotion: *He shot some promos for his syndicated TV show*—New Yorker

promote 1 *v* underworld by about 1920 To get, esp by theft, hard persuasion, or begging: *We got to promote a boat to run the stuff in*—American Mercury **2** *v* by 1934 To accost in an acquisitive spirit; =HIT: *. . . begun promoting him for something to drink*—James M Cain

promotion *See* MEXICAN PROMOTION

◁**prong**▷ by 1969 **1** *n* The penis; =PRICK **2** *v* To do the sex act to or with; =SCREW: . . . *every guy who had ever pronged her*—Earl Thompson

◁**prong on**▷ *n phr by 1970s* A penile erection; =HARD-ON: *I got this huge prong on*—George V Higgins

pronto *adv by 1850* Immediately; quickly; =PDQ [fr Spanish]

prop[1] *n theater by 1841* An article used on stage or in a film; property

prop[2] *n by 1914* A propeller

propeller head *n phr by middle 1980s* A computer expert or enthusiast; =GEEK, NERD: *Interactive multimedia software? The propeller heads live for this stuff*—New York Times [fr their visualization as wearing ridiculous little beanies with propellers on top]

property *See* HOT PROPERTY

proposition *by 1924* **1** *v* To request sexual favors; =COME ON TO someone, MAKE A PASS AT someone: *He propositioned every woman at the party* **2** *n* An invitation or request for sexual favors; =PASS: *He made a rude proposition and got his ears pinned back* [defined as "a proposal of marriage" in a 1908 source]

props[1] **1** *n theater by about 1900* The property manager at a theater or movie studio **2** *n* =FALSIES
See KNOCK THE PROPS FROM UNDER

props[2] *n 1990s black teenagers* Proper respect: *. . . the boys. . . described how they gain "props," or popularity, by yelling explicit propositions or fondling girls who pass by. . .* —New York Times

prosty *n* (also **prostie** or **pross** or **prossy** or **prossie**) *by 1930; pross and prossy variants by 1896* A prostitute: *. . . a retired prosty*—Playboy/ *. . . the dedicated pross with a meter ticking under her skirt*—New York Magazine

prowl *v by 1914* To search by running the hands over the person; =FRISK: *. . . prowled me over carefully with his left hand*—Raymond Chandler
See ON THE PROWL

prowl car *n phr by 1940s* A police squad car

prune **1** *n by 1895* A pedantic, stiff, and prudish person; =PRISSY **2** *v 1940s hot rodders* To accelerate faster than another car in a race **3** *n medical by 1980s* Dehydrated nursing home patient

prune-picker *n by 1918* A Californian

prunes *See* FULL OF BEANS

pruno *n by 1940s* Any fermented fruit juice, esp prune juice

prushon or **prushun** *hoboes by 1893* **1** *n* A boy tramp who begs for an adult tramp: *. . . a prushon, who averaged. . . $3 a day*—J Flynt **2** *n* A young homosexual who lives with tramps [origin unknown]

ps and qs *See* MIND one's PS AND QS

pseud (SooD) **1** *n by 1968* Someone or something false; a fraud; =FAKE, PHONY **2** *adj by 1962*: *That guy is really pseud, with all his big talk* [fr pseudo]

psych **1** *n college students by 1895* Psychology, esp as an academic study **2** *modifier by 1940s* Psychiatry; psychiatric: *. . . makes it down from the psych ward on the 15th floor*—Maclean's **3** *v* (also

psych out) *college students by 1934* To outsmart another person: *The bastards psyched me* **4** *v* (also **psych out**) *by 1961* To sense or infer the motives, behavior, etc, of others; feel out a situation: *. . . an uncanny ability to "psych out" audiences and make them love her*—Saturday Review **5** *v* (also **psych out**) *by 1960s* To unnerve someone; cause someone to lose composure, will, skill, etc: *He won't psych me as he did her*—New York Post

psych oneself or **psych** oneself **up** *v phr by 1972* To arouse oneself emotionally, spiritually, mentally, etc, to a maximum effort; raise oneself to a state of keen readiness and capability; =PUMP oneself UP: *That's almost a whole year of psyching yourself up as high as you can go*—Esquire/ *. . . I tried to psyche myself for this new challenge*—Anne Bernays

psyched or **psyched up** *adj* or *adj phr by 1968* In a state of excited preparedness and heightened keenness; =PUMPED UP: *They were all psyched up to carry the blue and white banner of Catawba College*—Charlotte Observer/ *. . . are generally so psyched that elation becomes their bottom line*—S Shapiro
See GET PSYCHED

psych-jockey *n by 1970s* The host and consultant of a radio or television call-in program on personal, emotional, sexual, and general psychological subjects [fr blend of *psychology* and *disc jockey*]

psycho **1** *n by 1942* A crazy person; maniac; psychopath; =NUT: *. . . no buzzing broad, no nympho, no psycho, no bitch*—Pauline Kael **2** *adj*: *. . . a special psycho channel that I know nothing about*—New York Magazine [probably fr *psychotic*; the form *psychot*, "psychopath," is found by the 1940s]

psychobabble **1** *n by 1976* Talk about self, feelings, motives, etc, esp in psychological jargon: *His characters have absorbed the attitudes of post–1960s psychobabble, and tend to say things like "Viet Nam is a reality warp. . . "*—New York Times **2** *v*: *"If you want space," she tells a psychobabbling boyfriend, "go to Utah"*—Village Voice

psych up *v phr by 1957* To bring to a state of keen attention; excite and incite; =PUMP UP

psywar (SĪ wawr) **1** *n by 1954* Psychological warfare **2** *modifier*: *. . . an impressively orchestrated psywar operation*—New Republic

◁**pt** or **PT**▷ (pronounced as separate letters) *n by 1960s* =PRICK-TEASER

pub[1] *n British by 1859* A saloon; bar; tavern: *. . . a round of Long Island pubs*—New York Daily News [fr British *public*, fr *public house*]

pub[2] *n by 1990s* Publicity: *You know Dallas is going to get all that pub*—Milwaukee Journal

pub crawl **1** *v British by about 1910* To carouse about from one saloon to another **2** *n*: *They went on a memorable pub crawl afterwards* [*gin crawl* is found by 1883, and *beer crawl* by 1902]
See BARHOP

pubes (PYoo beez) *n students by 1960s* Adolescent females; =TEENYBOPPER [fr *pubescent*]

pucker 1 *n by 1741* Fear; state of fright: *Don't get into such a pucker* **2** *modifier*: *The U.S. ships were taking no chances: as Capt. Mathis told his crew members, one mine is enough to keep the pucker factor up*—Time

◁**pucker-assed**▷ *adj by 1970s* Timid; fearful; =CHICKEN [fr *pucker*]

◁**pud**▷ (PUHD, PooD) **1** *n by 1939* The penis **2** *n 1980s teenagers* An obnoxious person; =JERK, DORK: *A dexter, that's your basic nerd, dork, or pud*—North Jersey Herald and News [fr slang sense of *pudding*]
See PULL one's PUD

◁**pudding**▷ *n by 1719* The penis: *You can't even come off unless you pull your own pudding*—Philip Roth

puddinghead *n by 1851* A stupid person, esp one who is also amiable: *. . . a natural nitwit, a puddinghead, a stand-up comedian*—WT Tyler

puddle-jumper *by 1932* **1** *n* A small or rickety vehicle: *I wouldn't ride in that puddle-jumper* **2** *n* An aircraft that makes several stops along a cross-country route

◁**pudlicker**▷ *n by 1990s* A person who does fellatio; =COCKSUCKER, DICKLICKER: *. . . asking when my new column, "Pudlicker to the Celebrated," was going to start*—New Yorker

◁**pud-pulling**▷ **1** *n by 1939* Masturbation: *. . . a frenzied bout of pud-pulling*—Village Voice **2** *modifier*: *a stupid pud-pulling jerk*

puff 1 *n* (also **puffery** or **puff job**) *by 1732*, puffery *by 1782* A specimen of extravagant praise, esp for commercial or political purposes; =PLUG **2** *v by 1858*: *There is little need for us to puff this book*—Saturday Review
See CREAM PUFF, POWDERPUFF

puffer **See** PINK PUFFER

puff piece *n phr by 1980s* Something written in extravagant praise, esp for sales purposes; =HYPE: *But as my brassy page-one editor would say, those portrayals are puff pieces*—Entertainment Weekly

puffy 1 *adj by 1664* Obese; bloated: *. . . these strutting athletes and puffy officials. . .* —New York Times **2** *adj by 1980* Very favorable; adulatory; drum-beating: *Even the stern* People's Daily *ran extraordinarily puffy coverage of Reagan*—Time

pug *n by 1858* A prizefighter or boxer; pugilist [fr *pugilist*]

puke 1 *v by 1600* To vomit **2** *n* Vomit; spew **3** *n by 1961* Something so disgusting that it might be vomit and the cause of vomit: *Who wrote this puke?*

puke-in *n by 1960s* A public occasion where participants vomit together in order to make some point or other

puker *n Pacific Northwest by 1970s* A charter fishing boat

puky or **pukey** *adj by 1965* Nasty; inferior; disgusting: *It's a pukey sort of ballad*

pull 1 *n by 1886* Influence; special power or favor; =CLOUT: *. . . irregularities and instances of political pull*—Associated Press **2** *v by 1436* To drink; take a swallow: *. . . a 17-year-old kid pulling on a beer*—

Toronto Life **3** *n by 1575* A gulp of a drink, a puff on a cigarette, etc: *I took a big pull at my drink and looked up* **4** *v* (also **pull down**) *by 1937*, variant *by 1917* To earn; receive;: *I pulled an A on the quiz/ The seven magazines. . . pull down nearly $700 million a year. . .* —Wired **5** *v by 1916* To do; perform; effect, esp a trick or shady act: *What are they trying to pull now?*
See LEG-PULL

pull a boner (or **a bonehead play**) *v phr by 1913* To blunder; commit an error, esp an egregious one: *I'm afraid you've pulled a boner this time; the thing sank*

pull a fast one *v phr by 1933* To execute or attempt a deception; achieve a clever fraud or swindle; =PULL something ON someone: *You're accusing me of trying to pull a fast one?*—Saul Bellow [probably fr *fast shuffle*]

pull a line *v phr by 1940s* To try to persuade or deceive someone with a false, overelaborate story, appeal, etc; =BULLSHIT: *She's honest, never pulls a line*

pull an all-nighter *v phr 1980s teenagers & students* To study all night

pull (or **do**) **an el foldo** *v phr by 1962* To lose energy; wilt; fade; =FOLD: *The Saints chose that time to pull an el foldo*—Sports Illustrated
See EL FOLDO

pull a one-eighty *v phr* Make a complete change of direction; make an about-face: *Of course the right quickly found itself obliged to pull a one-eighty. . .* —New Yorker [because *180* degrees indicates an exactly opposite heading on an azimuth compass]

pull a swifty (or **swiftie**) *v phr Australian by 1960s* =PULL A FAST ONE

◁**pull a train** (or **the train** or **the choo-choo**)▷ *v phr motorcyclists by 1965* Of a woman, to do the sex act with several men serially: *. . . taking some dame in the woods and making her pull a train*—TV show Rockford Files

pull a vanishing act *v phr by 1981* To disappear; =TAKE A POWDER: *That may be exactly why he's pulled a vanishing act. . .* —Hugh Pentecost [fr a magician's *vanishing* or causing someone to do so; in the form *do a vanishing act* found by 1923]

pull someone's **chain** (Variations: **jerk** or **rattle** may replace **pull**; **string** may replace **chain**) *by 1980s* **1** *v phr* To deceive; fool; =PULL A FAST ONE: *. . . too busy trying to figure out if I had been pulling his chain*—Richard Price **2** *v phr* To upset someone; anger someone: *I did not know you can rattle his chain with marvelous results*—Washington Post/ *He was insecure and sensitive. It was easy to pull his string*—New York Times [probably fr the image of a person who upsets a captive animal by *pulling* or *jerking* at its *chain*]

puller **See** WIRE-PULLER

pull (or **drag**) one's **freight** *v phr by 1895* To leave; depart quickly: *This bird's gonna pull his freight*—W R Burnett

pull one's **head out** *v phr* 1960s students To pay attention to one's affairs; wake up: *You better pull your head out and get to studying or you won't graduate*—Current Slang [shortening and euphemizing of *pull your head out of your ass*]

pull in *v phr* by 1905 To arrive: *She pulled in about noon* [fr railroad]

pull someone **in** *v phr* by 1891 To arrest someone; =RUN someone IN

pull in one's **ears** by 1940s **1** *v phr* To be cautious; watch out for oneself **2** *v phr* To be less aggressive; moderate oneself: *You better pull in your ears a little or you'll scare them away* [origin uncertain; perhaps in some cases an alteration of *pull in one's horns*]

pull in one's **horns** *v phr* by 1589 To moderate or retract one's behavior; =BACK OFF: *The USFL Pulled In Its Financial Horns*—Inside Sports [fr the way an anxious snail behaves]

pull it off *v phr* by 1887 To accomplish something; succeed; =MAKE IT: *. . . pull it off and keep the patients coming back for more*—San Francisco

pull someone's **leg** *v phr* by 1886 To deceive in fun; fool; =KID: *I suspected that he was pulling my leg*—F Scott Fitzgerald [fr the act of playfully tripping someone]

Pullman *See* SIDE-DOOR PULLMAN

pull numbers or **get digits** *v phr* by 1990s To succeed in getting the telephone numbers of potential dates, escorts, etc

pull off 1 *v phr* by 1883 To succeed in or at; achieve: *Fegley managed to pull off a hat trick for this issue*—Playboy ◁**2**▷ *v phr* by 1922 To masturbate: *At Smolka's signal, each begins to pull off*—Philip Roth

◁**pull** oneself **off**▷ *v phr* by about 1900 To masturbate; =JACK OFF

◁**pull** someone **off**▷ *v phr* by about 1900 To cause someone to ejaculate semen by manipulating the penis

pull something **on** someone *v phr* by 1916 To deceive or cheat; take advantage of; =PULL A FAST ONE: *At first she thought I was trying to pull a slick scam on her*

pull out 1 *v phr* by 1884 To leave; depart: *He pulled out after 45 minutes and disappeared*—Associated Press **2** *v phr* by 1887 To withdraw; terminate one's association: *He threatened to pull out if we didn't raise the ante*

◁**pull** something **out of** one's **ass**▷ *v phr* Army by 1970s To produce something, esp information or an idea, unexpectedly

pull something **out of the fire** *v phr* by 1893 To salvage something; rescue: *They got hot and pulled the game out of the fire*

◁**pull** one's **pud**▷ (PUHD, PŏŏD) *v phr* (Variations: **dong** or **joint** or **wang** or any other word for "**penis**" may replace **pud**) by 1944 To masturbate; =JACK OFF

pull one's **punches** *v phr* prizefighting by 1934 To soften one's blows; be lenient and moderate: *Ouch. . . You don't pull your punches*—Xaviera Hollander

pull rank *v phr* by 1923 To overwhelm with one's authority; be officiously arrogant: *Each was frightened that the other would pull rank*—Eldridge Cleaver

pull strings (or **wires**) *v phr* entry form by 1860s, variant by 1893 To exert influence; use one's power, esp clandestinely: *If she pulls a few wires I think I might get the job* [probably fr the use of *strings* or *wires* to control marionettes; *work wire* is found by 1886]

pull teeth through the armpit *v phr* armed forces by 1970s To do something in the most difficult way; do something the hard way

pull the plug[1] **1** *v phr* by 1940s To terminate something; end support or cooperation: *. . . if the affiliates. . . rise up in rebellion and pull the plug*—New Yorker **2** *v phr* by 1960s To terminate various mechanical and electronic efforts being used to keep life in a moribund patient [fr the disconnecting of an electrical *plug*]

pull the plug[2] *v phr* Navy by 1970s To dive in a submarine; submerge [fr the withdrawing of a bathtub *plug*]

pull the rug from under (or **out from under**) *v phr* by 1946 To undermine or disable; put opponents at a great and often sudden disadvantage: *They were intended to pull the rug out from under left-wing critics*—Nation

pull the string 1 *v phr* baseball by 1937 To pitch a change-of-pace ball, a very slow ball after the motion for a fast one **2** *v phr* by 1928 To rudely reveal the truth, previously kept hidden; unveil true intentions; reveal the catch ●The full form is *pull the string of the shower bath*: *They doubled their efforts, showering her with affection, then they pulled the string*—Playboy [perhaps fr the use of a *string* to fasten and release a concealing sheet on something about to be unveiled; perhaps fr *pull the lanyard*, "to fire a cannon"]

pull the wool over someone's **eyes** *v phr* by 1842 To deceive; mislead: *The whole indignant act was an attempt to pull the wool over the voters' eyes* [a slightly earlier form is *spread the wool over someone's eyes*]

pull up one's **socks** *v phr* by 1893 To correct one's behavior; look to one's performance; =GET ON THE BALL: *Whittingham was terminated after having failed to pull up his socks enough during six months on probation*—Toronto Life

pull up stakes *v phr* by 1817 To depart; decamp: *If things don't get better we'll pull up stakes*

pulp 1 *n* by 1931 A magazine printed on rough paper and devoted to adventure, science fiction, cowboy stories, rude erotica, etc **2** *modifier*: *a pulp romance*

the pulps *n phr* by 1931 Pulp magazines collectively: *He used to write sci-fi for the pulps*

pulverize *v* by 1631 To defeat thoroughly; punish; =CLOBBER

pump ◁1▷ *v* by *1730* To do the sex act; =FUCK, HUMP: *Duffy wondered if Jert had been pumping Tish*—Harry Crews **2** *v* by *1667* To question long and closely; extract information: *The cops pumped him for three days straight* **3** *n* (also **pumper**) by *1885* The heart; =TICKER: *He had a hole through his pump*—movie *Asphalt Jungle* **4** *v* *1980s* students To excite; =AMP, HYPE, PUMP UP, TURN ON: *That stripper at the party last night really pumped me*—UCLA Slang **5** *n* baseball by *1980s* A home run; =TATER: *He had three pumps yesterday. Three home runs!*—Jane Leavy
See SLUSH PUMP

pump-and-dump *modifier* by *1990s*: *Investigators reported two "pump-and-dump" schemes in which Canadian companies were heavily hyped on computer bulletin board services. Their stock prices tripled or more in a short time, then collapsed*—Milwaukee Journal

pumped and dumped *adj phr* by *1990s* Exploited then rejected; used and discarded: *Poor Emmett is feeling "pumped and dumped"*—Douglas Coupland

pumped up 1 *adj phr* (also **pumped**) by *1980s* Excited and expectant; =PSYCHED UP ●Used often of athletes in or before competition: *The girls were really pumped up*—Playboy/ *. . . was returning to play in his first game in more than two years and this city was pumped*—Milwaukee Journal **2** *adj phr* by *1904* Exaggerated; artificial; =PHONY: *. . . a pumped-up conviviality. Concannon didn't like it*—Barry Reed **3** *adj* *1960s* students Pregnant: *She got pumped and had to quit her job*—Current Slang

pump iron *v phr* by *1980s* To lift weights; do body-building

pumpkin or **pumkin** or **punkin 1** *n* by *1890s* The head **2** *n* by *1940s* One's sweetheart, beloved, spouse, etc; =DOLL, HONEY, SWEETIE: *We're allies in everything, pumpkin*—Robert B Parker

pumpkinhead or **punkinhead** *n* by *1848* A stupid person

pumpkinheaded or **punkinheaded** *adj* by *1607* Stupid; doltish

◁**pumpkin (or punkin) roller**▷ *n phr* by about *1905* A rural person; farmer: *Like as not the feller is a punkin roller*—Time

the **pumpkins** *n phr* circus & carnival by *1950s* A small town; a rural site: *I never worked the pumpkins*—New Yorker

pump ship (or bilge) *v phr* by *1788* To urinate: *The Duke of Wellington's most cogent advice was "Never lose an opportunity to pump ship"*

pump up 1 *v phr* by *1970s* To exaggerate; assign too much importance to; =BLOW UP: *. . . wanted a scandal and wanted to fry Maxine Waters. . . They wanted to pump it up*—Los Angeles Times **2** *v phr* by *1980s* To persuade to keen excitement; =AMP, HYPE, TURN ON: *Experts like Dr Edward Teller. . . have steadily "pumped up" Reagan. . .*

about the potential of such defensive-weapons systems—Newsweek

pump oneself **up** *v phr* by *1970s* To arouse oneself emotionally, spiritually, mentally, etc, to a maximum effort; =PSYCH oneself ●Much used by sports commentators, esp by baseball announcers of pitchers: *The big lefthander's really pumped himself up for this crucial encounter*

punch *n* by *1911* Power; force; impact; =CLOUT: *This article has no punch*
See BEAT someone TO THE DRAW, CAN'T FIGHT one's WAY OUT OF A PAPER BAG, ONE-TWO, SUCKERPUNCH, SUNDAY PUNCH

Punch-and-Judy hitter *n* baseball by *1965* A hitter who depends on punching weak hits rather than swinging for long ones: *. . . not because I was a wimp, or some Punch-and-Judy hitter*—Milwaukee Journal

punchboard *n* by *1930s* A very promiscuous woman; =ROUNDHEEL [fr a gambling or lottery device where one paid to *punch* a round scroll of paper out of a hole in a *board* for a possible prize; related to 1700s *punch*, "deflower"]

punch cows (or cattle) *v phr* by *1890* To herd or drive cattle

punch-drunk by *1915* **1** *adj* Exhibiting brain damage from repeated blows to the head; slow in movement, slurring in speech, disoriented and shambling; =PUNCHY, SLAP-HAPPY **2** *adj* Dazed from overwork, excessive stress, etc: *He was punch-drunk after the annual meeting*

punched **See** GET one's CARD PUNCHED, HAVE one's TICKET PUNCHED

punched-up *adj* by *1950s* Improved; increased in energy, impressiveness, impact, etc: *. . . no more than a punched-up form of the sentiment that the prose style of most social scientists "is Greek to me"*—New York Times

puncher *n* cowboys by *1890* =COWPUNCHER

punches **See** PULL one's PUNCHES, ROLL WITH THE PUNCHES, TELEGRAPH one's PUNCHES

punch in (or out) *v phr* by *1934* To come or go at a certain time, esp to or from a job; =CLOCK IN (or OUT) [fr the stamping of one's work-card at a time-clock]

punching bag *n phr* by *1980s* A target; butt; whipping boy; scapegoat: *Milken has come to be regarded as a handy punching bag for everything that went wrong in the 1980s*—Vanity Fair

punch someone's **lights out** *v phr* by *1970s* To beat or defeat someone severely; trounce; =CLOBBER: *Sugar Ray Leonard punched Thomas Hearns's lights out*—Sports Illustrated [fr the earlier *beat out someone's liver and lights*, where *lights* reflects a Middle English word for "lungs, esp of a slaughtered animal or game animal," now certainly interpreted as "eyes" and as "electric lights"]

punch line *n phr* by *1921* The last line or part of a joke, which makes it funny; =KICKER, ZINGER: *I remember the jokes, but not the punch lines*

punch out 1 *v phr* by *1970s* To beat, esp with the

fists; =BEAT UP, CLOBBER: *Oh. . . I punched out this guy*—Armistead Maupin **2** *v phr* Air Force *by 1970s* To use the ejection seat for escape from a aircraft

punch-out *n by 1970s* A fist fight; brawl; fisticuffs

punch the clock *v phr by 1940s* To do the minimum routinely required: *The public has good instincts for when people are doing significant or courageous things in space and when merely punching the clock*—New Republic

punch up 1 *v phr by 1950s* To improve; increase the energy, impressiveness, etc, of; =JAZZ something UP: *I guess they hired me because their material needed punching up*—National Lampoon **2** *v phr* To bring a specified part of a recording tape into view, into place at the playing head, etc **3** *v phr* computers *by 1980s* To call up a software program

punchy 1 *adj by 1937* Exhibiting brain damage from repeated blows to the head; =PUNCH-DRUNK: *Sailor Bob, a punchy stumble-bum*—John O'Hara **2** *adj by 1940s* Feeling somewhat confused and battered, as if punch-drunk: *Even if she's a little punchy and hyper from doing a dozen interviews that day*—react **3** *adj by 1926* Having force, impact, energy, etc; potent; =JAZZY, ZINGY: *The English language may someday be as colorful and punchy as it was in Elizabethan times*—Literary Digest

punk[1] 1 *n by 1904* A catamite; young companion of a sodomite; =GUNSEL ◁2▷ *v by 1970s* To sodomize; do anal sex to; =BUGGER, CORNHOLE: *The guy peeled off Tate's pants and punked him*—Tom Aldibrandi **3** *n by middle 1920s* Any young or inexperienced person; boy; =KID: *Sparky was always a fresh punk*—John O'Hara **4** *n by 1917* A petty hoodlum; meager minor tough or criminal: *to emphasize just how tough a Division Street punk could be*—Nelson Algren **5** *n by 1917* Any inferior, insignificant person, like an ineffective fighter, jockey, pool player, waiter, porter, etc **6** *n* circus *by 1926* Any young circus animal [ultimately fr 1500s British, "prostitute, harlot," of unknown origin]

punk[2] 1 *adj by 1896* Inferior; poor; bad: *The idea strikes me as punk*—Westbrook Pegler **2** *n by 1891* Bread **3** *n by 1940s* A patent medicine **4** *modifier*: *. . . the punk workers who sell corn removers*—M Zolotow [probably early 1700s, "rotting wood, touchwood," of unknown origin, usu taken to be fr *spunk,* of the same meaning, fr Gaelic *spong,* "tinder"]

punk[3] 1 *n* (also **punker**) *by 1976* An adherent to a style of dress and behavior marked by seemingly threatening, dangerous, and aggressive attributes, such as safety pins worn through ear lobes, razor blades around the neck, and torn clothes: *. . . in the beginning, punk wasn't just fashion. Punk was outrage*—New York Times **2** *adj*: *The atmosphere in North London's pubs is really punk* [originally meant to be reminiscent of the hoodlums called punks in the 1950s, but soon an independent style]

punk day *n phr* circus *by about 1930* A day when children are admitted free

punked out *adj phr by 1980s* Having the style of dress and behavior marked by seemingly threatening, dangerous, and aggressive attributes: *I am a punked-out loner boy-repellent*—Sassy

punkette *n by 1980s* A young woman who adopts the manners and appearance of the punk milieu: *. . . a scruffy, androgynous punkette with close-cropped hair and dressed all in black except for a pair of electric-red socks*—New York Magazine

punkin *See* PUMPKIN

punkoid 1 *n by 1980s* =PUNK[3], PUNK ROCKER **2** *adj*: *his punkoid slouch and sneer*

punk out 1 *v phr by 1920* To quit, esp from fear; =CHICKEN OUT, FOLD: *The Soho News punked out*—Philadelphia **2** *v phr by 1980s* To adopt the style of a punk rocker

punk rock *n phr by 1976* Loud and crude rock and roll music played by persons who purport, in their dress, vile behavior and language, repellent names, and ugly appearance, to be loathsome louts: *The bad equivalent of "bubble-gum," it was called punk-rock, and it was totally utilitarian music*—Changes

punk rocker *by 1976* **1** *n phr* A player of loud and crude rock and roll music who purports to be a loathsome lout **2** *n phr* A person who adheres to a style of dress and behavior marked by seemingly threatening, dangerous, and aggressive attributes; =PUNK

punt[1] *v by 1706* To gamble; bet [fr French *ponte,* Spanish *punta,* "point," used for playing against the banker in faro and other games]

punt[2] *1970s* college students **1** *v* To drop a course in order not to fail it **2** *v* To give up; withdraw; =COP OUT: *I hate to punt, but I just don't have time to finish this job* **3** *v* To return something; throw (or kick) something back: *The high court punted the usetax issue back to Congress and cleared the way for future legislative action*—Time **4** *v* To stall for time; to delay; to relinquish control: *Clinton suddenly punted on health reform and shifted to welfare*—New Republic [fr the kick out of danger in football, fr middle–1800s Rugby football, "kick the ball before it hits the ground," of unknown origin; perhaps echoic]

punter *n by 1706* A gambler; a bettor: *Inside the clubhouse, the punters sit enraged on their slatted benches*—Village Voice [fr French *punter,* "to place a bet against the bank in a card game," of uncertain origin]

punt someone or something off *v phr 1970s* college students To deliberately forget; ignore and evade; =BAG: *He decided to punt the whole problem off*

pup 1 *n by 1890* A young, inexperienced person; =KID, PUNK **2** *n by 1940s* =HOT DOG **3** *n* truckers *by 1940s* A small four-wheeled truck trailer **4** *n* (also **puppy**) *by 1980s* A thing; =BABY, SUCKER: *I guess we turn this pup around*—Don Metz/ *You can mail this puppy in or you can appear at the tribal court*—movie Thunderheart [ultimately fr French *poupée,* "doll"]

See GUTTERSNIPE, SNUGGLE-PUP

puppies or **pups** *n* by 1923 The feet; =DOGS

puppy love *n phr* by 1834 Love or infatuation of very young persons; =CALF LOVE

pup (or dog) tent *n phr* by 1863 A small tent; an Army shelter tent: *The crew loaded pup tents and cooking equipment into motorcycle sidecars*—King Vidor

purp *n* by 1863 A dog; pup: *. . . after the purp solved a few simple problems*—Billy Rose

purple heart *n phr* 1960s narcotics Any barbiturate, or a mixture of a barbiturate and morphine; =NIMBY, GOOFBALL [fr the US decoration awarded for a combat wound]

purpose pitch *n phr* baseball by 1920s A pitch purposely thrown intimidatingly close to a batter [said to have been coined by the manager Branch Rickey]

◁**pus bag**▷ *n phr* by 1970s A despicable person; a filthy wretch; =SCUMBAG: *He hissed that I was "a goddam scum-sucking pus bag"*—Peter Gent

pus-gut or **pustle-gut** by 1940s, but probably much earlier **1** *n* A protuberant belly; =POTBELLY **2** *n* A person with a pus-gut: *. . . some pus-gut in an American Legion cap*—Time **3** *modifier*: *. . . they do the job without a lot of pus-gut shop stewards grieving everything you try to do*—Robert B Parker [origin unknown; probably fr a dialect pronunciation of *purse*, suggesting a full, baggy gut; many related dialectal variants are found, including *bussen gutted* by the 1770s, *bus-bellied* by 1840, and more recently *pussy-gutted, pustle-gutted,* and *puzzle-gutted*]

push 1 *n* 1940s street gang A fight between street gangs; =RUMBLE **2** *n* loggers by 1930 A supervisor: *Jigger's first season as a camp push*—Stewart Holbrook **3** *n* Army by 1970s A radio frequency, such as is tuned by pressing a push-button **4** *n* by 1940s An intense sustained effort: *They made a big push to get the damn thing done* **5** *v* (also **push across**) by 1940s To kill someone: *. . . when one of our boys gets pushed*—J Evans/ *He might have pushed Foster across*—movie *The Sleeping City* **6** *v* by 1937 To approach a specified age: *You're pushing 50*—Earl Wilson **7** *v* by 1894 To advertise; publicize; promote: *They don't have to push reference books too much* **8** *v* (also **push for**) by 1888 To recommend; boost; =GET BEHIND: *He decided to push my idea, and pushed for two new labs* **9** *v* by 1940s To sell, esp in an aggressive way; hawk: *Push the specials today, okay?* **10** *v* by 1578 To press or importune, esp too often and too hard: *I'll probably do what you want, just stop pushing* **11** *v* 1930s narcotics To sell narcotics; peddle; =DEAL: *Funny cigarettes ain't all that one pushes*—Nelson Algren **12** *v* underworld by 1940s To distribute and pass counterfeit money

push a pen *v phr* by 1911 To do office work: *Why should I want to push a pen in an office?*—New Yorker

push a button *v phr* by 1980s To provoke a response; reach one's feelings; hit a "hot button": *Don't push my button. I haven't exactly been behind him, pushing and clapping*—Washington Post/ *The issue of domestic disputes pushes buttons, summons up personal emotions*—Time

push comes to shove *sentence* by 1958 A touchy situation becomes actively hostile; a quarrel becomes a fight; =the CHIPS ARE DOWN: *If push comes to shove, can you count on him?*

pusher 1 *n* narcotics by 1935 A narcotics peddler or distributor; =CANDY MAN, CONNECTION: *. . . queen of the Broadway narcotics pushers*—Associated Press **2** *n* underworld by 1940s A distributor or passer of counterfeit money; =PAPERHANGER *See* COOKIE-PUSHER, GOSPEL-PUSHER, GREASE-PUSHER, PENCIL-PUSHER, PEN-PUSHER, PILL-PUSHER, WOOD-PUSHER

push-in robbery (or crime) *n phr* by 1976 A violent burglary or mugging done as the victim opens the door

push one's **luck** *v phr* by 1911 To take additional risks when things are going well: *He pushed his luck and lost the whole bundle*

push off 1 *v phr* by 1918 To leave; =SHOVE OFF **2** *v phr* underworld by 1940s To kill; murder; =PUSH

pushover 1 *n* by 1926 A person who is easily defeated, imposed upon, convinced, etc: *. . . an eight-round preliminary with some pushover*—H Witwer **2** *modifier*: *He wasn't a pushover kind of cat*—Claude Brown **3** *n* by 1906 =PUNCHBOARD, ROUNDHEEL **4** *n* by 1906 An easy job or task; =CINCH, DUCK SOUP: *. . . two ways to do it. One was a pushover*—Jerome Weidman

push poll *n phr* by 1990s: *It's called a "push poll" because the idea is to see whether certain "information" can "push" voters away from the opposition candidate. . . to the candidate supported by the people paying for the poll*—David Broder

◁**push-push**▷ *n* The sex act: *If they don't go where she wants, it's no push-push for him that night*—Lawrence Sanders

push the envelope *v phr* by late 1980s To expand possibilities; innovate boldly; take risks: *What we want. . . is to create the next computing revolution. We want to push the envelope*—New York Times

push the panic button *See* HIT THE PANIC BUTTON

push up daisies *v phr* by about 1860 To be dead; be buried

push water *n phr* by 1938 Gasoline

pushy *adj* by 1936 Assertive in a repellent way; aggressive: *Pushy people alarmed him*—Ira Wolfert

puss[1] *n* by 1890 The face: *. . . one sock in the puss*—American Mercury [fr Irish *pus*, "lip, mouth"] *See* GLAMOR-PUSS, PICKLEPUSS, SOURPUSS

puss[2] *adj* by 1990s Excellent; wonderful; =GREAT, RAD, TITS [fr *pussy*]

pussy ◁**1**▷ *n* by 1879 The vulva or vagina ◁**2**▷ *n* by 1879 A woman as a sex object or partner; =ASS, TAIL: *Where I come from we call that kind of stuff table pussy*—Calder Willingham ◁**3**▷ *n* by 1859 A harmless person, either gentle or timid or both;

=PUSSYCAT: *Space Invaders are pussies compared to the marketing aggression of the major producers*—Toronto Life **4** *adj* by 1970s Harmless and undemanding; fit for the timid: *The bumper cars are pussy*—Cameron Crowe [fr *pussy*, "cat," found by 1726]

See EATIN' STUFF, WOOD-PUSSY

◁**pussy butterfly**▷ *n phr* by 1980s An intrauterine contraceptive device; IUD

pussycat by 1859 **1** *n* A harmless, gentle, or timid person: *Iacocca is no closet pussycat masquerading as a tiger*—Washington Post **2** *n* A pleasant and amiable person; =DOLL, HONEY

pussyfoot or **pussyfoot around** *v* or *v phr* by 1903 To be careful and hesitant; be evasive; tergiversate: *Please stop pussyfooting and get to the point* [fr the nickname of W E Johnson, given because of his catlike stealth as a law-enforcement officer in the Indian Territory (Oklahoma); Johnson became a famous advocate of Prohibition, and the term briefly meant "prohibitionist"]

◁**pussy posse (**or **squad)**▷ *n phr* by 1963 A police morals or vice squad

◁**pussy-whipped**▷ *adj* by 1956 Dominated by one's wife or female lover; obsequiously uxorious; henpecked: *Francie. . . had had it with bore-ass "pussy-whipped" men*—Village Voice

pustle-gut *See* PUS-GUT

◁**put**▷ *v* by 1930s To proffer or do the sex act; =LAY: *With men buyers, you get them put and you can sell them the Brooklyn Bridge*—Jerome Weidman [a shortening of *put out*]

See KNOW WHAT one CAN DO WITH something, TELL someone WHAT TO DO WITH something

◁**puta**▷ (Poō tah) by 1950s **1** *n* A prostitute: *A white puta like you got to have more money than that*—High Times **2** *n* =PUNCHBOARD [fr Spanish]

put a bug in someone's **ear** *v phr* by 1940s To give someone a special and private piece of information, esp in the hope of favorable action

put a cork in it *v phr* by 1990s To keep silent; =SHUT UP •Often an irritated command: *A New York judge has mercifully told Woody and Mia to put a cork in it*—New Republic

put a crimp in someone or something *v phr* by 1896 To thwart or hamper; block or interfere with; =STYMIE: *How can we put a crimp in this guy's plans?* [fr the notion of a severe pinching-in as an obstacle]

put something **across (**or **over)** by 1917 **1** *v phr* =GET something ACROSS **2** *v phr* To succeed; =PULL IT OFF: *Ask her, she knows how to put it across*

put a fork into someone *v phr* by 1990s To show that someone or something is definitively finished; confirm failure: *If American businesses don't catch up. . . you can "put a fork into 'em. They're done"*—Ann Landers [fr the cook's way of testing whether something baked or roasted is ready to serve]

put a lid on someone or something *v phr* by 1970s To suppress; quiet; quell: *Putting a Lid on The Kid*—Washington Post

put a move on someone *v phr* (Variations: **make** can replace **put**; **the move** or **the moves** can replace **a move**) 1980s students To make a sexual advance to someone; =PROPOSITION: *Why don't you put a move on that Tuck girl?*—John Irving/ *. . . tryin' to put the moves on every girl in the place*—John Sayles

put (or **stick) a sock in it** *v phr* by 1919 To keep silent; =SHUT UP: *Would you please be so kind as to force the media to put a sock in it*—Milwaukee Journal/ *And they can stick a sock in it. Or maybe a bratwurst*—Milwaukee Journal

◁**put** one's **ass in a sling**▷ *See* HAVE one's ASS IN A SLING

◁**put** one's **ass on the line**▷ *v phr* by 1940 To assume risk and responsibility; put oneself in peril: *I agreed with him, but I wasn't going to put my ass on the line to prove the point*

put a verb in it *sentence* by 1990s To get into action; stop loafing and wasting time; =GET one's ASS IN GEAR: *Make up your bed, and put a verb in it; we don't have all day!*—Knight-Ridder Newspapers

put away *v phr* by 1878 To eat or drink, esp heartily or excessively: *They were able to put away a lot of noodles, turkey hash, corn, Jell-O, bread, peanut butter, jelly, and water*—Playboy

put someone or something **away 1** *v phr* by 1872 To commit to an asylum or send to jail, an old age home, nursing home, etc **2** *v phr* by 1588 To kill someone **3** *v phr* by 1970s To please someone enormously; =KNOCK someone's SOCKS OFF: *It put me away. It destroyed me*—Washington Post

◁**put balls (**or **hair) on**▷ *v phr* by 1970s To make more emphatic, effective, etc; add impact to: *Rewrite that paragraph and put balls on it*

put daylight between *v phr* by 1970s To separate things, esp to separate oneself from someone or something disadvantageous: *The President is trying hard to put daylight between himself and the National Rifle Association*

put-down *n* by late 1950s Something disparaging, humiliating, or deflating; a reducing insult; =KNOCK: *. . . since it is such a neat put-down of the arrogant administrator*—Fortune

put someone or something **down 1** *v phr* by 1560 To kill: *Criticizing Jim Brady's wife. . . Mohan said, "Because of all her barking and complaining, she really needs to be put down. A humane shot at a veterinarian's would be an easy way to do it"*—New York Times **2** *v phr* by late 1950s To criticize adversely and severely; denigrate; =DUMP ON, KNOCK: *Not that I mean to put down the Old Masters*—D Gillespie

put someone or something **down for** something *v phr* by 1950s To identify or classify; recognize; =PEG: *When I see a guy with a pull-over sweater under a double-breasted suit, I put him down for an Englishman*—Joe Cannon

put one's **finger on** something *v phr* by 1889

To recall or specify a desired matter with precision; define exactly: *I remember it, but can't quite put my finger on the outcome*

put one's **foot in it** *v phr by 1856* To get into difficulties, esp by blundering: *Trying to be delicate, I put my foot right in it*

put one's **foot in** one's **mouth** *v phr by 1940s* To make an embarrassing comment; say something stupid: *... part of the same hysterical syndrome that caused me to put my foot in my mouth*—Saul Bellow

put someone **in the picture** *v phr by 1942* To give necessary orienting data; brief; =BRING someone UP TO SPEED: *Nobody put me in the picture, and I was confused for weeks*

put in one's **two cents worth** *See* PUT one's TWO CENTS IN

put it in your ear or **take it in the ear** *v phr by 1940s* To insert something figuratively into one's ear as a means of contemptuous disposal; =STICK IT •Mild euphemistic forms of *stick it up your ass,* used for reduced effect and among friends: *It was easy to say things like "take it in the ear" to them. . . they didn't get it*—John Irving

put it on ice *v phr by 1918* To make victory certain; insure success: *Back-to-back doubles put it on ice in the ninth inning*

put it on the line *See* LAY IT ON THE LINE

put it on the street *v phr by 1970s* To disclose something, esp rather publicly: *So we put it on the street that she was leaving*

put it over on someone *v phr by 1913* To deceive; fool: *Be careful, nobody puts it over on her* [found slightly earlier as *put it all over on*]

put it past someone *See* NOT PUT IT PAST someone

◁**put it to** someone▷ *v phr by 1940s* To do the sex act with or to; =SCREW

put one's **money where** one's **mouth is** *sentence by 1942* Support your statements, brags, opinions, etc, with something tangible; =PUT UP OR SHUT UP: *I won't believe he's leaving until he puts his money where his mouth is and goes away*

put someone's **nose out of joint** *v phr by 1581* To make someone envious or jealous

put one's **oar in** *v phr by 1779* =PUT one's TWO CENTS IN

put-on 1 *n by 1896* An act, remark, etc, intended to fool someone; a more or less amiable deception: *a master of the "put-on," a mildly cruel art*—Time/ *They nudge us that what they're doing is just a "put-on"*—Pauline Kael **2** *n* (also **put-on artist**) *by 1960s* A pretender; =PHONY: *to equate an original talent like Kenneth Anger with a put-on like Andy Warhol*—Jack Newfield **3** *adj by 1621* Feigned; affected: *his put-on machismo*

put someone **on** *v phr by 1896* To fool someone, esp by pretending; tease: *The Countess who adores the poet pities him and puts him "on"*—Wallace Stevens

put on airs *by 1781* **1** *v phr* To affect a refinement and hauteur one is not born to: *Now that I have the Rolls Royce I'll put on airs* **2** *v phr* To be snobbish and aloof

put on an act *v phr by 1934* To behave misleadingly, esp pretentiously; =SHOOT someone A LINE

put one over on someone *v phr by 1912* To deceive someone; best someone by a trick

put something or someone **on hold** *v phr by 1960s* To defer an immediate decision; postpone consideration: *I'm afraid that whole matter is on hold just now* [fr the *hold* function of a telephone, with which one can close off a conversation temporarily]

put on the feedbag (or **the nosebag**) *v phr by 1874* To eat; have a meal

put someone **on the floor** *v phr by 1970s* To please someone enormously; =PUT someone or something AWAY, KNOCK someone OUT: *Schaefer said the strip "put me on the floor"*—Washington Post

put something **on the line** *See* LAY something ON THE LINE

put on the ritz (or **the dog**) *entry form by 1926, variant by 1934* **1** *v phr* To make a display of wealth and luxury: *... everything they could. . . to put on the ritz*—Car and Driver/ *. . . put on the dog and give him the ritz like this*—Ira Wolfert **2** *v phr* To dress stylishly and flashily **3** *v phr* =PUT ON AIRS [fr the name of the Swiss César *Ritz* and the various luxurious European hotels he built; *put on the dog* fr a late–1800s college, esp Yale, expression] *See* DOGGY

put someone **on the spot** *by 1929* **1** *v phr* To require action, a solution, etc, at once: *It had to be ready tomorrow, which put our department on the spot* **2** *v phr* To embarrass; put in a difficult position: *I don't want her to put us on the spot again*—New Yorker

put someone **on to** someone or something *v phr by 1887* To introduce someone; get someone access to: *... that little Andronica you put me onto*—Lawrence Sanders

putout *n baseball* An out, other than a strikeout

put-out *adj by 1887* Angry; upset; offended: *I know you will be put out at my not writing*—The Lantern

◁**put** (or **give**) **out**▷ *v phr* To proffer sexual favors, esp do so readily; be promiscuous: *A guy gives a dame a string of beads. . . and she puts out*—Lawrence Sanders/ *As a Yale woman I am resented because I will not "put out" for Yale men*—Yale Alumni Magazine/ *A guy buys a gift for his wife because he knows she won't give out if he don't*—Lawrence Sanders

put someone **out** *v phr by 1940s* To impose upon; cause inconvenience

put someone or something **out to pasture** *v phr by 1930s* To retire; take out of active use, practice, etc, usu after long service: *That old machine's about shot, and we should put it out to pasture* [fr the farm practice of letting an old horse graze at will, and work no longer]

put over *See* PUT something OFF

put one's **pants on one leg at a time** *v phr* by 1960s To have traits of ordinary humanity: . . . *even giants put their pants on one leg at a time*—New Yorker

put one's **papers in** by 1950s **1** *v phr teenagers* To apply for admission, enlistment, etc **2** *v phr police* To retire or resign

putter-offer *n* by 1940s A procrastinator: *No, admitted Franklin Roosevelt, as weakly as any putter-offer*—Time [found as *putter-off* by 1803]

put the arm (or **the sleeve**) **on** someone by 1930s **1** *v phr* To detain or arrest, esp by force: *It was a signal for the waiter to hustle over and put the arm on the customer who was trying to stiff him*—M Zolotow **2** *v phr* To hit; beat up: . . . *in case a tough greengrocer tries to put the arm on you*—Robert B Parker **3** *v phr* To ask for a loan; =PUT THE BITE ON someone or something: . . . *writing a letter to my friend Ted without putting the arm on him for a couple of bucks*—John O'Hara

put the bite (or **the bee**) **on** someone or something by 1933 **1** *v phr fr early 1900s* To ask for money, esp for a loan: *And how. . . do you put the ite on me*—Elmore Leonard **2** *v phr* To make a request; solicit: *Sullivan continues putting the bee on other government agencies*—Variety

◁**put the blocks to** someone▷ *v phr loggers by about 1900* To do the sex act with or to; =SCREW: . . . *putting the blocks to the Winnipeg whore*—Canadian folk song [fr the logging practice of placing *blocks* on a tree that is to be felled, perhaps with the reinforcing sense that *blocks* suggests "testicles"]

put the clamps on *v phr* by 1940s To seize, esp to steal

put the eye on someone by 1940s **1** *v phr* To look at invitingly or seductively; =GIVE someone THE EYE: *I was having the eye put on me*—Raymond Chandler **2** *v phr* To look at; look over; examine; =SCOPE OUT

put the finger on someone *underworld by 1926* **1** *v phr* To locate and identify a victim; =FINGER **2** *v phr* To provide evidence leading to the arrest of a criminal; betray a criminal to the police: *He put the finger on my husband*—New York Daily News

put the freeze on someone *v phr* by 1960s To reject; treat very coldly: *Women are quick to put the freeze on free loaders*—Hal Boyle

put the hammer down *v phr car-racing by 1960, fr truckers* To accelerate; go full speed: *Guerrero put the hammer down and passed Unser a few laps later. . .* —Milwaukee Journal

put the heat on someone *v phr* by 1936 To use coercive pressure; =LEAN ON someone: *He put the heat on me to vote that way*

put the icing on the cake *See* ICE THE CAKE

put the kibosh on someone or something (KĪ bahsh) *v phr* by 1836 To quash or stifle; put the quietus to: *I was praying that the kid wouldn't. . . put the "kibosh" on me*—Jack London [origin unknown and richly speculated upon; many regard it as probably fr Yiddish because it sounds as if it ought to be; Padraic Colum, however, attributed it to Irish *cie bais,* "cap of death," presumably the black cap donned by a judge before pronouncing the death sentence, which is a semantically appealing suggestion; the phrase was used by Dickens in his first published book, in 1836, and put into the mouth of a London urchin]

put the make on someone *v phr* by 1970s To make sexual advances; =MAKE A PASS AT someone: *The codger was horny and put the make on the lady cop*—Playboy

put them in the aisles *See* LAY THEM IN THE AISLES

put the pedal to the metal **1** *v phr* by 1980s To accelerate; go fast; =GIVE IT THE GUN: *Bolan. . . settled back on creaky springs, and put the pedal to the metal*—Don Pendleton **2** *modifier* Regulating or deregulating highway speeds: *President Clinton will sign what friends and foes alike call "the pedal to the metal bill"*—New York Times

put the screws to someone *v phr* by 1940s To use extreme coercive pressure; harass; =PUT THE HEAT ON someone: *The only reason Fidel agreed. . . was to put the screws to Reagan*—Art Buchwald [fr a torturer's use of *thumbscrews; put the screws on* is found by 1834]

put the skids under someone or something *v phr* by 1917 To cause to fail, be defeated, be rejected, etc: *They put the skids under him when they found out he had cheated*

put the slug on someone by 1940s **1** *v phr* To hit or attack; =SLUG: . . . *fined for putting the slug on a heckling fan*—Arthur Daley **2** *v phr* To criticize harshly; =KNOCK: . . . *needn't think he can get away with putting the slug on rummies*—Red Smith

put the snatch on someone or something *v phr* by 1940s To take or commandeer; seize; kidnap: *The Treasury Department is going to put the snatch on virtually the entire 40 grand*—Billy Rose

put the squeeze on someone *v phr* by 1941 To put under heavy pressure or exigency; =LEAN ON someone, PUT THE HEAT ON someone: *She hired me to put the squeeze on Linda for a divorce*—Raymond Chandler

put the spurs to someone *v phr* by 1898 To urge and goad; prod; =GOOSE: . . . *had been critic of the Pentagon and had "put the spurs to us from time to time"*—Milwaukee Journal

put the wood to someone *v phr* by 1970s To punish; coerce by threat of punishment: *Why can't Mayor Barry put the wood to school administrators and demand more caring than this?*—Washingtonian

put (or **run**) someone **through the mill** *v phr* by 1818 To subject to an arduous experience; be rough on someone: *She's quite eager to try again, although they really put her through the mill* *See* GO THROUGH THE MILL, THROUGH THE MILL

put someone **through the wringer** *v phr* by 1942 To subject to harsh treatment, esp by severe interrogation [fr the image of squeezing something out by passing it through a clothing *wringer*]

putting *See* OFF-PUTTING

put-together *adj by 1970*: *Calm, cool, and collected. Never blew his stack. Never raised his voice. A real put-together guy*—Lawrence Sanders

putt-putt *by 1905* **1** *n* A small marine engine **2** *n* A motorboat, esp a slow one: *A sneaker's no good. Got to use a putt-putt*—American Mercury **3** *v*: *We'll putt-putt over to the island* **4** *n* Any small motor vehicle [fr the sound of a two-cycle engine]

put (or **add**) one's **two cents** (or **two cents worth**) **in** *v phr by 1930s* To volunteer one's advice, esp when it is not solicited; =KIBITZ: *If I may put my two cents in, I think we should shut up*

putty *n by 1924* A very malleable or biddable person or persons: *. . . they'll be putty and do exactly what you want (as they should)*—Sassy

putty-head *n by 1856* A stupid person; =PUDDINGHEAD

put someone **under** *v phr police by 1990s* To arrest someone; =COLLAR, HOOK SOMEONE UP, PINCH [shortening of *put someone under arrest*]

put up *v phr by 1865* To contribute or pay money, esp money bet or promised

put someone **up** *v phr by 1800* To provide lodging for

put-up job *n phr by 1838* A prearranged matter; a contrived affair: *The surprise award was a put-up job*

put up or shut up *sentence by 1878* =PUT one's MONEY WHERE one's MOUTH IS

put someone **up to** something *v phr by 1824* To incite or persuade someone: *I know who did it, but not who put him up to it*

put up with someone or something *v phr by 1755* To tolerate or accept: *I'll put up with it if you think I should*

put someone **wise** *v phr by 1896* To make aware; inform, esp of something shrewd and elementary or covert: *The kindly old clerk put me wise to how things were done around there*

◁**putz**▷ **1** *n by 1964* A detestable person; obnoxious wretch; =PRICK, SCHMUCK: *Here comes the Moravian putz*—Joseph Heller **2** *n by 1964* An ineffectual person; =NEBBISH: *There wasn't much that worried him. Dying like a putz in a fucked-up gag was one thing that did*—Carsten Stroud **3** *n by 1934* The penis [fr Yiddish, literally "ornament"]

putz around *v phr by 1970s* To behave idly; putter around; =FOOL AROUND, FUTZ AROUND: *Dad was putzing around in the background*—Douglas Coupland [fr *putz* and semantically related to *dick around, fuck around,* though less coarse than these to any but, probably, Jewish ears]

puzzle palace *Army by 1970s* **1** *n phr* Any higher headquarters, including the Pentagon **2** *n phr* A place, like the White House, where vital decisions are made in great and pompous secrecy: *. . . some kind of puzzle palace on the Potomac*—Ronald Reagan *See* FIVE-SIDED PUZZLE PALACE

pyramids *See* PLATFORMS

Q

the **Q** *n phr* *hoboes by 1940s* The Chicago, Burlington, and Quincy Railroad

the **QT** *See* ON THE QT

Q sign *n phr* *medical by 1980s* A sign of death: the patient's mouth is wide open with tongue hanging out

quack *n by 1659* An incompetent and fraudulent doctor [a shortening of *quacksalver*, "a person who boasts about the virtues of his worthless remedies"; fr Dutch and found by 1579]

quackery *n by 1709* The practices of "quacks": *. . . and knew it was "world-class quackery"*—Associated Press

quad 1 *n by 1820* Any architectural quadrangle, esp one at a college or university **2** *n by 1804* =QUOD **3** *n 1950s hot rodders* A car having four headlights **4** *n 1990s Canadian students* An idiot; fool; =SPAZ, TARD: *I feel like such a quad, falling on my face while skating with those cute boys*—Slang Bag 93 [said to be a shortening of *quadrilateral*, "square"]

quads *n 1950s hot rodders* A set of four headlights on a car

quadzillion *See* JILLION

quail 1 *n students by 1859* An attractive young woman; =CHICK: *. . . a lovely little quail from Arkansas*—Arthur Godfrey **2** *n jazz musicians by 1950s* A cornet or trumpet: *. . . listen to that kid blow that quail*—Louis Armstrong
See SAN QUENTIN QUAIL

quail-roost *n college students by about 1900* A women's dormitory

quant or **quant jock** *n* or *n phr by 1990s* An expert in quantitative analysis of stock market and other business trends: *While not all the students entering business school can be classified as "quant jocks," those whose strengths lie in their quantitative abilties. . .*—Macon Telegraph

quarterback *v by 1945* To lead or direct; control; manage: *. . . and quarterbacking the rise of Action News at Channel 6*—Philadelphia
See MONDAY MORNING QUARTERBACK

queen 1 *n by 1900* A woman, esp a wealthy and gracious one: *Wouldn't it be luck if some ritzy queen fell for him!*—James T Farrell **2** *v* (also **queen it**) *by 1611* To behave in a refined and haughty way **3** *n homosexuals by 1924* A male homosexual, esp one who ostentatiously takes a feminine role: *The queens look great strutting along the boardwalk*—Albert Goldman [homosexual sense probably a late–1800s alteration of *quean*, "harlot, prostitute," influenced by connotations of *queen*, "aged, dignified, tawdry, and overadorned"]
See CLOSET QUEEN, DRAG QUEEN, MAIN QUEEN, SIZE QUEEN, TEAROOM QUEEN, TOE-JAM QUEEN

queer 1 *adj by 1740* Counterfeit **2** *n* (also **the queer**) *underworld fr early 1900s by 1812* Counterfeit money: *. . . eagle-eyed concessionaires always on the lookout for the queer*—W&F Simpson ◁3▷ *adj by 1922* Homosexual; =CAMP, GAY •In the early 1990s *queer* was adopted as a non-pejorative designation by some homosexuals, in the spirit of "gay pride": *Some girls said that I was queer*—New York Post ◁4▷ *n* (also **queerie**) *by 1932: . . . a lot of queeries in the State Department*—Westbrook Pegler **5** *v fr late 1700s British by 1812* To spoil; ruin; =GOOF UP: *Food is what queered the party*—F Scott Fitzgerald

queer fish *n phr by 1750* A strange or weird person; odd fellow; =WACK, WEIRDO

quetor *See* CUTER

quick-and-dirty 1 *n by 1968* =GREASY SPOON **2** *adj by 1977* Hastily done as an expedient; slipshod: *The gossip in this quick-and-dirty, self-pitying memoir. . .*—New York Times

quick buck *See* FAST BUCK

quick fix *n phr by 1966* A hasty repair or relief job: *He called my idea a quick fix at best, but he'd do it* [fr *fix* as "repair" influenced by *fix* as "dose of narcotics"]

quickie 1 *n* (also **quick one**) *entry form by 1940, variant by 1928* A quick drink of liquor **2** *n by 1926* Anything taken or done very hastily; something rushed: *. . . a "quickie," one of those overnight film concoctions*—Picture Play **3** *modifier: . . . the new "quickie divorce" law*—Selden Rodman **4** *n by 1940s* The sex act done very hastily: *We may have time for a quickie* **5** *n by 1943* An unauthorized strike; =WILDCAT

quick like a bunny *adv phr early 1940s students* Very quickly [possibly a reference to the rapid copulation of rabbits]

quick on the draw (or **the trigger** or **the uptake**) *adj phr by 1940s* Quick to respond or react; touchy; sensitive

quick-over *n by 1950s* A quick glance or inspection; =the ONCE-OVER

quiff *n by 1923* A prostitute or promiscuous woman; =ROUNDHEEL: *. . . because some quiff is going to give you head*—Lawrence Sanders [origin obscure;

probably related to the sense "copulate," found by 1719]

quill *n 1960s narcotics* A folded matchbook cover used to hold heroin or cocaine for sniffing

◁**quim**▷ *n by 1613* The vulva or vagina; =CUNT [origin unknown]

quits *See* CALL IT A DAY

quiz *n by 1867* A brief examination in college
   See POP QUIZ

quod (KWAHD) *n by 1700* A prison [perhaps fr *quadrangle*; perhaps fr Romany *quaid*, "prison"]

quux *interj computer by 1983* A exclamation of disgust; =FEH, YUCK [said to have been coined by Guy Steele, editor of the 1983 *The Hacker's Dictionary*]

R

RA (pronounced as separate letters) *n by 1942* Anger; =the RED ASS

rabbi *n by 1932* An influential sponsor; a patron: *I see you got the gold tin; who's your rabbi?*—New York Times [the dated instance has to do with post-office workers]

rabbit *v by 1887* To run away fast; escape in a hurry; =LAM: *The man who had rabbited was later identified*—Ann Rule

rabbit ball *n phr baseball by 1910* An especially lively baseball

rabbit ears 1 *n phr by middle 1960s* A V-shaped television antenna **2** *n phr by 1930s* Exceptionally keen hearing: *. . . he was a terrific umpire, although he had one of the worst cases of rabbit ears I've ever seen*—Whitey Herzog

rabbit food *See* BUNNY FOOD

rabbit-foot *prison by 1940s* **1** *n* A convict who escapes from prison **2** *v* =RABBIT, LAM

race *See* BOAT RACE, DRAG RACE, HORSE-RACE, RAT RACE

rack 1 *v* (also **rack out**) *1960s teenagers* To sleep; nap; =COP ZS: *I'll rack out for awhile on the grass till I get it together*—Perception & Persuasion **2** *v by 1990s* To denigrate severely; =TRASH: *Why rack Clinton?*—Denver radio talk show [probably fr torture on the *rack*, a stetching machine, the verb found by 1433]

See MEAT RACK, OFF-THE-RACK, PANIC RACK

the **rack** *n Navy by 1940s* Bed; =SACK: *Jeanne is pretty good in the rack*—George V Higgins

rack duty (or **time**) *n phr Navy by 1940s* Sleep; time spent in one's bunk; =SACK TIME

racked *adv by 1960s* For certain; under control; =TAPED: *As for the next step, I have that racked* [probably fr the *racking* of the balls before a pool game, putting them in a precise pattern]

racked out *adj phr 1960s teenagers* Asleep; in bed

racket 1 *n by 1785* Any illegal concern or enterprise; a criminal business; =DODGE, GRIFT: *G Marks and Abe Cohn have a new racket now of promenading Clinton Street dock*—New York Owl **2** *n by 1745* A party or dance, esp a noisy one •In recent usage this is most common among the police: *. . . passing evidence around like a pretzel tray at a retirement racket*—Carsten Stroud **3** *v by 1760* To lead a busy life professionally and socially: *Monk's seesawing years, from 1935 to 1940, were spent racketing endlessly back and forth between Europe and New York, an itinerant pianist and boulevardier*—New Yorker **4** *n circus & carnival by 1940s* Any concession, stand, etc [fr early–1800s British underworld fr *racket,* "noise, confusion," etc]

racketeer *n by late 1920s* A person who works in an illegal racket; a member of the rackets; =GANGSTER, MOBSTER, WISE GUY

the **rackets** *n phr by late 1920s* Organized crime; the syndicate; the Mafia; =the MOB

rack up¹ *v phr by 1960s* To register or post; accumulate; achieve: *. . . more representative of actual consumer use than 60,000 miles would have been if racked up in short order*—Popular Science [probably fr the *racking up* of pool balls in a triangular frame before a game]

rack up² *v phr by 1970s* To wreck; ruin; damage severely; =TOTAL: *. . . got caught raping a nine-year-old Japanese girl. He got racked up*—Lawrence Sanders

See RACK

racy *adj by 1901* Somewhat indecent; =RAUNCHY: *The movie has a lot of racy dialogue*

rad 1 *n by 1820* A radical **2** *adj teenagers by late 1970s* Extraordinary; wonderful; =AWESOME, CHILL, GNARLY: *Want to go to this way rad party?*—Levi's 501 Report

radio *See* THUNDERBOX RADIO

raft *n by 1833* A large number; =OODLES, SLEW: *I have rafts of reasons for not doing that* [fr earlier uses of *raft* to mean a dense flight of waterfowl, a mass of logs in a river, etc]

rag 1 *n by 1855* An article of clothing: *She got into her rags*—John O'Hara **2** *n circus by 1940s* A tent **3** *n baseball by 1908* The pennant awarded to the annual winner of a league championship **4** *n by 1734* A newspaper or magazine, esp one that the speaker does not like: *This so-called revolutionary organ is a horrible rag*—O Chubb **5** *n by 1897* =RAGTIME **6** *n by 1897* A piece of ragtime music **7** *v by 1897* To play in a ragtime style: *The street bands ragged a tune by taking one note and putting two or three in its place*—Stephen Longstreet **8** *v by 1808* To tease; banter disparagingly with; =NEEDLE, RIDE: *Sometimes we'd rag one another in the rough manner that is safe only for friends*—F G Patton

See the BIG RAG, DAMP RAG, GLAD RAGS

◁the **rag**▷ *by 1930s* **1** *n* A sanitary napkin; a vaginal tampon: *She told him she had the rag on, which cooled his ardor some* **2** *n* Menstruation; =the CURSE

See CHEW THE FAT, HAVE THE RAG ON, ON THE RAG, TAKE THE RAG OFF THE BUSH

rag bag 1 *n phr by 1820* Any miscellany, esp a very random and confusing one: *What he calls his philosophy is a rag bag of trite trivialities* **2** *modifier*: *a rag-bag collection, but an interesting one*

rag-chewing *n by 1885* Talking, esp of an amiable and idle sort

rage *n Australian by 1980, Canadian by 1990s* A good party: *This is a rage, man*—Slang Bag 93

ragged *See* RUN someone RAGGED

◁**raggedy-ass**▷ (or **raggedy-pants**) *adj WWI armed forces* Inferior; sloppy; =HALF-ASSED: *. . . some kinda raggedy-ass agreement she thinks is a legal will*—Joseph Wambaugh/ *. . . picked up from some raggedy-pants US trackside*—Sports Illustrated [found as *ragged-arse* by 1896]

◁**raggedy-ass militia**▷ *n phr WWI armed forces* A sloppy or inept military unit [found as *ragged-arse brigade* by 1896]

raggle-taggle *See* TAKE THE RAG OFF THE BUSH

◀**raghead**▶ *by 1921* **1** *n* A Hindu or other Eastern or Middle Eastern person: *speaks Arab like a raghead*—W T Tyler **2** *n* A gypsy: *You let that raghead touch your hand*—Harry Crews

rag on someone or something *v phr 1980s students* To disparage; strongly deprecate; =TRASH: *. . . and Ivey, who was hosting the show, began ragging on him*—Milwaukee Journal Sentinel/ *. . . he overheard Mel ragging on one of his shots*—Sassy

rag out (or **up**) *v phr entry form by 1875, variant by 1934* To dress in one's best clothes; =DOLL UP

rags *See* GLAD RAGS

rag-tag and bobtail *n phr by 1820* The rabble; hoi polloi: *Oh Lord, deliver me from the rag-tag and bobtail*—Ray Bradbury [*tag-rag and bobtail* is found by 1659; *bobtail*, "cur, lout," by 1619]

ragtime 1 *n by 1897* A highly syncopated style of music, esp for the piano, having a heavily accented tempo and a melody consisting of many short rapid notes **2** *modifier*: *a ragtime classic*

ragtop or **rag-roof 1** *n by 1955* A convertible car: *It's been a while since the ragtops rolled off the assembly line*—Aquarian/ *Return of the rag roofs*—Time **2** *modifier*: *I sure wouldn't sleep in that rag-top car*—Earl Thompson

the **rag trade** *n phr by 1890* The clothing and fashion industry; the garment industry; =SEVENTH AVENUE: *. . . the enormously canny middle-aged men of the rag trade*—New Yorker

rah-rah 1 *adj by 1911* Naively enthusiastic and hortatory, esp in a partisan collegiate context: *Some are rah-rah types, some are hard-ass disciplinarians. . .* —Whitey Herzog **2** *n*: *I just couldn't see myself spending four years of my life with rah-rahs like them* [a shortening of *hurrah*, found by 1877 as used in cheers]

rail 1 *n 1960s narcotics* A thin row of powdered narcotic to be sniffed; =LINE: *I snorted the rails that Hondo offered*—Peter Gent **2** *n 1970s hot rodders* An elongated sort of competition hot rod

railbird *n by 1890* An ardent horse-racing devotee: *. . . another three-year old. . . that set the railbirds agog*—Audax Minor

railroad *by 1884* **1** *v* To convict and imprison someone very rapidly, perhaps unjustly or illegally: *The prisoner is railroaded to jail*—E Lavine **2** *v* To force a resolution of something quickly, perhaps without due process: *if all cases were railroaded through that quick*—James M Cain

See a HELL OF A WAY TO RUN A RAILROAD

railroad tracks 1 *n phr WWII Army* An Army captain's two silver bars, the insignia of rank **2** *n phr by 1970s* Braces on teeth: *. . . a chubbette with "railroad tracks" across her teeth*—New York Magazine

rain *v black by 1960s* To complain; =BITCH

rain cats and dogs *v phr* (Variations: **chicken coops** or **darning needles** or **pitchforks** may replace **cats and dogs**) *entry form by 1738,* pitchforks *by 1850* To rain very hard [origin unknown, although many improbable derivations have been proposed, from classical Greek to pagan Scandinavian; *rain dogs and polecats* is found by 1652]

rain check *n phr baseball by 1884* A postponement or delay, with promise of renewal, of a sports event, dinner, party, date, receipt of a sale item at a store, etc [fr the ticket stub that permits one to see another baseball game if the game one has a ticket for is not played on account of rain]

See TAKE A RAIN CHECK

raincoat *n by 1980s* A condom; =RUBBER: *If a guy said "I ride bareback," I'd tell him he needs a raincoat. Instead of gonorrhea, I'd talk about the clap*—US News & World Report

rain dance *n phr by 1970s* An impressive political reception or banquet

rainmaker *n by 1968* A powerful and successful representative or agent, esp for a law firm: *. . . to a six-figure "rainmaker" generating fees for one of the most politically connected law firms in the state*—Village Voice

rain on someone's **parade** *v phr by 1941* To spoil someone's day, performance, special occasion, etc

raise *v black by 1990s* To leave; =CUT OUT, SPLIT

See MEXICAN PROMOTION

raise a stink *v phr by 1970s* =RAISE CAIN: *I didn't even raise a stink when Bradley's stylist guy came over. . .* —Stan Cutler [*kick up a stink* is found by 1948; *stink*, "fuss, disturbance," is found by 1812]

raise Cain (or **a ruckus**) *v phr by 1840* To make a disturbance; complain loudly and bitterly; =KICK UP A FUSS

raise hell *by 1896* **1** *v phr* (Variations: **living hell** or **unshirted hell** may replace **hell**) *first variant by 1980s* =RAISE CAIN: *They raised living hell—*

Milwaukee Journal Sentinel/ . . . *cold frosts raise unshirted hell with fishing*—Milwaukee Journal **2 v phr** To carouse and celebrate boisterously **3 v phr** To rebuke strongly; castigate: *He raised hell with me when he found out*

raiser *See* HELL-RAISER

raise sand *v phr* *black by about 1930* =RAISE CAIN

raise the roof 1 *v phr* *by 1860* To complain angrily and bitterly; issue a strong rebuke: *When the president sees this fuck-up, she'll raise the roof* **2 v phr** *by 1894* To make a boisterous noise; carouse raucously

raked *adj* *1960s hot rodders* Of a customized car, having the front end lower than the rear

rake in *v phr* *by 1583* To acquire large sums of money: *The Yosemite Fund has so far raked in $200,000 from the sale of 15,000 plates*—Los Angeles Times

rake-off *by 1888* **1 n** A gambling house's percentage of each pot or stake **2 n** An illegal or unethical share or payment [fr the *rake* used by casino croupiers]

rake on someone *v phr* *1980s students* To denigrate and humiliate someone

rake someone **over the coals** *See* HAUL someone OVER THE COALS

rally *See* PEP RALLY

ralph *v* (also **Ralph** or **ralph up** or **rolf**) *teenagers by 1967* To vomit; =BARF: *He ralphs up the downers and the quarts of beer*—J Gallick [probably echoic]

-rama or **-arama** or **-orama** *suffix used to form nouns* *by 1824* A spectacular display or instance of what is indicated: *boatarama/ bunsorama/ videorama* [fr *panorama*, ultimately fr Greek *horama*, "sight"]

ram-bam thank you ma'am *See* WHAM-BAM THANK YOU MA'AM

Rambo *modifier* *by 1985* Violent; loutishly aggressive: *Each day Bush ratchets up the Rambo rhetoric and closes more alleys of diplomatic escape for Saddam Hussein*—Nation [fr the main character of the movie *Rambo*]

rambunctious *adj* *by 1859* Boisterous; obstreperous; wild [origin unknown; *rumbunctious* is found by 1830]

◁**ram it**▷ *v phr* *by 1950s* =STICK IT

rammer *See* MOTHERFUCKER

ranch *See* BUY THE FARM, HENCOOP

random *adj* *1980s student fr computers* Inferior; undesirable: *This is one random pen I'm writing with*—College Slang 101

randy *by 1847* **1 adj** Sexually aroused; =HORNY: . . . *a desperately randy brain surgeon*—Time **2 adj** Desirous; yearning: . . . *randy for the smell of setting cement*—Washingtonian [origin unknown; various dialect senses suggest a possible derivation fr "wild movement," "boisterousness," "wantonness"]

rank 1 *v* *underworld by 1920s* To say or do something that reveals another's guilt: *She ranked him by busting out with that new fur so soon after the robbery*—E Booth **2** *v* *by 1934* To harass; annoy; =KID,

NEEDLE: . . . *the fine, foul art of "ranking." Light insults were his way of making friends*—Time [second sense used by 1960s teenagers in the preferred variant *rank out*, both as a verb phrase and a noun phrase]

See PULL RANK

rank on someone *v phr* *1980s students* To insult; disparage; =PUT DOWN: *Fred ranked on Dawn after the fight was broken up*—Delcastle Dictionary of Slang

rap¹ 1 n *by 1777* A rebuke; blame; responsibility; =KNOCK: *Who'll take the rap for this?* **2 n** *by 1903* Arrest, indictment, or arraignment for a crime: *Gangs with influence can beat about 90 percent of their "raps"*—E Lavine **3 n** *by 1928* An official complaint or reprimand: *Honest cops will often take a "rap" or complaint rather than testify against a fellow cop*—E Lavine

See BEAT THE RAP, TAKE THE RAP

rap² 1 v *by 1929* To converse; chat and exchange views, esp in a very candid way: . . . *drugs, youth cult, ecstasy questing, rapping*—New York Times **2 n** *by 1929* Informal talk; candid conversation and communion **3 v** *black by 1970s* To chant a rap song **4 n** *black by 1970s* =RAP SONG [origin unknown; perhaps related to *repartee*, perhaps to *rapport*, perhaps to *rapid*]

a **rap** *n phr* *by 1834* Nothing; zero; =ZIP: *She didn't care a rap for the whole bunch of them* [fr a counterfeit coin of the 1700s]

rap club (or **parlor** or **studio**) *by 1973* **1 n phr** A place that offers sexual services in the guise of conversation and companionship: . . . *"rap clubs," which have replaced massage parlors*—New York Post **2 n phr** A nightclub, discotheque, etc, featuring rap music

◁**rape wagon**▷ *n phr* *by 1970s* =PIMPMOBILE, SEX WAGON

rap someone's **knuckles** *v phr* *by 1749* To give a light and insufficient punishment; =GIVE someone A SLAP ON THE WRIST: *Tokyo had been rapped over the knuckles*—New York Review of Books [the dated instance might indicate a more severe punishment than modern use does]

rapper¹ 1 n *by 1904* A person who charges or identifies another as a criminal **2 n** *by 1904* A judge or prosecutor **3 n** *by 1940* A crime for which someone not guilty has been punished: . . . *a couple of gang murders solved, but they were just rappers*—Raymond Chandler [first senses fr early–1700s *rap*, "charge with a crime"]

rapper² 1 n *1960s counterculture* A person who converses and chats, esp a member of a rap (discussion) group **2 n** *black by 1970s* The chanter of a rap song **3 n** *black by 1970s* A devotee of rap music and its attendant styles of dressing, dancing, etc: . . . *as rappers pick up on a little new wave style. . . and make their moves*—Time **4 modifier**: . . . *rapper talk, which pulls in language from. . . 40s hipsters, 60s hippies, and even cockney rhyming slang*—Time

rap session *by 1970* **1** *n phr* A conversation; a bout of candid chat: *... talk shows featuring rap sessions between hosts and listeners*—Newsweek **2** *n phr* A meeting of a discussion group: *I was asked to lead a rap session*—Betty Friedan

rap sheet *n phr by 1960* *Their rap sheets listed convictions for the possession or sale of controlled substances*—Village Voice **See** RAPPER[1]

rap song (or **music**) *n phr black by 1970s* A song that is rapidly spoken rather than actually sung, usu with an electronic rhythm accompaniment

rare back *v phr by 1930s* To gather one's strength; poise oneself for action: *She rared back and let him have it* [fr the verb *rear*, and the image of a horse *rearing* on its hind legs]

be **raring to go** *v phr by 1927* To be very eager and keen to begin; =LEAN FORWARD IN THE SADDLE [fr the image of a *rearing*, mettlesome horse]

raspberries or **razzberries** (RAZ behr *eez*) *interj by about 1925* An exclamation of disbelief, defiance, disgust, etc; =NUTS

raspberry *n by about 1880* A rude labial flatulation: *You should expect an occasional heathen to utter a raspberry*—Washington Post **See** FLIP ONE'S LID

the **raspberry** (or **razzberry**) (RAZ beh ree) *n phr by about 1880* A rude and contemptuous expulsion of breath through vibrating lips; =the BIRD: *... that staccato sputter of derision known as the Bronx cheer, or raspberry*—Newsweek [fr Cockney rhyming slang *raspberry tart*, "fart"]

rat 1 *n by 1629* A treacherous and disgusting person: *He's acting like a prime rat on this* **2** *v by 1812* To betray; desert; turn one's coat **3** *n by 1902* An informer; =STOOL PIGEON: *In most cases they were "rats" and the best tools the keepers had*—PL Quinlan **4** *v by 1910: ... an inmate, rankled by Angelo's attempts to woo his daughter, ratted on them*—Time **5** *combining word by 1970s* A frequenter and devotee of the place indicated: *arcade rat/ rink rat* **6** *v by 1980s* =HOODGE **See** BRIG RAT, DESERT RAT, DOCK RAT, LOOK LIKE A DROWNED RAT, PACK RAT, RUG APE, SACK RAT, SHACK MAN, SMELL A RAT, WINTER RAT

rat around *v phr by 1960s* To idle about; loaf; =BAT AROUND: *Oh, I don't know. Ratting around*—John O'Hara

ratchet *v by 1977* To change by increments in one direction: *Gold... had ratcheted down to 385*—New York Times [fr the *ratchet* action of a winch or of a wrench, where an increasing pressure, torque, pull, etc, is registered by the clicking of a pawl on a gear wheel]

ratchet-mouth or **ratchet-jaw** *n by 1970s* A person who is constantly talking; =MOTOR-MOUTH [perhaps because a *ratchet* wrench can be operated without pause, and makes a constant rapid rasping, clacking noise]

rate 1 *v by 1920* To merit; deserve: *He rates a big cheer, folks* **2** *v by 1940s* To be highly esteemed: *What stunt did he ever pull that makes him rate?*—Billy Rose **See** FIRST-RATE

rated **See** X-RATED

rate with someone *v phr by 1928* To be highly regarded, cherished, trusted, etc, by someone: *That sort of persuasion doesn't rate a damn with me*

rat fink 1 *n phr teenagers by 1963* A treacherous and disgusting person; =BASTARD, SHITHEEL: *... that rat-fink Danny's kid*—TV Guide **2** *modifier*: *the rat-fink Eastern press*—New Yorker [perhaps originally fr labor union use, since both terms mean "scab"]

◀**rat fuck**▶ *college students by 1950s* **1** *adj phr* Unacceptable to conventional moral traditions **2** *adj phr* =FAR OUT **3** *v phr* To have a good time; =JAM **4** *v phr* To loaf and idle about; =RAT AROUND **5** *n phr* A despicable person; =RAT FINK: *You lousy bastard rat-fuck*—Barry Reed

rathole 1 *n by 1812* A wretched, messy place; a filthy hovel; =DUMP: *Those days we lived in a rathole* **2** *v by 1950s* To store up food and supplies; stockpile; =STASH **See** POUR MONEY DOWN THE DRAIN

rations **See** GROUND RATIONS

rat on someone *v phr by 1932* To inform on someone; give evidence against someone; =SQUEAL: *No power on earth can keep her from ratting on you*—James M Cain

rat out *v phr by 1941* To abandon or desert; withdraw; =FINK OUT: *I wouldn't feel you were ratting out*—Budd Schulberg [fr the *rats* that desert a sinking ship]

rat someone **out** *v phr by 1990s* To betray or inform on someone; =RAT ON someone: *My little brother ratted me out, though. . .* —Young and Modern

rat pack *n phr by 1951* A teenage street gang: *... juvenile gangs, sometimes called rat packs*—R S Prather

rat race *n phr by 1939* A job, situation, milieu, etc, marked by confusion and stress; futile and enervating hyperactivity: *... the rat-race of ordinary social gatherings*—E Wilder [found by 1937 as the name of a dance]

the **rat race** *n phr by 1956* The everyday world of toil and struggle; the routine workaday world

rats *interj by 1886* An exclamation of disgust, disappointment, dismay, etc

◁a **rat's ass**▷ **See** NOT GIVE A DAMN

◁**rat's asshole**▷ *n phr by 1970s* A despicable person; =BASTARD, RAT-FINK: *You rat's asshole*—John Irving

rattle 1 *v* (also **rattle on**) *by 1594* To talk on and on, esp foolishly or pointlessly; babble **2** *v by 1869* To confuse; upset; disturb concentration: *I rattled him with veiled menaces*

rattlebrain or **rattlehead** *n first form by 1709, second by 1641* A silly or stupid person; =SCATTERBRAIN: *Mother would like to travel around but not with an old rattlebrain like you driving*—Ring Lardner

rattle someone's **cage** (or **caboose**) by 1980s
1 *v phr* To criticize; needle; sting; =BUG: *Reiner and friends affectionately rattle the cage of rock music and its every pretension—Washingtonian*
2 *v phr* To make a scene or disturbance; =RAISE CAIN: *I'm going into his office and rattle his cage*

rattle cages *v phr* by 1980s To cause excitement; shake things up: *"You like to rattle cages," the saleswoman observed, explaining that it was a California expression—Village Voice*

rattle someone's **chain** *See* PULL someone's CHAIN

rattler 1 *n* by 1903 A railroad train: . . . *a very luxurious rattler—W Davenport* **2** *n* hoboes by 1913 A fast freight train or a freight car **3** *n* by 1827 A rattlesnake [in the first sense, *rattler,* "coach," is found by 1630]
See CAGE RATTLER

rattlesnakes *See* UP TO one's ASS IN something

rattletrap *n* by 1822 A ramshackle coach or other vehicle, esp an old car

rattling 1 *adv* by 1829 Very; extremely: . . . *a rattling good story—A Hays* **2** *adj* by 1690 Good; =GREAT: *a rattling party*

ratty or ◁**rat-ass**▷ *adj* by 1867 Shabby; slovenly; =SCRUFFY, TACKY: *The skinny Berkley, with her ratty hair and sharp teeth. . . —Newark Star-Ledger/ . . . the rat-ass rags he's always wearing—National Lampoon*

raunch 1 *n* by 1964 Vulgarity; smut; =PORN: . . . *no obscenities in Glen's Bar. . . Too tired for raunch—Herbert Kastle/ . . . the latest batch of 8mm raunch—Playboy* **2** *v* by 1970s To do the sex act with or to; =SCREW: . . . *just because she's raunched a few law students—National Lampoon* [back formation fr *raunchy*]

raunch radio (or **television**) *n phr* by middle 1980s Radio or television shows featuring vulgarity, obscenity, sensation, etc: *Howard Stern is the paragon of raunch radio*

raunchy or **ronchie 1** *adj* by 1939 Sloppy; slovenly; careless: . . . *depending on how good or how "raunchy" we were—R Hubler* **2** *adj* (also **rotchy**) *teenagers* by about 1950 Inferior; cheap; =CRUMMY, GRUNGY: . . . *my raunchy old jeans* **3** *adj* by 1967 Vulgar; salacious; =DIRTY: *In the beginning there was Playboy, then came raunchy Penthouse—Time* [origin uncertain; the pronunciation and the early currency among aviation cadets in Texas suggest a possible origin in Spanish *rancho,* "ranch," found by 1857, and called by 1864 "a place of evil report"; a ranch, of course, may be regarded as a place of animal filth, odors, etc]

rave 1 *v* by 1816 To commend or applaud enthusiastically: *He's raving over this new book* **2** *n* by 1926: *The critics gave it a rave* **3** *modifier*: *rave notices* **4** *n* by early 1990s: *Organized on the fly (sometimes by electronic mail) and often held in warehouses, raves are huge, nomadic dance parties that tend to last all night, or until the police show up—Time/ . . . all-night, Ecstasy-fueled parties*

known as raves—New York Times/ *Rave head dictates nonviolent fashion and dancing spasmodically to very fast "techno" music—New York Times* [*rave* meant "party" in British slang by 1960]
See FAVE

rave-up 1 *n* British by 1940 A wild party **2** *n* by 1967 Something loud and exciting: . . . *in "Take Me Back," a lively rave-up—Time*

raw 1 *adj* by 1561 Inexperienced; unfledged; callow: *a raw young actress* **2** *adj* by 1546 Harsh; inhospitable: *a raw reception* **3** *adj* by 1931 Nude; naked; =IN THE RAW: *You can't go raw on this beach, ma'am* **4** *adj* by 1940s Vulgar; salacious; dirty; raunchy: *He offended us all with a very raw story*

raw deal *n phr* by 1912 A case of harsh, unfair, or injurious treatment; =a ROYAL FUCKING: *The Academy officers were heaping raw deal after raw deal on him—Sloan Wilson*

rays *n* by 1980s Sunshine: *soaking up some rays*
See BAG SOME RAYS

razorback *n circus & hoboes* by 1940s A manual laborer; roustabout

razz *v* by 1920 To insult and ridicule; =NEEDLE, RIDE: *Is there ever any razzing about the fact that you report to your wife?—Washington Post* [fr *raspberry*; found in the form *razoo* by 1890]

the razz *n phr* by 1920 Mocking insults; rude splatting sounds; =the RASPBERRY: *They begin to give him the razz—H Witwer*

the razzberry *See* the RASPBERRY

razzle-dazzle 1 *n* by 1898 Adroit deception; slick dodging and feinting; =DIPSY-DOODLE, RAZZMATAZZ: . . . *suspecting some sort of razzle-dazzle—New Yorker* **2** *modifier*: *a razzle-dazzle quarterback* **3** *n* by 1889 Excitement; gaudiness; spectacular show: . . . *put razzle-dazzle into the grocery business—This Week* **4** *adj*: . . . *its razzle-dazzle weapons and command and control systems—Newsweek* **5** *n carnival* by 1935 An exciting carnival ride [probably a reduplication of *dazzle*]

razzmatazz or **razzamatazz 1** *n* by 1894 Swift and adroit deception; slick jugglery; =RAZZLE-DAZZLE: . . . *more glitter, more razzmatazz, more false human interest—Washington Post* **2** *adj* Spectacular; showy; dazzling; =RAZZLE-DAZZLE: *a razzmatazz New Year's Eve bash—Philadelphia* **3** *n jazz talk* by 1950s Anything outdated, esp old and sentimental; =CORN, RICKY-TICK: *"Razzmatazz" is corny jazz—Stephen Longstreet*

reach-me-down by 1862 **1** *adj* Inferior; shoddy: . . . *the nice and the reach-me-down manners—Raymond Chandler* **2** *n* =HAND-ME-DOWN

reaction *See* GUT REACTION

read 1 *v WWI Army* To inspect clothing for lice **2** *v radio operators* by 1940s To receive and interpret a radio signal; understand: *He's breaking up and I can't read him* **3** *v* by 1956 To understand; =DIG: *I read you, baby, and I flatly agree* **4** *n* by 1958 A book or other printed matter: *Ultimately, it's Maas' reporter's eye for detail. . . that makes "China White" a great read—Milwaukee Journal* **5** *n* by

1990s Understanding; interpretation; =TAKE: *What's your read on this?*—Curtis Sliwa

read 'em and weep *sentence* gambling by *1940s* Here is some probably unwelcome information for you; here is the truth [fr the crapshooter's or poker player's injunction that his opponents look carefully at a winning roll or hand]

reader *See* METER-READER, MITT-READER

readers *n* gambling by *1894* Marked playing cards: *The cards and dice were crooked, the cards being readers*—W & F Simpson

read from the same page *v phr* by *1990s* To agree; see eye to eye: *Tom Hauge. . . and Francis William (Bill) Murphy. . . reading from the same page for the first time in years, signed the pact*—Milwaukee Journal

read someone his rights *See* GIVE someone HIS RIGHTS

read someone **like a book** *v phr* by *1844* To know and understand someone thoroughly, including deep motives and likely actions: *She thinks she's pretty clever, but I read her like a book*

read someone **loud and clear** *v phr* radio operators by *1940s* To understand someone very well; comprehend perfectly: *Do you read me loud and clear, mister?*—Pat Conroy

read my lips or **can you read lips** by *1980s* **1** *sentence* I am thinking but not uttering something obscene, insulting, or otherwise not for the public ear: *Psst. Hey, parents! Read my lips*—Erma Bombeck **2** *v phr* You seem to be too stupid to understand what I'm saying, so look at me very attentively and try

read the riot act *v phr* by *1819* To rebuke firmly; reprove severely, esp in the vein of a stern warning

the **ready** *n phr* by *1688* Money: *Take the ready and send it along*—John Kieran [fr *ready* money]

real *adv* by *1658* Really; truly
See FOR REAL, IT'S BEEN REAL

the **real cheese** *See* the CHEESE

the **real George** *n phr* *1950s* teenagers Anything superb and genuine; the best or greatest: *She's real George all the way*—Newsweek

real gone *adj phr* *1950s* students Excellent; wonderful; =COOL, FUNKY FRESH: *a real gone chick*

reality check *n phr* by *1990s* A confirmation of fact, esp when compared with fantasy: *Proxmire's pronouncements provided a reality check on spending requests*—New Republic

reality-impaired *adj phr* *1990s* students Stupid; dim; =DUMB •A wicked imitation of "mentally challenged" and other such euphemisms

really pick 'em *See* one CAN REALLY PICK 'EM

the **real McCoy (**or the **McCoy) *n phr* by *1922* Any genuine and worthy person or thing; the genuine article: *. . . egg bagels, a sweeter variety of the real McCoy*—New York Times/ *You can trust her, she's the McCoy* [origin uncertain; *the real Mackay* is found by *1883*; revived during Prohibition times to describe liquor]

real money *See* HEAVY MONEY

real pro *See* PRO

ream 1 *v* (also **rim**) by *1914* To cheat; swindle, esp by unfair business practice; =SCREW: *A new technique for reaming the customers*—A J Liebling **2** *v* (also **ream out**) *WWII armed forces* To rebuke harshly; =BAWL SOMEONE OUT, CHEW OUT: *I've seen him just ream guys out for not getting the job done*—Time ◁**3**▷ *v* (also **rim**) *homosexuals* by *1942* To stimulate the anus, either orally or with the penis

rear end 1 *n phr* (also **rear**) by *1937*, variant by *1796* The buttocks; =ASS: *She's a pain in the rear end*—Jerome Weidman **2** *v* by *middle 1970s* To hit a car from the rear: *. . . his Grand Am was rear-ended*—New Yorker

rearrange the deck chairs on the Titanic *v phr* by *1990s* To behave with appalling futility; =FUCK THE DOG: *The Administration seems quite willing to rearrange the chairs on the deck of the Titanic while money and confidence flow out of the deposit insurance system*—New York Times

reat *See* ALL REET, REET

Rebel or **Reb** *n* by *1862* A white Southerner

rebop *n* by *1940s* =BOP

recap (REE kap) **1** *v* by *1940s* To repeat, esp in a summary form; recapitulate; =REHASH **2** *n*: *I gave her a quick recap of the incident*

recharge one's **batteries** *v phr* by *middle 1970s* To replenish one's energies, resources, etc: *I came to New York to recharge my cultural batteries*—American Scholar

record *See* BROKEN RECORD, OFF THE RECORD, TRACK RECORD

red 1 *adj* *1990s* narcotics Intoxicated with narcotics, esp with marijuana; =HIGH **2** *n* by *1990s* Chili con carne: *. . . places to consider when I need a bowl of red*—Milwaukee Journal
See IN THE RED, MEXICAN RED, PAINT THE TOWN RED, SEE RED

Red or **Red Devil** *n* or *n phr* *1960s* narcotics Seconal™, a barbiturate capsule: *. . . dropping Reds and busting heads*—Eldridge Cleaver

the **red ass** *n phr* Southern by *1940s* Anger; =PISS-OFF, PUCKER
See GET THE RED ASS

◁**red-assed**▷ *adj* Southern by *1940s* Very angry; livid; =PISSED OFF

red ball 1 *n phr* railroad by *1927* A fast freight train **2** *n phr* by *1940s* Any train, bus, or truck running fast and given priority [fr the pole-mounted *red ball* used as a controlling signal on early railroads; in WWII the *Red Ball Express* was a military transport outfit carrying supplies fr the ports to the front in Europe]

◁**redbone**▷ *n* black by *1980s* A light-skinned black person

red carpet 1 *n phr* by *1934* A sumptuous welcome: *He was sort of expecting the red carpet and not the fish-eye* **2** *adj phr* by *1950s* Luxurious; plush; =RITZY: *Jewelry gives you a red carpet elegance*—Life [fr an ancient custom, at least as old as

Aeschylus's *Agamemnon,* of putting down a *red car-pet* over which a welcomed dignitary would walk]
See ROLL OUT THE RED CARPET

a (or one) **red cent** *n phr* (Variation: a (or one) **red**) by 1839 A cent; the least amount of money; =a THIN DIME: *The poor man claimed he didn't have a red cent* [fr the fact that a copper *cent* is *red*]

red dog *n phr* football by 1966 A defensive assault in which the linebacker goes directly for the quarterback

redd up *v phr* by 1718 To make neat and clean; put in order: *. . . workers are redding up after the gale*—Albert Payson Terhune [fr Scots dialect, of uncertain origin]

redeye **1** *n* by 1819 Raw and inferior whiskey; =PANTHER PISS, ROTGUT: *Barrow put down a slug of redeye*—A Hynd **2** *n* by 1927 Ketchup

the **red-eye** or the **red-eye special** *n phr* by 1968 An airline flight from coast to coast, esp from west to east, that leaves one coast late at night and arrives early in the morning: *I just flew in on the red-eye*—Vincent Canby [fr the bleary sleepless look of overnight passengers]

red face See HAVE A RED FACE

red-faced *adj* by 1950s Embarrassed; abashed; guilty-looking

redflag *v* narcotics by 1990s To inject narcotics by hypodermic needle; =MAINLINE, SHOOT UP: *. . . take it home and redflag the works into your arm*—Carsten Stroud

red flag *modifier* by 1976 Subject of a special warning or suspicion: *His article identifies several "red flag" professions that have a higher-than-usual chance of being audited*—Milwaukee Journal [found as a sign of warning by 1777]

red herring *n phr* by 1884 Something used to divert attention from the real issue or matter: *All this talk of deficits is just a red herring* [fr the use of a dead *red herring* to confuse or test the scent of hunting dogs, found by 1686]

red hot **1** *adj phr* by 1758 Very hot; sizzling •An intensive of all slang senses of *hot* **2** *n phr* by 1892 A frankfurter; =HOT DOG

red-hot mama **1** *n phr* by 1926 A type of heavy, loud, and somewhat vulgar woman singer of the 1920s **2** *n phr* by 1936 An especially lively, amorous, and attractive woman

red ink **1** *n phr* by 1919 Red wine, esp of an inferior sort; =DAGO RED: *A pint of red ink still sells for two bits*—NY Confidential **2** *n phr* by 1929 Financial loss or losses: *. . . a flood of red ink totaling close to $80 billion*—Fortune

redleg *n* Army by 1900 An artillery soldier

redlight **1** *v* circus & carnival To push someone off a moving train; kill by pushing off a train: *Who'd you red-light, Ferris?*—Dashiell Hammett **2** *v* To eject someone from a car

the **red light** *n phr* by 1931 A warning or command to stop: *We were all set, but the boss gave us the red light* [found by 1849 in the time before traffic lights]

redline **1** *v* WWII Army To cross a soldier's name off the payroll for some wrongdoing **2** *v* by 1973: *. . . aimed at preventing redlining, the practice of denying loans to entire neighborhoods based on the predominant race or economic class of their residents*—Milwaukee Journal **3** *v* by 1990s To achieve maximum speed; push the dial up to the red line: *He had the car redlined*—Carsten Stroud **4** *v* computers : *Comparerite also does what's called "redlining," which allows you to add notes and comments that won't become part of the final document but can be seen by the next reader*—Bob Schwabach

redneck **1** *n* by 1893 =CRACKER **2** *modifier*: *This is a redneck rural county*—Newsweek **3** *n* by 1975 A bigoted and conventional person; a loutish ultra-conservative: *Fred is a crude redneck, and Carol is his latest bimbo*—Time [perhaps fr the characteristic ruddy *neck* of an angry person, and influenced by the image of a bigoted rural Southern white person; perhaps fr the fact that pellagra, a deficiency disease associated with poor Southern whites, produces a dermatitis that turns the neck red; first sense found by 1830 in a more specialized derogatory use, "the Presbyterians in Fayetteville"]

red-necked *adj* by 1940s Angry; =RED-ASSED

red paint *n phr* by 1900 Ketchup

redshirt sports by 1955 **1** *v* To extend a college student's period of athletic eligibility **2** *n* A student whose period of athletic eligibility has been extended **3** *n* An act of redshirting: *Indiana forward Alan Henderson is recovering from knee surgery, so a medical redshirt is a possibility*—New York Times **4** *v* Various non-college and non-sports instances of providing an extra year of eligibility: *It is a capricious misuse of scarce resources when public schools provide redshirting, borrowing the term used in college athletics*—New York Times/ *To get them eligibility for additional schooling: Under the redshirt plan, special education students could extend their high school program by at least one year*—LDA Newsbriefs [fr the *red shirts* worn by such athletes in contrast with varsity players]

red-tag *v* by 1990s To label a house officially as damaged and uninhabitable: *Because of the Northridge earthquake, a Pacoima house I rented out was red-tagged*—Los Angeles Times

red tape *n phr* by 1736 Delay and complication; bureaucratic routine; petty officious procedure [fr the tape used for tying up legal and official documents]

red totem poles See KNOCK someone or something FOR A LOOP

red zone *n phr* football by 1990s The part of the field closest to the defender's goal line: *We wouldn't be talking about a lull if we wouldn't have made the mistakes in the red zone*—Milwaukee Journal

reeb *n* by 1990s Beer [an interesting modern case of back slang]

reef See TAKE A REEF IN IT

reefer[1] *n* by 1914 A refrigerated railroad car, truck, ship, etc; =FREEZE: *A malfunction in a refrigerated* *trailer, or reefer, raises the temperature*— Smithsonian [fr *refrigerated*]

reefer² or **reefer weed** *1920s narcotics* **1** *n* A marijuana cigarette; =JOINT **2** *n* A person who smokes marijuana; =POTHEAD [origin unknown; perhaps originally *rifa* fr Mexican Spanish *grifa,* "marijuana," the *g-* lost because it is not aspirated or exploded in Spanish pronunciation and hence not readily heard by English speakers]

reefer³ or **refer** *n 1990s newspaper office* A front-page paragraph referring to a story on an inside page: *The Times ran a reefer with the new term for "change of mind" subtly noted*—New York Times/ *The Timeses of New York or LA could produce front pages of refers, meaning concise summaries that resemble the tops of articles*—New York Times

reeler *n by 1930s* A spree; drunken carouse: *. . . before he realizes he is off on a reeler*— J Alexander

reenter *v narcotics* To cease feeling the effects of a narcotic; descend from a narcotic ecstasy [fr the *reentry* of a space vehicle into the Earth's atmosphere]

reentry *n 1960s narcotics* The act of descent from a narcotic ecstasy

reet or **reat** *adj* (also **reet** and **compleat**) *1930s jazz musicians* Good; proper; excellent; right: *With her good looks, she was still "reet" with me*—Louis Armstrong/ *. . . looking extremely reet and compleat*—Stephen King
See ALL REET

reet pleat *n phr 1940s jive talk* A long, narrow pleat in a zoot suit

ref **1** *n by 1899* A referee **2** *v by 1929: I started reffing basketball in southern Illinois in 1957*— Whitey Herzog

refrigerator mom *n phr by 1990s* A working or absentee mother who communicates with her children by notes on the refrigerator door: *Autistic kids are not due to refrigerator moms*—TV program *This Morning*

register *v by 1901* To express with the face and body: *I jumped up and registered horror*

regs *n by 1940s* Regulations; rules: *All regs say you can't*

regular 1 *adj by 1821* Real; genuine: *He thinks he's a regular Casanova* **2** *n fr lunch counter by 1950s* A cup of coffee with the usual moderate amount of cream and sugar •In New York City no sugar is included **3** *adj: regular coffee*

regular fellow (or guy) *n phr* first form by 1920, second by 1840 An honest, pleasant, convivial person, esp of the moral bourgeoisie: *I know I'm not a regular fellow, yet I loathe anybody else that isn't*—F Scott Fitzgerald/ *She's like Wallace. . . . A real fighter. A regular guy*—New York Magazine

rehab (REE hab) **1** *n by 1948* Rehabilitation, esp of a drug addict, alcoholic, etc: *After a few weeks' rehab they sent him back home* **2** *modifier: . . . more work-release and rehab centers*—L J Berry **3** *v by 1970s* To rehabilitate, esp a building,

factory, etc: *Williams has worked for minimum wage, rehabbing houses*—Philadelphia/ *. . . had to give up a sublease because the building was rehabbed*—Village Voice

rehash *by 1880* **1** *v* To review; discuss again; repeat; =RECAP: *. . . the things. . . they had hashed and rehashed for many a frugal conversational meal*—F Scott Fitzgerald **2** *n: . . . a rehash of stale political charges*—Associated Press [called vulgar in the dated source]

◁**Reilly's balls**▷ **See** TIGHT AS KELSEY'S NUTS

reinvent the wheel *v phr by 1980s* To go laboriously and unnecessarily through elementary stages in some process or enterprise; waste time on tediously obvious fundamentals

rejigger or **rejig** *v* first form by 1940s, second by 1960 To alter or readjust; tinker with: *. . . sought to raise output this year by rejiggering its agricultural policies*—Time [fr mid-1800s *jigger,* "shake or jerk rapidly," related to *jig* as a rapid movement, dance, etc, hence "rearrange or readjust by shaking," semantically similar to *shake up*]

religion **See** GET RELIGION

reloading *n by 1940s: In one of the worst scams, called "reloading," consumers who have already lost money are bilked again by companies that offer to recover their losses. . .* —Milwaukee Journal

◁**reltney**▷ *n* The penis: *My reltney was ready for action*—Playboy [origin unknown]

reno (REH noh) **1** *n Canadian by 1970s* A renovated house: *Buying an off-the-rack reno is expensive and not very adventurous*—Toronto Life **2** *modifier: Today a boarded-up construction site, tomorrow a reno Parthenon*—Toronto Life

rent **See** BET THE FARM, HIGH-RENT

rent-a-cop or ◁**rent-a-pig**▷ *n by 1970s* A uniformed security guard; =SQUARE BADGE: *. . . a part-time rent-a-cop, somebody's doorman*—Elmore Leonard [coined on the model of *rent-a-car,* on which model depends also the coinage *Rent-a-Kvetch* and many others]

rent party *n phr black by 1925* A party where one's friends and neighbors buy drinks, food, etc, and help one pay the rent; =PERCOLATOR, SHAKE

rents or **'rents** *n 1960s teenagers* Parents: *. . . I'm sure your only salvation is to hit up your rents*— Sassy

rep¹ *n by 1705* Reputation: *gettin' the rep a not havin' a big schnozz*—Jimmy Durante
See DEMI-REP

rep² **1** *n by 1896* A representative: *The sales rep from Kokomo* **2** *v: Both of whom are repped by yours truly. . .* —Gary Trudeau

rep³ **1** *n theater by 1925* Repertory: *She played in rep a couple years* **2** *modifier: a rep company*

rep⁴ *n by 1864* A repetition: *I mused on this while I did 15 reps at 250*—Robert B Parker

repeaters *n gambling by 1950s* Loaded dice

repeat on someone *v phr by 1930s* To cause eructation or belching: *I never eat chili because it always repeats on me*

repellent *See* CESSNA REPELLENT

replay *See* INSTANT REPLAY

repo[1] (REE poh) **1** *n* by 1970s A car repossessed for nonpayment of installments **2** *v*: . . . *when the best times are to repo or rip off cars*—*Time*

repo[2] (REE poh) *n* by 1963 A type of investment: . . . *investments known as retail repurchase agreements, or repos for short*—*Newsweek*

repo (or **snatch**) **man** (REE poh) *n phr* by 1970s A person employed to confiscate repossessed cars: *He had become unpopular as a result of his work as a repo man, work that had required him to carry a sawed-off shotgun*—*New Yorker*/ *Baraka gave young black artists a place to go outside of white bohemia and black academia, though some of us still landed in those two purgatories to stay ahead of the snatch man*—*Nation*

report *See* SUGAR REPORT

repple-depple or **rep-dep** or **reppo-depot** *n* WWII Army A military replacement center or depot where soldiers await assignment, processing, etc: . . . *the Naples "repple depple"*—J McKnight

res (REHZ) *n* by 1990s An Indian reservation: *He won't get off the res*—movie *Thunderheart*

resin *See* KISS THE CANVAS

rest *See* GIVE IT A REST

restless *See* the NATIVES ARE RESTLESS

◁**retard**▷ (REE tard) *n* by 1960s A stupid person; =AIRHEAD, SPAZ: . . . *the stereotype of the crazy retard*—*Philadelphia* [fr mentally *retarded*]

retread (REE tred) **1** *n* by 1914 A used tire with new tread **2** *n* WWII armed forces A former military person recalled or accepted for additional service

retro by 1974 **1** *n* A retrospective art exhibit, movie festival, etc: . . . *the Bleecker's current Godard retro*—*Village Voice* **2** *adj* Nostalgic; historically resurrectional: *I'm going to give them retro names like Madge or Verna or Ralph*—Douglas Coupland [fr *retrospective*]

Reuben *n* carnival & circus by 1905 =HAYSEED, HICK, RUBE

re-up Army by 1906 **1** *v* To re-enlist: *Are you really going to re-up and go to that chopper school?*—Earl Thompson **2** *v* To obligate or engage oneself again: . . . *paying him $6,000,000 to re-up with the Cubs*—KYW radio news [fr the requirement of holding up one's right hand while taking an oath]

rev or **rev up 1** *v* or *v phr* by 1916 To speed up a motor; increase the rpms **2** *v* or *v phr* by 1956 To stir up; stimulate; enliven; =JAZZ something UP: . . . *seems to think he has to really rev his prose every now and again*—*Washington Post*

revamp *v* by 1850 To improve by remaking; renovate; revise: *We can't just patch it up; we need to revamp the whole proposal* [fr shoemakers, "to replace the upper front part of a shoe"]

revolving-door *modifier* Of short duration; helter-skelter; transient: . . . *revolving-door presidents and prime ministers, that's what's happening*—W T Tyler

revved up *adj phr* by 1931 Excited; expectant;

=PUMPED UP: . . . *we were really revved up that here was somebody who was going to try to run up the middle*—*Milwaukee Journal*

RF (pronounced as separate letters) 1960s college students **1** *n* =RAT FINK **2** *n* =RAT FUCK **3** *n* =a ROYAL FUCKING

RHIP (pronounced as separate letters) *sentence* Army by 1930s Rank hath its privileges

rhubarb[1] *n* baseball by 1938 A loud quarrel or squabble; a controversy of riotous potential, esp among baseball players on the field: . . . *beanball throwing, rhubarbs, and umpire baiting*—J Durant [origin unknown and richly speculated on; said to have been first used in a broadcast by Garry Schumacher]

rhubarb[2] **1** *n* WWII Air Forces A low-level aerial strafing mission **2** *v*: *flying for rhubarbing*—C Macon [an arbitrary code name]

the rhubarbs *n phr* baseball by 1915 Small towns; rural venues; the provinces: *what the game meant as it's played out in the rhubarbs*—G Patten [fr a humorous alteration of *suburbs*]

rib 1 *v* by 1930 To tease; make fun of; =KID, RAG, RIDE: *His trick is gently ribbing the audience* **2** *n*: *Carson sensed that he was the victim of a rib*—Russell Baker [origin unknown; perhaps fr a symbolic nudge in the *ribs*]

ribbie or **ribby** or **rib-eye steak** *n* first forms baseball by 1960s, third form by 1990s A run batted in; RBI: . . . *had two other big ribbies*—*Sports Illustrated*/ *Brandon. . . had two homers and seven rib-eye steaks (RBI)*—*Milwaukee Journal Sentinel*

rib joint *n phr* by 1943 A brothel: . . . *fracas in a Minneapolis rib joint*—Max Shulman [probably fr earlier *rib*, "woman," fr *Adam's rib*, influenced by the designation of a restaurant specializing in barbecued spare *ribs*]

ribs *n* 1950s bop & cool talk Food; a meal [extension of barbecued spare *ribs*, semantically similar to the extension of *grits*]

rib-tickler *n* by 1933 Something amusing, esp a joke

rice-burner or **rice-grinder** *n* motorcyclists by 1980s A motorcycle of Japanese manufacture

rich *See* STRIKE IT RICH, TOO RICH FOR someone's BLOOD

Richard Roe *See* JOHN DOE

◁**rich bitch**▷ **1** *n phr* by 1940s A wealthy woman **2** *adj phr*: . . . *his rich-bitch mother-in-law*—*Newsweek*

rich rich *adj phr* by 1963 Very rich: *They're rich, OK, but not rich rich* [found by 1725 in a poem of Edward Taylor, but the meaning is not clearly the same]

rickety-tick *See* MOST RICKETY-TICK

ricky-tick[1] (also **ricky-ticky** or **rinky-tink**) **1** *n* jazz musicians about 1930 Bouncy ragtime music of the 1920s **2** *adj* jazz musicians about 1930 Old-fashioned; outworn; =CORNY: . . . *a brassy, ricky-ticky big band sound*—*Life*

ricky-tick[2] *adj* =RINKY-DINK

ride 1 *v by 1912* To tease; heckle; make fun of; =NEEDLE, RIB: *I can remember riding Pete Rose to death from the bench*—Inside Sports ◁**2**▷ *v by 1250* To do the sex act with or to a woman; mount; =SCREW **3** *n by 1937: He asked her for a ride and she slapped him* **4** *n jazz musicians by 1930* An improvised passage; =BREAK, RIFF **5** *n by 1787* A saddle horse **6** *n 1960s narcotics* A psychedelic narcotic experience; =TRIP **7** *n by 1929* A car: *This you ride, man?*—Robert B Parker **8** *v baseball by 1929* To hit the ball hard; =POWDER: *Goslin rode it right out of the park*

See FULL RIDE, GO ALONG FOR THE RIDE, GRAVY RIDE, HITCH A RIDE, JOY RIDE, LET something RIDE, SLEIGHRIDE, TAKE someone FOR A RIDE, THUMB

◁**ride** someone's **ass**▷ *v phr by 1980s* To harass someone; =BUG, HASSLE: *... somebody wants to bother you, man, really ride your ass*—George V Higgins [*ride* is found by 1583 in the stronger sense "to dominate cruelly, oppress"]

ride cymbal or **ride** *n phr* or *n jazz musicians by about 1925* A drummer's cymbal used for keeping up a constant tintinnabulation, as distinct from a crash

ride herd on someone or something *v phr by 1897* To keep someone or something under control; monitor and correct; manage: *.... Chief Suarez hasn't been riding herd on his guys*—Lawrence Sanders

rideout *v jazz musicians by about 1925* To play the last chorus of a jazz number in a free and lively way

rider 1 *n cowboys by 1894* A cowboy **2** *n by 1795* A jockey

See BAREBACK RIDER, BUG BOY, EASY RIDER, FREE-RIDER, JOY-RIDER, LOW RIDER, SLEIGHRIDER

ride (or **go**) **shank's mare** *v phr by 1846* To walk

ride shotgun 1 *v phr by 1963* To act as a guard, esp on a vehicle; keep a vigilant eye peeled; insure safety: *... beefing up security and changing the pattern of deliveries, although nobody will start to ride shotgun*—Time/ *Several wives have gotten wise and are riding shotgun on who checks in and out*—Amsterdam News **2** *v phr 1960s teenagers* To ride in the front passenger seat of a car [fr the Old West practice of having an armed guard with a *shotgun riding* beside the driver on the stagecoaches]

ride the arm *v phr cabdrivers by 1970s* To collect a fare without using the meter; =ARM IT, HIGHFLAG

ride the blinds *v phr hoboes by 1920s* To ride a train in the spaces at the locked or doorless ends of baggage cars

ride the gravy train (or **gravy boat**) *v phr by 1927* To enjoy a good and effortless life; bask in prosperous ease

ride the lightning *v phr prison by 1935* To be executed in the electric chair; =BURN, FRY

ride the pine (or **pines**) *v phr sports by 1980s* To sit idle on the player's bench: *... who right now seems destined to ride the pine a lot behind Mark Jackson*—Milwaukee Journal/ *I'd rather ride the pines on Mars than play the outfield for these mo'-fuckers*—Jane Leavy

ride (or **hit**) **the rods** *v phr hoboes by 1920s* To ride trains as a hobo, esp to ride perilously in the steel reinforcing struts beneath a freight car

ridge-runner 1 *n by 1917* A southern Appalachian mountain dweller; =HILLBILLY **2** *n black by 1960s* A white person; =OFAY, GRAY

ridic *adj students by 1925* Ridiculous

rif (pronounced as separate letters or as an acronym RIF) *by 1953* **1** *v* To notify an employee of dismissal or layoff: *... when he receives his Reduction in Force letter, and he will say, "I've been riffed"*—New York Times **2** *n* A dismissal; layoff **3** *v* To demote: *... had been "rif'd" back to sergeants*—C Bryan **4** *n* A demotion [fr *reduction in force*]

riff¹ 1 *n jazz musicians by about 1917* An improvised passage, esp a solo; =BREAK, LICK: *... an initially funky bass riff*—Rolling Stone **2** *n jazz musicians by about 1917* A solo passage of any sort: *He never inflates a movement, never accelerates into showy riffs of excess energy*—Time **3** *n by 1990s* A particular variation or version: *I have actually eaten something called a pastrami burrito dog, sort of a riff on the oki dog...*—Los Angeles Times **4** *n by 1980s* A piece of personal behavior, esp of entertainment; =SHTICK: *... allow the star to do character riffs... that approximate the sort of things she does as monologues in her one-woman show*—New York Times/ *He can make out the riffs and scams of the inner city like a dog picking up a scent*—Scott Turow [origin unknown; perhaps echoic; perhaps fr *refrain*; perhaps fr *riffle* or *ripple* in the sense of "try, shot, crack"]

riff² *n railroad by 1950s* A refrigerator car; =REEFER¹

riffle¹ *n baseball by 1932* A hard swing at the ball; =RIPPLE: *... gives it a really good solid riffle*—H Lobert [probably fr *ripple* fr *rip*]

riffle² 1 *v cardplaying by 1894* To shuffle playing cards **2** *n*: *Give that deck a good riffle* [probably echoic]

riff on someone *v phr 1980s students* To take advantage of someone: *Hey, don't riff on me, man, just because I'm sick*—College Slang 101

rig 1 *v by 1930s* To prearrange or tamper with a result or process; =FIX: *Prizefights or horse-races have been rigged*—Literary Digest **2** *n* (also **rig-out**) *by 1843* Clothing; outfit: *How come you're wearing that rig?/... a waiter's or a chef's rig-out*—Niven Busch **3** *n bus drivers & truckers by 1930s* A truck, bus, ambulance, etc

right 1 *adj by 1856* Reliable; safe: *He assured them his partner was all right* **2** *affirmation by 1588* Yes; correct: *Did you say left? Right!* **3** *question by 1961* Am I not right?; =CAPEESH, OK: *He's in charge, right?*

See ALL RIGHT, ALL RIGHT ALREADY, DEAD TO RIGHTS, FLY RIGHT, HANG A RIGHT

Right *See* MISTER RIGHT

righteous *adj jazz musicians by about 1900* Excellent; genuine; =the GREATEST: *... what we used* *to call the righteous jazz*—National Review/ *"Is that righteous gold?" "Righteous it ain't, but gold it is"*—Harry Crews

righteous moss *n phr* black by 1942 Hair of a Caucasian sort; nonkinky hair; =GOOD HAIR: . . . *it looked just like that righteous moss*—Zora Neale Hurston

right guy *by 1906* **1** *n phr* A reliable and helpful person; =SQUARE GUY: *You was a right guy*—J Lilienthal **2** *n phr* A person who can be trusted, esp not to inform to the police

right-handed *adj by 1970s* Heterosexual; =STRAIGHT: *He was about 60 percent right-handed and he ended up as a male go-go dancer*—George V Higgins

right joint *underworld by 1950s* **1** *n phr* A trustworthy gambling place, criminal haunt, etc **2** *n phr* prison A prison, reformatory, etc, where prisoners are treated fairly: *Great Meadow. . . a "right joint"*—John Lardner

right money *n phr by 1941* =the SMART MONEY: *It's the combination of likely lad and a good horse that makes "right money" dig down in its jeans*—J Lilienthal

right-o *affirmation* (also **righto** or **right-ho** or **rightho**) British by 1896 Yes; correct; all right

right off the bat *adv phr by 1914* Immediately; without delay: *I normally get four cars right off the bat*—Philadelphia [*hot from the bat* is found by 1888]

right on 1 *interj* black by 1925 An exclamation of approval, encouragement, agreement, etc: *Oh mercy, baaabeh, riiight onnnn!*—Time **2** *adj phr by 1960s* Precisely right; very effective: *Michael Caine. . . is right on as the medic*—Judith Crist [first sense popularized as a Black Panther usage in the middle 1960s]

rights See DEAD TO RIGHTS, GIVE someone HIS RIGHTS

the **right stuff** *n phr by 1848* The best human ingredients, such as fortitude and resolution: . . . *a heart that was made of the right stuff to set off to advantage his iron frame*—Illustrated London News [popularized by Tom Wolfe's 1979 book about the first astronauts]

right there See IN THERE PITCHING, THERE

right up there *adv phr by 1970* Among the leaders, the most distinguished, etc; in contention: *Two weeks to go and the Mets are still right up there*

righty *n by 1940s* A righthanded person, esp a baseball player; =NORTHPAW
See ALL RIGHTY

rigmatick *n by 1970s* A complicated procedure; rigmarole: *We went through the whole rigmatick*—Xaviera Hollander

rig out *v phr by 1616* To dress; clothe: *Then they rigged me out in a uniform*

◁**rim**▷ *v* homosexuals by 1959 To lick or suck the anus
See REAM

rims See ON THE RIMS

rinctum *n* black by 1950s The rectum
See SPIZZERINCTUM

ring 1 *v* horse-racing by 1812 To substitute one horse illegally for another in a race: . . . *to attempt ringing*—A Hynd **2** *v* (also **ring up**) by 1940s, variant by 1880 To call on the telephone; =GIVE someone A RING: *I rang him the next day, but he was out*
See THROW one's HAT IN THE RING

ring a bell *v phr by 1934* To remind one of something; sound familiar: *"Nineteen seventy-six. June 25" "Ring a bell?"*—Carsten Stroud

ring-a-ding-ding or **ring-a-ding** by 1970s **1** *n* Glamour and show; spectacular impressiveness; =RAZZLE-DAZZLE: . . . *an aura of breathless showbiz ring-a-ding-ding*—Albert Goldman **2** *adj*: *Our new stack addition is a huge brick building full of metal, a ring-a-ding book box*—American Libraries

ring someone's **bell** (or **chimes**) *v phr by 1970s* To be sexually attractive to someone; =TURN someone ON

ring changes *v phr by 1614* To make or try out variations, esp ingeniously: *Berle could do the same mugging bits. . . and ring many more changes on them*—Pauline Kael [fr *change-ringing*, the elaborate esp British ringing of sets of church bells]

ring-dang-do (RING DANG Do͞o) *n by 1970s* A complicated process, scene, affair, etc; rigmarole; =RIGMATICK: . . . *the whole ring-dang-do of moral Darwinism*—Village Voice

ring-ding *n by 1970s* A stupid person; =DING-A-LING: . . . *that South American ring-ding with his sequined rodeo shirt*—Richard Fariña

ringer 1 *n* horse-racing by 1890 A person or animal substituted for another, esp a racehorse put in to run in place of an inferior beast: . . . *"ringers," good horses masquerading as poor ones*—Fortune **2** *n* horse-racing by 1890 A person who arranges the illegal substitution of a horse: . . . *the master horse ringer of them all*—A Hynd **3** *n by 1891* A person or thing that closely resembles another; =DEAD RINGER: *With the mustache and glasses, Blackmer is a ringer for Teddy*—Associated Press [fr the expression *ring someone in*, "announce or herald someone"]

ringmaster *n* railroad by 1940s A yardmaster

ring off 1 *v phr by 1882* To end a telephone conversation; hang up **2** *v phr by about 1895* To stop talking; =SHUT UP

ring off the hook (or **the wall**) *v phr by 1970s* To ring constantly and often: *Says the director of the hotline: "The phones have been ringing off the hook"*—Time

ringtail 1 *n* hoboes by 1931 A grouch **2** *n* underworld by 1931 An offensive person; =BASTARD, JERK ◀**3**▶ *n* dockworkers by 1940s An Italian dockworker or one of Italian extraction ◀**4**▶ *n* WWII Navy A Japanese [origin unknown]

ringtailed snorter *n phr by 1840s* A vigorous, impressive person; =HUMDINGER: *He's a ringtailed snorter*—Ithaca Journal [*ringtailed* was an early–1800s US superlative, perhaps fr the *ringtailed painter*, a fierce wild cat of the Western US, or perhaps fr the coonskin caps, with *ringed tails* appended, worn by frontiersmen]

ring the bell *v phr* by 1900 To succeed; be a winner: *That last contribution rang the bell* [fr the carnival machine where one wins, esp a cigar, by *ringing a bell* with a hard hammer stroke]

rink rat *n phr* Canadian by 1945 A person who frequents hockey rinks, does odd jobs there for free admission, etc

rinktum *See* SPIZZERINKTUM

rinky-dink 1 *n* carnival by 1912 Cheap and gaudy merchandise; =DRECK, JUNK **2** *n* by 1913 Used merchandise; secondhand articles: *Let's go see what sort of rinky-dink the Salvation Army has this week* **3** *n* by 1912 A small, cheap nightclub, cabaret, etc; =HONKY-TONK: *... as she was called when she played the rinky-dinks*—Edward Weeks **4** *adj* (also **ricky-tick**) by 1913 Inferior; cheap; =CRUMMY: *... described by federal attorneys as rinky dink and a very strange document*—Wall Street Journal/ *... its deserted beaches, summer houses, and ricky-tick towns*—Denison Hatch **5** *n* by 1912 A deception; swindle; =RUNAROUND: *Don't give me the rinkydink*—Sherman Billingsley

See RICKY-TICK

rinky-tink *See* RICKY-TICK

a riot *n phr* by 1909 A very amusing person or thing, joke, occasion, etc; =a HOOT, a SCREAM

See LAFF RIOT

the riot act *See* READ THE RIOT ACT

riot grrrl *n phr* by 1990s A militant female feminist: *Watching this magazine drool like a dirty old man over riot grrrls is very amusing. Like a riot grrrl would ever have sex with an Esquire reader*—Sassy

rip¹ *n* by 1797 A debauched and dissolute person; libertine: *... the proper way to treat a rip*— J Stephens [perhaps a variant of *rep* fr *reprobate*]

rip² **1** *n* police by 1939 An official demerit or fine **2** *n* by 1940s An insult; a disparagement; •Common in baseball talk; =KNOCK: *... master of the off-field rip*—Milwaukee Journal **3** *v* British dialect by 1857: *William Proxmire... who is usually ripped for refusing to bring home the bacon*— Milwaukee Journal **4** *v* (also **rip-ass**) by 1853 To speed; =BARREL, TEAR: *... cars rip-assing up and down the street*—Stephen King **5** *n* by 1970s A joy; a pleasure: *What a rip it is to know there are still people... who feel for the cars they put together*—Car and Driver **6** *n* by 1940s A try; attempt; =CRACK, RIPPLE, SHOT: *I'll have a rip at that old record* **7** *n* by 1990s =RIPOFF [all, one way or another, fr *rip*, "tear"; fifth sense perhaps related to *ripping*, "excellent, first-rate," found by 1846]

See GIVE something A SHOT, HAVE A CRACK AT something

a rip *n phr* by 1940s The smallest quantity; =ZILCH: *Doesn't have a rip to do with your health...* —Bill Clinton

See NOT GIVE A DAMN

ripoff 1960s black **1** *n* A theft; an act of stealing **2** *n* A fraud; swindle; =SCAM: *The whole arms-reduction policy is a big ripoff* **3** *n* (also **ripoff**

artist) A person or company that steals or swindles: *He was the biggest ripoff ever seen, even in Congress*

rip off 1960s black **1** *v phr* To steal: *Somebody ripped off my bike* **2** *v phr* To swindle; defraud; =GYP: *I don't know who rips us off more, business or government* [*rip*, "to steal," is found by 1200]

rip on someone *v phr* 1960s black To harass and insult; =RIP: *When those two get together they totally rip on Jeff*—UCLA Slang

ripped 1 *adj* by 1971 Intoxicated, either from narcotics or alcohol; =HIGH: *I'm ripped to the tits as it is*—Armistead Maupin **2** *adj* 1980s students Showing well-defined muscles: *So ripped you can see her liver, or think you can...* —Harry Crews

ripple *n* A try; an attempt; =CRACK, RIP, SHOT: *I'll never figure out how these pieces fit, so why don't you have a ripple?* [origin uncertain; perhaps fr *rip* in the sense of a strong action, attempt, or blow; perhaps fr 1800s *make a riffle* or *ripple*, "to succeed, make it," based on crossing or getting through dangerous rapids in a river]

See GIVE something A SHOT, HAVE A CRACK AT something

◁**ripshit**▷ *adj* by 1980s Very angry; =PISSED OFF, STEAMED: *Michael was ripshit*—Jane Leavy

ripsnorter *n* by 1840 A person or thing that is remarkable, wonderful, superior; etc; =BEAUT, HUMDINGER: *The villain is a real ripsnorter*—S J Perelman

a rise *See* GET A RISE OUT OF someone

the ritz *See* PUT ON THE RITZ

ritzy by 1920 **1** *adj* Elegant; luxurious; =CLASSY, POSH: *The ritziest dance hall was the Haymarket*— E Lavine **2** *adj* Haughty; supercilious; =STUCK-UP

river *See* SELL someone DOWN THE RIVER, SEND UP, UP THE RIVER

rivethead *n* Army by 1970s A member of a tank crew

rivets *n* by 1846 Money

roach 1 *n* prison & black by 1932 A police officer **2** *n* horse-racing by 1940s A racehorse, esp an inferior one; =BEETLE **3** *n* narcotics by 1938 The stub or butt of a marijuana cigarette: *He lighted the toke again, a roach now that he impaled on a thin wire*—Lawrence Sanders **4** *n* 1960s students An unattractive woman [narcotics sense perhaps fr earlier *roach mane*, a horse's mane clipped very short and tied; perhaps fr the insect]

roach clip (or **holder) *n phr* 1960s narcotics Any tweezerlike device for holding a marijuana cigarette stub too short to be held in the fingers; =CRUTCH: *... necessitating the invention of the "roach clip," which holds roaches*—New York Times

roach-coach *n* by 1990s: *At lunch time he spots a roach-coach lunch wagon that dispenses burgers, hot dogs, french fries*—US News & World Report

road *modifier* theater by 1900 Traveling; touring; itinerant: *a road show*

See BURN THE ROAD, GO THE HANG-OUT ROAD, HARD-ROAD FREAK, HIT THE ROAD, LET'S GET THE SHOW ON

THE ROAD, ONE FOR THE ROAD, ON THE ROAD, SKID ROAD, WHERE THE RUBBER MEETS THE ROAD, WIDE PLACE IN THE ROAD

road apple *See* ALLEY APPLE

road dog *n phr* 1980s *Philadelphia black* A good friend; best friend; =ACE BOON COON

road hog *n phr* by 1891 A driver who takes more than his or her share of the road

roadie *n* (also **roadster**) by 1969 A person who travels with a musical, political, theatrical, or other group to handle booking, business arrangements, equipment, etc: *Microphones tossed by Chapman land in unlikely places, one on a roadie, another in the lap of the audience*—Changes

road kill 1 *n phr* by 1980s A person or animal struck by a car and killed; =ROAD PIZZA: *After screeching to check for roadkill, these. . . young motorists started howling, laughing it up*—Sassy **2** *n phr* by 1980s Something undesirable and unpalatable, like the meat of an animal killed in traffic: *Plagiarism proclaims that some written words are valuable enough to steal. But what if the borrowed stuff is a flat, lifeless mess, the road kill of passing ideas?*—Time **3** *n phr* *sports* by 1990s : *Nothing like a road kill. For our young guys who are new to the team, nothing is better than getting a road win*—Milwaukee Journal

road people *n phr* by 1960s Persons, esp young, who travel about in vans or with backpacks; itinerants: *Some road people tend to display a continual inability to adjust*—A Miller

road pizza 1 *n phr* by 1980s A dead animal smashed in traffic **2** *n phr* *cyclists* by 1990s (also **road rash**) Abrasions from a crash

road-stake *n* *hoboes* by 1940s Money for traveling

roam *v* by 1990s To use a cellular phone outside of one's own service area: *Hi honey. I'm roaming in San Francisco*—Los Angeles Times

roast 1 *v* by 1710 To make fun of; ridicule; insult, often in an affectionate way: *. . . had been roasted often by the critics as a ham*—Russell Baker **2** *n*: *. . . this national love for a good "roast," this spirit of mockery*—H Spencer

robber *See* BELLY-ROBBER, CRADLE-ROBBER, DOG-ROBBER

Robin Hood's barn *See* GO AROUND ROBIN HOOD'S BARN

robocop *n* by 1990s A robot police officer

rob the cradle by 1940s **1** *v phr* To marry or date someone much younger than oneself **2** *v phr* To recruit, use, or exploit young persons

robuck *v* *prison* by 1970s To instigate something; get something going [fr a mispronunciation of *robot*, with the notion that one performs certain provocative actions as one would push a button or throw a switch to activate a robot]

rock 1 *n* by 1840 A dollar; =BUCK: *I want to see you make twenty rocks*—R Starnes **2** *n* *underworld* by 1908 Any precious stone, esp a diamond **3** *v* by about 1900 To do the sex act with or to; =SCREW, RIDE: *My man rocks me with one steady roll*—

Metronome **4** *n* by early 1950s A rock and roll devotee: *. . . teenagers called "rocks"*—Herbert Mitgang **5** *n* by early 1950s Rock and roll music: *hard rock* **6** *v* by early 1950s To move, dance, writhe, etc, to rock and roll music; =BOOGIE, BOP: *Soon just one couple was rocking in the middle of the floor* **7** *v* by early 1950s To be resonant with and physically responsive to rock and roll music; =JUMP: *Soon the whole room was rocking* **8** *n* 1980s *narcotics* A small cube of very pure cocaine, intended for smoking rather than inhalation: *Dealers sell pellet-size "rocks". . . in small plastic vials*—Time **9** *n* *prison* by 1970s A cellblock: *When is the wagon due back on this rock, Pops?*—Donald Goines **10** *n* *basketball* by 1980s A basketball

See ACID ROCK, EIGHT-ROCK, GLITTER ROCK, HARD ROCK, HOT ROCK, PUNK ROCK

the Rock 1 *n phr* by 1940s Alcatraz Island and its (former) federal penitentiary **2** *n* *fr middle 1800s* Gibraltar

rockabilly 1 *n* by 1956 A blend of black rhythm and blues with white hillbilly music **2** *modifier*: *. . . showing up at rockabilly dances and clubs in full '50s regalia*—Newsweek

rock and roll or **rock 'n' roll 1** *n phr* by early 1950s A style of heavily accented music evolved from blues, folk, and country music, usu having sung lyrics, and played on very highly amplified electronic instruments **2** *modifier*: *a rock and roll group* **3** *n phr* by early 1950s Dancing done to such music

rock 'em, sock 'em *adj phr* by 1970s Violent and energetic; concussive: *. . . the rock 'em, sock 'em action that goes on inside a full-sized truck*—Car and Driver

rocker[1] by early 1950s **1** *n* A rock and roll musician, singer, radio station, etc: *. . . general manager of rhythm-and-blues rocker WOL in Washington, DC*—National Observer **2** *n* A rock and roll song: *. . . classic country rockers, sometimes with an old-timey flavor*—Playboy

See PUNK ROCKER, TEENYBOPPER

rocker[2] *See* OFF one's NOODLE

rocket *n* by 1941 A complaint or rebuke; =BEEF, DING •Chiefly British: *. . . you get a rocket from one of the parties*—Time

rocket scientist *See* YOU DON'T HAVE TO BE A BRAIN SURGEON

rockhead by 1950s **1** *n* A stupid person **2** *modifier*: *. . . some rockhead hoodlums*—I, Mobster

rock jock *n phr* by 1980 A rock-climber; mountain-climber; Alpinist: *In about a year she's gone from novice climber to total rock jock*—Sassy

rocks 1 *n* by 1946 Ice cubes ◁2▷ *n* by 1948 The testicles; =FAMILY JEWELS, NUTS [*stones* in the second sense is found by 1154]

See GET one's ROCKS, HAVE ROCKS IN one's HEAD, HOT ROCKS, ON THE ROCKS, TOUGH SHIT

rocks in one's **(or the) head** *n phr* by 1951 Stupidity; foolishness; mental incapacity: *. . . dedi-*

cated to whiny losers with rocks in their heads—Village Voice

See HAVE ROCKS IN one's HEAD

rock the boat *v phr by* 1931 To cause trouble; create inconveniences; disrupt things: *Fritz Mondale doesn't want to rock the boat*—Associated Press

rocky 1 *adj* Drunk **2** *adj by* 1895 Weak and unsteady; groggy; =WOOZY: *. . . came back to work, looking pale and rocky*—Hal Boyle **3** *adj by* 1873 Difficult; trying; =TOUGH: *That was a very rocky time for our family*

Rocky Mountain canary *See* MOUNTAIN CANARY

Rocky Mountain oyster *n phr by* 1889 A lamb's testicles used as food

rod 1 *n underworld by* 1903 A pistol: *Here's a rod, blow your brains out*—Ernest Boyd **2** *n* 1940s *hot rodders* A car, esp a specially prepared car; =HOT ROD: *A restless youth buys a broken-down rod*—New York Times ◁3▷ *n by* 1902 The penis; =SHAFT

See GRAB A HANDFUL OF RODS, HAVE A ROD ON, JOHNSON ROD

rod-man *n underworld by* 1929 A gunman; =TORPEDO

rod up *v phr underworld by* 1940s To arm; provide with a pistol: *They do not rod up or arm themselves*—E DeBaun

Roe *See* JOHN DOE

Roger or **Roge** or **Rodger-dodger** *affirmation WWII armed forces* Yes; I understand; =OK: *Get your asses over there. . . Roge*—New York Times [fr the US military phonetic alphabet word designating *R* for "received," said also to have been used by the Royal Air Force by 1938]

rogues' gallery *by* 1859 **1** *n phr* A police collection of photographs of criminals; =MUG SHOTS **2** *n phr* Any group or collection of unsavory persons; den of thieves: *The new building commission is a plain rogues' gallery*

'roid or **roid** *n by late* 1980s A steroid drug used for body-building: *'Roids, dude. The Wheaties of the '80s*—Milwaukee Journal

'roid (or **roid) rage** *n phr by late* 1980s: *Normally easygoing, he recalls bouts of roid rage, an urge to destroy that often strikes steroid users*—Los Angeles Times

Rok (RAHK) *n Korean War armed forces* A South Korean, esp a soldier [fr *Republic of Korea*]

rolf *See* RALPH

roll 1 *v by* 1873 To rob, esp a stuporous or helpless drunkard who is literally rolled over for access to pockets: *. . . rolling a stiff*—Jack London/ *. . . the less perilous profession of rolling lushes*—Wolcott Gibbs **2** *v railroad by* 1950s To displace another worker: *Negro firemen on the good runs should be "rolled" by whites*—Survey Graphic **3** *v movie studio by* 1939 To run or start a movie camera: *Quiet, and roll 'em*—King Vidor **4** *n by* 1846 Money; funds; =BANKROLL **5** *n by* 1940s The sex act; =ROLL IN THE HAY

See CRUMB-ROLL, JACKROLL, JELLY-ROLL, LOG ROLL,

MICHIGAN ROLL, ON A ROLL, PRESS ROLL, ROCK AND ROLL

rollback *n by* 1942 A reduction, esp of wages or production

roller 1 *n prison by* 1940s A prison guard **2** *n black by* 1964 A police officer **3** *n by* 1915 A thief who robs drunks [first two senses fr late–1700s British *rollers,* "horse and foot patrols of police"]

See DOWN THE GOODYEARS, HIGH ROLLER, LUSH ROLLER, PILL-PUSHER, PUMPKIN ROLLER, STEAMROLLER

roller skate *n phr truckers by* 1980s: *Cars are "four-wheelers," small cars are "roller skates"*—Brian Di Salvatore

roll in *v phr by* 1940s To arrive; =SHOW UP: *What time did you finally roll in?*

roll in money *v phr by* 1773 To be very rich

rolling doughnut *See* TAKE A FLYING FUCK

rolling off a log *See* EASY AS PIE

roll in the hay *n phr by* 1940s The sex act, esp when regarded as casual and joyous: *A roll in the hay with Seattle Slew cost $710,000*—Philadelphia

roll out the red carpet *v phr by* 1952 To give someone a very sumptuous or ceremonious welcome

rollover *n prison by* 1940s The last night of a prison sentence

roll over 1 *v phr by* 1957 To reinvest bonds, certificates of deposit, or other monetary instruments upon maturity, rather than liquidating them **2** *v phr police by* 1973 To inform on one's criminal associates; =SQUEAL: *It was the easiest flip Stone ever made. The man rolled over like a puppy and proceeded to hand up his associates so fast that Stone had to tell him to slow down*—Carsten Stroud

roll over and play dead *v phr by* 1940s To surrender or acquiesce, esp without resisting: *We're not about to roll over and play dead while the Republicans rubber stamp their extremist agenda*—Time [fr a trick one would teach a dog]

roll the bones *v phr by* 1929 To play craps [*bones,* "dice," is found by 1386]

roll with the punches *v phr by* 1951 To behave so as to defend oneself against damage and surprise; absorb punishment and survive: *"You roll with the punches. . . My experience was, I was going to lose her. . . . But I'm thankful for what I've gotten so far"*—Washington Post [fr the evasive action of a boxer who does not avoid a *punch* but reduces its effect by moving in the direction of the blow]

romp 1 *n* 1960s *street gang* A fight, esp between street gangs; =RUMBLE **2** *v*: *The gangs romped on Thursday*

ronchie *See* RAUNCHY

-roo *See* -EROO

roof *See* FALL OFF THE ROOF, RAISE THE ROOF

the roof falls (or **caves) in** *v phr by* 1958 A sudden and total catastrophe occurs; one's joy and world collapses: *. . . long before the roof fell in on Gossage*—Village Voice/ *But then the roof caved in on the Bucks*—Milwaukee Journal

rook 1 *v by* 1577 To cheat; defraud; =GYP: *. . . who would rook them for two dollars*—Abel Green **2** *n: Balcony seats for 40 bucks are a real rook* [probably fr the thieving habits of the *rook,* which it shares with other corvine birds like the crow and magpie]

rookie or **rookey** or **rooky 1** *n by 1892* A newcomer; recruit; tyro: . . . *the rookies and substitutes*—Babe Ruth **2** *modifier*: *The shooting of "rookie" patrolman James A Broderick*—E Lavine [probably fr shortening of *recruit;* perhaps fr the black, *rook*-colored coat worn by some British army recruits]

room *n show business by 1950s* A nightclub; =BOITE, NITERY

See BALLOON ROOM, BUCKET SHOP, CRYING ROOM, ELBOW ROOM, HORSE ROOM, LIVING-ROOM GIG, RUMPUS ROOM, TEAROOM

roost *n by 1940s* One's home; =PAD
See QUAIL-ROOST

root¹ *v by 1888* To cheer; applaud; urge on: *We rooted and rooted, but our side folded* [origin obscure]

root² **1** *n by about 1900* A cigarette **2** *n 1960s narcotics* A marijuana cigarette [perhaps fr *cheroot* or *cigaroot*]

◁**root³**▷ *n by 1846* The penis [fr something that is or can be planted]

rooter *n by 1890* A supporter or fan, esp of a team, fighter, school, etc

root for 1 *v phr by 1889* To be a regular supporter of; be a fan of: *He rooted for the Giants* **2** *v phr by 1922* To urge hopefully: *I'm rooting for the tax bill* [perhaps fr British dialect *route,* "roar, bellow"]

root hog or die *sentence by middle 1834* Work extremely hard, or fail; =the CHIPS ARE DOWN: *A red-faced rookie tackle from the University of Michigan. . . screamed, "Root hog or die!"*—Peter Gent

rootin'-tootin' *adj by 1924* Boisterous; noisy; vigorous: *He's a hifalutin' rootin'-tootin' son of a gun from Arizona*—song Ragtime Cowboy Joe [probably fr *rooting,* "cheering loudly," and *tooting,* "blowing a horn"]

rootle out *v phr* To root or grub out; seek and eliminate ●Chiefly British: . . . *rootle out Government fraud and waste*—Village Voice [an 1809 source says "to dig up roots like swine"]

rooty *adj by 1960s* Sexually aroused; =HORNY [fr *root,* "penis"]

rooty-toot *n musicians by 1936* Old-fashioned music; =CORN, RICKY-TICK

rope 1 *n by 1934* A cigar; =EL ROPO, HEMP **2** *v* (also **rope in**) *by 1848* To ensnare someone with amity and concern, as a means of swindling **3** *n baseball by 1960s* A hard-hit line drive; =CLOTHESLINE, FROZEN ROPE **4** *v*: . . . *Surhoff roped an RBI double to the gap in left-center*—Milwaukee Journal
See FROZEN ROPE, GOAT FUCK, GO PISS UP A ROPE, KNOW THE ROPES, SUCK

ro-ro *n by 1955* A roll-on roll-off ship, whose cargo is driven on and off

Roscoe or **roscoe** or **John Roscoe** *n by 1914* A pistol; =HEAT [a pet name, used for dissimulation]
See JOHN ROSCOE

rose *n medical* A comatose and dying patient [fr the color and the perilous frailty of such a patient]
See COME UP SMELLING LIKE A ROSE, SMELL LIKE A ROSE

◁**rosebud**▷ *n homosexuals by 1970s* The anus

rose garden *See* FRUIT SALAD

rose room *n phr medical by 1970s* A room where comatose and dying patients are treated

rosewood *n by 1950s* A police officer's nightstick; =BILLY CLUB

rosy 1 *adj by 1905* Slightly drunk; =TIDDLY **2** *adj by 1887* Promising; favorable; =COPACETIC: *Things look rosy now*

rot 1 *n by 1848* Nonsense; =BALONEY, BULLSHIT **2** *v 1960s teenagers* To be deplorable, nasty, inept, bungled, etc; =STINK, SUCK: *This idea of yours rots*

Rotacy (ROH tə see, RAH-) *n* (also **rot-see** or **rotasie** or **Rot-corps**) *college students by 1940s* The Reserve Officers Training Corps

rotchy *adj students by 1960s* =RAUNCHY

rotgut *n by 1597* Inferior liquor; =PANTHER PISS: . . . *re Prohibition rotgut*—H Allen Smith

rotorhead *n Army by 1970s* A helicopter pilot or crew member

Roto-Rooter *by 1980s* **1** *n* Any medical device that clears or cleans out obstructions in tubes: *More than 100,000 Americans had a surgical procedure known as carotid endartectomy, a kind of Roto-Rooter for cleaning out clogged arteries*—Nation **2** *n*: *The number of computers directly connected to the Internet is updated periodically by sending a computer program crawling around like a Roto-Rooter tallying the number of connections*—Time [fr a trademarked plumber's device for cleaning out clogged pipe]

rotten *adj by 1880* Deplorable; nasty; inept and bungled: *This is a rotten situation altogether*

rotten apple *n phr by 1940s* A corrupt or unfit person, who may corrupt others: *But a certain number of rotten apples, predisposed to brutality, make it through psychological testing that can be woefully inadequate*—Time [fr the saying "one rotten apple can spoil a barrel"; stated in a 1528 source as "For one rotten apple lytell and lytell putrifieth an whole heape"]

rough 1 *adj by 1958* Lewd; salacious; =DIRTY, RAUNCHY: *Some of the jokes were pretty rough* **2** *adj by 1856* Difficult; dangerous; =TOUGH: *Conditions were very rough that winter* **3** *n salespersons by 1950s* A used car that has been in a wreck
See PLAY FOR KEEPS

rough-and-tumble *adj by 1832* Free and uninhibited; with no limits or reservations; =NO HOLDS BARRED: *It was a rough-and-tumble confrontation* [originally of a fight where the usual rules were not observed; an article of 1810 says that "in roughing and tumbling it is allowable to peel the skull, tear out the eyes, and smooth away the nose"]

rough around the edges *adj phr by 1940s* Somewhat crude; unpolished: . . . *a slightly rough-around-the-edges New York manner*—Toronto Life

rough as a cob *adj phr* by 1940s Very rough [fr the rural use of *corncobs* as toilet paper]

◁**rough-ass**▷ *adj* by 1940s Harsh; crude; =KICK-ASS: *She liked his rough-ass ways for a while*

roughhouse 1 *n* by 1897 Boisterous and rowdy behavior; more or less harmless scuffling **2** *v* by 1900: *The kids roughhoused half the night* **3** *n* by 1887 Physical violence; mayhem **4** *adj*: . . . *roughhouse work for the political boss*—E Lavine **5** *v* by 1902: *Gun-toting bodyguards roughhoused Swedish citizens*—Associated Press

roughneck 1 *n* by 1836 A thug and brawler; =PLUG-UGLY, TOUGH: *The so-called roughneck is hit with everything*—E Lavine **2** *n* by 1917 A worker or laborer, esp in a circus or on an oil-drilling rig **See** RUFFNECK

rough stuff 1 *n phr* by 1913 Physical violence; mayhem: . . . *have graduated from the "rough stuff" class*—E Lavine **2** *n phr* by 1950s Obscenity; profanity; =PORN

rough trade *n phr* homosexuals by 1935 A sadistic or violent sex partner, often heterosexual; ruffianly partner of a homosexual: *I hope the next time he meets some rough trade from uptown*—Lawrence Sanders

rough someone **up** by 1920 **1** *v phr* To hit or pummel, esp as intimidation: *He told it like a good citizen, and got roughed up for his pains* **2** *v phr* To injure someone: *The wreck roughed me up some*

roulette **See** VATICAN ROULETTE

rounder *n* by 1854 A debauchee; habitual carouser: . . . *some rich "rounders" of the town*—Theodore Dreiser [one who "makes the rounds" of saloons]

round-eye 1 *n* Korean War armed forces A Caucasian as distinct from an Asian **2** *modifier*: *a round-eye woman*

roundheel or **roundheels 1** *n* by about 1920 An inferior prizefighter; =PALOOKA **2** *n* by 1926 A promiscuous woman; =PUNCHBOARD: . . . *little roundheels over there*—Raymond Chandler [because such persons readily topple over backwards]

roundheeled *adj* by 1980 Willing; complaisant; easily induced; like a "roundheel": *The chronically roundheeled US Congress is a wholly owned subsidiary of the huge Japanese real estate and industrial investments*—Time

roundhouse 1 *n* prizefighting by 1920 A long, looping punch to the head **2** *modifier*: *He swung a roundhouse left*—H Witwer **3** *n* baseball by 1910 A sweeping curveball **4** *modifier*: *a roundhouse pitch*

round the bend 1 *adj phr* by 1929 =AROUND THE BEND **2** *adj phr* WWII prisoners of war =STIR-CRAZY

round the horn **See** AROUND THE HORN

round-tripper *n* baseball by 1950s A home run: . . . *a round-tripper in the ninth*—D Parker

round up *v phr* by 1885 To find and bring together, esp to a police station or lockup: *Round up the usual suspects*—movie *Casablanca* [found by 1847 of the collection and corralling of animals]

roust by 1970s **1** *v* Esp of police officers, to harass someone; =CHIVVY, ROUGH UP: . . . *always being rousted by cops*—movie *The Gauntlet* **2** *v* To arrest: . . . *try rousting me and see what real resistance is like*—Robert B Parker **3** *v* To raid: *They're rousting all the gay bars*—Lawrence Sanders **4** *n* *What's the roust? You gonna close this place?*—Herbert Kastle [fr *rouster* or *rooster*, "a deckhand or waterfront laborer," attested fr the mid–1800s, hence with connotations of roughness; related to *roustabout,* fr British dialect *rous-about,* "unwieldy," *rousing,* "rough, shaggy," and *rousy,* "filthy"; the semantic core seems to combine roughness with laziness, in the old heroic mold, and to be associated with the behavior of the *rooster,* who combines rough vigor with long periods on the perch; first sense found in 1904 prison slang in the sense "to jostle," and by the 1940s in the sense "to jostle so as to pick a pocket"]

routine 1 *n* show business by 1926 A passage of behavior; act; =BIT, RIFF, SHTICK: *They did a Laurel and Hardy routine* **2** *n* 1950s cool talk An evasive or contrived response: *I look for revelation and get routine*

row *n* 1960s narcotics An elongated pile of narcotic, esp cocaine, for sniffing; =LINE: . . . *and snorted a row of coke*—Harry Crews **See** BALD-HEADED ROW, a HARD ROW TO HOE, HAVE one's DUCKS IN A ROW, KNOCK someone or something FOR A LOOP, SKID ROW

row-dow (ROU dou) *n* 1920s jazz musicians Exaggerated syncopation; ragtime

rowdy-dow (also **rowdy-dowdy** or **row-de-dow** or **row-de-dowdy** or **row-dow**) by 1790 in form row-de-dow **1** *n* Boisterousness; excitement; =RUMPUS, WHOOP-DE-DO: . . . *the old rowdy-dow of burlesque*—Brooks Atkinson **2** *adj*: . . . *this rowdy-dow round-up*—Time **3** *n* A brawl; fight [fr *row,* "fuss, disturbance," of obscure origin, found by 1746, and now standard]

row with one oar *v phr* (Variation: **in the water** may be added) by 1970s To behave irrationally; be crazy or stupid: *Ellis sounds as if he is rowing with one oar*—Ann Landers

royal *adj* by 1940s Thorough; definitive: . . . *gives me a royal pain in the ass*—J D Salinger

◀a **royal fucking**▶ *n phr* by 1940s Very rough and unfair treatment; =RAW DEAL

RTFM (pronounced as separate letters) *sentence*: . . . *"RTFM" for "Read the Fucking Manual," which is a message people often send back to you when you ask them for technical help*—New Yorker

rub 1 *n* 1920s students A dancing party **2** *n* 1930s students A session of hugging and kissing **3** *v* by 1848 =RUB OUT **4** *n* by 1990s A complaint; =BEEF, BITCH: *What's your rub?*—TV show *Larry King* **See** CHIEF ITCH AND RUB

rubber[1] **1** *n* by 1896 To gaze; gape: *Don't be rubbering at McCorn*—P Dunning & G Abbott ◁**2**▷ *n* by 1930s A condom: *"Rubbers,"* Cushie told him—John Irving **3** *n* by 1961 Automobile tires: *The thing's a wreck but has good rubber* **See** BURN RUBBER, LAY RUBBER

rubber² *n underworld by 1934* A professional killer; =HIT MAN

rubber boots *n phr by 1970s* Condoms: *My husband don't like rubber boots*—George V Higgins

rubber check *n phr by 1927* A check that cannot be cashed, because not enough money is on deposit [because it "bounces"]

rubber-chicken *modifier by 1959* Featuring the unappetizing usual sort of banquet food occupationally eaten by politicians, lecturers, etc: *She's on the rubber-chicken circuit*

rubber duck *See* TAKE A FLYING FUCK

rubber gun (or rubber) squad *n phr police by 1980s* An innocuous police assignment given as punishment, its inefficacy symbolized by the rubber gun: *Pike would get a year on a rubber gun squad*—Carsten Stroud

rubber heel *n phr* A detective; =GUMSHOE

rubber meets the road *See* WHERE THE RUBBER MEETS THE ROAD

rubberneck **1** *n* (also **rubbernecker**) *by 1896* A person who stares and gapes; gawking spectator: *The courtroom was full of rubbernecks/ These were rubberneckers, staring curiously at a bloody accident*—Hugh Pentecost **2** *v*: *They all slowed down and rubbernecked at the wreck*

rubbernecking delay *n phr by 1980s* A traffic slowdown due to drivers staring at a wreck

rubberneck wagon (or bus) *n phr by early 1900s* A sightseeing bus

rube or Rube **1** *n* A rustic; farmer; =HAYSEED **2** *n* An unsophisticated person, esp a newcomer; =GREENHORN **3** *n circus* A member of the audience or public; =CITIZEN: *Mr Todd knows how to panic the rubes*—Brooks Atkinson **4** *adj*: *. . . a rube police force*—R Starnes [short for *Reuben*]
See HEY RUBE

Rube Goldberg *n phr by 1940* A much overcomplicated machine or arrangement: *The public's got the idea that this is a boondoggle, a Rube Goldberg*—Time [fr the fancifully articulated machines drawn by the cartoonist Rube Goldberg (1883–1970); the British artist Heath Robinson (1872–1944) amused his public with similar gadgets]

rub (or nudge) elbows *v phr* To meet and consort; spend time together; mingle: *. . . colleagues with whom we rub elbows in the course of a day's work*—New York Times

rub it in *v phr by 1870* To increase the pain or embarrassment of something; exacerbate something: *. . . always trying to rub it in*—W T Tyler

rub someone's nose in it *v phr by 1940s* To punish or chide with undue harshness: *I screwed up that one time, and they rubbed my nose in it for years* [fr the punishment of a puppy or kitten that has irresponsibly evacuated]

◁**rub off**▷ *v phr by 1903* To masturbate

rub out *v phr by 1846* To murder; kill; =HIT: *. . . whose husband you rubbed out*—Samuel Liebowitz

rubout *n underworld by 1927* A murder; gangster-style killing: *. . . the hombre she blamed for Paddy's rub-out*—Dashiell Hammett

rub parlor *n phr by 1970s* A massage parlor: *. . . the rub parlors, kiddy porn*—Neal Travis

◁**rub the bacon**▷ *v phr by 1980s* To do the sex act; =FUCK, SCREW: *January and Trumball are rubbing the bacon*—Lawrence Sanders

rub someone the wrong way *v phr by 1883* To be distasteful or obnoxious to someone's sensibilities; regularly displease: *I don't quite know why, but that woman rubs me the wrong way* [rub the hair the wrong way is found by 1868]

ruckus *n by 1890* A disturbance; uproar; brawl; =RUMPUS [perhaps fr *ruction* plus *rumpus*]

ructious *adj by 1893* Vexed and violent; turbulent: *the long and ructious road that is life* [fr *ruction*, found by 1825, and perhaps dialect for *insurrection*]

ruffneck *1990s black* **1** *n* A devotee of rap music; =B-BOY: *He is also a B-boy. That's right, a ruffneck*—Advocate **2** *modifier* Violent; rabble-rousing; =GANGSTA: *Even some rappers are having trouble drawing a line between their "ruffneck" lyrics and real life*—Mesa Tribune

rug *n fr theater by 1940s* A toupee; hair piece; =DIVOT: *I even wear a little rug up front*—John O'Hara
See CUT THE RUG, PULL THE RUG OUT FROM UNDER

rug ape or rug rat or carpet rat *n phr* (Variations: **yard** may replace **rug** or **carpet**) *by 1960s* An infant or small child: *He lived with his wife and their two rug apes*

rug-cut **1** *v black by 1930s* To dance at rent parties and other fairly cheap occasions **2** *v 1930s jive talk* To dance to swing music; =JITTERBUG

rug-cutter *n jive talk by 1938* A person who dances to swing music: *. . . the rug-cutter's way of saying "all right"*—New Yorker

rugged *adj by 1730* Very trying; dangerous; =ROUGH •Very popular with WWII armed forces: *They had a real rugged time getting away*

rug joint *n phr* An elegant club, hotel, etc: *. . . not a rug joint (a lavishly decorated casino)*—J Scarne

rum bag *n phr by 1940s* A drunkard; =LUSH: *. . . a lot of cowardly rum bags*—Joe Cannon

rumble **1** *n underworld by 1911* Information or notification given to the police: *The cops had gotten a rumble that gangsters were holed up*—A Hynd **2** *n police by 1940s* A police search or raid; =ROUST: *If there's a rumble, we do the time*—movie *Johnny Stool Pigeon* **3** *n 1940s street gang* A fight between street gangs: *Teenagers Injured in Brooklyn Rumble*—New York World-Telegram **4** *v airline by 1970s* To steal; loot: *. . . ending a run by rumbling. . . everything from airline glasses to grub*—Philadelphia Journal

rum-dum *by 1891* **1** *n* A stupid person, esp one slow-witted from habitual drunkenness: *The murmuring rum-dums were being let out to wash*—Nelson Algren **2** *adj* Stupefied by liquor; =DEAD DRUNK

rummy or rummie *n by 1851* A drunkard; =LUSH: *He spotted the old rummy at the corner*

rumor *See* LATRINE RUMOR

rumor mill *n phr by 1973* The source of rumors, esp those that seem to be deliberately passed along: *There has been a rumor mill on him for years—*New York Times

rumpot *n by 1933* A heavy drinker; drunkard; =LUSH

rumpus *n by 1764* A disturbance; uproar; =RUCKUS [origin unknown]

rumpus room *n phr by 1939* A family room used for games, parties, etc

run 1 *v by 1864* To be in charge of; manage; supervise: *Who's running this operation, anyway?* **2** *v by 1864* To drive; convey; transport: *. . . if you keep jerking me around, I'm going to run your ass down to the drunk tank. . .* —Lawrence Sanders **3** *n by 1925* A route followed by a vehicle, esp regularly: *In the middle of her run, the bus driver was attacked by a gang of thugs* **4** *v 1980s black* To play basketball on a pick-up basis: *Enough of this crap, let's run—*Chuck Klosterman **5** *v by 1374* To go on; proceed; happen; =SHAKE OUT, WORK OUT: *. . . that's the way it'll run. They'll throw me the bone—*Scott Turow

See CUT AND RUN, DRY RUN, IN THE LONG RUN, MEAT RUN, MILK RUN, TAKE A RUN AT someone

run a game on *v phr fr black* =DO A NUMBER ON: *Then he had to run a game on Iris—*Elmore Leonard [perhaps fr *running* a whole *game* of pool without yielding the cue]

run a make *v phr police & prison by 1970s* To perform a checking procedure for identifying someone, that is, for "making" an identification

run-and-gun 1 *v basketball by 1970s* To play in an aggressive single-handed way, for high scoring: *. . . as a big city ball player looking to run-and-gun—*Philadelphia **2** *adj:* . . . *the Lakers' run-and-gun offense—*Newsweek

run-and-shoot *modifier football by 1980s* Combining running and passing, in an offense: *The Lions' run-and-shoot offense almost exclusively uses four receivers—*Milwaukee Journal

run a number on *See* DO A NUMBER ON

the runaround *n by 1915* Deceptive, evasive, and diversionary treatment, esp in response to a request: *All he gets is a polite runaround—*Drew Pearson

See GIVE someone THE RUNAROUND

◁**run around with** one's **finger up** one's **ass**▷ *v phr by 1970s* To be frantically ineffectual: *. . . you and your little band of merry men scoff up truckloads of narcotics while we run around with our fingers up our asses—*Michael Grant

run something **by again** *v phr by 1980s* To repeat; =COME AGAIN: *Just run that name and address by me again, will you?*

run circles around someone or something *v phr by 1940s* To be much faster or more effective than someone or something: *. . . they follow directions and they run circles around other teams—*New York Times

rundown *n by 1945* A summary or account: *. . . a brief rundown of what happened—*Associated Press

run someone **down** *v phr by 1668* To disparage; denigrate; =BAD-MOUTH: *He's your pal, so I won't run him down*

run something **down** *v phr black by 1964* To tell or explain completely: *Maybe one day I'll run it down to you—*Donald Goines

run hog-wild *See* GO HOG-WILD

run hot 1 *v phr police by 1970s* To drive a police car with siren, lights, etc, turned on: *Wager didn't bother with running hot—*Rex Burns **2** *v phr bus drivers by 1990s* To be ahead of one's schedule: *I have to slow down because I'm running hot—*Los Angeles Times

run in *v phr by 1919* To run an engine at a special rate, with special fuel, etc, to prepare it for full operation

run-in *n by 1905* A quarrel; an unpleasant confrontation: *. . . sorry we had the run-in—*H McHugh

run someone **in** *v phr by 1859* To arrest; =PULL someone IN: *Am I going to have to run you in?—*Nathaniel Benchley

run interference *v phr by 1947* To provide justification, protection, etc: *The average personnel department merely pushes paper, occasionally running interference for the line managers who actually make hiring decisions—*New York Times [the primary football use is found by 1929]

run into a buzz saw *v phr by 1990s* To get into trouble; encounter fierce resistance: *The House. . . ran into a buzz saw when GOP leaders tried to adjourn until Monday afternoon without first working out a deal to reopen the entire government—*David Hess [*buzz saw* is found by 1886 as "a characteristic and picturesque Americanism"]

run (or **work**) something **into the ground** *v phr by 1826* To overdo; carry too far: *You already warned us, so now don't run it into the ground*

runner *See* FRONT RUNNER, RIDGE-RUNNER, TENNIES

running dog *n phr Army by 1970s* A subordinate with little authority [fr abusive Chinese and North Korean Communist phrases like "a *running dog* of Western imperialism," fr Mandarin *zou gou,* "running dog," a dog that runs at its master's command]

running gag *n phr by 1980s* A recurrent thematic pleasantry: *. . . which are actually just a running gag that allows Martin to stammer, stumble and mug appealingly—*Milwaukee Journal Sentinel

running shoes *See* GIVE someone HIS WALKING PAPERS

run off at the mouth *v phr by 1909* To talk too much; =SHOOT OFF one's MOUTH: *I'm not about to run off at the mouth to the tabloids—*Lawrence Sanders

run-of-the-mill or **run-of-the-mine** *adj by 1930* Ordinary; average; =GARDEN-VARIETY

run on empty (or **on fumes**) *by 1980s* **1** *v phr* To be ineffectual; fail: *As televison, "The Africans". . . is sometimes stunning; as scholarship it runs on empty—*Washington Post **2** *v phr* To be nearly devoid of resources: *The school system is running on empty, too, with a $400 million deficit—*

Time/ Our bank account must be running on fumes again—Douglas Coupland [fr the needle of a fuel gauge indicating "Empty"]

run-out *n* *by 1928* A fleeing; desertion; escape: *. . . has taken a run-out with the bankroll*—E Booth

run out of gas (or **steam**) *v phr by 1920s* To lose impetus, effect, etc; fail; stall: *He ran out of gas a lot slower*—Village Voice/ *A succès d'estime is a success that's run out of steam*—George S Kaufman

run-out powder *See* TAKE A POWDER

run over someone *v phr by 1836* To treat arrogantly, slightingly, or flippantly

run someone **ragged** *v phr by 1918* To exhaust; wear out

the **runs** *n phr by 1962* Diarrhea; =the GIS

run scared *v phr by 1950s* To show signs of panic and fear; try to escape: *Members. . . aren't exactly running scared*—New York Times

run short *v phr by 1752* To lack resources; exhaust one's supply: *Please send me two dollars. I run short*—The Lantern

run the table *v phr football by 1990s* To finish a season undefeated: *. . . when a team runs the table in a major conference and then wins one of the big bowl games. . . it usually finds a national title at the end*—Newark Star-Ledger [fr the feat of sinking all the balls on the table successively in pool]

run through *v phr by 1923* To rehearse: *I ran through my story once more, to polish it*

run-through *n by 1923* A rehearsal; =DRY RUN: *After the first run-through, Mr Berlin casually tossed out three songs*—New York Times

run up against *v phr by 1821* To meet someone or something as an opponent or obstruction: *We were doing fine until we ran up against those real scumbags*

run something **up the flagpole** *v phr* (Variation: **and see if anybody salutes** may be added) *by 1960s* To test the reaction to; to try out an idea, concept, etc: *Television runs these vapidities up the flagpole and we salute as though we had been programmed to do so*—Washington Post [an expression attributed to the Madison Avenue advertising milieu, along with others like "Put it on a train and see if it gets off at Westport"]

run with it *v phr by 1980s* To grasp and capitalize on something: *". . . say nothing about this, until I can get something solid in our hands." "Please. Take it and run with it"*—Carsten Stroud [fr the notion of seizing and *running with* a football]

ruptured (or **pregnant**) **duck** *n phr WWII armed forces* A lapel pin, featuring an eagle rather than a duck, given to veterans honorably discharged after World War 2

rush 1 *v by 1899* To court a woman ardently: *He had "rushed" her, she said, for several months*—Ellery Queen **2** *n*: *. . . appears to want to give her a big rush*—F Blake **3** *v 1890s college students* To entertain and cultivate a student wanted as a fraternity or sorority member **4** *n movie studio by 1924* A motion picture print made immediately after the scene is shot **5** *n 1960s narcotics* An intense flood of pleasure, with quickened heart rate, felt soon after ingestion of a narcotic: *He didn't have to wait long for the rush* **6** *n by 1960s* A surge of pleasure; an ecstacy: *To Friend, it's a kind of a rush. . . the last big high*—Chicago Tribune/ *. . . gives her a unique rush*—Time

rushee *n by 1916* A person being rushed, esp by a college fraternity or sorority

rush hour *n phr by 1890* The times when people are going to or leaving work, notable for heavy traffic

rushing *See* GROWLER-RUSHING

Russian *n black by 1942* A Southern black in the North: *One of them Russians, eh? Rushed up North here to get away*—Zora Neale Hurston

rust bowl (or **belt**) **1** *n phr by 1984* The beleaguered and declining industrial areas, esp of the Middle West: *. . . in the midwestern middle, the "rust bowl"*—Time/ *Breaking the Rust Belt loose*—Milwaukee Journal **2** *modifier*: *Wall Street, Chrysler, high-tech enterprises vs "rust bowl" basic industries* [modeled on the 1930s term *dust bowl* and the 1970s term *sun belt*]

rust bucket 1 *n phr WWII Navy* An old worn vessel **2** *modifier*: *. . . the recent grounding in New York of a rust-bucket freighter. . .*—Milwaukee Journal **3** *n phr by 1969* An old car •Originally Australian: *Has your old rust bucket driven its last mile?*—Milwaukee Journal Sentinel

rustle 1 *v* (also **rustle** one's **bustle**) *by 1882* To bestir oneself; =GET OFF one's ASS **2** *v* (also **rustle up**) *by 1844* To find and produce: *. . . where I knew I could rustle up the Lompoc phone book. . .*—Sue Grafton [origin unknown; perhaps fr *rush* plus *hustle*]

rusty-dusty *n black by 1930s* The buttocks; rump; =ASS •Nearly always with the suggestion of torpor or laziness: *. . . the necessity of welfare recipients getting off their rusty dusties. . .*—Newark Star-Ledger [fr the notion that something not in frequent use or active motion will become *rusty* and *dusty*]

rusty gate *See* SWING LIKE A RUSTY GATE

rutabaga *n by 1940s* A dollar: *We've spent 60,000 rutabagas*—S J Perelman

S

-s *suffix used to form singular nouns* by 1936 in ducks A diminutive or affectionate version of what is indicated, used as a term of address: *babes/ ducks/ moms/ sweets*

SA (pronounced as separate letters) *n* by 1927 Sex appeal

sac fly *n phr baseball* by 1980s A sacrifice fly, a fly ball that permits a runner to score [the unshortened form is found by 1908]

sack¹ 1 *v* by 1841 To discharge; dismiss; =CAN, FIRE: *. . . by refusing to sack his aide*—Philadelphia Bulletin **2** *n* by 1829 A bed, bunk, sleeping bag, etc; sleeping place; =RACK: *Let me stay in the sack all day*—Hal Boyle **3** *n* by 1940s Sleep; =SACK TIME: *He needed some sack* **4** *modifier*: *sack duty* **5** *n* by 1957 A dress that fits loosely over the shoulders, waist, and hips, and is gathered at the hem line **6** *n baseball* by 1891 A base; =BAG, PILLOW: *He slid into the sack* [first sense probably fr the notion of giving a discharged person a traveling bag or *sack*, since the earliest expression was *get the sack*]

See FART SACK, HIT THE HAY, the KEYSTONE, SAD SACK

sack² 1 *v football* by 1969 To tackle the quarterback behind the line of scrimmage **2** *n football* by 1972: *The Lions made 18 sacks in the first half* **3** *n* by 1990s An assault or blow: *You have to credit Dim Rome for hanging in there and taking the sack he accused Everett of being afraid to take. . .*—Los Angeles Times [fr *sack*, "to assault and pillage"]

the sack 1 *n phr* by 1825 Discharge from a job; dismissal; =the BOOT: *He was late once too often and got the sack* **2** *n phr* by 1980s Bed as the site of sexual activity: *Was this guy also a miracle worker in the sack?*—Robert B Parker [first sense apparently fr an old practice of giving someone a *sack* when sending him away; corresponding expressions are found in French: *donner son sac à quelqu'un*]

sack artist 1 *n phr WWII armed forces* A chronic loafer; =GOLDBRICK, GOOF-OFF **2** *n phr* by 1990s A sexual virtuoso: *Goddess, riot grrrl, warrior, tattooed love child, sack artist, leader of men: The 21st Century Woman*—Esquire

sack duty (or **drill** or **time)** *n phr WWII armed forces* Sleeping time; sleep; loafing: *. . . get in some sack drill*—J L Riordan

sacker *See* FIRST SACKER, SECOND SACKER, THIRD SACKER

sack out (or **in** or **up** or **down)** *v phr WWII armed forces* To go to bed; sleep; =HIT THE HAY: *Well, it's time to sack out*—Hal Boyle

sack rat *n phr WWII armed forces* =SACK ARTIST

sack time *fr WWII armed forces* **1** *n phr* =SACK DUTY **2** *n phr* Bedtime; time to retire

sacred cow *n phr* by 1910 Someone or something that may not be questioned or altered: *Everything is on the table. . . There are no sacred cows*—New York Times [fr the venerated status of *cows* in Hinduism]

sad or ◁**sad-ass**▷ *adj* first form by 1899, second by 1971 Inferior; botched or bungled; =CRUMMY: *It's a sad dump: What a sad-ass town*

sad apple *n phr* by 1941 An obnoxious individual; a contemptible person; =DRIP, JERK, a PAIN IN THE ASS

saddle *See* LEAN FORWARD IN THE SADDLE

sadie-maisie *See* S AND M

sad sack *n phr students fr 1920s & esp WWII armed forces* An awkward, unfortunate, harried, and maladjusted person; =EIGHTBALL, SCHLEMAZEL: *. . . nevertheless stuck with an inexplicable sad sack of a leading man*—Washington Post [fr the unflattering image of a human being as primarily a container for feces]

safe or **safety** or **French safe** *n* or *n phr* by 1897 A condom; =FRENCH LETTER, RUBBER

safecracker *n* by 1930s A person who blows or breaks open safes; =BOX MAN, PETE-MAN

sagebrusher *n* by 1950s =HORSE OPERA: *Horse operas, also known as sagebrushers. . .*—Bob Thomas

someone said a mouthful *sentence* by 1922 Someone spoke accurately and cogently; someone said something very important •Often an expression of vehement agreement: *Daisy sure said a mouthful*

said it *See* YOU SAID IT

sail in *v phr* by 1856 To go boldly to the attack or to the rescue

sailing *See* CLEAR SAILING

sail into *v phr* by 1856 To attack; criticize severely; =LAMBASTE: *He quickly sails into anyone that complains*

Saint Elsewhere *See* MOUNT SAINT ELSEWHERE

Sal or **Sally** or **Sally Ann** *n* or *n phr hoboes* by 1930s The Salvation Army, or any other mission or place that gives food and shelter

salad *See* FRUIT SALAD

salary wing *n phr baseball* by 1892 A pitcher's throwing arm

Sale *See* CHIC SALE

salt 1 *n* by 1840 A sailor, esp an old and seasoned one **2** *n* 1960s narcotics Heroin in powder form *See* GO POUND SALT

salt and pepper 1 *n phr* 1960s narcotics Impure or low-grade marijuana **2** *adj phr* by 1950s Interracial; =BLACK AND TAN: *a salt and pepper neighborhood in Detroit* **3** *adj phr* by 1915 Referring to hair that is turning gray

salt away *v phr* by 1902 To save or store, esp money; hoard: *... tapping the millions he had salted away to finance the company's renaissance*—Wired

salt horse *n phr* by 1836 Corned beef; dried or chipped beef, salted [*horse* used as a derogatory term for the unappetizing meat]

the salt mines *See* BACK TO THE SALT MINES

salts *See* LIKE SHIT THROUGH A TIN HORN

salty 1 *adj* Navy by 1920 Audacious; daring; aggressive: *I relaxed, smiled. Salty little bugger*—Stan Cutler **2** *adj* 1940s jive talk Terrible; nasty; unpalatable **3** *adj* black by 1938 Angry; hostile *See* JUMP SALTY

salute *See* RUN something UP THE FLAGPOLE

salvage *v* WWI Army To steal; loot; =LIBERATE

salve 1 *n* hoboes by about 1915 Butter **2** *n* by 1864 Cajolement; flattery; =SOFT SOAP: *I handed him a little salve*—Erle Stanley Gardner **3** *n* by 1940s A bribe; =PALM OIL **4** *n* by 1940s Money, esp as a remedy or reward for something unpleasant

Sam or **sam** *n* 1960s narcotics A federal narcotics agent; =NARC [fr *Uncle Sam*]

the same difference *n phr* by 1945 The same thing; something exactly equal: *So they fire him or he quits, it's the same difference*

same here *interj* by 1895 An exclamation of agreement

the same wavelength *See* ON THE SAME WAVELENGTH

Sam Hill *n phr* by 1839 Hell: *Where in Sam Hill do you think you're going?* [an echoic euphemism]

sand *See* CRATE OF SAND, GO POUND SALT

sandbag 1 *v* by 1887 To attack someone viciously, esp with a blackjack or similar bludgeon; =BUSHWHACK: *I was sandbagged from behind*—Life **2** *v* by 1901 To intimidate; cow; =BULLDOZE: *Persuasion didn't work, so they tried to sandbag her* **3** *v* gambling by 1940 To check and then to raise the bet **4** *v* by 1970s To pretend weakness or ineptitude; mislead an opponent by apparent inferiority: *He charged that the Aussies were "sand bagging" (deliberately losing) to take the limelight off their disputed keel*—Time **5** *v* 1950s hot rodders To drive a hot rod very fast **6** *n* WWII Navy A type of life preserver

sandbagged *adj* 1980s students Temporarily evicted from one's dormitory room so that one's roommate can entertain a lover: *Bill's girlfriend came up for the weekend and Bob got sandbagged again*—College Slang 101

sand biter *n phr* Gulf War Army A soldier in the desert: *... held in similar disregard by "sand*

biters," those troopers who were sweltering in the desert heat—The Retired-Officer Magazine

sandlot baseball by about 1890 **1** *n* A rough or improvised baseball field; =HOGAN'S BRICKYARD **2** *modifier*: *sandlot ball*

S and M or **S/M** or **sadie-maisie** *n phr* or *n* by 1960s Sado-masochism; perverse sexual practices featuring whips, chains, etc

sandwich *See* HERO SANDWICH

sandwich bag *n phr* 1990s narcotics A $40 bag of marijuana

sandwich board *n phr* by 1864 A board bearing advertising messages, and worn one in front and one behind by a sandwich man

sandwich man *n phr* by 1864 A person paid to walk about bearing sandwich boards

San Quentin quail *n phr* by 1939 A girl below the legal age of sexual consent; =JAIL BAIT [fr the name of a California state penitentiary]

Santa Claus 1 *n phr* airline by 1970s A check pilot who is very lenient and agreeable on a pilot check flight **2** *n phr* by 1970s A male donor or benefactor; a very generous man: *What the orphanage needed was a Santa Claus to pay the debts*

sao (SOU) *n* Vietnam War armed forces A repulsive, obnoxious, or dishonorable person; =BASTARD [fr Vietnamese]

sap¹ *n* by 1815 A stupid person; fool, esp a gullible one: *Quit acting like a sap* [fr British dialect, short for *sapskull*, "person with a head full of soft material"; probably influenced by early–1800s British schoolboy slang, "compulsive studier, grind," which is probably fr *sap* as an ironic abbreviation of Latin *sapiens*, "wise," and is hence semantically akin to *sophomore*]

sap² 1 *n* by 1899 A blackjack; bludgeon: *... the sap... a nice little tool about five inches long, covered with woven brown leather*—Raymond Chandler **2** *v* by 1926: *One of the others sapped him from behind with the blackjack*—Life [perhaps fr Middle English *sappe*, "shovel," the shovel being for ages a popular club]

sapfu (SAP foo) WWII armed forces **1** *adj* Surpassingly and incredibly botched **2** *n*: *a stupefying sapfu we had* [fr *surpassing all previous fuck-ups*]

saphead *n* by 1798 A stupid person; =BLOCKHEAD, SAP: *... one young woman who just seems to be a saphead*—Wolcott Gibbs

sapheaded *adj* by 1665 Stupid; =GOOFY, SAPPY

sappy 1 *adj* by 1670 Stupid; foolish; =GOOFY: *... lay off them sappy songs*—W R Burnett **2** *adj* Sentimental; mawkish; =SCHMALTZY: *... the Velveeta-voiced crooner of sappy tunes*—Seventeen

sarge *n* by 1867 A sergeant

sashay *v* by 1836 To go; walk; flounce: *... after a great deal of extravagantly publicized sashaying about*—Washington Post [fr the square-dance gait, fr French *chasser*, "chase"]

sass 1 *n* by 1835 Impudence; impertinent backtalk: *... if this reporter was going to give her any sass*—

Washington Post **2** *v*: *He kept sassing his mama till she decked him* [fr *sauce*, "rude and impudent language or action"]

sassy *adj by 1831* Impudent; impertinent; =IN-YOUR-FACE

satch *by 1940s* **1** *n* (also **satchelmouth**) A man with a large mouth **2** *n* An overly talkative man; =WINDBAG: . . . *in the days when I was fearlessly denouncing old satch*—Westbrook Pegler

satchel *by 1940s* **1** *n* The buttocks; rump; =KEISTER: . . . *a chance to rest my satchel*—G Moore **2** *n* =SATCH **3** *n* A jazz musician who plays a horn **4** *v* To prearrange the outcome of a fight, race, etc; =FIX, RIG: *It was satcheled against him*—D Egan [verb sense fr in the bag]

saturated *adj by 1902* Drunk: . . . *to keep them saturated indefinitely*—American Mercury

Saturday night special 1 *n phr by 1968* A cheap, small-caliber revolver quite easy to obtain: *Detroit lawmen began to refer to the weapons as "Saturday night specials"*—B Kaiser **2** *n phr* medical *by 1970s* A person, often an alcoholic, who comes to a hospital on weekends seeking a bed and board [*Saturday night pistol*, "25-caliber semi-automatic," is found by 1929]

sauce 1 *n by 1835* Impudence; impertinence; =LIP, SASS **2** *n by middle 1980s* A steroid drug used for body-building; ='ROID
See APPLESAUCE

the **sauce** *n by 1940* Liquor; whiskey; =BOOZE: *It made him sad and he almost began hitting the sauce*—John O'Hara
See HIT THE BOTTLE, ON THE SAUCE

sausage 1 *n by 1930s* A prizefighter, esp one with a swollen and battered face **2** *n by 1940s* A stupid person; =MEATHEAD

sausage hound *n phr by 1940s* A dachshund; =WIENER DOG

savage *n* police *by 1940s* A young police officer eager to make arrests

save someone's **ass** *v phr by 1980s* To rescue someone: . . . *and I figure I better come down and save your ass*—Robert B Parker

save one's **bacon** *v phr by 1654* To save oneself; work one's preservation: *We'd better act right now if we want to save our bacon*

saved by the bell *adj phr by 1950s* Rescued, relieved, or preserved at the last moment: *Some Republicans argue that the threat of recession makes serious deficit cutting unwise right now. Saved by the bell!*—New Republic [fr the plight of a boxer who is being severely punished when the *bell* rings to end the round]

savvy or **savvey 1** *v by 1785* To understand; know; grasp: *I'm the honcho here, savvy?* **2** *n by 1785* Comprehension; intelligence; =BRAINS, SMARTS: *He's a guy with much savvy* **3** *adj*: *a very savvy lady* [fr West Indian pidgin fr Spanish *sabe usted*, "do you know?"; modern use influenced by French *savez*, "you know"]

saw 1 *n by 1940s* =SAWBUCK **2** *n* black *by 1950s* The landlord of a rooming house
See DOUBLE SAWBUCK

sawbones *n by 1830* A surgeon; a physician: . . . *without being able to rouse a sawbones*—R Ruark

sawbuck *n by 1850* A ten-dollar bill; ten dollars [fr the resemblance of the Roman numeral X to the ends of a *sawhorse*]
See DOUBLE SAWBUCK

sawdust eater *n phr* loggers *by 1940s* A sawmill worker or lumberjack

sawdust parlor *n phr by 1950s* A cheap night-club, restaurant, etc: . . . *not a rug joint. . . but rather a sawdust parlor*—J Scarne [fr the former use of *sawdust* as a floor covering]

sawed-off *adj by 1887* Short of stature: . . . *sawed-off fight manager from Newark*—J Cuddy

saw wood *by 1940s* **1** *v phr* To sleep, esp very soundly **2** *v phr* To snore [fr the sound of snoring]

sawyer *n 1920s* underworld A sawed-off shotgun

sax 1 *n by 1923* A saxophone **2** *modifier*: *a sax virtuoso*

say *See* WHAT DO YOU SAY

say a mouthful *v phr by 1918* To say something true, important, etc ●Usu a conversational response: *He is stupid? You said a mouthful*
See someone SAID A MOUTHFUL

say boo *v phr by 1932* To make an innocuous threat ●Often in the negative: *No politician will say boo to the tobacco industry*—New Yorker

say-so *n by 1637* One's word, report, recommendation, etc: *No jury'll convict Manny on your say-so alone*—Raymond Chandler

says which *question 1920s* students What did you say?: *Says which? I don't believe what I heard*

says you or **says who** *interj* (Variations: **sez** or **sezz** may replace **says**) *by 1926* An exclamation of defiance, disbelief, mere pugnacity, etc; =IZZATSO: *I'm in the wrong seat? Says who?*

say that again *See* YOU CAN SAY THAT AGAIN

say uncle *v phr by 1918* To surrender; give up; =KNUCKLE UNDER

say what *interj 1970s* black A request for more information; excuse me? ●Sometimes with the sense of not believing what one has heard: *Marvella put her apple down. "Say whuuut?"*—Harry Crews

scab *n by 1777* A nonunion worker, esp one who attempts to break a strike; =FINK

scads 1 *n by 1890* A large quantity of money **2** *n by 1809* A large quantity of anything; =BAGS, OODLES: *I have scads of studying to do*—Philadelphia Bulletin [origin unknown; perhaps fr British dialect, "shed," and hence semantically akin to a *shithouse full*]

scag *See* SKAG

scag jones *n phr 1960* narcotics A heroin addiction: . . . *sell them to janitors for a quarter to support their "scag jones"*—Claude Brown

scairdy cat *See* SCAREDY CAT

scalp *v by 1883* To sell tickets at a higher than normal or legal price

scalper 1 *n* by 1869 A person who scalps tickets **2** *n* gambling by 1960s A person who places bets and backs bets in such a way that he will win whether the horse wins or loses

scam 1 *n* (also **scambo**) by 1963 A swindle; confidence game; fraud; =CON: *It was a full scam*—Time/ *Looking for a good scambo for April Fool's Day. . .*—Milwaukee Journal **2** *v* (also **scam on**) : *You guys are scamming me*—Joseph Wambaugh **3** *n* by 1964 The information; =the LOWDOWN, the SCOOP: *Here's the scam. . . We're holing in for the night*—Patrick Mann [origin unknown; perhaps related to early–1800s British *scamp,* "cheater, swindler"] *See* WHAT'S THE SCAM

◀**Scandahoovian** or **Scandanoovian**▶ **1** *n* by 1931 A Scandinavian or person of Scandinavian extraction **2** *adj*: *murky Scandanoovian movies*

scandal sheet *n phr* by 1939 A sensationalistic and vulgar newspaper, magazine, etc; cheap tabloid; =RAG
See SWINDLE SHEET

◀**scank**▶ *n* black teenagers by 1970s An unattractive girl

scankie *adj* black teenagers by 1970s Disheveled; sloppy

the **scare** *n phr* 1930s underworld Extortion based on menaces: *We build the sap for the scare*—American Mercury

scare badge *n phr* Army by 1970s A badge given in recognition of paratroop or other rigorous and prestigious training

◀**scared shitless**▶ *adj phr* by 1936 Very frightened; terrified: *And the producer is scared shitless of the sponsor*—Sterling Hayden [based on the expression *scare the shit out of* someone]

scared spitless (or witless) *adj phr* by 1930s Very frightened; terrified; =SCARED SHITLESS: *They were scared spitless at the prospect of appearing in a play*—Richard Wright [two plausible euphemisms for *scared shitless*]

scared stiff *adj phr* by 1900 Very frightened; paralyzed by terror [fr the notion of being *scared to death*]

scaredy (or scairdy) cat *n phr* by 1933 =FRAIDY CAT

scarehead *n* newspaper office by 1900 A very large and conspicuous headline; =SCREAMER

◀**scare** someone **shitless**▶ (or **spitless** or **witless**) *v phr* by 1936 To frighten very much; terrify: *It scared me shitless, but that didn't stop me from watching it again and again*—Edward I Koch

◀**scare the shit out of** someone▶ *v phr* (Variations: **living shit** or **bejesus** or **daylights** may replace **shit**) entry form by 1930s, others perhaps earlier To frighten very much; terrify: *Their strategy was to maximize the threat of bloodshed, to scare the shit out of the KGB*—New Yorker/ *It scares the living shit out of them*—National Lampoon/ *. . . these complexities would scare the bejesus out of David Cronenberg*—Village Voice

scare up *v phr* by 1853 To find and produce; =RUSTLE: *. . . was among the goodies scared up at a flea market*—Casper Star-Tribune [fr the rising or starting of wildlife, which sense is found by 1846]

scarf 1 *n* 1930s teenagers fr black Food; a meal; =CHOW, SCOFF **2** *v* (also **scarf down** or **scarf up**) by 1950 To eat or drink, esp voraciously; consume: *. . . puffing on his morning joint, eating cereal, and scarfing up a beer*—Easyriders/ *People scarf up food after truck overturns*—Casper Star-Tribune/ *. . . or scarfed down Milky Ways flambe*—Macon Telegraph **3** *v* by 1960s To do cunnilingus: *Scarf her a few times: eat her box, in other words*—Candy Murder Case

scarf out by 1970s **1** *v phr* To eat very heartily; overeat; =PIG OUT: *I took the band there and we scarfed out*—Vegetarian Times **2** *n phr*: *. . . eat all I wanted in the cafeteria. . . really a scarf out*—Kathy Hogan Trocheck

scary *adj* musicians by 1990s Very good; first-rate: *And there are some pretty scary community players out there; it's not as if just anyone can come in and play*—Los Angeles Times

scat[1] jazz musicians by about 1926 **1** *n* Pattering staccato gibberish sung to songs, esp jazz songs: *Then I'd carry on some of my scat*—Jelly Roll Morton **2** *modifier*: *. . . precise "scat" singing*—F Grunfeld **3** *v*: *Scatting has almost always been used by jazz singers as an interlude*—San Francisco [origin unknown; probably one of the nonsense syllables used]

scat[2] *v* teenagers by 1950s To drive or otherwise move very fast [fr early–1800s ss *cat,* a hissing address designed to drive away a cat; the earliest occurrence is in the expression *quicker than ss'cat*]

scatback *n* football by 1946 A very fast and agile backfield runner

scatterbrain *n* by 1790 A silly or stupid person, esp one who cannot attend properly to a subject or get simple things done; =DITZ, RATTLEBRAIN: *He's such a scatterbrain I don't look for a plausible theory from him*

scatterbrained *adj* by 1804 Silly or stupid; mentally unstable; =DITSY ●The dated form *scattered-brained* is found by 1747]

scattergun 1 *n* by 1836 A shotgun **2** *n* WWII Army A machine gun, submachine gun, or machine pistol; =BURP GUN **3** *modifier* by 1952 Broadly and imprecisely directed; crudely comprehensive; =SHOTGUN: *. . . the scattergun memo*—New York Daily News

scatter market *n phr* television advertising by 1990s : *The time that is not sold up front. . . will be sold later in smaller blocks and presumably at higher rates, on the so-called scatter market*—Milwaukee Journal

scatty *adj* British by 1911 Irrational; crazy; =GOOFY, SCATTERBRAINED: *. . . the ferociously ambitious, slightly scatty Louise Bryant*—Vincent Canby [probably fr *scatterbrained*; said to be a Cockney use]

scenario *n* by 1962 A reasoned or imagined pattern of events in the future; a possible plan: *According to*

one scenario we only kill 87 percent of the population
See WORST-CASE SCENARIO

scene *1960s counterculture* **1** *n* The setting or milieu of a specific activity or group; specialized venue: . . . *the rock "scene"*—E Willis/ *It is really quite difficult. . . to understand their scene*—Trans-Action **2** *n* One's particular preference, activity, etc; =BAG, THING: *I mean that's not my own scene or anything*—Changes
See ALL-ORIGINALS SCENE, BAD SCENE, LAY A TRIP ON someone, MAKE A SCENE, MAKE THE SCENE, MOB SCENE, SPLIT THE SCENE

scenery **See** CHEW UP THE SCENERY

scenester *n by 1990s* A person who is often seen at a particular scene; a publicity monger: . . . *the new Hollywood club is going to make some local bands, as well as local scenesters, happy*—Los Angeles Times

Schaffner **See** HART, SCHAFFNER AND MARX

schizo (SKITSO, SKIH zoh) **1** *n* (also **schiz**) *by 1945, variant by 1955* A schizophrenic: *Docs find he's a schizo*—New York Daily News **2** *adj*: . . . *a schizo drug addict* **3** *adj* (also **schizy** or **schizzy** or **schizie**) *by 1920s fr hospital* Crazy; demented, esp in a self-contradictory way; psychotic; =NUTTY: *People in democracies. . . are a little schizzy about authority*—Newsweek/ . . . *this same schizy little brain*—Esquire [fr *schizophrenic, schizophrenia*]

schiz out *v phr 1980s students* To go crazy; become schizophrenic; =FLIP: *She thought he'd schizzed out completely*—Cyra McFadden/ . . . *on the perpetual verge of schizing out*—Richard Merkin

schlang **See** SCHLONG

schlemazel or **schlemasel** or **shlemozzle** (shlə MAH zəl) *n by 1940s, but probably earlier* An awkward, unfortunate, maladjusted person; =SAD SACK [fr Yiddish *shlimazel* fr *shlim mazel*, "rotten luck"; British slang *shemozzle, shlemozzle*, "a muddle, an unhappy plight," is found by 1889, and is probably related]

schlemiel or **schlemihl** or **shlemiel** (shlə MEEL) *n by 1892* A stupid person; fool; oaf; esp, a naive person often victimized: *Don't talk like a schlemiel, you schlemiel*—Budd Schulberg/ . . . *playing the lovable schlemiel to Brooklyn Jews*—Esquire [fr Yiddish *shlemiel*, probably fr the name of the main character in A von Chamisso's German fable *The Wonderful History of Peter Schlemihl*, 1813]

schlep or **schlepp** or **shlep 1** *v by 1922* To carry; drag along: . . . *schlepping the male's genetic material so his baby inherits half its genes from each parent. . .* —Harper's Bazaar **2** *v by 1922* To move or advance with difficulty; drag: . . . *then I'd have to schlep around to the Quarter Note*—Nashville **3** *n by 1964*: . . . *even with the four-flight schlep to the editorial office*—New York Magazine **4** *n* (also **schlepper** or **shlepper**) *by 1939* A stupid person; oaf; =LOSER, KLUTZ, SLOB:

. . . *dead schleps playing behind him*—Rolling Stone/ *Poor John was a schlepper of the first order*—Scott Turow [fr Yiddish *shleppen*]

schleppable *adj by 1990s* Portable: *The Canon BJ–20 portable printer at 6.6 pounds is certainly more schleppable than its main competitor*—PC World

schleppy or **shleppy** *adj by 1940s* Awkward; stupid; =KLUTZY

schlock 1 *n* (also **schlack** or **schlag** or **shlock**) *by 1915* Inferior merchandise; an inferior product; =CRAP, JUNK: . . . *that "Macbird" is a piece of schlock*—Russell Baker/ . . . *are bringing out schlock so they can pay for the books they care about*—Pauline Kael **2** *adj*: . . . *unlike all those schlock films*—C L Westerbeck Jr [fr Yiddish fr German *schlag*, "a blow," perhaps because the merchandise has been knocked around, or knocked down, or perhaps because as Eric I Bromberg wrote in *American Speech* in 1938, "to schlach is to cut or raise a price according to a customer"; the *New York Times* speculated in 1922 that the underworld use *schlock*, "a broken lot of loot," was adopted because *junk* had recently come to mean "narcotics, dope"]

schlockmeister *n by 1965* A successful maker or seller of schlock: *Low-budget, high-profit exploitation has solidified their position as Hollywood's premier schlockmeisters*—Newsweek [fr *schlock* plus German *Meister*, "master"]

schlock shop (or **joint)** *n phr by 1940s* A store that sells inferior merchandise, esp a junk shop, thrift store, etc [in the 1930s, a store that varies its prices according to the customer]

schlockudrama *n by 1990s* An inferior and exploitive movie or television play: . . . *Fox's schlockudrama "Madonna: Innocence Lost"*—Milwaukee Journal

schlocky or **shlocky** *adj by 1968* Inferior; shoddy; cheap and gaudy; =JUNKIE

◁**schlong**▷ *n* (also **schlang** or **shlang** or **shlong**) *by 1969* The penis; =PRICK: . . . *you know with his schlong hanging out there*—Rolling Stone [fr Yiddish *shlang*, literally "snake"]

◁**schlontz** or **shlontz**▷ *n by 1970s* The penis [perhaps a blend of Yiddish *shlong* and *shwants*]

schloomp (SHLooMP) (also **schlump** or **shloomp** or **shlump**) *by 1930s* **1** *n* A stupid person; =KLUTZ: *For openers, he looks like a shlump*—Philadelphia Journal **2** *v* (also **shalump** or **schloomp around**) To loaf; idle about; =GOOF OFF: *She shalumps around the Ritz in her loose clothes and sneakers*—Washington Post [fr Yiddish *shlump*, related to German *Schlumpe*, "a slovenly woman"]

schlub **See** ZHLUB

schmaltz or **shmaltz** (SHMAWLTS) *n swing musicians by 1935* Blatant sentimentality, esp musical or theatrical material of a cloyingly sweet and maudlin sort; =CORN: . . . *happy combination of good theater and good pathos known as schmaltz*—New Yorker [fr Yiddish *shmalts*, literally "rendered fat"]

schmaltzy or **schmalzy** or **shmaltzy** *adj by 1935* Sentimental; sweetly melancholy; =CORNY, ICKY: . . . *this schmaltzy king of schlock and roll*—Rolling Stone

schmancy *See* FANCY-SCHMANCY

schmatte (SHMAH tə) *n* (also **schmattah** or **schmatteh** or **shmatte** or **shmotte**) *by 1970* A shabby or unstylish garment: *She had on a tired old schmattah*—Xaviera Hollander [fr Yiddish *shmatte*, literally "rag"]

schmear¹ or **shmear** or **shmeer 1** *v by 1909* To bribe; =GREASE someone's PALM: . . . *see this here Rabbi and schmear him a thousand dollars*—Potash and Perlmutter **2** *n*: *Since the rest of the tables were all unoccupied, it would seem to call for a bit of a shmear*—Stan Cutler **3** *v by 1930* To flatter and cajole someone; =SOFT SOAP [fr Yiddish *shmeer*, literally "grease"]

schmear² *by 1950s* **1** *v* To treat someone very roughly; =CLOBBER, CREAM, SMEAR **2** *n* An accusation or innuendo meant to harm someone's reputation; a slander [fr a humorous mispronunciation of *smear*]

the schmear *n phr by 1940s* =the WHOLE SCHMEAR [fr Yiddish *shmeer*]

schmeck or **shmeck 1** *n by 1968* A taste; a bite: *How about a little schmeck?*—Esquire **2** *n 1930s* narcotics Heroin; =SMACK: *She's hustling right now, schmeck, tail, abortion, the whole bit*—Lawrence Sanders [fr Yiddish *shmek*, "a smell, sniff," related to German *schmecken*]

Schmedlap *n Army by 1970s* An inept soldier

schmegeggy or **shmegeggy** or **schmegegge** (shmə GEG gee) *by 1964* **1** *n* A stupid person; oaf; =SCHLEMIEL: . . . *the shmegeggy she lives with*—Philip Roth/ . . . *a new story. . . about some gringo schmegegge exchanging his dollars for a worthless mess of Batista money*—Village Voice **2** *n* Nonsense; foolishness; =BALONEY [fr Yiddish *shmegegi* of unknown origin, perhaps coined in American Yiddish]

schmendrick or **shmendrick** *n by 1951* A stupid person, *esp* an awkward and inept nonentity; =SCHLEMIEL: . . . *a schmendrick with a noodle for a brain*—A Hirschfeld [fr Yiddish *shmendrik*, fr the name of a character in an operetta by A Goldfaden]

schmo (also **schmoe** or **shmo** or **shmoe**) *by 1947* **1** *n* A naive and hapless person; fool; =GOOF: *I've been standing here like a schmoe for 20 minutes*—Fred Allen **2** *n* A person; man; =GUY: *Them bigtime schmoes was stockholders*—Saturday Evening Post [perhaps a euphemistic alteration of Yiddish *shmok* "penis"; perhaps a quasi-Yiddish coinage for amusing effect; the term has been adopted into American Yiddish]

See JOE SCHMO

schmooz (SHMOOS or SHMOOZ) (also **schmoo** or **schmooze** or **schmoos** or **schmoose** or **schmoozl** or **schmoozle** or **schmoosl** or **schmoosle** or **schmuss** or any of these spelled with **sh-**) **1** *v by 1897* To converse, *esp* lengthily and cozily: . . . *stop and chat (Schmoos, he calls it)*—New York Times/

. . . *lawyers schmoozing in the halls*—Village Voice **2** *n*: *Two buddies enjoying a quiet schmooz* **3** *v by 1990s* To seduce with flattery; =SOFT SOAP: *What he does. . . is he hooks up with these dumb women whom he schmoozes and lives off*—Macon Telegraph [fr Yiddish fr Hebrew *schmuos*, "things heard"]

schmoozefest *n by 1990s* A meeting, conference, etc, where people chat; =GABFEST: . . . *where they're on their way to yet another promotional schmoozefest*—Milwaukee Journal

schmoozer *n by 1909* A person who schmoozes, *esp* as an aspect of personality: *He has none of the small coin of politics. He's not a schmoozer*—Washington Post

schmoozoisie *n by 1990s* A set of persons who are habitually and professionally garrulous; =CHATTERING CLASSES: . . . *the drag-orients throwaway zine leaves behind outraged member of the gay schmoozoisie. . .* —Los Angeles Weekly [fr *schmooze* plus *bourgeoisie*]

schmuck or **shmuck** *n by 1892* A detestable person; an obnoxious man; =BASTARD, PRICK: *You must be a real schmuck*—Nora Ephron [fr Yiddish *shmok*, "penis," literally "ornament"]

schmucky *adj by 1975* Detestable; obnoxious: *The fact that this kid might be schmucky hurt his chances*—Sassy

schmutz or **shmutz** *n by 1967* Filth; smut [fr Yiddish]

schneider or **schneid 1** *v* To win before one's opponent has scored; =SHUT OUT **2** *n*: *The Yanks took four straight, a schneider/ . . . the AFC might have teams capable of breaking the Super Bowl schneid*—Sports Illustrated **3** *v* To defeat decisively; trounce; =CLOBBER [fr German, literally "tailor," probably by way of Yiddish; the term is used in various card games for a clean sweep]

schnockered or **snockered** *adj by 1955* Drunk: *Better quit before you get schnockered/ . . . while all the male guests get snockered*—Philadelphia [origin uncertain; perhaps fr Irish *snagaireact*, pronounced with initial *sh-*, "tippling, stammering"]

schnook or **shnook** (SHNöoK) *n by 1940s* An ineffectual person; a naive person often victimized; =PATSY ●A more affectionate and compassionate way of designating a schlemiel: *Don't be such an apologetic schnook*—Jack Benny [fr American-Yiddish *shnook*, said to be fr German *Schnucke*, "small sheep"; probably related to the pet names *snooks, snookums, etc*]

schnorrer or **shnorrer 1** *n by 1892* A beggar, *esp* one who counts parasitically on a family or community; =MOOCHER: *"Hooray for Captain Spaulding, the African explorer!" "Did someone call me schnorrer?"*—movie Animal Crackers **2** *n* A person who habitually haggles; niggard [fr Yiddish *shnorrer*]

schnozz *n* (also **schnoz** or **schnozzle** or **schnozzola** or any of these spelled with **sh-** or **snozzle**) *entry* *form by 1942,* schnozzle *by 1934,* schnozzola *and* snozzle *by 1930* The nose, esp a large one; =BUGLE: *. . . the rep of not havin' a big schnozz*—Jimmy Durante/ *Five players broke their schnozzolas*—Associated Press [fr Yiddish *shnoz* fr *shnoitsl* fr German *Schnauze,* "snout"]

school *n underworld by 1950s* A state penitentiary; =the BIG HOUSE
> *See* the BIG SCHOOL, LITTLE SCHOOL, PREP SCHOOL

schpritz *See* SHPRITZ

schtarker *See* SHTARKER

schtick *See* SHTICK

schtoonk (SHT○○NK) *n* (also **schtunk** or **shtoonk** or **shtunk**) *by 1968* A person one detests or despises; =JERK, STINKER [fr Yiddish *shtunk,* "stink, scandal"]

schtup *See* SHTUP

schussboom (SH○○S b○○m) *v by 1959* To ski very fast downhill [fr German *Schuss,* literally, "shot" plus American English *boom,* "speed"]

schvantz or **schvontz** *See* SHVANTZ

◄**schvartze**► (SHVAHR tsə) *n* (also **shvartzeh** or **shvartze** or **schwartze** or **schvartzer** or **shvartzer** or **schwartzer**) *by 1961* A black person: *. . . irons even better than the schvartze*—Philip Roth/ *A shwartze. Some wife killer who'd faked it. . .*—Robert B Parker [fr Yiddish fr *shvartz,* "black"]

schwing *interj by early 1990s* An exclamation of delight, esp sexual; =HUBBA-HUBBA: *As a child, he found cartoon characters (in particular Bugs Bunny) arousing. Schwing!*—People Weekly [popularized by the 1992 movie *Wayne's World*]

science *See* HARD SCIENCE

sci-fi or **sciffy** (SĪ FĪ) **1** *n by 1955* Science fiction **2** *modifier: sci-fi fans. . . secretly crave*—Rolling Stone

scillion *See* SKILLION

scissorbill or **scissorsbill 1** *n by 1871* A person whose income is not from wages; a wealthy or privileged person **2** *n labor union by 1913* A worker who will not join a union; =SCAB **3** *n hoboes by 1940s* A railroad detective or police officer; =CINDER DICK: *Paoli is a dirty scissorbill!* [origin unknown; first attested fr late–1800s lumberjacks as a generalized term of contempt, perhaps alluding to the bird; attested in early–20th-century hobo use with gloss "a farmer who can clip coupons," hence perhaps used contemptuously to designate bondholders and others inimical to workers and labor unions]

scoff 1 *v by 1846* To eat or drink, esp voraciously; =SCARF: *I'll take you over. . . so you can scoff*—Jim Tully **2** *n by 1846* Food: *Beef heart is their favorite scoff* **3** *v by 1893* To steal; seize; plunder; =SWIPE: *Who scoffed my butts?* [origin uncertain; perhaps fr Afrikaans *schoft,* defined in a 1600s dictionary as "eating free for labourers or workmen foure times a day"; perhaps fr British dialect *scaff*; South African use in current senses is attested in late 1700s]

scoffings *n hoboes by 1892* Food; meals: *A hard town for "scoffings"*—Jack London

scooch *See* SCRUNCH

scoop 1 *v newspaper office by 1884* To publish or file a news story before another newspaper or another reporter: *I was afraid of being scooped, because I knew a lot of reporters were on the same story*—New York Post **2** *n newspaper office by 1874* : *The paper scored a major scoop with that revelation* **3** *n lunch counter by 1950s* A standard hemispherical portion of ice cream, mashed potatoes, etc; =DIP **4** *v by 1927* In singing, to attain a desired note by beginning lower and sliding up to pitch: *In the video* Forza del Destino, *Renata Tebaldi sometimes scoops and has occasional bouts of flatness*—New York Times **5** *n politics by 1990s* A fund-raising event that allows many contributions to be given at once; =DUMP **6** *v 1960s students* To steal; pilfer **7** *n 1990s narcotics* A designer drug, gamma hydroxybutyrate; =GHB, GRIEVOUS BODILY HARM

the **scoop** *n phr 1940s students & armed forces* News or data, esp when anxiously awaited, heretofore secret, etc; =POOP: *Oh, come on. What's the scoop?*—Sue Grafton

scooper *See* POOPER SCOOPER

scoop on someone *v phr 1980s students* To make sexual advance; =HIT ON someone: *. . . I saw him trying to scoop on Nancy at the party*—UCLA Slang

scoot 1 *v by 1841* To move rapidly, esp in fleeing or escaping: *When they saw the cops they scooted right out of there* **2** *v by 1838* To slide, esp suddenly as on a slippery surface: *Let's scoot this thing into the corner* **3** *n by 1970s* A dollar: *Greg could have the sixty scoots, the guns, everything*—Joseph Wambaugh **4** *n 1960s students* A motorcycle; =BIKE, IRON [origin unknown; perhaps ultimately fr a Scandinavian cognate of *shoot,* by way of Scottish dialect; British naval *scout,* in the first sense, is found by 1758; the third sense may have an entirely different derivation than the first two]

scope a vic *See* VIC

scope on (or **out**) *v phr 1980s teenagers fr black* To look at; examine; =CHECK OUT, DIG: *. . . scoping on the foxy sisters*—New York Times/ *. . . I'd scoped him out pretty well*—Richard Merkin [probably fr *periscope*]

scorch 1 *v by 1891* To travel very fast; =BARREL: *I proceed to scorch to make up for lost time*—Jack London **2** *v baseball by 1940s* To throw the ball very fast and hard; =BURN: *You had to love how he scorched Buddy Ryan. . .*—New York Times

scorched earth *n phr business by 1990s* : *Scorched Earth: a self-destructive strategy in which a company seeks to discourage a takeover by making itself less attractive*—Time [translation of Chinese *jiaotu,* describing the 1930s strategy adopted in defense against the invasion by Japan, under which retreating troops destroyed everything useful]

scorcher 1 *n by 1842* A very harsh remark, review, etc; =ZINGER **2** *n by 1874* A very hot day **3** *n baseball by 1900* A very hard-hit ball

score 1 *n by 1970s* A success or coup: *This was the big score for him, the chance he'd been waiting for*

all his life—Stan Cutler **2** *n* underworld by 1914 The loot or proceeds from a robbery, swindle, gamble, etc; also, the amount of such loot; =HAUL **3** *n* 1930s underworld A share of loot; =CUT **4** *v* by 1884 To succeed, esp to please an audience, interviewer, or others who judge; =RATE: *The show didn't score with the TV critics* **5** *v* by 1960 To do the sex act with or to someone; =MAKE IT WITH someone **6** *n* by 1960: *He was always looking for an easy score* **7** *v* prostitutes by 1960s To find a client for prostitution **8** *n* prostitutes by 1960s: *The little hooker got only five scores all evening* **9** *n* underworld by 1970s A planned murder; =HIT **10** *v* 1950s narcotics To buy or get narcotics: *You go score what you need for the trip*—Harry Crews **11** *n* 1950s narcotics : *He's out looking for a score* **12** *v* students by 1970s To get; acquire: *Most of them score their clothes as gifts from parents*—Time **13** *n* New York City police by 1990s: *The Mollen Commission focused on clusters of officers who profited from scores, a code word for stealing and extorting narcotics and cash from drug dealers*—New York Times
See EVEN THE SCORE, MAKE A SCORE

the **score** *n* by 1938 The main point; crux; =the BOTTOM LINE: *I heard the facts, now what's the score?*
See KNOW THE SCORE

scosh *See* SKOSH

scow *n* truckers by 1940s A large truck

scrag[1] **1** *v* by 1930 To kill; murder: *. . . overshoot or undershoot and scrag some scared civilian*—Robert Ruark **2** *v* by 1835 To destroy or severely damage; ruin: *The beet sugar people. . . try to scrag the cane sugar people*—R Starnes ◁**3**▷ *v* by 1970s To do the sex act with or to; =SCREW, SCROG: *. . . the middle-American hobby of scragging the random housewife at any opportunity*—John D MacDonald [fr earlier slang, "hang by the neck"]

◁**scrag**[2]▷ *n* 1940s students An unattractive woman; =DOG [probably fr *hag* reinforced by the name of the ugly *Scraggs* family in the comic strip "Li'l Abner" and possibly by earlier slang, "a raw-bones; a skinny person," found by 1542]

scraggy *adj* by 1611 Gaunt and wasted; lean; bony: *. . . snapshot of a scraggy Sindona as an apparent captive*—Time

scram **1** *v* by 1928 To leave quickly; flee; =BEAT IT: *Customers scrammed screaming when the trailer went on*—Village Voice/ *Scram, you kids* **2** *n*: *I got ready for a sudden scram* [fr *scramble*]

scramble *v* 1980s teenagers : *Some girls I know "scramble," which means sell drugs, to get it*—New York Times

scrambled eggs WWII armed forces **1** *n* Gold braid, embroidery, etc, on the uniform of a senior officer, esp on the bill of a hat **2** *n* Senior officers; =BRASS, the TOP BRASS

scrambler *n* motorcyclists by 1970s A motorcycle used for mountain or hill riding

scrap **1** *n* by 1846 A fight; quarrel; =DUSTUP **2** *v*: *They scrapped for days over the appointment* [origin uncertain; probably fr *scrape*]

scrape along (or **by**) *v phr* by 1884 To survive; carry on; =GET BY, MAKE OUT: *I'm not flourishing, but I'm scraping along, barely*

scrape the bottom of the barrel *v phr* by 1942 To use one's last and worst resources; be forced to desperate measures: *He scraped the bottom of the barrel when he proposed that topic for his paper*

scrape (or **scratch**) **up** *v phr* first form by 1617, variant by 1922 To get, esp laboriously and bit by bit: *Dollar by dollar they scraped up a million: . . . even if you can't scratch up all of that cash now*—Sports Afield

scrap iron *n phr* by 1942 Inferior whiskey; =ROTGUT

scrappy *adj* by 1895 Inclined to fight; pugnacious

scratch **1** *n* by 1914 Money; =BREAD, DOUGH: *If the mayor doesn't come up with the scratch*—Saturday Review **2** *n* by 1930s A loan; an act of borrowing money: *. . . where they are going to make a scratch for tomorrow's operations*—Damon Runyon **3** *v* horse-racing by 1902 To cancel a horse from a race **4** *n*: *two scratches in the third race* **5** *n* horse-racing by 1970s : *She had found one "scratch," a ticket. . . bet on a horse that had not started*—New York Times **6** *v* by 1685 To cancel a plan, an entrant, someone on a list, etc; =SCRUB: *Looks like our tête-à-tête will have to be scratched* **7** *v* (also **itch**) billiards by 1909 To put the cue ball into a pocket inadvertently **8** *n* (also **itch**) billiards by 1909: *He made a scratch at a crucial juncture: And when the cue ball goes into the pocket, you call that an itch*—Max Shulman **9** *adj* by 1851 Hastily arranged; impromptu; spur of the moment; =PICKUP: *a scratch jazz ensemble* **10** *n* by late 1930s A mention of one's name in the news media, esp when this is useful publicity
See FROM SCRATCH; START FROM SCRATCH; UP TO SCRATCH; YOU SCRATCH MY BACK, I SCRATCH YOURS

scratcher *n* underworld by 1859 A forger

scratch (or **scratch around**) **for** something *v phr* by 1509 To acquire something, esp something hard to find or get: *I was scratching around for whatever work I could get* [fr the food-seeking action of chickens]

scratch hit *n phr* baseball by 1876 A lucky base hit that is nearly an out

scratch house *n phr* merchant marine & hoboes by about 1930 A cheap lodging house; =FLEABAG, FLOPHOUSE

scratch sheet *n phr* horse-racing by 1939 A daily publication giving betting data, including the cancellations, on races to be run that day: *. . . the first scratch sheet that ever appeared. The year was 1917*—T Betts

scrawny *adj* by 1833 Lean; bony; =SCRAGGY

a **scream** *n phr* by 1903 Someone or something that is hilariously funny; =a HOOT, a RIOT: *Isn't this decor a scream?*

scream (or **yell**) **bloody murder** *v phr* entry form by 1882, variant by 1931 To make a raucous outcry; complain noisily: *They'll scream bloody murder if we even suggest that*

screamer 1 *n print shop by 1895* An exclamation point; =BANG, SHRIEK **2** *n show business by 1920s* A murder mystery, horror show, or thriller **3** *n by 1940s* A very conspicuous advertising plaque or banner **4** *n newspaper office by 1926* =SCAREHEAD

screaming *See* DRAG someone KICKING AND SCREAMING INTO THE TWENTIETH CENTURY

screaming meemie 1 *modifier by 1927* Resembling or causing a state of nervous hysteria: *. . . rather than endure another minute of screaming-meemie loneliness*—New York Times **2** *n phr WWII Army* A small rocket launched from a jeep or truck

the **screaming meemies** or the **meemies** *n phr fr WWI Army* A state of nervous hysteria; =the HEEBIE-JEEBIES, the JITTERS: *. . . a town that would give the ordinary thrill-seeker the screaming meemies*—G S Perry/ *Knowing (a chimpanzee) was on the loose gave him the meemies*—F Brown [apparently fr the soldier's echoic name for a very loud and terrifying German artillery shell, and then the battle fatigue caused by exposure to such materiel; the name may reflect a soldier's pattern of giving feminine names, here the French *Mimi*, to projectiles and weapons, such as *Betsy, Big Bertha, Moaning Minnie*, etc]

screech *n by 1902* Inferior whiskey; =PANTHER PISS

a **screeching halt** *n phr by 1970s* A sudden and definitive stop: *I'll know when it's coming to a screeching halt*—Lawrence Sanders/ *Let's bring this conversation to a screeching halt*

screenager *n by 1990s Did you hear about Bobby? He downloaded Windows 95 from his counselor's computer and then sold it to his Dad's accounting firm. What a screenager*—Macon Telegraph

◁**screw¹**▷ **1** *v by 1785* To do the sex act with or to someone; =FUCK •Felt by many to be excusable when *fuck* is the term really intended, and used as an attenuated form in nearly the whole range of *fuck* senses and compounds: *At last people are screwing like minks*—Saturday Review **2** *n by 1929*: *She loves a good screw* **3** *n by 1937* A person regarded merely as a sex object: *She's only a medium screw* **4** *v by 1900* To take advantage of; swindle; maltreat; =FUCK •Rapidly losing all offensive impact: *The city's taxpayers get screwed*—Village Voice [*screw*, "strumpet, prostitute," is found by 1725]

See GOAT FUCK, PUT THE SCREWS TO someone, THROW A FUCK INTO someone

screw² *n underworld by 1812* A prison guard or warden; turnkey: *. . . a hard-boiled screw*—E Lavine [fr 1700s underworld, "a skeleton key," then turnkey, the bearer of such a key]

screw³ or **screw out** *v entry form by 1896, variant by 1908* To leave hastily; flee; =SCRAM: *Now go on. Screw*—Nathaniel Benchley [perhaps imitative of *scram*; perhaps semantically derived fr *fuck off* "leave, depart," by way of less taboo *screw off*]

screw around *by 1939* **1** *v phr* To pass one's time idly and pleasantly; potter about; =GOOF AROUND **2** *v phr* To joke and play when one should be serious; =FUCK AROUND: *Quit screwing around and take this call* **3** *v phr* To flirt or dally, esp promiscuously; =SWINGER: *After he met Janet, he stopped screwing around*

screw around with something *v phr by 1970s* To play or tinker with; =MESS AROUND WITH: *I told her to stop screwing around with the TV dial*

screwball¹ or **screwhead 1** *n by 1933* An eccentric person; =FREAK, ODDBALL: *. . . a catchall for screwballs and semi-screwballs from all over*—Saturday Evening Post/ *He's just another screwhead too big for his britches*—Milwaukee Journal **2** *adj*: *. . . screwball antics*—Time **3** *n jazz musicians by 1936* Inferior, commercial jazz played for indifferent faddists [fr *screwy* and probably based on *screwball²*; the *-ball* of this term is the source of the very productive combining word that yields *oddball, nutball,* etc]

screwball² *n baseball by 1928* A pitched ball that moves to the right from a righthanded pitcher and the left from a lefthanded pitcher, unlike a curve ball [said to have been coined by the pitcher Carl Hubbell]

screwed *adj British & 1980s students* Drunk *See* HALF-STEWED

screwed, blued, and tattooed *by 1940s* **1** *adj phr* Thoroughly cheated; victimized; maltreated **2** *adj phr Navy*: *In the Pacific Fleet, screwed, blued, and tattooed means that you've hit a foreign port and have done everything of importance in that port. . . you have gotten laid, had a new set of dress blues hand made, and added to your already prodigious collection of tattoos*—LCDR Grey Chisholm [in the first sense, *blued* is probably fr earlier *blewed*, "robbed"; *tattooed* has the standard sense "struck rapidly and repeatedly"]

screwed up *WWII armed forces* **1** *adj phr* Confused; tangled; spoiled, esp by bungling; =BALLED UP, FUCKED UP: *He screwed up the punch line* **2** *adj phr* Mentally and emotionally disturbed; neurotic; =FUCKED UP: *Hamlet was a sad, screwed-up type guy*—J D Salinger

◁**screwee**▷ *n by 1970s* A sex partner; a person being screwed: *My screwee was so angry that nothing would distract her*—Playboy

screw-loose *n by 1940s* An eccentric person; =NUT, SCREWBALL

a **screw loose** *See* HAVE A SCREW LOOSE

◁**screw off**▷ **1** *v phr by 1950s* To masturbate; =JACK OFF **2** *v phr WWII Army* =FUCK OFF

screw-off *n WWII Army* A person who evades work; idler; loafer; =FUCK-OFF

screw someone **over** *v phr by 1960s* To take advantage of; swindle and victimize; =FUCK OVER: *. . . don't trust the Government. They feel it screwed them over*—Time

screws *See* PUT THE SCREWS TO someone

◁**screw the pooch**▷ *v phr* =FUCK THE DOG

screw up 1 *v phr WWII Army* To fail by blundering; ruin one's prospects, life, etc; =FUCK UP: *I* screwed up and got canned **2** **v phr** by 1938 To confuse; tangle; spoil by bungling; =BALL UP, FUCK UP: *It really screws up my sex life*—J D Salinger

screw-up 1 *n* WWII Army A chronic bungler; a consistently inept person; =FUCK-UP **2** *n* by 1950s A confused situation; a botch; =FUCK-UP: *The program's a total screw-up*

screwy *adj* by 1887 Very eccentric; crazy; =NUTTY, SCREWBALL: *Newspaper guys are mostly screwy*—Joel Sayre [fr the gait of a drunk person suggested by the twistiness of a *screw* thread, whence the various senses of deviation; influenced by the notion of having a *screw loose* in one's head]

◁**screw you**▷ *interj* by 1940s An exclamation of strong defiance and contempt; =FUCK YOU: *Screw you all*—New York Magazine

script¹ *n* 1960s narcotics A doctor's prescription, often a forged or stolen one

script² *n* theater by 1897, also publishing A manuscript

◁**scrog**▷ **1** *v* by 1970s To do the sex act with or to; =SCRAG, SCREW: *You guys gotta scrog the sociable cervix*—Samuel Shem **2** *modifier*: *All that scroggin' material out there*—Calvin Trillin [origin uncertain; perhaps fr *scrag*]

scrooch or **scrooge** or **scrouge** See SCRUNCH

scrooched *adj* by about 1925 Drunk

Scrooge by 1940 **1** *n* A miser; =PINCHPENNY, TIGHTWAD **2** *n* A spoiler of Christmas; =GRINCH [fr the Dickens character in the 1843 story *A Christmas Carol*]

scrooge up *v phr* by 1909 To tense and narrow one's eyelids: *I find myself scrooging up my eyes*—Sports Afield

scroogie or **screwgie** (SKRōō jee) *n* baseball by 1953 An unconventional pitch, esp a screwball thrown with a change of pace: *It was some sort of a scroogie. . . a changeup screwball*—Associated Press [said to have been coined by Mickey Mantle, probably fr *screwball* and *screwy*]

scrounge or **scrounge up** 1909 **1** *v* (also **scrounge up**) To acquire by such dubious ways as habitual borrowing, begging, foraging, scavenging, pilfering, etc; =CADGE, MOOCH ●Popularized by military use during World War I: *. . . eating what little he could scrounge*—Louis Armstrong **2** *v* (also **scrounge up**) To seek and collect; =SCRAPE UP: *Let's see what we can scrounge up for supper* **3** *n* (also **scrounger**) A person who acquires by begging, borrowing, or pilfering; =CADGER, MOOCHER, SCHNORRER [probably fr British dialect *scrunge,* "squeeze," hence "steal," semantically parallel with pinch]

scroungy or **scrounging** or **scrungy** *adj* by 1950s Inferior; wretched; =CRUMMY, GRUNGY: *I'd tell my own children to wear something scroungy*—Time/ *The musical has a scroungy book*—New York Magazine *. . . could have bundled all this scrungy stuff into my car*—John D MacDonald [probably fr the notion of inferior things *scavenged* and *scrounged,* with the form now influenced by *grungy*]

scrub¹ *v* by 1828 To cancel or eliminate: *They were forced to scrub the whole plan* [popularized by military use during World War II]

scrub² **1** *n* by 1589 A contemptible person; =BUM: *Ed is a scrub*—Delcastle Dictionary of Slang **2** *n* by 1892 An athlete who is not on the first or varsity team; a lowly substitute [ultimately fr scrub, "shrub, a low, stunted tree"; the quoted 1990s teenager use is an interesting survival or perhaps a revival based on the second sense]

scrub club *n phr* by 1970s A uniformly ineffectual group, business, project, etc

scrubs *n* medical by 1970s Loose-fitting garments, slippers, etc, worn by surgeons, nurses, and others in a sterile environment: *Finally, Bill emerged from the delivery room in green scrubs, cradling a seven-pound baby, saying he was "bonding" with his new daughter*—Vanity Fair

scrud or **double scrud** 1930s Army **1** *n* or *n phr* Any disease, esp something quite serious and painful; =CRUD **2** *n* or *n phr* Any venereal disease; =CRUD

scruff¹ or **scruff along** *v* or *v phr* by 1940s To make a bare living; =SCRAPE ALONG

scruff² *adj* teenagers by 1970s =SCRUFFY [fr *scruffy*]

scruffy *adj* by 1871 Dirty and unkempt; shabby; slovenly: *The scruffy little city, Knoxville, did it*—Wall Street Journal/ *. . . one bearded, sad-eyed, scruffy-looking lad*—Albert Goldman [fr obsolete British *scruff,* "valueless, contemptible," probably an alteration of *scurf,* "scabbiness of the skin," hence related to *scurvy*]

scrump or **scromp** *v* 1980s students To do the sex act; =BOFF, JAZZ [perhaps a blend of *screw* and *hump*]

scrumptious *adj* by 1836 Excellent; superior; luxurious: *What a scrumptious dessert!* [perhaps a humorous alteration of *sumptuous*]

scrunch (also **ooch** or **oonch** or **scooch** or **scrooch** or **scrooge** or **scrouge**) **1** *v* entry form by 1844 To squeeze oneself into a tighter space: *I scrunched into the corner and covered my ears/ She scrooged over and patted the sofa beside her. Ooch over*—WR Burnett **2** *v* by 1880 To squeeze: *He scrunched the paper into a ball* [ultimately fr late–16th-century *scruze,* "squeeze," perhaps a blend of *screw* and *squeeze*]

scrunge *n* 1970s students Dirt; filth; a nasty substance; =GRUNGE: *Wipe the scrunge off your shoe* [probably fr *grunge*]

scrungy *adj* by 1974 Dirty; =SCUZZY: *. . . and being with a bunch of scrungy addicts*—Stan Cutler

scuffle or **scuffle along** **1** *v* or *v phr* jazz musicians by 1939 To make one's modest living the best one can; struggle along; =GET BY, SCRAPE ALONG, SCRUFF **2** *v* or *v phr* 1950s jive talk To dance

◁**scum**▷ *n* by 1960s Semen; =COME

◁**scumbag**▷ by 1960s **1** *n* A condom; =RUBBER **2** *n* (also **scumbucket** or **scummer** or **scumsack** or **scumster** or **scumwad**) A despicable person; =ASSHOLE, BASTARD, SLEAZEBAG: *. . . calls. . . Charlton*

Heston a scumbag—National Review/ *Everybody says he was a scumbucket*—movie *Columbo*/ *The scummers were dressed sleeveless now*—Elmore Leonard/ *And another opportunistic scumsack limps straight to a lawyer. . .* —Carsten Stroud **3 modifier**: . . . *accused us of practicing scumbag journalism*—Village Voice [fr *scum,* "semen"]

◁**scumsucker**▷ *by 1970s* **1 n** A person who does fellatio; =COCKSUCKER: . . . *strumpet called Tony a scumsucker*—San Francisco **2 n** A despicable person; =SCUMBAG

◁**scumsucking**▷ *adj by 1970s* Despicable; disgusting: *You scum-sucking dog, you think everybody in town. . . doesn't know you keep this whore up here?*—Harry Crews

a **scunner** *n by 1500* Extreme dislike; hostility: . . . *had taken a scunner against the main competitor*—Atlantic Monthly [fr Scots dialect]

scunnion *See* BRING SCUNNION

scupper *n WWII Navy* A prostitute [probably fr the sewerish connotations of *scupper,* "deck drain on a ship"]

scurve *n teenagers by 1951* A despicable person; =CRUMB, SCUMBAG, DIRTBAG: *A beer-bottle-in-pocket, fast-talking scurve pushes through the crowd*—Village Voice/ *The scurves are on the street again tonight*—Harpers [fr *scurvy*]
See SCRUFFY

scut 1 n *by 1873* A detestable or contemptible person; =CRUMB, LOUSE: *You bloody scut!*—Lawrence Sanders **2 n** *by 1950s* A novice; recruit; neophyte: *The fraternity was famous for treating scuts very roughly* **3 n** (also **scud** or **scut work**) *by 1950s* Menial work such as would be given to a novice: . . . *a detention company doing scut work around the fort*—Newsweek **4 n** (also **scut dog** or **scut monkey** or **scut puppy**) *medical by 1940s* A junior intern or physician **5 n** (also **scut work**) *medical by 1940s* Routine and tedious medical procedures usually relegated to the least senior members of the staff [the 1500s slang use, "vulva, cunt," and the standard use "tail of a hare or deer," suggest a core sense "tail, buttocks, ass," reinforced by British dialect *skut,* "crouch down," and perhaps related to Old Norse *skutr,* "stern of a ship"; *scut* meant "little boy," perhaps fr Scots *scudler,* "scullion, kitchen boy," among Scotch-Irish settlers in Pennsylvania]

◀**scuttle**▶ *n 1920s cabdrivers* A black person, esp a black taxi passenger; =HOD [because a *scuttle* is a container for coal, which, as the taboo sense recalls, is black]

scuttlebutt *n Navy by 1901* Rumors; gossip; presumed confidential information: . . . *worry about a slump, according to business scuttlebutt*—Associated Press [fr the chit-chat around the *scuttlebutt,* "drinking fountain, water cask," on naval vessels]

scuzz *1960s teenagers* **1 n** (also **scuzzo**) Dirt; filth; a nasty substance; =GRUNGE, MUNG, SCRUNGE: *He has scuzz all over his pants and in his mind* ◁**2**▷ **n** An unattractive young woman; =SCANK, SKAG [origin unknown; a blend of *scum* with *fuzzy* has been suggested, but most such suggestions are mere ingenuity]

scuzzbag *n* (also **scuzzball** or **scuzzbucket**) *by 1983* A despicable person; =CRUMB, SCURVE, SLEAZEBAG: *He calls a minister a "scuzzbag"*—Time/ *As Johnny Depp. . . and countless other West Coast scuzzballs are proving. . .* —Milwaukee Journal

scuzz-food *n by 1970s* Food like potato chips, popcorn, sugar-coated cereal, etc; =JUNK FOOD: *I will take a back seat to no one as a scuzz-food fanatic*—Car and Driver

scuzz someone **out** *v phr teenagers by 1970s* To disgust mightily; nauseate; =GROSS someone OUT: *With-it slanguists are scuzzed out at the squared-out weirdos who still use grossed out*—William Safire

scuzzy or **scuz** *adj 1960s teenagers* Dirty; filthy; repellent; =GRUNGY: . . . *a bunch of scuzzy Moroccan A-rabs*—Village Voice [origin unknown]
See SCUZZ

sea cow *n phr WWII Navy* Milk, esp canned milk

seagoing bellhop *n phr Navy by 1940s* A US Marine [fr the colorful and elaborate dress uniform]

seagull *v WWII Navy* To travel by airplane; fly

sea gull *WWII Navy* **1 n phr** Chicken, esp canned or frozen chicken **2 n phr** A woman, wife, sweetheart, etc, who follows the fleet **3 n phr** A very hearty or gluttonous eater

sea lawyer *See* FORECASTLE LAWYER

seams *See* COME APART AT THE SEAMS

seam squirrel *n phr by 1899* A body louse; =COOTIE

search me *interj by 1900* An exclamation or acknowledgment of ignorance; =BEATS ME: *Who said it? Search me, I couldn't say*

season *See* SILLY SEASON

seas over *See* HALF SEAS OVER

seat *n by 1607* The buttocks; =ASS
See BUDDY SEAT, CATBIRD SEAT, the HOT SEAT, SMOKY SEAT, TAKE A BACK SEAT

seat-of-the-pants *adj by 1970s* Inclined to work by instinct, feel, impulse, etc, rather than by precise rules; practical: *The news had seat-of-the-pants editors who knew their audience*—Washingtonian
See FLY BY THE SEAT OF one's PANTS

sec[1] *n by 1860* A second of time: *Come here a sec, Billy*—Sinclair Lewis

sec[2] *n by 1934* A secretary: *His femme secs open the mail*—Variety

second banana *n phr show business by 1940s* A supporting comedian: *Who was second banana, Laurel or Hardy?*
See TOP BANANA

second fiddle 1 n *by 1809* A person or thing that is not the most favored, the best, the leader, etc: . . . *definitely second fiddle before the Convention started*—Pete Martin **2 adj**: *a sort of second-fiddle appointment*
See PLAY SECOND FIDDLE

second john (or **looey**) *n phr WWII Army* A second lieutenant; =SHAVETAIL

second line *v phr musicians by about 1900* To follow the leader or first rank, esp in hope of advancement: *I was "second lining". . . following the brass bands in parades*—Louis Armstrong

second off *adv phr by 1970s* Second in order; secondly: *. . . and, second off, readers and authors both*—New York Times [based on *first off*]

second sacker *n phr* baseball *by 1911* A second baseman

second thought *See* DON'T GIVE IT A SECOND THOUGHT

secret *See* DIRTY LITTLE SECRET

section eight or **section 8** *WWII Army* **1** *n phr* A military discharge given for emotional or psychological disability, defective character, or military inaptitude **2** *n phr* A crazy or eccentric person; a neurotic; =NUT [fr *Section VIII*, Army Regulation 615–360]

security blanket *n phr by 1971* A thing or person that provides someone with a sense of safety and emotional comfort: *Zeigler instead is. . . Mr Nixon's "security blanket"*—Newsweek [fr the *blanket* or token fragment of blanket that some small children carry about as a source of comforting familiarity; Charles M Schulz, creator of the comic strip "Peanuts," popularized and may have coined the term]

see 1 *n* police *by 1950s* Recognition; complimentary notice by a superior: *He was a good cop ten years, but never got a see* **2** *n* police *by 1930* A visit of inspection: *. . . numerous "sees" or visits from the sergeant*—E Lavine **3** *v* police *by 1930* To pay protection money or graft: *. . . doing business without "seeing the cops"*—E Lavine **4** *v* gambling *by 1599* To equal a bet or a raise rather than dropping out of the game [first sense perhaps an abbreviation of *commendation*]
  See LONG TIME NO SEE, LOOK SEE, a LOOK-SEE

see a man about a dog *v phr by 1927* To take one's leave for some urgent purpose, esp to go to the bathroom or in earlier times to go have a drink or to meet one's bootlegger •Usu a smiling apology for one's departure; a bland euphemism to conceal one's true purpose

seed *n 1960s* narcotics =ROACH
  See HAYSEED

seeing-eye hit *n phr* baseball *by 1950s* A batted ball that seems to have the power of choosing its elusive course: *We should have been out of the inning, but they had some seeing-eye hits*—Milwaukee Journal [fr Seeing Eye, Incorporated™ of Morristown NJ, which trains guide dogs for the blind]

see pink elephants *v phr by 1940* To have hallucinations from alcoholism [said to have been originated by P G Wodehouse]

see red *v phr by 1897* To become very angry: *Politics make him see red*

see the chaplain *sentence WWII Army* Stop complaining; I can't help you with your problems

see the light at the end of the tunnel *v phr Vietnam War period* To see at last the beginning of the end of a difficult struggle, period, etc: *The Flower People of Saigon. . . invite you to see the light at the end of the tunnel*—New York Times

see-through 1 *adj by 1950* Transparent; made of a very sheer fabric; =PEEKABOO: *a see-through blouse* **2** *n by 1990s*: *While empty office buildings (colorfully called "see-throughs") cluttered the skylines, investors did manage to cut their overall tax bills*—New Republic

see someone's **wheels turning** *v phr by 1990s* To observe that someone is thinking, analyzing, etc: *When my dog is in obedience class, I can see his wheels turning*—Healthy Pets

see you *interj by 1891* A casual farewell; =SO LONG •Often with *around, soon, later,* or another modifier: *. . . the careless "see you's" that people say*—Life

see-you *n 1920s* salespersons A customer who always asks to be waited on by a certain person

segue or **seg** (SEHG way or SEHG) **1** *n* musicians *by 1937* Transition from one piece of music, record, etc, to the next without an obvious break **2** *v* musicians *by 1958* To make a "segue": *Then they segued to "Body and Soul"* **3** *v by 1972* To go smoothly from one thing to another: *His features seg rapidly from fascination to fear*—Playgirl **4** *n* college students *by 1970s* A sequel; something that follows or follows up [fr Italian, "now follows," an instruction on musical scores, found by 1740]

seg unit *n phr* prison *by 1990s*: Expand segregation space. Inmates who habitually break rules or assault staff are sent to "seg" units—On the Move

sell 1 *v by 1597* To cheat; swindle; hoax: *I've tunneled, hydraulicked, and cradled, and I have been frequently sold*—folk song Acres of Clams **2** *n by 1838* A hoax or swindle; a deception: *The Cardiff Giant was a "sell"*—A T Vance **3** *v by 1916* To convince someone of the value of something: *But would it sell anybody else? I doubt it*—Hugh Pentecost [first sense said in an article of 1810 to be derived from *sell a bargain*, "the dexterous transfer of any unmarketable commodity for a high price to an unwary customer"]
  See HARD SELL, SOFT SELL, be SOLD ON

sell oneself *v phr by 1920s* To make oneself appealing and successful with an audience, a potential employer, etc

sell someone **down the river** *v phr by 1927* To betray someone; take victimizing advantage [fr slavery days, when a black person or escaped slave *sold down the river* was sent to or returned to the South, a use found by 1851]

selling plater *n phr* horse-racing *by 1940s* An inferior race horse: *. . . these selling platers with a shot of dope in them*—Ernest Hemingway

sell like hot cakes *v phr by 1839* To enjoy very brisk sales: *The General's book sold like hot cakes*

sell out[1] *v phr by 1888* To become a traitor, esp to prostitute one's ideals, talents, etc, for money or other comforts: *. . . are often labeled Toms and mammies who sold out*—Saturday Review/ *. . . accuse them of selling out Chiang Kai-shek*—David Halberstam

sell out² *v phr* by 1796 To dispose of entirely by sale: *You can't get that here, we sold out*

sell-out *n* by 1862 for betrayal, 1859 for disposition of tickets, etc An act or instance of selling out, in either sense: *He disappointed us, but he was honest enough and it was no sell-out/ The new bathing suits should be a quick sell-out*

semolia *n black by 1950s* A stupid person; fool

send *v jazz talk by 1932* To arouse keen admiration, esp as an ecstatic response; excite; =TURN someone ON: *Bessie Smith really sent him*—Stephen Longstreet

sender *See* SOLID SENDER

send-off *n* by 1872 A funeral: *. . . give a man a classy send-off*—Billy Rose

send someone **to the showers 1** *v phr* baseball by 1940s To remove or eject a player, esp a pitcher, from a game **2** *v phr* by 1940s To dismiss or reject someone

send up 1 *v phr* (also **send up the river**) by 1901 To send someone to prison: *He got sent up for grand theft* **2** *v phr* by 1950s To ridicule, esp by parody; mock; lampoon; =SPOOF: *. . . cracking jokes, sending up everyone and everything in sight*—Rolling Stone [first sense fr or influenced by the course from New York City *up* the Hudson *River* to Sing Sing Prison at Ossining]

send-up *n* fr British by 1958 A mocking, teasing parody; lampoon; =SPOOF: *. . . just another stupid soap send-up*—People Weekly/ *. . . a relentless send-up of attitudes and gestures*—Vincent Canby

send someone **up the wall** *v phr* by 1966 To make someone furious: *Mention of Picasso sends her up the wall*

sensaysh (sen SAYSH) *adj* by 1951 Sensational: *I had a sensaysh time*—Max Shulman

separate the men from the boys *v phr* by 1962 To show who is effective and who is not; separate the sheep from the goats: *Every mayor knows snow can separate the men from the boys, or the two-termers from the one-termers*—New York Times

sergeant *See* BUCK SERGEANT

serious 1 *adj black by 1940s* Very commendable; excellent; superb **2** *adj* Intended to make a good and sober impression; overtly conformistic; =SINCERE: *. . . in a serious suit and striped tie*—Dan Jenkins **3** *adj by 1980s* Impressive; imposing; =HEAVY, IMPORTANT: *He pushed a button activating some serious chimes*—Stan Cutler

See FOR SERIOUS

server *n 1990s narcotics: As many as 10 "servers," slang for dealers, worked out of the Keefe house. . .* —Milwaukee Journal Sentinel

serve up grapefruits *v phr* baseball by 1990s To pitch balls that are easy to hit: *Garner was asked why his pitching staff continued to serve up grapefruits. . .* —Milwaukee Journal [because the ball seems as big as a *grapefruit; serve* and *serve up,* "to pitch," are found by 1913, and are possibly from tennis]

session 1 *n 1950s teenagers* A dance or party; =HOP **2** *n 1960s narcotics* The period of intoxication from a dose of narcotics, esp of LSD; =TRIP **3** *n musicians by 1927* An occasion at which a recording is made in a studio; a studio rehearsal or performance: *Horn is from an earlier session*—Swing **4** *modifier*: *He used to do a lot of session playing but hardly ever worked for an audience*

See BITCH SESSION, BULL SESSION, GRIPE SESSION, HASH SESSION, JAM SESSION, RAP SESSION, SKULL SESSION

set 1 *adj by 1844* Ready; prepared: *We were all set to go* **2** *n by 1590* The group of pieces musicians perform during about a 45-minute period at a club, show, etc: *. . . clarinetist Scott opened his set*—Metronome **3** *n 1960s jazz musicians* An improvisatory musical interchange of about half an hour **4** *n black & jazz talk by 1960s* A small party or friendly conversational gathering; =SCENE: *Don't stop belly rubbing just because we showed on the set*—Donald Goines **5** *n black by 1960s* A discussion; =RAP: *He never said get those Panthers out. . . all through the whole set*—Bobby Seale **6** *n 1960s narcotics* A narcotic dose of two Seconals™ and one amphetamine **7** *n 1990s street gang* A gang or sub-gang: *Mr Shakur was initiated into the Eight Trays, a "set" of the Crip gang based in his neighborhood. . .* —New York Times [second sense in modern use since about 1925]

See the BUBBLE-GUM SET, the JET SET

setaside *n by 1990s: Taking advantage of government setasides. . . that are designed to benefit small businesses, those owned by women and minorities, and historically black colleges and universities and minority institutions*—Macon Telegraph

set someone **back** *v phr by 1900* To cost: *How much will it set me back if I order a plain steak?*—H McHugh/ *. . . set us back what was then an astonishing $18 a person*—San Francisco

set in concrete *See* not carved in stone

set of pipes *See* PIPES

set of threads (or **drapes**) *n phr by 1926* A suit of clothing, esp a new and stylish one: *. . . the smart set of threads*—Stephen Longstreet

set of wheels *n phr by 1940s* A car: *. . . if you're feverish for a great set of wheels*—Playboy

set someone **over** *v phr 1920s underworld* To kill; murder; =RUB OUT: *They have to set a guy over*—W R Burnett

set someone or something **straight** *v phr by 1849* To determine or specify the truth: *Let me set you straight on that allegation/ I've come to set the whole thing straight*

settle *v by 1899* To imprison, esp for a life sentence: *Foley was "pinched" and "settled" in San Quentin*—Literary Digest

settle (or **fix**) someone's **hash** *British universities & schools by 1803* **1** *v phr* To injure or ruin someone definitively; =FINISH, COOK someone's GOOSE: *I'll check you out after I settle his hash*—Pulpsmith **2** *v phr* To deflate; humiliate; defeat;

=FIX someone's WAGON [origin unknown; semantically related to such similar and ironic expressions as *clean* someone's *clock, cook* someone's *goose,* and *fix* someone's *wagon*]

set-to *n boxing by 1743* A contention; fight; bout: *Another venomous set-to among the politicians*

setup 1 *n by 1926* A person who is easily duped, tricked, etc; =PATSY, SUCKER: . . . *a set-up, a tout's dream come true*—J Lilienthal **2** *n 1920s underworld* A one-day jail sentence **3** *n by 1930* A glass, ice, soda, etc, to be mixed with liquor: *They supplied the set-ups*—NY Confidential **4** *n lunch counter & restaurant by 1934* Dishes, utensils, etc, constituting a place setting for a meal **5** *n by 1890* Arrangement; organization; situation; mode of operation: . . . *except its size and its co-op set-up*—New York Times **6** *n by 1940s* A house, office, apartment, etc: *He has a very comfy setup in a rehabbed brownstone* [most senses apparently fr the *setting up* of billiard or pool balls to insure a special or a trick shot]

set up[1] *adj by about 1930* Gratified; elated; braced: *He looks real set up now that they've published his book*

set up[2] *v phr by 1865* To arrange; prepare for: . . . *set up a meet with the crook*—Lawrence Sanders

set someone **up 1** *v phr by about 1875* To prepare and maneuver someone for swindling, tricking, etc; =BUILD: *He was so vain it was easy to set him up* **2** *v phr by 1526* To gratify and encourage; brace: *Finishing first for a change really set me up* **3** *v phr by 1880* To treat someone; provide food or drink

set-up pitcher *n phr baseball by 1980s* A relief pitcher who usually works fairly late in the game and prepares the situation for another relief pitcher known as a "closer"

seventeen *See* FILE 17

Seventh Avenue *n phr by 1960s* The garment and fashion industry; =the RAG TRADE [fr the fact that New York City's *Seventh Avenue* is the traditional center of the garment industry]

seventy-'leven 1 *n by 1914* An indefinite large number; =FORTY-'LEVEN **2** *modifier*: *about seventy-'leven years*

sewer *n 1960s narcotics* A vein or artery: . . . *if I had put it right in the sewer instead of skin popping*—R V Winslow

sew something **up 1** *v phr by 1904* To finish; put the finishing touches on: *They sewed up the contract today* **2** *v phr by 1960* To insure a victory; make a conclusive score, stroke, etc; =CLINCH, ICE: *The last-period goal sewed it up for the Drew Rangers*

sex *See* UNISEX

sex bomb *n phr by 1962* A sensationally sexy person, esp a woman

sex goddess *n phr by 1970s* A woman, usu a movie star, who is a provocative and famous sexual object

sex someone **in** *v phr 1990s street gang* To initiate a woman into a gang by enjoying her sexually: *Given the choice. . . of being "beat in" or "sexed in" she chooses the former but insists that both are merely ways of showing "love"*—LA Weekly

sex job *n phr by 1940s* A sexually attractive, provocative, or available person

sex kitten (or **bunny** or **doll)** *n phr entry form by 1958, variants by 1970s* A young woman who is highly attractive, provocative, and seemingly available sexually

sexpert *n by 1924* A sex expert, esp a therapist who treats persons complaining of sexual dysfunction: *The behavioristic sexpert would call this situation homosexuality*—Playboy

sexploitation 1 *n by 1940s* Commercial exploitation of sex: *Female chauvinist sexploitation will reach a new level*—Time **2** *modifier*: . . . *a camp sexploitation horror musical*—Esquire

sexpot *n by 1954* A person, esp a woman, who is especially attractive and provocative sexually: *How pitiful the American who cannot command the smile of a sexpot*—Frederic Morton

sex wagon *n phr by 1970s* =PIMPMOBILE

sexy *adj by 1970* Very appealing; exciting; desirable; stimulating: *Acid rain is politically sexy, but it hasn't half the allure of jobs*—Toronto Life

-sey *See* -IE

sez (or **sezz) you** *See* SAYS YOU

shack 1 *n railroad, hoboes & circus by 1899* The caboose of a freight train **2** *n railroad, hoboes & circus by 1899* A railroad brake operator, who rode in the caboose **3** *n by 1940s* =SHACK JOB **4** *v by 1940s* =SHACK UP [fr *shack*, "hut, shanty," found by 1878, probably fr earlier *shackle* fr American Spanish *jacal* fr Aztec *xacalli*]

◁**shack job**▷ *n phr WWII Army* A woman one lives with adulterously; common-law wife; mistress: *This was an early shack-job, not the girl mentioned above*—New Yorker

shack man (or **rat)** *n phr WWII Army* A man who lives with or does the sex act with a woman who is not his wife; a man who keeps a mistress

shack up 1 *v phr by 1935* To live with, do the sex act with, and support a woman who is not one's wife; keep a mistress: *The medicine man had shacked up with a half-breed cook*—Time/ *When I was 13 I shacked up with a Puerto Rican chick of 38*—New York Magazine **2** *v phr by 1940s* To do the sex act; esp, to lead a promiscuous sex life; =SLEEP AROUND: *If you drink and shack up with strangers you get old at thirty*—Tennessee Williams **3** *v phr by 1950* To live; reside, esp in a nonpermanent place: . . . *got rid of his home and shacked up in a hotel*—Westbrook Pegler

shade ◀**1**▶ *n by 1865* A black person **2** *n underworld by 1925* A receiver of stolen goods; =FENCE: *It is sold to a "fence" or "shade"*—Collier's **3** *v by 1865* To defeat by a narrow margin: . . . *Michigan shaded Iowa. The final score was 98 to 96*

shades *n 1950s bop musicians* Sunglasses

◁**shad-mouth**▷ *black by about 1935* **1** *n* A person with a prominent upper lip **2** *n* A black person

shadow 1 *v by 1872* To follow a person secretly; do physical surveillance; =TAIL **2** *n*: *They put a shadow on the suspect* [verb sense found by 1602 in an isolated instance]

shadow gazer *n phr medical by 1970s* A radiologist

◁**shaft**▷ *v by 1950s* To treat unfairly or cruelly; victimize: *When do you shaft a pal, when do you hand him the poison cup?*—Saul Bellow/ *The oil companies you leased the land to shafted you out of an estimated $650 million*—Art Buchwald [fr the notion of sodomizing a victim]

◁**the shaft** or **a shafting**▷ *n phr by 1950s* Unfair or cruel treatment: *Jamaicans have learned from past experience to expect the shaft from foreign journalists*—Newsweek

See GET THE SHAFT, GIVE someone THE SHAFT

shag 1 *v by 1788* To do the sex act; =BOFF, SCREW **2** *v by 1851* To depart; leave, esp quickly; =SHAG ASS: *You'd best shag now*—W Henry **3** *v by 1912* To chase: *I was allowed to "shag" foul balls*—C H Claudy . . . *shagging rabbits*—E Kasser **4** *v 1930s teenagers* To tease and harass; =HASSLE, HOUND **5** *n 1930s teenagers* A party or session where boys and girls experiment sexually **6** *n by 1950s* A person's date or escort; =DRAG: *He didn't have a shag for the prom* **7** *adj by 1940s* With a date or escort: *Did you go to the party stag or shag?* **8** *adj 1950s teenagers* Excellent; wonderful [origin unknown; perhaps fr *shake* by way of *shack*]

See GANG BANG

◁**shag ass**▷ *v phr by 1940s* To depart; leave, esp hurriedly; =HAUL ASS, SCRAM

shagger *n by 1940s* A person who follows another secretly; =SHADOW, TAIL [fr *shag*, "chase"]

shake 1 *n by 1940s* A rent party: . . . *charge a few coins and have a shake*—Louis Armstrong **2** *n by 1839* A moment; =SEC: *Be ready in two shakes* **3** *v by 1873* To come to an agreement; shake hands: *Let's shake and call it done* **4** *n by 1930* Blackmail or extortion; =SHAKEDOWN: *This isn't any kind of a shake*—Raymond Chandler **5** *v by 1930*: . . . *tried to shake one of the big boys*—Raymond Chandler **6** *v by 1960s* To search a person or place thoroughly; =SHAKE DOWN **7** *n*: *We'd better give the entire house a shake; I know it's here somewhere* **8** *v by 1883* =GIVE someone THE SHAKE

See a FAIR SHAKE, HALF A SHAKE, ON THE SHAKE, SKIN-SEARCH, TWO SHAKES

shake a leg *v phr by 1904* To hurry; speed up

shake and bake *v phr by 1990s* To go very fast: . . . *but we gotta shake and bake through Pennsylvania, down 95, and you can't make time back here*—New Yorker/ *Roffe-Steinrotter, first among 56 skiers in a giant slalom course, told herself "whoever shakes and bakes the best is going to get the gold"*—Time [fr the trademark name of a brand of pre-baking crumb coating for meats, used by putting the meat and the coating into a bag and shaking; probably referring to the quickness of the operation]

shake-and-bake shelter *n phr by 1990s* An emergency shelter for firefighters: . . . *they struggled to get into their lightweight aluminum "shake-and-bake" shelters*—Wisconsin State Journal

See SHAKE AND BAKE

shake a wicked calf *v phr* (Variations: **mean** may replace **wicked**; **hoof** or **leg** may replace **calf**) *by 1920* To dance well, impressively, or joyfully: *Phoebe and I are going to shake a wicked calf*—F Scott Fitzgerald

shakedown 1 *n by 1730* A night's lodging; an impromptu bed: *I'll get a shakedown on the couch*—movie *The Thirty-Nine Steps* **2** *n underworld by 1902* An instance of or a demand for blackmail, extortion, etc; victimization by the protection racket: *Listen, I know this is a shakedown*—New York Magazine **3** *n by 1914* A thorough search of a person or place; =SHAKE: *We gave the room a first-class shakedown*—R Starnes **4** *n by 1930s* A trying-out or first tentative use, esp of a machine, ship, process, etc: *Let's give this new idea a shakedown and see if it works* [final sense fr *shakedown cruise*; all senses fr the notion of a vigorous *shaking* of a person or place to reveal something hidden, a flaw, etc]

shake down 1 *v phr by 1872* To blackmail or extort; demand protection money: . . . *shaking down poor peddlers, newsboys*—E Lavine **2** *v phr by 1915* To search a person or place thoroughly; =SHAKE: . . . *a couple of policemen to shake down the neighborhood*—R Starnes

shakedown cruise *n phr Navy by 1927* A cruise or sea trial for a new or a newly repaired ship

shake in one's **shoes** *v phr by 1818* To be terrified; fear greatly: *The mere thought has me shaking in my shoes*

shake it or **shake it up** *v phr by 1871* To hurry; =SHAKE A LEG: *We've got to shake it*—Dashiell Hammett

shakeout *n by 1895* A business upheaval, esp a reduction in the number of competitors in a field; a spate of failures and bankruptcies: *The central event was a major shakeout and contraction of the Eurodollar market*—Fortune/ . . . *The recorded-music business is going through a significant shakeout*—New York Magazine

shake out *v phr by 1990s* To develop; come to fruition; eventuate; =COME OUT: *Let's just wait and see how it shakes out*

shaker *See* BONE-SHAKER

the **shakes** *n phr by 1837* An attack of trembling, esp one due to alcoholism or drug abuse; =the CLANKS

shake the money tree *v phr by 1970s* To produce profit, esp in great amounts: *It took two to shake the money tree*—Village Voice

shake one's **tree** *v phr by 1980s* To engage and please one; =TURN someone ON: . . . *I have no problem with prostitution. If it shakes your tree, go for it*—Milwaukee Journal

shake-up *n* by 1899 The reorganization of a working group, its methods, etc, usu including some dismissals: *The remedy is a shake-up in the Bureau of the Budget*—Ithaca Journal

shaking *See* WHAT'S SHAKING

shalump *See* SCHLOOMP

shame *See* A DIRTY SHAME

shamus (SHAH məs, SHAY-) (also **shammus** or **shamos** or **shommus**) **1** *n* by 1925 A police officer, private detective, security guard, etc; =COP: . . . *a British-accented burlesque of the tough American shamus*—New York Times/ *Soon a character began to develop: a shamus named Marlowe*—New York Times **2** *n* by 1940s A police informer; =STOOL PIGEON [fr Yiddish, "sexton of a synagogue," fr Hebrew *shamash*, "servant"; perhaps influenced by the Celtic name *Seamus*, "James," as a typical name of an Irish police officer]

Shangri La *n phr* by 1930s An ideal place of leisure and secure remoteness; an earthly paradise [fr the fictional Himalayan country in James Hilton's 1933 novel *Lost Horizon*]

shank 1 *n* prison & street gang by 1950s A stiletto-like weapon: *We'd yoke him with a shank*—New York Post/ *looks like a large screwdriver and is known in prison parlance as a shank*—Philadelphia Journal **2** *v*: . . . *that dude the dicks want for shanking his old lady*—Joseph Wambaugh **3** *v* football by 1970s To kick: . . . *is shanking punts all over the lot*—Philadelphiã **4** *n* by 1828 The end or last part of a period of time, esp of the evening •Also interpreted as the early or chief part of a period of time: *Let's have one for the road, my friends; it's the shank of the evening* [all senses reflect the basic notion of something long and thin, like a leg bone]

shank it *v phr* by 1862 To walk; hike

shank's mare *See* RIDE SHANK'S MARE

shanty 1 *n* by 1820 A rickety hut; a hovel; a shack **2** *n* railroad A caboose [origin uncertain; perhaps fr Irish *sean-tig*, "old house"; perhaps fr Canadian French *chantier*, although this is more probably a borrowing of *shanty*]

◁**shanty Irish**▷ *n phr* by 1928 Poor or disreputable Irish people: . . . *oh, not shanty Irish*—Stephen Longstreet

shantytown by 1876 **1** *n* A poor, dilapidated neighborhood **2** *n* A cluster of makeshift dwellings, often on the edge of a town and inhabited by the vagrant or the very poor; =HOOVERVILLE

shape *n* by 1865 Condition; state of fitness: *I have to find out what shape they're in*
See BENT OUT OF SHAPE, DRAPE SHAPE

shape up 1 *v phr* by 1865 To progress; go along: *How are your plans shaping up?* **2** *v phr* (also **shape up or ship out**) WWII armed forces, but found by 1938 To correct one's behavior; conform and perform •Often a firm command or admonition: *From this day on you're going to shape up or ship out. Is that understood?*—Art Buchwald

shape someone **up** *v phr* WWII armed forces To cause someone to conform and perform; correct someone's behavior: . . . *praying for a good depression that could shape these kids up*—World

shark 1 *n* by 1599 A confidence man or swindler; =HUSTLER, SHARP **2** *n* students by 1895 A very able student, esp one who does not seem to work hard **3** *n* by 1920s An expert, esp a somewhat exploitive or unscrupulous one •Usually preceded by a modifier showing the field of skill: . . . *the gun-shark's report*—Raymond Chandler [all senses fr the predaceous fish, except that the oldest sense may originally have been fr German *schurke*, "rascal"]
See CARD SHARP, LOAN SHARK

sharp 1 *n* by 1840 An expert, esp at card games; =PRO: *Hurstwood's a regular sharp*—Theodore Dreiser **2** *n* (also **sharper**) by 1688 A confidence trickster; a swindler, esp a dishonest card player; =CARD SHARP **3** *adj* jive talk by 1940 Stylish; of the latest and most sophisticated sort: *He wore bow ties and sharp suits*—Truman Capote **4** *adj* jive talk by 1940 Good; excellent; admirable; =COOL: *I sound like everything was sharp*—John O'Hara
See CARD SHARP

sharp as a tack 1 *adj phr* by 1922 Very intelligent and perceptive **2** *modifier*: *Becker is a Hollywood type: a driven, sharp-as-a-tack intelligence devoted to a completely second-rate subject*—Nation [*sharp as tacks* is found by 1912]

sharpie 1 *n* 1940s jive talk A devotee of swing music, esp one who dances well to swing **2** *n* jazz musicians by about 1925 A stylish dresser in the flashy modes: . . . *and not just among the sharpies*—Associated Press **3** *modifier*: . . . *an incredible sharpie opulence of leather pockets and hand-wrought belt loops*—New York Magazine **4** *n* by 1940s A shrewd person watchful of his or her profit: . . . *an open invitation for a sharpie to have the free use of a new car for 30 days*—Time **5** *n* by 1942 A confidence trickster; a swindler; =SHARP, SHARK: *They were outwitted. . . by three "sharpies"*—Associated Press **6** *n* by 1970 Something desirable; =DOOZIE: *He got himself a new bike, a real sharpie*

◁**shat on**▷ *v phr* by 1960s Maltreated; victimized: *Because women have been shat on for centuries*—Off Our Backs [fr a humorous past tense form of *shit*, found in the 1700s]

◁**shatting on** one's **uppers**▷ *adj phr* by 1894 Entirely out of money; =BROKE: *She has to blow and she's shatting on her uppers*—Raymond Chandler [fr *shat*, humorous past tense form of *shit*, and *uppers*, "shoes so worn they have no soles"]

shave *v* by 1898 To reduce: *They've shaved the estimate a little*

shaved 1 *adj* by 1851 Drunk **2** *adj* 1950s hot rodders Having the ornamental and other nonfunctional parts removed; =STRIPPED DOWN

shave points or **shave** *v phr* or *v* sports & gambling by 1971 To get a gambling or money advantage by failing to score as much as one could; fraudulently lose a game: *Did they think I liked shaving the points?*—Stan Cutler

shaver *See* LITTLE SHAVER

shavetail *n Army by 1891* A second lieutenant, esp a newly commissioned one [perhaps fr an early–1800s sense, "unbroken Army mule"; perhaps also fr the fact that a newly commissioned officer might have shoulder straps made with material cut off the shirttail]

shaving *See* POINT-SHAVING

shay *See* GANG BANG

shazam (shə ZAM) *interj by 1940* An exclamation of triumphant and delighted announcement, emphasis, etc: *SHAZAM! He was up on the table*—Richard Fariña/ *Go ahead and say it, Shazam!, juice it up*—Tom Wolfe [fr the operative or command word of a magician, similar to *presto change-o*]

the shebang (shə BANG, shee-) *n by 1869* Everything; =the WHOLE SHEBANG: *You can have the shebang* [fr *shebang*, "shanty, hut," found by 1862, of obscure origin; perhaps fr an approximate pronunciation of French *char-à-banc*, "bus-like wagon with many seats," in which case the semantics of *the whole shebang* would depend upon the hiring of the whole vehicle rather than one or two seats]

◄**she can sit on my face anytime**► *sentence by 1970s* She attracts me very powerfully in a basic sexual way

shed *See* WOODSHED

she-devil *n by 1840* A wicked and difficult woman; harridan; harpie: *Hell, I practically had the she-devil cornered*

◄**shee-it**► (SHEE ət) *interj by 1960s* =SHIT [humorous imitation of a drawled Southern pronunciation]

◄**sheeny** or **sheenie**► *by 1816* **1** *n* A Jew **2** *adj*: *. . . one of those Sheeny employment bureaus*—Sinclair Lewis **3** *n* A pawnbroker, tailor, junkman, or member of another traditionally Jewish occupation [origin unknown; perhaps fr non-Jewish hearing of Yiddish *miesse meshina*, a curse; perhaps fr Yiddish *shayn* or *sheen*, "beautiful," because this is the way a merchant would praise his wares]

sheepskin *n by 1804* A college or university diploma [fr the fact that diplomas were once made of sheepskin]

sheesh[1] *interj by 1970s* An exclamation of disgust, frustration, etc: *Sheesh! I mean, really! You know?*—Lee K Russell [a euphemism for *shit*]

sheesh[2] *n 1960s narcotics* Hashish

sheet **1** *n by 1749* A newspaper: *Both morning sheets have written it up*—J Evans **2** *n police* =RAP SHEET: *He's a con man with a sheet as long as your arm*—Lawrence Sanders *See* DOPE SHEET, POOP SHEET, RAP SHEET, SCRATCH SHEET, SWINDLE SHEET, THREE SHEETS TO THE WIND

sheik (SHEEK) *by 1924* **1** *n* A handsome, sleek, romantic male lover; a ladies' man **2** *v* To attempt to captivate; charm; seduce: *Are you sheiking me, Ralph?*—New York Times [fr the 1921 movie *The Sheikh,* starring Rudolph Valentino]

sheive *See* SHIV

shekels (SHEK əls) *n by 1871* Money; wealth [fr the Hebrew name of a unit of weight and money]

shelf *See* ON THE SHELF

shell *v by 1948* To pay; =SHELL OUT: *. . . to shell at least a buck*—NY Confidential *See* HARD-SHELL

shellac or **shellack** *v sports by 1930* To defeat decisively; trounce; =CLOBBER: *The Giants were shellacked again Monday* [perhaps fr the use of *shellac* as a finish]

shellacked *adj by 1922* Drunk: *One of the boys got beautifully shellacked*—Philadelphia Bulletin

shellacking *by 1931* **1** *n* A beating: *"Shellacking" . . . and numerous other phrases are employed by the police as euphemisms*—E Lavine **2** *n* A decisive defeat; a drubbing; an utter rout: *Should Black take a shellacking, the National Leaguers are in bad trouble*—Associated Press

shell game *n phr by 1890* A swindle; confidence game; =SCAM: *I'm afraid this proposed merger looks like a shell game* [fr a version of three-card monte played with a pea or other token under walnut shells]

shell out *v phr by 1801* To pay; put out; contribute; =FORK OVER: *. . . get ready to shell out again*—Associated Press/ *. . . or shell out the enormous amounts of money it takes to market software*—Douglas Coupland

shells *See* CLAM SHELLS

◁**shemale**▷ **1** *n by 1854* A female **2** *n by 1972* A tough woman or aggressive lesbian; =BULLDYKE

shemozzle (also **shimozzle** or **shlamozzle** or **shlemozzle**) **1** *n by 1899* A difficult and confused situation; an uproar; melee; =MESS, RHUBARB ●Chiefly British: *It became clear that the whole shlamozzle, introns and exons, are transcribed into RNA*—Gordon Rattray Taylor **2** *v by 1903* To depart; =POWDER, SCRAM [ultimately probably fr Yiddish *shlim mazel*, "rotten luck," hence "a difficulty or misfortune," and related to *shlemazel*]

shenanigan or **shenanigans** *n by 1855* A trick or bit of foolery; a mild cheat or deception [origin unknown; perhaps fr Irish *sionnachuighim*, "play tricks, be foxy"]

sherm or **Sherman** **1** *n 1960s narcotics* Phencyclidine, an animal tranquilizer smoked as a narcotic; =ANGEL DUST, PCP **2** *v* To use phencyclidine: *He felt his heart bound, his stomach lunged, like the time he shermed at Venice Beach*—Buzz [said to be a prison term for *Sherman* cigarettes soaked in phencyclidine]

Sherpa or **sherpa** *n by 1980* A high-ranking assistant of a head of state, esp one who makes the arrangements for a summit meeting: *. . . high-level civil servants known in the diplomatic community as Sherpas*—New York Times [fr the Himalayan tribe that specializes in guiding and assisting mountain climbers to summits]

she-she *n WWII armed forces* A young woman; =CHICK [based on Pidgin English; the term originated in the Pacific area]

shet or **shed** *adj by 1871* Free of; unencumbered

by: *There it was again: "risk." I wondered if I'd ever be shed of it*—New York Times

shiever (SHEEVER) *n 1920s underworld* A traitor or informer: *The worst thing you can call a crook is a "shiever"*—H McLellan [probably fr the notion of being stabbed in the back with a *shieve* or *shiv*]

shift *See* GRAVEYARD SHIFT, LOBSTER SHIFT, SWING SHIFT

shift (or **move**) **into high gear** *v phr by 1970* To begin to work at top speed; become serious: *. . . although the Senate hearings are just shifting into high gear*—George Will

shift the goal posts *v phr by 1970s* To change the rules or conditions disingenuously in order to win

shikker or **shicker** *adj Australia & New Zealand by 1898* Drunk: *We'll eat good, then we'll get shikker*—A J Liebling [fr Yiddish fr Hebrew *shikkur*]

shill 1 *n* (also **shillaber**) *circus by 1916* An associate of an auctioneer, gambler, hawker, etc, who pretends to be a member of the audience and stimulates it to desired action: *The shill is innocuous-looking*—New York Times 2 *v by 1914*: *That summer he shilled for a sidewalk hawker* 3 *n by 1940s* A barker, hawker, advertising or public relations person, or anyone else whose job is to stimulate business; =FLACK [origin unknown; perhaps, since it is a shortening of *shillaber*, ultimately fr *Shillibeer*, the name of an early–1800s British owner of a large bus company, the reference being to persons hired as decoys to sit in buses and attract passengers]

shilly-shally *v by 1782* To vacillate; be irresolute: *For god sake, stop shilly-shallying and make up your mind* [found by 1700 in form *shill I shall I*]

shim *n 1950s rock and roll* A person not appreciative of rock and roll; =CLYDE

shimmy[1] *n* (also **shimmy shirt**) *by 1837* A woman's chemise: *. . . to persuade the young matron to doff her wet shimmy*—S J Perelman [fr *chemise*]

shimmy[2] *by 1918* 1 *n* A very energetic vibrational dance and dancing style 2 *v*: *I wish that I could shimmy like my sister Kate* 3 *n* A flick or flirting of the buttocks: *She calls to the owner, with a little shimmy*—New York Magazine

shimmy[3] *n gambling by 1960s* Chemin de fer: *. . . a "shimmy" (chemin de fer) table*—J Scarne

shimozzle *See* SHEMOZZLE

shindig *n by 1871* A party, reception, festival, etc, esp a noisy dancing party; =CLAMBAKE [probably fr *shin dig*, "a blow on the shin incurred while dancing," found by 1859; perhaps by folk etymology fr the older *shindy*]

shindy *n nautical by 1821* An uproar; a confused struggle; =DONNYBROOK [origin unknown; perhaps fr Irish *sinteag*, "skip, caper"; perhaps fr *shinny*, the name of a rough hockey-like schoolboy game; perhaps fr Romany *chindi*, "a cut, a cutting up"]

shine ◄1► *n by 1908* A black person ◄2► *modifier*: *. . . another shine killing*—Raymond Chandler 3 *n by 1929* Bootleg whiskey; =MOONSHINE: *. . . non-blinding shine sold in fruit jars*—Robert Ruark 4 *v teenagers by 1970s* To reject; disregard; avoid; =SKIP: *But I always end up

shining the rad guys who like me. . .* —Sassy [the racial sense may have originated among blacks, may refer to the glossiness of a very black skin, and hence may reflect the caste system based upon color; among white speakers, this sense was surely influenced by the fact that most *shoeshine* persons were black; the teenager sense has a black parallel, *shine on,* and the origin may be the poetic notion that when one turns one's back on something one is letting his "moon (that is, buttocks) *shine on"* it]
See MONKEYSHINES, STICK IT, TAKE A SHINE TO someone or something, WHERE THE SUN DOESN'T SHINE

◄**shine box**► *n phr by 1940s* A black bar, nightclub, etc

shine someone **on** *by 1970s* 1 *v phr* To reject and ignore someone; abandon someone: *I gotta cut this maniac loose. I gotta shine him on*—Joseph Wambaugh 2 *v phr* To deceive someone; beguile; =BAMBOOZLE, SCAM: *Don't shine me on, buddy boy. I've been yessed by the best*—Stan Cutler
See SHINE

shiner 1 *n by 1904* A bruise near the eye; =BLACK EYE, MOUSE: *. . . a pip of a shiner*—John McNulty 2 *n gambling by 1909* A shiny table top or other mirror-like surface a dealer can use to see the faces of the cards he deals

shine up to someone *v phr by 1891* To court and flatter someone; curry favor; =SUCK UP TO someone

shingle *n by 1847* A signboard, esp one designating professional services: *He got him a shingle and started practice last year*
See HANG UP one's SHINGLE, SHIT ON A SHINGLE

shinny or **shinny up** *v by 1888* To climb a rope, pole, wall, etc [fr the use of *shins* and ankles in climbing a rope or pole]

Shinola *See* NOT KNOW SHIT FROM SHINOLA

ship *See* PUMP SHIP, SHAPE UP

shirt *See* BET YOUR BOOTS, BOILED SHIRT, GIVE someone THE SHIRT OFF one's BACK, KEEP one's SHIRT ON, SHIMMY, SKIVVY, STUFFED SHIRT

shirtsleeve *adj by 1908* Simple and unpretentious; down-to-earth: *Here's what that means in shirtsleeve English. . .* —Paul Harvey

shirttail 1 *adj by 1929* Impoverished; mean; paltry: *My brother and I had a pretty shirttail existence as kids*—Playboy 2 *n newspaper office by 1944* An editorial column: *The boss blurbed the story in his shirttail*—Collier's [both senses depend on the *shirttail* being a short appendage to a shirt; the first sense derives fr the shortness, hence meagerness; the second fr the appendedness, the editor's personal addition]

shirttail kin *n phr Southern & Midwestern by 1930s* Distant relations; third and fourth cousins, etc

shirty *adj by 1846* Angry; very upset; =HUFFY, PISSED OFF •Chiefly British: *He was a little ashamed of himself for getting shirty with Ivar*—Lawrence Sanders [said to be fr the dishevelment resulting when one is actively angry, since a verb variant was *get someone's shirt out,* found by 1859]

◄**shit**► 1 *n by 800s or earlier* Feces; excrement;

=CRAP, POO **2** *v* by 1308: *They diurnally shit, shave, and shower* **3 interj** *by* 1920 An exclamation of disbelief, disgust, disappointment, emphasis, etc: *Oh, shit, I missed the bus!* **4** *n* by 1940s Nonsense; pretentious talk; bold and deceitful absurdities; =BULLSHIT: *Neighborhood watch, public vigil, shit like that*—Robert B Parker **5** *v* by 1934 To lie; exaggerate; try to deceive: *"Don't shit me," said Dina*—Joseph Heller/ *"You're shitting me, baby," he said*—Lawrence Sanders/ *The sky's the limit, Wilson, I shit you not*—W R Tyler **6** *n* by 1903 Offensive and contemptuous treatment; disrespect; insults: *She don't take no shit from nobody* **7** *n* by 1930 Anything of shoddy and inferior quality; pretentious and meretricious trash; =CRAP, DRECK: . . . *that ricegrinding piece of shit*—Bryan Di Salvatore **8 modifier**: . . . *as well as shit loans to companies like Massey-Ferguson and Turbo Resources*—Toronto Life **9** *n* by 1970s One's possessions; one's personal effects: *Get your shit, both of you are moving*—Donald Goines **10** *n* by 1508 An obnoxious, disgusting, or contemptible person; a despicable wretch; =PRICK, SHITHEEL **11** *v* by 1960s To respond powerfully, esp with alarm, anger, or panic; =SHIT A BRICK: *He'll shit when we tell him about this* **12** *n* 1940s narcotics Heroin; =HORSE: . . . *insisted on retaining the word "shit" as junkie slang for heroin*—Dwight MacDonald **13** *n* by 1922 Nothing; the least quantity; =DIDDLY: . . . *of whom I hadn't seen shit*—R Grossbach/ *Engine's froze up, frame's out of line, not worth shit*—W T Tyler **14** *n* by 1937 Misfortune; hardship; =GRIEF: . . . *if you can keep those fucking maggots quiet, you're not going to get any shit from us*—Robert B Parker
See ACT LIKE one's SHIT DOESN'T STINK, ALL THAT KIND OF CRAP, BAD SHIT, BEAT THE SHIT OUT OF someone or something, as BLAZES, BULLSHIT, CHICKENSHIT, CLEAN UP one's ACT, CROCK, the DAY THE EAGLE SHITS, DEEP TROUBLE, DIDDLY, DOES A BEAR SHIT IN THE WOODS, DOODLESHIT, EAT SHIT, FULL OF SHIT, GOOD SHIT, HAVE SHIT FOR BRAINS, HORSESHIT, HOT SHIT, I'LL BE DAMNED, LIKE HELL, PIGS IN CLOVER, LIKE SHIT THROUGH A TIN HORN, NO SHIT, NOT GIVE A DAMN, NOT KNOW BEANS, NOT KNOW SHIT FROM SHINOLA, PIECE OF SHIT, PILE OF SHIT, SCARE THE SHIT OUT OF someone, SHOOT THE BULL, SHOVEL THE SHIT, STRONGER THAN PIG SHIT, TAKE A DUMP, TAKE SHIT, THINK one's SHIT DOESN'T STINK, TICKLE THE SHIT OUT OF someone, TOUGH SHIT, TREAT someone LIKE A DOORMAT

◁**shit a brick (or bricks)**▷ *v phr* by 1961 To be very upset and angry; have an emotional crisis; =SWEAT BULLETS: *At Cheri's, Mott was shitting a brick*—Richard Price/ *I had a few scenes where I was really shittin' bricks*—Rolling Stone

◁**shit-all**▷ *adj* by 1970s Not any; none at all;: *Monica, we have shit-all evidence of what the killer looks like*—Lawrence Sanders [related to and perhaps derived from 1930s British *bugger-all* and *fuck-all* in the same sense, used as intensives and based on *not at all*; Dylan Thomas's mythical Welsh village *Llareggub* has a pseudo-Welsh name, which is *bugger-all* spelled backwards]

◁**shit a shitter**▷ **See** DON'T SHIT A SHITTER

◁**shit-ass**▷ *by* 1940s **1** *n* An insignificant, contemptible person; =JERK, POOTBUTT **2** *n* =SHITHEEL **3** *v* To behave like a despicable or contemptible person, esp by betrayal of a duty or promise: *I don't want anybody shitassing out of it*—Jackie Collins

◁**shit bullets**▷ **See** SWEAT BULLETS

◁**shitbum**▷ *n* by 1980s =SHITHEEL: *Mooney was a shitbum*—George V Higgins

◁**shitcan**▷ *v* by 1970s To discard; throw away; abandon: *If it rained before he entered the tunnel, he would have to, shitcan his plans*—Easyriders/ *I'd already kind of shitcanned the idea*—Stephen King [fr *shitcan*, "refuse can"]

◁**shit creek**▷ **See** UP SHIT CREEK

◁**one's shit doesn't stink**▷ **See** THINK one's SHIT DOESN'T STINK

◀**shiteater**▶ *n* by 1940s A contemptible person; =DILDO, JERK, PECKERHEAD: *Those shiteaters accepted the deal. The Communist Party of Cuba was now demanding dues in dollars*—Harper's

◁**shiteating**▷ *adj* by 1960s Stupid; self-satisfied: . . . *he has eased himself into a series of chuckling, expansive, shit-eating parts*. . . —New Yorker

◁**shit-eating (or turd-eating) grin**▷ *n phr* by 1960s An expression of smug satisfaction; a stupid gloating look: *Go ahead, sit there with that shit-eating grin on your face*—Earl Thompson/ . . . *stood with them, a stupid turd-eating grin on my face*. . . —William Bayer

◁**shit-faced**▷ *adj* 1960s students Drunk: *We'd get totally shitfaced*—Vanity Fair

◁**shit fit**▷ **See** HAVE A SHIT FIT

◁**shit-for-brains**▷ *n* by 1950s A very stupid person: *What's old Shit-for-brains trying to say?* **See** HAVE SHIT FOR BRAINS

◁**shit for the birds**▷ *n phr* WWII armed forces Nonsense; lies and exaggerations; =BULLSHIT: *This thing, this war thing between us, it's shit for the bird*—Loren Estleman [probably because birds eat the excrement of horses and cattle] **See** FOR THE BIRDS

◁**shit green**▷ *v phr* by 1960s To be alarmed, shocked, or enraged; =SHIT A BRICK: *The second the going gets jumpy, you shit green*—Patrick Mann

◁**shit happens**▷ *sentence* by 1980s Bad things come to pass in this sad world: *Another shrug. "Shit happens"*—Robert B Parker

◁**shithead** or **shitface**▷ *by* 1940s **1** *n* A stupid, confused, and blundering person; =FUCK-UP: *And you'll look like a shithead for backing him in the first place*—Lawrence Sanders **2** *n* =SHITHEEL: . . . *and this shithead comes sneaking around, asking questions*—W T Tyler

◁**shitheel**▷ *n* by 1935 A despicable person; a scoundrel and blackguard; =BASTARD, PRICK [probably an intensive form of *heel*; in a tradition of scorn for people who have excrement on their shoes, for example, *shit-shoe*, found by 1903, and *shit-kicker*, by 1960s]

◁the **shit hits the fan**▷ *sentence by 1930s* Trouble breaks out; a fearful crisis ensues; things turn nasty ●Often part of a time clause beginning with when or then: *The shit is going to hit the fan, buddy*—Philip Roth/ *The shit didn't hit the fan till this guy, Eddie Jaffe, takes the pad*—Rocky Graziano [fr the classical joke about the man who, finding no toilet, defecated into a hole in the floor; back downstairs, finding the barroom emptied of its celebrants, he inquired why, and was asked, "Where were you when the shit hit the fan?"]

◁**shithole**▷ **1** *n by 1903* The anus; =ASSHOLE, POOP CHUTE **2** *n by 1960s* A disgusting place; =SHITHOUSE: *You must move out of this shithole*

◁**shithook**▷ *n by 1960s* =SHITHEEL

◁**shit-hot**▷ *by 1918* **1** *adj* Very effective; supremely confident: *The band was shit-hot last night* **2** *n* An especially gifted and effective person; a notably successful person; =BALL OF FIRE, HOT SHOT, WINNER: *The greatest of the greats, the makers of legends, the "shit-hots"*—American Speech [fr *hot shit*]

◁**shithouse**▷ *by 1795* **1** *n* A toilet: *This ain't no shithouse, man*—John R Powers **2** *n* A filthy, sloppy place; a shambles: *The kid's room was always a shithouse*
See BUILT LIKE A BRICK SHITHOUSE

◁a **shithouse full**▷ *n phr by 1960s* A very large number or amount; =OODLES: *He had to wade through a shithouse full of people to get here*

◁**shit in high cotton**▷ *v phr by 1950s* To live well and opulently; enjoy prosperity, esp newly; =EAT HIGH ON THE HOG, PISS ON ICE [fr the notion that well-grown *cotton* means wealth]

◁**shit (or go shit) in your hat**▷ *sentence by 1950s* =GO TO HELL, GO FUCK oneself: *It's unfair, but say so and people tell you to go shit in your hat*—Village Voice [the similar *shit in your teeth* is found by 1903]

◁**shitkicker** or **turd-kicker**▷ *by 1966* **1** *n* A farmer or other rural person; =HICK, RUBE: *. . . looked like he'd just come off the farm and was nothing but a Midwest shitkicker*—Washingtonian/ *. . . why should she waste time with a turd-kicker like him. . .* —Lawrence Sanders **2** *adj* Rural; country; country and western: *. . . the old shitkicker country guitarist*—George Warren **3** *n* A cowboy movie; =HORSE OPERA

◁**shitkickers** or **shit stompers**▷ *n* or *n phr by 1960s* Heavy boots such as farm, cowboy, or hiking boots: *I never see you in anything but those old shit-kickers*—Stephen King

◁**shit-kicking**▷ *adj* Rough and rural; crude; stupid: *It's down-home, shit-kickin', ball-scratchin' country*—Aquarian/ *. . . gets to carry a piece. . . and wear that shit-kicking grin*—Carsten Stroud

◁**shitless**▷ **See** SCARED SHITLESS, SCARE someone SHITLESS

◁**shit (or crap) list**▷ *n phr by 1942* One's fancied or real list of persons who are hated, not trusted, to be avoided, etc: *. . . you're going to be on Professor What's-Her-Face's shit list when she finds you*—T Coraghessan Boyle

◁a **shitload (or shitpot)**▷ *n by 1970s* A very large number or amount; =a SHITHOUSE FULL: *They sure sell a shitload of them*—San Francisco/ *make a shitload of noise*—Richard Merkin/ *. . . a whole shitpot of that stuff*—George Warren

◁**shit money**▷ *v phr by 1980s* To be extremely lucrative: *Well, he owns that bakery, which just shits money*—Lawrence Sanders

◁**shit on** someone or something▷ *interj* An exclamation of powerful disgust, contempt, rejection, etc: *Shit on his suggestions!*

◁**shit on a shingle**▷ *n phr WWII Army* Creamed chipped beef on toast, or some similar delicacy

◁**shit on wheels**▷ *n phr* =HOT SHIT

◁**shit or get off the pot**▷ **1** *sentence* (Variation: **piss** may replace **shit**) *by 1950s* =FISH OR CUT BAIT **2** *modifier*: *It's shit-or-get-off-the-pot time*—Armistead Maupin

◁the **shit out of** someone▷ **See** BEAT THE SHIT OUT OF someone

◁**shit out of luck**▷ *adv phr WWI armed forces* Having no chance of success; already too late for what one wants; very ill-starred; =OUT OF LUCK, SOL: *I guess I'm shit out of luck on this one*

◁**shit** one's **pants (or in** one's **pants)**▷ *v phr* (Variations: **drawers** may replace **pants**) *by 1940s* To become frightened; be scared; panic: *Don't shit your pants, it's only the cat/ Michael was shitting in his drawers*—Richard Merkin

◁the **shits**▷ *n phr by 1930* Diarrhea; =the TROTS
See the GIS

◁**shitstick**▷ *n by 1903* A contemptible, stupid person; =SHIT-ASS [the dated for is *shitsticks*]

◁**shitstorm**▷ *n by 1970s* A very confused situation or affair; a crazy jumble: *. . . an artist trying to turn the shitstorm of his life into music*—Village Voice/ *Nothing like a shit storm to improve his mood*—Jane Leavy [perhaps modeled on *firestorm*]

◁**shitsure**▷ *adv* Very certainly; definitely: *Shitsure it's gonna be a rough winter*—Village Voice [probably modeled on *sure as shit*]

◁**shitter**▷ *n by 1960s* A toilet: *Know where the movie of the week went? Right in the old shitter*—Dan Jenkins

◁**shit through a tin horn**▷ **See** LIKE SHIT THROUGH A TIN HORN

◁**shitty**▷ *by 1920s* **1** *adj* Mean; malicious; nasty: *. . . accepted what he characterized as his "shitty offer"*—Inside Sports **2** *adj* Tedious and unpleasant; futile; wearing: *a real shitty day* **3** *adj* Unwell; ill: *Ralph, I feel shitty tonight*—Joseph Heller

◁**shitty-britches**▷ *n by 1930s* An infant or child; =POOTBUTT: *So what has little shitty-britches been up to?* [*shit-brich*, a translation from Dutch, is found by 1648]

◁the **shitty (or shit) end of the stick**▷ **See** GET THE SHITTY END OF THE STICK

◁**shitwork**▷ **1** *n by 1960s* Menial and tedious work; degrading routine work: *. . . the boredom, the shit-*

work, the perpetual deadlines—Armistead Maupin **2** *modifier*: . . . *something better than shitwork jobs*—Ms

shiv (Variations: **chev** or **chib** or **chiv** or **chive** or **sheive** or **shive**) by 1912 **1** *n* A knife, esp a clasp-knife or similar weapon: *She gets this anonymous letter sticking the shiv in my back*—John O'Hara/ *The big knife called the chib*—Louis Armstrong **2** *v*: . . . *being shivved by Johnny Mizzoo*—Damon Runyon **3** *n* A razor; anything with a sharp cutting edge [fr Romany *chiv*, "blade," by way of British underworld slang]

shlamozzle *See* SHEMOZZLE

shlang or **shlong** *See* SCHLONG

shlemiel *See* SCHLEMIEL

shlemozzle *See* SCHLEMAZEL, SHEMOZZLE

shlep *See* SCHLEP

shleppy *See* SCHLEPPY

shlock *See* SCHLOCK

shlocky *See* SCHLOCKY

shlontz *See* SCHLONTZ

shloomp or **shlump** *See* SCHLOOMP

shlub or **shlubbo** *See* ZHLUB

shlunk *v* by 1970s To cover in a viscid and repellent way: *He dumped the bucket of slime and let it shlunk all over me*—Time [apparently a quasi-Yiddish echoism]

shmaltz *See* SCHMALTZ

shmaltzy *See* SCHMALTZY

shmatte *See* SCHMATTE

shmear or **shmeer** *See* SCHMEAR[1], the WHOLE SCHMEAR

shmeck or **shmack** *See* SCHMECK, SMACK

shmee *n* 1960s narcotics Heroin [perhaps a shortening of *shmeck*]

shmegeggy *See* SCHMEGEGGY

shmendrick *See* SCHMENDRICK

shmo or **shmoe** *See* SCHMO

shmooz *See* SCHMOOZ

shmotte *See* SCHMATTE

shmuck *See* SCHMUCK

shnook *See* SCHNOOK

shnorrer *See* SCHNORRER

shnozz *See* SCHNOZZ

shock jock *n phr* by late 1980s A radio entertainer who uses vulgar and sensational language: *The Federal Communications Commission is warning "shock jocks" that they will be fined if they broadcast indecent material during daylight hours*—Milwaukee Journal

shoe *See* BLACKSHOE, GUMSHOE, MARSHMALLOW SHOES, WHITE SHOE

shoehorn *v* To insinuate by effort; force or fit in: *Attorney General Griffin Bell managed to shoehorn an energy pitch into a speech*—Time

shoestring catch *n phr* baseball by 1912 A catch made near the ground, usu by an outfielder while running, stooping, and lunging

shommus *See* SHAMUS

sho-nuff *adv* by 1880 Surely; certainly: . . . *but Tip (a peaceful Nubian sho-nuff) setled his beef*. . . —

The Source [presumed black pronunciation of *sure enough*]

shoo-fly *n* police by 1877 A police officer, often in plainclothes, set to watch other police officers: *Fuck the shooflies. . . I never took a nickel from anybody*—Ed McBain [fr a common admonition to a fly or other pest, popularized by a Dan Bryant minstrel song about 1870, and which according to H L Mencken "afflicted the American people for at least two years" as a catch phrase]

shoo-in or **shoe-in 1** *n* horse-racing by 1928 A horse that wins a race by prearrangement **2** *n* by 1939 A person, team, candidate, etc, certain to win; =CINCH, SURE THING: *The big, powerful Trojans were the shoo-ins*—Associated Press **3** *modifier*: . . . *to be a shoe-in candidate*—Ms [this spelling may simply be a misspelling, but it is probably based on a misunderstanding of the origin of the term; it is a sort of folk etymology]

shoo in *v phr* horse-racing by 1908 To cause a particular horse, esp an inferior one, to win a race [fr the notion that the beast, not caring to run and not needing to, can be shooed over the finish line, and win]

shook up (also **shook** or **all shook** or **all shook up**) **1** *adj phr* or *adj* entry form by 1897, first variant by 1891 In a state of high excitement or extreme disturbance; very much upset: *So Woody kept his voice down, but he was all shook up*—Saul Bellow **2** *adj phr* or *adj* teenagers & rock and roll fr 1950s Very happy; exhilarated; =HIGH: *I expected years in prison. . . they let me go free, boy was I shook up*—New York Post [revived and popularized in 1950s by Elvis Presley]

shooper *See* SHUPER

shoot 1 *v* by 1890 To photograph, esp to make a movie: *They were shooting over in Jersey* **2** *n* by 1970s A photographic or movie-making session: *It was not an easy shoot*—National Public Radio **3** *interj* by 1915 An invitation to speak, explain, etc: *Just a minute. . . okay. Shoot*—Carsten Stroud **4** *interj* by late 1800s A mild exclamation of disgust, disappointment, distress, etc •A euphemism for shit: *Shoot, it's just the whiskey*—Joseph Wambaugh **5** *n* by 1940s =SHOOT THE BREEZE **6** *v* narcotics by 1914 =SHOOT UP ◁**7**▷ *v* (also **shoot off**) by 1922 To ejaculate semen; =COME **8** *v* by 1926 To play certain games: . . . *watch the flamingos, shoot a little golf, grow a little garden*—W T Tyler [eighth sense by 1891 in the case of *craps*] *See* TURKEY-SHOOT

shoot someone a line *v phr* by 1938 To boast; speak pretentiously; =PUT ON AN ACT: *Don't trust that guy; he's always shooting you a line*

shoot (or **fire**) **blanks** *v phr* To do the sex act without causing pregnancy; suffer male infertility: *This guy was shooting blanks. . . this guy's wad's all dead*—Scott Turow

shoot bricks *v phr* basketball by 1990s To throw the ball ineptly: *Especially the free throws. I mean, we were shooting some bricks out there tonight*—Milwaukee Journal

shoot one's **cookies** *v phr* (Variations: **breakfast** or **dinner** or **lunch** or **supper** may replace **cookies**; **toss** or **lose** may replace **shoot**) *entry form by 1920s* To vomit; =BARF, RALPH: *If I'm any judge of color, you're going to shoot your cookies*—Raymond Chandler/ *... smelled like someone just tossed his cookies*—J D Salinger

shoot someone **down** (or **down in flames**) *v phr by 1940s* To defeat someone; thwart or ruin someone's efforts; =BLOW someone OUT OF THE WATER: *Woody, who had been flying along, level and smooth, was shot down in flames*—Saul Bellow

shoot-'em-up 1 *n by 1953* A movie or TV program with much gunplay and violence: *... gambled for cigarettes, slurped Tang or watched shoot-'em-ups on TV*—New York Times **2** *modifier*: *... an exaggerated reaction to the male-oriented "shoot-'em-up games"*—Washington Post

shooter *See* BEAVER-SHOOTER, HIP SHOOTER, PEA-SHOOTER, SIX-SHOOTER, SQUARE SHOOTER

shoot from the hip *v phr by 1970s* To act or respond impulsively and aggressively; be recklessly impetuous; =HAVE A SHORT FUSE: *A politician should seldom shoot from the hip* [fr the image of a gunfighter who fires his weapon without aiming, as just drawn from the holster]

shoot hoops *v phr by 1980s* To play impromptu basketball; try for baskets: *The Boys shoot hoops and zip around on skateboards*—New Yorker

shooting gallery *1950s narcotics* **1** *n phr* A place where a narcotics user can get a dose or injection **2** *n phr* A party or gathering where narcotics users take injections: *... in a fellow musician's hotel room during a "shooting gallery" (dope party)*—New York Daily News

shooting iron *n phr by 1775* A firearm, esp a pistol

shooting match *See* the WHOLE SHOOTING MATCH

shooting war *n phr by 1941* =HOT WAR

shoot oneself **in the foot** *v phr by 1970s* To wound or injure oneself by ineptitude; attack wildly and hurt oneself: *Ted Turner has taken to shooting himself in the foot*—Village Voice/ *... a situation, Vance writes, "where we were shooting ourselves in the foot"*—Newsweek

◁**shoot** one's **load**▷ *v phr by 1920s* To ejaculate semen; have an orgasm; =COME

shoot off one's **mouth** *v phr* (Variations: **bazoo** or **face** or **gab** or **yap** may replace **mouth**) *entry form by 1864* To talk irresponsibly and inappropriately, esp to bluster and brag; =TALK BIG: *You come busting in here and shoot off your bazoo at me*—J Evans

shoot-out 1 *n* (also **shoot-up**) *by 1950s* A gunfight: *... the justly famous shoot-out between the Earps and the Clantons in the O-K Corral*—New York Times/ *The shoot-up may have been a skirmish between Mafia factions*—New York Times **2** *n by 1970s* Any fight or violent confrontation; a hotly contested game or issue: *... the simple corporate shoot-out reported by the newspapers*—New York Magazine *... another sociological shoot-out, with men as the heroes this time*—New Yorker **3** *n soccer by 1978* A form of tie-breaker used in the North American Soccer League, in which five players from each team have five seconds each to attempt goals one-on-one against the goalkeeper **4** *n basketball by 1990s* An invitational basketball tournament

shoot the breeze (or **the fat**) *v phr by 1941* To chat amiably and casually; =CHEW THE FAT: *... making transatlantic calls just to shoot the breeze*—Village Voice/ *... enjoying ourselves and shooting the breeze*—Billy Rose/ *... sit down on a bench and shoot the fat*—Village Voice

◁**shoot the bull** (or **crap** or **shit**)▷ *by 1928* **1** *v phr* To lie and exaggerate; talk grandly but emptily; =BULLSHIT: *And they weren't just shooting the crap*—J D Salinger **2** *v phr* To chat amiably; =SHOOT THE BREEZE: *... stand on a corner, shoot the bull*—Langston Hughes/ *The basketball guys shoot the shit during timeouts*—Village Voice

shoot the lights out *v phr sports by 1970s* To excel; perform superbly: *These kids will jump right up and shoot the lights out on you*—Sports Illustrated/ *He shoots the lights out in physics, calculus, biology*—Sports Illustrated [perhaps fr the accuracy of marksmanship implied if one is to hit a small target like a *lightbulb*; certainly influenced by the notion of knocking the *daylights*, or earlier the *liver and lights*, "liver and lungs, innards," out of someone or something]

shoot the works *v phr by 1922* To act, give, spend, etc, without limit; =GO FOR BROKE: *In whatever pertains to comfort, shoot the works*—James M Cain [fr the *shooting* of dice in craps, with its extended sense of betting or gambling all one has]

shoot up *v phr 1920s narcotics* To take an injection of narcotics; =JAB A VEIN, MAINLINE

shoot-up *n 1920s narcotics* A narcotics injection *See* SHOOT-OUT

shoot one's **wad** *by 1914* **1** *v phr* To commit or bet everything one has; =GO FOR BROKE, SHOOT THE WORKS **2** *v phr* To say everything one can on a subject; have one's say **3** *v phr* To exhaust one's resources; be unable to persist ◁**4**▷ *v phr* =SHOOT one's LOAD [fr the *wad* of cloth formerly stuffed into a gun barrel to keep the shot and powder in place]

shop *v 1980s* To sell; promote; merchandise: *Sid says I need a lawyer to shop me to the non-paying media*—Gary Trudeau/ *Jacoby ... has shopped this event around since the day he got here. . .*—Mesa Tribune *See* BUCKET SHOP, CHOP SHOP, GUZZLE SHOP, HEAD SHOP, HOCKSHOP, HOOKSHOP, JUNK SHOP, SCHLOCK SHOP, SMOKE SHOP

shopaholic *n by 1990s* A person addicted to shopping: *He accuses me of being a shopaholic. I admit that sometimes I spend more than I should. . .*—Los Angeles Times

shop around *by 1922* **1** *v phr* To search for something or someone: *I heard he was shopping around for a new Secretary of the Interior* **2** *v phr*

To compare prices, services, etc: *I really wish I had more time to shop around before buying that yacht*

shopping bag lady *See* BAG LADY

shopping list *See* LAUNDRY LIST

short 1 *n by about 1925* A prisoner, soldier, etc, near the end of his term **2** *n by 1932* A car; =WHEELS **3** *v 1960s narcotics* To inhale a narcotic in crystal or powder form; =SNORT [automobile sense apparently fr *hot short*, "a stolen car," *short* having come to mean "streetcar," and then "car"; *streetcar* because its runs were *short* compared with those of a train]
See HOT SHORT

short-arm[1] *n armed forces by about 1918* =SHORT-ARM INSPECTION

short-arm[2] *v football by 1980s* To pass the ball with a short, chopped motion, without follow-through: *To short-arm it or do things halfway is not worthwhile*—Milwaukee Journal

◁**short-arm inspection**▷ *n phr* (also **short-arm drill**) *armed forces by about 1910* Medical inspection of the squeezed, milked penis for a discharge symptomatic of gonorrhea [fr the notion that the penis is a limb, combined with the notion that it is a weapon]

short block *n phr by 1990s*: *A "long block" is a complete engine minus the oil pump and oil pan (there's also something called a "short block," which is the same thing without a cylinder head)*—Car Talk

short-change artist *n phr circus & carnival by 1940s* A ticket-seller skillful at returning less change than is due

short cut *n phr by 1618* A quicker or shorter way to do something, go somewhere, etc: *The job is easier if you know a few short cuts*

short dog *n phr by 1960s* A bottle of cheap wine: *. . . staggering down Broadway sucking on a short dog*—Joseph Wambaugh

short end of the stick *See* GET THE SHITTY END OF THE STICK

short eyes *n phr prison by 1970s* A sexual molester of children: *. . . end up in the punk tank with the free-world queers and the short eyes*—Ezra Hannon

short fuse *See* HAVE A SHORT FUSE

short hairs *See* HAVE someone BY THE SHORT HAIRS

short heist *n phr underworld by 1970s* Petty theft, shoplifting, purse-snatching, etc

a **short one** *n phr by 1859* A single shot of whiskey, often drunk quickly; a small drink

the **shorts** *n phr by 1932* Lack of money; a shortage of funds: *He is troubled with the shorts with regard to dough*—Damon Runyon

short-sheet *v* To play a nasty trick; maltreat: *. . . headed for big things until the Reagan crowd short-sheeted you*—W T Tyler/ *England's favorite recreational activity, shortsheeting the royals*—Milwaukee Journal [fr a student and barracks practical joke in which a *bedsheet* is folded in half and made to appear as an upper and lower sheet, so

when the victim gets into bed the stretching legs and toes are painfully arrested]

shortstop *by 1940s* **1** *v* To take food being passed to someone else at the table **2** *n*: *I avoided that table where the shortstop always sat* **3** *v* To wait on another salesperson's customer

the **short strokes** *v phr by 1980s* The detailed end of a process: *. . . a book tells you all about that thing. . . Gets into all the short strokes*—Carsten Stroud [origin uncertain; perhaps the opposite of *broad strokes, broad brush*; perhaps a reference to the percussive end of the male orgasm, described in one source in 1916 as *the short jerks*]

shorty or **shortie** *n by 1888* A very short person; =DUSTY BUTT

Shorty George *n phr by 1930s* A jazz dance: *. . . all the famous dances of the jitterbugging Thirties: the Big Apple, the Shag, the Boogie, the Shorty George, Truckin', Peckin'. . . the Lindy Hop*—Albert Goldman

shot 1 *n by 1676* A drink of straight liquor **2** *n Southern & Western lunch counter by 1950s* A glass or other serving of Coca-Cola™ **3** *n 1920s narcotics* An injection of narcotics; =FIX **4** *n by 1950s* An atomic explosion, a rocket or missile launching, or some other complex sort of military and technological blasting **5** *n by 1960s* A person's particular preference, style, etc; =BAG, THING: *That's our shot. That's who we are*—Rolling Stone **6** *n by 1840* A try; an attempt, esp at something rather difficult: *He didn't make it, but he gave it a hell of a shot* **7** *adj by 1864* Drunk **8** *adj* (also **shot to hell**) *by 1930* Worn out or out of repair: *This old machine is shot* **9** *adj by 1939* Exhausted; ill; in bad shape: *Say, am I shot?*—James T Farrell **10** *n baseball by 1880* A very hard-hit ball, usu a line drive, and often a home run **11** *n by 1980s* A television appearance: *But it was the exposure on television that seemed to count most. . . with a shot on "Good Morning America" believed to be worth its weight in votes*—Village Voice **12** *n by 1980s* Interpretation; understanding; opinion; guess; =TAKE: *Gimme your shot on Leon. . . You know, tell me about him*—Scott Turow [the drinking senses are shortenings of an early–1800s expression *shot in the neck* meaning both "a drink" and "drunk"; *shoot*, "to guess," in the twelfth sense is found by 1864]
See BEAVER SHOT, CALL THE SHOTS, CHEAP SHOT, DROP CASE, GIVE something A SHOT, GIVE something one's BEST SHOT, GRAB SHOT, HALF-SHOT, HAVE A CRACK AT something, HOT SHOT, LONG SHOT, MUG SHOT, NOT BY A LONG SHOT, ONE-SHOT, UNGODLY SHOT

a **shot across the bow** *n phr by 1990s* A warning or admonition: *White House dithering led the Republican whip to fire a warning shot across the Administration's bow*—Time [fr an old naval practice]

shot glass *n phr by 1940s* =JIGGER

shotgun[1] **1** *n WWII Army* A machine gun or other rapid-fire gun **2** *n 1960s narcotics* A type of pipe used for smoking marijuana; =BONG **3** *n football by*

1966 An offensive formation in which the quarterback lines up well behind instead of immediately behind the center **4** *modifier* (also **blunderbuss**) *by 1930s* Very diffuse and general; indiscriminate; done in haste; =SCATTERGUN: *I hate it when the administrators make shotgun accusations/ But this is a blunderbuss technique. . .* —Scott Turow
See RIDE SHOTGUN, SIT SHOTGUN

shotgun² *n by 1950s* A matchmaker; a marriage broker [fr Yiddish *shadchen*, which is pronounced something like *shotgun*; perhaps reinforced by the notion of a *shotgun wedding*]

shotgun approach *n phr by 1960s* A very broad and undiscriminating judgment or action: *It's no good taking a shotgun approach to this matter of addiction* [similarly, *shotgun prescription* is found by 1903]

shotgun house *n phr by 1930s* A house of connected rooms without a corridor: *He grew up in a tarpaper "shotgun" house, built on tree stumps. . .* —Milwaukee Journal

shotgun quiz *See* POP QUIZ

shotgun wedding (or **marriage**) *n phr by 1927* A wedding under duress, esp when the bride is pregnant; a forced marriage; =MILITARY WEDDING

a **shot in the arm** *n phr by 1922* Something that stimulates and enlivens; an invigorating influence or event: *. . . has given his campaign for the Democratic presidential nomination a shot in the arm*—Washington Post

shot John *See* PLAY WHO SHOT JOHN

shoulda coulda woulda *sentence by 1970s* One ought to have and would have done something •An expression of regret: *"Shoulda, coulda, woulda," the First Lady replied. "We didn't"*—New York Times

shoulder *See* COLD SHOULDER, STRAIGHT FROM THE SHOULDER

shoulder surfer *n phr by 1990s* A person who peers over the shoulder of someone using an automatic teller machine in order to steal a PIN (personal identification number)

one **should have stood in bed** *sentence by 1940s* This has been a complete disaster or a waste of time, and one should not have bothered to get up in the morning

shouldn't happen to a dog *See* IT SHOULDN'T HAPPEN TO A DOG

shout 1 *n 1930s jazz musicians* A hymn or traditional blues song, esp when sung with a heavily accented beat **2** *n print shop by 1950s* An exclamation point **3** *n by 1980s* A call, esp on the telephone: *Stradazzi. . . wants you to give him a shout*—Carsten Stroud [in the musical sense, *shout*, "a black religious song and dance," is found by 1862]

shove 1 *v by about 1850* To pass counterfeit money **2** *v underworld by 1940s* To kill; =HIT: *Who shoved her?*—J Evans **3** *v by 1856* =SHOVE OFF
See KNOW WHAT one CAN DO WITH something, PUSH COMES TO SHOVE, TELL someone WHAT TO DO WITH something

shove it *See* STICK IT

◁**shovel shit** (or **the shit**)▷ *v phr by 1930s* To lie and exaggerate; =BULLSHIT, SHOOT THE BULL: *I was just fooling, shoveling the shit a little/ . . . no varsity letters for shoveling shit*—John Irving

shove off 1 *v phr by 1844* To leave; depart; =SCRAM: *. . . when we shoved off*—James M Cain **2** *v phr underworld by 1939* To kill; murder: *People got shoved off for their money*—Agatha Christie [fr the boating term for pushing the craft away from a dock, ship's side, etc]

shover *See* PENCIL-PUSHER

show *v by 1300* To arrive; appear; =SHOW UP: *You suppose he'll show?*—W R Burnett
See BALLY SHOW, CATTLE SHOW, DOG SHOW, GRIND SHOW, KID SHOW, LEG SHOW, LET'S GET THE SHOW ON THE ROAD, MEAT SHOW, NO-SHOW, ONE-MAN SHOW, PEEP SHOW

show-and-tell *n by 1970s* An elaborate display, usu for selling or other persuasion; =DOG AND PONY ACT: *There just hasn't been time to arrange the kind of show-and-tell that attracts media attention*—Village Voice/ *No one seems to have been impressed by the show-and-tell*—New Yorker [fr the name of an elementary-school teaching technique of the late 1940s where pupils exhibit and explain things]

show biz *n phr by 1940s* The entertainment industry; show business

showboat 1 *v by 1951* To behave in a showy, flamboyant way; =GRANDSTAND, HOT DOG: *And, please, no showboating, fist-pounding, breast-beating, or blame-casting*—Washingtonian **2** *n* (also **show-boater**) *by 1953*: *. . . even your most hardassed right wingers had some showboat in them*—Elmore Leonard/ *Jesse is a showboater, privately*—Amsterdam News **3** *v by 1960s* =PULL RANK

show business *See* THAT'S SHOW BUSINESS

showcase 1 *n theater by 1937* A theater, performance, etc, where a major aim is to exhibit relatively unknown performers and work **2** *v by 1940s* To feature or exhibit a relatively unknown player, performer, work, etc: *You don't showcase a guy by sending him smack into the middle of the line*—Sports Illustrated

showdown 1 *n poker by 1901* A hand where the cards are dealt face up and the best hand wins at once **2** *n by 1904* A confrontation, esp a last one **3** *modifier*: *. . . the opening game of the showdown Yankee-Red Sox series*—Associated Press

shower *See* GOLDEN SHOWER, SEND someone TO THE SHOWERS

show off *v phr by 1793* To behave in an ostentatiously skilled and assured way in order to impress others; =GRANDSTAND, HOT DOG: *He ran a quick eight miles, just showing off*

show-off *n* A person who habitually shows off; =HOT DOG, SHOWBOAT: *Speedo swimsuit and a globe tied to his shoulder. Show-off*—Douglas Coupland

show someone **the door** *v phr by 1778* To dismiss someone summarily; eject someone

show-up 1 *n police by 1929* =LINE-UP **2** *modifier*: *. . . a group about to be shoved into the show-up line*—W R Burnett

show up *v phr by 1888* To arrive; be present; appear: *I had to show up to make a touch*—Erle Stanley Gardner

show someone or something **up** *v phr by 1826* To reveal; expose: *That slip showed him up for a fraud*

shpos (SHPAHS) *n medical by 1970s* An obnoxious patient [fr *subhuman piece of shit*]

shpritz *n by 1970s* A bit or touch; a dose: *. . . each a free-associational shpritz of surreal hi-de-ho*—Village Voice [fr Yiddish, literally, "a squirt"]

shriek 1 *n print shop by 1864* An exclamation point; =BANG, SHOUT **2** *n by middle 1980s* Distilled and concentrated heroin; =BLACK TAR

shrimp *n by 1386* A very short or small person; =PEANUT

shrink *n by about 1960* A psychiatrist, psychoanalyst, or other psychotherapist; =HEADSHRINKER

shrinking violet *n phr by 1915* A self-effacing person: *Theodore Roosevelt was no shrinking violet* [fr the presumed shyness of the *violet*]

'shroom or **shroom** *n narcotics by 1980s* A hallucinogenic mushroom, Psilocybe mexicana: *Shroom seekers have bumper crop*—Macon Tribune

shtarker or **schtarker** or **starker** (SHTAHR kə, -kər or STAHR kər) *n by 1908* A strong person; =TOUGH GUY: *I went from dealing with shtarkers to intellectual bullies*—Playboy [fr Yiddish]

shtick or **schtick** or **shtik 1** *n show business by 1961* A small theatrical role or part of a role; a piece of theatrical "business"; =BIT: *It turned out to be a nice little "shtick"*—New York Post **2** *n show business by 1968* A characteristic trait of performance or behavior; a typical personal feature: *To each his own schtick. Chapman performs his with gusto*—Changes **3** *n by 1966* A clever device; =GADGET, GIMMICK: *The "shtick" is that the taped remarks of a number of political figures are tacked onto questions dreamed up by writers*—Playboy **4** *n by 1968* One's special area of interest or activity; =BAG, SCENE: *Post-post literary theory is not my shtick* [fr Yiddish, literally, "piece, bit"]

shtoonk or **shtunk** *See* SCHTOONK

◁**shtup** or **schtup** or **stup**▷ (SHToŏP) **1** *v by 1952* To annoy; pressure **2** *v by 1967* To do the sex act with or to; =FUCK: *Why of course he was shtupping her*—Philip Roth **3** *modifier by 1967*: *. . . take a big video plunge, coming closer than any outfit yet to breaking the shtup barrier*—Village Voice **4** *n by 1967* A person regarded merely as a sex partner; =ASS **5** *n* The sex act; copulation [fr Yiddish, literally, "push, shove"]

shuck 1 *v by 1848* To undress; strip oneself **2** *v* (also **shuck and jive**) *black by 1966* To joke; tease; =FOOL AROUND: *. . . 22 percent of each trash-truck crew's workday is spent shucking and jiving and shadowboxing*—Philadelphia/ *We ain't got no time for shuckin'*—Joseph Wambaugh **3** *modifier*: All

he has to sell is a shuck and jive caricature of Blackness—The Source **4** *v* (also **shuck and jive**) *black & student by 1959* To swindle; cheat; deceive; esp to bluff verbally and counterfeit total sincerity **5** *v cool musicians by 1957* To improvise chords, esp to a piece of music one does not know; =FAKE IT, VAMP **6** *n black by 1950s* A theft or fraud; =RIPOFF: *Linear thinking was a total shuck*—Cyra McFadden [black senses probably fr the fact that black slaves sang and shouted gleefully during *corn-shucking* season, and this behavior, along with lying and teasing, became a part of the protective and evasive behavior normally adopted towards white people in "traditional" race relations; the sense of "swindle" is perhaps related to the mid–1800s term *to be shucked out*, "be defeated, be denied victory," which suggests that the notion of stripping someone as an ear of corn is stripped may be basic in the semantics]

shucks *See* AW SHUCKS

shuffle 1 *v 1960s street gang* To have a gang fight; =RUMBLE **2** *v black by about 1880* To behave in the stereotypical obsequious way of a black person in "traditional" race relations; =TOM: *A lot of brothers and sisters died. So. . . are we just going to shuffle and jive?*—Ebony
See DOUBLE SHUFFLE

shuffler *n underworld by 1950s* A confidence trickster, hawker, etc; =GRIFTER [fr older *shuffle*, "deceive, defraud," probably fr the shuffling of cards cheatingly by a professional gambler]
See PAPER-PUSHER

shunt *n car-racing by 1959* An accident; a collision

shuper or **shooper** or **shupper** (SHoŏ pər) *n by 1907* A large glass or stein for beer: *. . . spent for "shupers" of beer*—Jack London [perhaps fr German *Shüppe*, "scoop"]

shush *v by 1905* To tell someone to be quiet and stop talking •Very often a command: *"Shush!" he shouted, uselessly, to the large noisy hound* [the dated form is spelled *sush*]

shutdown *n by 1884* A complete cessation; a stoppage: *. . . assembly line shutdowns*—Associated Press

shut down *v phr by 1950s* To defeat; outdo; =BEAT: *Gore shut down Perot in the debate*—TV show Front Page/ *. . . we're gonna shut 'em down*—song Hey Little Cobra

shut-eye *n by 1899* Sleep: *I'll give Betsy the first crack at some shut-eye*—Hugh Pentecost

shut one's **face** *v phr by 1899* To stop talking; =SHUT UP •Often an irritated command

shutout *n sports by 1940s* A game in which one side is held scoreless

shut out *v phr sports by 1881* To hold an opponent scoreless; =BLANK, SCHNEIDER, SKUNK: *The last time Princeton was shut out, Penn did it*—Associated Press

shutterbug *n by 1940* A photographer, esp an enthusiastic amateur: *Two of the more prominent Senate-shutterbugs are Sens. Patrick J Leahy. . . and John C Danforth*—Washington Post

shut one's **trap** *v phr* by 1776 =SHUT one's FACE

shut up *v phr* by 1860 To be quiet; stop talking •Very often a stern or angry command

shut someone's **water off** *v phr* by 1940s To defeat or incapacitate someone: *Harry just shut his water right off*—Milwaukee Journal

◁**shvantz**▷ (SHVAHNTS) *n* (also **schvantz** or **schvanz** or **schwantz** or **schwanz** or **schvontz** or **shvonce** or **shvuntz**) by 1970s The penis; =SCHLONG [fr Yiddish, literally, "tail"; hence semantically analogous with *penis,* literally, "tail"]
See STEP ON IT

◀**shvartze** or **shvartzer**▶ *See* SCHVARTZE

shy *n* by 1970s A usu criminal usurer; =LOAN SHARK, SHYLOCK: *. . . a shy on East Houston who lent money*—Fran Lebowitz/ *I don't know who's got the markers. . . . It's some shy*—George V Higgins

shylock or **Shylock 1** *n* by 1786 A usurer; =LOAN SHARK, SHY: *In Toronto and Hamilton both, loan sharks ("shylocks") appeared in the gambling clubs*—Maclean's **2** *v* by 1930: *. . . the shylocking that went with it as hot dogs go with baseball*—Mario Puzo/ *numbers games, shylocking, and other illegal operations*—Gay Talese **3** *modifier* by 1980s: *. . . that were into them for shylock money and couldn't make the payments*—Elmore Leonard [fr the character in Shakespeare's *The Merchant of Venice*]

shy of a load *See* THREE BRICKS SHY OF A LOAD

shyster 1 *n* by 1844 A dishonest and contemptible lawyer, politician, or businessperson: *You lousy little shyster bastard*—Ira Wolfert ◁**2**▷ *n* Any lawyer [origin unknown and hotly disputed; perhaps fr the name of a Mr Sheuster, a New York City lawyer of the early 1800s; perhaps fr German *Scheisse,* "shit," or *Scheisser,* "shitter," by way of anglicized forms *shice* and *shicer* attested fr the mid–1800s, with the addition of the agentive suffix -*ster*; perhaps because prisoners were said and advised to *fight shy of,* "avoid," lawyers who frequented jails, esp the Tombs in New York City; perhaps fr earlier sense of *shy,* "disreputable, not quite honest," and -*ster*]

the **Siberian Express** *n phr* by 1980s A spell of very cold weather

sick 1 *adj* (also **sicko** or **sicksicksick**) by 1551 Mentally twisted; psychopathic, esp in a sadistic vein: *. . . a rapist or a sicko father who abuses his teenage daughters*—Philadelphia Journal **2** *adj* by 1853 Disgusted; surfeited; =FED UP: *Sick to the gills of the Simpson trial?*—New York Times **3** *adj* (also **sicko** or **sicksicksick**) by about 1955 Gruesome; morbid; mentally and spiritually unhealthy: *Label it S for Sicko*—Philadelphia/ *He is even better at establishing a sicksicksick atmosphere*—New York Times **4** *adj* narcotics by 1940s Needing a dose of narcotics **5** *n* narcotics by 1940s The craving and misery of an addict in need of a narcotic dose [modern use of first sense from about 1955 is probably not a survival]

sick him or **sic 'em** *sentence* by 1845 Attack that person or animal •A command [fr a dialect pronunciation of *seek*]

sickie or **sicko** *n* by 1973 A mentally unhealthy person; a psychopath: *It was not considered very kosher to toss out the sickies once they had taken their final vows*—John R Powers/ *Only sickies get involved with married women*—New York Magazine

sick joke *n phr* by 1959 A joke with a grimly morbid tone or point; a nasty sort of jape: *Wouldn't it be a sick joke if I got something without understanding the financial underpinnings. . .* —Douglas Coupland

sick someone **on** someone or something *v phr* by 1845 To incite someone against someone or something: *They've decided to sick the voters on the whole government*
See SICK HIM

sick-out *n* by 1970 A form of job action in which employees declare themselves ill and unable to work; =BLUE FLU

sickroom *adj* by 1970s Unhealthy; repellent; =SICK: *I have something to tell you. . . . It's kind of sickroom*—Armistead Maupin

side 1 *n* theater by 1933 A sheet containing the lines and cues for one performer **2** *n* by 1936 A phonograph record **3** *n* by 1936 The music on one side of a phonograph record, one band of a long-playing record, one segment of a cassette or other tape, etc •Usu plural: *He had never heard these classic sides until recently*—San Francisco
See ON THE SIDE, STATESIDE, SUNNY SIDE UP, the WRONG SIDE OF THE TRACKS

sidearms *n* armed forces by about 1925 Salt and pepper, cream and sugar, or other regular adjuncts to a meal

sidebar 1 *n* news media by 1948 A news or feature story serving as a supplement or background to a main story: *Banner headlines and sidebar after sidebar flashed in front of our eyes*—New York Times/ *. . . the wandering sidebars and frivolous frolicking of the Post*—Washingtonian **2** *adj* by 1950s Auxiliary; supplementary: *Now he has a sidebar job, hustling beer or sports equipment*—Robert Ruark **3** *n* courtroom by 1980s A conference held between lawyers and a judge unheard by the jury: *Some judges hold these meetings, known as sidebars, in the courtroom at the side of the bench away from the jury*—Scott Turow [first two senses probably fr the late–1800s use of *sidebar buggy* or *wagon* for a vehicle having longitudinal reinforcements along the *sides;* perhaps fr *side-bar,* "an auxiliary toll-gate on a road leading into a main toll-road"; third sense fr auxiliary *bars,* legal or courtroom sites and barriers, formerly found in the Scottish and English parliaments, and so noted by 1708]

side-door Pullman *n phr* hoboes by 1887 A railroad freight car: *I rode into Niagara Falls in a "side-door Pullman"*—Jack London

sidekick 1 *n* by 1906 A close friend, partner, associate, etc: *Wayne and his side-kick James Arness*—New York Herald-Tribune **2** *n* pickpockets by 1916 A side pocket [origin uncertain; *side-pal* in the first sense is found by 1886]

the side of a barn *See* someone CAN'T HIT THE SIDE OF A BARN

side of one's **face** *See* LAUGH ON THE OTHER SIDE OF one's FACE

sider *See* PORTSIDER

sides of the street *See* WORK BOTH SIDES OF THE STREET

sideswipe *n by 1924* A critical observation, esp an oblique one: . . . *took a sideswipe at "restrictive court decisions"*—New York Times [fr *sideswipe,* "a glancing blow," found by 1917]

sidewalk *See* POUND THE PAVEMENT

sidewalk hostess *n phr by 1980s* A prostitute •An arch euphemism: . . . *a leather miniskirt and. . . black hose, you know, the typical accoutrements of the typical sidewalk hostess*— Milwaukee Journal

sidewalk superintendent *by 1930s* **1** *n phr* A person who watches excavation or other construction work, usu through a hole in the surrounding fence **2** *n phr* Any amateur critic or observer

side-wheeler **1** *n baseball by 1910* A lefthanded pitcher; =SOUTHPAW **2** *n* (also **sidewinder**) *horseracing by 1940s* A pacing horse; a pacer [fr the *sidewheel* steamboat]

sidewinder¹ **1** *n by 1840* A wide, looping blow with the fist; =ROUNDHOUSE **2** *n loggers by 1940s* A tree that does not fall where it was intended to [both senses literally from a *winding* at or to a *side,* and the second sense probably influenced by *sidewinder²*]

sidewinder² **1** *n by 1940s* A dangerous and pugnacious man **2** *n underworld by 1940s* A gangster's bodyguard; =GORILLA: *Eddy Prue, Morny's sidewinder*—Raymond Chandler [fr the dangerous *sidewinder* rattlesnake, so called fr its lateral locomotion, and presumed to be treacherous]

-sie *See* -IE

sieve *n* A leaky boat or ship: *That frog-eating sieve. . .* —Nathaniel Benchley
See HAVE A MIND LIKE A SIEVE

◁**siff** or **the siff**▷ *See* SYPH

sight gag *n phr by 1957* A joke or comic turn that depends entirely on what is seen

sightseer handle *n phr horse-racing by 1970s* A small total amount of money bet on a horse race: *The handle. . . much less than $100 per capita, was described as a "sightseer" handle by an employee of the calculating room*—New York Times

sign *See* the HIGH SIGN, the INDIAN SIGN

signify *v black by 1932* To make provocative comments in a gamelike manner; =SNAP, SOUND: . . . *any black kid who has stood in a school yard or on a street corner engaging in the mock-hostile banter that blacks call "signifying"*—Mike Royko/ *In Chicago you still get people doing the old-style rhyming; that's called signifying*—John Tierney

sign off *v phr by 1928* To stop talking; =SHUT UP [fr radio broadcasting, "to end transmission and go off the air"]

sign off on something *v phr by 1970s* To agree to or approve of a proposal, a legislative bill, etc, esp without actual formal endorsement: *When enough Senators had signed off on the treaty, the President announced it* [*sign off,* "to relinquish a right or claim," is found by 1859]

sign up *v phr by 1903* To join; enroll; enlist: *They signed up for a course in hands-on interpersonal relations*

sigoggling *See* SKYGODLIN

silent rap *n phr black by 1980s: Where talking is not possible, a man may indicate his sexual interest in a woman nonverbally, with what black men call a "silent rap" or "pimp eye"*—Milwaukee Journal

Silicon Valley *n phr by 1974* The Santa Clara Valley south of San Francisco in California: . . . *smack in the middle of Silicon Valley*—San Francisco [fr the concentration of manufacturers of *silicon* chips for computers, watches, etc, in the Santa Clara *Valley*]

◁**silk**▷ *n black by 1960s* A white person: *So did the silks on the Knapp Commission ever ask about the rate of drug busts?*—Carsten Stroud
See HIT THE SILK

silk-stocking *adj by 1812* Wealthy; affluent: *a silkstocking neighborhood*

silly billy *n phr 1834* A foolish man

silly season *n phr by 1861* Any period when people do silly things, esp when these are reported in the news media [fr a term designating the months of August and September, when Parliament was not sitting and valid and useful news was scarce, and the newspapers resorted to reporting frivol and trivialities]

silver bullet *n phr by 1808* A very effective, quasimagical agent, remedy, etc: . . . *Stokovich looked on Kennedy as his "silver bullet," his absolute best man. . .* —Carsten Stroud/ *No single silver bullet is going to do the job*—Mesa Tribune [reflecting an ancient belief that silver weapons can conquer any foe, found, for example, in the Delphic Oracle's advice to Philip of Macedon, "With silver weapons you may conquer the world"]

silver Jeff *n phr 1950s rock and roll* A quarter or a nickel [fr the image of Thomas Jefferson on the nickel coin, apparently transferred to the quarter by confusion with George Washington]

silver wing *n phr 1950s rock & roll* A fifty-cent piece [fr the image of an eagle with spread *wings* on the coin]

simmer down *v phr by 1871* To become calm and quiet, esp after anger; =COOL IT, LIGHTEN UP •Often a command or a bit of advice

simoleon or **samoleon** (sih MOH lee ən) *n by 1895* A dollar [origin unknown; found in form *sambolio* by 1886]

Simon Legree *n phr by 1849* A cruel, unsympathetic person, esp a tyrannical superior; a slave-driver [fr the character in *Uncle Tom's Cabin,* somewhat unfairly]

simon-pure *adj by 1840* Genuine; unadulterated [the name of a virtuous Quaker in Susanna Centlivre's 1717 play *A Bold Stroke for a Wife*]

simp *n* by 1903 A simpleton; a stupid person; =KLUTZ: *Simps with mustaches are a menace to society*—Playboy/ *I really thought it would be till death do us part. I was such a simp*—Lawrence Sanders

simpatico by 1864 **1** *adj* Nice; pleasant; sympathetic and congenial **2** *n* Sympathy; affinity: *Alan Keyes has as much simpatico with the Christian right as I do*—Nation [fr Italian or Spanish]

simple *See* COW-SIMPLE, STIR-CRAZY

sincere *adj* 1940s *students* Intended to make a good and winning impression; overtly ingratiating: *. . . packaged in a sincere apothecary-type bottle*—New York Times

since the year one *adv phr* by 1970s For a very long time: *. . . they've known each other since the year one*—Stan Cutler/ *This is Mozab. I've known him since the Year One*—New Yorker

sing *v underworld* by 1710 To inform; incriminate oneself and others; =SQUEAL: *Vice Prisoners Ready To Sing*—New York Daily News [perhaps related to the expression *a little bird told me*; a variant, *chant*, is found by 1883]
See HEAR THE BIRDIES SING, the OPERA AIN'T OVER TILL THE FAT LADY SINGS

singer *n underworld* by 1935 =CANARY, STOOL PIGEON

single **1** *n* by 1936 A dollar bill **2** *n underworld* by 1940s A person, esp a criminal, who works alone: *Dillinger now becomes a single*—A Hynd **3** *n show business* by 1940s A solo performer; a one-person act **4** *n* by 1964 An unmarried person: *The place tried to attract singles* **5** *n* by 1949 A phonograph record having only one piece of music on each side: *The single sold about three million*
See SWINGING SINGLE

single-o **1** *adj* by 1932 Unmarried; single **2** *adj underworld* by 1930 Working alone; unpartnered: *There are "single-o" heist-men*—E DeBaun **3** *n underworld* by 1930 A person, esp a criminal, who works alone; =SINGLE **4** *adv* by 1948 Alone; solo: *. . . instead of working single-o as was the custom*—Billy Rose

singles *modifier* by 1960s For unmarried persons: *a singles bar/ a singles party*

sing out **1** *v phr* by 1813 To speak up; make oneself known and heard; =PIPE UP: *If anybody doesn't like it, just sing out* **2** *v phr* by 1815 To inform; =SQUEAL: *. . . and get him to sing out*—J Roeburt

sink *v* by 1613 To destroy; ruin; =TORPEDO: *I'm afraid we're sunk this time*

sinker[1] *n* by 1870 A biscuit or doughnut [fr the lead weight used by fishermen to *sink* line and bait, probably an ironic reference to the weight of the biscuit or doughnut]

sinker[2] or **sinkerball** *baseball* by 1920s **1** *n* A pitch that dips downward as it nears home plate **2** *n* A line drive or other batted ball that sinks suddenly toward the ground

sink-or-swim *adj* by 1668 Risky; succeed-or-be-ruined: *Playing cornerback in the National Football League, particularly for a young player, is a sink-or-swim proposition*—Milwaukee Journal

sin tax *n phr* by 1963 A tax on some activity or product regarded as immoral: *Then there are the always popular so-called sin taxes, which could be slapped on cigarettes and liquor*—Mike Royko

sis **1** *n* by 1656 A sister: *That's his sis with him* **2** *n* by 1835 Woman; girl; =CHICK ●Used in direct address: *What's up, sis?* [a shortening of *sister*]

sissified *adj* by 1905 Timorous; weak and effeminate; =CHICKENHEARTED, PANSIFIED

sissy **1** *n* by 1887 A timorous, weak, and effeminate male; =DAISY, LILY, PANSY **2** *adj* by 1891: *wearing sissy clothes* **3** *n* by 1970s A male homosexual; =PANSY: *No more sissies for Jimmy Smith*—Joseph Wambaugh [fr *sis* fr *sister*]

sissy bar *n phr* by 1969 A high metal projection at the back of a bicycle to prevent it from rolling over backwards [fr the fact that someone adopting such a device is timorous]

sister **1** *n* by 1906 Woman; girl ●Used in direct address: *Hey, sister, you'd better leave* **2** *n black* by 1926 A black woman **3** *n* by 1912 A fellow feminist
See JOHN WAYNE'S SISTER, SOB SISTER, WEAK SISTER

sister act *n phr homosexuals* by 1972 The sex act between a homosexual man and a heterosexual woman

sit *v* by about 1945 To take care of; attend and watch over: *Who'll sit your house while you're gone?*
See BABY-SIT, HOUSE-SIT

sitcom *n* by 1964 A situation comedy series on television: *. . . the new family of sitcoms*—Newsweek

sit-down **1** *n hoboes* by 1919 A meal, usu a free one, eaten at a table **2** *n* by 1861 A settling for a chat; meeting; =SCHMOOZ: *The voice suggested that we have a little "sit-down" over lunch at Chianti. . .*—Stan Cutler/ *Zilber was supposed to go to a sit-down with Pagano in Brooklyn*—New York Magazine **3** *n* (also **sit-down strike**) by 1936 A strike in which the workers occupy their job sites but do not work

sit in **1** *v phr musicians* by 1936 To join and play with other musicians, esp on one occasion or temporarily: *. . . had the very good fortune of sitting in with him*—Metronome **2** *v phr* fr 1960s To occupy a place as a participant in a sit-in [found by 1599 in the first sense "to participate in a game"]

sit-in *n* by 1960s An illegal occupation of a place, in order to make a political or philosophical statement [the term was popularized during the movement for black civil rights and has many offspring: *be-in, love-in, puke-in,* etc]

sit in the catbird seat *v phr* by 1930s To be in the position of advantage; =be SITTING PRETTY: *. . . willing to give us a hundred seventy million in preferred notes. We're sitting in the catbird seat*—Art Buchwald [fr a term used by a poker opponent of the late sportscaster Red Barber to explain his situation with two aces in the hole at stud poker; Mr Barber adopted the term, which was afterwards used by James Thurber in a story called "The Catbird Seat" with attribution to Red Barber; probably a Southern dialect term based on a folk notion of the cleverness and masterfulness of *catbirds* and/or their high and superior perch]

sit on someone *v phr* by 1865 To suppress or squelch someone: *When I opened my mouth they all sat on me*

sit on one's **ass** *v phr* by 1940s To remain inactive; esp, to fail to cope or deal with a responsibility: *The congressman sat on his ass while the neighborhood hospital deteriorated*

sit on one's **hands 1** *v phr* by 1926 To refrain from applauding; be an unresponsive or adverse audience: *They sat on their hands until he started waving the flag* **2** *v phr* by 1950s To do nothing; be passive; =SIT ON one's ASS: *Even when the thing fell down they just sat on their hands*

sit on my face *See* SHE CAN SIT ON MY FACE ANY TIME

sit on threes *v phr* basketball by 1990s To make three-point scores: *But he's out there sitting on threes, and that's all she wrote*—Milwaukee Journal

sitrep *n* by 1943 A situation report: *That seems to be the sitrep, Beau*—Carsten Stroud

sit shotgun *v phr* by 1960s To sit in the passenger seat of a car; =RIDE SHOTGUN: *I sat shotgun in my pop's flower truck*—Philadelphia

sitski *v* by 1990s To ski sitting down: *. . . Pagels has dedicated himself to wheelchair racing and sitskiing. . . and earning a reputation as a fierce competitor*—Milwaukee Journal

sit (or **stand**) **still for** something *v phr* by 1940s To accept or condone; tolerate something provocative: *The nation will simply not sit still for. . . the years of slow growth*—Time

sitter *n* by about 1945 A person who baby-sits, house-sits, etc

sit the pines *v phr* sports by 1980s To sit on the bench rather than play: *Of course I'm disappointed. . . I'm not used to sitting the pines*—Milwaukee Journal

◁**sit there with** one's **finger** (or **thumb**) **up** one's **ass**▷ *v phr* by 1040s To be passive and unresponsive; fail to cope; be useless: *I suppose you think I'm just sitting around every day with my thumb up my ass*—Village Voice

sit tight 1 *v phr* by 1890 To keep one's present position, stance, convictions, etc; refuse to be moved; =STAND PAT **2** *v phr* by 1903 To wait patiently: *Be up as quickly as I can, Vicky. Sit tight*—Hugh Pentecost

sitting duck *n phr* by 1944 An easy target; a totally defenseless person

be **sitting pretty** *v phr* by 1921 To be in a superior and very pleasant position: *He's just the same genial idiot whether he is out of luck or sitting pretty*—W W Rose

situash (sit yōō AYSH) *n* by 1934 Situation

situation *See* ON TOP OF

sit up and take notice *v phr* by 1889 To pay attention; become aware; =WAKE UP AND SMELL THE COFFEE: *Let's do something that'll make him sit up and take notice*

Siwash or **old Siwash** (SĪ wahsh) **1** *n* or *n phr* by 1910 Any small college; the archetypical small college; =EAST JESUS STATE: *. . . collegians (from Harvard to Siwash) and their professors*—Time **2** *v* Canadian by 1980s To prohibit from buying liquor [fr Chinook jargon "north Pacific Coast Indian," fr French *sauvage*, "savage, native," adopted as a term of contempt by cowboys; used in *Saturday Evening Post* short stories by George Fitch in 1910–11, probably because some provincial colleges have similar Indian names]

six *See* DEEP SIX, EIGHTY-SIX, FIFTY-SIX, HIT ON ALL SIX

six-bit *modifier* by 1840 Worth or costing seventy-five cents: *a six-bit sandwich*

six bits *n phr* by 1840 Seventy-five cents

six-by *n* truckers by 1973 A truck, esp a large one [fr *six-by-six*, the designation of a truck with six wheels and a six-speed transmission]

sixer *n* underworld by 1950s A six-month prison sentence

six feet under *adj phr* by 1940s Dead

six-hundred-pound gorilla *n phr* (also **eight-hundred-pound gorilla** or **nine-hundred-pound gorilla**) by 1970s A powerful force; a virtually irresistible influence: *She is a 600-pound gorilla. . . . She can intimidate anybody*—Time/ *. . . likens Spielberg to an "800-pound gorilla," which can be defined as a high-priced Hollywood species that makes its own decisions*—Los Angeles Times/ *. . . there were no obvious 900-pound gorillas like Forrest Gump or Schindler's List*—Wisconsin State Journal [fr a joke in which the question "Where does a *six-hundred-pound gorilla* sleep?" is answered "Anywhere it wants"]

six-pack 1 *n* circus by 1970s Three performances a day for two days: *Fridays and Saturdays. . . he has three [shows], the two days' stint known as a six-pack*—New Yorker **2** *n* police by 1990s A set of six photographs from which a witness is asked to identify a suspect **3** *n* by 1970s Any set of six **4** *v* beach volleyball by 1990s : *. . . elevates in a spray of sand, and "six-packs" her opponents, spiking the ball so savagely that it knocks the defender down*—Buzz [fr a set of cans or bottles of beverage, most notably of beer, sold as a unit; the term is found by 1952]

See JOE SIX-PACK

six-shooter or **six-gun** *n* by 1844 A revolver with a cylinder holding six cartridges

sixty *See* LIKE SIXTY

the **sixty-four dollar question** *n phr* by 1942 The crucial question or issue •The dollar amount has increased over the years: *To flee or not to flee, that's the sixty-four dollar question/ "What will the European Community do?" "Well, that's really the sixty-four-thousand dollar question"*—radio program Morning Edition/ *Are baby boomers going to want a smaller car? That's the $64 million ques-*

tion for Ford—New York Times [fr a radio quiz show where the top prize was $64]

◁**sixty-nine** or **69**▷ *n by 1888* Simultaneous oral sex between two persons, whose reciprocally inverse positions suggest the numeral 69

six ways to Sunday *See* FORTY WAYS TO SUNDAY

size *See* KING-SIZE

◁**size queen**▷ *n phr homosexuals by 1972* A homosexual who is particularly and nearly exclusively concerned with the length of penises

size up *v phr by 1847* To estimate or assess: *How do you size up his chances?*

sizzle 1 *v* =FRY **2** *n by 1980s* Persuasive pressure; =HEAT: *That's the sizzle*—National Public Radio

sizzler 1 *n by 1901* A very hot day **2** *n baseball by 1910* A very fast pitch or hard-hit ground ball **3** *n loggers by 1940s* A cook

sizzling *adj by 1845* Hot, in any sense: *... sell some of the sizzling green at a discount*—Abel Green

ska (SKAH) *n by 1964* An early form of reggae music: *... various musical trends, punk, New Wave, power-pop, ska*—Aquarian [origin unknown]

skag or **scag 1** *n armed forces by 1915* A cigarette or cigarette butt **2** *n 1960s teenagers fr black* A despicable person or thing; =JERK **3** *n black by 1920s* An unattractive woman; =BAT, SKANK **4** *n 1960s narcotics* Cheap, low-quality heroin

skaggy *adj by 1960s* Ugly; unkempt; nasty; =SKANKY: *She's too skaggy for your average john*—Michael Connelly

◁**skank**▷ **1** *n* An unattractive woman; a malodorous woman; =SKAG **2** *n black by 1970s* A prostitute; =HOOKER: *How long would it take for them to find them f— skanks (the hookers) again?*—New York Times **3** *n by 1980s* Copulation; coition; =ASS: *... how 'bout witnessing some skank*—Jane Leavy **4** *n by 1980s* A despicable person; =GRUNGE, SLEAZEBAG: *Julie gets used and humiliated by the lens-wielding skank*—Sassy **5** *n 1990s teenagers* A slovenly style of dress, possibly imitative of disheveled heroin adicts: *Some teenagers prefer a grungier, if equally tasteless, look known as "skank"...*—New York Times **6** *v by 1976* To do a sort of reggae dancing in which the body bends forward, the knees are raised, and the hands claw the air: *They move in sympathetic response to the music, skankin' from side to side*—Village Voice/ *They mosh. They slam. They skank and thrash, too*—Capitol Times **7** *n*: *... then back to that gentle skank*—Village Voice

skanky or **skank-o-rama** *adj 1980s teenagers fr black* Nasty; repellent; =GROTTY, SCUZZY, TRASHY: *The girls were somewhat skanky, with lank hair and rotten posture*—Richard Price/ *... you moved, the earth moved. Skank-o-rama*—Sassy

skate 1 *v 1930s black* To default a debt; avoid paying **2** *v by 1915* To leave; =SPLIT **3** *v WWII armed forces* To evade duty; =GOLDBRICK, GOOF OFF: *The gunny... accuses you of trying to skate*—New York Times **4** *n by 1894* An inferior horse: *They'd kill that bunch of skates for their hides*—Ernest Hemingway

sked *See* ON SKED

skedaddle *v by 1861* To run away; flee; fly; depart hastily: *... the verb "to skedaddle," which was revived during the war to suggest precipitous flight, and has held its own ever since*—Encyclopedia Britannica [origin unknown; perhaps fr an attested Scots dialect sense, "spill," which could suggest "scatter, disperse"; the example from 1884 supposes an earlier origin]

skeeter *n by 1839* A mosquito

skeevy *adj 1990s students* Nasty; repellent; =GROTTY, SCUZZY, TRASHY: *How's your skeevy pal?*

skeezer *n 1980s students fr black* A promiscuous woman; slut: *That skeezer has no self-respect*—Delcastle Dictionary of Slang/ *... nice women, those who are neither sluts nor skeezers (women who use men for money), should take no offense*—Milwaukee Journal

skell *n New York City police by 1980s* A street derelict who may be a villain: *Perp:... also a mutt, a mope, a skid, or a skell*—Street News [ultimately fr Dutch *schelm*, "scoundrel, villain," found in English as *skelum* by 1611]

sketch *See* HOT SKETCH, THUMBNAIL SKETCH

skewgee (SKoo jee) *by 1893* **1** *adj* Rattled and confused **2** *adj* Disorderly; =MESSY

◀**skibby**▶ **1** *n by 1926* A Japanese or Chinese; Asian **2** *n WWII armed forces fr Pacific Northwest* An Asian prostitute [second sense fr Japanese *sukebi*, "a bawdy person, hot stuff"]

ski bum *n phr by 1960* A person who frequents ski resorts habitually, often doing casual jobs, for the sake of skiing

ski bunny *See* SNOW BUNNY

skid *n New York City police by 1980s* =SKELL

skid lid *n phr motorcyclists by 1970s* A motorcyclist's helmet: *... suffered severe brain damage while wearing one of the company's skid lids*—Easyriders

skidoo or **skiddoo** *v by 1905* To depart hastily; =SCRAM ●Often a command or a bit of advice: *We heard the shooting and we skiddooed quick/ Skidoo, skidoo, and quit me*—H McHugh [perhaps fr *skedaddle*]

skid road or **skidroad 1** *n phr* or *n loggers by 1880* A forest track over which logs are dragged **2** *n phr* or *n* (also **Skid Road** or **Skidroad**) *lumberjacks, hoboes & underworld by about 1915* A street or district of cheap shops and resorts; a relatively disreputable district: *I headed towards the Skidroad and its cheap eating joints*—Atlantic Monthly/ *no skid road for the professor*—Westword **3** *modifier*: *... a tightwad with latent skid-road tendencies*—Washington Post [fr the log-paved path on which the Seattle lumberman Henry Yesler skidded logs to his sawmill]

skid row or **Skid Row** *n by 1931* A street or district frequented by derelicts, hoboes, drifters, etc, such as the Bowery in New York City [fr *skid road*]

Skid Row bum *n phr by* 1930s A usu alcoholic derelict or drifter who frequents a street or district frequented by many such types and who lives by begging and pilfering; =BOWERY BUM, STUMBLEBUM, WINO

the **skids** *See* HIT THE SKIDS, ON THE SKIDS, PUT THE SKIDS UNDER someone or something

skillet *n black by* 1940s A black person: *You skillets is trying to promote a meal on me*—Zora Neale Hurston

skillion or **scillion** *n by* 1970s An indefinite very large number; =BAZILLION, GAZILLION: *I have a scillion things to say*—Philadelphia Bulletin
See JILLION

skim 1 *n gambling by* 1960 Income not reported for tax purposes, esp from the gross earnings of a gambling casino or other such enterprise; =BLACK MONEY: *. . . allegedly "cleansed" in the neighborhood of $2 million in "skim," untaxed gambling profits*—New York Times/ *Caltronics is in on the skim*—WT Tyler **2** *v gambling by* 1961 : *. . . "appropriate, conceal, and skim" part of the winnings*—New York Times

skimpies *n by* 1990s Underwear panties: *Once again, Roseanne is pushing the envelope, not to mention the skimpies*—Los Angeles Times

skin 1 *n black by* 1942 The hand as used in hand-shaking or hand-slapping as a salutation •Nearly always in the expression *some skin*: *My man!. . . Gimme some skin!*—Malcolm X/ *Slip me some skin*—Ray Noble **2** *n by* 1923 An inferior racehorse; =BEETLE: *They take the first bunch of skins out to gallop*—Ernest Hemingway **3** *n by* 1790 A pocketbook, wallet, etc **4** *n by* 1930 One dollar; a dollar bill; =FROGSKIN: *One laid out 190 skins*—New Yorker ◁**5**▷ *n by about* 1935 A condom; =RUBBER **6** *modifier by* 1960s Featuring nudity; indecently exposing; =GIRLIE: *a skin flick* **7** *n jazz musicians by* 1938 A drum **8** *v by* 1862 To defeat decisively; trounce; =SKUNK: *They skinned the Wolverines 20–zip* **9** *v by* 1819 To cheat or swindle; victimize: *You got skinned in that deal*—C Kuhn **10** *v by* 1876 To slip away; =SKEDADDLE: *. . . and then skin out the window*—Harold Robbins
See FROGSKIN, GET UNDER someone's SKIN, GIVE SOME SKIN, NO SKIN OFF MY ASS, PIGSKIN, PRESS THE FLESH, SHEEPSKIN

skin someone **alive** *v phr by* 1975 To punish someone severely; castigate roundly: *She'll skin me alive if I'm late again*

skin-beater *n jazz musicians by about* 1925 A drummer: *. . . the reefer-smitten skin beater*—New York Times

skin (or flesh) flick *n phr by* 1968 A movie featuring nudity and more or less patent sexual activity; =BLUE MOVIE, FUCK FILM

◁**skin flute**▷ *n phr by* 1940s The penis
See PLAY THE SKIN FLUTE

a **skinful** *n phr by* 1788 One's intoxicating fill of liquor; =a SNOOT FULL: *Dey bot' got a skinful*—Eugene O'Neill

skin game *n phr by* 1868 A confidence game; =SCAM

skinhead 1 *n by* 1940s A bald person or person with a shaved or cropped head **2** *n Marine Corps by* 1950s A Marine recruit **3** *n fr* 1960s *British* A close-cropped person with neo-Nazi, racist, and other extreme right sentiments: *A mob enraged by the appearance of a nationally known racist chased and beat a group of teenage white supremacist "skinheads". . .* —Associated Press

skin house *n phr by* 1970 A theater featuring nude shows, sex movies, etc

skin magazine (or **mag**) **1** *n phr by* 1960 A magazine featuring nudity, more or less explicit sexual activity, etc; =NUDIE **2** *modifier*: *Asked whether the skin-mag ban would apply to other magazines in which women are scantily clad or naked. . .* —Milwaukee Journal

skinner *See* MULE-SKINNER

the **skinny** *n phr fr WWII armed forces* The truth; =the LOWDOWN, the SCOOP: *Are you giving me the straight skinny?*—Rex Burn/ *Here's the skinny: the show's an old-fashioned formula musical*—Village Voice [origin unknown; perhaps an alteration of *the naked truth*]
See the STRAIGHT SKINNY

skinny-dip *v phr by* 1950s To swim naked: *Andrew went skinny-dipping in rocky pools*—Newsweek

skinny something **down** *v phr by* 1970s To reduce something, esp to a minimum: *We were told to skinny the budget down still more*

skinnymalink or **skinny marink** *n* or *n phr entry form by* 1916 A very thin person: *If a self-confessed skinny marink like Mayer dared have summer dreams, why not a muscular woman?*—New York Times [fr Scottish dialect]

skin pop *v phr* 1950s *narcotics* To inject narcotics into the skin or muscles, rather than into the circulatory system: *I'll have to skin pop*—H Braddy

skins 1 *n jazz musicians by* 1938 A set of drums **2** *n* 1950s *hot rodders & truckers* Automotive tires: *Protect your present skins*—Playboy

skin-search or **body-shake 1** *n police by* 1935 A thorough scrutiny of a naked person, esp for hypodermic needle marks, concealed narcotics, etc **2** *v by* 1970: *They skin-searched both couples*

skint *adj by* 1925 Lacking money; =BROKE •Still chiefly British[fr *skinned*]

skip 1 *v by* 1905 To fail to attend; absent oneself; =SHINE: *. . . if I let you skip school this afternoon*—J D Salinger **2** *v* (also **skip out**) *by* 1590 To depart hastily, escape, abscond, esp to avoid paying a bill, being arrested, etc: *They skipped out of the motel at 2 AM* **3** *n by* 1915 A person who absconds, esp to avoid paying a bill: *The skip took off. . . with a girl friend*—John D MacDonald **4** *n by* 1830 =SKIPPER

skip it *v phr by* 1934 To drop or ignore some matter: *If you can't remember, let's skip it for now*

skipper 1 *n nautical by* 1390 The captain of a ship or boat **2** *n Army by* 1906 Any commanding officer; =the OLD MAN

◄**skippy**► *n WWII Army* A Japanese woman, esp a prostitute
See SKIBBY

skip tracer *n phr by 1950s* An investigator who tries to find persons who have absconded from debts, marriages, etc: *Stern hired some sort of skip tracer and he came back with a complete zip*—Scott Turow

skirt *n by 1906* A woman, esp a young woman; =BROAD, CHICK ●Regarded by some women as offensive: *. . . a real skirt*—Eugene O'Neill/ *. . . never give any skirt a tumble*—Sinclair Lewis

skirt-chaser *n by 1942* A ladies' man; =LOVER-BOY

skitch *v 1990s students* : *. . . some hanging on the sides of the Jeep, "skitching," or dragging their feet through the powder*—Milwaukee Journal

ski-trip *n 1960s narcotics* The taking of cocaine; a dose of cocaine [by extension fr *snow,* "cocaine"]

skitter *v by 1845* To move about rapidly; scamper: *. . . where the poor skitter around the doll's house on the hill like so many rats among garbage*—New Yorker

skitz *v 1990s teenagers* To go crazy; =FLIP OUT, SCHIZ OUT: *No, I'm not driving you past Gary's house again. You are skitzin over this guy*—Macon Telegraph
See SCHIZO

skiv *n* =SHIV

skivvies 1 *n by 1932* Underwear; underpants and undershirt ●Originally a nautical use: *. . . stripped down to his skivvies and played his harmonica*—Playboy **2** *n by about 1945* A pair of sandal-like slippers

skivvy 1 *n* (also **skivvy shirt**) *by 1932* A man's undershirt, esp a T-shirt: *. . . pants, sneakers, some skivvy shirts*—Harper's **2** *n by 1947* A pair of mens' underpants, esp of the boxer type

skivvy-waver *n WWII Navy* A naval signal operator

skookum *adj by 1847* Effective; powerful [fr Chinook jargon, "powerful evil spirit," fr Chehalis *skukum*]

skosh or **scosh** (SKOHSH) *n Korean War armed forces* A little bit; =SMIDGEN: *You need a skosh more room here for your desk* [fr Japanese *sukoshi*]

◁**skull**▷ *n homosexuals by 1970s* Fellatio; =BLOW JOB
See GO OUT OF one's SKULL, OUT OF one's HEAD, POP-SKULL

skull-buster 1 *n 1930s black* A police officer **2** *n 1920s students* A very difficult course in school

skullcap *n 1980s motorcyclists* A helmet; =BRAIN DISH

skullduggery or **skulduggery** *n by 1867* Shady behavior; =DIRTY WORK, HANKY-PANKY [a US alteration of Scots *sculduddery,* "bawdry, obscenity," which is attested from the early–18th century]

skull popper *n phr by 1980s* Liquor; =BOOZE, POP-SKULL, the SAUCE: *. . . his vices are slow horses and fast bookies, rather than 86-proof skull popper. . .* —Milwaukee Journal

skull practice *n phr sports by 1930s* The learning of plays, patterns, etc, esp in football by blackboard demonstrations

skull session *n phr by 1959* An intensive learning and teaching period, esp a briefing session: *. . . two separate "skull sessions" with six members of the US negotiating team*—Newsweek

skunk 1 *n by 1840* A despicable person; =BASTARD, LOUSE **2** *v by 1849* To defeat utterly, esp to hold the opponent scoreless in sports; trounce; =CLOBBER: *They're saying I'm going to get skunked in the black community*—Time **3** *v football by 1980s* To learn by deduction the signals used by an opposing team telling the quarterback what play to call **4** *v windsurfers by 1990s* To lack wind for sailing: *We went to Baja last month, but got skunked every day*—Los Angeles Times **5** *n 1990s narcotics* Marijuana; =POT, GRASS
See DRUNK AS A SKUNK

skunk someone **out of** something *v phr students by 1890* To cheat someone out of something

sky 1 *v sports by 1909* To hit or kick or throw a ball very high: *See me skying out there?*—Milwaukee Journal/ *This time he skied the punt right over the end zone* **2** *v 1980s basketball* To jump high in order to slam-dunk the ball; =AIR
See PIE IN THE SKY

sky bear *n phr by 1975* =BEAR IN THE AIR

skycap *n by 1950* A porter at an air terminal [modeled on *red cap,* "a railroad terminal porter"]

skygodlin or **sigoggling** (SKĪ gahd lən, SĪ gahg ling) *adj by 1869* Slantwise; askew; =COCKEYED, SLONCHWAYS [origin unknown; perhaps the original form was *skygoggling* or *sidegoggling,* where *goggle* means "eye," and the term would be an exact synonym of *cockeyed*]

skyhook 1 *n by 1915* An imaginary hook in the sky, which explains why some things stay up, which solves the problems of keeping some things up, etc: *How will I hold up the roof when I fix the wall? On a skyhook, of course* **2** *n basketball by 1980s* A high hook shot at the basket

the **sky is the limit** *sentence* No limits exist: *Yeltsin proudly proclaims that today in Russia the sky is the limit to what a person can earn*—Nation

skyjack 1 *v by 1961* To take control of an aircraft illegally, usu by claiming to have a weapon or a bomb; commit air piracy **2** *n by 1968*: *the week's third skyjack to Cuba* [modeled on *hijack*]

sky-pilot *n by 1883* A member of the clergy; preacher

skyrocket *v by 1895* To increase rapidly: *Profits are expected to skyrocket after the announcement*

skyscraper *n baseball by 1866* A very high fly ball, esp near home plate

skywest *See* KNOCK someone or something GALLEY-WEST

slab 1 *n 1930s jive talk* A bed **2** *n by 1950s* One dollar; a dollar bill: *Ten slabs for two days' work!*—Merrill Blosser **3** *n baseball by 1919* The pitcher's "rubber" at the top of the mound, against which the pitcher braces his foot when throwing
See SUPER SLAB

slack 1 *n by 1851* A period of inertness or decreased activity: *He'd pulled his weight long enough to get some slack*—Carsten Stroud/ *. . . a channel surfer trapped in his own den of slack*—Seventeen **2** *v*: *Witness the 40,000 or so Americans here now, a lot of them teaching English or just slacking, drinking 50-cent beers in the pubs, grooving to acid jazz at the Roxy. . .* —Sassy

slacker 1 *n by 1898* An indolent and detached person; shirker; idler: *The epitome of the slang-slinging, wise-cracking slacker*—New York Times **2** *modifier*: *. . . this lame "slacker" attitude a la Jeff Spicoli from* Fast Times at Ridgemont High—Los Angeles Times [revived in the 1990s to describe a sort of cultural anomie]

slag 1 *v (also* **slag off***) by 1971* To denigrate; =BAD-MOUTH, PUT DOWN: *Everybody was getting slagged*—Rolling Stone/ *I don't mean to slag the girls at Douglas*—Aquarian/ *This time I can't give it to you, can't totally slag you off*—Village Voice **2** *n*: *. . . its purposeful indie-rock slag at commerciality*—Village View [origin unknown; perhaps fr German *schlagen,* "beat, whip"]

slam 1 *n by 1884* An uncomplimentary comment; a jibe; =KNOCK: *. . . took a slam at the male stars who dress like "ranch hands"*—Associated Press **2** *v by 1916*: *Thrifty Slams Riordan on Its Way Out of Town*—Los Angeles Times **3** *v by 1905* To hit; =CLOBBER ◁4▷ *v 1980s students* To do the sex act with; =BOFF, SCREW: *Did you slam her, Jon?*—UCLA Slang **5** *v (also* **slam-dance***) by 1980s* To do a physically colliding and athletic sort of rock-and-roll dancing, esp in the vein of punk rock: *The music is hardcore, the dance is slamming*—Village Voice **6** *v 1980s students* To consume or use: *He slammed two beers and then went out on his date*—UCLA Slang/ *Did they ever slam heroin?* *See* GRAND SLAM

the **slam** *n phr by 1960* =the SLAMMER

slam-bang 1 *n prizefighting by 1920s* A wild and vicious fight **2** *adv by 1840* Violently: *They went at it slam-bang* **3** *adj by 1823* Raucous, violent, vigorous, etc: *. . . in climaxes as slam-bang as a four-horse stretch drive*—Heywood Hale Broun/ *. . . a couple of slam-bang musical numbers*—Playboy *See* SLAP

slam-book *n by 1922* A sort of notebook or autograph book into which one's friends would write genial insults

slam dunk 1 *v phr basketball by 1976* To score a field goal by leaping up and thrusting the ball violently down through the hoop **2** *n phr by 1990s* A spectacular success; winner: *Both pro- and antimerger members have been equally taken with the new rabbi. "It's a slam dunk,"* enthuses *Corwin. . .* —Buzz **3** *modifier*: *Welfare reform should have been a slam-dunk issue for the Republicans. But last week they allowed tax cuts to get in the way*—Time/ *The bombing is not a slam-dunk case. It's going to require a really good presentation by the government to convince the jury*—

New York Times **4** *n phr (also* **slam-dunk landing***)*: *The safety board said that Flight 2268 didn't need to dive abruptly toward the runway. It contended the pilot elected to quickly slow down the plane for a slam dunk landing by reversing the engines*—Milwaukee Journal

slammer *n basketball by 1970s* =SLAM DUNK *See* GRAND SLAMMER

the **slammer 1** *n phr 1930s jive talk* A door: *. . . twister to the slammer*—Variety **2** *n phr (also* **the slams***) black by 1952* A jail, prison, etc: *Drunk drivers go to the slammer in this town*

**slammin' ** *adj 1990s teenagers* Excellent; superb; =COOL, FUNKY FRESH: *That food was slammin'*—New York Times/ *. . . in my opinion the most slammin' song on the album. . .* —Milwaukee Journal [*slamming* is found in a similar sense, "large, exceptional," by about 1900]

slamming *n by 1990s*: *. . . federal regulators plan to adopt tougher rules against switching customers' long-distance companies without their knowledge, a practice known as "slamming"*—Associated Press

slam the door on someone or something *v phr by 1786* To put an end to something as if by slamming a dismissive door: *Ray Floyd slammed the door on any would-be challengers with a string of 14 consecutive pars. . .* —Milwaukee Journal Sentinel

slang *n fr middle 1700s British* A style or register of language consisting of terms that can be substituted for standard terms of the same conceptual meaning but having stronger emotive impact than the standard terms, in order to express an attitude of self-assertion towards conventional order and moral authority and often an affinity with or membership in occupational, ethnic, or other social groups, and ranging in acceptability from sexual and scatological crudity to audacious wittiness (see *Preface*) [origin unknown; probably related to *sling,* which has cognates in Norwegian that suggest the abusive nature of slang; the British dialect original term *slang* meant both "a kind of projectile-hurling weapon" and "the language of thieves and vagabonds," reinforcing the connection with "sling"]

slant 1 *n by 1905* An opinion or point of view; =ANGLE: *. . . something about his tone or his "slant" that irritated his contemporaries*—Joseph Wood Krutch **2** *n by 1911* A look; an ocular inspection: *Take a slant at dat*—Eugene O'Neill/ *The prowl car takes a slant down now and then*—Raymond Chandler

◀**slant-eye**▶ *n by 1929* An Asian person or person of Asian descent

slap or **slap-bang** or **slam-bang** *adv first form by 1829, second by 1885, third by 1940s* Precisely; directly: *Streets that ended slap in a courtyard*—Sinclair Lewis/ *The storm was pointed slam-bang at Tampa*—Associated Press

slap and tickle *n phr by 1928* Amorous dalliance; playful fondling ●Chiefly British: *. . . a spot of slap and tickle*—Peter De Vries

slapdash *adj* by 1792 Hasty and careless; heedless of the fine details; =SLOPPY

slap someone **five** *See* GIVE someone FIVE

slap-happy 1 *adj* by 1936 Disoriented and stuporous, esp from being hit too often about the head: . . . *a slap-happy bum*—Jim Tully **2** *adj* Vertiginous; off balance: . . . *designed to knock philologists slap-happy*—Newsweek **3** *adj* Euphoric; intoxicated; =HIGH: *He was slap-happy a whole week after the baby came*

a **slap in the face** *n phr* by 1898 An insult or rebuke, esp when unexpected; a rebuff: *His not saying anything is a slap in the face*

slapman *n* 1920s underworld A plainclothes police officer

a **slap on the wrist** *n phr* by 1914 A very mild punishment ●Usu said when the punishment is felt to be unjustly lenient
See GIVE someone A SLAP ON THE WRIST

slapper *See* KNEE-SLAPPER

slapstick 1 *adj* show business by 1906 Featuring rowdy humor, both physical and conceptual; low comedy: *The old burlesque loved slapstick routines* **2** *n* show business by 1926 : *The Marx Brothers depended a lot on slapstick* [fr the *slapstick*, two wooden slats joined at one end, which made a loud splatting noise when used as a comic weapon, the term found by 1907]

slap-up *adj* by 1843 Excellent; =GREAT

slash-and-burn *adj* by 1980s Crudely violent; irresponsibly vitriolic: . . . *behavior on Echo tends to be fairly compared with the slash-and-burn style of other BBSs*—Elle [fr a type of transitory cultivation in which a forest area is cleared and the undergrowth burned for planting, the term found by 1939]

slasher *n* by 1980s A gory thriller movie; =SLICE AND DICE FILM

slat *n* skiers by 1960s A ski

slathers *n* by 1857 A large quantity; =OODLES: *It cost the railroads slathers of money*—Jack London [ultimately fr Irish *sliotar*]

slats 1 *n* by 1895 The ribs: . . . *pokes him in the slats*—Ben Hecht **2** *n* by 1935 The buttocks; =ASS: *She gives him a swift kick in the slats*

slave *n* black by 1930s A job: *You got a job, man. You got a slave*—New York Magazine

slave market *n phr* by 1911 An employment office or a place or occasion where jobs are sought and candidates present themselves: *Their annual convention is essentially a slave market*

slaves and masters *n phr* by 1970s Sadists and masochists, in sexual taste: . . . *referred to by the cognoscenti as "S and M," or "slaves and masters,"*. . . *the most prevalent of the freak syndrome*—Xaviera Hollander

slay *v* by 1593 To impress someone powerfully, esp to provoke violent and often derisive laughter: *Pardon me, this will slay you*—Heywood Hale Broun/ *The boys who slay me are the ones who have set pieces to recite when they answer the phone*—H Allen Smith

sleaze 1 *n* by 1976 Anything shabby and disgusting; particularly revolting trash; =CRAP, SCHLOCK, SHIT: . . . *a paragon of Dorothy Malone low-fashion sleaze*—Village Voice **2** *modifier*: *the sleaze factor* **3** *n* by 1976 =SLEAZEBAG **4** *v* by 1976 To be sexually promiscuous and disreputable **5** *v* students by 1970s To scrounge; =MOOCH [a back-formation from *sleazy*; *sleaze*, "a sleazy quality or appearance," is found by 1954]

sleazebag or **sleazeball** *n* by 1970s A despicable person; =DIRTBAG, SCUZZBAG: *Tartikoff calls the character "a total sleazebag"*—Time/ *If you're a sleaze-ball, you deserve a recall*—Newsweek

sleaze-bucket *adj* by 1970s Nasty; degradingly repellent: *sleaze-bucket movies*

sleazemonger *n* by 1970s A producer or seller of nasty entertainment: . . . *one of Hollywood's lowlier sleazemongers*—Washington Post

sleazy or **sleazo** or **sleazoid** *adj* entry form by 1941, second form by 1972, third by 1970s Disgusting; filthy; nasty; =GRUNGY, SCUZZY: . . . *dirty buildings in sleazy sections*—New York Daily News/ . . . *a tremendous evocation of the sleazoid speed-freak scene*—Rolling Stone/ . . . *who makes sleazo blood films*—Pauline Kael [fr the late–1600s British *sleasie*, "thin, flimsy, threadbare," of uncertain origin, whence it came to mean "of inferior workmanship, shoddy"; perhaps fr *Sleasie*, "Silesian," used of linen cloth from that part of Germany]

sled *n* motorcyclists by 1980s A car; =CAGE: *I don't know these little sleds*—George V Higgins

sleep around *v phr* by 1928 To be sexually promiscuous; =PLAY AROUND

sleeper 1 *n* by 1892 Anything, esp a low-budget movie, a show, or a book, which achieves or probably will achieve success after a time of obscurity; =DARK HORSE: *My Name is Julia Ross is the first "sleeper" to come to Philadelphia in months*—Philadelphia Bulletin/ . . . *whose Return of the Secaucus Seven. . . ranked among the more astute sleepers of 1980*—Playboy **2** *modifier*: *a sleeper play* **3** *n* football by 1953 A player who unexpectedly and cunningly gets the ball and runs **4** *n* 1960s narcotics A sleeping pill or a sedative [the first sense may be fr gambling term *sleeper*, found by 1856 and meaning both "an unexpected winning card" and "a pot whose owner has ignored it, and hence is free to anyone who takes it"]

sleep like a top *v phr* by 1693 To sleep very soundly [fr the stasis of a spinning *top*]

sleepville or **Sleepville** *adj* cool talk by 1950s Sleepy; comatose

sleep with someone *v phr* by 1400 To do the sex act with someone; =GO TO BED WITH someone ●Perhaps not so much slang as a much-needed euphemism: *No girl could love a man unless she had slept with the man over a period of time*—Calder Willingham

sleeve *See* ACE UP one's SLEEVE, PUT THE ARM ON someone

sleighride narcotics by 1915 **1** *n* Intoxication from cocaine **2** *v* To use cocaine [fr the association of *sleighrides* with *snow*, "cocaine"]

sleighrider *n* narcotics by 1915 A cocaine addict; also, a user of cocaine; =COKEHEAD

slew *n* by 1839 A large quantity; =OODLES, SLATHERS: . . . *a slew of cops*—G Homes [probably fr Irish *sluagh*, "host, multitude"]

slewed *adj* by 1801 Drunk [fr *slew*, "veer, swing around, hence, walk erratically"]

slewfoot 1 *n* by 1896 A clumsy, stumbling person; a person who moves awkwardly **2** *v* (also **sloughfoot**) by 1950 To walk with the feet turned away from the straight direction: *The Airedale sloughfooted away*—Richard Starnes **3** *n* (also **sleufoot**) by 1940s A police officer or detective [fr the awkwardness of a person whose feet *slew* outwards overmuch or are otherwise ill-controlled; police sense probably modeled on *flatfoot*]

slice *n* by 1550 A portion or share; =PIECE: *Five grand wouldn't get you a slice of her*—Fredric Brown

slice and dice *v phr* by 1970s To reduce to smaller pieces, inferentially by cutting up: *Congress is the single most unpopular American institution other than the income tax; slicing and dicing its committees. . . will bring the GOP only high praise. . . —Newark Star-Ledger/ Derivatives allow people to transfer risk, to slice and dice it into little pieces and pass it on—New York Times/ The Court decided that this broad requirement could be sliced and diced. . . —Nation* [fr the preparation of cooking ingredients by *slicing and dicing* them]

slice-and-dice film *n phr* by 1970s A horror movie, esp one featuring bloody mutilation; =SLASHER: *Mr De Palma's movies are distinguished from "slice and dice films"*—New York Times

sliced bread *See* the BEST THING SINCE SLICED BREAD

slick 1 *adj* by 1599 Smooth and clever; smart: *She's a very slick talker* **2** *adj* by 1807 Cunning; crafty: *. . . more than a match for any slick city lawyer*—Erle Stanley Gardner **3** *adj* by 1843 Excellent; =NIFTY: *The soup was "simply slick"*—Sinclair Lewis **4** *adj* by 1920 Glib and superficial; without real substance: *They turn out people with slick plastic personalities* **5** *n* by 1934 A magazine printed on glossy paper and usu having some artistic or intellectual pretensions, as distinguished from pulp magazines: *. . . magazines. . . from top slicks to minor pulps*—New York Times **6** *n* 1950s hot rodders An automobile tire with a very smooth tread: *My Sting Ray is light, the slicks are startin' to spin*—song "Shut Down" **7** *n* New York City police by 1980s A police bureaucrat regarded as self-serving by the rank and file: *But no way am I hanging around to talk to the slicks on this one*—Carsten Stroud [earlier 1800s uses were in comparative phrases like *slick as bear's grease* and *slick as molasses*]

slick as a whistle *adv phr* by 1830 Very adroitly; cleverly: *She played that horn slick as a whistle*

slick chick *n phr* 1930s jive talk An attractive young woman, esp one who is notably up-to-date and au courant: *. . . the "slick chicks" at Sequoia Union High*—Life/ *. . . a slick chick, a pretty girl*—Meyer Berger

slicker 1 *n* by 1900 A clever and crafty person, esp a confidence trickster, a dishonest business executive, a shrewd and predatory lawyer, etc; =CROOK: *I don't admire slickers who peddle get-rich-quick bubbles*—comic strip "Major Hoople" **2** *n* by 1920 A socially smooth and superficially attractive person; =SMOOTHIE: *The slicker was good-looking and clean-looking*—F Scott Fitzgerald **3** *v* by 1935 To cheat; =CON, SCAM: *. . . outsmarted and slickered by Moscow*—C V Jackson/ *A fox tried to slicker him out of the cheese*—Bing Crosby *See* CITY SLICKER

slickum *n* by 1940s Hair oil; pomade

slick someone or something **up** *v phr* by 1828 To make neat and more attractive; furbish; =GUSSY UP: *What are they all slicked up for?*

slide 1 *v* by 1859 To depart; =SPLIT **2** *n* by 1990s A delay in collecting a debt: *How about a slide on my rent?* **3** *n* Something easily done; =CINCH, PIECE OF CAKE

slim *n* jazz musicians by 1960s A cigarette

Slim *See* JERUSALEM SLIM

slime 1 *n* by 1950s =SLIMEBAG: *"I think he's a slime," Louise Hartley. . . said*—Milwaukee Journal **2** *v* by 1990s Denigrate harshly and often falsely; =SMEAR: *James Earl Jones gets slimed*—People Weekly **3** *v* by 1990s To speak in an unctuous and cajoling way: *"May I personally take your order, Mr Goodman," he slimed*—Stan Cutler

◁**slimebag** or **slimeball** or **slimebucket**▷ *n* by 1970s A despicable person; a repugnant wretch; =GEEK, SCUMBAG, SLEAZEBAG: *I'm a disgusting slime bag, but I don't grovel*—Washington Post/ *I remember when the slime-balls used to be packed in there so solid*—Joseph Wambaugh/ *If you chill out, those low-life slime buckets will sew your fingers inside your mouth*—Washington Post

slim pickings *n phr* by 1940s Very little to be had or earned; extremely unprofitable returns: *You'll find it's slim pickings there, if you're looking for a fast buck*

sling *v* 1990s narcotics To sell narcotics; =DEAL: *. . . gang-bangers. . . make careers of slingin' 'caine*—Los Angeles Times/ *I caught my first case for slinging (selling) drugs*—Macon Telegraph *See* HAVE one's ASS IN A SLING

sling beer *v phr* by 1903 To be a bartender or waiter: *. . . would look at home slinging beer at any tavern*—Toronto Life

slinger *n* by 1934 A waiter or waitress; a food server: *Anybody but a California Bar-B-Q slinger would know that*—James M Cain [fr *sling*, "to pass something from one person to another," found by 1860] *See* GRUB-SLINGER, GUNSLINGER, HASH-SLINGER, INK-SLINGER

sling hash *v phr* by 1906 To work as a waiter or waitress: *I used to sling their hash*—Joseph Auslander/ *She slung hash for a couple of weeks*—Life

slinging *See* MUD-SLINGING

sling ink *v phr* by 1864 To write, esp as a newspaper reporter or otherwise professionally

sling it or **sling the bull** *v phr* by 1940s To exaggerate and lie; talk smoothly and persuasively; =BULLSHIT, SHOOT THE BULL: *The chief reason for the conversational effectiveness of many individuals is their inherent ability to sling it*—A H Marckwardt and F G Cassidy

slinky *adj* by 1921 Sinuous and sexy: *... one of those slinky glittering females*—Raymond Chandler

slip 1 *v* by 1841 To give; hand: *So I slip him a double Z*—Lawrence Sanders **2** *v* by 1914 To lose one's competence or touch; decline: *Only six pages today? I must be slipping*
See BUCK SLIP, PINK SLIP

slip someone **a mickey** (or **a Mickey**) *v phr* by 1951 To give knockout drops, esp chloral hydrate, secretly in a drink: *He passed out as if someone had slipped him a Mickey*

slip between the cracks *See* FALL BETWEEN THE CRACKS

slip-horn *n* jazz musicians by about 1900 A slide trombone

slip (or **give**) **me five** *sentence* by 1926 Shake hands with me: *Slip me five so I know you're alive*

slip something **over on** someone *v phr* by 1912 To deceive someone; =CON, FLIMFLAM: *You can't slip this fraud over on the whole town* [fr baseball, "to pitch the ball deceptively over the plate"]

slippery slope *n phr* by 1951 A disastrous course; irrecoverable commitment: *Active euthanasia brings with it many dicey procedural questions, and, ultimately, a slippery slope*—New Republic

slippy *adj* by 1847 Quick; fast

slipstick *n* students by 1920s A slide rule

slip the blocks to someone *v phr* by 1980s To punish or injure; hamper: *Meanwhile, he's trying to devise a way to slip the blocks to Martin Gardow, that monster*—Lawrence Sanders
See PUT THE BLOCKS TO someone

slip one's **trolley** *v phr* by 1895 To lose one's rational composure; =FLIP OUT, FREAK OUT: *She was going around babbling like she slipped her trolley* [fr the condition of a trolley car that has lost contact with the electrical cable]

slip-up *n* by 1874 A miscalculation; an accident; =GLITCH: *There must have been a hell of a slip-up somewhere along the line*

◁**slit**▷ *n* by 1648 The vulva; =CUNT

slob by 1861 **1** *n* A pudgy, generally unattractive, and untidy person: *You great, fat slob!*—Owen Johnson/ *... a big slob with a chin that stuck out like a shelf*—Raymond Chandler **2** *n* A slovenly and disorderly person; a sloppy and disheveled person: *What a slob! You'd think his room was the town dump* **3** *n* A mediocre person, esp one who is likely to fail or be victimized: *... just another poor slob*—Jerome Weidman [fr Anglo-Irish, used affectionately of a quiet, fat, slow child]

slo-mo 1 *adv* by 1970s In slow-motion; slowly: *A man named Ahmed skated slo-mo*—Village Voice **2** *adj*: *She had a lot of things on her desk top, including a mondo-size slo-mo printer*—radio station WABC/ *... chock-full of slo-mo sequences of hunks running along the water*—Buzz

slonchways or **slaunchways** *adj* by 1913 =SKYGODLIN

slope[1] 1 *v* (also **slope out**) by 1830 To run away; depart; =LAM, SKEDADDLE **2** *v* underworld & hoboes by 1940s To escape from jail [perhaps fr Dutch *sloop*, "sneaked away"]

◀**slope[2]** or **slopehead**▶ *n* Vietnam War armed forces An Asian; =DINK, GOOK [fr the apparent slanting of eyes caused by the typical epicanthic fold of Asian peoples]

slopped *adj* by 1907 Drunk

sloppy by 1825 **1** *adj* Slovenly; disorderly; =MESSY **2** *adj* Careless; =SLAPDASH

sloppy Joe 1 *n phr* 1940s students A long, loose pullover sweater worn by women **2** *n phr* by 1961 A dish made from ground meat cooked in a barbecue sauce and spread on an open bun **3** *n phr* by 1970s A multidecked sandwich served in small thick triangles and filled with meats, cheeses, and mayonnaise, such that it is difficult to eat while keeping the fingers and face clean

sloppy Joe's *n phr* by 1940s A cheap restaurant or lunch counter; =GREASY SPOON

sloppy seconds by 1970s ◁**1**▷ *n phr* A sex act performed immediately after someone else's act: *Victoria denies having sex in the same bed as Heidi: "I like sex, but who wants sloppy seconds?"*—Vanity Fair **2** *n phr* The inferior position; =SECOND FIDDLE: *Lowden and Wood argued about who would be the top of the Chicago ticket and who would get sloppy seconds*—New Republic

slops *n* hoboes by about 1910 Beer

sloshed *adj* by about 1900 Drunk: *... a youngish man in a bar, a little sloshed and pouring out his troubles to the bartender*—New Yorker/ *You'll spend the night... getting sloshed on 3.2 salmon piss*—Village Voice [fr slosh, "a drink," found by the 1880s]

slot *n* by 1950 A slot machine; =ONE-ARM BANDIT: *The slots are going day and night*—Richard Bissell

slouch *See* NO SLOUCH

sloughfoot *See* SLEWFOOT

slough in (or **up**) (SLŌO) *v phr* hoboes by 1894 To arrest; imprison: *I've boozed around this town for seven years, and I've not been sloughed up yet*—J Flynt

slow burn 1 *n phr* by 1930s A gradually increasing anger: *He remembered Edgar Kennedy and his slow burns* **2** *modifier*: *Slow-burn resentment gave rise to a flinty local jargon*—Bryan Di Salvatore
See DO A SLOW BURN

slow coach *n phr* by 1837 A dull fellow; a stupid person

slowly in the wind *See* TWIST SLOWLY IN THE WIND

slow off the mark *adj phr* by 1972 Late in starting; dilatory; behind-hand: *If anything, the Clinton Administration has been a bit slow off the regulatory mark*—New Yorker [fr the *mark* from which foot-racers start]

slow on the draw (or **the uptake**) *adj phr* by 1940s Dull and dilatory; mentally sluggish [fr the action of drawing one's pistol, in the classical cowboy context]

slowpoke *n* by 1848 A slow, sluggish, slothful person: . . . *an old slowpoke*—Philip Wylie [fr *slow* used for vowel rhyme with the early–1800s *poke*, "behave dilatorily, potter, saunter," perhaps influenced by 16th-century *slowback*, "sluggard"]

sludd *v* Gulf War armed forces To suffer the terrible effects of chemical attack [acronym fr *salivate, lachrymate, urinate,* and *defecate*]

sludgeball *n* by 1970s A slovenly person; =DIRTBAG, SLOB: *I saw her drink beer out of a paper cup. . . I thought she was a sludgeball*—Washington Post [probably based in part on the increased currency of *sludge* as the product of sewer treatment plants]

sluff *v* by 1951 To avoid work and responsibility; shirk: *No one accused Bo of sluffing*—People Weekly [fr *slough off*]

slug¹ 1 *n* by 1622 A bullet: *Doctors said they're still unable to remove the slug*—New York Post **2** *n* by 1887 A dollar: . . . *do the job at 125 slugs a week*—Associated Press **3** *n* by 1762 A drink of liquid, esp of whiskey; =SNORT: . . . *ordering a slug of Old Stepmother*—Westbrook Pegler **4** *v* by 1940s (also **slug down**) : . . . *the crowd cheered and jeered and slugged beers*—Milwaukee Journal [origin uncertain; perhaps fr the resemblance of a lump of metal to the snail-like creature the *slug;* the earliest attested US senses are "gold nugget, lump of crude metal"; the drink and drinking senses appear to be derived fr phrases like *fire a slug* and *cast a slug,* "take a drink of liquor," found as metaphors in late–18th-century British sources, and may be fr Irish *slog,* "a drink; a swallow"]

slug² 1 *v* by 1862 To hit hard, esp with the fist; =CLOBBER: *He tried to make peace, but he got slugged* **2** *v* baseball by 1888 To make or try for long base hits, esp regularly; =GO FOR THE FENCES [fr British dialect *slog,* probably ultimately fr Old English *slagan,* cognate with German *schlagen*]

See PUT THE SLUG ON someone

slugfest 1 *n* by 1916 A hard and vicious fight, esp a prizefight more marked by powerful blows than by skillful boxing **2** *n* baseball by 1930s A baseball game in which many base hits are made

slugged *adj* by 1951 Drunk: *I want you really slugged when we shoot the scene*—S J Perelman

slugger 1 *n* baseball by 1883 A consistent long-ball hitter: *He's no slugger, he likes to place his hits* **2** *n* by 1877 A boxer more notable for hard hitting than for artistic finesse

See CIRCUIT SLUGGER

slug it out *v phr* by 1943 To fight with powerful blows; try to smash one another; =GO TOE TO TOE: *The principals were slugging it out in the alley*

slug-nutty *adj* by 1933 Stuporous or uncoordinated mentally and physically from taking too many blows on the head; =PUNCH-DRUNK: *"Slug-nutty" fighters are often very talkative*—Literary Digest

slum¹ or **go slumming** *v* or *v phr* by 1884 To visit places or consort with persons below one's place or dignity; mix with one's inferiors: *So we went slumming over in Philadelphia* [fr *slum,* "wretched poor area," origin unknown]

slum² or **slumgullion** or **slumgudgeon** *n* by 1847 Any inferior and esp unidentifiable food or drink; a nasty nameless stew; slop [origin unknown; perhaps a vaguely echoic denigrating coinage related to *slum¹*]

slump 1 *n* by 1888 A sudden decline or collapse, esp of economic value or activity: *The stock market is in a dangerous slump* **2** *n* baseball by 1895 A period of bad performance: *The whole team's in a hitting slump*

slurb *n* by 1962 A suburb of cheap mass-produced houses, ugly business places, etc: *The towns all merged in one faceless, undifferentiated slurb*—George Warren [probably a blend of *slum* and *suburb*]

slurp or **slup 1** *v* by 1648 To eat or drink with greed: . . . *slurping porridge from a wooden spoon*—Ogden Nash/ *The cat slupped up the milk in no time*—Christian Science Monitor **2** *n* by 1949: *Take a slurp of this soup, it's great!* **3** *n* musicians by 1940s A glissando passage [echoic]

slush *n* by 1916 Blatant sentimentality; =GOO, SCHMALTZ: *He sort of wept and uttered a lot of slush*

slush fund *n phr* by 1839 In politics, money used for shady enterprises like buying votes, bribing officials, etc: . . . *the use of slush funds to defeat selected victims*—Westbrook Pegler [fr the armed forces and especially nautical practice of selling grease and other garbage to accumulate a *fund* to buy little luxuries for the troops or crew]

slush pump *n phr* jazz musicians by 1937 A trombone; =SLIP-HORN

slut's wool *n phr* by 1864 The tufts and whorls of dust that accumulate under beds, tables, etc; =BEGGAR'S VELVET, GHOST TURDS, HOUSE MOSS

smack¹ 1 *n* by 1746 A blow; a slap: *He gave her a smack on the kisser* **2** *v* by 1835: *She smacked him hard* **3** *v* by 1570 To kiss, esp noisily: *She smacked him square on the lips* **4** *n* by 1604 A kiss; =SMACKER **5** *n* by 1889 A try; =CRACK: *Let's have a smack at it, shall we?* **6** *adv* (also **smack dab**) by 1892 Exactly; precisely: *What he said was smack on the mark/ . . . Rosenthal was seated smack-dab next to the Prez in a relatively cozy dinner. . .* —Milwaukee Journal **7** *n* sports by 1990s: *Rome. . . throughout the 45-minute interview, kept mentioning "smack," which isn't heroin, but a synonym for trash-talking*—Milwaukee Journal [probably ultimately echoic]

smack² or **shmack** or **shmeck** *n* narcotics by 1942 Heroin; =HORSE, SHIT: *The cocaine pulled from the front while the smack pushed from the*

back. It was an incredibly intense high—High
Times [fr Yiddish *shmek*, "a smell, sniff"; an earlier
sense was "a small packet of drugs," hence merely a
sniff or whiff]

smack³ *n* 1980s teenagers: Smart people who are
only interested in school are called "nerds" or
"smacks"—New York Times

smacker 1 *n* (also **smackeroo**) entry form by
1921, variant by 1940s A dollar; =BUCK: . . . having
to cough up a thousand smackers—Lowell
Thomas/ That car's not worth a single smackeroo
2 *n* by 1775 A kiss; =SMACK: Slip me a smacker,
sister—Jimmy Durante [the money sense, attested
also of pesos and pounds sterling, may echo the slapping down of a bill on a counter, gambling table, etc,
and hence be semantically related to *plank* and
plunk for coins]

smacky lips *See* PLAY KISSIE

smadge *n* Army by 1970s A sergeant major [fr *smaj*,
abbr for *sergeant major*]

small change *n phr* by 1902 Something of little
value: So I am now small change in Mamie's
scorn—Wallace Irwin **2** *modifier*: This is small-
change stuff—movie The Blue Brothers [fr coins of
small value]

small fry by 1866 **1** *n phr* Children or a child
•Often used as a term of address, either affectionate or
derogatory **2** *n phr* An insignificant person or persons; nonentities: . . . conveniences not enjoyed by
the small fry overhead—Theodore Dreiser **3** *adj*:
small-fry writers like me—Budd Schulberg [fr *fry*,
"small or immature fish"]

small potatoes by 1840 **1** *n phr* A trivial amount
of money; =CHICKEN FEED, PEANUTS: I received
$120,000, which is no small potatoes—Danny
Thomas **2** *n phr* An insignificant person, enterprise, etc: From the tuber is derived the term "small
potatoes," applied with more or less humor to anything mean or petty—Encyclopedia Britannica

the **small** (or **fine**) **print** *n phr* entry form by
1944, variant by 1960 Unsuspected and possibly
injurious conditions or requirements, esp when part
of a contract, an insurance policy, etc: Be sure you
look at the small print if you make any deals with
that guy/ Does the mayor read the fine print?—
Philadelphia

small talk *n phr* by 1751 Talk, esp relaxed and idle
conversation; phatic communion; =CHIN MUSIC,
CHITCHAT: He's very serious and has a hard time
making small talk

the **small time** *n phr* show business by 1910
Mediocre or inferior businesses, enterprises, enter-
tainment or sports circuits, etc; =the BUSH LEAGUES:
After six years in the small time she finally went to
Broadway

small-time *adj* show business by 1910 Characteristic
of the small time; inferior; petty; second-rate; =BUSH
LEAGUE: . . . a small-time political power—E Lavine

smarm *n* by 1937 The quality of something
"smarmy": How to write pet stories, then, while
skirting the swamps of smarm?—New York Times

smarmy by 1924 **1** *adj* Smooth and flattering; unc-
tuously ingratiating; fulsome: . . . a rather smarmy
doctor and a highly officious nurse—Time **2** *adj*
Rich and sonorous; orotund and fruity; =PLUMMY: an
announcer with a smarmy voice **3** *adj* Smug and
self-righteous: Uncle Sam's Smarmy Look Into
Employee Sex Lives—Nashville [origin unknown;
since the earliest attested uses have to do with hair
oil, it may be a vague blend of *smooth, smear, palm
oil, cream,* etc]

smart 1 *adj* by 1718 Fashionable; stylish; modish
2 *adj* armed forces fr Vietnam War Guided toward
a target by laser beams, television signals, etc, rather
than simply aimed: The subs are equipped with
smart torpedoes—New York Times/ . . . the potential accuracy of "smart" bombs and missiles—
Foreign Affairs [the first sense was revived in the
1880s and much reprehended]
See GET WISE, STREET-SMART

smart aleck 1 *n phr* by 1865 =SMART-ASS
2 *modifier*: I asked you to come here to give us
advice. . . not smart-aleck talk—Hugh Pentecost
[perhaps fr *Aleck* Hoag, a thief whose fate was
described in an 1844 book by George Wilkes]

smart (or **one smart**) **apple** *n phr* by 1940s
An intelligent person; sagacious person: I told you.
You're up against a smart apple—Lawrence
Sanders

◁**smart-ass** or **wise-ass**▷ **1** *n* by 1960 A person
who is quick to offer an often abrasive opinion or
comment from a posture of superior intelligence and
learning; =BIG-MOUTH, KNOW-IT-ALL, WISE GUY: You're
a real wiseass sometimes, Mary Anne—Pat Conroy
2 *adj*: That's a smart-ass question—Newsweek

smart bomb 1 *n phr* by 1972 An aerial bomb that
can be guided directly to its target **2** *n phr* Any similarly precise and directed agent: Researchers exper-
imenting with mice have created a cancer "smart
bomb" that attacks and kills leukemia cells without
harming normal cells—Newark Star-Ledger

smart card *n phr* by 1980 An identity card that
provides extensive information on a person by means
of a tiny microchip

smart cookie *n phr* by 1948 An intelligent person;
sagacious judge: Joanna was a very smart cookie,
and she was apt to put two and two together. . . —
Ed McBain

smart drug *n phr* by 1980s: Americans have
taken to smart drugs to prepare for tests, prime
themselves for business meetings or just burn a little brighter at parties—Time

smart guy *n* by 1940s =SMART-ASS: Well, I've got
news for you, smart guy—Joseph Heller

the **smart money** *n phr* by 1926 The predictions,
expectations, and bets of those who know best: Try
to stick where the smart money is

smartmouth *n* by 1968 An annoyingly impudent,
assertive, and critical person; =SMART-ASS: . . . keeps
getting beaten up because he's a smartmouth at
school—Philadelphia

smarts *n by 1970* Intelligence; =BRAINS, SAVVY: *If they had any smarts, they would have put a silencer on a gun and pumped a bullet in his head*—Playboy [probably on analogy with *brains* and *wits*]
***See* STREET SMARTS**

smarty or **smartie** *n by 1861* A smart aleck; =SMART-ASS, WISE-ASS •Most often used in address: *I will bid seven on hearts, smarty*—Sinclair Lewis

smarty-pants *n by 1930s* A smart aleck; =SMART-ASS, SMARTY: *That smarty-pants always gives a flip answer*

smash 1 *n by 1839* A total failure; a disaster, esp a financial collapse **2** *n* (also **smash hit**) *show business by 1923* A great success; =HIT: *Key Largo is an unqualified smash*—Variety **3** *n* black *by 1959* Wine

smash and grab *by 1927* **1** *n phr* A crude and violent robbery: *The smash and grab guys break through your closed window and grab your valuables, knowing that you're going to be stunned and perhaps blinded by bits of flying glass*—Harper's **2** *modifier* (also **crash and dash**) Similar to a "smash and grab" robbery in crudeness and violence: *There's a major difference between the smash-and-grab tactics of the tabloids and the relatively sober treatment these stories get on the networks*—Time/ *Deregulation promoted the casino economy, with its leveraged buyouts and smash-and-grab finance*—New Yorker/ *The attempted burglary was like scores of other "crash-and-dash" thefts*—Milwaukee Journal

smashed *adj by 1962* Drunk: *I'm really able to go into a bar without getting smashed*—Stan Cutler

smasher or **smasheroo** *n entry form by 1800, variant by 1940s* Something remarkably impressive and successful: *I thought the book was a smasher*—A J Liebling/ *... sequel to 1994's surprise smasheroo*—Milwaukee Journal Sentinel
***See* BAGGAGE SMASHER**

smashing *adj by 1911* Excellent; wonderful •Still chiefly British: *I told her she had a smashing figure*

smash-mouth football *n phr by 1990s* A particularly violent sort of football: *The Chiefs... who play smash-mouth football as well as anyone, were beaten at their own game*—Milwaukee Journal

smear[1] **1** *v prizefighting by about 1920* To knock unconscious; =KAYO **2** *v by 1900* To defeat decisively; trounce; =CLOBBER, SKUNK: *The Rangers got smeared 12–zip* **3** *v by 1847* To attack someone's reputation, esp with false or vague charges of the ad hominem sort; defame: *His technique was always to smear his opponent and avoid talking about issues of substance* **4** *n by 1943*: *His whole campaign was a vile smear of the other party's man* •The current term is "negative campaigning" **5** *modifier*: *They never stoop to smear tactics* [revived in the 1930s in the political context]

smear[2] *v by 1950s* =SCHMEAR[1]

smell 1 *v by 1933* To be nasty and contemptible; =STINK, SUCK: *The whole damn situation smells*

2 *v by 1949* To take narcotics by inhaling; =SNIFF: *You must be smelling the stuff*—John Roeburt

smell a rat *v phr by 1550* To be suspicious: *... impossible for Schwartz not to have smelled a rat if he had day-to-day contact*—Village Voice

smell blood *v phr by 1970s* To be aroused and exhilarated by the imminent destruction of one's prey or opponent: *The Democrats "smelled blood" over the trade issue*—New York Times [fr the behavior of predators who attack prey, esp wounded prey]

smeller *n by 1700* The nose: *... a sock on his smeller*—Charles MacArthur

smelling *See* GOAT-SMELLING

smell like a rose *See* COME UP SMELLING LIKE A ROSE

smell something **out** *v phr by 1538* To look for something as if by smelling: *... I figure I can't do any worse than the others by coming out here in the street and trying to smell it out*—Hugh Pentecost

smidgen or **smidge** or **smitch** *n by 1886* A little bit; =CUNT-HAIR, SKOSH: *The deck may be stacked a smidgen against Lianna's husband*—Playboy/ *... I was a smidge stressed as a result of a call from Mother...*—Stan Cutler [origin unknown; possibly fr Scots Gaelic *smidin*, "small syllable, hence tiny quantity"; found by 1845 as *smitchin* and by 1878 as *smidgeon*]

smile *See* CRACK A SMILE

smiley *See* EMOTICON

smiley face or **smiley** *n phr computer by 1990s* A computer "emoticon," (:—), used to express happiness or approval: *... messages studded with smiley faces...*—New Yorker

-smith *combining word by 1813* A person who makes or skillfully uses what is indicated; =ARTIST: *jokesmith/ tunesmith/ wordsmith/ wafflesmith*

smoke 1 *n by 1882* A cigarette or cigar: *I mooched a couple of smokes* **2** *n* narcotics *by 1940s* Marijuana; =POT: *... something called smoke or snow*—Carson McCullers **3** *n* hoboes *by 1904* Inferior liquor, esp denatured alcohol: *... drink that smoke, then pass out petrified*—Harper's **4** *n* (also **smoke and mirrors**) *by 1565* Artful lies; talk meant to deceive; =BULLSHIT: *Those sections of the article are pure smoke*—New York Times ◀**5**▶ *n by 1913* A black person **6** *v* underworld & police *by 1926* To shoot someone dead; =PLUG: *This wasn't a Jamaican whore got smoked in some vacant lot...*—Robert B Parker **7** *v* underworld and police *by 1970s* To be executed in a gas chamber: *... still faced death and might one day be smoked*—Joseph Wambaugh **8** *n* baseball *by 1912* A very fast fastball: *Has Joe lost his smoke?*—Newsweek/ *... the Yankees' smoke-throwing reliever*—Aquarian **9** *v*: *... pitchers are supposed to be cranked up and smoking*—Sports Illustrated **10** *v by 1548* To be very angry; =BURN, STEAM: *He was smoking for about an hour after she called him that* **11** *v* (also **smoke off**) *by 1980s* To defeat utterly; trounce; =CLOBBER: *He didn't simply beat*

Carl Lewis. He smoked him—Milwaukee Journal/ *The dreaded Bostons came to town, and the Brewers smoked 'em on opening day*—Milwaukee Journal/ *For a time...... we "smoked off" our rivals*—Biker **12** *n by 1980s* A very fast runner, vehicle, etc: *He's no smoke as for speed*—Milwaukee Journal **13** *v by 1980s* To hit very hard; =CLOBBER: *"Just let me take my jacket off," and bang, the guy from Chicago smokes him...*—Milwaukee Journal/ *... Alomar smoked a single to left...*—Milwaukee Journal

See BLOW SMOKE, BRING SCUNNION, GO UP IN SMOKE, HOLY CATS, J, JOY SMOKE

a **smoke** *n by 1882* Tobacco and a smoking of tobacco

the **smoke** *n phr narcotics by 1884* Opium: *He went for the smoke himself*—Stephen Longstreet

smoked out *adj phr narcotics by 1990s* Intoxicated by narcotics; =HIGH, STONED

smoke-eater *n by about 1930* A firefighter

smoke factory *n phr narcotics by 1905* An opium den: *... a No 9 pill in Hop Lee's smoke factory*—H McHugh

smoke out *v phr by 1720* To find out: *I'll try to smoke out where the bodies are hidden* [fr the use of *smoke* in order to get bees and other animals *out* of their domiciles]

smoker 1 *n* Something thrown, moving, played, etc, very fast: *... a number which is a quartet smoker*—Down Beat **2** *n* (also **smokeball**) *entry form by 1912, variant by 1940s* A very fast fastball

smoke (or **chiba**) **shop** *n phr 1960s narcotics* A place where one may buy marijuana, esp a shop where it is sold rather openly: *Smoke shops are taking over our streets*—New York Times/ *Thousands of clerks operate more than 800 smoke shops around the city*—New York Magazine

Smokey Bear or **Smokey the Bear** or **Smoky** *n phr* or *n 1970s citizens band & truckers* A police officer, esp a state highway patrol officer: *Keep Don advised for the location of "Smokies"*—Rolling Stone [fr the fact that many state highway patrol police wear a broad-brimmed ranger's hat like that worn by the US Forest Service's ursine symbol]

smokin' *adj by 1980s* Attractive; good-looking; desirable; =COOL, HOT: *What's smokin' in collectibles? Tobacco jars!*—Newark Star-Ledger/ *That is a smokin' car*—Delcastle Dictionary of Slang [a synonym of *hot*]

smoking *adj by 1980s* Providing evidence of crime or guilt: *smoking bed/ smoking bimbo/ smoking checkbook* [modeled on *smoking gun*]

smoking gun *n phr by early 1970s* Incontestable evidence; =the GOODS: *They had discovered the "smoking gun" that would destroy the general's case*—New York Times/ *In fact, there may be no "smoking gun," no incontrovertible, black-and-white evidence of wrongdoing*—Time [fr the image of a murderer caught with the fatal *smoking* firearm still in hand]

◀**smoky**▶ *adj by 1940s Black*; Negroid: *The spades*

are moving in and it's getting smokier every day—Nelson Algren

Smoky *See* OLD SMOKY

smoky seat *n phr by 1940s* The electric chair; =OLD SMOKY

smooch or **smooge** or **smouge 1** *v by 1941* To steal; pilfer; =MOOCH: *Then she went over to the cash box and smooched four $20 bills*—James M Cain **2** *v by 1588* To kiss and caress; =NECK, PET: *College kids are still smooching*—Max Shulman/ *... a few minutes of torrid hugging and smooching*—Calder Willingham **3** *n*: *I'd rather have hooch, and a bit of a smooch*—Hal Boyle [the pilfering sense probably derives from the kissing sense by way of *mooch*; the kissing sense may be fr German *schmutzen*, "to kiss, to smile"; the dated instance is spelled *smouch*; the term was reestablished as *smooch* in the 1930s]

smoosh or **smush** *v by 1914* To mash: *The one piece of Spandex flattens the curves as it squashes the bulges, so that your top and bottom weight get smooshed together evenly...*—comic strip "Cathy"

smooth *adj students by 1893* Excellent; pleasing; attractive: *Boy, she was smooth*—Jerome Weidman *See* JUMP SMOOTH

smoothie or **smooth article** or **smooth operator** *n* or *n phr students by 1933* A person who is attractive, pleasant, and full of finesse: *... thought of Dr Hugo Barker as a smooth article*—A R Hilliard/ *You think you're such a smoothie*—Sinclair Lewis [*smoothie* is like *slicker*, but today lacks the connotations of dishonesty and trickiness]

smurf *by 1980s* **1** *n*: *... and the husband and wife were "smurfs," a type of drug-money launderer. A husband-and-wife smurfing team will travel from bank to bank, posing as strangers...*—New Yorker **2** *v*: *To avoid being reported by banks, criminals often make numerous deposits of slightly less than $10,000, a practice known as smurfing*—New York Times

snaffle *v by 1725* To steal; appropriate; =SWIPE: *A streetwalker would have snaffled the lot*—Lawrence Sanders

snafu (SNA Foo) *WWII armed forces* **1** *n* A very confused situation; =FUCK-UP, MESS: *The snafu occurred at Markwood Road*—New York Daily News **2** *adj*: *It's a very snafu set-up here* **3** *n* A blunder; an egregious mistake; =BLOOPER: *My attempt to set things right was a total snafu* **4** *v*: *He gave it a good shot, but snafued horribly* [fr situation normal, all fucked up]

snail mail *n phr early 1980s computer* Mail sent through regular postal service: *Acrobat has the potential to pay for itself rather quickly by eliminating the need to send documents by courier or even regular mail (snail mail, as it is charmingly called by computer aficionados)*—New York Times [referring to the slowness of the *snail*]

snake 1 *n WWI Navy* A young woman **2** *n* (also **Snake**) *by 1934* A native or resident of West Virginia **3** *v by 1848* To depart, esp unobtrusively; sneak:

He snakes out of here without an overcoat—Leslie Ford **4** *n* by 1980s: . . . *US banks, railways, airlines . . and some fast-food restaurants have switched over almost entirely to what is known as the "snake," where all stations are served by one single-file line*—Milwaukee Journal

snake-bitten or **snake-bit** *adj* by 1940s Helplessly incapacitated; ineffective: *O'Neal seems particularly snake-bitten these days*—Playboy/ *I suppose when you're snakebit you feel lousy. And I sure feel lousy*—Milwaukee Journal

snake (or **tree**) **eater** *n phr* Army by 1970s A special forces soldier trained in survival and commando tactics, the initiates of which actually kill and eat snakes; =TREE EATER

snake eyes *n phr* crapshooting by 1929 The point or the roll of two

snakehead *n* by 1990s Agents who arrange illegal immigration of Chinese: *Sung and the elders in the family raised thousands of dollars to pay the snakeheads to smuggle the young to America*—New York Times

snake-hips or **swivel-hips** *n* by 1932 A person whose hips move smoothly and effectively, such as a clever runner in football, a hula dancer, etc

snake oil by 1927 **1** *n phr* A fraudulent remedy: *But I have to admit he sounded sincere, like he really believes in that snake oil he's peddling*—Lawrence Sanders **2** *modifier*: *Kenosha officials watch out for the "snake-oil salesmen"*—Milwaukee Journal

snake poison *n phr* by 1889 Whiskey

snap 1 *n* by 1865 Energy; vim; dash; =PIZZAZZ **2** *n* by 1894 A photograph; snapshot **3** *v*: *The photographer snapped him making a rude gesture* **4** *n* by 1990s An insult, esp a public taunt: . . . *in the relative privacy of the dugout, the quick-tempered wreak havoc with what some teams call "snaps"*—Milwaukee Journal **5** *v* black by 1960s To mock or tease; =SNAP ON someone **6** *v* by 1970s To go crazy; =FREAK OUT: . . . *that Richard Herrin should have snapped*—Ms [the fourth sense is found by 1648, but the current street and sports use is probably not a survival; the last sense is fr the cliché "something *snapped* in his mind"]

a **snap** *n phr* by 1845 Something easily done; =BREEZE, CINCH: *Winning next time will be a snap* [fr mid–1800s *a soft snap*, "something *snapped* up easily, a bargain"]

snap course *n phr* students by 1900 An easy course; =CRIP: *His heavily attended snap course is good for a laugh*—Atlantic Monthly

snap someone's **head off** *v phr* by 1886 To make a quick, angry retort: *When I suggested that, she snapped my head off*

snap it up *v phr* by 1940s To hurry; act faster; =SNAP TO IT: *Drop over to the main drag and snap it up*—Raymond Chandler

snap on someone *v phr* by 1990s To insult, esp publicly and in a sort of competitive way: *After Ivey spent five minutes on stage snapping on a white*

man in the audience, they conducted snapping sessions to get contributions from professionals*—New York Times [the general sense is found by 1578, but the current use is probably not a survival]

snap out of it *v phr* by 1928 To recover, esp from gloom or sluggardy; become energetic

snapper *n* by 1857 The point or risible climax of a story or joke; =PUNCH LINE, ZINGER: *With Neil Simon's vaudeville snappers what matters is that they come on schedule*—Pauline Kael/ *The final snapper was that Lubben never got his income tax paid by his ex-partners, either*—Fargo Forum [fr *snapper*, "a cracker on the end of a whip," found by 1817]

See BRONCO BUSTER

snapping or **snaps** *n* 1990s teenagers: *Ragging, bagging, snapping, and cracking, these are all word games teens use as a way of competing with one another*—NEA Today/ *Many blacks regard "snapping," a back-and-forth, can-you-top-this insult contest, as part of their cultural heritage*—People Weekly/ *I used to think this game was called "playing the dozens," but I recently learned that the '90s term for these insults is "snaps"*—Mesa Tribune

snappy 1 *adj* by 1831 Quick; brisk; energetic: *Be snappy about it* **2** *adj* by 1881 Trim and attractive; fashionable; smart: . . . *wearing a snappy light gray suit*—Associated Press

See MAKE IT SNAPPY

snap to *v phr* by 1940s To become sharply attentive and responsive: *His soldiers snapped to and did what they were told*—New York Times [fr the quick way a military person *snaps to attention* on command]

snap to (or **into**) **it** *v phr* by 1967 To hurry; go faster; =MAKE IT SNAPPY: *Get that floor clean and snap to it*

snarf *v* early 1980s computer To take or grab: *How to Keep Bandits From "Snarfing" Your Passwords*—New York Times

snarf up (or **down**) *v phr* by 1968 To eat; gobble; =SCARF: *We can think of a lot of places we would like to eat chocolate, snarf down a few burgers, and gawk at shiny cars*—Milwaukee Journal [in early 1980s computer slang, defined in the *Hacker's Dictionary* as "to snarf, sometimes with the connotation of absorbing, processing, or understanding"]

snarky *adj* by 1906 Irritable; touchy: *She's just in a snarky mood, that's all*—Noel B Gerson/ . . . *a snarky, no-illusions, but far-from-hopeless comedy*—Ms [fr British dialect *snark*, "to find fault, complain," fr the basic sense "snort, snore"; of echoic origin, with cognates in many Germanic languages]

snatch 1 *v* by 1932 To kidnap: *The kid was snatched as he left school* **2** *n*: . . . *a $50,000 ransom to get him back from a snatch*—Westbrook Pegler **3** *v* by 1765 To steal **4** *n*: *A piece of paper covering the slit was rolled aside in the course of a snatch*—Forum ◁**5**▷ *n* by 1903 The vulva; =CUNT:

Put the goddamned piece up her snatch and pulled the trigger—Robert B Parker

See PUT THE SNATCH ON someone or something

snatcher *n* by 1932 A kidnapper

See CRADLE-ROBBER

snazz *n* by 1930s Elegance; smartness; =CLASS: *. . . parading his tricks with skill and snazz*—Time

snazz something **up** *v phr* by 1970s To make something smarter and more elegant; enhance; =GUSSY UP: *. . . and snazzes them up with appliqués*—Philadelphia/ *Install a new loo, or snazz up your current water closet*—Philadelphia

snazzy 1 *adj* by 1932 Elegant; smart and fashionable; clever and desirable; =NIFTY, RITZY: *mounted on snazzy mag-type wheels*—New Yorker/ *While they may appear snazzy now. . . time will take its toll*—Sports Afield **2** *adj* by 1970s Gaudy and meretricious; =HOKEY, JAZZY: *TV's wittiest, toughest, least snazzy news strip*—Time [perhaps a blend of *snappy* and *jazzy*]

sneak 1 *v* movie studio by 1960s To show a movie unexpectedly to an audience in order to assess its appeal: *We sneaked it in several cities*—Psychology Today **2** *n* (also **sneak preview**): *After a sneak in Chicago they decided to shelve it*

sneakers or **sneaks** *n* by 1895 Rubber-soled sports shoes: *. . . wearing a sweater, a shirt, short socks, and sneakers*—E B White/ *Anybody see my old sneaks?* [because one can usually move noiselessly in such footwear]

sneaky *adj* by 1833 Furtive; shifty; deceptive: *I never trusted that sneaky little weasel*

sneaky pete (or **Pete**) **1** *n phr* by 1940s Inferior liquor, often homemade or bootleg; =PANTHER PISS: *. . . discussing the effects of "sneaky-pete"*—Collier's/ *. . . piled into the Ritz bar and polished off a whole row of "sneaky pete"*—Life **2** *n phr* by 1940s A cheap fortified wine sold in pint bottles called "jugs": *. . . full of that cheap wine they call "sneaky pete"*—A Lomax **3** *n phr* by 1940s Any cheap and inferior wine **4** *n phr* by 1950s Marijuana mixed in wine

snerting *n* by 1990s Sexual harassment by men: *. . . instituted strict rules against men hounding women (aka "snerting"). . .*—Elle

snide *adj* by 1859 Contemptible; mean; nasty, esp in an insinuating way ●Now used nearly exclusively in reference to remarks and persons who make them: *A woman gets nothing but snide remarks about her driving skills*—Associated Press [origin unknown]

sniff *v* 1920s narcotics To inhale a narcotic powder; =SNORT

sniffer or **snifter** *n* 1920s narcotics A cocaine user or addict: *The Baron was "a sniffer" himself*—American Mercury

sniff out *v phr* by 1940s To seek as if by following a scent: *Mike hopes his kids may sniff out something faster than the police*—Hugh Pentecost

sniffy or **snifty** *adj* by 1871 Disdainful; haughtily fastidious; fault-finding: *. . . even the sniffiest of lexicographers*—H L Mencken [fr the mien of a person who often seems to be smelling something nasty]

snifter 1 *n* by 1844 A drink of liquor; dram; =SLUG, SNORT: *. . . plastered on a couple of snifters*—New Yorker **2** *n* by 1937 A large, bulbous, stemmed glass used for drinking brandy [origin uncertain; perhaps fr the common upper-respiratory reaction to taking a strong swallow of liquor, also noted in the earlier term *sneezer* and in *snorter*; *snifter, sneezer* and *snorter* were all three used to mean "a strong breeze, gale," and all three came to mean "something large and impressive, something very strong," apparently after the drinking senses were established; before the drinking senses, the terms applied to snuff-taking, with its even more pronounced nasal spasms]

snipe 1 *n* by 1889 A cigarette or cigar butt **2** *n* Navy by about 1920 An engine-room hand, aircraft mechanic, or other below-decks crew member: *"Snipes". . . service and maintain their flying crews' birds*—New York Times [origin obscure, although apparently these, along with several other slang uses, both British and US, all refer somehow to the long-billed bird and its habits]

sniptious *adj* by 1829 Neat; elegant; spruce

snit or **snit-fit** *n* A fit of angry agitation; =SWIVET: *He goes into such a snit that he ploughs the car into a wall*—Saturday Review/ *He has a reputation for throwing considerable snits*—Car and Driver/ *And we forget about our little snit-fit in there. . .*—Carsten Stroud

snitch 1 *n* by 1785 An informer; =RAT, STOOL PIGEON: *Maybe some of my old snitches have run across something new*—Rex Burns **2** *v* by 1801 To inform; =SING, SQUEAL: *The little rat snitched and the little snitch ratted* **3** *v* by 1904 To steal; pilfer; =SWIPE: *He snitched a couple of cookies* [first senses probably fr underworld slang *snitch*, "nose"]

snitzy *adj* by 1934 Elegant; =POSH, RITZY: *. . . who becomes a cabana boy at a snitzy beach club*—Rolling Stone [perhaps a blend of *snooty* or *snazzy* and *ritzy*]

snog *v* by 1945 To flirt; court; make love; =MAKE OUT, NECK ●Chiefly British [origin unknown]

snooker (SNŏŏ kər, SNōō-) *v* fr early 1900s To cheat; swindle; =SCAM: *The Chinese clearly believe that they snookered Nixon*—National Review/ *I've been snookered before, and it'll happen again*—Book World/ *The simple arithmetic shows that Koch and the city were snookered*—Village Voice [fr the pool game called *snooker*, apparently because a novice at the game can easily be tricked and cheated by an expert; compare *euchre*]

snookums *n* by 1919 Precious one; sweet and dear one ●Used to address small dogs, babies, etc: *Yes, you are. You're my little snookums*—New Yorker

snoop *n* A detective: *Private snoop, hunh?*—J Evans [ultimately fr Dutch *snoepen*, "pry"]

snoose (SNŌŌS) *n* loggers by 1912 Snuff, esp a strong moist kind [fr Swedish *snus*, "snuff," fr *snustobak*]

snoot 1 *n* by 1861 The nose; snout; =SCHNOZZ: *Pokin' him one in the snoot*—Arthur Kober **2** *v* by

1928 To behave haughtily toward; disdain: . . . *people who snoot goat milk*—R Starnes

a **snoot full** or **snootful 1** *n phr by 1918* One's intoxicating fill of liquor; =a SKINFUL: *I met a lot of other reporters and I got a snoot full*—Jim Tully/ *You've had a snoot full*—Robert Ready **2** *n phr by 1940s* More than enough of something; one's fill: *By that time I'd had a snootful of good advice*

snooty *adj by 1919* Snobbish; haughty and disdainful; supercilious; =HOITY-TOITY, SNIFFY: . . . *the snootiest madame in America*—H Asbury/ . . . *a generally vain and snooty class of men*—H L Mencken [fr the mien of a person who smells something nasty and holds the nose high]

snooze 1 *v by 1789* To sleep; =COP ZS, SACK OUT **2** *n*: . . . *not comfortable enough to suit me for a snooze*—Jack London **3** *n by 1960s* Something that induces sleep; a soporific event, person, etc: *The concert was a snooze*—William Goldman [origin unknown; perhaps echoic of a snore]

snop *n 1960s narcotics* Marijuana [origin unknown]

snork *v by 1990s* To drink: *So we sat around snorking beers* [probably a variant of *snort*; found as such by 1807 in British dialect]

snort 1 *n by 1889* A drink of liquor, esp of plain whiskey; =HOOKER: *Who's ready for another short snort?*—K Brush/ *All hands had another snort*—H Allen Smith **2** *v narcotics by 1935* To inhale narcotics, esp cocaine; =SNIFF: . . . *since ma was a viper, and daddy would snort*—H Braddy **3** *n narcotics by 1951* A dose of narcotic for inhaling; =LINE [drinking sense fr earlier *snorter* of same purport]

See SNIFTER

snorter *See* RINGTAILED SNORTER, RIPSNORTER

◁**snot**▷ **1** *n by 1425* Nasal mucus **2** *n by 1809* A despicable person, esp a self-important nonentity: *Tell that little snot to get lost* **3** *v by 1970s* To treat someone disdainfully; be haughty: *I should not be "snotted" by an owner, maitre d', or waiter*—Time [ultimately fr a common Germanic term for "nose," also represented by *schnozzle, snout, snoot,* etc; the last two senses probably influenced by *snooty*]

◁**snotnose** or **snottynose**▷ **1** *n by 1941* An importunate upstart; a neophyte, esp a knowing one: . . . *some snot-nose in New York*—Washington Post **2** *modifier*: *He's just a snotnose kid*

◁**snot-rag**▷ *n by 1895* A handkerchief or tissue

◁**snotty**▷ *adj by 1926* Supercilious and disdainful: *I won't give that snotty bastard the time of day* [fr *snot* and influenced by *snooty*]

snow 1 *n narcotics by 1914* Cocaine: *And he was also snorting snow* **2** *v by 1945* To persuade in a dubious cause, esp by exaggeration, appeals to common sentiment, etc; =BLOW SMOKE: *The electorate will not be snowed into supporting that silly measure* **3** *n*: *I thought his rationale was pure snow* [second sense fr the idea of snowing someone *under* with articulate reasons]

See EYES LIKE PISS-HOLES IN THE SNOW

snowball 1 *v by 1929* To increase rapidly: *Soon the racket began to snowball*—Time **2** *v by 1850*

To dominate and crush; =STEAMROLLER: *He's less sensitive to people's feelings. He runs over them, snowballs them*—Time [first sense fr the fact that a snowball rolled downhill becomes larger and larger; second sense fr the notion of attacking someone with snowballs]

a **snowball's chance in hell** *n phr by 1934* No possibility whatever; =CHINAMAN'S CHANCE: *He doesn't have a snowball's chance in hell of getting that degree in time*

snowbird 1 *n hoboes by 1923* A person, esp a migratory worker or a hobo, who goes south in the winter to escape the cold **2** *n by 1980s* A retired person, usu elderly, who winters in the sunny South: *A Connecticut pharmaceutical firm hires elder "snowbirds" during the warmer months and holds their jobs open while they winter in Florida*—ISEA Retirees **3** *n* (also **snowblower**) *narcotics by 1914* A cocaine user or addict; =COKEHEAD: *Nelly's eyes had a glassy, faraway look. Snowbird, he thought to himself*—William Weeks **4** *n narcotics by 1931* Any narcotic addict

snow (or **ski**) **bunny** *n phr by 1953* A young woman who frequents skiing resorts

snowed in (or **up**) *adj phr 1920s narcotics* Intoxicated with narcotics; =HIGH

snow job 1 *n phr WWII armed forces* Strong and persistent persuasion, esp in a dubious cause; an overwhelming advocacy: *This is no snow job, either. I wish I had 25 Jerry Koosmans*—Inside Sports/ *Don't let Slattery give you a snow job and get you into trouble*—movie *Halls of Montezuma* **2** *v*: *I was snow-jobbed into giving the maximum* [fr the idea of *snowing under* with insistent reasons; now probably reinforced by the narcotics sense of *snow*]

snowman *n golf by 1980* : *Watson took a snowman, as golfers call an 8, here on the fifteenth, ruining what otherwise might have been the low round of the day*—New Yorker/ *"Whaddya have?" A snowman (an 8 on the hole)*—Esquire

snow queen *n phr homosexuals by 1971* A black homosexual who prefers white sex partners: *Zane, of course, was white, as were all the men Jones slept with in those years; in the parlance of the subculture, Jones was a "snow queen"*—New Yorker

snow someone or something **under** *v phr by 1880* To burden or assail with excessive demands, work, etc; overwhelm: . . . *until a frailer man than he would have been snowed under*—F Scott Fitzgerald

snozzle *See* SCHNOZZ

snubby or **snubbie** *n by 1970s* A cheap, short-barreled revolver; =SATURDAY NIGHT SPECIAL: . . . *cheap, concealable guns with short barrels called "snubbies"*—Atlantic/ . . . *the short-barreled handguns known as "snubbies"*—New York Times

snuff 1 *v by 1973* To kill: . . . *more chillingly, STRESS snuffed at least 20 civilians*—Ramparts/ *Garlic never snuffed me*—Cyra McFadden **2** *modifier by 1975* Showing or doing murder, esp the killing of women in sadistic shows or orgies:

. . . the snuff murder of an abused and homeless teenaged girl—Penthouse/ *. . . the vogue of the snuff film* [fr the idea of *snuffing* out a flame; found by 1884 in the form *snuff out*]
See UP TO SNUFF

snuff film (or movie) *n phr* by 1975 A movie in which the actual killing of a person is shown •Filmed murder is very likely a lurid idea rather than a fact: *Year Zero has the shock value of a snuff film*—Village Voice/ *If he'd told them he was making a snuff movie he would have been treated better*—New York Review of Books

snuffing *n* by 1970s A killing, esp a murder: *. . . too eager to put together two unconnected snuffings*—Lawrence Sanders

snuffy *adj* by 1823 Drunk

snuggle-bunnies See PLAY SNUGGLE-BUNNIES

snuggle-pup *n* by 1922 A boyfriend or girlfriend

snuggy *n* by 1970s A sexually interesting and interested woman: *It's a snuggy. No, too young, a snugette. Fourteen years old and hot to trot*—Flare

so See SAY-SO

soak 1 *v* by 1896 To hit; =SOCK: *. . . to soak you in the midriff*—J McHugh/ *Why don't you soak him?*—Sinclair Lewis **2** *v* by 1895 To overcharge; make someone pay exorbitantly: *. . . a good case of how soak-the-rich corporation taxes wind up right in the pocketbooks of all of us*—Associated Press **3** *n* by 1820 A drunkard; =LUSH, SOUSE

soaked *adj* by 1722 Drunk [one of Benjamin Franklin's catalog of words for "drunk"]

◁**soak** one's **hose**▷ *v phr* by 1990s To do the sex act; =SCREW: *I think maybe he soaking his hose*—Robert B Parker

soak yourself See GO SOAK YOURSELF

so-and-so *n* A despicable person; =BASTARD, JERK: *I think I'll sue the so-and-so*—Heywood Hale Broun
See SON OF A BITCH

soap 1 *v* by 1853 To flatter and cajole; =SWEET-TALK: *. . . one of those Republicans who soaped Vivien*—Westbrook Pegler **2** *n* by 1854 =SOFT SOAP **3** *n* by 1943 =SOAP OPERA
See NO SOAP

soapbox *n* by 1907 The attitude from which one orates, pontificates, counsels urgently, etc: *Be careful or she'll get on the old soapbox and preach about fiscal iniquity*

soaper or **soper** or **sopor** *n* 1960s narcotics A sedative drug, methaqualone; Quaalude™: *. . . an apparently insatiable market for the "sopers"*—Newsweek [fr *Sopor*, the trademark of a brand of the drug, fr the Latin root for "sleep"]

soap opera by 1939 **1** *n phr* A radio or television daily dramatic series typically showing the painful, passionate, and riveting amours and disasters of more or less ordinary people: *. . . a new soap opera. . . which threatens to out-misery all the others*—John Crosby **2** *modifier*: *The average man and woman in this country live a soap-opera existence*—Robert Ruark **3** *n phr* A life or incidents in life that resemble such shows: *You want to hear the latest in my*

never-ending soap opera? [fr the fact that in radio days such shows were typically sponsored by *soap* manufacturers]

the soaps *n phr* by 1943 Radio or television daily dramatic series collectively

◁**sob** or **SOB**▷ (pronounced as separate letters) *n* by 1918 =SON OF A BITCH

so bad one **can taste it** *adv phr* by 1960s Very urgently; very keenly: *She wanted the book so bad she could taste it* [fr the earlier expression *I have to piss so bad I can taste it*, implying that the urine had risen in one to the level of the throat and tongue]

sober See COLD SOBER, STONE COLD SOBER

sob sister *n phr* by 1912 A woman news reporter or writer who specializes in sentimental or human-interest material

sob story *n phr* by 1913 A very affecting tale, esp an account of one's disabling troubles; a story that disingenuously appeals to one's charitable nature: *. . . do not weep crocodile tears over media sob stories. . .* —Milwaukee Journal

sob stuff *n phr* by 1918 Affecting stories collectively, or the material of which they are made: *Eppingham had prepared to lay on the sob stuff*—William Weeks

sock[1] **1** *v* by 1700 To strike; hit hard; =CLOBBER, PASTE: *. . . bein' socked to dreamland*—H Witwer **2** *n* by 1700: *To land another sock on Mr Renault's nose*—Ben Hecht **3** *n* musicians by about 1920 A set of mounted cymbals sounded by tramping on a foot-pedal; =HIGH-HAT [probably echoic]

sock[2] **1** *n* by 1924 A place where money is kept, esp saved; also, savings collectively: *Every dollar that he will receive for the current four-year term will go into the family sock*—Westbrook Pegler **2** *n* underworld by 1930s A box, bag, safe, etc, where money is kept [fr the use of a *sock* as a container; one reference of 1698 indicates that *sock* meant "pocket" in underworld slang]

sock away *v phr* To save or horde; put away as savings: *Last year that group socked away $128 billion in savings bonds*—Time/ *The American people socked away $3,200,000 in the year's second quarter*—B Garrett [perhaps fr the notion of concealing money in a *sock*; but *sock*, "sew up and conceal," is attested fr the alteration of 1800s *sock* or *sock down*, "pay, dispose of money"]

sockdollager or **socdollager** **1** *n* by 1830 A decisive blow **2** *n* by 1838 A person or thing that is remarkable, wonderful, superior, etc; =HUMDINGER: *. . . his Dauntless Quest to lay his Sockdollager of a Product at the feet of the Public*—Washington Post [fr a metathesis of *doxology*, "the finish or finishing part of a religious service," as suggesting something that terminates, like a heavy blow; influenced by *sock*[1]]

socked in *adj phr* by 1953 Plagued by adverse weather, esp by fog, heavy rain or snow, etc: *You may find yourself partly socked in if you're coming down the Jersey Turnpike this morning*—radio station WCAU [probably fr the adverse weather indications given by the *wind sock* at early or small airports; perhaps influenced by the notion of being closed up in a *sock* as money is when it is *socked away*]

sock 'em *See* ROCK 'EM, SOCK 'EM

socker *See* BOBBY-SOXER

sockeroo 1 *n* by 1942 A great success; something with extraordinary power and impact; esp, a lavish and popular film, show, etc; =BLOCKBUSTER: . . . *an old-fashioned Hippodrome sockeroo*—Time/ . . . *with Paramount's "Dear Ruth" . . . the only sockeroo*—Variety **2** *modifier*: . . . *putting some sockeroo catches in the president's plan*—Drew Pearson

sock hop 1 *n phr* 1950s teenagers An lively and informal party where young people typically dance in their stockinged feet: *I feel like a kid at a sock hop, sneaking in here*—Philadelphia Journal/ . . . *many side forays to the drive-in burger stand, the sock hop, lover's lane*—Village Voice **2** *modifier*: . . . *a kind of sock-hop benefit for Approaching Middle Age*—Time

sock it to someone *v phr* by 1877 To attack someone vigorously and effectively; =LET someone HAVE IT: *Some congressional liberals would like to sock it to business by taking away the tax reductions*—Fortune/ *Thanks for socking it to Barbie, that all-American plastic tart*—Rolling Stone

socko 1 *n* by about 1925 A hard punch **2** *interj* by 1924 An exclamation imitating the impact of a hard blow, and expressing abrupt force: *Socko! . . . he punches the villain in the jaw*—Waverly Root **3** *adj* by 1939 Very powerful; explosively impressive; terrific: *Okay, now a socko surprise*—Xaviera Hollander/ . . . *the socko effect, recorded here by . . . camera*—New York Magazine **4** *adv* by 1948: . . . *find they do socko in their native heath*—Variety

socks *See* BOBBY SOCKS, DROP YOUR COCKS AND GRAB YOUR SOCKS, KNOCK someone's SOCKS OFF

the **socks off** *adv phr* by 1845 Very thoroughly
•Always used, like the semantically similar *the brains out* and *the pants off*, to intensify a verb: . . . *undressed her and screwed the socks off her*—George V Higgins/ . . . *a theoretical homily on the true meaning of Eros that, I am forced to admit, absolutely bored the socks off me*—Washington Post [the earliest recorded form is *knock the socks off*, and the usage has been revived recently]
See BEAT THE SOCKS OFF someone

sod 1 *n* 1818 A male; man; =GUY •Chiefly British, but beginning to invade the US: *Your lodge brother, your neighbor, the guy on the beat who's just a plain good sod*—Scott Turow **2** *v* To curse and vilify; revile extremely; =DAMN, FUCK, PISS ON someone or something: *You do not send the Prime Minister to China to bargain for just an airport. Sod the airport*—New Yorker [fr *sodomite* and *sodomize*]

soda jerk (or **jerker**) *n phr* by 1883 A person who makes ice cream sodas and other treats at a soda fountain: *She worked for a while as a soda jerk*—

Life/ . . . *the champion soda jerker of the United States*—Ernie Pyle [fr earlier *beer jerk,* "tapster," perhaps fr the action of drawing back on the vertical handle that controlled the flow of beer; perhaps also related to *jerkwater*]
See JERK SODA

sod off *v phr* by 1960 To leave; depart; =FUCK OFF
•Often an irritated command: *Well, that's that. If you don't like it, sod off*—New Republic

soft *See* WALK SOFT

◁**soft-ass**▷ *adj* by 1970s Slack and feeble; ineffectual; =WIMPY: . . . *basic economic psychology, not the soft-ass welfarism of Down East*—Toronto Life

softball *adj* by 1970s Trivial and contemptible; nonserious; =PISS-ELEGANT: . . . *a softball question if ever there was one*—New York Magazine/ *This softball performance by Democrats on the Judiciary Committee in the Thomas hearings left many in a huge TV audience wondering what legitimate claim to national power this bumbling crowd could possibly have*—New York Times [based on *hardball*]

soft-core by 1966 **1** *adj* Somewhat less than extreme; moderated; slightly ameliorated: *The fashion magazine is soft-core pornography*/ . . . *a soft-core picture of a bare-chested woman*—radio program *All Things Considered* **2** *n* Something that is not extreme, esp a sexually arousing but not carnally explicit movie, magazine, etc: *She doesn't care for X-rated, but enjoys a little soft-core now and then* [based on *hard-core*]

soft drug *n phr* by 1959 A narcotic like marijuana and some hallucinogens, thought of as nonaddictive and only slightly damaging to health [based on *hard drug*]

soft hands *n phr* baseball by 1980s The particular ability to field ground balls, esp those hit very hard: *He has "soft hands," baseball slang for an uncanny ability to field ground balls*—Washingtonian

softie or **softy** *n* by 1886 A person who is amiably and quickly compliant; someone easy to cajole and victimize: *You are a patsy, a quick push, a big softie*—W R Burnett

soft in the head *adj phr* by 1938 Stupid; dim-witted; =LAMEBRAINED [*soft* is found by 1621 in the sense "silly, simple, foolish"]

soft landing *n phr* by 1980s A slowing of the economy without a crash or recession: *A weakening dollar clearly holds risks for the White House, where prospects of a soft landing after 48 months of economic growth offered some hope*—Time

soft money (or **currency**) **1** *n phr* by about 1940 Currency that is highly inflated or likely to become less and less valuable: *During the first two months of this year, soft money contributions, chiefly from industry, flowed into the coffers of the Republican National Committee at the rate of $123,121 per day*—Harper's **2** *n phr* politics by 1980s Campaign donations that are not regulated by the Federal Election Commission: . . . *raising millions of dollars of what is known in election-financ-*

ing language as "soft money"—Washington Post National Weekly Edition/ Clinton is behind in the collection of soft money, funds that are supposed to go for "party-building activities" but can make a big difference in a Presidential contest—New Yorker **3** *n phr* universities by 1976 Money from research grants, which may run out if the grant is not renewed [modeled on *hard money*]

soft-pedal *v* by 1915 To make less prominent; de-emphasize; =DOWNPLAY: *Even my friends advised me to soft-pedal my criticisms*—New York Daily News [fr the *pedal* on a piano that *softens* the notes played]

soft sell *n phr* by 1955 Selling or advertising in a nonstrident, noninsistent tone [modeled on *hard sell*]

soft soap 1 *n phr* by 1830 Flattery; cajolement; =SWEET-TALK: *I won her over finally with a lot of soft soap* **2** *v* 1840: *We had to soft-soap the electorate pretty shabbily*

soft touch 1 *n phr* by 1939 A person from whom it is easy to borrow or wheedle something: *You get the reputation of being a soft touch*—John O'Hara **2** *n phr* by 1940s =SOFTIE **3** *n phr* by 1955 An easy job; a sinecure: *He spent his life seeking the ultimate soft touch*

SoHo *n* by 1970s The area in New York City that is located south of Houston Street

so hot *See* NOT SO HOT

sol (SAHL) *n* by 1930 Solitary confinement in prison: *He draws sol till he's crazy*—American Mercury

Sol *See* OLD SOL

◁**SOL**▷ (pronounced as separate letters) *adv* WWI *armed forces* Ruined; =KAPUT: *If the press gets ahold of this we're SOL* [fr *shit out of luck*]

sold *adj* by 1876 Cheated; deceived; =SCREWED: *I've tunneled, hydraulicked, and cradled, and I have been frequently sold*—song "Acres of Clam" [one source traces the use to 1597 in Shakespeare]

soldier 1 *n* by 1917 =DEAD SOLDIER **2** *v* nautical by 1840 To avoid work; idle; shirk; =FUCK THE DOG, GOLDBRICK: *He soldiered on the job and the place was deserted*—Carson McCullers **3** *n* underworld by 1963 A low-ranking member of the Mafia; an ordinary thug or gangster *See* FIRST MAN, SUNDAY SOLDIER

soldier on *v phr* by 1954 To persist doggedly: *A little warning bell went off, but I soldiered on*—Sue Grafton

be **sold on** *v phr* by 1928 To be convinced of the value of something or someone; strongly favor or accept: *It took me a half hour to get sold on the job*—James M Cain

solid *adj* jazz musicians by about 1920 Wonderful; remarkable; =GREAT, GROOVY ●Said to have been used regularly by Louis Armstrong: *Man, what solid jive*—Max Shulman/ *That's solid, Willie, let's get together and blow*—Slim Gaillard

solid sender *n phr* jazz musicians by about 1936 An admirable and effective person, esp a swing or jazz musician: *. . . a drag one minute and a solid sender the next*—Louis Armstrong

so long *interj* by 1865 A parting salutation [origin unknown; perhaps fr German *adieu so lange*; perhaps fr Hebrew *shalom* and related Arabic *salaam*, both greetings meaning "peace"; perhaps fr Irish *slan*, "health," used as a toast and a salutation]

some *adj* by 1808 Very good; very effective; real ●Often used ironically: *. . . in three weeks England will have her neck wrung like a chicken. Some neck! Some chicken!*—Winston S Churchill

somebody *n* by 1566 A consequential person: *Leroy was a somebody*—New York Post/ *I could have been a somebody, Charley. I could have been a contender*—movie On the Waterfront

some jeans *See* STRETCH SOME JEANS

some kind of *adj phr* by 1970 Very good; very effective; =SOME: *God, isn't she some kind of a singer?*

some pumpkins *n phr* by 1846 Something or someone very effective, impressive, etc: *He is some pumpkins*—F K Secrist

some skin *See* GIVE SOME SKIN, SKIN

something *n* by 1582 A remarkable person or thing: *Did you see his shirt? It's something!* *See* MAKE SOMETHING OUT OF

something else *n phr* by 1909 =SOMETHING [an intensive of *something*]

something else again *n phr* by 1949 Something quite different; something contrasting; =DIFFERENT ANIMAL: *The question of wages is something else again*

something fierce (or awful) *adv phr* entry form by 1909, variant by 1898 In a harsh and pronounced way; severely: *He cusses her out something fierce*—Sinclair Lewis/ *She came at me something awful*

something on the ball *n phr* by 1912 Talent; skill; ability: *. . . a guy with something on the ball*—Budd Schulberg [fr the curve, speed, etc, that a baseball pitcher puts *on the ball*]

some Zs *See* COP SOME ZS

song *See* RAP SONG, TORCH SONG

song and dance or song *n phr* or *n* by 1895 A prepared account or speech aimed at persuasion, apology, advocacy, wheedling, etc: *A flimsy excuse or transparent lie is called "a song and dance"*—Harper's Weekly/ *Some bum will brace you with a long song of utter inconsequence*—Robert Ruark *See* GO INTO one's DANCE

◁**son of a bitch or sumbitch**▷ (also **son of a b** or **son of a buck** or **son of a gun** or **son of a so-and-so**, all euphemistic) **1** *n phr* or *n* entry form by 1707, variants by 1975; gun by 1786 A despicable person; =BASTARD, SHITHEEL: *I told the son of a bitch what I thought of him* **2** *n phr* or *n* Something very difficult or vexatious, esp a hard task: *Getting that thing fitted was a son of a bitch* **3** *n phr* or *n* A person or thing that is remarkable, wonderful, superior, etc; =BITCH: *Their new album is a son of a bitch, I tell you*/ *. . . a big son of a buck*—movie Thunderheart **4** *interj* An exclamation of anger, annoyance, amazement, disappointment, etc:

Son of a bitch! The thing's busted again! [the *son of a gun* variant was said by Admiral Smythe to have been "originally applied to boys born afloat," at a time when women could accompany men to sea, and when children could be born and cradled under a gun or gun carriage, hence have no proper legitimate parentage]

◁**son-of-a-bitching** or **sumbitching**▷ *adj by 1970s* Wretched; accursed: *I'm going to have a son-of-a-bitching press conference of my own*—Senator Alan Simpson

Sooner 1 *n by 1930* A native or resident of Oklahoma **2** *modifier*: *the Sooner football team* [fr the fact that some settlers entered the public land and staked their claims *sooner* than the legal date and hour in 1889]

SOP or **sop** (pronounced as separate letters) *n WWII armed forces* The way things are properly and usually done: *The SOP here is that you ask the chairman first* [fr *standard operating procedure*]

soper or **sopor** *See* SOAPER

soph (SAHF) *n university by 1778* A sophomore

soppy *adj by 1918* Sentimental; maudlin; =MUSHY, SCHMALTZY: . . . *the soppy story of a rich-boy dropout*—Judith Crist

sore *adj by 1738* Angry; irritated; =PISSED OFF: *I was sore*—Eugene O'Neill

sorehead *n by 1848* An irritable person; a constant complainer; a grouch

soreheaded *adj by 1844* Angry; resentful; irritable

sore thumb *See* STICK OUT

sorrow *See* DROWN one's SORROWS

sorry or ◁**sorry-ass**▷ *adj entry form by 1250, variant by 1970s* Wretched; worthless; inferior; =HALF-ASSED: . . . *this one kid, and he was a sorry shit*—George V Higgins/ *The reputation of the Barclay. . . has been one of sorry-ass service*—Philadelphia/ *One more sorry-ass useless killing*—Carsten Stroud

sorry about that *sentence by 1960s* I am sorry; please forgive me •Most often an ironic understatement, as when one has been responsible for making a big mistake [popularized in the 1960s TV program *Get Smart*]

SOS[1] (pronounced as separate letters) *n WWII armed forces* The usual tedious exaggerations, pieties, wretched food, etc [fr *same old shit*]

SOS[2] (pronounced as separate letters) *n WWII armed forces* Chipped beef on toast or some similar food; =SHIT ON A SHINGLE: *It was commonly referred to in the service as SOS*—Prison [fr *shit on a shingle*]

so-so *adj by 1530* Average; ordinary: *It's a so-so movie*

so's your old man *interj by 1925* An exclamation of contempt and defiance, usu reciprocal: . . . *the most desperate exercise of so's-your-old-man since polemics began*—National Review

soul *jazz musicians by 1946* **1** *n* An instinctive, sensitive, humorous, and sympathetic quality felt by black persons to be inherent and to constitute their essential and valuable attribute: *He's got soul when he dances! I mean Super Soul!*—New York Post **2** *adj*:

. . . *program content on soul radio stations*—Black Week/ *That's what the Soul scene taught everybody*—Albert Goldman **3** *n* (also **soul music**) This quality in music, and music having this quality: *When Aretha Franklin pours forth a thousand cups of soul*—S Leaks **4** *adj*: . . . *a soul ballad*—Playboy/ . . . *a soul-jazz-blues quintet*—Saturday Review

See BLUE-EYED SOUL, BODY AND SOUL, GRIPE one's ASS

soul brother *n phr black by 1957* A male black person; =BLOOD, BROTHER

Soul City or **Soulville** *n phr black by 1959* Harlem

soul food *n phr black by about 1957* Food characteristic of and preferred by black persons, esp of Southern culture

soul kiss 1 *n phr by 1953* An intraoral and interlingual osculation, usu of a steamy sort; =FRENCH KISS **2** *v phr*: *The blissful pair soul-kissed the evening away*

soul sister *n phr black by 1957* A female black person; =SISTER

sound *1950s street gangs* **1** *v* To taunt or provoke; goad; =RAZZ **2** *v* =SIGNIFY

sound bite *n phr by late 1980s* A very brief excerpt of speech or film used esp in political campaigns to make a quick impression: *They present him chiefly in a staccato series of sound bites*

sound off 1 *v phr WWI Army* To talk, esp to complain, loud and long; bluster: *Its leaders have sounded off on various issues*—Philadelphia Bulletin **2** *v phr WWII Army* To boast; brag: *He was sounding off again about what a big shot he is*

soup 1 *n by 1902* Nitroglycerine; =NITRO **2** *n by 1940s* Fuel, esp that used in fast cars, airplanes, etc **3** *v by 1940s* =SOUP UP **4** *n surfers by 1962* The foamy part of a wave: . . . *a big wave with lots of soup, or white water*—Houston Chronicle **5** *n photography by 1929* Developing fluid or bath **6** *v*: *I had the lab soup my test roll normal, and the first frame was perfect*—Photo District News

See DUCK SOUP, IN THE SOUP, JERKWATER, LAUGHING SOUP, PEA SOUP

soup-and-fish *n by 1908* A man's formal evening dress: . . . *getting into the soup-and-fish*—Sinclair Lewis [fr the formality of a dinner that commences with the *soup* and then the *fish* course]

soupbone or **souper** *n baseball by 1930* A pitcher's pitching arm [probably fr the notion that *soup* represents one's sustenance; found by 1910 as "the pitcher"]

souped up *by 1949* **1** *adj phr* Producing a higher power or acceleration than the normal: . . . *a Ford with a souped-up motor*—A Hynd/ . . . *teen-age infatuation. . . with souped-up cars in which speed-crazy kids raced*—Life **2** *adj phr* Increased or heightened in value, attraction, production, etc: . . . *the souped-up Premium Bonds are also designed to this end*—N Ridley [fr *supercharged*, referring to a pump that forces additional air into the cylinders of an engine to increase its power; perhaps reinforced by *soup*, "fuel for a powerful engine," and "material injected into a horse with a view to changing its speed or temperament," the latter attested fr 1911 and earlier]

soup job *n phr* teenagers by 1940s A car that has been altered mechanically for increased power and speed

soup jockey *n phr* by 1940s A waiter or waitress

soup-strainer *n* by 1932 A mustache, esp a luxuriant one

soup up *v phr* by 1931 To increase power and speed above the normal; supercharge: *He souped up the motors*—A Hynd
See SOUPED UP

soupy *adj* by 1953 =SOPPY

sour *See* GO SOUR

sourball or **sourbelly 1** *n* by 1900 =SOREHEAD **2** *modifier*: *Everyone thought it was funny except the sour-balls instructor*—Michael Grant

sourpuss or **sourpan** *n* entry form by 1937, variant by 1942 A morose person; a chronic complainer and moaner; =PICKLEPUSS: . . . *the regular assortment of first-night sourpusses and professional runners down*—Philadelphia Bulletin/ *He'd change into a sour-pan*—American Mercury

souse 1 *n* by 1906 A drunkard; =LUSH: *A wonderful thyroid substance. . . sobered up the souse in 30 minutes*—New York Post **2** *n* by 1903 Drunkenness; intoxication: *Economic and religious saviors give a new kind of emotional souse*—American Mercury [fr an extension of *souse*, "pickle brine, something pickled," hence semantically akin to *soak*, "drunkard," and *pickled*, "drunk"]

soused *adj* (Variation: **to the gills** may be added) by 1613 Drunk [probably fr the image of a pickled herring or other pickled fish]

South *See* a MOUTH FULL OF SOUTH

south of the border *adj phr* by 1970s Failed and ineffective; rejected; =NG ●The phrase is similar to and enacted by the thumbs-down sign: *As performances go, yours was somewhat south of the border* [apparently a blend of the general notion of down as the direction of failure and rejection, with the legendary significance of the Mexican *border* as the demarcation *south* of which a hunted or rejected person may disappear]
See GO SOUTH

southpaw 1 *n* baseball by 1885 A lefthanded player, esp a pitcher; =FORKHANDER: *Southpaw Warren Spahn pitched his 17th victory*—Associated Press **2** *n* by 1940s Any lefthanded person: *Many brilliant persons are southpaws, although perhaps only coincidentally* **3** *modifier*: . . . *switched to a southpaw stance for his 11th round*—Associated Press [apparently coined by the humorist Finley Peter Dunne, "Mr Dooley," when he was a Chicago sports journalist and baseball diamonds were regularly oriented with home plate to the west]

sow-belly *n* by 1867 Fat salt pork, or bacon

so what by 1934 **1** *interj* An exclamation of specified indifference; =BIG DEAL: *When she heard the president was outside, she said, "So what?"*

2 *interj* An exclamation of defiance, reciprocal challenge, etc: *He told me I had screwed the affair up, and I said, "So what?"*

so what else is new or **what else is new** *sentence* by 1950s Do you have any other startling information? =TELL ME ABOUT IT ●Always used with heavy irony: *We are told that Stalin's was an exceptionally evil mind. So what else is new?*—New Republic/ *Once again, headlines warn of a trade war between the U.S. and Japan. So what else is new?*—Time

soxer *See* BOBBY-SOXER

sozzled *adj* by 1886 Drunk

space or **space out** *v* or *v phr* teenagers by 1968 To daydream; wool-gather; not attend to what one is doing: *He'd space on calling, break plans with me to hang out with his friends. . .*—Seventeen
See SPACE CADET

space bandit *n phr* 1940s show business A press agent [fr the fact that the press agent would strive, even unscrupulously, to have newspaper column *space* devoted to his or her clients]

space cadet or **space-case** or **space-out** *n phr* or *n* by 1980s A mad or eccentric person, esp one who seems stuporous or out of touch with reality as if intoxicated by narcotics; =NUT, SPACED-OUT: *Alda presents her as such a space cadet that the agony of divorce is tempered*—Kings Courier/ . . . *meant to convince the jury that he is an unreliable space-out, that perhaps he was hallucinating*—Washington Post [probably fr the 1950s TV program *Tom Corbett, Space Cadet*, which followed the adventures of a group of teenage cadets at a 24th-century space academy, thought of humorously as being *far out, way out*, etc]

spaced-out by 1968 **1** *adj* (also **spaced** or **spacey** or **spacy**) Stuporous from narcotic intoxication; in a daze: . . . *queerly bashful, shy, respectful, or spaced-out*—New York Magazine/ . . . *with very spaced-out movements, examines the parts of her body*—New York Times/ *You get into a trance, spaced, makin' plans*—Esquire **2** *adj* Crazy or eccentric; =NUTTY: . . . *the teacher, a spacey and sweetly strange spinster*—Richard Peck/ *He is not spaced-out, a point he makes clear in his new book*—T G Harris [probably fr black usage *space* or *space out*, "go, depart," reinforced by the notion of distance and remoteness in *outer space* and by the notion of blanks, gaps, and *spaces* in an otherwise sane and reasonable train of thought, speech, etc]

space opera *n phr* by 1941 A movie or show about interplanetary exploration, warfare, sex, etc [coined by Wilson Tucker]

space out *v phr* by 1968 To become stuporous from narcotic intoxication; be in a daze

◀**spade**▶ *n* by 1928 A black person: *The spades inhabited Harlem and let the ofays have Wall Street to themselves*—American Mercury [fr the color of the playing-card symbol and fr the phrase *black as the ace of spades*]

spades *See* IN SPADES

spaghetti ◀1▶ *n by 1931* An Italian or person of Italian descent **2** *n firefighters by 1941* Fire hose: *A foreman will always "Lay Spaghetti" when running out the hose*—New Yorker **3** *n by 1940s* Tubular insulation that may be cut and fitted over a wire conductor in radio or other electronic work **4** *n 1980s computers* An unreadable computer program **5** *modifier football by 1990s: George is a rookie, but he's got presence of mind, knowing that when they're in a "spaghetti" situation, when the receivers are in close, they're going to run crossing routes, like they scored on last week*—Milwaukee Journal [the taboo sense is semantically similar to Yiddish *luksh,* "an Italian," fr *lukshen,* "noodle"]

spaghetti Western *n phr by 1969* A cowboy movie usu made by Italian directors and producers, often in Europe: *. . . reacquaint yourself with films that made the spaghetti Western a grindhouse phenomenon*—Village Voice/ *The best turkeys, he went on, were spaghetti Westerns, because they earned a lot of bread*—Russell Baker

spaldeen or **Spaldeen** (spawl DEEN) *n New York City by 1930s* A small pink rubber ball used in various street games, esp stickball: *Only New York kids call it "Spaldeen"*—New York Magazine [fr a mispronunciation of *Spalding,* the name of the manufacturer, perhaps influenced by *balleen* fr Italian *pallino,* "little ball," the target ball used in the game of bocce]

spam *v computer by 1990s* To send a computer message out to myriad people: *. . . the cost to spam an advertisement in thousands of news groups. . . is typically less than $50*—New York Times/ *Spamming. Sending out on the Internet the cyberspace equivalent of junk mail. . .* —US News & World Report [fr *Spam,* trademark for a brand of canned meat, which acquired a probably undeserved unsavory reputation among WWII troops]

spang *by 1843* **1** *adv* Precisely; exactly; =SMACK: *Abilene was spang on a new westering railroad line*—advertisement for Time-Life books **2** *adv* Entirely; totally: *I had got spang through the job before they interrupted me* [fr British dialect, "spring, leap," and so semantically similar to an expression like *jump on the hour he got there,* because of the sharp precipitousness of a leap]

Spanish walk *See* FRENCH WALK

spanking *adv by 1666* Very; extremely, esp in an admirable sense [origin uncertain]

◁**spank the monkey**▷ *v phr by 1990s* To masturbate; =JACK OFF, MILK THE LIZARD

spare tire **1** *n phr by about 1925* Flab about the waist; a certain embonpoint; =BULGE **2** *n phr by 1940s* A superfluous and unwelcome person: *I didn't come, because I knew I'd be a spare tire in that crowd* **3** *n phr by 1940s* A tedious person; a bore

spark *v by 1912* To initiate and stimulate; trigger: *Willy Mays sparked an eighth inning Giant drive by stealing second*—Associated Press

sparkler *n by 1822* A gem, esp a diamond

spark plug *n phr by 1941* The most stimulating and energetic member of a group, team, etc; =LIVE WIRE: *Mr Fadiman himself is a splendid spark-plug*—H Allen Smith

Sparks *n merchant marine by about 1915* A ship's radio officer or operator

Sparky *See* OLD SMOKY

sparrow cop *n phr by 1896* A park policeman

◁**spaz** or **spastic**▷ (also **spas**) **1** *n teenagers by 1965* A strange and stupid person; =WEIRDO: *The man's a spaz, a total spaz*—Joseph Wambaugh **2** *adj: . . . only the spastic twits in competition*—Village Voice **3** *n by 1977* A nonathletic person, esp an awkward one **4** *n by 1990s* A fit of anger; =HISSY FIT: *Well, they threw a spaz and said we can talk on the phone, but I can't see him or have him over*—Seventeen [cruelly, fr the plight of cerebral palsy patients exhibiting constant body *spasms*]

spaz out *v phr teenagers by 1980s* To lose control of oneself; =FLIP OUT: *I spazzed out during the Chem final*—College Slang 101

spazwhiz *n 1980s computers* A clumsy, inept computer programmer

spazzed out *adj phr by 1980s* =SPACED-OUT: *A couple of spazzed out bikers*—Elmore Leonard

◁**spazzy** or **spassy**▷ *adj 1960s teenagers* Stupid; =WEIRD: *You gotta be spassy if you think that, just because kids aren't admitted to the casinos, they can't have a groovy. . . time in Atlantic City*—Philadelphia Inquirer [fr *spastic*]

speakeasy or **speak** or **speako** *n by 1889* A cheap saloon, esp an illegal or after-hours place: *It had been a speakeasy once*—L Ford/ *All they give you in these speaks is smoke*—James M Cain/ *. . . one thing that puts a speako over*—Joel Sayre [Samuel Hudson, a journalist, says in a 1909 book that he used the term in Philadelphia in 1889 after having heard it used in Pittsburgh by an old Irish woman who sold liquor clandestinely to her neighbors and enjoined them to "spake asy"; hence related to early–1800s Irish and British dialect *spake-aisy* or *speak softly* shop, "smugglers' den"]

spear carrier *n phr by 1960* An unimportant participant; supernumerary: *What helped me most was having been a catcher and a "spear carrier". . . definitely not a star*—Joe Garagiola/ *. . . like last-minute walk-ons in the closing scene. . . spear-carriers in Valhalla*—New Yorker [fr the persons who appear on stage, esp in operas, as soldiers in the background]

◀**spear chucker**▶ *n phr by late 1960s: When whites refer to blacks as spear chuckers, they're not thinking about the Olympics*—Milwaukee Journal/ *Where are the defenders of social stability when prime-time demagogues like Howard Stern deride African Americans as spear-chuckers?*—Time

spec[1] *n circus by 1926* The spectacular opening procession of a circus: *Mrs Webster rode an elephant in the "spec"*—Hamilton Basso

spec[2] *See* ON SPEC

special *See* the RED-EYE, SATURDAY NIGHT SPECIAL

Special K *n phr* 1990s *narcotics*: *The pre-voting-age enthusiasts come out of the stalls pie-eyed after a few lines of Special K, a snortable combination of horse tranquilizers, heroin, and coke—* New Yorker [fr the trademark name of a brand of breakfast cereal]

specs[1] *n by* 1807 Spectacles; glasses: *Oh Lord, I broke my new specs*

specs[2] *n by* 1940s The specifications of a blueprint, architectural plan, printing order, etc

speechifier *n by* 1778 A person who "speechifies": *Her presentations bear touches of an experienced speechifier*—New York Times

speechify *v by* 1723 To talk, esp in a pompous, pontifical way

speed *n* 1960s *narcotics* An amphetamine, esp Methedrine™

   See BRING someone UP TO SPEED

speedball 1 *n narcotics by* 1909 A dose of a stimulant and a depressant mixed, esp of heroin and cocaine: *. . . smack, coke, reefers, acid, speedballs (snorting cocaine and heroin together), a "luxury"*—New York Magazine **2** *v by* 1980s To produce rapidly; expedite: *I could have the agency speedball you a nice layout*—Elmore Leonard

speed bump 1 *n phr by* 1975 A transverse hump in a road made to slow the traffic **2** *n phr by* 1990s: *Aloe vera extract, fast on its way to becoming an all-purpose medicinal herb, has run into its first speed bump: a study suggesting that it delays the healing of some major surgical wounds—* Hippocrates/ *Instead, the drive toward integration has been stymied by the speedbump of crime*—Los Angeles Times

speedfreak or **speedo** *n* 1960s *narcotics* A habituated user of amphetamines and other such stimulants: *Well, you know about speedos*—Stan Cutler

speed merchant 1 *n phr baseball by* 1910 A very fast runner: *The little guy could really scoot, a speed merchant* **2** *n phr by* 1940s A very good fastball pitcher: *He had a glass arm and he certainly was no speed merchant*—Ithaca Journal

spell out 1 *v phr by* 1707 To explain; define: *. . . commission of distinguished citizens to spell out the difference between right and wrong—* Associated Press **2** *v phr by* 1940 To explain very patiently in great detail: *Are you a schoolboy I have to spell out everything for you?*—Ira Wolfert

spender *See* BIG SPENDER

spheroid *n baseball by* 1874 A baseball: *Hitting the ball is just as important as slugging the spheroid*—Associated Press

◄**spick** or **spic**► **1** *n by* 1913 A Latino or person of such descent: *. . . female spick, short, fat*—Ira Wolfert **2** *adj*: *Jill don't want anyone to know she got a spic baby*—Robert B Parker **3** *n by* 1933 The Spanish language [fr the presumed protestation *"No spick English"*]

spicy *adj by* 1886 Scandalous; mildly salacious: *. . . a spicy bit of gossip*—The Lantern

spiel 1 *n by* 1896 A barker's or hawker's persuasive talk **2** *n by* 1896 A speech meant to persuade by force and eloquence; a sales patter; =LINE: *I'll give his honor a spiel*—Jack London **3** *n by* 1940s An advertising monologue on radio or television [fr German *spielen,* "play"]

spieler *n by* 1894 A person who makes a persuasively eloquent speech: *. . . a real accomplished spieler*—Outlook

spiff *n by* 1859: *. . . a top-of-the-line washer and dryer that would bring not only a nice commission but a spiff (bonus) as well*—Milwaukee Journal

spiffed *adj by* 1918 Drunk

spiffed out *adj phr by* 1877 Fancily and formally dressed

spiffing *adj by* 1872 =SPIFFY

spifflicated *adj by* 1906 Drunk: *. . . a slightly spifflicated gent*—Hy Gardner/ *. . . a spifflicated patient entangling himself in a revolving door—* Time [fr British dialect *spifflicate,* "confound, dumbfound, crush," of obscure origin, found by 1785]

spiffy 1 *adj by* 1853 Elegant; excellent; =SNAZZY: *They wear spiffy red-and-gold scarves*—Time/ *New Model Buggy for Amish Is Spiffy*—Cleveland Plain Dealer **2** *adv by* 1937 Well; elegantly: *They don't translate so spiffy*—Arthur Baer

spike 1 *v by* 1889 To strengthen a drink by adding alcohol or liquor: *He spiked his coffee with brandy* **2** *n narcotics by* 1934 A hypodermic needle **3** *v by* 1960s To rise to a high level, esp rapidly: *He also. . . spikes into the upper registers*—Down Beat/ *. . . push fluids when the patient has spiked a temp*—American Speech **4** *v by* 1908 To reject; quash: *The spiking of Schanberg's column at The Times drew hundreds of angry letters from readers. . .*—Washington Post/ *. . . confident the man's disbelieving New York editors will spike the story*—People Weekly **5** *v baseball by* 1885 To injure a player, most often a defending baseman, with the spikes on one's shoes **6** *v volleyball by* 1970s To punch a volleyball powerfully and unreturnably down **7** *v football by* 1970s To slam the ball down, usu done by a player who has just scored a touchdown **8** *v black by* 1990s To shoot: *Figure whoever spiked Porter probably did us a favor*—Robert B Parker [all senses fr *spike,* "large nail," hence "sharp point"; the sense "to reject" may be fr the earlier phrase *spike a gun,* "render a cannon useless by driving a spike into the touchhole," or fr the notion of dealing with a paper, bill, manuscript, etc, by impaling it on a spindle or spindle file]

spike up *v phr* 1960s *narcotics* To inject narcotics; =SHOOT UP: *. . . if he came home and found her spiking up*—Richard Merkin

spill 1 *v by* 1731 To upset; down; dump: *I'll spill you in the drink*—Atlantic Monthly **2** *v by* 1574 To utter or confess something, esp something damaging; =SPILL THE BEANS

spill one's **guts** *v phr by* 1927 To tell everything one knows; be totally and lengthily candid: *"Can I be* *perfectly frank with you?" "Good. Spill your guts"*—Armistead Maupin

spill the beans *v phr* by 1919 To tell something inadvertently; blurt out a secret

spin *n* by 1979: *Turner. . . had suggested the spin she put on it*—Lawrence Sanders [fr the notion of *spin* on a baseball or pool ball, which gives a deviant rather than a straight track; semantically related to throwing someone a curve]

spinach 1 *n* by 1900 A beard **2** *n* by 1929 Nonsense; worthless matter; =JUNK: *You could put up with this spinach*—Richard Bissell

spin control *n phr* by middle 1980s: *Spin control is the subtle art of massaging reporters' minds after the event has taken place. The "doctors" try to control the interpretation, or "spin," the reporters will put on their stories*—Los Angeles Times

spin someone's **dials** *v phr* by 1990s To excite or stimulate someone; arouse someone; =TURN someone ON: *. . . a seemingly great guy who for some reason does not spin your dials*—Sassy

spin doctor or **spinmeister** *n phr* by middle 1980s An advisor or agent, esp of a politician, who imparts a partisan analysis or slant to a story for the news media: *Just after the debate, Johnson took his place with the other "spin doctors"*—Washington Post

spinner 1 *n* truckers by 1940s A truck driver **2** *n* by 1980s: *Did you know that professional "spinners" are responsible for setting back the true mileage on used cars?*—Consumer Reports

spin off by 1959 **1** *v phr* To produce as an entity separated from the whole: *The conglomerate spun off five new companies* **2** *n*: *This store is a spin-off from the big one downtown* **3** *v phr* To dispose of; rid oneself of; =DITCH: *Why didn't he spin off this stupid cunt?*—Saul Bellow

spin one's **wheels** *v phr* by 1940s To waste time; work fruitlessly: *Nobody spun his wheels. I'm proud of them*—Washington Post/ *Stop spinning your wheels, get yourself in gear*—W T Tyler

spit *n* by 1960s Nothing; =ZILCH, ZIP: *"What'd she come up with?" "Spit"*—Scott Turow [a euphemism for *shit*]
See HOT SPIT, NOT COUNT FOR SPIT, NOT WORTH A BUCKET OF WARM SPIT, SWAP SPIT

spitball 1 *n* baseball by 1905 A pitch thrown using a ball wetted with spit or otherwise illegally besmeared **2** *v* by 1955 To speculate; propose conclusions or possibilities: *Well, I'm just spit-balling*—Paul Theroux/ *You're just spitballing*—Lawrence Sanders **3** *n* by 1970s A nasty but feeble attack: *. . . despite the spitballs he keeps getting from the critical liberal media*—Philadelphia Journal [second and third senses fr the mischievous schoolboy's vice of throwing bits of paper soaked in saliva; second sense fr the notion of tossing such spitballs more or less idly]

spit in someone's **eye** *v phr* by 1908 To show extreme contempt and ingratitude: *What I hate is when you pay for it and they spit in your eye*—Stan Cutler

spit it out *v phr* by 1855 To speak out; reveal; disclose: *If you've got any more to tell me, spit it out right now*

spitless *See* SCARED SPITLESS, SCARE someone SHITLESS

spit tacks *v phr* by 1970s To become very upset and angry; =SHIT A BRICK: *I expected Eartha to spit tacks over the injustice*—Village Voice

spitter *n* baseball by 1908 =SPITBALL

spizzerinktum or **spizzerrinctum** *n* by 1940s Vigor; pep; =PIZZAZZ: *. . . the fellow who put foresight, science, and spizzerinktum into their business*—H E Babcock [origin unknown; since the earliest meaning is "money," perhaps a coinage fr Latin *specie rectum*, "the right sort"]

splash *See* MAKE A SPLASH

splat 1 *v* by 1922 To hit with a smacking sound; slap: *I wouldn't be at all concerned that a tomato would splat me in the face*—Mike Royko **2** *n* by 1958 A slap or smack [echoic]

splat movie or **splatterfest** *n phr* by 1970s A movie that features a major catastrophe or other event where things and people are severely damaged: *When he was working on the 1974 splatterfest The Texas Chainsaw Massacre. . .* —Los Angeles Times

◀**splib**▶ *n* black by 1964 A black person who opposes discrimination, etc, but will not challenge the status quo; a liberal black: *Don't nobody want no nice nigger anymore. They want an angry splib*—Al Young [fr *spade* plus *liberal*]

splice *v* by 1751 To marry ●Most often in the passive: *. . . crying to be spliced*—Joseph Auslander

splice the main brace *v phr* nautical by 1850 To have a drink of liquor

spliff *n* narcotics by 1936 A marijuana cigarette: *Smoking a spliff of high-octane chronic. . .* —People Weekly [a West Indian term]
See ENGLISH SPLIFF

splinter *See* KNEE-HIGH TO A GRASSHOPPER

split *v* jazz musicians by 1956 To leave; depart; =CUT OUT: *This party is dullsville, let's split*
See HELL TO SPLIT, LICKETY-SPLIT

split a gut *v phr* by 1940s To try very, very hard; make a maximum effort; =BUST one's ASS

◁**split beaver**▷ *n phr* by 1972 A photograph or view of a woman's vulva between spread legs; =SPREAD BEAVER: *I can toss off phrases like "split beaver" with almost devil-may-care abandon*—Esquire

splitsville *n* by 1980s A parting or dissolution; separation: *. . . teach the little chickadees to fly and then. . . it's splitsville*—Milwaukee Journal/ *Splitsville. . . Fergie and Prince Andrew are calling it quits*—Milwaukee Journal

splitter *See* LIP-SPLITTER

split the difference *v phr* by 1750 To compromise, esp when agreement is near: *We're almost agreed, so let's split the difference/ She may have to realize that the philosophical difference between* *herself and Rome remains one that finally just can't be split*—New Republic

split the scene *v phr* black musicians by about 1952 To leave; depart; =CUT OUT, SPLIT: *. . . just as I was about to split the scene*—Tennessee Williams

split the sheets *v phr* by 1980s To get a divorce: *They split the sheets*—TV show Hogan Family [fr the division of property after a divorce]

split-up 1 *n* by 1908 An angry separation: *Me and the old man had a split-up*—W R Burnett **2** *n* by 1975 A divorce or legal separation of a married couple

split week *n phr* poker by 1940s A potential straight with the middle card missing [fr show business use, where a *split week* is one in which a performer works in two towns, theaters, etc, serially]

spoil *v* by 1980s To kill; =WASTE: *You wanted to hate his guts so it would be easier to spoil him?*—Lawrence Sanders

spoil someone **rotten** *v phr* by 1970 To indulge and pamper someone to an extreme: *Spoiling your kid rotten from the start?*—New York Times

spondulics or **spondulix** (spahn Dōō liks) *n* by 1856 Money [said by Tony Thorne to be fr Greek *spondylikos* fr *spondylos*, a seashell used as currency]

sponge 1 *n* (also **sponger**) by 1598 A parasite; =FREELOADER, MOOCHER, SCHNORRER: *You avoided college boys, sponges*—F Scott Fitzgerald **2** *v* by 1676: *We were able to sponge lots of meals off his parents* **3** *n* by 1900 A drunkard; =SOAK
See THROW IN THE SPONGE

spoof 1 *v* by 1889 To fool; hoax; tease: *He was just spoofing*—Sinclair Lewis **2** *n* by 1884: *Don't take it seriously, it was just a spoof* **3** *n* by 1958 A parody or pastiche: *The show was a spoof of a TV sit-com* [coined by the British comedian Arthur Roberts, born 1852, as the name of a nonsense game he invented]

spoofing *n* 1990s computer To gain access electronically to a computer deceptively and perhaps illegally: *I thought someone might be electronically impersonating him, a practice that is known online as "spoofing"*—New Yorker/ *The technique is called "spoofing" because it fools a computer into thinking that another, friendly computer is requesting access*—Reid Kanaley

spooge *v* 1990s computer To squeeze something into an operating system, to its detriment: *Consumers don't know it yet, but Microsoft is going to spooge a lot of the interface of Word for Windows into the Word for Mac 6.0 version. . . and the new Mac version will operate slow as a glacier. . .* —Douglas Coupland

spook ◀1▶ *n* by 1945 A black person: *Some are just spooks by the door, used to give the organization a little color*—Amsterdam News **2** *n* espionage by 1942 A spy; secret agent: *Mr. Wolfson isn't a spook for the CIA*—Wall Street Journal **3** *v* by 1935 To put on edge; make apprehensive; frighten: *"It's the first time in my life I've ever been*

spooked," says a Byrd staffer—Washington Post [fr Dutch]

spoon *v* by 1831 =NECK, PET
See GREASY SPOON

spoony or **spooney 1** *adj* by 1836 Amorous; romantic: *I guess we got kind of spoony*—Ring Lardner **2** *n* by 1795 A foolish or silly person: *I don't believe a cock-and-bull story like that. Quiz was no spooney*—Stanley Elkin

sport 1 *v* by 1778 To wear: *He sported a Day-glo necktie* **2** *n* by 1923 A stylish and rakish man •Often used as a term of address, sometimes with an ironical tinge: *What did she tell you, sport?* **3** *n* by 1920 =GOOD SPORT

sport a woody *v phr* 1980s students To have an erection

sporting house *n phr* by 1857 A place for gambling and dissipation, esp a brothel

sport-ute *n* by 1990s: *There's about as much sport in most sport-utility trucks as there is in a professional wrestling match. Isuzu is doing its part to change this. Its sport-ute, the Trooper, is sporty*—Milwaukee Journal

spot 1 *v* sports & gambling by 1961 To give odds or a handicap: *They spotted Pittsburgh five runs before getting down to serious business*—New York Times **2** *v* by 1848 To recognize or identify: *I spotted her as a phony long ago* **3** *n* by 1937 A short commercial or paid political announcement on radio or television: *How do you like the spots, Senator?*—New York Magazine **4** *n* by 1940s A night club, restaurant, or other such venue of pleasure: *They were often seen in a fashionable spot uptown* [found by 1718 in the second sense as "identify as a wrongdoer"]
See DEUCE SPOT, FIVE-SPOT, HIT THE SPOT, HOT SPOT, JOHNNY-ON-THE-SPOT, NIGHT SPOT, ON THE SPOT, PUT someone ON THE SPOT, SWEET SPOT, TWO-SPOT, X MARKS THE SPOT

spotlight *v* by 1942 To single out prominently; focus on for emphasis: *He was trying to spotlight the danger of high deficits*
See IN THE SPOTLIGHT

spot market *n phr* by 1982 The free market in petroleum, outside the price scales set by the producers' organization [*spot oil* is found by 1888]

spot-on *adj* by 1956 Exact; precise; faithful; =ON THE BUTTON, ON THE MONEY •Chiefly British: *Elwood's spot-on use of an argot, half G.I. and half cokehead, infuses the book with surprise and a screeching undercurrent of despair*—New York Times [found in adverbial use by 1920]

spout *See* GO UP THE SPOUT

sprawl *n* by 1980s Spreading overdevelopment of urban areas: *The state can put the brakes on senseless sprawl*—Gordon Bishop

spread 1 *n* by 1858 Coverage in a newspaper or magazine, esp the full use of facing pages: *Do you know how much a two-page spread in the New York Times costs these days?* **2** *n* by 1822 A copious meal; a feast

spread oneself *v phr* by 1857 To make a great effort; do one's utmost: *You may be sure the staff will spread itself to accommodate you*

◁**spread beaver**▷ *n phr* by 1970s =SPLIT BEAVER

◁**spread for** someone▷ *v phr* by 1950s For a woman, to do or offer to do the sex act with someone; spread her legs for coital access

spread it thick *v phr* by 1940s To exaggerate; overstate; =BULLSHIT ●Very often used with *on*: *To say it was for the good of humanity is spreading it a bit thick*

spread oneself **thin** (or **too thin**) *v phr* by 1960s To attempt more than one can do; strain one's resources: *It's a good idea to get involved in a lot of activities, but don't spread yourself too thin*—American Idioms Dictionary

spring 1 *v underworld* by 1900 To get out of or be released or escape from prison: *The proprietor knew how to "spring" them, that is, get them out of jail*—Louis Armstrong/ *When's he springing?*—Lawrence Sanders **2** *v* by 1876 To reveal or do something as a surprise ●Very often used with *on*: *John L Lewis is preparing to spring a dramatic move*—Lowell Thomas/ *If we spring it on them suddenly they won't know how to react*

spring chicken *n phr* by 1906 A young person, esp a woman: . . . *Maggie Smith is the spring chicken among them. . .*—New Yorker [fr the market name for a small young chicken]

See NO SPRING CHICKEN

spring for something *v phr* To pay for, esp a treat of food or drink; =POP: . . . *always more than glad to guzzle the pitchers of Michelob you sprung for on payday*—Philadelphia/ *We'll spring for the gas*—Carsten Stroud

spring (or **pop**) someone **to** something *v phr* by 1941 To treat someone to something: *I sprang him to a couple of beers*

spritz 1 *v* by 1976 To spray or sprinkle: . . . *the fixative with which he spritzed it so it would not smear*—Earl Thompson/ *She spritzed a little scent behind her ear and was ready* **2** *n* by 1960s A serving of carbonated water, esp an addition of carbonated water to a glass of wine: *She asked for white wine with a spritz* **3** *n* by 1970s A slight rain or shower: *We may get just a wee spritz this afternoon* [fr Yiddish, "spray"]

spritzer *n* by 1961 A glass of wine mixed with carbonated water

spritzy *adj* by 1970s Light and volatile; airy; frothy: *She now does a string of spritzy little jetés that barely get her off the ground*—New Yorker/ . . . *the hair-trigger switch between Nathan's spritzy charm and the scary violence of his anger*—Newsweek

sprout *n* by 1934 A child, esp an infant: *A girl out your way has married. . . and is coming home with a sprout*—Harper's

sproutsy *adj* by 1970s Unconventional, unorthodox in habits and opinions: *I joined a sorority; now I'm seen as a sister, not as a sproutsy type*—Ms [fr the

eating of *bean-sprouts* as symbolizing radical or nonconformist behavior]

sprung *adj* by 1833 Drunk

spud *n* by 1845 A potato [origin unknown; perhaps related to the fact that in British dialect use *spud* means "a weeding instrument" and in US dialect it means "a spade," hence potatoes would be something *spudded* or dug; a relation has been seen between the fact that potatoes are also the nickname of men named Murphy, or indeed of any Irishman]

spudge around *v phr* by 1880s To exert oneself; apply oneself: *If she would only spudge around, get her work done*—Scribner's [origin unknown; perhaps related to British dialect *spuddle*, "move about busily"; perhaps to *pudge up*, "prod, stimulate"]

spunk 1 *n* by 1773 Energetic courage; mettle; =BALLS, GUTS: . . . *little girl's got a lot of spunk* ◁**2**▷ *n* by 1888 Semen: . . . *rushing with their hot spunk in their hands to the microscope*—John Irving ◁**3**▷ *v* by 1970s To ejaculate semen; =COME: . . . *the filthy pigs spunking into women*—Herbert Kastle [apparently fr Celtic *spong*, "tinder, touchwood, punk," fr Latin *spongia*, "sponge"; apparently semantically fr a resemblance between semen and a spongy excrescence found on trees, in which sense the word is found in British dialect]

squad *See* BEEF SQUAD, GOON SQUAD, PUSSY POSSE, TAXI SQUAD

square 1 *n* (also **square meal**) by 1882 A copious meal: *I've had my three squares every day*—J Flynt **2** *n jazz musicians* by about 1925 A conventional person, esp one with musical tastes not extending to jazz, swing, bop, etc; =CLYDE: *That GL. . . strictly a square*—Max Shulman/ *I do a little vocal number for the squares*—Mary Lou Williams **3** *adj jazz musicians* by about 1925 =UNCOOL: *You do not try to convert the square world*—Eugene Burdick **4** *n* (also **square joint**) 1960s *narcotics* A tobacco cigarette; =SLIM, STRAIGHT **5** *adj* by 1872 Fair; even-handed; just: *I'll be square with you* **6** *v* by 1859 To make things right, just, proper, etc: *He could never square himself with the police after that* [the sense "conventional person, etc," is said to come fr a jazz musician's and standard conductor's hand gesture that beats out regular and unsyncopated four-beat rhythm, the hand doing so describing a *square* figure in the air]

square badge *n phr* by 1980s A security guard; =RENT-A-COP: *You don't want to wind up a square badge emptying waste baskets in a bank, now do you?*—Michael Grant

square broad *n phr* by 1970s A woman who is not a prostitute: *He takes a "square broad" (a nonprostitute) and "turns her out"*—Time

the **squared circle** *n phr* by 1927 A boxing ring; =the CANVAS

a **square deal** *n phr* by 1876 Fair and honest treatment: *Don't look for a square deal from them crooks*

square guy *n phr* by 1908 An honest and reliable man; =RIGHT GUY: *Trust him; he's a square guy*

◀**squarehead**▶ *n by 1903* A Scandinavian or person of Scandinavian descent; =SCANDAHOOVIAN

square John (or **john**) *n phr underworld by 1920s* An ordinary honest person; a good citizen; a noncriminal person who can be victimized by, and is contemptuously regarded by, criminals

square off *v phr by 1837* To put oneself in a fighting posture: *The two biggest companies are squaring off over the microchip market*

square one *n phr by 1960* The place where some process begins or has begun; the original configuration: *So after all this fuss we are at square one again* [fr board games where a token is moved off the *first square* after the shake of a die, drawing of a card, etc]
See GO BACK TO SQUARE ONE

square peg *n phr by 1901* A misfit; an inconvenient and intractable person: *They were square pegs who weren't succeeding*—E Lavine [fr the earlier expression *put* or *drive a square peg in a round hole,* fr carpentry or joinery]

squares *See* THREE SQUARES

square shooter *n phr by 1914* An honest and candid person; =STRAIGHT ARROW •Now used nearly always with the conscious irony of archaic sincerity

Squaresville or **squaresville 1** *n 1960s bop talk* A putative city inhabited entirely by dull, conventional people: *The Innocent Nihilists Adrift in Squaresville*—The Reporter/ *Unintimidated by being in the squaresville, which is also the power center of the free world*—Hugh Sidey **2** *adj*: *. . . on campus, where it once was squaresville to flip for the rock scene*—Time

square the beef *v phr by 1940s* To repair a grievous situation; resolve a complaint

squat 1 *v by 1768* To sit: *Hey, squat there a minute and I'll be right with you* ◁**2**▷ *v by 1940s* To defecate; =SHIT, TAKE A DUMP ◁**3**▷ *n by 1930s* Excrement: *Don't step in the squat* **4** *n by 1934* Nothing; zero; =DIDDLY, ZILCH, ZIP: *She's got squat to do with that kind of shit*—Richard Fariña/ *You can't do squat anyway these days*—George V Higgins
See the HOT SQUAT, NOT GIVE A DAMN, NOT KNOW BEANS, TAKE A DUMP

squat hot *v phr by 1943* To be executed in the electric chair; =FRY: *If the crook ever squatted hot, that would be doing something for the country*—James M Cain

◁**squaw**▷ *n by 1934* A woman, esp one's wife

squawk 1 *v by 1875* To complain; =BEEF, BITCH: *Will you stop squawking about the food, please?* **2** *n by 1909*: *Okay, what's your squawk this morning?* **3** *v underworld by 1872* To inform; =SQUEAL: *Joe squawked*—W R Burnett [echoic of an unpleasant sound, esp the grating screech of a bird]

squawk box *n phr WWII Navy* A military public address system; =BITCH BOX

squeak by (or **through**) *v phr by 1938* To pass, succeed, achieve a goal, etc, by the narrowest of margins: *He just barely squeaked through his medical boards*

squeaker 1 *n by 1960s* A very closely contested and uncertain game, contest, etc: *They met in a squeaker that year, 23 to 24* **2** *n by 1960s* Something poised on the edge of one result or another, esp a success versus a disaster: *"It'll be a squeaker," Bartow said. "This is a nervous time for us"*—Washington Post

squeaky-clean *adj phr by 1972* Perfectly clean; white, sanitary, and untarnished •Sometimes used ironically to emphasize conventionality and unimaginativeness: *. . . this English band, made up of six squeaky-clean men in their early twenties*—Westword/ *. . . one of the most squeaky-clean and buttoned-down of US corporations*—Wall Street Journal [fr the *squeaky* sound produced by rubbing a finger across chinaware free of grease or dirt]

squeal 1 *v by 1825* To inform; =RAT, SING, SQUAWK **2** *n* (also **squeel**) *by about 1750* An informer; =RAT, SNITCH, STOOL PIGEON: *He was working on a case with a squeal, and he knifed him*—New York Post **3** *n* (also **squeak**) *by 1908* A complaint to the police: *. . . cop at stationhouse took the squeal*—Ed McBain/ *The young cops who had caught the squeal didn't know what to do*—Lawrence Sanders

squealer *n by 1865* An informer; =RAT, SNITCH, SQUEAL

squeegee operator (or **man**) *n phr by 1980s* A person who cleans one's windshield unbidden and then asks for payment: *Giuliani's mayoral campaign was directed at aggressive panhandlers, squeegee operators, brazen drug dealers*—New Yorker

squeeze *n* A situation of great pressure or peril; =CRUNCH: *I'm afraid we're in something of a squeeze just now*
See MAIN SQUEEZE, PUT THE SQUEEZE ON someone

squeeze-box *n by 1936* An accordion

squeezer *See* DUCK SQUEEZER

squib *n by 1739* A brief, sometimes witty piece of material in a newspaper or magazine, usu a space-filler: *A friend of mine, he writes those witty "squibs"*—Westbrook Pegler [fr *squib,* "a small firecracker," of unknown origin]

squid *n 1980s students* An obnoxious person, esp one who studies too hard; =DWEEB, GRIND, LOSER, NERD

squiffy or **squiffy-eyed** or **squiffed** *adj entry form by 1855, second variant by 1890* Drunk: *. . . so-and-so's getting "squiffy" at a dance*—Robert Lynd/ *. . . one of Frenise's squiffy-eyed nieces*—Paul Theroux

squiggle *n 1980s computer* The tilde, a sinuous diacritical mark

squillion *n by 1990s* A very large number; myriad; =ZILLION: *. . . the Beat Farmers have played in a zillion bars here and overseas*—Macon Telegraph

squillionaire *n by 1990s*: *The once aggressive squillionaires are staying away from contemporary art, and the mood at auction houses is glum*—Time

squinch *v by 1840* To distort the face; squint: *The eyes are squinched with innocence and glint*—Lawrence Sanders

squinchy *adj by middle 1800s* Like one who "squinches": *You've got that squinchy look around the eyes, and you're gritting your teeth*—Lawrence Sanders

squirrel 1 *v* (also **squirrel away**) *by 1939* To hoard or cache something; hide and save something for later **2** *n by 1940s* A crazy or eccentric person; =NUT, WEIRDO: *I seen some squirrels in my life, but you got 'em all beat*—H Allen Smith **3** *n 1950s* hot rodders A hesitant or confused hot rod driver **4** *v 1950s* hot rodders To weave about the road while driving, esp a hot rod

See SEAM SQUIRREL

squirrel-bait (or -food) *n first form by 1919, second by about 1915* A crazy or eccentric person; =NUT, SQUIRREL: *I'm afraid the old mentor is squirrel-food by now* [fr the fact that *squirrels eat nuts*]

squirrely *adj by 1934* Crazy; eccentric; =NUTTY: *I tell you, working out alone can make you squirrely*—Erma Bombeck

squirt 1 *n by 1839* A short or small person, esp an insignificant, contemptible little male; =PEANUT: *Ah, what a little squirt is there*—W H Auden **2** *n* (also **young squirt**) *by 1848* A young man, esp a presumptuous or foppish youth

squish 1 *n by 1980s*: *It wasn't that I was becoming a "squish" (That's a Washington term for a softy)*—Nation **2** *v* (also **squush** [*by 1846*] or **squoosh**) *by 1647* To squeeze; compress: *This universe he had built was a Guggenheim and a Toy-R-Us squished into one/ . . . some mondobra engineering breakthrough, to squoosh your breasts together and push them up under your chin*—Milwaukee Journal

squishy *adj by 1953* Sentimental; =SCHMALTZY, SOPPY: *The sentiment may sound squishy to those who have never been close to him*—Washington Post/ *. . . the squishy sentimentality attributed to him by most critics*—Village Voice

squooshy (SKWŏŏ shee) *adj by 1970s* Soft; yielding and insubstantial: *Support for Reagan is "all very squooshy"*—Newsweek [the date should probably be earlier; *sqush*, "to collapse into a soft, pulpy mass," is found by 1884]

SRO (pronounced as separate letters) **1** *n* theater *by 1890* Standing room only, usu indicating a full house and a successful production **2** *n by 1941* Single room occupancy residence hotel: *They're planning to demolish the SROs on this street*

stab *n by 1895* A try; =CRACK, SHOT, WHACK: *Well, I'll have a stab at it*

stable *n by 1937* The group of people performing similar work, managed by one person: *She's part of his stable of writers*

stache *See* STASH

'stache *n by 1980s* A mustache: *If they didn't, Garner would trash his own 'stache*—Milwaukee Journal

stack *See* BLOW one's TOP

◁**stack asses**▷ *v phr by 1980s* To play or behave violently; knock and throw people to the ground: *Let the other side know you've come to stack asses*—Dan Jenkins

stacked *adj by 1942* Very well-built in the sexual sense; having an attractive body, esp a large bosom: *She's well-stacked and sort of young*—Lionel Stander [found in the form *stacked up nicely* at Stanford University in 1931]

stack of Bibles *See* SWEAR ON A STACK OF BIBLES

stack the cards (or the deck) *v phr by 1825* To prearrange something dishonestly; assure one's advantage fraudulently; =COLD DECK: *I should have had the job, but they stacked the cards against me*

stack up 1 *v phr by 1911* To transpire; go along; succeed: *How are things stacking up for you this year?* **2** *v phr by 1903* To compare; measure against: *I'd like for somebody to begin stacking up Native Son with some of Frank Norris's stuff*—American Scholar **3** *v 1950s* teenagers To wreck a car; =RACK UP **4** *n 1950s* teenagers A multiple car wreck [first two senses fr the *stacking up* of one's poker chips to show winnings or for comparison]

stack Zs *See* COP ZS

staff *See* CHIEF OF STAFF

stag 1 *n by 1905* A man who goes to a party alone, without a woman partner **2** *adj by 1873* For men only; without women: *a stag function/ Several of the brothers were going to the dance stag*—P Marks **3** *n* (also **stag party**) *by 1904* A party for men only, as a bachelor party: *. . . as broad as the jokes at a Legion stag*—J Evans

stage *See* UPSTAGE

stagedoor Johnny *n phr by 1912* A man who haunts the stagedoor of a theater in order to meet actresses, chorus girls, etc

stage mother *n phr by 1919* A person who is aggressively overzealous in promoting the success of offspring, proteges, etc: *Once there were stage mothers, the legendary behind-the-scenes forces who achieved Broadway immortality as Rose in Gypsy*—New York Times/ *Many in the thin Dodger front line were pressed into larger roles, and they were cajoled and hugged and implored and cursed by Lasorda, their loud and unabashedly emotional manager, a stage mother if there ever was one*—New Yorker

stagflation *n by 1965* A simultaneous stagnation and inflation in the economy

the staggers *n phr by 1599* A faltering and unsteady physical state, esp from liquor or narcotics intoxication: *The next day you've got the staggers and your fine coordination is destroyed for 72 hours*—Albert Goldman [originally a disease of animals]

stag line *n phr by 1934* The group of unescorting males at a dance, thought of as a line beside the floor, studying the women as possible dance partners

stairs *See* UPSTAIRS

stake *See* GRUBSTAKE, ROAD-STAKE

stake out *v phr* police by 1942 To put someone or something under constant police surveillance: *He's been staked out often enough*—Mickey Spillane [fr earlier senses, as old as the 1600s, where *stake out* meant "mark off a territory, a line, a track, etc, with stakes"]

stake-out *n* police by 1942 A police surveillance: *. . . as silently as only a cop on a stake-out knows how to stand*—Raymond Chandler/ *The stake-outs continued*—radio program *Dragnet*

stakes *See* PULL UP STAKES

stake someone **to** something *v phr* by 1853 To give or provide something to someone, inferentially as a loan: *Could you stake me to a new suit so I can get a job?* [fr the earlier senses where *stake* meant someone's basic provisions for farming, prospecting, etc]

stalk *v* by 1980s To harass someone, esp a woman, in a menacing way: *During the first week at Wimbledon, a German stalking Steffi Graf had to be expelled*—New Yorker/ *The clinics have recourse to local laws against blocking an entrance and stalking doctors and nurses*—Time/ *A 9-year old boy who left a message for a 10-year old girl. . . has been accused of violating the state's anti-stalking law. . .* —New York Times

stall[1] **1** *v* by 1903 To delay; temporize; consume time and delay action; =BUY TIME: *I told him to quit stalling and give us a decision* **2** *v* (also **stall off**) by 1906 To subject someone to delay; make excuses for inaction: *You stall her while I try to find her original letter*—A Hynd **3** *n* by 1889 A pretext or excuse for delaying; a reason for inaction: *His claim of illness is only a stall* **4** *n* by 1851 A pretense or false indication, esp as part of a criminal alibi: *"I'd take meals up to him. I think that was just a stall." "You mean the meals were for someone else?"*—Erle Stanley Gardner [fr Old English *steall*, "standing, state, place, animal stall," whence the notion of stubbornly holding one's place]

stall[2] **1** *n* by 1591 A pickpocket's accomplice who in one way or another maneuvers the victim **2** *n* underworld by 1930 A criminal's accomplice who primarily diverts attention, obstructs pursuit, keeps watch, etc: *. . . an excellent lookout or "stall" for her male companions*—A Lavine [fr earlier *stale* or *stall*, "decoy bird," probably fr Anglo-French *estale* or *estal*, "a pigeon used to lure a hawk into a nest"; since delaying and misleading are involved in both, this derivation and that of *stall*[1] have probably intermingled over the centuries, as illustrated by the fact that *stand* meant "a thief's assistant" in the late–16th century]

stall and dip *n phr* by 1990: *The "stall and dip," where the "stall" drops change and, when the traveler bends down to help, the "dip" snatches the bags*—Newsday

stallion **1** *n* by 1553 =STUD **2** *n* black by 1970s A sexually attractive and/or active woman; =FOX

stamping ground (or **grounds**) *n phr* by 1821 One's particular domain or territory; one's native heath: *Ann Arbor used to be my stamping ground* [fr 1700s sense, "a place frequented by animals"]

stand **1** *v* by 1821 To give or pay for as a treat: *She stood him tea and muffins*—Sinclair Lewis **2** *v* by 1362 To cost; =SET someone BACK: *The suit I got on stood me ten cents*—A J Liebling **3** *n* by 1787 A shop or store; a place of business: *You can get it at the Brooks Brothers stand on Fifth Avenue*
See BALLY STAND, ONE-NIGHT STAND

◁**stand around with** one's **finger up** one's **ass**▷ (or **in** one's **ear**) *v phr* by 1940s To be idle and helpless; fail to cope; be useless: *If you're just standing around with your finger up your ass you might as well lend a hand here*

standee *n* by 1856 A person forced to stand because all seats are sold or occupied: *. . . long lines of standees waiting their turns*—Philadelphia Inquirer

stand (or **stand still**) **for** something *v phr* entry form by 1626, variant by 1970s To tolerate or abide something; swallow something •Usu in the negative: *He said he wouldn't stand for being replaced*

stand in *v phr* show business by 1904 To substitute; act as a proxy: *I'll have to stand in for her and run the meeting*

stand-in **1** *n* by 1938 A performer who takes the place of another **2** *n* by 1937 A substitute or proxy; a deputy: *Naive Stingo, as stand-in for us*—Philadelphia [perhaps fr the use of a substitute to replace a performer during such tedious procedures as adjusting lights, arranging the stage or set, etc; perhaps also fr the earlier notion of a deputy or placeholder, literally a lieutenant, in French, "a place-holder"]

standing O *n phr* by 1990s A standing ovation: *The audience greeted John Harbison's new cello concerto with a standing O*—Philadelphia radio station/ *Thiede. . . got a standing O*—Milwaukee Journal

standing on one's **head** *See* DO something ON TOP OF one's HEAD

standing up *See* DIE STANDING UP

standoff *n* by 1843 A balanced and static conflict; stalemate; deadlock: *The union and the company are locked in a standoff*
See MEXICAN STANDOFF

standoffish *adj* by 1860 Haughty; aloof; reserved and snobbish: *He gave us all a standoffish look*

stand on one's **brakes** *v phr* by 1970s To apply the brakes of a car very hard: *The guy on my right stood on his brakes*—Philadelphia Journal

stand-out *n* by 1928 A person or thing that is extraordinary, usu uncommonly good or talented; an outstanding person or thing: *Her performance of Amanda is the stand-out of the season*

stand pat **1** *v phr* poker by 1882 To keep one's original five cards in draw poker, without drawing new ones **2** *v phr* by 1890 To retain one's position; refuse to shift; carry on as one is; =SIT TIGHT: *The President stood pat on his decision to cut taxes* [fr the adverb *pat*, "exactly, precisely to the purpose"]

stand tall *v phr* Army by 1970s To be proud and ready; have an imposing and confident stance

stand the gaff *v phr* by 1896 To persist and endure against rigors; =TAKE IT: *I've had. . . at least seven lifetimes on Seventh Avenue, mainly because I've learned to stand the gaff*—New York Times [fr *gaff,* the steel spur attached to the leg of a fighting cock]

stand the heat *See* IF YOU CAN'T STAND THE HEAT STAY OUT OF THE KITCHEN

stand-up 1 *adj* by 1841 Courageous and personally accountable; bold; =GUTSY •Most often in the expression *stand-up guy: He handled the humiliating defeat like a stand-up guy*—Philadelphia/ *And he's very, very stand-up*—George V Higgins **2** *n* televison by 1990s A live interview at the scene of a news event: *I hang a left past the faded Rose law firm and the networks doing evening stand-ups at the entrance*—Esquire [first sense perhaps fr *stand up and be counted*]

stand someone **up** *v phr* fr late 1800s To fail to keep an appointment, esp a date, with someone: *You won't stand me up, now will you?*—Jerome Weidman [perhaps related to *stand up* in the sense of "go through a wedding ceremony," the image being the forsaken bride or groom left standing alone at the altar]

stand up and be counted *v phr* fr early 1900s To announce and be accountable for one's convictions, opinions, etc; not be afraid to speak up: *Maybe a lot agree with you, but they won't stand up and be counted*

stand-up comic (or **comedian**) *n phr* A performer who typically stands alone before the audience in a nightclub, telling jokes, engaging in patter, etc: *We saw Woody Allen way back when he was a rather obscure stand-up comic*

stand up for someone *v phr* To defend and support someone; =GO TO BAT FOR: *Nobody stood up for her, so she had to back off*

stanza *n* sports by 1933 A period, an inning, a round, a chukker, or some other division of a game or contest; =CANTO: *The Jets pulled an el foldo in the third stanza*

starboard slinger (or **flinger**) *n* baseball by 1908, variant by 1913 A righthanded pitcher

◀**starfucker▶ 1** *n* by 1970s A person, esp a young woman, who spends time with star performers and relishes the sex act with them; =GROUPIE: *"She was promiscuous." "The queen of the star fuckers"*—Robert B Parker **2** *modifier*: *Mellencamp appears to revel in the starfucker mentality he pokes fun at*—Village Voice

starker *See* SHTARKER

starkers 1 *adj* by 1923 Naked; stark naked; =BARE-ASS: *. . . sitting there at the bar starkers from the waist up*—Ed McBain/ *You jog about, absolutely starkers, and then dive straight into a swimming pool*—Vogue **2** *adj* by 1962 Crazy; =BONKERS, NUTS: *The doctor told me I was starkers to do that* [fr *stark naked* and *stark, staring mad,* with the British slang suffix *-ers*]

star-struck *adj* by 1990s Enchanted by entertainment stars; enamored of glamour: *I don't get star-struck*—New York Times

starters *See* FOR OPENERS

start from scratch by 1936 **1** *v phr* To begin on an even footing, with no advantage or handicap: *We're gonna have a good life together starting from scratch*—Inside Sports **2** *v phr* To begin with the very first and simplest steps; build from the ground: *So they threw their plans away and started from scratch* [fr the *scratch-line,* the starting line for races, often scratched in the earth]

Star Wars defense *n phr* by 1983 A system of defense against guided missiles that depends on orbiting laser-beam weapons: *. . . to spend between $22 billion to $29 billion over the next four years to build a "Star Wars" defense*—Scripps-Howard News Service [fr the name of a very popular science fiction movie of 1977]

stash[1] or **stache 1** *v* (also **stash away**) by 1797 To hide; hoard; save up: *I had not stashed any dough away*—John O'Hara/ *I'd stash that jug*—James T Farrell **2** *n* by 1914 A hoard or cache: *She had a little stash of money in her bureau drawer* **3** *n* by 1930 A hiding place: *. . . if he wasn't home or in his stash, people would say. . .*—Claude Brown/ *I have some here, in a stash downstairs* **4** *n* 1960s narcotics A supply of narcotics, esp one's personal supply: *. . . meeting him at the airport with samples of their "special stash"*—New York Times **5** *n* 1960s narcotics A place where narcotics and associated paraphernalia are hidden, esp by a dealer [origin unknown; perhaps a blend of *stow* or *store* with *cache*]

stash[2] *n* by 1940 A mustache; ='STACHE: *He had a little red stash*—David W Maurer

stash bag *n phr* 1960s narcotics A small bag for carrying personal possessions, esp one used for marijuana

state *See* EAST JESUS STATE, IN A STATE

state-o *n* prison by 1950s A convict's prison uniform: *It griped me to have to put on "state-o" or official clothes*—Life [perhaps fr *state official*]

state of the art *adj phr* by 1967 The latest; the very newest and most advanced: *Many of the escort services are so state-of-the-art that they make Toner's look primitive*—Philadelphia [found by 1889 in the form *present status of the art,* which anticipates the modern use]

Stateside or **stateside 1** *n* WWII armed forces The United States itself as distinct from foreign places, overseas possessions, etc **2** *adj*: *. . . a genuine Stateside flavor to the celebration*—Yank

static *n* by 1953 Complaints, backtalk, trivial objections, etc: *Here's the policy, and let's not have any static about it* [fr the atmospheric interference that makes unwanted noise in radio transmissions]

station *See* FILLING STATION

stats *n* by 1962 Figures or statistics, esp relating to sports; =NUMBERS: *They are the kind of stats that a college powerhouse. . . might covet*—Time/ *An* *extraordinary cornucopia of mathematical data. Still, the line had to be drawn. No stats—* Philadelphia

◁**stay**▷ *v by 1960s* To maintain a penile erection

stay loose *See* HANG LOOSE

stay out of the kitchen *See* IF YOU CAN'T STAND THE HEAT STAY OUT OF THE KITCHEN

stay put *v phr by 1843* To stay where one is; not budge: *No, stay put. I won't be but a minute—*Elmore Leonard

steady *n by 1897* One's constant and only boyfriend or girlfriend
  See GO STEADY

steak *See* AUSSIE STEAK, TUBE STEAK

steal *n by 1940s* A great bargain: *I got that for half price, a real steal*

steal someone **blind** *v phr by 1974* To rob someone thoroughly and subtly; strip someone [fr the notion that the person being robbed must or might as well be *blind*]

stealth *adj by late 1980s* Covert; clandestine; =SNEAKY: *His piece of stealth journalism was an exercise in character assassination—*New Republic/ *The Republicans are turning Dan Quayle into a virtual stealth Vice President; not even any pictures of him on the Bush-Quayle re-election posters—*Time [fr the US *Stealth* fighter plane, activated in 1983, which, along with a bomber version, was designed to be invisible to radar detection]

steam **1** *v by 1922* To anger; make furious: *I steam easily—*Richard Starnes/ *It steams me to hear that our fair burg is the Crime Capital of the World—*Washington Post **2** *v by 1970s* To make someone hotly amorous: *Be thrilled by. . . chilled by. . . and steamed by Gilbert and Garbo—*San Francisco
  See LET OFF STEAM

steamed *adj by 1935* Angry; =PISSED OFF: *I'm too steamed to sleep, Lacey—*comic strip "Doonesbury"/ *O'Neill wasn't the only member of Congress to be steamed—*CBS News

steamed up **1** *adj phr by 1923* Angry; =HOT AND BOTHERED, PISSED OFF: *The first thing she does is get all steamed up about it—*Hal Boyle **2** *adj phr by 1936* Eager; excited: *He's really steamed up about the new initiative*

steam fiddle *n phr circus by 1940s* A steam calliope

steamroller *v by 1912* To dominate and crush; achieve by sheer force; =SNOWBALL: *The governor tried to steamroller the bill through*

steam someone **up** *v phr by 1930s* To excite and stimulate; incite enthusiasm

steam was (or is) coming out of someone's **ears** *sentence by 1960s* He or she was or is very angry: *Houk. . . was red-faced with anger. Steam was coming out of his ears—*Inside Sports

steamy *adj by 1970* Excitingly carnal; sexually arousing; =HOT, SEXY: *Hollywood's steamiest starlet—*Esquire

steel pot *n phr Army by 1970s* A military helmet

steer **1** *v underworld by 1889* To take or inveigle someone to a place or person where gamblers or confidence men might victimize him: *I been steerin' for Schwiefka all day—*Nelson Algren **2** *n (also* **steerer**) *entry form by 1939, variant by 1873* A person who steers patrons and victims: *He is nothing but a steer for a bust-out joint—*Damon Runyon **3** *n by 1899* Advice or information; a bit of useful data
  See BUM STEER

steerer *See* BUNCO-STEERER

Steinway *See* STOMACH STEINWAY

stem **1** *n hoboes by 1914* A street, often the main street of a town or city **2** *v hoboes by 1927* =PANHANDLE **3** *n narcotics by 1940s* An opium pipe
  See MAIN DRAG

stems *n by 1891* The legs, esp the attractive legs of a woman

stem-winding **1** *n by 1970s* Strong persuasion; powerful rhetoric: *Any arguments are exercises in stem-winding—*Car and Driver **2** *modifier*: *Reagan delighted the crowd with a stem-winding speech—*Washington Journal [fr extension of *stem-winder*, "something excellent," found by 1892, in turn related to the *stem-winding watch*, very advanced and first-rate when introduced]

stephen *See* EVEN-STEPHEN

step on someone *v phr by 1970s* To break into a CB or VHF radio transmission: *You'll have to say that again; we're being stepped on*

step on it **1** *v phr (also* **step on the gas**) *entry form by 1923, variant by 1920* To accelerate; hurry; speed up: *We better step on it; there's only five minutes left* **2** *v phr (Variations: one's* **dick** *or one's* **shvantz** *may replace* **it**) *Army by 1970* To blunder; make a serious mistake: *It was only a matter of time before he stepped on his cock and another rising star would be looking for a police chief's job in Iowa—*Michael Grant

step out **1** *v phr by 1907* To go out socially, esp to a dance or a party: *I haven't stepped out much lately, too busy* **2** *v phr by 1918* To escort someone socially; =DATE: *Who is she stepping out with these days?*

step out on someone *v phr by 1940s* To be romantically or sexually unfaithful to someone; =CHEAT, TWO-TIME

stepping *n by 1990s*: *That's stepping. Until recently, this dance form, which is said to have its roots in South African boot dances, has been performed only in African-American fraternities and sororities. . . —*Los Angeles Times

-ster *suffix used to form nouns by 1000* A person involved with, doing, or described by what is indicated: *clubster/ gridster/ mobster/ oldster* [this Old English suffix, always common, has lately become very popular; for instance, forms like *The Newtster*, "Newt Gingrich," are found]

steven *See* EVEN-STEPHEN

stew[1] **1** *n by 1908* A drunkard; =STEWBUM **2** *n by 1806* Confusion; chaos; =MESS
  See IN A STEW

stew² or **stewie** *n* by 1970 An airline cabin attendant, esp a female one: *Aeroflot personnel, beefy pilots and no-nonsense stewies*—Village Voice

stewbum *n* by 1902 A drunken derelict; =SKID ROW BUM: *... about the kid, as, say, compared to an old stewbum*—Earl Thompson/ *Get up and go home, you stewbum*—William Kennedy

stewed or **stewed to the gills** *adj* or *adj phr* entry form by 1737, variant by 1922 Drunk: *He knew where the colonel lived from the time he'd taken him home stewed*—Peter De Vries/ *He came in stewed to the gills*—Nelson Algren See HALF-STEWED

stick 1 *n* baseball by 1868 A baseball bat **2** *n* by 1688 A baton or rod of office, now esp a conductor's baton **3** *n* by 1857 A golf club: *The golf dudes had their bag of sticks*—Sinclair Lewis **4** *n* by 1674 A billiard cue: *I lived off the stick three months*—Nelson Algren **5** *n* by 1802 The mast of a ship or boat: *The gale blew the sticks right out of her* **6** *n* by 1914 A control lever or handle; =JOY-STICK **7** *n* (also **stick shift**) by 1971 A manual gearshift lever, esp one mounted on the floor **8** *n* by 1920s A slide rule; =SLIPSTICK **9** *n* by 1961 A ski pole **10** *n* jazz musicians by about 1920 A clarinet; =LICORICE STICK **11** *n* narcotics by 1938 A marijuana cigarette; =JOINT, STICK OF GAGE, STICK OF TEA: *Marijuana was easy to get, 25 cents a "stick"*—New York Post **12** *n* by 1940s A tall, thin person; =BEANPOLE **13** *n* by 1800 A stiff, awkward person; an overformal person **14** *n* by 1733 A dull person; =STICK IN THE MUD **15** *n* gambling by 1940s A casino croupier **16** *n* carnival & underworld by 1926 An assistant who poses as an ordinary innocent person; =SHILL: *The man who won the $246 was a shill, sometimes referred to as a "stick"*—John Scarne/ *One operator, known as a "stall" or "stick," distracts or frames the sucker in some way*—New York Magazine **17** *v* by 1699 To cheat; swindle; esp, to overcharge; =SHAFT: *... runs the Bowie garage, routinely sticking what customers come his way*—Washington Post See BOOM STICK, CARRY THE STICK, DIPSHIT, DOPE STICK, FIRE STICK, GET ON THE STICK, GOB-STICK, HAVE A BROOM UP one's ASS, INKSTICK, JIVE STICK, JOY-STICK, KICK STICK, KNOW WHAT one CAN DO WITH something, MAKE something STICK, OLD STICK, SHITSTICK, SWIZZLE-STICK, TEA-STICK, TELL someone WHAT TO DO WITH something, WORK BEHIND THE STICK

stick a fork in someone *sentence* baseball by 1959 The person is finished, ready for removal: *Well, I guess we can stick a fork in him, he's done*—Los Angeles Times [fr the usual way of telling whether a roasted bird is ready to eat]

stick around *v phr* by 1912 To stay at or near a place; =HANG AROUND: *I asked the cops to stick around for a few minutes*

sticker See FROG-STICKER, PIG-STICKER

sticker shock *n phr* by 1970s The nasty impact of a price sticker, esp one on a new car, in inflationary times: *We're seeing more in the way of sticker shock lately*—New York Times/ *... lawmakers are*

suffering from "sticker shock" at the potential costs of health reform—Macon Telegraph

stick in the mud *n phr* by 1733 A dull, conservative person; =FOGY: *Be cautious, but don't be a stick in the mud*

stick it ◁1▷ *v phr* (Variations: **cram** or **ram** or **shove** or **stuff** may replace **stick**; **up** one's **ass** or **in** one's **ear** or **where the sun doesn't shine** may be added) entry form by 1922, shove by 1941, stuff by 1955 To dispose of or deal with something one vehemently rejects; take back something offered and scorned •Very often used as a rude interjection conveying both rejection and insult: *You can shove your coke up your ass*—Ed McBain/ *Cram it, will you?*—John Irving/ *He told them to take the money and ram it*—Interview/ *You can send them to President Carter or stick them in your ear*—Atlantic Monthly **2** *v phr* (also **stick it out**) by 1900, variant by 1876 To endure; =HANG IN: *It's rough as hell, but I'll stick it*

stick it to someone or something *v phr* by 1970s To assault violently and definitively; =SOCK IT TO someone or something: *Pickett has really been sticking it to us in the press*—Michael Grant

stick one's **neck out** *v phr* by 1926 To put oneself at risk; invite trouble: *Don't stick your neck out too far*—Budd Schulberg

stick of gage *n phr* narcotics by 1950s A cigarette, either of marijuana or of tobacco

stick of tea *n phr* narcotics by 1935 A marijuana cigarette; =JOINT

stick out *v phr* (Variations: **like a sore thumb** or **a mile** may be added) entry form by 1842, sore thumb by 1936, mile by 1933 To be very conspicuous; stand out starkly: *She really sticks out in that bunch/ Low profile? He sticks out like a sore thumb*

sticks 1 *n* musicians by about 1900 Drumsticks: *... the snare drummer throwing his sticks up*—A Lomax **2** *n* musicians by about 1900 A drummer •A standard nickname See BOOM STICKS

the sticks *n phr* by 1905 Rural or suburban places; the provinces; =the BOONDOCKS, the RHUBARBS: *A cop was transferred to the "sticks"*—A Lavine/ *... a revue being tried out in the sticks*—H I Phillips [fr *sticks*, "trees," representing the backwoods]

stick shift See STICK

stick to one's **knitting** *v phr* by 1970s To attend strictly to one's own affairs; not interfere with others; be singleminded: *I'm not a personal confidant. I stick to my knitting*—Washington Post [perhaps fr the indefatigable *knitting* of Madame De Farge in Dickens's *A Tale of Two Cities*]

stickum by 1909 **1** *n* Glue; paste; cement **2** *n* Any viscous fluid; =GLOP, GUNK

stickup 1 *n* by 1887 An armed robbery; =HOLDUP: *... a robbery or a "stick-up"*—John Gunther **2** *n* by 1905 An armed robber: *Mallory looked at the dark stick-up*—Raymond Chandler

stick up *v phr* by 1846 To rob, esp at gunpoint;

=HOLD UP: . . . *being "stuck up" by highwaymen*—Nation/ *They're liable to go out and stick up a bank if they owe you*—Jimmy Cannon [apparently fr the command *stick 'em up*, "hold up your hands"]

stick up for someone or something *v phr* by 1837 To defend and support: *If his own family won't, who will stick up for him?*

sticky 1 *adj* by 1864 Sentimental; =SCHMALTZY, SOPPY: *a sticky little song about a crippled puppy* **2** *adj* by 1915 Difficult; tricky; nasty: *He considered himself a tap dancer, because he was very agile at gliding away from any sticky situation*—Ed McBain

See ICKY

sticky floor (or **bottom**) **1** *n phr* by 1990s: *Sticky floor, the inability to rise above an entry-level position, the plight of hundreds of thousands of women trapped in low-wage, low-mobility jobs (the other end of the glass ceiling)*—Los Angeles Times/ . . . *sticky bottom, an entry-level job that workers can't seem to rise above*—Toronto Globe & Mail **2** *modifier*: *A sociologist at Skidmore proposes the sticky floor image to encapsulate the plight of hundreds of thousands of women trapped in low-wage, low-mobility jobs*—New York Times

sticky-fingered *adj* by 1890 Prone to steal or pilfer; larcenous; =LIGHT-FINGERED: *What are you, sticky-fingered?*—James Thurber

sticky wicket *n phr* by 1952 A very difficult or awkward situation; a nasty affair: *"It's a sticky wicket," he said, but he left open the possibility that it could be orchestrated in a few cases*—Philadelphia Journal/ *It's the original sticky wicket*—Car and Driver [fr the British phrase *bat on* (or *at*) *a sticky wicket*, "contend with great difficulties," fr the game of cricket]

stiff 1 *adj* by 1737 Drunk: . . . *when the regular piano player got stiff and fell from the stool*—Westbrook Pegler **2** *n* by 1907 A drunken person: *Robbing a drunken man they call "rolling a stiff"*—Jack London **3** *n* (also **stiffie**) by 1859 A corpse: . . . *a final chapter narrated by the stiff*—New Yorker/ *So we scope out the stiffie and everybody says you know, like it was too bad*—Carsten Stroud **4** *n* by 1900 A hobo; tramp; vagabond: *He bore none of the earmarks of the professional "stiff"*—Jack London **5** *n* by 1899 A migratory worker; =OKIE **6** *n* by 1930 A working man or woman; a nonclerical and nonprofessional employee; =WORKING STIFF: *Coolidge always seemed unreal to the ordinary stiff*—Robert Ruark **7** *n* underworld by 1889 A clandestine letter, esp one passed around among prisoners **8** *n* underworld by 1823 A forged check, banknote, etc **9** *adj* underworld by 1940s Forged; =PHONY: *"I put over a couple of stiff ones" is the way a paper-hanger describes an operation*—Saturday Evening Post **10** *n* by 1890 A team, fighter, contestant, etc, that is bound to lose; esp, a race horse that will not, cannot, or is not permitted to win: *There is also a rumor that Follow You is a stiff in the race*—Damon Runyon **11** *n* by 1960s Any fail-

ure; =FLOP, TURKEY: . . . *gets a million dollars worth of hype, and I hear it's a stiff*—Aquarian **12** *v* horse-racing by 1940s To cause a horse to lose a race: *He admitted that he himself had stiffed horses for a fee*—Sports Illustrated **13** *v* by 1939 To fail to tip a waiter or other employee: *But he was slow about getting our orders, so we stiffed him*—National Lampoon/ . . . *who not only stiffs waiters and cab drivers, but golf caddies as well*—Art Buchwald **14** *n* A person who "stiffs" a waiter: *The maitre d', knowing a stiff when he saw one, shrugged*—Stan Cutler **15** *v* by 1950 To cheat, esp out of money, fair wages, etc: *The company defends its plan as a business decision and denies it was trying to stiff the women*—Newsweek/ . . . *which creditors he could stiff, which he could stall, which had to be paid at once*—Lawrence Sanders **16** *v* by 1950 To swindle; defraud; =SCAM: *Some of the lessons were not as palatable, though, such as the one about a young woman who stiffed him*—Morris County Daily Record/ *In other words, New York City got stiffed*—Village Voice **17** *v* by 1974 To kill; =OFF: *Nobody was supposed to stiff a member of the family the way Vinnie had stiffed his niece's boy*—Patrick Mann **18** *v* (also **stiff-arm**) by 1973 To treat unfairly and harshly; rebuff or push aside brutally: *He had stiffed a Philadelphia charity golf tournament without explanation*—Sports Illustrated/ . . . *didn't want to stiff him or send him sniffing along false trails*—Lawrence Sanders/ *I'll just stiff-arm them*—James Watt [the underworld senses having to do with forged and clandestine papers, cheating, etc, are derived fr an early–1800s British sense, "paper, a document," probably based on the *stiffness* of official documents and document paper; the senses having to do with failure, etc, are related to the *stiffness* of a corpse; the sense of harsh snubbing, etc, is fr the *stiff-arm* in football, where a player, usu a runner, straightens out his arm and pushes it directly into the face or body of an intending tackler]

See BIG STIFF, BINDLESTIFF, BLANKET STIFF, BORED STIFF, JUNGLE STIFF, KNOCK someone OUT, SCARED STIFF, WORKING STIFF

still wet behind the ears **See** NOT DRY BEHIND THE EARS

sting 1 *v* by 1812 To cheat; swindle; defraud; =SCAM **2** *v* by 1927 To overcharge; =STICK: *He got stung at the corner market* **3** *n* by 1975 A tricking or entrapment, either in a confidence scheme or as part of a law enforcement operation: . . . *have used sting to describe undercover operations that use a bogus business operation as a front*—New York Times/ *Let's contrast Abscam with traditional law-enforcement stings*—Village Voice

stinger *n* by 1950s An unpleasant or adverse element; =CATCH: *Seems like a good proposition, but there's a stinger in it*

stink 1 *v* (also **stink on ice**) by 1225 To be deplorable, nasty, totally inept or bungling, disgusting, etc; =ROT, SUCK: *The whole idea stinks, if you ask me*/ *The group and its main man stunk on*

ice—Rolling Stone **2** *n phr* (also **big stink**) by 1812 An extensive fuss; huge brouhaha; scandal: *"I never made a big stink about it,"* says Righetti—Village Voice
See ACT LIKE one's SHIT DOESN'T STINK, THINK one's SHIT DOESN'T STINK

stink bomb *n phr* by 1970s Something that fails badly: *. . . the stink bomb of a film,* Flashdance—Village Voice/ *The Chevy Chase Show was really a stink bomb*—Los Angeles Times [fr *bomb*, "a failure"]

stinker 1 *n* by 1898 A despicable person; =BASTARD: *Stop acting like a stinker* **2** *n* (also **stinkeroo**) by 1917 Something disgusting, nasty, badly done, etc: *If it proves to be a "stinkeroo" leave the theater quietly or suffer in silence*—Coronet

◁**stink-finger**▷ *See* PLAY STINKY-PINKY

stinking 1 *adj* by 1926 Despicable; wretched; =LOUSY: *It was a stinking way to treat her* **2** *adj* (also **stinking rich**) by 1956 Very wealthy; =FILTHY RICH, LOADED: *The family, in those years, was stinking* **3** *adj* (also **stinko**) entry form by 1887, variant by 1927 Drunk: *. . . and he got pretty stinking*—Max Shulman

stinkpot *n sailors* by 1960s A motorboat, esp a cabin cruiser [used in the early 1800s for a steamboat]

stink to high heaven *v phr* by 1963 To be very disgusting, inept, nasty, etc: *. . . filler items that definitely stunk to high heaven*—Village Voice

stink with *v phr* by 1960s To have much of; be oversupplied with: *He stinks with confidence, certainly*

stinky *adj* by 1940s Despicable; nasty; =STINKING

stinky-pinky *See* PLAY STINKY-PINKY

stir 1 *n* by 1851 A jail or prison: *John went to stir*—E DeBaun **2** *modifier*: *. . . with the stir haircuts*—Damon Runyon [perhaps fr Romany *steriben*; the mid–1800s *sturaban* or *sturbin*, "state prison," may be a transitional form]

stir-crazy *adj* (Variations: **bugs** or **daffy** or **simple** may replace **crazy**) by 1908 Insane, stuporous, hysterical, or otherwise affected mentally by imprisonment: *Any number of others were what we call stir-crazy, going about their routine like punch-drunk boxers*—American Mercury

stir one's **stumps** *v phr* by 1832 To hurry; =GET THE LEAD OUT, HUSTLE

stir-wise *adj prison* by 1930s Having the sort of cunning, patience, etc, instilled by imprisonment: *Johnson was stir-wise, a tough man to question*—Fact Detective Mysteries

a **stitch** *n phr* by 1968 An amusing or hilarious person or thing; =a HOOT: *The Gossages were a stitch, playing it very loose*—Sports Illustrated/ *What a stitch*—Paul Theroux/ *Calling this tarty turn an "interpretation" really is a stitch*—Washington Post [fr the expression *in stitches*, "laughing uncontrollably," perhaps fr the notion of laughing so much that it gives one *stitches*, "sudden sharp pains," found by 1601 in Shakespeare]

stocking *See* SILK-STOCKING

stocking stuffer *n phr* by 1976 A small, usu cheap present to be put into the Christmas stocking

stoked *adj* by 1963 Enthusiastic; happily surprised: *Everyone's stoked that he's here and. . . would he do a couple of tunes*—Playboy [from surfer talk]

stoked on *adj phr* by 1969 Enthusiastic over; very much pleased with: *Stoked on cats? If you like catamarans*—Yachting/ *I was really stoked on that chick, man*—Dan Jenkins [fr the notion of being fueled and hot like a furnace]

stomach Steinway *n phr* by 1940s A piano accordion

stomp 1 *n jazz musicians* by 1906 A jazz number with a heavy rhythmic accent **2** *v* by 1946 To assault viciously; savage; =CLOBBER **3** *n* 1960s students A student who wears cowboy clothing and boots [fr a dialect pronunciation of "stamp"; second sense found by 1803 in the sense "stamp on someone"]

◁**stomp-ass**▷ *adj* by 1970s Violent and pugilistic; rough and vicious: *I never even touched the slut and now there's gonna be some sort of stompass scene*—Easyriders

stompers *n* by 1899 Heavy boots [revived in the 1960s]
See SHITKICKERS, WAFFLE-STOMPERS

stone *black* by 1935 **1** *adj* Thorough; perfect; total: *Reba's a stone psycho, I tell you*—Joseph Wambaugh/ *People think it's a stone groove being a superstar*—Esquire **2** *adv* Totally; genuinely: *He is one stone crazy dude* [fr earlier adverbial sense "like or as a stone," in phrases like *stone* blind or *stone* deaf]
See NOT CARVED IN STONE

stone broke *adj phr* by 1886 Penniless; impoverished: *. . . the money that is made out of stone-broke tramps*—Jack London

stone cold sober *adj phr* by 1937 Totally unintoxicated; =COLD SOBER

stoned or **stoned-out** *adj* 1940s *cool talk* Intoxicated with narcotics or liquor; =BOMBED OUT, ZONKED: *They get themselves stoned on beer*—Dorothy Parker/ *The old man was stoned mad*—Robert Stone/ *. . . giggling in that mutually exclusive stoned-out way*—San Francisco

stone dead *adj phr* by 1290 As dead as can be

stoned to the eyes *adj phr* by 1970s Completely intoxicated; =HIGH: *Under that tree, stoned to the eyes, I wolf down Daybreak, Joan Baez's autobiography*—Village Voice
See TO THE EYES

stoner *adj* by 1960s An intoxicated or stuporous person: *. . . mumbles a stoner performance that's sidesplittingly funny*—Village Voice/ *It's different than it was in the '60s because it's not just your obvious stoner types. It's the jocks and the A-plus students. It's just about everybody*—New York Times

stonewall by 1914 **1** *v* To delay and obstruct, esp by stubbornly keeping silent: *I want you all to* *stonewall it*—Richard M Nixon **2** *n*: *A sustained stonewall, no one's been willing to answer questions for a week*—Village Voice [fr a cricket term used of a determined batsman who blocked everything as if he were a *stone wall*; in the US probably influenced by the stolid reputation of the Confederate general Thomas J *"Stonewall"* Jackson; the term became prominent during the early 1970s Watergate scandal]

stonies *n by 1970s* Urgent sexual desire: *They passed a local law prohibiting a dude with stonies from soliciting a woman-of-the-night for a piece of ass*—Easyriders [semantically similar to *hard up*, with its suggestion of penile erection; probably transferred because of the hardness of *stone* and the sense of *stones* as "testicles"]

stony *adj 1980s teenagers* Especially good; =SUPER

stood in bed *See* ONE SHOULD HAVE STOOD IN BED

stooge 1 *n by 1913* A servile assistant; a mere flunky or tool: *Whenever Gulliver is not acting as a stooge there is a sort of continuity in his character*—George Orwell/ . . . *his bail-bond stooges*—Erle Stanley Gardner **2** *v by 1939*: *We're glad to stooge for him*—Raymond Chandler [origin unknown; perhaps an alteration of *student,* humorously mispronounced as STŌŌ jənt, in the sense of an apprentice, especially one unskilled at or learning a theatrical turn of some sort while serving as the underling of a master]

stool 1 *n* (also **stoolie**) *underworld by 1906,* variant *by 1924* A police informer; =STOOL PIGEON: *He's nothing but a cop's stool*—James M Cain **2** *v by 1911*: . . . *to make me stool on a friend*—J Evans [back formation fr *stool pigeon*]

stool pigeon *n phr underworld by 1930* A police informer; =SNITCH, SQUEALER: *In New York he is also called a stool-pigeon*—J Flynt [fr earlier sense "decoy," fr the early–1800s practice of fastening *pigeons* and other birds to *stools* or stands as decoys; this term was applied to the decoy or "hustler" for a faro bank]

stoop *See* STUPE

stooper *n by 1974* A person who looks on the ground at betting parlors and race tracks for betting tickets that may be valuable: *The girl said she had become a stooper*—New York Times

stop *n underworld by 1940s* A receiver of stolen goods; =FENCE
See PIT STOP, WHISTLE STOP

stop and smell the roses (or **flowers**) *v phr* To relax from the hurly-burly; enjoy an interval of simple enjoyment: *It's not a total consuming vocation with him as it is with most other members of Congress. So consequently he tends to stop and smell the flowers a lot more*—Los Angeles Times

stop-by *n by 1990s* A very brief visit, esp by a politician: *Capitol Hill types at this particular bar even include Sen Bill Bradley. . . , who just did a "stop-by," and Rep Richard Gephardt. . .* —Milwaukee Journal

stop someone or something **dead in** some-

one's or something's **tracks** *v phr by 1950s* To stop someone or something very definitely and abruptly: *The economy could be stopped dead in its tracks*—Art Buchwald [fr the image of a person or animal dropping straight down on being struck; "to shoot or kill someone dead in his tracks" is found by 1824]

stop on a dime *v phr by 1964* To stop quickly and neatly: *The car corners smoothly and stops on a dime*

stopper *n baseball by 1948* A dependable relief pitcher: *I had hoped he'd settle down and be the stopper. . .* —Whitey Herzog/ *And a bullpen stopper means even more in the confidence he can give the rest of the pitching staff and the entire team*—Milwaukee Journal

storage *See* IN COLD STORAGE

storch *by 1960s* **1** *n* An easy victim; dupe; =MARK, PATSY **2** *n* An ordinary person; =GUY, JOE

Storch *See* JOE BLOW

store *n circus & carnival by 1940s* A concession
See BUDDY STORE, MIND THE STORE

storm *v 1950s hot rodders* To speed; drive very fast
See BARNSTORM, BLOW UP A STORM, BRAINSTORM, SHITSTORM, UP A STORM

stormer *See* BARNSTORMER

story *See* FISH STORY, LOOSE IN THE BEAN, SOB STORY, TOP STORY, UPPER STORY

the story of my life *n phr by 1938* The sad truth of my earthly career: *Our plans. . . our hopes. . . what becomes of them? Nothing. . . story of my life*—Thornton Wilder

stove *See* HOT STOVE LEAGUE, POTBELLY STOVE

stow it *v by 1676* To stop doing something ●Often an irritated command

STP (pronounced as separate letters) *n 1960s narcotics* A powerful hallucinogen: . . . *a strictly contemporary folk drug, called STP by its Haight-Ashbury discoverers*—Scientific American [fr *Serenity Tranquility Peace,* named in imitation of the oil additive STP™]

strack *adj Army by 1970s* Very strict in one's military appearance and grooming [fr *STRAC,* acronym for *Strategic Army Corps,* chosen units in constant combat readiness, hence elite troops]

straddler *See* FENCE-STRADDLER

straight 1 *adj by 1874* Unmixed; undiluted; =NEAT: *He takes his liquor straight* **2** *adj 1950s narcotics* Not using narcotics; not addicted; =CLEAN **3** *adj narcotics by 1946* Having had a narcotics dose, esp the first one of the day: *Once the addict has had his shot and is "straight" he may become. . . industrious*—Reader's Digest **4** *n musicians & students by 1960s* A tobacco cigarette; =SQUARE **5** *adj fr homosexuals by 1941* Heterosexual; not sexually deviant **6** *adj by 1530* True; honest and direct: . . . *from straight-poop tough to moral*—Village Voice
See GO STRAIGHT

straight-ahead *adj by 1836* Unflinching; undeviating: *Bill was a straight-ahead guy*—Philadelphia

straight arrow *by 1969* **1** *n phr* A person who observes the social norms of decency, honesty, legality, heterosexuality, etc; a nondeviant: *It turns out the boy is a straight arrow underneath his finery*—Richard Schickel/ *This is a supervisory job that ordinarily is won by the group Straight Arrow, the Eagle Scout type*—Harper's **2** *adj*: *The distraught heroine murmured. . . to the straight-arrow hero*—Studs Terkel [fr an archetypical upright Native American brave named *Straight Arrow,* mythically associated with a similar Caucasian who is a *straight shooter*]

straight-edge *adj* *1990s teenagers* Not using narcotics; =CLEAN, STRAIGHT: *If you're a teenager and you don't do drugs, you're a straight-up, straight-edge*—Wisconsin State Journal

straighten someone *v phr* *1960s narcotics* To get or administer a narcotic for someone

straighten someone **out** *v phr* *by 1894* To give the correct information, explanation, etc: *First let me straighten you out about where we were when it happened*

straighten up *v phr* *by 1907* =CLEAN UP one's ACT

straight face *n phr* *by 1897* A face revealing no ironic amusement or disbelief: *He couldn't tell me that story with a straight face*

straight-faced *adj* *by 1975* Maintaining a straight face; =POKER-FACED: *It was a big lie, straight-faced, but a lie*

straight from Central Casting *adj phr* *by 1990s* Typical; true to appearance; undevious: *. . . a man described by one of his own attorneys as "straight from Central Casting"*—Los Angeles Times

straight from the horse's mouth *See* FROM THE HORSE'S MOUTH

straight from the shoulder *adv phr* *by 1856* Honestly and directly; unflinchingly; =STRAIGHT: *He gave it to us straight from the shoulder* [perhaps from the notion of an honest blow delivered *straight from the shoulder* rather than deviously, from the side, etc]

straight goods (or **dope**) *n phr* *by 1892* The truth: *Is all dat straight goods?*—Eugene O'Neill

straight job *n phr* *truckers by 1940s* An ordinary truck as distinct from a semitrailer

straight lane *See* IN THE STRAIGHT LANE

straight man *n* *show business by 1923* A comedian's interlocutor and companion, who acts as the foil; =STOOGE: *The late George Burns was the archetypal straight man*

the **straight skinny** *n phr* *by 1970s* The truth; =STRAIGHT GOODS: *. . . lame enough to have told me the straight skinny about that*—Richard Merkin *See* the SKINNY

straight shooter *n phr* *by 1928* A direct and honest person; =STRAIGHT ARROW: *. . . declares that she is "the straightest shooter you ever saw"*—USExpress

straight talk *n phr* *by about 1900* Direct and honest discourse; =STRAIGHT GOODS

straight-up **1** *adj* *by 1910* Honest; upright; =STRAIGHT ARROW: *They were straight-up, nice people*—Claude Brown/ *. . . doesn't believe the women's product can compete with men's volleyball, not straight up, not on the basis of skills or popularity*—Buzz **2** *adj* *by 1975* Of cocktails, served without ice cubes; =NEAT [*straight-up-and-down* in the first sense is found by 1903]

strainer *See* SOUP-STRAINER

strangioso *adj* *by 1970s* Very strange; weird: *. . . a strangioso publication like* Raw—Village Voice [fr the Italian or Spanish intensive form with *strange*]

strap **1** *n* *students by 1970s* A student interested primarily in sports; =JOCK **2** *n* *by 1990s* A condom; =RUBBER [first sense fr *jock strap,* "athletic supporter"]

strapped **1** *adj* *by 1857* Short of money; penniless; =BROKE: *He happens to be strapped financially*—Ellery Queen **2** *adj* *by 1990s*: *. . . we never had a word for carrying a gun. Today, that is what "strapped" means*—TV Guide/ *They exist in a world of "strapped" (gun-wielding) teenagers. . .*—Los Angeles Times [*strap,* "credit, tick," in the financial sense is found by 1828]

strapper *See* BOOT STRAPPER

strategist *See* ARMCHAIR GENERAL

straw boss *by 1894* **1** *n phr* The foreman of a work crew **2** *n phr* Any assistant chief or subordinate director [said to be fr the arrangement of a threshing crew, where the chief would superintend the grain itself, and the second the *straw;* perhaps fr Dutch *stroodekkerbaas*]

straw hat *n phr* *show business by 1935* A summer theater: *. . . a new play that's. . . at a straw hat*—Abel Green

straw-hat circuit *n phr* *show business by 1948* Summer theaters collectively

streak *by 1973* **1** *v* To run naked in public **2** *n*: *The students did a streak across the square* *See* a BLUE STREAK

streaker *n* *by 1973* A person who "streaks": *She complained that several streakers marred her view of the campus*

street *modifier* *by 1967* Having to do with the streets and the street life of a city, esp of a ghetto: *Curtis Sliwa, founder of the street-tough Guardian Angels*—Philadelphia Journal/ *The defendant was not some street punk with a long criminal record*—Playboy *See* ON EASY STREET, NOT A ONE-WAY STREET, TWO-WAY STREET

the **street** *See* PUT IT ON THE STREET, WORK BOTH SIDES OF THE STREET

street (or **garbage**) **furniture** *n phr* *by 1960s* Furniture put in the street for the trash collectors, and sometimes taken for use

street people *by 1967* **1** *n phr* Ghetto dwellers **2** *n phr* Homeless people such as transient hippies, bag ladies, and the like; drifters

the **streets** *See* POUND THE PAVEMENT

street-smart or **street-bright** or **street-wise**

adj by 1976 Cunning and clever in various practical ways, esp in the street culture of the urban ghetto: *. . . a place for very sophisticated, street-bright people*—Toronto Life/ *. . . supplanting preppie glamour with what's euphemistically called a "streetwise" look. Supertramp is more like it*—Us

street smarts *n phr by* 1972 Cunning and cleverness of a very practical sort, esp that useful in the urban ghetto: *. . . that raging philosophical conflict between street smarts and pinstripes*—Philadelphia

streetsweeper *n by* 1990s A kind of shotgun: *. . . a bill that would ban the sale of two kinds of assault weapons. . . the "streetsweeper" shotgun and the Tec–9 pistol. . .*—Milwaukee Journal

street time *prison by* 1960s **1** *n phr* The period when a convict is not imprisoned, but is on parole or probation **2** *n phr* The time between prison terms

stressed or **stressed out** *adj* or *adj phr by* 1980s Suffering from nervous stress: *I'm sorry. I'm just very stressed*—Robert B Parker/ *He had to take a two-week leave because he was completely stressed out*

stress out *v phr by* 1990s To succumb to nervous stress: *Whenever. . . are at the point of stressing out, inevitably one of them will say to the other, "Want a bugle?"*—Macon Telegraph

stretch 1 *v by* 1595 To hang or be hanged **2** *n by* 1821 A prison term: *. . . a stretch in the Big House*—A Lavine **3** *n by* 1973 =STRETCH LIMO **4** *n by* 1990s An unwarranted extension or inference; stretch of the imagination: *Earlier I mentioned Huck Finn and, though it sounds like a stretch, I'm convinced that Pamela Trowel is his direct descendant*—New York Times/ *It was not, as they say in Hollywood, a stretch. Throughout those years, Simpson was the good guy*—Macon Telegraph [prison sense originally "a one-year prison sentence"; fourth sense found by 1710 in the very similar "an exaggerated statement"]

stretch limo *n phr by* 1973 A limousine that has been lengthened to provide more seating and more luxurious surroundings: *. . . certified designer fashions, eye-popping jewelry, stretch limos*—Philadelphia/ *. . . a bar the length of a few stretch limos*—Washingtonian [probably modeled on the earlier term *stretch* or *stretched* applied to a jetliner with a lengthened fuselage providing more seating]

◁**stretch some jeans**▷ *n phr prison by* 1970s To do the sex act, esp homosexually

strictly *adv by* 1938 Totally; entirely: *Everything about it is strictly from yuck*—Washington Post

stride 1 *n jazz musicians by* 1935 A jazz piano style of alternating bass with treble notes in particular patterns **2** *modifier*: *. . . stride piano, Harlem's version of ragtime*—Albert Goldman

strike *See* SIT-DOWN, WILDCAT

strike it rich *v phr by* 1854 To have a sudden financial success

strike oil *v phr by* 1866 To succeed: *I worked at the problem eight days before I struck oil*

striker 1 *n Army by* 1867 An officer's servant or

orderly; =DOG-ROBBER **2** *n WWII Navy* An assistant; a helper **3** *n WWII Navy* A sailor on the lookout for his own advancement, even by flattering means; =EAGER BEAVER **4** *n motorcyclists by* 1980s: *. . . Mokie had talked about his friend who was a striker, a recruit, for a motorcycle gang in the Bronx*

string *v by* 1812 To deceive; fool; hoax: *Who are you trying to string, anyhow?*—Elmer Rice [fr the notion of getting somone on a string, under one's control]

See PULL someone's CHAIN, PULL THE STRING

string along *v phr by* 1877 To agree; follow; join in: *As long as you string along with me, your cafeteria days are over*—Jerome Weidman

string someone **along** *v phr by* 1902 To deceive; fool, esp into a continuing adherence, cooperation, etc; =STRING: *I'm afraid that he's just stringing me along, trying to encourage me*—P Marks [probably fr early–1800s British *string on*, in the same sense]

stringbean *n by* 1936 A tall, thin person; =BEANPOLE

string someone **out** *by* 1960s **1** *v phr* To intoxicate someone: *I couldn't figure what she had done in there to string him out so bad*—Harry Crews **2** *v phr* To disturb someone; upset someone: *The one thing that strings me out. . . is punks who travel in packs*—Noel Gerson

strings *See* PULL STRINGS

string someone **up** *v phr by* 1872 To hang someone

strip *See* DRAG STRIP, LEAVE A STRIP

Strip *See* SUNSET STRIP

the **Strip** *n phr* Any of various main streets in US cities, esp the street in Las Vegas where most of the gambling casinos are found

stripe *See* HASH MARK

striper *See* BROKEN-STRIPER, CANDY STRIPER, FOUR-STRIPER, ONE-AND-A-HALF-STRIPER, ONE-STRIPER

stripes 1 *n circus by* 1940s A tiger **2** *n by* 1827 Chevrons worn as insignias of noncommissioned rank; =CROW TRACKS

stripped down 1 *adj phr by* 1946 Of a car, divested of ornaments and other unnecessary parts; =SHAVED **2** *adj phr by* 1961 Reduced to the essentials; disencumbered: *a stripped-down version of the Oedipus myth*

stripper or **strippeuse** *n entry form by* 1930, variant by 1939 A striptease dancer: *Norma Vincent Peel, the noted stripper*

strippers *n gamblers by* 1887 A deck of fraudulent playing cards from which narrow strips have been trimmed off certain cards; a marked deck

See LOW-BELLY STRIPPERS

strip-search *n by* 1947 =SKIN-SEARCH

stroke 1 *v by* 1561 To praise and please; caress the ego of; flatter; cosset: *Mr Hoover should be called in privately for a stroking session*—Cal McCrystal/ *. . . and ads in Rolling Stone were more for the purpose of stroking recording artists*—Wall Street Journal **2** *n by* 1969: *Everybody needs a stroke or* two every once in a while **3 modifier** by 1969: Two things are at stake for employees who parrot their bosses or who always are in stroke mode—Milwaukee Journal ◁**4**▷ **v** by 1970 To masturbate [stroker, "flatterer" is found by 1632]

◁**stroke book**▷ **n phr** by 1970 A lewd or suggestive publication; a pornographic book or magazine; =FUCK BOOK: It took a stroke book for me to break the ice—Richard Price [fr stroke, "masturbate"]

◁**stroke house**▷ **n phr** by 1970 A pornographic movie theater [fr stroke, "masturbate"]

stroll **n** by 1990s An area or route favored by prostitutes for solicitation: Ms Lopez, a 38-year-old streetwalker, said she had been chased by packs of youngsters who descended at night on the stroll, where prostitutes ply their trade in the industrial park—New York Times

strong **See** COME ON STRONG

strong-arm **1 modifier** by 1901 Using threats of violence; physically brutal: . . . strong-arm work around election time—E Lavine/ We reprehended his strong-arm tactics **2 v** by 1903 To use force and intimidation: We can't strong-arm them into voting our way

strong-arm man **n phr** by 1897 A man who uses physical force, usu as a hired agent; a thug; =ENFORCER, GOON

◁**stronger than pig shit**▷ **adj phr** by 1970s Very strong: . . . beautiful and a genius. . . stronger than pig shit—Dan Jenkins

struggle **v** sports by 1970s To have difficulty winning or holding the pace; be in athletic travail: Mets struggling; Cardinals soaring—New York Times/ Lendl Struggles to Win—New York Times [in the general sense "strive despite difficulties," found by 1597]

See BUN-STRUGGLE

struggle-buggy **n** by 1925 A car [fr the use of cars as sites for sexual endeavor]

strung out **1 adj phr** 1950s narcotics Using or addicted to narcotics; intoxicated with narcotics: The entire college population is "strung out" thrice weekly—New York Post/ . . . got fairly well strung out, fairly well addicted—Esquire **2 adj phr** by 1959 Emotionally disturbed; psychologically tense, brittle, and vulnerable; =UPTIGHT: She got herself strung way out. . . just one more little push and she was a dead duck—Changes/ . . . or slung low and strung-out on drugs or inner tensions—Ramparts **3 adj** black by 1960s Infatuated; in love: He's strung out on her [apparently by extension fr the black term on a tight leash, "in love, addicted," stressing the tethered helplessness of each condition]

strut one's **stuff** **v phr** black by 1926 To display one's virtuosity, esp in a saucy provocative way [fr dances featuring a strut like the turkey cock's, popular from around 1900]

stuck on someone or something **part phr** by 1886 In love with; infatuated: That feller was stuck on yuh, Bess—H Witwer

stuck-up **adj** by 1839 Haughty and conceited; snobbish; =HINCTY: We didn't like her at first because we thought she acted stuck-up

stuck with **past part phr** by 1848 Burdened with; saddled with: Imagine being stuck with a moniker like that all your life—Leslie Ford

stud **1 n** by 1929 A man, esp one who is stylish, au courant, etc; =DUDE **2 n** by 1895 A sexually prodigious man; =COCKSMAN **3 n** by early 1950s An attractive man; =HUNK: Everyone knows Mike, he's the total stud of his class—UCLA Slang **4 n** medical by 1980s A medical student [fr stud or studhorse, "stallion, esp one kept for breeding," the term found by 1903; first sense popularized by 1940s jive talk]

student **n** 1930s narcotics A newly addicted and still lightly addicted drug user: On a quarter grain a week a man was still a student—Nelson Algren

studio **See** RAP CLUB

studly by 1960s **1 adj** Masculine; sexually keen; =MACHO: In one episode Ross is flustered when a new girlfriend wants him to talk dirty to her. For advice he goes to studly friend Joey—Time/ Gay men at their pagan-studliest celebrate play, physicality, pretense, not to mention Greco-Roman grappling—Vanity Fair **2 adj** Excellent; good; =COOL: . . . it seemed like a studly thing at the time. Microsoft got what it wanted, and I got what I wanted. . . —Douglas Coupland

studmuffin **n** 1980s students An attractive young man; =HUNK, STUD: The vixen can't stop chasing stud-muffins around the old conference table—New York Times/ Stud-muffin David Charvet cannot be coaxed from his trailer for a chat—Buzz

stuff **1 n** 1920s prohibition era Liquor, esp boot-leg liquor: The stuff is here and it's mellow **2 n** 1920 narcotics Any narcotic: Where's the stuff?—Saturday Evening Post/ He came out and seemed to be off the stuff—New York Post ◁**3**▷ **n** by 1909 A woman regarded as a sex object; =ASS, COOZ, PUSSY: . . . classiest stuff this side of Denver—Stephen Longstreet ◁**4**▷ **v** by 1960 To do the sex act; =FUCK ●Chiefly British and most often heard in the passive imperative form get stuffed, a rude insult; used in any sense of fuck: No women, no children, no fun. Stuff this—John Leonard **5 n** baseball by 1912 The various ways a pitcher throws the ball, esp curves, sliders, etc **6 v** baseball by 1990s To pitch using effective "stuff": "He'd stuffed us pretty good before," said Brewers manager Phil Garner—Milwaukee Journal

See ALL THAT KIND OF CRAP, BLACK STUFF, EATIN' STUFF, the GREEN STUFF, HARD STUFF, HOT STUFF, KID STUFF, KNOW one's ONIONS, KNOW WHAT one CAN DO WITH something, ROUGH STUFF, SOB STUFF, TELL someone WHAT TO DO WITH something, WHITE STUFF

stuff cuff **n phr** 1940s jive talk A padded cuff on the pants of a zoot suit: . . . zoot suit, reet pleat, stuff cuff—Leonard Feather

stuffed **See** GET STUFFED

stuffed shirt **n phr** by 1913 A pompous person; a stiff, self-important bore

stuffer *See* STOCKING STUFFER

the **stuffing** *See* BEAT THE SHIT OUT OF someone or something

stuff it *See* STICK IT

stuff the ballot box *v phr by 1854* To cast or record fraudulent votes in an election

stuffy *adj by 1895* Tediously conventional; pompous and self-righteous: *He was inclined to be a bit stuffy in sexual matters* [fr *stuffy*, "stale, lacking freshness," influenced by *stuffed shirt*]

stumble *v underworld by 1950s* To be arrested; =FALL

stumblebum *n by 1932* An alcoholic derelict; a drunken drifter; =SKID ROW BUM: *. . . to bemoan the lack of charisma and to paint the candidates as a wrangling collection of stumblebums*—Washington Post

stump *1 v by 1807* To baffle; perplex; nonplus: *The problem's got me stumped* *2 v by 1838* To make speeches, esp on a political tour: *The candidate is stumping today in Illinois* *3 v line repairers by 1940s* A telephone or other wire-carrying pole [first sense fr the notion of being blocked by *stumps* in one's way; second sense fr standing up on a *stump* to make a speech]

stump for someone or something *v phr by 1878* To advocate or support, esp very actively [fr the notion of giving speeches from *stumps*]

◁**stump-jumper**▷ *n by 1936* A rural person; farmer; =HILLBILLY, SHITKICKER

stumps *n by 1460* The legs: *Everybody stir your stumps when Pa calls*

stunner *n by 1847* Something very attractive or impressive, esp a good-looking woman

stunning *adj by 1849* Attractive; impressive: *Isn't that a stunning little dress?*

stunt *n by 1878* Act; bit of behavior; thing to do: *. . . vulgar "stunts" designed to be easily comprehended and greedily relished*—Time

◁**stup**▷ *See* SHTUP

stupe or **stoop** *n by 1762* A stupid person: *"Don't call me stupe," Humphrey said*—G Homes/ *Surprised that we're not total stupes?*—Lawrence Sanders

stupid or **stupid fresh** *adj* or *adj phr black by 1980s* Excellent; splendid; =COOL, RAD: *That's stupid*—Delcastle Dictionary of Slang/ *Yep. Cool, mellow and stupid fresh*—comic strip "Curtis"

◁**stupid-assed**▷ *adj by 1980s* Stupid; =DUMB: *. . . a stupid-assed honor student*—Jane Leavy

stutter-stepping *n football by 1970s* To run with rapid short steps: *Never mind all that stutter-stepping and looking for daylight*—Sports Illustrated

style *1 v black by 1970s* To act or play in a showy, flamboyant way; =HOT DOG, SHOWBOAT: *You got an A in physics! You're styling!*—UCLA Slang *2 modifier*: *The proper reward for a styling player is a fast ball in the ribs*—Philadelphia Journal/ *His favorite stylin'-and-bombin' wall. . .*—Los Angeles Times [*put on style*, "to act in a boastful way," is found by 1871]

See CRAMP someone's STYLE, DOG FASHION, LIKE IT'S GOING OUT OF STYLE

stymie *v golf by 1857* To block or thwart; frustrate: *Instead, the drive toward integration has been stymied by the speedbump of crime*—Los Angeles Times [origin uncertain; perhaps fr British dialect *stimey*, "dim-sighted person," fr *stime*, "ray or bit of light"; adopted in golf for situations where the player or, as it were, the ball, cannot "see" a clear path ahead]

suave or **swave** *1960s teenagers* *1 adj* Excellent; fine; =COOL *2 n* Smooth skill; polished adroitness: *He has plenty of suave when it comes to girls* *3 v*: *Then I took her off her feet. I suaved her*—New York Times/ *I guess old Buck suaved her off her feet*—Jane Leavy

sub[1] *1 n by 1830* A substitute of any sort, esp an athlete who replaces another or an athlete not on the first team *2 v by 1853*: *Who'll sub for me when I go on leave?*

sub[2] *1 n by 1917* A submarine: *Saw sub, sank same* *2 n* =HERO SANDWICH

sub[3] *n by 1990s*: *He sells systems for subs, the street name for the cars that go Booma Booma Booma until your house windows rattle*—Milwaukee Journal [fr *sub-woofer*, a low-bass audio speaker]

sub- prefix for forming adjectives *by 1963* Inferior to or imitative of what is indicated: *sub-Woody Allen*

submarine sandwich or **sub** or **submarine** *n phr* or *n by 1960s* =HERO SANDWICH [fr the shape of the bread cut lengthwise for the sandwich]

◁**suck**▷ *1 v by 1928* To do fellatio; =EAT *2 v* (also **suck rope**, **suck eggs**) *by 1971* To be disgusting or extremely reprehensible; be of wretched quality; =ROT, STINK: *. . . a failure as an album. It sucks*—Rolling Stone/ *Life irretrievably sucks, and what's the use*—Village Voice/ *Your decision sucks rope*—TV show *Bob Newhart*/ *. . . his own pet phrase, "That sucks eggs," for expressing disdain*—Washington Post *3 v by 1900* =SUCK ASS *4 n by 1960s* =SUCTION [*Sucks!* as a contemptuous interjection used by Beritich schoolboys is found by 1913]

suck air *v phr by 1970s* To be afraid or alarmed, so as to pant; hyperventilate with anxiety: *Were you afraid? I was sucking air a couple of times*—Bernard Arkules/ *Whereas the FDIC claimed to have $13.2 billion on hand to help failing banks, in fact the fund was sucking air*—Nation

suck around *v phr by 1931* To loiter about; frequent a place, esp with a view to currying favor: *What's the kid sucking around the clubhouse for?*

◁**suck ass**▷ *v phr by 1940s* To curry favor; flatter and cajole; =BROWN-NOSE, POLISH APPLES: *He sucks ass with everybody in the front office*

suck canal water *v phr Army by 1970s* To be in trouble; be in a bad situation

suck eggs *1 v phr by 1906* To be mean and irritable: *We've sucked on these eggs long enough*—Peter Gent *2 v phr by 1970s* To do something very nasty, esp when invited to; =GO FUCK oneself •A euphemism: *Tell your husband to suck huge eggs*—Village Voice

sucker 1 *n* by 1838 An easy victim; dupe; =MARK, PATSY: *I'm no sucker*—Theodore Dreiser/ *I'm a sucker for a beautiful blonde*—George Sanders **2** *v* by 1939 To victimize or dupe someone: . . . *if I can sucker him into drawing first*—Mickey Spillane **3** *n* by 1978 Any specified object, esp one that is prodigious, troublesome, effective, etc; =MOMMA, MOTHER-FUCKER •A euphemism for *cocksucker*: *It took me 90 days to get that sucker straightened out*—New York Magazine [origin uncertain; perhaps fr the *sucker*, a fish supposed to be easily caught; perhaps fr the notion of an unweaned and relatively helpless creature, as suggested by an earlier sense, "greenhorn, simpleton"]
See COCKSUCKER, EGG-SUCKER

Sucker *n* by 1833 A native or resident of Illinois [said to be fr the custom of Illinois people to go upriver to work in the mines in Wisconsin, and then return home downriver, like a migrating fish]

sucker bait *n phr* by 1939 Something offered to lure unsuspecting victims: *That discount TV set is plain sucker bait*

sucker list *n phr* by 1910 A list of prospective customers, victims, etc: *The directory is not intended to be a sucker list*—Philadelphia Bulletin

suckerpunch 1 *n* by 1947 A blow that surprises the recipient, who might have dodged or parried it **2** *v*: *He suckerpunched me*—Peter Gent/ *I'll sucker punch a man in a second to get what I want*—Rolling Stone

suck face *v phr* by 1970s To kiss and caress; =NECK, PET: *You know, kiss. Suck face, kiss*—Ernest Thompson

suck someone's **flava** *v phr* 1990s *teenagers* To copy someone's style

◁**suck hind tit**▷ *v phr* by late 1930s To be in a disadvantageous situation; get the worst and least of things: *The plum assignments are there. The press coverage is there. We're up here sucking hind tit*—Robert B Parker [fr the presumed disadvantage of a *suckling* at the *nethermost teat*]

suck someone **in** *v phr* by 1842 To deceive; befool or dupe, esp with false promises [said to be fr the action of quicksand]

sucking *See* COCKSUCKING

suck it up *v phr* by 1980s To become serious; stop dallying or loafing: . . . *forced the 76ers to suck it up for game four, which they did to beat L.A.*—Sports Illustrated/ *No matter. He'd suck it up and go*—Harry Crews [fr the military expression *suck up* or *suck in your guts*, "pull in your stomach and look trim, as a soldier should"]

◁**suck off**▷ *v phr* by 1928 To do fellatio or cunnilingus; =BLOW, GO DOWN ON someone

◁**suck-off**▷ by 1950s **1** *n* A despicable person, esp a flatterer; =BROWN-NOSE **2** *adj* Despicable; nasty; =SCUZZY: *We did a suck-off thing*—Stephen King

suck up *v phr* by 1970s To defeat in a speed race; pass in a drag race: *I have also sucked up plenty of cherry red Vettes*—Car and Driver [fr the notion of drawing the passed car along in one's turbulence behind]

suck (or **kiss**) **up to** someone *v phr entry form* by 1860, *variant* by 1990s To flatter and cajole someone; curry favor with someone; =BROWN-NOSE, SUCK ASS: *He gets ahead by sucking up to the mayor/ They are boss kisser-uppers. They kiss up to the boss*—Saundra Smokes

sucky *adj* by 1990s Repellent; inferior; =LOW-RENT: *I was a real sucky waitress*—Jeannine Orban/ *"The Tyler Set" can be real sucky, too. . .* —Douglas Coupland

suction *n* by 1940s Influence; =DRAG, PULL

sudden death 1 *n phr* *sports* by 1927 Any of several arrangements for breaking a tie by playing an extra period during which the first team to score wins the game: *They went into sudden death overtime* **2** *modifier*: *It's like playing a sudden death inning at the beginning of a game*—Walter Mondale

suds *n* by 1904 Beer

sudser *n* by 1969 A soap opera or soap-opera-like show; =SOAP: *Harvey Fierstein's savvy sudser about a not-so-gay drag queen*—Time

Sudsville or **Suds City** *n* or *n phr* by 1980s Milwaukee, Wisconsin: *Sudsville 10 easily cops tilt*—Milwaukee Journal [fr the prevalence of breweries]

sugar 1 *n* by 1859 Money; =BREAD: *I'd take a trip if I had the requisite sugar* **2** *n* by 1930 Dear one; sweetheart •Most often a term of address: *I hear you, sugar* **3** *n* *narcotics* by 1930s Heroin, cocaine, or morphine **4** *n* 1950s *narcotics* LSD; =ACID [second narcotics sense fr the taking of LSD soaked in a *sugar* cube]
See HEAVY MONEY

Sugar *See* UNCLE SUGAR

sugar-coat something *v phr* by 1870 To make something more acceptable or palatable: *We played bad. I'm not going to sugar-coat it*—Milwaukee Journal

sugar daddy *n phr* by 1926 A man who provides money, esp one who supports a clandestine sweetheart or a gold-digger: *Mrs Shawsky must have had a sugar daddy on the side*—Fact Detective Mysteries/ *The Pentagon seems to be playing sugar daddy to a lot of American workers*—Newsweek
See DADDY

sugar report *n phr* WWII *armed forces* A letter from one's sweetheart

◁**sugar tit**▷ *n phr* by 1892 Something that gives comfort and security; =SECURITY BLANKET [fr the use of a cloth soaked in *sugar* water to appease a suckling infant; *sugar-teat* is found by 1847]

suit *n* by 1979 A serious business or professional person: . . . *some slick suit comes along and sets him free*—Carsten Stroud/ . . . *turned as the suits from the Housing Authority approached*—Robert B

Parker [fr the wearing of a *suit,* shirt, tie, etc, at work]
See BIRTHDAY SUIT, JUMP SUIT, MONKEY SUIT, ZOOT SUIT

suitcase *n* jazz musicians by about 1935 A drum

suiter *See* ZOOT SUITER

◁**sumbitch**▷ *See* SON OF A BITCH

◁**sumbitching**▷ *See* SON-OF-A-BITCHING

sun *See* STICK IT

Sunday 1 *modifier* by 1794 The best; one's best: *Sunday punch* **2** *modifier* by 1925 Amateur; occasional: *For a Sunday painter he's not bad* [the first date refers to the phrase *Sunday best,* "one's best clothes"]
See FORTY WAYS TO SUNDAY

Sunday clothes or **Sunday-go-to-meeting clothes** *n phr* entry form by 1779, variant by 1831 One's best clothes; =BEST BIB AND TUCKER: *. . . both wearing what Delaney descibed as Sunday-go-to-meeting clothes*—Lawrence Sanders [fr the earlier *Sunday-go-to-meeting clothes*]

Sunday driver *n phr* by 1925 A slow and careless driver, like one out for a leisurely Sunday drive

Sunday punch 1 *n phr* prizefighting by 1929 A very hard and effective blow or assault, with the fist or otherwise: *. . . and lay his Sunday punch on your snoot*—Damon Runyon **2** *modifier*: *. . . rockets, the "Sunday punch" weapon of the war*—Associated Press **3** *n phr* baseball by 1952 A strong and effective pitch, esp an overpowering fastball

Sunday soldier or **weekend warrior** *n phr* by 1950s A military reservist or member of the National Guard, who typically goes on uniformed duty on the weekend

sundowner *n* medical by 1980s: A patient who suffers delusions and disorientation at night, but not by daylight

sunny side up *adj phr* by 1900 Of eggs, fried on one side only with the yolk showing yellow

sunset *v* by 1978 To subject a government agency, a legislative provision, etc, to automatic termination after a specified period: *Many senior members of the CAB favor legislative proposals to "sunset" the agency earlier*—New York Times [fr *sunset law*]

sunset law *n phr* by 1976 A law requiring a government agency to be reviewed periodically, or to be automatically terminated after a specified period

Sunset Strip *n phr* by 1962 A section of Los Angeles, along Sunset Boulevard, frequented by alienated teenagers, drug users, derelicts, and other sub- and counterculture persons

sunshades *n* by 1965 Sunglasses; =SHADES

sunshine *n* 1960s narcotics LSD, esp taken as an orange tablet; =ACID, ORANGE SUNSHINE: *. . . powerful as a tab of "sunshine" dropped before you step in the cab*—Albert Goldman [fr the yellow-orange color]
See YELLOW SUNSHINE

Sunshine *n* 1913 Term of address for a sour person
See ORANGE SUNSHINE

sunshine law *n phr* by 1972 A law requiring that meetings of legislative bodies be opened to the public: *After the sunshine law the city council had to open its doors*

super[1] *n* by 1857 A superintendent, esp one who is custodian of an apartment building

super[2] *adj* by 1895 Wonderful; excellent; very superior: *America's Teenage Girls Speak Language of Their Own That Is Too Divinely Super*—Life [perhaps fr *superior* or *superfine*; revitalized in the 1960s]

super- by 1930s **1** *prefix used to form nouns* A superbly qualified and prodigious specimen of what is indicated: *superjerk/ superjock/ superchick/ Supermom* **2** *prefix used to form adjectives* Having the indicated quality to an extraordinary degree: *superhappy/ superwonky* [noun prefix stimulated from 1938 by the comic book character *Superman*]

super-duper or **sooper-dooper** *adj* by 1940 Excellent; wonderful; splendid; superb: *. . . this new MGM sooper-dooper musical smash*—New York Times [rhyming]

superfly *adj* black by 1971 Superior; wonderful; =SUPER: *He really thinks he's superfly when he gets into his thing*—Richard Woodley
See FLY

superintendent *See* SIDEWALK SUPERINTENDENT

super slab *n phr* truckers by 1970s A superhighway; an interstate highway

superwoman *n* by 1976 A woman who successfully undertakes marriage, motherhood, and a full working life all at the same time

supper *See* SHOOT one's COOKIES

the **Supremes** *n phr* by 1990s The Supreme Court: *If the Supremes agree to take it*—Dan Caplis [fr the name of a popular female singing group]

sure *affirmation* by 1842 Yes; certainly: *Sure, I'll support you*
See SHITSURE

◀**sure as fuck**▶ *adv phr* by 1980s Surely; certainly; =SURE AS SHOOTING: *Sure as fuck, you didn't tell me you were in there handling her glassware*—Scott Turow

sure as God made little green apples *adj phr* by 1940s Certain; definite: *It's sure as God made little green apples that they'll never get here*

sure as shooting by 1847 **1** *affirmation* Yes; certainly **2** *adj phr* Certain; definite **3** *adv phr*: *Thousands of them are sent by civic leaders. . . and, sure as shooting, by other federal judges*—Saul Bellow

sure as you're a foot high *adv phr* by 1930s =SURE AS SHOOTING

sure-fire *adj* by 1901 Unfailing; certain to succeed, happen, etc: *His election is a sure-fire thing*

sure thing *affirmation* by 1896 Yes; certainly; willingly: *Sure thing I'll go with you*

a **sure thing** *n phr* by 1836 A certainty, esp a bet which one cannot lose: *His election is a sure thing, right?*

surf *v* by 1990s To move or pass through some range of choices, such as television channels: *. . . I surfed from your show*—New York Times/ *They're surfing the same part of the zeitgeist*—Time [fr the ease

and rapidity of movement while *surfing* on waves]
See CHANNEL SURF

surf bunny *n phr* by 1960s =BEACH BUNNY

surfer *n* by 1990s A person who "surfs": . . . *people are taking the trouble to put the professional sports schedules on line, to be consulted by any surfer of cyberspace*—New York Times

surprise or **surprise surprise** *interj* by 1953 An exclamation of feigned astonishment over something perfectly obvious or predictable: *A study conducted by university researchers a year ago found that the Family Support Act was failing to change the welfare culture. Surprise*—New Republic/ *There were two favorite spots for tots. Surprise surprise. The boys loved the little bosom rose.* . . —Sassy

suss out *v phr* by 1966 To discover by intuition or inquiry; find out; learn: *I sussed out Whoosh was the chief my first time. . . here*—Richard Price/ *I've got to start sussing out nonscuzzy places to pee all along our most-traveled routes*—Village Voice [fr *suspect* or *suspicion*, attested as *sus* in British sources by 1930s; perhaps popularized and brought to the US by British rock-and-roll groups]

-sville or **-ville** by 1891 **1** *suffix used to form adjectives* Characterized by what is indicated: *dragsville/ splitsville/ squaresville* **2** *suffix used to form nouns* Place characterized by what is indicated: *Derbyville/ Motorsville*

swab or **swabby** or **swabbie** *n* by 1798 A sailor, esp a Navy seaman: . . . *better fitting dress uniforms for the hard-to-fit doughboy or swabbie*—Milwaukee Journal Sentinel [probably fr the characteristic activity of using *swabs* for cleaning the decks and other features of a ship]

swacked *adj* by 1932 Drunk: *Besides, you're swacked all the time*—Saul Bellow

swag 1 *n* by 1794 Stolen goods, money, etc; loot **2** *n* by 1990s Souvenirs, etc, sold at rock'n'roll concerts: *Somehow, these trifling collectibles came to be known as swag*—Los Angeles Times [probably fr the *swag*, "sack," in which loot might be carried]

swagging *n* by 1846 Getting money or property illegally, esp by pilfering government property or by taking illegal payoffs or tips: . . . *a lack of hard evidence that "swagging" or tipping had actually taken place*—Philadelphia [apparently revived in the 1960s]

swak or **SWAK** (pronounced as separate letters) *sentence* by 1925 Sealed with a kiss

swallow something *v* by 1591 To accept or endure reluctantly; stomach: *What I can't swallow is that he was then promoted*

swallow the anchor *v phr* nautical by 1907 To leave the sea and settle down ashore

swallow the apple (or **the olive**) *v phr* sports by 1970s To become tense and ineffective; =CHOKE UP: *I flat-out swallowed the apple and blew it*—Philadelphia Journal

swallow (or **eat**) **the Bible** *v phr* by 1930 To lie; forswear oneself: *The police will. . . "swallow the Bible". . . to protect some grafter*—E Lavine

swamper 1 *n* by 1929 for a trucker, 1870 for a teamster A trucker's or teamster's helper or loader: *The cops want to know if any of the wives knew which swampers their husbands were using*—George Warren **2** *n* by 1980s The second in command of a white-water raft

swank 1 *v* by 1809 To behave ostentatiously: *I saw her swanking up the avenue in furs* **2** *adj* (also **swanky**) by 1913 Elegant; stylish; =POSH, RITZY: *Carroll's swank office*—Associated Press **3** *n* by 1920s: *the. . . swank of his riding clothes*—F Scott Fitzgerald [origin unknown; perhaps fr Middle English *swanken*, "to sway," cognate with German *schwenken*, "to flourish"]

swap notes *v phr* by 1970s To exchange information: *I thought we might be swapping notes on that by now*—Armistead Maupin

swap spit *v phr* college students by 1938 To kiss

swarming *n* by 1990s: *She has surprised her listeners by not seeking social or psychological explanations for a recent rash of "swarming" crimes. . . where gangs of young men descend upon convenience stores and terrorize clerks and customers*—New York Times

swat *v* by 1796 To strike; hit: *He spoke up and got swatted for it*

swat (or **SWAT**) **team** *n phr* by 1969 A police unit wearing militarylike uniforms and using military assault weapons on assignments requiring extraordinary coordination and force: *When the terrorists took over the whole building, the commissioner sent in the SWAT team* [fr abbreviation of *special weapons and tactics* used as a modifier]

swave **See** SUAVE

swear off *v phr* by 1898 To desist from something, with or as if with an abstemious vow: *He swore off cheese and crackers for a whole week*

swear (or **swear to**) **on a stack of Bibles** *v phr* by 1866 To affirm with absolute confidence and considerable vehemence: *Don called all those short-term signals for Joe. I'd swear to that on a stack of Bibles*—New York Magazine

swear up and down *v phr* by 1906 =SWEAR ON A STACK OF BIBLES

sweat 1 *v* by 1610 To suffer; stew; =COOK **2** *v* by 1592 To work very hard and meticulously: *Clinton did not sweat buckets to gain a minimum wage increase, fund extensive job training, or stop budget-busting tax breaks for the well-to-do*—Nation **3** *v* by 1764 To interrogate a prisoner roughly: *We hauled a bunch of them in, sweated them, nobody would give us anything*—Robert B Parker
See FLOP SWEAT, IN A SWEAT, NO SWEAT, PANTHER PISS, PIG SWEAT, TIGER SWEAT

sweat bullets 1 *v phr* by 1970s To be very worried; be apprehensive; =SHIT A BRICK: *They've been sweating bullets since they heard he was looking for them* **2** *v phr* (also **sweat blood**) by 1970s, variant by 1911 To work very hard: *Their father has to sweat bullets to make a living*—People Weekly

sweat equity *n phr by 1968* An equity or stake earned by hard work rather than purchase: *They've demonstrated with sweat equity that they're team players*—National Public Radio news

sweater (or **pin-up**) **girl** *n phr entry form by late 1930s, variant by 1941* A young woman, esp a movie actress or a model, with a notably attractive body, which she features by wearing tight and short clothing

sweat hog *college students by 1970s* ◁1▷ *n phr* A heavy and unattractive woman ◁2▷ *n phr* A sexually promiscuous woman **3** *n phr* A difficult and incompetent high school or college student

sweat it *v phr by 1963* To be apprehensive; =UPTIGHT •Most often used in the negative: *Well, don't sweat it. Look, is a buck and a quarter okay?*—New York Magazine

sweat something **out** *v phr by 1876* To endure or suffer, esp with nervous anticipation: *. . . a young writer sweating out the creation of his first short stories*—Village Voice [revived during WWII]

sweat something **out of** someone *v phr by 1940s* To discover by intimidation or harsh questioning

sweats *n by 1990s* Athletic clothing; warm-up suits: *. . . several court reporting firms. . . a T-shirt and sweats distributor. . .* —Milwaukee Journal

Sweeney *See* TELL IT TO SWEENEY

sweep 1 *n sports by 1940s* The winning of a tournament, series, etc, without losing a single game: *He took the match in a sweep, straight sets* **2** *v*: *The Giants swept the World Series that year*

sweeps 1 *n television by 1980s* Audience ratings and their announcement: *She plans to stay through the May ratings "sweeps"*—Milwaukee Journal **2** *modifier*: *. . . a bunch of mealy-mouthed wimps who'd break bread with Adolf fucking Hitler if it meant some kind of rating during sweeps week*—Stan Cutler [perhaps fr *sweepstakes*]

sweep something **under the rug** *v phr by 1961* To avoid or conceal something: *They just swept the whole race matter under the rug*

sweet *See* BLONDE AND SWEET

sweet ass *See* BUST one's ASS

sweeten *v cardplaying by 1896* To make something more attractive, esp more remunerative: *Then they sweetened the offer by several thousand dollars*

sweeten someone **up** *by 1950s* **1** *v phr* To bribe or otherwise recompense someone in exchange for something: *He had to sweeten the cops up even after he had the license* **2** *v phr* To flatter and cajole someone; =SUCK UP TO someone: *He sweetened the audience up a little by praising the town*

sweetheart 1 *n by 1942* Something excellent; a cherished and valuable object; =HONEY: *See that sweetheart of a car?* **2** *n by 1940s* A pleasant person; =DOLL: *Wait'll you meet her father, he's a sweetheart*

sweetheart contract (or **agreement**) *n phr labor union by 1950s* A labor contract that particu-

larly favors the employer, and is usually negotiated by a corrupt union official

sweetheart deal *n phr by 1959* A mutually profitable and either unethical or illegal arrangement, usu involving a public agency: *. . . what the cable companies now term a "sweetheart deal." The Port Authority just turned over the whole thing to Merrill Lynch*—Village Voice

sweetie *n by 1903* A sweetheart, in all senses •Often a term of endearment in address: *And Tom's the first sweetie she ever had*—F Scott Fitzgerald/ *Ain't my new computer a sweetie?* [an isolated instance, *sweet-ee* is found by 1778]

sweetie-pie *n by 1928* A sweetheart, in all senses: *His sweetie pie came home in the early hours*—Associated Press

sweet mama *n phr 1920s black* A female lover

sweet man (or **papa**) *n phr 1920s black* A male lover

sweet on someone *adj phr by 1740* Enamored of someone; in love with someone: *He was never really sweet on Miss Carlisle*—Agatha Christie/ *. . . very sweet on a handsome young man*—Frederic Morton

sweet patootie *See* PATOOTIE

sweet pea *n phr by 1940s* A sweetheart [perhaps a shortening of *sweet patootie,* influenced by the name of the garden plant]

sweet potato *n phr by 1930s* An ocarina

sweets or **sweetums** *n by about 1930* =SWEETHEART, SWEETIE •A term of endearment: *I'll get it for you, sweets*

Sweet 16 *n phr sports by 1990s* The last sixteen teams left in the annual college basketball playoffs: *Maryland to the Sweet 16*—Milwaukee Journal [fr the traditional phrase for a young girl, found by 1826, and still much in use]

sweet spot *n phr by 1974* The best area on a tennis racket, hockey stick, golf club, or baseball bat for contact with the ball or puck: *. . . they will find the sweet spot with greater frequency with the Slotz*—Milwaukee Journal Sentinel

sweet-talk 1 *v phr by 1936* To seek to persuade or soften someone, esp by flattery and endearments; =FAT-MOUTH **2** *n by 1945*: *He listened to her sweet-talk very receptively*

sweet-tooth *n 1960s narcotics* Narcotic addiction or craving

swell 1 *n by 1786* A stylish and well-groomed person; =DUDE **2** *n by 1786* A wealthy, elegant person; a socialite; =NOB: *. . . up on the hill where the swells live* **3** *adj by 1888* Excellent; wonderful; superb: *The hotels are swell*—Theodore Dreiser/ *He was a hell of a swell fellow*—Charles MacArthur **4** *adv by 1920s*: *The new owners have treated me swell*—Associated Press [perhaps fr the late–18th-century phrase *cut a swell,* "swagger," describing the behavior of a person who *swells* with arrogance]

swellelegant *adj* =SWELL

swellhead 1 *n by 1845* A conceited person; a person whose head is swollen with pride: *She acted like* a swellhead after she got the prize **2** *n by 1867* Conceit: *I was afraid you'd get the swellhead*—W R Burnett

swig *n by 1621* A swallow of liquor; =PULL, SLUG [origin unknown]

swill *n by 1570* Nasty and inferior food or drink; =BELLY-WASH: *What is this swill they've placed before us?*

swim *v by 1970s* To perform well; succeed; =FLY: *I didn't think the Harptones quite swam last time I saw them*—Village Voice [perhaps fr *sink or swim*]

swimming in *See* ROLL IN

swindle sheet *n phr* (also **cheat sheet, scandal sheet**) entry form *by 1923* An expense account: *Only one goes on the swindle sheet*—A R Hilliard

swing 1 *n by 1899* A style of white jazz music of the 1930s and '40s, developed from hot jazz and usu played by big bands: *That pastime was called Swing, and its king, Benny Goodman, and most of its greatest exponents and exploiters were quartered here in New York*—Albert Goldman **2** *v musicians by about 1935* To have a strong but easy and pleasant impetus: *Chaucer and Jazz are quite similar; they both swing, they both have the same punch, vitality, and guts*—Jazz World **3** *v by 1918* To perform very well, as a good jazz musician does: *It is appropriate that gifted, gravel-voiced Herschel Bernardi should swing eight times a week in this particular hit*—Walter Wager **4** *v black by 1957* To have a good time; enjoy oneself hugely, as at a good party **5** *v by 1964* To do the sex act, esp promiscuously with various partners either seriatim or at once: *The sexual revolution is not new; people have been swinging as long as they are on this earth*—Rona Jaffe **6** *v by about 1961* To be stylish, au courant, sophisticated, etc: *"Songs for Swingin' Lovers"*—Frank Sinatra album title **7** *v 1960s street gang* To be a member of a teenage street gang **8** *n by 1943* An interval between work periods: *... with two hours' swing in the afternoon for lunch*—Ira Wolfert

swing (or go) both ways *v phr by 1960s* To be bisexual; =AC-DC: *Do you go both ways?*—TV show Geraldo

swinger *n by about 1961* A person who "swings," esp in the mode of sexual promiscuity: *Kissinger, who enjoyed a reputation as a swinger, was asked to explain his oft-quoted remark*—Joseph Heller/ *Many swingers even pride themselves on preserving their marriages through these arrangements*—S Rudikoff

swinging single *n phr by 1967* A merry and celebratory unmarried person, esp one who is sexually promiscuous as well as au courant: *... entertaining other couples every weekend and making jokes about the "swinging singles" all around them*—Albert Goldman

swing for the fences 1 *v phr baseball by 1970s* To swing very hard, trying for a home run: *As the Babe knew, swinging for the fences often brings more strikeouts than four-baggers*—New York Times **2** *v phr by 1980s* To make a maximum

effort; =GO FOR BROKE: *What was striking about Clinton's first week in office was the way he swung for the fences on the domestic front*—New York Times/ *This stockbroker prefers to invest his own money in issues more risky than the ones Morgan Stanley recommends; he is willing to swing for the fences with his own investments*—New York Times

swingle *n* =SWINGING SINGLE

swing like a rusty gate 1 *v phr by 1950s* To swing at a baseball awkwardly or wildly **2** *v phr fr 1930s* To play swing music well

swingman *n 1960s narcotics* A narcotics dealer; =CONNECTION

swing shift *n phr by 1941* A work shift between the regular day and night shift, typically from four to midnight

swipe[1] 1 *v by 1889* To steal, esp something small or trivial; pilfer: *... nix on swiping anything*—E B White **2** *n by 1807* A stroke or blow, esp a strong one ●Most often in the phrase *take a swipe at*: *Let somebody... take a swipe at him*—Bennett Cerf **3** *v by 1990s* To run a credit card, identification card, etc, through an electronic detector groove: *Swipe your card there and the door will open* [all senses perhaps fr alterations of *sweep* or *swoop* and the actions of sweeping or swooping up, or of hitting a sweeping blow; second sense perhaps fr dialect preservation of Old English *swippan*, "beat, scourge"] *See* SIDESWIPE

swipe[2] *n by 1960s* Inferior liquor, esp of the homemade sort: *... the homemade bootleg mess made by the natives out of fruit and called "swipe"*—James Jones [probably related to several late 1780s and early 1800s British senses of *swipe*, "to gulp liquor quickly and deeply," of *swipes*, "small beer," and of *swipey*, "tipsy," all of which may be related to the British nautical *swipes*, "rinsings of the beer barrel," and hence to a sibilation of *wipe*]

swish[1] 1 *adj homosexuals by 1930s* Showing the traits of an effeminate male homosexual; mincing; limp-wristed; =NELLIE: *His walk was quite swish* **2** *n* An effeminate male homosexual; =QUEEN: *... that fat swish*—Budd Schulberg **3** *v fr homosexuals* To move, walk, speak, etc, in the manner or presumed manner of effeminate male homosexuals [perhaps fr the swinging movements of the hips in a mincing walk; perhaps fr *swish[2]*]

swish[2] *adj by 1879* Elegant; fancy; =POSH, RITZY: *You can get a very swish version... or a very basic version*—New York Times [fr British dialect, an apparent variant of *swash*, "a swaggerer," hence semantically related to *swank*]

switch 1 *n by 1920* A change, esp a reversal or major alteration: *This is a big switch for the reigning party* **2** *n by 1935* An exchange, esp an illicit substitution: *He made a switch, giving her the empty purse and taking the valuable one* **3** *v underworld by 1940s* To inform; =SNITCH **4** *n by about 1945* =SWITCHBLADE

See ASLEEP AT THE SWITCH, CHICKEN SWITCH, NOT HAVE ALL one's SWITCHES ON

switchblade *n* by 1932 A knife with a blade that springs out when a switch is pressed

switched *See* I'LL BE DAMNED

switched-off *adj* by 1966 Not in the current fashion; unconventional; =OUT OF SYNC: *... responding... to his unconventional (at that time), bohemian, "switched-off" quality*—Garry O'Conor

switched on by 1964 **1** *adj phr* Fashionable and admirable; au courant; up-to-date; =GEAR: *A larger number of the women were in short, switched-on dresses*—New Yorker/ *They are among the current drop of switched-on young matrons*—Enid Nemy **2** *adj phr* Exhilarated; stimulated; =HIGH, PLUGGED IN, TURNED ON: *He has powerful friends and you don't, switched-on in-crowd celebrity friends, high-all-the-time-and-getting-away-with-it friends*—T G Harris

switcheroo *n* by 1933 A switch or shift; a reversal: *For people in search of titillating diversion from their daily lives, switcheroos may seem exciting*—American Scholar/ *We'll pull a switcheroo. We'll use olives instead of cherries*—H T Webster

switch-hitter 1 *n* baseball by 1930s A player who bats both righthanded and lefthanded **2** *n* by 1950s A versatile person **3** *n* by 1956 A bisexual person: *... some people thought he was a switch-hitter. But a nice guy*—Elmore Leonard

switch on 1 *v phr* by 1960s To join the current trends, tastes, etc; become up-to-date **2** *v phr* by 1960s To excite and exhilarate; arouse sexually; =TURN ON: *He didn't see any girls that switched him on much* **3** *v phr* 1960s narcotics To become intoxicated with narcotics; =TURN ON

swivel-hips *See* SNAKE-HIPS

swivet *n* by 1892 A fit of angry agitation; =SNIT: *You can't get yourself in a swivet over some isolated instances*—Robert Ruark [origin unknown]

swizzled or **swozzled** *adj* by 1843 Drunk; tipsy

swizzle-stick *n* by 1879 A stick for stirring a mixed drink [fr earlier *swizzle*, "stir a drink," fr *swizzle*, "a drink, to drink," perhaps related to *switchel*, "drink of molasses and water, often mixed with rum"]

swoopy *See* ULTRASWOOPY

-sy *See* -IE

sync 1 *v* by 1950s To synchronize: *Let's sync our plans, okay?* **2** *n* by 1929 Synchronism; synchronization
See IN SYNC, LIP-SYNC, OUT OF SYNC

◁**syph** or the **syff**▷ *n* or *n phr* (Variations: **siff** or **the siff**) by 1914 Syphilis: *... syphilis, not siff*—Calder Willingham/ *They found out he had the syph while he was doin' time*—Rocky Graziano

syrup *See* COUGH SYRUP

sysadmin (SISS uhd MIN) *n* 1980s computer The computer operator who supervises a network: *... system administrators are the unacknowledged legislators of the net. Sysadmins are really the only authority figures that exist on the net*—New Yorker

sysop (SISS ahp) *n* 1980s computer The computer operator who manages a computer bulletin board, a computer display where those with access may get or convey information: *People look up to the sysop*—New York Times [fr *system operator*]

system *See* OLD BOY NETWORK

T

T¹ 1 *n* narcotics by 1940s Marijuana; =TEA **2** *n* 1960s narcotics A gram of methamphetamine

T² *n* basketball by 1990s A technical foul: *The "T" was absolutely ridiculous*—Milwaukee Journal

◁**TA** or **T and A**▷ (pronounced as separate letters) **1** *n phr* by 1972 A display of female bosoms and bottoms; a show featuring such display; =CHEESECAKE: *. . . the realm of feminine esthetics or, as it is known in the profession, TA*—Playboy/ *. . . to enliven their product they call for T and A*—Toronto Life **2** *adj phr*: *They turned it into a T and A show*—Philadelphia Journal [fr *tits* plus *ass*]

tab¹ 1 *n phr* by 1942 The bill or check for something, esp for food or drink: *. . . three- or four-hundred-dollar tabs for unpaid liquor*—Stephen Longstreet **2** *n* by 1950s A written acknowledgment of debt; =IOU: *They're liable to go out and stick up a bank if they owe you a tab*—Jimmy Cannon [origin unknown; perhaps a shortening of *tabulation*] *See* PICK UP THE TAB

tab² *v* by 1924 To identify or designate; label: *I tabbed him immediately as a crook* [fr *tab*, "a tied-on baggage label," of unknown origin; perhaps an alteration of *tag*]

tab³ 1960s narcotics **1** *n* A tablet **2** *n* A dose of LSD; =HIT

tab⁴ *n* by 1990s A tabloid newspaper: *. . . just be sure the other tabs and the London papers don't have track pictures either. . .* —New York Times

tabby *n* by 1990s =PUSSYCAT: *The 348 is a tabby by comparison. . .* —New York Times

table *See* UNDER THE TABLE

table grade *See* EATIN' STUFF

table-hop *v* by 1956 To go from table to table in a restaurant, night club, etc, visiting and chatting: *Linda goes to Elaine's to table-hop, not to eat*

tablet *See* BRAIN TABLET

tabs *See* KEEP TABS ON

tach *n* by 1966 A tachometer

tack *n* by 1924 An equestrian's equipment for riding [an abbreviation of *tackle*, "equipment"]

tacks *See* SPIT TACKS

tacky *adj* by 1862 Inferior; shabby; vulgar; =ICKY, RATTY: *She talked in a manner that would be considered a bit countrified, if not slightly tacky*—Calder Willingham/ *The girl's hunger for validation, however tacky. . .* —Newark Star-Ledger [apparently fr *tacky*, "small, useless horse," and later "hillbilly, cracker"] *See* TICKY-TACKY

◀**taco**▶ *n* by 1970s A Mexican or person of Mexican descent

◁**Taco**▷ *See* TIO TACO

tad 1 *n* by 1877 A small boy; a child: *I've liked reading since I was just a tad* **2** *n* by 1915 A small amount; =CUNT-HAIR, SKOSH, SMIDGEN: *. . . may be taking his new series. . . just a tad too seriously*—People Weekly/ *. . . seem white to me even if they are a tad deformed*—Harry Crews [origin uncertain; perhaps a shortening of *tadpole*; perhaps fr British dialect *tadde*, "toad"]

ta-da or **tah-dah** *interj* show business by 1940s An exclamation announcing one's arrival or some revelation: *She said "Ta da," and dropped the bath towel, and seduced me*—Robert B Parker/ *So, one-oh-two West a Hundred Sixteenth Street is, tah-dah!, Mohammed Temple Number Seven. . .* —Carsten Stroud [originally a two-note musical phrase introducing a performer]

tag 1 *n* by 1934 A person's name **2** *n* underworld by 1934 An arrest warrant: *Is there a tag out for me?*—Raymond Chandler **3** *n* by 1935 An automobile license plate: *The Seminoles get special tags*—Associated Press **4** *v* by 1940 To hit; =BELT, SOCK **5** *v* by 1980 To write graffiti on walls, etc: *. . . tagged with the rebellious urban scrawl of graffiti artists. . .* —Los Angeles Times [final sense fr the fact that many such graffiti are the names, or *tags*, of the painter] *See* DOG TAGS

tag along *v phr* by 1900 To accompany someone, esp when not invited: *If you don't mind. . . I'll just tag along with you*—W E B Griffin/ *Which I can do on my own, or whatever; you want to tag along*—Stan Cutler

tagger or **tag banger** *n* or *n phr* entry form by 1986, variant by 1990s A person, esp a street gang member, who defaces walls, etc, with graffiti: *. . . promised Sunday would be a new crackdown on graffiti "taggers"*—Milwaukee Journal Sentinel/ *Taggers. . . gang members and visitors who spray-paint graffiti in national parks*—ABC Radio news/ *. . . focussing on graffiti as a crime and tag bangers and killing. . .* —Los Angeles Times

tagging crew *n phr* by 1990s: *Frighteningly aggressive panhandlers. "Tagging crews" that cover a city with graffiti*—Milwaukee Journal

tail 1 *n* by 1303 The buttocks; =ASS: *. . . if all of us parked ourselves on our tails*—P Marks/ *I hadn't* *tossed him out on his tail*—Jerome Weidman ◁2▷ **n** *by* 1933 A woman regarded solely as a sex partner, object, or organ; =ASS: *a nice piece of tail* ◁3▷ **n** *by* 1920 Sexual activity or gratification; =ASS, FUCKING: *It was said that the freshmen up at Yale got no tail* **4 n** *by* 1914 A person who follows another for surveillance; =SHADOW: *The security officer was even going to put a tail on the children*— John McCarten **5 v** *by* 1907: *... tailing a jewelry salesman*—American Mercury [in the second sense, *tail*, "sex organ," is found by 1362]

See one's ASS OFF, DRAG-TAIL, DRAG one's TAIL, GET one's TAIL IN A GATE, HAVE A BROOM UP one's ASS, HAVE A TIGER BY THE TAIL, HAVE someone or something BY THE TAIL, PIECE OF ASS, RINGTAIL, SHAVETAIL, WORK one's ASS OFF

tail bone *n phr by* 1940s The buttocks; =ASS

tailed *See* RINGTAILED SNORTER

tail-end Charlie *WWII air forces n* =BUTT-END CHARLIE

tailgate 1 v To follow another car, truck, etc, dangerously closely; =HIGHTAIL: *... drove her car behind him, tailgating him between red walls of dead brick*—Saul Bellow **2 v** *college students* To watch girls go by **3 v** *Army* To join what one says closely to what has just been said; =DOVETAIL

tailgate party 1 n phr An outdoor party or picnic, typically in the parking lot of a sports stadium, and served on the tailgates of station wagons **2 n phr** *jazz musicians* A style of jazz said to resemble the early New Orleans sort [musical sense fr the fact that the *tailgate* of the band's wagon was left down to give slide-room for the trombone]

tailor-made 1 adj Exactly fitting or appropriate: *... a situation tailor-made for that sort of intervention* **2 adj** Made especially for someone or something; custom-made: *He had his own tailor-made piano stool* **3 n** A ready-made cigarette, as distinct from a hand-rolled one

tailpipe *See* BLOW IT OUT

tails *n* Men's formal dress

take 1 n *by* 1931 The money taken in for a sporting event, at a gambling casino, etc; =GROSS: *Nevada's take has been hit by a recession*—New York Post **2 v** *by* 1920 To cheat or defraud someone; swindle; =SCAM: *The old couple got taken for their life savings* **3 v** (also **take** someone **into camp** or **take** someone **downtown**) *by* 1939 To defeat someone utterly; trounce; =CLOBBER: *UCLA took Illinois in the Rose Bowl/ Last year Tanner took Borg downtown in the same round*—Sports Illustrated/ *In his heart, Gingrich thinks, "I can take them all"*— Newark Star-Ledger **4 n** *by* 1922 An acceptable portion of movie or TV recording, musical recording, taping, etc: *The director said okay, it was a take* **5 n** *by* 1847 A portion; extract; bit; =OUTTAKE: *... fast takes from the latest research that may change your life*—Working Woman **6 n** *by* 1980s One's interpretation or reaction: *What's your take?... You think he was telling the truth or was*

it just drunken bragging?—Lawrence Sanders **7 v** *by* 1633 To succeed; =COME OFF, CUT IT: *I tried to apologize, but I guess it didn't take* [the fifth sense dated example refers to a portion of reporter's copy set in type]

See CUT A TAKE, DOUBLE-TAKE, ON THE TAKE

take a back seat *v phr by* 1888 To assume or accept a subordinate position; demote or degrade oneself: *He said he wouldn't take a back seat to anybody but the president himself*

take a bath *v phr by* 1940s To suffer a financial or other loss; =GO TO THE CLEANERS, TAKE A BEATING: *Is it possible to take a bath on items previously thought to be incapable of depreciation?*—Toronto Life/ *Though the Republicans didn't take a bath, they did not end up breaking even in this election*—New Yorker [fr Yiddish, where *er haut mikh gefirt in bod arayn,* literally "he led me to the bath," means "he tricked me"; the sense is derived fr the deception of persons reluctant to take a steam bath and have their clothing decontaminated and who hence had to be tricked; probably reinforced by *cleaned out* and *taken to the cleaners* as terms for loss of money in gambling or business]

take a beating 1 v phr *by* 1940s =TAKE A BATH **2 v phr** *by* 1970s To be bested in a transaction; pay too much: *You really took a beating if you paid $2 a pound*

take a break *v phr by* 1940s To rest or cease temporarily from working; =CAULK OFF, KNOCK OFF: *Why don't you guys take a break while I figure this out?*

take a bye *v phr by* 1880s To decline; choose not to take; =PASS something UP: *The kid took a bye on breakfast*—Tom Aldibrandi [fr the term *bye* used when a participant in a tournament passes to the next level without playing, since he or she has drawn no opponent]

take a crack at something *See* HAVE A CRACK AT something

take a D *v phr by* 1970s To commit suicide [said to be fr the dramatic mythical sort of suicide where the unhappy person, usu a disappointed movie actor, leaped off the letter D in the HOLLYWOOD sign on Mount Lee, but suspiciously like an abbreviation of *take a dive*]

take a dig at someone *v phr by* 1970s To make an irritating or contemptuous comment; =BAD-MOUTH: *When he took a dig at his mother, his brother decked him*

take a dim view of something or someone *v phr by* 1941 To regard as not especially hopeful, delightful, etc; greet with less than buoyant enthusiasm: *Her parents take a decidedly dim view of me*

take a dive *v phr sports by* 1942 To fall in a feigned knockdown or knockout; lose a fight, game, etc, dishonestly; =TANK: *He refused to take a dive, so they took him out*

take a drink *v phr baseball by* 1916 To strike out [fr the fact that the player can then go to the *drinking fountain* in the dugout]

◁**take a dump**▷ *v phr* (Variations: **crap** or **shit** or

squat may replace **dump**) *by 1940s* To defecate; =SHIT: . . . *two dogs taking a dump in a restaurant*—Village Voice/ . . . *like taking a dump on Mom's apple pie*—National Lampoon

take a fall *v phr* underworld *by 1940s* To be arrested; =FALL: *He took a fall, Duke*—Lawrence Sanders/ . . . *who had already taken two falls for burglary*—Ed McBain

take a flyer (or **flier) *v phr* by 1885* To take an ambitious gamble; take a risky chance or chancy risk, esp financially: *I don't believe you, but what the hell, I'll take a flyer* [fr *flyer*, "jump, leap"]

◀**take a flying fuck▶** *v phr* (Variations: **frig** may replace **fuck**; **at a rubber duck** or **at a rolling doughnut** may be added) May you be accursed, confounded, humiliated, rejected, etc; =GO FUCK oneself, GO TO HELL: . . . *about four guys who could really tell me to go take a flying frig and make it stick*—Larry Niven & Jerry Pournelle/ *And if I was to tell you to go take a flying fuck at a rolling doughnut, what would be your reaction, Sid?*—Lawrence Sanders [*flying fuck* is explained in a source of about 1800 as "copulation done on horseback," found in a broadside ballad *New Feats of Horsemanship*]

take a gander *v phr* by 1914* To have a look; scrutinize; inspect: *I go over and take a gander into it*—Raymond Chandler

take a hike *sentence* by 1960s* Leave me alone; go away; =GET LOST: *He took one look at my clothes and told me to take a hike*

take a hinge at *See* GET A HINGE AT

take a (or **the) hit (**or **chop) *v phr* by 1990s* To be punished, damaged, etc, esp when not solely responsible; be the scapegoat: *Your standard of living will take a big hit over the short term*—New York Times/ *Those accounts aren't even insured; the fund can't keep taking hits like that*—Time/ *The Government winds up taking the hit for Resolution Trust*—New York Times/ *I was vice president of the institute, so he thought I should take the chop for those demonstrations*—Time

take a hosing *v phr* by 1940s* To be cheated or duped; be unfairly used: *The average worker and his family think they're taking a hosing*—Walter Mondale

take a knee *v phr* football *by 1990s* Of the quarterback, simply to kneel rather than execute a play: . . . *he told Brett Favre to take a knee on the final play of the game because "I didn't want anybody to get hurt"*—Milwaukee Journal

◁**take a leak▷** *v phr* by 1934* To urinate; =PISS, WHIZ: . . . *fella has to take a leak*—Tom Wolfe/ *You worry you'd miss it if you took a leak and went to the refrigerator*—Village Voice

take a load off (or **off your feet) *v phr* by 1945* To sit down; rest; relax: . . . *he waved Vito into a chair. . . "Take a load off. You take anything in your coffee?"*—W E B Griffin

take a meet *v phr* by 1990s* To meet; collogue: *Get down here, Babe! I need you to take a meet*—Gary Trudeau [*meet*, "meeting," is found by 1879; it

often refers to a clandestine or criminal activity]

take a number *sentence* by 1980s* Don't be impatient; take your place in line: *"Tall enough to kick you in the balls," he said. "Take a number," I said*—Robert B Parker [fr the practice at a busy shop or office, where petitioners are invited to *take* a printed *number* card to ensure their serial priority]

take a page from someone's **book** *v phr* by 1970s* To imitate or emulate someone: *I think I'll take a page from Castro's book and grow a beard and cigar*

take a peek *v phr* by 1836* To look; examine: *Shall we just take a peek at that sore?*

take a pew *sentence* by 1898* Sit down; take a seat: *Now that you're here, you may as well take a pew*

take a potshot at someone *v phr* by 1927* To criticize harshly; assault critically: *I don't want to take potshots at Frank*—Changes [fr the notion of a *shot* taken merely to put game in the cooking *pot*, hence not sportsmanlike or punctilious but crudely practical]

take a powder (or **a run-out powder) *v phr* by 1930s* To leave; depart hastily, esp to avoid arrest or detection; =POWDER: . . . *and take a powder out of here that day*—John O'Hara/ . . . *that goddamned Matthews, who took a powder to Florida*—W T Tyler [fr the magical *powder* of a magician or sorcerer, capable of making a person disappear or change form, a use found by 1688]

take a rain check *v phr* by 1950s* To arrange postponement or delay of some occasion that one cannot attend at the invited time: *Thanks awfully, Syl, but we're booked that night and will have to take a rain check*
See RAIN CHECK

take a run at someone *v phr* by 1970s* To approach or assault with a view to capture or seduction: *I wouldn't take a client of mine. . . into the place, unless he was such a close associate that nobody was going to take a run at him*—Toronto Life

take a shine to someone or something *v phr* by 1839* To incur a liking for; like: *May Venus. . . take such a shine to you both*—W H Auden

◁**take a shit (**or **a squat)▷** *See* TAKE A DUMP

take a walk *v phr* by 1871* To leave; absent oneself; abscond

take care of business *v phr* 1950s* black To perform stylishly and effectively; deal well with what one needs to: *I got up and took care of business*—Time

take care of Numero Uno *v phr* by 1970s* To devote oneself to one's own profit and well-being; see to oneself; =FEATHER one's NEST: *The Lord helps them that take care of Numero Uno*
See NUMERO UNO

take someone **down a peg** *v phr* by 1664* To deflate or reduce someone; esp, to humiliate someone pompous or vainglorious; =CUT someone OFF AT

THE KNEES: *Somebody ought to take that cocky bastard down a peg* [said to be fr the fact that a ship's flag or ensign was belayed on pegs, hence a lower peg meant less dignity in a salute; *take a peg lower* is found by 1589]

take someone **downtown** *See* TAKE

take five *v phr by 1929* To take a short respite from work; =TAKE A BREAK [about the time it takes to smoke a cigarette]

take someone **for a ride 1** *v phr by 1927* To murder by kidnapping and disposing of the body in a remote place, in gangster fashion **2** *v phr by 1929* To cheat or swindle someone

take gas or **catch a rail** *v phr 1960s surfers* To lose control of one's surfboard and fall off: *To "take gas". . . is to lose a board in the curl of a wave*—Time

take heat *v phr by 1940s* To endure punishment, complaints, etc: *I took a lot of heat and I stayed in the kitchen*—New York Post/ *They think they're taking the heat for being unaware and not doing anything*—New York Times [fr *if you can't stand the heat stay out of the kitchen,* attributed to President Harry S Truman]

take in *v phr by 1727* To perceive and understand: *I can't quite take in what he's saying*

take someone **into camp** *See* TAKE

take it *v phr by 1920* To endure pain, violent attack, the buffets of fate, etc; =HANG TOUGH, TOUGH IT OUT: *Valley Forge proved the Continentals could take it*

take it easy *by 1880* **1** *v phr* To keep one's anger and excitement under check; be calm: *Take it easy, Mac, nobody's hurt* **2** *v phr* To work slowly and smoothly: *Hurry and you're dead, take it easy and you survive* **3** *v phr* To stop working; relax; loaf: *I got to take it easy for a few minutes* [*take it easy* is most often used as a parting salutation or a bit of advice for living, in each case intending all senses at once]

take it hard (or **big) *v phr by 1894* To react very strongly to something: *I thought she'd ignore it, but she took it big/ We were surprised he took the news so hard*

take it in the ear *See* PUT IT IN YOUR EAR

take it on the chin *v phr by 1928* To be soundly defeated; be trounced: *They took it on the chin badly in the last period*

take it on the lam *v phr underworld by 1897* To leave, esp hastily; escape; =LIGHT OUT: *The girl. . . "took it on the lam"*—Atlantic Monthly

take it out of someone's **hide** *v phr by 1940s* To exact the harshest kind of compensation, even physical punishment, usu in place of a gentler or a monetary one: *He'll pay up, by God, or I'll take it out of his hide!*

take it out on someone or something *v phr by 1903* To punish or mistreat an innocent subject for wrongs one has suffered: *Whenever his boss yells at him, he takes it out on his secretary* [perhaps fr *take it out of someone's hide*]

take one's **lumps** *v phr by 1949* To accept and endure severe treatment; =TAKE IT: *The boys were taking their lumps trying to stay on wild Brahma bulls*—New York Daily News [*get the lumps,* "to be beaten up," is found by 1935]

take something **lying down** *v phr by 1860s* To accept something submissively

take one's **medicine** *v phr by 1903* To accept and endure what one has deserved; =FACE THE MUSIC

taken *See* be HAD

take names *See* KICK ASS AND TAKE NAMES

take-no-prisoners *modifier by 1990s* Ruthless; uncompromising: *. . . Ciarelli's take-no-prisoners approach earned her fifty-five thousand dollars on the sand last year*—Buzz [fr the putative command of a combat officer that all enemies be killed, none captured]

◁**take no shit**▷ *See* TAKE SHIT

be **taken to the cleaners** *See* GO TO THE CLEANERS

takeoff 1 *n by 1846* An imitation, esp of a famous person, actor, etc; an impression: *You should hear her takeoff of Liz Taylor* **2** *n by 1960s* A robbery, esp an armed street robbery or mugging: *He always uses the mugger's jargon for a street robbery: "take-off"*—New York Post **3** *modifier*: *. . . and if it comes to a take-off thing in the street*—New York Magazine

take off 1 *v phr by 1813* To leave; depart; =SPLIT: *They all took off for Houston* **2** *v phr by 1963* To have a sudden success, spurt of activity, etc: *. . . but nonsense that doesn't take off can be a trial*—Edith Oliver/ *Phase 2 of PAC face lift is taking off with a bang*—Milwaukee Journal Sentinel **3** *v phr by 1970* To rob; commit burglary; =HOLD UP, RIP OFF: *We took off a bar*—Clarence Cooper/ *They want to keep dealing, not just take off two dudes for a little cash*—New York Magazine **4** *v phr black by 1970s* To kill; =WASTE, ZAP **5** *v phr 1960s narcotics* To give oneself a narcotic injection; =SHOOT UP **6** *v phr by 1940s* To leave work for a time: *I'm going to take off without pay for a week or so* **7** *v phr by 1750* To imitate; mimic; parody: *She takes off a drunk hilariously* [first sense based on the rising and departure of an airplane]

takeoff artist *See* RIPOFF

◁**take off like a bigass bird (**or **like a bat out of hell)**▷ *v phr WWII armed forces* To depart hastily; leave in a hurry; =CUT OUT

take on 1 *v phr by 1430* To behave angrily; make a fuss: *How you do take on!* **2** *v phr police by 1970s* To stop and search someone, demand identification, question harshly, etc; =JACK UP, ROUST: *We were also taught that good cops take on a lot of people*—Rolling Stone

take someone or something **on 1** *v phr by 1300* To accept an assignment, job, role, etc: *I'm a bit diffident about my qualifications, but I'll take the chairmanship on* **2** *v phr by 1885* To accept combat or confrontation with someone or something: *The Knights took over the Philadelphia Inquirer. . . and later took on the Morning Journal head-to-head*—San Francisco

takeout *modifier* by 1940s Having to do with food bought to be eaten away from the place where it is prepared: . . . *pies she hoped to sell to the "take-out" trade*—James M Cain

take someone or something **out** *v phr* by 1939 To kill; destroy; totally disable: . . . *asked Col Beckwith what he intended to do with the Iranian guards. "Take them out," said Col Beckwith. . . they would each get two 45 caliber rounds between the eyes*—Wall Street Journal/ *The Brits were just seeking to reassure themselves that we were not planning to take out a country*—Time [perhaps fr the football term *take out*, "block an opponent decisively"]

takeover *n* by 1958 The buying of the control of one company by another, usu by the wooing and rewarding of stockholders and often against the wishes of the acquired company's management: . . . *a popular means of conducting corporate takeovers*—New York Times

taker *n* by 1810 A person who accepts a bet, challenge, offer, etc: *I dared them all but got no takers*

◁**take (or eat) shit**▷ *v phr* by 1940s To accept or endure humiliation, victimization, bullying, etc; =EAT DIRT •Often in the negative: *Yeah, but at least you don't take any shit from anybody*—Elmore Leonard/ *Do I have to take this shit from my own partner?*—Stuart Woods

take some doing *v phr* by 1891 To be very difficult; be arduous: *It took some doing, but they got there inside an hour*

it **takes two to tango** *See* IT TAKES TWO TO TANGO

take the cake *v phr* by 1847 To win or deserve the highest award and admiration: *His new sonnets quite take the cake* [fr the prize awarded in a *cakewalk* dancing contest]

take the money and run *sentence* by 1960s If a chance for profit comes, legally or not, accept it: *An objective person would say, if you can get the state out for 73 million, take the money and run!*—New Yorker [the title of a 1969 Woody Allen movie]

take the pipe *v phr* by 1970s To become ineffective under pressure; =CHOKE UP, SWALLOW THE APPLE: *He could have taken the pipe after that horrendous first half, but he didn't*—Sports Illustrated

take the plunge *v phr* by 1876 To act decisively, despite prior apprehension: *He took the plunge and bought a new computer*

take the rag off the bush *v phr* by 1870s To surprise one; be a wonder; =BEAT ALL [said to be fr shooting competitions in the western US, where the target was a *rag* to be shot off a *bush*]

take the rap (or the fall or the jump) *v phr* by 1930 To accept or suffer the punishment for something, esp for something one did not do: *If she gets caught, I'll take the rap for her/ Make sure Brewster doesn't come unglued. He has to take the fall right along with Beck*—Hannibal & Boris/ *Marcus got to take the jump for it*—Robert B Parker

take someone **to the cleaners** *v phr* by 1949 To win or otherwise acquire all or very much of someone's money, esp at gambling, in a lawsuit or business deal, etc; =CLEAN someone OUT: *Smarten up, Chrystie, take him to the cleaners*—People Weekly/ *Ephron did not take him to the cleaners in the divorce*—Washingtonian

take someone **to the woodshed** *v phr* by 1940s To punish or rebuke someone: *Baker spent more than an hour with Sharaa, and the lore around the press center was that he took him to the woodshed, but the Syrians were still not nailed down after the recess*—New Yorker [fr the tradition that a father takes a son to the *woodshed* to give him a disciplinary spanking]

tale *See* FISH STORY

tale of woe *n phr* by 1790 A distressing story •Most often used ironically: *Well, let's hear your current tale of woe, Mr Kvetch*

talk 1 *v* by 1924 To inform; confess and implicate others; =SQUEAL: *Socks would never never talk* **2** *v* To talk about; have as one's topic •Always in the progressive tenses: *The administrators aren't talking toga parties*—Macon Telegraph/ *What we're talking here. . . is seventy-five a key. . .* —Ed Mc Bain
    See BACK TALK, BIG TALK, FAST TALK, HAPPY TALK, LOUD-TALK, PEP TALK, PILLOW TALK, STRAIGHT TALK, SWEET-TALK

talk a blue streak *v phr* by 1895 To talk rapidly and copiously: *I left him talking a blue streak about his persecution*

talk a good game *v phr* by 1973 To speak, if not to perform, impressively: *These political embarrassments helped to establish that the Clinton people talked a good game but weren't up to the grownup job of governing*—New Yorker

talk someone's **arm (or ear) off** *v phr* entry form by 1833, variant by 1935 To address someone at very great length; =GAS: *Donna talked his ear off*—New York Daily News

talk big *v phr* by 1584 To boast and exaggerate; be self-aggrandizing; =SHOOT OFF one's MOUTH: *He was talking pretty big about how they treated him*

talkie *n* by 1913 A talking movie
    See WALKIE-TALKIE

talking head (or hairdo) *n phr* by 1968 A person, esp a news reporter, an interviewer, an expert, etc, who appears on television in a close-up, hence essentially as a bodiless head: . . . *using the medium as something more than a static platform for talking heads*—John J O'Connor/ . . . *what the TV experts term a talking head, just Ronnie in an easy chair*—Time/ . . . *one of those plays for which talking hairdos go to the videotape*—Sports Illustrated

talk jockey *n phr* by 1972 The "host" of a radio talk show [modeled on *disc jockey*]

talk out of turn *v phr* by 1934 To speak too candidly; be too bold verbally; =SHOOT OFF one's MOUTH: *I may be talking out of turn, but I think you ought* *to make the decision right now, and live with it*

talk poor mouth *v phr* by 1941 To deny one's wealth, advantages, etc; depreciate one's assets; =POOR-MOUTH: *And it is hard to talk poor mouth just after the papers have written of your daughter's coming-out party for 2,000 guests*—New York Times

talk radio *n phr* by 1985 Radio programs on which callers speak with a "host": *QVC is talk radio taken to its most shallow, most comforting limits*—Philadelphia [*talk show* is found by 1965]

talk shop *v phr* 1854 To discuss work or business rather than have social conversation

talk-talk or **talky-talk** *n* by 1902 Mere talk, esp bombast or idle chatter

talk the hind leg off a donkey *v phr* by 1861 To talk excessively; prate [*talk a horse's hind leg off* was called "old" and "vulgar" in 1808]

talk the talk and walk the walk *v phr* by 1990s To be both sincere and effective: *They Talk the Talk and Walk the Walk*—New York Times/ *In the end Perot could talk the talk, but he couldn't walk the walk*—New Republic

talk through one's **hat** *v phr* by 1887 To lie and exaggerate; talk nonsense; =BULLSHIT [said to be fr the deceptive demeanor of men who hold their *hats* over their faces on entering church, and are supposed to be praying]

talk turkey *v phr* by 1824 To speak candidly and cogently; =LAY IT ON THE LINE, LEVEL: *Do you want to talk turkey, or just bullshit?* [fr a story of the white man who said to the Native American, Wampum, that in dividing the game he would give him the choice: "You take the crow and I'll take the turkey, or I'll take the turkey and you take the crow," whereupon Wampum declared that the white man was not *talking turkey* to him]

talk up a storm *v phr* by 1970s To talk loud, long, impressively, incessantly, etc; =CHEW someone's EAR OFF: *City Teen-Agers Talking Up a "Say What?" Storm*—New York Times

tall *See* STAND TALL

tall can of corn *See* CAN OF CORN

tall red totem poles *See* KNOCK someone or something FOR A LOOP

the **tall timbers** *n phr* show business by about 1920 Rural areas; =the BOONDOCKS, the RHUBARBS

tan or **tan** someone's **hide** *v* or *v phr* by 1670 To beat someone severely; thrash: *Fetch me my gin, son, 'fore I tan your hide*—song "Old Rocking Chair's Got Me" [fr the making of a hide into leather by *tanning*]

See BLACK AND TAN

◁**T and A**▷ *See* TA

tang *See* POON TANG

tangle *v* by 1928 To fight; =MIX IT UP

◁**tangle assholes**▷ *v phr* by 1970s To come into conflict; disagree; quarrel; fight: *. . . remind them how it was the first time we tangled assholes*—Stan Cutler

tangle-foot or **tangle-leg 1** *n* by 1859 Liquor, esp cheap whiskey **2** *modifier*: *. . . a Western*

writer describing the effects of tangle-foot whiskey—Brander Matthews

tango *See* IT TAKES TWO TO TANGO

tang out *v phr* 1980s students To cease; make an end of; =BAG: *I'm going to tang out on studying*—College Slang 101

tank 1 *n* (also **fish tank, fish bowl, holding tank**) *entry form* by 1912 A detention cell; a jail cell: *. . . when he goes into the tank as a prisoner*—Erle Stanley Gardner/ *I'm in the fish tank. . . There are forty of us in the diagnostic center*—Ann Rule **2** *v* (also **tank up**) by 1902 To drink liquor, esp heavily: *I think he'd tanked up a good deal at luncheon*—F Scott Fitzgerald **3** *v* sports by 1976 To lose a game, match, etc, deliberately; =THROW: *He lost so implausibly they were sure he had tanked/ . . . the "tanking" of unlucrative doubles matches merely to catch a plane*—Time **4** *v* by 1980s To fall precipitately; collapse: *At FBI headquarters, morale has tanked after the Idaho investigation*—Time/ *Analysts say Texaco shares could tank to $25–$30 in bankruptcy*—US News & World Report

See DRUNK TANK, GO INTO THE TANK, THINK TANK

tanked or **tanked up** *adj* or *adj phr* by 1893 Drunk

tanker *n* by 1990s A competitive swimmer: *The Lady Hawk tankers sprinted to nine first-place finishes. . . —Milwaukee Journal Sentinel*

tank top *n phr* by 1968 A style of sleeveless woman's blouse resembling the top of the swimming suit called a "tank suit"

tank town *n phr* by 1906 A small town, such as one featuring mainly a water tank for locomotives; =JERK TOWN

tanky *adj* by 1970s Drunk: *Behind me sat four tanky guys*—Richard Price

tap 1 *v* by 1879 To rob; burgle: *Only chicks this guy taps*—Ed McBain **2** *n* basketball by 1980s: *Tap. . . Also tap-off and tip-off. A jump ball. The center jump which begins the game. . . —New York Daily News* **3** *v* by 1952 To select; designate: *When she was tapped for the job, Reno was in her 15th year as State Attorney for Dade County*—New York Times

See HEELTAP

Tap City *adj* by 1970s Lacking money; penniless; =BROKE: *You're Tap City? No problem*—Philadelphia Journal

tap dance *v phr* Army by 1970s To improvise, tergiversate, etc, in order to hide one's ignorance: *I didn't read the poop sheet, so I had to tap dance when the question came*

tap dancer *n phr* by 1970s A person who "tap dances": *He considered himself a tap dancer because he was very agile at gliding away from any sticky situation*—Ed McBain

tape *See* RED TAPE

taped *adv* by 1933 For certain; under control; =IN THE BAG, RACKED: *By the third round he had the fight taped* [the dated instance is *taped out* in the same sense]

See HAVE something CINCHED

tap someone **for** something *v phr by 1940s* To solicit money from; beg or borrow from; =HIT someone, TOUCH: *I tapped my brother for another two hundred*

tap out *v phr gambling by 1940s* To lose all one's money, esp in a gambling game: *"It's tapping me out," he says*—Philadelphia Journal [perhaps fr having *tapped* everyone available for a loan and found none]

tapped out 1 *adj phr gambling by 1940s* Penniless; =BROKE, TAP CITY: *Tapped out, a. . . bank goes under*—Time/ *. . . the tapped-out underdog he is supposed to be*—Sports Illustrated **2** *adj phr by 1940s* Exhausted; =FRAZZLED, POOPED: *. . . thought he looked terrible, haggard, pale, tapped out*—Time

tar[1] *n by 1676* A sailor [fr the *tarpaulin* garments they made and wore]

tar[2] *See* BEAT THE SHIT OUT OF someone or something

◁**tard** or **'tard** or **tart**▷ *n by 1983* =RETARD: *. . . the stupid shit. What a 'tard*—Elmore Leonard

tarfu (TAR Fōō) *adj WWII armed forces* Totally botched and confused; =SNAFU [fr *things are really fucked up*]

Tarheel *n by 1864* A native or resident of North Carolina [origin uncertain; perhaps fr the gummy resins of the pine barrens, which would cling to their feet; perhaps because a North Carolina unit that lost a hilltop position in the Civil War were jestingly told they had not *tarred their heels* to make them stick]

tarp *n by 1906* A tarpaulin, esp a weatherproof cover for a car, boat, etc

tart *n by 1887* A promiscuous woman, esp a prostitute; harlot; =HOOKER: *. . . nothing cheap for us like the grimy tarts on Mercury Street*—Stephen Longstreet [fr *tart*, the pastry confection, esp the English *jam-tart;* in original early–1800s use it meant any pleasant or attractive woman, and only specialized at the end of the century]

tart cart or **tartmobile** *n phr* or *n 1990s teenagers* A school bus for special education students *See* TARD

tart up *v phr by 1938* To decorate; prettify; bedizen; =GUSSY UP: *. . . go the glam route or tart it up or punk it down*—Village Voice/ *American directors feel obliged to tart up Shakespeare*—San Francisco

taste 1 *n theater by 1960s* A share or percentage of profits; =a PIECE OF THE ACTION **2** *n 1960s narcotics* A dose of a narcotic; =HIT **3** *n by 1919* Liquor in general; a drink of liquor *See* SO BAD one CAN TASTE IT

tat *n by 1990s* A skin tattoo: *There were two favorite spots for tats*—Sassy

ta-ta *interj by 1823* A parting salutation; a farewell [fr nursery talk]

tater or **long tater** *n baseball by 1960s* A home run: *. . . the man who hit all those taters in the American League*—Sports Illustrated/ *. . . Bolton . . . insisted the outfield fences be moved in, thus allowing his own team's heavy hitters to launch their taters*—Milwaukee Journal [perhaps fr earlier

Negro League use revived by George "Boomer" Scott when he joined the Boston Red Sox in 1966]

tater trap *n phr by 1843* The mouth; =FLY TRAP, MUSH: *There is no need to explain why. . . a 'tater trap is a mouth. . .*—E B Tylor

tattooed *See* SCREWED, BLUED, AND TATTOOED

tatty *adj by 1933* Inferior; cheap; shoddy; =TACKY: *. . . have met over lunch in tatty banquet halls to press the flesh*—Village Voice

taxi *See* TIJUANA TAXI

taxi dancer *n phr by 1941* A woman at a public dance hall who dances for hire

taxi squad *n phr football by 1966* A group of professional football players who are not officially members of a team, although they may be paid to be available as a reserve [fr the fact that a former owner of the Cleveland Browns would give such players jobs with his *taxicab* company to support them and keep them available]

T-bone *v by 1980s* To hit a car, bus, etc, from the side: *All the bus would have had to have been was another 8 or 10 feet into the intersection and that truck would have T-boned it*—Milwaukee Journal/ *. . . hit the wall almost head-on and was T-boned by Eddie Cheever's car*—Wisconsin State Journal

TCB (pronounced as separate letters) *v black by 1970s* To perform very well what one needs to do: *. . . where he is always to be found TCBing*—New Times [fr *take care of business,* found by 1955 among jazz musicians, apparently originally meaning "to copulate"]

tchotchke (CHAHCH kə, TSAHTS kə) (Variations: **tchatchka** or **tchotzke** or **tsatske** or **chotchke** or **chatchke**) *by 1964* **1** *n* Something trivial, esp a gew-gaw or decorative trifle; bagatelle; plaything: *. . . little rainbows and neon tchatchkas found in California neon boutiques*—New Times/ *. . . you know, the tchotzkes, the jewelry*—Boston Globe/ *. . . his job at the mall vending Watusi chatchkes*—Stan Cutler **2** *n* A precious or adorable person, usu a child: *The baby is a tchotchke* **3** *n* A woman considered as a plaything: *She's Harry's tsatske* [fr Yiddish *tsatske* fr Slavic]

TD or **Tee Dee** (pronounced as separate letters) *n football by 1940s* A touchdown

t'd off *See* TEE'D OFF

tea 1 *n* (also **T**) *narcotics by 1935* Marijuana **2** *n narcotics by 1935* A marijuana cigarette; =JOINT, TEA-STICK **3** *n horse-racing by 1951* A stimulant, often cocaine or strychnine, given to a racehorse to increase its speed [the narcotics senses probably fr use of *tea* as winking and ironic concealment] *See* CUP OF TEA, PINK TEA, STICK OF TEA, WEED TEA

teacups *See* ASS OVER TINCUPS

tea'd up *adj narcotics by 1940s* Intoxicated with marijuana; =GOWED UP, HIGH

tea head *n phr by 1953* A habitual user of marijuana

teakettle *See* ASS OVER TINCUPS

team *See* SWAT TEAM

team up *v phr by 1956* To join together in some effort; =BUDDY UP

tea pad *n phr narcotics by 1950s* A place where marijuana smokers gather

tea party 1 *n phr narcotics by 1940s* A gathering where marijuana is smoked: *Marijuana "tea parties" are little things. . .* —Eugene Burdick **2** *n phr by 1960s* An easy, pleasant, safe occasion •Most often used in the negative: *It wasn't exactly a brawl, but the meeting was no tea party either*

tear[1] (TAIR) *n by 1869* A drinking spree; =BENDER, BINGE: *Fred wanted to go on a little tear in the big town* —Fact Detective Mysteries
See ON A TEAR

tear[2] or ◁**tear-ass**▷ *v entry form by 1599, variant by 1940s* To go very fast; rush around rapidly: *McAllister had no inclination to go tear-assing up the slope and into the hills* —Carsten Stroud

tear[3] (TEER) *n* A pearl [fr the *tear* shape of some pearls]

tear-jerker *by 1921* **1** *n* A sentimental story, movie, song, etc: *. . . see the old tear-jerker* —H R Hoyt **2** *n* A person who appeals to sentimentality; a fomenter of pathos: *. . . a magniloquent tear-jerker named Delmas* —American Mercury

tear off *v phr by 1940s* To play or perform: *The musicians began to tear off a La Conga* —Richard Starnes

◁**tear off a piece** (or **a piece of ass**)▷ *v phr by 1941* To do the sex act; =FUCK [Tony Thorne dates the phrase to the late 1800s]

tearoom or **t-room** *n homosexuals by 1970s* A public toilet

tearoom queen *n phr homosexuals by 1970s* A male homosexual who frequents public toilets seeking sexual encounters

teaser 1 *n by 1895* A woman who invites or offers sexual activity but refuses to do the sex act; =COCK-TEASER: *Maybe Bella was right in calling his "uptown lady" a "teaser"* —Stephen Longstreet **2** *n by 1934* Anything offered as a sample and intended to increase appetite or desire: *He showed them one chapter as a teaser*

tea-stick *n narcotics by 1950s* A marijuana cigarette: *There isn't much record that he went for tea-sticks himself* —Stephen Longstreet

tea (or **tearoom**) **trade** *homosexuals by 1970s* **1** *n phr* Male homosexuals who seek encounters in public toilets **2** *n phr* Sexual encounters in public toilets

tec or **teck 1** *n by 1879* A detective; =DICK **2** *n by 1934* A detective story [a shortening of *detective*]
See TOUGH-TEC

TEC *sentence medical by 1980s* Transfer to Eternal Care

tech[1] *n by 1906* An engineering or technology college [fr *technology*]
See HIGH TECH

tech[2] *n by 1942* A technician, esp an electronics expert: *I got a guy to do it, a tech named Ernie Mann* —Lawrence Sanders

tech head *n phr by 1990s* A musician who has a huge amount of sound equipment: *That tech head's racks are taller than he is* —Los Angeles Times

techie *n by 1980s* A computer enthusiast, expert, etc: *But nerds these days aren't what they used to be. Many of these techies who grew up with computers have gotten older and gotten a life* —Milwaukee Journal/ *Or maybe it was when Conde Nast invested in the glossy techies' magazine Wired* —Milwaukee Journal

Technicolor yawn *n phr by 1963* The act and product of vomiting [fr *Technicolor,* trademark for a color-film process]

techno- *prefix used to form nouns* Having the indicated knowledge of, involvement with, or attitude towards technology, esp advanced and computer technology: *technobuddy/ technofreak/ technogood/ technopeasant*

technoklutz *n by 1990s* A person ignorant or clumsy where computers are concerned: *Another technoklutz. She softens her voice, sounding almost motherly* —Elle

technonerd *n by 1990s* A computer expert or enthusiast:*. . . the Electronic Frontier Foundation. . . an eclectic Washington lobby group (mostly business people and technonerds)* —New Yorker/ *Once considered strictly Dweeb City and frequented only by technonerds* —Sassy

technopop or **techno** *n by 1990s* Popular music using much technical equipment: *. . . manages to hammer enough melody into the wall of technopop he has erected. . .* —People Weekly

teddy *n by 1924* A one-piece women's undergarment serving as both chemise and panties [perhaps fr *teddy bear*]

tee'd (or **teed** or **t'd**) **off** *adj phr by 1950s* Angry; =PISSED OFF: *When people get teed off they want to march* —Time [perhaps fr *ticked off*; perhaps a euphemism for *pee'd off,* "pissed off"]

Tee Dee *See* TD

teed up *adj phr by 1928* Drunk [probably fr 1920s black *teed,* "drunk," probably related to marijuana or *tea* intoxication, and to *tea,* "whiskey," a use attested fr the 17th century]

teen (also **teener** *by 1894* or **teenie** or **teeny** *by 1969*) *entry form by 1818* A teenage person; *teenager: . . . a really interesting biz for a teen who loves being busy* —Deseret News/ *. . . a robust health that would be remarkable on a teener* —Robert Ruark/ *"You only pass this way once," he tells a teenie in persuading her to come along for a ride* —Terry Southern

teensy-weensy or **teeny-weeny** *adj entry form by 1906, variant by 1894* Very small; tiny: *. . . the teensy-weensy kind that small-town dailies like* —Philadelphia

teenybopper *n* (also **teenie bopper** or **teenybop** or **teeny-rocker**) *by 1966* A teenager or preteenager, esp one who undertakes the hippie or rock-and-roll culture and way of life: *Teenyboppers opt for zodiac signs* —Village Voice/ *. . . attract shady* *record promoters like rock stars attract teeny-bop-pers*—National Observer

teenzine (TEEN ZEEN) *n* by 1970s A magazine for teenagers: . . . *this teen-zine cover boy*—Rolling Stone

tee off *v phr* by 1953 To hit someone or something very hard: *He hit a homer, really teed off* [fr the opening shot of each hole in golf, off the *tee*]

tee someone **off** *v phr* by 1961 To make angry; =PISS someone OFF: . . . *and this moping is teeing me off*—Hannibal & Boris [probably a euphemism for *pee* or *piss* someone *off*, influenced by *tee off on* someone, fr golf]

tee off on someone or something **1** *v phr* by 1955 To verbally assault someone, esp to reprimand: *The critic really teed off on my book, alas* **2** *v phr* baseball by 1932 To hit the ball very hard: *He teed off on it and it went right over the wall*

teeth *See* DRESSED TO THE TEETH, DROP one's TEETH, PULL TEETH THROUGH THE ARMPIT

Teflon *modifier* Immune to criticism; sacrosanct or elusive: *They called Reagan the Teflon president* [fr a trademark brand of plastic coating]

Tejano 1 *n* by 1990s A Texan of Mexican origin or descent: *The Texas Ranger myths legitimized Anglo dispossession and then exploitation of Tejanos*—New Yorker **2** *adj*: *Tejano music combines the accordion-driven polkas and cumbias of Mexican conjunto music with synthesizers and rock songs*—New York Times

telecommute *v* by 1990s To work from one's home, working with a computer, and often hooked up to the main office: *Thakker is one of nearly 50 area employees who "telecommute" to jobs at JCPenney Co, hooked up by telephone and computer to the massive Penney customer service center in Wauwatosa*—Milwaukee Journal

telegraph *v* by 1925 To signal one's intentions, often inadvertently: *The tone of her voice telegraphed it*—J Evans

telegraph one's **punches** *v phr* prizefighting by 1936 To let an opponent know one's intentions inadvertently: . . . *never get to the top, he telegraphs his punches*—Jim Tully

telephone (or **phone**) **tag** *n phr* by 1990s The repeated exchange of recorded telephone messages: *I don't feel like playing telephone tag with her*—Lee K Russell/ *"Having computers in our volunteers' homes has eliminated phone tag," says Power, referring to the pervasive round-robin of messages left and phone calls missed*—Modern Maturity

teleporn *n* by 1980 Obscene matter broadcast on television

tell *See* SHOW-AND-TELL

tell it like it is *v phr* black by 1964 To be candid and cogent; tell the truth, even though it be unpleasant; =GIVE IT TO someone: . . . *by Negro psychiatrists William H Grier and Price M Cobbs, who tell it like it is*—McCall's

tell it to Sweeney *sentence* by 1926 =TELL IT TO THE MARINES [*Sweeney* is one of a group of surely

mythical Irishmen, like Riley, Kelsey, and Kilroy, whose names are used apparently for some humorous effect]

tell it to the Marines *sentence* by 1806 I do not believe what you have just told me; what you say is false and futile [the usage, esp in the form "tell it to the marines, but the sailors won't believe him," reflects the contempt in which *marines* were held by naval seamen]

tell me about it *sentence* by 1980s What you are saying is obvious; so what else is new: *"Put the water on. . . while I shower. I smell like a goat." "Tell me about it"*—Lawrence Sanders

tell someone **off** *v phr* by 1919 To reprimand; =CHEW someone OUT: *The man had just been told off, and told off plenty*—G Homes

tell the world *See* I'LL TELL THE WORLD

tell someone **what to do with** something *v phr* (Variations: **where to put** [or **shove** or **stick** or **stuff**] may replace **what to do with**) entry form by 1946 To reject something vehemently and defiantly •A euphemism for *stick it up your ass*: *She told me rudely what to do with my proffered assistance/ The first thing I did when I got home was to tell my old boss where to stick my old job*—Max Shulman

tell someone **where to get off** (or **to go**) *v phr* by 1900 To rebuke, rebuff, or deflate firmly; =LET someone HAVE IT •A euphemism for *go to hell*: *I advised Alice to tell him where to get off when he tries that big-shot stuff*

telly *See* BELLY TELLY

temp *n* by 1923 A temporary employee: *Instead of a full-time secretary he kept hiring temps*

ten *See* FIVE-AND-TEN, HANG TEN

a **ten** *n phr* by 1980s A young woman who is maximally sexually attractive; a perfect female specimen [perhaps fr *ten-carat;* perhaps fr the conventional question "Where would you put her (him, it) on a scale of one to ten?"]

ten-carat *adj* Big; impressive; imposing: *No more ten-carat heels were going to tell me sorry*—Jerome Weidman

ten cents *n phr* 1960s narcotics A ten-dollar packet of narcotics; =DIME BAG

tenderfoot *n* by 1881 A newcomer; neophyte; callow person; =GREENHORN

ten feet tall *adj phr* by 1962 Hugely impressive; menacing: *Iraq had an extremely large military force, and we gave them credit for being ten feet tall in certain areas*—New Republic

ten-foot pole *See* NOT TOUCH someone or something WITH A TEN-FOOT POLE

ten four 1 *n phr* citizens band by 1962 The signal that a message has been received, the equivalent of the earlier and military "roger" **2** *affirmation* fr citizens band That is correct: *That's a ten four, you have it just right* [fr a code of conventional procedure signals used esp by the police, where *ten* was a sort of prefix, and the numeral following bore the message; *ten seven,* for example, meant "transmissions finished"]

tenner 1 *n* by *1887* A ten-dollar bill: *. . . spent the tenner on Jersey applejack*—Billy Rose **2** *n* prison by *1866* A ten-year prison sentence

tennies or **tenny runners** *n* or *n phr* by *1969* Tennis shoes, running shoes, or other such rubber-soled footwear: *. . . grateful that my tennies were rubber-soled and silent*—Sue Grafton/ *. . . a plain black T-shirt and beige tennies*—Rolling Stone

◁**ten pounds of shit in a five-pound bag**▷ *See* BLIVIT

tense up *phr* by *1973* To become stiff, ineffective, and semiparalyzed from nervous tension

ten-spot 1 *n* by *1848* A ten-dollar bill; ten dollars; =DIME-NOTE, TENNER: *A ten-spot can't get you past two counters in a grocery store without limping*—Hal Boyle **2** *n* prison by *1928* A ten-year prison sentence: *. . . after having served a ten-spot*—D Purroy

tent *See* PUP TENT

-teria *See* -ATERIA

terminal *adj* by *1990s* Extreme; unmitigated: *Terminal cuteness is the dread disease of too much Southern writing*—New York Times [based on the medical sense "fatal, incurable"]

terminally *adv* by *1990s* Intractably; hopelessly: *All but the terminally high-minded should try to get to see the Blue Man Group*—Nation

tern *n* medical by *1970s* An intern

terps 1 *n* (also **turps**) by *1823* Turpentine **2** *n* narcotics by *1970s* Elixir of terpin hydrate with codeine, a cough syrup prized as a narcotic

terrific *1888* **1** *adj* Excellent; wonderful; =GREAT: *The script is apt to be terrific*—Time **2** *adj* Prodigious; extreme; amazing: *Times Square hotel biz is on the terrific fritz*—Variety

territory *See* GO WITH THE TERRITORY

terror *See* HOLY TERROR

test *See* POP QUIZ

test the waters *v phr* by *1970s* To make a preliminary assessment: *I've tested the waters, and this product works*—Stan Major/ *One sign of this is the number of. . . vice presidents who are testing the union's political waters*—Newsweek [an example from 1888 may refer to such an assessment or may refer to an actual testing of well-water]

tetchy *adj* by *1592* Irritable; irascible; testy: *. . . the days when tetchy film crews invaded the center of soporific conferences*—Washington Post [fr dialect *tetched,* "crazy, touched in the head"]

Texas leaguer *n phr* baseball by *1905* A hit that falls out of reach between the infielders and the outfielders; =BANJO HIT, BLOOPER [fr the fact that such hits were used in minor-league baseball's *Texas League* as trick plays]

Tex-Mex by *1949* **1** *adj* Texan-Mexican **2** *n* A native of the Texas-Mexico border region: *Fender. . . who calls himself a Tex-Mex, was born in the south Texas valley border town of San Benito*—Washington Post **3** *n* A style of cooking characteristic of the Texas-Mexico border region: *. . . exemplars of Tex-Mex, the mongrel cuisine*

that has grown up along America's southern border—Newsweek

TGIF (pronounced as separate letters) *sentence* by *1970s* Thank God it's Friday: *When I came out of the Wheaton Liquor Store I didn't see a cruiser. TGIF*—Robert B Parker

thanks a lot (or **a bunch)** *sentence* entry form by *1940s,* variant by *1980s* Thank you very much •Often used ironically: *Well thanks a lot; that kick in the face was just what I needed/ Thanks a bunch*—Elmore Leonard

thanks for nothing *sentence* by *1960s* Thank you very much for what you have not done for me: *Willie has an assortment of bumper stickers: To All You Virgins, Thanks For Nothing*—Harper's

thank you ma'am *n phr* by *1849* A bump or hole in the road [because riders bounce up and down as if they were bowing thanks]
See WHAM-BAM THANK YOU MA'AM

that ain't (or **isn't) hay** *sentence* by *1943* That is a large sum; that is not insignificant •*Chopped liver* is very commonly used analogously; *cornflakes* and *zucchini* are also found, but rarely: *And what they pay me in addition ain't hay*—John O'Hara

that dog will hunt *sentence* by *1980s* The idea is a good one; success is probable: *"Let's order out for pizza." "That dog'll hunt"*—College Slang 101/ *Looks like this dog will hunt, to use Clinton's own phrase*—Wisconsin State Journal

that dog won't (or **don't) hunt (**or **bark)** *sentence* Southern by *1930s* That proposition is invalid; the explanation will not do: *Then they got that crazy bullet zigzagging all over the place, so it hit Kennedy and Connolly seven times. . . That dog won't hunt*—movie JFK [the folk saying is certainly older than the quoted date; such sayings about inadequate animals are found by 1789, "That cock won't fight"; 1838, "That cat won't jump"; 1860s, "That cat won't fight"]

that does (or **tears) it** *sentence* entry form by *1968,* variant by *1909* That ruins things; that's the last straw [by 1837 in the form "Now you have done it"]

that'll hold you *sentence* by *1900* That will care for your needs; that will keep you from being troublesome: *So I gave him the ten thou and said "That'll hold you"*

that's all someone needs *sentence* by *1930s* That is precisely what someone does not need; that is excessive, fatal, very ill-timed, etc: *Another tax increase is all I need right now/ A speeding ticket? Brother, that's all you needed* [perhaps fr a translation of the ironical Yiddish lament *Dos felt mir nokh,* "I still lack that"]

that's all she wrote *sentence* by *1940s* That is the sum and end of it; that is the bitter end: *Tell him that's it, brother, that's all she wrote*—Hannibal & Boris [fr the sad case of someone, esp a World War II soldier, who got a *Dear John* letter from his sweetheart, ending the affair]

that's big of you *sentence* by *1920* Your behavior is very generous ●Often used ironically: *That's big of you, to help him up after you knock him down*

that's close *sentence* **1950s teenagers** That's nonsense; that's not so: *"She's real George all the way". . . "Huh, that's close"*—Newsweek

that's my boy (or **girl**) *sentence* **by 1930s** You have done very well; I'm proud of you; =WAY TO GO

that's show business (or **show biz**) *sentence* **by 1947** Such is the unpredictable or grim nature of things; =THAT'S THE WAY THE BALL BOUNCES: *We didn't get invited, but that's show business*

that's the ball game *sentence* That's the end of the affair ●Usu spoken by the loser

that's the ticket *sentence* **by 1838** That's just what is needed: *You have a spare blanket? That's just the ticket* [origin uncertain]

that's the way the ball bounces (or **the cookie crumbles**) *sentence* **entry form by 1951, variant by 1957** Such is life; such are the buffetings of fate; c'est la vie: *. . . guess that's the way the ball bounces*—Sidney Skolsky

that way *adj phr* **by 1929** In love; enamored: *He decided he was that way about her*

the goods 1 *n phr* **by 1904** Competent and genuine; =the REAL CHEESE: *They told me she was the goods, and I believed them* **2** *n phr* **by 1913** Convincing evidence against someone: *He turned himself in when he knew the cops had the goods on him* [second sense fr *goods*, "stolen property"]

the hang *n phr* **by 1845** A useful knowledge and command of something: *He fired me just when I was getting the hang of the operation*

the limit *n phr* **by 1885** As much as one can tolerate: *He's the limit in this town*—Slang-Dic

the man upstairs *n phr* **by 1961** God: *I'm talking about the man upstairs. God himself*—Milwaukee Journal

them apples *See* HOW DO YOU LIKE THEM APPLES

the pits *n phr* **by 1953** The most loathsome place or situation imaginable: *The Soviet "government is the pits"*—Edward I Koch [fr *armpits*]

therapy *See* GREYHOUND THERAPY

there or **right there** *adj* or *adj phr* **by 1849** Very competent; very well informed; =WITH IT

there ain't no such animal *sentence* **by 1922** No such person or thing exists: *. . . those looking for New Jersey farm-raised certified organic turkeys. . . are out of luck. There ain't no such animal*—New York Times

there's no (or **no such thing as a**) **free lunch** *sentence* **by 1980s** The world is a hard place and one must work for what one gets (and even then one may not get it): *Rep David Obey. . . believes there is no such thing as a free lunch*—Milwaukee Journal [fr the memory of old-time saloons, where one could eat from a copious *free lunch* on the bar, even with a minimal liquor purchase]

there's no way *adv phr* **by 1975** Under no conceivable circumstances: *There's no way I'll ever see it your way*

there you are or **there you go** **entry form by 1883, variant by 1897 1** *sentence* That is, unfortunately, the way things happen; =THAT'S THE WAY THE BALL BOUNCES: *Beau started to laugh softly, at the absurdity of everything. "Well, there you go," said Beau*—Carsten Stroud **2** *sentence* Things happen as expected; results follow actions: *You push this one, see? There you go, it turned on* **3** *sentence* You have done something wrong again, of your habitual sort: *There you go, meddling again*

thick 1 *adj* (also **thickheaded**) **by 1597, variant by 1801** Stupid; dull-witted **2** *adj* (also **thick as thieves**) **by 1756, variant by 1833** Intimate; very well acquainted: *The two of them are very thick* **3** *adj* **1980s teenagers** Shapely; =CURVACEOUS
See SPREAD IT THICK

thicko *n* **by 1976** A stupid person; =DIMWIT: *Charlie doesn't know anything. He's a thicko*—Paul Theroux

thighs *See* THUNDER THIGHS

thinclad *n* **by 1940s** A track-and-field athlete: *Local thinclads prepare for state meet*—A J Gates

a (or **one**) **thin dime** **by 1918 1** *n phr* The least amount of money; =a RED CENT: *He was stony broke, not a thin dime could he produce* **2** *n phr* A dime; ten cents: *. . . which sells old-fashioned ice cream sundaes for one thin dime*—Associated Press [fr the fact that the *dime* is the *thinnest* and smallest of US coins]

thing *n* **by 1841** One's particular predilection, skill, way of living or perceiving, etc: *He ignored the world and stuck to his thing* [revived in the 1960s]
See the BEST THING SINCE SLICED BREAD, DO one's THING, HAVE A THING ABOUT, JUST ONE OF THOSE THINGS, OLD THING, SURE THING, a SURE THING

a thing *n phr* **by 1943** An amorous couple: *I just found out you and he are a thing*

thingamajig *n* (also **thingumabob** or **thingumadoodle** or **thingummy** or **thingamadoger** or **thingamadudgeon** or **thingumbob** or **thingamananny**) **entry form by 1824, first variant by 1832, others late 1700s or early 1800s** An unspecified or unspecifiable object; something one does not know the name of or does not wish to name; =DINGUS, DOODAD, GADGET: *When you want to go down you push this thingamajig up as high as it will go/. . . a thingummy so addicted to lethal violence*—W H Auden

thingy *n* **by 1968** A thing; =GIZMO, THINGAMAJIG: *. . . one of those thingies on the roofs of churches that the water spouts through*—Patrick Mann

think *See* DEEP-THINK

think something *v phr* **by 1980s** To concentrate on; aspire to; desire: *A fashion magazine could tell its readers to "think pink" one season, because they'd been thinking navy blue or yellow or aqua the season before*—New Yorker

think-box *n* **by 1917** The brain

think-piece *n* **by 1947** A newspaper or magazine article of intellectual virtue or pretension; a thoughtful essay: *The Knightly Quest drifts off into a think-piece on the nature of romantics and the state of the nation*—Partisan Review

◁**think** one's **shit doesn't stink**▷ *v phr by 1940s* To be very conceited; be stuck up and self-impressed: *The way she looks down her nose you know she thinks her shit doesn't stink*

think tank *n phr by 1959* An institute or institution that specializes in the custody of interpretive intellectuals, esp in the social sciences, and usu caters to and is financed by a government in return for studies, prognostications, etc: *A peace academy would be part graduate school, part think tank*—George F Will [think-tank, "the brain," is found by 1905]

third base *See* GET TO FIRST BASE

third degree or **third** *n phr* or *n by 1900* Long and harsh, even brutal, questioning, esp by the police: *The Third Degree, A Detailed and Appalling Exposé of Police Brutality*—A Lavine/ *He's giving me a third about some gun he says I had*—Raymond Chandler [origin uncertain]

third leg *See* MIDDLE LEG

third lieutenant *n phr WWII armed forces* A commissioned officer, such as a warrant officer or a flight officer, ranking below a second lieutenant

third sacker *n phr baseball by 1911* A third baseman

thirty or **30** *See* OH-DARK-THIRTY

this *n by 1940s* My penis •Accompanied by a gesture toward the indicated part: *Hey Vanessa, how about the bailiffs seize this?*—Carsten Stroud/ *"Mom said to go walk the dogs" "Walk this, John! You walk the dogs!"*—Slang Bag 93

this is it *sentence by 1942* The final crisis is here; the unavoidable has come; prepare for the worst: *He held her hand fast and said "This is it, kid"*—Saul Bellow

thou (THOU) *n by 1867* A thousand, esp a thousand dollars; =GRAND: *A hundred and fifty thou is business*—Dashiell Hammett

thought *See* DON'T GIVE IT A SECOND THOUGHT

threads *n by 1926* Clothes, esp a suit of clothes; =DUDS *See* SET OF THREADS

the Three *n phr airline by 1970* The Douglas DC–3 airplane; =GOONEY BIRD: *The airlines call it simply, "the Three"*—New York Post

three-bagger *n baseball by 1940s* A three-base hit; a triple

three bricks shy of a load *adj phr by 1970s* Stupid; =NOT ALL THERE: *A fine man, all right. It's too bad he was three bricks shy of a load*—Harry Crews

three D or **3-D** *by 1952* **1** *n phr* or *n* The technique of making or showing stereoscopic, three-dimensional movies: *They started making a lot of dreadful splat movies in three D* **2** *adj* Three-dimensional: *a three-D turkey of a movie*

three-dollar bill *See* PHONY AS A THREE-DOLLAR BILL

three-dollar pistol *See* HOT AS A THREE-DOLLAR PISTOL

◁**three-letter man**▷ *n phr 1930s college students* A homosexual [fr the fact that *fag* has three letters, and based on the custom of gauging athletic distinction by the number of varsity letters]

three-peat *n by 1990s* The third repetition of a feat; something like a "hat trick": *... won the match and with it a chance for the rare three-peat*—Newark Star-Ledger/ *Streisand's return to Broadway leaves one hungry for yet another album, a three-peat*—Time [modeled on *repeat*]

three-point landing *See* CHINESE THREE-POINT LANDING

three sheets to (or **in) the wind** *adj phr by 1821* Drunk [fr the fact that a drunken person is as helpless and disorganized as a sailboat with its *sheets*, that is, with its sails, flying, and hence its course and movement entirely out of control]

three squares or **three hots and a cot** *n phr by 1899* Enough to eat; an acceptable standard of living: *He isn't rich, but he gets his three squares every day/ ... homeless men do break the law to get "three hots and a cot"*

three-time loser *n phr by 1914* A criminal who has been convicted several times, and is in jeopardy of an automatic life sentence in some states if convicted again; hence, a hardened and perhaps dangerous criminal

thrift *n by 1980s* A savings and loan association

thriller *n by 1889* An exciting movie, play, etc, esp a horror show; =CHILLER

thriller-diller *n by 1950s* A very effective thriller; =CHILLER-DILLER

throat *n college students by 1970s* A very intense and competitive student, esp a premedical student: *... throat, a person who is overcompetitive about grades*—Rutgers Alumni Magazine [fr cutthroat] *See* CUT one's OWN THROAT, JUMP DOWN someone's THROAT

throb *See* HEART-THROB

throne *n by 1922* A toilet; =JOHN, SHITTER

throttle *See* BEND THE THROTTLE

through a tin horn *See* LIKE SHIT THROUGH A TIN HORN

through one's **hat** *See* TALK THROUGH one's HAT

through the mill *adv phr by 1818* By the course of hard experience; where the most difficult and practical experience is to be had: *He knows just where it's at; he's been through the mill* *See* GO THROUGH THE MILL, PUT someone THROUGH THE MILL

throw 1 *v by 1844* To confuse and incapacitate; amaze; confound; =FLABBERGAST: *When he called me that it just about threw me* **2** *v by 1868* To lose a game, race, etc, deliberately; =TANK: *Basketball players confess that they have accepted bribes to "throw" games*—Arthur Daley **3** *v* (also **pitch** or **toss**) *by 1922* To be host or hostess at; arrange for: *The president has to throw him a luncheon*—P Edson/ *One of his assistants actually pitched a party for me*—Robert Ruark/ *Kendall tossed a*

cocktail party for a group of us visiting writers—
New York Daily News

a **throw** *adv phr* by 1896 For each; apiece; =PER
EACH: *The meetings were a dollar "a throw"—*
P Marks [probably fr carnival games where the customer pays so much for several *throws* of a ball, a
ring, etc, trying to win a prize]

throw a bird *v phr* by 1963 =FLIP THE BIRD

throw someone **a curve** *v phr* by 1940s To do
something quite unexpected; deceive by the unpredicted: *But Spicoli threw him a curve*—Cameron
Crowe

throw a fit (or **spaz**) *v phr* entry form by 1896,
variant by 1990s To behave or react very angrily;
=HAVE KITTENS: *She just about threw a fit when I
told her we weren't going/ Well, they threw a spaz
and said I can't see him or have him over*—
Seventeen

◀**throw a fuck into** someone▶ *v phr* (Variations:
bop or **boff** or **screw** may replace **fuck**) entry form
by 1940s To do the sex act with someone; =FUCK: *It's
inevitable that someone is going to want to throw a
bop into someone else's wife*—Esquire

throw a monkey wrench into something *v
phr* by 1920 To confuse or disable something: *Hot-
eyed radicals eager to throw a monkey wrench into
the social machinery*

throw something **at** something *v phr* by 1970s
To cover or pelt a problem with some usu futile remedy: *Experience with throwing bureaucrats at such
problems does not presage success*—New York
Times

throwaway 1 *n* show business by 1955 A line,
joke, etc, deliberately spoken unemphatically, thus
increasing its effect **2** *modifier*: *He had a sort of
throwaway casualness about him* **3** *modifier* by
1928 Designed to be thrown away; disposable: *It
came in throwaway bottles* **4** *modifier* by 1970s
Useless; superfluous; cruelly neglected: *. . . a three-
times convicted killer, a throwaway man now*—Ann
Rule/ *Haiti has always been a throwaway
nation. . .* —Vanity Fair

throw away *v phr* show business by 1934 To deliver a "throwaway" line, joke, etc: *I love the way he
threw away that misquotation from Plato*

throwaway gun *See* DROP GUN

throw down 1 *v phr* by 1950s To threaten or
challenge; start trouble: *I told him about Sam throwing down on me with a gun*—R Starnes/ *. . . irate
macho mesomorphs about to throw down*—Village
Voice **2** *v phr* 1980s black teenagers To challenge
a rival break dancer by performing a particularly difficult feat or gyration **3** *v phr* 1980s teenagers To
have fun; =GET DOWN, PARTY: *I'm going to throw
down at the party Saturday night*—Delcastle
Dictionary of Slang [first two senses perhaps fr
late–1800s *throw down on,* "aim one's pistol at";
perhaps fr *throw down the gauntlet,* "issue a challenge," found by 1548]

throw someone or something **for a loop** *See*
KNOCK someone or something FOR A LOOP

throw one's **hat in the ring** *v phr* by 1917 To
issue a challenge, esp to announce one's candidacy in
an election, for an appointment, etc

throw in the sponge (or **the towel**) *v phr* by
1940s To concede defeat; give up; =FOLD [fr the signal of surrender given by a defeated boxer's manager
or associate when he tosses a *sponge* or a *towel* in
the air or into the ring; found by 1960 in the form
throw up the sponge]

throw leather *v phr* by 1930s To box; fight, esp
with gloves: *I was throwin' leather before you could
crawl*—Jim Tully

throw money at something *v phr* by 1970s To
spend extravagant amounts of money, in the hope of
solving some problem: *The answer to the quality of
schools is not just to throw money at the problem*

◁**throw** someone **out on** someone's **ass**▷ (or
ear) *v phr* To eject someone, esp violently; =BUM-
RUSH: *I just raised a little question and they threw
me out on my ass*

throw the book at someone *v phr* by 1932 To
impose a severe punishment, esp to assign a maximum sentence to a criminal; treat mercilessly: *If he
catches you one more time he'll throw the book at
you* [fr the image of a judge *throwing* the whole *law-
book* full of punishment indiscriminately at the convicted person]

throw the bull *v phr* =SHOOT THE BULL

throw together *See* KNOCK TOGETHER

throw one's **weight around** *v phr* by about
1916 To use one's influence, esp in a crude way;
exploit one's authority: *You'll never get picked if
you start throwing your weight around*

thumb 1 *v* (also **thumb a ride**) by 1939 To solicit
rides along a highway by pointing with one's thumb
in the direction one wishes to travel; =HITCHHIKE **2** *n*
1960s narcotics A marijuana cigarette; =JOINT
[narcotics sense fr the fact that one sucks the cigarette
as a baby does its *thumb*]
See a GREEN THUMB, STICK OUT

a **thumb in** one's **eye 1** *n phr* by 1970s An
annoyance; a constant irritant: *Yeah, he's been a
thumb in my eye for a long time*—Rolling Stone
2 *modifier*: *The underside of Gramm's conser-
vatism and thumb-in-your-eye individualism is a
brutal political style. . .* —GQ [fr a tactic in rough-
and-tumble fighting, scorned by the traditionalists]

thumbnail sketch *n phr* by 1852 A very brief
account; esp, a quick biography [so brief, that is, as
to be written on a *thumbnail*]

thumbprint *n* theater by 1951 What is characteristic and individual about one's personality, work, etc;
one's seal or cachet: *The director has achieved what
is known in the theater as his thumbprint*—Al
Hirschfeld

thumbs *See* ALL THUMBS, TWIDDLE one's THUMBS

thumbs down *n phr* by 1906 A negative response;
a negation: *It's thumbs down on his promotion this
year* [fr the *pollice verso* gesture of the audience at a
Roman gladiatorial show, indicating that a defeated
gladiator was to be killed rather than spared]

thumbsucker *n journalists by 1974* A newspaper or magazine article with pretensions of gravity and authority: . . . *appeared in the* Whole Earth Review *in a misty-eyed thumbsucker by Kevin Kelley. . .* —Village Voice/ *. . . story known in the trade as a thumbsucker. . . the desperate resort of editorial writers everywhere. . .* —James J Kilpatrick

thumbs up *n phr by 1887* A positive response; an affirmation; =the NOD: *We go, the answer is thumbs up* [the opposite of *thumbs down*]
> *See* THUMBS DOWN

thumper *See* IVORY-THUMPER

thunderbox radio *n phr by 1970s* A large stereo radio, esp one played very loud in public places; =GHETTO BOX: . . . *the thunderbox radios blaring trumpet fanfares* —Village Voice

thunder thighs *n phr by 1970s* Heavy thighs, esp when regarded as ugly and undesirable: *Bye-bye thunder thighs. You can have slimmer legs in 30 days* —People Weekly/ . . . *the sinewy thunder thighs of marathoner Gayle Olinekova* —Time

thusly *adv by 1865* Thus: . . . *content to sum up his contribution thusly: "It was the toughest thing I ever attempted"* —New York Times

tick[1] *n by 1642* Credit: . . . *plenty of canned goods and plenty of tick at the store* —Westbrook Pegler [fr *ticket*]
> *See* ON TICK

tick[2] **1** *n by 1970* A degree, esp of upward motion or increase; a discrete amount: . . . *if the price would have stayed where it was or skipped up a few more ticks* —Nicholas von Hoffman **2** *n by 1879* A second; =a JIFFY: *I'll be there in a couple of ticks*
> *See* RICKY-TICK, UPTICK, WHAT MAKES someone TICK

tick[3] *See* TIGHT

ticked off *or* **ticked** *adj phr or adj by 1959* Angry; =PISSED OFF, TEE'D OFF: *Steve Kemp is ticked off* —Village Voice

ticker **1** *n by 1883* A telegraphic printing machine for stock quotations, news reports, etc: *It's just coming in on the AP ticker* **2** *n by 1930* The heart: . . . *tapped the left side of his chest. "Ticker," he said* —J D Salinger

ticket *n fr late 1800s* An official license or certificate, esp one for a ship's officer, a radio operator, etc
> *See* BIG TICKET, BLUE TICKET, HAVE one's TICKET PUNCHED, MEAL TICKET, TS TICKET, WALKING PAPERS

the ticket *n phr by 1838* Exactly what is wanted: *That's the ticket, my dear, at last* [perhaps fr *the winning ticket* in a lottery, a race, etc]

tickety-boo **1** *adv* WWII British armed forces Very well; splendidly: *Weitz's report just after liftoff that "everything's going tickety-boo so far"* —Newsweek **2** *adj*: *The sergeant reported that all was tickety-boo* [origin uncertain; perhaps fr *the ticket;* more likely fr the slightly earlier Royal Air Force *tiggerty boo* in the same sense, fr Hindi *teega* plus unexplained but euphonious *boo*]

tickle *See* SLAP AND TICKLE

tickled *adj by 1586* Pleased; happy: *She says she's tickled to be off her soap in New York* —Buzz

tickled to death (or **pink) ** *adj phr* entry form *by 1834, variant by 1922* Very much pleased; happy as can be: *They were tickled to death with the suggestion/ I am tickled pink to have been asked*

tickler *See* FRENCH TICKLER, RIB-TICKLER

tickle the ivories *v phr by 1906* To play the piano, esp to play it well

◁**tickle the shit (** or **piss) out of** someone▷ *v phr by 1940s* To please someone very much; overjoy someone

tick someone **off** *v phr by 1915* To anger someone; =PISS someone OFF: *Just the slightest thing could tick off Harold* —Philadelphia

tick over *v phr by 1916* To idle; barely run; operate very slowly: *The motor was just ticking over*

ticky-tacky **1** *n by 1962* Shabby materials; insubstantial and inferior goods: *little houses made of ticky-tacky* **2** *adj* (also **ticky-tack**) *by 1969* Inferior; shabbily made or done; =TACKY: . . . *oil rigs and ticky-tack motels* —advertisement for Time-Life Books/ . . . *draw their energy from the ticky-tacky-taco style of curio shops* —Newsweek [coined by Malvina Reynolds and used in "Little Boxes," a 1960s satirical song about California housing tracts where the houses are described as little boxes made of *ticky-tacky*]

tiddly *adj by 1905* Drunk, esp slightly drunk: . . . *a little tiddly, which is to say, shot or blind* —Philip Wylie

◁**tiddy**▷ *See* TOUGH SHIT

tie (or **get) a bag on** *v phr by 1940s* To go on a drinking spree; get drunk: *You still tie a bag on now and again* —Westbrook Pegler

tie a can to (or **on)** someone *v phr by 1926* To dismiss; discharge; =CAN, FIRE: *First it was the Braves who tied a can to Tommy Hughes* —Raymond Johnson [probably fr *can,* "discharge"]

tie-in **1** *n by 1934* A connection: *I wonder if there's any tie-in with organized crime* **2** *n by 1943* An item sold because of the existence of another item: *The book is a movie tie-in*

tie someone or something **in knots** *v phr by 1957* To immobilize or paralyze with complications: . . . *lobbyists had helped tie the Energy and Commerce Committee in knots. . .* —New York Times

tie into *v phr by 1904* To assault; attack or deal with vigorously: *She put her head back and tied into her drink* —J Evans/ *No sooner had I said it but both of them tied into me*

tie it up *v phr by 1954* =WRAP UP

tie one on *v phr by 1940s* To get drunk; go on a spree

ties *See* HIT THE TIES

tie up *v phr 1960s narcotics* To inject narcotics into a vein, or tie a rubber tubing around one's arm in order to find a vein; =SHOOT UP: . . . *pop a handful of bennies, then tie up, smoking a joint at the same time* —Harper's

tiger *n by 1940s* A strong, virile man; a dangerous man ●Often used in direct address, either admiring-

ly or ironically: *He's switched from being a pussycat to being a regular tiger*
See BLIND PIG, BLIND TIGER, HAVE A TIGER BY THE TAIL

tiger sweat *n phr by 1950s* Cheap, raw liquor; =PANTHER PISS, ROTGUT: *. . . cheap alcohol, also known as tiger-sweat*—Stephen Longstreet

tight 1 *adj by 1805* Parsimonious; tightfisted; stingy: *He is tight in his dealings*—A Lavine **2** *adj* (Variations: **as a drum** (or **a lord** or **a mink**) may be added) *by 1830* Drunk: *Little tight, honey?*—Dorothy Parker/ *I wasn't especially tight*—Gene Fowler **3** *adj by 1956* Close; sympathetic: *John and Mary are very tight* **4** *adj 1980s students* Attractive; =COOL: *Renee's wig is tight*—College Slang 101
See SIT TIGHT

tight as a tick *adj phr by 1927* Very drunk [fr the inflated tightness of an engorged tick, found in reference to fullness by 1678]

◁**tight as Kelsey's nuts** (or **Reilly's balls** or **O'Reilly's balls**)▷ *adj phr by 1950s* Very parsimonious; stingy; close; =TIGHT

◁**tight-ass**▷ **1** *n by 1970* A tense and morally rigid person: *I know that one. . . a real tight-ass*—Erich Segal **2** *adj*: *That is Dr Nathan Schlemmer, very uptight, very tight-ass*—Ed McBain

tight-assed 1 *adj by 1903* Not disposed to sexual promiscuity; chaste: *Washington, I saw, was full of tight-assed women*—Irwin Shaw **2** *adj by 1967* Tense; overly formal: *. . . tightassed British film critic*—Changes

tighten someone **up** *v phr black by 1980s* To discipline someone; rectify someone's life: *There were actually men on the block that if you did something wrong they were going to catch you and tighten you up. . .*—Milwaukee Journal

tightly wrapped **See** NOT TIGHTLY WRAPPED

tight money *n phr by 1866* Money when the supply is scarce, esp during a period of high interest rates

the **tights** *n phr by 1970s* A penniless or financially grim condition; =the SHORTS: *No go. Everyone's got the tights*—Herbert Kastle

tight spot *n phr by 1852* A difficult situation; =JAM: *I'm in a tight spot and would appreciate your help*

tightwad 1 *n by 1900* A parsimonious person; a stingy person; a miser: *. . . the "tightwads" who have saved money*—New Republic **2** *adj*: *Don't be so tightwad with that hootch*—Sinclair Lewis [fr the forbidding *tightness* of his *wad* of money]

Tijuana Bible *n phr by 1950s* A pornographic book of the most revolting sort

Tijuana taxi *n phr 1960s citizens band* A police car [probably because of the relatively colorful decoration of such cars]

till **See** WITH one's HAND IN THE TILL

till (or **until**) one **is blue in the face** *adv phr by 1864* Until one is able to do no more; to the point of helpless exhaustion: *Hail and beware the dead who will talk life until you are blue in the face*—Charles Olson [fr the *facial blueness* or darkening symptomatic of choking]

till the fat lady sings **See** the OPERA AIN'T OVER TILL THE FAT LADY SINGS

timber *interj by 1912* An exclamation of triumph, achievement, etc [fr the cry of loggers as a tree begins to fall]
See the TALL TIMBERS

time **See** BAD TIME, BEAT someone's TIME, BIG TIME, DOUBLE-TIME, FLYING TIME, GIVE someone A HARD TIME, GOOD TIME, HAVE oneself A TIME, MAKE TIME, MAKE TIME WITH someone, RACK DUTY, SACK TIME, the SMALL TIME, STREET TIME

the **time of day** **See** NOT GIVE someone THE TIME OF DAY

timer **See** OLD TIMER

times **See** HARD TIMES

time warp *n phr by 1954* A blank, an inordinate rapidity or slowness, a blatant discontinuity, a seeming anachronism, or some other anomaly of time: *The case of five people indicted more than four years ago. . . has been "lost in a time warp" of delays, state prosecutors say*—Arizona Republic [fr science fiction notions of instantaneous eons and the like, devised to legitimize travel over enormous distances within conceivable and dramatically useful periods of time, and based on Albert Einstein's concept of "curved space"]

timey **See** OLD-TIMEY

tin 1 *n police by 1949* A police officer's badge; =POTSY: *Boone had to flash his tin*—Lawrence Sanders **2** *n 1960s narcotics* A few grains of cocaine **3** *n by 1836* Money

tin can 1 *n phr WWII Navy* A depth charge **2** *n phr Navy by 1937* A naval warship, esp a destroyer **3** *n phr by 1923* A car, esp a Model T Ford

tin ear *n phr by 1909* Unselective and unmusical hearing; auditory tastelessness: *He sometimes has a tin ear for dialogue*—Village Voice/ *I have a tin ear*—Studs Terkel

tin fish *n phr Navy by 1925* A torpedo

tin hat *n phr by 1903* A soldier's helmet

tinhorn or **tinhorn gambler** *n or n phr entry form by 1857, variant by 1885* A petty but flashy gambler, or any person with those characteristics: *. . . denunciations of punks, tin-horns, and gyps*—Westbrook Pegler [fr the *horn*-shaped metal can used by chuck-a-luck operators for shaking the dice; the notion of inferiority comes fr the presumed superiority of other, more sophisticated kinds of gambling, and fr the generalized inferiority of *tin* to other metals]

tin horn **See** LIKE SHIT THROUGH A TIN HORN

tinkle 1 *n by 1938* A telephone call ●Chiefly in the expression *give someone a tinkle* **2** *v by 1950* To urinate; =PEE ●A nursery use

tin Lizzie (or **lizzie**) *n phr by 1915* An early Ford car, esp a Model T: *It is as simple and homely as an old tin Lizzie*—Reader's Digest [perhaps because such vehicles were sturdy, dependable, and black, like the traditional ideal Southern servant, called *Elizabeth*]

Tin Pan Alley *n phr by 1908* The site where popular music was composed, arranged, published, recorded, etc, designating the neighborhood on Seventh Avenue between 48th and 52d Streets in New York City; also, the realm of popular music composition, publishing, etc [fr the late–1800s musicians' term *tin pan,* "cheap, tinny piano"]

tin parachute *n phr* by 1980s: . . . *a novel type of severance pay that adds a new wrinkle to the takeover game and advances the art of the takeover defense: it is called the "tin parachute." A play on the term "golden parachute," which guarantees fat payments to key executives. . . this new arrangement assures the entire rank and file of similar goodies*—New York Times

tinpot *adj* by 1838 Inferior; petty: . . . *tinpot Napoleons*—Richard Starnes/ . . . *individual liberty from coercive tin-pot bigots*—Toronto Life [apparently in part fr the image of a ludicrous military figure wearing a grandiose *tin* helmet, a sort of *tin* soldier]

tinselly *adj* by 1811 Gaudy; coruscating but insubstantial; =FLASHY: . . . *tinselly telecasts from CBS in Los Angeles*—Los Angeles Times

Tinseltown 1 *n* by 1975 Hollywood; the Los Angeles–Hollywood movie and TV area and culture: . . . *if he couldn't nab a ride to Tinsel Town in an hour's time*—George Warren/ *It sometimes seems that the whole society has spiritually decamped for Tinseltown*—Richard Schickel **2** *modifier*: *With familiar Tinseltown inventiveness, the new film has been entitled* Grease 2—Time [fr *tinsel,* "gaudy, glittering decoration," plus *town*]

◁**Tio Taco**▷ *n phr* by 1970s A Chicano who emulates or truckles to the values of the non-Hispanic majority [fr Spanish, literally "Uncle Taco," using the name of the Mexican fried tortilla; modeled on *Uncle Tom*]

tip 1 *v* (also **tip off**) by 1749, variant by 1891 To give useful information or advice, esp advance information that gives an advantage of some sort: *The room clerk tipped him*—movie Scene of the Crime/ *Who tipped Larkin off?*—Erle Stanley Gardner **2** *n* by 1845: . . . *our tip to Doc Jansen would be. . .* —New York Daily News [origin uncertain; perhaps fr the notion of *tipping,* that is, tilting something in someone's direction]

tip one's **mitt** (or **hand**) *v phr* entry form by 1917 To disclose one's plans, secrets, etc, esp inadvertently: *That would be tipping her mitt too much*—Heywood Broun/ . . . *somehow, even with best the intentions, you'd tip my hand*—Hugh Pentecost [fr the revealing of one's *hand,* that is, *mitt* in a card game; *tip,* "give, exhibit," is found in underworld slang by 1610]

tip-off *n* by 1901 A revealing, esp a warning; a particularly useful clue: . . . *the tip-off on what's ahead*—Associated Press

tip over *v phr* underworld by 1935 To rob; =HEIST, KNOCK OVER: *Ya wanta help us tip over this bank?*—radio show The Big Heist

tippy-toe *v* by 1901 To walk silently: *God-damn it,*

Hubert! *Don't tippy-toe around like that*—Carsten Stroud

tipster *n* by 1862 A person who gives tips, esp on horse races

tip the elbow *See* BEND THE ELBOW

tip-top *adj* by 1722 Excellent; first-rate: *He assured me his health was tip-top*

tire *See* FLAT TIRE, SPARE TIRE

◁**tired-ass**▷ *adj* by 1970s Tedious; overused; tired: . . . *thinking in tired-ass racial cliches*—Philadelphia Journal

◁**tit**▷ *n* by 1928 A woman's breast: *She couldn't make it out there.* . . . *No tits*—Calder Willingham [a respelling of *teat*]

See COLD AS HELL, GET one's TAIL IN A GATE, SUCK HIND TIT, SUGAR TIT

◁**tit art**▷ *n phr* newspaper office by 1970s Appealing photographs of young women; =CHEESECAKE

◁**tit man**▷ *n phr* by 1940s A man whose favorite part of the female body is the breasts

◁**tits**▷ **1** *adj* by 1960s Excellent; wonderful; =GREAT, NEAT: *What a tits car she's got!* **2** *adj* 1960s college students Easy; simple: *a real tits quiz*

See WITH BELLS ON

◁**tits and ass**▷ **1** *n phr* by 1972 A display of female bosoms and bottoms; also, a show, dance, etc, featuring such a display; =CHEESECAKE, TA: *Tits and ass, that's what the attraction is. . . An Apache team and tits and ass*—Lenny Bruce **2** *modifier*: *The magazine had a tits-and-ass section purporting to be a review of bathing-suit styles*

◁**tits-and-zits**▷ *modifier* by 1970s Dealing with teenage love and sex: . . . *yet another entry in the lamentable tits-and-zits genre of teenage sex comedies*—Time [modeled on *tits-and-ass*]

tittle-tattle *n* by 1542 Empty chatter; prattle and gossip: *An example is the press in Britain, where the tittle-tattle has lately infected. . . the quality papers*—Milwaukee Journal

◁**titty**▷ *n* by 1746 A breast; =TIT: *His dipping titties touched the floor before his chin did*—Saul Bellow *See* TOUGH SHIT

tizzy *See* IN A TIZZY

TKO (pronounced as separate letters) **1** *n* prizefighting by 1940s A technical knockout, declared when one fighter is judged unfit to continue, although still conscious **2** *v*: *He was TKO'd in the fourth round*

TO (toh) *n* by 1970s Toronto, Ontario: *What makes you so sure Holden Caulfield is in TO?*—Toronto Life

toad *n* by 1568 A repellent person; =ASSHOLE: . . . *the only time you want the guy to ask first is if he's a toad*—Los Angeles Times

See CAR TOAD, KNEE-HIGH TO A GRASSHOPPER

to a fare-you-well *adv phr* by 1884 Thoroughly; completely; =TO THE MAX: *That new hairdo suits you to a fare-you-well*

to a frazzle *adv phr* by 1865 Completely; totally; to a ruined condition: *After the marathon I was beat to a frazzle* [fr dialect *frazzle,* "frayed end of a rope"]

toast 1 *v* musicians by 1970s To talk or chant in the

reggae music mode: . . . *not exactly toasting, it was a kind of primitive rapping, consisting mainly of new slang words and an occasional joke*—Village Voice **2** *adj* teenagers fr black by 1970s Excellent; wonderful; =COOL, TITS, TUBULAR: *She told me my clothes were real toast* **3** *adj* by 1980s Ruined; actually or occupationally destroyed; =KAPUT: . . . *finished in one's career*, as in "He's toast"—Los Angeles Times/ . . . *much of the punditocracy that once embraced Clinton is declaring him dead. Buried. Toast*—Milwaukee Journal

toaster *n* musicians by 1970s A person who "toasts": . . . *an albino reggae rapper or "toaster"*—Rolling Stone

to beat the band (or the Dutch) *adv phr* entry form by 1897, variant by 1775 In an unrestrained way; to the highest pitch; very much; =ALL-OUT: *I hollered to beat the band/ We ran to beat the Dutch* [fr the notion that such extreme effort could even drown out *the band;* or, in the mid–1700s version, *this beats the Dutch,* could convince even a stolid, phlegmatic *Dutch* man]

to boot *adv phr* by 1000 In addition; in extra measure: *She has lots of talent and more to boot* [fr Old English, "as profit, to the good"]

to-die-for *adj* by 1990s Very desirable; extremely attractive; =DISHY: . . . *constant companion of the to-die-for Marilyn Montgomery*—Nation

to-do *n* by 1827 A disturbance; fuss; =FLAP: *What's all the to-do?*—Nation

toe *See* GO TOE TO TOE, PINK-TOES, TURN UP one's TOES

toehold *See* GET A TOEHOLD

◁**toe jam**▷ *n phr* by 1934 Malodorous matter and filth under and around the toenails

◁**toe-jam queen**▷ *n phr* homosexuals by 1972 A male homosexual foot-fetishist

toe the mark (or the line) *v phr* entry form by 1813, variant by 1895 To behave properly; =KEEP one's NOSE CLEAN: *If he doesn't toe the mark, fire him* [fr the *mark* or *line* indicating the starting point of a race]

toe to toe *See* GO TOE TO TOE

together 1 *adj* 1960s counterculture fr black Composed and effective; free of tension and anxiety: *Now they're together, unless they're strung out*—William Zinsser **2** *adj* black by 1960s Stylish and au courant; socially adept

See GET IT TOGETHER, HAVE IT ALL TOGETHER

togs *n* by 1779 Clothing, esp that worn for a specific purpose: *riding togs* [fr *tog,* "coat," ultimately fr Latin *toga*]

to hell by 1912 **1** *adv phr* (also **to hell and gone**) Thoroughly; irretrievably: *This thing's busted to hell/ The plan's wrecked to hell and gone* **2** *adv phr* (also **to heaven** or **to high heaven**) Very strongly; fervently; sincerely: *He swore to hell he'd never do it again/ I wish to heaven she'd leave*

toity *See* HOITY-TOITY

toke[1] by 1950s **1** *n* A puff or drag at a cigarette, cigar, etc, esp a marijuana cigarette: *He still took a toke of marijuana from time to time*—Norman

Mailer **2** *v*: . . . *to toke vigorously on an oversize cigar*—Rocky Mountain Magazine **3** *n* A cigarette, esp a marijuana cigarette: *Elaborately, I lit a toke*—Easyriders [probably fr Spanish *tocar* in its sense "touch," or "tap, hit," or "get a shave or part," or a combination of these]

toke[2] **1** *n* gambling by 1961 A gambling chip or token, esp one given to a dealer as a tip **2** *n* gambling by 1971 A gratuity given by a gambling casino, brothel, or other business to cab drivers for bringing in clients: *Cab drivers have long been paid "tokes". . . when they deliver customers to a long list of varied business establishments*—Toronto Globe and Mail

tokus (TOH kəs, Tŏŏ kəs) *n* (also **tokis** or **tuchis** or **tuckus** or **tush** or **tushie** or **tushy**) by 1914 The buttocks; =ASS, BOTTOM ●A frequent euphemism for ass: . . . *knocked him right square on his tokus/ He shakes his tushie with elegant languor*—New York Post/ . . . *bumps her tush gently along*—Village Voice [fr Yiddish; *tush* forms are affectionate, used esp with children]

told *See* FUCKING WELL TOLD

◁**Tom** or **tom**▷ **1** *n* black by 1959 A black person who emulates or truckles to the white majority taste and culture; =OREO, UNCLE TOM **2** *v*: . . . *sleeping, resisting, tomming, killing the enemy*—Amiri Baraka/ *You too young to be Tomming*—John Godey

See AUNT TOM, BLIND TOM, MISTER TOM, UNCLE TOM

Tomahawk *See* UNCLE TOMAHAWK

tomato *n* by 1922 An attractive young woman; =BABE, CHICK: *I was telling you about this kraut and the English tomato*—Russell Baker [fr the connotations of lusciousness, tautness, full color, etc]

tomboy or **tomgirl** *n* by 1592 A young girl who prefers boyish pursuits, looks, etc, to the presumed feminine ones

tomcat by 1927 **1** *v* To pursue male sexual activity avidly **2** *n*: *In his younger days he was a notorious tomcat* [fr the common name for a male cat, popularized by the 1760 book *The Life and Adventures of a Cat,* in which the creature was named *Tom*]

Tom, Dick, and Harry *See* EVERY TOM, DICK, AND HARRY

tomfool *adj* by 1762 Stupid; foolish; =NUTTY: . . . *some tomfool scientist*—Newsweek [found by 1356 as the actual name of a man, also called Thomas fatuus, "foolish Tom"]

tommy *n* by 1940s =TOMBOY: *The red-haired tommy. . . she'd put him over the jumps*—W R Burnett

Tommy *n* by 1884 A private in the British army; =TOMMY ATKINS: *He met three Tommys in a bar*

Tommy Atkins *n phr* by 1883 A private in the British army; =TOMMY [fr the name *Mr Thomas Atkins* used on sample forms of the British army]

Tommy (or tommy) gun *n phr* by 1929 A handheld automatic repeating firearm; a sub-machine gun; =BURP GUN, CHOPPER [fr the name of the .45-caliber *Thompson* submachine gun, the earliest well-known weapon of this sort, and a favorite arm of the gangster era]

Tommy man *n phr* by about 1930 A gangster armed with a Tommy gun

tommyrot *n* by 1884 Nonsense; balder-dash; =BALONEY, BULLSHIT [origin unknown; perhaps fr British *tommy,* "goods, esp food, supplied to workers in lieu of wages"]

ton *n teenagers & car-racing* by 1954 A speed of 100 miles an hour; a high speed

toned *See* HIGH-TONED

tonk *n* =HONKY-TONK

ton of bricks *See* HIT someone LIKE A TON OF BRICKS

◀**Tonto**▶ *n* by 1980s Any male American Indian [fr the faithful Indian companion of the cowboy hero the Lone Ranger, who first appeared in a 1930s Detroit radio series]

tony or **toney 1** *adj* by 1877 Stylish; very elegant; =RITZY: . . . *the tony St Regis hotel*—GQ **2** *n*: *St Michael's alley, still inhabited by the tony*—H L Mencken [probably fr French *bon ton,* "high fashion, chic"]
See HIGH-TONED

too-bad *adj black* by 1934 Excellent; good; =GREAT: *That was a too-bad game*—American Speech

toodle-oo *interj* by 1907 A parting salutation •Thought of as a humorous affectation, like "cheerio"[perhaps an alteration of French *à tout à l'heure,* "see you soon, so long"]

too hot to handle *adj phr* by 1940s Very delicate or explosive; very controversial: *The March was rejected by PBS as "not suitable to their programming" (nobody actually said it was too hot to handle)*—Atlantic Monthly [found in baseball by 1932, designating a very hard-hit ball]

took *See* be HAD

tool ◁**1**▷ *n* by 1553 The penis **2** *v* by 1980s To do the sex act with or to; =BOP, BOFF, SCREW: *Hit the man in the ass with a board while he was tooling your old lady*—Harry Crews **3** *n underworld* by about 1920 A pickpocket **4** *n* (also **dull tool**) by 1700 An incompetent person **5** *n students* A diligent student; =NERD, GREASY GRIND: *Nerds can also be "goobs" or "tools"*—New York Times **6** *v* (also **tool along**) by 1853 To speed; =BARREL: *I climbed into the Buick and tooled it down the ramp*—Raymond Chandler [underworld sense perhaps fr the practice of using a small boy as a sort of *tool* in pickpocketing, or perhaps fr Romany *tool,* "handle, take"; last sense fr *earlier tool,* "a whip"]

toolie *n students* by 1970s An engineering student: *My friends are engineers, or, as they call themselves, toolies*—New York Times

tools *See* FIGHTIN' TOOLS

the **tools of ignorance** *n phr baseball* by 1937 A catcher's gear [said to have been coined by the catcher Muddy Ruel, or the catcher Bill Dickey]

too many *See* ONE TOO MANY

too many chiefs and not enough Indians *sentence* Nobody wants to work around here,

though everybody wants to be a boss; the project suffers from a surplus of directors and advisers

too much *1930s jazz musicians* **1** *adj phr* Wonderful; superb; =the MOST: *The way she blows that horn is too much* **2** *adj phr* Excessively good, bad, wonderful, incredible, etc; prodigious; overwhelming: *You ate 23 hot dogs in one sitting? Man, you're too much* **3** *n* =FAR OUT

toon *n* by 1990s A cartoon: *"What are you, man, some kind of visionary?" "No, no, I'm just an ordinary toon. . . "*—Gary Trudeau
See LOONY-TUNE

'toonville *n* by 1990s The cartoons, esp the regular syndicated series: *And Garfield now ranks at the top in 'toonville*—Milwaukee Journal Sentinel

too rich for someone's **blood** *adj phr* by 1884 Exceeding someone's capabilities, purse, desires, etc; too much: *I don't go out with them anymore; it's too rich for my blood*

toot 1 *n* by 1790 A spree, esp of drinking; =BENDER, BINGE, KICK: *It gave me an excuse to go off on a four-day toot*—Humphrey Bogart/ *He got a bonus and went on a shopping toot* **2** *n 1960s narcotics* Cocaine: *Am I witnessing mere incompetence or too much toot?*—Playboy/ . . . *made it easier for the press to imagine him doing a little toot in the basement of. . . Studio 54*—Washingtonian **3** *n narcotics* by 1977 A whiff of cocaine into the nose; =SNORT: . . . *I don't suppose you have a toot till pay-day?*—Stan Cutler **4** *v narcotics* by 1975: *He was himself tooting cocaine on a daily basis*—New York Magazine **5** *v* by 1930s To flatulate; =LAY A FART: *"What's that smell?" "Oh, Andrea tooted again"*—UCLA Slang **6** *n* by 1930s A flatulation; =FART [the drinking sense is probably fr the image of someone *tooting* on a drinking horn, that is, holding a glass up as if it were a horn one were blowing; *toot* or *tout,* "drink deeply, quaff" are attested fr the 1600s; narcotics sense probably related to *honker,* "horn, nose," as something to be *tooted*]

tooth *See* CLEAN AS A WHISTLE, LONG IN THE TOOTH, SWEET-TOOTH

tooth fairy *See* BELIEVE IN THE TOOTH FAIRY

toothpick *n* by 1844 A knife, esp a switchblade: *Any of her roomers handy with a toothpick?*—J Evans

tootie fruitie *n phr* by 1970s A weak and ineffective male; =SISSY, WIMP: *We're all a bunch of Goddamned tootie fruities*—Dan Jenkins [fr *tutti-frutti,* "ice cream containing candied fruit," fr Italian, literally "all fruits," with a punning on *fruity,* "homosexual, gay"]

tootin' *See* ROOTIN'-TOOTIN', YOU'RE DAMN TOOTIN'

too too *adj phr* by 1881 Excessive, esp in social elegance, fastidiousness, affectation, etc: *Well, isn't his caring just too too!*

toot (or blow) one's **own horn (or trumpet)** *v phr entry form* by 1940, *blow form* by 1859, *trumpet form* by 1854 To praise and flatter oneself; advertise one's virtues; boast: *I am not ashamed of the text, but of being thought to "toot my own* horn"—Washington Post [the phrase *sound the trumpet of mine own merits* is found by 1576]

toots (TŏŏTS) *n* (also **tootsy** or **tootsy** or **tootsie-wootsie** or **tootsy-wootsy**) entry form by 1936, tootsie-wootsie by 1895 A woman; =DOLL •Often used in address, often disparagingly, and as a nickname: *Not any more, toots, not any more, my precious darling angel*—Raymond Chandler/ *How about one of those tootsie-wootsies?*—Saturday Evening Post/ *He was also paying for a penthouse apartment on Park Avenue for his tootsie*—Art Buchwald [perhaps fr *tootsie*]

tootsie *n* by 1854 A foot •A nursery use: *Pull up a chair and warm your tootsies*

top 1 *v* by 1718 To hang someone: *A colleague sent to the gallows has been topped*—H L Mencken **2** *v* by 1930s To kill; =BUMP OFF, HIT **3** *v* by 1586 To surpass; better; =CAP: *I'll top that story with one of my own* **4** *n* WWI Army =TOP SERGEANT **5** *v* black by 1960s To be executed for a capital crime **6** *n* by 1593 The best; most superior: *You're the top, you're the Louvre Museum*—Cole Porter song **7** *modifier* by 1714: *He got the top recommendation*
See the BIG TOP, BLOW one's TOP, BONE-TOP, CHOPPED TOP, COME OUT AHEAD, FROM THE TOP, GO someone or something ONE BETTER, KID TOP, MUTTONHEAD, OFF THE TOP, ON TOP OF, POP-TOP, RAG-TOP, TANK TOP, TIP-TOP

top banana 1 *n phr* show business by 1950s The leading or featured comedian in a burlesque show; the chief comic **2** *n phr* by 1970s The leader, president, manager, etc; =BOSS, BIG ENCHILADA: . . . *refuses its members. . . opportunity to become top banana*—Fran Lebowitz [said to have originated fr a burlesque routine having to do with a bunch of *bananas*]

the **top brass 1** *n phr* by 1940s The highest of military officers: *They went to the top brass at the Pentagon* **2** *n phr* by 1949 The highest of executives, managers, etc: *The top brass at Xerox liked the idea*

top dog *n phr* by 1900 The most important person; the chief; =BOSS: *Who's top dog around this place?*

top dollar *n phr* by 1970 The highest sum of money offered or given: *They pay top dollar over there*

top-drawer *adj* by 1920 Of the highest quality; most superior; =TOPS: *The drinks they serve are absolutely top-drawer* [fr a British expression *out of the top drawer,* "upper-class, well-bred"]

top-kick *n* WWI Army A first sergeant; =FIRST MAN, TOP: *The Top Kick was caught shorthanded*—American Legion Magazine

topless 1 *modifier* by 1966 Not wearing anything on the upper body; with breasts exposed: *a topless dancer* **2** *modifier* by 1967 Having to do with entertainment, bars and clubs, etc, featuring women bare from the waist up: . . . *only at bars and only if they were topless*—Rolling Stone

topline *v* by 1980s To feature as the main attraction: . . . *bio-pic that was expected to topline Elizabeth*

Taylor and Lauren Bacall. . . —New York Times [found as a noun, "a regular top-line combination," by 1906]

top-notch *adj phr* by 1900 Superior; of the highest quality; =TOP-DRAWER: *She's a top-notch racquetball player* [fr *notch* as representing position, rank, etc; found as a noun phrase, "the highest degree of excellence," by 1833]

top of one's **head** *See* OFF THE TOP OF one's HEAD

top of the (or one's**) head** *adj phr* by 1959 Without thought or calculation; impromptu: . . . *the doc's top-of-the-head opinion*—Lawrence Sanders

topper 1 *n* by 1820 A top hat **2** *n* by 1939 Something that surpasses something else, usu a joke, comments, etc; esp, a remark that both surpasses and perfects something already said: *I have a topper for that dirty crack* **3** *n* by 1960s =TOPSIDER
See BLOW one's TOP

tops *adj* by 1935 Best; most superior; absolutely first rate; =the TOPS: *I wish you could print Mencken every month; he's tops*—American Mercury/ *Sanitation Service Is Tops*—New York Times

the **tops** *n phr* by 1937 The best; the acme: *The English department is the tops here*

top sergeant 1 *n phr* by 1898 A first sergeant; =TOP-KICK **2** *n phr* homosexuals by 1950s A lesbian who takes the dominant, masculine role; =BUTCH, DYKE

topsider *n* by 1960s A high executive, officer, manager, etc: . . . *sighed one Pentagon topsider last week*—Newsweek/ . . . *and also "delightfully puzzled," as one topsider put it*—Newsweek [related to late–1800s British *topside,* "in control, commanding," in turn related to the nautical term *topside,* by the suggestion that the master of a ship works on the bridge, which is the highest deck of the ship]

top story *n phr* by 1932 The head

torch 1 *v* by 1931 To set a fire deliberately; burn a building: *The lumberyard at 12th and C was torched, for the insurance*—Village Voice **2** *n* by 1938 An arsonist; an incendiary; =FIREBUG: *If your suspicions are right, the torch will be close by*—L Turner
See CARRY THE TORCH

torch job *n phr* by 1970s An instance of arson: . . . *mob-linked torch jobs for a 10 percent cut of insurance proceeds*—New York Times

torch song *n phr* by 1927 A popular song bemoaning one's unrequited love: *If it is unrequited, the song is a torch song*—Haskin News Service
See CARRY THE TORCH

torchy *adj* by 1941 In love with someone who does not reciprocate; hopelessly enamored: *Junie, still torchy for the Ragtime Kid*—S J Perelman [fr *carry the torch*]

-torium *See* -ATORIUM

torp *n* WWI Navy A torpedo; =TIN FISH

torpedo 1 *n* underworld by 1929 A gunman, esp a hired killer; =HIT MAN: . . . *the torpedoes who worked for Ciro Terranova*—Time **2** *v* by 1895 To destroy; annihilate; =SINK: . . . *in an offensive that* *torpedoed cease-fire talks. . .* —Los Angeles Times **3** *n* by 1970s =HERO SANDWICH

torpedo (or **torp**) **juice** *n phr* WWII *armed forces* Liquor made from whatever ingredients are available; improvised alcoholic military drink [fr the fact that *torpedoes* were fueled with very pure grain alcohol, and *juice* commonly means "fuel"]

torqued *adj* black by 1960s Angry; upset; =PISSED OFF: *She was all torqued because he took someone else out*—Current Slang [probably somehow fr the sense "twisted," found by 1572, and hence semantically akin to *bent out of shape*]

to save one's **neck** *adv phr* by 1940s Even in extremity; =FOR SHIT, NO WAY: *I couldn't remember the date to save my neck*

toss 1 *v* by 1939 To search, esp a person for weapons, drugs, etc; =SHAKE DOWN: *How do you think Leo will react to getting tossed in the apartment?*—Robert B Parker **2** *v* by 1833 To determine by throwing up a coin for "heads or tails": *I'll toss you for the drinks*
See THROW

toss one's **cookies** (or **lunch**) *See* SHOOT one's COOKIES

toss in the sponge *v phr* =THROW IN THE SPONGE

toss off 1 *v phr* by 1874 To do something easily and casually: *They sat down and tossed off a couple of limericks* **2** *v phr* by 1590 To drink, esp at one gulp; =KNOCK BACK: *She tossed off three double Scotches*

a **toss-up** *n* by 1809 An even matter; a case of even probabilities, values, etc: *It's a toss-up between those two candidates/ I don't know which way to bet; it's a toss-up* [fr the fact that the choice might as well be made by *tossing up* a coin]

total 1 *v* by 1954 To destroy; totally wreck, esp a car: *It didn't look like much of a wreck, but his car was totaled* **2** *v* by 1895 To maim or kill; grievously injure; =WASTE: *Mightn't a tile have fallen off a roof and totaled us by dinnertime?*—National Lampoon [first sense fr the phrase *a total loss,* having to do with something insured]

totaled 1 *adj* by 1954 Destroyed; wrecked completely: *The totaled car made you wonder how they survived the wreck* **2** *adj* by 1960s Stuporous from narcotics, liquor, etc; =STONED, WASTED

a **total loss** *n phr* by 1940s A person or thing that is hopelessly futile; =LOSER

totally clueless *adj phr* teenagers by 1970s Uninformed; ignorant; in the dark [*Clueless* is a late–1930s Royal Air Force term]

tote[1] or **tote bag** *n* by 1900 A carrying sack or shoulder bag, usu strongly made and decorated with some attractive label or symbol: *He was carrying a canvas tote bag bearing the portrait of Geoffrey Chaucer* [fr Southern dialect, "carry," perhaps fr Gullah *tot,* "carry"; cognates are found in several African languages]

tote[2] or **tot** *v* by 1760 Total; add up to: *How much does it tote?*—James M Cain

tote[3] *n* (also **tote board**) by 1950 A totalizator, a machine that displays odds at a race track [*totalizator* is found by 1879]

totem poles *See* KNOCK someone or something FOR A LOOP

to the eyes (or **the eyeballs**) *adv phr* by 1778 Entirely; thoroughly; =UP TO HERE: *Carlotta keeps her doped to the eyeballs on Thorazine all her adult life*—New York Times
See STONED TO THE EYES

to the gills *See* SOUSED, STEWED

to the ground *See* BEAT TO THE GROUND, DOWN TO THE GROUND

to the mark *See* UP TO SCRATCH

to the max *adv phr* 1970s teenagers & Army To the highest degree; utterly; totally: *Many of these were obscure to the max*—Philadelphia [fr a shortening of *to the maximum*]
See GROTTY

to the nines *See* DRESSED TO THE TEETH

to the salt mines *See* BACK TO THE SALT MINES

to the teeth *See* DRESSED TO THE TEETH

to the tune of *adv phr* by 1716 In the amount of; to the extent of: *It'll cost him a bundle, to the tune of sixty grand or so*

to the wall *See* BALLS TO THE WALL

totsie *See* HOTSIE-TOTSIE

touch 1 *v* (also **touch up**) by 1760 To get or borrow money, a loan, etc; =HIT: *Who better to touch up than the richest guys in town?*—Philadelphia **2** *n* by 1846: *. . . . a quick ten- or twenty-dollar touch*— E Lavine [*touch up* variant may be influenced by British *touch up,* "to grope a woman"]
See SOFT TOUCH

touch all bases by 1980s **1** *v phr* To be thorough; leave nothing undone, esp in matters of consultation, communication, etc: *The plan flopped because you didn't touch all bases on the way* **2** *v phr* To be very versatile; be apt for various experiences: *Humphrey is a man to touch all bases*— Toronto Life [fr the necessity of *touching all bases* in baseball when one makes a home run]

touch base with someone *v phr* by 1980s To consult with or inform as to an impending matter: *Before you sign it you'd better touch base with your lawyer* [fr *touch all bases*]

touch dancing *n phr* by 1950s Kinds of dancing in which partners hold one another

touches *See* CUT UP THE TOUCHES

touchie-feelie or **touchy-feely** *adj* by 1970s Having to do with sensitivity training and other such goings-on where people touch and feel each other: *They're all part of the touchie-feelie movement*— National Review/ *It's not going to be a touchy-feely thing*—Milwaukee Journal

not **touch** someone or something **with a ten-foot pole** *See* NOT TOUCH someone or something WITH A TEN-FOOT POLE

tough 1 *adj* by 1883 Difficult; regrettable; unfortunate: *That's a tough break, pardner* **2** *adj* by 1906 Physically menacing; vicious: *Don't act tough with me, you little jerk* **3** *n* by 1866 A hard and menac-

ing person **4** *adj* black by 1937 Excellent; superb; =the MOST •Sometimes spelled *tuff*: *That's a really tough set of wheels*
See TOUGH IT OUT

a **tough** (or **hard**) **act to follow** *n phr* by 1980s A challenging or daunting prelude: . . . *her portrayal of Catwoman. . . was a tough act for Michelle Pfeiffer to follow*—New Yorker [fr the vaudeville ambiance where one performer succeeded another; one truism was "Never follow a dog act"]

tough call *n phr* by 1990s A hard decision or prediction: *This next election is bound to be a tough call* [fr the decisions made by sports officials and football quarterbacks]

tough cookie by 1928 **1** *n phr* =TOUGH GUY **2** *n phr* A stubborn and durable person: *He's a tough cookie. He isn't going to talk, threats or no threats*—Hugh Pentecost

tough cop **See** GOOD COP BAD COP

tough guy (or **baby**) *n phr* entry form and baby by 1932 A menacing man; a hoodlum; =BIMBO, ROUGHNECK, TOUGHIE: *Bogart used to play tough guys a lot*

toughie or **toughy** **1** *n* by 1929 A menacing person, esp a man; =TOUGH, TOUGH GUY: . . . *getting the toughies off the streets*—New Republic/ *That servant will talk her out of it. She's a toughie*—Saul Bellow **2** *n* by 1945 Something difficult; a severe test: *This is a toughie*—Max Shulman/ . . . *has 3 toughies barring its way to a perfect season*—Associated Press

tough it out *v phr* by 1830 To endure something doggedly and bravely; persist and survive against rigors; =HANG TOUGH: *He's never really had to tough it out in this world of ours*—J Bell/ *He is toughing out a feeling that since Mom divorced he is essentially homeless*—Richard Schickel

a **tough nut to crack** *n phr* by 1970s A difficult problem; =BITCH, TOUGHIE: *Getting them all here on time will be a tough nut to crack*

a **tough row to hoe** **See** a HARD ROW TO HOE

tough sell *n phr* by 1990s Something difficult to advocate or "sell": *High-tech warehousing a tough sell*—Milwaukee Journal Sentinel

◁**tough shit**▷ *sentence* (Variations: **luck** or **nibs** or **noogies** or **patootie** or **rocks** or **tiddy** or **titty** may replace **shit**) entry form by 1940s, luck by 1886, noogies by 1960s, tiddy by 1934 That's too bad; that's a terrible shame •Often ironical and mocking: *Lord, what tough luck*—The Lantern/ *"Tough tiddy,"* the Boss said—Robert Penn Warren/ . . . *to which one has to say, with whatever empathy. . . tough nibs*—Village Voice/ *"And guess what they had the nerve to tell me." "Tough patootie"*—comic strip "Blondie"/ *That's tough shit, man, my heart really bleeds*—W T Tyler/ *Well. . . tough titty*—Armistead Maupin [most forms probably fr black or Southern; the mammary forms seem based on a black folk-saying, "It's tough titty, but the milk is good"]

tough-tec *modifier* by 1960s Having to do with the "hard-boiled school" and style of crime fiction: . . . *a*

darn good tough-tec mystery—New York Magazine

tour guide *n phr* 1960s narcotics A person who aids and supports someone having a psychedelic drug experience or "trip"; =GURU

tourist trap by 1939 **1** *n phr* A museum, pageant, shop, etc, of minimal significance established to attract transient visitors **2** *n phr* A restaurant, nightclub, etc, in a tourist resort, that charges exorbitant prices for often inferior goods or services: *We had to eat in a shabby tourist trap, and it cost far too much money*

tout **1** *n* by 1865 A person who sells betting advice at a race track; =TIPSTER **2** *n*: *He makes a slender living with his touting at Belmont* **3** *v* by 1920 To advocate aggressively; publicize; =BALLYHOO, FLACK: *He's now touting acupuncture* [ultimately fr Middle English *tuten*, "look around, peer," by way of *tout*, "be on the lookout"]

towel **See** CRYING TOWEL, THROW IN THE SPONGE

town **See** GO TO TOWN, HICK TOWN, MAN-ABOUT-TOWN, ONE-HORSE TOWN, ON THE TOWN, PAINT THE TOWN, SHANTYTOWN, TANK TOWN, TINSELTOWN

Town **See** BEAN TOWN

toy boy *n phr* by 1981 Male lover of an older woman

track **1** *v* Army by 1970s To agree with other information; chime: *What you say doesn't track with what I know* **2** *v* by 1970s To make sense; be plausible; =FIGURE: *It does not necessarily track that because Son of Sam sells papers in New York he will sell books in Seattle*—California Magazine/ *She's practically out of her mind. Like, she isn't even tracking*—Cyra McFadden [probably fr *track*, "the groove of a phonograph record, a continuous line or passage of a tape recording," influenced by earlier *track*, "follow, come closely and directly behind"]

See FAST LANE, GO ON TRACK, HAVE THE INSIDE TRACK, ONE-TRACK MIND

the **track** **See** the TURF

Track One *n phr* Canadian police by 1970 The brothel district of a city; the red-light district

track record *n phr* by 1965 Any record of performance, esp of success; =CHART, FOOTPRINT, FORM: *I have a lot of relevant experience and a good track record*—New York Times/ *Voluntary organizations have a much better track record in the third world*—New York Times [fr the *record* of performance of a racehorse on the race *track*]

tracks **1** *n* WWII Army =RAILROAD TRACKS **2** *n* 1960s narcotics The scars or puncture-marks caused by narcotics injections: . . . *wear long sleeves (to cover their "tracks," needle marks)*—Reader's Digest

See CROW TRACKS, HEN TRACKS, PECKER TRACKS, RAILROAD TRACKS, STOP someone DEAD IN someone's or something's TRACKS, the WRONG SIDE OF THE TRACKS

Track Two *n phr* Canadian police by 1970 The homosexual quarter of a city; the gay ghetto

trade *n* homosexuals by 1935 : . . . *most White gay men use it to mean a heterosexual male who has* sex with men for money or other consideration ("He can be done for trade"; "Watch out for him; he's rough trade")—The Journal of Sex Research/ . . . is flashy, precise, and humpy as decidedly sexy trade in a Czardas with six girls—Village Voice **See** PIECE OF TRADE, the RAG TRADE, ROUGH TRADE, TEA TRADE

trademark *n by 1869* A person's particular trait or strong point; =someone's MIDDLE NAME: *Shyness is not my trademark*

tragic magic *n phr 1960s narcotics* Heroin: . . . *you know, duji, scag, tragic magic*—Richard Woolley

trailer *n movie studio by 1928* A preview of a coming movie, a brief travelogue, or another short film shown before or after a feature movie

◁**train**▷ **1** *v by 1970s* To do the sex act on a woman serially, man after man, in a gang; =GANG BANG: . . . *announced that they were going to train her*—Philadelphia Journal **2** *n*: . . . *popularly known as gang bangs or trains*—Ms [related to *pull a train;* perhaps influenced by earlier *train,* "romp, carry on wildly"] **See** the GRAVY TRAIN, ON THE GRAVY TRAIN, PULL A TRAIN, RIDE THE GRAVY TRAIN

train with *v phr by 1871* To associate with; consort with; =HANG OUT: . . . *the money it required to train with such*—Theodore Dreiser/ . . . *and I don't train with lawyers*—Leslie Ford [probably fr the notion of linking up with or even riding on the *train* with; perhaps influenced by the prizefighter's close association with those he *trains with*]

train wreck 1 *n phr* (also **crump**) *medical by 1980s* A person with many medical problems and in failing condition **2** *n phr by 1980s* An extremely harrowing situation or condition: *The special prosecutor's office is a worthy institution, but it will leave behind a legal train wreck*—New York Times/ *Demographers refer to collisions between rising demand and diminishing resources as train wrecks*—Time

tramp *n by 1922* A promiscuous woman; a harlot; =PUNCHBOARD

trank 1 *n by 1967* A tranquilizer; a tranquilizer tablet or capsule **2** *v* (also **trank out**) *by 1972: Last I heard, still at some pricey Rambler's Retreat, tranked to the tits*—Stan Cutler/ *The idea was to keep me tranked out so that everything would sort of stabilize*—New Yorker

trannie *n by 1983* A transvestite; =CROSS-DRESSER, TV: *A slicked-back platinumed, pirouetting trannie takes over the dance floor*—New Yorker

tranquilizer **See** ELEPHANT TRANQUILIZER

trans *n black teenagers by 1970s* A car; =TRANSPORTATION

transportation *n by 1940s* An old or decrepit car; an unappealing car: *It ain't pretty, but it's transportation*

trap 1 *n by 1776* The mouth; =YAP: *When she opens her trap she has an accent that is British*—John O'Hara **2** *n by 1932* A night club: . . . *a pretty good East Side trap*—Gilbert Milstein **3** *n black*

by 1970s An amount of money earned by a prostitute, and usu given to her pimp: *Ray's woman got in the car. Her trap was fat*—Donald Goines **4** *modifier black by 1970s* : . . . *to figure out why my trap money was shitty*—Donald Goines **See** BEAR TRAP, BLOW OFF one's MOUTH, BOOB TRAP, BOOBY TRAP, CLAM SHELLS, FLEABAG, FLY TRAP, KISSING TRAP, POTATO-TRAP, SHUT one's TRAP, TOURIST TRAP

traps *n by 1990s* The trapezius muscles: *Billitzer's lats, delts, traps and quads are ready for anything. Three or four days a week he runs through a 90-minute workout that has left him tuned and tough*—New York Times

trash 1 *n by 1604* A despicable, ill-bred person or group: *Don't mind them, they're just trash* **2** *v by 1970* To vandalize; mutilate or destroy, sometimes as an act of political protest; =WASTE: *They have also made it a practice to "trash" (wreck) restaurants, publishing houses, and other businesses that discriminate against the third world of sex*—Saturday Review/ *One year we were trashed three times*—Time **3** *v by 1975* To vilify; excoriate; =BAD-MOUTH, DUMP ON: . . . *the other mayoralty that Koch likes to trash whenever he gets the chance*—New York Magazine/ *Much given to the rave-pan approach to her craft, she can trash in a flash*—Toronto Life **4** *v by 1960s* To scavenge discarded furniture and other items that have been thrown away [first sense fr *white trash,* a black term of opprobrium] **See** WHITE TRASH

trashing *n by late 1960s* The act or an act of those who trash in the senses of wrecking and vilification: . . . *the Weathermen favoring of trashing was a ridiculous concept*—New York Times/ *In my experience the public contributes every bit as much to the trashing of our presidents as we grimy ones do*—Newsweek

trash talk (or **talking**) *n phr sports by 1990s* Provocative insults addressed by one athlete to others: *They learn about intimidation, bullying, bad call, trash talk, and that ends justify means*—New York Times/ *Trash talking is littering the air at NBA stadiums*—Milwaukee Journal

trash talker *n phr sports by 1990s* A person who does "trash talk": *If Muhammad Ali was the first trash-talker in boxing, Floyd Patterson was the last gentleman*—New Yorker

trashy *adj by 1620* Despicable; inferior; =LOW-RENT, LOW-RIDE

traveler **See** FELLOW TRAVELER

trawler *n by 1990s* =CHANNEL SURFER, GRAZER

treadhead *n Army by 1970s* A member of a tank crew

treat someone **like a doormat** (or ◁**like shit**▷) *v phr by 1970s* To deal with in a humiliating, haughty, or oppressive manner: *We treated poor old Uncle Bob like a doormat/* . . . *and is also a fucking nitwit imbecile who treats me like shit and makes me talk about vultures*—Joseph Heller

tree **See** CHRISTMAS TREE, LIT UP, OUT OF one's TREE, SHAKE THE MONEY TREE, UP A TREE

tree eater *See* SNAKE EATER

tree-hugger *n by late 1980s* An environmentalist; =DUCK-SQUEEZER: *TBS owner Ted Turner is a tree-hugger from way back*—Milwaukee Journal [said to have been used of Celia Harbeck, a Chicago woman who actually hugged trees in Jackson Park to prevent their being cut down]

tree jumper *n phr prison by 1970s* A sexual molester: *He was, in prison parlance, a tree jumper*—Milwaukee Journal

Trekkie or **Trekker** *n by 1976* A devotee of the television science-fiction series *Star Trek*: *Star Trek II. The Wrath of Khan. Come, all ye Trekkers*—Playboy/ *Trekkies hate being called Trekkies . . . They call themselves "Trekkers"*—Lee K Russell

trenches *See* IN THE TRENCHES

trendy 1 *adj* (also **trendacious** or **trendoid**) *by 1962* Following new trends in fashion, art, literature, etc; anxiously au courant: *Fetch a tumbril for these fellows, or at least a trendy tailor*—Saturday Review/ *A trendacious couple wear head-to-toe charcoal black*—Sassy/ *Your trendoid older sister gives you all her hand-me-downs on the 5th*—Sassy **2** *n* (also **trendoid**) *by 1968*: *That will undoubtedly have great appeal to all you trendies out there*—East Side Express/ *. . . and even a few tough trendoid from the East Village and Soho. . .* —Carsten Stroud

trey or **tray** *n 1960s narcotics* A $3 packet of narcotics

Tribeca or **TriBeCa** (trī BEK ə) *n New York City by early 1980s* An area in Manhattan being developed as an artist's and residential neighborhood: *They've traipsed all over Lower Manhattan, from Greenwich Village to Tribeca*—Playboy [fr *triangle below Canal* Street]

trick 1 *n by about 1915* A prostitute's client or sexual transaction: *. . . woman walking the streets for tricks to take to her room*—Louis Armstrong **2** *v prostitutes by 1965* To serve a customer: *She had tricked a john from Macon*—Playboy **3** *n homosexuals by 1970s* A casual homosexual partner; =NUMBER **4** *v* (also **trick out**) *by 1970s* To do the sex act, either hetero- or homosexually; =FUCK: *They can go "tricking out" with other gay people*—Deviant Reality **5** *n nautical by 1669* A shift or duty-period: *She doesn't require any breaks at her eight-hour trick*—New York Daily News

See CHAMPAGNE TRICK, HAT TRICK, LOBSTER SHIFT, TURN A TRICK

trickledown 1 *n by 1944* The stimulation of a whole economic system by the enrichment and encouragement of those in the upper reaches **2** *modifier*: *The planners counted on a trickledown effect when they relieved the rich of all taxation*

tricks *See* DIRTY TRICKS, GO DOWN AND DO TRICKS, HOW'S TRICKS

trigger 1 *n underworld by about 1935* A gunman; =HIT MAN, TRIGGER MAN: *He's a trigger*—movie Scene of the Crime **2** *v by 1950s* To commit a robbery:

Police said Sims has triggered dozens of holdups—Associated Press **3** *v by 1938* To initiate something; provoke something: *My innocent remark triggered a strange reaction*

See QUICK ON THE DRAW

trigger man *n phr underworld by 1920s* A gunman; =HIT MAN, TRIGGER

trikini *n by 1967* A woman's bathing suit with two top parts [fr *bikini*, based on the amusing assumption that *bi-* is Greek for "two," to be replaced with *tri-*, "three"]

trim 1 *v by 1950s* To defeat utterly; trounce; =CLOBBER: *They got trimmed 8–zip* **2** *n by 1955* A woman, esp one regarded as an object of sexual conquest ◁**3**▷ *n by 1960s* The sex act with a woman; =ASS, CUNT, GASH: *. . . you looking for some trim*—Ed McBain

trip[1] *n underworld by 1920s* An arrest; a prison sentence; =FALL [fr *trip*, "stumble, fall"]

trip[2] **1** *n narcotics by 1959* A psychedelic narcotics experience: *. . . users like beat poet Allen Ginsberg (30 trips)*—New York Post **2** *v* (also **trip out**) *narcotics by 1959* To have a psychedelic narcotics experience or comparable experience: *That film really tripped me out*—College Slang 101 **3** *n by 1966* Any experience comparable with a psychedelic experience: *The park is an icon. A nostalgia trip back into a youth*—Boston Magazine/ *I've known Chuck for many years and he's a trip. He's fun to be around*—Milwaukee Journal Sentinel **4** *v 1980s teenagers* To act stupidly: *He was trippin' at the party*—Delcastle Dictionary of Slang/ *If you're crazy, east side teens may say you're "trippin,'" "postal," or "gerpin'"*—KRT News Service

See BAD TRIP, EGO TRIP, HEAD TRIP, LAY A TRIP ON someone, POWER TRIP, SKI-TRIP

tripe *n by 1895* Contemptible material; worthless stuff; =CRAP, JUNK: *What the hell do they have to give us that tripe for?*—P Marks/ *. . . anyone who could make money on "such tripe"*—Time [fr *tripe*, "animal stomach used as food," because it is held in low regard]

tripes *n by 1529* The intestines; =GUTS, INNARDS, KISHKES: *He doesn't put their tripes in an unproar*—Westbrook Pegler

triple whammy *n phr by 1940s* A three-part attack, difficulty, threat, etc: *Triple Whammy on the Farm*—Newsweek

tripped out *adj phr 1960s narcotics* Having or symptomatic of a psychedelic narcotics experience: *. . . a tripped-out laughing jag*—Crawdaddy

tripper 1 *n by 1813* An excursionist; a tourist: *. . . the tripper class*—Sinclair Lewis **2** *n 1960s narcotics* A person who takes psychedelic narcotics

See PACKTRIPPER, ROUND-TRIPPER

trippy *1960s narcotics* **1** *adj* Intoxicated with narcotics; dazed; =SPACED-OUT, STONED: *. . . allowing the band to be tagged as a "trippy" band*—Los Angeles Times **2** *adj* Bizarre; phantasmal; surreal: *. . . a trippy fantasy, the Harvard University Press version of Instant Wingo*—Village Voice

Trojan horse *n phr* *1990s computers* A kind of computer virus: *"Trojan horse" programing lies in wait to be triggered later, either at a certain day, hour, or minute or when system use or storage reaches a certain level*—Milwaukee Journal [fr the wooden *horse* full of soldiers used by the Greeks to end the siege of Troy]

troll[1] *n Army by 1970s* A stupid person; a dullard [probably fr the dwarf or demon of Norse mythology]

troll[2] **1** *v by 1967* To go about looking for sexual encounters; =CRUISE •Tony Thorne dated this to the 1930s, without verification: *Women who are out trolling bars do not deserve the protection of the law*—Ms **2** *v 1990s computers* To seek respondents on the Internet; =SURF: *The firm was trolling for green card applicants in need of legal help*—Los Angeles Times [fr the action of fishing by *trolling*]

trolley *See* OFF one's TROLLEY, SLIP one's TROLLEY

trophy wife (or **husband) *n phr by 1984* A mate, often a younger person, chosen for decorative and prestige value: *Apparently the Senator and she have a private vision. . . that might make him as much a trophy husband as she a trophy wife*—Los Angeles Times [said to have been coined by Julie Connelly of *Fortune*]

trot out *v phr by 1845* To produce and display for admiration: *Oh Lord, he's trotting out his war record again*

the trots *n phr by 1904* Diarrhea; =the SHITS

trotter *See* BOG-TROTTER

trouble *See* DOUBLE-TROUBLE, DROWN one's SORROWS, HAND TROUBLE

trough *See* GREASE TROUGH

troupe *n police by 1950s* A team of cooperating pickpockets

trouser *See* DUST someone's JACKET •

truck 1 *v by 1681* To carry; haul; lug: *Why are you trucking all that weight around?* **2** *v jazz musicians by 1925* To leave; go along **3** *v 1930s jive talk* To dance the jitterbug; esp, to do a jitterbug dance called "Truckin" *See* MACK TRUCK

trucking *See* KEEP ON TRUCKING

Trues *n by 1980s*: *A white Cadillac Fleetwood. . . with blue-tinted windows and "Trues" and "Vogues," street talk for chrome-spoked wheels and tires with a thin gold stripe around the whitewalls. . .* —Milwaukee Journal

trumped up *adj phr by 1728* False; concocted; fabricated; =PHONY: *The indictment was trumped up for revenge*

trust *See* BEEF TRUST

try *See* the OLD COLLEGE TRY

try it on for size *v phr by 1956* To accept or attempt something tentatively: *Let's try this scenario on for size. . . And see if it binds in the crotch*—W E B Griffin

try-out *n by 1903* A trial, esp of someone's skill, acting or singing ability, etc

try out *v phr fr early 1900s* To apply for something; become a candidate: *I think I may try out for the*

choir this year

TS *n WWII armed forces* =TOUGH SHIT

tsatske *See* TCHOTCHKE

tsk-tsk *v by 1967* To use a mildly deprecating tone: *Editorial writers have been tsk-tsking over the fact that there are fewer and fewer union members*—Newsweek

TS ticket *n phr WWII Army* A putative ticket that a soldier could take to the chaplain, who, upon hearing the soldier's tale of woe, would punch the ticket [fr *tough shit*]

tsuris or **tsoris** or **tzuris** (TSŏŏR əs, TSAWR əs) *n by 1960s* Troubles; tribulations; anxieties; sufferings: *. . . if Samuels, with all his tsuris, wins the Democratic nomination*—New York Magazine/ *There is a tsoris, which is a kind of trouble spot*—New York Times/ *. . . during a long streak of tzuris*—T Betts [fr Yiddish fr Hebrew *tsarah*, "trouble"]

tub *See* IN THE TUB

tubby or **tubbo** *n entry form by 1891, variant by 1980s* A fat person: *. . . the ex-tubbies trying to live on lettuce leaves*—Hal Boyle/ *Hey, you're kind of a tubbo, ain't you?*—Mike Royko

the tube 1 *n phr by 1959* Television, as an industry, a medium, a television set, etc: *. . . making a name for herself as a singer on the tube*—New York Sunday News/ *. . . not a chance, unless you were back at the hotel watching on the tube*—Time **2** *n phr Los Angeles police by 1990s* A police shotgun [first sense a shortening of *cathode ray tube* or *picture tube*] *See* the BOOB TUBE, DOWN THE TUBE

tube it *v phr students by 1966* To fail an examination, course, etc

tube steak 1 *n phr by 1963* A frankfurter; =HOT DOG ◁**2**▷ *n phr* (also **tubesteak of love**) *by 1980s* The penis; =WEENIE

Tubesville *adj by 1980s* Rejected; =DEAD IN THE WATER, KAPUT: *Looks like your idea is Tubesville* [fr *down the tube*]

tub of guts (or **lard) *n phr by 1940* A fat person, esp a repulsive one: *. . . that tub-o'-guts*—G Holmes

tubular *adj 1970s teenagers* Wonderful; excellent; =AWESOME, GREAT [fr surfing term describing a wave with a *tube*, that is, a cylindrical space around which the crest is curling as the wave breaks, and inside which the surfer happily rides]

tuchis or **tuckus** *See* TOKUS

tuck *See* NIP AND TUCK

tucker *See* BEST BIB AND TUCKER

tude *n 1970s teenagers fr black* Attitude; view of things; typical reaction •Usually negative, sour, or surly [fr *attitude*]

tuff *See* TOUGH

tuifu (Tōō EE Fōō) *n WWII armed forces* A totally botched situation; an incredible blunder [fr *the ultimate in fuckups*]

tumble *v underworld by 1901* To be arrested; =FALL, TRIP *See* GIVE someone A TUMBLE

tumble to something *v phr by 1846* To discover; suddenly understand: *I tumbled to what she was* *really up to*—James M Cain [fr the notion of falling upon something, perhaps by stumbling over it]

tummy or **tum-tum** *n by 1869* The stomach: *. . . eliminating the protruding tummy*—Syracuse Post-Standard [fr a childish pronunciation of *stomach*]

See GYPPY TUMMY

tummyache *n by 1926* A stomachache: *An elephant died of an outsize tummyache at London Airport*—Associated Press

tumor **See** MILWAUKEE GOITER

◁**tuna** or **tuna fish**▷ *black by 1970s* **1** *n or n phr* The vulva; =CUNT **2** *n or n phr* A woman; a female [fr the similarity, recognized esp in black slang, between the odor of the vulva and that of fish or other seafood; perhaps somehow influenced by *Tiny Tuna*, homosexual slang for a sailor as a sex object]

tuna wagon *n phr by 1970s* An old, decrepit car; =HEAP, JUNKER: *the title of an article. . . in Vermont Life, "Junkers, Beaters, and Tuna Wagons"*—New York Times

tune **See** FINE-TUNE, LOONY-TUNE, TO THE TUNE OF

tuned *past part* Canadian teenagers *by 1970s* Possessed or practiced upon sexually; =be HAD [perhaps related to earlier British and Australian *tune,* "beat, hit," hence semantically to *bang*]

tune in *v phr esp 1960s counterculture* To become aware, au courant, involved, etc: *Tune in, turn on, drop out*—Timothy Leary

tune out *v phr esp 1960s counterculture* To cease being aware, au courant, etc; the opposite of "tune in"

tune up *v phr by 1901* To bring something, esp a car motor, to its best state of effectiveness; tinker with to improve: *. . . tuning up for the race at Santa Ana*—Life [fr the process of *tuning* a musical instrument, suggested by the fact that the performance of motors can be gauged by their sound]

tunnel *v underworld by 1950s* To go into hiding

See SEE THE LIGHT AT THE END OF THE TUNNEL

tunnel vision *n phr by 1949* Very narrow and restricted vision or perception; the inability to see anything except what is directly in front

T someone **up** *v phr basketball by 1990s* To call the maximum permissible number of technical fouls: *He had already T'd Barkley up for a technical foul. Now he did the same for Oakley, and summarily threw him out of the arena*—New Yorker

turbocharge or **turbo** *n 1980s narcotics: Grade school kids are introduced to cocaine along with marijuana. "It's called a turbocharge. . . They think turbo is not addicting. . .*—Newsweek

◁**turd**▷ **1** *n by 1000* A piece of excrement **2** *n by 1518* A despicable person; =PRICK, SHIT

See GHOST TURDS

turd in the punchbowl **See** GO OVER LIKE A LEAD BALLOON

turf **1** *n 1930s jive talk* The sidewalk; the street **2** *n street gang by 1953* The territory claimed or controlled by a street gang: *I tried to imagine my Deacons pacing the turf or talking about me*—Life

3 *n by 1970* A particular specialized concern; =THING: *Counterterrorism is not their exclusive turf*—Newsweek/ *I never thought of myself as pretty, that was my sister's turf*—Village Voice **4** *v medical by 1970s* To transfer a patient to another ward or service in order to evade responsibility, decisions, irritations, etc [*turf,* "the road," in the first sense is found in hobo use by 1899]

the **turf (or track)** *n phr by 1860* The work and venue of a prostitute; the street: *During early years "on the turf," as the saying went, she was. . . thrifty and ambitious*—H Asbury/ *I didn't want to lose her, now that she was ready for the track*—Donald Goines [fr an analogy between the prostitute's work and that of a racehorse]

turf war (or battle) *n phr by 1950s* A contention over the rights to a certain activity, location, etc: *We get eye-glazing accounts of turf wars between the Council on Economic Policy and the Commission on International Trade and Economic Policy*—New York Times/ *Faget suspected a turf battle for control of the Mercury program*—New Yorker

turista *n by 1970* Diarrhea; =AZTEC TWO-STEP, MONTEZUMA'S REVENGE [fr Spanish, "tourist"]

turk **See** YOUNG TURK

turkey **1** *n show business by 1927* An inferior show, esp a failure; =BOMB, FLOP: *Management prudently kept the turkey out of town*—Gene Fowler **2** *n by 1941* Anything inferior, stupid, or futile; =LEMON, LOSER: *For all ordinary purposes it was simply a turkey*—James M Cain/ *. . . calling the bill a turkey. . . said it would send the wrong signal*—New York Times **3** *n by 1951* A stupid, ineffectual person; =JERK: *You'd be stuck with that turkey practically until he died*—D Larsen **4** *n underworld & teenagers by 1970s* The victim of a mugging or street robbery: *On an average night, they. . . attacked eight victims or "turkeys," taking a total of about $300*—Time **5** *n bowling by 1940s* Three consecutive strikes [fr the common and perhaps accurate perception of the *turkey* as a stupid creature, an avian loser; the bowling sense is exceptional]

See CAPE COD TURKEY, COLD TURKEY, DEEPSEA TURKEY, FULL OF SHIT, IRISH TURKEY, TALK TURKEY

turkey-shoot *n phr by 1970s* Something very easy; =CINCH, PIECE OF CAKE: *Getting a job is no turkey-shoot anymore* [fr the marksmanship contests where *turkeys* are tied behind a log with their heads showing as targets]

turn someone *v police by 1980s* To cause a suspect to change his testimony and implicate others: *We tried to turn Rowe, but he was too scared. He said he'd do life before he'd hand up his associates*—Michael Grant

See TALK OUT OF TURN

turn someone **around** *v phr by 1970s* To change someone's attitude, behavior, etc: *You fuck it up, that's turning me around*—Robert Stone

turn a trick *v phr by 1946* To do the sex act for profit; do one piece of work as a prostitute; =TRICK:

*Many of the prostitutes were students, models, or would-be actresses who turned tricks part-time—*Washington Post

turned off 1 *adj phr* 1960s narcotics No longer using narcotics; =CLEAN **2** *adj phr by 1960s* Indifferent; bored **3** *adj phr by 1960s* Tired; =FED UP

turned on 1 *adj phr* 1950s narcotics Intoxicated, esp from narcotics; =HIGH: *I'm really turned on, man. . . I'm higher than a giraffe's toupee—*Stephen Longstreet **2** *adj phr by 1960s* Stimulated; aroused; excited; switched on: *You are so sexualized, and so turned on—*Sexual Behavior **3** *adj phr by 1960s* Aware and up-to-date; au courant; =HIP, PLUGGED IN: *. . . flower children who flock to New York's turned-on Macdougal Street—*Trans-Action/ *. . . an outlaw lobbyist, a turned-on Nader—*New York Times

turner *See* PAGE TURNER

turn in *v phr by 1833* To go to bed

turnkey job *n phr by 1934* A good job that will not need to be done again; a definitive treatment: *Scott has given us something less than a turnkey job—*Chronicle of Higher Education [fr the phrase *that locks it up,* "that ends it and achieves it definitively"]

turn someone's **lights out** *v phr by 1980s* To punish someone severely; incapacitate someone: *Man, if I sued every guy who ever turned my lights out, I wouldn't have time to do anything else—*Harry Crews/ *It looked like we started out with a bang, but then the kid turned our lights out—*Milwaukee Journal

turn-off *n by 1975* Something that damps one's spirits; a sexual or emotional depressant; =WET BLANKET: *The film is in fact a sexual turnoff—*Saturday Review

turn off *v phr by 1970s* To become indifferent; lose concern: *When he found he couldn't hack it, he just turned off*

turn someone **off** *v phr* 1950s beat talk To depress someone; be a deterrent to someone's spirits: *It seems like everybody turns you off—*New York Times/ *Policies and practices that are not "relevant," to use his language, "turn him off"—*US News & World Report

turn off someone's **water** *See* CUT OFF someone's WATER

turn on *fr* 1960s counterculture & narcotics **1** *v phr* To use narcotics, esp to begin to do so: *Tune in, turn on, drop out—*Timothy Leary **2** *v phr* To take or inject narcotics: *Do you turn on with any of the local heads?—*Trans-Action

turn-on *by 1960s* **1** *n* Something that arouses and excites; a sexual or emotional stimulant: *. . . which physical attributes of men are a turn-on for women—*Saturday Review/ *Reluctance is often a turn-on—*New York Times **2** *n* Excitement; ecstasy; elation: *He'd never felt a turn-on like that*

turn someone **on 1** *v phr by 1903* To excite or stimulate someone; arouse someone: *The professor was trying to find out what turns women on* **2** *v*

phr by 1960s To introduce someone to something; pique someone's curiosity: *He turned me on to Zen—*Lawrence Lipton

turn on a dime *v phr by 1970s* To be able to turn around in a very short radius: *That car corners very sweetly, and turns on a dime*

turn on the waterworks *v phr by 1885* To weep; begin to cry; =BLUBBER: *I turned on the waterworks—*Paul Theroux

turnout 1 *n by 1816* An audience, the participants at a meeting, etc: *We always get a good turnout for the council sessions* **2** *n by 1859* Clothing; dress; =GET-UP, TOGS **3** *n* homosexuals by 1970s A heterosexual man who turns homosexual: *A Navy turnout is one who went in heterosexual but came out dreaming of pecker—*Gay Talk

turn someone **out** *v phr by 1970s* To introduce someone to something; initiate someone, esp to narcotics, sex, prostitution, etc: *He takes a "square broad" (a nonprostitute) and "turns her out"—*Time

turnover *n* prison by 1934 The eve of one's release from prison: *He told me next Sunday was his turnover and I should meet him at the gate*

turn turtle *v phr by 1860* To turn upside down; capsize: *. . . in the heavier puffs, they thought she would turn turtle—*Robert Louis Stevenson [fr earlier *turn the turtle,* found by 1818, referring to making a turtle helpless by turning it on its back]

turn up *v phr by 1755* To arrive; =SHOW UP: *When do you want us to turn up?*

turn someone **up** *v phr* underworld by 1872 To inform; in effect, to turn someone over to the police; =HAND UP: *Maybe you better turn me up—*W R Burnett/ *Somebody turned him up—*Raymond Chandler

turn up one's **toes** *v phr by 1950s* To die

turpentine *See* UP THINE WITH TURPENTINE

turtle *See* TURN TURTLE

turtledoves *n by 1940s* A pair of sweethearts

tush or **tushie** or **tushy** *See* TOKUS

the **tush push** *n phr by 1990s* A dance: *. . . it's the individual dances that are most popular: the tush push, slapping leather, and the electric horseman—*Milwaukee Journal [fr Yiddish *tush,* "bottom, buttocks"]
See TOKUS

tux *n by 1922* A tuxedo

tuzzy-muzzy *n by 1440* A nosegay or bouquet: *A tuzzy-muzzy is a cone-shaped Victorian decoration with dried flowers—*Milwaukee Journal

TV *n by 1965* A transvestite; =TRANNIE: *TVs are not as feminine as they themselves think they are—*The Realist

◁**twat**▷ (TWAHT) *by 1656* **1** *n* The vulva; =CUNT **2** *n* A woman considered merely as a sex object or organ; =ASS, PIECE OF ASS

tweak 1 *v* computer by 1980s To adjust a computer program slightly; refine; fine-tune: *Michael's code is elegant stuff, really fun to tweak—*Douglas Coupland **2** *v by 1990s* To make minor adjustments; perfect: *Is the President going to tweak* *emissions for seven years and then let them rip?*—Time/ . . . *he used the core of the President's plan, and from that he did some tweaking*—Los Angeles Times [perhaps a memory of the days when a crystal was *tweaked* with a "cat's whisker" in order to tune a primitive radio receiver]

tweaked or **tweaky** *adj by 1980s* Odd; crazy; =FLAKY: *Julie is tweaked; first she says she loves Doug and then she fully grovels with Bill*—UCLA Slang/ . . . *"Twin Peaks" without the dwarves, the demons, and the tweaky humor*—Newark Star-Ledger

twee *adj by 1905* Tiny; dainty; miniature; cute: . . . *no tiny, twee money to dole out*—Village Voice [fr *tweet*, a childish pronunciation of *sweet*]

tweener *n by 1990s* A person poised between two major categories: *Yes, Bennett is a tweener, too small for fullback in most systems, but not Green Bay's, and too slow for halfback*—Milwaukee Journal/ . . . *"tweeners" are trapped in a sociological limbo-land, too big to be considered little kids but not old or mature enough to be looked upon as true adolescents*—Milwaukee Journal [fr *between*]

tweeter *n by 1934* A small loudspeaker for the higher tones

twenty-five *n 1960s narcotics* LSD [fr the fact that 25 is part of its chemical designation]

twenty-four seven or **24/7** or **24–7** *adv phr by late 1980s* Twenty-four hours a day seven days a week; always: . . . *they founded 24–7: Notes from the Inside. (The title, if you have been living under a rock, refers to being locked up 24 hours a day, 7 days a week)*—Sassy/ *If I could I would stay on vacation twenty-four-seven*—Delcastle Dictionary of Slang [said to have initiated by street gangs selling crack cocaine, available always]

twentysomething *See* GEN-X

twenty-twenty (or **20–20**) **hindsight** *n phr by 1962* Perfect foresight of what has already been seen: . . . *observers empowered with 20–20 hindsight wanted to know*—New York Times

twerp or **twirp** *n by 1874* A contemptible person; =JERK, NERD: . . . *ill-mannered, foul-mouthed little twirp*—Westbrook Pegler/ *Wrangel may have been a pretentious twerp*—Saul Bellow [origin uncertain]

twiddle *computer by 1980s* **1** *v* To change something in a small way; =TWEAK **2** *n* The tilde, a diacritical mark used especially in Spanish

twiddle one's **thumbs** *v phr by 1846* To waste time; be forced to sit idly and perhaps rotate one's thumbs about one another: *I was anxious to help, but all I could do was twiddle my thumbs while they debated*

twink or **twinkie** or **twinky** *by 1963* **1** *n* A young, sexually attractive person; tempting teenager: *You know, the twink who used to be Fielding's lover*—Armistead Maupin/ *The Weemawee twinkies troop out to the kickoff line*—New York Magazine **2** *modifier*: *I found this gorgeous twink carpenter in the Mission*—Armistead Maupin ◁**3**▷ *n by 1963* A weird or deviant person, esp a homo-

sexual; a social outcast: *They think "twinky" or sissy or something like that*—Washington Post/ *Rafi comes on strong, but he's a twink at heart*—Elmore Leonard **4** *adj*: *Quentin Crisp. . . croaks in a nasal monotone like a twinkie Mr Magoo*—Village Voice [origin uncertain]

twin pots *1950s hot rodders* **1** *n phr* Dual carburetors **2** *n phr* A car with dual carburetors

twirl *n underworld by 1979* A skeleton key or duplicate key

twirler *n baseball by 1883* A pitcher

twist *n by 1928* A young woman: . . . *sexy little twist. . . but a kook*—Joseph Wambaugh/ . . . *a tough, smart twist who got away with murder*—Lawrence Sanders [perhaps fr rhyming slang *twist and twirl*, "girl," attested in a poem of E E Cummings]

twist someone's **arm** *v phr by 1940s* To induce or persuade someone very strongly; importune someone powerfully, as if by physical force: *You grab this opportunity to twist my arm*—Saul Bellow

twisted *adj* **1** *1960s narcotics* Very much intoxicated with narcotics; =HIGH: *twisted. . . so high he doesn't know where the hell he is*—Clarence L Cooper **2** Unusual; perverted: *My Twisted World of Convoluted Music*

twister **1** *n by 1897* A tornado **2** *n 1930s jive talk* A key **3** *n by 1940s* A spree; =BENDER: . . . *their periods of sobriety between twisters*—Saturday Evening Post

See BRONCO BUSTER

twist slowly (or **twist**) **in the wind** *v phr by 1973* To suffer protracted humiliation, obloquy, regret, etc: *The second mistake was to let Sherrill twist slowly in the wind*—Washington Post/ . . . *just letting you twist slowly, slowly in the wind*—New York Times [perhaps coined by John Ehrlichman, an aide of President Richard Nixon, fr the gruesome image of a hanging body]

twisty *adj by 1970s* Attractively feminine; =SEXY: *Most female doctors aren't as, uh. . . young. No, ah, say twisty might be more like it*—William Brashler

twit *n by 1934* A contemptible and insignificant person; a trivial idiot: *Craig Stevens as her twit of a husband*—Village Voice/ *I've got the authorization, you fucking twit*—Stephen King [origin unknown; rapidly adopted in the 1970s, perhaps because of the popularity of the British television series *Monty Python's Flying Circus*, on which the term was often employed]

two *See* FIFTY-TWO, NUMBER TWO, ONE-TWO

Two *See* TRACK TWO

two-bagger **1** *n baseball by 1880* A two-base hit; a double **2** *n by 1970s* A very ugly person; =DOUBLE-BAGGER: . . . *two-bagger, a girl who needs exactly that to cover her ugliness*—Time

two-bit *adj by 1929* Cheap; tawdry; trivial; =TACKY: . . . *the two-bit bureaucrats*—Billy Rose/ *Congressmen were panic-stricken, running around like two-*

bit whores—Washingtonian [literally, worth only *two bits*]

two bits *n phr* by 1730 A quarter; twenty-five cents [fr the quarter part of a Mexican *real,* which had eight *bits*]

two-by-four or **two-by-twice** *adj* entry form by 1896, variant by 1930s Small; insignificant; inferior; =TWO-BIT: *We stopped at a two-by-four hotel near the tracks*

two cents *See* PUT one's TWO CENTS IN

two cents' worth *n phr* by 1942 A little; a trivial amount: *I'll give you two cents' worth of advice about that*

twofer (Tōō fər) **1** *n* by 1911 A cheap cigar **2** *n* by 1948 A theater ticket sold at half the normal price [fr the phrase *two for,* in these cases *two for a nickel* and *two for the price of one*]

two hats *See* WEAR TWO HATS

two shakes or **two shakes of a lamb's tail** *n phr* by 1883 A moment; a wink; =a JIFFY: *Hold it, I'll just be two shakes* [by 1840 in the form *a couple of shakes*]

two-spot *n* by 1904 A two-dollar bill

two-step *See* AZTEC TWO-STEP

two-time *v* by 1924 To deceive and betray someone; esp, to betray one's proper sweetheart by consorting with someone else: *Two-Timing Boy Wrecks Girl's Dream*—New York Daily News [perhaps fr *two at a time;* perhaps fr *making time with two at once*]

two-time loser 1 *n phr* underworld by 1931 A person who has been convicted twice, and therefore risks a higher sentence another time **2** *n phr* by 1970s A person who has been divorced twice: *Nora Ephron. . . funny two-time loser*—Time

two to tango *See* IT TAKES TWO TO TANGO

two ways *See* WORK BOTH WAYS

two-way street *n phr* by 1951 A situation that cannot or should not be handled by only one person: *After all, Sam, keeping a marriage happy is a two-way street*

typewriter *n* by 1915 A machine gun, esp a submachine gun; =TOMMY GUN

tzuris *See* TSURIS

U

ugly *See* PLUG-UGLY

ugly as sin *adj phr* (Variations: **galvanized sin** or **catshit** may replace **sin**) *entry form by 1821* Very ugly; extremely repellent

ugly gun *n phr by 1990s*: *Gun lovers call. . . semi-automatic weapons. . . "ugly guns"*—New York Times

uie or **u-ey** *n by 1976* A U-turn

ultraswoopy *adj by 1970s* Very fast: *. . . a down-sized, hitech, ultraswoopy model next year*—Car and Driver

umlaut *n by 1970s* Half of a bottle of Löwenbräu™ beer: *Slick ordered four more umlauts for himself*—Dan Jenkins [two *umlauts* is a bottle, since the name has two diereses]

ump *n baseball by 1888* An umpire

umpteen *modifier fr WWI* Of any large unspecified number: *. . . exhausted all the encomia in your vocabulary on umpteen reviews*—Anthony Boucher [said to have been first used by British military signalers during World War I to disguise the number designations of units]

umpteenth *modifier fr WWI* The ordinal form of "umpteen": *Here's the umpteenth development in the battle*—Associated Press

umpty *modifier by 1905* Of an unspecified number of the decimal order: *. . . the umpty-fifth regiment*—Bill Mauldin

umpty-umpth *modifier fr WWI* Of a large and unspecified ordinal number:. . . *making the same speech for the umpty-umpth time*—Eleanor Roosevelt/. . . *the umpty-umpth revision*—Bennett Cerf

unc or **unk** or **unky** *n by 1905* Uncle

uncle 1 *n by 1756* A pawnbroker **2** *n underworld by 1924* A receiver of stolen goods; =FENCE **3** *n underworld & narcotics by about 1920* A federal narcotics agent; =NARC [last sense fr *Uncle Sam*] *See* SAY UNCLE

Uncle Dudley *See* YOUR UNCLE DUDLEY

Uncle Sam 1 *n phr by 1813* The US Government; the US as a nation **2** *n phr underworld by 1940s* A federal agent or agency; =FED [said to have originated during the War of 1812 when Samuel Wilson of Troy, New York, locally known as *Uncle Sam,* stamped US on supplies he provided for the government, and this was jocularly taken to be his own initials]

Uncle Sugar *n phr WWII armed forces* The United States government; =UNCLE SAM [fr the military phonetic alphabet words for *U* and *S*]

Uncle Tom *n phr black by 1922* A black man who emulates or adopts the behavior of the white majority; a servile black man; =AFRO-SAXON, OREO [fr the title character of Harriet Beecher Stowe's novel *Uncle Tom's Cabin,* who was stigmatized as a dishonorably submissive black]

Uncle Tomahawk *n phr Native American by 1970s* A Native American who emulates or adopts the behavior of the majority culture; a servile Native American

Uncle (or Mister) Whiskers *n phr underworld by 1933* The federal government or one of its agents or agencies: *. . . do we get our percent of the gross, but Charley said not with Mr Whiskers at the gate*—John O'Hara/ *You can't do business with Uncle Whiskers*—NY Confidential [fr the bewhiskered image of *Uncle Sam*]

uncool *adj cool talk by 1953* Not cool; wrong, excited, rude, etc

under *See* GET OUT FROM UNDER

under one's **belt** *adj phr by 1954* Successfully achieved or survived: *Get a couple more months' experience under your belt and we'll talk about a promotion*

underground 1 *adj by 1953* Apart from and opposed to conventional society; esp, advocating and representing the hippie and narcotics subculture: *The Voice started as a sort of underground newspaper* **2** *adj by 1820* In hiding; concealing one's identity and whereabouts, esp to escape arrest

the **underground** *n phr WWII & 1960s counter-culture* Political or cultural dissenters collectively who lead a partly or wholly clandestine life and resist the dominant regime; also, their arena of life and operations [term first applied to the various resistance movements against German occupation in World War II, and then was adopted by the 1960s counter-culture, which saw the US government and culture as analogous with the Hitlerian]

underground comic *See* HEAD COMIC

under one's **hat** *adj phr by 1885* Secret; in confidence: *Here it is, but it's strictly under the hat, see?*—Joel Sayre

under one's **nose** *adv phr by 1548* In plain sight, although unnoticed: *. . . I'm afraid I may be missing something that's right under my nose*—Lawrence Sanders

under the collar *See* HOT UNDER THE COLLAR

under the gun *adj phr* *by 1940s* In a position of danger; urgently called on to take action: *Under the economic gun*—Denver talk show guest [fr a poker term for the player called upon to open, bet, fold, raise, etc]

under the table 1 *adj phr* *by 1921* Very drunk **2** *adv phr* *by 1940s* Illegal; secret and illicit; unethical: *He would never make any deals under the table* **3** *adj phr*: *What was the best under-the-table offer you got?*—Playboy

under someone's **thumb** *adj phr* *by 1754* Entirely in someone's control: *Our boss likes to keep us under his thumb*

underwear *See* LONG-HANDLE UNDERWEAR, LONG UNDERWEAR

underwhelm *v* *by 1956* To impress very little; be quite insignificant; be less than overwhelming: *Her performance rather underwhelmed the audience*

under wraps *adv phr* *by 1939* In secrecy; in obscurity: *We had better keep this under wraps for a while*

undies *n* *by 1906* Underwear, esp women's panties: *. . . a glimpse of her undies*—Morris Bishop
See FUDGE one's PANTS

unflappable *adj* *by 1958* Calm; imperturbable; cool: *They admired Mrs Thatcher's unflappable mien*
See FLAP

◀**unfuckingbelievable▶** *adj* *by 1940s* Unbelievable
•A fairly common use of the "fucking" infix: *"Totally unfuckingbelieveable," said Duffy*—Harry Crews

unglued *See* COME UNGLUED

ungodly shot *n phr* baseball *by 1970s* A hard line drive: *A hard line drive is a blue darter, frozen rope, or an ungodly shot*—Jim Bouton

unhep or **unhipped** *adj* *1930s* jive talk Conventional; unstylish; unimaginative; =UNCOOL: *. . . faith, devotion, and other such unhep subjects*—Billy Rose

unisex *adj* *by 1968* Intended for or fitting for both sexes: *The unisex trend was launched by the era's pacesetters, the teenagers*—Life

unleaded coffee *n phr* *by 1980s* Decaffeinated coffee: *Feel like having a big decaffeinated espresso with lots of milk and no foam? In java jive, that's an unleaded grande latte without*—New York Times

unmentionables *n* *by 1910* Underwear; undergarments: *. . . required to don upper and lower unmentionables*—Owen Johnson

uno *See* NUMERO UNO, TAKE CARE OF NUMERO UNO

unreal *adj* *by 1965* Excellent; wonderful; =GREAT: *Like great. She's real unreal*—Harper's Bazaar

unshirted hell *n phr* *by 1932* Serious trouble: *. . . cold fronts raise unshirted hell with fishing*—Milwaukee Journal/ *Then it's pure unshirted hell*—George V Higgins

unstuck *See* COME UNGLUED

until one **is blue in the face** *See* TILL one IS BLUE IN THE FACE

until the last dog dies *adv phr* *by 1990s* Until the bitter end: *In Dover, New Hampshire, Clinton promised voters that if they gave him a second chance, he would be with them until the last dog dies*—Esquire/ *But no—he swore a blood oath that he was one of us, and would stay until the last dog died*—Vanity Fair

untogether black *by 1960s* **1** *adj* Ineffectual; confused; =SCREWED UP: *. . . leading us to think you are so untogether that you want other blacks to go through the same thing*—Ebony **2** *adj* Not fashionable or stylish **3** *adj* Not smooth and effective socially

up 1 *adj* *by 1815* Exhilarated; happy; sparkling; hopeful: *I was feeling up. I thought it had been a very successful evening*—Lawrence Sanders **2** *adj* *by 1970s* Encouraging; hopeful; =UPBEAT: *I don't like down movies, I like up movies*—New Yorker **3** *n* *by 1966* A source of excitement; a pleasurable thrill; =LIFT: *Her words gave me a huge up* **4** *v* *by 1925* To raise; increase: *My confidence has upped itself*—New York Post **5** *adj* *by 1972* Ready and effective; keyed up; in one's best form: *Obviously, Kennedy wanted to be "up" for the meeting*—Village Voice **6** *adj* *1960s* narcotics Intoxicated by narcotics, esp amphetamines; =HIGH: *. . . as it does when you're up on bennie*—Hubert Selby Jr **7** *n* *1960s* narcotics An amphetamine dose, capsule, etc; =UPPER: *Let's do some ups tonight* **8** *adj* (also **up and rolling** or **up and running**) *1980s* computer Functioning; in operation; active: *English-only is a phony issue raised only to get folks' bile up and running in time for the presidential race*—Lawrence Hall [first sense is based on *up*, "effervescent, bubbling," used of beer and other drinks; later similar uses, from the 1940s, are based on the "high" produced by narcotics]

up against it *adj phr* *by 1896* In a difficult situation; in serious trouble: *When they saw the gap they knew they were really up against it*

up against the wall *sentence* *1960s* counterculture Prepare to be humiliated, attacked, robbed, despised, etc; =GO FUCK oneself: *. . . our commune motto, "Up against the wall, motherfuckers"*—James Simon Kunen/ *Up against the wall, IBM and General Electric and Xerox and Procter & Gamble and American Express*—Wall Street Journal [fr a line in a poem by Leroi Jones (Amiri Baraka), "Up against the wall, motherfuckers," fr the command of a holdup man to his victim, or of the police to a person being arrested, forcing him to immobilize himself by leaning forward arched with hands against a wall; probably influenced by the fact that people are executed by being shot against a wall]

up someone's **alley** *See* DOWN someone's ALLEY

up-and-coming *adj* *by 1848* Promising and energetic: *I gathered a few up-and-coming young writers for my staff*

up-and-down *n* *by 1924* A close look; scrutiny: *The tray-toter gave me the slow up-and-down*—Billy Rose [found by 1820 in Byron's *Don Juan*, "a survey up and down"]

up and up or **on the up and up** *adj phr* *by*

1863 Honest; reliable; =STRAIGHT-UP: *It's an up and up place*—W R Burnett/ *I almost wonder if the whole bunch of 'em are on the up and up*—Sinclair Lewis

up a rope *See* GO PISS UP A ROPE

◁**up** one's **ass**▷ *See* SIT THERE WITH one's FINGER UP one's ASS, STICK IT

up a storm *adv phr by 1953* Very intensively; very diligently; very competently: *. . . and they're really dancing up a storm*—Washingtonian

up a tree *adj phr by 1825* In a predicament; faced with a dilemma; helpless

upbeat *adj by 1947* Optimistic; encouraging; positive: *They use catchy, upbeat phrases*—Saturday Review/ *A triumph of upbeat pictures over the downbeat*—Associated Press [apparently fr the musical term *upbeat*, "a beat on which a conductor raises his baton," but since such beats have no emotional connotations, the coiner must have seized on the general positive notion of *up* and taken *beat* to mean "stroke, movement"]

upchuck *v by about 1925* To vomit; throw up; =BARF, RALPH: *It is enough to make one upchuck*—Wisconsin Journal [fr *up* plus *chuck*, "throw"]

update 1 *v by 1948* To give, add, record, etc, the latest information: *He updated me on a couple of gimmicks*—John Crosby **2** *n by 1967*: *I'll give you a quick update* **3 modifier**: *Is this the update material?*

up for grabs *by 1940s* **1** *adj phr* Available, esp newly available: *"High Haven," Luke repeated sonorously, "is up for grabs"*—John Le Carré/ *I got two doozies up for grabs*—Esquire **2** *adj phr* Problematical or undecided, esp newly so: *The whole question of one-man-one-vote is up for grabs again*

up front 1 *adv phr* (also **in front**) *by 1972* In advance; before any deductions: *His twin wasn't getting enough cash (something like $1,000) up front*—Pulpsmith/ *Don't pay your money up front*—Consumers Digest **2** *adj phr by 1980* From the beginning; first; at once: *. . . we knew right up front that if I did the film. . .*—Rolling Stone **3** *adj phr by 1972* Honest; open; truthful: *. . . very up-front about who she is and what she thinks*—J Nolan/ *"These people are not being up-front and honest," the Mayor said*—New York Times

up in the air *adj phr by 1933* Unsettled; undecided; uncertain: *When he left, the whole project was up in the air for a while*

upmanship *See* ONE-UPMANSHIP

upmarket *adj by 1972* Appealing to or created for wealthy people: *. . . a daily newspaper which would make even the Sun look up-market*—Guardian

upper or **uppie 1** *n 1960s narcotics* An amphetamine; a stimulant narcotic;: *. . . the effect of mixing "uppers" and "downers"*—New Republic **2** *n by 1973* A source of excitement; a pleasurable thrill; =UP: *It may not be the same kind of thrill as winning a hand of poker at a casino, but it's definitely an upper*—Games

See PEPPER-UPPER, PICKER-UPPER, WARMER-UPPER

the **upper crust (**or **drawer)** *by 1835* **1** *n phr* The social aristocracy; the elite **2** *adj phr* (also **upper-drawer**) : *His manners were silkily uppercrust/ . . . the upper-drawer voters*—Lawrence Sanders

See ON one's UPPERS, SHATTING ON one's UPPERS

upper story *n phr by 1699* The brain; the mind: *. . . definite shortcomings in the upper story*—D Nowinson

See LOOSE IN THE BEAN

uppity *adj black by 1880* Conceited; arrogant; snobbish; =HINCTY ●Once used almost exclusively of black people felt to be too self-assertive by the white speaker: *. . . the most uppity colored fellow I ever ran into in my life*—Calder Willingham/ *. . . to estimate if this reporter was going to give her any sass or put on any uppity airs*—Washington Post

uproar *See* NOT GET one's BALLS IN AN UPROAR

upscale *adj by 1966* Having to do with upper social and economic reaches; wealthy; aristocratic; =RITZY: *The killing. . . by Jean Harris was. . . an upscale crime*—Time

◁**up shit (**or **shit's) creek**▷ or **up the creek** *adj phr* (Variation: **without a paddle** may be added) *entry form by 1937, variant by 1941* In serious difficulty; very unfortunate; ruined: *Then you guys'll be up the creek for good*—Jerome Weidman [perhaps related to the early-1800s term *up Salt River*, of much the same meaning, and which may refer to the Salt River in Kentucky, a legendary abode of violent and brutal people; but the term is attested in British armed forces use without US attribution fr the early 1900s]

upside or **upside of** *prep black by 1970* On the side of; in: *He got whacked upside the head with a board*—William Brashler

the **upside** *n phr by 1980s* The hopeful aspect; the good news: *The upside is that she's still conscious* [both *upside* and *downside* originally referred to the fluctuations of the stock market]

upside one's **face** *See* GO UPSIDE one's FACE

up one's **sleeve** *See* ACE UP one's SLEEVE

up-South *n black by 1970s* The North, esp with respect to its racism

upstage 1 *v theater by 1933* To attract attention to oneself and away from other performers, esp by standing upstage so that they must look at you and turn their backs to the audience **2** *v by 1921* To demand and receive inordinate attention at the cost of others: *The secretary was trying to upstage the president on this, so he had to act at once* **3** *adj by 1918* Haughty; aloof; snobbish: *"Upstage" has taken on the additional meaning of "ritzy," that is, arrogantly proud and vain*—B Sobel

upstairs *adv by 1932* In the brain; mentally: *. . . became a little balmy upstairs*—Hal Boyle

See KICK someone UPSTAIRS

uptake *See* QUICK ON THE DRAW, SLOW ON THE DRAW

up the ante *v phr by 1970s* To raise the price, offer, sum in question, etc; increase; make a higher demand: *I think I may up the ante to a cool fifty*—

Pat Conroy/ *The trader decides to up the ante*—Philadelphia [fr the *ante* in poker, which gives one the right to take part]

◁**up the ass**▷ *by 1971* **1** *adv phr* Thoroughly; perfectly well: *I know country music up the ass on the guitar*—Rolling Stone **2** *adv phr* (Variations: **butt** or **kazoo** or **gazoo** or **gazool** may replace **ass**) To a very great extent; in excess; =UP TO HERE: *They want vision? Vision up the kazoo!*—New Yorker/ *Bob Gottlieb has class up the gazoo*—New Yorker/ *I've got lawsuits up the gazool, which is one thing that disillusions me about writing*—Billy Joel
See KAZOO

up the flagpole *See* RUN something UP THE FLAGPOLE

up the river *adv phr by 1924* In prison [fr the fact that Ossining Correctional Facility, formerly called Sing Sing, is *up the Hudson River* from New York City; from 1891 the term referred only to Sing Sing]
See SEND UP

up the spout *See* GO UP THE SPOUT

up the wall *adj phr by 1951* Crazy; wild; =NUTTY: *It doesn't drive us crazy. At least, I don't know anybody who is up the wall about it*—Washingtonian [fr the image of insane persons, frantic and deprived drug addicts, wild animals, etc, trying to climb a wall, to escape]
See DRIVE someone UP THE WALL

◁**up thine with turpentine**▷ *interj by 1950s* An exclamation of very strong defiance and rejection; =FUCK YOU, STICK IT

uptick *by 1970* **1** *n* A rise, esp in stock prices; an increase of value: *. . . the strongest and broadest uptick in the history of the company*—Time/ *Another 10 percent uptick and you double up again*—Forbes **2** *n* Improvement; raising: *His apparent uptick in spirit was contagious*—Newsweek [fr the use, on boards above stock-market stations, of a plus sign (compare British *tick*, "check mark") beside a stock of which the last sale represented a rise in price; a minus sign represents a *down tick*; probably influenced by the *tick*, like *click*, or *notch*, representing one degree of change; compare *ratchet up*]

uptight **1** *adj by 1934* Tense; anxious: *He was all uptight about student plagiarism* **2** *adj by 1962* Excellent; =COOL, GREAT

up to one's **ass** *See* one HAS HAD IT

◁**up to** one's **ass (or neck) in** something▷ *adj phr* (Variations: **in alligators** or **in rattlesnakes** may be added for emphasis) *by 1940s* Deeply involved; overwhelmed: *Every time I turn around we're up to our asses in something*—Leslie Hollander/ *You're up to your ass in alligators, get a bigger alligator*—Carsten Stroud/ *. . . we're going to be up to our necks in soccer. . .*—New York Times

up to one's **eyeballs (or eyebrows)** *adv phr by 1940s* To a very great extent; totally; =UP TO HERE: *. . . one smaller outfit. . . which is in farm equipment smack up to its corporate eyeballs*—Barron's

up to one's **eyebrows** *See* one HAS HAD IT

up to here *by 1940s* **1** *adv phr* To the utmost; excessively; in great quantity: *Look, my friend, I've had it up to here with your bitching* **2** *adj phr* Surfeited; disgusted; =FED UP: *I'm so up-to-here with the primaries and the TV news interviews*—Washington Post [fr the notion of being fed to excess, fed up, and with the implicit gesture of indicating one's throat as the place up to which one has had it]
See one HAS HAD IT

up to scratch (or the mark) *adj phr by 1911* Satisfactory; acceptable; qualified: *I'm afraid this story isn't quite up to scratch* [fr the early custom of drawing a line across a boxing ring and requiring that the able and willing fighter stand with his toe touching the *mark* or *scratch-line*]

up to snuff *by 1811* **1** *adj phr* Satisfactory; acceptable; =UP TO SCRATCH: *His work doesn't come anywhere near up to snuff* **2** *adj phr* In good health; feeling well: *I don't feel quite up to snuff this morning* [origin uncertain; the original British sense was "shrewd, not gullible," apparently referring to the fact that one could be blinded with *snuff* in the eyes, and victimized; the early 1800s US phrases *in high* (or *great*) *snuff*, "in good form, high fettle, etc," perhaps having to do with *snuff* as an aristocratic commodity and symbol, may also be related]

up to speed *adj phr by 1980s* Informed; au courant; aware of the situation: *Ballard was up to speed now*—Carsten Stroud
See BRING someone UP TO SPEED

up to the wire *See* COME UP TO THE WIRE

uptown *n 1960s narcotics* Cocaine; =the LADY [fr the aristocratic and wealthy overtones of cocaine as compared with other narcotics, fr the earlier sense of *uptown*, "affluent, swanky," as distinct fr *downtown*; the topography and demography of Manhattan Island underlies these senses]
See the BOYS UPTOWN

◁**up yours**▷ *interj* (Variations: **you** or **your ass** or **your butt** or **your gig** or **your giggy** or any other synonym of **ass** may replace **yours**) *by 1950s* An exclamation of strong defiance, contempt, rejection, etc: *Up yours, sister, he thought tardily as the barbs quivered home*—W T Tyler [a shortening of *stick it up your ass*]

use *v 1950s narcotics* To use narcotics; take a dose or injection of a narcotic: *I used this morning and I'm still nice*—Clarence Cooper

use one's **head (or** one's **bean)** *v phr by 1828* To think; reason out one's actions: *. . . teaches a man to use his head and to do the best he can*—Hal Boyle/ *You certainly used the old bean*—P Marks

◁**useless as tits on a boar**▷ *adj phr by 1940s* Absolutely futile

user *n 1950s narcotics* A person who uses narcotics, esp an addict

ush *v by 1890* To be an usher: *. . . the rancid troglodytes who ush at the Knicks' games*—Playboy

usual *See* AS PER USUAL

the usual suspects *n phr by 1943* The persons

one would expect: *The amusing Rossini concert was well executed by the usual suspects (Hampson, Marilyn Horne, Samuel Ramey, June Anderson)*—Nation/ *We are given new perspectives on those who are the usual suspects in any consideration of modern lesbian writing: Willa Cather, Virginia Woolf, H.D. and Djuna Barnes*—Nation [fr an order given by Claude Rains as the French police official in the 1943 movie *Casablanca*]

ute *n* by 1943 A utility or sports-utility vehicle: *The San Clemente is the first sport ute created especially for the mature market*—New York Times/ *Sport-utes, which are four-wheel-drive trucks outfitted like boxy station wagons, are being scarfed up by buyers in record numbers*—Milwaukee Journal [the dated instance is from WWII Australia-New Zealand use]

V

vacation *n* underworld by about 1920 A prison sentence: . . . *who won a 20 years' vacation in the Big House*—E Lavine

vag (VAYG) **1** *n* by 1859 A drifter; derelict; vagrant; vagabond; =BAG LADY: *America can almost compete with England in the number of her "city vags"*—J Flynt **2** *n* by 1877 Vagrancy, as a legal offense: *We'll book him on vag*—movie *Asphalt Jungle*

vamoose or **vamose** (va MOOS) *v* by 1834 To leave; depart, esp hastily; =LAM, SCRAM, SPLIT: *We better vamoose, Moose* [fr Spanish *vamos,* "let us depart"]

vamp[1] *v* musicians by 1789 To improvise, esp an accompaniment; play casually and extemporaneously; =FAKE, SHUCK [probably fr 1500s *vamp,* "provide with a new (shoe) vamp, renovate," ultimately fr conjectured Anglo-French *vampé* fr Old French *avant-pié,* "foot-sock"; a refooted sock or a *revamped* shoe were felt to be in a way false, or improvised, hence the sense of "fake"]

vamp[2] **1** *n* by 1911 A seductive, sexually aggressive woman; a temptress: *The flirt had become the "baby vamp"*—F Scott Fitzgerald **2** *v* by 1904: *I haven't tried to vamp Sam*—Elmer Rice [fr *vampire,* and esp fr the 1914 movie *A Fool There Was,* in which Theda Bara played a seductive woman, the title and concept coming fr Rudyard Kipling's poem "The Vampire"]

vamp[3] *n* by 1877 A volunteer firefighter [origin unknown; said to be fr *Voluntary Association of Master Pumpers*]

vamp[4] or **vamp on** black by 1970s **1** *v* or *v phr* To assault; trounce; =BEAT someone UP, CLOBBER: *They knew that he'd vamp on them if they got wrong*—Bobby Seale/ *Chairman, chairman wake up, the Pigs are vampin'*—New York Times **2** *v* or *v phr* To arrest; =BUST [perhaps related to black English *vamp* someone, "come at someone suddenly and aggressively"; perhaps fr *vamp*[2] reinforced by the murderous aggression of Count Dracula, a genuine and popular *vampire* in Bram Stoker's novel and the movies made from it]

vanilla 1 *n* black by 1970s A white person, esp a white woman **2** *adj* by 1970s Conventional; usual; bland; =WHITE BREADY **3** *n* by 1970s A person of ordinary sexual preferences; a usual heterosexual; =STRAIGHT: *They called women who did not proclaim joy at being chained to the bedposts or chaining someone else "vanilla"*—Village Voice **4** *adj* by 1970s: *As a self-confessed vanilla-sexual*—Village Voice **5** *adj* by 1970s =PLAIN VANILLA [fr the white color and the perhaps unimaginative choice of *vanilla* ice cream]

vanilla wafer *n phr* by 1990s A very conventional man; =STRAIGHT

vanner *n* by 1970s A person who drives a van, esp as a symbol of a somewhat alienated and independent social attitude: *A vanner is tough to put your finger on. . . some are former bikers*—US News & World Report

vaporware *n* computer by 1990s Computer software that is advertised but still nonexistent: *We have a new name for vaporware. . .* —Douglas Coupland

varnish *See* COFFIN VARNISH

varnish remover *n phr* by 1950s Raw and inferior whiskey; =PANTHER PISS

varoom *See* VROOM

Vatican roulette *n phr* by 1962 The rhythm method of birth control

va-voom or **va-va-voom** by 1960s **1** *interj* An exclamation of delight, esp of excited sexual interest **2** *adj* (also **voomy**): *. . . pressing the tits of this va-va-voom sophomore and shtupping her pussy*—National Lampoon/ *Under that icky mask, I think you're the voomiest*—comic strip "Spiderman" [probably fr *vroom* and *varoom*]

VC *n* Vietnam War armed forces The Vietcong or a member of the Vietcong; =VICTOR CHARLIE [fr *Vietcong*]

veeno *See* VINO

veep *n* by 1949 A vice president: *Veep Fresco Thomas, Coach Jake Pitler, and Dressen*—Associated Press [fr pronunciation of *vp*]

veg[1] (VEJ) **1** *n* by 1918 A vegetable **2** *n* by 1970s =VEGETABLE

veg[2] (VEJ) *v* (also **vedge** or **veg out**) 1980s college students To relax luxuriously and do nothing; vegetate; =GOOF OFF, MELLOW OUT: *. . . . I'm going to vanish up to someplace beautiful. . . and just veg for two solid days*—Douglas Coupland/ *. . . when you could escape from the world by vegging out in front of the tube. . .* —Milwaukee Journal [fr *vegetate*]

vegan (VEHG uhn) *n* by 1990s: *This is especially important for vegan vegetarians who eliminate milk and eggs from their diet, in addition to meat, fish, and chicken*—Mesa Tribune

vegetable *n* A person lacking normal senses,

579

responses, intelligence, etc; =BASKET CASE, GOMER, GORK, RETARD: *He was fine the first couple of years of marriage, but then he turned into a vegetable*

vegetable patch *See* FRUIT SALAD

veggie 1 *n by 1975* A vegetarian **2** *modifier*: *a veggie pal of ours* **3** *n 1980s college* A person who relaxes and does nothing: *When I finish this paper, I'm just going to be a veggie*—College Slang 101

veggies or **vegies** *n by 1955* Vegetables

vein *See* JAB A VEIN

velvet *n by 1901* Profit, esp an easy and unexpected profit; gambler's winnings; money in general: *There are substantial money returns, "velvet,". . . for those who secure places*—Oskar von Engeln *See* BEGGAR'S VELVET, BLUE VELVET, ON VELVET

vent *v* (also **ventilate**) *by 1990s* To relieve one's feelings by vehement expression; =LET IT ALL HANG OUT: *Last year. . . the critics vented madly about all the great shows the networks killed*—USA Today/ *Alvin ventilated, complaining about the prosecutors, his business partners, the intolerance of his wife*—Scott Turow

ventilate *v by 1875* To shoot; =PLUG [fr the notion of letting air into someone]

vent man *n phr by 1970s* A homeless drifter who typically sleeps on the warm sidewalk air-vents from subways and other underground places: *There are the bag ladies and the vent men*—Philadelphia

verbal (or **oral**) **diarrhea** *n phr* (also **diarrhea of the mouth**) *by 1940s* Logorrhea; uncontrollable loquaciousness: *You've got verbal diarrhea*—Calder Willingham

Veronica *n 1990s computer* A computer search tool *See* ARCHIE

verse *See* CHAPTER AND VERSE

vest *n by 1976* An important person; =SUIT *See* PLAY CLOSE TO THE VEST

vet[1] **1** *n by 1869* A veteran, esp a former member of the armed forces: *I'm a combat vet*—Nelson Algren **2** *modifier*: *. . . the vet producer of scouting plays*—Esquire

vet[2] **1** *n by 1862* A veterinarian **2** *modifier* Veterinary: *the vet school* **3** *v by 1904* To examine closely; scrutinize critically •*Chiefly British: Random House plans a review of its procedures for "vetting" or checking a book prior to publication*—Washington Post/ *The hosts are a carefully vetted collection of bubble brains*—Time [third sense fr the close examination of an animal by a *veterinarian*]

vette or **'vette** *n by 1960s* A Corvette™ car

V-girl *n WWII* A woman who more or less freely made love to soldiers, sailors, etc, from patriotic motives [fr *victory girl*]

vibes[1] *n jazz musicians by about 1937* A vibraphone or vibraharp

vibes[2] or **vibrations** *n by 1967* What emanates from or inheres in a person, situation, place, etc, and is sensed; =CHEMISTRY, KARMA: *The vibes were good that morning for our reunion*—Saturday Review

vic[1] *n underworld by 1925* A convict

vic[2] *n by 1921* A phonograph; Victrola™

vic[3] *1960s black teenagers* **1** *n* A victim; =MARK, PATSY: *There were no "poppy loves" or "vics" in the car, no white people at all. . .* —Carsten Stroud **2** *v* (also **scope a vic**) To look for someone to rob, mug, etc **3** *v* To steal: *I told them not to vic the car, because I knew they would get caught*—Delcastle Dictionary of Slang **4** *v* To cheat: *I was vicked by the people that gave me only one dollar for a tip*—Delcastle Dictionary of Slang

vicious *adj 1970s teenagers* Excellent; superb; wonderfully attractive

Victor Charlie *n phr Vietnam War armed forces* Vietcong; =VC [fr the military phonetic alphabet words for *V* and *C*]

vidaholic *n by 1970s* An addict of television: *. . . a lifelong vidaholic, the 33-year-old Simmons*—Newsweek [fr *video* plus *-aholic*]

video jock or **VJ** *n phr by 1970s* A television performer who plays and comments on music videos: *. . . record-company executives, V J's, directors, agents, and managers*—New York Times

vidiot *n by 1980s* A person addicted to television; =VIDAHOLIC: *Daytime? That's when you give America's vidiots pure junk food. . .* —Milwaukee Journal

vidkid *n by 1990s*: *. . . even preadolescent vidkids fused like Krazy Glue to their Super Nintendo and Sega Genesis games, the training wheels of cyberpunk*—Time

Vietnik 1 *n 1960s and 70s* A person who actively protested US military involvement in Vietnam **2** *modifier*: *. . . the latest Vietnik demonstration*—Time

vig or **vigorish** or **viggerish** *n fr gambling by 1908* Profits of a bookmaker, a usurer, a criminal conspirator, a casino, etc: *I'm not nailing you no vig for last week*—George V Higgins/ *About 180 percent a year in interest, known in the trade as vigorish, vig, or juice*—Wall Street Journal [probably fr Yiddish fr Russian *vyigrysh*, "profit, winnings"]

vig ounce *n phr 1960 narcotics* An ounce of narcotics; =PIECE

-ville *See* -SVILLE

vinegar *See* FULL OF PISS AND VINEGAR

vines *n jive talk by 1932* Clothing; a suit, esp a stylish one; =THREADS [fr earlier prison *vine*, "civilian clothes, nonprison clothes"; perhaps fr a semantic extension of *weeds*, "clothing"]

vino or **veeno** (VEE noh) *n by 1919* Wine, esp red jug wine [fr Italian, "wine"]

vinyl *by 1976* **1** *n* Phonograph records; recording: *Now this disco graffiti has found its way to vinyl and created quite a bit of excitement*—Variety **2** *modifier*: *. . . woman who rides the vinyl grooves*—New York Daily News **3** *modifier* Having to do with discotheques, the dancing done there, etc: *The only vinyl junkies were the nattily-suited variety*—Circus [fr the chemical material used for phonograph records, semantically analogous with earlier *wax*]

VIP (pronounced as separate letters) *n by 1933* A very important person; =BIG SHOT

viper *n* *1930s narcotics* A marijuana dealer or user

virus or **computer virus** *n* *1980s computers*: *"Viruses" have the goal of self-propagation, seeking to spread from program to program within a computer's storage area. . . Eventually they spread to other computers as well when an infected program is transferred*—Milwaukee Journal

vision *See* TUNNEL VISION

visiting fireman *n phr* *by 1926* An out-of-town visitor, esp a dignitary: *He meets a good many distinguished visiting firemen*—New Yorker [fr the earlier sense *fireman* or *fire maker,* "a Native American ceremonial dignitary who was responsible for lighting the fires"]

VJ *See* VIDEO JOCK

vogue *v* *by 1980s* To do the "vogueing" dance or performance: *She vogued in the West Village. Disappeared in San Diego with a porn filmmaker*—Washington Post/ *. . . commenced vogueing official International Body-Building Federation poses. . . Such brazen posing!*—Douglas Coupland

vogueing *n* *by 1980s* To do a dance involving poses similar to glamour magazine models: *Vogueing, an unusual dance fad popular in New York's underground clubs. . .* —Macon Telegraph

Vogues *n* *by 1980s*: *A white Cadillac Fleetwood. . . with blue-tinted windows and "Trues" and "Vogues," street talk for chrome-spoked wheels and tires with a thin gold stripe around the whitewalls. . .* —Milwaukee Journal

volume *n* *by 1970s* A dose or capsule of Valium™, a tranquilizer: *I'd take maybe five volumes in the morning*—New York Times

vomity or **vomitrocious** *adj* *by 1970s* So nasty as to cause one to vomit: *Gross and even grossening are out. Vomitrocious is in*—George F Will [longer form fr *vomit* plus *(a)trocious*]

voomy *See* VA-VOOM

vote with one's **feet** *v phr* *by 1965* To escape; become a refugee or emigrant: *Nearly three million people voted with their feet*—New York Times

vroom or **varoom** *by 1967* **1** *n* The noise of a powerful car **2** *modifier* (also **vroom-vroom**): *. . . if you drive a sporty, vroom-vroom model*—Washingtonian **3** *v* To speed, esp in a roaring car: *. . . as we vroomed up and down the Watchung Mountains*—Esquire

W

wack or **whack 1** *n* by 1938 A crazy or eccentric person; =NUT, SCREWBALL, WEIRDO: *Two wacks if I ever saw one. . .* —John O'Hara/ *. . . a father who was so abrasive and married now to such a wack—* Joseph Heller **2** *adj* Worthless; stupid; "wimpish": *. . . you'll have to deal with some really wack people. . .* —Sassy
See WACKY

wack off *See* WHACK OFF

wacky or **whacky** *adj* (also **wacked-out** or **wacko** or **whacked** or **whacked-out**) by 1935 Crazy; eccentric; =NUTTY: *You think I'm going wacky?*—John O'Hara/ *. . . annually collects whacky accidents*—NEA Service/ *. . . the most wacked-out cop game anybody had ever seen any cops play*—Tom Wolfe/ *. . . the wacked-out hustler who talks Winkler into running a call-girl service out of the morgue*—People Weekly/ *. . . she tried to convert me to her religion! She was whacked—* Sassy [fr British dialect *whacky*, "fool," attested fr the early 1900s; *whacky*, "a person who fools around," is attested in British tailors' talk fr the late 1800s; perhaps fr being *whacked* over the head too often; perhaps influenced by *whack off* "masturbate," and semantically akin to *jerk*]

-wacky *combining word* by middle 1940s =CRAZY, NUTTY: *car-wacky/ chick-wacky*

wad *n* by 1864 A roll of money: *My grandmother'd just sent me this wad about a week before*—J D Salinger
See SHOOT one's LOAD, SHOOT one's WAD

-wad *combining word* 1980s & 90s teenagers A disgusting or unpleasant person ●Used as second formative in *dickwad, dipwad, dripwad, phlegmwad, jerkwad, scumwad,* and *tightwad; -wad* joins *-bag, -ball* and *-head* as very productive elements for forming insults [fr several sources: *wad* as defined above; *wad,* "an unattractive or unpopular person," in late 1800s college slang; *wad,* "a quantum of semen," fr 1920s; *wad,* "a mass or lump of something"; *wad,* "the male genitals," recently attested but not widespread]

waddie or **cow-waddie** *n* late 1800s A cowboy

wader *See* HIGH WATERS

waffle¹ 1 *v* by 1803 To speak or behave evasively; tergiversate; equivocate: *When asked for specifics, I demur, I waffle*—New York Magazine/ *. . . unlike the windy, waffling, anonymous editorial writers—*

Philadelphia **2** *n*: *I was tired of all the candidates' waffle* [fr northern British dialect, "waver, fluctuate," perhaps related to another dialect sense, "yelp, yap"]

waffle² *v* by 1970s To trample viciously; =STOMP: *No player called out at second threatened to waffle an umpire*—Philadelphia Daily News [fr *waffle-stompers*]

waffle-iron *n* A sidewalk grating

waffle-stompers *n* early 1970s Heavy hiking boots; =SHITKICKERS [fr the pattern of the soles, which make a *waffle*-like print]

wag *See* CHIN-WAG

wag one's **chin** *v phr* by 1920 To talk: *. . . to be seen waggin' your chin with a sleuth*—Dashiell Hammett

wagon *n* Navy fr WWI A naval vessel
See BEAN WAGON, BUZZ-BUGGY, COVERED WAGON, DEAD WAGON, DOG-WAGON, FALL OFF THE WAGON, FIX someone's WAGON, FRUIT WAGON, HONEY WAGON, MEAT WAGON, MILK WAGON, OFF THE WAGON, ON THE WAGON, PADDY WAGON, PIE WAGON, RAPE WAGON, RUBBERNECK WAGON, SEX WAGON, TUNA WAGON

wah-wah 1 *n* 1920s musicians A pronounced wavering, scooping sound from an instrument, the voice, etc: *. . . imitations of animal sounds. . . such as wah-wahs on trumpets and trombones*—A Lomax/ *Then Wah-Wah Waddy breaks into his best funkadelic solo*—Village Voice **2** *n* A pedal-operated electronic device for producing wah-wahs, esp on electric guitars: *the same kind of highly-perfected control over use of the wah-wah, distortion, and amplifier*—Peter Occhiogrosso **3** *modifier*: *By passing his vocal sounds through an amplifier with the aid of a wah-wah pedal, he has achieved spectacular effects*—Ebony/ *Mike McCready's wah-wah pedaling?*—Sassy [echoic; interestingly similar to Chinook jargon *wawa,* "speech, talk," and to Cree *wawa,* an echoic name for the snow goose, Canada goose, and gray goose]

wail 1 *v* 1930s jazz musicians To play jazz well and feelingly: *We were wailing, but nobody had a tape machine*—Nat Hentoff **2** *v* (also **whale**) 1950s college students fr cool talk fr jazz musicians To do very well; perform well [fr the notion of a well-performed blues number, with its melodious lamentations]

wailing or **whaling** *adj* black musicians by about 1954 Excellent; wonderful; =GREAT

waist *See* PANTYWAIST

wait up *v phr* by 1920s To pause, when well ahead, for someone to overtake one ●Often a panting request

wake up and smell the coffee (or something else**)** *sentence* early 1990s Become aware before it's too late: *. . . the legislators had better wake up and smell the coffee*—radio talk-show host Curtis Sliwa/ *Why Bond Bulls Need to Wake Up, Smell the Coffee*—Los Angeles Times/ *Wake up and smell where the money's going*—National Public Radio

wake-up call *n phr* by 1970s A summons to action; clarion call: *The vote should be taken as a wake-up call to the civil rights movement that it better reinvigorate its leadership*—New York Times/ *I sure hope this hurricane is a wake-up call*—New York Times

walk 1 *v* (also, earlier, **walk free**) by 1970s To be released from prison **2** *v* late 1950s To be acquitted of or otherwise freed from a criminal indictment: *. . . more killers walk because of the incompetence of arresting officers*—Carsten Stroud/ *Actually, I'm gonna cop a plea. A $15 fine and I'll walk*—New York Times **3** *v* (also, fr 1890s, **walk out**) 1970s *labor unions* To go out on strike: *Several more Caterpillar locals have decided to walk* **4** *v* To leave someone, esp a spouse or lover; =GET LOST, TAKE A HIKE: *She said if he didn't straighten out he could walk*

See FRENCH WALK, TAKE A WALK, WIN IN A WALK

walk all over someone *v phr* 1890s *college students* To intimidate and maltreat someone [based on middle 1800s *walk over*]

walkaway or **walkover** *n* An easy victory; =CINCH, PUSHOVER: *It looked like a walkover for Clarence*—H McHugh/ *The odds were on the Redskins in a walkaway*

walk away from *v phr* 1960s To turn one's back on; fail to respond to when needed: *The offer promises motorists who switch to a Ford that they can walk away from the lease, no questions asked, after trying the car for six months*—New York Times

walk away with *v phr* by 1899 To win easily: *That year the Tigers walked away with the pennant*

walk back *v phr* by 1990s To reverse: *These may be developments we have to walk back*—National Public Radio news

walk back the cat *v phr* 1980s *espionage* To reexamine a case to diagnose errors: *In walking back the cat to seek the genesis, do we exaggerate the human element?*—William Safire

walkboy *n* 1970s *black* A good male friend; =HOME BOY: *. . . to groove on emotional intersubjectivication with a woman more than you groove on hanging with your walkboys*—Village Voice

walker *See* HOT WALKER

walk heavy *v phr black* by 1960s To be important and influential; =CLOUT

walkie-talkie *n WWII Army* A small and portable radio transmitter and receiver

walk-in 1 *n* by 1970s A customer, patient, etc, who enters without an appointment: *Our hair-styling boutique welcomes walk-ins* **2** *modifier*: *He found a walk-in clinic just outside town*

walking-around money *n phr* (also **street money**) by 1970s Political petty-cash used in promoting party candidates

walking papers (or **ticket)** *n phr* by 1820s A dismissal or discharge; esp, a rejection; =PINK SLIP: *Two baseball veterans got their walking papers today*—Associated Press

See GIVE someone HIS WALKING PAPERS

walking timebomb *n phr* A person who is likely to explode into violence [fr *timebomb*, an explosive device with the detonator set to go off]

walking wounded *n phr* by 1960s Persons who are injured, esp in a psychological or spiritual way, but still functional; depressed people: *. . . by the end of the year the salesmen are "walking wounded". . . just plain going bonkers*—New York Times [fr a WWI military medical term for a *wounded* person who is ambulatory]

walk-on 1 *n theater* about 1900 A very minor, usu nonspeaking, role; an insignificant or minimal sort of participation: *. . . looking like last-minute walk-ons in the closing scene of "Götterdammerung"*—New Yorker **2** *modifier*: *Since antiquity the figure of the black has played far more than a walk-on part in Western culture*—New York Review of Books

walk on *v phr* (also **step on**) 1970s *citizen's band radio* To interfere with a radio transmission by transmitting at the same time

walk on air *v phr* by 1887 To be ecstatic: *for a week after the promotion she was walking on air*

walk on eggs *v phr* by 1859 To proceed very carefully; go gingerly and warily: *I always feel as if I'm walking on eggs around her*

walk on water *v phr* by 1970s To do miraculous things; emulate Jesus Christ: *Not everybody thinks Colin Powell walks on water*

walkout *n* late 1880s *labor union* A strike: *There's a walkout at the supermarkets right now*

walk out on someone or something *v phr* by 1890s To abandon; =TAKE A WALK: *She was fed up, and just walked out on the whole deal*

walkover *See* WALKAWAY

walk soft *v phr black* by 1960s To behave quietly and peacefully; be modest: *I told him he was acting like an ass, and he walks a lot softer now*—Eugene E Landy

walk Spanish *See* FRENCH WALK

walk the plank *v phr* by 1835 To be destroyed or sacrificed: *Rostow's Deputy Walks the Plank; Rostow Hangs In*—New York Times/ *If you don't have the votes, you don't make your friends walk the plank*—Senator J Bennett Johnston [fr the pirate practice of forcing unwanted persons to *walk* out on a *plank* and plunge into the sea]

walk the talk *v phr* by 1980s To conform; not rock the boat; =GO STRAIGHT: . . . *a man or woman. . . asks a man or woman in prison fatigues if they intend "to walk the talk"*—Mesa (Arizona) Tribune

walk the walk *v phr* by 1980s =WALK THE TALK: . . . *the department is "walking the walk" of reengineering government*—New York Times

walk through *v phr* middle 1800s theater To explain something carefully and gradually; learn something by going slowly through the steps: *I'll walk you through it one more time; you nearly have it right* [fr the practice of learning a role partly by moving about onstage without speaking the lines]

walk-through *n* by 1959 A rehearsal, in the theater, sports, etc; =DRY RUN

walk-up *n* by 1919 A room, apartment, building, etc, without an elevator: . . . *second-floor walk-ups above stores*—Raymond Chandler

wall *See* BALLS TO THE WALL, BOUNCE OFF THE WALLS, CLIMB THE WALL, DRIVE someone UP THE WALL, GO TO THE WALL, HOLE IN THE WALL, NAIL someone TO THE CROSS, OFF THE WALL, PING OFF THE WALLS, UP AGAINST THE WALL, UP THE WALL

wallbanger **1** *n phr* 1950s teenagers & narcotics A dose or capsule of methaqualone; =LUDE: *called wall bangers by the kids*—Albert Goldman **2** *n* (also **Harvey Wallbanger**) by late 1960s A drink made of vodka or gin and juice [presumably fr the effect of the drug or potion on the consumer]

wallbangin' *n* 1990s California street gangs Writing one's name on a wall as a form of personal advertising

wallet biopsy (or **X-ray**) *n phr* 1980s medical Determination of who is to pay for medical services: . . . *the first examination performed is a wallet biopsy*—National Public Radio/ . . . *we don't perform a wallet X-ray before giving treatment*—Atlanta Constitution

wall-eyed *adj* by 1920s Drunk

wallflower *n* by 1820 A person, esp a woman, who is peripheral and uncourted at a dance, party, etc: *the homely and ugly girls who were called wall-flowers*—James T Farrell

wallop *by* 1823 **1** *n* A hard blow; a severe and resounding stroke: *She gave him a wallop on the chin* **2** *v*: *He walloped the ball right over the wall* **3** *v* To defeat utterly; =CLOBBER **4** *n* Power; =CLOUT, MOXIE: *She'd be good if she had a little more wallop* [fr British dialect, "beat, thrash," apparently fr Old Norman French *walop,* "gallop"]
See CIRCUIT CLOUT

walloper *See* DOCK-WALLOPER, POT-WALLOPER

wallpaper charges *n phr* by 1990s Many counts filed against a defendant, to make sure of some sort of conviction

wall-to-wall *adj* by 1967 Total; all-encompassing: . . . *a wall-to-wall nightmare in which society dissolves*—S Kanfer/ . . . *wall-to-wall hookers, niggers, and junkies*. . .—W T Tyler/ *It was wall-to-wall people*—Time [fr the phrase *wall-to-wall carpeting,* found by 1953]

wally or **Wally** or **wallie** 1990s students fr British rock groups **1** *n* Stupid person; moron **2** *n* An awkward person; =KLUTZ **3** *n* An unfashionable person: *The Arnolds call anyone who wears conventional clothes. . . a Wally*—Brisbane Telegraph **4** *n* The penis; =DORK, PRICK: *No wonder men are in awe of their wallies. First thing in the morning, a penis is a pretty magnificent sight*—Vanity Fair [origin unknown; perhaps fr the nickname for Walter or Wallace, suggesting, as Clyde does, someone like a wally; perhaps, improbably, fr British *wally,* "pickle"; *wally* in current senses appears to be borrowed from British use; however, it is attested in the US in the early 1900s meaning "A small-town sport," and in 1915–22 in college (Bryn Mawr) and flapper slang meaning "a goof with patent-leather hair"]

walsy *See* PALSY-WALSY

Walter Mitty *n phr* by 1939 An unimpressive person who regularly has daydreams of glory: *Walter Cronkite is a Walter Mitty in reverse*—Playboy [fr the title character in *The Secret Life of Walter Mitty,* a story by James Thurber]

waltz **1** *v* by 1862 To move in a smooth, unhurried, yet sprightly manner: *Jesse James could have waltzed in there and carted off the patio furniture*—Lawrence Sanders/ . . . *some one. . . waltzing into that wreck that we've grown old with searching*—Robert Louis Stevenson **2** *n* by 1968 Something easily accomplished; =CINCH, PIECE OF CAKE

waltz someone **around** *v phr* by 1950s To evade or deceive: *Have you been waltzing me around for three months*—TV show Murder She Wrote

walyo or **wallyo** or **Wally-O** (WAHL yoh) upper New York State by 1930s **1** *n* A young man; =GUY •Like *goombah,* used in affectionate address, often by an older man to a younger: *how the walyo had kept his muscles so finely tuned on health food*—Paul Sann **2** *n* An Italian or a male of Italian descent: *Did you hear how the Wally-Os stole a ballot box in the Fifth Ward?*—William Kennedy [origin uncertain; perhaps fr Italian dialect *uaglio* or *uaiu,* pronounced wah Yŏŏ, meaning something like "young squirt," but nearly always used affectionately; perhaps fr Naples dialect *guaglione,* "street urchin, corner boy"]

wampum *n* by 1897 Money; cash; =BREAD [short for Algonquin *wampumpeag,* "beads made from quahog shells and used as money"]

◁**wang** or **whang** or **whanger**▷ *n* by 1935 The penis; =COCK, PRICK: *I can see your whang. Your dong is visible*—William Goldman/ . . . *a trigger that was bigger than an elephant's proboscis or the whanger of a whale*—John Steinbeck [probably fr *whangdoodle,* "something of uncertain name, gadget"; many such terms, like *diddlywhacker, dingus, doodle,* and *thingy,* are euphemisms for the penis]
See PULL one's PUD

wangdoodle *See* WHANGDOODLE

wangle **1** *v* 1880s British printer's slang To get or arrange by shrewd maneuvering; contrive cunningly: *President Truman has given Ching a free hand in trying to wangle agreements*—Associated Press **2** *n*: *made a precise science out of the wangle*—

H Allen Smith [origin unknown; perhaps a form of *waggle,* "overcome, get the better of"; popularized by WWI soldiers]

wank ◁1▷ *v* (also **wank off**) *late 1940s British* To fondle one's own penis; =JACK OFF, BEAT one's MEAT **2** *n*: *He had a good wank as he watched her* **3** *n* *by 1970* A contemptible person; =GEEK, JERK, DORK: *. . . he got what he wanted needed. Which was a little badoom-badoom. Ugh. Complete wank*—Sassy **4** *v* *1990s Canadian students* To have fun; =PARTY, HAVE A BALL

wanker ◁1▷ *n* chiefly British fr late 1940s A masturbator, either literally or figuratively; =JERK-OFF: *There I was, this clubfooted wanker sitting on the organ seat*—Playboy/ *. . . all manner of artsy bubbleheads and academic wankers*—Village Voice/ *It was just wankers*—Us **2** *n* *1990s Canadian students* A fun-loving person; =PARTY ANIMAL **3** *n* *1990s students* The penis [origin unknown; perhaps fr British dialect *wank,* "a violent blow," and semantically analogous with *beat* one's *meat, whack off, pound* one's *peenie,* etc]

wannabe or **wannabee** or **wanna-be** or **wanta be** (WAW nuh bee) *1980s California surfers & black street gangs* **1** *n* Someone who aspires to be someone else, esp a star or hero: *Rambo Wanna-be's*—Milwaukee Journal/ *A "poser" or a "wanta be" is someone who tries to be like someone else*—New York Times [fr imprecise or dialectal pronunciation of "*want to be*"]

want list *See* WISH LIST

war *See* HOT WAR, PSYWAR, SHOOTING WAR

warbler *n* *by 1946* A woman singer; =CANARY [found by 1633 as "singer"]

ward heeler *n phr* *by 1890* A low-ranking associate or flunky of a political boss; a menial crony [fr *heeler,* "a loafer, one on the lookout for shady work"; in the 1870s the ward heeler was known simply as *heeler,* or as *ward-bummer*]

warhorse *n* *by 1837* A seasoned and reliable veteran; a grizzled doyen

warm body *n phr* *by 1960s* A person regarded as merely such, without individual qualities, virtues, vices, etc; an animate person who occupies space; =CHAIR-WARMER: *I'll look you up if all I need is a warm body*

warm someone's **ear** *v phr* To talk insistently and passionately to someone, esp about scandals and the like

warmed over *adj phr* *by 1970* Derivative and only slightly changed; revived unimaginatively: *The president, he wrote, had "offered the poor the Protestant Ethic warmed over"*—Daniel Patrick Moynihan/ *out of the mouths of bunnies and gulls, some warmed-over Gibran*—Irving Kolodin *See* LOOK LIKE DEATH WARMED OVER

warmer *See* BENCH WARMER, CHAIR-WARMER

warmer-upper *n* Something that warms or starts: *wonderful warmer-upper, four-button coat sweater*—New York Herald Tribune/ *Now try it as a warmer-upper*—Saturday Evening Post

warm fuzzy *fr 1970s* **1** *n phr* A compliment; a word of praise; also, such praise collectively; =STROKE: *You need some warm fuzzy*—Time **2** *n phr* Pleasant feelings, esp when tinged with nostalgia: *This was the sort of evening that gave you the warm fuzzies. . . cherished memories. . . funny lines*—Daily Jefferson County Union/ *Although foster parenting can provide plenty of warm fuzzies, the job is always challenging. . .* —Los Angeles Times [probably fr the notion of a snuggling small animal, like Charles Schulz's *warm puppy*]

warm spit *See* NOT WORTH A BUCKET OF WARM SPIT

warm the bench *v phr* *sports by 1907* To be held in reserve

warm up *v phr* *sports by 1868* To do exercises and preparatory maneuvers before some activity, esp some sports effort

warm someone **up** *v phr* *by 1950s* To induce a receptive and approving attitude in someone, esp by joking and cajoling: *The second banana warmed the audience up before the star appeared*

Warner *See* MARY WARNER

warp *See* TIME WARP

war paint *n phr* *by 1869* Cosmetics [fr the facial paint worn by Native American warriors]

warp factor *n phr* *by 1970s* A very large factor of multiplication; a high exponent: *We feel it won't increase by warp factor five, either*—Toronto Life [fr the notion of *warp speed,* a velocity greater than the speed of light, popularized in science fiction and especially by the TV series *Star Trek;* it is necessary to imagine such enormous speeds in order to keep fictional cosmic travel more or less in the realm of the humanly compassable] *See* TIME WARP

warp out *v phr* To move, esp to leave, very rapidly; =CUT OUT

warrior *See* SUNDAY SOLDIER

wart *n* A flaw; an imperfection: *The new format has some warts, but no integrity warts*—Philadelphia Journal [probably from *warts and all*] *See* WORRY WART

warts and all *n phr* *by 1763* The accurate totality of someone or something, including the imperfections: *Audiences hearing the local orchestra week after week hear it with warts and all*—Village Voice/ *Your friends see Doherty, warts and all*—George V Higgins/ *Lyndon Johnson, warts and all*—Washington Post [fr the putative remark of Oliver Cromwell to his portraitist Peter Lely: "Remark all these roughnesses, pimples, warts, and everything as you see me"]

was *See* BE, NEVER-WAS

wash 1 *n* *by 1950s* A drink to follow another, to wash it down; =CHASER: *. . . what for a wash?*—Richard Bissell **2** *v* *by 1849* To prove acceptable; bear testing ●Usually in the negative: *Well, it just won't wash*—Atlantic Monthly/ *The stereotype of gay males as child molesters just doesn't wash any more*—Village Voice/ *That washes. I'll buy it*—

Lawrence Sanders **3** *n by 1950s* An elaborate justification; =WHITEWASH: *It looked like a wash to me*—George V Higgins **4** *n stock market by 1870s* A balance between opposing values, cases, effects, etc; a moot situation; =STANDOFF, a TOSS-UP: *The net effect of the medical testimony was a wash*—Legal Times/ *I'd have to go to bed at the same time as my 6-year-old. So it's pretty much a wash*—Philadelphia Journal/ *the Ferraro factor. Was it a political plus, a minus, a wash?*—Washington Post [second sense said to be fr a defective printed calico that could not be *washed*; final sense perhaps fr the notion that equal opposing elements *wash* each other out or away, or *wipe the slate clean*]
See HANG OUT THE WASH, WHITEWASH

wash (or air) one's **dirty linen** *v phr* (Variation: **in public** may be added) *by 1867* To talk or argue about intimate matters in public [probably a translation of earlier French *Il faut laver ton linge sale en famille*]

washed up or **all washed up** *adj phr theater by 1923* No longer valid or active as a performer, competitor, worker, etc; =AUSGESPIELT, FINISHED: *I'm all washed up*—Ben Hecht & Charles MacArthur/ *Borden is all washed up*—G Homes [fr the notion of *washing up* one's hands at the finish of a job or a day's work]

washing *n 1990s police* A technique of evading surveillance by taking an absurdly indirect route from one place to another

wash someone's **mouth out with soap** *v phr by 1920s* To punish someone for using offensive language: *Ma Gingrich ought to wash Newtie's mouth out with soap. He owes the First Lady big time*—Nation

washout *WWI British military* **1** *n* A failure; a total fiasco; =FLOP: *I'm afraid our big birthday bash was a washout* **2** *n* A student pilot or aviation cadet who fails to complete the course and become a qualified pilot: *the major cause for the large number of "washouts"*—New York Times [origin unknown; perhaps because the student's name was *washed* or scrubbed from the roster]

wash out **1** *v phr WWI flyers* To fail, esp to fail to finish a pilot-training course and be qualified: *Then I was washed out on a slight technicality*—Max Shulman **2** *v phr* To eliminate or cancel; =SCRATCH, SCRUB **3** *v phr early 1900s* To lose all one's money; =TAP OUT: *hustlers who really knew how to gamble. I always got washed out*—Louis Armstrong

WASP or **wasp** **1** *n sociologists by 1962* A person of nonminority or nonethnic background, ancestry, etc, as conceived in the United States; a White Anglo-Saxon Protestant: *The Republican Party is run largely by "wasps"*—Stewart Alsop **2** *adj*: *Westchester and Darien and places like that, WASP country*—New York Herald Tribune [said to have been coined by the Philadelphia author E Digby Baltzell]

waspish *adj* Dominated by and characteristic of

WASPs: *This town is naughty and waspish and expensive*—Village Voice

waste **1** *v teenagers fr 1950s street gang* To defeat utterly; trounce; =CLOBBER **2** *v by 1450* To wreck; destroy; mutilate; =TRASH: *. . . Stallone wastes everything in his path*—Los Angeles Times **3** *v by 1964* To kill; =BLOW someone AWAY, TAKE someone or something OUT

wasted **1** *adj 1950s cool talk* Penniless; =BROKE **2** *adj 1950s narcotics & cool talk* Intoxicated by narcotics or alcohol; =STRUNG OUT: *Everybody was getting kind of high on acid, wasted, in fact*—Tom Wolfe **3** *adj fr middle 1950s* Exhausted; =POOPED **4** *adj fr late 1950s* Wrecked; ruined; destroyed: *Like, I'm wasted. . . I can't lose no more*—Claude Brown

watch *See* GRAVEYARD WATCH, ON someone's WATCH

watcher *See* CLOCK-WATCHER

watch one's **mouth** *v phr by 1970s* To be careful of what one says, esp to stop being provocative, obscene, presumptuous, etc ●Often an irritated command: *Watch your mouth, white boy*—Harry Crews

watch my lips **1** *sentence 1970s Army* Listen very carefully to me: *Hey. . . watch my lips. You. Me. . . Her. That's it*—Scott Turow **2** *sentence* Do you read lips? [second sense is a euphemism for a silently spoken obscenity or insult]

watch the submarine races *v phr 1980s teenagers* To do sex play in a parked car [fr the fact that no submarine races are in progress to be watched]

water *See* BLOW someone OUT OF THE WATER, COME HELL or HIGH WATER, CUT OFF someone's WATER, DEAD IN THE WATER, FIREWATER, HIGH WATERS, HOLD one's WATER, HOT WATER, IN DEEP WATER, IN HOT WATER, JERKWATER, a LONG DRINK OF WATER, ON THE WAGON, SUCK CANAL WATER

water-cooler story *n phr early 1990s* A piece of gossip; =LATRINE RUMOR

waterfront *See* COVER THE WATERFRONT

Watergate *early 1970s* **1** *n* A scandal usu involving corruption **2** *v* To find or publicize instances of corruption: *The news media have been Watergating the Department pretty good*—CBS Television News [fr the name of the Washington building complex where Democratic headquarters were burglarized in 1972, an act that led finally to the resignation of Richard M. Nixon as President of the US]

waterhole or **watering hole** (or **spot**) *n* or *n phr by 1960s* A bar; a saloon; a drinking place: *That place is the waterhole of choice for aspiring actors/ . . . a posh watering hole on Madison Avenue/ . . . gathering for the school's alums and their friends at selected watering spots. . .* —Milwaukee Journal Sentinel

water wagon *See* ON THE WAGON

waterworks *See* TURN ON THE WATERWORKS

Wausau wagon *n phr by 1980s* A pickup truck [fr *Wausau*, Wisconsin; these trucks tend to have local or regional names, like *cowboy* or *Navajo Cadillac*, *Grantsburg gondola* and many others] the **wave** *n phr* 1980s *sports fans* A stadium demonstration in which sections of spectators successively stand up and sit in synchronism, for no apparent reason

wavelength *See* ON THE SAME WAVELENGTH

wave-maker *n by* 1960s A person who raises questions, imposes difficulties and objections, etc: *said that he is a wave-maker whose troubles arose from his insistence on injecting moral values*—Philadelphia Journal [perhaps from an old joke in which a set of persons in Hell, immersed up to their mouths in feces, are heard to chant "Don't *make waves,*" very melodiously]

waver *See* FLAG-WAVER, SKIVVY-WAVER

wax 1 *v by* 1884 To defeat; outdo; =BEAT, CLOBBER, ZAP **2** *v by* 1884 To assault and maul; injure or kill: *I've always got a few bucks to wax Red Gs*—Soldier of Fortune **3** *v* (also **put on wax**) 1920s *jazz musicians* To make a phonograph recording; record: *Louis Armstrong waxed "Beale Street Blues"/ put the Stone Age stuff of jazz on wax*—Stephen Longstreet **4** *n*: *. . . play the tune and cut a wax of it*—John O'Hara [the origin of the violent senses is unknown; perhaps semantically analogous with *polish off*, referring to *wax* as a polish; recording senses fr the material used, as *vinyl* was used later]
See the WHOLE BALL OF WAX

waxing *n by* 1920s A phonograph record or other recording: *Their waxing made the charts about eight months before Manfred Mann's*—Milwaukee Journal

way 1 *adv by early* 1980s Very; extremely; absolutely; = TO THE MAX: *. . . one of the way coolest in the US*—Wisconsin State Journal **2** *affirmation* 1990s Yes; on the contrary •Used as a response to the negative "No way!" [the intensifier may have developed from *all the way*, attested along with *way*, both meaning "very" in prison slang of the 1980s]
See BEAT one's WAY, the FRENCH WAY, GO OUT OF one's WAY, GO THE LIMIT, the GREEK WAY, the HARD WAY, IN A BIG WAY, KNOW one's WAY AROUND, NOT A ONE-WAY STREET, NO WAY, RUB someone THE WRONG WAY, THERE'S NO WAY

the **way it plays 1** *adv phr* According to the usual pattern: *The way it plays in there, you can't plead the Fifth*—Paul Sann **2** *n phr* The usual pattern; what is to be expected: *Well, I guess that's the way it plays when you get old*

way out 1 *adj phr* 1940s *jazz musicians* Imaginative; original and bold, esp successfully and admirably so **2** *adj phr* 1950s *cool talk fr jazz musicians* Excellent; wonderful; =FAR OUT, GREAT, OUT OF SIGHT **3** *adj phr* 1960s *narcotics* Intoxicated with narcotics; =HIGH, OUT OF IT [probably fr earlier *out of this world* or *out of sight*]

ways *See* FORTY WAYS TO SUNDAY, HAVE IT BOTH WAYS, SWING BOTH WAYS, WORK BOTH WAYS

way the ball bounces (or **the cookie crumbles)** *See* THAT'S THE WAY THE BALL BOUNCES

way to go *sentence* You are doing extremely well; that is splendid •An exclamation of praise and encouragement: *Ron, stick that old hand out. . . .*

Way to go, Prez—Washingtonian [a shortening of *that's the way to go*]

the wrong **way to run a railroad** *n phr* (Variations: **a hell of a** or **a stupid** or **what a** or other deprecative modifiers may precede **way**) *by* 1980s Not the best way to do something: *Mfune blasted the White House for not including the Black Caucus in the formulation of policy: "This isn't any way to run a railroad"*—New Yorker/ *Arafat's flawed technique in governing Jericho and Gaza is an awful way to run a railroad*—Washington Week in Review

wazoo *n* 1970s The buttocks; anus; =ASS [perhaps a variant of *kazoo*]

weak sister *n phr by* 1857 An unreliable person, esp a male

wear a wire *v phr by* 1950s To be fitted with a concealed listening or recording device: *. . . and wear a hidden tape recorder, what do they call it? Wear a wire*—Scott Turow

wear cement shoes *v phr by* 1990s To be killed and disposed of by the crime syndicate, esp by being sunk in the water

wear goat's horns *v phr by* 1980s To be responsible for a defeat or other misfortune: *. . . did miss three free throws. . . and came close to wearing goat's horns*—Milwaukee Journal

the **wearies** *n phr* Fatigue and depression; ennui: *I'm getting the evening wearies*—Nelson Algren

wear the pants (or **trousers** or **britches)** *v phr by* 1931 To be the dominant one in a marriage, household, etc •Nearly always said of a woman [*wear the breeches* can be traced to the 1400s in a French version (*braies*) and to the 1500s in English]

wear two hats *v phr by* 1966 To have two separate jobs or functions •The phrase may specify more than two hats: *three hats, several hats: Each of these men wears two hats: one as topbraid officer. . . the other as a member of the Joint Chiefs*—Time/ *Rockefeller to Wear Two Hats*—New York Post

weasel 1 *v by* 1956 To evade and equivocate; use deceptive language; deceive: *They told the candidate to stop weaseling and get to the substance/ I was trying to weasel some bank from you*—comic strip "Curtis" **2** *v underworld by* 1920s To inform; =SING, SQUEAL **3** *n*: *Little Joe turned weasel* [the first sense is said to be based on the *weasel's* habit of sucking the meat or substance from an egg, leaving only the shell; the other senses reflect the more general nasty reputation of the *weasel*, which has meant "contemptible person" since at least the 1500s]

weasel out *v phr by* 1956 To withdraw from or evade, esp a promise or obligation, in a sneaky, underhanded way: *I coulda cut them loose, coulda made some excuse, even coulda weaseled out*—Joseph Wambaugh

weasel words *n phr by* 1900 Language designed to deceive; empty talk; self-serving verbiage [words as empty as an eggshell that a *weasel* has sucked]

web-foot *modifier by* 1970s Devoted to and advocating preservation of the environment: *Anyone favoring the bottle bill must be web-foot conservationist*—Boston Globe [presumably fr the notion that lovers of wild life are thus adapted to walking about in swamps; similar to *web-foot,* "a native of the wet state of Oregon," and British "a dweller in the fens of East Anglia"]

wedding *See* MILITARY MARRIAGE, SHOTGUN WEDDING

wedged *adj 1980s computers* Behaving as if frozen; not responding to the keyboard

wedgie or **wedgy** *n 1970s children* The prank of pulling the underwear upward from behind by the waistband; =MELVIN, MURPHY: . . . *the impression of leaping through the camera lens and giving the viewers a wedgie.* . . —Newsweek/ . . . *haze.* . . *by pulling up their underpants to give them "wedgies"*—Milwaukee Journal [presumably fr *wedging* the underpants between the buttocks]

weed 1 *n* (also **the weed**) *by 1606* Tobacco **2** *n by 1847* A cigar, esp an inferior one: *Throw that weed away and have a good one*—Earl Wilson **3** *n* (also **the weed**) *narcotics by 1920s* A marijuana cigarette; =JOINT
See REEFER

weedhead *n 1960s narcotics* A user of marijuana; =POTHEAD

weed tea *n phr 1920s narcotics* Marijuana

wee hours *n phr by 1890s fr Scottish* The hours just after midnight: . . . *the story of what happened.* . . *in the wee hours of Dec 2, 1985*—Milwaukee Journal [Scottish *wee sma' hours* is attested in the late 1700s]

weejuns *n 1980s teenagers* Moccasins; loafers [fr *Weejuns,* trademark of a brand of such shoes]

week *See* KNOCK someone or something INTO THE MIDDLE OF NEXT WEEK, SPLIT WEEK

weekend warrior *See* SUNDAY SOLDIER

weenchy *adj by about 1900* Very small; tiny: . . . *just a weenchy.* . . *little dash of perfume*—Ira Wolfert [fr *wee*]

weenie (also **weeny** or **weeney** or **weinie** or **wienie**) **1** *n* (also **wiener** or **weener**) *by 1911* A frankfurter; =HOT DOG: . . . *this wienie and kraut combination*—New York Daily News ◁**2**▷ *n* (also **wiener** or **weener**) The penis; esp, the relaxed penis **3** *n* (also **weeniehead** or **weiner-head**) *by 1960s* An ineffectual, despised person; =JERK, WIMP: *She plans to be a weenie, is a weenie, asks to be loved anyway, and is loved anyway*—Village Voice/ . . . *anybody who zips their coat when the temperature is higher than zero is an automatic weenie*—Los Angeles Times **4** *modifier:* . . . *you'd never know that weenie voice belonged to a gorilla*—Michael Grant **5** *n* (also **ween**) *1970s college students* A very serious student; =GREASY GRIND, THROAT: *Premeds.* . . *known to their less pressurized campus colleagues as throats and weenies*—Newsweek/ *Weens are strange creatures with pallid faces, glassy eyes, and calculators strapped to their belts*—Dirk Johnson [fr German *Wienerwurst,* "Vienna sausage,"* with pejorative senses developing fr its penile shape]
See PLAY HIDE THE WEENIE

weenie bin *n phr 1970s college students* An academic library carrel, where a serious student spends time studying

◁**weenie-wagger** or **wienie-wagger**▷ *n 1980s police* A male who exposes his genitals; =FLASHER

weensy *See* TEENSY-WEENSY

weep *See* READ 'EM AND WEEP

weeper or **weepie** *n by 1940s* A sentimental or otherwise tearful movie, play, etc; =TEAR-JERKER: *It was the weepers that established her as a top Hollywood star*—Bob Thomas/ *The day-time weepies have been greatly enriched by a new soap opera*—John Crosby

Weepers *interj 1950s teenagers* A mild, euphemistic exclamation of surprise, distress, etc [fr *Jeepers Creepers,* a euphemism for *Jesus Christ*]

weevil *See* BOLL WEEVIL

wee-wee *by 1930* **1** *v* To urinate **2** *n:* . . . *specimen of wee-wee*—Carson McCullers **3** *modifier:* . . . *the Cuomo family dog and her controversial weewee pads*—New Yorker **4** *n* The penis [perhaps a euphemism for the euphemism *pee-pee* for *piss,* used in talking to small children]

weigh in *v phr by 1909* To make a contribution to something, esp to a debate, quarrel, etc; present an addition: . . . *Ellen Goodman and Meg Greenfield also weighed in with women's rights polemics*—Milwaukee Journal [perhaps fr the formal *weighing in* of a prizefighter before a match, as an earnest of participation; perhaps fr the notion of bringing weight to bear]

weight *n 1960s narcotics* The amount of narcotics an addict needs for a week: *I'm going up there to give her her weight for the week, you know*—Claude Brown
See CARRY A LOT OF WEIGHT, THROW one's WEIGHT AROUND

weighter *See* PENNYWEIGHTER

weight man *n phr 1990s narcotics: Inside the drug house.* . . *worked three "servers" and a "weight man".* . . *who packaged the cocaine, according to police*—Milwaukee Journal Sentinel

weird *adj 1940s bop talk & cool talk* Excellent; wonderful; =COOL [also attested as 1920s British upper-class use]

weirdo or **weirdie** or **weirdy** *n by 1955* A very strange, eccentric, repellent person; =BIRD, CREEP, GEEK: *He's a weirdy, all right*—W R Burnett [*weirdie* is attested from 1894, but was probably Scots dialect]

weird out *v phr* To become hallucinatory or intoxicated; to feel a loss of reality because of a strange experience: *Talk to me. I'm weirding out*—Armistead Maupin/ *You're weirding me out already, Dag*—Douglas Coupland

welcome to the club *sentence by 1970s* Now you have joined me in adversity; now you see how badly things turn out: *So you've been fired? Welcome to the club, old buddy*

◁**welldigger's ass**▷ *See* COLD AS HELL

well-heeled 1 *adj* by 1897 Having much money; rich: . . . *the average, fairly well-heeled, middle-aged American male*—New Yorker **2** *adj* by 1873 Well armed: *He's always well-heeled*—radio program Gangbusters

◁**well-hung**▷ *adj* by 1611 Having large genitals: *Death takes the innocent young. And those who are very well hung*—W H Auden/ *A guy with 640K of RAM is the electronic equivalent of well-hung*—New Republic

well-oiled *adj* fr early 1900s Drunk: *He happened to be well-oiled, as was usually the case*—Stewart Holbrook

well told *See* FUCKING WELL TOLD

welsh or **welch 1** *v* by 1857 To default on or evade an obligation, esp paying a gambling debt: *Say, are you going to welsh on me?*—H McHugh/ *Some American officials feel that the Syrians welshed on their promise*—New York Times **2** *n*: *Link can't take a welsh, so he looks around for a way to get his dough*—Mickey Spillane [apparently fr the same bigoted stereotype of the *Welsh* reflected in the English nursery rhyme "Taffy was a Welshman, Taffy was a thief," although perhaps a borrowing of German *Welsch,* "foreigner"]

west *See* TO KNOCK someone or something GALLEY-WEST

West *See* MAE WEST

western or **Western** *n* by 1909 A book, movie, etc, about the Old West
See EASTERN WESTERN, SPAGHETTI WESTERN

wet 1 *adj* by 1870 Permitting or advocating the sale of liquor: *This is a wet county* **2** *adj* by 1916 Inferior; stupid and unappealing; =WIMPISH: *A man is "wet" if he isn't a regular guy*—P Marks **3** *adj* 1970s police Bloody; gory: . . . *he's criminally liable. . . even if Willoughby did the wet work*—Carsten Stroud **4** *adj* by 1940s Sexually aroused: *Simon is a smoothie who likes to woo women with fast rides: "The 'vette gets 'em wet"*—New Yorker/ *Elvis dreamed of belting "All Shook Up" for strange, wet women*—Esquire
See ALL WET, GET one's FEET WET

◁**wetback**▷ *n* by 1929 A Mexican who enters the US illegally, esp as a migratory worker •The term may be generalizing to include all illegal immigrants: *An American's as good as a wetback, who is a Mexican whom we don't know how he got here*—James M Cain [fr the fact that they get their *backs wet* in wading across the Rio Grande; the terms *wet pony, wet cow,* etc, were used earlier for animals brought illegally across the border]

wet behind the ears *See* NOT DRY BEHIND THE EARS

wet blanket *n phr* by 1879 A person who dampens and smothers all enthusiasm; a person who prevents fun; a pessimist; =KILLJOY, PARTY POOPER

◁**wet deck**▷ *n phr* by 1940s A woman, often a prostitute, who does serial sex acts

◁**wet dream**▷ *n phr* by 1851 A male's erotic dream during which he has an orgasm

wet hen *See* MAD AS A WET HEN

wetware *n* 1980s computer The human brain: *Slip a microchip into snug contact with your gray matter (a.k.a. wetware)*—Time/ *wetware: the human brain and its DNA code*—Los Angeles Times

wet one's **whistle** (or **goozle**) *v phr* fr late 1300s To have a drink, esp of liquor [Chaucer says of a drunken miller's comely wife: "Her pretty whistle was well wetted"]

whack 1 *v* by 1721 To strike; hit **2** *n* by 1737: . . . *to explore their manhood and give and take a few whacks*—People **3** *n* by 1891 A try; =BASH, CRACK, SHOT: *He was given a whack at drama reviewing*—Bennett Cerf **4** *v* (also **whack out**) 1980s mobsters To kill; execute, gangland style: . . . *the lieutenant took it personal when they whacked the witness*—Carsten Stroud **5** *v* (also **wack**) 1960s narcotics To dilute a narcotic; cut a narcotic **6** *n* =WACK [probably echoic; in fourth sense, the use of *whacks,* "any form of force," is attested among Chicago gunmen in 1932]
See HAVE A CRACK AT something, OUT OF WHACK, WACK

whacked or **whacked out** *adj* by 1919 Exhausted; tired out; =BEAT, BUSHED, POOPED: *You were whacked-out. Want to take a hot shower?*—Lawrence Sanders

whacking *adj* by 1806 Very big; =WHOPPING: *After that she got a whacking big raise*

◁**whack** (or **wack**) **off**▷ *v phr* by 1960s To masturbate; =JERK OFF [one of the many terms equating masturbation with *banging, beating,* or *pounding*]

whack out *v phr* gambling by 1950s To lose all one's money; =GO BROKE, TAP OUT

whacky *See* WACKY

whale[1] *n* by about 1900 A large or fat person; =BEACHED WHALE

whale[2] **1** *v* by 1790 To hit; thrash; trounce: *They whaled us six–zip/ She hauled off and whaled him a shrewd blow* **2** *n* A heavy blow: *She gave him a hard whale to the nose* **3** *v* (also **wail**) 1980s students To do extremely well; excel [fr British dialect spelling of *wale,* "strike, beat," perhaps related to Old English *wæl,* "slaughter, carnage, death"]

whale away *v phr* by 1897 To attack or do something vigorously and persistently: *I was whaling away at the cleaning job/ He's best when he's whaling away at the other candidates*

whale into (or **on**) someone or something *v phr* by 1790 To attack vigorously: *He'd barely met me when he whaled into me for not answering his letter/ Instead of whaling on the ball. . . Agassi should hit low, dipping topspin returns*—New York Times

a **whale of a** someone or something *n phr* students by about 1900 An excellent or large example; a very superior specimen: *That woman is a whale of a politician* [fr the prodigious size of the *whale*]

whale (or **wail) on** something or someone *1980s students* **1** *v phr* To perform extremely well **2** *v phr* To criticize severely; denigrate; =CLOBBER: *. . . and he just wailed on a chunk of code Michael had written*—Douglas Coupland

whaling *n by 1852* A beating
See WAILING

wham *by 1925* **1** *v* To hit; strike; =SOCK: *And the whamming continues*—E Lavine **2** *interj* (also **whammo**) *by 1932* An exclamation signaling the suddenness, violence, surprise, etc, of a quick, sharp blow: *Wham! suddenly the meaning hit me/ . . . and then—whammo—she was blindsided*—Milwaukee Journal [echoic, and related in sound symbolism to *whip, whale, whack, whomp, whop* and other *wh-* words denoting blows]

wham-bam (or **ram-bam** or **slam-bam) thank you ma'am** *n phr WWII armed forces* A very quick sex act, esp a casual coupling: *And short it was: a regular "wham, bam, thank you, Ma'am"*—CoEvolution Quarterly/ *He's not a wham bam thank you ma'am, he's a thriller*—Harper's Bazaar/ *They're more slam-bam-thank-you-ma'am type guys*—Milwaukee Journal Sentinel

whambang *adj by 1950s* Huge; loud and vigorous; =WHOPPING

the **whammy** *n phr by 1932* The evil eye; a crippling curse; =HEX, THE INDIAN SIGN: *. . . with a whammy of ordinary indebtedness over his head*—Robert Ruark [origin unknown; popularized in the comic strip "Li'l Abner" by Al Capp, beginning in 1941, where a character named Evil-Eye Fleegle can paralyze with a stare; the dated example is spelled *wami*]
See DOUBLE WHAMMY, TRIPLE WHAMMY

whams **See** the WHIM-WHAMS

whang *v by 1684* To hit; =WHAM: *She whanged him a shrewd one*
See WANG

whangdoodle or **wangdoodle** or **wingdoodle** *n by 1931* An unspecified or unspecifiable object; something one does not know the name of or does not wish to name; =GIZMO, THINGAMAJIG: *Push in this dingus, step on this wingdoodle*—Billy Rose [fr mid–1800s sense, "a mythical beast of strange but indefinite traits"]

whanger **See** WANG

what **See** SAY WHAT

what are you giving me? *sentence early 1880s Western* What kind of nonsense are you asking me to believe?/ *What are you giving me? Don't try to bullshit a bullshitter*

whatchamacallit or **what-you-may-call-it** or **what-d'ye-call-it** (WHUT chə mə CAWL it) *n about 1920* An unspecified or unspecifiable object; something one does not know the name of or does not wish to name; =GIZMO, THINGAMAJIG: *. . . lady in a robe and a white whatchamacallit around her head appeared. . .*—WEB Griffin [*what-d'ye-call-it* is attested from 1573, and *what-ye-call-'em* as London slang in 1710]

◁**what crawled up your ass** or **what crawled up your ass and died**▷ *sentence 1990s students* What is troubling you?

what do you say *sentence early 1900s Western* How are you?; how have things been?: *What do you say, Ed? Long time no see*

what else is new **See** SO WHAT ELSE IS NEW

whatever *adv by 1900* Perhaps; possibly •Often a reply to an unanswerable question, with the force of "Could be" or "We'll see": *Well, whatever. The point was, he was dead. . .*—Carsten Stroud/ *Which I can do on my own, or whatever. . .*—Stan Cutler [perhaps a shortening of *whatever's fair* attested in 1960 student use]

whatever turns you on or **whatever floats your boat** *sentence by 1980s* Enjoy whatever you enjoy; *chacun à son goût: You listen to Russ Limburger? Whatever turns you on/ So do I, but there isn't a wrong way or a right way to do either. Whatever floats your boat, Anatole*—New York Times

what for *n phr by 1873* A drubbing, either physical or verbal; a thrashing; severe punishment: *. . . a sadistic desire to watch the big shots get what for*—John Crosby [fr the startled question *what for? why?* asked by someone being assaulted]
See GIVE someone WHAT FOR

what gives *by 1940* **1** *sentence* What is going on?; =WHAT'S UP: *What gives, I asked her*—John O'Hara **2** *sentence* How are you?; how have things been with you?; =WHAT DO YOU SAY **3** *sentence* What is wrong?; I do not understand: *"What gives?" he croaked in an annoyed tone*—Raymond Chandler •Since the early 1960s, this sense is often referred to a person: *"What gives with Joe?"*; and is often an exasperated inquiry: *"What's bothering you? Why are you behaving this way?"* [a translation of Yiddish or German *was gibt*, "what's going on"]

what goes around comes around *1970s black* **1** *sentence* Retribution follows wrongdoing; justice may take time, but it will prevail: *"What goes around comes around," Young said*—Philadelphia/ *Always remember this, what goes around comes around*—Donald Goines **2** *sentence* Things have a tendency to recur: *So once again in the world of music, everything that goes around comes around*—The Nation

what one **is driving at** *n phr by 1762* What one means; what one is trying to say: *The persons may know what you are driving at*—CoEvolution Quarterly

what it takes *n phr by 1929* The desirable strength, character, appeal, etc: *I wonder if he has what it takes to get this job done*

what makes someone **tick (**or **run)** *n phr by 1947* Someone's motives, inner psychology, system of principles, etc: *It's the gambling instinct that makes me tick*—Esquire/ *What Makes Sammy Run?*—Budd Schulberg [fr the analogy of human motivation with the mechanism of a clock]

what say *sentence* by 1825 =SAY WHAT, WHAT DO YOU SAY

what's been shaking *See* WHAT'S SHAKING

what's buzzin', cousin *sentence* 1930s *jive talk* What is happening?; =WHAT'S COOKING

what's cooking or **what cooks 1** *sentence* 1930s *jive talk* What is happening?; =WHAT'S GOING DOWN: *What cooks, Jimmy?*—Lionel Stander/ *"What's cooking?," I asked Cardoza*—Hugh Pentecost **2** *sentence* How have you been?; =WHAT DO YOU SAY

what's eating (or **what's got into**) someone *sentence* first form by 1893, second by 1876 What is troubling someone; why is someone behaving this way; =WHAT'S WITH someone: *What's eating you today? I can't get a civil word from you*

what's going down *sentence* 1940s *black* What is happening?; =WHAT'S COOKING

what she wrote *See* THAT'S ALL SHE WROTE

what's-his-name *n* (Variations: **her** or **its** or **your** may replace **his; face** or ◁**ass**▷ may replace **name**) first form by 1757, second fr 1967 An unspecified or unspecifiable person or thing; someone or something one does not know or remember the name of or does not wish to name; =WHOOZIS: *What did old what's-his-face have to tell you?/ But aren't you afraid you're going to get on Professor What's-Her-Face's shit list. . .*—T Coraghessan Boyle

what's-it or **whatsis** or **whatzis** (WHUT sit, -səs) *n* by 1882 An unspecified or unspecifiable object; something one does not know the name of or does not wish to name; =DINGUS, THINGAMAJIG: *the world's tallest free-standing what's-it*—Toronto Life/ *What's that whatsis he's playing with?*

what's it to you *sentence* by 1896 It's none of your business; don't butt in: *What's it to you if I want to go?*

what's shaking or **what's been shaking** *sentence* 1950s *jazz musicians* What is happening?; =WHAT'S GOING DOWN: *Hello, what's shakin'?*—TV show *Buffalo Bill* [perhaps fr an analogy between *shaking* and being vigorously alive; the *shake* was a jazz dance known fr about 1900]

what's the big idea *sentence* by 1917 Why are you being so presumptuous, aggressive, etc?; account for your behavior at once

what's the good word *sentence* by 1920s How are things going with you?; what have you to tell me about yourself? •A cordial greeting

what's the haps *sentence* 1990s *teenagers* What is happening?; =WHAT'S GOING DOWN, WHAT'S THE SCAM

what's the scam *sentence* by 1960s What is the latest information?

what's up or **wass up** *sentence* by 1881 What is happening?; what is the matter, question, problem, etc?

what's what *n phr* by 1553 The current state of reality; basic truth

what's with someone or something *late 1930s* **1** *sentence* What is the problem, difficulty, etc?: *What's with this guy? All I did was say hello* **2** *sentence* What is the explanation?; why is this?: *What's with the free food? Explain*—John O'Hara [fr Yiddish *vos iz mit,* "what is with"]

what the doctor ordered *See* JUST WHAT THE DOCTOR ORDERED

what the hell (or **hey**) **1** *interj* (also **what the fuck**) by 1872 An exclamation of surprise, puzzlement, resentment, etc: *What the hell! Who does this clown think he is, anyhow?/ Is five successive base hits enough? Let's make it seven, what the hey*—New Yorker/ *What the fuck, Boyce!*—William Bayer **2** *interj* (also **what the hay**) by 1872 An exclamation of resignation, acceptance, etc: *What the hell, it isn't the greatest, but it'll do* **3** *n phr* (also **what the fuck** or **what in hell**) by 1836 What? •Lengthened for emphasis and euphony: *What the hell do you think you're doing?/ So what the fuck is this about?*—Scott Turow

what the Sam Hill *interj* by 1927 =WHAT THE HELL •A euphemistic form

what-you-may-call-it *See* WHATCHAMACALLIT

what you see is what you get *sentence* by 1980s The situation, thing, person, etc, is precisely as it appears to be; no trickery, decoration, glowing promises, etc, are involved here [probably fr the supposed statement of a salesperson both assuring and warning a customer about the wares]

whatzis *See* WHAT'S-IT

whee *n* by 1980s Urine; =PISS, WHIZZ: *that will scare the whee out of you*—Car and Driver [probably fr wee-wee]

wheel *See* BIG WHEEL, INVENT THE WHEEL, REINVENT THE WHEEL

wheel and deal *v phr* by 1950s To make many and frequent arrangements and agreements, esp in business and aggressively [perhaps fr the baseball phrase describing a pitchers wind-up and throw]

wheeler *See* EIGHTEEN WHEELER, FOUR-WHEELER, SIDE-WHEELER

wheeler-dealer *n* by 1950s A person who wheels and deals; =BIG-TIME OPERATOR, GANZE MACHER

wheelhouse *n baseball* by 1959 A batter's preferred hitting zone over the plate; =KITCHEN [probably fr the controlling prominence of the *wheelhouse* on a river boat or a ship]

wheelie 1 *n* 1960s *motorcyclists & bicyclists* A riding on the rear wheel only, with the front wheel raised off the ground **2** *n* 1970s *skateboarders* To ride a skateboard on one pair of wheels *See* POP A WHEELIE

wheeling *See* FREE-WHEELING

wheel man *n phr* 1930s *underworld* The driver of a car used in a robbery or other criminal endeavor: *Like, I'm a pretty good wheel man, you know what I mean?*—Joseph Wambaugh

wheels 1 *n* by 1940s The legs: *His wheels are good. His arm is probably better than it was. . .*—Milwaukee Journal/ *. . . even the veiny old wheels*—Joseph Wambaugh **2** *n* 1950s *hot rod-*

ders A car: . . . *he tried to convince them that their wheels belonged to someone else*—Milwaukee Journal Sentinel
See SET OF WHEELS, SHIT ON WHEELS

the **wheels fall off** *sentence by 1990s* Trouble breaks out; a fearful crisis ensues; things turn nasty; =the SHIT HITS THE FAN: *We were in good shape until that play, and then the wheels kind of fell off*—Associated Press

wheeze *n by 1864* An old joke; =CHESTNUT: . . . *even remembered a wheeze I pulled*—Groucho Marx/ . . . *this tired little wheeze*—Billy Rose [origin unknown; perhaps fr a *wheezing* delivery used by clowns in telling jokes; the earliest attested use refers to a circus clown's joke]

when the balloon goes up *adv phr* Army fr WWI British Army When war, action, etc, begins [fr a *balloon* released to signal the beginning of a barrage]

when the bell rings *adv phr by 1990s* At the beginning; when the time comes: *When the bell rings, we'll work hard and let the chips fall where they may*—Milwaukee Journal Sentinel

when the hammer comes down *adv phr by 1990s* When the decision is made; when all is said and done: *I just hope that when the hammer comes down, that they will look at my performance on the field*—Milwaukee Journal [probably fr the terminating blow of the auctioneer's *hammer*]

where does one **get off** doing something *sentence by about 1900* How does he or she dare?; what right has he or she?: *Where does she get off being so snotty?/ Where does he get off, saying I'd do that?* [fr *get off,* "cease, stop," probably fr the notion of getting off a train; so the question is "When does one desist?"]

where someone's **head is at** *adv phr by 1960s* One's mental condition; one's attitudes, thoughts, aberrations, etc: *They have the maturity to understand where a freak's head is at*—Xaviera Hollander

where I sit *See* FROM WHERE I SIT

where someone **is at** *n phr 1960s black* Someone's essential nature, current value system, attitudes, etc: *might make sense in evaluating where you are all at*—New York Times/ *everything from Woody Guthrie to the country blues. That's where I was at*—Rolling Stone

where someone **is coming from** 1 *n phr by 1977* What someone means; what someone is saying 2 *n phr* =WHERE someone IS AT

where it's at *by about 1960* 1 *n phr* The essential locus of the truth; the core of things: *A lot of cats are finding out where it's at in the joint*—Claude Brown 2 *adv phr*: *Why should only book writers write books?. . . They're not where it's at*—James Simon Kunen/ *TV is where it's at*—Village Voice 3 *adv phr* At the site of stimulating and modish events, trends, etc; =WHERE THE ACTION IS: *Where the important stuff is going on. This is where it's at*—New York Times
See KNOW WHERE IT'S AT

where someone **lives** *adv phr by 1860* At a vital

or crucial place; in one's most essential nature, feelings, etc; profoundly: *Let them hear the click when you cock it. And point it right where they live*—Joseph Wambaugh/ . . . *an ability to capture the moment and zap you where you live*—Playgirl/ *Her appeal hit me where I live*
See HIT someone WHERE HE LIVES

where the action is *by 1970s* 1 *n phr* The site of stimulating and modish events, trends, etc; a place of excitement; =WHERE IT'S AT: *Don't come here if you're looking for where the action is* 2 *adv phr*: *Do you want to live where the action is?* [probably fr *action,* "gambling"]

where the bodies are buried *See* KNOW WHERE THE BODIES ARE BURIED

where the rubber meets the road *n phr* Army by 1980s Where the action is most immediate; the place of the nitty-gritty: *Assembly lines like this one at Northrop are like living things. This is where the rubber meets the road*—New Yorker

where the sun doesn't shine *by 1980s* 1 *n phr* One's anus; =ASS, ASSHOLE 2 *adv phr*: *Put it and all his other contributions where the sun doesn't shine*—Car and Driver/ *Give you a hickey where the sun doesn't shine*—National Lampoon
See STICK IT

where to get off (or **to go**) *See* TELL someone WHERE TO GET OFF

where to put (or **shove** or **stick** or **stuff**) something *See* KNOW WHAT one CAN DO WITH something, TELL someone WHAT TO DO WITH something

the **wherewithal** *n phr by 1833* Money; =the NEEDFUL

whew or **whooee** (hw EE OO) *interj by 1890* An exclamation of astonishment, relief, incredulity, etc: . . . *and face ABC's not-nearly-so-formidable Ellen. Whew*—USExpress/ "*Woooeee!*" says Dahl in mock terror—People [probably echoic fr the whistling exhalation of a relieved person]

which *See* SAYS WHICH

whiff 1 *v baseball by 1916* To strike at a ball and miss 2 *v baseball by 1916* To strike out: . . . *surpassed Sandy Koufax's single-season strikeout record, whiffing 383 batters*—Inside Sports 3 *n narcotics by 1970s* Cocaine; =SNOW: *Hey, man, know where I can score some whiff?*—Dan Jenkins 4 *v narcotics by 1970s* To inhale cocaine into the nose; =SNORT, TOOT

whimp *See* WIMP

the **whim-whams** (or **wim-wams**) *n phr by 1940s* Nervousness; =JIM-JAMS, the JITTERS: . . . *gives Pavarotti the whim-whams before every performance*—Time/ *Kittenish dames give us the wim-wams*—Time

whingding *See* WINGDING

whip *See* BUGGY WHIP

whip-out *n by 1980s* Money, esp a first payment, investment, etc: . . . *a whole lot of what you call your up-front whip-out*—Dan Jenkins

whip out *v phr by 1980s* To pay; expend; =FORK

OVER: *But if you're waiting for the Yankees' principal owner to whip out some new Ben Franklin $100 bills. . . don't hold your breath*—New York Times

whipped *See* PUSSY-WHIPPED

whipped up *adj phr* (also **whipped**) late 1930s jazz musicians Exhausted; =BEAT, POOPED: . . . *found the controllers dangerously whipped up*—Time/ *Leading one of those late-night bands, I'm whipped when I get off that bandstand*—New York Times

whipsaw 1 *v* by 1873 To attack or operate by letting rival parties attack one another, to the benefit of the more or less passive manipulator: . . . *pit one plant against another, using interplant rivalries to spur production, a tactic called "whipsawing"*—Time **2** *v* by 1970s To assault; defeat; =CLOBBER: *I'm not trying to sandbag anybody, and I'm not trying to whipsaw anybody*—George V Higgins/ *Tormented? Driven Witless? Whipsawed by Confusion?*—Elle [first sense perhaps fr the reciprocal action of the *whipsaw,* a pit saw operated by one person above and one in the pit below; in an earlier slang use *whipsaw* meant "to take bribes from two political sources at once"; second sense probably fr the cutting efficiency of this two-person saw]

whip the dog *v phr* nautical by 1950s =FUCK THE DOG

whip up *v phr* To make hurriedly: *Let's whip up a new policy on this/ Just relax while I whip up dinner*

whirlpool 1 *n* (also **whirlpooling**) 1980s teenagers A rowdy boys'prank of surrounding a girl in a swimming pool and roiling the water while chanting rap lyrics •The game has often led to sexual violence against the trapped girl **2** *v* by 1990s To dispose of someone or something as if by tossing into a whirlpool: . . . *what music was Bill Clinton listening to when he whirlpooled Lani Guinier?*—Milwaukee Journal

whirlybird *n* by 1951 A helicopter; =CHOPPER •Along with *egg-beater,* nearly obsolete

whiskers *See* BET YOUR BOOTS, the CAT'S MEOW, UNCLE WHISKERS

whispering campaign *n phr* by 1920 An effort at discrediting someone or something, esp by starting false rumors: . . . *start a whispering campaign against your product*—S J Perelman

whistle *v* by 1813 To move very rapidly, as if with a whistling sound; =BARREL: . . . *two bills whistled through the Montana legislature. . .* —New York Times

See BELLS AND WHISTLES, BLOW THE WHISTLE, DOODAD, NOT JUST WHISTLING DIXIE, WET one's WHISTLE, WHISTLE DIXIE, WOLF WHISTLE

whistle blower *n* by 1970 A person who makes an accusation of wrongdoing, illegality, etc: *Thanks to yet another whistle blower, it is now known that even the cost of the one-inch square plastic caps. . . has flown as high as the planes*—Time/ *. . . trading inside information with whistle-blowers and publicity seekers*—Washingtonian

whistle Dixie *by 1940s* **1** *v phr* To say something of no consequence in order to make a positive impression **2** *v phr* To engage in wishful thinking [fr the effect of Dan Emmett's 1859 minstrel song *Dixie,* which became the favorite of the Confederates]

whistle stop *n phr* railroad by 1934 A small town [fr the fact that the train does not regularly stop at such a town, or stops only when signaled by a *whistle*]

white *n* 1940s narcotics Cocaine

See BLACK AND WHITE, BLEED someone WHITE, CHINA WHITE, LILY-WHITE

white bready or **white bread** or **white-bread** *adj phr* or *adj* by 1980s Conventional; bourgeois; =PLASTIC, SQUARE: *Some of the sequences are Middle American. Evans calls them white bready*—Time/ . . . *two normal white bread all-American boys. . .* —William Bayer/ *He taught them to give up the safe, white-bread types*—Playboy [fr the marketing fact that most Americans prefer soft, factory-baked *white bread*]

white buck *See* WHITE SHOE

white-collar *by 1919* **1** *modifier* Employed as clerks, office workers, etc: *The white collar workers don't strike very often/ As early as the 1920s they were called white-collar slaves . . . and by the 1950s nine-to-fivers*—The City in Slang **2** *modifier* Performed by people who work in offices, esp by managers, high executives, etc: *White-collar crime has become a serious problem*

white elephant *n phr* by 1851 Something putatively valuable, often a gift, that one does not want; an embarrassing piece of bric-a-brac: *a wonderful collection of white elephants, trash, treasures*—Washington Post [fr the *white elephant* of Thailand which, although it is sacred and royal, is also a clumsy sort of possession for one's house]

white-face *n* 1890s circus A clown

white flight *n phr* by 1967 The moving by white persons into the suburbs to avoid the hazards of urban life and esp to avoid living among various racial and ethnic minorities: *By the mid-Sixties, the rate of white flight in Crown Heights had increased dramatically, largely because of real-estate speculators' use of blockbusting techniques*—New Yorker

white-haired boy *See* FAIRHAIRED BOY

white hat *by 1970s* **1** *n phr* A law-abiding, morally upright, and heroic person, as distinct from the villainous black hat **2** *modifier*: *I told them they were the white-hat guys*—Larry Hagman [fr the conventional dress of heroes in cowboy movies]

white knight *n phr* by 1981 A person or company that intervenes to thwart a hostile takeover bid: *Miami firm calls $1.6 billion bid "inadequate"; seeks white knight for rescue*—Newark Star-Ledger [fr the *White Knight* in Lewis Carroll's *Through the Looking Glass*]

white knuckle 1 *n phr* by 1980s Something tense, uncertain, frightening, very suspenseful, etc; =CLIFFHANGER: *It was a white knuckle*—CBS News **2** *v*: . . . *"just plain folks" can white knuckle it* *around Mugello's tight curves*—New York Times [fr the pallor of knuckles on an anxiously clenched hand]

white-knuckle *adj* by 1980s Marked by tension, suspense, fear, etc: *Invocations of a Soviet threat have become so common. . . He calls it "the white-knuckle show"*—Washingtonian/ *A genuine white-knuckle road*—William Least Heat Moon

white-knuckled *adj phr* by 1980s Tense; anxious; frightened: *Are you as white knuckled as I am when traveling as an airline passenger?*—Newsweek/ *Metro's countless thousands of white-knuckled motorists*—Toronto Life

white knuckler 1 *n phr* by 1980s An airplane flight, esp an anxious one on a commuter airline: *You take a white-knuckler. Smilin' Jack at the controls*—Paul Theroux 2 *n phr* A tense and anxious person; someone or something frightened: *A list of companies in trouble: The white knucklers*—New Jersey Monthly

white lightning 1 *n phr* by 1921 Inferior whiskey; =PANTHER PISS, ROTGUT: *He had a pint of bootleg white lightning*—Carson McCullers 2 *n phr* 1970s narcotics LSD; =ACID

◁**white meat**▷ *n phr* A white person, esp a woman, regarded solely as a sex partner [immediately fr the *white meat* and *dark meat* of cooked fowl; *meat*, "the vulva," is attested fr the late 1500s]

white money *n phr* by 1980s Money, esp an illegal political contribution, that has been provided with a legitimate history and provenience

white mule *n phr* by 1889 Strong bootleg liquor, esp nearly pure grain alcohol [because it had a kick like a *mule*]

white picket fence *n phr* A comfortable, peaceful, and affluent sort of life; rural paradise: *What do I want after this rat-race? The white picket fence* [fr the frequent depiction of such life in such dwellings by film-makers of the 1930s and '40s]

white shoe (or **buck)** by 1980s 1 *n phr* A typical Ivy League student 2 *adj phr* (also **white-shoe**) Having the attitudes, appearance, etc, of the Ivy League: *Do I look white shoe?*—New York Times/ *. . . a Harvard-educated bluestocking who practiced white-shoe corporate law. . .*—Wisconsin State Journal [fr the *white buckskin shoes* that were part of that student's dress]

white stuff 1 *n phr* by about 1920 Grain alcohol used for making bootleg liquor 2 *n phr* narcotics by 1908 Cocaine or morphine; =SNOW

◁**white trash**▷ *n phr* (often **poor white trash**) black by 1855 =PECKERWOOD, REDNECK

whitewash 1 *v* by 1851 To win decisively, esp not permitting the opponent to score; =SKUNK 2 *v* by 1762 To make something unsavory, damaging, etc, seem to be legitimate and acceptable, usu by falsification or concealment; decontaminate someone's actions or reputation 3 *n*: *Several Republican senators reported that the report was a "whitewash" of McCarthy's charges*—Associated Press

whitewater *n* 1990s corporate Frequent changes in the structure and environment of a company, like mergers, cutbacks, and reengineering: *Some whitewater is fun, but it takes a lot out of you*—Wall Street Journal [fr rafting or kayaking in turbulent and dangerous *white water*]

white wrapper *See* PLAIN WRAPPER

◁**Whitey** or **whitey**▷ *n* 1940s black A white person; =MISTER CHARLIE, OFAY

whiz[1] *n* by 1914 A very successful performer; an outstanding expert; =HUMDINGER: *the town's most promising high school football whiz*—Associated Press/ *a whiz at exterior (as opposed to psychological) characterization*—New York Times [perhaps a shortened form of *wizard*]

whiz[2] or **whizz** 1 *v* by 1929 To urinate; =PISS: *exactly twenty-five minutes after whizzing in his pants for the last time*—Stephen King/ *I gotta whiz. Will you just cover me at the register for a minute?*—Cameron Crowe 2 *n* by 1971: *I just came down for a whizz*—Paul Theroux [perhaps echoic; perhaps related to late–1800s British *hold your whiz,* "be quiet, shut up," similar to *hold your water*]

whiz[3] *v* underworld by 1925 To pick pockets [apparently fr the *whizzing* speed with which an expert pickpocket works]

whiz[4] *See* GEE WHIZ[2]

whizbang 1 *n* by about 1915 A person or thing that is remarkable, wonderful, superior, etc; =BEAUT, HUMDINGER: *It's a whizbang of an idea* 2 *modifier*: *definitely has been a whiz-bang franchise-winning tool*—Village Voice 3 *n* by about 1915 A very successful performer; an outstanding expert; =WHIZ: *In time we'll all be varsity whizbangs*—Arthur Daley/ *The TV whizbangs were sweating through their pancake makeup*—Washington Post 4 *n* 1920s narcotics A mixture of cocaine and morphine; an injection of this mixture [fr an intensification of *whiz* either due to or influenced by the echoic use of *whizbang* to designate an artillery shell in World War I]

◁**whiz bitch**▷ *n phr* by 1920s Anything arduous or very disagreeable; =BITCH: *Wasn't that test a whiz bitch?*

whiz kid 1 *n phr* by 1930s A very clever young person; a youthful prodigy: *. . . the physics whiz kid*—W T Tyler 2 *modifier*: *Then the whiz-kid lawyers collided with a tougher adversary*—Village Voice [fr *whiz*[1] blended with *quiz kid,* "very bright child or young person," used of participants in a 1930s radio quiz program]

whizzer *n* underworld by 1925 A pickpocket; =WHIZ

who *See* SAYS YOU

whoa or **woah** 1 *interj* by 1980s An exclamation of surprise and delight; =WOW •This interjection appears to be replacing the very popular *wow* of the 1960s: *Unsolicited confession: woah!*—Douglas Coupland 2 *interj* (also **whoa there, whoa Nelly**) by 1940s An exhortation to wait, go slow, not be hasty •The expression must be quite old in this use: *Whoa, Nelly. Two aliens are heading this way*—

comic strip "Sherman's Lagoon" [fr *whoa!* "Stop, horse!" attested fr the 1840s]

who died and made someone something *sentence* by 1990s Where did you get your authority?; what makes you presume?: *Who died and made Louis Farrakhan the judge of every other black person's racial loyalty?*—New York Times/ *Who died and made you marriage counselor to the Broncos?* —Steve Kelly radio show

whodunit *n* by 1937 A mystery or detective story, play, movie, etc, esp a novel: *a conventional whodunit*—Anthony Boucher [fr *who done it* , "who committed the crime?"; claimed as a coinage by and of various persons]

the **whole ball of wax** *n phr* by 1950s The totality; everything; the whole thing; =the WHOLE SHEBANG: *For that price you get the whole ball of wax* [origin unknown; perhaps fr a manner of distributing the land of an estate to heirs, described in the early 1600s, in which the amount of each portion is concealed in a *ball of wax* that is drawn out of a hat in a sort of lottery. If so, the term went unrecorded for a very long time]

the **whole enchilada** *n phr* The totality; everything; the whole thing: *We're talking best seller, mini-series, the whole enchilada*—Stan Cutler

whole famn damily *n phr* by 1940s The whole family •An amusing euphemism: *I hate him and his whole famn damily*
See CHUCK YOU, FARLEY

whole hog *adv phr* Utterly; without reservation: *He believed me whole hog* [fr early–1800s *go the whole hog*, "act, give, etc, without reservation," explained in 1852 as fr the butcher's question whether the customer wants the whole slaughtered animal, at a cheaper price than the prime parts only]

the **whole megillah** **See** the MEGILLAH

a **whole new ball game** *n phr* by 1960s A totally new situation; something completely different from what has been the case: *Since the government got into it this has been a whole new ball game*

the **whole nine yards** *n phr* 1960s Army & Air Force The totality; everything; the whole thing; =the WHOLE SHEBANG: *... went with the odd-looking ship, built a press platform in front of it, had power brought in for press lights, "the whole nine yards"*—Washingtonian/ *... guys in black tie passing champagne and the whole nine yards*—Washington Post/ *Floods. Fires. The whole nine yards*—New Yorker [origin unknown; perhaps based on the load of a concrete mixing and hauling truck, which normally comes in a *nine-yard* and a ten-yard size; perhaps based on *yard*, "one hundred dollars," rather than on the linear or cubic measure]

a **whole 'nother** *n phr* by 1980s Completely different; new: *... getting in would be a whole nother thing*—Stan Cutler/ *That's a whole 'nother question; we'll get to it later*—Jim Lehrer

the **whole schmear** *n phr* (Variations: **schmier** or **schmeer** or **shmear** or **shmeer** or **shmier** **smear** may replace **schmear**) by 1940s The totali-

ty; everything; the whole thing; =the WHOLE SHEBANG: *... names, ages, business they're in, daily schedules, the whole schmear*—Lawrence Sanders/ *... the whole fucking schmear*—George Warren [fr Yiddish *shmeer* fr *shmeeren*, "spread"; probably immediately fr the spreading out of the hand in a pinochle or rummy game]

the **whole shebang** *n phr* by 1895 The totality; everything; the whole thing; =the WHOLE SCHMEAR: *We could move the whole shebang*—Washington Post/ *The whole shebang is festive, pleasantly show-offy and communal*—Village Voice [fr middle 1800s *shebang*, "hut, hovel," perhaps fr Irish *shebeen*, "cheap saloon," hence, "the house and everything in it"]

the **whole shooting match** *n phr* by 1896 The totality; everything; the whole thing; =the WHOLE SCHMEAR [probably fr the crowd that would gather at a frontier *shooting match*, hence, "the whole crowd"; perhaps influenced by earlier British *the whole shoot* of the same meaning, fr *the whole shot*, "the whole cost or price"; noted in 1900 as a favorite expression of children]

the **whole works** **See** the WORKS

wholly owned subsidiary *n phr* by 1990s Someone or something in the complete control of another person or entity: *Public transportation in Boston is practically a wholly owned subsidiary of Bill Bulger's*—New Yorker/ *We must put on a happy face and embrace George Pataki, a wholly owned subsidiary of Alfonse D'Amato*—New York Times [fr the phrase used to describe one company owned by another]

whomp or **whump 1** *v* by 1952 To defeat utterly; =CLOBBER: *The Tigers got badly whomped* **2** *v* by 1973 To hit; =BASH: *sturdily whumped at the New Deal's "insane deficit policy"*—Life [echoic fr the sound of a blow, perhaps influenced by dialect *whup* and *whop*, "whip"]

whomp up *v phr* by 1950 To make; devise or build: *I whomped me up one heck of a nightmare*—Billy Rose

whoomp, there it is or **whoot, there it is** (WOOMP, WOOT) *interj* Atlanta nightclub about 1990 An exclamation of pleasure, approval, and enthusiasm; =WOW [*there it is* is said to be a reference to women's buttocks]

whoop-de-do (HooP dee doo) (also **hoopty-doo** or **hoopty-do** or **hoop-de-doo** or **hoop-a-doop** or **hoop-de-doop** or **whoop-de-doo** or **whoop-de-doodle**) **1** *n* by 1929 Raucous confusion; noisy celebration; jolly fuss: *... a gay sense of flossy whoop-de-doo*—Esquire/ *... but, in spite of this whoop-de-doo*—Time/ *Cowboys and soldiers created a deafening hoop-a-doop*—New York Times **2** *adj* by 1920s: *The racketeering, gossiping, whoop-de-doodle thing, it is a piece of stinking fish*—Thomas Wolfe **3** *n* 1980s motorcyclists & highway engineers A series of ruts or bumps in a road: *A department analysis of the ripples, called whoopdedoos by engineers...*—Milwaukee Journal [echoic]

whoopee (WHoo pee) **1** *n by 1928* Exuberant merriment; wild celebration; =WHOOP-DE-DO: *"Whoopee" seems to have entered New York with the accent on the first syllable*—American Speech **2** *interj by 1862* An exclamation of joy and approval; hurrah [based on *whoop*, which is found the late 1300s; popularized and perhaps coined by the colmnist Walter Winchell]

whoopee (or **whoopie) cushion** *n phr by late 1950s* A bladder that makes a loud flatulating sound when sat upon: *It's Grandma's whoopie cushion. I thought you'd like that, you little fart*—National Lampoon

whooper-dooper *n by about 1930* A carouse; a wild party: *He finds himself off on a rousing whooper-dooper*—Saturday Evening Post

whoop it up *v phr by 1884* To celebrate; carouse; have raucous fun: *It's natural the Boys should whoop it up for so huge a phallic triumph*—W H Auden

whoopla *See* HOOPLA

whoops **1** *v* (also **whoops up**) *by 1980s* To vomit; =OOPS: *A man. . . had whoopsed into his National Observer*—Stephen King **2** *n by 1980s* A blunder; serious mistake; =GOOF, OOPS: *"I think we got a whoops," said a police inspector*—Milwaukee Journal

whoosh *See* IN A WHOOSH

whoota joint *n phr by 1990s* A marijuana cigarette containing crack: *. . . with these guys smoking that damn whoota joint*—Sassy

whoozis or **whozis** or **whoozit** (Hoo zəs) *n by 1929* An unspecified or unspecifiable object; something one does not know the name of or does not wish to name; =THINGAMAJIG: *Is impotence in the whoozis?*—San Francisco/ *There should be a whozis over the first* n—A H Holt/ *What do you call this whoozis on top here?*

whoozit (Hoo zət) *n by 1931* A person whose name one does not know; =WHAT'S-HIS-FACE: *Hello to Fred and Whoozit*—Village Voice

whop **1** *v by 1575* To hit; =WHACK **2** *n by 1440*: *Give a good whop this time* **3** *n by 1980s* A try or chance; =CRACK, POP, SHOT: *. . . politicians, judges, people from out of town, $50 to $100 a whop*—Milwaukee Journal [echoic]

whopper *by 1785* **1** *n* Something huge and powerful: *. . . the Mauritius tortoise must have been a whopper*—J Williams/ *You know, come up with the whopper before Election Day*—Scott Turow **2** *n* A very bold lie: *He told a whopper and got away with it* [fr *whop*]

See BELLY-WHOPPER

whopping *adj by 1706* Huge; very impressive: *It was a whopping idea she had*

whore (or **whore's) bath** *n phr by 1940s* A very perfunctory washing of oneself: *Living conditions on the front were brutal—filthy clothes, cold food, "whore's baths," in which we rinsed ourselves off with frigid water*—New York Times

◁**whorehouse**▷ *adj by 1940s* Of a gaudiness or bad taste befitting a cheap brothel; =HONKY-TONK: *The room is painted a sort of whorehouse pink*

◁**whose names end in vowels**◁ *adj phr by 1980s* Having Italian surnames, hence members of organized crime families: *. . . a contractor whom Tooley desperately wanted to testify against two gentlemen whose names ended in vowels*—Scott Turow

who shot John *See* PLAY WHO SHOT JOHN

who's on first *n phr by 1950s* The most basic facts; =WHAT'S WHAT: *With the energy tax seemingly changing every few minutes, many corporate executives say they don't know who's on first*—New York Times [fr a confusing comedy baseball routine of Bud Abbott and Lou Costello]

whump *See* WHOMP

wicked *by 1920* **1** *adj* Impressive; prodigious; =MEAN: *He can shake a wicked spatula*—A L Bass/ *Look at the wicked bat he swings!* **2** *adj* Excellent; wonderful; =BAD, GREAT

See SHAKE A WICKED CALF

wicket *See* STICKY WICKET

wickey *See* ICKY

wide *See* HIGH, WIDE, AND HANDSOME

wide ones *See* FOUR WIDE ONES

wide open **1** *adj phr by 1892* Free of police hindrance; hospitable to profitable vice: *Phoenix City was a famous wide-open town* **2** *adj phr* boxing *by 1915* Vulnerable; open to attack **3** *adj phr* Going at full speed; =FLAT OUT, LIKE SIXTY **4** *adv phr*: *He always drove his bike wide open* [third sense from *wide-open throttle*, probably fr railroading]

wide place (or **spot) in the road** *n phr 1930s* truckers fr Western A small town; =JERK TOWN: *A Wide Place in the Road*—Look

widget or **widgit** **1** *n by about 1920* A mechanical, electrical, or electronic device; =GADGET, GIZMO: *It's three floors of sights, sounds, illusions, movements, gadgets, widgets, and gizmos*—Westword/ *not an activity I would recommend to anyone daunted by a widgit more complicated than a stapler*—Village Voice **2** *modifier*: *as though it were read aloud from the press release of a widget manufacturer*—Time [an alteration of *gadget*, perhaps based on hypothetical *which it* on the model of *whatzit* and *whoozis*]

widow **1** *n* print shop & publishing *by 1904* A short line of type, esp an isolated one at the top of a column or page **2** *n* cardplaying *by 1891* A spare hand dealt in certain card games

See GOLF WIDOW, GRASS WIDOW

widow-maker *n* loggers *by 1945* Anything that is lethally dangerous, esp a falling bough or a dead tree

wiener *See* WEENIE

wiener dog *n phr by 1990s* A dachshund; =SAUSAGE HOUND: *For wiener dogs across Wisconsin. . .* —Wisconsin State Journal

wife **1** *n* prostitutes *by about 1900* A member of a pimp's group of prostitutes: *She is his favorite "wife" at the moment*—New York Times **2** *n by 1883* The more passive of a homosexual couple

wiff or **wif** (WIF) **1** *n* A wife **2** *n* =WHIFF

wig 1 *n* *1930s jive talk* One's head; one's mind **2** *v* *1930s jive talk* To talk, esp casually and freely; =RAP: *We stood around wigging* **3** *v* *1930s jive talk* To annoy someone; =BUG: *She ordered me to stop wigging her* **4** *n* *1950s jazz musicians* A cool jazz musician **5** *v* *1950s jazz musicians* To play cool or progressive jazz **6** *v* *1950s cool talk* To behave more or less hysterically; =FLIP, FREAK OUT, WIG OUT: *I realized my goddamn father wasn't there, again, and I wigged*—Richard Price **7** *v* *1950s cool talk* To be happy and in harmony; =DIG **8** *adj* *early 1960s teenagers* Excellent; wonderful; =GREAT, NEAT: *a real wig rock trio*

See BLOW one's TOP, FLIP one's LID

wigged out or **wigged 1** *adj phr* *1950s students* Out of touch with reality; deluded; =OUT OF IT: *one of whom is comically wigged out on cleanliness and ecology*—Richard Schickel/ *... if you're really feeling wigged out by any and all contact. . .*—Sassy **2** *adj phr* *narcotics by 1950s* Intoxicated with narcotics; =HIGH

◁**wigger**▷ or **yo-boy** *n* *early 1990s* A white person, esp a teenager, who imitates the style and behavior of inner-city blacks: *When I was wearing my permanent-press Lees with matching Adidas sneakers, kids I went to school with were calling me a wigger*—New Republic [apparently a shortening of *white nigger*; perhaps influenced by *wigger*, "a very crazy person," fr jazz talk]

wiggle *See* GET A MOVE ON

wiggle room *n phr* *by middle 1980s* Space, either real or figurative, in which to maneuver; =ELBOW ROOM: *Clinton's health plan gives Congress wiggle room*—National Public Radio

wiggle one's **way out** *v phr* *by 1685* To extricate oneself from difficulty, often by devious means: *. . . men who are just trying to wiggle their way out of their obligations*—Morris County Daily Record

wiggy 1 *adj* *1960s cool talk* Exciting and up-to-date; =COOL, FAR OUT: *But I have some really wiggy experiences*—Dayton Daily News **2** *adj* Intoxicated on or using narcotics; =OUT OF IT, SPACED-OUT, WIGGED OUT: *one of whom is so wiggy that she got fired from her job*—Newsweek **3** *adj* Crazy; weird; strange: *Things were wiggy*—Robert Stone/ *. . . neither a wiggy sexual penitent. . . nor a kohl-eyed tough cookie. . .*—Vogue

See WIG OUT

wig out *1950s cool talk fr jazz musicians* **1** *v phr* To become ecstatic; enjoy oneself hugely; =FLIP, FREAK OUT, WIG: *The first time I read The Collected Stories I wigged out*—Saturday Review **2** *n phr* To become mentally unbalanced; lose one's sanity: *. . . whose guiding genius, Brian Wilson, spent years wigging out in a sandbox*—Rolling Stone [fr a complex set of jazz uses, mostly based on the idea of *flipping* one's *wig*, "losing one's head"]

wild *adj* *1950s cool talk* Excellent; exciting; wonderful; =COOL

wild about (or **over**) **1** *adj phr* *by 1879* Enthusiastically approbatory of; =CRAZY ABOUT: *the new lemon flavored cough drop everyone's wild about*—New York Post **2** *adj phr* In love with

wild and woolly *adj phr* *by 1884* Crude and raucous; untamed; uncouth: *. . . a couple of good old country boys having a wild and woolly time* [fr an alliterating phrase *wild and woolly West*, the *woolly* perhaps referring to range steers, to range horses, or to the unkempt heads of cowboys and frontiersmen]

◁**wild-ass** or **wild-assed**▷ *adj* *by 1960s* Madly exuberant; untamed; =CRAZY, WILD: *Shepard tops himself as a wild-ass country boy*—Playboy/ *. . . and for goddamned sure a wild-assed warrior*—Don Pendleton/ *Ijah was a kind of wild-ass type*—Saul Bellow [an example of the use of *ass*, "the whole person"]

wild card 1 *n phr* *card games by 1920s* Something outside of the normal rules, category, etc; an unpredictable thing, event, etc: *Being from Princeton wasn't like being from Jersey, it was a wild card*—Philadelphia **2** *n phr* *sports by 1950s* A team picked for a playoff by some more or less arbitrary method, not having won its championship during the season: *We can always hope the Lions will be the wild card* **3** *modifier*: *the wild-card slot/ last year's wild-card team* [fr poker and other games, where in some cases one or more *wild cards*, having any value the player desires, may be designated]

wildcat 1 *v* *by 1877* To drill for oil, esp without strong corporate and financial backing **2** *modifier* *by 1883* Done or ventured individually, apart from ordinary corporate structures: *a wildcat well/ a wildcat cab* **3** *n* *early 1990s narcotics* A mixture of the drugs cat (metcathenone) and cocaine **4** *n* (also **wildcat strike**) *labor union by 1937* A strike not authorized by the union authorities [fr the independent behavior of feral felines; in the 1840s a western bank issued banknotes picturing a *wildcat*, and then suspended payment; in early 1900s show business, to *wild-cat* meant to book a theater tour day-by-day]

wilding *n* *late 1980s urban black* Concerted violent behavior by groups of usu black teenagers: *. . . a pack of 33 teenagers swept out of Harlem for a night of. . . wilding, attacking anyone. . . who looks vulnerable*—Los Angeles Times [the word became widespread after a particular attack in April 1989]

wild out *v phr* *1990s urban black* To go on a damaging rampage; riot; go wilding: *Some brothers is like "I'm going to wild out, cause I have nothing positive to look for"*—Los Angeles Times

willie or **willy 1** *n* *by 1905* The penis; =WEENIE •Adopted in US slang fairly recently: *The notion that some small part of the cosmic order hung on our teenage willies was a heavy load for us young soldiers in St. Ignatius' Army of Christ*—New Yorker/ *The plethysmograph, basically a strain gauge wrapped around the willy, electronically reg-*

isters the pulls and tugs of arousal and then draws them as jagged peaks and valleys on a line graph— Philadelphia **2 n** =CORN WILLIE
See DOODAD

Willie Fudd n phr *Vietnam War Navy* A WF–2 propeller-driven naval radar aircraft [fr the name of a cartoon character, whose initials are *WF* like the designation of the aircraft]

the **willies n phr** *by 1896* Acute nervousness; a spell of uneasiness; =the JITTERS: . . . *the thought of an intense daily association with this troglodyte gave me the willies*—Stan Cutler/ *The willies or the creeps. Call it what you like*—Scott Turow/ *For years her friends' shoptalk gave him the willies*— Geoffrey T Hellman [perhaps fr *the woollies*, a dialect term for nervousness and uneasiness, perhaps suggested by the itchy sensation of wool on the skin]

willikers *See* GEE[2]

will the real someone **please stand up question** *by 1950s* May the actual claimant now be identified: *After listening to Mr. Brown and Mr. Christopher, it was tempting to ask: Would the real Secretary of Commerce please stand up?*—New York Times [fr a television panel show, *To Tell the Truth,* where three different people claimed to have a certain identity, and the real one was finally asked to stand up]

wilma n *1980s college students* An ugly or stupid woman [fr the name of a character in the television show and movie *The Flintstones*]

wimp or **whimp n** *early 1960s college students* An ineffectual person; a soft, silly person; a weakling; =DRIP, NEBBISH: . . . *unmacho. Short hair, glasses, awkward, uncertain. WIMP*—New York Sunday News/ . . . *his unfortunate and unfounded charge that Thompson portrayed him as a "wimp"*— Newsweek/ *Apparently whimps complained it was too hot*—Nashville [origin unknown; perhaps fr J Wellington *Wimpy,* a relatively unaggressive character in the comic strip "Popeye"; perhaps fr the early–1900s British University *wimp* "young woman," perhaps fr *whimper;* occurs in a 1920 George Ade story, which may be the source of the term, used more in intervening years in the adjective form *wimpish*]

wimp out or **wimp v phr** *early 1980s* To cancel or withdraw from an action or place because of fear; =CHICKEN OUT: *I could feel for my friend because I've wimped out on the assertive front. . .* —Sassy/ *"I know it seems disrespectful to you," I wimped*— Stan Cutler

wimpish or **wimpy** or **wimpo** or **wimpoid adj** *entry form by 1925, first variant by 1967, others fr 1960s and later* Having the traits of a wimp; soft; weak: . . . *less wimpy version of the husband she leaves*—Ms/ . . . *seats that go wimpo during cornering*—Car and Driver/ *a wimpoid ballad with the refrain "the doggone girl is mine"*—Rolling Stone

Wimpy n A hamburger sandwich [fr J Wellington

Wimpy, an obsessive lover and seeker of such sandwiches]
See WIMP

win a few lose a few or **win some lose some sentence** One cannot always be victorious or successful; =YOU CAN'T WIN 'EM ALL: *Manning fought from within Luce's empire against the Republicanizing of the news, and as Theodore White predicted in urging him to take the job, he won some and lost some*—Nation

wind *See* BAG OF WIND, BREAK WIND, a LOAD OF VW RADIATORS, PISS AND WIND, TWIST SLOWLY IN THE WIND

windage *See* KENTUCKY WINDAGE

windbag n *by 1827* A person who talks too much, esp a pompous prater; =BAG OF WIND, GASBAG: . . . *a windbag who shoots the gab*—J R Williams

wind down 1 v phr *by 1952* To come or bring to a gradual halt or conclusion: *The campaign has begun to wind down/ Shall we wind down our collection drive?* **2 v phr** *by 1958* To relax gradually: *Let me sit here for a few minutes, to wind down* [modeled on the *winding down* of a clock or other machine]

winder *See* SIDEWINDER, STEM-WINDING

window n *by 1967* A time period when something may be accomplished; a critical period: *We now have a window of opportunity to try for peace in Bosnia again/ They're worried about a window of vulnerability* [fr the 1960s astronautics term for the exact time and directional limits governing the launching of a rocket to achieve a certain orbit or destination, which were pictured as a *window* through which the rocket must be shot]
See BAY WINDOW, OUT THE WINDOW

wind up v phr *by 1825* To finish: *We wind up learning less*—Philadelphia Journal

wind something **up v phr** *by 1825* To finish; bring to a conclusion: *I suggest we wind this discussion up and go home*

windy adj *by 1513* Given to talking too much; overly garrulous, esp pompously so: *It's another one of his windy orations*

wine *See* JUG WINE, POP WINE

win for losing *See* someone CAN'T WIN FOR LOSING

wing 1 n *by 1297* An arm, esp a baseball pitcher's throwing arm **2 v** *fr middle 1800s* To shoot someone, not necessarily in the arm: *You were winged by something big, 45 maybe*—R Starnes **3 v** *by 1885* =WING IT
See PAY-WING, PING-WING, SALARY WING, SILVER WING

wingding or **whingding 1 n** *hoboes, prison, and narcotics by 1927* An epileptic or drug-induced fit, esp as counterfeited to attract sympathy **2 n** *by 1933* A fit of anger; a violent outburst of feeling: . . . *going to throw a wingding they'll hear in Detroit*—J Evans **3 n** (also **wingdinger**) *by 1949* An energetic celebration or commotion; a noisy party; =RUCKUS: *Then they did their wingding out in front of the West Wing*—Washington Post

wingdoodle *See* WHANGDOODLE

wing it or **wing v phr** *first form by 1933, second*

by 1885 To improvise; extemporize; act without sufficient preparation; =FAKE IT: *Winging It, Coping Without Controllers*—Time/ *He was confident of his ability to wing it, adjusting. . . to counter her responses*—Lawrence Sanders [fr the notion that an actor could learn his lines in the stage's *wings*, or be coached while standing there; *wing the part* is found by 1886]

wingnut *n* by 1980s A weird or insane person; =WEIRDO: *. . . too weird for me. You guys are wingnuts*—Carsten Stroud [probably fr *wingy* and *nut*]

win going away *v phr* horse-racing by 1940s To win easily, increasing one's lead to the end; =WIN IN A WALK: *We saw the results in Pennsylvania—the Democrat won going away*—National Public Radio

wings *See* EARN ONE'S WINGS

wingy *adj* by 1980s Intoxicated with narcotics; =HIGH [fr *wings*, "cocaine, heroin, or morphine"]

◁**Wingy**▷ *n* by 1880 Nickname for a one-armed person

win in a walk *v phr* by 1896 To win easily; be a confident victor

winkie 1 *n* (also **winkle**) by 1970s The penis: *Had Kaufman discovered a bump on his winkie, he probably would have shared that with us, too*—Village Voice **2** *n* (also **winker**) by 1916 The vulva [both the penis and vulva have been likened to eyes: *upright wink* is recorded as a fanciful term for the vulva, and *one-eyed snake* for the penis]

winks *See* FORTY WINKS

winner *n* A very promising and successful person or thing; =HOT SHOT: *Your new poem is a winner/ Hire this guy, he looks like a winner/ That passing shot was a winner*

wino *n* early 1900s hoboes A habitual drunkard, esp a derelict who drinks cheap wine; =STUMBLEBUM: *a couple of "winos" who had been drinking cheap sherry in the bar*—G Homes/ *patronized largely by vagrants, winos, dehorns, grifters*—Max Shulman

win out *v phr* by 1896 To win; prevail: *De Bird of Time will win out in a walk*—L Coley

winter rat *n phr* An old car; =JALOPY: *old cars known as clunkers, lunkers, winter rats*—New York Times

wiped *adj* by 1950s Exhausted; =POOPED, BEAT

wiped out 1 *adj phr* Drunk: *Everybody had been too wiped out to watch*—Washington Post **2** *adj phr* Tired; exhausted: *At the end of that hearing she felt wiped out*

be wiped out *v phr* To be wrecked, ruined, finished; =GET IT IN THE NECK, SHOOT someone DOWN

wipe it off *v phr* WWII armed forces To force oneself to stop smirking or joking; stop larking •Very often a stern command: *Wipe it off, Mister, this is no comic routine*

wipeout 1 *n* 1960s surfers A fall from the surfboard, esp a spectacular one **2** *n* (also **wipe**) by about 1925 A killing, esp a gangland execution; =RUBOUT: *I don't know a goddam thing about this goddam Covino wipe*—Rex Burns

wipe out *v phr* 1960s surfers To lose control of the surfboard during a ride and be thrown off into the water: *About six of them wiped out on one big wave*

wipe someone **out** *v phr* by 1577 To kill; =ICE, OFF, RUB OUT

wipe the slate clean *v phr* by 1921 To cancel or ignore what has gone before; begin anew; =GO BACK TO SQUARE ONE: *Let's just wipe the slate clean and pretend it never happened*

wipe (or **clean** or **mop**) **up the floor with** someone *v phr* first form by 1875 To defeat utterly and abjectly; trounce easily; =CLOBBER

wire 1 *v* by 1859 To send a telegram: *Wire me when you get there* **2** *n*: *Send me a wire if you get the job* **3** *v* by 1950s To place eavesdropping devices in a room, office, etc, or concealed on someone's body; =BUG: *She quietly checked to see if her bedroom was wired/ The FBI wired me before they sent me to see the suspect* **4** *n*: *They checked to see whether she was wearing a wire* **5** *n* An overstimulated person; an anxious, excitable person: *You know I'm a natural wire. . . . What I need is a drink to calm me down*—Harry Crews

See COME UP TO THE WIRE, DOWN TO THE WIRE, GO TO THE WIRE, HAYWIRE, HOT-WIRE

wired 1 *adj* (also **wired up**) 1970s narcotics Intoxicated by narcotics, esp cocaine or amphetamines; =HIGH, SPACED-OUT: *"If you're wired, you're fired," is how Willie Nelson warns band members about cocaine usage*—Chicago Tribune/ *That night Elvis was wired for speed*—Albert Goldman **2** *adj* (also **wired up**) by 1970s Eagerly excited; overstimulated; =HIGH, HYPER, JACKED UP: *Keeping the people wired with a mix of Sixties vines and Eighties technology*—Rolling Stone/ *They have him wired up tight with the slogans of TV and the World Series*—Eldridge Cleaver **3** *adj* by 1970s Anxious; nervous; =UPTIGHT: *I got wired when Myrt was sneaking a break and Jerry showed up*—Ms **4** *adj* (also **wired up**) by 1950s fr poker Certain and secure; totally under control; assured; =RACKED, TAPED: *Mention of all those other top contenders is just a smokescreen and Brown's got it wired*—Washington Post/ *Then I get this wired up and I think, well*—George V Higgins **5** *adj* by 1957 Wearing an eavesdropping device; having such a device planted; =BUGGED: *He's wired. He's wearing a tape recorder*—Scott Turow [fr *wire* as conducting an electrical charge or stimulus, or as used for binding; *wired up* is recorded as a US term for "irritated, provoked" in the late 1800s, and may be related to the sense "anxious, nervous"]

See COOL AS A CHRISTIAN WITH ACES WIRED, HAVE something CINCHED

wired into *adj* by 1970s Intimately involved in; closely and sympathetically connected with; =INTO: *"I'm wired into Marin Transit right now." "That's cool. . . if you get off on buses"*—Cyra McFadden/ *for the first time, I really felt wired into that* poem—Adrienne Rich [fr *wire* as creating a close connection]

wirehead *n* *computer by late 1980s* A nearly obsessional computer user: *. . . a cross-country quest in search of the wirehead's answer to an amusement park*—Omni

wire-puller *n* *by 1833* A person who exerts influence, esp in a covert way; =OPERATOR: *Grunewald, bigtime wire-puller in the tangled Washington bureaucracy*—New York Daily News

wires *See* PULL STRINGS

wise *adj* *by 1896* Aware; cunningly knowing; =HEP: *Get wise, son!*—Sinclair Lewis/ *He's close-mouthed and wise, stir-wise*—Erle Stanley Gardner
   See CRACK WISE, GET WISE, PUT someone WISE, STREET-SMART

◁**wise-ass**▷ *early 1970s* **1** *n* =SMART-ASS **2** *modifier*: *And I don't need any big-deal Boston wiseass dick to come out here and piss all over my town, you understand*—Robert B Parker
   See NOBODY LIKES A WISE-ASS

wisecrack *n* *by 1924* A witty remark, esp one with a knowing, sarcastic edge; a joke; =GAG, ONE-LINER: *. . . at least two wisecracks in the first paragraph*—Nation/ *. . . makers of wars and wise-cracks, a rum creature*—W H Auden [perhaps fr the theatrical term *crack a wheeze,* "tell a joke"]

wise guy or **wiseguy** **1** *n phr* (also **wise apple**) *by 1896* A person who is ostentatiously and smugly knowing; a smart aleck; =SMART-ASS: *My little brother is an irrepressible wise guy* **2** *n phr* (also **wise hombre**) *by 1896* A shrewd and knowing person; a person who is "wised up": *The wise guys said Frank didn't stand a chance*—Philadelphia Bulletin **3** *n phr* *1970s underworld* A professional criminal, esp a mob member: *The wiseguys like places they're known*—1973 movie *The Seven-Ups/ Hanging out at a neighborhood restaurant in the Italian section of Queens, the first thing he learned is that the wiseguys never talk about what they do*—New Yorker

wisenheimer (WĬ zən hī mər) *n* *by 1904* A person who is ostentatiously and smugly knowing; a smart aleck; =SMART-ASS: *the way an old-time carny handles a tough wisenheimer with the aid of a hammer*—New York Times [fr *wise* plus the German or Yiddish element *-enheimer* found in surnames based on German place names ending in *-heim;* the coinage may be motivated by the humorous attempt to add weight to the term, and is perhaps tinged with anti-Semitism]

wise to *adj phr* *by 1915* Aware of, esp of something shady or forbidden: *They soon became wise to his little deceptions*

wise up *v phr* *by 1914* To become shrewdly aware; =GET SMART, GET WITH IT •Often an exhortation: *Wise up or you'll lose this opportunity/ Now, however, the industry is wising up*—New York Times

wise someone **up** *v phr* *by 1905* To give useful and usu covert particulars; =PUT someone WISE: *My adviser was a good scout and wised me up*—P Marks

wishbone *n* *football fr early 1970s* A football formation in which the quarterback and three other backs line up in a Y pattern with the quarterback at the base and directly behind the center

wish (or **want**) **list** *n phr* A presumed list of things one wants: *. . . intent on buying every weapon the generals and admirals put on their wish lists*—Time

wishy-washy *adj* *by 1873* Marked by imprecision and vacillation; inconstant; uncertain: *The wishy-washy player keeps putting off the evil day*—Oswald Jacoby/ *It's not overpowering like Opium and not wishy-washy*—Washington Post [fr a rhythmic reduplication of *washy,* "weak, diluted, watered-down," probably influenced by *wishy* as suggesting vacillating desires; the original sense was "weak, insubstantial, trashy," found by 1703]

wit *See* NITWIT

witch *n* *by 1940s* A vicious woman •A euphemism for *bitch*: *She's being very nasty about it, a real witch*

◁**witch's tit**▷ *See* COLD AS HELL

with *adj phr* *lunch counter fr 1930s* Having the usual accompaniment, that is, onions with hamburger, cream with coffee, etc: *We ordered two coffees with, to go*

with a full deck *See* PLAY WITH A FULL DECK

with something **and a dime I can get a cup of coffee** *sentence* *by 1970s* The honor, award, compliment, etc I have received is not worth much: *She likes me? With that and a dime I can get a cup of coffee*

with a ten-foot pole *See* NOT TOUCH someone or something WITH A TEN-FOOT POLE

with someone's **bare face hanging out** *v phr* *by 1930s* To speak openly and brazenly; behave without shame or reticence: *My boss, his bare face hanging out, suggested it would be a nice idea*—Modern Maturity [fr *bare-faced,* "audacious, shameless," found by 1712]

with bells on *adv phr* (Variations: **on** may be dropped; **knobs** or **tits** may replace **bells**) *early 1900s theater* Very definitely; without any doubt; emphatically •Used especially in affirming that one will be present at a certain time and place: *Don't worry, I'll be there with bells on/ I'll be here Thursday. With bells*—James M Cain [perhaps the suggestion is that one will be very conspicuous, like a train or a fire engine *with bells*]

with one's **feet** *See* VOTE WITH one's FEET

◁**with** one's **finger up** one's **ass**▷ *See* SIT THERE WITH one's FINGER UP one's ASS

with flying colors *adv phr* *by 1706* In a bold and assured way; grandly; =HIGH, WIDE, AND HANDSOME: *She won nicely, in fact with flying colors* [probably fr the image of a naval vessel with the national flag bravely *flying*]

with one's **hand in the till** (or **the cookie jar**) *adv phr* *by 1970s* With no possibility of escape or evasion; in flagrante delicto; =DEAD TO RIGHTS: *Most people think all members of Congress* *have their hands in the till. Last week's indictment of Rostenkowski simply confirms it*—Time/ *I got caught with my hand in the cookie jar*—Scott Turow [fr the situation of a thief caught *with his hand in the money-box* or *cash register*]

within an ace *See* COME WITHIN AN ACE

with it 1 *adj phr* 1930s black Coolly cognizant; absolutely in touch; stylish and au courant; =HEP: *He affects clothes that carefully cultivate the "with-it" image*—New York Times/ *to spend less time attempting to be "with it" and to exert greater effort to communicate with our deprived and our outcast*—New York Times/ *Shadows of course there are, Porn-Ads, with-it clergy*—W H Auden **2** *adj phr* carnival & circus fr 1920s Working in a carnival as a full-time professional: *. . . had previous short experiences traveling with carnivals. . . before becoming fully "with it" (as carnival workers describe the fully-initiated member)*—Society *See* GET WITH IT

with one's **left hand** *adv phr* At less than full efficiency; more or less casually: *Talese said, "The Frank Sinatra piece is something I dashed off with my left hand"*—Vanity Fair [the *Oxford English Dictionary* in the 1903 volume lists *work with the left hand,* "implying inefficiency of performance," as obsolete, without dates or examples]

with one hand tied behind one's **back (**or **behind** one**) 1** *adv phr* by 1890 Very easily; readily and neatly: *I can do that job with one hand tied behind my back* •The phrase originally referred to fistfights **2** *adv phr* by 1990s At a great disadvantage; under a handicap: *This is what Lord Owen calls "negotiating with one hand tied behind your back"*—New York Times

◁**without a pot to piss in**▷ *See* NOT HAVE A POT TO PISS IN

without skipping (or **missing) a beat** *adv phr* by 1940s With no pause or discontinuity; smoothly: *She segued to the tricky point without skipping a beat/ Without missing a beat, she plucked the pipe from Dolan's mouth. . .* —Loren Estleman [fr *heartbeat* and musical *beat*]

with one's **pants down** *See* CATCH someone WITH THEIR PANTS DOWN

with the bark on *adv phr* by 1870s Unedited; unaltered: *President Johnson read news right off the teletype because he wanted the news with the bark on*—C-SPAN TV

with the punches *See* ROLL WITH THE PUNCHES

with the territory *See* GO WITH THE TERRITORY

witless *See* SCARED SPITLESS, SCARE someone SHITLESS

wizard *adj* by 1922 Excellent; =GREAT, TITS, SUPER [first recorded in Sinclair Lewis, but afterwards chiefly British]

wizmo-gizmo *n* 1990s =GIZMO

wobble weed *n* 1970s narcotics =ANGEL DUST

wobbly or **Wobbly** *n* esp 1920s A member of the Industrial Workers of the World or IWW, a radical labor organization [said to be fr a Chinese-American pronunciation of *w* as "wobble", in IWW]

woe *See* TALE OF WOE

◄**wog** or **Wog**► *n* WWII armed forces fr British A native of India, esp a laborer [the British usage, "any native of an Eastern country," is said to derive fr an arch acronym for *Worthy Oriental Gentleman* or *Westernized Oriental Gentleman*; some think it is more likely to be a shortening of *golliwog,* "a black doll with wild frizzy hair and staring eyes," fr the name of such a doll in late–1800s childrens' stories by Bertha Upton, and a popular toy in British nurseries]

wolf 1 *n* by 1847 A sexually aggressive man; an ardent womanizer; =COCKSMAN: *Mary considered him quite a wolf* **2** *v*: *I give with the vocals and wolf around in a nite club*—John O'Hara **3** *n* prison & hoboes by about 1915 An aggressive male homosexual; a homosexual rapist: *the sodomist, the degenerate, the homosexual "wolf"*—New Republic *See* LONER

wolf whistle *n phr* by 1940s A two-note whistled expression, esp of male appreciation for the sexual attributes of a woman

woman *See* BAG LADY, BOTTOM WOMAN, the LITTLE WOMAN, OLD WOMAN

woman-chaser *n* by 1890s A womanizer; =LADIES' MAN, SKIRT-CHASER, WOLF

wombat *n* 1980s teenagers An eccentric person; =FREAK, NUT [probably fr the inherently amusing name of the *wombat,* a pudgy Australian marsupial, and the occurrence of *bat,* "crazy person, nut," as an element of the name]

wonder *See* NINE-DAYS' WONDER, NINETY-DAY WONDER

Wonder Bread *adj phr* 1980s Conventional; =WHITE BREADY: *Of course, the president's a little too Wonder Bread. . .* —Washington Post [fr the trademark of a popular brand of white bread]

wonk *n* 1990s college students An overstudious student; an intellectual; =GREASY GRIND: *I had a real wonk of a roommate. The guy drove me bats*—National Lampoon/ *Along come these wonks with slide rules sewn into their sports jackets*—John Leonard [origin unknown; perhaps fr British *wanker,* "masturbator"; in British sailor slang, *wonk* meant "midshipman"; the term became suddenly common in the phrase *policy wonk* during the first year of the Clinton administration, 1993]

wonkily *adv* 1990s college students In a halting and unsteady way: *We commended him on his performance and sent him wonkily tottering back onto the floor. . .* —Douglas Coupland

wonkish *adj* 1990s Redolent of policy, theory, discussion, etc: *Greenberg felt that a wonkish tone had pervaded the transition*—Bob Woodward

wonky[1] **1** *adj* by 1923 Badly done or made; ineffective; weird; =COCKEYED: *. . . the wonky clutter of a Victorian parlor*—Toronto Life/ *Only the steering feels wonky to me*—Car and Driver **2** *adj* 1990s computer Out of order; needing repair; =DOWN [fr British dialect *wanky* or *wankle,* "weak, unsteady"; perhaps related to *wanky,* "spurious, doubtful", said of coins, and attested by 1913]

wonky² *adj* students by 1970s Tedious and serious, esp anxious and overstudious in an academic situation: *"Jenny Cavilleri," answered Ray. "Wonky music type"*—Erich Segal/ *. . . a class which I have long dismissed as hopelessly wonky*—Illinois Times [fr *wonk*]

someone **won't eat you** *sentence* by 1738 Don't worry, that person will not harm you: *Answer the question; we won't eat you*

woo *See* PITCH WOO

◁**wood¹**▷ *n* black by 1970s A white person; =PECKERWOOD, REDNECK: *. . . just because they find some cum in that wood's ass*—Donald Goines [fr a shortening of *peckerwood*]

◁**wood²** or **woody**▷ *n* 1980s prison An erect penis; =BLUE VEINER, HARD-ON
See SAW WOOD

wood butcher 1 *n phr* by 1883 A carpenter, esp an incompetent one **2** *n phr* WWI Navy A carpenter's mate

◁**woodchuck**▷ *n* by 1980s =CRACKER, REDNECK

woodenhead *n* A stupid person; =BLOCKHEAD, KLUTZ

wooden kimono *n phr* by 1926 =PINE OVERCOAT

wooden nickels *See* DON'T TAKE ANY WOODEN NICKELS

wooden overcoat *n phr* by 1903 =PINE OVERCOAT

woodpile *n* 1930s jazz musicians A xylophone

wood-pusher *n* by 1950s A chess player, esp an unskilled one; =PATZER: *. . . enough to make any parlor wood-pusher loosen his collar and roll up his sleeves*—Time

wood-pussy *n* by 1920s A skunk; a polecat

the **woods are full of** someones or somethings *sentence* by 1940s The named things or persons are in plentiful supply; these things are cheap and available: *Look, the woods are full of computer programmers; I want one that's a real whiz*

woodshed or **shed** *v* 1930s jazz musicians To rehearse; practice one's part, role, etc, esp to do so alone and rigorously: *Bix did plenty of woodshedding, playing alone*—Stephen Longstreet/ *I just learned a new technique and I've got to shed on it*—Los Angeles Times [fr the *woodshed* as the traditional place where one could be alone to work, think, smoke, etc]

woodshedder *n* 1930s jazz musicians A person who woodsheds: *I've always been a "woodshedder." What I do is go off alone and think things out and practice*—Good Housekeeping

woodwork *See* CRAWL OUT OF THE WOODWORK

woody *n* 1950s surfers A station wagon with wooden outside trim: *Get your woody working*—Rocky Mountain Magazine

woof 1 *v* black by 1934 To talk idly; chatter meaninglessly: *I ain't woofin'. I'm not fooling*—Life **2** *v* black by 1934 To boast, esp menacingly; bluff: *The extreme of arguing is "woofing," like Ali and Frazier*—Washington Post [echoic fr the idle or menacing barking of a dog]

woofer 1 *n* black by 1934 A person who woofs

2 *n* by 1935 A loudspeaker designed to reproduce bass notes faithfully

woofty *adj* by 1990s Unkempt; shaggy, like a dog: *I need a haircut. I look awfully woofty* [probably fr *woof*, "dog's bark"]

wool *See* PULL THE WOOL OVER someone's EYES

◁**wool hat**▷ *n phr* by 1828 A rural person; a bumpkin; =REDNECK

woolies or **woollies** *n* by 1940s Long woolen underwear; =LONG JOHNS

woolly *See* WILD AND WOOLLY

woolly-headed *adj* 1883 Inclined to idealism and hopeful fantasy; impractical: *She dismissed it as another woolly-headed scheme of mine*

wootsie or **wootsy** *See* TOOTS

woozily *adv* 1911 In a woozy manner: *I balanced myself woozily on the flats of my hands*—Raymond Chandler/ *. . . tottered woozily off a plane from Tripoli*—Associated Press

woozy by 1897 **1** *adj* Not fully alert and conscious; half-asleep; befuddled: *You'll just get woozy if you stay up any longer*—P Marks/ *. . . some woozy tourist*—Gene Fowler **2** *adj* Dizzy; faint; unwell [origin unknown; perhaps fr *oozy*, suggesting the insolidity and limpness of mud]

◀**wop** or **Wop**▶ **1** *n* by 1912 An Italian or a person of Italian extraction; =DAGO **2** *adj*: *. . . big wop tenor*—James M Cain [apparently fr southern Italian dialect *guappo*, "dandy, dude, stud," used as a greeting by male Neapolitans]

word 1 *interj* 1980s black teenagers An exclamation of agreement and appreciation, used when someone has said something important or profound: *If it's really meaningful, "Word, man, word" should be used*—New York Times **2** *interj* =WORD UP
See EAT one's WORDS, FIGHTIN' WORDS, FROM THE WORD GO, WEASEL WORDS, WHAT'S THE GOOD WORD

-word *combining word* by early 1980s Used in real or mock euphemisms to avoid saying a taboo or repulsive word: *C-word, "cancer"/ F-word, "fuck"/ L-word, "liberal"/ T-word, "taxes"*

word up *interj* 1980s black An exhortation to listen, to pay attention: *Word up, fool. We be fresh tonight*—Carsten Stroud [probably based on *listen up*]

work 1 *v* by 1851 To go about a place begging, selling, stealing, etc; ply one's often dishonest trade: *She did not deserve charity. She worked the town*—TV show The State of Colorado **2** *v* by 1851 To exert one's charm, power, persuasiveness, etc, esp on an audience; manipulate: *To watch Dick Engberg work the crowd and Al McGuire tossing peanuts to the spectators. . . .*—Milwaukee Journal/ *We watched him work the room a bit*—Stan Cutler
See BULLWORK, DIRTY WORK, DONKEYWORK, GRUNT WORK, NICE WORK IF YOU CAN GET IT, NOODLEWORK, SCUT

workaholic 1 *n* by 1968 A person whose primary and obsessive interest is work; a compulsive worker: *This type of person is a work freak, a workaholic*—National Observer **2** *modifier*: *I made a hardy* attempt to suppress my workaholic tendency [coined fr work plus -aholic (fr alcoholic) by the pastoral counselor W E Oates]

◁**work** one's **ass** (or **buns** or **tail**) **off**▷ *v phr* by 1940s To work very hard; =BUST one's ASS: *They work their ass off all year*—Elmore Leonard/ *The dead acoustics of the room force. . . the students to work their tails off*—Esquire/ *Complains one Apple staffer, "People are working their buns off"*—Time

work behind the stick *v phr* by 1970s To be an active police officer, esp a patrolling officer: *I used to work behind the stick in the afternoons*—Lawrence Sanders [fr the patrolling officer's *nightstick*]

work blue *v phr* by 1990s To use obscene language; peddle smut: *Deane does not, in the parlance of stand-up comics, "work blue" when he bench coaches*—Milwaukee Journal

work both sides of the street *v phr* 1930s politics To take two contrary positions at once; =HAVE IT BOTH WAYS: *Most politicians have a good instinct for working both sides of the street* [probably fr the notion of a hoboes' or beggars' agreement to parcel out the territory]

work both ways or **cut two ways** *v phr* variant by 1605 To suggest or entail a necessary contrary; have double and opposite application: *Most often the claim of mental cruelty works both ways in a marriage: I see your point, but don't you see it cuts two ways?* [originally fr the notion of a two-edged sword]

worked up *adj phr* by 1883 Angry; excited; distraught: *The whole town was worked up over the shooting incident*

worker *See* LUSH ROLLER

working *See* HAVE something GOING FOR someone or something

working girl *n phr* 1960s prostitutes A prostitute; =HOOKER: *. . . an old white pimp named Tony Roland who was known to handle the best-looking "working" girls in New York*—Xaviera Hollander/ *The customer. . . was a working girl just like Jenny. . .* —Ed McBain

working stiff *n phr* by 1930 A common working man; an ordinary worker: *. . . made good cars cheap and paid working stiffs $5 a day*—Stewart Holbrook/ *The author has been a novelist. . . he has also been a movie and TV working stiff*—Time

work it *v phr* by 1980s To behave in a blatantly seductive way; engage in high-pressure salesmanship: *Meanwhile, De Luca and Saperstein are working it hard from the conference room*—Los Angeles Times [propagated from a scene in the 1990 movie *Pretty Woman*, in which one prostitute urges another to *Work it, girl*, "activate your derriere," as she approaches a possible client]

work it into the ground *See* RUN something INTO THE GROUND

work one's **nerves** *v phr* by 1990s =GET ON someone's NERVE: *More energy going nowhere. It's working my nerves*—Sassy

workout 1 *n* by 1909 A session of strenuous physi-

cal exercises, practice athletic efforts, etc: *He came in sweating after his morning workout* **2** *n* A hard job; an exhausting effort: *She told us that handling that kid all day is one hell of a workout*

work out 1 *v phr* by 1885 To end; eventuate; =PLAY OUT, RUN, SHAKE OUT: *How's this plan going to work out?* **2** *v phr* by 1909 To do strenuous exercises; have a hard session of physical conditioning: *The president works out every day in the palace gym*

work something **out** *v phr* by 1970s To achieve an agreement, esp by compromise: *We'll just stay at it until we work something out* [found by 1849 in the sense "to solve"]

work someone **over** *v phr* by 1927 To beat someone, esp cruelly and systematically; =MESS someone UP: *. . . he tells me to work this guy over, do a number on him*—Milwaukee Journal

works *n* 1930s narcotics The devices used for injecting narcotics; drug paraphernalia; =FIT: *When he awakes in the morning he reaches instantly for his "works," eyedropper, needle,. . . and bottle top*—Reader's Digest

the **works** or the **whole works** *n phr* by 1912 Everything; the totality of resources; =the WHOLE SCHMEAR, the WHOLE NINE YARDS: *. . . the works, shave, haircut, massage, and tonic*—Hal Boyle [perhaps like *kit and caboodle* in referring to an entire outfit of equipment, conceived as a *works*, "factory, workplace and equipment"; perhaps referring to the entirety of a mechanism like that in *gum up the works*]

See GIVE someone THE WORKS, GUM UP, IN THE PIPELINE, SHOOT THE WORKS

work up *v phr* middle 1800s To devise; =WHOMP UP: *We'll have to work up a good story to explain this one*

the **world** *n phr* Army by 1970s The territorial US

See DEAD TO THE WORLD, GO AROUND THE WORLD, HAVE THE WORLD BY THE BALLS, I'LL TELL THE WORLD

world-beater *n* by 1893 A very effective person; a winner; a champion: *Sometimes I think you're a world-beater*—Raymond Chandler

worldclass *See* FREEWORLD, OUT OF THIS WORLD

world-class *adj* by 1950 Very superior; outstanding; super-excellent: *. . . a few of the nasties. . . are scenery-chomping world-class scum*—Los Angeles Times/ *. . . took one look at me and bolted off in world-class time!*—Stan Cutler [fr the superiority of an athlete who competes successfully in the Olympic Games or other world-wide events]

the **world is** one's **oyster** *sentence* The person referred to is doing very well, is prosperous, is happy, has great prospects, etc: *Before the crash his rich grandfather figured the world was his oyster*

worm ◁**1**▷ *n* fr 800s A despicable person; =BASTARD, JERK: *Cut that out, you little worm* **2** *n* (also **tapeworm**) late 1980s computer A program that copies itself from one computer to another in a network, does not destroy data but can clutter up a system: *. . . which is now classified as a "worm"* because the writer of the program did not mean to do damage—Time/ *A worm, in computerese, is one of the many varieties of viruses that infect computers*—New Yorker

See CAN OF WORMS

worm hole *n phr late 1980s computer* An unauthorized way into a computer system: *. . . an unknown hacker burrowed electronically through a "worm hole" of the World Wide Web. . .* —Newark Star-Ledger

worm out of something *v phr by 1893* To evade or avoid an unpleasant situation, esp by ignominious means: *This time we have him dead to rights, and he won't worm out of it*

worm one's **way** *v phr by 1845* To enter or penetrate stealthily, like a worm or snake: *. . . has used his sophisticated skill. . . to worm his way into many of the nation's telephone networks*—New York Times

worry *See* NOT TO WORRY

worry wart *n phr by 1956* A person who worries excessively; a constantly apprehensive person [fr the designation of such a person in the comic strip "Out Our Way" by J R Williams]

worst-case scenario *n phr 1960s armed forces* A speculation or prediction as to what would happen if everything turned out as badly as possible: *our worst-case scenario in Western Europe*—Time

worth *See* TWO CENTS' WORTH

would you buy a used car from this man question *by 1960s* Can this person really be trusted; is this an honest face [fr the belief that used-car salesmen are notoriously dishonest; popularized as applied to President Richard M Nixon]

wound or **wound up** *adj phr by 1788* Tense; anxious; on edge: *She was a tall, angular woman, tightly wound, with a Nefertiti profile and hands made for scratching*—Lawrence Sanders

wounded *See* WALKING WOUNDED

wounded duck *1980s sports* **1** *n phr* In baseball, a short looping fly that falls for a hit; =TEXAS LEAGUER **2** *n phr* In football, a wobbling forward pass, which might be intercepted

wow[1] **1** *interj* (also **wowee-kazowee** or **wowie-kazowie**) *entry form by 1513, variants by 1990s* An exclamation of pleasure, wonder, admiration, surprise, etc ●This old interjection had a new popularity in the early 1900s and again during the 1960s and later: *Wow, what a nice voice you have!/ Oh, wow, far out!/ Hey, wow!/ I have a PhD in communications from UCLA. . . Well, wowee-kazowee!*—New York Times/ *Big rock-'n'-roll concerts are often as much about wowie-kazowie production values, video, neon, fireworks, suggestively costumed young men and women, as music*—Time **2** *n by 1920* Something very exciting and successful; a sensation: *It would be a wow of a scrap*—H Witwer/ *. . . a wow of a line!*—Katharine Brush **3** *n 1920s show business* A theatrical success; =BOFFOLA, HIT **4** *v 1920s show business* To impress someone powerfully and favorably; =KNOCK someone DEAD,

LAY THEM IN THE AISLES: *. . . wondering whether he'll make a fraternity and whether or not he'll wow the girls*—Saturday Evening Post/ *. . . all self-proclaimed poets who, to wow an audience, utter some resonant line*—W H Auden [echoic of a bark or howl of approval]

See POW-WOW

wow[2] *n 1930s electronics* An intrusive wavering sound from a record player, usu caused by uneven running of the turntable [echoic of a howl or yowl]

wowser[1] *n by 1928* Something very successful and impressive; a sensation; =WOW[1]: *It would make a wowser of a movie*—Pittsburgh Press/ *The four-beat peroration is a wowser*—National Review [fr wow, perhaps influenced by rouser]

wowser[2] *n by 1899* A stiff and puritanical person; a prude and prig; =KILLJOY, PARTY POOPER ●Now outdated and sure to be confused with *wowser*[1]: *. . . men of letters, who would swoon at the sight of a split infinitive, such wowsers they are in regard to pure English*—Robert Lynd [origin unknown; claimed in 1899 by John Norton, an Australian muck-raking publisher, as his coined acronym for the name of his organization *We Only Want Social Evils Righted*]

wrap 1 *v 1970s movies and television* To complete; finish; =WRAP UP: *Filming, based on Bob Randall's 1977 thriller, wrapped last summer*—People Weekly/ *Because when it wraps, they strike the sets and you're stuck*—GQ **2** *n*: *Well, it's a wrap on the squash*—Dan Jenkins [possibly fr the shrouding of a corpse]

wrapped *adj by 1980s* Under control; in hand; =TOGETHER: *. . . got everything wrapped, whole fuckin' world on the half-shell*—George V Higgins

wrapped around the axle *adj phr 1980s Army* Tangled in complex and trivial matters; involved in pointless discussion [fr the plight of a person whose vehicle *axle* has become ensnarled in a tangle of rope or some other material]

wrapper *See* PLAIN WRAPPER

wraps *See* UNDER WRAPS

wrap up *v phr by 1926* To complete; finish: *Let's wrap the matter up now and call it a day*

wrap-up *n by 1950s* A completion; a final treatment, summary, etc; =RECAP: *This is the 11:30 pm wrap-up of the news*

wreck 1 *n by 1930s* An old car or other vehicle; =HEAP, JALOPY **2** *n by 1795* An exhausted or dissipated person; a human ruin: *He's pretty smart, but physically a wreck*

wrecked *adj 1960s narcotics* Intoxicated with or addicted to narcotics

wringer *See* GET one's TAIL IN A GATE, PUT someone THROUGH THE WRINGER

wrinkle 1 *n by 1817* An idea, device, trick, notion, style, etc, esp a new one: *Wearing that thing sideways is a nice wrinkle* **2** *n by 1643* A defect or problem, esp a minor one; =BUG: *The plan's still got a few wrinkles, nothing we can't handle* [origin of first sense unknown; perhaps fr the same semantic impulse as *twist* in a similar sense, referring to a quick shift in course; perhaps a reference to a lack of plain simplicity in dress or decoration, and the prevalence of stylish pleats, folds, etc, since the earliest form is *without all wrinkles*; second sense fr the notion of *ironing the wrinkles out* of something]

Wrinkle City *1980s* **1** *n phr* Old age; the golden years: *Women live with an unspoken fear of Wrinkle City*—Time/ *I mean, 45 isn't exactly Wrinkle-City*—comic strip "For Better or for Worse" **2** *n phr* (also **Wrinkle Village**) A place inhabited or frequented by old people: *I'm not quite ready to dodder around Wrinkle Village*—Mike Royko

◁**wrinkly** or **wrinklie**▷ *n by 1972* An old person: *I tried to help this wrinkly cross the street*

wrist *See* GIVE someone A SLAP ON THE WRIST, LIMP WRIST

write someone **a blank check** *See* GIVE someone A BLANK CHECK

write home about *See* NOTHING TO WRITE HOME ABOUT

write the book *v phr by 1980s* To be very authoritative or seasoned; be an expert •Usu in the past tense: *Can she sing? Hell, she wrote the book*

write-up *n by 1885* A written article, news story, etc: *I figure you have seen the write-ups*—John O'Hara/ *The papers gave his book a good write-up*

wrong guy (or **gee**) *n phr 1920s underworld* A man who cannot be trusted; a devious and corrupt man: *You're guilty the second that spotlight hits you 'cause you're a wrong guy*—Nelson Algren

wrongo *1937* **1** *n* A wicked or criminal person; a villain **2** *n* An undesirable person; a person of the wrong sort: *a "closet for wrongos" on the second floor that "looks like an attic decorated by a cross-eyed paper hanger in a hurry"*—Playboy **3** *n* Something wrong or improper; an error, lie, misstatement, etc: *They haven't hit me with a wrongo yet, although they did miss a whopper this morning*—Paul Sann **4** *adj* Prone to error; inept: *an almost endearingly wrong-o, sloppily managed outfit*—Washington Post

wrong side of the bed *See* GOT UP ON THE WRONG SIDE OF THE BED

the **wrong side of the tracks** *adv phr* A socially and economically inferior neighborhood; the slums: *He did very well for a boy from the wrong side of the tracks*/ *I was born on the wrong side of the tracks* [fr the fact that poor and industrial areas were often located on one side of the railroad *tracks*, partly because prevailing wind patterns would carry smoke into them and away from the better-off neighborhoods]

the **wrong way** *See* RUB someone THE WRONG WAY

wrote *See* THAT'S ALL SHE WROTE

wuss or **wussy** (Woŏ see) *n 1960s teenagers* A weak person; =PUSSYCAT, WIMP: *6 Ways Not to be a Wuss*—Sassy/ *"Wussy" was a particularly expressive word. . . the handy combination of wimp and pussy*—Cameron Crowe [perhaps a shortening of hypothetical *pussy-wussy*]

wussiness *n by 1980s* Weakness; ineffectuality: *. . . Paglia wants to get the wussiness out of culture. . .*—Macon Telegraph

X

X¹ *n* A person's signature: *Just put your X on this and we're in business* [fr the custom of an illiterate person to make an X in place of a written signature]

X² **1** *n* narcotics by 1990s Ecstasy, a variety of amphetamine narcotic **2** *v* To use the narcotic ecstasy: *Many of us have had the experience of being around someone who is X-ing*—Homol

X amount *n phr* by 1970s An indefinite number: *There's always X amount of people out there laughing and talking*—Milwaukee Journal [fr the algebraic symbol X]

X-er *n* by 1990s A member of Generation X: *. . . a 25-year-old self-proclaimed champion of the X-ers. . .* —Buzz

X marks the spot *sentence* by 1813 This is the place; here is the exact location: *I pointed to the map and told her "X marks the spot"* [fr the graphic convention of designating a precise location on a picture, map, etc, with an X; the date refers to the earliest example found where a particular place is marked with an X]

X-rated *adj* Lewd; obscene; pornographic; =BLUE, DIRTY: *He uttered a few well-chosen X-rated words* [fr the now-superseded early 1950s system of rating movies according to the amount of sex, verbal obscenity, violence, etc, they contain, X being the most censorious rating]

Xs and Os *n phr* sports by 1990s Symbols used to chart plays with Xs and Os representing players: *He gets the job done; he's a great "X" and "O" guy. . .* —Milwaukee Journal/ *"You coach a mentality," Kotite said before today's game. "It's not just Xs and Os"*—New York Times

XX (duh bəl EKS) *n* by 1930s A betrayal; =DOUBLE CROSS: *I know you gave me the XX*—John O'Hara

Y

-y *See* -IE

the Y *n phr* by 1915 One of the recreational, social and athletic organizations or facilities for young persons, such as the YMCA, the YMHA, the YWCA, etc: *He lives in a room at the Y*

yadda yadda *adv phr* by 1990s And so on; so they say repeatedly: *. . . Snyder is too old, too abrasive, yadda yadda, on and on*—Milwaukee Journal

yak (also **yack** or **yack-yack** or **yack-yack-yack** or **yackety-yack** or **yackety-yak** or **yak-yak** or **yak-yak-yak** or **yakitty-yack** or **yakkity-yak** or **yock** or **yock-yock** or **yock-yock-yock** or **yok** or **yok-yok** or **yok-yok-yok** or **yuck** or **yuck-yuck** or **yuck-yuck-yuck** or **yuk** or **yuk-yuk** or **yuk-yuk-yuk**) **1** *n* by 1958 Talk, esp idle or empty chatter; mere babbling: *All they can talk about. . . yack-yack-yack is their own specialty*—Associated Press/ *I don't care how owlish you look, how convincing you sound, this is just yak yak yak until you do it*—John McPhee/ *. . . in the midst of all the political yuk-yuk that dins around us*—New York Times/ *. . . if the State Department would stop its incessant yakitty-yak*—Associated Press **2** *v* (also **yack it up** or **yak it up** or **yock it up** or **yuk it up**) by 1950: *Everybody is yakking out an opinion on whether he should now reconsider his candidacy*—Life/ *. . . sparing the rod and yak-yakking and explaining all the time*—Associated Press/ *The students were seated on the floor, still yocking away*—Max Shulman/ *I'll be 75 and hanging around bars yocking it up*—Newsweek **3** *n* by 1938 A laugh; a guffaw: *"Take off your clothes." Pause for audience yuks*—Judith Crist/ *It makes me furious when I have a corny line and it gets a yock*—New York Times **4** *v* (also **yack it up** or **yak it up** or **yock it up** or **yuk it up**) by 1938: *Ken Gaul is yukking, tugging at his pointy satyr's beard*—Changes/ *There'd be Don, yockin' it up like crazy. . . he's so hysterical with laughter*—Arthur Kober/ *. . . former senator George McGovern, yukking it up with. . . Paul Volcker*—Washington Post [echoic, perhaps of Yiddish origin]

yakky by 1950s **1** *adj* Talkative; garrulous; noisy **2** *n*: *. . . a welcome antidote to the yakkies who can't be bothered by anybody else*—John Leonard

yak show 1 *n phr* by 1980s A radio talk show **2** *modifier*: *. . . despite what you may have heard from Ralph Nader or some radio yak-show host. . .* —Milwaukee Journal

Yale *See* JOE YALE

yammer 1 *v* by 1513 To talk loudly; =YAK: *They were yammering away about taxes* **2** *n* by about 1500: *He kept up his tedious yammer* **3** *v* by about 1786 To complain; whine and nag; =BITCH: *They are always yammering about mere details* [fr Scots dialect, related to German *Jammer,* "lamentation, misery"]

yang or **yang-yang** *n* by 1970s The penis; =JANG, WANG: *A macho. . . machine. . . a celebration of the yang, bang. . . whang*—Penthouse/ *Like I need a three-foot yang-yang*—Elmore Leonard

See YING-YANG

yank *v* by 1970s To victimize or harass; dupe; mislead: *The detective uses expressions like "You gotta be yankin' me"*—Washington Post [an alteration and shortening of *yank someone's chain* or *jerk someone around* or *jack someone around*]

Yank 1 *n* by 1778 A US citizen; an American: *. . . inquiring after the "Yank" and swearing to have his life*—Life **2** *n* WWI British army A US soldier: *Some Tommies resented the Yanks for being overpaid* [a shortening fr *Yankee* for both senses]

yank someone's chain *See* JERK someone's CHAIN

yantsy *adj* by 1970s Excited; nervous; aroused; =ANTSY [probably an alteration of *antsy*]

yap[1] **1** *n* by 1894 A stupid person; a half-wit; =BOOB: *. . . just a no-account yap*—W R Burnett **2** *n* hoboes by about 1900 A rural person; =HICK, YOKEL **3** *n* underworld by 1912 A criminal's victim; =MARK, PATSY [probably fr British dialect, "half-wit"]

yap[2] **1** *n* by 1900 The mouth; =BAZOO: *. . . every time you open your yap to say something*—Jerome Weidman **2** *v* by 1886 To talk, esp idly or naggingly; =YAMMER: *You've been yapping away*—Jerome Weidman [probably echoic, and similar to the sense "yelp," esp as a small dog does]

See BLOW OFF one's MOUTH, OPEN one's YAP

YAP (pronounced as separate letters) *n* by 1970s A young person in one of the learned and well-paid professions [fr *Young American Professional*]

yard[1] *n* by 1926 A hundred dollars; a $100 bill: *"Mac, what you payin' for this?" Stony looked around the room. "A yard and a half"*—Richard Price [fr the unit of measure]

See GO THE FULL YARD, HALF A YARD

yard[2] *v* black by 1960 To be sexually unfaithful; =CHEAT: *She told him she didn't like to yard on her*

man—Clarence L Cooper [said to be fr the phrase *backyard woman,* "mistress, illicit sex partner"]
See the BACK YARD

yard ape **See** RUG APE

yardbird 1 *n* by 1956 A convict **2** *n* WWII armed forces A recruit; a basic trainee **3** *n* WWII armed forces A soldier who because of ineptitude or misdemeanor is confined to a certain area, and often ordered to keep it clean and neat [fr the fact that convicts exercise in the *yard* of the prison, and that neophyte soldiers are confined to the grounds of the training post during their first weeks; the basic metaphor is probably based on the behavior of urban pigeons]

yard bull 1 *n phr* by 1940s A railroad police officer, guard, or detective **2** *n phr* (also **yard hack**) by 1950s A prison guard; =SCREW

yards **See** the WHOLE NINE YARDS

yarf *v* by 1990s: . . . *the kid was yarfing at me, I mean, Pete was whining and complaining about the shift. Kid complained a lot, ma'am.* . . —Carsten Stroud

yatata (YA tə tə) by 1940s **1** *n* Talk, esp idle talk and chatter; =YAK **2** *v*: . . . *mustn't yatata yatata yatata in the public library*—William Saroyan [echoic]

yatter 1 *n* by 1825 Incessant talk; chatter; =YATATA **2** *n* by 1827 Talk, esp loud talk; chatter; =YAK, YAMMER: . . . *the yatter against a military man in the White House*—Time [echoic]

yawn **See** TECHNICOLOR YAWN

yawner *n* by 1940s Something boring; a tedious account: *Most of the time, stories about child care are a snooze, total yawners*—Los Angeles Times

yawn in Technicolor *v phr* by 1980s To vomit; =BARF, RALPH: *John was sick. He yawned in Technicolor all over Mary's lap*—Washington Post

yay or **yea** (YAY) *adv* by 1950s To this extent; this; so •A sort of demonstrative adverb used with adjectives of size, height, extent, etc, and often accompanied by a hand gesture indicating size: *Dorsey almost did him in yea years ago*—W T Tyler/ *Helen Venable said she'd swear on a stack of Bibles yea high*—Lawrence Sanders [perhaps fr *yea,* "yes," specialized fr an earlier sense "even, truly, verily" to something like "even so, truly so, verily so"; perhaps fr Pensylvania German, based on German *je*]

yeah (YE, YE ə) *affirmation* by 1905 Yes; certainly; right: *Don't say "yeah." It's common*—Raymond Chandler
See OH YEAH

yeah man *interj* by 1934 An exclamation of agreement, pleasure, affirmation, etc

year *n* underworld by 1935 One dollar; a dollar bill
See OUT YEAR

yecch or **yech** **See** YUCK

yegg *n* underworld by 1903 A thief or burglar, esp an itinerant thief or safecracker [origin unknown; said to be fr the name of John *Yegg,* a Swedish tramp and safebreaker; perhaps fr German *Jäger,* "huntsman," applied to a safecracker's advance scouts, but originally *yeggman*]

yell bloody (or **blue) murder** *v phr* entry form by 1931, variant by 1859 To shout and complain loudly: *The crowd in the kitchen was yelling bloody murder* [*scream bloody murder* is found by 1882]

yell one's **head off** *v phr* by 1940s To complain loudly and persistently; express oneself forcefully

yellow 1 *adj* by 1856 Cowardly; faint-hearted; =CHICKEN: *Don't get into this race if you're yellow* **2** *n* by 1896 Cowardice; poltroonery; excessive timidity •Most often in the expression "yellow streak" or "streak of yellow": *I'm afraid he has a streak of yellow in him* **3** *adj* by 1808 Having light skin for a black person: *You know that baker we hired. The yellow boy*—Calder Willingham [the origin of the coward sense is unknown; perhaps it is derived fr the traditional symbolic meanings of *yellow,* among which were "deceitfulness, treachery, degradation, the light of hell"]
See HIGH YELLOW

yellow-bellied *adj* by 1924 Cowardly; =YELLOW: . . . *you yellow-bellied jerk*—Joseph Mitchell

yellow-belly *n* by 1930 A coward; a poltroon: *He is a contemptible yellow-belly, scared of his own shadow* [probably a rhyming expansion of *yellow;* influenced by the early–1800s sense, "a Mexican, esp a Mexican soldier," perhaps fr the color of their uniforms]

yellow dog 1 *n phr* by 1881 A contemptible person; scoundrel; cur; =BASTARD **2** *n phr* underworld by 1980s An informer; =RAT

yellow dog contract *n phr* labor union by 1920 An employee's work contract that forbids membership in a union

◄**yellowfish**► *n* Pacific Coast by 1970s An illegal Chinese immigrant: . . . *a thoughtful man for whom yellowfish begin as a commodity to be hauled for pay and end as tragic figures*—Time

yellow jacket *n phr* 1960s narcotics A capsule of Nembutal™, a barbiturate narcotic

yellow sunshine *n phr* 1960s narcotics LSD; =ACID

yelper *n* by 1970s The screaming and wavering warning signal used on police cars, ambulances, and other emergency vehicles: . . . *two police cars going north.* . . *with yelpers wide open*—John Farris

yen 1 *n* by 1906 A strong craving; a keen desire; a passion: *He's got a yen for faro*—W R Burnett . . . *a yen to put on paper what I was saying in class*—AAUP Bulletin **2** *v* by 1919: *I yenned to own a Rolls Royce*—Billy Rose [fr a Peking dialect Chinese word, "smoke," hence opium, perhaps reinforced by *yearn;* found by 1876 as "the craving of a narcotic addict"]
See PEN YEN

yenta or **yente** (YEN tə) *n* by 1923 A garrulous and gossipy person, usu a woman; =BLABBERMOUTH: *Terrible Tom and Rampaging Rona stopped talking to each other, which is something small-screen yentas should never do*—Us [fr a Jewish woman's given name perhaps derived fr Italian *Gentile* or French *Gentille,* degraded by its association with a humorous character *Yente* Telebende in a regular column of the New York Yiddish newspaper the *Jewish Daily Forward*]

yentz **1** *v* by 1930 To cheat; swindle; =EUCHRE, SCAM: *Don't trust him, he'll yentz you*—Leo Rosten ◁**2**▷ *v* To do the sex act with or to; =SCREW **3** *v* prison by 1950 To abuse [fr Yiddish fr German *jenes*, "that thing, the unmentionable thing"]

yep *affirmation* by 1891 Yes; certainly; sure; =YEAH **See** NOPE

yesca *n narcotics* by 1950s Marijuana; =POT

yes-man *n* by 1913 An obsequious and flattering subordinate; =ASS-KISSER: *Joe Davies, Roosevelt's yes-man at the Kremlin*—Westbrook Pegler/ *This president doesn't want yes-men*—Joseph Heller [said to have appeared first in a 1913 drawing by the sports cartoonist T A Dorgan, showing a group of newspaper assistants, each labeled *yes-man*, all firmly agreeing with their chief; perhaps fr German *Jaherr*, cited in 1941 as "long current"]

yes siree or **yes siree bob** *affirmation* 1846: *I'll take that, yes siree bob, I'll take that any day of the week*—New York Times

◀**Yid** or **yid**▶ (YID) *n* by 1874 A Jew •Not felt to be offensive if pronounced (YEED) by Jews themselves: *Some boy was not admitted to a secret society. . . because he was a "Yid"*—Stephen Longstreet [fr Yiddish, ultimately fr Hebrew *Yehuda*, "Judea"]

yike or **yikes** *interj* first form by 1940s, variant by 1971 An exclamation of alarm or surprise: *"There are people next door," she said." "Yikes," Hawk said*—Robert B Parker

ying-yang or **yin-yang** **1** *n* by 1970s The anus; =ASS, ASSHOLE, WHERE THE SUN DOESN'T SHINE •Nearly always in the expression *up the ying-yang*, "in great abundance": *A mother-jumper of a winter. Snow up the ying-yang*—George V Higgins **2** *n* by early 1960s The penis; =PRICK: *. . . a peek at one of my troopers with tubes up his ying-yang*—Richard Merkin **3** *n Army* by 1970s A stupid or foolish person [origin uncertain; perhaps coined because of the increasing currency of the Chinese term *yin and yang*, "the female and male principles in nature," influenced by *wang*, "penis"; perhaps fr Louisiana French *yan-yan*, "ass"]

yin-yang *n* by 1990s Nonsense; cant; =BULLSHIT: *. . . talking all this yin-yang about us women. . .* —Sassy

yip *v* by 1907 To talk in an insistent, petulant, and annoying way: *Will you please stop yipping about your rights?* [echoic of the high-pitched bark of a small dog]

yipe or **yipes** or **yikes** *interj esp teenagers* An exclamation of dismay, alarm, emphatic response, etc: *Yipes, it's a rattlesnake! Yipe, that hurt!* [probably fr the spontaneous interjection *yi*, a cry of pain or dismay, with the *p* or *k* stop intruding after lip closure, as it does in *nope* and *yep*]

yippee (yip EE) *interj* by 1920 An exclamation of pleasure, approval, triumph, etc: *Yippee, all my candidates won!*

yippie *n* by 1969 A member of the Youth International Party, a left-wing group espousing values of the counterculture movement of the 1960s and early '70s [fr the acronym of the name of the group, reinforced by the rhyme with *hippie*]

yips *n golf* by 1963 : *. . . the president mused about his "yips," anxiety when putting*

yo *interj* by 1859 A greeting; =HEY: *Yo, dudes and babes!*—Philadelphia Inquirer [even though *yo* and *yoho* are very old utterances, found by 1420, the recent revival of *yo* as a primarily black interjection has spawned comment; Ernest Paolino of Philadelphia, indignant because a New York writer had claimed the syllable for New York, recalls it from the 1930s as shortening of *walyo*; in the WWII Army it was the common form of *here!* used in responding to roll-calls]

YO *v* 1990s computer : *He YOed me (sent an electronic message), and I asked him if he wanted to have phone sex*—Elle

yo-boy **See** WIGGER

yock **See** HON-YOCK, YAK

yok **See** YAK

yoke *v* by early 1900s To rob with violence; rob and mutilate; =MUG: *They decided to "yoke" the old man with the hearing aid*—New York Post [said to be fr the seizing of the *yoke* of a sailor's collar from behind in order to subdue and rob him]

yokel *n* by 1812 A rural person; a bumpkin; =HAYSEED, HICK [perhaps fr a dialect name for a woodpecker, hence semantically similar to British dialect *gowk*, "cuckoo, simpleton"] **See** LOCAL YOKEL

yoker *n* by early 1900s A person who "yokes" criminally: *In Washington, muggers are called "yokers"*—New York Post

yold or **yolt** (YUHld) *n* by 1968 An easy victim; =SUCKER, PATSY: *Yold, which rhymes with cold. . . means a chump*—New York Daily News/ *. . . we called them yolts and morons when I was growing up*—Washington Post [fr Yiddish, "simpleton, fool," fr Hebrew *yeled*, "boy"]

yonder **See** DOWN YONDER

Yooper *n* by 1990 A resident of the Upper Peninsula of Michigan: *. . . Michigan's distant Upper Peninsula, aka "The Land Above the Bridge" or home of the "Yoopers". . .*—Sports Illustrated

you **See** SAYS YOU

you ain't seen nothing yet *sentence* by early 1920s What follows is much better than what you have had before: *. . . put her mouth lightly against mine and said "You ain't seen nothing yet"*—Robert B Parker [this was a catch-line of the singer and comedian Al Jolson, and the first words in his 1927 movie *The Jazz Singer*]

you bet (or **betcha)** *affirmation* by 1857 Yes; certainly; surely; =BET YOUR BOOTS [*betcha* form fr *you bet you* or *you bet your life*]

you (or **you'd) better believe** something *sentence* by 1856 Something is absolutely certain; something is assured; you are absolutely right: *Am I* *ready to try? You better believe it/ You'd better believe she's the best*

you can say that again *sentence by 1941* That is absolutely right; I totally agree with you

you can't fight city hall *sentence by 1970s* It is futile to pit yourself against the political or other chiefs and their establishment; it is foolish to take on a battle you cannot possibly win

you can't get there from here 1 *sentence by 1930s* The place referred to is very remote and the route hard to describe **2** *sentence* The problem described is insoluble

you can't make an omelet without breaking eggs *sentence by 1898* One must sometimes do evil or cause damage and inconvenience to accomplish good; the end justifies the means [in the form "an omelet cannot be made without breaking eggs" found by 1859]

you can't win 'em all *sentence sports by 1910* One cannot always be successful; =WIN A FEW LOSE A FEW •Often said ruefully after one has failed, or comfortingly to someone else who has failed [attributed to a pitcher named Clifton G Curtis, after losing his 23rd game of the season]

you don't have to be a brain surgeon *sentence* (Variations: **It doesn't take** or **You don't need** may replace **you don't have to be; Harvard MBA** or **rocket scientist** may replace **brain surgeon**) *by 1990s* This problem is not very difficult; superintelligence is not required: *. . . it does-n't take a brain surgeon to realize that some viewers might be uncomfortable with this subject*—New York Times/ *You don't need an MBA from Harvard to understand the long-term consequences*—New York Times/ *We didn't have to be rocket scientists to understand that this would put us on the leading edge*—New York Times

you foul *n phr 1990s teenagers* Your fault or mistake

you go *See* THERE YOU ARE

you got a problem with that *question by 1990s* Does something about my true and useful statement bother you •A very truculent response: *So she's not Mother Teresa in a tut, you got a problem with that?*—Milwaukee Journal/ *Evander Holyfield, who'll defend his heavyweight title this week, loosens up with ballet exercises. You got a problem with that?*—People Weekly

you-know-what (or **-who)** *n by 1605* Something or someone one does not wish to name, usu because it is both obvious and indelicate or taboo; =WHATSIS: *They were knocked on their you-know-what/ A Rhodes scholar, he earned his law degree at Yale (like you-know-who). . .* —Nation

you name it *sentence by 1962* You cannot designate anything not included here; =the WHOLE SCHMEAR: *Casinos, giant water slides, aquariums, old-time steam engines, wine tasting, you name it: attracting tourists has become the gold rush of the '90s*—Utne Reader [fr the retailing locution *you name it, we got it*]

youngblood *n by 1970s* A young black man; =BLOOD, BROTHER: *. . . youngbloods from Bed-Stuy looking for a reputation*—Village Voice

young squirt *See* SQUIRT

Young Turk *n phr by 1908* A person, usu a young one, who threatens to overthrow an established system or order; an active rebel or reformer: *He scrutinizes the new staff very carefully, and is dreadfully fearful of potential Young Turks* [originally, a member of *Young Turkey,* a revolutionary party of late–1800s Turkey, which finally established constitutional government in 1908]

you pays your money and you takes your choice *sentence by 1883* The proposition is very uncertain; take a good guess: *"How many shots were fired at the OK Corral?" "No one knows. Just pay your money and take your choice*—Glenn G Boyer

your basic *adj phr by 1980s* Definite; unquestionable •Used with a negating irony or slight sense of disbelief: *Now that would be your basic clue, right?*—Carsten Stroud/ *He had your basic heart of gold*—Whitey Herzog

you're another *sentence by 1534* A contemptuous response to an insult: *Oh yeah, big shot? Well, you're another!*

your ear *See* PUT IT IN YOUR EAR

you're damn (or **darn) tootin'** *affirmation by 1932* That is emphatically true; you are absolutely right: *Did I run? You're damn tootin' I did*

you're the doctor *sentence by 1920* I defer to your authority: *You're the doctor. But I wouldn't do it that way*

your money is no good here *sentence by 1900* You are our guest; you get everything free •Modified to a clause in the example: *The FBI agents began to discover that their money was no good in Wright City, and this made them uncomfortable*—New Yorker

yours truly *pron phr by 1844* I; me; myself; =YOUR UNCLE DUDLEY: *Both of whom are repped by yours truly. . .* —Gary Trudeau [fr the conventional parting salutation of a letter]

your Uncle Dudley *n phr by 1922* Oneself; I or me; =YOURS TRULY: *If you want to know about that, just ask your uncle Dudley*

you said it *affirmation by 1919* You are absolutely right; that is correct; =DEF, RIGHT ON

you scratch my back, I scratch yours *sentence by 1858* Let us cooperate; let us be reciprocally and mutually helpful: *I'd love the whole country to get a good gander at how a labor union's supposed to run! You scratch my back, I'll scratch yours!*—Hannibal & Boris [*scratch me and I'll scratch thee* is found by 1704]

yowza or **yowsah** *affirmation by 1934* Yes, sir; certainly: *Recycling tax. Camping fees. State park fees. License plate renewal tax. Yowza*—Milwaukee Journal [popularized by the band leader Ben Bernie]

yo-yo 1 *n by 1958* A vacillating person; one who has no firm convictions: *Feldstein's sudden turn-around. . . makes the president look like a yo-yo*—

Newsweek **2** *n* *teenagers by 1970* A stupid and obnoxious person; =JERK, NERD: *Some yo-yo yells "What happened, you bum. . . "*—Inside Sports

yuck (also **ech** or **yecch** or **yech**) **1** *interj* *by 1969* An exclamation of disgust: *"Those women on the PBS specials seem to love it." "Yuck,"* Connie *mugged*—Armistead Maupin **2** *n* *by 1943* A disgusting substance, person, or thing; someone or something nasty: *. . . precipitation in the form of rain, snow, and assorted other atmospheric yuck*—Washington Post/ *. . . clean all the yecch out of her system*—Cyra McFadden/ *Mario is an intellectually dishonest person. He's just yecch*—New York Magazine [perhaps echoic of gagging or vomiting] **See** YAK

Yucko City *adj phr* *by 1970s* Disgusting; nasty; =YUCKY: *Have you ever tried any popular American beer warm?. . . Yucko City*—Illinois Times

yucky or **yecchy** or **yucko** *adj* *by 1970* Disgusting, esp in a filthy and viscous way; thoroughly nasty: *Some of it is awful yucky*—Philadelphia Daily News/ *Cripes, what's that yucko bulging overhead object?*—New Yorker

yuk *See* YAK

yukdom *n* *by 1990s* The realm of comedy; humor: *Their credits run the gamut of TV yukdom. . .* —Entertainment Weekly

yukmeister or **yukster** *n* *first form by 1990s, variant by 1980s* A comedian: *. . . every yukmeister, including Prior, starts somewhere*—Milwaukee Journal/ *. . . scored some points as a yukster during his pre-meal prayer Thursday*—Milwaukee Journal

yummy *adj* *by 1899* Pleasant, esp sensually; delicious; delightful: *What a yummy cake!/ a yummy prospect*

Yumpie *n* *by 1984* =YUPPIE: *. . . the highly desirable*

"Yumpies," young, upwardly mobile professionals—Washingtonian [fr *young upwardly mobile professional*]

yum-yum 1 *interj* *by 1878* An exclamation of pleasure, esp of sensual delight **2** *n* *by 1889* Something sweet or pleasant, esp to eat [perhaps fr a locution used with children, hence contextually as well as phonetically related to *tummy* or *tum-tum*]

yup *affirmation* *by 1906* =YEP

Yuppie *n* (also **Yup** or **yuppoid** or **yupster**) *by 1984* An affluent, usu city-dwelling, professional in his or her 20s and 30s; a prosperous and ambitious young professional: *Yuppies are dedicated to the twin goals of making piles of money and achieving perfection through physical fitness and therapy*—Time/ *The narrow dance floor is soon crammed with "Yuppies," young urban professionals taking time out from social climbing*—Washingtonian/ *The Yups discover that the locals have been putting up with this. . . for years*—Philadelphia/ *His death must have made more than a few Madison yupsters check their calendars*—Wisconsin State Journal *. . . photos of two generically cheerful yuppoids holding scotch glasses. . .*—Milwaukee Journal [fr *young urban professional,* and modeled on *yippie;* perhaps coined for a 1983 book called *The Yuppie Handbook,* which was modeled on the earlier book *The Official Preppy Handbook*]

yutz ◁1▷ *n* *by 1980s* The penis; =COCK, PRICK, SCHLONG: *. . . as I was sticking my yutz into her Dark Place*—Richard Price **2** *n* (also **yotz**) *1980s students* A fool; =LOSER: *My ex-boyfriend was such a yutz*—UCLA Slang/ *. . . some sweaty, exhausted, dignity-free yutz in a grotesquely unnatural pose. . .*—Dave Barry [origin unknown]

Z

Z¹ or **Zee** *by 1960s* **1** *v* To sleep; snooze; =COP ZS: *Gotta Z a little while* **2** *n* Some sleep; a nap: *If he wants a few zees we can go on automatic*—Robert Stone [fr the conventional sibilant or buzzing sound attributed to a sleeping or snoring person]

Z² *n 1960s narcotics* An ounce of a narcotic: *. . . trips to the rundown neighborhood to purchase Zs (ounces) and even Ks (kilograms) of cocaine*—New York Times [fr the conventional abbreviation of ounces, "oz"]

za or **'za** (ZAH) *n teenagers by 1968* Pizza: *Rents are parents. . . . Za is pizza*—Philadelphia Inquirer [a shortening of *pizza*]

zaftig *See* ZOFTIG

zap **1** *v by 1942* To kill or disable; strike violently; =CLOBBER, WASTE: *Sitcom Zaps Boardroom Bozos*— Time **2** *v medical by 1980s* To administer electroshock therapy **3** *interj by 1929* An exclamation imitating sudden impact; =WHAM: *It's a gradual thing. It ain't zap, you're healed*—Philadelphia Journal **4** *n by 1968* Vitality; force; =PIZZAZZ, ZIP **5** *v by 1990s* To cook or heat in a microwave oven; =NUKE: *Zap one minute, open the microwave door, stir and break up the meat pieces with a fork. . .* — Pittsburgh Post-Gazette [fr the echoic word used to convey the sound of a ray gun in the comic strip "Buck Rogers in the Twenty-Fifth Century"]

zappy *adj by 1969* Having force, impact, energy, etc; =PUNCHY, ZINGY: *. . . black outlines, comic book blonde, and zappy words*—Village Voice

zazz *modifier by 1970s* Having to do with the world of high or jaunty fashion: *. . . everything very haut couture, of course, the whole zazz world*—Ray Smith [perhaps fr unattested *zazzy* fr *jazzy* influenced by *pizzazz*]

zazz something **up** *v phr by 1970s* To make more decorative and impressive; =GUSSY UP, JAZZ something UP: *. . . relied heavily on somewhat musty shadings, zazzing them up, however, with bursts of dusty mauve*—Cosmopolitan [perhaps fr *jazz* something *up*, influenced by *pizzazz*]

zazzy *adj by 1961* Energetic; stylish

zebra **1** *n sports by 1978* A referee or other sports official who wears a striped shirt on the playing field: *Pro football zebras point immediately toward the offending team*—New York Daily News/ *. . . a crooked Zebra (also known as an umpire)*— Washington Post **2** *n medical by 1980s* An unlikely, arcane, or obscure diagnosis **3** *n by 1980s* A per-

son of mixed black and white race: *I've been called a "zebra" and an "Oreo"*—React [the medical sense is fr the saying "If you hear horse's hoofbeats going by outside, don't look for *zebras*"]

zerking *adj teenagers by 1970s* Behaving in a strange way; =GOOFY, WACKY

zero cool *adj phr by 1980s* Extremely aware, alert, up-to-date, relaxed, etc; =COOL [probably fr the concept of *absolute zero*]

zero in *v phr by 1944* To aim at or concentrate on a specific person, thing, etc; single out: *We're trying to zero in on the problem* [fr the *zeroing* of the sights of a rifle, that is, adjusting the sights so that the round hits the exact point aimed at and the shooter needs to make no, or *zero*, estimated correction in aiming]

zero out *v phr by 1990s* To eliminate; reduce to nothing: *When Gingrich threatens to zero out all funding for public broadcasting, there's every reason to believe he can make good on the threat*— Washington Post

zetz *n by 1940s* A blow; a punch: *I'd love to give that guy such a zetz*—National Lampoon/ *Although Mifune gives the proceedings a zetz, everyone else seems tired*—Village Voice [fr Yiddish, related to German *Zurücksetzung*, "a setting back"]

zhlub *n* (also **schlub** or **shlub** or **shlubbo** or **zhlob** or **zshlub**) *by 1964* A coarse person; a boorish man; =JERK, SLOB: *. . . the presence of fine wines and the absence of shlubs*—Philadelphia/ *. . . replied Angela as she glided off to cut the poor schlub out of her will*—Newsweek/ *Lieberman was the worst. Lieberman was a real zshlub*—Joseph Heller [fr Yiddish fr Slavic, "coarse fellow"]

zhlubby *adj by 1964* Having the qualities of a "zhlub"; coarse; boorish: *. . . booze station for the zhlubby middle-aged boat owners from the other side*—New York Magazine

◀**zig** or **zigabo** or **zigaboo**▶ *See* JIGABOO

ziggety *See* HOT DIGGETY

zig-zig *See* JIG-JIG

zilch **1** *n by 1960s* Nothing; zero; =ZIP: *The city. . . has turned its smaller islands into zilch*— New York Magazine/ *. . . got the jeep for practically zilch*—George V Higgins **2** *modifier*: *York has close to zilch industry*—Toronto Life **3** *v sports by 1960s* To hold an opponent scoreless; =BLANK, SKUNK **4** *n teenagers by 1970s* =STORCH **5** *n teenagers by 1970s* A minor skin lesion; =ZIT [probably fr *zero*, and like *zip¹*, primarily a variant coined from a familiar word beginning with *z*; notice, in this regard, how *zilch* has become a variant of *zit*; in British use, but not US, *zilch* might be reinforced by *nil*, "zero"; all senses may derive fr the early–1900s US college use *Joe Zilsch,* "any insignificant person," popularized during the 1930s by ubiquitous use in the humor magazine *Ballyhoo* with the spelling *Zilch,* an actual German surname of Slavic origin]

See JOE BLOW, NOT KNOW BEANS

zillion *See* JILLION

zillionaire *n by 1940* An enormously rich person; a supertycoon: *. . . and Larry Dunlap will become an instant zillionaire*—Village Voice/ *. . . his earlier piece about how the Hong Kong zillionaires are buying up San Francisco*—San Francisco

zine 1 *n by 1965* A magazine **2** *modifier*: *Marr, 32, has been a part of San Francisco's zine scene*—Milwaukee Journal

-zine (ZEEN) *suffix used to form nouns by 1949* Magazine: *teenzine/ fanzine*

zing 1 *n by 1918* Energetic vitality; power; vigor; =OOMPH, PEP, PIZZAZZ, ZIP: *Rock. . . adds zing*—Toronto Star/ *. . . with plenty of zing in both the. . . V–8 engine and the powerful Six*—Philadelphia Bulletin **2** *v* (also **zing along**) *by 1961* To move rapidly and strongly; =ZIP: *The movie zings right along*—Playboy **3** *v by 1960s* To throw; inject, esp rapidly and strongly: *. . . like the Beatles every once in a while can zing it in there*—Rolling Stone **4** *v by 1974* To insult; assault verbally, esp with bitter humor: *King Caen, who zings everyone, gets a taste of his own medicine*—California/ *A woman on the editorial board merrily zinged the winking minister*—Village Voice [probably echoic of the whishing sound of rapid movement, like *zip* and *zoom*]

zinger *by 1950* **1** *n* A quip, esp one that is somewhat cruel and aggressive; a funny crack or punch line: *Watt's off-the-cuff zingers have been a frequent source of pain for the Reagan Administration*—Time/ *The plump little actor is polished and funny; his zingers stay zung*—Washington Post **2** *n* A quick and sharp response; a sturdy retort: *. . . get right in there with Williams, stand eyeball to eyeball, and plant the zinger on him, bang, or else you would be dismissed*—Harper's

zingy *adj by 1948* Full of energy and vigor; =PEPPY, ZIPPY: *. . . written by no less than the zingy Nora Ephron*—Philadelphia/ *Zingy Zeroes, Wall Street's hot bonds*—Time

zip¹ or **zippo** *students by 1900* **1** *n* A mark or grade of zero **2** *n* Zero; nothing; a score of zero; =ZILCH: *People aren't exactly beating down the doors to buy California port. "The market. . . is zip, zero, and not too much"*—San Francisco/ *. . . dipped into your moneybag and found zippo*—Washington Post [like *zilch*, probably coined from a familiar word beginning with *z*]

See NOT GIVE A DAMN, NOT KNOW BEANS, ZILCH

zip² or **zippo** *n by 1900* Energy; vitality; vim; =PIZZAZZ, ZING: *There is a zip and a zing here*—NY Confidential/ *. . . bounced back with the real zippo*—Joseph Wambaugh [echoic of the sound of something swishing rapidly through the air, giving an impression of force, and also of the tearing of cloth; such a use is attested fr 1875]

◀**zip³**▶ *n Vietnam War* A Vietnamese; =DINK [said to be fr *zero intelligence*]

zip gun *n phr by 1950* A homemade pistol: *. . . a zip gun, the kind kids make themselves*—Pageant

zip one's **lip** (or one's **mouth**) *v phr by 1942* To stop talking, esp abruptly and completely; =SHUT UP: *I just had to zip my mouth and do what I could*—Toronto Life [fr the notion that one has a *zipper* fastener on one's mouth]

zippo *v Army by 1970s* To set something on fire; ignite something [fr *Zippo,* trademark of a cigarette lighter, probably fr the sound made as one turns the sparking wheel, and the speed with which the lighter ignites]

zippy *adj by 1904* Energetic; =PEPPY, ZINGY: *. . . and the zippy pacing by Russell. . .* —Macon Telegraph [fr *zip²*]

zit *teenagers by 1966* **1** *n* A minor skin lesion; a pimple; a blackhead: *First Arnie's zits mysteriously clear up*—Newsweek **2** *n* A mark left by a love-bite, a strong kiss, etc; =HICKEY: *She tried to conceal the big zit on her neck* [origin unknown; perhaps echoic of the squishy pop made when the pus is squeezed from a blackhead]

zit doctor *n phr medical by 1960s* A dermatologist

zits *See* TITS-AND-ZITS

zizz 1 *v 1920s British armed forces* To sleep; snooze; nap; =COP ZS **2** *n*: *She stretched out for a short zizz* [echoic of the sibilance or buzzing of one who sleeps, hence semantically akin to the notion of *sawing wood*]

zizzy¹ *n WWII armed forces fr British* A sleep; a nap; a snooze [fr *zizz*]

zizzy² *adj by 1966* Showy and frivolous; light; frothy [perhaps a thinning of *zazzy*; perhaps an alteration of *fizzy*]

zod *n 1970s teenagers* An eccentric and obnoxious person; =CREEP, NERD [origin unknown; perhaps related to the alligator represented on *Izod™* apparel]

zoftig or **zaftig** (ZAWF tik, ZAHF-) *adj by 1937* Sexually appealing or arousing to males, esp in a plump and well-rounded way; curvaceous; =BUILT LIKE A BRICK SHITHOUSE: *. . . zoftig. . . pleasantly plump and pretty*—New York Daily News/ *The legs of the Red Suit are cut so high and deep, even the leanest female bum looks like a zaftig peach*—Buzz [fr Yiddish, literally "juicy"]

zoid *n by 1970s* A nonconforming person; a misfit: *Andie doesn't "fit in". . . she's an outsider, a "zoid"*—Washington Post

zombie (ZAHM bee) **1** *n 1930s students* A very strange person, esp one with a vacant corpse-like manner; =WEIRDO **2** *n by 1936* An unresponsive person; a mentally numb or dead person: *My stu-*

dents are all zombies this term [origin uncertain; perhaps fr an African word akin to *nzambi*, "god"; perhaps fr Louisiana Creole, "phantom, ghost," fr Spanish *sombra*, "shade, ghost"; popularized by horror stories and movies featuring the walking dead persons of voodoo belief]

zombie someone **out** *v phr* by 1980s To make someone stuporous like a zombie: . . . the medication I received for a couple of years "zombied me out" so bad I couldn't work—Daily Jefferson County Union

zone[1] *See* IN A ZONE, OZONE

zone[2] **1** *n* (also **zoner**) 1960s narcotics A person intoxicated with narcotics, esp habitually so; =SPACE CADET **2** *v* 1980s To be inattentive; be hazily preoccupied: He zoned so bad he didn't even hear the teacher call his name—UCLA Slang/ I was kind of zonin', checking things out—Milwaukee Journal [fr *ozone*, "a very high level of the atmosphere"]

zoned or **zoned out** *adj* or *adj phr* 1960s narcotics Intoxicated with narcotics; =HIGH [fr *zone*; influenced by *spaced out*]

zone something **out** or **zone out** *v phr* by 1960s To omit from consciousness; shut out of the mind: I can just zone everything out and keep going—New York Sunday News

zonk or **zonk out 1** *v* or *v phr* by 1968 To lose consciousness, esp from alcohol or narcotics; fall asleep; become stuporous: He suddenly zonked and went rigid **2** *v* or *v phr* by 1950 To strike a stupefying blow; =CLOBBER: "We've been zonked," said Jim Robbins—Washington Post [fr *zonked*]

zonked or **zonked out** or **zonkers 1** *adj* or *adj phr* 1960s narcotics Intoxicated by narcotics or alcohol; =HIGH, STONED: . . . zonked, one step past being stoned—E Horne/ . . . either while I was still zonked out or in the shower—Stan Cutler **2** *adj* or *adj phr* by 1970s Very enthusiastic; excited; =HIGH: Rene Carpenter remembers Gilruth as "a kindly, wonderful man who was zonked on this project"—Washingtonian **3** *adj* or *adj phr* by 1972 Exhausted; =BEAT, POOPED: After just an hour of that I was zonked [echoic of a heavy blow; a 1929 Bookman article on sound effects is entitled "Socko, Whamo, and Sonk!"]

zonky *adj* by 1972 Odd; strange; =FREAKY, WEIRD

zoo *n* by 1935 A crowded and chaotic place: Opening Day is always a zoo—Jane Leavy/ The emergency room at Bellevue was usually a zoo—Stuart Woods

zoo daddy *n phr* by 1970s A divorced or separated father who sees his children rarely; =DISNEYLAND DADDY

zooey *adj* by 1970s Like a zoo; nasty; barbaric: It's been zooey down here. . . it's been hectic—Philadelphia Daily News

zoomy *adj* by 1970s Fast and stylish; high-flying; showy and flaunting: . . . and it isn't just a matter of zoomy looks, either—Car and Driver/ . . . jet-setters, sort of really zoomy people—George V Higgins [fr *zoom*, "fly up spectacularly"]

zoot suit *n phr* by 1942 A man's suit with a jacket having very wide lapels, heavily padded shoulders, and many-buttoned sleeves, with very high-waisted trousers full in the leg and tapering to narrow cuffs •Such garments were worn as symbols of status and defiance, esp by urban black hipsters and Los Angeles Chicanos: Some were garbed in short sleeve shirts, others in zoot suits—Associated Press/ Jelly got into his zoot suit with the reet pleats—Zora Neale Hurston [origin unknown; probably in essence a rhyming phrase of the sort common in black English and slang; perhaps related to other jive and cool talk terms like *vootie*]

zoot suiter *n phr* by 1942 A man, esp a young black hipster or a Chicano, who wears a zoot suit and/or exemplifies the values symbolized by such a garment

zorch *v* 1980s computer To convey or transfer quickly: This file transfer program. . . really zorches those files through the network—Hacker's Dictionary

zot or **zotz** *n* 1960s students Nothing; zero; =ZILCH, ZIP: Zero. Nothing. Absolutely zotz—Psychology Today [like *zip* and *zilch* based mainly on the initial *z* suggesting *zero*; perhaps influenced by *squat* in the same sense]

zowie 1 *interj* by 1913 An exclamation imitating sudden impact; =POW, WHAM: I ducked, but zowie, it caught me on the nose **2** *n* by 1940s Energy; vitality; vim; =ZING, ZIP: . . . full of zing, full of zest, full of zowie—movie Mad Wednesday

some **Zs** *See* COP ZS

zshlub *See* ZHLUB